- Chapter One's **fold-out case exhibit** presents a full annotated court case. This two-page feature labels the various parts of a case so the student can see a complete case.

- ***A Student's Guide to Case Analysis and Online Research*** is shrink-wrapped with every new copy of ***West's Business Law: A Case Study Approach***. This guide helps students learn how to read and analyze case law, research case law, and conduct online legal research.

- **Case updates**, organized by topic and cross-referenced to relevant chapters within the text, can be found at **http://wbl-cs.westbuslaw.com**.

- **Interactive online quizzes** are available through the text's Web site to prepare students for exams and to test their knowledge.

For the Student

Your Web Resources at a Glance—

Explore the text's companion Web site at **http://wbl-cs.westbuslaw.com**. There you will find the following resources:

- **Westlaw cases** Westlaw—Click on the Westlaw icon on the left side of the screen to register and find the full Westlaw text of each case presented in your textbook!
- **Internet exercises for every chapter**—Go to the "Interactive Study Center" on the text's Web site to find these exercises that you can perform to become familiar with important legal sources on the Web!
- **Interactive quizzes for every chapter**—Don't forget to try these quizzes to test your knowledge of topics covered in each chapter, especially before an exam!
- **Court case updates**—Find out about recent court decisions in an area that you are studying by going to this section of the text's Web site!
- **Talk to the authors**—From the Web site, you can e-mail us any questions you may have about your text or its supplements!

Congratulations!

Your purchase of ***Miller/Jentz/Cross West's Business Law: A Case Study Approach*** entitles you to the full Westlaw Cases Online. You will have unlimited access to these cases throughout the semester. These cases are the ones utilized and referenced throughout the entire text, including end-of-chapter questions by the authors. **The duration of the subscription is one year.**

To get started, please complete the following steps:

1. Make sure you have Internet connectivity and open a Web browser. Go to this textbook's Web site at **http://wbl-cs.westbuslaw.com**. Click on the "Westlaw" icon that will appear to the left of your screen.

2. You must first register for the Westlaw cases using the serial number on this card. This serial number identifies you as a purchaser of this textbook. Click on the "Register" button. You will be asked to enter your serial number and a new or existing user name. Take care to enter your serial number exactly as it appears on this card.

   Here is your serial number:

   SC-000035E3-WLCA

   This serial number can only be used one time.

   Make sure you type the dashes. In between the hyphens is a collection of letters and numbers. A "o(zero)" with a slash through it is a "zero".

3. While registering your serial number, you will choose a username and password for use in accessing the Westlaw cases. Make a note of your username and password as you will need those to return to the cases.

If you have purchased a used textbook and the subscription has expired, you can purchase access to the full Westlaw cases online by visiting **http://wbl-cs.westbuslaw.com** and clicking on the Westlaw icon.

WEST'S BUSINESS LAW

A CASE STUDY APPROACH

Roger LeRoy Miller
Institute for University Studies
Arlington, Texas

Gaylord A. Jentz
Herbert D. Kelleher Emeritus Professor in Business Law
University of Texas at Austin

Frank B. Cross
Herbert D. Kelleher Centennial Professor in Business Law
University of Texas at Austin

Australia · Canada · Mexico · Singapore · Spain · United Kingdom · United States

West's Business Law

A CASE STUDY APPROACH

Roger LeRoy Miller
Institute for University Studies
Arlington, Texas

Gaylord A. Jentz
Herbert D. Kelleher Emeritus Professor in Business Law
University of Texas at Austin

Frank B. Cross
Herbert D. Kelleher Centennial Professor in Business Law
University of Texas at Austin

Vice President and Team Director:
Michael P. Roche

Sr. Acquisitions Editor:
Rob Dewey

Sr Developmental Editor:
Jan Lamar

Marketing Manager:
Nicole C. Moore

Production Manager:
Bill Stryker

Manufacturing Coordinator:
Rhonda Utley

Compositor:
Parkwood Composition, New Richmond, WI

Printer:
RR Donnelley & Sons Company
Willard Manufacturing Division

Design Project Manager:
Michelle Kunkler

Internal Designer:
Bill Stryker

Cover Designer:
Jennifer Lambert/Jen2Design, Cincinnati, OH

Printed in the
United States of America
1 2 3 4 5 04 03 02

For more information
contact South-Western,
5191 Natorp Boulevard,
Mason, Ohio 45040.
Or you can visit our Internet
site at:
http://www.westbuslaw.com

**Library of Congress
Cataloging-in-Publication
Data**
Miller, Roger LeRoy.
West's Business Law: a case
study approach/ Roger LeRoy
Miller, Gaylord A. Jentz,
Frank B. Cross.
p. cm.
Includes bibliographical
references and index.
ISBN 0–324–16096–8
1. Commercial law—United
States—Cases. 2. Business
law—United States. I. Jentz,
Gaylord A. II. Title.
KF888.M5543 2003
346.7307—dc21
99–21224
CIP

Contents in Brief

UNIT SIX
AGENCY 621

UNIT SEVEN
BUSINESS ORGANIZATIONS 663

UNIT EIGHT
LABOR AND EMPLOYMENT RELATIONS 827

UNIT NINE
GOVERNMENT REGULATION 873

UNIT TEN
PROPERTY 945

UNIT ELEVEN
SPECIAL TOPICS 1015

APPENDICES

Contents

Preface to the Instructor

For many instructors of business law and the legal environment, there can be no better way to teach the law than through the study and analysis of actual cases in the exact words of the court. We have created *West's Business Law: A Case Study Approach* to satisfy such professors.

In so doing, we have sacrificed none of the accessibility that has been one of the hallmarks of all previous editions of *West's Business Law. West's Business Law* remains accessible for many reasons, not the least being its clear, straightforward writing style. In addition, the book remains accessible because of the numerous pedagogical features that help guide the student reader through the sometimes complex learning process that makes up the study of law and the legal environment. Additionally, as you will read below, we have followed the tradition of all other versions of *West's Business Law* by making sure that all information included in this edition is the most up-to-date possible.

• Emphasis on Case Study and Analysis

To facilitate case study and analysis, the *West's Business Law: A Case Study Approach* teaching/learning package includes a number of special components, including those discussed below.

Extensive Case Excerpts within the Text

Each chapter contains excerpts, ranging from one to two pages in length, from court opinions relating to topics covered in the chapter. We have made sure that each excerpt clearly conveys to the student the background and facts of the case, the procedural history when relevant, the issue before the court, and the court's reasoning and conclusion regarding that issue. In order to prevent the case excerpts from interfering with the discussion of the law within the chapter, the cases are presented together at the end of the chapter, just following the *Chapter Summary*. For each case, the order of presentation is as follows:

- A case number assigned by the authors, followed by a brief heading indicating the general topic or issue involved in the case.
- Case title.
- Citations, including parallel citations when available.
- The name of the judge or justice who authored the opinion.
- A dissenting opinion (in some cases).

The cases include both classic cases and contemporary cases showing the most recent trends in case law. Virtually every chapter in *West's Business Law: A Case Study Approach* includes at least one case from the early 2000s.

Westlaw. Westlaw Cases on the Text's Web Site

The full text of all cases presented in the text can be accessed by going to this book's Web site at http://wbl-cs.westbuslaw.com and clicking on the Westlaw icon on the left side of the screen.

Whenever a case is presented, students are directed to the Web site to view the full text of each case, as prepared by West editors for the Westlaw database. Each Westlaw case includes the following:

- The names of all plaintiffs and defendants.
- The dates on which the case was argued and decided.
- A brief summary of the issues and decisions in the case.

• Headnotes classifying specific issues in each case according to the West Key Number System.
• The court's opinion.
• Concurring and dissenting opinions, when they exist.

An Annotated Court Case

To help students learn how to read cases, we have included in Chapter 1 a special fold-out exhibit showing excerpts from an actual case decided by the United States Supreme Court in 2001. Margin annotations define and describe the various elements contained in the case, as displayed on Westlaw.

Fifteen Case Problems in Each Chapter

To further emphasize case study and analysis, we have included *fifteen case problems at the end of every chapter.* Each case problem deals with a topic covered in the chapter's text.

Focus on Legal Reasoning

In addition to the cases presented within the chapters, at the end of each unit we have included a feature entitled *Focus on Legal Reasoning*. Each of these features includes the following elements:

• A brief opening paragraph linking the case to a topic covered in a specific chapter within the unit.
• A *Case Background* section, in which the background and facts of the case are presented.
• The name of the judge or justice who authored the court's opinion.
• The majority opinion of the court, including all legal sources cited by the judge or justice.
• A series of questions for analysis that ask the student to perform tasks involving legal analysis, legal reasoning, and legal research.
Westlaw. • A concluding section titled *Westlaw Online Research,* in which students are referred to the full Westlaw text of the case on the book's companion Web site. Students are asked to answer a series of questions that can only be answered by viewing the full Westlaw text of the particular case. Often, these questions address issues raised in dissenting opinions.

A Student's Guide to Case Analysis and Online Research

Shrink-wrapped with every new copy of *West's Business Law: A Case Study Approach* is a booklet entitled *A Student's Guide to Case Analysis and Online Research.* The purpose of this guide is to help students learn how to read and understand cases and how to find legal resources and information on the Internet. Sections in the guide offer instructions and tips to the student in the following areas:

• *Reading and Analyzing Cases*—The guide opens with a section on how to read and analyze cases. Included in this opening section are subsections discussing the components of a case and how to analyze a case.
• *Analyzing Case Problems*—The student is then given tips on how to analyze case problems using the IRAC method. This method, which was discussed briefly in Chapter 1 of the text, is again described and illustrated by an example showing how the method can be applied.
• *Researching Case Law*—This section looks at primary and secondary sources of case law, the basic steps in the legal research process, how to find cases on point, and the difference between mandatory and persuasive authorities.
• *Online Legal Research*—The booklet also contains a section that indicates how online legal resources can be used in the legal research process. Subsections instruct the student on the nature of the Internet, how to access and navigate the Internet, the types of legal and information resources available online, online research techniques, and some of the best legal resource sites on the Internet. In the final pages of this section, students are shown how to evaluate online resources.
• *Using a Commercial Database: westlaw.com*—We conclude the handbook with a discussion of the Westlaw legal research service. Students are instructed in the types of legal materials available on Westlaw, the browser and editorial enhancements available through Westlaw, and how to perform searches.

Case Analysis Handbook for Instructors

We have also prepared a special handbook, called *Case Analysis Handbook for Instructors,* which is available free to adopters. The handbook includes the following elements:

• *Case Summaries*—Each case in the text is presented here in a summarized form so that instructors can quickly review what issue was addressed in the case and how the court decided the issue.

• *Classroom Case Discussion Questions*—Following each case summary are two brief essay questions with answers. The questions are designed to elicit classroom discussion. The issues addressed in these questions are also the focus of two multiple-choice questions in the *Test Bank* that accompanies this text and two multiple-choice questions in the interactive quizzes on the text's companion Web site at http://wbl-cs.westbuslaw.com.

• *Public Policy Implications*—After the case summary and the sample question/answer sets, we present, when applicable, a section discussing the public policy implications of the case.

Case Printouts

For each case presented in the text, we have included the full printed text of the majority opinion in the *Case Printouts* that accompany *West's Business Law: A Case Study Approach*. The *Case Printouts* can be accessed in electronic form on the *Instructor's Resource CD-ROM* (discussed later in this preface).

Case-Problem Cases

The full texts of all cases used in the chapter-ending *Case Problems* sections of the text are also included on the *Instructor's Resource CD-ROM*.

• Other Key Areas of Emphasis

To provide a framework for the study of case law relating to business topics, *West's Business Law: A Case Study Approach* not only offers comprehensive and authoritative coverage of "black letter" law but also emphasizes significant legal trends in the contemporary world. Throughout the text, we discuss how traditional (and, sometimes, newly enacted) laws apply to online transactions. In addition to a chapter devoted solely to electronic contracts (Chapter 23), this text includes sections discussing Internet law with respect to jurisdictional issues, cyber torts and crimes, intellectual property, banking, electronic agents, online securities offerings, consumer transactions, electronic performance monitoring in the employment context, and other topics.

You will find that this text reflects the most recent developments in other areas of the law as well. For example, to ensure that *West's Business Law: A Case Study Approach* offers the most up-to-date coverage possible, the chapter covering secured transactions (Chapter 28) is based entirely on the revised Article 9. Because all of the states have now adopted the revised version of Article 9, we do not make references to the unrevised Article 9 within this text, nor do we include it in the most current version of the Uniform Commercial Code included at the end of this text as Appendix B. Similarly, the chapter on bankruptcy law (Chapter 30) reflects the current dollar amounts specified in various provisions of the Bankruptcy Code. If the bankruptcy reform bill currently before Congress becomes law, updates will be posted on the text's Web site in the Instructor's Resource section of the site.

• The Companion Web Site

When you visit our Web site at **http://wbl-cs.westbuslaw.com**, you will find, as already mentioned, a collection of cases from the Westlaw database that your students can access to view the full text of every case presented in this text. We also include on the Web site a continually updated set of briefed cases, specifically keyed to each chapter in the text. Other resources on the Web site include the following:

• Internet activities, which include at least one Internet activity for every chapter in the text.
• Interactive quizzes for each chapter in the text, including two questions specifically addressing each case presented in the text.
• Links to other important legal resources available for free on the Web.
• A "Talk to the Authors" feature that allows you to e-mail your questions about the text to the authors.

• A Complete Supplements Package

Numerous supplements make up the complete *West's Business Law: A Case Study Approach* teaching/learning package. We have already mentioned two of them—the *Student's Guide to Case Analysis and Online Research* and the *Case Analysis Handbook for Instructors*—as well as the supplemental teaching/learning materials available on this text's Web site at http://wbl-cs.westbuslaw.com. Other supplements are listed below. For further information on what supplements are available and how to obtain them, contact your local West sales representative. An additional source of information is the Web site for this text.

Printed Supplements

- *Study Guide* (including "Change the Facts" question/answer sets for selected cases presented in the text).
- *Instructor's Manual* (also available on the *Instructor's Resource CD-ROM,* or IRCD).
- *Test Bank* (including essay questions for each chapter and two questions on each case presented in the text; also available on the IRCD).
- *Answers to Case Problems*; (also available on the IRCD).
- *Case Printouts*; (also available on the IRCD).
- *Business Law and the CPA Exam.*
- *Handbook of Landmark Cases and Statutes in Business Law and the Legal Environment.*
- *Handbook on Critical Thinking and Writing in Business Law and the Legal Environment.*
- *A Guide to Personal Law.*
- *Instructor's Manual* for the *Drama of the Law* video series; (also available on the IRCD).

Software, Video, and Multimedia Supplements

- *Instructor's Resource CD-ROM* (IRCD)—Includes the following supplements: Case Analysis Handbook for Instructors, Answers to Case Problems, Case-Problem Cases, Instructor's Manual, Instructor's Manual for the *Drama of the Law,* ExamView, Test Bank, and Case Printouts.
- ExamView Testing Software.
- Web Tutor (on WebCT or Blackboard)—Features chat, discussion groups, testing, student progress tracking, and business law course materials.
- Westlaw.
- Video Library—Including Court TV® and the *Drama of the Law* videos. (For further information on video supplements, go to http://www.westbuslaw.com.)
- InfoTrac® College Edition.

Dedication

We dedicate this book to Clyde Perlee, Jr., who served as an inspiration to us during almost three decades of publishing. He has also honored us with his continuing friendship, for which we remain forever grateful.

R.L.M.

G.A.J.

F.B.C.

UNIT ONE

The Legal Environment of Business

CONTENTS

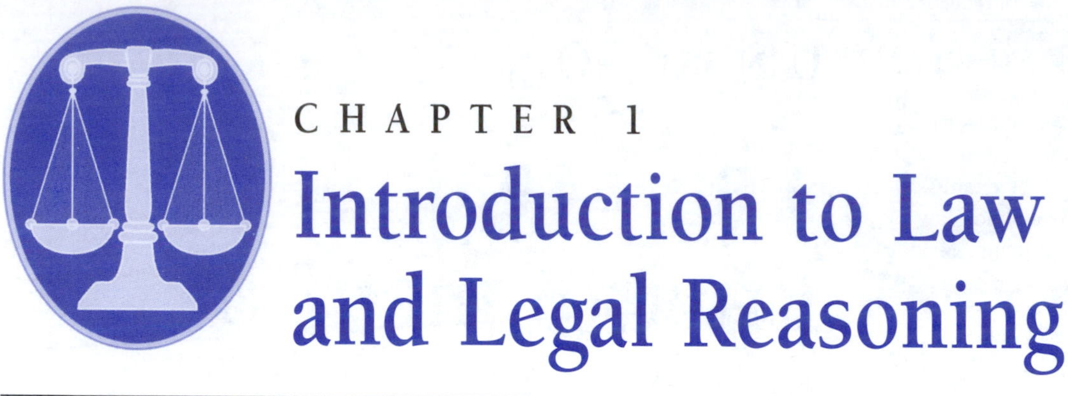

CHAPTER 1

Introduction to Law and Legal Reasoning

One of the important functions of law in any society is to provide stability, predictability, and continuity so that people can be sure of how to order their affairs. If any society is to survive, its citizens must be able to determine what is legally right and legally wrong. They must know what sanctions will be imposed on them if they commit wrongful acts. If they suffer harm as a result of others' wrongful acts, they need to know how they can seek redress. By setting forth the rights, obligations, and privileges of citizens, the law enables individuals to go about their business with confidence and a certain degree of predictability. The stability and predictability created by the law provide an essential framework for all civilized activities, including business activities.

In this introductory chapter, we first look at the nature of law and then examine the foundation and fundamental characteristics of the American legal system. We next describe the basic sources of American law and some general classifications of law. We conclude with sections offering practical guidance on several topics, including how to find the sources of law discussed in this chapter (and referred to throughout the text), how to read and understand court opinions, and why a basic knowledge of the law is important for those who contemplate a career in business.

SECTION 1

What Is Law?

There have been and will continue to be different definitions of law. Although the definitions of law vary in their particulars, they all are based on the general observation that, at a minimum, **law** consists of *enforceable rules governing relationships among individuals and between individuals and their society.* These "enforceable rules" may consist of unwritten principles of behavior established by a nomadic tribe. They may be set forth in a law code, such as the Code of Hammurabi in ancient Babylon or the law code of one of today's European nations. They may consist of written laws and court decisions created by modern legislative and judicial bodies, as in the United States. Regardless of how such rules are created, they all have one thing in common: they establish rights, duties, and privileges that are consistent with the values and beliefs of their society or its ruling group.

While few legal philosophers and scholars would disagree with these general observations about the law, those who embark on a study of law will find that these broad statements leave unanswered some important questions concerning the nature of law. Part of the study of law, often referred to as **jurisprudence**, involves learning about different schools of jurisprudential thought and discovering how the approaches to law characteristic of each school can affect judicial decision making.

Schools of Jurisprudential Thought

You may think that legal philosophy is far removed from the practical study of business law and the legal environment. In fact, it is not. As you will learn in the chapters of this text, how judges apply the law to specific disputes, including disputes relating to the business world, depends in part on their philosophical approaches to law. We look now at some of the significant schools of legal, or jurisprudential, thought that have evolved over time.

The Natural Law School. An age-old question about the nature of law has to do with the finality of a nation's laws, such as the laws of the United States at the present time. For example, what if a particular law is deemed to be a "bad" law by a substantial number of that nation's citizens? Must a citizen obey the law if it goes against his or her conscience to do so? Is there a higher or universal law to which individuals can appeal? One who adheres to the natural law tradition would answer this question in the affirmative. **Natural law** denotes a system of moral and ethical principles that are inherent in human nature and that people can discover through the use of their natural intelligence.

The natural law tradition is one of the oldest and most significant schools of jurisprudence. It dates back to the days of the Greek philosopher Aristotle (384–322 B.C.E.), who distinguished between natural law and the laws governing a particular nation. According to Aristotle, natural law applies universally to all humankind.

The notion that people have "natural rights" stems from the natural law tradition. Those who claim that a specific foreign government is depriving certain citizens of their human rights implicitly are appealing to a higher law that has universal applicability. The question of the universality of basic human rights also comes into play in the context of international business operations. Should rights extended to workers in this country, such as the right to be free of discrimination in the workplace, be applied to a U.S. firm doing business in another country that does not provide for such rights? This question is rooted implicitly in a concept of universal rights that has its origins in the natural law tradition.

The Positivist School. In contrast, **positive law**, or national law (the written law of a given society at a particular point in time), applies only to the citizens of that nation or society. Those who adhere to the **positivist school** believe that there can be no higher law than a nation's positive law. According to the positivist school, there is no such thing as "natural rights." Rather, human rights exist solely because of laws. If the laws are not enforced, anarchy will result. Thus, whether a law is "bad" or "good" is irrelevant. The law is the law and must be obeyed until it is changed—in an orderly manner through a legitimate lawmaking process. A judge with positivist leanings probably would be more inclined to defer to an existing law than would a judge who adheres to the natural law tradition.

The Historical School. The **historical school** of legal thought emphasizes the evolutionary process of law by concentrating on the origin and history of the legal system. Thus, this school looks to the past to discover what the principles of contemporary law should be. The legal doctrines that have withstood the passage of time—those that have worked in the past—are deemed best suited for shaping present laws. Hence, law derives its legitimacy and authority from adhering to the standards that historical development has shown to be workable. Adherents of the historical school are more likely than those of other schools to strictly follow decisions made in past cases.

Legal Realism. In the 1920s and 1930s, a number of jurists and scholars, known as legal realists, rebelled against the historical approach to law. **Legal realism** is based on the idea that law is just one of many institutions in society and that it is shaped by social forces and needs. The law is a human enterprise, and judges should take social and economic realities into account when deciding cases. Legal realists also believe that the law can never be applied with total uniformity. Given that judges are human beings with unique personalities, value systems, and intellects, obviously different judges will bring different reasoning processes to the same case.

Legal realism strongly influenced the growth of what is sometimes called the **sociological school** of jurisprudence. This school views law as a tool for promoting justice in society. In the 1960s, for example, the justices of the United States Supreme Court played a leading role in the civil rights movement by upholding long-neglected laws calling for equal treatment for all Americans, including African Americans and other minorities. Generally, jurists who adhere to the sociological school are more likely to depart from past decisions than are those jurists who adhere to the other schools of legal thought.

Judicial Interpretation of the Law

Because of our common law tradition (which will be discussed shortly), the courts—and thus the personal views and philosophies of judges—play a paramount role in the American legal system. This is particularly true of the United States Supreme Court, which has the final say on how a particular law or legal principle should be interpreted and applied. Indeed, Oliver Wendell Holmes, Jr., once stated that law was a set of rules that allowed one to predict how a court would resolve a particular dispute—"the prophecies [predictions] of what the courts will do in fact, and nothing more pretentious, are what I mean by the law."

Clearly, judges are not free to decide cases solely on the basis of their personal philosophical views or their opinions on the issues before the court. A judge's function is not to make the laws—that is the function of the legislative branch of government—but to interpret and apply them. From a practical point of view, however, the courts play a significant role in defining what the law is. This is because laws enacted by legislative bodies tend to be expressed in general terms. Judges thus have some flexibility in interpreting and applying the law. It is because of this flexibility that different courts can, and often do, arrive at different conclusions in cases that involve nearly identical issues, facts, and applicable laws. This flexibility also means that each judge's unique personality, legal philosophy, set of values, and intellectual attributes necessarily frame the judicial decision-making process to some extent.

SECTION 2

The Common Law Tradition

Because of our colonial heritage, much of American law is based on the English legal system, which originated in medieval England and continued to evolve in the following centuries. A knowledge of this system is necessary to an understanding of the American legal system today.

EARLY ENGLISH COURTS

The origins of the English legal system—and thus the U.S. legal system as well—date back to 1066, when the Normans conquered England. William the Conqueror and his successors began the process of unifying the country under their rule. One of the means they used to this end was the establishment of the king's courts, or *curiae regis*. Before the Norman Conquest, disputes had been settled according to the local legal customs and traditions in various regions of the country. The king's courts sought to establish a uniform set of customs for the country as a whole. What evolved in these courts was the beginning of the **common law**—a body of general rules that prescribed social conduct and applied throughout the entire English realm.

Courts of Law and Remedies at Law.

In the early English king's courts, the kinds of **remedies** (the legal means to recover a right or redress a wrong) that could be granted were severely restricted. If one person wronged another in some way, the king's courts could award as compensation one or more of the following: (1) land, (2) items of value, or (3) money. The courts that awarded this compensation became known as **courts of law**, and the three remedies were called **remedies at law**. (Today, the remedy at law normally takes the form of money **damages**—money given to a party whose legal interests have been injured.) Even though the system introduced uniformity in the settling of disputes, when a complaining party wanted a remedy other than economic compensation, the courts of law could do nothing, so "no remedy, no right."

Courts of Equity and Remedies in Equity.

Equity is a branch of law, founded on what might be described as notions of justice and fair dealing, that seeks to supply a remedy when no adequate remedy at law is available. When individuals could not obtain an adequate remedy in a court of law because of strict technicalities, they petitioned the king for relief. Most of these petitions were decided by an adviser to the king, called a **chancellor**, who was said to be the "keeper of the king's conscience." When the chancellor thought that the claims were fair, new and unique remedies were granted. Eventually, formal chancery courts, or **courts of equity**, were established.

The remedies granted by equity courts became known as **remedies in equity**, or equitable remedies. These remedies include *specific performance* (ordering a party to perform an agreement as promised), an *injunction* (ordering a party to cease engaging in a specific activity or to undo some wrong or injury), and *rescission* (the cancellation of a contractual obligation). We discuss these and other equitable remedies in more detail at appropriate points in the chapters that follow. As a general rule, today's courts, like the early English courts, will not grant equitable remedies unless the remedy at law—money damages—is inadequate.

In fashioning appropriate remedies, judges often were (and continue to be) guided by so-called **equitable maxims**—propositions or general statements of equitable rules. Exhibit 1–1 lists some important equitable maxims. The last maxim listed in that exhibit—"Equity aids the vigilant,

EXHIBIT 1–1 EQUITABLE MAXIMS

1. *Whoever seeks equity must do equity.* (Anyone who wishes to be treated fairly must treat others fairly.)
2. *Where there is equal equity, the law must prevail.* (The law will determine the outcome of a controversy in which the merits of both sides are equal.)
3. *One seeking the aid of an equity court must come to the court with clean hands.* (Plaintiffs must have acted fairly and honestly.)
4. *Equity will not suffer a wrong to be without a remedy.* (Equitable relief will be awarded when there is a right to relief and there is no adequate remedy at law.)
5. *Equity regards substance rather than form.* (Equity is more concerned with fairness and justice than with legal technicalities.)
6. *Equity aids the vigilant, not those who rest on their rights.* (Equity will not help those who neglect their rights for an unreasonable period of time.)

not those who rest on their rights"—merits special attention. It has become known as the equitable doctrine of **laches** (a term derived from the Latin *laxus*, meaning "lax" or "negligent"), and it can be used as a defense. A **defense** is an argument raised by the **defendant** (the party being sued) indicating why the **plaintiff** (the suing party) should not obtain the remedy sought. (Note that in equity proceedings, the party bringing a lawsuit is called the **petitioner**, and the party being sued is referred to as the **respondent**.)

The doctrine of laches arose to encourage people to bring lawsuits while the evidence was fresh. What constitutes a reasonable time, of course, varies according to the circumstances of the case. Time periods for different types of cases are now usually fixed by **statutes of limitations.** After the time allowed under a statute of limitations has expired, no action can be brought, no matter how strong the case was originally.

LEGAL AND EQUITABLE REMEDIES TODAY

The establishment of courts of equity in medieval England resulted in two distinct court systems: courts of law and courts of equity. The systems had different sets of judges and granted different types of remedies. Parties who sought legal remedies, or remedies at law, would bring their claims before courts of law. Parties seeking equitable relief, or remedies in equity, would bring their claims before courts of equity. During the nineteenth century, however, most states in the United States adopted rules of procedure that resulted in combined courts of law and equity—although some states, such as Arkansas, still retain the distinction. A party now may request both legal and equitable remedies in the same action, and the trial court judge may grant either or both forms of relief.

The distinction between legal and equitable remedies remains relevant to students of business law, however, because these remedies differ. To seek the proper remedy for a wrong, one must know what remedies are available. Additionally, certain vestiges of the procedures used when there were separate courts of law and equity still exist. For example, a party has the right to demand a jury trial in an action at law, but not in an action in equity. In the old courts of equity, the chancellor heard both sides of an issue and decided what should be done. Juries were considered inappropriate. In actions at law, however, juries participated in determining the outcome of cases, including the amount of damages to be awarded. Exhibit 1–2 summarizes the procedural differences (applicable in most states) between an action at law and an action in equity.

THE DOCTRINE OF *STARE DECISIS*

One of the unique features of the common law is that it is *judge-made* law. The body of principles and

EXHIBIT 1–2 PROCEDURAL DIFFERENCES BETWEEN AN ACTION AT LAW AND AN ACTION IN EQUITY

PROCEDURE	ACTION AT LAW	ACTION IN EQUITY
Initiation of lawsuit	By filing a complaint	By filing a petition
Parties	Plaintiff and defendant	Petitioner and respondent
Decision	By jury or judge	By judge (no jury)
Result	Judgment	Decree
Remedy	Monetary damages	Injunction, specific performance, or rescission

doctrines that form the common law emerged over time as judges decided actual legal controversies.

Case Precedents and Case Reporters. When possible, judges attempted to be consistent and to base their decisions on the principles suggested by earlier cases. They sought to decide similar cases in a similar way and considered new cases with care, because they knew that their decisions would make new law. Each interpretation became part of the law on the subject and served as a legal **precedent**—that is, a decision that furnished an example or authority for deciding subsequent cases involving similar legal principles or facts.

By the early fourteenth century, portions of the most important decisions of each year were being gathered together and recorded in *Year Books,* which became useful references for lawyers and judges. In the sixteenth century, the *Year Books* were discontinued, and other forms of case publication became available. Today, cases are published, or "reported," in volumes called **reporters**, or *reports*. We describe today's case reporting system in detail later in this chapter.

Stare Decisis* and the Common Law Tradition.** The practice of deciding new cases with reference to former decisions, or precedents, became a cornerstone of the English and American judicial systems. The practice forms a doctrine called ***stare decisis[1] (a Latin phrase meaning "to stand on decided cases"). Under this doctrine, judges are obligated to follow the precedents established within their jurisdictions (areas over which they have the power to apply the law—see Chapter 2).

For example, suppose that the lower state courts in California have reached conflicting conclusions on whether drivers are liable for accidents they cause while merging into freeway traffic, even though the drivers looked and did not see any oncoming traffic and even though witnesses (passengers in their cars) testified to that effect. To settle the law on this issue, the California Supreme Court decides to review a case involving this fact pattern. The court rules that in such a situation, the driver who is merging into traffic is liable for any accidents caused by the driver's failure to yield to freeway traffic—regardless of whether the driver looked carefully and did not see an approaching vehicle.

The California Supreme Court's decision on this matter will influence the outcome of all future cases on this issue brought before the California state courts. Similarly, a decision on a given question by the United States Supreme Court (the nation's highest court) is binding on all courts. Case precedents, as well as statutes and other laws that must be followed, are referred to as **binding authorities.** (Nonbinding legal authorities on which judges may rely for guidance, such as precedents established in other jurisdictions, are referred to as *persuasive authorities.*)

The doctrine of *stare decisis* helps the courts to be more efficient, because if other courts have carefully analyzed a similar case, their legal reasoning and opinions can serve as guides. *Stare decisis* also makes the law more stable and predictable. If the law on a given subject is well settled, someone bringing a case to court can usually rely on the court to make a decision based on what the law has been in the past.

Departures from Precedent. Although courts are obligated to follow precedents, sometimes a court will depart from the rule of precedent if it decides that the precedent should no longer be followed. If a court decides that a ruling precedent is simply incorrect or that technological or social changes have rendered the precedent inapplicable, the court might rule contrary to the precedent. Cases that overturn precedent often receive a great deal of publicity.[2]

Note that judges have some flexibility in applying precedents. For example, a trial court may avoid applying a Supreme Court precedent by arguing that the facts of the case before the court are distinguishable from the facts in the Supreme Court case. Therefore, the Supreme Court's ruling on the issue does not apply to the case before the court.

When There Is No Precedent. Occasionally, cases come before the courts for which no precedents exist. Such cases, called *cases of first impression*, often result when new practices or technological developments in society create new types of legal disputes. In

1. Pronounced *ster*-ay dih-*si*-ses.

2. For example, when the United States Supreme Court held in the 1950s that racial segregation in the public schools was unconstitutional, it expressly overturned a Supreme Court precedent upholding the constitutionality of "separate-but-equal" segregation. The Supreme Court's departure from precedent received a tremendous amount of publicity as people began to realize the ramifications of this change in the law. See *Brown v. Board of Education of Topeka,* 347 U.S. 483, 74 S.Ct. 6896, 98 L.Ed. 873 (1954). (Legal citations are explained later in this chapter.)

the last several years, for example, the courts have had to deal with disputes involving transactions conducted via the Internet. When existing laws governing free speech, pornography, fraud, jurisdiction, and other areas were drafted, cyberspace did not exist. Although new laws are being created to govern such disputes, in the meantime the courts have to decide, on a case-by-case basis, what rules should be applied.

Generally, in deciding cases of first impression, courts may consider a number of factors, including persuasive authorities (such as cases from other jurisdictions, if there are any), legal principles and policies underlying previous court decisions or existing statutes, fairness, social values and customs, **public policy** (governmental policy based on widely held societal values), and data and concepts drawn from the social sciences. Which of these sources is chosen or receives the greatest emphasis depends on the nature of the case being considered and the particular judge or judges hearing the case. As mentioned previously, judges are not free to decide cases on the basis of their own personal views. In cases of first impression, as in all cases, judges must have legal reasons for ruling as they do on particular issues. When a court issues a written opinion on a case (we discuss court opinions later in this chapter), the opinion normally contains a carefully reasoned argument justifying the decision.

STARE DECISIS AND LEGAL REASONING

Legal reasoning is the reasoning process used by judges in deciding what law applies to a given dispute and then applying that law to the specific facts or circumstances of the case. Through the use of legal reasoning, judges harmonize their decisions with those that have been made before—which the doctrine of *stare decisis* requires.

Students of business law also engage in legal reasoning. For example, you may be asked to provide answers for some of the case problems that appear at the end of every chapter in this text. Each problem describes the facts of a particular dispute and the legal question at issue. If you are assigned a case problem, you will be asked to determine how a court would answer that question and why. In other words, you will need to give legal reasons for whatever conclusion you reach. We look here at the basic steps involved in legal reasoning and then describe some forms of reasoning commonly used by the courts in making their decisions.

Basic Steps in Legal Reasoning. At times, the legal arguments set forth in court opinions are relatively simple and brief. At other times, the arguments are complex and lengthy. Regardless of the brevity or length of a legal argument, however, the basic steps of the legal reasoning process remain the same in all cases. These steps, which you also can follow when analyzing cases and case problems, form what is commonly referred to as the *IRAC method* of legal reasoning. IRAC is an acronym comprising the first letters of the following words: Issue, Rule, Application, and Conclusion. To apply the IRAC method, you would ask the following questions:

1. *What are the key facts and issues?* For example, suppose that a plaintiff comes before the court claiming *assault* (a wrongful and intentional action, or tort, in which one person makes another fearful of immediate physical harm). The plaintiff claims that the defendant threatened her while she was sleeping. Although the plaintiff was unaware that she was being threatened, her roommate heard the defendant make the threat. The legal issue, or question, raised by these facts is whether the defendant's actions constitute the tort of assault, given that the plaintiff was not aware of those actions at the time they occurred.
2. *What rules of law apply to the case?* A rule of law may be a rule stated by the courts in previous decisions, a state or federal statute, or a state or federal administrative agency regulation. In our hypothetical case, the plaintiff **alleges** (claims) that the defendant committed a tort. Therefore, the applicable law is the common law of torts—specifically, tort law governing assault (see Chapter 5 for more detail on torts). Case precedents involving similar facts and issues thus would be relevant. Often, more than one rule of law will be applicable to a case.
3. *How do the rules of law apply to the particular facts and circumstances of this case?* This step is often the most difficult one, because each case presents a unique set of facts, circumstances, and parties. Although there may be similar cases, no two cases are ever identical in all respects. Normally, judges (and lawyers and law students) try to find **cases on point**—previously decided cases that are as similar as possible to the one under consideration. (Because of the difficulty—and importance—of this step in the legal reasoning process, we discuss it in more detail in the next subsection.)
4. *What conclusion should be drawn?* This step normally presents few problems. Usually, the conclusion

is evident if the previous three steps have been followed carefully.

Forms of Legal Reasoning. Judges use many types of reasoning when following the third step of the legal reasoning process—applying the law to the facts of a particular case. Three common forms of reasoning are deductive reasoning, linear reasoning, and reasoning by analogy.

Deductive Reasoning. Deductive reasoning is sometimes called syllogistic reasoning because it employs a **syllogism**—a logical relationship involving a major premise, a minor premise, and a conclusion. For example, consider the hypothetical case presented earlier, in which the plaintiff alleged that the defendant committed assault by threatening her while she was sleeping. The judge might point out that "under the common law of torts, an individual must be *aware* of a threat of danger for the threat to constitute civil assault" (major premise); "the plaintiff in this case was unaware of the threat at the time it occurred" (minor premise); and "therefore, the circumstances do not amount to a civil assault" (conclusion).

Linear Reasoning. A second important form of legal reasoning that is commonly employed might be thought of as "linear" reasoning, because it proceeds from one point to another, with the final point being the conclusion. An analogy will help make this form of reasoning clear. Imagine a knotted rope, with each knot tying together separate pieces of rope to form a tight length. As a whole, the rope represents a linear progression of thought logically connecting various points, with the last point, or knot, representing the conclusion. For example, suppose that a tenant in an apartment building sues the landlord for damages for an injury resulting from an allegedly dimly lit stairway. The court may engage in a reasoning process involving the following "pieces of rope":

1. The landlord, who was on the premises the evening the injury occurred, testifies that none of the other nine tenants who used the stairway that night complained about the lights.
2. The fact that none of the tenants complained is the same as if they had said the lighting was sufficient.
3. That there were no complaints does not prove that the lighting was sufficient but proves that the landlord had no reason to believe that it was not.
4. The landlord's belief was reasonable, because no one complained.
5. Therefore, the landlord acted reasonably and was not negligent in respect to the lighting in the stairway.

On the basis of this reasoning, the court concludes that the tenant is not entitled to compensation on the basis of the stairway's lighting.

Reasoning by Analogy. Another important type of reasoning that judges use in deciding cases is reasoning by *analogy.* To reason by **analogy** is to compare the facts in the case at hand to the facts in other cases and, to the extent that the patterns are similar, to apply the same rule of law to the present case. To the extent that the facts are unique, or "distinguishable," different rules may apply. For example, in case A, it is held that a driver who crosses a highway's center line is negligent. In case B, a driver crosses the line to avoid hitting a child. In determining whether case A's rule applies in case B, a judge would consider what the reasons were for the decision in A and whether B is sufficiently similar for those reasons to apply. If the judge holds that B's driver is not liable, that judge must indicate why case A's rule does not apply to the facts presented in case B.

There Is No One "Right" Answer

Many persons believe that there is one "right" answer to every legal question. In most situations involving a legal controversy, however, there is no single correct result. Good arguments can often be made to support either side of a legal controversy. Quite often, a case does not present the situation of a "good" person suing a "bad" person. In many cases, both parties have acted in good faith in some measure or have acted in bad faith to some degree.

Additionally, as already mentioned, each judge has his or her own personal beliefs and philosophy, which shape, at least to some extent, the process of legal reasoning. What this means is that the outcome of a particular lawsuit before a court can never be predicted with absolute certainty. In fact, in some cases, even though the weight of the law would seem to favor one party's position, judges, through creative legal reasoning, have found ways to rule in favor of the other party in the interests of preventing injustice.

SECTION 3

Sources of American Law

There are numerous sources of American law. *Primary sources of law,* or sources that establish the law, include the following:

1. The U.S. Constitution and the constitutions of the various states.
2. Statutory law—including laws passed by Congress, state legislatures, or local governing bodies.
3. Regulations created by administrative agencies, such as the Food and Drug Administration.
4. Case law and common law doctrines.

We describe each of these important sources of law in the following pages.

Secondary sources of law are books and articles that summarize and clarify the primary sources of law. Examples are legal encyclopedias, treatises, articles in law reviews, and compilations of law, such as the *Restatements of the Law* (which will be discussed shortly). Courts often refer to secondary sources of law for guidance in interpreting and applying the primary sources of law discussed here.

CONSTITUTIONAL LAW

The federal government and the states have separate written constitutions that set forth the general organization, powers, and limits of their respective governments. **Constitutional law** is the law as expressed in these constitutions.

According to Article VI of the U.S. Constitution, the Constitution is the supreme law of the land. As such, it is the basis of all law in the United States. A law in violation of the Constitution, if challenged, will be declared unconstitutional and will not be enforced, no matter what its source. Because of its importance in the American legal system, we present the complete text of the U.S. Constitution in Appendix A.

The Tenth Amendment to the U.S. Constitution reserves all powers not granted to the federal government to the states. Each state in the union has its own constitution. Unless it conflicts with the U.S. Constitution or a federal law, a state constitution is supreme within the state's borders.

STATUTORY LAW

Laws enacted by legislative bodies at any level of government, such as the statutes passed by Congress or by state legislatures, make up the body of law generally referred to as **statutory law.** When a legislature passes a statute, that statute ultimately is included in the federal code of laws or the relevant state code of laws (these codes are discussed later in this chapter).

Statutory law also includes local **ordinances**—statutes (laws, rules, or orders) passed by municipal or county governing units to govern matters not covered by federal or state law. Ordinances commonly have to do with city or county land use (zoning ordinances), building and safety codes, and other matters affecting the local unit.

A federal statute, of course, applies to all states. A state statute, in contrast, applies only within the state's borders. State laws thus may vary from state to state. No federal statute may violate the U.S. Constitution, and no state statute or local ordinance may violate the U.S. Constitution or the relevant state constitution.

Uniform Laws.

The differences among state laws were particularly notable in the 1800s, when conflicting state statutes frequently made trade and commerce among the states very difficult. To counter these problems, in 1892 a group of legal scholars and lawyers formed the National Conference of Commissioners on Uniform State Laws (NCCUSL) to draft **uniform laws,** or model laws, for the states to consider adopting. The NCCUSL still exists today and continues to issue uniform laws.

Each state has the option of adopting or rejecting a uniform law. *Only if a state legislature adopts a uniform law does that law become part of the statutory law of that state.* Note that a state legislature may adopt all or part of a uniform law as it is written, or the legislature may rewrite the law however the legislature wishes. Hence, even when a uniform law is said to have been adopted in many states, those states' laws may not be entirely "uniform."

The earliest uniform law, the Uniform Negotiable Instruments Law, had been completed by 1896 and adopted in every state by the early 1920s (although not all states used exactly the same wording). Over the following decades, other acts were drawn up in a similar manner. In all, over two hundred uniform acts have been issued by the NCCUSL since its inception. The most ambitious uniform act of all, however, was the Uniform Commercial Code.

The Uniform Commercial Code. The Uniform Commercial Code (UCC), which was created through the joint efforts of the NCCUSL and the American Law Institute,[4] was first issued in 1952. The UCC has been adopted in all fifty states,[5] the District of Columbia, and the Virgin Islands. The UCC facilitates commerce among the states by providing a uniform, yet flexible, set of rules governing commercial transactions. The UCC assures businesspersons that their contracts, if validly entered into, normally will be enforced.

As you will read in later chapters, from time to time the NCCUSL revises the articles contained in the UCC and submits the revised versions to the states for adoption. During the 1990s, for example, four articles were revised (Articles 3, 4, 5, and 9). Additionally, new articles were added (Articles 2A and 4A). Because of its importance in the area of commercial law, we cite the UCC frequently in this text. We also present the UCC in its entirety in Appendix B.

ADMINISTRATIVE LAW

An important source of American law is **administrative law**—which consists of the rules, orders, and decisions of administrative agencies. An **administrative agency** is a federal, state, or local government agency established to perform a specific function. Administrative law and procedures, which will be examined in detail in Chapter 43, constitute a dominant element in the regulatory environment of business. Rules issued by various administrative agencies now affect virtually every aspect of a business's operation, including the firm's capital structure and financing, its hiring and firing procedures, its relations with employees and unions, and the way it manufactures and markets its products.

At the national level, numerous **executive agencies** exist within the cabinet departments of the executive branch. The Food and Drug Administration, for example, is an agency within the Department of Health and Human Services. Executive agencies are subject to the authority of the president, who has the power to appoint and remove officers of federal agencies. There are also major **independent regulatory agencies** at the federal level, such as the Federal Trade Commission, the Securities and Exchange Commission, and the Federal Communications Commission. The president's power is less pronounced in regard to independent agencies, the officers of which serve for fixed terms and cannot be removed without just cause.

There are administrative agencies at the state and local levels as well. Commonly, a state agency (such as a state pollution-control agency) is created as a parallel to a federal administrative agency (such as the Environmental Protection Agency). Just as federal statutes take precedence over conflicting state statutes, so federal agency regulations take precedence over conflicting state regulations.

CASE LAW AND COMMON LAW DOCTRINES

As is evident from the earlier discussion of the common law tradition, another basic source of American law comprises the rules of law announced in court decisions. These rules of law include interpretations of constitutional provisions, of statutes enacted by legislatures, and of regulations created by administrative agencies. Today, this body of law is referred to variously as the common law, judge-made law, or **case law.**

The Relationship between the Common Law and Statutory Law. Common law doctrines and principles govern all areas not covered by statutory or administrative law. In a dispute concerning a particular employment practice, for example, if a statute regulates that practice, the statute will apply rather than the common law doctrine that applied prior to the enactment of the statute.

Even though the body of statutory law has expanded greatly since the beginning of this nation, thus narrowing the applicability of common law doctrines, there is a significant overlap between statutory law and the common law. For example, many statutes essentially codify existing common law rules, and thus the courts, in interpreting the statutes, often rely on the common law as a guide to what the legislators intended.

Additionally, how the courts interpret a particular statute determines how that statute will be applied. If you wanted to learn about the coverage and applicability of a particular statute, for example, you would, of course, need to locate the statute and study it. You would also need to see how the courts

4. This institute was formed in the 1920s and consists of practicing attorneys, legal scholars, and judges.

5. Louisiana has not adopted Articles 2 and 2A (covering contracts for the sale and lease of goods), however.

in your jurisdiction have interpreted the statute—in other words, what precedents have been established in regard to that statute. Often, the applicability of a newly enacted statute does not become clear until a body of case law develops to clarify how, when, and to whom the statute applies.

Restatements of the Law. The American Law Institute (ALI) has drafted and published compilations of the common law called *Restatements of the Law,* which generally summarize the common law rules followed by most states. There are *Restatements of the Law* in the areas of contracts, torts, agency, trusts, property, restitution, security, judgments, and conflict of laws. The *Restatements,* like other secondary sources of law, do not in themselves have the force of law but are an important source of legal analysis and opinion on which judges often rely in making their decisions.

Many of the *Restatements* are now in their second or third editions. For example, as you will read in Chapter 6, the ALI has recently published the first volume of the third edition of the *Restatement of the Law of Torts.* We refer to the *Restatements* frequently in subsequent chapters of this text, indicating in parentheses the edition to which we are referring. For example, we refer to the second edition of the *Restatement of the Law of Contracts* simply as the *Restatement (Second) of Contracts.*

SECTION 4

Classifications of Law

Because the body of law is so large, one must break it down by some means of classification. A number of classification systems have been devised. For example, one classification system divides law into substantive law and procedural law. **Substantive law** consists of all laws that define, describe, regulate, and create legal rights and obligations. **Procedural law** consists of all laws that establish the methods of enforcing the rights established by substantive law.

Another classification system divides law into civil law and criminal law. **Civil law** is concerned with the duties that exist between persons or between citizens and their governments, excluding the duty not to commit crimes. Typically, in a civil case, a private party sues another private party (although the government can also sue a party for a civil law violation) to make that other party comply with a duty or pay for the damage caused by failure to comply with a duty. Much of the law that we discuss in this text is civil law. Contract law, for example, covered in Chapters 9 through 17, is civil law. The whole body of tort law (see Chapters 5 and 6) is civil law.

Criminal law, in contrast, is concerned with wrongs committed *against the public as a whole.* Criminal acts are defined and prohibited by local, state, or federal government statutes and prosecuted by public officials, such as a district attorney (D.A.), on behalf of the state, not by their victims or other private parties. (See Chapter 8 for a further discussion of the distinction between civil law and criminal law.)

Other classification systems divide law into federal law and state law, private law (dealing with relationships between private entities) and public law (addressing the relationship between persons and their governments), national law and international law, and so on.

SECTION 5

Cyberlaw

Increasingly, traditional laws are being applied to new legal issues stemming from the use of the Internet to conduct business transactions. Additionally, new laws are being created to deal specifically with such issues. Frequently, people use the term **cyberlaw** to designate the emerging body of law (consisting of court decisions, newly enacted or amended statutes, and so on) that governs cyberspace transactions. Note that *cyberlaw* is not really a classification of law; rather, it is an informal term used to describe how traditional classifications of law, such as civil law and criminal law, are being applied to online activities.

Realize, too, that cyberlaw is not a new *type* of law. For the most part, it consists of traditional legal principles that have been modified and adapted to fit situations that are unique to the online world. Of course, in some areas new statutes have been enacted, at both the federal and state levels, to cover specific types of problems stemming from online communications.

Anyone preparing to enter today's business world will find it useful to know how old and new laws are being applied to activities conducted online, such as advertising, contracting, banking, filing documents with the courts or government agencies, employment relations, and a variety of other transactions. For that reason, many sections in this text are devoted to this topic.

SECTION 6

How to Find Primary Sources of Law

This text includes numerous citations to primary sources of law—federal and state statutes, regulations issued by administrative agencies, and court cases. (A **citation** is a reference to a publication in which a legal authority—such as a statute or a court decision or other source—can be found.) In this section, we explain how you can use citations to find primary sources of law.

FINDING STATUTORY LAW

When Congress passes laws, they are collected in a publication titled *United States Statutes at Large*. When state legislatures pass laws, they are collected in similar state publications. Most frequently, however, laws are referred to in their codified form—that is, the form in which they appear in the federal and state codes.

In these codes, laws are compiled by subject. The *United States Code* (U.S.C.) arranges all existing federal laws of a public and permanent nature by subject. Each of the fifty subjects into which the U.S.C. arranges the laws is given a title and a title number. For example, laws relating to commerce and trade are collected in Title 15, "Commerce and Trade." Titles are subdivided by sections. A citation to the U.S.C. includes title and section numbers. Thus, a reference to "15 U.S.C. Section 1" means that the statute can be found in Section 1 of Title 15. ("Section" may also be designated by the symbol §, and "Sections," by §§.) Sometimes a citation includes the abbreviation *et seq.*, as in "15 U.S.C. Sections 1 *et seq.*" The term is an abbreviated form of *et sequitur*, which in Latin means "and the following"; when used in a citation, it refers to sections that concern the same subject as the numbered section and follow it in sequence.

State codes follow the U.S.C. pattern of arranging law by subject. They may be called codes, revisions, compilations, consolidations, general statutes, or statutes, depending on the preferences of the states. In some codes, subjects are designated by number. In others, they are designated by name. For example, "13 Pennsylvania Consolidated Statutes Section 1101" means that the statute can be found in Title 13, Section 1101, of the Pennsylvania code. "California Commercial Code Section 1101" means the statute can be found under the subject heading "Commercial Code" of the California code in Section 1101. Abbreviations may be used. For example, "13 Pennsylvania Consolidated Statutes Section 1101" may be abbreviated "13 Pa. C.S. §1101," and "California Commercial Code Section 1101" may be abbreviated "Cal. Com. Code §1101."

Commercial publications of these laws and regulations are available and are widely used. For example, West Group publishes the *United States Code Annotated* (U.S.C.A.). The U.S.C.A. contains the complete text of laws included in the U.S.C., plus notes on court decisions that interpret and apply specific sections of the statutes, as well as the text of presidential proclamations and executive orders. The U.S.C.A. also includes research aids, such as cross-references to related statutes, historical notes, and library references. A citation to the U.S.C.A. is similar to a citation to the U.S.C.: "15 U.S.C.A. Section 1."

FINDING ADMINISTRATIVE LAW

Rules and regulations adopted by federal administrative agencies are initially published in the *Federal Register*, a daily publication of the U.S. government. Later, they are incorporated into the *Code of Federal Regulations* (C.F.R.). Like the U.S.C., the C.F.R. is divided into fifty titles. Rules within each title are assigned section numbers. A full citation to the C.F.R. includes title and section numbers. For example, a reference to "17 C.F.R. Section 230.504" means that the rule can be found in Section 230.504 of Title 17.

FINDING CASE LAW

To understand how to read citations to court cases, we need first to look briefly at the court system. As will be discussed in Chapter 2, there are two types of courts in the United States, federal courts and state courts. Both the federal and state court systems consist of several levels, or tiers, of courts.

Trial courts, in which evidence is presented and testimony given, are on the bottom tier (which also includes lower courts handling specialized issues). Decisions from a trial court can be appealed to a higher court, commonly an intermediate *court of appeals*, or an *appellate court*. Decisions from these intermediate courts of appeals may be appealed to an even higher court, such as a state supreme court or the United States Supreme Court.

When reading the cases presented in this text, you will note that most of the state court cases are from state appellate courts. This is because most state trial court opinions are not published. Except in New York and a few other states that publish selected opinions of their trial courts, decisions from the state trial courts are merely filed in the office of the clerk of the court, where they are available for public inspection. Many of the federal trial (district) courts do publish their opinions, however, and you will find that several of the cases set forth in this book are from these courts, as well as the federal appellate courts.

State Court Decisions. Written decisions of the state appellate, or reviewing, courts are published and distributed in volumes called *Reports,* which are numbered consecutively.

State Reporters. Decisions of the appellate courts of a particular state are found in the reporters of that state. A few states—including those with intermediate appellate courts, such as California, Illinois, and New York—have more than one reporter for opinions given by their courts.

Additionally, state court opinions appear in regional units of the National Reporter System, published by West Group. Most lawyers and libraries have the West reporters because they report cases more quickly, and are distributed more widely, than the state-published reporters. In fact, many states have eliminated their own reporters in favor of West's National Reporter System. The National Reporter System divides the states into the following geographical areas: *Atlantic* (A. or A.2d), *South Eastern* (S.E. or S.E.2d), *South Western* (S.W., S.W.2d, or S.W.3d), *North Western* (N.W. or N.W.2d), *North Eastern* (N.E. or N.E.2d), *Southern* (So. or So.2d), and *Pacific* (P., P.2d, or P.3d). (The *2d* and *3d* in the preceding abbreviations refer to *Second Series* and *Third Series,* respectively.) The states included in each of these regional divisions are indicated in Exhibit 1–3 on page 14, which illustrates West's National Reporter System.

Case Citations. After an appellate decision has been published, it is normally referred to (cited) by the name of the case (called the *style* of the case); the volume, name, and page of the state's official reporter (if different from West's National Reporter System); the volume, unit, and page number of the National Reporter; and the volume, name, and page number of any other selected reporter. (Citing a reporter by volume number, name, and page number, in that order, is common to all citations; often, as in this book, the year the decision was made will be included in parentheses, just following the citations to reporters.) When more than one reporter is cited for the same case, each reference is called a *parallel citation.*[6]

For example, consider the following case citation: *Crews v. Hollenbach,* 126 Md.App. 609, 730 A.2d 742 (1999). We see that the opinion in this case may be found in Volume 126 of the official *Maryland Appellate Reports,* on page 609. The parallel citation is to Volume 730 of the *Atlantic Reporter, Second Series,* page 742. In reprinting appellate opinions in this text, in addition to the reporter, we give the name of the court hearing the case and the year of the court's decision.

Sample citations to state court decisions are explained in Exhibit 1–4, starting on page 16.

Federal Court Decisions. Federal district (trial) court decisions are published unofficially in West's *Federal Supplement* (F.Supp. or F.Supp.2d), and opinions from the circuit courts of appeals are reported unofficially in West's *Federal Reporter* (F., F.2d, or F.3d). Cases concerning federal bankruptcy law are published unofficially in West's *Bankruptcy Reporter* (Bankr.).

The official edition of all decisions of the United States Supreme Court for which there are written opinions is the *United States Reports* (U.S.), which is published by the federal government. The series includes reports of Supreme Court cases dating from the August term of 1791, although many of the Supreme Court's decisions were not reported in the early volumes.

Unofficial editions of Supreme Court cases include West's *Supreme Court Reporter* (S.Ct.), which includes cases dating from the Court's term in October 1882; and the *Lawyers' Edition of the Supreme Court Reports* (L.Ed. or L.Ed.2d), published by the Lawyers Cooperative Publishing Company

6. Note that Wisconsin has adopted a "public domain citation system" in which the format is somewhat different. For example, a Wisconsin Supreme Court decision might be designated "2002 WI 40," meaning that the case was decided in the year 2002 by the Wisconsin Supreme Court and was the fortieth decision issued by that court during that year. (Parallel citations to the *Wisconsin Reports* and West's *North Western Reporter* are still required when citing Wisconsin cases, but they must follow the public domain citation.)

EXHIBIT 1–3 NATIONAL REPORTER SYSTEM—REGIONAL/FEDERAL

Regional Reporters	Coverage Beginning	Coverage
Atlantic Reporter (A. or A.2d)	1885	Connecticut, Delaware, Maine, Maryland, New Hampshire, New Jersey, Pennsylvania, Rhode Island, Vermont, and District of Columbia.
North Eastern Reporter (N.E. or N.E.2d)	1885	Illinois, Indiana, Massachusetts, New York, and Ohio.
North Western Reporter (N.W. or N.W.2d)	1879	Iowa, Michigan, Minnesota, Nebraska, North Dakota, South Dakota, and Wisconsin.
Pacific Reporter (P., P.2d, or P.3d)	1883	Alaska, Arizona, California, Colorado, Hawaii, Idaho, Kansas, Montana, Nevada, New Mexico, Oklahoma, Oregon, Utah, Washington, and Wyoming.
South Eastern Reporter (S.E. or S.E.2d)	1887	Georgia, North Carolina, South Carolina, Virginia, and West Virginia.
South Western Reporter (S.W., S.W.2d, or S.W.3d)	1886	Arkansas, Kentucky, Missouri, Tennessee, and Texas.
Southern Reporter (So. or So.2d)	1887	Alabama, Florida, Louisiana, and Mississippi.
Federal Reporters		
Federal Reporter (F., F.2d, or F.3d)	1880	U.S. Circuit Courts from 1880 to 1912; U.S. Commerce Court from 1911 to 1913; U.S. District Courts from 1880 to 1932; U.S. Court of Claims (now called U.S. Court of Federal Claims) from 1929 to 1932 and since 1960; U.S. Courts of Appeals since 1891; U.S. Court of Customs and Patent Appeals since 1929; and U.S. Emergency Court of Appeals since 1943.
Federal Supplement (F.Supp. or F.Supp.2d)	1932	U.S. Court of Claims from 1932 to 1960; U.S. District Courts since 1932; and U.S. Customs Court since 1956.
Federal Rules Decisions (F.R.D.)	1939	U.S. District Courts involving the Federal Rules of Civil Procedure since 1939 and Federal Rules of Criminal Procedure since 1946.
Supreme Court Reporter (S.Ct.)	1882	U.S. Supreme Court since the October term of 1882.
Bankruptcy Reporter (Bankr.)	1980	Bankruptcy decisions of U.S. Bankruptcy Courts, U.S. District Courts, U.S. Courts of Appeals, and U.S. Supreme Court.
Military Justice Reporter (M.J.)	1978	U.S. Court of Military Appeals and Courts of Military Review for the Army, Navy, Air Force, and Coast Guard.

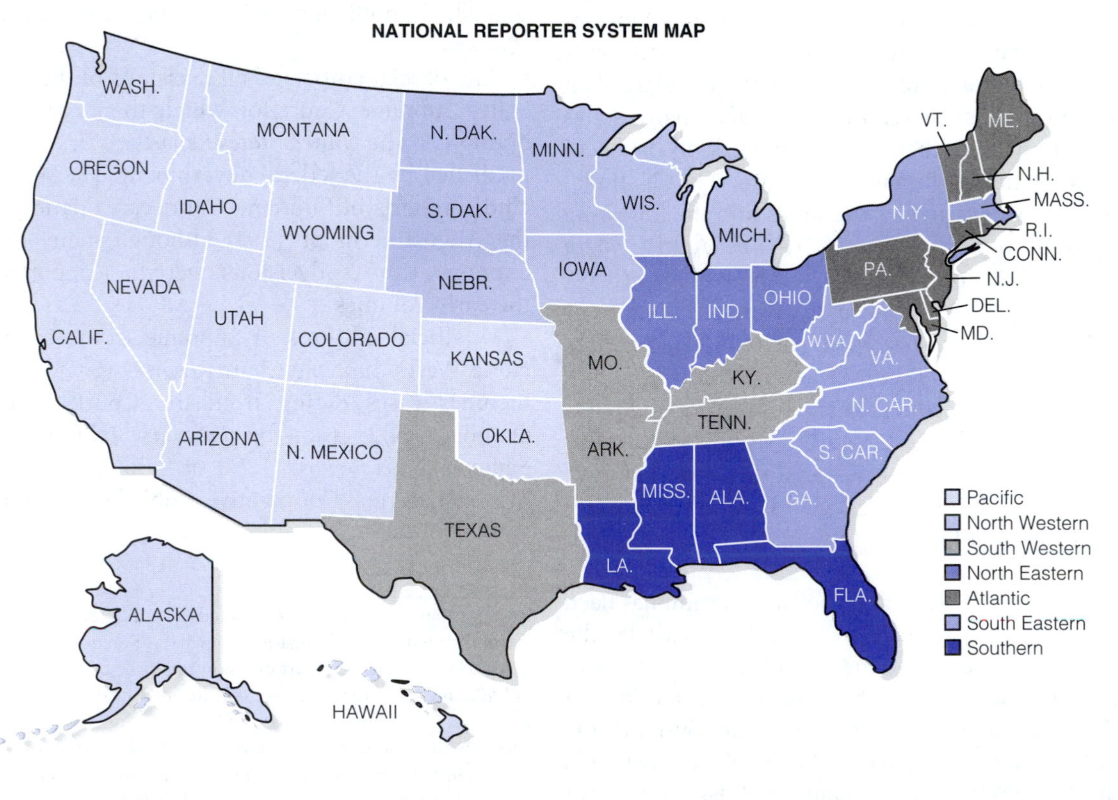

(now a part of West Group). The latter contains many of the decisions not reported in the early volumes of the *United States Reports*.

Sample citations for federal court decisions are also listed and explained in Exhibit 1–4.

Old Case Law. On a few occasions, this text cites opinions from old, classic cases dating to the nineteenth century or earlier; some of these are from the English courts. The citations to these cases appear not to conform to the descriptions given above, because the reporters in which they were published were often known by the name of the person who compiled the reporter and have since been replaced.

Case Digests and Legal Encyclopedias. The body of American case law consists of over five million decisions, to which more than forty thousand decisions are added each year. Because judicial decisions are published in chronological order, finding relevant precedents would be a Herculean task if it were not for secondary sources of law that classify decisions according to subject. Two important "finding tools" that are helpful when researching case law are case digests, such as West's *American Digest System*, and legal encyclopedias, such as *American Jurisprudence, Second Edition*, and *Corpus Juris Secundum*, both published by West Group.

SECTION 7

How to Read and Understand Case Law

The decisions made by the courts establish the boundaries of the law as it applies to business firms and business relationships. It thus is essential that businesspersons know how to read and understand case law. The cases that we present in this text have been condensed from the full text of the courts' opinions—that is, in each case we have summarized the background and facts, as well as the court's decision and remedy, in our own words and have included only selected portions of the court's opinion ("in the language of the court"). For those who wish to review court cases to perform research projects or to gain additional legal information, however, the following sections will provide useful insights into how to read and understand case law.

CASE TITLES

The title of a case, such as *Adams v. Jones*, indicates the names of the parties to the lawsuit. The v. in the case title stands for *versus*, which means "against." In the trial court, Adams was the plaintiff—the person who filed the suit. Jones was the defendant. If the case is appealed, however, the appellate court will sometimes place the name of the party appealing the decision first, so that the case may be called *Jones v. Adams* if Jones is appealing. Because some appellate courts retain the trial court order of names, it is often impossible to distinguish the plaintiff from the defendant in the title of a reported appellate court decision. You must carefully read the facts of each case to identify the parties. Otherwise, the discussion by the appellate court will be difficult to understand.

TERMINOLOGY

The following terms, phrases, and abbreviations are frequently encountered in court opinions and legal publications. Because it is important to understand what is meant by these terms, phrases, and abbreviations, we define and discuss them here.

Parties to Lawsuits. As mentioned previously, the party initiating a lawsuit is referred to as the *plaintiff* or *petitioner*, depending on the nature of the action, and the party against whom a lawsuit is brought is the *defendant* or *respondent*. Lawsuits frequently involve more than one plaintiff and/or defendant. When a case is appealed from the original court or jurisdiction to another court or jurisdiction, the party appealing the case is called the **appellant**. The **appellee** is the party against whom the appeal is taken. (In some appellate courts, the party appealing a case is referred to as the petitioner, and the party against whom the suit is brought or appealed is called the respondent.)

Judges and Justices. The terms *judge* and *justice* are usually synonymous and represent two designations given to judges in various courts. All members of the United States Supreme Court, for example, are referred to as justices, and justice is the formal title usually given to judges of appellate courts, although this is not always the case. In New York, a *justice* is a judge of the trial court (which is called the Supreme Court), and a member of the Court of Appeals (the state's highest court) is called a *judge*. The term *justice* is

EXHIBIT 1–4 HOW TO READ CITATIONS

State Courts

261 Neb. 943, 627 N.W.2d 118 (2001)[a]

N.W. is the abbreviation for West s publication of state court decisions rendered in the *North Western Reporter* of the National Reporter System. *2d* indicates that this case was included in the *Second Series* of that reporter. The number 627 refers to the volume number of the reporter; the number 118 refers to the first page in that volume on which this case can be found.

Neb. is an abbreviation for *Nebraska Reports,* Nebraska s official reports of the decisions of its highest court, the Nebraska Supreme Court.

89 Cal.App.4th 675, 107 Cal.Rptr.2d 542 (2001)

Cal.Rptr. is the abbreviation for West s unofficial reports titled *California Reporter* of the decisions of California courts.

96 N.Y.2d 51, 749 N.E.2d 192, 725 N.Y.S.2d 617 (2001)

N.Y.S. is the abbreviation for West s unofficial reports titled *New York Supplement* of the decisions of New York courts.

N.Y. is the abbreviation for *New York Reports,* New York s official reports of the decisions of its court of appeals. The New York Court of Appeals is the state s highest court, analogous to other states supreme courts. In New York, a supreme court is a trial court.

105 Wash.App. 937, 21 P.3d 1165 (2001)

Wash.App. is the abbreviation for *Washington Appeals Reports,* Washington s official reports of the decisions of its court of appeals.

Federal Courts

532 U.S. 318, 121 S.Ct. 1536, 149 L.Ed.2d 549 (2001)

L.Ed. is an abbreviation for *Lawyers Edition of the Supreme Court Reports,* an unofficial edition of decisions of the United States Supreme Court.

S.Ct. is the abbreviation for West s unofficial reports titled *Supreme Court Reporter* of decisions of the United States Supreme Court.

U.S. is the abbreviation for *United States Reports,* the official edition of the decisions of the United States Supreme Court.

a.˚The case names have been deleted from these citations to emphasize the publications. It should be kept in mind, however that the name of a case is as important as the specific numbers of the volumes in which it is found. If a citation is incorrect, the correct citation may be found in a publication s index of case names. The date of a case is also important because, in addition to providing a check on errors in citations, the value of a recent case as an authority is likely to be greater than that of earlier cases.

EXHIBIT 1–4 HOW TO READ CITATIONS (CONTINUED)

Federal Courts (continued)

252 F.3d 712 (5th Cir. 2001)

5th Cir. is an abbreviation denoting that this case was decided in the United States Court of Appeals for the Fifth Circuit.

38 F.Supp.2d 1233 (E.D.Ark. 1998)

E.D.Ark. is an abbreviation indicating that the United States District Court for the Eastern District of Arkansas decided this case.

English Courts

9 Exch. 341, 156 Eng.Rep. 145 (1854)

Eng.Rep. is an abbreviation for *English Reports, Full Reprint,* a series of reports containing selected decisions made in English courts between 1378 and 1865.

Exch. is an abbreviation for *English Exchequer Reports,* which included the original reports of cases decided in England's Court of Exchequer.

Statutory and Other Citations

18 U.S.C. Section 1961(1)(A)

U.S.C. denotes *United States Code,* the codification of *United States Statutes at Large.* The number 18 refers to the statute's U.S.C. title number and 1961 to its section number within that title. The number 1 refers to a subsection within the section and the letter A to a subdivision within the subsection.

UCC 2–206(1)(b)

UCC is an abbreviation for *Uniform Commercial Code.* The first number 2 is a reference to an article of the UCC and 206 to a section within that article. The number 1 refers to a subsection within the section and the letter b to a subdivision within the subsection.

Restatement (Second) of Torts, Section 568

Restatement (Second) of Torts refers to the second edition of the American Law Institute's *Restatement of the Law of Torts.* The number 568 refers to a specific section.

17 C.F.R. Section 230.505

C.F.R. is an abbreviation for *Code of Federal Regulations,* a compilation of federal administrative regulations. The number 17 designates the regulation's title number, and 230.505 designates a specific section within that title.

EXHIBIT 1–4 HOW TO READ CITATIONS (CONTINUED)

Westlaw® Citations

2001 WL 12345

WL is an abbreviation for Westlaw□. The number 2001 is the year of the document that can be found with this citation in the Westlaw□ database. The number 12345 is a number assigned to a specific document. A higher number indicates that a document was added to the Westlaw□ database later in the year.

Uniform Resource Locators[b]

www.westlaw.com

The suffix *com* is the top-level domain (TLD) for this Web site. The TLD *com* is an abbreviation for commercial, which usually means that a for-profit entity maintains this Web site.

westlaw is the host name the part of the domain name selected by the organization that registered the name. In this case, West Group registered the name. This Internet site is the Westlaw database on the Web.

www is an abbreviation for World Wide Web. The Web is a system of Internet servers[c] that support documents formatted in *HTML* (hypertext markup language). HTML supports links to text, graphics, and audio and video files.

www.uscourts.gov

This is The Federal Judiciary Home Page. The host is the Administrative Office of the U.S. Courts. The TLD *gov* is an abbreviation for government. This Web site includes information and links from, and about, the federal courts.

www.law.cornell.edu/index.html

This part of a URL points to a Web page or file at a specific location within the host s domain. This page, at this Web site, is a menu with links to documents within the domain and to other Internet resources.

This is the host name for a Web site that contains the Internet publications of the Legal Information Institute (LII), which is a part of Cornell Law School. The LII site includes a variety of legal materials and links to other legal resources on the Internet. The TLD *edu* is an abbreviation for educational institution (a school or a university).

www.ipl.org.ref/RR

RR is an abbreviation for this Web site s Ready Reference Collection, which contains links to a variety of Internet resources.

ref is an abbreviation for Internet Public Library Reference Center, which is a map of the topics into which the links at this Web site have been categorized.

ipl is an abbreviation for Internet Public Library, which is an online service that provides reference resources and links to other information services on the Web. The IPL is supported chiefly by the School of Information at the University of Michigan. The TLD *org* is an abbreviation for organization (usually nonprofit).

b.˚The basic form for a URL is service://hostname/path. The Internet service for all of the URLs in the text is *http* (hypertext transfer protocol. Most Web browsers will add this prefix automatically when a user enters a host name or a hostname/path.
c.˚A *server* is hardware that manages the resources on a network. For example, a network server is a computer that manages the traffic on the network, and a print server is a computer that manages one or more printers.

commonly abbreviated to J., and *justices,* to JJ. A Supreme Court case might refer to Justice Kennedy as Kennedy, J., or to Chief Justice Rehnquist as Rehnquist, C.J.

Decisions and Opinions. Most decisions reached by reviewing, or appellate, courts are explained in written **opinions.** The opinion contains the court's reasons for its decision, the rules of law that apply, and the judgment.

When all judges or justices unanimously agree on an opinion, the opinion is written for the entire court and can be deemed a *unanimous opinion.* When there is not a unanimous opinion, a *majority opinion* is written; it outlines the views of the majority of the judges or justices deciding the case. If a judge agrees, or concurs, with the majority's decision, but for different reasons, that judge may write a *concurring opinion.* A *dissenting opinion* is written by one or more judges who disagree with the majority's decision. The dissenting opinion is important because it may form the basis of the arguments used years later in overruling the precedential majority opinion.

Occasionally, a court issues a *per curiam* opinion. *Per curiam* is a Latin phrase meaning "of the court." In *per curiam* opinions, there is no indication of which judge or justice authored the opinion. This term may also be used for an announcement of a court's disposition of a case that is not accompanied by a written opinion. Sometimes, the cases presented in this text are *en banc* decisions. When an appellate court reviews a case *en banc,* which is a French term (derived from a Latin term) for "in the bench," generally all of the judges sitting on the bench of that court review the case.

A Sample Court Case

Knowing how to read and understand court opinions and the legal reasoning used by the courts is an essential step in undertaking accurate legal research. A further step is "briefing," or summarizing, the case. Legal researchers routinely brief cases by reducing the texts of the opinions to their essential elements.

Each case presented in this text consists of excerpts from the court's opinion. The full text of each case can also be accessed in the Westlaw cases included on this text's companion Web site at **http://wbl-cs.westbuslaw.com**. Each Westlaw case includes the names of all plaintiffs and defendants, the dates on which the case was argued and decided, a brief summary of the issues and decisions in the case, headnotes classifying specific issues in the case according to the West Key Number System, and the court's opinion. Concurring and dissenting opinions, if any, are included as well.

The *fold-out exhibit* in this chapter illustrates the various elements contained in a court case, as displayed on Westlaw. The case presented in the exhibit is an actual case that the United States Supreme Court decided in 2001. Ms. Breeden initiated the lawsuit against Clark County School District, Nevada, claiming in part that she was a victim of alleged sexual harassment in violation of federal law. The Court granted a summary judgment in favor of the school district. When the U.S. Court of Appeals for the Ninth Circuit reversed this ruling, the school district appealed to the United States Supreme Court. The primary issue before the Court was whether a single incident of offhand comments being made constitutes illegal sexual harassment.

SECTION 8

Businesspersons and the Law

Those entering into the world of business will find that laws and government regulations affect virtually all business activities—from hiring and firing decisions, to the manufacturing and marketing of products, to financing matters, and so on. To make good business decisions, a basic knowledge of the laws and regulations governing these activities is beneficial—if not essential. The study of business law is thus a sound investment for anyone who wishes to succeed in today's business arena.

As you will note, each of the chapters in this text covers a specific area of the law and shows how the legal rules in that area of law affect businesses. While compartmentalizing the law in this fashion promotes conceptual clarity, it does not indicate the extent to which one area of law overlaps with another.

Consider an example. Net Systems, Inc., creates and maintains computer network systems for its clients, including business firms. Net Systems also markets software for customers who need an internal computer network but cannot afford an individually designed intranet. Mark is the president of Net Systems. Janet, an operations officer for Southwest Distribution Corporation (SDC), contacts Mark by e-mail about a possible contract concerning SDC's computer network. In deciding whether to enter into a contract with SDC, Mark needs to consider, among other things, the legal requirements for an enforceable contract. Are there different requirements for a contract for services and a contract for products? What are the options if SDC **breaches** (breaks, or fails to perform) the contract? The answers to these questions are part of contract law and sales law.

Other questions might concern payment under the contract. How can Net Systems guarantee that it will be paid? If a payment is made with, for example, a check that is returned for insufficient funds, what are Net Systems's options? Answers to these questions can be found in the laws that relate to negotiable instruments (such as checks) and creditors' rights. Also, a dispute may occur over the rights to Net Systems's software, or there may be a question of liability if the software is defective. There may be an issue regarding the authority of Mark or Janet to make a deal. A disagreement may arise from such circumstances as an accountant's evaluation of the contract. Resolutions of these questions may be found in areas of the law that relate to intellectual property, e-commerce, torts, product liability, agency, business organizations, or professional liability.

Finally, if any dispute cannot be resolved amicably, then the laws and the rules concerning courts and court procedures spell out the steps of a lawsuit. Exhibit 1–5 illustrates the various areas of law that may influence business decision making.

EXHIBIT 1–5 AREAS OF THE LAW THAT MAY AFFECT BUSINESS DECISION MAKING

Terms and Concepts to Review

administrative agency 10
administrative law 10
allege 7
analogy 8
appellant 15
appellee 15
binding authority 6
breach 20
case law 10
case on point 7
chancellor 4
citation 12
civil law 11
common law 4
constitutional law 9
court of equity 4
court of law 4
criminal law 11
cyberlaw 11
damages 4
defendant 5
defense 5
equitable maxims 4
executive agency 10
historical school 3
independent regulatory agency 10
jurisprudence 2
laches 5
law 2
legal realism 3
legal reasoning 7
natural law 3
opinion 19
ordinance 9
petitioner 5
plaintiff 5
positive law 3
positivist school 3
precedent 6
procedural law 11
public policy 7
remedy 4
remedy at law 4
remedy in equity 4
reporter 6
respondent 5
sociological school 3
stare decisis 6
statute of limitations 5
statutory law 9
substantive law 11
syllogism 8
uniform law 9

Chapter Summary

What Is Law?	Law can be defined as a body of rules of conduct with legal force and effect, prescribed by the controlling authority (the government) of a society. Three important schools of legal thought, or legal philosophies, are the following: 1. *The natural law school*—One of the oldest and most significant schools of legal thought. Those who believe in natural law hold that there is a universal law applicable to all human beings and that this law is of a higher order than positive, or conventional, law. 2. *The positivist school*—A school of legal thought centered on the assumption that there is no law higher than the laws created by the government. Laws must be obeyed, even if they are unjust, to prevent anarchy. 3. *The historical school*—A school of legal thought that stresses the evolutionary nature of law and that looks to doctrines that have withstood the passage of time for guidance in shaping present laws. 4. *Legal realism*—A school of legal thought, popular during the 1920s and 1930s, that left a lasting imprint on American jurisprudence. Legal realists generally advocated a less abstract and more realistic approach to the law, an approach that would take into account customary practices and the circumstances in which transactions take place.
The Common Law Tradition	1. *Common law*—Law that originated in medieval England with the creation of the king's courts, or *curiae regis*, and the development of a body of rules that were common to (or applied throughout) the land.

CHAPTER SUMMARY—CONTINUED

The Common Law Tradition—continued	2. *Remedies*— a. Remedies at law—Money or something else of value. b. Remedies in equity—Remedies that are granted when the remedies at law are unavailable or inadequate. Equitable remedies include specific performance, an injunction, and contract rescission (cancellation). 3. *Stare decisis*—A doctrine under which judges "stand on decided cases"—or follow the rule of precedent-in deciding cases. *Stare decisis* is the cornerstone of the common law tradition. 4. *Stare decisis and legal reasoning*—Legal reasoning refers to the reasoning process used by judges in applying the law to the facts and issues of specific cases. In linking the legal rules to the facts of a case, judges may use deductive reasoning, linear reasoning, or reasoning by analogy.
Sources of American Law	1. *Constitutional law*—The law as expressed in the U.S. Constitution and the various state constitutions. The U.S. Constitution is the supreme law of the land. State constitutions are supreme within state borders to the extent that they do not violate the U.S. Constitution or a federal law. 2. *Statutory law*—Laws or ordinances created by federal, state, and local legislatures and governing bodies. None of these laws can violate the U.S. Constitution or the relevant state constitutions. Uniform laws, when adopted by a state legislature, become statutory law in that state. 3. *Administrative law*—The rules, orders, and decisions of federal or state government administrative agencies. Federal administrative agencies are created by enabling legislation enacted by the U.S. Congress. Agency functions include rulemaking, investigation and enforcement, and adjudication. 4. *Case law and common law doctrines*—Judge-made law, including interpretations of constitutional provisions, of statutes enacted by legislatures, and of regulations created by administrative agencies. The common law—the doctrines and principles embodied in case law—governs all areas not covered by statutory law (or agency regulations issued to implement various statutes).
Classifications of Law	The law may be broken down according to several classification systems, such as substantive or procedural law, federal or state law, and private or public law. Two broad classifications are civil and criminal law, and national and international law.
Cyberlaw	*Cyberlaw* is an informal term used to describe how traditional classifications of law, such as civil law and criminal law, are being applied to online activities.
How to Find Primary Sources of Law	See Section 6 of this chapter for a detailed summary of how to find statutory, administrative, and case law.
How to Read and Understand Case Law	See Section 7 of this chapter and the fold-out exhibit showing an annotated sample court case for instructions on how to read and understand case law.
Businesspersons and the Law	Laws and government regulations affect virtually all business activities. Although the chapters in this text cover various legal topics separately, in fact areas of the law overlap considerably (see Exhibit 1–5).

E-LINKS

Today, business law professors and students can go online to access information on virtually every topic covered in this text. A good point of departure for online legal research is the Web site for *West's Business Law: A Case Study Approach*, at http://wbl-cs.westbuslaw.com. There you will find numerous materials relevant to this text and to business law generally, including links to various legal resources on the Web. Additionally, every chapter in this text ends with an *E-Links* feature that contains selected Web addresses.

You can access many of the sources of law discussed in Chapter 1 at the FindLaw Web site, which is probably the most comprehensive source of free legal information on the Internet. Go to

http://www.findlaw.com

The Legal Information Institute (LII) at Cornell Law School, which offers extensive information about U.S. law, is also a good starting point for legal research. The URL for this site is

http://www.law.cornell.edu

The Library of Congress offers extensive links to state and federal government resources at

http://www.loc.gov

The Virtual Law Library Index, created and maintained by the Indiana University School of Law, provides an index of legal sources categorized by subject at

http://www.law.indiana.edu

LEGAL RESEARCH EXERCISES ON THE WEB

The text's Web site also offers online research exercises. These exercises will help you find and analyze specific types of legal information available at specific Web sites. There is at least one of these exercises for each chapter in *West's Business Law: A Case Study Approach*. To access these exercises, go to this book's Web site at http://wbl-cs.westbuslaw.com and click on "Interactive Study Center." When that page opens, select the relevant chapter to find the exercise or exercises relating to topics in that chapter. The following activity will direct you to some of the important sources of law discussed in Chapter 1:

Activity 1–1: Internet Sources of Law

CHAPTER 2
Traditional and Online Dispute Resolution

Today in the United States there are fifty-two court systems—one for each of the fifty states, one for the District of Columbia, and a federal system. Keep in mind that the federal courts are not superior to the state courts; they are simply an independent system of courts, which derives its authority from Article III, Section 2, of the U.S. Constitution. By the power given to it under Article I of the U.S. Constitution, Congress has extended the federal court system beyond the boundaries of the United States to U.S. territories such as Guam, the Virgin Islands, and Puerto Rico.[1] As we shall see, the United States Supreme Court is the final controlling voice over all of these fifty-two systems, at least when questions of federal law are involved.

Every businessperson will likely face a lawsuit at some time in his or her career. It is thus important for anyone involved in business to have an understanding of the American court systems, as well as the various methods of dispute resolution that can be pursued outside the courts. In this chapter, after examining the judiciary's general role in the American governmental scheme, we discuss some basic requirements that must be met before a party may bring a lawsuit before a particular court. We then look at the court systems of the United States in some detail. We conclude the chapter with an overview of some alternative methods of settling disputes.

1. In Guam and the Virgin Islands, territorial courts serve as both federal courts and state courts; in Puerto Rico, they serve only as federal courts.

Section 1

The Judiciary's Role in American Government

As you learned in Chapter 1, the body of American law includes the federal and state constitutions, statutes passed by legislative bodies, administrative law, and the case decisions and legal principles that form the common law. These laws would be meaningless, however, without the courts to interpret and apply them. This is the essential role of the judiciary—the courts—in the American governmental system: to interpret the laws and apply them to specific situations.

As the branch of government entrusted with interpreting the laws, the judiciary can decide, among other things, whether the laws or actions of the other two branches are constitutional. The process for making such a determination is known as **judicial review**. The power of judicial review enables the judicial branch to act as a check on the other two branches of government, in line with the checks and balances system established by the U.S. Constitution.[2]

The power of judicial review is not mentioned in the Constitution (although many constitutional scholars conclude that the founders intended the ju-

2. In a broad sense, judicial review occurs whenever a court "reviews" a case or legal proceeding—as when an appellate court reviews a lower court's decision. When referring to the judiciary's role in American government, however, the term *judicial review* is used to indicate the power of the judiciary to decide whether the actions of the other two branches of government do or do not violate the Constitution.

diciary to have this power). Rather, this power was established by the United States Supreme Court in 1803 by its decision in *Marbury v. Madison,*[3] in which the Supreme Court stated, "It is emphatically the province and duty of the Judicial Department to say what the law is. . . . If two laws conflict with each other, the courts must decide on the operation of each. . . . So if the law be in opposition to the Constitution . . . [t]he Court must determine which of these conflicting rules governs the case. This is the very essence of judicial duty." Since the *Marbury v. Madison* decision, the power of judicial review has remained unchallenged. Today, this power is exercised by both federal and state courts.

SECTION 2

Basic Judicial Requirements

Before a lawsuit can be brought before a court, certain requirements must be met. These requirements relate to jurisdiction, venue, and standing to sue. We examine each of these important concepts here.

JURISDICTION

In Latin, *juris* means "law," and *diction* means "to speak." Thus, "the power to speak the law" is the literal meaning of the term **jurisdiction.** Before any court can hear a case, it must have jurisdiction over the person against whom the suit is brought or jurisdiction over the property involved in a lawsuit. The court must also have jurisdiction over the subject matter. Keep in mind throughout this discussion of jurisdiction that we are talking about jurisdiction over the *defendant* in a lawsuit.

Jurisdiction over Persons. Generally, a particular court can exercise ***in personam* jurisdiction** (personal jurisdiction) over residents of a certain geographical area. A state trial court, for example, normally has jurisdictional authority over residents of a particular area of the state, such as a county or district. A state's highest court (often called the state supreme court)[4] has jurisdictional authority over all residents within the state.

In some cases, under the authority of a state **long arm statute,** a court can exercise personal jurisdiction over nonresident defendants as well. Before a court can exercise jurisdiction over a nonresident defendant under a long arm statute, though, it must be demonstrated that the defendant had sufficient contacts, or *minimum contacts,* with the state to justify the jurisdiction.[5] For example, if an individual has committed a wrong within the state, such as injuring someone in an automobile accident or selling defective goods, a court can usually exercise jurisdiction even if the person causing the harm is located in another state. Similarly, a state may exercise personal jurisdiction over a nonresident defendant who is sued for breaching a contract that was formed within the state.

In regard to corporations,[6] the minimum-contacts requirement is usually met if the corporation does business within the state, advertises or sells its products within the state, or places its goods into the "stream of commerce" with the intent that the goods be sold in the state. Suppose that a business incorporated under the laws of Maine and headquartered in that state has a branch office or manufacturing plant in Georgia. Does this corporation have sufficient contacts with the state of Georgia to allow a Georgia court to exercise jurisdiction over the corporation? Yes, it does. If the Maine corporation advertises and sells its products in Georgia, or places goods within the stream of commerce with the expectation that the goods will be purchased by Georgia residents, those activities may also suffice to meet the minimum-contacts requirement.

Westlaw. See Case 2.1 at the end of this chapter. To view the full, unedited case from Westlaw,® go to this text's Web site at **http://wbl-cs.westbuslaw.com.**

Jurisdiction over Property. A court can also exercise jurisdiction over property that is located within its boundaries. This kind of jurisdiction is known as ***in rem* jurisdiction**, or "jurisdiction over the thing." For example, suppose a dispute arises over the ownership of a boat in dry dock in Fort Lauderdale, Florida. The boat is owned by an Ohio resident, over whom a Florida court normally cannot exercise personal

3. 5 U.S. (1 Cranch) 137, 2 L.Ed. 60 (1803).

4. As will be discussed shortly, a state's highest court is often referred to as the state supreme court, but there are exceptions. For example, in New York the supreme court is a trial court.

5. The minimum-contacts standard was established in *International Shoe Co. v. State of Washington,* 326 U.S. 310, 66 S.Ct. 154, 90 L.Ed. 95 (1945).

6. In the eyes of the law, corporations are "legal persons"—entities that can sue and be sued. See Chapter 34.

jurisdiction. The other party to the dispute is a resident of Nebraska. In this situation, a lawsuit concerning the boat could be brought in a Florida state court on the basis of the court's *in rem* jurisdiction.

Jurisdiction over Subject Matter. Jurisdiction over subject matter is a limitation on the types of cases a court can hear. In both the federal and state court systems, there are courts of *general* (unlimited) *jurisdiction* and courts of *limited jurisdiction*. A court of general jurisdiction can decide cases involving a broad array of issues. An example of a court of general jurisdiction is a state trial court or federal district court. An example of a state court of limited jurisdiction is a probate court. **Probate courts** are state courts that handle only matters relating to the transfer of a person's assets and obligations after that person's death, including issues relating to the custody and guardianship of children. An example of a federal court of limited subject-matter jurisdiction is a bankruptcy court. **Bankruptcy courts** handle only bankruptcy proceedings, which are governed by federal bankruptcy law (discussed in Chapter 30).

A court's jurisdiction over subject matter is usually defined in the statute or constitution creating the court. In both the federal and state court systems, a court's subject-matter jurisdiction can be limited not only by the subject of the lawsuit but also by how much money is in controversy, whether the case is a felony (a more serious type of crime) or a misdemeanor (a less serious type of crime), or whether the proceeding is a trial or an appeal.

Original and Appellate Jurisdiction. The distinction between courts of original jurisdiction and courts of appellate jurisdiction normally lies in whether the case is being heard for the first time. Courts having original jurisdiction are courts of the first instance, or trial courts—that is, courts in which lawsuits begin, trials take place, and evidence is presented. In the federal court system, the *district courts* are trial courts. In the various state court systems, the trial courts are known by different names, as will be discussed shortly.

The key point here is that normally, any court having original jurisdiction is known as a trial court. Courts having appellate jurisdiction act as reviewing courts, or appellate courts. In general, cases can be brought before appellate courts only on appeal from an order or a judgment of a trial court or other lower court.

Jurisdiction of the Federal Courts. Because the federal government is a government of limited powers, the jurisdiction of the federal courts is limited. Article III of the U.S. Constitution establishes the boundaries of federal judicial power. Section 2 of Article III states that "[t]he judicial Power shall extend to all Cases, in Law and Equity, arising under this Constitution, the Laws of the United States, and Treaties made, or which shall be made, under their Authority." In effect, this clause means that whenever a plaintiff's cause of action is based—at least in part—on the U.S. Constitution, a treaty, or a federal law, a **federal question** arises, and the case comes under the judicial authority of the federal courts. Any lawsuit involving a federal question can originate in a federal court. People who claim that their constitutional rights have been violated can begin their suits in a federal court.

Federal district courts can also exercise original jurisdiction over cases involving **diversity of citizenship.** This term applies whenever a federal court has jurisdiction over a case that does not involve a question of federal law. The most common type of diversity jurisdiction has two requirements:[7] (1) the plaintiff and defendant must be residents of different states, and (2) the dollar amount in controversy must exceed $75,000. For purposes of diversity jurisdiction, a corporation is a citizen of both the state in which it is incorporated and the state in which its principal place of business is located. A case involving diversity of citizenship can be filed in the appropriate federal district court. If the case starts in a state court, it can sometimes be transferred, or "removed," to a federal court. A large percentage of the cases filed in federal courts each year are based on diversity of citizenship.

Note that in a case based on a federal question, a federal court will apply federal law. In a case based on diversity of citizenship, however, a federal court will apply the relevant state law (which is often the law of the state in which the court sits).

Exclusive versus Concurrent Jurisdiction. When both federal and state courts have the power to hear a case, as is true in suits involving diversity of citizenship, **concurrent jurisdiction** exists. When cases

---

7. Diversity jurisdiction also exists in cases between (1) a foreign country and citizens of a state or of different states and (2) citizens of a state and citizens or subjects of a foreign country. These bases for diversity jurisdiction are less commonly used.

can be tried only in federal courts or only in state courts, **exclusive jurisdiction** exists. Federal courts have exclusive jurisdiction in cases involving federal crimes, bankruptcy, patents, and copyrights; in suits against the United States; and in some areas of admiralty law (law governing transportation on the seas and ocean waters). The states also have exclusive jurisdiction in certain subject matters—for example, divorce and adoption.

JURISDICTION IN CYBERSPACE

The Internet's capacity to bypass political and geographic boundaries undercuts the traditional basis for a court to assert personal jurisdiction. This basis includes a party's contacts with a court's geographic jurisdiction. As already discussed, for a court to compel a defendant to come before it, there must be at least minimum contacts—the presence of a salesperson within the state, for example. Are there sufficient minimum contacts if the only connection to a jurisdiction is an ad on the Web originating from a remote location?

The "Sliding-Scale" Standard. Gradually, the courts are developing a standard—called a "sliding-scale" standard—for determining when the exercise of jurisdiction over an out-of-state defendant is proper. In developing this standard, the courts have identified three types of Internet business contacts: (1) substantial business conducted over the Internet (with contracts, sales, and so on); (2) some interactivity through a Web site; and (3) passive advertising. Jurisdiction is proper for the first category, improper for the third, and may or may not be appropriate for the second.[8]

International Jurisdictional Issues. Because the Internet is international in scope, international jurisdictional issues have understandably come to the fore. What seems to be emerging in the world's courts is a standard that echoes the requirement of "minimum contacts" applied by the U.S. courts. To compel a defendant to appear, most courts are indicating that a physical presence is not necessary but that minimum contacts—doing business within the jurisdiction, for example—are enough. The effect of this standard is that a business firm has to comply with the laws of any jurisdiction in which it targets customers for its products.[9]

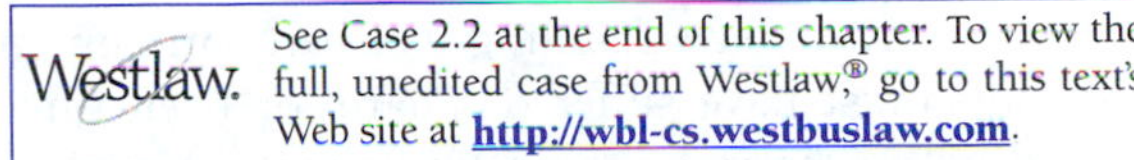

See Case 2.2 at the end of this chapter. To view the full, unedited case from Westlaw,® go to this text's Web site at **http://wbl-cs.westbuslaw.com**.

VENUE

Jurisdiction has to do with whether a court has authority to hear a case involving specific persons, property, or subject matter. **Venue**[10] is concerned with the most appropriate location for a trial. For example, two state courts (or two federal courts) may have the authority to exercise jurisdiction over a case, but it may be more appropriate or convenient to hear the case in one court than in the other.

Basically, the concept of venue reflects the policy that a court trying a suit should be in the geographical neighborhood (usually the county) in which the incident leading to the lawsuit occurred or in which the parties involved in the lawsuit reside. Pretrial publicity or other factors, though, may require a change of venue to another community, especially in criminal cases in which the defendant's right to a fair and impartial jury has been impaired.

For example, a change of venue from Oklahoma City to Denver, Colorado, was ordered for the trials of Timothy McVeigh and Terry Nichols after they had been indicted in connection with the 1995 bombing of the federal building in Oklahoma City. As a result of the bombing, more than 160 persons were killed, and hundreds of others were wounded. In view of these circumstances, it was felt that to hold the trial in Oklahoma City could prejudice the rights of the defendants to a fair trial. (McVeigh was later sentenced to death and was executed by lethal injection in 2001. Nichols was sentenced to life imprisonment.)

STANDING TO SUE

In order to bring a lawsuit before a court, a party must have **standing to sue**, or a sufficient "stake" in

8. For a leading case on this issue, see *Zippo Manufacturing Co. v. Zippo Dot Com, Inc.*, 952 F.Supp. 1119 (W.D.Pa. 1997).

9. Currently under negotiation is the Hague Convention on Jurisdiction, which is an international treaty the intention of which is to make civil judgments enforceable across national borders. One issue being considered is whether to require that all disputes be settled in the country of the seller or the country of the buyer. It has also been suggested that mandatory jurisdiction provisions be left out of the treaty.

10. Pronounced *ven*-yoo.

a matter to justify seeking relief through the court system. In other words, a party must have a legally protected and tangible interest at stake in the litigation in order to have standing. The party bringing the lawsuit must have suffered a harm or been threatened with a harm by the action about which he or she has complained. In some circumstances, a person can have standing to sue on behalf of another person. For example, suppose that a child suffers serious injuries as a result of a defectively manufactured toy. Because the child is a minor, a lawsuit can be brought on his or her behalf by another person, such as the child's parent or legal guardian.

Standing to sue also requires that the controversy at issue be a **justiciable**[11] **controversy**—a controversy that is real and substantial, as opposed to hypothetical or academic. For instance, in the above example, the child's parent could not sue the toy manufacturer merely on the ground that the toy was defective. The issue would become justiciable only if the child had actually been injured due to the defect in the toy as marketed. In other words, the parent normally could not ask the court to determine what damages might be obtained if the child had been injured, because this would be merely a hypothetical question.

11. Pronounced jus-*tish*-a-bul.

SECTION 3

The State and Federal Court Systems

As mentioned earlier in this chapter, each state has its own court system. Additionally, there is a system of federal courts. Although no two state court systems are exactly the same, the left-hand side of Exhibit 2–1 illustrates the basic organizational framework characteristic of the court systems in many states. The exhibit also shows how the federal court system is structured. We turn now to an examination of these court systems, beginning with the state courts.

STATE COURT SYSTEMS

Typically a state court system includes several levels, or tiers, of courts. As indicated in Exhibit 2–1, state courts may include (1) trial courts of limited jurisdiction, (2) trial courts of general jurisdiction, (3) intermediate appellate courts, and (4) the state's highest court (often called the state supreme court). Judges in the state court system are usually elected by the voters for specified terms.

Generally, any person who is a party to a lawsuit has the opportunity to plead the case before a trial court and then, if he or she loses, before at least one level of appellate court. Finally, if a federal statute or

EXHIBIT 2–1 THE STATE AND FEDERAL COURT SYSTEMS

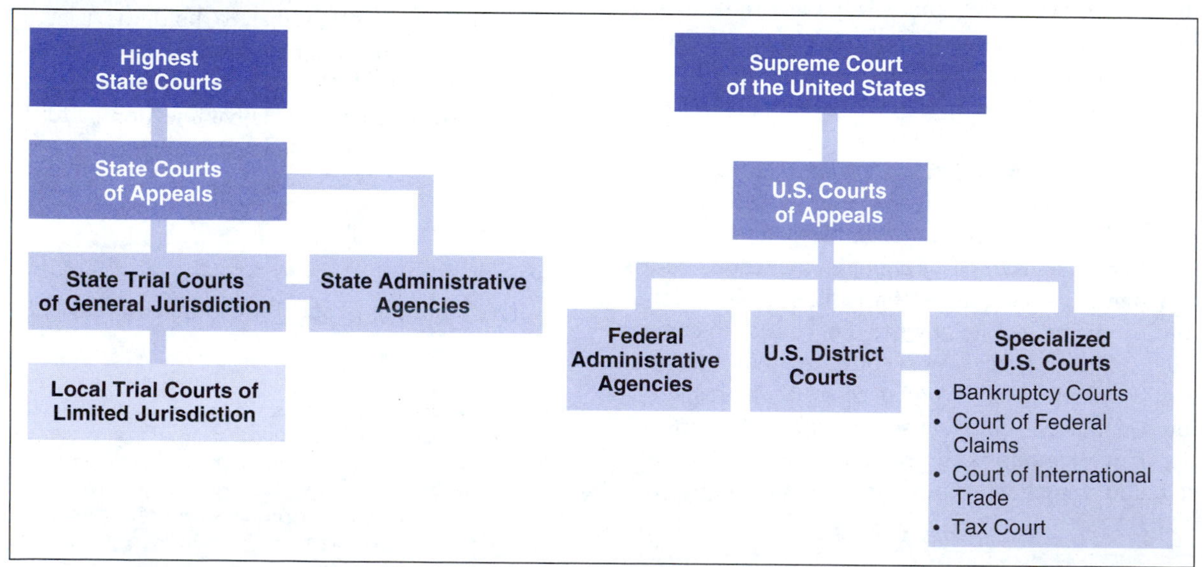

federal constitutional issue is involved in the decision of a state supreme court, that decision may be further appealed to the United States Supreme Court.

Trial Courts. Trial courts are exactly what their name implies—courts in which trials are held and testimony taken. State trial courts have either general or limited jurisdiction. Trial courts that have general jurisdiction as to subject matter may be called county, district, superior, or circuit courts.[12] State trial courts of general jurisdiction have jurisdiction over a wide variety of subjects, including both civil disputes and criminal prosecutions. In some states, trial courts of general jurisdiction may hear appeals from courts of limited jurisdiction.

Courts of limited jurisdiction as to subject matter are often called special inferior trial courts or minor judiciary courts. **Small claims courts** are inferior trial courts that hear only civil cases involving claims of less than a certain amount, such as $2,500 (the amount varies from state to state). Suits brought in small claims courts are generally conducted informally, and lawyers are not required. In a minority of states, lawyers are not even allowed to represent people in small claims courts for most purposes. Decisions of small claims courts may be appealed to a state trial court of general jurisdiction.

Other courts of limited jurisdiction include domestic relations courts, which handle only divorce actions and child-custody cases; local municipal courts, which mainly handle traffic cases; and probate courts, as mentioned earlier.

Courts of Appeals. Every state has at least one court of appeals (appellate court, or reviewing court). A court of appeals may be an intermediate appellate court or the state's highest court. About three-fourths of the states have intermediate appellate courts. Generally, courts of appeals do not conduct new trials, in which evidence is submitted to the court and witnesses are examined. Rather, an appellate court panel of three or more judges reviews the record of the case on appeal, which includes a transcript of the trial proceedings, and then determines whether the trial court committed an error.

12. The name in Ohio and Pennsylvania is Court of Common Pleas; the name in New York is Supreme Court, Trial Division.

Appellate courts look at questions of law and procedure. Usually, they do not look at questions of fact. A **question of law** is a question concerning the application or interpretation of the law, on which only a judge, not a jury, can rule. A **question of fact** is a question about what really happened in regard to the dispute being tried. Questions of fact are decided by a trial judge (in a nonjury trial) or by a jury (in a jury trial) based on the evidence presented. Normally, an appellate court will defer to the trial court's judgment on questions of fact because the trial court judge and jury were in a better position to evaluate testimony. They directly observed witnesses' gestures, demeanor, and other nonverbal behavior during the trial. At the appellate level, the judges review the written transcript of the trial, which does not include these nonverbal elements.

An appellate court will tamper with a trial court's finding of fact only when the finding is clearly erroneous (that is, when it is contrary to the evidence presented at trial) or when there is no evidence to support the finding. For example, if at trial a jury concluded that a manufacturer's product had harmed the plaintiff but no evidence was submitted to the court to support that conclusion, the appellate court would hold that the trial court's decision was erroneous. The options exercised by appellate courts will be further discussed in Chapter 3.

State Supreme (Highest) Courts. The highest state courts usually are called simply supreme courts, but they may be designated by other names. For example, in both New York and Maryland, the highest state court is called the court of appeals. In Maine and Massachusetts, the highest court is labeled the supreme judicial court. In West Virginia, the highest state court is the supreme court of appeals. The decisions of each state's highest court on all questions of state law are final. Only when issues of federal law are involved can a decision made by a state's highest court be overruled by the United States Supreme Court.

The Federal Court System

The federal court system is basically a three-tiered model consisting of (1) U.S. district courts (trial courts of general jurisdiction) and various courts of limited jurisdiction, (2) U.S. courts of appeals (intermediate courts of appeals), and (3) the United States Supreme Court.

Unlike state court judges, who are usually elected, federal court judges—including the justices of the Supreme Court—are appointed by the president of the United States, subject to confirmation by the U.S. Senate. Article III of the Constitution states that federal judges "hold their offices during good Behaviour." In effect, this means that federal judges have lifetime appointments. Although they can be impeached (removed from office) for misconduct, this is rarely done. In the entire history of the United States, only seven federal judges have been removed from office through impeachment proceedings.

U.S. District Courts. At the federal level, the equivalent of a state trial court of general jurisdiction is the district court. U.S. district courts have original jurisdiction in federal matters, and federal cases typically originate in district courts. There are other federal courts with original, but special (or limited), jurisdiction, such as the federal bankruptcy courts and others shown earlier in Exhibit 2–1.

There is at least one federal district court in every state. The number of judicial districts can vary over time, primarily owing to population changes and corresponding changes in caseloads. Currently, there are ninety-four federal judicial districts. Exhibit 2–2 shows the boundaries of U.S. district courts, as well as the U.S. courts of appeals (discussed next).

U.S. Courts of Appeals. In the federal court system, there are thirteen U.S. courts of appeals—referred to as U.S. circuit courts of appeals. Twelve of the federal courts of appeals (including the Court of Appeals for the D.C. Circuit) hear appeals from the federal district courts located within their respective judicial "circuits," or geographical boundaries (shown in Exhibit 2–2). The court of appeals for the thirteenth circuit, called the Federal Circuit, has national appellate jurisdiction over certain types of cases, such as cases involving patent law and cases in which the U.S. government is a defendant. The decisions of a circuit court of appeals are binding on all courts within the circuit court's jurisdiction and are final in most cases, but appeal to the United States Supreme Court is possible.

United States Supreme Court. At the highest level in the three-tiered federal court system is the United States Supreme Court. According to the language of Article III of the U.S. Constitution, there is only one national Supreme Court. All other courts in the federal system are considered "inferior." Congress is empowered to create other inferior courts as it deems necessary. The inferior courts that Congress has created include the second tier in our model—the U.S. circuit courts of appeals—as well as the district courts and the various federal courts of limited, or specialized, jurisdiction.

The United States Supreme Court consists of nine justices. Although the Supreme Court has original, or trial, jurisdiction in rare instances (set forth in Article III, Section 2), most of its work is as an appeals court. The Supreme Court can review any case decided by any of the federal courts of appeals, and it also has appellate authority over cases involving federal questions that have been decided in the state courts. The Supreme Court is the final arbiter of the Constitution and federal law.

How Cases Reach the Supreme Court. To bring a case before the Supreme Court, a party requests the Court to issue a writ of *certiorari*. A **writ of *certiorari***[13] is an order issued by the Supreme Court to a lower court requiring the latter to send it the record of the case for review. The Court will not issue a writ unless at least four of the nine justices approve of it. This is called the **rule of four.**

Whether the Court will issue a writ of *certiorari* is entirely within its discretion. The Court is not required to issue one, and most petitions for writs are denied. (Thousands of cases are filed with the Supreme Court each year, yet it hears, on average, less than one hundred of these cases.[14]) A denial is not a decision on the merits of a case, nor does it indicate agreement with the lower court's opinion. Furthermore, denial of the writ has no value as a precedent. A denial of the writ simply means that the decision of the lower court remains the law within that court's jurisdiction.

Typically, the petitions granted by the Court involve cases that raise important constitutional questions or cases that conflict with other state or federal court decisions. For example, if federal appellate

13. Pronounced sur-shee-uh-*rah*-ree.

14. From the mid-1950s through the early 1990s, the Supreme Court reviewed more cases per year than it has in the last few years. In the Court's 1982–1983 term, for example, the Court issued written opinions in 151 cases. In contrast, during the Court's 2000–2001 term, the Court issued written opinions in only 79 cases.

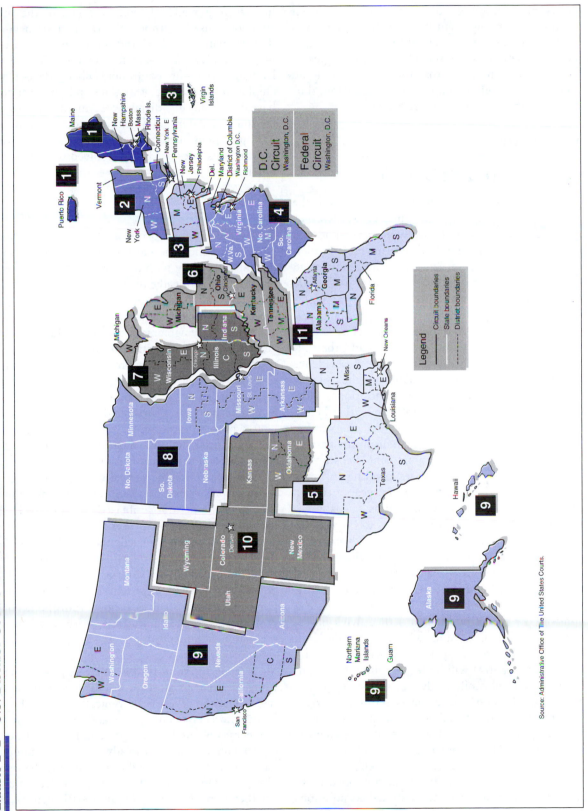

EXHIBIT 2–2 U.S. DISTRICT COURTS AND COURTS OF APPEALS

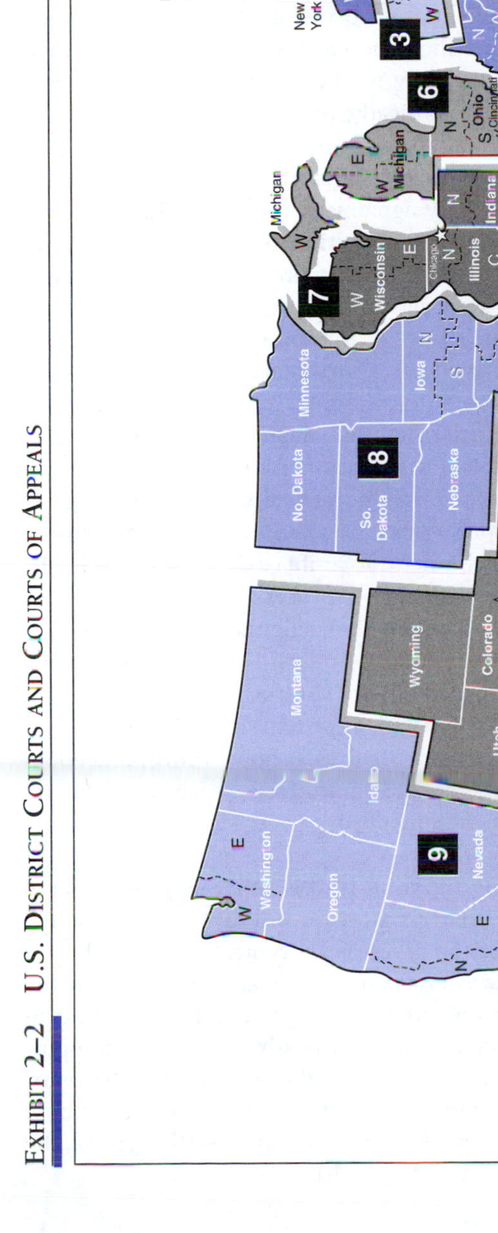

courts are rendering conflicting or inconsistent opinions on an important issue, such as how a particular federal statute should be applied to a specific factual situation, the Supreme Court may agree to review a case involving that issue. The Court can then render a definitive opinion on the matter, thus clarifying the law for the lower courts.

SECTION 4

Alternative Dispute Resolution

Alternative dispute resolution (ADR) refers to the various methods by which disputes are settled outside the court system. Typically, to save time and money for all parties involved, attorneys advise their clients to attempt a settlement before resorting to **litigation**—the process of resolving a dispute through the court system. Frequently, a settlement is achieved after a lawsuit has been initiated and pretrial investigations undertaken, but before a trial takes place. At this point, the parties and their attorneys have an opportunity to assess the evidence and attempt a settlement based on the relative strengths or weaknesses of their positions. Most civil lawsuits (about 95 percent) are settled before they go to trial.

ADR offers many advantages to disputing parties. Litigating even the simplest complaint is costly, and because of the backlog of cases pending in many courts, it may sometimes be several years before a case is actually tried. ADR, in contrast, usually entails fewer costs and allows disputes to be resolved relatively quickly. ADR also offers the advantage of privacy. Court proceedings are public, whereas ADR allows the parties to come together privately and work out an agreement. Another advantage of ADR is its flexibility. Normally, the parties themselves can control how the dispute will be settled, what procedures will be used, and whether the decision reached (either by the parties themselves or by a neutral third party) will be legally binding or nonbinding. ADR also offers advantages for the courts. To ease the burden on the courts and reduce costs, both the state and federal court systems have implemented programs that encourage or even require some form of ADR prior to trial.

Methods of ADR range from neighbors sitting down over a cup of coffee in an attempt to work out their differences to huge multinational corporations agreeing to resolve a dispute through a formal hearing before a panel of experts. Some of the most commonly used methods of ADR include negotiation, mediation, and arbitration. Keep in mind that new methods of ADR—or new combinations of existing methods—are continuously being devised and employed. In recent years, several organizations have been offering dispute-resolution services via the Internet. After looking at the traditional forms of ADR just mentioned, we examine some of the ways in which disputes are being resolved in various online forums.

NEGOTIATION

One of the simplest forms of ADR is **negotiation**, a process in which the parties attempt to settle their dispute informally, with or without attorneys to represent them. Typically, during the pretrial stages of litigation, the parties and/or their attorneys may meet informally one or more times to see if a mutually satisfactory agreement can be reached. In some courts, pretrial negotiation is mandatory. In these courts, before parties may proceed to trial, they must first meet with each other and attempt to negotiate a settlement. Only if the parties cannot reach an agreement will the court decide the issue. In other courts, negotiation is one of a menu of ADR options that the parties may (or must, in some cases and in some courts) pursue prior to trial.

In working out a mutually satisfactory agreement, disputing parties often find it helpful to have the input of a neutral (unbiased) third party. In the traditional negotiation process, however, attorneys act as advocates for their clients, which means that they put their clients' interests first. In recent years, to facilitate negotiation, various forms of what might be called "assisted negotiation" have been employed. Forms of ADR associated with the negotiation process include mini-trials, early neutral case evaluation, summary jury trials, and conciliation.

Mini-Trials. A **mini-trial** is a private proceeding in which each party's attorney briefly argues the party's case before the other party. Typically, a neutral third party, who acts as an adviser and an expert in the area being disputed, is also present. If the parties fail to reach an agreement, the adviser renders an opinion as to how a court would likely decide the issue. The proceeding assists the parties in determining whether they should negotiate a settlement of the dispute or take it to court.

Early Neutral Case Evaluation. In **early neutral case evaluation**, the parties select a neutral third party (generally an expert in the subject matter of the dispute) to evaluate their respective positions. The parties explain their points of view to the case evaluator however they wish. The case evaluator then assesses the strengths and weaknesses of the parties' positions, and this evaluation forms the basis for negotiating a settlement.

Summary Jury Trials. A form of ADR that has been successfully employed in the federal court system is the **summary jury trial (SJT)**. In an SJT, which occurs after a lawsuit has been initiated but before the trial, the litigants present their arguments and evidence to a jury. The jury then renders a verdict. The jury's verdict, however, is not binding. Rather, it serves as a guide to both sides in reaching an agreement during the mandatory negotiations that immediately follow the trial. Because no witnesses are called, the SJT is much speedier than a regular trial, and frequently the parties are able to settle their dispute without resorting to an actual trial. If no settlement is reached, both sides have the right to a full trial later.

Conciliation. Disputes may also be resolved in a friendly, nonadversarial manner through **conciliation**, in which a third party assists parties to a dispute in reconciling their differences. The conciliator helps to schedule negotiating sessions and carries offers back and forth between the parties when they refuse to face each other in direct negotiations. Technically, conciliators are not to recommend solutions. In practice, however, they often do. In contrast, a mediator is expected to propose solutions.

MEDIATION

Mediation, one of the oldest forms of ADR, is essentially a form of assisted negotiation, but one in which the mediator plays a more active role than the neutral third parties in negotiation-associated forms of ADR. In the **mediation** process, the parties themselves attempt to negotiate an agreement, but with the assistance of a neutral third party, called a mediator. The mediator need not be a lawyer. The mediator may be a single person, such as a paralegal, an attorney, or a volunteer from the community. Alternatively, a panel of mediators may be used. Usually, a mediator charges a fee, which can be split between the parties.

As with negotiation, some courts may encourage or require the parties to undertake mediation prior to a trial. Some states offer mediation as the only ADR method that may (or must) be undertaken before proceeding to trial. Florida, for example, has a comprehensive statewide mediation program to facilitate pretrial settlements.

The Mediator's Role. The mediator's role is basically to help the parties evaluate their positions and clarify the issues on which they do and do not agree. A mediator will try to discern what the parties' real interests are, as opposed to the stances that the parties have put forward. This is often done by holding private sessions with each party, in which the mediator learns what information the parties are unwilling to disclose to each other. Through joint and individual sessions with the parties, the mediator obtains information to assess realistically the alternative ways in which the dispute might be resolved. The mediator then proposes a solution, or alternative solutions, including what compromises will be necessary to reach agreement.

The Advantages of Mediation. Unlike litigation (and, to a certain extent, negotiation), mediation is not adversarial in nature. Rather, a mediator tries to find common ground on which an agreement can be based. Therefore, the process tends to reduce the antagonism between the disputants and to allow them to resume their former relationship. For this reason, mediation is often the preferred form of ADR for business disputes involving parties who either must or would like to continue an ongoing relationship. For example, business partners may be able to work out their differences through mediation more satisfactorily than through other forms of ADR or through litigation. Mediation is also beneficial in settling differences between employers and employees or other parties involved in long-term relationships.

ARBITRATION

A more formal method of alternative dispute resolution is **arbitration**, in which an arbitrator (a neutral third party or a panel of experts) hears a dispute and renders a decision. The key difference between arbitration and the forms of ADR just discussed is that in arbitration, the third party's decision may be legally binding, depending on the wishes of the parties.

Many courts, in both the federal and state court systems, require the pretrial arbitration of disputes. When pretrial arbitration is mandated by a court, normally the arbitrator's decision is not legally binding. If either of the parties is not satisfied with the decision, the court will try the case.

The Arbitration Process. In some respects, formal arbitration resembles a trial, although usually the procedural rules are much less restrictive than those governing litigation. In the typical hearing format, the parties present opening arguments to the arbitrator and state what remedies should or should not be granted. Next, evidence is presented, and witnesses may be called and examined by both sides. The arbitrator then renders a decision, called an **award**.

An arbitrator's award is usually the final word on the matter. Although the parties may appeal an arbitrator's decision, a court's review of the decision will be much more restricted in scope than an appellate court's review of a trial court's decision. The general view is that because the parties were free to frame the issues and set the powers of the arbitrator at the outset, they cannot complain about the results. The award will only be set aside if the arbitrator's conduct or "bad faith" substantially prejudiced the rights of one of the parties, if the award violates an established public policy, or if the arbitrator exceeded his or her powers (by arbitrating issues that the parties did not agree to submit to arbitration).

Arbitration Clauses and Statutes. Virtually any commercial matter can be submitted to arbitration. Frequently, parties include an **arbitration clause** in a contract specifying that any dispute arising under the contract will be resolved through arbitration rather than through the court system. Parties can also agree to arbitrate a dispute after it arises.

Most states have statutes (often based in part on the Uniform Arbitration Act of 1955) under which arbitration clauses will be enforced, and some state statutes compel arbitration of certain types of disputes, such as those involving public employees. At the federal level, the Federal Arbitration Act (FAA), enacted in 1925, enforces arbitration clauses in contracts involving maritime activity and interstate commerce—activities that the federal government has the authority to regulate through legislation (see Chapter 4).

Arbitrability. When a dispute arises as to whether the parties to a contract with an arbitration clause have agreed to submit a particular matter to arbitration, one party may file suit to compel arbitration. The court before which the suit is brought will not decide the basic controversy but must decide the issue of *arbitrability*—that is, whether the matter is one that must be resolved through arbitration.

Even when a claim involves a violation of a statute passed to protect a certain class of people, a court may determine that the parties must nonetheless abide by their agreement to arbitrate the dispute. Usually, a court will allow the claim to be arbitrated if the court, in interpreting the statute, can find no legislative intent to the contrary.

No party, however, will be ordered to submit a particular dispute to arbitration unless the court is convinced that the party has consented to do so.[15] Additionally, the courts will not compel arbitration if it is clear that the prescribed arbitration rules and procedures are inherently unfair to one of the parties. For example, in one case, an employer asked a court to issue an order compelling a former employee to submit to arbitration in accordance with an arbitration agreement that the parties had signed. Under that agreement, it was the employer's responsibility to establish the procedure and the rules for the arbitration. The court held that the employee did not have to submit her claim to arbitration because the rules were so one-sided that their only possible purpose was "to undermine the neutrality of the proceeding." According to the court, the biased rules created "a sham system unworthy even of the name of arbitration" in violation of the parties' contract to arbitrate.[16]

Mandatory Arbitration in the Employment Context. A significant question in the last several years has concerned mandatory arbitration clauses in employment contracts. Many claim that employees' rights are not sufficiently protected when they are forced, in order to be hired, to agree to arbitrate

15. See, for example, *Wright v. Universal Maritime Service Corp.*, 525 U.S. 70, 119 S.Ct. 391, 142 L.Ed.2d 361 (1998). In this case, the United States Supreme Court held that an arbitration clause in a collective bargaining agreement between a union and an employer did not clearly waive a union member's right to have a court rule on federal claims of employment discrimination; thus, an employee who was a member of the union was not required to submit his claim to arbitration.

16. *Hooters of America, Inc. v. Phillips*, 173 F.3d 933 (4th Cir. 1999).

all disputes and thus waive their rights under statutes specifically designed to protect workers. The Supreme Court, however, has generally held that mandatory arbitration clauses in employment contracts are enforceable.

For example, in a landmark 1991 decision, *Gilmer v. Interstate/Johnson Lane Corp.*,[17] the Supreme Court held that a claim brought under a federal statute prohibiting age discrimination (see Chapter 42) could be subject to arbitration. The Court concluded that the employee had waived his right to sue when he agreed, as part of a required registration application to be a securities representative with the New York Stock Exchange, to arbitrate "any dispute, claim, or controversy" relating to his employment.

The *Gilmer* decision was—and remains—controversial. In the years following that decision, the Equal Employment Opportunity Commission, which administers federal laws prohibiting employment discrimination, and some lower courts concluded that employment agreements mandating the arbitration of all disputes should not be enforced. By the early 2000s, whether the Federal Arbitration Act even applied to employment contracts was at issue. Some lower courts claimed that Congress, when passing the FAA, intended to exempt such contracts from coverage. In 2001, the Supreme Court rendered its opinion on this issue—see Case 2.3.

See Case 2.3 at the end of this chapter. To view the full, unedited case from Westlaw,® go to this text's Web site at **http://wbl-cs.westbuslaw.com**.

Providers of ADR Services

ADR services are provided by both government agencies and private organizations. A major provider of ADR services is the **American Arbitration Association (AAA).** Most of the largest law firms in the nation are members of this nonprofit association. Founded in 1926, the AAA now handles about 150,000 claims each year in its numerous offices around the country and in other nations. Cases brought before the AAA are heard by an expert or a panel of experts in the area relating to the dispute and are usually settled quickly. Generally, about half of the panel members are lawyers. To cover its costs, the AAA charges a fee, paid by the party filing the claim. In addition, each party to the dispute pays a specified amount for each hearing day, as well as a special additional fee in cases involving personal injuries or property loss.

Hundreds of for-profit firms around the country also provide dispute-resolution services. Typically, these firms hire retired judges to conduct arbitration hearings or otherwise assist parties in settling their disputes. Private ADR firms normally allow the parties to decide on the date of the hearing, the presiding judge, whether the judge's decision will be legally binding, and the site of the hearing—which may be a conference room, a law school office, or a leased courtroom. The judges follow procedures similar to those of the federal courts and use similar rules. Usually, each party to the dispute pays a filing fee and a designated fee for a hearing session or conference.

There are also international organizations, such as the International Chamber of Commerce, that provide forums for the arbitration of disputes between parties to international contracts. These organizations, as well as some of the advantages and disadvantages of arbitrating disputes in the international context, will be discussed in Chapter 52.

SECTION 5

Online Dispute Resolution

An increasing number of companies and organizations now offer dispute-resolution services using the Internet. **Online dispute resolution (ODR)** refers to the settlement of disputes in these online forums. To date, the most common types of disputes resolved in these forums have involved disagreements over the rights to domain names (Web site addresses—see Chapter 7) and disagreements over the quality of goods marketed via the Internet, including goods sold through Internet auction sites.

Currently, ODR may be best for resolving small- to medium-sized business liability claims, which may not be worth the expense of litigation or traditional methods of alternative dispute resolution. Rules being developed in online forums, however, may ultimately become a code of conduct for all of those who do business in cyberspace. In most online forums, there is no automatic application of the law of any specific jurisdiction. Instead, outcomes are often based on general, universal legal principles. As with offline methods of dispute resolution, any party may appeal to a court at any time.

17. 500 U.S. 20, 111 S.Ct. 1647, 114 L.Ed.2d 26 (1991).

Negotiation and Mediation Services

The online negotiation of a dispute is generally simpler and more practical than litigation. Typically, one party files a complaint, and the other party is notified by e-mail. Password-protected access is possible twenty-four hours a day, seven days a week. Fees are sometimes nominal; otherwise, they are low (often 2 percent to 4 percent, or less, of the disputed amount).

CyberSettle.com, Inc., clickNsettle.com, U.S. Settlement Corp. (ussettle.com), and other Web-based firms offer online forums for negotiating monetary settlements. The parties to a dispute may agree to submit offers that, if they fall within a previously determined range, will end the dispute, and the parties will split the difference. Special software keeps secret any offers that are not within the range. If there is no agreed-on range, typically an offer includes a deadline by which the other party must respond before the offer expires. The parties can drop the negotiations at any time.

Mediation providers have also tried resolving disputes online. SquareTrade, one of the mediation providers that has been used by eBay, the online auction site, mediates disputes involving $100 or more among eBay customers, currently for no charge. SquareTrade, which also resolves disputes among other parties, uses Web-based software that walks participants through a five-step e-resolution process. Negotiation between the parties occurs on a secure page within SquareTrade's Web site. The parties may consult a mediator. The entire process takes as little as ten to fourteen days, and there is no fee unless the parties use a mediator.

Arbitration Programs

A number of organizations and companies offer online arbitration programs. The Internet Corporation for Assigned Names and Numbers (ICANN), a nonprofit corporation that the federal government set up to oversee the distribution of domain names, has issued special rules for the resolution of domain name disputes.[18] ICANN has also authorized several organizations to arbitrate domain name disputes in accordance with ICANN's rules. Recently, the American Arbitration Association announced that it will soon be launching technology-based arbitration services as well.

Resolution Forum, Inc. (RFI), is a nonprofit organization associated with the Center for Legal Responsibility at South Texas College of Law. RFI offers arbitration services through its CAN-WIN conferencing system. Using standard browser software and an RFI password, the parties to a dispute access an online conference room. When multiple parties are involved, private communications and break-out sessions are possible via private messaging facilities. RFI also offers mediation services.

The Virtual Magistrate Project (VMAG) is affiliated with the American Arbitration Association, Chicago-Kent College of Law, Cyberspace Law Institute, National Center for Automated Information Research, and other organizations. VMAG offers arbitration for disputes involving users of online systems; victims of wrongful messages, postings, and files; and system operators subject to complaints or similar demands. VMAG also arbitrates intellectual property, personal property, real property, and tort disputes related to online contracts. VMAG attempts to resolve a dispute within seventy-two hours. The proceedings occur in a password-protected online newsgroup setting, and private e-mail among the participants is possible. A VMAG arbitrator's decision is issued in a written opinion. A party may appeal the outcome to a court.

18. ICANN's Rules for Uniform Domain Name Dispute Resolution Policy are online at **http://www.icann.org/udrp/udrp-rules-24oct99.htm**. Domain names will be discussed in more detial in Chapter 7, in the context of trademark law.

Terms and Concepts to Review

alternative dispute resolution (ADR) 32
American Arbitration Association (AAA) 35
arbitration 33
arbitration clause 34
award 34
bankruptcy court 26
conciliation 33
concurrent jurisdiction 26
diversity of citizenship 26
early neutral case evaluation 33

exclusive jurisdiction 27
federal question 26
in personam jurisdiction 25
in rem jurisdiction 25
judicial review 24
jurisdiction 25
justiciable controversy 28
litigation 32
long arm statute 25
mediation 33
mini-trial 32
negotiation 32
online dispute resolution (ODR) 35
probate court 26
question of fact 29
question of law 29
rule of four 30
small claims court 29
standing to sue 27
summary jury trial (SJT) 33
venue 27
writ of *certiorari* 30

Chapter Summary

The Judiciary's Role in American Government

The role of the judiciary—the courts—in the American governmental system is to interpret and apply the law. Through the process of judicial review—determining the constitutionality of laws—the judicial branch acts as a check on the executive and legislative branches of government.

Basic Judicial Requirements

1. *Jurisdiction*—Before a court can hear a case, it must have jurisdiction over the person against whom the suit is brought or the property involved in the suit, as well as jurisdiction over the subject matter.
   a. Limited versus general jurisdiction—Limited jurisdiction exists when a court is limited to a specific subject matter, such as probate or divorce. General jurisdiction exists when a court can hear any kind of case.
   b. Original versus appellate jurisdiction—Original jurisdiction exists with courts that have authority to hear a case for the first time (trial courts). Appellate jurisdiction exists with courts of appeals, or reviewing courts; generally, appellate courts do not have original jurisdiction.
   c. Federal jurisdiction—Arises (1) when a federal question is involved (when the plaintiff's cause of action is based, at least in part, on the U.S. Constitution, a treaty, or a federal law) or (2) when a case involves diversity of citizenship (citizens of different states, for example) and the amount in controversy exceeds $75,000.
   d. Concurrent versus exclusive jurisdiction—Concurrent jurisdiction exists when two different courts have authority to hear the same case. Exclusive jurisdiction exists when only state courts or only federal courts have authority to hear a case.
2. *Jurisdiction in cyberspace*—Because the Internet does not have physical boundaries, traditional jurisdictional concepts have been difficult to apply in cases involving activities conducted via the Web. Gradually, the courts are developing standards to use in determining when jurisdiction over a Web owner or operator in another state is proper.
3. *Venue*—Venue has to do with the most appropriate location for a trial, which is usually the geographic area where the event leading to the dispute took place or where the parties reside.
4. *Standing to sue*—A requirement that a party must have a legally protected and tangible interest at stake sufficient to justify seeking relief through the court system. The controversy at issue must also be a justiciable controversy—one that is real and substantial, as opposed to hypothetical or academic.

The State and Federal Court Systems

1. *Trial courts*—Courts of original jurisdiction, in which legal actions are initiated.
   a. State—Courts of general jurisdiction can hear any case; courts of limited jurisdiction include divorce courts, probate courts, traffic courts, small claims courts, and so on.

Chapter Summary—continued

The State and Federal Court Systems—(continued)	**b.** Federal—The federal district court is the equivalent of the state trial court. Federal courts of limited jurisdiction include the U.S. Tax Court, the U.S. Bankruptcy Court, and the U.S. Court of Federal Claims. **2.** *Intermediate appellate courts*—Courts of appeals, or reviewing courts; generally without original jurisdiction. Many states have an intermediate appellate court; in the federal court system, the U.S. circuit courts of appeals are the intermediate appellate courts. **3.** *Supreme (highest) courts*—Each state has a supreme court, although it may be called by some other name, from which appeal to the United States Supreme Court is possible only if a federal question is involved. The United States Supreme Court is the highest court in the federal court system and the final arbiter of the Constitution and federal law.
Alternative Dispute Resolution	**1.** *Negotiation*—The parties come together, with or without attorneys to represent them, and try to reach a settlement. Traditionally, no third party was involved in the process. Today, several forms of "assisted negotiation"—negotiation involving a neutral (unbiased) third party—are used, including mini-trials, early neutral case evaluation, and (in some federal courts) summary jury trials, or SJTs. The opinion of a third party (or "jury," in an SJT) forms the basis for negotiating a settlement. **2.** *Mediation*—The parties themselves reach an agreement with the help of a neutral third party, called a mediator, who proposes solutions. At the parties' request, a mediator may make a legally binding decision. **3.** *Arbitration*—A more formal method of ADR in which the parties submit their dispute to a neutral third party, the arbitrator, who renders a decision. The decision may or may not be legally binding, depending on the circumstances. **4.** *Providers of ADR services*—The leading nonprofit provider of ADR services is the American Arbitration Association. Hundreds of for-profit firms also provide ADR services.
Online Dispute Resolution	A number of organizations and firms are now offering negotiation, mediation, and arbitration services through online forums. To date, these forums have been a practical alternative for the resolution of domain name disputes and e-commerce disputes in which the amount in controversy is relatively small.

Cases for Analysis

Westlaw. You can access the full text of each case presented below by going to the Westlaw cases on this text's Web site at http://wbl-casebook.westbuslaw.com. Each Westlaw case includes the names of all plaintiffs and defendants, the dates on which the case was argued and decided, a brief summary of the issues and decisions in the case, headnotes classifying the specific issues in the case according to the West Key Number System, and the court's opinion. Concurring and dissenting opinions, if any, are included as well.

Case 2.1 Jurisdiction

Cole v. Mileti
United States Court of Appeals,
Sixth Circuit, 1998.
133 F.3d 433.

MERRITT, Circuit Judge.

In this diversity case, defendant Mileti appeals the Magistrate's judgment in favor of plaintiff Cole, arguing that the Magistrate, * * * improperly assert[ed] personal jurisdiction over him * * * . We conclude that the Magistrate had jurisdiction over Mileti * * * .

I.

This dispute arises from * * * [an] agreement between defendant Mileti and plaintiff's decedent, Joseph

Cole. In 1983, Mileti co-produced a motion picture with Robert Altman called "Streamers" and organized Streamers International Distributors, Inc., a California corporation, to purchase and distribute the film. Cole was an initial investor in the corporation. He purchased two hundred shares of Streamers stock, lent the corporation $475,000, and became one of its officers and directors. To fund his investment, Cole secured a loan from Equitable Bank of Baltimore. The film was not a success. Mileti offered to buy Cole's share of the corporation in exchange for Cole's resignation as an officer and director. Accordingly on September 4, 1984, the parties executed the * * * agreement at issue in which Cole transferred his stock and indebtedness to Mileti, who in return agreed to repay the Bank by June 16, 1985.

Mileti and Cole were business associates in Cleveland, Ohio in the 1970s. In 1979, Mileti moved to California where he became a movie producer. He was a California resident at all times relevant to the negotiation of this surety agreement. Cole continued to live in Cleveland throughout the Streamers project. He was therefore an Ohio resident when he executed this contract. When "Streamers" failed at the box office in early 1984, Mileti began negotiating with Cole to buy out his share of the corporation. On February 6, 1984, Cole's lawyer sent Mileti a written draft integrating their agreement. Thereafter, telephone calls concerning the September 4, 1984 agreement were exchanged between California and Ohio. The record also contains a letter dated August 17, 1984, that refers to these negotiations and to Cole's resignation. Mileti subsequently signed the contract in California and sent it back to Ohio, where Cole executed it. The parties agreed that the contract would "be governed and construed in accordance with the laws of the State of California."

Mileti failed to repay the loan by June 16, 1985, as required by the contract, so Cole continued to make sporadic payments to the Bank until 1992, when the Bank sued him to recover the balance. Cole settled that dispute with the Bank for $310,000. He eventually brought this diversity action in the Northern District of Ohio on May 24, 1994, nine years after the alleged breach. Cole's widow, Marcia Cole, was substituted as the plaintiff in this action after Cole died on January 8, 1995.

After the district court rejected Mileti's motion to dismiss this suit for lack of personal jurisdiction, the parties consented to the jurisdiction of a U.S. Magistrate and filed simultaneous motions for summary judgment. The Magistrate granted summary judgment to Ms. Cole after concluding that personal jurisdiction existed * * * . [T]he Magistrate entered a final judgment against Mileti for damages of $988,861.89 and prejudgment interest of $470,728.66. Mileti appealed the Magistrate's judgment directly to this Court.

II.

Mileti first argues that the Magistrate's assertion of personal jurisdiction over him was fundamentally unfair and therefore unconstitutional. To determine whether personal jurisdiction exists over a nonresident defendant, federal courts apply the law of the forum state [the state in which the court sits], subject to the constitutional limits of due process. The Magistrate below therefore properly applied the Ohio long-arm statute, which provides:

> A court may exercise personal jurisdiction over a person who acts directly or by an agent, as to a cause of action arising from the person's:
>
> (1) Transacting any business in this state * * * .

* * * [O]ur central inquiry is whether Mileti established certain minimum business contacts with Ohio so that the Magistrate's exercise of personal jurisdiction over him did not offend traditional notions of fair play and substantial justice.

The [U.S. Court of Appeals for the] Sixth Circuit [whose decisions bind this court] has established a three-part test to determine whether specific jurisdiction exists over a nonresident defendant like Mileti. First, the defendant must purposefully avail himself of the privilege of conducting activities within the forum state; second, the cause of action must arise from the defendant's activities there; and third, the acts of the defendant or consequences caused by the defendant must have a substantial enough connection with the forum state to make its exercise of jurisdiction over the defendant fundamentally fair.

If, as here, *a nonresident defendant transacts business by negotiating and executing a contract via telephone calls and letters to an Ohio resident, then the defendant has purposefully availed himself of the forum by creating a continuing obligation in Ohio.* Furthermore, if the cause of action is for breach of that contract, as it is here, then the cause of action naturally arises from the defendant's activities in Ohio. Finally, when we find that a defendant like Mileti purposefully availed himself of the forum and that the cause of action arose directly from that contact, we presume the specific assertion of personal jurisdiction was proper. In light of this precedent, we have no doubt that the Magistrate's assertion of jurisdiction over Mileti was fundamentally fair and constitutional. [Emphasis added.]

* * * *

Accordingly, we affirm the Magistrate's judgment below.

WELLFORD, Circuit Judge, dissenting.

I believe that the assertion of personal jurisdiction over Mileti offends traditional notions of fair play and substantial justice. Mileti moved to California from Ohio in 1979. Calls and correspondence between Mileti in California and Cole in Ohio took place in 1984, resulting in the subject contract which the parties agreed would be construed in accordance with California law. It was not until 1994 that the plaintiff sought to hold Mileti responsible for breach of contract in Ohio.

* * * Jurisdiction over a foreign corporation doing some degree of business within a state involves entirely different jurisdictional considerations than personal jurisdiction over a nonresident individual with few contacts within the forum state. Even a corporation's conducting a single activity or isolated items of activities were not considered to be sufficient to establish personal jurisdiction if it maintained no property, business, or agency in the state. * * * The existence of a contract with a citizen of the forum state, standing alone, will not suffice to confer personal jurisdiction over a foreign defendant. Rather, prior negotiations and contemplated future consequences, along with the terms of the contract and the parties' actual course of dealing * * * must be evaluated in determining whether the defendant purposefully established minimum contacts within the forum. Further, the unilateral activity of those who claim some relationship with a non-resident defendant cannot satisfy the requirement of contact with the forum State.

* * * Cole bears the burden of establishing jurisdiction over Mileti in Ohio. The defendant must be amenable to suit under the forum state's long-arm statute and the due process requirements of the Constitution. This court must examine the limits of the statute and due process.

The majority sets out the tests this court adopts in these situations, but they are usually applied to corporations conducting some modicum of business in the forum state. * * *

* * * *

The two related functions of the minimum contacts requirement are that it protects a defendant from the burden of litigating in an inconvenient forum and prevents the states from reaching out, through their courts, beyond the limits imposed on them by their status as coequal sovereigns in a federal system.

This is a case between two individuals. It does not involve an Ohio corporation whose activities with nonresidents may occasion special interests or concerns in Ohio. I would find that Mileti has not been shown by the plaintiff to have any substantial connection in or with Ohio, nor that he would have been led reasonably to believe that he was subjecting himself to the processes of the Ohio jurisdiction.

For the foregoing reasons, I believe personal jurisdiction in Ohio over California resident Mileti offends notions of fairness and equity in this case. Accordingly, I DISSENT because Mileti's motion to dismiss should have been granted. Plaintiff has simply failed in her burden of proof.

CASE 2.2 JURISDICTION

INTERNATIONAL LEAGUE AGAINST RACISM AND ANTISEMITISM V. YAHOO! INC.

Tribunal de Grande Instance de Paris, 2000.

[*JEAN-JACQUES GOMEZ*] the Presiding Justice,

Considering our order of 22nd May 2000, to which reference shall expressly be made and wherein we ordered:

1/ YAHOO Inc.: to take all necessary measures to dissuade and make impossible any access via yahoo.com to the auction service for Nazi merchandise as well as to any other site or service that may be construed as an apology for Nazism or contesting the reality of Nazi crimes

2/ YAHOO France: to issue to all Internet surfers, even before use is made of the link enabling them to proceed with searches on yahoo.com, a warning informing them of the risks involved in continuing to view such sites;

3/ continuance of the proceeding in order to enable YAHOO Inc. to submit for deliberation by all interested parties the measures that it proposes to take to put an end to the trouble and damage suffered and to prevent any further trouble;

Considering our order of 11th August 2000, to which reference shall be made insofar as it sets out the facts of the case as well as the arguments and claims of the parties.

Considering the submissions made by [the International League Against Racism and Antisemitism and others] and reiterated at the hearing of 6th November 2000 in pursuit of their case * * *;

Considering the submissions in defence presented both by Yahoo France and by Yahoo Inc. in pursuit of their case * * *;

Considering the report by the consultants [whom the court appointed to consider technical solutions];

* * * *

On the demands placed on YAHOO Inc.

Whereas in the opinion of the company YAHOO Inc.:

—this court is not competent to make a ruling in this dispute;

—there are no technical means capable of satisfying the terms of the order of 22nd May 2000;

* * * *

Whereas it is true that the "Yahoo Auctions" site is in general directed principally at surfers based in the United States having regard notably to the items posted for sale, the methods of payment envisaged, the terms of delivery, the language and the currency used, the same cannot be said to apply to the auctioning of objects representing symbols of Nazi ideology which may be of interest to any person;

Whereas, furthermore, and as already ruled, the simple act of displaying such objects in France constitutes a violation of [French law] and therefore a threat to internal public order;

Whereas, in addition, this display clearly causes damage in France to the plaintiff associations who are justified in demanding the cessation and reparation thereof;

Whereas YAHOO is aware that it is addressing French parties because upon making a connection to its auctions site from a terminal located in France it responds by transmitting advertising banners written in the French language;

Whereas a sufficient basis is thus established in this case for a connecting link with France, which renders our jurisdiction perfectly competent to rule in this matter;

* * * *

Whereas this plea will therefore be rejected;

* * * *

Whereas it emerges from the [findings of the consultants whom the court appointed to consider technical solutions] that it is possible to determine the physical location of a surfer from the [Internet Protocol (IP)] address;

* * * *

Whereas it should be borne in mind that YAHOO Inc. already carries out geographical identification of French surfers or surfers operating out of French territory and visiting its auctions site, insofar as it routinely displays advertising banners in the French language targeted at these surfers, in respect of whom it therefore has means of identification; * * *

Whereas in addition to the geographical identification * * *, the consultants' report suggests that a request be made to surfers whose IP address is ambiguous * * * to provide a declaration of nationality, which in effect amounts to a declaration of the surfer's geographical origin, which YAHOO could ask for when the home page is reached, or when a search is initiated for Nazi objects if the word "Nazi" appears in the user's search string, immediately before the request is processed by the search engine;

Whereas the consultants * * * estimate that a combination of two procedures, namely geographical identification and declaration of nationality, would enable a filtering success rate approaching 90% to be achieved;

* * * *

Whereas * * * even if YAHOO had been unable to identify with certainty the surfer's geographical origin, in this case France, it would know the place of delivery, and would be in a position to prevent the delivery from taking place if the delivery address was located in France;

Whereas, furthermore, YAHOO Inc. could obtain additional nationality information from the language version of the surfer's browser;

* * * *

Whereas the combination of these technical measures at its disposal * * * therefore afford it the opportunity of satisfying the injunctions contained in the order of 22nd May 2000 in respect of the filtering of access to the auctions service for Nazi objects and to the service relating to the work *Mein Kampf* which was included in the wording of the aforementioned order by the phrase "and any other site or service constituting an apology for Nazism";

* * * *

ON THESE GROUNDS

Ruling in public hearing, with the possibility of appeal, by order following full discussion by all parties,

We reject the plea of incompetence reiterated by YAHOO Inc.;

We order YAHOO Inc. to comply within 3 months from notification of the present order with the injunctions contained in our order of 22nd May 2000 subject to a penalty of 100,000 Francs per day of delay effective from the first day following expiry of the 3 month period;

* * * *

We order YAHOO Inc. to pay to each of the plaintiffs the sum of 10,000 Francs * * *.

Made at Paris on 20th November 2000

CASE 2.3 ARBITRATION

CIRCUIT CITY STORES, INC. V. ADAMS

Supreme Court of the United States, 2001.
532 U.S. 105,
121 S.Ct. 1302,
149 L.Ed.2d 234.

Justice *KENNEDY* delivered the opinion of the Court.

Section 1 of the Federal Arbitration Act (FAA) excludes from the Act's coverage "contracts of employment of seamen, railroad employees, or any other class of workers engaged in foreign or interstate commerce." * * *

* * * *

I

In October 1995, respondent Saint Clair Adams applied for a job at petitioner Circuit City Stores, Inc., a national retailer of consumer electronics. Adams signed an employment application which included the following provision:

> "I agree that I will settle any and all previously unasserted claims, disputes or controversies arising out of or relating to my application or candidacy for employment, employment and/or cessation of employment with Circuit City, *exclusively* by final and binding *arbitration* before a neutral Arbitrator. By way of example only, such claims include claims under federal, state, and local statutory or common law, such as the Age Discrimination in Employment Act, Title VII of the Civil Rights Act of 1964, as amended, including the amendments of the Civil Rights Act of 1991, the Americans with Disabilities Act, the law of contract and the law of tort." ([E]mphasis in original.)

Adams was hired as a sales counselor in Circuit City's store in Santa Rosa, California.

Two years later, Adams filed an employment discrimination lawsuit against Circuit City in state court, asserting claims under * * * California law. Circuit City filed suit in the United States District Court for the Northern District of California, seeking to enjoin the state-court action and to compel arbitration of respondent's claims pursuant to the FAA. The District Court entered the requested order. Respondent, the court concluded, was obligated by the arbitration agreement to submit his claims against the employer to binding arbitration. An appeal followed.

* * * [T]he Court of Appeals held the arbitration agreement between Adams and Circuit City was contained in a "contract of employment," and so was not subject to the FAA. Circuit City petitioned this Court * * * . We granted *certiorari* to resolve the issue.

II

A

* * * [T]he FAA compels judicial enforcement of a wide range of written arbitration agreements. * * *

* * * *

The instant case * * * involves * * * the exemption from coverage under [Section] 1. * * * Most Courts of Appeals conclude the exclusion provision is limited to transportation workers, defined, for instance, as those workers "actually engaged in the movement of goods in interstate commerce." * * * [T]he Court of Appeals for the Ninth Circuit takes a different view and interprets the [Section] 1 exception to exclude all contracts of employment from the reach of the FAA. * * *

B

* * * *

Respondent, endorsing the reasoning of the Court of Appeals for the Ninth Circuit that the provision excludes all employment contracts, relies on the asserted breadth of the words "contracts of employment of . . . any other class of workers engaged in * * * commerce." * * * [R]espondent contends [Section] 1's interpretation should have a like reach, thus exempting all employment contracts. The two provisions, it is argued, are coterminous; under this view the "involving commerce" provision brings within the FAA's scope all contracts within the Congress' commerce power, and the "engaged in . . . commerce" language in [Section] 1 in turn exempts from the FAA all employment contracts falling within that authority.

This reading of [Section] 1, however, runs into an immediate and, in our view, insurmountable textual obstacle [a problem in interpeting the text of Section 1 of the FAA]. * * * [T]he words "any other class of workers engaged in * * * commerce" constitute a residual phrase, following, in the same sentence, explicit reference to "seamen" and "railroad employees." Construing the residual phrase to exclude all employment contracts fails to give independent effect to the statute's enumeration of the specific categories of workers which precedes it; there would be no need for Congress to use the phrases "seamen" and "railroad employees" if those same classes of workers were subsumed within the meaning of the "engaged in * * * commerce" residual clause. The wording of [Section] 1 calls for the application of * * * the statutory canon that "[w]here general words follow specific words in a statutory enumeration, the general words are construed to embrace only objects similar in nature to those objects enumerated by the preceding specific words." Under this rule of construction the residual clause should be read to give effect to the terms "seamen" and "railroad employees," and should itself be controlled and defined by reference to the enumerated categories of workers which are recited just before it; the interpretation of the clause pressed by respondent fails to produce these results.

* * * [E]ven if the term "engaged in commerce" stood alone in [Section] 1, we would not construe the provision to exclude all contracts of employment from the FAA. Congress uses different modifiers to the word "commerce" in the design and enactment of its statutes. The phrase "affecting commerce" indicates Congress' intent to regulate to the outer limits of its authority under the Commerce Clause. The "involving commerce" phrase, the operative words for the reach of the basic coverage provision in [Section] 2, was at issue in [a previous Supreme Court case]. * * * Considering the usual meaning of the word "involving," and the pro-arbitration purposes of the FAA, [we] held the word "involving," like "affecting," signals an intent to exercise Congress' commerce power to the full. Unlike those phrases, however, the general words "in commerce" and the specific phrase "engaged in commerce" are understood to have a more limited reach. * * * [T]he words "in commerce" are often-found words of art that we have not read as expressing congressional intent to regulate to the outer limits of authority under the Commerce Clause.

* * * *

In sum, the text of the FAA forecloses the construction of [Section] 1 followed by the Court of Appeals in the case under review, a construction which would exclude all employment contracts from the FAA. * * *

* * * *

For the foregoing reasons, the judgment of the Court of Appeals for the Ninth Circuit is reversed, and the case is remanded for further proceedings consistent with this opinion.

It is so ordered.

Justice *STEVENS* * * *, dissenting.

* * * *

* * * History amply supports the proposition that [the exclusion] was an uncontroversial provision that merely confirmed the fact that no one interested in the enactment of the FAA ever intended or expected that [Section] 2 would apply to employment contracts. * * *

The irony of the Court's reading of [Section] 2 to include contracts of employment is compounded by its cramped interpretation of the exclusion inserted into [Section] 1. As proposed and enacted, the exclusion fully responded to the concerns of the Seamen's Union and other labor organizations that [Section] 2 might encompass employment contracts by expressly exempting not only the labor agreements of "seamen" and "railroad employees," but also of "*any other class of workers* engaged in foreign or interstate commerce" [emphasis added]. Today, however, the Court fulfills the original—and originally unfounded—fears of organized labor by essentially rewriting the text of [Section] 1 to exclude the employment contracts solely of "seamen, railroad employees, or any other class of *transportation* workers engaged in foreign or interstate commerce" [emphasis added] In contrast, whether one views the legislation before or after the amendment to [Section] 1, it is clear that it was not intended to apply to employment contracts at all.

* * * *

Justice *SOUTER* * * *, dissenting.

* * * [In the FAA] Congress used language intended to go as far as Congress could go, whatever that might be over time.

* * * *

[In the majority's opinion] exemption language is to be read as petrified when coverage language is read to grow. * * *

The Court has no good reason * * * to reject a reading of "engaged in" as an expression of intent to legislate to the full extent of the commerce power over employment contracts. The statute is accordingly entitled to a coherent reading as a whole by treating the exemption for employment contracts as keeping pace with the expanded understanding of the commerce power generally.

CASE PROBLEMS

2–1. George Noonan, a Boston police detective and a devoted nonsmoker, has spent most of his career educating Bostonians about the health risks of tobacco use. In 1992, an ad for Winston cigarettes featuring Noonan's image appeared in several French magazines. Some of the magazines were on sale at newsstands in Boston. Noonan filed a suit in a federal district court against The Winston Co., Lintas:Paris (the French advertising agency that created the ads), and others. Lintas:Paris and the other French defendants claimed that they did not know the magazines would be sold in Boston and filed a motion to dismiss the suit for lack of personal jurisdiction. Does the court have jurisdiction? Why, or why not? [*Noonan v. The Winston Co.*, 135 F.3d 85 (1st Cir. 1998)]

2–2. Aldo Uberti and Co., an Italian corporation, manufactures a six-shot, single-action revolver known as the Cattleman. Uberti made the gun primarily for the American market and sells its guns to a U.S. distributor for sale throughout the country. Henry Pacho, a resident of Arizona, bought one of the guns, wrapped it in a towel, and put it under the seat of his car. His two-year-old niece, Corrina, was helping to clean the car when the gun fell out of the towel, hit the pavement, and discharged. The bullet struck Corrina in the head and killed her. Corrina's parents filed a suit in an Arizona state court against Uberti, alleging that the company was liable for the "design, manufacture, sale, and distribution of a defective and unreasonably dangerous product." Uberti asked the court to dismiss the suit on the ground that the court did not have personal jurisdiction over Uberti. Can an Arizona state court exercise jurisdiction over Uberti in this case? Why, or why not? [*A. Uberti and Co. v. Leonardo,* 892 P.2d 1354 (Ariz. 1995)]

2–3. Gates worked for Arizona Brewing Co. and was a member of the International Union of United Brewers, Flour, Cereal, and Soft Drink Workers of America. A contract between Gates's employer and the union stated that in any employment-related disputes the employer and the union were to try to settle their differences, but if the parties could not reach a settlement, the matter was to be decided by arbitration. Claiming that the arbitration clause was void under an Arizona arbitration statute, Gates brought a lawsuit against Arizona Brewing Co. to recover wages. Gates had not made any attempt to submit the dispute between him and the employer to arbitration. The employer argued that Gates could not bring a lawsuit until after arbitration had occurred. A provision in the Arizona arbitration statute, which generally enforced arbitration clauses in contracts, stated that "this act shall not apply to collective contracts between employers and . . . associations of employ[ees]." Must Gates participate in arbitration before bringing a lawsuit? Explain. [*Gates v. Arizona Brewing Co.,* 54 Ariz. 266, 95 P.2d 49 (1939)

2–4. When Roger and Susan Faherty divorced, they entered into a property settlement agreement that was incorporated into the final divorce decree. The property settlement agreement contained a clause that mandated arbitration of any dispute arising out of the agreement. Roger failed to make several alimony and child-support payments, and Susan sought court enforcement of the property settlement agreement. Roger's consequent motion to have the court compel arbitration was granted by the court, and the dispute was arbitrated. The arbitrator's decision required Roger to pay Susan $37,648 for back alimony payments and $12,284 for overdue child support. Roger, although he had been the one to petition the court for arbitration, now challenged the validity of the arbitration clause in alimony and child-support matters. He claimed that as a matter of public policy, such issues should be settled by the courts, not by arbitration. Will the court agree with Roger? Discuss. [*Faherty v. Faherty,* 97 N.J. 99, 477 A.2d 1257 (1984)]

2–5. Colorado's Mandatory Arbitration Act required that all civil lawsuits involving damages of less than $50,000 be arbitrated rather than tried in court. The statutory scheme, which was a pilot project, affected eight judicial districts in the state. It provided for a court trial for any party dissatisfied with an arbitrator's decision. It also provided that if the trial did not result in an improvement of more than 10 percent in the position of the party who demanded the trial, that party had to pay the costs of the arbitration proceeding. The constitutionality of the act was challenged by a plaintiff who maintained in part that it violated litigants' rights of access to the courts and to trial by jury. What will the court decide? Explain your answer. [*Firelock, Inc. v. District Court, 20th Judicial District,* 776 P.2d 1090 (Colo. 1989)]

2–6. A few years ago, New York State revised its new car "lemon law" to allow consumers who complained of purchasing a "lemon" to have their disputes arbitrated before a professional arbitrator appointed by the New York attorney general. Before it was revised, the lemon law allowed for the arbitration of disputes, but the forum in which arbitration took place was sponsored by trade associations within the automobile industry, and consumers often complained of unfair awards. The revised law also provided that consumers were not required to arbitrate but, if they wished, could sue a manufacturer in court. Manufacturers, however, were *compelled* to arbitrate claims if a consumer chose to do so and could not resort to the courts. Trade associations representing automobile manufacturers and importers brought an action seeking a declaration that the alternative arbitration mechanism of the lemon law was unconstitutional because it deprived them of their right to trial by jury. How will the court decide? Discuss. [*Motor Vehicle Manufacturers Association of the United States v. State,* 551 N.Y.S.2d 470, 550 N.E.2d 919, 75 N.Y.2d 175 (1990)]

2–7. Alex Sutton, a professional golfer living in Middleburg, Florida, entered into a sponsorship agreement with ARS & Associates, a Michigan partnership. Among other things, the agreement provided that (1) ARS would sponsor Sutton on a Professional Golfing Association (PGA) tour, (2) ARS would pay all of Sutton's expenses, (3) ARS and Sutton would split the proceeds (whatever remained after ARS had been reimbursed for expenses) fifty-fifty, and (4) ARS would provide health insurance for Sutton. Preliminary negotiations were carried out mostly over the phone. ARS drew up the agreement in Michigan and sent it to Sutton in Florida; Sutton signed the contract and returned it to ARS. ARS then signed the agreement and sent a copy of it to Sutton. Sutton subsequently participated in several senior PGA events, including two tournaments in Florida. While playing golf in a senior PGA tournament in Palm Springs, California, Sutton suffered a heart attack and, as a result, later incurred costs of more than $100,000 for open-heart surgery and related medical expenses. Because ARS had not obtained health-insurance coverage for Sutton, Sutton sued ARS in a Florida state court for breach of the agreement. ARS moved to dismiss the action for lack of personal jurisdiction. Can the Florida court, under its long arm statute, exercise personal jurisdiction over the Michigan defendant in this case? Discuss. [*Sutton v. Smith*, 603 So.2d 693 (Fla.App. 1992)]

2–8. Crown Central Petroleum Corporation does business as La Gloria Oil & Gas Company. Under a permit issued by the Environmental Protection Agency (EPA), La Gloria's oil refinery discharges storm-water run-off into Black Fork Creek. Black Fork Creek flows into Prairie Creek, which flows into the Neches River, which flows into Lake Palestine eighteen miles downstream. Friends of the Earth, Inc. (FOE), is a not-for-profit corporation dedicated to the protection of the environment. FOE filed a suit in a federal district court against La Gloria under the Federal Water Pollution Control Act. FOE claimed that La Gloria had violated its EPA permit and that this conduct had directly affected "the health, economic, recreational, aesthetic and environmental interests of FOE's members" who used the lake. La Gloria filed a motion for summary judgment, arguing that FOE lacked standing to bring the suit. The court granted the motion, and FOE appealed. Does FOE have standing to sue La Gloria with respect to this issue? Explain. [*Friends of the Earth, Inc. v. Crown Central Petroleum Corp.*, 95 F.3d 358 (5th Cir. 1996)]

2–9. A former probationary employee of the Ohio Department of Mental Retardation brought a suit against her employer in the Ohio Court of Claims. The employee claimed that her discharge constituted a violation of her right to freedom of speech, guaranteed by the First Amendment to the U.S. Constitution, in that she was fired because she vocally disagreed about the treatment received by a particular mentally retarded person. Without ruling on her constitutional claims, the state court dismissed her action, holding that her discharge was a valid personnel decision. Following the dismissal by the Ohio court, the plaintiff sued in a federal district court. The federal court dismissed the constitutional claim against the state officials on the ground that the employee's previous state action constituted "a knowing, intelligent, and voluntary waiver" of her federal action. An Ohio statute provides that "filing a civil action in the Court of Claims results in a complete waiver of any cause of action, based on the same act or omission . . . against any state officer or employee." The employee appealed. The question before the appellate court is whether a state statute can limit jurisdiction granted by federal law. What should the court decide, and why? [*Leaman v. Johnson*, 794 F.2d 1148 (6th Cir. 1986)]

2–10. George Rush, a New York resident and columnist for the New York *Daily News*, wrote a critical column about Berry Gordy, the founder and former president of Motown Records. Gordy, a California resident, filed suit in a California state court against Rush and the newspaper (the defendants), alleging defamation (a civil wrong, or tort, that occurs when the publication of false statements harms a person's good reputation). Most of the newspaper's subscribers are in the New York area, and the paper covers mostly New York events. Thirteen copies of its daily edition are distributed to California subscribers, however, and the paper does cover events that are of nationwide interest to the entertainment industry. Because of its focus on entertainment, the newspaper also routinely sends reporters to California to gather news from California sources. Can a California state court exercise personal jurisdiction over the New York defendants in this case? What factors will the court consider in deciding this question? If you were the judge, how would you decide the issue, and why? Discuss fully. [*Gordy v. Daily News, L.P.*, 95 F.3d 829 (9th Cir. 1996)]

2–11. In 1989, Kidder, Peabody & Co. (KP) hired Alphonse Fletcher, an African American, to work as a trader analyst. His annual salary was tied to a percentage of his trading profits. Fletcher contended that for 1990 he was entitled to between $5 million and $6.5 million in compensation. Fletcher alleged that KP concluded that the amount "was simply too much money to pay a young black man." The company purportedly deferred payment of half of his compensation and applied other terms relating to his compensation agreement to which his white counterparts were not subject. Fletcher resigned and filed a lawsuit against the firm in a New York state court, charging the firm with racial discrimination in violation of state law. KP asked the court to compel arbitration on the basis of an arbitration clause in the form that Fletcher had signed as part of his application for registration with the New York Stock Exchange and securities exchanges (which he had been required to do as a condition of working for KP). Will the court require Fletcher to arbitrate his claim of unlawful discrimination? Discuss. [*Fletcher v. Kidder, Peabody & Co.*, 81 N.Y.2d 623, 619 N.E.2d 998, 601 N.Y.S. 686 (1993)]

2–12. Randall Fris worked as a seaman on an Exxon Shipping Co. oil tanker for eight years without incident. One night, he boarded the ship for duty while intoxicated, in violation of company policy. This policy also allowed Exxon to discharge employees who were intoxicated and thus unfit for work. Exxon discharged Fris. Under a contract with Fris's union, the discharge was submitted to arbitration. The arbitrators ordered Exxon to reinstate Fris on an oil tanker. Exxon filed a suit against the union, challenging the award as contrary to public policy, which opposes having intoxicated persons operate seagoing vessels. Can a court set aside an arbitration award on the ground (legal basis) that the award violates public policy? Should the court set aside the award in this case? Explain. [*Exxon Shipping Co. v. Exxon Seamen's Union*, 11 F.3d 1189 (3d Cir. 1993)]

2–13. Phillip Beaudry, who suffered from mental illness, worked in the Department of Income Maintenance for the state of Connecticut. Beaudry was fired from his job when it was learned that he had misappropriated approximately $1,640 in state funds.

Beaudry filed a complaint with his union, Council 4 of the American Federation of State, County, and Municipal Employees (AFSCME), and eventually the dispute was submitted to an arbitrator. The arbitrator concluded that Beaudry had been dismissed without "just cause," because Beaudry's acts were caused by his mental illness and "were not willful or volitional or within his capacity to control." Because Beaudry had a disability, the employer was required, under state law, to transfer him to a position that he was competent to hold. The arbitrator awarded Beaudry reinstatement, back pay, seniority, and other benefits. The state appealed the decision to a court. What public policies must the court weigh in making its decision? How should the court rule? [*State v. Council 4, AFSCME*, 27 Conn.App. 635, 608 A.2d 718 (1992)]

2–14. Cal-Ban 3000 is a weight loss drug made by Health Care Products, Inc., a Florida corporation, and marketed through CKI Industries, another Florida corporation. Enticed by North Carolina newspaper ads for Cal-Ban, the wife of Douglas Tart bought the drug at Prescott's Pharmacies, Inc., in North Carolina for her husband. Within a week, Tart suffered a ruptured colon. Alleging that the injury was caused by Cal-Ban, Tart sued Prescott's Pharmacies, CKI, the officers and directors of Health Care, and others in a North Carolina state court. CKI and the Health Care officers and directors argued that North Carolina did not have personal jurisdiction over them because CKI and Health Care were Florida corporations. How will the court rule? Why? [*Tart v. Prescott's Pharmacies, Inc.*, 118 N.C.App. 516, 456 S.E.2d 121 (1995)]

2–15. Blue Cross and Blue Shield insurance companies (the Blues) provide 68 million Americans with health-care financing. The Blues have paid billions of dollars for care attributable to illnesses related to tobacco use. In an attempt to recover some of this amount, the Blues filed a suit in a federal district court against tobacco companies and others, alleging fraud, among other things. The Blues claimed that beginning in 1953, the defendants conspired to addict millions of Americans, including members of Blue Cross plans, to cigarettes and other tobacco products. The conspiracy involved misrepresentation about the safety of nicotine and its addictive properties, marketing efforts targeting children, and agreements not to produce or market safer cigarettes. Their success caused lung, throat, and other cancers, as well as heart disease, stroke, emphysema, and other illnesses. The defendants asked the court to dismiss the case on the ground that the plaintiffs did not have standing to sue. Do the Blues have standing in this case? Why, or why not? [*Blue Cross and Blue Shield of New Jersey, Inc. v. Philip Morris, Inc.*, 36 F.Supp.2d 560 (E.D.N.Y. 1999)]

E-LINKS

For updated links to resources available on the Web, as well as a variety of other materials, visit this text's Web site at

http://wbl-cs.westbuslaw.com

The decisions of the United States Supreme Court and of all of the U.S. courts of appeals are now published online shortly after the decisions are rendered (often within hours). You can find these decisions and obtain information about the federal court system by accessing the Federal Court Locator at

http://vls.law.vill.edu/Locator/fedcourt.html

For information on the justices of the United States Supreme Court, links to opinions they have authored, and other information about the Supreme Court, go to the Supreme Court's official Web site at

http://supremecourtus.gov

The Web site for the federal courts offers information on the federal court system and links to all federal courts at

http://www.uscourts.gov

The National Center for State Courts (NCSC) offers links to the Web pages of all state courts. Go to

http://www.ncsc.dni.us/court/sites/courts.htm

For information on alternative dispute resolution, go to the American Arbitration Association's Web site at

http://www.adr.org

Legal Research Exercises on the Web

Go to http://wbl-cs.westbuslaw.com, the Web site that accompanies this text. Select "Interactive Study Center," and then click on "Chapter 2." There you will find the following Internet research exercises that you can perform to learn more about alternative dispute resolution and the judiciary's role in American government:

Activity 2–1: Alternative Dispute Resolution

Activity 2–2: The Judiciary's Role in American Government

CHAPTER 3
Court Procedures

AMERICAN AND ENGLISH COURTS follow the *adversary system of justice*. Although clients are allowed to represent themselves in court (called *pro se* representation),[1] most parties to lawsuits hire attorneys to represent them. Each lawyer acts as his or her client's advocate, presenting the client's version of the facts in such a way as to convince the judge (or the judge and jury, in a jury trial) that this version is correct.

Most of the judicial procedures that you will read about in this chapter are rooted in the adversarial framework of the American legal system. In this chapter, after a brief overview of judicial procedures, we illustrate the steps involved in a lawsuit with a hypothetical civil case (criminal procedures will be discussed in Chapter 8).

Broadly speaking, there are three phases of the litigation process: pretrial, trial, and posttrial. Each phase involves specific procedures. Although civil lawsuits may vary greatly in terms of complexity, cost, and detail, they typically progress through the specific stages charted in Exhibit 3–1.

We now turn to our hypothetical civil case. The case arose from an automobile accident, which occurred when a car driven by Antonio Carvello, a resident of New Jersey, collided with a car driven by Jill Kirby, a resident of New York. The accident took place at an intersection in New York City. Kirby suffered personal injuries, incurring medical and hospital expenses as well as lost wages for four months. In all, she calculated that the cost to her of the accident was $100,000.[3] Carvello and Kirby have been unable to agree on a settlement, and Kirby now must decide whether to sue Carvello for the $100,000 compensation she feels she deserves.

SECTION 1

Procedural Rules

The parties to a lawsuit must comply with the procedural rules of the court in which the lawsuit is filed. These rules specify what must be done at each stage of the litigation process. All civil trials held in federal district courts are governed by the **Federal Rules of Civil Procedure (FRCP)**.[2] Each state also has rules of civil procedure that apply to all courts within that state. In addition, each court has its own local rules of procedure that supplement the federal or state rules.

SECTION 2

Consulting with an Attorney

The first step taken by virtually anyone contemplating a lawsuit is to obtain the advice of a qualified attorney. In the hypothetical Kirby-Carvello case, Kirby may consult with an attorney, who will advise her as to what she can expect to gain from a lawsuit, her probability of success if she sues, what procedures will be involved, and how long it may take to

1. This right was definitively established in *Faretta v. California*, 422 U.S. 806, 95 S.Ct. 2525, 45 L.Ed.2d 562 (1975).

2. The United States Supreme Court's authority to promulgate these rules is set forth in 28 U.S.C. Sections 2071–2077.

3. We are ignoring in this example damages for pain and suffering or for permanent disabilities. Plaintiffs often seek such damages in personal injury cases.

EXHIBIT 3–1 STAGES IN A TYPICAL LAWSUIT

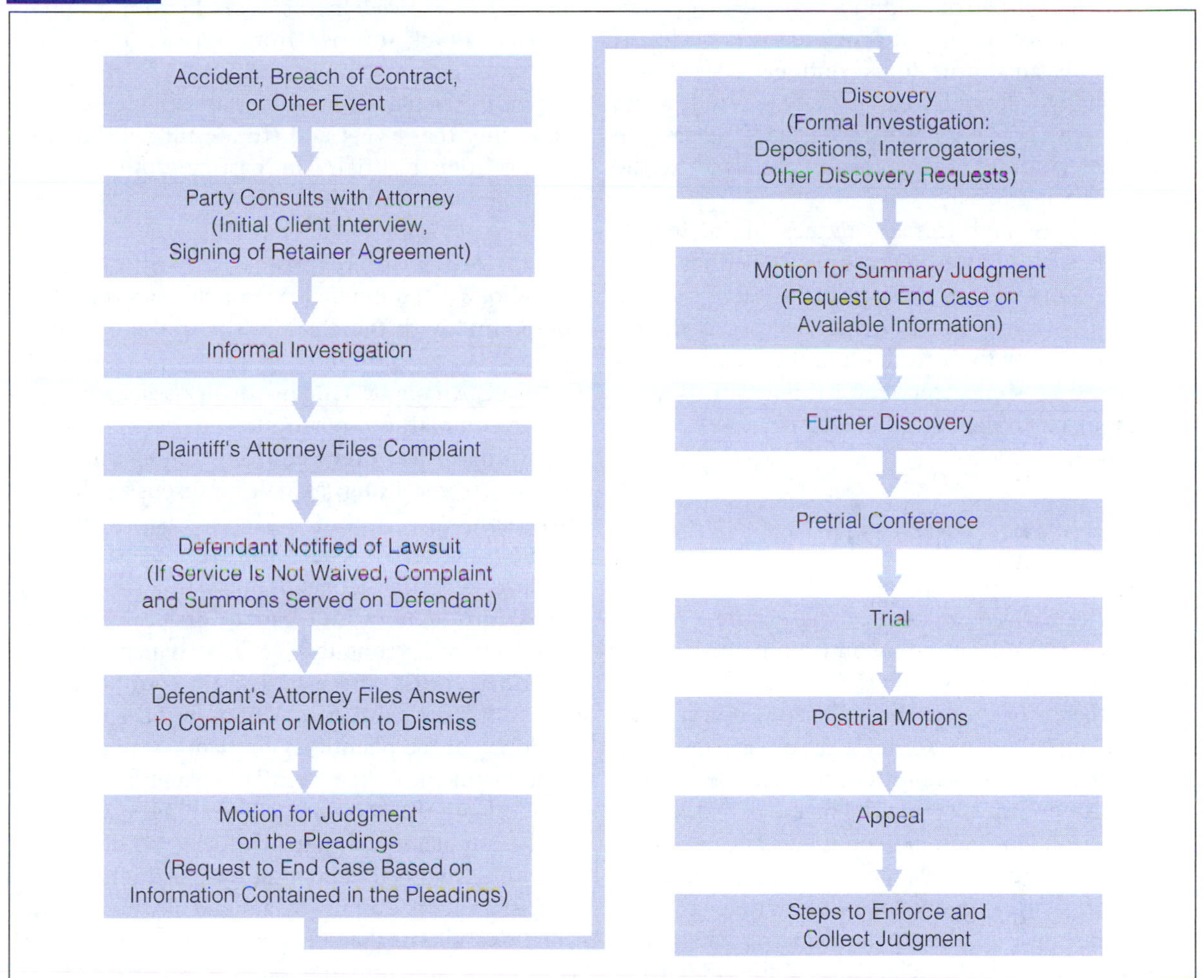

resolve the issue through the judicial process. Depending on the court hearing the case, the time costs of the litigation may be significant. Personal injury cases may take two to three years to resolve, and this is an important factor for Kirby to consider.

LEGAL FEES

Another crucial factor that Kirby must consider is, of course, the cost of the attorney's time—the legal fees that she will have to pay to collect damages from the defendant, Carvello. Attorneys base their fees on such factors as the difficulty of a matter, the amount of time involved, the experience and skill of the attorney in the particular area of the law, and the cost of doing business. In the United States, legal fees range from $60 per hour to $500 per hour (the average fee per hour is between $150 and $170). Not included in attorneys' fees are various expenses relating to a case, often called "out-of-pocket" costs, that the attorneys must pay. These costs include court filing fees, travel expenses, the cost of expert witnesses and investigators, and so on.

A particular legal matter may include one type or a combination of several types of fees. *Fixed fees* may be charged for the performance of such services as drafting a simple will. *Hourly fees* may be computed for matters that will involve an indeterminate period of time. Any case brought to trial, for example, may involve an expenditure of time that cannot be precisely estimated in advance. *Contingency fees* are fixed as a percentage (usually between 25 and 40 percent) of a client's recovery in certain types of lawsuits, such as a personal injury lawsuit. If the lawsuit is unsuccessful, the attorney receives no fee. If Kirby retains an attorney on a contingency-fee basis, she normally will not have to pay any fees unless she wins the case. (She will, however, have to pay the court fees and any other expenses incurred by the attorney on her behalf.)

Many state and federal statutes allow for an award of attorneys' fees in certain legal actions, such as probate matters. In these cases, a judge sets the amount of the fee, based on such factors as the results obtained by the attorney and the fee customarily charged for similar services. In some situations, a client may receive an award of attorneys' fees as part of his or her recovery.

SETTLEMENT CONSIDERATIONS

Frequently, the most important factor in determining the extent to which an attorney will pursue a resolution of a legal problem is how much time and money the client wishes to invest in the process. If the client decides that he or she can afford a lengthy trial and one or more appeals, the attorney may pursue those actions. Often, once a client learns the extent of the costs involved in litigating a claim, he or she may decide to settle the claim for a lower amount by using one of the methods of alternative dispute resolution discussed in Chapter 2, such as negotiation or mediation.

Another important factor in deciding whether to pursue litigation is the defendant's ability to pay the damages sought. Even if Kirby is awarded damages, it may be difficult to enforce the court's judgment. (We will discuss the problems involved in enforcing a judgment later in this chapter.)

SECTION 3

Pretrial Procedures

The pretrial litigation process involves the filing of the *pleadings*, the gathering of evidence (called *discovery*), and possibly other procedures, such as a pretrial conference and jury selection.

THE PLEADINGS

The *complaint* and *answer* (and other documents discussed below), taken together, are known as the **pleadings.** The pleadings notify each party of the claims of the other and specify the issues (disputed questions) involved in the case. Pleadings remove the element of surprise from a case. They allow lawyers to gather the most persuasive evidence and to prepare better arguments, thus increasing the probability that a just and true result will be forthcoming from the trial. The basic pleadings are the complaint and answer.

The Plaintiff's Complaint. Kirby's action against Carvello will commence when her lawyer files a **complaint**[4] with the clerk of the trial court in the appropriate geographical area—the proper venue. (Typically, the lawyer or his or her assistant delivers the complaint in person to the trial court clerk. Increasingly, however, courts are experimenting with electronic filing, as will be discussed later in this chapter.

In most states, the court would be one having general jurisdiction; in others, it might be a court having special jurisdiction with regard to subject matter. The complaint will contain (1) a statement alleging (asserting) the facts necessary for the court to take jurisdiction, (2) a short statement of the facts necessary to show that the plaintiff is entitled to a remedy, and (3) a statement of the remedy the plaintiff is seeking. A typical complaint is shown in Exhibit 3–2.

The complaint will state that Kirby was driving her car through a green light at the specified intersection, exercising good driving habits and reasonable care, when Carvello negligently drove his vehicle through a red light and into the intersection from a cross street, striking Kirby and causing serious personal injury and property damage. The complaint will go on to state that Kirby is seeking $100,000 in damages. (Note that in some state civil actions, the amount of damages sought is not specified.)

Service of Process. Before the court can exercise jurisdiction over the defendant (Carvello)—in effect, before the lawsuit can begin—the court must have proof that the defendant was notified of the lawsuit. The process of notifying the defendant of a lawsuit is called **service of process.** Service of process involves serving the defendant with a summons and a copy of the complaint—that is, delivering these items to the defendant. The **summons** notifies defendant Carvello that he is required to

4. Sometimes, the document filed with the court is called a petition or a declaration instead of a complaint.

EXHIBIT 3–2 A TYPICAL COMPLAINT

IN THE UNITED STATES DISTRICT COURT
FOR THE Southern DISTRICT OF New York

CIVIL NO. 2-1047

Jill Kirby

Plaintiff

vs.

COMPLAINT

Antonio Carvello

Defendant.

The plaintiff brings this cause of action against the defendant, alleging as follows:

1. This action is between the plaintiff, who is a resident of the State of New York, and the defendant, who is a resident of the State of New Jersey. There is diversity of citizenship between the parties.
2. The amount in controversy, exclusive of interest and costs, exceeds the sum of $75,000.
3. On September 10th, 2001, the plaintiff, Jill Kirby, was exercising good driving habits and reasonable care in driving her car through the intersection of Boardwalk and Pennsylvania Avenue, New York City, New York, when the defendant, Antonio Carvello, negligently drove his vehicle through a red light at the intersection and collided with the plaintiff's vehicle.
4. As a result of the collision, the plaintiff suffered severe physical injury, which prevented her from working, and property damage to her car.

WHEREFORE, the plaintiff demands judgment against the defendant for the sum of $100,000 plus interest at the maximum legal rate and the costs of this action.

By Joseph Roe

Joseph Roe
Attorney for Plaintiff
100 Main Street
New York, New York

1/2/02

prepare an answer to the complaint and to file a copy of his answer with both the court and the plaintiff's attorney within a specified time period (twenty days in the federal courts).

The summons also informs Carvello that if he fails to answer or respond to the plaintiff's complaint within the required time period (unless he can provide a convincing reason to the court why he could not do so), the result will be a default judgment for the plaintiff. A **default judgment** in Kirby's favor would mean that she would be awarded the damages alleged in her complaint. A typical summons is shown in Exhibit 3–3.

How service of process occurs depends on the rules of the court or jurisdiction in which the lawsuit is brought. Under the Federal Rules of Civil Procedure (FRCP), service of process in federal court cases may be effected by anyone who is not a party to the lawsuit and who is at least eighteen years of age. In state courts, the process server is often a county sheriff or deputy. Usually, the server effects the service by handing the summons to the defendant personally or by leaving it at the defendant's residence or place of business. In a few states, a summons can be served by mail if the defendant so agrees. When the defendant cannot be reached, special rules sometimes permit serving the summons by leaving it with a designated person, such as the secretary of state.

Serving Corporate Defendants. In cases involving corporate defendants, the summons and complaint may be served on an officer or *registered agent* (representative) of the corporation. The name of a corporation's registered agent can usually be obtained from the secretary of state's office in the state in which the company incorporated its business (and, usually, from the secretary of state's office in any state in which the corporation does business).

Waiver of Formal Service of Process. The FRCP allow formal service of process to be waived by defendants in federal cases, providing that certain procedures are followed. Kirby's attorney, for example, could mail to defendant Carvello a copy of the complaint, along with "Waiver of Service of Summons" forms for Carvello to sign. If Carvello signs and returns the forms within thirty days, formal service of process is waived. To encourage defendants to waive formal service of process, the FRCP provide that defendants who sign and return the waiver are not required to respond to the complaint for sixty days after the date on which the request for waiver of service was sent, instead of the twenty days allowed if formal service of process is undertaken.

The Defendant's Response. The defendant's response to the plaintiff's complaint may take the form of an **answer**, in which the defendant either admits the statements or allegations set out in the complaint or denies them and sets out any defenses that the defendant may have. If Carvello admits to all of Kirby's allegations in his answer, a judgment will be entered for Kirby. If Carvello denies Kirby's allegations, the matter will proceed further.

Carvello can also admit the truth of Kirby's complaint but raise new facts to show that he should not be held liable for Kirby's damages. This is called raising an **affirmative defense.** As will be discussed in subsequent chapters, there are affirmative defenses that can be raised by defendants in both civil and criminal cases. For example, a defendant accused of physically harming another might claim that he or she acted in self-defense. A defendant charged with breach of contract might defend on the ground (legal basis) of mistake or the fact that the contract was oral when it was required by law to be in writing. In the Kirby-Carvello case, assume that Carvello has obtained evidence that Kirby was not exercising good driving habits at the time the accident occurred (she was looking at a child in the back of her car instead of watching the road). Carvello could assert Kirby's own negligence as a defense. In some states, a plaintiff's contributory negligence operates as a complete defense. In most states, however, the plaintiff's own negligence constitutes only a partial defense (see Chapter 5).

Carvello could also deny Kirby's allegations and set forth his own claim that the accident occurred as a result of Kirby's negligence, and therefore Kirby owes Carvello money for damages to his car. This is appropriately called a **counterclaim.** If Carvello files a counterclaim, Kirby will have to submit an answer to the counterclaim.

DISMISSALS AND JUDGMENTS BEFORE TRIAL

Many actions for which pleadings have been filed never come to trial. The parties may, for example, negotiate a settlement of the dispute at any stage of

EXHIBIT 3–3 A TYPICAL SUMMONS

SUMMONS IN A CIVIL ACTION

United States District Court

FOR THE Southern **DISTRICT OF:** New York

CIVIL ACTION FILE NO. 2-1047

Jill Kirby

Plaintiff

v.

Antonio Carvello

Defendant

SUMMONS

To the above named Defendant:

You are hereby summoned and required to serve upon Joseph Roe

plaintiff's attorney, whose address is 100 Main Street New York, New York

an answer to the complaint which is herewith served upon you, within 20 days after service of this summons upon you, exclusive of the day of service. If you fail to do so, judgment by default will be taken against you for the relief demanded in the complaint.

Samuel Raeburn

Clerk of Court

Mary Doakes

Deputy Clerk.

Date: 1/10/02

[Seal of Court]

NOTE:—This summons is issued pursuant to Rule 4 of the Federal Rules of Civil Procedure.

the litigation process. There are also numerous procedural avenues for disposing of a case without a trial. Many of them involve one or the other party's attempts to get the case dismissed through the use of various motions.

A **motion** is a procedural request submitted to the court by an attorney on behalf of his or her client. When one party files a motion with the court, that party must also send to, or serve on, the opposing party a *notice of motion*. The notice of motion informs the opposing party that the motion has been filed. **Pretrial motions** include the motion to dismiss, the motion for judgment on the pleadings, and the motion for summary judgment.

Motion to Dismiss. If the defendant challenges the sufficiency of the plaintiff's complaint, the defendant can present to the court a **motion to dismiss** for failure to state a claim for which relief (a remedy) can be granted, or a *demurrer.* (The rules of civil procedure in many states do not use the term *demurrer;* they use only *motion to dismiss.*) The motion to dismiss for failure to state a claim for which relief can be granted is an allegation that even if the facts presented in the complaint are true, their legal consequences are such that there is no reason to go further with the suit and no need for the defendant to present an answer. If, for example, Kirby's complaint had alleged facts that excluded the possibility of negligence on Carvello's part, Carvello could move to dismiss the case.

Defendant Carvello could also file a motion to dismiss if he believed that he had not been properly served, that the complaint had been filed in the wrong court (for example, that the court lacked personal or subject-matter jurisdiction or the venue was improper), or for other specific reasons.

A motion to dismiss may be—and often is—filed with the court by a defendant instead of an answer. If the court denies the motion, the defendant generally is given an extension of time to file an answer (or further pleading). If the defendant fails to file the appropriate pleading, a judgment will normally be entered for the plaintiff. If the court grants the motion to dismiss, the defendant is not required to answer the complaint. The plaintiff generally is given time to file an amended complaint. If the plaintiff does not file this amended complaint, a judgment will be entered against the plaintiff solely on the basis of the pleadings, and the plaintiff will not be allowed to bring suit on the matter again.

If Kirby wishes to discontinue the suit because, for example, an out-of-court settlement has been reached, she can likewise move for dismissal. The court can also dismiss a case on its own motion.

Motion for Judgment on the Pleadings. After the pleadings are closed—after the complaint, answer, and any other pleadings have been filed—either of the parties can file a **motion for judgment on the pleadings.** This motion may be filed when it appears from the pleadings that the plaintiff has failed to state a cause of action for which relief may be granted. The motion may also be filed when the pleadings indicate that no facts are in dispute and the only question is how the law applies to a set of agreed-on facts. For example, assume for a moment that in the Kirby-Carvello case, defendant Carvello admitted to all of Kirby's allegations in his answer and raised no affirmative defenses. In this situation, Kirby would file a motion for judgment on the pleadings in her favor.

The difference between this motion and a motion for summary judgment, discussed next, is that the party requesting the motion may support a motion for summary judgment with sworn statements and other materials that will be admissible as evidence at trial; on a motion for a judgment on the pleadings, however, a court may consider only what is contained in the pleadings.

Motion for Summary Judgment. The **motion for summary judgment** is similar to a motion for judgment on the pleadings in that the party filing the motion is asking the court to grant a judgment in its favor without a trial. As with a motion for judgment on the pleadings, a court will grant a motion for summary judgment only if it determines that no facts are in dispute and the only question is how the law applies to the facts.

To support a motion for summary judgment, one party can submit, prior to trial, sworn evidence obtained at any point prior to trial (including during the discovery stage of litigation—to be discussed shortly) that refutes the other party's factual claim. The evidence may consist of **affidavits** (sworn statements by parties or witnesses), as well as documents, such as a contract. The evidence must be *admissible* evidence—that is, evidence that the court would allow to be presented during the trial. Hearsay, for example, normally would not be admissible. As mentioned, the use of this additional evidence is one of the features that distinguishes the motion for summary judgment from the motion to dismiss and the motion for judgment on the pleadings.

In the Kirby-Carvello accident, whether or not the light was red is a question of fact. Assume that during discovery, Carvello obtained undisputable evidence that the stoplight was not working when he drove through the intersection. Assume further that Carvello has evidence (a witness's testimony) that he was not exceeding the legal speed limit. Carvello could file a motion for summary judgment on the ground that there was no evidence in the record to support Kirby's claim. The court might grant Carvello's motion, because there would be no genuine factual dispute and Carvello would be entitled to judgment as a matter of law.

A motion for summary judgment can be made before or during a trial, but it will be granted only if, when the evidence is viewed in the light most favorable to the other party, it is clear that there are no factual disputes in contention.

Westlaw. See Case 3.1 at the end of this chapter. To view the full, unedited case from Westlaw,® go to this text's Web site at http://wbl-cs.westbuslaw.com.

Discovery

Before a trial begins, the parties can use a number of procedural devices to obtain information and gather evidence about the case. Kirby, for example, will want to know how fast Carvello was driving, whether he had been drinking or was under the influence of any medication, whether he was wearing corrective lenses if he was required by law to do so while driving, and so on. The process of obtaining information from the opposing party or from witnesses prior to trial is known as **discovery.**

The Federal Rules of Civil Procedure and similar rules in the states set forth the guidelines for discovery activity. Discovery includes gaining access to witnesses, documents, records, and other types of evidence. The rules governing discovery are designed to make sure that a witness or a party is not unduly harassed, that privileged material is safeguarded, and that only information relevant to the case at hand—or likely to lead to the discovery of relevant information—is discoverable.

Of course, there are limits as to what a party can obtain as part of the discovery process. For example, a business firm in litigation with a competitor normally will not be given unrestricted access to the competitor's trade secrets, customer lists, and other confidential records. A court may order that only the firm's attorneys and certain experts can view such sensitive information.

Discovery prevents surprises by giving both parties access to evidence that might otherwise be hidden. This allows the litigants to learn as much as they can about what to expect at a trial before they reach the courtroom. Discovery also serves to narrow the issues so that trial time is spent on the main questions in the case. Currently, the trend is toward allowing more discovery and thus fewer surprises.[5]

Depositions and Interrogatories. At a minimum, discovery involves the use of depositions, interrogatories, or both. A **deposition** is sworn testimony by a party to the lawsuit or by any witness, recorded by an authorized court official. The person deposed gives testimony and answers questions asked by the attorneys from both sides. The questions and answers are recorded, sworn to, and signed. These answers, of course, will help the attorneys prepare their cases. Depositions also give attorneys the opportunity to evaluate how their witnesses will conduct themselves at trial. In addition, depositions can be employed in court to impeach (challenge the credibility of) a party or a witness who changes testimony at the trial. A deposition can also be used as testimony if the witness is not available at trial.

Interrogatories are written questions for which written answers are prepared and then signed under oath. Interrogatories are addressed only to parties directly involved in a lawsuit (plaintiffs or defendants), not to witnesses, and the parties can prepare their answers with the aid of attorneys. Whereas depositions are useful for eliciting candid responses from a party and answers not prepared in advance, interrogatories are designed to obtain accurate information about specific topics, such as how many contracts were signed, the specific dates on which certain contracts were signed, and so on.

Requests for Admissions. One party can serve a written request to the other party for an admission of the truth of matters relating to the trial. Any fact admitted under such a request is conclusively

5. This is particularly evident in the 1993 revision of the Federal Rules of Civil Procedure. The revised rules provide that each party must disclose to the other, on an ongoing basis, the types of evidence that will be presented at trial, the names of witnesses that may or will be called, and other relevant information.

established as true for the trial. For example, Kirby can ask Carvello to admit that his driver's license was suspended at the time of the accident. A request for admission shortens the trial, because the parties will not have to spend time proving facts on which they already agree.

Requests for Documents, Objects, and Entry upon Land. A party can gain access to documents and other items not in his or her possession in order to inspect and examine them. Likewise, a party can gain "entry upon land" to inspect the premises. Carvello, for example, can gain permission to inspect and copy Kirby's repair bills.

Request for Examinations. When the physical or mental condition of one party is in question, the opposing party can ask the court to order a physical or mental examination by an independent examiner. If the court is willing to make the order, the opposing party can obtain the results of the examination. Note that the court will make such an order only when the need for the information outweighs the right to privacy of the person to be examined.

Pretrial Conference

After discovery has taken place and before the trial begins, the attorneys may meet with the trial judge in a **pretrial conference.** The purpose of this conference is to clarify the issues that remain in dispute after discovery has taken place and to explore the possibility of settling the conflict without a trial. If a settlement is not possible at this time, the parties and the judge discuss the manner in which the trial will be conducted. In particular, the parties may attempt to establish ground rules to restrict such things as the number of expert witnesses or the admissibility of certain types of evidence. Once the pretrial conference concludes, both parties will have to turn their attention to the trial itself and, if the trial is to be a jury trial, to the selection of jurors who will hear the case.

The Right to a Jury Trial

The Seventh Amendment to the U.S. Constitution guarantees the right to a jury trial for cases at law in federal courts when the amount in controversy exceeds $20. Most states have similar guarantees in their own constitutions, although many states restrict the guarantee to a higher minimum amount. For example, Iowa requires the dollar amount of damages to be at least $1,000 before there is a right to a jury trial. The right to a trial by jury does not have to be exercised, and many cases are tried without a jury. If there is no jury, the judge determines the truth of the facts alleged in the case. In most states and in federal courts, one of the parties must request a jury, or the right is presumed to be waived.

Jury Selection

Prior to the commencement of any jury trial, a panel of jurors must be assembled. The clerk of the court will usually notify local residents by mail that they have been selected for jury duty. The process of selecting the names of these prospective jurors varies, but often they are randomly chosen by the court clerk from lists of registered voters or those within the state to whom driver's licenses have been issued. These persons then report to the courthouse on the date specified in the notice. There they are gathered into a single pool of jurors, and the process of selecting those jurors who will actually hear the case begins. Although some types of trials require twelve-person juries, most civil matters can be heard by six-person juries.

Voir Dire. The process by which the jury is selected is known as ***voir dire.***[6] In most jurisdictions, *voir dire* consists of oral questions that attorneys for the plaintiff and the defendant ask a group of prospective jurors to determine whether a potential juror is biased or has any connection with a party to the action or with a prospective witness. Usually, jurors are questioned one at a time, although when large numbers of jurors are involved, the attorneys may direct their questions to groups of jurors instead to minimize the amount of time spent in jury selection. Sometimes, jurors are asked to fill out written questionnaires. Some trial attorneys use psychologists and other professionals to help them select jurors.

6. Pronounced *vwahr deehr.* Literally, these French verbs mean "to see, to speak." During the *voir dire* phase of litigation, attorneys do in fact see the jurors speak. In legal language, however, the phrase refers to the process of interrogating jurors to learn about their backgrounds, attitudes, and so on.

Challenges during *Voir Dire*. During *voir dire,* a party may challenge a certain number of prospective jurors *peremptorily*—that is, ask that these individuals not be sworn in as jurors without providing any reason. The total number of peremptory challenges allowed each side is determined by statute or by the court. Furthermore, a party may challenge any juror *for cause*—that is, provide a reason why an individual should not be sworn in as a juror. If the judge grants the challenge, the individual is asked to step down. A prospective juror may not be excluded from participation in the trial process, however, by use of discriminatory challenges, such as those based on racial criteria[7] or gender.[8]

After both sides have completed their challenges, those jurors who have been excused will be permitted to leave. The remaining jurors—those who have been found acceptable by the attorneys for both sides—will be seated in the jury box.

Alternate Jurors. Because unforeseeable circumstances or illness may necessitate that one or more of the sitting jurors be dismissed, the court, depending on the rules of the particular jurisdiction and the expected length of the trial, might choose to have two or three alternate jurors present throughout the trial. If a juror has to be excused in the middle of the trial, then an alternate may take his or her place without disrupting the proceedings. Once the jury members are seated, the judge will swear in the jury members, and the trial itself can begin.

SECTION 4

The Trial

Various rules and procedures govern the trial phase of the litigation process. There are rules governing what kind of evidence will or will not be admitted during the trial, as well as specific procedures that the participants in the lawsuit must follow.

Rules of Evidence

Whether evidence will be admitted in court is determined by the **rules of evidence**—a series of rules that have been created by the courts to ensure that any evidence presented during a trial is fair and reliable. The Federal Rules of Evidence govern the admissibility of evidence in federal courts.

Evidence will not be admitted in court unless it is relevant. **Relevant evidence** is evidence that tends to prove or disprove a fact in question before the court or to establish the degree of probability of a fact or action. For example, evidence that a suspect's gun was in the home of another person when a victim was shot would be relevant—because the evidence would tend to prove that the suspect did not shoot the victim.

Even relevant evidence may not be admitted in court if its reliability is questionable or if its probative (proving) value is substantially outweighed by other important considerations of the court. For example, a video or a photograph that shows in detail the severity of a victim's injuries would be relevant evidence, but the court might exclude this evidence on the ground that it would emotionally inflame the jurors.

Generally, hearsay is not admissible as evidence. **Hearsay** is defined as any testimony given in court about a statement made by someone else. Literally, it is what someone heard someone else say. For example, if a witness in the Kirby-Carvello case testified in court concerning what he or she heard another observer say about the accident, that testimony would be hearsay—secondhand knowledge. Admitting hearsay into evidence carries many risks because, even though it may be relevant, there is no way to test its reliability.

Opening Statements

At the commencement of the trial, both attorneys are allowed to make **opening statements** concerning the facts that they expect to prove during the trial. The opening statement provides an opportunity for each lawyer to give a brief version of the facts and the supporting evidence that will be used during the trial.

Examination of Witnesses

Because Kirby is the plaintiff, she has the burden of proving that her claim is correct. Kirby's attorney

7. *Batson v. Kentucky,* 476 U.S. 79, 106 S.Ct. 1712, 90 L.Ed.2d 69 (1986).

8. *J.E.B. v. Alabama ex rel. T.B.,* 511 U.S. 127, 114 S.Ct. 1419, 128 L.Ed.2d 89 (1994). (*Ex rel.* is an abbreviation of the Latin *ex relatione.* The phrase refers to an action brought on behalf of the state, by the attorney general, at the instigation of an individual who has a private interest in the matter.)

begins the presentation of Kirby's case by calling the first witness for the plaintiff and examining (questioning) the witness. (For both attorneys, the types of questions and the manner of asking them are governed by the rules of evidence.) This questioning is called **direct examination.** After Kirby's attorney is finished, the witness is subject to **cross-examination** by Carvello's attorney. Then Kirby's attorney has another opportunity to question the witness in *redirect examination,* and Carvello's attorney may follow the redirect examination with a *recross-examination.* When both attorneys have finished with the first witness, Kirby's attorney calls the succeeding witnesses in the plaintiff's case, each of whom is subject to examination by the attorneys in the manner just described.

At the conclusion of the plaintiff's case, the defendant's attorney has the opportunity to ask the judge to direct a verdict for the defendant on the ground that the plaintiff has presented no evidence to support the plaintiff's claim. This is called a **motion for a directed verdict** (federal courts use the term *judgment as a matter of law* instead of *directed verdict*). In considering the motion, the judge looks at the evidence in the light most favorable to the plaintiff and grants the motion only if there is insufficient evidence to raise an issue of fact. (Motions for directed verdicts at this stage of trial are seldom granted.)

The defendant's attorney then presents the evidence and witnesses for the defendant's case. Witnesses are called and examined by the defendant's attorney. The plaintiff's attorney has the right to cross-examine them, and there may be a redirect examination and possibly a recross-examination. At the end of the defendant's case, either attorney can move for a directed verdict, and the test again is whether the jury can, through any reasonable interpretation of the evidence, find for the party against whom the motion has been made. After the defendant's attorney has finished introducing evidence, the plaintiff's attorney can present a **rebuttal,** which includes additional evidence to refute the defendant's case. The defendant's attorney can, in turn, refute that evidence in a **rejoinder.**

Closing Arguments

After both sides have rested their cases, each attorney presents a **closing argument.** In the closing argument, each attorney summarizes the facts and evidence presented during the trial, indicates why the facts and evidence support the client's claim, reveals the shortcomings of the points made by the opposing party during the trial, and generally urges a verdict in favor of the client. Each attorney's comments must be relevant to the issues in dispute.

Jury Instructions

After the closing arguments, the judge instructs the jury (assuming it is a jury trial) in the law that applies to the case. The instructions to the jury are often called *charges.* A charge is a document that includes statements of the applicable laws, as well as a review of the facts as they were presented during the case. Because the jury's role is to serve as the fact finder, the factual account contained in the charge is not binding on them. Indeed, the jurors may disregard the facts as noted in the charge entirely. They are not free to ignore the statements of law, however. The charge will help to channel the jurors' deliberations.

The Jury's Verdict

Following its receipt of instructions, the jury retires to the jury room to deliberate the case. In a civil case, the standard of proof is a *preponderance of the evidence.* That is, the plaintiff (Kirby in our hypothetical case) need not provide indisputable proof that she is entitled to a judgment. She need only show that her factual claim is more likely to be true than the defendant's. (As you will read in Chapter 8, in a criminal trial, the prosecution has a higher standard of proof to meet—it must prove its case *beyond a reasonable doubt.*)

Note that some civil claims must be proved by a "clear and convincing evidence" standard, under which the evidence must show that the truth of the party's claim is highly probable. This standard applies in suits involving charges of fraud, suits to establish the terms of a lost will, some suits relating to oral contracts, and other suits involving circumstances in which there is thought to be a particular danger of deception.

Once the jury has reached a decision, it may issue a **verdict** in favor of one party, which specifies the jury's factual findings and the amount of damages to be paid by the losing party. After the announcement of the verdict, which marks the end of the trial itself, the jurors will be discharged.

SECTION 5

Posttrial Motions

After the jury has rendered its verdict, either party may make a posttrial motion. The prevailing party usually files a motion for a judgment in accordance with the verdict. The nonprevailing party frequently files one of the motions discussed next.

MOTION FOR A NEW TRIAL

At the end of the trial, a motion can be made to set aside an adverse verdict and any judgment and to hold a new trial. The **motion for a new trial** will be granted only if the judge (1) is convinced, after looking at all the evidence, that the jury was in error but (2) does not feel it is appropriate to grant judgment for the other side. This will usually occur when the jury verdict is the obvious result of a misapplication of the law or a misunderstanding of the evidence presented at trial.

A new trial can also be granted on the grounds of newly discovered evidence, misconduct by the participants (such as the attorneys, the judge, or the jury) during the trial, or error by the judge. If a motion for a new trial is denied, the judge's denial may be appealed to a higher court.

See Case 3.2 at the end of this chapter. To view the full, unedited case from Westlaw,® go to this text's Web site at http://wbl-cs.westbuslaw.com.

MOTION FOR JUDGMENT *N.O.V.*

If Kirby wins, and if Carvello's attorney has previously moved for a directed verdict, Carvello's attorney can now make a **motion for judgment** ***n.o.v.*** (from the Latin *non obstante veredicto*, meaning "notwithstanding the verdict"; federal courts use the term *judgment as a matter of law* instead of judgment *n.o.v.*). The standards for granting a judgment *n.o.v.* often are the same as those for granting a motion to dismiss or a motion for a directed verdict. Carvello can state that even if the evidence is viewed in the light most favorable to Kirby, a reasonable jury should not have found in Kirby's favor. If the judge finds this contention to be correct or decides that the law requires the opposite result, the motion will be granted. If the motion is denied, Carvello may then appeal the case. (Kirby may also appeal the case, even though she won at trial. She might appeal, for example, if she received a smaller money award than she had sought.)

SECTION 6

The Appeal

Either party may appeal not only the jury's verdict but also any pretrial or posttrial motion. Many of the appellate court cases that appear in this text involve appeals of motions to dismiss, motions for summary judgment, or other motions that were denied by trial court judges. Note that few trial court decisions are reversed on appeal. In most appealed cases (approximately 90 percent), the trial court's decision is affirmed and thus becomes final.

FILING THE APPEAL

If Carvello decides to appeal the verdict in Kirby's favor, then his attorney must file a *notice of appeal* with the clerk of the trial court within a prescribed period of time. Carvello then becomes the *appellant*. The clerk of the trial court sends to the reviewing court (usually an intermediate court of appeals) the *record on appeal*, which contains the following: (1) the pleadings, (2) a transcript of the trial testimony and copies of the exhibits, (3) the judge's rulings on motions made by the parties, (4) the arguments of counsel, (5) the instructions to the jury, (6) the verdict, (7) the posttrial motions, and (8) the judgment order from which the appeal is taken.

Carvello's attorney will file a **brief** with the reviewing court. The brief contains (1) a short statement of the facts; (2) a statement of the issues; (3) the rulings by the trial court that Carvello contends are erroneous and prejudicial (biased in favor of one of the parties); (4) the grounds for reversal of the judgment; (5) a statement of the applicable law; and (6) arguments on Carvello's behalf, citing applicable statutes and relevant cases as precedents. The attorney for the *appellee* (Kirby, in our hypothetical case) usually files an answering brief. Carvello's attorney can file a reply, although it is not required. The reviewing court then considers the case.

APPELLATE REVIEW

As mentioned in Chapter 2, a court of appeals does not hear any evidence. Its decision concerning a case is based on the record on appeal and the briefs. The attorneys can present oral arguments, after which the case is taken under advisement. The court then issues a written opinion. In general, the appellate courts do not reverse findings of fact unless the findings are unsupported or contradicted by the evidence.

An appellate court has several options after reviewing a case: it can *affirm* the trial court's decision; it can *reverse* the trial court's judgment if it concludes that the trial court erred or that the jury did not receive proper instructions; or it can *remand* (send back) the case to the trial court for further proceedings consistent with its opinion on the matter. The court might also affirm or reverse a decision *in part*. For example, the court might affirm the jury's finding that Carvello was negligent but remand the case for further proceedings on another issue (such as the extent of Kirby's damages). An appellate court can also *modify* a lower court's decision. If the appellate court decided that the jury awarded an excessive amount in damages, for example, the court might reduce the award to a more appropriate, or fairer, amount.

HIGHER APPELLATE COURTS

If the reviewing court is an intermediate appellate court, the losing party may be allowed by the court to appeal the decision to the state supreme court. Such a petition corresponds to a petition for a writ of *certiorari* in the United States Supreme Court. If the petition is granted (in some states, a petition is automatically granted), new briefs must be filed before the state supreme court, and the attorneys may be allowed or requested to present oral arguments. Like the intermediate appellate courts, the supreme court may reverse or affirm the appellate court's decision or remand the case.

If a federal question is involved, the losing party (or the winning party, if that party is dissatisfied with the relief obtained) may appeal the decision to the United States Supreme Court by petitioning the Court for a writ of *certiorari*. (As discussed in Chapter 2, the Supreme Court may or may not grant the writ, depending on the significance of the issue in dispute.)

SECTION 7

Enforcing the Judgment

The uncertainties of the litigation process are compounded by the lack of guarantees that any judgment will be enforceable. Even if the jury awarded Kirby the full amount of damages requested ($100,000), for example, she might not, in fact, "win" anything at all. Carvello's auto insurance coverage might have lapsed, in which event the company would not pay any of the damages. Alternatively, Carvello's insurance policy might be limited to $50,000, meaning that Carvello would have to pay personally the remaining $50,000.

If Carvello did not have that amount of money available, then Kirby would need to go back to court and request that the court issue a *writ of execution*—an order, usually issued by the clerk of the court, directing the sheriff to seize and sell Carvello's nonexempt assets (certain assets are exempted by law from creditors' actions). The proceeds of the sale would then be used to pay the damages owed to Kirby. Any excess proceeds of the sale would be returned to Carvello. Alternatively, the nonexempt property itself could be transferred to Kirby in lieu of an outright payment. (Creditors' remedies, including those of judgment creditors, and exempt and nonexempt property will be discussed in more detail in Chapter 29.)

The problem of collecting a judgment is less pronounced, of course, when a party is seeking to satisfy a judgment against a defendant, such as a major corporation, that has substantial assets that can be easily located. Usually, one of the factors considered before a lawsuit is initiated is whether the defendant has sufficient assets to cover the amount of damages sought, should the plaintiff win the case.

SECTION 8

Technology and the Courts

We mentioned in Chapter 2 how the courts have attempted to adapt traditional jurisdictional concepts to the online world. Not surprisingly, the Internet has also brought about changes in court procedures and practices, including new methods for filing pleadings and other documents and the online publication of decisions and opinions. Several courts are experimenting with electronic delivery, such as via the Internet or CD-ROM. Some jurisdictions are exploring the possibility of cyber courts, in which legal proceedings could be conducted totally online.

Electronic Filing

The federal court system first experimented with an electronic filing system in January 1996, in an asbestos case heard by the U.S. District Court for the Northern District of Ohio. Currently, a number of federal courts permit attorneys to file documents electronically in certain types of cases. At last count, more than 130,000 documents in approximately 10,000 cases had been filed electronically in federal courts. The Administrative Office of the U.S. Courts has recently announced that it is considering permitting electronic filing in all U.S. district courts on a nationwide basis.

State and local courts are also setting up electronic court filing systems. Since the late 1990s, the court system in Pima County, Arizona, has been accepting pleadings via e-mail. The supreme court of the state of Washington also now accepts online filings of litigation documents. In addition, electronic filing projects are being developed in other states, including Kansas, Virginia, Utah, and Michigan. Notably, the judicial branch of the state of Colorado recently implemented the first statewide court e-filing system in the United States. E-filing is now an option in over sixty courts in that state. In California, Florida, and a few other states, some court clerks offer docket information and other searchable databases online.

Typically, when electronic filing is made available, it is optional. In early 2001, however, a trial court judge in the District of Columbia launched a pilot project that *required* attorneys to file electronically all documents relating to certain types of civil cases.

Courts Online

Most courts today have sites on the Web. Of course, it is up to each court to decide what to make available at its site. Some courts display only the names of court personnel and office phone numbers. Others add court rules and forms. Some include judicial decisions, although generally the sites do not feature archives of old decisions. Instead, decisions are available online for only a limited time. For example, California keeps opinions online for only sixty days.

Appellate court decisions are often posted online immediately after they are rendered. Recent decisions of the U.S. courts of appeals, for example, are available online at their Web sites. The United States Supreme Court has also launched an official Web site and publishes its opinions there immediately after they are announced to the public.

Cyber Courts and Proceedings

Someday, litigants may be able to use cyber courts, in which judicial proceedings take place only on the Internet. The parties to a case could meet online to make their arguments and present their evidence. This might be done with e-mail submissions, through video cameras, in designated "chat" rooms, at closed sites, or through the use of other Internet facilities. These courtrooms could be efficient and economical. We might also see the use of virtual lawyers, judges, and juries—and possibly the replacement of court personnel with computers or software.

The governor of Michigan recently proposed that separate cyber courts be created for cases involving technology and high-tech businesses. In these courts, everything would be done via computer and the Internet, rather than in a courtroom. The state of Maryland is also planning a separate judicial division for cases involving high-tech businesses. Many lawyers predict that other states will do likewise.

The courts may also use the Internet in other ways. In a ground-breaking decision in early 2001, for example, a Florida county court granted "virtual" visitation rights in a couple's divorce proceeding. Although the court granted custody rights to the father of the couple's ten-year-old daughter, the court also ordered each parent to buy a computer and a videoconferencing system so that the mother could "visit" with her child via the Internet at any time.[9]

9. For a discussion of this case, see Shelley Emling, "After the Divorce, Internet Visits?" *Austin American-Statesman*, January 30, 2001, pp. A1 and A10.

Terms and Concepts to Review

affidavit 54	answer 52	closing argument 58
affirmative defense 52	brief 59	complaint 50

counterclaim 52
cross-examination 58
default judgment 52
deposition 55
direct examination 58
discovery 55
Federal Rules of Civil Procedure (FRCP) 48
hearsay 57
interrogatories 55
motion 54
motion for a directed verdict 58
motion for a new trial 59
motion for judgment *n.o.v.* 59
motion for judgment on the pleadings 54
motion for summary judgment 54
motion to dismiss 54
opening statement 57
pleadings 50
pretrial conference 56
pretrial motion 54
rebuttal 58
rejoinder 58
relevant evidence 57
rules of evidence 57
service of process 50
summons 50
verdict 58
voir dire 56

Chapter Summary

Procedural Rules	Rules of procedure prescribe the way in which disputes are handled in the courts. Rules differ from court to court, and separate sets of rules exist for federal and state courts, as well as for criminal and civil cases.
Consulting with an Attorney	Attorney's fees and other "out-of-pocket" costs (filing fees, expert witnesses, etc.) involved in a lawsuit can be significant. Even if an attorney is retained on a contingency basis—the attorney receives fees contingent on winning the case—the other expenses involved in the suit are still the responsibility of the litigant. The high costs of bringing or defending against a lawsuit often lead the parties to pursue a settlement outside of court.
Pretrial Procedures	1. *The pleadings*— a. Plaintiff's complaint—Filed by the plaintiff with the court to initiate the lawsuit; served with a summons on the defendant. b. Defendant's response—An answer to the complaint in which the defendant admits or denies allegations made by the plaintiff; may assert a counterclaim or an affirmative defense. 2. *Pretrial motions*— a. Motion to dismiss—A motion made by the defendant—often prior to filing an answer to the complaint—requesting the court to dismiss the case for stated reasons, such as the plaintiff's failure to state a claim for which relief can be granted. b. Motion for judgment on the pleadings—May be made by either party; will be granted if the parties agree on the facts and the only question is how the law applies to the facts. The judge bases the decision solely on the pleadings. c. Motion for summary judgment—May be made by either party; will be granted if the parties agree on the facts. The judge applies the law in rendering a judgment. The judge can consider evidence outside the pleadings when evaluating the motion. 3. *Discovery*—The process of gathering evidence concerning the case. Discovery involves depositions (sworn testimony by a party to the lawsuit or any witness), interrogatories (written questions and answers to these questions made by parties to the action with the aid of their attorneys), and various requests (for admissions, documents, medical examination, and so on). 4. *Pretrial conference*—Either party or the court can request a pretrial conference to identify the matters in dispute after discovery has taken place and to plan the course of the trial.

CHAPTER SUMMARY—CONTINUED

Pretrial Procedures—continued	5. *Jury selection*—The federal and most state constitutions guarantee the right to a jury trial for disputes involving a minimum dollar amount of damages. If the right is not exercised, the judge determines the truth of the facts alleged in the case. In a jury trial, members of the jury are selected from a pool of prospective jurors. During a process known as *voir dire*, the attorneys for both sides may challenge prospective jurors either for cause or peremptorily (for no cause).
The Trial	Following jury selection, the trial begins with opening statements from the attorneys for both parties. The following events then occur: 1. The plaintiff's introduction of evidence (including the testimony of witnesses) that supports the plaintiff's position. The defendant's attorney can challenge the evidence and cross-examine witnesses. 2. The defendant's introduction of evidence (including the testimony of witnesses) that supports the defendant's position. The plaintiff's attorney can challenge the evidence and cross-examine witnesses. 3. Closing arguments by the attorneys in favor of their respective clients' positions, the judge's instructions to the jury, and the jury's verdict.
Posttrial Options	1. *Motion for a new trial*—Will be granted if the judge is convinced that the jury was in error; can also be granted on the grounds of newly discovered evidence, misconduct by the participants during the trial, or error by the judge. 2. *Motion for judgment n.o.v. ("notwithstanding the verdict")*—Will be granted if the judge is convinced that the jury was in error. 3. *Appeal*—Either party can appeal the trial court's judgment to an appropriate court of appeals. a. Filing the appeal—The appealing party must file a notice of appeal with the clerk of the trial court, who forwards to the appellate court the record on appeal. Attorneys' briefs are filed. b. Appellate review—The appellate court does not hear evidence but bases its opinion, which it issues in writing, on the record on appeal and the attorneys' briefs and oral arguments. The court may affirm or reverse all (or part) of the trial court's judgment and/or remand the case for further proceedings consistent with its opinion. Most decisions are affirmed on appeal. c. In some cases, further review may be sought from a higher appellate court, such as a state supreme court. Ultimately, if a federal question is involved, the case may be appealed to the United States Supreme Court.
Technology and the Courts	A number of state and federal courts now allow parties to file litigation-related documents with their courts via the Internet or other electronic means. The federal courts are considering the implementation of electronic filing systems in all federal district courts. Virtually every court now has a Web page offering information about the court and its procedures, and an increasing number of courts publish their opinions online. In the future, we may see "cyber courts," in which all trial proceedings are conducted online.

CASES FOR ANALYSIS

Westlaw. You can access the full text of each case presented below by going to the Westlaw cases on this text's Web site at http://wbl-cs.westbuslaw.com. Each Westlaw case includes the names of all plaintiffs and defendants, the dates on which the case was argued and decided, a brief summary of the issues and decisions in the case, headnotes classifiying specific issues in the case according to the West Key Number System, and the court's opinion. Concurring and dissenting opinions, if any, are included as well.

CASE 3.1 MOTION FOR SUMMARY JUDGMENT

AUSLEY V. BISHOP

Court of Appeals of North Carolina, 1999.
515 S.E.2d 72.

EDMUNDS, Judge.

Plaintiff [Andrew Ausley] is a state-certified appraiser of real estate. Defendant [Bryan Bishop], seeking to become a certified appraiser, was employed by plaintiff in November 1994 as an apprentice, a requisite step in defendant's training and certification process. Between November 1994 and April 1997, defendant prepared and signed appraisal reports, as required by the North Carolina Appraisal Board (the Board). For each report, defendant also prepared and retained a log sheet. The Board required that these log sheets be signed and stamped by a supervising appraiser to certify that each apprentice's report was completed under his or her general supervision.

In November 1994, plaintiff signed and stamped the first report and log sheet prepared by defendant. Plaintiff instructed defendant to let subsequent reports accumulate, however, and plaintiff would sign them simultaneously. In June 1996, defendant passed the State registered trainee examination. In April 1997, defendant was qualified to receive a license, subject only to plaintiff forwarding the supervising appraiser's certification. However, on 12 April 1997, at a meeting of the parties, plaintiff conditioned his certification of defendant's reports upon defendant's signing a newly drafted employment contract, which included a provision relating to compensation and a non-compete clause. After examining the contract and having an attorney review it, defendant, claiming to have "no other choice," signed on 14 April 1997. Plaintiff then signed and stamped defendant's log sheets, and on 30 April 1997, the State issued defendant his official license.

On 1 June 1997, plaintiff opened a new branch office, which was to be run by defendant, and placed a new trainee there to work under defendant's supervision. It was only at this point that defendant began receiving the compensation guaranteed him pursuant to the April 14 contract. On 22 September 1997, plaintiff called for another meeting with defendant. During this meeting, after expressing concerns about misspellings and outdated data in some of defendant's reports, plaintiff proposed renegotiating their contract under terms that would result in decreased income to defendant. Defendant declined to agree to the new terms, and the employment relationship between the parties ended. On 24 September 1997, defendant began to operate his own appraisal business.

On 13 October 1997, plaintiff filed a complaint against defendant alleging breach of contract [among other things]. On 17 November 1997, defendant filed an answer and counterclaim, asserting * * * slander [and other claims]. On 5 December 1997, defendant filed a motion for partial summary judgment against plaintiff, which was granted on 11 February 1998. This summary judgment order has not been appealed. On 23 April 1998, plaintiff filed a motion for summary judgment as to defendant's counterclaim, which was granted on 11 May 1998. From the judgment dismissing his counterclaim, defendant appeals.

A trial court's grant of summary judgment is fully reviewable by this Court. *The standard of review for whether summary judgment is proper is whether the trial court properly concluded that there was no genuine issue of material fact and that the moving party was entitled to judgment as a matter of law.* The record is to be viewed in the light most favorable to the non-movant, giving it the benefit of all inferences reasonably arising therefrom. After reviewing each claim in accordance with this standard, we conclude that the trial court correctly granted summary judgment as to most of defendant's claims; however, we also conclude that summary judgment was improper as to one claim and as to parts of two others, and reverse in part and remand for further proceedings. [Emphasis added.]

* * * *

* * * Defendant alleged in his counterclaim that plaintiff committed slander by communicating to defendant's personal mortgage lender statements to the effect that defendant had committed loan fraud. This Court has held that among statements which are slanderous *per se* are accusations of crimes or offenses involving moral turpitude, defamatory statements about a person with respect to his trade or profession, and imputation that a person has a loathsome disease. When a statement falls into one of these categories, a *prima facie* presumption of malice and a conclusive presumption of legal injury and damage arise; allegation and proof of special damages are not required.

Defendant avers that the statements allegedly made by plaintiff adversely affected defendant's business and personal reputation. Plaintiff admitted in his deposition that he made statements that impeached defendant in his trade. During a line of questions pertaining to a form signed by plaintiff and submitted by defendant to mortgage broker Southern Fidelity to finance defendant's own home, plaintiff was asked, "Did you suggest, infer, or imply to Robert [Phillips] at Southern Fidelity that your signature was procured by fraud or some other unlawful means on that appraisal report?" Plaintiff responded, "Correct." However, other questioning revealed that there was no evidence that the signature had been obtained improperly; instead, plaintiff admitted voluntarily signing the form without reading it. Further, plaintiff also admitted telling the same Robert Phillips at Southern Fidelity that "Mr. Bishop had not been truthful about his income in qualifying for the loan that Southern Fidelity brokered, arranged or gave to the Bishops," when there was evidence that plaintiff previously had verified defendant's income to Southern Fidelity. Additionally, defendant stated in his affidavit that "[plaintiff] contacted several of my clients and potential clients and advised them, untruthfully, that I had engaged in various unethical conduct." Because defendant was launching his own business as an appraiser, plaintiff's incorrect statements to defendant's clients and potential clients undoubtedly had the capacity to harm defendant in his trade or profession.

In a second episode, plaintiff admitted reporting to police that defendant had stolen client files. The evidence to support plaintiff's report was that defendant was seen leaving his old office at plaintiff's business with a box, and that later a Rolodex was no longer on defendant's desk, and files containing defendant's resumes and sample appraisal files were also missing from a file cabinet. Although the investigation subsequently was dropped without any charges being brought, plaintiff admitted communicating to at least one person at Piedmont Home Equity that he suspected defendant had taken files, and had called the police. Again, this statement to a potential client of defendant was capable of harming him in his trade or profession. We therefore conclude that defendant has forecast sufficient evidence of all essential elements of his claim to make a *prima facie* case at trial to survive plaintiff's motion for summary judgment. We reverse as to this issue and remand for further proceedings.

CASE 3.2 MOTION FOR A NEW TRIAL

LEBLANC V. AMERICAN HONDA MOTOR CO.

Supreme Court of New Hampshire, 1997.
141 N.H. 579,
688 A.2d 556.

BROCK, Chief Justice.

The defendant, American Honda Motor Co., Inc. (Honda), appeals the special jury verdict of the Superior Court, holding Honda liable for injuries caused by the defective design and failure to warn of the braking and steering properties of its product, the Honda Odyssey. For the reasons that follow, we reverse and remand.

On January 16, 1988, the plaintiff, Thomas LeBlanc, while riding on the back of a snowmobile driven by his friend, was injured when the snowmobile collided with an off-road vehicle driven by Stephen Beaulieu and manufactured by Honda. The impact of the collision severely injured the plaintiff's leg.

The plaintiff sued Beaulieu and Honda alleging negligent operation of the Odyssey by Beaulieu and asserting a products liability claim against Honda. The jury rendered its verdict * * * . The superior court ordered judgment against Honda for $1,487,196 plus statutory interest and costs, and against Beaulieu for $590,504 plus statutory interest and costs.

On appeal, Honda argues * * * that the plaintiff's trial counsel, Vincent C. Martina, made improper and inflammatory remarks during the trial and during closing arguments in an attempt to cultivate in the jury a racial and national bias against Honda, a subsidiary of a Japanese corporation * * * .

Honda * * * argues that certain remarks made by Martina so tainted the proceedings as to deprive Honda of a fair trial and that denial of its * * * motion for a new trial on this ground was reversible error. We agree.

* * * *

The defendant points to several statements made by Martina as grounds for reversal. The first, directed at Honda's vehicle design expert, focused on the color scheme of the Odyssey. Martina asked the expert if he knew the color of the Japanese flag. After Honda objected, Martina explained that he was curious about how the machine's color happened to be designed. The court decided to give Martina "some latitude." Martina then questioned the expert about whether the expert had ever wondered why the Odyssey is "red, white and blue, the color of the American flag."

The second series of statements highlighted by Honda occurred during the plaintiff's closing argument:

> What's this case about? It's not about Honda making great automobiles or Sony making good Walkmans. But also it's not about Pearl Harbor or the Japanese prime minister saying Americans are lazy and stupid.
>
> * * * *
>
> What this case is about is not American xenophobia; it's about corporate greed.

Counsel for Honda again objected * * * . At the bench conference, Martina explained that he was certain that the fact that the defendant is a foreign corporation had entered the minds of the jurors, and he was trying to tell them that that was irrelevant to the case. The court * * * warned Martina: "I am, however, Mr.

Martina, cautioning you that there's a limit to how far argument can go, and I think you're right at the wall on it. So please back away from it and focus on the issues in the case." The court did not strike the remarks or issue a curative instruction to the jury.

At the conclusion of the trial, the court instructed the jury: * * *

> [Y]ou should decide this case without passion, without prejudice, and without sympathy. It is your highest duty as officers of this court to conscientiously determine a fair and just result in this case.

The court never instructed the jury specifically with regard to Attorney Martina's above-quoted remarks.

Although the decision whether to grant * * * the motion for a new trial falls within the trial court's discretion, in some circumstances * * * counsel's remarks may be so prejudicial as to mandate reversal.

We do not expect advocacy to be devoid of passion. But jurors must ultimately base their judgment on the evidence presented and the natural inferences therefrom. Thus, *there must be limits to pleas of pure passion and there must be restraints against blatant appeals to bias and prejudice.* [Emphasis added.]

A * * * new trial may be warranted where counsel attempts to appeal to the sympathies, passions, and prejudices of jurors grounded in race or nationality, by reference to the opposing party's religious beliefs or lack thereof, or by reference to a party's social or economic condition or status. Such an appeal was attempted in this case.

The remarks, when viewed in isolation and outside of the context of the trial, may not seem to be so explicit and brazen as to warrant the severe remedy of reversal. This sort of argument, which may be indirect or implied, as well as direct or express, is nonetheless an affront to the court. * * *

Honda invites us to declare appeals to racial bias *per se* incurable. Although we have considered seriously the adoption of a *per se* rule of reversal in such cases, we believe it better at this time to leave these matters to the sound discretion of the trial court. Such appeals, although extremely unprofessional and deplorable, must be considered in light of the circumstances of the particular case. When a racial or ethnic appeal has been made, as in this case, the trial judge must examine, on a case-by-case basis, the totality of the circumstances, including the nature of the comments, their frequency, their possible relevancy to the real issues before the jury, the manner in which the parties and the court treated the comments, the strength of the case (e.g. whether it is a close case), and the verdict itself.

In reaching this conclusion, we keep in mind that it will be an unusual case in which the invocation of racial or ethnic bias should not result in a mistrial or sanctions, and that attorneys and judges have authority to refer these matters to the committee on professional conduct or the committee on judicial conduct when appropriate.

In denying Honda's motion for a new trial, the trial court recognized that Martina's remarks "raised irrelevant and potentially prejudicial issues," but nonetheless concluded that "the jury followed the Court's instructions, and based its verdict only on the evidence and the law." * * * Plaintiff's counsel's remarks, however, were not only improper but reflect disregard * * * of his duty to the court and to the adversary system which supposes a fair contest, not under-handed blows. Under the circumstances of this case, we conclude that Martina's remarks, calculated as they were to encourage the jury to make a decision based on * * * bias rather than reason and the presented evidence, were so prejudicial as to require a new trial.

* * * *

HORTON, Justice, dissenting:

The plurality correctly asserts that the plaintiff's arguments regarding the color of the Honda Odyssey and the need to ignore Japanese transgressions in favor of attention to corporate greed were "extremely unprofessional and deplorable," but the plurality also correctly states that these arguments "must be considered in light of the circumstances of the particular case." The plurality further notes correctly that "the decision whether to grant the mistrial motion or the motion for a new trial falls within the trial court's discretion." The actual rule is because the trial court is in the best position to gauge prejudicial impact, it has broad discretion to determine whether a mistrial or other remedial action is necessary. I would hold that the trial court's actions relative to these arguments were within its broad discretion.

Neither comment was directly related to an issue in the case. Although completely uncalled for, the arguments were, at best, a weak attempt to engender nationalistic (rather than racial) prejudice, the former suggesting that it might be unfair for a Japanese manufacturer to use the colors of the American flag, and the latter pointing out (albeit in the context of suggesting that the jury should not consider this fact) that the Japanese had bombed Pearl Harbor and criticized American workers. These comments are so unrelated to the basis of the case and so lame in their obvious intent to move the jury to act on prejudice that the trial court could make a fair assessment that any prejudice would be cured by its general instructions. In the words of the trial court, the plaintiff "raised irrelevant and potentially prejudicial issues * * * . The Court must evaluate the statements in the context of the entire trial and determine whether they * * * rendered the trial unfair." The trial court specifically found that the jury followed the court's instructions and based its verdict on the evidence and the law. A review of the record demonstrates that the verdict is, in all other respects, consistent with the evidence and the law. There is no indication that the verdict was based on national prejudice.

CASE PROBLEMS

3–1. Benjamin Omoruyi was convicted in a federal district court of the possession of counterfeit securities in violation of federal law. Omoruyi appealed his conviction to the U.S. Court of Appeals for the Ninth Circuit, arguing that the district court erred by permitting the government to peremptorily challenge female prospective jurors on the basis of gender. (In a previous case decided by the Ninth Circuit, that court had held that equal-protection principles prohibit striking potential jurors on the basis of gender.) The first government peremptory challenge was exercised against an unmarried white woman, and the second was exercised against an unmarried black woman. Omoruyi objected to the second challenge on the basis that it was racially discriminatory. In response to the district court's request to explain the challenge, the government counsel responded: "Because she was a single female and my concern, frankly, is that she, like the other juror I struck, is single and given defendant's good looks would be attracted to the defendant." The district court denied Omoruyi's motion for a new jury. In response to Omoruyi's allegations on appeal, the government argued that the peremptory strikes were based on marital status, not gender. How should the court decide? Discuss fully. [*United States v. Omoruyi*, 7 F.3d 880 (9th Cir. 1993)]

3–2. Joseph Stout, while on the job as a construction worker, fell from a beam that he was attempting to secure to a steel column. As a result of the fall, Stout sustained injuries that rendered him a paraplegic. Stout brought a suit against his employer, A. M. Sunrise Construction Co., and Central Rent-A-Crane, Inc., for damages. Prior to the trial, a number of discovery motions were filed by the defendants, who sought detailed information on the nature of the accident and the injuries incurred. Stout repeatedly failed to respond to these requests, even when the trial court ordered him to do so. Finally, the trial court dismissed the action because of Stout's failure to respond. Stout appealed the dismissal. On appeal, Stout claimed that the trial court had abused its discretion by dismissing his action against the defendants, thus depriving him of his right to be heard in court. What will the appellate court decide? [*Stout v. A. M. Sunrise Construction Co.*, 505 N.E.2d 500 (Ind.App. 1987)]

3–3. Mary Sabo suffered injuries in an automobile accident caused by Daniel Hoag, an intoxicated driver. Hoag had just left Peoples Restaurant after having consumed a large number of drinks. Sabo sued Peoples for damages, alleging that the restaurant had violated a state statute that provided that any person who "knowingly serves" an individual who is "habitually addicted" to alcohol may be held liable for any injuries or damages caused by the intoxication of that individual. In spite of evidence indicating that for the two years prior to the accident, Hoag had gone to Peoples twice a week and on each occasion had drunk liquor until he was intoxicated, the trial court granted Peoples's motion for summary judgment. The court held that Sabo had failed to show that Peoples had knowledge that Hoag was an alcoholic and the bar had therefore not "knowingly" served an alcohol addict. Sabo appealed. The appellate court reversed the trial court's ruling, and Peoples appealed the case to the Supreme Court of Florida. Was summary judgment for Peoples appropriate in this case? [*Sabo v. Peoples Restaurant*, 591 So.2d 907 (Fla. 1991)]

3–4. Ms. Hummel sued Dr. James Strittmatter and his professional corporation, the Gainesville Radiology Group, P.C. ("the Group"), for medical malpractice. Hummel alleged that the Group was negligent in failing to timely diagnose her breast cancer after a mammogram examination. During *voir dire*, jurors were asked if any of them had family members who had been diagnosed with breast cancer or other forms of cancer, how the cancer had been diagnosed, and whether there had been any recurrence. One juror made no response, but it was later discovered that the juror's wife had died of breast cancer some years before. When the trial court jury returned a verdict for the Group, Hummel moved for a new trial on the ground that the juror had violated his oath and failed to disclose pertinent information during *voir dire*. In opposing the motion, the Group submitted an affidavit signed by the juror in which the juror averred that he had not answered the question because he had not heard it and that the cause of his wife's death had not influenced his judgment in the case. Did the juror's failure to hear the question about cancer constitute juror misconduct to the extent that Hummel's motion for a new trial should be granted? [*Gainesville Radiology Group v. Hummel*, 428 S.E.2d 786 (Ga. 1993)]

3–5. Martin Wohl worked for Spectrum Manufacturing, Inc., as the firm's controller. His responsibilities included financial and cost accounting. Billing, which would normally fall under a controller's supervision, was handled by Greg Reuhs, Spectrum's general manager. According to Wohl, Reuhs's unorthodox billing policy (involving "stealing" billing from, and allocating labor to, subsequent months) made it difficult for Wohl to obtain accurate information for his accounting reports. It also prevented management from obtaining an accurate picture of department profit and loss. Wohl discussed the problem with Spectrum's president and others, but he was told to "get along with" Reuhs and to work out their differences. Wohl later stated that it was clear to him "that the company considered Reuhs, who was the younger man, to be a key player in the organization, and that he was to be appeased." When Spectrum fired Wohl, who was then fifty-four years old, and replaced him with a man who was twenty years younger, Wohl sued the company in a federal district court for age discrimination in violation of federal law. Spectrum moved for summary judgment, arguing that it had fired Wohl not because of his age but because of his inability to produce certain accounting reports. Is summary judgment appropriate in this case, or is a question of fact involved? How should the court rule on Spectrum's motion? Discuss. [*Wohl v. Spectrum Manufacturing, Inc.*, 94 F.3d 353 (7th Cir. 1996)]

3–6. Chabad House-Lubavitch of Palm Beach County, Inc., purchased some real estate from Vannoy and Christian Banks. When a dispute arose, the Bankses sued Chabad House in a Florida state court, claiming breach of contract. The jury charges included the following questions: First, did either party breach the contract, and if so, what amount of damages should be awarded to the nonbreaching party? Second, if neither party breached an essential term of the contract, should the contract be rescinded (canceled) on the basis of mistake? The jury decided that Chabad House had breached the contract, and it awarded the Bankses $17,000 in damages. The jury also found that the contract should be rescinded on the basis of mistake. In other words, the jury decided that a canceled contract had been breached. The trial court entered a judgment in favor of the Bankses, and Chabad House appealed. What will happen on appeal? Discuss fully. (Recall from Chapter 1 that when a plaintiff seeks a remedy in equity, such as contract rescission, or cancellation, a judge—not a jury—decides whether the remedy should be granted.) [*Chabad House-Lubavitch of Palm Beach County, Inc. v. Banks*, 602 So.2d 670 (Fla.App. 1992)]

3–7. Ronald Metzgar placed his fifteen-month-old son Matthew, awake and healthy, in his playpen. Ronald left the room for five minutes and on his return found Matthew lifeless. A purple toy block had lodged in the boy's throat, choking him to death. Ronald called 911, but efforts to revive Matthew were to no avail. There was no warning of a choking hazard on the box containing the block. Matthew's parents sued Playskool, Inc., the manufacturer of the block, and others in a federal district court. They alleged, among other things, negligence (the failure to exercise reasonable care, as required by law) in failing to warn of the hazard of the block. Playskool filed a motion for summary judgment, arguing that the danger of a young child choking on a small block was obvious. The court entered a summary judgment in favor of Playskool. The parents appealed. Is summary judgment appropriate in these circumstances, or is the question of the obviousness of the danger, in the context of a negligence claim, a question of fact for the jury to decide? Explain. [*Metzgar v. Playskool, Inc.*, 30 F.3d 459 (3d Cir. 1994)]

3–8. Derrick and Eugenia Powell, American citizens of Jamaican birth, were in an automobile accident with another motorist, whose insurance liability policy limit was $10,000. Claiming damages in excess of $200,000, the Powells sued their own insurer, Allstate Insurance Company, in a Florida state court to recover the difference. A jury awarded Derrick $29,320 and Eugenia nothing. The next day, one of the jurors—all of whom were white—told the Powells' attorney and the judge that some of the jurors had made racial jokes and statements about the Powells during the trial and the jury deliberations. The Powells filed a motion for a new trial. The court denied the motion, and the appellate court affirmed. The Powells appealed to the Supreme Court of Florida. Do explicit statements of racial bias made by jurors concerning the parties in a case constitute juror misconduct requiring a new trial? Discuss. [*Powell v. Allstate Insurance Co.*, 652 So.2d 354 (Fla. 1995)]

3–9. Machelle Brungart brought a suit in a Louisiana state court against a K-Mart store located in Baton Rouge, Louisiana, for injuries that she had sustained while shopping at the store. Brungart alleged that she had been looking at some rugs when a rug on the top shelf of the display rolled off the shelf and hit her head, knocking her to the floor, and that, while on the floor, a second rug fell on top of her. Brungart also stated that she had not touched the rugs on the top shelf, only on some of the lower shelves. A store manager who met with Brungart at the time of the incident, however, testified that she told him immediately following the accident that she was moving some Oriental rugs when one of them started to fall toward her. The Oriental rugs were on the top shelf. The jury found that Brungart was 80 percent at fault and that the store was 20 percent at fault. Brungart moved for a judgment *n.o.v.* Under Louisiana's Code of Civil Procedure, a judgment *n.o.v.* is warranted only when "the evidence points so strongly in favor of the moving party that reasonable men could not reach different conclusions." The trial court granted the motion, and the store appealed. Will the appellate court uphold the trial court's judgment? Discuss. [*Brungart v. K-Mart Corp.*, 668 So.2d 1335 (La.App. 1st Cir. 1996)]

3–10. Cheryl Lessin, a member of the Revolutionary Communist Party, participated in a political demonstration protesting the U.S. president's ordering of American troops to the Persian Gulf in 1990. Lessin made prepared political statements to the crowd; assisted in the burning of an American flag to illustrate her own and her party's disapproval of the president's decision; and then pushed, shoved, and punched her way through the crowd until she was arrested by the police. In 1989, prior to Lessin's trial, the United States Supreme Court had decided that burning an American flag to convey a political message is protected under the First Amendment's guarantee of freedom of speech. The trial court in Lessin's case, however, failed to instruct the jury on the law set forth by the Supreme Court on this issue. The jury returned a guilty verdict, and Lessin appealed. Should Lessin be entitled to a new trial in view of the trial court's failure to accurately and thoroughly set forth jury instructions with respect to the law on flag burning, as decided by the United States Supreme Court? Discuss. [*Ohio v. Lessin*, 67 Ohio St.3d 487, 620 N.E.2d 72 (1993)]

3–11. Martin brought a civil rights action against his employer, the New York Department of Mental Hygiene, when it failed to promote him on several occasions. His complaint stated only that the defendant had discriminated against him on the basis of race by denying him "the authority, salary, and privileges commensurate with this position." The employer made a motion to dismiss the claim for failure to state a cause of action. Discuss whether the employer could be successful. [*Martin v. New York State Department of Mental Hygiene*, 588 F.2d 371 (2d Cir. 1978)]

3–12. On June 16, 1986, the director of the Administrative Office of the U.S. Courts notified all federal district courts that no civil jury trials could be initiated until the end of the fiscal year (September 30) due to lack of funds with which to pay the jurors. Armster and others claimed that the consequent delay (of three and a half months) in scheduling a jury trial violated the Seventh Amendment right to a civil jury trial. The Justice Department maintained that although the Sixth Amendment guarantees a speedy criminal jury trial, the Seventh Amendment does not guarantee a speedy civil jury trial. The Justice Department further noted that district courts have postponed civil jury trials before, although for other reasons—such as court-calendar congestion, the lack of a sufficient number of judges, and the priority accorded to trying criminal cases before civil actions. Discuss whether the suspension of civil jury trials for a period of three and a half months due to lack of funds to pay jurors violates the constitutional right to a trial by jury. Are people always entitled to a jury trial in civil lawsuits? [*Armster v. U.S. District Court for the Central District of California*, 792 F.2d 1423 (9th Cir. 1986)]

3–13. Washoe Medical Center, Inc., admitted Shirley Swisher for the treatment of a fractured pelvis. During her stay, Swisher suffered a fatal fall from her hospital bed. Gerald Parodi, the administrator of her estate, and others filed an action against Washoe in which they sought damages for the alleged lack of care in treating Swisher. During *voir dire*, when the plaintiffs' attorney returned a few minutes late from a break, the trial judge led the prospective jurors in a standing ovation. The judge joked with one of the prospective jurors, whom he had known in college, about his fitness to serve as a judge and personally endorsed another prospective juror's business. After the trial, the jury returned a verdict in favor of Washoe. The plaintiffs moved for a new trial, but the judge denied the motion. The plaintiffs then appealed, arguing that the tone set by the judge during *voir dire* prejudiced their right to a fair trial. Should the appellate court agree? Why, or why not? [*Parodi v. Washoe Medical Center, Inc.*, 111 Nev. 365, 892 P.2d 588 (1995)]

3–14. Advance Technology Consultants, Inc. (ATC), contracted with RoadTrac, L.L.C., to provide software and client software systems for the products for global positioning satellite system (GPS) technology being developed by RoadTrac. RoadTrac agreed to provide ATC hardware with which ATC's software would interface. Problems soon arose, however. ATC claimed that RoadTrac's hardware was defective, making it difficult to develop the software. RoadTrac contended that its hardware was fully functional and that ATC simply failed to provide supporting software. ATC told RoadTrac that it considered their contract terminated. RoadTrac filed a suit in a Georgia state court against ATC, charging, among other things, breach of contract. During discovery, RoadTrac requested ATC's customer lists and marketing procedures. Before producinthe court rule regarding RoadTrac's discovery request? [*Advance Technology Consultants, Inc. v. RoadTrac, L.L.C.*, 236 Ga.App. 582, 512 S.E.2d 27 (1999)]

3–15. Ms. Thompson filed a suit in a federal district court against her employer, Altheimer & Gray, seeking damages for alleged racial discrimination in violation of federal law. During *voir dire*, the judge asked the prospective jurors whether "there is something about this kind of lawsuit for money damages that would start any of you leaning for or against a particular party?" Ms. Leiter, one of the prospective jurors, raised her hand and explained that she had "been an owner of a couple of businesses and am currently an owner of a business, and I feel that as an employer and owner of a business that will definitely sway my judgment in this case." She explained, "I am constantly faced with people that want various benefits or different positions in the company or better contacts or, you know, a myriad of issues that employers face on a regular basis, and I have to decide whether or not that person should get them." Asked by Thompson's lawyer whether "you believe that people file lawsuits just because they don't get something they want," Leiter answered, "I believe there are some people that do." In answer to another question, she said, "I think I bring a lot of background to this case, and I can't say that it's not going to cloud my judgment. I can try to be as fair as I can, as I do every day." Thompson filed a motion to strike Leiter for cause. Should the judge grant the motion? Explain. [*Thompson v. Altheimer & Gray*, 248 F.3d 621 (7th Cir. 2001)]

E-LINKS

For updated links to resources available on the Web, as well as a variety of other materials, visit this text's Web site at

http://wbl-cs.westbuslaw.com

If you are interested in learning more about the Federal Rules of Civil Procedure (FRCP) and the Federal Rules of Evidence (FRE), they can now be accessed via the Internet at the following Web site:

http://www.cornell.edu

Procedural rules for several of the state courts are now also online and can be accessed via the courts' Web pages. You can find links to the Web pages for state courts at the Web site of the National Center for State Courts. Go to

http://www.ncsc.dni.us/court/sites/courts.htm

LEGAL RESEARCH EXERCISES ON THE WEB

Go to http://wbl-cs.westbuslaw.com, the Web site that accompanies this text. Select "Interactive Study Center," and then click on "Chapter 3." There you will find the following Internet exercises that you can perform to learn more about the court procedures involved in civil lawsuits and in small claims courts:

Activity 3–1: Civil Procedure

Activity 3–2: Small Claims Courts

CHAPTER 4

Constitutional Authority to Regulate Business

THE U.S. CONSTITUTION IS THE SUPREME law in this country.[1] As mentioned in Chapter 1, neither Congress nor any state may pass a law that conflicts with the Constitution. Laws that govern business have their origin in the lawmaking authority granted by this document.

Before the Constitution was written, a *confederal form* of government existed. The Articles of Confederation, which went into effect in 1781, established a confederation of independent states and a central government of very limited powers. The central government could handle only those matters of common concern expressly delegated to it by the member states, and the national congress had no authority to make laws directly applicable to individuals unless the member states explicitly supported such laws. In short, the *sovereign power*[2] to govern rested essentially with the states. The Articles of Confederation clearly reflected the central tenet of the American Revolution—that a national government should not have unlimited power.

After the Revolutionary War, however, the states began to pass laws that hampered national commerce and foreign trade by preventing the free movement of goods and services. Consequently, in 1787, the Constitutional Convention assembled to **amend** (change, alter) the Articles of Confederation. Instead, the delegates to the Convention created the Constitution and a completely new type of federal government, which they believed was much better equipped than its predecessor to resolve the problems of the nation.

1. See Appendix A for the full text of the U.S. Constitution.
2. Sovereign power refers to that supreme power to which no other authority is superior or equal.

SECTION 1

The Constitutional Powers of Government

The U.S. Constitution established a federal form of government. A **federal form of government** is one in which the states form a union and the sovereign power is divided between a central governing authority and the member states. The Constitution delegates certain powers to the national government, and the states retain all other powers. The relationship between the national government and the state governments is a partnership—neither partner is superior to the other except within the particular area of exclusive authority granted to it under the Constitution.

To prevent the possibility that the national government might use its power arbitrarily, the Constitution provided for three branches of government. The legislative branch makes the laws, the executive branch enforces the laws, and the judicial branch interprets the laws. Each branch performs a separate function, and no branch may exercise the authority of another branch.

Each branch, however, has some power to limit the actions of the other two branches. Congress, for example, can enact legislation relating to spending and commerce, but the president can veto that legislation. The executive branch is responsible for foreign affairs, but treaties with foreign governments require the advice and consent of members of the Senate. Although Congress determines the jurisdiction of the federal courts, the federal courts have the power to hold acts of the other branches of the federal government unconstitutional.[3] Thus, with this system of **checks and balances**, no one branch of government can accumulate too much power.

THE COMMERCE CLAUSE

Article I, Section 8, of the U.S. Constitution expressly permits Congress "[t]o regulate Commerce with foreign Nations, and among the several States, and with the Indian Tribes." This clause, referred to as the **commerce clause**, has had a greater impact on business than any other provision in the Constitution. This power was delegated to the federal government to ensure the uniformity of rules governing the movement of goods through the states.

One of the questions posed for the courts by the commerce clause is whether the word *among* in the phrase "among the several States" meant *between* the states or *between and within* the states. For some time, the federal government's power under the commerce clause was interpreted to apply only to commerce between the states (*interstate* commerce) and not commerce within the states (*intrastate* commerce). In 1824, however, in *Gibbons v. Ogden,*[4] the United States Supreme Court held that commerce within the states could also be regulated by the national government as long as the commerce concerned more than one state.

The Breadth of the Commerce Clause. As a result of the Supreme Court's interpretation of the commerce clause in *Gibbons v. Ogden,* the national government exercised increasing authority over all areas of economic affairs throughout the land. In a 1942 case,[5] for example, the Court held that wheat production by an individual farmer intended wholly for consumption on his own farm was subject to federal regulation. The Court reasoned that the home consumption of wheat reduced the demand for wheat and thus could have a substantial effect on interstate commerce. Today, at least theoretically, the power over commerce authorizes the national government to regulate every commercial enterprise in the United States. The breadth of the commerce clause permits the national government to legislate in areas in which there is no explicit grant of power to Congress.

In the last decade, however, the Supreme Court has begun to curb somewhat the national government's regulatory authority under the commerce clause. In a 1995 case, *United States v. Lopez,*[6] the Court held—for the first time in sixty years—that Congress had exceeded its regulatory authority under the commerce clause. The Court stated that the Gun-Free School Zones Act (passed in 1990), which banned the possession of guns within one thousand feet of any school, was unconstitutional because it attempted to regulate an area that had "nothing to do with commerce."

Two years later, in 1997, the Court struck down portions of the Brady Handgun Violence Prevention Act of 1993, which obligated state and local law enforcement officers to do background checks on prospective handgun buyers until a national instant check system could be implemented. The Court stated that Congress lacked the power to "dragoon" state employees into federal service through an unfunded mandate of this kind.[7] In 2000, the Court invalidated key portions of the federal Violence Against Women Act of 1994, which allowed women to sue in federal court when they were victims of gender-motivated violence, such as rape. According to the Court, the commerce clause did not justify national regulation of noneconomic, criminal conduct.[8] Nonetheless, the commerce clause continues to serve as the constitutional backbone for national laws regulating a broad number of activities.

The Regulatory Powers of the States. A problem that frequently arises under the commerce clause concerns a state's ability to regulate matters within its own borders. The U.S. Constitution does not expressly exclude state regulation of commerce, and there is no doubt that states have a strong interest in regulating activities within their borders. As part of their inherent sovereignty, states possess **police powers.** The term does not relate solely to criminal law enforcement but rather refers to the broad right of state governments to regulate private activities to protect or promote the public order, health, safety,

3. As discussed in Chapter 2, the power of judicial review was established by the United States Supreme Court in *Marbury v. Madison,* 5 U.S. (1 Cranch) 137, 2 L.Ed. 60 (1803).

4. 22 U.S. (9 Wheat.) 1, 6 L.Ed. 23 (1824).

5. *Wickard v. Filburn,* 317 U.S. 111, 63 S.Ct. 82, 87 L.Ed. 122 (1942).

6. 514 U.S. 549, 115 S.Ct. 1624, 131 L.Ed.2d 626 (1995).

7. *Printz v. United States,* 521 U.S. 898, 117 S.Ct. 2365, 138 L.Ed.2d 914 (1997).

8. *United States v. Morrison,* 529 U.S. 598, 120 S.Ct. 1740, 146 L.Ed.2d 658 (2000).

morals, and general welfare. Fire and building codes, antidiscrimination laws, parking regulations, zoning restrictions, licensing requirements, and thousands of other state statutes covering virtually every aspect of life have been enacted pursuant to states' police powers.

When state regulations impinge on interstate commerce, courts must balance the state's interest in the merits and purposes of the regulations against the burden placed by the regulations on interstate commerce. Generally, state laws enacted pursuant to a state's police powers carry a strong presumption of validity. If state laws *substantially* interfere with interstate commerce, however, they will be held to violate the commerce clause of the Constitution.

In *Raymond Motor Transportation, Inc. v. Rice,*[9] for example, the United States Supreme Court invalidated Wisconsin administrative regulations limiting the length of trucks traveling on the state's highways. The Court weighed the burden on interstate commerce against the benefits of the regulations and concluded that the challenged regulations "place a substantial burden on interstate commerce and they cannot be said to make more than the most speculative contribution to highway safety." Because courts balance the interests involved, it is extremely difficult to predict the outcome in a particular case.

THE SUPREMACY CLAUSE AND FEDERAL PREEMPTION

Article VI of the Constitution provides that the Constitution, laws, and treaties of the United States are "the supreme Law of the Land." This article, commonly referred to as the **supremacy clause**, is important in the ordering of state and federal relationships. When there is a direct conflict between a federal law and a state law, the state law is rendered invalid. Because some powers are *concurrent* (shared by the federal government and the states), however, it is necessary to determine which law governs in a particular circumstance.

Federal Preemption. When Congress chooses to act exclusively in an area in which the federal government and the states have concurrent powers, it is said to have *preempted* the area. When federal **preemption** occurs, a valid federal statute or regulation will take precedence over a conflicting state or local law or regulation on the same general subject.

Whether the federal government has preempted a certain area can have important implications for businesspersons. For example, for some time it was not clear whether tobacco companies that complied with federal cigarette-labeling requirements could be sued under state laws requiring cigarette manufacturers to sufficiently warn consumers of the potential dangers associated with cigarette smoking. In a 1992 case, *Cipollone v. Liggett Group, Inc.,*[10] the United States Supreme Court held that the Federal Cigarette Labeling and Advertising Act of 1965, which requires specific warnings to be included on cigarette packages, preempted the state laws requiring warnings. The Court declared, however, that there was no indication that Congress had intended to preempt state laws that fall *outside* the scope of the federal law, such as laws governing fraudulent misrepresentation.

Determining Congressional Intent. In *Cipollone* and other cases involving preemption issues, the courts must decide whether Congress, when enacting a particular statute, *intended* to preempt the area and thus preclude plaintiffs from bringing claims under state law. In determining congressional intent, courts look at the wording of the statute itself, as well as at the legislative history of the statute (such as congressional committee reports on the topic).

For example, in *Tebbetts v. Ford Motor Co.,*[11] a plaintiff alleged that a 1988 Ford Escort was defectively designed because it did not contain an air bag on the driver's side. The defendant-manufacturer contended that it had complied with federal safety regulations authorized by the National Traffic and Motor Vehicle Safety Act (NTMVSA) of 1966 and that those regulations preempted recovery under state product-safety laws. The court interpreted House and Senate reports on the issue, as well as a clause included in the act itself, to mean that not all state law claims were preempted by the federal regulations. (The relevant clause stated that "[c]ompliance with any Federal motor vehicle safety standard issued under this [act] does not exempt any person from any liability under common law.") Thus, the plaintiff in *Tebbetts* was not precluded by the NTMVSA from suing Ford under state product-liability laws (see Chapter 6).

9. 434 U.S. 429, 98 S.Ct. 787, 54 L.Ed.2d 664 (1978).

10. 505 U.S. 504, 112 S.Ct. 2608, 120 L.Ed.2d 407 (1992).

11. 665 A.2d 345 (N.H. 1995).

Generally, it is difficult to predict whether a defendant will be subject to liability under state laws notwithstanding the defendant's compliance with federally mandated product-safety standards. Courts differ in their interpretations of congressional intent, and the outcomes in cases involving similar facts can thus also differ.

THE TAXING AND SPENDING POWERS

Article I, Section 8, provides that Congress has the "Power to lay and collect Taxes, Duties, Imposts, and Excises." Section 8 further provides that "all Duties, Imposts and Excises shall be uniform throughout the United States." The requirement of uniformity refers to uniformity among the states, and thus Congress may not tax some states while exempting others.

Traditionally, if Congress attempted to regulate indirectly, by taxation, an area over which it had no authority, the tax would be invalidated by the courts. Today, however, if a tax measure is reasonable, it is generally held to be within the national taxing power. Moreover, the expansive interpretation of the commerce clause almost always provides a basis for sustaining a federal tax.

Under Article I, Section 8, Congress has the power "to pay the Debts and provide for the common Defence and general Welfare of the United States." Through the spending power, Congress disposes of the revenues accumulated from the taxing power. Congress can spend revenues not only to carry out its enumerated powers but also to promote any objective it deems worthwhile, so long as it does not violate the Bill of Rights. For example, Congress could not condition welfare payments on the recipients' agreement not to criticize government policies. The spending power necessarily involves policy choices, with which taxpayers may disagree.

SECTION 2

Business and the Bill of Rights

The importance of a written declaration of the rights of individuals eventually caused the first Congress of the United States to submit twelve amendments to the Constitution to the states for approval. The first ten of these amendments, commonly known as the **Bill of Rights**, were adopted in 1791 and embody a series of protections for the individual against various types of interference by the federal government.[12] These protections are summarized in Exhibit 4–1.[13] Some of these constitutional protections apply to business entities as well. For example, corporations exist as separate legal entities, or *legal persons*, and enjoy many of the same rights and privileges as *natural persons* do.

As originally intended, the Bill of Rights limited only the powers of the national government. Over time, however, the United States Supreme Court "incorporated" most of these rights into the protections against state actions afforded by the Fourteenth Amendment to the Constitution. That amendment, passed in 1868 after the Civil War, provides in part that "[n]o State shall . . . deprive any person of life, liberty, or property, without due process of law." Starting in 1925, the Supreme Court began to define various rights and liberties guaranteed in the national Constitution as constituting "due process of law," which was required of state governments under the Fourteenth Amendment. Today, most of the rights and liberties set forth in the Bill of Rights apply to state governments as well as the national government. In other words, neither the federal government nor state governments can deprive individuals of those rights and liberties.

The rights secured by the Bill of Rights are not absolute. Many of the rights guaranteed by the first ten amendments are described in very general terms (see Exhibit 4–1). For example, the Fourth Amendment prohibits *unreasonable* searches and seizures, but it does not define what constitutes an unreasonable search or seizure. Similarly, the Eighth Amendment prohibits excessive bail or fines, but no definition of *excessive* is contained in that amendment. Ultimately, it is the United States Supreme Court, as the final interpreter of the Constitution, that defines our rights and determines their boundaries.

FREEDOM OF SPEECH

A democratic form of government cannot survive unless people can freely voice their political opinions and criticize government actions or policies. Freedom of speech, particularly political speech, is

12. Another of these proposed amendments was ratified 203 years later (in 1992) and became the Twenty-seventh Amendment to the Constitution. See Appendix A.

13. See the Constitution in Appendix A for the complete text of each amendment.

EXHIBIT 4–1 PROTECTIONS GUARANTEED BY THE BILL OF RIGHTS

First Amendment: Guarantees the freedoms of religion, speech, and the press and the rights to assemble peaceably and to petition the government.	**Sixth Amendment:** Guarantees the accused in a criminal case the right to a speedy and public trial by an impartial jury and with counsel. The accused has the right to cross-examine witnesses against him or her and to solicit testimony from witnesses in his or her favor.
Second Amendment: Guarantees the right to keep and bear arms.	
Third Amendment: Prohibits, in peacetime, the lodging of soldiers in any house without the owner's consent.	**Seventh Amendment:** Guarantees the right to a trial by jury in a civil case involving at least twenty dollars.[a]
Fourth Amendment: Prohibits unreasonable searches and seizures of persons or property.	**Eighth Amendment:** Prohibits excessive bail and fines, as well as cruel and unusual punishment.
Fifth Amendment: Guarantees the rights to indictment by grand jury, to due process of law, and to fair payment when private property is taken for public use; prohibits compulsory self-incrimination and double jeopardy (trial for the same crime twice if the first trial ends in acquittal or conviction).	**Ninth Amendment:** Establishes that the people have rights in addition to those specified in the Constitution.
	Tenth Amendment: Establishes that those powers neither delegated to the federal government nor denied to the states are reserved for the states.

a. Twenty dollars was forty days' pay for the average person when the Bill of Rights was written.

thus a prized right, and traditionally the courts have protected this right to the fullest extent possible.

Symbolic speech—gestures, movements, articles of clothing, and other forms of expressive conduct—is also given substantial protection by the courts. For example, in a 1989 case, *Texas v. Johnson,*[14] the United States Supreme Court ruled that state laws that prohibited the burning of the American flag as part of a peaceful protest violated the freedom of expression protected by the First Amendment. Congress responded by passing the Flag Protection Act of 1989, which was ruled unconstitutional by the Supreme Court in 1990.[15] Congress and George Bush, who was then president, pledged immediately to work for a constitutional amendment to "protect our flag"—an effort that has yet to be successful. In a subsequent case, the Supreme Court ruled that a city statute banning bias-motivated disorderly conduct (including, in this case, the placing of a burning cross in another's front yard as a gesture of hate) was an unconstitutional restriction of speech.[16]

Governments can and do place restraints on free speech, of course, but such restraints are permissible only when they are necessary to protect other substantial interests and rights. It is up to the courts—and ultimately, the United States Supreme Court—to determine the point at which laws restricting free speech can be justified by the need to protect other rights.

Commercial Speech. Speech and communications—primarily advertising—made by business firms are called *commercial speech.* Although commercial speech is protected by the First Amendment, it is not protected as extensively as noncommercial speech. A state may restrict certain kinds of advertising, for example, in the interest of preventing consumers from being misled by the advertising practices. States also have a legitimate interest in the beautification of roadsides, and this interest allows states to place restraints on billboard advertising.

Generally, a restriction on commercial speech will be considered valid as long as it meets the following three criteria: (1) it must seek to implement a substantial government interest, (2) it must directly advance that interest, and (3) it must go no further than necessary to accomplish its objective.

See Case 4.1 at the end of this chapter. To view the full, unedited case from Westlaw,® go to this text's Web site at **http://wbl-cs.westbuslaw.com**.

Corporate Political Speech. Political speech that otherwise would fall within the protection of the

14. 491 U.S. 397, 109 S.Ct. 2533, 105 L.Ed.2d 342 (1989).

15. *United States v. Eichman,* 496 U.S. 310, 110 S.Ct. 2804, 110 L.Ed.2d 287 (1990).

16. *R.A.V. v. City of St. Paul, Minnesota,* 505 U.S. 377, 112 S.Ct. 2538, 120 L.Ed.2d 305 (1992).

First Amendment does not lose that protection simply because its source is a corporation. For example, in *First National Bank of Boston v. Bellotti,*[17] national banking associations and business corporations sought United States Supreme Court review of a Massachusetts statute that prohibited corporations from making political contributions or expenditures that individuals were permitted to make. The Court ruled that the Massachusetts law was unconstitutional because it violated the right of corporations to freedom of speech. Similarly, the Court has held that a law forbidding a corporation from using bill inserts to express its views on controversial issues violates the First Amendment.[18] Although in 1990 a more conservative Supreme Court reversed this trend somewhat,[19] corporate political speech continues to be given significant protection under the First Amendment.

Unprotected Speech. The United States Supreme Court has made it clear that certain types of speech will not be protected under the First Amendment. Speech that harms the good reputation of another, or defamatory speech (see Chapter 5), is not protected under the First Amendment. Speech that violates criminal laws (threatening speech, pornography, and so on) is not constitutionally protected. Other unprotected speech includes "fighting words" (speech that is likely to incite others to respond violently). Many people think that the "hate speech" exchanged between members of different groups on college campuses should be included in the category of "fighting words." Courts, however, have been reluctant to uphold university codes banning hate speech, concluding that the codes go too far in restricting the free speech of students.[20]

Another category of unprotected speech is obscene speech. Numerous state and federal statutes make it a crime to disseminate obscene materials. The United States Supreme Court has grappled from time to time with the problem of trying to establish an operationally effective definition of obscene speech. Frequently, this determination is left to state and local authorities, who customarily base their definitions of obscenity on community standards. Generally, obscenity is still a constitutionally unsettled area. In the interest of preventing the abuse of children, however, the Supreme Court has upheld state laws prohibiting the sale and possession of child pornography.[21] In the interest of protecting women against sexual harassment on the job, at least one court has banned lewd speech and pornographic pinups in the workplace.[22]

In recent years, obscenity issues have also arisen in relation to television shows, movies, the lyrics and covers of music albums, and the content of monologues by "shock" comedians. In addition, a challenging legal issue today is how to regulate the availability of obscene materials on the Internet.

Online Obscenity. Congress has passed several laws in an attempt to protect minors from pornographic materials on the Internet. Most of these laws, though, have been challenged as unconstitutional restraints on free speech. For example, the Communications Decency Act (CDA) of 1996 made it a crime to make available to minors online any "obscene or indecent" message that "depicts or describes, in terms patently offensive as measured by contemporary community standards, sexual or excretory activities or organs." Ultimately, the United States Supreme Court ruled that portions of the act were unconstitutional, because the terms *indecent* and *patently offensive* covered large amounts of nonpornographic material with serious educational or other value. Moreover, said the Court, "the 'community standards' criterion as applied to the Internet means that any communication available to a nationwide audience will be judged by the standards of the community most likely to be offended by the message."[23]

Later attempts by Congress to curb pornography on the Internet have also encountered constitutional stumbling blocks. For example, the Child Online

17. 435 U.S. 765, 98 S.Ct. 1407, 55 L.Ed.2d 707 (1978).

18. *Consolidated Edison Co. v. Public Service Commission,* 447 U.S. 530, 100 S.Ct. 2326, 65 L.Ed.2d 319 (1980).

19. See *Austin v. Michigan Chamber of Commerce,* 494 U.S. 652, 110 S.Ct. 1391, 108 L.Ed.2d 652 (1990), in which the Court upheld a state law prohibiting corporations from using general corporate funds for independent expenditures in state political campaigns.

20. See, for example, *Doe v. University of Michigan,* 721 F.Supp. 852 (1989); and *The UWM Post v. Board of Regents of the University of Wisconsin System,* 774 F.Supp. 1163 (E.D.Wis. 1991).

21. See *Osborne v. Ohio,* 495 U.S. 103, 110 S.Ct. 1691, 109 L.Ed.2d 98 (1990).

22. *Robinson v. Jacksonville Shipyards, Inc.,* 760 F.Supp. 1486 (M.D.Fla. 1991).

23. *Reno v. American Civil Liberties Union,* 521 U.S. 844, 117 S.Ct. 2329, 138 L.Ed.2d 874 (1997).

Privacy Protection Act (COPPA) of 1998 imposed criminal penalties on those who distribute material that is "harmful to minors" without using some kind of age-verification system to separate adult and minor users. The act has been tied up in the courts since its passage, and in 2001 the Supreme Court agreed to review the case. In 2000, Congress enacted the Children's Internet Protection Act, which requires public schools and libraries to block adult content from access by children by installing **filtering software.** Such software is designed to prevent persons from viewing certain Web sites at specific times by responding to a site's uniform resource locator (URL), or Internet address, or its **tags**, or key words. The 2000 act has also been challenged in court as unconstitutional, on the ground that it blocks access to too much information, including information of educational value.

Recently, the Supreme Court agreed to review a case challenging the constitutionality of another federal act attempting to protect minors in the online environment—the Child Pornography Prevention Act of 1996. This act made it illegal to distribute or possess computer-generated images that appear to depict minors engaging in lewd and lascivious behavior. At issue in the case is whether digital child pornography should be considered a crime, given that no actual children take part in the production of digital child pornography. In the case pending before the Supreme Court, the U.S. Court of Appeals for the Ninth Circuit held that the CPPA was unconstitutional. The court emphasized that the government can place significant restraints on free speech rights only if the restraints are necessary to promote a compelling government interest. In the court's eyes, the government has a compelling interest in protecting children only from actual, not "fake," child pornography.[24] Other courts, however, have held that there is little difference, in effect, between digital and real pornography.

Other Forms of Online Speech. On the Internet, extreme hate speech is known as **cyber hate speech.** Racist materials and Holocaust denials on the Web, for example, are cyber hate speech. Can the federal government restrict this type of speech? Should it? Are there other forms of speech that the government should restrict?[25] Content restrictions generally amount to censorship and can be difficult to enforce. Even if it were possible to impose content restrictions online, U.S. federal law is only "local" law in cyberspace—less than half of the users of the Internet are in the United States. Speech that may be legal in one country may not be legal in another, thus making it extremely difficult for any one nation to regulate Internet speech.

Freedom of Religion

The First Amendment states that the government may neither establish any religion nor prohibit the free exercise of religious practices. The first part of this constitutional provision is referred to as the **establishment clause,** which has to do with the separation of church and state. The second part of the provision is known as the **free exercise clause.**

The Establishment Clause. The establishment clause prohibits the government from establishing a state-sponsored religion, as well as from passing laws that promote (aid or endorse) religion or that show a preference for one religion over another. Establishment clause issues often involve such matters as the legality of allowing or requiring school prayers, the teaching of evolutionary versus creationist theory, and state and local government aid to religious organizations and schools.

Federal or state laws that do not promote or place a significant burden on religion are constitutional even if they have some impact on religion. "Sunday closing laws," for example, make the performance of some commercial activities on Sunday illegal. These statutes, also known as "blue laws" (from the color of the paper on which an early Sunday law was written), have been upheld on the ground that it is a legitimate function of government to provide a day of rest. The United States Supreme Court has held that the closing laws, although originally of a religious character, have taken on the secular purpose of promoting the health and welfare of workers.[26] Even though closing laws admittedly make it easier for Christians to attend religious services, the Court has viewed this effect as an incidental, not a primary, purpose of Sunday closing laws.

24. *Free Speech Coalition v. Reno,* 198 F.3d 1083 (9th Cir. 1999); rehearing denied, 220 F.3d 1113 (2000).

25. The content of some speech is regulated to a certain extent by tort law, copyright law, trademark law, and other laws. See Chapters 5 and 7 for a discussion of these topics.

26. *McGowan v. Maryland,* 366 U.S. 420, 81 S.Ct. 1101, 6 L.Ed.2d 393 (1961).

The First Amendment does not require a complete separation of church and state. On the contrary, it affirmatively mandates accommodation of all religions and forbids hostility toward any.[27] An ongoing challenge for the courts is determining the extent to which governments can accommodate a religion without appearing to promote that religion, which would violate the establishment clause. For example, in *Lynch v. Donnelly*,[28] the United States Supreme Court held that a municipality could include religious symbols, such as a Nativity scene, or crèche, in its annual holiday display as long as the religious symbols constituted just one part of a display in which other, nonreligious symbols (such as reindeer and candy-striped poles) were also featured. The Court has applied this same reasoning in subsequent cases and continues to face such issues.[29]

The Free Exercise Clause. The free exercise clause guarantees that no person can be compelled to do something that is contrary to his or her religious beliefs. For this reason, if a law or policy is contrary to a person's religious beliefs, exemptions are often made to accommodate those beliefs. When, however, religious practices work against public policy and the public welfare, the government can act. For example, children of Jehovah's Witnesses are not required to say the Pledge of Allegiance at school, but their parents cannot prevent these children from accepting medical treatment (such as blood transfusions) if the children's lives are in danger.

For business firms, an important issue involves the accommodation that businesses must make for the religious beliefs of their employees. For example, if an employee's religion prohibits him or her from working on a certain day of the week or at a certain type of job, the employer must make a reasonable attempt to accommodate these religious requirements. Employers must reasonably accommodate an employee's religious belief even if the belief is not based on the tenets or dogma of a particular church, sect, or denomination. The only requirement is that the belief be religious in nature and sincerely held by the employee.[30] (See Chapter 42 for a further discussion of religious freedom in the employment context.)

SELF-INCRIMINATION

The Fifth Amendment guarantees that no person "shall be compelled in any criminal case to be a witness against himself." Thus, in any federal proceeding, an accused person cannot be compelled to give testimony that might subject him or her to any criminal prosecution. Nor can an accused person be forced to testify against himself or herself in state courts, because the due process clause of the Fourteenth Amendment (discussed later in this chapter) incorporates the Fifth Amendment provision against self-incrimination.

The Fifth Amendment's guarantee against self-incrimination extends only to natural persons. Because a corporation is a legal entity and not a natural person, the privilege against self-incrimination does not apply to it. Similarly, the business records of a partnership do not receive Fifth Amendment protection.[31] When a partnership is required to produce these records, it must give the information even if it incriminates the persons who constitute the business entity. In contrast, sole proprietors and sole practitioners (those who fully own their businesses) who have not incorporated cannot be compelled to produce their business records. These individuals have full protection against self-incrimination, because they function in only one capacity; there is no separate business entity.

Westlaw. See Case 4.2 at the end of this chapter. To view the full, unedited case from Westlaw,® go to this text's Web site at **http://wbl-cs.westbuslaw.com**.

SEARCHES AND SEIZURES

The Fourth Amendment protects the "right of the people to be secure in their persons, houses, papers, and effects." Before searching or seizing private property, law enforcement officers must obtain a **search warrant**—an order from a judge or other public official authorizing the search or seizure.

27. *Zorach v. Clauson*, 343 U.S. 306, 72 S.Ct. 679, 96 L.Ed. 954 (1952).

28. 465 U.S. 668, 104 S.Ct. 1355, 79 L.Ed.2d 604 (1984).

29. See, for example, *County of Allegheny v. American Civil Liberties Union*, 492 U.S. 573, 109 S.Ct. 3086, 106 L.Ed.2d 472 (1989); and *Capitol Square Review and Advisory Board v. Pinette*, 515 U.S. 753, 115 S.Ct. 2440, 132 L.Ed.2d 650 (1995).

30. *Frazee v. Illinois Department of Employment Security*, 489 U.S. 829, 109 S.Ct. 1514, 103 L.Ed.2d 914 (1989).

31. The privilege has been applied to some small family partnerships. See *United States v. Slutsky*, 352 F.Supp. 1005 (S.D.N.Y. 1972).

Search Warrants and Probable Cause. To obtain a search warrant, the officers must convince a judge that they have reasonable grounds, or probable cause, to believe a search will reveal a specific illegality. **Probable cause** requires law enforcement officials to have trustworthy evidence that would convince a reasonable person that the proposed search or seizure is more likely justified than not. Furthermore, the Fourth Amendment prohibits *general* warrants. It requires a particular description of that which is to be searched or seized. General searches through a person's belongings are impermissible. The search cannot extend beyond what is described in the warrant.

There are exceptions to the requirement for a search warrant, as when it is likely that the items sought will be removed before a warrant can be obtained. For example, if a police officer has probable cause to believe an automobile contains evidence of a crime and it is likely that the vehicle will be unavailable by the time a warrant is obtained, the officer can search the vehicle without a warrant.

Searches and Seizures in the Business Context. Constitutional protection against unreasonable searches and seizures is important to businesses and professionals. As federal and state regulation of commercial activities increased, frequent and unannounced government inspections were conducted to ensure compliance with the regulations. Such inspections were at times extremely disruptive. In *Marshall v. Barlow's, Inc.*,[32] the United States Supreme Court held that government inspectors do not have the right to enter business premises without a warrant, although the standard of probable cause is not the same as that required in nonbusiness contexts. The existence of a general and neutral enforcement plan will justify issuance of the warrant.

Lawyers and accountants frequently possess the business records of their clients, and inspecting these documents while they are out of the hands of their true owners also requires a warrant. A warrant is not required, however, for the seizure of spoiled or contaminated food. In addition, warrants are also not required for searches of businesses in such highly regulated industries as liquor, guns, and strip mining. General manufacturing is not considered to be one of these highly regulated industries, however.

32. 436 U.S. 307, 98 S.Ct. 1816, 56 L.Ed.2d 305 (1978).

Of increasing concern to many government employers is how to maintain a safe and efficient workplace without jeopardizing the Fourth Amendment rights of employees "to be secure in their persons." Requiring government employees to undergo random drug tests, for example, may be held to violate the Fourth Amendment. In Chapter 41, we will discuss Fourth Amendment issues in the employment context, as well as employee privacy rights in general, in greater detail.

SECTION 3

Other Constitutional Protections

Other constitutional guarantees of great significance to Americans are mandated by the *privileges and immunities clause* and the *full faith and credit clause* of Article IV of the Constitution, the *due process clauses* of the Fifth and Fourteenth Amendments, and the *equal protection clause* of the Fourteenth Amendment.

THE PRIVILEGES AND IMMUNITIES CLAUSE

Article IV, Section 2, of the Constitution provides that the "Citizens of each State shall be entitled to all Privileges and Immunities of Citizens in the several States." This clause is often referred to as the interstate **privileges and immunities clause.**[33] When a citizen of one state engages in basic and essential activities in another state (the "foreign state"), such as transferring property, seeking employment, or accessing the court system, the foreign state must have a *substantial reason* for treating the nonresident differently from its own residents. The foreign state must also establish that its reason for the discrimination is substantially related to the state's ultimate purpose in adopting the legislation or activity.[34]

Charging nonresidents $2,500 for a shrimp-fishing license, for example, while residents are charged only $25 for the same license, may be considered unconstitutional discrimination against nonresidents who are pursuing the essential activity of making a

33. The terms *privilege* and *immunity* are commonly used synonymously with regard to the interpretation of this clause. Generally, the terms refer to certain rights, benefits, or advantages enjoyed by individuals.

34. *Supreme Court of New Hampshire v. Piper,* 470 U.S. 274, 105 S.Ct. 1272, 84 L.Ed.2d 205 (1985).

living.[35] Similarly, attempting to limit the practice of law to residents only (on the premise that it would help reduce the state's unemployment rate) may unconstitutionally restrict a nonresident's professional pursuit without substantial justification.[36]

The Fourteenth Amendment provides that "[n]o State shall make or enforce any law which shall abridge the privileges or immunities of citizens of the United States." This clause also protects all individuals, as citizens of the United States, from *state* action that might infringe on their privileges or immunities.[37]

The Full Faith and Credit Clause

Article IV, Section 1, of the Constitution provides that "Full Faith and Credit shall be given in each State to the public Acts, Records, and judicial Proceedings of every other State." This clause, which is referred to as the **full faith and credit clause**, applies only to civil matters. It ensures that rights established under deeds, wills, contracts, and the like in one state will be honored by other states. It also ensures that any judicial decision with respect to such property rights will be honored and enforced in all states.

The full faith and credit clause originally was included in the Articles of Confederation to promote mutual friendship among the people of the various states. In fact, it has contributed to the unity of American citizens, because it protects their legal rights as they move about from state to state. It also protects the rights of those to whom they owe obligations, such as judgment creditors. This is extremely important for the conduct of business in a country with a very mobile citizenry.

Due Process

Both the Fifth and the Fourteenth Amendments provide that no person shall be deprived "of life, liberty, or property, without due process of law." The **due process clause** of these constitutional amendments has two aspects—procedural and substantive. Note that the due process clause applies to "legal persons" (that is, corporations) as well as to individuals.

Procedural Due Process.

Procedural due process requires that any government decision to take life, liberty, or property must be made equitably. For example, fair procedures must be used in determining whether a person will be subjected to punishment or have some burden imposed on him or her. Fair procedure has been interpreted as requiring that the person have at least an opportunity to object to a proposed action before a fair, neutral decision maker (which need not be a judge). Thus, for example, if a driver's license is construed as a property interest, some sort of opportunity to object to its suspension or termination by the state must be provided.

Substantive Due Process.

Substantive due process focuses on the content, or substance, of legislation. If a law or other governmental action limits a *fundamental right*, it will be held to violate substantive due process unless it promotes a *compelling* or *overriding state interest*. Fundamental rights include interstate travel, privacy, voting, and all First Amendment rights. Compelling state interests could include, for example, the public's safety. Thus, laws designating speed limits may be upheld even though they affect interstate travel, if they are shown to reduce highway fatalities, because the state has a compelling interest in protecting the lives of its citizens.

In all other situations, a law or action does not violate substantive due process if it rationally relates to any legitimate government purpose. It is almost impossible for a law or action to fail this "rational basis" test. Under this test, virtually any business regulation will be upheld as reasonable—the United States Supreme Court has upheld insurance regulations, price and wage controls, banking controls, and controls of unfair competition and trade practices against substantive due process challenges.

Suppose that a state legislature enacted a law imposing a fifteen-year term of imprisonment without a trial on all businesspersons who appeared in their own television commercials. This law would be unconstitutional on both substantive and procedural grounds. Substantive review would invalidate the legislation because it abridges freedom of speech, a fundamental right. Procedurally, the law is constitutionally invalid because it imposes a penalty without giving the accused a chance to defend his or her actions.

---

35. *Toomer v. Witsell*, 334 U.S. 385, 68 S.Ct. 1156, 92 L.Ed. 1460 (1948).

36. *Hicklin v. Orbeck*, 437 U.S. 518, 98 S.Ct. 2482, 57 L.Ed.2d 397 (1978).

37. Unlike the due process and equal protection clauses (to be discussed shortly), the privileges and immunities clause of the Fourteenth Amendment does not apply to the individual rights found in the Bill of Rights.

Equal Protection

Under the Fourteenth Amendment, a state may not "deny to any person within its jurisdiction the equal protection of the laws." The United States Supreme Court has used the due process clause of the Fifth Amendment to make the **equal protection clause** applicable to the federal government. Equal protection means that the government must treat similarly situated individuals in a similar manner.

Both substantive due process and equal protection require review of the substance of the law or other governmental action rather than review of the procedures used. When a law or action limits the liberty of all persons to do something, it may violate substantive due process; when a law or action limits the liberty of some persons but not others, it may violate the equal protection clause. Thus, for example, if a law prohibits all persons from buying contraceptive devices, it raises a substantive due process question; if it prohibits only unmarried persons from buying the same devices, it raises an equal protection issue.

In an equal protection inquiry, when a law or action distinguishes between or among individuals, the basis for the distinction—that is, the classification—is examined by the courts. The courts may use one of three standards: strict scrutiny, intermediate scrutiny, or the "rational basis" test.

Strict Scrutiny. If a law or action prohibits or inhibits some persons from exercising a fundamental right, the law or action will be subject to "strict scrutiny" by the courts. Under this standard, the classification must be necessary to promote a *compelling state interest.* Also, if the classification is based on a *suspect trait*—such as race, national origin, or citizenship status—the classification must be necessary to promote a compelling state interest. Compelling state interests include remedying past unconstitutional or illegal discrimination but do not include correcting the general effects of "society's" discrimination. Thus, for example, if a city gives preference to minority applicants in awarding construction contracts, the city normally must identify the past unconstitutional or illegal discrimination against minority construction firms that it is attempting to correct. Generally, few laws or actions survive strict-scrutiny analysis by the courts.

Intermediate Scrutiny. Another standard, that of "intermediate scrutiny," is applied in cases involving discrimination based on gender or legitimacy. Laws using these classifications must be *substantially related to important government objectives.*

For example, an important government objective is preventing illegitimate teenage pregnancies. Therefore, because males and females are not similarly situated in this regard—only females can become pregnant—a law that punishes men but not women for statutory rape will be upheld, even though it treats men and women unequally. A state law requiring illegitimate children to bring paternity suits within six years of their births, however, will be struck down if legitimate children are allowed to seek support from their parents at any time. An important objective behind statutes of limitations is to prevent persons from bringing stale or fraudulent claims, but distinguishing between support claims on the basis of legitimacy has no relation to this objective.

The "Rational Basis" Test. In matters of economic or social welfare, the classification will be considered valid if there is any conceivable *rational basis* on which the classification might relate to a legitimate government interest. It is almost impossible for a law or action to fail the rational basis test. Thus, for example, a city ordinance that in effect prohibits all pushcart vendors except a specific few from operating in a particular area of the city will be upheld if the city provides a rational basis—perhaps regulation and reduction of traffic in the particular area—for the ordinance. In contrast, a law that provides unemployment benefits only to people over six feet tall would violate the guarantee of equal protection. There is no rational basis for determining the distribution of unemployment compensation on the basis of height. Such a distinction could not further any legitimate government objective.

Westlaw. See Case 4.3 at the end of this chapter. To view the full, unedited case from Westlaw,® go to this text's Web site at **http://wbl-cs.westbuslaw.com**.

Privacy Rights

Until relatively recently, most privacy concerns involved the public's belief that personal information collected by government agencies posed a threat to individual privacy. In other words, typical privacy issues in the past related to personal information that government agencies, including the Federal Bureau of Investigation (FBI), might obtain and keep about an individual. Later, worries about what banks and insurance companies might know and transmit to others about individuals became an issue. One of the major concerns of individuals in recent years has been the increasing value of personal information for online marketers—who are willing to pay a high price to those who collect and sell them such information—and how to protect privacy rights in cyberspace.

Indeed, in today's online world, some people believe that privacy rights are quickly becoming a thing of the past. "Cookies" on their hard drives allow Internet users' Web movements to be tracked. Technology is now available that makes it possible to connect previously anonymous Internet users to actual geographic locations. Furthermore, any individual who wants to purchase goods from online merchants or auctions inevitably must reveal some personal information, which may include the purchaser's name, address, and credit-card number.

Clearly, an area of pressing concern today is how to secure privacy rights in an online world. In this section, we look at the protection of privacy rights under the U.S. Constitution and various federal statutes. Note that state constitutions and statutes also protect individuals' privacy rights, often to a significant degree. Privacy rights are also protected under tort law (see Chapter 5). Additionally, the Federal Trade Commission has played an active role in protecting the privacy rights of online consumers (see Chapter 44). The protection of employees' privacy rights, particularly with respect to electronic monitoring practices, is another area of growing concern (see Chapter 41).

Constitutional Protection of Privacy Rights. The U.S. Constitution does not explicitly mention a general right to privacy, and only relatively recently have the courts regarded the right to privacy as a constitutional right. In a 1928 Supreme Court case, *Olmstead v. United States,*[38] Justice Louis Brandeis stated in his dissent that the right to privacy is "the most comprehensive of rights and the right most valued by civilized men." The majority of the justices at that time did not agree, and it was not until the 1960s that a majority on the Supreme Court endorsed the view that the Constitution protected individual privacy rights.

In a landmark 1965 case, *Griswold v. Connecticut,*[39] the Supreme Court invalidated a Connecticut law that effectively prohibited the use of contraceptives. The Court held that the law violated the right to privacy. Justice William O. Douglas formulated a unique way of reading this right into the Bill of Rights (the first ten amendments to the Constitution). He claimed that "emanations" from the rights guaranteed by the First, Third, Fourth, Fifth, and Ninth Amendments formed and gave "life and substance" to "penumbras" (partial shadows) around these guaranteed rights. These penumbras included an implied constitutional right to privacy.

When we read these amendments, we can see the foundation for Justice Douglas's reasoning. Consider the Fourth Amendment. By prohibiting unreasonable searches and seizures, the amendment effectively protects individuals' privacy. Consider also the words of the Ninth Amendment: "The enumeration in the Constitution of certain rights, shall not be construed to deny or disparage others retained by the people." In other words, just because the Constitution, including its amendments, does not specifically mention the right to privacy does not mean that this right is denied to the people. Indeed, in a recent survey of America Online subscribers, respondents ranked privacy second behind freedom of speech and ahead of freedom of religion when listing the most important rights guaranteed by the Constitution. A recent Harris poll showed that almost 80 percent of those questioned believed that if the framers were writing the Constitution today, they would add privacy as an important right.[40]

Federal Statutes Protecting Privacy Rights. In the last several decades, Congress has enacted a number of statutes that protect the privacy of individuals in various areas of concern. In the 1960s, Americans were sufficiently alarmed by the accumulation of personal information in government files that they pressured Congress to pass laws permitting individuals to access their files. Congress responded in 1966 with the Freedom of Information Act, which allows any person to request copies of any information on him or her contained in federal government files. In 1974, Congress passed the Privacy Act, which also gives persons the right to access such information. These and other major federal laws protecting privacy rights are listed and described in Exhibit 4–2.

Westlaw. See Case 4.4 at the end of this chapter. To view the full, unedited case from Westlaw,® go to this text's Web site at **http://wbl-cs.westbuslaw.com**.

38. 277 U.S. 438, 48 S.Ct. 564, 72 L.Ed. 2d 944 (1928).
39. 381 U.S. 479, 85 S.Ct. 1678, 14 L.Ed. 2d 510 (1965).

40. *Public Perspective,* November/December 2000, p. 9.

EXHIBIT 4–2 FEDERAL LEGISLATION RELATING TO PRIVACY

TITLE	PROVISIONS CONCERNING PRIVACY
Freedom of Information Act (1966)	Provides that individuals have a right to obtain access to information about them collected in government files.
Fair Credit Reporting a Act (1970)	Provides that consumers have the right to be informed of the nature and scope of credit investigation, the kind of information that is being compiled, and the names of the firms or individuals who will be receiving the report.
Crime Control Act (1973)	Safeguards the confidentiality of information amassed for certain state criminal systems.
Family and Educational Rights and Privacy Act (1974)	Limits access to computer-stored records of education-related evaluations and grades in private and public colleges and universities.
Privacy Act (1974)	Protects the privacy of individuals about whom the federal government has information. Specifically, the act provides as follows: 1. Agencies originating, using, disclosing, or otherwise manipulating personal information must ensure the reliability of the information and provide safeguards against its misuse. 2. Information compiled for one purpose cannot be used for another without the concerned individual's permission. 3. Individuals must be able to find out what data concerning them are being compiled and how the data will be used. 4. Individuals must be given a means by which to correct inaccurate data.
Tax Reform Act (1976)	Preserves the privacy of personal financial information.
Right to Financial Privacy Act (1978)	Prohibits financial institutions from providing the federal government with access to customers' records unless a customer authorizes the disclosure.
Electronic Fund Transfer Act (1978)	Prohibits the use of a computer without authorization to retrieve data in a financial institution's or consumer reporting agency's files.
Cable Communications Policy Act (1984)	Regulates access to information collected by cable service operators on subscribers to cable services.
Electronic Communications Privacy Act (1986)	Prohibits the interception of information communicated by electronic means.
Driver's Privacy Protection Act (1994)	Prevents states from disclosing or selling a driver's personal information without the driver's consent.
Health Insurance Portability and Accountability Act (1996)	Prohibits the use of a consumer's medical information for any purpose other than that for which such information was provided, unless the consumer expressly consents to the use. Final rules under the act, issued by the Department of Health and Human Services, became effective on April 14, 2001.
Children's Online Privacy Protection Act (1998)	Requires operators of Web sites aimed at children under the age of thirteen to clearly provide notice about the information being collected and how it will be used; requires verifiable parental consent for certain types of information about children.
Financial Services Modernization Act (Gramm-Leach-Bliley Act) (1999)	Requires all financial institutions to provide customers with information on their privacy policies and practices; prohibits the disclosure of nonpublic personal information about a consumer to an unaffiliated third party unless strict disclosure and opt-out requirements are met. Final rules under the act, issued by the Federal Trade Commission, became mandatory on July 1, 2001.

Terms and Concepts to Review

Chapter Summary

The Constitutional Powers of Government	The U.S. Constitution established a federal form of government, in which government powers are shared by the national government and the state governments. At the national level, government powers are divided among the legislative, executive, and judicial branches.
The Commerce Clause	1. *The expansion of national powers*—The commerce clause expressly permits Congress to regulate commerce. Over time, courts expansively interpreted this clause, thereby enabling the national government to wield extensive powers over the economic life of the nation. 2. *The commerce power today*—Today, the commerce power authorizes the national government, at least theoretically, to regulate every commercial enterprise in the United States. In recent years, the Supreme Court has reined in somewhat the national government's regulatory powers under the commerce clause. 3. *The regulatory powers of the states*—The Tenth Amendment reserves all powers not expressly delegated to the national government to the states. Under their police powers, state governments may regulate private activities to protect or promote the public order, health, safety, morals, and general welfare. If state regulations substantially interfere with interstate commerce, however, they will be held to violate the commerce clause of the U.S. Constitution.
The Supremacy Clause	The U.S. Constitution provides that the Constitution, laws, and treaties of the United States are "the supreme Law of the Land." Whenever a state law directly conflicts with a federal law, the state law is rendered invalid.
The Taxing and Spending Powers	The U.S. Constitution gives Congress the power to impose uniform taxes throughout the United States and to spend revenues accumulated from the taxing power. Congress can spend revenues to promote any objective it deems worthwhile, so long as it does not violate the Bill of Rights.
Business and the Bill of Rights	The Bill of Rights, which consists of the first ten amendments to the U.S. Constitution, was adopted in 1791 and embodies a series of protections for individuals—and in some cases, business entities—against various types of interference by the federal government. Some of the key protections that affect businesses include the following: 1. *Freedom of speech*—Speech, including symbolic speech, is given the fullest possible protection by the courts. Corporate political speech and commercial speech also receive substantial protection under the First Amendment. Certain types of speech, such as defamatory speech and lewd or obscene speech, are not protected. Government attempts to regulate unprotected forms of speech in the online environment have, to date, met with little success. 2. *Freedom of religion*—Under the First Amendment, the government may neither establish any religion (the establishment clause) nor prohibit the free exercise of religion (the free exercise clause).

CHAPTER SUMMARY—CONTINUED

Business and the Bill of Rights—continued	**5.** *Self-incrimination*—The Fifth Amendment guarantees that no person "shall be compelled in any criminal case to be a witness against himself." This protection extends only to natural persons, not to corporations or business records of a partnership. **6.** *Searches and Seizures*—The Fourth Amendment protects the "right of the people to be secure in their persons, houses, papers, and effects." A search warrant is required to search people, businesses, or business records. A search warrant is not required for searches of businesses in such highly regulated industries as liquor, guns, and strip mining.
Other Constitutional Protections	The Constitution contains other protections important to businesses, including the following: **1.** *Privileges and Immunities Clause and Full Faith and Credit Clause*—These two clauses of the Constitution protect the legal rights of citizens who move about (or do business in) the various states. **2.** *Due process*—Both the Fifth and the Fourteenth Amendments provide that no person shall be deprived of "life, liberty, or property, without due process of law." Procedural due process requires that any government decision to take life, liberty, or property must be made using fair procedures. Substantive due process is violated if a law that is not compatible with the Constitution, unless the law promotes a compelling state interest, such as public safety. **4.** *Equal protection*—Under the Fourteenth Amendment, a law or action that limits the liberty of some persons but not others may violate the equal protection clause. Such a law may be deemed valid, however, if there is a rational basis for the discriminatory treatment of a given group or if the law substantially relates to an important government objective. **5.** *Privacy Rights*—Americans are increasingly becoming concerned over privacy issues raised by Internet-related technology. The Constitution does not contain a specific guarantee of a right to privacy, but such a right has been derived from guarantees found in several constitutional amendments. A number of federal statutes protect privacy rights. Privacy rights are also protected by many state constitutions and statutes, as well as under tort law.

CASES FOR ANALYSIS

Westlaw. You can access the full text of each case presented below by going to the Westlaw cases on this text's Web site at http://wbl-cs.westbuslaw.com. Each Westlaw case includes the names of all plaintiffs and defendants, the dates on which the case was argued and decided, a brief summary of the issues and decisions in the case, headnotes classifying specific issues in the case according to the West Key Number System, and the court's opinion. Concurring and dissenting opinions, if any, are included as well.

CASE 4.1 FREEDOM OF SPEECH

BAD FROG BREWERY, INC. V. NEW YORK STATE LIQUOR AUTHORITY

U.S. Court of Appeals,
Second Circuit, 1998.
134 F.3d 87.

JON O. NEWMAN, Circuit Judge:

A picture of a frog with the second of its four unwebbed "fingers" extended in a manner evocative of a well known human gesture of insult has presented this Court with significant issues concerning First Amendment protections for commercial speech. The frog appears on labels that Bad Frog Brewery, Inc. ("Bad Frog") sought permission to use on bottles of its beer products. The New York State Liquor Authority ("NYSLA" or "the Authority") denied Bad Frog's application.

Bad Frog appeals from the * * * judgment of the [United States] District Court for the Northern District of New York * * * granting summary judgment in favor of NYSLA * * * and rejecting Bad Frog's commercial free speech challenge to NYSLA's decision. We conclude that the State's prohibition of the labels from use in all circumstances does not materially advance its asserted interests in insulating children from vulgarity or promoting temperance, and is not narrowly tailored to the interest concerning children. We therefore reverse the judgment insofar as it denied Bad Frog's federal claims for injunctive relief with respect to the disapproval of its labels. * * *

* * * *

Bad Frog is a Michigan corporation that manufactures and markets several different types of alcoholic beverages under its "Bad Frog" trademark. This action concerns labels used by the company in the marketing of Bad Frog Beer, Bad Frog Lemon Lager, and Bad Frog Malt Liquor. Each label prominently features an artist's rendering of a frog holding up its four-"fingered" right "hand," with the back of the "hand" shown, the second "finger" extended, and the other three "fingers" slightly curled. The membranous webbing that connects the digits of a real frog's foot is absent from the drawing, enhancing the prominence of the extended "finger." Bad Frog does not dispute that the frog depicted in the label artwork is making the gesture generally known as "giving the finger" and that the gesture is widely regarded as an offensive insult, conveying a message that the company has characterized as "traditionally * * * negative and nasty." Versions of the label feature slogans such as "He just don't care," "An amphibian with an attitude," "Turning bad into good," and "The beer so good * * * it's bad." * * *

Bad Frog's labels have been approved for use by the Federal Bureau of Alcohol, Tobacco, and Firearms, and by authorities in at least 15 states and the District of Columbia, but have been rejected by authorities in New Jersey, Ohio, and Pennsylvania.

In May 1996, Bad Frog's authorized New York distributor, Renaissance Beer Co., made an initial application to NYSLA for brand label approval and registration * * *. NYSLA denied that application in July. Bad Frog filed a new application in August * * *. The second application, like the first, included promotional material making the extravagant claim that the frog's gesture, whatever its past meaning in other contexts, now means "I want a Bad Frog beer," and that the company's goal was to claim the gesture as its own and as a symbol of peace, solidarity, and good will.

In September 1996, NYSLA denied Bad Frog's second application, finding Bad Frog's contention as to the meaning of the frog's gesture "ludicrous and disingenuous." Explaining its rationale for the rejection, the Authority found that the label "encourages combative behavior" and that the gesture and the slogan, "He just don't care," placed close to and in larger type than a warning concerning potential health problems,

> foster a defiance to the health warning on the label, entice underage drinkers, and invite the public not to heed conventional wisdom and to disobey standards of decorum.

In addition, the Authority said that it

> considered that approval of this label means that the label could appear in grocery and convenience stores, with obvious exposure on the shelf to children of tender age

and that it

> is sensitive to and has concern as to [the label's] adverse effects on such a youthful audience.

* * * *

Bad Frog filed the present action in October 1996 * * *.

The parties * * * filed cross motions for summary judgment, and the District Court granted NYSLA's motion. * * *

* * * *

Advertising, however tasteless and excessive it sometimes may seem, is nonetheless dissemination of information as to who is producing and selling what product, for what reason, and at what price.

* * * *

Bad Frog's label attempts to function, like a trademark, to identify the source of the product. The picture on a beer bottle of a frog behaving badly is reasonably to be understood as attempting to identify to consumers a product of the Bad Frog Brewery. In addition, the label serves to propose a commercial transaction. *Though the label communicates no information beyond the source of the product, we think that minimal information, conveyed in the context of a proposal of a commercial transaction, suffices to invoke the protections for commercial speech* * * *. [Emphasis added.]

* * * *

* * * At the outset, we must determine whether the expression is protected by the First Amendment. For commercial speech to come within that provision, it at least must concern lawful activity and not be misleading. Next, we ask whether the asserted government interest is substantial. If both inquiries yield positive answers, we must determine whether the regulation directly advances the government interest asserted, and whether it is not more extensive than is necessary to serve that interest.

* * * *

* * * Bad Frog's labels pass [the] threshold requirement that the speech must concern lawful activity and not be misleading. The consumption of beer (at least by adults) is legal in New York, and the labels cannot be said to be deceptive, even if they are offensive. Indeed, although NYSLA argues that the labels convey no useful information, it concedes that "the commercial speech at issue * * * may not be characterized as misleading or related to illegal activity."

* * * *

* * * [T]o support its asserted power to ban Bad Frog's labels [NYSLA advances] * * * the State's inter-

est in "protecting children from vulgar and profane advertising" * * *.

[This interest is] substantial * * *. States have a compelling interest in protecting the physical and psychological well-being of minors and this interest extends to shielding minors from the influence of literature that is not obscene by adult standards. * * *

* * * *

* * * NYSLA endeavors to advance the state interest in preventing exposure of children to vulgar displays by taking only the limited step of barring such displays from the labels of alcoholic beverages. In view of the wide currency of vulgar displays throughout contemporary society, including comic books targeted directly at children, barring such displays from labels for alcoholic beverages cannot realistically be expected to reduce children's exposure to such displays to any significant degree.

* * * If New York decides to make a substantial effort to insulate children from vulgar displays in some significant sphere of activity, at least with respect to materials likely to be seen by children, NYSLA's label prohibition might well be found to make a justifiable contribution to the material advancement of such an effort, but its currently isolated response to the perceived problem, applicable only to labels on a product that children cannot purchase, does not suffice. * * * [A] state must demonstrate that its commercial speech limitation is part of a substantial effort to advance a valid state interest, not merely the removal of a few grains of offensive sand from a beach of vulgarity.

* * * *

* * * Even if we were to assume that the state materially advances its asserted interest by shielding children from viewing the Bad Frog labels, it is plainly excessive to prohibit the labels from all use, including placement on bottles displayed in bars and taverns where parental supervision of children is to be expected. Moreover, to whatever extent NYSLA is concerned that children will be harmfully exposed to the Bad Frog labels when wandering without parental supervision around grocery and convenience stores where beer is sold, that concern could be less intrusively dealt with by placing restrictions on the permissible locations where the appellant's products may be displayed within such stores.

CASE 4.2 SELF-INCRIMINATION

VERNIERO V. BEVERLY HILLS, LTD., INC.

Superior Court of New Jersey,
Appellate Division, 1998.
316 N.J.Super. 121,
719 A.2d 713.

SKILLMAN, J.A.D. [Judge, Appellate Division]

The issue presented by this appeal is whether a corporation which produces documents in compliance with an administrative subpoena issued by the Attorney General [Peter Verniero] [of the state of New Jersey] under the Consumer Fraud Act, N.J.S.A. [New Jersey Statutes Annotated] 56:8-1 to -20, is entitled to absolute immunity from any criminal prosecution arising out of and related to the subject matter of the administrative proceedings.

The Attorney General, acting in his capacity as attorney for the Division of Consumer Affairs (Division), served an administrative subpoena upon defendant Beverly Hills Ltd., Inc. (Beverly Hills), directing it to produce certain business records, including advertisements and/or solicitations of consumers, marketing agreements with other companies and documentation pertaining to its corporate status. This subpoena was issued in connection with an investigation into advertisements, solicitations and other commercial practices used by Beverly Hills in marketing and selling goods and services. In response, Beverly Hills' attorney, on behalf of the corporation * * *, sent a letter to the Attorney General which asserted that [the corporation was] entitled to "exemption from both civil and criminal punishment in the event demanded documents would in any way result in self-incrimination," and demanded such immunity "prior to the turnover of any documents." The Attorney General replied by a letter which stated that Beverly Hills has no privilege against self-incrimination with respect to its business records and insisted upon compliance with the subpoena. * * *

The Attorney General then filed this action to enforce compliance with the subpoena. The matter was brought before the trial court * * *. After hearing argument, the court issued a brief oral opinion which concluded that N.J.S.A. 56:8-7 provides absolute immunity from any criminal prosecution arising out of or related to administrative proceeding in connection with which a subpoena has been issued. Accordingly, the court entered a final judgment which provides in pertinent part:

> If the Attorney General fails to withdraw his administrative subpoena or subsequent to withdrawal he renews his demand for corporate documents, and Beverly Hills complies with such non-withdrawn or renewed request, Beverly Hills shall be exempt from being prosecuted or subjected to any penalty or forfeiture in any

criminal proceeding which arises out of and relates to the subject matter of the administrative proceeding pursuant to N.J.S.A. 56:8-7, *without having to make a showing that the production of the corporate documents by the corporation may tend to incriminate the corporation.* [Emphasis added.]

* * * *

The subpoena for the production of Beverly Hills' records was issued pursuant to N.J.S.A. 56:8-4, which authorizes the Attorney General to issue subpoenas "[t]o accomplish the objectives and to carry out the duties prescribed by [the Consumer Fraud Act]." In refusing to comply with this subpoena unless it was granted immunity from prosecution, Beverly Hills invoked N.J.S.A. 56:8-7, which provides in pertinent part:

> If any person shall refuse to testify or produce any book, paper or other document in any proceeding under this act for the reason that the testimony or evidence, documentary or otherwise, required of him may tend to incriminate him, convict him of a crime, or subject him to a penalty or forfeiture, and shall, notwithstanding, be directed to testify or to produce such book, paper or document, he shall comply with such direction.
>
> *A person who is entitled by law to,* and does *assert such privilege,* and who complies with such direction shall not thereafter be prosecuted or subjected to any penalty or forfeiture in any criminal proceeding which arises out of and relates to the subject matter of the proceeding. [Emphasis added.]

By its terms, N.J.S.A. 56:8-7 only provides immunity from prosecution to "[a] person who is entitled by law to * * * assert [the] privilege [against self-incrimination.]" Therefore, the determination whether defendants would be entitled to immunity from prosecution if they complied with the subpoena turns on whether the privilege applies to Beverly Hills' business records.

* * * *

The Fifth Amendment to the United States Constitution provides that "[n]o person * * * shall be compelled to be a witness against himself." Although the New Jersey Constitution does not contain a similar privilege, New Jersey has a common law privilege against self-incrimination which is now codified in the rules of evidence [N.J.S.A. 2A:84-17 through 2A:84-19]. *It is firmly established that a corporation may not invoke either the Fifth Amendment or the New Jersey privilege against self-incrimination. Moreover, a custodian of corporate records may not rely upon his or her personal privilege against self-incrimination as a basis for refusing to produce corporate records.* [Emphasis added.]

Beverly Hills is admittedly a corporation, and the subpoena issued by the Division only sought the production of Beverly Hills' records. Therefore, it is clear that * * * Beverly Hills * * * could [not] invoke the Fifth Amendment or the New Jersey privilege against self-incrimination incorporated in N.J.S.A. 2A:84-17 to 19 as a basis for refusing to produce the records.

Nevertheless, the trial court concluded that N.J.S.A. 56:8-7 provides a more expansive immunity from a prosecution arising out of or related to the subject matter of the compelled production of corporate documents than is mandated by the Fifth Amendment or N.J.S.A. 2A:84-17 to 19. The court stated, without further explanation, that N.J.S.A. 56:8-7 is "a legislative enactment superimposed upon a criminal common law privilege." We discern no basis in the language of N.J.S.A. 56:8-7 or the policies of the Consumer Fraud Act for this conclusion.

N.J.S.A. 56:8-7 does not itself provide any immunity from prosecution with respect to the compelled production of documents or testimony; it only confers immunity upon a person who is "entitled by law to * * * assert [the] privilege" against self-incrimination. Thus, a person claiming immunity under N.J.S.A. 56:8-7 must identify some "law" other than N.J.S.A. 56:8-7 as the source of a privilege against self-incrimination. By construing N.J.S.A. 56:8-7 to provide immunity from prosecution to a party who is not entitled to invoke the privilege against self-incrimination, the trial court effectively read the words "entitled by law to * * * assert such privilege" out of the statute. However, it is a fundamental principle of statutory interpretation that a court should try to give effect to every word of the statute, and should not assume that the Legislature used meaningless language. Therefore, N.J.S.A. 56:8-7 must be read to provide immunity from prosecution solely to a person who is entitled to assert the privilege against self-incrimination under the Fifth Amendment or N.J.S.A. 2A:84-17 to 19.

Moreover, the trial court's interpretation of N.J.S.A. 56:8-7 would undermine enforcement of the Consumer Fraud Act. Because a corporation or custodian of corporate records cannot invoke the privilege against self-incrimination as a basis for refusing to produce documents relevant to a criminal investigation, the Attorney General would be faced with a dilemma if his investigatory powers under the Consumer Fraud Act were circumscribed by a more expansive immunity from criminal prosecution than applies in a criminal investigation. He would be compelled either to delay issuance of a subpoena for the production of documents which may be needed to seek injunctive relief to prevent continuation of sales practices which violate the Consumer Fraud Act or to immunize the corporation and its principals from criminal prosecution by issuing the subpoena. Such an interpretation of N.J.S.A. 56:8-7, which would force the Attorney General to choose at the outset of an investigation whether to pursue civil or criminal remedies with respect to conduct that may violate both the Consumer Fraud Act and criminal statutes, would be inconsistent with the legislative intent to confer on the Attorney General the broadest kind of power to act in the interest of the consumer public.

Accordingly, the judgment of the trial court is reversed and the case is remanded to the trial court for the entry of an order compelling Beverly Hills to produce the subpoenaed documents.

CASE 4.3 EQUAL PROTECTION

WHS REALTY CO. v. TOWN OF MORRISTOWN

Superior Court of New Jersey,
Appellate Division, 1999.
323 N.J.Super. 553,
733 A.2d 1206.

HAVEY, P.J.A.D. [Presiding Judge, Appellate Division]

This appeal presents a challenge to Morristown's garbage collection ordinance which provides free collection service to all residential dwellings of three or less units as well as condominium developments where no more than 50% of the units are owned by one person or entity. Excluded from the ordinance are all multi-family dwellings of four or more units. Therefore, plaintiff's garden apartment complex, consisting of 140 units, does not receive collection service.

Plaintiff [WHS Realty Co.] filed a complaint * * * claiming that the ordinance violates its right to * * * equal protection of the laws guaranteed by the United States * * * Constitution. It demands the same garbage collection service provided to all other residents * * *.

* * * *

After a four-day hearing, the trial court [determined] that the ordinance was unconstitutional, finding it was not rationally related to the fostering of home ownership or any other legitimate state interest. The court ordered the Town to collect garbage and recyclable materials from plaintiff's apartment complex subject to the same terms and conditions as it collects from condominium complexes. It denied plaintiff's demand for damages * * *.

The Town defendants now appeal from the judgment invalidating the ordinance. * * * We affirm the judgment invalidating the ordinance, but we reverse the dismissal of plaintiff's claim for damages * * *, and remand for further proceedings.

* * * *

If a legislative classification neither burdens a fundamental right nor targets a suspect class, we must uphold the constitutionality of legislation so long as it bears a rational relation to some legitimate end. *Under the federal rational basis test, a classification made by legislation is presumed to be valid and will be sustained if it is rationally related to a legitimate state interest.* * * * [Emphasis added.]

* * * *

The parties agree that, since the Town's ordinance does not implicate a suspect class or fundamental right, the rational basis test applies. Therefore, plaintiff has the burden of demonstrating that classification by the ordinance lacks a rational basis. * * *

* * * *

A municipality is not mandated to provide for municipal garbage removal. * * *

However, once the service is provided by a municipality, * * * [t]here is a violation of equal protection of the laws unless the service is available to all persons in like circumstances upon the same terms and conditions. Persons situated alike shall be treated alike.

* * * *

* * * [T]here is nothing about the mechanics or costs of solid waste collection that justifies differentiating between apartment complexes and other residents within the community. As the trial court observed during an early stage of the proceedings, "people are people," and the type and quality of solid waste generated by all types of residential dwellings is the same. In fact, the evidence demonstrated that because there are fewer residents living in individual apartment units than single-family or condominium units, apartment units generate less solid waste. Moreover, the Town's Director of Public Works conceded that it would be more cost-effective to pick up solid waste from four dumpsters serving 140 apartment units than picking up solid waste from 140 separate single-family residential units at curbside. He also acknowledged that the mechanics for collection from dumpsters is the same for apartment units and condominiums.

* * * *

The Town defendants nevertheless argue that the * * * ordinance is rationally related to fostering home ownership. * * *

* * * *

* * * Here, * * * the facts established that approximately 42% of the dwelling units receiving garbage collection service are not occupied by their owners. Only 27% and 11.7% of the two- and three-family dwelling units are owner-occupied. If the disputed classification in fact promotes home ownership, particularly among the two- and three-family owners, there is no question that the percentages of owner-occupancy would be significantly higher. The low percentages of owner-occupants necessarily indicates that the disputed classification is irrational.

* * * [T]he only service involved is collection of solid waste, which, according to the [facts], costs approximately $400 per residential unit per year. * * * The Town performed no studies or surveys indicating that people are more inclined to purchase a home if free garbage

collection service is provided. No interviews of homeowners were conducted.

Moreover, * * * [the Town's own Master Plan expresses] a clear countervailing policy to fostering home ownership: the provision of affordable housing to young married couples, senior citizens and other low and medium-income residents. * * * In view of this competing policy expressed in the Master Plan, we cannot say that the plan supports disparate treatment to apartment dwellers in the provision of garbage collection service.

* * * *

The Town defendants also advance, as a rational basis for the ordinance, the fact that condominiums are taxed differently than apartment units. The Town's real estate appraiser testified that residential condominium units generally sell for a substantially larger unit value than the equivalent value of rental type units. Therefore, the assessed value, based merely on the form of ownership, can be as much as two or three times greater for a condominium. * * *

* * * *

* * * The Town concedes that * * * apartment complexes, condominium complexes, and single-family residences are all assessed at true value for taxation purposes. In other words, both apartment and single-family residences and condominiums are being taxed based upon what their individual units are worth. If apartment owners are paying less taxes per unit, it is only because the units are worth less for assessment purposes. It cannot seriously be argued that just because apartment units have a lesser value for tax assessment purposes, they should be entitled to less municipal services. We conclude that the methodology of taxing apartment complexes and condominium units is not a rational basis for upholding the ordinance.

CASE 4.4 PRIVACY RIGHTS

RENO V. CONDON

United States Supreme Court, 2000.
528 U.S. 141,
120 S.Ct. 666,
145 L.Ed.2d 587.

Chief Justice *REHNQUIST* delivered the opinion of the Court.

The Driver's Privacy Protection Act of 1994 (DPPA or Act) regulates the disclosure of personal information contained in the records of state motor vehicle departments (DMVs). * * *

* * * State DMVs require drivers and automobile owners to provide personal information, which may include a person's name, address, telephone number, vehicle description, Social Security number, medical information, and photograph, as a condition of obtaining a driver's license or registering an automobile. Congress found that many States, in turn, sell this personal information to individuals and businesses. These sales generate significant revenues for the States.

The DPPA establishes a regulatory scheme that restricts the States' ability to disclose a driver's personal information without the driver's consent. The DPPA generally prohibits any state DMV, or officer, employee, or contractor thereof, from "knowingly disclos[ing] or otherwise mak[ing] available to any person or entity personal information about any individual obtained by the department in connection with a motor vehicle record." The DPPA defines "personal information" as any information "that identifies an individual, including an individual's photograph, social security number, driver identification number, name, address (but not the 5-digit zip code), telephone number, and medical or disability information," but not including "information on vehicular accidents, driving violations, and driver's status." A "motor vehicle record" is defined as "any record that pertains to a motor vehicle operator's permit, motor vehicle title, motor vehicle registration, or identification card issued by a department of motor vehicles."

The DPPA's ban on disclosure of personal information does not apply if drivers have consented to the release of their data. * * * States may not imply consent from a driver's failure to take advantage of a state-afforded opportunity to block disclosure, but must rather obtain a driver's affirmative consent to disclose the driver's personal information for use in surveys, marketing, solicitations, and other restricted purposes.

The DPPA's prohibition of nonconsensual disclosures is also subject to a number of statutory exceptions. For example, the DPPA *requires* disclosure of personal information "for use in connection with matters of motor vehicle or driver safety and theft, motor vehicle emissions, motor vehicle product alterations, recalls, or advisories, performance monitoring of motor vehicles and dealers by motor vehicle manufacturers, and removal of non-owner records from the original owner records of motor vehicle manufacturers to carry out the purposes of * * * the Anti Car Theft Act of 1992, the Automobile Information Disclosure Act, the Clean Air Act, and [other statutes]." The DPPA *permits* DMVs to disclose personal information from motor vehicle records for a number of purposes.

* * * *

* * * [A] state agency that maintains a "policy or practice of substantial noncompliance" with the Act may be subject to a civil penalty imposed by the United States Attorney General of not more than $5,000 per day of substantial noncompliance.

South Carolina law conflicts with the DPPA's provisions. Under that law, the information contained in the State's DMV records is available to any person or entity that fills out a form listing the requester's name and address and stating that the information will not be used for telephone solicitation. South Carolina's DMV retains a copy of all requests for information from the State's motor vehicle records, and it is required to release copies of all requests relating to a person upon that person's written petition. State law authorizes the South Carolina DMV to charge a fee for releasing motor vehicle information, and it requires the DMV to allow drivers to prohibit the use of their motor vehicle information for certain commercial activities.

Following the DPPA's enactment, South Carolina and its Attorney General, respondent [Charles] Condon, filed suit in the United States District Court for the District of South Carolina, alleging that the DPPA violates the Tenth * * * Amendment to the United States Constitution. The District Court concluded that the Act is incompatible with the principles of federalism inherent in the Constitution's division of power between the States and the Federal Government. The court accordingly granted summary judgment for the State and permanently enjoined the Act's enforcement against the State and its officers. The Court of Appeals for the Fourth Circuit affirmed, concluding that the Act violates constitutional principles of federalism. We granted *certiorari*, and now reverse.

* * * *

The United States asserts that the DPPA is a proper exercise of Congress' authority to regulate interstate commerce under the Commerce Clause. The United States bases its Commerce Clause argument on the fact that the personal, identifying information that the DPPA regulates is a "thin[g] in interstate commerce," and that the sale or release of that information in interstate commerce is therefore a proper subject of congressional regulation. We agree with the United States' contention. The motor vehicle information which the States have historically sold is used by insurers, manufacturers, direct marketers, and others engaged in interstate commerce to contact drivers with customized solicitations. The information is also used in the stream of interstate commerce by various public and private entities for matters related to interstate motoring. Because drivers' information is, in this context, an article of commerce, its sale or release into the interstate stream of business is sufficient to support congressional regulation. * * *

But the fact that drivers' personal information is, in the context of this case, an article in interstate commerce does not conclusively resolve the constitutionality of the DPPA. In [other cases] we held federal statutes invalid, not because Congress lacked legislative authority over the subject matter, but because those statutes violated the principles of federalism contained in the Tenth Amendment. * * * While Congress has substantial powers to govern the Nation directly, including in areas of intimate concern to the States, the Constitution has never been understood to confer upon Congress the ability to the require the States to govern according to Congress' instructions.

* * * Congress cannot compel the States to enact or enforce a federal regulatory program. * * * Congress cannot circumvent that prohibition by conscripting the States' officers directly. *The Federal Government may neither issue directives requiring the States to address particular problems, nor command the States' officers, or those of their political subdivisions, to administer or enforce a federal regulatory program.* [Emphasis added.]

South Carolina contends that the DPPA violates the Tenth Amendment because it "thrusts upon the States all of the day-to-day responsibility for administering its complex provisions" and thereby makes "state officials the unwilling implementors of federal policy." South Carolina emphasizes that the DPPA requires the State's employees to learn and apply the Act's substantive restrictions and notes that these activities will consume the employees' time and thus the State's resources. South Carolina further notes that the DPPA's penalty provisions hang over the States as a potential punishment should they fail to comply with the Act.

We agree with South Carolina's assertion that the DPPA's provisions will require time and effort on the part of state employees, but reject the State's argument that the DPPA violates [constitutional] principles * * *.

* * * Any federal regulation demands compliance. That a State wishing to engage in certain activity must take administrative and sometimes legislative action to comply with federal standards regulating that activity is a commonplace that presents no constitutional defect.

* * * [T]he DPPA does not require the States in their sovereign capacity to regulate their own citizens. The DPPA regulates the States as the owners of databases. It does not require the South Carolina Legislature to enact any laws or regulations, and it does not require state officials to assist in the enforcement of federal statutes regulating private individuals. We accordingly conclude that the DPPA is consistent with * * * constitutional principles * * *.

CASE PROBLEMS

4–1. Thomas worked in the nonmilitary operations of a large firm that produced both military and nonmilitary goods. When the company discontinued the production of nonmilitary goods, Thomas was transferred to a plant producing war materials. Thomas left his job, claiming that it violated his religious principles to participate in the manufacture of materials to be used in destroying life. In effect, he argued, the transfer to the war-materials plant forced him to quit his job. He was denied unemployment compensation by the state because he had not been effectively "discharged" by the employer but had voluntarily terminated his employment. Did the state's denial of unemployment benefits to Thomas violate the free exercise clause of the First Amendment? Explain. [*Thomas v. Review Board of the Indiana Employment Security Division,* 450 U.S. 707, 101 S.Ct. 1425, 67 L.Ed.2d 624 (1981)]

4–2. South Dakota Disposal Systems, Inc. (SDDS), applied to the South Dakota Department of Water and Natural Resources (DWNR) for a permit to operate a solid waste disposal facility (Lonetree). It was estimated that 90 to 95 percent of the waste would come from out of state. The DWNR determined that Lonetree would be environmentally safe and issued a permit. Later, a public referendum was held. The state attorney general issued a pamphlet to accompany the referendum that urged the public to vote against "the out-of-state dump" because "South Dakota is not the nation's dumping grounds." The measure was defeated. SDDS filed a suit against the state, challenging the referendum as a violation of, among other things, the commerce clause. Was the referendum unconstitutional? Why, or why not? [*SDDS, Inc. v. State of South Dakota,* 47 F.3d 263 (8th Cir. 1995)]

4–3. With the objectives of preventing crime, maintaining property values, and preserving the quality of urban life, New York City enacted an ordinance to regulate the locations of commercial establishments that featured adult entertainment. The ordinance expressly applied to female, but not male, topless entertainment. Adele Buzzetti owned the Cozy Cabin, a New York City cabaret, that featured female topless dancers. Buzzetti and an anonymous dancer filed a suit in a federal district court against the city, asking the court to block the enforcement of the ordinance. The plaintiffs argued in part that the ordinance violated the equal protection clause. Under the equal protection clause, what standard applies to the court's consideration of this ordinance? Under this test, how should the court rule? Why? [*Buzzetti v. City of New York,* 140 F.3d 134 (2d Cir. 1998)]

4–4. The City of Tacoma, Washington, enacted an ordinance that prohibited the playing of car sound systems at a volume that would be "audible" at a distance greater than fifty feet. Dwight Holland was arrested and convicted for violating the ordinance. The conviction was later dismissed, but Holland filed a civil suit in a Washington state court against the city. He claimed in part that the ordinance violated his freedom of speech under the First Amendment. On what basis might the court conclude that this ordinance is constitutional? (Hint: In playing a sound system, was Holland actually expressing himself?) [*Holland v. City of Tacoma,* 90 Wash.App. 533, 954 P.2d 290 (1998)]

4–5. The members of Greater New Orleans Broadcasting Association, Inc., operate radio and television stations in New Orleans. They wanted to broadcast ads for private, for-profit casinos that are legal in Louisiana. A federal statute banned casino advertising, but other federal statutes exempted ads for tribal, government, nonprofit, and "occasional and ancillary" commercial casinos. The association filed a suit in a federal district court against the federal government, asking the court to hold that the statute, as it applied to their ads, violated the First Amendment. The government argued that the ban should be upheld, because "[u]nder appropriate conditions, some broadcast signals from Louisiana broadcasting stations may be heard in neighboring states including Texas and Arkansas," where private casino gambling is unlawful. What is the test for whether a regulation of commercial speech violates the First Amendment? How might it apply in this case? How should the court rule? [*Greater New Orleans Broadcasting Association, Inc. v. United States,* 527 U.S. 173, 119 S.Ct. 1923, 144 L.Ed.2d 161 (1999)]

4–6. A 1988 Minnesota statute required all operators of slow-moving vehicles to display on their vehicles a fluorescent orange-red triangular emblem or, as an alternative, a dull black triangle with a white reflective border, plus seventy-two square inches of permanent red reflective tape. A vehicle operator who chose the alternate emblem still had to carry a regular orange-red emblem in the vehicle and display it externally during times of darkness or low visibility. The state brought charges against Hershberger and other members of the Amish religion (the defendants) because they refused to comply with the statute. The defendants claimed that the statute violated their freedom of religion under the First Amendment because displaying the "loud" colors and "worldly symbols" on their slow-moving vehicles (black, boxlike buggies) compromised their religious belief that they should remain separate and apart from the modern world. The defendants stated that they would not object to displaying a sign similar to the alternate symbol if they could use silver, instead of red, reflective tape, and if they did not have to display the "regular" emblem at night. The state argued that although the silver tape was as effective as the red in terms of visibility, vehicles, and therefore the Amish, should comply with the statute as written. What will the court hold? Discuss. [*State v. Hershberger,* 444 N.W.2d 282 (Minn. 1989)]

4–7. In 1957, Rhodes and several other Georgia landowners entered into a sixty-five-year timber purchase contract with Inland-Rome, Inc. Thereafter, Inland-Rome cut timber from the landowners' land and then removed it for processing in certain Georgia facilities, after which it was shipped as lumber products to points throughout the country. In 1986, the landowners claimed that Inland-Rome had breached the contract, and they filed suit. Inland-Rome moved to compel arbitration because the parties had agreed, in their contract, to arbitrate any disputes arising thereunder. Georgia law enforces arbitration clauses only if they are contained in construction contracts. Arbitration clauses are enforceable under the Federal Arbitration Act only if the contracts in which they appear affect interstate commerce. Inland-Rome contended that because lumber products from the cut timber were shipped throughout the nation, the contract related to interstate commerce, and therefore the Federal Arbitration Act should apply. Will the court agree? Discuss. [*Rhodes v. Inland-Rome, Inc.*, 195 Ga.App. 39, 392 S.E.2d 270 (1990)]

4–8. In response to rapidly rising property taxes, California voters approved a statewide ballot initiative, Proposition 13, that added Article XIIIA to the state constitution. Among other things, Article XIIIA embodied an "acquisition value" system of taxation, whereby property was reassessed up to the current appraised value on new construction or at the time of a change in ownership. Exemptions from the reassessment existed for two types of transfers: (1) exchanges of principal residences by persons over the age of fifty-five and (2) transfers between parents and children. Over time, the acquisition-value system created dramatic disparities in the taxes paid by persons owning similar parcels of property. Long-term owners paid lower taxes reflecting historic property values, whereas new owners paid higher taxes reflecting more recent values. Faced with such a disparity, Stephanie Nordlinger, who had recently bought a house in Los Angeles County, sued the county and Kenneth Hahn, the county tax assessor, claiming that Article XIIIA's reassessment scheme violated the equal protection clause. The complaint was dismissed, and ultimately Nordlinger appealed to the United States Supreme Court. Will the Court hold that the California property tax system violates the equal protection clause? [*Nordlinger v. Hahn*, 505 U.S. 1, 112 S.Ct. 2326, 120 L.Ed.2d 1 (1992)]

4–9. Adela Izquierdo Prieto, age forty-two, had worked for a government-owned and -operated radio and television station in Puerto Rico for over a decade when, without any prior notice, she was suddenly transferred from her television program to a position in radio. Her replacement on the television program was a twenty-eight-year-old woman with less experience. Agustin Mercado Rosa (Mercado), the administrator of the television channel, explained to a newspaper reporter that Izquierdo was removed because "we need new faces" and because Izquierdo's replacement "is young, attractive and refreshing." Izquierdo sued Mercado, alleging in part that the transfer discriminated against her on the basis of age and therefore violated her rights under the equal protection clause. Mercado claimed that the transfer was rationally related to furthering a legitimate state interest in maximizing viewership for the public television channel and therefore was a permissible action. Will the court agree with Mercado? (In forming your answer, disregard the fact that Prieto could have sued Mercado under a federal law prohibiting age discrimination in employment. She based her claim only on the equal protection clause. The sole issue here is whether the state's interest was sufficient to justify replacing Prieto.) [*Izquierdo Prieto v. Mercado Rosa*, 894 F.2d 467 (1st Cir. 1990)]

4–10. Taylor owned a bait business in Maine and arranged to have live baitfish imported into the state. The importation of the baitfish violated a Maine statute. Taylor was charged with violating a federal statute that makes it a federal crime to transport fish in interstate commerce in violation of state law. Taylor moved to dismiss the charges on the ground that the Maine statute unconstitutionally burdened interstate commerce. Maine intervened to defend the validity of its statute, arguing that the law legitimately protected the state's fisheries from parasites and nonnative species that might be included in shipments of live baitfish. Were Maine's interests in protecting its fisheries from parasites and nonnative species sufficient to justify the burden placed on interstate commerce by the Maine statute? Discuss. [*Maine v. Taylor*, 477 U.S. 131, 106 S.Ct. 2440, 91 L.Ed.2d 110 (1986)]

4–11. In 1988, the Nebraska legislature enacted a statute that required any motorcycle operator or passenger on Nebraska's highways to wear a protective helmet. Eugene Robotham, a licensed motorcycle operator, sued the state of Nebraska to block enforcement of the law. Robotham asserted, among other things, that the statute violated the equal protection clause, because it placed requirements on motorcyclists that were not imposed on other motorists. Will the court agree with Robotham that the law violates the equal protection clause? Why, or why not? [*Robotham v. State*, 241 Neb. 379, 488 N.W.2d 533 (1992)]

4–12. Isaiah Brown was the director of the information services department for Polk County, Iowa. During department meetings in his office, he allowed occasional prayers and, in addressing one meeting, referred to Bible passages related to sloth and "work ethics." There was no apparent disruption of the work routine, but the county administrator reprimanded Brown. Later, the administrator ordered Brown to remove from his office all items with a religious connotation. Brown sued the county, alleging that the reprimand and the order violated, among other things, the free exercise clause of the First Amendment. Could the county be held liable for violating Brown's constitutional rights? Discuss. [*Brown v. Polk County, Iowa*, 61 F.3d 650 (8th Cir. 1995)]

4–13. Carol Elewski, a resident of Syracuse, New York, brought an action to enjoin (prevent) the city from displaying a crèche in a city park during the holidays. The crèche, accompanied by a religious banner, was situated at the foot of a decorated evergreen tree and surrounded by sawhorse barricades containing the names of the mayor and a municipal agency. The downtown merchants supported the display to attract shoppers. There were secular decorations in neighboring areas of the park, and a menorah was displayed in another city park located a block away. Does the display of the crèche and the religious banner on city property violate the establishment clause? How might the precedents established by the Supreme Court on this issue apply to this set of facts? [*Elewski v. City of Syracuse*, 123 F.3d 51 (2d Cir. 1997)]

4–14. In February 1999, Carl Adler mailed a driver's license renewal application form and a check for $28 to the New York Department of Motor Vehicles (DMV). The form required Adler's Social Security number, which he intentionally omitted. The DMV returned the application and check, and told him to supply his Social Security number or send proof that the Social Security Administration could not give him a number. Claiming a right to privacy, Adler refused to comply. The DMV responded that federal law authorizes the states to obtain Social Security numbers from individuals in the context of administering certain state programs, including driver's license programs, and that Adler's application would not be processed until he supplied the number. Adler filed a suit in a New York state court against the DMV, asserting in part that it was in violation of the federal Privacy Act of 1974. Adler asked the court to, among other things, order the DMV to renew his license. Should the court grant Adler's request? Why, or why not? [*Adler v. Jackson*, 712 N.Y.S.2d 240 (Sup. 2000)]

4–15. A Question of Ethics

In 1999, in an effort to reduce smoking by children, the attorney general of Massachusetts issued comprehensive regulations governing the advertising and sale of tobacco products. Among other things, the regulations banned cigarette advertisements within one thousand feet of any elementary school, secondary school, or public playground and required retailers to post any cigarette advertising in their stores at least five feet off the floor, out of the immediate sight of young children. A group of tobacco manufacturers and retailers filed suit against the state, claiming that the regulations were preempted by the federal Cigarette Labeling and Advertising Act of 1965, as amended. That act sets uniform labeling requirements and bans broadcast advertising for cigarettes. Ultimately, the case reached the United States Supreme Court, which held that the federal law on cigarette ads preempted the cigarette advertising restrictions adopted by Massachusetts. The only portion of the Massachusetts regulatory package to survive was the requirement that retailers had to place tobacco products in an area accessible only by the sales staff. In view of these facts, consider the following questions. [Lorillard Tobacco Co. v. Reilly, *533 U.S.525, 121 S.Ct. 2404, 150 L.Ed.2d 532 (2001)*]

1. Some argue that having a national standard for tobacco regulation is more important than allowing states to set their own standards for tobacco regulation. Do you agree? Why, or why not?
2. According to the Court in this case, the federal law does not restrict the ability of state and local governments to adopt general zoning restrictions that apply to cigarettes, as long as those restrictions are "on equal terms with other products." How would you argue in support of this reasoning? How would you argue against it?

E-Links

For updated links to resources available on the Web, as well as a variety of other materials, visit this text's Web site at

http://wbl-cs.westbuslaw.com

An ongoing debate in the United States concerns whether the national government exercises too much regulatory control over intrastate affairs. To find current articles on this topic, go to

http://www.vote-smart.org/issues/FEDERALISM_STATES_RIGHTS

For an online version of the Constitution that provides hypertext links to amendments and other changes, go to http://www.law.cornell.edu/constitution/constitution.overview.html

For discussions of current issues involving the rights and liberties contained in the Bill of Rights, go to the Web site of the American Civil Liberties Union at

http://www.aclu.org

Summaries and the full texts of constitutional law decisions by the United States Supreme Court are included at the following site:

http://oyez.nwu.edu

Legal Research Exercises on the Web

Go to http://wbl-cs.westbuslaw.com, the Web site that accompanies this text. Select "Interactive Study Center," and then click on "Chapter 4." There you will find the following Internet research exercises that you can perform to learn more about free speech issues:

Activity 4–1: Flag Burning

Activity 4–2: Begging and the First Amendment

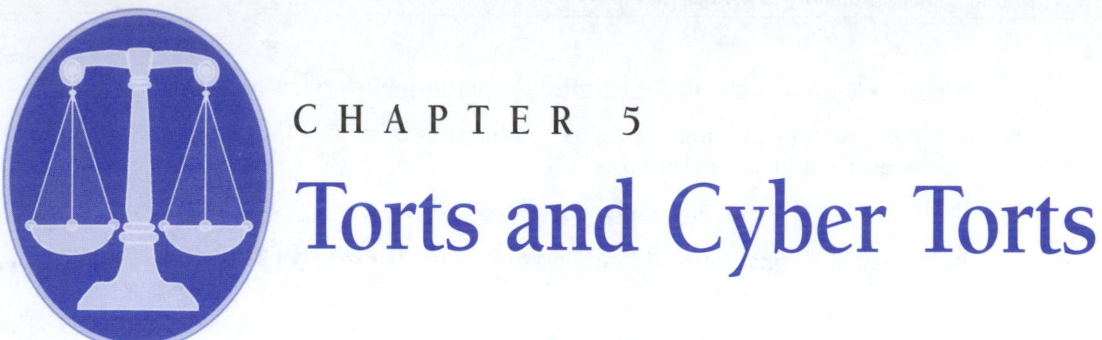

CHAPTER 5

Torts and Cyber Torts

PART OF DOING BUSINESS TODAY—and, indeed, part of everyday life—is the risk of being involved in a lawsuit. The list of circumstances in which businesspersons can be sued is long and varied. An employee injured on the job may attempt to sue the employer because of an unsafe working environment. A consumer who is injured while using a product may attempt to sue the manufacturer because of a defect in the product. At issue in these examples is alleged wrongful conduct by one person that causes injury to another. Such wrongful conduct is covered by the law of **torts** (the word *tort* is French for "wrong").

Of course, a tort is not the only type of wrong that exists in the law. Crimes also involve wrongs. A crime, however, is an act so reprehensible that it is considered a wrong against the state or against society as a whole, as well as against the individual victim. Therefore, the *state* prosecutes and punishes (through fines and/or imprisonment—and possibly death) persons who commit criminal acts. A tort action, in contrast, is a civil action in which one party brings a suit against another to obtain compensation (money damages) or other relief for the harm suffered. Some wrongs, however, provide a basis for both a criminal prosecution and a tort action—see Chapter 8.

As you will see in later chapters of this book, many of the lawsuits brought by or against business firms are based on the tort theories discussed in this chapter. Some of the torts examined here can occur in any context, including the business environment. Others traditionally have been referred to as **business torts**, which are defined as wrongful interferences with the business rights of others. Torts committed via the Internet are sometimes referred to as **cyber torts.** We look at how the courts have applied traditional tort law to wrongful actions in the online environment in the concluding pages of this chapter. Because so many of today's lawsuits against businesses involve product liability (liability for defective products) and strict liability, we devote all of Chapter 6 to a discussion of those tort theories.

SECTION 1

The Basis of Tort Law

The basic purpose of tort law is to provide remedies for the invasion of various *protected interests.* Society recognizes an interest in personal physical safety, and tort law provides remedies for acts that cause physical injury or that interfere with physical security and freedom of movement. Society recognizes an interest in protecting property, and tort law provides remedies for acts that cause destruction or damage to property. Society also recognizes an interest in protecting certain intangible interests, such as personal privacy, family relations, reputation, and dignity, and tort law provides remedies for invasion of these interests.

In the remainder of this chapter, we examine two broad classifications of torts: *intentional torts* and *unintentional torts* (torts involving negligence). The classification of a particular tort depends largely on how the tort occurs (intentionally or negligently) and the surrounding circumstances. (Under the doctrine of strict liability discussed in the following chapter, liability may be imposed regardless of fault.)

SECTION 2

Intentional Torts against Persons and Business Relationships

An **intentional tort**, as the term implies, requires *intent*. The **tortfeasor** (the one committing the tort) must intend to commit an act, the consequences of which interfere with the personal or business interests of another in a way not permitted by law. An evil or harmful motive is not required—in fact, the actor may even have a beneficial motive for committing what turns out to be a tortious act. In tort law, intent only means that the actor intended the consequences of his or her act or knew with substantial certainty that certain consequences would result from the act. The law generally assumes that individuals intend the *normal* consequences of their actions. Thus, forcefully pushing another—even if done in jest and without any evil motive—is an intentional tort (if injury results), because the object of a strong push can ordinarily be expected to go flying.

Intentional torts against persons and business relationships include assault and battery, false imprisonment, infliction of emotional distress, defamation, invasion of the right to privacy, appropriation, misrepresentation, and wrongful interference.

ASSAULT AND BATTERY

Any intentional, unexcused act that creates in another person a reasonable apprehension or fear of immediate harmful or offensive contact is an **assault**. Note that apprehension is not the same as fear. If a contact is such that a reasonable person would want to avoid it, and if there is a reasonable basis for believing that the contact will occur, then the plaintiff suffers apprehension whether or not he or she is afraid. The interest protected by tort law concerning assault is the freedom from having to expect harmful or offensive contact. The arousal of apprehension is enough to justify compensation.

The *completion* of the act that caused the apprehension, if it results in harm to the plaintiff, is a **battery**, which is defined as an unexcused and harmful or offensive physical contact *intentionally* performed. For example, Ivan threatens Jean with a gun, then shoots her. The pointing of the gun at Jean is an assault; the firing of the gun (if the bullet hits Jean) is a battery. The interest protected by tort law concerning battery is the right to personal security and safety.

Essentially, any unpermitted, offensive contact, whether harmful or not, is a battery. The contact may be merely an unwelcome kiss or smoke intentionally blown in one's face. The contact can involve any part of the body or anything attached to it—for example, a hat or other item of clothing, a purse, or a chair or an automobile in which one is sitting. Whether the contact is offensive is determined by the *reasonable person standard.*[1] The contact can be made by the defendant or by some force the defendant sets in motion—for example, a rock thrown, food poisoned, or a stick swung. If the plaintiff shows there was contact, and the jury agrees that the contact was offensive, the plaintiff has a right to compensation. There is no need to establish that the defendant acted out of malice; in fact, proving a motive is never necessary.

A number of legally recognized defenses can be raised by a defendant who is sued for assault, battery, or both:

1. *Consent.* When a person consents to the act that damages him or her, there is generally no liability for the damage done.
2. *Self-defense.* An individual who is defending his or her life or physical well-being can claim self-defense. In a situation of either *real* or *apparent* danger, a person may normally use whatever force is *reasonably* necessary to prevent harmful contact (see Chapter 8 for a more detailed discussion of self-defense).
3. *Defense of others.* An individual can act in a reasonable manner to protect others who are in real or apparent danger.
4. *Defense of property.* Reasonable force may be used in attempting to remove intruders from one's home, although force that is likely to cause death or great bodily injury normally cannot be used just to protect property.

FALSE IMPRISONMENT

False imprisonment is defined as the intentional confinement or restraint of another person's activities without justification. It involves interference with the freedom to move without restriction. The confinement can be accomplished through the use of physical barriers, physical restraint, or threats of physical

1. The reasonable person standard is an objective test of how a reasonable person would have acted under the same circumstances. See the subsection entitled "The Duty of Care and Its Breach" later in this chapter.

force. Moral pressure does not constitute false imprisonment. Furthermore, it is essential that the person being restrained not comply with the restraint willingly. In other words, the person being restrained must not agree to the restraint.

Businesspersons are often confronted with suits for false imprisonment after they have attempted to confine a suspected shoplifter for questioning. Under the privilege to detain granted to merchants in some states, a merchant can use the defense of *probable cause* to justify delaying a suspected shoplifter. Probable cause exists when the evidence to support the belief that a person is guilty outweighs the evidence against that belief. The detention, however, must be conducted in a *reasonable* manner and for only a *reasonable* length of time.

Intentional Infliction of Emotional Distress

The tort of *intentional infliction of emotional distress* can be defined as an intentional act that amounts to extreme and outrageous conduct resulting in severe emotional distress to another. For example, a prankster telephones an individual and says that the individual's spouse has just been in a horrible accident. As a result, the individual suffers intense mental pain or anxiety. The caller's behavior is deemed to be extreme and outrageous conduct that exceeds the bounds of decency accepted by society and is therefore **actionable** (capable of serving as the ground for a lawsuit).

Emotional distress claims pose several problems. One major problem is that such claims must be subject to some limitation, or the courts could be flooded with lawsuits alleging emotional distress. A society in which individuals are rewarded if they are unable to endure the normal emotional stresses of day-to-day living is obviously undesirable. Therefore, the law usually focuses on the nature of the acts that fall under this tort. Indignity or annoyance alone is usually not sufficient to support a lawsuit based on intentional infliction of emotional distress.

Many times, however, repeated annoyances (such as those experienced by a person who is being stalked), coupled with threats, are enough. In a business context, for example, the repeated use of extreme methods to collect an overdue debt may be actionable. Also, an event causing an unusually severe emotional reaction, such as the severe distress of a woman incorrectly informed that her husband and two sons have been killed, may be actionable. Because it is difficult to prove the existence of emotional suffering, a court may require that the emotional distress be evidenced by some physical symptom or illness or a specific emotional disturbance that can be documented by a psychiatric consultant or other medical professional.

See Case 5.1 at the end of this chapter. To view the full, unedited case from Westlaw,® go to this text's Web site at **http://wbl-cs.westbuslaw.com**.

Defamation

As discussed in Chapter 4, the freedom of speech guaranteed by the First Amendment is not absolute. In interpreting the First Amendment, the courts must balance the vital guarantee of free speech against other pervasive and strong social interests, including society's interest in preventing and redressing attacks on reputation.

Defamation of character involves wrongfully hurting a person's good reputation. The law imposes a general duty on all persons to refrain from making false, defamatory statements of fact about others. Breaching this duty orally involves the tort of **slander**; breaching it in writing involves the tort of **libel**. The tort of defamation also arises when a false statement of fact is made about a person's product, business, or title to property. We deal with these torts later in this chapter.

The Publication Requirement. The basis of the tort of defamation is the publication of a statement or statements that hold an individual up to contempt, ridicule, or hatred. *Publication* here means that the defamatory statements are communicated to persons other than the defamed party. If Thompson writes Andrews a private letter falsely accusing him of embezzling funds, the action does not constitute libel. If Peters falsely states that Gordon is dishonest and incompetent when no one else is around, the action does not constitute slander. In neither case was the message communicated to a third party.

The courts have generally held that even dictating a letter to a secretary constitutes publication, although the publication may be privileged (a concept that will be explained shortly). Moreover, if a third party overhears defamatory statements by chance, the courts usually hold that this also constitutes publication. Defamatory statements made via the

Internet are actionable as well, as you will read later in this chapter. Note also that any individual who repeats (republishes) defamatory statements normally is liable even if that person reveals the source of the statements.

Damages for Defamation. Once a defendant's liability for libel is established, "general damages" are presumed as a matter of law. General damages are designed to compensate the plaintiff for nonspecific harms such as disgrace or dishonor in the eyes of the community, humiliation, injured reputation, emotional distress, and so on—harms that are difficult to measure. In other words, to recover damages in a libel case, the plaintiff need not prove that he or she was actually injured in any way as a result of the libelous statement.

In a case alleging slander, however, the plaintiff must prove "special damages" to establish the defendant's liability. The plaintiff must show that the slanderous statement caused the plaintiff to suffer actual economic or monetary losses. Unless this initial hurdle of proving special damages is overcome, a plaintiff alleging slander normally cannot go forward with the suit and recover any damages. This requirement is imposed in cases involving slander because slanderous statements have a temporary quality. In contrast, a libelous (written) statement has the quality of permanence, can be circulated widely, and usually results from some degree of deliberation on the part of the author.

Exceptions to the burden of proving special damages in cases alleging slander are made for certain types of slanderous statements. If a false statement constitutes "slander *per se*," no proof of special damages is required for it to be actionable. The following four types of utterances are considered to be slander *per se*:

1. A statement that another has a loathsome communicable disease.
2. A statement that another has committed improprieties while engaging in a profession or trade.
3. A statement that another has committed or has been imprisoned for a serious crime.
4. A statement that an unmarried woman is unchaste.

Defenses to Defamation. Truth is almost always a defense against a defamation charge. In other words, if a defendant in a defamation case can prove that the allegedly defamatory statement of fact was actually true, normally no tort has been committed. Other defenses to defamation may exist if the speech is privileged or concerns a public figure.

Privileged Speech. In some circumstances, a person will not be liable for defamatory statements because he or she enjoys a **privilege**, or immunity. Privileged communications are of two types: absolute and qualified. Only in limited cases, such as in judicial and legislative proceedings, is *absolute* privilege granted. For example, statements made by attorneys and judges in the courtroom during a trial are absolutely privileged. So are statements made by legislators during congressional floor debate, even if the legislators make such statements maliciously—that is, knowing them to be untrue. An absolute privilege is granted in these situations because judicial and legislative personnel deal with matters that are so much in the public interest that the parties involved should be able to speak out fully and freely and without restriction.

In other situations, a person will not be liable for defamatory statements because he or she has a *qualified*, or conditional, privilege. For example, statements made in written evaluations of employees are qualifiedly privileged. Generally, if the communicated statements are made in good faith and the publication is limited to those who have a legitimate interest in the communication, the statements fall within the area of qualified privilege. The concept of conditional privilege rests on the common law assumption that in some situations, the right to know or speak is equal in importance to the right not to be defamed. If a communication is conditionally privileged, to recover damages, the plaintiff must show that the privilege was abused.

Public Figures. In general, false and defamatory statements that are made about **public figures** (public officials who exercise substantial governmental power and any persons in the public limelight) and published in the press are privileged if they are made without "actual malice." To be made with **actual malice**, a statement must be made *with either knowledge of falsity or a reckless disregard of the truth.*[2]

Statements made about public figures, especially when they are communicated via a public medium, are usually related to matters of general public

2. *New York Times Co. v. Sullivan*, 376 U.S. 254, 84 S.Ct. 710, 11 L.Ed.2d 686 (1964).

interest; they refer to people who substantially affect all of us. Furthermore, public figures generally have some access to a public medium for answering disparaging falsehoods about themselves; private individuals do not. For these reasons, public figures have a greater burden of proof in defamation cases (they must prove actual malice) than do private individuals.

Invasion of Privacy

A person has a right to solitude and freedom from prying public eyes—in other words, to privacy. As mentioned in Chapter 4, the courts have held that certain amendments to the U.S. Constitution imply a right to privacy. Some state constitutions explicitly provide for privacy rights. Additionally, a number of federal and state statutes have been enacted to protect individual privacy rights in specific areas. Tort law also safeguards these rights through the tort of *invasion of privacy.* Four acts qualify as invasion of privacy:

1. *The use of a person's name, picture, or other likeness for commercial purposes without permission.* For example, using without permission someone's picture to advertise a product or someone's name to enhance a company's reputation invades the person's privacy. (This tort, which is usually referred to as the tort of *appropriation,* will be examined shortly.)
2. *Intrusion on an individual's affairs or seclusion.* For example, invading someone's home or illegally searching someone's briefcase is an invasion of privacy. This tort has been held to extend to eavesdropping by wiretap, unauthorized scanning of a bank account, compulsory blood testing, and window peeping.
3. *Publication of information that places a person in a false light.* This could be a story attributing to someone ideas not held or actions not taken by that person. (The publication of such a story could involve the tort of defamation as well.)
4. *Public disclosure of private facts about an individual that an ordinary person would find objectionable.* A newspaper account of a private citizen's sex life or financial affairs could be an actionable invasion of privacy.

A pressing issue in today's online world has to do with the privacy rights of Internet users. As noted in Chapter 4, this is particularly true with respect to personal information collected not only by government agencies but by online merchants. Another area in which Internet users face significant privacy concerns is in the employment context. In *Tiberino v. Spokane County* (Case 5.2) for example, a state government agency threatened to disclose to the media the personal e-mail messages that an employee had sent or received over the Internet from her work computer. The same rules concerning public disclosure do not apply in the context of private employment. The case illustrates, however, the problems associated with sending and receiving personal e-mail in any workplace in which it is prohibited. (See Chapter 41 for a more detailed examination of privacy rights in the employment context.)

See Case 5.2 at the end of this chapter. To view the full, unedited case from Westlaw,® go to this text's Web site at **http://wbl-cs.westbuslaw.com**.

Appropriation

The use of another person's name, likeness, or other identifying characteristic, without permission and for the benefit of the user, constitutes the tort of **appropriation.** Under the law, normally an individual's right to privacy includes the right to the exclusive use of his or her identity. For example, in a case involving a Ford Motor Company television commercial in which a Bette Midler "sound-alike" sang a song that Midler had made famous, the court held that Ford "for their own profit in selling their product did appropriate part of her identity."[3]

A court ruled similarly in a case brought by Vanna White, the hostess of the popular television game show *Wheel of Fortune,* against Samsung Electronics America, Inc. Without White's permission, Samsung included in an advertisement for Samsung videocassette recorders a depiction of a robot dressed in a wig, gown, and jewelry, posed in a scene that resembled the *Wheel of Fortune* set, in a stance for which White is famous. The court held in White's favor, holding that the tort of appropriation does not require the use of a celebrity's name or likeness. The court stated that Samsung's robot ad left "little doubt" as to the identity of the celebrity that the ad was meant to depict.[4]

3. *Midler v. Ford Motor Co.*, 849 F.2d 460 (9th Cir. 1988).
4. *White v. Samsung Electronics America, Inc.*, 971 F.2d 1395 (10th Cir. 1992).

Cases of wrongful appropriation, or misappropriation, may also involve the rights of those who invest time and money in the creation of a special system, such as a method of broadcasting sports events. Commercial misappropriation may also occur when a person takes and uses the property of another for the sole purpose of capitalizing unfairly on the goodwill or reputation of the property owner.

FRAUDULENT MISREPRESENTATION

A misrepresentation leads another to believe in a condition that is different from the condition that actually exists. This is often accomplished through a false or an incorrect statement. Misrepresentations may be innocently made by someone who is unaware of the facts. The tort of **fraudulent misrepresentation**, or *fraud,* however, involves intentional deceit for personal gain. The tort includes several elements:

1. A misrepresentation of material facts or conditions with knowledge that they are false or with reckless disregard for the truth.
2. An intent to induce another party to rely on the misrepresentation.
3. A justifiable reliance on the misrepresentation by the deceived party.
4. Damages suffered as a result of that reliance.
5. A causal connection between the misrepresentation and the injury suffered.

For fraud to occur, more than mere **puffery**, or *seller's talk,* must be involved. Fraud exists only when a person represents as a fact something he or she knows is untrue. For example, it is fraud to claim that the roof of a building does not leak when one knows it does. Facts are objectively ascertainable, whereas seller's talk is not. "I am the best architect in town" is seller's talk. The speaker is not trying to represent something as fact, because the term *best* is a subjective, not an objective, term.

Normally, the tort of fraudulent misrepresentation occurs only when there is reliance on a *statement of fact.* Sometimes, however, reliance on a *statement of opinion* may involve the tort of fraudulent misrepresentation if the individual making the statement of opinion has a superior knowledge of the subject matter. For example, when a lawyer, in a state in which he or she is licensed to practice, makes a statement of opinion about the law, a court would construe reliance on such a statement to be equivalent to reliance on a statement of fact.

Fraudulent and nonfraudulent misrepresentation will be examined further in Chapter 13, in the context of contract law. A growing problem in the online era is fraudulent misrepresentation in Internet transactions, a topic we examine in Chapter 44.

WRONGFUL INTERFERENCE

Torts involving wrongful interference with another's business rights generally fall into two categories—interference with a contractual relationship and interference with a business relationship.

Wrongful Interference with a Contractual Relationship. The body of tort law relating to *wrongful interference with a contractual relationship* has increased greatly in recent years. A landmark case in this area involved an opera singer, Joanna Wagner, who was under contract to sing for a man named Lumley for a specified period of years. A man named Gye, who knew of this contract, nonetheless "enticed" Wagner to refuse to carry out the agreement, and Wagner began to sing for Gye. Gye's action constituted a tort, because it interfered with the contractual relationship between Wagner and Lumley.[5] (Of course, Wagner's refusal to carry out the agreement also entitled Lumley to sue Wagner for breach of contract.)

In principle, any lawful contract can be the basis for an action of this type. The plaintiff must prove that the defendant actually knew of the contract's existence and *intentionally induced* the breach of the contractual relationship, not merely that the defendant reaped the benefits of a broken contract. For example, suppose that Carlin has a contract with Sutter that calls for Sutter to do gardening work on Carlin's large estate every week for fifty-two weeks at a specified price per week. Mellon, who needs gardening services, contacts Sutter and offers to pay Sutter a wage that is substantially higher than that offered by Carlin—although Mellon knows nothing about the Sutter-Carlin contract. Sutter breaches his contract with Carlin so that he can work for Mellon. Carlin cannot sue Mellon, because Mellon knew nothing of the Sutter-Carlin contract and was totally unaware that the higher wage he offered induced Sutter to breach that contract.

Three elements are necessary for wrongful interference with a contractual relationship to occur:

5. *Lumley v. Gye,* 118 Eng.Rep. 749 (1853).

1. A valid, enforceable contract must exist between two parties.
2. A third party must know that this contract exists.
3. This third party must *intentionally* cause one of the two parties to the contract to breach the contract, and the interference must be for the purpose of advancing the economic interest of the third party.

The contract may be between a firm and its employees or a firm and its customers, suppliers, competitors, or other parties. Sometimes a competitor of a firm draws away a key employee. If the original employer can show that the competitor induced the breach of the employment contract—that is, that the employee would not normally have broken the contract—damages can be recovered.

In a famous case in the 1980s, Texaco, Inc., was found to have wrongfully interfered with an agreement between the Pennzoil Company and the Getty Oil Company. After Pennzoil had agreed to purchase a portion of Getty Oil, Texaco made an offer to purchase Getty Oil, and Getty Oil accepted Texaco's offer. Pennzoil then successfully sued Texaco for wrongful interference with Pennzoil's contractual relationship with Getty Oil.[6]

Wrongful Interference with a Business Relationship. Individuals devise countless schemes to attract business, but they are forbidden by the courts to interfere unreasonably with another's business in their attempts to gain a share of the market. There is a difference between *competitive practices* and *predatory behavior.* The distinction usually depends on whether a business is attempting to attract customers in general or to solicit only those customers who have already shown an interest in the similar product or service of a specific competitor.

For example, if a shopping center contains two shoe stores, an employee of Store A cannot be positioned at the entrance of Store B for the purpose of diverting customers to Store A. This type of activity constitutes the tort of wrongful interference with a business relationship, often referred to as interference with a prospective (economic) advantage, and it is commonly considered to be an unfair trade practice. If this type of activity were permitted, Store A would reap the benefits of Store B's advertising.

Generally, a plaintiff must prove the following elements to recover damages for the tort of wrongful interference with a business relationship:

1. There was an established business relationship.
2. The tortfeasor, by use of predatory methods, *intentionally* caused this business relationship to end.
3. The plaintiff suffered damages as a result of the tortfeasor's actions.

Defenses to Wrongful Interference. A person will not be liable for the tort of wrongful interference with a contractual or business relationship if it can be shown that the interference was justified, or permissible. Bona fide competitive behavior is a permissible interference even if it results in the breaking of a contract.

For example, if Jerrod's Meats advertises so effectively that it induces Sam's Restaurant to break its contract with Burke's Meat Company, Burke's Meat Company will be unable to recover against Jerrod's Meats on a wrongful interference theory. After all, the public policy that favors free competition in advertising definitely outweighs any possible instability that such competitive activity might cause in contractual relations. Therefore, although luring customers away from a competitor through aggressive marketing and advertising strategies obviously interferes with the competitor's relationship with its customers, such activity is permitted by the courts.

SECTION 3

Intentional Torts against Property

Intentional torts against property include trespass to land, trespass to personal property, and conversion. These torts are wrongful actions that interfere with individuals' legally recognized rights with regard to their land or personal property. The law distinguishes real property from personal property (see Chapter 46). *Real property* is land and things permanently attached to the land. *Personal property* consists of all other items, which are basically movable. Thus, a house and lot are real property, whereas the furniture inside a house is personal property. Money and securities are also personal property.

6. *Texaco, Inc. v. Pennzoil Co.*, 725 S.W.2d 768 (Tex.App.–Houston [1st Dist.] 1987, writ ref'd n.r.e.). (Generally, a complete Texas Court of Appeals citation includes a writ-of-error history showing the Texas Supreme Court's disposition of the case. In this case, "writ ref'd n.r.e." is an abbreviation of "writ refused, no reversible error," which means that Texas's highest court refused to grant the appellant's request to review the case, because the court did not consider there to be any reversible error.)

TRESPASS TO LAND

The tort of **trespass to land** occurs any time a person, without permission, enters onto, above, or below the surface of land that is owned by another; causes anything to enter onto the land; or remains on the land or permits anything to remain on it. Note that actual harm to the land is not an essential element of this tort, because the tort is designed to protect the right of an owner to exclusive possession. Common types of trespass to land include walking or driving on the land; shooting a gun over the land; throwing rocks or spraying water on a building that belongs to someone else; building a dam across a river, thus causing water to back up on someone else's land; and placing part of one's building on an adjoining landowner's property.

In the past, the right to land gave exclusive possession of a space that extended from "the center of the earth to the heavens," but this rule has been relaxed. Today, reasonable intrusions are permitted. Thus, aircraft can normally fly over privately owned land. Society's interest in air transportation preempts the individual's interest in the airspace.

Trespass Criteria, Rights, and Duties. Before a person can be a trespasser, the real property owner (or other person in actual and exclusive possession of the property) must establish that person as a trespasser. For example, "posted" trespass signs expressly establish as a trespasser a person who ignores these signs and enters onto the property. Any person who enters onto another's property to commit an illegal act (such as a thief entering a lumberyard at night to steal lumber) is established impliedly as a trespasser, without posted signs.

A guest in one's home is not a trespasser—unless he or she has been asked to leave but refuses. A *licensee* (a person who has a revocable right to come onto another person's land—see Chapter 47) who is asked to leave and refuses to do so is also a trespasser. For example, one who purchases a ticket to a play has a right to enter the theater, but the theater manager may revoke (take back) that right—if the playgoer becomes rowdy during the play's performance, for instance.

At common law, a trespasser is liable for damages caused to the property and generally cannot hold the owner liable for injuries that the trespasser sustains on the premises. This common law rule is being abandoned in many jurisdictions in favor of a "reasonable duty" rule that varies depending on the status of the parties. For example, a landowner may have a duty to post a notice that the property is patrolled by guard dogs. Also, under the "attractive nuisance" doctrine, a landowner may be held liable for injuries sustained by young children on the landowner's property if the children were attracted to the premises by some object, such as a swimming pool or an abandoned building. Finally, an owner can remove a trespasser from the premises—or detain a trespasser on the premises for a reasonable time—through the use of reasonable force without being liable for assault and battery or false imprisonment.

Defenses against Trespass to Land. Trespass to land involves wrongful interference with another person's real property rights. If it can be shown that the trespass was warranted, however, as when a trespasser enters to assist someone in danger, a defense exists.

TRESPASS TO PERSONAL PROPERTY

Whenever any individual, without consent, harms the personal property of another or otherwise interferes with the personal property owner's right to exclusive possession and enjoyment of that property, **trespass to personal property**—also called *trespass to personalty*—occurs. Trespass to personal property involves intentional meddling. If Kelly takes Ryan's business law book as a practical joke and hides it so that Ryan is unable to find it for several days prior to a final examination, Kelly has engaged in a trespass to personal property.

If it can be shown that trespass to personal property was warranted, then a complete defense exists. Most states, for example, allow automobile repair shops to hold a customer's car (under what is called an *artisan's lien,* discussed in Chapter 29) when the customer refuses to pay for repairs already completed.

CONVERSION

Conversion is defined as any act that deprives an owner of personal property without that owner's permission and without just cause. Conversion is the civil side of crimes related to theft. A store clerk who steals merchandise from the store commits a crime and engages in the tort of conversion at the same time. When conversion occurs, the lesser offense of trespass to personal property usually occurs as well. If the initial taking of the property was a trespass, retention of that property is conversion. If the initial taking of the property was permitted by the owner or for some other reason is not a trespass, failure to return it may still be conversion.

Even if a person mistakenly believed that he or she was entitled to the goods, a tort of conversion may still have occurred. In other words, good intentions are not a defense against conversion; in fact, conversion can be an entirely innocent act. Someone who buys stolen goods, for example, has committed the tort of conversion even if he or she did not know the goods were stolen.

A successful defense against the charge of conversion is that the purported owner does not in fact own the property or does not have a right to possess it that is superior to the right of the holder. Necessity is another possible defense against conversion. If Abrams takes Mendoza's cat, Abrams is guilty of conversion. If Mendoza sues Abrams, Abrams must return the cat or pay damages. If, however, the cat had rabies and Abrams took the cat to protect the public, Abrams has a valid defense—necessity.

DISPARAGEMENT OF PROPERTY

Disparagement of property occurs when economically injurious falsehoods are made not about another's reputation but about another's product or property. *Disparagement of property* is a general term for torts that can be more specifically referred to as *slander of quality* or *slander of title.*

Slander of Quality. Publishing false information about another's product, alleging it is not what its seller claims, constitutes the tort of **slander of quality.** This tort has also been given the name **trade libel.** The plaintiff must prove that actual damages proximately resulted from the slander of quality. That is, it must be shown not only that a third person refrained from dealing with the plaintiff because of the improper publication but also that the plaintiff suffered damages because the third person refrained from dealing with him or her. The economic calculation of such damages—they are, after all, conjectural—is often extremely difficult.

It is possible for an improper publication to be both a slander of quality and a defamation. For example, a statement that disparages the quality of a product may also, by implication, disparage the character of a person who would sell such a product. In one case, for instance, the claim that a product that was marketed as a sleeping aid contained "habit-forming drugs" was held to constitute defamation.[7]

Slander of Title. When a publication falsely denies or casts doubt on another's legal ownership of property, and when this results in financial loss to the property's owner, the tort of **slander of title** may exist. Usually, this is an intentional tort in which someone knowingly publishes an untrue statement about another's ownership of certain property with the intent of discouraging a third person from dealing with the person slandered. For example, it would be difficult for a car dealer to attract customers after competitors published a notice that the dealer's stock consisted of stolen autos.

SECTION 4

Negligence

In contrast to intentional torts, in torts involving **negligence**, the tortfeasor neither wishes to bring about the consequences of the act nor believes that they will occur. The actor's conduct merely creates a risk of such consequences. If no risk is created, there is no negligence. Moreover, the risk must be foreseeable; that is, it must be such that a reasonable person engaging in the same activity would anticipate the risk and guard against it. In determining what is reasonable conduct, courts consider the nature of the possible harm. A very slight risk of a dangerous explosion might be unreasonable, whereas a distinct possibility of someone's burning his or her fingers on a stove might be reasonable.

To succeed in a negligence action, the plaintiff must prove the following:

1. That the defendant owed a duty of care to the plaintiff.
2. That the defendant breached that duty.
3. That the plaintiff suffered a legally recognizable injury.
4. That the defendant's breach caused the plaintiff's injury.

We discuss here each of these four elements of negligence.

7. *Harwood Pharmacal Co. v. National Broadcasting Co.*, 9 N.Y.2d 460, 174 N.E.2d 602, 214 N.Y.S.2d 725 (1961).

THE DUTY OF CARE AND ITS BREACH

Central to the tort of negligence is the concept of a **duty of care.** This concept arises from the notion that if we are to live in society with other people, some actions can be tolerated and some cannot; some actions are right and some are wrong; and some actions are reasonable and some are not. The basic principle underlying the duty of care is that people are free to act as they please so long as their actions do not infringe on the interests of others.

The law of torts defines and measures the duty of care by the **reasonable person standard.** In determining whether a duty of care has been breached, for example, the courts ask how a reasonable person would have acted in the same circumstances. The reasonable person standard is said to be (though in an absolute sense it cannot be) objective. It is not necessarily how a particular person would act. It is society's judgment on how an ordinarily prudent person should act. If the so-called reasonable person existed, he or she would be careful, conscientious, prudent, even tempered, and honest. That individuals are required to exercise a reasonable standard of care in their activities is a pervasive concept in business law, and many of the issues dealt with in subsequent chapters of this text have to do with this duty.

In negligence cases, the degree of care to be exercised varies, depending on the defendant's occupation or profession, his or her relationship with the plaintiff, and other factors. Generally, whether an action constitutes a breach of the duty of care is determined on a case-by-case basis. The outcome depends on how the court judge (or jury, if it is a jury trial) decides a reasonable person in the position of the defendant would act in the particular circumstances of the case. In the following subsections, we examine the degree of care typically expected of landowners and professionals.

Duty of Landowners. Landowners are expected to exercise reasonable care to protect from harm individuals coming onto their property. As mentioned earlier in this chapter, in some jurisdictions, landowners are held to have a duty to protect even trespassers against certain risks. Landowners who rent or lease premises to tenants are expected to exercise reasonable care to ensure that the tenants and their guests are not harmed in common areas, such as stairways, entryways, and laundry rooms (see Chapter 48).

Retailers and other firms that explicitly or implicitly invite persons to come onto their premises are usually charged with a duty to exercise reasonable care to protect these **business invitees.** For example, if you entered a supermarket, slipped on a wet floor, and sustained injuries as a result, the owner of the supermarket would be liable for damages if, when you slipped, there was no sign warning that the floor was wet. A court would hold that the business owner was negligent because the owner failed to exercise a reasonable degree of care in protecting the store's customers against foreseeable risks about which the owner knew or *should have known.* That a patron might slip on the wet floor and be injured as a result was a foreseeable risk, and the owner should have taken care to avoid this risk or warn the customer of it.[8]

Some risks, of course, are so obvious that an owner need not warn of them. For example, a business owner does not need to warn customers to open a door before attempting to walk through it. Other risks, however, even though they may seem obvious to a business owner, may not be so in the eyes of another, such as a child. For example, a hardware store owner may not think it is necessary to warn customers that, if climbed, a stepladder leaning against the back wall of the store could fall down and harm them. It is possible, though, that a child could tip the ladder over while climbing it and be hurt as a result.

See Case 5.3 at the end of this chapter. To view the full, unedited case from Westlaw,® go to this text's Web site at **http://wbl-cs.westbuslaw.com**.

Duty of Professionals. If an individual has knowledge, skill, or intelligence superior to that of an ordinary person, the individual's conduct must be consistent with that status. Professionals—including physicians, dentists, psychiatrists, architects, engineers, accountants, and lawyers, among others—are required to have a standard minimum level of special knowledge and ability. Therefore, in determining what constitutes reasonable care in the case of professionals, the court takes their training and expertise

8. A business owner can warn of a risk in a number of ways—for example, by placing a sign, traffic cone, sawhorse, board, or the like near a hole in the business's parking lot. See *Hartman v. Walkertown Shopping Center, Inc.,* 113 N.C.App. 632, 439 S.E.2d 787 (1994).

into account. In other words, an accountant cannot defend against a lawsuit for negligence by stating, "But I was not familiar with that general principle of accounting."

If a professional violates his or her duty of care toward a client, the client may bring a **malpractice** suit against the professional. For example, a patient might sue a physician for *medical malpractice.* A client might sue an attorney for *legal malpractice.* The liability of professionals will be examined in further detail in Chapter 51.

No Duty to Rescue. Although the law requires individuals to act reasonably and responsibly in their relations with others, if a person fails to come to the aid of a stranger in peril, that person will not be considered negligent under tort law. For example, assume that you are walking down a city street and notice that a pedestrian is about to step directly in front of an oncoming bus. You realize that the person has not seen the bus and is unaware of the danger. Do you have a legal duty to warn that individual? No. Although most people would probably concede that in this situation, the observer has an *ethical* or *moral* duty to warn the other, tort law does not impose a general duty to rescue others in peril. Duties may be imposed in regard to certain types of peril, however. For example, most states require a motorist involved in an automobile accident to stop and render aid. Failure to do so is both a tort and a crime.

The Injury Requirement and Damages

To recover damages (receive compensation), the plaintiff in a tort lawsuit must prove that he or she suffered a *legally recognizable* injury. That is, the plaintiff must have suffered some loss, harm, wrong, or invasion of a protected interest. This is true in lawsuits for intentional torts as well as lawsuits for negligence. Essentially, the purpose of tort law is to compensate for legally recognized harms and injuries resulting from wrongful acts. If no harm or injury results from a given negligent action, there is nothing to compensate—and no tort exists.

For example, if you carelessly bump into a passerby, who stumbles and falls as a result, you may be liable in tort if the passerby is injured in the fall. If the person is unharmed, however, there normally can be no suit for damages, because no injury was suffered. Although the passerby might be angry and suffer emotional distress, few courts recognize negligently inflicted emotional distress as a tort unless it results in some physical disturbance or dysfunction.

As already mentioned, the purpose of tort law is not to punish people for tortious acts but to compensate the injured parties for damages suffered. **Compensatory damages** are intended to compensate, or reimburse, a plaintiff for actual losses—to make the plaintiff whole. Occasionally, however, punitive damages are also awarded in tort lawsuits. **Punitive damages**, or *exemplary damages,* are intended to punish the wrongdoer and deter others from similar wrongdoing. Punitive damages are rarely awarded in lawsuits for ordinary negligence and usually are given only in cases involving intentional torts. They may be awarded, however, in suits involving *gross negligence,* which can be defined as an intentional failure to perform a manifest duty in reckless disregard of the consequences of such a failure for the life or property of another.

Causation

Another element necessary to a tort is *causation.* If a person breaches a duty of care and someone suffers injury, the wrongful activity must have caused the harm for a tort to have been committed.

Causation in Fact and Proximate Cause. In deciding whether the requirement of causation is met, the court must address two questions:

1. *Is there causation in fact?* Did the injury occur because of the defendant's act, or would it have occurred anyway? If an injury would not have occurred without the defendant's act, then there is causation in fact. **Causation in fact** can usually be determined by use of the *but for* test: "but for" the wrongful act, the injury would not have occurred.
2. *Was the act the proximate cause of the injury?* Theoretically, causation in fact is limitless. One could claim, for example, that "but for" the creation of the world, a particular injury would not have occurred. Thus, as a practical matter, the law has to establish limits, and it does so through the concept of proximate cause. **Proximate cause**, or *legal cause,* exists when the connection between an act and an injury is strong enough to justify imposing liability. Consider an example. Ackerman carelessly leaves a campfire burning. The fire not only burns down the forest but also sets off an explosion in a nearby chemical plant

that spills chemicals into a river, killing all the fish for a hundred miles downstream and ruining the economy of a tourist resort. Should Ackerman be liable to the resort owners? To the tourists whose vacations were ruined? These are questions of proximate cause that a court must decide.

Foreseeability. Questions of proximate cause are linked to the concept of foreseeability, because it would be unfair to impose liability on a defendant unless the defendant's actions created a foreseeable risk of injury. Probably the most cited case on the concept of foreseeability as a requirement for proximate cause—and as a measure of the extent of the duty of care generally—is the *Palsgraf* case, which is presented in Case 5.4.

See Case 5.4 at the end of this chapter. To view the full, unedited case from Westlaw®, go to this text's Web site at http://wbl-cs.westbuslaw.com.

Defenses to Negligence

The basic defenses to liability in negligence cases are (1) assumption of risk, (2) superseding cause, and (3) contributory negligence.

Assumption of Risk. A plaintiff who voluntarily enters into a risky situation, knowing the risk involved, will not be allowed to recover. This is the defense of **assumption of risk.** For example, a driver entering an automobile race knows there is a risk of being injured or killed in a crash. The driver has assumed the risk of injury. The requirements of this defense are (1) knowledge of the risk and (2) voluntary assumption of the risk.

The risk can be assumed by express agreement, or the assumption of risk can be implied by the plaintiff's knowledge of the risk and subsequent conduct. Of course, the plaintiff does not assume a risk different from or greater than the risk normally carried by the activity. In our example, the race driver assumes the risk of being injured in the race but not the risk that the banking in the curves of the racetrack will give way during the race because of a construction defect.

Risks are not deemed to be assumed in situations involving emergencies. Neither are they assumed when a statute protects a class of people from harm and a member of the class is injured by the harm. For example, courts have generally held that an employee cannot assume the risk of an employer's violation of safety statutes passed for the benefit of employees.

Superseding Cause. An unforeseeable intervening event may break the causal connection between a wrongful act and an injury to another. If so, it acts as a *superseding cause*—that is, it relieves a defendant of liability for injuries caused by the intervening event. For example, suppose that Derrick, while riding his bicycle, negligently hits Julie, who is walking on a sidewalk. As a result of the impact, Julie falls and fractures her hip. While she is waiting for help to arrive, a small aircraft crashes nearby and explodes, and some of the fiery debris hits her, causing her to sustain severe burns. Derrick will be liable for damages caused by Julie's fractured hip, but normally he will not be liable for the wounds caused by the plane crash—because the risk of a plane crashing nearby and injuring Julie was not foreseeable.

Contributory Negligence. Traditionally, under the common law, if a plaintiff's own negligence contributed to his or her injury, the defendant could raise the defense of **contributory negligence.** Contributory negligence on the part of the plaintiff was a complete defense to liability for negligence. Today, contributory negligence can be used as a defense in only a very few states.

In those jurisdictions that do allow the defense of contributory negligence, the *last clear chance* doctrine can excuse the effect of a plaintiff's negligence. The last clear chance doctrine allows the plaintiff to recover full damages despite his or her failure to exercise care. This rule operates when, through his or her own negligence, the plaintiff is endangered (or his or her property is endangered) by a defendant who has an opportunity to avoid causing damage but fails to take advantage of that opportunity. For example, if Murphy walks across the street against the light, and Lewis, a motorist, sees her in time to avoid hitting her but hits her anyway, Lewis (the defendant) is not permitted to use Murphy's (the plaintiff's) prior negligence as a defense. The defendant negligently missed the opportunity to avoid injuring the plaintiff.

Neither the complete defense of contributory negligence nor the last clear chance doctrine applies in states that have adopted a comparative negligence standard, as the majority of states have done. Under the doctrine of **comparative negligence**, both the plaintiff's negligence and the defendant's negligence are taken into consideration, and damages are awarded accordingly. Some jurisdictions have adopted a "pure" form of comparative negligence that allows the plaintiff to recover damages even if his or her fault is greater than that of the defendant. For example, if the plaintiff was 80 percent at fault and the defendant was 20 percent at fault, the plaintiff may recover 20 percent of his or her damages. Many states' comparative negligence statutes, however, contain a "50 percent" rule, under which the plaintiff recovers nothing if he or she was more than 50 percent at fault.

Special Negligence Doctrines and Statutes

There are a number of special doctrines and statutes relating to negligence that are important. We examine a few of them here.

Res Ipsa Loquitur. Generally, in lawsuits involving negligence, the plaintiff has the burden of proving that the defendant was negligent. In certain situations, the courts may presume that negligence has occurred, in which case the burden of proof rests on the defendant—that is, the defendant must prove that he or she was *not* negligent. The presumption of the defendant's negligence is known as the doctrine of ***res ipsa loquitur,***[9] which translates as "the facts speak for themselves."

This doctrine is applied only when the event creating the damage or injury is one that ordinarily does not occur in the absence of negligence. For example, if a person undergoes knee surgery and following the surgery has a severed nerve in the knee area, that person can sue the surgeon under a theory of *res ipsa loquitur.* In this case, the injury would not have occurred but for the surgeon's negligence.[10] For the doctrine of *res ipsa loquitur* to apply, the event must have been within the defendant's power to control, and it must not have been due to any voluntary action or contribution on the part of the plaintiff.

Negligence *Per Se.* Certain conduct, whether it consists of an action or a failure to act, may be treated as **negligence *per se*** ("in or of itself"). Negligence *per se* may occur if an individual violates a statute or an ordinance providing for a criminal penalty and that violation causes another to be injured. The injured person must prove (1) that the statute clearly sets out what standard of conduct is expected, when and where it is expected, and of whom it is expected; (2) that he or she is in the class intended to be protected by the statute; and (3) that the statute was designed to prevent the type of injury that he or she suffered. The standard of conduct required by the statute is the duty that the defendant owes to the plaintiff, and a violation of the statute is the breach of that duty.

For example, a statute may require a landowner to keep a building in safe condition and may also subject the landowner to a criminal penalty, such as a fine, if the building is not kept safe. The statute is meant to protect those who are rightfully in the building. Thus, if the owner, without a sufficient excuse, violates the statute and a tenant is thereby injured, then a majority of courts will hold that the owner's unexcused violation of the statute conclusively establishes a breach of a duty of care—that is, that the owner's violation is negligence *per se.*

"Danger Invites Rescue" Doctrine. Under the "danger invites rescue" doctrine, if a person commits an act that endangers another, the person committing the act will be liable for any injuries the other party suffers as well as any injuries suffered by a third person in an attempt to rescue the endangered party. For example, suppose that Ludlam, while driving down a street, fails to see a stop sign because he is trying to stop a squabble between his two young children in the car's back seat. Salter, on the curb near the stop sign, realizes that Ludlam is about to hit a pedestrian walking across the street at the intersection. Salter runs into the street to push the pedestrian out of the way, and Ludlum's vehicle hits Salter instead. In this situation, Ludlam will be liable for Salter's injury, as well as for any injuries the other pedestrian sustained. Rescuers can injure themselves, or the persons rescued, or even bystanders, but the original wrongdoers will still be liable.

Special Negligence Statutes. A number of states have enacted statutes prescribing duties and responsibilities in certain circumstances. For example, most states now have what are called **Good Samaritan statutes.** Under these statutes, persons whom others aid voluntarily cannot turn around and sue the "Good Samaritans" for negligence. These laws were

9. Pronounced *rihz ihp*-suh *low*-kwuh-duhr.

10. *Edwards v. Boland,* 41 Mass.App.Ct. 375, 670 N.E.2d 404 (1996).

passed largely to protect physicians and medical personnel who voluntarily render their services in emergency situations to those in need, such as individuals hurt in car accidents.

Many states have also passed **dram shop acts**, under which a tavern owner or bartender may be held liable for injuries caused by a person who became intoxicated while drinking at the bar or who was already intoxicated when served by the bartender. Some states have statutes that impose liability on *social hosts* (persons hosting parties) for injuries caused by guests who became intoxicated at the hosts' homes. Under these statutes, it is unnecessary to prove that the tavern owner, bartender, or social host was negligent. Sometimes, the definition of a "social host" is fashioned broadly. For example, in a New York case, the court held that the father of a minor who hosted a "bring your own keg" party could be held liable for injuries caused by an intoxicated guest.[11]

SECTION 5

Cyber Torts

A significant issue that has come before the courts in recent years relates to the question of who should be held liable for *cyber torts*, or torts committed in cyberspace. For example, who should be held liable when someone posts a defamatory message online? Should an Internet service provider (ISP), such as Yahoo! or AOL, be liable for the remark if the ISP was unaware that it was being made?

Other questions involve matters of proof. How, for example, can it be proved that an online defamatory remark was "published" (which requires that a third party see or hear it)? How can the identity of the person who made the remark be discovered? Can an ISP be forced to reveal the source of an anonymous comment? We explore some of these questions in this section, as well as some of the legal issues that have arisen with respect to bulk e-mail advertising.

DEFAMATION ONLINE

Online forums allow anyone—customers, employees, or crackpots—to complain about a business firm. The complaint could concern the firm's personnel, policies, practices, or products, and it might have an impact on the firm's business. This is possible regardless of whether the complaint is justified or whether it is true. One of the early questions arising in the online legal arena was whether the providers of such forums could be held liable for defamatory statements made in those forums.

Liability of Internet Service Providers. Newspapers, magazines, and television and radio stations may be held liable for defamatory remarks that they disseminate, even if those remarks are prepared or created by others. Under the Communications Decency Act (CDA) of 1996, however, Internet service providers (ISPs), or "interactive computer service providers," are not liable with respect to such material.[12] An ISP typically provides access to the Internet through a local phone number and may furnish other services, including access to databases available only to the ISP's subscribers.

The CDA Shields ISPs from Liability. In a number of key cases, the ISP provisions of the CDA have been invoked to shield ISPs from liability for defamatory postings on their bulletin boards. In a leading case, decided the year after the CDA was enacted, America Online, Inc. (AOL), was not held liable even though it did not promptly remove defamatory messages of which it had been made aware. In upholding a district court's ruling in AOL's favor, a federal appellate court stated that the CDA "plainly immunizes computer service providers like AOL from liability for information that originates with third parties." The court explained that the purpose of the statute is "to maintain the robust nature of Internet communication and, accordingly, to keep government interference in the medium to a minimum." The court added, "None of this means, of course, that the original culpable party who posts defamatory messages would escape accountability."[13]

Most of the cases concerning the issue of ISP immunity under the CDA have involved bulletin boards and other forums provided by ISPs. In 2000, however, a California state court extended the 1996 CDA further into the realm of e-commerce when it ruled that eBay, the online auction house, could not

11. *Rust v. Reyer*, 693 N.E.2d 1074, 670 N.Y.S.2d 822 (1995).

12. 47 U.S.C. Section 230.

13. *Zeran v. America Online, Inc.*, 129 F.3d 327 (4th Cir. 1997); cert. denied, 118 S.Ct. 2341 (1998).

be held liable for the sale of pirated sound recordings on its Web site.[14]

Piercing the Veil of Anonymity. A threshold barrier to anyone who seeks to bring an action for online defamation is discovering the identity of the person who posted a defamatory message online. ISPs can disclose personal information about their customers only when ordered to do so by a court. Because of this, businesses and individuals are increasingly resorting to lawsuits against "John Does." Then, using the authority of the courts, they can obtain from ISPs the identities of the persons responsible for the messages.

In one case, for example, Eric Hvide, a former chief executive of a company called Hvide Marine, sued a number of "John Does" who had posted allegedly defamatory statements about his company on various online message boards. Hvide, who eventually lost his job, sued the John Does for libel in a Florida court. The court ruled that Yahoo! and America Online had to reveal the identities of the defendant Does.[15]

In another case, however, discovering the identity of a person who posted an online defamatory message was more difficult. The case involved a physician, Dr. Sam D. Graham, Jr., who at the time was the chair of the urology department at Emory University's School of Medicine. A posting on a Yahoo! message board suggested that Graham had taken kickbacks from a urology company after giving his department's pathology business to the firm. Graham resigned from his position and sued the anonymous poster for libel. Because the person posting the message was not actually a Yahoo! customer, an extensive investigation and, according to Graham's attorney, a lot of "dumb luck" was required to learn the identity of the person who posted the message. The case went to trial, and a federal district court awarded Graham $675,000 in damages.[16]

SPAM

Bulk, unsolicited e-mail ("junk" e-mail) sent to all of the users on a particular e-mailing list is often called **spam.**[17] Typical spam consists of a product ad sent to all of the users on an e-mailing list or all of the members of a newsgroup.

Spam can waste user time and network bandwidth (the amount of data that can be transmitted within a certain time). It can also impose a burden on an ISP's equipment. For example, Cyber Promotions, Inc., sent bulk e-mail to subscribers of CompuServe, Inc., an ISP. CompuServe subscribers complained to the service about Cyber Promotions's ads, and many canceled their subscriptions. Handling the ads also placed a tremendous burden on CompuServe's equipment. CompuServe told Cyber Promotions to stop using CompuServe's equipment to process and store the ads—in effect, to stop sending the ads to CompuServe subscribers. Ignoring this demand, Cyber Promotions stepped up the volume of its ads. After CompuServe attempted unsuccessfully to block the flow with screening software, it filed a suit against Cyber Promotions in a federal district court, seeking an injunction on the ground that the ads constituted trespass to personal property. The court agreed and ordered Cyber Promotions to stop sending its ads to e-mail addresses maintained by CompuServe.[18]

Because of the problems associated with spam, some states have taken steps to prohibit or regulate its use. For example, a few states, such as Washington, prohibit unsolicited e-mail that has the purpose of promoting goods, services, or real estate for sale or lease. In California, an unsolicited e-mail ad must state in its subject line that it is an ad ("ADV:"). The ad must also include a toll-free phone number or return e-mail address through which the recipient can contact the sender to request that no more ads be e-mailed.[19] An Internet service provider (ISP) can bring a successful suit in a California state court against a spammer who violates the ISP's policy that prohibits or restricts unsolicited e-mail ads. The court can award damages of up to $25,000 per day.[20] The Internet is a public forum, however, and thus free speech issues may be involved—see Chapter 4.

14. *Stoner v. eBay,* Cal.Super.Ct. 2000. For further details on this unpublished decision, see "California Judge Finds eBay Immune under CDA," *e-commerce Law & Strategy,* November 2000, p. 9.

15. *Does v. Hvide,* 770 So.2d 1237 (Fla.App.3d 2000).

16. *Graham v. Oppenheimer* (E.D. Va. 2000). For details on this unpublished decision, see "Net Libel Verdict Is Upheld," *The National Law Journal,* December 25, 2000, p. A19.

17. The term *spam* is said to come from a Monty Python song with the lyrics, "Spam spam spam spam, spam spam spam spam, lovely spam, wonderful spam." Like these lyrics, spam online is often considered to be a repetition of worthless text.

18. *CompuServe, Inc. v. Cyber Promotions, Inc.,* 962 F.Supp.2d 1015 (S.D.Ohio 1997).

19. Ca. Bus. & Prof. Code Section 17538.4.

20. Ca. Bus. & Prof. Code Section 17538.45.

WHO SHOULD BE HELD LIABLE FOR COMPUTER VIRUSES?

As everybody knows, viruses sent into cyberspace can cause significant damage to computer systems "infected" by the viruses. To date, adapting tort law to virus-caused damages has been difficult because it is not all that clear who should be held liable for these damages. For example, who should be held liable for damages caused by the "ILOVEYOU" virus that spread around the globe in 2000 and caused an estimated $10 billion in damages? Of course, the person who wrote the virus is responsible. But what about the producer of the e-mail software that the virus accessed to spread itself so rapidly? What about the antivirus software companies? Were they negligent in failing to market products that were capable of identifying and disabling the virus before damage occurred? Another question is whether the users themselves should share part of the blame. After all, even after the virus had received widespread publicity, users continued to open e-mail attachments containing the virus.

Generally, determining what tort duties apply in cyberspace and the point at which one of those duties is breached is not an easy task for the courts.

TERMS AND CONCEPTS TO REVIEW

CHAPTER SUMMARY

Intentional Torts against Persons and Business	**1.** *Assault and battery*—An assault is an unexcused and intentional act that causes another person to be apprehensive of immediate harm. A battery is an assault that results in physical contact. **2.** *False imprisonment*—The intentional confinement or restraint of another person's movement without justification. **3.** *Intentional infliction of emotional distress*—An intentional act that amounts to extreme and outrageous conduct resulting in severe emotional distress to another.

CHAPTER SUMMARY—CONTINUED

Intentional Torts against Persons and Business Relationships —continued	**4.** *Defamation*—A false statement of fact, not made under privilege, that is communicated to a third person and that causes damage to a person's reputation. For public figures, the plaintiff must also prove actual malice. **5.** *Invasion of privacy*—The use of a person's name or likeness for commercial purposes without permission, wrongful intrusion into a person's private activities, publication of information that places a person in a false light, or disclosure of private facts that an ordinary person would find objectionable. **6.** *Appropriation*—The use of another person's name, likeness, or other identifying characteristic, without permission and for the benefit of the user. **7.** *Fraudulent misrepresentation*—A false representation made by one party, through misstatement of facts or through conduct, with the intention of deceiving another and on which the other reasonably relies to his or her detriment. **8.** *Wrongful interference*—The knowing, intentional interference by a third party with an enforceable contractual relationship or an established business relationship between other parties for the purpose of advancing the economic interests of the third party.
Intentional Torts against Property	**1.** *Trespass to land*—The invasion of another's real property without consent or privilege. Specific rights and duties apply once a person is expressly or impliedly established as a trespasser. **2.** *Trespass to personal property*—Unlawfully damaging or interfering with the owner's right to use, possess, or enjoy his or her personal property. **3.** *Conversion*—A wrongful act in which personal property is taken from its rightful owner or possessor and placed in the service of another. **4.** *Disparagement of property*—Any economically injurious falsehood that is made about another's product or property; an inclusive term for the torts of *slander of quality* and *slander of title*.
Negligence	**1.** *Definition of negligence*—The careless performance of a legally required duty or the failure to perform a legally required act. Elements that must be proved are that a legal duty of care exists, that the defendant breached that duty, and that the breach caused damage or injury to another. **2.** *Defenses to negligence*—The basic affirmative defenses in negligence cases are (a) assumption of risk, (b) superseding cause, (c) contributory negligence, and (d) comparative negligence. **3.** *Special negligence doctrines and statutes*— **a.** *Res ipsa loquitur*—A doctrine under which a plaintiff need not prove negligence on the part of the defendant because "the facts speak for themselves." **b.** Negligence *per se*—A type of negligence that may occur if a person violates a statute or an ordinance providing for a criminal penalty and the violation causes another to be injured. **c.** Special negligence statutes—State statutes that prescribe duties and responsibilities in certain circumstances, the violation of which will impose civil liability. Dram shop acts and Good Samaritan statutes are examples of special negligence statutes.
Cyber Torts	General tort principles are being extended to cover cyber torts, or torts that occur in cyberspace, such as online defamation or spamming (which may constitute trespass to personal property). Federal and state statutes may also apply to certain forms of cyber torts. For example, under the federal Communications Decency Act of 1996, Internet service providers (ISPs) are not liable for defamatory messages posted by their subscribers. Some states restrict the use of direct e-mail, or spam. Certain types of online wrongs, such as the transmission of computer viruses, pose unique legal challenges.

CASES FOR ANALYSIS

Westlaw. You can access the full text of each case presented below by going to the Westlaw cases on this text's Web site at http://wbl-cs.westbuslaw.com. Each Westlaw case includes the names of all plaintiffs and defendants, the dates on which the case was argued and decided, a brief summary of the issues and decisions in the case, headnotes classifiying specific issues in the case according to the West Key Number System, and the court's opinion. Concurring and dissenting opinions, if any, are included as well.

CASE 5.1 INTENTIONAL INFLICTION OF EMOTIONAL DISTRESS

ROACH V. STERN

Supreme Court of New York,
Appellate Division,
Second Department, 1998.
252 A.D.2d 488,
675 N.Y.S.2d 133.

MEMORANDUM BY THE COURT.

* * * *

This lawsuit concerns events that occurred during a radio show hosted by the defendant Howard Stern, which was videotaped and later aired on a cable television station. The participants in the program handled and made crude remarks about the cremated remains of the plaintiffs' sister, Deborah Roach. We conclude that the plaintiffs have sufficiently pleaded a cause of action to recover damages for the intentional infliction of emotional distress and therefore the [lower court] erred in dismissing their complaint.

The deceased, Deborah Roach, who used the name Debbie Tay, was described in a newspaper article following her death as a topless dancer, cable-access TV host, and perennial guest on Howard Stern's radio show. Stern gave her the label "Space Lesbian" based on her stories of encounters with aliens. After Tay's death in April 1995 her sister, the plaintiff Melissa Roach Driscol, had the body cremated and gave a portion of the remains to the defendant Chaunce Hayden, Tay's close friend. Driscol asserted that she did so with the understanding that Hayden would "preserve and honor said remains in an appropriate and private manner."

According to the complaint, sometime in July 1995 Hayden engaged in certain "on air" conversations with Stern during his radio show about Tay's death and the disposition of her remains. Upon learning that Stern had encouraged Hayden to appear on the radio show and to bring Tay's remains with him, her brother, the plaintiff Jeff Roach, telephoned the producer of the show and the manager of the radio station to demand that such conversations cease. Nevertheless, on July 18, 1995, Hayden brought a box containing Tay's cremated remains to the radio station. Thereafter Stern, Hayden, and other participants in the broadcast made comments about the remains while handling various bone fragments. The radio show was videotaped and later broadcast on a national cable television station.

The transcript and videotape of the show, which were made available to the court, corroborate the allegations in the complaint that Stern at one point donned rubber gloves and held up certain bone fragments while he guessed whether they came from Tay's skull or ribs. * * *

The plaintiffs commenced this action against Stern, Infinity Broadcasting, Inc. (hereinafter Infinity), the owner of the radio station, and Hayden, in which they alleged, *inter alia,* that the defendants' conduct caused them severe emotional distress. Stern and Infinity moved to dismiss the complaint * * * on the ground that the allegations failed to state a cause of action. The Supreme Court granted the motion and dismissed the complaint.

We agree with the Supreme Court that the allegations in the complaint fail to state a cause of action against the moving defendants to recover damages for interference with or mishandling of a corpse. In general, such a cause of action requires a showing of interference with the right of the next-of-kin to dispose of the body. The moving defendants did not interfere with the plaintiffs' decision to cremate the body and divide the ashes with Hayden.

The Supreme Court further determined that, while the conduct complained of in the complaint was "vulgar and disrespectful," it did not rise to the level of outrageousness necessary to maintain a cause of action to recover damages for the intentional infliction of emotional distress. In order to impose liability for this intentional tort, the conduct complained of must be so outrageous in character, and so extreme in degree, as to go beyond all possible bounds of decency, and to be regarded as atrocious, and utterly intolerable in a civilized community. *The element of outrageous conduct is rigorous, and difficult to satisfy, and its purpose is to filter out trivial complaints and assure that the claim of severe emotional distress is genuine.* A court may determine, as a matter of law, that the alleged behavior is not sufficiently outrageous to warrant the imposition of liability. [Emphasis added.]

Upon our review of the allegations in the case at bar, we conclude that the Supreme Court erred in determining that the element of outrageous conduct was not satisfied as a matter of law. Although the defendants contend that the conduct at issue was not particularly shocking, in light of Stern's reputation for vulgar humor and Tay's actions during her guest appearances on his program, a jury might reasonably conclude that the manner in which Tay's remains were handled, for entertainment purposes and against the express wishes of her family, went beyond the bounds of decent behavior.

We further conclude that the remaining elements necessary to establish a cause of action to recover damages for the intentional infliction of emotional distress were also sufficiently pleaded in the complaint.

Accordingly, the appellants' motion to dismiss the complaint is denied.

KRAUSMAN, J., dissents and votes to affirm the order appealed from, with the following memorandum:

The majority decision amply demonstrates that Howard Stern and his cohorts behaved in a manner that some would find inappropriate when Chaunce Hayden came on the show with the decedent's remains. Certainly, many would consider their remarks and conduct in handling the decedent's remains tasteless, offensive, and insensitive to the feelings of the plaintiffs, who lost their sister to a drug overdose at the age of 27. However, I disagree with the majority's view that Stern's actions give rise to a cognizable legal right to recover damages for emotional distress.

At common law, emotional injury was not recognized as an independent basis for the recovery of damages, primarily because of the ease with which emotional injury could be feigned without detection. While modern tort law now permits recovery for emotional distress, the historical reluctance to allow damages for purely psychic injury is reflected in the formulation of the tort, which demands a showing that the defendant has engaged in extreme and outrageous conduct, with the intent to cause, or disregard of a substantial possibility of causing, severe emotional distress.

* * * [T]he first element—outrageous conduct—serves the dual function of filtering out petty and trivial complaints that do not belong in court, and assuring that plaintiff's claim of severe emotional distress is genuine * * * . In practice, courts have tended to focus on the outrageousness element, the one most susceptible to determination as a matter of law. * * * Indeed, liability has been found only where the conduct has been so outrageous in character, and so extreme in degree, as to go beyond all possible bounds of decency, and to be regarded as atrocious, and utterly intolerable in a civilized community.

The issue of whether the decedent's brother and sister may recover tort damages cannot be considered in a vacuum, with total disregard for who Debbie Tay was. Debbie Tay rose to fame by spinning outrageous tales of sexual encounters with female aliens on the Howard Stern show, and used the notoriety she had achieved to launch her own cable access show. While the plaintiffs now claim that Stern's conduct following their sister's untimely death caused them extreme emotional distress, the defendants note that on one occasion, the decedent's own mother appeared on the show, describing her daughter as an unusual young woman who was "a lot of fun."

The record also reflects the fact that the plaintiff Melissa Roach Driscoll voluntarily gave a portion of her sister's remains to the decedent's close friend, the defendant Chaunce Hayden. Hayden brought the decedent's remains on the air as a memorial to her because "the only happiness Debbie had was the Howard Stern show." Once on the air, Hayden encouraged cast members to examine the remains, believing that since the decedent had so enjoyed Stern's irreverent brand of humor during her lifetime, she "would love this." Although the plaintiffs allege that the show's producer ignored their request to cease discussing the disposition of the remains, there is no indication that Stern or Infinity acted out of a desire to cause the plaintiffs distress. Indeed, at the end of the show, Stern advised Hayden that he should have the decedent's remains properly buried or turned into ashes, telling him to "remember her in your mind." Closing credits announced that the show was "dedicated in loving memory of Debbie Tay." Considering these circumstances, I would find, as a matter of law, that the conduct of Stern and Infinity was not so extreme and outrageous in nature as to be "utterly intolerable in a civilized community."

CASE 5.2 INVASION OF PRIVACY

TIBERINO v. SPOKANE COUNTY

Court of Appeals of Washington,
Division 3, 2000.
13 P.3d 1104.

KURTZ, C.J. [Chief Judge]

* * * *

On August 26, 1998, Gina Tiberino was hired as a secretary in the [Spokane County] Prosecuting Attorney's Office and assigned to the Special Assault Unit. Spokane County provided Ms. Tiberino with a personal computer equipped with electronic communications applications (e-mail). As part of her employee orientation, Ms. Tiberino attended a program that advised employees about their use of electronic communications. Employees were told that (i) Spokane County Information Systems Department had the capability of monitoring all e-mail; (ii) not to put anything on e-mail that they would not want on the front page of the newspaper, and (iii) County equipment was not for personal use. These admonitions were consistent with e-mail policies formally adopted by both the County and the Prosecutor.

In the early part of October 1998, the Prosecutor's Office Administrator, Travis Jones, received complaints from Ms. Tiberino's co-workers that she was using her computer to send personal e-mail via the Internet. One co-worker indicated that excessive amounts of personal e-mail were being sent by Ms. Tiberino and that the e-mail contained coarse and vulgar language. On October 13, 1998, Mr. Jones observed that when Ms. Tiberino left for the day, she failed to turn off her computer. As a result of the complaints from her co-workers, he viewed her "sent" mail folder.

Mr. Jones did not read the contents of all Ms. Tiberino's e-mail, but only randomly selected e-mail messages to determine whether or not they were work-related or of a personal nature. The "sent" mail folder revealed that approximately 214 e-mail messages had been sent. Of those messages, 200 were sent via the Internet to Ms. Tiberino's sister or mother. Approximately 10 to 15 appeared to be work-related. Mr. Jones recommended to Ms. Tiberino's supervisor that she be given an Event Report reminding her that County computers were not to be used for personal business and informing her that the volume of her personal e-mail strongly suggested that she was compromising her job responsibilities.

On November 10, 1998, Ms. Tiberino was discharged for unsatisfactory work performance. At the time of her discharge, Ms. Tiberino was told that she had alienated co-workers with her preoccupation with personal issues. Specifically, she was told that her co-workers resented performing her assigned job responsibilities while she was spending her time using the e-mail for nonbusiness purposes.

* * * *

On December 1, 1998, Ms. Tiberino's attorney sent a letter to the Prosecutor's Office claiming that Ms. Tiberino had been unlawfully discharged and demanding reinstatement. The letter threatened litigation. Ms. Tiberino ultimately filed a complaint with the Washington State Human Rights Commission.

As a result of Ms. Tiberino's threatened litigation, the Prosecutor's Office printed all e-mails in Ms. Tiberino's "sent" mail folder. The "sent" mail folder now contained 551 sent items. Of those, 467 were personal messages sent to a total of five addresses. Each of the 467 messages were time-stamped over a 40 working-day time frame between September 18, 1998, and November 10, 1998.

On December 16, 1998, a reporter for Cowles Publishing Company made a public record request to the Prosecutor's Office requesting release and copies of all e-mail correspondence received and generated by Ms. Tiberino. Thereafter, the Prosecutor's Office advised Ms. Tiberino's attorney that the 3,805 paginated/printed e-mails, with 147 pages redacted [edited; prepared for publication] in whole or in part, would be made available to the newspaper. However, Ms. Tiberino was afforded sufficient time to obtain injunctive relief to prohibit the release of her e-mails.

At Ms. Tiberino's request, [a state] court issued a temporary restraining order preventing the Prosecutor from releasing her e-mail. * * * Following oral argument and [a] review performed at the request of the Prosecutor, the * * * court held that Ms. Tiberino's e-mail communications were public records and, except for the 147 redacted [edited] pages, were subject to disclosure * * * .

* * * Ms. Tiberino filed this appeal * * * .

* * * *

* * * In reviewing an agency's action with regard to a public disclosure request, we must consider the [state] public records act's policy that "free and open examination of public records is in the public interest, even though such examination may cause inconvenience or embarrassment[.]" * * *

Generally, the Act requires disclosure of public records by governmental entities upon request unless exempted.

A "public record," subject to disclosure under the Act

> includes [1] any writing [2] containing information relating to the conduct of government or the performance of any governmental or proprietary function [3] prepared, owned, used, or retained by any state or local agency regardless of physical form or characteristics.

Ms. Tiberino does not dispute that the e-mail records are writings and that they are prepared, owned, used or retained by a state agency. She contends that the e-mails are not "public records" because the second element of the definition of public record is not met. She argues that the e-mails do not contain any information relating to the conduct of governmental or proprietary function.

* * *

Ms. Tiberino's excessive personal use of e-mail was a reason for her discharge. The County printed the e-mails in preparation for litigation over her termination, a proprietary function. Consequently, they contain information relating to the conduct of a governmental or proprietary function. The second element is met and the e-mails are "public records" within the scope of the public records act.

* * * *

Once documents are determined to be within the scope of the Act, disclosure is required unless a specific statutory exemption is applicable. Ms. Tiberino contends that even if her e-mails are public records, they are exempt from disclosure * * * .

* * * *

A person's right to privacy is violated only if disclosure of information about the person: (1) [w]ould be highly offensive to a reasonable person, and (2) is not of legitimate concern to the public. * * *

* * * *

The right of privacy applies only to the intimate details of one's personal and private life. * * *

Ms. Tiberino argues that the purely personal nature of her e-mails to her mother, sister and friends makes it clear that public disclosure would be highly offensive to any reasonable person. Ms. Tiberino's e-mails contain intimate details about her personal and private life and do not discuss specific instances of misconduct. An individual has a privacy interest whenever information which reveals unique facts about those named is linked to an identifiable individual. * * * Any reasonable person would find disclosure of Ms. Tiberino's e-mails to be highly offensive.

* * * *

For the e-mails to be exempt from disclosure, Ms. Tiberino must also show that the public has no legitimate concern requiring release of the e-mails. Ms. Tiberino contends that the disclosure of private e-mails could decrease the efficiency and morale of government employees. The County argues that the County employees were on notice that the computers should not be used for personal business, so the disclosure of their e-mail would not affect the efficient administration of government.

* * * *

Generally, records of governmental agency expenditures for employee salaries, including vacation and sick leave, and taxpayer-funded benefits are of legitimate public interest and therefore not exempt from disclosure. Certainly, there exists a reasonable concern by the public that government conduct itself fairly and use public funds responsibly.

* * * *

However, * * * [t]he content of Ms. Tiberino's e-mails is personal and is unrelated to governmental operations. Certainly, the public has an interest in seeing that public employees are not spending their time on the public payroll pursuing personal interests. But it is the amount of time spent on personal matters, not the content of personal e-mails or phone calls or conversations, that is of public interest. The fact that Ms. Tiberino sent 467 e-mails over a 40 working-day time frame is of significance in her termination action and the public has a legitimate interest in having that information. But what she said in those e-mails is of no public significance. The public has no legitimate concern requiring release of the e-mails and they should be exempt from disclosure.

* * * *

Reversed.

CASE 5.3 DUTY OF CARE

MARTIN v. WAL-MART STORES, INC.

United States Court of Appeals,
Eighth Circuit, 1999.
183 F.3d 770.

BEAM, Circuit Judge.

* * * *

* * * Harold Martin was shopping in the sporting goods department of Wal-Mart on the afternoon of September 16, 1993. In front of the sporting goods section, in the store's main aisle, called the "action alley," there was a large display consisting of several pallets stacked with cases of shotgun shells. On top of the cases were individual boxes of shells. As Martin walked past the display with his shopping cart, he slipped on some loose shotgun shell pellets and fell to the floor. Martin lost both feeling [in] and control of his legs. Sensation and control soon returned. However, during the following week, he lost the use of his legs several times, and the paralysis would last for ten to fifteen minutes. Following the last paralytic episode, sensation and control did not return to the front half of his left foot. Martin's doctors have diagnosed the condition as permanent and can offer no treatment.

Just prior to Martin's fall, a Wal-Mart employee walked past the display in the same area where Martin fell. At the time, the sporting goods department should have been staffed with two people, however, only one was in the department. Martin had been in the sporting goods department for ten to fifteen minutes prior to his fall and did not notice anyone handling or tampering with the shotgun shells.

After Martin's fall, the sporting goods clerk searched for the source of the pellets and found a box of shells with one shell missing, and a single shell sitting on top of the display with some of the pellets missing. These were given to his manager. However, Wal-Mart lost the shell and it was unavailable as an exhibit at trial.

* * * *

A United States District Court sitting in diversity jurisdiction applies the substantive law of the forum state, in this case, Missouri. The parties dispute the proper interpretation and application of Missouri law pertaining to slip and fall cases. * * * [T]he traditional rule * * * required a plaintiff in a slip and fall case to establish that the defendant store had either actual or constructive notice of the dangerous condition. The defendant store is deemed to have actual notice if it is shown that an employee created or was aware of the hazard. Constructive notice could be established by showing that the dangerous condition had existed for a sufficient length of time that the defendant should reasonably have known about it.

* * * *

* * * [R]etail store operations have evolved since the traditional liability rules were established. In modern self-service stores, customers are invited to traverse the same aisles used by the clerks to replenish stock, they are invited to retrieve merchandise from displays for inspection, and to place it back in the display if the item is not selected for purchase. Further, a customer is enticed to look at the displays, thus reducing the chance that the customer will be watchful of hazards on the floor. The storeowner necessarily knows that customers may take merchandise into their hands and may then lay articles that no longer interest them down in the aisle * * * . The storeowner, therefore, must anticipate and must exercise due care to guard against dangers from articles left in the aisle. The risk of items creating dangerous conditions on the floor, previously created by employees, is now created by other customers as a result of the store's decision to employ the self-service mode of operation. Therefore, an owner of a self-service operation has actual notice of these problems. In choosing a self-service method of providing items, he [or she] is charged with the knowledge of the foreseeable risks inherent in such a mode of operation. Thus, in slip and fall cases in self-service stores, the inquiry of whether the danger existed long enough that the store should have reasonably known of it (constructive notice) is made in light of the fact that the store has notice that certain dangers arising through customer involvement are likely to occur, and the store has a duty to anticipate them.

Because of this self-service exception, * * * the precise amount of time a dangerous substance has been on the floor will not be so important a factor. More important will be the method of merchandising and the nature of the article causing the injury. The amount of time is even less important if there is evidence that employees of the store were regularly in the area where the accident occurred.

* * * *

Wal-Mart * * * claims that Martin failed to * * * establish that Wal-Mart had actual or constructive notice of the pellets in the action aisle. We disagree. We find there is substantial evidence of constructive notice in the record. Martin slipped on shotgun shell pellets on the floor which were next to a large display of shotgun shells immediately abutting the sporting goods department. *The chance that merchandise will wind up on the floor (or merchandise will be spilled on the floor) in the department in which that merchandise is sold or displayed is exactly the type of foreseeable risk [that is part of the self-service exception to the traditional rule].* Under [this exception] Wal-Mart has notice that merchandise is likely to find its way to the floor and create a dangerous condition, and it must exercise due care to discover this hazard and warn customers or protect them from the danger. Watching for hazards on the floor is part of the job duties of every Wal-Mart employee. They are trained to anticipate and protect customers from these hazards. The sporting goods department was understaffed at the time. Five minutes before Martin fell, the sporting goods clerk had walked through the same part of the aisle where the fall occurred. Just before Martin fell, a Wal-Mart employee walked through the same area and did not notice the hazard, or did nothing about it. The sporting goods clerk testified that the pellets could have been on the floor for up to an hour. The department was not extremely busy, and though the clerk had inspected and straightened up the exercise equipment area, he had not inspected the display in the action aisle. The black pellets were scattered on a white tile floor with gray stripes. The display and the pellets were in the action alley, the highest traffic area of the store, where the risk was presumably greatest, thus calling for greater vigilance in order to meet the standard of ordinary care. Even assuming that the hazard was created by a customer, a jury could easily find, given that it had notice that merchandise is often mishandled or mislaid by customers in a manner that can create dangerous conditions, that, had Wal-Mart exercised due care under the circumstances, it would have discovered the shotgun pellets on the floor. [Emphasis added.]

* * * *

For the foregoing reasons, the judgment of the district court is affirmed.

CASE 5.4 FORESEEABILITY AND PROXIMATE CAUSE

PALSGRAF V. LONG ISLAND RAILROAD CO.

Court of Appeals of New York, 1928.
248 N.Y. 339,
162 N.E. 99.

CARDOZO, C. J. [Chief Justice].

Plaintiff was standing on a platform of defendant's railroad after buying a ticket to go to Rockaway Beach. A train stopped at the station, bound for another place. Two men ran forward to catch it. One of the men reached the platform of the car without mishap, though the train was already moving. The other man, carrying a package, jumped aboard the car, but seemed unsteady as if about to fall. A guard on the car, who had held the door open, reached forward to help him in, and another guard on the platform pushed him from behind. In this act, the package was dislodged, and fell upon the rails. It was a package of small size, about fifteen inches long, and was covered by a newspaper. In fact it contained fireworks, but there was nothing in its appearance to give notice of its contents. The fireworks when they fell exploded. The shock of the explosion threw down some scales at the other end of the platform many feet away. The scales struck the plaintiff, causing injuries for which she sues.

The conduct of the defendant's guard, if a wrong in its relation to the holder of the package, was not a wrong in its relation to the plaintiff, standing far away. Relatively to her it was not negligence at all. Nothing in the situation gave notice that the falling package had in it the potency of peril to persons thus removed. Negligence is not actionable unless it involves the invasion of a legally protected interest, the violation of a right. Proof of negligence in the air, so to speak, will not do. Negligence is the absence of care, according to the circumstances. The plaintiff, as she stood upon the platform of the station, might claim to be protected against intentional invasion of her bodily security. Such invasion is not charged. She might claim to be protected against unintentional invasion by conduct involving in the thought of reasonable men an unreasonable hazard that such invasion would ensue. These, from the point of view of the law, were the bounds of her immunity, with perhaps some rare exceptions, survivals for the most part of ancient forms of liability, where conduct is held to be at the peril of the actor. If no hazard was apparent to the eye of ordinary vigilance, an act innocent and harmless, at least to outward seeming, with reference to her, did not take to itself the quality of a tort because it happened to be a wrong, though apparently not one involving the risk of bodily insecurity, with reference to some one else. *In every instance, before negligence can be predicated of a given act, back of the act must be sought and found a duty to the individual complaining, the observance of which would have averted or avoided the injury.* The ideas of negligence and duty are strictly correlative. The plaintiff sues in her own right for a wrong personal to her, and not as the vicarious beneficiary of a breach of duty to another. [Emphasis added.]

* * * *

The argument for the plaintiff is built upon the shifting meanings of such words as "wrong" and "wrongful," and shares their instability. What the plaintiff must show is "a wrong" to herself; i. e., a violation of her own right, and not merely a wrong to some one else, nor conduct "wrongful" because unsocial, but not "a wrong" to any one. We are told that one who drives at reckless speed through a crowded city street is guilty of a negligent act and therefore of a wrongful one, irrespective of the consequences. Negligent the act is, and wrongful in the sense that it is unsocial, but wrongful and unsocial in relation to other travelers, only because the eye of vigilance perceives the risk of damage. If the same act were to be committed on a speedway or a race course, it would lose its wrongful quality. The risk reasonably to be perceived defines the duty to be obeyed, and risk imports relation; it is risk to another or to others within the range of apprehension. This does not mean, of course, that one who launches a destructive force is always relieved of liability, if the force, though known to be destructive, pursues an unexpected path. It was not necessary that the defendant should have had notice of the particular method in which an accident would occur, if the possibility of an accident was clear to the ordinarily prudent eye. Some acts, such as shooting are so imminently dangerous to any one who may come within reach of the missile however unexpectedly, as to impose a duty of prevision not far from that of an insurer. * * * Here, * * * there was nothing in the situation to suggest to the most cautious mind that the parcel wrapped in newspaper would spread wreckage through the station. If the guard had thrown it down knowingly and willfully, he would not have threatened the plaintiff's safety, so far as appearances could warn him. His conduct would not have involved, even then, an unreasonable probability of invasion of her bodily security. Liability can be no greater where the act is inadvertent.

Negligence, like risk, is thus a term of relation. Negligence in the abstract, apart from things related, is surely not a tort, if indeed it is understandable at all. Negligence is not a tort unless it results in the commission of a wrong, and the commission of a wrong imports the violation of a right, in this case, we are told, the right to be protected against interference with one's bodily security. But bodily security is protected, not against all forms of interference or aggression, but only against some. One who seeks redress at law does not make out a cause of action by showing without more that there has been damage to his person. If the harm was not willful, he must show that the act as to him had possibilities of danger so many and apparent as to entitle him to be protected against the doing of it though the harm was unintended. Affront to personality is still the keynote of the wrong. * * *

The law of causation, remote or proximate, is thus foreign to the case before us. The question of liability is always anterior to the question of the measure of the consequences that go with liability. If there is no tort to be redressed, there is no occasion to consider what damage might be recovered if there were a finding of a tort. * * *

The judgment of the [state intermediate appellate court] and that of the [trial court] should be reversed, and the complaint dismissed, with costs in all courts.

ANDREWS, J. [Justice] (dissenting).

* * * *

* * * [W]hen injuries * * * result from our unlawful act, we are liable for the consequences. It does not matter that they are unusual, unexpected, unforeseen, and unforeseeable. But there is one limitation. The damages must be so connected with the negligence that the latter may be said to be the proximate cause of the former.

* * * *

* * * What we * * * mean by the word "proximate" is that, because of convenience, of public policy, of a rough sense of justice, the law arbitrarily declines to trace a series of events beyond a certain point. This is not logic. It is practical politics. Take our rule as to fires. Sparks from my burning haystack set on fire my house and my neighbor's. I may recover from a negligent railroad. He may not. Yet the wrongful act as directly harmed the one as the other. We may regret that the line was drawn just where it was, but drawn somewhere it had to be. We said the act of the railroad was not the proximate cause of our neighbor's fire. Cause it surely was. The words we used were simply indicative of our notions of public policy. * * *

* * * *

* * * The act upon which defendant's liability rests is knocking an apparently harmless package onto the platform. The act was negligent. For its proximate consequences the defendant is liable. If its contents were broken, to the owner; if it fell upon and crushed a passenger's foot, then to him; if it exploded and injured one in the immediate vicinity, to him also as to A in the illustration. Mrs. Palsgraf was standing some distance away. How far cannot be told from the record—apparently 25 or 30 feet, perhaps less. Except for the explosion, she would not have been injured. We are told by the appellant in his brief, "It cannot be denied that the explosion was the direct cause of the plaintiff's injuries." So it was a substantial factor in producing the result—there was here a natural and continuous sequence—direct connection. The only intervening cause was that, instead of blowing her to the ground, the concussion smashed the weighing machine which in turn fell upon her. There was no remoteness in time, little in space. And surely, given such an explosion as here, it needed no great foresight to predict that the natural result would be to injure one on the platform at no greater distance from its scene than was the plaintiff. Just how no one might be able to predict. Whether by flying fragments, by broken glass, by wreckage of machines or structures no one could say. But injury in some form was most probable.

Under these circumstances I cannot say as a matter of law that the plaintiff's injuries were not the proximate result of the negligence. * * *

The judgment appealed from should be affirmed, with costs.

CASE PROBLEMS

5–1. Jim Meads had a VISA credit-card account with Citibank, a subsidiary of Citicorp. Meads fell behind in his payments on the $5,000 owing on the account, and in July 1986 Citibank closed Meads's account and notified him that the account would be referred to the Collection Group of Citicorp Credit Services, Inc. (CCSI), for collection. Thereafter, Meads wrote to CCSI, explaining that because of medical problems and related medical expenses, he was unable to meet the minimum-payment requirements but would make partial payments on the account. Meads's attorney also wrote to CCSI, requesting that CCSI not contact Meads again about the account and instead direct all future inquiries to the attorney's office. Nevertheless, CCSI continued to contact Meads, by telephone and letter, at frequent intervals (at times more often than once per week) over a four-month period. Calls were made not only to Meads's home but also to his place of work. Meads alleged that the callers were so abusive as to reduce his wife to tears. Meads finally sued CCSI for intentional infliction of emotional distress. Although Meads did not deny the validity of his debt to Citicorp, he felt that the collection attempts were abusive and stated that both he and his wife had suffered verifiable emotional and physical problems as a direct result of the actions of CCSI. Was CCSI's conduct sufficiently outrageous to warrant an emotional distress claim? [*Meads v. Citicorp Credit Services, Inc.*, 686 F.Supp. 330 (S.D.Ga. 1988)]

5–2. George Giles was staying at a Detroit hotel owned by the Pick Hotels Corp. While a hotel employee was removing luggage from the back seat of Giles's car, Giles reached into the front seat to remove his briefcase. As he did so, he supported himself by placing his left hand on the center pillar to which the rear door was hinged, with his fingers in a position to be injured if the rear door was closed. The hotel employee closed the rear door, and a part of Giles's left index finger was amputated. Giles sued the hotel for damages. The hotel claimed that it was not liable because Giles, by placing his hand on the car as he did, contributed to the injury. (Under state law, contributory negligence was an absolute defense to liability.) Discuss whether the hotel will succeed in its defense. [*Giles v. Pick Hotels Corp.*, 232 F.2d 887 (6th Cir. 1956)]

5–3. While Charles and Esther Kveragas were in a rented motel room at the Scottish Inns, Inc., in Knoxville, Tennessee, three intruders kicked open the door, shot Charles, and injured Esther. The intruders also took $3,000 belonging to the Kveragases. The Kveragases brought an action against the motel owners, claiming that the owners had been negligent in failing to provide adequately for the safety of the motel's guests. At trial, the evidence showed that the door had a hollow core and that it fit poorly into the door frame. There was no deadbolt lock on the door, although such locks were easily available and commonly used in motels. The only lock on the door was one fitted into the door handle, which was described as a grade three lock, although a security chain was attached to the door. The Kveragases had both locked and chained the door, but still, a single kick on the part of the intruders was all that was necessary to open it. Evidence at trial also indicated that a deadbolt lock would have withstood the force that was applied to the door. Did the motel owners have a duty to protect their guests from criminal acts on the motel premises, and if so, did the owners breach that duty of care by failing to provide more secure locks on the doors of the motel rooms? [*Kveragas v. Scottish Inns, Inc.*, 733 F.2d 409 (6th Cir. 1984)]

5–4. George Ward entered a K-Mart department store in Champaign, Illinois, through a service entrance near the home improvements department. After purchasing a large mirror, Ward left the store through the same door. On his way out the door, carrying the large mirror in front and somewhat to the side of him, he collided with a concrete pole located just outside the door about a foot and a half from the outside wall. The mirror broke, and the broken glass cut his right cheek and eye, resulting in reduced vision in that eye. He later stated that he had not seen the pole, had not realized what was happening, and only knew that he felt "a bad pain, and then saw stars." Ward sued K-Mart Corp. for damages, alleging that the store was negligent. The issue before the court is whether the store should have foreseen the risk to its customers posed by the poles and guarded against it. What should the court decide? Discuss fully. [*Ward v. K-Mart Corp.*, 136 Ill.2d 132, 554 N.E.2d 223, 143 Ill.Dec. 288 (1990)]

5–5. Lofton Johnson, a police officer employed by the West Virginia University Security Police, was called to the emergency room of the university's hospital to help subdue an unruly patient. Prior to Johnson's arrival, the patient had informed the doctors and nurses in the emergency room that he was infected with acquired immune deficiency syndrome (AIDS). While Johnson assisted medical personnel in restraining the patient, the patient bit Johnson on the forearm. The patient had previously bitten himself, and his blood was in and around his mouth when he bit Johnson. On previous occasions, the officer had assisted in restraining AIDS patients, but it was always the hospital's procedure to inform him that these patients were infected with AIDS so that proper precautions could be taken. The hospital did not inform Johnson on this occasion, however. Although Johnson tested negative for AIDS on several subsequent occasions, he claimed that he suffered severe emotional distress as a result of the AIDS exposure—he was shunned by his family and co-workers and generally felt like a social outcast with an uncertain future. In his suit against the hospital to recover for emotional distress, what will the court decide? Explain. [*Johnson v. West Virginia University Hospitals, Inc.*, 186 W.Va. 648, 413 S.E.2d 889 (1991)]

5–6. In 1963, Pacific Gas and Electric Co. (PG&E) entered into a contract with the Placer County Water Agency (Agency) under which PG&E would purchase hydroelectric power from the Agency. The contract provided that the agreement would terminate in the year 2013 or at the end of the year in which the Agency completed the retirement of its project bonds, whichever occurred first. As energy prices rose, the Agency wished it could terminate the contract and sell its hydroelectric power in a more favorable market, but it felt it could not do so without breaching its contract with PG&E. Bear Stearns & Co., an investment brokerage firm, approached the Agency and spent several years overcoming the Agency's resistance to making any effort to terminate the contract. Finally it succeeded, and in 1983 the Agency entered into an agreement with Bear Stearns in which Bear Stearns agreed to pay for legal, engineering, and marketing studies on the feasibility of terminating the power contract, in return for 15 percent of any resulting increase in the Agency's revenues above $2.5 million for twenty years. Bear Stearns retained legal counsel to draw up a plan by which the Agency could retire its project bonds and to litigate the question of whether the Agency could terminate the contract. PG&E sued Bear Stearns for tortious interference with PG&E's contract with the Agency. What will the court decide? Explain. [*Pacific Gas and Electric Co. v. Bear Stearns & Co.*, 50 Cal.3d 1118, 270 Cal.Rptr. 1, 791 P.2d 587 (1990)]

5–7. East Bay Limited Partnership purchased a shopping center for the purpose of renovating the center and reselling it to a third party. The purchase was financed through a loan from American General Life & Accident Insurance Co. (American). The parties agreed in writing that during the first six months of the loan, the property could be sold to a buyer approved by the lender and the loan assumed without payment of any fee, but after six months a 1 percent fee would be required. Prepayment of the loan was precluded during the first six years. The written agreement specifically provided that American had the right to approve a proposed buyer based on the buyer's "net worth, credit worthiness and management expertise." About one and a half years into the loan, East Bay requested American's approval to sell the shopping center to the James W. Hall Corp. In a letter to East Bay, American stated that it would not allow Hall to assume the loan because of the "lack of experience of the company buying the property." East Bay wished to pay off the loan in full so that it could then sell the shopping center without American's approval. American told East Bay that the latter could pay the loan in full only if a prepayment fee of 24.25 percent was paid. In the end there was no sale and no prepayment. East Bay went into default, and American obtained ownership rights in the shopping center, which had been given as security for the loan. East Bay sued American for, among other things, intentional interference with a business relationship and breach of its duty to act in good faith and deal fairly with East Bay. Will the court hold for East Bay on either of these counts? Discuss. [*East Bay Limited Partnership v. American General Life & Accident Insurance Co.*, 744 F.Supp. 1118 (M.D.Fla. 1990)]

5–8. As pedestrians exited at the close of an arts and crafts show, Jason Davis, an employee of the show's producer, stood near the exit. Suddenly and without warning, Davis turned around and collided with Yvonne Esposito, an eighty-year-old woman. Esposito was knocked to the ground, fracturing her hip. After hip-replacement surgery, she was left with a permanent physical impairment. Esposito filed a suit in a federal district court against Davis and others, alleging negligence. What are the factors that indicate whether Davis owed Esposito a duty of care? What do those factors indicate in these circumstances? [*Esposito v. Davis*, 47 F.3d 164 (5th Cir. 1995)]

5–9. A North Carolina Department of Transportation regulation prohibits the placement of telephone booths within public rights of way. Despite this regulation, GTE South, Inc., placed a booth in the right of way near the intersection of Hillsborough and Sparger Roads in Durham County. Laura Baldwin was using the booth when an accident at the intersection caused a dump truck to cross the right of way and smash into the booth. To recover for her injuries, Baldwin filed a suit in a North Carolina state court against GTE and others. Was Baldwin within the class of persons protected by the regulation? If so, did GTE's placement of the booth constitute negligence *per se*? Explain. [*Baldwin v. GTE South, Inc.*, 335 N.C. 544, 439 S.E.2d 108 (1994)]

5–10. On the morning of October 2, 1989, a fire started by an arsonist broke out in the Red Inn in Provincetown, Massachusetts. The inn had smoke detectors, sprinklers, and an alarm system, all of which alerted the guests, but there were no emergency lights or clear exits. Attempting to escape, Deborah Addis and James Reed, guests at the inn, found the first-floor doors and windows locked. Ultimately, they forced open a second-floor window and jumped out. To recover for their injuries, they filed a suit in a Massachusetts state court against Tamerlane Corp., which operated the inn under a lease, and others (including Duane Steele, who worked for the owner of the inn). Under what tort theory discussed in this chapter might Addis and Reed recover damages from Tamerlane and the others? What must they prove to recover damages under this theory? Discuss fully. [*Addis v. Steele*, 38 Mass.App.Ct. 433, 648 N.E.2d 773 (1995)]

5–11. The Oklahoma State Board of Cosmetology inspected the equipment of the Poteau Beauty College and found it to be in satisfactory condition. A month later, Marilyn Sue Weldon, a student at Poteau, was injured when a salon chair failed to work properly. Weldon had washed the hair of a woman with the chair in a reclining position. The chair did not spring back, and due to a previous injury, the client had to be helped into an upright position. The chair was close to a manicure table, and in maneuvering around the table, Weldon twisted her back. Weldon filed a suit in an Oklahoma state court against Poteau and others, claiming in part that the college was negligent. Assuming that Weldon was an invitee, what duty did Poteau, as the owner of the premises, owe to her? On what basis might the court rule that Poteau was not liable? [*Weldon v. Dunn*, 962 P.2d 1273 (Okla.Sup. 1998)]

5–12. The United States Golf Association (USGA) was founded in 1894. In 1911, the USGA developed the Handicap System, which was designed to enable individual golfers of different abilities to compete fairly with one another. The USGA revised the system and implemented new handicap formulas between 1987 and 1993. The USGA permits any entity to use the system free of charge as long as it complies with the USGA's procedure for peer review through authorized golf associations of the handicaps issued to individual golfers. In 1991, Arroyo Software Corp. began marketing software known as EagleTrak, which incorporated the USGA's system, and used its name in Arroyo's ads without the USGA's permission. Arroyo's EagleTrak did not incorporate any means for obtaining peer review of handicap computations. The USGA filed a suit in a California state court against Arroyo, alleging, among other things, misappropriation. The USGA asked the court to stop Arroyo's use of its system. Should the court grant the injunction? Why, or why not? [*United States Golf Association v. Arroyo Software Corp.*, 69 Cal.App.4th 607, 81 Cal.Rptr.2d 708 (1999)]

5–13. Flora Gonzalez visited a Wal-Mart store. While walking in a busy aisle from the store's cafeteria toward a refrigerator, Gonzalez stepped on some macaroni that came from the cafeteria. She slipped and fell, sustaining injuries to her back, shoulder, and knee. She filed a suit in a Texas state court against Wal-Mart, alleging that the store was negligent. She presented evidence that the macaroni had "a lot of dirt" and tracks through it and testified that the macaroni "seemed like it had been there awhile." What duty does a business have to protect its patrons from dangerous conditions? In Gonzalez's case, should Wal-Mart be held liable for a breach of that duty? Why, or why not? [*Wal-Mart Stores, Inc. v. Gonzalez*, 968 S.W.2d 934 (Tex.Sup. 1998)]

5–14. America Online, Inc. (AOL), provides services to its customers (members), including the transmission of e-mail to and from other members and across the Internet. To become a member, a person must agree not to use AOL's computers to send bulk, unsolicited, commercial e-mail (spam). AOL uses filters to block spam, but bulk e-mailers sometimes use other software to thwart the filters. National Health Care Discount, Inc. (NHCD), sells discount optical and dental service plans. To generate leads for NHCD's products, sales representatives, who included AOL members, sent more than 300 million pieces of spam through AOL's computer system. Each item cost AOL an estimated

$.00078 in equipment expenses. Some of the spam used false headers and other methods to hide the source. After receiving more than 150,000 complaints, AOL asked NHCD to stop. When the spam continued, AOL filed a suit in a federal district court against NHCD, alleging in part trespass to chattels—an unlawful interference with another's rights to possess personal property. AOL asked the court for a summary judgment on this claim. Did the spamming constitute trespass to chattels? Explain. [*America Online, Inc. v. National Health Care Discount, Inc.*, 121 F.Supp.2d 1255 (N.D.Iowa, 2000)]

5–15. A Question of Ethics

Patsy Slone, while a guest at the Dollar Inn, a hotel, was stabbed in the thumb by a hypodermic needle concealed in the tube of a roll of toilet paper. Slone, fearing that she might have been exposed to the virus that causes acquired immune deficiency syndrome (AIDS), sued the hotel for damages to compensate her for the emotional distress she suffered after the needle stab. An Indiana trial court held for Slone and awarded her $250,000 in damages. The hotel appealed, and one of the issues before the court was whether Slone had to prove that she was actually exposed to AIDS to recover for emotional distress. The appellate court held that she did not and that her fear of getting AIDS was reasonable in these circumstances. [*Slone v. Dollar Inn, Inc.*, 395 N.E.2d 185 (Ind.App. 1998)]

1. Should the plaintiff in this case have been required to show that she was actually exposed to the AIDS virus in order to recover for emotional distress? Should she have been required to show that she actually acquired the AIDS virus as a result of the needle stab?
2. In some states, plaintiffs are barred from recovery in emotional distress cases unless the distress is evidenced by some kind of physical illness. Is this fair?

E-LINKS

For updated links to resources available on the Web, as well as a variety of other materials, visit this text's Web site at

http://wbl-cs.westbuslaw.com

You can find cases and articles on torts, including business torts, in the tort law library at the Internet Law Library's Web site. Go to

http://www.lawguru.com/ilawlib/index.html

Legal Research Exercises on the Web

Go to http://wbl-cs.westbuslaw.com, the Web site that accompanies this text. Select "Interactive Study Center," and then click on "Chapter 5." There you will find the following Internet research exercises that you can perform to learn more about privacy rights in an online world and the elements of negligence:

Activity 5–1: Privacy Rights in Cyberspace

Activity 5–2: Negligence and the *Titanic*

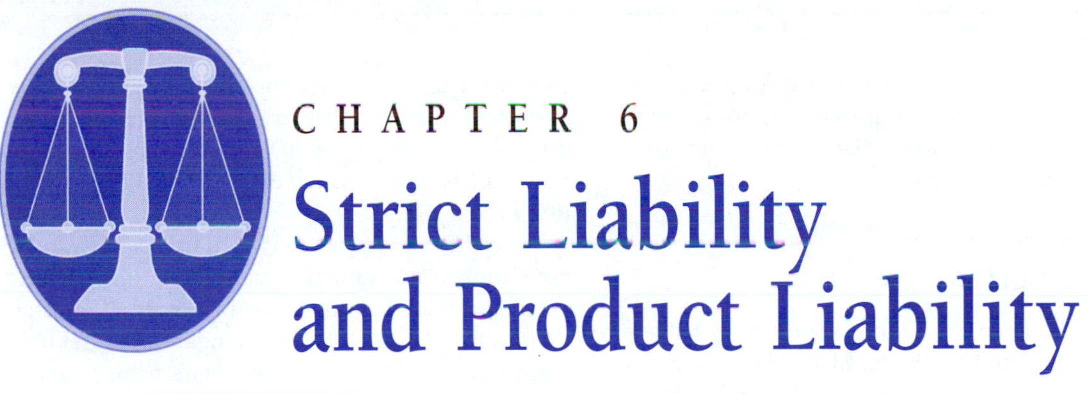

CHAPTER 6

Strict Liability and Product Liability

THE INTENTIONAL TORTS AND TORTS of negligence discussed in Chapter 5 involve acts that depart from a reasonable standard of care and cause injuries. In this chapter, we look at another basis for liability in tort—strict liability. Under the tort doctrine of **strict liability**, liability for injury is imposed for reasons other than fault. We open this chapter with an examination of this doctrine. We then look at an area of tort law of particular importance to businesspersons—product liability. **Product liability** refers to the liability incurred by manufacturers and sellers of products when product defects cause injury or property damage to consumers, users, or **bystanders** (people in the vicinity of the product).

SECTION 1

Strict Liability

The modern concept of strict liability traces its origins, in part, to the 1868 English case of *Rylands v. Fletcher.*[1] In the coal-mining area of Lancashire, England, the Rylands, who were mill owners, had constructed a reservoir on their land. Water from the reservoir broke through a filled-in shaft of an abandoned coal mine nearby and flooded the connecting passageways in an active coal mine owned by Fletcher. Fletcher sued the Rylands, and the court held that the defendants (the Rylands) were liable, even though the circumstances did not fit within existing tort liability theories.

In justifying its decision, the court compared the situation to the trespass of dangerous animals: "the true rule of law is, that the person who for his own purposes brings on his land and collects and keeps there anything likely to do mischief if it escapes, must keep it at his peril, and, if he does not do so, is *prima facie* [at first sight; on the face of it] answerable for all the damage which is the natural consequence of its escape."

The doctrine that emerged from *Rylands v. Fletcher* was liberally applied by British courts. Initially, few U.S. courts accepted this doctrine, presumably because the courts were worried about its effect on the expansion of American businesses. Today, however, the doctrine of strict liability is the norm rather than the exception.

ABNORMALLY DANGEROUS ACTIVITIES

The influence of *Rylands v. Fletcher* can be seen in the strict liability rule for abnormally dangerous activities, which is one application of the strict liability doctrine. Abnormally dangerous activities have three characteristics:

1. The activity involves potential harm, of a serious nature, to persons or property.
2. The activity involves a high degree of risk that cannot be completely guarded against by the exercise of reasonable care.
3. The activity is not commonly performed in the community or area.

Clearly, the primary basis of liability is the creation of an extraordinary risk. For example, even if blasting with dynamite is performed with all reasonable care, there is still a risk of injury. Balancing that risk against the potential for harm, it seems reasonable to ask the

1. L.R. 3 H.L. 330 (1868).

person engaged in the activity to pay for any injury it causes. Although there is no fault, there is still responsibility because of the dangerous nature of the undertaking.

OTHER APPLICATIONS OF STRICT LIABILITY

Persons who keep wild animals are strictly liable for any harm inflicted by the animals. The basis for applying strict liability is the fact that wild animals, should they escape from confinement, pose a serious risk of harm to persons in the vicinity. An owner of domestic animals (such as dogs, cats, cows, or sheep) may be strictly liable for harm caused by those animals if the owner knew, or should have known, that the animals were dangerous or had a propensity to harm others.

A significant application of strict liability is in the area of product liability, which we discuss next. Strict liability is also applied in certain types of *bailments* (a bailment exists when goods are transferred temporarily into the care of another—see Chapter 46).

SECTION 2

Product Liability

Product liability encompasses the tort theories of negligence and misrepresentation, which were discussed in Chapter 5, as well as strict liability. Product liability can also be based on warranty theory, a topic we treat in Chapter 22.

PRODUCT LIABILITY BASED ON NEGLIGENCE

In Chapter 5, *negligence* was defined as the failure to exercise the degree of care that a reasonable, prudent person would have exercised under the circumstances. If a manufacturer fails to exercise "due care" to make a product safe, a person who is injured by the product may sue the manufacturer for negligence.

Due care must be exercised in designing the product, in selecting the materials, in using the appropriate production process, in assembling and testing the product, and in placing adequate warnings on the label informing the user of dangers of which an ordinary person might not be aware. The duty of care also extends to the inspection and testing of any purchased components that are used in the final product sold by the manufacturer. A manufacturer's negligence *per se*—which occurs when a manufacturer violates a duty imposed by statute, such as a labeling statute (see Chapter 5)—may also serve as a ground for a tort action for damages.

A product liability action based on negligence does not require the injured plaintiff and the negligent defendant-manufacturer to be in **privity of contract**. That is, the plaintiff and the defendant need not be directly involved in a contractual relationship. A manufacturer is liable for its failure to exercise due care to *any person* who sustains an injury proximately caused by a negligently made (defective) product. Relative to the long history of the common law, this exception to the privity requirement is a fairly recent development, dating to the early part of the twentieth century.[2]

PRODUCT LIABILITY BASED ON MISREPRESENTATION

When a fraudulent misrepresentation has been made to a user or consumer and that misrepresentation ultimately results in an injury, the basis of liability may be the tort of fraud. In this situation, the misrepresentation must have been made knowingly or with reckless disregard for the facts. An example is the intentional concealment of a product's defects. In contrast to actions based on negligence and strict liability, in a suit based on fraudulent misrepresentation, the plaintiff does not have to show that the product was defective or that it malfunctioned in any way.[3]

Nonfraudulent misrepresentation, which occurs when a merchant *innocently* misrepresents the character or quality of goods, can also provide a basis of liability. In this situation, the plaintiff does not have to prove that the misrepresentation was made knowingly. A famous example involved a drug manufacturer and a victim of addiction to a prescription medicine called Talwin. The manufacturer, Winthrop Laboratories, a division of Sterling Drug, Inc., innocently indicated to the medical profession that the drug was not physically addictive. Using this information, a physician prescribed the drug for his patient, who developed an addiction that turned out to be fatal. Even though the addiction was a highly uncommon reaction resulting from the victim's unusual

2. A landmark case in this respect is *MacPherson v. Buick Motor Co.*, 217 N.Y. 382, 111 N.E. 1050 (1916).

3. See, for example, *Khan v. Shiley, Inc.*, 217 Cal.App.3d 848, 266 Cal.Rptr. 106 (1990).

susceptibility to this product, the drug company was still held liable.[4]

Whether fraudulent or nonfraudulent, the misrepresentation must be of a material fact (a fact concerning the quality, nature, or appropriate use of the product on which a normal buyer may be expected to rely). There must also have been an intent to induce the buyer's reliance on the misrepresentation. Misrepresentation on a label or advertisement is enough to show an intent to induce the reliance of anyone who may use the product. The buyer also must rely on the misrepresentation. If the buyer is not aware of the misrepresentation or if it does not influence the transaction, there is no liability.

SECTION 3

Strict Product Liability

As explained earlier in this chapter, under the doctrine of strict liability people may be liable for the results of their acts regardless of their intentions or their exercise of reasonable care. In several landmark cases involving manufactured goods in the 1960s, courts applied the doctrine of strict liability, and it has since become a common method of holding manufacturers liable. Some states, however, including Massachusetts and Virginia, have refused to recognize strict product liability. Additionally, some courts limit the application of the doctrine only to cases involving personal injuries, not property damage. Until recently, recovery for economic loss was not available in an action based on strict liability; even today, it is rarely available.

STRICT PRODUCT LIABILITY AND PUBLIC POLICY

Strict product liability is imposed by law as a matter of public policy. This public policy rests on the threefold assumption that (1) consumers should be protected against unsafe products; (2) manufacturers and distributors should not escape liability for faulty products simply because they are not in privity of contract with the ultimate user of those products; and (3) manufacturers, sellers, and lessors of products are in a better position to bear the costs associated with injuries caused by their products—costs that they can ultimately pass on to all consumers in the form of higher prices.

California was the first state to impose strict product liability in tort on manufacturers. In the landmark decision presented as Case 6.1, the California Supreme Court sets out the reason for applying tort law rather than contract law (including laws governing warranties—guarantees made by sellers and lessors to those who buy or lease their products) to cases in which consumers are injured by defective products.

Westlaw. See Case 6.1 at the end of this chapter. To view the full, unedited case from Westlaw,® go to this text's Web site at **http://wbl-cs.westbuslaw.com**.

THE REQUIREMENTS FOR STRICT PRODUCT LIABILITY

As mentioned in Chapter 1, the courts often look to the *Restatements of the Law* for guidance, even though the *Restatements* are not binding authorities. Section 402A of the *Restatement (Second) of Torts* indicates how it was envisioned that the doctrine of strict product liability should be applied. This *Restatement* was issued in 1964, and during the decade following its release it became a widely accepted statement of the liabilities of sellers of goods (including manufacturers, processors, assemblers, packagers, bottlers, wholesalers, distributors, retailers, and lessors). Section 402A reads as follows:

> (1) One who sells any product in a defective condition unreasonably dangerous to the user or consumer or to his property is subject to liability for physical harm thereby caused to the ultimate user or consumer or to his property, if
> (a) the seller is engaged in the business of selling such a product, and
> (b) it is expected to and does reach the user or consumer without substantial change in the condition in which it is sold.
>
> (2) The rule stated in Subsection (1) applies although
> (a) the seller has exercised all possible care in the preparation and sale of his product, and
> (b) the user or consumer has not bought the product from or entered into any contractual relation with the seller.

The bases for an action in strict liability as set forth in Section 402A of the *Restatement (Second) of Torts*, and as the doctrine came to be commonly applied, can

4. *Crocker v. Winthrop Laboratories, Division of Sterling Drug, Inc.*, 514 S.W.2d 429 (Tex. 1974).

be summarized as a series of six requirements, which are listed here. Depending on the jurisdiction, if these requirements were met, a manufacturer's liability to an injured party could be virtually unlimited.[5]

1. The product must be in a defective condition when the defendant sells it.
2. The defendant must normally be engaged in the business of selling (or otherwise distributing) that product.
3. The product must be unreasonably dangerous to the user or consumer because of its defective condition (in most states).
4. The plaintiff must incur physical harm to self or property by use or consumption of the product.
5. The defective condition must be the proximate cause of the injury or damage.
6. The goods must not have been substantially changed from the time the product was sold to the time the injury was sustained.

Thus, under these requirements, in any action against a manufacturer, seller, or lessor, the plaintiff does not have to show why or in what manner the product became defective. To recover damages, however, the plaintiff must show that the product was so "defective" as to be "unreasonably dangerous"; that the product caused the plaintiff's injury; and that at the time the injury was sustained, the condition of the product was essentially the same as when it left the hands of the defendant manufacturer, seller, or lessor.

A court could consider a product so defective as to be an **unreasonably dangerous product** if either (1) the product was dangerous beyond the expectation of the ordinary consumer or (2) a less dangerous alternative was economically feasible for the manufacturer, but the manufacturer failed to produce it. As will be discussed later, a product may be unreasonably dangerous due to a flaw in the manufacturing process, a design defect, or an inadequate warning.

MARKET-SHARE LIABILITY

Generally, in cases involving product liability, a plaintiff must prove that the defective product that caused his or her injury was the product of a specific defendant. In recent decades, however, in cases in which plaintiffs could not prove which of many distributors of a harmful product supplied the particular product that caused their injuries, courts have dropped this requirement.

This has occurred, for example, in several cases involving DES (diethylstilbestrol), a drug administered in the past to prevent miscarriages. DES's harmful character was not realized until, a generation later, daughters of the women who had taken DES developed health problems, including vaginal carcinoma, that were linked to the drug. Partly because of the passage of time, a plaintiff-daughter often could not prove which pharmaceutical company—out of as many as three hundred—had marketed the DES her mother had ingested. In these cases, some courts applied **market-share liability**, holding that all firms that manufactured and distributed DES during the period in question were liable for the plaintiffs' injuries in proportion to the firms' respective shares of the market.[6]

Market-share liability has also been applied in other situations.[7] In one case, the New York Court of Appeals (that state's highest court) held that even if a firm can prove that it did not manufacture the particular product that caused injuries to the plaintiff, the firm can be held liable based on the firm's share of the national market.[8]

OTHER APPLICATIONS OF STRICT PRODUCT LIABILITY

Strict product liability also applies to suppliers of component parts. For example, suppose that General Motors buys brake pads from a subcontractor and puts them in Chevrolets without changing their composition. If those pads are defective, both the supplier of the brake pads and General Motors will be held strictly liable for the damages caused by the defects. Under the *Restatement (Third) of Torts: Products Liability,* which will be discussed shortly, a component supplier may be liable if the component is defective "at the time of sale or distribution." A supplier may also be liable if it "substantially

5. In a number of states, *statutes of repose* (discussed later in this chapter) place a limit on the time period within which product liability actions may be brought.

6. See, for example, *Martin v. Abbott Laboratories,* 102 Wash.2d 581, 689 P.2d 368 (1984).

7. See, for example, *Smith v. Cutter Biological, Inc.,* 72 Haw. 416, 823 P.2d 717 (1991).

8. *Hymowitz v. Eli Lilly and Co.,* 73 N.Y.2d 487, 539 N.E.2d 1069, 541 N.Y.S.2d 941 (1989).

participates in the integration of the component into the design of the product," the "integration" causes the product to be defective, and the defect causes harm.[9]

Although the drafters of Section 402A of the *Restatement (Second) of Torts* did not take a position on bystanders, all courts extend the strict liability of manufacturers and other sellers to injured bystanders. For example, in one case, an automobile manufacturer was held liable for injuries caused by the explosion of a car's motor. A cloud of steam that resulted from the explosion caused multiple collisions because other drivers could not see well.[10]

Westlaw. See Case 6.2 at the end of this chapter. To view the full, unedited case from Westlaw,® go to this text's Web site at **http://wbl-cs.westbuslaw.com**.

SECTION 4

The Restatement (Third) of Torts

Because Section 402A of the *Restatement (Second) of Torts* did not clearly define such terms as "defective" and "unreasonably dangerous," these terms have been subject to different interpretations by different courts. To address these concerns, the American Law Institute (ALI) drafted a new restatement of the principles and policies underlying product liability law. In particular, the ALI attempted to respond to questions that had not been part of the legal landscape thirty-five years earlier. The result was the *Restatement (Third) of Torts: Products Liability*, which was released in 1997.

Traditionally, the law has categorized product defects into three types: manufacturing defects, design defects, and warning defects—each of which will be discussed shortly. The *Restatement (Third) of Torts: Products Liability* defines the three types of defects and integrates the applicable legal principles into the definitions. By defining defects in this manner, the new *Restatement* eliminates some of the hard-to-understand distinctions that developed when different theories of liability were applied to the same defects.

For example, in one case, a court upheld a verdict that found a product "not defective" on a theory of strict liability but its manufacturer liable for harm caused by the product on a theory of breach of warranty.[11] The court based its decision on the various tests that exist under the different legal theories. The new *Restatement* sets out a single test to be applied for each type of defect regardless of the kind of legal claim involved.

MANUFACTURING DEFECTS

According to Section 2(a) of the new *Restatement*, a product "contains a manufacturing defect when the product departs from its intended design even though all possible care was exercised in the preparation and marketing of the product." This statement imposes liability on the manufacturer (and on the wholesaler and retailer) whether or not the manufacturer acted "reasonably." This is strict liability, or liability without fault.

DESIGN DEFECTS

A determination that a product has a design defect (or a warning defect, discussed later in this chapter) can affect all of the units of a product. A product "is defective in design when the foreseeable risks of harm posed by the product could have been reduced or avoided by the adoption of a reasonable alternative design by the seller or other distributor, or a predecessor in the commercial chain of distribution, and the omission of the alternative design renders the product not reasonably safe."[12]

Different states have applied different tests to determine whether a product has a design defect under Section 402A of the *Restatement (Second) of Torts*. There has been much controversy regarding the different tests, particularly about one that focused on the "consumer expectations" concerning a product. The test prescribed by the *Restatement (Third) of Torts: Products Liability* focuses on a product's actual design and the reasonableness of that design.

To succeed in a product liability suit alleging a design defect, a plaintiff has to show that there is a reasonable alternative design. In other words, a manufacturer or other defendant is liable only when

9. *Restatement (Third) of Torts: Products Liability*, Section 5.

10. *Giberson v. Ford Motor Co.*, 504 S.W.2d 8 (Mo. 1974).

11. *Denny v. Ford Motor Co.*, 87 N.Y.2d 248, 662 N.E.2d 730, 639 N.Y.S.2d 250 (1995). The *Restatement* has not eliminated all of these distinctions, however, because in some cases they may be necessary.

12. *Restatement (Third) of Torts: Products Liability*, Section 2(b).

the harm was reasonably preventable. According to the Official Comments accompanying the new *Restatement,* factors that a court may consider on this point include

> the magnitude and probability of the foreseeable risks of harm, the instructions and warnings accompanying the product, and the nature and strength of consumer expectations regarding the product, including expectations arising from product portrayal and marketing. The relative advantages and disadvantages of the product as designed and as it alternatively could have been designed may also be considered. Thus, the likely effects of the alternative design on production costs; the effects of the alternative design on product longevity, maintenance, repair, and esthetics; and the range of consumer choice among products are factors that may be taken into account.

Note that the "consumer expectations" element, instead of being the whole test, is only one factor taken into consideration. Another factor is the warning that accompanies a product.

WARNING DEFECTS

A product may also be deemed defective because of inadequate instructions or warnings. Section 2(c) of the *Restatement (Third) of Torts: Products Liability* states that a product "is defective because of inadequate instructions or warnings when the foreseeable risks of harm posed by the product could have been reduced or avoided by the provision of reasonable instructions or warnings by the seller or other distributor, or a predecessor in the commercial chain of distribution, and the omission of the instructions or warnings renders the product not reasonably safe."[13]

Important factors for a court to consider under the *Restatement (Third) of Torts: Products Liability* include the risks of a product, the "content and comprehensibility" and "intensity of expression" of warnings and instructions, and the "characteristics of expected user groups."[14] For example, children would likely respond readily to bright, bold, simple warning labels, while educated adults might need more detailed information.

There is no duty to warn about risks that are obvious or commonly known. Warnings about such risks do not add to the safety of a product and could even detract from it by making other warnings seem less significant. The obviousness of a risk and a user's decision to proceed in the face of that risk may be a defense in a product liability suit based on a warning defect. (Defenses to product liability will be discussed shortly.)

Generally, a seller must warn those who purchase its product of the harm that can result from the foreseeable misuse of the product as well. The key is the foreseeability of the misuse. According to the Official Comments accompanying the new *Restatement,* sellers "are not required to foresee and take precautions against every conceivable mode of use and abuse to which their products might be put."

See Case 6.3 at the end of this chapter. To view the full, unedited case from Westlaw,® go to this text's Web site at **http://wbl-cs.westbuslaw.com**.

SECTION 5

Defenses to Product Liability

Defendants in product liability suits can raise a number of defenses. One defense, of course, is to show that there is no basis for the plaintiff's claim. For example, in a product liability case based on negligence, if a defendant can show that the plaintiff has not met the requirements (such as causation) for an action in negligence, the defendant will not be liable. In regard to strict product liability, a defendant can claim that the plaintiff failed to meet one of the requirements for an action in strict liability. For example, if the defendant establishes that the goods have been subsequently altered, the defendant will not be held liable.[15] Defendants may also assert the defenses discussed next.

ASSUMPTION OF RISK

Assumption of risk can sometimes be used as a defense in a product liability action. To establish such a defense, the defendant must show that (1) the plaintiff knew and appreciated the risk created by the product defect, and (2) the plaintiff voluntarily assumed the risk, even though it was unreasonable to do so. For example, if a buyer failed to heed a

13. *Restatement (Third) of Torts: Products Liability,* Section 2(c).

14. *Restatement (Third) of Torts: Products Liability,* Section 2, Comment h.

15. Under some state laws, the failure to properly maintain a product may constitute a subsequent alteration. See, for example, *LaPlante v. American Honda Motor Co.,* 27 F.3d 731 (1st Cir. 1994).

seller's product recall, the buyer may be deemed to have assumed the risk of the product defect that the seller offered to cure. (See Chapter 5 for a more detailed discussion of assumption of risk.)

PRODUCT MISUSE

Similar to the defense of voluntary assumption of risk is that of **product misuse.** Here, the injured party *does not know that the product is dangerous for a particular use* (contrast this with assumption of risk), but the use is not the one for which the product was designed. The courts have severely limited this defense, however. Even if the injured party does not know about the inherent danger of using the product in a wrong way, if the misuse is reasonably foreseeable, the seller must take measures to guard against it.

For example, in one case two men were using a crane to retrieve drilling pipe from beneath power lines when the crane cable touched one of the lines. The cable did not have an insulated link and thus conducted electricity from the line to the pipe, electrocuting one of the men. The man's widow sued the crane manufacturer, alleging that the crane—without the insulated link—was defectively designed and unreasonably dangerous. The manufacturer argued that the men had been using the crane to sideload (a practice that causes the crane's cable to extend its slack in unpredictable ways) and that sideloading was an unreasonable misuse of the product. The court held that although sideloading was a misuse, the misuse was reasonably foreseeable. Because the manufacturer had failed to guard against this foreseeable misuse, it was liable to the widow for damages.[16]

CONTRIBUTORY NEGLIGENCE

As discussed in Chapter 5, under the doctrine of contributory negligence, a defendant in a negligence suit may avoid liability in whole or in part if the plaintiff's own negligence contributed to the injury for which the plaintiff seeks damages. Whereas earlier the plaintiff's conduct was not a defense to strict liability, today some jurisdictions consider the negligent or intentional actions of both the plaintiff and the defendant in the apportionment of liability and damages. In other words, in those jurisdictions a comparative negligence standard is applied in strict liability cases.

Westlaw. See Case 6.4 at the end of this chapter. To view the full, unedited case from Westlaw,® go to this text's Web site at **http://wbl-cs.westbuslaw.com**.

COMMONLY KNOWN DANGERS

The dangers associated with certain products (such as matches and guns) are so commonly known that manufacturers need not warn users of those dangers. If a defendant succeeds in convincing the court that a plaintiff's injury resulted from a *commonly known danger,* the defendant will not be liable.

A classic case on this issue involved a plaintiff who was injured when an elastic exercise rope she had purchased slipped off her foot and struck her in the eye, causing a detachment of the retina. The plaintiff claimed that the manufacturer should be liable because it had failed to warn users that the exerciser might slip off a foot in such a manner. The court stated that to hold the manufacturer liable in these circumstances "would go beyond the reasonable dictates of justice in fixing the liabilities of manufacturers." After all, stated the court, "[a]lmost every physical object can be inherently dangerous or potentially dangerous in a sense. . . . A manufacturer cannot manufacture a knife that will not cut or a hammer that will not mash a thumb or a stove that will not burn a finger. The law does not require [manufacturers] to warn of such common dangers."[17]

A related defense is the *knowledgeable user* defense. If a particular danger is or should be commonly known by particular users of a product, the manufacturer need not warn these users of the danger.

STATUTES OF LIMITATIONS AND REPOSE

As discussed in Chapter 1, *statutes of limitations* restrict the time within which an action may be brought. A typical statute of limitations provides that an action must be brought within a specified period of time after the cause of action accrues. Generally, a cause of action is held to accrue when some damage occurs. Sometimes, the running of the prescribed period is *tolled* (that is, suspended) until the party suffering an injury has discovered it or should have discovered it.

16. *Lutz v. National Crane Corp.*, 884 P.2d 455 (Mont. 1994).

17. *Jamieson v. Woodward & Lothrop*, 247 F.2d 23 (D.C. 1957).

Many states have passed laws placing outer time limits on some claims so that the defendant will not be left vulnerable to lawsuits indefinitely. These **statutes of repose** may limit the time within which a plaintiff can file a product liability suit. Typically, a statute of repose begins to run at an earlier date and runs for a longer time than a statute of limitations. For example, a statute of repose may require that claims must be brought within twelve years from the date of sale or manufacture of the defective product. It is immaterial that the product is defective or causes an injury if the injury occurs after this statutory period has lapsed. In addition, some of these legislative enactments have limited the application of the doctrine of strict liability to new goods.

Terms and Concepts to Review

bystander 123	product liability 123	strict liability 123
market-share liability 126	product misuse 129	unreasonably dangerous product 126
privity of contract 124	statute of repose 130	

Chapter Summary

Strict Liability	Under the doctrine of strict liability, a person may be held liable, regardless of the degree of care exercised, for damages or injuries caused by her or his product or activity. Strict liability includes liability for harms caused by abnormally dangerous activities, by dangerous animals, and by defective products (product liability).
Product Liability Based on Negligence	**1.** Due care must be used by the manufacturer in designing the product, selecting materials, using the appropriate production process, assembling and testing the product, and placing adequate warnings on the label or product. **2.** Privity of contract is not required. A manufacturer is liable for failure to exercise due care to any person who sustains an injury proximately caused by a negligently made (defective) product.
Product Liability Based on Misrepresentation	Fraudulent misrepresentation of a product may result in product liability based on the tort of fraud.
Strict Product Liability	**1.** *Strict product liability and public policy*—Strict product liability is imposed by law as a matter of public policy under the assumption that consumers should be protected against unsafe products and that manufacturers, sellers, and lessors of products are in a better position to bear the costs associated with injuries caused by their products. **2.** *Requirements for strict liability*— **a.** The defendant must sell the product in a defective condition. **b.** The defendant must normally be engaged in the business of selling that product. **c.** The product must be unreasonably dangerous to the user or consumer because of its defective condition (in most states). **d.** The plaintiff must incur physical harm to self or property by use or consumption of the product. (Courts will also extend strict liability to include injured bystanders.) **e.** The defective condition must be the proximate cause of the injury or damage. **f.** The goods must not have been substantially changed from the time the product was sold to the time the injury was sustained. **3.** *Market-share liability*—In cases in which plaintiffs cannot prove which of many distributors of a defective product supplied the particular product that caused the plaintiffs' injuries,

CHAPTER SUMMARY—CONTINUED	
Strict Product Liability—continued	some courts have applied market-share liability. All firms that manufactured and distributed the harmful product during the period in question are then held liable for the plaintiffs' injuries in proportion to the firms' respective shares of the market, as directed by the court. 4. *Other applications of strict product liability*— a. Manufacturers and other sellers are liable for harms suffered by injured bystanders due to defective products. b. Suppliers of component parts are strictly liable for defective parts that, when incorporated into a product, cause injuries to users.
The *Restatement (Third) of Torts*	The *Restatement (Third) of Torts* defines three basic ways in which a product may be defective: 1. In its manufacture. 2. In its design. 3. In the instructions or warnings that come with it.
Defenses to Product Liability	1. *Assumption of risk*—The user or consumer knew of the risk of harm and voluntarily assumed it. 2. *Product misuse*—The user or consumer misused the product in a way unforeseeable by the manufacturer. 3. *Comparative negligence*—Liability may be distributed between plaintiff and defendant under the doctrine of comparative negligence if the plaintiff's misuse of the product contributed to the risk of injury. 4. *Commonly known dangers*— If a defendant succeeds in convincing the court that a plaintiff's injury resulted from a commonly known danger, such as the danger associated with using a sharp knife, the defendant will not be liable. 5. *Statutes of limitation and repose*—These statutes specify a period of time after which an action in product liability may not be brought.

CASES FOR ANALYSIS

Westlaw. You can access the full text of each case presented below by going to the Westlaw cases on this text's Web site at http://wbl-cs.westbuslaw.com. Each Westlaw case includes the names of all plaintiffs and defendants, the dates on which the case was argued and decided, a brief summary of the issues and decisions in the case, headnotes classifying specific issues in the case according to the West Key Number System, and the court's opinion. Concurring and dissenting opinions, if any, are included as well.

CASE 6.1 STRICT PRODUCT LIABILITY

GREENMAN V. YUBA POWER PRODUCTS, INC.

Supreme Court of California, 1963.
59 Cal.2d 57,
377 P.2d 897,
27 Cal.Rptr. 697.

TRAYNOR, Justice.

Plaintiff brought this action for damages against the retailer and the manufacturer of a Shopsmith, a combination power tool that could be used as a saw, drill, and wood lathe. He saw a Shopsmith demonstrated by the retailer and studied a brochure prepared by the manufacturer. He decided he wanted a Shopsmith for his home workshop, and his wife bought and gave him one for Christmas in 1955. In 1957 he bought the necessary attachments to use the Shopsmith as a lathe for turning a large piece of wood he wished to make into a chalice. After he had worked on the piece of wood several times without difficulty, it suddenly flew out of the machine and struck him on the forehead, inflicting serious injuries. About ten and a half months later, he gave the retailer and the manufacturer written notice of claimed breaches of warranties and filed a complaint against them alleging such breaches and negligence.

After a trial before a jury, the court ruled that there was no evidence that the retailer was negligent or had breached any express warranty and that the manufacturer was not liable for the breach of any implied warranty. Accordingly, it submitted to the jury only the cause of action alleging breach of implied warranties against the retailer and the causes of action alleging negligence and breach of express warranties against the manufacturer. The jury returned a verdict for the retailer against plaintiff and for plaintiff against the manufacturer in the amount of $65,000. The trial court denied the manufacturer's motion for a new trial and entered judgment on the verdict. The manufacturer and plaintiff appeal. * * *

Plaintiff introduced substantial evidence that his injuries were caused by defective design and construction of the Shopsmith. His expert witnesses testified that inadequate set screws were used to hold parts of the machine together so that normal vibration caused the tailstock of the lathe to move away from the piece of wood being turned permitting it to fly out of the lathe. They also testified that there were other more positive ways of fastening the parts of the machine together, the use of which would have prevented the accident. The jury could therefore reasonably have concluded that the manufacturer negligently constructed the Shopsmith. The jury could also reasonably have concluded that statements in the manufacturer's brochure were untrue, that they constituted express warranties, and that plaintiff's injuries were caused by their breach.

* * * *

* * * [T]o impose strict liability on the manufacturer under the circumstances of this case, [however,] it was not necessary for plaintiff to establish an express warranty * * *. *A manufacturer is strictly liable in tort when an article he places on the market, knowing that it is to be used without inspection for defects, proves to have a defect that causes injury to a human being.* Recognized first in the case of unwholesome food products, such liability has now been extended to a variety of other products that create as great or greater hazards if defective. [Emphasis added.]

Although in these cases strict liability has usually been based on the theory of an express or implied warranty running from the manufacturer to the plaintiff, the abandonment of the requirement of a contract between them, the recognition that the liability is not assumed by agreement but imposed by law and the refusal to permit the manufacturer to define the scope of its own responsibility for defective products make clear that the liability is not one governed by the law of contract warranties but by the law of strict liability in tort. Accordingly, rules defining and governing warranties that were developed to meet the needs of commercial transactions cannot properly be invoked to govern the manufacturer's liability to those injured by their defective products unless those rules also serve the purposes for which such liability is imposed.

* * * The purpose of such liability is to insure that the costs of injuries resulting from defective products are borne by the manufacturers that put such products on the market rather than by the injured persons who are powerless to protect themselves. Sales warranties serve this purpose fitfully at best. In the present case, for example, plaintiff was able to plead and prove an express warranty only because he read and relied on the representations of the Shopsmith's ruggedness contained in the manufacturer's brochure. Implicit in the machine's presence on the market, however, was a representation that it would safely do the jobs for which it was built. Under these circumstances, it should not be controlling whether plaintiff selected the machine because of the statements in the brochure, or because of the machine's own appearance of excellence that belied the defect lurking beneath the surface, or because he merely assumed that it would safely do the jobs it was built to do. It should not be controlling whether the details of the sales from manufacturer to retailer and from retailer to plaintiff's wife were such that one or more of the implied warranties of the sales act arose. The remedies of injured consumers ought not to be made to depend upon the intricacies of the law of sales. To establish the manufacturer's liability it was sufficient that plaintiff proved that he was injured while using the Shopsmith in a way it was intended to be used as a result of a defect in design and manufacture of which plaintiff was not aware that made the Shopsmith unsafe for its intended use.

* * * *

The judgment is affirmed.

CASE 6.2 STRICT PRODUCT LIABILITY

EMBS V. PEPSI-COLA BOTTLING CO. OF LEXINGTON, KENTUCKY, INC.

Court of Appeals of Kentucky, 1975.
528 S.W.2d 703.

JUKOWSKY, Justice.

* * * *

On the afternoon of July 25, 1970 plaintiff-appellant entered the self-service retail store operated by the defendant-appellee, Stamper's Cash Market, Inc., for the purpose of "buying soft drinks for the kids." She went to an upright soft drink cooler, removed five bottles and placed them in a carton. Unnoticed by her, a carton of Seven-Up was sitting on the floor at the edge of the produce counter about one foot from where she was standing. As she turned away from the cooler she heard an explosion that sounded "like a shotgun." When she looked down she saw a gash in her leg, pop on her leg, green pieces of a bottle on the floor and the Seven-Up carton in the midst of the debris. She did not kick or otherwise come into contact with the carton of Seven-Up prior to the explosion. Her son, who was with her, recognized the green pieces of glass as part of a Seven-Up bottle.

She was immediately taken to the hospital by Mrs. Stamper, a managing agent of the store. Mrs. Stamper told her that a Seven-Up bottle had exploded and that several bottles had exploded that week. * * *

The defendant-appellee, Arnold Lee Vice, was the distributor of Seven-Up in the Clark County [Kentucky] area. As such, he supplied Stamper's Cash Market, Inc., with its entire stock of Seven-Up. He would deliver it with his truck to the store and place it in the store and the cooler. Employees of the store would also place Seven-Up in the cooler from other locations in the store. His truck was loaded with Seven-Up by the bottler at the plant.

The defendant-appellee, Pepsi-Cola Bottling Co. of Lexington, Kentucky, Inc., was the bottler who produced and supplied Vice with his entire stock of Seven-Up.

The foregoing narrative is a fair summary of the evidence introduced by the plaintiff-appellant in support of her claim for bodily injury. When she rested her case, the defendants-appellees moved for a directed verdict in their favor. The trial court granted the motion on the grounds that the doctrine of strict product liability in tort does not extend beyond users and consumers * * *.

* * * *

Comment f [to the *Restatement (Second) of Torts,* Section 402A] makes it abundantly clear that [the rule expressed in Section 402A] applies to any person engaged in the business of supplying products for use or consumption, including any manufacturer of such a product and any wholesale or retail dealer or distributor.

Comment c points out that on whatever theory, the justification for the rule has been said to be that the seller, by marketing his product for use and consumption, has undertaken and assumed a special responsibility toward any member of the consuming public who may be injured by it; that the public has the right to and does expect that reputable sellers will stand behind their goods; that public policy demands that the burden of accidental injuries caused by products intended for consumption be placed upon those who market them, and be treated as a cost of production against which liability insurance can be obtained; and that the consumer of such products is entitled to the maximum of protection at the hands of someone, and the proper persons to afford it are those who market the products.

The *caveat* [a warning or caution] to the section provides that the Institute expresses no opinion as to whether the rule may not apply to harm to persons other than users or consumers. * * * [T]he Institute expresses neither approval nor disapproval of expansion of the rule to permit recovery by casual bystanders and others who may come in contact with the product, and admits there may be no essential reason why such plaintiffs should not be brought within the scope of protection afforded, other than they do not have the same reasons for expecting such protection as the consumer who buys a marketed product, and that the social pressure which has been largely responsible for the development of the rule has been a consumer's pressure, and there is not the same demand for the protection of casual strangers.

The *caveat* articulates the essential point: Once strict liability is accepted, bystander recovery is *fait accompli* [an accomplished and presumably irreversible deed or fact]. Moreover, with but one exception no jurisdiction which has adopted strict tort liability has rejected the bystanders claim. * * *

Our expressed public policy will be furthered if we minimize the risk of personal injury and property damage by charging the costs of injuries against the manufacturer who can procure liability insurance and distribute its expense among the public as a cost of doing business; and since the risk of harm from defective products exists for mere bystanders and passersby as well as for the purchaser or user, there is no substantial reason for protecting one class of persons and not the other. The same policy requires us to maximize protection for the injured third party and promote the public interest in discouraging the marketing of products having defects that are a menace to the public by imposing strict liability upon retailers and wholesalers in the distributive chain responsible for marketing the defective product which injures the bystander. The imposition of strict liability places no unreasonable burden upon sellers because they can adjust the cost of insurance protection among themselves in the course of their continuing business relationship.

We must not shirk from extending the rule to the manufacturer for fear that the retailer or middleman will be impaled on the sword of liability without regard to fault. Their liability was already established under Section 402 A of the *Restatement of Torts 2d. As a matter of public policy the retailer or middleman as well as the manufacturer should be liable since the loss for injuries resulting from defective products should be placed on those members of the marketing chain best able to pay the loss, who can then distribute such risk among themselves by means of insurance and indemnity agreements.* Any inclination to relieve the retailer must have in mind the little corner grocery store but in these days the dealer is more likely to be Safeway Stores or some other nationwide enterprise which is the prime mover in marketing the goods and the manufacturer only a small concern which feeds it to order. [Emphasis added.]

The result which we reach does not give the bystander a "free ride." When products and consumers are considered in the aggregate, bystanders, as a class, purchase most of the same products to which they are exposed as bystanders. Thus, as a class, they indirectly subsidize the liability of the manufacturer, middleman and retailer and in this sense do pay for the insurance policy tied to the product.

Public policy is adequately served if parameters are placed upon the extension of the rule so that it is limited to bystanders whose injury from the defect is reasonably foreseeable.

For the sake of clarity we restate the extension of the rule. The protections of Section 402 A of the *Restatement of Torts 2d* extend to bystanders whose injury from the defective product is reasonably foreseeable.

* * * *

The motions for a directed verdict should have been denied and the defendants-appellees should have been required to come forward with their evidence.

The judgment is reversed and the cause is remanded to the [trial court] for further proceedings consistent herewith.

* * * *

STEPHENSON, Justice (dissenting).

I respectfully dissent from the majority opinion to the extent that it subjects the seller to liability. Every rule of law in my mind should have a rational basis. I see none here.

Liability of the seller to the user, or consumer, is based upon warranty. To extend this liability to injuries suffered by a bystander is to depart from any reasonable basis and impose liability by judicial fiat upon an otherwise innocent defendant. I do not believe that the expression in the majority opinion which justifies this rule for the reason that the seller may procure liability insurance protection is a valid legal basis for imposing liability without fault.

CASE 6.3 WARNING DEFECTS

LIRIANO V. HOBART CORP.

United States Court of Appeals,
Second Circuit, 1999.
170 F.3d 264.

CALABRESI, Circuit Judge:

* * * *

BACKGROUND

* * * *

Luis Liriano was severely injured on the job in 1993 when his hand was caught in a meat grinder manufactured by Hobart Corporation ("Hobart") and owned by his employer, Super Associated ("Super"). The meat grinder had been sold to Super with a safety guard, but the safety guard was removed while the machine was in Super's possession and was not affixed to the meat grinder at the time of the accident. The machine bore no warning indicating that the grinder should be operated only with a safety guard attached.

Liriano sued Hobart under several theories, including failure to warn. Hobart brought a third-party claim against Super. The United States District Court for the Southern District of New York * * * dismissed all of Liriano's claims except the one based on failure to warn, and the jury returned a verdict for Liriano on that claim. * * *

Hobart and Super appealed, arguing * * * [in part] that even if there had been a duty to warn, the evidence presented was not sufficient to allow the failure-to-warn claim to reach the jury. * * *

* * * *

DISCUSSION

* * * *

* * * With respect to the asserted clarity of the danger, the question is when a danger is so obvious that a court can determine, as a matter of law, that no additional warning is required. * * *

* * * *

If the question before us were * * * simply whether meat grinders are sufficiently known to be dangerous so that manufacturers would be justified in believing that further warnings were not needed, we might be in doubt [that the jury should consider whether an additional warning was needed]. On the one hand, * * * most New Yorkers would probably appreciate the danger of meat grinders * * * . Any additional warning might seem superfluous. On the other hand, Liriano was only seventeen years old at the time of his injury and had only recently immigrated to the United States. He had been on the job at Super for only one week. He had never been given instructions about how to use the meat grinder, and he had used the meat grinder only two or three times. And * * * the mechanism that injured Liriano would not have been visible to someone who was operating the grinder. It could be argued that such a combination of facts was not so unlikely that a court should say, as a matter of law, that the defendant could not have foreseen them or, if aware of them, need not have guarded against them by issuing a warning. * * *

Nevertheless, it remains the fact that meat grinders are widely known to be dangerous. * * *

* * * *

* * * [A] warning can do more than exhort its audience to be careful. It can also affect what activities the people warned choose to engage in. And where the function of a warning is to assist the reader in making choices, the

value of the warning can lie as much in making known the existence of alternatives as in communicating the fact that a particular choice is dangerous. It follows that *the duty to warn is not necessarily obviated merely because a danger is clear.* [Emphasis added.]

To be more concrete, a warning can convey at least two types of messages. One states that a particular place, object, or activity is dangerous. Another explains that people need not risk the danger posed by such a place, object, or activity in order to achieve the purpose for which they might have taken that risk. Thus, a highway sign that says "Danger—Steep Grade" says less than a sign that says "Steep Grade Ahead—Follow Suggested Detour to Avoid Dangerous Areas."

If the hills or mountains responsible for the steep grade are plainly visible, the first sign merely states what a reasonable person would know without having to be warned. The second sign tells drivers what they might not have otherwise known: that there is another road that is flatter and less hazardous. A driver who believes the road through the mountainous area to be the only way to reach her destination might well choose to drive on that road despite the steep grades, but a driver who knows herself to have an alternative might not, even though her understanding of the risks posed by the steep grade is exactly the same as those of the first driver. Accordingly, a certain level of obviousness as to the grade of a road might, in principle, eliminate the reason for posting a sign of the first variety. But no matter how patently steep the road, the second kind of sign might still have a beneficial effect. As a result, the duty to post a sign of the second variety may persist even when the danger of the road is obvious and a sign of the first type would not be warranted.

One who grinds meat, like one who drives on a steep road, can benefit not only from being told that his activity is dangerous but from being told of a safer way. As we have said, one can argue about whether the risk involved in grinding meat is sufficiently obvious that a responsible person would fail to warn of that risk, believing reasonably that it would convey no helpful information. But if it is also the case—as it is—that the risk posed by meat grinders can feasibly be reduced by attaching a safety guard, we have a different question. Given that attaching guards is feasible, does reasonable care require that meat workers be informed that they need not accept the risks of using unguarded grinders? Even if most ordinary users may—as a matter of law—know of the risk of using a guardless meat grinder, it does not follow that a sufficient number of them will—as a matter of law—also know that protective guards are available, that using them is a realistic possibility, and that they may ask that such guards be used. It is precisely these last pieces of information that a reasonable manufacturer may have a duty to convey even if the danger of using a grinder were itself deemed obvious.

Consequently, the instant case does not require us to decide the difficult question of whether New York would consider the risk posed by meat grinders to be obvious as a matter of law. A jury could reasonably find that there exist people who are employed as meat grinders and who do not know (a) that it is feasible to reduce the risk with safety guards, (b) that such guards are made available with the grinders, and (c) that the grinders should be used only with the guards. Moreover, *a jury can also reasonably find that there are enough such people, and that warning them is sufficiently inexpensive, that a reasonable manufacturer would inform them that safety guards exist and that the grinder is meant to be used only with such guards.* Thus, even if New York would consider the danger of meat grinders to be obvious as a matter of law, that obviousness does not substitute for the warning that a jury could, and indeed did, find that Hobart had a duty to provide. It follows that we cannot say, as a matter of law, that Hobart had no duty to warn Liriano in the present case. We therefore decline to adopt appellants' argument that the issue of negligence was for the court only and that the jury was not entitled, on the evidence, to return a verdict for Liriano. [Emphasis added.]

* * * *

The district court did not err. We affirm its decision in all respects.

CASE 6.4 COMPARATIVE NEGLIGENCE

SMITH V. INGERSOLL-RAND CO.

Alaska Supreme Court, 2000.
14 P.3d 990.

MATTHEWS, Chief Justice.

* * * *

II. *FACTS AND PROCEEDINGS*

A. *Facts*

On August 12, 1987, Dan Smith was injured at Prudhoe Bay [Alaska] while attempting to start the diesel engine of an Ingersoll Rand portable air compressor. Smith, a light duty mechanic, was not wearing a hard hat when he was dispatched by his supervisor to start the air compressor's engine.

The air compressor was an older model that required the mechanic to open its door in order to start the engine. There was no latch on the door to hold it open. Instead, the mechanic had to prop the door open * * *.

* * * Smith does not remember how he propped the door open. All that he remembers is that he opened the door, started the engine, and the "next thing [he] knew, [he] was picking the door up off the top of [his] head." Somehow—whether from wind, vibration, or improper placement—the door had fallen from its open position and hit Smith's head. Initially, despite some blood and swelling, Smith did not think that he was seriously injured.

However, eleven days after the accident, Smith suffered a generalized motor seizure. He had no history of seizures in his adult life. On the medevac plane out of Prudhoe Bay, he suffered another seizure. He was later diagnosed with traumatic epilepsy, presumably caused by the compressor door hitting his head.

Since the accident, Smith has continued to suffer from repeated seizures, fatigue, difficulty concentrating, lapses in memory, and other related medical problems. He lost his job because of these medical problems and remains unemployed.

B. *Proceedings*

In 1988, Smith filed a products liability suit against Ingersoll-Rand in [an Alaska] state court, alleging that the company had designed a defective product. Smith claimed that the compressor was defective because it did not include a latch to hold its doors open and because there was no warning in the manual or on the compressor regarding the risk of falling doors.

Ingersoll-Rand removed the case to federal district court based on diversity jurisdiction. * * *

* * * *

* * * The jury found Smith forty percent responsible for the accident and Ingersoll Rand sixty percent responsible. The jury assessed Smith's total damages at $668,000.

Both parties appealed to the Ninth Circuit. * * *

The Ninth Circuit * * * noted, however, that the question of whether ordinary negligence could constitute comparative negligence in a products liability case presented a "novel issue of Alaska law," particularly in light of [Alaska's] 1986 Tort Reform Act. The circuit court therefore recommended that the district court consider certifying this question to the Alaska Supreme Court.

On remand, the federal district court certified [the question] to this court * * * .

III. *STANDARD OF REVIEW*

A decision by this court upon certification from another court involves determinative questions of Alaska law for which there is no controlling precedent. In determining questions of law, we exercise our independent judgment and adopt the rule of law that is most persuasive in light of precedent, reason, and policy.

* * * *

IV. *DISCUSSION*

A. *Prior to the 1986 Tort Reform Act, Alaska Allowed Comparative Negligence as a Defense in Products Liability Actions Only Under Limited Circumstances.*

In 1975 this court judicially adopted the doctrine of comparative negligence for fault-based tort actions and abolished the older, harsher doctrine of contributory negligence, which completely barred a plaintiff's recovery if he was to some degree at fault for his injuries. Under the "pure" system of comparative fault adopted by the court, a plaintiff would still be able to recover if he was comparatively at fault for his injuries, but his recovery would be reduced in proportion to his percentage of fault.

Less than a year later, we held that comparative negligence principles also apply to products liability actions based on strict liability. But we held that comparative negligence in strict products liability cases was limited to two specific situations: (1) when the plaintiff knows that the product is defective and unreasonably and voluntarily proceeds to use it; and (2) when the plaintiff misuses the product and the misuse is a proximate cause of the injuries.

* * * Ordinary negligence [was] generally not sufficient to establish comparative negligence on the part of a products liability plaintiff.

* * * *

B. *The 1986 Tort Reform Act Modified the Definition of Comparative Negligence in Products Liability Actions to Include Ordinary Negligence.*

In 1986 the Alaska Legislature passed the Tort Reform Act. Modeled after the Uniform Comparative Fault Act, the Tort Reform Act was intended to create a more equitable distribution of the cost and risk of injury and increase the availability and affordability of insurance. The legislature hoped to reduce the costs of the tort system while still ensuring that adequate and appropriate compensation for persons injured through the fault of others remained available.

As part of the Act, the legislature enacted a rule of comparative fault similar to the doctrine of comparative negligence which this court had adopted a decade earlier:

In an action based on fault seeking to recover damages for injury or death to a person or harm to property, contributory fault chargeable to the claimant diminishes proportionally the amount awarded as compensatory damages for the injury attributable to the claimant's contributory fault, but does not bar recovery.

The Act defined "fault" as

> acts or omissions that are in any measure negligent or reckless toward the person or property of the actor or others, or that subject a person to strict tort liability. The term also includes breach of warranty, unreasonable assumption of risk not constituting an enforceable express consent, misuse of product for which the defendant otherwise would be liable, and unreasonable failure to avoid injury or to mitigate damages. Legal requirements of causal relation apply both to fault as the basis for liability and to contributory fault.

The question before us is whether these two provisions modified the existing case law on comparative negligence in products liability cases. We conclude that they did.

The Act clearly applies to strict products liability cases. The Act applies to tort actions "based on fault." Fault is defined to include * * * "acts or omissions * * * that subject a person to strict liability." Products liability cases in Alaska are typically based on a strict liability theory. Thus the Act applies to strict products liability actions.

The Act's definition of comparative fault is broader than the comparative fault recognized in pre-1986 strict products liability cases. * * * [I]n addition to "misuse of product" and "unreasonable assumption" of risk, the Act also defined "fault" as including "acts or omissions that are in any measure negligent or reckless * * * ." Thus, the Act modifies the pre-1986 products liability case law by expanding the type of conduct that will trigger a proportional reduction of damages to include ordinary negligence—"acts or omissions that are in any measure negligent."

The Act's modification of comparative negligence in strict products liability cases reflects a general trend occurring across the nation. The recently published *Third Restatement of Torts, Products Liability,* observes that *a "strong majority" of courts now apply comparative negligence principles in strict products liability cases. Moreover, most of these courts do not limit comparative negligence to instances of product misuse or unreasonable and voluntary assumption of risk. Instead, they allow a plaintiff's ordinary negligence to constitute comparative fault.* [Emphasis added.]

In addition, legislatures in other states have enacted tort reform statutes similar to the one here, incorporating a universal definition of "contributory fault" for all tort cases, including strict products liability cases. Courts in other jurisdictions have generally interpreted these statutes as incorporating an ordinary negligence framework into the comparative fault analysis in strict liability cases.

V. *CONCLUSION*

* * * *

We therefore answer the * * * certified question in the affirmative.

CASE PROBLEMS

6–1. During the 1960s, Aluminum Co. of America (Alcoa) designed, patented, manufactured, and marketed a closure system for applying aluminum caps to carbonated soft-drink bottles. In 1969, Alcoa sold a capping machine to Houston 7-Up Bottling Co. On June 3, 1976, James Alm suffered a severe eye injury when an aluminum bottle cap exploded off a thirty-two-ounce bottle of 7-Up that had come from the Houston 7-Up Bottling Co. Alm sued Alcoa, alleging that, as the manufacturer, Alcoa had a duty to warn consumers of the dangers of a possible bottle-cap explosion. Alcoa argued that it had not had a duty to warn Alm, because it had not manufactured or sold any component part or the final product that injured Alm. Alcoa had mentioned possible cap explosions in the machine users' manual, wall charts, and technical information that it had provided to the Houston 7-Up Bottling Co. Which allegation is correct? Explain. [*Alm v. Aluminum Co. of America,* 717 S.W.2d 588 (Tex. 1986)]

6–2. William Mackowick, who had worked as an electrician for thirty years, was installing high-voltage capacitors in a switchgear room in a hospital when he noticed that a fellow electrician had removed the cover from an existing capacitor manufactured by Westinghouse Electric Corp. Westinghouse had placed a warning label inside the cover of the metal box containing the capacitor on which users were instructed to ground the electricity before handling. Nothing was said on the label about the propensity of electricity to "arc." (Arcing occurs when electricity grounds itself by "jumping" to a nearby object or instrument.) Mackowick walked over to warn the other electrician of the danger associated with the exposed capacitor, and while talking, pointed his screwdriver toward the capacitor box. The electricity flowing through the fuses arced to the screwdriver and sent a high-voltage electric current through Mackowick's body. As a result, he sustained severe burns and was unable to return to work for three months. Should Westinghouse be held liable because it failed to warn users of arcing—a principle of electricity? Discuss. [*Mackowick v. Westinghouse Electric Corp.,* 575 A.2d 100 (Pa. 1990)]

6–3. On February 16, 1986, David Jordon, a ten-year-old boy, lost control of his sled, hit a tree, and was injured. The sled was a plastic toboggan-like sled that had been purchased from K-Mart. David's parents brought suit against K-Mart, alleging that the sled was defective and unreasonably dangerous because (1) the sled contained design defects (the molded runners on the sled rendered the sled unsteerable, and the sled lacked any independent steering or braking mechanisms), and (2) there were no warnings of the dangers inherent in the use of the sled. K-Mart moved for summary judgment. Should the court grant K-Mart's motion? Discuss fully. [*Jordon v. K-Mart Corp.,* 611 A.2d 1328 (Pa.Sup. 1992)]

6–4. George Nesselrode lost his life in an airplane crash. The plane had been manufactured by Beech Aircraft Corp. and sold to Executive Beechcraft, Inc. Shortly before the crash occurred, Executive Beechcraft had conducted a routine inspection of the plane and found that some of the parts needed to be replaced. The new parts were supplied by Beech Aircraft but installed by Executive Beechcraft. These particular airplane parts could be installed backwards, and if they were, the plane would crash. In Nesselrode's case, the crash resulted from just such an incorrect installation of the airplane parts. Nesselrode's estate sued both Executive Beechcraft and Beech Aircraft for damages. Beech Aircraft claimed that it was not at fault because it had not installed the parts. Will Beech Aircraft be held liable for Nesselrode's death? Discuss. [*Nesselrode v. Executive Beechcraft, Inc.*, 707 S.W.2d 371 (Mo. 1986)]

6–5. Danny and Marion Klein were injured when an aerial shell at a public fireworks exhibit went astray and exploded near them. They sued Pyrodyne Corp., the pyrotechnic company that was hired to set up and discharge the fireworks, alleging, among other things, that the company should be strictly liable for damages caused by the fireworks display. Will the court agree with the Kleins? What factors will the court consider in making its decision? Discuss fully. [*Klein v. Pyrodyne Corp.*, 117 Wash.2d 1, 810 P.2d 917 (1991)]

6–6. Frances Ontai entered the Straub Clinic and Hospital to have an X-ray examination of the colon. Ontai was placed in a vertical position on a table manufactured by General Electric. The footrest on the table broke, and Ontai fell to the floor of the examination room, suffering injuries. Ontai filed suit against Straub and General Electric. Ontai's suit against General Electric was based on negligence and strict liability in tort. Discuss briefly each of these theories of liability. Should General Electric be held liable under either theory? Discuss fully. [*Ontai v. Straub Clinic and Hospital, Inc.*, 66 Haw. 237, 659 P.2d 734 (1983)]

6–7. James Patterson, who worked as a clerk in a convenience store in Dallas, was shot and killed during a robbery of the store in 1980. The revolver used by the robber was a .38 caliber "Saturday Night Special" manufactured by a West German company, Rohm Gesellschaft. Patterson's mother brought a product liability action against Rohm and the Florida distributor of the handgun, claiming that the handgun was "defective and unreasonably dangerous" in design because its potential for injury and death far outweighed any social utility it might have. The defendant moved for summary judgment, contending that it could not be liable for Patterson's death because the handgun was not defective—the gun did not malfunction, nor did it lack any essential safety features. What was the result? Discuss fully. [*Patterson v. Rohm Gesellschaft,* 608 F.Supp. 1206 (N.D.Tex.—Dallas Div. 1985)]

6–8. A water pipe burst, flooding a switchboard at the offices of RCA Global Communications, Inc. This tripped the switchboard circuit breakers. RCA employees assigned to reactivate the switchboard included an electrical technician with twelve years of on-the-job training, a licensed electrician, and an electrical engineer with twenty years of experience who had studied power engineering in college. The employees attempted to switch one of the circuit breakers back on without testing for short circuits, which they later admitted they knew how to do and should have done. The circuit breaker failed to engage but ignited an explosive fire. RCA filed a claim with its insurer, the Travelers Insurance Company. Travelers paid the claim and filed a suit in a New York state court against, among others, the Federal Pacific Electric Company, the supplier of the circuit breakers. Travelers alleged that Federal had been negligent in failing to give RCA adequate warnings and instructions regarding the circuit breakers. The court apportioned 15 percent of the responsibility for the fire to Federal. Federal appealed. Did Federal fail to give RCA adequate warnings and instructions regarding the circuit breakers? Discuss. [*Travelers Insurance Co. v. Federal Pacific Electric Co.*, 211 A.D.2d 40, 625 N.Y.S.2d 121 (1995)]

6–9. John Whitted bought a Chevrolet Nova from General Motors Corp. (GMC). Six years later, Whitted crashed the Nova into two trees. During the impact, the seat belt broke, and Whitted was thrust against the steering wheel, which broke, and the windshield, which shattered. He suffered fractures in his left arm and cuts to his forehead. Whitted sued GMC and the manufacturer, asserting, among other things, that because the seat belt broke, the defendants were strictly liable for his injuries. What does Whitted have to show in order to prove his case? [*Whitted v. General Motors Corp.*, 58 F.3d 1200 (7th Cir. 1995)]

6–10. A two-year-old child lost his leg when he became entangled in a grain auger on his grandfather's farm. The auger had a safety guard that prevented any item larger than 4⅝ inches from coming into contact with the machine's moving parts. The child's foot was smaller than the openings in the safety guard. Was such an injury reasonably foreseeable? Discuss. [*Richelman v. Kewanee Machinery & Conveyor Co.,* 59 Ill.App.3d 578, 375 N.E.2d 885, 16 Ill.Dec. 778 (1978)]

6–11. The Campbell Soup Co. manufactured, sold, and shipped packages of chicken-flavored Campbell's Ramen Noodle Soup to a distributor. The distributor sold and shipped the packages to Associated Grocers. Associated Grocers shipped the packages to Warehouse Foods, a retail grocer. Six weeks after Campbell first shipped the soup to the distributor, Warehouse Foods sold a package of the soup to Kathy Jo Gates. Gates prepared the soup. Halfway through eating her second bowl, she discovered beetle larvae in the noodles. She filed a product liability suit against Campbell and others. Gates argued, in effect, that the mere presence of the bugs in the soup was sufficient to hold Campbell strictly liable. How might Campbell defend itself? [*Campbell Soup Co. v. Gates,* 319 Ark. 54, 889 S.W.2d 750 (1994)]

6–12. When Mary Bresnahan drove her Chrysler LeBaron, she sat very close to the steering wheel—less than a foot away from the steering-wheel enclosure of the driver's-side air bag. At the time, Chrysler did not provide any warning that a driver should not sit close to the air bag. In an accident with another car,

Bresnahan's air bag deployed. The bag caused her elbow to strike the windshield pillar and fracture in three places, resulting in repeated surgery and physical therapy. Bresnahan filed a suit in a California state court against Chrysler to recover for her injuries, alleging in part that they were caused by Chrysler's failure to warn consumers about sitting near the air bag. At the trial, an expert testified that the air bag was not intended to prevent arm injuries, which were "a predictable, incidental consequence" of the bag's deploying. Should Chrysler pay for Bresnahan's injuries? Why or why not? [*Bresnahan v. Chrysler Corp.*, 76 Cal.Rptr.2d 804, 65 Cal.App.4th 1149 (1998)]

6–13. New England Ecological Development, Inc. (NEED), a recycling station in Rhode Island, needed a conveyor belt system and gave the specifications to Colmar Belting Co. Colmar did not design or make belts but distributed the component parts. For this system, Emerson Power Transmission Corp. (EPT) manufactured the wing pulley, a component of the nip point (the point at which a belt moves over the stationary part of the system). Kenneth Butler, a welder, assembled the system with assistance from Colmar. Neither Colmar nor EPT recommended the use of a protective shield to guard the nip point, and as finally built, NEED's system did not have a shield. Later, as Americo Buonanno, a NEED employee, was clearing debris from the belt, his arm was pulled into the nip point. The arm was severely crushed and later amputated at the elbow. Buonanno filed a suit in a Rhode Island state court against Colmar and EPT, alleging in part strict liability. The defendants filed a motion for summary judgment, arguing that as sellers of component parts, they had no duty to ensure the proper design of the final product. On what grounds might the court deny the motion? [*Buonanno v. Colmar Belting Co.*, 733 A.2d 712 (R.I. 1999)]

6–14. Among the equipment that Ingersol-Rand makes is a milling machine. In the maintenance manual that accompanies the machine are warnings that users should stay ten feet away from the rear of the machine when it is operating, verify that the back-up alarm is working, and check the area for the presence of others. There is also a sign on the machine that tells users to stay ten feet away. While using the machine to strip asphalt from a road being repaved, Terrill Wilson backed up. The alarm did not sound, and Cosandra Rogers, who was standing with her back to the machine, was run over and maimed. Rogers filed a suit in a federal district court against Ingersoll-Rand alleging in part strict liability on the basis of a design defect. The jury awarded Rogers $10.2 million in compensatory damages and $6.5 million in punitive damages. Ingersoll-Rand appealed, emphasizing the adequacy of its warnings. Can an adequate warning immunize a manufacturer from any liability caused by a defectively designed product? Discuss fully. [*Rogers v. Ingersoll-Rand Co.*, 144 F.3d 841 (D.C.Cir. 1998)]

6–15. In May 1995, Ms. McCathern and her daughter, together with McCathern's cousin, Ms. Sanders, and her daughter, were riding in Sanders's 1994 Toyota 4Runner. Sanders was driving, McCathern was in the front passenger seat, and the children were in the back seat. Everyone was wearing a seat belt. While the group was traveling south on Oregon State Highway 395 at a speed of approximately 50 miles per hour, an oncoming vehicle veered into Sanders's lane of travel. When Sanders tried to steer clear, the 4Runner rolled over and landed upright on its four wheels. During the rollover, the roof over the front passenger seat collapsed and, as a result, McCathern sustained serious, permanent injuries. McCathern filed a suit in an Oregon state court against Toyota Motor Corp. and others, alleging in part that the 1994 4Runner "was dangerously defective and unreasonably dangerous in that the vehicle, as designed and sold, was unstable and prone to rollover." What is the test for product liability based on a design defect? Applying that test, what would McCathern have to prove to succeed? [*McCathern v. Toyota Motor Corp.*, 332 Or. 59, 23 P.3d 320 (2001)]

E-LINKS

For updated links to resources available on the Web, as well as a variety of other materials, visit this text's Web site at

http://wbl-cs.westbuslaw.com

For information on the *Restatements of the Law*, including the *Restatement (Second) of Torts* and the *Restatement (Third) of Torts: Products Liability*, go to the Web site of the American Law Institute at

http://www.ali.org

The law firm of Horvitz & Levy offers a review of recent judicial decisions in the area of product liability at

http://www.horvitzlevy.com/annrev/an5in.html

For information on product liability suits against tobacco companies and recent settlements, go to

http://www.usatoday.com/news/smoke/smoke00.htm

LEGAL RESEARCH EXERCISES ON THE WEB

Go to http://wbl-cs.westbuslaw.com, the Web site that accompanies this text. Select "Interactive Study Center," and then click on "Chapter 6." There you will find the following Internet research exercise that you can perform to learn more about product liability litigation.

Activity 6–1: Product Liability Litigation

CHAPTER 7
Intellectual Property and Internet Law

Most people think of wealth in terms of houses, land, cars, stocks, and bonds. Wealth, however, also includes **intellectual property**, which consists of the products that result from intellectual, creative processes. Although it is an abstract term for an abstract concept, intellectual property is nonetheless wholly familiar to virtually everyone. *Trademarks, service marks, copyrights,* and *patents* are all forms of intellectual property. The book you are reading is copyrighted. Undoubtedly, the personal computer you use at home is trademarked. Exhibit 7–1 on the next two pages offers a comprehensive summary of these forms of intellectual property, as well as intellectual property that consists of trade secrets. In this chapter, we examine each of these forms in some detail.

The study of intellectual property law is important because intellectual property has taken on increasing significance, not only within the United States but globally as well. Today, ownership rights in intangible intellectual property are more important to the prosperity of many U.S. companies than are their tangible assets. As you will read in this chapter, a major challenge to businesspersons today is how to protect these valuable rights in the online world.

The need to protect creative works was voiced by the framers of the U.S. Constitution over two hundred years ago: Article I, Section 8, of the U.S. Constitution authorized Congress "[t]o promote the Progress of Science and useful Arts, by securing for limited Times to Authors and Inventors the exclusive Right to their respective Writings and Discoveries." Laws protecting patents, trademarks, and copyrights are explicitly designed to protect and reward inventive and artistic creativity. Although intellectual property law limits the economic freedom of some individuals, it does so to protect the freedom of others to enjoy the fruits of their labors—in the form of profits.

SECTION 1
Trademarks and Related Property

A **trademark** is a distinctive mark, motto, device, or implement that a manufacturer stamps, prints, or otherwise affixes to the goods it produces so that they may be identified on the market and their origin vouched for. At common law, the person who used a symbol or mark to identify a business or product was protected in the use of that trademark. Clearly, if one used the trademark of another, it would lead consumers to believe that one's goods were made by the other. The law seeks to avoid this kind of confusion. We examine in this section various aspects of the law governing trademarks.

Westlaw. See Case 7.1 at the end of this chapter. To view the full, unedited case from Westlaw,® go to this text's Web site at **http://wbl-cs.westbuslaw.com**.

STATUTORY PROTECTION OF TRADEMARKS

Statutory protection of trademarks and related property is provided at the federal level by the Lanham Trade-Mark Act of 1946.[1] The Lanham Act was enacted in part to protect manufacturers from losing business to rival companies that used confusingly

1. 15 U.S.C. Sections 1051–1127.

EXHIBIT 7–1 FORMS OF INTELLECTUAL PROPERTY

	PATENT	COPYRIGHT	TRADEMARKS (SERVICE MARKS AND TRADE DRESS)	TRADE SECRETS
Definition	A grant from the government that gives an inventor exclusive rights to an invention.	An intangible property right granted to authors and originators of a literary work or artistic production that falls within specified categories.	Any distinctive word, name, symbol, or device (image or appearance), or combination thereof, that an entity uses to identify and distinguish its goods or services from those of others.	Any information (including formulas, patterns, programs, devices, techniques, and processes) that a business possesses and that gives the business an advantage over competitors who do not know the information or processes.
Requirements	An invention must be: 1. Novel. 2. Not obvious. 3. Useful.	Literary or artistic works must be: 1. Original. 2. Fixed in a durable medium that can be perceived, reproduced, or communicated. 3. Within a copyrightable category.	Trademarks, service marks, and trade dress must be sufficiently distinctive (or must have acquired a secondary meaning) to enable consumers and others to distinguish the manufacturer's, seller's, or business user's products or services from those of competitors.	Information and processes that have commercial value, that are not known or easily ascertainable by the general public or others, and that are reasonably protected from disclosure.
Types or Categories	1. Utility (general). 2. Design. 3. Plant (flowers, vegetables, and so on).	1. Literary works (including computer programs). 2. Musical works. 3. Dramatic works. 4. Pantomime and choreographic works. 5. Pictorial, graphic, and sculptural works. 6. Films and audiovisual works. 7. Sound recordings.	1. Strong, distinctive marks (such as fanciful, arbitrary, or suggestive marks). 2. Marks that have acquired a secondary meaning by use. 3. Other types of marks, including certification marks and collective marks. 4. Trade dress (such as a distinctive decor, menu, or style or type of service).	1. Customer lists. 2. Research and development. 3. Plans and programs. 4. Pricing information. 5. Production techniques. 6. Marketing techniques. 7. Formulas. 8. Compilations.
How Acquired	By filing a patent application with the U.S. Patent and Trademark Office and receiving that	Automatic (once in tangible form); to recover for infringement, the copyright must be	1. At common law, ownership is created by use of mark. 2. Registration (either with the U.S. Patent and Trademark Office or with the	Through the originality and development of information and processes that are

EXHIBIT 7–1 FORMS OF INTELLECTUAL PROPERTY (CONTINUED)

	PATENT	COPYRIGHT	TRADEMARKS (SERVICE MARKS AND TRADE DRESS)	TRADE SECRETS
How Acquired (continued)	office's approval.	registered with the U.S. Copyright Office.	appropriate state office) gives constructive notice of date of use. 3. Federal registration is permitted if the mark is currently in use *or* if the applicant intends use within six months (period can be extended to three years). 4. Federal registration can be renewed between the fifth and sixth years and, thereafter, every ten years.	unique to a business, that are unknown by others, and that would be valuable to competitors if they knew of the information and processes.
Rights	An inventor has the right to make, use, sell, assign, or license the invention during the duration of the patent's term. The first to invent has patent rights.	The author or originator has the exclusive right to reproduce, distribute, display, license, or transfer a copyrighted work.	The owner has the right to use the mark or trade dress and to exclude others from using it. The right of use can be licensed or sold (assigned) to another.	The owner has the right to sole and exclusive use of the trade secrets and the right to use legal means to protect against misappropriation of the trade secrets by others. The owner can license or assign a trade secret.
Duration	Twenty years from the date of application; for design patents, fourteen years.	1. For authors: the life of the author, plus 70 years. 2. For publishers: 95 years after the date of publication or 120 years after creation.	Unlimited, as long as it is in use. To continue notice by registration, the registration must be renewed by filing.	Unlimited, as long as not revealed to others. (Once revealed to others, they are no longer trade secrets.)
Civil Remedies for Infringement	Monetary damages, which include reasonable royalties and lost profits, *plus* attorneys' fees. (Treble damages are available for intentional infringement.)	Actual damages, plus profits received by the infringer; *or* statutory damages of not less than $500 and not more than $20,000 ($100,000, if infringement is willful); *plus* costs and attorneys' fees.	1. Injunction prohibiting future use of mark. 2. Actual damages, plus profits received by the infringer (can be increased to three times the actual damages under the Lanham Act). 3. Impoundment and destruction of infringing articles. 4. *Plus* costs and attorneys' fees.	Monetary damages for misappropriation (the Uniform Trade Secrets Act permits punitive damages up to twice the amount of actual damages for willful and malicious misappropriation); *plus* costs and attorneys' fees.

similar trademarks. The Lanham Act incorporates the common law of trademarks and provides remedies for owners of trademarks who wish to enforce their claims in federal court. Many states also have trademark statutes.

In 1995, Congress amended the Lanham Act by passing the Federal Trademark Dilution Act,[2] which extended the protection available to trademark owners by creating a federal cause of action for trademark **dilution.** Until the passage of this amendment, federal trademark law only prohibited the unauthorized use of the same mark on competing—or on noncompeting but "related"—goods or services when such use would likely confuse consumers as to the origin of those goods and services. Trademark dilution laws, which have also been enacted by about half of the states, protect "distinctive" or "famous" trademarks (such as Jergens, McDonald's, RCA, and Macintosh) from certain unauthorized uses of the marks *regardless* of a showing of competition or a likelihood of confusion.

In one of the first cases to be decided under the 1995 act's provisions, a federal court held that a famous mark may be diluted not only by the use of an *identical* mark but also by the use of a *similar* mark. The lawsuit was brought by Ringling Bros.–Barnum & Bailey, Combined Shows, Inc., against the state of Utah. Ringling Bros. claimed that Utah's use of the slogan "The Greatest Snow on Earth"—to attract visitors to the state's recreational and scenic resorts—diluted the distinctiveness of the circus's famous trademark, "The Greatest Show on Earth." Utah moved to dismiss the suit, arguing that the 1995 provisions only protect owners of famous trademarks against the unauthorized use of identical marks. The court disagreed and refused to grant Utah's motion to dismiss the case.[3]

Trademark Registration

Trademarks may be registered with the state or with the federal government. To register for protection under federal trademark law, a person must file an application with the U.S. Patent and Trademark Office in Washington, D.C. Under current law, a mark can be registered (1) if it is currently in commerce or (2) if the applicant intends to put it into commerce within six months.

2. 15 U.S.C. Section 1125.

3. *Ringling Bros.–Barnum & Bailey, Combined Shows, Inc. v. Utah Division of Travel Development,* 935 F.Supp. 736 (E.D.Va. 1996).

Under extenuating circumstances, the six-month period can be extended by thirty months, giving the applicant a total of three years from the date of notice of trademark approval to make use of the mark and file the required use statement. Registration is postponed until the mark is actually used. Nonetheless, during this waiting period, any applicant can legally protect his or her trademark against a third party who previously has neither used the mark nor filed an application for it. Registration is renewable between the fifth and sixth years after the initial registration and every ten years thereafter (every twenty years for those trademarks registered before 1990).

Registration of a trademark with the U.S. Patent and Trademark Office gives notice on a nationwide basis that the trademark belongs exclusively to the registrant. The registrant is also allowed to use the symbol ® to indicate that the mark has been registered. Whenever that trademark is copied to a substantial degree or used in its entirety by another, intentionally or unintentionally, the trademark has been *infringed* (used without authorization). When a trademark has been infringed, the owner of the mark has a cause of action against the infringer. A person need not have registered a trademark in order to sue for trademark infringement, but registration does furnish proof of the date of inception of the trademark's use.

Distinctiveness of Mark

A central objective of the Lanham Act is to reduce the likelihood that consumers will be confused by similar marks. For that reason, only those trademarks that are deemed sufficiently distinctive from all competing trademarks will be protected. A trademark must be sufficiently distinct to enable consumers to identify the manufacturer of the goods easily and to distinguish between those goods and competing products.

Strong Marks. Fanciful, arbitrary, or suggestive trademarks are generally considered to be the most distinctive (strongest) trademarks. This is because these types of marks are normally taken from outside the context of the particular product and thus provide the best means of distinguishing one product from another.

Fanciful trademarks include invented words, such as Xerox for one manufacturer's copiers and

Kodak for another company's photographic products. Arbitrary trademarks include actual words used with products that have no literal connection to the words, such as English Leather used as a name for an after-shave lotion (and not for leather processed in England). Suggestive trademarks are those that suggest something about a product without describing the product directly. For example, the trademark Dairy Queen suggests an association between the products and milk, but it does not directly describe ice cream.

Secondary Meaning. Descriptive terms, geographic terms, and personal names are not inherently distinctive and do not receive protection under the law until they acquire a secondary meaning. A secondary meaning may arise when customers begin to associate a specific term or phrase (such as London Fog) with specific trademarked items (coats with London Fog labels). Whether a secondary meaning becomes attached to a term or name usually depends on how extensively the product is advertised, the market for the product, the number of sales, and other factors. Once a secondary meaning is attached to a term or name, a trademark is considered distinctive and is protected. Even a shade of color can qualify for trademark protection, once customers associate the color with the product.[4]

Generic Terms. Generic terms, such as *bicycle* and *computer*, receive no protection, even if they acquire secondary meanings. A particularly thorny problem arises when a trademark acquires generic use. For example, *aspirin* and *thermos* were originally the names of trademarked products, but today the words are used generically. Other examples are *escalator, trampoline, raisin bran, dry ice, lanolin, linoleum, nylon,* and *corn flakes*. Even so, the courts will not allow another firm to use those marks in such a way as to deceive a potential consumer.

> Westlaw. See Case 7.2 at the end of this chapter. To view the full, unedited case from Westlaw,® go to this text's Web site at http://wbl-cs.westbuslaw.com.

Trade Dress

The term **trade dress** refers to the image and overall appearance of a product—for example, the distinctive decor, menu, layout, and style of service of a particular restaurant. Basically, trade dress is subject to the same protection as trademarks. In cases involving trade dress infringement, as in trademark infringement cases, a major consideration is whether consumers are likely to be confused by the allegedly infringing use.

Service, Certification, and Collective Marks

A **service mark** is similar to a trademark but is used to distinguish the services of one person or company from those of another. For example, each airline has a particular mark or symbol associated with its name. Titles and character names used in radio and television are frequently registered as service marks.

Other marks protected by law include certification marks and collective marks. A **certification mark** is used by one or more persons other than the owner to certify the region, materials, mode of manufacture, quality, or accuracy of the owner's goods or services. When used by members of a cooperative, association, or other organization, it is referred to as a **collective mark.** Examples of certification marks are the phrases "Good Housekeeping Seal of Approval" and "UL Tested." Collective marks appear at the ends of motion picture credits to indicate the various associations and organizations that participated in the making of the film. The union marks found on the tags of certain products are also collective marks.

Trade Names

Trademarks apply to *products*. The term **trade name** is used to indicate part or all of a business's name, whether the business is a sole proprietorship, a partnership, or a corporation. Generally, a trade name is directly related to a business and its goodwill. A trade name may be protected as a trademark if the trade name is the same as the name of the company's trademarked product—for example, Coca-Cola. Unless also used as a trademark or service mark, a trade name cannot be registered with the federal government. Trade names are protected under the common law, however. As with trademarks, words must be unusual or fancifully used if they are to be protected as trade names. The word *Safeway*, for example, was held by the courts to be sufficiently

4. *Qualitex Co. v. Jacobson Products Co.*, 514 U.S. 159, 115 S.Ct. 1300, 131 L.Ed.2d 248 (1995).

fanciful to obtain protection as a trade name for a foodstore chain.[5]

SECTION 2

Cyber Marks

In cyberspace, trademarks are sometimes referred to as **cyber marks**. We turn now to a discussion of trademark-related issues in cyberspace and how new laws and the courts are addressing these issues. One concern relates to the rights of a trademark's owner to use the mark as part of a domain name (Internet address). Other issues have to do with cybersquatting, meta tags, and trademark dilution on the Web. The use of licensing as a way to avoid liability for infringing on another's intellectual property rights in cyberspace will be discussed later in this chapter.

DOMAIN NAMES

In the real world, one business can often use the same name as another without causing any conflict, particularly if the businesses are small, their goods or services are different, and the areas within which they do business are far apart. In the online world, however, there is only one area of business—cyberspace. Thus, disputes between parties over which one has the right to use a particular domain name have become common. A **domain name** is part of an Internet address, such as "westlaw.com." The top level domain (TLD) is the part of the name to the right of the period and represents the type of entity that operates the site (for example, "com" is an abbreviation for "commercial"). The second level (the part of the name to the left of the period) is chosen by the business entity or individual registering the domain name.

Conflicts over rights to domain names emerged during the 1990s as e-commerce expanded on a worldwide scale. Of the TLDs then available (*.com, .org, .net, .edu, .int, .mil,* and *.gov*), only one—*.com*—was typically used by commercial enterprises. As e-commerce grew, the *.com* TLD became widely used by businesses on the Web. Competition among firms with similar names and products for the second level domains preceding the *.com* TLD led, understandably, to numerous disputes over domain name rights. Disputes that have arisen over the same, or similar, domain names have involved parties' attempts to profit from the goodwill of a competitor, to sell pornography, to offer for sale another party's domain name, and to otherwise infringe on others' trademarks.

As noted in Chapter 2, the Internet Corporation for Assigned Names and Numbers (ICANN), a nonprofit corporation set up by the federal government to oversee the distribution of domain names, has played a leading role in facilitating the settlement of domain name disputes worldwide. ICANN has also attempted to reduce domain name conflicts by approving seven additional TLDs for use in domain names.[6]

ANTICYBERSQUATTING LEGISLATION

In the late 1990s, Congress passed legislation prohibiting another practice that had given rise to numerous disputes over domain names: cybersquatting. **Cybersquatting** occurs when a person registers for a domain name that is the same as, or confusingly similar to, the trademark of another and then offers to sell the domain name back to the trademark owner. During the 1990s, cybersquatting became a contentious topic and led to much litigation. Often in controversy in these cases was whether cybersquatting constituted a commercial use of the mark so as to violate federal trademark law. Additionally, it was not always easy to separate cybersquatting from legitimate business activity. Although no clear rules emerged from this litigation, many courts held that cybersquatting violated trademark law.[7]

In 1999, Congress addressed this issue by passing the Anticybersquatting Consumer Protection Act (ACPA), which amended the Lanham Act (the federal law protecting trademarks, discussed earlier in this chapter). The ACPA makes it illegal for a person to "register, traffic in, or use" a domain name if (a) the name is identical or confusingly similar to the trademark of another and (b) if the one registering, trafficking in, or using the domain name has a "bad faith intent" to profit from that trademark. The act does not define what constitutes bad faith. Instead, it lists several factors that the courts can consider in deciding whether bad faith exists. Some of these factors are the trademark rights of the other

5. *Safeway Stores v. Suburban Foods,* 130 F.Supp. 249 (E.D.Va. 1955).

6. The new TLDs, which were approved by ICANN in November 2000, are *.biz, .info, .name, .pro, .museums, .coop,* and *.aero.*

7. See, for example, *Panavision International, L.P. v. Toeppen,* 141 F.3d 1316 (9th Cir. 1998).

person, the intent to divert consumers in a way that could harm the goodwill represented by the trademark, whether there is an offer to transfer or sell the domain name to the trademark owner, and whether there is an intent to use the domain name to offer goods and services.

The ACPA applies to all domain name registrations, even domain names registered before the passage of the act. Successful plaintiffs in suits brought under the act can collect actual damages and profits, or elect to receive statutory damages of from $1,000 to $100,000.

META TAGS

Search engines compile their results by looking through a Web site's key words field. **Meta tags**, or key words, may be inserted in this field to increase a site's appearance in search engine results, even though the site has nothing to do with the inserted words. Using this same technique, one site may appropriate the key words of other sites with more frequent hits, so that the appropriating site appears in the same search engine results as the more popular site. Using another's trademark in a meta tag without the owner's permission, however, constitutes trademark infringement.

DILUTION IN THE ONLINE WORLD

As discussed earlier, trademark *dilution* occurs when a trademark is used, without authorization, in a way that diminishes the distinctive quality of the mark. Unlike trademark infringement, a dilution cause of action does not require proof that consumers are likely to be confused by a connection between the unauthorized use and the mark. For this reason, the products involved do not have to be similar. In the first case alleging dilution on the Web, a court precluded the use of "candyland.com" as the URL for an adult site. The suit was brought by the maker of the "Candyland" children's game and owner of the "Candyland" mark.[8]

SECTION 3

Patents

A **patent** is a grant from the government that gives an inventor the exclusive right to make, use, and sell an invention for a period of twenty years from the date of filing the application for a patent. Patents for a fourteen-year period are given for designs, as opposed to inventions. For either a regular patent or a design patent, the applicant must demonstrate to the satisfaction of the U.S. Patent and Trademark Office that the invention, discovery, process, or design is genuine, novel, useful, and not obvious in light of current technology. A patent holder gives notice to all that an article or design is patented by placing on it the word *Patent* or *Pat.* plus the patent number. In contrast to patent law in other countries, in the United States patent protection is given to the first person to invent a product or process, even though someone else may have been the first to file for a patent on that product or process.

A significant development relating to patents is the availability online of the world's patent databases. The U.S. Patent and Trademark Office provides at its Web site searchable databases covering U.S. patents granted since 1976. The European Patent Office (EPO) maintains at its Web site databases covering all patent documents in sixty-five nations and the legal status of patents in twenty-two of those countries.

PATENT INFRINGEMENT

If a firm makes, uses, or sells another's patented design, product, or process without the patent owner's permission, the tort of patent infringement occurs. Patent infringement may arise even though the patent owner has not put the patented product in commerce. Patent infringement may also occur even though not all features or parts of an invention are copied. (With respect to a patented process, however, all steps or their equivalents must be copied in order for infringement to occur.)

Often, litigation for patent infringement is so costly that the patent holder will instead offer to sell to the infringer a license to use the patented design, product, or process (licensing will be discussed later in this chapter). Indeed, in many cases, the costs of detection, prosecution, and monitoring are so high that patents are valueless to their owners, because the owners cannot afford to protect them.

In the past, parties involved in patent litigation also faced another problem: it was often hard to predict the outcome of litigation because jurors found it difficult to understand the issues in dispute. This was particularly true when the claims involved patents on

8. *Hasbro, Inc. v. Internet Entertainment Group, Ltd.*, 1996 WL 84853 (W.D.Wash. 1996).

complicated products—such as sophisticated technological or biotechnological products. In a significant case decided in 1996, *Markman v. Westview Instruments, Inc.*,[9] the United States Supreme Court held that it is the responsibility of judges, not juries, to interpret the scope and nature of patent claims. In other words, before a case goes to the jury, the judge must interpret the nature of the claim and give the jury instructions based on that interpretation.

Patents for Software

At one time, it was difficult for developers and manufacturers of software to obtain patent protection because many software products simply automate procedures that can be performed manually. In other words, the computer programs do not meet the "novel" and "not obvious" requirements previously mentioned. Also, the basis for software is often a mathematical equation or formula, which is not patentable. In 1981, however, the United States Supreme Court held that it is possible to obtain a patent for a process that incorporates a computer program—providing, of course, that the process itself is patentable.[10] Subsequently, many patents have been issued for software-related inventions.

Another obstacle to obtaining patent protection for software is the procedure for obtaining patents. The process can be expensive and slow. The time element is a particularly important consideration for someone wishing to obtain a patent on software. In light of the rapid changes and improvements in computer technology, the delay could undercut the product's success in the marketplace.

Despite these difficulties, patent protection is used in the computer industry. If a patent is infringed, the patent holder may sue for an injunction, damages, and the destruction of all infringing copies, as well as attorneys' fees and court costs.

Business Process Patents

Traditionally, patents have been granted to inventions that are "new and useful processes, machines, manufacturers, or compositions of matter, or any new and useful improvements thereof." The Patent and Trademark Office (PTO) routinely rejected computer systems and software applications because they were deemed not to be useful processes, machines, articles of manufacture, or compositions of matter. They were simply considered mathematical algorithms, abstract ideas, or "methods of doing business." In a landmark 1998 case, however, *State Street Bank & Trust Co. v. Signature Financial Group, Inc.*,[11] the U.S. Court of Appeals for the Federal Circuit ruled that only three categories of subject matter will always remain unpatentable: (1) the laws of nature; (2) natural phenomena; and (3) abstract ideas. This decision meant, among other things, that business processes were patentable.

After this decision, numerous technology firms applied for business process patents. Walker Digital applied for a business process patent for its "Dutch auction" system, which allowed consumers on the Internet to make offers for airline tickets and led to the creation of Priceline.com. About.com obtained a patent for its "Elaborative Internet Data Mining System," which creates and pulls together Web content on a large range of topics onto a single Web site. Amazon.com obtained a business process patent for its "one-click" ordering system, a method of processing credit-card orders securely without asking, more than once, for the customer's card number or other personal information, such as the customer's name and address. Indeed, since the *State Street* decision, there has been a more than 800 percent increase in the number of Internet-related patents issued by the U.S. Patent and Trademark Office.

SECTION 4

Copyrights

A **copyright** is an intangible property right granted by federal statute to the author or originator of a literary or artistic production of a specified type. Currently, copyrights are governed by the Copyright Act of 1976,[12] as amended. Works created after January 1, 1978, are automatically given statutory copyright protection for the life of the author plus 70 years. For copyrights owned by publishing houses, the copyright expires 95 years from the date of publication or 120 years from the date of creation, whichever is first. For works by more than one au-

9. 517 U.S. 370, 116 S.Ct. 1384, 134 L.Ed.2d 577 (1996).
10. *Diamond v. Diehr,* 450 U.S. 175, 101 S.Ct. 1048, 67 L.Ed.2d 155 (1981).
11. 149 F.3d 1368 (Fed. Cir. 1998).
12. 17 U.S.C. Sections 101 *et seq.*

thor, the copyright expires 70 years after the death of the last surviving author.

Copyrights can be registered with the U.S. Copyright Office in Washington, D.C. A copyright owner no longer needs to place the symbol © or the term *Copr.* or *Copyright* on the work, however, to have the work protected against infringement. Chances are that if somebody created it, somebody owns it.

What Is Protected Expression?

Works that are copyrightable include books, records, films, artworks, architectural plans, menus, music videos, product packaging, and computer software. To obtain protection under the Copyright Act, a work must be original and fall into one of the following categories: (1) literary works; (2) musical works; (3) dramatic works; (4) pantomimes and choreographic works; (5) pictorial, graphic, and sculptural works; (6) films and other audiovisual works; and (7) sound recordings. To be protected, a work must be "fixed in a durable medium" from which it can be perceived, reproduced, or communicated. Protection is automatic. Registration is not required.

Section 102 of the Copyright Act specifically excludes copyright protection for any "idea, procedure, process, system, method of operation, concept, principle, or discovery, regardless of the form in which it is described, explained, illustrated, or embodied." Note that it is not possible to copyright an *idea*. The underlying ideas embodied in a work may be freely used by others. What is copyrightable is the particular way in which an idea is expressed. Whenever an idea and an expression are inseparable, the expression cannot be copyrighted. Generally, anything that is not an original expression will not qualify for copyright protection. Facts widely known to the public are not copyrightable. Page numbers are not copyrightable, because they follow a sequence known to everyone. Mathematical calculations are not copyrightable.

Compilations of facts, however, are copyrightable. Section 103 of the Copyright Act defines a compilation as "a work formed by the collection and assembling of preexisting materials or data that are selected, coordinated, or arranged in such a way that the resulting work as a whole constitutes an original work of authorship." The key requirement in the copyrightability of a compilation is originality. Therefore, the White Pages of a telephone directory do not qualify for copyright protection when the information that makes up the directory (names, addresses, and telephone numbers) is not selected, coordinated, or arranged in an original way.[13] In one case, even the Yellow Pages of a telephone directory did not qualify for copyright protection.[14]

Copyright Infringement

Whenever the form or expression of an idea is copied, an infringement of copyright has occurred. The reproduction does not have to be exactly the same as the original, nor does it have to reproduce the original in its entirety. If a substantial part of the original is reproduced, there is copyright infringement.

Those who infringe copyrights may be liable for damages or criminal penalties. These range from actual damages or statutory damages, imposed at the court's discretion, to criminal proceedings for willful violations. Actual damages are based on the harm caused to the copyright holder by the infringement, while statutory damages, not to exceed $150,000, are provided for under the Copyright Act. Criminal proceedings may result in fines and/or imprisonment.

An exception to liability for copyright infringement is made under the "fair use" doctrine. In certain circumstances, a person or organization can reproduce copyrighted material without paying royalties (fees paid to the copyright holder for the privilege of reproducing the copyrighted material). Section 107 of the Copyright Act provides as follows:

> [T]he fair use of a copyrighted work, including such use by reproduction in copies or phonorecords or by any other means specified by [Section 106 of the Copyright Act], for purposes such as criticism, comment, news reporting, teaching (including multiple copies for classroom use), scholarship, or research, is not an infringement of copyright. In determining whether the use made of a work in any particular case is a fair use the factors to be considered shall include—
>
> (1) the purpose and character of the use, including whether such use is of a commercial nature or is for nonprofit educational purposes;
> (2) the nature of the copyrighted work;

13. *Feist Publications, Inc. v. Rural Telephone Service Co.*, 499 U.S. 340, 111 S.Ct. 1282, 113 L.Ed.2d 358 (1991).

14. *Bellsouth Advertising & Publishing Corp. v. Donnelley Information Publishing, Inc.*, 999 F.2d 1436 (11th Cir. 1993).

(3) the amount and substantiality of the portion used in relation to the copyrighted work as a whole; and
(4) the effect of the use upon the potential market for or value of the copyrighted work.

Because these guidelines are very broad, the courts determine whether a particular use is fair on a case-by-case basis. Thus, anyone reproducing copyrighted material may still be subject to a violation. In determining whether a use is fair, courts have often considered the fourth factor to be the most important.

Copyright Protection for Software

In 1980, Congress passed the Computer Software Copyright Act, which amended the Copyright Act of 1976 to include computer programs in the list of creative works protected by federal copyright law. The 1980 statute, which classifies computer programs as "literary works," defines a computer program as a "set of statements or instructions to be used directly or indirectly in a computer in order to bring about a certain result."

Because of the unique nature of computer programs, the courts have had many difficulties in applying and interpreting the 1980 act. In a series of cases decided in the 1980s, the courts held that copyright protection extended not only to those parts of a computer program that can be read by humans, such as the high-level language of a source code, but also to the binary-language object code of a computer program, which is readable only by the computer.[15] Additionally, such elements as the overall structure, sequence, and organization of a program were deemed copyrightable.[16]

By the early 1990s, the issue had evolved into whether the "look and feel"—the general appearance, command structure, video images, menus, windows, and other screen displays—of computer programs should also be protected by copyright. Although the courts have disagreed on this issue, the tendency has been not to extend copyright protection to look-and-feel aspects of computer programs. For example, in 1995 the Court of Appeals for the First Circuit held that Lotus Development Corporation's menu command hierarchy for its Lotus 1-2-3 spreadsheet was not protectable under the Copyright Act. The court deemed that the menu command hierarchy is a "method of operation," and Section 102 of the Copyright Act specifically excludes methods of operation from copyright protection.[17] The decision was affirmed by the United States Supreme Court in 1996.[18]

15. See *Stern Electronics, Inc. v. Kaufman*, 669 F.2d 852 (2d Cir. 1982); and *Apple Computer, Inc. v. Franklin Computer Corp.*, 714 F.2d 1240 (3d Cir. 1983).

16. *Whelan Associates, Inc. v. Jaslow Dental Laboratory, Inc.*, 797 F.2d 1222 (3d Cir. 1986).

SECTION 5

Copyrights in Digital Information

Copyright law is probably the most important form of intellectual property protection on the Internet. This is because much of the material on the Internet consists of works of authorship (including multimedia presentations, software, and database information). These works are the traditional focus of copyright law. Copyright law is also important because the nature of the Internet requires that data be "copied" to be transferred online. Copies are a significant part of the traditional controversies arising in this area of the law.

The Copyright Act of 1976

When Congress drafted the principal U.S. law governing copyrights, the Copyright Act of 1976, cyberspace did not exist for most of us. The threat to copyright owners was posed not by computer technology but by unauthorized *tangible* copies of works and the sale of rights to movies, television, and other media.

Some of the issues that were unimagined when the Copyright Act was drafted have posed thorny questions for the courts. For example, to sell a copy of a work, permission of the copyright holder is necessary. Because of the nature of cyberspace, however, one of the early controversies was determining at what point an intangible, electronic "copy" of a work has been made. The courts have held that loading a file or program into a computer's random access memory, or RAM, constitutes the making of a "copy" for purposes of copyright law.[19] RAM is a portion of a computer's

17. *Lotus Development Corp. v. Borland International, Inc.*, 49 F.3d 807 (1st Cir. 1995).

18. *Lotus Development Corp. v. Borland International, Inc.*, 517 U.S. 843, 116 S.Ct. 804, 113 L.Ed.2d 610 (1996). This issue may again come before the Supreme Court for a decision, because only eight justices heard the case, and there was a tied vote; the effect of the tie was to affirm the lower court's decision.

19. *MAI Systems Corp. v. Peak Computer, Inc.*, 991 F.2d 511 (9th Cir. 1993).

memory into which a file, for example, is loaded so that it can be accessed (read or written over). Thus, a copyright is infringed when a party downloads software into RAM if that party does not own the software or otherwise have a right to download it.[20]

Other rights, including those relating to the revision of "collective works" such as magazines, were acknowledged thirty years ago but were considered to have only limited economic value. Today, technology has made some of those rights vastly more significant.

Westlaw. See Case 7.3 at the end of this chapter. To view the full, unedited case from Westlaw,® go to this text's Web site at http://wbl-cs.westbuslaw.com.

THE NO ELECTRONIC THEFT ACT OF 1997

In the last several years, Congress has enacted legislation designed specifically to protect copyright holders in a digital age. For example, prior to 1997 criminal penalties under copyright law could be imposed only if unauthorized copies were exchanged for financial gain. Yet much piracy of copyrighted materials was "altruistic" in nature; that is, unauthorized copies were made and distributed not for financial gain but simply for reasons of generosity—to share the copies with others.

To combat altruistic piracy and for other reasons, Congress passed the No Electronic Theft (NET) Act of 1997. This act extends criminal liability for the piracy of copyrighted materials to persons who exchange unauthorized copies of copyrighted works, such as software, even though they realize no profit from the exchange. The act also imposes penalties on those who make unauthorized electronic copies of books, magazines, movies, or music for *personal* use, thus altering the traditional "fair use" doctrine. The criminal penalties for violating the act are steep; they include fines as high as $250,000 and incarceration for up to five years.

THE DIGITAL MILLENNIUM COPYRIGHT ACT OF 1998

As you will read later in this chapter, to curb the unauthorized copying of copyrighted materials, the World Intellectual Property Organization (WIPO) enacted a treaty in 1996 to upgrade global standards of copyright protection, particularly for the Internet. In 1998, Congress implemented the provisions of the WIPO treaty to update U.S. copyright law. Among other things, the new law—the Digital Millennium Copyright Act of 1998—created civil and criminal penalties for anyone who circumvents (bypasses, or gets around—through clever maneuvering, for example) encryption software or other technological antipiracy protection. Also prohibited are the manufacture, import, sale, or distribution of devices or services for circumvention.

There are exceptions to fit the needs of libraries, scientists, universities, and others. In general, the new law does not restrict the "fair use" of circumvention for educational and other noncommercial purposes. For example, circumvention is allowed to test computer security, to conduct encryption research, to protect personal privacy, or to allow parents to monitor their children's use of the Internet. The exceptions are to be reconsidered every three years.

The 1998 act also limited the liability of Internet service providers (ISPs). Under the act, an ISP is not liable for any copyright infringement by its customer *unless* the ISP is aware of the subscriber's violation. An ISP may be held liable only after learning of the violation and failing to take action to shut the subscriber down. A copyright holder has to act promptly, however, by pursuing a claim in court, or the subscriber has the right to be restored to online access.

MP3 AND FILE-SHARING TECHNOLOGY

At one time, music fans swapped compact disks (CDs) and recorded the songs that they liked from others' CDs onto their own cassettes. This type of "file-sharing" was awkward at best. After the Internet became popular, it was not long before a few enterprising programmers created software to compress large data files, particularly those associated with music. The reduced file sizes make transmitting music over the Internet fast and easy. The most widely known compression and decompression system is MP3. With MP3, music fans can download songs or entire CDs onto their computers or onto a portable listening device, such as Rio. The MP3 system also allows music fans to access other files via the Internet through file-sharing.

File-sharing via the Internet is accomplished by what is called **peer-to-peer (P2P) networking.** The concept is simple. Rather than going through a central Web server, P2P involves numerous personal

20. *DSC Communications Corp. v. Pulse Communications, Inc.*, 170 F.3d 1354 (Fed. Cir. 1999).

computers (PCs) that are connected to the Internet. Files stored on one PC can be accessed by other members of the same network. Sometimes this is called a **distributed network.** In other words, parts of the network are distributed all over the country or the world. File-sharing offers an unlimited number of uses for distributed networks. Currently, for example, many researchers allow their home computers' computing power to be accessed through file-sharing software so that very large mathematical problems can be solved quickly. Additionally, those who collaborate on a project but who are dispersed throughout the country or the world use file-sharing programs in order to advance their project rapidly.

When file-sharing is used to download others' stored music files, however, copyright issues arise. Recording artists and their labels stand to lose large amounts of royalties and revenues if relatively few CDs are purchased and then made available on distributed networks, from which everyone can then get them for free.

See Case 7.4 at the end of this chapter. To view the full, unedited case from Westlaw,® go to this text's Web site at **http://wbl-cs.westbuslaw.com**

SECTION 6

Trade Secrets

Some business processes and information that are not, or cannot be, patented, copyrighted, or trademarked are nevertheless protected against appropriation by competitors as trade secrets. **Trade secrets** consist of customer lists, plans, research and development, pricing information, marketing techniques, production techniques, and generally anything that makes an individual company unique and that would have value to a competitor.

Unlike copyright and trademark protection, protection of trade secrets extends both to ideas and to their expression. (For this reason, and because a trade secret involves no registration or filing requirements, trade secret protection may be well suited for software.) Of course, the secret formula, method, or other information must be disclosed to some persons, particularly to key employees. Businesses generally attempt to protect their trade secrets by having all employees who use the process or information agree in their contracts, or in confidentiality agreements, never to divulge it.

State and Federal Law on Trade Secrets

Under Section 757 of the *Restatement of Torts,* "One who discloses or uses another's trade secret, without a privilege to do so, is liable to the other if (1) he discovered the secret by improper means, or (2) his disclosure or use constitutes a breach of confidence reposed in him by the other in disclosing the secret to him." The theft of confidential business data by industrial espionage, as when a business taps into a competitor's computer, is a theft of trade secrets without any contractual violation and is actionable in itself.

Until recently, virtually all law with respect to trade secrets was common law. In an effort to reduce the unpredictability of the common law in this area, a model act, the Uniform Trade Secrets Act, was presented to the states in 1979 for adoption. Parts of the act have been adopted in more than twenty states. Typically, a state that has adopted parts of the act has adopted only those parts that encompass its own existing common law. Additionally, in 1996 Congress passed the Economic Espionage Act, which made the theft of trade secrets a federal crime. We will examine the provisions and significance of this act in Chapter 8, in the context of crimes related to business.

Trade Secrets in Cyberspace

The nature of the new technology undercuts a business firm's ability to protect its confidential information, including trade secrets.[21] For example, a dishonest employee could e-mail trade secrets in a company's computer to a competitor or a future employer. If e-mail is not possible, the employee might walk out with the information on a computer disk. Dissatisfied former employees have resorted to other options as well. For example, in one case, a former employee of Intel Corporation, Ken Hamidi, became a thorn in Intel's side when he criticized the company's policies in e-mail sent to current employees. Hamidi, an engineer who had operated an Intel employee Web site, e-mailed from 25,000 to 35,000 messages at a time to Intel employees. Intel

21. Note that in a recent case, the court indicated that customers' e-mail addresses may constitute trade secrets. See *T-N-T Motorsports, Inc. v. Hennessey Motorsports, Inc.*, 965 S.W.2d 18 (Tex.App.—Hous. [1 Dist.] 1998); rehearing overruled (1998); petition dismissed (1998).

eventually took Hamidi to court, and the court ordered Hamidi to cease sending e-mails to Intel employees.[22]

SECTION 7

Licensing

One of the ways to make use of another's trademark, copyright, patent, or trade secret, while avoiding litigation, is to obtain a license to do so. A license in this context is essentially an agreement to permit the use of a trademark, copyright, patent, or trade secret for certain purposes. For example, a licensee (the party obtaining the license) might be allowed to use the trademark of the licensor (the party issuing the license) as part of the name of its company, or as part of its domain name, without otherwise using the mark on any products or services.

The National Conference of Commissioners on Uniform State Laws approved the Uniform Computer Information Transactions Act (UCITA) in 1999 and submitted it to the states for adoption. The act was drafted to address problems unique to electronic contracting and to the purchase and sale (licensing) of computer information, such as software. We will look at some of the key provisions of this act in Chapter 23, in the context of electronic contracts.

SECTION 8

International Protection for Intellectual Property

For many years, the United States has been a party to various international agreements relating to intellectual property rights. For example, the Paris Convention of 1883, to which about ninety countries are signatory, allows parties in one country to file for patent and trademark protection in any of the other member countries. Other international agreements in this area include the Berne Convention and the TRIPS agreement.

The Berne Convention

Under the Berne Convention of 1886, an international copyright agreement, if an American writes a book, his or her copyright in the book must be recognized by every country that has signed the convention. Also, if a citizen of a country that has not signed the convention first publishes a book in a country that has signed, all other countries that have signed the convention must recognize that author's copyright. Copyright notice is not needed to gain protection under the Berne Convention for works published after March 1, 1989.

Currently, the laws of many countries as well as international laws are being updated to reflect changes in technology and the expansion of the Internet. Copyright holders and other owners of intellectual property generally agree that changes in the law are needed to stop the increasing international piracy of their property. The World Intellectual Property Organization (WIPO) Copyright Treaty of 1996, a special agreement under the Berne Convention, attempts to update international law governing copyright protection to include more safeguards against copyright infringement via the Internet. The United States, which signed the WIPO treaty in 1996, implemented its terms in the Digital Millennium Copyright Act of 1998, as previously discussed.

The Berne Convention and other international agreements have given some protection to intellectual property on a global level. Another significant worldwide agreement to increase such protection is the Trade-Related Aspects of Intellectual Property Rights agreement—or, more simply, the TRIPS agreement.

The TRIPS Agreement

The TRIPS agreement was signed by representatives from over one hundred nations in 1994. It was one of several documents that were annexed to the agreement that created the World Trade Organization, or WTO, in 1995. The TRIPS agreement established, for the first time, standards for the international protection of intellectual property rights, including patents, trademarks, and copyrights for movies, computer programs, books, and music.

Prior to the TRIPS agreement, one of the difficulties faced by U.S. sellers of intellectual property in the international market was that another country might either lack laws to protect intellectual property rights or fail to enforce what laws it had. To address this problem, the TRIPS agreement provides

22. *Intel Corp. v. Hamidi*, 1999 WL 450944 (Cal.Super. 1999).

that each member country must include in its domestic laws broad intellectual property rights and effective remedies (including civil and criminal penalties) for violations of those rights.

Generally, the TRIPS agreement provides that member nations must not discriminate (in terms of the administration, regulation, or adjudication of intellectual property rights) against foreign owners of such rights. In other words, a member nation cannot give its own nationals (citizens) favorable treatment without offering the same treatment to nationals of all member countries. For example, if a U.S. software manufacturer brings a suit for the infringement of intellectual property rights under Japan's national laws, the U.S. manufacturer is entitled to receive the same treatment as a Japanese domestic manufacturer. Each member nation must also ensure that legal procedures are available for parties who wish to bring actions for infringement of intellectual property rights. Additionally, as part of the agreement creating the WTO, a mechanism for settling disputes among member nations was established.

Particular provisions of the TRIPS agreement refer to patent, trademark, and copyright protection for intellectual property. The agreement specifically provides copyright protection for computer programs by stating that compilations of data, databases, and other materials are "intellectual creations" and are to be protected as copyrightable works. Other provisions relate to trade secrets and the rental of computer programs and cinematographic works.

Terms and Concepts to Review

certification mark 145	domain name 146	trade dress 145
collective mark 145	intellectual property 141	trade name 145
copyright 149	meta tags 147	trade secret 152
cyber mark 146	patent 147	trademark 141
cybersquatting 146	peer-to-peer (P2P) networking 151	
dilution 144	service mark 145	
distributed network 152		

Chapter Summary

Trademarks and Related Property	1. A *trademark* is a distinctive mark, motto, device, or emblem that a manufacturer stamps, prints, or otherwise affixes to the goods it produces so that they may be identified on the market and their origin vouched for. 2. The major federal statutes protecting trademarks and related property are the Lanham Trade-Mark Act of 1946 and the Federal Trademark Dilution Act of 1995. Generally, to be protected, a trademark must be sufficiently distinctive from all competing trademarks. 3. *Trademark infringement* occurs when one uses a mark that is the same as, or confusingly similar to, the protected trademark, service mark, trade name, or trade dress of another without permission when marketing goods or services. 4. Trade dress, trade names, and service, certification, and collective marks are also protected forms of intellectual property.

CHAPTER SUMMARY—CONTINUED

Cyber Marks	A *cyber mark* is a trademark in cyberspace. Trademark infringement in cyberspace occurs when one person uses a name that is the same as, or confusingly similar to, the protected mark of another in a domain name or in meta tags. To protect the rights of trademark owners, Congress passed the Anticybersquatting Consumer Reform Act in 1999. This act makes it illegal for a person to use another's domain name under certain conditions.
Patents	1. A *patent* is a grant from the government that gives an inventor the exclusive right to make, use, and sell an invention for a period of twenty years from the date of filing the application for a patent. To be patentable, an invention (or a discovery, process, or design) must be genuine, novel, useful, and not obvious in light of current technology. Computer software may be patented. 2. *Patent infringement* occurs when one uses or sells another's patented design, product, or process without the patent owner's permission. 3. Business process patents give protection to methods of doing business, such as the "Dutch auction" system used by Priceline.com and the "one-click" ordering system developed by Amazon.com.
Copyrights	1. A *copyright* is an intangible property right granted by federal statute to the author or originator of certain literary or artistic productions. Computer software may be copyrighted. 2. *Copyright infringement* occurs whenever the form or expression of an idea is copied without the permission of the copyright holder. An exception applies if the copying is deemed a "fair use." 3. Copyrights are governed by the Copyright Act of 1976, as amended. To protect copyrights in digital information, Congress passed the No Electronic Theft Act of 1997 and the Digital Millennium Copyright Act of 1998.
Trade Secrets	*Trade secrets* include customer lists, plans, research and development, pricing information, and so on. Trade secrets are protected under the common law and, in some states, under statutory law against misappropriation by competitors. The Economic Espionage Act of 1996 made the theft of trade secrets a federal crime (see Chapter 8).
Licensing	In the context of intellectual property rights, a *license* is an agreement in which the owner of a trademark, copyright, patent, or trade secret permits another person or entity to use that property for certain purposes. In 1999, the National Conference of Commissioners of Uniform State Laws approved the Uniform Computer Information Transactions Act and submitted it to the states for adoption. The act addresses problems unique to electronic contracting and to the licensing of computer information, such as software (see Chapter 23).
International Protection for Intellectual Property	International protection for intellectual property exists under various international agreements. A landmark agreement is the 1994 agreement on Trade-Related Aspects of Intellectual Property Rights (TRIPS), which provides for enforcement procedures in all countries signatory to the agreement.

CASES FOR ANALYSIS

Westlaw. You can access the full text of each case presented below by going to the Westlaw cases on this text's Web site at http://wbl-cs.westbuslaw.com. Each Westlaw case includes the names of all plaintiffs and defendants, the dates on which the case was argued and decided, a brief summary of the issues and decisions in the case, headnotes classifying specific issues in the case according to the West Key Number System, and the court's opinion. Concurring and dissenting opinions, if any, are included as well.

CASE 7.1 TRADEMARK INFRINGEMENT

COCA-COLA CO. V. KOKE CO. OF AMERICA

Supreme Court of the United States, 1920.
254 U.S. 143,
41 S.Ct. 113,
65 L.Ed. 189.

Mr. Justice *HOLMES* delivered the opinion of the Court.

This is a [case] in equity brought by the Coca-Cola Company to prevent the infringement of its trade-mark Coca-Cola and unfair competition with it in its business of making and selling the beverage for which the trade-mark is used. The District Court gave the plaintiff a decree. This was reversed by the Circuit Court of Appeals. Subsequently a writ of *certiorari* was granted by this Court.

It appears that after the plaintiff's predecessors in title had used the mark for some years it was registered under the Act of Congress of March 3, 1881, and again under the Act of February 20, 1905. Both the [lower courts] * * * agree that subject to the one question to be considered the plaintiff has a right to equitable relief. Whatever may have been its original weakness, the mark for years has acquired a secondary significance and has indicated the plaintiff's product alone. It is found that defendant's mixture is made and sold in imitation of the plaintiff's and that the word "Koke" was chosen for the purpose of reaping the benefit of the advertising done by the plaintiff and of selling the imitation as and for the plaintiff's goods. The only obstacle found by the Circuit Court of Appeals in the way of continuing the injunction granted below was its opinion that the trade-mark in itself and the advertisements accompanying it made such fraudulent representations to the public that the plaintiff had lost its claim to any help from the Court. That is the question upon which the writ of *certiorari* was granted and the main one that we shall discuss.

Of course a man is not to be protected in the use of a device the very purpose and effect of which is to swindle the public. But the defects of a plaintiff do not offer a very broad ground for allowing another to swindle him. The defence relied on here should be scrutinized with a critical eye. The main point is this: Before 1900 the beginning of the good will was more or less helped by the presence of cocaine, a drug that, like alcohol or caffein or opium, may be described as a deadly poison or as a valuable item of the pharmacopoeia according to the rhetorical purposes in view. The amount seems to have been very small, but it may have been enough to begin a bad habit and after the Food and Drug Act of June 30, 1906, if not earlier, long before this suit was brought, it was eliminated from the plaintiff's compound. Coca leaves still are used, to be sure, but after they have been subjected to a drastic process that removes from them every characteristic substance except a little tannin and still less chlorophyl. The cola nut, at best, on its side furnishes but a small portion of the caffein, which now is the only element that has appreciable effect. That comes mainly from other sources. It is argued that the continued use of the name imports a representation that has ceased to be true and that the representation is reinforced by a picture of coca leaves and cola nuts upon the label and by advertisements, which however were many years before this suit was brought, that the drink is an "ideal nerve tonic and stimulant," etc., and that thus the very thing sought to be protected is used as a fraud.

The argument does not satisfy us. We are dealing here with a popular drink not with a medicine, and although what has been said might suggest that its attraction lay in producing the expectation of a toxic effect the facts point to a different conclusion. Since 1900 the sales have increased at a very great rate corresponding to a like increase in advertising. The name now characterizes a beverage to be had at almost any soda fountain. It means a single thing coming from a single source, and well known to the community. *It hardly would be too much to say that the drink characterizes the name as much as the name the drink.* In other words "Coca-Cola" probably means to most persons the plaintiff's familiar product to be had everywhere rather than a compound of particular substances. * * * [W]e see no reason to doubt that, as we have said, *it has acquired a secondary meaning in which perhaps the product is more emphasized than the producer but to which the producer is entitled.* The coca leaves and whatever of cola nut is employed may be used to justify the continuance of the name or they may affect the flavor as the plaintiff contends, but before this suit was brought the plaintiff had advertised to the public that it must not expect and would not find cocaine, and had eliminated everything tending to suggest cocaine effects except the name and the picture of the leaves and nuts, which probably conveyed little or nothing to most who saw it. It appears to us that it would be going too far to deny the plaintiff relief against a palpable fraud because possibly here and there an ignorant person might call for the drink with the hope for incipient cocaine intoxication. The plaintiff's position must be judged by the facts as they were when the suit was begun, not by the facts of a different condition and an earlier time. [Emphasis added.]

The decree of the District Court restrains the defendant from using the word "Dope." The plaintiff illustrated in a very striking way the fact that the word is one of the most featureless known even to the language of those who are incapable of discriminating speech. In some places it would be used to call for Coca-Cola. It equally would have been used to call for anything else having about it a faint aureole of poison. It does not suggest Coca-Cola by similarity and whatever objections there may be to its use, objections which the plaintiff equally makes to its application to Coca-Cola, we see no ground on which the plaintiff can claim a personal right to exclude the defendant from using it.

The product including the coloring matter is free to all who can make it if no extrinsic deceiving element is present. The injunction should be modified also in this respect.

Decree reversed.

Decree of District Court modified and affirmed.

CASE 7.2 TRADEMARK INFRINGEMENT

AMERICA ONLINE, INC. v. AT&T CORP.

United States Court of Appeals,
Fourth Circuit, 2001.
243 F.3d 812.

NIEMEYER, Circuit Judge:

* * * *

Founded in 1985, [America Online, Inc. (AOL)] is now the world's largest Internet service provider, claiming more than 18 million members who pay a monthly fee for its services. These services include the facility to transmit and receive electronic mail ("e-mail") * * * .

* * * *

Also, in connection with its e-mail service, AOL advises its subscribers that they have received e-mail by displaying the words "You Have Mail," by playing a recording that announces, "You've got mail," and by depicting an icon of a traditional mailbox with the red flag raised. AOL contends that it has used these marks to describe its e-mail service since 1992, that it has promoted them extensively, and that it now has a proprietary interest in them.

AT&T [Corporation], a competing Internet service provider, uses * * * the [term] * * * "You have Mail!" * * *

In December 1998, AOL commenced this action, seeking preliminary and permanent injunctive relief against AT&T to prohibit it from using marks similar to those asserted by AOL. In its complaint, it alleged that AT&T's use of similar marks * * * infringes AOL's marks in violation of [federal trademark law.] * * * In its answer, AT&T contended, among other things, that AOL's asserted marks were "common, generic terms for the e-mail * * * services." * * *

The district court denied preliminary injunctive relief and, following discovery, granted AT&T summary judgment on the ground that * * * the claimed marks were generic and therefore incapable of functioning as trademarks. * * *

* * * *

* * * We agree with the district court * * * .

First, the record establishes, without contradiction, that "You Have Mail" has been used to inform computer users since the 1970s, a decade before AOL came into existence, that they have electronic mail in their electronic "mailboxes." AT&T has noted, for example, that the UNIX operating system, one of the most widely used in the computer industry, has, since before AOL was formed, displayed the phrase "You Have Mail" or "You Have New Mail" whenever a user has received electronic mail. * * *

* * * *

Furthermore, other companies that provide e-mail services have used "You Have Mail," or derivations thereof, to notify their subscribers of the arrival of e-mail messages. * * * [For example,] Qualcomm has used "You Have New Mail" since the late 1980s in its Eudora Pro and Eudora Light e-mail programs to notify users of new e-mail. * * *

It is significant in the context of this usage that AOL has never registered "You Have Mail," nor has it attempted to enforce it as a mark prior to this action.

Second, in addition to the long and uninterrupted use by others of "You Have Mail," AOL's own use of "You Have Mail" has been inconsistent with its claim that the phrase is a trademark. Rather than describing a service that AOL offers—and indicating that it is describing such a service—AOL simply uses "You Have Mail" when the subscriber *in fact* has mail in the electronic mailbox. Once the user opens the new message, the phrase "You Have Mail" disappears from the user's screen. Moreover, if the subscriber does not have mail when he logs on, the screen does not display "You Have Mail." AOL's use of the phrase, conditioned on whether mail is present, does not describe AOL's e-mail service, but rather simply informs subscribers, employing common words to express their commonly used meaning, of the ordinary fact that they have new electronic mail in their mailboxes.

This functional manner in which AOL uses "You Have Mail" is consistent with a *public perception* of the phrase as describing whether or not mail is in an electronic mailbox, rather than as describing a service associated with AOL. * * *

Indeed, AOL itself has made no claim that "You Have Mail" has been used to indicate anything but the information that the subscriber has mail. Even in its complaint, it asserts little more, alleging that it has used "You Have Mail * * * in connection with its automatic e-mail notification services for AOL Service members." The scope of this asserted use—to give notice of mail to subscribers—is no broader than the words' common meaning.

* * * *[W]hen words are used in a context that suggests only their common meaning, they are generic and may not be appropriated as exclusive property*. But a debate over whether a word or phrase is being used in a context that communicates merely its common meaning can quickly become as metaphysical as the study of language itself. At the basic level, we can conclude that when a fruit merchant sells fruit as "apples" or "blackberries," he should never be able to exclude competitors from similarly using the words "apple" or "blackberries" to sell their fruit. But if the common word "apple" or "blackberry" is used by a computer merchant in selling computers, we conclude that the usage, not the word, is so uncommon and therefore "distinctive," that the computer merchant should be entitled to exclude other competitors from using "apple" or "blackberry" in the sale of its computers. While this example readily demonstrates the principle, its application can become difficult when words or phrases are used in a context *close* to their common meaning. And because our dynamic economy, characterized by extensive creativity and inventiveness, produces new products and services for which no words of description have previously existed, *entrepreneurs and the public are engaged in a continual tug of war over naming these new products and services—entrepreneurs wishing to gain some exclusive rights to the names of their inventions and the public wishing merely to have a convenient term by which to refer to the new product, or service to facilitate communication.* The words "Internet," "pixel," "chip," "software," "byte," or "e-mail" might well have become marks distinguishing one entrepreneur's product or service from all other electronic networks, screen density aspects, transistorized components, sets of computer commands, groups of digital information, or electronic communications. Yet, because of pervasive use, these terms have become generic. And *even when created words for new products have become strong marks, the public's pervasive use of these marks sometimes creates a real risk that their distinctiveness will disappear,* a process [referred to as] "genericide," as occurred with earlier trademarks such as "Thermos," "Aspirin," "Cellophane," and "Escalator." [Emphasis added.]

The task of distinguishing words or phrases functioning as trademarks from words or phrases in the "linguistic commons" begins with the development of an understanding of the common meaning of words and their common usage and then proceeds to a determination of whether the would-be trademark falls within this heartland of meaning and usage. The farther a would-be mark falls from the heartland of common meaning and usage, the more "distinctive" the would-be mark can become. * * *

When a word or phrase does not fall within the heartland of common meaning and usage, but is nevertheless close, its distinctiveness is strengthened by the entrepreneur's use. Thus, words or phrases that are not directly descriptive of a company, product, or service, but rather suggest, through operation of the consumer's imagination, the company, product, or service, can become trademarks. Similarly, well-recognized slogans used without any direct context can, through use, become marks because with such a generalized application, they are not used in the context of their common meaning, but rather suggestively. Witness "Just do it!" and "We try harder."

* * * *

In the case before us, the record context of "You Have Mail" permits us to conclude as a matter of law that AOL's usage of the would-be mark falls within the heartland of common meaning and usage and therefore that AOL may not exclude others from using the same words in connection with their e-mail service. * * *

* * * *

* * * Because AOL has failed to establish its exclusive right to "You Have Mail," we affirm the district court's conclusion that AOL may not exclude others from use of those words in connection with its e-mail service.

LUTTIG, Circuit Judge, * * * dissenting * * * :

* * * *

* * * I would not decide the question of whether AOL is entitled to protection for its unregistered e-mail notification feature that includes the phrase "YOU HAVE MAIL" because it is my understanding that AOL

no longer informs its customers that they have e-mail through use of the phrase "YOU HAVE MAIL." Rather, it now informs them that they have e-mail with the different message "YOU'VE GOT MAIL." And, as the district court explicitly found, it is undisputed that AT&T never has used, and "has claimed no future plans to use," this phrase to inform its customers of the arrival of e-mail.

CASE 7.3 COPYRIGHT INFRINGEMENT

NEW YORK TIMES CO. V. TASINI

Supreme Court of the United States, 2001.
533 U.S. 483,
121 S.Ct. 2381,
150 L.Ed.2d 500.

Justice *GINSBURG* delivered the opinion of the Court.

* * * *

Respondents Jonathan Tasini, Mary Kay Blakely, Barbara Garson, Margot Mifflin, Sonia Jaffe Robbins, and David S. Whitford are authors (Authors). Between 1990 and 1993, they wrote the 21 articles (Articles) on which this dispute centers. Tasini, Mifflin, and Blakely contributed 12 Articles to *The New York Times*, the daily newspaper published by petitioner The New York Times Company (Times), [and 9 articles to other periodicals, including *Newsday* and *Time*]. * * * The Authors registered copyrights in each of the Articles. The Times [and the other publishers] (Print Publishers) registered collective work copyrights in each periodical edition in which an Article originally appeared. The Print Publishers engaged the Authors as independent contractors (freelancers) under contracts that in no instance secured consent from an Author to placement of an Article in an electronic database.

At the time the Articles were published, all three Print Publishers had agreements with petitioner LEXIS/NEXIS (formerly Mead Data Central Corp.), owner and operator of NEXIS, a computerized database that stores information in a text-only format. NEXIS contains articles from hundreds of journals (newspapers and periodicals) spanning many years. The Print Publishers have licensed to LEXIS/NEXIS the text of articles appearing in the three periodicals. The licenses authorize LEXIS/NEXIS to copy and sell any portion of those texts.

* * * *

The Times * * * also has licensing agreements with petitioner University Microfilms International (UMI). The agreements authorize reproduction of Times materials on two CD-ROM products, the *New York Times OnDisc* (NYTO) and *General Periodicals OnDisc* (GPO).

* * * *

On December 16, 1993, the Authors filed this civil action in the United States District Court for the Southern District of New York. The Authors alleged that their copyrights were infringed when, as permitted and facilitated by the Print Publishers, LEXIS/NEXIS and UMI (Electronic Publishers) placed the Articles in the NEXIS, NYTO, and GPO databases (Databases). The Authors sought declaratory and injunctive relief, and damages. In response to the Authors' complaint, the Print and Electronic Publishers raised the reproduction and distribution privilege accorded collective work copyright owners by [the Copyright Act]. After discovery, both sides moved for summary judgment.

The District Court granted summary judgment for the Publishers * * *.

The Authors appealed, and the [U.S. Court of Appeals for the] Second Circuit reversed. * * *

We granted *certiorari* to determine whether the copying of the Authors' Articles in the Databases is privileged by [the Copyright Act.] * * *

* * * *

Under the Copyright Act, as amended in 1976, "*[c]opyright protection subsists * * * in original works of authorship fixed in any tangible medium of expression * * * from which they can be perceived, reproduced, or otherwise communicated.*" When, as in this case, a freelance author has contributed an article to a "collective work" such as a newspaper or magazine, the statute recognizes two distinct copyrighted works: "Copyright in *each separate contribution to a collective work* is distinct from copyright in *the collective work as a whole* * * *" [emphasis added]. Copyright in the separate contribution "vests initially in the author of the contribution" (here, the freelancer). Copyright in the collective work vests in the collective author (here, the newspaper or magazine publisher) and extends only to the creative material contributed by that author, not to "the preexisting material employed in the work." [Emphasis added.]

* * * *

A newspaper or magazine publisher is thus privileged to reproduce or distribute an article contributed by a freelance author, absent a contract otherwise providing, only "as part of" any (or all) of three categories of collective works: (a) "that collective work" to which the author contributed her work, (b) "any revision of that collective work," or (c) "any later collective work in the same series." In accord with Congress' prescription, a publishing company could reprint a contribution from one issue in a later issue of its magazine, and could reprint an article from a 1980 edition of an encyclopedia in a 1990 revision of it; the publisher could not revise the contribution itself or include it in a new anthology or an entirely different magazine or other collective work.

* * * *

In determining whether the Articles have been reproduced and distributed "as part of" a "revision" of the collective works in issue, we focus on the Articles as presented to, and perceptible by, the user of the Databases. In this case, the three Databases present articles to users clear of the context provided either by the original periodical editions or by any revision of those editions. The Databases first prompt users to search the universe of their contents: thousands or millions of files containing individual articles from thousands of collective works (*i.e.*, editions), either in one series (the *Times,* in NYTO) or in scores of series (the sundry titles in NEXIS and GPO). When the user conducts a search, each article appears as a separate item within the search result. In NEXIS and NYTO, an article appears to a user without the graphics, formatting, or other articles with which the article was initially published. In GPO, the article appears with the other materials published on the same page or pages, but without any material published on other pages of the original periodical. In either circumstance, we cannot see how the Database perceptibly reproduces and distributes the article "as part of" either the original edition or a "revision" of that edition.

One might view the articles as parts of a new compendium—namely, the entirety of works in the Database. In that compendium, each edition of each periodical represents only a miniscule fraction of the ever-expanding Database. The Database no more constitutes a "revision" of each constituent edition than a 400-page novel quoting a sonnet in passing would represent a "revision" of that poem. * * *

* * * *

We conclude that the Electronic Publishers infringed the Authors' copyrights by reproducing and distributing the Articles in a manner not authorized by the Authors and not privileged by [the Copyright Act]. We further conclude that the Print Publishers infringed the Authors' copyrights by authorizing the Electronic Publishers to place the Articles in the Databases and by aiding the Electronic Publishers in that endeavor. We therefore affirm the judgment of the Court of Appeals.

It is so ordered.

Justice *STEVENS* * * * dissenting.

* * * *

The record indicates that what is sent from the New York Times to the Electronic Databases * * * is simply a collection of ASCII text files representing the editorial content of the *New York Times* for a particular day. * * *

* * * *

No one doubts that the New York Times has the right to reprint its issues in Braille, in a foreign language, or in microform, even though such revisions might look and feel quite different from the original. Such differences, however, would largely result from the different medium being employed. Similarly, the decision to convert the single collective work newspaper into a collection of individual ASCII files can be explained as little more than a decision that reflects the different nature of the electronic medium. Just as the paper version of the *New York Times* is divided into "sections" and "pages" in order to facilitate the reader's navigation and manipulation of large batches of newsprint, so too the decision to subdivide the electronic version of that collective work into individual article files facilitates the reader's use of the electronic information.

CASE 7.4 COPYRIGHT INFRINGEMENT

A&M RECORDS, INC. V. NAPSTER, INC.

United States Court of Appeals,
Ninth Circuit, 2001.
239 F.3d 1004.

BEEZER, Circuit Judge:

Plaintiffs are engaged in the commercial recording, distribution and sale of copyrighted musical compositions and sound recordings. The complaint alleges that Napster, Inc. ("Napster") is a contributory and vicarious copyright infringer. On July 26, 2000, the district court granted plaintiffs' motion for a preliminary injunction. * * * The district court preliminarily enjoined Napster "from engaging in, or facilitating others in copying, downloading, uploading, transmitting, or distributing plaintiffs' copyrighted musical compositions and sound recordings, protected by either federal or state law, without express permission of the rights owner." * * *

We entered a temporary stay of the preliminary injunction pending resolution of this appeal. * * *

* * * *

We have examined the papers submitted in support of and in response to the injunction application and it appears that Napster has designed and operates a system which permits the transmission and retention of sound recordings employing digital technology.

* * * *

In 1987, the Moving Picture Experts Group set a standard file format for the storage of audio recordings in a digital format called MPEG-3, abbreviated as "MP3." Digital MP3 files are created through a process colloquially called "ripping." Ripping software allows a computer owner to copy an audio compact disk ("audio CD") directly onto a computer's hard drive by compressing the audio information on the CD into the MP3 format. The MP3's compressed format allows for rapid transmission of digital audio files from one computer to another by electronic mail or any other file transfer protocol.

Napster facilitates the transmission of MP3 files between and among its users. Through a process commonly called "peer-to-peer" file sharing, Napster allows its users to: (1) make MP3 music files stored on individual computer hard drives available for copying by other Napster users; (2) search for MP3 music files stored on other users' computers; and (3) transfer exact copies of the contents of other users' MP3 files from one computer to another via the Internet. These functions are made possible by Napster's MusicShare software, available free of charge from Napster's Internet site, and Napster's network servers and server-side software. Napster provides technical support for the indexing and searching of MP3 files, as well as for its other functions, including a "chat room," where users can meet to discuss music, and a directory where participating artists can provide information about their music.

* * * *

* * * *In the context of copyright law, vicarious [indirect] liability extends* * * *to cases in which a defendant has the right and ability to supervise the infringing activity and also has a direct financial interest in such activities.* [Emphasis added.]

* * * *

The ability to block infringers' access to a particular environment for any reason whatsoever is evidence of the right and ability to supervise. Here, plaintiffs have demonstrated that Napster retains the right to control access to its system. Napster has an express reservation of rights policy, stating on its website that it expressly reserves the "right to refuse service and terminate accounts in [its] discretion, including, but not limited to, if Napster believes that user conduct violates applicable law * * * or for any reason in Napster's sole discretion, with or without cause."

To escape imposition of vicarious liability, the reserved right to police must be exercised to its fullest extent. Turning a blind eye to detectable acts of infringement for the sake of profit gives rise to liability.

The district court correctly determined that Napster had the right and ability to police its system and failed to exercise that right to prevent the exchange of copyrighted material. * * *

Napster, however, has the ability to locate infringing material listed on its search indices, and the right to terminate users' access to the system. The file name indices, therefore, are within the "premises" that Napster has the ability to police. We recognize that the files are user-named and may not match copyrighted material exactly (for example, the artist or song could be spelled wrong). For Napster to function effectively, however, file names must reasonably or roughly correspond to the material contained in the files, otherwise no user could ever locate any desired music. As a practical matter, Napster, its users and the record company plaintiffs have equal access to infringing material by employing Napster's "search function."

Our review of the record requires us to accept the district court's conclusion that plaintiffs have demonstrated a likelihood of success on the merits of the vicarious copyright infringement claim. Napster's failure to police the system's "premises," combined with a showing that Napster financially benefits from the continuing availability of infringing files on its system, leads to the imposition of vicarious liability.

* * * *

The district court correctly recognized that a preliminary injunction against Napster's participation in copyright infringement is not only warranted but required. We believe, however, that the scope of the injunction needs modification in light of our opinion. Specifically, we reiterate that contributory liability may potentially be imposed only to the extent that Napster: (1) receives reasonable knowledge of specific infringing files with copyrighted musical compositions and sound recordings; (2) knows or should know that such files are available on the Napster system; and (3) fails to act to prevent viral distribution of the works. The mere existence of the Napster system, absent actual notice and Napster's demonstrated failure to remove the offending material, is insufficient to impose contributory liability.

Conversely, Napster may be vicariously liable when it fails to affirmatively use its ability to patrol its system and preclude access to potentially infringing files listed in its search index. Napster has both the ability to use its search function to identify infringing musical recordings and the right to bar participation of users who engage in the transmission of infringing files.

The preliminary injunction which we stayed is overbroad because it places on Napster the entire burden of ensuring that no "copying, downloading, uploading, transmitting, or distributing" of plaintiffs' works occur on the system. As stated, we place the burden on plaintiffs to provide notice to Napster of copyrighted works and files containing such works available on the Napster system before Napster has the duty to disable access to the offending content. Napster, however, also bears the burden of policing the system within the limits of the system. Here, we recognize that this is not an exact science in that the files are user named. In crafting the injunction on remand, the district court should recognize that Napster's system does not currently appear to allow Napster access to users' MP3 files.

* * * *

We direct that the preliminary injunction fashioned by the district court prior to this appeal shall remain stayed until it is modified by the district court to conform to the requirements of this opinion. We order a partial remand of this case on the date of the filing of this opinion for the limited purpose of permitting the district court to proceed with the settlement and entry of the modified preliminary injunction.

* * * *

AFFIRMED IN PART, REVERSED IN PART AND REMANDED.

Case Problems

7–1. Nike, Inc., manufactures and markets footwear, apparel, and related accessories. To identify its products, Nike uses the word "Nike" and/or a "swoosh" design as its trademarks. From 1977 through 1991, Nike spent more than $300 million advertising the trademarks. Since 1971, sales revenues for items bearing the trademarks have exceeded $10 billion. Nike began using the phrase "Just Do It" in 1989 as a slogan for its sweatshirts, T-shirts, caps, and other accessories. Sales revenues for "Just Do It" items have exceeded $15 million. "Nike," the swoosh design, and "Just Do It" have gained widespread public acceptance and recognition. Michael Stanard is an award-winning commercial artist whose works include, among others, the trademark "Louisville Slugger" printed on baseball bats. As a summer project, he and his daughter decided to market his first name, Mike, as a takeoff on the Nike logo. They named their project "Just Did It" Enterprises and concentrated on marketing T-shirts and sweatshirts to members of the general public with the given (first) name of Michael. They also mailed brochures to college athletes and celebrities named Michael. Sales were entirely by mail order. Approximately two-thirds of those purchasing the shirts were named Mike. Stanard believed that the other third probably bought a T-shirt for a friend, relative, or loved one named Mike. Ultimately, the project lost money. Nike sued Stanard for trademark infringement. Stanard argued that the word play was humorous and constituted a fair use of the trademarks as a parody. Should the court rule that Nike's trademark had been infringed? Explain. [*Nike, Inc. v. "Just Did It" Enterprises*, 6 F.3d 1225 (7th Cir. 1993)]

7–2. Jonathan Caven-Atack had been a member of the Church of Scientology for nine years when he decided that the church was a dangerous cult and its leader, L. Ron Hubbard, a vindictive and profoundly disturbed man. Caven-Atack spent the next several years investigating, and then writing a book about, Hubbard and the church. Caven-Atack's purpose was to expose what he believed was the pernicious nature of the church and the deceit on which its teachings were based. Approximately 3 percent of Caven-Atack's book consisted of quotations from Hubbard's published works. When New Era Publications International, which held exclusive copyright rights in all of Hubbard's works, learned that the Carol Publishing Group planned to publish Caven-Atack's book, it sued Carol Publishing for copyright infringement. The Carol Publishing Group claimed that Caven-Atack's use of Hubbard's works was a "fair use" of the copyrighted materials. What factors must the court consider in making its decision? What will its decision be? Discuss. [*New Era Publications International, ApS v. Carol Publishing Group*, 904 F.2d 152 (2d Cir. 1990)]

7–3. Nintendo of America, Inc., manufactures a home video game system, the Nintendo Entertainment System (NES). Nintendo designed the NES to prevent it from accepting unauthorized video game cartridges. Microprocessor chips in the NES consoles were coded to accept only Nintendo cartridges. Atari Games Corp. wanted to sell video game cartridges that could be used in the NES consoles. Atari attempted to analyze the NES lockout program through reverse engineering. Unable to do so successfully, Atari obtained a copy of the human-readable source code of the NES program from the U.S. Copyright Office by means of false representations. Atari was then able to decode the NES lockout program through reverse engineering and develop a program to place in its cartridges to allow its games to be played on the NES. Nintendo filed a lawsuit against Atari, alleging that Atari had infringed Nintendo's copyright in the NES program when it made copies of the program code during the course of its reverse engineering. Atari argued that copying for the purposes of reverse engineering is a fair use. What will result in court? Discuss. [*Atari Games Corp. v. Nintendo of America, Inc.*, 975 F.2d 832 (Fed. Cir. 1992)]

7–4. Sega Enterprises, Ltd., develops and markets video entertainment systems, including the "Genesis" console and video game cartridges. Accolade, Inc., is an independent developer, manufacturer, and marketer of computer entertainment software, including game cartridges that are compatible with Genesis and other computer systems. Sega licenses its copyrighted computer code and its trademark to developers of Genesis-compatible games in competition with Sega. Accolade chose not to purchase a license from Sega, however, but to reverse-engineer Sega's games to discover the requirements of the code that would make Accolade's games compatible with Genesis. As part of the reverse engineering, Accolade transformed the machine-readable object code contained in Sega's game cartridges into human-readable source code using a process called "disassembly." At the end of the process, Accolade created a manual that incorporated the information it had discovered about the requirements for a Genesis-compatible game. The manual did not include any of Sega's code. With the manual, Accolade created a new computer code; with this code, Accolade developed Genesis-compatible games. Sega sued Accolade, claiming, among other things, that Accolade's disassembly of its computer program constituted copyright infringement. Accolade contended that its disassembly of the code was a fair use. How should the court rule? Discuss fully. [*Sega Enterprises, Ltd. v. Accolade, Inc.*, 977 F.2d 1510 (9th Cir. 1992)]

7–5. Texaco, Inc., conducts research to develop new products and technology in the petroleum industry. As part of the research, Texaco employees routinely photocopy articles from scientific and medical journals without the permission of the copyright holders. The publishers of the journals brought a copyright infringement action against Texaco in a federal district court. Texaco argued that its photocopying of the articles constituted a fair use. What should the court decide? Explain. [*American Geophysical Union v. Texaco, Inc.*, 37 F.3d 881 (2d Cir. 1994)]

7–6. In 1987, Quality Inns International, Inc., announced a new chain of economy hotels to be marketed under the name McSleep Inns. McDonald's wrote Quality Inns a letter stating that the use of this name infringed on the McDonald's family of trademarks characterized by the prefix Mc attached to a generic term. Quality Inns claimed that Mc had come into generic use as a prefix and therefore McDonald's had no trademark rights to the prefix itself. Quality Inns filed an action seeking a declaratory judgment from the court that the mark McSleep Inns did not infringe on McDonald's federally registered trademarks or common law rights to its marks and would not constitute an unfair trade practice. What factors must the court consider in deciding this issue? What will be the probable outcome of the case? Explain. [*Quality Inns International, Inc. v. McDonald's Corp.*, 695 F.Supp. 198 (D.Md. 1988)]

7–7. CBS, Inc., owns and operates Television City, a television production facility in Los Angeles that is home to many television series. The name Television City is broadcast each week in connection with each show. CBS sells T-shirts, pins, watches, and so on emblazoned with "CBS Television City." CBS registered the name Television City with the U.S. Patent and Trademark Office as a service mark "for television production services." David and William Liederman wished to open a restaurant in New York City using the name Television City. Besides food, the restaurant would sell television memorabilia such as T-shirts, sweatshirts, and posters. When CBS learned of the Liedermans' plans, it asked a federal district court to order them not to use the name Television City in connection with their restaurant. Does CBS's registration of the Television City mark ensure its exclusive use in all markets and for all products? If not, what factors might the court consider to determine whether the Liedermans can use the name Television City in connection with their restaurant? [*CBS, Inc. v. Liederman*, 866 F.Supp. 763 (S.D.N.Y. 1994)]

7–8. William Redmond, as the general manager for PepsiCo, Inc., in California, had access to the company's inside information and trade secrets. In 1994, Redmond resigned to become chief operating officer for the Gatorade and Snapple Co., which makes and markets Gatorade and Snapple and is a subsidiary of the Quaker Oats Co. PepsiCo brought an action in a federal district court against Redmond and Quaker Oats, seeking to prevent Redmond from disclosing PepsiCo's secrets. The court ordered Redmond not to assume new duties that were likely to trigger disclosure of those secrets. The central issue on appeal was whether a plaintiff can obtain relief for trade secret misappropriation on showing that a former employee's new employment will inevitably lead him or her to rely on the plaintiff's trade secrets. How should the court rule on this issue? Discuss fully. [*PepsiCo v. Redmond*, 54 F.3d 1262 (7th Cir. 1995)]

7–9. James Smith, the owner of Michigan Document Services, Inc. (MDS), a commercial copyshop, concluded that it was unnecessary to obtain the copyright owners' permission to reproduce copyrighted materials in coursepacks. Smith publicized his conclusion, claiming that professors would not have to worry about any delay in production at his shop. MDS then compiled, bound, and sold coursepacks to students at the University of Michigan without obtaining the permission of copyright owners. Princeton University Press and two other publishers filed a suit in a federal district court against MDS, alleging copyright infringement. MDS claimed that its course-packs were covered under the fair use doctrine. Were they? Explain. [*Princeton University Press v. Michigan Document Services, Inc.*, 99 F.3d 1381 (6th Cir. 1996)]

7–10. Elvis Presley Enterprises, Inc. (EPE), owns all of the trademarks of the Elvis Presley estate. None of these marks is registered for use in the restaurant business. Barry Capece registered "The Velvet Elvis" as a service mark for a restaurant and tavern with the U.S. Patent and Trademark Office. Capece opened a nightclub called "The Velvet Elvis" with a menu, décor, advertising, and promotional events that evoked Elvis Presley and his music. EPE filed a suit in a federal district court against Capece and others, claiming, among other things, that "The Velvet Elvis" service mark infringed on EPE's trademarks. During the trial, witnesses testified that they thought the bar was associated with Elvis Presley. Should Capece be ordered to stop using "The Velvet Elvis" mark? Why, or why not? [*Elvis Presley Enterprises, Inc. v. Capece,* 141 F.3d 188 (5th Cir. 1998)]

7–11. A&H Sportswear Co., a swimsuit maker, obtained a trademark for its MIRACLESUIT in 1992. The design of MIRACLESUIT makes the wearer appear slimmer. The MIRACLESUIT, which was widely advertised and discussed in the media, was also sold for a brief time in the Victoria's Secret (VS) catalogue, which is published by Victoria's Secret Catalogue, Inc. In 1993, Victoria's Secret Stores, Inc., began selling a cleavage-enhancing bra, which was named THE MIRACLE BRA and for which a trademark was obtained. The next year, THE MIRACLE BRA swimwear debuted in the VS catalogue and stores. A&H filed a suit in a federal district court against VS Stores and VS Catalogue, alleging in part that MIRACLE BRA mark, when applied to swimwear, infringed on the MIRACLESUIT mark. A&H argued that there was a "possibility of confusion" between the marks. The VS entities contended that the appropriate standard was "likelihood of confusion" and that in this case, there was no likelihood of confusion. In whose favor will the court rule, and why? [*A&H Sportswear, Inc. v. Victoria's Secret Stores, Inc.,* 166 F.3d 197 (3d Cir. 1999)]

7–12. Sara Lee Corp. manufactures pantyhose under the L'eggs trademark. Originally, L'eggs were sold in egg-shaped packaging, a design that Sara Lee continues to use with its product. Sara Lee's only nationwide competitor in the same pantyhose markets is Kayser-Roth Corp. When Kayser-Roth learned of Sara Lee's plan to introduce L'eggs Everyday, a new line of hosiery, Kayser-Roth responded by simultaneously introducing a new product, Leg Looks. Sara Lee filed a complaint in a federal district court against Kayser-Roth, asserting that the name Leg Looks infringed on the L'eggs mark. Does Kayser-Roth's Leg Looks infringe on Sara Lee's L'eggs? Why, or why not? [*Sara Lee Corp. v. Kayser-Roth Corp.,* 81 F.3d 455 (4th Cir. 1996)]

7–13. Playboy Enterprises, Inc. (PEI), owns the rights to the cyber marks "Playboy," "Playboy magazine," and "Playmate." Without authorization, Calvin Designer Label used the terms as meta tags for its Web sites on the Internet. As tags, the terms were invisible to viewers (in black type on a black background), but they caused the Web sites to be returned at the top of the list of a search engine query for "Playboy" or "Playmate." PEI filed a suit in a federal district court against Calvin Designer Label, alleging, among other things, trademark infringement. Should the court order the defendant to stop using the terms as tags? Why, or why not? [*Playboy Enterprises, Inc. v. Calvin Designer Label,* 985 F.Supp. 1220 (N.D.Cal. 1997)]

7–14. Webbworld operates a Web site called Neptics, Inc. The site accepts downloads of certain images from third parties and makes these images available to any user who accesses the site. Before being allowed to view the images, however, the user must pay a subscription fee of $11.95 per month. Over a period of several months, images were available that were originally created by or for Playboy Enterprises, Inc. (PEI). The images were displayed at Neptics's site without PEI's permission. PEI filed a suit in a federal district court against Webbworld, alleging copyright infringement. Webbworld argued in part that it should not be held liable because, like an Internet service provider that furnishes access to the Internet, it did not create or control the content of the information available to its subscribers. Do you agree with Webbworld? Why, or why not? [*Playboy Enterprises, Inc. v. Webbworld,* 968 F.Supp. 1171 (N.D.Tex. 1997)]

7–15. In 1999, Steve and Pierce Thumann and their father, Fred, created Spider Webs, Ltd., a partnership, to, according to Steve, "develop Internet address names." Spider Webs registered nearly two thousand Internet domain names for an average of $70 each, including the names of cities, the names of buildings, names related to a business or trade (such as air conditioning or plumbing), and the names of famous companies. It offered many of the names for sale on its Web site and through eBay.com. Spider Webs registered the domain name "ERNESTANDJULIOGALLO.COM" in Spider Webs's name. Gallo filed a suit against Spider Webs, alleging, in part, violations of the Anticybersquatting Consumer Protection Act (ACPA). Gallo asked the court for, among other things, statutory damages. Gallo also sought to have the domain name at issue transferred to Gallo. During the suit, Spider Webs published anticorporate articles and opinions, and discussions of the suit at the URL "ERNESTANDJULIOGALLO.COM." Should the court rule in Gallo's favor? Why, or why not? [*E. & J. Gallo Winery v. Spider Webs, Ltd.,* 129 F.Supp.2d 1033 (S.D.Tex. 2001)]

E-LINKS

For updated links to resources available on the Web, as well as a variety of other materials, visit this text's Web site at

http://wbl-cs.westbuslaw.com

You can find answers to frequently asked questions (FAQs) about trademark and patent law—and links to registration forms, statutes, international patent and trademark offices, and numerous other related materials—at the Web site of the U.S. Patent and Trademark Office. Go to

http://www.uspto.gov

To access the federal database of registered trademarks directly, go to

http://tess.uspto.gov

To perform patent searches and to access information on the patenting process, go to

http://www.bustpatents.com

You can also access information on patent law at the following Internet site:

http://www.patents.com

For information on copyrights, go to the U.S. Copyright Office at

http://www.loc.gov/copyright

You can find extensive information on copyright law—including United States Supreme Court decisions in this area and the texts of the Berne Convention and other international treaties on copyright issues—at the Web site of the Legal Information Institute at Cornell University's School of Law. Go to

http://www.law.cornell.edu/topics/copyright.html

The Cyberspace Law Institute (CLI) offers articles and information on such topics as copyright infringement, privacy, trade secrets, and trademarks. To access the CLI's Web site, go to

http://www.cli.org

LEGAL RESEARCH EXERCISES ON THE WEB

Go to **http://wbl-cs.westbuslaw.com**, the Web site that accompanies this text. Select "Interactive Study Center," and then click on "Chapter 7." There you will find the following Internet research exercises that you can perform to learn more about intellectual property rights:

Activity 7–1: The Price of Free Speech

Activity 7–2: Gray-Market Goods

CHAPTER 8 Criminal Law and Cyber Crimes

THE LAW IMPOSES VARIOUS sanctions in attempting to ensure that individuals engaging in business in our society can compete and flourish. These sanctions include those imposed by civil law, such as damages for various types of tortious conduct (discussed in Chapters 5 and 6); damages for breach of contract (to be discussed in Chapter 17); and the equitable remedies discussed in Chapter 1. Additional sanctions are imposed under criminal law. Indeed, many statutes regulating business provide for criminal as well as civil penalties. Therefore, criminal law joins civil law as an important element in the legal environment of business.

In this chapter, after examining some essential differences between criminal law and civil law, we look at how crimes are classified, the basic requirements that must be met for criminal liability to be established, the various types of crimes, the defenses that can be raised to avoid criminal liability, and criminal procedures.

Since the advent of computer networks and, more recently, the Internet, new types of crimes or new variations of traditional crimes have been committed in cyberspace. For that reason, they are often referred to as **cyber crimes.** Generally, the term *cyber crime* refers more to the way a particular crime is committed than to a new category of crime. We devote the concluding pages of this chapter to a discussion of this increasingly significant area of criminal activity.

SECTION 1

Civil Law and Criminal Law

Recall from Chapter 1 that *civil law* pertains to the duties that exist between persons or between persons and their governments. Criminal law, in contrast, has to do with crime. A **crime** can be defined as a wrong against society proclaimed in a statute and punishable by a fine and/or imprisonment—or, in some cases, death. As mentioned in Chapter 1, because crimes are *offenses against society as a whole,* they are prosecuted by a public official, such as a district attorney (D.A.) or an attorney general (A.G.), not by victims.

MAJOR DIFFERENCES BETWEEN CIVIL LAW AND CRIMINAL LAW

Because the state has extensive resources at its disposal when prosecuting criminal cases, there are numerous procedural safeguards to protect the rights of defendants. One of these safeguards is the higher standard of proof that applies in a criminal case. As you can see in Exhibit 8–1, which summarizes some of the key differences between civil law and criminal law, in a civil case the plaintiff usually must prove his or her case by a *preponderance of the evidence.* Under this standard, the plaintiff must convince the court that, based on the evidence presented by both parties, it is more likely than not that the plaintiff's allegation is true.

In a criminal case, in contrast, the state must prove its case **beyond a reasonable doubt.** Every juror in a criminal case must be convinced, beyond a reasonable doubt, of the defendant's guilt. The higher standard of proof in criminal cases reflects a fundamental social value—a belief that it is worse to convict an innocent individual than to let a guilty person go free. We will look at other safeguards later in the chapter, in the context of criminal procedure.

The sanctions imposed on criminal wrongdoers are also harsher than those that are applied in civil cases. Remember from Chapter 5 that the purpose of tort law

EXHIBIT 8–1 CIVIL AND CRIMINAL LAW COMPARED

ISSUE	CIVIL LAW	CRIMINAL LAW
Area of concern	Rights and duties between individuals and between persons and their government	Offenses against society as a whole
Wrongful act	Harm to a person or to a person's property	Violation of a statute that prohibits some type of activity
Party who brings suit	Person who suffered harm	The state
Standard of proof	Preponderance of the evidence	Beyond a reasonable doubt
Remedy	Damages to compensate for the harm or an equitable remedy	Punishment (fine and/or imprisonment)

is to allow persons harmed by the wrongful acts of others to obtain compensation, or money damages, from the wrongdoer or to enjoin (prevent) a wrongdoer from undertaking or continuing a wrongful action. Rarely are tortfeasors subject to punitive damages—damages awarded simply to *punish* the wrongdoer. In contrast, criminal sanctions are designed to punish those who commit crimes in order to deter others from committing similar acts in the future.

CIVIL LIABILITY FOR CRIMINAL ACTS

Some torts, such as assault and battery, provide a basis for a criminal prosecution as well as a tort action. For example, Jonas is walking down the street, minding his own business, when suddenly a person attacks him. In the ensuing struggle, the attacker stabs Jonas several times, seriously injuring him. A police officer restrains and arrests the wrongdoer. In this situation, the attacker may be subject both to criminal prosecution by the state and to a tort lawsuit brought by Jonas to compensate Jonas for his injuries. Exhibit 8–2 on the next page shows how the same wrongful act can result in both a civil (tort) action and a criminal action against the wrongdoer.

SECTION 2

Classification of Crimes

Depending on their degree of seriousness, crimes are classified as felonies or misdemeanors.

FELONIES

Felonies are serious crimes punishable by death or by imprisonment in a federal or state penitentiary for one year or longer.[1] The Model Penal Code[2] provides for four degrees of felony:

1. Capital offenses, for which the maximum penalty is death.
2. First degree felonies, punishable by a maximum penalty of life imprisonment.
3. Second degree felonies, punishable by a maximum of ten years' imprisonment.
4. Third degree felonies, punishable by up to five years' imprisonment.

Although criminal laws vary from state to state, some general rules apply when grading crimes by degree. For example, most jurisdictions punish a burglary that involves a forced entry into a home at night more harshly than a burglary that takes place during the day and involves a nonresidential building or structure. A homicide—the taking of another's life—is classified according to the degree of intent involved.

For example, first degree murder requires that the homicide be premeditated and deliberate, instead of being a spontaneous act of violence. When no premeditation or deliberation is present but the offender acts with *malice aforethought* (that is, with wanton disregard of the consequences of his or her actions for the victim), the homicide is classified as second degree

1. Some states, such as North Carolina, consider felonies to be punishable by incarceration for at least two years.

2. The American Law Institute issued the Official Draft of the Model Penal Code in 1962. The Model Penal Code is not a uniform code. Uniformity in criminal law among the states is not as important as uniformity in other areas of the law. Crime varies with local circumstances, and it is appropriate that punishments vary accordingly. The Model Penal Code contains four parts: (1) general provisions, (2) definitions of special crimes, (3) provisions concerning treatment and corrections, and (4) provisions on the organization of corrections.

EXHIBIT 8–2 TORT LAWSUIT AND CRIMINAL PROSECUTION FOR THE SAME ACT

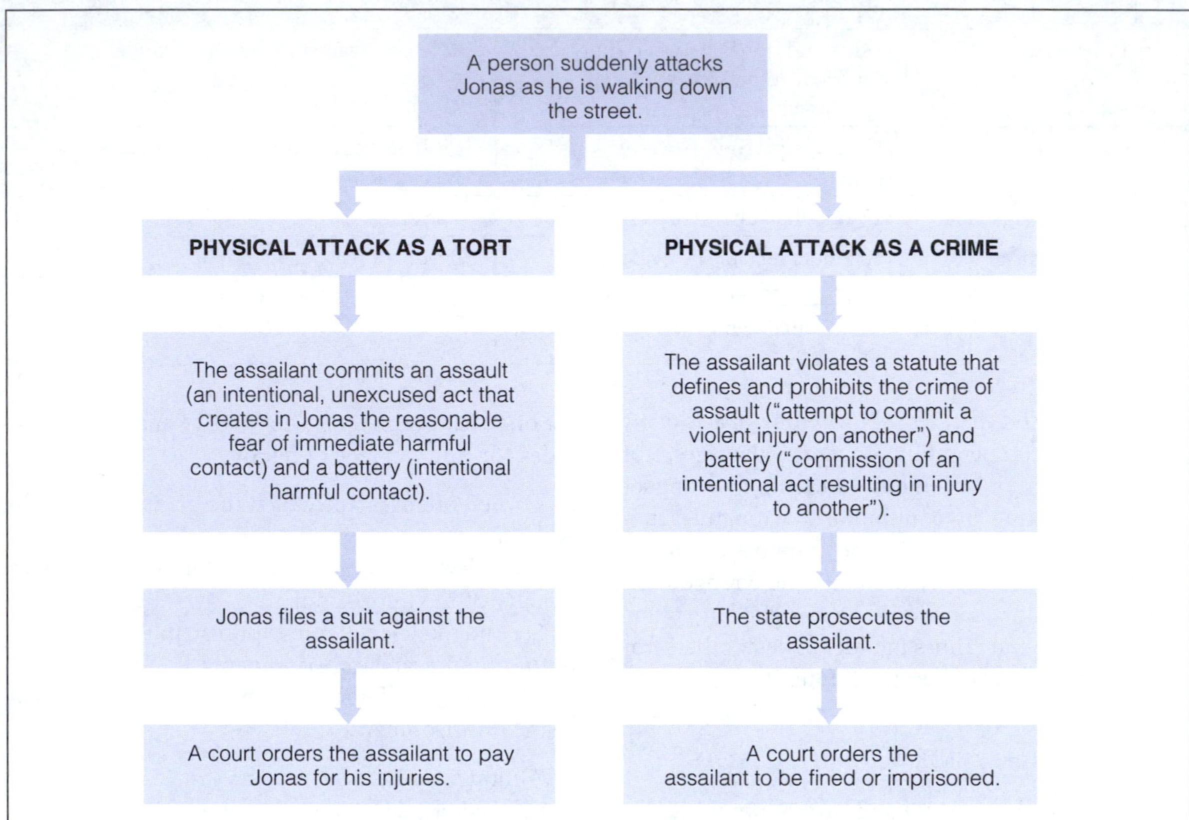

murder. A homicide that is committed without malice toward the victim is known as *manslaughter. Voluntary manslaughter* occurs when the intent to kill may be present, as in a crime committed in the heat of passion, but malice is lacking. A homicide is classified as *involuntary manslaughter* when it results from an act of negligence, such as when a drunk driver causes the death of another person, and there is no intent to kill.

MISDEMEANORS AND PETTY OFFENSES

Under federal law and in most states, any crime that is not a felony is considered a **misdemeanor.** Misdemeanors are crimes punishable by a fine or by incarceration (imprisonment) for up to one year. If confined, the guilty party goes to a local jail instead of a penitentiary. Disorderly conduct and trespass are common misdemeanors. Some states have several classes of misdemeanors. For example, in Illinois, misdemeanors are either Class A (confinement for up to a year), Class B (not more than six months), or Class C (not more than thirty days). Whether a crime is a felony or a misdemeanor can also determine if the case is tried in a magistrate's court (for example, by a justice of the peace) or a general trial court.

In most jurisdictions, **petty offenses** are considered to be a subset of misdemeanors. Petty offenses are minor violations, such as violations of building codes or driving under the influence of alcohol. Even for petty offenses, however, a guilty party can be put in jail for a few days, fined, or both, depending on state law.

Probation and community service are often imposed on those who commit misdemeanors, especially juveniles. Also, most states have decriminalized all but the most serious traffic offenses. These infractions are treated as civil proceedings, and civil fines are imposed. In many states, "points" are assessed against the violator's driving record.

SECTION 3

The Essentials of Criminal Liability

Two elements must exist for a person to be convicted of a crime: (1) the performance of a prohibited act and (2) a specified state of mind, or intent, on the part of the actor. Additionally, to establish criminal liability, there must be a *concurrence* between the act and the intent. In other words, these two elements must occur together.

For example, suppose that a woman plans to kill her husband by poisoning him. On the day she plans to do so, she is driving her husband home from work and swerves to avoid hitting a cat crossing the road. The car crashes into a tree as a result, killing her husband. Even though she had planned to murder her husband, the woman would not be guilty of murder in this situation because she had not planned to kill him by driving the car into a tree.

The Criminal Act

Every criminal statute prohibits certain behavior. Most crimes require an act of *commission;* that is, a person must *do* something in order to be accused of a crime. In criminal law, a prohibited act is referred to as the ***actus reus,***[3] or guilty act. In some cases, an act of omission can be a crime, but only when a person has a legal duty to perform the omitted act. Failure to file a tax return is an example of an omission that is a crime.

The *guilty act* requirement is based on one of the premises of criminal law—that a person should be punished for harm done to society. Thus, for a crime to exist, the guilty act must cause some harm to a person or to property. Thinking about killing someone or about stealing a car may be wrong, but the thoughts do no harm until they are translated into action. Of course, a person can be punished for *attempting* murder or robbery, but only if substantial steps toward the criminal objective have been taken. Additionally, the punishment for an attempt to commit a crime is normally less severe than it would be if the act had been completed.

State of Mind

A wrongful mental state (***mens rea***)[4] is as necessary as a wrongful act in establishing guilt. The mental state, or requisite intent, required to establish guilt of a crime is indicated in the applicable statute or law. Murder, for example, involves the guilty act of killing another human being, and the guilty mental state is the desire, or intent, to take another's life. For theft, the guilty act is the taking of another person's property, and the mental state involves both the awareness that the property belongs to another and the desire to deprive the owner of it.

A guilty mental state can be attributed to acts of negligence or recklessness as well. *Criminal negligence* involves the mental state in which the defendant deviates from the standard of care that a reasonable person would use under the same circumstances. The defendant is accused of taking an unjustified, substantial, and foreseeable risk that resulted in harm. Under the Model Penal Code, a defendant is negligent even if he or she was not actually aware of the risk but *should have been aware* of it.[5] The Model Penal Code defines *criminal recklessness* as "consciously disregard[ing] a substantial and unjustifiable risk."[6] In other words, a defendant is reckless if he or she is *actually aware* of the risk. A defendant who commits an act recklessly is more blameworthy than one who is criminally negligent.

3. Pronounced *ak*-tuhs *ray*-uhs.

4. Pronounced *mehns ray*-uh.

SECTION 4

Corporate Criminal Liability

As will be discussed in Chapter 34, a corporation is a legal entity created under the laws of a state. Both the corporation as an entity and the individual directors and officers of the corporation are potentially subject to liability for criminal acts.

Liability of the Corporate Entity

At one time, it was thought that a corporation could not incur criminal liability because, although a corporation is a legal person, it can act only through its agents (corporate directors, officers, and employees). Therefore, the corporate entity itself could not "intend" to commit a crime. Under modern criminal law, however, a corporation may be held liable for crimes. Obviously, corporations cannot be imprisoned, but they can be fined or denied certain legal privileges (such as a license).

5. Model Penal Code Section 2.02(2)(d).

6. Model Penal Code Section 2.02(2)(c).

The Model Penal Code provides that a corporation may be convicted of a crime in the following situations:

1. The criminal act by the corporation's agent or employee is within the scope of his or her employment, and the purpose of the statute defining the act as a crime is to impose liability on the corporation.
2. The crime consists of a failure to perform a specific affirmative duty imposed on corporations by law.
3. The crime was authorized, requested, commanded, committed, or recklessly tolerated by one of the corporation's high managerial agents.[7]

As implied by the first statement in the above list, corporate criminal liability is vicarious—the corporation as an entity may be liable for the criminal acts of its employees when the acts are committed within the scope of employment. Thus, the corporation that is found to be criminally responsible for an act committed by an employee can be fined for that offense. Through the fine, stockholders and other employees suffer because of the vicarious liability of the corporation. The justification for such criminal liability involves a showing that the corporation could have prevented the act or that there was authorized consent to or knowledge of the act by persons in supervisory positions within the corporation.

LIABILITY OF CORPORATE OFFICERS AND DIRECTORS

Corporate directors and officers are personally liable for the crimes they commit, regardless of whether the crimes were committed for their private benefit or on the corporation's behalf. Additionally, corporate directors and officers may be held liable for the actions of employees under their supervision. Under what has become known as the "responsible corporate officer" doctrine, a court may impose criminal liability on a corporate officer regardless of whether he or she participated in, directed, or even knew about a given criminal violation.

For example, in *United States v. Park,*[8] the chief executive officer of a national supermarket chain was held personally liable for sanitation violations in corporate warehouses, in which the food was exposed to contamination by rodents. The court imposed personal liability on the corporate officer not because he intended the crime or even knew about it. Rather, liability was imposed because the officer was in a "responsible relationship" to the corporation and had the power to prevent the violation. Since the *Park* decision, courts have applied this "responsible corporate officer" doctrine on a number of occasions to hold corporate officers liable for their employees' statutory violations.

7. Model Penal Code Section 2.07.
8. 421 U.S. 658, 95 S.Ct. 1903, 44 L.Ed.2d 489 (1975).

Westlaw. See Case 8.1 at the end of this chapter. To view the full, unedited case from Westlaw,® go to this text's Web site at **http://wbl-cs.westbuslaw.com**.

SECTION 5

Types of Crimes

The number of actions that are designated as criminal is nearly endless. Federal, state, and local laws provide for the classification and punishment of hundreds of thousands of different criminal acts. Generally, though, criminal acts can be grouped into five broad categories: violent crime (crimes against persons), property crime, public order crime, white-collar crime, and organized crime. Cyber crime—which consists of crimes committed in cyberspace with the use of computers—is, as mentioned earlier in this chapter, less a category of crime than a new way to commit crime. We will examine cyber crime later in this chapter.

VIOLENT CRIME

Some types of crime are called *violent crimes,* or crimes against persons, because they cause others to suffer harm or death. Murder is a violent crime. So is sexual assault, or rape. Assault and battery, which were discussed in Chapter 5, are also classified as violent crimes. **Robbery**—defined as the taking of money, personal property, or any other article of value from a person by means of force or fear—is also a violent crime. Typically, states have more severe penalties for *aggravated robbery*—robbery with the use of a deadly weapon.

Each of these violent crimes is further classified by degree, depending on the circumstances surrounding the criminal act. These circumstances include the intent of the person committing the crime, whether a weapon was used, and (in cases other than murder) the level of pain and suffering experienced by the victim.

PROPERTY CRIME

The most common type of criminal activity is property crime, or those crimes in which the goal of the offender is some form of economic gain or the damaging of property. Robbery is a form of property crime, as well as a violent crime, because the offender seeks to gain the property of another. We look here at a number of other crimes that fall within the general category of property crime.

Burglary. Traditionally, **burglary** was defined under the common law as breaking and entering the dwelling of another at night with the intent to commit a felony. Originally, the definition was aimed at protecting an individual's home and its occupants. Most state statutes have eliminated some of the requirements found in the common law definition. The time at which the breaking and entering occurs, for example, is usually immaterial. State statutes frequently omit the element of breaking, and some states do not require that the building be a dwelling. *Aggravated burglary*—which is defined as burglary with the use of a deadly weapon, burglary of a dwelling, or both—incurs a greater penalty.

Larceny. Any person who wrongfully or fraudulently takes and carries away another person's personal property is guilty of **larceny.** Larceny includes the fraudulent intent to deprive an owner permanently of property. Many business-related larcenies entail fraudulent conduct. Whereas robbery involves force or fear, larceny does not. Therefore, picking pockets is larceny, not robbery.

In most states, the definition of property that is subject to larceny statutes has been expanded to cover relatively new forms of theft. For example, stealing computer programs may constitute larceny even though the "property" consists of magnetic impulses. Stealing computer time may also be considered larceny. So, too, may the theft of natural gas. Trade secrets may be subject to larceny statutes. Obtaining another's phone card number, without authorization, and then using that number to place long-distance calls is a form of property theft. These types of larceny are covered by "theft of services" statutes in many jurisdictions.

The common law makes a distinction between grand and petit larceny based on the value of the property taken. Many states have abolished this distinction, but in those that have not, grand larceny (theft above a certain amount) is a felony and petit larceny, a misdemeanor.

Arson. The willful and malicious burning of a building (and in some states, personal property) owned by another is the crime of **arson.** At common law, arson traditionally applied only to burning down another person's house. The law was designed to protect human life. Today, arson statutes have been extended to cover the destruction of any building, regardless of ownership, by fire or explosion.

Every state has a special statute that covers a person's burning a building for the purpose of collecting insurance. If Shaw owns an insured apartment building that is falling apart and sets fire to it himself or pays someone else to do so, he is guilty not only of arson but also of defrauding insurers, which is an attempted larceny. Of course, the insurer need not pay the claim when insurance fraud is proved.

Receiving Stolen Goods. It is a crime to receive stolen goods. The recipient of such goods need not know the true identity of the owner or the thief. All that is necessary is that the recipient knows or should know that the goods are stolen, which implies an intent to deprive the owner of those goods.

Forgery. The fraudulent making or altering of any writing in a way that changes the legal rights and liabilities of another is **forgery.** If, without authorization, Severson signs Bennett's name to the back of a check made out to Bennett, Severson is committing forgery. Forgery also includes changing trademarks, falsifying public records, counterfeiting, and altering a legal document.

Obtaining Goods by False Pretenses. It is a criminal act to obtain goods by false pretenses—for example, to buy groceries with a check, knowing that one has insufficient funds to cover it. Using another's credit-card number to obtain goods is another example of obtaining goods by false pretenses. Statutes dealing with such illegal activities vary widely from state to state. For example, in some states an intent to defraud must be proved before a person is criminally liable for writing a bad check. Some states define the theft and use of another's credit card as a separate crime, while others consider credit-card crime as a form of forgery.

Public Order Crime

Historically, societies have always outlawed activities that are considered contrary to public values and morals. Today, the most common public order crimes include public drunkenness, prostitution, gambling, and illegal drug use. These crimes are sometimes referred to as *victimless crimes* because they often harm only the offender. From a broader perspective, however, they are deemed detrimental to society as a whole because they often create an environment that may give rise to property and violent crimes.

White-Collar Crime

Crimes occurring in the business context are popularly referred to as white-collar crimes. Although there is no official definition of **white-collar crime**, the term is commonly used to mean an illegal act or series of acts committed by an individual or business entity using some nonviolent means to obtain a personal or business advantage. Usually, this kind of crime takes place in the course of a legitimate business occupation. The crimes discussed next normally occur only in the business environment and thus fall into the category of white-collar crimes. Note, though, that certain property crimes, such as larceny and forgery, may also fall into this category if they occur within the business context.

Embezzlement. When a person entrusted with another person's property or funds fraudulently appropriates that property or those funds, **embezzlement** occurs. Typically, embezzlement involves an employee who steals funds from his or her employer. Banks face this problem, and so do a number of businesses in which corporate officers or accountants "doctor" the books to cover up the fraudulent conversion of funds for their own benefit. Embezzlement is not larceny, because the wrongdoer does not physically take the property from the possession of another, and it is not robbery, because no force or fear is used.

It does not matter whether the accused takes the money from the victim or from a third person. If, as the financial officer of a large corporation, Carlson pockets a certain number of checks from third parties that were given to her to deposit into the corporate account, she is embezzling.

Ordinarily, an embezzler who returns what has been taken will not be prosecuted, because the owner usually will not take the time to make a complaint, give depositions, and appear in court. That the accused intended eventually to return the embezzled property, however, does not constitute a sufficient defense to the crime of embezzlement.

Mail and Wire Fraud. One of the most potent weapons against white-collar criminals is the Mail Fraud Act of 1990.[9] Under this act, it is a federal crime to use the mails to defraud the public. Illegal use of the mails must involve (1) mailing or causing someone else to mail a writing—something written, printed, or photocopied—for the purpose of executing a scheme to defraud and (2) contemplating or organizing a scheme to defraud by false pretenses. If, for example, Johnson advertises by mail the sale of a cure for cancer that he knows to be fraudulent because it has no medical validity, he can be prosecuted for fraudulent use of the mails.

Federal law also makes it a crime (wire fraud) to use wire, radio, or television transmissions to defraud.[10] Violators may be fined up to $1,000, imprisoned for up to five years, or both. If the violation affects a financial institution, the violator may be fined up to $1 million, imprisoned for up to thirty years, or both.

Bribery. Basically, three types of bribery are considered crimes: commercial bribery, bribery of public officials, and bribery of foreign officials. As an element of the crime of bribery, intent must be present and proved. The bribe can be anything the recipient considers to be valuable. Realize that the *crime of bribery occurs when the bribe is offered.* It does not matter whether the person to whom the bribe is offered accepts the bribe or agrees to perform whatever action is desired by the person offering the bribe. *Accepting a bribe* is a separate crime.

Typically, people make commercial bribes to obtain proprietary information, cover up an inferior product, or secure new business. Industrial espionage sometimes involves commercial bribes. For example, a person in one firm may offer an employee in a competing firm some type of payoff in exchange for trade secrets or pricing schedules. So-called kickbacks, or payoffs for special favors or services, are a form of commercial bribery in some situations.

The attempt to influence a public official to act in a way that serves a private interest is a crime. Bribing

9. 18 U.S.C. Sections 1341–1342.
10. 18 U.S.C. Section 1343.

foreign officials to obtain favorable business contracts is also a crime. This crime is discussed in detail in Chapter 40, along with the Foreign Corrupt Practices Act of 1977, which was passed to curb the use of bribery by American businesspersons in securing foreign contracts.

Bankruptcy Fraud. Today, federal bankruptcy law (see Chapter 30) allows individuals and businesses to be relieved of oppressive debt through bankruptcy proceedings. Numerous white-collar crimes may be committed during the many phases of a bankruptcy action. A creditor, for example, may file a false claim against the debtor, which is a crime. Also, a debtor may fraudulently transfer assets to favored parties before or after the petition for bankruptcy is filed. For example, a company-owned automobile may be "sold" at a bargain price to a trusted friend or relative. Closely related to the crime of fraudulent transfer of property is the crime of fraudulent concealment of property, such as the hiding of gold coins.

Insider Trading. An individual who obtains "inside information" about the plans of publicly held corporations can often make stock-trading profits by using the information to guide decisions relating to the purchase or sale of corporate securities. *Insider trading* is a violation of securities law and will be considered more fully in Chapter 37. At this point, it may be said that one who possesses inside information and who has a duty not to disclose it to outsiders may not profit from the purchase or sale of securities based on that information until the information is available to the public.

The Theft of Trade Secrets. As discussed in Chapter 7, trade secrets constitute a form of intellectual property that for many businesses can be extremely valuable. The Economic Espionage Act of 1996[11] makes the theft of trade secrets a federal crime. The act also makes it a federal crime to buy or possess another person's trade secrets, knowing that the trade secrets were stolen or otherwise acquired without the owner's authorization.

Violations of the act can result in steep penalties. The act provides that an individual who violates the act can be imprisoned for up to ten years and fined up to $500,000. If a corporation or other organization violates the act, it can be fined up to $5 million. Additionally, the law provides that any property acquired as a result of the violation and any property used in the commission of the violation is subject to criminal forfeiture—meaning that the government can take the property. A theft of trade secrets conducted via the Internet, for example, could result in the forfeiture of every computer, printer, or other device used to commit or facilitate the violation.

11. 18 U.S.C. Sections 1831–1839.

Organized Crime

White-collar crime takes place within the confines of the legitimate business world. Organized crime, in contrast, operates *illegitimately* by, among other things, providing illegal goods and services. For organized crime, the traditional preferred markets are gambling, prostitution, illegal narcotics, pornography, and loan sharking (lending money at higher than legal interest rates), along with more recent ventures into counterfeiting and credit-card scams.

Money Laundering. The profits from organized crime and other illegal activities amount to billions of dollars a year, particularly the profits from illegal drug transactions and, to a lesser extent, from racketeering, prostitution, and gambling. Under federal law, banks, savings and loan associations, and other financial institutions are required to report currency transactions of over $10,000. Consequently, those who engage in illegal activities face difficulties in depositing their cash profits from illegal transactions.

As an alternative to simply placing cash from illegal transactions in bank deposits, wrongdoers and racketeers have invented ways to launder "dirty" money to make it "clean." This **money laundering** is done through legitimate businesses. For example, a successful drug dealer might become a partner with a restaurateur. Little by little, the restaurant shows an increasing profit. As a shareholder or partner in the restaurant, the wrongdoer is able to report the "profits" of the restaurant as legitimate income on which federal and state taxes are paid. The wrongdoer can then spend those monies without worrying about whether his or her lifestyle exceeds the level possible with his or her reported income.

The Federal Bureau of Investigation estimates that organized crime alone has invested tens of billions of dollars in as many as a hundred thousand business establishments in the United States for the purpose of money laundering. Globally, it is estimated that

$300 billion in illegal money moves through the world banking system every year.

RICO. In 1970, in an effort to curb the apparently increasing entry of organized crime into the legitimate business world, Congress passed the Racketeer Influenced and Corrupt Organizations Act (RICO).[12] The act, which was enacted as part of the Organized Crime Control Act, makes it a federal crime to (1) use income obtained from racketeering activity to purchase any interest in an enterprise, (2) acquire or maintain an interest in an enterprise through racketeering activity, (3) conduct or participate in the affairs of an enterprise through racketeering activity, or (4) conspire to do any of the preceding activities.

Racketeering activity is not a new type of substantive crime created by RICO; rather, RICO incorporates by reference twenty-six separate types of federal crimes and nine types of state felonies[13] and declares that if a person commits two of these offenses, he or she is guilty of "racketeering activity." The act provides for both civil and criminal liability.

Civil Liability under RICO. The penalties for violations of the RICO statute are harsh. In the event of a violation, the statute permits the government to seek civil penalties, including the divestiture of a defendant's interest in a business (called forfeiture) or the dissolution of the business. Perhaps the most controversial aspect of RICO is that in some cases, private individuals are allowed to recover three times their actual losses (treble damages), plus attorneys' fees, for business injuries caused by a violation of the statute.

The broad language of RICO has allowed it to be applied in cases that have little or nothing to do with organized crime, and an aggressive trial attorney may attempt to show that any business fraud constitutes "racketeering activity." In its 1985 decision in *Sedima, S.P.R.L. v. Imrex Co.,*[14] the United States Supreme Court interpreted RICO broadly and set a significant precedent for subsequent applications of the act. Plaintiffs have used the RICO statute in numerous commercial fraud cases because of the inviting prospect of being awarded treble damages if they win. The most frequent targets of civil RICO lawsuits are insurance companies, employment agencies, commercial banks, and stockbrokerage firms.

One of the requirements of RICO is that there be more than one offense—there must be a "pattern of racketeering activity." What constitutes a "pattern" has been the subject of much litigation. According to the interpretation of some courts, a pattern must involve, among other things, continued criminal activity. This is known as the "continuity" requirement. Part of this requirement is that the activity occur over a "substantial" period of time.

Criminal Liability under RICO. Many criminal RICO offenses, such as gambling, arson, and extortion, have little, if anything, to do with normal business activities. But securities fraud (involving the sale of stocks and bonds) and mail and wire fraud also may constitute criminal RICO violations, and RICO has become an effective tool in attacking these white-collar crimes in recent years. Under the criminal provisions of RICO, any individual found guilty of a violation is subject to a fine of up to $25,000 per violation, imprisonment for up to twenty years, or both.

SECTION 6

Defenses to Criminal Liability

In certain circumstances, the law may allow a person to be excused from criminal liability because he or she lacks the required mental state. Criminal defendants may also be relieved of criminal liability if they can show that their criminal actions were justified, given the circumstances. Among the most important defenses to criminal liability are infancy, intoxication, insanity, mistake, consent, duress, justifiable use of force, necessity, entrapment, and the statute of limitations. Also, in some cases, defendants are given *immunity* from prosecution and thus relieved, at least in part, of criminal liability for their actions. We look next at each of these defenses.

Note that procedural violations (such as obtaining evidence without a valid search warrant) may operate as defenses also—because evidence obtained in violation of a defendant's constitutional rights may not be admitted in court. If the evidence is suppressed, then there may be no basis for prosecuting the defendant.

INFANCY

The term *infant,* as used in the law, refers to any person who has not yet reached the age of majority (see

12. 18 U.S.C. Sections 1961–1968.

13. See 18 U.S.C. Section 1961(1)(A).

14. 473 U.S. 479, 105 S.Ct. 3275, 87 L.Ed.2d 346 (1985).

Chapter 12). In all states, certain courts handle cases involving children who are alleged to have violated the law. In some states, juvenile courts handle children's cases exclusively. In most states, however, courts that handle children's cases also have jurisdiction over other matters, such as traffic offenses.

Originally, juvenile court hearings were informal, and lawyers were rarely present. Since 1967, however, when the United States Supreme Court ordered that a child charged with delinquency must be allowed to consult with an attorney before being committed to a state institution,[15] juvenile court hearings have become more formal. In some states, a child may be treated as an adult and tried in a regular court if he or she is above a certain age (usually fourteen) and is guilty of a felony, such as rape or murder.

INTOXICATION

The law recognizes two types of intoxication, whether from drugs or from alcohol: involuntary and voluntary. *Involuntary intoxication* occurs when a person either is physically forced to ingest or inject an intoxicating substance or is unaware that a substance contains drugs or alcohol. Involuntary intoxication is a defense to a crime if its effect was to make a person incapable of understanding that the act committed was wrong or incapable of obeying the law.

Using voluntary drug or alcohol intoxication as a defense is based on the theory that extreme levels of intoxication may negate the state of mind that a crime requires. Many courts are reluctant to allow *voluntary intoxication* as a defense to a crime, however. After all, the defendant, by definition, voluntarily chose to put himself or herself into an intoxicated state.

INSANITY

Just as a child is often judged incapable of the state of mind required to commit a crime, so also may be someone suffering from a mental illness. Thus, insanity may be a defense to a criminal charge. The courts have had difficulty deciding what standards should be used to measure sanity for the purposes of a criminal trial. One of the oldest standards, or tests, for insanity is the *M'Naghten* test,[16] which is still used in about one-third of the states. Under this test, which is sometimes called the "right-wrong" test, a criminal defendant is not responsible if, at the time of the offense, he or she did not know the nature and quality of the act or did not know that the act was wrong.

Several other jurisdictions use the less restrictive irresistible-impulse test to determine sanity. Under this test, a person may be found insane even if he or she was aware that a criminal act was wrong, providing that some "irresistible impulse" resulting from a mental deficiency drove him or her to commit the crime.

Today, almost all federal courts and about half of the states use the relatively liberal standard set forth in the Model Penal Code:

> A person is not responsible for criminal conduct if at the time of such conduct as a result of mental disease or defect he lacks *substantial capacity* either to appreciate the wrongfulness of his conduct or to conform his conduct to the requirements of the law.[17] [Emphasis added.]

This "substantial-capacity" standard is considerably easier to meet than the *M'Naghten* test or the irresistible-impulse test.

Under any of these tests, it is extremely difficult to prove insanity. For this reason, the insanity defense is rarely used. It is raised in only about 1 percent of felony cases and is unsuccessful in about three-fourths of those cases.

MISTAKE

Everyone has heard the saying "Ignorance of the law is no excuse." Ordinarily, ignorance of the law or a mistaken idea about what the law requires is not a valid defense. In some states, however, that rule has been modified. People who claim that they honestly did not know that they were breaking a law may have a valid defense if (1) the law was not published or reasonably made known to the public or (2) the people relied on an official statement of the law that was erroneous.

A *mistake of fact*, as opposed to a *mistake of law*, operates as a defense if it negates the mental state necessary to commit a crime. If, for example, Oliver Wheaton mistakenly walks off with Julie Tyson's briefcase because he thinks it is his, there is no theft. Theft requires knowledge that the property belongs to another.

---

15. *In re Gault*, 387 U.S. 1, 87 S.Ct. 1428, 18 L.Ed.2d 527 (1967).
16. A rule derived from *M'Naghten's Case*, 8 Eng.Rep. 718 (1843).
17. Model Penal Code Section 4.01.

CONSENT

What if a victim consents to a crime or even encourages the person intending a criminal act to commit it? Depending on the circumstances, the law may allow **consent** as a defense. In each case, one question is whether the law forbids an act committed against the victim's will or forbids the act without regard to the victim's wish. The law forbids murder, prostitution, and drug use whether the victim consents or not. Also, if the act causes harm to a third person who has not consented, there is no escape from criminal liability. Consent or forgiveness given after a crime has been committed is not really a defense, although it can affect the likelihood of prosecution. Consent operates as a defense most successfully in crimes against property.

DURESS

Duress exists when the *wrongful threat* of one person induces another person to perform an act that he or she would not otherwise have performed. In such a situation, duress is said to negate the mental state necessary to commit a crime. For duress to qualify as a defense, the following requirements must be met:

1. The threat must be of serious bodily harm or death.
2. The harm threatened must be greater than the harm caused by the crime.
3. The threat must be immediate and inescapable.
4. The defendant must have been involved in the situation through no fault of his or her own.

One crime that cannot be excused by duress is murder. It is difficult to justify taking a life as a result of duress even if one's own life is threatened.

JUSTIFIABLE USE OF FORCE

Probably the most well-known defense to criminal liability is **self-defense**. Other situations, however, also justify the use of force: the defense of one's dwelling, the defense of other property, and the prevention of a crime. In all of these situations, it is important to distinguish between the use of deadly and nondeadly force. *Deadly force* is likely to result in death or serious bodily harm. *Nondeadly force* is force that reasonably appears necessary to prevent the imminent use of criminal force.

Generally speaking, people can use the amount of nondeadly force that seems necessary to protect themselves, their dwellings, or other property or to prevent the commission of a crime. Deadly force can be used in self-defense if there is a *reasonable belief* that imminent death or grievous bodily harm will otherwise result, if the attacker is using unlawful force (an example of lawful force is that exerted by a police officer), and if the defender has not initiated or provoked the attack. Deadly force can be used to defend a dwelling only if the unlawful entry is violent and the person believes deadly force is necessary to prevent imminent death or great bodily harm or—in some jurisdictions—if the person believes deadly force is necessary to prevent the commission of a felony in the dwelling.

NECESSITY

Sometimes criminal defendants can be relieved of liability by showing that a criminal act was necessary to prevent an even greater harm. According to the Model Penal Code, the defense of **necessity** is justifiable if "the harm or evil sought to be avoided by such conduct is greater than that sought to be prevented by the law defining the offense charged."[18] For example, in one case a convicted felon was threatened by an acquaintance with a gun. The felon grabbed the gun and fled the scene, but subsequently he was arrested under a statute that prohibits convicted felons from possessing firearms. In this situation, the necessity defense succeeded because the defendant's crime avoided a "greater evil."[19]

ENTRAPMENT

Entrapment is a defense designed to prevent police officers or other government agents from encouraging crimes in order to apprehend persons wanted for criminal acts. In the typical entrapment case, an undercover agent *suggests* that a crime be committed and somehow pressures or induces an individual to commit it. The agent then arrests the individual for the crime. For entrapment to be considered a defense, both the suggestion and the inducement must take place. The defense is intended not to prevent law enforcement agents from setting a trap for an unwary criminal but rather to prevent them from pushing the individual into that trap. The crucial issue is whether a person who committed a crime was pre-

18. Model Penal Code Section 3.02.
19. *United States v. Paolello*, 951 F.3d 537 (3d Cir. 1991).

disposed to commit the crime or did so because the agent induced it.

STATUTE OF LIMITATIONS

With some exceptions, such as for the crime of murder, statutes of limitations apply to crimes just as they do to civil wrongs. In other words, criminal cases must be prosecuted within a certain number of years. If a criminal action is brought after the statutory time period has expired, the accused person can raise the statute of limitations as a defense. The running of the time period in a statute of limitations may be tolled—that is, suspended or stopped temporarily—if the defendant is a minor or is not in the jurisdiction. When the defendant reaches the age of majority or returns, the statute revives—that is, its time period begins to run or to run again.

IMMUNITY

At times, the state may wish to obtain information from a person accused of a crime. Accused persons are understandably reluctant to give information if it will be used to prosecute them, and they cannot be forced to do so. The privilege against self-incrimination is granted by the Fifth Amendment to the Constitution, which reads, in part, "nor shall [any person] be compelled in any criminal case to be a witness against himself." In cases in which the state wishes to obtain information from a person accused of a crime, the state can grant *immunity* from prosecution or agree to prosecute for a less serious offense in exchange for the information. Once immunity is given, the person can no longer refuse to testify on Fifth Amendment grounds because he or she now has an absolute privilege against self-incrimination.

Often a grant of immunity from prosecution for a serious crime is part of the **plea bargaining** between the defending and prosecuting attorneys. The defendant may be convicted of a lesser offense, while the state uses the defendant's testimony to prosecute accomplices for serious crimes carrying heavy penalties.

SECTION 7

Criminal Procedures

Criminal law brings the force of the state, with all of its resources, to bear against the individual. Criminal procedures are designed to protect the constitutional rights of individuals and to prevent the arbitrary use of power on the part of the government.

The U.S. Constitution provides specific safeguards for those accused of crimes. The United States Supreme Court has ruled that most of these safeguards apply not only in federal but also in state courts by virtue of the due process clause of the Fourteenth Amendment. These safeguards include the following:

1. The Fourth Amendment protection from unreasonable searches and seizures.
2. The Fourth Amendment requirement that no warrant for a search or an arrest be issued without probable cause.
3. The Fifth Amendment requirement that no one be deprived of "life, liberty, or property without due process of law."
4. The Fifth Amendment prohibition against **double jeopardy** (trying someone twice for the same criminal offense).[20]
5. The Fifth Amendment requirement that no person be required to be a witness against (incriminate) himself or herself.
6. The Sixth Amendment guarantees of a speedy trial, a trial by jury, a public trial, the right to confront witnesses, and the right to a lawyer at various stages in some proceedings.
7. The Eighth Amendment prohibitions against excessive bail and fines and cruel and unusual punishment.

THE EXCLUSIONARY RULE

Under what is known as the **exclusionary rule**, all evidence obtained in violation of the constitutional rights spelled out in the Fourth, Fifth, and Sixth Amendments normally is not admissible at trial. All evidence derived from the illegally obtained evidence is known as the "fruit of the poisonous tree,"

20. The prohibition against double jeopardy means that once a criminal defendant is found not guilty of a particular crime, the government may not reindict the person and retry him or her for the same crime. The prohibition against double jeopardy does not preclude a *civil* suit's being brought against the same person by the crime victim to recover damages, however. For example, a person found not guilty of assault and battery in a criminal case may be sued by the victim in a civil tort case for damages. Additionally, a state's prosecution of a crime will not prevent a separate federal prosecution of the same crime, and vice versa. For example, a defendant found not guilty of violating a state law can be tried in federal court for the same act, if the act is also defined as a (perhaps different) crime under federal law.

and such evidence normally must also be excluded from the trial proceedings. For example, if a confession is obtained after an illegal arrest, the arrest is the "poisonous tree," and the confession, if "tainted" by the arrest, is the "fruit."

The purpose of the exclusionary rule is to deter police from conducting warrantless searches and from other misconduct. The rule is sometimes criticized because it can lead to injustice. Many a defendant has "gotten off on a technicality" because law enforcement personnel failed to observe procedural requirements based on the above-mentioned constitutional amendments. Even though a defendant may be obviously guilty, if the evidence of that guilt is obtained improperly (without a valid search warrant, for example), it cannot be used against the defendant in court.

Over the last several decades, however, the United States Supreme Court diminished the scope of the exclusionary rule by creating some exceptions to its applicability. For example, in 1984 the Court held that if illegally obtained evidence would have been "inevitably" discovered and obtained by the police using lawful means, the evidence will be admissible at trial.[21] In another case decided in the same year, the Court held that a police officer who used a technically incorrect search warrant form to obtain evidence had acted in good faith and therefore the evidence was admissible. The Court thus created the "good faith" exception to the exclusionary rule.[22] Additionally, the courts can exercise a certain amount of discretion in determining whether evidence has been obtained improperly, thus somewhat balancing the scales.

THE *MIRANDA* RULE

In regard to criminal procedure, one of the questions many courts faced in the 1950s and 1960s was not whether suspects had constitutional rights—that was not in doubt—but how and when those rights could be exercised. Could the right to be silent (under the Fifth Amendment's prohibition against self-incrimination) be exercised during pretrial interrogation proceedings, or only during the trial? Were confessions obtained from suspects admissible in court if the suspects had not been advised of their right to remain silent and other constitutional rights?

To clarify these issues, the United States Supreme Court issued a landmark decision in 1966 in *Miranda v. Arizona,* presented as Case 8.2. The procedural rights required by the Court in this case are familiar to virtually every American.

Westlaw. See Case 8.2 at the end of this chapter. To view the full, unedited case from Westlaw,® go to this text's Web site at **http://wbl-cs.westbuslaw.com**.

Exceptions to the *Miranda* Rule. As part of a continuing attempt to balance the rights of accused persons against the rights of society, the Supreme Court has made a number of exceptions to the *Miranda* ruling. In 1984, for example, the Court recognized a "public safety" exception to the *Miranda* rule. The need to protect the public warranted the admissibility of statements made by the defendant (in this case, indicating where he placed the gun) as evidence in a trial, even when the defendant had not been informed of his *Miranda* rights.[23]

In 1986, the Court further held that a confession need not be excluded even though the police failed to inform a suspect in custody that his attorney had tried to reach him by telephone.[24] In an important 1991 decision, the Court stated that a suspect's conviction will not be automatically overturned if the suspect was coerced into making a confession. If the other evidence admitted at trial was strong enough to justify the conviction without the confession, then the fact that the confession was obtained illegally can be, in effect, ignored.[25] In yet another case, in 1994, the Supreme Court ruled that a suspect must unequivocally and assertively request to exercise the right to counsel in order to stop police questioning. Saying, "Maybe I should talk to a lawyer" during an interrogation after being taken into custody is not enough. The Court held that police officers are not required to decipher the suspect's intentions in such situations.[26]

21. *Nix v. Williams,* 467 U.S. 431, 104 S.Ct. 2501, 81 L.Ed. 377 (1984).

22. *Massachusetts v. Sheppard,* 468 U.S. 981, 104 S.Ct. 3424, 82 L.Ed.2d 737 (1984).

23. *New York v. Quarles,* 467 U.S. 649, 104 S.Ct. 2626, 81 L.Ed.2d 550 (1984).

24. *Moran v. Burbine,* 475 U.S. 412, 106 S.Ct. 1135, 89 L.Ed.2d 410 (1986).

25. *Arizona v. Fulminante,* 499 U.S. 279, 111 S.Ct. 1246, 113 L.Ed.2d 302 (1991).

26. *Davis v. United States,* 512 U.S. 452, 114 S.Ct. 2350, 129 L.Ed.2d 362 (1994).

Section 3501 of the Omnibus Crime Control Act of 1968. In 1999, the U.S. Court of Appeals for the Fourth Circuit stunned the nation's legal establishment by enforcing a long-forgotten provision, Section 3501, of the Omnibus Crime Control Act of 1968. Congress passed the act two years after the Supreme Court's *Miranda* decision in an attempt to reinstate a rule that had been in effect for 180 years before *Miranda*—namely, that statements by defendants can be used against them as long as they are voluntarily made. The Justice Department immediately disavowed Section 3501 as unconstitutional and continued to hold that position.

The Fourth Circuit's attempt to enforce the provision was overturned by the Supreme Court in 2000, however. The Court held that the rights enunciated by the Court in the 1966 *Miranda* case were constitutionally based and thus could not be overruled by a legislative act.[27]

Videotaped Interrogations. There are no guarantees that *Miranda* will survive indefinitely—particularly in view of the numerous exceptions that are made to the rule. Additionally, law enforcement personnel are increasingly using videotapes to record interrogations. According to some scholars, the videotaping of *all* custodial interrogations would satisfy the Fifth Amendment's prohibition against coercion and in the process render the *Miranda* warnings unnecessary.

Criminal Process

As mentioned earlier in this chapter, a criminal prosecution differs significantly from a civil case in several respects. These differences reflect the desire to safeguard the rights of the individual against the state. Exhibit 8–3 on page 180 shows the major steps in processing a criminal case. We discuss below in more detail three phases of the criminal process—arrest, indictment or information, and trial.

Arrest. Before a warrant for arrest can be issued, there must be probable cause for believing that the individual in question has committed a crime. As discussed in Chapter 4, *probable cause* can be defined as a substantial likelihood that the person has committed or is about to commit a crime. Note that probable cause involves a likelihood, not just a possibility. Arrests may sometimes be made without a warrant if there is no time to get one, but the action of the arresting officer is still judged by the standard of probable cause.

Indictment or Information. Individuals must be formally charged with having committed specific crimes before they can be brought to trial. If issued by a grand jury, such a charge is called an **indictment.**[28] A **grand jury** does not determine the guilt or innocence of an accused party; rather, its function is to determine, after hearing the state's evidence, whether a reasonable basis (probable cause) exists for supposing that a crime has been committed and whether a trial ought to be held.

Usually, grand juries are called in cases involving serious crimes, such as murder. For lesser crimes, an individual may be formally charged with a crime by an **information**, or criminal complaint. An information will be issued by a magistrate (a public official vested with judicial authority) if the magistrate determines that there is sufficient evidence to justify bringing the individual to trial.

Trial. At a criminal trial, the accused person does not have to prove anything; the entire burden of proof is on the prosecutor (the state). As discussed at the beginning of this chapter, the burden of proof in a criminal case is higher than that in a civil case. The prosecution must show that, based on all the evidence, the defendant's guilt is established *beyond a reasonable doubt*. If there is any reasonable doubt as to whether a criminal defendant did, in fact, commit the crime with which he or she has been charged, then the verdict must be "not guilty." Note that giving a verdict of "not guilty" is not the same as stating that the defendant is innocent; it merely means that not enough evidence was properly presented to the court to prove guilt beyond all reasonable doubt.

Courts have complex rules about what types of evidence may be presented and how the evidence may be brought out in criminal cases, especially in jury trials. These rules are designed to ensure that evidence presented at trials is relevant, reliable, and not prejudicial against the defendant.

27. *Dickerson v. United States*, 530 U.S. 428, 120 S.Ct. 2326, 147 L.Ed.2d 405 (2000).

28. Pronounced in-*dyte*-ment.

EXHIBIT 8–3 MAJOR STEPS IN PROCESSING A CRIMINAL CASE

BOOKING
After arrest, at the police station, the suspect is searched, photographed, fingerprinted, and allowed at least one telephone call. After the booking, charges are reviewed, and if they are not dropped, a complaint is filed and a judge or magistrate examines the case for probable cause.

INITIAL APPEARANCE
The suspect appears before the judge, who informs the suspect of the charges and of his or her rights. If the suspect requests a lawyer, one is appointed. The judge sets bail (conditions under which a suspect can obtain release pending disposition of the case).

PRELIMINARY HEARING
In a proceeding in which both sides are represented by counsel, the judge determines whether there is probable cause to believe that the suspect committed the crime, based on the evidence.

GRAND JURY REVIEW
The federal government and about half of the states require grand jury indictments for at least some felonies. In those states, a grand jury determines whether the evidence justifies a trial on the charges sought by the prosecutor.

PROSECUTORIAL REVIEW
In jurisdictions that do not require grand jury indictments, a prosecutor issues an information. An information is similar to an indictment: both indicate that there is sufficient evidence to justify bringing an individual to trial.

ARRAIGNMENT
The suspect is brought before the trial court, informed of the charges, and asked to enter a plea.

PLEA BARGAIN
A plea bargain is a prosecutor's promise of concessions (or promise to seek concessions) in return for the defendant's guilty plea. Concessions include a reduced charge and/or a lesser sentence.

GUILTY PLEA
In a majority of jurisdictions, most cases that reach the arraignment stage do not go to trial but are resolved by a guilty plea, often as the result of a plea bargain. The judge sets the case for sentencing.

TRIAL
If the defendant refuses to plead guilty, he or she proceeds to either a jury trial (in most instances) or a bench trial.

FEDERAL SENTENCING GUIDELINES

Traditionally, persons who had committed the same crime might have received very different sentences, depending on the judge hearing the case, the jurisdiction in which it was heard, and many other factors. In 1984, however, Congress passed the Sentencing Reform Act. This act created the U.S. Sentencing Commission, which was charged with the task of standardizing sentences for federal crimes. The commission's guidelines, which became effective in 1987, established a range of possible penalties for each federal crime. Judges must select a sentence from within this range when sentencing criminal defendants, taking into consideration the defendant's criminal record, the seriousness of the offense, and other factors specified in the guidelines.

The commission also created specific guidelines for the punishment of crimes committed by corporate employees (white-collar crimes). These guidelines, which went into effect in 1991, established stiffer penalties for mail and wire fraud, commercial bribery and kickbacks, and money laundering, as well as for criminal violations of securities laws (see Chapter 37), employment laws (see Chapters 41 and 42), and antitrust laws (see Chapter 45). The guidelines allow judges to take into consideration a number of factors when selecting from the range of possible penalties for a specified crime. These factors include the defendant company's history of past violations, the extent of management's cooperation with federal investigators, and the extent to which the firm has undertaken specific programs and procedures to prevent criminal activities by its employees.

SECTION 8

Cyber Crime

Some years ago, the American Bar Association defined **computer crime** as any act that is directed against computers and computer parts, that uses computers as instruments of crime, or that involves computers and constitutes abuse. Today, because much of the crime committed with the use of computers occurs in cyberspace, many computer crimes fall under the broad label of cyber crime.

Realize that most cyber crimes are not "new" crimes. Rather, they are existing crimes in which the Internet is the instrument of wrongdoing. The challenge for law enforcement is to apply traditional laws—which were designed to protect persons from physical harm or to safeguard their physical property—to crimes committed in cyberspace. Here we look at several types of activity that constitute cyber crimes against persons or property. Other cyber crimes will be discussed in later chapters of this text as they relate to particular topics, such as banking or consumer law.

CYBER THEFT

In cyberspace, thieves are not subject to the physical limitations of the "real" world. A thief can steal data stored in a networked computer with dial-in access from anywhere on the globe. Only the speed of the connection and the thief's computer equipment limit the quantity of data that can be stolen.

Financial Crimes. Computer networks also provide opportunities for employees to commit crimes that can involve serious economic losses. For example, employees of a company's accounting department can transfer funds among accounts with little effort and often with less risk than that involved in transactions evidenced by paperwork.

Generally, the dependence of businesses on computer operations has left firms vulnerable to sabotage, fraud, embezzlement, and the theft of proprietary data, such as trade secrets or other intellectual property. As noted in Chapter 7, the theft of intellectual property via the Internet is one of the most serious legal challenges facing lawmakers and the courts today.

Identity Theft. A form of cyber theft that has become particularly troublesome in recent years is **identity theft.** Identity theft occurs when the wrongdoer steals a form of identification—such as a name, date of birth, or Social Security number—and uses the information to access the victim's financial resources. This crime did exist to a certain extent before Internet use became widespread. Thieves would "steal" calling-card numbers by watching over people using public telephones, or they would rifle through garbage in order to find bank account or credit-card numbers. The identity thieves would then use the calling-card or credit-card number or withdraw funds from the victims' accounts until he or she was discovered.

The Internet, however, has turned identity theft into perhaps the fasting-growing financial crime in the United States. Primarily, it provides those who steal information offline with an easy arena in which to use items such as stolen credit-card numbers or e-mail addresses while protected by anonymity. An estimated 500,000 Americans are victims of identity theft each year.

CYBER STALKING

California enacted the first stalking law in 1990, in response to the murders of six women—including Rebecca Schaeffer, a television star—by the men who had harassed them. The law made it a crime to harass or follow a person while making a "credible threat" that puts that person in reasonable fear for his or her safety or the safety of the person's immediate family.[29] Most other states have also enacted stalking laws, yet in about half of the states these stalking laws require a physical act (following the victim). **Cyber stalkers** (stalkers who commit their crimes in cyberspace), however, find their victims through Internet chat rooms, Usenet newsgroups or other bulletin boards, or e-mail. To close this "loophole" in existing stalking laws, over three-fourths of the states now have laws specifically designed to combat cyber stalking and other forms of online harassment.

Note that cyber stalking is usually easier to commit and harder for law-enforcement officers to prevent than traditional stalking. Physically stalking someone takes a great deal of effort, while harassing a victim with electronic messages is relatively easy. Many stalkers fear personal confrontations with their victims, so they turn to the anonymity and safety of the Internet to harass and threaten. This makes it difficult for law-enforcement officers to identify or locate them. It also presents a problem for victims, for how can one obtain a restraining order against a cyber stalker whose identity is unknown? Additionally, there is always the possibility that a cyber stalker will eventually pose a physical threat to his or her target.

HACKING

Persons who use one computer to break into another are sometimes referred to as **hackers.** Hackers who break into computers without authorization often commit cyber theft. Sometimes, however, their principal aim is to prove how smart they are by gaining access to others' password-protected computers and causing random data errors or making unpaid-for telephone calls.[30]

The Computer Crime and Security Survey polled 538 companies and large government institutions and found that 85 percent had experienced security breaches through computer-based means in 2000. It is difficult to know, however, just how frequently hackers succeed in breaking into databases across the United States. The FBI estimates that only 25 percent of all corporations that suffer such security breaches report the incidents to a law enforcement agency. For one thing, corporations do not want it to become publicly known that the security of their data has been breached. For another, acknowledging such a breach would be admitting to a certain degree of incompetence, which could damage their business reputations.

CYBER TERRORISM

Cyber terrorists are hackers who aim not to gain attention but to remain undetected in order to exploit computers for a more serious impact. Just as "real" terrorists destroyed the World Trade Center towers and a portion of the Pentagon in September 2001, cyber terrorists might explode "logic bombs" to shut down central computers. Such activities can pose a danger to national security. After an American surveillance airplane collided with a Chinese military jet, hackers from China bombarded American Web sites with messages such as "Hack the USA" and "For our pilot Wang." Over a period of several weeks, these hackers were able to destroy or deface hundreds of Web sites, including some from the White House, the FBI, and NASA.

Businesses may also be targeted by cyber terrorists. The goal of a hacking operation might include a wholesale theft of data, such as a merchant's customer files, or the monitoring of a computer to discover a business firm's plans and transactions. A cyber terrorist might want to insert false codes or data. For example, the processing control system of a food manufacturer could be changed to alter the levels of ingredients so that consumers of the food would become ill. A cyber terrorist attack on a major financial institution such as the New York Stock Exchange or a large bank could leave monetary markets in flux and seriously affect the daily lives of mil-

29. Cal. Penal Code Section 646.9.

30. The total cost of crime on the Internet is estimated to be several billion dollars annually, but two-thirds of that total is said to consist of unpaid-for toll calls.

lions of citizens. Similarly, any prolonged disruption of computer, cable, satellite, or telecommunications systems due to the actions of expert hackers would have serious repercussions on business operations—and national security—on a global level. Computer viruses (see Chapter 5) are another tool that can be used by cyber terrorists to cripple communications networks.

PROSECUTING CYBER CRIMES

The "location" of cyber crime (cyberspace) has raised new questions in the investigation of crimes and the prosecution of offenders. A threshold issue is, of course, jurisdiction. A person who commits an offense against a business in California, where the act is a cyber crime, might never have set foot in California but might instead reside in New York, or even in Canada, where the act may not be a crime. If the crime were committed via e-mail, the question arises as to whether the e-mail would constitute sufficient "minimum contacts" (see Chapter 2) for the victim's state to exercise jurisdiction over the perpetrator.

Another problem is identifying the wrongdoers. Cyber criminals do not leave physical traces, such as fingerprints or DNA samples, as evidence of their crimes. Even electronic "footprints" can be hard to find and follow. For example, e-mail may be sent through a remailer, an online service that guarantees that a message cannot be traced to its source.

For these reasons, laws written to protect physical property are difficult to apply in cyberspace. Nonetheless, governments at both the state and federal levels have taken significant steps toward controlling cyber crime, both through applying existing criminal statutes and enacting new laws that specifically address wrongs committed in cyberspace.

The Computer Fraud and Abuse Act. Perhaps the most significant federal statute specifically addressing cyber crime is the Counterfeit Access Device and Computer Fraud and Abuse Act of 1984 (commonly known as the Computer Fraud and Abuse Act, or CFAA). This act, as amended by the National Information Infrastructure Protection Act of 1996,[31] provides, among other things, that a person who accesses a computer online, without authority, to obtain classified, restricted, or protected data, or attempts to do so, is subject to criminal prosecution. These data could include financial and credit records, medical records, legal files, military and national security files, and other confidential information in government or private computers. The crime has two elements: accessing a computer without authority and taking the data.

This theft is a felony if it is committed for a commercial purpose or for private financial gain, or if the value of the stolen data (or computer time) exceeds $5,000. Penalties include fines and imprisonment for up to twenty years. A victim of computer theft can also bring a civil suit against the violator to obtain damages, an injunction, or other relief.

The CFAA defines *damage* as a "loss aggregating at least $5,000 in value during any one-year period to one or more individuals." At issue in Case 8.3 was whether the term *individual* in this definition included a corporation.

> Westlaw. See Case 8.3 at the end of this chapter. To view the full, unedited case from Westlaw,® go to this text's Web site at **http://wbl-cs.westbuslaw.com**.

Other Federal Statutes. The federal wire fraud statute, the Economic Espionage Act of 1996, and RICO, all of which were discussed earlier in this chapter, extend to crimes committed in cyberspace as well. Other federal statutes that may apply include the Electronic Fund Transfer Act of 1978, which makes unauthorized access to an electronic fund transfer system a crime; the Anticounterfeiting Consumer Protection Act of 1996, which increased penalties for stealing copyrighted or trademarked property; and the National Stolen Property Act of 1988, which concerns the interstate transport of stolen property. Recall from Chapter 4 that the federal government has also enacted laws (many of which have been challenged on constitutional grounds) to protect minors from online pornographic materials. In later chapters of this text, you will read about other federal statutes and regulations that are designed to address wrongs committed in cyberspace in specific areas of the law.

31. 18 U.S.C. Section 1030.

Terms and Concepts to Review

actus reus 169
arson 171
beyond a reasonable doubt 166
burglary 171
computer crime 181
consent 176
crime 166
cyber crimes 166
cyber stalker 182
cyber terrorists 182
double jeopardy 177
duress 176
embezzlement 172
entrapment 176
exclusionary rule 177
felony 167
forgery 171
grand jury 179
hackers 182
identity theft 181
indictment 179
information 179
larceny 171
mens rea 169
misdemeanor 168
money laundering 173
necessity 176
petty offense 168
plea bargaining 177
robbery 170
self-defense 176
white-collar crime 172

Chapter Summary

Civil Law and Criminal Law	1. *Civil law*—Spells out the duties that exist between persons or between citizens and their governments, excluding the duty not to commit crimes. 2. *Criminal law*—Has to do with crimes, which are defined as wrongs against society proclaimed in statutes and, if committed, punishable by society through fines, removal from public office, and/or imprisonment—and, in some cases, death. Because crimes are offenses against society as a whole, they are prosecuted by a public official, not by victims. 3. *Key differences*—An important difference between civil and criminal law is that the standard of proof is higher in criminal cases (see Exhibit 8–1 for other differences between criminal and civil laws). 4. *Civil liability for criminal acts*—A criminal act may give rise to both criminal liability and tort liability (see Exhibit 8–2 for an example of criminal and tort liability for the same act).
Classification of Crimes	1. *Felonies*—Serious crimes punishable by death or by imprisonment in a penitentiary for more than one year. 2. *Misdemeanors and petty offenses*—Under federal law and in most states, any crimes that are not felonies are either misdemeanors (crimes punishable by a fine or imprisonment for up to one year) or petty offenses (minor violations, such as violations of building codes).
The Essentials of Criminal Liability	1. *Criminal act*—In general, some form of harmful act *(actus reus)* must be committed for a crime to exist. 2. *State of mind*—An intent to commit a crime, or a wrongful mental state *(mens rea)*, is required for a crime to exist.
Corporate Criminal Liability	1. *Liability of the corporate entity*—Corporations normally are liable for the crimes committed by their agents and employees within the course and scope of their employment. Corporations cannot be imprisoned, but they can be fined or denied certain legal privileges. 2. *Liability of corporate officers and directors*—Corporate directors and officers are personally liable for the crimes they commit and may be held liable for the actions of employees under their supervision.

CHAPTER SUMMARY—CONTINUED

Types of Crimes	1. *Violent crime*—Crimes that cause others to suffer harm or death. Examples include murder, assault and battery, rape, and robbery. 2. *Property crime*—Crimes in which the goal of the offender is some form of economic gain or the damaging of property. Examples include burglary, larceny, arson, receiving stolen goods, forgery, and obtaining goods by false pretenses. 3. *Public order crime*—Crimes contrary to public values and morals. Examples include public drunkenness, prostitution, gambling, and illegal drug use. 4. *White-collar crime*—Nonviolent crimes committed in the course of a legitimate occupation to obtain a personal or business advantage. Examples include embezzlement, mail and wire fraud, bribery, bankruptcy fraud, insider trading, and the theft of trade secrets. 5. *Organized crime*—Crime committed by groups operating illegitimately to satisfy the public's demand for illegal goods and services (such as narcotics or pornography). Often, organized crime involves *money laundering*—the establishment of legitimate enterprises through which "dirty" money obtained through criminal activities can be "laundered" and made to appear as legitimate income. The Racketeer Influenced and Corrupt Organizations Act (RICO) of 1970, which prohibits racketeering activity, was passed, in part, to control organized crime.
Defenses to Criminal Liability	1. *Infancy.* 2. *Intoxication.* 3. *Insanity.* 4. *Mistake.* 5. *Consent.* 6. *Duress.* 7. *Justifiable use of force.* 8. *Necessity.* 9. *Entrapment.* 10. *Statute of limitations.* 11. *Immunity.*
Criminal Procedures	1. *Exclusionary rule*—A criminal procedural rule that prohibits the introduction at trial of all evidence obtained in violation of constitutional rights, as well as any evidence derived from the illegally obtained evidence. 2. Miranda *rule*—A rule set forth by the Supreme Court in *Miranda v. Arizona* that individuals who are arrested must be informed of certain constitutional rights, including their right to counsel. 3. *Criminal procedures*— a. Arrest, indictment, and trial—Procedures governing arrest, indictment, and trial for a crime are designed to safeguard the rights of the individual against the state. See Exhibit 8–3 for the steps involved in prosecuting a criminal case. b. Sentencing guidelines—Both the federal government and the states have established sentencing laws or guidelines. The federal sentencing guidelines indicate a range of penalties for each federal crime; federal judges must abide by these guidelines when imposing sentences on those convicted of federal crimes.
Cyber Crime	Cyber crime is any crime that occurs in cyberspace. Examples include cyber theft (financial crimes committed with the aid of computers, as well as identity theft), cyber stalking, hacking, and cyber terrorism. Significant federal statutes addressing cyber crimes include the Electronic Fund Transfer Act of 1978 and the Counterfeit Access Device and Computer Fraud and Abuse Act of 1984, as amended by the National Information Infrastructure Protection Act of 1996.

CASES FOR ANALYSIS

Westlaw. You can access the full text of each case presented below by going to the Westlaw cases on this text's Web site at http://wbl-cs.westbuslaw.com. Each Westlaw case includes the names of all plaintiffs and defendants, the dates on which the case was argued and decided, a brief summary of the issues and decisions in the case, headnotes classifying specific issues in the case according to the West Key Number System, and the court's opinion. Concurring and dissenting opinions, if any, are included as well.

CASE 8.1 LIABILITY OF CORPORATE OFFICERS AND DIRECTORS

UNITED STATES v. HANOUSEK
United States Court of Appeals,
Ninth Circuit, 1999.
176 F.3d 1116.

DAVID R. THOMPSON, Circuit Judge:

* * * *

[Edward] Hanousek was employed by the Pacific & Arctic Railway and Navigation Company (Pacific & Arctic) as roadmaster of the White Pass & Yukon Railroad, which runs between Skagway, Alaska, and Whitehorse, Yukon Territory, Canada. As roadmaster, Hanousek was responsible under his contract "for every detail of the safe and efficient maintenance and construction of track, structures and marine facilities of the entire railroad . . . and [was to] assume similar duties with special projects."

One of the special projects under Hanousek's supervision was a rock-quarrying project at a site alongside the railroad referred to as "6-mile," located on an embankment 200 feet above the Skagway River. The project was designed to realign a sharp curve in the railroad and to obtain * * * rock for a ship dock in Skagway. The project involved blasting rock outcroppings alongside the railroad, working the fractured rock toward railroad cars, and loading the rock onto railroad cars with a backhoe. Pacific & Arctic hired Hunz & Hunz, a contracting company, to provide the equipment and labor for the project.

At 6-mile, a high-pressure petroleum products pipeline owned by Pacific & Arctic's sister company, Pacific & Arctic Pipeline, Inc., runs parallel to the railroad at or above ground level, within a few feet of the tracks. To protect the pipeline during the project, a work platform of sand and gravel was constructed on which the backhoe operated to load rocks over the pipeline and into railroad cars. The location of the work platform changed as the location of the work progressed along the railroad tracks. In addition, when work initially began in April, 1994, Hunz & Hunz covered an approximately 300-foot section of the pipeline with railroad ties, sand, and ballast material to protect the pipeline, as was customary. After Hanousek took over responsibility for the project in May, 1994, no further sections of the pipeline along the 1,000-foot work site were protected, with the exception of the movable backhoe work platform.

On the evening of October 1, 1994, Shane Thoe, a Hunz & Hunz backhoe operator, used the backhoe on the work platform to load a train with rocks. After the train departed, Thoe noticed that some fallen rocks had caught the plow of the train as it departed and were located just off the tracks in the vicinity of the unprotected pipeline. At this location, the site had been graded to finish grade and the pipeline was covered with a few inches of soil. Thoe moved the backhoe off the work platform and drove it down alongside the tracks between 50 to 100 yards from the work platform. While using the backhoe bucket to sweep the rocks from the tracks, Thoe struck the pipeline causing a rupture. The pipeline was carrying heating oil, and an estimated 1,000 to 5,000 gallons of oil were discharged over the course of many days into the adjacent Skagway River, a navigable water of the United States.

Following an investigation, Hanousek was charged with [among other things] one count of negligently discharging a harmful quantity of oil into a navigable water of the United States, in violation of the Clean Water Act [CWA]. * * *

After a twenty-day trial, the jury convicted Hanousek of negligently discharging a harmful quantity of oil into a navigable water of the United States * * * . The district court imposed a sentence of six months of imprisonment, six months in a halfway house and six months of supervised release, as well as a fine of $5,000. This appeal followed.

* * * *

The criminal provisions of the CWA constitute public welfare legislation. Public welfare legislation is designed to protect the public from potentially harmful or injurious items and may render criminal a type of conduct that a reasonable person should know is subject to stringent public regulation and may seriously threaten the community's health or safety.

It is well established that a public welfare statute may subject a person to criminal liability for his or her ordinary negligence without violating due process.

* * * [T]he government [is] not required to prove that the [defendant] knew [his] conduct violated the law. * * * *[W]here * * * dangerous or deleterious [harmful] devices or products or obnoxious waste materials are involved, the probability of regulation is so great that anyone who is aware that he is in possession of them or dealing with them must be presumed to be aware of the regulation.* [Emphasis added.]

Hanousek argues that * * * he was simply the roadmaster of the White Pass & Yukon railroad charged with overseeing a rock-quarrying project and was not in a position to know what the law required under the CWA. * * * In the context of a public welfare statute, as long as a defendant knows he is dealing with a dangerous device of a character that places him in responsible relation to a public danger, he should be alerted to the probability of strict regulation. Although Hanousek was not a permittee under the CWA, he does not dispute that he was aware that a high-pressure petroleum products pipeline owned by Pacific & Arctic's sister company ran close to the surface next to the railroad tracks at 6-mile, and does not argue that he was unaware of the dangers a break or puncture of the pipeline by a piece of heavy machinery would pose. Therefore, Hanousek should have been alerted to the probability of strict regulation.

In light of [the fact] that the criminal provisions of the CWA constitute public welfare legislation, and the fact that a public welfare statute may impose criminal penalties for ordinary negligent conduct without offending due process, we conclude that [the CWA] does not violate due process by permitting criminal penalties for ordinary negligent conduct.

* * * *

In light of the plain language of [the CWA] we conclude Congress intended that a person who acts with ordinary negligence in violating [the CWA] may be subjected to criminal penalties. These sections, as so construed, do not violate due process. * * *

AFFIRMED.

CASE 8.2 CRIMINAL PROCEDURE

MIRANDA V. ARIZONA

Supreme Court of the United States, 1966.
384 U.S. 436,
86 S.Ct. 1602,
16 L.Ed.2d 694.

Mr. Chief Justice *WARREN* delivered the opinion of the Court.

The [case] before us [raises] questions which go to the roots of our concepts of American criminal jurisprudence: the restraints society must observe consistent with the Federal Constitution in prosecuting individuals for crime. * * *

* * * *

An understanding of the nature and setting of * * * in-custody [police] interrogation is essential to our decisions today. * * * From extensive factual studies undertaken in the early 1930's, including the famous Wickersham Report to Congress by a Presidential Commission, it is clear that police violence and the "third degree" flourished at that time. In a series of cases decided by this Court long after these studies, the police resorted to physical brutality—beatings, hanging, whipping—and to sustained and protracted questioning incommunicado in order to extort confessions. The Commission on Civil Rights in 1961 found much evidence to indicate that "some policemen still resort to physical force to obtain confessions." The use of physical brutality and violence is not, unfortunately, relegated to the past or to any part of the country. Only recently in Kings County, New York, the police brutally beat, kicked and placed lighted cigarette butts on the back of a potential witness under interrogation for the purpose of securing a statement incriminating a third party.

The examples given above are undoubtedly the exception now, but they are sufficiently widespread to be the object of concern. *Unless a proper limitation upon custodial interrogation is achieved—such as these decisions will advance—there can be no assurance that practices of this nature will be eradicated in the foreseeable future.* * * * [Emphasis added.]

* * * Interrogation still takes place in privacy. Privacy results in secrecy and this in turn results in a gap in our knowledge as to what in fact goes on in the interrogation rooms. * * *

Even without employing brutality, the "third degree" or the specific stratagems [maneuvers or deceptions] described above, the very fact of custodial interrogation exacts a heavy toll on individual liberty and trades on the weakness of individuals. * * *

* * * *

* * * Unless adequate protective devices are employed to dispel the compulsion inherent in custodial surroundings, no statement obtained from the defendant can truly be the product of his free choice.

* * * *

At the outset, if a person in custody is to be subjected to interrogation, he must first be informed in clear and unequivocal terms that he has the right to remain silent. * * *

* * * *

The warning of the right to remain silent must be accompanied by the explanation that anything said can and will be used against the individual in court. This warning is needed in order to make him aware not only of the privilege, but also of the consequences of forgoing it. * * *

The circumstances surrounding in-custody interrogation can operate very quickly to overbear the will of one merely made aware of his privilege by his interrogators. Therefore, the right to have counsel present at the interrogation is indispensable to the protection of the Fifth Amendment privilege under the system we delineate today. * * *

* * * *

In order fully to apprise a person interrogated of the extent of his rights under this system then, it is necessary to warn him not only that he has the right to consult with an attorney, but also that if he is indigent a lawyer will be appointed to represent him. * * * The warning of a right to counsel would be hollow if not couched in terms that would convey to the indigent—the person most often subjected to interrogation—the knowledge that he too has a right to have counsel present. * * *

* * * *

Once warnings have been given, the subsequent procedure is clear. *If the individual indicates in any manner, at any time prior to or during questioning, that he wishes to remain silent, the interrogation must cease.* * * * *If the individual states that he wants an attorney, the interrogation must cease until an attorney is present.* * * * [Emphasis added.]

* * * *

On March 13, 1963, petitioner, Ernesto Miranda, was arrested at his home and taken in custody to a Phoenix police station. He was there identified by the complaining witness. The police then took him to "Interrogation Room No. 2" of the detective bureau. There he was questioned by two police officers. The officers admitted at trial that Miranda was not advised that he had a right to have an attorney present. Two hours later, the officers emerged from the interrogation room with a written confession signed by Miranda. At the top of the statement was a typed paragraph stating that the confession was made voluntarily, without threats or promises of immunity and "with full knowledge of my legal rights, understanding any statement I make may be used against me."

At his trial before a jury, the written confession was admitted into evidence over the objection of defense counsel, and the officers testified to the prior oral confession made by Miranda during the interrogation. Miranda was found guilty of kidnapping and rape. He was sentenced to 20 to 30 years' imprisonment on each count, the sentences to run concurrently. On appeal, the Supreme Court of Arizona held that Miranda's constitutional rights were not violated in obtaining the confession and affirmed the conviction. In reaching its decision, the court emphasized heavily the fact that Miranda did not specifically request counsel.

We reverse. From the testimony of the officers and by the admission of respondent, it is clear that Miranda was not in any way apprised of his right to consult with an attorney and to have one present during the interrogation, nor was his right not to be compelled to incriminate himself effectively protected in any other manner. Without these warnings the statements were inadmissible. The mere fact that he signed a statement which contained a typed-in clause stating that he had "full knowledge" of his "legal rights" does not approach the knowing and intelligent waiver required to relinquish constitutional rights.

* * * *

Mr. Justice *CLARK*, dissenting * * * .

* * * I am unable to join the majority because its opinion goes too far on too little * * * . [T]he examples of police brutality mentioned by the Court are rare exceptions to the thousands of cases that appear every year in the law reports. The police agencies—all the way from municipal and state forces to the federal bureaus—are responsible for law enforcement and public safety in this country. I am proud of their efforts, which in my view are not fairly characterized by the Court's opinion.

* * * *

Rather than employing the arbitrary Fifth Amendment rule which the Court lays down I would follow the more pliable dictates of the Due Process Clauses of the Fifth and Fourteenth Amendments which we are accustomed to administering and which we know from our cases are effective instruments in protecting persons in police custody. In this way we would not be acting in the dark nor in one full sweep changing the traditional rules of custodial interrogation which this Court has for so long recognized as a justifiable and proper tool in balancing individual rights against the rights of society. It will be soon enough to go further when we are able to appraise with somewhat better accuracy the effect of such a holding.

I would affirm the [conviction] in *Miranda v. Arizona* * * * .

Mr. Justice *HARLAN* * * * dissenting.

I believe the decision of the Court represents poor constitutional law and entails harmful consequences for the country at large. How serious these consequences may prove to be only time can tell. But the basic flaws in the Court's justification seem to me readily apparent now once all sides of the problem are considered.

* * * *

* * * [T]he thrust of the new rules is to negate all pressures, to reinforce the nervous or ignorant suspect, and ultimately to discourage any confession at all. The aim in short is toward "voluntariness" in a utopian sense, or to view it from a different angle, voluntariness with a vengeance.

To incorporate this notion into the Constitution requires a strained reading of history and precedent and a disregard of the very pragmatic concerns that alone may on occasion justify such strains. I believe that * * * the Due Process Clauses provide an adequate tool for coping with confessions and that, even if the Fifth Amendment privilege against self-incrimination be invoked, its precedents taken as a whole do not sustain the present rules. * * *

* * * *

Applying the traditional standards to the cases before the Court, I would hold these confessions voluntary.

CASE 8.3 COMPUTER CRIME

UNITED STATES V. MIDDLETON

United States Court of Appeals,
Ninth Circuit, 2000.
231 F.3d 1207.

GRABER, Circuit Judge:

* * * *

Defendant [Nicholas Middleton] worked as the personal computer administrator for Slip.net, an Internet service provider. His responsibilities included installing software and hardware on the company's computers and providing technical support to its employees. He had extensive knowledge of Slip.net's internal systems, including employee and computer program passwords. Dissatisfied with his job, Defendant quit. He then began to write threatening e-mails to his former employer.

Slip.net had allowed Defendant to retain an e-mail account as a paying customer after he left the company's employ. Defendant used this account to commit his first unauthorized act. After logging in to Slip.net's system, Defendant used a computer program called "Switch User" to switch his account to that of a Slip.net receptionist, Valerie Wilson. This subterfuge allowed Defendant to take advantage of the benefits and privileges associated with that employee's account, such as creating and deleting accounts and adding features to existing accounts.

Ted Glenwright, Slip.net's president, discovered this unauthorized action while looking through a "Switch User log," which records all attempts to use the Switch User program. Glenwright cross-checked the information with the company's "Radius Log," which records an outside user's attempt to dial in to the company's modem banks. The information established that Defendant had connected to Slip.net.'s computers and had then switched to Wilson's account. Glenwright immediately terminated Defendant's e-mail account.

Nevertheless, Defendant was able to continue his activities. Three days later, he obtained access to Slip.net's computers by logging in to a computer that contained a test account and then using that test account to gain access to the company's main computers. Once in Slip.net's main system, Defendant accessed the account of a sales representative and created two new accounts, which he called "TERPID" and "SANTOS." Defendant used TERPID and SANTOS to obtain access to a different computer that the company had named "Lemming." Slip.net used Lemming to perform internal administrative functions and to host customers' websites. Lemming also contained the software for a new billing system. After gaining access to the Lemming computer, Defendant changed all the administrative passwords, altered the computer's registry, deleted the entire billing system (including programs that ran the billing software), and deleted two internal databases.

Glenwright discovered the damage the next morning. He immediately contacted the company's system administrator, Bruno Connelly. Glenwright and Connelly spent an entire weekend repairing the damage that Defendant had caused to Slip.net's computers, including restoring access to the computer system, assigning new passwords, reloading the billing software, and recreating the deleted databases. They also spent many hours investigating the source and the extent of the damage. Glenwright estimated that he spent 93 hours repairing the damage; Connelly estimated that he spent 28 hours; and other employees estimated that they spent a total of 33 hours. Additionally, Slip.net bought new software to replace software that Defendant had deleted, and the company hired an outside consultant for technical support.

Defendant was arrested and charged with a violation of [The Computer Fraud and Abuse Act (CFAA)]. * * *

* * * *

The jury convicted Defendant. The district court sentenced him to three years' probation, subject to the condition that he serve 180 days in community confinement. The court also ordered Defendant to pay $9,147 in restitution. This timely appeal ensued.

* * * *

[The CFAA] prohibits a person from knowingly transmitting "a program, information, code, or command, and as a result of such conduct, intentionally caus[ing] damage without authorization, to a protected computer." A "protected computer" is a computer "which is used in interstate or foreign commerce or communication." Defendant concedes that Slip.net's computers fit within that definition. The statute defines "damage" to mean "any impairment to the integrity or availability of data, a program, a system, or information, that causes loss aggregating at least $5,000 in value during any 1-year period to one or more individuals." Defendant argues that Congress intended the phrase "one or more individuals" to exclude corporations. We disagree.

* * * *

According to Defendant, in common usage the term "individuals" excludes corporations. He notes that the [federal] "Dictionary Act," which provides general rules of statutory construction, defines the word "person" to include "corporations, companies, associations, firms, partnerships, societies, and joint stock companies, as well as individuals." That definition, argues Defendant, implies that the word "person" includes "corporations," but that the word "individuals" does not. Defendant reasons that, if Congress had intended [the CFAA] to cover damage to corporations, Congress would have used the word "persons," not "individuals." For several reasons, we are not persuaded.

We examine first the ordinary meaning of "individuals." That word does not necessarily exclude corporations. *Webster's Third New Int'l Dictionary* * * * (unabridged ed. 1993) provides five definitions of the noun "individual," the first being "a single or particular being or *thing or group of beings or things.*" [Emphasis added.] To the extent that a word's dictionary meaning equates to its "plain meaning," a corporation can be referred to as an "individual."

Neither is "individual" a legal term of art that applies only to natural persons. As *Black's Law Dictionary* * * * (6th ed. 1990) states:

> Individual. As a noun, this term denotes a single person as distinguished from a group or class, and also, very commonly, a private or natural person as distinguished from a partnership, corporation, or association; *but it is said that this restrictive signification is not necessarily inherent in the word, and that it may, in proper cases, include artificial persons.* [Emphasis added.]

* * * *

In 1996, Congress amended [the CFAA] to its current form, using the term "protected computer" and concomitantly expanding the number of computers that the statute "protected." The 1996 amendments also altered the definition of damage to read, "loss aggregating at least $5,000 in value during any 1-year period to one or more individuals." We have found no explanation for this change. We do not believe, however, that this change evidences an intent to limit the statute's reach.

To the contrary, Congress has consciously broadened the statute consistently since its original enactment. The Senate Report on the 1996 amendments notes:

> As intended when the law was originally enacted, the Computer Fraud and Abuse statute facilitates addressing in a single statute the problem of computer crime. * * * *As computers continue to proliferate in businesses and homes, and new forms of computer crimes emerge, Congress must remain vigilant to ensure that the Computer Fraud and Abuse statute is up-to-date and provides law enforcement with the necessary legal framework to fight computer crime* [emphasis added].

The report instructs that "the definition of 'damage' is amended to be sufficiently broad to encompass the types of harm against which people should be protected." The report notes that the interaction between * * * the provision that prohibits conduct causing damage * * * and * * * the provision that defines damage * * * will prohibit a hacker from stealing passwords from an existing log-on program, when this conduct requires "all system users to change their passwords, *and requires the system administrator to devote resources to resecuring the system.* * * * If the loss to the victim meets the required monetary threshold, the conduct should be criminal, and the victim should be entitled to relief" [emphasis added]. The reference to a "system administrator" suggests that a corporate victim is involved. That is, if Congress intended to limit the definition of the crime to conduct causing financial damage to a natural person only, its report would not use the example of a "system administrator" devoting resources to fix a computer problem as illustrative of the "damage" to be prevented and criminalized. The Senate Report's reference to the proliferation of computers in businesses as well as homes provides additional evidence of the Senate's intent to extend the statute's protections to corporate entities.

* * * [W]e conclude that [the CFAA] criminalizes computer crime that damages natural persons and corporations alike. The district court did not err in so ruling.

* * * *

AFFIRMED.

Case Problems

8–1. In 1965, Rybicki failed to pay the federal government the total amount of income tax he owed. Attempts by the Internal Revenue Service (IRS) to collect the tax proved fruitless. Therefore, the IRS obtained (through lawful means) a tax lien on Rybicki's personal property, which included his truck. In February 1967, Rybicki's wife, on hearing the truck's motor, awakened her sleeping husband. Wielding a shotgun, Rybicki went to his front door and told the two men who were attempting to take his truck to stop. Rybicki claimed that he did not know the two men were IRS agents. Subsequently, the federal government indicted Rybicki for obstructing justice. Can Rybicki be held criminally liable if he did not know that the men were IRS agents performing their duty? [*United States v. Rybicki*, 403 F.2d 599 (6th Cir. 1968)]

8–2. Khoury went to a department store, spent some time shopping, and eventually filled a large, empty chandelier box with approximately $900 worth of tools. When he went to the check-out counter, the cashier indicated that she wanted to look inside the box before accepting Khoury's payment for the chandelier. Khoury then pushed the cart back into the store and departed from the premises. Khoury was convicted of grand larceny by the trial court. On appeal, Khoury alleged that because he had not actually removed any goods from the store, he had not committed larceny. Is Khoury correct? [*People v. Khoury*, 108 Cal.App.3d, 166 Cal.Rptr. 705 (1980)]

8–3. Gomez, an informant for the police who was posing as an ex-convict, urged Saldana on several occasions to sell cocaine to make money. But Saldana, although he used cocaine, did not wish to sell any. Finally, to get Gomez to stop pestering him, Saldana agreed to sell some cocaine to Castello, who turned out to be a police officer. May Saldana successfully claim an entrapment defense? Discuss. [*Saldana v. State*, 732 S.W.2d 701 (Tex.App.—Corpus Christi 1987)]

8–4. While at a grocery store, Moses Racquemore stuffed two packages of meat into his pants and was just pulling his shirt down over them when he noticed that the store manager and a security guard were watching him. He returned the meat to the counter, but he was arrested for shoplifting anyway. Had Racquemore committed a criminal act? Were Racquemore's actions in the store sufficient to prove the element of intent? Discuss. [*Racquemore v. State*, 204 Ga.App. 88, 418 S.E.2d 448 (1992)]

8–5. Slemmer, who had been a successful options trader, gave lectures to small groups about stock options. Several persons who attended his lectures decided to invest in stock options and have Slemmer advise them. They formed an investment club called Profit Design Group (PDG). Slemmer set up an account for PDG with a brokerage firm. Slemmer had control of the PDG account and could make decisions on which stock options to buy or sell. He was not authorized to withdraw money from the account for his own benefit. Nonetheless, he withdrew money from the PDG account to make payments on personal loans. Slemmer made false representations to the members of PDG, and he eventually lost all the money in their account. A jury found him guilty of first degree theft by embezzlement. Slemmer objected to the trial court's failure to instruct the jury that an intent to permanently deprive was an element of the crime charged. Is intent to permanently deprive another of property a required element for the crime of embezzlement? Discuss fully. [*State v. Slemmer*, 48 Wash.App. 48, 738 P.2d 281 (1987)]

8–6. Bernardy came to the defense of his friend Harrison in a fight with Wilson. Wilson started the fight, and after Harrison knocked Wilson down, Bernardy (who was wearing tennis shoes) kicked Wilson several times in the head. Bernardy stated that he did so because he believed an onlooker, Gowens, would join forces with Wilson against Harrison. Bernardy maintained that his use of force was justifiable because he was protecting another (Harrison) from injury. Discuss whether Bernardy's use of force to protect Harrison from harm was justified. [*State v. Bernardy*, 25 Wash.App. 146, 605 P.2d 791 (1980)]

8–7. The Child Protection Act of 1984 makes it a crime to receive knowingly through the mails sexually explicit depictions of children. After this act was passed, government agents found Keith Jacobson's name on a bookstore's mailing list. (Jacobson previously had ordered and received from a bookstore two *Bare Boys* magazines containing photographs of nude preteen and teenage boys.) To test Jacobson's willingness to break the law, government agencies sent mail to him, through five fictitious organizations and a bogus pen pal, over a period of two and a half years. Many of these "organizations" claimed that they had been founded to protect sexual freedom, freedom of choice, and so on. Jacobson eventually ordered a magazine. He testified at trial that he ordered the magazine because he was curious about "all the trouble and the hysteria over pornography and I wanted to see what the material was." When the magazine was delivered, he was arrested for violating the 1984 act. What defense discussed in this chapter might Jacobson raise to avoid criminal liability under the act? Explain fully. [*Jacobson v. United States*, 503 U.S. 540, 112 S.Ct. 1535, 118 L.Ed.2d 174 (1992)]

8–8. A troublesome issue concerning the constitutional privilege against self-incrimination has to do with "jail plants"—that is, placing undercover police officers in cells with criminal suspects to gain information from the suspects. For example, in one case the police placed an undercover agent, Parisi, in a jail cell block with Lloyd Perkins, who had been imprisoned on charges unrelated to the murder that Parisi was investigating. When Parisi asked Perkins if he had ever killed anyone, Perkins made statements implicating himself in the murder. Perkins was then charged with the murder. Should Perkins's statements be suppressed—that is, not be treated as admissible evidence at trial—because he was not "read his rights," as required by the *Miranda* decision, prior to making his self-incriminating statements? Does *Miranda* apply to Perkins's situation? Discuss. [*Illinois v. Perkins,* 496 U.S. 914, 110 S.Ct. 2394, 110 L.Ed.2d 243 (1990)]

8–9. Britt was convicted of second degree homicide for the shooting death of his neighbor, Cavell. The victim was killed by a .44 caliber revolver that was part of a trap set by Britt to prevent forcible entry into his home from the back door. The booby trap was set to discharge if the door was opened a distance of two to four inches. The relevant Louisiana law reads as follows: "A homicide is justifiable . . . when committed by a person lawfully inside a dwelling against a person who is attempting to make an unlawful entry into the dwelling or who has made an unlawful entry into the dwelling and the person committing the homicide reasonably believes that the use of deadly force is necessary to prevent the entry or to compel the intruder to leave the premises. The homicide shall be justifiable even though the person committing the homicide does not retreat from the encounter." Britt argued on appeal that the shooting of Cavell was justified because, had Britt been present, he would have been authorized to use deadly force and to use a mechanical contrivance. Will Britt's appeal be successful? Explain. [*State v. Britt,* 510 So.2d 670 (La.App. 1st Cir. 1987)]

8–10. Keith and Stephanie Cannon sold crack cocaine to a deputy sheriff, who was operating undercover as a drug buyer. The Cannons asked the undercover officer to help them procure some handguns. The officer arranged for an agent of the U.S. Bureau of Alcohol, Tobacco, and Firearms (BATF) to pose as an illegal gun seller. The BATF agent, on his own initiative, brought a machine gun to the meeting with the Cannons. At that meeting, the Cannons again sold crack to the sheriff and bought three handguns from the agent. After the undercover officers exercised some persuasive sales tactics, the Cannons also bought the machine gun. They were promptly arrested and later tried and convicted for using firearms during and in relation to drug trafficking. Because one of the weapons was a machine gun, their convictions required minimum prison sentences of thirty years—instead of the five-year minimum term imposed for the use of a firearm generally. At their sentencing hearing, the Cannons argued that they were victims of entrapment. Were they? Discuss fully. [*United States v. Cannon,* 886 F.Supp. 705 (D.N.Dak. 1995)]

8–11. Faulkner, a truck driver, was hauling a load of refrigerators from San Diego to New York for the trucking company that employed him. He departed from his assigned route and stopped in Las Vegas, where he attempted to display and sell some of the refrigerators to a firm. Although the refrigerators never left the truck, to display them he had to break the truck's seals, enter the cargo department, and open two refrigerator cartons. The store owner refused to purchase the appliances, and when Faulkner left the store, he was arrested. He was later convicted under federal law for the embezzlement of an interstate shipment. Faulkner appealed, claiming that the charge of embezzlement should not apply because the property had not been physically removed from the owner's possession. Will the appellate court agree with Faulkner? Explain. [*United States v. Faulkner,* 638 F.2d 129 (9th Cir. 1981)]

8–12. In January 1988, David Ludvigson was hired as chief executive officer of Leopard Enterprises, a group of companies that owned funeral homes and cemeteries in Iowa and sold "pre-need" funeral contracts. Under Iowa law, 80 percent of the funds obtained under such a contract must be set aside in trust until the death of the person for whose benefit the funds were paid. Shortly after Ludvigson was hired, the firm began having financial difficulties. Ludvigson used money from the funeral contracts to pay operating expenses until the company went bankrupt and was placed in receivership. Ludvigson was charged and found guilty on five counts of second degree theft stemming from the misappropriation of these funds. He appealed, alleging, among other things, that he was not guilty of any crime, because he had not intended to permanently deprive any of the clients of their trust funds. Furthermore, because none of the victims whose trust funds were used to cover operating expenses was denied services, no injury was done. Will the court agree with Ludvigson? Explain. [*State v. Ludvigson,* 482 N.W.2d 419 (Ia. 1992)]

8–13. On the grounds of a school, Gavin T., a fifteen-year-old student, was eating lunch. He threw a half-eaten apple toward the outside wall of a classroom some distance away. The apple sailed through a slowly closing door and struck a teacher who was in the room. The teacher was knocked to the floor and lost consciousness for a few minutes. Gavin was charged, in a California state court, with assault by "any means of force likely to produce great bodily injury." The court found that he did not intend to hit the teacher but only intended to see the apple splatter against the outside wall. To send a "message" to his classmates that his actions were wrong, however, the court convicted him of the charge. Should Gavin's conviction be reversed on appeal? Why, or why not? [*In re Gavin T.,* 66 Cal.App.4th 238, 77 Cal.Rptr.2d 701 (1998)]

8–14. The federal government was investigating a corporation and its employees. The alleged criminal wrongdoing, which included the falsification of corporate books and records, occurred between 1993 and 1996 in one division of the corporation. In 1999, the corporation pled guilty and agreed to cooperate in an investigation of the individuals who might have been involved in the improper corporate activities. "Doe I," "Doe II," and "Doe III" were officers of the corporation during the period in which the illegal activities occurred and worked in the division where the wrongdoing took place. They were no longer working for the corporation, however, when, as part of the subsequent investigation, the government asked them to provide specific corporate documents in their possession. All three asserted the Fifth Amendment privilege against self-incrimination. The government asked a federal district court to order the three to produce the records. Corporate employees can be compelled to produce corporate records in a criminal proceeding, because they hold the records as representatives of the corporation, to which the Fifth Amendment privilege against self-incrimination does not apply. Should *former* employees also be compelled to produce corporate records in their possession? Why, or why not? [*In re Three Grand Jury Subpoenas* Duces Tecum *Dated January 29, 1999,* 191 F.3d 173 (2d Cir. 1999)]

8–15. The District of Columbia Lottery Board licensed Soo Young Bae, a Washington, D.C., merchant, to operate a terminal that prints and dispenses lottery tickets for sale. Bae used the terminal to generate tickets with a face value of $525,586, for which he did not pay. The winning tickets among these had a total redemption value of $296,153, of which Bae successfully obtained all but $72,000. Bae pleaded guilty to computer fraud, and the court sentenced him to eighteen months in prison. In sentencing a defendant for fraud, a federal court must make a reasonable estimate of the victim's loss. The court determined that the value of the loss due to the fraud was $503,650—the market value of the tickets less the commission Bae would have received from the lottery board had he sold those tickets. Bae appealed, arguing that "[a]t the instant any lottery ticket is printed," it is worth whatever value the lottery drawing later assigns to it; losing tickets, that is, have no value. Bae thus calculated the loss at $296,153, the value of his winning tickets. Should the U.S. Court of Appeals for the District of Columbia Circuit affirm or reverse Bae's sentence? Why? [*United States v. Bae,* 250 F.3d 774 (C.A.D.C. 2001)]

E-LINKS

For updated links to resources available on the Web, as well as a variety of other materials, visit this text's Web site at

http://wbl-cs.westbuslaw.com

The Bureau of Justice Statistics in the U.S. Department of Justice offers an impressive collection of statistics on crime at the following Web site:

http://www.ojp.usdoj.gov/bjs

For summaries of famous criminal cases and documents relating to these trials, go to Court TV's Web site at

http://www.courttv.com/index.html

If you would like to learn more about criminal procedures, the following site offers an "Anatomy of a Murder: A Trip through Our Nation's Legal Justice System":

http://tqd.advanced.org/2760/home.htm

At the above site, you can also find a glossary of terms used in criminal law, view actual forms that are filled out during the course of an arrest, and learn about some controversial issues in criminal law.

Many state criminal codes are now online. To find your state's code, go to

http://www.findlaw.com

and select "State" under the link to "Laws: Cases and Codes."

LEGAL RESEARCH EXERCISES ON THE WEB

Go to http://wbl-cs.westbuslaw.com, the Web site that accompanies this text. Select "Interactive Study Center," and then click on "Chapter 8." There you will find the following Internet research exercise that you can perform to learn more about criminal procedures:

Activity 8–1: Revisiting *Miranda*

Focus on Legal Reasoning

Kyllo v. United States

Introduction

We explained, in Chapter 4, that the Fourth Amendment protects the "right of the people to be secure in their persons, houses, papers, and effects." In this *Focus on Legal Reasoning*, we examine *Kyllo v. United States,*[1] a decision that considered the requirement that law enforcement officers obtain a search warrant before searching private property. The question was whether police officers are required to obtain a warrant before using sense-enhancing technology that reveals information about the inside of a home, which the officers would otherwise be able to learn only if they physically entered the house.

1. 533 U.S. 27, 121 S.Ct. 2038, 150 L.Ed.2d 94 (2001).

Case Background

Suspicious that marijuana was being grown in Danny Lee Kyllo's home in a triplex in Florence, Oregon, federal agents used an Agema Thermovision 210, a thermal imaging device, to scan the building to determine if the amount of heat emanating from it was consistent with the high-intensity lamps often used to grow marijuana indoors. The scan showed that Kyllo's garage roof and a side wall were relatively hot compared to the rest of his home and substantially warmer than the neighboring units. Based in part on the thermal imaging, a judge issued a warrant to search Kyllo's home, where the agents found marijuana growing. Kyllo was indicted for violations of federal law. He filed a motion to suppress the evidence seized from his home. The court denied the motion. Kyllo pled guilty, and appealed the court's ruling to the U.S. Court of Appeals for the Ninth Circuit.

The appellate court affirmed the trial court's decision. The appellate court upheld the thermal imaging on the ground that Kyllo had no subjective expectation of privacy because he made no attempt to conceal the heat escaping from his home. The court ruled that even if he had, there was no objectively reasonable expectation of privacy, because the thermal imager did not expose any intimate details of Kyllo's life, only hot spots on the outside of his home. Kyllo appealed to the United States Supreme Court.

Majority Opinion

Justice *SCALIA* delivered the opinion of the Court.

* * * *

The Fourth Amendment provides that "[t]he right of the people to be secure in their persons, houses, papers, and effects, against unreasonable searches and seizures, shall not be violated." At the very core of the Fourth Amendment stands the right of a man to retreat into his own home and there be free from unreasonable governmental intrusion. With few exceptions, the question whether a warrantless search of a home is reasonable and hence constitutional must be answered no.

On the other hand, the antecedent question of whether or not a Fourth Amendment "search" has occurred is not so simple * * *. The permissibility of ordinary visual surveillance of a home used to be clear because, well into the 20th century, our Fourth Amendment jurisprudence was tied to common-law trespass. Visual surveillance was unquestionably lawful because the eye cannot * * * be guilty of a trespass. We have since decoupled violation of a person's Fourth Amendment rights from trespassory violation of his property, but the lawfulness of warrantless visual surveillance of a home has still been preserved. The Fourth Amendment protection of the home has never been extended to require law enforcement officers to shield their eyes when passing by a home on public thoroughfares.

One might think that the new validating rationale would be that examining the portion of a house that is in plain public view, while it is a "search" despite the absence of trespass, is not an "unreasonable" one under the Fourth Amendment. But in fact we have held that visual observation is no "search" at all—perhaps in order to preserve somewhat more intact our doctrine that warrantless searches are presumptively unconstitutional. In assessing when a search is not a search, we have applied somewhat in reverse the principle first enunciated in *Katz v. United States,* 389 U.S. 347, 88 S.Ct. 507, 19 L.Ed.2d 576 (1967). *Katz* involved eavesdropping by means of an electronic listening device placed on the outside of a telephone booth—a location not within the catalog ("persons, houses, papers, and effects") that the Fourth Amendment protects against unreasonable searches. We held that the Fourth Amendment nonetheless protected Katz from the warrantless eavesdropping because he "justifiably relied" upon the privacy of the telephone booth. * * * [A] Fourth Amendment search occurs when the government violates a subjective expectation of privacy that society recognizes as reasonable. * * *

The present case involves officers on a public street engaged in more than naked-eye surveillance of a home. We have previously reserved judgment as to how much technological enhancement of ordinary perception from such a vantage point, if any, is too much. * * *

* * * *

It would be foolish to contend that the degree of privacy secured to citizens by the Fourth Amendment has been entirely unaffected by the advance of technology.

* * * The question we confront today is what limits there are upon this power of technology to shrink the realm of guaranteed privacy.

The *Katz* test—whether the individual has an expectation of privacy that society is prepared to recognize as reasonable—has often been criticized as circular, and hence subjective and unpredictable. While it may be difficult to refine *Katz* when the search of areas such as telephone booths, automobiles, or even the curtilage and uncovered portions of residences are at issue, in the case of the search of the interior of homes—the prototypical and hence most commonly litigated area of protected privacy—there is a ready criterion, with roots deep in the common law, of the minimal expectation of privacy that exists, and that is acknowledged to be reasonable. To withdraw protection of this minimum expectation would be to permit police technology to erode the privacy guaranteed by the Fourth Amendment. We think that obtaining by sense-enhancing technology any information regarding the interior of the home that could not otherwise have been obtained without physical intrusion into a constitutionally protected area, constitutes a search—at least where (as here) the technology in question is not in general public use. This assures preservation of that degree of privacy against government that existed when the Fourth Amendment was adopted. On the basis of this criterion, *the information obtained by the thermal imager in this case was the product of a search.* [Emphasis added.]

The Government maintains, however, that the thermal imaging must be upheld because it detected "only heat radiating from the external surface of the house." * * * But just as a thermal imager captures only heat emanating from a house, so also a powerful directional microphone picks up only sound emanating from a house—and a satellite capable of scanning from many miles away would pick up only visible light emanating from a house. We rejected such a mechanical interpretation of the Fourth Amendment in *Katz,* where the eavesdropping device picked up only sound waves that reached the exterior of the phone booth. Reversing that approach would leave the homeowner at the mercy of advancing technology—including imaging technology that could discern all human activity in the home. While the technology used in the present case was relatively crude, the rule we adopt must take account of more sophisticated systems that are already in use or in development. * * *

The Government also contends that the thermal imaging was constitutional because it did not "detect private activities occurring in private areas." * * * The Fourth Amendment's protection of the home has never been tied to measurement of the quality or quantity of information obtained. * * * [A]ny physical invasion of the structure of the home, by even a fraction of an inch, [is] too much, and there is certainly no exception to the warrant requirement for the officer who barely cracks open the front door and sees nothing but the nonintimate rug on the vestibule floor. *In the home, our cases show, all details are intimate details, because the entire area is held safe from prying government eyes.* * * * [Emphasis added.]

* * * *

Where, as here, the Government uses a device that is not in general public use, to explore details of the home that would previously have been unknowable without physical intrusion, the surveillance is a "search" and is presumptively unreasonable without a warrant.

Since we hold the Thermovision imaging to have been an unlawful search, it will remain for the [trial court] to determine whether, without the evidence it provided, the search warrant issued in this case was supported by probable cause—and if not, whether there is any other basis for supporting admission of the evidence that the search pursuant to the warrant produced.

QUESTIONS FOR ANALYSIS

1. **Legal Analysis.** The Court cites, in its opinion, *Katz v. United States,* 389 U.S. 347, 88 S.Ct. 507, 19 L.Ed.2d 576 (1967) (see the *E-Links* feature at the end of Chapter 2 for instructions on how to access opinions of the United States Supreme Court). Do the facts and issues in that case compare to the facts and issues of the *Kyllo* case? How do the holdings in the two cases compare? Why did the Court refer to the *Katz* case in its opinion?

2. **Legal Reasoning.** What reasons does the majority provide to justify its conclusion? Which, if any, of the forms of legal reasoning described in Chapter 1 did the majority use to reach its conclusion?

3. **International Considerations.** To what extent should U.S. law regarding search and seizure be applied to foreign persons that reside, visit, or do business in the United States?

4. **Implications for the Business Owner.** Is there a sufficient difference between the expectation of privacy in a person's place of business and that in his or her home that could allow the police to use technology to search the business, but not the home, without a warrant?

WESTLAW ONLINE RESEARCH

Westlaw. Go to this text's companion Web site, at http://wbl-cs.westbuslaw.com, and click on the Westlaw icon. Use your special password to access the full text of this case, including the dissenting opinions. Read through the case, and then answer the following questions.

1. Contrast the conclusion of the majority with that of the dissent. What arguments did the dissent make to support its assertion that the majority's conclusions were incorrect? What legal sources did the dissent cite to justify its position?
2. Compare the first three headnotes to the related portions of the Court's opinion. How do the headnotes differ from the opinion? What are some advantages to scanning headnotes before reading a case?
3. Considering the decision in this case, can law enforcement officers ever use a thermal imaging device without obtaining a warrant? If so, when? What effect might the decision in this case have on the government's use of the DCS-1000 system (popularly known as Carnivore)?[2]

---

2. DCS-1000 is a modified version of software known as a packet sniffer that Internet service providers (ISPs) use to maintain their networks. DCS-1000 taps the traffic coming through an ISP's networks in search of data from the target of an investigation.

UNIT TWO

Contracts

CONTENTS

CHAPTER 9

Nature and Terminology

THE NOTED LEGAL SCHOLAR Roscoe Pound once said that "[t]he social order rests upon the stability and predictability of conduct, of which keeping promises is a large item."[1] A **promise** is an assurance that one will or will not do something in the future. A **contract** is "a promise or a set of promises for the breach of which the law gives a remedy, or the performance of which the law in some way recognizes as a duty."[2] Put simply, a contract is an agreement (based on a promise or an exchange of promises) that can be enforced in court.

Like other types of law, contract law reflects our social values, interests, and expectations at a given point in time. It shows, for example, to what extent our society allows people to make promises or commitments that are legally binding. It distinguishes between promises that create only *moral* obligations (such as a promise to take a friend to lunch) and promises that are legally binding (such as a promise to pay for merchandise purchased). Contract law also demonstrates what excuses our society accepts for breaking certain types of promises. In addition, it indicates what promises are considered to be contrary to public policy—against the interests of society as a whole—and therefore legally invalid. When a promise is made by a child or a mentally incompetent person, for example, a question will arise as to whether the promise should be enforced. Resolving such questions is the essence of contract law.

The common law governs all contracts except when it has been modified or replaced by statutory law, such as the Uniform Commercial Code (UCC),[3] or by administrative agency regulations. Contracts relating to services, real estate, employment, insurance, and so on generally are governed by the common law of contracts. Contracts for the sale and lease of goods, however, are governed by the UCC—to the extent that the UCC has modified general contract law. The relationship between general contract law and the law governing sales and leases of goods will be explored in detail in Chapter 18. In the discussion of general contract law that follows, we indicate in footnotes the areas in which the UCC has significantly altered common law contract principles.

SECTION 1

The Function of Contract Law

The law encourages competent parties to form contracts for lawful objectives. Indeed, no aspect of modern life is entirely free of contractual relationships. Even the ordinary consumer in his or her daily activities acquires rights and obligations based on contract law. You acquire rights and obligations, for example, when you borrow money to make a purchase or when you buy a DVD or a house. Contract law is designed to provide stability and

1. R. Pound, *Jurisprudence*, Vol. 3 (St. Paul: West Publishing Co., 1959), p. 162.

2. *Restatement (Second) of Contracts*. The *Restatement of the Law of Contracts* is a nonstatutory, authoritative exposition of the common law of contracts compiled by the American Law Institute in 1932. The *Restatement*, which is now in its second edition (a third edition is being drafted), will be referred to throughout the following chapters on contract law.

3. See Chapter 1 and Chapter 18 for further discussions of the significance and coverage of the Uniform Commercial Code. The UCC is presented in Appendix B at the end of this book.

predictability, as well as certainty, for both buyers and sellers in the marketplace.

Contract law deals with, among other things, the formation and enforcement of agreements between parties (in Latin, *pacta sunt servanda*—"agreements shall be kept"). By supplying procedures for enforcing private contractual agreements, contract law provides an essential condition for the existence of a market economy. Without a legal framework of reasonably assured expectations within which to plan and venture, businesspersons would be able to rely only on the good faith of others. Duty and good faith are usually sufficient, but when price changes or adverse economic factors make it costly to comply with a promise, these elements may not be enough. Contract law is necessary to ensure compliance with a promise or to entitle the innocent party to some form of relief.

SECTION 2

Elements of a Contract

The many topics that will be discussed in the following chapters on contract law require an understanding of the basic elements of a contract and the way in which a contract is created. The following list briefly describes these elements. Each element will be explained more fully in subsequent chapters.

1. *Agreement.* An agreement to form a contract includes an *offer* and an *acceptance.* One party must offer to enter into a legal agreement, and another party must accept the terms of the offer.
2. *Consideration.* Any promises made by the parties to the contract must be supported by legally sufficient and bargained-for *consideration* (something of value received or promised, such as money, to convince a person to make a deal).
3. *Contractual capacity.* Both parties entering into the contract must have the contractual *capacity* to do so; the law must recognize them as possessing characteristics that qualify them as competent parties.
4. *Legality.* The contract's purpose must be to accomplish some goal that is legal and not against public policy.

These four elements constitute what are normally known as the requirements that must be met for a valid contract to exist. If any of these elements is lacking, no contract will have been formed. Even if all of these elements exist, however, a contract may be unenforceable if the following requirements are not met. These requirements typically are raised as *defenses* to the enforceability of an otherwise valid contract.

1. *Genuineness of assent.* The apparent consent of both parties must be genuine. For example, if a contract was formed as a result of fraud, undue influence, mistake, or duress, the contract may not be enforceable.
2. *Form.* The contract must be in whatever form the law requires; for example, some contracts must be in writing to be enforceable.

SECTION 3

The Objective Theory of Contracts

Sometimes, parties claim that they should not be bound in contract because they did not *intend* to form an agreement that would be legally binding. Although the element of intent is of prime importance in determining whether a contract has been formed, it is not the party's *subjective* intent that a court looks to in deciding the issue. In contract law, intent is determined by what is called the **objective theory of contracts,** not by the personal or subjective intent, or belief, of a party. The theory is that intention to enter into a legally binding agreement, or contract, is judged by outward, objective facts as interpreted by a *reasonable* person, rather than by the party's own secret, subjective intentions. Objective facts include (1) what the party said when entering into the contract, (2) how the party acted or appeared (intent may be manifested by conduct as well as by oral or written words), and (3) the circumstances surrounding the transaction.

Consider an example. Jaffe has just purchased a new car for $28,000. A number of his neighbors are admiring his car, and one neighbor, Logan, states that he would like to own a car exactly like Jaffe's. Jaffe, in front of all of his neighbors, says to Logan, "I'll sell you this car for $20,000 in cash." Logan agrees to buy the car, and they put the agreement in writing and sign it. Jaffe immediately tells everyone that his agreement to sell the car to Logan was only a joke. Is the agreement legally binding? In other words, do Jaffe and Logan have a contract?

The answer depends on whether the circumstances (Jaffe's just having purchased a new car, the price of the new car, and the fact that Jaffe agreed in writing to sell the car) and Jaffe's words would, to a reasonable person, manifest Jaffe's intention to form a contract. It is not Jaffe's inner belief or intent to make a joke that determines the answer. If a person in Logan's position could reasonably believe that Jaffe intended to form the contract with him, Jaffe would be legally required to sell the car to Logan.

SECTION 4

Types of Contracts

There are many types of contracts. The categories into which contracts are placed involve legal distinctions as to formation, enforceability, and performance.

BILATERAL VERSUS UNILATERAL CONTRACTS

Every contract involves at least two parties. The **offeror** is the party making the offer. The **offeree** is the party to whom the offer is made. Whether the contract is classified as *unilateral* or *bilateral* depends on what the offeree must do to accept the offer and to bind the offeror to a contract. If to accept the offer the offeree must only *promise* to perform, the contract is a **bilateral contract**. Hence, a bilateral contract is a "promise for a promise." No performance, such as payment of money or delivery of goods, need take place for a bilateral contract to be formed. The contract comes into existence at the moment the promises are exchanged.

For example, Jeff offers to buy Ann's digital camera for $200. Jeff tells Ann that he will give her the money for the camera next Friday, when he gets paid. Ann accepts Jeff's offer and promises to give him the camera when Jeff pays her on Friday. Jeff and Ann have formed a bilateral contract.

In a **unilateral contract**, in contrast, the offer is phrased so that the offeree can accept the offer only by completing the contract performance. Hence, a unilateral contract is a "promise for an act."[4] A classic example of a unilateral contract is as follows: O'Malley says to Parker, "If you carry this package across the Brooklyn Bridge, I'll give you $10." Only on Parker's complete crossing with the package does she fully accept O'Malley's offer to pay $10. If she chooses not to undertake the walk, there are no legal consequences. Contests, lotteries, and other competitions involving prizes are examples of offers for unilateral contracts. If a person complies with the rules of the contest—such as by submitting the right lottery number at the right place and time—a unilateral contract is formed, binding the organization offering the prize to a contract to perform as promised in the offer.

A problem arises in unilateral contracts when the **promisor** (the one making the promise) attempts to *revoke* (cancel) the offer after the **promisee** (the one to whom the promise was made) has begun performance but before the act has been completed. The promisee can accept the offer only on full performance, and under traditional contract principles, an offer may be revoked at any time before the offer is accepted. The present-day view, however, is that an offer to form a unilateral contract becomes irrevocable once performance has begun. Thus, even though the offer has not yet been accepted, the offeror is prohibited from revoking it for a reasonable time period.

For instance, in the Brooklyn Bridge example, suppose that Parker is walking across the bridge and has only three yards to go when O'Malley calls out to her, "I revoke my offer." Under traditional contract law, O'Malley's revocation would terminate the offer. Under the modern view of unilateral contracts, however, O'Malley will not be able to revoke his offer because Parker has undertaken performance and walked all but three yards of the bridge. In these circumstances, Parker can finish crossing the bridge and bind O'Malley to the contract.

EXPRESS VERSUS IMPLIED CONTRACTS

An **express contract** is one in which the terms of the agreement are fully and explicitly stated in words, oral or written. A signed lease for an apartment or a house is an express written contract. If a classmate calls you on the phone and agrees to buy your textbooks from last semester for $75, an express oral contract has been made.

A contract that is implied from the conduct of the parties is called an **implied-in-fact contract** or an implied contract. This type of contract differs from an express contract in that the *conduct* of the parties,

4. Clearly, a contract cannot be "one sided," because, by definition, an agreement implies the existence of two or more parties. Therefore, the phrase *unilateral contract,* if read literally, is a contradiction in terms. As traditionally used in contract law, however, the phrase refers to the kind of contract that results when only one promise is being made (the promise made by the offeror in return for the offeree's performance).

rather than their words, creates and defines the terms of the contract. (Note that a contract may be a mixture of an express contract and an implied-in-fact contract. In other words, a contract may contain some express terms, while others are implied.) Normally, if the following conditions exist, a court will hold that an implied contract was formed:

1. The plaintiff furnished some service or property.
2. The plaintiff expected to be paid for that service or property, and the defendant knew or should have known that payment was expected.
3. The defendant had a chance to reject the services or property and did not.

For example, suppose that you need an accountant to complete your tax return this year. You look through the Yellow Pages and find an accountant at an office in your neighborhood, so you drop by to see her. You go into the accountant's office and explain your problem, and she tells you what her fees are. The next day you return and give her secretary all the necessary information and documents—canceled checks, W-2 forms, and so on. You say nothing expressly to the secretary; rather, you walk out the door. In this situation, you have entered into an implied-in-fact contract to pay the accountant the usual and reasonable fees for her services. The contract is implied by your conduct and by hers. She expects to be paid for completing your tax return, and by bringing in the records she will need to do the work, you have implied an intent to pay her.

See Case 9.1 at the end of this chapter. To view the full, unedited case from Westlaw,® go to this text's Web site at **http://wbl-cs.westbuslaw.com**.

Quasi Contracts—Contracts Implied in Law

Quasi contracts, or contracts *implied in law*, are wholly different from actual contracts. Whereas express contracts and implied-in-fact contracts are actual contracts formed by the words or conduct of the parties, quasi contracts are fictional contracts created by courts and imposed on parties in the interests of fairness and justice. Quasi contracts are therefore equitable, rather than contractual, in nature. Usually, quasi contracts are imposed to avoid the *unjust enrichment* of one party at the expense of another. Under the doctrine of quasi contract, a plaintiff may recover in ***quantum meruit***,[5] a Latin phrase meaning "as much as he deserves." *Quantum meruit* essentially describes the extent of compensation owed under a contract implied in law.

For example, suppose that a vacationing doctor is driving down the highway and encounters Potter lying unconscious on the side of the road. The doctor renders medical aid that saves Potter's life. Although the injured, unconscious Potter did not solicit the medical aid and was not aware that the aid had been rendered, Potter received a valuable benefit, and the requirements for a quasi contract were fulfilled. In such a situation, the law will impose a quasi contract, and Potter normally will have to pay the doctor for the reasonable value of the medical services rendered.

A Limitation on Quasi Contracts. Although quasi contracts exist to prevent unjust enrichment, the party obtaining the unjust enrichment is not liable in some situations. Basically, the quasi-contractual principle cannot be invoked by a party who has conferred a benefit on someone else unnecessarily or as a result of misconduct or negligence.

Consider the following example. You take your car to the local car wash and ask to have it run through the washer and to have the gas tank filled. While it is being washed, you go to a nearby shopping center for two hours. In the meantime, one of the workers at the car wash has mistakenly believed that your car is the one that he is supposed to hand wax. When you come back, you are presented with a bill for a full tank of gas, a wash job, and a hand wax. Clearly, a benefit has been conferred on you. But this benefit has been conferred because of a mistake by the car-wash employee. You have not been *unjustly* enriched under these circumstances. People cannot normally be forced to pay for benefits "thrust" on them.

When an Actual Contract Exists. The doctrine of quasi contract generally cannot be used when there is an *actual contract* that covers the area in controversy. For example, Bateman contracts with Cameron to deliver a furnace to a building owned by Jones. Bateman delivers the furnace, but Cameron never pays Bateman. Jones has been unjustly enriched in this situation, to be sure. Bateman, however, cannot recover from Jones in quasi contract, because Bateman had

5. Pronounced *kwahn*-tuhm *mehr*-oo-wit.

an actual contract with Cameron. Bateman already has a remedy—he can sue for breach of contract to recover the price of the furnace from Cameron. No quasi contract need be imposed by the court in this instance to achieve justice.

Westlaw. See Case 9.2 at the end of this chapter. To view the full, unedited case from Westlaw,® go to this text's Web site at **http://wbl-cs.westbuslaw.com**.

FORMAL VERSUS INFORMAL CONTRACTS

Another classification system divides contracts into formal contracts and informal contracts. **Formal contracts** are contracts that require a special form or method of creation (formation) to be enforceable. One type of formal contract is the **contract under seal**, a formalized writing with a special seal attached. The seal may be actual (made of wax or some other durable substance) or impressed on the paper or indicated simply by the word *seal* or the letters *L.S.* at the end of the document. *L.S.* stands for *locus sigilli* and means "the place for the seal."[6]

A written contract may be considered sealed if the promisor *adopts* a seal already on it. A standard-form contract purchased at the local office supply store, for example, may have the word *seal* (or something else that qualifies as a seal) printed next to the blanks intended for the signatures. Unless the parties who sign the form indicate a contrary intention, when they sign the form, they adopt the seal.

Informal contracts include all other contracts. Such contracts are also called *simple contracts*. No special form is required (except for certain types of contracts that must be in writing), as the contracts are usually based on their substance rather than their form. Typically, businesspersons put their contracts in writing to ensure that there is some proof of a contract's existence should problems arise.

EXECUTED VERSUS EXECUTORY CONTRACTS

Contracts are also classified according to the degree to which they have been performed. A contract that has been fully performed on both sides is called an **executed contract**. A contract that has not been fully performed on either side is called an **executory contract**. If one party has fully performed but the other has not, the contract is said to be executed on the one side and executory on the other, but the contract is still classified as executory.

For example, assume that you agree to buy ten tons of coal from the Northern Coal Company. Further assume that Northern has delivered the coal to your steel mill, where it is now being burned. At this point, the contract is executed on the part of Northern and executory on your part. After you pay Northern for the coal, the contract will be executed on both sides.

VALID, VOID, VOIDABLE, AND UNENFORCEABLE CONTRACTS

A **valid contract** has the elements necessary to entitle at least one of the parties to enforce it in court. Those elements, as mentioned earlier, consist of (1) an agreement consisting of an offer and an acceptance of that offer, (2) supported by legally sufficient consideration, (3) made by parties who have the legal capacity to enter into the contract, and (4) made for a legal purpose.

A **void contract** is no contract at all. The terms *void* and *contract* are contradictory. A void contract produces no legal obligations on the part of any of the parties. For example, a contract can be void because the purpose of the contract was illegal.

A **voidable contract** is a valid contract but one that can be avoided at the option of one or both of the parties. The party having the option can elect either to avoid any duty to perform or to *ratify* (make valid) the contract. If the contract is avoided, both parties are released from it. If it is ratified, both parties must fully perform their respective legal obligations.

As a general rule, but subject to exceptions, contracts made by minors are voidable at the option of the minor (see Chapter 12). Contracts entered into under fraudulent conditions are voidable at the option of the defrauded party. In addition, contracts entered into under duress or undue influence are voidable (see Chapter 13).

An **unenforceable contract** is one that cannot be enforced because of certain legal defenses against it. It is not unenforceable because a party failed to satisfy a legal requirement of the contract; rather, it is a valid contract rendered unenforceable by some

6. The contract under seal has been almost entirely abolished under such provisions as UCC 2–203 (Section 2–203 of the Uniform Commercial Code). In sales of real estate, however, it is still common to use a seal (or an acceptable substitute).

statute or law. For example, some contracts must be in writing (see Chapter 14), and if they are not, they will not be enforceable except in certain exceptional circumstances.

SECTION 5

Interpretation of Contracts

Sometimes parties agree that a contract has been formed but disagree on the meaning or the legal effect of the contract. This may happen if one of the parties is not familiar with the legal terminology used in the contract. To an extent, "plain language" laws have helped to avoid this difficulty. Today, the federal government and a majority of the states have enacted special laws to regulate legal writing. Additionally, however, a dispute over the meaning of a contract may arise simply because the rights or obligations under the contract are not expressed clearly—no matter how "plain" the language used.

In this section, we look at some common law rules of contract interpretation. These rules, which have evolved over time, provide the courts with guidelines for deciding disputes over how contract terms or provisions should be interpreted.

THE PLAIN MEANING RULE

When a contract's writing is clear and unequivocal, a court will enforce it according to its obvious terms. This is sometimes referred to as the *plain meaning rule.* Under this rule, if a contract's words appear to be clear and unambiguous, a court cannot consider *extrinsic evidence,* which is any evidence not contained in the document itself. If a contract's terms are unclear or ambiguous, however, extrinsic evidence may be admissible to clarify the meaning of the contract. The admissibility of such evidence can significantly affect the court's interpretation of ambiguous contractual provisions and thus the outcome of litigation.

Westlaw. See Case 9.3 at the end of this chapter. To view the full, unedited case from Westlaw,® go to this text's Web site at **http://wbl-cs.westbuslaw.com**.

INTERPRETATION OF AMBIGUOUS TERMS

When the writing contains ambiguous or unclear terms, a court will interpret the language to give effect to the parties' intent *as expressed in their contract.* This is the primary purpose of the rules of interpretation—to determine the parties' intent from the language used in their agreement and to give effect to that intent. Usually, a court will not make or remake a contract, nor will it interpret the language according to what the parties *claim* their intent was when they made it. The following rules are used by the courts in interpreting ambiguous contractual terms:

1. Insofar as possible, a reasonable, lawful, and effective meaning will be given to all of a contract's terms.
2. A contract will be interpreted as a whole; individual, specific clauses will be considered subordinate to the contract's general intent. All writings that are a part of the same transaction will be interpreted together.
3. Terms that were the subject of separate negotiation will be given greater consideration than standardized terms and terms that were not negotiated separately.
4. A word will be given its ordinary, commonly accepted meaning, and a technical word or term will be given its technical meaning, unless the parties clearly intended something else.
5. Specific and exact wording will be given greater consideration than general language.
6. Written or typewritten terms will prevail over preprinted ones.
7. Because a contract should be drafted in clear and unambiguous language, a party who uses ambiguous expressions is held to be responsible for the ambiguities. Thus, when the language has more than one meaning, it will be interpreted against the party who drafted the contract.
8. Evidence of trade usage, prior dealing, and course of performance may be admitted to clarify the meaning of an ambiguously worded contract (these terms are defined and discussed in Chapter 18). When considering custom and usage, a court will look at what is common to the particular business or industry and to the locale in which the contract was made or is to be performed.

Terms and Concepts to Review

bilateral contract 200
contract 198
contract under seal 202
executed contract 202
executory contract 202
express contract 200
formal contract 202
implied-in-fact contract 200
informal contract 202
objective theory of contracts 199
offeree 200
offeror 200
promise 198
promisee 200
promisor 200
quantum meruit 201
quasi contract 201
unenforceable contract 202
unilateral contract 200
valid contract 202
void contract 202
voidable contract 202

Chapter Summary

The Definition of a Contract	A contract is an agreement that can be enforced in court. It is formed by two or more competent parties who agree to perform or to refrain from performing some act now or in the future.
The Function of Contract Law	Contract law establishes what kinds of promises will be legally binding and supplies procedures for enforcing legally binding promises, or agreements.
Elements of a Contract	1. *Elements of a valid contract*—Agreement, consideration, contractual capacity, and legality. 2. *Possible defenses to the enforcement of a contract*—Genuineness of assent and form.
The Objective Theory of Contracts	The intention to enter into a legally binding agreement, or contract, is judged by outward, objective facts as interpreted by a reasonable person, rather than by the party's own secret, subjective intentions.
Types of Contracts	1. *Bilateral*—A promise for a promise. 2. *Unilateral*—A promise for an act (acceptance is the completed—or substantial—performance of the contract by the offeree). 3. *Express*—Formed by words (oral, written, or a combination). 4. *Implied in fact*—Formed at least in part by the conduct of the parties. 5. *Quasi contract (contract implied in law)*—Imposed by law to prevent unjust enrichment. 6. *Formal*—Requires a special form for creation. 7. *Informal*—Requires no special form for creation. 8. *Executed*—A fully performed contract. 9. *Executory*—A contract not yet fully performed. 10. *Valid*—The contract has the necessary contractual elements of offer and acceptance, consideration, parties with legal capacity, and having been made for a legal purpose. 11. *Void*—No contract exists, or there is a contract without legal obligations. 12. *Voidable*—A party has the option of avoiding or enforcing the contractual obligation. 13. *Unenforceable*—A contract exists, but it cannot be enforced because of a legal defense.
Interpretation of Contracts	When the terms of a contract are unambiguous, a court will enforce the contract according to its plain terms, the meaning of which must be determined from the written document alone. (Plain language laws enacted by the federal government and the majority of the states require contracts to be clearly written and easily understandable.) When the terms of a contract are ambiguous, the courts use the following rules in interpreting the terms:

CHAPTER SUMMARY—CONTINUED

Interpretation of Contracts—continued	1. A reasonable, lawful, and effective meaning will be given to all contract terms. 2. A contract will be interpreted as a whole, specific clauses will be considered subordinate to the contract's general intent, and all writings that are a part of the same transaction will be interpreted together. 3. Terms that were negotiated separately will be given greater consideration than standardized terms and terms not negotiated separately. 4. Words will be given their commonly accepted meanings and technical words their technical meanings, unless the parties clearly intended otherwise. 5. Specific wording will be given greater consideration than general language. 6. Written or typewritten terms prevail over preprinted terms. 7. A party that uses ambiguous expressions is held to be responsible for the ambiguities. 8. Evidence of prior dealing, course of performance, or usage of trade is admissible to clarify an ambiguously worded contract. In these circumstances, express terms are given the greatest weight, followed by course of performance, course of dealing, and custom and usage of trade—in that order.

CASES FOR ANALYSIS

Westlaw. You can access the full text of each case presented below by going to the Westlaw cases on this text's Web site at http://wbl-cs.westbuslaw.com. Each Westlaw case includes the names of all plaintiffs and defendants, the dates on which the case was argued and decided, a brief summary of the issues and decisions in the case, headnotes classifying specific issues in the case according to the West Key Number System, and the court's opinion. Concurring and dissenting opinions, if any, are included as well.

CASE 9.1 IMPLIED CONTRACTS

HOMER V. BURMAN
Indiana Court of Appeals, 2001.
743 N.E.2d 1144.

DARDEN, Judge

STATEMENT OF THE CASE

Dave and Annette Homer ("the Homers") appeal the trial court's negative judgment in favor of J.M. Burman d/b/a Burman Electric Service ("Burman Electric").

We reverse and remand.

ISSUE

Whether the trial court's judgment is contrary to law.

FACTS

During the month of August 1999, the Homers hired Burman Electric to perform electrical work on their rental property located at 432 North Boots in Marion. Burman was initially hired to install an electric box at the rear of the house. However, after Stephanie Clevenger ("Clevenger"), the Homers' tenant, complained of malfunctioning lights in the kitchen and dining room, the Homers hired Burman Electric to rewire the entire house. The Homers took out a loan and paid Burman Electric $2,650.00 to complete the project.

During the home improvement project, problems developed. First, when power was reconnected to the house, Clevenger's "T.V., VCR, [her] son's Playstation," and her satellite receiver were destroyed. Burman's insurance carrier reimbursed her in the amount of $1,096.13. Subsequently, Clevenger's hair dryers, clocks, and lamps would repeatedly burn out. She and the Homers also noticed holes from drilling were left uncovered in the ceiling. The Homers also noticed that the furnace was not reconnected and that "plaster was damaged around the electrical outlets." Mr. Homer also noticed exposed wires, not rated for exterior use, running from the attic across the roof line and down, along aluminum siding, to the back porch.

Believing that the required permits had been acquired, Mr. Homer then called Michael Bowen ("Bowen"), a building inspector, to look over the property. Bowen stated that no permit had been issued and that the outdoor wiring was not consistent with the electrical building code. He said that if the outdoor wiring ever became worn or cut, the aluminum siding could become electrified. When Mr. Homer contacted Burman Electric about the problems, Burman Electric offered to return and "fix some of the problems." However, Mr. Homer declined the offer fearing that further damage would be done.

On October 26, 1999, the Homers filed a complaint in [an Indiana state small claims court] alleging breach of contract and seeking unspecified damages, plus reasonable attorney fees. Evidence was heard * * * on May 12, 2000.

At trial, the Homers introduced photographs documenting the shoddy work done to the house. They also introduced as plaintiff's exhibit 2, a four-page document containing (1) the building inspector's reasons why the house did not pass inspection; (2) copies of the estimates; and (3) cancelled checks. Clevenger testified about the difficulties she experienced and the property she had lost. She also detailed the locations of the holes left in the ceiling. Carl Burman, Jr. ("Mr. Burman") admitted that the required building permit was not obtained before rewiring the house and that the house did not pass inspection. Further, he testified that "[b]ecause of this job," employees that performed most of the work were no longer employed by Burman Electric. Mr. Burman also admitted that he was unaware of the Indiana Home Improvement Contracts Act ("the Act"), and he did not provide the Homers with a home improvement contract.

Additionally, Mr. Homer testified that he received an estimate of $2,500.00 from Dick Garriott, another electrician, to repair the work done by Burman Electric. He also testified that because the house could not be occupied, he had lost two months rental income at a rate of $300 per month.

* * * On May 24, 2000, judgment was entered against the Homers.

DECISION

The Homers argue that the judgment of the trial court is contrary to law because "the evidence presented at trial clearly established that Burman's workmanship was poor" and that they are entitled to damages. We agree.

Indiana Small Claims Rule 8(A) provides for informal hearings with relaxed rules of procedure in order that speedy justice can be dispensed. As a result, we are particularly deferential to [respectful of, willing to abide by] the trial court's judgment. However, we will reverse a negative judgment when it is contrary to law. A judgment is contrary to law when the evidence is without conflict and leads to but one conclusion which is opposite from that reached by the trial court.

The law concerning contracts is well settled in Indiana. An offer, acceptance, plus consideration make up the basis for a contract. A mutual assent or a meeting of the minds on all essential elements or terms must exist in order to form a binding contract. Assent to those terms of a contract may be expressed by acts which manifest acceptance.

The goal of contract interpretation is to give effect to the parties' intent. Unless the contract provides otherwise, it is implied that the parties intend to comply with all applicable statutes and city ordinances in effect at the time of the contract. Further, in a contract for work, there is an implied duty to do the work skillfully, carefully, and in a workmanlike manner. Negligent failure to do so is a tort, as well as a breach of contract. [Emphasis added.]

In this case, we first examine whether a contract existed. Although the estimate (contract) is not in the record, the evidence shows that the Homers paid Burman Electric $2,650.00 to rewire their home. Burman Electric accepted the payment and began work. Therefore, because we have an offer, acceptance, consideration, and a manifestation of mutual assent, a contract was in existence.

Next, we determine what duties were imposed upon Burman Electric. When this contract was executed, Burman Electric became duty bound to perform the work skillfully, carefully, and in a workmanlike manner. Furthermore, it was bound to abide by the applicable electric code and the Act, both of which were in existence when the contract was formed.

Concerning Burman Electric's duty to perform the work in a skillful and workmanlike manner, the evidence clearly shows a breach of that duty. There were photographs and testimony from the Homers and Clevenger about drilling holes left in the ceiling, the unconnected furnace, and damaged plaster. Further, Clevenger testified about the damage to her property and the continuing problem of hair dryers, clocks, and lamps burning out. Burman Electric clearly breached the contract to rewire the Homers' house by not performing the work in a skillful and workmanlike manner.

Concerning Burman Electric's duty to follow the electric code, the evidence clearly shows multiple violations. Mr. Burman admitted that Burman Electric did not acquire the appropriate building permits. He also testified that the project did not pass inspection by Mr. Bowen. Again, the evidence is clear that a breach of contract occurred because the parties impliedly intended the work to be completed in accordance with the appropriate electric code.

Concerning Burman Electric's duty to follow the Act, the evidence shows that the statute was violated. Through the Act, the legislature sought to protect consumers by placing specific minimum requirements on the contents of home improvement contracts. Accordingly, we will hold the contractor to a strict standard. The Act requires home improvement suppliers performing any alteration, repair, or modification to a residential property in an amount greater than $150.00 to provide the customer with a home improvement contract. The Act also makes the home improvement contract "subject to obtaining the necessary licenses or permits prior to any work commencing." The Act further requires the following provisions to be included in the contract before it is signed by the consumer: (1) the name and address of the consumer and the residential property; (2) the name and address of the home improvement supplier; (3) the date of the contract; (4) a reasonably detailed description of the work to be done; (5) the approximate start and stop dates; (6) a statement of contingencies; (7) the contract price; and (8) signature lines. Further, before the consumer signs the contract, the home improvement supplier must agree to the terms by signing the contract. Finally, "[a] home improvement supplier who violates this chapter commits a deceptive act that is actionable by the attorney general or by a consumer under [Indiana Code (IC)] 24-5-0.5-4 and is subject to the remedies and penalties under IC 24-5-0.5."

In this case, the evidence clearly shows that Burman Electric did not comply with the Act. Mr. Burman not only testified that he was unaware of the Act, but that he did not provide a home improvement contract; nor did he acquire the appropriate building permits. As a result, Burman Electric committed a deceptive act, and the Homers were entitled to bring an "action for the damages actually suffered * * * ."

The evidence shows that Burman Electric did not perform the work in a skillful and workmanlike manner, and it failed to follow the appropriate electric code and the Act. As a result, the trial court's judgment for Burman Electric was contrary to law. We reverse and enter judgment for the Homers, and remand for a hearing on the issue of damages and reasonable attorney fees.

CASE 9.2 QUASI CONTRACTS

INDUSTRIAL LIFT TRUCK SERVICE CORP. V. MITSUBISHI INTERNATIONAL CORP.

Appellate Court of Illinois,
First District, Fourth Division, 1982.
104 Ill.App.3d 357,
432 N.E.2d 999,
60 Ill.Dec. 100.

LINN, Justice:

* * * *

Plaintiff, Industrial Lift [Truck Service Corporation], is an Illinois corporation in the business of selling and servicing fork-lift trucks. Defendant, Mitsubishi International Corporation, is the United States distributor of fork-lift trucks manufactured by Nippon Yusoki Corporation of Japan. In 1973, plaintiff and defendant entered into a dealership agreement under which plaintiff would purchase fork-lift trucks from defendant and use its best efforts to sell the trucks to plaintiff's customers. Plaintiff was also required to service the trucks it sold under the manufacturer's warranty.

In November 1976, the original agreement was terminated and replaced by a new agreement under which plaintiff would use its best efforts to sell and service defendant's product. The agreement contained numerous terms and was designated to be the entire and exclusive agreement of the parties and could be amended only by written agreement. The terms in the contract important to this case were the following:

> (1) defendant could terminate the agreement without cause by giving 90 days written notice except that such termination could not occur during the first year of the agreement;
> (2) following termination, defendant would not be liable for any losses incurred by plaintiff as a result of termination.

From 1973 through 1977, plaintiff enjoyed success in selling defendant's product and allegedly became the nation's largest dealer in the product as a result of "great expenditures of time, effort, and money." Among the "great expenditures of time, effort, and money" were expenditures that went into making several design changes, which we need not detail, in defendant's product. These design changes were made by plaintiff because it believed them necessary to adapt defendant's Japanese product to an American market. The changes were not made because of any express or implied request or demand by defendant. Apparently, plaintiff sold many trucks with the design changes and eventually defendant incorporated the changes into the products it sold to its other dealers.

In August 1978, defendant sent plaintiff notice of termination of the dealership agreement. Defendant cited as cause plaintiff's declining sales in the previous year, but indicated that it was exercising its right to terminate under the 90 day notice of termination without cause term in the contract. Thereafter, plaintiff brought this action. * * *

* * * *

* * * [Plaintiff sought recovery based on quasi-contract principles] alleg[ing] that defendant was profitting from the design changes made by plaintiff, that defendant had failed to reimburse plaintiff for the costs incurred in developing the design changes, that defendant's retention of the benefits accruing to it as a result of the design changes was unjust, and that plaintiff should receive restitution for those benefits including the reasonable value of the expenses plaintiff had incurred in developing the design changes. The quasi-contract [allegations] were dismissed as failing to state a cause of action.

* * * *

A contract implied in law, or a quasi-contract, is fictitious and arises by implication of law wholly apart from the usual rules relating to contract. Quasi-contractual claims involving services usually arise when there is no contract, either express or implied, between the parties. One party performs a service that benefits another. The benefitting party has not requested the service but accepts the benefit. Circumstances indicate that the services were not intended to be gratuitous. As a result, the law will sometimes impose a duty on the benefiting party to pay for the services rendered despite the lack of a contract.

Difficulties arise with quasi-contractual claims when there is an express contract between the parties. *The general rule is that no quasi-contractual claim can arise when a contract exists between the parties concerning the same subject matter on which the quasi-contractual claim rests.* The reason for this rule is not difficult to discern. When parties enter into a contract they assume certain risks with an expectation of a return. Sometimes, their expectations are not realized, but they discover that under the contract they have assumed the risk of having those expectations defeated. As a result, they have no remedy under the contract for restoring their expectations. In desperation, they turn to quasi-contract for recovery. This the law will not allow. Quasi-contract is not a means for shifting a risk one has assumed under contract. [Emphasis added.]

Plaintiff asserts its complaint states a valid cause of action in quasi-contract despite the existence of a contract because the contract does not cover the specific service plaintiff rendered—the development of the design changes. It is perhaps true that the contract did not expressly cover the design changes, but it does not follow that an action in quasi-contract is therefore allowable. If a quasi-contract action could be brought every time a party under contract performs a service not precisely covered by the contract, then the rule preventing quasi-contract actions when a contract exists would have little meaning. Parties to a contract often perform services not expressly demanded by the contract. They do so to enhance their position under the contract and not because they expect a different remuneration for those services from what they could receive under the contract.

In the present case, plaintiff obviously made the design changes with a view to being compensated pursuant to the contract terms. By its own admission, the design changes allowed plaintiff to become one of the nation's largest dealers in defendant's product. When the changes were made, plaintiff knew the risk involved. It knew the contract could be terminated as it was terminated, and thus knew when it made the changes that it might not be compensated under the contract to the extent it hoped to be compensated. Now that a situation plaintiff knew could occur has occurred, plaintiff seeks to shift a risk it assumed in light of the contract to defendant. In essence, plaintiff is seeking to use quasi-contract as a means to circumvent the realities of a contract it freely entered into.

Moreover, the contract was declared to be the entire agreement of the parties and could only be amended by express agreement of the parties. Plaintiff was forewarned that any changes in the agreement could only be made with the express consent of defendant. If the services rendered bore a reasonable relationship to the contract, it was incumbent upon plaintiff to seek an amendment to the agreement if plaintiff expected more compensation than it could recover pursuant to the contract terms.

The contract defined the entire relationship of the parties with respect to its general subject matter—the sale and servicing of defendant's products. Plaintiff's attempt here to bring a quasi-contract action is nothing more than an attempt to unilaterally amend the agreement in a manner prohibited by the agreement. In such circumstances, the benefit received by defendant can hardly be considered unjust. Defendant had a right to assume that the contract defined the entire relationship of the parties with respect to all matters related to defendant's product. Defendant had a right to assume, absent a valid amendment to the agreement, that it should not have to compensate plaintiff for any acts done in relation to the subject matter of the contract except pursuant to the contract terms. [Emphasis added.]

Accordingly, we must hold that the contract in this case barred plaintiff's action in quasi-contract and that plaintiff's [allegations] in quasi-contract were properly dismissed.

* * * *

Affirmed.

CASE 9.3 INTERPRETATION OF CONTRACTS

UNITED AIRLINES, INC. v. GOOD TASTE, INC.
Supreme Court of Alaska, 1999.
982 P.2d 1259.

BRYNER, Justice.

* * * *

In 1987, United contacted Saucy Sisters' President and invited her to bid on United's in-flight catering contract. Shortly after United's invitation, Saucy Sisters entered into discussions/negotiations with United regarding the particulars of the catering contract and the obligations of the parties. On March 14, 1988, United awarded Saucy Sisters the catering contract. As a result of being awarded the contract, and in order to meet United's operation requirements for contracting caterers, Saucy Sisters expanded its operation extensively, spending roughly one million dollars in the process. A "Catering Agreement" ("Agreement") was signed by the parties and was performed for approximately one year. On May 18, 1989, United gave Saucy Sisters a ninety (90) day notice of termination by which it notified Saucy Sisters that its performance under the Agreement would terminate as of August 15, 1989. The Agreement was terminated August 15, 1989.

United's ninety day termination notice was in accordance with a no-cause termination provision found in the Catering Agreement. The provision states:

> *Term:* The term of this Agreement shall commence on May 1, 1988, and shall continue for a period of 3 years(s) [*sic*]; provided, however, either party may terminate this Agreement upon ninety (90) days' prior written notice.

The facts surrounding this termination provision are at the center of this dispute. In its version of the facts, Saucy Sisters alleges that Roger Groth, United's contracting representative, assured Saucy Sisters that United had never used the ninety day termination provision in the past and that the provision existed only to provide United with an "out" in the event United chose not to fly to Anchorage in the future. Saucy Sisters claims it would not have undertaken such a massive and expensive expansion effort at the risk of a no-cause, ninety day termination notice but for Roger Groth's allegedly fraudulent representations regarding the restrictions on the termination provision. United fails to dispute these facts anywhere in the record, but stated during oral argument that Roger Groth would testify that he never made such statements regarding the termination provision.

Saucy Sisters sued United, alleging wrongful termination of the Catering Agreement, fraud, and breach of the covenant of good faith and fair dealing. The parties filed opposing motions for summary judgment[which the Alaska state court denied]. * * *

* * * *

* * * The jury returned a verdict finding that United had not engaged in fraud but had breached the covenant of good faith and fair dealing. The jury awarded Saucy Sisters $1,541,000 in damages. After adding prejudgment interest, costs, and attorney's fees to the verdict, [the judge] entered judgment in Saucy Sisters' favor for $3,604,843.57. * * *

* * * *

* * * Saucy Sisters [appeals], claiming that, because the Agreement was ambiguous and extrinsic evidence concerning its meaning differed, the trial court erred in granting summary judgment against Saucy Sisters on its breach of contract claim. * * *

* * * *

Saucy Sisters asserts that the Agreement's ninety-day termination clause was ambiguous and allowed for varying interpretations, one of which might have sustained a breach of contract claim. Saucy Sisters asserts that this ambiguity created a genuine issue of material fact as to its claim for breach of contract, precluding summary judgment and requiring the claim to be submitted to the jury.

This court reviews trial court orders granting summary judgment *de novo*, drawing all inferences in favor of the opposing party, to determine whether genuine issues of material fact exist and whether the moving party [the party who made the motion for summary judgment] is entitled to judgment as a matter of law * * *

The [trial] court found [the termination] provision clear and unambiguous, ruling that it "has only one reasonable interpretation, which is that the contract period is for three years unless one of the parties decides to take affirmative action to end it early." Accordingly, the court determined as a matter of law that United did not breach the express terms of the contract when it terminated the catering contract upon ninety days' written notice.

* * * [T]he question of whether a contract is ambiguous is ordinarily one for the court to determine. A disagreement as to contract terms does not in itself create an ambiguity; the reviewing court must initially seek to ascertain the meaning of the contract from the provisions of the contract itself. *Contract terms are to be given their plain, ordinary, popular, and natural meaning.* And when the language of a contract is unambiguous, the express provision governs and there is no need for construction or inquiry as to the intention of the parties. [Emphasis added.]

Here, the meaning of the disputed termination clause is clear and unambiguous on its face when its words are given their plain, ordinary, popular, and natural meaning. This provision clearly fixes the Agreement's term at three years, but allows each party to end it earlier by doing nothing more than giving the other party ninety days' notice. As the [trial] court aptly noted, such termination clauses are hardly uncommon:

> Anyone familiar with real world business practices would instantly recognize this provision as a no-cause termination provision that is often used to limit an otherwise definite term. No-cause termination clauses like the one considered here are widely used, and this one in particular would not cause anyone to second-guess its clear and unambiguous terms.

Because the Agreement's no-cause termination provision was clear and unambiguous on its face, the trial court * * * had no occasion to consider extrinsic evidence supporting Saucy Sisters' assertion that it actually understood the provision to have a different meaning. And because United undisputedly abided by the literal terms of the provision—terminating the Agreement upon ninety days' written notice to Saucy Sisters—the trial court properly concluded that no genuine issue of material fact existed and that United was entitled to summary judgment on Saucy Sisters' breach of contract claim.

* * * *

We AFFIRM the trial court's order granting United summary judgment on Saucy Sisters' breach of contract claim * * * .

Case Problems

9–1. Nichols is the principal owner of Samuel Nichols, Inc., a real estate firm. Nichols signed an exclusive brokerage agreement with Molway to find a purchaser for Molway's property within ninety days. This type of agreement entitles the broker to a commission if the property is sold to any purchaser to whom it is shown during the ninety-day period. Molway tried to cancel the brokerage agreement before the ninety-day term had expired. Nichols had already advertised the property, put up a "for sale" sign, and shown the property to prospective buyers. Molway claimed that the brokerage contract was unilateral and that she could cancel at any time before Nichols found a buyer. Nichols claimed that the contract was bilateral and that Molway's cancellation breached the contract. Discuss who should prevail at trial. [*Samuel Nichols, Inc. v. Molway,* 25 Mass.App. 913, 515 N.E.2d 598 (1987)]

9–2. Weichert Co. Realtors sought damages from Thomas Ryan and his partner because they refused to pay a commission to William Tackaberry, one of Weichert's agents, for work done on a sale of property. Tackaberry had contacted Ryan about the property and subsequently met with him to discuss the sale. At that time and during subsequent discussions, Tackaberry informed Ryan that his commission was to be 10 percent of the purchase price of the property, payable at closing. Despite Tackaberry's continued efforts to get Ryan to sign a letter that spelled out the terms of the commission, Ryan refused to sign it. Ryan offered several times to negotiate with Tackaberry the amount and terms of the commission, but Tackaberry insisted that his commission must be 10 percent of the final price and that it was due at closing. When the deal was finalized, Weichert sent Ryan and his partner a bill for Tackaberry's commission. When the bill remained unpaid, Weichert filed suit for breach of an implied-in-fact contract or, failing that, for quasi-contractual recovery. Did an implied-in-fact contract exist between Tackaberry and Ryan? If not, could Weichert recover in quasi contract for the value of Tackaberry's services? What should the court decide? [*Weichert v. Ryan,* 128 N.J. 427, 608 A.2d 280 (1992)]

9–3. Garris Briggs died on October 11, 1990, leaving $782 in unpaid medical bills. Following his death, insurance checks in the amount of $676.72, payable to Briggs, were sent to his widow, Beatrice Briggs. The Briggses had been living apart for the previous five years and during that time had not had any financial connections. Under state law, a surviving spouse, on the execution of an affidavit before the appropriate county official, was entitled to all of the estate's assets without administration, and the assets of the estate up to $5,000 were free from all debts of the decedent (the one who died). Garris Briggs's estate was worth less than $5,000, so Beatrice Briggs signed the necessary affidavit, cashed the checks, and deposited the funds. The physicians who had provided medical services for Garris Briggs sued the widow to recover the insurance proceeds. The widow claimed that because she had not lived with her husband for five years, she should not be liable for his debts. Should the physicians be allowed to recover the insurance proceeds from Beatrice Briggs? Discuss fully. [*Drs. Laves, Sarewitz and Walko v. Briggs,* 259 N.J.Super. 368, 613 A.2d 506 (1992)]

9–4. William Greene began working for Grant Building, Inc., in 1959. Greene allegedly agreed to work at a pay rate below union scale in exchange for a promise that Grant would employ him "for life." In 1975, Oliver Realty, Inc., took over the management of Grant Building. Oliver Realty's president assured former Grant employees that existing employment contracts would be honored. During that same year, Greene explained the terms of his agreement to an Oliver Realty supervisor. The supervisor stated that he would look into the matter but never got back to Greene. After twenty-four years of service, Greene was fired by the new owners of the business. Greene sued Oliver Realty for breach of a unilateral contract. Discuss fully whether Greene and Oliver Realty had a unilateral contract. [*Greene v. Oliver Realty, Inc.,* 363 Pa.Super. 534, 526 A.2d 1192 (1987)]

9–5. Engelcke Manufacturing, Inc., planned to design and manufacture Whizball, an electronic parlor game. Engelcke asked Eaton to design the electronic schematic for it. Engelcke told Eaton that he would be paid for the reasonable value of his services on the project's completion, but no written contract was signed. The specific amount and terms were also not discussed. Eaton had produced a plan that represented 90 percent of the finished design when Engelcke terminated his employment. Eaton sued Engelcke for breach of an implied-in-fact contract. Engelcke claimed that they had an express contract. Why did Engelcke claim an express contract rather than an implied-in-fact contract? [*Eaton v. Engelcke Manufacturing, Inc.,* 37 Wash.App. 677, 681 P.2d 1312 (1984)]

9–6. Ashton Co., which was engaged in a construction project, leased a crane from Artukovich & Sons, Inc., and hired the Reliance Truck Co. to deliver the crane to the construction site. Reliance, while the crane was in its possession and without permission from either Ashton or Artukovich, used the crane to install a transformer for a utility company, which paid Reliance for the job. Reliance then delivered the crane to the Ashton construction site at the appointed time of delivery. When Artukovich learned of the unauthorized use of the crane by Reliance, it sued Reliance for damages. What equitable doctrine could be used as a basis for awarding damages to Artukovich? [*Artukovich & Sons, Inc. v. Reliance Truck Co.,* 126 Ariz. 246, 614 P.2d 327 (1980)]

9–7. In 1982, in the closing days of Minnesota's gubernatorial campaign, Dan Cohen offered a reporter from the *Minneapolis Star and Tribune* some documents—copies of two public court records of a rival party's candidate for lieutenant governor—if the reporter promised not to reveal the source of the information. The reporter promised to keep the source confidential. The editor of the *Tribune*, however, in spite of the reporter's objections, decided to name Cohen as the source of the information so as not to mislead the public into thinking that the information came from an unbiased source. On the day the newspaper article was published, Cohen was fired by his employer. Cohen sued the newspaper's owner, Cowles Media Co., for breach of contract. Had the newspaper's owner breached a contract? Discuss fully. [*Cohen v. Cowles Media Co.*, 501 U.S. 663, 111 S.Ct. 2513, 115 L.Ed.2d 586 (1991)]

9–8. Financial & Real Estate Consulting Co. (Financial) contracted with Regional Properties, Inc. (Regional), to sell to investors limited partnership interests (ownership interests) in some ventures being undertaken by Regional. Regional promised to pay Financial for its brokerage services. Financial sold a number of partnership interests and was paid the stipulated fee for some (but not all) of the sales. Regional later discovered that Financial was not registered with the Securities and Exchange Commission as a broker-dealer, as required by law. Regional brought an action before the court to rescind (cancel) the contract with Financial. Financial counterclaimed for the unpaid fees. Is the contract between Financial and Regional enforceable? Why, or why not? [*Regional Properties, Inc. v. Financial & Real Estate Consulting Co.*, 678 F.2d 552 (5th Cir. 1982)]

9–9. Nancy Mollinedo's house was damaged in a fire. Her insurance company, Sentry Insurance, hired GAB Business Services, Inc., an independent insurance claims adjuster, to investigate the claim. GAB hired ServiceMaster of St. Cloud to repair the damage. While ServiceMaster was working on the house, Sentry decided to deny Mollinedo's claim on the ground that she had deliberately set the fire. Sentry allowed the repairs to continue, however, without informing either ServiceMaster or GAB that it would deny the claim. When the work was done, Sentry sent a check for the amount ServiceMaster charged for the work (a little more than $30,000) to the Federal Housing Administration (FHA), Mollinedo's mortgagee (the holder of the mortgage), as required under the insurance policy's mortgagee clause. Sentry received in return a partial mortgage on the house. ServiceMaster received nothing. ServiceMaster filed a suit in a Minnesota state court against Sentry and GAB for, among other things, unjust enrichment. Will ServiceMaster prevail in court? Discuss. [*ServiceMaster of St. Cloud v. GAB Business Services, Inc.*, 530 N.W.2d 558 (Minn.App.1995)]

9–10. In 1976, Kerr-McGee Corporation issued an employee handbook that listed examples of misconduct that could result in discipline or discharge and spelled out specific procedures that would be used in those instances. This handbook was in effect when LeRoy McIlravy began working for Kerr-McGee. In 1992, as part of a reduction in Kerr-McGee's work force, McIlravy was laid off. He and other former employees filed a suit in a federal district court against Kerr-McGee, contending, among other things, that the handbook implied that employees would not be dismissed without "cause." The plaintiffs argued that Kerr-McGee breached this implied term when it discharged them. Did the statements in the handbook create an implied contract? Discuss. [*McIlravy v. Kerr-McGee Corp.*, 119 F.3d 876 (10th Cir. 1997)]

9–11. Sosa Crisan, an eighty-seven-year-old widow, collapsed while shopping at a local grocery store. The Detroit police took her to the Detroit city hospital by ambulance. She was admitted, and she remained there fourteen days. Then she was transferred to another hospital, at which she died some eleven months later. Crisan had never regained consciousness after her collapse at the grocery store. After she died, the city of Detroit sued her estate to recover the expenses of both the ambulance that took her to the Detroit city hospital and her Detroit city hospital stay. Is there a contract between Sosa Crisan and the Detroit city hospital? If so, how much can the hospital recover? [*In re Estate of Crisan*, 362 Mich. 569, 107 N.W.2d 907 (1961)]

9–12. After Walter Washut had suffered a heart attack and could no longer take care of himself, he asked Eleanor Adkins, a friend who had previously refused his proposal of marriage, to move to his ranch. For the next twelve years, Adkins lived with Washut, although she retained ownership of her own house and continued to work full-time at her job. Adkins took care of Washut's personal needs, cooked his meals, cleaned and maintained his house, cared for the livestock, and handled other matters for Washut. According to Adkins, Washut told her on numerous occasions that "everything would be taken care of" and that she would never have to leave the ranch. After Washut's death, Adkins sought to recover in quasi contract for the value of the services she had rendered to Washut. Adkins stated in her deposition that she had performed the services because she loved Washut, not because she had expected to be paid for them. What will the court decide, and why? [*Adkins v. Lawson*, 892 P.2d 128 (Wyo. 1995)]

9–13. Jerilyn Dawson hired Michael Shaw of the law firm of Jones, Waldo, Holbrook, and McDonough to represent her in her divorce. Dawson signed an agreement to pay the attorneys' fees. The agreement did not include an estimate of how much the divorce would cost. When Dawson failed to pay, the firm filed a suit in a Utah state court to collect, asking for an award of more than $43,000. During the trial, Shaw testified that he had told Dawson the divorce would cost "something in the nature of $15,000 to $18,000." The court awarded the firm most—but not all—of what it sought. Both parties appealed: Dawson contended that the award was too high, and the firm complained that it was too low. What rule of interpretation discussed in this chapter might the appellate court apply in deciding the appropriate amount of damages in this case? If this rule is applied, what will the court likely decide? Explain. [*Jones, Waldo, Holbrook & McDonough v. Dawson,* 923 P.2d 1366 (Utah 1996)]

9–14. Thomas Rinks and Joseph Shields developed Psycho Chihuahua, a caricature of a Chihuahua dog with a "do-not-back-down" attitude. They promoted and marketed the character through their company, Wrench, L.L.C. Ed Alfaro and Rudy Pollak, representatives of Taco Bell Corp., learned of Psycho Chihuahua and met with Rinks and Shields to talk about using the character as a Taco Bell "icon." Wrench sent artwork, merchandise, and marketing ideas to Alfaro, who promoted the character within Taco Bell. Alfaro asked Wrench to propose terms for Taco Bell's use of Psycho Chihuahua. Taco Bell did not accept Wrench's terms, but Alfaro continued to promote the character within the company. Meanwhile, Taco Bell hired a new advertising agency, which proposed an advertising campaign involving a Chihuahua. When Alfaro learned of this proposal, he sent the Psycho Chihuahua materials to the agency. Taco Bell made a Chihuahua the focus of its marketing but paid nothing to Wrench. Wrench filed a suit against Taco Bell in a federal district court, claiming in part that it had an implied contract with Taco Bell, which the latter breached. Do these facts satisfy the requirements for an implied contract? Why, or why not? [*Wrench L.L.C. v. Taco Bell Corp.,* 51 F.Supp.2d 840 (W.D.Mich. 1999)]

9–15. Professor Dixon was an adjunct professor at Tulsa Community College (TCC) in Tulsa, Oklahoma. Each semester, near the beginning of the term, the parties executed a written contract that always included the following provision: "It is agreed that this agreement may be cancelled by the Administration or the instructor at any time before the first class session." In the spring semester of Dixon's seventh year, he filed a complaint with TCC alleging that one of his students, Meredith Bhuiyan, had engaged in disruptive classroom conduct. He gave her an incomplete grade and asked TCC to require her to apologize as a condition of receiving a final grade. TCC later claimed, and Dixon denied, that he was told to assign Bhuiyan a grade if he wanted to teach in the fall. Toward the end of the semester, Dixon was told which classes he would teach in the fall, but the parties did not sign a written contract. The Friday before classes began, TCC terminated him. He filed a suit in an Oklahoma state court against TCC and others, alleging breach of contract. Did the parties have a contract? If so, did TCC breach it? Explain. [*Dixon v. Bhuiyan,* 10 P.3d 888 (Okla. 2000)]

E-LINKS

For updated links to resources available on the Web, as well as a variety of other materials, visit this text's Web site at

http://wbl-cs.westbuslaw.com

The 'Lectric Law Library provides information on contract law, including a definition of a contract, the elements required for a contract, and so on. Go to

http://www.lectlaw.com

Then go to the Laypeople's Law Lounge, and scroll down to Contracts.

You can keep abreast of recent and planned revisions of the *Restatements of the Law,* including the *Restatement (Second) of Contracts,* by accessing the American Law Institute's Web site at

http://www.ali.org

LEGAL RESEARCH EXERCISES ON THE WEB

Go to http://wbl-cs.westbuslaw.com, the Web site that accompanies this text. Select "Interactive Study Center," and then click on "Chapter 9." There you will find the following Internet research exercises that you can perform to learn more about contracts and contract provisions:

Activity 9–1: Contracts and Contract Provisions

Activity 9–2: Contracts in Ancient Mesopotamia

CHAPTER 10
Agreement

AN ESSENTIAL ELEMENT for contract formation is **agreement**—the parties must agree on the terms of the contract and manifest to each other their **mutual assent** to the same bargain. Ordinarily, agreement is evidenced by two events: an *offer* and an *acceptance.* One party offers a certain bargain to another party, who then accepts that bargain. The agreement does not necessarily have to be in writing. Both parties, however, must manifest their assent to the same bargain. Once an agreement is reached, if the other elements of a contract are present (consideration, capacity, and legality—discussed in subsequent chapters), a valid contract is formed, generally creating enforceable rights and duties between the parties.

Note that not all agreements are contracts. John and Kevin may agree to play golf on a certain day, but a court would not hold that their agreement is an enforceable contract. A *contractual* agreement only arises when the terms of the agreement impose legally enforceable obligations on the parties.

As you read through this chapter, keep in mind that the contract requirement of agreement applies to all contracts, regardless of how they are formed. Many contracts continue to be formed in the traditional way—through the exchange of paper documents. Increasingly, contracts are also being formed online—through the exchange of electronic messages or documents. We will examine contracts formed online in Chapter 23.

SECTION 1

Requirements of the Offer

As mentioned in Chapter 9, the parties to a contract are the *offeror,* the one who makes an offer or proposal to another party, and the *offeree,* the one to whom the offer or proposal is made. An **offer** is a promise or commitment to do or refrain from doing some specified thing in the future. Under the common law, three elements are necessary for an offer to be effective:

1. The offeror must have a serious intention to become bound by the offer.
2. The terms of the offer must be reasonably certain, or definite, so that the parties and the court can ascertain the terms of the contract.
3. The offer must be communicated by the offeror to the offeree, resulting in the offeree's knowledge of the offer.

Once an effective offer has been made, the offeree has the power to accept the offer. If the offeree accepts, an agreement is formed (and thus a contract, if other essential elements are present).

INTENTION

The first requirement for an effective offer is a serious intent on the part of the offeror. Serious intent is not determined by the *subjective* intentions, beliefs, and assumptions of the offeror. As discussed in Chapter 9, courts generally adhere to the *objective theory of contracts* in determining whether a contract has been formed. Under this theory, a party's words and conduct are held to mean whatever a reasonable person in the offeree's position would think they meant. The court will give words their usual meanings even if "it were proved by twenty bishops that [the] party . . . intended something else."[1]

1. Judge Learned Hand in *Hotchkiss v. National City Bank of New York,* 200 F. 287 (2d Cir. 1911), aff'd 231 U.S. 50, 34 S.Ct. 20, 58 L.Ed. 115 (1913).

Offers made in obvious anger, jest, or undue excitement do not meet the intent test, because a reasonable person would realize that a serious offer was not being made. Because these offers are not effective, an offeree's acceptance does not create an agreement. For example, suppose that you and three classmates ride to school each day in Davina's new automobile, which has a market value of $20,000. One cold morning, the four of you get into the car, but Davina cannot get the car started. She yells in anger, "I'll sell this car to anyone for $500!" You drop $500 in her lap. Given these facts, a reasonable person, taking into consideration Davina's frustration and the obvious difference in worth between the market value of the car and the proposed purchase price, would declare that her offer was not made with serious intent and that you did not have an agreement.

The concept of intention can be further clarified through an examination of the types of expressions and statements that are not offers. We look at these expressions and statements in the subsections that follow.

Westlaw. See Case 10.1 at the end of this chapter. To view the full, unedited case from Westlaw,® go to this text's Web site at **http://wbl-cs.westbuslaw.com**.

Expressions of Opinion. An expression of opinion is not an offer. It does not evidence an intention to enter into a binding agreement. Consider an example. Hawkins took his son to McGee, a doctor, and asked McGee to operate on the son's hand. McGee said that the boy would be in the hospital three or four days and that the hand would *probably* heal a few days later. The son's hand did not heal for a month, but the father did not win a suit for breach of contract. The court held that McGee had not made an offer to heal the son's hand in three or four days. He had merely expressed an opinion as to when the hand would heal.[2]

Statements of Intention. If Arif says, "I *plan* to sell my stock in Novation, Inc., for $150 per share," a contract is not created if John "accepts" and tenders the $150 per share for the stock. Arif has merely expressed his intention to enter into a future contract for the sale of the stock. If John accepts and tenders the $150 per share, no contract is formed, because a reasonable person would conclude that Arif was only *thinking about* selling his stock, not *promising* to sell it.

Preliminary Negotiations. A request or invitation to negotiate is not an offer. It only expresses a willingness to discuss the possibility of entering into a contract. Included are statements such as "Will you sell Blythe Estate?" or "I wouldn't sell my car for less than $1,000." A reasonable person in the offeree's position would not conclude that these statements evidenced an intention to enter into a binding obligation. Likewise, when construction work is done for the government and private firms, contractors are invited to submit bids. The *invitation* to submit bids is not an offer, and a contractor does not bind the government or private firm by submitting a bid. (The bids that the contractors submit are offers, however, and the government or private firm can bind the contractor by accepting the bid.)

Agreements to Agree. During preliminary negotiations, the parties may form an agreement to agree to a material term of a contract at some future date. Traditionally, such "agreements to agree" were not considered to be binding contracts. More recent cases illustrate the view that agreements to agree serve valid commercial purposes and can be enforced if the parties clearly intended to be bound by such agreements.

For example, suppose Zahn Consulting leases office space from Leon Properties, Inc. Their lease agreement includes a clause permitting Zahn to extend the lease at an amount of rent to be agreed on when the lease is extended. Under the traditional rule, because the amount of rent is not specified in the lease clause itself, the clause would be too indefinite in its terms to enforce. Under the current view, a court could hold that the parties intended the future rent to be a reasonable amount and could enforce the clause.[3] In other words, under the current view, the emphasis is on the parties' intent rather than on form.

Advertisements, Catalogues, Price Lists, and Circulars. In general, advertisements, mail-order catalogues, price lists, and circulars are treated not as offers to contract but as invitations to negotiate.

2. *Hawkins v. McGee,* 84 N.H. 114, 146 A. 641 (1929).

3. *Restatement (Second) of Contracts,* Section 33. See also UCC 2–204 and 2–305.

Suppose that Loeser advertises a used paving machine. The ad is mailed to hundreds of firms and reads, "Used Loeser Construction Co. paving machine. Builds curbs and finishes cement work all in one process. Price $42,350." If Star Paving calls Loeser and says, "We accept your offer," no contract is formed. Any reasonable person would conclude that Loeser was not promising to sell the paving machine but rather was soliciting offers to buy it. If such an ad were held to constitute a legal offer, and fifty people accepted the offer, there would be no way for Loeser to perform all fifty of the resulting contracts. He would have to breach forty-nine contracts. Obviously, the law seeks to avoid such unfairness.

Price lists are another form of invitation to negotiate or trade. A seller's price list is not an offer to sell at that price; it merely invites the buyer to offer to buy at that price. In fact, the seller usually puts "prices subject to change" on the price list. Only in rare circumstances will a price quotation be construed as an offer.[4]

Although most advertisements and the like are treated as invitations to negotiate, this does not mean that an advertisement can never be an offer. If the advertisement makes a promise so definite in character that it is apparent that the offeror is binding himself or herself to the conditions stated, the advertisement is treated as an offer.[5]

Auctions. Sometimes, what appears to be an offer is not sufficient to serve as the basis for contract formation. Particularly problematic in this respect are "offers" to sell goods at auctions. In an auction, a seller "offers" goods for sale through an auctioneer. This is not, however, a *contractual* offer. Instead, the seller is only expressing a willingness to sell. Unless the terms of the auction are explicitly stated to be *without reserve*, the seller (through the auctioneer) may withdraw the goods at any time before the sale is closed by announcement or by fall of the auctioneer's hammer. The seller's right to withdraw goods characterizes an auction with reserve; all auctions are assumed to be of this type unless a clear statement to the contrary is made.[6] At auctions without reserve, the goods cannot be withdrawn and must be sold to the highest bidder.

In an auction with reserve, there is no obligation to sell, and the seller may refuse the highest bid. The bidder is actually the offeror. Before the auctioneer strikes the hammer, which constitutes acceptance of the bid, a bidder may revoke his or her bid, or the auctioneer may reject that bid or all bids. Typically, an auctioneer will reject a bid that is below the price the seller is willing to accept. When the auctioneer accepts a higher bid, he or she rejects all previous bids. Because rejection terminates an offer (as pointed out later in the chapter), if the highest bidder withdraws his or her bid before the hammer falls, none of the previous bids is reinstated. If the bid is not withdrawn or rejected, the contract is formed when the auctioneer announces, "Going once, going twice, sold" (or something similar) and lets the hammer fall.

In auctions with reserve, the seller may reserve the right to confirm or reject the sale even after the "hammer has fallen." In this situation, the seller is obligated to notify those attending the auction that sales of goods made during the auction are not final until confirmed by the seller.

DEFINITENESS OF TERMS

The second requirement for an effective offer involves the definiteness of its terms. An offer must have terms that are reasonably definite so that, if a contract is formed, a court can determine if a breach has occurred and can provide an appropriate remedy. What specific terms are required depends, of course, on the type of contract. Generally, a contract must include the following terms, either expressed in the contract or capable of being reasonably inferred from it:

1. The identification of the parties.
2. The identification of the object or subject matter of the contract (also the quantity, when appropriate), including the work to be performed, with specific identification of such items as goods, services, and land.
3. The consideration to be paid.
4. The time of payment, delivery, or performance.

Courts sometimes are willing to supply a missing term in a contract when the parties have clearly manifested an intent to form a contract. If, in contrast, the parties have attempted to deal with a particular term of the contract but their expression of intent is too vague or uncertain to be given any precise meaning, the court will not supply a "reasonable" term, because to do so might conflict with the intent of the

4. See, for example, *Fairmount Glass Works v. Grunden-Martin Woodenware Co.*, 106 Ky. 659, 51 S.W. 196 (1899).

5. See, for example, *Lefkowitz v. Great Minneapolis Surplus Store, Inc.*, 251 Minn. 188, 86 N.W.2d 689 (1957).

6. See UCC 2–328.

parties. In other words, the court will not rewrite the contract.[7]

An offer may invite an acceptance to be worded in such specific terms that the contract is made definite. For example, suppose that Marcus Business Machines contacts your corporation and offers to sell "from one to ten MacCool copying machines for $1,600 each; state number desired in acceptance." Your corporation agrees to buy two copiers. Because the quantity is specified in the acceptance, the terms are definite, and the contract is enforceable.

COMMUNICATION

A third requirement for an effective offer is communication of the offer to the offeree, resulting in the offeree's knowledge of the offer. Ordinarily, one cannot agree to a bargain without knowing that it exists. Suppose that Estrich advertises a reward for the return of his lost dog. Hoban, not knowing of the reward, finds the dog and returns it to Estrich. Hoban cannot recover the reward, because she did not know it had been offered.[8]

SECTION 2

Termination of the Offer

The communication of an effective offer to an offeree gives the offeree the power to transform the offer into a binding, legal obligation (a contract) by an acceptance. This power of acceptance, however, does not continue forever. It can be terminated either by the action of the parties or by operation of law.

TERMINATION BY ACTION OF THE PARTIES

An offer can be terminated by the action of the parties in any of three ways: by revocation, by rejection, or by counteroffer.

Revocation of the Offer by the Offeror. The offeror's act of withdrawing an offer is known as **revocation.** Unless an offer is irrevocable, the offeror usually can revoke the offer (even if he or she has promised to keep it open), as long as the revocation is communicated to the offeree before the offeree accepts. Revocation may be accomplished by an express repudiation of the offer (for example, with a statement such as "I withdraw my previous offer of October 17") or by the performance of acts inconsistent with the existence of the offer, which are made known to the offeree.

The general rule followed by most states is that a revocation becomes effective when the offeree or offeree's agent (a person acting on behalf of the offeree) actually receives it. Therefore, a letter of revocation mailed on April 1 and delivered at the offeree's residence or place of business on April 3 becomes effective on April 3.

An offer made to the general public can be revoked in the same manner in which the offer was originally communicated. Suppose that a department store offers a $10,000 reward to anyone giving information leading to the apprehension of the persons who burglarized the store's downtown branch. The offer is published in three local papers and in four papers in neighboring communities. To revoke the offer, the store must publish the revocation in all of the seven papers in which it published the offer. The revocation is then accessible to the general public, even if some particular offeree does not know about it.

Irrevocable Offers. Although most offers are revocable, some can be made irrevocable. One type of irrevocable offer involves the option contract. Increasingly, courts also refuse to allow an offeror to revoke an offer when the offeree has changed position because of justifiable reliance on the offer. (In some circumstances, an offer for the sale of goods made by a merchant may also be considered irrevocable—see the discussion of the "merchant's firm offer" in Chapter 18.)

Option Contract. An **option contract** is created when an offeror promises to hold an offer open for a specified period of time in return for a payment (consideration) given by the offeree. An option contract takes away the offeror's power to revoke the offer for the period of time specified in the option. If no time is specified, then a reasonable period of time is implied. For example, suppose that you are in the

7. See Chapter 18 and UCC 2–204. Article 2 of the UCC specifies different rules relating to the definiteness of terms used in a contract for the sale of goods. In essence, Article 2 modifies general contract law by requiring less specificity.

8. A few states allow recovery of the reward, but not on contract principles. Because Estrich wanted his dog to be returned, and Hoban returned it, these few states would allow Hoban to recover on the basis that it would be unfair to deny her the reward just because she did not know it had been offered.

business of writing movie scripts. Your agent contacts the head of development at New Line Cinema and offers to sell New Line your latest movie script. New Line likes your script and agrees to pay you $10,000 for a six-month option. In this situation, you (through your agent) are the offeror, and New Line is the offeree. You cannot revoke your offer to sell New Line your script for the next six months. If after six months no contract has been formed, however, New Line loses the $10,000, and you are free to sell the script to another firm.

Option contracts are also frequently used in conjunction with the sale or lease of real estate. For example, you might agree with a landowner to lease a home and include in the lease contract a clause stating that you will pay $2,000 for an option to purchase the home within a specified period of time. If you decide not to purchase the home after the specified period has lapsed, you forfeit the $2,000, and the landlord is free to sell the property to another buyer.

Additionally, contracts to lease business premises often include options to renew the leases at certain intervals, such as after five years. Typically, a lease contract containing a renewal option requires notification—that is, the person leasing the premises must notify the property owner of his or her intention to exercise the renewal option within a certain number of days or months before the current lease expires.

Detrimental Reliance. When the offeree justifiably relies on an offer to his or her detriment, the court may hold that this *detrimental reliance* makes the offer irrevocable. For example, assume that Angela has rented commercial property from Jake for the past thirty-three years under a series of five-year leases. Under business conditions existing as their seventh lease nears its end, the rental property market is more favorable for tenants than landlords. Angela tells Jake that she is going to look at other, less expensive properties as possible sites for her business. Wanting Angela to remain a tenant, Jake promises to reduce the rent in their next lease. In reliance on the promise, Angela does not look at other sites but continues to occupy and do business on Jake's property. When they sit down to negotiate a new lease, however, Jake says he has changed his mind and will increase the rent. Can he effectively revoke his promise?

Normally, he cannot, because Angela has been relying on his promise to reduce the rent. Had the promise not been made, she would have relocated her business. This is a case of detrimental reliance on a promise, which therefore cannot be revoked. In this situation, the **doctrine of promissory estoppel** comes into play. To **estop** means to bar, impede, or preclude someone from doing something. Thus, promissory estoppel means that the promisor (the offeror) is barred from revoking the offer, in this case because the offeree has already changed her actions in reliance on the offer. We look again at the doctrine of promissory estoppel in Chapter 11, in the context of consideration.

Detrimental reliance on the part of the offeree can also involve partial performance by the offeree in response to an offer looking toward formulation of a unilateral contract. As discussed in Chapter 9, the offer to form a unilateral contract invites acceptance only by full performance; merely promising to perform does not constitute acceptance. Injustice can result if an offeree expends time and money in partial performance, and then the offeror revokes the offer before performance can be completed. Many courts will not allow the offeror to revoke the offer after the offeree has performed some substantial part of his or her duties.[9] In effect, partial performance renders the offer irrevocable, giving the original offeree reasonable time to complete performance. Of course, once the performance is complete, a unilateral contract exists.

Rejection of the Offer by the Offeree. The offer may be rejected by the offeree, in which case the offer is terminated. Any subsequent attempt by the offeree to accept will be construed as a new offer, giving the original offeror (now the offeree) the power of acceptance. A rejection is ordinarily accomplished by words or conduct evidencing an intent not to accept the offer. As with revocation, rejection of an offer is effective only when it is actually received by the offeror or the offeror's agent.

Merely inquiring about an offer does not constitute rejection. Suppose that a friend offers to buy your CD-ROM library for $300, and you respond, "Is that your best offer?" or "Will you pay me $375 for it?" A reasonable person would conclude that you had not rejected the offer but had merely made an inquiry for further consideration of the offer. You can still accept and bind your friend to the $300 purchase price. When the offeree merely inquires as to the firmness of the offer, there is no reason to presume that he or she intends to reject it.

9. *Restatement (Second) of Contracts,* Section 45.

Counteroffer by the Offeree. A rejection of the original offer and the simultaneous making of a new offer is called a **counteroffer.** Suppose that Duffy offers to sell her home to Wong for $170,000. Wong responds, "Your price is too high. I'll offer to purchase your house for $160,000." Wong's response is a counteroffer, because it terminates Duffy's offer to sell at $170,000 and creates a new offer by Wong to purchase at $160,000.

At common law, the **mirror image rule** requires the offeree's acceptance to match the offeror's offer exactly—to mirror the offer. Any material change in, or addition to, the terms of the original offer automatically terminates that offer and substitutes the counteroffer. The counteroffer, of course, need not be accepted; but if the original offeror does accept the terms of the counteroffer, a valid contract is created.[10]

Termination by Operation of Law

The power of the offeree to transform the offer into a binding, legal obligation can be terminated by operation of law through the occurrence of the following events:

1. Lapse of time.
2. Destruction of the specific subject matter of the offer.
3. Death or incompetence of the offeror or the offeree.
4. Supervening illegality of the proposed contract.

Lapse of Time An offer terminates automatically by law when the period of time specified in the offer has passed. For example, suppose Alejandro offers to sell his camper to Kelly if she accepts within twenty days. Kelly must accept within the twenty-day period, or the offer will lapse (terminate). The time period specified in an offer normally begins to run when the offer is actually received by the offeree, not when it is sent or drawn up. When the offer is delayed (through the misdelivery of mail, for example), the period begins to run from the date the offeree would have received the offer, but only if the offeree knows or should know that the offer is delayed.[11]

If no time for acceptance is specified in the offer, the offer terminates at the end of a *reasonable* period of time. What constitutes a reasonable period of time depends on the subject matter of the contract, business and market conditions, and other relevant circumstances. An offer to sell farm produce, for example, will terminate sooner than an offer to sell farm equipment because farm produce is perishable and subject to greater fluctuations in market value.

Destruction of the Subject Matter. An offer is automatically terminated if the specific subject matter of the offer is destroyed before the offer is accepted.[12] If Johnson offers to sell his prize greyhound to Rizzo, for example, but the dog dies before Rizzo can accept, the offer is automatically terminated. Johnson does not have to tell Rizzo that the animal has died for the offer to terminate.

Death or Incompetence of the Offeror or Offeree. An offeree's power of acceptance is terminated when the offeror or offeree dies or is deprived of legal capacity to enter into the proposed contract. If the offer is irrevocable, however, the death of the offeror or offeree does not terminate the offer.[13] A revocable offer is personal to both parties and cannot pass to the heirs, guardian, or estate of either. Furthermore, this rule applies whether or not the other party had notice of the death or incompetence.

Supervening Illegality of the Proposed Contract. When a statute or court decision makes an offer illegal, the offer is automatically terminated.[14] For example, Lee offers to loan Kim $10,000 at an annual interest rate of 12 percent. Before Kim can accept the offer, a law is enacted that prohibits interest rates higher than 10 percent. Lee's offer is automatically terminated. If the law had been passed after Kim accepted the offer, a valid contract would have been formed, because the offer would still have been legal when it was accepted. In some circumstances, such a contract might be unenforceable, however, as when a statute or law is retroactively applied.

10. The mirror image rule has been greatly modified in regard to sales contracts. Section 2–207 of the UCC provides that a contract is formed if the offeree makes a definite expression of acceptance (such as signing the form in the appropriate location), even though the terms of the acceptance modify or add to the terms of the original offer (see Chapter 18).

11. *Restatement (Second) of Contracts,* Section 49.

12. *Restatement (Second) of Contracts,* Section 36.

13. *Restatement (Second) of Contracts,* Section 48. If the offer is such that it can be accepted by the performance of a series of acts, and those acts began before the offeror died, the offeree's power of acceptance is not terminated.

14. *Restatement (Second) of Contracts,* Section 36.

SECTION 3

Acceptance

Acceptance is a voluntary act (either words or conduct) by the offeree that shows assent (agreement) to the terms of an offer. The acceptance must be unequivocal and communicated to the offeror.

UNEQUIVOCAL ACCEPTANCE

To exercise the power of acceptance effectively, the offeree must accept unequivocally. This is the *mirror image rule* previously discussed. If the acceptance is subject to new conditions or if the terms of the acceptance materially change the original offer, the acceptance may be deemed a counteroffer that implicitly rejects the original offer. An acceptance may be unequivocal even though the offeree expresses dissatisfaction with the contract. For example, "I accept the offer, but I wish I could have gotten a better price" is an effective acceptance. So, too, is "I accept, but can you shave the price?" In contrast, the statement "I accept the offer but only if I can pay on ninety days' credit" is not an unequivocal acceptance and operates as a counteroffer, rejecting the original offer.

Certain terms when added to an acceptance will not qualify the acceptance sufficiently to constitute rejection of the offer. Suppose that in response to an offer to sell a piano, the offeree replies, "I accept; please send a written contract." The offeree is requesting a written contract but is not making it a condition for acceptance. Therefore, the acceptance is effective without the written contract. If the offeree replies, "I accept if you send a written contract," however, the acceptance is expressly conditioned on the request for a writing, and the statement is not an acceptance but a counteroffer. (Notice how important each word is!)[15]

SILENCE AS ACCEPTANCE

Ordinarily, silence cannot constitute acceptance, even if the offeror states, "By your silence and inaction you will be deemed to have accepted this offer." This general rule applies because an offeree should not be obligated to act affirmatively to reject an offer when no consideration has passed to the offeree to impose such a duty.

In some instances, however, the offeree does have a duty to speak, in which case his or her silence or inaction will operate as an acceptance. For example, silence may be an acceptance when an offeree takes the benefit of offered services even though he or she had an opportunity to reject them and knew that they were offered with the expectation of compensation. Suppose that Sayre watches while a stranger rakes his leaves, even though the stranger has not been asked to rake the yard. Sayre knows the stranger expects to be paid and does nothing to stop her. Here, his silence constitutes an acceptance, and an implied-in-fact contract is created (see Chapter 9). He is bound to pay a reasonable value for the stranger's work. This rule normally applies only when the offeree has received a benefit from the goods or services rendered.

Silence can also operate as acceptance when the offeree has had prior dealings with the offeror. Suppose that a merchant routinely receives shipments from a certain supplier and always notifies the supplier when defective goods are rejected. In this situation, silence regarding a shipment will constitute acceptance. Additionally, if a person solicits an offer specifying that certain terms and conditions are acceptable, and the offeror makes the offer in response to the solicitation, the offeree has a duty to reject—that is, a duty to tell the offeror that the offer is not acceptable. Failure to reject (silence) operates as an acceptance.

COMMUNICATION OF ACCEPTANCE

Whether the offeror must be notified of the acceptance depends on the nature of the contract. In a bilateral contract, communication of acceptance is necessary because acceptance is in the form of a promise (not performance) and the contract is formed when the promise is made (rather than when the act is performed). The offeree must communicate the acceptance to the offeror. Communication of acceptance is not necessary, however, if the offer dispenses with the requirement. Additionally, if the offer can be accepted by silence, no communication is necessary. Because in a unilateral contract the full performance of some act is called for, acceptance is usually evident, and notification is therefore unnecessary. Exceptions do exist, however. When the offeror requests notice of acceptance or has no

15. As noted in footnote 10, in regard to sales contracts the UCC provides that an acceptance may still be valid even if some terms are added. The new terms are simply treated as proposals for addition to the contract.

adequate means of determining whether the requested act has been performed, or when the law requires notice of acceptance, then notice is necessary.[16]

Mode and Timeliness of Acceptance

Acceptance in bilateral contracts must be timely. The general rule is that acceptance in a bilateral contract is timely if it is made before the offer is terminated. Problems arise, however, when the parties involved are not dealing face to face. In such cases, acceptance takes effect, thus completing formation of the contract, at the time the acceptance is communicated via the mode expressly or impliedly authorized by the offeror. According to the *Restatement (Second) of Contracts,* unless the offeror provides otherwise, "an acceptance made in a manner and by a medium invited by an offer is operative and completes the manifestation of mutual assent as soon as put out of the offeree's possession, without regard to whether it ever reaches the offeror."[17]

This rule traditionally has been referred to as the **mailbox rule,** also called the "deposited acceptance rule," because once an acceptance has been deposited into a mailbox, it is "out of the offeree's possession." Under this rule, if the authorized mode of communication is the mail, then an acceptance becomes valid when it is dispatched by mail (even if it is never received by the offeror). Thus, whereas a revocation becomes effective only when it is received by the offeree, an acceptance becomes effective on *dispatch,* providing that *authorized* means of communication are used.

Authorized Means of Acceptance. An authorized means of communication may be either expressly authorized—that is, expressly stipulated in the offer—or impliedly authorized by the facts and circumstances surrounding the situation or by law. When an offeror specifies how acceptance should be made (for example, by overnight delivery), *express authorization* is said to exist, and the contract is not formed unless the offeree uses that specified mode of acceptance. Moreover, both offeror and offeree are bound in contract the moment this means of acceptance is employed. If overnight delivery is expressly authorized as the only means of acceptance, a contract is created as soon as the offeree delivers the message to the express delivery company. The contract would still exist even if the delivery company failed to deliver the message.

Many offerors, for one reason or another, do not indicate their preferred method of acceptance. When the offeror does not specify expressly that the offeree is to accept by a certain means, or that the acceptance will be effective only when received, acceptance of an offer may be made by any medium that is *reasonable under the circumstances.*[18] When two parties are at a distance, for example, mailing is impliedly authorized because it is a customary mode of dispatch.[19] Several factors determine whether the acceptance was reasonable: the nature of the circumstances as they existed at the time the offer was made, the means used by the offeror to transmit the offer to the offeree, and the reliability of the offer's delivery. If, for example, an offer was sent by FedEx overnight delivery because an acceptance was urgently required, then the offeree's use of first-class mail (which may take three days or more to deliver) might not be deemed reasonable.[20]

An acceptance sent by means not expressly or impliedly authorized is normally not effective until it is received by the offeror. If an acceptance is timely sent and timely received, however, despite the means by which it is transmitted, it is considered to have been effective on its dispatch.[21] If, in the previous example, the acceptance that was sent by first-class mail was actually delivered to the offeror the next day (the same as FedEx overnight delivery), then the court would recognize the acceptance as operative.

Westlaw. See Case 10.2 at the end of this chapter. To view the full, unedited case from Westlaw,® go to this text's Web site at **http://wbl-cs.westbuslaw.com**.

16. Under UCC 2–206(1)(b), an order or other offer to buy goods for prompt shipment may be treated as an offer contemplating either a bilateral or a unilateral contract and may be accepted by either a promise to ship or actual shipment. If the offer is accepted by actual shipment of the goods, the offeror must be notified of the acceptance within a reasonable period of time, or the offeror may treat the offer as having lapsed before acceptance [UCC 2–206(2)]. See also Chapter 18.

17. *Restatement (Second) of Contracts,* Section 63(a).

18. *Restatement (Second) of Contracts,* Section 30. This is also the rule under UCC 2–206(1)(a).

19. *Adams v. Lindsell,* 106 Eng.Rep. 250 (K.B. 1818); *Restatement (Second) of Contracts,* Section 65, Comment c.

20. See, for example, *Defeo v. Amfarms Associates,* 161 A.D.2d 904, 557 N.Y.2d 469 (1990).

21. *Restatement (Second) of Contracts,* Section 67.

Exceptions. There are three basic exceptions to the rule that a contract is formed when an acceptance is sent by authorized means.

1. If the acceptance is not properly dispatched by the offeree (if it was sent to an incorrect address, for example), in most states it will not be effective until it is received by the offeror.[22] For example, if mail is the authorized means for acceptance, the offeree's letter must be properly addressed and have the correct postage. Nonetheless, if acceptance is timely sent and timely received, despite the offeree's carelessness in sending it, it is still considered to have been effective on dispatch.[23]
2. The offeror can stipulate in the offer that an acceptance will not be effective until it is received by the offeror.
3. Sometimes an offeree sends a rejection first, then later changes his or her mind and sends an acceptance. Obviously, this chain of events could cause confusion and even detriment to the offeror, depending on whether the rejection or the acceptance arrived first. Because of this, the law cancels the rule of acceptance on dispatch in such situations, and the first communication to be received by the offeror determines whether a contract is formed. If the rejection is received first, there is no contract.[24]

22. *Restatement (Second) of Contracts,* Section 66.
23. *Restatement (Second) of Contracts,* Section 67.
24. *Restatement (Second) of Contracts,* Section 40.

ONLINE ACCEPTANCES

Technology, and particularly the Internet, has changed profoundly the way in which contracts are formed. While online offers are not significantly different from conventional offers contained in paper documents, some elements of traditional contract law do not apply to online acceptances. In the cyber environment, for example, offers are presented online, and acceptance is typically indicated by clicking on a box stating "I agree" or "I accept." Clearly, the mailbox rule is not applicable to online acceptances, because the acceptance is communicated virtually instantaneously to the offeror.

An initial question in the cyber age was whether contracts formed using click-on acceptances were even enforceable. Generally, the courts have concluded that a click-on acceptance essentially constitutes acceptance by conduct and results in a valid contract. (For a more detailed discussion of how traditional contract law is being applied to online acceptances, see Chapter 23.)

TERMS AND CONCEPTS TO REVIEW

acceptance 219	**mailbox rule 220**	**option contract 216**
agreement 213	**mirror image rule 218**	**promissory estoppel 217**
counteroffer 218	**mutual assent 213**	**revocation 216**
estop 217	**offer 213**	

CHAPTER SUMMARY

Requirements of the Offer	1. *Intent*—There must be a serious, objective intention by the offeror to become bound by the offer. Nonoffer situations include (a) expressions of opinion; (b) statements of intention; (c) preliminary negotiations; (d) generally, advertisements, catalogues, price lists, and circulars; (e) solicitations for bids made by an auctioneer; and (f) traditionally, agreements to agree in the future. 2. *Definiteness*—The terms of the offer must be sufficiently definite to be ascertainable by the parties or by a court. 3. *Communication*—The offer must be communicated to the offeree.

CHAPTER SUMMARY—CONTINUED

Termination of the Offer	1. *By action of the parties—* a. Revocation—Unless the offer is irrevocable, it can be revoked at any time before acceptance without liability. Revocation is not effective until received by the offeree or the offeree's agent. Some offers, such as the merchant's firm offer and option contracts, are irrevocable. b. Rejection—Accomplished by words or actions that demonstrate a clear intent not to accept the offer; not effective until received by the offeror or the offeror's agent. c. Counteroffer—A rejection of the original offer and the making of a new offer. 2. *By operation of law—* a. Lapse of time—Terminates the offer (1) at the end of the time period specified in the offer or (2) if no time period is stated in the offer, at the end of a reasonable time period. b. Destruction of the specific subject matter of the offer—Automatically terminates the offer. c. Death or incompetence—Terminates the offer unless the offer is irrevocable. d. Illegality—Supervening illegality terminates the offer.
Acceptance	1. Can be made only by the offeree or the offeree's agent. 2. Must be unequivocal. Under the common law (mirror image rule), if new terms or conditions are added to the acceptance, it will be considered a counteroffer. 3. Acceptance of a unilateral offer is effective on full performance of the requested act. Generally, no communication is necessary. 4. Acceptance of a bilateral offer can be communicated by the offeree by any authorized mode of communication and is effective on dispatch. Unless the mode of communication is expressly specified by the offeror, the following methods are impliedly authorized: a. The same mode used by the offeror or a faster mode. b. Mail, when the two parties are at a distance. c. In sales contracts, by any reasonable medium. 5. When forming electronic contracts, acceptance is normally indicated by clicking on a box or icon stating "I agree" or "I accept." The courts have generally held that such click-on acceptances are a form of acceptance by conduct and result in valid contracts (see Chapter 23).

CASES FOR ANALYSIS

Westlaw. You can access the full text of each case presented below by going to the Westlaw cases on this text's Web site at http://wbl-cs.westbuslaw.com. Each Westlaw case includes the names of all plaintiffs and defendants, the dates on which the case was argued and decided, a brief summary of the issues and decisions in the case, headnotes classifying specific issues in the case according to the West Key Number System, and the court's opinion. Concurring and dissenting opinions, if any, are included as well.

CASE 10.1 INTENTION

LUCY V. ZEHMER

Supreme Court of Appeals of Virginia, 1954.
196 Va. 493,
84 S.E.2d 516.

BUCHANAN, J. [Judge], delivered the opinion of the court.

This suit was instituted by W. O. Lucy and J. C. Lucy, complainants, against A. H. Zehmer and Ida S. Zehmer, his wife, defendants, to have specific performance of a contract by which it was alleged the Zehmers had sold to W. O. Lucy a tract of land owned by A. H. Zehmer in Dinwiddie County containing 471.6 acres, more or less, known as the Ferguson farm, for $50,000. J. C. Lucy, the other complainant, is a brother of W. O.

Lucy, to whom W. O. Lucy transferred a half interest in his alleged purchase.

The instrument sought to be enforced was written by A. H. Zehmer on December 20, 1952, in these words: "We hereby agree to sell to W. O. Lucy the Ferguson Farm complete for $50,000.00, title satisfactory to buyer," and signed by the defendants, A. H. Zehmer and Ida S. Zehmer.

* * * *

Depositions were taken and the decree appealed from was entered holding that the complainants had failed to establish their right to specific performance * * *.

W. O. Lucy, a lumberman and farmer, thus testified in substance:

He had known Zehmer for fifteen or twenty years and had been familiar with the Ferguson farm for ten years. Seven or eight years ago he had offered Zehmer $20,000 for the farm which Zehmer had accepted, but the agreement was verbal and Zehmer backed out. On the night of December 20, 1952, around eight o'clock, he took an employee to McKenney, where Zehmer lived and operated a restaurant, filling station and motor court. While there he decided to see Zehmer and again try to buy the Ferguson farm. He entered the restaurant and talked to Mrs. Zehmer until Zehmer came in. He asked Zehmer if he had sold the Ferguson farm. Zehmer replied that he had not. Lucy said, "I bet you wouldn't take $50,000.00 for that place." Zehmer replied, "Yes, I would too; you wouldn't give fifty." Lucy said he would and told Zehmer to write up an agreement to that effect. Zehmer took a restaurant check and wrote on the back of it, "I do hereby agree to sell to W. O. Lucy the Ferguson Farm for $50,000 complete." Lucy told him he had better change it to "We" because Mrs. Zehmer would have to sign it too. Zehmer then tore up what he had written, wrote the agreement quoted above and asked Mrs. Zehmer, who was at the other end of the counter ten or twelve feet away, to sign it. Mrs. Zehmer said she would for $50,000 and signed it. Zehmer brought it back and gave it to Lucy, who offered him $5 which Zehmer refused, saying, "You don't need to give me any money, you got the agreement there signed by both of us."

The discussion leading to the signing of the agreement, said Lucy, lasted thirty or forty minutes, during which Zehmer seemed to doubt that Lucy could raise $50,000. Lucy suggested the provision for having the title examined and Zehmer made the suggestion that he would sell it "complete, everything there," and stated that all he had on the farm was three heifers.

Lucy took a partly filled bottle of whiskey into the restaurant with him for the purpose of giving Zehmer a drink if he wanted it. Zehmer did, and he and Lucy had one or two drinks together. Lucy said that while he felt the drinks he took he was not intoxicated, and from the way Zehmer handled the transaction he did not think he was either.

* * * *

* * * Zehmer testified in substance as follows:

He bought this farm more than ten years ago for $11,000. He had had twenty-five offers, more or less, to buy it, including several from Lucy, who had never offered any specific sum of money. He had given them all the same answer, that he was not interested in selling it. On this Saturday night before Christmas it looked like everybody and his brother came by there to have a drink. He took a good many drinks during the afternoon and had a pint of his own. When he entered the restaurant around eight-thirty Lucy was there and he could see that he was "pretty high." He said to Lucy, "Boy, you got some good liquor, drinking, ain't you?" Lucy then offered him a drink. "I was already high as a Georgia pine, and didn't have any more better sense than to pour another great big slug out and gulp it down, and he took one too."

After they had talked a while Lucy asked whether he still had the Ferguson farm. He replied that he had not sold it and Lucy said, "I bet you wouldn't take $50,000.00 for it." Zehmer asked him if he would give $50,000 and Lucy said yes. Zehmer replied, "You haven't got $50,000 in cash." Lucy said he did and Zehmer replied that he did not believe it. They argued "pro and con for a long time," mainly about "whether he had $50,000 in cash that he could put up right then and buy that farm."

Finally, said Zehmer, Lucy told him if he didn't believe he had $50,000, "you sign that piece of paper here and say you will take $50,000.00 for the farm." He, Zehmer, "just grabbed the back off of a guest check there" and wrote on the back of it. At that point in his testimony Zehmer asked to see what he had written to "see if I recognize my own handwriting." He examined the paper and exclaimed, "Great balls of fire, I got 'Firgerson' for Ferguson. I have got satisfactory spelled wrong. I don't recognize that writing if I would see it, wouldn't know it was mine."

After Zehmer had, as he described it, "scribbled this thing off," Lucy said, "Get your wife to sign it." Zehmer walked over to where she was and she at first refused to sign but did so after he told her that he "was just needling him [Lucy], and didn't mean a thing in the world, that I was not selling the farm." Zehmer then "took it back over there * * * and I was still looking at the dern thing. I had the drink right there by my hand, and I reached over to get a drink, and he said, 'Let me see it.' He reached and picked it up, and when I looked back again he had it in his pocket and he dropped a five dollar bill over there, and he said, 'Here is five dollars payment on it.' * * * I said, 'Hell no, that is beer and liquor talking. I am not going to sell you the farm. I have told you that too many times before."

* * * *

In his testimony Zehmer claimed that he "was high as a Georgia pine," and that the transaction "was just a bunch of two doggoned drunks bluffing to see who could talk the biggest and say the most." That claim is inconsistent with his attempt to testify in great detail as to what was said and what was done. It is contradicted by other evidence as to the condition of both parties, and rendered of no weight by the testimony of his wife that when Lucy left the restaurant she suggested that Zehmer drive him home. *The record is convincing that Zehmer was not intoxicated to the extent of being unable to comprehend the nature and consequences of the instrument he executed, and hence that instrument is not to be invalidated on that ground.* It was in fact conceded by defendants' counsel in oral argument that under the evidence Zehmer was not too drunk to make a valid contract. [Emphasis added.]

The evidence is convincing also that Zehmer wrote two agreements, the first one beginning "I hereby agree to sell." Zehmer first said he could not remember about that, then that "I don't think I wrote but one out." Mrs. Zehmer said that what he wrote was "I hereby agree," but that the "I" was changed to "We" after that night. The agreement that was written and signed is in the record and indicates no such change. Neither are the mistakes in spelling that Zehmer sought to point out readily apparent.

The appearance of the contract, the fact that it was under discussion for forty minutes or more before it was signed; Lucy's objection to the first draft because it was written in the singular, and he wanted Mrs. Zehmer to sign it also; the rewriting to meet that objection and the signing by Mrs. Zehmer; the discussion of what was to be included in the sale, the provision for the examination of the title, the completeness of the instrument that was executed, the taking possession of it by Lucy with no request or suggestion by either of the defendants that he give it back, are facts which furnish persuasive evidence that the execution of the contract was a serious business transaction rather than a casual, jesting matter as defendants now contend.

* * * *

In the field of contracts, as generally elsewhere, *[w]e must look to the outward expression of a person as manifesting his intention rather than to his secret and unexpressed intention.* The law imputes to a person an intention corresponding to the reasonable meaning of his words and acts. [Emphasis added.]

* * * *

Whether the writing signed by the defendants and now sought to be enforced by the complainants was the result of a serious offer by Lucy and a serious acceptance by the defendants, or was a serious offer by Lucy and an acceptance in secret jest by the defendants, in either event it constituted a binding contract of sale between the parties.

* * * *

The complainants are entitled to have specific performance of the contracts sued on. The decree appealed from is therefore reversed and the cause is remanded for the entry of a proper decree requiring the defendants to perform the contract * * * .

CASE 10.2 MODE AND TIMELINESS OF ACCEPTANCE

OSPREY L.L.C. v. KELLY-MOORE PAINT CO.

Supreme Court of Oklahoma, 1999.
1999 OK 50,
984 P.2d 194.

KAUGER, J. [Judge]:

* * * *

FACTS

The appellant, Osprey, an Oklahoma limited liability company (Osprey), owns commercial property in Edmond, Oklahoma. On March 18, 1977, the appellee, Kelly-Moore Paint Company (Kelly-Moore), a California corporation, negotiated a fifteen-year lease for its Edmond, Oklahoma, store with Osprey's predecessors James and Victoria Fulmer. The lease contained two five-year renewal options which required that the lessee give notice of its intent to renew the lease at least six months prior to its expiration date. The lease also provided that all notices "shall be given in writing and may be delivered either personally or by depositing the same in United States mail, first class postage prepaid, registered or certified mail, return receipt requested."

It is undisputed that after the first fifteen years, Kelly-Moore timely informed Osprey's predecessors by certified letter of its intent to extend the lease an additional five years. The first five-year extension was due to expire on August 31, 1997. According to the property manager of Kelly-Moore, she telephoned one of the owners of Osprey in January of 1997, to inform him that Kelly-Moore intended to extend its lease for the remaining five-year period. On Friday, February 28, 1997, the last day of the six-month notification deadline, Kelly-Moore faxed a letter of renewal notice to Osprey's office at 5:28 P.M., Oklahoma time. Kelly-Moore also sent a copy of the faxed renewal notice letter by Federal Express the same day.

Although the fax activity report and telephone company records confirm that the fax was transmitted successfully and that it was sent to Osprey's correct facsimile number, Osprey denies ever receiving the fax. The Federal Express copy of the notice was scheduled for delivery on Saturday, March 1, 1997. However, Osprey actually received it on Monday, March 3, 1997. In a letter dated March 6, 1997, Osprey acknowledged that it had received Kelly-Moore's Federal Express notice; denied that the notice was timely according to the terms of the lease; and it rejected the notice as untimely. In July of 1997, Osprey wrote Kelly-Moore reminding it to vacate the premises by August 31, 1997. Kelly-Moore refused to vacate, insisting that it had effectively extended the lease term for the remaining five years.

On September 2, 1997, Osprey filed an action * * * in the district court of Oklahoma County. It alleged that Kelly-Moore wrongfully possessed the property and that it refused to vacate the premises. Kelly-Moore argued that it was entitled to possession of the property because of its timely renewal of the lease. After a trial on the merits, the trial court granted judgment in favor of Kelly-Moore, finding that the faxed notice was effective. Osprey appealed. The Court of Civil Appeals reversed, determining that the plain language of the lease required that it be renewed for an additional term by delivering notice either personally or by mail, and that Kelly-Moore had done neither. We granted *certiorari* on April 13, 1999, to address the question of first impression.

* * * *

The contested portions of the lease provide in pertinent part:

> " * * * 20. OPTION TO RENEW * * * The Lessee must, in order to exercise each such renewal option give to the Lessor at least six (6) months prior to the expiration of the term hereof or the extended term, written notice of the Lessee's intention to renew this lease as by this paragraph provided * * * .
>
> 26. NOTICES. All notices required to be given hereunder by Lessee or Lessor *shall* be given in writing and *may* be delivered either personally or by depositing the same in the United States mail, first class postage prepaid, registered or certified mail, return receipt requested, addressed to the party to receive the same at that party's address hereinabove first written or to such changed address as the party may have from time to time during the term hereof notified the other party. Notices which are mailed shall be deemed delivered three (3) days after having been deposited in the United States mail as herein. * * *
>
> 29. TIME. Time is hereby expressly declared to be the essence of this lease and of all the covenants, agreements, terms, conditions, restrictions and obligations herein contained." [Emphasis added.]

Osprey argues that: 1) the lease specifically prescribed limited means of acceptance of the option, and it required that the notice of renewal be delivered either personally or sent by United States mail, registered or certified; 2) Kelly-Moore failed to follow the contractual requirements of the lease when it delivered its notice by fax; and 3) because the terms for extending the lease specified in the contract were not met, the notice was invalid and the lease expired on August 31, 1997. Kelly-Moore counters that: 1) the lease by the use of the word "shall" mandates that the notice be written, but the use of the word "may" is permissive; and 2) although the notice provision of the lease permits delivery personally or by United States mail, it does not exclude other modes of delivery or transmission which would include delivery by facsimile. Kelly-Moore also asserts that the lease specified that time was of the essence and that faxing the notice was the functional equivalent of personal delivery because it provided virtually instantaneous communication.

Although the question tendered is novel in Oklahoma, the sufficiency of the notice given when exercising an option contract or an option to renew or extend a lease has been considered by several jurisdictions. A few have found that delivery of notice by means other than hand delivery or by certified or registered mail was insufficient if the terms of the contract specifically referred to the method of delivery. However, the majority have reached the opposite conclusion. These courts generally recognize that, despite the contention that there must be strict compliance with the notice terms of a lease option agreement, *use of an alternative method does not render the notice defective if the substituted method performed the same function or served the same purpose as the authorized method.* [Emphasis added.]

A lease is a contract and in construing a lease, the usual rules for the interpretation of contractual writings apply. Generally, the terms of the parties' contract, if unambiguous, clear, and consistent, are accepted in their plain and ordinary sense and the contract will be enforced to carry out the intention of the parties as it existed at the time the contract was negotiated. The interpretation of a contract, and whether it is ambiguous is a matter of law for the Court to determine and resolve.

Language in a contract is given its plain and ordinary meaning, unless some technical term is used in a manner meant to convey a specific technical concept. A contract term is ambiguous only if it can be interpreted as having two different meanings. Nevertheless, the Court will not create an ambiguity by using a forced or strained construction, by taking a provision out of context, or by narrowly focusing on provision. The lease does not appear to be ambiguous. "Shall" is ordinarily construed as mandatory and "may" is ordinarily construed as permissive. The contract clearly requires that notice "shall" be in writing. The provision for delivery, either personally or by certified or registered mail, uses the permissive "may" and it does not bar other modes of transmission which are just as effective.

The purpose of providing notice by personal delivery or registered mail is to insure the delivery of the notice, and to settle any dispute which might arise between the parties concerning whether the notice was received. *A substituted method of notice which performs the same function and serves the same purpose as an authorized method of notice is not defective.* Here, the contract provided that time was of the essence. Although Osprey denies that it ever received the fax, the fax activity report and telephone company records confirm that the fax was transmitted successfully, and that it was sent to Osprey's correct facsimile number on the last day of the deadline to extend the lease. The fax provided immediate written communication similar to personal delivery and, like a telegram, would be timely if it were properly transmitted before the expiration of the deadline to renew. Kelly-Moore's use of the fax served the same function and the same purpose as the two methods suggested by the lease and it was transmitted before the expiration of the deadline to renew. Under these facts, we hold that the faxed or facsimile delivery of the written notice to renew the commercial lease was sufficient to exercise timely the renewal option of the lease. [Emphasis added.]

CONCLUSION

Use of an alternative method of notification of the exercise of a lease option does not render the notice defective if the substituted notice performed the same function or served the same purpose as the authorized method. Here, the lease provision concerned uses the permissive "may" rather than the mandatory "shall" and refers to personal delivery or registered or certified mail, but it does not require these methods of delivery, to the exclusion of other modes of transmission which serve the same purpose.

* * * **COURT OF CIVIL APPEALS OPINION VACATED; TRIAL COURT AFFIRMED.**

CASE PROBLEMS

10–1. Dodds signed and delivered to Dickinson the following memorandum on Wednesday, June 10:

> I hereby agree to sell to Mr. George Dickinson the whole of the dwelling-houses, garden ground, stabling, and outbuildings thereto belonging, situated at Croft, belonging to me, for the sum of £800 [£ is the symbol for British pounds]. As witness my hand this tenth day of June, 1874.
> £800 [signed] John Dodds.
>
> P.S. This offer to be left over until Friday, 9 o'clock A.M. J.D. (the twelfth) 12th June, 1874
> [Signed] J. Dodds.

The next afternoon (Thursday), Dickinson's agent told Dickinson that Dodds had decided to sell the property to a man named Allan and was negotiating with Allan for that purpose. That evening, Dickinson went to the house of Dodds's mother-in-law and left her a written acceptance. This document never reached Dodds. The next morning, at 7 A.M., Dickinson's agent gave Dodds a copy of the acceptance. Dodds replied that it was too late, as he had already sold the property. Did Dickinson's knowledge that Dodds was negotiating to sell the property to Allan revoke Dodds's offer to Dickinson? Explain. [*Dickinson v. Dodds,* 2 Ch.D. 463 (1876)]

10–2. Central Properties, Inc., entered into a contract with Robbinson and Westside (Westside), a real estate development company, whereby Central Properties purchased sixty acres of land. The contract included a "right of first refusal" to purchase the water and sewage system on the remaining property of Westside. Westside wanted to sell the sewage system and over the course of three months exchanged letters with Central asking whether it wished to exercise its "right." Central Properties never affirmatively accepted in any of its responses but requested different terms, price, and so on. Central now wishes to hold Westside to a contract for the system. Westside states that no contract was formed. Discuss who is right. [*Central Properties, Inc. v. Robbinson,* 450 So.2d 277 (Fla.App. 1st Dist. 1984)]

10–3. On July 31, 1966, Lee Calan Imports, Inc. (the defendant), advertised a 1964 Volvo station wagon for sale in the *Chicago Sun Times.* The defendant had instructed the newspaper to advertise the price of the automobile at $1,795. Due to the newspaper's mistake, however, and without fault on the part of the defendant, the newspaper inserted a price of $1,095 for the automobile in the advertisement. Christopher O'Brien (the plaintiff) visited the defendant's place of business, examined the automobile, and stated that he wished to purchase it for $1,095. One of the defendant's sales agents at first agreed, but then refused to sell the car for the erroneous price listed in the advertisement. O'Brien sued Lee Calan Imports for breach of contract, claiming the ad constituted an offer that had been accepted by O'Brien. O'Brien died before the trial, and his administrator (O'Keefe) continued the suit. Discuss whether there is a contract. [*O'Keefe v. Lee Calan Imports, Inc.,* 128 Ill.App.2d 410, 262 N.E.2d 758 (1970)]

10–4. In August 1984, James and Barbara Gibbs submitted an offer for $180,000 to American Savings & Loan Association to purchase a house. The Gibbses submitted another offer on March 27, 1985, after learning from an American Savings employee, Dorothy Folkman, that their original offer had been lost. On the morning of June 6, 1985, the Gibbses received a counteroffer from American Savings containing several additional terms and conditions, but nothing was mentioned about the purchase price. Barbara Gibbs later claimed that she and her husband immediately signed the counteroffer—which American Savings had requested her to do if she wished to accept it—and at 10 A.M. on that same day handed an envelope containing the signed counteroffer to the mail clerk at her office, with instructions to mail it for her. (The mail clerk was not an employee of the U.S. Postal Service but an employee of Barbara's firm who handled the firm's mail.) An hour later, at 11 A.M., Barbara had a telephone conversation with Dorothy Folkman in which Folkman said that the counteroffer was in error, since American Savings had intended to increase the sales price to $198,000. Folkman said that because of this error the counteroffer was revoked. The Gibbses insisted that they had accepted the counteroffer before it was revoked. The trial court held that no contract had been formed because the actual postmark on the envelope was not June 6 but June 7. The Gibbses appealed, contending that they had placed the acceptance in the "course of transmission" at 10 A.M. on June 6 when Barbara handed the letter to the mail clerk in her office. Does handing the counteroffer to the mail clerk in her office constitute dispatch by mail in this case? Discuss. [*Gibbs v. American Savings & Loan Association,* 217 Cal.App.3d 1372, 266 Cal.Rptr. 517 (1990)]

10–5. Chia and Shin Chang read First Colonial Bank's advertisement about the bank's saving certificates, which stated that a depositor could deposit $14,000, receive a gift immediately, and collect $20,136.12 in three and a half years when the certificate matured. The Changs, in reliance on the ad, deposited $14,000 at First Colonial and received a color television and a certificate of deposit. When they cashed in the certificate on its maturity, however, they received only $18,823.93 instead of the promised $20,136.12. First Colonial informed the Changs that the advertisement had contained a typographical error and that they would have had to deposit $15,000, not $14,000, to receive $20,136.12. The Changs filed suit to recover $1,312.19, the difference between the amount they received and the amount they had expected. Did the newspaper advertisement constitute an offer that, when accepted, created a legally enforceable contract? Explain. [*Chang v. First Colonial Savings Bank,* 242 Va. 388, 410 S.E.2d 928 (1991)]

10–6. John H. Surratt was one of John Wilkes Booth's alleged accomplices in the murder of President Lincoln. On April 20, 1865, the Secretary of War issued and caused to be published in newspapers the following proclamation: "$25,000 reward for the apprehension of John H. Surratt and liberal rewards for any information that leads to the arrest of John H. Surratt." On November 24, 1865, President Johnson revoked the reward and published the revocation in the newspapers. Henry B. St. Marie learned of the reward but left for Rome prior to its revocation. In Rome, St. Marie discovered Surratt's whereabouts. In April 1866, unaware that the reward had been revoked, he reported this information to U.S. officials. Based on this information, the officials were able to arrest Surratt. Should St. Marie have received the reward? If so, was he entitled to the full $25,000? [*Shuey v. United States,* 92 U.S. (2 Otto) 73, 23 L.Ed. 697 (1875)]

10–7. The Olivers were planning to sell some of their ranch land and mentioned this fact to Southworth, a neighbor. Southworth expressed interest in purchasing the property and later notified the Olivers that he had the money available to buy it. The Olivers told Southworth they would let him know shortly about the details concerning the sale. The Olivers later sent a letter to Southworth—and (unknown to Southworth) to several other neighbors—giving information about the sale, including the price, the location of the property, and the amount of acreage involved. When Southworth received the letter, he sent a letter to the Olivers "accepting" their offer. The Olivers stated that the information letter had not been intended as an "offer" but merely as a starting point for negotiations. Southworth brought suit against the Olivers to enforce the "contract." Did a contract exist? Explain. [*Southworth v. Oliver,* 284 Or. 361, 587 P.2d 994 (1978)]

10–8. The Jewish War Veterans of the United States placed in the newspaper an offer of a reward of $500 "to the person or persons furnishing information resulting in the apprehension and conviction of the persons guilty of the murder of Maurice L. Bernstein." Mary Glover gave police information that led to the arrest and conviction of the murderers, not knowing that a reward had been offered and not learning of it until the next day. In an action brought before a District of Columbia trial court, the court held that Glover was not entitled to the reward because no contract existed. Why would the court reach this conclusion? Will the trial court's decision be upheld on appeal? Discuss fully. [*Glover v. Jewish War Veterans of the United States, Post No. 58,* 68 A.2d 233 (D.C.App. 1949)]

10–9. Treece, a vice president of Vend-A-Win, Inc., was testifying before the Washington State Gambling Commission concerning an application his firm had made for a temporary license to distribute punchboards (gambling devices). The Gambling Commission was conducting an investigation into gambling practices, and Treece's testimony was given during a televised hearing. Treece made the following statement at the hearing: "I'll pay $100,000 to anyone to find a crooked board. If they find it, I'll pay it." The audience laughed, and Treece thought no more about the offer until he received a telephone call from Barnes. Barnes had watched Treece's television appearance and later read about Treece's statement in a newspaper. Barnes asked Treece if Treece had been serious when he made the statement, and Treece affirmed that he had been serious. Barnes then brought a crooked board into Vend-A-Win's offices and delivered another crooked board to the Gambling Commission. When Vend-A-Win and Treece refused to pay Barnes $100,000, Barnes sued them for the promised amount, claiming that Treece had made an offer for a unilateral contract. What will the court decide? Explain. [*Barnes v. Treece,* 15 Wash.App. 437, 549 P.2d 1152 (1976)]

10–10. Cora Payne was involved in an automobile accident with Don Chappell, an employee of E & B Carpet Cleaning, Inc. E & B's insurance company offered Payne $18,500 to settle her claim against E & B. Payne did not accept the offer at that time but instead filed suit against E & B and its insurance company (the defendants). Later, Payne offered to settle the case for $50,000, but the defendants refused her offer. Ultimately, Payne told the defendants that she would accept the insurance company's original settlement offer of $18,500, but the insurance company stated that the offer was no longer open for acceptance. When Payne sought to compel the defendants to perform the original settlement offer, the defendants contended that Payne's filing of her lawsuit terminated the insurance company's earlier settlement offer. Will the court agree with the defendants? Discuss. [*Payne v. E & B Carpet Cleaning, Inc.,* 896 S.W.2d 650 (Mo.App. 1995)]

10–11. The corporate manual of Great Plains Supply, Inc., (GPS) states that employees can be discharged at any time for any reason. This manual constitutes an employment contract between GPS and its employees. Kevin Ruud was a store manager for GPS. Before accepting an offer to transfer to an unprofitable store, he expressed worries about job security to Michael Wigley, GPS's owner, and Ronald Nelson, a GPS vice president. Wigley and Nelson each responded, "Good employees are taken care of." Ruud accepted the transfer, but when the store closed as he had feared, he was offered only lesser jobs at lower pay. Ruud quit his job and filed a suit in a Minnesota state court against GPS, Wigley, and Nelson for, among other things, breach of contract. Ruud alleged that their statements modified the terms of his contract with GPS to include permanent employment. Were the statements of Wigley and Nelson sufficiently definite to modify the terms of Ruud's employment contract? Explain. [*Ruud v. Great Plains Supply, Inc.,* 526 N.W.2d 369 (Minn. 1995)]

10–12. James sent invitations to a number of potential buyers to submit bids for some timber he wanted to sell. Two bids were received as a result; the higher bid was submitted by Eames. James changed his mind about selling the timber, however, and did not accept Eames's bid. Eames claimed that a contract for sale existed and sued James for breach. Did a contract exist? Discuss. [*Eames v. James,* 452 So.2d 384 (La.App.3d Cir. 1984)]

10–13. Ameritrust Co. employed Rosen & Co. to conduct an auction. Included in Rosen's extensive advertisements of the sale was the announcement that the sale was subject to confirmation by Ameritrust. The auctioneer made a similar announcement at the time of the sale. At the auction, the auctioneer first offered the equipment in bulk, but only one bid—from Alpine Co. for $50,000—was received. Then the equipment was offered piecemeal, and total bids of $139,000 were received. Two bids—one from Lawrence Paper Co. and one from American Corrugated Machine Corp. (ACMC)—were accepted, and both companies submitted checks for 25 percent of their bid totals, as requested. Subsequent to the auction, Alpine offered $175,000 for the equipment, and Ameritrust sold the entire lot to Alpine. Lawrence and ACMC sued for breach of contract. Will they succeed in their suit? Why, or why not? [*Lawrence Paper Co. v. Rosen & Co.,* 939 F.2d 376 (6th Cir. 1991)]

10–14. Before an employee convention, Nationwide Mutual Insurance Co. created a committee, whose members included Mary Peterson, to select a theme. The committee announced a contest for theme suggestions: "Here's what you could win: His and Hers Mercedes. An all expense paid trip for two around the world. Additional prize to be announced. (All prizes subject to availability.)" David Mears submitted the theme "At the Top and Still Climbing." At a dinner of Nationwide employees, Peterson told Mears that he had won two Mercedes. Mears and others who heard this believed that he had won the cars. Nationwide never gave him the cars, however, and he filed a suit in a federal district court, alleging breach of contract. At the trial, Peterson claimed that she spoke with a facetious tone and, in reality, had no intention of awarding the cars. Is Mears entitled to the cars? Why, or why not? [*Mears v. Nationwide Mutual Insurance Co.,* 91 F.3d 1118 (8th Cir. 1996)]

10–15. Air Jamaica Vacations (AJV) requested bids from printing firms to produce travel brochures. Moore Graphic Services responded with an offer quoting prices and terms for an agreement to produce between 100,000 and 250,000 brochures. The offer stated that sales tax would be charged and requested that AJV indicate its acceptance by signing and returning the offer. Moore then contacted one of its vendors, Starr Printing Co., about producing the brochures and sent AJV samples of the work to be performed. Meanwhile, AJV returned the offer with some modified terms, including a handwritten notation, "no tax." Moore then told Starr it was putting "the job" on hold and told AJV that it could not perform "the job" because of the dispute about the tax. Starr printed the brochures and demanded payment. AJV refused, claiming in part that the brochures were of "poor quality." Starr filed a suit in a federal district court against AJV. AJV filed a suit against Moore, claiming breach of contract for giving the job to Starr. Moore filed a motion for summary judgment, on the ground that there was no contract. Did Moore and AJV have a contract? Why, or why not? [*Starr Printing Co. v. Air Jamaica,* 45 F.Supp.2d 625 (W.D.Tenn. 1999)]

E-LINKS

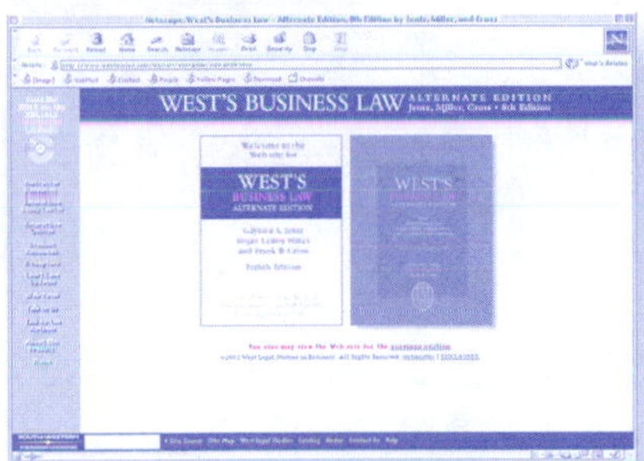

For updated links to resources available on the Web, as well as a variety of other materials, visit this text's Web site at

http://wbl-cs.westbuslaw.com

Select the topic of Business and Commercial Law from the Law Knowledgebase list on the right-hand side of the home page.

To view the terms of a sample contract, go to the "forms" pages of the 'Lectric Law Library at

http://www.lectlaw.com/form.html

For information on and examples illustrating the common law requirements governing offer and acceptance, go to FindLaw's Web site at

http://profs.lp.findlaw.com/contracts/index.html

LEGAL RESEARCH EXERCISES ON THE WEB

Go to http://wbl-cs.westbuslaw.com, the Web site that accompanies this text. Select "Interactive Study Center," and then click on "Chapter 10." There you will find the following Internet research exercise that you can perform to learn more about contract terms:

Activity 10–1: Contract Terms

CHAPTER 11
Consideration

THE FACT THAT A PROMISE has been made does not mean the promise can or will be enforced. Under Roman law, a promise was not enforceable without some sort of *causa*—that is, a reason for making the promise that was also deemed to be a sufficient reason for enforcing it. Since the beginning of the common law tradition in England, good reasons for enforcing informal promises (promises made in contracts that are not under seal) have been held to include something given as an agreed-on exchange, a benefit that the promisor received, and a detriment that the promisee incurred. Over time, these reasons came to be referred to legally as "consideration."

Thus, for centuries, it has been said that no informal promise is enforceable without consideration. **Consideration** is usually defined as the value (such as money) given in return for a promise (such as the promise to sell a stamp collection on receipt of payment). Often, consideration is broken down into two parts: (1) something of *legal value* must be given in exchange for the promise, and (2) there must be a *bargained-for* exchange. The "something of legal value" may consist of a return promise that is bargained for. If it consists of performance, that performance may be (1) an act (other than a promise); (2) a forbearance (a refraining from action); or (3) the creation, modification, or destruction of a legal relation.[1]

For example, Anita says to her son, "When you finish painting the garage, I will pay you $100." Anita's son paints the garage. The act of painting the garage is the consideration that creates Anita's contractual obligation to pay her son $100. Suppose, however, that Anita says to her son, "In consideration of the fact that you are not as wealthy as your brothers, I will pay you $500." This promise is not enforceable, because Anita's son has not given any consideration for the $500 promised.[2] Anita has simply stated her motive for giving her son a gift. The fact that the word *consideration* is used does not, alone, mean that consideration has been given.

SECTION 1

Legal Sufficiency of Consideration

For a binding contract to be created, consideration must be *legally sufficient*. To be legally sufficient, consideration for a promise must be either *legally detrimental to the promisee* (the one receiving the promise) or *legally beneficial to the promisor* (the one making the promise). Recall from Chapter 9 that in a bilateral contract, each party is both a promisor and a promisee. A party can incur legal detriment by either promising to give legal value (such as the payment of money) or by forbearance or a promise of forbearance—that is, by refraining from or promising to refrain from undertaking an action that the party had a legal right to undertake.

Suppose that Sue Ray owns the right to use the name "Sue's Kitchen." Susan Katz (the promisor) offers Ray $5,000 to stop using the name for her restaurant, and Ray (the promisee) agrees. A bilateral contract is formed by this exchange of promises. The

1. *Restatement (Second) of Contracts*, Section 71.

2. See *Fink v. Cox*, 18 Johns. 145, 9 Am.Dec. 191 (N.Y. 1820).

consideration flowing from Ray to Katz is Ray's promise to refrain from doing something that she is legally entitled to do—use the name "Sue's Kitchen." The consideration flowing from Katz to Ray is Katz's promise to pay Ray $5,000.

See Case 11.1 at the end of this chapter. To view the full, unedited case from Westlaw,® go to this text's Web site at **http://wbl-cs.westbuslaw.com**.

SECTION 2

Adequacy of Consideration

Adequacy of consideration refers to the fairness of the bargain. In general, a court will not question the adequacy of consideration if the consideration is legally sufficient. Under the doctrine of freedom of contract, parties are normally free to bargain as they wish. If people could sue merely because they had entered into an unwise contract, the courts would be overloaded with frivolous suits.

In extreme cases, a court may consider the adequacy of consideration in terms of its amount or worth because inadequate consideration may indicate fraud, duress, undue influence, or a lack of bargained-for exchange. It may also reflect a party's incompetence (for example, an individual might have been too intoxicated or simply too young to make a contract). Suppose that Dylan has a house worth $100,000 and he sells it for $50,000. A $50,000 sale could indicate that the buyer unduly pressured Dylan into selling the house at that price or that Dylan was defrauded into selling the house at far below market value. (Of course, it might also indicate that Dylan was in a hurry to sell and that the amount was legally sufficient.)

See Case 11.2 at the end of this chapter. To view the full, unedited case from Westlaw,® go to this text's Web site at **http://wbl-cs.westbuslaw.com**.

SECTION 3

Contracts That Lack Consideration

Sometimes, one of the parties (or both parties) to a contract may think that consideration has been exchanged when in fact it has not. Here we look at some situations in which the parties' promises or actions do not qualify as contractual consideration.

PREEXISTING DUTY

Under most circumstances, a promise to do what one already has a legal duty to do does not constitute legally sufficient consideration, because no legal detriment is incurred.[3] The preexisting legal duty may be imposed by law or may arise out of a previous contract. A sheriff, for example, cannot collect a reward for providing information leading to the capture of a criminal if the sheriff already has a legal duty to capture the criminal. Likewise, if a party is already bound by contract to perform a certain duty, that duty cannot serve as consideration for a second contract. To illustrate, suppose that Bauman-Bache, Inc., begins construction on a seven-story office building and after three months demands an extra $75,000 on its contract. If the extra $75,000 is not paid, it will stop working. The owner of the land, having no one else to complete construction, agrees to pay the extra $75,000. The agreement is not enforceable, because it is not supported by legally sufficient consideration; Bauman-Bache was under a preexisting contract to complete the building.

Unforeseen Difficulties. The rule regarding preexisting duty is meant to prevent extortion and the so-called holdup game. What happens, though, when an honest contractor who has contracted with a landowner to construct a building runs into extraordinary difficulties that were totally unforeseen at the time the contract was formed? In the interests of fairness and equity, the courts sometimes allow exceptions to the preexisting duty rule. In the example just mentioned, if the landowner agrees to pay extra compensation to the contractor for overcoming unforeseen difficulties, the court may refrain from applying the preexisting duty rule and enforce the agreement. When the "unforeseen difficulties" that give rise to a contract modification involve the types of risks ordinarily assumed in business, however, the courts will usually assert the preexisting duty rule.[4]

Rescission and New Contract. The law recognizes that two parties can mutually agree to rescind their contract, at least to the extent that it is executory

3. See *Foakes v. Beer,* 9 App.Cas. 605 (1884).

4. Note that under Article 2 of the UCC, an agreement modifying a contract needs no consideration to be binding. See UCC 2–209(1).

(still to be carried out). **Rescission**[5] is defined as the unmaking of a contract so as to return the parties to the positions they occupied before the contract was made. When rescission and the making of a new contract take place at the same time, without a change in the duties of both parties as required in their rescinded contract, the courts frequently are given a choice of applying the preexisting duty rule or allowing rescission and letting the new contract stand.

PAST CONSIDERATION

Promises made in return for actions or events that have already taken place are unenforceable. These promises lack consideration in that the element of bargained-for exchange is missing. In short, you can bargain for something to take place now or in the future but not for something that has already taken place. Therefore, **past consideration** is no consideration.

Suppose, for example, that Elsie, a real estate agent, does her friend Judy a favor by selling Judy's house and not charging any commission. Later, Judy says to Elsie, "In return for your generous act, I will pay you $3,000." This promise is made in return for past consideration and is thus unenforceable; in effect, Judy is stating her intention to give Elsie a gift.

SECTION 4

Problem Areas Concerning Consideration

Problems concerning consideration usually fall into one of the following categories:

1. Promises exchanged when total performance by the parties is uncertain.
2. Settlement of claims.
3. Promises enforceable without consideration.

The courts' solutions to these types of problems give insight into how the law views the complex concept of consideration.

UNCERTAIN PERFORMANCE

If the terms of the contract express such uncertainty of performance that the promisor has not definitely promised to do anything, the promise is said to be *illusory*—without consideration and unenforceable. For example, suppose that the president of Tuscan Corporation says to her employees, "All of you have worked hard, and if profits continue to remain high, a 10 percent bonus at the end of the year will be given—if management thinks it is warranted." The employees continue to work hard, and profits remain high, but no bonus is given. This is an *illusory promise,* or no promise at all, because performance depends solely on the discretion of the president (the management). There is no bargained-for consideration. The statement declares merely that the management may or may not do something in the future. The president is not obligated (incurs no detriment) now or later.

Option-to-cancel clauses in term contracts sometimes present problems in regard to consideration. For example, suppose that I contract to hire you for one year at $5,000 per month, reserving the right to cancel the contract at any time. On close examination of these words, you can see that I have not actually agreed to hire you, as I could cancel without liability before you started performance. I have not given up the opportunity of hiring someone else. This contract is therefore illusory. Suppose, however, that I am required to give you thirty days' notice to exercise the option. The thirty days' notice entitles you to at least one month's salary of $5,000, which is consideration. Thus, until I give you notice, you are entitled to $5,000 per month until the contract is terminated at the end of the year.

There are other types of contracts in which problems with consideration may arise because of uncertainty of performance. Uncertain performance is characteristic of requirements and output contracts, for example. In a *requirements contract,* a buyer and a seller agree that the buyer will purchase from the seller all of the goods of a designated type that the buyer needs, or requires. In an *output contract,* the buyer and seller agree that the buyer will purchase from the seller all of what the seller produces, or the seller's output. These types of contracts will be discussed further in Chapter 18.

SETTLEMENT OF CLAIMS

Businesspersons or others can settle legal claims in several ways, and it is important to understand the nature of consideration given in these kinds of settlement agreements, or contracts. A common means of settling a claim is through an *accord and satisfaction,*

5. Pronounced reh-*sih*-zhen.

in which a debtor offers to pay a lesser amount than the creditor purports to be owed. Other methods that are commonly used to settle claims include the *release* and the *covenant not to sue.*

Accord and Satisfaction. The concept of **accord and satisfaction** deals with a debtor's offer of payment and a creditor's acceptance of a lesser amount than the creditor originally purported to be owed. The *accord* is defined as the agreement under which one of the parties undertakes to give or perform, and the other to accept, in satisfaction of a claim, something other than that on which the parties originally agreed. *Satisfaction* takes place when the accord is executed. A basic rule is that there can be no satisfaction unless there is first an accord.

For accord and satisfaction to occur, the amount of the debt *must be in dispute.* If a debt is *liquidated,* accord and satisfaction cannot take place. A liquidated debt is one the amount of which has been ascertained, fixed, agreed on, settled, or exactly determined. For example, if Baker signs an installment loan contract with her banker in which she agrees to pay a specified rate of interest on a specified sum of borrowed money at monthly intervals for two years, that is a liquidated debt. The total obligation is precisely known to both of the parties, and reasonable persons will not differ over the amount owed.

Suppose that Baker has missed her last two payments on the loan and the creditor demands that she pay the overdue debt. Baker makes a partial payment and states that she believes this payment is all she should have to pay and that, if the creditor accepts the payment, the debt will be satisfied, or discharged. In the majority of states, acceptance of a lesser sum than the entire amount of a liquidated debt is not satisfaction, and the balance of the debt is still legally owed. The rationale for this rule is that no consideration is given by the debtor to satisfy the obligation of paying the balance to the creditor—because the debtor has a preexisting legal obligation to pay the entire debt.

An *unliquidated debt* is the opposite of a liquidated debt. Here, reasonable persons may differ over the amount owed. It is not settled, fixed, agreed on, ascertained, or determined. In these circumstances, acceptance of payment of the lesser sum operates as satisfaction, or discharge, of the debt. For example, suppose that Devereaux goes to the dentist's office. The dentist tells him that he needs three special types of gold inlays. The price is not discussed, and there is no standard fee for this type of work. Devereaux has the work done and leaves the office. At the end of the month, the dentist sends him a bill for $3,000. Devereaux, believing that this amount is grossly out of proportion with what a reasonable person would believe to be the debt owed, sends a check for $2,000. On the back of the check he writes "payment in full for three gold inlays." The dentist cashes the check. Because the situation involves an unliquidated debt—the amount has not been agreed on—payment accepted by the dentist normally will eradicate the debt. One argument to support this rule is that the parties give up a legal right to contest the amount in dispute, and thus consideration is given.

Release. A **release** bars any further recovery beyond the terms stated in the release. Assume that you are involved in an automobile accident caused by Donovan's negligence. Donovan offers to give you $1,000 if you will release him from further liability resulting from the accident. You believe that this amount will cover your damages, so you agree, in writing, to the release. Later you discover that it will cost $1,500 to repair your car. Can you collect the balance from Donovan? The answer is normally no; you are limited to the $1,000 specified in the release because the release represents a valid contract. You and Donovan both assented to the bargain (hence, agreement existed), and sufficient consideration was present. The consideration was the legal detriment you suffered (by releasing Donovan from liability, you forfeited your right to sue to recover damages, should they be more than $1,000).

Clearly, you are better off if you know the extent of your injuries or damages before signing a release. Releases will generally be binding if they are (1) given in good faith, (2) stated in a signed writing (which is required in many states), and (3) accompanied by consideration.[6]

Covenant Not to Sue. A **covenant not to sue** is an agreement to substitute a contractual obligation for some other type of legal action based on a valid claim. Unlike a release, a covenant not to sue does not always bar further recovery. Suppose (continuing the earlier example) that you agree with Donovan not to sue for damages in a tort action if he

6. Under the UCC, a written, signed waiver or renunciation by an aggrieved party discharges any further liability for a breach, even without consideration.

will pay for the damage to your car. If Donovan fails to pay, you can bring an action against him for breach of contract.

PROMISES ENFORCEABLE WITHOUT CONSIDERATION

There are some exceptions to the rule that only promises supported by consideration are enforceable. The following types of promises may be enforced despite the lack of consideration:

1. Promises to pay debts that are barred by a statute of limitations.
2. Promises inducing detrimental reliance, under the doctrine of promissory estoppel.
3. Promises to make charitable contributions.

Promises to Pay Debts Barred by a Statute of Limitations. Statutes of limitations in all states require a creditor to sue within a specified period to recover a debt. If the creditor fails to sue in time, recovery of the debt is barred by the statute of limitations. A debtor who promises to pay a previous debt even though recovery is barred by the statute of limitations makes an enforceable promise. *The promise needs no consideration.* (Some states, however, require that it be in writing.) In effect, the promise extends the limitations period, and the creditor can sue to recover the entire debt, or at least the amount promised. The promise can be implied if the debtor acknowledges the barred debt by making a partial payment.

Detrimental Reliance and Promissory Estoppel. As discussed in Chapter 10, under the doctrine of *promissory estoppel,* a person who has reasonably and substantially relied on the promise of another may be able to obtain some measure of recovery. This doctrine is applied in a wide variety of contexts in which a promise is otherwise unenforceable, such as when a promise is not supported by consideration. Under this doctrine, a court may enforce an otherwise unenforceable promise to avoid the injustice that would therefore result. For the doctrine to be applied, the following elements are required:

1. There must be a clear and definite promise.
2. The promisee must justifiably rely on the promise.
3. The reliance normally must be of a substantial and definite character.
4. Justice will be better served by enforcement of the promise.

If these requirements are met, a promise may be enforced even though it is not supported by consideration. In essence, the promisor will be *estopped* (prevented) from asserting the lack of consideration as a defense. For example, suppose that your uncle tells you, "I'll pay you $150 a week so you won't have to work anymore." In reliance on your uncle's promise, you quit your job, but your uncle refuses to pay you. Under the doctrine of promissory estoppel, you may be able to enforce such a promise.[7]

See Case 11.3 at the end of this chapter. To view the full, unedited case from Westlaw,® go to this text's Web site at **http://wbl-cs.westbuslaw.com**.

Charitable Subscriptions. Subscriptions to religious, educational, and charitable institutions are promises to make gifts and are unenforceable on traditional contract grounds because they are not supported by legally sufficient consideration. A gift, after all, is the opposite of bargained-for consideration.

There have been cases in which it was held that a promise to give money to a charity was supported by consideration. For example, the promisor may have bargained for and received a promise from the charity that the gift would be used in a specific way or that it would be memorialized with the promisor's name. The modern view, however, is to enforce these promises under the doctrine of promissory estoppel or to find consideration simply as a matter of public policy.

The premise for enforcement is that a promise is made and an institution changes its position because of reliance on that promise. For example, suppose a church solicits and receives pledges (commitments to contribute funds) from church members to erect a new church building. On the basis of these pledges, the church purchases land, employs architects, and makes other contracts that change its position. Courts may enforce the pledges under promissory estoppel. Alternatively, they may find consideration in the fact that each promise was made in reliance on the other promises of support or that the trustees, by accepting the subscriptions, impliedly promised to complete the proposed undertaking.

Such cases represent exceptions to the general rule that consideration must exist for a contract to be formed. These exceptions come about as a result of public policy.

7. *Ricketts v. Scothorn,* 57 Neb. 51, 77 N.W. 365 (1898).

Terms and Concepts to Review

accord and satisfaction 234	covenant not to sue 234	release 234
consideration 231	past consideration 233	rescission 233

Chapter Summary

Legal Sufficiency of Consideration	Consideration is broken down into two parts: (1) something of *legally sufficient value* must be given in exchange for the promise, and (2) there must be a *bargained-for exchange.* To be legally sufficient, consideration must involve a legal detriment to the promisee, a legal benefit to the promisor, or both. One incurs a legal detriment by doing (or refraining from doing) something that one had no prior legal duty to do (or to refrain from doing).
Adequacy of Consideration	Legal sufficiency of consideration relates to the first element of consideration just mentioned—something of legal value must be given in exchange for a promise. Adequacy of consideration relates to "how much" consideration is given and whether a fair bargain was reached. Courts will inquire into the adequacy of consideration (if the consideration is legally sufficient) only when fraud, undue influence, duress, or unconscionability may be involved.
Contracts That Lack Consideration	Consideration is lacking in the following situations: 1. *Preexisting duty*—Consideration is not legally sufficient if one is either by law or by contract under a *preexisting duty* to perform the action being offered as consideration for a new contract. 2. *Past consideration*—Actions or events that have already taken place do not constitute legally sufficient consideration.
Problem Areas Concerning Consideration	1. *Uncertain performance*—When the nature or extent of performance is too uncertain, the promise is rendered illusory (without consideration and unenforceable). 2. *Settlement of claims*— a. Accord and satisfaction—An *accord* is an agreement in which a debtor offers to pay a lesser amount than the creditor purports to be owed. *Satisfaction* may take place when the accord is executed. b. Release—An agreement by which, for consideration, a party is barred from further recovery beyond the terms specified in the release. c. Covenant not to sue—An agreement not to sue on a present, valid claim. 3. *Promises enforceable without consideration*— a. Promises to pay debts barred by a statute of limitations. b. Promises inducing detrimental reliance (under the doctrine of promissory estoppel). c. Charitable subscriptions.

CASES FOR ANALYSIS

Westlaw. You can access the full text of each case presented below by going to the Westlaw cases on this text's Web site at http://wbl-cs.westbuslaw.com. Each Westlaw case includes the names of all plaintiffs and defendants, the dates on which the case was argued and decided, a brief summary of the issues and decisions in the case, headnotes classifying specific issues in the case according to the West Key Number System, and the court's opinion. Concurring and dissenting opinions, if any, are included as well.

CASE 11.1 LEGAL SUFFICIENCY OF CONSIDERATION

HAMER v. SIDWAY

Court of Appeals of New York, Second Division, 1891.
124 N.Y. 538,
27 N.E. 256.

PARKER, J. [Judge] * * *

The question which provoked the most discussion by counsel on this appeal, and which lies at the foundation of plaintiff's [Hamer's] asserted right of recovery, is whether by virtue of a contract defendant's [Sidway's] testator, William E. Story, became indebted to his nephew, William E. Story, 2d, on his twenty-first birthday in the sum of $5,000. The trial court found as a fact that "on the 20th day of March, 1869, * * * William E. Story agreed to and with William E. Story, 2d, that if he would refrain from drinking liquor, using tobacco, swearing, and playing cards or billiards for money until he should become twenty-one years of age, then he, the said William E. Story, would at that time pay him, the said William E. Story, 2d, the sum of $5,000 for such refraining, to which the said William E. Story, 2d, agreed," and that he "in all things fully performed his part of said agreement." The defendant contends that the contract was without consideration to support it, and therefore invalid. He asserts that the promisee, by refraining from the use of liquor and tobacco, was not harmed, but benefited; that that which he did was best for him to do, independently of his uncle's promise,—and insists that it follows that, unless the promisor was benefited, the contract was without consideration,—a contention which, if well founded, would seem to leave open for controversy in many cases whether that which the promisee did or omitted to do was in fact of such benefit to him as to leave no consideration to support the enforcement of the promisor's agreement. Such a rule could not be tolerated, and is without foundation in the law. * * * *A valuable consideration, in the sense of the law, may consist either in some right, interest, profit, or benefit accruing to the one party, or some forbearance, detriment, loss, or responsibility given, suffered, or undertaken by the other.* Courts will not ask whether the thing which forms the consideration does in fact benefit the promisee or a third party, or is of any substantial value to any one. It is enough that something is promised, done, forborne, or suffered by the party to whom the promise is made as consideration for the promise made to him. *In general a waiver of any legal right at the request of another party is a sufficient consideration for a promise. Any damage, or suspension, or forbearance of a right will be sufficient to sustain a promise.* * * * Now, applying this rule to the facts before us, the promisee used tobacco, occasionally drank liquor, and he had a legal right to do so. That right he abandoned for a period of years upon the strength of the promise of the testator that for such forbearance he would give him $5,000. We need not speculate on the effort which may have been required to give up the use of those stimulants. It is sufficient that he restricted his lawful freedom of action within certain prescribed limits upon the faith of his uncle's agreement, and now, having fully performed the conditions imposed, it is of no moment whether such performance actually proved a benefit to the promisor, and the court will not inquire into it; but, were it a proper subject of inquiry, we see nothing in this record that would permit a determination that the uncle was not benefited in a legal sense. * * * [Emphasis added.]

In further consideration of the questions presented, then, it must be deemed established for the purposes of this appeal that on the 31st day of January, 1875, defendant's testator was indebted to William E. Story, 2d, in the sum of $5,000; and, if this action were founded on that contract, it would be barred by the statute of limitations, which has been pleaded, but on that date the nephew wrote to his uncle as follows: "Dear Uncle: I am 21 years old to-day, and I am now my own boss; and I believe, according to agreement, that there is due me $5,000. I have lived up to the contract to the letter in every sense of the word." A few days later, and on February 6th, the uncle replied, and, so far as it is material to this controversy, the reply is as follows: "Dear Nephew: Your letter of the 31st ult. came to hand all right, saying that you had lived up to the promise made to me several years ago. I have no doubt but you have, for which you shall have $5,000, as I promised you. I had the money in the bank the day you was 21 years old that I intend for you, and you shall have the money certain. Now, Willie, I don't intend to interfere with this money in any way until I think you are capable of taking care of it, and the sooner that time comes the better it will please me. I would hate very much to have you start out in some adventure that you thought all right, and lose this money in one year. * * * This money you have earned much easier than I did, besides acquiring good habits at the same time; and you are quite welcome to the money. Hope you will make good use of it. * * * W. E. STORY. P. S. You can consider this money on interest." The trial court found as a fact that "said letter was received by said William E. Story, 2d, who thereafter consented that said money should remain with the said William E. Story in accordance with the terms and conditions of said letter." And further, "that afterwards, on the 1st day of March, 1877, with the knowledge and consent of his said uncle, he duly sold, transferred, and assigned all his right, title, and interest in and to said sum of $5,000 to his wife, Libbie H. Story, who thereafter duly sold, transferred, and assigned the same to the plaintiff in this action." * * * The order appealed from should be reversed, and the judgment of the special term affirmed, with costs payable out of the estate.

CASE 11.2 ADEQUACY OF CONSIDERATION

POWELL v. MVE HOLDINGS, INC.

Court of Appeals of Minnnesota, 2001.
626 N.W.2d 451.

LANSING, Judge

MVE Holdings, Inc. (Holdings), appeals from judgment and denial of its new-trial motion in a breach-of-contract action brought by R. Edwin Powell, its former employee and shareholder. The district court found that Holdings contracted to redeem Powell's stock and then breached that contract. Holdings appeals, claiming [in part] * * * that any agreement * * * is void for lack of consideration * * * . We conclude that the evidence supports the district court's findings and affirm.

FACTS

From 1993 until January 23, 1997, R. Edwin Powell was CEO and president of CAIRE, Inc., a Delaware company based in Burnsville, Minnesota. CAIRE manufactures home health-care products, including portable oxygen tanks. Powell had worked for CAIRE, a subsidiary of Holdings, for the preceding 13 years as an at-will employee. In addition, Powell and the Powell Family Limited Partnership were minority shareholders in Holdings, owning 63,747 shares or 11.9% of the company. Trial testimony established that Powell paid $114,000 to $344,000 for the stock during his employment.

In 1996, a group of investors decided to acquire Holdings and CAIRE. They formed MVE Investors, LLC (Investors), a Delaware limited-liability company with its principal place of business in New York. Investors, organized solely to acquire a majority interest in Holdings, purchased the shares of three retiring Holdings shareholders in June 1996 as part of a recapitalization of the company. Investors paid the retiring shareholders $125.456 per share, investing $47 million in Holdings to become its primary owner.

Powell declined Investors' offer to sell his stock and retire with the shareholders who had accepted Investors' offer. Powell continued as CAIRE's CEO and president. To compensate Powell for losing his chance to sell his shares in the recapitalization, Holdings loaned Powell $1.5 million secured by 24,793 of Powell's shares of Holdings' common stock. Holdings called the loan in January 1998; at the time, an independent company valued the shares at $5.37 per share.

In response to CAIRE's financial setbacks, David O'Halloran, Holdings' CEO and president, met with Powell on January 23, 1997, to fire Powell. O'Halloran gave Powell the option to resign in lieu of termination, and Powell chose to resign, writing a resignation letter on January 28, 1997.

The critical factual issues in this litigation revolve around O'Halloran and Powell's January 23, 1997, meeting. The two men sharply disagree on the severance package O'Halloran offered Powell on behalf of Holdings at the meeting, the terms of which were to be included in a "separation agreement." Both men agree that O'Halloran offered Powell six months' salary and an additional six months' salary if Powell was not re-employed within the six months immediately following his departure. They also agree that O'Halloran offered Powell $30,000 in out-placement services, a continuation of Powell's health insurance and other benefits for a year, and a cash bonus if Powell was successful in lobbying Congress for particular legislation.

But the two men disagree on the terms for the disposition of Powell's stock. Powell testified that O'Halloran agreed, on behalf of Holdings, to buy Powell's stock at the same price that the retiring shareholders had been paid at the recapitalization that occurred in August 1996. According to Powell, O'Halloran told Powell that Holdings would be able to buy the shares within a few weeks and would buy them no later than August 1997.

O'Halloran maintains that he did not promise Powell that Holdings would buy Powell's stock. But O'Halloran concedes that at the meeting, he gave Powell a detailed chart showing the number of shares Powell owned on January 23, 1997, and how much money Powell would receive if those shares were sold or redeemed at a price of $125.456, the same price the retiring shareholders had received. O'Halloran also testified that he wrote a letter terminating Powell's employment if he chose not to resign. In the letter, O'Halloran expressed Holdings' intent to buy Powell's stock in the same manner as it had bought the retiring shareholders' stock.

After his termination, Powell continued to attend trade-association meetings and to lobby Congress on Holdings' behalf until April 1997. Holdings and Powell continued to discuss Powell's separation agreement until April 1997, when O'Halloran informed Powell in writing that Holdings would no longer reimburse Powell for any expenses he incurred on behalf of Holdings. Also, Powell testified that O'Halloran called Powell in April to tell him that O'Halloran had lost board support for the stock redemption and that the deal was off.

Holdings fired O'Halloran from his position as CEO and president of Holdings in August. As part of the separation agreement that followed O'Halloran's discharge, he agreed to represent that he did not "make any statements or provide any writings that [he] in good faith believe[d] could reasonably be construed to constitute any agreement, oral or written, concerning the payment of severance or similar payments to, or the redemption or other disposition of capital stock of, R. Edwin Powell."

Powell brought this action against Holdings in October 1997, claiming, among other things, that Holdings had contracted to buy back his shares and then breached that contract. Chart Industries merged with Holdings in February 1999, paying $78 million for Holdings' stock. The merger agreement specified that shareholders who released claims against Holdings would receive $45 per share, but shareholders refusing to release claims against Holdings would receive only $25 per share. Powell refused to drop his lawsuit, and Holdings redeemed his shares at $25 per share, paying him a total of about $860,000 and retaining about $680,000 for defense costs associated with Powell's lawsuit. Powell also received shares of stock in a Holdings subsidiary as a result of the merger.

* * * [T]he district court found that Holdings had contracted to buy Powell's stock and breached the contract. The district court awarded Powell $3,455,887.20, the amount that Powell would have received had he sold his non-pledged stock for $125.456 per share, less $860,050 Powell received for his shares after the Chart merger, and also ordered Powell to transfer to Holdings the Holdings subsidiary shares he had acquired in the Chart merger. * * * Holdings appeals, claiming [in part] that * * * any agreement [between O'Halloran and Powell] is void for lack of consideration * * * .

ISSUES

* * * *

III. Is the agreement between O'Halloran and Powell invalid because it * * * lacks consideration * * * ?

* * * *

ANALYSIS

* * * *

Holdings * * * argues that any agreement between Powell and Holdings is void because Powell did not furnish adequate consideration. When a contract is not supported by consideration, no valid contract is formed. Consideration is something of value given in return for a performance or promise of performance, and requires that a contractual promise be the product of a bargain. * * *

Powell asserts and O'Halloran concedes that, in exchange for the stock redemption, O'Halloran asked him to continue, even after he left CAIRE, to participate as a member of several trade-association boards, to attend trade-association meetings, and to lobby Congress on behalf of Holdings. Additionally, Powell and O'Halloran testified that to disrupt CAIRE's business as little as possible and because of his belief that customer goodwill might be affected if customers felt that Powell was fired, O'Halloran asked Powell to contact CAIRE's key customers and industry contacts to reassure them that Powell's departure was a positive, voluntary step. Powell performed these functions until April 1997, when O'Halloran wrote a letter requesting that Powell no longer make those efforts and telling Powell that Holdings would no longer pay him or offer reimbursement for any incurred expenses.

Holdings asserts that Powell's lobbying activities were not performed as consideration for stock redemption but, instead, for a cash bonus tied to those efforts and that the other tasks Powell claims to have performed were of no value to Holdings. But even if Powell's lobbying efforts are discounted, he performed other tasks for Holdings at Holdings' request. Also, *a court will not examine the adequacy of consideration so long as something of value has passed between the parties.* Although the consideration that Powell furnished may not have been as significant as the benefits that Holdings promised to confer, Powell provided adequate consideration, and the agreement between Powell and Holdings is not void for lack of consideration. [Emphasis added.]

* * * *

DECISION

The district court did not err in finding that * * * the parties formed a valid contract supported by consideration * * * .

Affirmed.

CASE 11.3 PROMISSORY ESTOPPEL

GOFF-HAMEL v. OBSTETRICIANS & GYNECOLOGISTS, P.C.

Supreme Court of Nebraska, 1999.
256 Neb. 19,
588 N.W.2d 798.

WRIGHT, J. [Justice]

NATURE OF CASE

Julie Goff-Hamel brought this action against Obstetricians & Gynecologists, P.C. (Obstetricians), seeking * * * damages for detrimental reliance on a promise of employment. The trial court granted summary judgment in favor of Obstetricians, and Goff-Hamel appeals.

* * * *

FACTS

Goff-Hamel worked for Hastings Family Planning for 11 years. Prior to leaving Hastings Family Planning, Goff-Hamel was earning $24,000 plus the following benefits: 6 weeks' paid maternity leave, 6 weeks' vacation, 12 paid holidays, 12 sick days, an educational reimbursement, and medical and dental insurance coverage.

In July 1993, Goff-Hamel met with representatives of Obstetricians regarding the possibility of employment. Present at the meeting were Janet Quackenbush, the office manager; Dr. George Adam, a part owner of Obstetricians; and Larry Draper, a consultant of Obstetricians involved in personnel decisions. Adam had approached Goff-Hamel in June 1993 about working for him as a patient relations and outreach coordinator at Obstetricians. Goff-Hamel initially declined the offer, explaining that she had made commitments to do some training in the fall and to hire and help train a new bookkeeper. Adam spoke to Goff-Hamel approximately 1 month later, asking her to reconsider and whether she was ready to "jump ship and come work for him." Goff-Hamel told Adam she would be interested in hearing some details, and an interview was set for July 27 at Adam's office.

At the meeting, Adam represented to Goff-Hamel that the position would be full time and would start at a salary of $10 per hour and that she would be provided 2 weeks' paid vacation, three or four paid holidays, uniforms, and an educational stipend. A retirement plan would start after the end of the second year, retroactive to the end of the first year. The job would not provide health insurance.

Goff-Hamel was offered a job with Obstetricians during the July 27, 1993, meeting, and she accepted the job offer at that time. She expressed concern that she be given time to finish some projects at Hastings Family Planning, and it was agreed that she would start her employment on October 4. Goff-Hamel gave notice to Hastings Family Planning in August, informing them that she would be resigning to take a job with Obstetricians.

Subsequently, Goff-Hamel went to Obstetricians' office and was provided with uniforms for her job. She was given a copy of her schedule for the first week of work, but did not receive a copy of the employee handbook.

On October 3, 1993, Goff-Hamel was told by Draper that she should not report to work the next morning as had been planned. Draper told her that Janel Foote, the wife of a part owner of Obstetricians, Dr. Terry Foote, opposed the hiring of Goff-Hamel.

The trial court found that there were no facts in dispute and that Goff-Hamel had not turned down any other employment opportunities between July and October 1993. The court found that she had terminated her employment at Hastings Family Planning in reliance on an offer of employment from Obstetricians; however, the prospective employment agreement was not for a specific term of employment. The court noted that Goff-Hamel sought replacement employment, but was unable to obtain employment until April 1995, when she was employed part time at the rate of $11 per hour.

The trial court concluded that since Goff-Hamel was to be employed at will, her employment could be terminated at any time, including before she began working. The court concluded that * * * Obstetricians was entitled to a judgment as a matter of law.

* * * *

ANALYSIS

* * * *

* * * The development of the law of promissory estoppel is an attempt by the courts to keep remedies abreast of increased moral consciousness of honesty and fair representations in all business dealings.

Promissory estoppel provides for damages as justice requires and does not attempt to provide the plaintiff damages based upon the benefit of the bargain. It requires only that reliance be reasonable and foreseeable. It does not impose the requirement that the promise giving rise to the cause of action must be so comprehensive in scope as to meet the requirements of an offer that would ripen into a contract if accepted by the promisee. [Emphasis added.]

We have not specifically addressed whether promissory estoppel may be asserted as the basis for a cause of action for detrimental reliance upon a promise of at-will employment. * * *

Other jurisdictions which have addressed the question of whether a cause of action for promissory estoppel can be stated in the context of a prospective at-will employee are split on the issue. Some have held that an employee can recover damages incurred as a result of resigning from the former at-will employment in reliance on a promise of other at-will employment. They have determined that when a prospective employer knows or should know that a promise of employment will induce an employee to leave his or her current job, such employer shall be liable for the reliant's damages. Recognizing that both the prospective new employer and the prior employer could have fired the employee without cause at any time, they have concluded that the employee would have continued to work in his or her prior employment if it were not for the offer by the prospective employer. Although damages have not been allowed for wages lost from the prospective at-will employment, damages have been allowed based upon wages from the prior employment and other damages incurred in reliance on the job offer.

In contrast, other jurisdictions have held as a matter of law that a prospective employee cannot recover damages incurred in reliance on an unfulfilled promise of at-will employment, concluding that reliance on a promise consisting solely of at-will employment is unreasonable as a matter of law because the employee should know that the promised employment could be terminated by the employer at any time for any reason without liability. These courts have stated that an anomalous result occurs when recovery is allowed for an employee who has not begun work, when the same employee's job could be terminated without liability 1 day after beginning work.

* * * *

Having reviewed and considered decisions from other jurisdictions, we conclude under the facts of this case that *promissory estoppel can be asserted in connection with the offer of at-will employment* and that the trial court erred in granting Obstetricians summary judgment. A cause of action for promissory estoppel is based upon a promise which the promisor should reasonably expect to induce action or forbearance on the part of the promisee which does in fact induce such action or forbearance. Here, promissory estoppel is appropriate where Goff-Hamel acted to her detriment in order to avail herself of the promised employment. [Emphasis added.]

* * * *

The facts are not disputed that Obstetricians offered Goff-Hamel employment. Apparently, at the direction of the spouse of one of the owners, Obstetricians refused to honor its promise of employment. It is also undisputed that Goff- Hamel relied upon Obstetricians' promise of employment to her detriment in that she terminated her employment of 11 years. Therefore, under the facts of this case, the trial court should have granted summary judgment in favor of Goff-Hamel on the issue of liability.

* * * *

We therefore reverse the judgment of the trial court and remand the case for further proceedings in accordance with this opinion.

REVERSED AND REMANDED FOR FURTHER PROCEEDINGS.

STEPHAN, J., dissenting.

I respectfully dissent. * * * I cannot reconcile the result reached by the majority or its rationale with our firmly established legal principles governing at-will employment. As succinctly and, in my view, correctly stated by the district court: "Since plaintiff could have been terminated after one day's employment without the defendant incurring liability, logic dictates she could also be terminated before the employment started."

* * * *

* * * I acknowledge that this reasoning would produce a seemingly harsh result from the perspective of Goff-Hamel under the facts of this case, but to some degree, this is inherent in the concept of at-will employment. * * * Similarly, an employer which has made a significant expenditure in training an at-will employee may feel harshly treated if, upon completing the training, the employee immediately utilizes his or her newly acquired skills to secure more remunerative employment with a competitor. If the law of at-will employment were regularly bent to circumvent what some may consider a harsh result in a particular case, its path would soon become hopelessly circuitous and impossible to follow.

CASE PROBLEMS

11–1. Ellen and Gabriel Fineman held MasterCards issued by Citibank. Holders of these cards paid an annual $15 fee. The issuance and use of the cards were governed by a retail installment credit agreement, which contained the following statement: "We can change this Agreement including the *finance charge* and the *annual percentage rate* at any time." The agreement did provide for thirty days' notice of any such changes, and the cardholder had a right to reject the changes in writing and return the credit card. Two months before the expiration of the Finemans' cards, Citibank notified them that it was increasing its annual fee to $20; however, Citibank was also providing its cardholders with extra services and benefits, such as "$100,000 common carrier travel insurance." The Finemans did not object in writing, nor did they return the cards. Citibank added 83 cents to the Finemans' next bill, the prorated portion of the increase for the two months remaining on their cards. The Finemans filed a suit (a class-action lawsuit on behalf of all cardholders) to recover the increased charges. Among other claims, the Finemans argued that the modification failed on the ground that the travel insurance was not adequate consideration for the modification because they never received any benefits from the insurance, and because its cost to Citibank was negligible. Was there adequate and legally sufficient consideration for Citibank's modification of the annual credit-card fee? Discuss. [*Fineman v. Citicorp USA, Inc.*, 137 Ill.App.3d 1055, 485 N.E.2d 591, 92 Ill.Dec. 780 (1985)]

11–2. The state of Connecticut offered a $20,000 reward to anyone providing information leading to the arrest and conviction of the individual responsible for the murder of a man who was killed during the course of a robbery. Robert DePretis, a private investigator hired by an attorney—Joseph Gallicchio—representing a co-defendant in the case, obtained a written and signed confession from James Avis, in which Avis admitted responsibility for the murder, and delivered the confession to the state police. This information eventually led to Avis's arrest, and Avis was later convicted for the crime. When DePretis tried to obtain the reward money, the state claimed, among other things, that DePretis was not eligible to collect the reward because, as Gallicchio's private investigator, he had a preexisting duty to investigate and report information relating to the crime. DePretis argued that although he commenced his activity in this matter as a result of his relationship with the attorney, he had no duty—as a police officer would—to continue his investigations. What will the court decide? Discuss. [*State v. Avis*, 41 Conn.Supp. 385, 577 A.2d 1146 (1990)]

11–3. Red Owl Stores, Inc., induced the Hoffmans to give up their current business and run a Red Owl franchise. Although no contract was ever signed, the Hoffmans incurred numerous expenses in reliance on Red Owl's representations. When the deal ultimately fell through because of Red Owl's failure to keep its promise concerning the operation of the franchise agency store, the Hoffmans brought suit to recover their losses. Will the Hoffmans succeed? Explain. [*Hoffman v. Red Owl Stores, Inc.*, 26 Wis.2d 683, 133 N.W.2d 267 (1965)]

11–4. Kowalsky, a contractor, was required to make periodic payments to a union pension fund administered by Kelly, trustee for the union. Kowalsky and Kelly disagreed over the amount of money Kowalsky owed the union. After a number of heated discussions Kowalsky sent Kelly four checks totaling $8,500 and enclosed them in a letter saying: "These checks are tendered with the understanding that they are full payment of all claims against Kowalsky." Immediately after receiving the checks, Kelly called Kowalsky and told him the checks were not going to be cashed but would simply be held and that Kowalsky still owed Kelly money because the $8,500 did not cover late charges on the deposited payments. Kowalsky did not ask for the return of the checks or stop payment. Kelly retained, but did not cash, the checks and sued Kowalsky for the late charges. Kowalsky claimed that retention of the checks constituted full accord and satisfaction of the debt. With whom did the court agree? Why? [*Kelly v. Kowalsky*, 186 Conn. 618, 442 A.2d 1355 (1982)]

11–5. Widener and Mozumder were employed as geophysicists by Arco Oil and Gas Co. On March 31, 1986, both employees were notified by letter that they were being placed on "surplus" status—which meant that if they were not assigned to another position in the company during the next sixty days, their employment would be terminated. On termination, they would become eligible for benefits, including lump-sum allowance payments, under either of two company termination and retirement programs. Their employment was subsequently terminated. To be eligible for payments under either plan, the employees were required to sign release documents. The employees were given informational packets outlining each plan in detail and advising the employees to contact the company's benefits specialist, Barbara Hough, about which plan they wished to elect. The employees went to Hough's office and signed various documents, among which was a general release that read, in part: "I release and discharge the Company . . . from all claims, liabilities, demands, and causes of action known or unknown, fixed or contingent, which I may have or claim to have against the Company as a result of this termination and do hereby covenant not to file a lawsuit to assert such claims." After signing the release, each employee received a lump-sum payment. When the employees later sued Arco, alleging wrongful discharge on the basis of age discrimination, Arco claimed that the release document signed by the employees relieved it of any liability. The employees contended that they had not voluntarily and knowingly given the releases. The release document was confusing because it was not called a "release," and Hough had never informed them of the significance of what they were signing. She only told them that they had to sign the various documents before they left. Will the court hold that the release was valid? Why, or why not? [*Widener v. Arco Oil and Gas Co.*, 717 F.Supp. 1211 (N.D.Tex. 1989)]

11–6. John and Alan Padgett sold their business, Econotax, Inc., to Taxpro, Inc. The terms of the sale required Taxpro to take over the Padgetts' payments to Wanda Austin under a promissory note as part of the purchase price. When Austin died, James Austin inherited the right to payment. A dispute arose over the exact amount owed. Taxpro sent Austin three checks and a new promissory note as a proposed settlement, asking Austin to sign and return the note to accept the settlement. Austin cashed the checks but did not return the note. Instead, he filed a suit in a Mississippi state court against the Padgetts. The Padgetts sued Taxpro. Did Austin's cashing the checks and keeping the note constitute an accord and satisfaction? Why, or why not? [*Austin v. Padgett*, 678 So.2d 1002 (Miss. 1996)]

11–7. Gordon Hayes and Winslow Construction Co. (Hayes) promised to hire Kathleen Hunter as a flag person on a construction job beginning June 14, 1971. Relying on the offer, Hunter left her position with the telephone company, as Hayes had asked her to do. When Hayes failed to hire her, she was unemployed for two months, in spite of her efforts to find another job. Hunter sued Hayes for damages in the amount of $700, which she would have earned during the two months had she not left the telephone company (she had been earning $350 a month). The trial court ruled for Hunter, awarding her $700 in damages. Hayes appealed, contending that it should not be liable because no valid employment contract existed between the plaintiff and the defendant. Discuss whether Hunter should be allowed to recover damages incurred by her reliance on Hayes's offer of employment, even in the absence of a valid employment contract. [*Hunter v. Hayes*, 533 P.2d 952 (Colo.App. 1975)]

11–8. An article written by Claudia Dreifus and published in *Glamour* magazine discussed therapists who sexually exploit their patients. Jill Ruzicka had told Dreifus that she (Ruzicka) had been sexually abused as a child by her father and later by her therapist. Dreifus had promised to withhold Ruzicka's identity from the article, and the published story identified Ruzicka by a fictitious name ("Lundquist"). In the article, Dreifus stated that "Lundquist" was an attorney who had served on the Minnesota Task Force against Sexual Abuse. Ruzicka claimed that this detail revealed her true identity because she was, in fact, the only woman on that task force. Ruzicka asserted that she had relied to her detriment on Dreifus's promise and sued Dreifus to recover damages under, among other theories, a theory of promissory estoppel. Under the relevant state law, to support a promissory estoppel theory the plaintiff must prove (1) that the promise was clear and definite, (2) that the promisor intended to induce reliance on the part of the promisee and such reliance occurred to the promisee's detriment, and (3) that the promise must be enforced to prevent injustice. What should the court decide? Discuss fully. [*Ruzicka v. Conde Nast Publications, Inc.*, 999 F.2d 1319 (8th Cir. 1993)]

11–9. In August 1982, James Bennett was driving his automobile when it was struck from behind by a Shinoda Floral, Inc., truck driven by George Wasilche in the course of his employment. Following the collision, Bennett was told by his physician that he had incurred a lumbosacral and dorsal sprain, which would only temporarily disable him; eventually he would be able to return to his job. Aetna Casualty and Surety Company, Shinoda Floral's insurance company, paid Bennett's medical expenses and lost wages until December 1982, at which time Aetna offered Bennett $5,000 to settle his claim, stating that this was all Aetna would pay. Bennett accepted the offer and signed a release "of all claims of every nature and kind whatsoever . . . that are known and unknown, suspected and unsuspected." Later, Bennett's back condition worsened, and medical examinations revealed a herniated intravertebral disc in Bennett's lower back—a much more serious condition than the sprain that was originally diagnosed. The examining physicians concluded that Bennett was permanently and totally disabled. Bennett brought an action for damages against Wasilche and Shinoda Floral, the defendants. The defendants asserted the release as a defense to liability. Is Bennett legally bound by the release? What will the court decide? Discuss fully. [*Bennett v. Shinoda Floral, Inc.*, 108 Wash.2d 386, 739 P.2d 648 (1987)]

11–10. Martino was a police officer in Atlantic City. Gray, who had lost a significant amount of her jewelry during a burglary of her home, offered a reward for the recovery of the property. Incident to his job, Martino possessed certain knowledge concerning the theft of Gray's jewelry. When Martino informed Gray of his knowledge of the theft, Gray offered Martino $500 to help her recover her jewelry. As a result of Martino's police work, the jewelry was recovered and returned to Gray. Martino sued Gray for the reward he claimed she had promised him. Was there a valid contract between Gray and Martino? Discuss fully. [*Gray v. Martino*, 91 N.J.L. 462, 103 A. 24 (1918)]

11–11. In 1972, Thomas L. Weinsaft signed a written agreement with his son, Nicholas L. Weinsaft. Thomas agreed that during his lifetime he would not transfer any interest in his 765 shares of stock of Crane Manufacturing Co. unless he first gave Nicholas an opportunity to purchase them, and on Thomas's death, Nicholas would have the "option and right to purchase all of the stock" from the estate. The agreement stated that it was entered into "In consideration of $10.00 and other good and valuable consideration, including the inducement of Second Party [Nicholas] to remain the chief executive officer of said company." Thomas died in 1980. Nicholas gave notice that he intended to buy the stock, but one of the beneficiaries under Thomas's will objected, contending that there was no consideration for Thomas's promises. Nicholas sued to force the estate to transfer the shares. Discuss whether this contract is supported by consideration. [*In re Estate of Weinsaft*, 647 S.W.2d 179 (Mo.App. 1983)]

11–12. Rivendell Forest Products, Ltd., had a computer program—the *Quote Screen* system—that allowed it to quote prices to its customers many times faster than its competitors. To keep the *Quote Screen* system a secret, Rivendell insisted that all of its employees, including Timothy Cornwell, sign a confidentiality agreement in 1988. Cornwell was employed by Rivendell from 1987 to 1990, when he left Rivendell to work as a marketing manager for the Georgia-Pacific Corp., a competitor. Cornwell introduced Georgia-Pacific to Rivendell's *Quote Screen* system. Rivendell sued Cornwell for, among other things, breach of the confidentiality agreement. The trial court held that the confidentiality agreement was not a valid contract because Rivendell had failed to provide consideration, such as a salary increase or a promotion, in exchange for Cornwell's promise to keep the *Quote Screen* system a secret. If Cornwell had signed the confidentiality agreement when he was first hired, would the result have been the same? Explain. [*Rivendell Forest Products, Ltd. v. Georgia-Pacific Corp.*, 824 F.Supp. 961 (D.Colo. 1993)]

11–13. E. S. Herrick Co. grows and sells blueberries. Maine Wild Blueberry Co. agreed to buy all of Herrick's 1990 crop under a contract that left the price unliquidated. Herrick delivered the berries, but a dispute arose over the price. Maine Wild sent Herrick a check with a letter that stated the check was the "final settlement." Herrick cashed the check but filed a suit in a Maine state court against Maine Wild, on the ground of breach of contract, alleging that the buyer owed more. Given these facts, consider the following questions: What will the court likely decide in this case? Why? [*E. S. Herrick Co. v. Maine Wild Blueberry Co.*, 670 A.2d 944 (Me. 1996)]

11–14. New England Rock Services, Inc., agreed to work as a subcontractor on a sewer project on which Empire Paving, Inc., was the general contractor. For drilling and blasting a certain amount of rock, Rock Services was to be paid $29 per cubic yard or on a time-and-materials basis, whichever was less. From the beginning, Rock Services experienced problems. The primary obstacle was a heavy concentration of water, which, according to the custom in the industry, Empire should have controlled but did not. Rock Services was compelled to use more costly and time-consuming methods than anticipated, and it was unable to complete the work on time. The subcontractor asked Empire to pay for the rest of the project on a time-and-materials basis. Empire signed a modification of the original agreement. On completion of the work, Empire refused to pay Rock Services the balance due under the modification. Rock Services filed a suit in a Connecticut state court against Empire. Empire claimed that the modification lacked consideration and was thus not valid and enforceable. Is Empire right? Why, or why not? [*New England Rock Services, Inc. v. Empire Paving, Inc.*, 53 Conn.App. 771, 731 A.2d 784 (1999)]

11–15. In 1995, Helikon Furniture Co. appointed Gaede as its independent sales agent for the sale of its products in parts of Texas. The parties signed a one-year contract that specified, among other things, the commissions that Gaede would receive. Over a year later, although the parties had not signed a new contract, Gaede was still representing Helikon when it was acquired by a third party. Helikon's new management allowed Gaede to continue to perform for the same commissions and sent him a letter stating that it would make no changes in its sales representatives "for at least the next year." Three months later, in December 1997, the new managers sent Gaede a letter proposing new terms for a contract. Gaede continued to sell Helikon products until May 1997 when he received a letter effectively reducing the amount of his commissions. Gaede filed a suit in a Texas state court against Helikon, alleging breach of contract. Helikon argued in part that there was no contract because there was no consideration. In whose favor should the court rule, and why? [*Gaede v. SK Investments, Inc.*, 38 S.W.3d 753 (Tex.App.—Houston [14 Dist.] 2001)]

E-LINKS

For updated links to resources available on the Web, as well as a variety of other materials, visit this text's Web site at

http://wbl-cs.westbuslaw.com

A good way to learn more about how the courts decide such issues as whether consideration was lacking for a particular contract is to look at relevant case law. To find recent cases on contract law decided by the United States Supreme Court and the federal appellate courts, access Cornell University's School of Law site at

http://www.law.cornell.edu/topics/contracts.html

LEGAL RESEARCH EXERCISES ON THE WEB

Go to http://wbl-cs.westbuslaw.com, the Web site that accompanies this text. Select "Interactive Study Center," and then click on "Chapter 11." There you will find the following Internet research exercise that you can perform to learn more about contracts that are enforceable without consideration:

Activity 11–1: Promissory Estoppel

CHAPTER 12
Capacity and Legality

In addition to agreement and consideration, for a contract to be deemed valid the parties to the contract must have **contractual capacity**—the legal ability to enter into a contractual relationship. Courts generally presume the existence of contractual capacity, but there are some situations in which capacity is lacking or may be questionable. In many situations, a party may have the capacity to enter into a valid contract but also have the right to avoid liability under it. For example, minors usually are not legally bound by contracts. We examine these situations in the first part of this chapter.

We then turn to the topic of legality—another element that is required for a valid contract to exist. The agreement must not call for the performance of an illegal act—that is, any act that is criminal, tortious, or otherwise opposed to public policy. In this section of the chapter, we consider illegal contracts, or contracts that are contrary to state or federal statutes or to public policy, and the effects of an illegal bargain. Such contracts are normally void—that is, they really are not contracts at all.

Realize that capacity and legality are not inherently related other than that they are both contract requirements. We treat these topics in one chapter merely for convenience and reasons of space.

Section 1

Contractual Capacity

Historically, the law has given special protection to those who bargain with the inexperience of youth or those who lack the degree of mental competence required by law. *Full competence* exists when both parties have complete legal capacity to enter into a contract and to have the contract enforced against them. *No competence* exists when one or both of the parties have been adjudged by a court to be mentally incompetent and therefore without legal capacity to contract. In this situation, an essential element for a valid contract is missing, and the contract is thus *void*. *Limited competence* exists when one or both of the parties are minors, intoxicated, or mentally incompetent but not yet adjudicated officially as such. These parties have full and legal capacity to enter into a contract; but if they wish, they can normally avoid liability under the contract, which is said to be *voidable*.

Minors

Today, in virtually all states, the **age of majority** (when a person is no longer a minor) for contractual purposes is eighteen years.[1] In addition, some states provide for the termination of minority on marriage. Minority status may also be terminated by a minor's **emancipation,** which occurs when a child's parent or legal guardian relinquishes the legal right to exercise control over the child. Normally, a minor who leaves home to support himself or herself is considered emancipated. Several jurisdictions permit minors to petition a court for emancipation themselves. For business purposes, a minor may petition a court to be treated as an adult.

The general rule is that a minor can enter into any contract that an adult can, provided that the contract is not one prohibited by law for minors (for

1. The age of majority may still be twenty-one for other purposes, such as the purchase and consumption of alcohol.

example, the sale of tobacco or alcoholic beverages). Indeed, any time a minor purchases goods, such as a car or a video game, he or she is entering into a contract. A contract entered into by a minor, however, is voidable at the option of that minor, subject to certain exceptions. To exercise the option to avoid a contract, a minor need only manifest an intention not to be bound by it. The minor "avoids" the contract by disaffirming it.

Minor's Right to Disaffirm. The technical definition of **disaffirmance** is the legal avoidance, or setting aside, of a contractual obligation. A contract can ordinarily be disaffirmed at any time during minority or for a reasonable period after the minor comes of age. Note that the minor must disaffirm the entire contract, not merely a portion of it. For example, the minor cannot decide to keep part of the goods purchased under a contract and return the remaining goods.

Minor's Obligations on Disaffirmance. Although all state laws permit minors to disaffirm contracts (with certain exceptions), states differ on the extent of a minor's obligations on disaffirmance. Courts in a majority of states hold that the minor need only return the goods (or other consideration) subject to the contract, provided the goods are in the minor's possession or control. For example, suppose that Jim Garrison, a seventeen-year-old, purchases a computer from Radio Shack. While transporting the computer to his home, Garrison negligently drops it, breaking the plastic casing. The next day, he returns the computer to Radio Shack and disaffirms the contract. Under the majority view, this return fulfills Garrison's duty even though the computer is now damaged. Garrison is entitled to receive a refund of the purchase price (if paid in cash) or to be relieved of any further obligations under an agreement to purchase the computer on credit.

An increasing number of states, either by statute or by court decision, place an additional duty on the minor—the duty to restore the adult party to the position he or she held before the contract was made. In the example above, Garrison would be required not only to return the computer but also to pay Radio Shack for the damage to the unit.

Westlaw. See Case 12.1 at the end of this chapter. To view the full, unedited case from Westlaw,® go to this text's Web site at **http://wbl-cs.westbuslaw.com**.

Exceptions to the Minor's Right to Disaffirm. State courts and legislatures have carved out several exceptions to the minor's right to disaffirm. Some contracts cannot be avoided simply as a matter of law, on the ground of public policy. For example, marriage contracts and contracts to enlist in the armed services fall into this category. Other contracts may not be disaffirmed for other reasons, including those discussed here.

Misrepresentation of Age. Suppose that a minor tells a seller she is twenty-one years old when she is really seventeen. Ordinarily, the minor can disaffirm the contract even though she has misrepresented her age. Moreover, the minor is not liable in certain jurisdictions for the tort of deceit (fraud) for such misrepresentation, the rationale being that such a tort judgment might indirectly force the minor to perform the contract.

Many jurisdictions, however, find circumstances under which a minor can be bound by a contract when the minor has misrepresented his or her age. First, several states have enacted statutes for precisely this purpose. In these states, misrepresentation of age is enough to prohibit disaffirmance. Other statutes prohibit disaffirmance by a minor who has engaged in business as an adult.

Second, some courts refuse to allow minors to disaffirm executed (fully performed) contracts unless they can return the consideration received. The combination of the minors' misrepresentation and their unjust enrichment has persuaded these courts to *estop* (prevent) minors from asserting contractual incapacity.

Third, some courts allow a misrepresenting minor to disaffirm the contract, but they hold the minor liable for damages in tort. Here, the defrauded party may sue the minor for misrepresentation or fraud. A split in authority exists on this point, because some courts, as previously noted, have recognized that allowing a suit in tort is equivalent to indirectly enforcing the minor's contract.

Contracts for Necessaries. A minor who enters into a contract for necessaries may disaffirm the contract but remains liable for the reasonable value of the goods. **Necessaries** are basic needs, such as food, clothing, shelter, and medical services, at a level of value required to maintain the minor's standard of living or financial and social status. Thus, what will be considered a necessary for one person may be a luxury for another. For example, if a minor from a low-income family contracts for the purchase of a $2,000 coat, a court may deem the coat a luxury. In this situation, the contract would not be for "necessaries."

Additionally, what is considered a necessary depends on whether the minor is under the care or control of his or her parents, who are required by law to provide necessaries for the minor. If a minor's parents provide him or her with shelter, for example, then a contract to lease shelter (such as an apartment) normally will not be classified as a contract for necessaries.

Generally, then, to qualify as a contract for necessaries, (1) the item contracted for must be necessary to the minor's subsistence, (2) the value of the necessary item must be up to a level required to maintain the minor's standard of living or financial and social status, and (3) the minor must not be under the care of a parent or guardian who is required to supply this item. Unless these three criteria are met, the minor can disaffirm the contract *without* being liable for the reasonable value of the goods used.

Insurance and Loans. Traditionally, insurance has not been viewed as a necessary, so minors can ordinarily disaffirm their insurance contracts and recover all premiums paid. Some jurisdictions, however, prohibit the right to disaffirm insurance contracts—for example, when minors contract for life insurance on their own lives. Financial loans are seldom considered to be necessaries, even if the minor spends the money borrowed on necessaries. If, however, a lender makes a loan to a minor for the express purpose of enabling the minor to purchase necessaries, and the lender personally makes sure the money is so spent, the minor normally is obligated to repay the loan.

Ratification. In contract law, **ratification** is the act of accepting and giving legal force to an obligation that previously was not enforceable. In relation to minors' contracts, ratification may be defined as an expression in words or an act by which a person, *on or after reaching majority,* indicates an *intention* to become bound by a contract made as a minor.

An *express* ratification takes place when the individual, on reaching the age of majority, states orally or in writing that he or she intends to be bound by the contract. For example, if Humphrey enters into a contract to sell his laptop computer to Lombard, a minor, Lombard can avoid her legal duty to pay for the laptop by disaffirming the contract. Suppose, though, that Lombard does not disaffirm the contract and on reaching the age of majority writes a letter to Humphrey stating that she still agrees to buy the laptop. Now Lombard has ratified the contract and is legally bound by its terms. An *implied* ratification takes place when the minor, on reaching the age of majority, evidences an intent to abide by the contract. For example, if Lombard takes possession of the laptop as a minor and continues to use it after reaching the age of majority, she has impliedly ratified the contract.

If a minor fails to disaffirm a contract within a reasonable time after reaching the age of majority, then the court must determine whether the conduct constitutes ratification or disaffirmance. Generally, a contract that is *executed* (fully performed by both parties) is presumed to be ratified. A contract that is still *executory* (not yet fully performed by both parties) is considered to be disaffirmed.

Parents' Liability for Minor Children's Contracts and Torts. As a general rule, parents are not liable for contracts made by minor children acting on their own. This is why businesses ordinarily require parents to sign any contract made with a minor. The parents then become personally obligated under the contract to perform the conditions of the contract, even if their child avoids liability.

Generally, minors are personally liable for their own torts. In some states, however, a parent may be liable if he or she failed to exercise proper parental control over the minor child and knew or should have known, from the minor's habits and tendencies, that failure to exercise control posed an unreasonable risk of harm to others. Other states have enacted statutes imposing on parents legal responsibility for the consequences of the tortious acts of their children. These statutes vary. For example, in some states, liability will be imposed on parents only for the willful, malicious, or wanton acts of their minor children. In other states, liability will also be imposed on parents for their children's negligent acts that result from the parents' negligence.

INTOXICATION

Intoxication is a condition in which a person's normal capacity to act or think is inhibited by alcohol or some other drug.[2] A contract entered into by an intoxicated person can be either voidable or valid. If the person was sufficiently intoxicated to lack mental capacity, then the transaction is voidable at the option of the intoxicated person even if the intoxication was purely voluntary. For the contract to be voidable, it must be proved that the intoxicated person's judgment and ability to reason were impaired to such an extent that he or she did not comprehend the legal consequences of entering into the contract. If, despite intoxication, the person understood these legal consequences, the contract will be enforceable.

The fact that the terms of the contract are foolish or obviously favor the other party does not make the contract voidable (unless the other party *fraudulently* induced the person to become intoxicated). Problems often arise in determining whether a party was intoxicated enough to avoid legal duties. Rather than inquire into the intoxicated person's mental state, many courts prefer to look at objective indications to determine whether the contract is voidable owing to intoxication.[3]

If a contract is voidable because of a person's intoxication, that person has the option of disaffirming it—the same option available to a minor. The vast majority of courts, however, require that the intoxicated person make full restitution (fully return any consideration received) as a condition of disaffirmance, except in cases involving necessaries (as explained below). For example, suppose that Briller, who is intoxicated, contracts to purchase a set of encyclopedias from Stevens. If the books are delivered, Briller can disaffirm the executed contract and recover the payment made to Stevens only by returning the encyclopedias.

An intoxicated person, after becoming sober, may ratify a contract expressly or impliedly, just as a minor may do on reaching majority. Implied ratification occurs when a person enters into a contract while intoxicated and fails to disaffirm the contract within a *reasonable* time after becoming sober. Acts or conduct inconsistent with an intent to disaffirm—such as the continued use of property purchased under a voidable contract—will also ratify the contract. In addition, contracts for necessaries are voidable, but the intoxicated person is liable in quasi contract for the reasonable value of the consideration received.

Mentally Incompetent Persons

Contracts made by mentally incompetent persons can be void, voidable, or valid. If a person has been adjudged mentally incompetent by a court of law and a guardian has been appointed, any contract made by the mentally incompetent person is *void*—no contract exists. Only the guardian can enter into binding legal obligations on the incompetent person's behalf.

If a mentally incompetent person not previously so adjudged by a court enters into a contract, the contract may be *voidable* if the person does not know he or she is entering into the contract or lacks the mental capacity to comprehend its nature, purpose, and consequences. In such a situation, the contract is voidable at the option of the mentally incompetent person but not the other party. The contract may then be disaffirmed or ratified. Like minors and intoxicated persons, mentally incompetent persons are liable (in quasi contract) for the reasonable value of any necessaries they receive.

A contract entered into by a mentally incompetent person not previously so adjudged by a court may also be *valid.* A person may be able to understand the nature and effect of entering into a certain contract yet simultaneously lack capacity to engage in other activities. In such cases, the contract will be valid, because the person is not legally mentally incompetent for contractual purposes.[4] Similarly, an otherwise mentally incompetent person may have a *lucid interval*—a temporary restoration of sufficient intelligence, judgment, and will to enter into contracts without disqualification—during which he or she will be considered to have full legal capacity. (Mental incompetence caused by age or disease, such as Alzheimer's disease, is often a problem facing older persons—see

2. The lack of contractual capacity of a person intoxicated while the contract is being made differs from the contractual capacity of an alcoholic. If an alcoholic makes a contract while sober, there is no lack of capacity. See *Olsen v. Hawkins,* 90 Idaho 28, 408 P.2d 462 (1965).

3. See, for example, Case 10.1 *(Lucy v. Zehmer)* in Chapter 10.

4. Modern courts no longer require a person to be completely irrational to disaffirm contracts on the basis of mental incompetence. A contract may be voidable if, due to a mental illness or defect, an individual was unable to act reasonably with respect to the transaction and the other party was aware of the condition. See *Ortelere v. Teachers' Retirement Board,* 25 N.Y.2d 196, 250 N.E.2d 460, 303 N.Y.S.2d 362 (1969).

Chapter 50 for a discussion of this difficulty and how individuals can prepare for such a situation.)

SECTION 2

Legality

A contract to do something that is prohibited by federal or state statutory law is illegal and, as such, void from the outset and thus unenforceable. Also, a contract that calls for a tortious act or an action contrary to public policy is illegal and unenforceable. It is important to note that a contract or a clause in a contract may be illegal even in the absence of a specific statute prohibiting the action promised by the contract.

CONTRACTS CONTRARY TO STATUTE

Statutes often prescribe the terms of contracts. We now examine several ways in which contracts may be contrary to statute and thus illegal.

Usury. Virtually every state has a statute that sets the maximum rate of interest that can be charged for different types of transactions, including ordinary loans. A lender who makes a loan at an interest rate above the lawful maximum is guilty of **usury**. The maximum rate of interest varies from state to state.

Although usury statutes place a ceiling on allowable rates of interest, exceptions have been made to facilitate business transactions. For example, many states exempt corporate loans from the usury laws. In addition, almost all states have adopted special statutes allowing much higher interest rates on small loans to help those borrowers who are in need of money but simply cannot get loans at interest rates below the normal lawful maximum.

In a few states, a usurious loan is a void transaction, and the lender cannot recover either the principal or the interest. A number of states allow the lender to recover only the principal of a usurious loan along with interest up to the legal maximum. In effect, the lender is denied recovery of the excess interest. In other states, the lender can recover the principal amount of the loan but not the interest.

Gambling. All states have statutes that regulate gambling—defined as any scheme that involves distribution of property by chance among persons who have paid a valuable consideration for the opportunity (chance) to receive the property.[5] Gambling is the creation of risk for the purpose of assuming it. Traditionally, state statutes have deemed gambling contracts to be illegal and thus void.

In several states, however, including Nevada, New Jersey, and Louisiana, casino gambling is now lawful. In other states, certain other forms of gambling are lawful. California, for example, has not defined draw poker as a crime, although criminal statutes prohibit numerous other types of gambling games. Several states allow gambling at horse races, and the majority of the states obtain substantial revenues from legalized state-operated lotteries. Many states also allow gambling on Native American reservations.

Sometimes it is difficult to distinguish a gambling contract from the risk sharing inherent in almost all contracts. Suppose that Isaacson takes out a life insurance policy on Donohue, naming himself as beneficiary under the policy. At first glance, this may seem entirely legal; but further examination shows that Isaacson is simply gambling on how long Donohue will live. To prevent that type of practice, insurance contracts can be entered into only by someone with an *insurable interest* (see Chapter 49).

Sabbath (Sunday) Laws. Statutes that are known as Sabbath (Sunday) laws prohibit the formation or performance of certain contracts on a Sunday. Under the common law, such contracts are legal in the absence of this statutory prohibition. Under a few state statutes, all contracts entered into on a Sunday are illegal. Statutes in other states prohibit only the sale of certain types of merchandise, particularly alcoholic beverages, on a Sunday.

These statutes, which date back to colonial times, are often called blue laws. **Blue laws** get their name from the blue paper on which New Haven, Connecticut, printed its Sabbath law in 1781. The ordinance prohibited all work on Sunday and required all shops to close on the "Lord's Day." A number of states enacted laws forbidding the carrying on of "all secular labor and business on the Lord's Day." Exceptions to Sunday laws permit contracts for necessities (such as food or drugs) and works of charity. A fully performed (executed) contract that was entered into on a Sunday, however, cannot be rescinded (canceled).

5. See *Wishing Well Club v. Akron*, 66 Ohio Law Abs. 406, 112 N.E.2d 41 (1951).

Sunday laws are often not enforced, and some of these laws have been held to be unconstitutional on the ground that they are contrary to the freedom of religion. Nonetheless, as a precaution, business owners contemplating doing business in a particular locality should check to see if any Sunday statutes or ordinances will affect their business activities.

Licensing Statutes. All states require that members of certain professions or occupations obtain licenses allowing them to practice. Physicians, lawyers, real estate brokers, architects, electricians, and stockbrokers are but a few of the people who must be licensed. Some licenses are obtained only after extensive schooling and examinations, which indicate to the public that a special skill has been acquired. Others require only that the particular person be of good moral character.

Generally, business licenses provide a means of regulating and taxing certain enterprises and protecting the public against actions that could threaten the general welfare. For example, in nearly all states, a stockbroker must be licensed and must file a bond with the state to protect the public from fraudulent stock transactions. Similarly, a plumber must be licensed and bonded to protect consumers against incompetent plumbers and to safeguard the public health. Only persons or businesses possessing the qualifications and complying with the conditions required by statute are entitled to licenses. Sometimes, for example, an owner of a saloon or tavern is required to sell food as a condition of obtaining a license to sell liquor for consumption on the premises.

When a person enters into a contract with an unlicensed individual, the contract may still be enforceable, depending on the nature of the licensing statute. Some states expressly provide that the lack of a license in certain occupations bars the enforcement of work-related contracts. If the statute does not expressly declare this, one must look to the underlying purpose of the licensing requirements for a particular occupation. If the purpose is to protect the public from unauthorized practitioners, a contract involving an unlicensed individual normally is illegal and unenforceable. If the underlying purpose of the statute is to raise government revenues, however, a contract entered into with an unlicensed practitioner generally is enforceable—although the unlicensed person is usually fined.

Contracts to Commit a Crime. Any contract to commit a crime is a contract in violation of a statute.[6] Thus, a contract to sell an illegal drug (the sale of which is prohibited by statute) is not enforceable. Should the object or performance of the contract be rendered illegal by statute *after* the contract has been entered into, the contract is said to be discharged by law. (See the discussion under "Impossibility or Impracticability of Performance" in Chapter 16.)

Contracts Contrary to Public Policy

Although contracts involve private parties, some are not enforceable because of the negative impact they would have on society. We look here at certain types of contracts that are often said to be *contrary to public policy.*

Contracts in Restraint of Trade. Contracts in restraint of trade (anticompetitive agreements) usually adversely affect the public (which favors competition in the economy) and typically violate one or more federal or state statutes.[7] An exception is recognized when the restraint is reasonable and is contained in an ancillary (subordinate) clause in a contract. Many such exceptions involve a type of restraint called a **covenant not to compete**, or a restrictive covenant.

Covenants (promises) not to compete are often contained as ancillary clauses in contracts concerning the sale of an ongoing business. A covenant not to compete is created when a seller agrees not to open a new store in a certain geographic area surrounding the old store. Such agreements enable the seller to sell, and the purchaser to buy, the goodwill and reputation of an ongoing business. If, for example, a well-known merchant sells his or her store and opens a competing business a block away, many of the customers will likely do business at the well-known merchant's new store. This, in turn, renders valueless the good name and reputation purchased by the new owner of the old store for a price. If a covenant not to compete is not ancillary to a sales agreement, however, it is void, because it unreasonably restrains trade and is contrary to public policy.

6. See, for example, *McConnell v. Commonwealth Pictures Corp.*, 7 N.Y.2d 465, 166 N.E.2d 494, 199 N.Y.S.2d 483 (1960).

7. Federal statutes that prohibit anticompetitive agreements include the Sherman Act, the Clayton Act, and the Federal Trade Commission Act (see Chapter 45).

Agreements not to compete can also be contained in employment contracts. It is common for people in middle-level and upper-level management positions to agree not to work for competitors or not to start competing businesses for a specified period of time after termination of employment. Such agreements are legal so long as the specified period of time (of restraint) is not excessive in duration and the geographic restriction is reasonable.

Westlaw. See Case 12.2 at the end of this chapter. To view the full, unedited case from Westlaw,® go to this text's Web site at **http://wbl-cs.westbuslaw.com**.

Unconscionable Contracts or Clauses. Ordinarily, a court does not look at the fairness or equity of a contract. For example, the courts generally do not inquire into the adequacy of consideration (see Chapter 11). Persons are assumed to be reasonably intelligent, and the courts will not come to their aid just because they have made an unwise or foolish bargain. In certain circumstances, however, bargains are so oppressive that the courts relieve innocent parties of part or all of their duties. Such bargains are called **unconscionable** because they are so unscrupulous or grossly unfair as to be "void of conscience."[8] There are two general types of unconscionability, procedural and substantial.

Procedural Unconscionability. *Procedural* unconscionability has to do with how a term becomes part of a contract and relates to factors that may make it difficult for a party to know or understand the contract terms due to inconspicuous print, unintelligible language ("legalese"), or the lack of an opportunity to read the contract or to ask questions about its meaning. Procedural unconscionability sometimes relates to purported lack of voluntariness due to a disparity in bargaining power between the two parties. Contracts entered into because of one party's vastly superior bargaining power may be deemed unconscionable. These situations usually involve an *adhesion contract,* which, as will be discussed in Chapter 13, is a contract drafted by the dominant party and then presented to the other—the adhering party—on a take-it-or-leave-it basis.[9]

Substantive Unconscionability. *Substantive* unconscionability characterizes those contracts, or portions of contracts, that are oppressive or overly harsh. Courts generally focus on provisions that deprive one party of the benefits of the agreement or leave that party without remedy for nonperformance by the other. For example, suppose that a person with little income and with only a fourth-grade education agrees to purchase a refrigerator for $2,000 and signs a two-year installment contract. The same type of refrigerator usually sells for $400 on the market. Some courts have held this type of contract to be unconscionable, despite the general rule that the courts will not inquire into the adequacy of the consideration, simply because the contract terms are so oppressive as to "shock the conscience" of the court.[10]

Exculpatory Clauses. Closely related to the concept of unconscionability are **exculpatory clauses,** defined as clauses that release a party from liability in the event of monetary or physical injury, no matter who is at fault. Indeed, some courts refer to such clauses in terms of unconscionability. Suppose, for example, that Jones and Laughlin Steel Company hires a laborer and has him sign a contract containing the following clause:

> Said employee hereby agrees with employer, in consideration of such employment, that he will take upon himself all risks incident to his position and will in no case hold the company liable for any injury or damage he may sustain, in his person or otherwise, by accidents or injuries in the factory, or which may result from defective machinery or carelessness or misconduct of himself or any other employee in service of the employer.

This contract provision attempts to remove Jones and Laughlin's potential liability for injuries to the employee, and it would usually be held contrary to public policy.[11] Exculpatory clauses found in rental agreements for commercial property are also frequently held to be contrary to public policy. Additionally, such clauses are almost universally held to be illegal and unenforceable when they are included in residential property leases.

8. The Uniform Commercial Code incorporated the concept of unconscionability in Sections 2–302 and 2A–108. These provisions, which apply to contracts for the sale or lease of goods, will be discussed in Chapter 18.

9. See, for example, *Henningsen v. Bloomfield Motors, Inc.*, 32 N.J. 358, 161 A.2d 69 (1960).

10. See, for example, *Jones v. Star Credit Corp.*, 59 Misc.2d 189, 298 N.Y.S.2d 264 (1969). This case is presented as Case 18.3 in Chapter 18.

11. For a case with similar facts, see *Little Rock & Fort Smith Railway Co. v. Eubanks*, 48 Ark. 460, 3 S.W. 808 (1887). In such a case, the exculpatory clause may also be illegal on the basis of a violation of a state workers' compensation law.

Generally, an exculpatory clause will not be enforced if the party seeking its enforcement is involved in a business that is important to the public interest. These businesses include public utilities, common carriers, and banks. Because of the essential nature of these services, a company offering them has an advantage in bargaining strength and could insist that anyone contracting for its services agree not to hold it liable. As a result, the company would tend to relax its carefulness and the number of injuries would increase. Imagine the results, for example, if all exculpatory clauses in contracts between airlines and their passengers were enforced.

Exculpatory clauses may be enforced, however, when the parties seeking their enforcement are private businesses that are not involved in enterprises considered important to the public interest. These businesses have included health clubs, amusement parks, skiing facilities, horse-rental concessions, golf-cart concessions, and skydiving organizations. Because these services are not essential, the firms offering them are sometimes considered to have no relative advantage in bargaining strength, and anyone contracting for their services is considered to do so voluntarily.

Westlaw. See Case 12.3 at the end of this chapter. To view the full, unedited case from Westlaw,® go to this text's Web site at **http://wbl-cs.westbuslaw.com**.

Other Contracts Contrary to Public Policy. Contracts in which a party promises to discriminate on the basis of race, color, national origin, religion, gender, age, or disability are contrary to statute and contrary to public policy.[12] For example, if a property owner promises in a contract not to sell the property to a member of a particular race, the contract is unenforceable. The public policy underlying these prohibitions is very strong, and the courts are quick to invalidate discriminatory contracts.

Contracts that require a party to commit a civil wrong, or tort, have been held to be contrary to public policy. Remember that a tort is an act that is wrongful to another individual in a private sense, even though it may not necessarily be criminal in nature (an act against society).

Contracts that interfere with the duties of a public officer, such as a city commissioner, are contrary to public policy. Agreements that involve a conflict of interest are also often illegal. Public officers cannot enter into contracts that cause conflict between their official duties as representatives of the people and their private interests. Statutes require many public officers to liquidate their interests in private businesses before serving as elected representatives. Other statutes merely require that while they are in office, they take no part in the operation of or decisions concerning any business in which they have an interest, so that private and public responsibilities remain separate.

Any agreement that is intended to delay, prevent, or obstruct the legal process is illegal. For example, an agreement to pay some specified amount if a criminal prosecution is terminated is illegal. Likewise, agreements to suppress evidence in a legal proceeding or to commit fraud on a court are illegal. Tampering with a jury by offering jurors money in exchange for their votes is illegal.

Effect of Illegality

In general, an illegal contract is void; that is, the contract is deemed never to have existed, and the courts will not aid either party. In most illegal contracts, both parties are considered to be ***in pari delicto***[13] (equally at fault). In such cases, the contract is void. If the contract is executory, neither party can enforce it. If it has been executed, there can be neither contractual nor quasi-contractual recovery.

That one wrongdoer who is a party to an illegal contract is unjustly enriched at the expense of the other is of no concern to the law—except under certain special circumstances that will be discussed below. The major justification for this hands-off attitude is that it is improper to place the machinery of justice at the disposal of a plaintiff who has broken the law by entering into an illegal bargain. Another justification is the hoped-for deterrent effect of this general "hands-off" rule. A plaintiff who suffers loss because of an illegal bargain should presumably be deterred from entering into similar illegal contracts.

Exceptions to the General Rule. There are some exceptions to the general rule that neither party to an illegal bargain can sue for breach and that neither party can recover for performance rendered.

12. The major federal statute prohibiting discrimination is the Civil Rights Act of 1964, 42 U.S.C. Sections 2000e–2000e-17. For a discussion of this act and other acts prohibiting discrimination in the employment context, see Chapter 42.

13. Pronounced in *paa*-ree deh-*lick*-tow.

Justifiable Ignorance of the Facts. When one of the parties is relatively innocent, that party can often recover any benefits conferred in a partially executed contract. In this case, the courts will not enforce the contract but will allow the parties to return to their original positions. An innocent party who has fully performed under the contract may sometimes enforce the contract against the guilty party. For example, a trucking company contracts with Gillespie to carry goods to a specific destination for a normal fee of $500. The trucker delivers the goods and later finds out that the contents of the shipped crates were illegal. Although the law specifies that the shipment, use, and sale of the goods were illegal, the trucker, being an innocent party, can still legally collect the $500 from Gillespie.

Members of Protected Classes. When a statute is clearly designed to protect a certain class of people, a member of that class can enforce a contract in violation of the statute even though the other party cannot. For example, flight attendants and pilots are subject to a federal statute that prohibits them from flying more than a certain number of hours every month. If an attendant or a pilot exceeds the maximum, the airline must nonetheless pay for those extra hours of service.

Other examples of statutes designed to protect particular classes of people include *blue sky laws*—state laws that regulate and supervise investment companies for the protection of the public (see Chapter 37)—and state statutes regulating the sale of insurance. If an insurance company violates a statute when selling insurance, the purchaser can nevertheless enforce the policy and recover from the insurer.

Withdrawal from an Illegal Agreement. If an agreement has been only partly carried out and the illegal portion of the bargain has not yet been performed, the party rendering performance can withdraw from the contract and recover the performance or its value. For example, Sam and Jim decide to wager (illegally) on the outcome of a boxing match. Each deposits money with a stakeholder, who agrees to pay the winner of the bet. At this point, each party has performed part of the agreement, but the illegal element of the agreement will not occur until the money is paid to the winner. Before such payment occurs, either party is entitled to withdraw from the bargain by giving notice of repudiation to the stakeholder.

Contract Illegal through Fraud, Duress, or Undue Influence. Often, illegal contracts involve two blameworthy parties, but one party is more at fault than the other. When a party has been induced to enter into an illegal bargain by fraud, duress, or undue influence on the part of the other party to the agreement, that party will be allowed to recover for the performance or its value.

Severable, or Divisible, Contracts. A contract that is *severable,* or divisible, consists of distinct parts that can be performed separately, with separate consideration provided for each part. An *indivisible* contract, in contrast, exists when the parties intended that complete performance by each party would be essential, even if the contract contains a number of seemingly separate provisions.

If a contract is divisible into legal and illegal portions, a court may enforce the legal portion but not the illegal one, so long as the illegal portion does not affect the essence of the bargain. This approach of the courts is consistent with the basic policy of enforcing the legal intentions of the contracting parties whenever possible. For example, if an overly broad and thus illegal covenant not to compete was drafted into an employment contract, the court might allow the employment contract to be enforceable but reform the unreasonably broad covenant by converting its terms into reasonable ones. Alternatively, the court could declare the covenant illegal (and thus void) and enforce the remaining employment terms.

Terms and Concepts to Review

age of majority 245	disaffirmance 246	necessaries 246
blue law 249	emancipation 245	ratification 247
contractual capacity 245	exculpatory clause 251	unconscionable 251
covenant not to compete 250	*in pari delicto* 252	usury 249

CHAPTER SUMMARY

CONTRACTUAL CAPACITY

Minors	A minor is a person who has not yet reached the age of majority. In most states, the age of majority is eighteen for contract purposes. Contracts with minors are voidable at the option of the minor. **1.** *Disaffirmance*—Defined as the legal avoidance of a contractual obligation. **a.** Disaffirmance can take place (in most states) at any time during minority and within a reasonable time after the minor has reached the age of majority. **b.** If a minor disaffirms a contract, the entire contract must be disaffirmed. **c.** When disaffirming executed contracts, the minor has a duty to return received goods if they are still in the minor's control or (in some states) to pay their reasonable value. **d.** A minor who has committed an act of fraud (such as misrepresentation of age) will be denied the right to disaffirm by some courts. **e.** A minor may disaffirm a contract for necessaries but remains liable for the reasonable value of the goods. **2.** *Ratification*—Defined as the acceptance, or affirmation, of a legal obligation; may be express or implied. **a.** Express ratification—Exists when the minor, through a writing or an oral agreement, explicitly assumes the obligations imposed by the contract. **b.** Implied ratification—Exists when the conduct of the minor is inconsistent with disaffirmance or when the minor fails to disaffirm an executed contract within a reasonable time after reaching the age of majority. **3.** *Parents' liability*—Generally, except for contracts for necessaries, parents are not liable for the contracts made by minor children acting on their own, nor are parents liable for minors' torts except in certain circumstances.
Intoxication	**1.** A contract entered into by an intoxicated person is voidable at the option of the intoxicated person if the person was sufficiently intoxicated to lack mental capacity, even if the intoxication was voluntary. **2.** A contract with an intoxicated person is enforceable if, despite being intoxicated, the person understood the legal consequences of entering into the contract.
Mentally Incompetent Persons	**1.** A contract made by a person adjudged by a court to be mentally incompetent is void. **2.** A contract made by a mentally incompetent person not adjudged by a court to be mentally incompetent is voidable at the option of the mentally incompetent person.

LEGALITY

Contracts Contrary to Statute	**1.** *Usury*—Usury occurs when a lender makes a loan at an interest rate above the lawful maximum. The maximum rate of interest varies from state to state. **2.** *Gambling*—Gambling contracts that contravene (go against) state statutes are deemed illegal and thus void. **3.** *Sabbath (Sunday) laws*—These laws prohibit the formation or the performance of certain contracts on Sunday. Such laws vary widely from state to state, and many states do not enforce them. **4.** *Licensing statutes*—Contracts entered into by persons who do not have a license, when one is required by statute, will not be enforceable *unless* the underlying purpose of the statute is to raise government revenues (and not to protect the public from unauthorized practitioners). **5.** *Contracts to commit a crime*—Any contract to commit a crime is a contract in violation of a statute and is thus not enforceable.
Contracts Contrary to Public Policy	**1.** *Contracts in restraint of trade*—Contracts to reduce or restrain free competition are illegal. Most such contracts are now prohibited by statutes. An exception is a *covenant not to compete.*

CHAPTER SUMMARY—CONTINUED

Contracts Contrary to Public Policy—continued	It is usually enforced by the courts if the terms are ancillary to a contract (such as a contract for the sale of a business or an employment contract) and are reasonable as to time and area of restraint. Courts tend to scrutinize covenants not to compete closely. If a covenant is overbroad, a court may either reform the covenant to fall within reasonable constraints and then enforce the reformed contract or declare the covenant void and thus unenforceable. 2. *Unconscionable contracts or clauses*—When a contract or contract clause is so unfair that it is oppressive to one party, it can be deemed unconscionable; as such, it is illegal and cannot be enforced. 3. *Exculpatory clauses*—An exculpatory clause is a clause that releases a party from liability in the event of monetary or physical injury, no matter who is at fault. In certain situations, exculpatory clauses may be contrary to public policy and thus unenforceable. 4. *Other contracts contrary to public policy*—Contracts that are illegally discriminatory, that require a party to commit a civil wrong, that interfere with the duties of a public officer, or that are intended to delay, prevent, or obstruct the legal process are illegal.
Effect of Illegality	1. *In general*—An illegal contract is void, and the courts will not aid either party when both parties are considered to be equally at fault (*in pari delicto*). If the contract is executory, neither party can enforce it. If the contract is executed, there can be neither contractual nor quasi-contractual recovery. 2. *Exceptions (situations in which recovery is allowed):* a. When one party to the contract is relatively innocent. b. When one party to the contract is a member of a group of persons protected by statute. c. When either party seeks to recover consideration given for an illegal contract before the illegal act is performed. d. When one party was induced to enter into an illegal bargain through fraud, duress, or undue influence.

CASES FOR ANALYSIS

Westlaw. You can access the full text of each case presented below by going to the Westlaw cases on this text's Web site at http://wbl-cs.westbuslaw.com. Each Westlaw case includes the names of all plaintiffs and defendants, the dates on which the case was argued and decided, a brief summary of the issues and decisions in the case, headnotes classifying specific issues in the case according to the West Key Number System, and the court's opinion. Concurring and dissenting opinions, if any, are included as well.

CASE 12.1 MINOR'S OBLIGATION ON DISAFFIRMANCE

DODSON v. SHRADER
Supreme Court of Tennessee, 1992.
824 S.W.2d 545.

O'BRIEN, Justice.

This is an action to disaffirm the contract of a minor for the purchase of a pick-up truck and for a refund of the purchase price. The issue is whether the minor is entitled to a full refund of the money he paid or whether the seller is entitled to a setoff for the decrease in value of the pick-up truck while it was in the possession of the minor.

In early April of 1987, Joseph Eugene Dodson, then 16 years of age, purchased a used 1984 pick-up truck from Burns and Mary Shrader. The Shraders owned and operated Shrader's Auto Sales in Columbia, Tennessee. Dodson paid $4,900 in cash for the truck, using money he borrowed from his girlfriend's grandmother. At the time of the purchase there was no inquiry by the Shraders, and no misrepresentation by Mr. Dodson, concerning his minority. However, Mr. Shrader did testify that at the time he believed Mr. Dodson to be 18 or 19 years of age.

In December 1987, nine (9) months after the date of purchase, the truck began to develop mechanical problems. A mechanic diagnosed the problem as a burnt valve, but could not be certain without inspecting the valves inside the engine. Mr. Dodson did not want, or did not have the money, to effect these repairs. He continued to drive the truck despite the mechanical problems. One month later, in January, the truck's engine "blew up" and the truck became inoperable.

Mr. Dodson parked the vehicle in the front yard at his parents' home where he lived. He contacted the Shraders to rescind [cancel] the purchase of the truck and requested a full refund. The Shraders refused to accept the tender of the truck or to give Mr. Dodson the refund requested.

Mr. Dodson then filed an action in [a Tennessee state] court seeking to rescind the contract and recover the amount paid for the truck. * * * Before the * * * court could hear the case, the truck, while parked in Dodson's front yard, was struck on the left front fender by a hit-and-run driver. At the time of the * * * trial, according to Shrader, the truck was worth only $500 due to the damage to the engine and the left front fender.

The case was heard * * * in November 1988. The trial judge, based on previous common-law decisions and, under the doctrine of *stare decisis* reluctantly granted the rescission. The Shraders were ordered, upon tender and delivery of the truck, to reimburse the $4,900 purchase price to Mr. Dodson. The Shraders appealed.

The [state intermediate] Court of Appeals * * * affirmed * * * .

* * * *

* * * [W]here the minor has not been overreached in any way, and there has been no undue influence, and the contract is a fair and reasonable one, and the minor has actually paid money on the purchase price, and taken and used the article purchased, * * * *he ought not to be permitted to recover the amount actually paid, without allowing the vendor of the goods reasonable compensation for the use of, depreciation, and willful or negligent damage to the article purchased, while in his hands.* If there has been any fraud or imposition on the part of the seller or if the contract is unfair, or any unfair advantage has been taken of the minor inducing him to make the purchase, then the rule does not apply. Whether there has been such an overreaching on the part of the seller, and the fair market value of the property returned, would always, in any case, be a question for the trier of fact [the trial judge or jury]. This rule * * * fully and fairly protect[s] the minor against injustice or imposition, and at the same time it [is] fair to a businessperson who has dealt with such minor in good faith. [Emphasis added.]

This rule is best adapted to modern conditions under which minors are permitted to, and do in fact, transact a great deal of business for themselves, long before they have reached the age of legal majority. Many young people work and earn money and collect it and spend it oftentimes without any oversight or restriction. The law does not question their right to buy if they have the money to pay for their purchases. It seems intolerably burdensome for everyone concerned if merchants and business people cannot deal with them safely, in a fair and reasonable way. Further, it does not appear consistent with practice of proper moral influence upon young people, tend to encourage honesty and integrity, or lead them to a good and useful business future, if they are taught that they can make purchases with their own money, for their own benefit, and after paying for them, and using them until they are worn out and destroyed, go back and compel the vendor to return to them what they have paid upon the purchase price. Such a doctrine can only lead to the corruption of principles and encourage young people in habits of trickery and dishonesty.

* * * *

We note that in this case, some nine (9) months after the date of purchase, the truck purchased by the plaintiff began to develop mechanical problems. Plaintiff was informed of the probable nature of the difficulty which apparently involved internal problems in the engine. He continued to drive the vehicle until the engine "blew up" and the truck became inoperable. Whether or not this involved gross negligence or intentional conduct on his part is a matter for determination at the trial level. It is not possible to determine from this record whether a counterclaim for tortious [wrongful] damage to the vehicle was asserted. After the first tender of the vehicle was made by plaintiff, and refused by the defendant, the truck was damaged by a hit-and-run driver while parked on plaintiff's property. The amount of that damage and the liability for that amount between the purchaser and the vendor, as well as the fair market value of the vehicle at the time of tender, is also an issue for the trier of fact.

The case is remanded to the trial court for further proceedings in accordance with this judgment.

CASE 12.2 CONTRACTS IN RESTRAINT OF TRADE

BRUNSWICK FLOORS, INC. v. GUEST

Court of Appeals of Georgia, 1998.
234 Ga.App. 298,
506 S.E.2d 670.

RUFFIN, Judge.

* * * *

The record shows that Brunswick Floors, [Inc.,] a retail floor covering business, employed [Brian] Guest as a floor covering installer. On September 14, 1995, after approximately five years of employment, Guest signed a covenant not to compete. The covenant prohibited Guest for two years from termination of employment from (1) "engag[ing] in the floor covering installation, or in floor covering services, directly or indirectly, as an individual, partner, adviser, stockholder, director, officer, clerk, principal, agent or employee, within an eighty (80) mile radius from Employer's location at 3550 Darien Highway, Brunswick, Georgia, 31520"; (2) soliciting business in the floor covering business from any customer or providing floor covering services to any customers who have dealt with Brunswick Floors; and (3) disclosing customer lists, records, statistics, or other information acquired by Guest and from aiding or being a party to any acts which would tend to divert, diminish, or prejudice the good will or business of Brunswick Floors.

After Guest signed the covenant, Brunswick Floors sent him to Kansas City for training in advanced carpet installation. Brunswick Floors paid the cost of lodging, airfare, and training, and $150 spending money. [It] also sent Guest to Atlanta for a certification course in floor installation, again bearing the costs of lodging and registration.

Guest terminated his employment with Brunswick Floors in May 1997. That same year, he installed carpet for a company in Savannah, Georgia, for approximately one month. Thereafter, Guest installed carpet as an independent contractor for two other flooring companies in Brunswick, Georgia.

Brunswick Floors filed the underlying action to enjoin Guest based on Guest's breach of the covenant not to compete. Guest responded that the covenant was invalid. The trial court, after conducting an evidentiary hearing, granted an injunction for the nonsolicitation and nondisclosure restrictions, but refused to enjoin Guest from "working for another employer as a carpet layer within an 80 mile radius of Brunswick." * * *

In this appeal, Brunswick Floors asserts that the restriction forbidding Guest from installing carpets for two years in an eighty-mile radius is valid and the trial court erred in denying the injunction. While a contract in general restraint of trade or which tends to lessen competition is against public policy and is void, a restrictive covenant contained in an employment contract is considered to be in partial restraint of trade and will be upheld if the restraint imposed is not unreasonable, is founded on a valuable consideration, and is reasonably necessary to protect the interest of the party in whose favor it is imposed, and does not unduly prejudice the interests of the public. Whether the restraint imposed by the employment contract is reasonable is a question of law for determination by the court, which considers the nature and extent of the trade or business, the situation of the parties, and all the other circumstances. *A three-element test of duration, territorial coverage, and scope of activity has evolved as a helpful tool in examining the reasonableness of the particular factual setting to which it is applied.* Applying this three-element test to the agreement before us, we find the covenant is overbroad with regard to its territorial coverage and scope of activity restrictions. [Emphasis added.]

In evaluating whether the territorial coverage restriction is overbroad, we acknowledge that the goal of a non-competition covenant is to balance two competing rights: first, the employee's right to earn a living and his ability to determine with certainty the prohibited territory; second, the employer's interest in customer relationships created or furthered by its former employee on its behalf and its right to protect itself from the former employee's possible unfair appropriation of contacts developed while working for the employer. Under this analysis, an employer is permitted to include in such a covenant the territory in which the employee has in fact performed work, thus protecting itself from the unfair appropriation of good will and information acquired in the course of that work. In contrast, a restriction relating to the area in which the employer does business is generally unenforceable due to overbreadth, unless the employer can show a legitimate business interest that will be protected by such an expansive geographic description.

In this case, the covenant restricts Guest from working within an 80-mile radius of Brunswick Floors' location in Brunswick. Guest testified at the evidentiary hearing that he performed work for Brunswick Floors as a carpet installer in Jacksonville, Florida, and had performed other jobs outside Glynn County, Georgia. Robert Blake, corporate executive officer and president of Brunswick Floors, testified that the company performed work in markets from Savannah, Georgia, to Jacksonville, Florida. Further, Blake testified that Brunswick Floors maintained store locations in St. Simons Island, and Kingsland in Camden County, Georgia. There was no testimony presented that Guest worked in the entire 80-mile radius of the company's Brunswick store location. The 80-mile radius relates to the area in which the employer, Brunswick Floors, and not the employee, Guest, did business. Consequently, unless Brunswick Floors can show a legitimate business interest for the restriction, the covenant is overbroad.

Blake testified that "if our employees start * * * doing business, working for our competitors, then certainly our market share would face, you know, diminishing status." *Avoidance of competition, however, is not a legitimate business interest.* [Emphasis added.]

Brunswick Floors contends the training and money expended on Guest legitimizes [its] interest. In determining the legitimacy of the interest the employer seeks to protect, the court will take into account the employer's time and monetary investment in the employee's skills and development of his craft. However, in the cases Brunswick Floors cites, the employers spent large sums of money, and the employees received extensive training. This factor, among others, outweighed the minimal harm imposed by the restrictions. Here, Guest's minimal training does not outweigh the substantial harm imposed by prohibiting him from installing carpet in an 80-mile radius. Thus, we find this to be an overbroad territorial limitation.

We also find the scope of activity prohibited in the non-compete provision is overbroad. The covenant provides that Guest may not "engage in the floor covering installation, or in floor covering services, directly or indirectly, as an individual, partner, adviser, stockholder, director, officer, clerk, principal, agent or employee * * * ." This imposes a greater limitation on the employee than is necessary because Guest is prohibited from being an officer or director or owning stock in other companies, activities which are very different from his work as a floor covering installer. As a result, this restriction is broader than necessary to protect the employer.

Accordingly, we affirm the trial court's refusal to enjoin Guest "from working for another employer as a carpet layer within an 80 mile radius of Brunswick."

CASE 12.3 EXCULPATORY CLAUSES

BEAVER v. GRAND PRIX KARTING ASSOCIATION, INC.

United States Court of Appeals for the Seventh Circuit, 2001.
246 F.3d 905.

TERENCE T. EVANS, Circuit Judge.

* * * [T]he sport of automobile racing is a hazardous activity, and drivers on the NASCAR circuit know very well that they risk life and limb every time they get into a race. The same can be said, though to a lesser degree, to be sure, of go kart racers. As karts have become faster and more maneuverable, the sport has matured from little more than child's play to a rather dangerous activity. Although the risks of negotiating a race course at high speeds in a vehicle that offers little protection seem obvious, organizers of go kart races have adopted the practice of requiring participants to sign a release flagging those risks and waiving claims arising from injuries sustained during a race. In this case we confront the question of whether such a release can be enforced against a racer who likely was aware of the requirement that she execute it, but somehow participated in the race without doing so.

First, a little bit of background. In July of 1994, plaintiff Dorothy Beaver participated in the annual Elkhart Grand Prix, a series of go kart races held in Elkhart, Indiana. During the event in which she drove, a piece of polyurethane foam padding used as a course barrier was torn from its base and ended up on the track. One portion of the padding struck Beaver in the head, and another portion was thrown into oncoming traffic, causing a multi-kart collision during which Beaver sustained severe injuries. In 1996 Beaver and her husband Stacy filed this diversity action [an action in which jurisdiction is based on diversity of citizenship, as occurs when the plaintiff and defendant reside in different states—see Chapter 2] against the race organizers (Grand Prix Karting Association, Inc., National Kart News, Inc., and Curt Paluzzi) and the manufacturers of the foam padding (Foamcraft, Inc. and, by later amendment, Foamex International, Inc. and Foamex L.P.) which the Beavers claimed was defective. The race organizers denied the material allegations of the complaint * * * and asserted the affirmative defense that Beaver "executed a valid and proper release and indemnification agreement."

Much to the race organizers' chagrin, discovery revealed that the release upon which they relied was executed by Beaver prior to the 1993 Elkhart Grand Prix, a race in which she participated one year before her accident. A search for a release executed by Beaver for the 1994 race turned up nothing. Despite this major setback, the race organizers pressed on with a motion for summary judgment, arguing (1) the evidence demonstrated Beaver had executed a release applicable to the 1994 race (notwithstanding their inability to find it) and, (2) even if she had not executed such a release, her actions manifested her intention to be bound by its terms.

* * * *

At the trial, Beaver testified that she had participated in a number of go kart races since taking up the sport in 1985, that many of these races required her to execute a release in order to participate, and that she had never refused to sign one. Beaver acknowledged her signature on the release for the 1993 Elkhart Grand Prix but could not remember executing a fresh copy at registration for the 1994 race. Although she participated in the 1994 race, and a photograph of her taken prior to the race shows her wearing a wristband she received at race registration, Beaver remembers nothing about the 1994 race due to the injuries she sustained.

Paluzzi, the race promoter, testified for the defense. He stated that all participants in the 1994 race were required to sign a release, identical to the one used in 1993, as part of the registration process. Paluzzi confirmed that Beaver had pre-registered and checked in at the race site. It was never brought to Paluzzi's attention that anyone refused to sign the release, and if anyone had done so, he or she would not have been permitted to race. Paluzzi admitted, however, that he had searched far and wide for Beaver's 1994 release before coming up dry. In addition, Paluzzi admitted that several race officials who entered a "restricted area" (i.e., the track, pit, and other potentially dangerous areas covered by the release) had not executed releases.

Paluzzi's testimony was corroborated by several other race officials who testified that race policy required a release and that they could conceive of no way a racer could complete registration without executing one. At least two of these individuals admitted that they did not sign releases themselves, however, despite the fact that they entered restricted areas. Finally, the race organizers called a host of witnesses who testified that in the dozens (or hundreds) of races in which they had participated, a release was always required.

Beaver's mother, father, and brother—all go kart racers themselves—testified by deposition. Although her mother could remember no race that did not require a release, her father and brother each named certain events that permitted drivers to race without executing a release. None of Beaver's family members had ever refused to sign a release when asked. In addition, an acquaintance of Beaver's named C.J. Van Dorn testified that he had gone to race-day registration with Beaver, and that neither she, her brother, nor Van Dorn had signed a release.

* * * *

* * * Based on the jury's determination that Beaver had agreed to be bound by the terms of the release, the district court entered summary judgment in favor of the race organizers. Beaver appeals.

Beaver raises a host of alleged errors committed by the district court, but her primary argument is that she may be bound by the release only if she expressly agreed to its terms. An express agreement, according to the sixth edition of *Black's Law Dictionary,* is one that is "[m]anifested by direct and appropriate language, as distinguished from that which is inferred from conduct." As the jury found (and the race organizers do not dispute on appeal), Beaver never executed a release applicable to the 1994 race. And there is no evidence that she ever orally indicated her assent to be bound by its terms. * * *

* * * [C]ourts repeatedly have held that assent to a contract—and that, in essence, is what a release is—may be established by acts which manifest acceptance. * * * Such a manifestation or expression of assent necessary to form a contract may be by work, act, or conduct which evinces the intention of the parties to contract.

Release and indemnification agreements are governed by the same rules as other contracts, including the rule that assent to the terms of a contract may be manifested by a party's actions. * * * [A]ssent to a limitation of liability may be assumed where a knowledgeable party enters into the contract, aware of the limitation and its legal effect, without indicating non-acquiescence [lack of agreement] to those terms. * * * [Emphasis added.]

The question of whether assent to an exculpatory clause can be gleaned from a party's actions is generally a question of fact. * * * Based on the evidence presented, the jury reasonably concluded that it is the custom and practice of the go kart industry, as well as the Elkhart Grand Prix, to require race participants to execute releases. The jury further reasonably concluded that Beaver was well aware of this requirement and chose to participate in the 1994 race anyway. * * * [T]hese facts sufficiently establish Beaver's assent to the release.

* * * *

In sum, we find a sufficient legal and factual basis to hold Beaver to the terms of the 1994 release. * * * [T]he district court's judgment is affirmed.

CASE PROBLEMS

12–1. Frank Feiden was diagnosed with Alzheimer's disease in 1982. On January 11, 1986, during a hospital stay for surgery, Feiden conveyed his farm to his sons, Harry and Norman. Harry was deeded a larger share of the property than Norman. Norman asked a court to set the deeds aside, alleging that his father was not mentally competent when the deeds were signed. Conflicting medical evidence was introduced at trial. A physician, a psychiatrist, and an attorney all testified that when they had seen Frank at various times during 1985 and early 1986, Frank had been unable to handle his financial affairs or understand the legal consequences of his actions. Another psychiatrist, however, testified that Frank "had lucid intervals." The attorney who obtained Frank's signatures on the deeds stated that Frank understood what he was signing and was aware that he was deeding more of the property to Harry than to Norman. The nursing summaries indicated that on the day that the deeds were signed, Frank was having lucid periods. How should the court rule? Explain fully. [*Feiden v. Feiden,* 151 A.D.2d 889, 542 N.Y.2d 860 (1989)]

12–2. Smith purchased a car on credit from Bobby Floars Toyota, Inc., a month before his eighteenth birthday. Smith made regular monthly payments for eleven months but then returned the car to the dealer and made no further payments on it. The dealer sold the car and sued Smith to recover the difference between the amount obtained by the sale of the car and the money Smith still owed to the dealer. Smith refused to pay on the ground that he had been a minor at the time of purchase and had disaffirmed the contract after he had reached the age of majority. Will the car dealer succeed in its claim that the ten monthly payments made after Smith turned eighteen constituted a ratification of the purchase contract? Discuss. [*Bobby Floars Toyota, Inc. v. Smith,* 48 N.C.App. 580, 269 S.E.2d 320 (1980)]

12–3. Robertson, a minor, entered into a conditional sales agreement whereby he purchased a pickup truck from Julian Pontiac Co. for $1,743.85. Robertson traded in a passenger car for which he was given a credit of $723.85 on the purchase price, leaving a balance of $1,020, which he agreed to pay in twenty-three monthly installments. Robertson had already paid one of the installments when the pickup truck began to experience electrical wiring difficulties. Less than a month after the purchase of the truck, Robertson turned eighteen. About two weeks later, as a result of the electrical wiring defects, the truck caught fire and was practically destroyed. Robertson refused to make any further payments under the installment agreement. Julian Pontiac sued Robertson to recover the truck. Robertson filed a complaint to rescind the contract and recover the amounts he had paid. Who prevailed? [*Robertson v. King*, 225 Ark. 276, 280 S.W.2d 402 (1955)]

12–4. Spaulding, a minor, entered into a contract with New England Furniture Co. for the purchase of bedroom furniture and a stove. The purchase included a three-piece bedroom set that was priced significantly higher than most other three-piece bedroom sets on the market and an expensive combination oil-and-gas stove. After making several payments, Spaulding defaulted, disaffirmed his contract, and allowed the company to remove all the furniture and the stove. New England Furniture, however, refused to return the money that Spaulding had already paid. Was Spaulding able to recover these payments? Why, or why not? [*Spaulding v. New England Furniture Co.*, 154 Me. 330, 147 A.2d 916 (1959)]

12–5. Johnny Hays, a sixteen-year-old minor, went to Quality Motors, Inc., seeking to purchase a car. The salesperson refused to sell the car unless the purchase was made by an adult. Shortly thereafter, Johnny returned with a young man of twenty-three whom Johnny had met that day for the first time. The sales agent then accepted Hays's cashier's check, and a bill of sale was made out to the twenty-three-year-old. The salesperson recommended a notary public who could prepare the necessary papers to transfer title from the young man to Johnny and then drove the two boys into town for this purpose. The young man transferred title to Johnny, and the salesperson delivered the car to Johnny. Johnny's father attempted to return the car to Quality Motors for a full refund, but Quality Motors refused it. The car was stored while Johnny's father sought to get Quality Motors to take it back, but Johnny found the keys and wrecked the car in an accident. Johnny, through his father, brought suit to disaffirm the contract and recover the purchase price. Can Johnny disaffirm this contract although it was nominally made by an adult? [*Quality Motors, Inc. v. Hays*, 216 Ark. 264, 225 S.W.2d 326 (1949)]

12–6. In 1983, Doughty contracted to sell a portion of his anticipated potato crop to Idaho Frozen Foods Corp. (IFF) to secure financing for the growing of the crop. To express the terms of their agreement, the parties used a "form" contract that had been developed through negotiations between IFF and the Potato Growers of Idaho (PGI), of which Doughty was not a member. Under the contract, Doughty was to receive a base price if the potato crop contained a certain percentage of potatoes weighing ten ounces or more. If the crop contained a higher percentage, the price would be increased. Conversely, if the crop contained a lower percentage, the price would be reduced. These provisions in the contract reflected IFF's desire to have potatoes a certain size in order to meet its processing needs. The contract also provided IFF with the option of accepting or refusing delivery of the potatoes if less than 10 percent of them weighed ten ounces or more. Doughty contracted to sell only a portion of his crop to IFF; the rest of his crop he sold to another processor on the "fresh pack" market—in which potatoes are packaged in sacks and sold for whole use, such as for baking potatoes—for $4.69 per hundredweight. In the fresh pack market, no preharvest contract is used. The potatoes are sold after harvest. Because of poor weather conditions, only 8 percent of Doughty's potato crop consisted of ten-ounce potatoes. Because of the small percentage of ten-ounce potatoes, Doughty was entitled to only $2.57 per hundredweight for his potatoes under the terms of the IFF contract. After four days of delivery under the contract, Doughty refused to deliver any more potatoes to IFF. IFF brought suit for breach of contract. Doughty claimed that the contract was not enforceable because it was unconscionable and therefore void. Will the court agree? Discuss. [*Doughty v. Idaho Frozen Foods Corp.*, 112 Idaho 791, 736 P.2d 460 (1987)]

12–7. George Aubin, the ex-president of a failed bank and a resident of Texas (where gambling debts are unenforceable), traveled to the Bahamas (where gambling debts are enforceable) to gamble at the Cable Beach Hotel and Casino, owned by Carnival Leisure Industries, Ltd. Aubin took more than $2,000, which he lost at blackjack. The casino then approved credit of up to $25,000 for Aubin, if he chose to take advantage of it. In less than two days, Aubin gambled away the entire $25,000, issued to him in exchange for drafts (instruments similar to checks that ordered Aubin's bank in Texas to pay a certain sum of money to the casino). On each draft was printed "I represent that I have received cash for the above amount and that said amount is on deposit in said financial entity in my name, is free and clear of claim and is subject to this check and is hereby assigned to payee, and I guarantee payment with exchange and costs in collecting." Aubin returned to Texas. Over the next six weeks, Carnival sent Aubin letters asking him to pay the $25,000. When Aubin did not respond, Carnival presented the drafts to Aubin's bank for payment. Aubin had already directed his bank to stop payment. Carnival sued Aubin for the $25,000, on the ground of fraud, among other things. Aubin claimed that he had signed only markers (IOUs), not drafts, and that he had had no intention of honoring any drafts. How should the court rule? Discuss. [*Carnival Leisure Industries, Ltd. v. Aubin*, 830 F.Supp. 371 (S.D.Tex. 1993)]

12–8. In 1982, Webster Street Partnership, Ltd. (Webster), entered into a lease agreement for an apartment with Matthew Sheridan and Pat Wilwerding. Webster was aware that both Sheridan and Wilwerding were minors. Both tenants were living away from home, apparently with the understanding that they could return home at any time. Sheridan and Wilwerding paid the first month's rent but then failed to pay the rent for the next month and vacated the apartment. Webster sued them for breach of contract. They claimed that the lease agreement was voidable because they were minors. Who will prevail, and why? [*Webster Street Partnership, Ltd. v. Sheridan*, 220 Neb. 9, 368 N.W.2d 439 (1985)]

12–9. When he was seventeen years old, Sean Power bought an automobile insurance policy from Allstate Insurance Co. At the time, he rejected Allstate's offer of underinsured motorist coverage. Three months later, Power was injured in an automobile accident. The other driver's insurance was not enough to pay for Power's injuries. Power filed a suit in a South Carolina state court against Allstate, claiming that he could disaffirm the part of his insurance contract in which he had rejected the underinsured motorist coverage. Will the court allow Power to disaffirm his contract only in part? Why, or why not? [*Power v. Allstate Insurance Co.*, 2312 S.C. 381, 440 S.E.2d 406 (1994)]

12–10. Tony's Tortilla Factory, Inc., had two checking accounts with First Bank. Owing to financial difficulties, Tony's wrote a total of 2,165 checks (totaling $88,000) for which there were insufficient funds in the accounts. First Bank covered the overdrawn checks but imposed an "NSF" (nonsufficient funds) fee of $20 for each check covered. The owners of Tony's sued First Bank and one of its officers, alleging, among other things, that the $20-per-check fee was essentially "interest" charged by the bank for Tony's use of the bank's money (the money the bank advanced to cover the bad checks); because the rate of "interest" charged by the bank ($20 per check) exceeded the rate allowed by law, it was usurious. First Bank claimed that its NSF fees were not interest but fees charged to cover its costs in processing checks drawn on accounts with insufficient funds. How should the court decide this issue? Discuss fully. [*First Bank v. Tony's Tortilla Factory, Inc.*, 877 S.W.2d 285 (Tex. 1994)]

12–11. No law prohibits citizens in a state that does not sponsor a state-operated lottery from purchasing lottery tickets in a state that does have such a lottery. Because Georgia did not have a state-operated lottery, Talley and several other Georgia residents allegedly agreed to purchase a ticket in a lottery sponsored by Kentucky and to share the proceeds if they won. They did win, but apparently Talley had difficulty collecting his share of the proceeds. In Talley's suit to obtain his portion of the funds, a Georgia trial court held that the "gambling contract" was unenforceable because it was contrary to Georgia's public policy. On appeal, how should the court rule on this issue? Discuss. [*Talley v. Mathis*, 265 Ga. 179, 453 S.E.2d 704 (1995)]

12–12. Sergei Samsonov is a Russian and one of the top hockey players in the world. When Samsonov was seventeen years old, he signed a contract to play hockey for two seasons with the Central Sports Army Club, a Russian club known by the abbreviation CSKA. Before the start of the second season, Samsonov learned that because of a dispute between CSKA coaches, he would not be playing in Russia's premier hockey league. Samsonov hired Athletes and Artists, Inc. (A&A), an American sports agency, to make a deal with a U.S. hockey team. Samsonov signed a contract to play for the Detroit Vipers (the corporate name of which was, at the time, Arena Associates, Inc.). Neither A&A nor Arena knew about the CSKA contract. CSKA filed a suit in a federal district court against Arena and others, alleging, among other things, wrongful interference with a contractual relationship. What effect will Samsonov's age have on the outcome of this suit? [*Central Sports Army Club v. Arena Associates, Inc.*, 952 F.Supp. 181 (S.D.N.Y. 1997)]

12–13. Norbert Eelbode applied for a job with Travelers Inn in the state of Washington. As part of the application process, Eelbode was sent to Laura Grothe, a physical therapist at Chec Medical Centers, Inc., for a preemployment physical exam. Before the exam, Eelbode signed a document that stated in part, "I hereby release Chec and the Washington Readicare Medical Group and its physicians from all liability arising from any injury to me resulting from my participation in the exam." During the exam, Grothe asked Eelbode to lift an item while bending from the waist using only his back with his knees locked. Eelbode experienced immediate sharp and burning pain in his lower back and down the back of his right leg. Eelbode filed a suit in a Washington state court against Grothe and Chec, claiming that he was injured because of an improperly administered back torso strength test. Grothe and Chec cited the document that Eelbode signed, and filed a motion for summary judgment. Should the court grant the motion? Why, or why not? [*Eelbode v. Chec Medical Centers, Inc.*, 984 P.2d 436 (Wash.App. 1999)]

12–14. In 1993, Mutual Service Casualty Insurance Co. and its affiliates (collectively, MSI) hired Thomas Brass as an insurance agent. Three years later, Brass entered into a career agent's contract with MSI. This contract contained provisions regarding Brass's activities after termination. These provisions stated that Brass could not solicit any MSI customers to "lapse, cancel, or replace" any insurance contract in force with MSI in an effort to take that business to a competitor, for a period of not less than one year. If he did, MSI could at any time refuse to pay the commissions that it otherwise owed him. The contract also restricted Brass from working for American National Insurance Co. for three years after termination. In 1998, Brass quit MSI and went immediately to work for American National, soliciting MSI customers. MSI filed a suit in a Wisconsin state court against Brass, claiming that he violated the noncompete terms of his MSI contract. Should the court enforce the covenant not to compete? Why, or why not? [*Mutual Service Casualty Insurance Co. v. Brass*, 625 N.W.2d 648 (Wis.App. 2001)]

12–15. A Question of Ethics

Nancy Levy worked for Health Care Financial Enterprises, Inc., and signed a noncompete agreement in June 1992. When Levy left Health Care and opened up her own similar business in 1993, Health Care brought a court action in a Florida state court to enforce the covenant not to compete. The trial court concluded that the noncompete agreement prevented Levy from working in too broad a geographic area and thus refused to enforce the agreement. A Florida appellate court, however, reversed the trial court's ruling and remanded the case with instructions that the trial court modify the geographic area to make it reasonable and then enforce the covenant. [*Health Care Financial Enterprises, Inc. v. Levy,* 715 So.2d 341 (Fla.App.4th 1998)]

1. What interests are served by refusing to enforce covenants not to compete? What interests are served by allowing them to be enforced?
2. What argument could be made in support of reforming (and then enforcing) illegal covenants not to compete? What argument could be made against this practice?

E-Links

For updated links to resources available on the Web, as well as a variety of other materials, visit this text's Web site at

http://wbl-cs.westbuslaw.com

For state statutory provisions governing the emancipation of minors, go to

http://www.law.cornell.edu/topics/Table_Emancipation.htm

If you are interested in reading about some "Sunday laws" in colonial America, go to

http://www.natreformassn.org/statesman/99/charactr.html

Legal Research Exercises on the Web

Go to http://wbl-cs.westbuslaw.com, the Web site that accompanies this text. Select "Interactive Study Center," and then click on "Chapter 12." There you will find the following Internet research exercise that you can perform to learn more about the law governing minors:

Activity 12–1: Minors and the Law

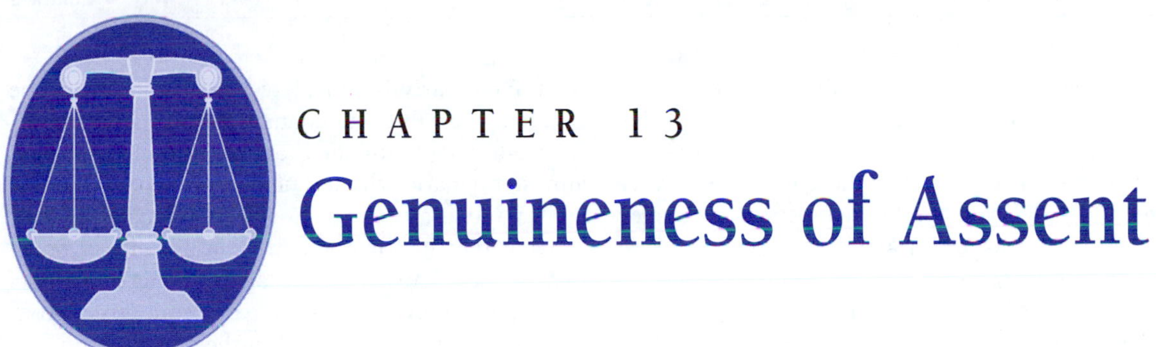

CHAPTER 13

Genuineness of Assent

A CONTRACT HAS BEEN ENTERED INTO by two parties, each with full legal capacity and for a legal purpose. The contract is also supported by consideration. The contract thus meets the four requirements for a valid contract that were specified in Chapter 9. Nonetheless, the contract may be unenforceable if the parties have not genuinely assented to its terms. As stated in Chapter 9, lack of **genuineness of assent** can be used as a defense to the contract's enforceability.

Genuineness of assent may be lacking because of a mistake, misrepresentation, undue influence, or duress—in other words, because there is no true "meeting of the minds." In this chapter, we examine problems relating to genuineness of assent.

SECTION 1

Mistakes

We all make mistakes, and it is therefore not surprising that mistakes are made when contracts are formed. It is important to distinguish between *mistakes of fact* and *mistakes of value or quality*. Only a mistake of fact allows a contract to be avoided.

MISTAKES OF FACT

Mistakes of fact occur in two forms—*unilateral* and *mutual (bilateral)*. A unilateral mistake is made by only one of the contracting parties; a mutual, or bilateral, mistake is made by both.

Unilateral Mistakes of Fact. A unilateral mistake occurs when one contracting party makes a mistake as to some *material fact*—that is, a fact important to the subject matter of the contract. The general rule is that a unilateral mistake does not afford the mistaken party any right to relief from the contract. For example, DeVinck intends to sell his motor home for $17,500. When he learns that Benson is interested in buying a used motor home, DeVinck faxes Benson an offer to sell the vehicle to him. When typing the fax, however, DeVinck mistakenly keys in the price of $15,700. Benson immediately sends DeVinck a fax, accepting DeVinck's offer. Even though DeVinck intended to sell his motor home for $17,500, his unilateral mistake falls on him. He is bound in contract to sell the motor home to Benson for $15,700.

There are at least two exceptions to this general rule.[1] First, if the *other* party to the contract knows or should have known that a mistake of fact was made, the contract may not be enforceable. In the above example, if Benson knew that DeVinck intended to sell his motor home for $17,500, then DeVinck's unilateral mistake (stating $15,700 in his offer) may render the resulting contract unenforceable. The second exception arises when a unilateral mistake of fact was due to a mathematical mistake in addition, subtraction, division, or multiplication and was made inadvertently and without gross (extreme) negligence. If a contractor's bid was low because he or she made a mistake in addition when totaling the estimated costs, any contract resulting from the bid may be rescinded. Of course, in both situations, the mistake must still involve some *material fact*.

Bilateral Mistakes of Fact. When both parties are mistaken about the same material fact, the contract can be rescinded by either party.[2] To illustrate:

1. The *Restatement (Second) of Contracts*, Section 153, liberalizes the general rule to take into account the modern trend of allowing avoidance even though only one party has been mistaken.
2. *Restatement (Second) of Contracts*, Section 152.

Assume that at Umberto's art gallery, Keeley buys a painting of a landscape. Both Umberto and Keeley believe that the painting is by the artist Van Gogh. Later, Keeley discovers that the painting is a very clever fake. Because neither Umberto nor Keeley was aware of this material fact when they made their deal, Keeley can rescind the contract and recover the purchase price of the painting.

A word or term in a contract may be subject to more than one reasonable interpretation. In that situation, if the parties to the contract attach materially different meanings to the term, their mutual mistake of fact may allow the contract to be rescinded because there has been no "meeting of the minds," or true assent, which is required for a contract to arise.

MISTAKES OF VALUE

If a mistake concerns the future market value or quality of the object of the contract, the mistake is one of *value,* and the contract normally can be enforced by either party. As with mistakes of fact, mistakes of value may be unilateral or bilateral. For example, suppose that Wong Sun plans to buy ten acres of land in Montana, believing that the land is worth $100,000. After he purchases the land, he learns that it is worth only $40,000. Wong Sun's unilateral mistake of value cannot be a basis for avoiding the contract.

Similarly, a bilateral mistake of value or quality will not serve as a basis for avoiding the contract. For example, suppose that Yu Chin, after seeing Bev Weiler's violin, buys it for $250. Although both parties know that it is very old, neither party believes that it is extremely valuable. An antiques dealer later informs the parties, however, that old violins in good condition, such as this one, are rare and worth thousands of dollars. Although Weiler may claim that a mutual mistake has been made, the mistake is not a mistake of fact that warrants contract rescission. Both Chin and Weiler mistook the *value* of that particular violin. Therefore, the contract cannot be rescinded.

The reason that mistakes of value or quality have no legal significance is that value is variable. Depending on the time, place, and other circumstances, the same item may be worth considerably different amounts. When parties contract, their agreement establishes the value of the object of their transaction—for the moment. At the next moment, the value may change. Either party may be mistaken as to the shape that change will take, but a mistake as to value will almost never justify voiding a contract. Each party is considered to have assumed the risk that the value will change or prove to be different from what he or she thought. Without this rule, almost any party who did not receive what he or she considered a fair bargain could argue mistake.

Note that in some situations a mistake of value may occur because of a mistake of material fact. As pointed out previously, if the parties are mistaken as to some fact that is material to their transaction, the transaction may be avoided. This rule applies when the fact affects the value of the subject matter of the parties' deal. For example, an early Michigan case, *Sherwood v. Walker,*[3] involved two farmers who entered into a contract for the purchase of a cow. The owner told the purchaser that the cow was barren (incapable of breeding and producing calves). Based on this belief, the parties negotiated a price several hundred dollars less than it would have been had the cow been capable of breeding. Just before delivery, the owner discovered the cow had conceived a calf, and he refused to deliver the much more valuable cow to the purchaser. In a split decision, the court held that "a barren cow is substantially a different creature than a breeding one," and the transaction was avoided.

SECTION 2

Fraudulent Misrepresentation

Although fraud is a tort (see Chapter 5), it also affects the genuineness of the innocent party's consent to the contract. Thus, the transaction is not voluntary in the sense of involving "mutual assent." When an innocent party is fraudulently induced to enter into a contract, the contract normally can be avoided because that party has not *voluntarily* consented to its terms.[4] Normally, the innocent party can either rescind the contract and be restored to his or her original position or enforce the contract and seek damages for any injuries resulting from the fraud.

The word *fraudulent* means many things in the law. Generally, fraudulent misrepresentation refers only to misrepresentation that is consciously false and is intended to mislead another. The perpetrator of the fraudulent misrepresentation knows or believes that the assertion is false or knows that he or she does not have a basis (stated or implied) for the assertion.[5]

3. 66 Mich. 568, 33 N.W. 919 (1887).

4. *Restatement (Second) of Contracts,* Sections 163 and 164.

5. *Restatement (Second) of Contracts,* Section 162.

What is at issue is whether the defendant believed that the plaintiff was substantially certain to be misled as a result of the misrepresentation. Dantzler, for example, makes a statement to the ABC Credit Rating Company about his financial condition that he knows is untrue. Dantzler realizes that ABC will publish this information for its subscribers. Marchetti, a subscriber, receives the published information. Relying on that information, Marchetti is induced to make a contract to lend money to Dantzler. Dantzler's statement is a fraudulent misrepresentation, and the contract is voidable by Marchetti.

Typically, fraudulent misrepresentation consists of the following elements:

1. A misrepresentation of a material fact must occur.
2. There must be an intent to deceive.
3. The innocent party must justifiably rely on the misrepresentation.

To collect damages, a party must also have been injured. To obtain rescission of a contract, or to defend against the enforcement of a contract on the basis of fraudulent misrepresentation, in most states a party need not have suffered an injury.

MISREPRESENTATION HAS OCCURRED

The first element of proving fraud is to show that misrepresentation of a material fact has occurred. This misrepresentation can occur by words or actions. For example, the statement "This sculpture was created by Michelangelo" is an express misrepresentation of fact if the statue was sculpted by another artist. The misrepresentation as to the identity of the artist would certainly be a material fact in the formation of a contract.

Representations of future facts (predictions) and statements of opinion are generally not subject to claims of fraud. Every person is expected to exercise care and judgment when entering into contracts, and the law will not come to the aid of one who simply makes an unwise bargain. Statements such as "This land will be worth twice as much next year" or "This car will last for years and years," for example, are statements of opinion, not fact. Contracting parties should recognize them as such and not rely on them. An opinion is usually subject to contrary or conflicting views; a fact is objective and verifiable. A seller of goods, then, is allowed to use *puffery* to sell his or her wares without liability for fraud.

In certain cases, however, particularly when a naïve purchaser relies on a so-called expert's opinion, the innocent party may be entitled to rescission or reformation. (*Reformation* is an equitable remedy granted by a court in which the terms of a contract are altered to reflect the true intentions of the parties—see Chapter 17.)

See Case 13.1 at the end of this chapter. To view the full, unedited case from Westlaw,® go to this text's Web site at **http://wbl-cs.westbuslaw.com**.

Misrepresentation by Conduct. Misrepresentation can also take place through the conduct of a party, such as concealment. Concealment involves preventing the other party from learning of a material fact.[6] Suppose, for example, that Rakas contracts to buy a new car from Bustamonte, a dealer in new automobiles. The car has been used as a demonstration model for prospective customers to test-drive, but Bustamonte has turned back the odometer. Rakas cannot tell from the odometer reading that the car has been driven nearly five hundred miles, and Bustamonte does not tell Rakas the distance the car has actually been driven. The concealment constitutes fraud because of Bustamonte's conduct.

Misrepresentation of Law. Misrepresentation of law does not *ordinarily* entitle a party to relief from a contract. For example, Camara has a parcel of property that she is trying to sell to Pye. Camara knows that a local ordinance prohibits building anything higher than three stories on the property. Nonetheless, she tells Pye, "You can build a condominium fifty stories high if you want to." Pye buys the land and later discovers that Camara's statement is false. Normally, Pye cannot avoid the contract, because at common law people are assumed to know state and local ordinances. Additionally, a layperson should not rely on a statement made by a nonlawyer about a point of law.

Exceptions to this rule occur, however, when the misrepresenting party is in a profession that is known to require greater knowledge of the law than the average citizen possesses. The courts are recognizing an increasing number of such professions. For example, the courts recognize that real estate brokers are expected by their clients to know the law governing real estate sales, land use, and so on. If Camara, in the

6. *Restatement (Second) of Contracts*, Section 160.

preceding example, were a lawyer or a real estate broker, her misrepresentation of the area's zoning status would probably constitute fraud.[7]

Misrepresentation by Silence. Ordinarily, neither party to a contract has a duty to come forward and disclose facts. Therefore, a contract cannot be set aside because certain pertinent information is not volunteered. For example, suppose you have an accident that requires extensive body work on one side of your car. After the repair, the car's appearance and operation are the same as they were before the accident. One year later you decide to sell your car. Do you have a duty to volunteer the information about the accident to the seller? The answer is no. In this case, silence does not constitute misrepresentation. In contrast, if the purchaser asks you if the car has had extensive body work and you lie, you have committed a fraudulent misrepresentation.

Some exceptions to this general rule exist. Generally, if a *serious* defect or a *serious* potential problem is known to the seller but could not reasonably be suspected by the buyer, the seller may have a duty to speak. For example, if a city fails to disclose to bidders subsoil conditions that will cause great expense in constructing a sewer, the city is guilty of fraud.[8] Similarly, if the manufacturer of a mechanical heart valve fails to disclose to a recipient the serious risks attending the use of the valve, of which the manufacturer has knowledge, the recipient has a cause of action for fraud.[9] Other exceptions involve duties imposed on parties involved in certain relationships. An attorney, for example, has a duty to disclose material facts to a client. Other such relationships include those between physicians and their patients, partners in a partnership, directors of corporations and shareholders, and guardians and wards.[10]

Statutes provide still other exceptions to the general rule of nondisclosure. The Truth-in-Lending Act, for example, requires disclosure of certain facts (see Chapter 44). Statutes may even specify the typeface size to be used in the document providing the information.

INTENT TO DECEIVE

The second element of fraud is knowledge on the part of the misrepresenting party that facts have been falsely represented. This element, normally called ***scienter,***[11] or "guilty knowledge," signifies that there was an *intent to deceive. Scienter* clearly exists if a party knows a fact is not as stated. *Scienter* also exists if a party makes a statement that he or she believes not to be true or makes a statement recklessly, without regard to whether it is true or false. Finally, this element is met if a party says or implies that a statement is made on some basis such as personal knowledge or personal investigation when it is not.

For example, assume that Meese, a securities broker, offers to sell BIM stock to Packer. Meese assures Packer that BIM shares are blue-chip securities—that is, they are stable, are limited in risk, and yield a high return on investment over time. Meese, however, knows nothing about the quality of BIM stock and does not believe the truth of what he is saying. Meese's statement is a misrepresentation because Meese does not believe the truth of what he has told Packer and because he knows that he does not have any basis for making such a statement. Therefore, if Packer is induced by Meese's intentional misrepresentation of a material fact to enter into a contract to buy the stock, normally he can avoid his obligations under the contract.

In many cases involving a seller's misrepresentation, courts have held that proving fault is unnecessary. That is, a buyer need prove only that the seller's representation was false, without regard to the seller's state of mind. In those cases—often involving sales of land or stock—the courts reason that it is the seller's duty to know the truth of what he or she says.

See Case 13.2 at the end of this chapter. To view the full, unedited case from Westlaw,® go to this text's Web site at **http://wbl-cs.westbuslaw.com**.

RELIANCE ON THE MISREPRESENTATION

The third element of fraud is reasonably *justifiable reliance* on the misrepresentation of fact. The deceived party must have a justifiable reason for relying

7. *Restatement (Second) of Contracts,* Section 170.

8. *City of Salinas v. Souza & McCue Construction Co.,* 66 Cal.2d 217, 424 P.2d 921, 57 Cal.Rptr. 337 (1967). Normally, the seller must disclose only "latent" defects—that is, defects that would not be readily discovered even by an expert. Thus, termites in a house would not be a latent defect, because an expert could normally discover their presence.

9. *Khan v. Shiley, Inc.,* 217 Cal.App.3d 848, 266 Cal.Rptr. 106 (1990).

10. *Restatement (Second) of Contracts,* Sections 161 and 173.

11. Pronounced sy-*en*-ter.

on the misrepresentation, and the misrepresentation must be an important factor (but not necessarily the sole factor) in inducing that party to enter into the contract.

Reliance is not justified if the innocent party knows the true facts or relies on obviously extravagant statements. Suppose a used-car dealer tells you, "This old Cadillac will get fifty miles to the gallon." You will not normally be justified in relying on the statement. Or suppose that Kovich, a bank director, induces Mallory, a co-director, to sign a guaranty that the bank's assets will satisfy its liabilities, stating, "We have plenty of assets to satisfy our creditors." If Mallory knows the true facts, he will not be justified in relying on Kovich's statement. If, however, Mallory does not know the true facts *and has no way of finding them out,* he normally will be justified in relying on the statement.

The same rule applies to defects in property sold. If the defects are of the kind that would be obvious on inspection, the buyer cannot justifiably rely on the seller's representations. If the defects are hidden or latent (that is, not apparent on the surface), the buyer is justified in relying on the seller's statements.

See Case 13.3 at the end of this chapter. To view the full, unedited case from Westlaw,® go to this text's Web site at **http://wbl-cs.westbuslaw.com**.

INJURY TO THE INNOCENT PARTY

Most courts do not require a showing of injury when the action is to *rescind* (cancel) the contract. These courts hold that because rescission returns the parties to the positions they held before the contract was made, a showing of injury to the innocent party is unnecessary.[12]

For a person to recover damages caused by fraud, proof of an injury is universally required. The measure of damages is ordinarily equal to the property's value had it been delivered as represented, less the actual price paid for the property. In actions based on fraud, courts often award *punitive damages,* or *exemplary damages,* which are granted to a plaintiff over and above the proved, actual compensation for the loss. As discussed in Chapter 5, punitive damages are based on the public-policy consideration of punishing the defendant or setting an example to deter similar wrongdoing by others.

SECTION 3

Nonfraudulent Misrepresentation

If a plaintiff seeks to rescind a contract because of *fraudulent* misrepresentation, the plaintiff must prove that the defendant had the intent to deceive. Most courts also allow rescission in cases involving *nonfraudulent* misrepresentation—that is, innocent or negligent misrepresentation—if all of the other elements of misrepresentation exist.

INNOCENT MISREPRESENTATION

If a person makes a statement that he or she believes to be true but that actually misrepresents material facts, the person is guilty only of an **innocent misrepresentation,** not of fraud. If an innocent misrepresentation occurs, the aggrieved party can rescind the contract but usually cannot seek damages. For example, Parris tells Roberta that a tract contains 250 acres. Parris is mistaken—the tract contains only 215 acres—but Parris does not know that. Roberta is induced by the statement to make a contract to buy the land. Even though the misrepresentation is innocent, Roberta can avoid the contract if the misrepresentation is material.

NEGLIGENT MISREPRESENTATION

Sometimes a party will make a misrepresentation through carelessness, believing the statement is true. This misrepresentation is negligent if he or she fails to exercise reasonable care in uncovering or disclosing the facts or does not use the skill and competence that his or her business or profession requires. For example, an operator of a weight scale certifies the weight of Sneed's commodity, even though the scale's accuracy has not been checked in more than a year. In virtually all states, such **negligent misrepresentation** is equal to *scienter,* or to knowingly making a misrepresentation. In effect, negligent misrepresentation is treated as fraudulent misrepresentation, even though the misrepresentation was not purposeful. In negligent misrepresentation, culpable ignorance of the truth supplies the intention to mislead, even if the defendant can claim, "I didn't know."

12. See, for example, *Kaufman v. Jaffe,* 244 App.Div. 344, 279 N.Y.S. 392 (1935).

SECTION 4

Undue Influence

Undue influence arises from special kinds of relationships in which one party can greatly influence another party, thus overcoming that party's free will. Minors and elderly people, for example, are often under the influence of guardians. If the guardian induces a young or elderly ward to enter into a contract that benefits the guardian, undue influence may have been exerted. Undue influence can arise from a number of confidential or fiduciary relationships:[13] attorney-client, physician-patient, guardian-ward, parent-child, husband-wife, or trustee-beneficiary. The essential feature of undue influence is that the party being taken advantage of does not, in reality, exercise free will in entering into a contract. A contract entered into under excessive or undue influence lacks genuine assent and is therefore voidable.[14]

To determine whether undue influence has been exerted, a court must ask, "To what extent was the transaction induced by domination of the mind or emotions of the person in question?" It follows, then, that the mental state of the person in question will often show to what extent the persuasion from the outside influence was "unfair."

When a contract enriches a party at the expense of another who is in a relationship of trust and confidence with, or who is dominated by, the enriched party, the court will often presume that the contract was made under undue influence. For example, if a person challenges a contract made by his or her guardian, the presumption will normally be that the guardian has taken advantage of the ward. To rebut (refute) this presumption successfully, the guardian has to show that full disclosure was made to the ward, that consideration was adequate, and that the ward received, if available, independent and competent advice before completing the transaction.

In a relationship of trust and confidence, such as between an attorney and a client, the dominant party (the attorney) is held to extreme or utmost good faith in dealing with the other party. Suppose that a long-time attorney for an elderly man induces him to sign a contract for the sale of some of his assets to a friend of the attorney at below-market prices. It is presumed that the attorney has not upheld good faith in dealing with the man. Unless this presumption can be rebutted, the contract will be voidable.

SECTION 5

Duress

Assent to the terms of a contract is not genuine if one of the parties is *forced* into the agreement. Recall from Chapter 8 that forcing a party to do something, including entering into a contract, through fear created by threats is legally defined as *duress*. In addition, blackmail or extortion to induce consent to a contract constitutes duress. Duress is both a defense to the enforcement of a contract and a ground for the rescission of a contract.

Generally, the threatened act must be wrongful or illegal. Threatening to exercise a legal right is not ordinarily illegal and usually does not constitute duress. Suppose that Donovan injures Jaworski in an auto accident. The police are not called. Donovan has no automobile insurance, but she has substantial assets. Jaworski is willing to settle the potential claim out of court for $3,000. Donovan refuses. After much arguing, Jaworski loses her patience and says, "If you don't pay me $3,000 right now, I'm going to sue you for $35,000." Donovan is frightened and gives Jaworski a check for $3,000. Later in the day, she stops payment on the check. Jaworski comes back to sue her for the $3,000. Although Donovan argues that she was the victim of duress, the threat of a civil suit is normally not considered duress.

Economic need is generally not sufficient to constitute duress, even when one party exacts a very high price for an item that the other party needs. If the party exacting the price also creates the need, however, *economic duress* may be found. The Internal Revenue Service, for example, assessed a large tax and penalty against Weller. Weller retained Eyman, the accountant who had filed the tax returns on which the assessment was based, to resist the assessment. Two days before the deadline for filing a reply with the Internal Revenue Service, Eyman declined to represent Weller unless he signed a very high contingency-fee agreement for his services. The agreement was unenforceable.[15] Although Eyman had threatened only to withdraw his services, something that he was legally entitled to do, he was re-

13. A fiduciary relationship is one involving a high degree of trust and confidence—see Chapter 31.

14. *Restatement (Second) of Contracts,* Section 177.

15. *Thompson Crane & Trucking Co. v. Eyman,* 123 Cal.App.2d 904, 267 P.2d 1043 (1954).

sponsible for delaying the withdrawal until the last days. Because it would have been impossible at that late date to obtain adequate representation elsewhere, Weller was forced either to sign the contract or to lose his right to challenge the IRS assessment.

SECTION 6

Adhesion Contracts and Unconscionability

Questions concerning genuineness of assent may arise when the terms of a contract are dictated by a party with overwhelming bargaining power and the signer must agree to those terms or go without the commodity or service in question. As mentioned in Chapter 12, such contracts are often referred to as *adhesion contracts*. An **adhesion contract** is written *exclusively* by one party (the dominant party, usually the seller or the creditor) and presented to the other party (the adhering party, usually the buyer or the borrower) on a take-it-or-leave-it basis. In other words, the adhering party has no opportunity to negotiate the terms of the contract.

Standard-form contracts often contain fine-print provisions that shift a risk naturally borne by one party to the other. Such contracts are used by a variety of businesses and include life insurance policies, residential leases, loan agreements, and employment agency contracts. To avoid enforcement of the contract or of a particular clause, the aggrieved party must show that the parties had substantially unequal bargaining positions and that enforcement would be manifestly unfair or oppressive. If the required showing is made, the contract or particular term is deemed *unconscionable* and not enforced. Technically, unconscionability under Section 2–302 of the Uniform Commercial Code (UCC) applies only to contracts for the sale of goods. Many courts, however, have broadened the concept and applied it in other situations.

Although unconscionability was discussed in Chapter 12, it is important to note here that the great degree of discretion permitted a court to invalidate or strike down a contract or clause as being unconscionable has met with resistance. As a result, some states have not adopted Section 2–302 of the UCC. In those states, the legislature and the courts prefer to rely on traditional notions of fraud, undue influence, and duress. On the one hand, this gives certainty to contractual relationships, because parties know they will be held to the exact terms of their contracts. On the other hand, public policy does require that there be some limit on the power of individuals and businesses to dictate the terms of contracts.

TERMS AND CONCEPTS TO REVIEW

CHAPTER SUMMARY

Mistakes	1. *Mistakes of fact*—Mistakes of fact may be either unilateral or bilateral. a. Unilateral mistake—Generally, the mistaken party is bound by the contract *unless* (a) the other party knows or should have known of the mistake or (b) the mistake is an inadvertent mathematical error—such as an error in addition or subtraction—committed without gross negligence. b. Bilateral (mutual) mistake—When both parties are mistaken about the same material fact, such as identity, either party can avoid the contract. If the mistake concerns value or quality, either party can enforce the contract. 2. *Mistakes of value*—A mistake of value is one that concerns the future market value or quality of the object of the contract. If a mistake (unilateral or bilateral) is one of value, normally the contract can be enforced by either party.

CHAPTER SUMMARY—CONTINUED

Fraudulent Misrepresentation	When fraud occurs, usually the innocent party can enforce or avoid the contract. The elements necessary to establish fraud are as follows: 1. A misrepresentation of a material fact must occur. 2. There must be an intent to deceive. 3. The innocent party must justifiably rely on the misrepresentation. 4. To recover damages, proof of an injury is universally required.
Nonfraudulent Misrepresentation	Most courts allow contracts to be rescinded (canceled) in cases involving nonfraudulent misrepresentation. 1. *Innocent misrepresentation*—A misrepresentation that occurs when a person makes a statement that he or she believes to be true but that actually misrepresents a material fact. 2. *Negligent misrepresentation*—A misrepresentation made through carelessness, or negligence. In virtually all states, negligent misrepresentation is equal to *scienter,* or to knowingly making a misrepresentation.
Undue Influence	Undue influence arises from special relationships, such as fiduciary or confidential relationships, in which one party's free will has been overcome by the undue influence exerted by the other party. Usually, the contract is voidable.
Duress	Duress is defined as the tactic of forcing a party to enter a contract under the fear of a threat—for example, the threat of violence or serious economic loss. The party forced to enter the contract can rescind the contract.
Adhesion Contracts and Unconscionability	Genuineness of assent may be lacking in certain adhesion contracts—contracts in which the terms are dictated by a party with overwhelming bargaining power and the signer must agree to those terms or go without the commodity or service in question. If such contracts are so one sided that enforcement would be manifestly unfair or oppressive, the courts may deem them to be unconscionable and refuse to enforce them.

CASES FOR ANALYSIS

Westlaw. You can access the full text of each case presented below by going to the Westlaw cases on this text's Web site at http://wbl-cs.westbuslaw.com. Each Westlaw case includes the names of all plaintiffs and defendants, the dates on which the case was argued and decided, a brief summary of the issues and decisions in the case, headnotes classifying specific issues in the case according to the West Key Number System, and the court's opinion. Concurring and dissenting opinions, if any, are included as well.

CASE 13.1 MISREPRESENTATION

VOKES V. ARTHUR MURRAY, INC.

District Court of Appeal of Florida, Second District, 1968.
212 So.2d 906.

PIERCE, Judge.

* * * *

Defendant Arthur Murray, Inc., a corporation, authorizes the operation throughout the nation of dancing schools under the name of "Arthur Murray School of Dancing" through local franchised operators, one of whom was defendant J. P. Davenport whose dancing establishment was in Clearwater [Florida].

Plaintiff Mrs. Audrey E. Vokes, a widow of 51 years and without family, had a yen to be "an accomplished dancer" with the hopes of finding "new interest in life." So, on February 10, 1961, a dubious fate, with the assist of a motivated acquaintance, procured her to attend a "dance party" at Davenport's "School of Dancing" where she whiled away the pleasant hours, sometimes in a private room, absorbing his accomplished sales technique, during which her grace and poise were elaborated upon and her rosy future as "an excellent dancer" was painted for her in vivid and glowing colors. As an incident to this interlude, he sold her eight 1/2-hour dance lessons to be utilized within one calendar month therefrom, for the sum of $14.50 cash in hand paid, obviously a baited "come on."

Thus she embarked upon an almost endless pursuit of the terpsichorean art [dancing art—the judge is referring to Terpsichore, the Greek muse of dancing and choral music] during which, over a period of less than sixteen months, she was sold fourteen "dance courses" totalling in the aggregate 2,302 hours of dancing lessons for a total cash outlay of $31,090.45, all at Davenport's dance emporium. All of these fourteen courses were evidenced by execution of a written "Enrollment Agreement—Arthur Murray's School of Dancing" with the addendum in heavy black print, "No one will be informed that you are taking dancing lessons. Your relations with us are held in strict confidence," setting forth the number of "dancing lessons" and the "lessons in rhythm sessions" currently sold to her from time to time, and always of course accompanied by payment of cash of the realm.

These dance lesson contracts and the monetary consideration therefor of over $31,000 were procured from her by means and methods of Davenport and his associates which went beyond the unsavory, yet legally permissible, perimeter of "sales puffing" and intruded well into the forbidden area of undue influence, the suggestion of falsehood, the suppression of truth, and the free exercise of rational judgment * * *. From the time of her first contact with the dancing school in February, 1961, she was influenced unwittingly by a constant and continuous barrage of flattery, false praise, excessive compliments, and panegyric encomiums [elaborate formal compliments] * * *.

She was incessantly subjected to overreaching blandishment [flattery] and cajolery. She was assured she had "grace and poise"; that she was "rapidly improving and developing in her dancing skill"; that the additional lessons would "make her a beautiful dancer, capable of dancing with the most accomplished dancers"; that she was "rapidly progressing in the development of her dancing skill and gracefulness," etc., etc. She was given "dance aptitude tests" for the ostensible purpose of "determining" the number of remaining hours [of] instructions needed by her from time to time.

At one point she was sold 545 additional hours of dancing lessons to be entitled to award of the "Bronze Medal" signifying that she had reached "the Bronze Standard," a supposed designation of dance achievement by students of Arthur Murray, Inc.

Later she was sold an additional 926 hours in order to gain the "Silver Medal," indicating she had reached "the Silver Standard," at a cost of $12,501.35.

At one point, while she still had to her credit about 900 unused hours of instructions, she was induced to purchase an additional 24 hours of lessons to participate in a trip to Miami at her own expense, where she would be "given the opportunity to dance with members of the Miami Studio."

She was induced at another point to purchase an additional 123 hours of lessons in order to be not only eligible for the Miami trip but also to become "a life member of the Arthur Murray Studio," carrying with it certain dubious emoluments [benefits or compensation], at a further cost of $1,752.30.

At another point, while she still had over 1,000 unused hours of instruction she was induced to buy 151 additional hours at a cost of $2,049.00 to be eligible for a '"Student Trip to Trinidad," at her own expense as she later learned.

Also, when she still had 1,100 unused hours to her credit, she was prevailed upon to purchase an additional 347 hours at a cost of $4,235.74, to qualify her to receive a "Gold Medal" for achievement, indicating she had advanced to "the Gold Standard."

On another occasion, while she still had over 1,200 unused hours, she was induced to buy an additional 175 hours of instruction at a cost of $2,472.75 to be eligible "to take a trip to Mexico."

Finally, sandwiched in between other lesser sales promotions, she was influenced to buy an additional 481 hours of instruction at a cost of $6,523.81 in order to "be classified as a Gold Bar Member, the ultimate achievement of the dancing studio."

All the foregoing sales promotions, illustrative of the entire fourteen separate contracts, were procured by defendant Davenport and Arthur Murray, Inc., by false representations to her that she was improving in her dancing ability, that she had excellent potential, that she was responding to instructions in dancing grace, and that they were developing her into a beautiful dancer, whereas in truth and in fact she did not develop in her dancing ability, she had no "dance aptitude," and in fact had difficulty in "hearing that musical beat." [Vokes's] complaint alleged that such representations to her "were in fact false and known by the defendant to be false and contrary to the plaintiff's true ability, the truth of plaintiff's ability being fully known to the defendants, but withheld from the plaintiff for the sole and specific intent to deceive and defraud the plaintiff and to induce her in the purchasing of additional hours of dance lessons." It was averred that the lessons were sold to her "in total disregard to the true physical, rhythm, and mental ability of the plaintiff." In other words, while she first exulted that she was entering the "spring of her life," she finally was awakened to the fact there was "spring" neither in her life nor in her feet.

The complaint [asked a Florida state court to] decree the dance contracts to be null and void and to be cancelled * * *. The Court held the complaint not to state a cause of action and dismissed it * * *.

* * * Defendants contend that contracts can only be rescinded for fraud or misrepresentation when the alleged misrepresentation is as to a material fact, rather than an opinion, prediction or expectation, and that the statements and representations set forth at length in the complaint were in the category of "trade puffing," within its legal orbit.

It is true that generally a misrepresentation, to be actionable, must be one of fact rather than of opinion. But this rule has significant qualifications, applicable here. It does not apply where there is a fiduciary relationship between the parties, or where there has been some artifice or trick employed by the representor, or where the parties do not in general deal at "arm's length" as we understand the phrase, or where the representee does not have equal opportunity to become apprised of the truth or falsity of the fact represented.

* * * *A statement of a party having * * * superior knowledge may be regarded as a statement of fact although it would be considered as opinion if the parties were dealing on equal terms.* [Emphasis added.]

It could be reasonably supposed here that defendants had "superior knowledge" as to whether plaintiff had "dance potential" and as to whether she was noticeably improving in the art of terpsichore. And it would be a reasonable inference from the undenied averments of the complaint that the flowery eulogiums [praises] heaped upon her by defendants as a prelude to her contracting for 1,944 additional hours of instruction in order to attain the rank of the Bronze Standard, thence to the bracket of the Silver Standard, thence to the class of the Gold Bar Standard, and finally to the crowning plateau of a Life Member of the Studio, proceeded as much or more from the urge to "ring the cash register" as from any honest or realistic appraisal of her dancing prowess or a factual representation of her progress.

Even in contractual situations where a party to a transaction owes no duty to disclose facts within his knowledge or to answer inquiries respecting such facts, the law is if he undertakes to do so he must disclose the whole truth. From the face of the complaint, it should have been reasonably apparent to defendants that her vast outlay of cash for the many hundreds of additional hours of instruction was not justified by her slow and awkward progress, which she would have been made well aware of if they had spoken the "whole truth."

* * * [W]hat is plainly injurious to good faith ought to be considered as a fraud sufficient to impeach a contract, and * * * an improvident agreement may be avoided * * * because of surprise, or mistake, want of freedom, undue influence, the suggestion of falsehood, or the suppression of truth.

* * * *

It accordingly follows that the order dismissing plaintiff's last amended complaint * * * should be and is reversed.

CASE 13.2 MISREPRESENTATION

SARVIS v. VERMONT STATE COLLEGES

Supreme Court of Vermont, 2001.
772 A.2d 494.

SKOGLUND, J. [Justice]

* * * *

The material facts in this case are not in dispute. On March 13, 1995, plaintiff was convicted of five counts of bank fraud and sentenced to serve forty-six months in prison. He was ordered to pay over $12 million in restitution to five banks in order of priority, including two million dollars to the Proctor Bank, a Vermont bank, which was given top payment priority. He was incarcerated from April 4, 1995 to August 17, 1998, at the Allenwood prison in Lewisburg, Pennsylvania, where he worked in the prison's electric department. In August of 1998, two weeks after he was released from prison, plaintiff applied for an adjunct professor position at Community College of Vermont (CCV), a division of defendant. Plaintiff provided defendant with a resume, in which he indicated that from 1984–1998 he was "President and Chairman of the Board" of "CMI International, Inc., Boston, Massachusetts." In describing his duties, plaintiff indicated he was "[r]esponsible for all operations and financial matters." He ended his summary with the following: "[f]rom 1995–1998 this company was sold off by various divisions and I have retired." Defendant replied, and asked plaintiff to fill out an "Instructor Information" form. On September 30, 1998, plaintiff submitted this form and, in the space provided to list applicant's "Most Recent Previous Employment," plaintiff referred his reader to the resume he submitted with his August letter.

Plaintiff also applied for a position as CCV's Coordinator of Academic Services, and submitted a second resume in connection with this application. The second resume was similar to the first, except he changed the last line of his description of duties at CMI to read: "From 1995–1998 this company was sold off by various divisions. I have since been semi-retired." Under the "Business Experience" heading, he also added a line, "1998–present" "Semi-retired. Adjunct Instructor of Business at Colby-Sawyer College and Franklin Pierce College." In a memorandum to a CCV administrator, plaintiff also advised that "I have not 'worked' for almost four years," and discouraged defendant from contacting management at Franklin Pierce for additional references.

Plaintiff provided defendant with additional application materials, attempting to secure a teaching position. Plaintiff listed for defendant the classes he believed defendant would find him "well equipped to teach." He highlighted business law and business ethics as courses in which he had "the highest level of capability and interest."

He alerted defendant that he had "a great interest and knowledge of business law" and that he believed he would do "an excellent job" teaching a business ethics class because this subject was "of particular concern" to him.

In response to the information plaintiff provided, defendant entered into three employment contracts with plaintiff, covering plaintiff's duties as academic coordinator, teacher, and independent studies instructor. After plaintiff commenced performance on the coordinator and independent study contracts, his probation officer alerted defendant to plaintiff's criminal history. Defendant terminated plaintiff before the expiration of his contracts of employment, citing,

> [t]he nature of the federal offenses (involving dishonesty), the gravity of the offenses (multiple counts of bank fraud, over $12 million dollars in restitution) the presence of local victims (Proctor Bank and any other Vermont victims) and the potential harm to CCV's reputation, [as] substantial factors contributing to the termination decision.

Plaintiff filed a complaint alleging that defendant was liable for breach of all three contracts and wrongful termination. * * * Plaintiff moved for summary judgment * * *. Defendant opposed the motion, and also moved for summary judgment on all claims. * * * The court granted defendant's motion, concluding that it was reasonable for defendant to discharge plaintiff because of his material misrepresentations about his criminal record, and that plaintiff had notice that dishonesty and fraud were just cause for dismissal.

* * * *

It is well established that a party induced into a contract by fraud or misrepresentation can rescind the contract and avoid liability for any breach thereon. A misrepresentation is fraudulent when made with knowledge of its falsity. *Where the procurer [in law, one who induces another to do something; as used here, the one making the statement] of a statement knew it was false, materiality is not required.* Materiality is required where the mistake or false statement was not intentionally made and may be proved where the statement is likely to induce a reasonable person to manifest his assent, or if the maker knows that it would be likely to induce such assent. * * * [Emphasis added.]

* * * *

* * * [M]isrepresentation during the hiring process can be a basis for rescission of an employment contract. Further, we hold as a matter of law, such misrepresentation can constitute misconduct sufficient to support a just cause dismissal.

Plaintiff fraudulently induced defendant into entering into the employment contracts. Plaintiff misrepresented material facts related to his candidacy upon which defendant relied in making its employment decision. In both resumes, plaintiff omitted the fact that he was in prison from 1995 through 1998. Instead, he misrepresented his work history with the intent of creating the false impression of how he spent those years. During that time, he claimed he was, as president and chairman of the board of CMI, "[r]esponsible for all operations and financial matters" of CMI. In reality, he was in prison and working in the prison's electric department. Also during the hiring process, in a written response to defendant's coordinator of academic services, plaintiff declared that he had not worked for almost four years and that he had not worked for someone else since 1984. Plaintiff knew this statement was false and deceptive because four months earlier, seeking district court approval for employment in Maine under a post-prison relocation plan, he admitted that "[a]t Allenwood FPC I currently work in the Electrical Department." Defendant's assertions and omissions were not in accord with the facts, and were offered for the sole purpose of affecting the employment decision.

Plaintiff seeks to avoid rescission and enforce the contracts by faulting defendant for failing to discover his criminal background. Plaintiff, however, cannot enforce the contract where his own actions hampered defendant's inquiry. Plaintiff discouraged defendant from contacting his current employers at Franklin Pierce for references. In a letter to defendant's academic services coordinator, plaintiff demurred that he did "not believe Franklin Pierce management could give an evaluation of me at this short date and I feel it would be unfair of me to ask that." What plaintiff failed to reveal to defendant was that he had disclosed his criminal history to Franklin Pierce. Plaintiff's effort to discourage defendant from contacting Franklin Pierce management for a reference succeeded in dissuading defendant from making full inquiry into his background.

Plaintiff also argues that his nondisclosure of his criminal history does not constitute fraud or misrepresentation because he had no duty to disclose his criminal past. Contrary to plaintiff's claim, plaintiff's misrepresentation involved more than nondisclosure. We have found fraud from partial disclosure.

Where one has full information and represents that he has, if he discloses a part of his information only, and by words or conduct leads the one with whom he contracts to believe that he has made a full disclosure and does this with intent to deceive and overreach and to prevent investigation, he is guilty of fraud against which equity will relieve, if his words and conduct in consequence of reliance upon them bring about the result which he desires.

The misrepresentation in this case occurred through plaintiff's partial disclosure of his past work history and references and his effort to limit defendant's inquiry into his past. Plaintiff was not silent; he carefully drafted his resumes and supplemental materials to lead defendant to believe he had made a full disclosure about his past and his qualifications. He listed classes in business ethics and law in which he claimed he had the highest level of capability and knowledge but failed to mention his felony bank fraud conviction. Plaintiff assured defendant that making additional inquiries into his background would have revealed "more of the same" type of information as that offered by the references plaintiff supplied. This was not true. Contact with plaintiff's probation officer or supervisor at the Allenwood prison would have notified defendant of plaintiff's fraud convictions, period of incarceration, and work history at the prison. We agree with the trial court's conclusion that plaintiff misrepresented material facts related to his candidacy upon which defendant relied in making its employment decision.

* * * *

Affirmed.

CASE 13.3 MISREPRESENTATION

MEADE v. CEDARAPIDS, INC.

United States Court of Appeals,
Ninth Circuit, 1999.
164 F.3d 1218.

EZRA, District Judge:

Factual Background

Plaintiffs William Meade, Leland S. Stewart, Doug Vierkant, and David Girard ("Plaintiffs") * * * appeal the [federal] district court's summary judgment in favor of Cedarapids and related corporations ("Defendants") in Plaintiffs' diversity action. Plaintiffs allege fraudulent misrepresentation * * *, arising from the closure of the El-Jay Division of Cedarapids ("El-Jay") in Eugene, Oregon.

The main factual dispute centers on when the decision to close El-Jay was made. Plaintiffs assert that it was made in July of 1994, long before any of them even applied for a job. Defendants contend that a *plan* (rather than a decision) was made at that time, and that the plan was contingent upon a number of factors * * *. Defendants further argue that [the] last contingency was not resolved until May 1, 1995 and that, therefore, the decision to close El-Jay was not made until that time. Both Plaintiffs and Defendants have produced evidence supporting the date on which each believes the decision to close El-Jay was made.

Each Plaintiff applied for and was offered a job at El-Jay between August 1994 and April 1995. Before accepting the positions, Plaintiffs each signed an at-will employment agreement stating that their employment was subject to termination by either party at any time. To accept the positions at El-Jay, each Plaintiff either quit the job he was then doing or passed up other employment opportunities. Each Plaintiff and his spouse moved to Eugene, Oregon, where El-Jay was located.

Plaintiffs assert that Defendants made intentional or reckless misrepresentations during the course of the hiring process. For instance, Plaintiffs allege that in response to specific questions about El-Jay's future growth, they were told how desirable it was to live in Eugene; that there would be growth in the parts business; that El-Jay would be growing 20% in the next year; that El-Jay was running out of office space; that sales were up and were expected to increase; that production rates were expanding; that El-Jay was a stable company with few downsizings and layoffs; that it would be hiring more staff and creating new positions; that the company was "ramping up"; that the future looked great for the company; and that the company's growth was a "long term situation."

The personnel who made these statements were unaware of the closure plan. Some of these persons stated that they would not have made these statements had they known of the closure decision. Plaintiffs contend they never would have interviewed with El-Jay had they known of the closure plans. Plaintiffs gave notice to their employers and prospective employers in reliance on Defendants' representations and omissions. * * *

On July 24, 1997, the district court granted summary judgment to Defendants, holding that Defendants had no duty to disclose their closure plan and that Plaintiffs could not, as a matter of law, reasonably have relied on the representations made to them. * * * We have jurisdiction over this timely filed appeal * * *. We affirm in part, and reverse in part.

* * * *

Discussion

I. *Intentional or Reckless Misrepresentation*

To support their claims of misrepresentation under Oregon law, Plaintiffs must establish 1) that Defendants made a false representation of material fact; 2) with the knowledge or belief that it was false, or with an insufficient basis for asserting that it was true; 3) with the intent that Plaintiffs rely on it; 4) that Plaintiffs justifiably relied; and 5) that Plaintiffs suffered consequent damages.

Reckless indifference to the truth or falsity of a statement can satisfy the state of mind requirement for a misrepresentation action. A party need not make an affirmative statement to be liable for fraud. *The mere nondisclosure of material facts can be a form of misrepresentation where the defendant has made representations which would be misleading without full disclosure.* The extent to which a representation is misleading and, therefore, imposes a duty of disclosure, is a question of fact. [Emphasis added.]

A. *False Representations*

* * * *

There are two bases on which Defendants could be found to have made false representations. First, the mere nondisclosure of material facts can be a form of misrepresentation where the defendant has concealed a known fact that is material to the transaction, or has made representations that would be misleading without full disclosure. Defendants argue that nondisclosure is actionable only where a defendant has made representations that would be misleading without full disclosure *and* there is a duty to disclose. The district court apparently agreed and held that since there was no duty to disclose, there was no actionable fraud. However, this is not entirely correct. One who makes a representation that is misleading because it is in the nature of a "half-truth" assumes the obligation to make a full and fair disclosure of the whole truth.

* * * *

Second, Plaintiffs contend that no duty to disclose is required when fraud is based upon active concealment, as opposed to nondisclosure. Plaintiffs allege Defendants actively concealed the closure by intentionally withholding material information from El-Jay management. The fact that El-Jay management did not know of the closure is irrelevant because a principal who deliberately withholds material facts from his agent in order that the agent may innocently misrepresent the facts is guilty of fraud if the agent does in fact make such a misrepresentation and it is relied on by the third party.

The district court erred in holding, as a matter of law, that no reasonable trier of fact could conclude that Defendants made false representations. Plaintiffs have put forth sufficient evidence to allow a jury reasonably to decide either way.

Defendants argue that they should not be forced to disclose sensitive business information. Defendants would not have been placed in this position, however, but for the false impression created by statements suggesting future growth and the "ramping up" of production. But for Defendants' affirmative misrepresentations, there would be no duty to disclose.

B. *Justified Reliance*

The district court held that Plaintiffs were not justified in relying on representations and omissions made during their pre-employment negotiations, as a matter of law, because Plaintiffs each signed an at-will employment agreement. That Plaintiffs' employment with Defendants was at-will does not defeat their justified reliance on Defendants' representations about El-Jay. *Even in the presence of language stating "no promises about employment have been made," an action for fraud in the inducement of a contract is possible.* The representation Plaintiffs relied upon in this case is that El-Jay was growing and expanding. Plaintiffs were not relying on representations as to the duration of their employment. Plaintiffs accepted at-will employment, but they accepted at-will employment with a company that represented its Eugene facility as growing while failing to disclose and/or concealing that it was closing. [Emphasis added.]

Furthermore, Plaintiffs contend that their injuries were suffered as a result of the fraudulent inducement to enter employment, not the premature termination of that employment. The district court apparently treated the claims as breach of contract claims rather than claims of fraudulent inducement to form a contract.

Finally, Plaintiffs maintain that allowing at-will employment to defeat Plaintiffs' reliance would effectively allow employers to make any representations to prospective employees and then not fulfill those representations once employment began. We agree. Although Plaintiffs had no reasonable expectations for employment of any particular duration, they reasonably relied on statements as to the company's future growth, particularly when given in response to Plaintiffs' concerns. If Plaintiffs can prove Defendants' representations were knowingly or recklessly false, then a reasonable trier of fact could find the requisite elements of the tort of fraudulent misrepresentation.

Therefore, because genuine issues of material fact exist as to whether Defendants made false representations and whether Plaintiffs justifiably relied on those representations, we reverse the district court's grant of summary judgment on this claim.

* * * *

* * * **REVERSED** * * * .

CASE PROBLEMS

13–1. In 1982, William Schmalz was hired by the Hardy Salt Co. under an employment contract that stated that he was entitled to six months' severance pay in the event that he was laid off. The company would not have to pay in the event of any voluntary separation or involuntary termination for other reasons, such as for poor performance or for cause. In mid-1983, Schmalz was asked to resign after having an affair with the chairman's executive secretary. Schmalz was told that if he did not resign he would be fired but that if he did resign the company would keep him on the payroll for another six weeks. Schmalz resigned and signed an agreement releasing Hardy Salt from any liability for breach of the employment contract. Schmalz later claimed that he had signed the release under duress and sued Hardy Salt for the six months' severance pay under his employment contract. Discuss whether Schmalz's claim for duress should succeed. [*Schmalz v. Hardy Salt Co.*, 739 S.W.2d 765 (Mo.App.1987)]

13–2. William and Lilly Adams obtained a divorce in 1985 and began the process of dividing their property. They inventoried their worldly possessions and decided that certain property would go to Mrs. Adams and the remainder, including the debts on the community property, would remain with Mr. Adams. Mrs. Adams later testified in legal proceedings that Mr. Adams had consistently told her that she must take the property as offered and agree not to seek alimony, that Mr. Adams had threatened to declare bankruptcy and force her to accept the responsibility for her share of the community debts if she did not agree, and that Mr. Adams frequently cursed her but did not in any way threaten physical harm. Mrs. Adams also testified that she had examined the subsequent formal community property settlement and that she basically understood it. At that time, she had casually spoken to two different attorneys about the settlement contract, but because both attorneys said that they would need time to investigate before giving advice, she went ahead and signed it. She later claimed that she had signed the agreement under duress and because of fraudulent misrepresentation. Discuss whether Mrs. Adams can rescind the settlement contract on these grounds. [*Adams v. Adams*, 503 So.2d 1052 (La.App. 2 Cir. 1987)]

13–3. In July 1965, Loral Corp. was awarded a $6 million contract to produce radar sets for the Navy. For this contract Loral needed to purchase forty precision gear parts. Loral awarded to Austin Instrument, Inc., a subcontract to supply twenty-three of the forty gear parts. In May of 1966 Loral was awarded a second contract to produce more radar sets. Loral solicited bids for forty more gear parts. Austin submitted a bid for all forty but was told by Loral that the subcontract would be awarded only for items for which Austin was the lowest bidder. Austin's president told Loral that it would not accept an order for less than forty gear parts and, one day later, told Loral that Austin would cease deliveries on the existing contract unless (1) Loral awarded Austin a contract for all forty gear part units and (2) Loral consented to substantial increases for the prices of all gear parts under the existing contract. Ten days later Austin ceased making deliveries. Loral tried to find other suppliers to furnish the gear parts, but none were available. Because of deadlines and liquidated damage clauses (clauses providing for money damages to be paid in the event of delays) in the Navy contract, plus the possible loss of reputation by Loral with the government, Loral agreed to Austin's terms. After Austin's last delivery, Loral filed suit to recover the increased prices Austin had charged on the ground that the agreement to pay these prices was based on duress. Discuss Loral's claim. [*Austin Instrument, Inc. v. Loral Corp.*, 29 N.Y.2d 124, 272 N.E.2d 533, 324 N.Y.S.2d 22 (1971)]

13–4. Division West Chinchilla Ranch made numerous TV advertisements that induced listeners to go into the business of raising chinchillas. The advertisements stated that, for a payment of $2,150 or more, Division would send one male and six female chinchillas and—for an additional sum—cages, feed, and supplies. Division's representations were that "chinchilla ranching can be done in the basement, [and] spare rooms, . . . with minor modifications" and that chinchillas were "odorless and practically noiseless" and "a profitable pastime that can explode into a FIVE FIGURE INCOME." All statements would lead one to believe that no special skill was needed in the raising of chinchillas. Based on these representations, Adolph Fischer and others (the plaintiffs) purchased chinchillas from Division. None of the plaintiffs was a sophisticated businessperson or highly educated. It soon became apparent that greater skill than that advertised was required to raise chinchillas and that certain statements made by Division's sales representatives as to the value of the pelts were untrue. None of the plaintiffs had financial success with their growing (ranching) of chinchillas over a three-year period. The plaintiffs sought to rescind the contracts to get their money back, claiming fraud on the part of Division. Discuss whether Division's statements constitute fraud. [*Fischer v. Division West Chinchilla Ranch*, 310 F.Supp. 424 (D.Minn. 1970)]

13–5. Jacobsen attended Columbia University from 1951 to 1954. During his years at Columbia, Jacobsen was an uncooperative student and critical of his professors. He shifted his academic interests a number of times—from physics to social work to creative writing and other areas. In his last year, he attended classes only as he chose, and he rejected the university's regimen requiring examinations and term papers. Ultimately, he failed to graduate because of poor scholastic standing. When Columbia sued Jacobsen for $1,000 in tuition still owed by him, Jacobsen countered with the allegation that the university had failed to impart the "wisdom" promised—by its motto, by its brochures, by the inscriptions over its buildings, in its presidential addresses, and so on. Because Columbia had promised something it could not deliver, it was guilty of misrepresentation and deceit and should return to Jacobsen all the tuition he had paid—$7,016. What exactly is the nature of a university's contractual duty to its students? Do you agree with Jacobsen that Columbia, by implicitly promising to impart wisdom, was guilty of misrepresentation? Discuss fully. [*Trustees of Columbia University v. Jacobsen*, 53 N.J.Super. 574, 148 A.2d 63 (1959)]

13–6. Robert and Wendy Pfister held one hundred shares of Tracor Computing Corp. stock. The stock was no longer being traded on the New York Stock Exchange, and they thought their shares were of little value. They asked a stockbrokerage firm, Foster & Marshall, Inc., to evaluate the shares for them. The brokerage firm advised the Pfisters that Tracor Computing had changed its name to Continuum Company, Inc., and that its stock was worth $49.50 a share; thus, the Pfisters' holdings were valued at $4,950. Robert Pfister suspected there might be an error in the valuation and asked Foster & Marshall to recheck the value, which was done. The Pfisters sold their shares to Foster & Marshall, which paid them $4,950 for the one hundred shares. Later, the brokerage firm discovered that the Tracor Computing stock had been exchanged for Continuum stock at a ten-to-one ratio, which meant that the Pfisters had owned only ten shares. The Pfisters refused to return the $4,455 overpayment they had received from the brokerage firm. Can Foster & Marshall recover the overpayment it made to the Pfisters resulting from its own unilateral mistake of fact? Discuss. [*Foster & Marshall, Inc. v. Pfister,* 66 Or.App. 685, 674 P.2d 1215 (1984)]

13–7. Kenneth and Linda Whitaker filed an action against Trans Union Corporation and others, alleging violations of the Fair Credit Reporting Act. The lawyer for Trans Union drafted an offer of settlement and presented it to the Whitakers' attorney. The amount of the settlement was supposed to be $500, but the first draft contained a typographical error showing the amount as $500,000. The error went undetected, and the $500,000 figure was typed into the second draft, which was forwarded to Linda Gosnell, Trans Union's attorney, who also did not detect the mistake. Gosnell filed the offer with the clerk of the court and mailed a copy to the Whitakers' lawyer. The Whitakers filed an acceptance of the settlement and forwarded it to Gosnell, who at that time noticed the typing error. The Whitakers refused a substitute offer, and Trans Union filed a motion to set aside the judgment. Can the settlement be set aside on the basis of mistake, notwithstanding the fact that the mistake was unilateral? Explain. [*Whitaker v. Associated Credit Services, Inc.*, 946 F.2d 1222 (6th Cir. 1991)]

13–8. Art Stone Theatrical Corporation bought a computer software system from Technical Programming & Systems Support of Long Island, Inc. After a dispute over the software's performance, a representative of Technical removed the source code from the system without Stone's knowledge or consent. Removing the source code made the system useless to Stone. Later the parties agreed that Technical would make the source code available and that Stone would release Technical from liability for any damages incurred by its removal of the source code. Stone signed the release but later sued Technical for damages in a New York state court, claiming that the release was void because it had been procured under duress. The trial court dismissed the action on the ground that the action was barred by the release. Stone appealed. What will the appellate court decide? Discuss fully. [*Art Stone Theatrical Corp. v. Programming & Systems Support of Long Island, Inc.*, 157 A.D.2d 689, 549 N.Y.S.2d 789 (Sup.Ct.App.Div. 1990)]

13–9. Mark Van Wagoner, an attorney experienced in real estate transactions, and his wife, Kathryn, were interested in buying certain property being sold by Carol Klas for her former husband, John Klas. When the Van Wagoners asked Carol Klas if there had been any appraisals of the property, she replied that there had been several appraisals, ranging from $175,000 to $192,000. (At trial, Carol claimed that she understood the term *appraisal* to mean any opinion as to the market value of the house.) The Van Wagoners did not request a written appraisal of the property until after signing an agreement to purchase the property for $175,000. Carol Klas then provided them with a written appraisal that listed the house's value as $165,000. When the Van Wagoners refused to go through with the deal, John Klas brought suit to recover the difference between the agreement price and the price for which the house was later sold. The Van Wagoners claimed that the contract should be rescinded on the basis of their mistaken assumption as to the value of the house. What kind of mistake was made in this situation (mutual or unilateral, mistake of value or mistake of fact)? How should the court rule on this issue? [*Klas v. Van Wagoner,* 829 P.2d 135 (Utah App.1992)]

13–10. When Michigan Health Care Corp. in Detroit offered Karen Clement-Rowe a position as a nurse, she accepted, sold her home, and moved to Detroit. One month later, in response to a financial crisis, Michigan Health terminated 150 employees, including Clement-Rowe. She filed a suit in a Michigan state court against the employer, claiming in part misrepresentation by silence. She asserted that Michigan Health had a duty to tell her of its financial condition but that the company had told her nothing—even though she had asked—and had intended to induce her to rely on the nondisclosure in accepting the job. Michigan Health responded that it had not been aware of the financial crisis until after Clement-Rowe had been hired. Michigan Health asked the court to grant summary judgment in its favor. What will the court decide? [*Clement-Rowe v. Michigan Health Care Corp.,* 212 Mich.App. 503, 538 N.W.2d 20 (1995)]

13–11. Steven Lanci was involved in an automobile accident with an uninsured motorist. Lanci was insured with Metropolitan Insurance Co., although he did not have a copy of the insurance policy. Lanci and Metropolitan entered settlement negotiations, during which Lanci told Metropolitan that he did not have a copy of his policy. Ultimately, Lanci agreed to settle all claims for $15,000, noting in a letter to Metropolitan that $15,000 was the "sum you have represented to be the . . . policy limits applicable to this claim." After signing a release, Lanci learned that the policy limits were actually $250,000, and he refused to accept the settlement proceeds. When Metropolitan sued to enforce the settlement agreement, Lanci argued that the release had been signed as the result of a mistake and therefore was unenforceable. Should the court enforce the contract? Explain. [*Lanci v. Metropolitan Insurance Co.*, 388 Pa.Super. 1, 564 A.2d 972 (1989)]

13–12. Nosrat, a citizen of Iran, owned a hardware store with his brother-in-law, Edwin. Edwin induced Nosrat to sign a promissory note for $11,400, payable to a third party, telling Nosrat that the document was a credit application for the hardware store. Although Nosrat could read and write English, he failed to read the note or to notice that the document was clearly entitled "PROMISSORY NOTE (SECURED) and Security Agreement." The money received from the third party in exchange for the note was spent by Edwin and others. When the third party sued for payment, Nosrat sought to void the note on the basis of Edwin's fraudulent inducement. Will Nosrat succeed in his attempt? Discuss. [*Waldrep v. Nosrat*, 426 So.2d 822 (Ala. 1983)]

13–13. Linda Lorenzo bought Lurlene Noel's home in 1988 without having it inspected. The basement started leaking in 1989. In 1991, Lorenzo had the paneling removed from the basement walls and discovered that the walls were bowed inward and cracked. Lorenzo then had a civil engineer inspect the basement walls, and he found that the cracks had been caulked and painted over before the paneling was installed. He concluded that the "wall failure" had existed "for at least thirty years" and that the basement walls were "structurally unsound." Does Lorenzo have a cause of action against Noel? If so, on what ground? Discuss. [*Lorenzo v. Noel*, 206 Mich.App. 682, 522 N.W.2d 724 (1994)]

13–14. W. B. McConkey owned commercial property, including a building that, as McConkey knew, had experienced flooding problems for years. McConkey painted the building, replaced damaged carpeting, and sold the property to M&D, Inc., on an "as is" basis. M&D did not ask whether there were flooding problems, and McConkey said nothing about them. M&D leased the property to Donmar, Inc., to operate a pet supplies store. Two months after the store opened, the building flooded following heavy rain. M&D and Donmar filed a suit in a Michigan state court against McConkey and others, claiming in part that McConkey had committed misrepresentation by silence. Based on this claim, will the court hold McConkey liable? Why, or why not? [*M&D, Inc. v. McConkey*, 585 N.W.2d 33 (Mich.App. 1998)]

13–15. In 1987, United Parcel Service Co. and United Parcel Service of America, Inc. (together known as "UPS"), decided to change its parcel delivery business from relying on contract carriers to establishing its own airline. During the transition, which took sixteen months, UPS hired 811 pilots. At the time, UPS expressed a desire to hire pilots who remained throughout that period with its contract carriers, which included Orion Air. A UPS representative met with more than fifty Orion pilots and made promises of future employment. John Rickert, a captain with Orion, was one of the pilots. Orion ceased operation after the UPS transition, and UPS did not hire Rickert, who obtained employment about six months later as a second officer with American Airlines, but at a lower salary. Rickert filed a suit in a Kentucky state court against UPS, claiming, in part, fraud based on the promises made by the UPS representative. UPS filed a motion for a directed verdict. What are the elements for a cause of action based on fraudulent misrepresentation? In whose favor should the court rule in this case, and why? [*United Parcel Service, Inc. v. Rickert*, 996 S.W.2d 464 (Ky. 1999)]

E-LINKS

For updated links to resources available on the Web, as well as a variety of other materials, visit this text's Web site at

http://wbl-cs.westbuslaw.com

To learn how the Australian government defines unconscionable conduct, go to

http://www.consumer.act.gov.au/CAB/publications/unconscionable.html

LEGAL RESEARCH EXERCISES ON THE WEB

Go to http://wbl-cs.westbuslaw.com, the Web site that accompanies this text. Select "Interactive Study Center," and then click on "Chapter 13." There you will find the following Internet research exercise that you can perform to learn more about fraudulent misrepresentation:

Activity 13–1: Fraudulent Misrepresentation

CHAPTER 14

The Statute of Frauds

As discussed in Chapter 13, a contract that is otherwise valid may still be unenforceable if the parties have not genuinely assented to its terms. An otherwise valid contract may also be unenforceable for another reason—because it is not in the proper form. For example, certain types of contracts are required to be in writing. If a contract is required by law to be in writing and there is no written evidence of the contract, it may not be enforceable. In this chapter, we examine the kinds of contracts that require a writing under what is called the **Statute of Frauds.**

The chapter concludes with a discussion of the *parol evidence rule,* under which courts determine the admissibility at trial of evidence that is extraneous, or external, to written contracts. The parol evidence rule is not inherently related to the Statute of Frauds but is a rule that has general application in contract law. We cover these topics within one chapter primarily for reasons of convenience and space.

SECTION 1

The Origins of the Statute of Frauds

At early common law, parties to a contract were not allowed to testify. This led to the practice of hiring third party witnesses. As early as the seventeenth century, the English recognized the many problems presented by this practice and enacted a statute to help deal with it. The statute, passed by the English Parliament in 1677, was known as "An Act for the Prevention of Frauds and Perjuries." The act established that certain types of contracts, to be enforceable, had to be evidenced by a writing and signed by the party against whom enforcement was sought.

Today, almost every state has a statute, modeled after the English act, that stipulates what types of contracts must be in writing. Although the statutes vary slightly from state to state, all states require certain types of contracts to be in writing or evidenced by a written memorandum signed by the party against whom enforcement is sought, unless certain exceptions apply. (These exceptions will be discussed later in this chapter.) In this text, we refer to these statutes collectively as the Statute of Frauds. The actual name of the Statute of Frauds is misleading because it neither applies to fraud nor invalidates any type of contract. Rather, it denies *enforceability* to certain contracts that do not comply with its requirements.

SECTION 2

Contracts That Fall within the Statute of Frauds

The following types of contracts are said to fall "within" or "under" the Statute of Frauds and therefore require a writing:

1. Contracts involving interests in land.
2. Contracts that cannot by their terms be performed within one year from the date of formation.
3. Collateral, or secondary, contracts, such as promises to answer for the debt or duty of another and promises by the administrator or executor of an estate to pay a debt of the estate personally—that is, out of his or her own pocket.
4. Promises made in consideration of marriage.
5. Under the Uniform Commercial Code (UCC), contracts for the sale of goods priced at $500 or more.

CONTRACTS INVOLVING INTERESTS IN LAND

A contract calling for the sale of land is not enforceable unless it is in writing or evidenced by a written memorandum. Land is real property and includes all physical objects that are permanently attached to the soil, such as buildings, fences, trees, and the soil itself. The Statute of Frauds operates as a *defense* to the enforcement of an oral contract for the sale of land. For example, if Sam contracts orally to sell Blackacre to Betty but later decides not to sell, under most circumstances Betty cannot enforce the contract. The Statute of Frauds also requires all contracts for the transfer of other interests in land, such as mortgages and leases (see Chapters 47 and 48), to be in writing, although most state statutes provide for the enforcement of short-term oral leases.

THE ONE-YEAR RULE

A contract that cannot, *by its own terms*, be performed within one year from the date it was formed must be in writing to be enforceable.[1] The one-year period begins to run *the day after the contract is made*. Suppose that on June 1 an employer orally contracts to hire you immediately (June 1) for one year at $4,000 per month. This contract is not subject to the Statute of Frauds (and thus need not be in writing to be enforceable) because the one-year period to measure performance begins on June 2. In contrast, if the oral contract is formed on March 1 for one year's work that is to begin on June 1, the contract cannot be performed within one year and thus falls under the Statute of Frauds—that is, it must be in writing to be enforceable.

The test for determining whether an oral contract is enforceable under the one-year rule of the Statute of Frauds is not whether an agreement is *likely* to be performed within a year but whether performance is *possible* within one year. Even if performance takes place more than one year after the date of contract formation, an oral contract is binding as long as performance was possible in less than a year.

For example, suppose that Bankers Life orally contracts to loan $40,000 to Janet Lawrence "as long as Lawrence and Associates operates its financial consulting firm in Omaha, Nebraska." The contract is not within the Statute of Frauds—no writing is required—because Lawrence and Associates could go out of business in one year or less. In this event, the contract would be fully performed within one year.[2] Exhibit 14–1 illustrates graphically the application of the one-year rule.

See Case 14.1 at the end of this chapter. To view the full, unedited case from Westlaw,® go to this text's Web site at **http://wbl-cs.westbuslaw.com**.

COLLATERAL PROMISES

A **collateral promise**, or secondary promise, is one that is ancillary (subsidiary) to a principal transaction or primary contractual relationship. In other words, a collateral promise is one made by a third party to assume the debts or obligations of a primary party to a contract if that party does not perform. Any collateral promise of this nature falls under the Statute of Frauds and therefore must be in writing to be enforceable. To understand this concept, it is important to distinguish between primary and secondary promises and obligations.

Primary versus Secondary Obligations. Suppose that Bancroft forms an oral contract with Harmony's Floral Boutique to send his mother a dozen roses for Mother's Day. Bancroft's oral contract with Harmony's Floral Boutique provides that he will pay for the roses when he receives the bill for the flowers. Bancroft is a direct party to this contract and has incurred a *primary* obligation under the contract. Because he is a party to the contract and has a primary obligation to Harmony's Floral Boutique, this contract does *not* fall under the Statute of Frauds and does not have to be in writing to be enforceable.

Now suppose that Bancroft's mother borrows $1,000 from the International Trust Company on a promissory note payable six months later. Bancroft promises the bank officer handling the loan that he will pay the $1,000 *only if his mother does not pay the loan on time*. Bancroft, in this situation, becomes what is known as a *guarantor* on the loan. That is, he is guaranteeing to the bank that he will pay back the loan if his mother fails to do so. This kind of collateral promise, in which the guarantor states that he or she will become responsible only if the primary

1. *Restatement (Second) of Contracts*, Section 130.

2. See *Warner v. Texas & Pacific Railroad Co.*, 164 U.S. 418, 17 S.Ct. 147, 41 L.Ed. 195 (1896).

EXHIBIT 14–1 THE ONE-YEAR RULE

Under the Statute of Frauds, contracts that by their terms are impossible to perform within one year from the date of contract formation must be in writing to be enforceable. Put another way, if it is at all possible to perform an oral contract within one year after the contract is made, the contract will fall outside the Statute of Frauds and be enforceable.

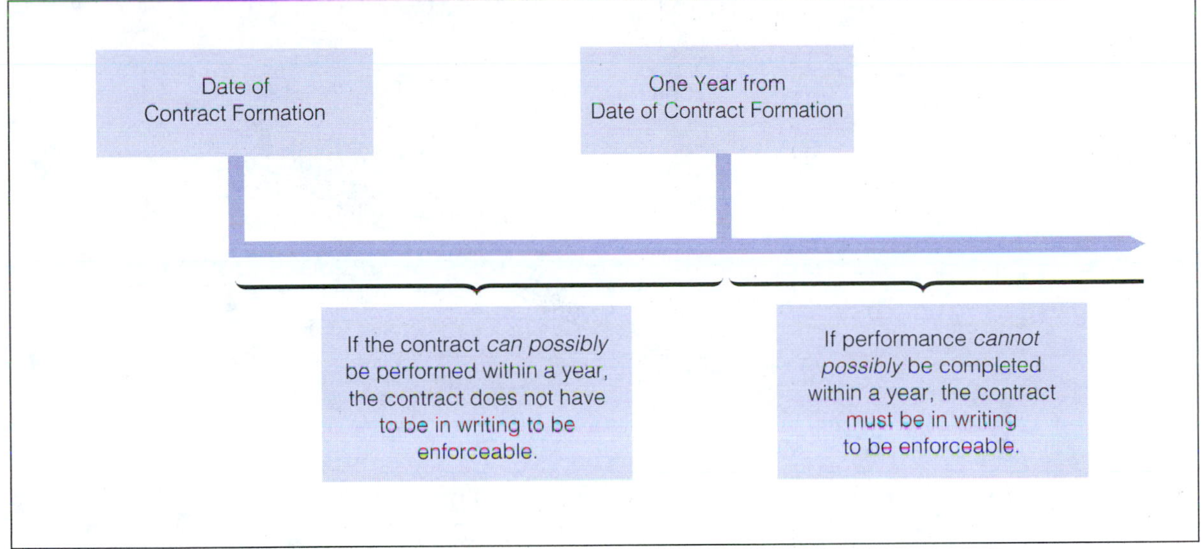

party does not perform, must be in writing to be enforceable. Exhibit 14–2 on the next page illustrates graphically the concept of a collateral promise. (We will return to the concept of guaranty and the distinction between primary and secondary obligations in Chapter 29, in the context of creditors' rights.)

An Exception—The "Main Purpose Rule." An oral promise to answer for the debt of another is covered by the Statute of Frauds unless the guarantor's main purpose in accepting secondary liability is to secure a personal benefit. This type of contract need not be in writing.[3] The assumption is that a court can infer from the circumstances of a particular case whether the "leading objective" of the promisor was to secure a personal benefit and thus, in effect, to answer for his or her own debt.

Consider an example. Braswell contracts with Custom Manufacturing Company to have some machines custom-made for Braswell's factory. She promises Newform Materials Supply Company, Custom Manufacturing's supplier, that if Newform continues to deliver the materials to Custom Manufacturing for the manufacture of the custom-made machines, she will guarantee payment. This promise need not be in writing, even though the effect may be to pay the debt of another. This is because Braswell's main purpose in forming the contract is to secure a benefit for herself.[4]

Another typical application of the main purpose rule is the situation in which one creditor guarantees the debtor's debt to another creditor to forestall litigation. This allows the debtor to remain in business long enough to generate profits sufficient to pay both creditors.

Estate Debts. The administrator (or executor) of an estate has the duty of paying the debts of the deceased and distributing any remainder to the deceased's heirs. The administrator can contract orally on behalf of the estate. Under the Statute of Frauds, promises made by the administrator or executor of an estate to pay *personally* the debts of the estate must be in writing to be enforceable, even though

3. *Restatement (Second) of Contracts*, Section 116.

4. See *Kampman v. Pittsburgh Contracting and Engineering Co.*, 316 Pa. 502, 175 A. 396 (1934); UCC 2–201(3)(c).

EXHIBIT 14–2 COLLATERAL PROMISES

A collateral (secondary) promise is one made by a third party (C, in this exhibit) to a creditor (B, in this exhibit) to pay the debt of another (A, in this exhibit), who is primarily obligated to pay the debt. Under the Statute of Frauds, collateral promises must be in writing to be enforceable.

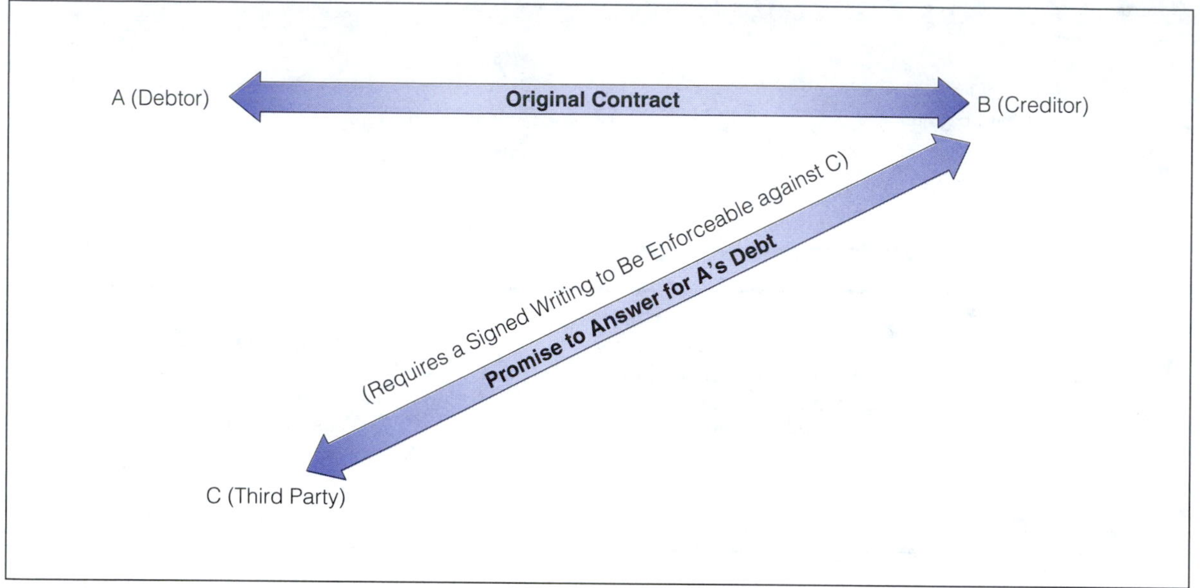

the nature of the promise is to assume a primary obligation to pay the creditor.

PROMISES MADE IN CONSIDERATION OF MARRIAGE

A unilateral promise to pay a sum of money or to give property in consideration of a promise to marry must be in writing. If Mr. Baumann promises to pay Joe Villard $10,000 if Villard promises to marry Baumann's daughter, the promise must be in writing. The same rule applies to **prenuptial agreements**—agreements made before marriage that define each partner's ownership rights in the other partner's property. A couple might make such an agreement if, for example, a prospective wife wished to limit the amount her prospective husband could obtain if the marriage ended in divorce. Prenuptial agreements must be in writing to be enforceable.[5]

5. To add certainty to the enforceability of prenuptial agreements, the National Conference of Commissioners on Uniform State Laws issued the Uniform Prenuptial Agreements Act (UPAA) in 1983. The act provides that prenuptial agreements must be in writing to be enforceable and that the agreements become effective when the parties marry.

Generally, courts tend to give more credence to prenuptial agreements that are accompanied by consideration. For example, assume that Maureen, who has little money, and Kaiser, who has a net worth of $300 million, plan to marry. Kaiser has several children, and he wants them to receive most of his wealth on his death. The couple forms a prenuptial agreement in which Kaiser promises to give Maureen $100,000 a year for the rest of her life should they divorce. Kaiser offers to give Maureen $200,000 if she consents to the agreement. If Maureen consents to the agreement and accepts the $200,000, very likely a court will hold this to be a valid prenuptial agreement should it ever be contested.

In some circumstances, a prenuptial agreement will not be enforceable even if it is in writing. For example, an agreement is not enforceable if the party against whom enforcement is sought proves that he or she did not sign the agreement voluntarily. In a growing number of jurisdictions, the advice of independent counsel is a significant factor in determining whether a party signed a prenuptial agreement voluntarily. In other words, if a prospective spouse did not have the advice of his or her own attorney before signing the agreement, that could indicate that the agreement was not signed voluntarily.

CONTRACTS FOR THE SALE OF GOODS

The UCC generally requires a writing or memorandum for the sale of goods priced at $500 or more. A writing that will satisfy the UCC requirement need only state the quantity term; other terms agreed on can be omitted or even stated imprecisely in the writing, as long as they adequately reflect both parties' intentions. The contract will not be enforceable, however, for any quantity greater than that set forth in the writing. In addition, the writing must have been signed by the person to be charged—that is, by the person who refuses to perform or the one being sued. Beyond these two requirements, the writing need not designate the buyer or the seller, the terms of payment, or the price. Requirements of the Statute of Frauds under the UCC will be discussed in more detail in Chapter 18.

EXCEPTIONS TO THE APPLICABILITY OF THE STATUTE OF FRAUDS

Exceptions to the applicability of the Statute of Frauds are made in certain circumstances. We look here at these exceptions.

Partial Performance. In cases involving contracts relating to the transfer of interests in land, if the purchaser has paid part of the price, taken possession, and made permanent improvements to the property and the parties cannot be returned to their *status quo* before the contract was formed, a court may grant *specific performance* (performance of the contract according to its precise terms). Whether the courts will enforce an oral contract for an interest in land when partial performance has taken place is usually determined by the degree of injury that would be suffered if the court chose not to enforce the oral contract. Under the UCC an oral contract is enforceable to the extent that a seller accepts payment or a buyer accepts delivery of the goods[6] (see Chapter 18 for a fuller discussion of this exception).

Admissions. In some states, if the party against whom the enforcement of an oral contract is sought admits in pleadings, testimony, or otherwise in court that a contract for sale was made, the contract will be enforceable.[7] Thus, if the president of Ashley Corporation admits under oath that an oral agreement was made with Com Best, Inc., to sell certain business premises, the agreement will be enforceable in those states. A contract subject to the UCC will be enforceable, but only to the extent of the quantity admitted.[8]

Promissory Estoppel. In some states, an oral contract that would otherwise be unenforceable under the Statute of Frauds may be enforced under the doctrine of promissory estoppel, based on detrimental reliance. Recall from Chapter 11 that if a promisor makes a promise on which the promisee justifiably relies to his or her detriment, a court may *estop* (prevent) the promisor from denying that a contract exists. Section 139 of the *Restatement (Second) of Contracts* provides that in these circumstances, an oral promise can be enforceable notwithstanding the Statute of Frauds if the reliance was foreseeable to the person making the promise and if injustice can be avoided only by enforcing the promise.

Special Exceptions under the UCC. Special exceptions to the applicability of the Statute of Frauds apply to sales contracts. Oral contracts for customized goods may be enforced in certain circumstances. Another exception has to do with oral contracts *between merchants* that have been confirmed in writing. These exceptions and those mentioned above will be examined in greater detail in the discussion of the UCC provisions regarding the Statute of Frauds in Chapter 18.

SECTION 3

Sufficiency of the Writing

The Statute of Frauds and the UCC require either a written contract or a written memorandum evidencing an oral contract signed by the party against whom enforcement is sought, except when there is a legally recognized exception, such as partial performance. The signature need not be placed at the end of the document but can be anywhere in the writing. It can even be an initial rather than the full

6. UCC 2–201(3)(c).

7. *Restatement (Second) of Contracts*, Section 133.

8. UCC 2–201(3)(b).

name. (A significant issue in today's business world has to do with how "signatures" can be created and verified on electronic contracts and other documents. For a discussion of this topic, see Chapter 23.)

A memorandum evidencing the oral contract need only contain the essential terms of the contract. Under the UCC, for contracts evidencing sales of goods, the writing need only name the quantity term and be signed by the party to be charged. Any confirmation, invoice, sales slip, check, fax, or e-mail—or such items in combination—can constitute a writing sufficient to satisfy the Statute of Frauds. Under most other provisions of the Statute of Frauds, for contracts evidencing transactions other than sales of goods, the writing must also name the parties, the subject matter, the consideration, and the essential terms with reasonable certainty. In some states, contracts for the sale of land must state the price and describe the property with sufficient clarity to allow them to be determined without reference to outside sources.[9]

SECTION 4

The Parol Evidence Rule

Sometimes, a written contract does not include—or contradicts—an oral understanding reached by the parties before or at the time of contracting. For example, consider the following situation. Laura is about to lease an apartment. As she is signing the lease, she asks the landlord whether cats are allowed in the building. The landlord says that they are and that Laura can keep her cat in the apartment. The lease that Laura actually signs, however, contains a provision prohibiting pets. Later, a dispute arises between Laura and the landlord over whether the landlord agreed that Laura could have a cat in the apartment. Will Laura be able to introduce evidence at trial to show that, at the time the written contract was formed, the landlord orally agreed that she could have a cat, or will the written contract absolutely control?

In determining the outcome of contract disputes such as the one between Laura and her landlord, the courts look to a common law rule governing the admissibility in court of oral evidence, or *parol evidence*. Under the **parol evidence rule**, if a court finds that the parties intended their written contract to be a complete and final embodiment of their agreement, a party cannot introduce in court evidence of any oral agreement or promise made prior to the contract's formation or at the time the contract was created.[10] Because of the rigidity of the parol evidence rule, the courts have created several exceptions:

1. *Contracts subsequently modified.* Evidence of *subsequent modification* (oral or written) of a written contract can be introduced into court. Keep in mind that the oral modifications may not be enforceable if they come under the Statute of Frauds—for example, if they increase the price of the goods for sale to $500 or more or increase the term for performance to more than one year. Also, oral modifications will not be enforceable if the original contract provides that any modification must be in writing.[11]
2. *Voidable or void contracts.* Oral evidence can be introduced in all cases to show that the contract was voidable or void (for example, induced by mistake, fraud, or misrepresentation). In this case, if deception led one of the parties to agree to the terms of a written contract, oral evidence attesting to the fraud should not be excluded. Courts frown on bad faith and are quick to allow such evidence when it establishes fraud.
3. *Contracts containing ambiguous terms.* When the terms of a written contract are ambiguous, evidence is admissible to show the meaning of the terms.
4. *Incomplete contracts.* When the written contract is incomplete in that it lacks one or more of the essential terms, the courts allow evidence to "fill in the gaps."
5. *Prior dealing, course of performance, or usage of trade.* Under the UCC, evidence can be introduced to explain or supplement a written contract by showing a prior dealing, course of performance, or usage of trade.[12] These terms will be discussed in further detail in Chapter 18, in the context of sales contracts. Here, it is sufficient to say that when buyers and sellers deal with each other over extended periods of time, certain customary practices develop. These practices are often overlooked in the writing of the contract, so courts allow the introduction of evidence to show how the parties have acted in the past.

9. *Rhodes v. Wilkins*, 83 N.M. 782, 498 P.2d 311 (1972).

10. *Restatement (Second) of Contracts*, Section 213.

11. UCC 2–209(2) and (3).

12. UCC 1–205 and 2–202.

6. *Contracts subject to orally agreed-on conditions.* The parol evidence rule does not apply if the existence of the entire written contract is subject to an orally agreed-on condition. Proof of the condition does not alter or modify the written terms but involves the enforceability of the written contract. A leading case concerning this exception is *Pym v. Campbell*,[13] in which the court stated that "evidence to vary the terms of an agreement in writing is not admissible, but evidence to show that there is not an agreement at all is admissible."

7. *Contracts with an obvious or gross clerical (or typographic) error that clearly would not represent the agreement of the parties.* Parol evidence is admissible to correct an obvious typographic error.

The key in determining whether evidence will be allowed basically depends on whether the written contract is intended to be a complete and final embodiment of the terms of the agreement. If it is so intended, it is referred to as an **integrated contract**, and extraneous evidence (evidence derived from sources outside the contract itself) is excluded. If it is only partially integrated, evidence of consistent additional terms is admissible to supplement the written agreement.[14]

See Case 14.2 at the end of this chapter. To view the full, unedited case from Westlaw,® go to this text's Web site at **http://wbl-cs.westbuslaw.com**.

13. 6 Ellis and Blackburn Reports 370 (Q.B. [Queen's Bench] 1856).

14. *Restatement (Second) of Contracts*, Section 216.

TERMS AND CONCEPTS TO REVIEW

CHAPTER SUMMARY

The Origins of the Statute of Frauds	In 1677, the English Parliament passed an act titled "An Act for the Prevention of Frauds and Perjuries," which required certain types of contracts to be in writing. Today, almost every state in the United States has a statute modeled after the English act.
Contracts that Fall within the Statute of Frauds	1. The following types of contracts fall under the Statute of Frauds and must be in writing to be enforceable: a. Contracts involving interests in land—The statute applies to any contract for an interest in realty, such as a sale, a lease, or a mortgage. b. Contracts whose terms cannot be performed within one year—The statute applies only to contracts objectively impossible to perform fully within one year from (the day after) the contract's formation. c. Collateral promises—The statute applies only to express contracts made between the guarantor and the creditor whose terms make the guarantor secondarily liable. *Exception:* the "main purpose" rule. d. Promises made in consideration of marriage—The statute applies to promises to pay money or give property in consideration of a promise to marry and to prenuptial agreements made in consideration of marriage. e. Contracts for the sale of goods priced at $500 or more—Under the UCC Statute of Frauds provision in UCC 2–201. 2. *Exceptions*—Partial performance, admissions, and promissory estoppel.

Chapter Summary—continued

Sufficiency of the Writing	To constitute an enforceable contract under the Statute of Frauds, a writing must be signed by the party against whom enforcement is sought, must name the parties, must identify the subject matter, and must state with reasonable certainty the essential terms of the contract. In a sale of land, the price and a description of the property may need to be stated with sufficient clarity to allow them to be determined without reference to outside sources. Under the UCC, a contract for a sale of goods is not enforceable beyond the quantity of goods shown in the contract.
Parol Evidence Rule	The parol evidence rule prohibits the introduction at trial of evidence of the parties' prior negotiations, prior agreements, or contemporaneous oral agreements that contradicts or varies the terms of the parties' written contract. The written contract is assumed to be the complete embodiment of the parties' agreement. Exceptions are made in the following circumstances: 1. To show that the contract was subsequently modified. 2. To show that the contract was voidable or void. 3. To clarify the meaning of ambiguous terms. 4. To clarify the terms of the contract when the written contract lacks one or more of its essential terms. 5. Under the UCC, to explain the meaning of contract terms in light of a prior dealing, course of performance, or usage of trade. 6. To show that the entire contract is subject to an orally agreed-on condition. 7. When an obvious clerical or typographic error was made.

Cases for Analysis

Westlaw. You can access the full text of each case presented below by going to the Westlaw cases on this text's Web site at http://wbl-cs.westbuslaw.com. Each Westlaw case includes the names of all plaintiffs and defendants, the dates on which the case was argued and decided, a brief summary of the issues and decisions in the case, headnotes classifying specific issues in the case according to the West Key Number System, and the court's opinion. Concurring and dissenting opinions, if any, are included as well.

Case 14.1 The One-Year Rule

McInerney v. Charter Golf, Inc.

Supreme Court of Illinois, 1997.
176 Ill.2d 482,
680 N.E.2d 1347,
223 Ill.Dec. 911.

Justice *HEIPLE* delivered the opinion of the court:

[Must] an employee's promise to forgo another job opportunity in exchange for a guarantee of lifetime employment * * * be in writing to satisfy the requirements of the statute of frauds? [This question] must be answered in plaintiff Dennis McInerney's appeal from an order of [a state intermediate] appellate court affirming a grant of summary judgment in favor of the defendant, Charter Golf, Inc. Although we conclude that a promise for a promise is sufficient consideration to modify a contract—even an employment contract—we further conclude that the statute of frauds requires that a contract for lifetime employment be in writing.

The facts are uncomplicated. * * * From 1988 through 1992, Dennis McInerney worked as a sales representative for Charter Golf, Inc., a company which manufactures and sells golf apparel and supplies. Initially, McInerney's territory included Illinois but was later expanded to include Indiana and Wisconsin. In 1989, McInerney allegedly was offered a position as an exclusive sales representative for Hickey-Freeman, an elite clothier which manufactured a competing line of golf apparel. Hickey-Freeman purportedly offered McInerney an 8% commission.

Intending to inform Charter Golf of his decision to accept the Hickey-Freeman offer of employment, McInerney called Jerry Montiel, Charter Golf's president. Montiel wanted McInerney to continue to work for Charter Golf and urged McInerney to turn down the Hickey-Freeman offer. Montiel promised to guarantee McInerney a 10% commission on sales in Illinois and Wisconsin "for the remainder of his life," in a position where he would be subject to discharge only for dishonesty or disability. McInerney allegedly accepted Charter Golf's offer and, in exchange for the guarantee of lifetime employment, gave up the Hickey-Freeman offer. McInerney then continued to work for Charter Golf.

In 1992, the relationship between Charter Golf and McInerney soured: Charter Golf fired McInerney. McInerney then filed a complaint in [an Illinois state court] alleging breach of contract. The trial court granted Charter Golf's motion for summary judgment after concluding that the alleged oral contract was unenforceable under the statute of frauds because the contract amounted to an agreement which could not be performed within a year from its making. The [state intermediate] appellate court affirmed * * * .

This court accepted McInerney's petition for leave [permission] to appeal, and for the reasons set forth below, we affirm * * * .

* * * *

* * * Charter Golf argues that the oral contract at issue in this case violates the statute of frauds and is unenforceable because it is not capable of being performed within one year of its making. By statute in Illinois, "[n]o action shall be brought * * * upon any agreement that is not to be performed within the space of one year from the making thereof, unless * * * in writing and signed by the party to be charged." Our statute tracks the language of the original English Statute of Frauds and Perjuries. The English statute enacted by Parliament had as its stated purpose the prohibition of those "many fraudulent practices, which are commonly endeavored to be upheld by perjury and subordination of perjury." Illinois' statute of frauds seeks to do the same by barring actions based upon nothing more than loose verbal statements.

The period of one year, although arbitrary, recognizes that with the passage of time evidence becomes stale and memories fade. The statute proceeds from the legislature's sound conclusion that while the technical elements of a contract may exist, certain contracts should not be enforced absent a writing. It functions more as an evidentiary safeguard than as a substantive rule of contract. As such, *the statute exists to protect not just the parties to a contract, but also—perhaps more importantly—to protect the fact finder from charlatans, perjurers and the problems of proof accompanying oral contracts.* [Emphasis added.]

There are, of course, exceptions to the statute of frauds' writing requirement which permit the enforcement of certain oral contracts required by the statute to be in writing. One such exception is the judicially created exclusion for contracts of uncertain duration. In an effort to significantly narrow the application of the statute, many courts have construed the words "not to be performed" to mean "not capable of being performed" within one year. These cases hold that if performance is possible by its terms within one year, the contract is not within the statute regardless of how unlikely it is that it will actually be performed within one year. Under this interpretation, the actual course of subsequent events and the expectations of the parties are entirely irrelevant. A contract for lifetime employment would then be excluded from the operation of the statute because the employee could, in theory, die within one year, and thus the contract would be capable of being performed.

We find such an interpretation hollow and unpersuasive. A "lifetime" employment contract is, in essence, a permanent employment contract. Inherently, it anticipates a relationship of long duration—certainly longer than one year. In the context of an employment-for-life contract, we believe that the better view is to treat the contract as one "not to be performed within the space of one year from the making thereof." To hold otherwise would eviscerate [take away an essential part of] the policy underlying the statute of frauds and would invite confusion, uncertainty and outright fraud. Accordingly, we hold that a writing is required for the fair enforcement of lifetime employment contracts.

* * * *

* * * Accordingly, we affirm the judgment of the appellate court.

* * * *

Justice *NICKELS*, dissenting:

* * * I disagree with the majority's holding that the employment contract in the case at bar must be in writing because it falls within the requirements of the statute of frauds.

* * * *

A contract of employment for life is necessarily one of uncertain duration. Since the employee's life may end within one year, and, as the majority acknowledges, the contract would be fully performed upon the employee's death, the contract is not subject to the statute of frauds' one-year provision. It is irrelevant whether the parties anticipate that the employee will live for more than a year or whether the employee actually does so.

* * * *

* * * I would reverse the judgments of the courts below. Accordingly, I respectfully dissent.

CASE 14.2 THE PAROL EVIDENCE RULE

COUSINS SUBS SYSTEMS, INC. v. MCKINNEY

United States District Court,
Eastern District of Wisconsin, 1999.
59 F.Supp.2d 816.

ADELMAN. District Judge.

This is a diversity action arising out of a dispute between the parties to a franchise agreement. Plaintiff, Cousins Subs Systems, Inc. ("Cousins"), a Wisconsin company, entered into several agreements with defendant, Michael R. McKinney, a Minnesota businessman, for McKinney to operate Cousins submarine sandwich shops in northern Minnesota and Wisconsin. McKinney owns the Best Oil Company, which operates a chain of gas station/convenience stores known as The Little Stores, in which the Cousins shops were placed.

On June 12, 1998, Cousins filed this lawsuit alleging that McKinney sold Cousins products and used Cousins confidential techniques in unauthorized ways, failed to pay fees owed to Cousins and wrongfully terminated his agreements with Cousins. * * * McKinney * * * filed a counterclaim * * * , alleging a number of claims against Cousins and its sales representatives, David K. Kilby and Daniel J. Sobiech. These claims include * * * breach of contract. Cousins then moved to dismiss McKinney's counterclaim * * * . This decision addresses Cousins's motion to dismiss.

I. FACTUAL BACKGROUND

In 1995 McKinney and Cousins began discussing the possibility of McKinney becoming a Cousins franchisee and area developer. Following negotiations and correspondence involving the parties and their lawyers, on May 9, 1996, McKinney and Cousins entered into an agreement for McKinney to operate a Cousins franchise in Carlton, Minnesota. Also on May 9, 1996, the parties signed an area development agreement authorizing McKinney to oversee the development of other franchises in the area. On January 7, 1997, the parties entered into an agreement for McKinney to operate a franchise in Superior, Wisconsin. Subsequently, however, McKinney became disillusioned with the arrangement, and on April 9, 1998, he notified Cousins that he was terminating all the agreements.

In his counterclaim * * * , McKinney's specific allegations [include] that Sobiech guaranteed that "annual sales at each of McKinney's franchises would range from $250,000 to $500,000 per franchise" * * * . McKinney alleges that these promises were not kept. * * *

* * * *

III. DISCUSSION

* * * *

The main problem with this claim and, for that matter, with all of McKinney's claims is that the oral promises allegedly made by Cousins are directly contradicted by the written terms of the agreements that he signed * * * . *Where the allegations of a complaint are inconsistent with the terms of a written contract * * * , the terms of the contract prevail * * * .* Unfortunately for McKinney, every oral representation that he alleges was made by Cousins is inconsistent with the written contracts he signed or the written circular he received. [Emphasis added.]

McKinney alleges first that Cousins through Sobiech orally guaranteed that annual sales at McKinney's franchises would be between $250,000 and $500,000, and that this level of sales was not realized. However, the Area Development Agreement states that McKinney "has not received any warranty or guaranty, express or implied, as to the potential volume, profits, or success of the business venture." The Franchise Agreement contains virtually identical language. Thus, McKinney's claim of guaranteed profits is directly contradicted by the written contracts. McKinney also claims that Cousins promised to provide "advertising * * * in excess of the amount paid by McKinney," and that Cousins failed to do so. But the Uniform Franchise Offering Circular states that "Cousins is not obligated to spend any specific amounts on advertising in the area where a particular franchisee is located * * * ." McKinney next alleges that Cousins "expressly guaranteed and promised to provide extensive assistance in recruitment of other franchisees in the development area," but that such assistance was not forthcoming. The Area Development Agreement, however, states, with respect to the recruitment issue, that "AREA DEVELOPER shall be responsible for advertising for, recruiting and screening prospects for SHOPS within the Exclusive Area." Thus, every single oral promise that McKinney asserts was made by Cousins is inconsistent with the documents appended to his complaint. * * *

McKinney's claims are further undermined by other language in the agreements. The area development and franchise agreements each contain integration clauses which expressly disavow any promises not included in the written agreements between the parties. The Area Development Agreement, for example, states that "this Agreement * * * constitutes the entire agreement of the parties, and there are no other oral or written understandings or agreements * * * relating to the subject matter of this agreement."

Finally, McKinney's attempt to invoke alleged oral agreements to contradict the terms of the written agreements is barred by the parol evidence rule * * * . The parol evidence rule prohibits the use of oral agreements of the type McKinney relies on to contradict written contracts if the written contract is intended by the parties to be the final expression of their agreement. The presence of the integration clauses in the written agreements makes clear that the contracts were intended to embody all of the agreed on terms. Thus, the parol evidence rule presents another fundamental bar to all of McKinney's claims.

* * * *

McKinney attempts to bolster his claim by referring in his pleadings to a questionnaire that he filled out, purportedly raising questions as to whether promises were made by Cousins employees contrary to the written contracts. However, this argument is unpersuasive. First, McKinney filled out the questionnaire prior to signing the contracts which expressly disavow oral promises of the type that he relies on. Second, McKinney acknowledges in his pleadings that Cousins gave him the opportunity to clarify his answers to the questionnaire but that he never bothered to respond to the Cousins inquiry. Third, six months after filling out the questionnaire, McKinney signed a second franchise agreement and again acknowledged that no promises had been made to him other than those contained in the document.

In sum, McKinney is an experienced businessman who made a deal which turned out to be less favorable than he anticipated. McKinney expressly acknowledged in detailed written agreements negotiated with the assistance of counsel that his purchase of a franchise was not a risk-free endeavor. He now makes allegations that are directly contrary to the agreements he signed. For the reasons stated, his claim * * * fails.

* * * *

For the foregoing reasons,

IT IS HEREBY ORDERED that Cousin's motion to dismiss McKinney's counterclaim * * * is **GRANTED**.

CASE PROBLEMS

14–1. The plaintiff, Young, formed an oral agreement with the defendant, Drury, to buy several carloads of tomatoes. Afterward, Drury wrote a memorandum concerning the agreement and all its terms for his own records and put it in his safe. The memo, which Drury did not sign, was created on Drury's letterhead (which is a sufficient signing in the eyes of the court) and contained Young's name in the text. Subsequently, Drury wrote a letter to Young stating he was not going to sell Young the tomatoes as agreed. When Young sued Drury in a Maryland state court for breach of contract, Drury used the Statute of Frauds as a defense. The trial court held in Young's favor, claiming that Drury's memo (even if it was never delivered to Young), combined with the subsequent letter, satisfied the writing requirement of the Statute of Frauds. Drury appealed. Does the memo written by Drury satisfy the writing requirement under the Statute of Frauds? Discuss. [*Drury v. Young*, 58 Md. 546 (1882)]

14–2. John Peck, an employee of V.S.H. Realty, Inc., asked Abdu Nessralla, his father-in-law, to act as a "straw" (a person who is put up in name only to take part in a deal) in V.S.H.'s acquisition of real property near Nessralla's farm. In return, Peck agreed to act as a straw to assist Nessralla in purchasing other nearby property—the Sturtevant farm. Nessralla purchased the property V.S.H. wanted and conveyed it to V.S.H. Subsequently, Peck purchased the Sturtevant farm and conveyed the property to himself and his cousin. Nessralla took no part in the purchase of the Sturtevant farm, provided none of the purchase price, and did not know that the purchase had taken place until about a month later. When Nessralla learned of the purchase and asked Peck to sell the farm to him, Peck refused. Nessralla filed a complaint seeking specific performance of Peck's oral agreement to convey the Sturtevant farm to him. The trial court dismissed Nessralla's action, concluding that the Statute of Frauds operated as a complete defense. Nessralla appealed, arguing that Peck was estopped from pleading the Statute of Frauds as a defense. Nessralla claimed that he suffered injury in reliance on the oral agreement, both because he purchased property on Peck's (V.S.H.'s) behalf and because he took no action to purchase the Sturtevant farm on his own behalf. Will the appellate court uphold the trial court's ruling? Explain. [*Nessralla v. Peck*, 403 Mass. 757, 532 N.E.2d 685 (1989)]

14–3. The plaintiffs—the Nicols, Hoerrs, Turners, and Andersons—purchased subdivision lots from Ken Nelson. The lots bordered an undeveloped tract and offered scenic views of an adjacent lake. When Nelson and his partners began taking steps to develop the previously undeveloped tract, the plaintiffs sued. The trial court found that the plaintiffs had purchased their lots only after receiving oral assurances from Nelson that (1) the tract would remain undeveloped open space, (2) the property was owned by a company that had no plans to build on the land, (3) he held an option to purchase the property if it became available, and (4) he would not develop the land if it came under his ownership. Concluding that the plaintiffs had reasonably relied on Nelson's oral promise, the trial court enjoined Nelson's development of the property. Nelson appealed, arguing that the Statute of Frauds, which requires that contracts involving interests in real property be in writing, barred enforcement of his oral promise. Will the appellate court affirm the trial court's judgment? Discuss fully. [*Nicol v. Nelson*, 776 P.2d 1144 (Colo.App. 1989)]

14–4. Carol Mann and Gerald Harris worked for Helmsley-Spear, Inc. (HSI), as account managers for various HSI properties. In 1983, each received a $50,000 bonus for work performed in converting an HSI apartment complex, known as Windsor Park, into a cooperative housing unit. The conversion had taken several years to complete. After they had finished the Windsor Park conversion, Mann and Harris were asked to work on another cooperative conversion of two HSI apartment buildings known as Park West Village. They were orally promised compensation, over and above their base salaries, on the basis of a formula similar to the one that had been orally agreed on with regard to the Windsor Park conversion. In 1987, after they had completed the conversion of Park West Village, they were fired, and HSI refused to pay them the additional compensation. Among other things, HSI contended that the oral agreement concerning the extra compensation was unenforceable under the Statute of Frauds. How should the court rule on this issue, and why? [*Mann v. Helmsley-Spear, Inc.*, 177 A.D.2d 147, 581 N.Y.S.2d 16 (1992)]

14–5. A 1965 bargaining agreement between employees and Wheelabrator Corp. clearly stated that the company would pay the cost of health insurance for employees who had retired prior to 1959. Later bargaining agreements also indicated that once employees reach the age of sixty-five, Wheelabrator would pay for their health insurance and that when they die, their spouses would continue to receive supplemental health benefits at the company's cost. Wheelabrator withdrew the health benefits of retired employees in 1988, when it closed its plant and the last agreement expired. Kenneth Bidlack and other retired employees sued the company to have their health benefits reinstated. The employees asserted that the agreements meant that they would be granted benefits for life. Wheelabrator contended that the agreements granted benefits only for years—during the duration of the agreements. The court was left to decide whether extrinsic evidence (including letters from the company to retirees indicating that the company would pay the cost of the health insurance throughout the retirees' lives) was admissible to clarify the terms of the contract. Should the court allow the employees to introduce extrinsic evidence to justify their claim? Discuss fully. [*Bidlack v. Wheelabrator Corp.*, 993 F.2d 603 (7th Cir. 1993)]

14–6. Michael Elrod, as agent for Kenneth Katz, offered in writing to purchase certain real estate owned by Joiner and his wife, the defendants. The written contract (offer) sent to Joiner provided an earnest money payment (deposit) by Katz of $1,000. Over the telephone, Joiner told Katz on October 13, 1985, that "everything was agreeable, that we had a deal, that [Joiner] was going to execute the contract and mail it back." Katz then pointed out to Joiner that the contract contained a provision by which the offer would be revoked unless the contract was executed (signed) and delivered by Joiner no later than October 14. Katz and Joiner agreed to disregard the provision. On October 20, Joiner mailed the executed contract, and Katz deposited the earnest money in a trust account with the title company. Joiner then sent a telegram that read, "I have signed and returned contract but have changed my mind. Do not wish to sell property." Elrod sued the Joiners for specific performance (to enforce the contract). The Joiners contended that no contract was ever formed and that any contract was unenforceable because the oral modification was material. The trial court found that a valid and enforceable contract existed, and the Joiners appealed. What will happen on appeal? Discuss. [*Joiner v. Elrod*, 716 S.W.2d 606 (Tex.App.—Corpus Christi, 1986)]

14–7. Thomas Frederick was a regional sales manager with Kahn's & Company and was not seeking any change of employment. Bernard Zilinskas, a vice president for a division of the Armour Processed Meat Company (a subsidiary of ConAgra, Inc.), contacted Frederick about coming to work for Armour as its northeast regional sales manager. Zilinskas made numerous representations about the job, including that Armour wanted to hire Frederick for a minimum of two years. Frederick accepted the position and began work for Armour, although no employment contract was signed. He moved his family from New York to Massachusetts and arranged to have a new home constructed. Three months later, he was fired on thirty days' notice for no stated cause. Frederick sued ConAgra in a federal district court for breach of contract, and ConAgra moved to dismiss the complaint, contending, among other things, that even if there was an employment contract, an action for its enforcement was barred by the Statute of Frauds. What should the court decide? Discuss fully. [*Frederick v. ConAgra, Inc.*, 713 F.Supp. 41 (D.Mass. 1989)]

14–8. Illinois Bell Telephone Co. (IBT) and the Reuben H. Donnelley Corp. (RHD) had by contract jointly produced telephone directories in Illinois for over sixty years. While in the process of oral negotiations to renew the contracts, IBT notified RHD by letter that the existing contracts were being canceled pursuant to contract terms. These contract terms required RHD to turn over records, to assign advertising contracts, to refrain from using certain information in any future directories RHD might publish, and so on. The termination clause under which IBT canceled stated that "either party may cancel this agreement by giving prior written notice to the other one year in advance of the effective date of cancellation." The requirements imposed on RHD were to take place on "termination." In anticipation that RHD's and IBT's interpretation of the contract terms and the time when RHD's obligations would become effective would differ, IBT filed a lawsuit, seeking specific performance of its demand for RHD to meet the termination requirements immediately. RHD moved to dismiss the suit, claiming that the words of the contract were clear and that such demands were not effective until one year after "the effective date of cancellation." Discuss who is correct. [*Illinois Bell Telephone Co. v. Reuben H. Donnelley Corp.*, 595 F.Supp. 1192 (N.D.Ill. 1984)]

14–9. Wilson Floors Company contracted to provide flooring materials for a development owned by the defendant bank, Sciota Park, Ltd. When the general contractor for Sciota fell behind in payments to Wilson, Wilson stopped work. Sciota assured Wilson that he would be paid if he returned to work. When Wilson's final bill was not paid, Wilson sued Sciota in an Ohio state court. The trial court held that the bank's assurances to Wilson that he would be paid did not fall under the Statute of Frauds because the bank assumed a "direct undertaking"—not a secondary obligation—when it guaranteed payment to Wilson. Therefore, the oral promise was enforceable. The appellate court reversed, finding that the bank became only secondarily liable to Wilson when it guaranteed payment; therefore, the oral promise was unenforceable. Wilson appealed. What will happen on appeal? Discuss. [*Wilson Floors Co. v. Sciota Park, Ltd.*, 54 Ohio St.2d 451, 377 N.E.2d 514 (1978)]

14-10. On November 11, 1988, Roberta Chafetz telephoned a United Parcel Service (UPS) office to inquire about shipping two packages containing diamonds from her home to New York City. She told the UPS representative that each package would need to be insured for $25,000. Arrangements were made to pick up the packages, and three days later, a UPS driver called at Chafetz's home, presented her with the standard "pick-up" form, and requested payment of $6.65. Chafetz paid the charge and signed the pick-up agreement form without reading it and without filling in the blank on the form that provided for extra insurance coverage. Subsequently, one of the two packages was lost or stolen during shipment. UPS claimed its liability was limited to $100—the standard package insurance specified on the shipping agreement that Chafetz signed. Chafetz contended that UPS was liable for $25,000—the amount of insurance on which the parties had orally agreed. Who will prevail in court, and why? [*Chafetz v. United Parcel Service, Inc.*, 1992 Mass.App.Div. 67 (1991)]

14–11. Fernandez orally promised Pando that if Pando helped her win the New York state lottery, she would share the proceeds equally with him. Pando agreed to purchase the tickets in Fernandez's name, select the lottery numbers, and pray for divine intervention from a saint to help them win. Fernandez won $2.8 million in the lottery, which was to be paid over a ten-year period. When Fernandez failed to share the winnings equally, Pando sued for breach of her contractual obligation. Fernandez countered that the contract was unenforceable under the Statute of Frauds because the contract could not be performed within one year. Could the contract be performed within a year? Explain. [*Pando by Pando v. Fernandez*, 127 Misc.2d 224, 485 N.Y.S.2d 162 (1984)]

14–12. Samuel DaGrossa and others were planning to open a restaurant. At some point prior to August 1985, DaGrossa orally agreed with Philippe LaJaunie that LaJaunie, in exchange for his contribution in designing, renovating, and managing the restaurant, could purchase a one-third interest in the restaurant's stock if the restaurant was profitable in its first year of operations. The restaurant opened in March 1986, and a few weeks later, LaJaunie's employment was terminated. LaJaunie brought an action to enforce the stock-purchase agreement. Is the agreement enforceable? Why, or why not? [*LaJaunie v. DaGrossa*, 159 A.D.2d 349, 552 N.Y.S.2d 628 (1990)]

14–13. Glenn Grove bought a 1936 Pontiac from Bernard Stanfield. Stanfield signed the certificate of title, which stated that the car was sold for $1,000. No other terms of sale were mentioned in the certificate, and none were incorporated by reference. Three years later, Stanfield filed a suit against Grove in a Missouri state court, claiming that Grove still owed $9,000 on the price of the car. At the trial, Stanfield testified that he and Grove had an oral agreement by which Grove was to pay $1,000 for the "title document" and $9,000 for the actual car. The court entered a judgment in Stanfield's favor. What will happen on appeal? Explain. [*Stanfield v. Grove*, 924 S.W.2d 611 (Mo.App.Div.4 1996)]

14–14. Vision Graphics, Inc., provides printing services to customers such as Milton Bradley Co. To perform its services, Vision agreed to buy or lease from E. I. du Pont de Nemours & Co. parts of a computer software system. Vision needed the system to accept files written in "PostScript," a computer language used in the printing industry. Du Pont orally represented to Vision that with three upgrades, its system would be completely "postscriptable." Promises regarding postscriptability were not included in any of the parties' written contracts. Each contract, however, included an integration clause stating that the contract contained the entire agreement of the parties. Before the three upgrades were complete, du Pont determined that for financial reasons, it could no longer support its system and told Vision that the software would not be made postscriptable. Vision lost customers and could not attract new accounts, and its reputation in the industry was damaged. Vision filed a suit in a federal district court against du Pont, alleging, among other things, breach of contract on the basis of the oral promises. Du Pont filed a motion for summary judgment, arguing that whether it breached any oral agreement was "immaterial." Will the court agree? Why, or why not? [*Vision Graphics, Inc. v. E. I. du Pont de Nemours & Co.*, 41 F.Supp.2d 93 (D.Mass. 1999)]

14–15. Robert Pinto, doing business as Pinto Associates, hired Richard MacDonald as an independent contractor in March 1992. The parties orally agreed on the terms of employment, including payment to MacDonald of a share of the company's income, but they did not put anything in writing. In March 1995,

MacDonald quit. Pinto then told MacDonald that he was entitled to $9,602.17—25 percent of the difference between the accounts receivable and the accounts payable as of MacDonald's last day. MacDonald disagreed and demanded more than $83,500—25 percent of the revenue from all invoices, less the cost of materials and outside processing, for each of the years that he worked for Pinto. Pinto refused. MacDonald filed a suit in a Connecticut state court against Pinto, alleging breach of contract. In Pinto's response and at the trial, he testified that the parties had an oral contract under which MacDonald was entitled to 25 percent of the difference between accounts receivable and payable as of the date of MacDonald's termination. Did the parties have an enforceable contract? How should the court rule, and why? [*MacDonald v. Pinto,* 62 Conn.App. 317, 771 A.2d 156 (2001)]

E-LINKS

For updated links to resources available on the Web, as well as a variety of other materials, visit this text's Web site at

http://wbl-cs.westbuslaw.com

The online version of UCC Section 2–201 on the Statute of Frauds includes links to definitions of certain terms used in the section. To access this site, go to

http://www.law.cornell.edu/ucc/2/2-201.html

Professor Eric Talley of the University of Southern California provides an interesting discussion of the history and current applicability of the Statute of Frauds, both internationally and in the United States, at the following Web site:

http://www-bcf.usc.edu/~etalley/frauds.html

LEGAL RESEARCH EXERCISES ON THE WEB

Go to http://wbl-cs.westbuslaw.com, the Web site that accompanies this text. Select "Interactive Study Center," and then click on "Chapter 14." There you will find the following Internet research exercise that you can perform to learn more about the Statute of Frauds:

Activity 14–1: The Statute of Frauds

CHAPTER 15

Third Party Rights

ONCE IT HAS BEEN DETERMINED that a valid and legally enforceable contract exists, attention can turn to the rights and duties of the parties to the contract. A contract is a private agreement between the parties who have entered into it, and traditionally these parties alone have rights and liabilities under the contract. This principle is referred to as *privity of contract.* A *third party*—one who is not a direct party to a particular contract—normally does not have rights under that contract.

There are exceptions to the rule of privity of contract. As we noted in Chapter 6, privity of contract between a seller and a buyer is no longer a requirement to recover damages under product liability laws. In this chapter, we look at two other exceptions. One exception allows a party to a contract to transfer the rights or duties arising from the contract to another person through an *assignment* (of rights) or a *delegation* (of duties). The other exception involves a *third party beneficiary contract*—a contract in which the parties to the contract intend that the contract benefit a third party. We look at both of these exceptions to the rule of privity of contract in this chapter, beginning with the law relating to assignments and delegations.

SECTION 1

Assignments and Delegations

In a bilateral contract, the two parties have corresponding rights and duties. One party has a *right* to require the other to perform some task, and the other has a *duty* to perform it. The transfer of contractual *rights* to a third party is known as an **assignment.** The transfer of contractual *duties* to a third party is known as a **delegation.** An assignment or a delegation occurs *after* the original contract was made.

ASSIGNMENTS

When rights under a contract are assigned unconditionally, the rights of the *assignor* (the party making the assignment) are extinguished.[1] The third party (the *assignee,* or party receiving the assignment) has a right to demand performance from the other original party to the contract.

For example, suppose that Brower is obligated by contract to pay Horton $1,000. In this situation, Brower is the *obligor,* because she owes an obligation, or duty, to Horton. Horton is the *obligee,* the one to whom the obligation, or duty, is owed. Now suppose that Horton assigns his right to receive the $1,000 to Kuhn. Horton is the assignor, and Kuhn is the assignee. Kuhn now becomes the obligee, because now Brower owes Kuhn the $1,000. Here, a valid assignment of a debt exists. Kuhn (the assignee-obligee) is entitled to enforce payment in court if Brower (the obligor) does not pay her the $1,000. These concepts are illustrated in Exhibit 15–1 on the next page.

The assignee takes only those rights that the assignor originally had. Furthermore, the assignee's rights are subject to the defenses that the obligor has against the assignor. For example, assume that in the above example, Brower owed Horton the $1,000 under a contract in which Brower agreed to buy Horton's personal computer. Brower, in deciding to

1. *Restatement (Second) of Contracts,* Section 317.

EXHIBIT 15–1 ASSIGNMENT RELATIONSHIPS

In the assignment relationship illustrated here, Horton assigns his *rights* under a contract that he made with Brower to a third party, Kuhn. Horton thus becomes the *assignor* and Kuhn the *assignee* of the contractual rights. Brower, the *obligor* (the party owing performance under the contract), now owes performance to Kuhn instead of Horton. Horton's original contract rights are extinguished after assignment.

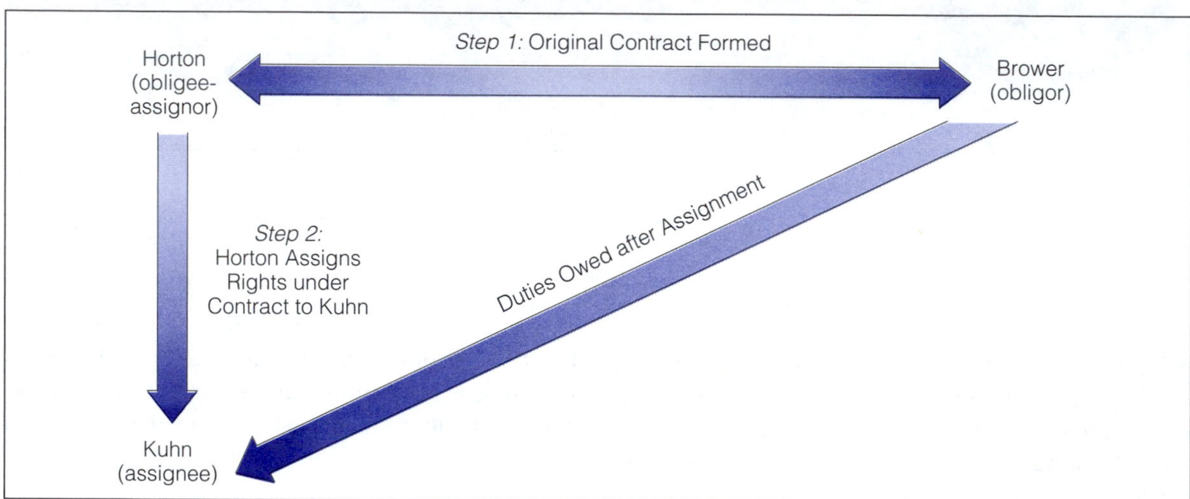

purchase the computer, relied on Horton's fraudulent misrepresentation that the computer's hard drive had a storage capacity of forty gigabytes. When Brower discovered that the computer could store only ten gigabytes, she told Horton that she was going to return the computer to him and cancel the contract. Even though Horton had assigned his "right" to receive the $1,000 to Kuhn, Brower need not pay Kuhn the $1,000—Brower can raise the defense of Horton's fraudulent misrepresentation to avoid payment.

How Assignments Function. Assignments are important because they are involved in much business financing. Banks, for example, frequently assign the rights to receive payments under their loan contracts to other firms, which pay for those rights. For example, if you obtain a loan from your local bank to purchase a car, you might later receive in the mail a notice from your bank stating that it has transferred (assigned) its rights to receive payments on the loan to another firm and that, when the time comes to repay your loan, you must make the payments to that other firm.

Banks that make *mortgage loans* (loans to allow prospective home buyers to purchase land or a home) often assign their rights to collect the mortgage payments to a third party, such as GMAC Mortgage Corporation. Following the assignment, the home buyers are notified that they must make future payments not to the bank that loaned them the funds but to the third party. Millions of dollars change hands daily in the business world in the form of assignments of rights in contracts. If it were not possible to transfer (assign) contractual rights, many businesses could not continue to operate.

Form of the Assignment. In general, an assignment can take any form, oral or written. Naturally, it is more difficult to prove that an oral assignment occurred, so it is practical to put all assignments in writing. Of course, assignments covered by the Statute of Frauds must be in writing to be enforceable. For example, an assignment of an interest in land must be in writing to be enforceable. In addition, most states require contracts for the assignment of wages to be in writing.[2]

Rights That Cannot Be Assigned. As a general rule, all rights can be assigned. Exceptions are made, however, in the following circumstances:

1. If a statute expressly prohibits assignment of a particular right, that right cannot be assigned. Suppose that Quincy is an employee of Specialty

2. See, for example, California Labor Code Section 300. There are other assignments that must be in writing as well.

Computer, Inc. Specialty Computer is an employer under workers' compensation statutes in this state, and thus Quincy is a covered employee. Quincy is injured on the job and begins to collect monthly workers' compensation checks (see Chapter 41 for a discussion of workers' compensation laws). In need of a loan, Quincy asks Draper to lend her some money and offers to assign to Draper all of her future workers' compensation benefits. The assignment of future workers' compensation benefits is prohibited by state statute, however, and thus such rights cannot be assigned.

2. When a contract is *personal* in nature, the rights under the contract cannot be assigned unless all that remains is a money payment.[3] Suppose that Brower signs a contract to be a tutor for Horton's children. Horton then attempts to assign to Kuhn his right to Brower's services. Kuhn cannot enforce the contract against Brower. Kuhn's children may be more difficult to tutor than Horton's; thus, if Horton could assign his rights to Brower's services to Kuhn, it would change the nature of Brower's obligation. Because personal services are unique to the person rendering them, rights to receive personal services are likewise unique and cannot be assigned.

3. A right cannot be assigned if assignment will materially increase or alter the risk or duties of the obligor.[4] Assume that Horton has a hotel, and to insure it, he takes out a policy with Southeast Insurance. The policy insures against fire, theft, floods, and vandalism. Horton attempts to assign the insurance policy to Kuhn, who also owns a hotel. The assignment is ineffective, because it substantially alters Southeast Insurance's *duty of performance*. An insurance company evaluates the particular risk of a certain party and tailors its policy to fit that risk. If the policy is assigned to a third party, the insurance risk is materially altered because the insurance company may have no information on the third party. Therefore, the assignment will not operate to give Kuhn any rights against Southeast Insurance.

4. If a contract stipulates that a right cannot be assigned, then *ordinarily* the right cannot be assigned. Whether an antiassignment clause is effective depends in part on how it is phrased. A contract that states that any assignment is "void" effectively prohibits any assignment. Note that restraints on the power to assign operate only against the parties themselves. They do not effectively prohibit an assignment by operation of law, such as an assignment pursuant to bankruptcy or death.

There are several exceptions to the fourth rule. These exceptions are as follows:

1. A contract cannot prevent an assignment of the right to receive money. This exception exists to encourage the free flow of money and credit in modern business settings.
2. The assignment of rights in real estate often cannot be prohibited, because such a prohibition is contrary to public policy. Prohibitions of this kind are called restraints against **alienation** (transfer of land ownership).
3. The assignment of *negotiable instruments* (see Chapter 24) cannot be prohibited.
4. In a contract for the sale of goods, the right to receive damages for breach of contract or for payment of an account owed may be assigned even though the sales contract prohibits such assignment.[5]

Westlaw. See Case 15.1 at the end of this chapter. To view the full, unedited case from Westlaw,® go to this text's Web site at **http://wbl-cs.westbuslaw.com**.

Notice of Assignment. Once a valid assignment of rights has been made, the assignee (the third party to whom the rights have been assigned) should notify the obligor (the one owing performance) of the assignment. For example, when Horton assigns to Kuhn his right to receive the $1,000 from Brower, Kuhn should notify Brower, the obligor, of the assignment. Giving notice is not legally necessary to establish the validity of the assignment, because an assignment is effective immediately, whether or not notice is given. Two major problems arise, however, when notice of the assignment is not given to the obligor.

1. If the assignor assigns the same right to two different persons, the question arises as to which one has priority—that is, which one has the right to the performance by the obligor. Although the rule most often observed in the United States is that the first assignment in time is the first in right, some states follow the English rule, which basically gives priority to the first assignee who gives notice.
2. Until the obligor has notice of assignment, the obligor can discharge his or her obligation by performance to the assignor, and performance by the

3. *Restatement (Second) of Contracts*, Sections 317 and 318.
4. UCC 2–210(2).
5. UCC 2–210(2).

obligor to the assignor constitutes a discharge to the assignee. Once the obligor receives proper notice, only performance to the assignee can discharge the obligor's obligations. To illustrate: In the Horton-Brower-Kuhn example, assume that Brower, the obligor, is not notified of Horton's assignment of his rights to Kuhn. Brower subsequently pays Horton the $1,000. Although the assignment was valid, Brower's payment to Horton discharges the debt. Kuhn's failure to give notice to Brower of the assignment has caused Kuhn to lose the right to collect the money from Brower. If Kuhn had given Brower notice of the assignment, Brower's payment to Horton would not have discharged the debt, and Kuhn would have had a legal right to require payment from Brower.

Westlaw. See Case 15.2 at the end of this chapter. To view the full, unedited case from Westlaw,® go to this text's Web site at **http://wbl-cs.westbuslaw.com**.

DELEGATIONS

Just as a party can transfer rights through an assignment, a party can also transfer duties. Duties are not assigned, however; they are *delegated.* Normally, a delegation of duties does not relieve the party making the delegation (the *delegator*) of the obligation to perform in the event that the party to whom the duty has been delegated (the *delegatee*) fails to perform. No special form is required to create a valid delegation of duties. As long as the delegator expresses an intention to make the delegation, it is effective; the delegator need not even use the word *delegate.* Exhibit 15–2 illustrates delegation relationships.

Duties That Cannot Be Delegated. As a general rule, any duty can be delegated. There are, however, some exceptions to this rule. Delegation is prohibited in the following circumstances:

1. When special trust has been placed in the obligor.
2. When performance depends on the personal skill or talents of the *obligor* (the person contractually obligated to perform).
3. When performance by a third party will vary materially from that expected by the obligee (the one to whom performance is owed) under the contract.
4. When the contract expressly prohibits delegation.

The following examples will help to clarify the kinds of duties that can and cannot be delegated:

1. Suppose that Brower contracts with Horton to tutor Horton in the various aspects of financial underwriting and investment banking. Brower, an experienced businessperson known for her expertise in finance, wants to delegate her duties to a third party, Kuhn. This delegation is ineffective because Brower has contracted to render a service that is founded on her expertise. The delegation would change Horton's expectations under the contract. Therefore, Kuhn cannot perform Brower's duties.
2. Suppose that Horton, who is impressed with Brower's ability to perform veterinary surgery, contracts with Brower to have Brower perform surgery on Horton's prize-winning stallion in July. Brower later decides that she would rather spend the summer at the beach, so she delegates her duties under the contract to Kuhn, who is also a competent veterinary surgeon. The delegation is not effective, no matter how competent Kuhn is, without Horton's consent. The contract is for *personal* performance.
3. Assume that Brower contracts with Horton to pick up and deliver heavy construction machinery to Horton's property. Brower delegates this duty to Kuhn, who is in the business of delivering heavy machinery. This delegation is effective. The performance required is of a *routine* and *nonpersonal* nature, and the delegation does not change Horton's expectations under the contract.

Effect of a Delegation. If a delegation of duties is enforceable, the obligee (the one to whom performance is owed) must accept performance from the delegatee (the one to whom the duties have been delegated). Consider the third example in the above list, in which Brower delegates to Kuhn the duty to pick up and deliver a heavy construction machine to Horton's property. In that situation, Horton (the obligee) must accept performance from Kuhn (the delegatee), because the delegation was effective. The obligee can legally refuse performance from the delegatee only if the duty is one that cannot be delegated.

As noted, a valid delegation of duties does not relieve the delegator of obligations under the contract.[6] Thus, in the above example, if Kuhn (the delegatee) fails to perform, Brower (the delegator) is still liable to Horton (the obligee). The obligee can also hold the delegatee liable if the delegatee made a

6. *Crane Ice Cream Co. v. Terminal Freezing & Heating Co.*, 147 Md. 588, 128 A. 280 (1925).

EXHIBIT 15–2 DELEGATION RELATIONSHIPS

In the delegation relationship illustrated here, Brower delegates her *duties* under a contract that she made with Horton to a third party, Kuhn. Brower thus becomes the *delegator* and Kuhn the *delegatee* of the contractual duties. Kuhn now owes performance of the contractual duties to Horton. Note that a delegation of duties normally does not relieve the delegator (Brower) of liability if the delegatee (Kuhn) fails to perform the contractual duties.

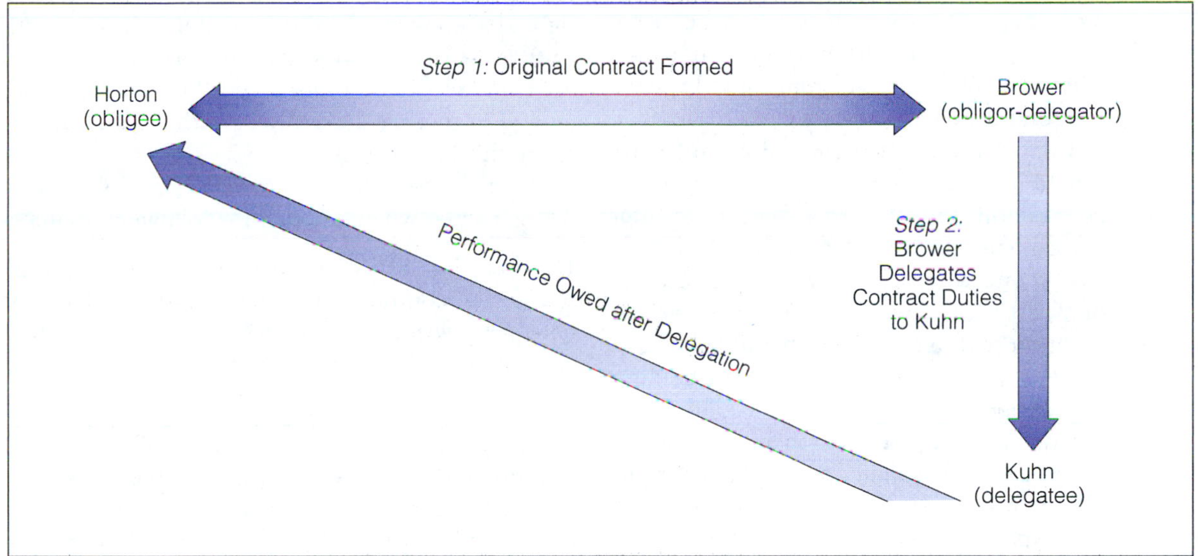

promise of performance that will directly benefit the obligee. In this situation, there is an "assumption of duty" on the part of the delegatee, and breach of this duty makes the delegatee liable to the obligee. For example, if Kuhn (the delegatee) promises Brower (the delegator), in a contract, to pick up and deliver the construction equipment to Horton's property but fails to do so, Horton (the obligee) can sue Brower, Kuhn, or both. Although there are many exceptions, the general rule today is that the obligee can sue both the delegatee and the delegator.

ASSIGNMENT OF "ALL RIGHTS"

When a contract provides for an "assignment of all rights," this wording may create both an assignment of rights and a delegation of duties.[7] Therefore, when general words are used (for example, "I assign the contract" or "I assign all my rights under the contract"), the contract normally is construed as implying both an assignment of the assignor's rights and a delegation of any duties of performance owed by the assignor under the contract being assigned. Thus, the assignor remains liable if the assignee fails to perform the contractual obligations.

SECTION 2

Third Party Beneficiaries

Another exception to the doctrine of privity of contract exists when the original parties to the contract intend at the time of contracting that the contract performance directly benefit a third person. In this situation, the third person becomes a **third party beneficiary** of the contract. As an **intended beneficiary** of the contract, the third party has legal rights and can sue the promisor directly for breach of the contract.

Who, though, is the promisor? In bilateral contracts, both parties to the contract are promisors, because they both make promises that can be enforced. In third party beneficiary contracts, courts will determine the identity of the promisor by asking which party made the promise that benefits the third party—that person is the promisor. Allowing a third party to sue the promisor directly in effect circumvents the "middle person" (the promisee) and thus reduces the burden on the courts.

7. *Restatement (Second) of Contracts*, Section 328; UCC 2–210(1) and (4).

Otherwise, a third party would sue the promisee, who would then sue the promisor.

TYPES OF INTENDED BENEFICIARIES

At one time, third party beneficiaries had no legal rights in contracts. Over time, however, the concept developed that a third party for whose benefit a contract was formed could sue the promisor to have the contract enforced. In a classic case decided in 1859, *Lawrence v. Fox*,[8] the court permitted a third party beneficiary to bring suit directly against a promisor. This case established the rule that a *creditor beneficiary* can sue the promisor directly. A creditor beneficiary is one who benefits from a contract in which one party (the promisor) promises another party (the promisee) to pay a debt that party owes to a third party (the creditor beneficiary). The creditor beneficiary, although not a party to the contract between the debtor and the other person, becomes the intended beneficiary and can thus enforce the promisor's promise to pay the debt.

Another type of intended beneficiary is a *donee beneficiary*. When a contract is made for the express purpose of giving a *gift* to a third party, the third party (the donee beneficiary) can sue the promisor directly to enforce the promise.[9] The most common donee beneficiary contract is a life insurance contract. Consider the following example of a typical life insurance contract: Akins (the promisee) pays premiums to Standard Life, a life insurance company, and Standard Life (the promisor) promises to pay a certain amount of money on Akins's death to anyone Akins designates as a beneficiary. The designated beneficiary is a donee beneficiary under the life insurance policy and can enforce the promise made by the insurance company to pay him or her on Akins's death.

As the law concerning third party beneficiaries evolved, numerous cases arose in which the third party beneficiary did not fit readily into either category—creditor beneficiary or donee beneficiary. Thus, the modern view, and the one adopted by the *Restatement (Second) of Contracts*, does not draw such clear lines and distinguishes only between intended beneficiaries (who can sue to enforce contracts made for their benefit) and incidental beneficiaries (who cannot sue, as will be discussed shortly).

8. 20 N.Y. 268 (1859).

9. *Seaver v. Ransom*, 224 N.Y. 233, 120 N.E. 639 (1918).

THE VESTING OF AN INTENDED BENEFICIARY'S RIGHTS

An intended third party beneficiary cannot enforce a contract against the original parties until the rights of the third party have *vested*, which means the rights have taken effect and cannot be taken away. Until these rights have vested, the original parties to the contract—the promisor and the promisee—can modify or rescind the contract without the consent of the third party.

When do the rights of third parties vest? Generally, the rights vest when either of the following occurs:

1. When the third party demonstrates manifest assent to the contract, such as by sending a letter or note acknowledging awareness of and consent to a contract formed for his or her benefit.
2. When the third party materially alters his or her position in detrimental reliance on the contract.

If the contract expressly reserves to the contracting parties the right to cancel, rescind, or modify the contract, the rights of the third party beneficiary are subject to any changes that result. In such a situation, the vesting of the third party's rights does not terminate the power of the original contracting parties to alter their legal relationships.[10] This is particularly true in most life insurance contracts, in which the right to change the beneficiary is reserved to the policyholder. Exhibit 15–3 summarizes third party rights in contracts generally, including when the rights of an intended beneficiary vest.

INTENDED VERSUS INCIDENTAL BENEFICIARIES

The benefit that an **incidental beneficiary** receives from a contract between two parties is unintentional. Because the benefit is *unintentional*, an incidental beneficiary cannot sue to enforce the contract. In determining whether a third party beneficiary is an intended or an incidental beneficiary, the courts generally use the *reasonable person* test. That is, a beneficiary will be considered an intended beneficiary if a reasonable person in the position of the beneficiary would believe that the promisee *intended* to confer on the beneficiary the right to bring suit to enforce the contract. The court also looks at a number of other factors. The presence of one or more of the

10. Defenses against third party beneficiaries are given in the *Restatement (Second) of Contracts*, Section 309.

EXHIBIT 15–3 THIRD PARTY RIGHTS IN CONTRACTS

	ASSIGNMENT	DELEGATION	THIRD PARTY BENEFICIARY CONTRACT
How are third party rights created?	After contract formation, rights are assigned to a third party.	After contract formation, duties are delegated to a third party.	Purpose of original contract is to benefit a third party. If purpose is: 1. To discharge a duty or debt owed, third party is a *creditor* beneficiary. 2. To confer a gift, third party is a *donee* beneficiary.
Is the assignment, delegation, or third party beneficiary contract effective?	To be effective, an assignment cannot involve: 1. Rights that a statute expressly prohibits from being assigned. 2. Rights to performance by personal service. 3. Rights the assignment of which will materially increase or alter the obligor's duties. 4. Rights that the contract stipulates cannot be assigned, except: a. Rights to receive money. b. Rights in real property (see Chapter 47). c. Rights to negotiable instruments (see Chapter 24). d. Rights to damages for breach of contract or for payment of an account.	To be effective, a delegation cannot involve: 1. Duties that involve special trust placed in the obligor. 2. Duties that depend on the personal skill or talent of the obligor. 3. Duties the delegation of which will materially increase or alter the performance expected by the obligee. 4. Duties that the contract stipulates cannot be delegated.	For a third party beneficiary contract to be effective, rights under the contract must vest by: 1. Third party's manifesting assent to the contract. 2. Third party's materially altering position in detrimental reliance on the contract.

following factors strongly indicates that the third party is an *intended* (rather than an incidental) beneficiary to the contract:

1. Performance is rendered directly to the third party.
2. The third party has the right to control the details of performance.
3. The third party is expressly designated as the beneficiary in the contract.

In contrast, the following are examples of incidental beneficiaries. The third party has no rights in the contract and cannot enforce it against the promisor.

1. Escobedo contracts with Monell to build a cottage on Monell's land. Escobedo's plans specify that All-Weather Insulation Company's insulation materials must be used in constructing the house. All-Weather is an incidental beneficiary and cannot enforce the contract against Escobedo by attempting to require that Escobedo purchase its insulation materials.
2. Bollow contracts with Coolidge to build a recreational facility on Coolidge's land. Once the facility is constructed, it will greatly enhance the property values in the neighborhood. If Bollow subsequently refuses to build the facility, Tran, Coolidge's neighbor, cannot enforce the contract against Bollow because Tran is an incidental beneficiary.

See Case 15.3 at the end of this chapter. To view the full, unedited case from Westlaw,® go to this text's Web site at **http://wbl-cs.westbuslaw.com**.

TERMS AND CONCEPTS TO REVIEW

alienation 295	delegation 293	intended beneficiary 297
assignment 293	incidental beneficiary 298	third party beneficiary 297

CHAPTER SUMMARY

Assignments	1. An assignment is the transfer of rights under a contract to a third party. The person assigning the rights is the *assignor,* and the party to whom the rights are assigned is the *assignee.* The assignee has a right to demand performance from the other original party to the contract. 2. Generally, all rights can be assigned, except in the following circumstances: a. When the assignment is expressly prohibited by statute (for example, workers' compensation benefits). b. When a contract calls for the performance of personal services. c. When the assignment will materially increase or alter the risks or duties of the *obligor* (the party that is obligated to perform). d. When the contract itself stipulates that the rights cannot be assigned (with some exceptions). 3. The assignee should give notice of the assignment to the obligor. a. If the assignor assigns the same right to two different persons, generally the first assignment in time is the first in right, although in some states the first assignee to give notice takes priority. b. Until the obligor is notified of the assignment, the obligor can tender performance to the assignor; and if performance is accepted by the assignor, the obligor's duties under the contract are discharged without benefit to the assignee.
Delegations	1. A delegation is the transfer of duties under a contract to a third party (the *delegatee*), who then assumes the obligation of performing the contractual duties previously held by the one making the delegation (the *delegator*). 2. As a general rule, any duty can be delegated, except in the following circumstances: a. When performance depends on the personal skill or talents of the obligor. b. When special trust has been placed in the obligor. c. When performance by a third party will vary materially from that expected by the obligee (the one to whom the duty is owed) under the contract. d. When the contract expressly prohibits delegation. 3. A valid delegation of duties does not relieve the delegator of obligations under the contract. If the delegatee fails to perform, the delegator is still liable to the obligee. 4. An "assignment of all rights" or an "assignment of contract" is often construed to mean that both the rights and the duties arising under the contract are transferred to a third party.
Third Party Beneficiaries	A third party beneficiary contract is one made for the purpose of benefiting a third party. 1. *Intended beneficiary*—One for whose benefit a contract is created. When the promisor (the one making the contractual promise that benefits a third party) fails to perform as promised, the third party can sue the promisor directly. Examples of third party beneficiaries are creditor and donee beneficiaries. 2. *Incidental beneficiary*—A third party who indirectly (incidentally) benefits from a contract but for whose benefit the contract was not specifically intended. Incidental beneficiaries have no rights to the benefits received and cannot sue to have the contract enforced.

CASES FOR ANALYSIS

Westlaw. You can access the full text of each case presented below by going to the Westlaw cases on this text's Web site at http://wbl-cs.westbuslaw.com. Each Westlaw case includes the names of all plaintiffs and defendants, the dates on which the case was argued and decided, a brief summary of the issues and decisions in the case, headnotes classifying specific issues in the case according to the West Key Number System, and the court's opinion. Concurring and dissenting opinions, if any, are included as well.

CASE 15.1 ASSIGNMENT

REYNOLDS AND REYNOLDS CO. V. HARDEE

United States District Court
Eastern District of Virginia, 1996.
932 F.Supp. 149.

REBECCA BEACH SMITH, District Judge.

* * * *

I. FACTUAL AND PROCEDURAL BACKGROUND

On March 9, 1988, defendant Thomas P. Hardee entered into an employment contract with Jordan Graphics, Inc. ("Jordan") as a sales representative for the territory in a sixty-mile radius of Virginia Beach. Jordan was in the business of manufacturing, buying, selling, trading, and dealing in business forms, such as stationery. Prior to January, 1996, Jordan had a substantial customer base throughout the mid-Atlantic region.

In Paragraph 2, the Employment Agreement between Mr. Hardee and Jordan contained a covenant not to compete:

> Sales Representative agrees that during the period of one (1) year next following the date of the termination for any reason of his employment with [Jordan], he will not * * * engage in or become financially interested in the business of manufacturing, buying, selling, trading and dealing in business forms, including printed matter, stationery, manifolding forms, books of account and pressure sensitive labels in the Territory; and it is hereby provided that if Sales Representative shall violate or attempt to violate any provision of this paragraph, he may be enjoined in an action to be brought in any court of competent jurisdiction and such action shall not be subject to the defense that there exists an adequate remedy at law.

In Paragraph 3 of the Employment Agreement, Mr. Hardee agreed

> that all sales files, customer records, and reports used, prepared or collected by him are the property of [Jordan] and agrees that in the event of the termination of his employment with [Jordan] for any reason, he will return and make available to [Jordan] prior to the last day of his employment all sales files, customer records [and] reports in his possession.

Plaintiff, The Reynolds and Reynolds Company ("Reynolds"), also deals in business forms. On January 23, 1996, Reynolds purchased a substantial portion of Jordan's assets and goodwill, including various contracts and agreements that Jordan had with third parties. Included in the sale was the Employment Agreement between Jordan and Mr. Hardee. However, on the same day as the sale to Reynolds, Jordan terminated Mr. Hardee's employment. Reynolds then offered Mr. Hardee a new contract of employment. The Reynolds contract contained a more restrictive covenant not to compete: it extended the territory covered by the covenant to a radius of 100 miles around Virginia Beach and it lasted for two years with respect to Reynolds' customers. Mr. Hardee rejected the contract, but stated that he would work for Reynolds under the same terms as his Employment Agreement with Jordan. Reynolds did not agree to those terms, but informed Mr. Hardee that it intended to enforce the covenant not to compete in Mr. Hardee's Employment Agreement with Jordan.

On March 29, 1996, Reynolds filed suit in this court against Mr. Hardee for breach of contract * * * . Jurisdiction is based on diversity of citizenship. The complaint alleges that in late January, 1996, Mr. Hardee began to sell and deal in business forms in the Virginia Beach area in violation of his covenant not to compete. As a result of Mr. Hardee's competition, several customers of Reynolds switched to Mr. Hardee. * * *

* * * Reynolds seeks an injunction to prevent Mr. Hardee from engaging in the business of buying, selling, trading, or dealing in business forms within a sixty-mile radius of Virginia Beach * * * . In addition, Reynolds asks for a sum in excess of $50,000 for compensatory damages, plus costs.

Mr. Hardee responded to Reynolds' complaint on April 22, 1996, with a motion to dismiss or, in the alternative, for summary judgment. * * *

Mr. Hardee asserts five grounds for dismissal or summary judgment, [including that] Reynolds is not the assignee of the Employment Agreement between Mr. Hardee and Jordan and, therefore, has no standing to sue under the agreement * * * .

* * * *

II. ANALYSIS

* * * *

The question of plaintiff's standing is whether covenants not to compete contained in employment contracts are assignable. * * *

Under Virginia law, [which applies in this case,] contracts for personal services are not assignable, unless both parties agree to the assignment. Defendant's Employment Agreement with Jordan is clearly a contract for personal services, based on trust and confidence. Defendant's position involved direct sales to clients; he acted as Jordan's agent in its dealings with customers. A person in such a position must necessarily obtain the trust and confidence of his or her employer. Defendant also placed considerable trust in Jordan by even agreeing to the non-compete clause, namely trusting that Jordan would not fire him and then invoke the covenant not to compete. Because the Employment Agreement was based on mutual trust and confidence, it is not assignable under Virginia law. [Emphasis added.]

No Virginia court, however, has expressly addressed whether a covenant not to compete contained *in an employment contract* may be assignable apart from the whole contract, despite the personal nature of the whole agreement and the non-assignability of the agreement as a whole. The court, therefore, looks to other jurisdictions for guidance.

Several courts have held that employment contracts in their entirety, including covenants not to compete, are non-assignable.

* * * [T]he reasoning for this position emphasiz[es] that employment contracts are personal in nature, based on mutual confidence. * * *

* * * The employer confide[s] to the [employee] important customer relationships and business confidences. The employee entrust[s] to his employer the important privilege of discharging him at will and without cause. This eventuality * * * at once invoke[s] the severe detriment of foreclosing him from employment elsewhere in that community in his chosen occupation. The restriction, in its own terms, [is] designed to protect a fiduciary relationship which emanate[s] solely from the master and servant relationship.

Knowing the character and personality of his master, the employee might be ready and willing to safeguard the trust which his employer had reposed in him by granting a restrictive covenant against leaving that employment. His confidence in his employer might be such that he could scarcely anticipate any rupture between them. As to that particular employer, if a break did occur, he might be willing to pledge that his fidelity would continue after the employment had ended, even at the cost of forsaking the vocation for which he was best suited. This does not mean that he was willing to suffer this restraint for the benefit of a stranger to the original undertaking.

* * * *

This court finds [this] reasoning * * * most persuasive. Without question, an employment contract of the sort involved in this case is not assignable under Virginia law. * * * This court, therefore, holds that the covenant not to compete contained in Mr. Hardee's employment contract is not assignable. Accordingly, this court **FINDS** that plaintiff is not an assignee of the contract between defendant and Jordan and, consequently, has no standing to sue on that contract. Defendant's motion to dismiss * * * is **GRANTED.**

CASE 15.2 NOTICE OF ASSIGNMENT

GOLD v. ZIFF COMMUNICATIONS CO.

Appellate Court of Illinois,
First District, 2001.
322 Ill.App.3d 32,
748 N.E.2d 198,
254 Ill.Dec. 752.

Justice *COUSINS* delivered the opinion of the court:

Plaintiffs Anthony Gold (Gold), PC Brand, Inc. (PC Brand), Software Communications, Inc. (SCI), and Hanson & Connors, Inc. (Hanson), sued defendant Ziff Communications Company, doing business as Ziff-Davis Publishing Company (Ziff), [in an Illinois state court] for breach of contract, seeking damages arising from Ziff's alleged breach of an agreement which provided that any company controlled by Gold could advertise in Ziff's publications at reduced rates.* * *

After a five-week trial, the jury found Ziff liable and awarded two verdicts: (1) $44,580,000 to PC Brand, Inc./Gold for future lost profits and business value damages; and (2) $10,800,000 to Hanson & Connors, Inc./SCI/Gold for future lost profits and business value damages. The trial court subsequently awarded prejudgment interest of $26,773,834.58 to PC Brand, Inc./Gold and $6,486,265.27 to Hanson & Connors, Inc./SCI/Gold.

Ziff now appeals * * * .

BACKGROUND

In 1981, Gold founded *PC Magazine* for users of personal computers. In 1982, Ziff, a publisher of specialty magazines, bought the magazine from Gold for more than $10 million. In connection with the purchase, Gold and Ziff signed a letter dated November 19, 1982, providing Gold or a company he "owned and controlled" a right to advertise at an 80% discount on a limited number of pages in *PC Magazine*, as well as free usage of Ziff's subscriber lists (collectively, the ad/list rights). Gold intended to use these ad/list rights as the foundation for computer mail order companies he planned to set up.

In 1983, Gold formed SCI to use the ad/list rights. SCI, wholly owned by Gold, conducted a mail order software business and advertised in *PC Magazine* at the 80% discount. * * *

* * * *

To maximize the use of the ad/list rights, Gold formed two new mail order companies in late 1987 and early 1988—Hanson and PC Brand. Gold formed Hanson to sell software by sending catalogs to names on Ziff's subscriber lists. Hanson took over SCI's business and assumed most of its assets. Gold hired Howard Gosman to operate Hanson as its president.

Gold also contacted Stephen Dukker and they negotiated a structure for a new business which became PC Brand. On January 15, 1988, Gold and Dukker signed a number of interrelated agreements drafted by their attorney, Richard Friedman. One agreement provided that Gold assigned ad/list rights to PC Brand and, in return, PC Brand was to pay Gold or SCI the cash value of the 80% discount used by PC Brand once it became profitable. Also, Gold owned 90% of PC Brand's stock while Dukker owned 10%. * * *

* * * *

* * * Several internal memoranda to Ziff's in-house counsel, Malcolm Morris, indicated that full-rate advertisers learned of Gold's ad/list rights and demanded similar treatment. Plaintiffs allege that complaints by full-rate advertisers motivated Ziff to breach the Ad/List Agreement as to PC Brand and Hanson.

* * * [C]ontract disputes arose between Gold and Ziff in 1988. The first dispute involved Hanson's use of the discounted space in *PC Magazine* to place full-page ads of other advertiser's products. On May 13, 1988, Morris declared a breach of the Ad/List Agreement based on these ads, stating that they constituted a transfer of Gold's discount to the manufacturers whose products appeared in the ads. Plaintiffs allege that the objectionable ads were nearly identical to ads Gold had run for several years through SCI without objection. In July 1988, Gold told Morris that Hanson was voluntarily refraining from placing the large ads for third-party products. At trial, Hanson claimed damages resulting from Ziff's refusal to run the large ads.

* * * *

[Another] dispute centered around the issue of whether Gold "controlled" PC Brand for purposes of utilizing the Ad/List Agreement. Ziff alleges that it first learned of PC Brand through a May 13, 1988, letter in which Gold stated he owned and controlled PC Brand. PC Brand began placing ads at the 80% discount rate in May 1988. After reviewing PC Brand's corporate records, Ziff informed Gold in a letter dated November 8, 1988, that "PC Brand is not eligible for allocation of the rights under the Ad/List Agreement" based on Ziff's conclusion that PC Brand was not controlled by Gold. The letter stated that Gold's 90% record ownership of stock was meaningless and that Dukker, as president, had greater control of the company. The letter also stated that PC Brand must pay full price for ads it had placed at the 80% discount and that if the matter was not resolved in 30 days, Ziff would have to consider other appropriate steps.

* * * Gold, Dukker, Morris and Ziff's senior vice president, Phil Sine, met on December 6, 1988, to discuss PC Brand. At the meeting, Sine stated that the 20% rate Gold's companies paid for advertising was too little and that Ziff wanted to double the price to 40% of the full rates.

* * * *

ANALYSIS

* * * *

II. PROPER PLAINTIFFS

Ziff contends that PC Brand and Hanson were not parties to the Ad/List Agreement and lacked standing to sue for its breach. *Generally, only a party to a contract or those in privy with him may sue to enforce it. In order for a third party to enforce a contract, it must be shown that there was a contractual intent to benefit the third person. A third-party beneficiary may sue to enforce the terms of the contract even though the beneficiary did not exist at the time of the contract's execution.* [Emphasis added.]

In the instant case, the agreement explicitly provided that the ad/list rights could be used by Gold "personally or by a company which [Gold] control[led]." It also stated that Gold could use the rights in a "business which [Gold] set up which is engaged in mail order sales or similar distribution of products." Mail order businesses like PC Brand and Hanson were the direct and intended beneficiaries of the contract. As such, they had standing to sue under the Ad/List Agreement.

Ziff also argues that Gold never properly reassigned his rights under the amended ad/list agreement from SCI to PC Brand and Hanson. We agree with plaintiffs that assignments can be implied from circumstances. *No particular mode or form * * * is necessary to effect a valid assignment, and any acts or words are sufficient which show an intention of transferring or appropriating the owner's interest.* [Emphasis added.]

In the instant case, it is undisputed that Gold owned 100% of SCI. In a letter dated May 13, 1988, Gold, as president of SCI, instructed Ziff that he was allocating the ad/list rights to Hanson and PC Brand. Additionally, SCI stopped using the ad/list rights when PC Brand and Hanson were formed. Dukker and Gosman both testified that Gold told them PC Brand and Hanson could use the ad/list rights. Gold's behavior toward his companies and his conduct toward the obligor, Ziff, implied that the ad/list rights were assigned to PC Brand and Hanson.

* * * *

IV. PC BRAND: DAMAGES

* * * *

* * * [O]n the issue of damages, we believe that a new trial limited to the question of damages is necessary to subtract recovery for lost profits and recompute business value damages for breach, commencing in December 1988.

V. HANSON: * * * DAMAGES

* * * *

* * * [W]e reverse Hanson's lost profit award because such damages were not within the reasonable contemplation of the parties. We also remand for a new trial limited to the issue of business value damages to be recomputed as of the date of breach, commencing in October 1988.

* * * *

For the foregoing reasons, the judgment of the trial court is affirmed in part and reversed in part, and the cause remanded to the trial court for a new trial limited to damages.

Affirmed in part and reversed in part; remanded with directions.

CASE 15.3 THIRD PARTY BENEFICIARIES

VOGAN v. HAYES APPRAISAL ASSOCIATES, INC.

Supreme Court of Iowa, 1999.
588 N.W.2d 420.

CARTER, Justice.

Hayes Appraisal Associates, Inc. (Hayes Appraisal), the defendant in the [state trial] court, had been hired by MidAmerica Savings Bank (MidAmerica) to monitor the progress of new home construction for plaintiffs, Susan J. Vogan and Rollin G. Vogan. The Vogans had obtained a construction loan from MidAmerica. The contractor defaulted after all of the original construction loan proceeds and a subsequent portion of a second mortgage loan had been paid out by the bank.

The Vogans recovered judgment against Hayes Appraisal on a third-party beneficiary theory based on its alleged failure to properly monitor the progress of construction, thus allowing funds to be improperly released by the lender to the defaulting contractor. The [state intermediate] court of appeals reversed the judgment on the basis that erroneous progress reports by Hayes Appraisal were not the cause of any loss to the Vogans. After reviewing the record and considering the arguments of the parties, we vacate the decision of the court of appeals and affirm the judgment of the [trial] court.

In June 1989 the Vogans moved to Des Moines. They wanted to build a home in West Des Moines. They met with builder Gary Markley of Char Enterprises, Inc. Markley agreed to build the home for $169,633.59. The Vogans contacted MidAmerica for a mortgage. MidAmerica orally contracted with Hayes Appraisal to do the initial appraisal and make periodic appraisals of the progress of the construction. The home, according to the plans, and lot were appraised at $250,000.

Thereafter, the Vogans obtained a $170,000 mortgage from MidAmerica. MidAmerica was to disburse progress payments to Markley based on progress reports received from Hayes Appraisal. On November 6, 1989, the Vogans purchased the lot for $66,000 with their own funds. Construction began on November 22, 1989. On December 28, 1989, Hayes Appraisal issued a progress report to MidAmerica that twenty-five percent of the home had been completed.

There were cost overruns on the job, and in February 1990 MidAmerica determined that there was less than $2,000 remaining of the $170,000 loan proceeds. Markley determined that at this point it would take another $70,000 to complete the home. The Vogans then took out a second mortgage on the home for $42,050 and turned that money plus some of their own funds over to the bank to continue making progress payments to Markley based on Hayes Appraisal's progress reports. Prior to completion of the home, the Vogans decided to sell it rather than to occupy it.

On March 20, 1990, Hayes Appraisal certified that the home was sixty percent complete. Only eight days later, Hayes Appraisal issued another progress report indicating that ninety percent of the work had been completed on the home. During the trial, witnesses testified for the Vogans that this was an inaccurate report overstating the extent of the contractor's progress on the job. As late as October 1990, substantial additional work was required on the house. At this point, Markley defaulted on the job after having been paid all of the initial $170,000 and much of the additional monies raised by the Vogans. Another contractor estimated the completion of the home would cost an additional $60,000.

* * * *

The Vogans * * * filed a petition against Hayes Appraisal * * * .

The case proceeded to jury trial on a contract theory. The court denied Hayes Appraisal's motions for directed verdict in which it argued the Vogans were not third-party beneficiaries of its contract with MidAmerica * * * . The jury returned a verdict for the Vogans. Hayes Appraisal's motion for judgment notwithstanding the verdict was denied.

Hayes Appraisal appealed. * * *

The court of appeals reversed. * * * We granted further review.

* * * *

* * * The Vogans argue that they presented ample evidence to generate a jury question concerning whether they were third-party beneficiaries of the contract between MidAmerica and Hayes Appraisal. The Vogans assert that the court should look to the intent of the parties and the surrounding circumstances and argue that the bank's intent was to protect the Vogans' money as construction progressed. The Vogans claim that Hayes Appraisal knew they were owners of the property and that they would benefit from the progress reports.

Hayes Appraisal, however, claims that the verbal contract between MidAmerica and Hayes had no provision or intent to make the Vogans third-party beneficiaries. Hayes Appraisal claims that the Vogans presented no evidence of intent on behalf of the bank to benefit the Vogans and so failed to meet their burden of proof. Hayes Appraisal argues that this failure of proof entitles them to a directed verdict or judgment notwithstanding the verdict on this issue.

* * * This court has adopted the following principles from the *Restatement (Second) of Contracts* that are applicable to third-party beneficiary cases:

> "(1) Unless otherwise agreed between promisor and promisee, a beneficiary of a promise is an intended beneficiary if recognition of a right to performance in the beneficiary is appropriate to effectuate the intention of the parties and either
>
> (a) the performance of the promise will satisfy an obligation of the promisee to pay money to the beneficiary; or
>
> (b) the circumstances indicate that the promisee intends to give the beneficiary the benefit of the promised performance.
>
> (2) An incidental beneficiary is a beneficiary who is not an intended beneficiary."

This court has determined that the primary question in a third-party beneficiary case is whether the contract manifests an intent to benefit a third party. However, this intent need not be to benefit a third party directly.

* * * When a contract is made, the two or more contracting parties have separate purposes; each is stimulated by various motives, [of] some of which he may not be acutely conscious. * * * *A third party who is not a promisee and who gave no consideration has an enforceable right by reason of a contract made by two others* * * * *if the promised performance will be of pecuniary benefit to the third party and the contract is so expressed as to give the promisor reason to know that such benefit is contemplated by the promisee as one of the motivating causes of his making the contract.* In the present case, MidAmerica is the promisee, who stands to benefit from Hayes Appraisal's performance, and Hayes Appraisal is the promisor, who agreed to provide periodic inspections to the bank. [Emphasis added.]

The promised performance of Hayes Appraisal to MidAmerica will be of pecuniary benefit to the Vogans, and the contract is so expressed as to give Hayes reason to know that such benefit is contemplated by MidAmerica as one of the motivating causes of making the contract. The inspection reports and invoices that Hayes Appraisal provided MidAmerica contained not only the location of the project, but also the Vogans' name as the home purchasers. This information gave Hayes Appraisal reason to know that the purpose of MidAmerica obtaining the periodic progress reports from Hayes was to provide the Vogans with some protection for the money they had invested in the project. * * * [In] these circumstances, the Vogans qualify as third-party beneficiaries of the agreement between MidAmerica and Hayes Appraisal.

* * * *

We * * * conclude that the decision of the court of appeals should be vacated. We affirm the judgment of the district court.

DECISION OF COURT OF APPEALS VACATED; DISTRICT COURT JUDGMENT AFFIRMED.

CASE PROBLEMS

15–1. Owens, a federal prisoner, was transferred from federal prison to the Nassau County Jail pursuant to a contract between the U.S. Bureau of Prisons and the county. The contract included a policy statement that required the receiving prison to provide for the safekeeping and protection of transferred federal prisoners. While in the Nassau County Jail, Owens was beaten severely by prison officials and suffered lacerations, bruises, and a lasting impairment that caused blackouts. Can Owens, as a third party beneficiary, sue the county for breach of its agreement with the U.S. Bureau of Prisons? Discuss fully. [*Owens v. Haas*, 601 F.2d 1242 (2d Cir. 1979)]

15–2. Rogers agreed with Newton to do the plumbing work as a subcontractor on a construction project. Their contract stipulated that Rogers was to receive $22,100 in three installments. Rogers secured a loan from the Merchants & Farmers Bank of Dumas for $15,500 to pay for the necessary expenses he would incur when he began work and before he had received his first installment from Newton. In return for the borrowed money, Rogers assigned to the bank his rights in the contract he had formed with Newton. On February 11, the bank sent Newton notice of the assignment and asked Newton to make his payment checks payable to Rogers and the bank *jointly*. Newton agreed in a letter to the bank to do this. On March 12, however, Newton wrote a check for $7,085 payable to Rogers only. Rogers completed the work for Newton and had paid all his expenses except for an amount owed to one of his suppliers, Southern Pipe and Supply Co. Rogers eventually defaulted on his payments to the bank, and the bank sued Newton for the balance on the note. Newton could not avoid his obligation to the assignee of the note (the bank), but he claimed that he should not be responsible for the bill from Southern Pipe and Supply. He claimed that Rogers's assignment of his contract with Newton to the bank obligated the bank to assume Rogers's duties under the contract (including payments to all suppliers) and that the bank should therefore pay the debt owed to Southern Pipe and Supply. Did Rogers's assignment of his rights in the contract with Newton include a delegation of his duties under the contract as well? Discuss. [*Newton v. Merchants & Farmers Bank of Dumas*, 11 Ark.App. 167, 668 S.W.2d 51 (1984)]

15–3. On August 8, 1978, Shirley Petry entered into a contract with Cosmopolitan Spa International, Inc. The contract was for a spa membership that was to include "processing, program counseling, and facilities usage." The written contract contained an exculpatory clause. The pertinent part of the clause stated, "Member fully understands and agrees that in participating in one or more of the courses, or using the facilities maintained by Cosmopolitan, there is the possibility of accidental or other physical injury. Member further agrees to assume the risk of such injury and further agrees to indemnify Cosmopolitan from any and all liability to Cosmopolitan by either the Member or third party as the result of the use by the Member of the facilities and instructions as offered by Cosmopolitan." On or around January 1, 1980, Cosmopolitan sold the spa to Holiday Spa of Tennessee, Inc. On February 25, 1980, Petry injured her back when she sat on an exercise machine and it collapsed under her. She brought suit against both Cosmopolitan and Holiday for damages for personal injuries resulting from the defendants' negligence in properly maintaining the exercise machine. The defendants claimed that the exculpatory clause negated their liability. Petry argued that Holiday could not use the exculpatory clause as a defense because it was part of a contract for personal services, and therefore the contract was not assignable. What will the court decide? Discuss fully. [*Petry v. Cosmopolitan Spa International, Inc.*, 641 S.W.2d 202 (Tenn.App. 1982)]

15–4. Abby's Cakes on Dixie, Inc., agreed in a lease contract to lease space in a shopping center from Colonial Palms Plaza, Inc. The contract included a provision in which Colonial agreed to pay Abby's a construction allowance of up to $11,250 after Abby's had satisfactorily completed certain improvements to the rented premises. The contract also contained a clause stating that Abby's agreed "not to assign, mortgage, pledge, or encumber this Lease" without first obtaining the written consent of Colonial and that any such "assignment, encumbrance or subletting without such consent shall be void." Prior to the improvements' completion, Abby's assigned its right to receive the initial $8,000 of the construction allowance to Robert Aldana (without first obtaining Colonial's consent). In return, Aldana loaned Abby's $8,000 to finance the construction. Aldana notified Colonial of the assignment by certified mail. After Abby's had completed the improvements to the rented premises, Colonial ignored the assignment and paid Abby's the construction allowance. In Aldana's suit against Colonial for the $8,000 due him pursuant to the assignment, Colonial claimed that the assignment was prohibited by the contract provision and therefore void. Who will win, and why? [*Aldana v. Colonial Palms Plaza, Ltd.*, 591 So.2d 953 (Fla.App. 1992)]

15–5. In October 1985, Beatriz Pino signed a five-year employment contract as a radio announcer and disc jockey with two radio stations. The contract provided that Pino would not "engage directly or indirectly in the broadcasting business * * * in Dade or Broward Counties, Florida, for a period of twelve (12) months after the termination of her employment by the stations." The contract also provided that it was assignable. In December 1986, the stations sold their assets to Spanish Broadcasting System of Florida, Inc. (SBS), and as part of the sale, Pino's contract was assigned to SBS. In October 1989, Pino contracted with Viva, a broadcasting competitor of SBS, to begin working for Viva when her SBS contract terminated in March 1990. SBS asked a Florida state court to grant a temporary injunction to enforce the agreement not to compete. Pino contended that the assignment of the clause containing the covenant not to complete was invalid. Although a Florida statute provided that covenants not to compete could be enforced, it said nothing about such covenants being assignable. Was the covenant not to compete assignable? Discuss. [*Pino v. Spanish Broadcasting System of Florida, Inc.*, 564 So.2d 186 (Fla.App. 3 Dist. 1990)]

15–6. Zoya International, Inc., operated a store on property owned by Peerless Weighing and Vending

Corporation. The lease required Zoya to carry insurance to "protect and indemnify" Peerless and Zoya against all claims arising out of the use of the property. Zoya never obtained the insurance. Linda Caswell, a Zoya customer, fell through a trap door inside the entrance to the store. When she learned that there was no insurance, she filed a suit in an Illinois state court against Zoya and Peerless. Peerless filed a motion to dismiss the claim against it. Caswell argued that she was an intended third party beneficiary of the insurance provision of the lease and thus could sue Peerless for failing to enforce it. The court dismissed the claim against Peerless, and Caswell appealed. What will happen on appeal? Discuss. [*Caswell v. Zoya International, Inc.*, 274 Ill.App.3d 1072, 654 N.E.2d 552, 211 Ill.Dec. 90 (1995)]

15–7. Mary Pratt contracted to buy Harold and Gladys Rosenberg's Dairy Queen franchise on February 8, 1980. The price was $62,000, with payments to be made over a fifteen-year period. In 1982, Pratt assigned her rights in the contract to Son, Inc. The Rosenbergs signed a "Consent to Assignment" clause at that time. Pratt then moved to Arizona and had nothing more to do with the business. In 1984, Son assigned the contract to the Merit Corporation. The assignment did not contain a consent clause for the Rosenbergs to sign, but they were aware of the transaction and accepted Merit's continued payments on the balance. Merit took out a bank loan, using the equipment and inventory as collateral for the loan. After June 1988, Merit ceased making payments to the Rosenbergs. Merit filed for bankruptcy, and the bank foreclosed on the loan. The Rosenbergs sued Son and Pratt in a North Dakota state court for the balance due ($17,326.24) under the original contract for the sale of the Dairy Queen. The trial court dismissed the Rosenbergs' claims, finding that Pratt was a guarantor and that the second assignment to Merit, Merit's pledging of the business assets as collateral for a loan, and other actions accomplished without Pratt's knowledge were sufficient alterations to the original contract to exonerate her. The Rosenbergs appealed. What will happen on appeal? Discuss. [*Rosenberg v. Son, Inc.*, 491 N.W.2d 71 (N.Dak. 1992)]

15–8. When Charles and Judy Orr were divorced in 1970, their divorce agreement included a provision that Charles would pay for the college or professional school education of the couple's two children, then minors. In 1990, when Charles's daughter Jennifer was attending college, Charles refused to pay her college tuition. Can Jennifer, who was not a party to her parents' divorce agreement, bring a court action to compel her father to pay her college expenses? Discuss fully. [*Orr v. Orr*, 228 Ill.App.3d 234, 592 N.E.2d 553, 170 Ill.Dec. 117 (1992)]

15–9. Rensselaer Water Co. was under contract to the city of Rensselaer, New York, to provide water to the city, including water at fire hydrants. A warehouse owned by H. R. Moch Co. was totally destroyed by a fire that could not be extinguished because of inadequate water pressure at the fire hydrants. Moch brought suit against Rensselaer Water Co. for damages, claiming that Moch was a third party beneficiary to the city's contract with the water company. Will Moch be able to recover damages from the water company on the ground that the water company breached its contract with the city? Explain. [*H. R. Moch Co. v. Rensselaer Water Co.*, 247 N.Y. 160, 159 N.E. 896 (1928)]

15–10. Don and Beulah DeVoss hired attorney James McGrath to handle the transfer of title to a farm they wished to give to Bobby and Barbara Holsapple. The transfer failed because McGrath did not have the new deed notarized. The DeVosses died before a corrected deed could be signed. The Holsapples filed a suit in an Iowa state court against McGrath, alleging negligence. McGrath filed a motion to dismiss for failure to state a claim, which the court granted on the ground that the Holsapples were not parties to the lawyer-client relationship between McGrath and the DeVosses and thus McGrath owed them no duty. The Holsapples appealed to the Supreme Court of Iowa. Can the Holsapples recover by establishing that they were intended beneficiaries of the DeVosses' transfer of their property and that the transfer failed only because of McGrath's negligence? Explain. [*Holsapple v. McGrath*, 521 N.W.2d 711 (Iowa 1994)]

15–11. Bath Iron Works (BIW) offered a job to Thomas Devine, contingent on Devine's passing a drug test. The testing was conducted by NorDx, a subcontractor of Roche Biomedical Laboratories. When NorDx found that Devine's urinalysis showed the presence of opiates, a result confirmed by Roche, BIW refused to offer Devine permanent employment. Devine claimed that the ingestion of poppy seeds can lead to a positive result and that he tested positive for opiates only because of his daily consumption of poppy seed muffins. In Devine's suit against Roche, Devine argued, among other things, that he was a third party beneficiary of the contract between his employer (BIW) and NorDx (Roche). Is Devine an intended third party beneficiary of the BIW–NorDx contract? In deciding this issue, should the court focus on the nature of the promises made in the contract itself or on the consequences of the contract for Devine, a third party? [*Devine v. Roche Biomedical Laboratories*, 659 A.2d 868 (Me. 1995)]

15–12. Clement was seriously injured in a car accident with King. Clement sued King. King retained Prestwich as her attorney. Because of the alleged negligence of Prestwich, Clement was able to obtain a $21,000 judgment on her claim against King. Clement received from King a purported written assignment of King's malpractice claim against Prestwich as settlement for the judgment against her. Can King assign her cause of action against Prestwich to Clement? Explain. [*Clement v. Prestwich*, 114 Ill.App.3d 479, 448 N.E.2d 1039, 70 Ill.Dec. 161 (1983)]

15–13. Fox Brothers Enterprises, Inc., agreed to convey to Canfield a lot, Lot 23, in a subdivision known as

Fox Estates, together with a one-year option to purchase Lot 24. The agreement did not contain any prohibitions, restrictions, or limitations against assignments. Canfield paid the price of $20,000 and took title to Lot 23. Thereafter, Canfield assigned his option right in Lot 24 to the Scotts. When the Scotts tried to exercise their right to the option, Fox Brothers refused to convey the property to them. The Scotts then brought a suit for specific performance. What was the result? Discuss fully. [*Scott v. Fox Brothers Enterprises, Inc.*, 667 P.2d 773 (Colo.App. 1983)]

15–14. Joseph LeMieux, of Maine, won $373,000 in a lottery operated by the Tri-State Lotto Commission. The lottery is sponsored by the three northern New England states and is administered in Vermont. In accordance with its usual payment plan, Tri-State was to pay the $373,000 to LeMieux in annual installments over a twenty-year period. LeMieux assigned his rights to the lottery installment payments for the years 1996 through 2006 to Singer Freidlander Corp. for the sum of $80,000. LeMieux and Singer Freidlander (the plaintiffs) sought a court judgment authorizing the assignment agreement between them despite Tri-State's regulation barring the assignment of lottery proceeds. The trial court granted Tri-State's motion for summary judgment. On appeal, the plaintiffs argued that Tri-State's regulation was invalid. Is it? Discuss fully. [*LeMieux v. Tri-State Lotto Commission,* 666 A.2d 1170 (Vt. 1995)]

15–15. John Castle and Leonard Harlan, who headed Castle Harlan, Inc., an investment firm, entered into an agreement with the federal government to buy Western Empire Federal Savings and Loan. Under the agreement, Castle Harlan was to invest a nominal amount in the bank and arrange for others to invest much more, in exchange for, among other things, a promise that for two years Western Empire would not be subject to certain restrictions in federal regulations. The government's enforcement of other regulations against Western Empire led to its going out of business. Castle, Harlan, and the other investors filed a suit in the U.S. Court of Federal Claims against the government, alleging breach of contract. The government filed a motion to dismiss all of the plaintiffs except Castle and Harlan, on the ground that the others did not sign the contract between the government and Castle and Harlan. Is the government correct? Should the court dismiss the claims brought by the other investors? Why, or why not? [*Castle v. United States,* 42 Fed.Cl. 859 (1999)]

E-LINKS

For updated links to resources available on the Web, as well as a variety of other materials, visit this text's Web site at

http://wbl-cs.westbuslaw.com

You can find a summary of the law governing assignments, as well as "SmartAgreement" forms that you can use for various types of contracts, at

http://www.smartagreements.com/gen1/lp75.htm

LEGAL RESEARCH EXERCISES ON THE WEB

Go to http://wbl-cs.westbuslaw.com, the Web site that accompanies this text. Select "Interactive Study Center," and then click on "Chapter 15." There you will find the following Internet research exercise that you can perform to learn more about third party rights in contracts:

Activity 15–1: Third Party Beneficiaries

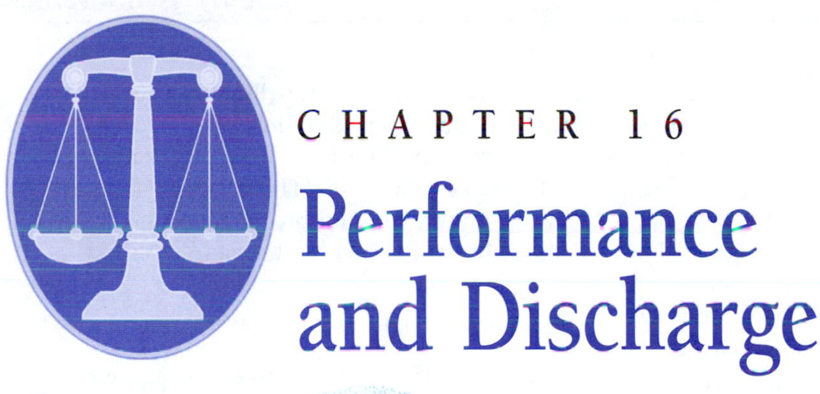

CHAPTER 16

Performance and Discharge

JUST AS RULES ARE NECESSARY to determine when a legally enforceable contract exists, so also are they required to determine when one of the parties can justifiably say, "I have fully performed, so I am now discharged from my obligations under this contract." The legal environment of business requires the identification of some point at which the parties can reasonably know that their duties are at an end.

The most common way to **discharge**, or terminate, one's contractual duties is by the **performance** of those duties. For example, a buyer and seller have a contract for the sale of a 2000 Buick for $28,000. This contract will be discharged on the performance by the parties of their obligations under the contract—the buyer's payment of $28,000 to the seller and the seller's transfer of possession of the Buick to the buyer.

The duty to perform under a contract may be *conditioned* on the occurrence or nonoccurrence of a certain event, or the duty may be *absolute*. In the first part of this chapter, we look at conditions of performance and the degree of performance required. We then examine some other ways in which a contract can be discharged, including discharge by agreement of the parties and discharge by operation of law.

SECTION 1

Conditions

In most contracts, promises of performance are not expressly conditioned or qualified. Instead, they are *absolute promises*. They must be performed, or the parties promising the acts will be in breach of contract. For example, Jerome contracts to sell Alfonso a painting for $3,000. The parties' promises—Jerome's transfer of the painting to Alfonso and Alfonso's payment of $3,000 to Jerome—are unconditional. The payment does not have to be made if the painting is not transferred.

In some situations, however, performance is contingent on the occurrence or nonoccurrence of a certain event. A **condition** is a possible future event, the occurrence or nonoccurrence of which will trigger the performance of a legal obligation or terminate an existing obligation under a contract.[1] If this condition is not satisfied, the obligations of the parties are discharged. Suppose that Alfonso, in the previous example, offers to purchase Jerome's painting only if an independent appraisal indicates that it is worth at least $3,000. Jerome accepts Alfonso's offer. Their obligations (promises) are conditioned on the outcome of the appraisal. Should the condition not be satisfied (for example, if the appraiser deems the value of the painting to be only $1,500), the parties' obligations to each other are discharged and cannot be enforced.

Three types of conditions can be present in contracts: conditions *precedent*, conditions *subsequent*, and *concurrent* conditions. Conditions are also classified as *express* or *implied*.

CONDITIONS PRECEDENT

A condition that must be fulfilled before a party's performance can be required is called a **condition precedent.** The condition precedes the absolute duty

1. The *Restatement (Second) of Contracts*, Section 224, defines a condition as "an event, not certain to occur, which must occur, unless its nonoccurrence is excused, before performance under a contract becomes due."

to perform, as in the Jerome-Alfonso example just discussed. Real estate contracts frequently are conditioned on the buyer's ability to obtain financing. For example, Fisher promises to buy Calvin's house if Salvation Bank approves Fisher's mortgage application. The Fisher-Calvin contract is therefore subject to a condition precedent—the bank's approval of Fisher's mortgage application. If the bank does not approve the application, the contract will fail because the condition precedent was not met. Insurance contracts frequently specify that certain conditions must be met before the insurance company will be obligated to perform under the contract.

Conditions Subsequent

When a condition operates to terminate a party's absolute promise to perform, it is called a **condition subsequent.** The condition follows, or is subsequent to, the arising of an absolute duty to perform. If the condition occurs, the party need not perform any further. For example, imagine that a law firm hires Koker, a recent law school graduate and newly licensed attorney. Their contract provides that the firm's obligation to continue employing Koker is discharged if Koker fails to maintain her license to practice law. This is a condition subsequent, because a failure to maintain the license would discharge a duty that has already arisen.

Generally, conditions precedent are common; conditions subsequent are rare. The *Restatement (Second) of Contracts* does not use the terms *condition subsequent* and *condition precedent* but refers to both simply as conditions.[2]

Concurrent Conditions

When each party's absolute duty to perform is conditioned on the other party's absolute duty to perform, there are **concurrent conditions.** Concurrent conditions occur only when the parties expressly or impliedly are to perform their respective duties *simultaneously.* For example, if a buyer promises to pay for goods when they are delivered by the seller, each party's absolute duty to perform is conditioned on the other party's absolute duty to perform. The buyer's duty to pay for the goods does not become absolute until the seller either delivers or tenders the goods. (**Tender** is an unconditional offer to perform by one who is ready, willing, and able to do so.) Likewise, the seller's duty to deliver the goods does not become absolute until the buyer tenders or actually makes payment. Therefore, neither can recover from the other for breach unless he or she first tenders his or her own performance.

Express and Implied Conditions

Conditions can also be classified as express or implied in fact. *Express conditions* are provided for by the parties' agreement. An express condition is usually prefaced by the word *if, provided, after,* or *when.*

Conditions *implied in fact* are similar to express conditions because they are understood to be part of the agreement, but they are not found in the express language of the agreement. The court infers them from the promises. For example, Wellbuilt Construction Company builds a house for Kirby, including in the contract a one-year warranty against defects in materials and construction—that is, Wellbuilt promises to fix or replace anything attributable to its work that goes wrong within a year. That Kirby must notify Wellbuilt of any defects is an implied-in-fact condition of Wellbuilt's duty to correct the defects.

SECTION 2

Discharge by Performance

The great majority of contracts are discharged by performance. The contract comes to an end when both parties fulfill their respective duties by performing the acts they have promised. Performance can also be accomplished by *tender.* Therefore, a seller who places goods at the disposal of a buyer has tendered delivery and can demand payment. A buyer who offers to pay for goods has tendered payment and can demand delivery of the goods. Once performance has been tendered, the party making the tender has done everything possible to carry out the terms of the contract. If the other party then refuses to perform, the party making the tender can sue for breach of contract.

Types of Performance

There are two basic types of performance—*complete performance* and *substantial performance.* A contract may stipulate that performance must meet the personal satisfaction of either the contracting party or a

2. *Restatement (Second) of Contracts,* Section 224.

third party. Such a provision must be considered in determining whether the performance rendered satisfies the contract.

Complete Performance. When a party performs exactly as agreed, there is no question as to whether the contract has been performed. When a party's performance is perfect, it is said to be complete.

Conditions expressly stated in a contract must be fully satisfied for complete performance to take place. For example, most construction contracts require the builder to meet certain specifications. If the specifications are conditions, complete performance is required to avoid material breach. (Material breach will be discussed shortly.) If the conditions are met, the other party to the contract must then fulfill his or her obligation to pay the builder. If the specifications are not conditions and if the builder, without the other party's permission, fails to comply with the standards, performance is not complete. What effect does such a failure have on the other party's obligation to pay? The answer is part of the doctrine of substantial performance.

Substantial Performance. A party who in good faith performs substantially all of the terms of a contract can enforce the contract against the other party under the doctrine of substantial performance. Note that good faith is required, which means that the failure to fully perform must not be willful. Willfully failing to comply with the terms is a breach of the contract. Generally, performance that provides a party with the important and essential benefits of a contract, in spite of any omission or deviation from the terms, is substantial performance.

Determining whether performance has provided the "important and essential benefits" of a contract requires taking into consideration all of the facts. For example, in a construction contract, these facts would include the intended purpose of the structure and the expense required to bring the structure into compliance with the contract. Thus, the exact point at which performance is considered substantial varies from case to case.

Because substantial performance is not perfect, the other party is entitled to damages to compensate for the failure to comply with the contract. The measure of the damages is the cost to bring the object of the contract into compliance with its terms, if that cost is reasonable under the circumstances. If the cost is unreasonable, the measure of damages is the difference in value between the performance that was rendered and the performance that would have been rendered if the contract had been performed completely.

Westlaw. See Case 16.1 at the end of this chapter. To view the full, unedited case from Westlaw,® go to this text's Web site at **http://wbl-cs.westbuslaw.com**.

Performance to the Satisfaction of One of the Parties. Contracts often state that completed work must personally satisfy one of the parties. The question then arises whether this satisfaction becomes a condition precedent, requiring actual personal satisfaction or approval for discharge, or whether the test of satisfaction is an absolute promise requiring such performance as would satisfy a "reasonable person" (substantial performance).

When the subject matter of the contract is personal, a contract to be performed to the satisfaction of one of the parties is conditioned, and performance must actually satisfy that party. For example, contracts for portraits, works of art, medical or dental work, and tailoring are considered personal. Therefore, only the personal satisfaction of the party will be sufficient to fulfill the condition. To illustrate: Suppose that Williams agrees to paint a portrait of Hirshon's daughter for $750. The contract provides that Hirshon must be satisfied with the portrait. If Hirshon is not, she will not be required to pay for it. The only requirement imposed on Hirshon is that she act honestly and in good faith. If Hirshon expresses dissatisfaction only to avoid paying for the portrait, the condition of satisfaction is excused, and her duty to pay becomes absolute. (Of course, the jury, or the judge acting as a jury, will have to decide whether she is acting honestly.)[3]

Contracts that involve mechanical fitness, utility, or marketability need only be performed to the satisfaction of a reasonable person. For example, construction contracts and manufacturing contracts are usually *not* considered to be personal, so the party's personal satisfaction is normally irrelevant. As long as the performance will satisfy a reasonable person, the contract is fulfilled.[4]

3. For a classic case illustrating this principle, see *Gibson v. Cranage*, 39 Mich. 49 (1878).

4. If, however, the contract specifically states that it is to be fulfilled to the "personal" satisfaction of one or more of the parties, and the parties so intended, the outcome will probably be different.

Performance to the Satisfaction of a Third Party. At times, contracts may require performance to the satisfaction of a third party (not a party to the contract). To illustrate: Assume that you contract to pave several city streets. The contract provides that the work will be done "to the satisfaction of Phil Hopper, the supervising engineer." In this situation, the courts are divided. A few courts require the personal satisfaction of the third party—in this example, Phil Hopper. If Hopper is not satisfied, you will not be paid, even if a reasonable person would be satisfied. Again, the personal judgment must be made honestly, or the condition will be excused. A majority of courts require the work to be satisfactory to a reasonable person. Thus, even if Hopper was dissatisfied with the paving work, you would be paid, as long as a qualified supervising engineer would have been satisfied. All of the above examples demonstrate the necessity for *clear, specific wording* in contracts.

MATERIAL BREACH OF CONTRACT

A **breach of contract** is the nonperformance of a contractual duty. The breach is *material* when performance is not at least substantial—in other words, when there has been a failure of consideration.[5] In such cases, the nonbreaching party is excused from the performance of contractual duties and has a cause of action to sue for damages caused by the breach.

If the breach is *minor* (not material), the nonbreaching party's duty to perform can sometimes be suspended until the breach has been remedied, but the duty to perform is not entirely excused. Once the minor breach has been cured, the nonbreaching party must resume performance of the contractual obligations undertaken. Any breach entitles the nonbreaching party to sue for damages, but only a material breach discharges the nonbreaching party from the contract. The policy underlying these rules allows contracts to go forward when only minor problems occur but allows them to be terminated if major difficulties arise.

Westlaw. See Case 16.2 at the end of this chapter. To view the full, unedited case from Westlaw,® go to this text's Web site at **http://wbl-cs.westbuslaw.com**.

5. *Restatement (Second) of Contracts,* Section 241.

ANTICIPATORY REPUDIATION

Before either party to a contract has a duty to perform, one of the parties may refuse to carry out his or her contractual obligations. This is called **anticipatory repudiation**[6] of the contract and can discharge the nonbreaching party from performance. Until the nonbreaching party treats an early repudiation as a breach, however, the repudiating party can retract his or her anticipatory repudiation by proper notice and restore the parties to their original obligations.[7] There are two reasons for allowing the nonbreaching party to treat an anticipatory repudiation as a present, material breach:

1. The nonbreaching party should not be required to remain ready and willing to perform when the other party has already repudiated the contract.
2. The nonbreaching party should have the opportunity to seek a similar contract elsewhere.[8]

Quite often, anticipatory repudiation occurs when performance of the contract would be extremely unfavorable to one of the parties because of a sharp fluctuation in market prices. For example, Martin Corporation contracts to manufacture and sell ten thousand personal computers to ComAge, a retailer of computer equipment that has five hundred outlet stores. Delivery is to be made six months from the date of the contract. The contract price is based on the seller's present costs of purchasing inventory parts from others. One month later, three inventory suppliers raise their prices to Martin.

Based on these prices, if Martin Corporation manufactures and sells the personal computers to ComAge at the contract price, Martin stands to lose $500,000. Martin immediately writes ComAge that it cannot deliver the ten thousand computers at the contract price. Martin's letter is an anticipatory repudiation of the contract. ComAge has the option of treating the repudiation as a material breach of contract and proceeding immediately to pursue remedies, even though the actual contract delivery date is still five months away.[9]

6. *Restatement (Second) of Contracts,* Section 253; UCC 2–610.
7. See UCC 2–611.
8. The doctrine of anticipatory repudiation first arose in the landmark case of *Hochster v. De La Tour,* 2 Ellis and Blackburn Reports 678 (1853), when the English court recognized the delay and expense inherent in a rule requiring a nonbreaching party to wait until the time of performance before suing on an anticipatory repudiation.
9. See *Reliance Cooperage Corp. v. Treat,* 195 F.2d 977 (8th Cir. 1952), as a further illustration.

Time for Performance

If no time for performance is stated in the contract, a *reasonable time* is implied.[10] If a specific time is stated, the parties must usually perform by that time. Unless time is expressly stated to be vital, however, a delay in performance will not destroy the performing party's right to payment. When time is expressly stated to be vital, or when it is construed to be "of the essence," the parties normally must perform within the stated time period. The time element becomes a condition.

SECTION 3

Discharge by Agreement

Any contract can be discharged by agreement of the parties. The agreement can be contained in the original contract, or the parties can form a new contract for the express purpose of discharging the original contract.

Discharge by Rescission

Rescission is the process by which a contract is canceled or terminated and the parties are returned to the positions they occupied prior to forming it. For **mutual rescission** to take place, the parties must make another agreement, which must also satisfy the legal requirements for a contract. There must be an *offer,* an *acceptance,* and *consideration.*

Ordinarily, in an executory contract in which neither party has yet performed, if the parties agree to rescind the original contract, their promises not to perform the acts stipulated in the original contract will be legal consideration for the second contract. The rescission agreement is generally enforceable even if made orally. An exception applies under the Uniform Commercial Code (UCC) to agreements rescinding a contract for the sale of goods regardless of price when the contract requires written rescission.[11]

When one party has fully performed, an agreement to call off the original contract normally will not be enforceable. Because the performing party has received no consideration for the promise to call off the original bargain, additional consideration will be necessary.

In sum, contracts that are *executory on both sides* (contracts on which neither party has performed) can be rescinded solely by agreement.[12] But contracts that are *executed on one side* (contracts on which one party has performed) can be rescinded only if the party who has performed receives consideration for the promise to call off the deal.

Discharge by Novation

A contractual obligation may also be discharged through novation. A **novation** occurs when both of the parties to a contract agree to substitute a third party for one of the original parties. The requirements of a novation are as follows:

1. A previous valid obligation.
2. An agreement of all the parties to a new contract.
3. The extinguishment of the old obligation (discharge of the prior party).
4. A new contract that is valid.

For example, suppose that Union Corporation contracts to sell its pharmaceutical division to British Pharmaceuticals, Ltd. Before the transfer is completed, Union, British Pharmaceuticals, and a third company, Otis Chemicals, execute a new agreement to transfer all of British Pharmaceutical's rights and duties in the transaction to Otis Chemicals. As long as the new contract is supported by consideration, the novation will discharge the original contract (between Union and British Pharmaceuticals) and replace it with the new contract (between Union and Otis Chemicals).

A novation expressly or impliedly revokes and discharges a prior contract.[13] The parties involved may expressly state in the new contract that the old contract is now discharged. If the parties do not expressly discharge the old contract, it will be impliedly discharged because of the change or because of the new contract's different terms, which are inconsistent with the old contract's terms.

10. See UCC 2–204.

11. UCC 2–209(2) and (4).

12. Certain sales made to a consumer at home can be rescinded by the consumer within three days for no reason at all. This three-day "cooling-off" period is designed to aid consumers who are susceptible to high-pressure door-to-door sales tactics. See Chapter 44 and 15 U.S.C. Section 1635(a).

13. It is this immediate discharge of the prior contract that distinguishes a novation from both an accord and satisfaction, discussed in the next subsection, and an assignment of all rights, discussed in Chapter 15. In an assignment of all rights, the original party to the contract (the assignor) remains liable under the original contract if the assignee fails to perform the contractual obligations. In contrast, in a novation, the original party's obligations are completely discharged.

DISCHARGE BY SUBSTITUTED AGREEMENT

A *compromise,* or settlement agreement, that arises out of a genuine dispute over the obligations under an existing contract will be recognized at law. Such an agreement will be substituted as a new contract, and it will either expressly or impliedly revoke and discharge the obligations under any prior contract. In contrast to a novation, a substituted agreement does not involve a third party. Rather, the two original parties to the contract form a different agreement to substitute for the original one.

DISCHARGE BY ACCORD AND SATISFACTION

For a contract to be discharged by accord and satisfaction, the parties must agree to accept performance that is different from the performance originally promised. As discussed in Chapter 11, an *accord* is defined as an executory contract to perform some act to satisfy an existing contractual duty.[14] The duty has not yet been discharged. A *satisfaction* is the performance of the accord agreement. An accord and its satisfaction discharge the original contractual obligation.

Once the accord has been made, the original obligation is merely suspended. The obligor (the one owing the obligation) can discharge the obligation by performing the obligation agreed to in the accord or the original obligation. If the obligor refuses to perform the accord, the obligee (the one to whom performance is owed) can bring action on the original obligation or seek a decree compelling specific performance on the accord.

SECTION 4

Discharge by Operation of Law

Under certain circumstances, contractual duties may be discharged by operation of law. These circumstances include material alteration of the contract, the running of the statute of limitations, bankruptcy, and the impossibility or impracticability of performance.

ALTERATION OF THE CONTRACT

To discourage parties from altering written contracts, the law operates to allow an innocent party to be discharged when the other party has materially altered a written contract without consent. For example, contract terms such as quantity or price might be changed without the knowledge or consent of all parties. If so, the party who was unaware of the alteration can treat the contract as discharged or terminated.[15]

STATUTES OF LIMITATIONS

As mentioned earlier in this text, statutes of limitations restrict the period during which a party can sue on a particular cause of action. After the applicable limitations period has passed, a suit can no longer be brought. For example, the limitations period for bringing suits for breach of oral contracts is usually two to three years; for written contracts, four to five years; and for recovery of amounts awarded in judgments, ten to twenty years, depending on state law.

Section 2–725 of the UCC deals with the statute of limitations applicable to contracts for the sale of goods. For purposes of applying this section, the UCC does not distinguish between oral and written contracts. Section 2–725 provides that an action for the breach of any contract for sale must be commenced within four years after the cause of that action has accrued. The cause of action accrues when the breach occurs, regardless of the aggrieved party's lack of knowledge of the breach. By original agreement, the parties can reduce this four-year period to one year. They cannot, however, extend it beyond the four-year limitation period.

Technically, the running of a statute of limitations bars access only to *judicial* remedies; it does not extinguish the debt or the underlying obligation. The statute precludes access to the courts for collection. If, however, the party who owes the debt or obligation agrees to perform (that is, makes a new promise to perform), the cause of action barred by the statute of limitations will be revived. For the old agreement to be restored by a new promise in this manner, many states require that the promise be in writing or that there be evidence of partial performance.

14. *Restatement (Second) of Contracts,* Section 281.

15. The contract is voidable, and the innocent party can also treat the contract as in effect, either on the original terms or on the terms as altered. A buyer who discovers that a seller altered the quantity of goods in a sales contract from 100 to 1,000 by secretly inserting a zero can purchase either 100 or 1,000 of the items.

BANKRUPTCY

A proceeding in bankruptcy attempts to allocate the assets the debtor owns to the creditors in a fair and equitable fashion. Once the assets have been allocated, the debtor receives a **discharge in bankruptcy.** A discharge in bankruptcy will ordinarily bar enforcement of most of a debtor's contracts by the creditors. Partial payment of a debt *after* discharge in bankruptcy will not revive the debt. (Bankruptcy will be discussed in detail in Chapter 30.)

IMPOSSIBILITY OR IMPRACTICABILITY OF PERFORMANCE

After a contract has been made, performance may become impossible in an objective sense. This is known as **impossibility of performance** and may discharge a contract.[16]

Objective Impossibility of Performance. *Objective impossibility* ("It can't be done") must be distinguished from *subjective impossibility* ("I'm sorry, I simply can't do it"). An example of subjective impossibility is a contract in which money cannot be paid on time because the bank is closed.[17] In effect, the party in this case is saying, "It is impossible for me to perform," not "It is impossible for anyone to perform." Accordingly, such excuses do not discharge a contract, and the nonperforming party is normally held in breach of contract. Three basic types of situations, however, generally qualify as grounds for the discharge of contractual obligations based on impossibility of performance:[18]

1. *When one of the parties to a personal contract dies or becomes incapacitated prior to performance.* For example, Fred, a famous dancer, contracts with Ethereal Dancing Guild to play a leading role in its new ballet. Before the ballet can be performed, Fred becomes ill and dies. His personal performance was essential to the completion of the contract. Thus, his death discharges the contract and his estate's liability for his nonperformance.
2. *When the specific subject matter of the contract is destroyed.* For example, A-1 Farm Equipment agrees to sell Gudgel the green tractor on its lot and promises to have it ready for Gudgel to pick up on Saturday. On Friday night, however, a truck veers off the nearby highway and smashes into the tractor, destroying it beyond repair. Because the contract was for this specific tractor, A-1's performance is rendered impossible owing to the accident.
3. *When a change in law renders performance illegal.* An example is a contract to build an apartment building, when the zoning laws are changed to prohibit the construction of residential rental property at this location. This change renders the contract impossible to perform.

Commercial Impracticability. Courts may excuse parties from their performance obligations when the performance becomes much more difficult or expensive than originally contemplated at the time the contract was formed. For someone to invoke successfully the doctrine of **commercial impracticability**, however, the anticipated performance must become *extremely* difficult or costly.[19] For example, in one case, a court held that a contract was discharged because a party would have had to pay ten times more than the original estimate to excavate a certain amount of gravel.[20] Caution should be used in invoking commercial impracticability. The added burden of performing must be *extreme* and, more important, *must not have been within the cognizance of the parties when the contract was made.*

Westlaw. See Case 16.3 at the end of this chapter. To view the full, unedited case from Westlaw,® go to this text's Web site at **http://wbl-cs.westbuslaw.com**.

Frustration of Purpose. A theory closely allied with the doctrine of commercial impracticability is the doctrine of **frustration of purpose.** In principle, a contract will be discharged if supervening circumstances make it impossible to attain the purpose both parties had in mind when making the contract. The origins of the doctrine lie in the old English "coronation cases." A coronation procession was planned for Edward VII when he became king of England following the death of his mother, Queen Victoria. Hotel rooms along the coronation route were rented at exorbitant prices for that day. When

16. *Restatement (Second) of Contracts,* Section 261.
17. *Ingham Lumber Co. v. Ingersoll & Co.,* 93 Ark. 447, 125 S.W. 139 (1910).
18. *Restatement (Second) of Contracts,* Sections 262–266; UCC 2–615.
19. *Restatement (Second) of Contracts,* Section 264.
20. *Mineral Park Land Co. v. Howard,* 172 Cal. 289, 156 P. 458 (1916).

the king became ill and the procession was canceled, a flurry of lawsuits resulted. Hotel and building owners sought to enforce the room-rent bills against would-be parade observers, and would-be parade observers sought to be reimbursed for rental monies paid in advance on the rooms. Would-be parade observers were excused from their duty of payment because the purpose of the room contracts had been "frustrated."

Temporary Impossibility. An occurrence or event that makes performance temporarily impossible operates to suspend performance until the impossibility ceases. Then, ordinarily, the parties must perform the contract as originally planned. If, however, the lapse of time and the change in circumstances surrounding the contract make it substantially more burdensome for the parties to perform the promised acts, the contract is discharged.

The leading case on the subject, *Autry v. Republic Productions,*[21] involved an actor who was drafted into the army in 1942. Being drafted rendered the actor's contract temporarily impossible to perform, and it was suspended until the end of the war. When the actor got out of the army, the value of the dollar had so changed that performance of the contract would have been substantially burdensome to the actor. Therefore, the contract was discharged.

21. 30 Cal.2d 144, 180 P.2d 888 (1947).

Terms and Concepts to Review

- anticipatory repudiation 312
- breach of contract 312
- commercial impracticability 315
- concurrent conditions 310
- condition 309
- condition precedent 309
- condition subsequent 310
- discharge 309
- discharge in bankruptcy 315
- frustration of purpose 315
- impossibility of performance 315
- mutual rescission 313
- novation 313
- performance 309
- tender 310

Chapter Summary

Conditions of Performance	Contract obligations may be subject to the following types of conditions: 1. *Condition precedent*—A condition that must be fulfilled before a party's promise becomes absolute. 2. *Condition subsequent*—A condition that operates to terminate a party's absolute promise to perform. 3. *Concurrent conditions*—In this case, each party's absolute duty to perform is conditioned on the other party's absolute duty to perform. 4. *Express and implied conditions*—Conditions may be classified as express or implied in fact.
Discharge by Performance	A contract may be discharged by complete (strict) performance or by substantial performance. In some cases, performance must be to the satisfaction of another. Totally inadequate performance constitutes a material breach of contract. An anticipatory repudiation of a contract allows the other party to sue immediately for breach of contract.
Discharge by Agreement	Parties may agree to discharge their contractual obligations in several ways: 1. *By rescission*—The parties mutually agree to rescind (cancel) the contract. 2. *By novation*—A new party is substituted for one of the primary parties to a contract. 3. *By substituted agreement*—A compromise (settlement) agreement is substituted for the old contract.

CHAPTER SUMMARY—CONTINUED

Discharge by Agreement—continued	4. *By accord and satisfaction*—The parties agree to render and accept performance different from that on which they originally agreed.
Discharge by Operation of Law	Parties' obligations under contracts may be discharged by operation of law owing to one of the following: 1. *Alteration of the contract.* 2. *Statutes of limitations.* 3. *Bankruptcy.* 4. *Impossibility or impracticability of performance.*

CASES FOR ANALYSIS

Westlaw. You can access the full text of each case presented below by going to the Westlaw cases on this text's Web site at http://wbl-cs.westbuslaw.com. Each Westlaw case includes the names of all plaintiffs and defendants, the dates on which the case was argued and decided, a brief summary of the issues and decisions in the case, headnotes classifying specific issues in the case according to the West Key Number System, and the court's opinion. Concurring and dissenting opinions, if any, are included as well.

CASE 16.1 SUBSTANTIAL PERFORMANCE

JACOBS & YOUNG, INC. V. KENT

Court of Appeals of New York, 1921.
230 N.Y. 239,
129 N.E. 889.

CARDOZO, J. [Judge]

The plaintiff built a country residence for the defendant at a cost of upwards of $77,000, and now sues to recover a balance of $3,483.46, remaining unpaid. The work of construction ceased in June, 1914, and the defendant then began to occupy the dwelling. There was no complaint of defective performance until March, 1915. One of the specifications for the plumbing work provides that—

> "All wrought-iron pipe must be well galvanized, lap welded pipe of the grade known as 'standard pipe' of Reading manufacture."

The defendant learned in March, 1915, that some of the pipe, instead of being made in Reading, was the product of other factories. The plaintiff was accordingly directed by the architect to do the work anew. The plumbing was then encased within the walls except in a few places where it had to be exposed. Obedience to the order meant more than the substitution of other pipe. It meant the demolition at great expense of substantial parts of the completed structure. The plaintiff left the work untouched, and asked for a certificate that the final payment was due. Refusal of the certificate was followed by this suit [in a New York state court].

The evidence sustains a finding that the omission of the prescribed brand of pipe was neither fraudulent nor willful. It was the result of the oversight and inattention of the plaintiff's subcontractor. Reading pipe is distinguished from Cohoes pipe and other brands only by the name of the manufacturer stamped upon it at intervals of between six and seven feet. Even the defendant's architect, though he inspected the pipe upon arrival, failed to notice the discrepancy. The plaintiff tried to show that the brands installed, though made by other manufacturers, were the same in quality, in appearance, in market value, and in cost as the brand stated in the contract—that they were, indeed, the same thing, though manufactured in another place. The evidence was excluded, and a verdict directed for the defendant. The [state intermediate appellate court] reversed, and granted a new trial.

We think the evidence, if admitted, would have supplied some basis for the inference that the defect was insignificant in its relation to the project. The courts never say that one who makes a contract fills the measure of his duty by less than full performance. They do say, however, that *an omission, both trivial and innocent, will sometimes be atoned for by allowance of the resulting damage, and will not always be the breach of a condition.* * * * [Emphasis added.]

Those who think more of symmetry and logic in the development of legal rules than of practical adaptation to the attainment of a just result will be troubled by a classification where the lines of division are so wavering and blurred. Something, doubtless, may be said on the score of consistency and certainty in favor of a stricter standard. The courts have balanced such considerations against those of equity and fairness, and found the latter to be the weightier. The decisions in this state commit us to the liberal view, which is making its way, nowadays, in jurisdictions slow to welcome it. Where the line is to be drawn between the important and the trivial cannot be settled by a formula. In the nature of the case precise boundaries are impossible. The same omission may take on one aspect or another according to its setting. Substitution of equivalents may not have the same significance in fields of art on the one side and in those of mere utility on the other. Nowhere will change be tolerated, however, if it is so dominant or pervasive as in any real or substantial measure to frustrate the purpose of the contract. There is no general license to install whatever, in the builder's judgment, may be regarded as "just as good." The question is one of degree, to be answered, if there is doubt, by the triers of the facts, and, if the inferences are certain, by the judges of the law. We must weigh the purpose to be served, the desire to be gratified, the excuse for deviation from the letter, the cruelty of enforced adherence. Then only can we tell whether literal fulfillment is to be implied by law as a condition. This is not to say that the parties are not free by apt and certain words to effectuate a purpose that performance of every term shall be a condition of recovery. That question is not here. This is merely to say that the law will be slow to impute the purpose, in the silence of the parties, where the significance of the default is grievously out of proportion to the oppression of the forfeiture. The willful transgressor must accept the penalty of his transgression. For him there is no occasion to mitigate the rigor of implied conditions. The transgressor whose default is unintentional and trivial may hope for mercy if he will offer atonement for his wrong.

In the circumstances of this case, we think the measure of the allowance is not the cost of replacement, which would be great, but the difference in value, which would be either nominal or nothing. Some of the exposed sections might perhaps have been replaced at moderate expense. The defendant did not limit his demand to them, but treated the plumbing as a unit to be corrected from cellar to roof. In point of fact, the plaintiff never reached the stage at which evidence of the extent of the allowance became necessary. The trial court had excluded evidence that the defect was unsubstantial, and in view of that ruling there was no occasion for the plaintiff to go farther with an offer of proof. We think, however, that the offer, if it had been made, would not of necessity have been defective because directed to difference in value. It is true that in most cases the cost of replacement is the measure. The owner is entitled to the money which will permit him to complete, unless the cost of completion is grossly and unfairly out of proportion to the good to be attained. When that is true, the measure is the difference in value. Specifications call, let us say, for a foundation built of granite quarried in Vermont. On the completion of the building, the owner learns that through the blunder of a subcontractor part of the foundation has been built of granite of the same quality quarried in New Hampshire. The measure of allowance is not the cost of reconstruction. There may be omissions of that which could not afterwards be supplied exactly as called for by the contract without taking down the building to its foundations, and at the same time the omission may not affect the value of the building for use or otherwise, except so slightly as to be hardly appreciable. The rule that gives a remedy in cases of substantial performance with compensation for defects of trivial or inappreciable importance has been developed by the courts as an instrument of justice. The measure of the allowance must be shaped to the same end.

The order should be affirmed, and judgment absolute directed in favor of the plaintiff upon the stipulation, with costs in all courts.

McLAUGHLIN, J. [Justice]

I dissent. The plaintiff did not perform its contract. Its failure to do so was either intentional or due to gross neglect which, under the uncontradicted facts, amounted to the same thing, nor did it make any proof of the cost of compliance, where compliance was possible.

* * * *

I am of the opinion the trial court was right in directing a verdict for the defendant. The plaintiff agreed that all the pipe used should be of the Reading Manufacturing Company. Only about two-fifths of it, so far as appears, was of that kind. If more were used, then the burden of proving that fact was upon the plaintiff, which it could easily have done, since it knew where the pipe was obtained. The question of substantial performance of a contract of the character of the one under consideration depends in no small degree upon the good faith of the contractor. If the plaintiff had intended to, and had, complied with the terms of the contract except as to minor omissions, due to inadvertence, then he might be allowed to recover the contract price, less the amount necessary to fully compensate the defendant for damages caused by such omissions. But that is not this case. It installed between 2,000 and 2,500 feet of pipe, of which only 1,000 feet at most complied with the contract. No explanation was given why pipe called for by the contract was not used, nor that any effort [was] made to show what it would cost to remove the pipe of other manufacturers and install that of the Reading Manufacturing Company. The defendant had a right to contract for what he wanted. He had a right before making payment to get what the contract called for.

CASE 16.2 MATERIAL BREACH OF CONTRACT

VAN STEENHOUSE v. JACOR BROADCASTING OF COLORADO, INC.

Supreme Court of Colorado, 1998.
958 P.2d 464.

Chief Justice *VOLLACK* delivered the Opinion of the Court.

* * * *

Jacor [Broadcasting of Colorado, Inc.] owns and operates Newsradio 85 KOA (KOA). [Dr. Andrea] Van Steenhouse is a radio personality and practicing psychologist. On June 18, 1991, Van Steenhouse signed a three-year agreement as a radio talk show host with KOA (the Agreement). The Agreement provided that Van Steenhouse was to render these services "on air from 2:00 P.M. to 4:00 P.M. Monday through Friday (any change in such hours to be mutually agreed upon)." Van Steenhouse was to receive a base salary of $100,000 for the first year, $105,000 for the second year, and $112,000 for the third year. In addition, Van Steenhouse was eligible for a performance bonus, depending on KOA's audience share during her show.

In October, 1993, Jacor acquired the rights to broadcast the *Rush Limbaugh Show,* which conflicted with the 2:00 P.M. to 4:00 P.M. time slot occupied by Van Steenhouse. As a result, Jacor proposed several alternatives to Van Steenhouse, including a two-hour time slot on AM 760 KTLK, Jacor's newly purchased station, with one hour to be broadcast simultaneously on KOA. However, none of Jacor's proposals included two consecutive hours on KOA. The parties failed to reach agreement, and on January 3, 1994, Jacor started broadcasting Rush Limbaugh in place of Van Steenhouse. Although Jacor paid her base salary until the expiration of the Agreement in August 1994, Van Steenhouse did not work as a radio talk show host for a period of approximately eight months.

On January 12, 1994, Van Steenhouse sued Jacor and KOA's general manager Lee Larsen in [a Colorado state court] (the trial court), alleging various claims, including breach of contract * * * .

The trial court concluded that although Jacor continued to pay Van Steenhouse's base salary, it materially breached the Agreement by preventing her from performing as a talk show host according to the terms of the Agreement. Consequently, the trial court awarded Van Steenhouse $3,518.00 plus costs, which represented the performance bonus that she could have received by broadcasting during the last eight months of the Agreement. * * *

The [state intermediate] court of appeals affirmed the trial court's finding that Jacor breached the Agreement. * * *

* * * *

Jacor argues that an employee's claim for breach of contract cannot be predicated solely on an employer's failure to provide an opportunity to work. We disagree.

Ordinarily, an employment agreement does not obligate an employer to furnish work for an employee. However, such an obligation may be inferred depending on the circumstances under which the agreement for employment is made or the nature of the employment. In particular, *an obligation to furnish work arises if the employee materially benefits from performing the duties described in the agreement* * * * . [S]everal courts have held that when an employer fails to furnish the kind of work specified in an employment agreement, the employee has a cause of action for breach of contract. [Emphasis added.]

* * * *

* * * [T]he trial court in this case held that Jacor breached the Agreement by depriving Van Steenhouse of the opportunity to perform as a talk show host on KOA. Pursuant to the Agreement, Van Steenhouse was to host her show on KOA Monday through Friday from 2:00 to 4:00 P.M. The Agreement specified that "any change in such hours [would] be mutually agreed upon." Nevertheless, Jacor refused to broadcast Van Steenhouse during this time slot and eventually removed her show from KOA's broadcast lineup. As a result, Van Steenhouse lost the opportunity to build and maintain her professional marketability. In addition, Van Steenhouse lost the opportunity to earn a 1994 performance bonus.

Jacor deprived Van Steenhouse of these benefits by refusing to broadcast her show in the time slot specified by the clear terms of the Agreement. Accordingly, we hold that Van Steenhouse stated a valid claim for breach of contract.

* * * *

* * * Accordingly, we affirm [this part of the lower court's decision].

CASE 16.3 COMMERCIAL IMPRACTICABILITY

SYROVY v. ALPINE RESOURCES, INC.

Court of Appeals of Washington,
Division 3, 1992.
841 P.2d 1279.

SWEENEY, Judge.

* * * *

On March 19, 1988, [the George Syrovy Trust] and Alpine Resources, Inc., entered into a "Timber Purchase Agreement" (TPA) drafted by Ken Reoh of Alpine. The term of the agreement was for 2 years, beginning April 15, 1988 and ending April 15, 1990. Mr. Syrovy agreed to sell and Alpine agreed to buy "all the merchantable timber (12" DBH and larger) produced during the term * * * ". The timber to be "sold, purchased, and delivered * * * [was to] be produced by Buyer [Alpine] from timber on Seller's land * * * ."

"The total purchase price for all the commercial timber * * * [was to] be * * * $140,000.00." One thousand dollars, in earnest money, was escrowed [placed in the hands of an escrow agent, a third party who holds the funds until certain conditions of the sale and purchase are met]. The earnest money was to be released to Mr. Syrovy on April 15, 1988, after Alpine completed the forest applications, verified access routes and determined that it could proceed with the harvest. The agreement then set out three different areas to be harvested and required that specified payments be made by Alpine before it commenced harvesting in the described areas. The agreement further provided:

> Time is of the essence of this agreement. The Buyer will commence with active harvesting on said land as soon as possible after the execution of this contract and will carry on a continuous operation to this end so that the road system and harvesting will be completed and delivered within the term of this contract.

On June 1, 1988, the parties entered into a "Supplement to Timber Purchase Agreement and Receipt of Payment." Again the document was drafted by Mr. Reoh. The supplement changed the harvesting and payment schedule. Alpine verified the access and haul routes and Mr. Syrovy received the earnest money. Alpine then paid the initial $50,000 and began harvesting the first area. Alpine continued harvesting until October 1989. It stopped prior to completing the first area because of weather and the arrival of hunting season, which precluded access to the area.

* * * *

On July 18, 1990, Mr. Syrovy filed suit [in a Washington state court] against Alpine for the balance of the contract payment ($90,000) plus interest, attorney fees, and costs. Alpine answered denying the obligation and asserting impossibility of performance because of problems with access to the timber and bad weather. * * *

* * * *

Mr. Syrovy * * * moved for summary judgment and the trial court granted the motion. Alpine appeals * * *.

* * * *

Alpine * * * contends its defense of impossibility of performance precludes summary judgment. The commercial transaction before us does not readily fit those anticipated by [Revised Code of Washington (RCW) Section 62A.2, Washington State's version of Article 2 of the Uniform Commercial Code]. Usually, the seller of goods is responsible for production. RCW 62A.2-615 affords a defense to the seller's performance based on impracticability. Here, the contract relegated control over production to the buyer. Accordingly, it is the buyer who asserts impracticability as a defense. Nevertheless, cases construing RCW 62A.2-615 are instructive because the operative term is "impracticability"—regardless of which party is responsible for production. Moreover, our analysis is in accord with general principles of contract law which control the issue of impracticability.

* * * Article 2 recognizes impracticability as a defense to performance when a seller is unable to deliver goods:

> Except so far as a seller may have assumed a greater obligation * * * :
>
> (a) Delay in delivery * * * is not a breach * * * if performance as agreed has been made impracticable by the occurrence of a contingency the non-occurrence of which was a basic assumption on which the contract was made * * *.

The Washington Comments to this code section suggest that performance is excused if events occur that are not foreseen or anticipated—a "wholly unexpected contingency." *Difficulties that are assumed by a party, at the time of contracting, cannot form the basis of an impracticability defense.* [Emphasis added.]

Alpine argues that the winters of 1988 and 1989 were so severe that harvesting became impossible. However, Mr. Reoh is a logger with considerable experience in purchasing timber. It would be unreasonable to suggest that weather conditions were an unforeseeable event. Also, there is no evidence to support the assertion that the weather was so remarkable that contract performance was impossible.

Alpine also argues that it did not have access to the property during hunting season. The terms of the contract provided Alpine with 30 days in which it could verify "access and haul routes." Having verified the routes, it accepted the risk of access problems when it proceeded with the contract. Access problems were foreseeable and the risk was allocated in the contract. The problems cannot be asserted as a basis for an impracticability defense. In sum, Alpine's defense presents no issue of fact.

* * * *

For the contract price, Alpine agreed to purchase all merchantable timber it could harvest during the 2-year period. These goods were delivered and Alpine is obligated to pay for them.

We affirm.

CASE PROBLEMS

16–1. John Agosta and his brother Salvatore had formed a corporation, but disagreements between the two brothers caused John to petition for voluntary dissolution of the corporation. According to the dissolution agreement, the total assets of the corporation, which included a warehouse and inventory, would be split between the brothers by Salvatore's selling his stock to John for $500,000. This agreement was approved, but shortly before the payment was made, a fire totally destroyed the warehouse and inventory, which were the major assets of the corporation. John refused to pay Salvatore the $500,000, and Salvatore brought suit for breach of contract. Discuss whether the destruction of the major assets of the corporation affects John's required performance. [*In the Matter of Fontana D'Oro Foods, Inc.*, 122 Misc.2d 1091, 472 N.Y.S.2d 528 (1983)]

16–2. Zilg is the author of *DuPont: Behind the Nylon Curtain*, a historical account of the duPont family in America's social, political, and economic affairs. Prentice-Hall, Inc., signed Zilg to an exclusive contract to publish the book. There was no provision to have Prentice-Hall use its best efforts to promote the book; rather, it was left up to the publisher to use its discretion regarding the number of volumes printed and the level of promotion. Prentice-Hall had originally planned a first printing of 15,000 copies and an advertising budget of $15,000 for the book. Later, having had second thoughts about the sales potential of the book, Prentice-Hall decided to do a first printing of only 10,000 copies and to reduce the amount it had allocated for advertising. In all, Prentice-Hall published a total of 13,000 volumes (3,000 beyond the sales volume at which it received the highest royalties), authorized an advertising budget of $5,500, distributed over 600 copies to reviewers, and purchased ads in major newspapers. Zilg later claimed that the reductions in the number of volumes printed and in the advertising budget were evidence that Prentice-Hall had not made a "best effort" to fully promote the book. Prentice-Hall claimed that its reduction came after careful review and was based on sound and valid business decisions. Based on these facts alone, discuss whether Prentice-Hall fulfilled its contractual duty to Zilg. [*Zilg v. Prentice-Hall, Inc.*, 717 F.2d 671 (2d Cir. 1983)]

16–3. Coker International, Inc., entered into a contract with Burlington Industries, Inc., under which Coker agreed to purchase 221 used textile looms from Burlington for a total price of $1,021,000. Under the contract, Coker was required to make a 10 percent down payment, with the balance to be paid prior to the removal of the looms. Coker planned to resell the looms to a customer in Peru, but the contract was not conditioned on any resale of the looms by Coker. Because of the Peruvian government's actions, Coker's plan to resell the equipment to the Peruvian buyer fell through. Coker sought to rescind the contract with Burlington and recover its down payment, asserting that it should be excused from performance under the doctrine of frustration of purpose. Discuss fully whether Coker can be excused from performance of the contract under this doctrine. [*Coker International, Inc. v. Burlington Industries, Inc.*, 747 F.Supp. 1168 (D.S.C. 1990)]

16–4. Edgar and Peggy Stacy owned a 588-acre farm in Mississippi County, Arkansas. In June 1985, the Williams family agreed to purchase the Stacys' farm for $882,000. The Stacys' real estate agent inserted into a preprinted contract (just after the provision stating the purchase price) the following typewritten statement: "Buyers to pledge approximately 900 acres of land in Tallahatchie County in Mississippi together with lands herein described for loan to pay purchase price." The Williams family failed to obtain financing for the property, in part because the farm in Tallahatchie County was subject to a long-term lease and because the value of the lands they held turned out to be less than they had assumed. The Williams family notified the Stacys' real estate broker of these facts, and the family members also wrote a letter to Edgar Stacy stating that they wanted to rescind the contract for these reasons. Several months later, the Stacys sold the farm to another party for $630,000 and sued the Williams family for breach of contract, seeking $252,000, which represented the difference between the $882,000 purchase price offered by the Williams family and the $630,000 paid by the property's ultimate purchaser. The issue before the court is whether the ability of the Williamses to obtain financing was a condition precedent to the Williamses' obligation to perform under the contract.

Assuming that parol evidence is admissible, how should the court rule? Discuss. [*Stacy v. Williams,* 38 Ark.App. 192, 834 S.W.2d 156 (1992)]

16–5. Sharon Russell's weight varied between 280 and 305 pounds while she was enrolled in a nursing program at Salve Regina College in Newport, Rhode Island. Her weight was never an issue until her sophomore year, at which time she began to be the target of cruel remarks by school officials. In her junior year, she received a failing grade in a clinical nursing course—not on the basis of her performance but simply because she was obese. The normal consequence of failing a clinical nursing course was expulsion from the college, but Russell was offered a deal: If she signed a "contract" in which she promised to attend Weight Watchers regularly and to submit proof of her attendance, and if she managed to lose two pounds a week steadily, she would remain in good standing. Russell attended Weight Watchers regularly but failed to lose the required two pounds a week, and the following year the college requested that she withdraw from the nursing program. Russell sued the college for damages for breach of contract. The jury found that Russell's relationship to the college was essentially a contractual one in which she was required to abide by disciplinary rules, pay tuition, and maintain a good academic record (which she did—except for the course that she failed because of her obesity) and the college was required to provide her with an education until graduation. The jury also found that Russell had "substantially performed" her side of the bargain and that the college's actions prevented Russell from rendering complete performance and constituted a breach. The college appealed, contending that the circumstances of Russell's situation did not justify the application of the principle of substantial performance. What will the appellate court decide? Discuss. [*Russell v. Salve Regina College,* 890 F.2d 484 (1st Cir. 1989)]

16–6. K & K Pharmacy, Inc., contracted to sell a pharmacy to James Barta. The pharmacy was in a shopping mall, and the pharmacy premises were leased from the owner of the mall, Larsen Enterprises. The contract between K & K and Barta provided: "This Agreement shall be contingent upon Buyer's ability to obtain a new lease from Larsen Enterprises, Inc., for the premises presently occupied by Seller. In the event Buyer is unable to obtain a new lease satisfactory to Buyer, this Agreement shall be null and void." Barta wanted to sell certain foods in the pharmacy as he did in his other stores, but another lessee in the mall had an exclusive right to sell groceries and refused to give the necessary permission. As a result, Barta refused to sign a lease with Larsen and notified K & K that he would not go through with the sale. K & K sued in a Nebraska state court to recover damages for Barta's alleged breach of contract. The trial court granted Barta's motion for summary judgment, and K & K appealed. What will happen on appeal? Discuss. [*K & K Pharmacy, Inc. v. Barta,* 222 Neb. 215, 382 N.W.2d 363 (1986)]

16–7. Frank and Carol Jacobs contracted with Eugene Plante for Plante to furnish the necessary materials and construct a house on their lot, in accordance with plans and specifications, for $26,765. During construction, Plante was paid $20,000. Disputes arose concerning the work, and the Jacobses refused to make further payments. Plante did not complete the house, and an allowance of approximately $1,600 was given the Jacobses. When Plante asked a Wisconsin state court to place a lien on the house for the rest of the money, the Jacobses counterclaimed for damages, complaining that there were cracks in the living room and kitchen ceilings, that a wall between the living room and the kitchen had been located incorrectly, and that there were numerous other problems. The trial court found that the contract had been substantially performed and required the Jacobses to pay $4,152.90 plus interest and court costs. The Jacobses appealed. What will happen on appeal? Discuss. [*Plante v. Jacobs,* 10 Wis.2d 567, 103 N.W.2d 296 (1960)]

16–8. In November 1950, Ryland Parker went to the Arthur Murray Dance Studio for three free dance lessons. During the free lessons, the instructor told Parker that he had "exceptional potential to become . . . [an] accomplished dancer" and encouraged him to take more lessons. Parker signed a contract for seventy-five hours of lessons at a cost of $1,000. At the bottom of the contract, "NON-CANCELLABLE NEGOTIABLE CONTRACT" was printed in boldface type. During the lessons the instructors praised Parker despite his lack of progress, and he signed several more contracts, each containing similar language. Some contained the statement, "I UNDERSTAND THAT NO REFUNDS WILL BE MADE UNDER THE TERMS OF THIS CONTRACT," also in boldface. Eventually, he contracted for 2,734 hours of lessons for which he paid $24,812.80. In September 1961, Parker was seriously injured in an accident, rendering him incapable of continuing the lessons. Despite his repeated written demands, the studio refused to return any of his money. He sued in an Illinois state court. The trial court ruled that Parker could recover his money under the impossibility of performance doctrine. Arthur Murray, Inc., and the studio appealed. What will happen on appeal? Discuss. [*Parker v. Arthur Murray, Inc.,* 10 Ill.App.3d 1000, 295 N.E.2d 487 (1973)]

16–9. Sun Maid Raisin Growers signed a contract to buy 1,800 tons of raisins from Victor Packing Co. in 1976. Victor planned to supply the raisins by purchasing them in the market very late in the year in order to get a good price. It waited too long. Because of heavy, "disastrous" rains that year, 50 percent of the crop was destroyed, and the price of raisins skyrocketed from $860 per ton to $1,600 per ton. Victor Packing could not meet Sun Maid's contract demand without sustaining equally "disastrous" losses, and it notified Sun Maid that it was repudiating the contract. Sun Maid sued for damages for breach of contract, and Victor

Packing claimed, among other things, that performance was impracticable. Discuss whether Victor Packing's defense should succeed. [*Sun Maid Raisin Growers v. Victor Packing Co.,* 146 Cal.App.3d 787, 194 Cal.Rptr. 612 (5 Dist. 1983)]

16–10. Larry Allen signed a contract with Weyerhaeuser, Inc., to work as a truck driver to haul timber. The contract provided the following: "Contractor agrees to comply with all operational safety and conservation rules and regulations promulgated by Weyerhaeuser." Billy Corey, the company's supervisor in charge of contract trucking, was responsible for informing contractors of safety regulations and ensuring that drivers complied with them. Before Allen signed the contract, Corey told him that Weyerhaeuser required its contract truckers to operate their trucks with headlights on while they were on the road. Initially, Allen complied. Occasionally, however, Corey had to remind him to turn on his lights. Allen's noncompliance became more frequent, even though Corey explained to him on several occasions that he had to comply with company policy. Finally, Allen told Corey that "he [wasn't] going to run with his lights on; that he was tired of it anyway and if [the company] would fire him it would do him a favor." Weyerhaeuser terminated Allen's contract. Allen sued, claiming that the contract had been wrongfully terminated. The trial court granted a directed verdict in Weyerhaeuser's favor, and Allen appealed. Discuss whether Allen's conduct constituted an anticipatory repudiation of his contract. [*Allen v. Weyerhaeuser, Inc.,* 95 N.C.App. 205, 381 S.E.2d 824 (1989)]

16–11. Grane, a homeowner, contracted with Butkovich & Sons, Inc., to enlarge Grane's basement and build a new room over the remodeled basement area. Butkovich was also to lay a new garage floor and construct a patio. The parties agreed to a price of $19,290 for the work. When the construction was completed, Grane refused to pay the contractor the $9,290 balance he still owed, claiming that Butkovich had failed to install water stops and reinforcing wire in one concrete floor, in accordance with Grane's specifications, and that the main floor of the addition was 8⅞ inches lower than the plans had called for. Butkovich sued Grane for recovery of the $9,290. As a mortgage holder on the property, the State Bank of St. Charles was named co-defendant by Butkovich, because its interests would be affected by a judgment against Grane if the latter could not pay. Butkovich claimed that it had substantially performed the contract. Grane claimed that performance was of poor quality and that failure to follow contract specifications constituted a material breach. Discuss who should prevail. [*Butkovich & Sons, Inc. v. State Bank of St. Charles,* 62 Ill.App.3d 810, 379 N.E.2d 837, 20 Ill.Dec. 4 (1978)]

16–12. Larry McLanahan's 1985 Lamborghini was stolen, and by the time McLanahan recovered the car, it had been extensively damaged. The car was insured by Farmers Insurance Co. of Washington under a policy providing comprehensive coverage, including coverage for theft. A provision in the policy stated that the coverage for theft damages was subject to certain terms and conditions, including the condition that any person claiming coverage under the policy must allow Farmers "to inspect and appraise the damaged vehicle before its repair or disposal." McLanahan, without notifying Farmers and without giving Farmers an opportunity to inspect the vehicle, sold the car to a wholesale car dealer. Farmers then denied coverage, and McLanahan brought suit to recover for the damages caused to his car by the theft. Did McLanahan have a valid claim against the insurance company? Explain. [*McLanahan v. Farmers Insurance Co. of Washington,* 66 Wash.App. 36, 831 P.2d 160 (1992)]

16–13. Heublein, Inc., makes wines and distilled spirits. Tarrant Distributors, Inc., agreed to distribute Heublein brands. When problems arose, the parties entered mediation. Under a settlement agreement, Heublein agreed to pay Tarrant the amount of its "net loss" as determined by Coopers & Lybrand, an accounting firm, according to a specified formula. The parties agreed that Coopers & Lybrand's calculation would be "final and binding." Heublein disagreed with Coopers & Lybrand's calculation, however, and refused to pay. The parties asked a federal district court to rule on the dispute. Heublein argued that the settlement agreement included an implied condition precedent that Coopers & Lybrand would correctly apply the specified formula before Heublein was obligated to pay. Tarrant pointed to the clause that the calculation would be "final and binding." With whom will the court agree, and why? [*Tarrant Distributors, Inc. v. Heublein, Inc.,* 127 F.3d 375 (5th Cir. 1997)]

16–14. Steven McPheters, a house builder and developer, hired Terry Tentinger, who did business as New Horizon Construction, to do some touching up and repainting on one of McPheters's new houses. Tentinger worked two days, billed McPheters $420 (a three-man crew for fourteen hours at $30 per hour), and offered to return to the house to remedy any defects in his workmanship at no cost. McPheters objected to the number of hours on the bill—although he did not express dissatisfaction with the work—and offered Tentinger $250. Tentinger refused to accept this amount and filed a suit in an Idaho state court to collect the full amount. McPheters filed a counterclaim, alleging that Tentinger failed to perform the job in a workmanlike manner, resulting in $2,500 in damages, which would cost $500 to repair. Tentinger's witnesses testified that although some touchup work needed to be done, the job had been performed in a workmanlike manner. McPheters presented testimony indicating that the workmanship was so defective as to render it commercially unreasonable. On what basis could the court rule in Tentinger's favor? Explain fully. [*Tentinger v. McPheters*, 132 Idaho 620, 977 P.2d 234 (Idaho App. 1999)]

16–15. In May 1996, O'Brien-Sheipe Funeral Home, Inc., in Hempstead, New York, hired Teramo & Co. to build an addition to O'Brien's funeral home. The parties' contract did not specify a date for the completion of the work. The city of Hempstead issued a building permit for the project on June 14, and Teramo began work about two weeks later. There was some delay in construction because O'Brien asked that no work be done during funeral services, but by the end of March 1997, the work was substantially complete. Hempstead issued a "Certificate of Completion" on April 15. During the construction, O'Brien made periodic payments to Teramo, but there was a balance due of $17,950, which O'Brien did not pay. To recover this amount, Teramo filed a suit in a New York state court against O'Brien. O'Brien filed a counterclaim to recover lost profits for business allegedly lost due to the time Teramo took to build the addition, and for $6,180 spent to correct problems caused by poor workmanship. Which, if any, party is entitled to an award in this case? Explain. [*Teramo & Co. v. O'Brien-Sheipe Funeral Home, Inc.*, 725 N.Y.S.2d 87 (A.D. 2 Dept. 2001)]

E-LINKS

For updated links to resources available on the Web, as well as a variety of other materials, visit this text's Web site at

http://wbl-cs.westbuslaw.com

Law Guru can lead you to other sources of law relating to contract performance and discharge. Go to

http://lawguru.com/lawlinks.index.html

LEGAL RESEARCH EXERCISES ON THE WEB

Go to http://wbl-cs.westbuslaw.com, the Web site that accompanies this text. Select "Interactive Study Center," and then click on "Chapter 16." There you will find the following Internet research exercise that you can perform to learn more about anticipatory repudiation:

Activity 16–1: Anticipatory Repudiation

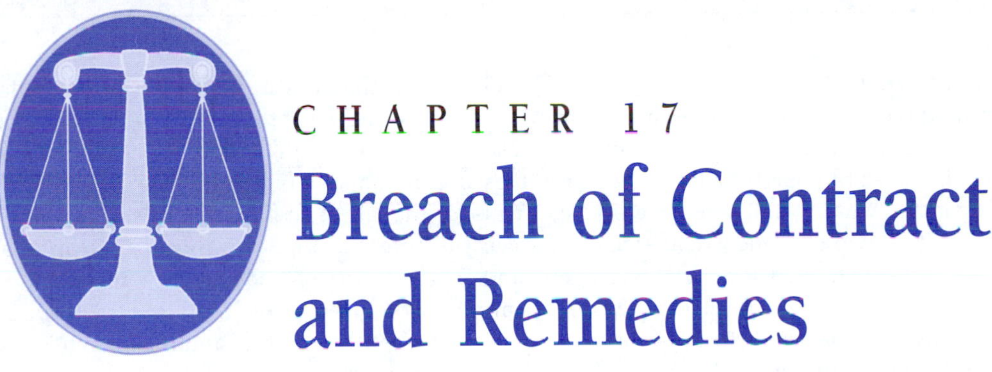

CHAPTER 17

Breach of Contract and Remedies

WHEN ONE PARTY BREACHES A CONTRACT, the other party—the nonbreaching party—can choose one or more of several remedies. A *remedy* is the relief provided for an innocent party when the other party has breached the contract. It is the means employed to enforce a right or to redress an injury.

The most common remedies available to a nonbreaching party include damages, rescission and restitution, specific performance, and reformation. As discussed in Chapter 1, a distinction is made between *remedies at law* and *remedies in equity.* Today, the remedy at law is normally money damages, which are discussed in the first part of this chapter. Equitable remedies include rescission and restitution, specific performance, and reformation, all of which will be examined later in the chapter. Usually, a court will not award an equitable remedy unless the remedy at law is inadequate. Special legal doctrines and concepts relating to remedies will be discussed in the final pages of this chapter.

SECTION 1

Damages

A breach of contract entitles the nonbreaching party to sue for money (damages). As discussed in Chapter 5, damages are designed to compensate a party for harm suffered as a result of another's wrongful act. In the context of contract law, damages compensate the nonbreaching party for the loss of the bargain.[1]

1. Bear in mind that although a nonbreaching party may succeed in obtaining damages from a court from the breaching party, the court's judgment may be difficult to enforce. As discussed in Chapter 3, the breaching party may not have sufficient funds or assets to pay the damages awarded.

Often, courts say that innocent parties are to be placed in the position they would have occupied had the contract been fully performed.[2] For example, in the famous case of the "hairy hand," a doctor promised to make a boy's scarred hand "a hundred percent perfect." Skin was taken from the boy's chest and grafted onto his thumb and fingers. The hand became infected, and the boy was hospitalized for three months. Use of the hand was greatly restricted, and hair grew out of the grafted skin. In hearing a suit against the doctor, the court explained that the amount of damages was to be determined by the difference between the value to the boy of the "perfect" hand that the doctor had promised and the value of the hand in its condition after the operation.[3]

TYPES OF DAMAGES

There are basically four broad categories of damages:

1. Compensatory (to cover direct losses and costs).
2. Consequential (to cover indirect and foreseeable losses).
3. Punitive (to punish and deter wrongdoing).
4. Nominal (to recognize wrongdoing when no monetary loss is shown).

Compensatory and punitive damages were discussed in Chapter 5 in the context of tort law. Here, we look at these types of damages, as well as consequential and nominal damages, in the context of contract law.

Compensatory Damages. Damages compensating the nonbreaching party for the *loss of the bargain* are

2. *Restatement (Second) of Contracts,* Section 347; UCC 1–106(1).
3. *Hawkins v. McGee,* 84 N.H. 114, 146 A. 641 (1929).

known as *compensatory damages.* These damages compensate the injured party only for damages actually sustained and proved to have arisen directly from the loss of the bargain caused by the breach of contract. They simply replace what was lost because of the wrong or damage. To illustrate: Wilcox contracts to perform certain services exclusively for Hernandez during the month of March for $2,000. Hernandez cancels the contract and is in breach. Wilcox is able to find another job during the month of March but can earn only $1,000. He can sue Hernandez for breach and recover $1,000 as compensatory damages. Wilcox can also recover from Hernandez the amount that he spent to find the other job. Expenses that are caused directly by a breach of contract—such as those incurred to obtain performance from another source—are known as *incidental damages.*

The measurement of compensatory damages varies by type of contract. Certain types of contracts deserve special mention. They are contracts for the sale of goods, land contracts, and construction contracts.

Sale of Goods. In a contract for the sale of goods, the usual measure of compensatory damages is an amount equal to the difference between the contract price and the market price.[4] For example, suppose that Chrysler Corporation contracts to buy ten model UTS 400 network servers from an XEXO Corporation dealer for $8,000 each. The dealer, however, fails to deliver the ten servers to Chrysler. The market price of the servers at the time the buyer learns of the breach is $8,150. Chrysler's measure of damages is therefore $1,500 (10 × $150) plus any incidental damages (expenses) caused by the breach. In a situation in which the buyer breaches and the seller has not yet produced the goods, compensatory damages normally equal lost profits on the sale, not the difference between the contract price and the market price.

Sale of Land. Ordinarily, because each parcel of land is unique, the remedy for a seller's breach of a contract for a sale of real estate is specific performance—that is, the buyer is awarded the parcel of property for which he or she bargained (specific performance is discussed more fully later in this chapter). When this remedy is unavailable (for example, when the seller has sold the property to someone else), or when the breach is on the part of the buyer, the measure of damages is ordinarily the same as in contracts for the sale of goods—that is, the difference between the contract price and the market price of the land. The majority of states follow this rule.

A minority of states follow a different rule when the seller breaches the contract and the breach is not deliberate.[5] In such a case, these states allow the prospective purchaser to recover any down payment plus any expenses incurred (such as fees for title searches, attorneys, and escrows). This minority rule effectively places purchasers in the position they occupied prior to the sale.

Construction Contracts. The measure of damages in a building or construction contract varies depending on which party breaches and when the breach occurs. The owner can breach at three different stages of the construction:

1. Before performance has begun.
2. During performance.
3. After performance has been completed.

If the owner breaches *before performance has begun,* the contractor can recover only the profits that would have been made on the contract (that is, the total contract price less the cost of materials and labor). If the owner breaches *during performance,* the contractor can recover the profits plus the costs incurred in partially constructing the building. If the owner breaches *after the construction has been completed,* the contractor can recover the entire contract price, plus interest.

When the construction contractor breaches the contract by stopping work partway through the project, the measure of damages is the cost of completion, which includes reasonable compensation for any delay in performance. If the contractor finishes late, the measure of damages is the loss of use. If the contractor substantially performs, the courts may use the cost-of-completion formula, but only if there is no substantial economic waste in requiring completion. Economic waste occurs when the cost

4. That is, the amount is the difference between the contract price and the market price at the time and place at which the goods were to be delivered or tendered. See UCC 2–708 and UCC 2–713.

5. "Deliberate" breaches include the seller's failure to convey the land because the market price has gone up. "Nondeliberate" breaches include the seller's failure to convey the land because an unknown easement (another's right of use over the property) has rendered title unmarketable. See Chapter 47.

of additional resources to finish the project exceeds any subjective value placed on the additional work done. For example, if a contractor discovers that it will cost $20,000 to move a large coral rock eleven inches as specified in the contract, and the change in the rock's position will alter the appearance of the project only a trifle, full completion will involve an economic waste. These rules concerning the measurement of damages in breached construction contracts are summarized in Exhibit 17–1.

Consequential Damages. Foreseeable damages that result from a party's breach of contract are called **consequential damages**, or *special damages*. They differ from compensatory damages in that they are caused by special circumstances beyond the contract itself. They flow from the consequences, or results, of a breach.

For example, if a seller fails to deliver goods, and the seller knows that a buyer is planning to use or resell those goods immediately, consequential damages will be awarded for the loss of profit from the planned resale. The buyer will also recover compensatory damages for the difference between the contract price and the market price of the goods.

To recover consequential damages, the breaching party must know (or have reason to know) that special circumstances will cause the nonbreaching party to suffer an additional loss. This rule was enunciated in the classic case of *Hadley v. Baxendale*,[6] which established the rule that when damages are awarded, compensation is given only for those injuries that the defendant could *reasonably have foreseen* as a probable result of the usual course of events following a breach.

Punitive Damages. Punitive, or exemplary, damages are generally not awarded in an action for breach of contract. Punitive damages are designed to punish a guilty party and to make an example of the party to deter similar conduct in the future. Such damages have no legitimate place in contract law because they are, in essence, penalties, and a breach of contract is not unlawful in a criminal or societal sense. A contract is simply a civil relationship between the parties. The law may compensate one party for the loss of the bargain, no more and no less.

In a few situations, a person's actions can constitute both a breach of contract and a tort. For example, the parties may establish by contract a certain reasonable standard or duty of care. Failure to live up to that standard is a breach of contract, and the act itself may constitute negligence. Additionally, some intentional torts, such as fraud, may be tied to a breach of the terms of a contract. In such cases, it is possible for the nonbreaching party to recover punitive damages for the commission of the tort, in addition to compensatory and consequential damages for breach of contract.

Nominal Damages. When no actual damages result from a breach of contract and only a technical injury is involved, the court may award **nominal damages** to the innocent party. Awards of nominal damages are often trifling, such as a dollar, but they do establish that the defendant acted wrongfully.

For example, suppose that Jackson contracts to buy potatoes from Stanley at fifty cents a pound. Stanley breaches the contract and does not deliver the potatoes. In the meantime, the price of potatoes has fallen. Jackson is able to buy them in the open market at half the price he contracted for with Stanley. He is clearly better off because of Stanley's breach. Thus, in a suit for breach of contract, Jackson may be awarded only nominal damages for the technical injury he sustained, because no monetary loss was involved. Most lawsuits for nominal damages are brought as a matter of principle under

6. 156 Eng.Rep. 145 (1854).

EXHIBIT 17–1 MEASUREMENT OF DAMAGES—BREACH OF CONSTRUCTION CONTRACTS

PARTY IN BREACH	TIME OF BREACH	MEASUREMENT OF DAMAGES
Owner	Before construction has begun	Profits (contract price less cost of materials and labor)
Owner	During construction	Profits plus costs incurred up to time of breach
Owner	After construction is completed	Contract price plus interest
Contractor	Before construction is completed	Generally, all costs incurred by owner to complete construction

the theory that a breach has occurred and some damages must be imposed regardless of actual loss.

MITIGATION OF DAMAGES

In most situations, when a breach of contract occurs, the innocent injured party is held to a duty to mitigate, or reduce, the damages that he or she suffers. Under this **mitigation of damages** doctrine, the duty owed depends on the nature of the contract.

For example, some states require a landlord to use reasonable means to find a new tenant if a tenant abandons the premises and fails to pay rent. If an acceptable tenant becomes available, the landlord is required to lease the premises to this tenant to mitigate the damages recoverable from the former tenant. The former tenant is still liable for the difference between the amount of the rent under the original lease and the rent received from the new tenant. If the landlord has not used the reasonable means necessary to find a new tenant, presumably a court can reduce the award made by the amount of rent he or she could have received had such reasonable means been used.

In the majority of states, persons whose employment has been wrongfully terminated owe a duty to mitigate damages suffered because of their employers' breach of the employment contract. The damages they receive are their salaries less the incomes they would have received in similar jobs that they could have obtained by reasonable means. The employer must prove both that such a job existed and that the employee could have been hired.

Westlaw. See Case 17.1 at the end of this chapter. To view the full, unedited case from Westlaw,® go to this text's Web site at **http://wbl-cs.westbuslaw.com**.

LIQUIDATED DAMAGES VERSUS PENALTIES

Unliquidated damages are damages that have not been calculated or determined. **Liquidated damages**, in contrast, are damages that are certain in amount. A liquidated damages provision in a contract specifies a certain amount to be paid in the event of a *future* default or breach of contract. For example, a provision requiring a construction contractor to pay $300 for every day he or she is late in completing the construction is a liquidated damages provision.

Liquidated damages differ from penalties. **Penalties** specify a certain amount to be paid in the event of a default or breach of contract and are designed to *penalize* the breaching party. Liquidated damages provisions are enforceable; penalty provisions are not.

To determine if a particular provision is for liquidated damages or for a penalty, two questions must be answered:

1. When the contract was entered into, was it apparent that damages would be difficult to estimate in the event of a breach?
2. Was the amount set as damages a reasonable estimate and not excessive?[7]

If the answers to both questions are yes, the provision will be enforced. If either answer is no, the provision will not be enforced. Section 2–718(1) of the Uniform Commercial Code (UCC) specifically permits the inclusion of liquidated damages clauses in contracts for the sale of goods as long as both of these tests are met. In construction contracts, it is difficult to estimate the amount of damages that would be caused by a delay in completing construction, so liquidated damages clauses are often used.

See Case 17.2 at the end of this chapter. To view the full, unedited case from Westlaw,® go to this text's Web site at **http://wbl-cs.westbuslaw.com**.

SECTION 2

Rescission and Restitution

As discussed in Chapter 16, *rescission* is essentially an action to undo, or terminate, a contract—to return the contracting parties to the positions they occupied prior to the transaction. When fraud, a mistake, duress, undue influence, misrepresentation, or lack of capacity to contract is present, unilateral rescission is available.[8] Rescission may also be available by statute.[9] The failure of one party to

7. *Restatement (Second) of Contracts*, Section 356(1).

8. In *unilateral* rescission, only one party wants to undo the contract. In *mutual* rescission, the type of rescission discussed in Chapter 16, both parties agree to undo the contract. Mutual rescission discharges the contract; unilateral rescission is generally available as a remedy for breach of contract.

9. The Federal Trade Commission and many states have rules or statutes allowing consumers to unilaterally rescind contracts made at home with door-to-door salespersons. Rescission is allowed within three days for any reason or for no reason at all. See, for example, California Civil Code Section 1689.5.

perform entitles the other party to rescind the contract. The rescinding party must give prompt notice to the breaching party. Generally, to rescind a contract, each party must make **restitution** to the other by returning goods, property, or money previously conveyed.[10] If the goods or property received can be restored *in specie*—that is, if the actual goods or property can be returned—they must be. If the goods or property have been consumed, restitution must be made in an equivalent amount of money.

Essentially, *restitution* refers to the plaintiff's recapture of a benefit conferred on the defendant through which the defendant has been unjustly enriched. For example, Katie pays $10,000 to Bob in return for Bob's promise to design a house for her. The next day Bob calls Katie and tells her that he has taken a position with a large architectural firm in another state and cannot design the house. Katie decides to hire another architect that afternoon. Katie can obtain restitution of the $10,000.

Restitution may be appropriate when a contract is rescinded, but the right to restitution is not limited to rescission cases. Restitution may be sought in actions for breach of contract, tort actions, and other actions at law or in equity. Usually, restitution of money or property transferred by mistake or because of fraud can be awarded. An award in a case may include restitution of money or property obtained through embezzlement, conversion, theft, copyright infringement, or misconduct by a party in a confidential or other special relationship.

SECTION 3

Specific Performance

The equitable remedy of **specific performance** calls for the performance of the act promised in the contract. This remedy is quite attractive to the nonbreaching party for three reasons:

1. The nonbreaching party need not worry about collecting the money damages awarded by a court (see the discussion in Chapter 3 of some of the difficulties that may arise when trying to enforce court judgments).
2. The nonbreaching party need not spend time seeking an alternative contract.
3. The performance is more valuable than the money damages.

Normally, however, specific performance will not be granted unless the party's legal remedy (money damages) is inadequate.[11] For this reason, contracts for the sale of goods rarely qualify for specific performance. The legal remedy, money damages, is ordinarily adequate in such situations, because substantially identical goods can be bought or sold in the market. If the goods are unique, however, a court of equity will decree specific performance. For example, paintings, sculptures, or rare books or coins are so unique that money damages will not enable a buyer to obtain substantially identical substitutes in the market.

SALE OF LAND

Specific performance is granted to a buyer in a contract for the sale of land. The legal remedy for breach of a land sales contract is inadequate, because every parcel of land is considered to be unique. Money damages will not compensate a buyer adequately, because the same land in the same location obviously cannot be obtained elsewhere. Only when specific performance is unavailable (for example, when the seller has sold the property to someone else) will money damages be awarded instead.

CONTRACTS FOR PERSONAL SERVICES

Personal-service contracts require one party to work personally for another party. Courts of equity normally refuse to grant specific performance of personal-service contracts. If a contract is not deemed personal, the remedy at law may be adequate if substantially identical service (for example, lawn mowing) is available from other persons.

In individually tailored personal-service contracts, courts will not order specific performance by the party who was to be employed because public policy strongly discourages involuntary servitude.[12] Moreover, the courts do not want to have to monitor

10. *Restatement (Second) of Contracts*, Section 370.

11. *Restatement (Second) of Contracts*, Section 359.

12. The Thirteenth Amendment to the U.S. Constitution prohibits involuntary servitude, and thus a court will not order a person to perform under a personal-service contract. A court may grant an order (injunction) prohibiting that person from engaging in similar contracts in the future for a period of time, however.

a continuing service contract if supervision would be difficult—as it would be if the contract required the exercise of personal judgment or talent. For example, if you contracted with a brain surgeon to perform brain surgery on you and the surgeon refused to perform, the court would not compel (and you certainly would not want) the surgeon to perform under those circumstances. A court cannot assure meaningful performance in such a situation.[13]

SECTION 4

Reformation

Reformation is an equitable remedy used when the parties have *imperfectly* expressed their agreement in writing. Reformation allows the contract to be rewritten to reflect the parties' true intentions. It applies most often when fraud or mutual mistake (for example, a clerical error) is present.

Reformation is almost always sought so that some other remedy may then be pursued. For example, if Gregory contracts to buy a certain parcel of land from Cavendish but their contract mistakenly refers to a parcel of land different from the one being sold, the contract does not reflect the parties' intentions. Accordingly, a court can reform the contract so that it conforms to the parties' intentions and accurately refers to the parcel of land being sold. Gregory can then, if necessary, show that Cavendish has breached the contract as reformed. She can at that time request an order for specific performance.

Two other examples deserve mention. The first involves two parties who have made a binding oral contract. They further agree to put the oral contract in writing, but in doing so, they make an error in stating the terms. Normally, the courts will allow into evidence the correct terms of the oral contract, thereby reforming the written contract. The second example deals with written agreements (covenants) not to compete (see Chapter 12). If the covenant is for a valid and legitimate purpose (such as the sale of a business) but the area or time restraints of the covenant are unreasonable, some courts will reform the restraints by making them reasonable and will enforce the entire contract as reformed. Other courts, however, will throw out the entire restrictive covenant as illegal.

SECTION 5

Recovery Based on Quasi Contract

As stated in Chapter 9, quasi contract is a legal theory under which an obligation is imposed in the absence of an agreement. The courts use this theory to prevent unjust enrichment. Hence, quasi contract provides a basis for relief when no enforceable contract exists. The legal obligation arises because the law considers that a promise to pay for benefits received is implied by the party accepting the benefits. Generally, when one party has conferred a benefit on another party, equity requires the party receiving the benefit to pay for its reasonable value. The party conferring the benefit can recover in *quantum meruit,* which means "as much as he deserves" (see Chapter 9).

Quasi-contractual recovery is useful when one party has partially performed under a contract that is unenforceable. It can be used as an alternative to a suit for damages and will allow the party to recover the reasonable value of the partial performance, measured in some cases according to the benefit received and in others according to the detriment suffered.

To recover on a quasi contract, the party seeking recovery must show the following:

1. The party conferred a benefit on the other party.
2. The party conferred the benefit with the reasonable expectation of being paid.
3. The party did not act as a volunteer in conferring the benefit.
4. The other party (the party receiving the benefit) would be unjustly enriched by retaining the benefit without making payment.

For example, suppose that Watson contracts to build two oil derricks for Energy Industries. The derricks are to be built over a period of three years, but the parties do not make a written contract. Enforcement of the contract will therefore be barred by the Statute of Frauds.[14] Watson completes one derrick, and then Energy Industries informs him that it will not pay for the derrick. Watson can sue in quasi

13. Similarly, courts often refuse to order specific performance of construction contracts because courts are not set up to operate as construction supervisors or engineers.

14. Contracts that by their terms cannot be performed within one year must be in writing to be enforceable. See Chapter 14.

contract because he conferred a benefit on Energy Industries with the expectation of being paid, and allowing Energy Industries to retain the derrick without paying would enrich the company unjustly. Therefore, Watson should be able to recover in *quantum meruit* the reasonable value of the oil derrick. The reasonable value is ordinarily equal to the fair market value.

Westlaw. See Case 17.3 at the end of this chapter. To view the full, unedited case from Westlaw,® go to this text's Web site at **http://wbl-cs.westbuslaw.com**.

SECTION 6

Election of Remedies

In many cases, a nonbreaching party has several remedies available. The party must choose which remedy to pursue. The purpose of the doctrine of *election of remedies* is to prevent double recovery.

Suppose that McCarthy agrees in writing to sell his land to Tally. Then McCarthy changes his mind and repudiates the contract. Tally can sue for compensatory damages *or* for specific performance. If Tally could seek compensatory damages in addition to specific performance, she would recover twice for the same breach of contract. The doctrine of election of remedies requires Tally to choose the remedy she wants, and it eliminates any possibility of double recovery. In other words, the election doctrine represents the legal embodiment of the adage "You can't have your cake and eat it, too."

The doctrine has often been applied in a rigid and technical manner, leading to some harsh results. For example, suppose that Wilson is fraudulently induced to buy a parcel of land for $150,000. He spends an additional $10,000 moving onto the land and then discovers the fraud. Instead of suing for damages, Wilson sues to rescind the contract. The court allows Wilson to recover only the purchase price of $150,000. The court denies recovery of the additional $10,000 because the seller, Martin, did not receive the $10,000 and is therefore not required to reimburse Wilson for his moving expenses. So Wilson suffers a net loss of $10,000 on the transaction. If Wilson had elected to sue for damages instead of seeking the remedy of rescission and restitution, he could have recovered the $10,000 as well as the $150,000.[15]

15. See, for example, *Carpenter v. Mason*, 181 Wis. 114, 193 N.W. 973 (1923).

Because of such problems, the UCC expressly rejects the doctrine of election of remedies.[16] As will be discussed in Chapter 21, remedies under the UCC are not exclusive but cumulative in nature and include all the available remedies for breach of contract.

SECTION 7

Waiver of Breach

Under certain circumstances, a nonbreaching party may be willing to accept a defective performance of the contract. This knowing relinquishment of a legal right (that is, the right to require satisfactory and full performance) is called a **waiver.** When a waiver of a breach of contract occurs, the party waiving the breach cannot take any later action on it. In effect, the waiver erases the past breach; the contract continues as if the breach had never occurred. Of course, the waiver of breach of contract extends only to the matter waived and not to the whole contract.

Businesspersons often waive breaches of contract to get whatever benefit is still possible out of the contract. For example, a seller contracts with a buyer to deliver to the buyer ten thousand tons of coal on or before November 1. The contract calls for the buyer's payment to be made by November 10 for coal delivered. Because of a coal miners' strike, coal is scarce. The seller breaches the contract by not tendering delivery until November 5. The buyer may be well advised to waive the seller's breach, accept delivery of the coal, and pay as contracted.

Ordinarily, the waiver by a contracting party will not operate to waive subsequent, additional, or future breaches of contract. This is always true when the subsequent breaches are unrelated to the first breach. For example, an owner who waives the right to sue for late completion of a stage of construction does not waive the right to sue for failure to comply with engineering specifications on the same job. A waiver will be extended to subsequent defective performance if a reasonable person would conclude that similar defective performance in the future will be acceptable. Therefore, a *pattern of conduct* that waives a number of successive breaches will operate as a continued waiver. To change this result, the nonbreaching party should give notice to the breaching party that full performance will be required in the future.

16. See UCC 2–703 and UCC 2–711.

The party who has rendered defective or less-than-full performance remains liable for the damages caused by the breach of contract. In effect, the waiver operates to keep the contract going. The waiver prevents the nonbreaching party from calling the contract to an end or rescinding the contract. The contract continues, but the nonbreaching party can recover damages caused by defective or less-than-full performance.

SECTION 8

Contract Provisions Limiting Remedies

A contract may include provisions stating that no damages can be recovered for certain types of breaches or that damages must be limited to a maximum amount. The contract may also provide that the only remedy for breach is replacement, repair, or refund of the purchase price. Provisions stating that no damages can be recovered are called *exculpatory clauses* (see Chapter 12). Provisions that affect the availability of certain remedies are called *limitation-of-liability clauses.*

Whether these contract provisions and clauses will be enforced depends on the type of breach that is excused by the provision. For example, a provision excluding liability for fraudulent or intentional injury will not be enforced. Likewise, a clause excluding liability for illegal acts or violations of law will not be enforced. A clause excluding liability for negligence may be enforced in certain cases, however. When an exculpatory clause for negligence is contained in a contract made between parties who have roughly equal bargaining positions, the clause usually will be enforced.

The UCC provides that in a contract for the sale of goods, remedies can be limited. We will examine the UCC provisions on limited remedies in Chapter 21, in the context of the remedies available on the breach of a contract for the sale or lease of goods.

TERMS AND CONCEPTS TO REVIEW

consequential damages 327	nominal damages 327	restitution 329
liquidated damages 328	penalty 328	specific performance 329
mitigation of damages 328	reformation 330	waiver 331

CHAPTER SUMMARY

COMMON REMEDIES AVAILABLE TO NONBREACHING PARTY

Damages

The legal remedy designed to compensate the nonbreaching party for the loss of the bargain. By awarding money damages, the court tries to place the parties in the positions that they would have occupied had the contract been fully performed. The nonbreaching party frequently has a duty to *mitigate* (lessen or reduce) the damages incurred as a result of the contract's breach. There are five broad categories of damages:

1. *Compensatory damages*—Damages that compensate the nonbreaching party for injuries actually sustained and proved to have arisen directly from the loss of the bargain resulting from the breach of contract.
   a. In breached contracts for the sale of goods, the usual measure of compensatory damages is an amount equal to the difference between the contract price and the market price.
   b. In breached contracts for the sale of land, the measure of damages is ordinarily the same as in contracts for the sale of goods.
   c. In breached construction contracts, the measure of damages depends on which party breaches and at what stage of construction the breach occurs.

CHAPTER SUMMARY—CONTINUED

Damages—continued	2. *Consequential damages*—Damages resulting from special circumstances beyond the contract itself; the damages flow only from the consequences of a breach. For a party to recover consequential damages, the damages must be the foreseeable result of a breach of contract, and the breaching party must have known at the time the contract was formed that special circumstances existed that would cause the nonbreaching party to incur additional loss on breach of the contract. Also called special damages. 3. *Punitive damages*—Damages awarded to punish the breaching party. Usually not awarded in an action for breach of contract unless a tort is involved. 4. *Nominal damages*—Damages small in amount (such as one dollar) that are awarded when a breach has occurred but no actual damages have been suffered. Awarded only to establish that the defendant acted wrongfully. 5. *Liquidated damages*—Damages that may be specified in a contract as the amount to be paid to the nonbreaching party in the event the contract is breached in the future. Clauses providing for liquidated damages are enforced if the damages were difficult to estimate at the time the contract was formed and if the amount stipulated is reasonable. If construed to be a penalty, the clause will not be enforced.
Rescission and Restitution	1. *Rescission*—A remedy whereby a contract is canceled and the parties are restored to the original positions that they occupied prior to the transaction. Available when fraud, a mistake, duress, or failure of consideration is present. The rescinding party must give prompt notice of the rescission to the breaching party. 2. *Restitution*—When a contract is rescinded, both parties must make restitution to each other by returning the goods, property, or funds previously conveyed. Restitution prevents the unjust enrichment of parties.
Specific Performance	An equitable remedy calling for the performance of the act promised in the contract. This remedy is available only in special situations—such as those involving contracts for the sale of unique goods or land—and when monetary damages would be an inadequate remedy. Specific performance is not available as a remedy in breached contracts for personal services.
Reformation	An equitable remedy allowing a contract to be "reformed," or rewritten, to reflect the parties' true intentions. Available when an agreement is imperfectly expressed in writing.
Recovery Based on Quasi Contract	An equitable theory imposed by the courts to obtain justice and prevent unjust enrichment in a situation in which no enforceable contract exists. The party seeking recovery must show the following: 1. A benefit was conferred on the other party. 2. The party conferring the benefit did so with the expectation of being paid. 3. The benefit was not volunteered. 4. Retaining the benefit without paying for it would result in the unjust enrichment of the party receiving the benefit.
CONTRACT DOCTRINES RELATING TO REMEDIES	
Election of Remedies	A common law doctrine under which a nonbreaching party must choose one remedy from those available. This doctrine prevents double recovery. Under the UCC, in contracts for the sale of goods, remedies are cumulative.
Waiver of Breach	The nonbreaching party's knowing relinquishment of the legal right to require satisfactory and full performance is known as a waiver of breach. When a waiver of a breach of contract occurs, the party waiving the breach cannot take any later action on it.

CHAPTER SUMMARY—CONTINUED

Contract Provisions Limiting Remedies	A contract may provide that no damages (or only a limited amount of damages) can be recovered in the event the contract is breached. Clauses excluding liability for fraudulent or intentional injury or for illegal acts cannot be enforced. Clauses excluding liability for negligence may be enforced if both parties hold roughly equal bargaining power. Under the UCC, in contracts for the sale of goods, remedies may be limited.

CASES FOR ANALYSIS

Westlaw. You can access the full text of each case presented below by going to the Westlaw cases on this text's Web site at http://wbl-cs.westbuslaw.com. Each Westlaw case includes the names of all plaintiffs and defendants, the dates on which the case was argued and decided, a brief summary of the issues and decisions in the case, headnotes classifying the specific issues in the case according to the West Key Number System, and the court's opinion. Concurring and dissenting opinions, if any, are included as well.

CASE 17.1 MITIGATION OF DAMAGES

FUJITSU LTD. V. FEDERAL EXPRESS CORP.
United States Court of Appeals,
Second Circuit, 2001.
247 F.3d 423.

SPATT, District Judge:

* * * *

BACKGROUND

On May 30, 1996, Plaintiff-Appellee Fujitsu Limited ("Fujitsu") shipped a container of silicon wafers from Narita, Japan to Ross Technologies, Inc. ("Ross") in Austin, Texas, using Defendant-Appellant Federal Express [Corporation] ("FedEx") as the cargo carrier. Accompanying the container was an air waybill—a document serving as a bill of lading for goods transported by air—designated as "AWB3691," specifying the consignor and consignee, weight, contents, destination, and route of the container.

On May 31, 1996, the container arrived in Austin and was placed in a bonded cargo cage to await clearance through [the U.S. Customs Service] by the Customs Agent for Ross. FedEx does not release goods to their consignees until the goods actually have cleared customs and all import and customs duties have been paid. In this case, Ross' Customs Agent faxed a notification to FedEx that Ross was rejecting the shipment. Pursuant to FedEx's procedures, it contacted Fujitsu and Ross to determine what should be done with the cargo. * * *

According to a June 3, 1996 comment in the FedEx computer tracking system concerning a telephone call, Fujitsu orally instructed FedEx to return the goods to Japan. However, a separate document in the record, on Ross letterhead and dated June 4, 1996, indicates that Ross issued written instructions to FedEx to return the goods to Fujitsu in Japan and informed FedEx that Ross would incur all shipping charges. On July 27, 1996, after the return shipment was completed, FedEx sent an invoice billing Ross $493.00 for the return of the shipment to Japan. * * *

FedEx proceeded to prepare the goods for shipment back by re-labeling and moving the cargo from the customs cage to an outbound staging area. The goods were flown from Austin to the main FedEx hub in Memphis [Tennessee]. * * *

* * * *

The goods apparently left Austin in good condition, but sat in Memphis for a week before being shipped to Japan. On June 24, 1996, the shipment arrived in Japan. At that time, Fujitsu observed that the outer container was broken and covered with an oily substance which had permeated into some of the interior boxes. Fujitsu opened one of the interior boxes and discovered that the oily substance was also on the exterior of the sealed aluminum bags containing the wafers. Fujitsu did not open any of the bags to determine whether the oily substance had penetrated any of the bags.

Fujitsu reported the damage to FedEx immediately. FedEx eventually acknowledged that the damage occurred to the container while in its possession. At some point in July 1996, upon instructions from its insurance carrier, Fujitsu disposed of the container and wafers. FedEx had not requested an opportunity to inspect the wafers prior to that time.

Fujitsu then brought this action [in a federal district court] against FedEx grounded [in part on] breach of contract * * * . [The court] found FedEx liable to Fujitsu for damages in the amount of $726,640.

FedEx appeals * * * .

DISCUSSION

* * * *

* * * FedEx challenges the court's findings on the mitigation of damages by Fujitsu.

* * * *

While FedEx is correct that the record contains no evidence that the wafers themselves were damaged, there was sufficient evidence adduced to support a finding by the court that the shipment was a total loss because the residue on the outer packaging made it impossible to access the wafers. According to the testimony, the bags containing the wafers could only be opened in a specially designed and maintained "clean room" so as to prevent dust contamination. However, because the bags themselves were coated with the oily residue, they could not be brought into a clean room for inspection, as the residue itself would contaminate the clean room. Consequently, the trial court found that even if the wafers were undamaged, Fujitsu was unable to extract them from the bags in an operable condition. This Court can discern no difference between damage rendering the wafers inoperable and damage that prevents otherwise operable wafers from being used or salvaged.

* * * *

In addition, with regard to mitigation, the trial court's factual finding that efforts to salvage the wafers would have been prohibitively expensive also suffices to reject FedEx's argument that Fujitsu failed to mitigate its damages.

* * * *

CONCLUSION

We hold that * * * the trial court was not clearly erroneous in finding that Fujitsu suffered damages in the amount of $726,400 * * * .

AFFIRMED.

CASE 17.2 LIQUIDATED DAMAGES

ATEL FINANCIAL CORP. V. QUAKER COAL CO.

United States District Court,
Northern District of California, 2001.
132 F.Supp.2d 1233.

THELTON E. HENDERSON, District Judge.

* * * *

FACTUAL AND PROCEDURAL BACKGROUND

Plaintiff, Atel Financial Corporation ("Atel"), and defendant, Quaker Coal Company ("Quaker"), entered into a Master Lease Agreement ("the Lease") on October 22, 1993. Atel is a California corporation that leases heavy industrial equipment. Quaker is a Kentucky corporation that engages in coal mining. The Lease states that Atel would provide Quaker with approximately twenty (20) pieces of heavy mining equipment, such as dump trucks, wheel loaders, drills, and bulldozers. The Lease provided for separate schedules identifying each particular piece of equipment, the lease term for each piece, the commencement date, and the amount of basic rent. Five separate schedules were entered into which form the basis of the instant suit; these are identified as Schedules 1, 7, 8, 9, and 10.

From 1993 to 1997, the leasing activity appears to have gone relatively smoothly, with the equipment being provided and with timely rental payments being made. However, in December 1997, Quaker requested a moratorium [delay or temporary suspension] from all of its lessors for a period of time to permit Quaker to refinance its outstanding debt. Atel responded to the forbearance request with a series of nine conditions, contained in a letter of December 31, 1997. By letter dated February 14, 1998, Quaker accepted certain of the conditions, and remitted a payment of $91,229.66, bringing the lease current as of December 31, 1997.

* * * *

On May 12, 1998, Atel sent another letter to Quaker, entitled "Notice of an Event of Default and Demand * * * ." In this letter, Atel triggered enforcement of sections 4 and 9 of the Lease, which govern late payment and liquidated damages. * * * By letter of May 26, 1998, Quaker expressed surprise at Atel's actions, offered to "make every effort to satisfy the requests" that Atel had initially made, and included the January 1998 lease payments. * * *

Shortly thereafter, on May 29 and June 1, 1998, Quaker made two payments, amounting to $674,985.99. * * * On June 4, 1998, Atel wrote to Quaker, stating that Quaker's May 26 response was inadequate, and that Atel was now formally declaring Quaker in default and was demanding liquidated damages. Atel noted that while Quaker had made partial payment on its past due obligations in the amount of $674,985.99, there remained an outstanding past due balance of an equal amount, as well as $50,221.52 in late charges, and that Quaker had been in "continuous default of its payment obligations under the Lease for six months." * * * Atel also reiterated its demand for liquidated damages, adding its recognition that the amount would be reduced by all future payments or proceeds from the disposition of the assets.

In the third week of June, 1998, Quaker closed on its loan restructuring. Quaker then sent Atel a check for all outstanding invoices, in the amount of $583,756.33, on June 22, 1998, by overnight service.

The day after Quaker sent the check for all outstanding invoices, Atel filed a Complaint in [a California state court]. The Complaint contains a single cause of action for breach of contract, and seeks liquidated damages in an amount it calculates at $4,624,357. The case was removed to federal [district] court on the basis of diversity of citizenship * * * .

The parties agree that by the time of trial, all past due payments had been made. Furthermore, at least to the time of trial, Quaker has made timely payment on all of Atel's subsequent invoices. In sum, Quaker paid approximately $4.8 million for the use of equipment commencing in January 1998. Furthermore, the equipment relating to Schedule 1 has been returned to Atel, which in turn has sold it. Schedules 8 and 10 were renewed and the renewals remained in effect at the time of trial.

* * * *

DISCUSSION

* * * *

Section 9(e) of the Lease provides as follows:

> Upon the occurrence of an Event of Default, Lessor may at its option * * * (iii) recover from Lessee, as liquidated damages for loss of a bargain and not as a penalty, an amount equal to the present value of all monies to be paid by Lessee during the remaining Basic Term or any successive period then in effect, plus the present value of any balloon payment and the anticipated residual of the Equipment, calculated by discounting at the rate of six percent (6%) per annum compounded monthly, which payment shall become immediately due and payable * * * .

"Anticipated residual value" is the lessor's estimate of its remaining ownership value at the end of the lease transaction.

Section 9 additionally provides:

> In the event that Lessee shall have first paid to Lessor * * * the liquidated damages * * * the party having received such liquidated damages shall pay to Lessee * * * all rentals or proceeds received from any reletting of the Equipment during the balance of the Basic Term (after deduction of all expenses incurred in connection therewith) * * * Lessee shall in any event remain fully liable for reasonable damages as provided by law and for all costs * * * on account of default including * * * court costs and reasonable attorney's fees.

* * * [L]iquidated damages are enforceable if at the formation of the contract: (1) it was mutually recognized that damages from a breach would be impracticable or extremely difficult to determine with certainty; and (2) the amount or formula stipulated by the parties represented a reasonable endeavor to ascertain what such damages might be. The burden of proof is on Quaker, as the party seeking invalidation, to show that the provision was unreasonable under the circumstances existing at the time the contract was made.

A liquidated damages clause will generally be considered unreasonable, and hence unenforceable, if it bears no reasonable relationship to the range of actual damages that the parties could have anticipated would flow from a breach. An amount disproportionate to the anticipated actual damages is termed a "penalty." * * * [Emphasis added.]

* * * *

* * * [T]he formula for calculating liquidated damages in this case constitutes a penalty. By requiring a defaulting lessee to pay the present value of all monies to be paid by lessee during the remaining term of the lease, plus the anticipated residual value of the equipment, implementation of the liquidated damages clause would multiply Atel's likely actual damages many times over. While such a formula might be reasonable in the event of destruction to the equipment, where no future value in the equipment remains, it is highly disproportionate to the loss of only a limited number of loan payments.

* * * *

* * * [B]y failing to anticipate at the time of contracting the situation that now exists—i.e. continuation of a significant portion of the Lease by Quaker—the parties agreed to a liquidated damages provision that, by its literal terms, entitles Atel to an amount grossly disproportionate to its actual damages. Thus, at the time of the formation of the contract, the amount of actual damages that could have been anticipated from the instant situation would have been far below the amount that results from the formula used in the Lease. Put another way, while it was foreseeable at the time of contracting that the lessee might miss a number of monthly payments and that both parties would desire to continue and/or to renew the lease, would it have been reasonable to impose on the lessee the full value of the equipment which it had never expressed any intention to own? The Court believes that such a drastic measure is disproportionate to the range of damages that reasonably could have been anticipated. * * *

* * * *

In conclusion, * * * this Court finds that defendant has met its burden of proving that the liquidated damages provision in [Section] 9 of the Lease between Atel and Quaker was unreasonable under the circumstances existing at the time the contract was made. On that basis, the Court rules that the liquidated damages provision shall not be enforced.

* * * *

CONCLUSION

For the aforementioned reasons, and with good cause appearing, IT IS HEREBY ORDERED and ADJUDGED, * * * that plaintiff's demand for liquidated damages is DENIED, and that JUDGMENT shall be entered in favor of Defendant Quaker Coal Company.

IT IS SO ORDERED.

CASE 17.3 RECOVERY BASED ON QUASI CONTRACT

MAGLICA V. MAGLICA

California Court of Appeal,
Fourth District, Division 3, 1998.
66 Cal.App.4th 442,
66 Cal.App.4th 1367C,
78 Cal.Rptr.2d 101.

SILLS, P.J. [Presiding Judge].

* * * *

I. Introduction

This case forces us to confront the legal doctrine known as *"quantum meruit"* in the context of a case about an unmarried couple who lived together and worked in a business solely owned by one of them. *Quantum meruit* is a Latin phrase, meaning "as much as he deserves," and is based on the idea that someone should get paid for beneficial goods or services which he or she bestows on another.

* * * *

II. Facts

The important facts in this case may be briefly stated. Anthony Maglica, a Croatian immigrant, founded his own machine shop business, Mag Instrument, in 1955. He got divorced in 1971 and kept the business. That year he met Claire Halasz, an interior designer. They got on famously, and lived together, holding themselves out as man and wife—hence Claire began using the name Claire Maglica—but never actually got married. And, while they worked side by side building the business, Anthony never agreed—or at least the jury found Anthony never agreed—to give Claire a share of the business. When the business was incorporated in 1974 all shares went into Anthony's name. Anthony was the president and Claire was the secretary. They were paid equal salaries from the business after incorporation. In 1978 the business began manufacturing flashlights, and, thanks in part to some great ideas and hard work on Claire's part (e.g., coming out with a purse-sized flashlight in colors), the business boomed. Mag Instrument, Inc., is now worth hundreds of millions of dollars.

In 1992 Claire discovered that Anthony was trying to transfer stock to his children but not her, and the couple split up in October. In June 1993 Claire sued Anthony for, among other things, * * * *quantum meruit*. The case came to trial in the spring of 1994. The jury awarded $84 million * * * , finding that $84 million was the reasonable value of Claire's services.

III. Discussion

* * * *

* * * The absence of a contract between Claire and Anthony * * * would not preclude her recovery in *quantum meruit:* As every first year law student knows or should know, recovery in *quantum meruit* does not require a contract.

* * * The measure of recovery in *quantum meruit* is the reasonable value of the services rendered provided they were of direct benefit to the defendant.

The underlying idea behind *quantum meruit* is the law's distaste for unjust enrichment. *If one has received a benefit which one may not justly retain, one should restore the aggrieved party to his or her former position by return of the thing or its equivalent in money.* [Emphasis added.]

The idea that one must be benefited by the goods and services bestowed is thus integral to recovery in *quantum meruit;* hence courts have always required that the plaintiff have bestowed some benefit on the defendant as a prerequisite to recovery.

* * * But the threshold requirement that there be a benefit from the services can lead to confusion, as it did in the case before us. It is one thing to require that the defendant be benefited by services, it is quite another to measure the reasonable value of those services by the value by which the defendant was "benefited" as a result of them. *Contract price and the reasonable value of services rendered are two separate things; sometimes the reasonable value of services exceeds a contract price. And sometimes it does not.* [Emphasis added.]

At root, allowing *quantum meruit* recovery based on "resulting benefit" of services rather than the reasonable value of beneficial services affords the plaintiff the best of both contractual and quasi-contractual recovery. Resulting benefit is an open-ended standard, which, as we have mentioned earlier, can result in the plaintiff obtaining recovery amounting to *de facto* ownership in a business all out of reasonable relation to the value of services rendered. After all, a particular service timely rendered can have * * * disproportionate value to what it would cost on the open market.

* * * *

The jury instruction given here allows the value of services to depend on their impact on a defendant's business rather than their reasonable value. True, the services must be of benefit if there is to be any recovery at all; even so, the benefit is not necessarily related to the reasonable value of a particular set of services. Sometimes luck, sometimes the impact of others makes the difference. Some enterprises are successful; others less so. Allowing recovery based on resulting benefit would mean the law imposes an exchange of equity for services, and that can result in a windfall—as in the present case—or a serious shortfall in others. Equity-for-service compensation packages are extraordinary in the labor market, and always the result of specific bargaining. To impose such a measure of recovery would make a deal for the parties that they did not make themselves. If courts cannot use *quantum meruit* to change the terms of a contract which the parties did make, it follows that neither can they use *quantum meruit* to impose a highly generous and extraordinary contract that the parties did not make.

* * * *

Telling the jury that it could measure the value of Claire's services by "[t]he value by which Defendant has benefited as a result of [her] services" was error. It allowed the jury to value Claire's services as having bought her a *de facto* ownership interest in a business whose owner never agreed to give her an interest. On remand, that part of the jury instruction must be dropped.

* * * *

Disposition

The judgment is reversed. The case is remanded for a new trial.

Case Problems

17–1. Vrgora, a general contractor, entered into a contract with the Los Angeles Unified School District (LAUSD) to construct an "automotive service shed" and an enclosed room outfitted with an electronic vehicle performance tester. The contract specified a price of $167,195.09, a completion time of 250 days from commencement, and a liquidated damages clause of $100 per day for late completion. Vrgora began construction on January 31, 1977, with an expected completion date of July 29, 1977. Delays in the project arose when the manufacturer of the tester did not receive approval for the tester until September 23, 1977 (a delay of over six months). The tester arrived on November 15, 1977, but because of a conflict over payment, the manufacturer removed the tester. On payment, the manufacturer redelivered the tester on December 2, 1977, and Vrgora completed the project on May 2, 1978. LAUSD assessed $20,700 as liquidated damages and eventually brought an action against Vrgora to collect the assessed amount, which Vrgora refused to pay. Given the circumstances of this case, will the court require Vrgora to pay the liquidated damages demanded by LAUSD? [*Vrgora v. Los Angeles Unified School District,* 152 Cal.App.3d 1178, 200 Cal.Rptr. 130 (1984)]

17–2. Teachers Insurance and Annuity Association of America (T.I.A.A.) agreed to lend City Centre One Associates $14.5 million for the construction of an office building in Salt Lake City. City Centre, however, refused to go through with the closing on the loan, and T.I.A.A. sued for specific performance of the contract. Courts have in the past granted specific performance of lending agreements when requested by the *borrower* if failure to go through with the loan would result in irreparable injury to the borrower, which may be unable to secure alternate financing. Should T.I.A.A., as a *lender,* succeed in its request for specific performance? Explain. [*City Centre One Associates v. Teachers Insurance and Annuity Association,* 656 F.Supp. 658 (D.Utah 1987)]

17–3. Roger and Lois Robinson bought a mobile home and lot subject to a promissory note secured by a deed of trust in favor of Delores Dorn and Elizabeth Britt. The note provided for monthly payments. The deed of trust provided that "by accepting payment of any sum secured hereby after its due date" Dorn and Britt would "not waive [their] right either to require prompt payment when due of all other sums so secured or to declare default for failure so to pay." For the first six months, none of the Robinsons' payments was more than a week late. Over the next seven months, their payments were consistently, on average, one or two weeks late. After they had missed two consecutive payments without explanation, Dorn and Britt initiated foreclosure proceedings. The Robinsons argued that since Dorn and Britt had accepted the previous late payments, they were required to give notice before filing to foreclose. Had Dorn and Britt, by their acceptance of late payments, waived their right to prompt payment, notwithstanding the nonwaiver clause in the deed of trust? Explain. [*Dorn v. Robinson,* 158 Ariz. 279, 762 P.2d 566 (1988)]

17–4. Southwestern Bell Telephone Co. executed a license agreement that gave United Video Cablevision of St. Louis, Inc., authority to construct and operate a cable television system using poles and conduits owned by Bell. The agreement specified that United Video would make a down payment for rent and telephone wire service. By law, Bell was required to locate and mark underground facilities, on request, before any excavation so that no disruption of the telephone lines would take place. Bell had provided this service free of charge for many years, and it performed the service for United Video before United Video installed its lines. After United Video had substantially completed its installation, Bell notified the company of its intention to charge for the locating and marking service. The charge was not a part of the oral or written contract, and United Video refused to pay. Bell sought to recover based on *quantum meruit.* Discuss whether Bell should succeed in its claim. [*Southwestern Bell Telephone Co. v. United Video Cablevision of St. Louis, Inc.,* 737 S.W.2d 474 (Mo.App. 1987)]

17–5. W. A. and Lola Dunn were payees of several installment promissory notes issued by General Equities of Iowa, Ltd. Each note contained an acceleration clause that permitted the holder of the note to accelerate and demand full payment of the note should any installment not be paid when due. Over a period of time the Dunns accepted late installment payments from

General Equities without invoking the acceleration clause. General Equities made a further late payment. The Dunns returned the General Equities check and demanded payment of the entire balance, with interest, in accordance with the acceleration clause. General Equities claimed that the acceptance of the previous late payments constituted a waiver of the Dunns' right to invoke the acceleration clause. Discuss whether General Equities was correct. [*Dunn v. General Equities of Iowa, Ltd.*, 319 N.W.2d 515 (Iowa 1982)]

17–6. Patricia Elsken leased an apartment in a large apartment complex. She signed a "Residential Alarm Security Agreement" in which she agreed to have security services provided by Network Multi-Family Security Corp. The contract contained a clause limiting Network's liability to $250 for any injury or damage caused by a failure of the alarm service or by Network's negligent performance. The agreement stated, in all capital letters, that Network was not an insurer and that "resident assumes all responsibility for obtaining insurance to cover losses of all types." The agreement also provided that "Resident may obtain from Network increased liability by paying an additional charge directly to Network." Network received an alarm signal indicating intrusion into Elsken's apartment at 10:33 A.M. on April 11, 1988. Network called Elsken's apartment and, receiving no answer, called the apartment manager instead of going to Elsken's apartment. The manager told Network to disregard the alarm. Later that day, Elsken was found dead in her apartment, the victim of an apparent homicide. The administrator of Elsken's estate brought an action for damages against Network, alleging negligence. Will the court hold that the contractual limitation of liability for personal injury is valid and enforceable? Discuss. [*Elsken v. Network Multi-Family Security Corp.*, 838 P.2d 1007 (Okla. 1992)]

17–7. Ballard was working for El Dorado Tire Co. He was discharged, and he sued El Dorado for breach of the employment contract. The trial court awarded damages to Ballard, and El Dorado appealed. In the appeal, El Dorado claimed that the trial court had failed to reduce Ballard's damages by the amount that he might have earned in other employment during the remainder of the period covered by the breached contract. El Dorado introduced as evidence the fact that there was an extremely low rate of unemployment for professional technicians and managers with Ballard's qualifications. The implication was that Ballard had not taken advantage of the opportunity to mitigate his damages. Was El Dorado correct? Explain. [*Ballard v. El Dorado Tire Co.*, 512 F.2d 901 (5th Cir. 1975)]

17–8. Dewerff was a teacher and basketball coach for Unified School District No. 315. The employment contract included a clause that read, in part: "Penalty for breaking contracts: . . . In all cases where a teacher under contract fails to honor the full term of his or her contract, a lump sum of $400 is to be collected if the contract is broken before August 1." Dewerff resigned on June 28, 1978, and he was told that the school would accept his resignation on his payment of the $400 stipulated in the contract. When Dewerff refused to make the $400 payment, the school district sued for $400 as "liquidated damages" on the basis of the contract clause. Dewerff argued that the contract provision was a penalty clause and unenforceable in this situation. Is Dewerff correct? Discuss. [*Unified School District No. 315, Thomas County v. Dewerff*, 6 Kan.App.2d 77, 626 P.2d 1206 (1981)]

17–9. Westinghouse Electric Corp. entered into a contract with New Jersey Electric to manufacture and install a turbine generator for producing electricity. The contract price was over $10 million. The parties engaged in three years of negotiations and bargaining before they agreed on a suitable contract. The ultimate contract provided, among other things, that Westinghouse would not be liable for any injuries to the utility's property or to its customers or employees. Westinghouse warranted only that it would repair any defects in workmanship and materials appearing within one year of installation. After installation, part of New Jersey Electric's plant was damaged and several of its employees were injured because of a defect in the turbine. New Jersey Electric sued Westinghouse, claiming that Westinghouse was liable for the damages because the exculpatory provisions in the contract were unconscionable. How will the court rule, and why? [*Royal Indemnity Co. v. Westinghouse Electric Corp.*, 385 F.Supp. 520 (S.D.N.Y. 1974)]

17–10. Kerr Steamship Co. delivered to Radio Corp. of America (RCA) a twenty-nine-word coded message to be sent to Kerr's agent in Manila. The message included instructions on loading cargo onto one of Kerr's vessels. Kerr's profits on the carriage of the cargo were to be about $6,600. RCA mislaid the coded message, and it was never sent. Kerr sued RCA for the $6,600 in profits that it lost because RCA never sent the message. Can Kerr recover? Explain. [*Kerr Steamship Co. v. Radio Corp. of America*, 245 N.Y. 284, 157 N.E. 140 (1927)]

17–11. Jeffrey Stambovsky was a resident of New York City. While looking at houses in the village of Nyack, New York, Stambovsky came across a riverfront Victorian house that he liked. He purchased it, only to discover later that the house had a local reputation for being haunted. The seller, Helen Ackley, had promoted this reputation herself by reporting to the *Reader's Digest* in 1977 and to the local press in 1982 that the house was haunted. By 1989, the house was included in a five-home walking tour of Nyack because of the purported presence of ghosts in the house. There was even a newspaper article describing it as "a riverfront Victorian (with ghost)." Stambovsky brought an action to rescind the contract, contending that the house's reputation for being haunted impaired the value of the property. What will the court decide? Discuss fully. [*Stambovsky v. Ackley*, 169 A.D.2d 254, 572 N.Y.S.2d 672 (1991)]

17–12. The Ivanovs, who were of Russian origin, agreed to purchase the Sobels' home for $300,000. A $30,000 earnest money deposit was placed in the trust account of Kotler Realty, Inc., the broker facilitating the transaction. Tiasia Buliak, one of Kotler's salespersons, negotiated the sale because she spoke fluent Russian. To facilitate the closing without the Ivanovs' having to be present, Buliak suggested they form a Florida corporation, place the cash necessary to close the sale in a corporate account, and give her authority to draw checks against it. The Ivanovs did as Buliak had suggested. Before the closing date of the sale, Buliak absconded with all of the closing money, which caused the transaction to collapse. Subsequently, because the Ivanovs had defaulted, Kotler Realty delivered the $30,000 earnest money deposit in its trust account to the Sobels. The Ivanovs then sued the Sobels, seeking to recover the $30,000. Was the clause providing that the seller could retain the earnest money if the buyer defaulted an enforceable liquidated damages clause or an unenforceable penalty clause? Discuss. [*Ivanov v. Sobel*, 654 So.2d 991 (Fla.App.3d 1995)]

17–13. Patricia Fair worked in a Red Lion restaurant. The employee manual provided that "[d]uring a medical leave of absence, every effort will be made to keep a position available for the employee's return." After sustaining an injury that was unrelated to her work, Fair was given a month's medical leave. On her return, she asked for, and was granted, additional time to submit a physician's release to return to work. She provided the release within the extra time, but before she went back to work she was terminated, effective as of her original return date. When she attempted to resolve the matter, Red Lion offered to reinstate her in her old job. Her response was to set several conditions for a return, including a different job. Red Lion said no, and Fair did not return. Fair filed a suit in a Colorado state court against Red Lion, alleging in part breach of contract. Red Lion argued that by rejecting its offer of reinstatement, Fair failed to mitigate her damages. Assuming that Red Lion was in breach of contract, did Fair fail to mitigate her damages? Explain. [*Fair v. Red Lion Inn, L.P.*, 943 P.2d 431 (Colo. 1997)]

17–14. In December 1992, Beys Specialty Contracting, Inc., contracted with New York City's Metropolitan Transportation Authority (MTA) for construction work. Beys subcontracted with Hudson Iron Works, Inc., to perform some of the work for $175,000. Under the terms of the subcontract, within seven days after the MTA approved Hudson's work and paid Beys, Beys would pay Hudson. The MTA had not yet approved any of Hudson's work when Beys submitted to the MTA invoices dated May 20 and June 21, 1993. Without proof that the MTA had paid Beys on those invoices, Hudson submitted to Beys an invoice dated September 10, claiming that the May 20 and June 21 invoices incorporated its work. Beys refused to pay, Hudson stopped working, and Beys paid another contractor $25,083 more to complete the job than if Hudson had completed its subcontract. Hudson filed a suit in a New York state court to collect on its invoice. Beys filed a counterclaim for the additional money spent to complete Hudson's job. In which firm's favor should the court rule, and why? What might be the measure of damages, if any? [*Hudson Iron Works, Inc. v. Beys Specialty Contracting, Inc.*, 691 N.Y.S.2d 132 (N.Y.A.D., 2 Dept. 1999)]

17–15. Ms. Vuylsteke, a single mother with three children, lived in Portland, Oregon. Cynthia Broan also lived in Oregon until she moved to New York City to open and operate an art gallery. Broan contacted Vuylsteke with an offer to manage the gallery under a one-year contract for an annual salary of $72,000. To begin work, Vuylsteke relocated to New York. As part of the move, Vuylsteke transferred custody of her children to her ex-husband, who lived in London, England. In accepting the job, Vuylsteke also forfeited her ex-husband's alimony and child-support payments, including unpaid amounts of nearly $30,000. Before Vuylsteke started work, Broan repudiated the contract. Unable to find employment for more than an annual salary of $25,000, Vuylsteke moved to London to be near her children. Vuylsteke filed a suit in an Oregon state court against Broan, seeking damages for breach of contract. Should the court hold, as Broan argued, that Vuylsteke did not take reasonable steps to mitigate her damages? Why, or why not? [*Vuylsteke v. Broan*, 172 Or.App. 74, 17 P.3d 1072 (2001)]

E-LINKS

For updated links to resources available on the Web, as well as a variety of other materials, visit this text's Web site at

http://wbl-cs.westbuslaw.com

The following sites offer information on contract law, including breach of contract and remedies:

http://www.nolo.com/category/cm_home.html

http://www.law.cornell.edu/topics/contracts.html

LEGAL RESEARCH EXERCISES ON THE WEB

Go to http://wbl-cs.westbuslaw.com, the Web site that accompanies this text. Select "Interactive Study Center," and then click on "Chapter 17." There you will find the following Internet research exercise that you can perform to learn more about breach of contract and damages:

Activity 17–1: Contract Damages and Contract Theory

Focus on Legal Reasoning

Kline v. Turner

Introduction

In Chapter 13, we discussed fraudulent misrepresentation in the context of entering into contracts. As with other causes of action, suits based on fraud are subject to statutes of limitations, which are covered in Chapter 16. In this *Focus on Legal Reasoning,* we examine *Kline v. Turner,*[1] a recent decision that concerned the application of a statute of limitations to a suit involving allegations of fraud.

Case Background

Thomas Kline, a talent agent, entered into an oral contract through Bryan Turner with Priority Records, Inc., for the services of a musical group, "Miss Allen and Nem." Priority agreed to immediately issue a check payable to Kline for $50,000, with an additional $50,000 to be paid after the completion of a master recording. On August 31, 1990, Kline sent a business associate, Marion Knight, to pick up the first check. When Knight did not soon return, Kline called Priority and learned that at Knight's insistence the check was made payable to Knight. Kline was told that Knight had said this was "okay with Mr. Kline." When Kline objected, Priority assured Kline that it would stop payment on the check.[2] On Monday, Priority told Kline that the check was cashed before payment was stopped. Later, Knight confronted Kline, showed him a gun, and told him to "back off." Fearful of Knight and assuming that Priority had either been intimidated or believed it appropriate to make the check payable to Knight, Kline did nothing.

In 1996, Kline learned that Priority and Knight had entered into a contract on August 31, 1990, for the services of "Miss Allen and Nem." Kline also saw a copy of the $50,000 check given to Knight on that date. A stamp on the check indicated that it was cashed on September 4, not on August 31. In 1999, Kline filed a suit in a California state court against Priority and Turner, alleging fraud. The defendants filed a motion for summary judgment, arguing that the suit was barred by a three-year state statute of limitations. Kline asserted that his suit was within the limitations period because he was not on notice of the fraud until 1996. The trial court granted the motion for summary judgment, and Kline appealed to a state intermediate appellate court.

1. 87 Cal.App.4th 1369, 105 Cal.Rptr.2d 699 (4 Dist. 2001).

2. Stop-payment orders on checks are discussed in detail in Chapter 27.

Majority Opinion

BENKE, Acting P.J.

* * * *

DISCUSSION

Kline argues the trial court erred in determining his causes of action time barred. He contends the date of the accrual of his causes of action is a factual issue and should be decided at trial.

A. *Standard of Review*

A motion for summary judgment is properly granted if the papers submitted show there is no triable issue as to any material fact and the moving party is entitled to a judgment as a matter of law. A defendant moving for summary judgment must show either one or more essential elements of the plaintiff's cause of action cannot be separately established or there is an affirmative defense which bars recovery. If the plaintiff fails to set forth specific facts showing a triable issue of material fact as to that cause of action or defense, summary judgment must be granted.

A three-step analysis is employed in ruling on motions for summary judgment. First, the court identifies the issues framed by the pleadings. Next, the court determines, when the moving party is the defendant, whether it has produced evidence showing one or more of the elements of the cause of action cannot be established or there is a complete defense to that cause of action. If the defendant does so, the burden shifts to the plaintiff to show the existence of triable issue of material fact as to that cause of action or defense.

We independently review the parties' papers supporting and opposing the motion, using the same method of analysis as the trial court. Essentially, we assume the role of the trial court and apply the same rules and standards.

B. *Statute of Limitations*

An action for relief on the grounds of fraud or mistake must be commenced within three years. However, such action is not deemed accrued until the discovery, by the aggrieved party, of the facts constituting the fraud or mistake. The courts interpret discovery in this context to mean not when the plaintiff became aware of the specific wrong alleged, but when the plaintiff suspected or should have suspected that an injury was caused by wrongdoing. *The statute of limitations begins to run when the plaintiff has information which would put a reasonable person on inquiry. A plaintiff need not be aware of the specific facts necessary to establish a claim since they can be developed in pretrial discovery.* Wrong and wrongdoing in this context are understood in their lay and not legal senses. [Emphasis added.]

* * * Under this rule constructive and presumed notice or knowledge are equivalent to knowledge. So, when the plaintiff has notice or information of circum-

stances to put a reasonable person on inquiry, or has the opportunity to obtain knowledge from sources open to her investigation (such as public records or corporation books), the statute commences to run.

Generally, statute of limitations issues raise questions of fact that must be tried, however, when the uncontradicted facts are susceptible of only one legitimate inference summary judgment is proper.

C. *Analysis*

The trial court correctly found Kline's lawsuit was time barred. The only legitimate inference based on the uncontroverted facts is that in September 1990 a reasonable person in Kline's position would conclude he was injured as the result not only of Knight's wrongdoing but Priority's as well. Priority had agreed to pay Kline $50,000 in the form of a check made payable to him. On the representation of Knight, who was acting merely as Kline's courier, Priority's staff, without clearing the change with Kline, gave Knight Kline's $50,000. Doing so was wrong and injurious in both a lay and legal sense. Kline was thus on inquiry. Discovery and/or investigation concerning the events would have revealed the fraud and the statute of limitations had begun to run.

The dissent argues our application of *Jolly [v. Eli Lilly & Co.,* 44 Cal.3d 1103, 245 Cal.Rptr. 658, 751 P.2d 923 (1988)] is insufficiently discriminating. Based on *Snow v. A.H.Robins Co.,* 165 Cal.App.3d 120, 211 Cal.Rptr. 271 (1985), it contends it is not the suspicion of a general wrong but rather the suspicion of a particular wrong that is crucial. In *Snow* the court found time barred negligence and products liability causes of action but not a fraud cause of action. The court so decided since in its view while the plaintiff was almost immediately on inquiry as to the negligence and products liability causes of action, she had no reason to suspect fraud until a much later date. The court concluded the fraud cause of action did not accrue until that later time.

We first note *Jolly* was decided three years after *Snow.* We agree with the dissent that *Jolly's* language defining the discovery rule is general and expansive but disagree the language applies only to the facts of that case, i.e., a cause of action accrues when the wrong is suspected even if its exact cause or the identity of the wrongdoer is unknown. We conclude the language is also applicable to ignorance concerning the specific causes of action arising from the wrong.

In any event, even if we were to accept the dissent's application of [the *Snow* case], we would still conclude the statute of limitations bars this action. We conclude as a matter of law that Kline was reasonably on inquiry that Priority was engaged in fraud. Priority had done an inexplicable act. With an agreement that Priority would pay him $50,000, it instead made the check out to Kline's courier. It told Kline it did so based on the courier's representation such a change was with Kline's approval. It did this without attempting to notify Kline there had been a change in plan. Kline should reasonably have suspected a possible explanation for Priority's action was something other than negligence. Kline's contract with Priority involved a continuing relationship between Kline, Priority and Miss Allen and Nem. A change in the representation of Miss Allen and Nem could not have been lost on Kline. Kline was on inquiry notice. Thus, the fraud cause of action accrued in 1990 and the fraud cause of action was time barred.

We also note Kline's claimed fear of Knight is of no legal consequence. The present case deals with a suit against Turner and Priority. When Kline discovered facts which led him to believe he had been defrauded by them, he sued, albeit not promptly. Kline asserts that until he discovered he had been defrauded by Turner and Priority, he believed they were also victims of Knight. However, this assertion does not advance his position. That Knight may have fooled Turner and Priority does not mean they had not, in both a lay and legal sense, also wronged Kline. Kline was on inquiry in 1990 concerning the actions of Turner and Priority. His suit for fraud filed against them in 1999 was time barred.

The judgment is affirmed.

QUESTIONS FOR ANALYSIS

1. **Legal Analysis.** In its opinion, the court cites *Jolly v. Eli Lilly & Co.*, 44 Cal.3d 1103, 245 Cal.Rptr. 658, 751 P.2d 923 (1988); and *Snow v. A.H.Robins Co.*, 165 Cal.App.3d 120, 211 Cal.Rptr. 271 (1985) (see the *E-Links* feature at the end of Chapter 2 for instructions on how to access the opinions of state courts). Why did the *Kline* court refer to these cases? With this purpose in mind, how do the facts and the holdings of the *Kline, Jolly,* and *Snow* cases compare?

2. **Legal Reasoning.** What was the plaintiff's major argument? Why did the court conclude that this argument was invalid?

3. **International Considerations.** How might the decision in this case affect the manner in which foreign parties do business in the United States?

4. **Implications for the Business Manager.** Would the result in this case have been different if the parties to the original contract had put their agreement in writing?

WESTLAW ONLINE RESEARCH

Westlaw. Go to this text's companion Web site, at http://wbl-cs.westbuslaw.com, and click on the Westlaw icon. Use your special password to access the full text of this case, including the dissenting opinions. Read through the case, and then answer the following questions.

1. Compare the conclusion of the majority to that of the dissent. What arguments does the dissent apply against the majority's conclusion? What legal sources does the dissent cite to support its position?
2. Consider the last headnote with regard to the related portion of the Court's opinion and to the other headnotes. How do the headnotes differ? What is an advantage of the last headnote compared to the others?
3. In light of the circumstances of the *Kline* case, what is a possible ethical basis for the majority's holding? What is an ethical basis for the dissent's disagreement with the majority's position?

UNIT THREE

Domestic and International Sales and Lease Contracts

CONTENTS

CHAPTER 18
The Formation of Sales and Lease Contracts

When we turn to contracts for the sale and lease of goods, we move away from common law principles and into the area of statutory law. State statutory law governing sales and lease transactions is based on the Uniform Commercial Code (UCC), which, as mentioned in Chapter 1, has been adopted as law by all states.[1] Relevant sections of the UCC are noted in the following discussion of sales and lease contracts. You should refer to Appendix B in the back of the book, which presents the most recent version of the UCC, while examining these notations.

We open this chapter with a discussion of the historical development of sales and lease law and the UCC's significance as a legal landmark. We then look at the scope of the UCC's Article 2 (on sales) and Article 2A (on leases) as a background to the topic of this chapter, which is the formation of contracts for the sale and lease of goods. Because international sales transactions are increasingly commonplace in the business world, the chapter concludes with an examination of the United Nations Convention on Contracts for the International Sale of Goods (CISG), which governs international sales contracts.

At the time UCC Article 2 was drafted, e-commerce as it exists today was not yet even envisioned. Thus, Article 2 does not provide specifically for electronic contracts. Nonetheless, Article 2's requirements relating to the formation of sales contracts apply to contracts formed online as well. We will discuss how the UCC (and other laws) apply to electronic contracts in Chapter 23.

1. Louisiana had not adopted Articles 2 and 2A, however.

SECTION 1

The Uniform Commercial Code

In the early years of this nation, sales law varied from state to state, and this made multistate sales contracts difficult. The problems became especially troublesome in the late nineteenth century as multistate contracts became the norm. For this reason, numerous attempts were made to produce a uniform body of laws relating to commercial transactions. The National Conference of Commissioners on Uniform State Laws (NCCUSL) drafted two uniform ("model") acts that were widely adopted by the states: the Uniform Negotiable Instruments Law (1896) and the Uniform Sales Act (1906). Several other proposed uniform acts followed, although most were not as widely adopted.

In the 1940s, the need to integrate the half-dozen or so uniform acts covering commercial transactions into a single, comprehensive body of statutory law was recognized. The NCCUSL developed the Uniform Commercial Code (UCC) to serve that purpose. First issued in 1949, the UCC facilitates commercial transactions by making the laws governing sales and lease contracts clearer, simpler, and more readily applicable to the numerous difficulties that can arise during such transactions.

COMPREHENSIVE COVERAGE OF THE UCC

The UCC is the single most comprehensive codification of the broad spectrum of laws involved in a total commercial transaction. The UCC views the entire "commercial transaction for the sale of and payment for goods" as a single legal occurrence having numerous facets.

As an example, first look at the titles of the articles of the UCC in Appendix B. Now consider a consumer who buys a deluxe, side-by-side refrigerator with an icemaker from an appliance store and agrees to pay for it on an installment plan. Several articles of the UCC can be applied to this single commercial transaction. Because there is a contract for the sale of goods, Article 2 will apply. If a check is given as the down payment on the purchase price, it will be negotiated and ultimately passed through one or more banks for collection. This process is the subject matter of Article 3, Negotiable Instruments, and Article 4, Bank Deposits and Collections. If the appliance store extends credit to the consumer through the installment plan, and if it retains a lien on the refrigerator (the collateral), then Article 9, Secured Transactions, will be applicable.

Suppose, in addition, that the appliance company must first obtain the refrigerator from its manufacturer's warehouse, after which it is to be delivered by common carrier to the consumer. The storage and shipment of goods are the subject matter of Article 7, Documents of Title. If the appliance company arranges to pay the manufacturer, located in another state, for the refrigerator supplied, a letter of credit, which is the subject matter of Article 5, may be used. Thus, the UCC attempts to provide a consistent and integrated framework of rules to deal with all the phases *ordinarily arising* in a commercial sales transaction from start to finish.

Two articles of the UCC seem not to apply to the "ordinary" commercial sales transaction. Article 6, Bulk Transfers, involves merchants who sell off the major part of their inventory (sometimes leaving creditors unpaid). Because bulk sales do not ordinarily arise in a commercial sales transaction, most states have repealed Article 6 entirely, although some states have adopted the revised version of Article 6 (see Appendix B). Article 8, Investment Securities, deals with transactions involving certain negotiable securities (stocks and bonds), transactions that do not involve a sale of (or payment for) *goods*. The subject matter of Articles 6 and 8, however, was considered by the UCC's drafters to be related *sufficiently* to commercial transactions to warrant the inclusion of these articles in the UCC.

Periodic Revisions of the UCC

Various articles and sections of the UCC are periodically changed or supplemented to clarify certain rules or to establish new rules when changes in business customs have rendered the existing UCC provisions inapplicable. For example, because of the increasing importance of leases of goods in the commercial context, Article 2A, governing leases, was added to the UCC. To clarify the rights of parties to commercial fund transfers, particularly electronic fund transfers, Article 4A was issued. Articles 3 and 4, covering negotiable instruments and banking, underwent a significant revision in the 1990s, as did Articles 5, 8, and 9. Because of other changes in business and in the law, the NCCUSL has recommended the repeal of Article 6, as mentioned earlier, and has offered a revised Article 6 to those states that prefer not to repeal it. Currently, the NCCUSL is in the process of revising Articles 2 and 2A. When those are complete, Article 1 is scheduled for revision.

SECTION 2

The Scope of Article 2—The Sale of Goods

Article 2 of the UCC governs **sales contracts**, or contracts for the sale of goods. To facilitate commercial transactions, Article 2 modifies some of the common law contract requirements that were discussed in the previous chapters. To the extent that it has not been modified by the UCC, however, the common law of contracts also applies to sales contracts. For example, the common law requirements for a valid contract—agreement (offer and acceptance), consideration, capacity, and legality—that were summarized in Chapter 9 and discussed at length in Chapters 10 through 12 are also applicable to sales contracts. Thus, you should reexamine these common law principles when studying the law of sales.

In general, the rule is that whenever there is a conflict between a common law contract rule and the UCC, the UCC controls. In other words, when a UCC provision addresses a certain issue, the UCC governs; when the UCC is silent, the common law governs. The relationship between general contract law and the law governing sales of goods is illustrated in Exhibit 18–1 on the following page.

In regard to Article 2, you should keep in mind two things. First, Article 2 deals with the sale of

EXHIBIT 18–1 LAW GOVERNING CONTRACTS

This exhibit graphically illustrates the relationship between general contract law and the law governing contracts for the sale of goods. Sales contracts are not governed exclusively by Article 2 of the Uniform Commercial Code but are also governed by general contract law whenever it is relevant and has not been modified by the UCC.

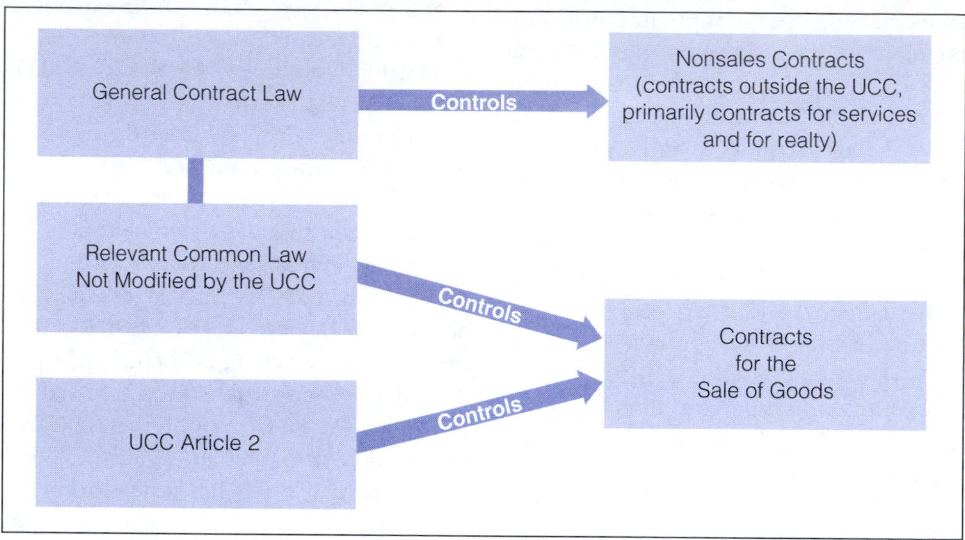

goods; it does not deal with real property (real estate), services, or intangible property such as stocks and bonds. Thus, if the subject matter of a dispute is goods, the UCC governs. If it is real estate or services, the common law applies. Second, in some cases, the rules may vary quite a bit, depending on whether the buyer or the seller is a *merchant.* We look now at how the UCC defines a *sale, goods,* and *merchant status.*

WHAT IS A SALE?

Section 2–102 of the UCC states that Article 2 "applies to transactions in goods." This implies a broad scope—covering gifts, bailments (temporary deliveries of personal property, discussed in Chapter 46), and purchases of goods. In this chapter, however, we treat Article 2 as being applicable only to an actual sale (as would most authorities and courts). The UCC defines a **sale** as "the passing of title from the seller to the buyer for a price," where *title* refers to the formal right of ownership of property [UCC 2–106(1)]. The price may be payable in money or in other goods, services, or realty (real estate).

WHAT ARE GOODS?

To be characterized as a *good,* an item of property must be *tangible,* and it must be *movable.* **Tangible property** has physical existence—it can be touched or seen. Intangible property—such as corporate stocks and bonds, patents and copyrights, and ordinary contract rights—have only conceptual existence and thus do not come under Article 2. A *movable* item can be carried from place to place. Hence, real estate is excluded from Article 2.

Two areas of dispute arise in determining whether the object of the contract is goods and thus whether Article 2 is applicable. One problem concerns *goods associated with real estate,* such as crops or timber, and the other concerns contracts involving a combination of *goods and services.*

Goods Associated with Real Estate. Goods associated with real estate often fall within the scope of Article 2. Section 2–107 provides the following rules:

1. A contract for the sale of minerals or the like (including oil and gas) or a structure (such as a building) is a contract for the sale of goods if *severance,* or separation, is to be made by the *seller.* If the *buyer* is

to sever (separate) the minerals or structures from the land, the contract is considered to be a sale of real estate governed by the principles of real property law, not the UCC.

2. A sale of growing crops or timber to be cut is a contract for the sale of goods *regardless of who severs them.*

3. Other "things attached" to realty but capable of severance without material harm to the land are considered to be goods *regardless of who severs them.*[2] Examples of "things attached" that are severable without harm to realty are a window air conditioner in a house and stools in a restaurant. Thus, removal of one of these things would be considered a sale of goods. The test is whether removal will cause substantial harm to the real property to which the item is attached.

Goods and Services Combined. In cases in which goods and services are combined, courts disagree. For example, is the furnishing of blood to a patient during an operation a "sale of goods" or the "performance of a medical service"? Some courts say it is a good; others say it is a service. The UCC does stipulate, however, that serving food or drink to be consumed either on or off restaurant premises is a "sale of goods," at least for the purpose of an implied warranty of merchantability (to be explained in Chapter 22) [UCC 2–314(1)]. Other special cases are also explicitly characterized as goods by the UCC, including unborn animals and rare coins.

Whether the transaction in question involves the sale of goods or services is important, because the majority of courts treat services as being excluded by the UCC. If the transaction is not covered by the UCC, then UCC provisions, including those relating to implied warranties, will not apply.

Westlaw. See Case 18.1 at the end of this chapter. To view the full, unedited case from Westlaw,® go to this text's Web site at **http://wbl-cs.westbuslaw.com**.

WHO IS A MERCHANT?

Article 2 governs the sale of goods in general. It applies to sales transactions between all buyers and sellers. In a limited number of instances, however, the UCC presumes that in certain phases of sales transactions involving merchants, special business standards ought to be imposed because of the merchants' relatively high degree of commercial expertise.[3] Such standards do not apply to the casual or inexperienced seller or buyer ("consumer"). Section 2–104 defines three ways in which merchant status can arise:

1. A merchant is a person who *deals in goods of the kind* involved in the sales contract. Thus, a retailer, a wholesaler, or a manufacturer is a merchant of those goods sold in the business. A merchant for one type of goods is not necessarily a merchant for another type. For example, a sporting-equipment retailer is a merchant when selling tennis equipment but not when selling a used computer.
2. A merchant is a person who, by occupation, holds himself or herself out as having knowledge and skill unique to the practices or goods involved in the transaction. This broad definition may include banks or universities as merchants.
3. A person who *employs a merchant as a broker, agent, or other intermediary* has the status of merchant in that transaction. Hence, if a "gentleman farmer" who ordinarily does not run the farm hires a broker to purchase or sell livestock, the farmer is considered a merchant in the transaction.

In summary, a person is a **merchant** when he or she, acting in a mercantile capacity, possesses or uses an expertise specifically related to the goods being sold. This basic distinction is not always clear-cut. For example, courts in some states have determined that farmers may be merchants, while courts in other states have determined that the drafters of the UCC did not intend to include farmers as merchants.

SECTION 3

The Scope of Article 2A—Leases

n the past few decades, leases of personal property (goods) have become increasingly common. Consumers and business firms lease automobiles,

2. The UCC avoids the term *fixtures* here because of the numerous definitions of the word. A fixture is anything so firmly or permanently attached to land or to a building as to become a part of it. Once personal property becomes a fixture, it is governed by real estate law. See Chapter 46.

3. The provisions that apply only to merchants deal principally with the Statute of Frauds, firm offers, confirmatory memoranda, warranties, and contract modification. These special rules reflect expedient business practices commonly known to merchants in the commercial setting. They will be discussed later in this chapter.

industrial equipment, items for use in the home (such as floor polishers), and many other types of goods. Until Article 2A was added to the UCC, no specific body of law addressed the legal problems that arose when goods were leased, rather than sold. In cases involving leased goods, the courts generally applied a combination of common law rules, real estate law, and principles expressed in Article 2 of the UCC.

Article 2A of the UCC was created to fill the need for uniform guidelines in this area. Article 2A covers any transaction that creates a lease of goods, as well as subleases of goods [UCC 2A–102, 2A–103(k)]. Article 2A is essentially a repetition of Article 2, except that it applies to leases of goods, rather than sales of goods, and thus varies to reflect differences between sales and lease transactions.

DEFINITION OF A LEASE

Article 2A defines a **lease agreement** as the bargain of the lessor and lessee, as found in their language and as implied by other circumstances [UCC 2A–103(k)]. A **lessor** is one who sells the right to the possession and use of goods under a lease [UCC 2A–103(p)]. A **lessee** is one who acquires the right to the possession and use of goods under a lease [UCC 2A–103(o)]. Article 2A applies to all types of leases of goods, including commercial leases and consumer leases. Special rules apply to certain types of leases, however, including consumer leases and finance leases.

CONSUMER LEASES

A *consumer lease* involves three elements: (1) a lessor who regularly engages in the business of leasing or selling, (2) a lessee (except an organization) who leases the goods "primarily for a personal, family, or household purpose," and (3) total lease payments that are less than $25,000 [UCC 2A–103(1)(e)]. In the interest of providing special protection for consumers, certain provisions of Article 2A apply only to consumer leases. For example, one provision states that a consumer may recover attorneys' fees if a court determines that a term in a consumer lease contract is unconscionable [UCC 2A–108(a)].

FINANCE LEASES

A *finance lease* involves a lessor, a lessee, and a supplier. The lessor buys or leases goods from a supplier and leases or subleases them to the lessee [UCC 2A–103(g)]. Typically, in a finance lease, the lessor is simply financing the transaction. For example, suppose that Marlin Corporation wants to lease a crane for use in its construction business. Marlin's bank agrees to purchase the equipment from Jennco, Inc., and lease the equipment to Marlin. In this situation, the bank is the lessor-financer, Marlin is the lessee, and Jennco is the supplier.

Article 2A, unlike ordinary contract law, makes the lessee's obligations under a commercial finance lease irrevocable and independent from the financer's obligations [UCC 2A–407]. That is, the lessee must perform whether or not the financer performs. The lessee also must look almost entirely to the supplier for warranties.

SECTION 4

The Formation of Sales and Lease Contracts

In regard to the formation of sales and lease contracts, the UCC modifies the common law in several ways. We look here at how Article 2 and Article 2A of the UCC modify common law contract rules. Remember that parties to sales contracts are free to establish whatever terms they wish. The UCC comes into play when the parties have not, in their contract, provided for a contingency that later gives rise to a dispute. The UCC makes this very clear time and again by its use of such phrases as "unless the parties otherwise agree" and "absent a contrary agreement by the parties."

OFFER

In general contract law, the moment a definite offer is met by an unqualified acceptance, a binding contract is formed. In commercial sales transactions, the verbal exchanges, the correspondence, and the actions of the parties may not reveal exactly when a binding contractual obligation arises. The UCC states that an agreement sufficient to constitute a contract can exist even if the moment of its making is undetermined [UCC 2–204(2), 2A–204(2)].

Open Terms. According to contract law, an offer must be definite enough for the parties (and the courts) to ascertain its essential terms when it is accepted. The UCC states that a sales or lease contract will not fail for indefiniteness even if one or more terms are left open as long as (1) the parties intended to make a contract and (2) there is a reasonably certain basis for the court to grant an appropriate remedy [UCC 2–204(3), 2A–204(3)].

For example, Mike agrees to lease from CompuQuik a highly specialized computer workstation. Mike and one of CompuQuik's sales representatives sign a lease agreement that leaves some of the details blank, to be "worked out" the following week, when the leasing manager will be back from her vacation. In the meantime, CompuQuik obtains the necessary equipment from one of its suppliers and spends several days modifying the equipment to suit Mike's needs. When the leasing manager returns, she calls Mike and tells him that his workstation is ready. Mike says he is no longer interested in the workstation, as he has arranged to lease the same equipment for a lower price from another firm. CompuQuik sues Mike to recover its costs in obtaining and modifying the equipment, and one of the issues before the court is whether the parties had an enforceable contract. The court will likely hold that they did, based on their intent and conduct, despite the blanks in their written agreement.

Although the UCC has radically lessened the requirement of definiteness of terms, keep in mind that if too many terms are left open, a court may find that the parties did not intend to form a contract. (This is also true with respect to online offers—see Chapter 23.)

Open Price Term. If the parties have not agreed on a price, the court will determine a "reasonable price at the time for delivery" [UCC 2–305(1)]. If either the buyer or the seller is to determine the price, the price is to be fixed (set) in good faith [UCC 2–305(2)].

Sometimes the price fails to be fixed through the fault of one of the parties. In that case, the other party can treat the contract as canceled or fix a reasonable price. For example, Johnson and Merrick enter into a contract for the sale of goods and agree that Johnson will fix the price. Johnson refuses to fix the price. Merrick can either treat the contract as canceled or set a reasonable price [UCC 2–305(3)].

Open Payment Term. When parties do not specify payment terms, payment is due at the time and place at which the buyer is to receive the goods [UCC 2–310(a)]. The buyer can tender payment using any commercially normal or acceptable means, such as a check or credit card. If the seller demands payment in cash, however, the buyer must be given a reasonable time to obtain it [UCC 2–511(2)]. This is especially important when the contract states a definite and final time for performance.

Open Delivery Term. When no delivery terms are specified, the buyer normally takes delivery at the seller's place of business [UCC 2–308(a)]. If the seller has no place of business, the seller's residence is used. When goods are located in some other place and both parties know it, delivery is made there. If the time for shipment or delivery is not clearly specified in the sales contract, then the court will infer a "reasonable" time for performance [UCC 2–309(1)].

Duration of an Ongoing Contract. A single contract might specify successive performances but not indicate how long the parties are required to deal with each other. Although either party may terminate the ongoing contractual relationship, principles of good faith and sound commercial practice call for reasonable notification before termination so as to give the other party sufficient time to seek a substitute arrangement [UCC 2–309(2), (3)].

Options and Cooperation Regarding Performance. When specific shipping arrangements have not been made but the contract contemplates shipment of the goods, the *seller* has the right to make these arrangements in good faith, using commercial reasonableness in the situation [UCC 2–311]. (The obligations of good faith and commercial reasonableness in sales and lease contracts are discussed in detail in Chapter 20.)

When terms relating to the assortment of goods are omitted from a sales contract, the buyer can specify the assortment. For example, Harley and Babcock contract for the sale of one thousand pens. The pens come in a variety of colors, but the contract is silent on which colors are ordered. Babcock, the buyer, has the right to take whatever colors he wishes. Babcock, however, must make the selection in good faith and must use commercial reasonableness [UCC 2–311].

Open Quantity Term. Normally, if the parties do not specify a quantity, a court will have no basis for determining a remedy. The UCC recognizes two exceptions in requirements and output contracts [UCC 2–306(1)].

In a **requirements contract**, the buyer agrees to purchase and the seller agrees to sell all or up to a stated amount of what the buyer *needs* or *requires*. There is implicit consideration in a requirements contract, for the buyer gives up the right to buy from any other seller, and this forfeited right creates a legal detriment. Requirements contracts are common in the business world and are normally enforceable. If, however, the buyer promises to purchase only if the buyer *wishes* to do so, or if the buyer reserves the right to buy the goods from someone other than the seller, the promise is illusory (without consideration) and unenforceable by either party.

In an **output contract**, the seller agrees to sell and the buyer agrees to buy all or up to a stated amount of what the seller *produces*. Again, because the seller essentially forfeits the right to sell goods to another buyer, there is implicit consideration in an output contract.

The UCC imposes a *good faith limitation* on requirements and output contracts. The quantity under such contracts is the amount of requirements or the amount of output that occurs during a *normal* production year. The actual quantity purchased or sold cannot be unreasonably disproportionate to normal or comparable prior requirements or output [UCC 2–306].

Merchant's Firm Offer. Under regular contract principles, an offer can be revoked at any time before acceptance. The major common law exception is an *option contract* (discussed in Chapter 10), in which the offeree pays consideration for the offeror's irrevocable promise to keep the offer open for a stated period. The UCC creates a second exception, which applies only to firm offers for the sale or lease of goods made by a merchant (regardless of whether the offeree is a merchant). A **firm offer** arises when a merchant-offeror gives assurances *in a signed writing* that the offer will remain open. The merchant's firm offer is irrevocable without the necessity of consideration[4] for the stated period or, if no definite period is stated, a reasonable period (neither to exceed three months) [UCC 2–205, 2A–205].

To illustrate: Daniels, a used-car dealer, writes a letter to Farad on January 1 stating, "I have a 1998 Pontiac on the lot that I'll sell you for $8,500 any time between now and January 31." By January 18, Daniels has heard nothing from Farad so he sells the Pontiac to another person. On January 23, Farad tenders $8,500 to Daniels and asks for the car. When Daniels tells him the car has already been sold, Farad claims that Daniels has breached a good contract. Farad is right. Daniels is a merchant of used cars and assured Farad in a signed writing that he would keep his offer open until the end of January. Farad's acceptance on January 23 thus created a contract, which Daniels breached.

It is necessary that the offer be both *written* and *signed* by the offeror.[5] When a firm offer is contained in a form contract prepared by the offeree, the offeror must also sign a separate firm-offer assurance. This requirement ensures that the offeror will be made aware of the offer. If the firm offer is buried amid copious language in one of the pages of the offeree's form contract, the offeror may inadvertently sign the contract without realizing that there is a firm offer, thus defeating the purpose of the rule—which is to give effect to a merchant's deliberate intent to be bound to a firm offer.

ACCEPTANCE

The following sections examine the UCC's provisions governing acceptance. As you will see, acceptance of an offer to buy, sell, or lease goods generally may be made in any reasonable manner and by any reasonable means.

Methods of Acceptance. The general common law rule is that an offeror can specify, or authorize, a particular means of acceptance, making that means the only one effective for contract formation. Even an unauthorized means of communication is effective, however, as long as the acceptance is received by the specified deadline. For example, suppose that an offer states, "Answer by fax within five days." If the offeree sends a letter, and the offeror receives it within five days, a valid contract is still formed. (For a review of the requirements relating to mode and timeliness of acceptance, see Chapter 10.)

As you will read in Chapter 23, online offers normally specify, or authorize, acceptance through "click-on" boxes or icons. To accept an online offer,

4. If the offeree pays consideration, then an option contract (not a merchant's firm offer) is formed.

5. "Signed" includes any symbol executed or adopted by a party with a present intention to authenticate a writing [UCC 1–201(39)]. A complete signature is not required. Therefore, initials, a thumbprint, a trade name, or any mark used in lieu of a written signature will suffice, regardless of its location on the document.

the offeree merely clicks on the box or icon stating "I agree" or "I accept."

Any Reasonable Means. When the offeror does not specify a means of acceptance, the UCC provides that acceptance can be made by any means of communication that are reasonable under the circumstances [UCC 2–206(1), 2A–206(1)]. This is also the basic rule under the common law of contracts (see Chapter 10).

For example, Anodyne Corporation writes a letter to Bethlehem Industries offering to lease $1,000 worth of goods. The offer states that Anodyne will keep the offer open for only ten days from the date of the letter. Before the ten days have lapsed, Bethlehem sends Anodyne an acceptance by fax. The fax is misdirected by someone at Anodyne's offices and does not reach the right person at Anodyne until after the ten-day deadline has passed. Is a valid contract formed? The answer is probably yes, because acceptance by fax appears to be a commercially reasonable medium of acceptance under the circumstances. Acceptance would be effective on Bethlehem's transmission of the fax, which occurred before the offer lapsed.

Promise to Ship or Prompt Shipment. The UCC permits acceptance of an offer to buy goods for current or prompt shipment by either a prompt *promise* to ship the goods to the buyer or the prompt shipment of conforming goods (that is, goods that accord with the contract's terms) to the buyer [UCC 2–206(1)(b)]. The prompt shipment of *nonconforming goods* constitutes both an *acceptance* (a contract) and a *breach* of that contract. This rule does not apply if the seller seasonably (within a reasonable amount of time) notifies the buyer that the nonconforming shipment is offered only as an *accommodation*, or as a favor. The notice of accommodation must clearly indicate to the buyer that the shipment does not constitute an acceptance and that, therefore, no contract has been formed.

For example, Barrymore orders one thousand *black* fans from Stroh. Stroh ships one thousand *blue* fans to Barrymore, notifying Barrymore that because Stroh has only blue fans in stock, these are sent as an *accommodation*. The shipment of blue fans is not an acceptance but a counteroffer, and a contract will be formed only if Barrymore accepts the blue fans. If, however, Stroh ships one thousand blue fans instead of black *without* notifying Barrymore that the goods are being shipped as an accommodation, Stroh's shipment acts as both an acceptance of Barrymore's offer and a *breach* of the resulting contract. Barrymore may sue Stroh for any appropriate damages.

Communication of Acceptance. Under the common law, because a unilateral offer invites acceptance by a performance, the offeree need not notify the offeror of performance unless the offeror would not otherwise know about it. The UCC is more stringent than the common law, stating that when the beginning of the requested performance is a reasonable mode of acceptance, an offeror who is not notified of acceptance within a reasonable time may treat the offer as having lapsed before acceptance [UCC 2–206(2), 2A–206(2)].

For example, Lee writes to Pickwick Bookstore on Monday, "Please send me a copy of *West's Best Law Text* for $95, C.O.D.," and signs it, "Lee." Pickwick receives the request but does not ship the book for four weeks. When the book arrives, Lee rejects it, claiming that it has arrived too late to be of value. In this situation, because Lee had heard nothing from Pickwick for a month, he was justified in assuming that the store did not intend to deliver the book. Lee could consider that the offer had lapsed because of the length of time Pickwick delayed shipment.

Additional Terms. Under the common law, if Alderman makes an offer to Beale, and Beale in turn accepts but adds some slight modification, there is no contract. Recall from Chapter 10 that the so-called *mirror image rule* requires that the terms of the acceptance exactly match those of the offer. Beale's modification of the terms of Alderman's offer makes Beale's action a rejection of—and a counteroffer to—the offer. This rule often led to what is known as the *battle of the forms*.

Say, for example, that a buyer contracts with a seller over the phone to purchase a certain piece of equipment. The parties agree to all of the specific terms of the sale—price, quantity, delivery date, and so on. The buyer then enters the terms of the agreement on its standard purchase order form and sends the form to the seller. At the same time, the seller enters the terms on its standard sales form. Because the parties presume that they have reached an oral agreement on the telephone, discrepancies in the terms and conditions contained in their respective forms may go unnoticed. If a dispute arises, however, the discrepancies become significant, and a "battle of the forms" begins, in which each party claims that its form represents the true terms of the agreement.

Under the common law, the courts tended to resolve this difficulty by holding that the last form to be sent was the final counteroffer. To avoid the battle of the forms, the UCC dispenses with the mirror image rule. The UCC generally takes the position that if the offeree's response indicates a *definite* acceptance of the offer, a contract is formed, even if the acceptance includes terms additional to or different from those contained in the offer [UCC 2–207(1)]. What happens to these additional terms? The answer to this question depends, in part, on whether the parties are nonmerchants or merchants.

Rules When One Party or Both Parties Are Nonmerchants. If one (or both) of the parties is a nonmerchant, the contract is formed according to the terms of the original offer submitted by the original offeror and not according to the additional terms of the acceptance [UCC 2–207(2)]. For example, Tolsen offers in writing to sell his personal computer to Valdez for $1,500. Valdez faxes a reply to Tolsen in which Valdez states, "I accept your offer to purchase your computer for $1,500. I *would like* a box of computer paper and ten diskettes to be included in the purchase price." Valdez has given Tolsen a definite expression of acceptance (creating a contract), even though Valdez's acceptance also suggests an added term for the offer. Because Tolsen is not a merchant, the additional term is merely a proposal (suggestion), and Tolsen is not legally obligated to comply with that term.

Rules When Both Parties Are Merchants. In contracts *between merchants*, the additional terms automatically become part of the contract unless (1) the original offer expressly limited acceptance to its terms, (2) the new or changed terms materially alter the contract, or (3) the offeror objects to the new or changed terms within a reasonable period of time [UCC 2–207(2)].

What constitutes a material alteration of the contract is frequently a question of fact that only a court can decide. Generally, if the modification involves no unreasonable element of surprise or hardship for the offeror, the court will hold that the modification did not materially alter the contract.

Westlaw. See Case 18.2 at the end of this chapter. To view the full, unedited case from Westlaw,® go to this text's Web site at **http://wbl-cs.westbuslaw.com**.

Conditioned on Offeror's Assent. Regardless of merchant status, the UCC provides that the offeree's expression cannot be construed as an acceptance if additional or different terms in the acceptance are expressly *conditioned* on the offeror's assent to the additional or different terms [UCC 2–207(1)]. For example, Philips offers to sell Hundert 650 pounds of turkey thighs at a specified price and with specified delivery terms. Hundert responds, "I accept your offer for 650 pounds of turkey thighs *on the condition that you agree that the weight will be evidenced by a city scale weight certificate.*" Hundert's response will be construed not as an acceptance but as a counteroffer, which Philips may or may not accept.

Additional Terms May Be Stricken. The UCC provides yet another option for dealing with conflicting terms in the parties' writings. Section 2–207(3) states that conduct by both parties that recognizes the existence of a contract is sufficient to establish a contract for sale even though the writings of the parties do not otherwise establish a contract. In this situation, "the terms of the particular contract will consist of those terms on which the writings of the parties agree, together with any supplementary terms incorporated under any other provisions of this Act." In a dispute over contract terms, this provision allows a court simply to strike from the contract those terms on which the parties do not agree.[6]

CONSIDERATION

The common law rule that a contract requires consideration also applies to sales and lease contracts. Unlike the common law, however, the UCC does not require a contract modification to be supported by new consideration. The UCC states that an agreement modifying a contract for the sale or lease of goods "needs no consideration to be binding" [UCC 2–209(1), 2A–208(1)].

Modifications Must Be Made in Good Faith.

Of course, any contract modification must be made in good faith [UCC 1–203]. For example, Jim agrees to lease certain goods to Louise for a stated price. Subsequently, a sudden shift in the market makes it

6. For an application of this solution to the "battle of the forms," see *Ionics, Inc. v. Elmwood Sensors, Inc.*, 896 F.Supp. 66 (D.Mass. 1995).

difficult for Jim to lease the items to Louise at the given price without suffering a loss. Jim tells Louise of the situation, and Louise agrees to pay an additional sum for the goods. Later, Louise reconsiders and refuses to pay more than the original price. Under the UCC, Louise's promise to modify the contract needs no consideration to be binding. Hence, Louise is bound by the modified contract.

In this example, a shift in the market is a *good faith* reason for contract modification. What if there really was no shift in the market, however, and Jim knew that Louise needed the goods immediately but refused to deliver them unless Louise agreed to pay an additional sum of money? This sort of extortion of a modification without a legitimate commercial reason would be ineffective, because it would violate the duty of good faith. Jim would not be permitted to enforce the higher price.

When Contract Modification without Consideration Requires a Writing. In some situations, modification of a sales or lease contract without consideration must be in writing to be enforceable. For example, if the contract itself prohibits any changes to the contract unless they are in a signed writing, only those changes agreed to in a signed writing are enforceable. If a consumer (nonmerchant buyer) is dealing with a merchant and the merchant supplies the form that contains the prohibition against oral modification, the consumer must sign a separate acknowledgment of the clause [UCC 2–209(2), 2A–208(2)].

Also, under Article 2, any modification that brings a sales contract under the Statute of Frauds must usually be in writing to be enforceable. Thus, if an oral contract for the sale of goods priced at $400 is modified so that the contract goods are priced at $600, the modification must be in writing to be enforceable [UCC 2–209(3)]. If, however, the buyer accepts delivery of the goods after the modification, he or she is bound to the $600 price [UCC 2–201(3)(c)]. Although Article 2 contains these provisions to govern modifications of sales contracts, Article 2A does not say whether a lease as modified needs to satisfy the Statute of Frauds.

THE STATUTE OF FRAUDS

The UCC contains Statute of Frauds provisions covering sales and lease contracts. Under these provisions, sales contracts for goods priced at $500 or more and lease contracts requiring payments of $1,000 or more must be in writing to be enforceable [UCC 2–201(1), 2A–201(1)].

Sufficiency of the Writing. The UCC has greatly relaxed the requirements for the sufficiency of a writing to satisfy the Statute of Frauds. A writing or a memorandum will be sufficient as long as it indicates that the parties intended to form a contract and as long as it is signed by the party (or agent of the party) against whom enforcement is sought. The contract normally will not be enforceable beyond the quantity of goods shown in the writing, however. All other terms can be proved in court by oral testimony. For leases, the writing must reasonably identify and describe the goods leased and the lease term.

Special Rules for Contracts between Merchants. Once again, the UCC provides a special rule for merchants. The rule, however, applies only to sales (under Article 2); there is no corresponding rule that applies to leases (under Article 2A).[7] Merchants can satisfy the requirements of a writing for the Statute of Frauds if, after the parties have agreed orally, one of the merchants sends a signed written confirmation to the other merchant. The communication must indicate the terms of the agreement, and the merchant receiving the confirmation must have reason to know of its contents. Unless the merchant who receives the confirmation gives written notice of objection to its contents within ten days after receipt, the writing is sufficient against the receiving merchant, even though he or she has not signed anything [UCC 2–201(2)].

For example, Alfonso is a merchant buyer in Cleveland. He contracts over the telephone to purchase $4,000 worth of goods from Goldstein, a New York City merchant seller. Two days later, Goldstein sends written confirmation detailing the terms of the oral contract, and Alfonso subsequently receives it. If Alfonso does not give Goldstein written notice of objection to the contents of the written confirmation within ten days of receipt, Alfonso cannot raise the Statute of Frauds as a defense against the enforcement of the oral contract.

7. According to the Comments accompanying UCC 2A–201 (Article 2A's Statute of Frauds), the "between merchants" provision was not included because "the number of such transactions involving leases, as opposed to sales, was thought to be modest."

Exceptions. The UCC defines three exceptions to the writing requirements of the Statute of Frauds. An oral contract for the sale of goods priced at $500 or more or the lease of goods involving payments of $1,000 or more will be enforceable despite the absence of a writing in the following circumstances [UCC 2–201(3), 2A–201(4)]. These exceptions and other ways in which sales law differs from general contract law are summarized in Exhibit 18–2 below.

Specially Manufactured Goods. An oral contract is enforceable if (1) it is for goods that are specially manufactured for a particular buyer or specially manufactured or obtained for a particular lessee, (2) these goods are not suitable for resale or lease to others in the ordinary course of the seller's or lessor's business, and (3) the seller or lessor has substantially started to manufacture the goods or has made commitments for the manufacture or procurement of the goods. In these situations, once the seller or lessor has taken action, the buyer or lessee cannot repudiate the agreement claiming the Statute of Frauds as a defense.

For example, suppose Womach orders custom-made draperies for her new boutique. The price is $1,000, and the contract is oral. When the merchant-seller manufactures the draperies and tenders delivery to Womach, Womach refuses to pay for them even though the job has been completed on time. Womach claims that she is not liable because the contract was oral. Clearly, if the unique style and color of the draperies make it improbable that the seller can find another buyer, Womach is liable to the seller. Note that the seller must have made a substantial beginning in manufacturing the specialized item prior to the buyer's repudiation. (Here, the manufacture was completed.) Of course, the court must still be convinced by evidence of the terms of the oral contract.

Admissions. An oral contract for the sale or lease of goods is enforceable if the party against whom en-

EXHIBIT 18–2 MAJOR DIFFERENCES BETWEEN CONTRACT LAW AND SALES LAW

	CONTRACT LAW	SALES LAW
Contract Terms	Contract must contain all material terms.	Open terms are acceptable, if parties intended to form a contract, but contract is not enforceable beyond quantity term.
Acceptance	Mirror image rule applies. If additional terms are added in acceptance, counteroffer is created.	Additional terms will not negate acceptance unless acceptance is made expressly conditional on assent to the additional terms.
Contract Modification	Modification requires consideration	Modification does not require consideration.
Irrevocable Offers	Option contracts (with consideration).	Merchants' firm offers (without consideration).
Statute of Frauds Requirements	All material terms must be included in the writing.	Writing is required only for sale of goods of $500 or more, but contract is not enforceable beyond quantity specified. *Exceptions:* 1. Contracts for specially manufactured goods are enforceable. 2. Contracts admitted to under oath by party against whom enforcement is sought are enforceable. 3. Contracts will be enforced to extent goods are delivered or paid for. 4. Confirmatory memorandum (between merchants): Contract is enforceable if merchant fails to object in writing to confirming memorandum within ten days of its receipt.

forcement is sought admits in pleadings, testimony, or other court proceedings that a sales or lease contract was made. In this situation, the contract will be enforceable even though it was oral, but enforceability will be limited to the quantity of goods admitted.

For example, Lane and Sanders negotiate an agreement over the telephone. During the negotiations, Lane requests a delivery price for five hundred gallons of gasoline and a separate price for seven hundred gallons of gasoline. Sanders replies that the price would be the same, $1.10 per gallon. Lane orally orders five hundred gallons. Sanders honestly believes that Lane ordered seven hundred gallons and tenders that amount. Lane refuses the shipment of seven hundred gallons, and Sanders sues for breach. In his pleadings and testimony, Lane admits that an oral contract was made, but only for five hundred gallons. Because Lane admits the existence of the oral contract, Lane cannot plead the Statute of Frauds as a defense. The contract is enforceable, however, only to the extent of the quantity admitted (five hundred gallons).

Partial Performance. An oral contract for the sale or lease of goods is enforceable if payment has been made and accepted or goods have been received and accepted. This is the "partial performance" exception. The oral contract will be enforced at least to the extent that performance *actually* took place.

Suppose that Allan orally contracts to lease Opus two thousand chairs at $1 each to be used during a one-day rock concert. Before delivery, Opus sends Allan a check for $500, which Allan cashes. Later, when Allan attempts to deliver the chairs, Opus refuses delivery, claiming the Statute of Frauds as a defense, and demands the return of his $500. Under the UCC's partial performance rule, Allan can enforce the oral contract by tender of delivery of five hundred chairs for the $500 accepted. Similarly, if Opus had made no payment but had accepted the delivery of five hundred chairs from Allan, the oral contract would have been enforceable against Opus for $500, the lease payment due for the five hundred chairs delivered.

PAROL EVIDENCE

If the parties to a contract set forth its terms in a confirmatory memorandum (a writing expressing offer and acceptance of the deal) or in a writing intended as their final expression, the terms of the contract cannot be contradicted by evidence of any prior agreements or contemporaneous oral agreements. As discussed in Chapter 14, this principle of law is known as the parol evidence rule. The terms of a contract may, however, be explained or supplemented by *consistent additional terms* or by *course of dealing, usage of trade,* or *course of performance* [UCC 2–202, 2A–202].

Consistent Additional Terms. If the court finds an ambiguity in a writing that is supposed to be a complete and exclusive statement of the agreement between the parties, it may accept evidence of consistent additional terms to clarify or remove the ambiguity. The court will not, however, accept evidence of contradictory terms. This is the rule under both the UCC and the common law of contracts.

Course of Dealing and Usage of Trade. Under the UCC, the meaning of any agreement, evidenced by the language of the parties and by their actions, must be interpreted in light of commercial practices and other surrounding circumstances. In interpreting a commercial agreement, the court will assume that the *course of prior dealing* between the parties and the *usage of trade* were taken into account when the agreement was phrased.

A **course of dealing** is a sequence of previous actions and communications between the parties to a particular transaction that establishes a common basis for their understanding [UCC 1–205(1)]. A course of dealing is restricted to the sequence of actions and communications between the parties that has occurred prior to the agreement in question. The UCC states, "A course of dealing between the parties and any usage of trade in the vocation or trade in which they are engaged or of which they are or should be aware give particular meaning to [the terms of the agreement] and supplement or qualify the terms of [the] agreement" [UCC 1–205(3)].

Usage of trade is defined as any practice or method of dealing having such regularity of observance in a place, vocation, or trade as to justify an expectation that it will be observed with respect to the transaction in question [UCC 1–205(2)]. Further, the express terms of an agreement and an applicable course of dealing or usage of trade will be construed to be consistent with each other whenever reasonable. When such a construction is *unreasonable,* however, the express terms in the agreement will prevail [UCC 1–205(4)].

Course of Performance. The conduct that occurs under the terms of a particular agreement is called a **course of performance.** Presumably, the parties themselves know best what they meant by their words, and the course of performance actually undertaken under their agreement is the best indication of what they meant [UCC 2–208(1), 2A–207(1)].

For example, suppose that Janson's Lumber Company contracts with Barrymore to sell Barrymore a specified number of two-by-fours. The lumber in fact does not measure 2 inches by 4 inches but rather 1⅞ inches by 3¾ inches. Janson's agrees to deliver the lumber in five deliveries, and Barrymore, without objection, accepts the lumber in the first three deliveries. On the fourth delivery, however, Barrymore objects that the two-by-fours do not measure 2 inches by 4 inches.

The course of performance in this transaction—that is, the fact that Barrymore accepted three deliveries without objection under the agreement—is relevant in determining that here a "two-by-four" actually means "1⅞ by 3¾." Janson's can also prove that two-by-fours need not be exactly 2 inches by 4 inches by applying usage of trade, course of dealing, or both. Janson's can, for example, show that in previous transactions, Barrymore took 1⅞-inch-by-3¾-inch lumber without objection. In addition, Janson's can show that in the trade, two-by-fours are commonly 1⅞ inches by 3¾ inches.

Rules of Construction. The UCC provides *rules of construction* for interpreting contracts. Express terms, course of performance, course of dealing, and usage of trade are to be construed together when they do not contradict one another. When such a construction is unreasonable, however, the following order of priority controls [UCC 1–205(4), 2–208(2), 2A–207(2)]:

1. Express terms.
2. Course of performance.
3. Course of dealing.
4. Usage of trade.

UNCONSCIONABILITY

As discussed in Chapter 12, an unconscionable contract is one that is so unfair and one sided that it would be unreasonable to enforce it. The UCC allows the court to evaluate a contract or any clause in a contract, and if the court deems it to have been unconscionable *at the time it was made,* the court can do any of the following [UCC 2–302, 2A–108]:

1. Refuse to enforce the contract.
2. Enforce the remainder of the contract without the unconscionable clause.
3. Limit the application of the unconscionable clause to avoid an unconscionable result.

The inclusion of Sections 2–302 and 2A–108 in the UCC reflects an increased sensitivity to certain realities of modern commercial activities. Classical contract theory holds that a contract is a bargain in which the terms have been worked out *freely* between parties that are equals. In many modern commercial transactions, this premise is invalid. Standard-form contracts and leases are often signed by consumer-buyers who understand few of the terms used and who often do not even read them. Virtually all of the terms are advantageous to the party supplying the standard-form contract or lease. The UCC's unconscionability provisions give the courts a powerful weapon for policing such transactions.

See Case 18.3 at the end of this chapter. To view the full, unedited case from Westlaw,® go to this text's Web site at **http://wbl-cs.westbuslaw.com**.

SECTION 5

Contracts for the International Sale of Goods

International sales contracts between firms or individuals located in different countries are governed by the 1980 United Nations Convention on Contracts for the International Sale of Goods (CISG). The CISG governs international contracts only if the countries of the parties to the contract have ratified the CISG and if the parties have not agreed that some other law will govern their contract. As of 2002, fifty-seven countries had ratified or acceded to the CISG, including the United States, Canada, Mexico, some Central and South American countries, and most of the European nations.

APPLICABILITY OF THE CISG

Essentially, the CISG is to international sales contracts what Article 2 of the UCC is to domestic sales contracts. As discussed in this chapter, in domestic transactions the UCC applies when the parties to a contract for a sale of goods have failed to specify in writing some important term concerning price, delivery, or the like. Similarly, whenever the parties to international transactions have failed to specify in writing the precise terms of a contract, the CISG will be applied. Unlike the UCC, the CISG does not apply to consumer sales, and neither the UCC nor the CISG applies to contracts for services.

Businesspersons must take special care when drafting international sales contracts to avoid problems caused by distance, including language differences and differences in national laws. The fold-out exhibit in this chapter, which shows an actual international sales contract used by Starbucks Coffee Company, illustrates many of the special terms and clauses that are typically contained in international contracts for the sale of goods. Annotations in the exhibit explain the meaning and significance of specific clauses in the contract. (See Chapter 52 for a discussion of other laws that frame global business transactions.)

A Comparison of CISG and UCC Provisions

The provisions of the CISG, although similar for the most part to those of the UCC, differ from them in some respects. In the event that the CISG and the UCC are in conflict, the CISG applies (because it is a treaty of the national government and therefore is supreme—see the discussion of the supremacy clause of the U.S. Constitution in Chapter 4).

The major differences between the CISG and the UCC in regard to contract formation concern the following:

1. The mirror image rule.
2. Irrevocable offers.
3. The Statute of Frauds.
4. The price term.
5. The time of contract formation.

CISG provisions relating to risk of loss, performance, remedies, and warranties will be discussed in the following chapters as those topics are examined.

The Mirror Image Rule. As discussed earlier in this chapter, the UCC relaxed substantially the rules governing contractual agreement. Under the UCC, a definite expression of acceptance that contains additional terms can still result in the formation of a contract, unless the additional terms are conditioned on the assent of the offeror.

Article 19 of the CISG provides the rules governing additional terms in international sales contracts. Article 19(1) states that if the terms of the acceptance vary from those of the offer, there is no contract: "A reply to an offer which purports to be an acceptance, but contains additions, limitations, or other modifications is a rejection of the offer and constitutes a counter-offer." Article 19(2), though, stipulates that an acceptance containing additional or different terms may still bind the offeror in contract if the additional or different terms do not materially alter the terms of the offer and if the offeror does not object to the discrepancy in a timely manner.

Note that the definition of a "material alteration" under the CISG involves virtually any differences in the terms relating to payment, quality, quantity, price, time and place of delivery, extent of one party's liability to the other, and settlement of disputes under the contract. In effect, then, Article 19 requires that the terms of the acceptance mirror those of the offer. As a practical matter, businesspersons undertaking international sales transactions therefore should not use the sale or purchase forms that they customarily use for transactions within the United States. Rather, such forms need to be specially drafted to suit the needs of the specific transactions.

Irrevocable Offers. UCC 2–205 requires that an irrevocable offer without consideration must be in writing. In contrast, Article 16(2) of the CISG provides that an offer will be irrevocable if the offeror simply states orally that the offer is irrevocable or if the offeree reasonably relies on the offer as being irrevocable. In both of these situations, the offer will be irrevocable even without a writing and without consideration.

Statute of Frauds. As mentioned previously, the UCC states that contracts for the sale of goods priced at $500 or more must be in writing [UCC 2–201]. The writing must be signed by the party against whom enforcement is sought and must be sufficient to show that a contract has been made. Article 11 of the CISG, however, states that a contract of sale "need not be concluded in or evidenced by writing and is not subject to any other requirements as to form. It may be proved by any means, including witnesses."

Article 11 of the CISG accords with the legal customs of most nations, in which contracts no longer need to meet certain formal or writing requirements to be enforceable. Ironically, even England, the nation that created the original Statute of Frauds in 1677, has repealed all of it except the provisions relating to collateral promises and to transfers of interests in land. Many other countries that once had such a statute have also repealed all or parts of it. Civil law countries, such as France, never had a writing requirement.

The Necessity of a Price Term. Under the UCC, if the parties to a contract have not agreed on a price, the contract will not fail if the parties intended to form a contract (had a "meeting of the minds"). If the price term is left open, the court will determine "a reasonable price at the time for delivery" [UCC 2–305(1)]. Under the CISG, however, the price term must be specified, or provisions for its specification must be included in the agreement; otherwise, normally no contract will exist. For example, if the contract states that the price of wheat to be delivered in two months will be its spot price at the Chicago Board of Trade on that day, that is a sufficient price term under the CISG.

Time of Contract Formation. Under the common law of contracts, an acceptance is effective on dispatch, and thus a contract is created when the acceptance is transmitted. The UCC does not alter this so-called mailbox rule. Under the CISG, however, a contract is created not at the time the acceptance is transmitted but only on its *receipt* by the offeror. (The offer becomes *irrevocable,* however, when the acceptance is sent.) Article 18(2) states that an acceptance by return promise "becomes effective at the moment the indication of assent reaches the offeror." Under Article 18(3), the offeree may also bind the offeror by performance even without giving any notice to the offeror. The acceptance becomes effective "at the moment the act is performed." The rule is therefore that it is the offeree's reliance, rather than the communication of acceptance to the offeror, that creates the contract.

Special Provisions in International Contracts

Language and legal differences among nations can create special problems for parties to international contracts when disputes arise. It is possible to avoid these problems by including in a contract special provisions relating to choice of language, choice of forum, choice of law, and the types of events that may excuse the parties from performance.

Choice of Language. A deal struck between a U.S. company and a company in another country normally involves two languages. One party may not understand complex contractual terms that are written in the other party's language. Translating the terms poses its own problems, as typically, many phrases are not readily translatable into another language. To make sure that no disputes arise out of this language problem, an international sales contract should have a **choice-of-language clause** designating the official language by which the contract will be interpreted in the event of disagreement.

A choice-of-language clause might state that the agreement is being written in English, which is to be regarded as the authoritative and official language of the contract's text. The clause may further allow that the agreement is to be translated into, say, Spanish; that the translation is to be ratified by both parties; and that the foreign company can rely on the translation. If arbitration is anticipated, an additional clause must be added to indicate that the arbitration will be conducted in, say, English, Spanish, or French—or whatever the case may be.

Choice of Forum. In international contracts, it is especially important to include a clause designating the **forum** (place, or court) in which any disputes that arise under the contract will be litigated. Including a **forum-selection clause** in an international contract is important because when several countries are involved, litigation may be sought in courts in different nations. There are no universally accepted rules regarding the jurisdiction of a particular court over subject matter or parties to a dispute. A forum-selection clause should specifically indicate the court that will have jurisdiction. The forum does not necessarily have to be within the geographic boundaries of either of the parties' nations.

Under certain circumstances, a forum-selection clause will not be valid. Specifically, if the clause denies one party an effective remedy, is the product of fraud or unconscionable conduct, causes substantial inconvenience to one of the parties to the contract, or violates public policy, the clause will not be enforced.

Choice of Law. A contractual provision designating the applicable law, called a **choice-of-law clause,** is typically included in every international contract. At common law (and in European civil law systems—see Chapter 52), parties are allowed to choose the law that will govern their contractual relationship, provided that the law chosen is the law of a jurisdiction that has a substantial relationship to the parties and to the international business transaction.

Under UCC 1–105, parties may choose the law that will govern the contract as long as the choice is "reasonable." Article 6 of the CISG, however, imposes no limitation on the parties in their choice of what law will govern the contract, and the 1986 Hague Convention on the Law Applicable to Contracts for the International Sale of Goods—often referred to as the Choice-of-Law Convention—allows unlimited autonomy in the choice of law. Whenever a choice of law is not specified in a contract, the Hague Convention indicates that the governing law is that of the country in which the seller's place of business is located.

Force Majeure Clause. Every contract, and particularly those involving international transactions, should have a ***force majeure*** clause. The definition of the French term *force majeure* is "impossible or irresistible force"—which sometimes is loosely identified as "an act of God." *Force majeure* clauses commonly stipulate that in addition to acts of God, a number of other eventualities (such as governmental orders or regulations, embargoes, or shortages of materials) may excuse a party from liability for nonperformance.

TERMS AND CONCEPTS TO REVIEW

choice-of-language clause 360	forum 360	output contract 352
choice-of-law clause 360	forum-selection clause 360	requirements contract 351
course of dealing 357	lease agreement 350	sale 348
course of performance 358	lessee 350	sales contract 347
firm offer 352	lessor 350	tangible property 348
force majeure clause 361	merchant 349	usage of trade 357

CHAPTER SUMMARY

The Uniform Commercial Code (UCC)	The UCC attempts to provide a consistent, uniform, and integrated framework of rules to deal with all phases *ordinarily arising* in a commercial sales or lease transaction, including contract formation, passage of title and risk of loss, performance, remedies, payment for goods, warehoused goods, and secured transactions. If there is a conflict between a common law rule and the UCC, the UCC controls.
The Scope of Article 2—The Sale of Goods	Article 2 governs contracts for the sale of goods (tangible, movable personal property). The common law of contracts also applies to sales contracts to the extent that the common law has not been modified by the UCC. Special rules apply to merchants.
The Scope of Article 2A—Leases	Article 2A governs contracts for the lease of goods. Article 2A is essentially a repetition of Article 2, except that it applies to leases, instead of sales, of goods. Article 2A thus varies from Article 2 only as necessary to reflect differences between sale and lease transactions.
The Formation of Sales and Lease Contracts	1. *Offer*— a. Not all terms have to be included for a contract to be formed (only the subject matter and quantity term must be specified). b. The price does not have to be included for a contract to be formed.

CHAPTER SUMMARY—CONTINUED

The Formation of Sales and Lease Contracts—continued	c. Particulars of performance can be left open. d. A written and signed offer by a *merchant,* covering a period of three months or less, is irrevocable without payment of consideration. 2. *Acceptance—* a. Acceptance may be made by any reasonable means of communication; it is effective when dispatched. b. The acceptance of a unilateral offer can be made by a promise to ship or by prompt shipment of conforming goods, or by prompt shipment of nonconforming goods if not accompanied by a notice of accommodation. c. Acceptance by performance requires notice within a reasonable time; otherwise, the offer can be treated as lapsed. d. A definite expression of acceptance creates a contract even if the terms of the acceptance vary from those of the offer. An exception to this rule is made when the acceptance is expressly conditioned on the offeror's assent to the varied terms.
Consideration	A modification of a contract for the sale of goods does not require consideration.
The Statute of Frauds	1. All contracts for the sale of goods priced at $500 or more must be in writing. A writing is sufficient as long as it indicates a contract between the parties and is signed by the party against whom enforcement is sought. A contract is not enforceable beyond the quantity shown in the writing. 2. When written confirmation of an oral contract *between merchants* is not objected to in writing by the receiver within ten days, the contract is enforceable. 3. Exceptions to the requirement of a writing exist in the following situations: a. When the oral contract is for specially manufactured goods not suitable for resale to others, and the seller has substantially started to manufacture the goods. b. When the defendant admits in pleadings, testimony, or other court proceedings that an oral contract for the sale of goods was made. In this case, the contract will be enforceable to the extent of the quantity of goods admitted. c. The oral agreement will be enforceable to the extent that payment has been received and accepted by the seller or to the extent that the goods have been received and accepted by the buyer.
Parol Evidence	1. The terms of a clearly and completely worded written contract cannot be contradicted by evidence of prior agreements or contemporaneous oral agreements. 2. Evidence is admissible to clarify the terms of a writing in the following situations: a. If the contract terms are ambiguous. b. If evidence of course of dealing, usage of trade, or course of performance is necessary to learn or to clarify the intentions of the parties to the contract.
Unconscionability	An unconscionable contract is one that is so unfair and one sided that it would be unreasonable to enforce it. If the court deems a contract to have been unconscionable at the time it was made, the court can (1) refuse to enforce the contract, (2) refuse to enforce the unconscionable clause of the contract, or (3) limit the application of any unconscionable clauses to avoid an unconscionable result.
Contracts for the International Sale of Goods	International sales contracts are governed by the United Nations Convention on Contracts for the International Sale of Goods (CISG)—if the countries of the parties to the contract have ratified the CISG (and if the parties have not agreed that some other law will govern their contract). Essentially, the CISG is to international sales contracts what Article 2 of the UCC is to domestic sales contracts. Whenever parties who are subject to the CISG have failed to specify in writing the precise terms of a contract for the international sale of goods, the CISG will be applied.

CASES FOR ANALYSIS

Westlaw. You can access the full text of each case presented below by going to the Westlaw cases on this text's Web site at http://wbl-cs.westbuslaw.com. Each Westlaw case includes the names of all plaintiffs and defendants, the dates on which the case was argued and decided, a brief summary of the issues and decisions in the case, headnotes classifying the specific issues in the case according to the West Key Number System, and the court's opinion. Concurring and dissenting opinions, if any, are included as well.

CASE 18.1 GOODS AND SERVICES COMBINED

MICRO DATA BASE SYSTEMS, INC. v. DHARMA SYSTEMS, INC.

United States Court of Appeals,
Seventh Circuit, 1998.
148 F.3d 649.

POSNER, Chief Judge.

We have before us an appeal and a cross-appeal in a diversity suit that presents issues of contract law * * * . The underlying dispute between the parties, two software companies that we'll call MDBS and Dharma, arises out of a four-way deal. The Internal Revenue Service requested bids for a contract to improve the Service's computer capabilities. Unisys Government Systems, Inc. wanted to bid on this contract. It made a contract with MDBS for the provision of a workstation database management system designed to be used by the IRS. MDBS in turn made the contract with Dharma that is in issue in this suit. In the contract, Dharma agreed to adapt its proprietary software program known as SQL Access for use in the system that MDBS would be providing to Unisys for sale to the IRS. MDBS agreed to pay a license fee of $125,000 for use of the SQL Access program plus $125,000 for Dharma's adapting the program to MDBS's needs. The license fee was to be paid immediately. The second $125,000, which is denominated "for professional services," was to be paid in three installments. The first installment, $50,000, was due upon "Project Start-up." The second installment, also $50,000, was due upon "Beta Release," that is, when the modified SQL Access program was sent to MDBS and Unisys for "beta testing." This is a term of art in the computer industry; but in the case of custom software (our case) as distinct from commercial software, the record is unclear whether it is the penultimate [next to the last] or ultimate performance test before the customer's acceptance of delivery of the software. The last installment, $25,000, was due upon "Acceptance by Unisys."

The contract terms that we have just summarized are the terms as stated in a letter that MDBS wrote Dharma on July 7, 1994. * * * [Previously] Dharma had sent MDBS a draft of a License Agreement designed to limit the distribution of the RDMS Emulation [software in which the SQL access program was incorporated] * * * . MDBS never signed the agreement, but continually reassured an increasingly anxious Dharma (which made repeated requests) that it would do so.

MDBS paid Dharma the $125,000 license fee, and Dharma went to work. MDBS also paid both the first installment of the adaptation fee—$50,000 upon project start-up—and, on November 8, 1994, when Dharma shipped the beta version of the RDMS Emulation, the second $50,000 installment. MDBS turned the beta version over to Unisys for testing. * * * The following May, Unisys landed the contract with the IRS, and it then asked MDBS to send it six copies of the RDMS Emulation—one for it to keep and the others to sell to the IRS. * * * Dharma * * * shipped the disks to MDBS on September 20, 1995. * * *

A few weeks after this, MDBS, without seeking or obtaining Dharma's consent, shipped the six copies of the RDMS Emulation to Unisys. MDBS's cover letter stated that the shipment was for "acceptance testing," was not "a distribution," and was to be used for "quality assurance and further testing only," and "any further duplication or distribution is strictly prohibited." Two weeks later Unisys notified MDBS of ten (later reduced to nine) defects in the RDMS Emulation. * * *

The defects apparently were minor and easy to correct. But Dharma refused to correct them until MDBS signed the License Agreement. Dharma was worried that once they were corrected, MDBS or Unisys could duplicate the disks and thus sell multiple copies to the Internal Revenue Service. It is true that Dharma's programs are copyrighted, so neither MDBS nor Unisys could lawfully have copied them. But Dharma was worried that MDBS or Unisys might be able through reverse engineering to extract noncopyrightable elements in the software from which it might be able to build a duplicate of the RDMS Emulation that would not infringe Dharma's copyright.

Despite the defects, Unisys turned over five of the six copies of the RDMS Emulation to the IRS, paid MDBS the $25,000 final installment for transmission to Dharma (which MDBS kept rather than remit to Dharma), and, pursuant to its contract with MDBS, paid MDBS $413,894 in prepaid royalties generated by Unisys's contract with the IRS. Unisys had been withholding this payment until it obtained the five copies of the RDMS

Emulation which it needed to satisfy its contractual obligations to the IRS.

MDBS brought this suit [in a federal district court] against Dharma seeking restitution of the $225,000 that it had paid Dharma under the contract. Dharma counterclaimed, seeking $25,000 (the unpaid final installment under the contract) in damages for breach of contract * * * . The district court ruled as a matter of law that the substantive issues in the case were governed by the law of New Hampshire [and] that MDBS and not Dharma had violated the contract and owed Dharma $25,000 for this breach * * * .

MDBS's business is in Indiana and Dharma's in New Hampshire. The contract was made by an exchange of letters and other communications, and so has no site. But the contract was performed entirely in New Hampshire, and we agree with the district court that under Indiana's choice of law rules, which are the rules applicable to this diversity case, the law applicable to both the contract and trade secrets issues is that of New Hampshire. The standards that state courts (including those of Indiana) use nowadays to resolve choice of law issues are widely and we think correctly believed to be nondirective, but their administration is usually pretty sensible. The important thing, especially in a contractual setting, is that the parties should have a clear idea of which state's law will apply, since once they know this they can if they wish change the state whose law is to govern their relation by including a choice of law provision in their contract. In a case in which the contract is made as it were nowhere, because the parties are in different states (or countries) and the contract is negotiated without a face-to-face meeting, but it is entirely performed in one state, the parties will expect the law of that state to govern any contractual dispute that arises during performance (for what other state would be a more plausible candidate?) unless they specify otherwise in the contract, which they did not do here. So the district court's choice of law ruling was clearly correct with respect to the contract issues. * * *

* * * *

The * * * significance of choice of law in this case is that the probability that the contract is governed by the Uniform Commercial Code is much greater under New Hampshire law than under Indiana law. Article 2, the relevant part of the Code, is limited to the sale of "goods." The only Indiana case holds that custom software is a service, while the only New Hampshire case holds that it is a good. * * * [Because the New Hampshire case] is consistent with the weight of authority and reaches the right result—for *we can think of no reason why the UCC is not suitable to govern disputes arising from the sale of custom software*—we'll follow it. [Emphasis added.]

That cannot be the end of the analysis, however. The contract between MDBS and Dharma was for the sale not only of a good (the RDMS Emulation), as we have just held, but also of a service—the creation of the RDMS Emulation by adaptation of Dharma's preexisting program, the SQL Access program. Under New Hampshire law, to determine whether such a "hybrid" transaction is governed by the Code requires deciding which aspect of the transaction, the sale of goods or the sale of services, predominates (unless, perhaps, the dispute is clearly assignable to either the goods or the services aspect, and it is not here). Here it is the sale of the goods that predominates. Although the contract recites that half the total contract price is for Dharma's "professional services," these were not services to be rendered to MDBS but merely the labor to be expended by Dharma in the "manufacture" of the "good" from existing software. It's no different than if MDBS were buying an automobile from Dharma, and Dharma invoiced MDBS $20,000 for the car and $1,000 for labor involved in customizing it for MDBS's special needs. It would still be the sale of a good within the meaning of the UCC. We doubt that it should even be called a "hybrid" sale, for this would imply that every sale of goods is actually a hybrid sale, since labor is a service and labor is an input into the manufacture of every good.

* * * *

We conclude that the district court's rulings were correct and that the jury's verdict was within the outer bounds of the lawful and the reasonable. The judgment is therefore

AFFIRMED.

CASE 18.2 ADDITIONAL TERMS

WILSON FERTILIZER & GRAIN, INC. v. ADM MILLING CO.

Court of Appeals of Indiana, 1995.
654 N.E.2d 848.

BARTEAU, Judge.

FACTS

Wilson [Fertilizer & Grain, Inc.] and ADM [Milling Company] entered into a contract under which Wilson shipped grain to ADM. A broker facilitated the deal between Wilson and ADM, and sent each party a confirmation of trade. The confirmation of trade did not contain an arbitration provision. ADM sent a purchase confirmation to Wilson that contained boiler plate language which states: "This contract is also subject to the Trade Rules of the National Grain and Feed Association currently in effect." Wilson did not object to this language and did not respond to ADM's purchase confirmation.

A dispute arose under the contract and Wilson filed suit against ADM in [an Indiana state court]. ADM moved to dismiss the action, claiming that the Trade Rules of the National Grain and Feed Association require the parties to arbitrate the dispute. Wilson argued that the arbitration provisions were not included within the terms of its agreement with ADM. The trial court granted ADM's motion and ordered the parties to arbitration.

DISCUSSION

A party seeking to compel arbitration must satisfy a two-prong burden of proof. First, the party must demonstrate an enforceable agreement to arbitrate the dispute. Second, the party must prove that the disputed matter is the type of claim that the parties agreed to arbitrate. In this case, the second prong of our analysis is not in dispute, since neither party contends that the arbitration provisions do not encompass Wilson's claim. The only question presented herein is under the first prong: whether the additional terms are included in the contract between Wilson and ADM.

Whether the additional provisions are part of the contract is controlled by [Indiana Code Section 26-1-2-207, Indiana's version of UCC 2–207], which provides in part:

> (1) A definite and seasonable expression of acceptance or a written confirmation which is sent within a reasonable time operates as an acceptance even though it states terms additional to or different from those offered or agreed upon, unless acceptance is expressly made conditional on assent to the additional or different terms.
>
> (2) The additional terms are to be construed as proposals for addition to the contract. Between merchants such terms become part of the contract unless:
>
> (a) the offer expressly limits acceptance to the terms of the offer;
>
> (b) they materially alter it; or
>
> (c) notification of objection to them has already been given or is given within a reasonable time after notice of them is received.

* * * *

The test for whether additional terms materially alter an agreement is whether their incorporation into the contract without express awareness by the other party would result in surprise or hardship. * * *

Some jurisdictions that have considered this issue have adopted the "New York rule" holding that additional arbitration provisions create a material alteration *per se*. This rule is based on New York's well-established law that parties will not be compelled to arbitrate in the absence of an express, unequivocal agreement to that effect; absent such an explicit commitment neither party may be compelled to arbitrate. * * *

* * * Wilson argues that we should follow the New York rule and find that * * * ADM's additional arbitration provisions materially alter the agreement as a matter of law.

* * * *

* * * [W]e reject Wilson's argument * * * and decline to adopt the New York rule. Instead, whether included arbitration provisions result in hardship or surprise depends upon the facts and circumstances of each case. * * *

* * * *

* * * [R]equiring a party to arbitrate a dispute does not *necessarily* place a hardship on the party. To the contrary, arbitration may work to the party's benefit by facilitating an efficient and potentially favorable resolution to a dispute. Many trades employ arbitration as a usual and customary dispute resolution mechanism. In light of this, even New York courts have deviated from their *per se* rule and have held that *an additional arbitration clause is not a material alteration if the party had reason to know that such a clause was customarily used in the trade.* [Emphasis added.]

* * * *

Turning to the facts presented, Wilson argues that the trial court erroneously determined that the additional provisions did not materially alter its agreement with ADM because the evidence conclusively shows that inclusion of the provisions imposes hardship on Wilson. Specifically, Wilson argues that the National Grain and Feed Association Rules of Arbitration significantly reduce the time period during which it may file its complaint against ADM from Indiana's six-year statute of limitation to one year. Wilson argues that this results in hardship because, now that its claim has been dismissed * * * , time has run for Wilson to file its claim under the arbitration rules. We disagree for two reasons.

First of all, contractually reducing the time period during which parties may bring complaints is permitted under the Uniform Commercial Code. * * * [The UCC] specifically permits parties to a contract for sale to reduce the time for filing claims to one year, and Wilson has not shown that the one-year limitation is not within the customary limits of the trade.

Second, and even more significantly, we are persuaded by Wilson's apparent ability to have submitted its claim for arbitration within the one-year limit. The contract between Wilson and ADM was formed on October 20, 1992. There is nothing in the record indicating when Wilson delivered its grain to ADM, or when ADM's alleged breach occurred. However, Wilson filed its complaint for damages * * * on September 24, 1993, within one year after the contract was formed. Thus, Wilson filed its complaint within one year after the cause of action accrued because, as a matter of logic, an action for breach of contract can only accrue after the contract was formed. If Wilson was able to file its complaint in court within one year after the cause of action accrued, we fail to see how a contract provision requiring Wilson to submit its claim for arbitration in the same time period imposes a hardship.

* * * *

The trial court's finding that the additional term in ADM's purchase confirmation did not materially alter the agreement is supported by the evidence and is not clearly erroneous.

AFFIRMED.

* * * *

KIRSCH, Judge, * * * dissenting.

I fully concur with the rule of law set forth in the majority opinion. From its application to the facts of this case, however, I respectfully dissent.

* * * *

* * * [T]here are two factual issues which should be determined by the trial court: The first issue is whether ADM's confirmation even constituted an acceptance within the meaning of UCC [Section] 2–207. If the confirmation sent by the broker to Wilson was sent prior to ADM's confirmation, it constitutes the acceptance of the offer; the contract was fully formed by that confirmation. The later confirmation sent by ADM would only be a proposal to modify the contract as formed and UCC [Section] 2–207 would not apply. Second, even if ADM's confirmation constitutes the acceptance and [Section] 2–207 does apply, there is an unresolved question of fact as to whether the additional term contained in such confirmation results in hardship or surprise and thus constitutes a material alteration. In either event, these unresolved factual issues make the dismissal of this case inappropriate.

ADM Milling Company played the latest version of "Legal Gotcha." And it won. It has received the grain which it ordered and escaped paying for it.

I would reverse the dismissal and remand to the trial court to conduct an evidentiary hearing.

CASE 18.3 UNCONSCIONABILITY

JONES V. STAR CREDIT CORP.

Supreme Court of New York, Nassau County, 1969.
59 Misc.2d 189,
298 N.Y.S.2d 264.

SOL M. *WACHTLER*, Justice.

On August 31, 1965 the plaintiffs, who are welfare recipients, agreed to purchase a home freezer unit for $900 as the result of a visit from a salesman representing Your Shop At Home Service, Inc. With the addition of the time credit charges, credit life insurance, credit property insurance, and sales tax, the purchase price totalled $1,234.80. Thus far the plaintiffs have paid $619.88 toward their purchase. The defendant claims that with various added credit charges paid for an extension of time there is a balance of $819.81 still due from the plaintiffs. The uncontroverted proof at the trial established that the freezer unit, when purchased, had a maximum retail value of approximately $300. The question is whether this transaction and the resulting contract could be considered unconsionable within the meaning of Section 2–302 of the Uniform Commercial Code which provides in part:

> (1) If the court as a matter of law finds the contract or any clause of the contract to have been unconscionable at the time it was made the court may refuse to enforce the contract, or it may enforce the remainder of the contract without the unconscionable clause, or it may so limit the application of any unconscionable clause as to avoid any unconscionable result.
> (2) When it is claimed or appears to the court that the contract or any clause thereof may be unconscionable the parties shall be afforded a reasonable opportunity to present evidence as to its commercial setting, purpose and effect to aid the court in making the determination.

There was a time when the shield of "*caveat emptor*" ["let the buyer beware"] would protect the most unscrupulous in the marketplace—a time when the law, in granting parties unbridled latitude to make their own contracts, allowed exploitive and callous practices which shocked the conscience of both legislative bodies and the courts.

The effort to eliminate these practices has continued to pose a difficult problem. On the one hand it is necessary to recognize the importance of preserving the integrity of agreements and the fundamental right of parties to deal, trade, bargain, and contract. On the other hand there is the concern for the uneducated and often illiterate individual who is the victim of gross inequality of bargaining power, usually the poorest members of the community.

Concern for the protection of these consumers against overreaching by the small but hardy breed of merchants who would prey on them is not novel. The dangers of inequality of bargaining power were vaguely recognized in the early English common law when Lord Hardwicke wrote of a fraud, which "may be apparent from the intrinsic nature and subject of the bargain itself; such as no man in his senses and not under delusion would make." * * * [T]he United States Supreme Court characterized [the English cases on this subject] as "cases in which one party took advantage of the other's ignorance of arithmetic to impose upon him, and the fraud was apparent from the face of the contracts."

The law is beginning to fight back against those who once took advantage of the poor and illiterate without risk of either exposure or interference. From the common law doctrine of intrinsic fraud we have, over the years, developed common and statutory law which tells not only the buyer but also the seller to beware. This body of laws recognizes the importance of a free enterprise system but at the same time will provide the legal armor to protect and safeguard the prospective victim from the harshness of an unconscionable contract.

Section 2–302 of the Uniform Commercial Code enacts the moral sense of the community into the law of commercial transactions. It authorizes the court to find, as a matter of law, that a contract or a clause of a contract was "unconscionable at the time it was made," and upon so finding the court may refuse to enforce the contract, excise the objectionable clause or limit the application of the clause to avoid an unconscionable result. The principle * * * is one of the prevention of oppression and unfair surprise. It permits a court to accomplish directly what heretofore was often accomplished by construction of language, manipulations of fluid rules of contract law and determinations based upon a presumed public policy.

There is no reason to doubt, moreover, that this section is intended to encompass the price term of an agreement. * * * [T]he statutory language itself makes it clear that not only a clause of the contract, but the contract *in toto* [in its entirety], may be found unconscionable as a matter of law. Indeed, *no other provision of an agreement more intimately touches upon the question of unconscionability than does the term regarding price.* [Emphasis added.]

Fraud, in the instant case, is not present; nor is it necessary under the statute. The question which presents itself is whether or not, under the circumstances of this case, the sale of a freezer unit having a retail value of $300 for $900 ($1,439.69 including credit charges and $18 sales tax) is unconscionable as a matter of law. The court believes it is.

Concededly, deciding the issue is substantially easier than explaining it. No doubt, the mathematical disparity between $300, which presumably includes a reasonable profit margin, and $900, which is exorbitant on its face, carries the greatest weight. Credit charges alone exceed by more than $100 the retail value of the freezer. These alone may be sufficient to sustain the decision. Yet, a *caveat* is warranted lest we reduce the import of Section 2–302 solely to a mathematical ratio formula. It may, at times, be that; yet it may also be much more. The very limited financial resources of the purchaser, known to the sellers at the time of the sale, is entitled to weight in the balance. Indeed, the value disparity itself leads inevitably to the felt conclusion that knowing advantage was taken of the plaintiffs. In addition, the meaningfulness of choice essential to the making of a contract can be negated by a gross inequality of bargaining power.

There is no question about the necessity and even the desirability of installment sales and the extension of credit. Indeed, there are many, including welfare recipients, who would be deprived of even the most basic conveniences without the use of these devices. Similarly, the retail merchant selling on installment or extending credit is expected to establish a pricing factor which will afford a degree of protection commensurate with the risk of selling to those who might be default prone. However, neither of these accepted premises can clothe the sale of this freezer with respectability.

* * * *

One final point remains. The defendant argues that the contract of June 15, 1966, upon which this suit is based, constitutes a financing agreement and not a sales contract. To support its position, it points to the typed words "Refinance of Freezer A/C #6766 and Food A/C #56788" on the agreement and to a letter signed by the plaintiffs requesting refinance of the same items. The request for "refinancing" is typed on the defendant's letterhead. The quoted refinance statement is typed on a form agreement entitled "Star Credit Corporation—Retail Installment Contract." It is signed by the defendant as "seller" and by the purchasers as "buyer." Above the signature of the buyers, they acknowledge "receipt of an executed copy of this RETAIL INSTALLMENT CONTRACT" (capitalization in original). The June 15, 1966 contract by defendant is on exactly the same form as the original contract of August 31, 1965. The original, too, is entitled "Star Credit Corporation—Retail Installment Contract." It is signed, however, by "Your Shop At Home Service, Inc." Printed beneath the signatures is the legend "Duplicate for Star." In substance and effect, the agreement of June 25, 1966 constitutes a novation and replacement of the earlier agreement. It is, in all respects, as it reads, a Retail Installment Contract.

Having already [been] paid more than $600 toward the purchase of this $300 freezer unit, it is apparent that the defendant has already been amply compensated. In accordance with the statute, the application of the payment provision should be limited to amounts already paid by the plaintiffs and the contract be reformed and amended by changing the payments called for therein to equal the amount of payment actually so paid by the plaintiffs.

CASE PROBLEMS

18–1. Fred and Zuma Palermo contacted Colorado Carpet Installation, Inc., for a price quotation on providing and installing new carpeting and tiling in their home. In response, Colorado Carpet submitted a written proposal to provide and install the carpet at a certain price per square foot of material, *including* labor. The total was in excess of $500. The proposal was never accepted in writing by the Palermos, and the parties disagreed over how much of the proposal had been agreed to orally. After the installation of the carpet and tiling had begun, Mrs. Palermo became dissatisfied and sought the services of another contractor. Colorado Carpet then sued the Palermos for breach of the oral contract. The trial court held that the contract was one for services and was thus enforceable (that is, it did not fall under the Statute of Frauds [UCC 2–201], which requires contracts for the sale of *goods* for the price of $500 or more to be in writing to be enforceable). Discuss fully whether the contract between the Palermos and Colorado Carpet was primarily for the sale of goods or the sale of services. [*Colorado Carpet Installation, Inc. v. Palermo,* 668 P.2d 1384 (Colo. 1983)]

18–2. Loeb & Co. entered into an oral agreement with Schreiner, a farmer, whereby Schreiner was to sell Loeb 150 bales of cotton, each weighing 480 pounds. Shortly thereafter, Loeb sent Schreiner a letter confirming the terms of the oral contract. Schreiner neither acknowledged receipt of the letter nor objected to its terms. When delivery came due, Schreiner ignored the oral agreement and sold his cotton on the open market, because the price of cotton had more than doubled (from 37 cents to 80 cents per pound) since the oral agreement had been made. In a lawsuit by Loeb & Co. against Schreiner, can Loeb & Co. recover? Explain. [*Loeb & Co. v. Schreiner,* 294 Ala. 722, 321 So.2d 199 (1975)]

18–3. Helvey received electricity from the Wabash County REMC, the county electrical utility. A mistake in the voltage delivered over the electrical line resulted in damage to Helvey's household appliances; households require only 110 volts, and Wabash delivered 135 volts or more. Some years later, Helvey sued Wabash County for breach of express and implied contractual warranties. Wabash County claimed that under UCC 2–725 a four-year statute of limitations existed and that Helvey had no claim because more than four years had elapsed since the accident. State law provided for a shorter statute of limitations period for sales of goods than for service contracts, however. Helvey claimed that the UCC provision did not apply because electricity is a service and not a good. Discuss whether the UCC should be applied in this case. [*Helvey v. Wabash County REMC,* 151 Ind.App. 176, 278 N.E.2d 608 (1972)]

18–4. R-P Packaging, Inc., is a manufacturer of cellophane wrapping material. The plant manager for Flowers Baking Co. decided to improve the company's packaging of cookies. The plant manager contacted R-P Packaging regarding the possible purchase of cellophane wrap imprinted with designed "artwork." R-P took measurements to determine the appropriate size of the wrap and submitted to Flowers a sample of wrap conforming to the measurements, along with a sample of the artwork to be imprinted. After agreeing that the artwork was satisfactory, Flowers gave a verbal order to R-P for the designed cellophane wrap at a price of $13,000. When the wrap was tendered, although it conformed to the measurements and design, Flowers complained that the wrap was too short and the design off-center. Flowers rejected the shipment. R-P sued. Flowers contended that the oral contract was unenforceable under the Statute of Frauds. Discuss this contention. [*Flowers Baking Co. v. R-P Packaging, Inc.,* 229 Va. 370, 329 S.E.2d 462 (1985)]

18–5. Monetti, S.P.A., is an Italian firm that makes decorative plastic trays and related products for the food services industry. In 1981, Monetti set up a wholly owned subsidiary, Melform U.S.A., to market its products in the United States. In 1984, after orally agreeing with Anchor Hocking Corp. (Anchor) that Anchor would become the exclusive U.S. distributor of Monetti products, Monetti terminated all of Melform's current distributors and informed all of Melform's customers that Anchor would be the exclusive distributor of its products in the future. Relations between Monetti and Anchor Hocking deteriorated over the next several months, and eventually Monetti sued for breach of contract. Anchor contended that their contract was unenforceable under the Statute of Frauds. Although their agreement had never been reduced to a writing, at one point Raymond Davis, the marketing director of Anchor, summarized the terms of the agreement in a memorandum on Anchor's letterhead that was sent to Anchor's law department. The memo included some handwritten notes by Davis, which, Davis stated, represented "more clearly our current position regarding the agreement." Will the memorandum signed by Davis constitute a sufficient writing under the UCC Statute of Frauds provisions? Discuss. [*Monetti, S.P.A. v. Anchor Hocking Corp.,* 931 F.2d 1178 (7th Cir. 1991)]

18–6. Ingram Meyers, a B. F. Goodrich Co. employee and agent, made an oral agreement with James Thomson of Thomson Printing Machinery Co. to sell Thomson some surplus printing machinery. Four days later, Thomson sent a "writing in confirmation" to Goodrich. The writing consisted of (1) a purchase order, which contained Thomson Printing's name, address, telephone number, and some details concerning the purchase of the machinery, and (2) a check that, by its notations, was specifically connected with the purchase order. Several weeks later, when Thomson called Goodrich about the machinery, it was revealed that the machinery had been sold to someone else. Thomson then brought suit against Goodrich to enforce the oral contract. Goodrich contended that the oral contract was not enforceable because the "writing" sent to Goodrich by Thomson had never been received by Ingram Meyers. Thus, Goodrich could not be held liable for the contract because it could not repudiate a writing that it had not received. Goodrich alleged that the written confirmation had never been received by its agent/seller because the envelope had not been properly sent to the attention of Meyers or to the surplus equipment department in which Meyers worked. Goodrich further contended that it made several attempts to "find a home" for the purchase order and check by sending copies of its contents to various divisions. Meyers stated that he did not learn of the purchase order until several weeks later, when Thomson called to arrange for the removal of the machines. Does the writing (the purchase order and check) sent by Thomson to Goodrich and received in Goodrich's mail room satisfy the writing requirements of the Statute of Frauds, thus making the oral contract enforceable? Discuss. [*Thomson Printing Machinery Co. v. B. F. Goodrich Co.*, 714 F.2d 744 (7th Cir. 1983)]

18–7. The Carpet Mart, a carpet dealer, telephoned an order (offer) for carpet to Collins & Aikman Corp., a carpet manufacturer. Collins & Aikman then sent Carpet Mart an acknowledgment form (acceptance), which specified the quantity and price agreed to in the telephone conversation. The reverse side of the printed acknowledgment form stated that Collins & Aikman's acceptance was subject to the buyer's agreement to submit all disputes to arbitration. Collins & Aikman shipped the carpet to Carpet Mart, which received the acknowledgment form and shipment without objection. Later, a dispute arose, and Carpet Mart brought a civil suit against Collins & Aikman, claiming misrepresentation as to the quality of the carpet. Collins & Aikman filed a motion to stay (cease all action on) the civil suit and to enforce the arbitration clause. Will the court enforce the arbitration clause? Discuss. [*Dorton v. Collins & Aikman Corp.*, 453 F.2d 1161 (6th Cir. 1972)]

18–8. Harry Starr orally contracted to purchase a new automobile from Freeport Dodge, Inc. Starr signed an order form describing the car and made a down payment of $25. The dealer did not sign the form, and the form stated that "this order is not valid unless signed and accepted by the dealer." The dealer deposited the $25, and that was noted on the order form. On the day scheduled for delivery, a sales representative for the dealer told Starr that an error had been made in determining the price and that Starr would be required to pay an additional $175 above the price on the order form. Starr refused to pay the additional amount and sued for breach of contract. Freeport Dodge claimed that the contract fell under the Statute of Frauds and that because Freeport Dodge had not signed the contract, the oral contract was not enforceable. Discuss Freeport Dodge's contention. [*Starr v. Freeport Dodge, Inc.*, 54 Misc.2d 271, 282 N.Y.S.2d 58 (Dist.Ct. 1967)]

18–9. John Schwanbeck entered into negotiations with Federal-Mogul Corp. to purchase Federal-Mogul's Vellumoid Division. The two parties drew up a letter of intent stating that "[n]o further obligation will arise until a definitive agreement is reduced to writing" and that it was the parties' intention "to proceed in good faith in the negotiation of such binding definitive agreement." At another place in the letter of intent were the words, "Of course, this letter is not intended to create, nor do you or we presently have any binding legal obligation whatever in any way relating to such sale and purchase." Federal-Mogul eventually sold the Vellumoid Division to another party. Schwanbeck sued Federal-Mogul, alleging, among other things, that Federal-Mogul had breached an agreement to negotiate in good faith the proposed contract with Schwanbeck. Did the letter of intent create a legally binding obligation, or was the letter merely an "agreement to agree" in the future? Discuss. [*Schwanbeck v. Federal-Mogul Corp.*, 412 Mass. 703, 592 N.E.2d 1289 (1992)]

18–10. Jane Pittsley contracted with Donald Houser, who was doing business as the Hilton Contract Carpet Co., for the installation of carpet in her home. Following installation, Pittsley complained to Hilton that some seams were visible, gaps had appeared, the carpet did not lie flat in all areas, and the carpet failed to reach the wall in certain locations. Although Hilton made various attempts to fix the installation by trying to stretch the carpet and other methods, Pittsley was not satisfied with the work and eventually sued Hilton to recover the $3,500 she had paid toward the $4,319.50 contract price for the carpet and its installation. Hilton had paid the installers $700 for the work done in laying Pittsley's carpet. One of the issues before the court was whether the contract was a contract for the sale of goods or a contract for the sale of services. How should the court decide this issue? Discuss fully. [*Pittsley v. Houser*, 125 Idaho 820, 875 P.2d 232 (1994)]

18–11. GPL Treatment, Ltd., orally agreed to sell a large quantity of cedar shakes to Louisiana-Pacific Corp. (L-P). GPL sent L-P order confirmation forms that stated the prices and quantities of shakes ordered. Each form also contained a "sign and return" clause, asking L-P to sign and return one copy. L-P did not sign or return any of the forms, but it also did not object to any of the terms. When L-P accepted only about 15 percent of the orders, GPL filed a suit in an Oregon state court against the buyer for breach of contract. Do GPL's confirmation forms satisfy the requirement of a writing under the Statute of Frauds? Are they enforceable against L-P? Discuss fully. [*GPL Treatment, Ltd. v. Louisiana-Pacific Corp.*, 323 Or. 116, 914 P.2d 682 (1996)]

18–12. Peggy Holloway, a real estate broker, guaranteed payment for a shipment of over $11,000 worth of mozzarella cheese sold by Cudahy Foods Co. to Pizza Pride in Jamestown, North Carolina. The entire arrangement was made orally. Cudahy mailed to Holloway an invoice for the order, and Holloway did not object in writing to the invoice within ten days of receipt. Later, when Cudahy demanded payment from Holloway, Holloway denied having guaranteed payment for the cheese and raised the Statute of Frauds as an affirmative defense. Cudahy claimed that the Statute of Frauds could not be used as a defense, as both Cudahy and Holloway were merchants and Holloway had failed to object in writing within ten days to Cudahy's invoice. Discuss Cudahy's argument. [*Cudahy Foods Co. v. Holloway*, 286 S.E.2d 606 (N.C.App. 1982)]

18–13. Ritz-Craft Corp. contracted with the Stanford Management Group (SMG) to "manufacture and install prefabricated multi-family housing units" for SMG. Ritz-Craft was also to set the units on the foundations constructed by SMG, as well as provide some connective work for electricity, plumbing, and so on. The original contract price for forty-nine units was $1,613,500, but a subsequent modification to the contract due to unforeseen circumstances raised the price by $45,000. SMG refused to pay the additional $45,000, arguing that the modification was not enforceable because it had not been accompanied by consideration. Ritz-Craft sued for breach of contract. If no consideration was given, is the agreement to modify the original contract binding? Does the manufacture and installation of modular homes involve goods or services? Discuss fully how the court should rule on each of these issues. [*Ritz-Craft Corp. v. Stanford Management Group*, 800 F.Supp. 1312 (D.Md. 1992)]

18–14. SNK, Inc., makes video arcade games and sells them to distributors, including Entertainment Sales, Inc. (ESI). Most sales between SNK and ESI were phone orders. Over one four-month period, ESI phoned in several orders for "Samurai Showdown" games. SNK did not fill the orders. ESI filed a suit against SNK and others, alleging, among other things, breach of contract. There was no written contract covering the orders. ESI claimed that it had faxed purchase orders for the games to SNK but did not offer proof that the faxes had been sent or received. SNK filed a motion for summary judgment. In whose favor will the court rule, and why? [*Entertainment Sales Co. v. SNK, Inc.*, 232 Ga.App. 669, 502 S.E.2d 263 (1998)]

18–15. Dennis Dahlmann and Dahlmann Apartments, Ltd., entered into contracts with Sulchus Hospitality Technologies Corp. and Hospitality Management Systems, Inc. (HMS), to buy property management systems. The systems included computer hardware and software, as well as installation, training, and support services, for the Bell Tower Hotel and the Campus Inn in Ann Arbor, Michigan. The software controlled the central reservations systems at both hotels. When Dahlmann learned that the software was not Y2K compliant—that it could not be used to post reservations beyond December 31, 1999—he filed a suit against Sulchus and HMS, alleging in part breach of contract. The defendants filed a motion for summary judgment. One of the issues was whether the contracts were subject to Article 2 of the UCC. Are they? Why, or why not? Explain fully. [*Dahlmann v. Sulchus Hospitality Technologies Corp.*, 63 F.Supp.2d 772 (E.D.Mich. 1999)]

E-LINKS

For updated links to resources available on the Web, as well as a variety of other materials, visit this text's Web site at

http://wbl-cs.westbuslaw.com

For information concerning the National Conference of Commissioners on Uniform State Laws (NCCUSL) and links to online uniform acts, go to

http://www.nccusl.org

The NCCUSL, in association with the University of Pennsylvania Law School, now offers an official site for in-process and final drafts of uniform and model acts. For an index of in-process drafts, go to

http://www.law.upenn.edu/bll/ulc/ulc.htm

For an index of final drafts, go to

http://www.law.upenn.edu/bll/ulc/ulc_final.htm

Cornell University's Legal Information Institute offers online access to the UCC, as well as to UCC articles as enacted by particular states and proposed revisions to articles, at

http://www.law.cornell.edu/ucc/ucc.table.html

The Pace University School of Law's Institute of International Commercial Law maintains a Web site that contains the full text of the CISG, as well as relevant cases and discussions of the law. Go to

http://cisgw3.law.pace.edu

LEGAL RESEARCH EXERCISES ON THE WEB

Go to http://wbl-cs.westbuslaw.com, the Web site that accompanies this text. Select "Interactive Study Center," and then click on "Chapter 18." There you will find the following Internet research exercise that you can perform to learn more about sales contracts:

Activity 18–1: Is It a Contract?

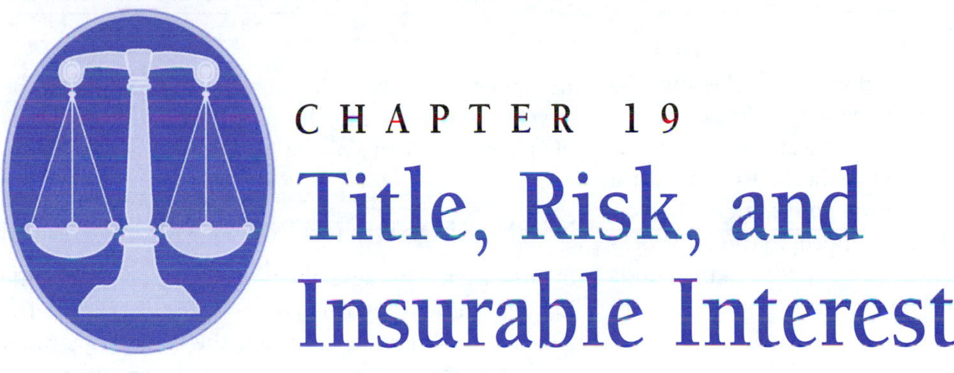

CHAPTER 19 Title, Risk, and Insurable Interest

BEFORE THE CREATION OF THE Uniform Commercial Code (UCC), *title*—the right of ownership—was the central concept in sales law, controlling all issues of rights and remedies of the parties to a sales contract. There were numerous problems with this concept. For example, frequently it was difficult to determine when title actually passed from seller to buyer, and therefore it was also difficult to predict which party a court would decide had title at the time of a loss. Because of such problems, the UCC divorced the question of title as completely as possible from the question of the rights and obligations of buyers, sellers, and third parties (such as subsequent purchasers, creditors, or the tax collector).

In some situations, title is still relevant under the UCC, and the UCC has special rules for locating title. These rules will be discussed in the sections that follow. In most situations, however, the UCC has replaced the concept of title with three other concepts: (1) identification, (2) risk of loss, and (3) insurable interest.

In lease contracts, of course, title to the goods is retained by the lessor-owner of the goods. Hence, the UCC's provisions relating to passage of title do not apply to leased goods. Other concepts discussed in this chapter, though, including identification, risk of loss, and insurable interest, relate to lease contracts as well as to sales contracts.

SECTION 1

Identification

Before any interest in specific goods can pass from the seller or lessor to the buyer or lessee, two conditions must prevail:

1. The goods must be in existence.
2. They must be identified as the specific goods designated in the contract.

Identification is a designation of goods as the subject matter of a sales or lease contract. Title and risk of loss cannot pass to the buyer from the seller unless the goods are identified to the contract [UCC 2–105(2)]. (As mentioned, title to leased goods remains with the lessor—or, if the owner is a third party, with that party. The lessee does not acquire title to leased goods.) Identification is significant because it gives the buyer or lessee the right to insure (or obtain an insurable interest in) the goods and the right to recover from third parties who damage the goods.

Once the goods are in existence, the parties can agree in their contract on when identification will take place. If they do not so specify, however, the UCC provisions discussed here determine when identification takes place [UCC 2–501(1), 2A–217].

EXISTING GOODS

If the contract calls for the sale or lease of specific and ascertained goods that are already in existence, identification takes place at the time the contract is made. For example, you contract to purchase or lease a fleet of five cars by the serial numbers listed for the cars.

FUTURE GOODS

If a sale involves unborn animals to be born within twelve months after contracting, identification takes place when the animals are conceived. If a lease involves any unborn animals, identification occurs when the animals are conceived. If a sale involves crops that are to be harvested within twelve months (or the next harvest season occurring after contracting, whichever is longer), identification takes place when the crops are planted or begin to grow. In a sale or lease of any other future goods, identification occurs when the goods are shipped, marked, or otherwise designated by the seller or lessor as the goods to which the contract refers.

Goods That Are Part of a Larger Mass

Goods that are part of a larger mass are identified when the goods are marked, shipped, or somehow designated by the seller or lessor as the particular goods to pass under the contract. Suppose that a buyer orders 1,000 cases of beans from a 10,000-case lot. Until the seller separates the 1,000 cases of beans from the 10,000-case lot, title and risk of loss remain with the seller.

A common exception to this rule deals with fungible goods. **Fungible goods** are goods that are alike naturally, by agreement, or by trade usage. Typical examples are specific grades or types of wheat, oil, and wine, usually stored in large containers. If these goods are held or intended to be held by owners in common (owners having shares undivided from the entire mass), a seller-owner can pass title and risk of loss to the buyer without an actual separation. The buyer replaces the seller as an owner in common [UCC 2–105(4)].

For example, Anselm, Braudel, and Carpenter are farmers. They deposit, respectively, 5,000 bushels, 3,000 bushels, and 2,000 bushels of grain of the same grade and quality in a bin. The three become owners in common, with Anselm owning 50 percent of the 10,000 bushels, Braudel 30 percent, and Carpenter 20 percent. Anselm could contract to sell her 5,000 bushels of grain to Tareyton and, because the goods are fungible, pass title and risk of loss to Tareyton without physically separating the 5,000 bushels. Tareyton now becomes an owner in common with Braudel and Carpenter.

SECTION 2

When Title Passes

Once goods exist and are identified, the provisions of UCC 2–401 apply to the passage of title. Unless an agreement is explicitly made,[1] title passes to the buyer at the time and the place the seller performs the *physical delivery* of the goods [UCC 2–401(2)].

Shipment and Destination Contracts

In the absence of agreement, delivery arrangements can determine when title passes from the seller to the buyer. In a **shipment contract**, the seller is required or authorized to ship goods by carrier, such as a trucking company. Under a shipment contract, the seller is required only to deliver the goods into the hands of a carrier, and title passes to the buyer at the time and place of shipment [UCC 2–401(2)(a)]. *Generally, all contracts are assumed to be shipment contracts if nothing to the contrary is stated in the contract.*

In a **destination contract**, the seller is required to deliver the goods to a particular destination, usually directly to the buyer, although sometimes the buyer designates that the goods should be delivered to another party. Title passes to the buyer when the goods are *tendered* at that destination [UCC 2–401(2)(b)]. A tender of delivery is the seller's placing or holding of conforming goods at the buyer's disposition (with any necessary notice), enabling the buyer to take delivery [UCC 2–503(1)].

Delivery without Movement of the Goods

When the contract of sale does not call for the seller's shipment or delivery of the goods (when the buyer is to pick up the goods), the passage of title depends on whether the seller must deliver a **document of title**, such as a bill of lading or a warehouse receipt, to the buyer. A *bill of lading* is a receipt for goods that is signed by a carrier and that serves as a contract for the transportation of the goods. A *warehouse receipt* is a receipt issued by a warehouser for goods stored in a warehouse.

When a document of title is required, title passes to the buyer *when and where the document is delivered.* Thus, if the goods are stored in a warehouse, title passes to the buyer when the appropriate documents are delivered to the buyer. The goods never move. In fact, the buyer can choose to leave the goods at the

1. In many sections of the UCC, the words "unless otherwise explicitly agreed" appear, meaning that any explicit agreement between the buyer and the seller determines the rights, duties, and liabilities of the parties, including when title passes.

same warehouse for a period of time, and the buyer's title to those goods will be unaffected.

When no documents of title are required, and delivery is made without moving the goods, title passes at the time and place the sales contract is made, if the goods have already been identified. If the goods have not been identified, title does not pass until identification occurs. Consider an example. Rogers sells lumber to Bodan. It is agreed that Bodan will pick up the lumber at the yard. If the lumber has been identified (segregated, marked, or in any other way distinguished from all other lumber), title passes to Bodan when the contract is signed. If the lumber is still in storage bins at the mill, title does not pass to Bodan until the particular pieces of lumber to be sold under this contract are identified [UCC 2–401(3)].

SALES OR LEASES BY NONOWNERS

Problems occur when persons who acquire goods with imperfect titles attempt to sell or lease them. Sections 2–402 and 2–403 of the UCC deal with the rights of two parties who lay claim to the same goods sold with imperfect titles. Generally, a buyer acquires at least whatever title the seller has to the goods sold.

These same UCC sections also protect lessees. Obviously, a lessee does not acquire whatever title the lessor has to the goods; rather, a lessee acquires a right to possess and use the goods—that is, a *leasehold interest.* A lessee acquires whatever leasehold interest the lessor has or has the power to transfer, subject to the lease contract [UCC 2A–303, 2A–304, 2A–305].

Void Title. A buyer may unknowingly purchase goods from a seller who is not the owner of the goods. If the seller is a thief, the seller's title is void—legally, no title exists. Thus, the buyer acquires no title, and the real owner can reclaim the goods from the buyer. The same result would occur if the goods were only leased, because the lessor would have no leasehold interest to transfer.

For example, if Jim steals goods owned by Maren, Jim has a *void title* to those goods. If Jim sells the goods to Shidra, Maren can reclaim them from Shidra even though Shidra acted in good faith and honestly was not aware that the goods were stolen. Article 2A contains similar provisions for leases.

Voidable Title. A seller has a *voidable title* if the goods that he or she is selling were obtained by fraud, paid for with a check that is later dishonored, purchased from a minor, or purchased on credit when the seller was *insolvent.* (Under the UCC, a person is **insolvent** when that person ceases to "pay his debts in the ordinary course of business or cannot pay his debts as they become due or is insolvent within the meaning of federal bankruptcy law" [UCC 1–201(23)].)

In contrast to a seller with void title, a seller with voidable title has the power to transfer a good title to a good faith purchaser for value. A **good faith purchaser** is one who buys without knowledge of circumstances that would make a person of ordinary prudence inquire about the validity of the seller's title to the goods. One who purchases *for value* gives legally sufficient consideration (value) for the goods purchased. The real owner normally cannot recover goods from a good faith purchaser for value [UCC 2–403(1)].[2] If the buyer of the goods is not a good faith purchaser for value, then the actual owner of the goods can reclaim them from the buyer (or from the seller, if the goods are still in the seller's possession).

The same rules apply in circumstances involving leases. A lessor with voidable title has the power to transfer a valid leasehold interest to a good faith lessee for value. The real owner cannot recover the goods, except as permitted by the terms of the lease. The real owner can, however, receive all proceeds arising from the lease, as well as a transfer of all rights, title, and interest as the lessor under the lease, including the lessor's interest in the return of the goods when the lease expires.

Westlaw. See Case 19.1 at the end of this chapter. To view the full, unedited case from Westlaw,® go to this text's Web site at **http://wbl-cs.westbuslaw.com**.

The Entrustment Rule. According to UCC 2–403(2), when goods are entrusted to a merchant *who deals in goods of that kind,* and the merchant sells the goods to a *buyer in the ordinary course of business,* that buyer obtains good title to the property. This is known as the entrustment rule. **Entrustment** includes both delivering the goods to the merchant and leaving the purchased goods with the merchant for later delivery or pickup [UCC 2–403(3)]. A buyer in the ordinary course of business is a person who, in good faith and without

2. The real owner could, of course, sue the purchaser who initially obtained voidable title to the goods.

knowledge that the sale violates the ownership rights or security interest of a third party, buys in ordinary course from a person (other than a pawnbroker) in the business of selling goods of that kind [UCC 1–201(9)].

For example, Jan leaves her watch with a jeweler to be repaired. The jeweler sells both new and used watches. The jeweler sells Jan's watch to Kim, a customer, who does not know that the jeweler has no right to sell it. Kim, as a good faith buyer, gets good title against Jan's claim of ownership.[3] Kim, however, obtains only those rights held by the person entrusting the goods (here, Jan). Suppose that in this example, Jan had stolen the watch from Greg and then left it with the jeweler to be repaired. The jeweler then sold it to Kim. Kim would have obtained good title against Jan, who entrusted the watch to the jeweler, but not against Greg (the real owner), who neither entrusted the watch to Jan nor authorized Jan to entrust it.

Article 2A provides a similar rule for leased goods. If a lessor entrusts goods to a lessee-merchant who deals in goods of that kind, and the lessee-merchant transfers the goods to a buyer or sublessee in the ordinary course of business, the buyer or sublessee acquires all of the rights that the lessor had in the goods [UCC 2A–305(2)].[4]

See Case 19.2 at the end of this chapter. To view the full, unedited case from Westlaw,® go to this text's Web site at **http://wbl-cs.westbuslaw.com**.

SECTION 3

Risk of Loss

Under the UCC, risk of loss does not necessarily pass with title. When risk of loss passes from a seller or lessor to a buyer or lessee is generally determined by the contract between the parties. Sometimes, the contract states expressly when the risk of loss passes. At other times, it does not, and a court must interpret the existing terms to ascertain whether the risk has passed. When no provision in the contract indicates when risk passes, the UCC provides special rules, based on delivery terms, to guide the courts, as will be discussed shortly.

Delivery with Movement of the Goods

When there is no specification in the agreement, the following rules apply to cases involving movement of the goods (carrier cases).

Shipment Contracts. In a shipment contract, if the seller or lessor is required or authorized to ship goods by carrier (but not required to deliver them to a particular destination), risk of loss passes to the buyer or lessee when the goods are duly delivered to the carrier [UCC 2–509(1)(a), 2A–219(2)(a)].

For example, a seller in Texas sells five hundred cases of grapefruit to a buyer in New York, F. O.B. Houston (free on board in Houston—that is, the buyer pays the transportation charges from Houston). The contract authorizes a shipment by carrier; it does not require that the seller tender the grapefruit in New York. Risk passes to the buyer when conforming goods are properly placed in the possession of the carrier. If the goods are damaged in transit, the loss is the buyer's. (Actually, buyers have recourse against carriers, subject to certain limitations, and they may insure the goods from the time the goods leave the seller.)

See Case 19.3 at the end of this chapter. To view the full, unedited case from Westlaw,® go to this text's Web site at **http://wbl-cs.westbuslaw.com**.

Destination Contracts. In a destination contract, the risk of loss passes to the buyer or lessee when the goods are tendered to the buyer or lessee at the specified destination [UCC 2–509(1)(b), 2A–219(2)(b)]. In the preceding example, if the contract had been F. O.B. New York, risk of loss during transit to New York would have been the seller's and would not pass to the buyer until the carrier tendered the goods to the buyer in New York.

Contract Terms. Specific terms in the contract help determine when risk of loss passes to the buyer. These terms, which are listed and defined in Exhibit 19–1, relate generally to the determination of which party will bear the costs of delivery, as well as which party will bear the risk of loss.

3. Jan, of course, can sue the jeweler for the tort of conversion (or trespass to personal property) to obtain the equivalent money value of the watch (see Chapter 5).

4. This rule is consistent with the common law of bailments (see Chapter 46).

EXHIBIT 19–1 CONTRACT TERMS—DEFINITIONS

F.O.B. (free on board)—Indicates that the selling price of goods includes transportation costs (and that the seller carries risk of loss) to the specific F.O.B. place named in the contract. The place can be either the place of initial shipment (for example, the seller's city or place of business) or the place of destination (for example, the buyer's city or place of business) [UCC 2–319(1)].

F.A.S. (free alongside)—Requires that the seller, at his or her own expense and risk, deliver the goods alongside the ship before risk passes to the buyer [UCC 2–319(2)].

C.I.F. or **C.&F.** (cost, insurance, and freight or just cost and freight)—Requires, among other things, that the seller "put the goods in possession of a carrier" before risk passes to the buyer [UCC 2–320(2)]. (These are basically pricing terms, and the contracts remain shipment contracts, not destination contracts.)

Delivery ex-ship (delivery from the carrying vessel)—Means that risk of loss does not pass to the buyer until the goods leave the ship or are otherwise properly unloaded [UCC 2–322].

DELIVERY WITHOUT MOVEMENT OF THE GOODS

The UCC also addresses situations in which the seller or lessor is required neither to ship nor to deliver the goods. Frequently, the buyer or lessee is to pick up the goods from the seller or lessor, or the goods are to be held by a bailee. A *bailment* is a temporary delivery of personal property, without passage of title, into the care of another, called a *bailee*. Under the UCC, a bailee is a party who, by a bill of lading, warehouse receipt, or other document of title, acknowledges possession of goods and contracts to deliver them. A warehousing company, for example, or a trucking company that normally issues documents of title for the goods it receives is a bailee.[5]

Goods Held by the Seller. If the goods are held by the seller, a document of title is usually not used. If the seller is a merchant, risk of loss to goods held by the seller passes to the buyer when the buyer *actually takes physical possession of the goods* [UCC 2–509(3)]. If the seller is not a merchant, the risk of loss to goods held by the seller passes to the buyer on *tender of delivery* [UCC 2–509(3)]. (As you will read in Chapter 20, tender of delivery occurs when the seller places conforming goods at the disposal of the buyer and gives the buyer whatever notification is reasonably necessary to enable the buyer to take possession.)

In respect to leases, the risk of loss passes to the lessee on the lessee's receipt of the goods if the lessor—or supplier, in a finance lease (see Chapter 18)—is a merchant. Otherwise, the risk passes to the lessee on tender of delivery [UCC 2A–219(c)].

5. See Chapter 46 for a detailed discussion of the law of bailments.

Goods Held by a Bailee. When a bailee is holding goods for a person who has contracted to sell them and the goods are to be delivered without being moved, the goods are usually represented by a negotiable or nonnegotiable document of title (a bill of lading or a warehouse receipt). Risk of loss passes to the buyer when (1) the buyer receives a negotiable document of title for the goods, (2) the bailee acknowledges the buyer's right to possess the goods, or (3) the buyer receives a nonnegotiable document of title *and* has had a *reasonable time* to present the document to the bailee and demand the goods. Obviously, if the bailee refuses to honor the document, the risk of loss remains with the seller [UCC 2–503(4)(b), 2–509(2)].

Whether a document of title is negotiable or nonnegotiable may have significant consequences. For example, suppose that Valley Food Products, Inc., delivers five lots of canned goods to a warehouser and receives five warehouse receipts, one for each lot of one hundred cases. The warehouse is open from 8:00 A.M. to 5:00 P.M., Monday through Friday. At 4:00 P.M. on Friday, Valley's sales representative contracts to sell Burdine one of the lots and transfers the warehouse receipt and a bill of sale to Burdine. Burdine does not pick up the cases that afternoon. During the weekend, the warehouse and all of its contents are destroyed by fire. In this situation, who bears the risk of loss, the seller (Valley) or the buyer (Burdine)?

The answer may depend on whether the warehouse receipt is negotiable or nonnegotiable. If the warehouse receipt is *negotiable,* title and risk passed to Burdine when Burdine received the document at 4:00 P.M. on Friday. Therefore, the loss caused by the warehouse fire over the weekend is on Burdine, the buyer. If the document is *nonnegotiable,* the result may be significantly different. Although title passed to Burdine on its receipt of the document, whether risk of loss had passed would depend on whether Burdine had failed to present the document to the bailee so that the bailee could honor it within a "reasonable time" after receipt. The issue here is whether one hour (between 4:00 P.M. and 5:00 P.M. on Friday) is a reasonable time. Very likely, a court would say no, particularly if the warehouse is located in a large city where rush-hour traffic would make it difficult for the buyer to present the document to the bailee within the hour.

With respect to leases, if goods held by a bailee are to be delivered without being moved, the risk of loss passes to the lessee on acknowledgment by the bailee of the lessee's right to possession of the goods [UCC 2A–219(2)(b)].

CONDITIONAL SALES

Buyers and sellers sometimes form sales contracts that are conditioned either on the buyer's approval of the goods or on the buyer's resale of the goods. Under such contracts, the buyer is in possession of the goods. Sometimes, however, problems arise as to whether the buyer or seller should bear the loss if, for example, the goods are damaged or stolen while in the possession of the buyer.

Sale or Return. A **sale or return** (sometimes called a *sale and return*) is a type of contract by which the buyer purchases the goods but has a conditional right to return the goods (undo the sale) within a specified time period. When the buyer receives possession at the time of sale, title and risk of loss pass to the buyer. Title and risk of loss remain with the buyer until the buyer returns the goods to the seller within the time period specified. If the buyer fails to return the goods within this time period, the sale is finalized. The return of the goods is made at the buyer's risk and expense. Goods held under a sale-or-return contract are subject to the claims of the buyer's creditors while they are in the buyer's possession.

The UCC treats a **consignment** as a sale or return. Under a consignment, the owner of goods (the *consignor*) delivers them to another (the *consignee*) for the consignee to sell or to keep. If the consignee sells the goods, the consignee must pay the consignor for them. If the consignee does not sell or keep the goods, they may simply be returned to the consignor. While the goods are in the possession of the consignee, the consignee holds title to them, and creditors of the consignee will prevail over the consignor in any action to repossess the goods [UCC 2–326(3)].

Sale on Approval. Usually, when a seller offers to sell goods to a buyer and permits the buyer to take the goods on a trial basis, a **sale on approval** is made. The term *sale* here is a misnomer, as only an *offer* to sell has been made, along with a bailment created by the buyer's possession.

Therefore, title and risk of loss (from causes beyond the buyer's control) remain with the seller until the buyer accepts (approves) the offer. Acceptance can be made expressly, by any act inconsistent with the *trial* purpose or the seller's ownership, or by the buyer's election not to return the goods within the trial period. If the buyer does not wish to accept, the buyer may notify the seller of that fact within the trial period, and the return is made at the seller's expense and risk [UCC 2–327(1)]. Goods held on approval are not subject to the claims of the buyer's creditors until acceptance.

It is often difficult to determine from a particular transaction which exists—a contract for a sale on approval or a contract for a sale or return. The UCC states that (unless otherwise agreed) "if the goods are delivered primarily for use," the transaction is a sale on approval; "if the goods are delivered primarily for resale," the transaction is a sale or return [UCC 2–326(1)].

RISK OF LOSS WHEN A SALES OR LEASE CONTRACT IS BREACHED

There are many ways to breach a sales or lease contract, and the transfer of risk operates differently depending on which party breaches. Generally, the party in breach bears the risk of loss.

When the Seller or Lessor Breaches. If the goods are so nonconforming that the buyer has the right to reject them, the risk of loss does not pass to the buyer until the defects are *cured* (that is, until the goods are repaired, replaced, or discounted in price by the seller—see Chapter 20) or until the buyer accepts the goods in spite of their defects (thus waiving the right to reject). For example, a buyer orders blue file cabinets from a seller, F.O.B. seller's plant. The seller ships black file cabinets instead. The black cabinets (nonconforming goods) are damaged in transit. The risk of loss falls on the seller. Had the seller shipped blue cabinets (conforming goods) instead, the risk would have fallen on the buyer [UCC 2–510(2)].

If a buyer accepts a shipment of goods and later discovers a defect, acceptance can be revoked. Revocation allows the buyer to pass the risk of loss back to the seller, at least to the extent that the buyer's insurance does not cover the loss [UCC 2–510(2)].

In regard to leases, Article 2A states a similar rule. If the lessor or supplier tenders goods that are so nonconforming that the lessee has the right to reject them, the risk of loss remains with the lessor or the supplier until cure or acceptance [UCC 2A–220(1)(a)]. If the lessee, after acceptance, revokes his or her acceptance of nonconforming goods, the revocation passes the risk of loss back to the seller or supplier, to the extent that the lessee's insurance does not cover the loss [UCC 2A–220(1)(b)].

When the Buyer or Lessee Breaches. The general rule is that when a buyer or lessee breaches a contract, the risk of loss *immediately* shifts to the buyer or lessee. There are three important limitations to this rule [UCC 2–510(3), 2A–220(2)]:

1. The seller or lessor must already have identified the contract goods.
2. The buyer or lessee bears the risk for only a *commercially reasonable time* after the seller or lessor has learned of the breach.
3. The buyer or lessee is liable only to the extent of any deficiency in the seller's or lessor's insurance coverage.

SECTION 4

Insurable Interest

Parties to sales and lease contracts often obtain insurance coverage to protect against damage, loss, or destruction of goods. Any party purchasing insurance, however, must have a sufficient interest in the insured item to obtain a valid policy. Insurance laws—not the UCC—determine sufficiency. The UCC is helpful, however, because it contains certain rules regarding insurable interests in goods.

Insurable Interest of the Buyer or Lessee

A buyer or lessee has an **insurable interest** in identified goods. The moment the contract goods are *identified* by the seller or lessor, the buyer or lessee has a special property interest that allows the buyer or lessee to obtain necessary insurance coverage for those goods even before the risk of loss has passed [UCC 2–501(1), 2A–218(1)].

Consider an example. In March, a farmer sells a cotton crop he hopes to harvest in October. The buyer acquires an insurable interest in the crop when it is planted, because those goods (the cotton crop) are identified to the sales contract between the seller and the buyer. The rule stated in UCC 2–501(1)(c) is that such buyers obtain an insurable interest in crops by identification, which occurs when the crops are planted or otherwise become growing crops, providing that the contract is for "the sale of crops to be harvested within twelve months or the next normal harvest season after contracting, whichever is longer."

Insurable Interest of the Seller or Lessor

A seller has an insurable interest in goods as long as he or she retains title to the goods. Even after title passes to a buyer, however, a seller who has a security interest in the goods (a right to secure payment—see Chapter 28) still has an insurable interest and can insure the goods [UCC 2–501(2)]. Hence, both a buyer and a seller can have an insurable interest in identical goods at the same time. Of course, the buyer or seller must sustain an actual loss to have the right to recover from an insurance company. In regard to leases, the lessor retains an insurable interest in leased goods until an option to buy has been exercised by the lessee and the risk of loss has passed to the lessee [UCC 2A–218(3)].

SECTION 5

Bulk Transfers

Article 6 of the UCC covers bulk transfers. A *bulk transfer* is defined as any transfer of a major part of the transferor's material, supplies, merchandise, or other inventory *not made in the ordinary course of the transferor's business* [UCC 6–102(1)]. Article 6 was designed to prevent certain difficulties with such transfers—such as when a business sold a substantial part of its equipment and inventories to a buyer and then failed to pay its creditors. Today, changes in the business and legal contexts in which bulk sales are conducted have largely made their regulation unnecessary. For this reason, the majority of the states have repealed Article 6. Those states that have not repealed the article follow either the original version of Article 6 or its alternative (see Appendix B).

Terms and Concepts to Review

consignment 376	fungible goods 372	insurable interest 377
destination contract 372	good faith purchaser 373	sale on approval 376
document of title 372	identification 371	sale or return 376
entrustment 373	insolvent 373	shipment contract 372

Chapter Summary

Shipment Contracts	In the absence of an agreement, title and risk pass on the seller's or lessor's delivery of conforming goods to the carrier [UCC 2–319(1)(a), 2–401(2)(a), 2–509(1)(a), 2A–219(2)(a)].
Destination Contracts	In the absence of an agreement, title and risk pass on the seller's or lessor's *tender* of delivery of conforming goods to the buyer or lessee at the point of destination [UCC 2–401(2)(b), 2–319(1)(b), 2–509(1)(b), 2A–219(2)(b)].
Delivery without Movement of the Goods	**1.** In the absence of an agreement, if the goods are not represented by a document of title: **a.** Title passes on the formation of the contract [UCC 2–401(3)(b)]. **b.** Risk passes to the buyer or lessee, if the seller or lessor (or supplier, in a finance lease) is a merchant, on the buyer's or lessee's receipt of the goods or, if the seller or lessor is a nonmerchant, on the seller's or lessor's *tender* of delivery of the goods [UCC 2–509(3), 2A–219(c)]. **2.** In the absence of an agreement, if the goods are represented by a document of title: **a.** If the document is negotiable and the goods are held by a bailee, title and risk pass on the buyer's *receipt* of the document [UCC 2–401(3)(a), 2–509(2)(a)]. **b.** If the document is nonnegotiable and the goods are held by a bailee, title passes on the buyer's receipt of the document, but risk does *not* pass until the buyer, after receipt of the document, has had a reasonable time to present the document to demand the goods [UCC 2–401(3)(a), 2–509(2)(c), 2–503(4)(b)]. **3.** In the absence of an agreement, if the goods are held by a bailee and no document of title is transferred, risk passes to the buyer when the bailee acknowledges the buyer's right to the possession of the goods [UCC 2–509(2)(b)]. **4.** In respect to leases, if goods held by a bailee are to be delivered without being moved, the risk of loss passes to the lessee on acknowledgment by the bailee of the lessee's right to possession of the goods [UCC 2A–219(2)(b)].
Sales or Leases by Nonowners	Between the owner and a good faith purchaser or sublessee: **1.** *Void title*—Owner prevails [UCC 2–403(1)]. **2.** *Voidable title*—Buyer prevails [UCC 2–403(1)]. **3.** *Entrusting to a merchant*—Buyer or sublessee prevails [UCC 2–403(2), (3); 2A–305(2)].
Sale-or-Return Contracts	When the buyer receives possession of the goods, title and risk of loss pass to the buyer, with the buyer's option to return the goods to the seller. If the buyer returns the goods to the seller, title and risk of loss pass back to the seller [UCC 2–327(2)].
Sale-on-Approval Contracts	Title and risk of loss (from causes beyond the buyer's control) remain with the seller until the buyer approves (accepts) the offer [UCC 2–327(1)].
Risk of Loss When a Sales or Lease Contract Is Breached	**1.** If the seller or lessor breaches by tendering nonconforming goods that are rejected by the buyer or lessee, the risk of loss does not pass to the buyer or lessee until the defects are cured (unless the buyer or lessee accepts the goods in spite of their defects, thus waiving the right to reject) [UCC 2–510(1), 2A–220(1)].

CHAPTER SUMMARY—CONTINUED

Risk of Loss When a Sales or Lease Contract Is Breached —continued	2. If the buyer or lessee breaches the contract, the risk of loss to identified goods immediately shifts to the buyer or lessee. Limitations to this rule are as follows [UCC 2–510(3), 2A–220(2)]: a. The seller or lessor must already have identified the contract goods. b. The buyer or lessee bears the risk for only a commercially reasonable time after the seller or lessor has learned of the breach. c. The buyer or lessee is liable only to the extent of any deficiency in the seller's or lessor's insurance coverage.
Insurable Interest	1. Buyers and lessees have an insurable interest in goods the moment the goods are identified to the contract by the seller or the lessor [UCC 2–501(1), 2A–218(1)]. 2. Sellers have an insurable interest in goods as long as they have (1) title to the goods or (2) a security interest in the goods [UCC 2–501(2)]. Lessors have an insurable interest in leased goods until an option to buy has been exercised by the lessee and the risk of loss has passed to the lessee [UCC 2A–218(3)].
Bulk Transfers	Article 6 of the UCC covers bulk transfers. A *bulk transfer* is defined as any transfer of a major part of the transferor's material, supplies, merchandise, or other inventory that is not made in the ordinary course of business [UCC 6–102(1)]. Changes in the business and legal contexts in which bulk sales are conducted have largely made their regulation unnecessary. As a result, the majority of the states have repealed Article 6.

CASES FOR ANALYSIS

Westlaw. You can access the full text of each case presented below by going to the Westlaw cases on this text's Web site at http://wbl-cs.westbuslaw.com. Each Westlaw case includes the names of all plaintiffs and defendants, the dates on which the case was argued and decided, a brief summary of the issues and decisions in the case, headnotes classifying the specific issues in the case according to the West Key Number System, and the court's opinion. Concurring and dissenting opinions, if any, are included as well.

CASE 19.1 VOIDABLE TITLE

MEMPHIS HARDWOOD FLOORING CO. V. DANIEL
Supreme Court of Mississippi, 2000.
771 So.2d 924.

MILLS, Justice, for the Court:

* * * *

Jamie Swann Daniel, a retired schoolteacher who was eighty-five years old at the time of the trial of this case, owns approximately 800 acres in Union County [Mississippi]. The land is divided by Wilhite Creek into a north tract and a south tract. She lives on the north tract. The tract immediately south of Wilhite Creek, where her best timber was found, contains about 243 acres. A third tract, known as "Darling Crossroads," lies about six miles south of the south tract and contains approximately 140 acres. A large part of this land, particularly the 243 acres and Darling Crossroads, was in timber.

A January 1994 ice storm in North Mississippi damaged some of Daniel's timber. After the ice storm, Lucky Easley [vice-president and secretary of Northern Hardwoods, Inc.] contacted Daniel about cutting her timber. He and William Heppler [also a Northern officer] made a videotape of the damaged timber on the 243 acres south of Wilhite Creek, showed the tape to Daniel, and convinced her to allow some cutting of the storm-damaged timber. Easley and Daniel reached an unrecorded written agreement on May 19, 1994, allowing Northern to cut the "disaster hardwood timber" on the 243 acres which was 20 inches in diameter and up. Eventually this agreement was verbally extended to include the same width of trees on the Darling Crossroads tract. * * *

* * * *

Sometime before November 1995 Easley approached Daniel about cutting more of her timber. Daniel agreed to the cutting of the timber remaining on the south tract and

Darling Crossroads. This [was] the area which had previously been cut down to 20 inches. Daniel * * * agreed to have it cut down to 16 inches. * * *

Rome Yarbrough and Robert Luther were * * * timber buyers [for Memphis Hardwood Flooring Company] at its Potts Camp mill * * * . Easley, Luther, and Yarbrough met on Daniel's land in late October or early November 1995. * * * Easley * * * told them that he had an agreement [to buy all of Daniel's timber]. * * *

* * * Luther and Easley agreed that Easley would act for both Northern and Memphis to buy Daniel's timber for Northern while concealing from Daniel that Northern was actually buying for Memphis.

* * * *

After Luther and another Memphis employee cruised the timber on all of Daniel's land, Luther offered Easley $400,000 for the timber. Easley countered with $410,000, and Luther accepted. * * * [W]hen Luther agreed to pay $410,000 for Daniel's timber, Daniel had already agreed to sell it to Easley for $150,000. Easley * * * told Daniel nothing about the fact he was going to sell the timber to Memphis that very same day for more than double what he was paying her.

* * * *

The deed conveyed, against Daniel's instructions, the timber down to a stump size of 16 inches on all of her land as opposed to only that land south of Wilhite Creek. In addition to conveying more timber than Daniel intended, the deed failed to include a non-assignment clause. Though she signed the deed without reading it, Daniel testified that she would not have done so had she known that there was not a provision preventing assignment. Daniel drove to Baldwyn to have the deed notarized, returned to her home where Easley was waiting, and gave the signed deed to him. Easley traveled to Memphis' Potts Camp office where he signed the second deed and gave both deeds to an employee. He was given two checks: one to Northern for $400,000 and one to himself for $10,000.

Memphis sold Stan Wilson, a timber buyer specializing in white oak who was familiar with the Daniel timber, $41,511 of veneer logs on December 29, 1995, and began cutting Daniel's other timber the first week of January 1996. The cutting continued until the preliminary injunction was granted on April 1, 1996.

* * * *

[Daniel filed a suit in a Mississippi state court against Memphis and the others, alleging fraud. The trial court] found a confidential relationship existed between Easley and Daniel; that Easley thus owed fiduciary duties to Daniel with reference to the timber deeds; and that Easley was guilty of fraud, even if there was no confidential relationship. The court further found that the consideration of $150,000 which Easley paid Daniel for her timber was grossly inadequate and in and of itself proof of fraudulent intent. The [court] also found that Memphis participated in the perpetration of frauds on Daniel and is equally guilty of defrauding her. In so holding the [court] stated, "Memphis' claim that it was not astride the horse of fraud may be so, but the evidence is clear that its left foot was in the stirrup, and that's sufficient to destroy its claim of innocent purchaser without notice." He determined that Daniel was entitled to a cancellation of both the deed from Daniel to Northern and the deed from Northern to Memphis. Judgment was entered, and Memphis timely perfected this appeal * * * .

* * * *

Memphis claims that it was a bona fide purchaser for value because it paid a valuable consideration for timber in good faith and in the absence of any notice of Easley's fraudulent acts. To the contrary, the [trial court] determined that Memphis did not act in good faith and charged it with notice of the plan to defraud Daniel. This finding is supported by substantial evidence and is, therefore, upheld by this Court.

Memphis' plea that it was a bona fide purchaser for value without notice constitutes an affirmative defense and must be sustained by competent proof. *The elements the innocent purchaser must prove are a valuable consideration, the presence of good faith, and the absence of notice.* * * * [Emphasis added.]

The first element is established in favor of Memphis. The record reveals that Memphis paid $410,000 to Northern for the timber.

The second element, the presence of good faith, was not adequately shown by Memphis. The fact that Easley made the deal with Daniel on behalf of both Northern and Memphis and that Memphis was a knowing participant in this scheme is supported by the testimony of Luther and Easley. Such actions reveal the absence of good faith. Even the circumstances surrounding the drafting of the deeds indicate the joint nature of the scheme and Memphis' lack of good faith. Luther, at the request of Easley, had Memphis' lawyer draft Northern's deed as well as Memphis'. Memphis paid for the drafting of the deed from Daniel to Northern. The closeness in time of the two transactions is a further indication of bad faith.

The third element is the absence of notice. Constructive notice of the intended fraud suffices. Even so, * * * Memphis was not only on actual notice, it was a knowing and willing participant in the defrauding of Daniel. Thus, Memphis fails to establish the third element. The record supports the [trial court's] finding that Memphis was not a bona fide purchaser.

* * * *

The [trial court's] findings are neither manifestly wrong nor clearly erroneous. They are supported by substantial evidence. For the foregoing reasons, the judgment of the [trial court] is affirmed.

AFFIRMED.

CASE 19.2 ENTRUSTMENT RULE

DEWELDON, LTD. V. MCKEAN
United States Court of Appeals,
First Circuit, 1997.
125 F.3d 24.

HILL, Senior Circuit Judge.

* * * *

I.

Felix DeWeldon is a well-known sculptor and art collector. He owned three paintings valued at $26,000. He displayed these, and other collection-grade paintings, on the walls of his home—Beacon Rock, in Newport, Rhode Island. He declared bankruptcy in 1991. In 1992, DeWeldon, Ltd. purchased all Felix DeWeldon's personal property from the bankruptcy trustee. In 1993, Nancy Wardell, the sole shareholder of DeWeldon, Ltd., sold all her DeWeldon, Ltd. stock to the Byron Preservation Trust, which in turn sold Felix DeWeldon an option to repurchase the paintings and a contractual right to continue to retain possession of the paintings until the option expired. At all times, Felix DeWeldon continued to possess and display the paintings at Beacon Rock. In 1994, his son Byron approached Robert McKean, an acquaintance, and told him that his father was interested in selling some of his paintings. McKean viewed the paintings at Beacon Rock and subsequently purchased the paintings at issue for $50,000. DeWeldon, Ltd. sued in [a federal] district court to recover the paintings. The district court entered judgment for McKean. For the following reasons, we affirm.

II.

We conclude that the evidence sufficiently establishes the following facts found by the district court. Felix DeWeldon was a "well-known artist" and "collector." After DeWeldon, Ltd. purchased Felix DeWeldon's paintings from his bankruptcy estate, Frederick Crevoiserat, director of DeWeldon, Ltd., entrusted the paintings to Felix DeWeldon as custodian. DeWeldon, Ltd. allowed Felix DeWeldon to maintain possession of the paintings; it put no signs on the premises, nor tags or labels on the paintings themselves to indicate that Felix DeWeldon no longer owned the paintings. The paintings remained on the walls of Beacon Rock.

McKean viewed the paintings on the walls at Beacon Rock. The only tags on the back of the paintings were those of Christie's—the auction house. McKean inquired of Christie's, and was informed that the paintings had not sold at auction and DeWeldon had "re-purchased" them. McKean paid more than the appraised value of the paintings and Felix DeWeldon gave him a bill of sale.

* * * *

III.

* * * *

As a general rule, a seller cannot pass better title than he has himself. Nevertheless, the Uniform Commercial Code (UCC) as adopted by Rhode Island provides that *an owner who entrusts items to a merchant who deals in goods of that kind gives him or her power to transfer all rights of the entruster to a buyer in the ordinary course of business.* "'Entrusting' includes any delivery and any acquiescence in retention of possession [agreement to retain possession] regardless of any condition expressed between the parties to the delivery or acquiescence and regardless of whether the procurement of the entrusting or the possessor's disposition of the goods have been such as to be larcenous under the criminal law," [according to Rhode Island General Laws Section 6A-2-403(3), Rhode Island's version of UCC 2–403(3)]. Under this provision, *a buyer in the ordinary course of business will prevail over the claim of a party who entrusted such items to the merchant.* [Emphasis added.]

In order for McKean to be protected * * * , DeWeldon, Ltd. must have allowed Felix DeWeldon to retain possession of the paintings. McKean must have bought the paintings in the ordinary course of business. He must have given value for the paintings, without actual or constructive notice of DeWeldon Ltd.'s claim of ownership to them. Finally, Felix DeWeldon must have been a merchant as defined by R.I. Gen. Laws [Section] 6A-2-104 [UCC 2–104]. Under this section, a merchant is one who has special knowledge or skill and deals in goods of the kind or "otherwise by his or her occupation holds him or herself out as having knowledge or skill peculiar to the practices or goods involved in the transaction * * * ."

Under the facts found by the district court, McKean's purchase of the paintings is protected by the entrustment doctrine. First, DeWeldon, Ltd. entrusted the paintings to Felix DeWeldon. After DeWeldon, Ltd. purchased the paintings, it acquiesced in Felix DeWeldon's retention of them. Although DeWeldon, Ltd. made some late efforts to regain possession of the paintings, these efforts were frustrated by its own prior grant to Felix DeWeldon of an option and right of possession until the expiration of the option.

Second, McKean was a buyer in the ordinary course of business. Byron informed McKean that Felix DeWeldon wished to sell some paintings. The paintings were hanging in Felix DeWeldon's home when McKean viewed and subsequently bought them. He knew that Felix DeWeldon had sold paintings out of his home before. McKean gave value for the paintings. In fact, he paid more than their appraised value.

McKean had no actual notice that Felix DeWeldon was no longer the true owner of the paintings. DeWeldon, Ltd. did nothing to shield the paintings in the cloak of its ownership. It did not place markings on the paintings, as

Christie's had when the paintings were in its possession; it posted no notice of ownership by or near the paintings; it failed to post the injunction it secured against transfer of the paintings by Felix DeWeldon; it posted, but then terminated, a security guard at DeWeldon's residence despite such a guard's being expressly permitted in the injunction; it posted no warnings against removal of the paintings from the residence. There were no markings on the paintings or other notice that Felix DeWeldon no longer owned the paintings. The paintings were hanging in Felix DeWeldon's home.

* * * *

Third, under the facts of this case, Felix DeWeldon acted as a merchant within the meaning of the [Uniform] Commercial Code. Under the Code, "merchant" is given an expansive definition. The Code provides that a merchant is "one who * * * by his occupation holds himself out as having knowledge or skill peculiar to the practices * * * involved in the transaction * * * ." Comment 2 to this section notes that "almost every person in business would, therefore, be deemed to be a 'merchant'."

The entrustment provision of the UCC is designed to enhance the reliability of commercial sales by merchants who deal in the kind of goods sold. It shifts the risk of resale to the one who leaves his property with the merchant.

The district court found that Felix DeWeldon was a "well-known" artist whose work was for sale commercially and a "collector." There was artwork all over Felix DeWeldon's home. He had recently sold paintings to a European buyer. By his occupation he held himself out as having knowledge and skill peculiar to art and the art trade. McKean viewed him as an art dealer.

We conclude from these facts that Felix DeWeldon was a "merchant" within the meaning of the entrustment provision of the UCC as adopted by the Rhode Island Commercial Code.

When a person knowingly delivers his property into the possession of a merchant dealing in goods of that kind, that person assumes the risk of the merchant's acting unscrupulously by selling the property to an innocent purchaser. The entrustment provision places the loss upon the party who vested the merchant with the ability to transfer the property with apparent good title. The entrustor in this case, DeWeldon, Ltd., took that risk and bears the consequences.

IV.

DeWeldon, Ltd. entrusted three paintings to the care of Felix DeWeldon. Felix DeWeldon was a merchant who bought and sold paintings. Robert McKean was a purchaser in the ordinary course of business who paid value for the paintings without notice of any claim of ownership by another. Under the law of Rhode Island, McKean took good title to the paintings. The judgment of the district court is ***affirmed.***

CASE 19.3 RISK OF LOSS

WINDOWS, INC. v. JORDAN PANEL SYSTEMS CORP.

United States Court of Appeals,
Second Circuit, 1999.
177 F.3d 114.

LEVAL, Circuit Judge:

* * * *

Windows, Inc. ("Windows" or "the seller") is a fabricator and seller of windows, based in South Dakota. Jordan Systems, Inc. ("Jordan" or "the buyer") is a construction subcontractor, which contracted to install window wall panels at an air cargo facility at John F. Kennedy Airport in New York City. Jordan ordered custom-made windows from Windows. The purchase contract specified that the windows were to be shipped properly packaged for cross country motor freight transit and "delivered to New York City."

Windows constructed the windows according to Jordan's specifications. It arranged to have them shipped to Jordan by a common carrier, Consolidated Freightways Corp. ("Consolidated" or "the carrier"), and delivered them to Consolidated intact and properly packaged. During the course of shipment, however, the goods sustained extensive damage. Much of the glass was broken and many of the window frames were gouged and twisted. Jordan's president signed a delivery receipt noting that approximately two-thirds of the shipment was damaged due to "load shift." Jordan, seeking to stay on its contractor's schedule, directed its employees to disassemble the window frames in an effort to salvage as much of the shipment as possible.

Jordan made a claim with Consolidated for damages it had sustained as a result of the casualty, including labor costs from its salvage efforts and other costs from Jordan's inability to perform its own contractual obligations on schedule. Jordan also ordered a new shipment from Windows, which was delivered without incident.

Jordan did not pay Windows for either the first shipment of damaged windows or the second, intact shipment. Windows filed suit to recover payment from Jordan for both shipments in the Supreme Court of the State of New York, Suffolk County. Jordan counterclaimed, seeking incidental and consequential damages resulting from the damaged shipment. Windows then brought a * * * claim against Consolidated, which removed the suit to the United States District Court for the Eastern District of New York.

Windows settled its claims against Consolidated. Windows later withdrew its claims against Jordan. The only remaining claim is Jordan's counterclaim against Windows for incidental and consequential damages.

The district court granted Windows' motion for summary judgment. * * *

* * * *

* * * This appeal followed.

DISCUSSION

* * * *

Jordan seeks to recover incidental and consequential damages pursuant to [New York Uniform Commercial Code Section 2-715, New York's version of UCC 2–715]. Under that provision, Jordan's entitlement to recover incidental and consequential damages depends on whether those damages "result[ed] from the seller's breach." A destination contract is covered by [NYUCC Section] 2-503(3); it arises where "the seller is *required to deliver* at a particular destination" [emphasis added]. In contrast, a shipment contract arises where "the seller is required * * * to send the goods to the buyer and the contract *does not require him to deliver* them at a particular destination" [emphasis added]. Under a shipment contract, the seller must "put the goods in the possession of such a carrier and make such a contract for their transportation as may be reasonable having regard to the nature of the goods and other circumstances of the case," [according to NYUCC Section 2-504(a)].

Where the terms of an agreement are ambiguous, there is a strong presumption under the U.C.C. favoring shipment contracts. *Unless the parties expressly specify that the contract requires the seller to deliver to a particular destination, the contract is generally construed as one for shipment.* [Emphasis added.]

Jordan's confirmation of its purchase order, by letter to Windows dated September 22, 1993, provided, "All windows to be shipped properly crated/packaged/boxed suitable for cross country motor freight transit and delivered to New York City." We conclude that this was a shipment contract rather than a destination contract.

To overcome the presumption favoring shipment contracts, the parties must have explicitly agreed to impose on Windows the obligation to effect delivery at a particular destination. The language of this contract does not do so. Nor did Jordan use any commonly recognized industry term indicating that a seller is obligated to deliver the goods to the buyer's specified destination.

Given the strong presumption favoring shipment contracts, and the absence of explicit terms satisfying both requirements for a destination contract, we conclude that the contract should be deemed a shipment contract.

Under the terms of its contract, Windows thus satisfied its obligations to Jordan when it put the goods, properly packaged, into the possession of the carrier for shipment. Upon Windows' proper delivery to the carrier, Jordan assumed the risk of loss, and cannot recover incidental or consequential damages from the seller caused by the carrier's negligence.

This allocation of risk is confirmed by the terms of NYUCC [Section] 2-509(1)(a), entitled "Risk of Loss in the Absence of Breach." It provides that where the contract "does not require [the seller] to deliver [the goods] at a particular destination, the risk of loss passes to the buyer when the goods are duly delivered to the carrier." As noted earlier, Jordan does not contest the court's finding that Windows duly delivered conforming goods to the carrier. Accordingly, as Windows had already fulfilled its contractual obligations at the time the goods were damaged and Jordan had assumed the risk of loss, there was no "seller's breach" as is required for a buyer to claim incidental and consequential damages. Summary judgment for Windows was therefore proper.

We are mindful of Jordan's concern that it not be left "holding the bag" for the damages it sustained through no fault of its own. The fact that Jordan had assumed the risk of loss under [NYUCC Section] 2-509(1)(a) by the time the goods were damaged does not mean it is without a remedy. Under * * * the Interstate Commerce Act, a buyer or seller has long been able to recover directly from an interstate common carrier in whose care their goods are damaged. * * *

CONCLUSION

The judgment of the district court is affirmed.

CASE PROBLEMS

19–1. Harold Shook agreed with Graybar Electric Co. to purchase three reels of burial cable for use in Shook's construction work. When the reels were delivered, each carton was marked "burial cable," although two of the reels were in fact aerial cable. Shook accepted the conforming reel of cable and notified Graybar that he was rejecting the two reels of aerial cable. Because of a trucker's strike, Shook was unsuccessful in arranging for the return of the reels to Graybar. He stored the reels in a well-lighted space near a grocery store owner's dwelling, which was close to his work site. About four months later, he noticed that one of the reels had been stolen. On the following day he notified Graybar of the loss and, worried about the safety of the second reel, arranged to have it transported to a garage for storage. Before the second reel could be transferred, however, it was also stolen, and Shook notified Graybar of the second theft. Graybar sued Shook for the purchase price, claiming that Shook had agreed to return to Graybar the nonconforming reels and had failed to do so. Shook contended that he had agreed only to contact a trucking company to return the reels and that, because he had contacted three trucking firms to no avail (owing to the strike), his obligation had been fulfilled. Discuss who bears the risk of loss for the stolen reels. [*Graybar Electric Co. v. Shook*, 283 N.C. 213, 195 S.E.2d 514 (1973)]

19–2. Bobby Locke, the principal stockholder and chief executive officer (CEO) of Worthco Farm Center,

Inc., hired Mr. Hobby as the company's manager. Subsequently, it was discovered that during the approximately thirteen months of Locke's tenure as CEO, Hobby had sold corn stored with Worthco to Arabi Grain & Elevator Co. and pocketed the proceeds. When Locke brought an action against Arabi to recover the corn, Arabi alleged, among other things, that Locke had entrusted the corn to Hobby and that because Arabi was a purchaser in the ordinary course of business, Hobby had transferred ownership rights in the corn to Arabi. Assuming that Arabi was a buyer in the ordinary course of business, how should the court rule? Discuss. [*Locke v. Arabi Grain & Elevator Co.*, 197 Ga.App. 854, 399 S.E.2d 705 (1991)]

19–3. Perez-Medina met Julio Lara at an auction at which they both bid on the same tractor. Perez-Medina purchased the tractor for $66,500. At a second auction, at which Lara was again present, Perez-Medina purchased equipment for installation on the tractor. Lara and Perez-Medina agreed that Lara would install the equipment for Perez-Medina at Lara's place of business, and the tractor was moved to Lara's shop. About four months later, Perez-Medina paid Lara $10,000 to make the installation. At that time, Perez-Medina thought Lara's business was a repair shop and not a "business dealing in heavy equipment." Lara, however, often purchased and sold heavy equipment at auction, and many people knew that Lara was a dealer. Lara sold the tractor to First Team Auction, Inc., for $54,000, representing to First Team that he was the tractor's true owner. Perez-Medina had no knowledge of the sale and received no payment from the transaction. First Team then sold the tractor to a dealer, who in turn sold it to a consumer. When the truth of Lara's deed became known, the dealer and consumer rescinded their contracts with First Team. Should First Team be required to return possession of the tractor to Perez-Medina? If Lara was a "merchant" and First Team a "buyer in the ordinary course of business," would your answer be different? Explain. [*Perez-Medina v. First Team Auction, Inc.*, 426 S.E.2d 397 (Ga.Ct.App. 1992)]

19–4. Tony Mangum contracted to purchase a 580C Case backhoe and loader from Liles Brothers & Son on November 25, 1977. The sales price was $20,561. Mangum wrote two checks in payment for the machine, one for $3,000 dated November 25 and one for $17,561 postdated to December 2. Liles checked with Mangum's bank and learned that there were sufficient funds to cover the $3,000 check, and Mangum assured Liles that by December 2 there would be sufficient funds in his account to cover the second check. Three days later, Mangum, posing as a heavy-equipment sales representative, sold the equipment for $11,000 to Carl Wright, who operated a septic-tank service. Wright had been looking for a backhoe and knew the market price for this equipment was around $20,000. Wright paid for the equipment with a certified check. On December 2, Liles learned that Mangum did not have sufficient funds in his bank account to cover the check dated December 2 and that Mangum was in jail. When Liles discovered that the backhoe was in Wright's possession, he sought the return of the backhoe from Wright. Does Wright have valid title to the backhoe? Explain. [*Liles Bros. & Son v. Wright*, 638 S.W.2d 383 (Tenn. 1982)]

19–5. Samuel Porter was the owner of a Maurice Utrillo painting entitled "Chateau de Lion-sur Mer." Harold Von Maker, who called himself Peter Wertz, bought a different painting from Porter, paying $50,000 cash and giving Porter ten promissory notes for $10,000 each. At the same time, Wertz talked Porter into allowing Wertz to hang the Utrillo painting in Wertz's home while he decided whether to buy it. When the first promissory note was not paid, Porter learned that he was dealing with Von Maker, a man with a history of arrests and judgments against him. Von Maker told Porter that the Utrillo painting was on consignment and would be returned or Porter would receive $30,000. Actually, the painting had already been sold to the Feigen Gallery, which had in turn sold it to Irwin Brenner, trading under the name Irwin Brenner Gallery. At the time of this lawsuit, the painting was in Venezuela. Porter filed suit against Wertz, the Feigen Gallery, and Irwin Brenner to recover either possession of the painting or its value. The Feigen Gallery and Irwin Brenner claimed that they had good title under UCC 2–403 and that Porter was estopped from repossessing the painting or its value. Discuss whether Porter was entitled to repossession or the value of the Utrillo painting. [*Porter v. Wertz*, 68 A.D.2d 141, 416 N.Y.S.2d 254 (1979)]

19–6. Isis Foods, Inc., located in St. Louis, wanted to purchase a shipment of food from Pocasset Food Sales, Inc. The sale of food was initiated by a purchase order from Isis stating that the shipment was to be made "F.O.B. St. Louis." Pocasset made the shipment by delivery of the goods to the carrier. Pocasset's invoices contained a provision stating "Our liability ceases upon delivery of merchandise to carrier." The shipment of food was destroyed in transit before reaching St. Louis. Discuss which party bears the risk of loss, and why. [*In re Isis Foods, Inc.*, 38 Bankr. 48 (Bankr.W.D.Mo. 1983)]

19–7. Donald Hayward agreed to buy a thirty-foot Revel Craft Playmate Yacht from Herbert F. Postma, a yacht dealer, on February 7, 1967. The boat was to be delivered to a slip on Lake Macatawa during April 1967. Hayward signed a security agreement on March 1, 1967, and gave a promissory note for $13,095.60 to Postma's dealership. The note was subsequently assigned to a bank. The security agreement contained clauses requiring the buyer to maintain the boat in first-class order or repair and to keep it fully insured at all times. After Hayward had made some payments but before the boat was delivered to Hayward, it was destroyed by fire. Neither Postma nor Hayward had insured the boat, and Hayward requested that Postma pay off the note or reimburse him for payments made. Postma refused, and Hayward sued. Discuss whether Hayward or Postma bears the risk of loss as to the boat destroyed in the fire. [*Hayward v. Postma*, 31 Mich.App. 720, 188 N.W.2d 31 (1971)]

19–8. A new car owned by a New Jersey car rental agency was stolen in 1967. The agency collected the full price of the car from its insurance company, Home Indemnity Co., and assigned all its interest in the automobile to the insurer. Subsequently, a thief sold the car to an automobile wholesaler, who in turn sold it to a retail car dealer. Schrier purchased the automobile from the car dealer without knowledge of the theft. Home Indemnity sued Schrier to recover the car. Can Home Indemnity recover? Discuss. [*Schrier v. Home Indemnity Co.*, 273 A.2d 248 (D.C.App. 1971)]

19–9. Kumar Corp. agreed to sell seven hundred television sets to Nava, a Venezuelan wholesaler. Kumar and Nava expressly agreed that Nava would not pay for the television sets until it received and actually sold the merchandise in Venezuela. Kumar loaded the goods from its Miami warehouse into a trailer and delivered the trailer to the freight handler but failed to procure insurance. The shipping documents reflected that the goods had been sold by Kumar to Nava for $144,417, C.I.F. Venezuela. Several days later, the trailer was discovered missing and was subsequently found abandoned and empty. Kumar sued the carrier. The carrier challenged Kumar's standing (right) to sue on the ground that the term *C.I.F.* (or its equivalent) required Kumar, the seller, to perform certain obligations with respect to the goods—including placing the goods in possession of the carrier—and that when these obligations had been properly performed, the risk of loss or damage to the goods passed to Nava, the buyer. Because Nava suffered the loss, only Nava had standing to sue. Discuss whether this argument is persuasive in light of all of the terms of the contract. [*Kumar Corp. v. Nopal Lines, Ltd.*, 462 So.2d 1178 (Fla.App. 1985)]

19–10. Hargo Woolen Mills had purchased bales of card waste, used in Hargo's manufacture of woolen cloth, from Shabry Trading Co. for many years. On this occasion, however, Shabry shipped twenty-four bales to Hargo without an order. Rather than pay for reshipment, both parties decided that Hargo would retain possession of the bales and pay for what it used. Hargo kept the bales separate inside its warehouse and eventually used, and was billed for, eight bales. The remaining sixteen bales were still kept separate by Hargo. Hargo went bankrupt, and everything in its warehouse was taken by the receiver, Meinhard-Commercial Corp. Shabry claimed that it was the owner and title holder of the bales and requested their return, but Meinhard refused. Discuss fully whether Shabry will be able to retake possession of the bales. [*Meinhard-Commercial Corp. v. Hargo Woolen Mills*, 112 N.H. 500, 300 A.2d 321 (1972)]

19–11. Ron Rasmus was a farmer in the business of buying, selling, and raising exotic animals, including ostriches. When Gene Baker began buying flightless birds for investment purposes, he entered into an agreement with Rasmus to board the animals at Rasmus's farm. Mike Pickard bought two pairs of adult breeding ostriches from Rasmus, unaware that they were Baker's. Pickard sold one of the pairs to Gary Prenger. Both Pickard and Prenger arranged to board the ostriches with Rasmus. When Baker removed the birds from Rasmus's farm, Pickard and Prenger filed a suit in an Iowa state court against him, seeking in part to recover the birds. To whom do the birds belong? Discuss fully. [*Prenger v. Baker*, 542 N.W.2d 805 (Iowa 1995)]

19–12. Roderick Cardwell owns Ticketworld, which sells tickets (a sale of goods, according to the court) to entertainment and sporting events to be held at locations throughout the United States. Ticketworld's Massachusetts office sold tickets to an event in Connecticut to Mary Lou Lupovitch, a Connecticut resident, for $125 per ticket, although each ticket had a fixed price of $32.50. There was no agreement that Ticketworld would bear the risk of loss until the tickets were delivered to a specific location. Ticketworld gave the tickets to a carrier in Massachusetts who delivered the tickets to Lupovitch in Connecticut. The state of Connecticut brought an action against Cardwell in a Connecticut state court, charging in part a violation of a state statute that prohibited the sale of a ticket for more than $3 over its fixed price. Cardwell contended in part that the statute did not apply because the sale to Lupovitch involved a shipment contract that was formed outside the state. Is Cardwell correct? How will the court rule? Why? [*State v. Cardwell*, 246 Conn. 721, 718 A.2d 954 (1998)]

19–13. Mark Olmstead sells trailers, doing business as World Cargo in St. Croix Falls, Wisconsin. In 1997, he also sold trailers from a site in Elk River, Minnesota. Gerald McKenzie ordered a custom-made trailer from Olmstead and mailed him a check for $3,620. McKenzie said that he would pick up the trailer at the Elk River site. After the trailer was made, Olmstead shipped it to Elk River and kept it within a locked, fenced area. He told McKenzie that the trailer could be picked up any Tuesday or Thursday before 6:00 p.m. Over Olmstead's protest, McKenzie asked for the trailer to be left outside the fenced area. Olmstead told McKenzie that the area was not secure and that the trailer could not be locked, except to chain the tires. McKenzie insisted, however, and Olmstead complied. When McKenzie arrived to pick up the trailer, it was gone—apparently stolen. McKenzie filed a suit in a Minnesota state court against Olmstead, to recover the amount of the check. Who bore the risk of loss in these circumstances? Why? [*McKenzie v. Olmstead*, 587 N.W.2d 863 (Minn.App. 1999)]

19–14. Phillip and Genevieve Carboy owned and operated Gold Hill Service Station in Fairbanks, Alaska. Gold Hill maintained underground storage tanks on its property to hold gasoline. When Gold Hill needed more fuel, Phillip placed an order with Petroleum Sales, Inc., which delivered the product by filling the tanks. Gold Hill and Petroleum Sales were separately owned companies. Petroleum Sales did not oversee or operate Gold Hill and did not construct, install, or maintain the station's tanks, and Gold Hill did not tell Petroleum Sales's personnel how to fill the tanks. Parks Hiway Enterprises, LLC, owned the land next to Gold Hill.

The Alaska Department of Environmental Conservation determined that benzene had contaminated the groundwater under Parks Hiway's property and identified the gasoline in Gold Hill's tanks as the probable source. Gold Hill promptly removed the tanks, but because of the contamination, Parks Hiway stopped drawing drinking water from its well. Parks Hiway filed a suit in an Alaska state court against Petroleum Sales, among others. Should the court hold the defendant liable for the pollution? Who had title to the gas when it contaminated the water? Explain. [*Parks Hiway Enterprises, LLC v. CEM Leasing, Inc.*, 995 P.2d 657 (Alaska 2000)]

19–15. A Question of Ethics

Toby and Rita Kahr donated some used clothing to Goodwill Industries, Inc. They were not aware that a small bag containing their sterling silver had been accidentally included within one of the sacks of donated clothing. The silverware, which was valued at over $3,500, had been given to them twenty-seven years earlier by Rita's father as a wedding present and had great sentimental value for them. The Kahrs realized what had happened shortly after Toby returned from Goodwill, but when Toby called Goodwill, he was told that the silver had immediately been sold to a customer, Karon Markland, for $15. Although Goodwill called Markland and asked her to return the silver, Markland refused to return it. The Kahrs then brought an action against Markland to regain the silver, claiming that Markland did not have good title to it. In view of these circumstances, discuss the following issues. [*Kahr v. Markland*, 187 Ill.App.3d 603, 543 N.E.2d 579, 135 Ill.Dec. 196 (1989)]

1. The basic issue in this case is whether the silver was "lost property" (defined as property unintentionally separated from its owner) or property entrusted to a merchant, Goodwill Industries. If the court decides that the silver was lost, this will mean that the party in possession of the property will have good title against all parties except the true owner—in which case the Kahrs will be able to recover the silver from Markland. If the court decides that the Kahrs entrusted the silver to Goodwill, then the entrustment rule will be applied—in which case the Kahrs will be unable to recover the silver from Markland, a good faith purchaser. If you were the judge, how would you decide the issue? Why?
2. The entrustment rule can sometimes result in unfair treatment of the entrustor, because the entrustor cannot recover the property from a good faith purchaser (although the entrustor can recover the value of the property from the merchant who wrongfully sold the entrusted property). Given this potential for unfair treatment, how can the entrustment rule be justified from an ethical point of view?

E-Links

For updated links to resources available on the Web, as well as a variety of other materials, visit this text's Web site at

http://wbl-cs.westbuslaw.com

To find information on the UCC, including the UCC provisions discussed in this chapter, refer to the Web sites listed in the *E-Links* feature in Chapter 18.

Information on current commercial law topics, including some of the topics discussed in this chapter, is available at the Web site of the law firm of Hale and Dorr. Go to

http://www.haledorr.com

To review bills of lading, access the following Web site:

http://www.showtrans.com/bl.htm

Legal Research Exercises on the Web

Go to http://wbl-cs.westbuslaw.com, the Web site that accompanies this text. Select "Interactive Study Center," and then click on "Chapter 19." There you will find the following Internet research exercise that you can perform to learn more about passage of title:

Activity 19–1: Passage of Title

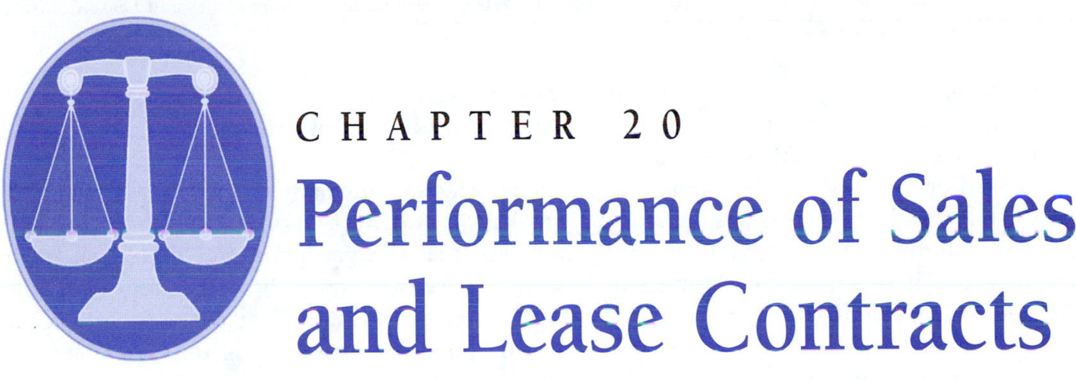

CHAPTER 20

Performance of Sales and Lease Contracts

To understand the obligations of the parties under a sales or lease contract, it is necessary to know the duties and obligations each party has assumed under the terms of the contract. Keep in mind that "duties and obligations" under the terms of the contract include those specified by the agreement, by custom, and by the UCC.

In the performance of a sales or lease contract, the basic obligation of the seller or lessor is to *transfer and deliver conforming goods*. The basic obligation of the buyer or lessee is to *accept and pay for conforming goods* in accordance with the contract [UCC 2–301, 2A–516(1)]. Overall performance of a sales or lease contract is controlled by the agreement between the parties. When the contract is unclear and disputes arise, the courts look to the UCC. In this chapter, after first scrutinizing the general requirement of good faith, we examine the basic performance obligations of the parties under a sales or lease contract.

SECTION 1

The Good Faith Requirement

The obligations of good faith and commercial reasonableness underlie every sales and lease contract within the UCC. These obligations can form the basis for a suit for breach of contract later on. The UCC's good faith provision, which can never be disclaimed, reads as follows: "Every contract or duty within this Act imposes an obligation of good faith in its performance or enforcement" [UCC 1–203]. Good faith means honesty in fact. In the case of a merchant, it means honesty in fact and the observance of reasonable commercial standards of fair dealing in the trade [UCC 2–103(1)(b)]. In other words, merchants are held to a higher standard of performance or duty than nonmerchants are.

Good faith can mean that one party must not take advantage of another party by manipulating contract terms. Good faith applies to both parties, even the nonbreaching party. The principle of good faith applies through both the performance and the enforcement of all agreements or duties within a contract. Good faith is a question of fact for the jury.

The standards of good faith and commercial reasonableness provide the framework within which the parties are to specify particulars of performance. If a sales contract leaves open some particulars of performance and permits one of the parties to specify them, "[a]ny such specification must be made in good faith and within limits set by commercial reasonableness" [UCC 2–311(1)]. Thus, when one party delays specifying particulars of performance for an unreasonable period of time or fails to cooperate with the other party, the innocent party is excused from any resulting delay in performance. In addition, the innocent party can proceed to perform in any reasonable manner.

SECTION 2

Obligations of the Seller or Lessor

The major obligation of the seller or lessor under a sales or lease contract is to tender conforming goods to the buyer or lessee. **Tender of delivery** requires that the seller or lessor have and hold **conforming goods** at the disposal of the buyer or lessee and give the buyer or lessee whatever notification is reasonably necessary to enable the buyer or lessee to take delivery [UCC 2–503(1), 2A–508(1)]. Conforming goods are goods that conform exactly to the description of the goods in the contract.

Tender must occur at a *reasonable hour* and in a *reasonable manner.* For example, a seller cannot call the buyer at 2:00 A.M. and say, "The goods are ready. I'll give you twenty minutes to get them." Unless the parties have agreed otherwise, the goods must be tendered for delivery at a reasonable hour and kept available for a reasonable period of time to enable the buyer to take possession of them [UCC 2–503(1)(a)].

All goods called for by a contract must be tendered in a single delivery unless the parties agree otherwise [UCC 2–612, 2A–510] or the circumstances are such that either party can rightfully request delivery in lots [UCC 2–307]. Hence, an order for 1,000 shirts cannot be delivered two shirts at a time. If, however, the seller and the buyer contemplate that the shirts will be delivered in four orders of 250 each, as they are produced (for summer, fall, winter, and spring stock), and the price can be apportioned accordingly, it may be commercially reasonable to deliver the shirts in this way.

PLACE OF DELIVERY

The UCC provides for the place of delivery pursuant to a contract if the contract does not do so. Of course, the parties may agree on a particular destination, or their contract's terms or the circumstances may indicate the place.

Noncarrier Cases. If the contract does not designate the place of delivery for the goods, and the buyer is expected to pick them up, the place of delivery is the *seller's place of business* or, if the seller has none, the *seller's residence* [UCC 2–308]. If the contract involves the sale of *identified goods,* and the parties know when they enter into the contract that these goods are located somewhere other than at the seller's place of business (such as at a warehouse), then the *location of the goods* is the place for their delivery [UCC 2–308].

For example, Laval and Boyd both live in San Francisco. In San Francisco, Laval contracts to sell Boyd five used trucks, which both parties know are located in a Chicago warehouse. If nothing more is specified in the contract, the place of delivery for the trucks is Chicago. The seller may tender delivery by either giving the buyer a negotiable or nonnegotiable document of title or by obtaining the bailee's (warehouser's) acknowledgment that the buyer is entitled to possession.[1]

Carrier Cases. In many instances, attendant circumstances or delivery terms in the contract make it apparent that the parties intend that a carrier be used to move the goods. There are two ways a seller can complete performance of the obligation to deliver the goods in carrier cases—through a shipment contract and through a destination contract.

Shipment Contracts. Recall from Chapter 19 that a *shipment contract* requires or authorizes the seller to ship goods by a carrier. The contract does not require that the seller deliver the goods at a particular destination [UCC 2–319, 2–509]. Unless otherwise agreed, the seller must do the following:

1. Place the goods into the hands of the carrier.
2. Make a contract for their transportation that is reasonable according to the nature of the goods and their value. (For example, certain types of goods need refrigeration in transit.)
3. Obtain and promptly deliver or tender to the buyer any documents necessary to enable the buyer to obtain possession of the goods from the carrier.
4. Promptly notify the buyer that shipment has been made [UCC 2–504].

If the seller fails to notify the buyer that shipment has been made or fails to make a proper contract for transportation, and a *material loss* of the goods or a *significant delay* results, the buyer can reject the shipment. Of course, the parties can agree that a lesser amount of loss or any delay will be grounds for rejection.

Destination Contracts. In a *destination contract,* the seller agrees to see that conforming goods will be duly tendered to the buyer at a particular destination. The goods must be tendered at a reasonable hour and held at the buyer's disposal for a reasonable length of time. The seller must also give the buyer appropriate notice. In addition, the seller must provide the buyer with any documents of title necessary

1. If the seller delivers a nonnegotiable document of title or merely writes instructions to the bailee to release the goods to the buyer without the bailee's acknowledgment of the buyer's rights, this is also a sufficient tender, unless the buyer objects [UCC 2–503(4)]. Risk of loss, however, does not pass until the buyer has had a reasonable amount of time in which to present the document or the instructions. See Chapter 19.

to enable the buyer to obtain delivery from the carrier. Sellers often do this by tendering the documents through ordinary banking channels [UCC 2–503].

The Perfect Tender Rule

As previously noted, the seller or lessor has an obligation to ship or tender *conforming goods,* and this entitles the buyer or lessee to accept and pay for the goods according to the terms of the contract. Under the common law, the seller was obligated to deliver goods in conformity with the terms of the contract in every detail. This was called the **perfect tender rule.** The UCC preserves the perfect tender doctrine by stating that if goods or tender of delivery fail *in any respect* to conform to the contract, the buyer or lessee has the right to accept the goods, reject the entire shipment, or accept part and reject part [UCC 2–601, 2A–509].

For example, a lessor contracts to lease fifty Comclear computers to be delivered at the lessee's place of business on or before October 1. On September 28, the lessor discovers that it has only thirty Comclear computers in inventory but will have another twenty Comclear computers within the next two weeks. The lessor tenders delivery of the thirty Comclear computers on October 1, with the promise that the other computers will be delivered within three weeks. Because the lessor has failed to make a perfect tender of fifty Comclear computers, the lessee has the right to reject the entire shipment and hold the lessor in breach.

Exceptions to the Perfect Tender Rule

Because of the rigidity of the perfect tender rule, several exceptions to the rule have been created, some of which we discuss here.

Agreement of the Parties.

Exceptions to the perfect tender rule may be established by agreement. If the parties have agreed, for example, that defective goods or parts will not be rejected if the seller or lessor is able to repair or replace them within a reasonable period of time, the perfect tender rule does not apply.

Cure.

The UCC does not specifically define the term **cure,** but it refers to the right of the seller or lessor to repair, adjust, or replace defective or nonconforming goods [UCC 2–508, 2A–513]. When any tender of delivery is rejected because of nonconforming goods and the time for performance has not yet expired, the seller or lessor can notify the buyer or lessee promptly of the intention to cure and can then do so *within the contract time for performance* [UCC 2–508(1), 2A–513(1)]. Once the time for performance under the contract has expired, the seller or lessor can still exercise the right to cure if he or she had *reasonable grounds to believe that the nonconforming tender would be acceptable to the buyer or lessee* [UCC 2–508(2), 2A–513(2)].

Sometimes, a seller or lessor will tender nonconforming goods with some type of price allowance, although this is not a requirement under the UCC. The allowance serves as the "reasonable grounds" for the seller or lessor to believe that the nonconforming tender will be acceptable to the buyer or lessee. Other reasons might also serve as the basis for the assumption that a buyer or lessee will accept a nonconforming tender. For example, if in the past a buyer frequently accepted a particular substitute for a good when the good ordered was not available, the seller has reasonable grounds to believe the buyer will again accept such a substitute. Even if the buyer rejects the substitute good on a particular occasion, the seller nonetheless had reasonable grounds to believe that the substitute would be acceptable. Therefore, the seller can cure within a *reasonable time,* even though conforming delivery will occur after the time limit for performance allowed under the contract.

The right to cure substantially restricts the right of the buyer or lessee to reject goods. For example, if a lessee refuses a tender of goods as nonconforming but does not disclose the nature of the defect to the lessor, the lessee cannot later assert the defect as a defense if the defect is one that the lessor could have cured. Generally, buyers and lessees must act in good faith and state specific reasons for refusing to accept goods [UCC 2–605, 2A–514].

Substitution of Carriers.

When an agreed-on manner of delivery (such as the use of a particular carrier to transport the goods) becomes impracticable or unavailable through no fault of either party, but a commercially reasonable substitute is available, this substitute performance is sufficient tender to the buyer and must be used [UCC 2–614(1)]. For example, a sales contract calls for the delivery of a large piece of machinery to be shipped by ABC Truck Lines on or before June 1. The contract terms clearly state the importance of the delivery date. The employees of ABC Truck Lines go on strike. The seller must make a reasonable substitute tender, perhaps by rail, if such is available. Note that the seller here is responsible for any additional shipping costs, unless contrary arrangements have been made in the sales contract.

Installment Contracts. An **installment contract** is a single contract that requires or authorizes delivery in two or more separate lots to be accepted and paid for separately. In an installment contract, a buyer or lessee can reject an installment *only if the nonconformity substantially impairs the value* of the installment and cannot be cured [UCC 2–307, 2–612(2), 2A–510(1)].

The entire installment contract is breached only when one or more nonconforming installments *substantially* impair the value of *the whole contract.* If the buyer or lessee subsequently accepts a nonconforming installment and fails to notify the seller or lessor of cancellation, however, the contract is reinstated [UCC 2–612(3), 2A–510(2)].

A major issue to be determined is what constitutes substantial impairment of the "value of the whole contract." For example, consider an installment contract for the sale of twenty carloads of plywood. The first carload does not conform to the contract because 9 percent of the plywood deviates from the thickness specifications. The buyer cancels the contract, and immediately thereafter the second and third carloads of plywood arrive at the buyer's place of business. If a lawsuit ensued, the court would have to grapple with the question of whether the nonconforming plywood, comprising 9 percent of one carload, substantially impaired the value of the whole.[2]

A more clear-cut example is an installment contract that involves parts of a machine. Suppose that the first part is delivered and is irreparably defective but is necessary for the operation of the machine. The failure of this first installment will be a breach of the whole contract. Even when the defect in the first shipment is such that it gives the buyer only a "reasonable apprehension" about the ability or willingness of the seller to complete the other installments properly, the breach on the first installment may be regarded as a breach of the whole.

The point to remember is that the UCC significantly alters the right of the buyer or lessee to reject the entire contract if the contract requires delivery to be made in several installments. The UCC strictly limits rejection to cases of *substantial* nonconformity (unless the parties agree that breach of an installment constitutes a breach of the entire contract).

Commercial Impracticability. As stated in Chapter 16, occurrences unforeseen by either party when a contract was made may make performance commercially impracticable. When this occurs, the rule of perfect tender no longer holds. According to UCC 2–615(a) and 2A–405(a), delay in delivery or nondelivery in whole or in part is not a breach when performance has been made impracticable "by the occurrence of a contingency the nonoccurrence of which was a basic assumption on which the contract was made." The seller or lessor must, however, notify the buyer or lessee as soon as practicable that there will be a delay or nondelivery.

Foreseeable versus Unforeseeable Contingencies. An increase in cost resulting from inflation does not in and of itself excuse performance, as this kind of risk is ordinarily assumed by a seller or lessor conducting business. The unforeseen contingency must be one that would have been impossible to contemplate in a given business situation. For example, a major oil company that receives its supplies from the Middle East has a contract to supply a buyer with 100,000 gallons of oil. Because of an oil embargo by the Organization of Petroleum Exporting Countries (OPEC), the seller is prevented from securing oil supplies to meet the terms of the contract. Because of the same embargo, the seller cannot secure oil from any other source. This situation comes fully under the commercial impracticability exception to the perfect tender doctrine [UCC 2–615, 2A–405].

See Case 20.1 at the end of this chapter. To view the full, unedited case from Westlaw,® go to this text's Web site at **http://wbl-cs.westbuslaw.com**.

Partial Performance. Sometimes the unforeseen event only *partially* affects the capacity of the seller or lessor to perform, and the seller or lessor is thus able to fulfill the contract *partially* but cannot tender total performance. In this event, the seller or lessor is required to allocate in a fair and reasonable manner any remaining production and deliveries among its

2. *Continental Forest Products, Inc. v. White Lumber Sales, Inc.*, 256 Or. 466, 474 P.2d 1 (1970). The court held that the deviation did not substantially impair the value of the whole contract. Additionally, the court stated that the nonconformity could be cured by an adjustment in the price.

regular customers and those to whom it is contractually obligated to deliver the goods [UCC 2–615(b), 2A–405(b)]. The buyer or lessee must receive notice of the allocation and has the right to accept or reject the allocation [UCC 2–615(c), 2A–405(c)].

For example, a Florida orange grower, Best Citrus, Inc., contracts to sell this season's production to a number of customers, including Martin's grocery chain. Martin's contracts to purchase two thousand crates of oranges. Best Citrus has sprayed *some* of its orange groves with a chemical called Karmoxin. The U.S. Department of Agriculture discovers that persons who eat products sprayed with Karmoxin may develop cancer and issues an order prohibiting the sale of these products. Best Citrus picks all the oranges not sprayed with Karmoxin, but the quantity does not fully meet all the contracted-for deliveries. In this situation, Best Citrus is required to allocate its production, so it notifies Martin's that it cannot deliver the full quantity agreed on in the contract and specifies the amount it will be able to deliver under the circumstances. Martin's can either accept or reject the allocation, but Best Citrus has no further contractual liability.

Destruction of Identified Goods. Sometimes, an unexpected event, such as a fire, totally destroys goods through no fault of either party and before risk passes to the buyer or lessee. In such a situation, *if the goods were identified at the time the contract was formed,* the parties are excused from performance [UCC 2–613, 2A–221]. If the goods are only partially destroyed, however, the buyer or lessee can inspect them and either treat the contract as void or accept the damaged goods with a reduction of the contract price.

Consider an example. Atlas Sporting Equipment agrees to lease to River Bicycles sixty bicycles of a particular model that has been discontinued. No other bicycles of that model are available. River specifies that it needs the bicycles to rent to tourists. Before Atlas can deliver the bikes, they are destroyed by a fire. In this situation, Atlas is not liable to River for failing to deliver the bikes. The goods were destroyed through no fault of either party, before the risk of loss passed to the lessee. The loss was total, so the contract is avoided. Clearly, Atlas has no obligation to tender the bicycles, and River has no obligation to pay for them.

Assurance and Cooperation. Two other exceptions to the perfect tender doctrine apply equally to parties to sales and lease contracts: the right of assurance and the duty of cooperation.

The Right of Assurance. The UCC provides that if one of the parties to a contract has "reasonable grounds" to believe that the other party will not perform as contracted, he or she may *in writing* "demand adequate assurance of due performance" from the other party. Until such assurance is received, he or she may "suspend" further performance without liability. What constitutes "reasonable grounds" is determined by commercial standards. If such assurances are not forthcoming within a reasonable time (not to exceed thirty days), the failure to respond may be treated as a *repudiation* of the contract [UCC 2–609, 2A–401].

For example, Zena has contracted to ship Jenkins one hundred shirts on or before October 1, with Jenkins's payment due within thirty days of delivery. Zena has made two previous shipments, neither of which has been paid for by Jenkins. On September 20, Zena demands in writing certain assurances of payment (including payment of the last two orders to bring the account up to date) before she will ship the shirts. If these desired assurances are reasonable, Zena can suspend shipment of the shirts without liability pending Jenkins's compliance. If Jenkins does not provide the assurances within a reasonable time (no longer than thirty days), Zena can hold Jenkins in breach of contract without having made the contracted-for shipment.

The Duty of Cooperation. Sometimes the performance of one party depends on the cooperation of the other. The UCC provides that when such cooperation is not forthcoming, the other party can suspend his or her own performance without liability and hold the uncooperative party in breach or proceed to perform the contract in any reasonable manner [see UCC 2–311(3)(b)].

For example, Amati is required by contract to deliver 1,200 model Z washing machines to locations in the state of California to be specified later by Farrell. Deliveries are to be made on or before October 1. Amati has repeatedly requested the delivery locations, and Farrell has not responded. The 1,200 model Z machines are ready for shipment on October 1, but Farrell still refuses to give Amati delivery locations. Amati does not ship on October 1. Can Amati be held liable? The answer is no. Amati is excused for any resulting delay of performance because of Farrell's failure to cooperate.

SECTION 3

Obligations of the Buyer or Lessee

Once the seller or lessor has adequately tendered delivery, the buyer or lessee is obligated to accept the goods and pay for them according to the terms of the contract.

PAYMENT

In the absence of any specific agreements, the buyer or lessee must make payment at the time and place the buyer or lessee *receives* the goods [UCC 2–310(a), 2A–516(1)]. When a sale is made on credit, the buyer is obliged to pay according to the specified credit terms (for example, 60, 90, or 120 days), not when the goods are received. The credit period usually begins on the *date of shipment* [UCC 2–310(d)]. Under a lease contract, a lessee must make the lease payment specified in the contract [UCC 2A–516(1)].

Payment can be made by any means agreed on between the parties—cash or any other method generally acceptable in the commercial world. If the seller demands cash when the buyer offers a check, credit card, or the like, the seller must permit the buyer reasonable time to obtain legal tender [UCC 2–511].

RIGHT OF INSPECTION

Unless otherwise agreed, or for C.O.D. (collect on delivery) transactions, the buyer or lessee has an absolute right to inspect the goods. This right allows the buyer or lessee to verify, before making payment, that the goods tendered or delivered are what were contracted for or ordered. If the goods are not what the buyer or lessee ordered, the buyer or lessee has no duty to pay. *An opportunity for inspection is therefore a condition precedent to the right of the seller or lessor to enforce payment* [UCC 2–513(1), 2A–515(1)].

Unless otherwise agreed, inspection can take place at any reasonable place and time and in any reasonable manner. Generally, what is reasonable is determined by custom of the trade, past practices of the parties, and the like. Costs of inspecting conforming goods are borne by the buyer unless otherwise agreed [UCC 2–513(2)].

C.O.D. Shipments. If a seller ships goods to a buyer C.O.D. (or under similar terms) and the buyer has not agreed to a C.O.D. shipment in the contract, the buyer can rightfully *reject* the goods. This is because a C.O.D. shipment does not permit inspection before payment, which is a denial of the buyer's right of inspection. When the buyer has agreed to a C.O.D. shipment in the contract, however, or has agreed to pay for the goods on the presentation of a bill of lading, no right of inspection exists, because it was negated by the agreement [UCC 2–513(3)].

Payment Due—Documents of Title. Under certain contracts, payment is due on the receipt of the required documents of title even though the goods themselves may not have arrived at their destination. With C.I.F. and C.&F. contracts,[3] payment is required on receipt of the documents unless the parties have agreed otherwise. Thus, payment is required prior to inspection, and payment must be made unless the buyer knows that the goods are nonconforming [UCC 2–310(b), 2–513(3)].

ACCEPTANCE

A buyer or lessee can manifest assent to the delivered goods in the following ways, each of which constitutes acceptance:

1. There is an acceptance if the buyer or lessee, after having had a reasonable opportunity to inspect the goods, signifies agreement to the seller or lessor that the goods are either conforming or are acceptable in spite of their nonconformity [UCC 2–606(1)(a), 2A–515(1)(a)].
2. Acceptance is presumed if the buyer or lessee has had a reasonable opportunity to inspect the goods and has failed to reject them within a reasonable period of time [UCC 2–602(1), 2–606(1)(b), 2A–515(1)(b)].
3. In sales contracts, the buyer will be deemed to have accepted the goods if he or she performs any act inconsistent with the seller's ownership. For example, any use or resale of the goods generally constitutes an acceptance. Limited use for the sole purpose of testing or inspecting the goods is not an acceptance, however [UCC 2–606(1)(c)].

If some of the goods delivered do not conform to the contract and the seller or lessor has failed to cure, the buyer or lessee can make a *partial* acceptance [UCC 2–601(c), 2A–509(1)]. The same is true if the nonconformity was not reasonably discover-

3. See Exhibit 19–1 in Chapter 19 for definitions of *C.I.F.* and *C.&F.*

able before acceptance.[4] A buyer or lessee cannot accept less than a single commercial unit, however. A *commercial unit* is defined by the UCC as a unit of goods that, by commercial usage, is viewed as a "single whole" for purposes of sale, division of which would materially impair the character of the unit, its market value, or its use [UCC 2–105(6), 2A–103(c)]. A commercial unit can be a single article (such as a machine), a set of articles (such as a suite of furniture or an assortment of sizes), a quantity (such as a bale, a gross, or a carload), or any other unit treated in the trade as a single whole.

Westlaw. See Case 20.2 at the end of this chapter. To view the full, unedited case from Westlaw,® go to this text's Web site at **http://wbl-cs.westbuslaw.com**.

SECTION 4

Anticipatory Repudiation

What if, before the time for contract performance, one party clearly communicates to the other the intention not to perform? Such an action is a breach of the contract by *anticipatory repudiation.*[5] When anticipatory repudiation occurs, the nonbreaching party has a choice of two responses. He or she can treat the repudiation as a final breach by pursuing a remedy; or he or she can wait to see if the repudiating party will decide to honor the obligations required by the contract despite the avowed intention to renege [UCC 2–610, 2A–402]. In either situation, the nonbreaching party may suspend performance.

Should the latter course be pursued, the UCC permits the breaching party (subject to some limitations) to "retract" his or her repudiation. This can be done by any method that clearly indicates an intent to perform. Once retraction is made, the rights of the repudiating party under the contract are reinstated [UCC 2–611, 2A–403].

To illustrate: Assume that Cora, who owns a small inn, purchases a suite of furniture from Horton's Furniture Warehouse on April 1. The contract states that "delivery must be made on or before May 1." On April 10, Horton informs Cora that he cannot make delivery until May 10 and asks Cora to consent to the modified delivery date. In this situation, Cora has the option of either treating Horton's notice of late delivery as a final breach of contract and pursuing a remedy or agreeing to the later delivery date. Suppose that Cora does neither for two weeks. On April 24, Horton informs Cora that he will be able to deliver the furniture by May 1, after all. In effect, Horton has retracted his repudiation, reinstating the rights and obligations of the parties under the original contract.

See Case 20.3 at the end of this chapter. To view the full, unedited case from Westlaw,® go to this text's Web site at **http://wbl-cs.westbuslaw.com**.

SECTION 5

Dealing with International Contracts—The Letter of Credit

Because buyers and sellers (or lessees and lessors) engaged in international business transactions may be separated by thousands of miles, special precautions are often taken to ensure performance under international contracts. Sellers and lessors want to avoid delivering goods for which they might not be paid. Buyers and lessees desire the assurance that sellers and lessors will not be paid until there is evidence that the goods have been shipped. Thus, **letters of credit** are frequently used to facilitate international business transactions.

In a simple letter-of-credit transaction, the *issuer* (a bank) agrees to issue a letter of credit and to ascertain whether the *beneficiary* (seller or lessor) performs certain acts. In return, the *account party* (buyer or lessee) promises to reimburse the issuer for the amount paid to the beneficiary. There may also be an *advising bank* that transmits information, and a *paying bank* may be involved to expedite payment under the letter of credit. Exhibit 20–1 on page 394 illustrates a letter-of-credit transaction.

Under a letter of credit, the issuer is bound to pay the beneficiary (seller or lessor) when the beneficiary has complied with the terms and conditions of the letter of credit. The beneficiary looks to the issuer, not to the account party (buyer or lessee), when it presents the documents required by the letter of credit. Typically, the letter of credit will require that the beneficiary deliver a *bill of lading* to prove that shipment has been made. Letters of credit assure

4. If the nonconformity was not reasonably discoverable before acceptance, the buyer or lessee may be able to revoke the acceptance, as will be discussed in Chapter 21.

5. Refer back to Chapter 16 for a discussion of the common law origins and application of the doctrine of anticipatory repudiation.

EXHIBIT 20–1 A LETTER-OF-CREDIT TRANSACTION

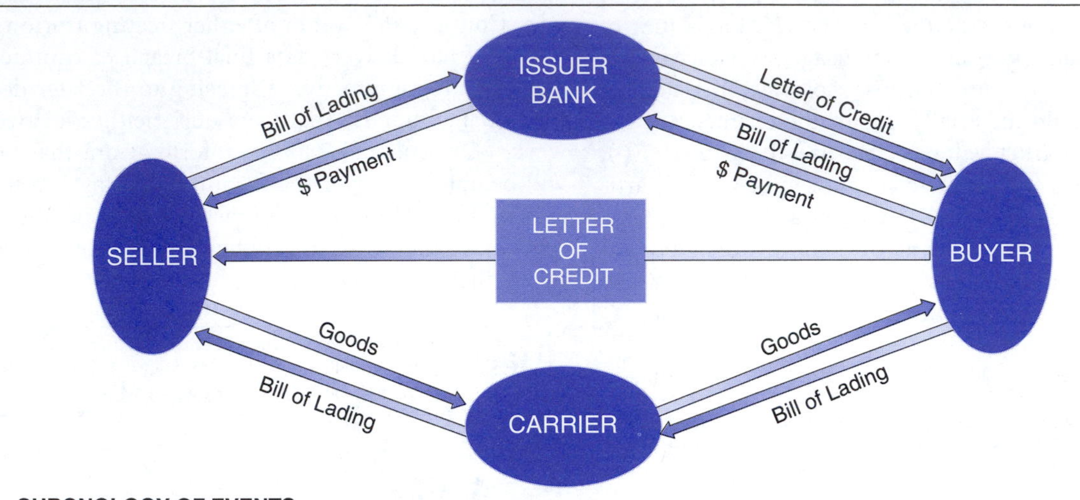

CHRONOLOGY OF EVENTS

1. Buyer contracts with issuer bank to issue a letter of credit; this sets forth the bank's obligation to pay on the letter of credit and buyer's obligation to pay the bank.
2. Letter of credit is sent to seller informing seller that on compliance with the terms of the letter of credit (such as presentment of necessary documents—in this example, a bill of lading), the bank will issue payment for the goods.
3. Seller delivers goods to carrier and receives a bill of lading.
4. Seller delivers the bill of lading to issuer bank and, if the document is proper, receives payment.
5. Issuer bank delivers the bill of lading to buyer.
6. Buyer delivers the bill of lading to carrier.
7. Carrier delivers the goods to buyer.
8. Buyer settles with issuer bank.

beneficiaries (sellers or lessors) of payment while at the same time assuring account parties (buyers or lessees) that payment will not be made until the beneficiaries have complied with the terms and conditions of the letter of credit.

The basic principle behind letters of credit is that payment is made against the documents presented by the beneficiary and not against the facts that the documents purport to reflect. Thus, in a letter-of-credit transaction, the issuer does not police the underlying contract; a letter of credit is independent of the underlying contract between the buyer and the seller. Eliminating the need for banks (issuers) to inquire into whether or not actual conditions have been satisfied greatly reduces the costs of letters of credit. Moreover, the use of a letter of credit protects all parties to a transaction.

TERMS AND CONCEPTS TO REVIEW

conforming goods 387	installment contract 390	perfect tender rule 389
cure 389	letter of credit 393	tender of delivery 387

Chapter Summary

Obligations of the Seller or Lessor	1. The seller or lessor must tender *conforming* goods to the buyer. Tender must take place at a *reasonable hour* and in a *reasonable manner.* Under the perfect tender doctrine, the seller or lessor must tender goods that conform exactly to the terms of the contract [UCC 2–503(1), 2A–508(1)]. 2. If the seller or lessor tenders nonconforming goods prior to the performance date and the buyer or lessee rejects them, the seller or lessor may *cure* (repair or replace the goods) within the contract time for performance [UCC 2–508(1), 2A–513(1)]. If the seller or lessor has reasonable grounds to believe the buyer or lessee would accept the tendered goods, on the buyer's or lessee's rejection the seller or lessor has a reasonable time to substitute conforming goods without liability [UCC 2–508(2), 2A–513(2)]. 3. If the agreed-on means of delivery becomes impracticable or unavailable, the seller must substitute an alternative means (such as a different carrier) if one is available [UCC 2–614(1)]. 4. If a seller or lessor tenders nonconforming goods in any one installment under an installment contract, the buyer or lessee may reject the installment only if its value is substantially impaired and cannot be cured. The entire installment contract is breached when one or more nonconforming installments *substantially* impair the value of the *whole* contract [UCC 2–612, 2A–510]. 5. When performance becomes commercially impracticable owing to circumstances unforeseen when the contract was formed, the perfect tender rule no longer holds [UCC 2–615, 2A–405].
Obligations of the Buyer or Lessee	1. On tender of delivery by the seller or lessor, the buyer or lessee must pay for the goods at the time and place the buyer or lessee *receives* the goods, even if the place of shipment is the place of delivery, unless the sale is made on credit. Payment may be made by any method generally acceptable in the commercial world unless the seller demands cash [UCC 2–310, 2–511]. In lease contracts, the lessee must make lease payments in accordance with the contract [UCC 2A–516(1)]. 2. Unless otherwise agreed, the buyer or lessee has an absolute right to inspect the goods before acceptance [UCC 2–513(1), 2A–515(1)]. 3. The buyer or lessee can manifest acceptance of delivered goods expressly in words or by conduct or by failing to reject the goods after a reasonable period of time following inspection or after having had a reasonable opportunity to inspect them [UCC 2–606(1), 2A–515(1)]. A buyer will be deemed to have accepted goods if he or she performs any act inconsistent with the seller's ownership [UCC 2–606(1)(c)]. 4. Following the acceptance of delivered goods, the buyer or lessee may revoke acceptance only if the nonconformity *substantially* impairs the value of the unit or lot and if one of the following factors is present: a. Acceptance was predicated on the reasonable assumption that the nonconformity would be cured and it was not cured within a reasonable time [UCC 2–608(1)(a), 2A–517(1)(a)]. b. The buyer or lessee did not discover the nonconformity before acceptance, either because it was difficult to discover before acceptance or because the seller's or lessor's assurance that the goods were conforming kept the buyer or lessee from inspecting the goods [UCC 2–608(1)(b), 2A–517(1)(b)].
Anticipatory Repudiation	If, before the time for performance, either party clearly indicates to the other an intention not to perform, under UCC 2–610 and 2A–402 the aggrieved party may do the following: 1. Await performance by the repudiating party for a commercially reasonable time. 2. Resort to any remedy for breach. 3. In either situation, suspend performance.

CASES FOR ANALYSIS

Westlaw. You can access the full text of each case presented below by going to the Westlaw cases on this text's Web site at http://wbl-cs.westbuslaw.com. Each Westlaw case includes the names of all plaintiffs and defendants, the dates on which the case was argued and decided, a brief summary of the issues and decisions in the case, headnotes classifying the specific issues in the case according to the West Key Number System, and the court's opinion. Concurring and dissenting opinions, if any, are included as well.

CASE 20.1 COMMERCIAL IMPRACTICABILITY

MAPLE FARMS, INC. V. CITY SCHOOL DISTRICT OF CITY OF ELMIRA

Supreme Court of New York, 1974.
76 Misc.2d 1080,
352 N.Y.S.2d 784.

CHARLES B. SWARTWOOD, Justice.

* * * *

The background of this dispute is that the price of raw milk at the farm site is and has been controlled for many years in this area by the United States Department of Agriculture through the New York–New Jersey Market Administrator. The president of the plaintiff milk dealer has for at least ten years bid on contracts to supply milk for the defendant school district and is thoroughly conversant with prices and costs. Though the plaintiff avers [declares] that the defendant was aware of the prices of raw milk and the profit picture, the fiscal officer of the defendant denies that either the price of raw milk or the profit structure of suppliers was known or of any concern to him or the defendant. The defendant's only concern was the assurance of a steady supply of milk for the school lunch program at an agreed price on which the school's budget had to be based.

The mandated price of raw milk has in the past fluctuated from a cost of $6.73 cwt. [hundredweight] in 1969 to a high of $7.58 cwt. in 1972, or 12%, with fluctuation within a calendar year ranging from 1% to 4.5%. The plaintiff agreed to supply milk to the defendant for the school year 1973–1974 by agreement of June 15, 1973 at a price of $.0759 per half pint, at which time the mandated price of raw milk was $8.03 cwt. By November of 1973 the price of raw milk had risen to $9.31 cwt. and by December 1973 to $9.89 cwt., an increase of 23% over the June 1973 price. However, it should be noted that there was an increase from the low price in 1972 to the June 1973 price (date of the contract) of 9.5%. Because of considerable increase in the price of raw milk, the plaintiff, beginning in October 1973, has requested the defendant to relieve the plaintiff of its contract and to put the contract out for rebidding. The defendant has refused.

The plaintiff spells out in detail its costs based on the June and December prices of raw milk and shows that it will sustain a loss of $7,350.55 if it is required to continue its performance on the same volume with raw milk at the December price. Its contracts with other school districts where it is faced with the same problem will triple its total contemplated loss.

* * * *

The plaintiff goes to great lengths to spell out the cause of the substantial increase in the price of raw milk, which the plaintiff argues could not have been foreseen by the parties because it came about in large measure from the agreement of the United States to sell huge amounts of grain to Russia and to a lesser extent to unanticipated crop failures.

The legal basis of the plaintiff's request for being relieved of the obligation under the contract award is the doctrine known variously as "impossibility of performance" and "frustration of performance" at common law and as "Excuse by Failure of Presupposed Conditions" under the Uniform Commercial Code, [Section] 2-615.

The common law rule is stated in [the *Restatement of Contracts,* Section 454] as follows:

> "[Section] 454. DEFINITION OF IMPOSSIBILITY.
> In the Restatement of this Subject impossibility means not only strict impossibility but impracticability because of extreme and unreasonable difficulty, expense, injury or loss involved."

Performance has been excused at common law where performance has become illegal; where disaster wipes out the means of production; [and] where governmental action prevents performance.

* * * *

* * * *[W]here economic hardship alone is involved performance will not be excused. This is so even where governmental acts make performance more expensive. Existing circumstances and foreseeability also play a part in determining whether a party should be relieved of his contracts.* [Emphasis added.]

The Uniform Commercial Code, [Section] 2-615 states in part:

> "Except so far as a seller may have assumed a greater obligation and subject to the preceding section on substituted performance:
> (a) Delay in delivery or non-delivery in whole or in part by a seller * * * is not a breach of his duty under a contract for sale if performance as agreed has been

made impracticable by the occurrence of a contingency the non-occurrence of which was a basic assumption on which the contract was made or by compliance in good faith with any applicable foreign or domestic governmental regulation or order whether or not it later proves to be invalid."

The Official Comment, Number "3" to that section points out that the test of impracticability is to be judged by commercial standards. Official Comment Number "4" states:

"Increased cost alone does not excuse performance unless the rise in cost is due to some unforeseen contingency which alters the essential nature of the performance. Neither is a rise or a collapse in the market in itself a justification, for that is exactly the type of business risk which business contracts made at fixed prices are intended to cover. But a severe shortage of raw materials or of supplies due to a contingency such as war, embargo, local crop failure, unforeseen shutdown of major sources of supply or the like, which either causes a marked increase in cost or altogether prevents the seller from securing supplies necessary to his performance, is within the contemplation of this section."

Official Comment Number "10" states in part that " * * * governmental interference cannot excuse unless it truly 'supervenes' in such a manner as to be beyond the seller's assumption of risk."

* * * *

* * * [The doctrine requires that] first, a contingency—something unexpected—must have occurred. Second, the risk of the unexpected occurrence must not have been allocated either by agreement or by custom. Finally, occurrence of the contingency must have rendered performance commercially impracticable.

Applying these rules to the facts here we find that the contingency causing the increase of the price of raw milk was not totally unexpected. The price from the low point in the year 1972 to the price on the date of the award of the contract in June 1973 had risen nearly 10% and any businessman should have been aware of the general inflation in this country during the previous years and of the chance of crop failures.

* * * [T]he very purpose of the contract was to guard against fluctuation of price of half pints of milk as a basis for the school budget. Surely had the price of raw milk fallen substantially, the defendant could not be excused from performance. We can reasonably assume that the plaintiff had to be aware of escalating inflation. It is chargeable with knowledge of the substantial increase of the price of raw milk from the previous year's low. It had knowledge that for many years the Department of Agriculture had established the price of raw milk and that that price varied. It nevertheless entered into this agreement with that knowledge. It did not provide in the contract any exculpatory clause to excuse it from performance in the event of a substantial rise in the price of raw milk. On these facts the risk of a substantial or abnormal increase in the price of raw milk can be allocated to the plaintiff.

* * * *

The plaintiff's motion is denied and the defendant is granted summary judgment dismissing the complaint.

CASE 20.2 ACCEPTANCE

INDUSTRIA DE CALCADOS MARTINI LTDA. v. MAXWELL SHOE CO.

Appeals Court of Massachusetts, 1974.
36 Mass.App.Ct. 268,
630 N.E.2d 299.

PORADA, Justice.

The plaintiff, Industria De Calcados Martini Ltda. (Martini), a Brazilian shoe manufacturer, filed an action in [a Massachusetts state court] against the defendant Maxwell Shoe Co., Inc. (Maxwell), a wholesale distributor of shoes, for breach of contract * * * arising out of the sale of 12,042 pairs of men's shoes by Martini to Maxwell. * * * The judge ruled that Maxwell was in breach of its contract and awarded damages to Martini in the sum of $25,890.30, the balance remaining due on the parties' contract. * * * Both Martini and Maxwell appealed from the judgment. We affirm.

We summarize the facts as found by the judge. * * * Louis Fingerhut, a shoe broker [showed a sample of Martini-made shoes to Maxwell's president]. The sample of shoes did not appear to have any defects * * * . After inspecting the shoes, Maxwell placed an order through Fingerhut's company, Fingerhut Footwear, Inc., for 12,042 pairs of men's shoes from Martini. The purchase order invoices indicated the order was for "regular" shoes "as sampled." The price to be paid for the shoes was $116,205.30 ($9.65 a pair), of which * * * $25,890.30 [was to be paid] by personal check. * * * [T]he shoes were to be inspected in Brazil by Southline, a trading company in Brazil chosen by Fingerhut to inspect the shoes. * * * [Payment] was contingent upon the issuance of a certificate of inspection by Southline. On or about February 8, 1988, Maxwell also sent its personal check to Martini in the sum of $25,890.30, which was received by Martini.

About February 1, 1988, Maxwell received a supplemental sample of the shoes from Brazil. Upon inspection, Maxwell discovered the shoes were cracked and peeling. As a result, Maxwell immediately contacted Fingerhut and informed him that if all the shoes were in that condition, he did not want the shoes shipped. Fingerhut in turn contacted his employees in Brazil to find out (1) if the shoes had been inspected by Southline, (2) whether there were any quality problems, and (3) if so, whether they could be corrected.

The shoes were shipped on February 10, 1988. A certificate of inspection was issued by Southline dated February 18, 1988, certifying that the shoes were in strict compliance with the specifications in the contract. The shoes arrived at Maxwell's warehouse on March 23, 1988. Upon inspection, Maxwell discovered the entire shipment was defective. All the shoes were cracked and peeling. Maxwell immediately contacted Fingerhut and told him that he did not want the shoes and wanted returned the [$90,315] already collected by Martini * * * . Maxwell had previously stopped payment on its check for $25,890.30, so Martini never received that payment. Fingerhut in turn contacted his associates at Southline in Brazil and informed them that Maxwell had rejected the shoes, but that he was trying to work out a solution to the problem. Subsequently, Maxwell notified Fingerhut by letter that the shoes had been misrepresented; that it considered Fingerhut responsible for recovering the money that it had paid Martini; and that if it did not have a positive response from Fingerhut by May 1, 1988, it would start selling the shoes at any price and would charge any expenses or losses to Fingerhut. Maxwell also offered to reship the goods provided it received a guaranty of payment of its shipping costs. When Maxwell did not receive word from anyone by May 1, 1988, as to whether the shoes were to be reshipped, it sent the shoes to Maine to be refinished at two dollars a pair. Maxwell then sold the refinished shoes over the next two years for the sum of $145,737, which it retained.

Martini never received notice directly from Maxwell itself regarding the quality of the shoes or that Maxwell wished to return the shoes. When Maxwell stopped payment on its check, Martini did ask Southline why Maxwell did so and was informed by Southline that Maxwell was dissatisfied with the shoes but that they were trying to work out a solution to the problem.

Based on these facts, the judge concluded that Maxwell, at first, properly rejected the shoes but once it shipped the goods to Maine to be refinished, it accepted them and, thus, was liable for the remaining balance due on its contract with Maxwell in the sum of $25,890.30. * * *

* * * *

The principal issue in this case is whether the shoes were accepted by Maxwell. The judge ruled that Maxwell accepted the shoes when it shipped the goods to Maine to be refinished on the grounds that an alteration or repair of a defect in goods is an act inconsistent with the seller's ownership, as it is not one of the prescribed remedies which a buyer is allowed to pursue once he rightfully rejects the goods [under Massachusetts General Laws Chapter 106, Section 2-604, Massachusetts's version of UCC 2-604]. Maxwell claims this was error because the judge applied too rigid an interpretation of [Section] 2-604.

Section 2-604 provides in pertinent part, "if the seller gives no instructions within a reasonable time after notification of rejection the buyer may store the rejected goods for the seller's account or reship them to him or resell them for the seller's account with reimbursement * * * ." Maxwell contends that these remedies are not exhaustive and that a buyer who acts in good faith should be allowed to take reasonable action to mitigate its damages. * * *

* * * Here, Maxwell received no * * * instructions from Martini. Instead, it acted on its own in sending the shoes for refinishing and then selling them and retaining the proceeds for its own benefit. Under [Section] 2-606(1)(c), a buyer accepts goods when it "does any act inconsistent with the seller's ownership." Accordingly, we do not think the judge's ruling, that Maxwell's shipment of the goods to Maine to be refinished was inconsistent with its claim that Martini retained ownership of the shoes, was clearly erroneous.

* * * *

Judgment affirmed.

CASE 20.3 ANTICIPATORY REPUDIATION

BANCO INTERNATIONAL, INC. v. GOODY'S FAMILY CLOTHING

United States District Court,
Eastern District of Tennessee, 1999.
54 F.Supp.2d 765.

MURRIAN, United States Magistrate Judge.

* * * *

II. *Findings of Fact*

In April, 1994, [Banco International, Inc., and Goody's Family Clothing, Inc.] entered into a series of purchase orders for the development and delivery of custom made, private label boys and girls windsuits (jogging suits). The contracts were for a total of 62,748 windsuits at a total contract price of $749,103.60. The first shipment of 26,640 windsuits had to be at Goody's distribution center in Knoxville, Tennessee, by September 30, 1994, or the order was subject to cancellation.

Goody's orally canceled the entire contract (*i.e.*, all six purchase orders) at approximately 3:00 P.M., Knoxville, Tennessee, time on August 23, 1994. This was accomplished by a telephone call to Banco's headquarters in

Humble, Texas. This notice was then immediately passed along to Muhammed Akhtar, the president and owner of Banco, who was in Bangladesh where the windsuits were to be manufactured. Bangladesh time is 12 hours ahead of Eastern Daylight Time and so Mr. Akhtar received notice of the cancellation around 3:00 A.M. in Bangladesh on August 24, 1994. Mr. Akhtar called Tom Baatz, Goody's boy's wear buyer, and asked if the contract was indeed canceled. Mr. Baatz told him it was due to Banco's dispute with its subcontractor. * * * Mr. Akhtar represented that although Banco was behind schedule, it could meet the September 30, 1994, delivery date for the first shipment if it shipped by air freight, it could meet the October 5 deadline for the second shipment if it shipped by air freight, and it could meet the delivery deadline for the third shipment by shipping by sea. Shipping by air freight was over six times more expensive than shipping by sea and Banco would have to absorb the cost.

Goody's did not accept Banco's assurances of performance and formally confirmed cancellation of the entire contract by letter dated August 29, 1994. [Banco then filed a suit in a federal district court against Goody's, alleging breach of contract.]

* * * *

In a letter to Goody's dated August 10, 1994, Mr. Akhtar acknowledged that Banco was "running around 25 days behind schedule due to one month delay in opening the [letter of credit]." Mr. Akhtar also stated in his letter that "[w]e have started the production and scheduled the first shipment to leave Bangladesh on the [*sic*] August 25, 1994 * * * . We have purchased around U.S. $450,000.00 piece goods, lining and accessories for the orders. Piece goods are cut and are in production." At the time the contract was canceled, Goody's had good reason to believe that these representations were false.

The only production that would take place before the contract was canceled was a "production run" done by Attune Garments, LTD ("Attune"), a subcontractor of Banco's and a "production run" done by City Apparel, another subcontractor and a factory owned by Mr. Akhtar and his brother. Mr. Akhtar stated that he rejected the production run done by Attune on the afternoon of August 10, 1994, due to poor quality. He said this was after he had already faxed his August 10, 1994, letter to Goody's stating * * * that the "piece goods are cut and are in production."

* * * *

At the inception of this contract, Mr. Akhtar had led Goody's to believe that the windsuits would be produced in Banco's factory. Goody's was not aware that production was going to be subcontracted to Attune or City Apparel. It therefore came as a shock and surprise when the Managing Director of Attune, Towhid Islam Ratan, spoke by telephone with Randy Hodge at Goody's on August 23, 1994, and told Hodge that Attune was in possession of all the fabric and other raw materials for the contract; that Attune and Banco were in a dispute over an alleged $70,000 debt Banco had to Attune; that Attune would not ship Goody's order through Banco; that the shipment had been "momentarily delayed"; but that Attune was willing to produce the garments for Goody's under certain conditions, including [payment to Attune] by Goody's. * * *

* * * *

III. *Conclusions of Law*

Anticipatory repudiation of a contract for the sale of goods is governed by [Tennessee Code Annotated Section 47-2-610, Tennessee's version of UCC 2-610].

> Anticipatory repudiation.—When either party repudiates the contract with respect to a performance not yet due the loss of which will substantially impair the value of the contract to the other, the aggrieved party may:
> (a) for a commercially reasonable time await performance by the repudiating party; or
> (b) resort to any remedy for breach ([Section] 47-2-703 or [Section] 47-2-711), even though he has notified the repudiating party that he would await the latter's performance and has urged retraction; and
> (c) in either case suspend his own performance or proceed in accordance with the provisions of this chapter on the seller's right to identify goods to the contract notwithstanding breach or to salvage unfinished goods ([Section] 47-2-704).

"[A]nticipatory repudiation centers upon an overt communication of intention or an action which renders performance impossible or demonstrates a clear determination not to continue with performance," [according to T.C.A. Section 47-2-610, Comment 1]. *"It is not necessary for repudiation that performance be made literally and utterly impossible. Repudiation can result from action which reasonably indicates a rejection of the continuing obligation,"* [according to T.C.A. Section 47-2-610, Comment 2]. [Emphasis added.]

Banco's failure to start actual production of the windsuits prior to cancellation of the contract on August 23, 1994, Banco's apparent inability to gain possession and control of the fabric and other raw materials necessary to perform the contract, Banco's false representations about production, and Banco's failure to give Goody's adequate assurances that it could perform the contract in a timely manner during the days following cancellation are the primary actions by Banco which reasonably indicated to Goody's that Banco had rejected its continuing obligation under the contract. These actions justified Goody's suspension of its own performance and cancellation of the contract.

In all contracts governed by Article 2 of the Uniform Commercial Code there is a continuing obligation of good faith and reasonableness. In this case, Goody's came to realize by August 23, 1994, that Mr. Akhtar had not been truthful with Goody's about the status of production of the windsuits; Goody's had reason to believe that the production samples were not production samples at all; Banco did not have possession of the fabric and raw materials to perform the contract; and, as far as Goody's knew, Banco had no prospects of obtaining possession and control of those raw materials. In the days subsequent to the cancellation, Banco's proffered "reasonable assurances" consisted of more promises from Mr. Akhtar (whose credibility had been severely damaged) but without an explanation of just how Banco proposed to perform because Mr. Akhtar believed it was "none of Goody's business."

* * * An act can be a repudiation of contract when it is a voluntary affirmative act which renders the obligor unable or apparently unable to perform without such a breach. Of course, no one will ever know if Banco could have delivered the first shipment to Goody's distribution center in Knoxville on or before September 30, 1994. That is beside the point, however. The critical question is whether Banco's actions reasonably indicated to Goody's that Banco had rejected its continuing obligation under the contract. It was this apparent inability to perform without a substantial breach of the contract that justified Goody's in canceling the contract and in refusing Banco's proffered "reasonable assurances" of performance.

I find that Goody's was justified in reasonably concluding that Banco could not deliver the windsuits to it by the date set in the first purchase order between the parties. Additionally, the failure to deliver the goods by that date would have substantially impaired the value of those goods to Goody's. A material inconvenience and injustice would have resulted if Goody's was forced to wait until Banco could actually deliver the goods. A late delivery of the windsuits would have substantially impaired the value of the windsuits to Goody's. Late delivery of the first shipment of goods would have substantially impaired the value to Goody's of the remaining goods yet to be shipped. Therefore, Goody's is not liable for canceling those remaining deliveries.

For the reasons indicated, judgment will enter in Goody's favor and Banco will take nothing on its claim.

CASE PROBLEMS

20–1. T.W. Oil, Inc., purchased fuel oil that was still at sea on a tanker. T.W. Oil then contracted to sell to Consolidated Edison Co. (Con Ed) this cargo of oil. When T.W. Oil purchased the shipment, it received a certificate from the foreign refiner that stated the sulfur content of the oil was 0.52 percent. When T.W. Oil contracted with Con Ed to sell the oil, T.W. Oil specified that the sulfur content was 0.5 percent, rounding off the 0.52 percent, as was the custom in the trade. During the negotiations with Con Ed, T.W. Oil learned that Con Ed was authorized to buy and burn oil with a sulfur content of up to 1 percent and would mix oils containing more and less than that amount to maintain that figure. When the oil shipment arrived, its sulfur content was found to be 0.92 percent. Con Ed rejected the shipment. T.W. Oil offered a reduced price, which was also rejected by Con Ed. The next day, T.W. Oil offered to cure with a substitute shipment of conforming oil on a tanker due to arrive approximately one month after the original delivery date. Con Ed rejected the offer to cure. T.W. Oil sued for breach of contract, and the trial court ruled in favor of T.W. Oil, holding that the plaintiff's "reasonable and timely offer to cure" was improperly rejected. Discuss whether Con Ed was required to accept the substitute shipment. [*T.W. Oil, Inc. v. Consolidated Edison Co.*, 57 N.Y.2d 574, 443 N.E.2d 932, 457 N.Y.S.2d 458 (1982)]

20–2. On March 18, 1975, Moulton Cavity & Mold, Inc., agreed to sell twenty-six innersole molds (molds for the manufacture of shoes) to Lyn-Flex Industries, Inc., for $600. Moulton understood that Lyn-Flex was in immediate need of the molds, and Moulton agreed to produce the molds within five weeks. The molds turned out to be quite complicated to manufacture, and Moulton had to make some thirty tests to meet Lyn-Flex's specifications and also to fit the molds to Lyn-Flex's machines. After ten weeks, Lyn-Flex indicated that the model was approved as far as the fit was concerned but that other problems remained unsolved. Moulton went ahead and produced the twenty-six molds, and Lyn-Flex rejected them. When Moulton sued for damages for Lyn-Flex's alleged breach of contract, the trial court instructed the jury that substantial performance was sufficient to issue a verdict in favor of Moulton. Discuss whether this is correct according to the UCC. [*Moulton Cavity & Mold, Inc. v. Lyn-Flex Industries, Inc.*, 396 A.2d 1024 (Me. 1979)]

20–3. In December 1985 and January 1986, Will Petroleum, Inc., and UPG Falco entered into agreements involving a sale of gasoline from Will Petroleum to Falco. BAII Banking Corp. provided financing to Will Petroleum for the agreements, which were to be performed before the end of January. During December and January, gasoline prices declined, and Falco determined that it would lose nearly $1.5 million if the agreements were performed. In mid-January, rumors circulated that Will Petroleum might be filing for bankruptcy. When the *Konpolis,* one of the ships carrying the gasoline, arrived ahead of schedule on January 23, Falco refused it permission to dock. Falco sent a telex to Will Petroleum requesting adequate assurances within twenty-three hours that Will Petroleum could perform the agreements. There was no response. The next evening, Falco sent Will Petroleum a telex stating that it considered the agreements repudiated. On January 28, Will Petroleum told Falco to contact BAII regarding Will Petroleum's ability to perform. Falco responded that it had already covered the agreements. The next day, Will Petroleum filed a petition for bankruptcy. The gasoline was sold for approximately $5.5 million less than the contract prices. In the subsequent suit against Falco and others, Falco contended that Will Petroleum had repudiated the agreements by failing to provide adequate assurances under UCC 2–609. How should the court rule? Discuss fully. [*BAII Banking Corp. v. UPG, Inc.*, 985 F.2d 685 (2d Cir. 1993)]

20–4. Can-Key Industries, Inc., manufactured a newly developed product, a turkey hatching unit, which it sold to Industrial Leasing Corp. (ILC). ILC agreed to buy the unit only on the condition that it was accepted by a customer, Rose-A-Linda, who would lease the unit from ILC. When Rose-A-Linda did not lease the unit because it failed to meet its specifications, ILC refused to go through with the contract of sale with Can-Key. Rose-A-Linda had tried four times to have the unit modified to meet its specifications and kept the hatching unit for over fifteen months. Can-Key sued ILC for breach of contract, alleging that ILC and Rose-A-Linda had accepted the hatching unit by keeping it in use for so long and by making several alterations in the goods that were inconsistent with the right of rejection. Discuss whether ILC and its lessee did accept the hatching unit or whether they still have the right to reject the goods offered by Can-Key. [*Can-Key Industries, Inc. v. Industrial Leasing Corp.*, 286 Or. 173, 593 P.2d 1125 (1979)]

20–5. Neptune Research & Development, Inc., contracted to purchase a high-precision drilling machine for approximately $55,000 from Teknics Industrial Systems, Inc. Although the contract specified a mid-June delivery date, nothing was included in the contract to indicate that time was of the essence. In addition, one of the paragraphs within the standard terms and conditions stated that shipping dates were approximate. By late August, the machine still had not been delivered, and Neptune desperately needed it. Contact with Teknics on August 29 resulted in both parties' agreeing to a September 5 delivery date, and Robertson, a Teknics representative, promised to call Neptune on September 3 so that delivery arrangements could be made. Robertson did not call Neptune on September 3. On September 4, Neptune's representative called Robertson, who allegedly said that under "no circumstances" would Teknics be able to have the machine ready for pickup until, at the earliest, September 9. As a result of this telephone conversation, Neptune canceled the contract on that same day. Later on September 4, Teknics informed Neptune that the machine could in fact be ready for pickup on September 5, but Neptune refused to go through with the transaction and instead filed suit against Teknics a few weeks later to recover the $3,000 deposit it had paid toward the price of the machine. The trial court held for Neptune, concluding that Teknics had anticipatorily breached the contract on September 4, giving Neptune the right to cancel the contract. Teknics appealed. What will the appellate court decide? Discuss. [*Neptune Research & Development, Inc. v. Teknics Industrial System, Inc.*, 235 N.J.Super. 522, 563 A.2d 465 (1989)]

20–6. Wilson purchased a new television set from Scampoli in 1965. When the set was delivered, Wilson found that it did not work properly; the color was defective. Scampoli's repairperson could not correct the problem, and Wilson refused to allow the repairperson to dismantle the set and take it back to the shop to determine the cause of the difficulty. Instead, Wilson demanded that Scampoli deliver a new television set or return the purchase price. Scampoli refused to refund Wilson's money and insisted that he receive the opportunity to correct the malfunctioning of Wilson's set before replacing it or issuing a refund. Discuss whether Scampoli has the right to attempt to cure the product, according to UCC 2–508. [*Wilson v. Scampoli,* 228 A.2d 848 (D.C.App. 1967)]

20–7. The Swiss Credit Bank issued a letter of credit in favor of Antex Industries to cover the sale of 92,000 electronic integrated circuits manufactured by Electronic Arrays. The letter of credit specified that the chips would be transported to Tokyo by ship. Antex shipped the circuits by air. Payment on the letter of credit was dishonored because the shipment by air did not fulfill the precise terms of the letter of credit. Should a court compel payment? Explain. [*Board of Trade of San Francisco v. Swiss Credit Bank,* 728 F.2d 1241 (9th Cir. 1984)]

20–8. Bobby Murray Chevrolet, Inc., contracted to supply 1,200 school bus chassis to local school boards. The contract stated that "products of any manufacturer may be offered," but Bobby Murray submitted its orders exclusively to General Motors Corp. (GMC). When a shortage in automatic transmissions occurred, GMC informed the dealer that it could not fill the orders. Bobby Murray told the school boards, which bought the chassis from another dealer. The boards filed a suit in a North Carolina state court against Bobby Murray on the ground of breach of contract. The dealer responded that its obligation to perform was excused under the doctrine of commercial impracticability, in part because of GMC's failure to fill its orders. Was it? Why, or why not? [*Alamance County Board of Education v. Bobby Murray Chevrolet, Inc.*, 121 N.C.App. 222, 465 S.E.2d 306 (1996)]

20–9. The Clark Dietz Division of CRS Group Engineers, Inc., set specifications for two waste-water treatment facilities for the Urbana and Champaign Sanitary District. Dietz's specifications required certain performance capabilities, as well as exact conformity of mechanical components, for all equipment, including belt filter presses. The specifications were outlined with reference to a press manufactured by the Ralph B. Carter Company. The Waldinger Corporation, a subcontractor on the project, took bids from four press manufacturers and selected Ashbrook-Simon-Hartley, Inc., to provide the presses. Ashbrook's presses could meet the performance specifications, but the mechanical components varied from those required by Dietz. Dietz did not approve Ashbrook's machine, and Waldinger was forced to buy the presses from Carter at a higher price. Waldinger sued Ashbrook in a federal district court for breach of contract (and CRS for wrongful interference with Waldinger's contract with Ashbrook). Ashbrook claimed that Dietz had intentionally or negligently drafted restrictive specifications that made it commercially impracticable for Ashbrook to fulfill its contract. The trial court agreed and excused Ashbrook from performance. Waldinger appealed. What will the appellate court decide? Explain. [*Waldinger Corp. v. CRS Group Engineers, Inc.,* 775 F.2d 781 (7th Cir. 1985)]

20–10. In 1973, Bernard and Elaine Zapatha entered into a franchise agreement with Dairy Mart, Inc. The agreement permitted either party to terminate the relationship without cause on ninety days' written notice. A second agreement was executed in 1974 when the Zapathas moved their store to a new location. In 1977, the Zapathas refused to sign a new agreement submitted by Dairy Mart because they believed that the provisions were too burdensome (they required the store to be open longer hours, required the Zapathas to pay future increases in the cost of utilities, and allowed Dairy Mart to relocate the Zapathas). Dairy Mart gave written notice that the contract would be terminated in ninety days. The Zapathas brought an action in a Massachusetts state court to enjoin termination of the agreement, alleging, among other things, that Dairy Mart had not acted in good faith. The trial court held for the Zapathas, and Dairy Mart appealed. What will happen on appeal? Discuss fully. [*Zapatha v. Dairy Mart, Inc.,* 408 N.E.2d 1370 (Mass. 1980)]

20–11. Bryant Lewis contracted to sell Ross Cattle Co. four hundred head of cattle at $47.50 per hundredweight. Ross made an $8,000 down payment. Before delivery, Lewis heard a rumor that Ross was in poor financial condition, and Lewis demanded that he receive full payment before delivering the animals. Ross told Lewis the balance would be paid on delivery, based on the weight of the cattle delivered. Lewis refused to deliver the cattle and sold them to a third party. Ross filed suit. Lewis claimed that the refusal of Ross to pay was an anticipatory repudiation of the contract. Discuss whether Lewis was correct and what action Lewis could have taken on the basis of the rumor. [*Ross Cattle Co. v. Lewis,* 415 So.2d 1029 (Miss. 1982)]

20–12. Rheinberg-Kellerei GMBH, a German wine producer and export seller, sold 1,245 cases of wine to Vineyard Wine Co., a U.S. company. The contract did not specify delivery to any particular destination, and Rheinberg, through its agent, selected the port of Wilmington for the port of entry. Rheinberg delivered the wine to the boat carrier in early December 1978. On or about January 24, 1979, Vineyard learned that the wine had been lost in the North Atlantic sometime between December 12 and December 22, when the boat sank with all hands aboard. Vineyard refused to pay Rheinberg. Rheinberg filed an action for the purchase price, claiming that risk of loss had passed to the buyer, Vineyard, on delivery of the wine to the carrier. Vineyard claimed that because of Rheinberg's failure to give prompt notice of shipment (notice had not been given until after the ship was lost at sea), risk of loss had not passed to the buyer. Discuss fully who is correct. [*Rheinberg-Kellerei GMBH v. Vineyard Wine Co.,* 281 S.E.2d 425 (N.C.App. 1981)]

20–13. E+E (US), Inc., Manley-Regan Chemicals Division, agreed to sell to Rockland Industries, Inc., three containers of antimony oxide for $1.80 per pound. At the time, both parties knew that there was a global shortage of the chemical, with rising prices, and that Manley-Regan would obtain its supply from GFI Chemicals, Inc. When GFI could not deliver, Manley-Regan told Rockland that it could not fulfill the contract. Rockland bought an equivalent amount of the chemical elsewhere at an increased price and filed a suit in a federal district court against Manley-Regan to recover the difference between the cost of the cover and the contract price. Manley-Regan argued that the failure of delivery by GFI, its sole source for the oxide, excused its failure to perform on the ground of commercial impracticability. Will the court agree? Why, or why not? [*Rockland Industries, Inc. v. E+E (US), Inc., Manley-Regan Chemicals Division,* 991 F.Supp. 468 (D.Md. 1998)]

20–14. OSHI Global Co. designs and sells novelty items, including a small children's plastic toy referred to as the "Number 89 Frog," a realistic replica of a frog that squeaks when it is squeezed. At a trade show in Chicago, Michael Osaraprasop, the owner of OSHI, sold a quantity of the frogs to Jay Gilbert, the president of S.A.M. Electronics, Inc. Gilbert asked Osaraprasop to design, make, and sell to S.A.M. a larger version of the frog with a motion sensor that would activate a "ribbit" sound. Osaraprasop agreed. OSHI delivered fourteen containers of the frogs, a number of which S.A.M. resold to its customers. When some of the buyers complained that the frogs were defective, S.A.M. had them repaired. S.A.M. refused to pay OSHI for any of the frogs and wrote a letter claiming to revoke acceptance of them. S.A.M. filed a suit in a federal district court against OSHI and others, alleging in part breach of contract, to which OSHI responded with a similar claim against S.A.M. OSHI argued that by reselling some of the frogs from the fourteen containers, S.A.M. had accepted all of them and must pay. In whose favor will the court rule? Discuss fully. [*S.A.M. Electronics, Inc. v. Osaraprasop,* 39 F.Supp.2d 1074 (N.D.Ill. 1999)]

20–15. Metro-North Commuter Railroad Co. decided to install a fall-protection system for elevated walkways, roof areas, and interior catwalks in Grand Central Terminal, in New York City. The system was needed to ensure the safety of Metro-North employees during work performed at great heights on the interior and exterior of the terminal. Sinco, Inc., proposed a system called "Sayfglida," which involved a harness worn by the worker, a network of cables, and metal clips or sleeves called "Sayflinks" that connected the harness to the cables. Metro-North agreed to pay $197,325 for the installation of this system by June 26, 1999. Because the system's reliability was crucial, the contract required certain quality control processes. During a training session for Metro-North employees on June 29, the Sayflink sleeves fell apart. Within two days, Sinco manufactured and delivered two different types of replacement clips without subjecting them to the contract's quality control process, but Metro-North rejected them. Sinco suggested other possible solutions, which Metro-North did not accept. In September, Metro-North terminated its contract with Sinco and awarded the work to Surety, Inc., at a price of about $348,000. Sinco filed a suit in a federal district court, alleging breach of contract. Metro-North counterclaimed for its cost of cover. In whose favor should the court rule, and why? [*Sinco, Inc. v. Metro-North Commuter Railroad Co.*, 133 F.Supp.2d 308 (S.D.N.Y. 2001)]

E-LINKS

For updated links to resources available on the Web, as well as a variety of other materials, visit this text's Web site at

http://wbl-cs.westbuslaw.com

To find information on the UCC, including the UCC provisions discussed in this chapter, refer to the Web sites listed in the *E-Links* feature in Chapter 18.

The Boeing Company has posted online a summary of the contract rights and duties of parties forming sales contracts with that company. To view the summary, go to

http://www.boeing.com/companyoffices/doingbiz.bluebook

To obtain information on performance requirements in relation to contracts for the international sale of goods, you can access the Institute of International Commercial Law at Pace University at

http://cisgw3.law.pace.edu

LEGAL RESEARCH EXERCISES ON THE WEB

Go to http://wbl-cs.westbuslaw.com, the Web site that accompanies this text. Select "Interactive Study Center," and then click on "Chapter 20." There you will find the following Internet research exercise that you can perform to learn more about performance requirements in the international context:

Activity 20–1: International Performance Requirements

CHAPTER 21

Remedies for Breach of Sales and Lease Contracts

BILLIONS OF SALES AND LEASE CONTRACTS are carried out every year in the United States. Most of these contracts involve virtually no problems. This is because most people try to fulfill their contractual obligations. Sometimes, however, circumstances make it difficult for a person to carry out the performance promised in a contract, in which case the contract may be breached. When breach occurs, the aggrieved party looks for remedies. These remedies range from retaining the goods to requiring the breaching party's performance under the contract. The general purpose of these remedies is to put the aggrieved party "in as good a position as if the other party had fully performed."

Recall from Chapter 17 that under the common law of contracts, the doctrine of election of remedies applies. Under this doctrine, a party must elect, or choose, one remedy to pursue. In contrast, remedies under the Uniform Commercial Code (UCC) are *cumulative* in nature. In other words, an innocent party to a breached sales or lease contract is not limited to one, exclusive remedy. (Of course, a party still may not recover twice for the same harm.)

SECTION 1

Remedies of the Seller or Lessor

Numerous remedies are available under the UCC to a seller or lessor when the buyer or lessee is in breach. Generally, the remedies available to the seller or lessor depend on the circumstances existing at the time of the breach, such as which party has possession of the goods, whether the goods are in transit, whether the buyer or lessee has rejected or accepted the goods, and so on.

WHEN THE GOODS ARE IN THE POSSESSION OF THE SELLER OR LESSOR

Under the UCC, if the buyer or lessee breaches the contract before the goods have been delivered to the buyer or lessee, the seller or lessor has the right to pursue the remedies discussed here.

The Right to Cancel the Contract. One of the options available to a seller or lessor when the buyer or lessee breaches the contract is simply to cancel the contract [UCC 2–703(f), 2A–523(1)(a)]. The seller must notify the buyer or lessee of the cancellation, and at that point all remaining obligations of the seller or lessor are discharged. The buyer or lessee is not discharged from all remaining obligations, however; he or she is in breach, and the seller or lessor can pursue remedies available under the UCC for breach.

The Right to Withhold Delivery. In general, sellers and lessors can withhold or discontinue performance of their obligations under sales or lease contracts when the buyers or lessees are in breach. If a buyer or lessee has wrongfully rejected or revoked acceptance of contract goods (rejection and revocation of acceptance will be discussed later in this chapter), failed to make proper and timely payment, or repudiated a part of the contract, the seller or lessor can withhold delivery of the goods in question [UCC 2–703(a), 2A–523(1)(c)]. If the breach results from the buyer's or the lessee's insolvency (inability to pay debts as they become due), the seller or lessor can refuse to deliver the goods unless the buyer or lessee pays in cash [UCC 2–702(1), 2A–525(1)].

The Right to Resell or Dispose of the Goods. When a buyer or lessee breaches or repudiates a sales contract while the seller or lessor is still in possession of the goods, the seller or lessor can resell or dispose of the goods, holding the buyer or lessee liable for any loss [UCC 2–703(d), 2–706(1), 2A–523(1)(e), 2A–527(1)].

When the goods contracted for are unfinished at the time of breach, the seller or lessor can do one of two things: (1) cease manufacturing the goods and resell them for scrap or salvage value or (2) complete the manufacture and resell or dispose of the goods, holding the buyer or lessee liable for any deficiency. In choosing between these two alternatives, the seller or lessor must exercise reasonable commercial judgment in order to mitigate the loss and obtain maximum value from the unfinished goods [UCC 2–704(2), 2A–524(2)]. Any resale of the goods must be made in good faith and in a commercially reasonable manner.

In sales transactions, the seller can recover any deficiency between the resale price and the contract price, along with *incidental damages*, defined as those costs to the seller resulting from the breach [UCC 2–706(1), 2–710]. The resale can be private or public, and the goods can be sold as a unit or in parcels. The seller must give the original buyer reasonable notice of the resale, unless the goods are perishable or will rapidly decline in value [UCC 2–706(2), (3)]. A good faith purchaser in a resale takes the goods free of any of the rights of the original buyer, even if the seller fails to comply with these requirements of the UCC [UCC 2–706(5)]. The UCC encourages the resale of the goods because although the buyer is liable for any deficiency, the seller is not accountable to the buyer for any profits made on the resale [UCC 2–706(6)].

In lease transactions, the lessor may lease the goods to another party and recover from the original lessee, as damages, any unpaid lease payments up to the beginning date of the lease term under the new lease. The lessor can also recover any deficiency between the lease payments due under the original lease contract and those under the new lease contract, along with incidental damages [UCC 2A–527(2)].

The Right to Recover the Purchase Price or Lease Payments Due. Under the UCC, an unpaid seller or lessor who is unable to resell or dispose of the goods can bring an action to recover the purchase price or the payments due under the lease contract, plus incidental damages [UCC 2–709(1), 2A–529(1)]. If a seller or lessor sues under these circumstances, the goods must be held for the buyer or lessee. The seller or lessor can resell or dispose of the goods at any time prior to collection of the judgment from the buyer or lessee, but in that situation the net proceeds from the sale must be credited to the buyer or lessee. This is an example of the duty to mitigate damages.

For example, suppose that Southern Realty contracts with Gem Point, Inc., to purchase one thousand pens with Southern Realty's name inscribed on them. Gem Point delivers the pens, but Southern Realty refuses to pay for them. In this situation, Gem Point has, as a proper remedy, an action for the purchase price. Gem Point has delivered conforming goods, and Southern Realty, because it has failed to pay, is in breach. Gem Point obviously cannot sell to anyone else the pens inscribed with the buyer's business name, so this situation falls under UCC 2–709.

The Right to Recover Damages. If a buyer or lessee repudiates a contract or wrongfully refuses to accept the goods, a seller or lessor can maintain an action to recover the damages sustained. Ordinarily, the amount of damages equals the difference between the contract price or lease payments and the market price or lease payments at the time and place of tender of the goods, plus incidental damages [UCC 2–708(1), 2A–528(1)]. The time and place of tender are frequently given by such terms as F.O.B., F.A.S., C.I.F.,[1] and the like, which determine whether there is a shipment or destination contract.

If the difference between the contract price or payments due under the lease contract and the market price or payments due under the lease contract is too small to place the seller or lessor in the position that he or she would have been in if the buyer or lessee had fully performed, the proper measure of damages is the lost profits of the seller or lessor, including a reasonable allowance for

1. See Exhibit 19–1 in Chapter 19 for a definition of these contract terms.

overhead and other expenses [UCC 2–708(2), 2A–528(2)].

When the Goods Are in Transit

If the seller or lessor has delivered the goods to a carrier or a bailee but the buyer or lessee has not yet received them, the goods are said to be *in transit.* If, while the goods are in transit, the seller or lessor learns that the buyer or lessee is insolvent, the seller or lessor can stop the carrier or bailee from delivering the goods, regardless of the quantity of goods shipped. If the buyer or lessee is in breach but is not insolvent, the seller or lessor can stop the goods in transit only if the quantity shipped is at least a carload, a truckload, a planeload, or a larger shipment [UCC 2–705(1), 2A–526(1)].

To stop delivery, the seller or lessor must *timely notify* the carrier or other bailee that the goods are to be returned or held for the seller or lessor. If the carrier has sufficient time to stop delivery, the goods must be held and delivered according to the instructions of the seller or lessor, who is liable to the carrier for any additional costs incurred [UCC 2–705(3), 2A–526(3)].

UCC 2–705(2) and 2A–526(2) provide that the right of the seller or lessor to stop delivery of goods in transit is lost when any of the following events occur:

1. The buyer or lessee obtains possession of the goods.
2. The carrier acknowledges the rights of the buyer or lessee by reshipping or storing the goods for the buyer or lessee.
3. A bailee of the goods other than a carrier acknowledges that he or she is holding the goods for the buyer or lessee.

Additionally, in sales transactions, the seller loses the right to stop delivery of goods in transit when a negotiable document of title covering the goods has been properly transferred to the buyer, giving the buyer ownership rights in the goods[2] [UCC 2–705(2)].

When the Goods Are in the Possession of the Buyer or Lessee

When the buyer or lessee breaches a sales or lease contract and the goods are in the buyer's or lessee's possession, the UCC gives the seller or lessor the right to choose among various remedies.

The Right to Recover the Purchase Price or Payments Due under the Lease Contract. If the buyer or lessee has accepted the goods but refuses to pay for them, the seller or lessor can sue for the purchase price of the goods or for the lease payments due, plus incidental damages [UCC 2–709(1), 2A–529(1)].

The Right to Reclaim Goods. In regard to sales contracts, if a seller discovers that the buyer has received goods on credit and is insolvent, the seller can demand return of the goods. Ordinarily, the demand must be made within ten days of the buyer's receipt of the goods; however, the seller can demand and reclaim the goods at any time if the buyer misrepresented his or her solvency in writing within three months prior to the delivery of the goods [UCC 2–702(2)]. The seller's right to reclaim the goods is subject to the rights of a good faith purchaser or other buyer in the ordinary course of business who purchases the goods from the buyer before the seller reclaims.

Under the UCC, a seller seeking to exercise the right to reclaim goods receives preferential treatment over the buyer's other creditors—the seller need only demand the return of the goods within ten days after the buyer has received them.[3] Because of this preferential treatment, the UCC provides that successful reclamation (reclaiming) of goods excludes all other remedies with respect to them [UCC 2–702(3)].

In regard to lease contracts, if the lessee is in default (fails to make payments that are due, for example), the lessor may reclaim the leased goods that are in the lessee's possession [UCC 2A–525(2)].

SECTION 2

Remedies of the Buyer or Lessee

Under the UCC, numerous remedies are available to the buyer or lessee when the seller or lessor breaches the contract. Like the remedies available to sellers and lessors, the remedies available to buyers and lessees depend on the circumstances existing at the time of the breach.

2. Negotiable and nonnegotiable documents of title were discussed in Chapter 19.

3. A seller who has delivered goods to an insolvent buyer also receives preferential treatment if the buyer enters into bankruptcy proceedings (discussed in Chapter 30).

When the Seller or Lessor Refuses to Deliver the Goods

If the seller or lessor refuses to deliver the goods to the buyer or lessee, the remedies available to the buyer or lessee include those discussed here.

The Right to Cancel the Contract. When a seller or lessor fails to make proper delivery or repudiates the contract, the buyer or lessee can cancel, or rescind, the contract. On giving notice of cancellation, the buyer or lessee is relieved of any further obligations under the contract but retains all rights to other remedies against the seller [UCC 2–711(1), 2A–508(1)(a)]. (The right to cancel the contract is also available to a buyer or lessee who has rightfully rejected goods or revoked acceptance, as will be discussed shortly.)

The Right to Recover the Goods. If a buyer or lessee has made a partial or full payment for goods that remain in the possession of the seller or lessor, the buyer or lessee can recover the goods if the seller or lessor becomes insolvent within ten days after receiving the first payment and if the goods are identified to the contract. To exercise this right, the buyer or lessee must tender to the seller any unpaid balance of the purchase price [UCC 2–502, 2A–522].

The Right to Obtain Specific Performance. A buyer or lessee can obtain specific performance when the goods are unique or when the remedy at law is inadequate [UCC 2–716(1), 2A–521(1)]. Ordinarily, an award of money damages is sufficient to place a buyer or lessee in the position he or she would have occupied if the seller or lessor had fully performed. When the contract is for the purchase of a particular work of art or a similarly unique item, however, money damages may not be sufficient. Under these circumstances, equity will require that the seller or lessor perform exactly by delivering the particular goods identified to the contract (a remedy of specific performance).

The Right of Cover. In certain situations, buyers and lessees can protect themselves by obtaining **cover**—that is, by buying or leasing substitute goods for those that were due under the sales contract. This option is available when the seller or lessor repudiates the contract or fails to deliver the goods.[4]

In obtaining cover, the buyer or lessee must act in good faith and without unreasonable delay [UCC 2–712, 2A–518]. After purchasing or leasing substitute goods, the buyer or lessee can recover from the seller or lessor the difference between the cost of cover and the contract price (or lease payments), plus incidental and consequential damages, less the expenses (such as delivery costs) that were saved as a result of the breach [UCC 2–712, 2–715, 2A–518]. Consequential damages are any losses suffered by the buyer or lessee that the seller or lessor could have foreseen (had reason to know about) at the time of contract and any injury to the buyer's or lessee's person or property proximately resulting from the contract's breach [UCC 2–715(2), 2A–520(2)].

Buyers and lessees are not required to cover, and failure to do so will not bar them from using any other remedies available under the UCC. A buyer or lessee who fails to cover, however, risks not being able to collect consequential damages that could have been avoided had he or she purchased or leased substitute goods.

> Westlaw. See Case 21.1 at the end of this chapter. To view the full, unedited case from Westlaw,® go to this text's Web site at http://wbl-cs.westbuslaw.com.

The Right to Replevy Goods. Buyers and lessees also have the right to replevy goods. **Replevin**[5] is an action to recover identified goods in the hands of a party who is unlawfully withholding them. Outside the UCC, the term *replevin* refers to a prejudgment process (a proceeding that takes place prior to a court's judgment) involving the seizure of specific personal property in which a party claims a right or an interest. Under the UCC, a buyer or lessee can replevy goods subject to the contract if the seller or lessor has repudiated or breached the contract. To maintain an action to replevy goods, buyers and lessees must usually show that they were unable to cover for the goods after making a reasonable effort [UCC 2–716(3), 2A–521(3)].

The Right to Recover Damages. If a seller or lessor repudiates the sales contract or fails to deliver the goods, the buyer or lessee can sue for damages. The measure of recovery is the difference between the contract price (or lease payments) and the market price of the goods (or lease payments that

4. The right to obtain cover is also available to a buyer or lessee who has rightfully rejected goods or revoked acceptance. Rejection and revocation of acceptance will be discussed shortly.

5. Pronounced ruh-*pleh*-vun.

could be obtained for the goods) at the time the buyer (or lessee) *learned* of the breach. The market price or market lease payments are determined at the place where the seller or lessor was supposed to deliver the goods. The buyer or lessee can also recover incidental and consequential damages less the expenses that were saved as a result of the breach [UCC 2–713, 2A–519].

Consider an example. Schilling orders 10,000 bushels of wheat from Valdone for $5.00 a bushel, with delivery due on June 14 and payment due on June 20. Valdone does not deliver on June 14. On June 14, the market price of wheat is $5.50 per bushel. Schilling chooses to do without the wheat. He sues Valdone for damages for nondelivery. Schilling can recover $0.50 × 10,000, or $5,000, plus any expenses the breach has caused him. The measure of damages is the market price on the day Schilling was to have received delivery less the contract price. (Any expenses Schilling saved by the breach would be deducted from the damages.)

When the Seller or Lessor Delivers Nonconforming Goods

When the seller or lessor delivers nonconforming goods, the buyer or lessee has several remedies available under the UCC.

The Right to Reject the Goods. If either the goods or the tender of the goods by the seller or lessor fails to conform to the contract in any respect, the buyer or lessee can reject the goods. If some of the goods conform to the contract, the buyer or lessee can keep the conforming goods and reject the rest [UCC 2–601, 2A–509]. If the buyer or lessee rejects the goods, he or she may then obtain cover or cancel the contract, just as if the seller or lessor had refused to deliver the goods (see the earlier discussion of these remedies).

Timeliness and Reason for Rejection Required. The buyer or lessee must reject the goods within a reasonable amount of time after delivery or tender of delivery, and the seller or lessor must be notified **seasonably**—that is, in a timely fashion or at the proper time [UCC 2–602(1), 2A–509(2)]. Furthermore, the buyer or lessee must designate defects that are ascertainable by reasonable inspection. Failure to do so precludes the buyer or lessee from using such defects to justify rejection or to establish breach when the seller or lessor could have cured the defects if they had been stated seasonably [UCC 2–605, 2A–514].

Westlaw. See Case 21.2 at the end of this chapter. To view the full, unedited case from Westlaw,® go to this text's Web site at **http://wbl-cs.westbuslaw.com**.

Duties of Merchant Buyers and Lessees When Goods Are Rejected. If a *merchant buyer* or *lessee* rightfully rejects goods, and the seller or lessor has no agent or business at the place of rejection, the buyer or lessee is required to follow any reasonable instructions received from the seller or lessor with respect to the goods controlled by the buyer or lessee. The buyer or lessee is entitled to reimbursement for the care and cost entailed in following the instructions [UCC 2–603, 2A–511]. The same requirements hold if the buyer or lessee rightfully revokes his or her acceptance of the goods at some later time [UCC 2–608(3), 2A–517(5)]. (Revocation of acceptance will be discussed shortly.)

If no instructions are forthcoming and the goods are perishable or threaten to decline in value quickly, the buyer or lessee can resell the goods in good faith, taking appropriate reimbursement and a selling commission (not to exceed 10 percent of the gross proceeds) from the proceeds [UCC 2–603(1), (2); 2A–511(1)]. If the goods are not perishable, the buyer or lessee may store them for the seller or lessor or reship them to the seller or lessor [UCC 2–604, 2A–512].

Buyers who rightfully reject goods (or who justifiably revoke acceptance of goods—discussed next) that remain in their possession or control have a *security interest* in the goods (basically, a legal claim to the goods to the extent necessary to recover expenses, costs, and the like—see Chapter 28). The security interest encompasses any payments the buyer has made for the goods, as well as any expenses incurred with regard to inspection, receipt, transportation, care, and custody of the goods [UCC 2–711(3)]. A buyer with a security interest in the goods is a "person in the position of a seller." This gives the buyer the same rights as an unpaid seller. Thus, the buyer can resell, withhold delivery of, or stop delivery of the goods. A buyer who chooses to resell must account to the seller for any amounts received in excess of the security interest [UCC 2–706(6), 2–711].

Revocation of Acceptance. Acceptance of the goods precludes the buyer or lessee from exercising the right of rejection, but it does not necessarily preclude the buyer or lessee from pursuing other remedies (discussed later). Additionally, in certain circumstances, a buyer or lessee is permitted to *revoke* his or her acceptance of the goods. Acceptance of a lot or a commercial unit can be revoked if the nonconformity *substantially* impairs the value of the lot or unit and if one of the following factors is present:

1. Acceptance was predicated on the reasonable assumption that the nonconformity would be cured, and it has not been cured within a reasonable period of time [UCC 2–608(1)(a), 2A–517(1)(a)].
2. The buyer or lessee did not discover the nonconformity before acceptance, either because it was difficult to discover before acceptance or because assurances made by the seller or lessor that the goods were conforming kept the buyer or lessee from inspecting the goods [UCC 2–608(1)(b), 2A–517(1)(b)].

Revocation of acceptance is not effective until notice is given to the seller or lessor. Notice must occur within a reasonable time after the buyer or lessee either discovers or *should have discovered* the grounds for revocation. Additionally, revocation must occur before the goods have undergone any substantial change (such as spoilage) not caused by their own defects [UCC 2–608(2), 2A–517(4)]. Once acceptance is revoked, the buyer or lessee can pursue remedies, just as if the goods had been rejected.

The Right to Recover Damages for Accepted Goods. A buyer or lessee who has accepted nonconforming goods may also keep the goods and recover for any loss "resulting in the ordinary course of events . . . as determined in any manner which is reasonable" [UCC 2–714(1), 2A–519(3)]. The buyer or lessee, however, must notify the seller or lessor of the breach within a reasonable time after the defect was or should have been discovered. Otherwise, the buyer or lessee cannot recover from the seller or lessor damages caused by defects in the goods [UCC 2–607(3), 2A–516(3)]. In addition, the parties to a sales or lease contract can insert a provision requiring that the buyer or lessee give notice of any defects in the goods within a prescribed period.

When the goods delivered are not as warranted, the measure of damages equals the difference between the value of the goods as accepted and their value if they had been delivered as warranted unless special circumstances show proximately caused damages of a different amount [UCC 2–714(2), 2A–519(4)]. For this and other types of breaches in which the buyer or lessee has accepted the goods, the buyer or lessee is entitled to incidental and consequential damages [UCC 2–714(3), 2A–519]. The UCC also permits the buyer or lessee, with proper notice to the seller or lessor, to deduct all or any part of the damages from the price or lease payments still due and payable to the seller or lessor [UCC 2–717, 2A–516(1)].

See Case 21.3 at the end of this chapter. To view the full, unedited case from Westlaw,® go to this text's Web site at **http://wbl-cs.westbuslaw.com**.

SECTION 3

Contractual Provisions Affecting Remedies

The parties to a sales or lease contract can vary their respective rights and obligations by contractual agreement. For example, a seller and buyer can expressly provide for remedies in addition to those provided in the UCC. They can also specifiy remedies in lieu of those provided in the UCC, or they can change the measure of damages. The seller can stipulate that the buyer's only remedy on the seller's breach be repair or replacement of the item, or the seller can limit the buyer's remedy to return of the goods and refund of the purchase price. In sales and lease contracts, an agreed-on remedy is in addition to those provided in the UCC unless the parties expressly agree that the remedy is exclusive of all others [UCC 2–719(1), 2A–503(1)].

If the parties state that a remedy is exclusive, then it is the sole remedy. When circumstances cause an exclusive remedy to fail in its essential purpose, however, it is no longer exclusive [UCC 2–719(2), 2A–503(2)]. For example, a sales contract that limits the buyer's remedy to repair or replacement fails in its essential purpose if the item cannot be repaired and no replacements are available.

A contract can limit or exclude consequential damages, provided the limitation is not unconscionable. When the buyer or lessee is a consumer, the limitation of consequential damages for personal injuries resulting from nonconforming goods is *prima facie* unconscionable. The limitation of consequential damages is not necessarily unconscionable when the loss is commercial in nature—for example, lost profits and property damage [UCC 2–719(3), 2A–503(3)].

SECTION 4

Lemon Laws

Some purchasers of defective automobiles—called "lemons"—found that the remedies provided by the UCC, after limitations had been imposed by the seller, were inadequate. In response to the frustration of these buyers, all of the states and the District of Columbia have enacted *lemon laws*. Basically, lemon laws provide that if an automobile under warranty possesses a defect that significantly affects the vehicle's value or use, and the defect has not been remedied by the seller within a specified number of opportunities (usually four), the buyer is entitled to a new car, replacement of defective parts, or return of all consideration paid.

In most states, lemon laws require an aggrieved new-car owner to notify the dealer or manufacturer of the problem and to provide the dealer or manufacturer with an opportunity to solve it. If the problem remains, the owner must then submit complaints to the arbitration program specified in the manufacturer's warranty before taking the case to court. Decisions by arbitration panels are binding on the manufacturer (that is, cannot be appealed by the manufacturer to the courts) but usually are not binding on the purchaser.

Most major automobile companies use their own arbitration panels. Some companies, however, subscribe to independent arbitration services, such as those provided by the Better Business Bureau. Although arbitration boards must meet state and/or federal standards of impartiality, industry-sponsored arbitration boards have been criticized for not being truly impartial in their decisions. In response to this criticism, some states have established mandatory government-sponsored arbitration programs for lemon-law disputes.

SECTION 5

Remedies for Breach of International Sales Contracts

The United Nations Convention on Contracts for the International Sale of Goods (CISG) provides international sellers and buyers with remedies very similar to those available under the UCC. Article 74 of the CISG provides for money damages, including foreseeable consequential damages, on a contract's breach. As under the UCC, the measure of damages is normally the difference between the contract price and the market price of the goods. Under Article 49, the buyer is permitted to avoid obligations under the contract if the seller breaches the contract or fails to deliver the goods during the time specified in the agreement or later agreed on by the parties. Similarly, under Article 64, the seller can avoid obligations under the contract if the buyer breaches the contract, fails to accept delivery of the goods, or fails to pay for the goods.

The CISG also allows for specific performance as a remedy under Article 28, which provides that "one party is entitled to require performance of any obligation by the other party." This statement is then qualified, however. Article 28 goes on to state that a court may only grant specific performance as a remedy if it would do so "under its own law in respect of similar contracts of sale not governed by this Convention." As already discussed, in the United States the equitable remedy of specific performance normally will be granted only if no adequate remedy at law (money damages) is available and the goods are unique in nature. In other countries, however, such as Germany, specific performance is a commonly granted remedy for breach of contract.

Terms and Concepts to Review

cover 407

replevin 407

seasonably 408

CHAPTER SUMMARY

Remedies of the Seller or Lessor	1. *When the goods are in the possession of the seller or lessor*—The seller or lessor may do the following: a. Cancel the contract [UCC 2–703(f), 2A–523(1)(a)]. b. Withhold delivery [UCC 2–703(a), 2A–523(1)(c)]. c. Resell or dispose of the goods [UCC 2–703(d), 2–706(1), 2A–523(1)(e), 2A–527(1)]. d. Sue to recover the purchase price or lease payments due [UCC 2–703(e), 2–709(1), 2A–529(1)]. e. Sue to recover damages [UCC 2–703(e), 2–708, 2A–528]. 2. *When the goods are in transit*—The seller may stop the carrier or bailee from delivering the goods [UCC 2–705, 2A–526]. 3. *When the goods are in the possession of the buyer or lessee*—The seller may do the following: a. Sue to recover the purchase price or lease payments due [UCC 2–709(1), 2A–529(1)]. b. Reclaim the goods. A seller may reclaim goods received by an insolvent buyer if the demand is made within ten days of receipt (reclaiming goods excludes all other remedies) [UCC 2–702]; a lessor may repossess goods if the lessee is in default [UCC 2A–525(2)].
Remedies of the Buyer or Lessee	1. *When the seller or lessor refuses to deliver the goods*—The buyer or lessee may do the following: a. Cancel the contract [UCC 2–711(1), 2A–508(1)(a)]. b. Recover the goods if the seller or lessor becomes insolvent within ten days after receiving the first payment and the goods are identified to the contract [UCC 2–502, 2A–522]. c. Obtain specific performance (when the goods are unique and when the remedy at law is inadequate) [UCC 2–716(1), 2A–521(1)]. d. Obtain cover [UCC 2–712, 2A–518]. e. Replevy the goods (if cover is unavailable) [UCC 2–716(3), 2A–521(3)]. f. Sue to recover damages [UCC 2–713, 2A–519]. 2. *When the seller or lessor delivers or tenders delivery of nonconforming goods*—The buyer or lessee may do the following: a. Reject the goods [UCC 2–601, 2A–509]. b. Revoke acceptance (in certain circumstances) [UCC 2–608, 2A–517]. c. Accept the goods and recover damages [UCC 2–607, 2–714, 2–717, 2A–519].
Contractual Provisions Affecting Remedies	Parties to sales and lease contracts can, by agreement, provide for remedies in addition to those provided in the UCC or limit the remedies that will be available under the contract. If the contract states that a remedy is exclusive, then that is the sole remedy—unless the remedy fails in its essential purpose. Sellers and lessors can also limit the rights of buyers and lessees to consequential damages—unless the limitation is unconscionable [UCC 2–719, 2A–503].
Lemon Laws	All of the states have "lemon laws" to protect purchasers of defective automobiles. These laws typically require that automobile purchasers, provided that they follow certain procedures (such as giving the dealer an opportunity to solve a problem with the automobile), can have their dispute arbitrated. Usually, the decision is binding on the dealer or manufacturer but not on the purchaser.
Remedies for Breach of International Sales Contracts	The United Nations Convention on Contracts for the International Sale of Goods (CISG) provides international sellers and buyers with remedies very similar to those available under the UCC.

CASES FOR ANALYSIS

Westlaw. You can access the full text of each case presented below by going to the Westlaw cases on this text's Web site at http://wbl-cs.westbuslaw.com. Each Westlaw case includes the names of all plaintiffs and defendants, the dates on which the case was argued and decided, a brief summary of the issues and decisions in the case, headnotes classifying the specific issues in the case according to the West Key Number System, and the court's opinion. Concurring and dissenting opinions, if any, are included as well.

CASE 21.1 REMEDIES OF THE BUYER OR LESSEE

KGM HARVESTING CO. V. FRESH NETWORK

California Court of Appeal,
Sixth District, 1995.
36 Cal.App.4th 376,
42 Cal.Rptr.2d 286.

COTTLE, P. J. [Presiding Judge]

California lettuce grower and distributor KGM Harvesting Company (hereafter seller) had a contract to deliver 14 loads of lettuce each week to Ohio lettuce broker Fresh Network (hereafter buyer). When the price of lettuce rose dramatically in May and June 1991, seller refused to deliver the required quantity of lettuce to buyer. Buyer then purchased lettuce on the open market in order to fulfill its contractual obligations to third parties. After a trial, the jury awarded buyer damages in an amount equal to the difference between the contract price and the price buyer was forced to pay for substitute lettuce on the open market. On appeal, seller argues that the damage award is excessive. We disagree and shall affirm the judgment. * * *

Facts

In July 1989 buyer and seller entered into an agreement for the sale and purchase of lettuce. Over the years, the terms of the agreement were modified. By May 1991 the terms were that seller would sell to buyer 14 loads of lettuce each week and that buyer would pay seller 9 cents a pound for the lettuce. (A load of lettuce consists of 40 bins, each of which weighs 1,000 to 1,200 pounds. Assuming an average bin weight of 1,100 pounds, 1 load would equal 44,000 pounds, and the 14 loads called for in the contract would weigh 616,000 pounds. At 9 cents per pound, the cost would approximate $55,440 per week.)

Buyer sold all of the lettuce it received from seller to a lettuce broker named Castellini Company who in turn sold it to Club Chef, a company that chops and shreds lettuce for the fast food industry (specifically, Burger King, Taco Bell, and Pizza Hut). Castellini Company bought lettuce from buyer on a "cost plus" basis, meaning it would pay buyer its actual cost plus a small commission. Club Chef, in turn, bought lettuce from Castellini Company on a cost plus basis.

Seller had numerous lettuce customers other than buyer, including seller's subsidiaries Coronet East and West. Coronet East supplied all the lettuce for the McDonald's fast food chain.

In May and June 1991, when the price of lettuce went up dramatically, seller refused to supply buyer with lettuce at the contract price of 9 cents per pound. Instead, it sold the lettuce to others at a profit of between $800,000 and $1.1 million. Buyer, angry at seller's breach, refused to pay seller for lettuce it had already received. Buyer then went out on the open market and purchased lettuce to satisfy its obligations to Castellini Company. Castellini covered all of buyer's extra expense except for $70,000. Castellini in turn passed on its extra costs to Club Chef which passed on at least part of its additional costs to its fast food customers.

In July 1991 buyer and seller each filed complaints [in a California state court] * * * . Seller sought the balance due on its outstanding invoices ($233,000), while buyer sought damages for the difference between what it was forced to spend to buy replacement lettuce and the contract price of nine cents a pound (approximately $700,000).

* * * At trial, the parties stipulated that seller was entitled to a directed verdict on its complaint for $233,000, the amount owing on the invoices. Accordingly, only the cross-complaint went to the jury, whose task was to determine whether buyer was entitled to damages from seller for the cost of obtaining substitute lettuce and, if so, in what amount. The jury determined that seller breached the contract, that its performance was not excused, and that buyer was entitled to $655,960.22, which represented the difference between the contract price of nine cents a pound and what it cost buyer to cover by purchasing lettuce in substitution in May and June 1991. * * * The court subtracted from buyer's award of $655,960.22 the $233,000 buyer owed to seller on its invoices, leaving a net award in favor of buyer in the amount of $422,960.22. * * *

Discussion

* * * *

In the instant case, buyer "covered" in order to fulfill its own contractual obligations to the Castellini Company. Accordingly, it was awarded the damages called for in cover cases—the difference between the contract price and the cover price [under Section 2712 of the California Uniform Commercial Code] [California's version of UCC 2–712].

* * * *

* * * [S]eller takes issue with [S]ection 2712 * * *, contending that despite the unequivocal language of [S]ection 2712, a buyer who covers should not necessarily recover the difference between the cover price and the contract price. Seller points out that because of buyer's "cost plus" contract with Castellini Company, buyer was eventually able to pass on the extra expenses (except for $70,000) occasioned by seller's breach and buyer's consequent purchase of substitute lettuce on the open market. It urges this court under these circumstances not to allow buyer to obtain a "windfall."

The basic premise of contract law is to effectuate the expectations of the parties to the agreement, to give them the "benefit of the bargain" they struck when they entered into the agreement. * * * [Emphasis added.]

The basic object of damages is compensation, and in the law of contracts the theory is that the party injured by breach should receive as nearly as possible the equivalent of the benefits of performance. A compensation system that gives the aggrieved party the benefit of the bargain, and no more, furthers the goal of predictability about the cost of contractual relationships * * * in our commercial system.

With these rules in mind, we examine the contract at issue in this case to ascertain the reasonable expectations of the parties. The contract recited that its purpose was "to supply [buyer] with a consistent quality raw product at a fair price to [seller], which also allows [buyer] profitability for his finished product." Seller promised to supply the designated quantity even if the price of lettuce went up ("We agree to supply said product and amount at stated price regardless of the market price or conditions") and buyer promised to purchase the designated quantity even if the price went down ("[Buyer] agrees to purchase said product and amounts at stated price regardless of the market price or conditions, provided quality requirements are met"). The possibility that the price of lettuce would fluctuate was consequently foreseeable to both parties.

Although the contract does not recite this fact, seller was aware of buyer's contract with the Castellini Company and with the Castellini Company's contract with Club Chef. This knowledge was admitted at trial and can be inferred from the fact that seller shipped the contracted for 14 loads of lettuce directly to Club Chef each week. Thus, seller was well aware that if it failed to provide buyer with the required 14 loads of lettuce, buyer would have to obtain replacement lettuce elsewhere or would itself be in breach of contract. This was within the contemplation of the parties when they entered into their agreement.

* * * *[T]he object of contract damages is to give the aggrieved party as nearly as possible the equivalent of the benefits of performance.* In the instant case, buyer contracted for 14 loads of lettuce each week at 9 cents per pound. When seller breached its contract to provide that lettuce, buyer went out on the open market and purchased substitute lettuce to fulfill its contractual obligations to third parties. However, purchasing replacement lettuce to continue its business did not place buyer in as good a position as if the other party had fully performed. This was because buyer paid more than 9 cents per pound for the replacement lettuce. Only by reimbursing buyer for the additional costs above 9 cents a pound could buyer truly receive the benefit of the bargain. This is the measure of damages set forth in [S]ection 2712. [Emphasis added.]

* * * *

In summary, we hold that where a buyer covers by making in good faith and without unreasonable delay any reasonable purchase of goods in substitution for those due from the seller, that buyer may recover from the seller as damages the difference between the cost of cover and the contract price. This gives the buyer the benefit of its bargain. What the buyer chooses to do with that bargain is not relevant to the determination of damages under [S]ection 2712.

* * * *

Disposition

* * * [As stated above] the judgment is affirmed.

CASE 21.2 REMEDIES OF THE BUYER OR LESSEE

CHINA NATIONAL METAL PRODUCTS IMPORT/EXPORT CO. v. APEX DIGITAL, INC.

United States District Court, 1974.
Central District of California, 2001.
141 F.Supp.2d 1013.

LARSON, United States Magistrate Judge.

* * * *

BACKGROUND

Apex [Digital, Inc.] is a company incorporated and headquartered in Ontario, California, whose principal business is importing consumer electronic goods and then distributing those goods under the "Apex Digital" brand name to national retailers, such as Circuit City, Best Buy, and K-Mart. Apex imports its line of DVD players from various Chinese manufacturers.

China National [Metal Products Import/Export Company] is a corporation organized under the laws of China and is based in Beijing, China. Chinese companies are permitted to import and export goods only if they have a government license granting them specific "foreign trading" rights. China National has been granted foreign trade rights and has made its principal business facilitating the import and export of goods between Chinese and foreign companies.

In the early part of 2000, Apex became interested in purchasing and importing into the United States DVD players manufactured by Jiangsu Shinco Electronic Group Company ("Shinco"), a Chinese company located in Changzhou, in the Chinese province of Jiangsu. Shinco, however, did not have foreign trading rights. Given China's foreign trade law, a three-way transaction between Apex, China National, and Shinco was required in order for Apex to purchase Shinco's DVD players. * * *

From July through October, 2000, Apex placed orders for AD-500A and AD-703 model DVD players from China National. The model AD-500A is a lower cost, single-disk unit capable of playing DVDs, CDs, and other digital media. The AD-703 model plays the same media disks, but also plays MP3 files and includes a disk loader and changer that will handle up to three disks at one time.

The purchase of the DVD players took the form of a series of separate but substantially identical written contracts. The contracts set forth the model number and quantity of the DVD players ordered, the price for each of the DVD players, the time of shipment, the port of destination, and the manner of payment. * * *

* * * *

China National's first shipments of Model AD-500A and AD-703 DVD players were delivered in July, 2000. Soon thereafter Apex began receiving reports from its retail distributors that customers were dissatisfied with the DVD players. The complaints covered a wide spectrum of structural and software problems, including disk loaders that did not open or that did not load the disk once it was inserted in the machine; the DVD player flashing a "no disk" signal even after the disk was inserted; the front panel of the DVD loader falling off after use; an inability to recognize or play MP3 music files; failure to play certain movies properly (some movies did not show at all, in others the picture was not clear, and with some the disks would skip from one part of the movie to another); the pause function self-activating during disk play; and finally, in a manner reminiscent of a badly dubbed martial-arts film, a delay of several seconds in the audio such that spoken words were heard well after an actor's lips moved. One customer, for example, wrote "Call me a dummy, [I] bought the Apex DVD player," while another observed that the only thing that the Apex DVD player was good for was as a boat anchor. * * *

With customer complaints mounting, so too was the return rates for the AD-500As and AD-703s. Through December, 2000, customers had returned approximately 4.2% of all AD-500A units sold, and over 6% of AD-703 units sold. Apex's DVD players normally enjoyed a return rate of almost 4%. Despite their knowledge of these defects, Apex continued to place orders for more DVD players from China National through November, 2000. Indeed, the quantity of goods ordered by Apex accelerated after the defects with the DVD players came to light.

Apex complained to representatives from China National about these defects as early as October, 2000. * * *

* * * *

Apex eventually elected (sometime after December 29, 2000) to withhold paying the remaining invoices submitted by China National for the AD-500As and AD-703s delivered from August until November. * * *

* * * *

In January, * * * Apex had returned a total of 21,069 AD-500A and 11,692 AD-703 units to China National, whose combined value, using the contract price, is \$3,767,281. * * *. Apex has also represented to the Court that it intends to return * * * 4,600 [more] AD-703 units to China National. The value of these remaining units, using the contract price, is \$611,800.

* * * [B]oth parties eventually filed applications for arbitration before CIETAC [China International Economic Trade Arbitration Commission]. In the interim, China National has filed a complaint in this [federal district] Court requesting that certain provisional remedies, namely a writ of attachment against Apex's property, be granted * * * .

ANALYSIS

* * * *

The outcome of the present dispute hinges on whether Apex rejected the DVD players described in the invoices mentioned above * * * . In [that] instance, Apex would have been relieved of its duty to pay for the goods thereby negating the probable validity of China National's claim.

The delivery of conforming goods is a condition to the buyer's duty to accept and pay for them. If the goods or the tender of delivery fail in any respect to conform to the contract, the buyer may reject the goods, accept the goods, or accept any commercial units and reject the rest of the goods delivered. There can be little doubt in this case that China National failed to deliver conforming goods. Whether it was loader doors falling off or the failure to play DVD movies or the pause function self-activating, many of the DVD players delivered by China National were more useful as doorstops, or as one creative consumer noted, as boat anchors, than as players of multimedia disks and files. These defects provided Apex with the option to reject the contract or contracts affected by the non-conformities or to reject the particular units containing those defects. [Emphasis added.]

Apex claims it did reject the contracts containing the defective goods. Nowhere in its pleadings, however, has Apex articulated how it rejected those goods. Instead, Apex simply states that the delivery of non-conforming goods *by itself* relieved its duty to pay for them. Apex is wrong. When a buyer is presented with non-conforming goods (or learns of the non-conformity of the goods after a reasonable inspection period), it *may* reject the entire contract, accept the entire contract, or accept those goods that do conform and reject the rest. Buyers therefore can accept non-conforming goods. Indeed, *if the buyer does nothing after receiving goods it learns are non-conforming, the law deems him to have accepted those goods. The simple fact that the goods are non-conforming does not obviate the need for the buyer to affirmatively reject those goods.* Once the non-conforming goods are accepted, the buyer is under a duty to pay for them. Apex must therefore demonstrate, given that it is the party asserting the defense that the goods' non-conformity relieved it of the duty to pay, that it affirmatively rejected the DVD players. [Emphasis added.]

Understanding this, Apex asserts that it rejected the DVD players in question by withholding payment for them upon first learning of the defects in the AD-500As and AD-703s. This assertion is contradicted by the declarations of Apex's own officers and by its course of conduct upon learning of the defects. Apex did not begin to withhold payment until the end of December, 2000. Apex's engineer, however, testified that he began testing the defective AD-500As and AD-703s towards the end of August, 2000, and initiated correspondence with Shinco's technical personnel regarding these defects as early as September, 2000. Moreover, Apex's President testified that he had numerous discussions from October, 2000, onward with China National officials regarding the unacceptable nature of the defects in the AD-500As and AD-703s. Yet despite knowing of these defects Apex continued and, in fact, accelerated the number of DVD players it ordered from China National and then sold to its retail distributors. To the extent one can view Apex's President's expressions of unacceptability as a form of rejection, those words were muted, to the point of ringing hollow, by Apex continuing to order more and more known defective DVD players from China National and by it continuing to sell those assertedly defective DVD players to retail distributors. In order to provide a proper rejection, a party must take such steps as may be reasonably required to inform the other in ordinary course that they have rejected the contract. Certainly continuing to order and then sell those goods you are complaining about would cause a seller to seriously question whether you in fact have rejected the contract.

* * * *

* * * [T]he Court hereby **GRANTS** China National's Application for a Writ of Attachment against Apex in the amount of $ 18,975,059 (representing the amount of the outstanding invoices minus the contract value of the DVD players Apex has returned to China National).

CASE 21.3 REMEDIES OF THE BUYER OR LESSEE

YATES V. PITMAN MANUFACTURING, INC.

Supreme Court of Virginia, 1999.
257 Va. 601,
514 S.E.2d 605.

STEPHENSON, Senior Justice.

* * * *

I

Eddie M. Yates sued Pitman Manufacturing, Inc. (Pitman), [on the basis of breach of warranty] seeking $3,000,000 in damages for injuries he sustained when an outrigger on a crane unit manufactured and sold by Pitman came down onto and crushed Yates' left foot. * * *

Prior to trial, Yates moved the court to exclude all evidence concerning whether he had provided reasonable notice to Pitman of its breach of warranty. The trial court overruled Yates' motion, holding that the notice provision of [Virginia Code Section 8.2–607(3), Virginia's version of UCC 2–607(3)] applied and required Yates, who was not the buyer of the crane unit, to give notice of breach of warranty to Pitman.

* * * *

* * * The jury returned its verdict in favor of Pitman, and the trial court entered judgment on the verdict. We awarded Yates this appeal.

II

In 1982, Pitman sold the crane unit to Shelton Witt Equipment, a distributor. At the time, Pitman certified that "these cranes meet applicable design and construction standards as prescribed in ANSI B30.5–1968." When the unit was sold, ANSI Standard B30.5–1968 mandated that "[e]ach outrigger shall be visible from its actuating [activating] location."

On July 19, 1991, when Yates was injured, Koch Carbon (Koch) owned the unit and was using it to deliver equipment to Baldwin Coal Corporation, Yates' employer. At the time Yates was injured, he was releasing restraining chains from the crane truck's bed when suddenly, without warning, one of the outriggers dropped onto his foot. Unbeknownst to Yates, Ira Stiltner, a Koch employee, had activated the outrigger from the front of the truck. When Stiltner activated the outrigger, he could not see either Yates or the outrigger.

III

* * * [W]hether the trial court erred in holding that Yates was required to provide Pitman with notice of breach of warranty as a prerequisite to recovery * * * [is an] issue * * * of first impression for this Court.

To resolve the issue, we look to [Virginia Code Section 8.2–607(3)] the only provision of the Sales title of the Uniform Commercial Code (the UCC) that requires notice to be given to a seller of goods. The section provides, in pertinent part, the following:

> Where a tender has been accepted * * * the buyer must within a reasonable time after he discovers or should have discovered any breach notify the seller of breach or be barred from any remedy.

It is firmly established that, when a statute is clear and unambiguous, a court must accept its plain meaning and not resort to extrinsic evidence or rules of construction. The pertinent language in [Va. Code Section 8.2–607(3)] is unambiguous and clearly states that "the *buyer* must * * * notify the seller of [the] breach." [Emphasis added.] Thus, accepting the statute's plain meaning, it is apparent that the notice of breach is required from the "buyer" of the goods.

In the present case, Yates was not the buyer of the crane unit. Therefore, the notice requirement of [Va. Code Section 8.2–607(3)] does not preclude Yates from maintaining a breach of warranty action.

We hold, therefore, that only buyers; *i.e.*, those who buy or contract to buy goods from a seller, must give notice of breach of warranty to the seller as a prerequisite to recovery. Consequently, the trial court erred in ruling that Yates was required to have given Pitman such notice.

* * * *

V

For the reasons stated, we will reverse the trial court's judgment and remand the case for a new trial consistent with the views expressed in this opinion.

Case Problems

21–1. Leemar Steel Co. manufactured counterweight inserts for CMI Corp. according to blueprints from CMI and shipped them to CMI. CMI prepared an internal memo rejecting the shipment for nonconformance two days after it was received. CMI did not send the rejection notice to Leemar. Instead, a few weeks later, it notified Leemar by phone that there was a "problem with the inserts." CMI paid for the inserts and attempted, with Leemar's aid, to have the inserts ground to the correct tolerances during the next few months. Because this could not be accomplished, CMI filed suit to cancel the contract and to recover the money that it had paid Leemar pursuant to the contract. Discuss whether CMI had accepted the goods. Could it still revoke its acceptance and get its money back? [*CMI Corp. v. Leemar Steel Co.*, 733 F.2d 1410 (10th Cir. 1984)]

21–2. In September 1982, Kathleen Inniss purchased a 1982 Buick Skylark from Methot Buick-Opel, Inc. The car, which was a demonstrator, had nearly six thousand miles on it but was accompanied by a new-car, twelve-month or twelve-thousand-mile warranty. It also had a history of significant mechanical and electrical problems, which Methot failed to mention to Inniss. Shortly after Inniss took possession, she experienced problems with the car. Between September and December 1982, she took the car back to Methot eight times for repairs. The horn, rear window defogger, throttle, and brakes were repaired, but by the end of the warranty period, several other problems still had not been fixed. The temperature gauge continued to malfunction, intermittently the car would not start, it vibrated in the front end, and the directional indicators intermittently flashed incorrectly when in use. In addition, although the purchase agreement had provided that the car would be rustproofed, much of it had not been. Before the twelve-month warranty had lapsed, Inniss sought to revoke her acceptance of the contract and asked for her money back. (The state of Maine did not have a lemon law at the time this case was brought.) Discuss fully whether Inniss could revoke her acceptance of the purchase contract and recover the purchase price of the automobile. [*Inniss v. Methot Buick-Opel, Inc.*, 506 A.2d 212 (Me. 1986)]

21–3. Lupofresh, Inc., contracted to sell a quantity of hops to Pabst Brewing Co. Lupofresh processed the hops and notified Pabst that the hops were ready for shipment. Pabst responded with a letter indicating acceptance of the hops but later refused to issue shipping orders, claiming that the price determination violated antitrust laws. Lupofresh sued for the full purchase price under UCC 2–709(1). Pabst claimed that the goods had not been accepted but merely identified to the contract and that Lupofresh was required to attempt to resell the hops before it was entitled to recover the purchase price. Discuss fully which party was correct. [*Lupofresh, Inc. v. Pabst Brewing Co.*, 505 A.2d 37 (Super.Ct.Del. 1985)]

21–4. Engineering Measurements Co. (EMCO) agreed to manufacture and deliver to International Technical Instruments, Inc. (ITI), a specified number of optical communication links (devices that allow wireless communication between two points). The links were to be delivered in stated installments. During a seven-month period, ITI continually complained that EMCO had failed to meet delivery schedules and had delivered some defective units.

ITI did not refuse any shipment during this period. Eventually ITI filed suit, claiming EMCO had breached its contract by failing to meet its delivery schedules and by delivering defective units. EMCO argued that ITI had accepted the goods and that by failing to revoke its acceptance and give notice, ITI was precluded from any remedy under UCC 2–607(3)(a). Discuss fully whether ITI was able to recover under its suit for breach of contract. [*International Technical Instruments, Inc. v. Engineering Measurements Co.*, 678 P.2d 558 (Colo.App. 1983)]

21–5. In 1968, Canal Electric Co. purchased a steam turbine generator from Westinghouse Corp. In 1983, Canal purchased some new rotating blades from Westinghouse to use in the generator. The contract covering the 1983 sale of the blades warranted that Westinghouse would repair or replace any defective parts for a one-year period and limited Westinghouse's total liability under the contract to the purchase price of the blades, which was $40,750. Liability for incidental and consequential damages was specifically disclaimed. A few months later, the blades developed cracks, and Canal had to shut down operations for 124 days while the blades were being replaced. As a result, Canal incurred costs (which were significantly higher than the purchase price of the blades) to obtain replacement power during this period. Ultimately, Canal sued Westinghouse for breach of warranty and negligence. Westinghouse claimed that its liability to Canal was limited to the purchase price of the blades, $40,750. Will the court enforce the limitation-of-liability clause? What factors will the court consider in deciding this issue? Discuss fully. [*Canal Electric Co. v. Westinghouse Electric Corp.*, 756 F.Supp. 620 (D.Mass. 1991)]

21–6. Rachel Hebron bought an Isuzu Trooper four-wheel-drive sport utility vehicle from American Isuzu Motors, Inc. Their contract required her to give notice of any defects in the car within two years of their discovery. In June 1991, Hebron was driving the Trooper when another vehicle pulled in front of her. She swerved to avoid hitting it, and the Trooper rolled over, causing her permanent injuries. Hebron waited, for no apparent reason, until July 1993 to file a suit in a federal district court against American, seeking damages for alleged defects in the car. She had already disposed of the Trooper, without notifying American. American filed a motion for summary judgment based on the contract requirement of notice within two years. How should the court rule? Discuss fully. [*Hebron v. American Isuzu Motors, Inc.*, 60 F.3d 1095 (4th Cir. 1995)]

21–7. In March 1985, Bruce Young purchased from Hessel Tractor & Equipment Co., a John Deere equipment dealer, a feller-buncher to shear trees in his logging business. The only warranty in the contract was a one-year warranty against defects in the equipment with an exclusive remedy of repair and replacement for any defect in material or assembly. All other warranties were expressly and conspicuously disclaimed. Young began to have serious problems with the equipment after less than a month of use. After over a year of continuing unsuccessful attempts at repair and after the one-year warranty had expired, Hessel, the seller, stopped repairing the machine. Is Young entitled to revoke his acceptance of the equipment? Explain. [*Young v. Hessel Tractor & Equipment Co.*, 782 P.2d 164 (Or.App. 1989)]

21–8. Royal Jones & Associates, Inc., ordered three steel rendering tanks from First Thermal Systems, Inc., for use in its business of constructing rendering plants (factories that process livestock carcasses into hides, fertilizer, and so on). The contract provided that First Thermal would manufacture the tanks according to Royal Jones's specifications for a price of $64,350. When the manufacture of the tanks was completed, Royal Jones refused to accept or pay for the tanks. First Thermal brought an action in a Florida state court for the contract price of the tanks. The trial court, finding that Royal Jones had breached the contract and that the specially manufactured goods were not suitable for sale in the ordinary course of First Thermal's business, awarded First Thermal the full contract price as damages. Royal Jones appealed. What will the appellate court decide? Explain. [*Royal Jones & Associates, Inc. v. First Thermal Systems, Inc.*, 566 So.2d 853 (Fla.App. 1990)]

21–9. McCalif Grower Supplies, Inc., provides for the supply and shipping of plants from growers to wholesale greenhouses. Wilbur Reed operates a small greenhouse in Missoula, Montana. Reed ordered poinsettias from McCalif. When the poinsettias were delivered, Reed discovered that many of them were damaged because they had not been packed properly. Reed refused to pay for any of the plants. McCalif filed an action in a Montana state court against Reed for the money. Reed claimed that McCalif owed him damages for, among other things, the nonconforming goods. The court awarded Reed nothing, and Reed appealed. What will happen on appeal? Discuss fully. [*McCalif Grower Supplies, Inc. v. Reed*, 272 Mont. 254, 900 P.2d 880 (1995)]

21–10. Innovative Computing Corporation (ICC) sold an International Business Machines Corporation (IBM) computer to TCA. As part of the deal, TCA expressly agreed to a disclaimer that stated, in part, "IN NO EVENT SHALL ICC BE LIABLE FOR ANY . . . CONSEQUENTIAL DAMAGES . . . IN CONNECTION WITH . . . THIS AGREEMENT." One year later, the computer failed. The downtime was nearly thirty-four hours. TCA spent more than $4,500 to replace unrecoverable data and lost nearly $470,000 in income while the computer was down. TCA filed a suit in a Minnesota state court against IBM and ICC, alleging, among other things, breach of warranty. The case was moved to a federal district court, and IBM and ICC filed a motion for summary judgment. The court granted the motion, based in part on the disclaimer. TCA appealed, arguing in part that the disclaimer was unconscionable. What will happen on appeal? Discuss. [*Transport Corp. of America, Inc. v. International Business Machines Corp.*, 30 F.3d 953 (8th Cir. 1994)]

21–11. In April 1988, Denis Tongish agreed to sell sunflower seeds grown on certain acres to the Decatur Cooperative Association (the co-op). One-third of the seeds were to be delivered by December 31, 1988, one-third on

March 31, 1989, and one-third on May 31, 1989. The co-op then entered into a contract to sell the seeds, when they had been delivered by Tongish, to Bambino Bean & Seed, Inc., for the same price plus a handling charge of 55 cents per hundredweight. Tongish delivered seeds to the co-op in October and November 1988. A smaller than normal crop, bad weather, and other factors caused the market price of sunflower seeds to double that winter from what it had been in April, and in January 1989, Tongish then sold 82,820 pounds of sunflower seeds to Danny Thomas for $14,714.89, which was $5,153.13 more than the co-op contract price. Thomas failed to pay the entire purchase price of the seeds, and Tongish sued him in a Kansas state court. The co-op intervened in the action, seeking damages for Tongish's breach of their contract. The trial court, finding that Tongish had breached the contract, awarded damages to the co-op in the amount of $455.51—the co-op's actual losses (the handling charges) resulting from the breach. The co-op appealed, contending that the damage award should have been the difference between the contract price of the seeds and the market price of the seeds at the time of the contract's breach. The appellate court agreed with the co-op and reversed the trial court's decision. Ultimately, the case was reviewed by the Supreme Court of Kansas. What will the Supreme Court decide? Discuss. [*Tongish v. Thomas,* 251 Kan. 728, 840 P.2d 471 (1992)]

21–12. Servbest Foods, Inc., had a contract with Emessee Industries, Inc., under which Emessee was to purchase 200,000 pounds of beef trimmings from Servbest at 52.5 cents per pound. Servbest delivered to Emessee the warehouse receipts and invoices for the beef trimmings. The price of beef trimmings then fell significantly, and Emessee returned the documents to Servbest and canceled the contract. Servbest then sold the beef trimmings for 20.25 cents per pound and sued Emessee for damages (the difference between the contract price and the market price at which it had been forced to sell the trimmings) for breach of contract, plus incidental damages. Discuss whether Servbest Foods exercised a proper remedy and was entitled to the damages alleged in its lawsuit. [*Servbest Foods, Inc. v. Emessee Industries, Inc.,* 82 Ill.App.3d 662, 403 N.E.2d 1, 37 Ill.Dec. 945 (1980)]

21–13. Bigelow-Sanford, Inc., entered into a contract to buy 100,000 yards of jute at $0.64 per yard from Gunny Corp. Gunny delivered 22,228 yards to Bigelow but informed the company that no more would be delivered. Several other suppliers to Bigelow defaulted, and Bigelow was forced to go into the market one month later to purchase a total of 164,503 yards of jute for $1.21 per yard. Bigelow sued Gunny for the difference between the market price and the contract price of the amount of jute that Gunny had not delivered. Discuss whether Bigelow could recover this amount from Gunny. [*Bigelow-Sanford, Inc. v. Gunny Corp.,* 649 F.2d 1060 (5th Cir. 1981)]

21–14. Wilk Paving, Inc., bought a street-paving asphalt roller from Southworth-Milton, Inc. In large capital letters, on the front of the contract, was printed, "ADDITIONAL TERMS AND CONDITIONS ON REVERSE SIDE." A clause on the back stated that "under no circumstances shall seller . . . be held liable for any . . . consequential damages." In a hurry to close the deal, Wilk's representative did not notice this clause, and Southworth's representative did not call attention to it. Within sixty days, the roller needed the first of what became continuous repairs for mechanical problems. Wilk asked Southworth for its money back. When Southworth refused, Wilk sued Southworth, seeking the purchase price and consequential damages. Was the clause limiting damages enforceable in these circumstances? Explain. [*Wilk Paving, Inc. v. Southworth-Milton, Inc.,* 649 A.2d 778 (Vt. 1995)]

21–15. Destileria Serralles, Inc., a distributor of rum and other products, operates a rum bottling plant in Puerto Rico. Figgie International, Inc., contracted with Serralles to provide bottle-labeling equipment capable of placing a clear label on a clear bottle of "Cristal" rum within a raised glass oval. The contract stated that Serralles's remedy, in case of a breach of contract, was limited to repair, replacement, or refund. When the equipment was installed in the Serralles plant, problems arose immediately. Figgie attempted to repair the equipment, but when it still did not work properly several months later, Figgie refunded the purchase price and Serralles returned the equipment. Serralles asked Figgie to pay for Serralles's losses caused by the failure of the equipment and by the delay in obtaining alternative machinery. Figgie filed a suit in a federal district court, asserting that it owed nothing to Serralles because its remedy for breach was limited to repair, replacement, or refund. Serralles responded that the limitation "fail[ed] of its essential purpose." In whose favor will the court resolve this dispute? Why? [*Figgie International, Inc. v. Destileria Serralles, Inc.,* 190 F.3d 252 (4th Cir. 1999)]

E-LINKS

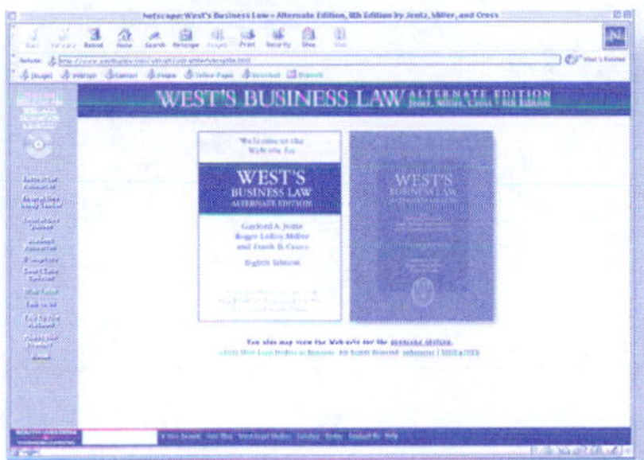

For updated links to resources available on the Web, as well as a variety of other materials, visit this text's Web site at

http://wbl-cs.westbuslaw.com

To find information on the UCC, including the UCC provisions discussed in this chapter, refer to the Web sites listed in the *E-Links* feature in Chapter 18.

For a discussion of "Lemon-Law Basics," go to Car Talk's Web site at

http://www.cartalk.cars.com/Got-A-Car/Lemon

For an example of a warranty providing for an exclusive remedy, see the "Warranty and Limited Remedy" of 3M Company, which is online at

http://www.mmm.com/promote/warranty.htm

LEGAL RESEARCH EXERCISES ON THE WEB

Go to http://wbl-cs.westbuslaw.com, the Web site that accompanies this text. Select "Interactive Study Center," and then click on "Chapter 21." There you will find the following Internet research exercise that you can perform to learn more about lemon laws:

Activity 21–1: Lemon Laws

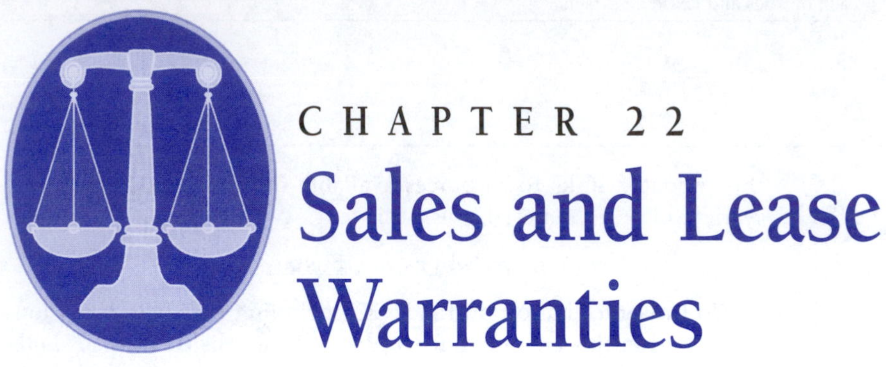

CHAPTER 22 Sales and Lease Warranties

WARRANTY IS AN AGE-OLD CONCEPT. In sales and lease law, a warranty is an assurance by one party of the existence of a fact on which the other party can rely. Article 2 (on sales) and Article 2A (on leases) of the Uniform Commercial Code (UCC) designate several types of warranties that can arise in a sales or lease contract. These warranties include warranties of title, express warranties, and implied warranties.

Because a warranty imposes a duty on the seller or lessor, a breach of warranty is a breach of the seller's or lessor's promise. If the parties have not agreed to limit or modify the remedies available to the buyer or lessee and if the seller or lessor breaches a warranty, the buyer or lessee can sue to recover damages from the seller or lessor. Under some circumstances, a breach can allow the buyer or lessee to rescind (cancel) the agreement.[1]

Recall from Chapter 6 that product liability lawsuits include those based on claims for breach of warranty. Warranty law is also part of the broad body of consumer protection law that will be discussed in Chapter 44.

SECTION 1

Warranty of Title

Title warranty arises automatically in most sales contracts. UCC 2–312 imposes the three types of warranties of title discussed here.

GOOD TITLE

In most cases, sellers warrant that they have good and valid title to the goods sold and that transfer of the title is rightful [UCC 2–312(1)(a)]. For example, Alice steals goods from Henry and sells them to Ona, who does not know that they are stolen. If Henry discovers that Ona has the goods, then Henry has the right to reclaim them from Ona. When Alice sold Ona the goods, Alice *automatically* warranted to Ona that the title conveyed was valid and that its transfer was rightful. Because a thief has no title to stolen goods, Alice breached the warranty of title imposed by UCC 2–312(1)(a) and became liable to the buyer for appropriate damages. (See Chapter 19 for a detailed discussion of sales by nonowners.)

NO LIENS

A second warranty of title provided by the UCC protects buyers who are *unaware* of any encumbrances (claims, charges, or liabilities—usually called *liens*[2]) against goods at the time the contract is made [UCC 2–312(1)(b)]. This warranty protects buyers who, for example, unknowingly purchase goods that are subject to a creditor's security interest (see Chapter 28). If a creditor legally repossesses the goods from a buyer *who had no actual knowledge of the security interest,* the buyer can recover from the seller for breach of warranty. (The buyer who has *actual knowledge of a security interest* has no recourse against a seller.)

To illustrate: Henderson buys a used boat from Loring for cash. A month later, Barish repossesses

1. Rescission restores the parties to the positions they were in before the contract was made.

2. Pronounced *leens*. Liens will be discussed in detail in Chapter 29.

the boat from Henderson, having proved that she, Barish, has a valid security interest in the boat and that Loring, who has missed five payments, is in default. Henderson demands his money back from Loring. Under Section 2–312(1)(b), Henderson has legal grounds to recover, because the seller of goods warrants that the goods shall be delivered free from any security interest or other lien of which the buyer has no knowledge.

Article 2A affords similar protection for lessees. Section 2A–211(1) provides that during the term of the lease, no claim of any third party will interfere with the lessee's enjoyment of the leasehold interest.

No Infringements

A merchant seller is also deemed to warrant that the goods delivered are free from any copyright, trademark, or patent claims of a third person[3] [UCC 2–312(3), 2A–211(2)]. If this warranty is breached and the buyer is sued by the party holding copyright, trademark, or patent rights in the goods, the buyer *must notify the seller* of litigation within a reasonable time to enable the seller to decide whether to defend the lawsuit. If the seller states in writing that he or she has decided to defend and agrees to bear all expenses, including that of an adverse judgment, then the buyer must let the seller undertake litigation; otherwise, the buyer loses all rights against the seller if any infringement liability is established [UCC 2–607(3)(b), 2–607(5)(b)].

Article 2A provides for the same notice of litigation in situations that involve leases rather than sales [UCC 2A–516(3)(b), 2A–516(4)(b)]. There is an exception for leases made by individual consumers for personal, family, or household purposes. A consumer who fails to notify the lessor within a reasonable time does not lose his or her remedy against the lessor for any liability established in the litigation [UCC 2A–516(3)(b)].

Disclaimer of Title Warranty

In an ordinary sales transaction, the title warranty can be disclaimed or modified only by *specific language* in a contract. For example, sellers may assert that they are transferring only such rights, title, and interest as they have in the goods. In a lease transaction, the disclaimer must "be specific, be by a writing, and be conspicuous" [UCC 2A–214(4)].

In certain cases, the circumstances surrounding the sale are sufficient to indicate clearly to a buyer that no assurances as to title are being made. The classic example is a sheriff's sale, when buyers know that the goods have been seized to satisfy debts, and the sheriff cannot guarantee title [UCC 2–312(2)].

SECTION 2

Express Warranties

A seller or lessor can create an **express warranty** by making representations concerning the quality, condition, description, or performance potential of the goods. Under UCC 2–313 and 2A–210, express warranties arise when a seller or lessor indicates any of the following:

1. That the goods conform to any *affirmation or promise* of fact that the seller or lessor makes to the buyer or lessee about the goods. Such affirmations or promises are usually made during the bargaining process. Statements such as "these drill bits will *easily* penetrate stainless steel—and without dulling" are express warranties.
2. That the goods conform to any *description* of them. For example, a label that reads "Crate contains one 150-horsepower diesel engine" or a contract that calls for the delivery of a "wool coat" creates an express warranty that the content of the goods sold conforms to the description.
3. That the goods conform to any *sample or model* of the goods shown to the buyer or lessee.

Express warranties can be found in a seller's or lessor's advertisement, brochure, or promotional materials, in addition to being made orally or in an express warranty provision in a sales or lease contract. To create an express warranty, a seller or lessor does not have to use formal words such as *warrant* or *guarantee*. It is only necessary that a reasonable buyer or lessee would regard the representation as part of the basis of the bargain [UCC 2–313(2), 2A–210(2)].

See Case 22.1 at the end of this chapter. To view the full, unedited case from Westlaw,® go to this text's Web site at http://wbl-cs.westbuslaw.com.

3. Recall from Chapter 18 that a *merchant* is defined in UCC 2–104(1) as a person who deals in goods of the kind involved in the sales contract or who, by occupation, presents himself or herself as having knowledge or skill peculiar to the goods involved in the transaction.

BASIS OF THE BARGAIN

The UCC requires that for an express warranty to be created, the affirmation, promise, description, or sample must become part of the "basis of the bargain" [UCC 2–313(1), 2A–210(1)]. Just what constitutes the basis of the bargain is hard to say. The UCC does not define the concept, and it is a question of fact in each case whether a representation was made at such a time and in such a way that it induced the buyer or lessee to enter into the contract. Therefore, if an express warranty is not intended, the marketing agent or salesperson should not promise too much.

Westlaw. See Case 22.2 at the end of this chapter. To view the full, unedited case from Westlaw,® go to this text's Web site at **http://wbl-cs.westbuslaw.com**.

STATEMENTS OF OPINION AND VALUE

If the seller or lessor merely makes a statement that relates to the value or worth of the goods, or makes a statement of opinion or recommendation about the goods, the seller or lessor is not creating an express warranty [UCC 2–313(2), 2A–210(2)].

For example, a seller claims that "this is the best used car to come along in years; it has four new tires and a 150-horsepower engine just rebuilt this year." The seller has made several *affirmations of fact* that can create a warranty: the automobile has an engine; it has a 150-horsepower engine; the engine was rebuilt this year; there are four tires on the automobile; and the tires are new. The seller's *opinion* that the vehicle is "the best used car to come along in years," however, is known as "puffing" and creates no warranty. (*Puffing* is an expression of opinion by a seller or lessor that is not made as a representation of fact.) A statement relating to the value of the goods, such as "it's worth a fortune" or "anywhere else you'd pay $10,000 for it," usually does not create a warranty.

Although the ordinary seller or lessor can give an opinion that is not a warranty, if the seller or lessor is an expert and gives an opinion as an expert to a layperson, then a warranty may be created. For example, Saul is an art dealer and an expert in seventeenth-century paintings. If Saul states to Lauren, a purchaser, that in his opinion a particular painting is a Rembrandt, Saul has warranted the accuracy of his opinion.

It is not always easy to determine what constitutes an express warranty and what constitutes puffing. The reasonableness of the buyer's or lessee's reliance appears to be the controlling criterion in many cases. For example, a salesperson's statements that a ladder will "never break" and will "last a lifetime" are so clearly improbable that no reasonable buyer should rely on them. Additionally, the context within which a statement is made might be relevant in determining the reasonableness of a buyer's or lessee's reliance. For example, a reasonable person is more likely to rely on a written statement made in an advertisement than on a statement made orally by a salesperson.

SECTION 3

Implied Warranties

An **implied warranty** is one that *the law derives* by inference from the nature of the transaction or the relative situations or circumstances of the parties. Under the UCC, merchants impliedly warrant that the goods they sell or lease are merchantable and, in certain circumstances, fit for a particular purpose. In addition, an implied warranty may arise from a course of dealing or usage of trade. We examine these three types of implied warranties in the following subsections.

IMPLIED WARRANTY OF MERCHANTABILITY

An **implied warranty of merchantability** automatically arises in every sale or lease of goods made *by a merchant* who deals in goods of the kind sold or leased [UCC 2–314, 2A–212]. Thus, a merchant who is in the business of selling ski equipment makes an implied warranty of merchantability every time the merchant sells a pair of skis, but a neighbor selling his or her skis at a garage sale does not.

Merchantable Goods. To be *merchantable,* goods must be "reasonably fit for the ordinary purposes for which such goods are used." They must be of at least average, fair, or medium-grade quality. The quality must be comparable to quality that will pass without objection in the trade or market for goods of the same description. To be merchantable, the goods must also be adequately packaged and labeled as provided by the agreement, and they must conform to the promises or affirmations of fact made on the container or label, if any.

An implied warranty of merchantability also imposes on the merchant liability for the safe performance of the product. It makes no difference whether the merchant knew of or could have discovered a defect that makes the product unsafe—he or she is liable in either situation. For example, Kaplan buys an ax at Enrique's Hardware Store. No express warranties are made. The first time she chops wood with it, the ax handle breaks, and she is injured. She immediately notifies Enrique. Examination shows that the wood in the handle was rotten but that the rottenness could not have been noticed by either Enrique or Kaplan. Nonetheless, Kaplan notifies Enrique that she will hold him responsible for her injuries. Enrique is responsible, because a merchant seller of goods warrants that the goods he or she sells are fit for the ordinary purposes for which such goods are used. This ax was obviously not fit for those purposes.

Of course, merchants are not absolute insurers against *all* accidents arising in connection with the goods. For example, a bar of soap is not unmerchantable merely because a user could slip and fall by stepping on it.

Merchantable Food. The UCC recognizes the serving of food or drink to be consumed on or off the premises as a sale of goods subject to the implied warranty of merchantability [UCC 2–314(1)]. "Merchantable" food is food that is fit to eat on the basis of consumer expectations. For example, the courts assume that consumers should reasonably expect to find on occasion bones in fish fillets, cherry pits in cherry pie, a nutshell in a package of shelled nuts, and so on—because such substances are natural incidents of the food. In contrast, consumers would not reasonably expect to find an inchworm in a can of peas or a piece of glass in a soft drink—because these substances are not natural to the food product.[4]

Implied Warranty of Fitness for a Particular Purpose

The **implied warranty of fitness for a particular purpose** arises when any *seller or lessor* (merchant or nonmerchant) knows the particular purpose for which a buyer or lessee will use the goods *and* knows that the buyer or lessee is relying on the skill and judgment of the seller or lessor to select suitable goods [UCC 2–315, 2A–213].

A "particular purpose" of the buyer or lessee differs from the "ordinary purpose for which goods are used" (merchantability). Goods can be merchantable but unfit for a particular purpose. For example, suppose that you need a gallon of paint to match the color of your living room walls—a light shade somewhere between coral and peach. You take a sample to your local hardware store and request a gallon of paint of that color. Instead, you are given a gallon of bright blue paint. Here, the salesperson has not breached any warranty of implied merchantability—the bright blue paint is of high quality and suitable for interior walls—but he or she has breached an implied warranty of fitness for a particular purpose.

A seller or lessor does not need to have actual knowledge of the buyer's or lessee's particular purpose. It is sufficient if a seller or lessor "has reason to know" the purpose. The buyer or lessee, however, must have *relied* on the skill or judgment of the seller or lessor in selecting or furnishing suitable goods for an implied warranty to be created.

For example, Bloomberg leases a computer from Future Tech, a lessor of technical business equipment. Bloomberg tells the clerk that she wants a computer that will run a complicated new engineering graphics program at a realistic speed. Future Tech leases Bloomberg an Architex One computer with a CPU speed of only 550 megahertz, even though a speed of at least 1200 megahertz would be required to run Bloomberg's graphics program at a "realistic speed." Bloomberg, after realizing that it takes her forever to run her program, wants her money back. Here, because Future Tech has breached the implied warranty of fitness for a particular purpose, Bloomberg normally will be able to recover. The clerk knew specifically that Bloomberg wanted a computer with enough speed to run certain software. Furthermore, Bloomberg relied on the clerk to furnish a computer that would fulfill this purpose. Because Future Tech did not do so, the warranty was breached.

Implied Warranty Arising from Course of Dealing or Trade Usage

Implied warranties can also arise (or be excluded or modified) as a result of course of dealing, course of performance, or usage of trade [UCC 2–314(3), 2A–212(3)]. In the absence of evidence to the contrary, when both parties to a sales or lease contract have knowledge of a well-recognized trade custom, the courts will infer that both parties intended for that custom to apply to their contract. For example, if it is

4. See, for example, *Mexicali Rose v. Superior Court,* 1 Cal.4th 617, 4 Cal.Rptr.2d 145, 822 P.2d 1292 (1992).

an industry-wide custom to lubricate a new car before it is delivered and a dealer fails to do so, the dealer can be held liable to a buyer for damages resulting from the breach of an implied warranty. (This, of course, would also be negligence on the part of the dealer.)

SECTION 4

Overlapping Warranties

Sometimes two or more warranties are made in a single transaction. An implied warranty of merchantability, an implied warranty of fitness for a particular purpose, or both, can exist in addition to an express warranty. For example, when a sales contract for a new car states that "this car engine is warranted to be free from defects for 36,000 miles or thirty-six months, whichever occurs first," there is an express warranty against all defects and an implied warranty that the car will be fit for normal use.

The rule under the UCC is that express and implied warranties are construed as *cumulative* if they are consistent with one another [UCC 2–317, 2A–215]. If the warranties are *inconsistent,* the courts usually hold as follows:

1. *Express* warranties displace inconsistent *implied* warranties, except implied warranties of fitness for a particular purpose.
2. Samples take precedence over inconsistent general descriptions.
3. Technical specifications displace inconsistent samples or general descriptions.

In the example described earlier, suppose that when Bloomberg leases the computer at Future Tech, the contract contains an express warranty concerning the speed of the CPU and the application programs that the computer is capable of running. Bloomberg does not realize that the speed expressly warranted in the contract is insufficient for her needs. When she tries to run the software with some engineering plans, the computer slows to a crawl. Bloomberg claims that Future Tech has breached the implied warranty of fitness for a particular purpose. Here, although the express warranty would take precedence over any implied warranty of merchantability, it would not take precedence over an implied warranty of fitness for a particular purpose. Bloomberg therefore has a good claim for the breach of implied warranty of fitness for a particular purpose, because she made it clear that she was leasing the computer to perform certain tasks.

SECTION 5

Warranties and Third Parties

One of the general principles of contract law is that a person who is not one of the parties to a contract has no rights under the contract. As discussed earlier in this text, the connection that exists between the contracting parties is called *privity of contract.* It was established at common law that privity must exist between a plaintiff and a defendant for any action based on a contract to be maintained. Notable exceptions to the rule of privity include product liability (see Chapter 6) and assignments and third party beneficiary contracts (see Chapter 15).

For example, I purchase a ham from retailer Bollinger. I invite you to my house that evening. I prepare the ham properly. You are served first, because you are my guest, and you become severely ill because the ham is spoiled. Can you sue retailer Bollinger for breach of the implied warranty of merchantability? Because warranty is based on a contract for the sale of goods, under the common law you would normally have warranty rights only if you were a party to the purchase of the ham. Therefore, the warranty would extend only to me, the purchaser.

There is sharp disagreement among the states as to how far warranty liability should extend, however. In view of this disagreement, the UCC offers three alternatives for liability to third parties [UCC 2–318, 2A–216]. All three alternatives are intended to eliminate the privity requirement with respect to certain enumerated types of injuries (personal versus property) for certain beneficiaries (for example, household members or bystanders).[5]

SECTION 6

Warranty Disclaimers

Because each type of warranty is created in a special way, the manner in which warranties can be disclaimed or qualified by a seller or lessor varies with the type of warranty.

5. For a case illustrating the alternative adopted by North Carolina, see *Crews v. W. A. Brown & Son, Inc.,* 106 N.C.App. 324, 416 S.E.2d 924 (1992). In this case, a teen-age volunteer working on a church's premises sustained severe frostbite while locked in a walk-in freezer with a malfunctioning door-release mechanism. She was unable to recover from the manufacturer of the freezer because she was neither the buyer nor a "family member" of the church.

EXPRESS WARRANTIES

As already stated, any affirmation of fact or promise, description of the goods, or use of samples or models by a seller or lessor creates an express warranty. Obviously, then, express warranties can be excluded if the seller or lessor carefully refrains from making any promise or affirmation of fact relating to the goods, describing the goods, or using a sample or model.

The UCC does permit express warranties to be negated or limited by specific and unambiguous language, provided that this is done in a manner that protects the buyer or lessee from surprise. Therefore, a written disclaimer in language that is clear and conspicuous, and called to a buyer's or lessee's attention, could negate all oral express warranties not included in the written sales or lease contract [UCC 2–316(1), 2A–214(1)]. This allows the seller or lessor to avoid false allegations that oral warranties were made, and it ensures that only representations made by properly authorized individuals are included in the bargain.

Note, however, that a buyer or lessee must be made aware of any warranty disclaimers or modifications *at the time the contract is formed.* In other words, any oral or written warranties—or disclaimers—made during the bargaining process cannot be modified at a later time by the seller or lessor without the consent of the buyer or lessee.

IMPLIED WARRANTIES

Generally speaking, unless circumstances indicate otherwise, the implied warranties of merchantability and fitness are disclaimed by the expressions "as is," "with all faults," and other similar expressions that in common understanding for *both* parties call the buyer's or lessee's attention to the fact that there are no implied warranties [UCC 2–316(3)(a), 2A–214(3)(a)].

The UCC also permits a seller or lessor to specifically disclaim an implied warranty either of fitness or of merchantability [UCC 2–316(2), 2A–214(2)]. To disclaim an implied warranty of fitness for a particular purpose, the disclaimer must be in writing and be conspicuous. The word *fitness* does not have to be mentioned in the writing; it is sufficient if, for example, the disclaimer states, "THERE ARE NO WARRANTIES THAT EXTEND BEYOND THE DESCRIPTION ON THE FACE HEREOF."

A merchantability disclaimer must be more specific; it must mention *merchantability.* It need not be written; but if it is, the writing must be conspicuous [UCC 2–316(2), 2A–214(4)]. According to UCC 1–201(10),

> A term or clause is conspicuous when it is so written that a reasonable person against whom it is to operate ought to have noticed it. A printed heading in capitals . . . is conspicuous. Language in the body of a form is conspicuous if it is in larger or other contrasting type or color.

For example, Forbes, a merchant, sells Maves a particular lawn mower selected by Forbes with the characteristics clearly requested by Maves. At the time of the sale, Forbes orally tells Maves that he does not warrant the merchantability of the mower, as it is last year's model. If the mower proves to be defective and does not work, Maves can hold Forbes liable for breach of the warranty of fitness for a particular purpose but not for breach of the warranty of merchantability. Forbes's oral disclaimer mentioning the word *merchantability* is a proper disclaimer. For Forbes to have disclaimed the implied warranty of fitness for a particular purpose, however, a conspicuous writing would have been required. Because he made no written disclaimer, Forbes can still be held liable.

See Case 22.3 at the end of this chapter. To view the full, unedited case from Westlaw,® go to this text's Web site at **http://wbl-cs.westbuslaw.com**.

BUYER'S OR LESSEE'S EXAMINATION OF THE GOODS

If a buyer or lessee actually examines the goods (or a sample or model) as fully as desired before entering into a contract, or, if the buyer or lessee refuses to examine the goods on the seller's or lessor's demand that he or she do so, *there is no implied warranty with respect to defects that a reasonable examination would reveal or defects that are found on examination* [UCC 2–316(3)(b), 2A–214(2)(b)].

For example, suppose that Joplin buys an ax at Gershwin's Hardware Store. No express warranties are made. Joplin, even after Gershwin asks, refuses to inspect the ax before buying it. Had she done so, she would have noticed that the handle of the ax was obviously cracked. If she is later injured by the defective ax, she normally will not be able to hold Gershwin liable for breach of the warranty of merchantability, because she would have spotted the defect during an inspection.

UNCONSCIONABILITY

The UCC sections dealing with warranty disclaimers do not refer specifically to unconscionability as a factor. Ultimately, however, the courts will test warranty disclaimers with reference to the UCC's unconscionability standards [UCC 2–302, 2A–108]. Such things as lack of bargaining position, "take-it-or-leave-it" choices, and a buyer's or lessee's failure to understand or know of a warranty disclaimer will become relevant to the issue of unconscionability.

SECTION 7

Statute of Limitations

An action for breach of contract under the UCC must be commenced *within four years after the cause of action accrues*—that is, within four years after the breach occurs. In addition to filing suit within the four-year period, the aggrieved party usually must notify the breaching party of the breach within a reasonable time, or the aggrieved party is barred from pursuing any remedy [UCC 2–607(3)(a), 2A–516(3)]. By agreement in the contract, the parties can reduce this period to not less than one year, but they *cannot* extend it beyond four years [UCC 2–725(1), 2A–506(1)].

The statute of limitations begins to run when a cause of action accrues (becomes an enforceable right). An action for breach of warranty accrues when the seller or lessor *tenders* delivery. This is the rule even if the aggrieved party is unaware that the cause of action has accrued [UCC 2–725(2), 2A–506(2)]. Remember that tender of delivery takes place under a shipment contract on delivery of the goods to the carrier and under a destination contract on tender of the goods at the specified destination delivery location. The statute of limitations in these cases can have a tremendous impact if the goods purchased are going to be stored primarily for future use. To avoid this effect, the UCC provides that when a warranty explicitly extends to future performance and discovery of its breach must await the time of that performance, the statute of limitations also begins to run at that time [UCC 2–725(2)].

For example, Hoover purchases a central air-conditioning unit for his restaurant. The unit is warranted specifically to keep the temperature below a certain level during the summer months. The unit is installed in the winter, but when summer comes, the restaurant does not stay cool. Because discovery of the warranty's breach is, of necessity, made in the summer and not when the unit is delivered in the winter, the statute of limitations does not begin to run until the summer.

When a buyer or seller brings suit on a legal theory unrelated to the UCC, the limitations periods specified above do not apply, even though the claim relates to goods. For example, Cane buys tires for his automobile. The tires prove to have an inherently dangerous defect. Four years and one month after purchasing the tires, Cane loses control of the car because of a defective tire and injures several passengers, as well as himself. Cane brings a suit against the tire manufacturer based on strict liability in tort (see Chapter 6). In this situation, the suit will not be governed by the UCC's statute of limitations but rather by the state's statute of limitations governing tort cases.

SECTION 8

Magnuson-Moss Warranty Act

The Magnuson-Moss Warranty Act of 1975[6] was designed to prevent deception in warranties by making them easier to understand. The act is enforced primarily by the Federal Trade Commission (FTC). Additionally, the attorney general or a consumer who has been injured can enforce the act if informal procedures for settling disputes prove to be ineffective. The act modifies UCC warranty rules to some extent when *consumer* transactions are involved. The UCC, however, remains the primary codification of warranty rules for industrial and commercial transactions.

No seller is *required* to give a written warranty for consumer goods sold under the Magnuson-Moss Warranty Act. If a seller chooses to make an express written warranty, however, and the cost of the consumer goods is more than $10, the warranty must be labeled as either "full" or "limited." In addition, if the cost of the goods is more than $15, by FTC regulation, the warrantor must make certain disclosures fully and conspicuously in a single document in "readily understood language." This disclosure states the names and addresses of the warrantor(s), what specifically is warranted, procedures for enforcement of the warranty, any limitations on warranty relief, and that the buyer has legal rights.

6. 15 U.S.C. Sections 2301–2312.

FULL WARRANTY

Although a *full warranty* may not cover every aspect of the consumer product sold, what it covers ensures some type of consumer satisfaction in the event that the product is defective. A full warranty requires free repair or replacement of any defective part; if the product cannot be repaired within a reasonable time, the consumer has the choice of either a refund or a replacement without charge. The full warranty frequently does not have a time limit on it. Any limitation on consequential damages must be *conspicuously* stated. Additionally, the warrantor need not perform warranty services if the problem with the product was caused by damage to the product or unreasonable use by the consumer.

LIMITED WARRANTY

A *limited warranty* arises when the written warranty fails to meet one of the minimum requirements of a full warranty. The fact that only a limited warranty is being given must be conspicuously designated. If it is only a time limitation that distinguishes a limited warranty from a full warranty, the Magnuson-Moss Warranty Act allows the warrantor to identify the warranty as a full warranty by such language as "full twelve-month warranty."

IMPLIED WARRANTIES

Implied warranties are not covered under the Magnuson-Moss Warranty Act; they continue to be created according to UCC provisions. When an express warranty is made, it may not, under the Magnuson-Moss Warranty Act, include disclaimers or modifications of the implied warranties of merchantability and fitness for a particular purpose. A warrantor can impose a time limit on the duration of an implied warranty, but it has to correspond to the duration of the express warranty.[7]

SECTION 9

Warranties under the CISG

The United Nations Convention on Contracts for the International Sale of Goods (CISG) does not use the term *warranty* in regard to the rights and obligations of parties to international sales contracts. Instead, the CISG prefers to phrase the concept of warranty in terms of "conformity of the goods." Although the CISG uses different language, it effectively provides for warranty protection similar to that available under the UCC. Article 35 of the CISG states that the seller "must deliver goods which are of the quantity, quality and description required by the contract and which are contained or packaged in the manner required by the contract." Other provisions of Article 35 are, in effect, equivalent to the UCC express and implied warranties.

7. This time limit must, of course, be reasonable, conscionable, and set forth in clear and conspicuous language on the face of the warranty.

TERMS AND CONCEPTS TO REVIEW

express warranty 421

implied warranty 422

implied warranty of fitness for a particular purpose 423

implied warranty of merchantability 422

CHAPTER SUMMARY

Warranties of Title	The UCC provides for the following warranties of title [UCC 2–312, 2A–211]: 1. *Good title*—A seller warrants that he or she has the right to pass good and rightful title to the goods. 2. *No liens*—A seller warrants that the goods sold are free of any encumbrances (claims, charges, or liabilities—usually called *liens*). A lessor warrants that the lessee will not be disturbed in his or her possession of the goods by the claims of a third party. 3. *No infringements*—A merchant seller warrants that the goods are free of infringement claims (claims that a patent, trademark, or copyright has been infringed) by third parties. Lessors make similar warranties.

CASES CASES CASES CASES CASES CASES CASES CASES CASES CASES CASES CASES CASES CASE

CHAPTER SUMMARY—CONTINUED

Express Warranties	1. *Under the UCC*—An express warranty arises under the UCC when a seller or lessor indicates any of the following as part of the sale or bargain [UCC 2–313, 2A–210]: a. An affirmation or promise of fact. b. A description of the goods. c. A sample or model shown as conforming to the contract goods. 2. *Under the Magnuson-Moss Warranty Act*—Express written warranties covering consumer goods priced at more than $10, *if made,* must be labeled as one of the following: a. Full warranty—Free repair or replacement of defective parts; refund or replacement for goods if they cannot be repaired in a reasonable time. b. Limited warranty—When less than a full warranty is being offered.
Implied Warranty of Merchantability	When a seller or lessor is a merchant who deals in goods of the kind sold or leased, the seller or lessor warrants that the goods sold or leased are properly packaged and labeled, are of proper quality, and are reasonably fit for the ordinary purposes for which such goods are used [UCC 2–314, 2A–212].
Implied Warranty of Fitness for a Particular Purpose	An implied warranty of fitness for a particular purpose arises when the buyer's or lessee's purpose or use is known by the seller or lessor, and the buyer or lessee purchases or leases the goods in reliance on the seller's or lessor's selection [UCC 2–315, 2A–213].
Implied Warranty Arising from Course of Dealing, Course of Performance, or Trade Usage	Other implied warranties can arise as a result of course of dealing, course of performance, or usage of trade [UCC 2–314(3), 2A–212(3)].
Warranties under the CISG	Article 35 of the United Nations Convention on Contracts for the International Sale of Goods (CISG), although it uses different terms, in effect provides warranties that are equivalent to the UCC express and implied warranties.

CASES FOR ANALYSIS

Westlaw. You can access the full text of each case presented below by going to the Westlaw cases on this text's Web site at http://wbl-cs.westbuslaw.com. Each Westlaw case includes the names of all plaintiffs and defendants, the dates on which the case was argued and decided, a brief summary of the issues and decisions in the case, headnotes classifying the specific issues in the case according to the West Key Number System, and the court's opinion. Concurring and dissenting opinions, if any, are included as well.

CASE 22.1 EXPRESS WARRANTIES

GENETTI V. CATERPILLAR, INC.
Supreme Court of Nebraska, 2001.
261 Neb. 98,
621 N.W.2d 529.

CONNOLLY, J. [Justice]

* * * *

I. BACKGROUND

On February 26, 1996, [Robert Genetti and Sherrie Genetti], who are in the business of delivering furniture nationwide, bought a new 1996 GMC truck and trailer from Omaha Truck Center, Inc. The truck was manufactured by General Motors [Corporation] and was equipped with a model 3116 diesel engine manufactured by Caterpillar [Inc.]. The model 3116 engine is generally described as a medium-duty engine. The purchase price for the truck was $97,043, and the Genettis took possession around March 8. The warranties issued by General Motors and Caterpillar stated that the truck was warranted for 3 years or 150,000 miles. From the time of purchase, it was serviced only through General Motors and Caterpillar dealerships.

Following a series of problems with the engine, the Genettis brought suit against both Caterpillar and General Motors seeking relief for breach of express warranty under the U.C.C. [and other causes of action. Among other things] [t]he Genettis * * * sought general damages and an award of attorney fees and costs.

* * * *

Genetti testified that he had 18 years of experience in driving, operating, and maintaining diesel engines and that it was his custom to check daily for engine problems such as leaking fluids. Furthermore, the truck was serviced according to the schedule provided by General Motors.

* * * *

[Genetti employee John] Seeley was driving the truck when the fourth [engine] failure occurred in March 1997. Seeley testified that he was driving over a mountain pass when he noticed that the truck lost power and that the temperature gauge was higher than normal. Seeley did not observe a sudden puff of smoke like he had noticed during the third breakdown, but he did observe some smoke. Seeley continued to drive the truck until the gauge indicated that the engine was warmer than it should be and then pulled over to the side of the road to allow it to cool down. After the truck had cooled down, Seeley checked the coolant level, found it to be about half full, and added more coolant. Seeley then waited for the truck to completely cool down before starting to drive again. After Seeley began to drive again, the truck continued to overheat. Seeley testified that he had to stop and allow the truck to cool down "quite a few" times.

* * * Seeley took the truck to a General Motors dealership in Commerce City, Colorado. * * *

* * * The dealership * * * repaired the truck * * * and issued an invoice [for almost $12,000] to the Genettis for the repairs on March 28, 1997.

On March 26, 1997, 2 days before the invoice for repairs was issued, the Genettis' attorney sent a letter to both General Motors and Caterpillar stating that the truck had experienced engine problems on four different occasions and that due to those problems, the truck had been out of service for a cumulative total of more than 40 days. The letter stated that the Genettis did not wish to retain the truck and demanded that the manufacturer either replace the truck with a comparable vehicle or refund the full purchase price, including taxes and fees paid. * * * [General Motors and Caterpillar refused.]

* * * *

At the conclusion of the Genettis' evidence, General Motors and Caterpillar moved for a directed verdict, arguing that there was an absence of proof of a defect in material or workmanship. The motions were overruled.

* * * *

The jury returned a verdict in favor of the Genettis on the breach of warranty claim. The jury found the total damages to be $105,000 with $36,500 allocated to Caterpillar and $68,500 allocated to General Motors. * * *

* * * *

* * * In its final order, the district court awarded prejudgment interest * * * , resulting in a judgment against Caterpillar of $39,600.47 and a judgment against General Motors of $74,319.88. Caterpillar appeals, * * * and General Motors cross-appeal[s].

* * * *

IV. ANALYSIS

* * * *

Caterpillar and General Motors argue that the district court should have directed a verdict in their favor because the Genettis failed to present expert testimony to prove that the fourth breakdown was caused by a defect in material and workmanship. * * * The Genettis contend that they need not prove the specific defect that caused the breakdowns in order to prove that the engine was defective.

* * * *

Of the few jurisdictions that have directly addressed the issue, the majority do not require proof of a specific defect under * * * the U.C.C. * * * . Rather, *it is generally held that a plaintiff is not required to prove the specific product defect and that the proof may be circumstantial in nature or inferred from the evidence.* [Emphasis added.]

* * * [U]nder many warranties, including the warranties at issue in this case, a consumer requiring warranty service on a vehicle may take the damaged vehicle only to a service department at an authorized dealer. * * * Placing the burden on the consumer to prove a precise defect is unfair and unconscionable since the dealer and manufacturer could tamper (whether intentionally or inadvertently) with the evidence. * * * To impose an unreasonably heavy burden on consumers is to deny them a meaningful remedy.

* * * *

We * * * hold that a precise or specific defect does not need to be proved in order to find a product defective under * * * the U.C.C. * * * . Although expert testimony pointing to a specific defect would be the best means of proving the existence of a defect in some cases, proof that the warranted product is defective may be circumstantial in nature and may be inferred from the evidence. We now turn to the question of whether the Genettis presented sufficient evidence of a defect in order to overcome Caterpillar's and General Motors' motions for a directed verdict.

Although Ervin Stepanek [an expert witness for the Genettis] could not specifically state what caused the fourth breakdown to occur, he did advance several reasons supported by the testimony and repair records.

Stepanek testified that he did not believe the breakdown was due to overheating, but was instead due to an engine failure, such as a cracked head gasket or cracked block that caused coolant to run into the engine. It was not required that Stepanek testify regarding a specific design defect. Further, the Genettis presented evidence that the actions of their employees during the fourth breakdown were proper * * * . Thus, the Genettis presented evidence eliminating abuse or misuse as the alternate cause of the breakdown. At that point, it was reasonable for a jury to conclude that if the breakdown was not due to improper use of the truck, then it was due to a defect such as one of those suggested by Stepanek. Looking at the evidence, a jury using common sense and experience could reasonably arrive at the conclusion that the fourth breakdown was caused by a defect in the engine and should have been covered by the warranty. Accordingly, we conclude that the district court did not err when it refused to direct a verdict.

* * * *

V. CONCLUSION

We conclude that the district court properly overruled General Motors' and Caterpillar's motions for a directed verdict. * * *

The record in this case reflects that the issue of damages under [a different cause of action] was not submitted to the jury. * * * Accordingly, we reverse, and remand for a new trial on the issue of damages under [this cause].

AFFIRMED IN PART, AND IN PART REVERSED AND REMANDED.

CASE 22.2 EXPRESS WARRANTIES

FELLEY v. SINGLETON

Appellate Court of Illinois,
Second District, 1999.
302 Ill.App.3d 248,
705 N.E.2d 930,
235 Ill.Dec. 747.

Presiding Justice *BOWMAN* delivered the opinion of the court:

Defendants, Thomas and Cheryl Singleton, appeal from an order entered by [an Illinois state court] in this small claims action. Defendants contend that the trial court erred when it found that statements they made to plaintiff, Brian D. Felley, when he purchased a used car from them constituted an express warranty. * * *

The relevant facts are not in dispute. On June 8, 1997, plaintiff went to defendants' home to look at a used car that defendants had offered for sale by newspaper advertisement. The car was a 1991 Ford Taurus and had about 126,000 miles on it. After test driving the car and discussing its condition with defendants, plaintiff purchased the car from defendants for $5,800.

At trial, plaintiff testified that he soon began experiencing problems with the car. On the second day after he bought the car, plaintiff noticed a problem with the clutch. Over the next few days, the clutch problem worsened to the point where plaintiff was unable to shift the gears no matter how far he pushed in the clutch pedal. Plaintiff presented an invoice dated June 18, 1997, showing that he paid $942.76 on that date for the removal and repair of the car's clutch.

Plaintiff further testified that the car developed serious brake problems within the first month that he owned it. Plaintiff presented two invoices for work he had done on the car's brakes. One of the invoices shows that on July 9, 1997, plaintiff paid $971.18 for brake work on the car. The second invoice shows that on September 16, 1997, plaintiff paid $429.09 for additional brake work on the car.

Plaintiff called Robert Hanover as an expert witness. Hanover is a technician at the Car X Muffler facility that performed the brake work on the car. Hanover is an underbody specialist with experience in diagnosing and repairing problems with clutches and brakes. Hanover examined the car when plaintiff brought it in on July 9, 1997. His examination revealed that the rear brakes on the car were not functioning because the calipers had locked up and that the car was only braking on the front brakes. In order to fix this problem, Car X installed new calipers on the rear brakes. Hanover also testified that both the front and rear brakes needed the pads and rotors replaced. Based on his experience, Hanover stated that problems such as those with the car's brakes take considerable time to develop. Hanover opined that the car's brake problems therefore probably existed when plaintiff purchased the car.

Hanover also testified that he was familiar with the type of work performed on the car's clutch and that he had experience with Rock River Ford, the facility that performed the clutch work on the car. Based on his experience, his discussions with plaintiff regarding the clutch problem, and the invoice showing the repair work that was performed on the clutch, Hanover opined that the clutch was not in good operating condition when plaintiff purchased the car from defendants.

* * * Thomas [Singleton] testified that he and his wife had owned the car for about three years when plaintiff bought it. He recalled discussing the condition of the car with plaintiff but did not recall if plaintiff asked about specific aspects of the car such as the condition of the brakes. He told plaintiff that the only thing known to be

wrong with the car was that it had a noise in the right rear and that a grommet (a connector having to do with a strut) was bad or missing. Thomas acknowledged that he told plaintiff that the car was in good condition.

* * * *

Plaintiff testified that the fact that defendants told him that the car was in good mechanical condition was a primary consideration in his decision to buy the car.

Defendant Cheryl Singleton (Cheryl) also testified at trial. Cheryl took care of all the maintenance on the car during the three years that she and her husband owned it. She had the oil changed every three months. In addition, she had a "stabilizing pin" installed on the front end, had a new battery installed, and had the front tires replaced with new tires. She did not experience any problems with the clutch or the brakes. * * * Cheryl acknowledged that she and her husband told plaintiff that the car was "in good mechanical condition."

* * * *

The trial court entered judgment for plaintiff in the amount of $2,343.03. This was the sum of the amounts shown on the three invoices presented by plaintiff. Defendants' timely appeal followed.

On appeal, defendants contend that the trial court erred when it determined that the statements that they made to plaintiff regarding the condition of the car constituted an express warranty. Defendants argue that their statements were nothing more than expressions of opinion in the nature of puffery that could not properly be deemed an express warranty.

Section 2–313 of the Uniform Commercial Code * * * governs the formation of express warranties by affirmation in the context of a sale of goods such as a used car. Section 2–313 provides, in relevant part:

> (1) Express warranties by the seller are created as follows:
>
> (a) Any affirmation of fact or promise made by the seller to the buyer which relates to the goods and becomes part of the basis of the bargain creates an express warranty that the goods shall conform to the affirmation or promise.
>
> * * * *
>
> (2) It is not necessary to the creation of an express warranty that the seller use formal words such as 'warrant' or 'guarantee' or that he have a specific intention to make a warranty, but an affirmation merely of the value of the goods or a statement purporting to be merely the seller's opinion or commendation of the goods does not create a warranty."

Defendants point to subsection (2) of [S]ection 2–313 as support for their argument that their statements to plaintiff did not constitute an express warranty. Defendants also cite the official comments to subsection (2) which state, in relevant part:

> "Concerning affirmations of value or a seller's opinion or commendation under subsection (2), the basic question remains the same: What statements of the seller have in the circumstances and in objective judgment become part of the basis of the bargain? As indicated above, all of the statements of the seller do so unless good reason is shown to the contrary. The provisions of subsection (2) are included, however, since common experience discloses that some statements or predictions cannot fairly be viewed as entering into the bargain."

In defendants' view, their statements to plaintiff cannot fairly be viewed as entering into the bargain. Defendants assert that they are not automobile dealers or mechanics with specialized knowledge of the brake and clutch systems of the car and therefore their statements were merely expressions of a vendor's opinion that did not constitute an express warranty.

* * * *

* * * *[A]ffirmations of fact made during a bargaining process regarding the sale of goods are presumed to be part of the basis of the bargain unless clear affirmative proof to the contrary is shown;* * * * *a showing of reliance on the affirmations by the buyer is not necessary for the creation of an express warranty; and* * * * *the seller has the burden to establish by clear affirmative proof that the affirmations did not become part of the basis of the bargain.* * * * [T]he seller may be held accountable for breach of warranty where affirmations are a basis of the bargain and the goods fail to conform to the affirmations. [Emphasis added.]

* * * [I]n the context of a used car sale, representations by the seller such as the car is "in good mechanical condition" are presumed to be affirmations of fact that become part of the basis of the bargain. Because they are presumed to be part of the basis of the bargain, such representations constitute express warranties, regardless of the buyer's reliance on them, unless the seller shows by clear affirmative proof that the representations did not become part of the basis of the bargain.

In this case, it is undisputed that plaintiff asked defendants about the car's mechanical condition and that defendants responded that the car was in good mechanical condition. Under the foregoing principles, defendants' representations are presumed to be affirmations of fact that became a part of the basis of the bargain. Nothing in the record indicates that defendants made a clear and affirmative showing that their representations did not become part of the basis of the bargain. Based on this record, we cannot say that the trial court's findings that defendants' representations were affirmations of fact that became a part of the basis of the bargain and created an express warranty were against the manifest weight of the evidence.

* * * *

The judgment of the [lower] court * * * is affirmed.

CASE 22.3 DISCLAIMER OF IMPLIED WARRANTIES

BORDEN, INC. v. ADVENT INK CO.

Superior Court of Pennsylvania, 1997.
701 A.2d 255.

SAYLOR, Judge.

* * * *

Advent [Ink Company], a Pennsylvania corporation, manufactured water-based inks for printers. Among those inks was a black ink that was sold to R.R. Donnelley & Sons Company ("Donnelley") for the printing of its telephone directories. In producing this ink, Advent used a water-based black dispersion, "Aquablak," which it purchased from Borden [Inc.]

In 1992, Borden sued Advent [in a Pennsylvania state court] to recover the sum of $16,227.50 on a book account for merchandise sold and delivered to Advent. In response, Advent asserted that it had rejected the shipments in question because prior shipments had failed to comply with implied warranties of merchantability and fitness for a particular purpose. Specifically, Advent alleged that Borden's failure to age the Aquablak resulted in material defects which, when the Aquablak was incorporated into the black ink, caused the ink to separate and to clog Donnelley's presses. As a result, Donnelley ceased buying water-based black ink from Advent. In its counterclaim Advent argued that it was "entitled to recover from Borden the profits which [it] lost and which [it had] reasonably expected to continue from the Donnelley contract which was cancelled solely as a result of Borden's failure to provide a merchantable black dispersion for use in the black ink."

* * * *

Following discovery, Borden filed a motion for summary judgment on the counterclaim. In its motion Borden argued that it was entitled to summary judgment on either of two bases: first, it had validly and conspicuously disclaimed the implied warranties of merchantability and of fitness for a particular purpose, as it was allowed to do under the Uniform Commercial Code ("UCC"), by means of language included in its sales invoices and in labels affixed to each drum of Aquablak that was shipped to Advent; second, by the same means it had validly excluded any liability for consequential damages * * * .

By order entered January 2, 1997, the trial court granted Borden's motion for summary judgment and dismissed the counterclaim. * * *

* * * *

In this appeal, Advent contends that summary judgment was not warranted on either of the two grounds advanced by Borden. As to the disclaimer of warranties on the invoices and drum labels, Advent argues that the disclaimer was inoperative because it was inconspicuous. * * *

I. Disclaimer of Warranties

In order to resolve Advent's first issue (namely, its challenge to the disclaimer of warranties), we turn first to the pertinent provisions of the UCC as adopted in this Commonwealth. The implied warranty of merchantability, as set forth in the UCC, is a warranty that the goods will pass without objection in the trade and are fit for the ordinary purposes for which such goods are used. Such a warranty serves to protect buyers from loss where the goods purchased are below commercial standards. * * * *[T]his warranty is so commonly taken for granted that its exclusion from a contract is recognized as a matter threatening surprise and therefore requiring special precaution.* The implied warranty that goods shall be fit for a particular purpose exists, under the UCC, where the seller at the time of contracting has reason to know of such purpose and of the buyer's reliance upon the seller's skill or judgment to select or furnish goods that are suitable for such purpose. [Emphasis added.]

The UCC sets forth the following requirements for excluding or modifying these implied warranties:

> Subject to subsection (c) [not relevant here], to exclude or modify the implied warranty of merchantability or any part of it the language must mention merchantability and in case of a writing must be conspicuous, and to exclude or modify any implied warranty of fitness the exclusion must be by a writing and conspicuous. Language to exclude all implied warranties of fitness is sufficient if it states, for example, that "There are no warranties which extend beyond the description on the face hereof."

In the present case, the attempted exclusions of both warranties appear in writings, and * * * the writings mention merchantability. The question to be decided, therefore, is whether those attempted exclusions are conspicuous. * * *

The UCC provides the following definition of the critical term "conspicuous":

> A term or clause is conspicuous when it is so written that a reasonable person against whom it is to operate ought to have noticed it. A printed heading in capitals * * * is conspicuous. Language in the body of a form is conspicuous if it is in larger or other contrasting type or color. But in a telegram any stated term is conspicuous.

* * * *

* * * [F]actors to be considered in determining whether a reasonable person should have noticed a

warranty disclaimer include: 1) the disclaimer's placement in the document, 2) the size of the disclaimer's print, and 3) whether the disclaimer was highlighted by being printed in all capital letters or in a type style or color different from the remainder of the document. The reasonableness test accords with the primary purpose of the conspicuousness requirement, which is to avoid fine print waiver of rights by the buyer.

* * * On the front of Borden's standard invoice, in red capital letters, is the phrase "SEE REVERSE SIDE." On the reverse side is the heading "CONDITIONS OF SALE," followed by nineteen conditions, the first of which is the following:

> 1. WARRANTIES AND DISCLAIMERS. SELLER MAKE [sic] NO WARRANTY, EXPRESS OR IMPLIED, CONCERNING THE PRODUCT OR THE MERCHANTABILITY OR FITNESS THEREOF FOR ANY PURPOSE, except: * * * that the product shall conform to the Seller's specifications, if any * * * .

At the top of the label affixed to each drum of dispersion is the Borden logo. Beneath the logo are [five] centered lines * * * .

* * * *

Below these lines is the centered heading "**DISCLAIMER**" and the following text:

> **SELLER MAKES NO WARRANTY, EXPRESS OR IMPLIED, CONCERNING THE PRODUCT OR THE MERCHANTABILITY OR FITNESS THEREOF FOR ANY PURPOSE OR CONCERNING THE ACCURACY OF ANY INFORMATION PROVIDED BY BORDEN, except that the product shall conform to contracted specifications.** * * *

* * * *

We agree with Advent that the sales invoice in the present case is * * * ineffective as a disclaimer of warranties. Advent asserts, and this court confirms, that the print on the reverse side of the invoice is no larger than one-sixteenth inch in height. All of the type appears to be boldfaced. Although the disclaimer of warranties is the first of nineteen numbered paragraphs, * * * nevertheless there is nothing to indicate that the first paragraph is any more significant than, for example, the seventh ("WEIGHTS") or the tenth ("CARRIER AND ROUTING").

Even more important, the reference on the front of the invoice to the terms on the reverse side is even less informative * * * . The reference in the present case simply states "SEE REVERSE SIDE"; there is absolutely no indication that among the terms on the reverse side is an exclusion of warranties, including a warranty (namely, the implied warranty of merchantability) so commonly taken for granted that its exclusion from a contract is recognized as a matter threatening surprise * * * .

* * * *

* * * Accordingly, we conclude that the disclaimer stated on Borden's invoice was inconspicuous and, consequently, ineffective.

Borden's argument that it disclaimed the warranties at issue therefore rests upon the language appearing on the drum labels. * * * As Advent points out, * * * the disclaimer is printed in very small type. In fact, it appears to this Court that the typeface, like that of the disclaimer on the back of the invoice, is one-sixteenth of an inch high. Moreover, all of the print on the label appears to be boldfaced; thus, the fact that the disclaimer and accompanying paragraph are boldfaced does not make them stand out. Finally, while the heading "DISCLAIMER" and the disclaimer itself are printed in capitals, so too are the preceding lines of text, and they are printed in larger sizes of type. Taking into account all of these factors, we conclude that this disclaimer, like that on the invoice, is inconspicuous and therefore ineffective.

* * * *

III. Conclusion

Although Advent has succeeded in demonstrating that Borden's disclaimers of warranties were inconspicuous and thus unenforceable, it has been unable to demonstrate that Borden's limitation of damages clause [is not enforceable]. Therefore, the clause is enforceable, and on that basis we affirm the order entering summary judgment in favor of Borden.

CASE PROBLEMS

22–1. Myrtle Carpenter purchased hair dye from a drugstore. The use of the dye caused an adverse skin reaction. She sued the local drugstore and the manufacturer of the dye, Alberto Culver Co. Carpenter claimed that a salesclerk had indicated that several of Carpenter's friends used the product and that their hair came out "very nice." The clerk purportedly also told Carpenter that she would get very fine results. On the package, there were cautionary directions instructing the user to make a preliminary skin test to determine if the user was sensitive in any unusual way to the product. Carpenter stated that she had not made the preliminary skin test. Did the seller make an express warranty about the hair dye? Explain. [*Carpenter v. Alberto Culver Co.,* 28 Mich.App. 399, 184 N.W.2d 547 (1970)]

22–2. In 1984, the Lindemann farm's cotton crop fared poorly because of lack of weed control. That year, and every year since the early 1960s, the Lindemanns had used Treflan, an herbicide manufactured by Eli Lilly and Co. The label specifically stated that Treflan would control weeds when used according to label instructions. The Treflan label recommended that the herbicide be incorporated into the soil twice after it had been sprayed. The purpose of the double incorporation was to provide greater uniformity in the herbicide's distribution. The Lindemanns, in an effort to create still greater uniformity in the distribution of the Treflan, made an application by spraying half the amount of a normal application in one direction and half in the opposite direction. Each spraying was incorporated into the soil after it had been applied. If the instructions did not contain a specific directive calling for a single application, could the Lindemanns recover for breach of express warranty of the herbicide to control weeds? Discuss. [*Lindemann v. Eli Lilly and Co.*, 816 F.2d 199 (5th Cir. 1987)]

22–3. On December 22, 1980, Jack M. Crothers purchased a used 1970 Dodge from Maurice Boyd, a sales agent employed by Norman Cohen, the owner of Norm's Auto Sales. On December 23, 1980, Crothers was seriously injured when the Dodge he had just purchased went out of control and crashed into a tree. Crothers filed suit, asserting breach of an express warranty based on Boyd's representation to Crothers that the 1970 Dodge had a rebuilt carburetor and was a "good runner." Did Boyd's representations amount to an express warranty? [*Crothers by Crothers v. Cohen*, 384 N.W.2d 562 (Minn.App. 1986)]

22–4. While passing by the American Kennels pet store, owned by defendant George Rosenthal, Ruby Dempsey, the plaintiff, decided to purchase a pedigreed white poodle. Dempsey told the salesperson that she wanted a dog suitable for breeding purposes. She purchased the poodle, whom she named Mr. Dunphy. Five days later, the dog was examined by a veterinarian and was discovered to have a congenital defect. Dempsey returned to the store and demanded a refund of the purchase price. The store refused, and Dempsey filed suit. Dempsey claimed that the defendant was liable for breach of the implied warranties of merchantability and fitness for a particular purpose. The defendant claimed that the poodle was still capable of breeding and thus no warranties had been breached. Discuss fully whether Dempsey was successful. [*Dempsey v. Rosenthal*, 121 Misc.2d 612, 468 N.Y.S.2d 441 (1983)]

22–5. In March 1986, Donald Laird discussed the purchase of corn with the manager of Scribner Cooperative, Inc., Gary Ruwe, whom Laird had trained for his job as manager. Ruwe told Laird that the co-op was having some heating problems in its corn storage bins, but Laird said that he would take four loads (about 1,300 bushels) of corn if Ruwe would "pull out the center and pull out all the damaged corn and get the fines [the fine bits of corn kernel knocked off during handling of the grain] out of the center." On inspecting the corn after it was delivered, Laird noticed damaged corn and a silage odor (which is the result of a fermentation process caused by heating). Although Laird was dissatisfied with the corn, he did not reject it. After Laird began feeding his hogs the corn, the hogs became ill. Eventually, it was concluded that the problem might be in the corn. In October 1986, Laird asked the University of Nebraska to test the corn, and traces of a toxic substance called vomitoxin were found in the corn. The veterinarian tending Laird's hogs testified that their symptoms were the direct result of feed containing vomitoxin. Laird sued the co-op for breach of the implied warranties of merchantability and fitness for a particular purpose. How should the court rule? Discuss. [*Laird v. Scribner Coop, Inc.*, 237 Neb. 532, 466 N.W. 2d 798 (1991)]

22–6. Arvo Lake, a retired seventy-one-year-old man, bought an air conditioner in May 1986. The unit was installed and operated according to the manufacturer's instructions. Unbeknownst to Lake, the unit contained a hole in the refrigeration system that allowed Freon, the coolant, to escape from the unit. By August, the unit had ceased cooling, and Lake's residence reached a temperature of at least ninety-six degrees Fahrenheit. The heat caused Lake to suffer from hypothermia, which led to circulatory failure and death. The executor of Lake's estate, David Garavalia, sued the manufacturer of the air conditioner for damages. For a manufacturer to be liable for consequential damages caused by a breach of warranty, the consequential damages must be foreseeable to the manufacturer. Was the risk of death from an air conditioner that failed to operate properly foreseeable, given Lake's age and the climate in southern Illinois in the summer? How should the court rule on this issue? Discuss fully. [*Garavalia v. Heat Controller, Inc.*, 212 Ill.App.3d 380, 570 N.E.2d 1227, 156 Ill.Dec. 505 (1991)]

22–7. Vertis Smith was considering buying a used car from Fitzner Pontiac-Buick-Cadillac, Inc. He particularly liked a 1982 Oldsmobile Cutlass on the lot and took it for a test drive. Smith then told Fitzner's sales representative that if Fitzner would fix a rattle he had heard and paint the car, he would purchase it for $7,475. The salesperson agreed to have these things done and assured Smith that when the car was delivered, it would be in "first class shape." Fitzner performed as agreed, and the car was delivered shortly thereafter to Smith. During the next few months, Smith had to install a new intake gasket, a new transmission, and a new radiator—repairs that were made by others, not Fitzner. Fitzner repaired a broken taillight and adjusted a window mechanism. In addition, Smith claimed that the car stalled frequently in traffic and got only eleven miles per gallon of gas. Nine months after he had purchased the car, Smith returned it to Fitzner and requested a refund of the purchase price plus the cost of the repairs, alleging, among other things, that Fitzner had breached an express warranty. Discuss fully whether Fitzner's statement that the car would be delivered in "first class shape" constituted an express warranty. [*Fitzner Pontiac-Buick-Cadillac, Inc. v. Smith,* 523 So.2d 324 (Miss. 1988)]

22–8. Khalid Ismael purchased a used 1985 Ford Tempo automobile from Goodman Toyota for $5,054 "as is," along with a Vehicle Service Agreement for $695. The service agreement was to cover repairs occurring during the first 24 months or first 24,000 miles, whichever came first. When Ismael test-drove the car prior to the purchase, it shook. Goodman's salesperson assured Ismael that the Tempo "probably just needed a tune-up and that Goodman would repair anything that was found wrong with the car at no charge." Ismael purchased the Tempo based on Goodman's assurances and the service agreement. During the first four months, Ismael was able to use the car for less than two weeks, and during the first six months the Tempo was in for repair six times. Having given up on Goodman's ability to repair the car, Ismael took it to a Ford dealer, who said the car was beyond repair due to "sludge in the engine." Ismael sued Goodman, asserting that Goodman had breached the implied warranty of merchantability. Goodman claimed that it should not be held liable, because the sale of the car "as is" effectively disclaimed the implied warranty of merchantability. Who will win in court, and why? Discuss fully. [*Ismael v. Goodman Toyota,* 106 N.C.App. 421, 417 S.E.2d 290 (1992)]

22–9. Robert Levondosky was a patron at Harrah's Marina Hotel Casino, an Atlantic City casino owned by Marina Associates. While playing at one of the casino's tables, he ordered a cocktail, which was served free of charge—it was the casino's custom to give complimentary drinks to patrons at the gambling tables. Levondosky alleged that he swallowed a few thin chips of glass from the rim of the glass in which the drink was served and, as a result, suffered internal injuries. Levondosky sued the casino, contending that the casino had breached an implied warranty of merchantability. In evaluating this claim, the court had to determine (1) whether a "sale" had in fact occurred, which is prerequisite to the creation of an implied warranty of merchantability, and (2) whether the casino gave an implied warranty as to the glass as well as to the drink within it. Review UCC 2–314, and discuss how the court should rule on both issues. [*Levondosky v. Marina Associates,* 731 F.Supp. 1210 (D.N.J. 1990)]

22–10. Hall Farms, Inc., in Knox County, Indiana, produces a variety of crops, including watermelons. In August 1988, Hall Farms ordered forty pounds of the Prince Charles variety of watermelon seeds from Martin Rispens & Son. At the top of Rispens's purchase order was the phrase "strictly high grade seeds." Rispens obtained the seeds from Petoseed and delivered them in February 1989, packaged in sealed one-pound cans. The labels on the cans stated that they contained "top quality seeds." Hall Farms stored the unopened cans until early April, when the seeds were germinated in two greenhouses. On April 25, Mark Hall, the owner of Hall Farms, noted that about fifteen seedlings were spotted with small yellow lesions. The lesions did not affect the plants' growth, however, and no plants died. The seedlings were transplanted to the fields in May. Hall monitored the plants every three or four days for the next several weeks. In early July, Hall spotted a watermelon blemished by a small purple blotch. By mid-July, the blotch had spread to other plants, and by harvest time ten days later, a significant portion of the watermelon crop had been ruined. Hall Farms sued Rispens and Petoseed, arguing, in part, that the phrases on Rispens's purchase order and Petoseed's cans constituted express warranties, which they breached. When Petoseed and Rispens were granted a summary judgment, Hall Farms appealed. Were Petoseed and Rispens entitled to summary judgment on this issue? Why, or why not? Discuss fully. [*Martin Rispens & Son v. Hall Farms, Inc.,* 621 N.E.2d 1078 (Ind. 1993)]

22–11. Blue Ship Tea Room, Inc., was located in Boston in an old building overlooking the ocean. Webster, who had been born and raised in New England, went to the restaurant and ordered fish chowder. The chowder was milky in color. After three or four spoonfuls, she felt something lodged in her throat. As a result, she underwent two esophagoscopies; in the second esophagoscopy, a fish bone was found and removed. Webster filed suit against the restaurant in a Massachusetts state court for breach of the implied warranty of merchantability. The jury rendered a verdict for Webster, and the restaurant appealed to the state's highest court. What will happen on appeal? Discuss. [*Webster v. Blue Ship Tea Room, Inc.,* 347 Mass. 421, 198 N.E.2d 309 (1964)]

22–12. On March 13, 1980, Judith Roth went to the hairdresser she had been using for the past seven years, at Ray-Stel's Hair Stylists, Inc., to have her hair bleached. The hair stylist used a new bleaching product, manufactured by Roux Laboratories, Inc., on Roth's hair. Although other Roux products had been used previously with excellent results, the use of the new product resulted in damage to Roth's hair that caused her embarrassment and anguish for the next several months as her hair grew back. The product's label had guaranteed it would not cause damage to a user's hair. Roth sued Ray-Stel's and Roux Laboratories, alleging, among other claims, breach of express warranty resulting in personal injuries to her. Discuss whether there was a breach of express warranty. [*Roth v. Ray-Stel's Hair Stylists, Inc.,* 18 Mass.App. 975, 470 N.E.2d 137 (1984)]

22–13. Prestige Motorcar Imports, Inc., advertised a used 1984 Aston Martin Lagonda for sale for $57,600. The car came with a written warranty that covered specific items. Gary Davenport had the car inspected, then bought it. Over the next couple of days, he had the car inspected further and learned that it needed $13,000 worth of repairs, none of which was covered by the written warranty. He complained to Irvin David, owner of Prestige, who offered to refund Davenport's money or fix the car. Davenport refused both and filed a suit in a Florida state court against David and Prestige, in part for breach of warranty. On what grounds might the court issue a judgment against Davenport? [*David v. Davenport,* 656 So.2d 952 (Fla.App.3d 1995)]

22–14. Marilyn Keaton entered an A.B.C. Drug store to buy a half-gallon bottle of liquid bleach. The bottles were stacked at a height above her eye level. She reached up, grasped the handle of one of the bottles, and began pulling it down from the shelf. The cap was loose, however, causing bleach to splash into her face, injuring her eye. Keaton filed a suit in a Georgia state court against A.B.C., alleging, in part, breach of the implied warranty of merchantability. She claimed that the bleach had not been adequately packaged. A.B.C. argued, in part, that Keaton had failed to exercise care for her own safety. Had A.B.C. breached the implied warranty of merchantability? Discuss. [*Keaton v. A.B.C. Drug Co.,* 266 Ga. 385, 467 S.E.2d 558 (1996)]

22–15. Ronald Anderson, Jr., a self-employed construction contractor, went to a Home Depot store to buy lumber for a construction project. It was raining, so Anderson bought a tarp to cover the bed of his pickup truck. To secure the tarp, Anderson bought a bag of cords made by Bungee International Manufacturing Corp. The printed material on the Bungee bag included the words "Made in the U.S.A." and "Premium Quality." To secure the tarp at the rear of the passenger's side, Anderson put one hook into the eyelet of the tarp, stretched the cord over the utility box, and hooked the other end in the drainage hole in the bottom of the box. As Anderson stood up, the upper hook dislodged and hit him in the left eye. Anderson filed a suit in a federal district court against Bungee and others, alleging in part breach of express warranty. Anderson alleged that the labeling on the bag of cords was an express warranty that "played some role in [his] decision to purchase this product." Bungee argued that, in regard to the cords' quality, the statements were puffery. Bungee filed a motion for summary judgment on this issue. Will the court grant the motion? Why, or why not? [*Anderson v. Bungee International Manufacturing Corp.,* 44 F.Supp.2d 534 (S.D.N.Y. 1999)]

E-LINKS

For updated links to resources available on the Web, as well as a variety of other materials, visit this text's Web site at

http://wbl-cs.westbuslaw.com

To find information on the UCC, including the UCC provisions discussed in this chapter, refer to the Web sites listed in the *E-Links* feature in Chapter 18.

For an example of an "as is" clause, see the warranty disclaimer provided by the University of Minnesota for one of its research software products at

http://www.cmrr.drad.umn.edu/stimulate/stimUsersGuide/node7.html

LEGAL RESEARCH EXERCISES ON THE WEB

Go to http://wbl-cs.westbuslaw.com, the Web site that accompanies this text. Select "Interactive Study Center," and then click on "Chapter 22." There you will find the following Internet research exercise that you can perform to learn more about warranty law:

Activity 22–1: Warranties

CHAPTER 23
E-Contracts

MANY OBSERVERS ARGUE that the development of cyberspace is revolutionary. Therefore, new legal theories, and new laws, are needed to govern **e-contracts**, or contracts entered into electronically. To date, however, most courts have adapted traditional contract law principles and, when applicable, provisions of the Uniform Commercial Code (UCC) to cases involving e-contract disputes.

In the first part of this chapter, we look at how traditional laws are being applied to contracts formed online. We then examine some new laws that have been created to apply in situations in which traditional laws governing contracts have sometimes been thought inadequate. For example, traditional laws governing signature and writing requirements are not easily adapted to contracts formed in the online environment. Thus, new laws have been promulgated to address these issues.

SECTION 1

Online Contract Formation

Today, numerous contracts are being formed online. Many of these contracts involve business-to-consumer sales, or **B2C transactions.** Consumers purchase books, CDs, software, airline tickets, clothing, computers, and a host of other goods via the Internet. An increasing number of transactions involve business-to-business sales, or **B2B transactions.** Although the medium through which these sales contracts are generated has changed, the age-old problems attending contract formation have not. Disputes concerning contracts formed online continue to center around contract terms and whether the parties voluntarily assented to those terms.

ONLINE OFFERS

Sellers doing business via the Internet can protect themselves against contract disputes and legal liability by creating offers that clearly spell out the terms that will govern their transactions if the offers are accepted. All important terms should be conspicuous and easily viewed by potential buyers. The seller's Web site should include a hypertext link to a page containing the full contract so that potential buyers are made aware of the terms to which they are assenting. An important rule to keep in mind is that the offeror controls the offer, and thus the resulting contract. This means that you should anticipate what terms you want to include in a contract and provide for them in the offer.

At a minimum, the following provisions should be included in an online offer:

1. A provision specifying the remedies available to the buyer if the goods turn out to be defective or if the contract is otherwise breached, or broken. Any limitation of remedies should be clearly spelled out.
2. The statute of limitations governing the transaction (that is, the time period within which a legal action can be brought over a dispute concerning the contract).
3. A clause that clearly indicates what constitutes the buyer's agreement to the terms of the offer.
4. A provision specifying how payment for the goods and of any applicable taxes must be made.
5. A statement of the seller's refund and return policies.
6. Disclaimers of liability for certain uses of the goods. For example, an online seller of business forms may add a disclaimer that the seller does not accept responsibility for the buyer's reliance on the forms rather than on an attorney's advice.

7. How the information gathered about the buyer will be used by the seller. (See the discussion of privacy rights in Chapter 4 for more information on this topic.)

Dispute-Settlement Provisions. In addition to the above provisions, many online offers include provisions relating to dispute settlement. For example, an arbitration clause might be included, specifying that if any dispute arises under the contract the dispute will be arbitrated in a designated forum.

Many online contracts also contain a forum-selection clause (indicating the forum, or location, for the resolution of any dispute that may arise under the contract). As discussed in Chapter 2, significant jurisdictional issues may arise when parties are at a great distance, as they often are when they form contracts via the Internet. This clause will help to avert future jurisdictional problems and also help ensure that the seller will not be required to appear in court in a distant state.

Displaying the Offer. The seller's Web site should include a hypertext link to a page containing the full contract so that potential buyers are made aware of the terms to which they are assenting. The contract generally must be displayed online in a readable format such as 12-point typeface. All provisions should be reasonably clear. For example, if a seller is offering certain goods priced according to a complex price schedule, that schedule must be fully provided and explained.

Indicating How the Offer Can Be Accepted. An online offer should also include some mechanism by which the customer may accept the offer. Typically, online sellers include boxes containing the words "I agree" or "I accept the terms of the offer" that offerees can click on to indicate acceptance.

Online Acceptances

In many ways, **click-on agreements** are the Internet equivalents of **shrink-wrap agreements** (or *shrink-wrap licenses,* as they are sometimes called). A *shrink-wrap agreement* is an agreement the terms of which are expressed inside a box in which the goods are packaged. (The term *shrink-wrap* refers to the plastic that covers the box.) Usually, the party who opens the box is told that he or she agrees to the terms by keeping whatever is in the box. When the purchaser opens the box, such as a software package, he or she agrees to abide by the terms of the limited license agreement.

For example, John orders a new computer from a national company, which ships the computer to John. The box contains an agreement setting forth the terms of the sale, including what remedies are available and so on. The document also states that John's retention of the computer for longer than thirty days will be construed as an acceptance of the terms.

In most cases, a shrink-wrap agreement is not between a retailer and a buyer, but between the manufacturer of the hardware or software and the ultimate buyer-user of the product. The terms generally concern warranties, remedies, and other matters associated with the use of the product.

We look next at how the law has been applied to both shrink-wrap and click-on agreements.

Shrink-Wrap Agreements—Enforceable Contract Terms. Section 2-204 of the Uniform Commercial Code (UCC), the law governing sales contracts, provides that any contract for the sale of goods "may be made in any manner sufficient to show agreement, including conduct by both parties which recognizes the existence of a contract." Thus, a buyer's failure to object to terms contained inside a shrink-wrapped software package (or in an online offer) may constitute an acceptance of the terms by conduct.

In many cases, the courts have enforced the terms of shrink-wrap agreements in the same way as the terms of other contracts. Some courts have reasoned that by including the terms with the product, the seller proposed a contract that the buyer could accept by using the product after having an opportunity to read the terms.

Also, it seems practical from a business's point of view to enclose a full statement of the legal terms of a sale with the product rather than to read the statement over the phone—for example, when a buyer calls in an order for the product.

See Case 23.1 at the end of this chapter. To view the full, unedited case from Westlaw,® go to this text's Web site at **http://wbl-cs.westbuslaw.com**.

Shrink-Wrap Agreements—Proposals for Additional Terms. Not all of the terms presented in shrink-wrap agreements have been enforced. One important consideration is whether the parties form their contract before or after the seller communicates the terms of the shrink-wrap agreement to the buyer. If a court finds that the buyer learned of the shrink-wrap terms *after* the parties entered into a contract, the court might conclude that those terms were proposals for additional terms, which were not part of the contract unless the buyer expressly agreed to them.

Westlaw. See Case 23.2 at the end of this chapter. To view the full, unedited case from Westlaw,® go to this text's Web site at **http://wbl-cs.westbuslaw.com**.

Click-On Agreements. As described earlier, a click-on agreement (also sometimes called a *click-on license* or *click-wrap agreement*) arises when a buyer, completing a transaction on a computer, is required to indicate his or her assent to be bound by the terms of an offer by clicking on a button that says, for example, "I agree." The terms may be contained on a Web site through which the buyer is obtaining goods or services, or they may appear on a computer screen when software is loaded. Exhibit 23–1 contains the language of a click-on agreement that accompanies a package of software made and marketed by Adobe Systems, Inc.

As noted, Article 2 of the UCC provides that acceptance can be made by conduct. The *Restatement (Second) of Contracts*, a compilation of common law contract principles, has a similar provision. It states that parties may agree to a contract "by written or spoken words or by other action or by failure to act."[1] The courts have used these provisions to conclude that a binding contract can be created by conduct, whether it be an acceptance of terms in a shrink-wrap agreement or those in a click-on agreement.

Generally, under the law governing contracts, including sales and lease contracts under the UCC, there is no requirement that all of the terms in a contract actually must have been read by all of the parties to be effective. For example, clicking on a button or box that states "I agree" to certain terms can be enough.

See Case 23.3 at the end of this chapter. To view the full, unedited case from Westlaw,® go to this text's Web site at **http://wbl-cs.westbuslaw.com**.

Browse-Wrap Terms. Like the terms of a click-on agreement, **browse-wrap terms** can be included in a transaction conducted over the Internet. The difference between a click-on agreement and browse-wrap terms is that the latter do not require an

1. *Restatement (Second) of Contracts*, Section 19.

EXHIBIT 23–1 A CLICK-ON AGREEMENT

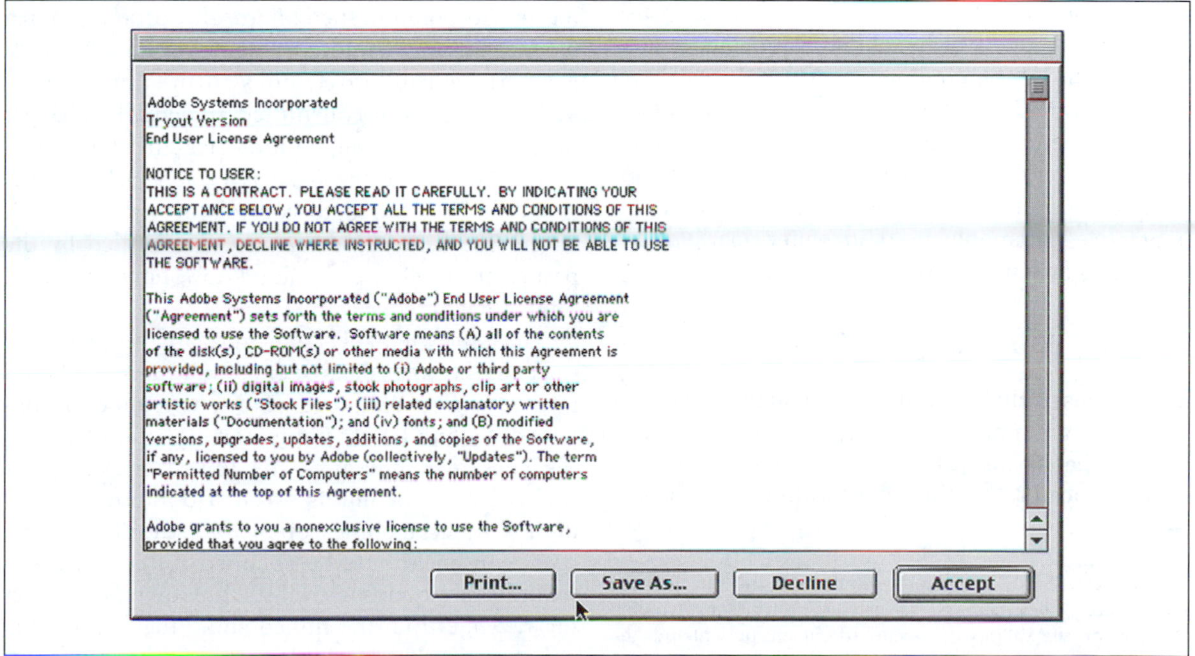
Adobe Systems Incorporated
Tryout Version
End User License Agreement

NOTICE TO USER:
THIS IS A CONTRACT. PLEASE READ IT CAREFULLY. BY INDICATING YOUR ACCEPTANCE BELOW, YOU ACCEPT ALL THE TERMS AND CONDITIONS OF THIS AGREEMENT. IF YOU DO NOT AGREE WITH THE TERMS AND CONDITIONS OF THIS AGREEMENT, DECLINE WHERE INSTRUCTED, AND YOU WILL NOT BE ABLE TO USE THE SOFTWARE.

This Adobe Systems Incorporated ("Adobe") End User License Agreement ("Agreement") sets forth the terms and conditions under which you are licensed to use the Software. Software means (A) all of the contents of the disk(s), CD-ROM(s) or other media with which this Agreement is provided, including but not limited to (i) Adobe or third party software; (ii) digital images, stock photographs, clip art or other artistic works ("Stock Files"); (iii) related explanatory written materials ("Documentation"); and (iv) fonts; and (B) modified versions, upgrades, updates, additions, and copies of the Software, if any, licensed to you by Adobe (collectively, "Updates"). The term "Permitted Number of Computers" means the number of computers indicated at the top of this Agreement.

Adobe grants to you a nonexclusive license to use the Software, provided that you agree to the following:

Internet user to assent to the terms before, say, downloading or using particular software. In other words, a person can install the software without clicking "I agree" to the terms of a license. Offerors of browse-wrap terms generally assert that the terms are binding without the users' active consent.

Critics contend that browse-wrap terms are not enforceable because they do not satisfy the basic elements of contract formation. It has been suggested that to form a valid contract online, a user must at least be presented with the terms before indicating assent.[2] In the case of a browse-wrap term, this would require that a user navigate past it and agree to it before being able to obtain whatever is being granted to the user.

Westlaw. See Case 23.4 at the end of this chapter. To view the full, unedited case from Westlaw,® go to this text's Web site at **http://wbl-cs.westbuslaw.com**.

SECTION 2

Linking and Framing

Generally, online sellers must be careful to operate within the parameters established by the laws covered in this text. For example, businesses are prohibited from making statements about their products or services that would deceive or mislead consumers. You will read about the laws prohibiting deceptive advertising in Chapter 44, in the context of consumer protection. Privacy laws (see Chapter 4) also place limits on how personal information about consumers who visit an online merchant's Web site can be utilized. Additionally, the unauthorized use of another's trademark in marketing, for example, could result in extensive liability under trademark law (see Chapter 7). Here we examine how the law applies to a practice commonly used in online marketing—linking to or framing others' Web pages.

Linking to Others' Web Pages

When a user clicks on an icon or highlighted text that is programmed to be a hypertext link, the user is immediately taken to a new online location. The link may lead to another point within the same site or to a different, unrelated site somewhere else in cyberspace.

Sometimes, a site owner asks the permission of other owners to link to their sites, but this is not generally done. Linking is legal and does not require permission. Linking is considered one of the primary factors in the success of Internet commerce and is part of the revolution of the new technology. Site owners are less agreeable to *framing*, however.

Framing Others' Web Pages

If a linking site is a framing site, the pages of the linked site will appear in a window of the original site. With frames, a single site can let users view several sites simultaneously. Using linking and framing technology, any site owner can divert traffic from another site. This may be desired because search engines base their results on the number of hits (visits to a site). More hits can mean more advertising revenue and more sales. An owner may even appropriate a competitor's content and hide it, so that an unsuspecting user is transported to the appropriator's site even though he or she cannot see the appropriated material. This is a violation of trademark law (and copyright law).

Although the law is not settled on this issue, framing has given rise to lawsuits alleging trademark violation. For example, in one case, Ticketmaster Corporation sued Microsoft Corporation in a federal district court, alleging that Microsoft Network's unauthorized links to interior pages of Ticketmaster's site constituted trademark infringement and unfair competition. Ticketmaster argued that its Web site is the same as a trademark and that it should be allowed to control the way in which others use it. Because the case was settled by the parties in 1999, we do not know how the court might have ruled.

The issue will likely come up again, however, and to be on the safe side, owners of linking sites should take several precautions. Consent should be obtained if a link falsely implies an affiliation between the sites, if a link uses the linked site's logo or trademark, if the link is "deep" (to internal pages), or if a frame modifies or distorts the linked site. Also, consent should be obtained if the linked site requests or requires it, or if the link diverts advertising revenue from the linked site. Finally, a linking site should include a disclaimer.

2. American Bar Association's Committee on the Law of Cyberspace, "Click-Through Agreements: Strategies for Avoiding Disputes on the Validity of Assent" (document presented at the annual American Bar Association meeting in August 2001).

SECTION 3

E-Signatures

In many cases a contract, to be enforced, requires the signature of the party against whom enforcement is sought. A significant issue in the context of e-commerce has to do with how electronic signatures, or **e-signatures**, can be created and verified on e-contracts.

Before the days when most people could write, they signed documents with an "X." Then came the handwritten signature, followed by typed signatures, printed signatures, and, most recently, digital signatures that are transmitted electronically. Throughout the evolution of signature technology, debates over what constitutes a valid signature have occurred, and with good reason—without some consensus on what constitutes a valid signature, little business or legal work could be accomplished.

E-SIGNATURE TECHNOLOGIES

Today, there are numerous technologies that allow electronic documents to be signed. These include digital signatures and alternative technologies.

Digital Signatures. The most prevalent e-signature technology is the *asymmetric cryptosystem,* which creates a digital signature using two different (asymmetric) cryptographic "keys." In such a system, a person attaches a digital signature to a document using a private key, or code. The key has a publicly available counterpart. Anyone can use it with the appropriate software to verify that the digital signature was made using the private key. A **cybernotary,** or legally recognized certification authority, issues the key pair, identifies the owner of the keys, and certifies the validity of the public key. The cybernotary also serves as a repository for public keys. Cybernotaries already are available, but they do not operate within any existing legal framework because they are so new.

Signature Dynamics. Another type of signature technology, known as *signature dynamics,* involves capturing a sender's signature using a stylus and an electronic digitizer pad. A computer program takes the signature's measurements, the sender's identity, the time and date of the signature, and the identity of the hardware. This information is then placed in an encrypted *biometric token* attached to the document being transmitted. To verify the authenticity of the signature, the recipient of the document compares the measurements of the signature with the measurements in the token. When this type of e-signature is used, it is not necessary to have a third party verify the signatory's identity.

Other Forms of E-Signature. Other forms of e-signature have been—or are now being—developed as well. For example, some e-signatures use "smart cards." A smart card is a credit-card–size device that is embedded with code and other data. As with credit and debit cards, this smart card can be inserted into computers to transfer information. Unlike those other cards, however, a smart card could be used to establish a person's identity as validly as a signature on a piece of paper. In addition, technological innovations now under way will allow an e-signature to be evidenced by an image of one's retina, fingerprint, or face that is scanned by a computer and then matched to a numeric code. The scanned image and the numeric code are registered with security companies that maintain files on an accessible server that can be used to authenticate a transaction.

STATE LAWS GOVERNING E-SIGNATURES

Most states have laws governing e-signatures. The problem is that the state e-signature laws are not uniform. Some states—California is a notable example—provide that many types of documents cannot be signed with e-signatures, while other states are more permissive in this respect. Additionally, some states recognize the validity of only digital signatures, while others permit other types of e-signatures.

In an attempt to create more uniformity among the states, the National Conference of Commissioners on Uniform State Laws promulgated the Uniform Electronic Transactions Act (UETA) in 1999. The UETA defines an *e-signature* as "an electronic sound, symbol, or process attached to or logically associated with a record and executed or adopted by a person with the intent to sign the record."[3] A **record** is "information that is inscribed on a tangible medium or that is stored in an electronic or other medium and is retrievable in perceivable [visual] form."[4]

This definition of *e-signature* includes encrypted digital signatures, names (intended as signatures) at

3. UETA 102(8).
4. UETA 102(15).

the ends of e-mail, and a click on a Web page if the click includes the identification of the person. The UETA also states, among other things, that a signature may not be denied legal effect or enforceability solely because it is in an electronic form. (Other aspects of the UETA will be discussed later in this chapter.)

FEDERAL LAW ON E-SIGNATURES AND E-DOCUMENTS

In 2000, Congress enacted the Electronic Signatures in Global and National Commerce Act (E-SIGN Act) to provide that no contract, record, or signature may be "denied legal effect" solely because it is in an electronic form. In other words, under this law, an electronic signature is as valid as a signature on paper, and an electronic document can be as enforceable as a paper one.

For an electronic signature to be enforceable, the contracting parties must have agreed to use electronic signatures. For an electronic document to be valid, it must be in a form that can be retained and accurately reproduced.

Contracts and documents that are exempt include court papers, divorce decrees, evictions, foreclosures, health-insurance terminations, prenuptial agreements, and wills. Also, the only agreements governed by the Uniform Commercial Code (UCC) that fall under this law are those covered by Articles 2 and 2A, and UCC 1-107 and 1-206.

Despite the limitations, the E-SIGN Act expands enormously the possibilities for contracting online. For example, from a remote location, a businessperson might open an account with a financial institution, obtain a mortgage or other loan, buy insurance, and purchase real estate over the Internet. Payments and transfers of funds could be done entirely online. This can avoid the time and costs associated with producing, delivering, signing, and returning paper documents.

SECTION 4

Partnering Agreements

One way that online sellers and buyers can prevent disputes over signatures in their e-contracts, as well as over the terms and conditions of those contracts, is to form partnering agreements. In a **partnering agreement**, a seller and a buyer who frequently do business with each other agree in advance on the terms and conditions that will apply to all transactions subsequently conducted electronically. The partnering agreement can also establish special access and identification codes to be used by the buyer and seller when transacting business electronically.

A partnering agreement reduces the likelihood that disputes under the contract will arise, because the buyer and the seller have agreed, in their partnering agreement, to the terms and conditions that will accompany each sale. Furthermore, if a dispute does arise, a court or arbitration forum will be able to refer to the partnering agreement when determining the parties' intent with respect to subsequent contracts. Of course, even with a partnering agreement there remains the possibility of fraud. If an unauthorized person uses a purchaser's designated access number and identification code, it may be some time before the problem is discovered.

SECTION 5

The Uniform Computer Information Transactions Act

In the early 1990s, with the continued development of the software industry, it became apparent that Article 2 of the Uniform Commercial Code (UCC), which deals with the sale of goods (tangible property), could not be applied to most transactions involving software.

There are two basic reasons for this. First, software is not a "good" (tangible property)—it is electronic information (intangible property). Second, the "sale" of software generally involves a license (right to use) rather than a sale (passage of title from the seller to the purchaser). The producer of the software either directly contracted with the licensee (user) or used a distribution system—for example, authorizing retailers to distribute (sell) copies of the producer's software to customers (end users). Because neither involved the sale of goods, new rules needed to be established.

These new rules were supplied by the Uniform Computer Information Transactions Act (UCITA). The UCITA is a uniform law created by the National Conference of Commissioners on Uniform State Laws (NCCUSL) and the American Law Institute (ALI). As noted earlier in this text, these organizations have initiated many of the most significant laws that apply to traditional commerce, including the Uniform Commercial Code (UCC). As with other uniform laws, the UCITA, as drafted in 1999 and amended in 2000, has been proposed to the states for adoption as law.

THE SCOPE AND APPLICABILITY OF THE UCITA

The UCITA establishes a comprehensive set of rules covering contracts involving computer information. **Computer information** is "information in electronic form obtained from or through use of a computer, or that is in digital or equivalent form capable of being processed by a computer."[5] Under this definition, the act covers contracts to license or purchase software, contracts to create a computer program, contracts for computer games, contracts for online access to databases, contracts to distribute information on the Internet, "diskettes" that contain computer programs, online books, and other similar contracts.

The UCITA, which consists of nine "parts," covers everything from the formation of a contract to construction rules, warranties available, transfer of interests and financing arrangements, performance rules, breach of contract, and remedies. This arrangement resembles that of UCC Article 2. The UCITA's Table of Contents is shown in Exhibit 23–2.

The UCITA resembles UCC Article 2. Both acts have similar general provisions, including definitions (approximately sixty-six) and formal requirements

5. UCITA 102(10).

EXHIBIT 23–2 UCITA'S TABLE OF CONTENTS

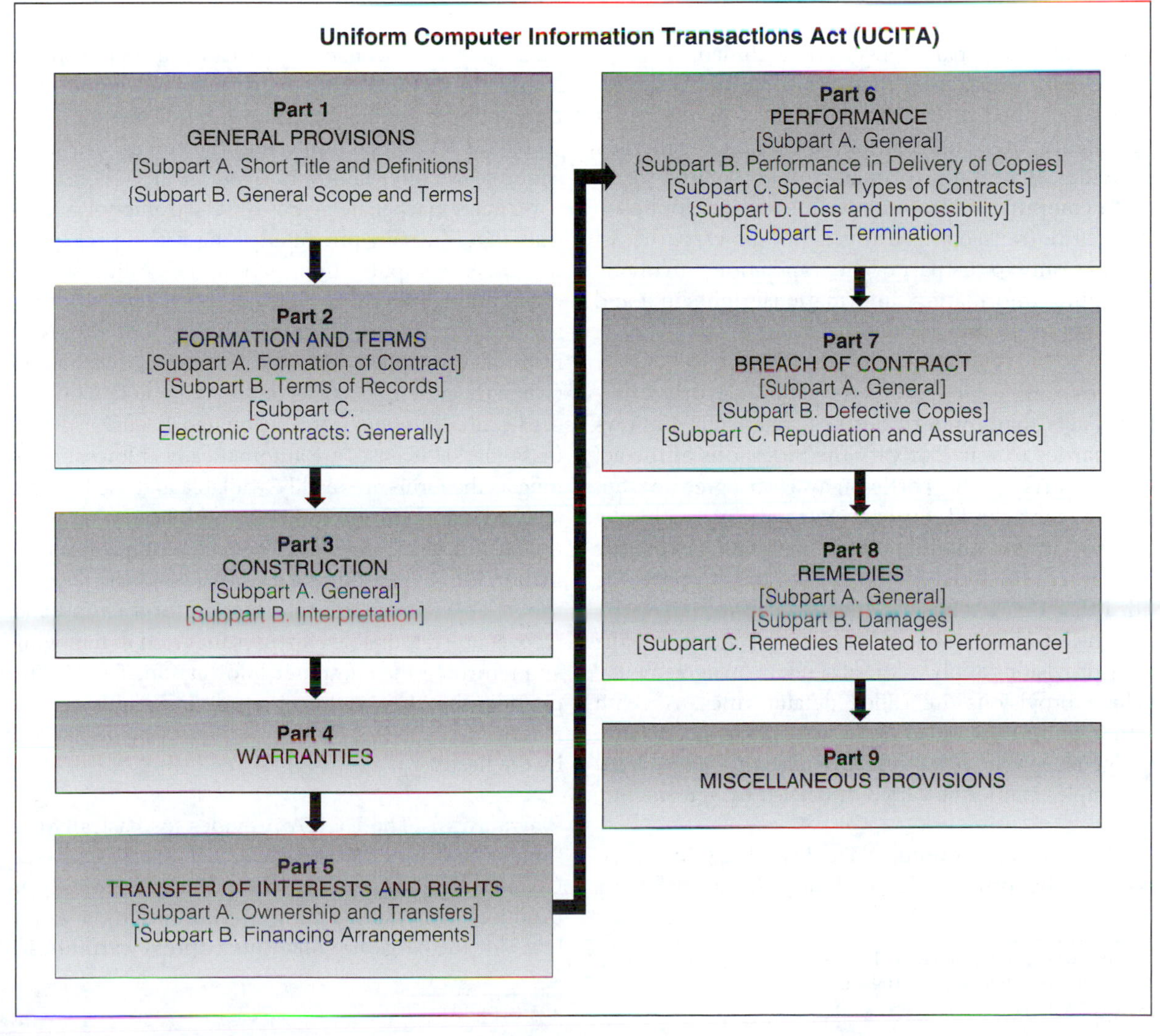

(such as a Statute of Frauds, which, in the case of the UCITA, requires a written memorandum when a contract requires a payment of $5,000 or more). The UCITA also includes rules for offer and acceptance, as well as other provisions comparable to those found in Article 2.[6] The UCITA goes further, however, with provisions covering the contracting parties' choice of law and choice of forum, the UCITA's relationship to federal law and other state laws, and many other areas.[7] These provisions make the UCITA more comprehensive in scope than UCC Article 2.

The UCITA May Apply to Only Part of a Transaction. The UCITA does not apply generally to the sale of goods even if software is embedded in or used in the production of the goods (except a computer). Examples are television sets, stereos, books, and automobiles. It also does not apply to traditional movies, records, or cable services. These industries are, for the most part, specifically excluded.

When a transaction includes computer information as defined in the act and subject matter other than computer information, the UCITA generally provides that if the primary subject matter deals with computer information rights, the act applies to the entire transaction. If this is not the case, the act applies only to the part of the transaction "involving computer information, informational rights in it and creation or modification of it."

Parties Can "Opt Out." As with most other uniform acts that apply to business, the UCITA allows the parties to waive or vary the provisions of the act by a contract. The parties may even agree to "opt out" of the act and, for contracts not covered by the act, to "opt in." In other words, the UCITA expressly recognizes the freedom to contract and supports the idea that this is a basic principle of contract law.

The UCITA stresses the parties' agreement, but the act's provisions apply in the absence of an agreement.[8] These provisions are called **default rules.** As with other uniform statutes, rules relating to good faith, diligence, public policy, unconscionability, and related principles cannot be varied or deleted by agreement.

Rights and Restrictions. The licensing of information is the primary method used for transferring computer information in business today. A license contract involves a transfer of computer information, such as software, from a seller (the licensor) to a buyer (the licensee). The licensee is given certain rights to use and control the computer information during the license period. Title does not pass, and quite often the license places restrictions on the licensee's use of, and rights to copy and control, the computer information. Many of the sections of the UCITA deal with the rights and restrictions that can be imposed on the parties in the license.

Highlights of the UCITA

In the following subsections, we describe some of the UCITA's highlights. Note that most of them address situations that arise due to the unique nature of licensing computer information.

Mass-Market Licenses. Basically, a *mass-market* transaction is either (1) a consumer contract or (2) a transaction in which the computer information is directed to the general public and the end user licensee acquires the information in a retail transaction.

A **mass-market license** is an electronic form contract that is usually presented along with a package of purchased computer information. These licenses are commonly received by having the license contract shrink-wrapped or, in the case of an online transaction, click-wrapped with the computer information (when the purchaser clicks on a certain link). These licenses are different from negotiated licenses in that mass-market licenses are automatically enforceable, as long as the terms are readily available and the licensee has had an opportunity to review the license terms.

If the licensee does not want the computer information for any reason, the UCITA allows the licensee to return the computer information for a refund and recover any reasonable expenses incurred in removing and returning the computer information. The UCITA provides that these rights of return and entitlement to reasonable expenses cannot be waived or disclaimed by the licensor.

Warranties. The UCITA provides for basically the same warranties as Article 2 of the UCC (see Chapter 22). Thus, a licensor's affirmations of fact or promises concerning computer information (as a basis for the bargain) constitute express warranties.[9]

6. See, for example, UCITA 111.
7. See, for example, UCITA 109 and 110.
8. UCITA 113.
9. UCITA 402.

Implied warranties are also provided for by the act (and can be disclaimed, as under UCC Article 2).[10] The UCITA's implied warranties of merchantability and fitness for a particular purpose are closely tailored to the information's content and the "compatibility of the computer systems."[11]

Authentication and Attribution. Before the emergence of electronic contracting, parties generally knew each other, and many contracts contained the signatures of the parties. Today, we deal with electronic signatures, or e-signatures. We want to be sure that the "person" sending the electronic message is in fact the person whose electronic message is being transmitted. For this reason, similar to the revisions of other statutes, the UCITA's rules were revised to provide for the authentication of e-signatures.

Authentication. To **authenticate** means to sign a record, or with the intent to sign a record, to execute or to adopt an electronic sound, symbol, or the like to link with the record. As noted earlier in this chapter, a *record* is information that is inscribed in either a tangible medium or stored in an electronic or other medium and that is retrievable. The UCITA uses the term *record* instead of *writing*.

Attribution Procedure. To ensure that the person sending the electronic computer information is the same person whose e-signature accompanies the information, the UCITA has a procedure, referred to as the *attribution procedure,* that sets forth steps for identifying a person who sends an electronic communication. These steps, which can be specified by the contracting parties, can be simple or complex as long as they are commercially reasonable.

Attribution procedures can also have an effect on liability for errors in the message content. If the attribution procedure is in place to detect errors, the party who conforms to the procedure is not bound by the error. Consumers who make unintended errors are not bound as long as the consumer notifies the other party promptly, returns the computer information received, and has not benefited from its use.

Access Contracts. The UCITA defines an **access contract** as "a contract to obtain by electronic means access to, or information from an information processing system of another person, or the equivalent of such access." This is important for most of us, if for no other reason than our ability to use the Internet. Section 611 of the UCITA, however, has special rules governing available times and manner of access.

Support and Service Contracts. The UCITA covers licensor support and service contracts, but no licensor is required to provide such support and service.[12] Computer software support contracts are common, and once made, the licensor is obligated to comply with the express terms of the support contract or, if the contract is silent on an issue, to do what is reasonable in light of ordinary business standards.

Electronic Self-Help. The UCITA allows the licensor to cancel, repossess, prevent continued use, and take similar actions on a licensee's breach of a license. The act permits the licensor to undertake "electronic self-help" to enforce the licensor's rights through electronic means. Outside the UCITA, "self-help" refers to the right of a lessor, for example, under Article 2A of the UCC, to repossess a leased computer if the lessee fails to make payments according to the terms of the lease. A lender may have this same right under UCC Article 9 if a borrower fails to make payments on a loan secured by a computer (for a discussion of the self-help provisions of Article 9, see Chapter 28).

In a transaction governed by the UCITA, electronic self-help includes the right of a software licensor to install a "turn-off" function in the software so that if the licensee violates the terms of the license, the software can be disabled from a distance. This right is most important to a small firm that licenses its software to a much larger company. Electronic self-help may be the licensor's only practical remedy if the license is breached.

Limitations on Electronic Self-Help. There are some limitations on this right.[13] For example, the UCITA prohibits electronic self-help in mass-market transactions. In addition, the remedy is not available unless the parties agree to permit electronic self-help. The licensor must give notice of the intent to use the self-help remedy at least fifteen days before doing so, along with full disclosure of the nature of the breach and information which will enable the licensee to cure

10. UCITA 401.
11. UCITA 403 adn 405.
12. See UCITA 612.
13. See UCITA 816.

the breach or to communicate with the licensor concerning the situation. Additionally, electronic self-help cannot be used if the licensor "has reason to know that its use will result in substantial injury or harm to the public health or safety or grave harm to the public interest affecting third persons involved in the dispute." These limitations on the use of electronic self-help cannot be waived or varied by contract.

SECTION 6

The Uniform Electronic Transactions Act

Another uniform law proposed by the NCCUSL concerning e-commerce is the Uniform Electronic Transactions Act (UETA). The goal of the UETA is not to create rules for electronic transactions—for example, the act does not require digital signatures—but to support the enforcement of e-contracts.

Under the UETA, contracts entered into online, as well as other electronic documents, are presumed valid. In other words, a contract is not unenforceable simply because it is in electronic form. The UETA does not apply to transactions governed by the UCC or the UCITA, or to wills or testamentary trusts.

There are many similarities between the UETA and the UCITA. There are also significant differences. The chief difference between the two uniform acts is that the UCITA addresses e-commerce not covered by the UETA.

SIMILARITIES BETWEEN THE UETA AND THE UCITA

The UETA and the UCITA are alike in many ways. The drafters of the laws attempted to make them consistent. Both proposals provide for such matters as the following:

1. The equivalency of records and writings.
2. The validity of e-signatures.
3. The formation of contracts by e-agents.
4. The formation of contracts between an e-agent and a natural person.
5. The attribution of an electronic act to a person if it can be proved that the act was done by the person or his or her agent.
6. A provision that parties do not need to participate in e-commerce to make binding contracts.

DIFFERENCES BETWEEN THE UETA AND THE UCITA

These two uniform laws, as mentioned, also have differences. Those differences include the following:

1. The UETA supports all electronic transactions, but it does not create rules for them. The UCITA concerns only contracts that involve computer information; for those contracts, however, the UCITA imposes rules.
2. The UETA does not apply unless contracting parties agree to use e-commerce in their transactions. The UCITA applies to any agreement that falls within its scope.

TERMS AND CONCEPTS TO REVIEW

access contract 445	click-on agreement 438	e-signature 441
authenticate 445	computer information 443	mass-market license 444
B2B transactions 437	cybernotary 441	partnering agreement 442
B2C transactions 437	default rules 444	record 441
browse-wrap terms 439	e-contract 437	shrink-wrap agreement 438

CHAPTER SUMMARY

Online Offers	Businesspersons who present contract offers via the Internet should keep in mind that the terms of the offer should be just as inclusive as the terms in an offer made in a written (paper) document. All possible contingencies should be anticipated and provided for in the offer. Because jurisdictional issues frequently arise with online transactions, it is particularly

Chapter Summary—Continued

Online Offers—continued	important to include dispute-settlement provisions in the offer, as well as a forum-selection clause. The offer should be displayed in such a way as to be easily readable and clear. An online offer should also include some mechanism, such as providing an "I agree" or "I accept" box, by which the customer may accept the offer.
Online Acceptances	**1.** *Shrink-wrap agreement—* **a.** Definition—An agreement the terms of which are expressed inside a box in which the goods are packaged. The party who opens the box is informed that, by keeping the goods in the box, he or she agrees to the terms of the shrink-wrap agreement. **b.** Enforceability—The courts have often enforced shrink-wrap agreements, even if the purchaser-user of the goods did not read the terms of the agreement. A court may deem a shrink-wrap agreement unenforceable, however, if the buyer learns of the shrink-wrap terms *after* the parties entered into the agreement. **2.** *Click-on agreement—* **a.** Definition—An agreement created when a buyer, completing a transaction on a computer, is required to indicate his or her assent to be bound by the terms of an offer by clicking on a button that says, for example, "I agree." The terms of the agreement may appear on the Web site through which the buyer is obtaining goods or services, or they may appear on a computer screen when software is downloaded. **b.** Enforceability—The courts have enforced click-on agreements, holding that by clicking "I agree," the offeree has indicated acceptance by conduct. Browse-wrap terms, however (terms in a license that an Internet user does not have to read prior to downloading the product, such as software), may not be enforced on the ground that the user is not made aware that he or she is entering into a contract.
E-Signatures	**1.** *Definition*—The Uniform Electronic Transactions Act (UETA) defines the term *e-signature* as an electronic sound, symbol, or process attached to or logically associated with a record and executed or adopted by a person with the intent to sign the record. **2.** *E-signature technologies*—These include the *asymmetric cryptosystem* (which creates a digital signature using two different cryptographic "keys"); *signature dynamics* (which involves capturing a sender's signature using a stylus and an electronic digitizer pad); a *smart card* (a device the size of a credit card that is embedded with code and other data); and, probably in the near future, scanned images of retinas, fingerprints, or other physical characteristics linked to numeric codes. **3.** *State laws governing e-signatures*—Although most states have laws governing e-signatures, these laws are not uniform. Two recently promulgated uniform acts—the UETA and the Uniform Computer Information Transactions Act (UCITA)—provide for the validity of e-signatures and may ultimately create more uniformity among the states in this respect. **4.** *Federal law on e-signatures and e-documents*—The Electronic Signatures in Global and National Commerce Act (E-SIGN Act) of 2000 gave validity to e-signatures by providing that no contract, record, or signature may be "denied legal effect" solely because it is in an electronic form.
The Uniform Computer Information Transactions Act (UCITA)	**1.** *Definition*—A uniform act submitted to the states for adoption by the National Conference of Commissioners on Uniform State Laws (NCCUSL). **2.** *Purpose*—To govern transactions involving the licensing of intangible property, such as computer information, which are not covered by Article 2 of the Uniform Commercial Code (UCC), because Article 2 deals with the sale of goods, defined as the passage of title to tangible goods from a seller to a buyer. **3.** *Coverage and content*—The act applies to contracts involving computer information, such as contracts to license or purchase software. *Computer information* is defined as "information in electronic form obtained from or through use of a computer, or that is in digital or equivalent

CHAPTER SUMMARY—CONTINUED

The Uniform Computer Information Transactions Act (UCITA)—continued	form capable of being processed by a computer." As with most other uniform acts that apply to business, the UCITA allows the parties to waive or vary its provisions by contract or even agree to "opt out" or "opt in" to UCITA provisions. The UCITA covers all aspects of e-contracts involving computer information, from contract formation to contract remedies.
The Uniform Electronic Transactions Act (UETA)	1. *Definition*—A uniform act submitted to the states for adoption by the NCCUSL. 2. *Purpose*—To create rules to support the enforcement of e-contracts. Under the UETA, contracts entered into online, as well as other documents, are presumed valid. The UETA does not apply to transactions governed by the UCC or the UCITA. 3. *The UETA and the UCITA compared*—The chief difference between the UETA and the UCITA is that the latter addresses e-commerce issues that the UETA does not. For example, the UETA does not apply unless contracting parties agree to use e-commerce in their transactions, while the UCITA applies to any agreement that falls within its scope.

CASES FOR ANALYSIS

Westlaw. You can access the full text of each case presented below by going to the Westlaw cases on this text's Web site at http://wbl-cs.westbuslaw.com. Each Westlaw case includes the names of all plaintiffs and defendants, the dates on which the case was argued and decided, a brief summary of the issues and decisions in the case, headnotes classifying specific issues in the case according to the West Key Number System, and the court's opinion. Concurring and dissenting opinions, if any, are included as well.

CASE 23.1 SHRINK-WRAP AGREEMENTS

M.A. MORTENSON CO. v. TIMBERLINE SOFTWARE CORP.
Supreme Court of Washington, 2000.
998 P.2d 305.

JOHNSON, J. [Justice]

* * * *

FACTS

Petitioner [M.A. Mortenson Company] is a nationwide construction contractor with its corporate headquarters in Minnesota and numerous regional offices, including a northwest regional office in Bellevue, Washington. Respondent Timberline [Software Corporation] is a software developer located in Beaverton, Oregon. Respondent Softworks [Data Systems, Inc.], an authorized dealer for Timberline, is located in Kirkland, Washington and provides computer-related services to contractors such as Mortenson.

Since at least 1990, Mortenson has used Timberline's *Bid Analysis* software to assist with its preparation of bids. * * * In early 1993, Mortenson installed a new computer network operating system at its Bellevue office and contacted Mark Reich (Reich), president of Softworks * * * . Reich informed Mortenson that *Precision*, a newer version of *Bid Analysis*, was compatible with its new operating system.

* * * *

After Reich provided Mortenson with a price quote, Mortenson issued a purchase order dated July 12, 1993, confirming the agreed upon purchase price, set up fee, delivery charges, and sales tax for eight copies of the software. The purchase order indicated that Softworks, on behalf of Timberline, would "[f]urnish current versions of Timberline *Precision Bid Analysis* Program Software and Keys" and "[p]rovide assistance in installation and system configuration for Mortenson's Bellevue Office." * * *

* * * *

All Timberline software is distributed to its users under license. * * * In the case of the Mortenson shipment, the full text of Timberline's license agreement was set forth on the outside of each diskette pouch and the inside cover of the instruction manuals. The first screen that appears each time the program is used also references the license and states, "[t]his software is licensed for exclusive use by: Timberline Use Only." Further, a license to use the protection device was wrapped around each of the devices shipped to Mortenson. The following warning preceded the terms of the license agreement:

> CAREFULLY READ THE FOLLOWING TERMS AND CONDITIONS BEFORE USING THE PROGRAMS. USE OF THE PROGRAMS INDICATES YOUR AC-

KNOWLEDGEMENT THAT YOU HAVE READ THIS LICENSE, UNDERSTAND IT, AND AGREE TO BE BOUND BY ITS TERMS AND CONDITIONS. * * *

Under a separate subheading, the license agreement limited Mortenson's remedies * * * .

* * * *

In December 1993, Mortenson utilized the *Precision Bid Analysis* software to prepare a bid for a project at Harborview Medical Center in Seattle. * * * After Mortenson was awarded the Harborview Medical Center project, it learned its bid was approximately $1.95 million lower than intended.

Mortenson filed an action in [a Washington state court] against Timberline and Softworks alleging breach of express and implied warranties. After the suit was filed, a Timberline internal memorandum surfaced, dated May 26, 1993. The memorandum stated, "[a] bug has been found [in the *Precision* software] * * *." Apparently, other Timberline customers had encountered the same problem and a newer version of the software was sent to some of these customers. * * *

Timberline moved for summary judgment of dismissal in July 1997, arguing the limitation on consequential damages in the licensing agreement barred Mortenson's recovery. Mortenson countered that its entire contract with Timberline consisted of the purchase order and it never saw or agreed to the provisions in the licensing agreement. The trial court granted Timberline's motion for summary judgment. * * *

Mortenson appealed the summary judgment order to [a state intermediate appellate court]. The Court of Appeals affirmed the trial court * * * . Mortenson petitioned this court for review, which we granted.

ANALYSIS

* * * *

Mortenson * * * argues * * * Timberline's delivery of the license terms merely constituted a request to add additional or different terms, which were never agreed upon by the parties. * * * Timberline responds that the terms of the license were not a request to add additional terms, but part of the contract between the parties. Timberline further argues that so-called "shrinkwrap" software licenses have been found enforceable by other courts, and that both trade usage and course of dealing support enforcement in the present case.

* * * *

[Revised Code of Washington Section 62A.2-204, Washington state's version of Uniform Commercial Code 2–204] states:

(1) A contract for sale of goods may be made *in any manner sufficient to show agreement,* including conduct by both parties which recognizes the existence of such a contract.

(2) An agreement sufficient to constitute a contract for sale may be found *even though the moment of its making is undetermined.*

(3) Even though one or more terms are left open a contract for sale does not fail for indefiniteness if the parties have intended to make a contract and there is a reasonably certain basis for giving an appropriate remedy. [Emphasis added.]

* * * *

* * * We conclude because RCW 62A.2-204 allows a contract to be formed "in any manner sufficient to show agreement * * * even though the moment of its making is undetermined," it allows the formation of "layered contracts" * * * . We, therefore, hold under RCW 62A.2-204 the terms of the license were part of the contract between Mortenson and Timberline, and Mortenson's use of the software constituted its assent to the agreement, including the license terms.

The terms of Timberline's license were either set forth explicitly or referenced in numerous locations. The terms were included within the shrinkwrap packaging of each copy of *Precision Bid Analysis;* they were present in the manuals accompanying the software; they were included with the protection devices for the software, without which the software could not be used. The fact the software was licensed was also noted on the introductory screen each time the software was used. Even accepting Mortenson's contention it never saw the terms of the license, as we must do on summary judgment, it was not necessary for Mortenson to actually read the agreement in order to be bound by it.

Furthermore, [UCC 1–201(3)] defines an "agreement" as "the bargain of the parties in fact as found in their language *or by implication from other circumstances including course of dealing or usage of trade* or course of performance * * * ." Mortenson and Timberline had a course of dealing; Mortenson had purchased licensed software from Timberline for years prior to its upgrade to *Precision Bid Analysis.* All Timberline software, including the prior version of *Bid Analysis* used by Mortenson since at least 1990, is distributed under license. Moreover, extensive testimony and exhibits before the trial court demonstrate an unquestioned use of such license agreements throughout the software industry. * * * [Emphasis added.]

As the license was part of the contract between Mortenson and Timberline, its terms are enforceable unless objectionable on grounds applicable to contracts in general.

* * * *

CONCLUSION

* * * *

We affirm the Court of Appeals, upholding the trial court's order of summary judgment of dismissal * * * .

* * * *

SANDERS, J. [Justice] (dissenting).

* * * [T]he majority abandons traditional contract principles governing offer and acceptance and relies on distinguishable cases with blind deference to software manufacturers' preferred method of conducting business. Instead of creating a new standard of contract formation—the majority's nebulous theory of "layered contracting"—I would look to the accepted principles of the Uniform Commercial Code (U.C.C.) and the common law to determine whether Timberline's licensing agreement is enforceable against Mortenson. Because the parties entered a binding and enforceable contract prior to the delivery of the software, I would treat Timberline's license agreement as a proposal to modify the contract requiring either express assent or conduct manifesting assent to those terms. * * * I would remand to the trial court to determine whether Mortenson manifested assent to the terms of Timberline's license agreement.

CASE 23.2 SHRINK-WRAP AGREEMENTS

KLOCEK V. GATEWAY, INC.
United States District Court,
District of Kansas, 2000.
104 F.Supp.2d 1332.

VRATIL, District Judge.

William S. Klocek brings suit against Gateway, Inc. * * * on claims arising from [the purchase] of a Gateway computer * * *. This matter comes before the Court on the *Motion to Dismiss* which Gateway filed November 22, 1999 * * *.

* * * *

* * * [P]laintiff * * * claims breach of contract and breach of warranty, in that Gateway breached certain warranties that its computer would be compatible with standard peripherals and standard Internet services.

Gateway asserts that plaintiff must arbitrate his claims under Gateway's Standard Terms and Conditions Agreement ("Standard Terms"). Whenever it sells a computer, Gateway includes a copy of the Standard Terms in the box which contains the computer battery power cables and instruction manuals. At the top of the first page, the Standard Terms include the following notice:

> NOTE TO THE CUSTOMER:
> This document contains Gateway 2000's Standard Terms and Conditions. By keeping your Gateway 2000 computer system beyond five (5) days after the date of delivery, you accept these Terms and Conditions.

The notice is in emphasized type and is located inside a printed box which sets it apart from other provisions of the document. The Standard Terms are four pages long and contain 16 numbered paragraphs. Paragraph 10 provides the following arbitration clause:

> DISPUTE RESOLUTION. Any dispute or controversy arising out of or relating to this Agreement or its interpretation shall be settled exclusively and finally by arbitration. The arbitration shall be conducted in accordance with the Rules of Conciliation and Arbitration of the International Chamber of Commerce. The arbitration shall be conducted in Chicago, Illinois, U.S.A. before a sole arbitrator. Any award rendered in any such arbitration proceeding shall be final and binding on each of the parties, and judgment may be entered thereon in a court of competent jurisdiction.

* * * *

The Uniform Commercial Code ("UCC") governs the parties' transaction * * *. Regardless whether plaintiff purchased the computer in person or placed an order and received shipment of the computer, the parties agree that plaintiff paid for and received a computer from Gateway. This conduct clearly demonstrates a contract for the sale of a computer. Thus the issue is whether the contract of sale includes the Standard Terms as part of the agreement.

* * * *

* * * [UCC 2–207] provides:

> Additional terms in acceptance or confirmation. (1) A definite and seasonable [timely] expression of acceptance or a written confirmation which is sent within a reasonable time operates as an acceptance even though it states terms additional to or different from those offered or agreed upon, unless acceptance is expressly made conditional on assent to the additional or different terms.
> (2) The additional terms are to be construed as proposals for addition to the contract [if the contract is not between merchants].

By its terms [UCC 2–207] applies to an acceptance or written confirmation. It states nothing which requires another form before the provision becomes effective. In fact, the official comment to the section specifically provides that [UCC 2–207](1) and (2) apply "where an agreement has been reached orally * * * and is followed by one or both of the parties sending formal memoranda embodying the terms so far agreed and adding terms not discussed." * * *

* * * The Court * * * assumes for purposes of the motion to dismiss that plaintiff offered to purchase the computer (either in person or through catalog order) and that Gateway accepted plaintiff's offer (either by completing the sales transaction in person or by agreeing to ship and/or shipping the computer to plaintiff).

Under [UCC 2–207] the Standard Terms constitute either an expression of acceptance or written confirmation. As an expression of acceptance, the Standard Terms would constitute a counter-offer only if Gateway expressly made its acceptance conditional on plaintiff's assent to the additional or different terms. The conditional nature of the acceptance must be clearly expressed in a manner sufficient to notify the offeror that the offeree is unwilling to proceed with the transaction unless the additional or different terms are included in the contract. Gateway provides no evidence that at the time of the sales transaction, it informed plaintiff that the transaction was conditioned on plaintiff's acceptance of the Standard Terms. Moreover, the mere fact that Gateway shipped the goods with the terms attached did not communicate to plaintiff any unwillingness to proceed without plaintiff's agreement to the Standard Terms.

Because plaintiff is not a merchant, additional or different terms contained in the Standard Terms did not become part of the parties' agreement unless plaintiff expressly agreed to them. Gateway argues that plaintiff demonstrated acceptance of the arbitration provision by keeping the computer more than five days after the date of delivery. Although the Standard Terms purport to work that result, Gateway has not presented evidence that plaintiff expressly agreed to those Standard Terms. Gateway states only that it enclosed the Standard Terms inside the computer box for plaintiff to read afterwards. It provides no evidence that it informed plaintiff of the five-day review-and-return period as a condition of the sales transaction, or that the parties contemplated additional terms to the agreement. The Court finds that the act of keeping the computer past five days was not sufficient to demonstrate that plaintiff expressly agreed to the Standard Terms. Thus, because Gateway has not provided evidence sufficient to support a finding under Kansas or Missouri law that plaintiff agreed to the arbitration provision contained in Gateway's Standard Terms, the Court overrules Gateway's motion to dismiss. [Emphasis added.]

* * * *

IT IS THEREFORE ORDERED that the *Motion to Dismiss* which defendant Gateway filed November 22, 1999 be and hereby is **OVERRULED**.

CASE 23.3 CLICK-ON AGREEMENTS

CASPI V. MICROSOFT NETWORK, L.L.C.

New Jersey Superior Court,
323 N.J.Super. 118,
732 A.2d 528.

KESTIN, J.A.D. [Judge, Appellate Division]

We are here called upon to determine the validity and enforceability of a forum selection clause contained in an on-line subscriber agreement of the Microsoft Network (MSN), an on-line computer service. The trial court granted defendants' motion to dismiss the complaint on the ground that the forum selection clause in the parties' contracts called for plaintiffs' claims to be litigated in the State of Washington. Plaintiffs appeal. * * *

The * * * complaint * * * sought * * * relief against two related corporate entities, The Microsoft Network, L.L.C. and Microsoft Corporation (collectively, Microsoft). Plaintiffs asserted various theories including breach of contract, common law fraud, and consumer fraud in the way Microsoft had "rolled over" MSN membership into more expensive plans. Among the claims was an accusation that Microsoft had engaged in "unilateral negative option billing," a practice condemned by the attorneys general of twenty-one states, including New Jersey's, with regard to a Microsoft competitor, America Online, Inc. Under the practice as alleged, Microsoft, without notice to or permission from MSN members, unilaterally charged them increased membership fees attributable to a change in service plans.

The four named plaintiffs are members of MSN. Two reside in New Jersey; the others in Ohio and New York. [They claim] to represent a nationwide class of 1.5 million similarly aggrieved MSN members * * * .

* * * [D]efendants moved to dismiss the * * * complaint for lack of jurisdiction and improper venue by reason of the forum selection clause which, defendants contended, was in every MSN membership agreement and bound all the named plaintiffs and all members of the class they purported to represent. That clause, paragraph 15.1 of the MSN membership agreement, provided:

> This agreement is governed by the laws of the State of Washington, USA, and you consent to the exclusive jurisdiction and venue of courts in King County, Washington in all disputes arising out of or relating to your use of MSN or your MSN membership.

* * * *

* * * [The trial court judge] in a written opinion, expressed his reasons for dismissing the complaint based upon the forum selection clause. * * *

The background of the matter was depicted in the * * * opinion:

> Before becoming an MSN member, a prospective subscriber is prompted by MSN software to view multiple computer screens of information, including a membership agreement which contains the above clause. MSN's membership agreement appears on the computer

> screen in a scrollable window next to blocks providing the choices "I Agree" and "I Don't Agree." Prospective members assent to the terms of the agreement by clicking on "I Agree" using a computer mouse. Prospective members have the option to click "I Agree" or "I Don't Agree" at any point while scrolling through the agreement. Registration may proceed only after the potential subscriber has had the opportunity to view and has assented to the membership agreement, including MSN's forum selection clause. No charges are incurred until after the membership agreement review is completed and a subscriber has clicked on "I Agree."

The trial court [judge] observed:

> Generally, forum selection clauses are *prima facie* valid and enforceable * * * . [C]ourts will decline to enforce a clause only if it fits into one of three exceptions to the general rule: (1) the clause is a result of fraud or "overweening" [excessive, overbearing] bargaining power; (2) enforcement would violate * * * public policy * * * ; or (3) enforcement would seriously inconvenience trial [make it very difficult for the parties to attend trial]. The burden falls on the party objecting to enforcement to show that the clause in question fits within one of these exceptions. Plaintiffs have failed to meet that burden here.

* * * *

The trial court opinion went on to analyze plaintiffs' contentions:

> Plaintiffs' consent to MSN's clause does not appear to be the result of fraud or overweening bargaining power. * * * [F]raud consists of (1) material misrepresentation of a past or present fact; (2) knowledge or belief by the declarant of its falsity; (3) an intention that the recipient rely on it; (4) reasonable reliance by the recipient; and (5) resulting damages. Plaintiffs have not shown that MSN's forum selection clause constitutes fraud. The clause is reasonable, clear and contains no material misrepresentation.
>
> Further, plaintiffs were not subjected to overweening bargaining power in dealing with Microsoft and MSN. * * * [A] corporate vendor's inclusion of a forum selection clause in a consumer contract does not in itself constitute overweening bargaining power. In order to invalidate a forum selection clause, something more than merely size difference must be shown. A court's focus must be whether such an imbalance in size resulted in an inequality of bargaining power that was unfairly exploited by the more powerful party.

Plaintiffs have shown little more than a size difference here. The on-line computer service industry is not one without competition, and therefore consumers are left with choices as to which service they select for Internet access, e-mail and other information services. Plaintiffs were not forced into a situation where MSN was the only available server. Additionally, plaintiffs and the class which they purport to represent were given ample opportunity to affirmatively assent to the forum selection clause. * * *

[The judge] opined that application of MSN's forum selection clause did not contravene public policy. * * * *[A]s a general matter, enforcement of forum selection clauses is not contrary to public policy* * * * . [Emphasis added.]

Finally, [the judge] held that enforcement of the forum selection clause would not inconvenience a trial. Given the fact that the * * * plaintiffs reside in several jurisdictions * * * "the inconvenience to all parties is no greater in Washington than anywhere else in the country."

* * * [W]e are in substantial agreement with the reasons for decision articulated by [the trial court judge]. We reject as meritless plaintiffs' arguments on appeal that the terms of the forum selection clause do not prevent plaintiffs from suing Microsoft outside of Washington or, alternatively, that the forum selection clause lacks adequate clarity. The meaning of the clause is plain and its effect as a limiting provision is clear. * * * As a general matter, none of the inherent characteristics of forum selection clauses implicate consumer fraud concepts in any special way. If a forum selection clause is clear in its purport and has been presented to the party to be bound in a fair and forthright fashion, no consumer fraud policies or principles have been violated. * * *

The only viable issues that remain bear upon the argument that plaintiffs did not receive adequate notice of the forum selection clause, and therefore that the clause never became part of the membership contract which bound them. * * * Defendants respond by arguing that 1) in the absence of fraud, a contracting party is bound by the provisions of a form contract even if he or she never reads them; 2) this clause met all reasonable standards of conspicuousness; and 3) the sign-up process gave plaintiffs ample opportunity to review and reject the agreement. * * *

* * * *

The scenario presented here is different [from a case in which a forum selection clause appeared in the fine print on the back of a cruise ticket] because of the medium used, electronic versus printed; but, in any sense that matters, there is no significant distinction. The plaintiffs in [the other case] could have perused [read] all the fine-print provisions of their travel contract if they wished before accepting the terms by purchasing their cruise ticket. The plaintiffs in this case were free to scroll through the various computer screens that presented the terms of their contracts before clicking their agreement.

Also, it seems clear that there was nothing extraordinary about the size or placement of the forum selection clause text. By every indication we have, the clause was presented in exactly the same format as most other provisions of the contract. It was the first item in the last paragraph of the electronic document. We note that a few paragraphs in the contract were presented in upper case typeface, presumably for emphasis, but most provisions, including the forum selection clause, were presented in lower case typeface. We discern nothing about the style or mode of presentation, or the placement of the provision, that can be taken as a basis for concluding that the forum selection clause was proffered unfairly, or with a design to conceal or de-emphasize its provisions. To conclude that plaintiffs are not bound by that clause would be equivalent to holding that they were bound by no other clause either, since all provisions were identically presented. Plaintiffs must be taken to have known that they were entering into a contract; and no good purpose, consonant with the dictates of reasonable reliability in commerce, would be served by permitting them to disavow particular provisions or the contracts as a whole.

The issue of reasonable notice regarding a forum selection clause is a question of law for the court to determine. We agree with the trial court that, in the absence of a better showing than has been made, plaintiffs must be seen to have had adequate notice of the forum selection clause. * * *

Affirmed.

CASE 23.4 BROWSE-WRAP AGREEMENTS

SPECHT V. NETSCAPE COMMUNICATIONS CORP.
United States District Court,
Southern District of New York, 2001.
150 F.Supp.2d 585.

HELLERSTEIN, District Judge.

Promises become binding when there is a meeting of the minds and consideration is exchanged. So it was at King's Bench in common law England; so it was under the common law in the American colonies; so it was through more than two centuries of jurisprudence in this country; and so it is today. *Assent may be registered by a signature, a handshake, or a click of a computer mouse transmitted across the invisible ether of the Internet. Formality is not a requisite; any sign, symbol or action, or even willful inaction, as long as it is unequivocally referable to the promise, may create a contract.* [Emphasis added.]

The [case] before me * * * involve[s] this timeless issue of assent, but in the context of free software offered on the Internet. If an offeree downloads free software, and the offeror seeks a contractual understanding limiting its uses and applications, under what circumstances does the act of downloading create a contract? * * *

* * * Plaintiffs allege that usage of the software transmits to Defendants private information about the user's file transfer activity on the Internet, thereby effecting an electronic surveillance of the user's activity in violation of [federal law]. Defendants move to compel arbitration and stay the proceedings, arguing that the disputes reflected in the Complaint, like all others relating to use of the software, are subject to a binding arbitration clause in the End User License Agreement ("License Agreement"), the contract allegedly made by the offeror of the software and the party effecting the download. * * *

I. Factual and Procedural Background

Defendant Netscape, a provider of computer software programs that enable and facilitate the use of the Internet, offers its "SmartDownload" software free of charge on its web site to all those who visit the site and indicate, by clicking their mouse in a designated box, that they wish to obtain it. SmartDownload is a program that makes it easier for its users to download files from the Internet without losing their interim progress when they pause to engage in some other task, or if their Internet connection is severed. * * *

Visitors wishing to obtain SmartDownload from Netscape's web site arrive at a page pertaining to the download of the software. On this page, there appears a tinted box, or button, labeled "Download." By clicking on the box, a visitor initiates the download. The sole reference on this page to the License Agreement appears in text that is visible only if a visitor scrolls down through the page to the next screen. * * *

Visitors are not required affirmatively to indicate their assent to the License Agreement, or even to view the license agreement, before proceeding with a download of the software. * * *

* * * *

The License Agreement * * * contains a term requiring that virtually all disputes be submitted to arbitration in Santa Clara County, California. * * *

* * * *

II. Applicable Law

* * * *

By its terms, Article 2 of the Uniform Commercial Code "applies to transactions in goods." The parties' relationship essentially is that of a seller and a purchaser of goods. Although in this case the product was provided free of charge, the roles are essentially the same as when an individual uses the Internet to purchase software from a company: here, the Plaintiff requested Defendant's product by clicking on an icon marked "Download," and Defendant then tendered the product. Therefore, in determining whether the parties entered into a contract, I look to * * * the Uniform Commercial Code * * * .

III. Did Plaintiffs Consent to Arbitration?

Unless the Plaintiffs agreed to the License Agreement, they cannot be bound by the arbitration clause contained therein. * * *

* * * *

* * * The sale of software, in stores, by mail, and over the Internet, has resulted in several specialized forms of license agreements. For example, software commonly is packaged in a container or wrapper that advises the purchaser that the use of the software is subject to the terms of a license agreement contained inside the package. The license agreement generally explains that, if the purchaser does not wish to enter into a contract, he or she must return the product for a refund, and that failure to return it within a certain period will constitute assent to the license terms. These [are] so-called "shrink-wrap licenses" * * * .

* * * *

For most of the products it makes available over the Internet (but not SmartDownload), Netscape uses another common type of software license, one usually identified as "click-wrap" licensing. A click-wrap license presents the user with a message on his or her computer screen, requiring that the user manifest his or her assent to the terms of the license agreement by clicking on an icon. The product cannot be obtained or used unless and until the icon is clicked. * * *

A third type of software license [is] "browse-wrap" * * * . Notice of a license agreement appears on [a] web site. Clicking on the notice links the user to a separate web page containing the full text of the license agreement, which allegedly binds any user of the information on the site. However, the user is not required to click on an icon expressing assent to the license, or even view its terms, before proceeding to use the information on the site. * * *

The SmartDownload License Agreement in the case before me differs fundamentally from both click-wrap and shrink-wrap licensing, and resembles more the browse-wrap license * * * .

* * * *

Netscape argues that the mere act of downloading indicates assent. However, downloading is hardly an unambiguous indication of assent. The primary purpose of downloading is to obtain a product, not to assent to an agreement. In contrast, clicking on an icon stating "I assent" has no meaning or purpose other than to indicate such assent. Netscape's failure to require users of SmartDownload to indicate assent to its license as a precondition to downloading and using its software is fatal to its argument that a contract has been formed.

Furthermore, unlike the user of Netscape Navigator or other click-wrap or shrink-wrap licensees, the individual obtaining SmartDownload is not made aware that he is entering into a contract. SmartDownload is available from Netscape's web site free of charge. Before downloading the software, the user need not view any license agreement terms or even any reference to a license agreement, and need not do anything to manifest assent to such a license agreement other than actually taking possession of the product. From the user's vantage point, SmartDownload could be analogized to a free neighborhood newspaper, readily obtained from a sidewalk box or supermarket counter without any exchange with a seller or vender. It is there for the taking.

The only hint that a contract is being formed is one small box of text referring to the license agreement, text that appears below the screen used for downloading and that a user need not even see before obtaining the product:

> Please review and agree to the terms of the *Netscape SmartDownload software license agreement* before downloading and using the software.

Couched in the mild request, "Please review," this language reads as a mere invitation, not as a condition. The language does not indicate that a user *must* agree to the license terms before downloading and using the software. While clearer language appears in the License Agreement itself, the language of the invitation does not require the reading of those terms or provide adequate notice either that a contract is being created or that the terms of the License Agreement will bind the user.

The case law on software licensing has not eroded the importance of assent in contract formation. Mutual assent is the bedrock of any agreement to which the law will give force. Defendants' position, if accepted, would so expand the definition of assent as to render it meaningless. Because the user Plaintiffs did not assent to the license agreement, they are not subject to the arbitration clause contained therein and cannot be compelled to arbitrate their claims against the Defendants. [Emphasis added.]

* * * *

VI. Conclusion

For the reasons stated, I deny Defendants' motion to compel arbitration.

CASE PROBLEMS

23–1. ProCD, Inc., compiles information from more than three thousand telephone directories into a computer database. ProCD sells a version of the database, called "SelectPhone," on CD-ROM. The data enables businesses to compile lists of potential customers. Ordinary consumers can use the database as, among other things, an electronic substitute for a local phone book. ProCD charges businesses a higher price for "SelectPhone" than it charges consumers. Every box containing the consumer version, however, declares that the CD comes with restrictions stated in an enclosed license. This license, which is encoded on the

CD and printed in the manual, and which appears on a user's screen every time the software runs, limits use of "SelectPhone" to noncommercial purposes. Matthew Zeidenberg bought a consumer "SelectPhone," but ignored the license. He formed Silken Mountain Web Services, Inc., to resell the information on the Internet for less than ProCD charges its business customers. ProCD filed a suit in a federal district court against Zeidenberg on the ground that he violated the license. Is Zeidenberg bound to terms that are located inside the packaging of "SelectPhone"? Explain. [*ProCD, Inc. v. Zeidenberg*, 86 F.3d 1447 (7th Cir. 1996)]

23–2. Over the phone, Rich and Enza Hill ordered a computer from Gateway 2000, Inc. Inside the box were the computer and a list of contract terms, which provided that the terms governed the transaction unless the customers returned the computer within thirty days. Among those terms was a clause that required any claims to be submitted to arbitration. The Hills kept the computer for more than thirty days before complaining to Gateway about the computer's components and its performance. When the matter was not resolved to their satisfaction, the Hills filed a suit in a federal district court against Gateway, arguing, among other things, that the computer was defective. Gateway asked the court to enforce the arbitration clause. The Hills claimed that this term was not part of a contract to buy the computer because the list on which it appeared had been in the box and they did not see the list until after the computer was delivered. Is the term a part of the contract? Why, or why not? [*Hill v. Gateway 2000, Inc.*, 105 F.3d 1147 (7th Cir. 1997)]

23–3. Hotmail Corporation provides free e-mail service to more than ten million subscribers. To obtain the service, at Hotmail's Web site a prospective subscriber clicks on an "I accept" button to agree to Hotmail's "Terms of Service." These terms prohibit a subscriber from using the service to send spam (junk e-mail). All of the millions of daily e-mail messages that subscribers send and receive automatically display Hotmail's domain name "hotmail.com" and its signature statement "Get Your Private, Free Email at *http://www.hotmail.com.*" Van$ Money Pie, Inc., and others began using Hotmail's service to send spam. Hotmail was soon inundated with hundreds of thousands of misdirected responses to the spam, including complaints from subscribers and returned e-mail that had been sent to nonexistent or incorrect addresses. This took up a substantial amount of Hotmail's computer space, threatened to adversely affect subscribers in sending and receiving e-mail, and resulted in significant costs to Hotmail in terms of increased personnel to sort and respond to the complaints. Hotmail filed a suit in a federal district court against the spammers, alleging, among other things, breach of contract and fraud. Hotmail asked the court to enjoin the defendants' use of Hotmail's service before the trial. Should the court issue the injunction? Why, or why not? [*Hotmail Corp. v. Van$ Money Pie, Inc.*, 47 U.S.P.Q.2d 1020 (N.D.Cal. 1998)]

23–4. Iomega Corp. makes and sells Zip drives—large-capacity drives for data storage on personal computers. Inside the packaging of each drive is a document labeled "IOMEGA LIMITED WARRANTY." Near the bottom of this document is a disclaimer of the implied warranty of merchantability. Some drives bought after January 1, 1995, contained a defect that, among some users of the drives, was known as the "Click of Death." This defect damaged the removable, magnetic storage disks on which the drives store data. Also, the defect sometimes rendered the data on the disks unreadable; and when a damaged disk was inserted into another drive, the defect could be transferred to the second drive, causing further damage. On behalf of all persons who bought the defective drives, Rinaldi and five other purchasers filed a suit in a Delaware state court against Iomega, alleging, among other things, breach of the implied warranty of merchantability. Iomega filed a motion to dismiss. On what ground might Iomega base its motion? How might the plaintiffs respond? How should the court rule? Why? [*Rinaldi v. Iomega Corp.*, __ A.2d __, 41 UCC Rep.Serv.2d 1143 (Del.Super. 1999)]

23–5. Management Computer Controls, Inc. (known as "MC 2"), is a Tennessee corporation in the business of selling software. Charles Perry Construction, Inc. (Perry), is a Florida corporation. Perry entered into two contracts with MC 2 to buy software designed to perform estimating and accounting functions for construction firms. Each contract was printed on a standard order form containing a paragraph that referred to a license agreement. The license agreement included a choice-of-forum clause and a choice-of-law provision: "Agreement is to be interpreted and construed according to the laws of the State of Tennessee. Any action, either by you or MC 2, arising out of this Agreement shall be initiated and prosecuted in the Court of Shelby County, Tennessee, and nowhere else." Each of the software packages arrived with the license agreement affixed to the outside of the box. Additionally, the boxes were sealed with an orange sticker bearing the following warning: "By opening this packet, you indicate your acceptance of the MC 2 license agreement." Alleging that the software was not suitable for use with Windows NT, Perry filed a suit against MC 2 in a Florida state court. MC 2 filed a motion to dismiss the complaint on the ground that the suit should be heard in Tennessee. How should the court rule? Why? [*Management Computer Controls, Inc. v. Charles Perry Construction, Inc.*, 743 So.2d 627 (Fla.App. 1 Dist. 1999)]

23–6. RealNetworks, Inc., offers free basic versions of two products, RealPlayer and RealJukebox, for users to download from RealNetworks's Web site. These products allow users to see and hear audio and video available on the Internet and to download, record, and play music. Before a user can install either of these products, he or she must accept the terms of RealNetworks's

"License Agreement," which appear on the user's screen. This agreement provides in part that "[a]ny and all unresolved disputes arising under this License Agreement shall be submitted to arbitration in the State of Washington." Michael Lieschke, a resident of Illinois, believed that RealNetworks's software products secretly allowed RealNetworks to access and intercept the users' electronic communications and stored information without their knowledge or consent. Lieschke and other Illinois residents filed a suit in a federal district court against RealNetworks, alleging, among other things, trespass to personal property. RealNetworks filed a motion to order the parties to arbitrate the dispute, under the License Agreement. Is the License Agreement unenforceable because it is not a "writing" (as required under the Federal Arbitration Act)? Explain. [*In re RealNetworks, Inc., Privacy Litigation,* __ F.Supp.2d __ (N.D.Ill. 2000)]

23–7. Register.com, Inc., is a domain name registrar. Like other registrars, Register.com collects data about its customers and provides, online, a "WHOIS" database that contains this data—customers' postal addresses, phone numbers, e-mail addresses, and fax numbers. The WHOIS database is accessible to the public via a Web page. On that page, to submit a WHOIS query, a user has to first read "Terms of Use," which state that "under no circumstances will you use this data to: . . . allow, enable, or otherwise support the transmission of mass unsolicited, commercial advertising or solicitations." Verio, Inc., provides comprehensive Internet services. To better target its sales efforts, Verio developed an automated software program to access the WHOIS database and solicit Register.com's customers. When the customers complained, Register.com filed a suit in a federal district court against Verio, alleging in part that it was violating the "Terms of Use" on the WHOIS Web page. Was Verio bound to those terms? Explain. [*Register.com, Inc. v. Verio, Inc.*, 126 F.Supp.2d 238 (S.D.N.Y. 2000)]

23–8. Ticketmaster Corp. operates a Web site that allows customers to buy tickets to concerts, ball games, and other events. On the site's home page are instructions and an index to internal pages (one page per event). Each event page provides basic information (a short description of the event, with the date, time, place, and price) and a description of how to order tickets over the Internet, by telephone, by mail, or in person. The home page contains—if a customer scrolls to the bottom—"terms and conditions" that proscribe, among other things, linking to Ticketmaster's internal pages. A customer need not view these terms to go to an event page. Tickets.Com, Inc., operates a Web site that also publicizes special events. Tickets.Com's site includes links to the internal events pages of Ticketmaster. These links bypass Ticketmaster's home page. Ticketmaster filed a suit in a federal district court against Tickets.Com, alleging in part breach of contract on the ground that Tickets.Com's linking violated Ticketmaster's "terms and conditions." Tickets.Com filed a motion to dismiss. Should the court grant the motion? Why, or why not? [*Ticketmaster Corp. v. Tickets.Com, Inc.*, 54 U.S.P.Q.2d 1344 (C.D.Cal. 2000)]

23–9. 1-A Equipment Co. signed a sales order to lease software made and marketed by ICode, Inc. The order stated, just above the signature line, "Thank you for your order. No returns or refunds will be issued for software license and/or services. All sales are final. Please read the End User License and Service Agreement." The software was delivered in a sealed envelope inside a box. On the outside of the envelope, an "End User Agreement" provided in part, "BY OPENING THIS PACKAGING, CLICKING YOUR ACCEPTANCE OF THE AGREEMENT DURING DOWNLOAD OR INSTALLATION OF THIS PRODUCT, OR BY USING ANY PART OF THIS PRODUCT, YOU AGREE TO BE LEGALLY BOUND BY THE TERMS OF THE AGREEMENT. . . . This agreement will be governed by the laws in force in the Commonwealth of Virginia . . . and exclusive venue for any litigation shall be in Virginia." Later, dissatisfied with the software, 1-A filed a suit in a Massachusetts state court against ICode, alleging breach of contract and misrepresentation. ICode asked the court to dismiss the case on the basis of the "End User Agreement." Is the agreement enforceable? Should the court dismiss the suit? Why, or why not? [*1-A Equipment Co. v. ICode, Inc.*, 43 UCC Rep.Serv.2d 807 (Mass.Dist. 2000)]

23–10. Peerless Wall & Window Coverings, Inc., is a small business in Pennsylvania. To run the cash registers in its stores, manage inventory, and link the stores electronically, in 1994 Peerless installed *Point of Sale V6.5* software produced by Synchronics, Inc., a small corporation in Tennessee that develops and markets business software. *Point of Sale V6.5* was written with code that used only a two-digit year field—for example, 1999 was stored as "99." This meant that all dates were interpreted as falling within the twentieth century (2001, stored as "01," would be mistaken for 1901). In other words, *Point of Sale V6.5* was not "Year 2000" (Y2K) compliant. The software was licensed under a shrink-wrap agreement printed on the envelopes containing the disks. The agreement included a clause that, among other things, limited remedies to replacement within ninety days if there was a defect in the disks. "The entire risk as to the quality and performance of the Software is with you." In 1995, Synchronics stopped selling and supporting *Point of Sale V6.5*. Two years later, Synchronics told Peerless that the software was not Y2K compliant and should be replaced. Peerless filed a suit in a federal district court against Synchronics, alleging, in part, breach of contract. Synchronics filed a motion for summary judgment. Who is most likely to bear the cost of replacing the software? Why? [*Peerless Wall & Window Coverings, Inc. v. Synchronics, Inc.*, 85 F.Supp.2d 519 (W.D.Pa. 2000), aff'd 234 F.3d 1265 (3d Cir. 2000)]

23–11. Melissa Westendorf bought Brian Pawlak a Gateway 2000, Inc., computer, which at her request, Gateway delivered directly to Pawlak. Several months later, Pawlak purchased a Gateway computer, which he requested be delivered directly to Westendorf. With each computer, Gateway included its "Standard Terms and Conditions Agreement," which contains a clause requiring that all disputes be submitted to arbitration. The agreement also states that retention of the computer beyond a thirty-day trial period equates to an acceptance of the terms. As part of its computer package, Gateway offers Internet access through its Gateway.net service. Only Gateway owners can use the service, which includes twenty-four-hour access and e-mail. After registering for the service, Westendorf complained of difficulties in using it—Gateway's access numbers were constantly busy, and she was otherwise unable to view her e-mail. Westendorf, on behalf of herself and other Gateway customers, filed a suit in a Delaware state court against Gateway, arguing that she and the others paid for services they did not receive. Gateway filed a motion to dismiss the complaint. What should the court decide? Explain. [*Westendorf v. Gateway 2000, Inc.*, __ A.2d __ (Del.Ch. 2000)]

23–12. Bell Atlantic Corp. (Verizon Communications, Inc.) provides Internet Digital Subscriber Line (DSL) service. Bell's Web site states that this service is "FAST—High speed Internet access service up to 126 times faster than your 56K modem" and "DEDICATED—You're always connected—no dialing in and no busy signals, ever!" A customer's testimonial adds, "The quality of the technical support staff is unbelievable; never have I experienced such prompt and responsive support." Bell's "Internet Access Service Agreement," which is on the installation CD-ROM, provides in part that "THE SERVICE IS PROVIDED ON AN 'AS IS' BASIS OR 'AS AVAILABLE' BASIS" and that Bell "DISCLAIM[S] ANY AND ALL WARRANTIES FOR THE SERVICE WHETHER EXPRESS OR IMPLIED." Customers are given thirty days to try the service and a right to otherwise cancel it at any time, without obligation. Subscribers who experienced disruptions in service filed a suit in a New York state court against Bell, alleging, among other things, fraud and breach of contract on the ground that the service was not of the quality advertised. Should the court dismiss the complaint? Discuss. [*Scott v. Bell Atlantic Corp.*, 726 N.Y.S.2d 60 (A.D. 1 Dept. 2001)]

23–13. Pollstar creates and develops up-to-the-day time-sensitive concert information and publishes this information daily on its Web site. On the home page is a notice, in small gray print on a gray background, declaring that use of the site is subject to a license agreement. Although not underlined, the text of this notice is a link to the terms of the license, one of which is that "[a]ll documents and information may only be used for non-commercial purposes." Gigmania, Ltd., downloaded from Pollstar's site information that Gigmania then placed on its own Web site for commercial purposes. On learning of this posting, Pollstar filed a suit in a federal district court against Gigmania, alleging in part breach of contract. Gigmania filed a motion to dismiss the complaint. Was Gigmania bound to the terms of the license? Why, or why not? [*Pollstar v. Gigmania, Ltd.*, __ F.Supp.2d __ (E.D.Cal. 2001)]

23–14. Al Mendoza lived in California. For a few years, Mendoza subscribed to the Internet service provided by America Online, Inc. (AOL). To initiate the service, Mendoza clicked on an "I agree" button on his computer screen, consenting to AOL's "Terms of Service" (TOS). The TOS included a clause designating Virginia as the jurisdiction in which any dispute between the parties would be litigated. Remedies afforded consumers under Virginia law are more limited than those available under California law. Mendoza paid for AOL's service by allowing AOL to debit his credit card monthly. Mendoza cancelled his subscription in October 1999, but AOL continued to charge monthly fees to his credit card through February 2000, when he canceled the card to stop the debits. Mendoza, on behalf of himself and others, filed a suit in a California state court against AOL, alleging, among other things, violations of state consumer protection statutes. AOL filed a motion to dismiss the suit. On what ground might the court grant the motion? Why might the court refuse to dismiss the suit? Discuss. [*America Online, Inc. v. Superior Court*, 90 Cal.App.4th 1, 108 Cal.Rptr.2d 699 (1 Dist. 2001)]

23–15. America Online, Inc. (AOL), is, among other things, an Internet service provider (ISP). AOL promotes its service through the mass distribution of its software. Mark Williams, a Massachusetts resident, installed on his computer the edition of the software known as "AOL Version 5.0." After it was loaded, a request appeared on Williams's computer screen, asking him to agree to "Terms of Service." To read the terms, Williams had to click "Read Now" boxes twice. The terms included a clause that stated all disputes were to be submitted to a Virginia state court. Williams later claimed that the installation of the software caused unauthorized changes to the configuration of his computer so he could no longer access non–AOL ISPs, was unable to run non–AOL e-mail programs, and was unable to access personal information and files. Williams and others filed a suit in a Massachusetts state court against AOL, alleging in part unfair or deceptive acts or practices in violation of state law. On the basis of the forum-selection clause in the "Terms of Service," AOL filed a motion to dismiss. Should the court grant the motion? Why, or why not? [*Williams v. America Online, Inc.*, 2001 WL 135825 (Mass.Super. 2001)]

E-LINKS

For updated resources available on the Web, as well as a variety of other materials, visit this text's Web site at

http://wbl-cs.westbuslaw.com

For a comprehensive review of the Uniform Computer Information Transactions Act, go to

http://www.ucitaonline.com

The Web site of the National Conference of Commissioners on Uniform States Laws (NCCUSL) includes an update of the list of the states that have adopted the UCITA and the UETA or have considered them for adoption. The site also contains summaries of the acts and "Question and Answer" sections concerning these laws. Go to

http://www.nccusl.org

LEGAL RESEARCH EXERCISES ON THE WEB

Go to http://wbl-cs.westbuslaw.com, the Web site that accompanies this text. Select "Interactive Study Center." There you will find the following Internet research exercise that you can perform to learn more about e-contracts:

Activity 23–1: E-Contracts

Focus on Legal Reasoning

Rheem Manufacturing Co. v. Phelps Heating & Air Conditioning, Inc.

Contractual provisions affecting remedies were discussed in Chapter 21, and express warranties were covered in Chapter 22. In this *Focus on Legal Reasoning*, we examine *Rheem Manufacturing Co. v. Phelps Heating & Air Conditioning, Inc.*,[1] a decision that involved an express warranty provision limiting a buyer's remedy to a replacement of parts and precluding consequential damages. If the limitation-of-remedy clause failed in its essential purpose, could the buyer recover consequential damages?

1. 746 N.E.2d 941 (Ind. 2001).

Case Background

Rheem Manufacturing Company makes furnaces for use in homes and offices. During the 1980s and 1990s, Rheem sold its furnaces through Federated Supply Corporation to Phelps Heating and Cooling, Inc., an Indiana contractor. The box in which each furnace was shipped contained an express warranty of "ANY PART of this furnace against failure under normal use and service." This warranty limited the remedies available for a breach of the warranty to replacement of parts, however, and disclaimed consequential damages. Many of the Rheem furnaces malfunctioned after Phelps installed them. Phelps asked Rheem to compensate it for the cost of servicing the furnaces. Rheem refused.

Phelps filed a suit in an Indiana state court against Rheem, claiming, in part, breach of warranty and seeking damages for lost customers, lost profits, and the cost of fixing the defective furnaces. Rheem filed a motion for summary judgment on this claim, pointing to the warranty's limitation of remedies and exclusion of consequential damages. The court denied the motion. Rheem appealed. A state intermediate appellate court affirmed the lower court's decision. Rheem appealed to the Indiana Supreme Court.

Majority Opinion

SULLIVAN, Justice.

* * * *

Rheem * * * argues that the trial court should have granted summary judgment as to Phelps's claim for lost profits under the express warranty because the warranty excluded consequential damages. This argument requires us to examine the interplay between Indiana Code [Sections] 26-1-2-719(2) and (3) [Indiana's versions of UCC 2-719(2) and (3)], the UCC subsections pertinent to damage exclusions and remedy limitations in express warranties: * * * .

* * * *

* * * [T]he question [is] whether an exclusion of consequential damages survives when a separate contract provision limiting a buyer's remedies has failed of its essential purpose. The courts that have faced this issue have fallen into two camps that are divided along the lines of the parties' arguments in this case. One group takes what is known as the "dependent" view and reads [Section] 2-719(2)'s reference to remedies provided in the UCC as overriding a contract's consequential damage exclusion. *See, e.g. Middletown Concrete Prod. v. Black Clawson Co.*, 802 F.Supp. 1135 (D.Del. 1992) * * * . This gloss on [Section] 2-719 makes an exclusion of consequential damages dependent on whether a limited remedy fails of its essential purpose. Other courts take an "independent" view and reason that because [Sections] 2-719(2) and (3) are separate subsections with separate language and separate standards, the failure of a limited remedy has no effect on an exclusion of consequential damages. *See Waters v. Massey-Ferguson, Inc.*, 775 F.2d 587 (4th Cir. 1985) * * * .

* * * *

Several aspects of Indiana Code [Sections] 26-1-2-719(2) and (3) point to a legislative intent consistent with the independent view. First, * * * the drafters of the UCC inserted distinct legal standards into each provision. A limited remedy will be struck when it fails of its essential purpose; an exclusion of consequential damages fails when it is unconscionable. Moreover, these subsections are distinct in *who* applies the standards they set out. *Whether a limited remedy fails of its essential purpose is an issue of fact that a jury may determine. Conversely, an exclusion of consequential damages stands unless it is unconscionable,* and unconscionability is determined by a court as a matter of law. These facial [readily apparent] distinctions between [Sections] 2-719(2) and (3) suggest a legislative intent that the provisions should function independently of one another.

Second, the independent view is consistent with the principle of statutory interpretation that where possible, we interpret a statute such that every word receives effect and meaning and no part is rendered meaningless if it can be reconciled with the rest of the statute. The dependent view renders [Section] 2-719(3) inoperative by deleting an exclusion of consequential damages without any analysis of its unconscionability. On the other hand, the independent view allows both provisions to operate * * *.

Third, [UCC 1-102] instructs us to construe its provisions with three specific legislative purposes in mind * * *. The independent view serves all of the enumerated purposes. The independent view supplies *simplicity* and *clarity* by allowing a clearly expressed agreement to control a transaction. The independent view is also the *modern* trend. The independent view aids sound *commercial practice* by allowing the parties to anticipate clearly the results of their transaction * * *.

Finally, the legislature's intent to follow the independent view is also supported by the UCC's general policy favoring the parties' freedom of contract. The UCC tells us that one of its paramount concerns is enabling contracting parties to control their own relationships. * * * However, the dependent view ignores the intent of the parties and allows a buyer to recover consequential damages despite an explicit contract term excluding them. The dependent courts essentially *presume* that the parties intended the exclusion of consequential damages to depend on the limited remedy. On the other hand, the independent view refuses to override categorically an exclusion of consequential damages and will give effect to the terms of the contract. Indeed, consistent with the principle of freedom of contract, the independent view allows the parties to *agree* to a dependent arrangement.

This freedom to set contract terms is especially important in the context of a commercial transaction. *Sophisticated commercial actors should be free to allocate risks as they see fit, and courts should not interfere simply because such risks have materialized.* * * * [Emphasis added.]

* * * *

* * * [W]e reverse the order of the trial court on Phelps's express warranty claims and remand this case for proceedings consistent with this opinion.

QUESTIONS FOR ANALYSIS

1. **Legal Analysis.** In its opinion, the court cites *Middletown Concrete Products v. Black Clawson Co.*, 802 F.Supp. 1135 (D.Del. 1992); and *Waters v. Massey-Ferguson, Inc.*, 775 F.2d 587 (4th Cir. 1985) (see the *E-Links* feature at the end of Chapter 2 for instructions on how to access the opinions of federal courts). Why did the *Rheem* court select these cases?

2. **Legal Reasoning.** What arguments did the *Rheem* court find most persuasive in choosing between the different views of UCC 2–719?

3. **Economic Dimensions.** How does the principle of freedom of contract, in the context of a deal between commercial parties, allocate the risk of consequential damages in a cost-effective way?

4. **Implications for the Seller.** Why did the drafters of the UCC expressly provide for the limitation or exclusion of consequential damages?

WESTLAW ONLINE RESEARCH

Westlaw. Go to this text's companion Web site, at http://wbl-cs.westbuslaw.com, and click on the Westlaw icon. Use your special password to access the full text of this case, including the dissenting opinions. Read through the case, and then answer the following questions.

1. Why, on the interpretation of UCC 2–719, is the dissent so short?
2. Should the editor's breakdown of the legal principles in this case into headnotes match the court's division of its opinion? Why, or why not?
3. According to the court in the *Rheem* case, what was the purpose of the limitation-of-remedy clause? Did it fail in this purpose?

UNIT FOUR
Negotiable Instruments

CONTENTS

CHAPTER 24
The Function and Creation of Negotiable Instruments

THE VAST NUMBER OF COMMERCIAL transactions that take place daily in the modern business world would be inconceivable without negotiable instruments. A **negotiable instrument** can be defined as a signed writing that contains an unconditional promise or order to pay an exact sum of money, either when demanded or at a specific future time. The checks you write to pay for groceries and other items are negotiable instruments.

The law governing negotiable instruments grew out of commercial necessity. In the medieval world, merchants dealing in foreign trade used negotiable instruments to finance and conduct their affairs. Problems in transportation and in the safekeeping of gold or coins had prompted this practice. Merchants deposited their precious metals with goldsmiths ("bankers") to avoid the dangers of loss or theft. When they needed funds to pay for the goods they were buying, they gave the seller a written order addressed to the "bank." This authorized the bank to deliver part (or all) of the precious metals to the seller. These orders, called *bills of exchange*, were sometimes used as a substitute for money. Because the English king's courts of those times did not recognize the validity of these bills, the merchants had to develop their own rules governing their use, and these rules were enforced by "fair" or "borough" courts. Eventually, these decisions became a distinct set of laws known as the *Lex Mercatoria* (Law Merchant).

The Law Merchant was codified in England in the Bills of Exchange Act of 1882. In 1896, in the United States, the National Conference of Commissioners on Uniform State Laws drafted the Uniform Negotiable Instruments Law. This law, which by 1920 had been adopted by all of the states, was the forerunner of Article 3 of the Uniform Commercial Code (UCC).

SECTION 1
Article 3 of the UCC

Negotiable instruments must meet special requirements relating to form and content. These requirements, which are imposed by Article 3 of the UCC, will be discussed at length in this chapter. When an instrument is negotiable, its transfer from one person to another is governed by Article 3. Indeed, UCC 3–104(b) defines *instrument* as a "negotiable instrument." For that reason, whenever the term *instrument* is used in this book, it refers to a negotiable instrument.

In 1990, a revised version of Article 3 was issued for adoption by the states. Many of the changes to Article 3 simply clarified old sections; some, however, significantly altered the former UCC Article 3 provisions. As of this writing, almost all of the states have adopted the revised article. Therefore, all references to Article 3 in this chapter and in the following chapters are to the *revised* Article 3. When the revised Article 3 has made important changes in the law, however, we discuss the previous law in footnotes.

Article 4 of the UCC, which governs bank deposits and collections, as well as bank-customer relationships (discussed in Chapter 27), was also revised in 1990. In part, these changes were necessary to reflect changes in Article 3 that affect Article 4 provisions. The revised Articles 3 and 4 are included in their entirety in Appendix B.

SECTION 2

The Function of Instruments

A negotiable instrument can function as a substitute for money or as an extension of credit. For example, when a buyer writes a check to pay for goods, the check serves as a substitute for money. When a buyer gives a seller a promissory note in which the buyer promises to pay the seller the purchase price within sixty days, the seller has essentially extended credit to the buyer for a sixty-day period.

For a negotiable instrument to operate *practically* as either a substitute for money or a credit device, or both, it is essential that the instrument be easily transferable without danger of being uncollectible. This is a fundamental function of negotiable instruments. Each rule described in the following pages can be examined in light of this function.

SECTION 3

Types of Negotiable Instruments

The UCC specifies four types of negotiable instruments: *drafts, checks, notes,* and *certificates of deposit (CDs).* These instruments, which are summarized in Exhibit 24–1, are frequently divided into the two classifications that we will discuss in the following subsections: *orders to pay* (drafts and checks) and *promises to pay* (promissory notes and CDs).

Negotiable instruments may also be classified as either demand instruments or time instruments. A *demand instrument* is payable on demand. "A promise or order is 'payable on demand' if it (i) states that it is payable on demand or at sight, or otherwise indicates that it is payable at the will of the holder, or (ii) does not state any time of payment" [UCC 3–108(a)]. (The UCC defines a **holder** as "the person in possession if the instrument is payable to bearer or, in the cases of an instrument payable to an identified person, if the identified person is in possession" [UCC 1–201(20)]. The term *bearer* will be explained later in this chapter.)

All checks are demand instruments, because by definition, they must be payable on demand. Therefore, checking accounts are sometimes called **demand deposits.** A demand instrument is payable immediately after it is *issued.* **Issue** is "the first delivery of an instrument by the maker or drawer, whether to a holder or nonholder [usually to the payee], for the purpose of giving rights on the instrument to any person" [UCC 3–105].[1] *Time instruments are payable at a future date.*

1. Under the unrevised UCC 3–102(1)(a), *issue* was limited to "the first delivery of an instrument to a holder or remitter."

EXHIBIT 24–1 BASIC TYPES OF INSTRUMENTS

INSTRUMENTS	CHARACTERISTICS	PARTIES
ORDERS TO PAY		
Draft	An order by one person to another person or to bearer [UCC 3–104(e)].	Drawer—The person who signs or makes the order to pay [UCC 3–103(a)(3)].
Check	A draft drawn on a bank and payable on demand [UCC 3–104(f)].[a] (With certain types of checks, such as cashier's checks, the bank is both the drawer and the drawee—see Chapter 27 for details.)	Drawee—The person to whom the order to pay is made [UCC 3–103(a)(2)]. Payee—The person to whom payment is ordered.
PROMISES TO PAY		
Note	A promise by one party to pay money to another party or to bearer [UCC 3–104(e)].	Maker—The person who promises to pay [UCC 3–103(a)(5)].
Certificate of deposit	A note made by a bank acknowledging a deposit of funds made payable to the holder of the note [UCC 3–104(j)].	Payee—The person to whom the promise is made.

a. Under UCC 4–105(1), banks include savings banks, savings and loan associations, credit unions, and trust companies.

DRAFTS AND CHECKS (ORDERS TO PAY)

A **draft** (bill of exchange) is an unconditional written order that involves *three parties*. The party creating the draft (the **drawer**) orders another party (the **drawee**) to pay money, usually to a third party (the **payee**). The most common type of draft is a check.

Time Drafts and Sight Drafts. A *time draft* is payable at a definite future time. A *sight draft* (or demand draft) is payable on sight—that is, when it is presented for payment. A sight draft may be payable on acceptance. **Acceptance** is the drawee's written promise to pay the draft when it comes due. The usual manner of accepting an instrument is by writing the word *accepted* across the face of the instrument, followed by the date of acceptance and the signature of the drawee. A draft can be both a time and a sight draft; such a draft is payable at a stated time after sight. Exhibit 24–2 shows a typical time draft.

Trade Acceptances. The trade acceptance is a type of draft that is frequently used in the sale of goods. In a **trade acceptance**, the seller of the goods is both the drawer and the payee. Essentially, the draft orders the buyer to pay a specified sum of money to the seller, usually at a stated time in the future. For example, Midwestern Style Fabrics sells $50,000 worth of fabric to D & F Clothiers, Inc., each fall on terms requiring payment to be made in ninety days. One year, Midwestern Style needs cash, so it draws a *trade acceptance* that orders D & F to pay $50,000 to the order of Midwestern Style Fabrics ninety days hence. Midwestern Style presents the draft to D & F, which *accepts* the draft by signing and dating the face of the instrument. D & F then returns the draft to Midwestern Style Fabrics. D & F's acceptance creates an enforceable promise to pay the draft when it comes due in ninety days. Midwestern Style can now sell the trade acceptance in the commercial money market to obtain the cash it needs. Trade acceptances are the standard credit instruments in sales transactions (see Exhibit 24–3).

When the draft is drawn by a seller on the buyer's bank for acceptance, it is called a banker's acceptance. A **banker's acceptance** is commonly used in international trade.

Checks. As mentioned, the most commonly used type of draft is a check. The writer of the **check** is the drawer, the bank on which the check is drawn is the drawee, and the person to whom the check is made payable is the payee. As stated earlier, checks, because they are payable on demand, are demand instruments.

Checks will be discussed more fully in Chapter 27, but it should be noted here that with certain types of checks, such as *cashier's checks*, the bank is both the drawer and the drawee. The bank customer

EXHIBIT 24–2 A TYPICAL TIME DRAFT—A BILL OF EXCHANGE

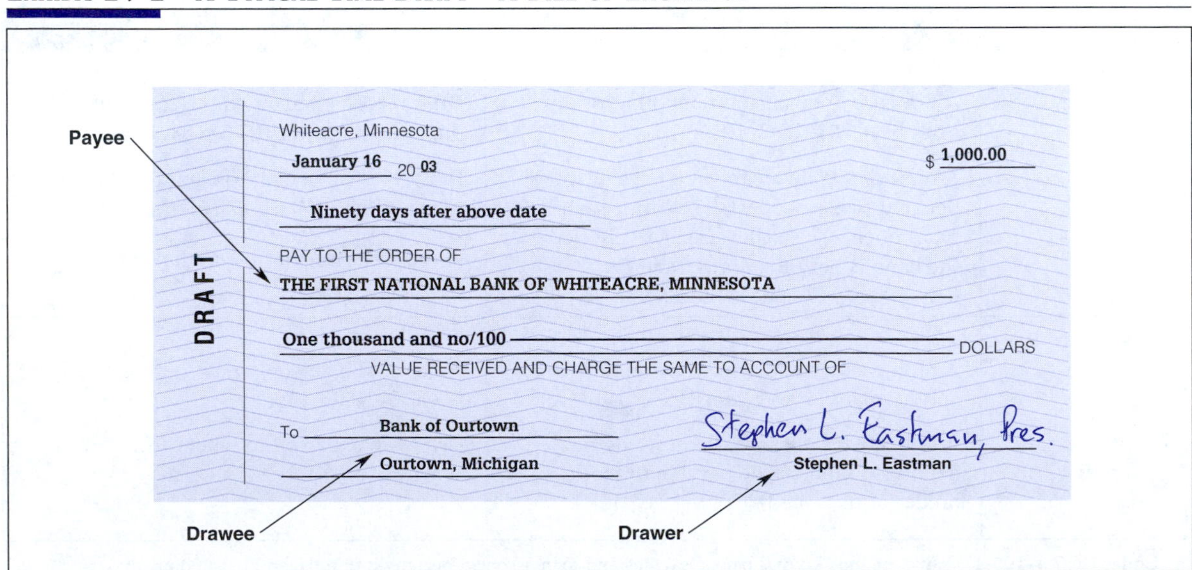
DRAFT

Whiteacre, Minnesota

January 16 20 03 $ 1,000.00

Ninety days after above date

PAY TO THE ORDER OF

THE FIRST NATIONAL BANK OF WHITEACRE, MINNESOTA

One thousand and no/100 DOLLARS

VALUE RECEIVED AND CHARGE THE SAME TO ACCOUNT OF

To Bank of Ourtown

Ourtown, Michigan

Stephen L. Eastman, Pres.

Stephen L. Eastman

EXHIBIT 24–3 A TYPICAL TRADE ACCEPTANCE

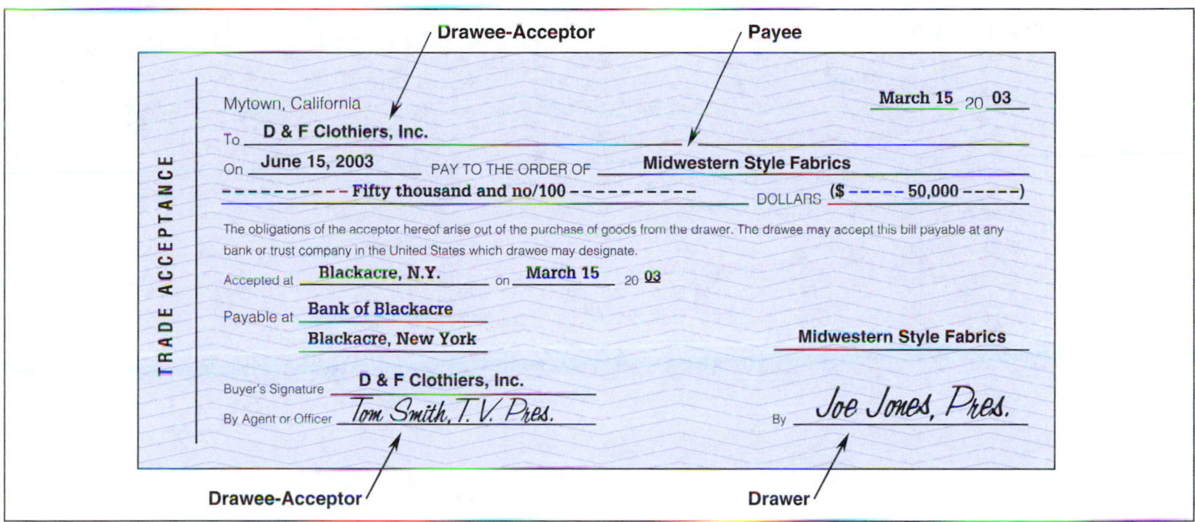

purchases a cashier's check from the bank—that is, pays the bank the amount of the check—and indicates to whom the check should be made payable. The bank, not the customer, is the drawer of the check, as well as the drawee.

Westlaw. See Case 24.1 at the end of this chapter. To view the full, unedited case from Westlaw,® go to this text's Web site at **http://wbl-cs.westbuslaw.com**.

PROMISSORY NOTES AND CDS (PROMISES TO PAY)

A **promissory note** is a written promise made by one person (the **maker** of the promise to pay) to another (usually a payee). A promissory note, which is often referred to simply as a *note,* can be made payable at a definite time or on demand. It can name a specific payee or merely be payable to bearer (bearer instruments are discussed later in this chapter). For example, on April 30, Laurence and Margaret Roberts sign a writing unconditionally promising to pay "to the order of" the First National Bank of Whiteacre $3,000 (with 8 percent interest) on or before June 29. This writing is a promissory note. A typical promissory note is shown in Exhibit 24–4 on the next page.

Notes are used in a variety of credit transactions and often carry the name of the transaction involved. For example, a note that is secured by personal property, such as an automobile, is called a *collateral note,* because the property pledged as security for the satisfaction of the debt is called *collateral.*[2] A note payable in installments, such as installment payments for a large-screen television over a twelve-month period, is called an *installment note.*

A **certificate of deposit (CD)** is a type of note. A CD is issued when a party deposits money with a bank, and the bank promises to repay the money, with interest, on a certain date [UCC 3–104(j)]. The bank is the maker of the note, and the depositor is the payee. For example, on February 15, Sara Levin deposits $5,000 with the First National Bank of Whiteacre. The bank promises to repay the $5,000, plus 5½ percent interest, on August 15.

Certificates of deposit in small denominations (for amounts up to $100,000) are often sold by savings and loan associations, savings banks, and commercial banks. Certificates of deposit for amounts over $100,000 are called large (or jumbo) CDs. Exhibit 24–5 on page 467 shows a typical small CD.

Westlaw. See Case 24.2 at the end of this chapter. To view the full, unedited case from Westlaw,® go to this text's Web site at **http://wbl-cs.westbuslaw.com**.

2. To minimize the risk of loss when lending money, a creditor often requires the debtor to provide some collateral, or security, beyond a promise that the debt will be repaid. When this security takes the form of personal property (such as a motor vehicle), the creditor has an interest in the property known as a *security interest.* Security interests are discussed in detail in Chapter 28.

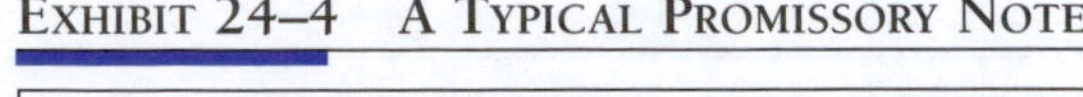

EXHIBIT 24–4 A TYPICAL PROMISSORY NOTE

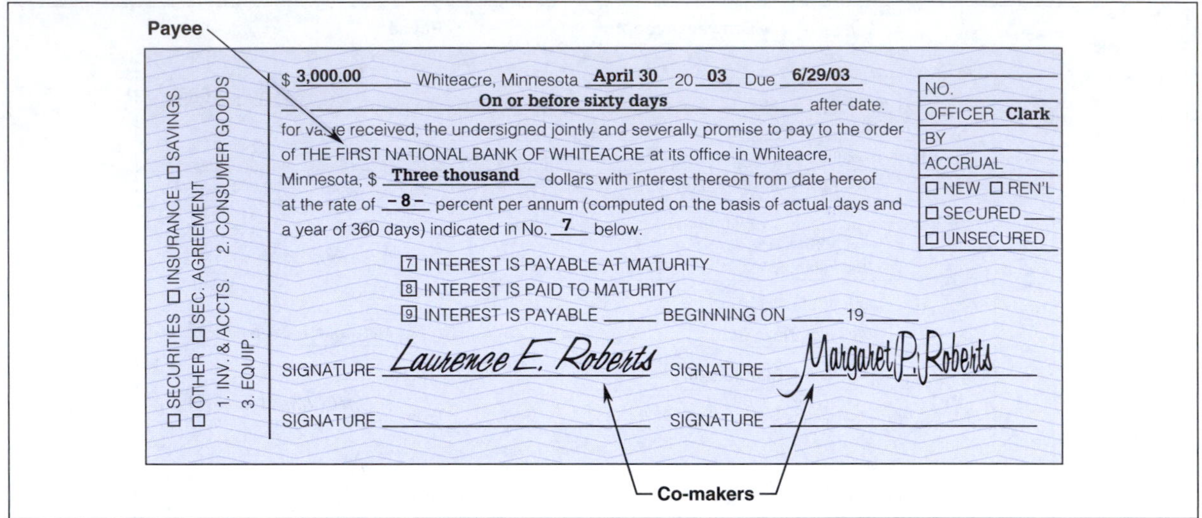

SECTION 4

Requirements for Negotiability

For an instrument to be negotiable, it must meet the following requirements:

1. Be in writing.
2. Be signed by the maker or the drawer.
3. Be an unconditional promise or order to pay.
4. State a fixed amount of money.
5. Be payable on demand or at a definite time.
6. Be payable to order or to bearer, unless it is a check.

WRITTEN FORM

Negotiable instruments must be in written form [UCC 3–103(a)(6)].[3] Clearly, an oral promise can create the danger of fraud or make it difficult to determine liability. Negotiable instruments must possess the quality of certainty that only formal, written expression can give. The writing must have the following qualities:

1. The writing must be on material that lends itself to *permanence*. Instruments carved in blocks of ice or recorded on other impermanent surfaces would not qualify as negotiable instruments. Suppose Shanda writes in the sand, "I promise to pay $500 to the order of Jason." This is not a negotiable instrument, because, although it is in writing, it lacks permanence.
2. The writing also must have *portability*. Although this is not a spelled-out legal requirement, if an instrument is not movable, it obviously cannot meet the requirement that it be freely transferable. For example, Cullen writes on the side of a cow, "I, Cullen, promise to pay to Merrill or her order $500 on demand." Technically, this meets the requirements of a negotiable instrument, but as a cow cannot easily be transferred in the ordinary course of business, the "instrument" is nonnegotiable.

SIGNATURES

For an instrument to be negotiable, it must be signed by (1) the maker if it is a note or a certificate of deposit or (2) the drawer if it is a draft or a check [UCC 3–103(a)(3), (5)]. If a person signs an instrument as an authorized *agent* for the maker or drawer, the maker or drawer has effectively signed the instrument. (Agents' signatures will be discussed in Chapter 26.)

The UCC grants extreme latitude in regard to what constitutes a signature. UCC 1–201(39) provides that a **signature** may include "any symbol executed or adopted by a party with present intention to authenticate a writing." UCC 3–401(b) expands on this by stating that a "signature may be made (i) manually or by means of a device or machine, and (ii) by the use

3. The writing requirement comes from the definitions of *order* and *promise* in UCC 3–103(a)(6), (9). In the unrevised Article 3, UCC 3–104(1) refers directly to "[a]ny writing."

EXHIBIT 24–5 A TYPICAL SMALL CD

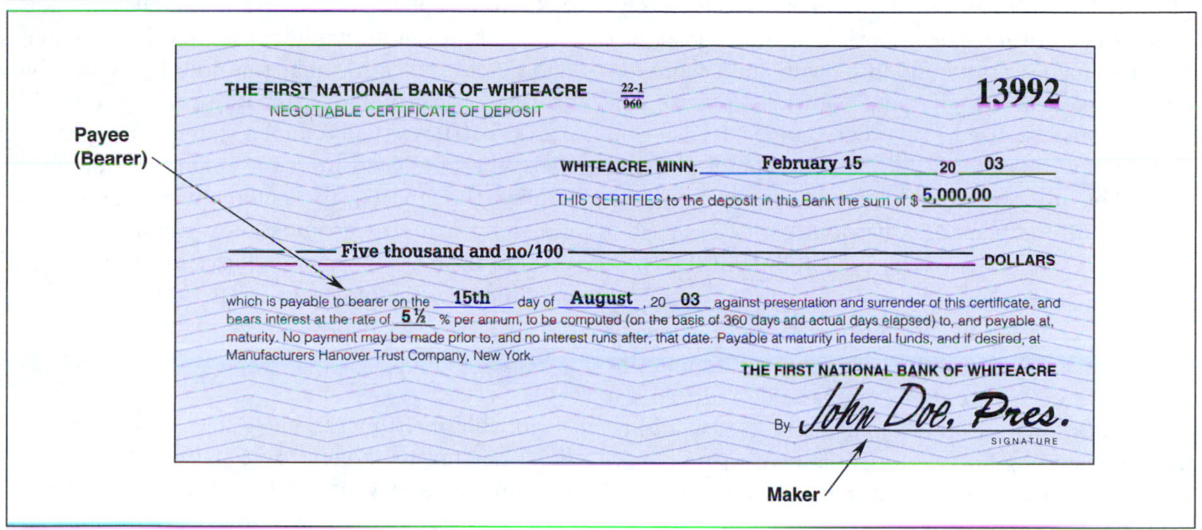
THE FIRST NATIONAL BANK OF WHITEACRE
NEGOTIABLE CERTIFICATE OF DEPOSIT
13992
WHITEACRE, MINN. February 15 20 03
THIS CERTIFIES to the deposit in this Bank the sum of $ 5,000.00
Five thousand and no/100 DOLLARS
which is payable to bearer on the 15th day of August, 20 03 against presentation and surrender of this certificate, and bears interest at the rate of 5 ½ % per annum, to be computed (on the basis of 360 days and actual days elapsed) to, and payable at, maturity. No payment may be made prior to, and no interest runs after, that date. Payable at maturity in federal funds, and if desired, at Manufacturers Hanover Trust Company, New York.
THE FIRST NATIONAL BANK OF WHITEACRE
By John Doe, Pres.
SIGNATURE

of any name, including a trade or assumed name, or by a word, mark, or symbol executed or adopted by a person with present intention to authenticate a writing." Thus, initials, an X (if the writing is signed by a witness), or a thumbprint will normally suffice as a signature. A trade name or an assumed name is also sufficient. Signatures that are placed onto instruments by means of rubber stamps are permitted and frequently used in the business world. If necessary, parol evidence (discussed in Chapter 14) is admissible to identify the signer. When the signer is identified, the signature becomes effective.

The location of the signature on the document is unimportant, though the usual place is the lower right-hand corner. A *handwritten* statement on the body of the instrument, such as "I, Kammie Orlik, promise to pay Janel Tan," is sufficient to act as a signature.

There are virtually no limitations on the manner in which a signature can be made, but one should be careful about receiving an instrument that has been signed in an unusual way. Furthermore, an unusual signature clearly decreases the *marketability* of an instrument, because it creates uncertainty.

UNCONDITIONAL PROMISE OR ORDER TO PAY

The terms of the promise or order must be included in the writing on the face of a negotiable instrument. The terms must also be *unconditional*—that is, they cannot be conditioned on the occurrence or nonoccurrence of some other event or agreement [UCC 3–104(a)].

Promise or Order. For an instrument to be negotiable, it must contain an express order or promise to pay. A mere acknowledgment of the debt, which might logically *imply* a promise, is not sufficient under the UCC, because the promise must be an *affirmative* (express) undertaking [UCC 3–103(a)(9)]. For example, the traditional I.O.U. is only an acknowledgment of indebtedness. Although the I.O.U. might logically *imply* a promise, it is not a negotiable instrument, because it does not contain an express promise to repay the debt. If such words as "to be paid on demand" or "due on demand" are added to the I.O.U., however, the need for an express promise is satisfied. Thus, if a buyer executes a promissory note using the words "I promise to pay $1,000 to the order of the seller for the purchase of X goods," then this requirement for a negotiable instrument is satisfied.

A certificate of deposit is exceptional in this respect. No express promise is required in a CD, because the bank's acknowledgment of the deposit and the other terms of the instrument clearly indicate a promise by the bank to repay the sum of money [UCC 3–104(j)].

An *order* is associated with three-party instruments, such as trade acceptances, checks, and drafts. An order directs a third party to pay the instrument as drawn. In the typical check, for example, the word *pay* (to the order of a payee) is a command to the drawee bank to pay the check when presented, and thus it is an order. The order is mandatory even if it is written in a courteous form with such words as "Please pay" or "Kindly pay." Generally, precise language must be used. An order stating "I wish you would pay" does not fulfill the requirement of precision. The order may be addressed to one person or to more than one person, either jointly ("to A *and* B") or alternatively ("to A *or* B") [UCC 3–103(a)(6)].

Unconditionality of Promise or Order. A negotiable instrument's utility as a substitute for money or as a credit device would be dramatically reduced if it had conditional promises attached to it. It would be time consuming and expensive to investigate conditional promises, and therefore the transferability of the negotiable instrument would be greatly restricted. Suppose that Granados promises in a note to pay McGraw $10,000 only if a certain ship reaches port. No one could safely purchase the promissory note without first investigating whether the ship had arrived. Even then, the facts disclosed by the investigation might be incorrect. To avoid such problems, the UCC provides that only instruments with unconditional promises or orders can be negotiable [UCC 3–104(a)].

A promise or order is conditional (and *not* negotiable) if it states any of the following:

1. That there is an express condition to payment.
2. That the promise or order is subject to or governed by another writing.
3. That the rights or obligations with respect to the promise or order are stated in another writing.

A reference to another writing, however, does not of itself make the promise or order conditional [UCC 3–106(a)]. For example, the words "as per contract" or "This debt arises from the sale of goods X and Y" do not render an instrument nonnegotiable.

Similarly, a statement in the instrument that payment can be made only out of a particular fund or source will not render the instrument nonnegotiable [UCC 3–106(b)(ii)].[4] Thus, for example, terms in a note that include the condition that payment will be made out of the proceeds of next year's cotton crop will not make the note nonnegotiable. (The payee of such a note, however, may find the note commercially unacceptable and refuse to take it.)

Finally, a simple statement in an otherwise negotiable note indicating that the note is secured by a mortgage does not destroy its negotiability [UCC 3–106(b)(i)]. Actually, such a statement might even make the note even more acceptable in commerce. Realize, though, that the statement that a note is secured by a mortgage must not stipulate that the maker's promise to pay is *subject to* the terms and conditions of the mortgage [UCC 3–106(a)(ii)].

A Fixed Amount of Money

Negotiable instruments must state with certainty a fixed amount of money to be paid at any time the instrument is payable [UCC 3–104(a)]. This requirement promises clarity and certainty in determining the value of the instrument.

Fixed Amount. The term *fixed amount* means an amount that is ascertainable from the face of the instrument. A demand note payable with 10 percent interest meets the requirement of a fixed amount because its amount can be determined at the time it is payable [UCC 3–104(a)].

The rate of interest may also be determined with reference to information that is not contained in the instrument if that information is readily ascertainable by reference to a formula or a source described in the instrument [UCC 3–112(b)]. For example, when an instrument is payable at the *legal rate of interest* (a rate of interest fixed by statute), the instrument is negotiable. Mortgage notes tied to a variable rate of interest (a rate that fluctuates as a result of market conditions) can also be negotiable.

Payable in Money. UCC 3–104(a) provides that a fixed amount is to be *payable in money*. The UCC defines money as "a medium of exchange authorized or adopted by a domestic or foreign government as a part of its currency" [UCC 1–201(24)].

Suppose that the maker of a note promises "to pay on demand $1,000 in U.S. gold." Because gold is not a medium of exchange adopted by the U.S. government, the note is not payable in money. The same result occurs if the maker promises "to pay $1,000 and fifty liters of 1994 Chateau Lafite-Rothschild wine," because the instrument is not payable *entirely* in money. An instrument payable in government bonds or in shares of IBM stock is not negotiable,

4. Section 3–105(2) of the unrevised Article 3 provided just the opposite: a term providing that payment could be made only out of a particular fund or source rendered the instrument nonnegotiable.

because neither is a medium of exchange recognized by the U.S. government. The statement "Payable in $1,000 U.S. currency or an equivalent value in gold" would render the instrument nonnegotiable if the maker reserved the option of paying in money *or* gold. If the option were left to the payee, some legal scholars argue that the instrument would be negotiable. Any instrument payable in the United States with a face amount stated in a foreign currency can be paid in the foreign money or in the equivalent in U.S. dollars [UCC 3–107].

Payable on Demand or at a Definite Time

A negotiable instrument must "be payable on demand or at a definite time" [UCC 3–104(a)(2)]. Clearly, to ascertain the value of a negotiable instrument, it is necessary to know when the maker, drawee, or acceptor is required to pay. It is also necessary to know when the obligations of secondary parties, such as *indorsers*[5] (to be discussed in Chapter 25), will arise. Furthermore, it is essential to know when an instrument is due in order to calculate when the statute of limitations may apply [UCC 3–118(a)]. Finally, with an interest-bearing instrument, it is necessary to know the exact interval during which the interest will accrue to determine the instrument's value today.

Payable on Demand. Instruments that are payable on demand include those that contain the words "Payable at sight" or "Payable upon presentment." **Presentment** occurs when a person presents an instrument to the party liable on the note to collect payment; presentment also occurs when a person presents an instrument to a drawee for acceptance—see the discussion of trade acceptances earlier in this chapter.

The very nature of the instrument may indicate that it is payable on demand. For example, a check, by definition, is payable on demand [UCC 3–104(f)]. If no time for payment is specified and the person responsible for payment must pay on the instrument's presentment, the instrument is payable on demand [UCC 3–108(a)].

Payable at a Definite Time. If an instrument is not payable on demand, to be negotiable it must be payable at a definite time. An instrument is payable at a definite time if it states that it is payable (1) on a specified date, (2) within a definite period of time (such as thirty days) after sight or acceptance, or (3) on a date or time readily ascertainable at the time the promise or order is issued [UCC 3–108(b)]. The maker or drawee is under no obligation to pay until the specified time.

Suppose that an instrument dated June 1, 2001, states, "One year after the death of my grandfather, Jeremy Adams, I promise to pay to the order of Lucy Harmon $500. [Signed] Jacqueline Wells." This instrument is nonnegotiable. Because the date of the grandfather's death is uncertain, the instrument is not payable at a definite time, even though the event is bound to occur or has already occurred.

When an instrument is payable on or before a stated date, it is clearly payable at a definite time, although the maker has the option of paying before the stated maturity date. This uncertainty does not violate the definite-time requirement. Suppose that John gives Ernesto an instrument dated May 1, 2003, that indicates on its face that it is payable on or before May 1, 2005. This instrument satisfies the requirement. In contrast, an instrument that is undated and made payable "one month after date" is clearly nonnegotiable. There is no way to determine the maturity date from the face of the instrument.

Westlaw. See Case 24.3 at the end of this chapter. To view the full, unedited case from Westlaw,® go to this text's Web site at **http://wbl-cs.westbuslaw.com**.

Acceleration Clause. An **acceleration clause** allows a payee or other holder of a time instrument to demand payment of the entire amount due, with interest, if a certain event occurs, such as a default in payment of an installment when due.

Assume that Martin lends $1,000 to Ruth. Ruth makes a negotiable note promising to pay $100 per month for eleven months. The note contains an acceleration provision that permits Martin or any holder to demand at once all the payments plus the interest owed to date if Ruth fails to pay an installment in any given month. If, for example, Ruth fails to make the third payment and Martin accelerates the unpaid balance, the note will be due and payable in full. Ruth will owe Martin the remaining principal plus any unpaid interest.

5. We should note here that because the UCC uses the spelling *indorse (indorsement,* and so on), rather than the more common spelling *endorse (endorsement,* and so on), we adopt the UCC's spelling here and in other chapters in the text.

Under the UCC, instruments that include acceleration clauses are negotiable regardless of the reasons for the accelerations, because (1) the exact value of the instrument can be ascertained and (2) the instrument will be payable on a specified date if the event allowing acceleration does not occur [UCC 3–108(b)(ii)]. Thus, the specified date is the outside limit used to determine the value of the instrument.

Extension Clause. The reverse of an acceleration clause is an **extension clause**, which allows the date of maturity to be extended into the future [UCC 3–108(b)(iii), (iv)]. To keep the instrument negotiable, the interval of the extension must be specified if the right to extend is given to the maker or the drawer of the instrument. If, however, the holder of the instrument can extend it, the extended maturity date does not have to be specified.

Suppose that a note reads, "The maker has the right to postpone the time of payment of this note beyond its definite maturity date of January 1, 2004. This extension, however, shall be for no more than a reasonable time." A note with this language is not negotiable, because it does not satisfy the definite-time requirement. The right to extend is the maker's, and the maker has not indicated when the note will become due after the extension.

In contrast, suppose that a note reads, "The holder of this note at the date of maturity, January 1, 2004, can extend the time of payment until the following June 1 or later, if the holder so wishes." This note is a negotiable instrument. The length of the extension does not have to be specified, because the option to extend is solely that of the holder. After January 1, 2004, the note is, in effect, a demand instrument.

PAYABLE TO ORDER OR TO BEARER

Because one of the functions of a negotiable instrument is to serve as a substitute for money, freedom to transfer is essential. To assure a proper transfer, the instrument must be "payable to order or to bearer" at the time it is issued or first comes into the possession of the holder [UCC 3–104(a)(1)]. An instrument is not negotiable unless it meets this requirement.

Order Instruments. An **order instrument** is an instrument that is payable (1) "to the order of an identified person" or (2) "to an identified person or order" [UCC 3–109(b)]. An identified person is the person "to whom the instrument is initially payable" as determined by the intent of the maker or drawer [UCC 3–110(a)]. The identified person, in turn, may transfer the instrument to whomever he or she wishes. Thus, the maker or drawer is agreeing to pay either the person specified on the instrument or whomever that person might designate. In this way, the instrument retains its transferability. Suppose an instrument states, "Payable to the order of James Jarrot" or "Pay to James Jarrot or order." Clearly, the maker or drawer has indicated that a payment will be made to Jarrot or to whomever Jarrot designates. The instrument is negotiable.

Except for bearer instruments (explained in the following paragraph), the person specified must be named with *certainty*, because the transfer of an order instrument requires an indorsement. (An **indorsement** is a signature placed on an instrument, such as on the back of a check, generally for the purpose of transferring one's ownership rights in the instrument. Indorsements will be discussed at length in Chapter 25.) If an instrument states, "Payable to the order of my kissing cousin," the instrument is nonnegotiable, because a holder could not be sure that the person who indorsed the instrument was actually the "kissing cousin" who was supposed to have indorsed it.

Bearer Instruments. A **bearer instrument** is an instrument that does not designate a specific payee [UCC 3–109(a)]. The term **bearer** refers to a person in possession of an instrument that is payable to bearer or indorsed in blank (with a signature only, as will be discussed in Chapter 25) [UCC 1–201(5), 3–109(a), 3–109(c)]. This means that the maker or drawer agrees to pay anyone who presents the instrument for payment. Any instrument containing one of the following terms is a bearer instrument:

1. "Payable to the order of bearer."
2. "Payable to Rocky Reed or bearer."
3. "Payable to bearer."
4. "Pay cash."
5. "Pay to the order of cash."

In addition, an instrument that "indicates that it is not payable to an identified person" is a bearer instrument [UCC 3–109(a)(3)]. Thus, an instrument that is "payable to X" can be negotiated as a bearer instrument, as though it were payable to cash. An instrument that is "payable to the order of the Camrod Company," however, if no such company exists, is not a bearer instrument, because the UCC does not accept an instrument issued to a nonexistent organization as payable to bearer [UCC 3–109, Comment 2].

SECTION 5

Factors Not Affecting Negotiability

Certain ambiguities or omissions will not affect the negotiability of an instrument. Article 3's rules for interpreting ambiguous terms include the following:

1. Unless the date of an instrument is necessary to determine a definite time for payment, the fact that an instrument is undated does not affect its negotiability. A typical example is a check that has no date [UCC 3–113(b)].
2. Postdating or antedating an instrument does not affect negotiability [UCC 3–113(a)].
3. Handwritten terms outweigh typewritten and printed terms (preprinted terms on forms, for example), and typewritten terms outweigh printed terms [UCC 3–114]. For example, if your check is printed "Pay to the order of," and in handwriting you insert in the blank "Anita Delgado or bearer," the check is a bearer instrument.
4. Words outweigh figures unless the words are ambiguous [UCC 3–114]. This is important when the numerical amount and written amount on a check differ.
5. When a particular interest rate is not specified but the instrument simply states "with interest," the interest rate is the judgment rate of interest (a rate of interest fixed by statute that is applied to a monetary judgment awarded by a court until the judgment is paid or terminated) [UCC 3–112(b)].
6. A notation on a check that it is "nonnegotiable" or "not governed by Article 3" has no effect on a check's negotiability. Any other instrument, however, even if it meets all of the requirements of negotiability, can be made nonnegotiable by the maker's or drawer's conspicuously noting on it that it is "nonnegotiable" or "not governed by Article 3" [UCC 3–104(d)].[6]

6. This is not true under the unrevised Article 3.

TERMS AND CONCEPTS TO REVIEW

acceleration clause 469	draft 464	negotiable instrument 462
acceptance 464	drawee 464	order instrument 470
banker's acceptance 464	drawer 464	payee 464
bearer 470	extension clause 470	presentment 469
bearer instrument 470	holder 463	promissory note 465
certificate of deposit (CD) 465	indorsement 470	signature 466
check 464	issue 463	trade acceptance 464
demand deposit 463	maker 465	

CHAPTER SUMMARY

Article 3 of the UCC	Article 3 of the Uniform Commercial Code governs the negotiability and transferability of negotiable instruments. Article 3 was significantly revised in 1990. Almost all of the states have adopted the revised article.
Function and Types of Negotiable Instruments	A negotiable instrument can function as a substitute for money or as an extension of credit. To operate practically as either, it is essential that the instrument be easily transferable without danger of being uncollectible. The UCC specifies four types of negotiable instruments: drafts, checks, promissory notes, and certificates of deposit (CDs). These instruments fall into two basic classifications:

CHAPTER SUMMARY—CONTINUED

Function and Types of Negotiable Instruments—continued	1. *Demand instruments versus time instruments*—A demand instrument is payable on demand (when the holder presents it to the maker or drawer). A time instrument is payable at a future date. 2. *Orders to pay versus promises to pay*—Checks and drafts are *orders* to pay. Promissory notes and certificates of deposit (CDs) are *promises* to pay.
Requirements for Negotiability	To be negotiable, an instrument must meet the following requirements: 1. Be in writing. 2. Be signed by the maker or drawer. 3. Be an unconditional promise or order to pay. 4. State a fixed amount of money. 5. Be payable on demand or at a definite time. 6. Be payable to order or bearer.
Factors Not Affecting Negotiability	1. The fact that an instrument is undated does not affect its negotiability unless the date is necessary to determine a definite time for payment. 2. Postdating or antedating an instrument does not affect negotiability. 3. Handwritten terms take priority over typewritten and printed terms. 4. Words outweigh figures unless the words are ambiguous. 5. An instrument that states "with interest" but that does not state the interest rate is payable at the judgment rate of interest.

CASES FOR ANALYSIS

Westlaw. You can access the full text of each case presented below by going to the Westlaw cases on this text's Web site at http://wbl-cs.westbuslaw.com. Each Westlaw case includes the names of all plaintiffs and defendants, the dates on which the case was argued and decided, a brief summary of the issues and decisions in the case, headnotes classifying the specific issues in the case according to the West Key Number System, and the court's opinion. Concurring and dissenting opinions, if any, are included as well.

CASE 24.1 CHECKS

FLATIRON LINEN, INC. V. FIRST AMERICAN STATE BANK
Colorado Supreme Court, 2001.
23 P.3d 1209.

Justice *KOURLIS* delivered the Opinion of the Court.

In this case, we granted *certiorari* to address questions related to the legal status of a cashier's check under Articles 3 and 4 of the Uniform Commercial Code (U.C.C.). Specifically, we address the issue of whether an obligated bank that accepts an endorsed personal check on the account of one of its customers and issues a cashier's check in the same amount can later refuse to honor that cashier's check on the basis that its customer had previously placed a stop payment order on the check and its employee, the cashier, failed to notice the stop payment order on the computer records. * * *

* * * *

I.

In 1996, Flatiron received a personal check for $4,100, drawn on an account at First American. Flatiron attempted to deposit the check the same day, but First American returned the check to Flatiron due to insufficient funds in the issuer's account. The next day, the issuer of the check contacted First American and requested a stop payment order on the dishonored check.

Five months later, without knowledge of the stop payment order, Flatiron contacted First American and inquired whether the dishonored check would clear. An employee of First American responded that the account contained sufficient funds for the check to clear. Flatiron then took the check to a First American branch and presented it for payment. A teller again verified that the account had sufficient funds to cover the check. The teller failed to notice the stop payment order on the check and, in exchange for the check, issued the plaintiff a cashier's check for $4,100.

Flatiron then went to its own bank, Colorado National Bank (CNB), deposited the cashier's check, and immediately withdrew the same amount of funds in the form of cash and a CNB cashier's check payable to Public Service Company of Colorado. Meanwhile, First American discovered the stop payment order on the original check. First American called and wrote to Flatiron, informing Flatiron of First American's mistake in issuing the cashier's check, asking for its return, and informing Flatiron that it intended to dishonor the cashier's check upon presentment.

The next day, CNB contacted Flatiron and informed it that First American had indeed dishonored the cashier's check. CNB charged back Flatiron's account for the amount of the cashier's check, resulting in an overdraft in Flatiron's account.

Flatiron filed this action [in a Colorado state court against] * * * First American to recover on First American's cashier's check * * *.

The trial court * * * granted summary judgment for First American * * *.

On appeal, the [state intermediate] court of appeals agreed * * *.

II.

We begin by discussing the proper classification of cashier's checks. *Our analysis of this case turns on whether we treat a cashier's check as an ordinary negotiable instrument or whether we treat it as equivalent to cash.* [Emphasis added.]

A.

Courts are split on this issue. A minority of courts treat a cashier's check as a note, subject to the provisions of the U.C.C.

Both the trial court and the court of appeals adopted this approach. Under this reasoning, courts then turn to the U.C.C. to determine which defenses the bank may assert against the holder of a cashier's check. [Colorado Revised Statutes] Section 4-3-305 [Colorado's version of UCC 3–305] outlines the availability of defenses to the payment of negotiable instruments under the revised U.C.C. and differentiates between defenses that may be asserted only against a holder in due course and those that may be asserted against a holder not in due course. The only defenses available against a holder in due course are the "real defenses." When the instrument is held by a holder not in due course, the obligor can raise not only the real defenses, but also the general contract defenses and the defenses included in the U.C.C. Failure of consideration is a defense that "would be available if the person entitled to enforce the instrument were enforcing a right to payment under a simple contract." Therefore, such a defense cannot be used against a holder in due course. Section 4-3-302 [UCC 3–302] outlines the requirements to establish the status of a holder in due course. The basic prerequisites of a holder in due course are: receiving the instrument for value, in good faith, and without notice of defects or claims against it. Hence, under this theory, in order for Flatiron to have holder in due course status, it must prove that it acted in good faith when it presented the personal check, that it had no knowledge of the stop payment order, and that the personal check had intrinsic value.

The majority of courts hold that a cashier's check is the equivalent of cash, accepted when issued. Those courts do not treat the cashier's check as a check on the bank's account, but rather as the equivalent of cash. Courts following this approach have held that a cashier's check is a bill of exchange drawn by a bank upon itself. Therefore, it is accepted in advance by the act of its issuance, and it cannot be dishonored by the issuing bank.

We agree with the majority of courts that a cashier's check is equivalent to cash.

B.

We begin with an analysis of the U.C.C.'s treatment of cashier's checks. Although the U.C.C. does not specifically state how cashier's checks should be classified, it does provide some guidance. Section 4-3-104(g) [UCC 3–104(g)] defines a cashier's check as "a draft with respect to which the drawer and drawee are the same bank or branches of the same bank." Because the bank serves as both the drawer and the drawee of the cashier's check, the check becomes a promise by the bank to draw the amount of the check from its own resources and to pay the check upon demand. Thus, the issuance of the cashier's check constitutes an acceptance by the issuing bank and the cashier's check itself becomes the primary obligation of the bank. Once the bank issues and delivers the cashier's check to the payee, the transaction is complete as far as the payee is concerned. *Because the issuing bank is obligated to pay the cashier's check upon presentment, we conclude that a cashier's check is essentially the same as cash.* [Emphasis added.]

* * * *

C.

* * * The commercial world treats cashier's checks as the equivalent of cash. People accept cashier's checks as a substitute for cash because the bank, not an individual, stands behind it. By issuing a cashier's check, the bank becomes a guarantor of the value of the check and pledges its resources to the payment of the amount represented upon presentation. To allow the bank to stop payment on such an instrument would be inconsistent with the representation it makes in issuing the check. Such a rule would undermine the public confidence in the bank and its checks and thereby deprive the cashier's check of the essential incident which makes it useful.

Cashier's checks play a unique role in the American economy because they are widely recognized as a cash equivalent. The public uses cashier's checks because they are a reliable vehicle for transferring funds, are as negotiable as cash, and are free of the risks of loss and theft that accompany cash.

In short, we conclude that cashier's checks represent the unconditional obligation of the issuing bank to pay, and therefore, banks may not dishonor their cashier's checks once issued.

* * * *

IV.

In conclusion, we hold that when First American issued the cashier's check, it became an unconditional promise to pay the amount of the check—as the equivalent of cash. Accordingly, First American was not entitled to stop payment on the cashier's check. * * * Therefore, we reverse the judgment of the court of appeals, and remand the case with directions to return it to the trial court for proceedings consistent with this opinion.

CASE 24.2 PROMISSORY NOTES

UNITED STATES V. DURBIN

United States District Court,
Southern District of Texas, 1999.
64 F.Supp.2d 635.

HUGHES, District Judge.

1. *Introduction.*

The government has sued for the amount due on a promissory note issued for a student loan that the government guaranteed. The government will recover its money.

2. *Student Loans.*

When the student borrowed money for his education, he issued a note. The bank lent the money under a federal program to assist students of post-secondary institutions. Ordinarily, repayment begins nine to twelve months after the student fails to carry at least one-half of the normal full-time course load. Lenders accept these notes because they are fully insured by the government.

When the student defaults on his repayment, the lender presents the current balance—principal, interest, and costs—to the government agency that guaranteed it. On paying the original lender, the government becomes the lender, and the borrower owes the government directly.

3. *Promissory Notes.*

A note is an unconditional promise to pay. It is an obligation of the borrower to the lender. *The practice and law of notes developed so that people could lend on the credit of a person with confidence that collecting the debt would not be complicated by side issues. As a result of their unconditional, absolute character, loans are both extended in the first place and traded among lenders with no direct knowledge of the original transaction, reducing their cost to the borrowers.* [Emphasis added.]

The government must show three things to win: (1) the defendant is the person who issued the note; (2) the government owns the note; and (3) the note is unpaid. In addition to the unpaid amount, the lender may collect attorney's fees under state and federal law. Federal law also allows reasonable administrative and collection costs.

4. *Defenses.*

The note may be enforced against the borrower unless he can show that he did not issue it or that he paid it. Unlike many other kinds of cases, the borrower largely has the responsibility to produce evidence. Evidence is not simply saying that something is true; evidence is specific facts of when, who, where, and how much as well as supporting records like canceled checks and tax returns. Under state law, a note is enforceable unless the borrower can show that he paid the note or that the note was forged.

A. Forgery is proof that the note was not issued by the apparent borrower nor issued under his authority. If the note was physically signed by another person—a parent or friend, say—the person who got the direct benefit of the funds is responsible for repayment.

B. Payment is proof that the debt represented by the note was returned to the lender from sources like cash, [a] check, or credit from tax refunds.

5. *Non-Defenses.*

Statute of limitations, laches, and failure of consideration are inapplicable in student loan cases.

A. No statute of limitations bars the government's right to collect on student loans. The government may have taken a long time to get around to collecting its debts, but while inconvenient, the delay does not affect the borrower's duty to make full payment. Federal law was changed to eliminate all restrictions on the time that the debts can be recovered.

B. In the law, when a person has waited a long time to enforce a right, courts sometimes do not enforce it. This is called laches, which is French for slackness. Laches is a second-guess supplied by judges under traditional law; however, traditional law does not apply when there is a statute that directly applies. The specific act of the legislative branch eliminates this implied limit. In 1991, Congress said that no delay is too long.

Even if no recent statute interfered, laches would not apply to the collection of a note. Laches requires the person claiming its benefit to have relied on the failure to enforce the right. In the case of a student loan, the borrower did all of his reliance shortly after signing the note—he spent the money. It has remained spent. In the years the government has not collected the debt, the borrower has done nothing with the money or about the debt.

C. Failure of consideration is the legal claim that a person did not get something of value in exchange for his promise to pay. In a student loan case, what the student got from the lender was money, and its value is unquestionable.

Sometimes students would like not to pay the loan because they now feel that the school they attended was not very good or that the education they got was not adequate to get them a good job. Even if these feelings are supported by solid evidence, they do not matter. The bank lent money, and the government promised the bank that the debt would be paid. Neither the bank nor the government guaranteed satisfaction with schools or educations. Because the choice of institution and curriculum was the student's, the responsibility for a bad choice rests with the student.

6. *Conclusion.*

The government has demonstrated that the defendant issued the promissory note, that the government owns the note, and that the note is in default and unpaid. The law requires that there be a judgment for the government for the principal, interest, costs, and attorney's fees.

Final Judgment

The United States of America recovers from Robert R. Durbin:

1. Principal of $3,670.25;
2. Prejudgment interest of $4,912.79;
3. Attorneys' fees of $1,200;
4. Administrative costs of $6.75; and
5. Post-judgment interest at 5.224% per annum.

CASE 24.3 PAYABLE ON DEMAND OR AT A DEFINITE TIME

BARCLAYS BANK PLC v. JOHNSON

Court of Appeals of North Carolina, 1998.
129 N.C.App. 370,
499 S.E.2d 768.

MCGEE, Judge.

Defendant executed a promissory note for $28,979.15 on 27 January 1993 in favor of Healthco International, Inc. to secure payment for dental supplies defendant purchased from Healthco for his dental practice. The pertinent language of the note provided that it was:

> [p]ayable in ____, Successive Monthly Installments of $ __________ Each, and in 11 Successive Monthly Installments of $2,414.92 Each thereafter, and in a final payment of $2,415.03 thereafter. The first installment being payable on the __ day of ______ 19 __, and the remaining installments on the same date of each month thereafter until paid.

The blank indicating the date of the initial installment payment was never filled in by either party.

Barclays Bank purchased this note on 5 February 1993. Defendant made six payments on the note with the first payment being on 22 March 1993. Defendant then defaulted on the note by failing to make the remaining six payments. Barclays Bank filed a complaint on 18 April 1995 seeking payment of the balance owed on the note. Defendant filed an answer alleging as a defense the failure of consideration as Healthco International did not complete delivery of the dental supplies purchased by defendant. The answer further alleged that Barclays Bank was not a holder in due course as the note was incomplete on its face, and Barclays Bank knew or should have known of this defect. * * * [T]he trial court entered summary judgment for defendant * * * . Barclays Bank appeals from this judgment.

* * * *

The main issue in this case is whether Barclays Bank, as purchaser of the promissory note, is a holder in due course and thus immune from the defense of failure of consideration asserted by defendant. This question is determined by whether the promissory note constitutes a negotiable instrument even though it does not state that it is payable on demand or at a definite time.

This case is governed by the pre-amended Article 3 of our Uniform Commercial Code, since the promissory note was executed prior to 1 October 1995.[7] *A holder in due course is one who takes an instrument for value, in good faith and without notice that it is overdue or has been dishonored or of any defense against or claim to it on the part of any person. One may only be a holder in due course of a negotiable instrument.* [Emphasis added.]

One of the requirements of a "negotiable instrument" is that it be "payable on demand or at a definite time." An instrument is "payable at a definite time" if by its terms it is payable:

> (a) on or before a stated date or at a fixed period after a stated date; or
> (b) at a fixed period after sight; or
> (c) at a definite time subject to any acceleration; or
> (d) at a definite time subject to extension at the option of the holder, or to extension to a further definite time at the option of the maker or acceptor or automatically upon or after a specified act or event.
> (2) An instrument which by its terms is otherwise payable only upon an act or event uncertain as to time of occurrence is not payable at a definite time even though the act or event has occurred.

Barclays Bank argues that the note is a negotiable instrument even though it does not state that it is payable on demand or at a definite time. We disagree. Historically, our courts have required strict compliance with the requirements set out under the Uniform Commercial Code defining negotiable instruments. The drafters of the Code encouraged the courts to strictly interpret the definitional

7. Although this case was decided under the unrevised UCC Article 3, the result under the revised Article 3 would likely be the same.

requirements to the extent that in doubtful cases the court's decision should be against negotiability. In this case it is undisputed that the note did not state either that it was payable on demand or at a definite time. For this reason, we hold that the note does not meet the requirements * * * for negotiability. Accordingly, Barclays Bank does not qualify as a holder in due course of a negotiable instrument and is not immune from the defense of failure of consideration.

* * * *

Affirmed.

Case Problems

24–1. Gilbert Ramirez claimed that he had purchased a winning lottery ticket, the prize for which was approximately $1.5 million. Unfortunately, Ramirez had lost the ticket itself and therefore could not claim the prize. Even though the evidence indicated that he very likely was indeed the purchaser of the winning ticket, under the state lottery rules, he could not claim the prize unless he produced the winning ticket. In a legal action brought by Ramirez against the state lottery bureau, Ramirez claimed, among other things, that the lottery ticket was a negotiable instrument because on the back of each lottery ticket were the following words: "THIS TICKET IS A BEARER INSTRUMENT SO TREAT IT AS IF IT WERE CASH." Because the owner of a lost negotiable instrument can collect on the instrument if certain requirements are met—such as establishing proof of ownership, the terms of the instrument, and so on—Ramirez argued that he should be allowed to claim the prize if he could meet these requirements. Discuss fully whether Ramirez will succeed in his claim that the lottery ticket was a negotiable instrument. [*Ramirez v. Bureau of State Lottery,* 186 Mich.App. 275, 463 N.W.2d 245 (1990)]

24–2. 1601 Partners, Ltd., executed a promissory note in the amount of $1,650,000. As collateral for the loan represented by the note, 1601 Partners executed a deed of trust (a mortgage) for certain property owned by 1601 Partners. The note stated that "the terms, agreements and conditions of [the deed of trust] are by reference made part of the note." Southmark subsequently assigned the note to San Jacinto Savings Association (SJSA). When 1601 Partners failed to make the payments due under the note, SJSA sold the collateral property for $1,050,000. SJSA subsequently failed, and the Resolution Trust Corp. (RTC) took over its accounts. To recover the deficiency between the amount of the loan and the price for which the collateral sold, RTC filed a lawsuit against 1601 Partners and others. One of the issues before the court was whether the note was negotiable. The defendants argued that it was not, because it incorporated the terms of the deed of trust. How should the court rule on this issue? Discuss. [*Resolution Trust Corp. v. 1601 Partners, Ltd.,* 796 F.Supp. 238 (N.D.Tex. 1992)]

24–3. Emil Amberboy and others invested in oil and gas partnerships formed by Vanguard Group International, Inc. Each investor made a down payment in cash and signed a promissory note payable to the partnership for the balance of the investment. Each note stated that its interest rate was to be determined by reference to a certain bank's published prime rate. Several months later, Vanguard sold the notes to Société de Banque Privée. Suspecting that the investments were being handled fraudulently, Amberboy and the other investors stopped making payments on the notes and filed a lawsuit against Société de Banque Privée and others. One of the issues before the court was whether the notes were negotiable. The plaintiffs contended that because the interest rate on the notes could be calculated only by reference to a source outside the notes, the notes could not be negotiable instruments. How should the court rule? [*Amberboy v. Société de Banque Privée,* 831 S.W.2d 793 (Tex. 1992)]

24–4. During a three-year period, Appliances, Inc., performed electrical heating and plumbing work for Yost Construction worth approximately $7,000. Yost never paid Appliances for any of these jobs. Yost, both in his capacity as president of the construction company and his individual capacity, signed an undated ninety-day promissory note in favor of Appliances to reduce Yost Construction's debt and to have Appliances perform services for Yost as an individual. Neither Yost in his individual capacity nor Yost Construction paid the note, and Appliances filed suit. The trial court held that the undated note was totally unenforceable. Should Appliances prevail on appeal by arguing that the note was negotiable? [*Appliances, Inc. v. Yost,* 181 Conn. 207, 435 A.2d 1 (1980)]

24–5. Thomas Fink, Donald Schroer, David Swanson, and Marie Swanson—doing business as F.S.S.S., a partnership—signed two promissory notes to borrow money from the Alaska Mutual Bank (AMB), providing the same real estate as collateral for both loans. Patricia Fink and LaVonne Schroer signed guaranties of repayment for the second note. AMB failed. The first note ended up in the hands of the First Interstate Bank of Oregon. The second fell into the possession of the Federal Deposit Insurance Corporation (FDIC). When Fink, Schroer, and the Swansons were unable to repay the first note, the Oregon bank agreed to accept a lesser amount if the FDIC would approve. The FDIC refused and filed a suit in a federal district court against the Finks, the Schroers, and the Swansons to collect the money due on the note that the FDIC now owned. On the FDIC's motion for summary judgment, one of the issues was whether Patricia and LaVonne's guaranties were negotiable instruments. If so, Patricia and LaVonne could have asserted a certain defense under which they might have been able to avoid liability. Did the guaranties satisfy the requirements for negotiable instruments? Explain. [*Federal Deposit Insurance Corp. v. F.S.S.S.*, 829 F.Supp. 317 (D.Alaska 1993)]

24–6. McDonald, the personal representative of the Marion Cahill estate, made out a check to himself on the estate checking account. The payee and the amount of the check read: "Pay to the order of Emmet E. McDonald $10,075.00 Ten hundred seventy-five . . . Dollars." The bank paid to McDonald and charged the estate account $10,075.00—the numerical rather than the written amount. McDonald absconded with the money. Yates, who succeeded McDonald as the personal representative of the estate, sued the bank to recover the $9,000 difference between $1,075 and $10,075, alleging that the bank should have paid only the amount expressed in words. The trial court dismissed the claim, and Yates appealed. Should Yates prevail on appeal? Discuss fully. [*Yates v. Commercial Bank & Trust Co.*, 432 So.2d 725 (Fla.App. 1983)]

24–7. Higgins, a used-car dealer, sold a 1977 Corvette to Holsonback, the defendant. Holsonback paid for the car with a draft drawn on First State Bank of Albertville, the plaintiff. On the draft were the following words: "ENCLOSED—TITLE ON 77 CHEV. VETT. FREE OF ALL LIENS AND ENCUMBRANCE." The bank paid Higgins. First State presented the draft to Holsonback for payment, but Holsonback refused to pay, claiming that Higgins was in breach of contract. First State Bank filed suit against Holsonback on his draft. Holsonback claimed that the draft was nonnegotiable because the draft's reference to the title rendered the draft conditional. Discuss Holsonback's contention. [*Holsonback v. First State Bank of Albertville*, 394 So.2d 381 Ala.Civ.App 1980)]

24–8. Walter Peffer loaned $125,000 to the Pefferoni Pizza Company. The note included a clause that allowed the maker (Pefferoni Pizza) to renegotiate the terms of repayment at any time and then extend the time for repayment by up to eighty-four months. Later, Peffer borrowed money from Northern Bank, using the Pefferoni Pizza note as collateral. When Peffer failed to repay his loan, the bank tried to collect on the collateral note, but the pizza company failed to pay. The bank filed a suit in a Nebraska state court against Pefferoni Pizza to recover on the collateral note. Pefferoni Pizza argued in part that its note was not a negotiable instrument because under the renegotiation clause, it was not payable at a definite time. Was the note a negotiable instrument? Explain. [*Northern Bank v. Pefferoni Pizza Co.*, 5 Neb.App. 50, 555 N.W.2d 338 (1996)]

24–9. Holly Hill Acres, Ltd., was the maker of a promissory note that named Rogers and Blythe as payees. Holly Hill Acres gave the note to Rogers and Blythe as payment for certain property, and Rogers and Blythe retained a mortgage (lien) on the property. (This type of mortgage is known as a purchase-money mortgage.) The note stated in part: "This note is secured by a mortgage on real estate. . . . The terms of said mortgage are by this reference made part hereof." Subsequently, Rogers and Blythe assigned the promissory note and the mortgage to Charter Bank of Gainesville. Holly Hill Acres defaulted on the note, and when the bank sued to recover, Holly Hill Acres claimed that Rogers and Blythe had fraudulently induced the company to purchase the land. Holly Hill Acres refused to pay on the note. The bank argued that it was a special type of assignee called a holder in due course because the promissory note was a negotiable instrument. This being the case, the bank claimed an unhampered right to recover on the note despite any underlying disputes between Holly Hill Acres and Rogers and Blythe. (A holder in due course takes a negotiable instrument free of most defenses to payment on it. This is the rule only when a negotiable instrument is involved.) The trial court held that the promissory note was negotiable and that the bank, as a holder in due course, could recover. Holly Hill Acres appealed, claiming that because the note was made subject to the mortgage agreement, the note was rendered nonnegotiable. What will happen on appeal? Discuss fully. [*Holly Hill Acres, Ltd. v. Charter Bank of Gainesville*, 314 So.2d 209 (Fla.App. 2d Dist. 1975)]

24–10. Walls purchased a car from Morris Chevrolet and signed a promissory note and security agreement on the same piece of paper. The note stated the amount owed and the finance charge, but it did not state the amount that would be owed if the note was prepaid. This amount, however, could be determined from the security agreement, which was on the same paper. (The promissory noted referred to the security agreement but did not incorporate its terms.) If Walls could show that the promissory note was negotiable, he could recover three times the amount of the credit charge under a statute that prohibits acceptance of a negotiable instrument except a check in conjunction with a consumer credit sale. The trial court held the note nonnegotiable and dismissed Walls's claim. What will happen on appeal? Discuss. [*Walls v. Morris Chevrolet, Inc.*, 515 P.2d 1405 (Okla.App. 1973)]

24–11. Briggs signed a note that read in part as follows: "*Ninety days* after date, I, we, or either of us, promise to pay to the order of *Three Thousand Four Hundred Ninety-Eight and 45/100—Dollars.*" The italic words and symbols were typed, and the remainder of the words in this quotation were preprinted. No blanks had been left on the face of the instrument; any unused space had been filled in with hyphens. The note contained several clauses that permitted acceleration in the event the holder deemed itself insecure. When the note was not paid at maturity, Broadway Management Corp. brought suit on the note for full payment, claiming that it (Broadway) was a holder. Is this an order or bearer instrument? What changes, if any, would have to be made on the note for it to be a negotiable instrument? [*Broadway Management Corp. v. Briggs*, 30 Ill.App.3d 403, 332 N.E.2d 131 (1975)]

24–12. Eugene Kindy, a seller of diesel engine parts, agreed to buy four diesel engines from Tony Hicks for $13,000. Kindy transferred $6,500 by wire and issued a check for the remainder. Kindy placed two different amounts on the check, because he did not want the check honored until Hicks had delivered the engine parts. Using a check-imprinting machine, Kindy imprinted $5,500 on the check in the space where the dollar amount is normally written in words, but he wrote $6,500 in figures in the box usually reserved for numbers. An employee of Galatia Community State Bank, noticing the discrepancy, altered the figures to read "$5,500," initialed the change, and accepted the check. The check was returned to Galatia by First National Bank at Kindy's request because Hicks had not delivered the engine parts. In the litigation that followed, a key issue was whether the machine-imprinted figure took precedence over the handwritten figure. What should the court decide on this issue? Discuss. [*Galatia Community State Bank v. Kindy*, 807 Ark. 467, 821 S.W.2d 765 (1991)]

24–13. William Bailey and William Vaught, as officers for Bailey, Vaught, Robertson, and Co. (BVR), signed a promissory note to borrow $34,000 from the Forestwood National Bank. The interest rate was variable: "the lender's published prime rate" plus 1 percent. Forestwood went out of business, and ultimately the note was acquired by Remington Investments, Inc. When BVR failed to make payments, Remington filed a suit in a Texas state court against BVR. BVR contended in part that the note was not negotiable because after Forestwood closed, there was no "published lender's prime rate" to use to calculate the interest. Did the note provide for payment of a "fixed amount of money"? Discuss fully. [*Bailey, Vaught, Robertson, and Co. v. Remington Investments, Inc.*, 888 S.W.2d 860 (Tex.App.—Dallas 1994)]

24–14. Regent Corp., U.S.A., an import company in New York, contracted with Azmat Bangladesh, Ltd., a textile company in Bangladesh, for the purchase of bed sheets and pillowcases for import into and resale in the United States. An essential condition of the sale was that the goods be manufactured in Bangladesh. The contract required payment by Regent within ninety days of the date on the bill of lading, and Regent issued promissory notes that indicated this term. After the goods were shipped, Azmat's bank presented drafts drawn against Regent to Regent's banks. Like the notes, each draft indicated that payment was to be made "at 90 days deferred from bill of lading date." The drafts were accompanied by dated bills of lading. On delivery of the goods, U.S. Customs refused to allow their entry because they were partially manufactured in Pakistan. Regent filed a suit in a New York state court against its banks, and Azmat, to stop payment on the drafts. One of the issues was whether the notes and drafts were "payable at a definite time." How should the court rule on this issue? Explain fully. [*Regent Corp., U.S.A. v. Azmat Bangladesh, Ltd.*, 253 A.D.2d 134, 686 N.Y.S.2d 24 (1 Dept. 1999)]

25–15. In October 1998, Somerset Valley Bank notified Alfred Hauser, president of Hauser Co., that the bank had begun to receive what appeared to be Hauser Co. payroll checks. None of the payees were Hauser Co. employees, however, and Hauser had not written the checks or authorized anyone to sign them on his behalf. Automatic Data Processing, Inc., provided payroll services for Hauser Co. and used a facsimile signature on all its payroll checks. Hauser told the bank not to cash the checks. In early 1999, Robert Triffin, who deals in negotiable instruments, bought eighteen of the checks, totaling more than $8,800, from various check-cashing agencies. The agencies stated that they had cashed the checks expecting the bank to pay them. Each check was payable to a bearer for a fixed amount, on demand, and did not state any undertaking by the person promising payment other than the payment of money. Each check bore a facsimile drawer's signature stamp identical to Hauser Co.'s authorized stamp. Each check had been returned to an agency marked "stolen check" and stamped "do not present again." When the bank refused to cash the checks, Triffin filed a suit in a New Jersey state court against Hauser Co. Were the checks negotiable instruments? Why, or why not? [*Triffin v. Somerset Valley Bank*, 777 A.2d 993 (N.J.Super.App.Div. 2001)]

E-LINKS

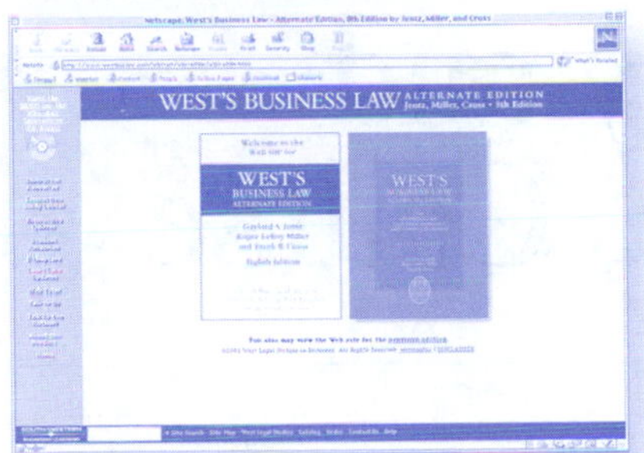

For updated links to resources available on the Web, as well as a variety of other materials, visit this text's Web site at

http://wbl-cs.westbuslaw.com

The National Conference of Commissioners on Uniform State Laws, in association with the University of Pennsylvania Law School, now offers an official site for in-process and final drafts of uniform and model acts. For an index of final acts, including UCC Articles 3 and 4, go to

http://www.law.upenn.edu/bll/ulc/ulc_final.htm

Cornell University's Legal Information Institute offers online access to the UCC, as well as to UCC articles as enacted by particular states and proposed revisions to articles, at

http://www.law.cornell.edu/ucc/ucc.table.html

British author Sir Alan Herbert has some fun with the "written form" requirement for a negotiable instrument in his entertaining (and fictitious) story entitled "The Negotiable Cow," which can be found online at

http://www.kmoser.com/herbert/herb04.htm

LEGAL RESEARCH EXERCISES ON THE WEB

Go to http://wbl-cs.westbuslaw.com, the Web site that accompanies this text. Select "Interactive Study Center," and then click on "Chapter 24." There you will find the following Internet research exercise that you can perform to learn more about negotiable instruments:

Activity 24–1: Overview of Negotiable Instruments

CHAPTER 25

Transferability and Holder in Due Course

ONCE ISSUED, A NEGOTIABLE instrument can be transferred to others by assignment or by negotiation. Recall from Chapter 15 that an assignment is a transfer of rights under a contract. Under general contract principles, a transfer by assignment to an assignee gives the assignee only those rights that the assignor possessed. Any defenses that can be raised against an assignor can normally be raised against the assignee. This same principle applies when an instrument, such as a promissory note, is transferred by assignment. The transferee is then an *assignee* rather than a *holder*. Sometimes, a transfer fails to qualify as a negotiation because it fails to meet one or more of the requirements of a negotiable instrument, discussed in Chapter 24. A transfer may also fail to qualify as a negotiation if the instrument is transferred by delivery only, without a required indorsement. In either of these situations, the transfer becomes an assignment.

Negotiation is the transfer of an instrument in such form that the transferee (the person to whom the instrument is transferred) becomes a holder [UCC 3–201(a)]. In the first part of this chapter, we look at the requirements for negotiation, which differ depending on whether the instrument is an order instrument or a bearer instrument. We then examine the various types of *indorsements* that are used when order instruments are negotiated.

Under Uniform Commercial Code (UCC) principles, a transfer by negotiation creates a holder who, at the very least, receives the rights of the previous possessor [UCC 3–203(b), 3–305]. Unlike an assignment, a transfer by negotiation can make it possible for a holder to receive *more* rights in the instrument than the prior possessor had [UCC 3–305]. A holder who receives greater rights is known as a *holder in due course,* a concept we discuss in the final pages of this chapter.

SECTION 1

Negotiation

There are two methods of negotiating an instrument so that the receiver becomes a holder. As just mentioned, the method used depends on whether the instrument is an order instrument or a bearer instrument.

NEGOTIATING ORDER INSTRUMENTS

An order instrument contains the name of a payee capable of indorsing, as in "Pay to the order of Elliot Goodseal." If an instrument is an order instrument, it is negotiated by delivery with any necessary indorsements. For example, the Carrington Corporation issues a payroll check "to the order of Elliot Goodseal." Goodseal takes the check to the supermarket, signs his name on the back (an indorsement), gives it to the cashier (a delivery), and receives cash. Goodseal has negotiated the check to the supermarket [UCC 3–201(b)].

NEGOTIATING BEARER INSTRUMENTS

If an instrument is payable to bearer, it is negotiated by delivery—that is, by transfer into another person's possession. Indorsement is not necessary [UCC 3–201(b)]. The use of bearer instruments thus involves more risk through loss or theft than the use of order instruments.

Assume that Alan Tyson writes a check payable to "cash," thus creating a bearer instrument, and hands the check to Blaine Parrington (a delivery). Parrington places the check in his wallet, which is subsequently stolen. The thief has possession of the check. At this point, the thief has no rights in the check. If the thief "delivers" the check to an innocent third person, however, negotiation will be complete. All rights to the check will be passed *absolutely* to that third person, and Parrington will lose all right to recover the proceeds of the check from that person [UCC 3–306]. Of course, Parrington can recover his money from the thief if the thief can be found.

CONVERTING ORDER INSTRUMENTS TO BEARER INSTRUMENTS AND VICE VERSA

The method used for negotiation depends on the character of the instrument *at the time the negotiation takes place*. For example, a check originally payable to "cash" but subsequently indorsed with the words "Pay to Arnold" must be negotiated as an order instrument (by indorsement and delivery), even though it was previously a bearer instrument [UCC 3–205(a)].

An instrument payable to the order of a named payee and indorsed in blank (by the holder's signature only, as will be discussed shortly) becomes a bearer instrument [UCC 3–205(b)]. For example, a check made payable to the order of Jessie Arnold is issued to Arnold, and Arnold indorses it by signing her name on the back. The instrument, which is now a bearer instrument, can be negotiated by delivery without indorsement. Arnold can negotiate the check to whomever she wishes merely by delivery, and that person can negotiate by delivery without indorsement. If Arnold loses the check after she indorses it, then a finder can negotiate it further. Exhibit 25–1 illustrates how indorsements can convert an order instrument into a bearer instrument and vice versa.

SECTION 2

Indorsements

An indorsement is required whenever an instrument being negotiated is classified as an order instrument. An *indorsement* is a signature with or without additional words or statements. It is most often written on the back of the instrument itself. If there is no room on the instrument, indorsements can be written on a separate piece of paper, called an **allonge**.[1] The allonge must be "so firmly affixed [to the instrument] as to become a part thereof" [UCC 3–204(a)]. Pins or paper clips will not suffice. Most courts hold that staples are sufficient.

1. Pronounced uh-*lohnj*.

EXHIBIT 25–1 CONVERTING AN ORDER INSTRUMENT TO A BEARER INSTRUMENT AND VICE VERSA

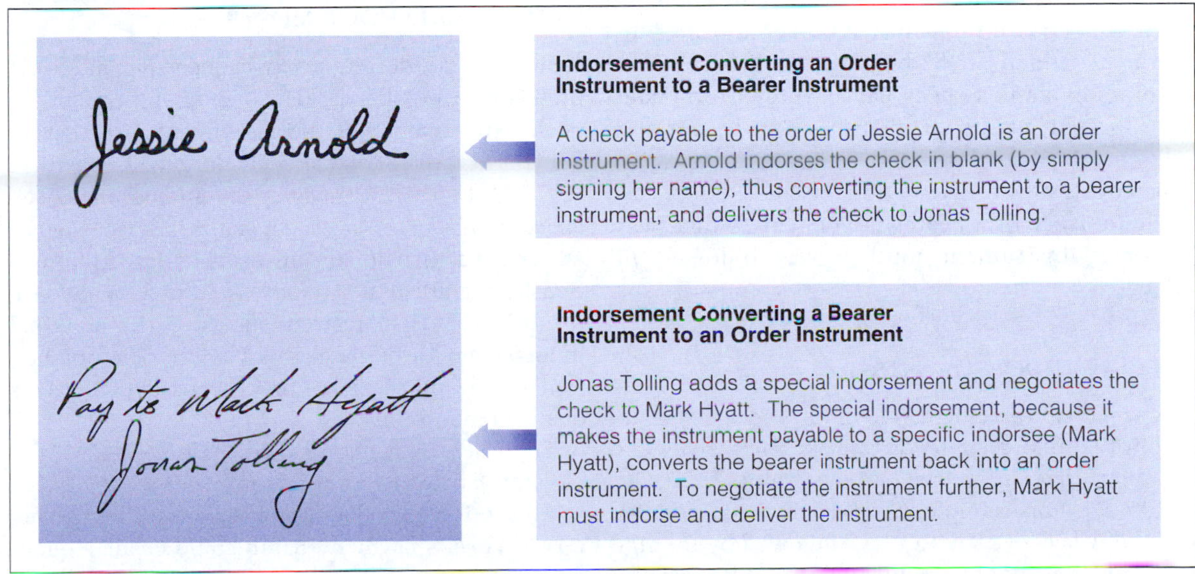

Jessie Arnold
Indorsement Converting an Order Instrument to a Bearer Instrument
A check payable to the order of Jessie Arnold is an order instrument. Arnold indorses the check in blank (by simply signing her name), thus converting the instrument to a bearer instrument, and delivers the check to Jonas Tolling.
Pay to Mark Hyatt
Jonas Tolling
Indorsement Converting a Bearer Instrument to an Order Instrument
Jonas Tolling adds a special indorsement and negotiates the check to Mark Hyatt. The special indorsement, because it makes the instrument payable to a specific indorsee (Mark Hyatt), converts the bearer instrument back into an order instrument. To negotiate the instrument further, Mark Hyatt must indorse and deliver the instrument.

A person who transfers a note or a draft by signing (indorsing) it and delivering it to another person is an **indorser.** For example, Luisa Parks receives a graduation check for $100. She can transfer the check to her mother (or to anyone) by signing it on the back. Luisa is an indorser. If Luisa indorses the check by writing "Pay to Aretha Parks," Aretha Parks is the **indorsee.**

We examine here four categories of indorsements: blank indorsements, special indorsements, qualified indorsements, and restrictive indorsements.

Blank Indorsements

A **blank indorsement** specifies no particular indorsee and can consist of a mere signature [UCC 3–205(b)]. Hence, a check payable "to the order of Mark Deitsch" can be indorsed in blank simply by having Deitsch's signature written on the back of the check. Exhibit 25–2 shows a blank indorsement.

Exhibit 25–2 A Blank Indorsement

Mark Deitsch

An instrument payable to order and indorsed in blank becomes a bearer instrument and can be negotiated by delivery alone [UCC 3–205(b)]. In other words, as discussed earlier, a blank indorsement converts an order instrument to a bearer instrument, which anybody can cash. If Rita Chou indorses in blank a check payable to her order and then loses it on the street, Coker can find it and sell it to Duncan for value without indorsing it. This constitutes a negotiation, because Coker has made delivery of a bearer instrument (which was an order instrument until it was indorsed in blank).

Special Indorsements

A **special indorsement** identifies the person to whom the indorser intends to make the instrument payable; that is, it names the indorsee [UCC 3–205(a)]. For example, words such as "Pay to the order of Clay" or "Pay to Clay," followed by the signature of the indorser, are sufficient. When an instrument is indorsed in this way, it is an order instrument.

To avoid the risk of loss from theft, a holder may convert a blank indorsement to a special indorsement. This changes the bearer instrument back to an order instrument. A holder may "convert a blank indorsement that consists only of a signature into a special indorsement by writing, above the signature of the indorser, words identifying the person to whom the instrument is made payable" [UCC 3–205(c)].

For example, a check is made payable to Hal Jones. He indorses his name by blank indorsement on the back of the check and negotiates the check to William Hunter. Hunter, not wishing to cash the check immediately, wants to avoid any risk should he lose the check. He therefore prints "Pay to William Hunter" above Jones's blank indorsement. In this manner, Hunter has converted Jones's blank indorsement into a special indorsement. Further negotiation now requires William Hunter's indorsement plus delivery. (See Exhibit 25–3.)

Exhibit 25–3 A Special Indorsement

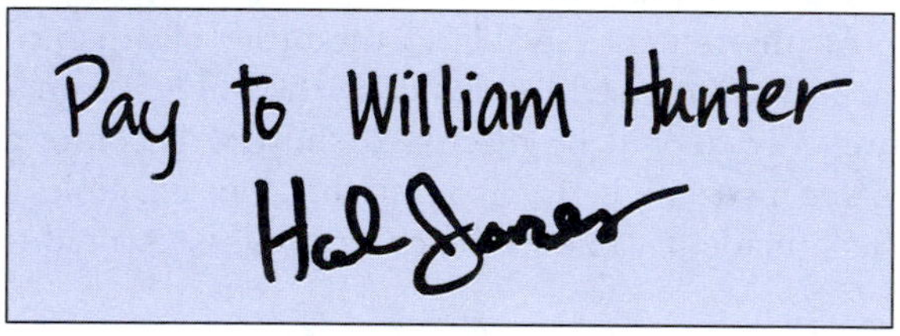

Pay to William Hunter
Hal Jones

Qualified Indorsements

Generally, an indorser, *merely by indorsing,* impliedly promises to pay the holder, or any subsequent indorser, the amount of the instrument in the event that the drawer or maker defaults on the payment [UCC 3–415(b)]. Usually, then, indorsements are *unqualified indorsements.* That is, the indorser is guaranteeing payment of the instrument in addition to transferring title to it. An indorser who does not wish to be liable on an instrument can use a **qualified indorsement** to disclaim this liability. The notation "without recourse" is commonly used to create a qualified indorsement.

Suppose that a check is made payable to the order of Sarah Jacobs. Sarah wants to negotiate the check to Allison Jong but does not want to assume liability for the check's payment. Sarah could create a qualified indorsement by indorsing the check as follows:

"Pay to Allison Jong, without recourse. [Signed] Sarah Jacobs." (See Exhibit 25–4.)

EXHIBIT 25–4 A QUALIFIED INDORSEMENT

Pay to Allison Jong, without recourse
Sarah Jacobs

Qualified indorsements are often used by persons acting in a representative capacity. For example, insurance agents sometimes receive checks payable to them that are really intended as payment to the insurance company. The agent is merely indorsing the payment through to the insurance company and should not be required to make good on the check if it is later dishonored. The "without recourse" indorsement relieves the agent from any liability on a check. If the instrument is dishonored, the holder cannot obtain recovery from the agent who indorsed "without recourse" unless the indorser has breached one of the transfer warranties discussed in Chapter 26, which relate to good title, authorized signature, no material alteration, and so forth.

A qualified indorsement ("without recourse") can be accompanied by a special indorsement or a blank indorsement. A special qualified indorsement includes the name of the indorsee as well as the words "without recourse," as in Exhibit 25–4. The special indorsement makes the instrument an order instrument, and it requires an indorsement plus delivery for negotiation. A blank qualified indorsement makes the instrument a bearer instrument, and only delivery is required for negotiation. In either situation, the instrument still transfers title to the indorsee and can be further negotiated.

RESTRICTIVE INDORSEMENTS

The **restrictive indorsement** requires indorsees to comply with certain instructions regarding the funds involved. A restrictive indorsement does not prohibit the further negotiation of an instrument [UCC 3–206(a)]. Restrictive indorsements come in many forms, some of which we discuss here.

Indorsements Prohibiting Further Indorsement. An indorsement such as "Pay to Julie Thrush only. [Signed] Thomas Fasulo" does not destroy negotiability. Thrush can negotiate the paper to a holder just as if it had read "Pay to Julie Thrush. [Signed] Thomas Fasulo" [UCC 3–206(a)]. If the holder gives value, this type of restrictive indorsement has the same legal effect as a special indorsement.

Conditional Indorsements. When payment depends on the occurrence of some event specified in the indorsement, the instrument has a conditional indorsement [UCC 3–204(a)]. For example, suppose that Ken Barton indorses a check as follows: "Pay to Lars Johansen if he completes the renovation of my kitchen by June 1, 2002. [Signed] Ken Barton." Article 3 states that an indorsement conditioning the right to receive payment "does not affect the right of the indorsee to enforce the instrument" [UCC 3–206(b)]. A person paying or taking an instrument for value (taking for value will be discussed later in the chapter) can disregard the condition without liability.[2]

A conditional indorsement does not prevent further negotiation of the instrument. If conditional language appears on the *face* of an instrument, however, the instrument is not negotiable, because it does not meet the requirement that a negotiable instrument must contain an unconditional promise to pay.

Indorsements for Deposit or Collection. A common type of restrictive indorsement is one that makes the indorsee (almost always a bank) a collecting agent of the indorser [UCC 3–206(c)]. Exhibit 25–5 on the next page illustrates this type of indorsement on a check payable and issued to Aimee St. Amant. In particular, the indorsements "Pay any bank or banker" and "For deposit only" have the effect of locking the instrument into the bank collection process. Only a bank can acquire the rights of a holder following one of the indorsements until the item has been specially indorsed by a bank to a person who is not a bank [UCC 3–206(c), 4–201(b)]. A bank's liability for payment of an instrument with a restrictive indorsement of this kind is discussed in Chapter 27.

2. Under Section 3–206(3) of the unrevised Article 3, the indorsement was enforceable (except against intermediary banks, defined in Chapter 27), and neither the indorsee nor any subsequent holder had the right to enforce payment against that indorser on the instrument before the condition was met.

EXHIBIT 25–5 FOR DEPOSIT/FOR TRUST INDORSEMENTS

For deposit only
Aimee St. Amant

or

For collection only
Aimee St. Amant

Trust Indorsements. Indorsements to persons who are to hold or use the funds for the benefit of the indorser or a third party are called **trust indorsements** (also known as agency indorsements). For example, assume that Ralph Zimmer asks his accountant, Stephanie Contento, to pay some bills for him while he is out of the country. He indorses a check, drawn by Bill Heise, to Stephanie Contento "as agent for Ralph Zimmer." This agency indorsement obligates Contento to use the funds from the Heise check only for the benefit of Zimmer [UCC 3–206(d), (e)].

The result of a trust indorsement is that legal rights in the instrument are transferred to the original indorsee. To the extent that the original indorsee pays or applies the proceeds consistently with the indorsement (for example, in an indorsement stating "Pay to Ellen Cook in trust for Roger Callahan"), the indorsee is a holder and can become a holder in due course (a status that will be described shortly). Sample trust (agency) indorsements are shown in Exhibit 25–6.

EXHIBIT 25–6 TRUST INDORSEMENTS

Pay to Stephanie Contento
as Agent for Ralph Zimmer
Ralph Zimmer

or

Pay to Ellen Cook
in trust for Roger Callahan
Roger Callahan

The fiduciary restrictions—restrictions mandated by a relationship involving trust and loyalty—on the instrument do not reach beyond the original indorsee [UCC 3–206(d), (e)]. Any subsequent purchaser can qualify as a holder in due course unless he or she has actual notice that the instrument was negotiated in breach of a fiduciary duty.[3]

SECTION 3

Miscellaneous Indorsement Problems

Of course, a significant problem in relation to indorsements occurs when an indorsement is forged or unauthorized. The UCC rules concerning unauthorized or forged signatures and indorsements will be discussed in Chapter 26 in the context of signature liability and again in Chapter 27 in the context of the bank's liability for payment of an instrument containing an unauthorized signature. Here we look at two other problems that may arise with indorsements.

An indorsement should be identical to the name that appears on the instrument. The payee or indorsee whose name is misspelled can indorse with the misspelled name, the correct name, or both [UCC 3–204(d)]. For example, if Marie Ellison receives a check payable to the order of Mary Ellison, she can indorse the check either "Marie Ellison" or "Mary Ellison." The usual practice is to indorse with the name as it appears on the instrument and follow it by the correct name.

An instrument payable to two or more persons *in the alternative* (for example, "Pay to the order of Ying or Mifflin") requires the indorsement of only one of the payees [UCC 3–110(d)]. If, however, an instrument is made payable to two or more persons *jointly* (for example, "Pay to the order of Bridgette and Tony VanHorn"), all of the payees' indorsements are necessary for negotiation. If an instrument payable to two or more persons does not clearly indicate whether it is payable in the alternative or payable jointly, then "the instrument is payable to the persons alternatively" [UCC 3–110(d)]. The same principles apply to special indorsements that identify more than one person to whom the indorser intends to make the instrument payable [UCC 3–205(a)].

3. See *In re Quantum Development Corp.*, 397 F.Supp. 329 (D.Virgin Islands 1975).

A negotiable instrument can be drawn payable to a legal entity such as an estate, a partnership, or an organization. For example, a check may read "Pay to the order of the Red Cross." An authorized representative of the Red Cross can negotiate this check. Similarly, negotiable paper can be payable to a public officer. For example, checks reading "Pay to the order of the County Tax Collector" or "Pay to the order of Larry White, Receiver of Taxes" can be negotiated by whoever holds the office [UCC 3–110(c)].

Westlaw. See Case 25.1 at the end of this chapter. To view the full, unedited case from Westlaw,® go to this text's Web site at **http://wbl-cs.westbuslaw.com**.

SECTION 4

Holder in Due Course

The body of rules contained in Article 3 of the UCC governs a party's right to payment of a check, draft, note, or certificate of deposit.[4] Problems arise when a holder seeking payment of a negotiable instrument learns that a defense to payment exists or that another party has a prior claim to the instrument. In such situations, for the person seeking payment, it becomes important to have the rights of a *holder in due course (HDC)*. An HDC takes a negotiable instrument free of all claims and most defenses of other parties.

SECTION 5

Holder versus Holder in Due Course

As pointed out in Chapter 24, the UCC defines a *holder* as a person in the possession of an instrument "if the instrument is payable to bearer or, in the cases of an instrument payable to an identified person, if the identified person is in possession" [UCC 1–201(20)]. An ordinary holder obtains only those rights that the transferor had in the instrument. In this respect, a holder has the same status as an assignee (see Chapter 15). A holder normally is subject to the same defenses that could be asserted against the transferor, just as an assignee is subject to the defenses that could be asserted against the assignor.

In contrast, a **holder in due course (HDC)** is a holder who, by meeting certain acquisition requirements (to be discussed shortly), takes the instrument free of most of the defenses and claims to which the transferor was subject. Stated another way, an HDC can normally acquire a higher level of immunity than can an ordinary holder in regard to defenses against payment on the instrument or ownership claims to the instrument by other parties.

An example will help to clarify the distinction between the rights of an ordinary holder and the rights of an HDC. Debby Morrison signs a $500 note payable to Alex Jerrod in payment for goods. Jerrod negotiates the note to Beverly Larson, who promises to pay Jerrod for it in thirty days. During the next month, Larson learns that Jerrod has breached his contract with Morrison by delivering defective goods and that, for this reason, Morrison will not honor the $500 note. Whether Larson can hold Morrison liable on the note depends on whether Larson has met the requirements for HDC status. If Larson has met these requirements and thus has HDC status, Larson is entitled to payment on the note. If Larson has not met these requirements, she has the status of an ordinary holder, and Morrison's defense against payment to Jerrod will also be effective against Larson.

SECTION 6

Requirements for HDC Status

The basic requirements for attaining HDC status are set forth in UCC 3–302. An HDC must first be a holder of a negotiable instrument and must have taken the instrument (1) for value; (2) in good faith; and (3) without notice that it is overdue, that it has been dishonored, that any person has a defense against it or a claim to it, or that the instrument contains unauthorized signatures or alterations or is so irregular or incomplete as to call into question its authenticity. We now examine each of these requirements.

TAKING FOR VALUE

An HDC must have given value for the instrument [UCC 3–302(a)(2)(i), 3–303]. A person who

4. Other kinds of documents, such as stock certificates and bills of lading, meet the requirements of negotiable instruments, but the rights and liabilities of the parties on these documents are covered by Articles 7 and 8 of the UCC. See Chapter 46 on bailments.

receives an instrument as a gift or who inherits it has *not* met the requirement of value. In these situations, the person normally becomes an ordinary holder and does not possess the rights of an HDC.

The concept of value in the law of negotiable instruments is not the same as the concept of consideration in the law of contracts. An executory promise (a promise to give value in the future) is clearly valid consideration to support a contract [UCC 1–201(44)]. It does not, however, normally constitute value sufficient to make one an HDC. UCC 3–303(a)(1) provides that a holder takes the instrument for value only to the extent that the promise has been performed. Therefore, if the holder plans to pay for the instrument later or plans to perform the required services at some future date, the holder has not yet given value. In that situation, the holder is not yet a holder in due course.

In the Larson-Morrison example presented earlier, Larson is not an HDC, because she did not take the instrument (Morrison's note) for value—she had not yet paid Jerrod for the note. Thus, Morrison's defense of breach of contract is valid not only against Jerrod but also against Larson. If Larson had paid Jerrod for the note at the time of transfer (which would mean she had given value for the instrument), she would be an HDC. As an HDC, she could hold Morrison liable on the note even though Morrison has a valid defense against Jerrod on the basis of breach of contract. Exhibit 25–7 illustrates these concepts.

Under UCC 3–303(a), a holder can take an instrument for value in one of five ways:

1. By performing the promise for which the instrument was issued or transferred.
2. By acquiring a security interest or other lien in the instrument (other than a lien obtained by a judicial proceeding).[5]
3. By taking an instrument in payment of, or as security for, an antecedent claim.
4. By giving a negotiable instrument as payment.
5. By giving an irrevocable commitment as payment.

Antecedent Claim. When an instrument is given in payment of—or as security for—an **antecedent claim** (a preexisting claim), the value requirement is met [UCC 3–303(a)(3)]. Here again, commercial law and contract law produce different results. An antecedent claim is not valid consideration under general contract law, but it does constitute value sufficient to satisfy the requirement for HDC status in commercial law. To illustrate: Cary owes Dwyer $2,000 on a past-due account. If Cary negotiates a $2,000 note signed by Gordon to Dwyer and Dwyer accepts it to discharge the overdue account balance, Dwyer has given value for the instrument.

Negotiable Instrument as Value. UCC 3–303(a)(4) provides that a holder takes the instrument for value if "the instrument is issued or transferred in exchange for a negotiable instrument." Suppose that Martin has issued a $500 negotiable promissory note to Paula. The note is due six months from the date issued. Paula's financial circumstances are such that she does not want to wait for the maturity date to collect. Therefore, she negotiates the note to her friend Susan,

5. Security interests will be discussed in Chapter 28. Other liens will be discussed in Chapter 29.

EXHIBIT 25–7 TAKING FOR VALUE

By exchanging defective goods for the note, Jerrod breached his contract with Morrison. Morrison could assert this defense if Jerrod presented the note to her for payment. Jerrod exchanged the note for Larson's promise to pay in thirty days, however. Because Larson did not take the note for value, she is not a holder in due course. Thus, Morrison can assert against Larson the defense of Jerrod's breach when Larson submits the note to Morrison for payment. If Larson had taken the note for value, Morrison could not assert that defense and would be liable to pay the note.

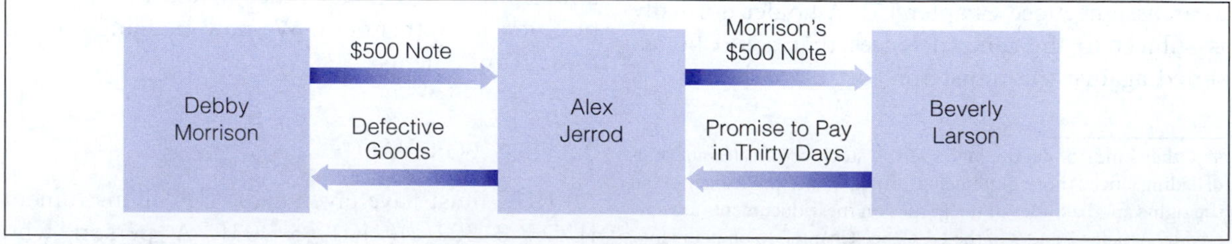

who pays her $200 in cash and writes her a check—a negotiable instrument—for the balance of $300. Susan has given full value for the note by paying $200 in cash and issuing Paula the check for $300. Note that a negotiable instrument has value when it is issued, not when the underlying obligation is finally paid.

Check Deposits and Withdrawals. Occasionally, a commercial bank can become an HDC when honoring other banks' checks for its own customers. In this situation, the bank becomes an "involuntary" HDC, in that at the time of giving value, the bank has no intention of becoming an HDC.

Assume that on Monday morning at the end of the month, Pat Stevens has $400 in her checking account at the First National Bank. That morning Stevens deposits her payroll check for $300, drawn by her employer on the Second Interstate Bank. During her lunch hour she issues a check to her landlord for $425. The landlord cashes the check at the First National Bank. Later, the Second Interstate Bank returns the payroll check marked "insufficient funds." In most cases, First National would charge this check against Stevens's account. If that cannot be done, however, is the First National Bank an HDC of the employer's check? The answer is yes. According to what is referred to as the *first-money-in, first-money-out rule,* First National Bank has paid to the landlord $25 of its own funds [UCC 4–210(b)]. Therefore, First National is an HDC to the extent it has given value—$25—and the bank can seek recovery of $25 from the employer (the drawer of the check).

Special Situations. In a few exceptional circumstances, a holder can take an instrument for value but still not be accorded HDC status. UCC 3–302(c) specifies that in the following situations, the rights of the holder will be limited to those of an ordinary holder:

1. Purchase at a judicial sale (for example, a bankruptcy sale) or acquisition by taking under legal process.
2. Acquisition when taking over an estate (as an administrator).
3. Purchase as part of a bulk transfer (as when a corporation buys the assets of another corporation).

TAKING IN GOOD FAITH

The second requirement for HDC status is that the holder take the instrument in *good faith* [UCC 3–302(a)(2)(ii)]. Under Article 3, *good faith* is defined as "honesty in fact and the observance of reasonable commercial standards of fair dealing" [UCC 3–103(a)(4)].[6] The good faith requirement applies only to the *holder.* It is immaterial whether the transferor acted in good faith. Thus, a person who in good faith takes a negotiable instrument from a thief may become an HDC.

Because of the good faith requirement, one must ask whether the purchaser, when acquiring the instrument, honestly believed that the instrument was not defective. If a person purchases a $10,000 note for $300 from a stranger on a street corner, the issue of good faith can be raised on the grounds of both the suspicious circumstances and the grossly inadequate consideration (value). The UCC does not provide clear guidelines to determine good faith, so each situation must be examined separately.

See Case 25.2 at the end of this chapter. To view the full, unedited case from Westlaw,® go to this text's Web site at **http://wbl-cs.westbuslaw.com**.

TAKING WITHOUT NOTICE

The final requirement for HDC status involves notice [UCC 3–302]. A person will not be afforded HDC protection if he or she acquires an instrument and is *on notice* (knows or has reason to know) that it is defective in any one of the following ways [UCC 3–302(a)]:

1. It is overdue.
2. It has been dishonored.
3. There is an uncured (uncorrected) default with respect to another instrument issued as part of the same series.
4. The instrument contains an unauthorized signature or has been altered.
5. There is a defense against the instrument or a claim to the instrument.
6. The instrument is so irregular or incomplete as to call into question its authenticity.[7]

What Constitutes Notice? Notice of a defective instrument is given whenever the holder (1) has actual

6. Before the revision of Article 3, the applicable definition of *good faith* was "honesty in fact in the conduct or transaction concerned" [UCC 1–201(19)].

7. Section 302(1)(c) of the unrevised Article 3 provided that HDC protection is lost if a holder has notice that an instrument is overdue or has been dishonored or if there is a claim to or defense against it.

knowledge of the defect; (2) has received a notice of the defect (such as a bank's receipt of a letter listing the serial numbers of stolen bearer instruments); or (3) has reason to know that a defect exists, given all the facts and circumstances known at the time in question [UCC 1–201(25)]. The holder must also have received the notice "at a time and in a manner that gives a reasonable opportunity to act on it" [UCC 3–302(f)]. A purchaser's knowledge of certain facts, such as insolvency proceedings against the maker or drawer of the instrument, does not constitute notice that the instrument is defective [UCC 3–302(b)].

Overdue Instruments. What constitutes notice that an instrument is overdue depends on whether it is a demand instrument (payable on demand) or a time instrument (payable at a definite time).

Demand Instruments. A purchaser has notice that a *demand instrument* is overdue if he or she either takes the instrument knowing that demand has been made or takes the instrument an unreasonable length of time after its date. A "reasonable time" for the presentment of a check is ninety days after its date, but for other demand instruments, what will be considered a reasonable time depends on the circumstances [UCC 3–304(a)].

Time Instruments. A holder of a *time instrument* who takes the instrument at any time after its expressed due date is on notice that it is overdue [UCC 3–304(b)]. Nonpayment by the due date should indicate to any purchaser that the instrument may be defective. Thus, a promissory note due on May 15 must be acquired before midnight on May 15. If it is purchased on May 16, the purchaser will be an ordinary holder, not an HDC. Sometimes, a time instrument reads, "Payable in thirty days." To count thirty days, you exclude the first day and count the last day. Thus, a note dated December 1 that is payable in thirty days is due by midnight on December 31. If the payment date falls on a Sunday or holiday, the instrument is payable on the next business day.

If a debt is to be paid in installments or through a series of notes, the maker's default on any one installment or on any one note of the series will constitute notice to the purchaser that the instrument is overdue [UCC 3–304(b)].

An instrument does not become overdue if there is a default on a payment of interest only [UCC 3–304(c)]. Most installment notes provide that any payment by the maker shall be applied first to interest and the balance to the principal. This serves as notice that any installment payment for less than the full amount results in a default on an installment payment toward the principal.

Also, when a series of notes with successive maturity dates is issued at a single time for a single indebtedness, a default on any one note of the series will constitute overdue notice for the entire series. In this way, prospective purchasers know that they cannot qualify as HDCs [UCC 3–302(a)(2)(iii)].

Suppose that a note reads, "Payable May 15, but may be accelerated if the holder feels insecure." A purchaser, unaware that a prior holder has elected to accelerate the due date on the instrument, buys the instrument before May 15. UCC 3–304(b)(3) provides that an instrument becomes overdue on the day after the accelerated due date. The purchaser may still qualify as an HDC, however, because he or she has no reason to know that acceleration has occurred [UCC 3–302(a)(2)(iii)].

Dishonored Instruments. An instrument is *dishonored* when the party to which the instrument is presented refuses to pay it. If a holder has actual knowledge that an instrument has been dishonored or has knowledge of facts that would lead him or her to suspect that an instrument has been dishonored, the holder is on notice [UCC 3–302(a)(2)]. Thus, a person who takes a check clearly stamped "insufficient funds" is put on notice.

For example, Schultz holds a demand note dated September 1 on Apfel, Inc., a local business firm. On September 17, she demands payment, and Apfel refuses (that is, dishonors the instrument). On September 22, Schultz negotiates the note to Brenner, a purchaser who lives in another state. Brenner does not know, and has no reason to know, that the note has been dishonored. Because Brenner is *not* put on notice, Brenner can become an HDC.

Notice of Claims or Defenses. A holder cannot become an HDC if he or she has notice of any claim to the instrument or defense against it [UCC 3–302(a)(2)(v), (vi)]. Knowledge of claims or defenses can be imputed to the purchaser if these claims or defenses are apparent on the face of the instrument—if the instrument is incomplete or irregular in any way, for example—or if the purchaser otherwise had reason to know of them from facts surrounding the transaction.[8]

Incomplete Instruments. A purchaser cannot expect to become an HDC of an instrument so incomplete on its face that an element of negotiability is lacking (for example, the amount is not filled in) [UCC 3–302(a)(1)]. Minor omissions (such as the omission of the date—see Chapter 24) are permissible, because these do not call into question the validity of the instrument [UCC 3–113(b)].

Similarly, when a person accepts an instrument that has been completed without knowing that it was incomplete when issued, the person can take it as an HDC [UCC 3–115(b), 3–302(a)(1)]. Even if an instrument is originally incomplete and later completed in an unauthorized manner, the unauthorized completion is not a good defense against an HDC, who can enforce the instrument as completed [UCC 3–407(c)].

To illustrate: Cosford asks Brittany to buy a textbook for him when she goes to the campus bookstore. Cosford writes a check payable to the campus store, leaves the amount blank, and tells Brittany to fill in the price of the textbook. The cost of the textbook is $85. If Brittany fills in the check for $115 before she gets to the bookstore, the bookstore cashier sees only a properly completed instrument. Therefore, the cashier will take the check as an HDC, and the store can enforce it for the full $115. The unauthorized completion is not a sufficient defense against the store in this situation. (Material alterations will be discussed more fully in Chapter 26.)

Irregular Instruments. Any irregularity on the face of an instrument that calls into question its validity or terms of ownership or that creates an ambiguity as to the party to pay will bar HDC status. A difference between the handwriting used in the body of a check and that used in the signature will not in and of itself make an instrument irregular. Postdating or antedating a check or stating the amount in digits but failing to write out the numbers will not make a check irregular [UCC 3–113(a)]. Visible evidence of forgery of a maker's or drawer's signature, however, or alterations to material elements of negotiable instruments will disqualify a purchaser from HDC status. Conversely, a careful forgery of a maker's or drawer's signature or a skillful alteration can go undetected by reasonable examination; therefore, the purchaser can qualify as an HDC [UCC 3–302(a)(1)].

Losses that result from careful forgeries usually fall on the party to whom the forger transferred the instrument (assuming, of course, that the forger cannot be found). Also, a forged indorsement (see Chapter 26) does not transfer title, and thus a person obtaining an instrument that has a forged indorsement of a name necessary to good title cannot normally become a holder or an HDC.

Voidable Obligations. It stands to reason that a purchaser who knows that a party to an instrument has a defense that entitles that party to avoid the obligation cannot be an HDC. At the very least, good faith requires *honesty in fact and the observance of reasonable commercial standards* on the part of the purchaser in a transaction. For example, a potential purchaser who knows that the maker of a note has breached the underlying contract with the payee cannot thereafter purchase the note as an HDC.

Knowledge of one defense precludes a holder from asserting HDC status in regard to all other defenses. For example, Litton, knowing that the note he has taken has a forged indorsement, presents it to the maker for payment. The maker refuses to pay on the grounds of breach of the underlying contract. The maker can assert this defense against Litton even though Litton had no knowledge of the breach, because Litton's knowledge of the forgery alone prevents him from being an HDC in *all* circumstances.

Knowledge that a fiduciary has wrongfully negotiated an instrument is sufficient notice of a claim against the instrument to preclude HDC status. Suppose that O'Banion, a trustee of a university, improperly writes a check on the university trust account to pay a personal debt. Lewis knows that the check has been improperly drawn on university funds, but she accepts it anyway. Lewis cannot claim to be an HDC. When a purchaser knows that a fiduciary is acting in breach of trust, HDC status is denied [UCC 3–307(b)].

8. If an instrument contains a statement required by a statute or an administrative rule to the effect that the rights of a holder or transferee are subject to the claims or defenses that the issuer could assert against the original payee, the instrument is negotiable, but there cannot be an HDC of the instrument. See UCC 3–106(d) and the discussion of federal limitations on HDC rights in the next chapter.

SECTION 7

Holder through an HDC

A person who does not qualify as an HDC but who derives his or her title through an HDC can acquire the rights and privileges of an HDC. According to UCC 3–203(b):

> Transfer of an instrument, whether or not the transfer is a negotiation, vests in the transferee any right of the transferor to enforce the instrument, including any right as a holder in due course, but the transferee cannot acquire rights of a holder in due course by a transfer, directly or indirectly, from a holder in due course if the transferee engaged in fraud or illegality affecting the instrument.

This rule, sometimes called the **shelter principle**, seems counter to the basic HDC philosophy. It is, however, in line with the concept of marketability and free transferability of negotiable instruments, as well as with contract law, which provides that assignees acquire the rights of assignors. The shelter principle extends the HDC benefits, and it is designed to aid the HDC in readily disposing of the instrument. Anyone, no matter how far removed from an HDC, who can trace his or her title ultimately back to an HDC comes within the shelter principle. Normally, a person who acquires an instrument from an HDC or from someone with HDC rights receives HDC rights on the legal theory that the transferee of an instrument receives at least the rights that the transferor had.

There are some limitations on the shelter principle, however. Certain persons who formerly held instruments cannot improve their positions by later reacquiring them from HDCs [UCC 3–203(b)]. Thus, if a holder was a party to fraud or illegality affecting the instrument or if, as a prior holder, he or she had notice of a claim or defense against the instrument, that holder is not allowed to improve his or her status by repurchasing the instrument from a later HDC.

To illustrate: Matthew and Carla collaborate to defraud Lorena. Lorena is induced to give Carla a negotiable note payable to Carla's order. Carla then specially indorses the note for value to Larry, an HDC. Matthew and Carla split the proceeds. Larry negotiates the note to Stuart, another HDC. Stuart then negotiates the note for value to Matthew. Matthew, even though he obtained the note through an HDC, is not a holder through an HDC, for he participated in the original fraud and can never acquire HDC rights in this note.

TERMS AND CONCEPTS TO REVIEW

allonge 481	indorsee 482	restrictive indorsement 483
antecedent claim 486	indorser 482	shelter principle 490
blank indorsement 482	negotiation 480	special indorsement 482
holder in due course (HDC) 485	qualified indorsement 482	trust indorsement 484

CHAPTER SUMMARY

Transfer of Instruments	1. *Transfer by assignment*—A transfer by assignment to an assignee gives the assignee only those rights that the assignor possessed. Any defenses against payment that can be raised against an assignor can normally be raised against the assignee. 2. *Transfer by negotiation*—An order instrument is negotiated by indorsement and delivery; a bearer instrument is negotiated by delivery only.
Indorsements	1. *Blank* (for example, "Mark Deitsch"). 2. *Special* (for example, "Pay to William Hunter. [Signed] Hal Jones"). 3. *Qualified* (for example, "Pay to Allison Jong, without recourse. [Signed] Sarah Jones"). 4. *Restrictive* (for example, "For deposit only. [Signed] Aimee St. Amant" or "Pay to Ellen Cook in trust for Roger Callahan. [Signed] Roger Callahan").

CHAPTER SUMMARY—CONTINUED

Miscellaneous Indorsement Problems	1. A payee or indorsee whose name is misspelled can indorse with the misspelled name, the correct name, or both. 2. An instrument payable to two or more persons in the alternative requires the indorsement of only one of the payees. 3. An instrument payable to two or more persons jointly requires all of the payees' indorsements for negotiation. 4. If an instrument payable to two or more persons does not clearly indicate whether it is payable in the alternative or jointly, it is payable to the persons alternatively. The same principle applies to special indorsements that contain multiple indorsees.
Holder versus Holder in Due Course (HDC)	1. *Holder*—A person in the possession of an instrument drawn, issued, or indorsed to him or her, to his or her order, or to bearer or in blank. A holder obtains only those rights that the transferor had in the instrument. 2. *Holder in due course (HDC)*—A holder who, by meeting certain acquisition requirements (summarized next), takes the instrument free of most defenses and claims to which the transferor was subject.
Requirements for HDC Status	To be an HDC, a holder must take the instrument: 1. *For value*—A holder can take an instrument for value in one of five ways [UCC 3–303]: a. By the complete or partial performance of the promise for which the instrument was issued or transferred. b. By acquiring a security interest or other lien in the instrument, excluding a lien obtained by a judicial proceeding. c. By taking an instrument in payment of (or as security for) an antecedent debt. d. By giving a negotiable instrument as payment. e. By giving an irrevocable commitment as payment. 2. *In good faith*—Good faith is defined as "honesty in fact and the observance of reasonable commercial standards of fair dealing" [UCC 3–103(a)(4)]. 3. *Without notice*—To be an HDC, a holder must not be on notice that the instrument is defective in any of the following ways [UCC 3–302, 3–304]: a. It is overdue. b. It has been dishonored. c. There is an uncured (uncorrected) default with respect to another instrument issued as part of the same series. d. The instrument contains an unauthorized signature or has been altered. e. There is a defense against the instrument or a claim to the instrument. f. The instrument is so irregular or incomplete as to call into question its authenticity.
Holder through an HDC	A holder who cannot qualify as an HDC has the *rights* of an HDC if he or she derives title through an HDC unless the holder engaged in fraud or illegality affecting the instrument [UCC 3–203(b)].

CASES FOR ANALYSIS

Westlaw. You can access the full text of each case presented below by going to the Westlaw cases on this text's Web site at http://wbl-cs.westbuslaw.com. Each Westlaw case includes the names of all plaintiffs and defendants, the dates on which the case was argued and decided, a brief summary of the issues and decisions in the case, headnotes classifying the specific issues in the case according to the West Key Number System, and the court's opinion. Concurring and dissenting opinions, if any, are included as well.

CASE 25.1 INDORSEMENTS

GENERAL MOTORS ACCEPTANCE CORP. V. ABINGTON CASUALTY INSURANCE CO.

Supreme Judicial Court of Massachusetts, 1992.
413 Mass. 583,
602 N.E.2d 1085.

NOLAN, Justice.

On April 13, 1990, General Motors Acceptance Corporation (GMAC) filed a complaint [in a Massachusetts state court] against Abington Casualty Insurance Company (Abington), alleging breach of contract and conversion. In response, Abington moved to dismiss the complaint for failure to state a claim on which relief can be granted. After a hearing, the trial judge granted Abington's motion to dismiss, and reported his decision to [a state intermediate appellate court] which dismissed the report. GMAC filed a timely claim of appeal on July 18, 1991. We transferred the case to this court on our own motion. We conclude that GMAC has presented a claim on which relief can be granted, and, therefore, we reverse the order of the [state intermediate appellate court] dismissing the report.

* * * *

In its complaint, GMAC alleges the following facts. Abington issued a physical damage insurance policy covering a 1984 Jeep motor vehicle to Robert A. Azevedo. GMAC, the holder of a security interest in the vehicle, was the loss payee beneficiary of that policy. In 1988 the vehicle sustained damage. Abington appraised the loss and issued a check on November 14, 1988, payable jointly "to the order of Robert A. Azevedo and G.M.A.C." The check was delivered to Azevedo who then presented it to the drawee bank without GMAC's [i]ndorsement. The check was drawn on an account with sufficient funds, and Azevedo received full payment. To date, GMAC has received none of the proceeds issued by Abington.

GMAC now seeks recovery of the insurance proceeds from neither the drawee bank, which mistakenly accepted the check without the necessary [i]ndorsements, nor Azevedo, who is subject to GMAC's lien, but instead from Abington, the drawer of the check. GMAC claims that in these circumstances, the payment on a check to only one of two joint payees does not discharge the underlying obligation of the payor to the remaining payee. This claim presents two novel issues to this court: (1) whether the delivery of a negotiable instrument to one joint payee operates as delivery to all joint payees, and (2) whether a drawer's underlying obligation to joint payees, who are not in an agency relationship, is discharged when one joint payee cashes a check without the endorsement of the other.

Although the issue has never been addressed in Massachusetts, other States have held that the delivery of a negotiable instrument to one joint payee constitutes delivery to all joint payees. The Uniform Commercial Code (U.C.C.)[9] expressly provides for instruments payable to two or more persons, and when, as in this case, the instrument is payable not in the alternative, it may be negotiated, discharged, or enforced only by consent of all the payees. To obtain the rights of a holder who may discharge or demand payment of the instrument * * * , one must take the instrument by negotiation. Negotiation of an instrument payable to order entails delivery of the instrument with all the necessary [i]ndorsements. Thus, since under Massachusetts law a person must seek the [i]ndorsements of every payee to negotiate, transfer, or discharge a negotiable instrument, delivery of the instrument to one payee does not jeopardize the rights of other payees. We hold, therefore, that Abington's delivery of the check to only one joint payee, Azevedo, nevertheless constitutes delivery to the remaining joint payee, GMAC.

Obligations on a negotiable instrument, however, do not end with delivery to a payee. *To discharge its liability, a party to an instrument must make payment or satisfaction to the holder. Once payment discharges the instrument, the underlying obligation is also discharged.* When a check is involved, final payment is made when it is accepted by the drawee bank. If a check is dishonored, then the drawer becomes obligated to pay the amount of the check or satisfy the underlying obligation. [Emphasis added.]

In this case, the drawee bank accepted the check, and payment was made to a payee. Ordinarily, an underlying debt is discharged when the check is drawn on an account with sufficient funds to cover it at a solvent bank and is delivered to the payee. * * * However, in this case, *where there are co-payees * * * , a negotiable instrument cannot be discharged by the actions of only one payee.* [Unrevised UCC] 3–116(b) [Revised UCC 3–110(d)] expressly prohibits the discharge of an instrument except by *all* the payees. * * * Without this rule, there would be no assurance that all the joint payees would receive payment and that the drawer's underlying obligation would be fully discharged. [Emphasis added.]

Prior to the adoption of [unrevised UCC] 3–116, the common law rule that any joint obligee has power to discharge the promisor by receipt of the promised performance had created particular incongruities when applied to negotiable instruments. The unpaid copayee could not collect from the *drawer* because the in-

9. This case was decided under unrevised UCC Article 3, but the result under the revised UCC Article 3 would likely be the same.

strument was deemed discharged; on the other hand, the unpaid co-payee could sue the *drawee* on a conversion of funds theory. [Unrevised UCC] 3–116 [Revised UCC 3–110(d)] settles the issue by requiring the endorsements of every joint payee before an instrument can be discharged. * * *

* * * Further, to hold that an instrument is discharged when payment is made to one co-payee without the endorsement of the other would effectively convert a "payable to A *and* B" instrument into one "payable to A *or* B." Thus, to protect the rights of all joint payees as well as the integrity of the commercial paper itself, we hold that payment of a check to one co-payee without the endorsement of the other co-payee does not discharge the drawer of either his liability on the instrument or the underlying obligation.

* * * *

For these reasons, we reverse the order of the [state intermediate appellate court] dismissing the report and remand the case to the [trial court].

So ordered.

CASE 25.2 TAKING IN GOOD FAITH

MAINE FAMILY FEDERAL CREDIT UNION V. SUN LIFE ASSURANCE CO. OF CANADA

Supreme Judicial Court of Maine, 1999.
1999 ME 43,
727 A.2d 335.

SAUFLEY, J. [Justice]

* * * *

Daniel, Joel, and Claire Guerrette are the adult children of Elden Guerrette, who died on September 24, 1995. Before his death, Elden had purchased a life insurance policy from Sun Life Assurance Company of Canada, through Sun Life's agent, Steven Hall, and had named his children as his beneficiaries. Upon his death, Sun Life issued three checks, each in the amount of $40,759.35, to each of Elden's children. The checks were drawn on Sun Life's account at Chase Manhattan Bank in Syracuse, New York. The checks were given to Hall for delivery to the Guerrettes.

The parties have stipulated that Hall and an associate, Paul Richard, then fraudulently induced the Guerrettes to indorse the checks in blank and to transfer them to Hall and Richard, purportedly to be invested in "HER, Inc.," a corporation formed by Hall and Richard. Hall took the checks from the Guerrettes and turned them over to Richard, who deposited them in his account at the Credit Union on October 26, 1995. The Credit Union immediately made the funds available to Richard.

The Guerrettes quickly regretted having negotiated their checks to Hall and Richard, and they contacted Sun Life the next day to request that Sun Life stop payment on the checks. Sun Life immediately ordered Chase Manhattan to stop payment on the checks. Thus, when the checks were ultimately presented to Chase Manhattan for payment, Chase refused to pay the checks, and they were returned to the Credit Union.

The Credit Union received notice that the checks had been dishonored on November 3, 1995, the sixth business day following their deposit. By that time, however, Richard had withdrawn from his account all of the funds represented by the three checks. The Credit Union was able to recover almost $80,000 from Richard, but there remained an unpaid balance of $42,366.56, the amount now in controversy.

The Credit Union filed a complaint [in a Maine state court] against Sun Life alleging that Sun Life was liable as drawer of the instruments * * * . The Credit Union then filed [claims] against * * * [the] Guerrette[s] and Richard, alleging that they were liable as indorsers of the checks * * * .

* * * *

At trial, the only issue presented to the jury was whether the Credit Union had acted in "good faith" when it gave value for the checks, thus entitling it to holder in due course status. * * * The jury found that the Credit Union had not acted in good faith and therefore was not a holder in due course. Therefore, the [court] entered judgment in favor of Sun Life, Daniel, Joel, and Claire, and against the Credit Union. * * * [T]he Credit Union filed this appeal.

* * * *

We * * * turn to the definition of "good faith" contained in Article 3-A of the Maine U.C.C. * * * [This] definition provides:

> "Good faith" means honesty in fact *and the observance of reasonable commercial standards of fair dealing.* [Emphasis added.]

* * * *

* * * It is undisputed that the Credit Union had no knowledge that Richard obtained the Sun Life checks by fraud. Nor was the Credit Union aware that a stop payment order had been placed on the Sun Life checks. The Credit Union expeditiously gave value on the checks, having no knowledge that they would be dishonored. In essence the Credit Union acted as banks have, for years, been allowed to act without risk to

holder in due course status. The Credit Union acted with honesty in fact.

* * * *

We turn then to the objective prong of the good faith analysis * * * .

* * * *

The factfinder must * * * determine, first, whether the conduct of the holder comported with industry or "commercial" standards applicable to the transaction and, second, whether those standards were reasonable standards intended to result in fair dealing. Each of those determinations must be made in the context of the specific transaction at hand. If the factfinder's conclusion on each point is "yes," the holder will be determined to have acted in good faith even if, in the individual transaction at issue, the result appears unreasonable. Thus a holder may be accorded holder in due course status where it acts pursuant to those reasonable commercial standards of fair dealing—even if it is negligent—but may lose that status, even where it complies with commercial standards, if those standards are not reasonably related to achieving fair dealing.

Therefore the jury's task here was to decide whether the Credit Union observed the banking industries' commercial standards relating to the giving of value on uncollected funds, and, if so, whether those standards are reasonably designed to result in fair dealing.

The evidence produced by the Credit Union in support of its position that it acted in accordance with objective good faith included the following: The Credit Union's internal policy was to make provisional credit available immediately upon the deposit of a check by one of its members. In certain circumstances—where the check was for a large amount and where it was drawn on an out-of-state bank—its policy allowed for a hold to be placed on the uncollected funds for up to nine days. The Credit Union's general written policy on this issue was reviewed annually—and had always been approved—by the National Credit Union Administration, the federal agency charged with the duty of regulating federal credit unions. In addition, the policy complied with applicable banking laws * * * .

The Credit Union also presented evidence that neither [federal banking regulations] nor the Credit Union's internal policy *required* it to hold the checks or to investigate the genesis [origin] of checks before extending provisional credit. It asserted that it acted exactly as its policy and the law allowed when it immediately extended provisional credit on these checks, despite the fact that they were drawn for relatively large amounts on an out-of-state bank. Finally, the Credit Union presented expert testimony that most credit unions in Maine follow similar policies.

In urging the jury to find that the Credit Union had not acted in good faith, Sun Life and the Guerrettes argued that the Credit Union's conduct did not comport with reasonable commercial standards of fair dealing when it allowed its member access to provisional credit on checks totalling over $120,000 drawn on an out-of-state bank without either: (1) further investigation to assure that the deposited checks would be paid by the bank upon which they were drawn, or (2) holding the instruments to allow any irregularities to come to light.

* * * *

The Credit Union's President admitted the risks inherent in the Credit Union's policy and admitted that it would not have been difficult to place a hold on these funds for the few days that it would normally take for the payor bank to pay the checks. He conceded that the amount of the checks were relatively large, that they were drawn on an out-of-state bank, and that these circumstances "could have" presented the Credit Union with cause to place a hold on the account. He also testified to his understanding that some commercial banks followed a policy of holding nonlocal checks for three business days before giving provisional credit. Moreover, the Credit Union had no written policy explicitly guiding its staff regarding the placing of a hold on uncollected funds. Rather, the decision on whether to place a temporary hold on an account was left to the "comfort level" of the teller accepting the deposit. There was no dispute that the amount of the three checks far exceeded the $5,000 threshold for a discretionary hold established by the Credit Union's own policy.

On these facts the jury could rationally have concluded that the reasonable commercial standard of fair dealing would require the placing of a hold on the uncollected funds for a reasonable period of time and that, in giving value under these circumstances, the Credit Union did not act according to commercial standards that were reasonably structured to result in fair dealing.

* * * *

Judgment in favor of Daniel, Joel, and Claire Guerrette and against Maine Family Federal Credit Union affirmed.

Judgment in favor of Sun Life Assurance Company of Canada and against Maine Family Federal Credit Union vacated [on other grounds] and remanded for further proceedings consistent with the opinion herein.

CASES PROBLEMS

25–1. Dennis Bowling was a friend and neighbor of David Dabney. Bowling had no indication that Dabney was financially troubled. Indeed, by all evidence, Dabney was quite well off: he owned four grocery stores, he drove a Cadillac, his wife owned a new sports car, he had racehorses and he lived in an expensive home. In the fall of 1983, Dabney admitted to Bowling that he had "cash flow" problems and borrowed $40,000 from Bowling. At the same time, Dabney proposed they become partners in his grocery business, and discussions concerning this prospect ensued over the following weeks. At one point, Dabney asked Bowling for a signed blank check that would be deposited with a new grocery supplier as "security" and would never be used without Bowling's consent. If it was, Dabney promised, he would reimburse Bowling's account appropriately. Shortly thereafter, Dabney dated and filled out Bowling's blank check for $10,606.79 and gave the check to his major supplier and creditor, E. Bierhaus & Sons. Dabney owed Bierhaus more than $400,000 for past deliveries; after having received ten to twenty bad checks from Dabney, Bierhaus required cash or cashier's checks from Dabney for any new shipments. Dabney had told Bierhaus about the supposedly imminent partnership with Bowling, and under those circumstances, Bierhaus's agent accepted the $10,606.79 check from Bowling in payment for a delivery of groceries. Bowling's check was returned to Bierhaus, as there were insufficient funds in Bowling's account to cover it. By this time, Dabney had filed for bankruptcy protection. Bierhaus sought to collect the amount of the check from Bowling. Is Bierhaus a holder in due course? [*E. Bierhaus & Sons v. Bowling,* 486 N.E.2d 598 (Ind.App. 1 Dist. 1985)]

25–2. In the fall of 1980, the Williams Brothers Asphalt Paving Co. contracted with two local communities in Michigan to resurface some of their streets. During the course of the jobs, Williams incurred debts to its supplier, Rieth-Riley Construction Co., in the amount of $45,960. When the work was completed, Williams received a total of $188,433 from the two communities and deposited the funds into its checking account at First Security Bank. Although the amount owed to Rieth-Riley ($45,960) was to have been set aside by the communities in a special trust (Michigan Builders Trust Fund), it was not. Williams owed a secured debt to First Security Bank and so immediately paid to the bank the entire amount it had received. The payment was in the form of checks drawn on Williams's checking account at the bank and made payable to the bank's order. Williams later filed for bankruptcy, and Rieth-Riley sought to get its money from the bank, contending that Williams Brothers had no right to the $45,960 still owed to Rieth-Riley and thus could not negotiate it to the bank (via the checks Williams Brothers had made payable to the bank). Is the bank a holder in due course in this instance? [*In re Williams Brothers Asphalt Paving Co.,* 59 Bankr. 71 (Bankr.W.D.Mich. 1986)]

25–3. James Liddell, who was doing business under the corporate name of JHL & Associates, Inc., agreed to invest Jan Mumma's funds in Fidelity, a nationally traded mutual fund management company. Mumma indorsed a cashier's check for $13,904.48 to "Fidelity/JHL & Associates." Liddell indorsed the check with JHL's indorsement stamp and deposited the check, without Fidelity's indorsement, into JHL's bank account at Rainier National Bank. Liddell never invested the funds in Fidelity. Mumma was unable to recover her money from JHL, which had become insolvent, or from Liddell, who was serving a jail sentence for fraud stemming from this incident and others like it. Mumma then attempted to recover from Rainier National Bank, claiming that the bank was negligent by not requiring *both* Fidelity and JHL & Associates to indorse the check. Was Mumma correct? Explain. [*Mumma v. Rainier National Bank,* 60 Wash.App. 937, 808 P.2d 767 (1991)]

25–4. Joseph Thomas stole two signed cashier's checks from a loan officer's desk at Chase Lincoln First Bank, N.A. Thomas wrote $200,000 as the amount of one check and $300,000 as the amount of the other, and made them payable to the order of his brother-in-law. Posing as his brother-in-law, Thomas presented the checks to the Tropicana Casino. A casino employee who contacted Chase was told that the $200,000 check was "good," that there were adequate funds to cover it, and that there was no stop-payment order on the $300,000 check. Thomas gambled away most of the money before Chase stopped payment on the checks. The owner of the Tropicana, Adamar of New Jersey, Inc., filed a suit in a New York state court against the bank to recover the $500,000. When the court denied Adamar's motion for summary judgment, Adamar appealed. Had Adamar taken the checks in good faith, as required for HDC status? Discuss. [*Adamar of New Jersey, Inc. v. Chase Lincoln First Bank, N.A.,* 615 N.Y.S.2d 550 (1994)]

25–5. Pamela Haas, an employee of Trail Leasing, Inc., had access to her employer's blank checks. Over a period of about two and a half years, Haas used the firm's checks to fraudulently obtain cash from the firm's bank, Drovers First American Bank. She carried out her scheme by writing checks payable to Drovers First, having the checks signed by an authorized officer of Trail Leasing, and then taking the checks to the bank. There she would fill out a "change order form"—a form used by bank customers to specify the coins and bill denominations in which they wished to take cash for business operations—and pocket the cash that she received. By the time the scheme was discovered (through a discrepancy in one of the change orders), Haas had negotiated fifty-five checks for a total of nearly $40,000. Trail Leasing sued the bank to recover the funds paid to Haas without its authorization, and the issue turned on whether the bank was a holder in due course of the checks delivered to it by Haas. Specifically, the issue was whether the bank had taken the checks for value. Trail Leasing argued that because the bank essentially paid Haas from Trail Leasing's funds (by debiting Trail Leasing's bank account), the bank had not given value for the instruments and therefore could not be an HDC. Will the court concur in this argument? Discuss. [*Trail Leasing, Inc. v. Drovers First American Bank*, 447 N.W.2d 190 (Minn. 1989)]

25–6. On September 9, 1976, Rob-Glen Enterprises, Inc., executed and delivered promissory notes payable to the Dolly Can Corp. in return for a loan of $46,000. In addition, to secure the loan a number of individual officers of Rob-Glen Enterprises executed identical guaranties of payment for the notes. Shortly thereafter, prior to the notes' maturity, Dolly Can indorsed the notes in blank and delivered them to the First National Bank of Long Island pursuant to an existing general loan and security agreement for past and future debts. Rob-Glen, at the date of maturity, refused to pay the notes held by the bank. The bank claimed that it was entitled to payment as a holder in due course. Rob-Glen claimed that the bank was not a holder in due course because it had given no value. Discuss whether the bank was a holder in due course. [*First National Bank of Long Island v. Rob-Glen Enterprises, Inc.*, 101 A.D.2d 848, 476 N.Y.S.2d (1984)]

25–7. Joe Morgan, Inc. (JMI), was in the telephone-utility contracting business in Alabama. JMI owed to AmSouth Bank money secured by JMI's accounts receivable. In September 1988, JMI obtained from Sunburst Bank loans also secured by JMI's accounts receivable. (Under the UCC, AmSouth and Sunburst were required to file certain documents in the office of the secretary of state to put all others on notice of their interests in JMI's accounts.) Utility Contractors Financial Services (UCON) was in the business of factoring (purchasing) accounts receivable from telephone-utility contractors. UCON factored a customer's receivable at a discount of the face value of the account and then collected the account from the account debtor. UCON began factoring JMI's accounts in the winter of 1989. JMI's customers always paid UCON, at first unaware of the need to check for UCC filings with the secretary of state. Also, although UCON occasionally ran credit checks on its customers, it did not do so with JMI's customers despite doubts about JMI's financial health. UCON soon learned of AmSouth's interest in JMI's accounts but did not contact AmSouth or investigate the matter further. UCON and Sunburst learned of each other's interests at a meeting on July 17. Two months later, when JMI filed for bankruptcy, UCON initiated proceedings to determine whether it or Sunburst was entitled to the proceeds from the accounts factored before July 17. (No one disputed that AmSouth was to be paid first.) The court held that UCON qualified as an HDC of the checks it had received in payment on those accounts and was therefore entitled to those proceeds. Sunburst appealed. One of the issues on appeal was whether UCON satisfied the objective standard for the good faith requirement for HDC status. How should the appellate court rule on this issue? Discuss. [*In re Joe Morgan, Inc.*, 985 F.2d 1554 (11th Cir. 1993)]

25–8. An employee of Epicycle Corp. cashed a payroll check at Money Mart Check Cashing Center, Inc. Money Mart deposited the check, with others, into its bank account. When the check was returned marked "Payment stopped," Money Mart sought to recover from Epicycle for the value of the check. Money Mart claimed that it was a holder in due course on the instrument because it had accepted the check for value, in good faith, and without notice that a stop-payment order had been made. Epicycle argued that Money Mart was not a holder in due course because it had failed to verify that the check was good before it cashed the check. Did Money Mart's failure to inquire into the validity of the check preclude it from being a holder in due course? Explain. [*Money Mart Check Cashing Center, Inc. v. Epicycle Corp.*, 667 P.2d 1372 (Colo. 1983)]

25–9. On October 25, 1983, in payment for cattle sold at auction, Fort Pierre Livestock Auction, Inc., issued check number 19074 for $31,730.23 to Gene Hunt. Later, Fort Pierre discovered that it had miscounted the cattle, and on October 31, it issued check number 19331 for $36,343.95 to Hunt. This check was meant to replace check 19074, but Fort Pierre made no notation to that effect on the check and did not ask Hunt to return check 19074. Fort Pierre tried to stop payment on check 19074, but its bank (American State Bank of Pierre) later could find no record of the attempt. On October 26, 1984, a representative of the Northwest South Dakota Production Credit Association (PCA) met with Hunt to arrange repayment of a delinquent loan. Hunt agreed to give PCA checks 19074 and 19331 in exchange for forgiveness of his remaining debt. PCA did not know that one check had replaced the other or that Fort Pierre had attempted to stop payment on check 19074. PCA told Fort Pierre that a couple of old "Hunt" checks would be deposited. Fort Pierre called its bank and warned it not to accept the checks without full indorsements. On discovering in January 1985 that both checks had cleared, Fort Pierre informed PCA that one check was meant to replace the other and demanded repayment for check 19074. PCA refused, asserting HDC status. Fort Pierre and its bank sued PCA, but the court ruled that PCA was an HDC and denied recovery. Fort Pierre and its bank appealed. What will happen on appeal? Discuss fully. [*American State Bank of Pierre v. Northwest South Dakota*

Production Credit Association, 404 N.W.2d 517 (S.Dak. 1987)]

25–10. An employee of J. M. Heinike Associates, Inc., on several occasions obliterated the restrictive words "for deposit only" from indorsements made by Heinike on checks. The checks thus became bearer instruments, which the employee cashed at the Liberty National Bank. When Heinike learned of these activities, it sued Liberty in a New York state court to recover the amount of the converted funds. Heinike contended that Liberty lacked HDC status because obliteration of the restrictive words served as notice that the indorsement had been materially altered. Liberty filed a motion for summary judgment. The trial court found Liberty to be an HDC and granted the motion. Heinike appealed. What will the appellate court decide? Discuss. [*J. M. Heinike Associates, Inc. v. Liberty National Bank,* 560 N.Y.S.2d 720 (1990)]

25–11. North Carolina National Bank (NCNB) made a long-term loan to Sharpe Hosiery Mill. In October 1974, NCNB issued a $20,000 certificate of deposit (CD) to Sharpe. A few days later Allen Stein bought Sharpe. As a result of the sale, NCNB called for payment of the long-term loan and stated that it was going to apply the CD, as well as Sharpe's checking account balance, toward the unpaid balance. Stein refused to return the CD and instead used it as partial collateral for a personal loan from Manufacturers Hanover Bank and Trust, which did not know of the NCNB claim. When the CD matured, Manufacturers sent it to NCNB for collection. NCNB dishonored and retained the CD. After paying the balance owed on the personal loan, Stein had Michael Rozen, his brother-in-law, purchase all of Manufacturers' rights in the CD from Manufacturers. Claiming the rights of an HDC, Rozen sued NCNB in a federal district court for the value of the CD. The trial court held that Rozen was not protected by the shelter principle. Rozen appealed. What will happen on appeal? Discuss fully. [*Rozen v. North Carolina National Bank,* 588 F.2d 83 (4th Cir. 1978)]

25–12. Dynamics Corp. and Marine Midland Bank had a long-standing agreement under which Marine Midland received checks payable to Dynamics and indorsed and deposited them into the Dynamics account. Dynamics never saw the checks. They were made out to the order of Dynamics and delivered directly to Marine Midland. Marine Midland stamped the backs of the checks with the Dynamics name and insignia and transferred them. Within the meaning of the UCC, is the act of sending checks to Marine Midland Bank a negotiation? If Marine Midland transfers the checks to other parties, will that be a negotiation? Discuss. [*Marine Midland Bank–New York v. Graybar Electric Co.,* 41 N.Y.2d 703, 363 N.E.2d 1139, 395 N.Y.S.2d 403 (1977)]

25–13. Universal Premium Acceptance Corp. issued more than $1 million in drafts, intending the payee to be Great American Insurance Co. When the drafts were issued, they were nonnegotiable instruments. Walter Talbot, an insurance agent, intercepted the drafts, forged Great American's indorsements in blank, and deposited the drafts in a phony account at York Bank & Trust Co. After Talbot was caught and convicted, Universal filed a suit in a federal district court against York to recover some of its losses. One of the issues was whether Talbot's indorsements converted the nonnegotiable drafts into negotiable bearer instruments. Did they? Why, or why not? [*Universal Premium Acceptance Corp. v. York Bank & Trust Co.,* 69 F.3d 695 (3d Cir. 1995)]

25–14. Stacey Dillabough presented two money orders for payment to Chuckie Enterprises, Inc., a check-cashing service in Philadelphia. Dillabough was known as a previous customer, the orders were presented within thirty days of the date on them, and there was nothing to indicate that they were not valid. Chuckie obtained photo identification from Dillabough, cashed the orders, and submitted them to the issuer, American Express, for payment. American Express recognized the orders as stolen and refused to pay. Chuckie assigned its right to payment to Robert Triffin, who filed a suit against American Express to collect. One of the issues was whether Chuckie was a holder in due course. One of the requirements of HDC status is good faith. Did Chuckie take the money orders in good faith? Discuss. [*Triffin v. Dillabough,* 552 Pa. 550, 716 A.2d 605 (1998)]

25–15. A QUESTION OF ETHICS

Richard Caliendo, an accountant, prepared tax returns for various clients. To satisfy their tax liabilities, the clients issued checks payable to various state taxing entities and gave them to Caliendo. Between 1977 and 1979, Caliendo forged indorsements on these checks, deposited them in his own bank account, and subsequently withdrew the proceeds. In 1983, after learning of these events and after Caliendo's death, the state brought an action against Barclays Bank of New York, N.A., the successor to Caliendo's bank, to recover the amount of the checks. Barclays moved for dismissal on the ground that because the checks had never been delivered to the state, the state never acquired the status of holder and therefore never acquired any rights in the instruments. The trial court held for the state, but the appellate court reversed. The state then appealed the case to the state's highest court. That court ruled that the state could not recover the amount of the checks from the bank because, although the state was the named payee on the checks, the checks had never been delivered to the payee. [*State v. Barclays Bank of New York, N.A.,* 561 N.Y.2d 533, 563 N.E.2d 11, 561 N.Y.S.2d 697 (1990)]

1. If you were deciding this case, would you make an exception to the rule and let the state collect the funds from Barclays Bank? Why, or why not?

What ethical policies must be balanced in this situation?

2. Under agency law, which will be discussed in Chapters 31 and 32, delivery to the agent of a given individual or entity constitutes delivery to that person or entity. The court deemed that Caliendo was not an agent of the state but an agent of the taxpayers. Does it matter that the taxpayers may not have known this principle of agency law and might have thought that, by delivering their checks to Caliendo, they were delivering them to the state? Discuss fully.

E-LINKS

For updated links to resources available on the Web, as well as a variety of other materials, visit this text's Web site at

http://wbl-cs.westbuslaw.com

To find information on the UCC, including the Article 3 provisions discussed in this chapter, refer to the Web sites listed in the *E-Links* feature in Chapter 24.

LEGAL RESEARCH EXERCISES ON THE WEB

Go to http://wbl-cs.westbuslaw.com, the Web site that accompanies this text. Select "Interactive Study Center," and then click on "Chapter 25." There you will find the following Internet research exercise that you can perform to learn more about concepts in negotiable instruments law:

Activity 25–1: Review of Negotiable Instruments

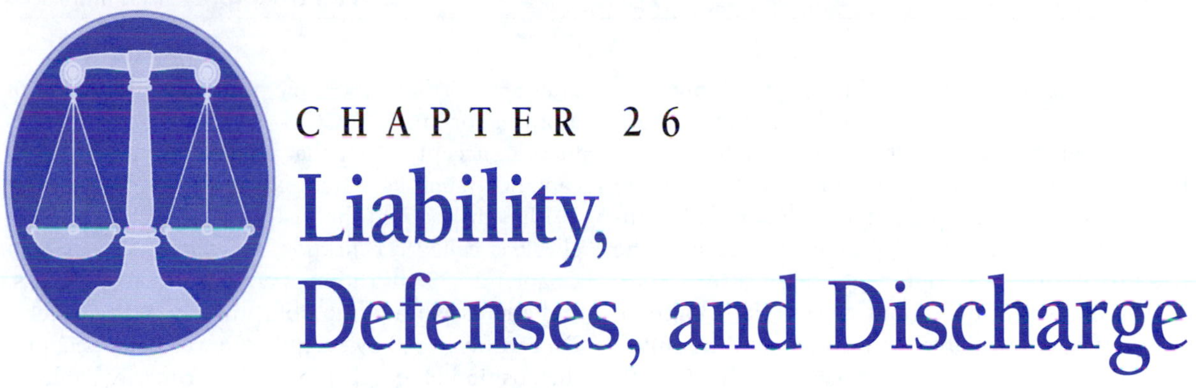

CHAPTER 26 Liability, Defenses, and Discharge

TWO KINDS OF LIABILITY ARE ASSOCIATED with negotiable instruments: signature liability and warranty liability. *Signature liability* relates to signatures on instruments. Those who sign negotiable instruments are potentially liable for payment of the amount stated on the instrument. *Warranty liability,* in contrast, extends to both signers and nonsigners. A breach of warranty can occur when the instrument is transferred or presented for payment.

Note that the focus is on liability *on the instrument itself or on warranties connected with transfer or presentment of the instrument* as opposed to liability on any underlying contract. Suppose, for example, that Donald agrees to buy one thousand compact discs from Luis and issues a check to Luis in payment. The liability discussed in this chapter does not relate directly to liability arising in connection with the contract (for instance, whether the compact discs are of proper quality or fit for the purpose for which they are intended). The liability discussed here relates to liability arising in connection with the *check* (such as what recourse Luis will have if Donald's bank refuses to pay the check—due to insufficient funds in Donald's account or Donald's order to his bank to stop payment on the check, for example).

The first part of this chapter covers the liability of the parties who sign instruments—for example, drawers of drafts and checks, makers of notes and certificates of deposit, and indorsers. It also covers the liability of accommodation parties and the warranty liability of those who transfer instruments and present instruments for payment. We then examine the defenses that can be raised to avoid liability on an instrument. As you will see, some defenses defeat payments to all holders, including holders in due course (HDCs). Others, however, can be asserted successfully only against ordinary holders. The final section in the chapter looks at some of the ways in which parties can be *discharged* from liability on negotiable instruments.

SECTION 1 Signature Liability

The key to liability on a negotiable instrument is a signature. As discussed in Chapter 24, a signature is "any name, including a trade or assumed name," or "a word, mark, or symbol executed or adopted by a person with present intention to authenticate a writing" [UCC 1–209(39), 3–401(b)]. A signature can be handwritten, typed, or printed; it also can be made by mark, by thumbprint, by machine, or in virtually any other manner. The general rule is as follows: "A person is not liable on an instrument unless (i) the person signed the instrument, or (ii) the person is represented by an agent or representative who signed the instrument and the signature is binding on the represented person" [UCC 3–401(a)].

The requirement of a signature is based on the need to know whose obligation the instrument represents. For example, Lamar writes a check for $1,000 on her account at Universal Bank payable to the order of Carerra. Carerra indorses and delivers the check, for value, to Deere. Deere deposits the check into his account at Universal Bank, but the bank returns the check to Deere marked "insufficient funds." Here the bank has dishonored the check. (**Dishonor** of an instrument occurs when payment or acceptance of the instrument—

whichever is required—is refused even though the instrument is presented in a timely and proper manner.) Given the bank's dishonor of the check, does Deere have any recourse against Lamar (the drawer) or Carerra (an indorser)? The UCC provides answers to these and similar questions concerning the liability of those who sign negotiable instruments.

The following subsections discuss the liability of the parties to negotiable instruments and the conditions that must be met before liability can arise. We begin by distinguishing between primary and secondary liability because every party, except a qualified indorser,[1] who signs a negotiable instrument is either primarily or secondarily liable for payment of that instrument when it comes due.

PRIMARY LIABILITY

A person who is primarily liable on a negotiable instrument is absolutely required to pay the instrument—unless, of course, he or she has a valid defense to payment [UCC 3–305]. The primary party's liability is immediate when the instrument is signed or issued and effective when the instrument becomes due. No action by the holder of the instrument is required. *Makers* and *acceptors* are primarily liable [UCC 3–412, 3–413].

The maker of a promissory note promises to pay the note. It is the maker's promise to pay that renders the note a negotiable instrument. The words "I promise to pay" embody the maker's obligation to pay the instrument according to the terms as written at the time of the signing or issue. If the instrument is incomplete when the maker signs it, then the maker's obligation is to pay it according to the terms written when it is completed as authorized (or as completed without authorization if it is later acquired by a holder in due course—see the discussion of defenses later in this chapter) [UCC 3–115, 3–407, 3–412].

An *acceptor* is a drawee that promises to pay an instrument when it is presented later for payment, as discussed in Chapter 24. When a drawee accepts a draft, the drawee becomes primarily liable to all subsequent holders of the instrument. In other words, the drawee's acceptance (promise to pay the instrument when presented for payment) places the drawee in virtually the same position as the maker of a promissory note [UCC 3–413]. A drawee that refuses to accept a draft that requires the drawee's acceptance (such as a trade acceptance—see Chapter 24) has dishonored the instrument. Acceptance of a check is called *certification,* as will be discussed in Chapter 27. Certification is not necessary on checks, and a bank is under no obligation to certify checks. On certification, however, the drawee bank occupies the position of an acceptor and is primarily liable on the check to any holder [UCC 3–409(d)].

The issuer of a cashier's check or other draft drawn on the drawer is also primarily liable on the instrument [UCC 3–412]. (Any "draft drawn on the drawer" is similar to a cashier's check, on which there are really only two parties. The first party is the payee, and the second party is a bank, which is both the drawer and the drawee. Of course, there is a third party—the person who pays the money to the bank for the check—but he or she is not a party to the instrument. Some courts view a bank money order as a "draft drawn on the drawer.")

SECONDARY LIABILITY

Drawers and *indorsers* have secondary liability. Secondary liability on a negotiable instrument is similar to the liability of a guarantor in a simple contract (described in Chapter 29) in the sense that it is *contingent liability.* In other words, a drawer or an indorser will be liable only if the party that is responsible for paying the instrument refuses to do so (dishonors the instrument). In regard to drafts and checks, a drawer's secondary liability does not arise until the drawee fails to pay or to accept the instrument, whichever is required. In regard to notes, an indorser's secondary liability does not arise until the maker, who is primarily liable, has defaulted on the instrument [UCC 3–412, 3–415].

Dishonor of an instrument thus triggers the liability of parties who are secondarily liable on the instrument—that is, the drawer and *unqualified* indorsers. In the Lamar-Carerra-Deere hypothetical discussed earlier, for example, the question for Deere is whether the drawer (Lamar) or the indorser (Carerra) can be held liable on the check after the bank has dishonored it. The answer to the question depends on whether certain conditions for secondary liability have been satisfied. According to the UCC, parties that are secondarily liable on a negotiable instrument, such as Lamar and Carerra in our

1. A qualified indorser—one who indorses "without recourse"—undertakes no obligation to pay [UCC 3–415(b)]. A qualified indorser merely assumes warranty liability, which is discussed later in this chapter.

example, promise to pay on that instrument only if the following events occur:[2]

1. The instrument is properly and timely presented.
2. The instrument is dishonored.
3. Timely notice of dishonor is given.[3]

Proper Presentment. The UCC spells out what constitutes a proper presentment. Basically, presentment by a holder must be made to the proper person, must be made in a proper manner, and must be timely [UCC 3–414(f), 3–415(e), 3–501]. The party to whom the instrument must be presented depends on what type of instrument is involved. A note or certificate of deposit (CD) must be presented to the maker for payment. A draft is presented by the holder to the drawee for acceptance, payment, or both, whichever is required. A check is presented to the drawee (bank) for payment [UCC 3–501(a), 3–502(b)].

Presentment can be properly made in any of the following ways, depending on the type of instrument involved [UCC 3–501(b)]:

1. By any commercially reasonable means, including oral, written, or electronic communication (but presentment is not effective until the demand for payment or acceptance is received).
2. Through a clearinghouse procedure used by banks, such as for deposited checks (discussed in Chapter 27).
3. At the place specified in the instrument for acceptance or payment.

One of the most crucial criteria for proper presentment is timeliness [UCC 3–414(f), 3–415(e), 3–501(b)(4)]. Failure to present on time is the most prevalent reason for improper presentment and consequent discharge of unqualified indorsers from secondary liability. For domestic checks, the holder must present the check for payment or collection within thirty days of its *date* to hold the drawer secondarily liable and within thirty days after an indorsement to hold the indorser secondarily liable [UCC–414(f), 3–415(e)].[4] Suppose, for example, that Deere did not deposit Lamar's check into his account until two months after Carerra indorsed it. If the bank dishonored the check, Deere could not hold Carerra liable and risks not being able to hold Lamar liable, because the check was not presented for payment within the time frame specified by the UCC.

Dishonor. As mentioned, an instrument is dishonored when presentment is properly and timely made and required acceptance or payment is refused or cannot be obtained within the prescribed time. An instrument is also dishonored when required presentment is excused (as it would be, for example, if the maker had died) and the instrument is not properly accepted or paid [UCC 3–502(e)].

Note that the postponement of payment or refusal to pay an instrument in certain situations will *not* dishonor the instrument. For example, payment can be postponed without dishonoring the instrument if presentment is made after an established cutoff hour (not earlier than 2:00 P.M.), but payment cannot be postponed beyond the close of the next business day after the day of presentment [UCC 3–501(b)(4)]. Banks frequently establish cutoff hours, after which payment will be postponed to the next business day (see Chapter 27).

In addition, the party to whom presentment is made may refuse payment without dishonoring the instrument if the holder refuses to exhibit the instrument, to give reasonable identification and/or authority to receive payment, or to sign on the instrument as a receipt for any payment made [UCC 3–501(b)(2)]. For example, suppose that Deere, instead of depositing Lamar's check into his bank account, demands payment from Universal Bank in cash. The bank requests identification, which Deere refuses to provide. In this situation, the bank would be within its rights to refuse payment to Deere, and the bank's refusal to pay would not create a dishonor of the check.

The UCC provides, in accordance with general banking practices, that returning an instrument because it lacks a proper indorsement also is not a dishonor [UCC 3–501(b)(3)(i)]. Assume that Carerra does not indorse Lamar's check before delivering it to Deere. Because at this point the check is an order

2. An instrument can be drafted to provide a waiver of the presentment and notice of dishonor requirements [UCC 3–504]. Presume, for simplicity's sake, that such waivers have *not* been incorporated into the instruments described in this chapter.

3. Note that these requirements are necessary for a secondarily liable party to have *signature* liability on a negotiable instrument, but they are not necessary for a secondarily liable party to have *warranty* liability (to be discussed later in this chapter).

4. Section 3–503(2) of the unrevised UCC *presumes* these periods to be thirty days after the date or issue of the instrument with respect to a drawer's liability and seven days after indorsement for an indorser's liability.

instrument—payable to Carerra or his order—Carerra's indorsement is required for further negotiation. If Carerra does not indorse the check, and Deere indorses it "For deposit only" into his account, the bank may return the check on the ground that it was not properly indorsed. In this situation, the return of the check is not a dishonor.

Proper Notice. The third requirement to hold secondary parties liable on an instrument is that those parties be properly notified of the dishonor. In our example, Deere would have to notify Carerra or Lamar of the dishonor to hold either party liable for the $1,000 payment. Again, the UCC specifies time frames for proper notice. Any necessary notice must be given by a bank before its midnight deadline (midnight of the next banking day after receipt) [UCC 3–503(c)]. Notice by any party other than a bank, such as Deere, must be given within thirty days following the day on which the person receives notice of dishonor [UCC 3–503(c)].[5]

Except for the dishonor of foreign drafts, notice may be given in any reasonable manner. This includes oral notice, written notice, electronic notice (notice by fax, e-mail, and the like), and notice written or stamped on the instrument itself [UCC 3–503(b)]. To give notice of dishonor of a foreign draft (a draft drawn in one country and payable in another country), a formal notice called a *protest* is required [UCC 3–505(b)]. In our example, Deere could telephone Lamar and inform her of the dishonor. Lamar, as the drawer, then would become liable for the check's payment. Similarly, Deere could notify Carerra, who indorsed the check, of the dishonor and request payment from Carerra.

Notice operates for the benefit of all parties who have rights in an instrument against the party notified [UCC 3–503(b)]. For example, assume that there are four indorsers on a note that its maker dishonors, and the holder gives timely notice to indorsers 1 and 4. If the holder collects payment from indorser 4, indorser 4 does not have to give notice to indorser 1 again to collect from indorser 1. (Indorsers 2 and 3 are not liable to indorser 4, because they were not given timely notice.) It is important to remember that if more than one indorsement appears on an instrument, each indorser is liable for the full amount to any subsequent indorser or to any holder.

5. Under Section 3–508(2) of the unrevised Article 3, notice by a person other than a bank has to be given "before midnight of the third business day after dishonor or receipt of notice of dishonor."

ACCOMMODATION PARTIES

In addition to the parties to instruments already discussed, accommodation parties may also be primarily or secondarily liable on instruments. An **accommodation party** is one who signs an instrument for the purpose of lending his or her name as credit to another party on the instrument [UCC 3–419(a)]. Accommodation parties are one form of security against nonpayment on a negotiable instrument. For example, a bank about to lend money wants some reasonable assurance that the debt will be paid. If the prospective borrower's financial condition is uncertain, the bank may be reluctant to rely solely on the borrower's ability to pay. To reduce the risk of nonpayment, the bank can require the joining of a third person as an accommodation party on the borrower's promissory note. When one person (such as a parent) cosigns a promissory note with the maker (such as the parent's son or daughter), the cosigner is an accommodation party.

If the accommodation party signs on behalf of the *maker,* he or she is an *accommodation maker* and is primarily liable on the instrument. For example, if Abe takes out a loan to purchase a car and has his uncle cosign the note, the uncle becomes primarily liable on the instrument. If, however, the accommodation party signs on behalf of a *payee or other holder* (usually to make the instrument more marketable), he or she is an *accommodation indorser* and, as an indorser, is secondarily liable. For example, if Abe's lender (who has possession of the note) has Mary sign the note so that Todd will buy it, Mary is an accommodation indorser and her liability is secondary.

Any indorsement not in the ordinary chain of title gives notice of its accommodation character [UCC 3–419(a), (b), (c)]. For example, an indorsement that appears on an instrument above that of the payee, who would normally be the first indorser, is outside the chain of title.

Westlaw. See Case 26.1 at the end of this chapter. To view the full, unedited case from Westlaw,® go to this text's Web site at **http://wbl-cs.westbuslaw.com**.

AUTHORIZED AGENTS' SIGNATURES

Questions often arise as to the liability on an instrument signed by an agent. An **agent** is a person who agrees to represent or act for another, who is known as the **principal.** Agents can sign negotiable instruments, just as they can sign contracts, and thereby bind their principals [UCC 3–401(a)(ii), 3–402(a)]. Without such a rule, all corporate commercial business would stop—as every corporation can and must act through its agents. (Agency law will be covered in detail in Chapters 31 and 32.) Certain requirements must be met, however, before the principal becomes liable on the instrument. A basic requirement to hold the principal liable on the instrument is that the agent be *authorized* to sign the instrument on the principal's behalf. We will assume here, for purposes of discussion, that such authority exists (unauthorized signatures will be dealt with shortly). Additionally, the UCC imposes certain requirements regarding the way in which the agent signs the instrument.

Liability of the Principal. Generally, an authorized agent binds a principal on an instrument if the agent *clearly names* the principal in his or her signature (by writing, mark, or some symbol). In this situation, the UCC presumes that the signature is authorized and genuine [UCC 3–308(a)]. The agent may or may not add his or her own name, but if the signature shows clearly that it is made on behalf of the principal, the agent is not liable on the instrument [UCC 3–402(b)(1)]. For example, either of the following two signatures by Sandra Binney as agent for Bob Aronson would bind Aronson on the instrument:

1. Aronson, by Binney, agent.
2. Aronson.

Liability of the Agent. What happens if an authorized agent signs just his or her own name on the instrument (such as "Binney") and does not name the principal? In this situation, normally the agent will be *personally* liable to a holder in due course who has no notice that the agent was not intended to be liable. For others, the agent can escape liability if the agent proves that the original parties did not intend the agent to be liable on the instrument [UCC 3–402(a), (b)(2)].[6] In either situation, the principal is bound if the party entitled to enforce the instrument can prove the agency relationship.

There are two other situations in which an authorized agent can be held personally liable on a negotiable instrument. When an instrument is signed in both the agent's name and the principal's name ("Sandra Binney, Bob Aronson" or "Aronson, Binney") but nothing on the instrument indicates the agency relationship (so the agent cannot be distinguished from the principal), the agent may be held personally liable. An agent may also be held personally liable if the agent indicates agency status in signing a negotiable instrument but fails to name the principal ("Sandra Binney, agent") [UCC 3–402(b)(2)]. Because these forms of signing are ambiguous, however, parol evidence is admissible to prove the agency relationship.

An important exception to the above rules is made for checks that are signed by agents. If an agent signs his or her own name on a check that is payable from the account of the principal, and the principal is identified on the check, the agent will not be personally liable on the check [UCC 3–402(c)]. For example, suppose that Binney, who is authorized to draw checks on Aronson Company's account, signs a check that is preprinted with Aronson Company's name. The signature reads simply "Sandra Binney." In this situation, Binney would not be personally liable on the check.

See Case 26.2 at the end of this chapter. To view the full, unedited case from Westlaw,® go to this text's Web site at http://wbl-cs.westbuslaw.com.

UNAUTHORIZED SIGNATURES

People normally are not liable to pay on negotiable instruments unless their signatures appear on the instruments. The general rule is that an unauthorized signature is wholly inoperative and will not bind the person whose name is forged. Assume, for example, that Pablo finds Veronica's checkbook lying on the street, writes out a check to himself, and forges Veronica's signature. If a bank negligently fails to ascertain that Veronica's signature is not genuine and cashes the check for Pablo, the bank will generally be liable to Veronica for the amount. (The liability of banks for paying instruments on which there are forged signatures will be discussed further in Chapter 27.)

Similarly, if an agent has no authority to sign the principal's name, the "unauthorized signature is ineffective except as the signature of the unauthorized signer" [UCC 3–403(a)]. Assume that Maya

6. See UCC 3–402, Comment 1. Under Section 3–401(1) of the unrevised UCC, the principal is not liable on an instrument unless his or her signature appears on it, even if the parties are aware of the agency relationship.

Campbell is the principal and Lena Shem is her agent. Shem, without authority, signs a promissory note as follows: "Maya Campbell, by Lena Shem, agent." Because Maya Campbell's "signature" is unauthorized, Campbell cannot be held liable, but Shem is liable to a holder of the note. This would be true even if Shem had merely signed the note "Maya Campbell," without indicating any agency relationship. In either situation, the unauthorized signer, Shem, is liable on the instrument.

There are two exceptions to the general rule that an unauthorized signature will not bind the person whose name is signed:

1. An exception is made when the person whose name is signed ratifies (affirms) the signature [UCC 3–403(a)]. For example, a principal can ratify an unauthorized signature made by an agent, either expressly, by affirming the validity of the signature, or impliedly, by other conduct, such as keeping any benefits received in the transaction or failing to repudiate the signature. The parties involved need not be principal and agent. For example, a mother may ratify her daughter's forgery of the mother's name so that her daughter will not be prosecuted for forgery.
2. Moreover, a person whose name is forged may be precluded from denying the effectiveness of the signature if the person's own negligence substantially contributed to the forgery. For example, Rob leaves his signature stamp and a blank check on an office counter. An employee, using the stamp, fills in and cashes the check. Rob can be estopped (prevented), on the basis of his negligence, from denying liability for payment of the check [UCC 3–115, 3–406, 4–401(d)(2)]. Whatever loss occurs may be allocated, however, between certain parties on the basis of comparative negligence [UCC 3–406(b)].[7] For example, if Rob can demonstrate that the bank was negligent in paying the check, the bank may bear a portion of the loss. The liability of the parties in this type of situation will be discussed further in Chapter 27.

An unauthorized signature operates as the signature of the unauthorized signer in favor of an HDC [UCC 3–403(a)]. For example, if Michel Vuillard signs "Paul Richaud" without Richaud's authorization, Vuillard is personally liable just as if he had signed his own name. Vuillard's liability is limited, however, to persons who take or pay the instrument in good faith. One who knew the signature was unauthorized would not qualify as an HDC and thus could not recover from Vuillard on the instrument. (The defenses that are effective against ordinary holders versus HDCs will be discussed in detail later in this chapter.)

Special Rules for Unauthorized Indorsements

Generally, when there is a forged or unauthorized indorsement, the burden of loss falls on the first party to take the instrument with the forged or unauthorized indorsement. This general rule is premised on the concept that the first party to take an instrument is in the best position to prevent the loss.

For example, suppose that a check drawn on Universal Bank and payable to the order of Inga Leed is stolen by Jenny Nilson. Nilson indorses the check "Inga Leed" and presents the check to Universal Bank for payment. The bank, without asking Nilson for identification, pays the check, and Nilson disappears. In this situation, Leed will not be liable on the check, because her indorsement was forged. The bank will bear the loss, which it might have avoided if it had requested identification from Nilson.

There are two important exceptions to this general rule. These exceptions arise when an indorsement is made by an imposter or by a fictitious payee. We look at these two situations here.

Imposters. An **imposter** is one who, by his or her personal appearance or use of the mails, telephone, or other communication, induces a maker or drawer to issue an instrument in the name of an impersonated payee. If the maker or drawer believes the imposter to be the named payee at the time of issue, the indorsement by the imposter is not treated as unauthorized when the instrument is transferred to an innocent party. This is because the maker or drawer *intended* the imposter to receive the instrument. In this situation, under the UCC's *imposter rule,* the imposter's indorsement will be effective-that is, not considered a forgery—insofar as the drawer or maker is concerned [UCC 3–404(a)].

The comparative negligence standard mentioned previously also applies in situations involving imposters [UCC 3–404(d)].[8] If, for example, a bank fails to exercise ordinary care in cashing a check

7. Section 3–406 of the unrevised Article 3 does not provide for an allocation of such a loss on a comparative negligence basis.

8. Section 3–405 of the unrevised Article 3 does not provide for an allocation of loss on a comparative negligence basis.

made out to an imposter—for example, if the bank fails to check the identity of the holder-payee and this failure substantially contributes to the drawer's loss—the drawer may have a cause of action against the bank and be able to recover a portion of the loss.

Fictitious Payees. Another situation in which an unauthorized indorsement will be effective occurs when a person causes an instrument to be issued to a payee who will have *no interest* in the instrument [UCC 3–404(b), 3–405]. In this situation, the payee is referred to as a **fictitious payee.** Situations involving fictitious payees most often arise when (1) a dishonest employee deceives the employer into signing an instrument payable to a party with no right to receive payment on the instrument or (2) a dishonest employee or agent has the authority to issue an instrument on behalf of the employer and issues a check to a party who has no interest in the instrument. Under the UCC's *fictitious payee rule,* the payee's indorsement is not treated as a forgery, and the employer can be held liable on the instrument by an innocent holder.

Assume that Goldstar Aviation, Inc., gives its bookkeeper, Leslie Rose, general authority to issue checks in the company name drawn on First State Bank so that Rose can pay employees' wages and other corporate bills. Rose decides to cheat Goldstar out of $10,000 by issuing a check payable to the Del Rey Company, a supplier of aircraft parts. Rose does not intend Del Rey to receive any of the money, nor is Del Rey entitled to the payment. Rose indorses the check in Del Rey's name and deposits the check in an account that she opened in West National Bank in the name "Del Rey Co." West National Bank accepts the check and collects payment from the drawee bank, First State Bank. First State Bank charges Goldstar's account $10,000. Rose transfers $10,000 out of the Del Rey account and closes the account. Goldstar discovers the fraud and demands that the account be recredited.

Who bears the loss? Because Rose's indorsement in the name of a payee with no interest in the instrument is "effective," there is no "forgery" [UCC 3–404(b)(2)]. Under this provision, West National Bank is protected in paying on the check, and the drawee bank is protected in charging Goldstar's account. Thus, it is the employer-drawer, Goldstar, that will bear the loss. Of course, Goldstar has recourse against Rose, if Rose has not absconded with the money. Additionally, if Goldstar can prove that the bank's failure to exercise reasonable care contributed substantially to the loss, the bank may be required to bear a proportionate share of the loss under the UCC's comparative negligence standard [UCC 3–404(d)]. Thus, West National Bank could be liable for a portion of the loss if it failed to exercise ordinary care when it allowed Rose to open an account in the name "Del Rey Co." and to deposit checks and withdraw funds from the account without requiring any proof that she was authorized to act for Del Rey.

Whether a dishonest employee actually signs the check or merely supplies his or her employer with names of fictitious creditors (or with true names of creditors having fictitious debts), the UCC makes no distinction in result. Assume that Dan Symes draws up the payroll list from which employees' salary checks are written. He fraudulently adds the name Penny Trip (a friend not entitled to payment) to the payroll, thus causing checks to be issued to her. Trip cashes the checks and shares the proceeds with Symes. Again, it is the employer-drawer who bears the loss.

SECTION 2

Warranty Liability

In addition to the signature liability discussed in the preceding section, transferors make certain implied warranties regarding the instruments that they are negotiating. Liability under these warranties is not subject to the conditions of proper presentment, dishonor, and notice of dishonor. These warranties arise even when a transferor does not indorse the instrument (as in delivery of a bearer instrument). Warranty liability is particularly important when a holder cannot hold a party liable on his or her signature.

Warranties fall into two categories: those that arise from the *transfer* of a negotiable instrument and those that arise on *presentment* [UCC 3–416, 3–417]. Both transfer and presentment warranties attempt to shift liability back to a wrongdoer or to the person who dealt face to face with the wrongdoer and thus was in the best position to prevent the wrongdoing.

TRANSFER WARRANTIES

There are five **transfer warranties** [UCC 3–416]. One who transfers an instrument for *consideration* makes the following warranties to all subsequent transferees and holders who take the instrument in good faith (with some exceptions, as will be noted shortly):

1. The transferor is entitled to enforce the instrument.
2. All signatures are authentic and authorized.
3. The instrument has not been altered.
4. The instrument is not subject to a defense or claim of any party that can be asserted against the transferor.[9]
5. The transferor has no knowledge of any insolvency proceedings against the maker, the acceptor, or the drawer of the instrument.

Parties to Whom Warranty Liability Extends. If the person who transfers an instrument receives consideration, the manner of transfer and the negotiation that is used determine how far and to whom a transfer warranty will run. Transfer of an order instrument by indorsement and delivery extends warranty liability to any subsequent holder who takes the instrument in good faith. The warranties of a person who, for consideration, transfers without indorsement (by delivery of bearer paper), however, will extend only to the immediate transferee [UCC 3–416(a)].

Suppose that Wylie forges Kim's name as a maker of a promissory note. The note is made payable to Wylie. Wylie indorses the note in blank, negotiates it for consideration to Bret, and then leaves the country. Bret, without indorsement, delivers the note for consideration to Fern. Fern, in turn without indorsement, delivers the note for consideration to Rick. On Rick's presentment of the note to Kim, the forgery is discovered. Rick can hold Fern (the immediate transferor) liable for breach of the warranty that all signatures are genuine. Rick cannot hold Bret liable, because Bret is not Rick's immediate transferor but is a prior nonindorsing transferor. This example shows the importance of the distinction between transfer by indorsement and delivery (of an order instrument) and transfer by delivery only, without indorsement (of a bearer instrument).

Recovery for Breach of Warranty. A transferee or holder who takes an instrument in good faith can sue on the basis of a breach of a warranty as soon as he or she has reason to know of the breach [UCC 3–416(d)]. Notice of a claim for breach of warranty must be given to the warrantor within thirty days after the transferee or holder has reason to know of the breach and the identity of the warrantor, or the warrantor is not liable for any loss caused by a delay [UCC 3–416(c)]. The transferee or holder can recover damages for the breach in an amount equal to the loss suffered (but not more than the amount of the instrument), plus expenses and any loss of interest caused by the breach [UCC 3–416(b)].

These warranties can be disclaimed with respect to any instrument except a check [UCC 3–416(c)]. In the check-collection process, banks rely on these warranties. For all other instruments, the immediate parties can agree to a disclaimer, and an indorser can disclaim by including in the indorsement such words as "without warranties."

PRESENTMENT WARRANTIES

Any person who presents an instrument for payment or acceptance makes the following presentment warranties to any other person who in good faith pays or accepts the instrument [UCC 3–417(a), 3–417(d)]:

1. The person obtaining payment or acceptance is entitled to enforce the instrument or is authorized to obtain payment or acceptance on behalf of a person who is entitled to enforce the instrument. (This is in effect a warranty that there are no missing or unauthorized indorsements.)
2. The instrument has not been altered.
3. The person obtaining payment or acceptance has no knowledge that the signature of the drawer of the instrument is unauthorized [UCC 3–417(a), (d)].

These warranties are referred to as **presentment warranties** because they protect the party to whom the instrument is presented. These warranties cannot be disclaimed with respect to checks, and a claim for breach must be given to the warrantor within thirty days after the claimant knows, or has reason to know, of the breach and the identity of the warrantor, or the warrantor is not liable for any loss caused by a delay [UCC 3–417(e)].

The second and third warranties do not apply in certain cases (to certain parties). It is assumed, for example, that a drawer will recognize his or her own signature and that a maker or an acceptor will recognize whether an instrument has been materially altered.

9. Under Section 3–417(3) of the unrevised UCC, a qualified indorser who indorses an instrument "without recourse" limits this warranty to a warranty that he or she has "no knowledge" of such a defense rather than that there is no defense. This limitation does not apply under the revised Article 3.

Westlaw. See Case 26.3 at the end of this chapter. To view the full, unedited case from Westlaw,® go to this text's Web site at http://wbl-cs.westbuslaw.com.

SECTION 3

Defenses

Depending on whether a holder or an HDC (or a holder through an HDC) makes the demand for payment, certain defenses can bar collection from persons who would otherwise be liable on an instrument. There are two general categories of defenses—*universal defenses* and *personal defenses*.

UNIVERSAL DEFENSES

Universal defenses (also called *real defenses*) are valid against all holders, including HDCs or holders through HDCs. Universal defenses include those described in the following subsections.

Forgery. Forgery of a maker's or drawer's signature cannot bind the person whose name is used unless that person ratifies (approves or validates) the signature or is precluded from denying it (because the forgery was made possible by the maker's or drawer's negligence, for example) [UCC 3–401(a), 3–403(a)]. Thus, when a person forges an instrument, the person whose name is used has no liability to pay any holder or any HDC the value of the forged instrument. In addition, a principal can assert the defense of unauthorized signature against any holder or HDC when an agent exceeds his or her authority to sign negotiable paper on behalf of the principal [UCC 3–403].

Fraud in the Execution. If a person is deceived into signing a negotiable instrument, believing that he or she is signing something other than a negotiable instrument (such as a receipt), *fraud in the execution*, or inception, is committed against the signer. For example, a consumer unfamiliar with the English language signs a paper presented by a salesperson. The salesperson says the paper is a request for an estimate, but in fact it is a promissory note. Even if the note is negotiated to an HDC, the consumer has a valid defense against payment [UCC 3–305(a)(1)(iii)]. This defense cannot be raised, however, if a reasonable inquiry would have revealed the nature and terms of the instrument.[10] Thus, the signer's age, experience, and intelligence are relevant, because they frequently determine whether the signer should have known the nature of the transaction before signing.

Material Alteration. An alteration is material if it changes the contract terms between any two parties in any way. Examples of material alterations include completing an instrument, adding words or numbers, or making any other change in an unauthorized manner that relates to the obligation of a party [UCC 3–407(a)]. Thus, cutting off part of the paper of a negotiable instrument, adding a clause, or making any change in the amount, the date, or the rate of interest—even if the change is only one penny, one day, or 1 percent—is material. But it is not a material alteration to correct the maker's address, to have a red line drawn across the instrument to indicate that an auditor has checked it, or to correct the total final payment due when a mathematical error is discovered in the original computation. If the alteration is not material, any holder is entitled to enforce the instrument according to its original terms.

Material alteration is a *complete defense* against an ordinary holder. An ordinary holder can recover nothing on an instrument if it has been materially altered [UCC 3–407(b)]. Material alteration may be at best only a partial defense against an HDC, however. When the holder is an HDC and an original term, such as the monetary amount payable, has been altered, the HDC can enforce the instrument against the maker or drawer according to the original terms but not for the altered amount [UCC 3–407(c)(i)].

If the instrument was originally incomplete and was later completed in an unauthorized manner, alteration can no longer be claimed as a defense against an HDC, and the HDC can enforce the instrument as completed [UCC 3–407(b), (c)]. This is because the drawer or maker of the instrument, as a result of issuing an incomplete instrument, will normally be held responsible for the alteration, which could have been avoided by the exercise of greater care. If the alteration is readily apparent, then obviously the holder has notice of some defect or defense and therefore cannot be an HDC [UCC 3–302(a)(1), (2)(iv)].

Discharge in Bankruptcy. Discharge in bankruptcy (see Chapter 30) is an absolute defense on any

10. *Burchett v. Allied Concord Financial Corp.*, 74 N.M. 575, 396 P.2d 186 (1964).

instrument regardless of the status of the holder, because the purpose of bankruptcy is to settle finally all of the insolvent party's debts [UCC 3–305(a)(1)(iv)].

Minority. Minority, or infancy, is a universal defense only to the extent that state law recognizes it as a defense to a simple contract. Because state laws on minority vary, so do determinations of whether minority is a universal defense against an HDC [UCC 3–305(a)(1)(i)]. See Chapter 12 for a further discussion of the contractual liability of minors.

Illegality. When the law declares that an instrument is void because it has been executed in connection with illegal conduct, then the defense is universal—that is, absolute against both an ordinary holder and an HDC. If the law merely makes the instrument voidable—as in the personal (rather than the universal) defense of illegality, discussed later—then it is still a defense against a holder, but not against an HDC. The courts are sometimes prone to treat the word *void* in a statute as meaning *voidable* to protect a holder in due course [UCC 3–305(a)(1)(ii)].

Mental Incapacity. If a person is adjudicated mentally incompetent by state proceedings, then any instrument issued by that person thereafter is null and void. The instrument is void *ab initio* (from the beginning) and unenforceable by any holder or any HDC [UCC 3–305(a)(1)(ii)]. (If a person has not been adjudicated mentally incompetent by state proceedings, mental incapacity is a personal, not a universal, defense.)

Extreme Duress. When a person signs and issues a negotiable instrument under such extreme duress as an immediate threat of force or violence (for example, at gunpoint), the instrument is void and unenforceable by any holder or HDC [UCC 3–305(a)(1)(ii)]. (Ordinary duress is a personal, not a universal, defense.)

PERSONAL DEFENSES

Personal defenses, such as those described here, are used to avoid payment to an ordinary holder of a negotiable instrument. Remember that an ordinary holder is a holder that has not met the requirements for HDC status.

Breach of Contract or Breach of Warranty. When there is a breach of the underlying contract for which the negotiable instrument was issued, the maker of a note can refuse to pay it, or the drawer of a check can stop payment. Breach of warranty can also be claimed as a defense to liability on the instrument.

For example, Elias purchases a dozen pairs of athletic shoes from De Soto. The shoes are to be delivered in six weeks. Elias gives De Soto a promissory note for $1,000, which is the price of the shoes. The shoes arrive, but many of the shoes are stained, and the soles of several pairs are coming apart. Elias has a defense to liability on the note on the basis of breach of contract and breach of warranty. (Under sales law, a seller impliedly promises that the goods are at least merchantable; see Chapter 22.) If, however, the note is no longer in the hands of the payee-seller (De Soto) but is presented for payment by an HDC, the maker-buyer (Elias) will not be able to plead breach of contract or warranty as a defense against liability on the note.

Lack or Failure of Consideration. The absence of consideration may be a successful defense in instances involving instruments [UCC 3–303(b), 3–305(a)(2)]. For example, Tony gives Cleo, as a gift, a note that states "I promise to pay you $100,000," and Cleo accepts the note. There is no consideration for Tony's promise, and a court will not enforce the promise.

Similarly, if delivery of goods becomes impossible, a party who has issued a draft or note under the contract has a defense for not paying it. Thus, in the hypothetical athletic-shoe transaction described above, if delivery of the shoes became impossible due to their loss in an accident, De Soto could not subsequently sue successfully to enforce Elias's promise to pay the $1,000 promissory note. If the note was in the hands of an HDC, however, Elias's defense would not be available against the HDC.

Fraud in the Inducement (Ordinary Fraud). A person who issues a negotiable instrument based on false statements by the other party will be able to avoid payment on that instrument, unless the holder is an HDC. To illustrate: Gerhard agrees to purchase Carla's used tractor for $26,500. Carla, knowing her statements to be false, tells Gerhard that the tractor is in good working order and that it has been used for only one harvest. In addition, she tells Gerhard that she owns the tractor free and clear of all claims. Gerhard pays Carla $4,500 in cash and issues a negotiable promissory note for the balance. As it turns out, Carla still owes the original seller $10,000 on the purchase of the tractor, and the tractor is subject to a filed security interest (discussed in Chapter 28). In addition, the tractor is three years old and has been used in three harvests. Gerhard can refuse to pay the note if it is held by an ordinary holder, but if Carla has negotiated the note to an HDC, Gerhard must pay the HDC. Of course, Gerhard can then sue Carla to recover the money.

Illegality. As mentioned, if a statute provides that an illegal transaction is void, a universal defense exists. If, however, the statute provides that an illegal transaction is voidable, the defense is personal. For example, a state may make gambling contracts illegal and void but be silent on payments of gambling debts. Thus, the payment of a gambling debt becomes voidable and is a personal defense.

Mental Incapacity. As mentioned, if a maker or drawer has been declared by a court to be mentally incompetent, any instrument issued by the maker or drawer is void. Hence, mental incapacity can serve as a universal defense [UCC 3–305(a)(1)(ii)]. If a maker or drawer issues a negotiable instrument while mentally incompetent but before a formal court hearing has declared him or her to be so, however, the instrument is voidable. In this situation, mental incapacity can serve only as a personal defense.

Other Personal Defenses. A number of other personal defenses can be used to avoid payment to an ordinary holder, but not an HDC, of a negotiable instrument, including the following:

1. Discharge by payment or cancellation [UCC 3–601(b), 3–602(a), 3–603, 3–604].
2. Unauthorized completion of an incomplete instrument [UCC 3–115, 3–302, 3–407, 4–401(d)(2)].
3. Nondelivery of the instrument [UCC 1–201(14), 3–105(b), 3–305(a)(2)].
4. Ordinary duress or undue influence rendering the contract voidable [UCC 3–305(a)(1)(ii)].

FEDERAL LIMITATIONS ON HDC RIGHTS

Because of the sometimes harsh effects of the HDC doctrine on consumers, the federal government limits HDC rights in certain circumstances. To understand the punitive effects of the doctrine, consider an example. A consumer purchases a used car under express warranty from an automobile dealer. The consumer pays $1,000 down and signs a promissory note to the dealer for the remaining $5,000 due on the car. The dealer sells the bank this promissory note, which is a negotiable instrument, and the bank then becomes the creditor, to whom the consumer makes payments.

The car does not perform as warranted. The consumer returns the car and requests return of the down payment and cancellation of the contract. Even if the dealer refunded the $1,000, however, under the traditional HDC rule, the consumer would normally still owe the remaining $5,000, because the consumer's claim of breach of warranty is a personal defense and the bank is a holder in due course.

Thus, the traditional HDC rule leaves consumers who have purchased defective products liable to HDCs. In order to protect consumers, the Federal Trade Commission (FTC) in 1976 issued Rule 433,[11] which effectively abolished the HDC doctrine in consumer credit transactions.

Requirements of FTC Rule 433. FTC Rule 433 limits the rights of an HDC in an instrument that evidences a debt arising out of a consumer credit transaction. Rule 433, entitled "Preservation of Consumers' Claims and Defenses," attempts to prevent a situation in which a consumer is required to make payment for a defective product to a third party (the bank, in the previous example) who is an HDC of a promissory note that formed part of the contract with the dealer who sold the defective good.

FTC Rule 433 applies to any seller of goods or services who takes or receives a consumer credit contract. The rule also applies to a seller who accepts as full or partial payment for a sale the proceeds of any purchase-money loan made in connection with any consumer credit contract. Under the rule, these parties must include in the consumer credit contract the following provision:

NOTICE

ANY HOLDER OF THIS CONSUMER CREDIT CONTRACT IS SUBJECT TO ALL CLAIMS AND DEFENSES WHICH THE DEBTOR COULD ASSERT AGAINST THE SELLER OF GOODS OR SERVICES OBTAINED PURSUANT HERETO OR WITH THE PROCEEDS HEREOF. RECOVERY HEREUNDER BY THE DEBTOR SHALL NOT EXCEED AMOUNTS PAID BY THE DEBTOR HEREUNDER.

11. 16 C.F.R. Section 433.2. The rule was enacted in 1976 pursuant to the FTC's authority under the Federal Trade Commission Act, 15 U.S.C. Sections 41–58.

Effect of the Rule. FTC Rule 433 allows a consumer who is a party to a consumer credit transaction to bring any defense he or she has against the seller of a product against a subsequent holder as well. In essence, FTC Rule 433 places an HDC of the instrument in the position of a contract assignee. The rule makes the buyer's duty to pay conditional on the seller's full performance of the contract. Both the seller and the creditor are responsible for the seller's misconduct. The rule also clearly reduces the degree of transferability of negotiable instruments resulting from consumer credit contracts. An instrument that contains this notice or a similar statement required by law may remain negotiable, but there cannot be an HDC of such an instrument [UCC 3–106(d)].

What if the seller does not include the notice in a promissory note and then sells the note to a third party, such as a bank? While the seller has violated the rule, the bank has not. Because the FTC rule does not prohibit third parties from purchasing notes or credit contracts that do *not* contain the required rule, the third party does not become subject to the buyer's defenses against the seller. Thus, some consumers remain unprotected by the FTC rule.

SECTION 4

Discharge

Discharge from liability on an instrument can occur in several ways, including by payment, cancellation, or, as previously discussed, material alteration. Discharge can also occur if a party reacquires an instrument, if a holder impairs another party's right of recourse, or if a holder surrenders collateral without consent.

Discharge by Payment or Tender of Payment

All parties to a negotiable instrument will be discharged when the party primarily liable on it pays to a holder the amount due in full [UCC 3–602, 3–603].[12] The same is true if the drawee of an unaccepted draft or check makes payment in good faith to the holder. In these situations, all parties on the instrument are usually discharged. In contrast, such payment made by any other party (for example, an indorser) will discharge only the indorser and subsequent parties on the instrument. The party making such a payment still has the right to recover on the instrument from any prior parties.

A party will not be discharged when paying in bad faith to a holder who acquired the instrument by theft or who obtained the instrument from someone else who acquired it by theft (unless, of course, the person has the rights of a holder in due course) [UCC 3–602(b)(2)].

If a tender of payment is made to a person entitled to enforce the instrument and the tender is refused, indorsers and accommodation parties with a right of recourse against the party making the tender are discharged to the extent of the amount of the tender [UCC 3–603(b)]. If a tender of payment of an amount due on an instrument is made to a person entitled to enforce the instrument, the obligor's obligation to pay interest after the due date on the amount tendered is discharged [UCC 3–603(c)].

Discharge by Cancellation or Surrender

Intentional cancellation of an instrument discharges the liability of all parties [UCC 3–604]. Intentionally writing "Paid" across the face of an instrument cancels it. Intentionally tearing up an instrument cancels it. If a holder intentionally crosses out a party's signature, that party's liability and the liability of subsequent indorsers who have already indorsed the instrument are discharged. Materially altering an instrument may discharge the liability of all parties, as previously discussed [UCC 3–407(b)]. (An HDC may be able to enforce a materially altered instrument against its maker or drawer according to the instrument's original terms, however.)

Destruction or mutilation of a negotiable instrument is considered cancellation only if it is done with the intention of eliminating obligation on the instrument [UCC 3–604(a)(i)]. Thus, if destruction or mutilation occurs by accident, the instrument is not discharged, and the original terms can be established by parol evidence [UCC 3–309].

A holder of a note may discharge the obligation by surrendering the note to the person to be discharged [UCC 3–604(a)(i)].

12. This is true even if the payment is made with knowledge of a claim to the instrument by another person unless the payor knows that "payment is prohibited by injunction or similar process of a court of competent jurisdiction" or, in most cases, "the party making payment accepted, from a person having a claim to the instrument, indemnity against loss resulting from refusal to pay the person entitled to enforce the instrument" [UCC 3–602(a), (b)(1)].

Discharge by Reacquisition

A person who reacquires an instrument that he or she held previously discharges all intervening indorsers against subsequent holders who do not qualify as holders in due course [UCC 3–207]. Of course, the person reacquiring the instrument may be liable to subsequent holders.

Discharge by Impairment of Recourse or of Collateral

Discharge can also occur when a party's right of recourse is impaired [UCC 3–605]. A right of recourse is a right to seek reimbursement. Ordinarily, when a holder collects the amount of an instrument from an indorser, the indorser has a right of recourse against prior indorsers, the maker or drawer, and accommodation parties. If the holder has adversely affected the indorser's right to seek reimbursement from these other parties, however, the indorser is not liable on the instrument (to the extent that the indorser's right of recourse is impaired). This occurs when, for example, the holder releases or agrees not to sue a party against whom the indorser has a right of recourse. It also occurs when a holder agrees to an extension of the instrument's due date or to some other material modification that results in a loss to the indorser with respect to the right of recourse [UCC 3–605(c), (d)].

Sometimes a party to an instrument gives collateral to secure that his or her performance will occur. When a holder "impairs the value" of that collateral without the consent of the parties who would benefit from the collateral in the event of nonpayment, those parties to the instrument are discharged to the extent of the impairment [UCC 3–605(e), (f)].

For example, suppose that Jerome and Donna sign a note as co-makers, putting up Jerome's property as collateral. The note is payable to Montessa. Montessa is required by law to file a financing statement with the state to put others on notice of Montessa's interest in Jerome's property as collateral for the note. If Montessa fails to file the statement and Jerome goes through bankruptcy—which results in Jerome's property's being sold to pay other debts and leaves him unable to pay anything on the note—Montessa has impaired the value of the collateral to Donna, who is discharged to the extent of that impairment. In other words, Montessa's failure to file the statement prevents Montessa, when Jerome goes through bankruptcy, from taking possession of the collateral, selling it, and crediting the amount owed on the note. Donna, as co-maker, is then responsible only for any remaining indebtedness, instead of the entire unpaid balance. Thus, Donna is discharged to the extent that the proceeds from the sale of the collateral would have discharged her liability on the note.

Terms and Concepts to Review

accommodation party 502	**imposter** 504	**transfer warranties** 505
agent 502	**personal defense** 508	**universal defense** 507
dishonor 499	**presentment warranties** 506	
fictitious payee 505	**principal** 503	

Chapter Summary

Signature Liability	Every party (except a qualified indorser) who signs a negotiable instrument is either primarily or secondarily liable for payment of the instrument when it comes due. 1. *Primary liability*—Makers and acceptors are primarily liable (an *acceptor* is a drawee that promises in writing to pay an instrument when it is presented for payment at a later time) [UCC 3–115, 3–407, 3–409, 3–412]. 2. *Secondary liability*—Drawers and indorsers are secondarily liable [UCC 3–412, 3–414, 3–415, 3–501, 3–502, 3–503]. Parties who are secondarily liable on an instrument promise to pay on that instrument if the following events occur:

CHAPTER SUMMARY—CONTINUED

Signature Liability—continued

- **a.** The instrument is properly and timely presented.
- **b.** The instrument is dishonored.
- **c.** Timely notice of dishonor is given to the secondarily liable party.

3. *Accommodation parties*—An accommodation party is one who signs his or her name as credit to another party on an instrument [UCC 3–419]. Accommodation *makers* are primarily liable; accommodation *indorsers* are secondarily liable.

4. *Authorized agents' signatures*—An agent is a person who agrees to represent or act for another, called the *principal*. Agents can sign negotiable instruments and thereby bind their principals. Liability on an instrument signed by an agent depends on whether the agent is authorized and on whether the agent's representative capacity and the principal's identity are both indicated on the instrument [UCC 3–401, 3–402, 3–403]. Agents need not indicate their representative capacity on *checks*—provided the checks clearly identify the principal and are drawn on the principal's account.

5. *Unauthorized signatures*—An unauthorized signature is wholly inoperative *unless:*

- **a.** The person whose name is signed ratifies (affirms) it or is precluded from denying it [UCC 3–115, 3–401, 3–403, 3–406].
- **b.** The instrument has been negotiated to an HDC [UCC 3–403].

6. *Special rules for unauthorized indorsements*—An unauthorized indorsement will not bind the maker or drawer except in the following circumstances:

- **a.** When an imposter induces the maker or drawer of an instrument to issue it to the imposter (*imposter rule*) [UCC 3–404(a)].
- **b.** When a person signs as or on behalf of a maker or drawer, intending that the payee will have no interest in the instrument, or when an agent or employee of the maker or drawer has supplied him or her with the name of the payee, also intending the payee to have no such interest (*fictitious payee rule*) [UCC 3–404(b), 3–405].

Warranty Liability

1. *Transfer warranties*—Any person who transfers an instrument for consideration makes the following warranties to all subsequent transferees and holders who take the instrument in good faith (but when a bearer instrument is transferred by delivery only, the transferor's warranties extend only to the immediate transferee) [UCC 3–416]:

- **a.** The transferor is entitled to enforce the instrument.
- **b.** All signatures are authentic and authorized.
- **c.** The instrument has not been altered.
- **d.** The instrument is not subject to a defense or claim of any party that can be asserted against the transferor.
- **e.** The transferor has no knowledge of any insolvency proceedings against the maker, the acceptor, or the drawer of the instrument.

2. *Presentment warranties*—Any person who presents an instrument for payment or acceptance makes the following warranties to any other person who in good faith pays or accepts the instrument [UCC 3–417(a), 3–417(d)]:

- **a.** The person obtaining payment or acceptance is entitled to enforce the instrument or is authorized to obtain payment or acceptance on behalf of a person who is entitled to enforce the instrument. (This is, in effect, a warranty that there are no missing or unauthorized indorsements.)
- **b.** The instrument has not been altered.
- **c.** The person obtaining payment or acceptance has no knowledge that the signature of the drawer of the instrument is unauthorized.

Defenses

1. *Universal (real) defenses*—The following defenses are valid against all holders, including HDCs and holders with the rights of HDCs [UCC 3–305, 3–401, 3–403, 3–407]:

- **a.** Forgery.
- **b.** Fraud in the execution.

CHAPTER SUMMARY—CONTINUED

Defenses — continued	**c.** Material alteration. **d.** Discharge in bankruptcy. **e.** Minority—if the contract is voidable under state law. **f.** Illegality, mental incapacity, or extreme duress—if the contract is void under state law. **2.** *Personal defenses*—The following defenses are valid against ordinary holders but not against HDCs or holders with the rights of HDCs [UCC 3–105, 3–115, 3–302, 3–305, 3–306, 3–407, 3–601, 3–602, 3–603, 3–604, 4–401]: **a.** Breach of contract or breach of warranty. **b.** Lack or failure of consideration (value). **c.** Fraud in the inducement. **d.** Illegality and mental incapacity—if the contract is voidable. **e.** Previous payment of the instrument. **f.** Unauthorized completion of the instrument. **g.** Nondelivery of the instrument. **h.** Ordinary duress or undue influence that renders the contract voidable.
Federal Limitations on HDC Rights	Rule 433 of the Federal Trade Commission, issued in 1976, limits the rights of HDCs who purchase instruments arising out of consumer credit transactions. Under the rule, a consumer who is a party to a consumer credit transaction is permitted to bring any defense he or she has against the seller against a subsequent holder as well, even if the subsequent holder is an HDC.
Discharge from Liability	All parties to a negotiable instrument will be discharged when the party primarily liable on it pays to a holder the amount due in full. Discharge can also occur in other circumstances (if the instrument has been canceled or materially altered, for example) [UCC 3–601 through 3–606].

CASES FOR ANALYSIS

Westlaw. You can access the full text of each case presented below by going to the Westlaw cases on this text's Web site at http://wbl-cs.westbuslaw.com. Each Westlaw case includes the names of all plaintiffs and defendants, the dates on which the case was argued and decided, a brief summary of the issues and decisions in the case, headnotes classifying the specific issues in the case according to the West Key Number System, and the court's opinion. Concurring and dissenting opinions, if any, are included as well.

CASE 26.1 ACCOMMODATION PARTIES

QUALITY WASH GROUP V, LTD. v. HALLAK
California Court of Appeal,
Fourth District,
Division 1, 1996.
50 Cal.App.4th 1687,
58 Cal.Rptr.2d 592.

PATE, Associate Justice.

This action arises out of the sale of a car wash business by defendants * * * Shawkat Hallak and Nahida Hallak (the Hallaks) to plaintiff * * * Quality Wash Group V, Ltd., a limited partnership. * * * Quality * * * sought to hold the Hallaks liable as joint and several co-obligors on a promissory note (the Allan note) Quality assumed as part of the purchase price of the car wash and eventually paid off in settlement of the collection action brought by its holders against Quality and the Hallaks. * * *

On appeal from a judgment in favor of the Hallaks * * *, Quality contends the court committed reversible error * * *.

FACTUAL AND PROCEDURAL BACKGROUND

The subject car wash was originally built by Harvey and Patricia Allan in 1962. The Allans held the car wash in the name of San Diego Oil Co., a corporation. In 1978, the Allans sold the car wash to Robert and Jo Lynn Brower, transferring to them all the shares of San Diego Oil Co. As part of the purchase price, the Browers executed a promissory note in favor of the Allans (the Allan note). In 1984, the Browers transferred all the shares of San Diego Oil Co. to the Hallaks. As part of that transaction, the Hallaks became obligated with the Browers under the Allan note.

In January 1986, Quality acquired the car wash by purchasing all the shares of San Diego Oil Co. from the Hallaks. Quality then dissolved the corporation and held the car wash directly as an asset of the limited partnership. Under the purchase agreement between Quality and the Hallaks, the Browers were relieved of liability under the Allan note and Quality became jointly and severally [individually] liable under the note with the Hallaks. * * *

During the course of negotiations between Larry E. Schaadt and the Hallaks regarding Quality's purchase of the car wash, Mr. Hallak and the original owner Harvey Allan, who was then a real estate broker acting on behalf of the Hallaks, pointed out what they thought to be the west boundary of the leasehold on which the car wash was situated. In 1987 the lessor of the car wash premises notified Quality that the car wash was encroaching on adjoining property. When Schaadt contested that notice, the lessor sent a surveyor to mark the boundaries according to the legal description of the leasehold property. The survey revealed the property line on the west side of the leasehold ran through the car wash building, cutting off vacuums and a substantial part of the business's area of operations.

Quality's lessor demanded Quality cease trespassing on the adjoining property and proposed Quality resolve the encroachment problem by entering into a new lease agreement. Since it was unable to operate the car wash under the existing lease, Quality entered into a new lease agreement which allowed it to use the encroachment area but required it to pay substantially higher rent. Thereafter, a dispute arose concerning, among other things, the Hallaks' and Harvey Allan's liability to Quality for the encroachment problem. As a result of that dispute, Quality refused to make any further payments on * * * the Allan note.

* * * On October 2, 1991, the Allans filed an action in [a California state court] against Quality and the Hallaks seeking to collect on the Allan note * * * .

Before trial, Quality settled with the Allans by paying off and taking an assignment of the Allan note. Following a bench trial * * * , the court * * * denied Quality any recovery against the Hallaks on the Allan note * * * .

* * * *

DISCUSSION

* * * *

Quality contends the court erred by * * * denying Quality contribution from the Hallaks as joint and several co-obligors under the Allan note. The Allan note was amended on December 23, 1985 to provide that the Hallaks and various other entities, along with Quality, were obligated to pay the note. * * *

* * * *

[As a result of signing the amendment to the note] the Hallaks fall within the definition of "accommodation party" under California Uniform Commercial Code section 3419, subdivision (a) [UCC 3-419(a)], which provides: "If an instrument is issued for value given for the benefit of a party to the instrument ('accommodated party') and another party to the instrument ('accommodation party') signs the instrument for the purpose of incurring liability on the instrument without being a direct beneficiary of the value given for the instrument, the instrument is signed by the accommodation party 'for accommodation.'" Having assumed the Allan note as part of the purchase price of the car wash, Quality was the direct beneficiary of the value given for the note and, therefore, was the "accommodated party" under California Uniform Commercial Code section 3419.

California Uniform Commercial Code section 3419, subdivision (e) [UCC 3–419(e)] provides: "An accommodation party who pays the instrument is entitled to reimbursement from the accommodated party and is entitled to enforce the instrument against the accommodated party. *An accommodated party who pays the instrument has no right of recourse against, and is not entitled to contribution from, an accommodation party.*" [Emphasis added.] Accordingly, as an accommodated party to the Allan note who paid the note, Quality has no right of recourse against, and is not entitled to contribution from the Hallaks, who are accommodation parties under the note.

The court did not err in denying Quality recovery against the Hallaks on the Allan note.

DISPOSITION

* * * The judgment [denying Quality the right to recover from the Hallaks] is * * * affirmed. The parties are to bear their own costs on appeal.

CASE 26.2 AGENTS' SIGNATURES

CARAWAY v. LAND DESIGN STUDIO

Texas Court of Appeals—Austin, 2001.
47 S.W.3d 696.

PURYEAR, Justice.

* * * *

FACTUAL AND PROCEDURAL BACKGROUND

[Internacional Realty, Inc.] hired Land Design [Studio] to perform landscaping services on an apartment complex development known as the Deerfield Project, resulting in a debt owed to Land Design for work completed on the project. Land Design later told [Hugh] Caraway that it needed to remove Realty's account receivable from Land Design's books in order to continue receiving working capital from its lender. The parties created a promissory note that essentially replaced Realty's account receivable. In September 1998, the parties executed the note, which states the following:

> In consideration of design services rendered, I(We) *Hugh Carraway* [sic], *Internacional Realty, Inc.* (hereinafter "Debtor") do hereby promise to pay *Land Design Studio* (hereinafter "Creditor"), the amount of *$42,639.82* * * *
> Hugh L. Caraway (Signature) 9/20/98 * * *

The note was to be paid in full no later than March 31, 1999; however, no payment was received.

Land Design demanded payment and brought suit [in a Texas state court] in July of 1999 to collect the amount due. * * * Caraway denied that he was personally liable for the note because he did not sign the note in his individual capacity. In support of his defense, Caraway presented his personal affidavit, which asserted * * * the fact that he did not intend to sign the note in his individual capacity. Caraway also relied on an unsigned contract entered into evidence by Land Design. According to Caraway, the unsigned contract, created in October 1996, indicates that Land Design knew Caraway acted on behalf of Realty when he contracted Land Design's services for the Deerfield Project and when he signed the promissory note. * * *

The trial court granted Land Design's summary judgment motion against Caraway * * * . Caraway * * * appeals the grant of summary judgment on the ground that a fact issue exists as to whether he signed the note in an individual capacity.

* * * *

DISCUSSION

* * * *

* * * Caraway contends, as evidenced by his affidavits, that he never intended to be liable on the note in his individual capacity, but rather signed only in his representative capacity. Caraway also claims that the unsigned contract between Land Design and Realty demonstrates that he did not sign the note in his individual capacity. In response, Land Design asserts that the note itself clearly indicates that both Realty and Caraway are liable. Land Design points out that Caraway did not indicate on the note that he signed only as an agent of Realty. According to Land Design, for Caraway to avoid liability, he must show that he disclosed to them his intent to sign only in a representative capacity.

* * * We do not have the instance of a note reflecting the name of the principal only, followed by the signature of a purported representative, but rather we have a note bearing the name of the signing party, Caraway, as one of the principals. In addition, the language of the instrument reflects that payment was promised from more than one source: "In consideration of design services received, I(We) * * * do hereby promise to pay * * * ." Either "We" refers to both Caraway and Realty, or exclusively to Realty, which leaves "I" to refer only to Caraway. In either event, Caraway has assumed liability. The note then bears the signature of "Hugh L. Caraway, Debtor." Given the language of the instrument, we find that the note, on its face, clearly obligates Caraway as the maker, or debtor.

Caraway would be in no different a position if the note did not bear his name as a principal. As previously mentioned, Caraway's signature on the note bears no indication of his representative capacity. According to [S]ection 3.402(b) of the [Texas] Business and Commerce Code [Texas's version of UCC 3–402(b)], an authorized representative who signs his name to an instrument "is liable on the instrument to a holder in due course that took the instrument without notice that the representative was not intended to be liable on the instrument if * * * the form of the signature does not show unambiguously that the signature is made in a representative capacity." Accordingly, *a person signing a promissory note is presumed to be personally liable unless he presents a defense.* [Emphasis added.]

In his response to Land Design's motion for summary judgment, Caraway used his affidavit as support for his agency defense. Caraway stated in his affidavit that he had not intended to sign the note in an individual capacity. This assertion of his subjective intent alone is not sufficient to defeat a grant of summary judgment. The intent must be disclosed or communicated to the other party. Under the plain language of [S]ection 3.402(b), the question is whether Land Design had notice that Caraway did not intend to sign in his individual capacity.

Caraway does not indicate in his affidavit that he told Land Design he intended to sign only in an individual capacity. Instead, Caraway asserted in his response to the motion for summary judgment that Land Design knew he acted only as an agent of Realty when he signed the note. Caraway based this assertion upon the unsigned contract submitted into evidence by Land Design.

The unsigned contract, created in October 1996, cannot be used to show that the parties understood that Caraway acted only as an agent of Realty when he signed the promissory note in September 1998. The creation of the note was a wholly separate transaction from the creation of the unsigned contract, with two years separating the events. What their intentions may have been at the time of the creation of the contract are irrelevant for the purpose of establishing the intent of the parties at the time of the creation of the note. The note itself is the best indicator of intent. Therefore, we conclude that this unsigned contract does not raise a question of fact sufficient to overcome summary judgment. We cannot speculate on whether Land Design was aware of Caraway's intention to sign the note as an agent rather than as an individual. Caraway must present some affirmative evidence that he communicated or disclosed his intent to Land Design to sign the note as an agent of Realty, and he failed to do this.

We conclude that the note identifies Caraway as a maker of the note. Moreover, because the note does not indicate that Caraway signed only in his representative capacity and because Caraway presents no other evidence that he disclosed his intent to Land Design to sign the note solely as an agent of Realty, we conclude that no factual question exists as to Caraway's capacity at the time he signed the note. * * *

CONCLUSION

* * * [T]he summary judgment of the trial court is affirmed.

CASE 26.3 PRESENTMENT WARRANTIES

FIRST NATIONAL BANK OF CHICAGO v. MIDAMERICA FEDERAL SAVINGS BANK

Appellate Court of Illinois,
First District,
Sixth Division, 1999.
303 Ill.App.3d 176,
707 N.E.2d 673,
236 Ill.Dec. 546.

Justice *QUINN* delivered the opinion of the court:

* * * *

The following facts are undisputed. Prior to June 21, 1995, [the First National Bank of Chicago (First Chicago)] mailed a maturity notice to its customer Muhamad Mustafa, at his home in Naperville, Illinois, informing him that his certificate of deposit was coming to maturity. The maturity notice allows a First Chicago customer to make a written election with respect to the handling of the certificate of deposit. Once the customer has made the election on the maturity notice form, the customer is required to return the form to First Chicago. The maturity notice form also includes a signature area that must be signed by the First Chicago customer in order to close the account. The form was returned to First Chicago with instructions to close the certificate of deposit account, apparently signed by Muhamad Mustafa.

On June 21, 1995, after receiving the maturity notice form, First Chicago issued a cashier's check in the amount of $157,611.30, payable to Muhamad S. Mustafa. First Chicago mailed the cashier's check to Muhamad Mustafa's address in Naperville via first class mail.

On or about June 26, 1995, Michael Mustafa deposited the check into his account at [MidAmerica Federal Savings Bank (MidAmerica)]. Michael Mustafa was a MidAmerica customer at the time and shared the same residential address as Muhamad Mustafa. Michael Mustafa is also the nephew of Muhamad Mustafa. When the check was deposited into Michael Mustafa's MidAmerica account, the purported signature of Muhamad Mustafa and the signature of Michael Mustafa both appeared on the reverse side of the check.

First Chicago paid the check on or about June 27, 1995. Approximately 10 days later, Michael Mustafa withdrew the funds from his MidAmerica account representing substantially all of the check proceeds. In the middle of July 1995, Michael Mustafa telephoned First Chicago and informed it that he had forged the signature of Muhamad Mustafa, taken the cash and lost it gambling at a riverboat casino.

On August 14, 1995, Muhamad Mustafa went to the First Chicago branch in Naperville, Illinois, to redeem the certificate of deposit. First Chicago informed Muhamad Mustafa that a cashier's check was already issued and that the account was closed. Muhamad Mustafa stated that he was out of the country at the time the cashier's check was issued. First Chicago then prepared and obtained Muhamad Mustafa's signature on a forged indorsement affidavit and issued a replacement check to him for the full amount.

First Chicago filed suit [in an Illinois state court] against MidAmerica alleging that MidAmerica breached certain warranties and was liable to First Chicago for $157,611.30. MidAmerica filed a * * * complaint against Michael Mustafa, alleging that he endorsed the check knowing that he was not authorized to do so and intended that MidAmerica rely on his endorsement to honor and pay the check.

* * * *

Following the filing of First Chicago's suit against MidAmerica, MidAmerica obtained a default judgment against Michael Mustafa in the amount of $157,611.30 in addition to $200,000 in punitive damages and $12,000 in attorney fees. Michael Mustafa also pleaded guilty to a federal crime arising out of this incident.

Both First Chicago and MidAmerica filed motions for summary judgment. The trial court granted summary judgment in favor of First Chicago. MidAmerica's timely appeal followed.

* * * *

MidAmerica argues that the trial court erred in granting summary judgment in favor of First Chicago because First Chicago has not demonstrated that MidAmerica breached any presentment warranties. First Chicago responds that it clearly established a *prima facie* case of breach of warranty under [UCC 3–417 and 4–208].

[UCC 3–417 and 4–208] provide in pertinent part:

"(a) If an unaccepted draft is presented to the drawee for payment or acceptance and the drawee pays or accepts the draft, (i) the person obtaining payment or acceptance, at the time of presentment, and (ii) a previous transferor of the draft, at the time of transfer,

warrant to the drawee making payment or accepting the draft in good faith that:
(1) the warrantor is or was, at the time the warrantor transferred the draft, a person entitled to enforce the draft or authorized to obtain payment or acceptance of the draft on behalf of a person entitled to enforce the draft;
(2) the draft has not been altered; and
(3) the warrantor has no knowledge that the signature of the purported drawer of the draft is unauthorized."

Each section further provides at subsection (c) as follows:

"(c) If a drawee asserts a claim for breach of warranty under subsection (a) based on an unauthorized indorsement of the draft or an alteration of the draft, the warrantor may defend by proving that the indorsement is effective under Section 3–404 or 3–405 or the drawer is precluded under Section 3–406 or 4–406 from asserting against the drawee the unauthorized indorsement or alteration."

Under [UCC 3–417(a)] a bank that accepts and pays a check with an unauthorized or forged indorsement warrants to subsequent transferees the validity of that indorsement and may be held liable on that warranty. The purpose of the warranty is to place on the bank taking an instrument from a person making an unauthorized indorsement the responsibility of collecting from that person. As explained in [a previous case] the reason for imposing the warranty is to:

"speed up the collection and transfer of checks and to take the burden off each bank to meticulously check the endorsements of each item transferred. Following that logic, the first bank taking in the item for collection is primarily responsible for checking the endorsements to make sure that they are proper. Each bank then warrants to each subsequent bank in the collection chain that the endorsements are good. Of course, the original bank has rights over against the person originally presenting the item.

"The rationale suggested puts the burden directly upon the first bank in the collection chain to make sure that the endorsements are valid. This is reasonable because the first bank is in a better position to insure that it is taking the item from someone with good title than are subsequent banks in the chain. If the rationale is to facilitate the speedy transfer and collection of items by removing the burden on each bank to inspect and verify each endorsement, subsequent banks are not negligent if they do not thoroughly inspect each item. In other words, the warranty feature of the statute is designed to remove the duty of each bank to check the endorsements, and, therefore, [the plaintiff bank] would not be negligent to fail to so inspect."

The rule recognizes that, while none of the parties may have had reason to suspect a fraud, the one who took from the forger was the closest to the person causing the loss and is presumed to have had the best opportunity to have prevented the loss.

In the instant case, the record establishes that the indorsement on the cashier's check issued to Muhamad Mustafa was unauthorized and ineffective. MidAmerica, as the first bank in the collection chain, had a responsibility to ensure that the indorsement was valid, and through acceptance and payment of the check, MidAmerica warranted that the indorsement was valid. As this indorsement was in fact, invalid, we hold that MidAmerica breached its presentment warranty to First Chicago under [UCC 3–417(a) and 4–208(a)].

* * * *

For the foregoing reasons, the judgment of the circuit court of Cook County is affirmed.

CASE PROBLEMS

26–1. F. Mitchell, assistant treasurer of Travco Corp., caused two checks payable to a fictitious company, L. and B. Distributors, to be drawn on the corporation's account. Mitchell took both checks to his personal bank, indorsed them "F. Mitchell," and gave them to the teller. The teller cashed them. When Travco learned of the embezzlement, it demanded reimbursement from the bank. The bank contended that under the rule concerning fictitious payees and imposters, Mitchell's indorsement was valid and that therefore the bank should be allowed to collect. Discuss whether the bank's contention is true. [*Travco Corp. v. Citizens Federal Savings & Loan Association*, 42 Mich.App. 291, 201 N.W.2d 675 (1972)]

26–2. First National Bank collected debts owed to Rock Island Bedding Co. and Berry Industries, Inc., and in turn paid those two firms the amounts collected by remitting checks to them drawn on First National Bank. On several occasions, Johns, an employee of First National, asked the bank's accounting department to prepare cashier's checks payable to Rock Island Bedding Co. and to Berry Industries, Inc. The requests did not appear to be irregular, because the bank had been making periodic payments to the two firms. Johns, however, forged the payees' indorsements on eighteen of the checks so issued and deposited them into an account at First City Bank of Dallas. Johns fraudulently obtained $903,300 in this way. First City indorsed the checks "P.I.G." (prior indorsements guaranteed) and presented them to First National for payment. First National paid the checks and later recovered from its insurer, Fidelity & Casualty Co. Fidelity sought recovery from First City, claiming that Johns's forged indorsements did not authorize First City to pay the checks and that First City should bear the loss. Do you agree? Why, or why not? [*Fidelity & Casualty Co. v. First City Bank of Dallas,* 675 S.W.2d 316 (Tex.App.—Dallas 1984, no writ)]

26–3. Mowatt worked as a bookkeeper for the law firm of McCarthy, Kenney & Reidy, P.C., which had several branch offices in the Boston area. Part of Mowatt's job involved preparing checks payable to the partners in other offices for the authorized signature of a partner of the firm. On numerous occasions, Mowatt wrote such checks with no intention of transmitting them to the payee-partners. Instead, after they had been signed by an authorized partner, Mowatt forged indorsements on the checks and then either cashed them or deposited them in one of three bank accounts that he had opened for this purpose. The fraudulent scheme went on for a year and a half, and when the forgeries were finally discovered, the law firm demanded that the bank credit its account with the full amount of the loss that it had sustained as a result of the forgeries. The bank refused to do so, and the law firm brought an action against the bank. Which party had to bear the loss arising from the forgeries, the law firm or the drawee-bank? Discuss. [*McCarthy, Kenney & Reidy, P.C. v. First National Bank of Boston,* 402 Mass. 630, 524 N.E.2d 390 (1988)]

26–4. While Wanda Snow was married to Cary Byron, Byron established an account with Shearson Lehman Hutton, Inc.—a securities brokerage firm—for Wanda's son by a previous marriage. Wanda was designated as the account custodian. After Wanda and Cary had separated but before their divorce became final, Byron wrote a letter to Shearson instructing Shearson to close the account and send the proceeds (about $44,000) to a Florida bank account. Byron forged Wanda's signature on the letter. Later, Byron called Shearson, identified himself, and asked that the proceeds be sent instead to Wanda Snow in care of Byron's cousin in Connecticut. Byron obtained the check, forged Wanda's indorsement on it, and deposited the check into his bank account, later using proceeds for his personal benefit. Wanda sued Byron, Shearson, and the bank to recover the funds. In her claim against the bank, Wanda alleged that the bank was liable for paying the check over a forged indorsement. The bank raised the "imposter rule" as a defense. Is the imposter rule applicable in these circumstances? Why, or why not? [*Snow v. Byron,* 580 So.2d 238 (Fla.App.1st 1991)]

26–5. Jerome Simon was the administrator of the Retail Shoe Health Commission, a jointly administered employee welfare fund ("the Fund"). Simon, who was an authorized signatory to the Fund's checking account at Manufacturers Hanover Trust Company, over a period of eight years embezzled approximately $675,000 from the Fund by preparing duplicate vouchers and signing checks payable to fictitious payees for medical benefit claims submitted by the Fund's beneficiaries. Simon then indorsed the fictitious payees' names on the backs of the checks and deposited the checks primarily into a bank account at Bankers Trust Company. Simon's scheme was not discovered until after his death, when various discrepancies in check vouchers surfaced. After discovering the embezzlement, the Fund's insurer sued Manufacturers Hanover and Bankers Trust to recover the full amount of the checks on the ground of forged indorsements. Are the banks liable to the Fund for the disputed checks? Explain. [*Retail Shoe Health Commission v. Manufacturers Hanover Trust Co.,* 160 A.D.2d 47, 558 N.Y.S.2d 949 (1st Dept. 1990)]

26–6. One day, while Ort, a farmer, was working alone in his field, a stranger approached him. The stranger said he was the state agent for a manufacturer of iron posts and wire fence. The two men conversed for some time, and eventually the stranger persuaded the farmer to accept a townshipwide agency for the same manufacturer. The stranger then completed two documents for Ort to sign, telling Ort that they were identical copies of an agency agreement. Because Ort did not have his glasses with him and could read only with great difficulty, he asked the stranger to read what the document said. The stranger then purported to read the document to Ort, not mentioning that it was a promissory note. Both men signed each document, Ort assuming that he was signing a document of agency. The stranger later negotiated the promissory note that he had fraudulently obtained from Ort to an HDC. When the HDC brought suit against Ort, Ort attempted to defend on the basis of fraud in the execution. Did Ort succeed in the universal defense of fraud? Explain. [*Ort v. Fowler,* 31 Kan. 478, 2 P. 580 (1884)]

26–7. On May 25, 1964, Kroyden Industries, Inc., a New Jersey corporation, was prohibited by court order from making certain representations to its customers in connection with the sale of carpeting. In August of 1964, in violation of this order, one of Kroyden's employees offered to give Anna Berenyi and her husband carpeting free of charge if they referred prospective buyers to Kroyden Industries. Mr. and Mrs. Berenyi agreed to this condition, and relying on the employee's offer, Anna Berenyi signed a promissory note for $1,521, from which "finder's fees" would be deducted when prospective buyers were referred to Kroyden Industries. Kroyden subsequently negotiated the note to the plaintiff in this case, New Jersey Mortgage & Investment Corp. When Berenyi refused to pay the note, the plaintiff brought this legal action against her to recover the debt. Berenyi claimed that she was not liable on the note because the contract with Kroyden was illegal, having been prohibited by court order. Can

Berenyi avoid her obligations on the note on the basis of illegality? Explain. [*New Jersey Mortgage & Investment Corp. v. Berenyi,* 140 N.J.Super. 406, 356 A.2d 421 (App.Div. 1976)]

26–8. Edward Bauerband contacted Minster State Bank by phone and requested a $25,000 loan, purportedly on behalf of himself and his wife, Michelle. The Bauerbands had a long-standing relationship with the bank, and the request was not so unusual as to put the bank on notice. The bank mailed a promissory note to Edward to be signed by both him and his wife. Edward forged his wife's signature on the note, signed it himself, and returned the note and other loan documents to the bank. On its receipt of the documents, the bank issued a cashier's check in the amount of $25,000, payable to Edward and Michelle jointly, and mailed the check to the Bauerbands' home. Edward indorsed the check in his name, forged his wife's indorsement, and deposited the check in his business account at another bank, Baybank Middlesex. Michelle knew nothing about the loan transaction or the check. Ultimately, the forgery was discovered, and Minster State Bank sued Baybank Middlesex to recover the funds. Baybank contended that it was precluded from liability under the UCC's "imposter rule." Was it? Explain. [*Minster State Bank v. Bauerband,* 1992 Mass.App.Div. 61 (1992)]

26–9. Nancy Gabbard was the office manager at Golden Years Nursing Home (No. 2), Inc. She was given a signature stamp to issue checks to the nursing home's employees for up to $100 as advances on their pay. The checks were drawn on Golden Years's account at the First National Bank. Over a seven-year period, Gabbard wrote a number of checks to employees exclusively for the purpose of embezzling the money. She forged the employees' indorsements on the checks, signed her name as a second indorser, and deposited the checks in her personal account at Star Bank. First National paid Star Bank for the deposited checks. The employees whose names were on the checks never actually requested them. When the scheme was uncovered, Golden Years filed a suit in an Ohio state court against Gabbard, Star Bank, and others to recover the money. Which party, Golden Years or Star Bank, will bear the loss in this situation? Why? [*Golden Years Nursing Home (No. 2), Inc. v. Gabbard,* 640 N.E.2d 1186 (Ohio App. 1994)]

26–10. James Liddell, the president of JHL & Associates, Inc., persuaded Clifford Marston and his wife to invest in Fidelity, a company that Liddell said he represented. To execute the transaction, Liddell had the Marstons issue a check for $15,000 payable to Seattle-First National Bank (Sea-First) for the purpose of obtaining cashier's checks, which would then be sent to Fidelity. Liddell, in Clifford Marston's presence, obtained three cashier's checks payable to "JHL & Associates, Trust." Liddell did not send the checks to Fidelity but rather indorsed them to different individuals as part of a fraudulent Ponzi scheme (a scheme in which the perpetrator uses funds of recent investors to pay previous investors—often referred to as pyramiding), signing the indorsements "JHL & Associates." Eventually, the Marstons sued Sea-First to recover their money, alleging that the bank was liable for the loss because the checks were indorsed by entities other than the named payee (JHL & Associates, Trust). Discuss fully whether Liddell's indorsements were ineffective and whether the bank should be liable to the Marstons. [*Marston Enterprises, Inc. v. Seattle-First National Bank,* 57 Wash.App 662, 789 P.2d 784 (1990)]

26–11. James Balkus died without leaving a will. A few days later, Ann Vesely, his sister, discovered in his personal effects two promissory notes made payable to her in the amount of $6,000. She presented the notes to the Security First National Bank of Sheboygan Trust Department, the personal representative for the estate of Balkus, for payment. The personal representative refused to pay the notes, claiming that Vesely was not a holder in due course and that nondelivery of the notes to her was a proper defense. The trial court upheld the personal representative's claim, and Vesely appealed. Discuss whether nondelivery is a proper defense against Vesely. [*Vesely v. Security First National Bank of Sheboygan Trust Department,* 128 Wis.2d 246, 381 N.W.2d 593 (1985)]

26–12. Richard and Coralea Triplett signed two promissory notes—one for $14,000 and one for $3,500—in favor of FirsTier Bank, N.A. The Tripletts sent the bank a check for $7,200 as payment on the notes. A clerk divided the $7,200 payment to pay the second note in full and to reduce the amount owed on the first note. The clerk then incorrectly stamped the first note "PAID," signed it, and mailed it to the Tripletts. Later, a different clerk stamped the second note "PAID," signed it, and returned it to the Tripletts. When FirsTier sued the Tripletts in a Nebraska state court for the rest of the money due on the first note, the Tripletts asserted that the bank had stamped "PAID" on the note and returned it. The bank contended that it had not intended to release both notes. In deciding whether the first note was discharged, what factors should the court take into consideration? [*FirsTier Bank, N.A. v. Triplett,* 242 Neb. 614, 497 N.W.2d 339 (1993)]

26–13. Mary Ann McClusky and her husband Curtis borrowed $75,000 and signed a note payable to Francis and Thomas Gardner. As collateral, Mary Ann gave the Gardners a mortgage on a farm owned in her name only. After the McCluskys divorced, Mary Ann found, in a file in the basement of her house, the note with the word "Paid" written across it. When the Gardners refused to cancel the mortgage, she filed a suit in an Indiana state court against them. During the trial, she testified that she did not know how the note came to be in her basement or who wrote "Paid" across it. The Gardners testified that they had not surrendered it. Should the court presume that the note had been discharged, given that it was in Mary Ann's possession and had the word "Paid" written across it? Discuss. [*Gardner v. McClusky,* 647 N.E.2d 1 (Ind.App. 1995)]

26–14. Telemedia Publications, Inc., publishes *Cablecast* magazine, a weekly guide for the listings of the cable television programming in Baton Rouge, Louisiana. Cablecast hired Jennifer Pennington as a temporary employee. Pennington's duties included indorsing subscription checks received in the mail with the Cablecast deposit stamp, preparing the deposit slip, and taking the checks to be deposited to City National Bank. John McGregor, the manager of Cablecast, soon noticed shortages in revenues coming into Cablecast. When he learned that Pennington had taken checks payable to Cablecast and deposited them in her personal account at Premier Bank, N.A., he confronted her. She admitted to taking $7,913.04 in Cablecast checks. Cablecast filed a suit in a Louisiana state court against Premier Bank. The bank responded in part that Cablecast was solely responsible for losses caused by the fraudulent indorsements of its employees. At trial, Cablecast failed to prove that Premier Bank had not acted in good faith or that it had not exercised ordinary care in its handling of the checks. What rule should the court apply here? Why? [*Cablecast Magazine v. Premier Bank, N.A.,* 729 So.2d 1165 (La.App. 1 Cir. 1999)]

26–15. Robert Helmer and Percy Helmer, Jr., were authorized signatories on the corporate checking account of Event Marketing, Inc. The Helmers signed a check drawn on Event Marketing's account and issued to Rumarson Technologies, Inc. (RTI), in the amount of $24,965. The check was signed on July 13, 1998, but dated August 14. When RTI presented the check for payment, it was dishonored due to insufficient funds. RTI filed a suit in a Georgia state court against the Helmers to collect the amount of the check. Claiming that the Helmers were personally liable on Event Marketing's check, RTI filed a motion for summary judgment. Can an authorized signatory on a corporate account be held personally liable for corporate checks returned for insufficient funds? Are the Helmers liable in this case? Discuss. [*Helmer v. Rumarson Technologies, Inc.,* 538 S.E.2d 504 (Ga.App. 2000)]

E-LINKS

For updated links to resources available on the Web, as well as a variety of other materials, visit this text's Web site at

http://wbl-cs.westbuslaw.com

To find information on the UCC, including the Article 3 provisions discussed in this chapter, refer to the Web sites listed in the *E-Links* feature in Chapter 24.

LEGAL RESEARCH EXERCISES ON THE WEB

Go to http://wbl-cs.westbuslaw.com, the Web site that accompanies this text. Select "Interactive Study Center," and then click on "Chapter 26." There you will find the following Internet research exercise that you can perform to learn more about fictitious payees:

Activity 26–1: Fictitious Payees

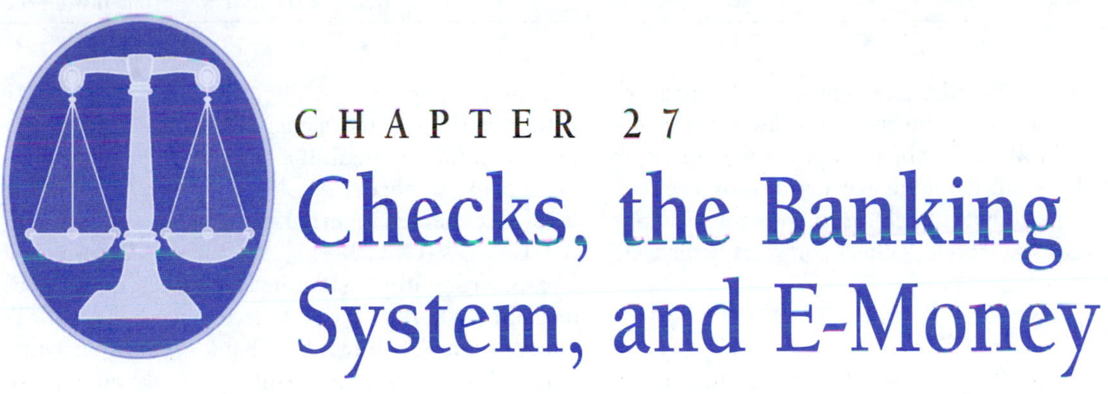

CHAPTER 27
Checks, the Banking System, and E-Money

CHECKS ARE THE MOST COMMON TYPE of negotiable instruments governed by the Uniform Commercial Code (UCC). Issues relating to checks are governed by Article 3 and Article 4 of the UCC. As noted in the preceding chapters, Article 3 establishes the requirements that all negotiable instruments, including checks, must meet. Article 3 also sets forth the rights and responsibilities of parties to negotiable instruments. Article 4 establishes a framework for deposit and checking agreements between a bank and its customers. Article 4 also governs the relationships of banks with one another as they process checks for payment. A check therefore may fall within the scope of Article 3 and yet be subject to the provisions of Article 4 while the check is in the course of collection. If a conflict arises between Article 3 and Article 4, Article 4 controls [UCC 4–102(a)].

In this chapter, we first identify the legal characteristics of checks and the legal duties and liabilities that arise when a check is issued. Then we examine the procedure by which the checks deposited into bank accounts move through banking channels, causing the underlying cash dollars to be shifted from one bank account to another. Increasingly, credit cards, debit cards, and other devices and methods to transfer funds electronically are being used to pay for goods and services. In the latter part of this chapter, we look at the law governing electronic fund transfers. We conclude the chapter with a discussion of recent innovations in money and banking practices, including electronic money and online banking.

SECTION 1

Checks

A **check** is a special type of draft that is drawn on a bank, ordering the bank to pay a fixed amount of money on demand [UCC 3–104(f)]. Article 4 defines a bank as "a person engaged in the business of banking, including a savings bank, savings and loan association, credit union or trust company" [UCC 4–105(1)].[1] If any other institution (such as a brokerage firm) handles a check for payment or for collection, the check is not covered by Article 4.

Recall from the preceding chapters that a person who writes a check is called the *drawer.* The drawer is usually a depositor in the bank on which the check is drawn. The person to whom the check is payable is the *payee.* The bank or financial institution on which the check is drawn is the *drawee.* If Anne Tomas writes a check from her checking account to pay her college tuition, she is the drawer, her bank is the drawee, and her college is the payee.

Between the time a check is drawn and the time it reaches the drawee, the effectiveness of the check may be altered by some event—for example, the

1. Under the unrevised Article 4, the term *bank* is not defined, except to distinguish among banks that deposit, collect, and pay instruments. The term is generally considered to include only commercial banks, which at the time the unrevised Article 4 was written were the only banks that could offer checking accounts. Revised Article 4's definition makes it clear that other depositary institutions now have the authority to issue and otherwise deal with checks.

drawer may die or order payment not to be made, or the account on which the check is drawn may be depleted. To avoid this problem, a payee may insist on payment by an instrument that has already been accepted by the drawee. Such an instrument may be a cashier's check, a traveler's check, or a certified check.

Cashier's Checks

Checks are usually three-party instruments, but on certain types of checks, the bank can serve as both the drawer and the drawee. For example, when a bank draws a check on itself, the check is called a **cashier's check** and is a negotiable instrument on issue (see Exhibit 27–1) [UCC 3–104(g)]. Normally, a cashier's check indicates a specific payee. In effect, with a cashier's check, the bank assumes responsibility for paying the check, thus making the check more readily acceptable in commerce.

For example, Blake needs to pay a moving company $7,000 for moving his household goods to a new home in another state. The moving company requests payment in the form of a cashier's check. Blake goes to a bank (he need not have an account at the bank) and purchases a cashier's check, payable to the moving company, in the amount of $7,000. Blake has to pay the bank the $7,000 for the check, plus a small service fee. He then gives the check to the moving company.

Cashier's checks are sometimes used in the business community as nearly the equivalent of cash. Except in very limited circumstances, the issuing bank must honor its cashier's checks when they are presented for payment. If a bank wrongfully dishonors a cashier's check, a holder can recover from the bank all expenses incurred, interest, and consequential damages [UCC 3–411]. This same rule applies if a bank wrongfully dishonors a certified check (to be discussed shortly) or a teller's check. (A **teller's check** is usually drawn by a bank on another bank; when drawn on a nonbank, it is payable at or through a bank [UCC 3–104(h)].)

Traveler's Checks

A **traveler's check** has the qualities of a teller's check or a cashier's check. It is an instrument that is payable on demand, drawn on or payable at a bank and designated as a traveler's check. The issuing institution is directly obligated to accept and pay its traveler's check according to the check's terms. The purchaser is required to sign the check at the time it is purchased and again at the time it is used [UCC 3–104(i)]. Most major banks today do not issue traveler's checks; rather, they purchase and issue American Express traveler's checks for their customers (see Exhibit 27–2).

Certified Checks

A **certified check** is a check that has been drawn by a depositor and then *accepted* by the bank on which

EXHIBIT 27–1 A CASHIER'S CHECK

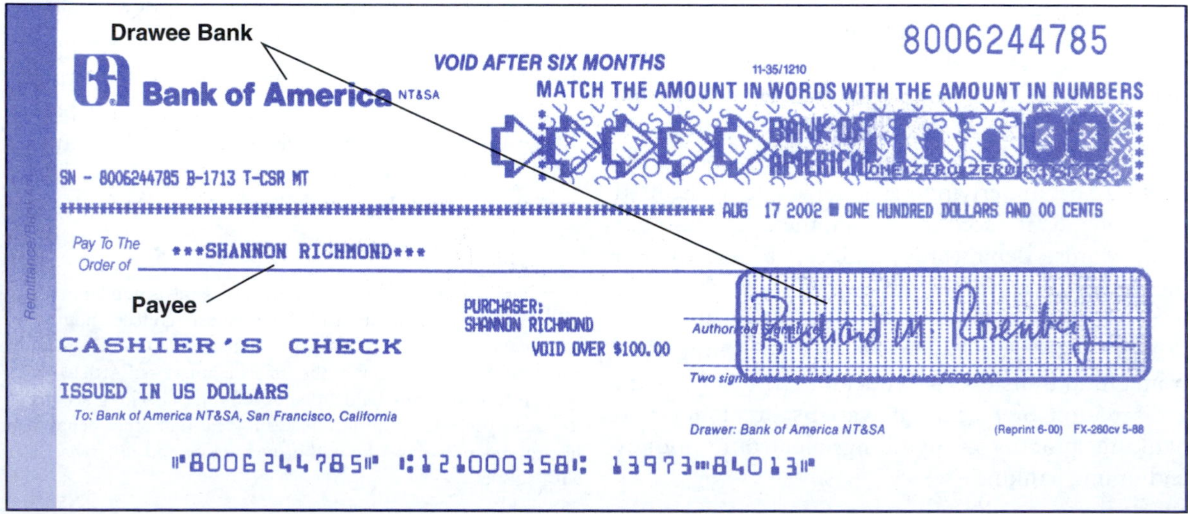

EXHIBIT 27–2 AN AMERICAN EXPRESS TRAVELER'S CHECK

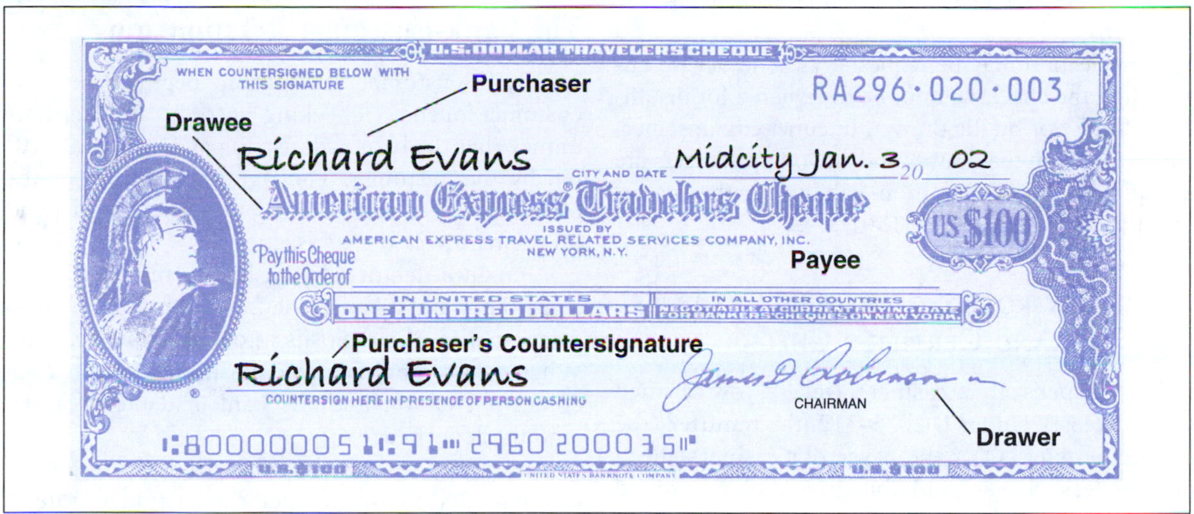

it is drawn [UCC 3–409(d)]. When a drawee bank agrees to certify a check, it immediately charges the drawer's account with the amount of the check and transfers those funds to its own certified check account. In effect, the bank is agreeing in advance to accept that check when it is presented for payment and to make payment from those funds reserved in the certified check account. Essentially, certification prevents the bank from denying liability. It is a promise that sufficient funds are on deposit and *have been set aside* to cover the check. Exhibit 27–3 illustrates a sample certified check.

A drawee bank is not obligated to certify a check, and failure to do so is not a dishonor of the check [UCC 3–409(d)]. If a bank does certify a check, however, the bank should write on the check the amount that it will pay. If the certification does not state an amount, and the amount is later increased and the instrument negotiated to a holder in due course (HDC), the obligation of the certifying bank is the amount of the instrument when it was taken by the HDC [UCC 3–413(b)]. If a certifying bank wrongfully refuses to pay a certified check, "the person asserting the right to enforce the check is entitled

EXHIBIT 27–3 A CERTIFIED CHECK

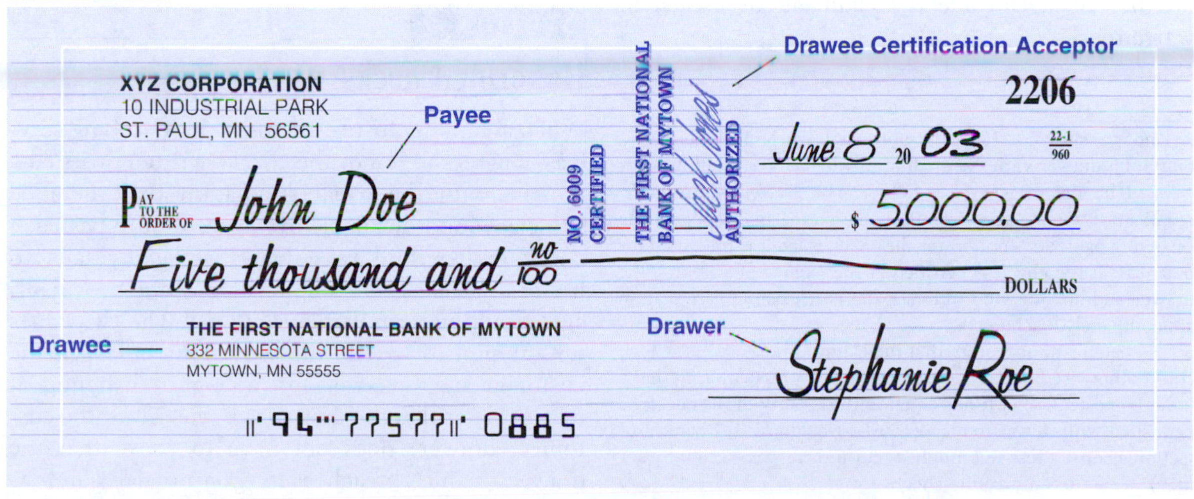

to compensation for expenses and loss of interest" and may also recover consequential damages [UCC 3–411(b)].

Certification may be requested by a holder (to ensure that the check will not be dishonored for insufficient funds) or by the drawer. In either circumstance, on certification the drawer and any prior indorsers are completely discharged from liability on the instrument [UCC 3–414(c), 3–415(d)].[2]

Lost, Destroyed, or Stolen Cashier's, Teller's, and Certified Checks

What happens if a cashier's, teller's, or certified check is lost? Under UCC 3–312, the **remitter** (the check's purchaser) or the payee of a cashier's check or a teller's check—and the drawer of a certified check—can get a refund of the amount of the check from the bank by asking for it before the check is paid. The bank may require reasonable identification of the claimant.[3]

The claim becomes enforceable ninety days after the date of the check [UCC 3–312(b)(1)]. If a person entitled to enforce the check presents it for payment within that ninety days and the bank pays, the bank is discharged [UCC 3–312(b)(2)]. If the claim becomes enforceable and no one entitled to enforce the check has presented it for payment, the bank's refund to the claimant discharges the bank-even if the claim was false [UCC 3–312(b)(4)]. (This is because a person who asks for a refund warrants to the bank, and to anybody else who might have a right to enforce the check, that the check was in fact lost, stolen, or destroyed. If it was not lost, stolen, or destroyed, a holder who cannot obtain payment on the check can sue the claimant for breach of warranty.)

2. Under Section 3–411 of the unrevised Article 3, the legal liability of a drawer varies according to whether certification is requested by the drawer or a holder. The drawer who obtains certification remains secondarily liable on the instrument if the certifying bank does not honor the check when it is presented for payment. If the check is certified at the request of a holder, the drawer and anyone who indorses the check before certification are completely discharged.

3. The bank cannot require that the claimant post a bond, which could otherwise be required under UCC 3–309. Requiring that a bond be posted—that funds equal in the amount of the check be deposited with, for example, a court—would give the bank protection against a loss that might occur if there was a claim by another person to enforce the check.

SECTION 2

The Bank-Customer Relationship

The bank-customer relationship begins when the customer opens a checking account and deposits money that the bank will use to pay for checks written by the customer. The rights and duties of the bank and the customer are contractual and depend on the nature of the transaction.

A creditor-debtor relationship is created between a customer and a bank when, for example, the customer makes cash deposits into a checking account. When a customer makes a deposit, the customer becomes a creditor, and the bank a debtor, for the amount deposited.

An agency relationship also arises between the customer and the bank when the customer writes a check on his or her account. In effect, the customer is ordering the bank to pay the amount specified on the check to the holder when the holder presents the check to the bank for payment. In this situation, the bank becomes the customer's agent and is obligated to honor the customer's request. Similarly, if the customer deposits a check into his or her account, the bank, as the customer's agent, is obligated to collect payment on the check from the bank on which the check was drawn. To transfer checkbook dollars among different banks, each bank acts as the agent of collection for its customer [UCC 4–201(a)].

Whenever a bank-customer relationship is established, certain contractual rights and duties arise. The respective rights and duties of banks and their customers are discussed in detail in the following pages.

SECTION 3

Honoring Checks

When a banking institution provides checking services, it agrees to honor the checks written by its customers, with the usual stipulation that there be sufficient funds available in the account to pay each check. When a drawee bank *wrongfully* fails to honor a check, it is liable to its customer for damages resulting from its refusal to pay. The UCC does not attempt to specify the theory under which the customer may recover for wrongful dishonor; it merely states that the drawee is liable. Thus, the customer (drawer) does not have to prove that the drawee (bank) breached its contractual commitment, slandered the customer's credit, or was negligent [UCC 4–402(b)].

The customer's agreement with the bank includes a general obligation to keep sufficient money on deposit to cover all checks written. The customer is liable to the payee or to the holder of a check in a civil suit if a check is not honored. If intent to defraud can be proved, the customer can also be subject to criminal prosecution for writing a bad check.

When the bank properly dishonors a check for insufficient funds, it has no liability to the customer. There are other circumstances as well in which the bank may rightfully refuse payment on a customer's check. We look here at the rights and duties of both the bank and its customers in relation to specific situations.

OVERDRAFTS

When the bank receives an item properly payable from its customer's checking account but there are insufficient funds in the account to cover the amount of the check, the bank has two options. It can either (1) dishonor the item or (2) pay the item and charge the customer's account, thus creating an **overdraft**, providing that the customer has authorized the payment and the payment does not violate any bank-customer agreement [UCC 4–401(a)].[4] The bank can subtract the difference from the customer's next deposit, because the check carries with it an enforceable implied promise to reimburse the bank.

When a check "bounces," a holder can resubmit the check, hoping that at a later date sufficient funds will be available to pay it. The holder must notify any indorsers on the check of the first dishonor, however; otherwise, they will be discharged from their signature liability, as discussed in Chapter 26.

Often, a bank will agree to provide overdraft protection for its customers. If a bank does make a special arrangement with its customer to accept overdrafts on an account, the bank can become liable to the customer for damages proximately caused by its wrongful dishonor of overdrafts [UCC 4–402(a), (b)].

See Case 27.1 at the end of this chapter. To view the full, unedited case from Westlaw,® go to this text's Web site at **http://wbl-cs.westbuslaw.com**.

4. If there is a joint account, the bank cannot hold any joint-account customer liable for payment of an overdraft unless the customer has signed the check or has benefited from the proceeds of the check [UCC 4–401(b)].

POSTDATED CHECKS

A bank may also charge a postdated check against a customer's account, unless the customer notifies the bank of the postdating in time to allow the bank to act on the notice before the bank commits itself to pay on the check [UCC 4–401(c)]. The notice is supposed to be treated like a stop-payment order—to be discussed shortly. If the bank fails to act on the customer's notice and charges the customer's account before the date on the postdated check, the bank may be liable for any damages incurred by the customer. Damages include those that result from the dishonor of checks that are subsequently presented for payment and are dishonored for insufficient funds.

STALE CHECKS

Commercial banking practice regards a check that is presented for payment more than six months from its date as a **stale check**. A bank is not obligated to pay an uncertified check presented more than six months from its date [UCC 4–404]. When receiving a stale check for payment, the bank has the option of paying or not paying the check. If a bank pays a stale check in good faith without consulting the customer, the bank has the right to charge the customer's account for the amount of the check.

DEATH OR INCOMPETENCE OF A CUSTOMER

UCC 4–405 provides that if, at the time a check is issued or its collection has been undertaken, a bank does not know of an adjudication of incompetence against the customer who wrote the check, the item can be paid and the bank will not incur liability. Neither death nor incompetence revokes the bank's authority to pay an item until the bank knows of the situation and has had reasonable time to act on the notice. Even when a bank knows of the death of its customer, for ten days *after the date of death* it can pay or certify checks drawn on or before the date of death—unless a person claiming an interest in that account, such as an heir or an executor of the estate, orders the bank to stop payment. Without this provision, banks would constantly be required to verify the continued life and competence of their drawers.

STOP-PAYMENT ORDERS

A **stop-payment order** is an order by a customer to his or her bank not to pay or certify a certain check.

Only a customer or a "person authorized to draw on the account" can order the bank not to pay the check when it is presented for payment [UCC 4–403(a)]. A customer has no right to stop payment on a check that has been certified or accepted by a bank, however. Also, a stop-payment order must be received within a reasonable time and in a reasonable manner to permit the bank to act on it [UCC 4–403(a)]. Although a stop-payment order can be given orally, usually by phone, it is binding on the bank for only fourteen calendar days unless confirmed in writing.[5] A written stop-payment order (see Exhibit 27–4) or an oral order confirmed in writing is effective for six months, at which time it must be renewed in writing [UCC 4–403(b)].

Bank's Liability for Wrongful Payment. If the bank pays the check over the customer's properly instituted stop-payment order, the bank will be obligated to recredit the customer's account, but only to the extent of the actual loss suffered by the drawer because of the wrongful payment [UCC 4–403(c)].

Assume that Toshio Murano orders one hundred cellular telephones from Advanced Communications, Inc., at $50 each. Murano pays in advance for the phones with a check for $5,000. Later that day, Advanced Communications tells Murano that it will not deliver the phones as arranged. Murano immediately calls the bank and stops payment on the check. Two days later, in spite of this stop-payment order, the bank inadvertently honors Murano's check to Advanced Communications for the undelivered phones. The bank will be liable to Murano for the full $5,000.

The result would have been different if Advanced Communications had delivered and Murano had accepted ninety-nine phones. Because Murano would have owed Advanced Communications $4,950 for the goods delivered, Murano would probably have been able to establish actual losses of only $50 resulting from the bank's payment over the stop-payment order. Consequently, the bank would have been liable to Murano for only $50.

Customer's Liability for Wrongful Stop-Payment Order. A stop-payment order has its risks for a customer. The drawer must have a *valid legal ground* for issuing such an order; otherwise, the holder can sue the drawer for payment. Moreover, defenses sufficient to refuse payment against a payee may not be valid grounds to prevent payment against a subsequent holder in due course [UCC 3–305, 3–306]. A person who wrongfully stops payment on a check

5. Some states do not recognize oral stop-payment orders; they must be in writing.

EXHIBIT 27–4 A STOP-PAYMENT ORDER

Bank of America

Checking Account Stop-Payment Order

To: Bank of America NT&SA
I want to stop payment on the following check(s).

ACCOUNT NUMBER: ______ – ______

SPECIFIC STOP

*ENTER DOLLAR AMOUNT: ______ *CHECK NUMBER: ______

THE CHECK WAS SIGNED BY: ______

THE CHECK IS PAYABLE TO: ______

THE REASON FOR THIS STOP PAYMENT IS: ______

STOP RANGE (Use for lost or stolen check(s) only.)

DOLLAR AMOUNT: 000

*ENTER STARTING CHECK NUMBER: ______ *END CHECK NUMBER: ______

THE REASON FOR THIS STOP PAYMENT IS: ______

BANK USE ONLY

TRANCODE:

☐ 21—ENTER STOP PAYMENT (SEE OTHER SIDE TO REMOVE)

NON READS: ______
UNPROC. STMT HIST: ______
PRIOR STMT CYCLE: ______
HOLDS ON COOLS: ______
REJECTED CHKS: ______
LARGE ITEMS: ______
FEE COLLECTED: ______
DATE ACCEPTED: ______
TIME ACCEPTED: ______

I agree that this order (1) is effective only if the above check(s) has (have) not yet been cashed or paid against my account, (2) will end six months from the date it is delivered to you unless I renew it in writing, and (3) is not valid if the check(s) was (were) accepted on the strength of my Bank of America courtesy-check guarantee card by a merchant participating in that program. I also agree (1) to notify you immediately to cancel this order if the reason for the stop payment no longer exists or (2) that closing the account on which the check(s) is (are) drawn automatically cancels this order.

IF ANOTHER BRANCH OF THIS BANK OR ANOTHER PERSON OR ENTITY BECOMES A "HOLDER IN DUE COURSE" OF THE ABOVE CHECK, I UNDERSTAND THAT PAYMENT MAY BE ENFORCED AGAINST THE CHECK'S MAKER (SIGNER).

*I CERTIFY THE AMOUNT AND CHECK NUMBER(S) ABOVE ARE CORRECT.

☐ I have written a replacement check (number and date of check).

______

(Optional—please circle one: Mr., Ms., Mrs., Miss) CUSTOMER'S SIGNATURE **X** ______ DATE ______

not only will be liable to the payee for the amount of the check but also may be liable for consequential damages incurred by the payee as a result of the wrongful stop-payment order.

Cashier's Checks and Teller's Checks. Cashier's checks and teller's checks, both of which were defined earlier in this chapter, are sometimes used in the business community as nearly the equivalent of cash. Except in very limited circumstances, the drawer bank will not stop payment on a cashier's check or a teller's check. Once it has been issued by a bank, the bank must honor it when it is presented for payment. If the bank issuing a cashier's check or a teller's check wrongfully refuses to pay it (whether as an accommodation to its customer or for other reasons), "the person asserting the right to enforce the check is entitled to compensation for expenses and loss of interest" as well as consequential damages [UCC 3–411(b)].

CHECKS BEARING FORGED SIGNATURES

When a bank pays a check on which the drawer's signature is forged, generally the bank suffers the loss.[6] A bank may be able to recover at least some of the amount of the loss, however, from a customer whose negligence substantially contributed to the forgery, from the forger of the check, or from a holder who presented the check for payment (if the holder knew that the signature was forged).

The General Rule. A forged signature on a check has no legal effect as the signature of a drawer [UCC 3–403(a)]. For this reason, banks require a signature card from each customer who opens a checking account so the bank can determine whether the signature on a customer's check is genuine. The general rule is that the bank must recredit the customer's account when it pays on a forged signature.

Customer Negligence. When a customer's negligence substantially contributes to a forgery, the bank normally will not be obliged to recredit the customer's account for the amount of the check [UCC 3–406(a)]. Suppose that CompuNet, Inc., uses a check-writing machine to write its payroll and business checks. A CompuNet employee uses the machine to write himself a check for $10,000, and CompuNet's bank subsequently honors it. CompuNet requests the bank to recredit $10,000 to its account for incorrectly paying on a forged check. If the bank can show that CompuNet failed to take reasonable care in controlling access to the check-writing equipment, CompuNet cannot require the bank to recredit its account for the amount of the forged check.

A customer's liability may be reduced, however, by the amount of a loss caused by negligence on the part of a bank (or other "person") paying the instrument or taking it for value or for collection if the negligence substantially contributes to the loss [UCC 3–406(b)].[7] Thus, in the preceding example, if CompuNet can show that the bank should have been alerted to possible fraud, the loss may be allocated between CompuNet and the bank.

Timely Examination of Bank Statements Required. Banks typically send or make available to their customers monthly statements detailing activity in their checking accounts. Banks are not obligated to include the canceled checks themselves with the statement sent to the customer. If the bank does not send the canceled checks, however, it must provide the customer with information (check number, amount, and date of payment) on the statement that will allow the customer to reasonably identify the checks that the bank has paid [UCC 4–406(a), (b)]. Often, banks send photocopies of the canceled checks with the statement. If the bank retains the canceled checks, it must keep the checks—or legible copies of the checks—for a period of seven years [UCC 4–406(b)]. The customer may obtain a canceled check (or a copy of the check) from the bank during this period of time.

The customer has a duty to examine bank statements (and canceled checks or photocopies, if they are included with the statements) promptly and with reasonable care when the statements are received or made available, and to report any alterations or forged signatures promptly [UCC 4–406(c)]. This includes forged signatures of indorsers, to be discussed later. If the customer fails to fulfill this duty and the bank suffers a loss as a result, the customer will be liable for the loss [UCC 4–406(d)]. Even if the customer can prove that he or she took reasonable care against forgeries, the UCC provides that discovery of such forgeries and

6. Each year, check fraud costs banks many billions of dollars—more than the combined losses from credit-card fraud, theft from automated teller machines, and armed robberies.

7. The unrevised Article 3 does not include a similar provision.

notice to the bank must take place within specific time frames in order for the customer to require the bank to recredit his or her account.

Consequences of Failing to Detect Forgeries. When a series of forgeries by the same wrongdoer has taken place, the UCC provides that the customer, to recover for all the forged items, must have discovered and reported the first forged check to the bank within thirty calendar days of the receipt or availability of the bank statement (and canceled checks or copies, if they are included) [UCC 4–406(d)(2)]. Failure to notify the bank within this period discharges the bank's liability for all forged checks that it pays prior to notification.

Westlaw. See Case 27.2 at the end of this chapter. To view the full, unedited case from Westlaw,® go to this text's Web site at **http://wbl-cs.westbuslaw.com**.

When the Bank Is Also Negligent. There is one situation in which a bank customer can escape liability, at least in part, for failing to notify the bank of forged or altered checks within the required thirty-day period. If the customer can prove that the bank was also negligent—that is, that the bank failed to exercise ordinary care—then the bank will also be liable, and the loss will be allocated between the bank and the customer on the basis of comparative negligence [UCC 4–406(e)]. In other words, even though a customer may have been negligent, the bank may still have to recredit the customer's account for a portion of the loss if the bank failed to exercise ordinary care.

Section 3–103(a)(7) of the UCC defines *ordinary care* to mean the "observance of reasonable commercial standards, prevailing in the area in which [a] person is located, with respect to the business in which that person is engaged." It is customary in the banking industry to manually examine signatures only on checks over a certain amount (such as $1,000, $2,500, or some higher amount). Thus, if a bank, in accordance with prevailing banking standards, fails to examine a signature on a particular check, the bank has not breached its duty to exercise ordinary care.[8]

8. Prior to the 1990 revision of Article 3, courts differed in their interpretation of what constituted ordinary care on the part of a bank. Some courts held that a bank had a duty to examine every signature on the checks it paid; other courts disagreed. The revised Article 3 put an end to the problem by clarifying the meaning of *ordinary care* in the context of today's banking system.

Regardless of the degree of care exercised by the customer or the bank, the UCC places an absolute time limit on the liability of a bank for paying a check with a forged customer signature. A customer who fails to report his or her forged signature within one year from the date that the statement was made available for inspection loses the legal right to have the bank recredit his or her account [UCC 4–406(f)].

See Case 27.3 at the end of this chapter. To view the full, unedited case from Westlaw,® go to this text's Web site at **http://wbl-cs.westbuslaw.com**.

Other Parties from Whom the Bank May Recover. As noted earlier, a forged signature on a check has no legal effect as the signature of a drawer; a forged signature, however, is effective as the signature of the unauthorized signer [UCC 3–403(a)]. Thus, when a bank pays a check on which the drawer's signature is forged, the bank has a right to recover from the party who forged the signature.

The bank may also have a right to recover from the person (its customer or a collecting bank) who transfers a check bearing a forged drawer's signature and receives a settlement. A customer or collecting bank guarantees that "all signatures on the item are authentic and authorized" [UCC 4–207(a)(2)]. If a drawee bank pays or accepts a check on the mistaken belief that the drawer's signature was authorized, the bank may recover the amount of the check from "the person to whom or for whose benefit payment was made" [UCC 3–418(a)(ii)].

This right is limited, however. A drawee bank cannot recover from "a person who took the instrument in good faith and for value or who in good faith changed position in reliance on the payment or acceptance" [UCC 3–418(c)]. This means that in most cases, a drawee bank will not recover from the person paid, because usually there is a person who took the check in good faith and for value or who in good faith changed position in reliance on the payment or acceptance.

Checks Bearing Forged Indorsements

A bank that pays a customer's check bearing a forged indorsement must recredit the customer's account or be liable to the customer (drawer) for breach of contract. Suppose that Carlo issues a $500 check "to the order of Sophia." Marcello steals the check, forges Sophia's indorsement, and cashes the check. When the check reaches Carlo's bank, the bank pays it and debits Carlo's account. The bank must recredit Carlo's account $500, because it failed to carry out Carlo's order to pay "to the order of Sophia" [UCC 4–401(a)]. (Carlo's bank will in turn recover—under principles regarding breach of warranty—from the bank that cashed the check [UCC 4–207(a)(2)].)

Eventually, the loss usually falls on the first party to take the instrument bearing the forged indorsement, because, as discussed in Chapter 26, a forged indorsement does not transfer title. Thus, whoever takes an instrument with a forged indorsement cannot become a holder.

The customer, in any case, has a duty to report forged indorsements promptly on discovery or notice. Failure to report forged indorsements within a three-year period after the forged items have been made available to the customer relieves the bank of liability [UCC 4–111].[9]

ALTERED CHECKS

The customer's instruction to the bank is to pay the exact amount on the face of the check to the holder. The bank must examine each check before making final payment. If it fails to detect an alteration, it is liable to its customer for the loss, because it did not pay as the customer ordered. The loss is the difference between the original amount of the check and the amount actually paid. Suppose that a check written for $11 is raised to $111. The customer's account will be charged $11 (the amount the customer ordered the bank to pay). The bank will normally be responsible for the $100 [UCC 4–401(d)(1)].

Customer Negligence. As in a case involving a forged drawer's signature, a customer's negligence can shift the loss when payment is made on an altered check. A common example occurs when a person carelessly writes a check, leaving large gaps around the numbers and words so that additional numbers and words can be inserted (see Exhibit 27–5).

Similarly, a person who signs a check and leaves the dollar amount for someone else to fill in is barred from protesting when the bank unknowingly and in good faith pays whatever amount is shown [UCC 4–401(d)(2)]. Finally, if the bank can trace its loss on successive altered checks to the customer's failure to discover the initial alteration, then the bank can reduce its liability for reimbursing the customer's account [UCC 4–406].[10] The law governing

9. The unrevised Article 4 limits this three-year period to the reporting of unauthorized indorsements. The revised Article 4 expands the limitation to cover any "action to enforce an obligation, duty, or right arising under this Article" [UCC 4–111]. In other words, under the revised Article 4, this is a general statute of limitations; it provides that any lawsuit must be begun within three years of the time that the cause of action occurs.

10. The bank's defense is the same whether the successive payments were made on a forged drawer's signature or on altered checks. The bank must prove that prompt notice would have prevented its loss. For example, notification might have alerted the bank not to pay further items or might have enabled it to catch the forger.

EXHIBIT 27–5 A POORLY FILLED-OUT CHECK

XYZ CORPORATION
10 INDUSTRIAL PARK
ST. PAUL, MINNESOTA 56561

2206

June 8 20 03

22-1/960

PAY TO THE ORDER OF John Doe $ 100.00

One hundred and no/100 DOLLARS

THE FIRST NATIONAL BANK OF MYTOWN
332 MINNESOTA STREET
MYTOWN, MINNESOTA 55555

Stephanie Roe

⑆94⑈ 77577⑆ 0885

the customer's duty to examine monthly statements and canceled checks, and to discover and report alterations to the bank, is the same as that applied to a forged drawer's signature.

In every situation involving a forged drawer's signature or an alteration, a bank must observe reasonable commercial standards of care in paying on a customer's checks [UCC 4–406(e)]. The customer's contributory negligence can be asserted only if the bank has exercised ordinary care.

Other Parties from Whom the Bank May Recover. The bank is entitled to recover the amount of loss (including expenses and any loss of interest) from the transferor who, by presenting the check for payment, warrants that the check has not been altered.[11]

There are two exceptions dealing with accepted drafts, however. If the bank is the drawer (as it is on a cashier's check and a teller's check), it cannot recover on this ground from the presenting party if the party is a holder in due course (HDC) acting in good faith [UCC 3–417(a)(2), 4–208(a)(2)]. The reason is that an instrument's drawer is in a better position than an HDC to know whether the instrument has been altered.

Similarly, an HDC, acting in good faith in presenting a certified check for payment, does not warrant to the check's certifier that the check was not altered before the HDC acquired it [UCC 3–417(a)(2), 4–208(a)(2)]. For example, Alan, the drawer, draws a check for $500 payable to Pam, the payee. Pam alters the amount to $5,000. The National City Bank, the drawee, certifies the check for $5,000. Pam negotiates the check to Don, an HDC. The drawee bank pays Don $5,000. On discovering the mistake, the bank cannot recover from Don the $4,500 paid by mistake, even though the bank was not in a superior position to detect the alteration. This is in accord with the purpose of certification, which is to obtain the definite obligation of a bank to honor a definite instrument.

11. Usually, the party presenting an instrument for payment is the payee, a holder, a bank customer, or a collecting bank. A bank's customers include its account holders, which may include other banks [UCC 4–104(a)(5)]. As will be discussed later in this chapter, a *collecting bank* is any bank handling an item for collection except the bank on which the check is drawn [UCC 4–105(5)].

SECTION 4

Accepting Deposits

A bank has a duty to its customer to accept the customer's deposits of cash and checks. When checks are deposited, the bank must make the funds represented by those checks available within certain time frames. A bank also has a duty to collect payment on any checks payable or indorsed to its customer and deposited by the customer into his or her account. Cash deposits made in U.S. currency are received into the customer's account without being subject to further collection procedures.

AVAILABILITY SCHEDULE FOR DEPOSITED CHECKS

The Expedited Funds Availability Act of 1987[12] and Regulation CC,[13] which was issued by the Federal Reserve Board of Governors (the Federal Reserve System will be discussed shortly) to implement the act, require that any local check deposited must be available for withdrawal by check or as cash within one business day from the date of deposit. A check is classified as a local check if the first bank to receive the check for payment and the bank on which the check is drawn are located in the same check-processing region (check-processing regions are designated by the Federal Reserve Board of Governors). For nonlocal checks, the funds must be available for withdrawal within not more than five business days.

In addition, the act requires the following:

1. That funds be available on the next business day for cash deposits and wire transfers, government checks, the first $100 of a day's check deposits, cashier's checks, certified checks, and checks for which the banks receiving and paying the checks are branches of the same institution.
2. That the first $100 of any deposit be available for cash withdrawal on the opening of the *next business day* after deposit. If a local check is deposited, the next $400 is to be available for withdrawal by no later than 5 P.M. the next business day. If, for example, you deposit a local check for $500 on Monday, you can with-

12. 12 U.S.C. Sections 4001-4010.
13. 12 C.F.R. Sections 229.1-229.42.

draw $100 in cash at the opening of the business day on Tuesday, and an additional $400 must be available for withdrawal by no later than 5 P.M. on Wednesday.

A different availability schedule applies to deposits made at *nonproprietary* automated teller machines (ATMs). These are ATMs that are not owned or operated by the bank receiving the deposits. Basically, a five-day hold is permitted on all deposits, including cash deposits, that are made at nonproprietary ATMs.

Other exceptions also exist. A banking institution has eight days to make funds available in new accounts (those open less than thirty days). It has an extra four days on deposits over $5,000 (except deposits of government and cashier's checks), on accounts with repeated overdrafts, and on checks of questionable collectibility (if the institution tells the depositor it suspects fraud or insolvency).

INTEREST-BEARING ACCOUNTS

Under the Truth-in-Savings Act (TISA) of 1991[14] and Regulation DD,[15] the act's implementing regulation, banks must pay interest based on the full balance of a customer's interest-bearing account each day. For example, Furman has an interest-bearing checking account with the First National Bank. Furman keeps a $500 balance in the account for most of the month but withdraws all but $50 the day before the bank posts the interest. The bank cannot pay interest on only the $50. The interest must be adjusted to account for all of the days, including those days when Furman's balance was higher.

Before opening a deposit account, new customers must be given certain information in a brochure, pamphlet, or other handout. The information, which must also appear in all advertisements, includes the following:

1. The minimum balance required to open an account and to be paid interest.
2. The interest, stated in terms of the annual percentage yield on the account.
3. How interest is calculated.
4. Any fees, charges, and penalties and how they are calculated. Also, under the TISA and Regulation DD, a customer's monthly statement must declare the interest earned on the account, any fees that were charged, how the fees were calculated, and the number of days that the statement covers.

14. 12 U.S.C. Sections 4301–4313.

15. 12 C.F.R. Sections 230.1–230.9.

THE COLLECTION PROCESS

Usually, deposited checks involve parties who do business at different banks, but sometimes checks are written between customers of the same bank. Either situation brings into play the bank collection process as it operates within the statutory framework of Article 4 of the UCC.

Designations of Banks Involved in the Collection Process. The first bank to receive a check for payment is the **depositary bank.**[16] For example, when a person deposits an IRS tax-refund check into a personal checking account at the local bank, that bank is the depositary bank. The bank on which a check is drawn (the drawee bank) is called the **payor bank.** Any bank except the payor bank that handles a check during some phase of the collection process is a **collecting bank.** Any bank except the payor bank or the depositary bank to which an item is transferred in the course of this collection process is called an **intermediary bank.**

During the collection process, any bank can take on one or more of the various roles of depositary, payor, collecting, and intermediary bank. To illustrate: A buyer in New York writes a check on her New York bank and sends it to a seller in San Francisco. The seller deposits the check in her San Francisco bank account. The seller's bank is both a *depositary bank* and a *collecting bank.* The buyer's bank in New York is the payor bank. As the check travels from San Francisco to New York, any collecting bank handling the item in the collection process (other than the ones acting as depositary bank and payor bank) is also called an *intermediary bank.* Exhibit 27–6 on page 532 illustrates how various banks function in the collection process in the context of this example.

Check Collection between Customers of the Same Bank. An item that is payable by the depositary bank that receives it (which in this case is also the payor bank) is called an "on-us item." If the bank does not dishonor the check by the opening of the second

16. All definitions in this section are found in UCC 4–105. The terms *depositary* and *depository* have different meanings in the banking context. A depository bank refers to a physical place (a bank or other institution) in which deposits or funds are held or stored.

EXHIBIT 27–6 THE CHECK-COLLECTION PROCESS

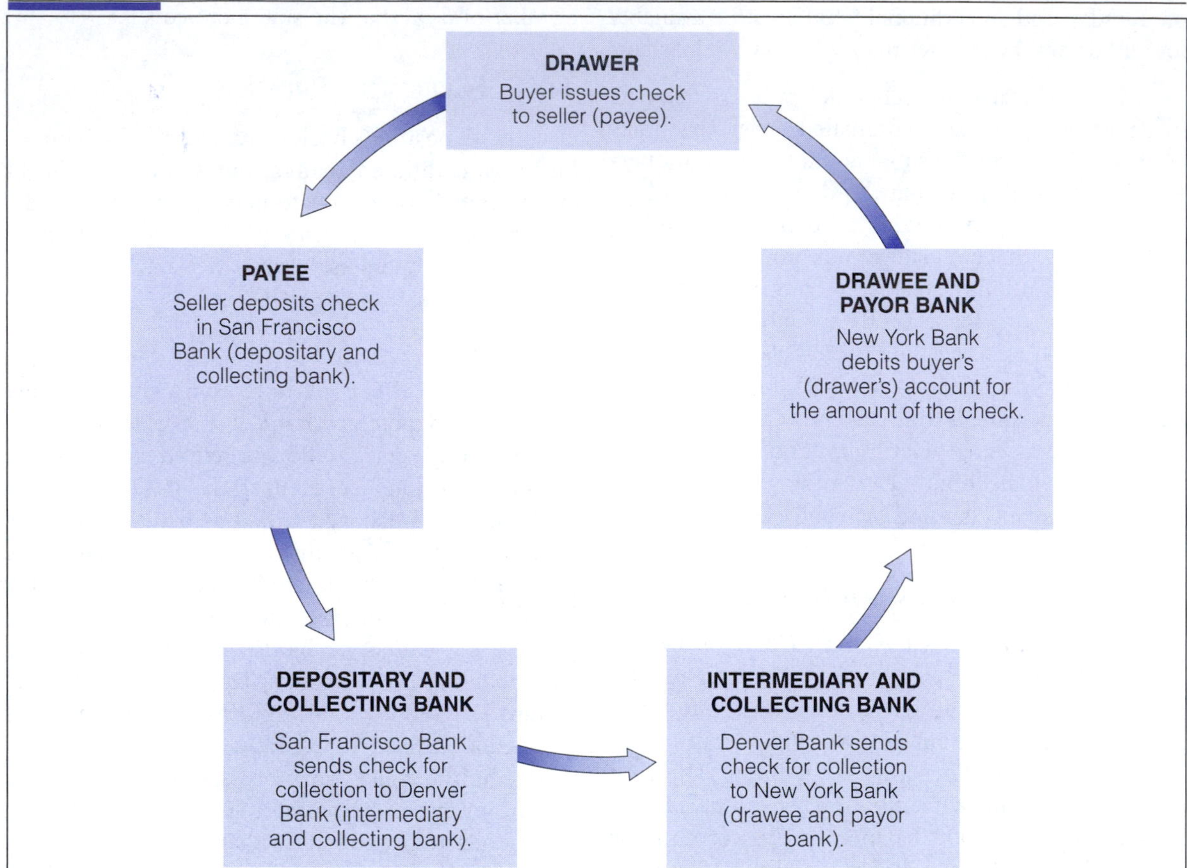

banking day following its receipt, the check is considered paid [UCC 4–215(e)(2)]. For example, Otterley and Martin both have checking accounts at First State Bank. On Monday morning, Martin deposits into his own checking account a $300 check from Otterley. That same day, the bank issues Martin a "provisional credit" for $300. When the bank opens on Wednesday, Otterley's check is considered honored, and Martin's provisional credit becomes a final payment.

Check Collection between Customers of Different Banks. Once a depositary bank receives a check, it must arrange to present it either directly or through intermediary banks to the appropriate payor bank. Each bank in the collection chain must pass the check on before midnight of the next banking day following its receipt [UCC 4–202(b)].[17] Thus, for example, a collecting bank that receives a check on Monday must forward it to the next collecting bank before midnight on Tuesday. When the check reaches the payor bank, unless the payor bank dishonors the check or returns it by midnight on the next banking day following receipt, the payor bank is accountable for the face amount of the check [UCC 4–302].[18]

Because of this deadline and because banks need to maintain an even work flow in the many items they handle daily, the UCC permits what is called *deferred posting.* According to UCC 4–108, "a bank may fix an afternoon hour of 2 P.M. or later as a cutoff hour for the handling of money and items and the

17. A bank may take a "reasonably longer time," such as when the bank's computer system is down because of a power failure [UCC 4–202(b)].

18. Most checks are cleared by a computerized process, and communication and computer facilities may fail because of weather, equipment malfunction, or other conditions. If such conditions arise and a bank fails to meet its midnight deadline, the bank is "excused" from liability if the bank has exercised "such diligence as the circumstances require" [UCC 4–109(d)].

making of entries on its books." Any checks received after that hour "may be treated as being received at the opening of the next banking day." Thus, if a bank's "cutoff hour" is 3 P.M., a check received by a payor bank at 4 P.M. on Monday will be deferred for posting until Tuesday. In this situation, the payor bank's deadline will be midnight Wednesday.

How the Federal Reserve System Clears Checks. The **Federal Reserve System** is a network of twelve central banks, located around the country and headed by the Federal Reserve Board of Governors. Most banks in the United States have Federal Reserve accounts. The Federal Reserve System has greatly simplified the check-collection process by acting as a **clearinghouse**—a system or a place where banks exchange checks and drafts drawn on each other and settle daily balances. Suppose that Pamela Moy of Philadelphia writes a check to Jeanne Sutton of San Francisco. When Jeanne receives the check in the mail, she deposits it in her bank. Her bank then deposits the check in the Federal Reserve Bank of San Francisco, which transfers it to the Federal Reserve Bank of Philadelphia. That Federal Reserve bank then sends the check to Moy's bank, which deducts the amount of the check from Moy's account. Exhibit 27–7 on page 534 illustrates this process.

Electronic Check Presentment. In the past, most checks were processed manually—the employees of each bank in the collection chain would physically handle each check that passed through the bank for collection or payment. Today, however, most checks are processed electronically. In contrast to manual check processing, which can take days, *electronic check presentment* can be done on the day of the deposit. With electronic check presentment, items may be encoded with information (such as the amount of the check) that can be read and processed by other banks' computers. In some situations, a check may be retained at its place of deposit, and only its image or information describing it is presented for payment under a Federal Reserve agreement, clearinghouse rule, or *truncation* agreement [UCC 4–110]. (The term *truncation* refers to presentment by notice rather than by delivery.)

Under UCC 4–209, any person who encodes information on an item, or with respect to an item, after the item has been issued warrants to any subsequent bank or payor that the encoded information is correct. This is also true for any person who retains an item while transmitting its image or description as presentation for payment. This person warrants that the retention and presentment of the item comply with the Federal Reserve or other agreement.

SECTION 5

Electronic Fund Transfers

The application of computer technology to banking, in the form of *electronic fund transfer systems*, has been helping to relieve banking institutions of the burden of having to move mountains of paperwork to process fund transfers. An **electronic fund transfer (EFT)** is a transfer of money made by the use of an electronic terminal, a telephone, a computer, or magnetic tape. The law governing EFTs depends on the type of transfer involved. Consumer fund transfers are governed by the Electronic Fund Transfer Act (EFTA) of 1978.[19] Commercial fund transfers are governed by Article 4A of the Uniform Commercial Code.

Types of EFT Systems

Most banks today offer EFT services to their customers. We look here at the four most common types of EFT systems used by bank customers.

Automated Teller Machines. Automated teller machines (ATMs) are located at banks and at convenient locations such as airports, shopping centers, and supermarkets. ATMs, which are connected online to the bank's computers, receive deposits, dispense funds from checking or savings accounts, make credit-card advances, and accept payments. To access an account through an ATM, the bank customer uses a plastic card (debit card or access card), issued to him or her by the bank, plus a secret *personal identification number (PIN)*.

Point-of-Sale Systems. Point-of-sale systems allow consumers to transfer funds to merchants to pay for purchases. Online terminals are located in, for example, grocery stores. When a purchase is made, the customer's *debit card* (issued by the bank to the customer) is inserted into the terminal, which reads the data encoded on it. The computer at the customer's

19. 15 U.S.C. Sections 1693–1693r. The EFTA amended Title IX of the Consumer Credit Protection Act.

EXHIBIT 27–7 HOW A CHECK IS CLEARED

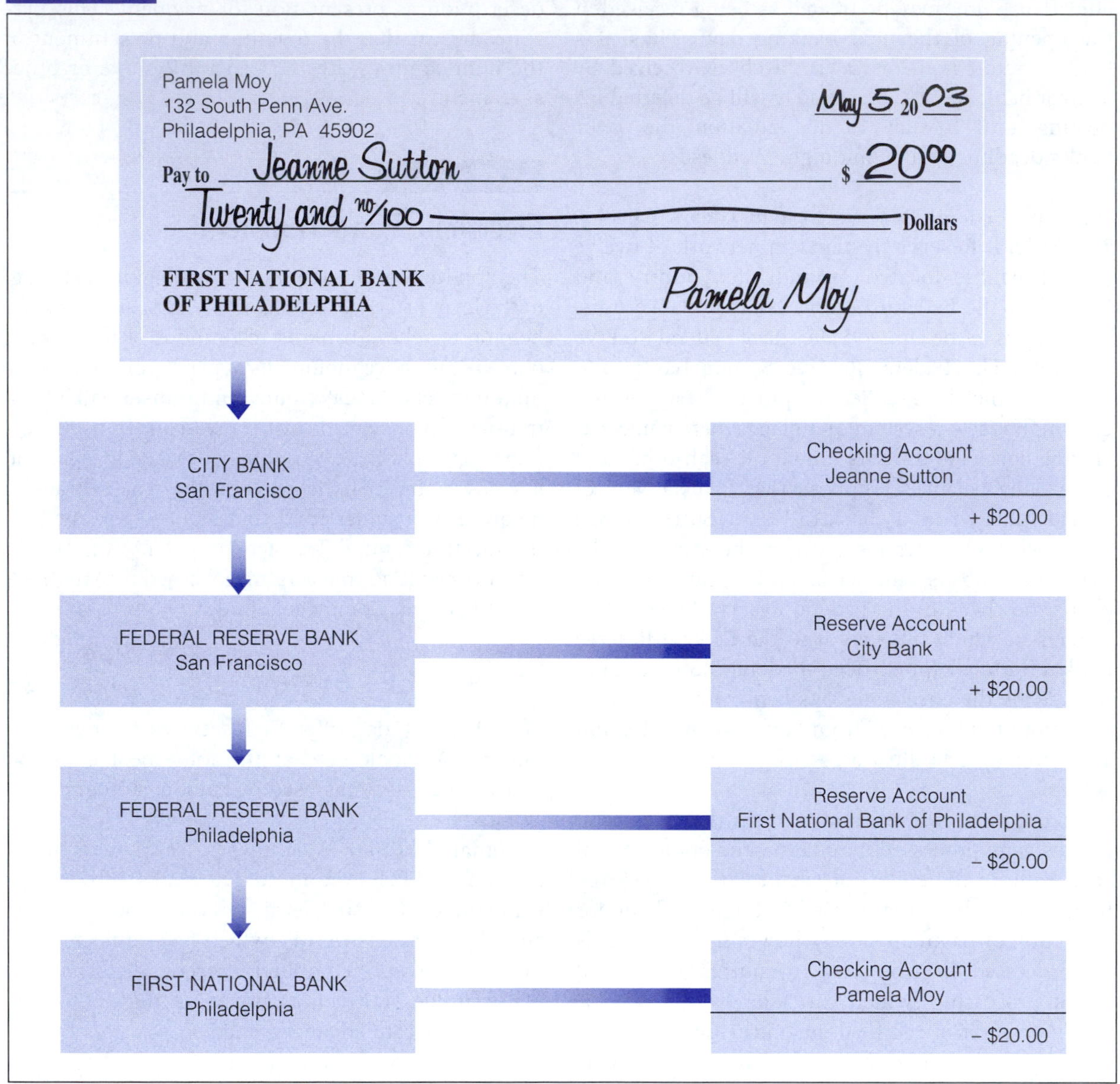

bank verifies that the card and identification code are valid and that there is enough money in the customer's account to cover the purchase. After the purchase is made, the customer's account is debited for the amount of the purchase.

Direct Deposits and Withdrawals. A direct deposit may be made to a customer's account through an electronic terminal when the customer has authorized the deposit in advance. Social Security payments are often deposited directly into beneficiaries' accounts. Similarly, an employer may agree to make payroll and pension payments directly into an employee's account at specified intervals. A customer may also authorize the bank (or other financial institution at which the customer's funds are on deposit) to make automatic payments at regular, recurrent intervals to a third party. For example, insurance premiums, utility bills, and automobile installment loan payments may often be made automatically.

Pay-by-Telephone Systems. Some financial institutions permit their customers to access the institution's computer system by telephone and direct a transfer of funds. Customers frequently pay utility bills directly using pay-by-telephone systems. Customers may also be permitted to transfer funds between accounts-for example, to withdraw funds from a savings account and make a deposit in a checking account—in this way.

CONSUMER FUND TRANSFERS

The Electronic Fund Transfer Act (EFTA) provided a basic framework for the rights, liabilities, and responsibilities of users of EFT systems. Additionally, the act gave the Federal Reserve Board authority to issue rules and regulations to help implement the act's provisions. The Federal Reserve Board's implemental regulation is called **Regulation E.**

The EFTA governs financial institutions that offer electronic fund transfers involving customer accounts. The types of accounts covered include checking accounts, savings accounts, and any other asset accounts established for personal, family, or household purposes. Note that telephone transfers are covered by the EFTA only if they are made in accordance with a prearranged plan under which periodic or recurring transfers are contemplated. Therefore, if an imposter, posing as an account holder, calls a bank official and requests a transfer of funds, the true account holder cannot hold the bank liable under the EFTA.[20] (The account holder may be able to recover the fraudulently transferred funds in a tort or contract lawsuit, however.)

Disclosure Requirements. The EFTA is essentially a disclosure law benefiting consumers. The act requires financial institutions to inform consumers of their rights and responsibilities, including those listed here, with respect to EFT systems.

1. If a customer's debit card is lost or stolen and used without his or her permission, the customer may be required to pay no more than $50. The customer, however, must notify the bank of the loss or theft within two days of learning about it. Otherwise, the liability increases to $500. The customer may be liable for more than $500 if he or she does not report the unauthorized use within sixty days after it appears on the customer's statement.
2. The customer must discover any error on the monthly statement within sixty days, and he or she must notify the bank. The bank then has ten days to investigate and must report its conclusions to the customer in writing. If the bank takes longer than ten days, it must return the disputed amount of money to the customer's account until it finds the error. If there is no error, the customer has to give the money back to the bank.
3. The bank must furnish receipts for transactions made through computer terminals, but it is not obligated to do so for telephone transfers.
4. The bank must send a monthly statement for every month in which there is an electronic transfer of funds. Otherwise, the bank must send statements every quarter. The statement must show the amount and date of the transfer, the names of the retailers or other third parties involved, the location or identification of the terminal, and the fees. Additionally, the statement must give an address and a phone number for inquiries and error notices.
5. Any preauthorized payment for utility bills and insurance premiums can be stopped three days before the scheduled transfer. To stop payment of a preauthorized EFT, a customer may notify the financial institution orally or in writing at any time up to three business days before the scheduled date of the transfer. The institution may require the customer to provide written confirmation within fourteen days of an oral notification.

Stopping Payment and Reversibility. As just mentioned, a customer may cancel a preauthorized transfer before the transfer is made, just as a drawer—the person who signs a check—may stop payment on a check before it is paid. For other EFT transactions, however, the EFTA does not provide for the reversal of an electronic transfer of funds once the transfer has occurred. This is because, unlike checks, the instantaneous nature of an EFT provides no "float time" (the time between a check's issuance and final payment) during which an effective reversal of an order to pay can be made.

Unauthorized Transfers. Because of the vulnerability of EFT systems to fraudulent activities, the EFTA of 1978 clearly defined what constitutes an unauthor-ized transfer. Under the act, a transfer is unauthorized if (1) it is initiated by a person who has no actual authority to initiate the transfer; (2) the consumer receives no benefit from it; and (3) the consumer did not furnish the person "with the card, code, or other means of access" to his or her

20. *Kashanchi v. Texas Commerce Medical Bank, N.A.*, 703 F.2d 936 (5th Cir. 1983).

account. The unauthorized use of EFT system access devices constitutes a federal felony, and unauthorized users of EFT systems are subject to criminal sanctions, including a $10,000 fine and ten years' imprisonment.

Violations and Damages. Banks are held to strict compliance with the terms of the EFTA. If they fail to adhere to the letter of the law of the EFTA, they will be held liable for violation. For a bank's violation of the EFTA, a consumer may recover actual damages, as well as punitive damages of not more than $1,000 or less than $100. (Unlike actual damages, punitive damages are assessed to punish a defendant or to set an example for similar wrongdoers.) In a class-action suit, the punitive-damage limit is the lesser of $500,000 or 1 percent of the institution's net worth. It is a federal misdemeanor to violate the EFTA. Criminal sanctions for violations of the EFTA by banking institutions may subject an institution or its officials to a $5,000 fine and up to one year's imprisonment.

Commercial Fund Transfers

The transfer of funds "by wire" between commercial parties is another way in which funds are transferred electronically. In fact, the dollar volume of payments made via wire transfers is more than $1 trillion a day-an amount that far exceeds the dollar volume of payments made by other means. The two major wire payment systems are the Federal Reserve wire transfer network (Fedwire) and the New York Clearing House Interbank Payments Systems (CHIPS).

In the past, any disputes arising as a result of unauthorized or incorrectly made transfers were settled by the courts under the common law principles of tort law or contract law. To clarify the rights and liabilities of parties involved in fund transfers not subject to the EFTA or other federal or state statutes, Article 4A of the UCC was issued in 1989. Most states have adopted this article.

The type of fund transfer covered by Article 4A is illustrated in the following example. American Industries, Inc., owes $5 million to Chandler Corporation. Instead of sending Chandler a check or some other instrument that would enable Chandler to obtain payment, American Industries tells its bank, North Bank, to credit $5 million to Chandler's account in South Bank. North Bank instructs South Bank to credit $5 million to Chandler's account. In more complex transactions, additional banks would be involved.

In these and similar circumstances, ordinarily a financial institution's instruction is transmitted electronically. Any means may be used, however, including first-class mail. To reflect this fact, Article 4A uses the term *funds transfer* rather than *wire transfer* to describe the overall payment transaction. The full text of Article 4A is presented in Appendix B, following the revised Article 4 of the Uniform Commercial Code.

Section 6

E-Money

New forms of electronic payments (e-payments) have the potential to replace *physical* cash—coins and paper currency—with *virtual* cash in the form of electronic impulses. This is the unique promise of **digital cash**, which consists of funds stored on microchips and other computer devices.

Stored-Value Cards

The simplest kind of **e-money** system is one that uses **stored-value cards**. These are plastic cards embossed with magnetic stripes containing magnetically encoded data. Using a stored-value card, a person purchases specific goods and services offered by the card issuer. For example, university libraries typically have copy machines that students operate by inserting a stored-value card. Each time a student makes copies, the machine deducts the per-copy fee from the card.

Smart Cards

Smart cards are plastic cards containing minute computer microchips that can hold far more information than a magnetic stripe. Because of microchip technology, a smart card can do much more than maintain a running cash balance in its memory or authorize the transfer of funds.

A smart card carries and processes security programming. This capability gives smart cards a technical advantage over stored-value cards. The microprocessors on smart cards can also authenticate the validity of transactions. Retailers can program electronic cash registers to confirm the authenticity of a smart card by examining a unique digital signature stored on its microchip. (Digital signatures were discussed in Chapter 23.) Exhibit 27–8 shows how digital encryption helps guarantee the security of e-payments.

Deposit Insurance for Smart-Card Balances. All depository institutions—including commercial banks and savings and loan associations—normally offer $100,000 of federally backed insurance for deposits. The Federal Deposit Insurance Corporation (FDIC) provides this insurance.

The FDIC has said that most forms of e-money do not qualify as deposits and thus are not covered by deposit insurance. If a bank becomes insolvent, an e-money holder would then be in the position of a general creditor. This means that he or she would be entitled to reimbursement only after nearly everyone else who is owed money is paid. At that point, there may not be any funds left.

Legal Protection for Smart Cards. There are some laws that extend to e-money and e-money transactions. The Federal Trade Commission Act of 1914[21] prohibits unfair or deceptive practices in, or affecting, commerce. Under this law, e-money issuers who misrepresent the value of their products or make other misrepresentations on which e-money consumers rely to their detriment may be liable for engaging in deceptive practices.

21. 15 U.S.C. Sections 41–58.

General common law principles also apply. For example, the rights and liabilities of e-money issuers and consumers are subject to the common law of contracts. This means that the parties' relationships are affected by the terms of the contracts to which they agree. On the whole, however, it is unclear how existing laws will apply to e-money.

Even without legal protection, e-money payment systems could be safer than cash and checks. Encryption (encoding) may solve some of the problems associated with e-money and with unprotected online exchanges. For example, the theft of encrypted e-money would be a waste of time because without the code a thief could not use the money. The failure of a merchant to give a customer a receipt may not matter if the e-money payment system provides proof of a transaction. Digital signatures could eliminate the problems associated with forged and bounced checks. Digital signatures can also increase the enforceability of contracts entered into online.

PRIVACY PROTECTION

Presently, it is not clear which, if any, laws apply to the security of e-money payment information and e-money issuers' financial records. This is partly because it is not clear whether e-money issuers fit within the traditional definition of a financial institution.

EXHIBIT 27–8 DIGITAL ENCRYPTION AND THE SECURITY OF ELECTRONIC PAYMENTS

An electronic payment instruction starts out in a form readable by a human being, called "plaintext." When this instruction is entered into a computer, it is secured, or encrypted, using an "encryption key," which is a software code. In computer-readable form, the payment instruction is called "ciphertext," which the computer transmits to another location. A computer at that location uses another software code, called a "decryption key," to read the data and turn it back into a plaintext form that a human operator can read.

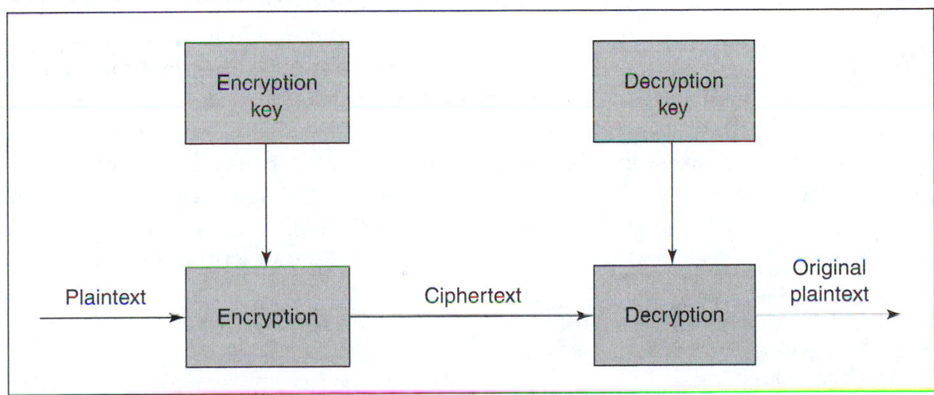

E-Money Payment Information. The Federal Reserve has decided not to impose Regulation E, which governs certain electronic fund transfers, on e-money transactions. Federal laws prohibiting unauthorized access to electronic communications might apply, however. For example, the Electronic Communications Privacy Act of 1986[22] prohibits any person from knowingly divulging to any other person the contents of an electronic communication while that communication is in transmission or in electronic storage.

E-Money Issuers' Financial Records. Under the Right to Financial Privacy Act of 1978,[23] before a financial institution may give financial information about you to a federal agency, you must explicitly consent. If you do not, a federal agency wishing to obtain your financial records must obtain a warrant. A digital cash issuer may be subject to this act if that issuer is deemed to be (1) a bank by virtue of its holding customer funds or (2) any entity that issues a physical card similar to a credit or debit card.

Consumer Financial Data. In 1999, Congress passed the Financial Services Modernization Act,[24] also known as the Gramm-Leach-Bliley Act, in an attempt to delineate how financial institutions can treat customer data. In general, the act and its implementing rules[25] place restrictions and obligations on financial institutions to protect consumer data and privacy. All financial institutions must provide their customers with information on their privacy policies and practices. No financial institution can disclose nonpublic personal information about a consumer to an unaffiliated third party unless the act's disclosure and opt-out requirements are met.

SECTION 7

Online Banking

Banks have an interest in promoting the widespread use of online banking because of its significant potential for profit. As in other areas of cyberspace, however, it is unclear which laws apply to online banking activities.

ONLINE BANKING SERVICES

Most online bank customers use three kinds of services. One of the most popular is bill consolidation and payment. Another is transferring funds among accounts. The third is applying for loans, which many banks permit customers to do over the Internet. Customers typically have to appear in person to finalize the terms of a loan, however.

Two important banking activities generally are not yet available online: depositing and withdrawing funds. With smart cards, people could transfer funds on the Internet, thereby effectively transforming their personal computers into ATMs. Many observers believe that online banking is the way to introduce people to e-money and smart cards.

Since the late 1990s, several banks, such as Bank of Internet (**http://www.bofi.com**), have operated exclusively on the Internet. These "virtual banks" have no physical branch offices. Because few people are equipped to send virtual banks funds via smart-card technology, the virtual banks have accepted deposits through physical delivery systems, such as the U.S. Postal Service or FedEx.

REGULATORY COMPLIANCE

A bank is required to define its market area. It must provide information to regulators about deposits and loans. All of these compliance efforts are pursuant to the Home Mortgage Disclosure Act (HMDA)[26] and the Community Reinvestment Act (CRA) of 1977.[27]

Under the CRA, banks establish market areas contiguous to their branch offices. The banks map these areas, using boundaries defined by counties or standard metropolitan areas, and annually review the maps. This is to prevent discrimination in lending practices.

How does a successful "cyberbank" delineate its community? If Bank of Internet becomes a tremendous success, does it really have any physical communities? Will the Federal Reserve Board simply allow a written description of a cybercommunity for Internet customers? Such regulatory issues are new,

22. 18 U.S.C. Sections 2510–2521.
23. 12 U.S.C. Sections 3401 *et seq.*
24. 12 U.S.C. Sections 24a, 248b, 1820a, 1828b, 1831v–1831y, 1848a, 2908, 4809; 15 U.S.C. Sections 80b–10a, 6701, 6711–6717, 6731–6735, 6751–6766, 6781, 6801–6809, 6821–6827, 6901–6910; and others.
25. 12 C.F.R. Part 40.
26. 12 U.S.C. Sections 2801–2810.
27. 12 U.S.C. Sections 2901–2908.

challenging, and certain to become more complicated as Internet banking widens its scope internationally.

SECTION 8

The Uniform Money Services Act

Over the past few years, many states have enacted one form of regulation or another on money services in a haphazard fashion. At the same time, e-money services that operate on the Internet—which, of course, cuts across jurisdictional lines—have been asking that these regulations be made more predictable.

In August 2001, the National Conference of Commissioners on Uniform State Laws recommended to state legislatures a new law that would subject traditional money services, as well as online and e-money services, to the same regulations that apply to other conventional financial service businesses. This new law is known as the Uniform Money Services Act (UMSA).[28]

TRADITIONAL MONEY SERVICES

Before the UMSA, traditional money service businesses were not subject to all of the same regulations that cover other conventional financial services. Money service businesses do not accept deposits, unlike banks. Money service businesses do, however, issue money orders, traveler's checks, and stored-value cards; exchange foreign currency; and cash checks. Immigrants often use these businesses to send money to their relatives in other countries.

Because these businesses often do not have continuing relationships with their customers, these customers have sometimes evaded federal law with respect to large currency transactions, or used the services to launder money (see Chapter 8). This has been particularly true with respect to financing terrorist activities.

The UMSA covers persons engaged in money transmission, check cashing, or currency exchange. The new law requires a money service business involved in these activities to obtain a license from a state, to be examined by state officials, to report on its activities to the state, and to comply with certain record-keeping requirements [UMSA 1–104]. Each of these areas has its provisions and exceptions.

Money service businesses would also be covered by rules that govern investments, including restrictions on the types of investments. They would be required to follow what are known as "safety and soundness rules," which concern the posting of bonds as a guaranty of their financial soundness, and the annual auditing of their books [see, for example, UMSA 2–204].

INTERNET-BASED MONEY SERVICES

Under the UMSA, Internet-based money services, and additional types of e-money services, would be treated the same as other money services.[29] To effect this coverage, the UMSA refers to *monetary value* instead of simply *money* [UMSA 1–102(c)(11)].

Internet-based monetary value systems subject to the new law may include:

- *E-money and Internet payment mechanisms*—Money, or its substitute, that is stored as data on a chip or a personal computer so that it can be transferred over the Internet or an intranet.
- *Internet scrip*—Monetary value that may be exchanged over the Internet but which could also be redeemed for cash.
- *Stored-value products*—Smart cards, prepaid cards, or value-added cards [UMSA 1–102(c)(21)].

28. Vermont enacted the UMSA in the same month. For a draft of the UMSA, go to the Web site of the National Conference of Commissioners on Uniform State Laws at **http://www.law.upenn.edu** and click on the appropriate links.

29. The UMSA does not apply to state governments, the federal government, securities dealers, banks, businesses that incidentally transport currency and instruments in the normal course of business, payday loan businesses, and others [UMSA 1–103].

TERMS AND CONCEPTS TO REVIEW

cashier's check 522
certified check 522
check 521
clearinghouse 533
collecting bank 531
depositary bank 531
digital cash 536
e-money 536
electronic fund transfer (EFT) 533
Federal Reserve System 533
intermediary bank 531

Chapter Summary

Checks

1. *Cashier's check*—A check drawn by a bank on itself (the bank is both the drawer and the drawee) and purchased by a customer. In effect, the bank lends its credit to the purchaser of the check, thus making the funds available for immediate use in banking circles.
2. *Traveler's check*—An instrument on which a financial institution is both the drawer and the drawee. The purchaser must provide his or her signature as a countersignature for a traveler's check to become a negotiable instrument.
3. *Certified check*—A check for which the drawee bank certifies in writing that it will set aside funds in the drawer's account to ensure payment of the check on presentation. On certification, the drawer and all prior indorsers are completely discharged from liability on the check.
4. *Lost, destroyed, or stolen cashier's, teller's, and certified checks*—Under UCC 3–312, the remitter (the check's purchaser) or the payee of a cashier's check or a teller's check—and the drawer of a certified check—can get a refund of the amount of the check from the bank by asking for it before the check is paid.

The Bank-Customer Relationship

1. *Contractual relationship*—The bank's relationship with its customer is contractual; both the bank and the customer assume certain contractual duties when a customer opens a bank account.
2. *Creditor-debtor relationship*—The relationship is also a creditor-debtor relationship (the bank is the debtor, because it holds the customer's funds on deposit).
3. *Agency relationship*—Because a bank must act in accordance with the customer's orders in regard to the customer's deposited money, an agency relationship also arises—the bank is the agent for the customer, who is the principal.

Honoring Checks

Generally, a bank has a duty to honor its customers' checks, provided that the customers have sufficient funds on deposit to cover the checks [UCC 4–401(a)]. The bank is liable to its customers for actual damages proved to be due to wrongful dishonor. The bank's duty to honor its customers' checks is not absolute. The following list summarizes the rights and liabilities of the bank and the customer in various situations.

1. *Overdrafts*—The bank has the right to charge a customer's account for any item properly payable, even if the charge results in an overdraft [UCC 4–401(a)].
2. *Postdated checks*—A bank may charge a postdated check against a customer's account as a demand instrument, unless the customer notifies the bank of the postdating in time to allow the bank to act on the notice before the bank commits itself to pay on the check [UCC 4–401(c)].
3. *Stale checks*—The bank is not obligated to pay an uncertified check presented more than six months after its date, but it may do so in good faith without liability [UCC 4–404].
4. *Death or incompetence of a customer*—So long as the bank does not know of the death or incompetence of a customer, the bank can pay an item without liability to the customer's estate. Even with knowledge of a customer's death, a bank can honor or certify checks (in the absence of a stop-payment order) for ten days after the date of the customer's death [UCC 4–405].
5. *Stop-payment orders*—The customer must make a stop-payment order in time for the bank to have a reasonable opportunity to act. Oral orders are binding for only fourteen days unless they are confirmed in writing. Written orders are effective for only six months unless renewed in writing. The bank is liable for wrongful payment over a timely stop-payment order, but only to the extent of the loss suffered by the drawer-customer [UCC 4–403].

CHAPTER SUMMARY—CONTINUED

Honoring Checks—continued

6. *Forged drawers' signatures, forged indorsements, and altered checks*—The customer has a duty to examine account statements with reasonable care on receipt and to notify the bank promptly of any forged signatures, forged or unauthorized indorsements, or alterations. On a series of unauthorized signatures or alterations by the same wrongdoer, examination and report must occur within thirty calendar days of receipt of the statement. Failure to notify the bank releases the bank from any liability unless the bank failed to exercise ordinary care. Regardless of care or lack of care, the customer is estopped from holding the bank liable after one year for unauthorized customer signatures or alterations and after three years for unauthorized indorsements [UCC 3–403, 4–111, 4–401(a), 4–406].

Accepting Deposits

A bank has a duty to accept deposits made by its customers into their accounts. Funds represented by checks deposited must be made available to customers according to a schedule mandated by the Expedited Funds Availability Act of 1987 and Regulation CC. A bank also has a duty to collect payment on any checks deposited by its customers. When checks deposited by customers are drawn on other banks, as they often are, the check-collection process comes into play (summarized next).

1. *Designations of banks involved in the collection process*—UCC 4–105 provides the following definitions of banks involved in the collection process:
    a. Depositary bank—The first bank to accept a check for payment.
    b. Payor bank—The bank on which a check is drawn.
    c. Collecting bank—Any bank except the payor bank that handles a check during the collection process.
    d. Intermediary bank—Any bank except the payor bank or the depositary bank to which an item is transferred in the course of the collection process.
2. *Check collection between customers of the same bank*—A check payable by the depositary bank that receives it is an "on-us item"; if the bank does not dishonor the check by the opening of the second banking day following its receipt, the check is considered paid [UCC 4–215(e)(2)].
3. *Check collection between customers of different banks*—Each bank in the collection process must pass the check on to the next appropriate bank before midnight of the next banking day following its receipt [UCC 4–108, 4–202(b), 4–302].
4. *How the Federal Reserve System clears checks*—The Federal Reserve System facilitates the check-clearing process by serving as a clearinghouse for checks.
5. *Electronic check presentment*—When checks are presented electronically, items may be encoded with information (such as the amount of the check) that is read and processed by other banks' computers. In some situations, a check may be retained at its place of deposit, and only its image or information describing it is presented for payment under a Federal Reserve agreement, clearinghouse rule, or other agreement [UCC 4–110].

Electronic Fund Transfers

1. *Types of EFT systems*—
    a. Automated teller machines (ATMs).
    b. Point-of-sale systems.
    c. Direct deposits and withdrawals.
    d. Pay-by-telephone systems.
2. *Consumer fund transfers*—Consumer fund transfers are governed by the Electronic Fund Transfer Act (EFTA) of 1978. The EFTA is basically a disclosure law that sets forth the rights and duties of the bank and the customer in respect to electronic fund transfer systems. Banks must comply strictly with EFTA requirements.
3. *Commercial fund transfers*—Disputes arising as a result of unauthorized or incorrectly made fund transfers between financial institutions are not covered under the EFTA. Article 4A of the UCC, which has been adopted by almost all of the states, governs fund transfers not subject to the EFTA or other federal or state statutes.

Chapter Summary—continued

E-Money	1. *New forms of e-payments*—These include stored-value cards and smart cards. 2. *Deposit insurance*—Most forms of e-money do not qualify as deposits and thus are not covered by federally guaranteed deposit insurance. 3. *Legal protection*—Statutes such as the Federal Trade Commission Act may cover e-money and e-payment transactions. General common law principles also apply. 4. *Privacy protection*—It is not entirely clear which, if any, laws apply to e-payment information and records. The Financial Services Modernization Act (the Gramm-Leach-Bliley Act) outlines how financial institutions can treat consumer data and privacy in general. The Right to Financial Privacy Act may also apply.
Online Banking	1. *Current online banking services*— a. Bill consolidation and payment. b. Transferring funds among accounts. c. Applying for loans. 2. *Regulatory compliance*—Banks must define their market areas, in communities contiguous to their branch offices, under the Home Mortgage Disclosure Act and the Community Reinvestment Act. It is not clear how an online bank would define its market area.
Uniform Money Services Act	In August 2001, the National Conference of Commissioners on Uniform State Laws recommended to state legislatures the Uniform Money Services Act. The purpose of the act is to subject online and e-money services to the same regulations that apply to conventional financial service businesses.

Cases for Analysis

Westlaw. You can access the full text of each case presented below by going to the Westlaw cases on this text's Web site at http://wbl-cs.westbuslaw.com. Each Westlaw case includes the names of all plaintiffs and defendants, the dates on which the case was argued and decided, a brief summary of the issues and decisions in the case, headnotes classifying the specific issues in the case according to the West Key Number System, and the court's opinion. Concurring and dissenting opinions, if any, are included as well.

Case 27.1 Overdrafts

Kendall Yacht Corp. v. United California Bank

Court of Appeal of California,
Fourth District,
Division 2, 1975.
50 Cal.App.3d 949,
123 Cal.Rptr. 848.

McDANIEL, Associate Justice.

* * * *

Lawrence and Linda Kendall were officers and the prospective principal shareholders of [Kendall Yacht] Corporation which was formed in May of 1969 to build and sell fiberglass cruising yachts. The Corporation never issued stock and was undercapitalized. Through the Corporation Mr. Kendall contracted to build yachts upon special order for customers. The customers were required to pay in advance for each stage of construction of their respective yachts, and these stage payments were the Corporation's sole source of income.

The Corporation had a payroll checking account and a general business checking account with [United California] Bank. On September 4, 1970, Kendall spoke with Ron Lamperts, a loan officer of the Bank, in an effort to obtain financing for the Corporation. The Corporation was in debt and was having serious financial problems. In order to gain a solid financial footing, it appeared that it would be necessary to arrange for substantial equity capital or long-term financing. * * *

* * * *

* * * Lamperts told Kendall that the Bank would honor certain of the Corporation's checks despite the lack of sufficient funds on deposit. The terms of this agreement were vague; Kendall contended that Lamperts promised to honor overdrafts until such time as the Corporation was "out of the woods." The Kendalls continued to write checks for supplies, payroll, and other operating expenses, and the Corporation's accounts were continuously overdrawn from mid-October through November and December. However, not all of the overdrafts were honored by the Bank.

By the end of October, the Corporation's accounts were overdrawn by approximately $6,000. The Corporation executed a note to the Bank for this amount, thus temporarily clearing the accounts. Also, at this time, the Kendalls executed a new guarantee whereby they assumed personal liability for the Corporation's debts up to $20,000.

On November 20, * * * Lamperts told Kendall that the Bank would not make [a] promised $25,000 loan. A check subsequently written by the Corporation * * * was dishonored by the Bank. The Bank did continue to honor some overdrafts through December. On December 30 Lamperts called Mrs. Kendall and told her that the Bank would no longer honor any of the Corporation's checks. Soon thereafter the Corporation's assets were seized and sold at auction by the Internal Revenue Service for nonpayment of taxes.

During October, November, and December, the Bank honored overdrafts of the Corporation totaling in excess of $15,000. There were also a number of overdrafts written during these months which were not honored by the Bank. Some of these were to suppliers and others were payroll checks to employees. In addition, the Bank failed to honor a check written to Insurance Company of North America to cover a premium for workmen's compensation insurance. The Kendalls were not aware that this check had been "bounced" until after one of their employees had been injured and they had been notified by Insurance Company of North America that their insurance had been terminated for nonpayment of premium.

* * * *

[The Corporation and the Kendalls filed a suit in a California state court against the Bank, seeking damages for the wrongful dishonor of the checks that the Bank had agreed to accept as overdrafts.] The trial court found that the Bank "encouraged, promised and represented to the plaintiffs to expect that (the Bank) would pay a large number of Kendall Yacht Corporation checks written by the plaintiffs" for the operation of the business without regard to whether there would be sufficient funds on deposit to cover the checks when they were presented for payment; that the Kendalls wrote numerous checks in reliance on the Bank's promises and with the expectation that they would be honored as overdrafts; that some such checks, including checks to suppliers, employee payroll checks, and the check for workmen's compensation coverage, were not honored by the Bank; that the Kendalls were induced by the promises of the Bank to endanger their credit and "to incur obligations that would not otherwise have been incurred, to violate the criminal law, and to suffer personal distress of varying kinds"; and that suppliers and employees were induced by the acts of the Bank to furnish supplies and labor to the Kendalls and to accept checks in payment which were subsequently not honored by the Bank. The court concluded that the failure of the Bank to honor the overdrafts constituted a "wrongful dishonor" under [California] Commercial Code [S]ection 4402 [California's version of UCC 4–402], and that as a proximate consequence thereof Mr. and Mrs. Kendall incurred attorney's fees in criminal and civil proceedings brought against them and suffered emotional distress and damage to their reputations. The court awarded $26,000 to each of the Kendalls as compensatory damages * * * .

On this appeal, the Bank does not challenge the sufficiency of the evidence to support the court's findings of fact, nor does it attack the court's conclusions that the Bank's acts constituted wrongful dishonoring of checks under Commercial Code [S]ection 4402, nor that the damages suffered by the Kendalls were proximately caused thereby. We therefore do not address these questions * * * .

The Bank contends * * * that under Commercial Code [S]ection 4402 the wrongful dishonor of a check of a Corporation does not give a cause of action for damages to individual officers and shareholders of the corporation. Commercial Code [S]ection 4402, which represents section 4–402 of the Uniform Commercial Code, reads as follows: "A payor bank is liable to its customer for damages proximately caused by the wrongful dishonor of an item. * * *" The Bank relies on [a previous case] where it was held that under Uniform Commercial Code [S]ection 4–402 individuals doing business as partners could not recover for damages to their personal credit, good reputation, and business standing which resulted from the wrongful dishonor of checks written on a partnership account. The court noted that Uniform Commercial Code [S]ection 4–402 states that a bank "is liable to its customer"; that Uniform Commercial Code [S]ection 4–104[(a)(5)] defines "customer" as "[a] person having an account with a bank"; that [S]ection 1–201(30) defines "person" as including "an individual or an organization"; and that under [S]ection 1–201(28) a "partnership" was embraced within the term "organization." After observing further that a partnership is recognized as a separate legal entity for at least some purposes, the court concluded that "[t]he partnership was the customer, and any damages arising from the dishonor belonged to the partnership and not to the partners individually."

It is not clear whether the * * * court meant to say that in every case where an account stands in the name of a partnership or a corporation, only the business entity may recover under [S]ection 4–402, regardless of the circumstances. Such a narrow and technical reading of the statute and the term "customer" does not seem warranted. The purpose of the statute—to hold banks accountable for damages proximately caused by wrongful dishonors—is more readily served by allowing a flexible and reasonable interpretation of the word "customer."

We would certainly not hold as a general proposition that the shareholders or officers of a corporation could recover under [S]ection 4402 for the wrongful dishonor of a corporation check. Here, however, it is difficult to avoid the conclusion that Mr. and Mrs. Kendall were as much "customers" of the Bank within the contemplation of the statute as was the Corporation. Lamperts and the Bank looked directly to the Kendalls to satisfy the obligations of the Corporation. They were required to execute a personal guarantee of * * * $20,000 to cover the additional credit the Bank was extending to the Corporation in the form of honoring its overdrafts. The reason the Bank required the guarantee is obvious. The Corporation had never issued shares and was undercapitalized; it was, in effect, nothing but a transparent shell, having no viability as a separate and distinct legal entity. The Kendalls alone were controlling its financial affairs and were personally vouching for its fiscal responsibility. Not only the Bank, but also the suppliers and employees of the Corporation knew that this was the situation. They too—in some cases at the behest of Lamperts—were placing their faith in the Kendalls to make good on the corporate debts. Thus it was entirely foreseeable that the dishonoring of the Corporation's checks would reflect directly on the personal credit and reputation of the Kendalls and that they would suffer the adverse personal consequences which resulted when the Bank reneged on its commitments. *Under these circumstances we would elevate form over substance if we were to hold that the wrong defined by [S]ection 4402 was done only to the Corporation and that the Kendalls as individuals could not recover therefor.* [Emphasis added.]

* * * *

* * * The judgment [of the award of compensatory damages to the Kendalls for the Bank's wrongful dishonor of the checks] is affirmed * * * .

CASE 27.2 FORGED SIGNATURES

MARX V. WHITNEY NATIONAL BANK

Supreme Court of Louisiana, 1998.
713 So.2d 1142.

MARCUS, Justice.

* * * *

* * * David Marx maintained a checking account at Whitney [National Bank] for which he received monthly statements. His January 1995 statement contained evidence of five forged checks totalling $2,373.00. He did not review his January 1995 statement. Nor did he review his statements for the months of February, March, and April of 1995. Had he reviewed the January through April 1995 statements, he would have discovered seventeen forged checks totalling almost $13,000.00. On April 24, 1995, two children of David Marx, Stanley Marx and Maxine Marx Goodman, were added as joint owners to the same account. Five additional checks were forged on the account in March, April, and May 1995 which first appeared on the May 1995 statement. Stanley Marx noticed these forged instruments when he reviewed the bank statement dated May 16, 1995 and the enclosed cancelled checks. At the behest of Stanley Marx, David Marx reported the forgeries to Whitney and executed an "Affidavit of Forgery, Alteration, Loss or Theft of Instrument and Subrogation and Hold Harmless Agreement" in which he identified his grandson, Joel Goodman, as both the maker and payee of the forged instruments. [David, Stanley, and Maxine] asked Whitney to credit back to their account the funds paid out on the last five forgeries discovered and reported upon receipt of the May 1995 statement. [They admitted] that Joel Goodman had access to David Marx's checkbook whenever he visited his grandfather, that he was the party who had forged all of the checks in question, and that David Marx was negligent for failing to review his January, February, March, and April 1995 statements. [The bank refused the request. David, Stanley, and Maxine filed a suit in a Louisiana state court against the bank, claiming that it was obligated to restore the funds. The plaintiffs filed a motion for summary judgment.]

The trial judge granted plaintiffs' motion for summary judgment, rendering judgment in plaintiffs' favor for $10,000, plus legal interest from date of judicial demand, and all costs of the proceedings. The [state intermediate] court of appeal affirmed. We [agreed] to review the correctness of that decision.

The sole issue for our review is whether the stipulated negligence of David Marx precludes recovery against Whitney by all joint owners on the account for the five forged checks honored by Whitney which were discovered and reported upon receipt of the May 1995 statement.

The law applicable to this case is found in Chapters Three and Four of the Louisiana Commercial Laws [Louisiana's version of Articles 3 and 4 of the UCC]. Pursuant to Louisiana's Commercial Laws as well as the established jurisprudence prior to their adoption, the relationship between a bank and its depositor is a debtor-creditor relationship that is contractual in nature. The initial deposit of funds gives rise to the contract between bank and depositor; the subsequent creation of rights of others to an interest in an account involves an amendment of the original contract.

During the course of the contract with its depositor, a bank has the right to use the funds on deposit and, in consideration thereof, it covenants to pay funds out of the depositor's account only on the depositor's orders. [UCC 3–401] specifically provides that a person is not liable on an instrument unless the person signed the instrument. [UCC 3–403] further provides that an unauthorized signature is ineffective except as the signature of the unauthorized signer in favor of a person who in good faith pays the instrument or takes it for value. Accordingly, the general rule is that a bank is liable when it pays based upon a forged signature. A charge against a customer's account based on a forged instrument is not an authorized charge under the contract between the parties because the order to pay was not given by the customer. For that reason, a banking customer can insist that the drawee bank recredit to his account any funds paid out on a forged instrument.

Notwithstanding the general rule that imposes the risk of loss for payment of a forged instrument on the drawee bank, the law provides that under certain circumstances a bank's customer may be *precluded* from asserting rights against the bank in connection with a forged check. * * *

* * * *

Whitney * * * defended against plaintiffs' motion for summary judgment by asserting that David Marx failed to discover and report the initial forgeries upon receipt of the January 1995 statement, thereby precluding recovery for any subsequent forgeries on the account by the same wrongdoer. [UCC 4–406] provides in pertinent part:

> (c) If a bank sends or makes available a statement of account or items pursuant to Subsection (a), *the customer must exercise reasonable promptness in examining the statement or the items to determine whether any payment was not authorized* because of an alteration of an item or because a purported signature by or on behalf of the customer was not authorized. If, based on the statement or items provided, the customer should reasonably have discovered the unauthorized payment, the *customer must promptly notify the bank* of the relevant facts.
> (d) If the bank proves that *the customer failed, with respect to an item, to comply with the duties imposed on the customer by Subsection (c), the customer is precluded from asserting against the bank:*
> (1) the customer's unauthorized signature or any alteration on the item, if the bank also proves that it suffered a loss by reason of the failure; and
> (2) *the customer's unauthorized signature* or alteration *by the same wrongdoer on any other item paid* in good faith by the bank *if the payment was made before the bank received notice* from the customer of the unauthorized signature or alteration and *after the customer had been afforded a reasonable period of time, not exceeding thirty days, in which to examine the item or statement of account and notify the bank.* [Emphasis added.]

The rule stated in Subsection (d)(2) imposes on the customer the risk of loss on all subsequent forgeries by the *same wrongdoer* after the customer had a reasonable time to detect an initial forgery if the bank has honored subsequent forgeries prior to notice. Even before the adoption of the Uniform Commercial Code, case law throughout the country reflected the view that the suppression of forgery required a cooperative approach. Rules developed which shifted the risk of loss on certain forgeries to a customer who failed to give notice to the bank of forgeries and alterations. Out of the duty imposed on the customer to review his statement grew the rule that successive forgeries result from the failure of the customer to discover and report the initial forgeries which he could have detected had he acted in accord with the duty imposed by law upon him.

* * * *

In this case, plaintiffs have stipulated that David Marx did not review the January 1995 bank statement for his account and that if he had done so the unauthorized signature of his grandson on several checks would have been detected. Since he did not do so, plaintiffs are precluded from asserting against the bank *all subsequent forgeries* by the *same* unauthorized signatory. That being the case, plaintiffs are not in a position to recover against Whitney for the five forged checks that were discovered in the May 1995 statement which were forged by the same wrongdoer.

* * * *

For the reasons assigned, the judgment of the court of appeal is reversed. Plaintiffs' motion for summary judgment is denied. The case is remanded to the district court for further proceedings.

CASE 27.3 FORGED SIGNATURES

HALIFAX CORP. v. FIRST UNION NATIONAL BANK

Supreme Court of Virginia, 2001.
262 Va. 91,
546 S.E.2d 696.

HASSELL, Justice.

I.

The primary issue that we consider in this appeal is whether a plaintiff's cause of action [in a Virginia state court] against a bank is precluded by [Virginia] Code [Section] 8.4–406(f) [Virginia's version of UCC 4–406(f)] * * * .

II.

* * * Halifax [Corporation] sought to recover against First Union [National Bank] for purported claims of negligence, gross negligence, and recklessness * * * .

First Union filed a motion for summary judgment alleging, among other things, that Halifax's claims were barred under Code [Section] 8.4–406(f). The [trial] court, in a written opinion, agreed with First Union and entered an order which granted the motion for summary judgment. Halifax * * * appeals the [trial] court's judgment in favor of First Union.

III.

* * * *

Halifax is a corporation organized and existing under the laws of Virginia. Between August 1995 and March 1999, Mary K. Adams served as Halifax's comptroller. Between August 1995 and January 1997, she wrote at least 88 checks on Halifax's account at Signet Bank, which was subsequently acquired by First Union National Bank. Adams used facsimile signatures on the checks, and she made the checks payable to herself or cash. Adams deposited these checks in her personal account at the former Central Fidelity Bank, which is now Wachovia Bank, N.A. First Union, as drawee bank, "paid each of these checks and debited [Halifax's] account despite the forged and/or unauthorized drawer's signatures."

First Union paid each check and debited Halifax's account even though most of these corporate checks "were drawn in large amounts exceeding $10,000 and $20,000, of which approximately one quarter were drawn in exceptionally large amounts of between $50,000 and $100,000 each, and payable to 'Mary Adams,' an individual who [First Union] knew to be an employee and Comptroller of [Halifax]." First Union paid these large checks "despite one, and in many instances, two levels of inspection of the individual checks for purposes of payment approval."

In January 1999, Halifax discovered accounting irregularities in certain check transactions and initiated an investigation. Subsequently, Halifax learned that Adams had embezzled at least $15,445,230.49 from its account. Halifax does not dispute that First Union sent Halifax monthly statements reflecting the unauthorized checks and that Halifax failed to notify First Union of the unauthorized signatures within one year after the statements were sent to Halifax.

IV.

A.

* * * *

Code [Section] 8.1-203 [Virginia's version of UCC 1–203] * * * states: "Every contract or duty within [the Uniform Commercial Code] imposes an obligation of good faith in its performance or enforcement."

B.

Halifax argues that the [trial] court erred in ruling that its claims * * * were barred by * * * Code [Section] 8.4-406(f) because First Union allegedly acted in bad faith. Halifax, relying upon Code [Section] 8.1-203, asserts that First Union had an obligation to act in good faith, and First Union failed to discharge that obligation when it paid checks which contained unauthorized signatures. * * *

* * * *

Code [Section] 8.4-406 imposes certain duties upon bank customers to discover and report unauthorized signatures or alterations. Code [Section] 8.4-406(a) provides that a bank which elects to send or make available to a customer a statement of account showing payment of items for the account must provide certain information to the customer.

Code [Section] 8.4-406(c) imposes a duty upon a customer to exercise reasonable promptness to examine the bank statement or items to determine whether any payment was not authorized because of an alteration or unauthorized signature. Code [Section] 8.4-406(c) also imposes a duty upon the customer to promptly notify the bank of the relevant facts. Code [Section] 8.4-406(c) does not limit the scope of the customer's duty to those items that the bank paid in good faith.

* * * *

* * * Code [Section] 8.4-406(d) which precludes a customer from asserting a claim against a bank for a loss caused by an unauthorized signature or alteration in certain prescribed circumstances, provides that this preclusion does not apply if the bank failed to pay an item in good faith. Code [Section] 8.4-406(d) explicitly limits the preclusion to items "paid in good faith by the bank." Additionally, * * * Code [Section] 8.4-406(e) * * * states in relevant part: "If the customer proves that the bank did not pay an item in good faith, the preclusion under subsection (d) does not apply."

Code [Section] 8.4-406(f) bars a customer, who received a statement or item from a bank but failed to discover or report the customer's unauthorized signature or alteration on the item to the bank within one year after the statement or item is made available to the customer, from asserting a claim against the bank for the unauthorized signature or alteration. The customer's compliance with this one-year statutory notice provision is a condition precedent to the customer's right to file an action against the bank to recover losses caused by the unauthorized signature or alteration. *Code [Section] 8.4-406(f) is devoid of any language which limits the customer's duty to discover and report unauthorized signatures and alterations to items paid in good faith by the bank.* The absence of the phrase, "good faith," * * * compels this Court to conclude that a bank's statutory right to assert a customer's failure to give the statutorily prescribed notice is not predicated upon whether the bank exercised good faith in paying the item which contained the unauthorized signature or alteration. If the General Assembly [the Virginia state legislature] had intended to limit the preclusion contained in Code [Section] 8.4-406(f) to items paid in good faith, the General Assembly would have done so explicitly. [Emphasis added.]

* * * *

V.

In summary, we hold that Halifax's claims * * * are barred because Halifax failed to satisfy the condition precedent in Code [Section] 8.4-406(f). * * *

* * * Accordingly, we will affirm the judgment of the [trial] court.

CASE PROBLEMS

27–1. MJZ Corp. had a checking account with Gulfstream First Bank & Trust. MJZ was unaware of the bank's policy of honoring checks for thirty days after a checking account had been closed. The policy was formed to prevent embarrassment on the part of customers whose checks would otherwise bounce if they were presented to the bank after the accounts had been closed. MJZ closed its checking account on April 2, 1980, and later that month, two outstanding checks written by the corporation were presented to the bank for payment. The bank paid the checks and requested reimbursement for the amounts from MJZ. When MJZ refused to reimburse the bank, the bank sued for recovery of the funds. Should the bank be able to recover from MJZ for the amounts of the checks paid after MJZ's account had been closed? [*MJZ Corp. v. Gulfstream First Bank & Trust,* 420 So.2d 396 (Fla.App. 1982)]

27–2. Lawrence Kruser and his wife maintained a joint checking account with the Bank of America. The bank issued to each of them a "Versatel" card and separate personal identification numbers so that they could access funds in their account from automated teller machines (ATMs). The Krusers believed that Mr. Kruser's card had been destroyed in September 1986. The December 1986 account statement mailed to the Krusers by the bank, however, reflected a $20 withdrawal of funds by someone using Mr. Kruser's card at an ATM. Mrs. Kruser underwent surgery in December 1986 and was in the hospital for eleven days. She spent the following months recuperating from the surgery. She therefore failed to examine the December bank statement promptly and did not discover the unauthorized December withdrawal until August or September of 1987, at which time she reported it to the bank. In September 1987, the Krusers received bank statements for July and August of 1987, which reflected forty-seven unauthorized withdrawals, totaling $9,020, made from an ATM by someone using Mr. Kruser's card. They notified the bank of these withdrawals within a few days of receiving the statements. Is the bank liable to the Krusers for the unauthorized withdrawals? Discuss. [*Kruser v. Bank of America NT & SA,* 230 Cal.App.3d 741, 281 Cal.Rptr. 463 (1991)]

27–3. Frank Quinn made out a check for $30,000 payable to Limetree Beach Associates, Ltd., a limited partnership formed for the purpose of investing in real estate. The check was delivered to Dan Wey, who served as the only general partner for the firm (in a limited partnership, general partners manage the firm, and those who invest in the firm are called *limited partners*). Wey was listed as an authorized signer for the partnership on its checking account with the American State Bank. Wey indorsed the check in his own name for deposit to his own personal account, which was also at American State. American State sent the check for collection to the drawee bank, National Bank, which paid the check. Quinn subsequently demanded that National Bank recredit his account for the amount of the check because the check had been improperly paid under UCC 4–401. Will the court agree with Quinn? [*National Bank v. Quinn,* 126 Ill.2d 129, 533 N.E.2d 846, 127 Ill.Dec. 764 (1988)]

27–4. Steven Gerber had a joint checking account with his mother at City National Bank of Florida. Between January and May 1990, a number of checks were allegedly forged on the account. Gerber asked City National to recredit the account for the amount of the checks, but the bank refused. In March 1992, Gerber filed a lawsuit against the bank. City National filed a motion to dismiss, claiming that the suit was barred because Gerber did not file it within a year of City National's making available to Gerber the bank statements that reflected the forged checks. Gerber argued that the only requirement was that he notify the bank of any unauthorized signatures within a year. How should the court rule? [*Gerber v. City National Bank of Florida,* 619 So.2d 328 (Fla.App. 1993)]

27–5. In July 1979, Read & Read, Inc., a corporation owned by Thomas and Emerson Read, hired Judy Bode as a sales secretary. She was promoted to executive secretary shortly thereafter and worked primarily for Emerson Read. Bode eventually assumed responsibility for overseeing nearly all of Read's checking accounts, including his personal account. She also reviewed the bank statements for each account and reconciled them to the corresponding checkbooks. As a result of a hunting accident, Emerson Read lost his hand; to facilitate check signing, he had a rubber signature stamp made. Bode had easy access to the stamp. From September 1980 until January 1981, Bode used the rubber stamp to forge a total of fourteen checks for her own purposes on Read's accounts, including one check for over $8,000. Read, who did not review any bank statements during this entire period of time, was unaware of the forgeries. When the forgeries were discovered in January 1981, Read sued his bank, the South Carolina National Bank, to recover the amount of the forged checks that he alleged had been wrongfully honored by the bank. The trial court held for the bank, and Read appealed. Can Read recover from the bank the funds lost as a result of Bode's forgeries? Discuss. [*Read v. South Carolina National Bank,* 286 S.C. 534, 335 S.E.2d 359 (1985)]

27–6. Robert Parrett was the principal shareholder, president, and chief operating officer of P & P Machinery, Inc., a farm machinery business located in Nebraska. On March 1, 1984, Parrett signed and delivered a check from P & P Machinery to a South Dakota firm. The check was dishonored by the bank even though P & P Machinery had sufficient funds in its account to cover the check. In addition, Parrett had a long-standing relationship with the bank as personal guarantor of corporate obligations to the bank and had never had any previous problems with the bank. As a result of the dishonored check, Parrett was charged with felony theft in South Dakota and extradited for trial in South Dakota. On learning that the bank had dishonored the check erroneously, the trial court dismissed the charge against Parrett. Parrett sued the bank for damages. The trial court held that Parrett had no standing to sue the bank because he was not the bank's "customer"—the corporation was. Will the appellate court agree that Parrett lacked standing to sue the bank? Discuss fully. [*Parrett v. Platte Valley State Bank & Trust Co.*, 236 Neb. 139, 459 N.W.2d 371 (1990)]

27–7. On August 23, 1983, Robert Porter tried to withdraw $100 from his checking account at an automated teller machine. When no money was dispensed from the machine after Porter had pushed the necessary buttons, he reported the incident to a bank official. A few weeks later, on September 5, Porter tried to withdraw $200. When no money appeared after two tries, he again reported the problem to a bank official. As a result of these two incidents, Porter's next bank statement showed one withdrawal of $100 and two of $200 each (for a total of $500). Porter filed suit against the bank to recover the $500 debit on his checking account for money he never received. Discuss whether Porter was able to recover the $500. [*Porter v. Citibank, N.A.*, 123 Misc.2d 28, 472 N.Y.S.2d 582 (1984)]

27–8. Shawmut Worcester County Bank in Massachusetts transferred $10,000 to First American Bank & Trust in Palm Beach, Florida, through Fedwire. Shawmut's payment order stated that the beneficiary of the transfer was Fernando Degan and that First American should credit account number 100 205 001 633. It turned out that the First American account under that number was held jointly by Degan and Joseph Merle. When Shawmut discovered its mistake 106 days after the erroneous transfer, it credited the account of its customer who had requested the transfer with the $10,000 and then asked First American to "reverse" the transfer. First American asked Merle, its customer, if he would authorize the reversal. Merle refused. Accordingly, First American told Shawmut it would not reverse the transfer. Shawmut then sued First American to recover the $10,000, alleging, among other claims, that the transaction fell under the EFTA, which prescribes specific requirements that must be followed in the event of error in an electronic fund transfer. Is Shawmut a consumer within the meaning of the EFTA? How should the court rule? [*Shawmut Worcester County Bank v. First American Bank & Trust*, 731 F.Supp. 57 (D.Mass. 1990)]

27–9. In September 1976, Edward and Christine McSweeney opened a joint checking account with the United States Trust Co. of New York. Between April 1978 and July 1978, 195 checks totaling $99,063 were written. In July 1978, activity in the account ceased. Ninety-five of the 195 checks, totaling $16,811, were written by Christine, and the rest of the checks were written by Edward. After deposits had been credited for that period, the checks created a cumulative overdraft of $75,983. Can a bank knowingly honor a check when payment creates an overdraft, or must the bank dishonor the check? If the bank pays a check and thereby creates an overdraft, can the bank collect the amount of the overdraft from its customer? [*United States Trust Co. of New York v. McSweeney*, 91 A.D.2d 7, 457 N.Y.S.2d 276 (1982)]

27–10. Parviz Haghighi Abyaneh and Iran Haghighi were co-owners of a savings account at First State Bank. On May 23, 1984, a person identifying himself as Abyaneh entered the Raleigh, North Carolina, office of Citizens Savings and Loan Association of Rocky Mount and opened a savings account. He then called the First State Bank and asked a bank employee to transfer funds from Abyaneh's First State account into the newly created account. As a result, $53,825.66 was transferred to the new account, and subsequently, the funds were withdrawn. When the true owners of the First State Bank account learned of the transfer, they filed suit against Merchants Bank, North, successor by merger to First State Bank, for violating the Electronic Fund Transfer Act. Discuss whether Abyaneh will be able to recover the $53,825.66. [*Abyaneh v. Merchants Bank, North*, 670 F.Supp. 1298 (M.D.Pa. 1987)]

27–11. Dr. As'ad M. Masri and his wife borrowed $150,000 from First Virginia Bank-Colonial (FVBC). Masri then signed a wire transfer request directing FVBC to transfer the funds to the Amro Bank in Amsterdam. The request also stated that the funds were to be deposited to the Lenex Corp.'s account in that bank. FVBC transferred the funds to the Bank of Nova Scotia, an intermediary bank, and sent disbursal instructions directly to Amro. The following day, the funds were credited to the Lenex account at the Amro Bank. They were withdrawn, however, by someone other than the person intended by Masri to withdraw them. When the Masris later defaulted on the loan, FVBC sought full repayment of the funds. The Masris claimed that FVBC had breached the wire transfer agreement. Did FVBC breach the wire transfer agreement? Where did FVBC's responsibility end? Discuss fully. [*First Virginia Bank-Colonial v. Masri, M.D.*, 245 Va. 461, 428 S.E.2d 903 (1993)]

27–12. Gary Morgan Chevrolet and Oldsmobile, Inc., issued four checks payable to General Motors Acceptance Corp. (GMAC) on Morgan's account with the Bank of Richmondville. There were insufficient funds in Morgan's account, and the bank gave GMAC oral notice of dishonor. The bank returned the checks two days later. GMAC filed a suit against the bank in a New York state court, claiming that the bank had failed to dishonor the checks before its midnight deadline, because notice of dishonor must be in writing under Article 4. The bank countered that notice of dishonor may be oral under Article 3. Which article controls—Article 3 or Article 4—when there is such a conflict? Explain. [*General Motors Acceptance Corp. v. Bank of Richmondville*, 203 A.D.2d 851, 611 N.Y.S.2d 338 (1994)]

27–13. On July 15, 1986, IBP, Inc., issued to Meyer Land & Cattle Co. a check for $135,234.18 payable to both Meyer and Sylvan State Bank for the purchase of cattle. IBP wrote the check on its account at Mercantile Bank of Topeka. Someone at the Meyer firm misplaced the check. In the fall of 1995, Meyer's president, Tim Meyer, found the check behind a desk drawer. Jana Huse, Meyer's office manager, presented the check for deposit at Sylvan, which accepted it. After Mercantile received the instrument and its computers noted the absence of any stop-payment order, it paid the check with funds from IBP's checking account. IBP insisted that Mercantile credit IBP's account. Mercantile refused. IBP filed a suit in a federal district court against Mercantile and others, claiming, among other things, that Mercantile had not acted in good faith because it had processed the check by automated means, without examining it manually. Mercantile responded that its check-processing procedures adhered to its own policies, as well as to reasonable commercial standards of fair dealing in the banking industry. Mercantile filed a motion for summary judgment. Should the court grant the motion? Why or why not? [*IBP, Inc. v. Mercantile Bank of Topeka,* 6 F.Supp.2d 1258 (D.Kan. 1999)]

27–14. On April 20, 1999, while visiting her daughter and her son-in-law, Michael Dowdell, Carol Farrow asked Dowdell to fix her car. She gave him her car keys, attached to which was a small wallet containing her debit card. Dowdell repaired her car and returned the keys. Two days later, Farrow noticed that her debit card was missing and contacted Auburn Bank, which had issued the card. Farrow reviewed her automatic teller machine (ATM) transaction record and noticed that a large amount of cash had been withdrawn from her checking account on April 22 and April 23. When Farrow reviewed the photos taken by the ATM cameras at the time of the withdrawals, she recognized Dowdell as the person using her debit card. Dowdell was convicted in an Alabama state court of the crime of fraudulent use of a debit card. What procedures are involved in a debit-card transaction? What problems with debit-card transactions are apparent from the facts of this case? How might these problems be prevented? [*Dowdell v. State,* 790 So.2d 359 (Ala.Crim.App. 2000)]

27–15. Robert Santoro was the manager of City Check Cashing, Inc., a check-cashing service in New Jersey, and Peggyann Slansky was the clerk. On July 14, Misir Koci presented Santoro with a $290,000 check signed by Melvin Green and drawn on Manufacturers Hanover Trust Co. (a bank). The check was stamped with a Manufacturers certification stamp. The date on the check had clearly been changed from August 8 to July 7. Slansky called the bank to verify the check and was told that the serial number "did not sound like one belonging to the bank." Slansky faxed the check to the bank with a query about the date, but received no reply. Slansky also called Green, who stated that the date on the check was altered before it was certified. Check Cashing cashed and deposited the check within two hours. The drawee bank found the check to be invalid and timely returned it unpaid. Check Cashing filed a suit in a New Jersey state court against Manufacturers and others, asserting that the bank should have responded to the fax before the midnight deadline delineated in UCC 4–302. Did the bank violate the midnight-deadline rule? Explain. [*City Check Cashing, Inc. v. Manufacturers Hanover Trust Co.,* 166 N.J. 49, 764 A.2d 411 (2001)]

E-LINKS

For updated links to resources available on the Web, as well as a variety of other materials, visit this text's Web site at

http://wbl-cs.westbuslaw.com

You can obtain an extensive amount of information on banking regulation from the Federal Deposit Insurance Corporation (FDIC) at

http://www.fdic.gov

The American Bankers Association is the largest banking trade association in the United States. To learn more about the banking industry, go to

http://www.aba.com

LEGAL RESEARCH EXERCISES ON THE WEB

Go to http://wbl-cs.westbuslaw.com, the Web site that accompanies this text. Select "Interactive Study Center," and then click on "Chapter 27." There you will find the following Internet research exercise that you can perform to learn more about check fraud and smart cards:

Activity 27–1: Check Fraud

Focus on Legal Reasoning

Maryott v. First National Bank of Eden

In Chapter 5, we discussed, in the context of negligence, proximate cause. In the same chapter, we covered the infliction of emotional distress. In Chapter 27, we focused on a bank's duty to honor its customers' checks and the bank's liability for wrongful dishonor of those checks. In this *Focus on Legal Reasoning,* we examine *Maryott v. First National Bank of Eden,*[1] a decision that involved all of these topics.

Case Background

Ned Maryott owned and operated Maryott Livestock Sales, a cattle-dealing business, near Britton, South Dakota. In July and August 1996, he shipped 887 head of cattle, worth about $480,000, to Oconto Cattle Company. In payment, he received two drafts from Oconto, but during the bank collection process the drafts were returned unpaid. First National Bank of Eden, Maryott's bank, then froze his checking account, although the account contained nearly $300,000. The bank applied the funds in the account against his outstanding loans and dishonored three of his checks, including one payable to Schaffer Cattle Company. The bank also told Central Livestock Company, which held a fourth Maryott check, that the check would not be honored. Schaffer and Central made claims against the bond that Maryott had filed with the state to obtain his dealer's license. The state took away Maryott's license, and he lost his business, which led him to suffer clinical depression.

Maryott filed a suit in a South Dakota state court against the bank, claiming, among other things, wrongful dishonor and emotional distress. The jury returned a verdict in Maryott's favor and awarded damages of more than $600,000. The bank appealed to the South Dakota Supreme Court.

1. 2001 SD 43, 624 N.W.2d 96 (2001).

Majority Opinion

GILBERTSON, Justice.

* * * *

[South Dakota Codified Laws Section 57A-4-402(b), South Dakota's version of UCC 4–402(b)] provides that "[a] payor bank is liable to its customer for damages proximately caused by the wrongful dishonor of an item." * * * Whether the wrongful dishonor proximately caused Maryott's damages is a question of fact for the jury to decide in all but the rarest of cases. Only when legal minds cannot differ as to the failure of proximate cause is judgment as a matter of law in favor of Bank appropriate. Bank claims this is one of those rarest cases. * * *

Bank's argument is based upon its claim that there is no connection between the three dishonored checks and the damage caused to Maryott, namely the loss of his dealer's license and the closing of his business after Central made a claim against his bond. * * *

Maryott * * * informed Central on the day he issued the check that he did not have enough funds to cover the check. Central personnel agreed to work with Maryott and hold the check until Maryott had sufficient funds. When Maryott discovered Bank had dishonored his checks and frozen his checking account, he informed Central of the situation. * * * Because of the freeze put on Maryott's account, he was essentially out of business at that time, as no future checks would be honored. In the words of [Central's president], "I had no recourse. I had nothing else I could do, I had to go against his bond at that time." When asked if he would have moved against the bond if the check had been honored, [Central's president] replied, "[m]ore than likely not because * * * that would have meant he was still in business and can continue in business and he could have probably worked out of his indebtedness to us."

* * * At trial, the owner of Schaffer testified he would not have filed a claim against Maryott's bond if Bank had honored that check. Bank argues that Schaffer's claim on the bond is irrelevant, as the bond would have been lost because of the actions of Central. * * * If the [Bank's] conduct was a substantial factor in causing [Maryott's] injury, it follows that [the Bank] will not be absolved from liability merely because other causes have contributed to the result, since such causes, innumerable, are always present. The wrongful dishonor by Bank was clearly a substantial factor causing the actions taken by Schaffer. * * * *[T]he proximate cause need not be the only cause, nor the last or nearest cause. It is sufficient if it concurs with some other cause acting at the same time, which in combination with it, causes injury.* * * * In addition, [Central's president] testified that but for Bank's actions, Central would not have moved against Maryott's bond. After reviewing the evidence in a light most favorable to the verdict, there is sufficient evidence to support the jury's verdict. Bank has failed to carry its burden of showing that no reasonable minds could differ as to the existence of proximate cause. [Emphasis added.]

* * * *

Bank [also] argues that the evidence fails to establish the necessary elements for recovery of damages for emotional distress. * * * Maryott argues that his emotional damages are recoverable under [UCC 4–402(b)] which provides that a bank is liable for "actual damages proved and may include * * * other consequential damages." Maryott argues that damages for emotional distress are part of his consequential damages, and he is therefore not required to establish the elements [separately, as an independent tort]. In the alternative, Maryott claims he has nevertheless met those requirements.

* * * *

* * * [T]he court in *First Nat'l Bank of New Castle v. Acra,* 462 N.E.2d 1345 (Ind.App.1984) examined a claim of emotional damages for wrongful dishonor in light of its state law requirements for * * * infliction of emotional distress. The Acra court noted that Indiana allowed recovery of damages for emotional distress only when intentionally inflicted or accompanied by a physical injury. In addition, the California courts require a plaintiff to prove either physical impact and resulting injury or intentional wrongdoing by the defendant before damages for emotional distress can be recovered under [UCC] 4–402. *Lee v. Bank of America,* 218 Cal.App.3d 914, 267 Cal.Rptr. 387 (1990). * * *

* * * South Dakota allows recovery of emotional damages only when intentionally inflicted or accompanied by actual physical injury. The U.C.C. provides that our common-law is effective in commercial transactions unless specifically displaced by a particular Code section. Because [UCC] 4–402 does not define the consequential damages that may be recovered and does not clearly indicate an independent right of recovery of emotional damages, we must interpret that section in light of our precedent which requires a plaintiff to prove either intentional or negligent infliction of emotional distress to recover emotional damages. * * * [T]hree principal concerns continue to foster judicial caution and doctrinal limitations on recovery for emotional distress: (1) the problem of permitting legal redress for harm that is often temporary and relatively trivial; (2) the danger that claims of mental harm will be falsified or imagined; and (3) the perceived unfairness of imposing heavy and disproportionate financial burdens upon a defendant, whose conduct was only negligent * * *. The best way to balance these concerns while still providing adequate relief for injured plaintiffs is to require plaintiffs to meet the standards already established in this state for the recovery of emotional damages. * * * Therefore, while emotional damages may be recoverable under [UCC 4–402(b)] they are not recoverable unless the plaintiff can establish the requirements * * * of emotional distress.

To recover for intentional infliction of emotional distress, Maryott must show:

> 1) an act by defendant amounting to extreme and outrageous conduct;
> 2) intent on the part of the defendant to cause plaintiff severe emotional distress;
> 3) the defendant's conduct was the cause in-fact of plaintiff's distress;
> 4) the plaintiff suffered an extreme disabling emotional response to defendant's conduct.

For conduct to be deemed "outrageous," it must be so extreme in degree as to go beyond all possible bounds of decency, and to be regarded as atrocious, and utterly intolerable in a civilized community. While Bank's actions were illegal and irresponsible, they do not rise to the level of outrageous conduct. Nor was any evidence introduced that Bank acted with the requisite intent. * * *

* * * [I]nfliction of emotional distress requires manifestation of physical symptoms. Maryott argues that his clinical depression and the symptoms thereof that resulted from Bank's wrongful dishonor are sufficient to establish manifestation of physical symptoms. The physical symptoms of his depression included shame, interruption of sleep, and humiliation. * * *

* * * Maryott's claim that clinical depression satisfies the requirement of physical symptoms is inconsistent with our established law. Nor can shame and humiliation be classified as physical symptoms. Finally, interruption of sleep on its own cannot be considered a physical symptom that would allow for recovery of emotional damages. Because Maryott has failed to establish the elements of * * * infliction of emotional distress, his claim for emotional damages under [UCC 4–402(b)] must fail as a matter of law.

* * * *

We affirm the trial court's denial of Bank's motion for judgment notwithstanding the verdict on the issue of proximate cause. The jury's award of emotional damages is reversed as a matter of law.

QUESTIONS FOR ANALYSIS

1. **Legal Analysis.** In its opinion, the court cites *First National Bank of New Castle v. Acra,* 462 N.E.2d 1345 (Ind.App.1984), and *Lee v. Bank of America,* 218 Cal.App.3d 914, 267 Cal.Rptr. 387 (1990) (see the *E-Links* feature at the end of Chapter 2 for instructions on how to access the opinions of state courts). Why did the *Maryott* court refer to these cases? How do the facts compare?

2. **Legal Reasoning.** What reasons did the *Maryott* court provide for

its ruling on the issue of proximate cause?

3. **Economic Dimensions.** What does the holding in this case say to small businesses?

4. **Implications for the Business Owner.** If a bank recredits its drawer-customer's account on the wrongful dishonor of a check, should the check's payee also be able to recover from the bank?

WESTLAW ONLINE RESEARCH

Go to this text's companion Web site, at http://wbl-cs.westbuslaw.com, and click on the Westlaw icon. Use your special password to access the full text of this case, including the dissenting opinions. Read through the case, and then answer the following questions.

1. Compare the conclusions of the majority and the dissent. With which of the majority's conclusions does the dissent disagree? Why?
2. Review the editors' summary of this case immediately following the citation. What is the value of this summary?
3. Considering the context of this case, what is the ethical basis for requiring that a bank honor the checks written by its customers?

Unit Five

Creditors' Rights and Bankruptcy

CONTENTS

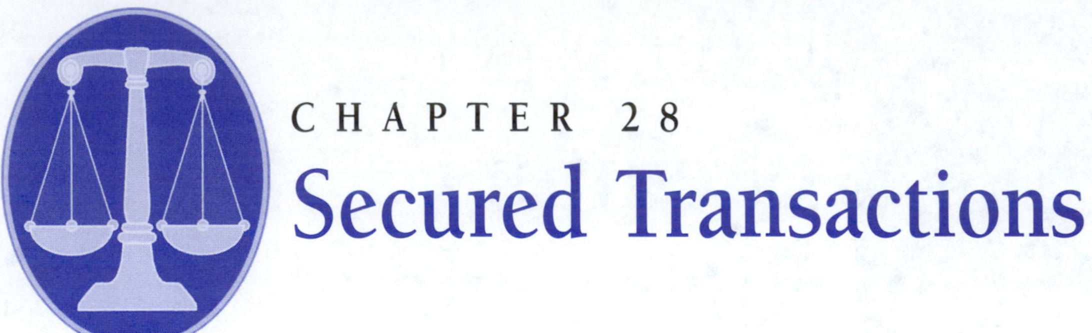

CHAPTER 28
Secured Transactions

WHENEVER THE PAYMENT OF A DEBT is guaranteed, or *secured,* by personal property owned by the debtor or in which the debtor has a legal interest, the transaction becomes known as a **secured transaction.** The concept of the secured transaction is as basic to modern business practice as the concept of credit. Logically, sellers and lenders do not want to risk nonpayment, so they usually will not sell goods or lend funds unless the promise of payment is somehow guaranteed. Indeed, business as we know it could not exist without laws permitting and governing secured transactions.

Article 9 of the Uniform Commercial Code (UCC) governs secured transactions relating to personal property, fixtures by contract, accounts, instruments, commercial assignments of $1,000 or more, *chattel paper* (any writing evidencing a debt secured by personal property), agricultural liens, and what are called general intangibles (such as patents and copyrights). Article 9 does not cover other creditor devices, such as landlord's liens, mechanic's liens, real estate mortgages, and the like [UCC 9–109]. In 1999, the National Conference of Commissioners of Uniform State Laws (NCCUSL) promulgated a revised version of Article 9. Because the revised version, which was later amended, has now been adopted by all of the states, we base this chapter's discussion of secured transactions entirely on the provisions of the revised version. The revised Article 9 is included in Appendix B at the end of this text.

In this chapter, we first look at the terminology of secured transactions. We then discuss how the rights and duties of creditors and debtors are created and enforced under Article 9. As will become evident, the law of secured transactions tends to favor the rights of creditors; but, to a lesser extent, it offers debtors some protections as well.

SECTION 1
The Terminology of Secured Transactions

The UCC's terminology is now uniformly adopted in all documents used in situations involving secured transactions. A brief summary of the UCC's definitions of terms relating to secured transactions follows.

1. A **secured party** is any creditor who has a *security interest* in the *debtor's collateral.* This creditor can be a seller, a lender, a cosigner, and even a buyer of accounts or chattel paper [UCC 9–102(a)(72)].
2. A **debtor** is the "person" who *owes payment* or other performance of a secured obligation [UCC 9–102(a)(28)].
3. A **security interest** is the *interest* in the collateral (personal property, fixtures, and so on.) that *secures payment or performance of an obligation* [UCC 1–201(37)].
4. A **security agreement** is an *agreement* that *creates* or provides for a *security interest* [UCC 9–102(a)(73)].
5. **Collateral** is the *subject* of the *security interest* [UCC 9–102(a)(12)].
6. A **financing statement**—referred to as the UCC–1 form—is the *instrument normally filed* to give *public notice* to *third parties* of the *secured party's security interest* [UCC 9–102(a)(39)].

These basic definitions form the concept under which a debtor-creditor relationship becomes a secured transaction relationship (see Exhibit 28–1).

EXHIBIT 28–1 SECURED TRANSACTIONS—CONCEPT AND TERMINOLOGY

In a security agreement, a debtor and creditor agree that the creditor will have a security interest in collateral in which the debtor has rights. In essence, the collateral secures the loan and ensures the creditor of payment should the debtor default.

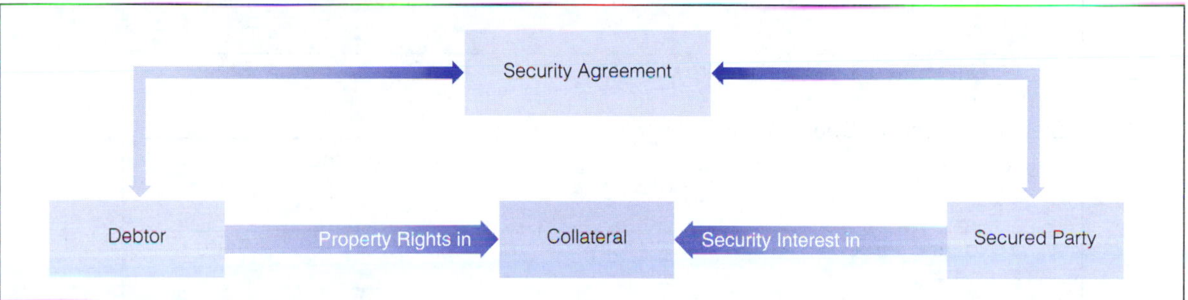

SECTION 2

Creating and Perfecting a Security Interest

A creditor has two main concerns if the debtor **defaults** (fails to pay the debt as promised): (1) satisfaction of the debt through the possession and (usually) sale of the collateral and (2) priority over any other creditors or buyers who may have rights in the same collateral. We look here at how these two concerns are met through the creation and perfection of a security interest.

CREATING A SECURITY INTEREST

To become a secured party, the creditor must obtain a security interest in the collateral of the debtor. Three requirements must be met for a creditor to have an enforceable security interest:

1. Either (a) the collateral must be in the possession of the secured party in accordance with an agreement, or (b) there must be a written or authenticated security agreement that describes the collateral subject to the security interest and is signed or authenticated by the debtor.
2. The secured party must give to the debtor something of value.
3. The debtor must have "rights" in the collateral.

Once these requirements have been met, the creditor's rights are said to attach to the collateral. **Attachment** gives the creditor an enforceable security interest in the collateral [UCC 9–203].[1]

Written or Authenticated Security Agreement. When the collateral is *not* in the possession of the secured party, the security agreement must be either written or authenticated, and it must describe the collateral. Note here that *authentication* includes any agreement or signature inscribed on a tangible medium or stored in an electronic or other medium (called a *record*) that is retrievable [UCC 9–102(a)(7)(69)]. If the security agreement is in writing or authenticated, only the debtor's signature or authentication is required to create the security interest. The reason authentication is acceptable is to provide for electronic filing (the filing process will be discussed later).

A security agreement must contain a description of the collateral that reasonably identifies it. Generally, such words as "all the debtor's personal property" or "all the debtor's assets" would *not* constitute a sufficient description [UCC 9–108(c)]. See Exhibit 28–2 on the following page for a sample security agreement.

See Case 28.1 at the end of this chapter. To view the full, unedited case from Westlaw,® go to this text's Web site at **http://wbl-cs.westbuslaw.com**.

1. Note that in the context of judicial liens, discussed in Chapter 29, the term *attachment* has a different meaning. In that context, it refers to a court-ordered seizure and taking into custody of property prior to the securing of a court judgment for a past-due debt.

EXHIBIT 28–2 AN EXAMPLE OF A SIMPLE SECURITY AGREEMENT

____
Date

____
Name No. and Street City County State

(hereinafter called "Debtor") hereby grants to __________________________
Name

____
No. and Street City County State

(hereinafter called "Secured Party") a security interest in the following property (hereinafter called the "Collateral"): ____

to secure payment and performance of obligations identified or set out as follows (hereinafter called the "Obligations"): ____

Default in payment or performance of any of the Obligations or default under any agreement evidencing any of the Obligations is a default under this agreement. Upon such default Secured Party may declare all Obligations immediately due and payable and shall have the remedies of a secured party under the __________ Uniform Commercial Code.

Signed in (duplicate) triplicate.

__________________________ __________________________
Debtor Secured Party
By________________________ By________________________

Secured Party Must Give Value. The secured party must give to the debtor something of value. Some examples would be a binding commitment to extend credit, a security, the satisfaction of a preexisting debt, or consideration to support a simple contract [UCC 1–201(44)]. Normally, the value given by a secured party is in the form of a direct loan, or it involves a commitment to sell goods on credit.

Debtor Must Have Rights in the Collateral. The debtor must have rights in the collateral; that is, the debtor must have some ownership interest or right to obtain possession of that collateral. The debtor's rights can represent either a current or a future legal interest in the collateral. For example, a retail seller-debtor can give a secured party a security interest not only in existing inventory owned by the retailer but also in *future* inventory to be acquired by the retailer.

One common misconception about having rights in the collateral is that the debtor must have title—this is *not* a requirement. A beneficial interest in a trust, when title to the trust property is held by the trustee, may be made the subject of a security interest for a loan made to the beneficiary by a secured party (a creditor).

CLASSIFICATIONS AND DEFINITIONS OF COLLATERAL

Where or how to perfect a security interest (perfection will be discussed shortly) sometimes depends on the classification or definition of the collateral.

Collateral is generally divided into two classifications: *tangible collateral* (collateral that can be seen, felt, touched, and so on) and *intangible collateral* (collateral that consists of or generates rights).

Exhibit 28–3 summarizes the various classifications of collateral and the methods of perfecting a security interest in collateral falling within each of those classifications.[2]

2. There are additional classifications, such as agricultural liens, investment property, and commercial tort claims. For definitions of these types of collateral, see UCC 9–102(a)(5), (a)(13), and (a)(49).

EXHIBIT 28–3 TYPES OF COLLATERAL AND METHODS OF PERFECTION

TYPE OF COLLATERAL	DEFINITION	PERFECTION METHOD	UCC SECTIONS
Tangible	All things that are movable at the time the security interest attaches or that are fixtures. These include timber to be cut, growing crops, and unborn animals.		
1. Consumer Goods	Goods used or bought primarily for personal, family, or household purposes—for example, household furniture [UCC 9–102(a)(23)].	For purchase-money security interest, attachment (that is, the creation of a security interest) is sufficient; for boats, motor vehicles, and trailers, there is a requirement of filing or compliance with a certificate-of-title statute; for other consumer goods, general rules of filing or possession apply.	9–301, 9–303, 9–309(1), 9–310(a), 9–313(a)
2. Equipment	Goods bought for or used primarily in business (and not part of inventory or farm products)—for example, a delivery truck [UCC 9–102(a)(33)].	Filing or (rarely) possession by secured party.	9–301, 9–310(a), 9–313(a)
3. Farm Products	Crops, including aquatic goods, livestock, or supplies produced in a farming operation—for example, ginned cotton, milk, eggs, and maple syrup [UCC 9–102(a)(34)].	Filing or (rarely) possession by secured party.	9–301, 9–310(a), 9–313(a)
4. Inventory	Goods held by a person for sale or under a contract of service or lease, or raw materials held for production and work in progress [UCC 9–102(a)(48)].	Filing or (rarely) possession by secured party.	9–301, 9–310(a), 9–313(a)
5. Accessions	Personal property that is so attached, installed, or fixed to other personal property (goods) that it becomes a part of the goods (the other personal property)—for example, a compact disc player installed in an automobile [UCC 9–102(a)(1)].	Filing or (rarely) possession by secured party (same as personal property being attached).	9–301, 9–310(a), 9–313(a)

EXHIBIT 28–3 TYPES OF COLLATERAL AND METHODS OF PERFECTION—CONTINUED

TYPE OF COLLATERAL	DEFINITION	PERFECTION METHOD	UCC SECTIONS
Intangible	Nonphysical property that exists only in connection with something else.		
1. Chattel Paper	A writing or writings (records) that evidence both a security interest in goods and software used in goods and a monetary obligation to pay—for example, a security agreement or a security agreement and promissory note. *Note:* If the record or records consist of information stored in an electronic medium, the collateral is called *electronic chattel paper.* If the information is inscribed on a tangible medium, it is called *tangible chattel paper* [UCC 9–102(a)(11), (a)(31), and (a)(78)].	Filing, or possession or control by secured party.	9–301, 9–310(a), 9–312(a), 9–313(a) 9–314(a)
2. Instruments	A negotiable instrument, such as a check, note, certificate of deposit, or draft, or other writing that evidences a right to the payment of money and is not a security agreement or lease, but rather a type that can ordinarily be transferred (after indorsement, if necessary) by delivery [UCC 9–102(a)(47)].	Except for temporary perfected status, filing or possession. For the sale of promissory notes, perfection can be by attachment (automatically on the creation of the security interest).	9–301, 9–309(4), 9–310(a), 9–312(a) and (e), 9–313(a)
3. Accounts	Any right to receive payment for the following: (a) any property, real or personal, sold, leased, licensed, assigned, or otherwise disposed of, including intellectual licensed property; (b) services rendered or to be rendered, such as contract rights; (c) policies of insurance; (d) secondary obligations incurred; (e) use of a credit card; (f) winnings of a government-sponsored or government-authorized lottery or other game of chance; and (g) health-care insurance receivables, defined as an interest or claim under a policy of insurance to payment for health-care goods or services provided [UCC 9–102(a)(2) and (a)(46)].	Filing required except for certain assignments that can be perfected by attachment (automatically on the creation of the security interest).	9–301, 9–309(2) and (5), 9–310(a)
4. Deposit Accounts	Any demand, time, savings, passbook, or similar account maintained with a bank [UCC 9–102(a)(29)].	Perfection by control.	9–104, 9–304, 9–312(b), 9–314(a)
5. General Intangibles	Any personal property (or debtor's obligation to pay money on such) other than that defined above [UCC 9–102(a)(42)], including software that is independent from a computer or a good [UCC 9–102(a)(44), (a)(61)], and (a)(75).	Filing only (for copyrights, with the U.S. Copyright Office), except a sale of a payment intangible by attachment (automatically on the creation of the security interest).	9–301, 9–309(3), 9–310(a) and (b)(8)

PERFECTING A SECURITY INTEREST

Perfection represents the legal process by which secured parties protect themselves against the claims of third parties who may wish to have their debts satisfied out of the same collateral. Usually, perfection is accomplished by filing a financing statement with the office of the appropriate government official. In some circumstances, however, a security interest becomes perfected without the filing of a financing statement.

Perfection by Filing.

The most common means of perfection is by filing a *financing statement*—a document that gives public notice to third parties of the secured party's security interest—with the office of the appropriate government official. The security agreement itself can also be filed to perfect the security interest. The financing statement must provide the names of the debtor and the secured party and indicate the collateral covered by the financing statement. There is now a uniform financing statement form that is to be used in all states [see UCC 9–521]. The uniform financing statement is shown in Exhibit 28–4 on the next page.

Communication of the financing statement to the appropriate filing office, together with the correct filing fee, or the acceptance of the financing statement by the filing officer constitutes a filing [UCC 9–516(a)]. The word *communication* means that the filing can be accomplished electronically [UCC 9–102(a)(18)]. Once completed, filings are indexed in the name of the debtor so that they can be located by subsequent searchers. A financing statement may be filed even before a security agreement is made or a security interest attaches [UCC 9–502(d)].

The Debtor's Name.

The UCC requires that a financing statement be filed under the name of the debtor [UCC 9–502(a)(1)]. Because of the use of electronic filing systems in most states, UCC 9–503 sets out some detailed rules for determining when the debtor's name as it appears on a financing statement is sufficient. For corporations, which are part of "registered organizations," the debtor's name on the financing statement must be "the name of the debtor indicated on the public record of the debtor's jurisdiction of organization" [UCC 9–503(a)(1)]. Slight variations in names normally will not be considered misleading if a search of the filing office's records, using a standard computer search engine routinely used by that office, would disclose the filings [UCC 9–506(c)]. Note that if the debtor is identified by the correct name at the time of the filing of a financing statement, the secured party's interest retains its priority even if the debtor later changes his or her name.

If the debtor is a trust, or a trustee with respect to property held in trust, this information must be disclosed on the filed financing statement, and it must provide the trust name as specified in its official documents [UCC 9–503(a)(3)]. In other cases, the filed financing statement must disclose "the individual or organizational name of the debtor" [UCC 9–503(a)(4)(A)]. The word *organization,* as used here, includes unincorporated associations, such as clubs and some churches, as well as joint ventures and general partnerships, even when these entities are organized without obtaining any official certificate of formation.

In general, providing only the debtor's trade name (or a fictitious name) in a financing statement is not sufficient for perfection [UCC 9–503(c)]. For example, assume that a loan is being made to a sole proprietorship owned by Peter Jones. The trade, or fictitious, name is Pete's Plumbing. A financing statement cannot use the trade name Pete's Plumbing; rather, it must be filed under the name of the actual debtor, who in this instance is Peter Jones. The reason for this rule is that a sole proprietorship is not a legal entity distinct from the person who owns it. The rule also furthers an important goal of Article 9: to ensure that the debtor's name on a financing statement is one that prospective lenders can locate and recognize in future searches.

Changes in the Debtor's Name.

A problem arises when the debtor subject to a filed perfected security interest changes his or her (or its) name. What happens if a subsequent creditor extends credit to the debtor and perfects its security interest under the debtor's new name? Obviously, a search by this subsequent creditor for filed security interests under the debtor's changed name may not disclose the previously filed security interest.

The UCC's revised Article 9 attempts to prevent potential conflicts caused by changes in the debtor's name if the debtor goes into default. First, UCC 9–503 states specifically what constitutes the "sufficiency" of the debtor's name in a financing statement. Second, if the debtor's name is insufficient, the filing is seriously

EXHIBIT 28–4 THE UNIFORM FINANCING STATEMENT

UCC FINANCING STATEMENT

FOLLOW INSTRUCTIONS (front and back) CAREFULLY

A. NAME & PHONE OF CONTACT AT FILER (optional)

B. SEND ACKNOWLEDGEMENT TO: (Name and Address)

THE ABOVE SPACE IS FOR FILING OFFICE USE ONLY

1. DEBTOR'S EXACT FULL LEGAL NAME - Insert only one debtor name (1a or 1b) - do not abbreviate or combine names

1a. ORGANIZATION'S NAME			
OR 1b. INDIVIDUAL'S LAST NAME	FIRST NAME	MIDDLE NAME	SUFFIX

1c. MAILING ADDRESS	CITY	STATE	POSTAL CODE	COUNTRY

1d. TAX ID# SSN OR EIN	ADDL INFO RE ORGANIZATION DEBTOR	1e. TYPE OF ORGANIZATION	1f. JURISDICTION OR ORGANIZATION	1g. ORGANIZATIONAL ID #, if any ☐ NONE

2. ADDITIONAL DEBTOR'S EXACT FULL LEGAL NAME - Insert only one debtor name (2a or 2b) - do not abbreviate or combine names

2a. ORGANIZATION'S NAME			
OR 2b. INDIVIDUAL'S LAST NAME	FIRST NAME	MIDDLE NAME	SUFFIX

2c. MAILING ADDRESS	CITY	STATE	POSTAL CODE	COUNTRY

2d. TAX ID# SSN OR EIN	ADDL INFO RE ORGANIZATION DEBTOR	1e. TYPE OF ORGANIZATION	1f. JURISDICTION OR ORGANIZATION	1g. ORGANIZATIONAL ID #, if any ☐ NONE

3. SECURED PARTY'S NAME - (or NAME of TOTAL ASSIGNOR S/P) Insert only one secured party name (3a or 3b)

3a. ORGANIZATION'S NAME			
OR 3b. INDIVIDUAL'S LAST NAME	FIRST NAME	MIDDLE NAME	SUFFIX

3c. MAILING ADDRESS	CITY	STATE	POSTAL CODE	COUNTRY

4. This FINANCING STATEMENT covers the following collateral:

5. ALTERNATIVE DESIGNATION (if applicable) ☐ LESSEE/LESSOR ☐ CONSIGNEE/CONSIGNOR ☐ BAILEE/BAILOR ☐ SELLER/BUYER ☐ AG. LIEN ☐ NON-UCC FILING

6. ☐ This FINANCING STATEMENT is to be filed [for record] (or recorded) in the REAL ESTATE RECORDS. Attach Addendum (if applicable) 7. Check to REQUEST SEARCH REPORT(S) on Debtor(s) (ADDITIONAL FEE) (optional) ☐ All Debtors ☐ Debtor 1 ☐ Debtor 2

OPTIONAL FILER REFERENCE DATA

NATIONAL UCC FINANCING STATEMENT (FORM UCC1) REV. 07/29/98)

misleading *unless* a search of records using the debtor's correct name by the filing officer's search engine would disclose the security interest [UCC 9–506(b) and (c)]. Third, even if the change of name renders the financing statement misleading, the financing statement is effective as a perfection of a security interest in collateral acquired by the debtor before *or* within four months after the name change. Unless an amendment is filed within this four-month period, collateral acquired by the debtor after the four-month period is unperfected [UCC 9–507(b) and (c)].

Description of the Collateral. The UCC requires that both the security agreement and the financing statement contain a description of the collateral in which the secured party has a security interest. The security agreement must include a description of the collateral because no security interest in goods can exist unless the parties agree on which goods are subject to the security interest. The financing statement must include a description of the collateral because the purpose of filing the statement is to give public notice of the fact that certain goods of the debtor are subject to a security interest. Other parties who might later wish to lend money to the debtor or buy the collateral can thus learn of the security interest by checking with the state or local office in which a financing statement for that type of collateral would be filed. For land-related security interests, a legal description of the realty is also required [UCC 9–502(b)].

Sometimes, the descriptions in the two documents vary, with the description in the security agreement being more precise than that in the financing statement, which is allowed to be more general. For example, a security agreement for a commercial loan to a manufacturer may list all of the manufacturer's equipment subject to the loan by serial number, whereas the financing statement may simply state "all equipment owned or hereafter acquired." The UCC permits broad, general descriptions in the financing statement, such as "all assets" or "all personal property." Generally, therefore, whenever the description in a financing statement accurately describes the agreement between the secured party and the debtor, the description is sufficient [UCC 9–504].

Where to File. In most states, a financing statement must be filed centrally in the appropriate state office, such as the office of the secretary of state, in the state where the debtor is located. County filings, where the collateral is located, are required only when the collateral consists of timber to be cut, fixtures, and collateral to be extracted—such as oil, coal, gas, and minerals [UCC 9–301(3) and (4), 9–502(b)].

The state office in which a financing statement should be filed depends on the *debtor's location,* not the location of the collateral (as was required under the unrevised Article 9) [UCC 9–301]. The debtor's location is determined as follows [UCC 9–307]:

1. For *individual debtors,* it is the state of the debtor's principal residence.
2. For a chartered entity created by a filing (such as a corporation), it is in the state of charter or filing. For example, if a debtor is incorporated in Maryland, with its chief executive office in New York, a secured party would file the financing statement in Maryland, which is the state of the debtor's organizational formation.
3. For all other entities, it is the state in which the business is located or, if the business is located in more than one state, the state in which the chief executive office is located.

Consequences of an Improper Filing. Any improper filing renders the secured party unperfected and reduces a secured party's claim in bankruptcy to that of an unsecured creditor. For example, if the debtor's name on the financing statement is inaccurate or if the collateral is not sufficiently described on the filing statement, the filing may not be effective.

Perfection without Filing. In two types of situations, security interests can be perfected without filing a financing statement. First, when the collateral is transferred into the possession of the secured party, the secured party's security interest in the collateral is perfected. Second, there are thirteen different types of security interests that can be perfected on attachment without a filing and without having to possess the goods [UCC 9–309]. (The phrase *perfected on attachment* means that these security interests are automatically perfected at the time of their creation.) Two of the most common security interests that are perfected on attachment are a *purchase-money security interest* in consumer goods (defined and explained below) and an assignment of a beneficial interest in a decedent's estate [UCC 9–309(1) and (13)].

Perfection by Possession. Under the common law, one of the most prevalent means of obtaining financing was to **pledge** certain collateral as security for the debt and transfer the collateral into the creditor's possession. When the debt was paid, the collateral was returned to the debtor. Usually, the transfer of collateral was accompanied by a written security agreement, but the agreement did not have to be in writing. In other words, an oral security agreement was effective as long as the secured party possessed the collateral. Article 9 of the UCC retained the common law pledge and the principle that the security agreement need not be in writing to be enforceable if the collateral is transferred to the secured party [UCC 9–310, 9–312(b), and 9–313].

For most collateral, possession by the secured party is impractical because it denies the debtor the right to use or derive income from the property to pay off the debt. For example, suppose that a farmer takes out a loan to finance the purchase of a piece of heavy farm equipment needed to harvest crops and uses the equipment as collateral. Clearly, the purpose of the purchase would be defeated if the farmer transferred the collateral into the creditor's possession. Certain items, however, such as stocks, bonds, instruments, and jewelry, are commonly transferred into the creditor's possession when they are used as collateral for loans.

Purchase-Money Security Interest. Often, sellers of consumer goods (defined as goods bought or used by the debtor primarily for personal, family, or household purposes [UCC 9–102(a)(23)]) agree to extend credit for part or all of the purchase price of those goods. Additionally, financial institutions that are not in the business of selling such goods often agree to lend consumers much of the purchase price for goods. The security interest that the seller or the lender obtains when such a transaction occurs is called a **purchase-money security interest (PMSI)** because the lender or seller has essentially provided a buyer with the "purchase money" to buy goods [UCC 9–103(a)(2)].

For example, suppose that Jamie wants to purchase a new large-screen TV from ABC Television, Inc. The purchase price is $2,500. Not being able to pay the entire amount in cash, Jamie signs a purchase agreement to pay $1,000 down and $100 per month until the balance plus interest is fully paid. ABC is to retain a security interest in the purchased goods until full payment has been made. Because the security interest was created as part of the purchase agreement, it is a PMSI.

A PMSI in consumer goods is perfected automatically at the time of a credit sale—that is, at the time the PMSI is created. The seller in this situation need do nothing more to perfect her or his interest.

Note that a PMSI may also exist with respect to goods sold to businesses or other entities that are not considered "consumers" for Article 9 purposes.

Effective Time Duration of Perfection. A financing statement is effective for five years from the date of filing [UCC 9–515]. If a **continuation statement** is filed within six months *prior to* the expiration date, the effectiveness of the original statement is continued for another five years, starting with the expiration date of the first five-year period [UCC 9–515(d) and (e)]. The effectiveness of the statement can be continued in the same manner indefinitely. Any attempt to file a continuation statement outside the six-month window will render the continuation ineffective, and the perfection will lapse at the end of the five-year period.

If a financing statement lapses, the security interest that had been perfected by the filing now becomes unperfected. It is as if it had never been perfected as against a purchaser for value [UCC 9–515(c)].

SECTION 3

The Scope of a Security Interest

In addition to covering collateral already in the debtor's possession, a security agreement can cover various other types of property, including the proceeds of the sale of collateral, after-acquired property, and future advances.

PROCEEDS

Proceeds include whatever is received when collateral is sold or disposed of in some other way [UCC 9–102(a)(64)]. A secured party's security interest in the collateral includes a security interest in the proceeds of the sale of that collateral. For example, suppose that a bank has a perfected security interest in the inventory of a retail seller of heavy farm machinery. The retailer sells a tractor out of this inventory to a farmer, who is by definition a buyer in the ordinary course of business. The farmer agrees, in a security agreement, to make monthly payments to the retailer for a period of twenty-four months. If the retailer should go into default on the loan from the bank, the bank is entitled to the remaining payments the farmer owes to the retailer as proceeds.

A security interest in proceeds perfects automatically on the *perfection* of the secured party's security interest in the original collateral and remains perfected for twenty days after receipt of the proceeds by the debtor. One way to extend the twenty-day automatic perfection period is to provide for such extended coverage in the original security agreement [UCC 9–315(c) and (d)]. This is typically done when the collateral is the type that is likely to be sold, such as a retailer's inventory—for example, of computers or DVD players. The UCC also permits a security interest in identifiable cash proceeds to remain perfected after twenty days [UCC 9–315(d)(2)].

AFTER-ACQUIRED PROPERTY

After-acquired property is property that the debtor acquired after the execution of the security agreement. The security agreement may provide for a security interest in after-acquired property [UCC 9–204(1)]. This is particularly useful for inventory financing arrangements because a secured party whose security interest is in existing inventory knows that the debtor will sell that inventory, thereby reducing the collateral subject to the security interest.

Generally, the debtor will purchase new inventory to replace the inventory sold. The secured party wants this newly acquired inventory to be subject to the original security interest. Thus, the after-acquired property clause continues the secured party's claim to any inventory acquired thereafter. This does not mean that the original security interest will be superior to the rights of all other creditors with regard to this after-acquired inventory, as will be discussed later.

For example, suppose that Amato buys factory equipment from Bronson on credit, giving as security an interest in all of her equipment—both what she is buying and what she already owns. The security interest with Bronson contains an after-acquired property clause. Six months later, Amato pays cash to another seller of factory equipment for more equipment. Six months after that, Amato goes out of business before she has paid off her debt to Bronson. Bronson has a security interest in all of Amato's equipment, even the equipment bought from the other seller.

FUTURE ADVANCES

Often, a debtor will arrange with a bank to have a *continuing line of credit* under which the debtor can borrow funds intermittently. Advances against lines of credit can be subject to a properly perfected security interest in certain collateral. The security agreement may provide that any future advances made against that line of credit are also subject to the security interest in the same collateral [UCC 9–204(c)]. Future advances do not have to be of the same type or otherwise related to the original advance to benefit from this type of cross-collateralization.[3]

For example, assume that Stroh is the owner of a small manufacturing plant with equipment valued at $1 million. He has an immediate need for $50,000 of working capital, so he obtains a loan from Midwestern Bank and signs a security agreement, putting up all of his equipment as security. The bank properly perfects its security interest. The security agreement provides that Stroh can borrow up to $500,000 in the future, using the same equipment as collateral for any future advances. In this situation, Midwestern Bank does not have to execute a new security agreement and perfect a security interest in the collateral each time an advance is made, up to a cumulative total of $500,000. For priority purposes, each advance is perfected as of the date of the original perfection.

THE FLOATING-LIEN CONCEPT

A security agreement that provides for a security interest in proceeds, in after-acquired property, or in collateral subject to future advances by the secured party (or in all three) is often characterized as a **floating lien**. This type of security interest continues in the collateral or proceeds even if the collateral is sold, exchanged, or disposed of in some other way. Floating liens commonly arise in the financing of inventories. A creditor is not interested in specific pieces of inventory, which are constantly changing, so the lien "floats" from one item to another, as the inventory changes.

Consider an example. Suppose that Cascade Sports, Inc., a corporation chartered in Oregon that operates as a cross-country ski dealer, has a line of credit with Portland First Bank to finance an inventory of cross-country skis. Cascade and Portland

3. See official Comment 5 to UCC 9–204.

First enter into a security agreement that provides for coverage of proceeds, after-acquired inventory, present inventory, and future advances. This security interest in inventory is perfected by filing centrally (with the office of the secretary of state in Oregon). One day, Cascade sells a new pair of the latest cross-country skis and receives a used pair in trade. That same day, Cascade purchases two new pairs of cross-country skis from a local manufacturer for cash. Later that day, Cascade borrows $2,000 from Portland First Bank under the security agreement to meet its payroll. Portland First gets a perfected security interest in the used pair of skis under the proceeds clause, has a perfected security interest in the two new pairs of skis purchased from the local manufacturer under the after-acquired property clause, and has the new amount of funds advanced to Cascade secured on all of the above collateral by the future-advances clause. All of this is accomplished under the original perfected security interest. The various items in the inventory have changed, but Portland First still has a perfected security interest in Cascade's inventory. Hence, it has a floating lien on the inventory.

The concept of the floating lien can also apply to a shifting stock of goods. The lien can start with raw materials; follow them as they become finished goods and inventories; and continue as the goods are sold and are turned into accounts receivable, chattel paper, or cash.

SECTION 4

Priorities

The importance of being perfected as a secured party cannot be overemphasized, particularly when another party is claiming an interest in the same collateral as covered by the perfected secured party's security interest.

The General Rule

The general rule is that a perfected secured party's interest has priority over the interests of the following parties [UCC 9–317, 9–322]:

1. An unsecured creditor.
2. An unperfected secured party.
3. A subsequent lien creditor, such as a judgment creditor who acquires a lien on the collateral by execution and levy—a process discussed later in this chapter.
4. A trustee in bankruptcy (see Chapter 30)—at least, the perfected secured party has priority to the proceeds from the sale of the collateral by the trustee.
5. Most buyers who *do not* purchase the collateral in the ordinary course of a seller's business.

In addition, whether a secured party's security interest is perfected or unperfected may have serious consequences for the secured party if the debtor defaults on the debt or files for bankruptcy. For example, what if the debtor has borrowed money from two different creditors, using the same property as collateral for both loans? If the debtor defaults on both loans, which of the two creditors has first rights to the collateral? In this situation, the creditor with a perfected security interest will prevail.

Buyers of the Collateral

Sometimes, the conflict is between a perfected secured party and a buyer of the collateral. The question then arises as to which party has priority to the collateral.

The UCC recognizes that there are five types of buyers whose interest in purchased goods could conflict with those of a perfected secured party on the debtor's default. These five types are as follows:

1. Buyers in the ordinary course of business—this type of buyer will be discussed in detail shortly.
2. Buyers *not* in the ordinary course of business of consumer goods.
3. Buyers of chattel paper [UCC 9–330].
4. Buyers of instruments, documents, or securities [UCC 9–330(d), 9–331(a)].
5. Buyers of farm products.[4]

Because buyers should not be required to find out if there is an outstanding security interest in, for example, a merchant's inventory, the UCC also provides that a person who buys "in the ordinary course of business" will take the goods free from any security interest created by the seller in the purchased

4. Under the Food Security Act of 1985, buyers in the ordinary course of business include buyers of farm products from a farmer. Under this act, these buyers are protected from prior perfected security interests unless the secured parties perfected centrally by a special form called an effective financing statement (EFS) or the buyers received proper notice of the secured party's security interest.

collateral. This is so even if the security interest is perfected and *even if the buyer knows of its existence* [UCC 9–320(a)].[5] The UCC defines a *buyer in the ordinary course of business* as any person who in good faith, and without knowledge that the sale is in violation of the ownership rights or security interest of a third party in the goods, buys in ordinary course from a person in the business of selling goods of that kind [UCC 1–201(9)].

To illustrate: On August 1, West Bank has a perfected security interest in all of ABC Television's existing inventory and any inventory thereafter acquired. On September 1, Carla, a student at Central University, purchases one of the TVs in ABC's inventory. If on December 1, ABC goes into default, can West Bank repossess the TV set sold to Carla? The answer is no, because Carla is a buyer in the ordinary course of business (ABC is in the business of selling goods of that kind) and takes free and clear of West Bank's perfected security interest.

Creditors or Secured Parties

Generally, the following UCC rules apply when more than one creditor claims rights in the same collateral.

1. *Conflicting perfected security interests.* When two or more secured parties have perfected security interests in the same collateral, generally the first to perfect (file or take possession of the collateral) has priority, unless the state's statute provides otherwise [UCC 9–322(a)(1)].
2. *Conflicting unperfected security interests.* When two conflicting security interests are unperfected, the first to attach has priority [UCC 9–322(a)(3)].
3. *Conflicting perfected security interests in commingled or processed goods.* When goods to which two or more perfected security interests attach are so manufactured or commingled into a product or mass that they lose their identities, the perfected parties' security interests attach to the new product or mass "according to the ratio that the cost of goods to which each interest originally attached bears to the cost of the total product or mass" [UCC 9–336].

Under certain circumstances, on the debtor's default, the perfection of a security interest will not protect a secured party against certain other third parties having claims to the collateral. For example, the UCC provides that in some instances a PMSI, properly perfected,[6] will prevail over another security interest in after-acquired collateral, even though the other was perfected first.

An important exception to the first-in-time rule deals with certain types of collateral, such as equipment, in which one of the perfected security parties has a PMSI [UCC 9–324(a)]. For example, suppose that Smith borrows funds from West Bank, signing a security agreement in which she puts up all of her present and after-acquired equipment as security. On May 1, West Bank perfects this security interest (which is not a PMSI). On July 1, Smith purchases a new piece of equipment from XYZ Company on credit, signing a security agreement. XYZ Company thus has a (nonconsumer) PMSI in the new equipment. The delivery date for the new equipment is August 1. If Smith defaults on her payments to both West Bank and XYZ, which party—West Bank or XYZ—has priority to the new piece of equipment? Generally, West Bank would have priority because its interest perfected first in time. In this situation, however, XYZ has a PMSI, and if it perfects its interest by filing before Smith takes possession on August 1, or within twenty days after that date, XYZ has priority.

Another important exception to the first-in-time rule has to do with security interests in inventory [UCC 9–324(b)]. For example, suppose that on May 1, ABC borrows funds from West Bank. ABC signs a security agreement, putting up all of its present inventory and any thereafter acquired as collateral. West Bank perfects its non-PMSI on that date. On June 10, ABC buys new inventory from Martin, Inc., a manufacturer, to use for its Fourth of July sale. ABC makes a down payment for the new inventory and signs a security agreement giving Martin a PMSI in the new inventory as collateral for the remaining debt. Martin delivers the inventory to ABC on June 28. Due to a hurricane in the area, ABC's Fourth of July sale is a disaster, and most of ABC's inventory remains unsold. In August, ABC defaults on its payments to both West Bank and Martin. As between West Bank and Martin, who has priority to the new inventory delivered on June 28? If Martin has not

5. Remember that there are generally three methods of perfection: by filing, by possession, or by attachment.

6. Recall that, with some exceptions (such as motor vehicles), a PMSI in consumer goods is automatically perfected—no filing is necessary.

perfected its security interest by June 28, West Bank's after-acquired collateral clause has priority because it was the first to be perfected. If, however, Martin has perfected *and* gives proper notice of its security interest to West Bank before ABC takes possession of the goods on June 28, Martin has priority.

The priority of claims to a debtor's collateral is detailed in Exhibit 28–5.

SECTION 5

Rights and Duties of Debtors and Creditors

The security agreement itself determines most of the rights and duties of the debtor and the secured party. The UCC, however, imposes some rights and duties

EXHIBIT 28–5 PRIORITY OF CLAIMS TO A DEBTOR'S COLLATERAL

PARTIES	PRIORITY
Unperfected Secured Party	An unperfected secured party prevails over unsecured creditors and creditors who have obtained judgments against the debtor but who have not begun the legal process to collect on those judgments [UCC 9–201(a)].
Purchaser of Debtor's Collateral	1. *Goods purchased in the ordinary course of the seller's business*—Buyer prevails over a secured party's security interest, even if perfected and even if the buyer knows of the security interest [UCC 9–320(a)]. 2. *Consumer goods purchased outside the ordinary course of business*—Buyer prevails over a secured party's interest, even if perfected by attachment, providing buyer purchased as follows: a. For value. b. Without actual knowledge of the security interest. c. For use as a consumer good. d. Prior to secured party's perfection by *filing* [UCC 9–320(b)]. 3. *Buyers of chattel paper*—Buyer prevails if the buyer: a. Gave new value in making the purchase. b. Took possession in the ordinary course of the buyer's business. c. Took without knowledge of the security interest [UCC 9–330]. 4. *Buyers of instruments, documents, or securities*—Buyers who are holders in due course, holders to whom negotiable documents have been duly negotiated, or bona fide purchasers of securities have priority over a previously perfected security interest [UCC 9–330(d), 9–331(a)]. 5. *Buyers of farm products*—Buyers from a farmer take free and clear of perfected security interests unless, where permitted, a secured party files centrally an effective financing statement (EFS) or the buyer receives proper notice of the security interest before the sale.
Perfected Secured Parties to the Same Collateral	1. *The general rule*—Between two perfected secured parties in the same collateral, the general rule is that first in time of perfection is first in right to the collateral [UCC 9–322(a)(1)]. 2. *Exception—Purchase-money security interest (PMSI)*—A PMSI, even if second in time of perfection, has priority, providing that the following conditions are met: a. Inventory—PMSI is perfected, and proper written or authenticated notice is given to the other security-interest holder *on* or *before* the time that debtor takes possession [UCC 9–324(b)]. b. Other collateral—PMSI has priority, providing it is perfected within twenty days after debtor receives possession [UCC 9–324(a)]. c. Software—Applies to a PMSI in software only if used in goods subject to a PMSI. Priority is determined the same as if the goods are inventory (if the goods are, in fact, inventory), or if not, as if the goods are other than inventory [UCC 9–103(c) and 9-324(f)].

that are applicable in the absence of a valid security agreement that states the contrary.

Information Requests

Under UCC 9–523(a), a secured party has the option, when making the filing, of furnishing a *copy* of the financing statement being filed to the filing officer and requesting that the filing officer make a note of the file number, the date, and the hour of the original filing on the copy. The filing officer must send this copy to the person designated by the secured party or to the debtor, if the debtor makes the request. Under UCC 9–523(c) and (d), a filing officer must also give information to a person who is contemplating obtaining a security interest from a prospective debtor. The filing officer must issue a certificate that provides information on possible perfected financing statements with respect to the named debtor. The filing officer will charge a fee for the certification and for any information copies provided [UCC 9–525(d)].

Release, Assignment, and Amendment

A secured party can release all or part of any collateral described in the filing, thereby terminating its security interest in that collateral. The release is recorded by filing a uniform amendment form [UCC 9–512 and 9–521(b)]. A secured party can assign all or part of the security interest to a third party (the assignee). The assignee can become the secured party of record if the assignment is filed by use of a uniform amendment form [UCC 9–514 and 9–521(a)].

If the debtor and secured parties so agree, the filing can be amended—by adding new collateral if authorized by the debtor, for example—by filing a uniform amendment form that indicates by file number the initial financing statement [UCC 9–512(a)]. The amendment does not extend the time period of perfection. If, however, the amendment adds collateral, the perfection date (for priority purposes) for the new collateral begins only on the date of the filing of the amendment [UCC 9–512(b) and (c)].

Confirmation or Accounting Request by Debtor

The debtor may believe that the unpaid debt amount or the listing of the collateral subject to the security interest is inaccurate. The debtor has the right to request a confirmation of his or her view of the unpaid debt or listing of collateral. The secured party must either approve or correct this confirmation request [UCC 9–210].

The secured party must comply with a debtor's confirmation request by authenticating and sending to the debtor an accounting within fourteen days after the request is received. Otherwise, the secured party will be held liable for any loss suffered by the debtor, plus $500 [UCC 9–210 and 9–625(f)].

The debtor is entitled to one request without charge every six months. For any additional requests, the secured party is entitled to the payment of a statutory fee of up to $25 per request [UCC 9–210(f)].

Termination Statement

When the debtor has fully paid the debt, if the secured party perfected the collateral by filing, the debtor is entitled to have a termination statement filed. Such a statement demonstrates to the public that the filed perfected security interest has been terminated [UCC 9–513].

Whenever consumer goods are involved, the secured party *must* file a termination statement (or, in the alternative, a release) within one month of the final payment or within twenty days of receipt of the debtor's authenticated demand, whichever is earlier [UCC 9–513(b)].

When the collateral is other than consumer goods, on an authenticated demand by the debtor, the secured party must either send a termination statement to the debtor or file such a statement within twenty days [UCC 9–513(c)]. Otherwise, when the collateral is other than consumer goods, the secured party is not required to file or, as required, send a termination statement. Whenever a secured party fails to file or send the termination statement as requested, the debtor can recover $500 plus any additional loss suffered [UCC 9–625(e)(4) and (f)].

SECTION 6

Default

Article 9 defines the rights, duties, and remedies of the secured party and of the debtor on the debtor's default. Should the secured party fail to comply with his or her duties, the debtor is afforded particular rights and remedies.

The topic of default is one of great concern to secured lenders and to the lawyers who draft security agreements. What constitutes default is not always clear. In fact, Article 9 does not define the term. Consequently, parties are encouraged in practice—and by the UCC—to include in their security agreements certain standards to be applied in determining when default has actually occurred. In so doing, parties can stipulate the conditions that will constitute a default [UCC 9–601 and 9–603]. Often, these critical terms are shaped by the creditor in an attempt to provide the maximum protection possible. The ultimate terms, however, are not allowed to go beyond the limitations imposed by the good faith requirement and the unconscionability provisions of the UCC. Article 9's definition of good faith includes "honesty in fact and the observance of reasonable commercial standards of fair dealing" [UCC 9–102(a)(43)].

Although any breach of the terms of the security agreement can constitute default, default occurs most commonly when the debtor fails to meet the scheduled payments that the parties have agreed on or when the debtor becomes bankrupt.

Basic Remedies

A secured party's remedies can be divided into two basic categories:

1. A secured party can take peaceful or judicial possession of the collateral covered by the security agreement [UCC 9–609(b)]. On taking possession, the secured party may choose either to retain the collateral for satisfaction of the debt [UCC 9–620] or resell the goods and apply the proceeds toward the debt [UCC 9–610].
2. A secured party can relinquish a security interest and use any judicial remedy available, such as proceeding to judgment on the underlying debt, followed by execution and levy. (**Execution** is the implementation of a court's decree or judgment. **Levy** is the obtaining of funds by legal process through the seizure and sale of noncollateralized property, usually done after a writ of execution has been issued.) Execution and levy are rarely undertaken unless the collateral is no longer in existence or has declined so much in value that it is worth substantially less than the amount of the debt and the debtor has other assets available that may be legally seized to satisfy the debt [UCC 9–601(a)].[7]

7. Some assets are exempt from creditors' claims—see Chapter 29.

The rights and remedies under UCC 9–601(a) are *cumulative* [UCC 9–601(c)]. Therefore, if a creditor is unsuccessful in enforcing rights by one method, she or he can pursue another method.[8]

When a security agreement covers both real and personal property, the secured party can proceed against the personal property in accordance with the remedies of Article 9. Alternatively, the secured party can proceed against the entire collateral under procedures set down by local real estate law, in which case the UCC does not apply [UCC 9–604(a)]. Determining whether particular collateral is personal or real property at times can prove difficult, especially when dealing with fixtures—things affixed to real property. Under certain circumstances, the UCC allows the removal of fixtures on default; such removal, however, is subject to the provisions of Article 9 [UCC 9–604(c)].

See Case 28.2 at the end of this chapter. To view the full, unedited case from Westlaw,® go to this text's Web site at **http://wbl-cs.westbuslaw.com**.

Repossession of Collateral—The Self-Help Remedy

On the debtor's default, the secured party is entitled to take peaceful possession of the collateral without the use of judicial process [UCC 9–609(b)]. The UCC does not define *peaceful possession,* however. The general rule is that the collateral has been taken peacefully if the secured party can take possession without committing (1) trespass onto realty, (2) assault and/or battery, or (3) breaking and entering.

Disposition of Collateral

Once default has occurred and the secured party has obtained possession of the collateral, the secured party may attempt to retain the collateral in full satisfaction of the debt or may sell, lease, or otherwise dispose of the collateral in any commercially reasonable manner [UCC 9–602(7), 9–603, 9–610(a), and 9–620]. Any sale is always subject to procedures established by state law.

8. See James J. White and Robert S. Summers, *Uniform Commercial Code,* 4th ed. (St. Paul: West Publishing Co., 1995), pp. 908–909.

Retention of Collateral by the Secured Party. The UCC acknowledges that parties are sometimes better off if they do not sell the collateral. Therefore, a secured party may retain the collateral unless it consists of consumer goods subject to a PMSI and the debtor has paid 60 percent or more of the purchase price or debt—as will be discussed shortly [UCC 9–620(e)].

This general right, however, is subject to several conditions. The secured party must send notice of the proposal to the debtor if the debtor has not signed a statement renouncing or modifying her or his rights *after default* [UCC 9–620(a) and 9–621]. If the collateral is consumer goods, the secured party does not need to give any other notice. In all other situations, the secured party must also send notice to any other secured party from whom the secured party has received written or authenticated notice of a claim of interest in the collateral in question and any other junior lien claimant (one holding a lien that is subordinate to a prior lien) who has filed a statutory lien (such as a mechanic's lien—see Chapter 29) or a security interest in the collateral ten days before the debtor consented to the retention [UCC 9–621].

If, within twenty days after the notice is sent, the secured party receives an objection sent by a person entitled to receive notification, the secured party must sell or otherwise dispose of the collateral in accordance with the provisions of UCC 9–602, 9–603, 9–610, and 9–613 (disposition procedures will be discussed shortly). If no such written objection is forthcoming, the secured party may retain the collateral in full or partial satisfaction of the debtor's obligation [UCC 9–620(a) and 9–621].

Consumer Goods. When the collateral is consumer goods with a PMSI and the debtor has paid 60 percent or more of the debt or the purchase price, the secured party must sell or otherwise dispose of the repossessed collateral within ninety days [UCC 9–620(e) and (f)]. Failure to comply opens the secured party to an action for conversion or other liability under UCC 9–625(b) and (c) unless the consumer-debtor signed a written statement *after default* renouncing or modifying the right to demand the sale of the goods [UCC 9–624].

Disposition Procedures. A secured party who does not choose to retain the collateral or who is required to sell it must resort to the disposition procedures prescribed under UCC 9–602(7), 9–603, 9–610(a), and 9–613. The UCC allows a great deal of flexibility with regard to disposition. UCC 9–610(a) states that after default, a secured party may sell, lease, license, or otherwise dispose of any or all of the collateral in its present condition or following any commercially reasonable preparation or processing. While the secured party may purchase the collateral at a public sale, it may not do so at a private sale—unless the collateral is of a kind customarily sold on a recognized market or is the subject of standard price quotations [UCC 9–610(c)].

One of the major limitations with respect to the disposition of collateral is that it be accomplished in a commercially reasonable manner. UCC 9–610(b) states:

> Every aspect of a disposition of collateral, including the method, manner, time, place, and other terms, must be commercially reasonable. If commercially reasonable, a secured party may dispose of collateral by public or private proceedings, by one or more contracts, as a unit or in parcels, and at any time and place and on any terms.

Unless the collateral is perishable or will decline rapidly in value or is a type customarily sold on a recognized market, a secured party must send to the debtor and other identified persons "a reasonable authenticated notification of disposition" [UCC 9–611(b) and (c)]. The debtor may waive the right to receive this notice, but only after default [UCC 9–624(a)].

See Case 28.3 at the end of this chapter. To view the full, unedited case from Westlaw,® go to this text's Web site at http://wbl-cs.westbuslaw.com.

Proceeds from Disposition. Proceeds from the disposition of collateral after default on the underlying debt are distributed in the following order:

1. Expenses incurred by the secured party in repossessing, storing, and reselling the collateral.
2. Balance of the debt owed to the secured party.
3. Junior lienholders who have made written or authenticated demands.
4. Unless the collateral consists of accounts, payment intangibles, promissory notes, or chattel paper, any surplus goes to the debtor [UCC 9–608(a) and 9–615(a) and (e)].

Noncash Proceeds. Whenever the secured party receives noncash proceeds from the disposition of collateral after default, the secured party must make a value determination and apply this value in a commercially reasonable manner [UCC 9–608(a)(3) and 9–615(c)].

Deficiency Judgment. Often, after proper disposition of the collateral, the secured party has not collected all that the debtor still owes. Unless otherwise agreed, the debtor is liable for any deficiency, and the creditor can obtain a **deficiency judgment** from a court to collect the deficiency. Note, however, that if the underlying transaction was, for example, a sale of accounts or of chattel paper, the debtor is entitled to any surplus or is liable for any deficiency only if the security agreement so provides [UCC 9–615(d) and (e)].

Whenever the secured party fails to conduct a disposition in a commercially reasonable manner or to give proper notice, the deficiency of the debtor is reduced to the extent that such failure affected the price received at the disposition [UCC 9–626(a)(3)].

Redemption Rights. At any time before the secured party disposes of the collateral or enters into a contract for its disposition, or before the debtor's obligation has been discharged through the secured party's retention of the collateral, the debtor or any other secured party can exercise the right of *redemption* of the collateral. The debtor or other secured party can do this by tendering performance of all obligations secured by the collateral and by paying the expenses reasonably incurred by the secured party in retaking and maintaining the collateral [UCC 9–623].

TERMS AND CONCEPTS TO REVIEW

CHAPTER SUMMARY

Creating a Security Interest	1. Unless the creditor has possession of the collateral, there must be a written or authenticated security agreement signed or authenticated by the debtor describing the collateral subject to the security interest. 2. The secured party must give value to the debtor. 3. The debtor must have rights in the collateral—some ownership interest or right to obtain possession of the specified collateral.
Perfecting a Security Interest	1. *Perfection by filing*—The most common method of perfection is by filing a financing statement containing the names of the secured party and the debtor and indicating the collateral covered by the financing statement. a. Communication of the financing statement to the appropriate filing office, together with the correct filing fee, constitutes a filing. b. The financing statement must be filed under the name of the debtor; fictitious (trade) names normally are not accepted. c. The classification of collateral determines whether filing is necessary and where to file (see Exhibit 28–3).

Chapter Summary—Continued

Perfecting a Security Interest—continued	2. *Perfection without filing*— a. By transfer of collateral—The debtor can transfer possession of the collateral to the secured party. For example, a *pledge* is this type of transfer. b. By attachment, such as the attachment of a purchase-money security interest (PMSI) in consumer goods. If the secured party has a PMSI in consumer goods (goods bought or used by the debtor for personal, family, or household purposes), the secured party's security interest is perfected automatically. In all, thirteen types of security interests can be perfected by attachment.
The Scope of a Security Interest	A security agreement can cover the following types of property: 1. *Collateral in the present possession or control of the debtor.* 2. *Proceeds from a sale, exchange, or disposition of secured collateral.* 3. *After-acquired property*—A security agreement may provide that property acquired after the execution of the security agreement will also be secured by the agreement. This provision often accompanies security agreements covering a debtor's inventory. 4. *Future advances*—A security agreement may provide that any future advances made against a line of credit will be subject to the initial security interest in the same collateral.
Priority of Claims to a Debtor's Collateral	See Exhibit 28–5.
Rights and Duties of Debtors and Creditors	1. *Information request*—On request by any person, the filing officer must send a statement listing the file number, the date, and the hour of the filing of financing statements and other documents covering collateral of a particular debtor; a fee is charged. 2. *Release, assignment, and amendment*—A secured party may (a) release part or all of the collateral described in a filed financing statement, thus ending the creditor's security interest; (b) assign part or all of the security interest to another party; and (c) amend a filed financing statement. 3. *Confirmation or accounting request by debtor*—If a debtor believes that the unpaid debt amount or the listing of the collateral subject to the security interest is inaccurate, the debtor has the right to request a confirmation of his or her view of the unpaid debt or listing of collateral. The secured party must authenticate and send to the debtor an accounting within fourteen days after the request is received. Only one request without charge is permitted per six-month period. 4. *Termination statement*—When a debt is paid, the secured party generally must send a *termination statement* to the debtor or file such a statement with the filing officer to whom the original financing statement was given. Failure to comply results in the secured party's liability to the debtor for $500 plus any loss suffered by the debtor. a. If the financing statement covers consumer goods, the termination statement must be filed by the secured party within one month after the debt is paid, or if the debtor makes an authenticated demand, it must be filed within twenty days of the demand or one month after the debt is paid, whichever is earlier. b. In all other cases, the termination statement must be filed or furnished to the debtor within twenty days after an authenticated demand is made by the debtor.
Default	On the debtor's default, the secured party may do either of the following: 1. Take possession (peacefully or by court order) of the collateral covered by the security agreement and then pursue one of two alternatives: a. Retain the collateral (unless the secured party has a PMSI in consumer goods and the debtor has paid 60 percent or more of the selling price or loan), in which case the secured party must— (1) Give notice to the debtor if the debtor has not signed a statement renouncing or modifying his or her rights after default. With consumer goods, no other notice is necessary.

CHAPTER SUMMARY—CONTINUED

Default—continued	**(2)** Send notice to any other secured party who has given written or authenticated notice of a claim to the same collateral or who has filed a security interest or a statutory lien ten days before the debtor consented to the retention. If an objection is received from the debtor or any other secured party given notice within twenty days, the creditor must dispose of the collateral according to the requirements of UCC 9–602, 9–603, 9–610, and 9–613. Otherwise, the creditor may retain the collateral in full or partial satisfaction of the debt. **b.** Dispose of the collateral in accordance with the requirements of UCC 9–602(7), 9–603, 9–610(a), and 9–613, in which case the secured party must— **(1)** Dispose of (sell, lease, or license) the goods in a commercially reasonable manner. **(2)** Notify the debtor and (except in sales of consumer goods) other identified persons, including those who have given notice of claims to the collateral to be sold (unless the collateral is perishable or will decline rapidly in value). **(3)** Apply the proceeds in the following order: **(a)** Expenses incurred by the secured party in repossessing, storing, and reselling the collateral. **(b)** The balance of the debt owed to the secured party. **(c)** Junior lienholders who have made written or authenticated demands. **(d)** Surplus to the debtor (unless the collateral consists of accounts, payment intangibles, promissory notes, or chattel paper). **2.** Relinquish the security interest and proceed with any judicial remedy available, such as reducing the claim to judgment on the underlying debt, followed by execution and levy on the nonexempt assets of the debtor.

CASES FOR ANALYSIS

Westlaw. You can access the full text of each case presented below by going to the Westlaw cases on this text's Web site at http://wbl-cs.westbuslaw.com. Each Westlaw case includes the names of all plaintiffs and defendants, the dates on which the case was argued and decided, a brief summary of the issues and decisions in the case, headnotes classifying the specific issues in the case according to the West Key Number System, and the court's opinion. Concurring and dissenting opinions, if any, are included as well.

CASE 28.1 WRITTEN SECURITY AGREEMENT

IN RE CANTU

United States Bankruptcy Appellate Panel,[9]
Eighth Circuit, 1999.
238 Bankr. 796.

SCHERMER, Bankruptcy Judge.

* * * *

Background

Prior to filing his Chapter 7 bankruptcy petition, [Jesus Cantu] purchased a truck with financing provided through the [Hormel Employees] Credit Union's open-end loan program. Under that loan program, employees complete one general loan agreement and thereafter are eligible to draw funds on either an unsecured or secured basis. Any advances taken from the Credit Union under this general program are called "Sub-accounts." With respect to secured Sub-accounts, the loan agreement grants a security interest to the Credit Union in personal property but does not describe the property that is to serve as collateral. Instead, the loan agreement refers to a second document, called a funds advance voucher, and states that the collateral will be described on that document. When issued, the funds advance voucher lists the amount of the loan, the amount of monthly payments, the applicable interest rate, and a detailed description of the property that

9. A *bankruptcy appellate panel*, with the consent of the parties, hears appeals from final judgments, orders, and decrees of bankruptcy judges.

serves as collateral for the specific Sub-account loan. The borrower/debtor signs the loan agreement but is not required to sign the funds advance voucher.

In the instant case, the Debtor signed the loan agreement on July 7, 1997, and on the same date, the Credit Union issued the funds advance voucher, fully describing the collateral by make, model, year, and vehicle identification number. The loan agreement specifically referred to the funds advance voucher stating: *"with respect to my secured Sub-accounts, * * * I am giving you a security interest in certain other personal property * * * which property will be individually identified in separate funds advance vouchers which I will receive at the time of each advance made under any Sub-account."* [Emphasis added]. On July 7, 1997, the Credit Union also issued a check for the loan proceeds payable to the Debtor and to the automobile dealer from whom Debtor intended to purchase the described vehicle. The funds advance voucher contained the following recitation on behalf of the Debtor concerning that loan proceeds check:

> *by endorsing my loan check, * * * I give you a security interest in the property identified above to secure my obligations with regard to Sub-account noted above in accordance with the minimum payment and security agreement provision of the [loan agreement]. Your rights to the security are governed by that Agreement.* [Emphasis added].

The funds advance voucher also contains a critical statement providing that all terms of the funds advance voucher are incorporated into the loan agreement and are binding upon the Debtor with the same effect as if the terms were set forth in the loan agreement. As stated, however, the Debtor was not required to sign the funds advance voucher.

Because no single document contained the Debtor's signature, language granting a security interest, and a description of the collateral, [Michael Dietz, the Bankruptcy] Trustee asserted that the Credit Union's security interest did not attach and sought to recover the vehicle for the benefit of the estate * * * . The bankruptcy court [ruled in favor of the Credit Union. The Trustee appealed to the U.S. Bankruptcy Appellate Panel for the Eighth Circuit.]

* * * *

Discussion

Unless collateral is in the possession of a secured party, for a security interest to attach and be enforceable, there must be a signed security agreement containing a description of the collateral, value must be given, and the debtor must have rights in the collateral. In this matter, the Trustee disputes only whether there is a signed security agreement that contains a description of the collateral. The Trustee urges that no such agreement exists because the loan agreement, although signed, does not contain a description of the collateral, and the funds advance voucher, although containing a description of the collateral, is unsigned. The Trustee asserts that strict construction of the statute requires the Debtor to sign the very document that contains a description of the collateral * * * . The Credit Union, conversely, urges that its documents are integrated, with cross-references from one to another, and that under a composite document theory, all of the loan documents may be taken together * * * .

* * * In this matter, the grant of a security interest is unequivocal. It is clearly stated in the loan agreement and echoed in the funds advance voucher. Here, the question is not whether there is a grant of a security interest, but whether the signed security agreement contains a description of the collateral * * * . To answer this question, we must first determine what documents comprise the security agreement.

Under Minnesota's adoption of the Uniform Commercial Code,[10] "security agreement" is defined as "an agreement which creates or provides for security." An "agreement" is "the bargain of the parties in fact as found in their language or by implication from other circumstances including course of dealing or usage of trade or course of performance as provided in this chapter * * * ." In this case, both the language used by the parties and their course of conduct demonstrate that the funds advance voucher and the loan agreement together create the security agreement. The loan agreement grants the Credit Union a security interest in property and expressly states that such property will be described in a separate funds advance voucher. The funds advance voucher, when issued thereafter, contains a full description of the collateral and provides that its terms are made part of the loan agreement. By cross-reference, the description of the collateral in the funds advance voucher is made part and parcel of the loan agreement bearing the debtor's signature. Together, these documents constitute the security agreement and satisfy the signed-writing requirement of Minnesota Statutes [Section] 336.9-203(1)(a) [Minnesota's version of unrevised UCC 9–203(1)(a), which applied here].

The course of conduct of the parties and the purpose of the open-end loan program, also support the conclusion that the loan agreement and funds advance voucher are to be read together as comprising the security agreement. The loan program is designed to operate in such a way that an employee has to sign only one loan agreement, * * * and thereafter, the employee may request advances, whether as secured or unsecured Sub-accounts, in person or by telephone. Unless the documents are taken together, the open-end agreement cannot operate as intended. It is the purpose of the Uniform Commercial Code to promote and facilitate commercial transactions, to simplify, clarify, and

10. This case was decided before the effective date of the revised version of Article 9, but the result would likely have been the same under the revised version.

modernize the law governing commercial transactions, and to permit the continued expansion of commercial practices through custom, usage and agreement of the parties. To deny enforcement of the security interest in this case would elevate form over substance and negate the underlying principles of the code.

* * * *

The drafters of the Uniform Commercial Code required a signed-writing describing the collateral pledged before a security interest could attach in order to address the very concerns raised by the Trustee. A signed-writing prevents disputes over precisely which items of property are covered by a security interest. A signed-writing, thus serves as a statute of frauds to prevent enforcement of claims based on wholly oral representations. * * * [T]he principal function of a description of the collateral in a security agreement is to enable the parties themselves * * * to identify it * * * .

In light of these purposes, and the flexible definition of "security agreement" which includes documents that are incorporated into one another, or clarify one another, where there is no question about the understanding of the parties, the court finds no reason to insist that the description of collateral must appear on the very same document which bears the debtor's signature. Provided a writing or writings, regardless of label, * * * adequately describes the collateral, carries the signature of the debtor, and establishes that in fact a security interest was agreed upon * * * the formal requirements of [Minn. Stat. Section 336.9-203(1)(a)] and the policies behind it are satisfied.

In this case, there is no question that the parties demonstrated in writing their purpose to create a security interest in the specified vehicle. We therefore conclude that the bankruptcy court did not err in holding that this transaction satisfied the requirements of Minn. Stat. [Section] 336.9-203(1)(a). The Credit Union was properly entitled to summary judgment.

Accordingly, the order of the bankruptcy court is affirmed.

CASE 28.2 RETENTION OF COLLATERAL

BANKS BROTHERS CORP. V. DONOVAN FLOORS, INC.

Wisconsin Court of Appeals, 2000.
200 WI App 253,
239 Wis.2d 381,
620 N.W.2d 631.

FINE, J. [Judge]

* * * *

I.

This case involves the interrelationship between a debt, collateral, and provisions of Wisconsin's version of Article 9 of the Uniform Commercial Code, specifically Wisconsin Statutes[Sections] 409.505(2) and 409.501(3) [unrevised UCC 9–505(2) and 9–501(3)].[11]

In 1990, Donovan Floors [Inc.] and Breakfall [Inc.], two companies controlled by [James and Jo-Ann Donovan], owed Bank One, Milwaukee, NA, some $245,000. * * * [T]he Donovans had * * * given to Bank One a mortgage on their house to secure the debt. Additionally, the companies gave to Bank One security interests in their property, also as security for the debt. * * *

Donovan Floors and Breakfall defaulted on the debt * * * . In late 1991, after the defaults, Bank One sued * * * the companies to recover on the collateral and the Donovans to foreclose on the mortgage. Subsequently, in early 1992, the case was settled when Bank One and the Donovans, Donovan Floors, and Breakfall stipulated to the entry of a judgment foreclosing on the Donovans' home and replevin in connection with the property given to Bank One as security for the debt. Bank One agreed to give the Donovans a chance to revitalize their business, and, pursuant to that arrangement, Bank One, the Donovans, Donovan Floors, and Breakfall executed two forbearance agreements pursuant to which Bank One deferred its immediate enforcement of the judgment.

In early 1993, Bank One assigned the debt and the security to the predecessor of Banks Bros. Corporation. A month later, Banks, the Donovans, Donovan Floors, and Breakfall signed an agreement entitled: "Notice of Assignment of Judgment, Security Interest, and Mortgage, and Agreement for Surrender of Collateral and Other Property, and Reduction of Indebtedness." [Uppercasing and underlining omitted.] Under that "Notice of Assignment," the parties agreed, as material here, that:

> The Notice of Assignment "shall also constitute notice * * * that BANKS intends to retain possession of certain collateral pledged and surrendered by BREAKFALL and DONOVAN FLOORS, and satisfies the debt as to BREAKFALL only." [Uppercasing in original.]

As consideration for the surrender of the property, the debt, which then stood at some $267,000, was to be "reduced by the sum of $25,000." In return for an additional $25,000 reduction of the debt owed by James Donovan and

11. This case was decided before the effective date of the revised version of Article 9, but the result would likely have been the same under the revised version.

Donovan Floors, Donovan Floors surrendered to Banks three cars, one van, and one truck. * * * Banks agreed to extend the Forbearance Agreement conditioned on its receipt of certain specified payments according to a payment schedule set out in the Notice of Assignment. The parties to the Notice of Assignment had a falling out, and Banks never received any money under the payment schedule. Ultimately, after some six years of strained relationships between Banks and the Donovans, Banks scheduled a sheriff's sale of the Donovans' home. The Donovans and their companies [filed a suit in a Wisconsin state court against Banks. The court ruled against the plaintiffs, who then appealed to a state intermediate appellate court.]

II.

* * * [T]he Donovans and their companies * * * contend * * * that "[t]he Foreclosure Judgment was completely satisfied when Banks Bros. retained the Personal Property." They argue that the satisfaction of the Breakfall debt that was memorialized in the Notice of Assignment operates, by virtue of Wis. Stat. [Section] 409.505(2), also as a satisfaction of the debt as to both Donovan Floors and the Donovans. Whether they are correct turns on an analysis of [Section] 409.505(2) and Wis. Stat. [Section] 409.501(3).

* * * *

Wis. Stat. [Section] 409.505(2) provides, as material to this appeal:

> [A] secured party in possession may, after default, propose to retain the collateral in satisfaction of the obligation. Written notice of such proposal shall be sent to the debtor if the debtor has not signed after default a statement renouncing or modifying the debtor's rights under this subsection * * * . If the debtor * * * objects in writing within 21 days from the receipt of the notification * * * the secured party must dispose of the collateral under [Section] 409.504. In the absence of such written objection the secured party may retain the collateral in satisfaction of the debtor's obligation.

* * * Acknowledging that they signed the Notice of Assignment, and thus agreed that the debt would be satisfied as to Breakfall only, the Donovans and Donovan Floors contend that their agreement is forbidden by Wis. Stat. [Section] 409.501(3), which as material here, provides:

> To the extent that they give rights to the debtor and impose duties on the secured party, the rules stated in the sections and subsections referred to in pars. (a) to (e) may not be waived or varied * * * but the parties may by agreement determine the standards by which the fulfillment of these rights and duties is to be measured if such standards are not manifestly unreasonable:
> * * *
> (c) Section 409.505(2) which deals with acceptance of collateral as discharge of obligation * * * .

Banks, on the other hand, argues that Wis. Stat. [Section] 409.505(2) *itself* gives to the creditor and debtor the authority to modify the rights fixed by that subsection, when it provides: "[A] secured party in possession may, after default, propose to retain the collateral in satisfaction of the obligation. Written notice of such proposal shall be sent to the debtor *if the debtor has not signed after default a statement renouncing or modifying the debtor's rights under this subsection*" [emphasis added].

Banks's syllogism is this: Wis. Stat. [Section] 409.505(2) permits the secured creditor to "propose to retain the collateral in satisfaction of the obligation," and, if the secured creditor seeks to do that, the secured creditor must send to the debtor "[w]ritten notice of such proposal." In such a case, the debt would be satisfied in full. Section 409.505(2), however, gives to the debtor the power to [renounce or modify] the rights that the debtor has under the subsection, so long as the agreement "renouncing or modifying" those rights is "signed" by the debtor "after default" on the debt. Thus, Banks argues, although the Notice of Assignment was described as a notice under [Section] 409.505(2), it was *also* a contemporaneous agreement (or, to use the terminology of [Section] 409.505(2), a "statement"), executed after default, between Banks, Donovan Floors, and the Donovans by which the Donovans and Donovan Floors renounced and modified their right under [Section] 409.505(2) to complete satisfaction of the debt, and by which they agreed that the satisfaction of the debt would run to Breakfall only. * * *

Somewhat surprisingly, there are no cases directly on point—that is, dealing with a situation where, as here, a secured creditor has satisfied a debt as to some but not all debtors, and where, after default, all the debtors agreed to that arrangement in a statement signed by them. Wis. Stat. [Section] 409.505(2), however, clearly grants to debtors the right to renounce or modify the normal *quid pro quo* for what is, in essence, strict foreclosure under [Section] 409.505(2): full satisfaction of the debt. * * * All judges appear to agree that if the debtor has expressly agreed after default that the secured creditor may take the collateral at an agreed valuation in *partial* satisfaction of the debt, the secured creditor may still recover the balance owing. This would be a "modification" permissible under 9–505(2), second sentence. But in the absence of such a modifying agreement, some courts appear to hold that the case automatically falls in 9–505(2) as a full strict foreclosure bars any further recovery by the secured creditor. Stated another way, in return for the relatively inexpensive and expeditious application of the secured property to the debt, the secured creditor forgoes the right to chase the debtor for any deficiency. After default on the debt, however, debtors may renounce that *quid pro quo* for something more valuable—time within which to reorganize a business with the hope of saving it. That is what was done here.

Understandably, the Donovans and Donovan Floors would love to have their cake (the chance to save their business given to them by Banks's agreement to hold off on its right to claim the assets pledged for the debt) and eat it also (keep those assets). But that is not the way Wis. Stat. [Section] 409.505(2) works. Banks had a right under that section to immediate strict foreclosure of all the pledged assets. It gave up that right in consideration for a partial payment on the debt and the concomitant partial satisfaction. The Donovans and Donovan Floors have no legal or moral ground to complain; they agreed to that arrangement, and did so in a statement signed after default. This makes the arrangement legal under [Section] 409.505(2).

Order affirmed.

CASE 28.3 NOTICE TO THE DEBTOR

FIELDER V. CREDIT ACCEPTANCE CORP.

United States District Court,
Western District of Missouri, 1998.
19 F.Supp.2d 966.

SMITH, District Judge.

* * * *

II. STATEMENT OF UNCONTROVERTED FACTS

* * * *

1. Defendant CAC is engaged in the business of financing, administering, servicing and collecting retail installments used in the purchase and sale of used automobiles.
2. Plaintiffs Marvin Fielder and Deborah Williams entered into an installment contract for the purchase of a vehicle from * * * Northeast Auto Credit, Inc., which contract contained a charge of $43.50 denominated as "Filing fees" and as "Other Charges" "To Public Officials."

* * * *

4. Plaintiffs Jerome Henderson and Lucy Henderson entered into an installment contract for the purchase of a vehicle from Charles Brock Oldsmobile.
5. The * * * installment contracts were assigned by the selling dealers to CAC.

* * * *

9. CAC supplied the above-mentioned installment sale contract forms to the selling dealers.
10. CAC took possession of a vehicle purchased by Plaintiffs Fielder and Williams, sold it and sued Plaintiffs Fielder and Williams on the installment contract for a deficiency.

* * * *

13. CAC filed suit [in a Missouri state court] against Plaintiffs Fielder and Williams and the Petition requested $4,177.42, including $88.72 in interest which was added to the balance of $4,088.70.

* * * *

15. In December of 1996, CAC filed an action for judgment in [a Missouri state court] against Jerome and Lucy Henderson requesting a judgment on the retail installment contract with interest in the amount of 18%.
16. CAC filed suit against Plaintiffs Jerome and Lucy Henderson and the Petition requested $4,354.71 including $394.50 in interest which was added to the balance of $3,960.21.
17. CAC obtained a default judgment against Plaintiffs Jerome and Lucy Henderson which included a provision for interest at 18%.

* * * *

19. CAC sent certain pre-sale notices to Plaintiffs Fielder, Williams, and the Hendersons.

* * * *

22. The balance stated in the Fielder/Williams and the Henderson pre-sale notice included unrebated charges.
23. * * * CAC did not sell the debtors' repossessed vehicles until some time after the sale date set by the pre-sale notice.

* * * *

[Fielder and others filed a suit in a federal district court against CAC and others.]

* * * *

III. DISCUSSION

* * * *

Plaintiffs claim CAC violated the Missouri UCC provisions for pre-sale notices and for redemption rights.[12] Plaintiffs claim the pre-sale notices violate the UCC by * * * falsely overstating the payment required to redeem the vehicles; * * * by making false and misleading statements about the date by which payment was required for redemption; and * * * by giving inadequate notice prior to the date of sale. Plaintiffs allege the violations of [Missouri Revised Statutes Sections] 400.9-504 and 400.9-506 [Missouri's version of unrevised UCC 9–504 and 9–506] give rise to the remedies in [Mo.Rev.Stat. Section] 400.9-507 [unrevised UCC 9–507]. CAC claims the pre-sale notices it sent to its debtors satisfy the "reasonable notification" requirement of Mo.Rev.Stat. [Section] 400.9-504(3).

Section 400.9-504(3) provides that:

> Disposition of the collateral may be by public or private proceedings and may be made by way of one or more contracts. Sale or other disposition may be as a

12. This case was decided before the effective date of the revised version of Article 9, but the result would likely have been the same. See UCC 9–613.

unit or in parcels and at any time and place and on any terms but every aspect of the disposition including the method, manner, time, place and terms must be commercially reasonable. Unless collateral is perishable or threatens to decline speedily in value or is of a type customarily sold on a recognized market, reasonable notification of the time and place of any public sale or reasonable notification of the time after which any private sale or other intended disposition is to be made shall be sent by the secured party to the debtor. If he has not signed after default a statement renouncing or modifying his right to notification of sale, but no such statement shall be effective in the case of consumer goods. [sic] In the case of consumer goods, no other notification need be sent. In other cases, notification shall be sent to any other secured party from whom the secured party has received (before sending his notification to the debtor) written notice of a claim of an interest in the collateral. The secured party may buy at any public sale and if the collateral is of a type customarily sold in a recognized market or is of a type which is the subject of widely distributed standard price quotations he may buy at a private sale.

Compliance with the notice provision of [Section] 400.9-504(3) is a prerequisite to recovery of a deficiency after resale of the collateral. *Any doubt as to what constitutes strict compliance with the notice requirement is resolved in favor of the debtor.* [Emphasis added.]

Under [Section] 400.9-506 a debtor has the right to redeem the collateral by tendering fulfillment of all the obligations secured by the collateral. Plaintiffs argue that CAC's pre-sale notices overstate the amount needed to redeem the collateral because the amount stated in the notices contain[s] unrebated and unearned finance charges. * * *

* * * [S]ome of the notices are deficient because the balance figures are overstated and the notices do not discuss redemption or unrebated charges at all. This issue also appears to be one of first impression in Missouri. Plaintiffs argue this Court should * * * [find] that insertion of an inflated redemption figure misled the debtors and violated the notice requirement. This Court accepts the premise * * * that the notice of resale may not contain such misleading information even if the other basic information required by the statute is included. The Court finds that some of the notices in this case violated the statute because CAC's figures were not only incorrect but were unreasonably misleading as to the principal debt and the notices did not inform the debtors that the stated balance might be inaccurate. Plaintiffs provided * * * sample notices that contain presumably unrebated figures with no reference in the notice that the redemption figures were inaccurate. Therefore, the debtors did not have reasonable notification of the sale because such notice is designed to ensure the debtors are aware of their rights which include redemption. Plaintiffs are granted summary judgment for those notices that contain inflated figures and no reference to the unrebated balance * * * .

* * * *

Lastly, Plaintiffs claim that the pre-sale notices suffer from a host of other defects. Some of the notices contained dates of sale that were prior to the actual date of the notice. One notice was blank as to any date of sale. Another notice shows that payment to redeem must be made three days before the scheduled sale and yet others provide less notice than provided for in the contracts. All of these pre-sale notices violate [Section] 400.9-504 and Plaintiffs' motion for summary judgment is granted. Plaintiffs are entitled to recover any loss caused by the failure to comply or "in any event an amount not less then the credit service charge plus ten percent of the principal amount of the debt or the time price differential plus ten percent of the cash price" [under Section 400.9-507(1)].

* * * *

IV. CONCLUSION

For the foregoing reasons Plaintiffs are granted * * * summary judgment * * * .

IT IS SO ORDERED.

CASE PROBLEMS

28–1. In 1969, Jones and Percell executed a promissory note and a security agreement covering a converted military aircraft built in the 1950s. On their default, the Bank of Nevada repossessed the aircraft. After providing the required notice to Jones and Percell, the bank placed advertisements in several trade journals, as well as in major newspapers in several large cities. In addition, the bank sent 2,000 brochures to 240 sales organizations. A sales representative was hired to market the aircraft. The plane was later sold for $71,000 to an aircraft broker, who in turn resold it for $123,000 after spending $33,000 on modifications. Because the price obtained on the sale of the plane was about $75,000 less than the amount Jones and Percell owed the bank, the bank initiated a lawsuit to obtain the amount of the deficiency. Can Jones and Percell object to the bank's manner of resale? Why, or why not? [*Jones v. Bank of Nevada,* 91 Nev. 368, 535 P.2d 1279 (1975)]

28–2. Calcote obtained an automobile loan from Citizens & Southern National Bank, with the bank maintaining a security interest in the car. On March 28, 1984, after Calcote had defaulted on the loan, the bank repossessed the vehicle. On the following day, the bank sent a certified letter, return receipt requested, to Calcote informing her of the repossession, of the bank's plans to sell the auto at a private sale in May 1984, and of her right to demand a public sale of the vehicle. Although the letter was sent to the address on the bank's records and at which the bank had repossessed the car, Calcote never received the letter. On April 19, 1984, it was returned to the bank stamped "unclaimed." On May 11, 1984, the car was sold at a private sale to which over 150 dealers had been invited. When Calcote learned that the car had been sold, she brought an action against the bank, claiming that she had not been properly notified of the repossession and sale and that the private sale was not a commercially reasonable method of disposition. Was sufficient notice given to Calcote, and was the private sale commercially reasonable? [*Calcote v. Citizens & Southern National Bank,* 179 Ga.App. 132, 345 S.E.2d 616 (1986)]

28–3. Barbara Wiegert and her daughter, Darcie Wiegert, went shopping at Sears, and Darcie bought a mattress and box spring for $396.11. Barbara later purchased from Sears a television set for $239.96. Both purchases of consumer goods were charged to the credit card of Barbara (and her husband, Harold). On both credit slips was printed the following statement: "I grant Sears a security interest or lien in this merchandise, unless prohibited by law, until paid in full." When the Wiegerts filed their bankruptcy petition, the balance due to Sears was $587.26, plus interest. The Wiegerts claimed that Sears was an unsecured creditor. Sears claimed that it was a secured creditor, arguing that the sales slip contained all of the information needed for a valid security agreement under UCC 9–203: (1) a description of the goods, (2) the signature of the debtor, and (3) language indicating that the debtor was granting Sears a security interest in the goods being purchased on credit. Sears further argued that it did not need to file a financing statement to perfect its security interest because UCC 9–302(1)(d) allows for automatic perfection for a purchase-money security interest in consumer goods. Was Sears correct in making these claims? Discuss fully. [*In the Matter of Wiegert,* 145 Bankr. 621 (D.Neb. 1991)]

28–4. Richard E. Walker, Kelly E. Walker, and Kenneth W. Walker were partners in the Walker Brothers Dairy, a general partnership located in Florida. The Walkers purchased a "Model 2955 utility tractor, a round bale saw, and a feed mixer box" from the John Deere Company. John Deere took a security interest in the equipment. The security agreement stated that the debtor was a partnership known as "Walker Brothers Dairy." John Deere filed a financing statement, however, that listed the debtors as "Richard Walker, Kelly Walker, and Kenneth Wendell Walker." The statement was signed by each of the three partners. Their signatures were followed by a typewritten declaration indicating that the partners were doing business as "Walker Brothers Dairy." When Walker Brothers Dairy voluntarily filed for bankruptcy, John Deere sought to repossess the equipment. The issue before the court was whether the financing statement, which listed the partners as debtors rather than the partnership, was sufficient to perfect John Deere's security interest in the partnership equipment. What should the court decide? Discuss. [*In re Walker,* 142 Bankr. 482 (M.D.Fla. 1992)]

28–5. In 1977, the Marcuses sold their drugstore business to Mistura, Inc. Mistura made a down payment on the purchase price, and the Marcuses took a security interest in the fixtures and personal property of the business for the unpaid portion of the debt. Arizona law requires that financing statements relating to security interests in personal property be filed with the secretary of state. Because the Marcuses had filed their statement with the Maricopa County Recorder, only their security interest in the fixtures was properly perfected. Mistura later obtained a loan from McKesson, using the same property secured by the Marcuse transaction as collateral. McKesson properly perfected a security interest in this same collateral by filing with the secretary of state. McKesson had actual knowledge at the time of the loan that the Marcuses had not properly perfected their security interest in the personal property of Mistura's business. A few days after McKesson's filing, the Marcuses filed a financing statement with the secretary of state. Which party had a superior security interest in the collateral, McKesson or the Marcuses? Explain. [*In re Mistura, Inc.,* 705 F.2d 1496 (9th Cir. 1983)]

28–6. In July 1978, Dr. Jose B. Namer executed to Citizens & Southern National Bank a note in the amount of $35,000 with an accompanying security agreement covering the following property: "All equipment of the debtor of every description used or useful in the conduct of the debtor's business, now or hereafter existing or acquired. . . . The listed assets held for collateral are presently located at 4385 Hugh Howell Rd, Tucker, Ga." In July 1980, Dr. Namer moved some of his equipment to a new office owned by Hudson Properties, Inc., in Fairburn, Georgia. To finance this move, Dr. Namer procured a loan from a Fairburn bank, and Hudson cosigned the note. The Fairburn bank prepared a security agreement covering the same equipment as the 1978 security agreement. In September 1980, Dr. Namer defaulted on the first note and absconded with the equipment from the Fairburn office. Hudson received an insurance payment as cash proceeds for the missing equipment. Citizens & Southern National Bank claimed priority rights to the missing equipment or the insurance proceeds even though the equipment had been moved to Fairburn. Did Citizens & Southern National Bank recover this insurance money from Hudson? [*Hudson Properties, Inc. v. Citizens & Southern National Bank,* 168 Ga.App. 331, 308 S.E.2d 708 (1983)]

28–7. The First National Bank of North Dakota loaned Freddie Mutschler, a prominent farmer in Jamestown, North Dakota, $3 million. Mutschler gave the bank a lien on his crops as partial security for the loan. The loan agreement provided that when Mutschler sold his grain, he would be obligated to turn over the proceeds to cover his indebtedness. Mutschler was also the owner, but not the manager, of the Jamestown Farmers Elevator, which bought and sold grain from various farmers. In the fall of 1982, Mutschler sold his crop to the Jamestown Farmers Elevator but did not apply the proceeds to the debt at the bank. The elevator, in turn, sold some of the grain to the Pillsbury Co., which knew of the bank's security interest but was unaware of the terms of the security agreement. The bank did not discover these events until Mutschler and the Jamestown Farmers Elevator filed for bankruptcy in early 1983. The bank sued Pillsbury for conversion of the collateral. Which party prevailed? [*First Bank of North Dakota v. Pillsbury Co.*, 801 F.2d 1036 (8th Cir. 1986)]

28–8. John and Melody Fish bought various pieces of expensive jewelry, including a diamond ring, a diamond necklace, and a wedding band, from Odom's Jewelers. The Fishes agreed to make monthly installment payments to Odom's until the purchase price was paid in full. In 1988, the Fishes fell behind in their monthly payments on the account. The Fishes and Odom's orally agreed that the Fishes would return the jewelry to Odom's and that Odom's would hold the items for the Fishes until the account was paid. In 1991, the Fishes filed for bankruptcy protection. The jewelry was still in the possession of Odom's. One of the issues before the bankruptcy court was whether Odom's had a security interest in the jewelry. Did it? Explain. [*In re Fish,* 128 Bankr. 468 (N.D.Okla. 1991)]

28–9. James Koontz bought a car and financed the purchase with a loan from Chrysler Credit Corporation. When Koontz failed to repay the loan, Chrysler sent M&M Agency to take possession of the vehicle. M&M entered Koontz's yard, where the vehicle was parked in the light of the front porch, to repossess the vehicle. While the repossession was in progress, Koontz, who was in his underwear, rushed outside and shouted, "Don't take it!" The repossessor did not respond and proceeded to remove the vehicle. Chrysler sold the car and then filed a suit in an Illinois state court against Koontz to recover the difference between the purchase price and the amount that Koontz owed on the loan. Koontz argued that Chrysler's repossession of the car over his oral protest was a breach of the peace. The court entered a judgment in favor of Chrysler, and Koontz appealed. What should the appellate court decide? Discuss. [*Chrysler Credit Corp. v. Koontz,* 277 Ill.App.3d 1078, 661 N.E.2d 1171, 214 Ill.Dec. 726 (1996)]

28–10. To pay for the purchases of several aircraft, Robert Wall borrowed funds from the Cessna Finance Corp., using the aircraft as collateral. Wall defaulted on the loans. Cessna took possession of the collateral (the aircraft) and sold it. Cessna filed a suit in a federal district court against Wall for the difference between the amount due on the loans and the amount received from the sale of the aircraft. Wall claimed that he could have obtained a higher price for the aircraft if he had sold them himself. How does the question of whether a better price could have been obtained affect the issue of whether the sale was commercially reasonable? Discuss. [*Cessna Finance Corp. v. Wall,* 876 F.Supp. 273 (M.D.Ga. 1994)]

28–11. Cambria Fuel Oil Co. sold its business to 306 Fuel Oil Corp. As part of the deal, Cambria Fuel took a security interest in 306 Fuel's assets and filed a financing statement that identified 306 Fuel as the debtor. Six weeks later, 306 Fuel changed its name to Cambria Petroleum Co. Cambria Fuel did not file a new financing statement. Fleet Factors Corp. loaned money to Cambria Petroleum and took a security interest in the same assets as those subject to Cambria Fuel's security interest. When Cambria Petroleum failed to repay the loan, Fleet Factors filed a suit in a New York state court to foreclose its security interest. Cambria Fuel claimed that its interest had priority. Whose security interest has priority? Why? [*Fleet Factors Corp. v. Bandolene Industries Corp.,* 86 N.Y.2d 519, 658 N.E.2d 202, 634 N.Y.S.2d 425 (1995)]

28–12. Leroy Headspeth bought a car under an installment sales contract that expressly permitted the creditor to repossess the car if the debtor defaulted on the payments. The seller assigned the contract to Mercedes-Benz Credit Corp. (MBCC). When Headspeth defaulted on the payments, an agent of Laurel Adjustment Bureau, Inc. (LAB), went onto Headspeth's property and repossessed the car on MBCC's behalf. Headspeth filed a suit against MBCC and LAB, contending in part that LAB trespassed onto his property to retake the car and that therefore the repossession was wrongful. Headspeth admitted that the repossession occurred without confrontation. Can a secured creditor legally retake possession of collateral, on the debtor's default, by entering onto the debtor's land, or would that be an illegal breach of the peace? How will the court rule? Explain. [*Headspeth v. Mercedes-Benz Credit Corp.,* 709 A.2d 717 (D.C.App. 1998)]

28–13. In 1994, SouthTrust Bank, N.A., loaned money to Environmental Aspecs, Inc. (EAI), and its subsidiary, EAI of NC. SouthTrust perfected its security interest by filing financing statements that listed only EAI as the debtor, described only EAI's assets as collateral, and was signed only on EAI's behalf. SouthTrust believed that both companies were operating as a single business represented by EAI. In 1996, EAI of NC borrowed almost $300,000 from Advanced Analytics Laboratories, Inc. (AAL). AAL filed financing statements that listed the assets of EAI of NC as collateral but identified the debtor as EAI. The statements referred, however, to attached copies of the security agreements, which were signed by the president of EAI of NC and identified the debtor as EAI of NC. One year later, EAI and EAI of NC renegotiated their loan with SouthTrust, and the bank filed financing statements listing both companies as debtors. In 1998, EAI and EAI of NC filed for bankruptcy. One of the issues was the priority of the security interests of SouthTrust and AAL. AAL contended that its failure to identify, on its financing statements, EAI of NC as the debtor did not give SouthTrust priority. Is AAL correct? Why, or why not? [*In re Environmental Aspecs, Inc.*, 235 Bankr. 378 (E.D.N.C., Raleigh Div. 1999)]

28–14. When a customer opens a credit-card account with Sears, Roebuck & Co., the customer fills out an application and sends it to Sears for review; if the application is approved, the customer receives a Sears card. The application contains a security agreement, a copy of which is also sent with the card. When a customer buys an item using the card, the customer signs a sales receipt that describes the merchandise and contains language granting Sears a purchase-money security interest (PMSI) in the merchandise. Dayna Conry bought a variety of consumer goods from Sears on her card. When she did not make payments on her account, Sears filed a suit against her in an Illinois state court to repossess the goods. Conry filed for bankruptcy and was granted a discharge. Sears then filed a suit against her to obtain possession of the goods through its PMSI, but it could not find Conry's credit-card application to offer into evidence. Is a signed Sears sales receipt sufficient proof of its security interest? In whose favor should the court rule? Explain. [*Sears, Roebuck & Co. v. Conry*, 321 Ill.App.3d 997, 748 N.E.2d 1248, 255 Ill.Dec. 178 (3 Dist. 2001)]

28–15. A QUESTION OF ETHICS

Raymond and Joan Massengill borrowed money from Indiana National Bank (INB) to purchase a van. Toward the end of the loan period, the Massengills were notified by mail that they were delinquent on their last two loan payments. Joan called INB and said that she and her husband would go to the bank the following Monday morning and take care of the matter. In the meantime, INB had made arrangements for the van to be repossessed. At 1:30 A.M. Sunday morning, two men appeared at the Massengills' driveway and began to hook up the van to a tow truck. Raymond, assuming that the van was being stolen, went outside to intervene and did so vociferously. During the course of events, Massengill became entangled in machinery at the rear of the tow truck and was dragged down the street and then run over by his towed van. The "repo men"—those hired by INB to repossess the van—knew of Massengill's plight but sped away. The trial court granted summary judgment for the bank, ruling that the bank was not liable for the injuries caused by the repossession company. On appeal, however, the court ruled that the bank could be liable for the acts of the repossession company and remanded the case for the determination of damages. [Massengill v. Indiana National Bank, *550 N.E.2d 97 (Ind.App. 1st Dist. 1990)*]

1. Frequently, courts must decide, as in this case, whether the secured party should be held liable for the wrongful acts of persons hired as independent contractors by the secured party to undertake an actual repossession effort. Is it fair to hold the secured party liable for acts that the creditor did not commit? Why, or why not?
2. Given the potential for violence during repossession efforts, why do you think Article 9 permits secured parties to resort to "self-help" repossessions?
3. Should repossession companies be prohibited from taking collateral from debtors' property during the middle of the night, when debtors are more likely to conclude that the activity is wrongful?

E-LINKS

For updated links to resources available on the Web, as well as a variety of other materials, visit this text's Web site at

http://wbl-cs.westbuslaw.com

The National Conference of Commissioners on Uniform State Laws, in association with the University of Pennsylvania Law School, now offers an official site for UCC articles. To keep abreast of changes in the UCC, including the recent revision of Article 9, go to

http://www.law.upenn.edu/bll/ulc/ulc.htm

The Web site of Cornell University's Legal Information Institute offers an overview and menu of sources on legal materials relating to secured transactions at

http://www.law.cornell.edu/topics/secured_transactions.html

LEGAL RESEARCH EXERCISES ON THE WEB

Go to http://wbl-cs.westbuslaw.com, the Web site that accompanies this text. Select "Interactive Study Center," and then click on "Chapter 28." There you will find the following Internet research exercise that you can perform to learn more about repossession of collateral under Article 9:

Activity 28–1: Repossession

CHAPTER 29

Other Creditors' Remedies and Suretyship

NORMALLY, CREDITORS HAVE NO PROBLEM collecting the debts owed to them. When disputes arise over the amount owed, however, or when the debtor simply cannot or will not pay, what happens? What remedies are available to creditors when debtors default? We have already discussed, in Chapter 28, the remedies available to secured creditors under Article 9 of the Uniform Commercial Code (UCC). In this chapter, we focus on other laws that assist the debtor and creditor in resolving their disputes without the debtor's having to resort to bankruptcy (discussed in Chapter 30).

SECTION 1

Laws Assisting Creditors

Both the common law and statutory laws other than Article 9 of the UCC create various rights and remedies for creditors. We discuss here some of these rights and remedies, including liens, garnishment, creditors' composition agreements, mortgage foreclosure, and a debtor's assignment of assets for the benefit of creditors.

LIENS

A **lien** is a claim or charge on a debtor's property that must be satisfied before the property (or its proceeds) is available to satisfy the claims of other creditors. As mentioned, liens may arise under the common law or under statutory law. Statutory liens include *mechanic's liens*. Liens created at common law include *artisan's liens* and *innkeeper's liens*. *Judicial liens* include those that represent a creditor's efforts to collect on a debt before or after a judgment is entered by a court.

Generally, a lien creditor has priority over an unperfected secured party but not over a perfected secured party. Thus, a person who becomes a lien creditor before another security interest in the same property is perfected has priority, but one who acquires the lien after perfection does not have priority. Mechanic's and artisan's liens, however, have priority over perfected security interests unless a statute provides otherwise.

Mechanic's Lien. When a person contracts for labor, services, or material to be furnished for the purpose of making improvements on real property but does not immediately pay for the improvements, the creditor can place a **mechanic's lien** on the property. This creates a special type of debtor-creditor relationship in which the real estate itself becomes security for the debt.

For example, a painter agrees to paint a house for a homeowner for an agreed-on price to cover labor and materials. If the homeowner cannot pay or pays only a portion of the charges, a mechanic's lien against the property can be created. The painter is the lienholder, and the real property is encumbered with a mechanic's lien for the amount owed. If the homeowner does not pay the lien, the property can be sold to satisfy the debt. Notice of the *foreclosure* (the enforcement of the lien) must be given to the debtor in advance, however.

The procedures by which a mechanic's lien is created are controlled by state law. Generally, the lienholder must file a written notice of lien against the particular property involved. The notice of lien must be filed within a specific time period, measured from the last date on which materials or labor were provided (usually within 60 to 120 days). Failure to pay the debt entitles the lienholder to foreclose on the real estate on which the improvements were made and to sell it to satisfy the amount of the debt. Of course, as mentioned, the lienholder is required by statute to give notice to the owner of the property prior to foreclosure and sale. The sale proceeds are used to pay the debt and the costs of the legal proceedings; the surplus, if any, is paid to the former owner.

Westlaw. See Case 29.1 at the end of this chapter. To view the full, unedited case from Westlaw,® go to this text's Web site at **http://wbl-cs.westbuslaw.com**.

Artisan's Lien. An **artisan's lien** is a security device created at common law through which a creditor can recover payment from a debtor for labor and materials furnished in the repair of personal property. For example, Whitney leaves her diamond ring at the jewelry shop to be repaired and to have her initials engraved on the band. In the absence of an agreement, the jeweler can keep the ring until Whitney pays for the services that the jeweler provides. Should Whitney fail to pay, the jeweler has a lien on Whitney's ring for the amount of the bill and can sell the ring in satisfaction of the lien.

In contrast to a mechanic's lien, an artisan's lien is *possessory.* The lienholder ordinarily must have retained possession of the property and have expressly or impliedly agreed to provide the services on a cash, not a credit, basis. The lien remains in existence as long as the lienholder maintains possession, and the lien is terminated once possession is voluntarily surrendered—unless the surrender is only temporary. With a temporary surrender, there must be an agreement that the property will be returned to the lienholder. Even with such an agreement, if a third party obtains rights in that property while it is out of the possession of the lienholder, the lien is lost.

Modern statutes permit the holder of an artisan's lien to foreclose and sell the property subject to the lien to satisfy payment of the debt. As with the mechanic's lien, the lienholder is required to give notice to the owner of the property prior to foreclosure and sale. In some states, holders of artisan's liens must give notice to title lienholders of automobiles prior to foreclosure. The sale proceeds are used to pay the debt and the costs of the legal proceedings, and the surplus, if any, is paid to the former owner. The artisan's lien has priority over a filed statutory lien (such as a title lien on an automobile or a lien filed under Article 9 of the UCC) as well as priority over a bailee's lien (such as a storage lien).

Innkeeper's Lien. An **innkeeper's lien** is another security device created at common law. An innkeeper's lien is placed on the baggage of guests for any agreed-on hotel charges that remain unpaid. If no express agreement has been made on the amount of those charges, the lien will be for the reasonable value of the accommodations furnished. The innkeeper's lien is terminated either by the guest's payment of the hotel charges or by the innkeeper's surrender of the baggage to the guest, unless the surrender is temporary. Most state statutes permit the innkeeper to satisfy the debt by means of a public sale of the guest's baggage. Some jurisdictions require that the guest first be given an impartial judicial hearing.[1]

Judicial Liens. A debt must be past due before a creditor can commence legal action against a debtor. Once legal action is brought, the debtor's property may be seized to satisfy the debt. If the property is seized prior to trial proceedings, the seizure is referred to as an *attachment* of the property. The seizure may also occur following a court judgment in the creditor's favor. In that case, the court's order to seize the property is referred to as a *writ of execution.*

Attachment. Under Article 9 of the UCC, as discussed in Chapter 28, *attachment* refers to the process through which a security interest becomes effective and enforceable against a debtor with respect to the debtor's collateral [UCC 9–203]. In the present context, **attachment** refers to a court-ordered seizure and taking into custody of property prior to the securing of a judgment for a past-due debt. Attachment rights are created by state statutes. Normally a *prejudgment* remedy, attachment occurs either at the time of or immediately after the commencement of a lawsuit and before the entry of a final judgment. By statute, the restrictions and requirements for a creditor to attach before judgment are specific and limited. The due process clause of the Fourteenth Amendment to the Constitution limits the courts' power to authorize seizure of a debtor's property without notice to the debtor or a hearing on

1. *Klim v. Jones,* 315 F.Supp. 109 (N.D.Cal. 1970).

the facts. In recent years, a number of state attachment laws have been held to be unconstitutional.

To use attachment as a remedy, the creditor must have an enforceable right to payment of the debt under law, and the creditor must follow certain procedures. Otherwise, the creditor can be liable for damages for wrongful attachment. He or she must file with the court an *affidavit* (a written or printed statement, made under oath or sworn to) stating that the debtor is in default and delineating the statutory grounds under which attachment is sought. A bond must be posted by the creditor to cover at least court costs, the value of the loss of use of the good suffered by the debtor, and the value of the property attached. When the court is satisfied that all the requirements have been met, it issues a **writ of attachment**, which is similar to a writ of execution (to be discussed shortly) in that it directs the sheriff or other public officer to seize nonexempt property. If the creditor prevails at trial, the seized property can be sold to satisfy the judgment.

Writ of Execution. If a creditor is successful in a legal action against a debtor, the court awards the creditor a judgment against the debtor (usually for the amount of the debt plus any interest and legal costs incurred in obtaining the judgment). Frequently, the creditor finds it easy to secure a judgment against the debtor but nevertheless fails to collect the awarded amount. If the debtor will not or cannot pay the judgment, the creditor is entitled to go back to the court and obtain a **writ of execution,** which is an order, usually issued by the clerk of the court, directing the sheriff to seize (levy) and sell any of the debtor's nonexempt real or personal property that is within the court's geographic jurisdiction (usually the county in which the courthouse is located). The proceeds of the sale are used to pay off the judgment and the costs of the sale. Any excess is paid to the debtor.

The debtor can pay the judgment and redeem the nonexempt property any time before the sale takes place. Because of exemption laws (which cover the debtor's homestead and designated items of personal property) and bankruptcy laws, however, many judgments are virtually uncollectible.

Garnishment. An order for **garnishment** permits a creditor to collect a debt by seizing property of the debtor (such as wages or money in a bank account) that is being held by a third party (such as an employer or a bank). Typically, a garnishment judgment is served on a debtor's employer so that part of the debtor's usual paycheck will be paid to the creditor.

The legal proceeding for a garnishment action is governed by state law. As a result of a garnishment proceeding, as noted, a third party (such as the debtor's employer) is ordered by the court to turn over property owned by the debtor (such as wages) to pay the debt. Garnishment can be a prejudgment remedy, requiring a hearing before a court, or a postjudgment remedy. According to the laws in some states, the judgment creditor needs to obtain only one order of garnishment, which will then continuously apply to the judgment debtor's weekly wages until the entire debt is paid. In other states, the judgment creditor must go back to court for a separate order of garnishment for each pay period.

Both federal laws and state laws limit the amount of money that can be taken from a debtor's weekly take-home pay through garnishment proceedings. Federal law provides a minimal framework to protect debtors from losing all their income in order to pay judgment debts.[2] State laws also provide dollar exemptions, and these amounts are often larger than those provided by federal law.[3] State and federal statutes can be applied together to help create a pool of funds sufficient to enable a debtor to continue to provide for family needs while also reducing the amount of the judgment debt in a reasonable way. Under federal law, garnishment of an employee's wages for any one indebtedness cannot be grounds for dismissal of an employee.

One of the questions courts have faced in recent years has to do with whether a debtor's pension fund can be attached by creditors, through garnishment or other proceedings, to satisfy a debt. Under the Employee Retirement Income Security Act (ERISA) of 1974,[4] certain types of pension funds "may not be alienated [transferred]," or attached. The law is less clear, however, on whether pension funds, after they

2. For example, the federal Consumer Credit Protection Act of 1968, 15 U.S.C. Sections 1601–1693r, provides that a debtor can retain either 75 percent of his or her disposable earnings per week or the sum equivalent to thirty hours of work paid at federal minimum wage rates, whichever is greater.

3. A few states (for example, Texas) do not permit garnishment of wages by private parties except under a child-support order.

4. 29 U.S.C. Sections 1001–1461.

have been received by a retiree, can be subject to attachment by creditors.

 See Case 29.2 at the end of this chapter. To view the full, unedited case from Westlaw,® go to this text's Web site at **http://wbl-cs.westbuslaw.com**.

Creditors' Composition Agreements

Creditors may contract with the debtor for discharge of the debtor's liquidated debts (debts that are definite, or fixed, in amount) on payment of a sum less than that owed. These agreements are referred to as *composition agreements* or **creditors' composition agreements** and, unless they are formed under duress, are usually held to be enforceable.

Mortgage Foreclosure

Mortgage holders have the right to foreclose on mortgaged property in the event of a debtor's default. The usual method of foreclosure is by judicial sale of the property, although the statutory methods of foreclosure vary from state to state. If the proceeds of the foreclosure sale are sufficient to cover both the costs of the foreclosure and the mortgaged debt, any surplus is received by the debtor. If the sale proceeds are insufficient to cover the foreclosure costs and the mortgaged debt, however, the **mortgagee** (the creditor-lender) can seek to recover the difference from the **mortgagor** (the debtor) by obtaining a deficiency judgment representing the difference between the mortgaged debt plus foreclosure costs and the amount actually received from the proceeds of the foreclosure sale. A deficiency judgment is obtained in a separate legal action that is pursued subsequent to the foreclosure action. It entitles the creditor to recover from other property owned by the debtor. Some states do not permit deficiency judgments for some types of real estate interests.

Before the foreclosure sale, a defaulting mortgagor can redeem the property by paying the full amount of the debt, plus any interest and costs that have accrued. This right is known as the **equity of redemption.** In some states, a mortgagor may even redeem the property within a certain period of time—called a **statutory period of redemption**—after the sale. In these states, the deed to the property usually is not delivered to the purchaser until the statutory period has expired.

Assignment for the Benefit of Creditors

Both common law and statutes may provide for a debtor's assignment of assets to a trustee or assignee for the benefit of the debtor's creditors. In these situations, that debtor voluntarily transfers title to assets owned to a trustee or assignee, who in turn sells or liquidates these assets, tendering payment to the debtor's creditors on a pro rata (proportionate) basis. Each creditor may accept the tender (and discharge the debt owed to him or her) or reject it (and attempt to collect the debt in another way).

The flexibility and informality of an assignment for the benefit of creditors may save creditors time and expense and result in better prices when a debtor's property is liquidated. Nevertheless, creditors may decide that this option does not adequately protect their rights. Under the bankruptcy laws, creditors may be able to force the debtor into involuntary bankruptcy, depending on the amount of their claims against the debtor and other factors (see Chapter 30). Thus, a debtor's bankruptcy may supersede assignment for the benefit of creditors-even if the bankruptcy is initiated by creditors.

SECTION 2

Suretyship and Guaranty

When a third person promises to pay a debt owed by another in the event the debtor does not pay, either a *suretyship* or a *guaranty* relationship is created. Exhibit 29–1 on the next page illustrates these relationships. The third person's credit becomes the security for the debt owed.

Suretyship

A contract of strict **suretyship** is a promise made by a third person to be responsible for the debtor's obligation. It is an express contract between the **surety** and the creditor. The surety in the strictest sense is primarily liable for the debt of the principal. The creditor can demand payment from the surety from the moment that the debt is due. A suretyship contract is not a form of indemnity; that is, it is not merely a promise to make good any loss that a creditor may incur as a result of the debtor's failure to pay. The creditor need not exhaust all legal remedies against

EXHIBIT 29–1 SURETYSHIP AND GUARANTY PARTIES

In a suretyship or guaranty arrangement, a third party promises to be responsible for a debtor's obligations. A third party who agrees to be responsible for the debt even if the primary debtor does not default is known as a surety; a third party who agrees to be *secondarily* responsible for the debt—that is, responsible only if the primary debtor defaults—is known as a guarantor. As noted in Chapter 14, normally a promise of guaranty (a collateral, or secondary, promise) must be in writing to be enforceable.

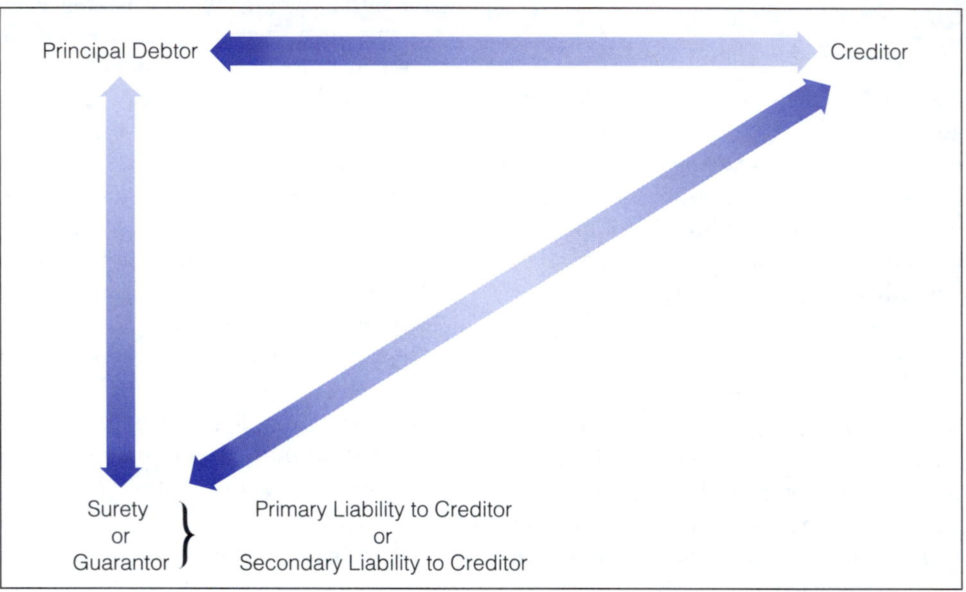

the principal debtor before holding the surety responsible for payment. Moreover, a surety agreement does not have to be in writing to be enforceable, although usually such agreements are in writing.

For example, Jason Oller wants to borrow money from the bank to buy a used car. Because Jason is still in college, the bank will not lend him the money unless his father, Stacey Oller, who has dealt with the bank before, will cosign the note (add his signature to the note, thereby becoming jointly liable for payment of the debt). When Mr. Oller cosigns the note, he becomes primarily liable to the bank. On the note's due date, the bank can seek payment from Jason Oller, Stacey Oller, or both jointly.

GUARANTY

A guaranty contract is similar to a suretyship contract in that it includes a promise to answer for the debt or default of another. With a suretyship arrangement, however, the surety is *primarily* liable for the debtor's obligation. With a guaranty arrangement, the **guarantor**—the third person making the guaranty—is *secondarily* liable. The guarantor can be required to pay the obligation only after the principal debtor defaults, and usually only after the creditor has made an attempt to collect from the debtor.

For example, a corporation, BX Enterprises, needs to borrow money to meet its payroll. The bank is skeptical about the creditworthiness of BX and requires Dawson, its president, who is a wealthy businessperson and owner of 70 percent of BX Enterprises, to sign an agreement making himself personally liable for payment if BX does not pay off the loan. As a guarantor of the loan, Dawson cannot be held liable until BX Enterprises is in default.

The Statute of Frauds requires that a guaranty contract between the guarantor and the creditor must be in writing to be enforceable unless the *main purpose exception* applies. Briefly, this exception provides that if the main purpose of the guaranty agreement is to benefit the guarantor, the contract need not be in writing to be enforceable. (See Chapter 14 for a more detailed discussion of this exception.)

The guaranty contract terms determine the extent and time of the guarantor's liability. For example, the guaranty can be *continuing*, designed to cover a series of transactions by the debtor. Also, the guaranty can be *unlimited* or *limited* as to time and amount. In addition, the guaranty can be *absolute,* in which case the guarantor becomes liable immediately on the debtor's default, or *conditional,* in which case the guarantor becomes liable only on the happening of a certain event.

Westlaw. See Case 29.3 at the end of this chapter. To view the full, unedited case from Westlaw,® go to this text's Web site at **http://wbl-cs.westbuslaw.com**.

Defenses of the Surety and the Guarantor

The defenses of the surety and the guarantor are basically the same. Therefore, the following discussion applies to both, although it refers only to the surety.

Actions Releasing the Surety. Certain actions will release the surety from the obligation. For example, making any material modification in the terms of the original contract between the principal debtor and the creditor, including the awarding of a binding extension of time for making payment, without first obtaining the consent of the surety will discharge a gratuitous surety (one who receives no consideration in return for acting as a surety) completely and a surety who is compensated to the extent that the surety suffers a loss.

Naturally, if the principal obligation is paid by the debtor or by another person on behalf of the debtor, the surety is discharged from the obligation. Similarly, if valid tender of payment is made, and the creditor for some reason rejects it with knowledge of the surety's existence, then the surety is released from any obligation on the debt.

Defenses of the Principal Debtor. Generally, any defenses available to a principal debtor can be used by the surety to avoid liability on the obligation to the creditor. Defenses available to the principal debtor that the surety *cannot* use include the principal debtor's incapacity or bankruptcy and the statute of limitations. The ability of the surety to assert any defenses the debtor may have against the creditor is the most important concept in suretyship, because most of the defenses available to the surety are also those of the debtor.

Surrender or Impairment of Collateral. In addition, if a creditor surrenders or impairs the debtor's collateral while knowing of the surety and without the surety's consent, the surety is released to the extent of any loss suffered from the creditor's actions. The primary reason for this is to protect the surety who agreed to become obligated only because the debtor's collateral was in the possession of the creditor.

Other Defenses. Obviously, a surety may also have his or her own defenses—for example, incapacity or bankruptcy. If the creditor fraudulently induced the surety to guarantee the debt, the surety can assert fraud as a defense. In most states, the creditor has a legal duty to inform the surety, prior to the formation of the suretyship contract, of material facts known by the creditor that would substantially increase the surety's risk. Failure to so inform is fraud and makes the suretyship obligation voidable.

Rights of the Surety and the Guarantor

The rights of the surety and the guarantor are basically the same. Therefore, again, the following discussion applies to both.

The Right of Subrogation. When the surety pays the debt owed to the creditor, the surety is entitled to certain rights. First, the surety has the legal **right of subrogation.** Simply stated, this means that any right the creditor had against the debtor now becomes the right of the surety. Included are creditor rights in bankruptcy, rights to collateral possessed by the creditor, and rights to judgments secured by the creditor. In short, the surety now stands in the shoes of the creditor and may pursue any remedies that were available to the creditor against the debtor.

The Right of Reimbursement. Second, the surety has a right to be reimbursed by the debtor. This **right of reimbursement** may stem either from the suretyship contract or from equity. Basically, the surety is entitled to receive from the debtor all outlays made on behalf of the suretyship arrangement. Such outlays can include expenses incurred, as well as the actual amount of the debt paid to the creditor.

The Right of Contribution. Third, in the case of **co-sureties** (two or more sureties on the same obligation owed by the debtor), the **right of contribution** allows a surety who pays more than his or her proportionate share on a debtor's default to recover from the co-sureties the amount paid above the surety's obligation. Generally, a co-surety's liability either is determined by agreement or, in the absence of agreement, is set at the maximum liability under the suretyship contract.

For example, assume that two co-sureties are obligated under a suretyship contract to guarantee the debt of a debtor. Together, the sureties' maximum liability is \$25,000. Surety A's maximum liability is \$15,000, and surety B's is \$10,000. The debtor owes \$10,000 and is in default. Surety A pays the creditor the entire \$10,000. In the absence of agreement, surety A can recover \$4,000 from surety B (\$10,000/\$25,000 × \$10,000 = \$4,000, surety B's obligation).

SECTION 3

Protection for Debtors

The law protects debtors, as well as creditors. Certain property of the debtor, for example, is exempt from creditors' actions. Consumer protection statutes also protect debtors' rights. Of course, bankruptcy laws, which will be discussed in the next chapter, are designed specifically to assist debtors in need of help.

EXEMPTIONS

In most states, certain types of real and personal property are exempt from levy of execution or attachment. Probably the most familiar of these exemptions is the **homestead exemption.** Each state permits the debtor to retain the family home, either in its entirety or up to a specified dollar amount, free from the claims of unsecured creditors or trustees in bankruptcy. The purpose is to ensure that the debtor will retain some form of shelter.

Suppose that Beere owes Veltman \$40,000. The debt is the subject of a lawsuit, and the court awards Veltman a judgment of \$40,000 against Beere. Beere's homestead is valued at \$50,000, and the homestead exemption is \$25,000. There are no outstanding mortgages or other liens on his homestead. To satisfy the judgment debt, Beere's family home is sold at public auction for \$45,000. The proceeds of the sale are distributed as follows:

1. Beere is given \$25,000 as his homestead exemption.
2. Veltman is paid \$20,000 toward the judgment debt, leaving a \$20,000 deficiency judgment (that is, "leftover debt") that can be satisfied from any other nonexempt property (personal or real) that Beere may have, if allowed by state law.

In a few states, statutes permit the homestead exemption only if the judgment debtor has a family. The policy behind this type of statute is to protect the family. If a judgment debtor does not have a family, a creditor may be entitled to collect the full amount realized from the sale of the debtor's home.

State exemption statutes usually include both real and personal property. Personal property that is most often exempt from satisfaction of judgment debts includes the following:

1. Household furniture up to a specified dollar amount.
2. Clothing and certain personal possessions, such as family pictures or a Bible.
3. A vehicle (or vehicles) for transportation (at least up to a specified dollar amount).
4. Certain classified animals, usually livestock but including pets.
5. Equipment that the debtor uses in a business or trade, such as tools or professional instruments, up to a specified dollar amount.

SPECIAL PROTECTION FOR CONSUMER-DEBTORS

Numerous consumer protection statutes and rules apply to debtor-creditor relationships involving **consumer-debtors** (defined as those whose debts are primarily consumer debts). We have already discussed the Federal Trade Commission's rule limiting the rights of a holder in due course (HDC) who holds a negotiable promissory note executed by a debtor-buyer as part of a consumer transaction. This rule, discussed in Chapter 26, provides basically that any personal defenses that the buyer can assert against the seller can also be asserted against an HDC. The seller must disclose this information clearly on the sales agreement.

Other laws regulating debtor-creditor relationships include the Truth-in-Lending Act, which protects consumers by requiring creditors to disclose specific types of information when making loans to consumers. This act, along with other consumer protection statutes, will be discussed in Chapter 44.

Terms and Concepts to Review

artisan's lien 583
attachment 583
consumer-debtor 588
co-surety 587
creditors' composition agreement 585
equity of redemption 585
garnishment 584
guarantor 586
homestead exemption 588
innkeeper's lien 583
lien 582
mechanic's lien 582
mortgagee 585
mortgagor 585
right of contribution 587
right of reimbursement 587
right of subrogation 587
statutory period of redemption 585
surety 585
suretyship 585
writ of attachment 584
writ of execution 584

Chapter Summary

Remedies Available to Creditors

Liens	**1.** *Mechanic's lien*—A nonpossessory, filed lien on an owner's real estate for labor, services, or materials furnished to or made on the realty. **2.** *Artisan's lien*—A possessory lien on an owner's personal property for labor performed or value added. **3.** *Innkeeper's lien*—A possessory lien on a hotel guest's baggage for hotel charges that remain unpaid. **4.** *Judicial liens*— **a.** Attachment—A court-ordered seizure of property prior to a court's final determination of the creditor's rights to the property. Attachment is available only on the creditor's posting of a bond and in strict compliance with applicable state statutes. **b.** Writ of execution—A court order directing the sheriff to seize (levy) and sell a debtor's nonexempt real or personal property to satisfy a court's judgment in the creditor's favor.
Garnishment	A collection remedy that allows the creditor to attach a debtor's money (such as wages owed or bank accounts) and property that are held by a third person.
Creditors' Composition Agreements	A contract between a debtor and his or her creditors by which the debtor's debts are discharged by payment of a sum less than the sum that is actually owed.
Mortgage Foreclosure	On the debtor's default, the entire mortgage debt is due and payable, allowing the creditor to foreclose on the realty by selling it to satisfy the debt.
Assignment for the Benefit of Creditors	In some situations, the debtor may voluntarily transfer title to assets owned to a trustee or assignee, who in turn sells or liquidates the assets and tenders payment to the creditors on a proportionate basis.
Suretyship or Guaranty	Under contract, a third person agrees to be primarily or secondarily liable for the debt owed by the principal debtor. A creditor can turn to this third person for satisfaction of the debt.

CHAPTER SUMMARY—CONTINUED

PROTECTION FOR DEBTORS	
Exemptions	Numerous laws, including consumer protection statutes, assist debtors. Additionally, state laws exempt certain types of real and personal property from levy of execution or attachment. 1. *Real property*—Each state permits a debtor to retain the family home, either in its entirety or up to a specified dollar amount, free from the claims of unsecured creditors or trustees in bankruptcy (homestead exemption). 2. *Personal property*—Personal property that is most often exempt from satisfaction of judgment debts includes the following: a. Household furniture up to a specified dollar amount. b. Clothing and certain personal possessions. c. Transportation vehicles up to a specified dollar amount. d. Certain classified animals, such as livestock and pets. e. Equipment used in a business or trade up to a specified dollar amount.
Special Protection for Consumer-Debtors	Numerous consumer protection statutes and rules provide special protection for consumer-debtors (those whose debts are primarily consumer debts).

CASES FOR ANALYSIS

Westlaw. You can access the full text of each case presented below by going to the Westlaw cases on this text's Web site at http://wbl-cs.westbuslaw.com. Each Westlaw case includes the names of all plaintiffs and defendants, the dates on which the case was argued and decided, a brief summary of the issues and decisions in the case, headnotes classifying the specific issues in the case according to the West Key Number System, and the court's opinion. Concurring and dissenting opinions, if any, are included as well.

CASE 29.1 MECHANIC'S LIEN

HERPEL, INC. V. STRAUB CAPITAL CORP.
District Court of Appeal of Florida,
Fourth District, 1996.
682 So.2d 661.

STEVENSON, Judge.

In this action to foreclose a mechanic's lien, the [Florida state] trial court granted summary judgment in favor of the defendants/appellees on the ground that the lien was not recorded within 90 days of the final furnishing of materials to the job site as required by [Florida Statutes Section] 713.08(5). * * *

The contract at issue called for appellant, Herpel, Inc. (Herpel), to specially fabricate a cast-stone mantel for installation in a newly constructed residence owned by appellee, The Blossom Estate, a limited partnership (Blossom). The contract was for materials only; no labor or other services were involved. The mantel was delivered sometime on or before November 30, 1994, and was installed in the residence. When the mantel was delivered, George Straub, the owner's authorized agent, was not satisfied with its appearance. On November 30, 1994, Herpel employees removed the mantel from the residence, leaving a large hole in the wall, and returned it to Herpel's work-yard to finish curing. The same mantel was reinstalled on January 5, 1995.

Herpel did not file its Claim of Lien until March 23, 1995; 113 days after the mantel was originally delivered to the property, but within 90 days of the date that the cured mantel was redelivered. Section 713.08(5) provides in pertinent part that:

> The claim of lien may be recorded at any time during the progress of the work or thereafter but not later than 90 days after the final furnishing of the labor or services or materials by the lienor * * * .

The trial court determined as a matter of law that the "final furnishing of materials" occurred on November 30, 1994, when the mantel was first placed on the job site. Consequently, the trial court concluded that the claim of lien had not been timely filed and granted judgment in favor of the defendants/appellees.

* * * We have uncovered no cases directly on point that explain the term "final furnishing" in the context of a materials-only contract. However, a number of cases, which involve contracts for the provision of both services and materials, are useful in our analysis of what constitutes the "final furnishing" of materials.

In contracts involving both services and materials, the courts have held that the time limit for filing a lien is not extended by repair, corrective, or warranty work; but that work done in fulfillment of the contract will extend the time for filing of the claim of lien. * * *

* * * The test to be applied is whether the work was done in good faith, within a reasonable time, in pursuance of the terms of the contract, and whether it was necessary to a "finished job."

It seems that the rationale * * * rests on the notion that work done in fulfillment of the contract is contemplated by the contract and extends the time for filing, since the contract is not complete until the work is done. Remedial work in the nature of correction or repair does not extend the time for filing the claim of lien since the contract is already complete, and any additional work performed is merely incidental to the executed contract. * * * Applying that reasoning, we have little difficulty determining that, as a matter of law, the final furnishing of the materials occurred when the mantel was reinstalled on January 5, 1995. The owner rejected the mantel as non-conforming to the contract when it was initially tendered. In response to the owner's objections, Herpel took the mantel back, allowed for further curing, and presented the mantel once again for acceptance. Under the circumstances, it is clear that the additional work on the mantel was performed to complete the job in compliance with the contract.

Accordingly, we find that appellant properly recorded its Claim of Lien within 90 days of the final furnishing of materials to the job site as required by [Florida Statutes Section] 713.08(5). We reverse and remand for entry of partial summary judgment in favor of the appellant on the issue of the timeliness of the lien.

REVERSED and REMANDED.

CASE 29.2 GARNISHMENT

UNITED STATES v. SMITH

United States Court of Appeals,
Fourth Circuit, 1995.
47 F.3d 681.

ERVIN, Chief Judge:

On September 24, 1992, a federal grand jury indicted Dr. Charles Smith on six counts of mail and wire fraud stemming from his nine-year campaign to solicit investments from numerous friends and acquaintances for fraudulent real estate schemes. Smith's fraud caused losses of over $200,000. On March 25, 1993, pursuant to a plea agreement, Smith pled guilty to count one of the indictment charging him with wire fraud * * * . The plea agreement called for a 21-month sentence and a recommendation that the sentencing court order restitution based on Smith's financial means. The [federal] district court ordered Smith to turn over upon receipt each month the entire amount of his pension benefits payable under an ERISA plan. Smith appeals the restitution order on the basis of ERISA's anti-alienability provisions. * * *

I.

* * * *

Beginning in 1983, Smith solicited at least fifty friends and acquaintances for investments in fraudulent business schemes, including investments in land deals in the "Caribbean Group." * * * The fraud victims made checks payable to Smith or wired money directly to accounts controlled by Smith. In one instance, a check was made out to Smith's landlord who credited the amount to Smith's rent bill. Smith converted the majority of the money collected to his personal use. He lied and made excuses when pressed by the investors, concealing his fraud. The amount of the loss was at least $200,000 and probably greater than $350,000.

Upon arrest, Smith expressed remorse for his crime and a desire to pay restitution upon his release from prison. * * * Smith receives $1,188 per month in pension benefits from two separate ERISA plans, * * * he [became] eligible on May 6, 1993 for social security benefits * * * amounting to $602 per month, and * * * his wife receives a net monthly salary of $1,900 from her employment as a third grade school teacher. * * * The district court * * * ordered Smith to turn over his pension benefits each month as he received them upon his release from prison.

II.

The Employee Retirement Income Security Act (ERISA) provides that "each pension plan shall provide that benefits provided under the plan may not be assigned or alienated." Binding Treasury Department Regulations further prohibit involuntary transfers of benefits from qualified plans by requiring that "benefits provided under the plan may not be anticipated, assigned (either at law or in equity), alienated [transferred to another] or subject to attachment, garnishment, levy, execution or other legal or equitable process."

This court has long recognized a strong public policy against the alienability of an ERISA plan participant's benefits. The [United States] Supreme Court, as well, has found that it is not "appropriate to approve any generalized equitable exception—either for employee malfeasance or for criminal misconduct—to ERISA's prohibition on the assignment or alienation of pension benefits." * * *

* * * The government's position is that once pension funds have been distributed, the anti-alienability statute no longer applies. * * *

We believe there is a distinction between funds disbursed from an ERISA plan before an employee has retired and such funds paid as an annuity for retirement purposes. The Supreme Court has noted that the purpose of ERISA is to safeguard a stream of income for pensioners. Where an employee elects to draw on her ERISA plan prior to her retirement, she forfeits the protection provided by the Act. Where, however, the funds are paid pursuant to the terms of the plan as income during retirement years, ERISA prohibits their alienation. * * *

* * * *

In the case at hand, the government attempted to require Smith to draw down his benefits due under the plans as a lump sum and turn it over intact as restitution. Upon discovering that Smith was not eligible for lump sum distribution, the government agreed to the recovery of his benefits as they are paid to him. It is clear that the government would not have been successful in requiring Smith to request a lump sum distribution. * * * [B]enefits in the hands of the fiduciary are beyond the reach of garnishment. The government should not be allowed to do indirectly what it cannot do directly; it cannot require Smith to turn over his pension benefits in a lump sum, nor can it require him to turn over his benefits as they are paid to him. Understandably, there may be a natural distaste for the result we reach here. The statute, however, is clear. Congress has made a policy decision to protect the ERISA income of retirees, even if that decision prevents others from securing relief for the wrongs done them.

* * * [A]s a general matter, courts should be loath to announce equitable exceptions to legislative requirements or prohibitions that are unqualified by the statutory text. * * * [There is a] danger in eroding through exception the anti-alienation policy of ERISA. That entire legislation was aimed at guaranteeing the security of retirement income for American workers. * * * We decline to participate in the diminution of these safeguards in circumstances which might seem harmless enough in particular instances but which, in the aggregate, might invite creditors to believe that ERISA funds are not, after all, inviolate.

The Government claims that the policy governing restitution under the [federal] Victim and Witness Protection Act obligates the defendant to make restitution payments regardless of the source of his income. This policy does not alter the * * * findings that ERISA funds are inviolate with exceptions only as announced by Congress. It is not for the courts to determine when exceptions to ERISA are appropriate.

III.

The restitution order in this case clearly required Smith to relinquish his pension benefits. The district court stated, "Well, he will be paying amounts, or pension [sic], and, once those sums are in his hands, it seems to me that they are subject to the existing order of this court announced today." That approach is impermissible. Smith cannot be forced to relinquish his ERISA pension benefits for restitution.

On remand the court must determine an appropriate amount of restitution that Smith must pay based on his financial resources. Although the court cannot mechanically deprive Smith of his pension benefits, it can determine restitution based on a balance of the victims' interest in compensation and Smith's other financial resources. Although the district court may determine an appropriate amount of restitution based on its findings * * * , it must make that determination while leaving Smith's ERISA-protected benefits in his possession. Congress requires that ERISA beneficiaries retain their pension benefits for retirement purposes.

IV.

The district court's restitution order is vacated and remanded for redetermination.

* * * *

WILLIAMS, Circuit Judge, dissenting:

* * * *

While I certainly agree with the majority that * * * the federal courts are not to fashion equitable exceptions to the assignment and alienation provision of ERISA, I conclude that * * * does not resolve the specific issue before us which *can* be decided under the statute: whether ERISA and the Department of Treasury's * * * Regulations prohibit a restitution order that may affect pension benefits that Smith will have received at the time a payment is to be made. * * *

* * * To begin, the relevant statutory text in [ERISA], "[e]ach pension plan shall provide that benefits provided under the plan may not be assigned or alienated," is ambiguous when one attempts to discern the meaning of benefits provided under the plan. Given the ambiguity in the text of the statute, the [court should turn] to the Department of Treasury regulation which define[s] "assignment" and "alienation" as:

> Any direct or indirect arrangement (whether revocable or irrevocable) whereby a party acquires from a participant or beneficiary a right or interest *enforceable against the plan* in, or to, all or any part of a plan benefit payment which is, or may become, payable to the participant or beneficiary. [Emphasis added.]

* * * I would hold that while there is admittedly some tension between the general principle under ERISA of protecting the beneficiary's retirement benefits and the Department of the Treasury's interpretation of the anti-alienation provision, the agency's interpretation is clear, reasonable, and entitled to deference. Under the above-stated regulatory provision, the restitution order against Smith's received retirement income is not an action against the plan; it is not prohibited by ERISA * * * .

CASE 29.3 GUARANTY

WILSON COURT LIMITED PARTNERSHIP v. TONY MARONI'S, INC.

Supreme Court of Washington, 1998.
134 Wash.2d 692,
952 P.2d 590.

TALMADGE, Justice.

* * * *

FACTS

Tony Maroni's, Inc. (Tony Maroni's) signed a written commercial lease (Lease) for Seattle [Washington] retail space owned by Wilson Court Limited Partnership (Wilson). Anthony L. Riviera (Riviera), Tony Maroni's President, signed the Lease. Tony Maroni's leased 1,676 square feet of space for a 60-month term. The Lease provided for extensive tenant improvements, estimated to be worth $45,520. Initially, Tony Maroni's contributed $5,000 toward those improvements, and then was to pay an additional $7,000 over the life of the Lease, amortized at $148.73 per month. Wilson contributed the balance of $33,520 toward the improvements.

Contemporaneously with the execution of the Lease, Riviera executed a guaranty agreement (Guaranty) which was incorporated by reference in the Lease. Riviera wrote the description "President" by hand after his name on the signature line of the Guaranty. The Guaranty stated:

* * *

GUARANTY

REFERENCE is made to lease dated the ____ day of __________, 19__, between Wilson Court Limited Partnership, as Landlord, and Tony Maroni's, Inc. as Tenant.

FOR VALUE RECEIVED and in condition for, and as an inducement to, the Landlord entering into said lease, which has been executed simultaneously herewith, the undersigned hereby guarantees to the Landlord, its successors and assigns, the full performance and observance of all covenants, conditions and agreements therein provided to be performed and observed by the Tenant, its successors and assigns, and expressly agrees that the validity of this agreement and the obligations of the Guarantor hereunder shall in no way be terminated, affected or impaired by reason of the assertion by the Landlord against the Tenant of any of the rights or remedies reserved to the Landlord pursuant to the provisions of said lease, or by reason of the waiver by the Landlord of, or failure to [sic] the Landlord to, enforce any of the terms, covenants or conditions of said lease, or the granting of any indulgence or extension of time to the Tenant, all of which may be given or done without notice to the Guarantor. The undersigned waives notice of default in the payment of rent, additional rent or any other amounts contained or reserved in said lease, or notice of a breach or non-performance on any of the covenants, conditions or agreements contained in said lease.

The undersigned further agrees that its liability under this agreement and guaranty shall be primary, and that in any right of action which shall accrue to the Landlord under the said lease, the Landlord may at its option, proceed against the undersigned without having commenced any action, or having obtained any judgment, against the Tenant and that the venue of any action against the undersigned may be in the county in which the premises are located.

WITNESS THE EXECUTION HEREOF THIS 23 day of December, 1992.

GUARANTOR:
By: */s/ Anthony L. Riviera President*

The Guaranty indicated its execution was a condition for Wilson to lease the space to Tony Maroni's. However, the Guaranty did not specifically identify in its text who was bound, referring only to "the undersigned" or "Guarantor."

In contrast with the Guaranty, Riviera also signed the Lease in a representative capacity, but the Lease contained numerous indicia that only Tony Maroni's was bound by the Lease terms. * * *

Shortly after the execution of the Lease, Tony Maroni's * * * assigned the Lease to M & R Foods (M & R), another Riviera company. Thereafter, M & R defaulted on the Lease. Wilson filed suit [in a Washington state court] against Tony Maroni's, M & R, and Riviera seeking a writ of restitution and damages. The trial court granted Wilson a writ of restitution. Wilson then moved for summary judgment against M & R for damages resulting from breach of the Lease and against Riviera on the Guaranty. Riviera also moved for summary judgment asserting he was not personally liable on the Guaranty because he signed only in his capacity as a corporate officer. The trial court granted summary judgment to Wilson and [a state intermediate appellate court] affirmed, holding the purpose and circumstances surrounding the Guaranty could lead only to the conclusion the parties intended to bind Riviera personally. We granted review.

ANALYSIS

* * * *

While the parties agree a guaranty here was intended and executed by the parties, they disagree as to who is bound by its terms. Riviera asserts he did not intend to be personally bound by the Guaranty and his signature on the Guaranty, he argues, is an objective manifestation of that intent. By adding the title "President" to his signature when he signed the Guaranty, he contends he was signing in a representative capacity only, on behalf of Tony Maroni's, making the Guaranty unenforceable against him personally. Wilson, on the other hand, contends the terms of the Guaranty itself, and the nature of guaranties generally, indicate the Guaranty was to be enforced against Riviera personally.

* * * *

* * * In this case, the Guaranty does not clearly specify the person to be bound in its text, referring generically to "the undersigned" or "Guarantor." In this context, Riviera's signature with the descriptive language of "President" creates a question as to whether the parties intended Riviera personally or Tony Maroni's to be bound by the Guaranty. This combination of circumstances renders the Guaranty ambiguous.

In construing the Guaranty in light of this ambiguity, we acknowledge contracts to answer for the debt of another must be explicit and are strictly construed, but we must also recognize the commercial context in which this Guaranty was signed. Where two commercial entities sign a commercial agreement, we will give such an agreement a commercially reasonable construction. In this case, such a construction leads us to the conclusion Riviera is personally liable on the Guaranty as a matter of law.

First, any ambiguity in the Guaranty was created by Riviera himself in adding the descriptive language to his signature. Such ambiguity will be construed against Riviera as the party who drafted this language.

Second, the language of the Guaranty itself compels the view Riviera is personally liable. We must interpret the Lease and Guaranty as a whole, giving reasonable effect to each of its parts. The plain language of the Guaranty clearly contemplates three separate entities, the Landlord, the Tenant and the Guarantor, and so designates them. It identifies Wilson as the Landlord, Tony Maroni's as the Tenant, and addresses the obligations of a separate third party, referred to interchangeably as the undersigned or Guarantor. * * * The only reasonable interpretation of these provisions is that the Landlord, Tenant and undersigned/Guarantor are three separate and distinct entities. If Riviera signed the Guaranty only in his representative capacity, Tony Maroni's would be both Tenant and Guarantor, rendering the Guaranty provisions absurd. For example, it would be impossible for the Landlord to proceed against the Guarantor without having commenced any action against the Tenant if they are the same entity.

Moreover, the Guaranty language stands in stark contrast to the language of the Lease where a corporate obligation was unambiguously contemplated. Riviera signed the Lease as president of Tony Maroni's to bind the company. No such intent can be gleaned from the Guaranty. * * *

Third, as the Court of Appeals correctly noted, the very nature of a guaranty is such that Riviera created personal liability by his signature. * * *

* * * *

Riviera is an experienced businessperson with prior experience in commercial leasing who dealt directly with Wilson in securing the Lease. There is no evidence or assertion of any improper conduct by Wilson. Given the commercial sophistication of the parties, the circumstances under which the Guaranty was entered into, and the nature of the Guaranty, a commercially reasonable approach to this case requires us to find the addition of "President" to Riviera's signature was merely *descriptio personae* and to hold Riviera personally liable under the Guaranty.

CONCLUSION

Although the descriptive language in Riviera's signature on the Guaranty created an ambiguity and our commercially reasonable construction of the Guaranty resolved the ambiguity by imposing personal liability on Riviera, we note the issue in this case could have been easily avoided by careful attention to the language of the Guaranty and communication between the parties. If Riviera did not intend personal liability, he should have said so. Wilson could have pressed Riviera to sign only in his individual capacity or modified its Guaranty to clearly specify Riviera as the Guarantor. As between commercial entities, we decline to write agreements for such entities they did not negotiate, but where they create ambiguities by their imprecise drafting, we will construe their agreements in a commercially reasonable manner to resolve any ambiguities.

We affirm the trial court's judgment in favor of Wilson * * * .

Case Problems

29–1. Chrysler Credit Corporation had a perfected security interest in a 1988 Dodge pickup truck that had been purchased by Robert Keeling. When Keeling defaulted on his payments, Chrysler attempted to repossess the vehicle but could not locate it for some time. Finally, the pickup was found in a lot operated by Joe Booth, doing business as Highway Tow Service. Booth had towed the pickup from an apartment complex parking lot to Booth's lot at the request of the apartment manager and had stored the pickup on his auto lot for over two months. Chrysler requested that Booth deliver possession of the truck to Chrysler, but Booth refused to do so until he was paid for the towing ($50) and storage ($1,235) services. Chrysler then sued Booth to gain possession of the pickup. Booth contended that he had an artisan's lien on the truck and that under Missouri law, the common law artisan's lien took priority over Chrysler's perfected security interest. The trial court held for Chrysler, and Booth appealed. What will happen on appeal? Discuss. [*Chrysler Credit Corp. v. Keeling,* 793 S.W.2d 222 (Mo.App. 1990)]

29–2. In June 1981, John Daniels agreed to purchase a used car from Lindsay Cadillac Company. Because John had a poor credit rating, his brother, Seymoure, agreed to cosign the installment sales contract. Seymoure signed the contract on the line designated "Buyer," and John signed on the line designated "Co-Buyer." Lindsay then assigned the contract to General Motors Acceptance Corporation (GMAC). In May 1982, GMAC declared the contract in default. After attempting to locate the car for several months, GMAC finally found it in a condition of total loss. GMAC brought an action for damages in a Maryland state court, but because service of process was never effected on John, the action proceeded only against Seymoure. The trial court found that Seymoure was a guarantor of the contract between John and GMAC and held that GMAC would have to attempt to bring suit first against John before it could proceed against Seymoure. GMAC appealed the ruling. What should the appellate court decide? Discuss fully. [*General Motors Acceptance Corp. v. Daniels,* 303 Md. 254, 492 A.2d 1306 (1985)]

29–3. Kloster-Madsen, Inc., a general contractor, entered into a contract with the owner of a building to do certain remodeling work. About a month later, pursuant to the contract, an electrical subcontractor removed several light fixtures from one of the ceilings, cut four new holes in the ceiling, and placed the removed light fixtures in these holes. Immediately after this work was begun, a new owner, Tafi's, Inc., purchased the building. Material and labor worth several thousand dollars were expended before Tafi's informed the general contractor that it did not wish to have the building remodeled. Discuss whether Kloster-Madsen can impose a mechanic's lien on the building even though it entered into the building contract with a different owner. [*Kloster-Madsen, Inc. v. Tafi's, Inc.,* 303 Minn. 59, 226 N.W.2d 603 (1975)]

29–4. In February 1973, Gladys Schmidt borrowed $4,120 from the National Bank of Joliet to finance the purchase of a Cadillac. The bank held a security interest in the automobile and perfected this interest by filing in the office of the secretary of state. In August 1973, Schmidt took the car to Bergeron Cadillac, Inc., for repairs, which cost approximately $2,000. When Schmidt failed to pay for the repairs, Bergeron Cadillac retained possession of the car and placed an artisan's lien on it. In September, Schmidt defaulted on her payments to the bank, and the bank later filed an action to gain possession of the Cadillac from Bergeron. Which party had a right to possession of the vehicle—Bergeron Cadillac or the National Bank? Discuss. [*National Bank of Joliet v. Bergeron Cadillac, Inc.,* 66 Ill.2d 140, 361 N.E.2d 1116, 5 Ill.Dec. 588 (1977)]

29–5. Allan Green worked for an Illinois engineering firm, Lewis, Yockey, and Brown (LYB), as an environmental engineer and project manager. Green was not, however, licensed as an engineer in Illinois. In October 1991, Green performed engineering work on a subsurface investigation for Snyder Development, Inc., concerning property on which a gas station had been located in Bloomington, Illinois. Snyder wanted to sell the property. Green discovered that the soil was contaminated and told Snyder that according to the regulations of the Illinois Environmental Protection Agency (IEPA), the contamination would have to be removed. Green left LYB in November to form his own company—Midwest Environmental Consulting & Remediation Services, Inc. At the end of November, Snyder asked Green if he would provide engineering services with regard to the clean-up. Green agreed. Midwest removed the contaminated soil according the IEPA specifications, but Snyder failed to pay for the removal. Midwest (Green) brought an action against Snyder and its bank, the Peoples Bank of Bloomington, to foreclose on the property on the basis of its filed mechanic's lien. The trial court issued a judgment that included an award of more that $40,000 in Midwest's favor, and the defendants appealed. Among the issues on appeal was whether Midwest could assert a mechanic's lien given the fact that Green was not licensed as an engineer in Illinois. Which party will prevail on appeal? Explain. [*Midwest Environmental Consulting & Remediation Services, Inc. v. Peoples Bank of Bloomington,* 251 Ill.App.3d 256, 620 N.E.2d 469, 189 Ill.Dec. 501 (1993)]

29–6. On October 1, 1985, Wallace and Helen Brunson contracted with Bear Park, Inc., to sell certain real estate in Taney County, Missouri, for $366,200. At the closing, Bear Park gave the Brunsons a promissory note for $285,000 in partial payment. Several of Bear Park's shareholders and directors, including Ronald Todd, signed a guaranty agreement on the back of the note. According to the terms of the note, Bear Park was to make quarterly payments of principal and interest, with the first payment of $68,800 due on January 7, 1986. The remaining quarterly payments, beginning April 7, 1986, would each be $7,226.80. When Bear Park failed to make the first payment, the Brunsons agreed to accept $7,000 in lieu of the full $68,800 and to increase the amount of the subsequent payments to cover the difference. Todd and the others knew nothing about the new terms. When Bear Park failed to make the next payment, the Brunsons declared the note in default and eventually demanded that the guarantors pay the amount due. No payments were made. The Brunsons assigned their interest in the note to Jake Kirkland, who foreclosed on the property. After the foreclosure sale, there was a deficiency of $36,454.84, plus interest, expenses, and attorneys' fees. Kirkland sued Todd and the others for this amount. Discuss the liability of Todd and the others in this situation. [*Kirkland v. Todd,* 856 S.W.2d 936 (Mo.App. 1993)]

29–7. Topjian Plumbing and Heating, Inc., the plaintiff, sought prejudgment writs of attachment to satisfy an anticipated judgment in a contract action against Bruce Topjian, Inc., the defendant. The plaintiff did not petition the court for permission to effect the attachments but merely completed the forms, served them on the defendant and on the Fencers (the owners of a parcel of land that had previously belonged to the defendant), and recorded them at the registry of deeds. On what grounds might the court invalidate the attachments? [*Topjian Plumbing and Heating, Inc. v. Bruce Topjian, Inc.,* 129 N.H. 481, 529 A.2d 391 (1987)]

29–8. John Shumate parked his car in a vacant lot where he had left it several times previously. When he returned, he was informed that the car had been towed at the property owner's request. Thomas Younger had a collision with another car. His car was towed from the scene of the accident at the request of the police while Younger was discussing the accident with the officers. The towing companies informed both vehicle owners that they must pay towing and storage charges before their autos would be returned. The car owners sued to challenge the towing companies' claim of a possessory lien. Could the owners be prevented from recovering their cars until payment was made? Discuss fully. [*Younger v. Plunkett,* 395 F. Supp. 702 (E.D.Pa 1975)]

29–9. A. J. Kellos Construction Co. was the general contractor for the construction of a building in Georgia. Kellos entered into a subcontract with Roofing Specialists, Inc., for the construction of the roof of this project. A bond was executed by Balboa Insurance Co. in favor of Kellos, underwriting Roofing Specialists's performance of its contract. When the roofing was condemned by the state architect, Kellos sued Balboa on the bond for damages resulting from Roofing Specialists's default on the contract. Was the bond executed by Balboa in favor of Kellos an insurance contract or a guaranty contract? [*A. J. Kellos Construction Co. v. Balboa Insurance Co.,* 495 F.Supp. 408 (S.D. Ga. 1980)]

29–10. John Johnson worked for the street department of the town of Trail Creek. In August 1989, Trail Creek received notice from a court that one of Johnson's creditors had been granted a court judgment against Johnson for an unpaid debt. The notice also stated that Johnson's wages would be subject to garnishment, pending a determination of whether Trail Creek owed any obligations or credits (for example, wages) to Johnson that could be garnished. Johnson was fired two days after this notice was received. Johnson brought an action against the town, the president of the town council, and the superintendent of the town's street department (the defendants), alleging, among other things, that the defendants had violated federal law because he was dismissed as a result of the notice of possible garnishment. The defendants moved to dismiss Johnson's complaint on the ground that they could not have violated the law because Johnson's wages were not actually being withheld at the time of his discharge—in other words, no garnishment proceeding had yet occurred. Must wages actually be withheld before a garnishment proceeding can be held to have occurred? How should the court rule? [*Johnson v. Town of Trail Creek,* 771 F.Supp. 271 (D.N.D.Ind. 1991)]

29–11. Harmony Unlimited, Inc., obtained a judgment against John Chivetta and his company, JMC Enterprises. At the time of the judgment, John lacked sufficient funds to pay. Just before Harmony obtained the judgment, John had transferred $126,000 to his mother, Nettie, who had signed a promissory note. The note for $126,000 was payable on demand, carried no interest, and contained a provision that barred John from obtaining a money judgment against his mother. Nettie paid some of John's bills after the transfer of money from her son to her. Harmony served a garnishment summons on Nettie, claiming that she was a party to a fraudulent scheme by her son to conceal his assets and was holding funds that belonged to her son. Nettie argued that Harmony's rights against her could not be any greater than John's rights against her and that because John could not obtain a judgment against her for the money, Harmony could not do so either. Discuss Harmony's right of garnishment against Nettie. [*Harmony Unlimited, Inc. v. Chivetta,* 743 S.W.2d 884 (Mo.App. 1987)]

29–12. Levinson and Johnson, who had both signed a promissory note, did not pay the note when it was due. Instead, American Thermex, Inc., a corporation in which Johnson had a controlling interest, voluntarily paid the note. American Thermex later brought suit against Levinson, seeking reimbursement for the payment. American Thermex argued, among other things, that because it had paid the note, it had the legal right of subrogation against the note's co-maker, Levinson. Will the court agree that American Thermex has a legal right of subrogation? Why, or why not? [*Levinson v. American Thermex, Inc.,* 196 Ga.App. 291, 396 S.E.2d 252 (1990)]

29–13. Hallmark Cards, Inc., sued Edward Peevy, who had guaranteed an obligation owed to Hallmark by Garry Peevy. At the time of Edward's guaranty, Hallmark had in its possession property pledged as security by Garry. Before the suit was filed, Hallmark sold the pledged property without notifying Edward and sued Edward for the remaining balance on the debt, seeking a deficiency judgment. Edward contended that because Hallmark had sold the property pledged by Garry as security for the obligation without notifying him (Edward), Hallmark was not entitled to a deficiency judgment against him. Hallmark contended that Edward was not entitled to notice of the sale of the collateral and was not required to give consent. Which party will prevail in court? Discuss. [*Hallmark Cards, Inc. v. Peevy,* 293 Ark. 594, 739 S.W.2d 691 (1987)]

29–14. Air Ruidoso, Ltd., operated a commuter airline and air charter service between Ruidoso, New Mexico, and airports in Albuquerque and El Paso. Executive

Aviation Center, Inc., provided services for airlines at the Albuquerque International Airport. When Air Ruidoso failed to pay more than $10,000 that it owed for fuel, oil, and oxygen, Executive Aviation took possession of Air Ruidoso's plane. Executive Aviation claimed that it had a lien on the plane and filed a suit in a New Mexico state court to foreclose. Do supplies such as fuel, oil, and oxygen qualify as "materials" for the purpose of creating an artisan's lien? Why, or why not? [*Air Ruidoso, Ltd. v. Executive Aviation Center, Inc.*, 122 N.M. 71, 920 P.2d 1025 (1996)]

29–15. In 1988, Jamieson-Chippewa Investment Co. entered into a five-year commercial lease with TDM Pharmacy, Inc., for certain premises in Ellisville, Missouri, on which TDM intended to operate a small drugstore. Dennis and Tereasa McClintock ran the pharmacy business. The lease granted TDM three additional five-year options to renew. The lease was signed by TDM and by the McClintocks individually as guarantors. The lease did not state that the guaranty was continuing. In fact, there were no words of guaranty in the lease other than the single word "Guarantors" on the signature page. In 1993, Dennis McClintock, acting as the president of TDM, exercised TDM's option to renew the lease for one term. Three years later, when the pharmacy failed, TDM defaulted on the lease. Jamieson-Chippewa filed a suit in a Missouri state court against the McClintocks for the rent for the rest of the term, based on their guaranty. The McClintocks filed a motion for summary judgment, contending that they had not guaranteed any rent payments beyond the initial five-year term. How should the court rule? Discuss fully. [*Jamieson-Chippewa Investment Co. v. McClintock*, 996 S.W.2d 84 (Mo.App.E.D. 1999)]

E-LINKS

For updated links to resources available on the Web, as well as a variety of other materials, visit this text's Web site at

http://wbl-cs.westbuslaw.com

The Legal Information Institute at Cornell University offers a collection of law materials concerning debtor-creditor relationships at

http://www.law.cornell.edu/topics/debtor_creditor.html

For an example of one state's (South Dakota's) laws on garnishment, go to

http://legis.state.sd.us/index.cfm

When the page opens, click on "Text Search" and key in "garnishment" in the search box that opens.

LEGAL RESEARCH EXERCISES ON THE WEB

Go to http://wbl-cs.westbuslaw.com, the Web site that accompanies this text. Select "Interactive Study Center," and then click on "Chapter 29." There you will find the following Internet research exercise that you can perform to learn more about debtor-creditor relations:

Activity 29–1: Debtor-Creditor Relations

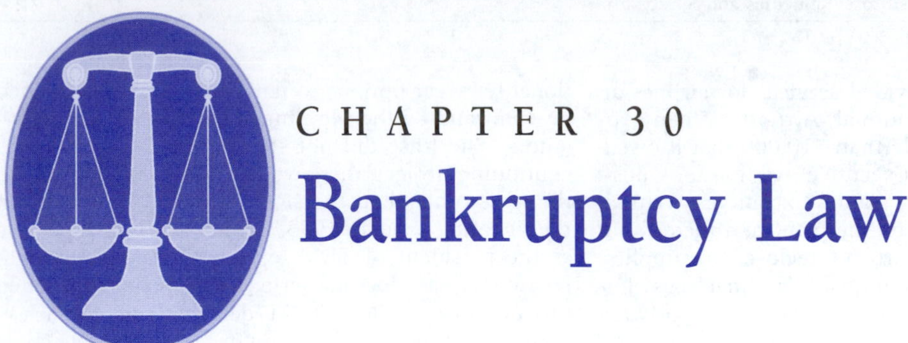

CHAPTER 30
Bankruptcy Law

HISTORICALLY, DEBTORS HAD FEW RIGHTS. Today, in contrast, debtors have numerous rights. Some of these rights were discussed in Chapter 29. In this chapter, we look at another significant right of debtors: the right to petition for bankruptcy relief. This right is established by federal law. Article I, Section 8, of the U.S. Constitution gave Congress the power to establish "uniform Laws on the subject of Bankruptcies throughout the United States."

Bankruptcy law in the United States has two goals—to protect a debtor by giving him or her a fresh start, free from creditors' claims, and to ensure equitable treatment to creditors who are competing for a debtor's assets. Federal bankruptcy legislation was first enacted in 1898 and since then has undergone several modifications. Current bankruptcy law is based on the Bankruptcy Reform Act of 1978, as amended—hereinafter called the Bankruptcy Code, or more simply, the Code (not to be confused with the Uniform Commercial Code, which is also sometimes called the Code). Significant changes to the Code were made by the Bankruptcy Reform Act of 1994; we discuss these changes in this chapter. Although bankruptcy law is federal law, state laws on secured transactions, liens, judgments, and exemptions also play a role in federal bankruptcy proceedings.

Bankruptcy proceedings are held in federal bankruptcy courts, which are under the authority of U.S. district courts, and rulings from bankruptcy courts can be appealed to the district courts. Essentially, a bankruptcy court fulfills the role of an administrative court for the federal district court concerning matters in bankruptcy. The bankruptcy court holds proceedings dealing with the procedures required to administer the estate of the debtor in bankruptcy. Bankruptcy court judges are federally appointed. A bankruptcy court can conduct a jury trial if the appropriate district court has authorized it and the parties to the bankruptcy consent.

SECTION 1

Types of Bankruptcy Relief

The Bankruptcy Code is contained in Title 11 of the *United States Code* (U.S.C.) and has eight chapters. Chapters 1, 3, and 5 of the Code include general definitional provisions and provisions governing case administration, creditors, the debtor, and the estate. These three chapters apply generally to all kinds of bankruptcies. The next five chapters of the Code set forth the different types of relief that debtors may seek. Chapter 7 provides for **liquidation** proceedings (the selling of all nonexempt assets and the distribution of the proceeds to the debtor's creditors). Chapter 9 governs the adjustment of debts of a municipality. Chapter 11 governs reorganizations. Chapters 12 and 13 provide for the adjustment of debts by parties with regular incomes (family farmers under Chapter 12 and individuals under Chapter 13).[1]

To fully inform a consumer-debtor of the various types of relief available, the Code requires that the clerk of the court give all consumer-debtors written notice of each chapter under which they may proceed prior to the commencement of a bankruptcy filing.

1. There are no Chapters 2, 4, 6, 8, or 10 in Title 11. Such "gaps" are not uncommon in the *United States Code*. This is because chapter numbers (or other subdivisional unit numbers) are sometimes reserved for future use when a statute is enacted. (A gap may also appear if a law has been repealed.)

(Recall from Chapters 28 and 29 that a consumer-debtor is a debtor whose debts result primarily from the purchase of goods for personal, family, or household use.)

In the following sections, we deal first with liquidation proceedings under Chapter 7 of the Code. We then examine the procedures required for Chapter 11 reorganizations and Chapter 12 and 13 plans. The latter three chapters are known as "rehabilitation" chapters.

SECTION 2

Liquidation Proceedings

Liquidation under Chapter 7 of the Bankruptcy Code is generally the most familiar type of bankruptcy proceeding and is often referred to as an *ordinary,* or *straight, bankruptcy.* Put simply, a debtor in a liquidation bankruptcy turns all assets over to a **trustee.** The trustee sells the nonexempt assets and distributes the proceeds to creditors. With certain exceptions, the remaining debts are then **discharged** (extinguished), and the debtors are relieved of their obligation to pay the debts.

Any "person"—defined as including individuals, partnerships, and corporations[2]—may be a debtor in a liquidation proceeding. Railroads, insurance companies, banks, savings and loan associations, investment companies licensed by the Small Business Administration, and credit unions cannot be debtors in a liquidation bankruptcy, however. Rather, other chapters of the Bankruptcy Code or federal or state statutes apply to them.

FILING THE PETITION

A straight bankruptcy may be commenced by the filing of either a voluntary or an involuntary **petition in bankruptcy**—the document that is filed with a bankruptcy court to initiate bankruptcy proceedings.

Voluntary Bankruptcy. When a voluntary petition in bankruptcy is brought by the debtor, he or she files official forms designated for that purpose in the bankruptcy court. The Code requires a consumer-debtor who has opted for liquidation bankruptcy proceedings to state in the petition, at the time of filing, that he or she understands the relief available under other chapters of the Code and has chosen to proceed under Chapter 7. If the consumer-debtor is represented by an attorney, the attorney must file an affidavit stating that he or she has informed the debtor of the relief available under each chapter. A debtor does not have to be insolvent[3] to file for bankruptcy relief. Anyone liable to a creditor can declare bankruptcy.

The voluntary petition contains the following schedules:

1. A list of both secured and unsecured creditors, their addresses, and the amount of debt owed to each.
2. A statement of the financial affairs of the debtor.
3. A list of all property owned by the debtor, including property claimed by the debtor to be exempt.
4. A listing of current income and expenses. (This schedule provides creditors and the court with relevant information on the debtor's ability to pay creditors a reasonable amount from future income. This information could permit a court, on its own motion, to dismiss a debtor's Chapter 7 petition after a hearing and to encourage the filing of a repayment plan under Chapter 13, when that would substantially improve the chances that creditors would be paid.)

The official forms must be completed accurately, sworn to under oath, and signed by the debtor. To conceal assets or knowingly supply false information on these schedules is a crime under the bankruptcy laws. If the voluntary petition for bankruptcy is found to be proper, the filing of the petition will itself constitute an **order for relief.** (An order for relief is a court's grant of assistance to a complainant. In the context of bankruptcy, relief consists of discharging a complainant's debts.) Once a consumer-debtor's voluntary petition has been filed, the clerk of the court or other appointee must give the trustee and creditors mailed notice of the order for relief not more than twenty days after entry of the order. A husband and wife may file jointly for bankruptcy under a single petition.

As mentioned above, debtors do not have to be insolvent to file for voluntary bankruptcy. Debtors

2. The definition of *corporation* includes unincorporated companies and associations. It also covers labor unions.

3. The inability to pay debts as they become due is known as *equitable* insolvency. A *balance sheet* insolvency, which exists when a debtor's liabilities exceed assets, is not the test. Thus, it is possible for debtors to voluntarily petition for bankruptcy or to be thrown into involuntary bankruptcy even though their assets far exceed their liabilities. This may occur when a debtor's cash flow problems become severe.

do not have unfettered access to bankruptcy proceedings under Chapter 7, however. Section 707(b) of the Bankruptcy Code allows a bankruptcy court to dismiss a petition for relief under Chapter 7 if the granting of relief would constitute "substantial abuse" of Chapter 7. There is no one, uniform standard, or test, for determining what constitutes substantial abuse.

Westlaw. See Case 30.1 at the end of this chapter. To view the full, unedited case from Westlaw,® go to this text's Web site at **http://wbl-cs.westbuslaw.com**.

Involuntary Bankruptcy. An involuntary bankruptcy occurs when the debtor's creditors force the debtor into bankruptcy proceedings. An involuntary case cannot be commenced against a farmer[4] or a charitable institution. For an involuntary action to be filed against other debtors, the following requirements must be met: If the debtor has twelve or more creditors, three or more of these creditors having unsecured claims totaling at least $11,625 must join in the petition. If a debtor has fewer than twelve creditors, one or more creditors having a claim of $11,625 may file.

If the debtor challenges the involuntary petition, a hearing will be held, and the bankruptcy court will enter an order for relief if it finds either of the following:

1. The debtor is generally not paying debts as they become due.
2. A general receiver, assignee, or custodian took possession of, or was appointed to take charge of, substantially all of the debtor's property within 120 days before the filing of the petition.

If the court grants an order for relief, the debtor will be required to supply the same information in the bankruptcy schedules as in a voluntary bankruptcy.

An involuntary petition should not be used as an everyday debt-collection device, and the Code provides penalties for the filing of frivolous petitions against debtors. Judgment may be granted against the petitioning creditors for the costs and attorneys' fees incurred by the debtor in defending against an involuntary petition that is dismissed by the court. If the petition is filed in bad faith, damages can be awarded for injury to the debtor's reputation. Punitive damages may also be awarded.

AUTOMATIC STAY

The moment a petition, either voluntary or involuntary, is filed, there exists an **automatic stay**, or suspension, of virtually all litigation and other action by creditors against the debtor or the debtor's property. In other words, once a petition has been filed, creditors cannot commence or continue most legal actions, such as foreclosure of liens, execution on judgments, trials, or any action to repossess property in the hands of the debtor. A secured creditor, however, may petition the bankruptcy court for relief from the automatic stay in certain circumstances. Also, the automatic stay does not apply to paternity, alimony, maintenance, and support debts, and to certain other actions, such as criminal proceedings, against the debtor. The Code provides that if a creditor knowingly violates the automatic stay (a willful violation), any party injured, including the debtor, is entitled to recover actual damages, costs, and attorneys' fees and may be entitled to recover punitive damages as well.

Underlying the Code's automatic stay provision for a secured creditor is a concept known as *adequate protection*. The **adequate protection doctrine,** among other things, protects secured creditors from losing their security as a result of the automatic stay. The bankruptcy court can provide adequate protection by requiring the debtor or trustee to make periodic cash payments or a one-time cash payment (or to provide additional collateral or replacement liens) to the extent that the stay may actually cause the value of the property to decrease. Or the court may grant other relief that is the "indubitable equivalent" of (that is, equivalent to, without any doubt) the secured party's interest in the property, such as a guaranty by a solvent third party to cover losses suffered by the secured party as a result of the stay.

PROPERTY OF THE ESTATE

On the commencement of a liquidation proceeding under Chapter 7, an *estate in property* is created. The estate consists of all the debtor's legal and equitable interests in property presently held, wherever located, together with community property, property transferred in a transaction voidable by the trustee,

4. The definition of *farmer* includes persons who receive more than 80 percent of their gross income from farming operations, such as tilling the soil, dairy farming, ranching, or the production or raising of crops, poultry, or livestock. Corporations and partnerships may qualify under certain conditions.

proceeds and profits from the property of the estate, and certain after-acquired property. Interests in certain property—such as gifts, inheritances, property settlements (divorce), and life insurance death proceeds—to which the debtor becomes entitled *within 180 days after filing* may also become part of the estate. Thus, the filing of a bankruptcy petition generally fixes a dividing line: property acquired prior to the filing of the petition becomes property of the estate, and property acquired after the filing of the petition, except as just noted, remains the debtor's.

Westlaw. See Case 30.2 at the end of this chapter. To view the full, unedited case from Westlaw,® go to this text's Web site at **http://wbl-cs.westbuslaw.com**.

CREDITORS' MEETING AND CLAIMS

Within a reasonable time after the order for relief has been granted (not less than ten days or more than thirty days), the bankruptcy court must call a meeting of the creditors listed in the schedules filed by the debtor. The bankruptcy judge does not attend this meeting.

The debtor is required to attend the meeting (unless excused by the court) and to submit to examination under oath by the creditors and the trustee. Failing to appear when required or making false statements under oath may result in the debtor's being denied a discharge in bankruptcy. At the meeting, the trustee ensures that the debtor is aware of the potential consequences of bankruptcy and of his or her ability to file for bankruptcy under a different chapter.

To be entitled to receive a portion of the debtor's estate, each creditor must normally file a *proof of claim* with the bankruptcy court clerk within ninety days of the creditors' meeting.[5] The proof of claim lists the creditor's name and address, as well as the amount that the creditor asserts is owed to the creditor by the debtor. If a creditor fails to file a proof of claim, the bankruptcy court or trustee may file the proof of claim on the creditor's behalf but is not obligated to do so.

Generally, any legal obligation of the debtor is a claim. In the case of a disputed, or unliquidated, claim, the bankruptcy court will set the value of the claim. Any creditor holding a debtor's obligation can file a claim against the debtor's estate. These claims are automatically allowed unless contested by the trustee, the debtor, or another creditor. A creditor who files a false claim commits a crime.

The Code, however, does not allow claims for breach of employment contracts or real estate leases for terms longer than one year. Such claims are limited to one year's wages or rent, despite the remaining length of either contract in breach.

EXEMPTIONS

The trustee takes control over the debtor's property, but an individual debtor is entitled to exempt certain property from the bankruptcy.[6] The Bankruptcy Code exempts the following property (the dollar amounts stated in the Bankruptcy Code were adjusted automatically on April 1, 1998, and will be adjusted every three years thereafter based on changes in the Consumer Price Index; the amounts stated in this chapter are in accordance with those computed on April 1, 2001):

1. Up to $17,425 in equity in the debtor's residence and burial plot (the homestead exemption).
2. Interest in a motor vehicle up to $2,775.
3. Interest, up to $450 for a particular item, in household goods and furnishings, wearing apparel, appliances, books, animals, crops, and musical instruments (the aggregate total of all items is limited, however, to $9,300).
4. Interest in jewelry up to $1,150.
5. Interest in any other property up to $925, plus any unused part of the $17,425 homestead exemption up to $8,725.
6. Interest in any tools of the debtor's trade up to $1,750.
7. Any unmatured life insurance contract owned by the debtor.
8. Certain interests in accrued dividends and interest under life insurance contracts owned by the debtor.
9. Professionally prescribed health aids.
10. The right to receive Social Security and certain welfare benefits, alimony and support, and certain pension benefits.
11. The right to receive certain personal injury and other awards up to $17,425.

Individual states have the power to pass legislation precluding debtors from using the federal exemptions

5. This ninety-day rule applies in Chapter 12 and Chapter 13 bankruptcies as well.

6. A debtor cannot avoid a judicial lien for paternity, alimony, maintenance, and support debts, however, even if the lien is imposed on exempt property.

within the state; a majority of the states have done this (see Chapter 29). In those states, debtors may use only state, not federal, exemptions. In the rest of the states, an individual debtor (or a husband and wife filing jointly) may choose either the exemptions provided under state law or the federal exemptions.[7]

THE TRUSTEE

Promptly after the order for relief in the liquidation proceeding has been entered, an interim, or provisional, trustee is appointed by the U.S. **Trustee** (a government official who performs appointing and other administrative tasks that a bankruptcy judge would otherwise have to perform). The interim, or provisional, trustee presides over the debtor's property until the first meeting of the creditors. At this first meeting, either a permanent trustee is elected or the interim trustee becomes the permanent trustee.

The basic duty of the trustee is to collect the debtor's available estate and reduce it to money for distribution, preserving the interests of both the debtor and unsecured creditors. This requires that the trustee be accountable for administering the debtor's estate. To enable the trustee to accomplish this duty, the Code gives the trustee certain powers, stated in both general and specific terms. These powers must be exercised within two years of the order for relief.

Trustee's Powers. The general powers of the trustee are described by the statement that the trustee occupies a position *equivalent* in rights to that of certain other parties. For example, the trustee has the same rights as a *lien creditor* who could have obtained a judicial lien on the debtor's property or who could have levied execution on the debtor's property. This means that a trustee has priority over an unperfected secured party (see Chapter 28) to the debtor's property. This right of a trustee, equivalent to that of a lien creditor, is known as the *strong-arm power.* A trustee also has power equivalent to that of a *bona fide purchaser* of real property from the debtor.

Nevertheless, in most states a creditor with a purchase-money security interest may prevail against a trustee, if the creditor files within ten days (twenty days, in most states) of the debtor's receipt of the collateral, even if the bankruptcy petition is filed before the creditor perfects. For example, Baker loaned Newbury $20,000 on January 1, taking a security interest in the machinery that Newbury purchased with the $20,000 and that was delivered on that same date. On January 27, before Baker had perfected her security interest, Newbury filed for bankruptcy. The trustee can invalidate Baker's security interest, because it was unperfected when Newbury filed the bankruptcy petition. Baker can only assert a claim as an unsecured creditor. But if Newbury had filed for bankruptcy on January 7, and Baker had perfected her security interest on January 8, she would have prevailed, because she would have perfected her purchase-money security interest within ten days of Newbury's receipt of the machinery.

The trustee has the power to require persons holding the debtor's property at the time the petition is filed to deliver the property to the trustee. (A trustee usually does not take actual possession of a debtor's property. Instead, a trustee's possession is constructive. For example, to obtain control of a debtor's business inventory, a trustee might change the locks on the doors to the business and hire a security guard.) The trustee also has specific powers of *avoidance*—that is, the trustee can set aside a sale or other transfer of the debtor's property, taking it back as a part of the debtor's estate. These powers include any voidable rights available to the debtor, preferences, certain statutory liens, and fraudulent transfers by the debtor. Each of these powers is discussed in more detail below.

The debtor shares most of the trustee's avoidance powers. Thus, if the trustee does not take action to enforce one of his or her rights (for example, to recover a preference), the debtor in a liquidation bankruptcy can nevertheless enforce that right.[8]

Voidable Rights. A trustee steps into the shoes of the debtor. Thus, any reason that a debtor can use to obtain the return of his or her property can be used by the trustee as well. These grounds include fraud, duress, incapacity, and mutual mistake.

---

7. State exemptions may or may not be limited with regard to value. Under state exemption laws, a debtor may enjoy an unlimited value exemption on a motor vehicle, for example, even though the federal bankruptcy scheme exempts a vehicle only up to a value of $2,775. A state's law may also define the property coming within an exemption differently than the federal law or may exclude, or except, specific items from an exemption, making it unavailable to a debtor who fits within the exception.

8. Under Chapter 11 (to be discussed later), for which no trustee other than the debtor generally exists, the debtor has the same avoidance powers as a trustee under Chapter 7. Under Chapters 12 and 13 (also to be discussed later), a trustee must be appointed.

For example, Ben sells his boat to Tara. Tara gives Ben a check, knowing that there are insufficient funds in her bank account to cover the check. Tara has committed fraud. Ben has the right to avoid that transfer and recover the boat from Tara. Thus, if Ben petitions for bankruptcy and the court enters an order for relief, the trustee can exercise the same right to recover the boat from Tara, and the boat becomes a part of the debtor's estate.

Preferences. A debtor is not permitted to transfer property or to make a payment that favors—or gives a **preference** to—one creditor over others. The trustee is allowed to recover payments made both voluntarily and involuntarily to one creditor in preference over another.

To have made a preferential payment that can be recovered, an *insolvent* debtor generally must have transferred property, for a *preexisting* debt, within *ninety days* of the filing of the petition in bankruptcy. The transfer must give the creditor more than the creditor would have received as a result of the bankruptcy proceedings. The trustee does not have to prove insolvency, as the Code provides that the debtor is presumed to be insolvent during this ninety-day period.

Sometimes the creditor receiving the preference is an **insider**—an individual, a partner, a partnership, a corporation, or an officer or a director of a corporation (or a relative of one of these) who has a close relationship with the debtor. If this is the situation, the avoidance power of the trustee is extended to transfers made within *one year* before filing; however, the *presumption* of insolvency is confined to the ninety-day period. Therefore, the trustee must prove that the debtor was insolvent at the time of a transfer that occurred prior to the ninety-day period.

Not all transfers are preferences. To be a preference, the transfer must be made for something other than current consideration. Therefore, it is generally assumed by most courts that payment for services rendered within ten to fifteen days prior to the payment of the current consideration is not a preference. If a creditor receives payment in the ordinary course of business, such as payment of last month's telephone bill, the payment cannot be recovered by the trustee in bankruptcy. To be recoverable, a preference must be a transfer for an antecedent (preexisting) debt, such as a year-old printing bill. In addition, the Code permits a consumer-debtor to transfer any property to a creditor up to a total value of $600 without the transfer's constituting a preference. Also, payment of paternity, alimony, maintenance, and support debts is not a preference.

If a preferred creditor has sold the property to an innocent third party, the trustee cannot recover the property from the innocent party. The creditor, however, generally can be held accountable for the value of the property.

Liens on Debtor's Property. The trustee has the power to avoid certain statutory liens against the debtor's property, such as a landlord's lien for unpaid rent. The trustee can avoid statutory liens that first became effective against the debtor when the bankruptcy petition was filed or when the debtor became insolvent. The trustee can also avoid any lien against a bona fide purchaser that was not perfected or enforceable on the date of the bankruptcy filing.

Fraudulent Transfers. The trustee may avoid fraudulent transfers or obligations if they are made within one year of the filing of the petition or if they are made with actual intent to hinder, delay, or defraud a creditor. Transfers made for less than reasonably equivalent consideration are also vulnerable if by making them, the debtor became insolvent, was left engaged in business with an unreasonably small amount of capital, or intended to incur debts that he or she could not pay. When a fraudulent transfer is made outside the Code's one-year limit, creditors may seek alternative relief under state laws. State laws often allow creditors to recover for transfers made up to three years prior to the filing of a petition.

Distribution of Property

The rights of perfected secured creditors were discussed in Chapter 28. The Code provides that a consumer-debtor, either within thirty days of filing a liquidation petition or before the date of the first meeting of the creditors (whichever is first), must file with the clerk a statement of intention with respect to the secured collateral. The statement must indicate whether the debtor will retain the collateral or surrender it to the secured party.[9] The trustee is obligated to enforce the debtor's statement within forty-five days after it is filed.

9. Also, if applicable, the debtor must specify whether the collateral will be claimed as exempt property and whether the debtor intends to redeem the property or reaffirm the debt secured by the collateral (the reaffirmation of debts will be discussed shortly).

If the collateral is surrendered to the perfected secured party, the secured creditor can enforce the security interest either by accepting the property in full satisfaction of the debt or by foreclosing on the collateral and using the proceeds to pay off the debt. Thus, the perfected secured party has priority over unsecured parties as to the proceeds from the disposition of the collateral. Indeed, the Code provides that if the value of the collateral exceeds the perfected secured party's claim and if the security agreement so provides, the secured party also has priority as to the proceeds in an amount that will cover reasonable fees and costs incurred because of the debtor's default. Fees include reasonable attorneys' fees. Any excess over this amount is used by the trustee to satisfy the claims of unsecured creditors. Should the collateral be insufficient to cover the secured debt owed, the secured creditor becomes an unsecured creditor for the difference.

Bankruptcy law establishes an order of priority for classes of debts owed to *unsecured* creditors, and they are paid in the order of their priority. Each class must be fully paid before the next class is entitled to any of the remaining proceeds. If there are insufficient proceeds to pay fully all the creditors in a class, the proceeds are distributed *proportionately* to the creditors in the class, and classes lower in priority receive nothing. The order of priority among classes of unsecured creditors is as follows:

1. Administrative expenses—including court costs, trustee fees, and attorneys' fees.
2. In an involuntary bankruptcy, expenses incurred by the debtor in the ordinary course of business from the date of the filing of the petition up to the appointment of the trustee or the issuance by the court of an order for relief.
3. Unpaid wages, salaries, and commissions earned within ninety days of the filing of the petition, limited to $4,650 per claimant. Any claim in excess of $4,650 or earned before the ninety-day period is treated as a claim of a general creditor (listed as item 9 below).
4. Unsecured claims for contributions to be made to employee benefit plans, limited to services performed during 180 days prior to the filing of the bankruptcy petition and $4,650 per employee.
5. Claims by farmers and fishers, up to $4,650, against debtor operators of grain storage or fish storage or processing facilities.
6. Consumer deposits of up to $2,100 given to the debtor before the petition was filed in connection with the purchase, lease, or rental of property or purchase of services that were not received or provided. Any claim in excess of $2,100 is treated as a claim of a general creditor (listed as item 9 below).
7. Paternity, alimony, maintenance, and support debts.
8. Certain taxes and penalties due to government units, such as income and property taxes.
9. Claims of general creditors.

If any amount remains after the priority classes of creditors have been satisfied, it is turned over to the debtor. Exhibit 30–1 illustrates graphically the collection and distribution of property in most voluntary bankruptcies.

In a bankruptcy case in which the debtor has no assets,[10] creditors are notified of the debtor's petition for bankruptcy but are instructed not to file a claim. In such a case, the unsecured creditors will receive no payment, and most, if not all, of these debts will be discharged.

DISCHARGE

From the debtor's point of view, the primary purpose of liquidation is to obtain a fresh start through a discharge of debts.[11] Certain debts, however, are not dischargeable in bankruptcy. Also, certain debtors may not qualify to have all debts discharged in bankruptcy. These situations are discussed below.

Exceptions to Discharge. Discharge of a debt may be denied because of the nature of the claim or the conduct of the debtor. Claims that are not dischargeable in a liquidation bankruptcy include the following:

1. Claims for back taxes accruing within three years prior to bankruptcy.
2. Claims for amounts borrowed by the debtor to pay federal taxes.
3. Claims against property or money obtained by the debtor under false pretenses or by false representations.
4. Claims by creditors who were not notified and did not know of the bankruptcy; these claims did not appear on the schedules the debtor was required to file.

10. This type of bankruptcy is called a "no asset" case.
11. Discharges are granted under Chapter 7 only to individuals, not to corporations or partnerships. The latter may use Chapter 11, or they may terminate their existence under state law.

EXHIBIT 30–1 COLLECTION AND DISTRIBUTION OF PROPERTY IN MOST VOLUNTARY BANKRUPTCIES

This exhibit illustrates the property that might be collected in a debtor's voluntary bankruptcy and how it might be distributed to creditors. Involuntary bankruptcies and some voluntary bankruptcies could include additional types of property and other creditors.

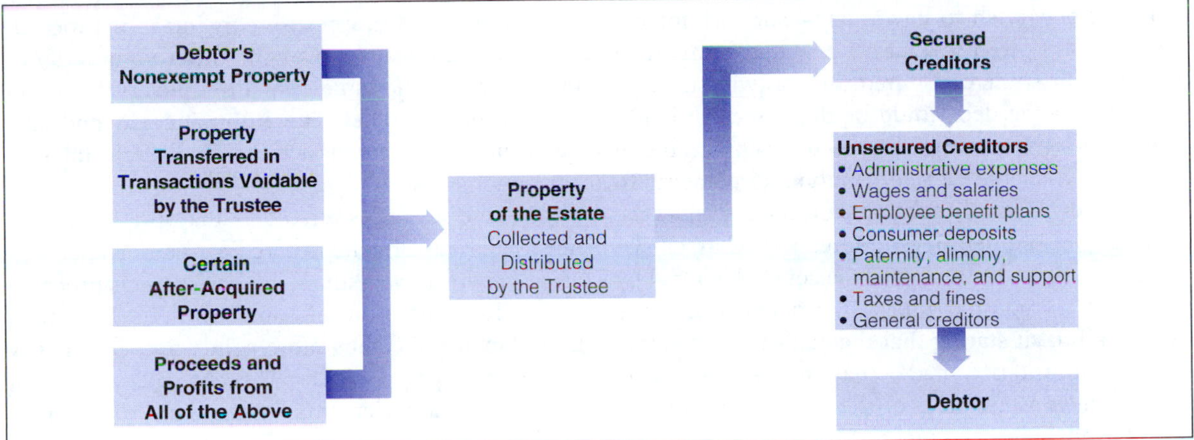

5. Claims based on fraud or misuse of funds by the debtor while he or she was acting in a fiduciary capacity or claims involving the debtor's embezzlement or larceny.

6. Alimony, child support, and (with certain exceptions) property settlements.

7. Claims based on willful or malicious conduct by the debtor toward another or the property of another.

8. Certain government fines and penalties.

9. Certain student loans, unless payment of the loans imposes an undue hardship on the debtor and the debtor's dependents.

10. Consumer debts of more than $1,150 for luxury goods or services owed to a single creditor incurred within sixty days of the order for relief. This denial of discharge is a rebuttable presumption (that is, the denial may be challenged by the debtor), however, and any debts reasonably incurred to support the debtor or dependents are not classified as luxuries.

11. Cash advances totaling more than $1,150 that are extensions of open-end consumer credit obtained by the debtor within sixty days of the order for relief. A denial of discharge of these debts is also a rebuttable presumption.

12. Judgments or consent decrees against a debtor as a result of the debtor's operation of a motor vehicle while intoxicated.

Westlaw. See Case 30.3 at the end of this chapter. To view the full, unedited case from Westlaw,® go to this text's Web site at **http://wbl-cs.westbuslaw.com**.

Objections to Discharge. In addition to the exceptions to discharge previously listed, a bankruptcy court may also deny the discharge of the *debtor* (as opposed to the debt). In the latter situation, the assets of the debtor are still distributed to the creditors, but the debtor remains liable for the unpaid portion of all claims. Some grounds for the denial of discharge of the debtor are the following:

1. The debtor's concealment or destruction of property with the intent to hinder, delay, or defraud a creditor.

2. The debtor's fraudulent concealment or destruction of financial records.

3. The granting of a discharge to the debtor within six years of the filing of the petition.

Effect of Discharge. The primary effect of a discharge is to void any judgment on a discharged debt and enjoin any action to collect a discharged debt. A discharge does not affect the liability of a co-debtor.

Revocation of Discharge. The Code provides that a debtor may lose his or her bankruptcy discharge by revocation on petition by the trustee or a creditor. The bankruptcy court may, within one year, revoke the discharge decree if it is discovered that the debtor acted fraudulently or dishonestly during the bankruptcy proceedings. The revocation renders the discharge void, allowing creditors not satisfied by the distribution of the debtor's estate to proceed with their claims against the debtor.

REAFFIRMATION OF DEBT

A debtor may wish to pay a debt—such as, for example, a debt owed to a family member, family doctor, bank, or some other creditor—notwithstanding the fact that the debt could be discharged in bankruptcy. An agreement to pay a debt dischargeable in bankruptcy is called a **reaffirmation agreement.** To be enforceable, reaffirmation agreements must be made before the debtor is granted a discharge. The agreement must be filed with the court. Approval by the court is required unless the debtor's attorney files an affidavit stating that the reaffirmation agreement is voluntarily made, that the debtor understands the consequences of the agreement and of a default under the agreement, and that the agreement will not result in an undue hardship on the debtor or the debtor's family. If court approval is required, a separate hearing will be held.

The agreement must contain a clear and conspicuous statement advising the debtor that reaffirmation is not required. The debtor can rescind, or cancel, the agreement at any time prior to discharge or within sixty days of the filing of the agreement, whichever is *later.* This rescission period must be stated *clearly* and *conspicuously* in the reaffirmation agreement.

SECTION 3

Reorganizations

The type of bankruptcy proceeding used most commonly by corporate debtors is the Chapter 11 *reorganization.* In a reorganization, the creditors and the debtor formulate a plan under which the debtor pays a portion of his or her debts and is discharged of the remainder. The debtor is allowed to continue in business. Although this type of bankruptcy is commonly a corporate reorganization, any debtors (including individuals but excluding stockbrokers and commodities brokers)[12] who are eligible for Chapter 7 relief are eligible for relief under Chapter 11.[13] In 1994, Congress established a "fast track" Chapter 11 for small-business debtors whose liabilities do not exceed $2 million and who do not own or manage real estate. This permits bankruptcy proceedings without the appointment of committees and can save time and costs.

The same principles that govern the filing of a liquidation petition apply to reorganization proceedings. The case may be brought either voluntarily or involuntarily. The same guidelines govern the entry of the order for relief. The automatic stay and adequate protection provisions are applicable in reorganizations as well.

In some instances, creditors may prefer private, negotiated adjustments of creditor-debtor relations, also known as **workouts**, to bankruptcy proceedings. Often, these out-of-court workouts are much more flexible and thus more conducive to a speedy settlement. Speed is critical, because delay is one of the most costly elements in any bankruptcy proceeding. Another advantage of workouts is that they avoid the various administrative costs of bankruptcy proceedings.

Under Section 305(a) of the Bankruptcy Code, a court, after notice and a hearing, may dismiss or suspend all proceedings in a case at any time if dismissal or suspension would better serve the interests of the creditors. Section 1112 also allows a court, after notice and a hearing, to dismiss a case under reorganization "for cause." Cause includes the absence of a reasonable likelihood of rehabilitation, the inability to effect a plan, and an unreasonable delay by the debtor that is prejudicial to (may harm the interests of) creditors.[14]

DEBTOR IN POSSESSION

On entry of the order for relief, the debtor generally continues to operate the business as a **debtor in possession (DIP).** The court, however, may appoint a trustee (often referred to as a *receiver*) to operate the debtor's business if gross mismanagement of the business is shown or if appointing a trustee is in the best interests of the estate.

The DIP's role is similar to that of a trustee in a liquidation. The DIP is entitled to avoid prepetition preferential payments made to creditors and prepetition fraudulent transfers of assets. The DIP has the power to decide whether to cancel or assume

12. In *Toibb v. Radloff,* 501 U.S. 157, 111 S.Ct. 2197, 115 L.Ed.2d 145 (1991), the United States Supreme Court ruled that a nonbusiness debtor may petition for relief under Chapter 11.

13. In addition, railroads are eligible for Chapter 11 relief.

14. See 11 U.S.C. Section 1112(b). Debtors are not prohibited from filing successive petitions, however. A debtor whose petition is dismissed, for example, can file a new Chapter 11 petition (which may be granted unless it is filed in bad faith).

prepetition executory contracts (those that are not yet performed) or unexpired leases.

Under the strong-arm clause[15] of the Bankruptcy Code, a DIP can avoid any obligation or any transfer of property of the debtor that could be avoided by certain parties. These parties include (1) a creditor who extended credit to the debtor at the time of bankruptcy (petition) and who consequently obtained a lien on the debtor's property; (2) a creditor who extended credit to the debtor at the time of bankruptcy and who consequently obtained a writ of execution against the debtor that was returned unsatisfied; and (3) a bona fide purchaser of real property from the debtor, if at the time of the bankruptcy the transfer was perfected.

COLLECTIVE BARGAINING AGREEMENTS

Under the Bankruptcy Reform Act of 1978, questions arose as to whether a reorganization debtor could reject a recently negotiated collectively bargained labor contract. In *National Labor Relations Board v. Bildisco and Bildisco*,[16] the United States Supreme Court held that a collective bargaining agreement subject to the National Labor Relations Act of 1935 (see Chapter 41) is an "executory contract" and thus subject to *rejection* by a debtor in possession. The Court emphasized that such a rejection should not be permitted unless there is a finding that the policy of Chapter 11 (successful rehabilitation of debtors) would be served by the action. Hence, when the bankruptcy court determines that rejection of a collective bargaining agreement should be permitted, it must make a reasoned finding *on the record* as to *why* it has determined that a rejection should be permitted.

The Code attempts to reconcile federal policies favoring collective bargaining with the need to allow a debtor company to reject executory labor contracts while trying to reorganize. The Code sets forth standards and procedures under which collective bargaining contracts can be assumed or rejected under a reorganization filing. In general, a collective bargaining contract can be rejected if the debtor has first proposed necessary contractual modifications to the union and the union has failed to adopt them without *good cause*. The company is required (1) to provide the union with the relevant information needed to evaluate this proposal and (2) to confer in *good faith* in attempting to reach a mutually satisfactory agreement on the modifications.

CREDITORS' COMMITTEES

As soon as practicable after the entry of the order for relief, a creditors' committee of unsecured creditors is appointed. The committee may consult with the trustee or the DIP concerning the administration of the case or the formulation of the plan. Additional creditors' committees may be appointed to represent special interest creditors. Orders affecting the estate generally will be entered only with either the consent of the committee or after a hearing in which the judge hears the position of the committee.

Certain small businesses that do not own or manage real estate can avoid creditors' committees. In these cases, orders can be entered without a committee's consent.

THE REORGANIZATION PLAN

A reorganization plan to rehabilitate the debtor is a plan to conserve and administer the debtor's assets in the hope of an eventual return to successful operation and solvency. The plan must be fair and equitable and must do the following:

1. Designate classes of claims and interests.
2. Specify the treatment to be afforded the classes. (The plan must provide the same treatment for all claims in a particular class.)
3. Provide an adequate means for execution.

Only the debtor may file a plan within the first 120 days after the date of the order for relief. If the debtor does not meet the 120-day deadline, however, or if the debtor fails to obtain the required creditor consent (discussed below) within 180 days, any party may propose a plan. If a small-business debtor chooses to avoid creditors' committees, the time for the debtor's filing is shortened to 100 days, and any other party's plan must be filed within 160 days.

Once the plan has been developed, it is submitted to each class of creditors for acceptance. Each class must accept the plan unless the class is not adversely affected by it. A class has accepted the plan when a majority of the creditors, representing two-thirds of the amount of the total claim, vote to approve it.

Even when all classes of claims accept the plan, the court may refuse to confirm it if it is not "in the

15. 11 U.S.C. Section 544(a).

16. 465 U.S. 513, 104 S.Ct. 1188, 79 L.Ed.2d 482 (1984).

best interests of the creditors."[17] A spouse or child of the debtor can block the plan if it does not provide for payment of their claims in cash.

The plan is binding on confirmation. The debtor is given a reorganization discharge from all claims not protected under the plan. This discharge does not apply to any claims that would be denied discharge under liquidation.

Even if only one class of claims has accepted the plan, the court may still confirm the plan under the Code's so-called **cram-down provision.** In other words, the court may confirm the plan over the objections of a class of creditors. Before the court can exercise this right of cram-down confirmation, it must be demonstrated that the plan does not discriminate unjustly against any creditors and that the plan is fair and equitable.

SECTION 4

Additional Forms of Bankruptcy Relief

In addition to bankruptcy relief through liquidation and reorganization, the Code also provides for individuals' repayment plans (Chapter 13) and family-farmer debt adjustments (Chapter 12).

INDIVIDUALS' REPAYMENT PLAN

Chapter 13 of the Bankruptcy Code provides for "Adjustment of Debts of an Individual with Regular Income." Individuals (not partnerships or corporations) with regular income who owe fixed unsecured debts of less than $290,525 or fixed secured debts of less than $871,550 may take advantage of bankruptcy repayment plans. This includes salaried employees; sole proprietors; and individuals who live on welfare, Social Security, fixed pensions, or investment income. Many small-business debtors have a choice of filing a plan for reorganization or for repayment. There are several advantages, however, with repayment plans. One advantage is that they are less expensive and less complicated than reorganization proceedings or, for that matter, even liquidation proceedings.

Filing the Petition. A repayment plan case can be initiated only by the filing of a voluntary petition by the debtor. Certain liquidation and reorganization cases may be converted to repayment plan cases with the consent of the debtor.[18] A trustee, who will make payments under the plan, must be appointed. On the filing of a repayment plan petition, the automatic stay previously discussed takes effect. Although the stay applies to all or part of a consumer debt, it does not apply to any business debt incurred by the debtor.

The Repayment Plan. A plan of rehabilitation by repayment must provide for the following:

1. The turnover to the trustee of such future earnings or income of the debtor as is necessary for execution of the plan.
2. Full payment in deferred cash payments of all claims entitled to priority.[19]
3. The same treatment of all claims within a particular class. (The Code permits the debtor to list codebtors, such as guarantors or sureties, as a separate class.)

Filing the Plan. Only the debtor may file for a repayment plan. This plan may provide either for payment of all obligations in full or for payment of a lesser amount. The time for payment under the plan may not exceed three years unless the court approves an extension. The term, with extension, may not exceed five years.

The Code requires the debtor to make "timely" payments, and the trustee is required to ensure that the debtor commences these payments. The debtor must begin making payments under the proposed plan within thirty days after the plan has been *filed.* If the plan has not been confirmed, the trustee is instructed to retain the payments until the plan is confirmed and then distribute them accordingly. If the plan is denied, the trustee will return the payments to the debtor less any costs. Failure of the debtor to make timely payments or to commence payments within the thirty-day period will allow the court to convert the case to a liquidation bankruptcy or to dismiss the petition.

Confirmation of the Plan. After the plan is filed, the court holds a confirmation hearing, at which inter-

17. The plan need not provide for full repayment to unsecured creditors. Instead, creditors receive a percentage of each dollar owed to them by the debtor.

18. A Chapter 13 case may be converted to a Chapter 7 case either at the request of the debtor or, under certain circumstances, "for cause" by a creditor. A Chapter 13 case may be converted to a Chapter 11 case after a hearing.

19. As with a Chapter 11 reorganization plan, full repayment of all claims is not always required.

ested parties may object to the plan. The court will confirm a plan with respect to each claim of a secured creditor under any of the following circumstances:

1. If the secured creditors have accepted the plan.
2. If the plan provides that creditors retain their liens and if the value of the property to be distributed to them under the plan is not less than the secured portion of their claims.
3. If the debtor surrenders the property securing the claims to the creditors.

Objection to the Plan. Unsecured creditors do not have a vote to confirm a repayment plan, but they can object to it. The court can approve a plan over the objection of the trustee or any unsecured creditor only in either of the following situations:

1. When the value of the property to be distributed under the plan is at least equal to the amount of the claims.
2. When all the debtor's projected disposable income to be received during the three-year plan period will be applied to making payments. Disposable income is all income received less amounts needed to support the debtor and dependents and/or amounts needed to meet ordinary expenses to continue the operation of a business.

Modification of the Plan. Prior to completion of payments, the plan may be modified at the request of the debtor, the trustee, or an unsecured creditor. If there is an objection to the modification by any interested party, the court must hold a hearing to determine approval or disapproval of the modified plan.

Discharge. After completion of all payments, the court grants a discharge of all debts provided for by the repayment plan. Except for allowed claims not provided for by the plan, certain long-term debts provided for by the plan, and claims for alimony and child support, all other debts are dischargeable. A discharge of debts under a Chapter 13 repayment plan is sometimes referred to as a "superdischarge." One of the reasons for this is that the law allows a Chapter 13 discharge to include fraudulently incurred debt and claims resulting from malicious or willful injury. Therefore, a discharge under Chapter 13 may be much more beneficial to some debtors than a liquidation discharge under Chapter 7.

Even if the debtor does not complete the plan, a hardship discharge may be granted if failure to complete the plan was due to circumstances beyond the debtor's control and if the value of the property distributed under the plan was greater than would have been paid in a liquidation. A discharge can be revoked within one year if it was obtained by fraud.

FAMILY FARMERS

In 1986, to help relieve economic pressure on owners of small farms, Congress created Chapter 12 of the Bankruptcy Code. For purposes of Chapter 12, a *family farmer* is one whose gross income is at least 50 percent farm dependent and whose debts are at least 80 percent farm related. The total debt must not exceed $1.5 million. A partnership or closely held corporation (at least 50 percent owned by the farm family) can also take advantage of this law.

The procedure for filing a family-farmer bankruptcy plan is very similar to the procedure for filing a repayment plan under Chapter 13. The farmer-debtor must file a plan not later than ninety days after the order for relief. The filing of the petition acts as an automatic stay against creditors' and co-obligors' actions against the estate.

The content of a family-farmer plan is basically the same as that of a Chapter 13 repayment plan. The plan can be modified by the farmer-debtor but, except for cause, must be confirmed or denied within forty-five days of the filing of the plan.

Court confirmation of the plan is the same as for a repayment plan. In summary, the plan must provide for payment of secured debts at the value of the collateral. If the secured debt exceeds the value of the collateral, the remaining debt is unsecured. For unsecured debtors, the plan must be confirmed if either the value of the property to be distributed under the plan equals the amount of the claim or the plan provides that all of the farmer-debtor's disposable income to be received in a three-year period (or longer, by court approval) will be applied to making payments. Disposable income is all income received less amounts needed to support the farmer-debtor and family and to continue the farming operation. Completion of payments under the plan discharges all debts provided for by the plan.

A farmer who has already filed a reorganization or repayment plan may convert the plan to a family-farmer plan. The farmer-debtor may also convert a family-farmer plan to a liquidation plan.

Terms and Concepts to Review

adequate protection doctrine 600
automatic stay 600
cram-down provision 608
debtor in possession (DIP) 606
discharge 599
insider 603
liquidation 598
order for relief 599
petition in bankruptcy 599
preference 603
reaffirmation agreement 606
trustee 599
U.S. Trustee 602
workout 606

Chapter Summary

FORMS OF BANKRUPTCY RELIEF COMPARED

Issue	Chapter 7	Chapter 11	Chapters 12 and 13
Purpose	Liquidation.	Reorganization.	Adjustment.
Who Can Petition	Debtor (voluntary) or creditors (involuntary).	Debtor (voluntary) or creditors (involuntary).	Debtor (voluntary) only.
Who Can Be a Debtor	Any "person" (including partnerships, corporations, and municipalities) except railroads, insurance companies, blanks, savings and loan institutions, investment companies licensed by the Small Business Administration, and credit unions. Farmers and charitable institutions also cannot be involuntarily petitioned.	Any debtor eligible for Chapter 7 relief; railroads are also eligible.	*Chapter 12*—Any family farmer (one whose gross income is at least 50 percent farm dependent and whose debts are at least 80 percent farm related) or any partnership or closely held corporation at least 50 percent owned by a farm family, when total debt does not exceed $1.5 million. *Chapter 13*—Any individual (not partnerships or corporations) with regular income who owes fixed unsecured debts of less than $290,525 or fixed secured debts of less than $871,550.
Procedure Leading to Discharge	Nonexempt property is sold with proceeds to be distributed (in order) to priority groups. Dischargeable debts are terminated.	Plan is submitted; if it is approved and followed, debts are discharged.	Plan is submitted and must be approved if the value of the property to be distributed equals the amount of the claims or if the debtor turns over disposable income for a three-year period; if the plan is followed, debts are discharged.
Advantages	On liquidation and distribution, most debts are discharged, and the debtor has an opportunity for a fresh start.	Debtor continues in business. Creditors can either accept the plan, or it can be "crammed down" on them. The plan allows for the reorganization and liquidation of debts over the plan period.	Debtor continues in business or possession of assets. If the plan is approved, most debts are discharged after a three-year period.

CASES FOR ANALYSIS

Westlaw. You can access the full text of each case presented below by going to the Westlaw cases on this text's Web site at http://wbl-cs.westbuslaw.com. Each Westlaw case includes the names of all plaintiffs and defendants, the dates on which the case was argued and decided, a brief summary of the issues and decisions in the case, headnotes classifying the specific issues in the case according to the West Key Number System, and the court's opinion. Concurring and dissenting opinions, if any, are included as well.

CASE 30.1 VOLUNTARY BANKRUPTCY

IN RE LAMANNA

United States Court of Appeals,
First Circuit, 1998.
153 F.3d 1.

LYNCH, Circuit Judge.

* * * *

I.

Richard Lamanna, a Rhode Island resident, filed for bankruptcy under Chapter 7 on February 18, 1997. Lamanna's schedules, filed with his voluntary petition, show that he has total unsecured debt of $15,911.96 which is primarily consumer debt, his monthly income is $1,350.96, and his monthly expenses are $580. Lamanna's income therefore exceeds his expenses by $770.96 per month, the amount of his disposable income.

On February 24, 1997, the bankruptcy court * * * ordered Lamanna to show * * * why his petition should not be dismissed as a "substantial abuse" of Chapter 7 under [Section] 707(b). * * * [T]he court noted that Lamanna's schedules showed that he was capable of paying 100% of his debts over three years under a Chapter 13 payment plan.

* * * Lamanna argued that his expenses were artificially low because he was living with his parents. Without that subsidy, he said, he could not limit his expenses to $580 per month and would thus have no disposable income with which to pay his debts. Yet Lamanna acknowledged that his scheduled expenses and income were accurate and that he did not anticipate a change in living circumstances, i.e., moving out of his parents' house, that would precipitate a rise in living expenses.

The [federal] bankruptcy court, applying the "totality of the circumstances" test, found "substantial abuse" and dismissed the case. The [U.S. Bankruptcy Appellate Panel for the First Circuit (BAP)] affirmed on the same grounds. Lamanna appeals.

II.

The question of whether allowing Lamanna's bankruptcy petition would constitute "substantial abuse" of Chapter 7 under [Section] 707(b) contains two components: first, the proper test by which "substantial abuse" is measured; second, whether, applying that test, the BAP correctly decided the issue. * * *

A. *The "totality of the circumstances" test*

* * * *

* * * Although tests employed by various [federal] courts of appeals do not employ precisely the same language, they share common elements. First and foremost, it is agreed that a consumer debtor's ability to repay his debts out of future disposable income is strong evidence of "substantial abuse". * * * In determining whether to apply [Section] 707(b) to an individual debtor, * * * a court should ascertain from the totality of the circumstances whether he is merely seeking an advantage over his creditors, or is "honest," in the sense that his relationship with his creditors has been marked by essentially honorable and undeceptive dealings, and whether he is "needy" in the sense that his financial predicament warrants the discharge of his debts in exchange for liquidation of his assets. *Substantial abuse can be predicated upon either lack of honesty or want of need.* * * * Among the factors to be considered in deciding whether a debtor is needy is his ability to repay his debts out of future earnings. That factor alone may be sufficient to warrant dismissal. For example, a court would not be justified in concluding that a debtor is needy and worthy of discharge, where his disposable income permits liquidation of his consumer debts with relative ease. Other factors relevant to need include whether the debtor enjoys a stable source of future income, whether he is eligible for adjustments of his debts through Chapter 13 of the Bankruptcy Code, whether there are state remedies with the potential to ease his financial predicament, the degree of relief obtainable through private negotiations, and whether his expenses can be reduced significantly without depriving him of adequate food, clothing, shelter and other necessities. * * * [T]he "totality of the circumstances" test demands a comprehensive review of the debtor's current and potential financial situation. [Emphasis added.]

* * * *

* * * [I]n assessing the totality of a debtor's circumstances, courts should regard the debtor's ability to repay out of future disposable income as the primary, but not necessarily conclusive, factor of "substantial abuse." * * *

B. *Application of the Standard*

Applying the "totality of the circumstances" test to Lamanna's case results in affirmance of the dismissal of his Chapter 7 petition for "substantial abuse." Lamanna's schedules showed that he has sufficient disposable income to repay his debts under a Chapter 13 repayment plan in three to five years. There is no evidence that Lamanna's living situation was unstable or likely to change in the near future. There is no evidence of other factors that cast doubt on the stability of Lamanna's future income and expenses. Although Lamanna's expenses are particularly low because he lives with his parents, this state of affairs, as the BAP noted, "is not artificial; it is actual." The court properly based its decision on the current and foreseeable facts. If Lamanna's circumstances dramatically change, he is free to seek relief anew.

Lamanna's argument that the court penalized him for living with his parents (and thus having exceptionally low monthly expenses) boils down to the notion that [Section] 707(b) requires the bankruptcy court to impute a minimum cost of living to a debtor and then measure the debtor's actual income against the higher of the imputed minimum and the debtor's actual expenses. [Section] 707 does not contain such an implicit requirement, and this court will not write such a requirement into the statute.

* * * *

III.

* * * The decision is *affirmed.* * * *

CASE 30.2 PROPERTY OF THE ESTATE

IN RE ANDREWS

United States Court of Appeals,
Fourth Circuit, 1996.
80 F.3d 906.

ELLIS, District Judge:

* * * *

I.

Appellant John A. Andrews ("Andrews") worked in the ready-mix concrete business most of his life. In 1974, he and various partners formed a ready-mix concrete company in Herndon, Virginia. The company, which ultimately came to be known as AMAX Corporation ("AMAX"), grew to be quite successful, with annual sales of approximately thirty million dollars. As a part owner of AMAX, Andrews was personally active in the company and consequently developed numerous and substantial customer contacts and relationships in the concrete business. He expanded these contacts in 1980 by forming a real estate development company, which allowed him to participate in joint ventures with builders and developers.

In 1989, Andrews and the other owners of the company negotiated with Tarmac Acquisition, Inc. ("Tarmac") for the latter to purchase the assets of AMAX and related entities. Both sides to the negotiations retained independent experts to value AMAX's assets. The final sale price of nine million dollars was based on these expert valuations. Tarmac also purchased AMAX's customer list, representing the good will of the company, for an additional one million dollars. At the same time, the principal owners of AMAX, including Andrews, entered into separate non-competition agreements with Tarmac. These agreements were an express condition of the asset sale because Tarmac was concerned about the AMAX principals' substantial customer relationships and contacts in the ready-mix concrete business.

Andrews's non-competition agreement with Tarmac ("NCA"), dated July 17, 1989, provided that he would not compete with Tarmac in the ready-mix concrete business in Northern Virginia, the District of Columbia, or the adjacent portions of Maryland for a period of four years. In exchange, Andrews was to receive one million dollars. * * * [T]his one million dollars was to be paid in quarterly installments of $62,500, plus ten percent annual interest. Andrews asserts that the payments were structured in this manner to approximate his AMAX salary. Yet, he also concedes that Tarmac arrived at the one million dollar figure based on its estimate of the value of eliminating future competition from Andrews.

* * * *

On October 14, 1992, Andrews filed a voluntary petition for relief under Chapter 7 in the United States Bankruptcy Court for the Eastern District of Virginia. On December 4, 1992, Andrews instituted this contested proceeding against the estate trustee * * * . The motion initiating the proceeding sought to exclude from Andrews's bankruptcy estate all post-petition payments due him under the NCA. The total of these payments is $250,000 plus interest. According to Andrews, the payments represented his only source of income while the NCA remained in effect because the NCA precluded him from engaging in the ready-mix concrete business. But for the NCA, Andrews asserts, he could have profitably re-entered the ready-mix concrete business.

The bankruptcy court denied Andrews's motion * * * . The [federal] district court affirmed, and this appeal followed.

II.

* * * *

* * * [T]he Bankruptcy Code * * * has two overarching purposes: (1) providing protection for the creditors of the insolvent debtor and (2) permitting the debtor to carry on and rebuild his life, that is, to make a "fresh start." The first purpose is effectuated through statutory provisions that marshal and consolidate the debtor's assets into a broadly defined estate from which, in an equitable and orderly process, the debtor's unsatisfied obligations to creditors are paid to the extent possible. The second purpose finds expression in the bright line the Bankruptcy Code draws between pre- and post-bankruptcy filing events. Thus, [the Code] provides that the estate includes the debtor's legal and equitable interests "as of the com-

mencement of the case," and leaves the bankrupt debtor free after that date to accumulate new wealth so that he might make a fresh start following bankruptcy. Similarly, [the Code] allows the debtor to exclude from his estate any compensation or salary he might earn after the date of the petition. Toward the same end, [the Code] facilitates the fresh start by ultimately discharging the balance of the debtor's unpaid obligations after the estate is exhausted.

Sometimes the Bankruptcy Code's two purposes appear to conflict, as when a debtor claims property to aid his fresh start while his creditors claim the same property to satisfy the debtor's obligations to them. Yet, this conflict is illusory, for by drawing the bright line between the debtor's pre- and post-petition assets, the Bankruptcy Code harmonizes the two purposes. * * * Pre-petition assets * * * are those assets rooted in the debtor's pre-petition activities, including any proceeds that may flow from those assets in the future. These assets belong to the estate and ultimately to the creditors. Post-petition assets are those that result from the debtor's post-petition activities and are his to keep free and clear of the bankruptcy proceeding.

* * * *

* * * [T]he NCA payments due Andrews fall clearly on the pre-bankruptcy or "past" side of the bright line. These payments are plainly rooted in, and grow out of, Andrews's pre-petition activities. Thus, it is undisputed that the NCA was more than just contemporaneous with Tarmac's purchase of the AMAX assets; it was an integral part of that purchase. This is precisely what the bankruptcy judge meant when he found that the NCA was "ancillary" to the sale of the business: but for the asset sale, there would have been no NCA and no quarterly payments to Andrews. * * * Given this close connection between the NCA and the pre-petition sale of the debtor's share in the concrete business, we are persuaded that the payments were well rooted in the pre-bankruptcy past. *We think they were also so little entangled with the bankrupt's ability to make a fresh start that they should be included in Andrews's estate.* [Emphasis added.]

* * * Were the rule otherwise, debtors would be able, indeed invited, to circumvent the bankruptcy laws through clever use of agreements not to compete. Specifically, a debtor selling a business, yet anticipating filing bankruptcy, could divert sale proceeds from the bankruptcy estate by shifting these proceeds from pre-petition sales payments to post-petition noncompetition payments. There, as here, the post-petition noncompetition payments are not part of the debtor's fresh start efforts, but rather payments that are rooted in the debtor's pre-petition conduct. As such, these are payments that [the Code] contemplates should be included in the bankruptcy estate.

* * * *

* * * The judgment of the district court is affirmed.

* * * *

WIDENER, Circuit Judge, dissenting:

I respectfully dissent.

I am of [the] opinion that since only Andrews can perform the noncompetition agreement, * * * the payments [due to him under the agreement should be] excluded from property of the estate. * * *

* * * *

The decision of the majority is that the [Bankruptcy] Trustee has the benefit of Andrews' noncompetition contract with Tarmac because payments under the contract are ordered to be given to the Trustee. Thus the effect of the majority decision is that the Trustee has assumed the [contract] in order that he might receive the benefits under it, that is to say, the $62,500 payments. What the majority does not mention, however, is [that under the Code:]

> (c) The trustee may not assume * * * any executory contract * * * if—
> (1)(A) Applicable law excuses a party, other than the debtor, to such contract * * * from accepting performance from or rendering performance to an entity other than the debtor * * * and
> (B) Such party does not consent to such * * * assumption.

* * * There is nothing in the noncompetition agreement about Tarmac accepting performance from anyone other than Andrews. * * *

Therefore, the attempted assumption of the noncompetition agreement by the Trustee, in order to get the payments, is a violation of [the Code].

CASE 30.3 DISCHARGE

IN RE JERCICH
United States Court of Appeals,
Ninth Circuit, 2001.
238 F.3d 1202.

T.G. NELSON, Circuit Judge:

* * * *

I.

* * * From June 1981 to January 1983, [James] Petralia was employed by George Jercich, Inc., a real estate company wholly owned and operated by debtor [George] Jercich. The company performed mortgage broker services, and Petralia's primary duty was to obtain investors to fund loans arranged by Jercich. Pursuant to an employment agreement between Petralia and Jercich, Petralia was to be paid a salary plus a commission for loans which were funded through his efforts. The commissions were to be paid on a monthly basis.

Jercich failed to pay Petralia his commissions as required under the employment agreement. Petralia quit his employment with Jercich in January 1983 and in February 1983 filed an action against Jercich in [a] California state court. * * *

After a bench trial, the state court granted judgment in favor of Petralia. The court found that Jercich had not paid Petralia commissions and vacation pay as required under the employment contract; that "Jercich had the clear ability to make these payments to Petralia, but chose not to"; that instead of paying Petralia and other employees the money owed to them, "Jercich utilized the funds from his company to pay for a wide variety of personal investments, including a horse ranch"; and that Jercich's behavior was willful and * * * deliberate and "constituted substantial oppression" * * * . The state trial court's judgment against Jercich was affirmed by [a state intermediate appellate court] * * * .

While the appeal of the state trial court judgment was pending, Jercich filed a Chapter 7 bankruptcy petition. * * * [A]fter the state trial court judgment had been affirmed on appeal, Petralia initiated the present adversary proceeding seeking to have the state court judgment excepted from discharge.

The [federal] bankruptcy court resolved the adversary proceeding in favor of Jercich. * * * The bankruptcy court therefore held that the debt was dischargeable.

[The U.S. Bankruptcy Appellate Panel for the Ninth Circuit (BAP)] affirmed * * * .

* * * *

III.

[The Bankruptcy Code] excepts from discharge debts resulting from "willful and malicious injury by the debtor to another entity or to the property of another entity." * * * An intentional breach of contract is excepted from discharge only when it is accompanied by malicious and willful *tortious conduct*. [Emphasis added.]

By holding, in the present case, that the debt was not excepted from discharge under [the Code], BAP imposed an additional requirement: not only must there be tortious conduct, but according to BAP, this conduct must be "tortious even if a contract between the parties did not exist." We disagree with the imposition of this additional requirement.

First, there is nothing in the language of [the Code] to indicate that a debt arising from a breach of contract is excepted from discharge only if the debtor's conduct would be tortious even if no contract existed. To the contrary, although * * * an intentional breach of contract *generally* will not give rise to a nondischargeable debt, where an intentional breach of contract is accompanied by tortious conduct which results in willful and malicious injury, the resulting debt is excepted from discharge * * * .

Moreover, *one of the fundamental policies of bankruptcy law is to give a fresh start only to the honest but unfortunate debtor.* * * * Allowing discharge of debts simply because the tortious conduct at issue would not be tortious in the absence of a contract would negate this fundamental policy. [Emphasis added.]

We therefore hold that to be excepted from discharge * * * , a breach of contract must be accompanied by some form of "tortious conduct" that gives rise to "willful and malicious injury." In so holding, we reject BAP's imposition of a requirement that the conduct at issue be tortious even if a contract between the parties did not exist.

IV.

A. *Tortious Conduct*

To determine whether Jercich's conduct was tortious, we look to California state law. Under California law, conduct amounting to a breach of contract becomes tortious only when it also violates an independent duty arising from principles of tort law.

Outside the area of insurance contracts, tort recovery for the bad faith breach of a contract is permitted only when, in addition to the breach of the covenant of good faith and fair dealing a defendant's conduct violates a fundamental public policy of the state. * * * [T]he prompt payment of wages due an employee is a fundamental public policy in California. * * *

In the present case, the state trial court found that Jercich had the "clear ability" to pay Petralia his wages when they were due, but willfully "chose not to" in violation of California law. The court also found that Jercich's acts amounted to oppression under [California law] * * * .

Based on these state court findings, we hold that Jercich's nonpayment of wages under the particular circumstances of this case constituted tortious conduct.

B. *Willful and Malicious Injury*

1. *Willfulness*

* * * *

We hold * * * that * * * the willful injury requirement * * * is met when it is shown either that the debtor had a subjective motive to inflict the injury or that the debtor believed that injury was substantially certain to occur as a result of his conduct. We believe that this holding comports with * * * bankruptcy law's fundamental policy of granting discharges only to the honest but unfortunate debtor.

Application of this standard to the state court's factual findings demonstrates that the injury to Petralia was willful. As the state court found, Jercich knew he owed the wages to Petralia and that injury to Petralia was substantially certain to occur if the wages were not paid; and Jercich had the clear ability to pay Petralia his wages, yet chose not to pay and instead used the money for his own personal benefit. He therefore inflicted willful injury on Petralia.

2. *Maliciousness*

A "malicious" injury involves (1) a wrongful act, (2) done intentionally, (3) which necessarily causes injury, and (4) is done without just cause or excuse. In the present case, the state court found Jercich knew he owed Petralia the wages and that injury to Petralia was substantially certain to occur if the wages were not paid; that Jercich had the clear ability to pay Petralia the wages; and that despite his knowledge, Jercich chose not to pay and instead used the money for his own personal benefit. Jercich has pointed to no just cause or excuse for his behavior. Moreover, Jercich's deliberate and willful failure to pay was found by the state trial court to constitute substantial oppression * * * which [under California law] is "despicable conduct that subjects a person to cruel and unjust hardship in conscious disregard of that person's rights." We hold that these state court findings are sufficient to show that the injury inflicted by Jercich was malicious * * * .

V.

The debt in this case arose from willful and malicious injury caused by the debtor's tortious conduct. It is therefore excepted from discharge * * * .

REVERSED.

CASE PROBLEMS

30–1. James Blair, Jr., owed primarily consumer debts of less than $7,000, and his income exceeded his living expenses by more than $200 a month. When he filed a petition for relief under Chapter 7, the court concluded that if he filed a repayment plan under Chapter 13, his debts would be paid off in forty months. The bankruptcy administrator filed a motion to dismiss Blair's petition. Should the court grant the motion to dismiss? Why, or why not? Discuss. [*Matter of Blair,* 180 Bankr. 656 (N.D.Ala. 1995)]

30–2. Mary Lou Baker attended three different institutions of higher learning, the University of Tennessee at Chattanooga, Cleveland State Community College, and the Baroness Erlanger School of Nursing. At these three schools, she received educational loans totaling $6,635. After graduation, she was employed, but her monthly take-home pay was less than $650. Monthly expenses for herself and her three children were approximately $925. Her husband had left town and provided no child or other financial support. She received no public aid and had no other income. In January 1981, just prior to this action, Mary Lou Baker's church paid her gas bill so that she and her children could have heat in their home. One child had difficulty reading, and another required expensive shoes. Baker had not been well and had been unable to pay her medical bills. She filed for bankruptcy in a federal bankruptcy court. In her petition, she sought a discharge of her educational loans based on the hardship provision, which is the issue before the court. Should Baker's debts be discharged? What will the court decide? Discuss fully. [*In re Baker,* 10 Bankr. 870 (E.D.Tenn. 1981)]

30–3. In 1983, Beech Acceptance Corp. financed the sale of three airplanes to Gull Air, Inc. Approximately three years later, Gull Air defaulted on its obligations to Beech Acceptance, and Beech filed suit. Before the trial, Gull Air and Beech negotiated a workout agreement that provided for large monthly payments over a certain period. Despite the workout agreement, Gull Air filed a Chapter 11 petition in bankruptcy. Gull Air claimed that payments made under the workout agreement during the ninety days prior to the filing of the Chapter 11 petition amounted to a preference and must be returned to the debtor in possession (Gull Air). There was no question that Beech had received more than it would have under a Chapter 7 liquidation. Beech claimed that the payments had been made in the ordinary course of business. Discuss who is correct. [*In re Gull Air, Inc.,* 82 Bankr. 1 (Bankr.D.Mass. 1988)]

30–4. Ellis and Bonnie Jarrell filed a Chapter 7 petition. The reason for the filing was not calamity, sudden illness, disability, or unemployment—both Jarrells were employed. Their petition was full of inaccuracies that understated their income and overstated their obligations. For example, they declared as an expense a monthly contribution to an investment plan. The truth was that they had monthly income of $3,197.45 and expenses of $2,159.44. They were attempting to discharge a total of $15,391.64 in unsecured debts. Most of these were credit-card debts, at least half of which had been taken as cash advances. Should the court dismiss the petition? If so, why? Discuss. [*In re Jarrell,* 189 Bankr. 374 (M.D.N.C. 1995)]

30–5. Prior to filing for bankruptcy, Bray was making loan payments to his company's credit union through payroll deductions. Bray's employer continued to deduct the loan payments from Bray's paychecks after being notified of the bankruptcy petition. Is this a violation of the Bankruptcy Code? Discuss. [*In re Bray,* 17 Bankr. 152 (Bankr.N.D.Ga. 1982)]

30–6. Ronald and Rhonda Harris filed a petition for liquidation under Chapter 7. They submitted a schedule that listed their debts at $9,735, their assets (other than real estate) at $7,295, their net monthly income at $2,249, and their monthly expenses at $1,973. The U.S. Trustee, concluding that the debtors could pay a significant portion of their unsecured debt under a three-year Chapter 13 plan, moved to dismiss the petition on the ground that to grant the Harrises relief would constitute a substantial abuse of Chapter 7 under Section 707(b) of the Bankruptcy Code. The bankruptcy court denied the U.S. Trustee's motion, holding that two conditions must be met before a case can be dismissed for substantial abuse and that the trustee had failed to establish the existence of these conditions. The two conditions were (1) that the debtors exhibited "egregious behavior" (such as repeated bankruptcy filings evidencing bad faith, fraud, or misconduct) and (2) that a significant portion of the unsecured debt could be paid under a three-year Chapter 13 plan. Assuming that the debtors had not committed any egregious acts and that they did have the ability to pay all of their debts over a three-year period, how should the court rule on appeal? What is the primary factor to be considered when determining whether a debtor's actions constitute "substantial abuse" of Chapter 7? Discuss. [*U.S. Trustee v. Harris*, 960 F.2d 74 (8th Cir. 1992)]

30–7. In 1987, Bank South repossessed and sold Jamie Lee Busbin's 1979 Ford LTD automobile. The price that the automobile brought at the sale was $1,450 short of the amount Busbin owed Bank South. Bank South obtained a deficiency judgment for the $1,450 and garnished Busbin's wages, collecting $896.46. Busbin filed a voluntary petition for a Chapter 7 bankruptcy discharge, listing Bank South's claim for $1,450 as his sole debt. Busbin told the court that he intended to file a complaint to recover the $896.46 Bank South had already collected on the ground that the sale had not been conducted so as to obtain the highest price for the car, but he offered no evidence to support his contention. Busbin showed that he had a monthly net income of $1,150, expenses of $970, and disposable income of $130 and that he expected an income tax refund of $500. A motion to dismiss Busbin's petition was filed, alleging that he had a present ability to pay his outstanding debts and that granting a discharge would be a substantial abuse of the provisions of Chapter 7. Will the court dismiss Busbin's petition? Explain. [*In re Busbin*, 95 Bankr. 240 (Bankr.N.D.Ga. 1989)]

30–8. Donald Lewis filed a voluntary petition for bankruptcy. One of the debts on which he sought discharge was a $1,500 judgment that had been entered against him for assault on Betty Dunson. Lewis testified in the bankruptcy court that he put both hands around Dunson's neck and told her to leave his wife alone or he would break her neck. Discuss whether the court will grant a discharge of the judgment claim. [*In re Lewis*, 17 Bankr. 341 (Bankr.S.D.Ohio 1982)]

30–9. John Patrick Goulding filed for Chapter 7 bankruptcy relief in 1987. In his schedules, he listed assets of $62,000 and debts of over $670,000. The majority of these debts were unsecured and were not consumer debts. The Federal Deposit Insurance Corp. (FDIC), as successor to two banks, was the largest unsecured creditor ($379,000). The FDIC and the trustee learned that Goulding was the beneficiary of three irrevocable spendthrift trusts (the assets of which cannot be reached by creditors) that provided him with $12,000 per month, and that he would receive from the corpus (principal) of one trust $200,000 on January 30, 1988. The trustee and the FDIC filed a joint motion requesting the court to dismiss Goulding's Chapter 7 petition. Discuss whether the court should have dismissed Goulding's petition and whether any payments made from the trusts were part of the debtor's estate. [*In re Goulding*, 79 Bankr. 874 (Bankr.W.D.Mo. 1987)]

30–10. Tracey Service Co. filed a petition for a Chapter 11 reorganization. Acar Supply Co., one of Tracey's creditors, filed a motion to convert the case to a Chapter 7 liquidation. The court found that the debtor corporation had no place of business, no inventory, no equipment, no employees, and no business phone. Should Tracey Service be permitted to reorganize under Chapter 11? Explain. [*In re Tracey Service Co.*, 17 Bankr. 405 (Bankr.E.D.Pa. 1982)]

30–11. Fred Currey purchased cattle from Itano Farms, Inc. As payment for the cattle, Currey gave Itano Farms worthless checks in the amount of $50,250. Currey was later convicted of passing bad checks, and the state criminal court ordered him to pay Itano Farms restitution in the amount of $50,250. About four months after this court order, Currey and his wife filed for Chapter 7 bankruptcy protection. During the ninety days prior to the filing of the petition, Currey had made three restitution payments to Itano, totaling $14,821. The Curreys sought to recover these payments as preferences. What should the court decide? Explain. [*In re Currey*, 144 Bankr. 490 (D.Ida. 1992)]

30–12. David Sisco had about $600 in an account in Tinker Federal Credit Union. Sisco owed DPW Employees Credit Union a little more than $1,100. To collect on the debt, DPW obtained a garnishment judgment and served it on Tinker. The next day, Sisco filed a bankruptcy petition. Tinker then told DPW that, because of the bankruptcy filing, it could not pay the garnishment. DPW objected, and Tinker asked an Oklahoma state court to resolve the issue. What effect, if any, does Sisco's bankruptcy filing have on DPW's garnishment action? [*DPW Employees Credit Union v. Tinker Federal Credit Union*, 925 P.2d 93 (Okla.App.4th 1996)]

30–13. The Securities and Exchange Commission (SEC) filed a suit in a federal district court against First Jersey Securities, Inc., and others, alleging fraud in First Jersey's sale of securities (stock). The court ordered the defendants to turn over to the SEC $75 million in illegal profits. This order made the SEC the largest unsecured creditor of First Jersey. First Jersey filed a voluntary petition in a federal bankruptcy court to declare bankruptcy under Chapter 11. On the same day, the debtor transferred 200,001 shares of stock to its law firm, Robinson, St. John, & Wayne (RSW), in payment for services in the SEC suit and the bankruptcy petition. The stock represented essentially all of the debtor's assets. RSW did not find a buyer for the stock for more than two months. The SEC objected to the transfer, contending that it was a voidable preference, and asked that RSW be disqualified from representing the debtor. RSW responded that the transfer was made in the ordinary course of business. Also, asserted RSW, the transfer was not in payment of an "antecedent debt," because the firm had not presented First Jersey with a bill for its services and therefore the debt was not yet past due. Was the stock transfer a voidable preference? Should the court disqualify RSW? Why or why not? [*In re First Jersey Securities, Inc.*, 180 F.3d 504 (3d Cir. 1999)]

30–14. Mr. Mallinckrodt earned an undergraduate degree from the University of Miami and, in 1995, a graduate degree from Barry University in mental health counseling. To finance this education, Mallinckrodt borrowed from the Education Resources Institute, Inc., and others. Unable to find a job as a counselor, Mallinckrodt worked as a tennis instructor and coach. (At one time, he had played professional tennis and was ranked among the top eight hundred players in the world.) In 1996, he ruptured his Achilles tendon and was unable to work. After a lengthy rehabilitation, he was employed on a part-time, hourly basis at Horizon Psychological Services, but the work was inconsistent and low paying. He continued to work as a tennis instructor and was also a licensed real estate broker, but had little income in either field. With monthly income of about $549 after taxes, and expenses of $544, Mallinckrodt filed a bankruptcy petition to discharge his student loan debt, which with interest totaled nearly $73,000. Is this debt dischargeable? Discuss. [*In re Mallinckrodt*, 260 Bankr. 892 (S.D. Fla. 2001)]

30–15. A Question of Ethics

In September 1986, Edward and Debora Davenport pleaded guilty in a Pennsylvania court to welfare fraud and were sentenced to probation for one year. As a condition of their probation, the Davenports were ordered to make monthly restitution payments to the county probation department, which would forward the payments to the Pennsylvania Department of Public Welfare, the victim of the Davenports' fraud. In May 1987, the Davenports filed a petition for Chapter 13 relief and listed the restitution payments among their debts. The bankruptcy court held that the restitution obligation was a dischargeable debt. On appeal, the district court reversed, holding that state-imposed criminal restitution obligations cannot be discharged in Chapter 13 bankruptcy. The Court of Appeals for the Third Circuit reversed the district court's decision, concluding that "the plain language of the chapter" demonstrated that restitution orders are debt within the meaning of the Code and hence dischargeable in proceedings under Chapter 13. Ultimately, the case was reviewed by the United States Supreme Court, which affirmed the Third Circuit's ruling. The Court noted that under the Bankruptcy Code, a debt is defined as a liability on a claim, and a claim is defined as a right to payment. Because the restitution obligations clearly constituted a right to payment, the Court held that the obligations were dischargeable in bankruptcy. [*Pennsylvania Department of Public Welfare v. Davenport*, 495 U.S. 552, 110 S.Ct. 2126, 109 L.Ed.2d 588 (1990)]

1. Critics of this decision contend that the Court adhered to the letter, but not the spirit, of bankruptcy law in arriving at its conclusion. In what way, if any, did the Court not abide by the "spirit" of bankruptcy law?
2. Do you think that individuals' repayment plans, which allow nearly all types of debts to be discharged, tip the scales of justice too far in favor of debtors?

E-Links

For updated links to resources available on the Web, as well as a variety of other materials, visit this text's Web site at

http://wbl-cs.westbuslaw.com

The U.S. Bankruptcy Code is online at

http://www.law.cornell.edu:80/uscode/11

You can find links to an extensive number of bankruptcy resources on the Internet by accessing the Bankruptcy Lawfinder at

http://www.agin.com/lawfind

Another good resource for bankruptcy information is the American Bankruptcy Institute (ABI) at

http://www.abiworld.org

Legal Research Exercises on the Web

Go to http://wbl-cs.westbuslaw.com, the Web site that accompanies this text. Select "Interactive Study Center," and then click on "Chapter 30." There you will find the following Internet research exercises that you can perform to learn more about bankruptcy and its alternatives:

Activity 30–1: Bankruptcy
Activity 30–2: Bankruptcy Alternatives

FOCUS ON LEGAL REASONING

In re Bentz Metal Products Co.

We covered creditor's liens in Chapter 29 and outlined the parameters of bankruptcy law in Chapter 30. Now, in this *Focus on Legal Reasoning*, we examine *In re Bentz Metal Products Co.*,[1] a decision that concerns the priority of a mechanic's lien[2] in the distribution of a debtor's property as part of a Chapter 7 bankruptcy proceeding. The specific dispute in this case concerned employees' vacation pay owed under a collective bargaining agreement. (Collective bargaining agreements are discussed in more detail in Chapter 41.)

1. 253 F.3d 283 (7th Cir. 2001).

2. Note that the type of mechanic's lien discussed in this case differs from the type of mechanic's lien discussed in Chapter 29.

CASE BACKGROUND

Twenty employees of Bentz Metal Products Company in Fort Wayne, Indiana, were members of the United Automobile, Aerospace and Agricultural Implement Workers of America, Local 2298. These employees, as union members, were parties to a collective bargaining agreement (CBA) with Bentz.

In 1996, an involuntary bankruptcy petition was filed in a federal bankruptcy court against Bentz. While the proceeding was pending, the employees filed liens under Indiana state law to secure $12,700.38 in unpaid vacation pay owed to them under the CBA. The employees then filed a suit in the same court against Bentz and its secured creditor, Bank One, to determine the validity and priority of their liens.

The court held that Section 301 of the federal Labor Management Relations Act (LMRA) of 1947 preempted the liens, lowering the employees' priority for collection of their vacation pay. (Preemption is explained in Chapter 4, and the LMRA is discussed in more detail in Chapter 41.) On the employees' appeal, a federal district court affirmed this holding. The employees appealed to the U.S. Court of Appeals for the Seventh Circuit.

MAJORITY OPINION

TERENCE T. EVANS, Circuit Judge.

Indiana law broadly protects the rights of workers ("mechanics and laborers employed in or about any shop, mill, wareroom, storeroom, * * * bridge, reservoir, * * * drainage ditch * * * or any other earth-moving operation * * * " in the charming, though antiquated, language of the old Hoosier [Indiana] statute) against losing wages due when an employer encounters tough economic times. It does so by moving workers to the front of the company's creditor queue [line] with a mechanic's lien that trumps [takes priority over] the rights of other creditors to the company's assets. Today we consider whether that lien protects unionized workers to the same extent it undoubtedly protects the rights of nonunionized workers. We find that it does, a determination that compels us to overrule *In re Bluffton Casting Corp.*, 186 F.3d 857 (7th Cir.1999).

* * * *

Two intertwined reasons compel the result we reach today. First, our examination of the relevant cases shows that this issue requires case-by-case factual analysis to determine the extent to which a state law claim will require interpretation of a CBA. The second is we believe that the controlling legal principle is stated too broadly in *Bluffton Casting*.

In *Bluffton Casting* the issue was, in part, whether a claim based on the same Indiana mechanic's lien statute at issue here was preempted under [Section] 301. The [court], relying on language in *Lingle v. Norge Division of Magic Chef, Inc.*, 486 U.S. 399, 108 S.Ct. 1877, 100 L.Ed.2d 410 (1988), concluded that it was. * * * [T]he [court] derived two alternative conditions under which preemption would result: "either because it depends on interpretation of a CBA or because the claim is founded on the CBA." * * * [T]he [court] held that the mechanic's lien claims were "founded on the CBA" and thus preempted. We now hold, consistent with *Lingle and Livadas v. Bradshaw*, 512 U.S. 107, 114 S.Ct. 2068, 129 L.Ed.2d 93 (1994), that a state law claim is not preempted if it does not require interpretation of the CBA even if it may require reference to the CBA.

* * * [Section] 301 expresses a policy that the substantive law to apply in [Section] 301 cases is federal law, which courts were directed to fashion from the policy of national labor laws. * * * The guiding principle behind [Section] 301 preemption was that a contract should not have different meanings under federal law and the laws of various states. Today, it is well understood that a claim for breach of a collective bargaining agreement is preempted. But in other cases, not based directly on a CBA [collective bargaining agreement], the scope of preemption continues to cause some bewilderment. The [United States] Supreme Court itself has noted, "We are aware * * * that the Courts of Appeals have not been entirely uniform in their understanding and application of the principles * * * ."

So we must do our best. While preemption is a strong federal policy, Congress has not exercised authority to occupy the entire field of labor legislation, and it did not explicitly declare the extent to which it intended [Section] 301 to preempt state law. What has become clear is that preemption can extend beyond contract disputes to other state law claims if resolution of those claims is sufficiently dependent on an interpretation of a CBA. * * * But the Supreme Court has often cautioned that "not every dispute concerning employment, or tangentially involving a provision of a collective-bargaining agreement, is pre-empted by [Section] 301 or other provisions of the federal labor law."

[In finding] a claim based on the Illinois tort of retaliatory discharge * * * not to be preempted, [the Supreme Court stated,] "[W]e hold that an application of state law is pre-empted by [Section] 301 of the Labor Management Relations Act of 1947 only if such application requires the interpretation of a collective-bargaining agreement." More recently, the Supreme Court said that a claim based on a California wage payment penalty statute should have been allowed to proceed even though the amount of the claim might be determined under the collective bargaining agreement. The mere need to look to the CBA for damage computation was said to be no reason to hold the state-law claim defeated by [Section] 301. The issue is whether a state law conflicts or interferes with federal law. These principles were applied in a case under the Railway Labor Act, in which a state wrongful discharge was allowed to proceed. Saying the standard under the RLA was "virtually identical" to that in LMRA cases, the Supreme Court again cautioned that [Section] 301 cannot be read broadly to preempt rights conferred on individual employees as a matter of state law. The principles set out in these cases, as other courts have noted, are sometimes easier to mouth than to apply, involving as they do, claims reaching far beyond those clearly founded on rights created by CBAs-for instance, those for breach of a collective bargaining agreement.

In our case, as in *Bluffton Casting,* the employees' rights to the monies due, and the precise amount, depend on the collective bargaining agreement. Here, that sum is undisputed. Nevertheless, it remains true that the entitlement to the money due is laid out in the CBA. * * * [W]hether the amount due is resolved, as here, by stipulation, or whether it is resolved through procedures set out in the CBA, the contract issues are separate from the claim the employees presented to the bankruptcy court. Once the contract issues are resolved, the employees can present their separate claim in bankruptcy for priority based on the Indiana mechanic's lien statute. The priority among creditors in a bankruptcy proceeding is not dependent on a CBA. It is not something which a collective bargaining agreement can or does dictate. *No amount of interpretation of a CBA and no arbitrator's decision would, independent of the state law lien, compel a bankruptcy court to let employees jump ahead of a bank in the money line* * * *. [Emphasis added.]

* * * *

To require that for preemption to exist, resolution of a claim must require interpretation of a CBA, not a mere glance at it, is consistent with recent cases in this circuit and in other circuits. * * * Other circuits require the same case-by-case analysis of the state-law claim as it relates to the CBA. As one would expect in case-by-case analysis, in some situations preemption is found and in others it is not. * * *

In summary, the overriding principle is that for preemption to apply, *interpretation* of the CBA and not simply a reference to it is required. If the entitlement to wages (or other employee pay) or the amount due were at issue, the CBA would control; almost certainly, interpretation of the agreement would be necessary and would be subject to the arbitration procedures in the contract. So as to that determination, preemption would apply. The mechanic's lien, however, is a benefit provided to workers based on a state policy protecting workers; it is a separate claim, not dependent on interpretation of the agreement for its existence even though the amount of the pay is dependent on the CBA. In this situation, the claim is not preempted.

Accordingly, the decision of the district court is REVERSED. This case is REMANDED for the entry of judgment in favor of the plaintiffs.

QUESTIONS FOR ANALYSIS

1. **Legal Analysis.** In its opinion, the court cites *In re Bluffton Casting Corp.,* 186 F.3d 857 (7th Cir.1999); *Lingle v. Norge Division of Magic Chef, Inc.,* 486 U.S. 399, 108 S.Ct. 1877, 100 L.Ed.2d 410 (1988); and *Livadas v. Bradshaw,* 512 U.S. 107, 114 S.Ct. 2068, 129 L.Ed.2d 93 (1994) (see the *E-Links* feature at the end of Chapter 2 for instructions on how to access the opinions of federal courts). Why did the court in the *Bentz* case cite these cases? How do the courts' statements of the "controlling legal principle" in these cases differ?

2. **Legal Reasoning.** What was the reasoning leading to the court's conclusion in the *Bentz* case?

3. **Economic Dimensions.** How might the result in this case affect a creditor's decision to lend to an employer with unionized employees?

4. **Implications for the Business Lender.** Under the holding in this case, can a lender ever have first priority to an employer's assets in a bankruptcy proceeding?

WESTLAW ONLINE RESEARCH

Westlaw.

Go to this text's companion Web site, at http://wbl-cs.westbuslaw.com, and click on the Westlaw icon. Use your special password to access the full text of this case, including the dissenting opinions. Read through the case, and then answer the following questions.

1. Review the dissenting opinion. What is the dissent's contention? On what does the dissent base its argument?
2. Look carefully at headnotes numbers 4, 5, and 6. Why do they each include two sets of editorial classifications?
3. In light of the facts of this case, what might be the ethical basis for holding, as the majority does, that the claims of unionized workers should be treated the same as those of nonunionized workers in a bankruptcy proceeding?

UNIT SIX
Agency

CONTENTS

CHAPTER 31

Agency Formation and Duties

One of the most common, important, and pervasive legal relationships is that of **agency.** As discussed in Chapter 26, in an agency relationship between two parties, one of the parties, called the *agent,* agrees to represent or act for the other, called the *principal.* The principal has the right to control the agent's conduct in matters entrusted to the agent. By using agents, a principal can conduct multiple business operations simultaneously in various locations. Thus, for example, contracts that bind the principal can be made at different places with different persons at the same time.

A familiar example of an agent is a corporate officer who serves in a representative capacity for the owners of the corporation. In this capacity, the officer has the authority to bind the principal (the corporation) to a contract. Indeed, agency law is essential to the existence and operation of a corporate entity, because only through its agents can a corporation function and enter into contracts. Because agency relationships permeate the business world, an understanding of the law of agency is crucial to understanding business law.

SECTION 1

Agency Relationships

Section 1(1) of the *Restatement (Second) of Agency*[1] defines *agency* as "the fiduciary relation which results from the manifestation of consent by one person to another that the other shall act in his behalf and subject to his control, and consent by the other so to act." The term **fiduciary** is at the heart of agency law. The term can be used both as a noun and as an adjective. When used as a noun, it refers to a person having a duty created by his or her undertaking to act primarily for another's benefit in matters connected with the undertaking. When used as an adjective, as in the phrase "fiduciary relationship," it means that the relationship involves trust and confidence.

Agency relationships commonly exist between employers and employees. Agency relationships may sometimes also exist between employers and independent contractors who are hired to perform special tasks or services.

Employer-Employee Relationships

Normally, all employees who deal with third parties are deemed to be agents. All employment laws (state and federal) apply only to the employer-employee relationship. Statutes governing Social Security, withholding taxes, workers' compensation, unemployment compensation, workplace safety laws, employment discrimination, and the like (see Chapters 41 and 42) are applicable only when an employer-employee relationship exists. *These laws do not apply to the independent contractor.*

Because employees may be deemed agents of their employers, agency law and employment law overlap considerably. Agency relationships, though, as will become apparent, can exist outside an employer-employee relationship and thus have a broader reach than employment laws do.

Employer–Independent Contractor Relationships

Independent contractors are not employees, because by definition, those who hire them have no control over the details of their work performance. Section

1. The *Restatement (Second) of Agency* is an authoritative summary of the law of agency and is often referred to by jurists in their decisions and opinions.

2 of the *Restatement (Second) of Agency* defines an **independent contractor** as follows:

> [An independent contractor is] a person who contracts with another to do something for him but who is not controlled by the other nor subject to the other's right to control with respect to his physical conduct in the performance of the undertaking. He may or may not be an agent.

Building contractors and subcontractors are independent contractors, and a property owner does not control the acts of either of these professionals. Truck drivers who own their equipment and hire out on a per-job basis are independent contractors, but truck drivers who drive company trucks on a regular basis are usually employees.

The relationship between a principal and an independent contractor may or may not involve an agency relationship. To illustrate: An owner of real estate who hires a real estate broker to negotiate a sale of his or her property not only has contracted with an independent contractor (the real estate broker) but also has established an agency relationship for the specific purpose of assisting in the sale of the property. Another example is an insurance agent, who is both an independent contractor and an agent of the insurance company for which he or she sells policies.

Criteria for Establishing Employee Status

A question that frequently comes before the courts is whether a worker should be deemed an employee or an independent contractor. How a court decides this issue can have a significant effect on the rights and liabilities of the parties.

For example, employers normally are held liable as principals for the actions of their employee-agents if those actions are carried out within the scope of employment. Additionally, federal and state statutory laws governing employment discrimination, workplace safety, and compensation for on-the-job injuries normally apply only to employees—not to independent contractors. The tax liability of employers is also affected by the determination of worker status. Whereas employers are responsible for certain taxes, such as Social Security and unemployment taxes, with respect to employees, they are not responsible for these taxes if their workers are classified as independent contractors.

In deciding whether a worker is categorized as an employee or an independent contractor, courts often consider the following questions:

1. How much control can the employer exercise over the details of the work? (If an employer can exercise considerable control over the details of the work and the day-to-day activities of the worker, this indicates employee status. This is perhaps the most important factor weighed by the courts in determining employee status.)
2. Is the worker engaged in an occupation or business distinct from that of the employer? (If so, this points to independent-contractor status, not employee status.)
3. Is the work usually done under the employer's direction or by a specialist without supervision? (If the work is usually done under the employer's direction, this indicates employee status.)
4. Does the employer supply the tools at the place of work? (If so, this indicates employee status.)
5. For how long is the person employed? (If the person is employed for a long period of time, this indicates employee status.)
6. What is the method of payment—by time period or at the completion of the job? (Payment by time period, such as once every two weeks or once a month, indicates employee status.)
7. What degree of skill is required of the worker? (If a great degree of skill is required, this may indicate that the person is an independent contractor hired for a specialized job and not an employee.)

Often, the criteria for determining employee status are established by a statute or administrative agency regulation. The Internal Revenue Service (IRS), for example, has guidelines for its auditors to follow in determining whether a worker is an independent contractor or an employee. In the past, auditors were to consider twenty factors in making such a decision. New guidelines effective in 1997, however, encourage IRS examiners to look closely at just one of those factors—the degree of control the business exercises over the worker.

The IRS tends to scrutinize closely a firm's classification of a worker as an independent contractor rather than an employee, because employers can avoid certain tax liabilities by hiring independent contractors instead of employees. Regardless of the firm's classification of a worker's status as an independent contractor, if the IRS decides that the worker should be classified as an employee, the employer will be responsible for paying any applicable Social Security, withholding, and unemployment taxes.

Sometimes, it is advantageous to have employee status—to take advantage of laws protecting employees, for example. At other times, it may be advantageous to have the status of an independent contractor—for instance, for tax purposes.

Under the Copyright Act of 1976, any copyrighted work created by an employee within the scope of his or her employment at the request of the employer is a "work for hire," and the employer owns the copyright to the work. When an employer hires an independent contractor, however, normally the contractor owns the copyright unless the parties agree in writing that the work is a "work for hire."

Westlaw. See Case 31.1 at the end of this chapter. To view the full, unedited case from Westlaw,® go to this text's Web site at http://wbl-cs.westbuslaw.com.

SECTION 2

Formation of the Agency Relationship

Agency relationships are *consensual;* that is to say, they come about by voluntary consent and agreement between the parties. Generally, the agreement need not be in writing,[2] and consideration is not required.

A principal must have contractual capacity. A person who cannot legally enter into contracts directly should not be allowed to do so indirectly through an agent. Because an agent derives the authority to enter into contracts from the principal and because a contract made by an agent is legally viewed as a contract of the principal, it is immaterial whether the agent personally has the legal capacity to make that contract. Thus, a minor can be an agent but in some states cannot be a principal appointing an agent.[3] (When a minor is permitted to be a principal, however, any resulting contracts will be voidable by the minor principal but not by the adult third party.) In sum, any person can be an agent, regardless of whether he or she has the capacity to contract. Even a person who is legally incompetent can be appointed an agent.

An agency relationship can be created for any legal purpose. An agency relationship created for a purpose that is illegal or contrary to public policy is unenforceable. If LaSalle (as principal) contracts with Burke (as agent) to sell illegal narcotics, the agency relationship is unenforceable, because selling illegal narcotics is a felony and is contrary to public policy. It is also illegal for medical doctors and other licensed professionals to employ unlicensed agents to perform professional actions.

Generally, an agency relationship can arise in four ways: by agreement of the parties, by ratification, by estoppel, and by operation of law. We look here at each of these possibilities.

AGENCY BY AGREEMENT

Because an agency relationship is, by definition, consensual, normally it must be based on an express or implied agreement that the agent will act for the principal and the principal agrees to have the agent so act. An agency agreement can take the form of an express written contract. For example, Arnstein enters into a written agreement with Vogel, a real estate agent, to sell Arnstein's house. An agency relationship exists between Arnstein and Vogel for the sale of the house and is detailed in a document that both parties sign.

Many express agency relationships are created by oral agreement and not based on a contract. If Arnstein asks Grace, a gardener, to contract with others for the care of his lawn on a regular basis, and Grace agrees, an agency relationship exists between Arnstein and Grace for the lawn care.

An agency relationship can also be implied by conduct. For example, a hotel expressly allows only Hans Cooper to park cars, but Hans has no employment contract there. The hotel's manager tells Hans when to work, as well as where and how to park the cars. The hotel's conduct amounts to a manifestation of its willingness to have Hans park its customers' cars, and Hans can infer from the hotel's conduct that he has authority to act as a parking valet. It can be inferred that Hans is an agent-employee of the hotel, his purpose being to provide valet parking services for hotel guests.

2. There are two main exceptions to the statement that agency agreements need not be in writing. An agency agreement must be in writing (1) whenever agency authority empowers the agent to enter into a contract that the Statute of Frauds requires to be in writing (this is called the *equal dignity rule,* to be discussed in the next chapter) and (2) whenever an agent is given power of attorney.

3. Some courts have granted exceptions to allow a minor to appoint an agent for the limited purpose of contracting for the minor's necessities of life. See *Casey v. Kastel,* 237 N.Y. 305, 142 N.E. 671 (1924).

AGENCY BY RATIFICATION

On occasion, a person who is in fact not an agent may make a contract on behalf of another (a principal). If the principal approves or affirms that contract by word or by action, an agency relationship is created by ratification. Ratification involves a question of intent, and intent can be expressed by either words or conduct. The basic requirements for ratification are discussed in Chapter 32.

AGENCY BY ESTOPPEL

When a principal causes a third person to believe that another person is the principal's agent, and the third person acts to his or her detriment in reasonable reliance on that belief, the principal is "estopped to deny" the agency relationship. In such a situation, the principal's actions have created the *appearance* of an agency that does not in fact exist. The third person must prove that he or she *reasonably* believed that an agency relationship existed, however.[4]

Suppose that Jerry accompanies Grant, a seed sales representative, to call on a customer, Palko, the proprietor of the Neighborhood Seed Store. Jerry has performed independent sales work but has never signed an employment agreement with Grant. Grant boasts to Palko that he wishes he had three more assistants "just like Jerry." Palko has reason to believe from Grant's statements that Jerry is an agent for Grant, because Grant's representation to Palko created the impression that Jerry was Grant's agent and had authority to solicit orders. Palko then places seed orders with Jerry.

If Grant does not correct the impression that Jerry is an agent, Grant will be bound to fill the orders just as if Jerry were really Grant's agent. The acts or declarations of a purported agent in and of themselves do not create an agency by estoppel. Rather, it is the deeds or statements of the principal that create an agency by estoppel. If Jerry walked into Palko's store and claimed to be Grant's agent, when in fact he was not, and Grant had no knowledge of Jerry's representations, Grant would not be bound to any deal struck by Jerry and Palko.

Westlaw. See Case 31.2 at the end of this chapter. To view the full, unedited case from Westlaw,® go to this text's Web site at **http://wbl-cs.westbuslaw.com**.

4. These concepts also apply when a person who is in fact an agent undertakes an action that is beyond the scope of his or her authority, as will be discussed in Chapter 32.

AGENCY BY OPERATION OF LAW

There are also other situations in which the courts will find an agency relationship in the absence of a formal agreement. This may occur in family relationships. For example, suppose one spouse purchases certain basic necessaries (such as food or clothing—see Chapter 12) and charges them to the other spouse's charge account. The courts will often rule that the latter is liable for payment of the necessaries, either because of a social policy of promoting the general welfare of the spouse or because of a legal duty to supply necessaries to family members.

Agency by operation of law may also occur in emergency situations, when the agent's failure to act outside the scope of his or her authority would cause the principal substantial loss. If the agent is unable to contact the principal, the courts will often grant this emergency power. For example, a railroad engineer may contract on behalf of his or her employer for medical care for an injured motorist hit by the train.

SECTION 3

Duties of Agents and Principals

Once the principal-agent relationship has been created, both parties have duties that govern their conduct. As discussed previously, the principal-agent relationship is *fiduciary*—one of trust. In a fiduciary relationship, each party owes the other the duty to act with the utmost good faith. In this section, we examine the various duties of agents and principals.

AGENT'S DUTIES TO THE PRINCIPAL

Generally, the agent owes the principal five duties—performance, notification, loyalty, obedience, and accounting.

Performance. An implied condition in every agency contract is the agent's agreement to use reasonable diligence and skill in performing the work. When an agent fails to perform his or her duties, liability for breach of contract may result. The degree of skill or care required of an agent is usually that expected of a reasonable person under similar circumstances. Generally, this is interpreted to mean ordinary care. An agent may, however, have represented himself or herself as possessing special skills or, by virtue of his or her profession, be expected to exercise certain skills (such as those that an accountant or attorney possesses—see Chapter 51). Similarly, a corporate director, as an agent of the corporation, is expected to exercise a reasonable degree of diligence and oversight in the performance of his or her duties (see Chapter 35). In these situations, the agent is expected to exercise the skill or skills claimed. Failure to do so constitutes a breach of the agent's duty.

Not all agency relationships are based on contract. In some situations, an agent acts gratuitously—that is, without payment. A gratuitous agent cannot be liable for breach of contract, as there is no contract; he or she is subject only to tort liability. Once a gratuitous agent has begun to act in an agency capacity, he or she has the duty to continue to perform in that capacity in an acceptable manner and is subject to the same standards of care and duty to perform as other agents. For example, Bower's friend Alcott is a real estate broker. Alcott offers to sell Bower's farm at no charge. If Alcott never attempts to sell the farm, Bower has no legal cause of action to force Alcott to do so. If Alcott does find a buyer, however, but fails to provide a sales contract within a reasonable period of time, thus causing the buyer to seek other property, Bower has a cause of action in tort against Alcott for negligence.

Notification. An agent is required to notify the principal of all matters that come to his or her attention concerning the subject matter of the agency. This is the *duty of notification,* or the duty to inform. For example, suppose that Lang, an artist, is about to negotiate a contract to sell a series of paintings to Barber's Art Gallery for $15,000. Lang's agent learns that Barber is insolvent and will be unable to pay for the paintings. Lang's agent has a duty to inform Lang of this knowledge because it is relevant to the subject matter of the agency—the sale of Lang's paintings. Generally, the law assumes that the principal knows of any information acquired by the agent that is relevant to the agency—regardless of whether the agent actually passes on this information to the principal.

Loyalty. Loyalty is one of the most fundamental duties in a fiduciary relationship. Basically stated, the agent has the duty to act solely for the benefit of his or her principal and not in the interest of the agent or a third party. For example, an agent cannot represent two principals in the same transaction unless both know of the dual capacity and consent to it. The duty of loyalty also means that any information or knowledge acquired through the agency relationship is confidential. It would be a breach of loyalty to disclose such information either during the agency relationship or after its termination. Typical examples of confidential information are trade secrets and customer lists compiled by the principal.

In short, the agent's loyalty must be undivided. The agent's actions must be strictly for the benefit of the principal and must not result in any secret profit for the agent. For example, suppose that Remington contracts with Averly, a real estate agent, to sell Remington's property. Averly knows that he can find a buyer who will pay substantially more for the property than Remington is asking. If Averly secretly purchased Remington's property, however, and then sold it at a profit to another buyer, Averly would breach his duty of loyalty as Remington's agent. Averly has a duty to act in Remington's best interests and can only become the purchaser in this situation with Remington's knowledge and approval.

Westlaw. See Case 31.3 at the end of this chapter. To view the full, unedited case from Westlaw,® go to this text's Web site at **http://wbl-cs.westbuslaw.com**.

Obedience. When an agent is acting on behalf of the principal, a duty is imposed on that agent to follow all lawful and clearly stated instructions of the principal. Any deviation from such instructions is a violation of this duty. During emergency situations, however, when the principal cannot be consulted, the agent may deviate from the instructions without violating this duty. Whenever instructions are not clearly stated, the agent can fulfill the duty of obedience by acting in good faith and in a manner reasonable under the circumstances.

Accounting. Unless an agent and a principal agree otherwise, the agent has the duty to keep and make available to the principal an account of all property and money received and paid out on behalf of the principal. The agent has a duty to maintain separate accounts for the principal's funds and the agent's personal funds, and no intermingling of these accounts is allowed. Whenever a licensed professional (such as an attorney) violates this duty to account, he or she may be subject to disciplinary proceedings carried out by the appropriate regulatory institution (such as the state bar association) in addition to being liable to the principal (the professional's client) for failure to account.

Principal's Duties to the Agent

The principal also has certain duties to the agent. These duties relate to compensation, reimbursement and indemnification, cooperation, and safe working conditions.

Compensation. In general, when a principal requests certain services from an agent, the agent reasonably expects payment. The principal therefore has a duty to pay the agent for services rendered. For example, when an accountant or an attorney is asked to act as an agent, an agreement to compensate the agent for this service is implied. The principal also has a duty to pay that compensation in a timely manner. Except in a gratuitous agency relationship, in which the agent does not act for money, the principal must pay the agreed-on value for the agent's services. If no amount has been expressly agreed on, the principal owes the agent the customary compensation for such services.

Reimbursement and Indemnification. Whenever an agent disburses sums of money to fulfill the request of the principal or to pay for necessary expenses in the course of a reasonable performance of his or her agency duties, the principal has the duty to reimburse the agent for these payments.[5] Agents cannot recover for expenses incurred by their own misconduct or negligence, however.

Subject to the terms of the agency agreement, the principal has the duty to *indemnify* (compensate) an agent for liabilities incurred because of authorized and lawful acts and transactions. For example, if the agent, on the principal's behalf, forms a contract with a third party, and the principal fails to perform the contract, the third party may sue the agent for damages. In this situation, the principal is obligated to compensate the agent for any costs incurred by the agent as a result of the principal's failure to perform the contract. Additionally, the principal must indemnify (pay) the agent for the value of benefits that the agent confers on the principal. The amount of indemnification is usually specified in the agency contract. If it is not, the courts will look to the nature of the business and the type of loss to determine the amount.

Cooperation. A principal has a duty to cooperate with the agent and to assist the agent in performing his or her duties. The principal must do nothing to prevent such performance. For example, when a principal grants an agent an exclusive territory, creating an exclusive agency, the principal cannot compete with the agent or appoint or allow another agent to so compete in violation of the *exclusive agency.* If the principal did so, he or she would be exposed to liability for the agent's lost sales or profits.

Safe Working Conditions. The common law requires the principal to provide safe working premises, equipment, and conditions for all agents and employees. The principal has a duty to inspect working areas and to warn agents and employees about any unsafe situations. When the agency is one of employment, the employer's liability is frequently covered by state workers' compensation insurance, which is the primary remedy for an employee's injury on the job (see Chapter 41).

SECTION 4

Remedies and Rights of Agents and Principals

It is said that every wrong has its remedy. In business situations, disputes between agents and principals may arise out of either contract or tort laws and carry corresponding remedies. These remedies include monetary damages, termination of the agency relationship, injunction, and required accountings.

AGENT'S RIGHTS AND REMEDIES AGAINST PRINCIPAL

For every duty of the principal, the agent has a corresponding right. Therefore, the agent has the right to be compensated, reimbursed, and indemnified and to work in a safe environment. An agent also has the right to perform agency duties without interference by the principal.

Remedies of the agent for breach of duty by the principal follow normal contract and tort remedies. For example, suppose that Aaron Hart, a builder who has just completed construction on a new house, contracts with a real estate agent, Fran Boller, to sell the house. The contract calls for the agent to have an exclusive, ninety-day listing and to receive 6 percent of the selling price when the home is sold. Boller holds several open houses and shows the property to a number of potential buyers. One month before the ninety-day listing terminates, Hart agrees to sell the house to another buyer—not one to whom Boller has shown the house—after the ninety-day listing expires. Hart and the buyer agree that Hart will reduce the price of

5. This principle applies to acts by gratuitous agents as well. If a finder of a dog that becomes sick takes the dog to a veterinarian and pays the required fees for the veterinarian's services, the agent is entitled to be reimbursed by the owner of the dog for those fees.

the house by 3 percent, because he will sell it directly and thus will not have to pay Boller's commission. In this situation, if Boller learns of Hart's actions, she can terminate the agency relationship and sue Hart for damages—including the 6 percent commission she should have earned on the sale of the house.

An agent can also withhold further performance and demand that the principal give an accounting. For example, a sales agent may demand an accounting if the agent and principal disagree on the amount of commissions the agent should have received for sales made during a specific period of time.

When the principal-agent relationship is not contractual, an agent has no right to specific performance. An agent can recover for past services and future damages but cannot force the principal to allow him or her to continue acting as an agent.

Principal's Rights and Remedies against Agent

In general, a principal has contract remedies for an agent's breach of fiduciary duties. The principal also has tort remedies for misrepresentation, negligence, fraud, deceit, libel, slander, and trespass committed by the agent. In addition, any breach of a fiduciary duty by an agent may justify the principal's termination of the agency. The main actions available to the principal are constructive trust, avoidance, and indemnification.

Constructive Trust. Anything an agent obtains by virtue of the employment or agency relationship belongs to the principal. It is a breach of an agent's fiduciary duty to retain secretly benefits or profits that, by right, belong to the principal. For example, Andrews, a purchasing agent, gets cash rebates from a customer. If Andrews keeps the rebates, he violates his fiduciary duty to his principal, Metcalf. On finding out about the cash rebates, Metcalf can sue Andrews and recover them.

An agent is also prohibited from taking advantage of the agency relationship to obtain goods or property that the principal wants to purchase. For example, Peterson (the principal) wants to purchase property in the suburbs. Cox, Peterson's agent, learns that a valuable tract of land has just become available. Cox cannot buy the land for herself. Peterson gets the right of first refusal. If Cox purchases the land for her own benefit, the courts will impose a constructive trust on the land; that is, the land will be held for, and on behalf of, the principal despite the fact that the agent attempted to buy it in her own name.

Avoidance. When an agent breaches the agency agreement or agency duties under a contract, the principal has a right to avoid any contract entered into with the agent. This right of avoidance is at the election of the principal.

Indemnification. In certain situations, when a principal is sued by a third party for an agent's negligent conduct, the principal can sue the agent for an equal amount of damages. This is called *indemnification.* The same holds true if the agent violates the principal's instructions. For example, Lewis (the principal) tells his agent Moore, who is a used-car salesperson, to make no warranties for the used cars. Moore is eager to make a sale to Walters, a third party, and makes a warranty for the car's engine. Lewis is not absolved from liability to Walters for engine failure, but if Walters sues Lewis, Lewis normally can then sue Moore for indemnification for violating his instructions.

Sometimes it is difficult to distinguish between instructions of the principal that limit an agent's authority and those that are merely advice. For example, Willis (the principal) owns an office supply company; Jones (the agent) is the manager. Willis tells Jones, "Don't order any more inventory this month." Willis goes on vacation. A large order comes in from a local business, and the present inventory is insufficient to meet it. What is Jones to do? In this situation, Jones probably has the inherent authority to order more inventory despite Willis's command. It is unlikely that Jones would be required to indemnify Willis in the event that the local business subsequently canceled the order.

Terms and Concepts to Review

agency 622	fiduciary 622	independent contractor 623

CHAPTER SUMMARY

Agency Relationships	In a *principal-agent* relationship, an agent acts on behalf of and instead of the principal in dealing with third parties. An employee who deals with third parties is normally an agent. An independent contractor is not an employee, and the employer has no control over the details of his or her physical performance. The independent contractor is not usually an agent.
Formation of the Agency Relationship	1. *By agreement*—An agency relationship may be formed through express consent (oral or written) or implied by conduct. 2. *By ratification*—The principal, either by act or agreement, ratifies the conduct of an agent who acted outside the scope of authority or the conduct of a person who is in fact not an agent. 3. *By estoppel*—When the principal causes a third person to believe that another person is his or her agent, and the third person deals with the supposed agent in reasonable reliance on the agency's existence, the principal is "estopped to deny" the agency relationship. 4. *By operation of law*—An agency relationship may arise based on a social duty (such as the need to support family members) or created in emergency situations when the agent is unable to contact the principal.
Duties of Agents and Principals	1. *Agent's duties to principal*— a. Performance—The agent must use reasonable diligence and skill in performing his or her duties or use the special skills that the agent has represented to the principal that the agent possesses. b. Notification—The agent is required to notify the principal of all matters that come to his or her attention concerning the subject matter of the agency. c. Loyalty—The agent has a duty to act solely for the benefit of his or her principal and not in the interest of the agent or a third party. d. Obedience—The agent must follow all lawful and clearly stated instructions of the principal. e. Accounting—The agent has a duty to make available to the principal records of all property and money received and paid out on behalf of the principal. 2. *Principal's duties to agent*— a. Compensation—Except in a gratuitous agency relationship, the principal must pay the agreed-on value (or reasonable value) for an agent's services. b. Reimbursement and indemnification—The principal must reimburse the agent for all sums of money disbursed at the request of the principal and for all sums of money the agent disburses for necessary expenses in the course of reasonable performance of his or her agency duties. c. Cooperation—A principal must cooperate with and assist an agent in performing his or her duties. d. Safe working conditions—A principal must provide safe working conditions for the agent-employee.

CASES FOR ANALYSIS

Westlaw. You can access the full text of each case presented below by going to the Westlaw cases on this text's Web site at http://wbl-cs.westbuslaw.com. Each Westlaw case includes the names of all plaintiffs and defendants, the dates on which the case was argued and decided, a brief summary of the issues and decisions in the case, headnotes classifying the specific issues in the case according to the West Key Number System, and the court's opinion. Concurring and dissenting opinions, if any, are included as well.

CASE 31.1 EMPLOYMENT STATUS

GRAHAM V. JAMES

United States Court of Appeals,
Second Circuit, 1998.
144 F.3d 229.

JACOBS, Circuit Judge.

* * * *

BACKGROUND

The facts * * * are as follows: [Richard] Graham, until recently doing business as Night Owl Computer Service [and now as Night Owl's Publisher, Inc.], markets CD-ROM disks containing compilations of computer programs known as "Shareware," "Freeware," and "Public Domain software." "Shareware" are programs that are created and released to the public to sample, with the understanding that anyone using the software will register with the author and remit a fee. "Freeware" is software available for free use. "Public Domain software" is software unprotected by copyright. Each of Graham's CD-ROM disk releases contains 5,000 to 10,000 such programs.

Graham's first CD-ROM disk release, called PDSI-001, was unwieldy because it lacked a file-retrieval program. * * *

* * * *

In March 1991, he contacted [Larry] James, a self-taught computer programmer, part-time taxi driver, and computer equipment salesman, and explained to him in general terms what was needed. James agreed to create a file-retrieval program in exchange for a CD-ROM disk drive and [author's] credit on the final product. * * *

Using "Borland's C++" language (said to be a superior programming language), James then developed a [file-retrieval program], which we will call the "C version." The C version was included in PDSI-004-1, released on August 2, 1991. * * * Graham's contribution was limited to communicating the general requirements of the program and collaborating on the organization of the files that the program retrieved.

In composing the C version, James built into it a notice attributing authorship and copyright to himself. In September 1991, Graham and James argued over the copyright notice, with Graham claiming the copyright under the work-for-hire doctrine. * * *

* * * Graham claimed that he made several payments to James for developing the C version, including $200 payments in July and August 1991, and three $250 payments in September 1991; Graham claimed that the last three payments were pursuant to a newly instituted "monthly" salary. James claimed that Graham orally agreed to a licensing arrangement under which Graham would pay James $1,000 for each CD-ROM release containing the program and $1 for each disk sold, that the five payments evidenced Graham's partial performance of the licensing agreement, and that Graham promised further payments pursuant to the agreement after he built up his cash reserve. * * *

* * * Graham removed James's copyright notice, repaired a "bug" in the program, and proceeded to release a new version of PDSI-004-1. In October 1991, Graham released PDSI-005. PDSI-006, PDSI-006-1 and PDSI-006-2 followed in early- to mid-1992, and NOPV-6 in the summer of 1992. All of these releases contained the C version * * * (or a slight modification of it).

Variants of the C version were used in NOPV 7, 8 and 9; but * * * these variants were created by other programmers, and * * * were not substantially similar to James's C version.

In September or October 1991, James sold the C version * * * to another CD-ROM publisher. Graham sued [James in a federal district court] and moved for a preliminary injunction, claiming ownership of the copyright in the C version under the work-for-hire doctrine and asserting that James had infringed Graham's copyright by selling the program. James counterclaimed, alleging that *he* owned the copyright and that Graham had infringed his copyright by installing the C version on his CD-ROM releases and removing James's copyright notice. * * *

After a bench trial, * * * the district court found for James on his * * * copyright infringement counterclaims. It concluded that James owned the C version copyright because he was an independent contractor when he developed the program, and that Graham's CD-ROM releases from PDSI-004-1 through NOPV-6 contained file-retrieval programs substantially similar to the C version, thereby infringing James's copyright. The court also rejected Graham's copyright infringement claim [and] permanently enjoined Graham from using the program * * * .

Damages [included] * * * actual damages and profits for copyright infringement of $119,542, representing: (a) $25,000 for Graham's failure to credit James with authorship; and (b) $112,258 of profits and actual damages on the six relevant CD-ROM releases * * * .

* * * *

DISCUSSION

* * * *

Graham challenges the finding—on which rests the conclusion that the C version was not a work for hire—that James developed the C version as an independent contractor rather than as an employee. * * *

The Copyright Act provides, *inter alia,* that "a work prepared by an employee within the scope of his or her employment" is a work for hire. "[T]he employer or other person for whom the work [for hire] was prepared is considered the author" and the employer owns the copyright, absent a written agreement to the contrary.

For this purpose, the term "employee" should be understood in light of the general common law of agency. * * * In determining whether a hired party is an employee under the general common law of agency, we consider the hiring party's right to control the manner and means by which the product is accomplished. Among the other factors relevant to this inquiry are the skill required; the source of the instrumentalities and tools; the location of the work; the duration of the relationship between the parties; whether the hiring party has the right to assign additional projects to the hired party; the extent of the hired party's discretion over when and how long to work; the method of payment; the hired party's role in hiring and paying assistants; whether the work is part of the regular business of the hiring party; whether the hiring party is in business; the provision of employee benefits; and the tax treatment of the hired party.

* * * We give greater weight to certain of the * * * factors: (i) the hiring party's right to control the manner and means of creation; (ii) the skill required; (iii) the provision of employee benefits; (iv) the tax treatment of the hired party; and (v) whether the hiring party had the right to assign additional projects to the hired party. * * *

We are persuaded by the district court's conclusion that James was an independent contractor. Almost all of the * * * factors line up in favor of that conclusion: James is a skilled computer programmer, he was paid no benefits, no payroll taxes were withheld, and his engagement by Graham was project-by-project. The only * * * factor arguably favoring Graham is his general control over the work; but the district court has found, plausibly, that Graham's participation in the development of the C version was minimal and that his instructions to James were very general. We affirm the district court's determination that the C version was not a work for hire, and that consequently James owns the copyright.

* * * *

CONCLUSION

We affirm the district court's finding that the file-retrieval program was not a work for hire * * * .

CASE 31.2 AGENCY BY ESTOPPEL

WILLIAMS v. INVERNESS CORP.

Supreme Judicial Court of Maine, 1995.
664 A.2d 1244.

DANA, Justice.

* * * *

I.

* * * Margaret Barrera owned and operated a jewelry cart at a Brunswick [Maine] mall. She sold items produced by a number of manufacturers, including earrings manufactured by Inverness [Corporation], a Delaware corporation headquartered in New Jersey. Barrera also offered ear piercing using exclusively the Inverness Ear Piercing System.

According to promotional material * * * , Inverness is the "world's largest producer of ear piercing products." The Inverness system is used "by more retailers throughout the world than any other system" and it "has pierced the ears of more than 50 million people." The Inverness system includes a "compact, professional work center [that] fits easily on the counter or under it. Everything [the vendor needs] is included: piercing instrument, sterile marking pen, sealed earring cassettes, aftercare instructions for customers and Ear Care Solution for an added sale." To "round out the Inverness Ear Piercing System," Inverness provides vendors with "a training program and an eye-catching assortment of selling aids[,] [i]ncluding * * * [f]ull-color counter displays, window displays and tent cards." Barrera had purchased the Inverness Ear Piercing System from a local beauty school, and she purchased sealed earring cassettes directly from Inverness. The sealed earring cassettes can only be used in conjunction with the Inverness ear piercing equipment.

Angela Williams, a seventeen-year-old high school student, had visited Barrera's stand "lots of times." She had observed the Inverness earring display, and had heard of Inverness. According to Angela, "[Inverness] was the only earring company that I knew of that pierced ears [in the cartilage area]."

In June 1991 Angela asked Barrera to pierce her left ear high in the cartilage area. Barrera produced a release form furnished by Inverness and bearing its name. The release form states at the top, in large letters, "The Only Completely Safe, Sterile Ear Piercing Method." In smaller print, the form states that "ear piercing should be limited to the earlobe area as piercing in the cartilage can result in redness, swelling and infection." Angela testified that she did not read the release form, but she did notice the Inverness name at the top. She also testified that she signed the release form *after* Barrera pierced her ear, and that Barrera did not tell her that ear piercing should be limited to the earlobe area.

Within two weeks Angela's ear swelled, became hot, and discharged green pus. She was subsequently admitted to the hospital where she received intravenous antibiotics. She was discharged after five days, but continued on intravenous therapy at home. Angela was pregnant when her ear was pierced. Her physicians told her that there was a "considerable risk" that the infection and the antibiotics would affect her fetus. Angela had an abortion in July 1991.

Angela's mother filed a complaint [in a Maine state court] on behalf of Angela in May 1992. The complaint alleged * * * liability for Barrera's negligence * * * against Inverness. * * *

* * * *

The [jury] set forth a verdict for Angela on [her] claim and an award of $90,000. A judgment was entered accordingly, and this appeal followed.

II.

* * * *

Angela's negligence claim against Inverness rests on an application of the doctrine of apparent agency. * * * Apparent authority is that which, though not actually granted, the principal knowingly permits the agent to exercise or which he holds him out as possessing. Apparent authority exists only when the *conduct of the principal* leads a third person to believe that a given party is his agent. We note that the *Restatement (Second) of the Law of Agency* § 267 (1958) provides,

> One who represents that another is his servant or other agent and thereby causes a third person justifiably to rely upon the care and skill of such apparent agent is subject to liability to the third person for harm caused by the lack of care or skill of the one appearing to be a servant or other agent as if he were such.

* * * *

The key issue here is whether it is a question for the jury whether Inverness either intentionally or negligently held Barrera out as its agent with respect to the ear piercing, and whether Inverness therefore could be held liable for Barrera's negligence. There are critical pieces of evidence in the record that can fairly be interpreted as leading to an inference that Inverness did hold Barrera out as its agent. Most important, a jury reasonably could infer that Inverness knew, or should have known, that Barrera distributed Inverness's release forms and after-care instructions. Indeed, a jury reasonably could infer that Inverness held Barrera out as its agent for the express purpose of securing releases from its end-users. A jury reasonably could infer, as well, that Inverness was aware that its vendors were piercing in the cartilage area and it, in fact, condoned the practice.

Inverness sold 36 sealed earring cassettes directly to Barrera. The sealed earring cassettes can only be used in conjunction with the Inverness ear piercing equipment. Inverness's assertion that "there is no evidence in the record that Inverness even knew that Barrera was using its earlobe piercing device before June 15, 1991," is arguably belied by the fact that she ordered the sealed earring cassettes in March 1991. A jury reasonably could infer, therefore, that Inverness knew, or should have known, that Barrera was using the Inverness Ear Piercing System, that she displayed Inverness's "eye-catching assortment of selling aids," and that she used Inverness's training program.

Finally, there was evidence that Angela believed that Barrera was Inverness's agent, that Angela relied on Inverness's manifestations of agency, and that Angela's reliance on Barrera's care and skill was justifiable. Angela testified, "[Inverness] was the only earring company that I knew of that pierced ears [in the cartilage area]." The release form and display promote the Inverness Ear Piercing System as "The Only Completely Safe, Sterile Ear Piercing Method." Given the evidence in the circumstances of this case, the court did not err in letting the jury decide whether Inverness either intentionally or negligently held Barrera out as its agent with respect to the ear piercing, and whether Inverness therefore could be held liable for Barrera's negligence based on an application of the doctrine of apparent agency.

* * * *

Judgment affirmed.

RUDMAN, Justice, * * * dissenting.

I respectfully dissent. The court has based its decision on Margaret Barrera's apparent authority to bind Inverness. * * * Apparent authority can * * * be created only by the principal's manifestation to a third party. Until there has been a communication from the principal to a particular person, and until that person learns facts from which he reasonably infers that the agent is authorized, there is no apparent authority * * * . The agent's representations of authority to a third person, standing alone, are insufficient to create apparent authority in the agent to act for the principal. * * *

Angela did not see nor was she provided the promotional material to which the court refers prior to her engaging Barrera to pierce the cartilage of her ears. Williams testified that Barrera's kiosk bore the sign "Inverness" indicating that earrings made by Inverness were sold at the kiosk and offered testimony that the release, she saw and signed *after* her ears were pierced, bore the word "Inverness." To establish apparent authority Williams had the burden to offer proof that Inverness *by its conduct* would cause a reasonable person to believe that Barrera was acting on Inverness's behalf. On the meager evidence offered by Williams one could neither actually nor reasonably believe that the purported agent (Ms. Barrera) had authority to act on behalf of the principal (Inverness). The court erred in submitting the issue of apparent authority to the jury.

* * * *

* * * I would vacate the judgment entered by the trial court and remand for entry of a judgment in favor of Inverness.

CASE 31.3 AGENT'S DUTIES TO THE PRINCIPAL

AMERICAN EXPRESS FINANCIAL ADVISORS, INC. v. TOPEL

United States District Court,
District of Colorado, 1999.
38 F.Supp.2d 1233.

BABCOCK, District Judge.

* * * *

For five years, [Stephen] Topel worked as a financial planner for [American Express Financial Advisors, Inc. (AMEX)] pursuant to a written contract with AMEX. (Planner Agreement). * * *

The Planner Agreement * * * prohibits [Mr. Topel], for a period of one year after resigning from AMEX, from soliciting or selling investments and financial services, directly or indirectly, to those AMEX customers in the territory he served or learned about through AMEX. * * *

According to AMEX, after Mr. Topel tendered his resignation in late May 1997, it learned that he was violating the terms of his Planner Agreement and was actively soliciting and diverting the AMEX customers he serviced on its behalf. [AMEX filed a suit in a federal district court against Mr. Topel, alleging, among other things, breach of fiduciary duty (the duty of loyalty) and seeking damages. AMEX filed a motion for summary judgment on this issue.]

* * * *

Mr. Topel's customers testified [in their depositions] that he contacted them while he was still affiliated with AMEX in an attempt to solicit their business on behalf of his new broker/dealer, Multi-Financial Securities Corporation. For example, customer James Hemming testified that Mr. Topel first contacted him in January 1997 to solicit his business for Mr. Topel's new venture. Mr. Hemming testified that he wanted to stay with AMEX and asked Mr. Topel on at least two occasions how he could stay with AMEX. Mr. Hemming testified that Mr. Topel "just blew right past" and "never honored" his requests to stay with AMEX. Mr. Hemming stated he went along with it because he "didn't want to press any issues with [Mr. Topel]." He explained that "when someone has access to anything I consider valuable, I don't want to cause any undue concern or aggravation." Mr. Hemming moved the full amount of his investments from AMEX to Mr. Topel's new venture. Mr. Hemming liquidated his AMEX accounts on May 12, 1997, nine days before Mr. Topel announced his resignation from AMEX.

Similarly, customer Amy Rogers testified that in April 1997, while Mr. Topel was still affiliated with AMEX, he recommended that she and her husband invest in non-AMEX products. The Rogers took Topel's advice and moved their funds out of AMEX. Ms. Rogers testified that Mr. Topel urged her and her husband to invest their funds with certain companies without fully advising them of his plans to leave AMEX. Ms. Rogers testified that their funds were transferred "before we really knew that he was leaving [AMEX]."

Ms. Rogers testified that, in reliance on Mr. Topel's advice, she and her husband sold a municipal bond they had previously held to invest in non-AMEX products. This transaction was completed on May 7, 1997, two weeks before Mr. Topel announced his resignation from AMEX. Ms. Rogers further testified that she and her husband signed all of the paperwork to invest in the non-AMEX products Mr. Topel had recommended on May 14, 1997, a week before he announced his resignation.

The evidence shows that on May 12, 1997, nine days before giving notice of his termination, Mr. Topel sent a letter on AMEX letterhead to Chris and Teresa Mammel, two of his AMEX customers. In the letter, Mr. Topel states that the Mammels "will have to transfer * * * accounts * * * out of AMEX into another family of funds * * * ." The letter indicates that Mr. Topel had previously made the Mammels aware of his decision to leave AMEX. In the letter, Mr. Topel states that AMEX will not allow its products to be brokered and that it was therefore necessary for the Mammels to liquidate their investments with AMEX.

* * * *

[The] law provides that unless otherwise agreed, an agent is subject to a duty to his principal to act solely for the benefit of the principal in all matters connected with the agency. *While an agent is entitled to make some preparations to compete with his principal after the termination of their relationship, an agent violates his duty of loyalty if he engages in pre-termination solicitation of customers for a new competing business.* [Emphasis added.]

As the undisputed facts make clear, Mr. Topel solicited customers for his new venture while he was still affiliated with AMEX. In some instances, there is evidence that Mr. Topel ignored his AMEX customers' requests to keep their investments with AMEX. He also sent correspondence to his AMEX customers to solicit them for his new venture while he was still employed by AMEX and, in at least one instance, on AMEX letterhead. There is no genuine issue regarding whether Mr. Topel's activities violated his fiduciary duty of loyalty to AMEX. * * *

* * * *

Nor does Mr. Topel create a genuine issue of material fact by offering the testimony of one customer, Theodore Benavidez, whose unrebutted testimony is that Mr. Topel did not solicit his business until after he left AMEX. Mr. Benavidez' testimony does not negate the testimony of other customers who testified that Mr. Topel solicited their business for Multi-Financial while he was still affiliated with AMEX. Furthermore, even if Mr. Topel sent a neutral letter regarding his resignation to the AMEX clients he serviced on its behalf, it does not follow that no solicitation occurred prior to that letter. In fact, many customers had already signed new account forms with Multi-Financial by the time this neutral letter was purportedly sent. Thus, that it is genuinely disputed whether Mr. Topel solicited improperly some of his customers is irrelevant when [it] is undisputed that he improperly solicited the [Hemmings], [Mr. and] Ms. Rogers, and [the Mammels] before he terminated his employment with AMEX. * * * Therefore, I grant AMEX' summary judgment motion on its claim * * * for breach of fiduciary duty.

CASE PROBLEMS

31–1. James Blatt hired Marilyn Scott to sell insurance for the Massachusetts Mutual Life Insurance Company. Their contract stated, "Nothing in this contract shall be construed as creating the relationship of employer and employee." The contract was terminable at will by either party. Scott hired and trained other agents according to Massachusetts Mutual's guidelines, but she financed her own office and staff, was paid according to performance, had no taxes withheld from her checks, and could sell products of Massachusetts Mutual's competitors. When Blatt terminated their contract, Scott filed a suit in a New York state court against him and Massachusetts Mutual. Scott claimed that she had been discriminated against on the basis of her gender, age, and marital status in violation of a state law prohibiting employment discrimination. The defendants filed a motion for summary judgment on the ground that the law applied only to employees and Scott was an independent contractor. The court granted the motion, which an appellate court upheld. Scott appealed to New York's highest state court. What will happen on appeal? Discuss fully. [*Scott v. Massachusetts Mutual Life Insurance Co.,* 86 N.Y.2d 429, 657 N.E.2d 769, 633 N.Y.S.2d 754 (1995)]

31–2. Ramsey, the plaintiff, was a licensed real estate broker and was also in the business of buying and holding land for resale. Gordon, the defendant, was the owner of approximately 181 acres of land and engaged Ramsey's services as a broker to find a buyer for the property. Ramsey, when he heard that the land was rapidly appreciating in value, told Gordon that he would buy the land himself. Gordon then agreed to sell Ramsey the tract of land for $800 per acre. A contract of sale to convey the property was drawn up; but before the contract was executed, Gordon conveyed the property to a third party for the same price ($800 per acre). Meanwhile, Ramsey, acting for himself, began negotiating for the resale of the property to another customer for a price of $1,250 per acre. Naturally, when Ramsey learned that Gordon had conveyed the property to another buyer, he blamed Gordon for his lost profits. Ramsey claimed that he had lost over $90,000 in profits on the resale of the property and brought an action against Gordon to recover this amount. Gordon maintained that that Ramsey had breached his fiduciary duties as Gordon's agent by not finding a purchaser for the best price available. The trial court held for Gordon, and Ramsey appealed. What will the appellate court decide? Discuss. [*Ramsey v. Gordon,* 567 S.W.2d 868 (Tex.App.—Waco 1978)]

31–3. Dr. George Hall hired Ivan Davey, who was Tom Amear's partner, to do landscaping and other household maintenance. Hall would tell Davey what needed to be done, and Davey, Amear, or others would do the work. Davey and Amear controlled their own hours and methods. Hall asked Davey to install fiberglass over four spaces formed by exposed beams connecting the carport and the house, but Hall did not instruct Davey in how to do the job. It was Amear's idea to climb out on a beam to install the fiberglass. The beams, however, were purely decorative and had no structural purpose. A beam collapsed under Amear, who fell and severely injured himself. In a suit against Hall in a Georgia state court, Amear claimed that he was an employee and that Hall had failed to provide and maintain safe working conditions. Hall claimed that Amear was an independent contractor. The trial court entered judgment in favor of Hall, and Amear appealed. What will result on appeal? Discuss fully. [*Amear v. Hall,* 164 Ga.App. 163, 296 S.E.2d 611 (1982)]

31–4. Broyles signed a sales representative's agreement with NCH Corp. that included covenants not to compete and not to solicit NCH customers after termination of the agreement. NCH maintained detailed and costly records of its routes and customers. It considered this information to be valuable and sensitive, although all the data were readily ascertainable from other sources. Broyles transcribed the names and information with intent to use this material after he left NCH's employ. He later voluntarily terminated his employment with NCH and went to work for a competing firm. Based on the information he had transcribed while an employee of NCH, he solicited business from some of his former customers. NCH sued Broyles, claiming that the use of his list was a breach of his employment contract and a breach of his fiduciary duty to NCH. Discuss whether NCH was successful in its claim that Broyles had breached his fiduciary duty. [*NCH Corp. v. Broyles,* 749 F.2d 247 (5th Cir. 1985)]

31–5. Sam Kademenos was about to sell a $1 million life insurance policy to a prospective customer when he resigned from his position with Equitable Life Assurance Society. Before resigning from the company, he had expended substantial amounts of company money and had utilized Equitable's medical examiners to procure the $1 million sale. After resigning,

Kademenos joined a competing insurance firm, Jefferson Life Insurance Co., and made the sale through it. Has he breached any duty to Equitable? [*Kademenos v. Equitable Life Assurance Society,* 513 F.2d 1073 (3d Cir. 1975)]

31–6. Clifford Aymes was hired by Jonathan Bonelli of Sun Island Sales, Inc., to create a computer program for Sun Island to use in maintaining records of its cash receipts, inventory, sales figures, and other data. No agreement was reached as to ownership rights in the program that Aymes developed, called CSALIB. Aymes did most of his programming at the Sun Island office. Although Bonelli gave Aymes frequent instructions as to what he wanted from the program, Aymes generally worked alone and enjoyed considerable autonomy in his work. He worked fairly regular hours, but he was not always paid by the hour—occasionally, he submitted bills (invoices) to Sun Island for his work. Aymes never received any employee benefits, such as health insurance, and Sun Island never withheld federal and state taxes from Aymes's paycheck; nor did it pay any Social Security taxes on Aymes's earnings. When Bonelli unilaterally cut Aymes's hours in violation of an alleged oral agreement, Aymes left Sun Island and demanded compensation for Sun Island's use of CSALIB. Bonelli refused to pay Aymes for the program's use and also stated that he would not pay Aymes $14,560 in back wages unless Aymes signed a form releasing all rights in CSALIB. Aymes then sued Bonelli and Sun Island for copyright infringement, and the court had to decide who owned the copyright in the program. Central to the determination of this issue was whether Aymes was an employee of Sun Island or an independent contractor. What should the court decide, and why? [*Aymes v. Bonelli,* 980 F.2d 857 (2d Cir. 1992)]

31–7. Evan Smith experienced a heart attack in the emergency room of Baptist Memorial Hospital after being given a dose of penicillin for a sore throat. Smith sued the attending physician as well as the hospital. The hospital called itself a full-service hospital with emergency room facilities. Baptist Memorial did not consider the doctors to be its agents. For tax and accounting purposes the doctors were not treated as employees of the hospital. Based on this information, discuss whether the doctors who treated patients in the emergency room were agents of the hospital. [*Smith v. Baptist Memorial Hospital System,* 720 S.W.2d 618 (Tex. App.—San Antonio 1986)]

31–8. Howard and Virginia Bankerd were having marital difficulties. In 1968 Howard decided to leave "for the West," but before he did so, he executed a power of attorney to his lawyer, Arthur King. Virginia continued to reside in their home in Maryland and assumed all expenses for the home. In 1975 Howard gave King an updated power of attorney and asked King to sell the property "on such terms as to him [King] seem best." In 1977 Virginia asked the lawyer to exercise his power of attorney and transfer her husband's interest in the property to her. She wished to sell the property and retire. After three letters failed to elicit any response from Howard, King concluded that Howard "didn't give a damn" about the property. King therefore transferred the property to Virginia by deed in 1978. Virginia paid no consideration for the transfer. Howard subsequently sued King, claiming that King had breached his duty of loyalty and trust by transferring the property gratuitously to Virginia. King argued that he had acted reasonably under the circumstances. The trial court held for Howard Bankerd, and King appealed. Had King breached his fiduciary duty of loyalty and trust by transferring the property gratuitously to Virginia? Discuss fully. [*King v. Bankerd,* 303 Md. 98, 492 A.2d 608 (1985)]

31–9. Brenda Tarver worked as an independent contractor with Dianne Landers's real estate agency. The agents in the firm worked on a commission basis, and Tarver's contract read that she would receive 30 percent of the agency's commissions to which she was "entitled as either listing and/or selling agent" in connection with a sale. In the spring of 1984, Charles Smith and his wife contacted the agency about a property for sale advertised in the local newspaper. The Smiths were referred to Tarver, who showed them the property and handled their offer to purchase the property and the seller's counteroffer. In all, Tarver negotiated three offers and three counteroffers between the seller and the buyer. Later, however, the Smiths returned to the agency and, because Tarver was out of the office, negotiated with Dianne Landers concerning the last counteroffer they had rejected. After some modifications were made, they reached an agreement with the seller and purchased the property. Landers would not pay Tarver a commission for the sale because Tarver had not negotiated the final purchase. Tarver sued to recover her commission on the ground that it was customary in the real estate office that when the initial selling agent was absent from the office, another agent would handle negotiations—but not receive the commission if a sale resulted. Who will prevail in court? Explain. [*Tarver v. Landers,* 486 So.2d 294 (La.App. 1986)]

31–10. Mallie Brackens consulted Dr. Floyd Jones in April 1983 because of stomach pains. Dr. Jones admitted her to the Detroit Osteopathic Hospital for the purpose of performing a gastrojejunostomy (a surgical joining of the middle section of the small intestine). After the surgery, Brackens was readmitted to the hospital twice because of dehydration and other problems and was seen by Drs. Taras and Tobes—whom she had never met be-fore—for upper gastrointestinal examinations. Her problems persisted and finally, in December 1983, she learned from physicians at another hospital that instead of a gastrojejunostomy, Dr. Jones had performed a gastroileostomy, which is a bypass procedure performed on an obese person. Brackens sued the Detroit Osteopathic Hospital, alleging that it was liable for the negligence of its agents, Drs. Taras and Tobes, who had failed to detect the improperly performed gastrojejunostomy when they examined her. The hospital claimed that Drs. Taras and Tobes were independent contractors who merely used the hospital's facilities to render treatment to their patients. Brackens, however, testified that during her confinement in the hospital, she at all times believed that Drs. Taras and Tobes were hospital physicians employed by the hospital. Should the court impose an agency by estoppel in this case? Why, or why not? Discuss fully. [*Brackens v. Detroit Osteopathic Hospital*, 174 Mich.App. 290, 435 N.W.2d 472 (1989)]

31–11. L.M.T. Steel Products, Inc., contracted with a school to install numerous room partitions. To accomplish this work, L.M.T. hired a man named Webster. Webster was not a regular employee of L.M.T., and it was stipulated that he was to be paid by the number of feet of partitions installed. Webster did not have a contractor's license. He hired other workers to do the installing, and these workers were paid by L.M.T. Webster was given blueprints by L.M.T., but he was not otherwise at any time actively supervised by L.M.T. on the job. Needing to place a telephone call to L.M.T., Webster drove his own personal vehicle to a public telephone. On the way, he negligently collided with another car, and an occupant of that car, Peirson, was injured. Peirson sued L.M.T., claiming that Webster was an employee. L.M.T. claimed that Webster was an independent contractor. Who was correct? Explain. [*L.M.T. Steel Products, Inc. v. Peirson*, 47 Md.App. 633, 425 A.2d 242 (1981)]

31–12. Douglas agreed to buy oil and gas leases for Aztec Petroleum Corp. In return for his services, Douglas was to receive an initial $5,000 plus a royalty interest in the leases he obtained. Douglas obtained a number of leases for Aztec but represented to Aztec that the prices paid for the leases were higher than they actually were. By sending Aztec photocopies of checks altered as to both payee and amount, along with forged receipts, Douglas was able to keep for himself a substantial amount of the money that Aztec had entrusted to him for payment of the leases. This money was used by Douglas for personal purchases, including two new cars, a boat, and other personal items. When Aztec refused to grant Douglas the promised royalty interest in the leases, Douglas brought suit to obtain it. The trial court held for Aztec, and Douglas appealed. In view of Douglas's deceptive activities, is Aztec required to grant the royalty interest? Discuss fully. [*Douglas v. Aztec Petroleum Corp.*, 695 S.W.2d 312 (Tex.App. 1985)]

31–13. Stephen Hemmerling was a driver for the Happy Cab Co. Hemmerling paid certain fixed expenses and abided by a variety of rules relating to the use of the cab, the hours that could be worked, the solicitation of fares, and so on. Rates were set by the state. Happy Cab did not withhold taxes from Hemmerling's pay. While driving a cab, Hemmerling was injured in an accident and filed a claim against Happy Cab in a Nebraska state court for workers' compensation benefits. Such benefits are not available to independent contractors. On what basis might the court hold that Hemmerling is an employee? Explain. [*Hemmerling v. Happy Cab Co.*, 247 Neb. 919, 530 N.W.2d 916 (1995)]

31–14. Ana Barreto and Flavia Gugliuzzi asked Ruth Bennett, a real estate salesperson who worked for Smith Bell Real Estate, to list for sale their house in the Pleasant Valley area of Underhill, Vermont. Diana Carter, a California resident, visited the house as a potential buyer. Bennett worked under the supervision of David Crane, an officer of Smith Bell. Crane knew, but did not disclose to Bennett or Carter, that the house was subject to frequent and severe winds, that a window had blown in years earlier, and that other houses in the area had suffered wind damage. Crane knew of this because he lived in the Pleasant Valley area, had sold a number of nearby properties, and had been Underhill's zoning officer. Many valley residents, including Crane, had wind gauges on their homes to measure and compare wind speeds with their neighbors. Carter bought the house, and several months later, high winds blew in a number of windows and otherwise damaged the property. Carter filed a suit in a Vermont state court against Smith Bell and others, alleging fraud. She argued in part that Crane's knowledge of the winds was imputable to Smith Bell. Smith Bell responded that Crane's knowledge was obtained outside the scope of employment. What is the rule regarding how much of an agent's knowledge a principal is assumed to know? How should the court rule in this case? Why? [*Carter v. Gugliuzzi*, 716 A.2d 17 (Vt. 1998)]

31–15. A Question of Ethics

In 1990, the Internal Revenue Service (IRS) determined that a number of independent contractors working for Microsoft Corp. were actually employees of the company for tax purposes. The IRS arrived at this conclusion based on the significant control that Microsoft exercised over the independent contractors' work performance. As a result of the IRS's findings, Microsoft was ordered to pay back payroll taxes for hundreds of independent contractors who should have been classified as employees. Rather than contest the ruling, Microsoft required most of the workers in question, as well as a number of its other independent contractors, to become associated with employment agencies and work for Microsoft as temporary workers ("temps") or lose the opportunity to work for Microsoft. Workers who refused to register with employment agencies, as well as some who did register, sued Microsoft. The workers alleged that they were actually employees of the company and, as such, entitled to participate in Microsoft's stock option plan for employees. Microsoft countered that it need not provide such benefits because each of the workers had signed an independent-contractor agreement specifically stating that the worker was responsible for his or her own benefits. In view of these facts, consider the following questions. [*Vizcaino v. Microsoft*, 173 F.3d 713 (9th Cir. 1999)]

1. If the decision were up to you, how would you rule in this case? Why?
2. Normally, when a company hires temporary workers from an employment agency, the agency—not the employer—is responsible for paying Social Security taxes and withholding other taxes. Yet the Court of Appeals for the Ninth Circuit held that being an employee of a temporary employment agency did not preclude the employee from having the status of a common law employee of Microsoft at the same time. Is this fair to the employer? Why, or why not?
3. Generally, do you believe that Microsoft was trying to "skirt the law"—and its ethical responsibilities—by requiring its employees to sign up as "temps"?
4. Each of the employees involved in this case had signed an independent-contractor agreement. In view of this fact, is this decision fair to Microsoft? Why, or why not?

E-LINKS

For updated links to resources available on the Web, as well as a variety of other materials, visit this text's Web site at

http://wbl-cs.westbuslaw.com

An excellent source for information on agency law, including court cases involving agency concepts, is the Legal Information Institute (LII) at Cornell University. You can access the LII's Web page on this topic at

http://www.law.cornell.edu/topics/agency.html

For a discussion of significant cases on fiduciary duties decided by the New York Court of Appeals (that state's highest court), go to the Web site of the *New York Law Journal* at

http://www.nylj.com/links/150sterk.html

and scroll down the page to "Fiduciary Duties."

LEGAL RESEARCH EXERCISES ON THE WEB

Go to http://wbl-cs.westbuslaw.com, the Web site that accompanies this text. Select "Interactive Study Center," and then click on "Chapter 31." There you will find the following Internet research exercise that you can perform to learn more about the distinction between employees and independent contractors:

Activity 31–1: Employees or Independent Contractors?

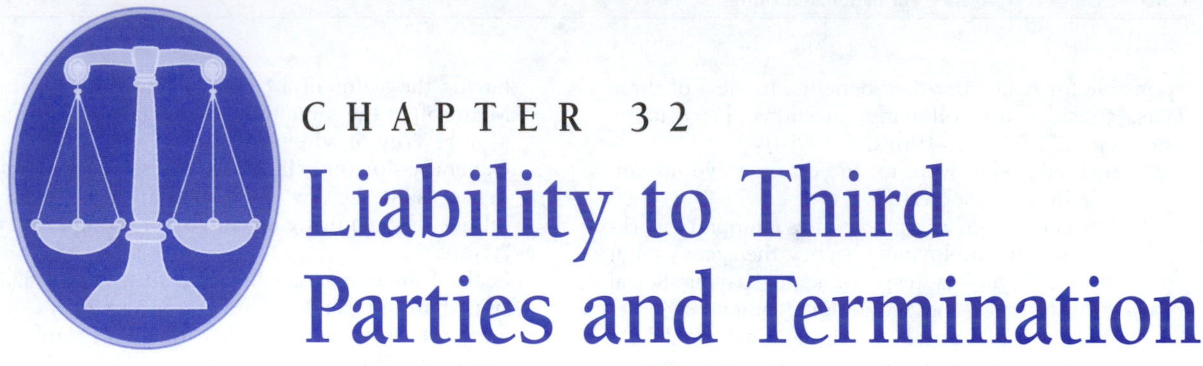

CHAPTER 32 Liability to Third Parties and Termination

AS DISCUSSED IN THE PREVIOUS CHAPTER, the law of agency focuses on the special relationship that exists between a principal and an agent—how the relationship is formed and the duties the principal and agent assume once the relationship is established. This chapter deals with another important aspect of agency law—the liability of principals and agents to third parties.

We first look at the rights of third parties who enter into contracts with agents. Such a contract will make an agent's principal liable to the third party only if the agent had authority to make the contract or if the principal ratified, or was estopped from denying, the agent's acts. The second part of the chapter will deal with an agent's liability to third parties in contract and tort and the principal's liability to third parties because of an agent's torts. The chapter concludes with a discussion of how agency relationships are terminated.

SECTION 1

Scope of Agent's Authority

A principal's liability in a contract with a third party arises from the authority given the agent to enter legally binding contracts on the principal's behalf. An agent's authority can be either *actual* (express or implied) or *apparent*.

EXPRESS AUTHORITY

Express authority is embodied in that which the principal has engaged the agent to do. Express authority can be given orally or in writing. The **equal dignity rule** in most states requires that if the contract being executed is or must be in writing, the agent's authority must also be in writing. Failure to comply with the equal dignity rule can make a contract voidable *at the option of the principal.* The law regards the contract at that point as a mere offer. If the principal decides to accept the offer, acceptance must be ratified, or affirmed, in writing. Assume that Pattberg (the principal) orally asks Austin (the agent) to sell a ranch that Pattberg owns. Austin finds a buyer and signs a sales contract (a contract for an interest in realty must be in writing) on behalf of Pattberg to sell the ranch. The buyer cannot enforce the contract unless Pattberg subsequently ratifies Austin's agency status in writing. Once the contract is ratified, either party can enforce rights under the contract.

An exception to the equal dignity rule exists in modern business practice. An executive officer of a corporation, when acting for the corporation in an ordinary business situation, is not required to obtain written authority from the corporation. In addition, the equal dignity rule does not apply when an agent acts in the presence of a principal or when the agent's act of signing is merely perfunctory. Thus, if Healy (the principal) negotiates a contract but is called out of town the day it is to be signed and orally authorizes Scougall to sign, the oral authorization is sufficient.

Giving an agent a **power of attorney** confers express authority.[1] The power of attorney is a written document and is usually notarized. (A document is notarized when a **notary public**—a public official au-

1. An agent who holds the power of attorney is called an *attorney-in-fact* for the principal. The holder does not have to be an attorney-at-law (and often is not).

thorized to attest to the authenticity of signatures—signs and dates the document and imprints it with his or her seal of authority.) A power of attorney can be special (permitting the agent to perform specified acts only), or it can be general (permitting the agent to transact all business for the principal). Because of the extensive authority granted to an agent by the latter (see Exhibit 32–1 on page 640), a general power of attorney should be used with great caution and usually only in exceptional circumstances.

An ordinary power of attorney terminates on the incapacity or death of the person giving the power. A *durable* power of attorney, however, provides an agent with very broad authority to act and make decisions for the principal and specifies that it is not affected by the principal's incapacity. An elderly person, for example, might grant a durable power of attorney to provide for the handling of property and investments or specific health-care needs should he or she become incompetent.

IMPLIED AUTHORITY

Implied authority is conferred by custom, can be inferred from the position the agent occupies, or is implied by virtue of being reasonably necessary to carry out express authority. For example, Carlson is employed by Packard Grocery to manage one of its stores. Packard has not specified (expressly stated) Carlson's authority to contract with third persons. In this situation, though, authority to manage a business implies authority to do what is reasonably required (as is customary or can be inferred from a manager's position) to operate the business. This includes making contracts for obtaining employee help, for buying merchandise and equipment, and even for advertising the products sold in the store.

Because implied authority is conferred on the basis of custom, it is important for third persons to be familiar with the custom of the trade. The list of rules that have developed to determine what authority is implied based on custom or on the agent's position is extensive. In general, implied authority is authority customarily associated with the position occupied by the agent or authority that can be inferred from the express authority given to the agent to perform fully his or her duties.

For example, an agent who has authority to solicit orders for goods sold by the principal has no authority to collect payments for the goods unless the agent possesses the goods. The test is whether it was reasonable for the agent to believe that he or she had the authority to enter into the contract in question.

Westlaw. See Case 32.1 at the end of this chapter. To view the full, unedited case from Westlaw,® go to this text's Web site at **http://wbl-cs.westbuslaw.com**.

APPARENT AUTHORITY AND ESTOPPEL

Actual authority (express or implied) arises from what the principal manifests *to the agent.* An agent has **apparent authority** when the principal, by either word or action, causes a *third party* reasonably to believe that the agent has authority to act, even though the agent has no express or implied authority. If the third party changes his or her position in reliance on the principal's representations, the principal may be *estopped* from denying that the agent had authority.

For example, assume that Adam is a traveling sales agent for a pesticide company. Adam neither possesses the goods ordered nor delivers them, and he has no express or implied authority to collect payments from customers. Now assume that a customer, Ling, pays Adam for a solicited order. Adam then takes the payment to the principal's accounting department. An accountant accepts payment and sends Ling a receipt. This procedure is thereafter followed for other orders solicited by Adam and paid for by Ling. Later, Adam solicits an order, and Ling pays Adam as before. This time, however, Adam absconds with the money.

Can Ling claim that the payment to Adam was authorized and thus, in effect, a payment to the principal? The answer is yes, because the principal's *repeated* acts of accepting Ling's payments through Adam led Ling reasonably to believe that Adam had authority to receive payments for goods solicited. Although Adam did not have express or implied authority, the principal's conduct gave Adam apparent authority to collect.

There are other ways in which agency by estoppel may arise based on apparent authority. If, for example, the principal has "clothed the agent" with both possession and apparent ownership of the principal's property, the agent has very broad powers and can deal with the property as if he or she were the true owner. For example, to deceive certain creditors, Sikora (the principal) and Hunter (the agent) agree verbally that Hunter will hold certain stock certificates for Sikora. Because the certificates are bearer paper (that is, they do not require indorsement to be transferred), Hunter's possession and apparent ownership of the

EXHIBIT 32–1 A SAMPLE GENERAL POWER OF ATTORNEY

POWER OF ATTORNEY

GENERAL

Know All Men by These Presents: That I, ______________________________

____

the undersigned (jointly and severally, if more than one) hereby make, constitute and appoint ______________

____

as a true and lawful Attorney for me and in my name, place and stead and for my use and benefit:

(a) To ask, demand, sue for, recover, collect and receive each and every sum of money, debt, account, legacy, bequest, interest, dividend, annuity and demand (which now is or hereafter shall become due, owing or payable) belonging to or claimed by me, and to use and take any lawful means for the recovery thereof by legal process or otherwise, and to execute and deliver a satisfaction or release therefore, together with the right and power to compromise or compound any claim or demand;

(b) To exercise any or all of the following powers as to real property, any interest therein and/or any building thereon: To contract for, purchase, receive and take possession thereof and or evidence of title thereto; to lease the same for any term or purpose, including leases for business, residence, and oil and/or mineral development; to sell, exchange, grant or convey the same with or without warranty; and to mortgage, transfer in trust, or otherwise encumber or hypothecate the same to secure payment of a negotiable or non-negotiable note or performance of any obligation or agreement;

(c) To exercise any or all of the following powers as to all kinds of personal property and goods, wares and merchandise, choses in action and other property in possession or in action: To contract for, buy, sell, exchange, transfer and in any legal manner deal in and with the same; and to mortgage, transfer in trust, or otherwise encumber or hypothecate the same to secure payment of a negotiable or non-negotiable note or performance of any obligation or agreement;

(d) To borrow money and to execute and deliver negotiable or non-negotiable notes therefore with or without security; and to loan money and receive negotiable or non-negotiable notes therefore with such security as he shall deem proper;

(e) To create, amend, supplement and terminate any trust and to instruct and advise the trustee of any trust wherein I am or may be trustor or beneficiary; to represent and vote stock, exercise stock rights, accept and deal with any dividend, distribution or bonus, join in any corporate financing, reorganization, merger, liquidation, consolidation or other action and the extension, compromise, conversion, adjustment, enforcement or foreclosure, singly or in conjunction with others, of any corporate stock, bond, note, debenture or other security; to compound, compromise, adjust, settle and satisfy any obligation, secured or unsecured, owing by or to me and to give or accept any property and/or money whether or not equal to or less in value than the amount owing in payment, settlement or satisfaction thereof;

(f) To transact business of any kind or class and as my act and deed to sign, execute, acknowledge and deliver any deed, lease, assignment of lease, covenant, indenture, indemnity, agreement, mortgage, deed of trust, assignment of mortgage or of the beneficial interest under deed of trust, extension or renewal of any obligation, subordination or waiver of priority, hypothecation, bottomry, charter-party, bill of lading, bill of sale, bill, bond, note, whether negotiable or non-negotiable, receipt, evidence of debt, full or partial release or satisfaction of mortgage, judgment and other debt, request for partial or full reconveyance of deed of trust and such other instruments in writing of any kind or class as may be necessary or proper in the premises.

Giving and Granting unto my said Attorney full power and authority to do so and perform all and every act and thing whatsoever requisite, necessary or appropriate to be done in and about the premises as fully to all intents and purposes as I might or could do if personally present, hereby ratifying all that my said Attorney shall lawfully do or cause to be done by virtue of these presents. The powers and authority hereby conferred upon my said Attorney shall be applicable to all real and personal property or interests therein now owned or hereafter acquired by me and wherever situated.

My said Attorney is empowered hereby to determine in his sole discretion the time when, purpose for and manner in which any power herein conferred upon him shall be exercised, and the conditions, provisions and covenants of any instrument or document which may be executed by him pursuant hereto; and in the acquisition or disposition of real or personal property, my said Attorney shall have exclusive power to fix the terms thereof for cash, credit and/or property, and if on credit with or without security.

The undersigned, if a married woman, hereby further authorizes and empowers my said Attorney, as my duly authorized agent, to join in my behalf, in the execution of any instrument by which any community real property or any interest therein, now owned or hereafter acquired by my spouse and myself, or either of us, is sold, leased, encumbered, or conveyed.

When the context so requires, the masculine gender includes the feminine and/or neuter, and the singular number includes the plural.

WITNESS my hand this ____________ day of ____________________, 20 ___

______________________ ______________________

______________________ ______________________

State of California
County of ______________ } SS.

On ______________________, before me, the undersigned, a Notary Public in and for said State, personally appeared ______________________

____

known to me to be the person __________ whose name ______________ subscribed to the within instrument and acknowledged that ______________ executed the same.

Witness my hand and official seal. (Seal) ______________________
Notary Public in and for said State.

stock certificates are such strong indications of ownership that a reasonable person would conclude that Hunter was the actual owner. If Hunter negotiates the stock certificates to a third person, Sikora will be estopped from denying Hunter's authority to transfer the stock.

When land is involved, courts have held that possession alone is not a sufficient indication of ownership (see Chapter 47 for details). If, however, the agent also possesses the deed to the property and sells the property against the principal's wishes to an unsuspecting buyer, the principal normally cannot cancel the sale or assert the claim to title.

Westlaw. See Case 32.2 at the end of this chapter. To view the full, unedited case from Westlaw,® go to this text's Web site at **http://wbl-cs.westbuslaw.com**.

EMERGENCY POWERS

When an unforeseen emergency demands action by the agent to protect or preserve the property and rights of the principal, but the agent is unable to communicate with the principal, the agent has emergency power.

For example, Fulsom is an engineer for Pacific Railroad. While Fulsom is acting within the scope of his employment, he falls under the train many miles from home and is severely injured. Dusky, the conductor, directs Thompson, a doctor, to give medical aid to Fulsom and to charge Pacific for the medical services. Dusky, an agent, has no express or implied authority to bind the principal, Pacific Railroad, for the services of Thompson. Because of the emergency situation, however, the law recognizes Dusky as having authority to act appropriately under the circumstances.

RATIFICATION

Ratification occurs when the principal affirms an agent's unauthorized act. Ratification binds the principal to the agent's act and creates a situation in which the act is treated as if it had been authorized by the principal *from the outset*. Ratification can be either express or implied.

With respect to a contract, if the principal does not ratify, the principal is not bound, and the third party's agreement with the agent is merely an unaccepted offer. Because the third party's agreement is an unaccepted offer, the third party can revoke it any time before the principal ratifies, without liability. The agent, however, may be liable to the third party for misrepresenting his or her authority.

To be effective, a ratification must meet certain requirements. These include the following:

1. The agent must act on behalf of an identified principal who subsequently ratifies the action.
2. The principal must affirm the agent's act in its entirety.
3. The principal's affirmance must occur before the third party withdraws from the transaction.
4. The principal must have the legal capacity to authorize the transaction at the time the agent engages in the act and at the time the principal ratifies. The third party must also have the legal capacity to engage in the transaction.
5. The principal must know all of the material facts involved in the transaction.

Regarding this last requirement, if a principal ratifies a contract *without knowing* all of the facts, the principal can rescind (cancel) the ratification. If the third party has changed his or her position in reliance on the apparent contract, however, the principal can rescind but must reimburse the third party for his or her costs.

For example, suppose that an agent, without authority, contracts with a third person on behalf of a principal for repair work to the principal's office building. The principal learns of the contract and agrees to "some repair work," thinking that it will involve only patching and painting the exterior of the building. In fact, the contract includes resurfacing the parking lot, which the principal does not want done. On learning of the additional provision, the principal rescinds the contract. If the third party has made preparations to do the work (such as purchasing materials, hiring additional workers, or renting equipment), in reliance on the principal's apparent ratification, the principal must reimburse the third party for the cost of those preparations.

SECTION 2

Liability for Contracts

Liability for contracts formed by an agent depends on how the principal is classified and on whether the actions of the agent were authorized or unauthorized.

Principals are classified as disclosed, partially disclosed, or undisclosed.[2] A **disclosed principal** is a principal whose identity is known by the third party at the time the contract is made by the agent. A **partially disclosed principal** is a principal whose identity is not known by the third party, but the third party knows that the agent is or may be acting for a principal at the time that the contract is made. An **undisclosed principal** is a principal whose identity is totally unknown by the third party, and the third party has no knowledge that the agent is acting in an agency capacity at the time the contract is made.

AUTHORIZED ACTS

If an agent acts within the scope of his or her authority, a disclosed or partially disclosed principal is liable to a third party for a contract made by the agent. If the principal is disclosed, an agent has no contractual liability for the nonperformance of the principal or the third party. If the principal is partially disclosed, in most states the agent is also treated as a party to the contract, and the third party can hold the agent liable for contractual nonperformance.[3]

When neither the fact of agency nor the identity of the principal is disclosed, the undisclosed principal is fully bound to perform just as if the principal had been fully disclosed at the time the contract was made. Exceptions to this rule are made in the following circumstances:

1. The undisclosed principal was expressly excluded as a party in the contract. For example, an agent contracts with a landlord for the lease of a building. The landlord does not know of the agency, and the lease specifically lists the agent as tenant, with no right of assignment without the landlord's consent. The undisclosed principal cannot enforce the lease.
2. The contract is a negotiable instrument. Here, the UCC provides that only the agent is liable if the instrument neither names the principal nor shows that the agent signed in a representative capacity.[4]
3. The performance of the agent is personal to the contract, allowing the third party to refuse the principal's performance. Typical examples involve extensions of credit and highly personal services, such as surgery.
4. The third party would not have entered into a contract with the principal had the third party known the principal's identity, the agent or the principal knew this, and the third party rescinds the contract.

When a principal's identity is undisclosed and the agent is forced to pay the third party, the agent is entitled to indemnification by the principal. It was the principal's duty to perform, even though his or her identity was undisclosed,[5] and failure to do so will make the principal ultimately liable. Once the undisclosed principal's identity is revealed, the third party generally can elect to hold either the principal or the agent liable on the contract.

UNAUTHORIZED ACTS

If an agent has no authority but nevertheless contracts with a third party, the principal cannot be held liable on the contract. It does not matter whether the principal was disclosed, partially disclosed, or undisclosed. The agent is liable, however. For example, Scammon signs a contract for the purchase of a truck, purportedly acting as an agent under authority granted by Johnson. In fact, Johnson has not given Scammon any such authority. Johnson refuses to pay for the truck, claiming that Scammon had no authority to purchase it. The seller of the truck is entitled to hold Scammon liable for payment.

If the principal is disclosed or partially disclosed, the agent's liability to the third party is based on the theory of breach of implied warranty of authority, not on breach of the contract itself.[6] The agent's implied warranty of authority can be breached intentionally or by a good faith mistake.[7] The agent is liable, as long as the third party relied on the agency status. Conversely, if the third party knows at the time the contract is made that the agent is mistaken about the extent of his or her authority, or the agent indicates to the third party *uncertainty* about the extent of authority, the agent is not personally liable for breach of warranty.

2. *Restatement (Second) of Agency,* Section 4.
3. *Restatement (Second) of Agency,* Section 321.
4. UCC 3–402(b)(2).

5. If the agent is a gratuitous agent, and the principal accepts the benefits of the agent's contract with a third party, the principal will be liable to the agent on the theory of quasi contract (see Chapter 9).
6. The agent is not liable on the contract because the agent was never intended personally to be a party to the contract.
7. If the agent intentionally misrepresents his or her authority, the agent can also be liable in tort for fraud.

SECTION 3

Liability for Agent's Torts

Obviously, an agent is liable for his or her own torts. A principal may also be liable for an agent's torts if they result from one of the following:

1. The principal's own tortious conduct.
2. The principal's authorization of a tortious act.
3. The agent's unauthorized but tortious misrepresentation made within the scope of the agency.

If the agent is an employee, whose conduct the principal-employer controls, the employer may also be liable for torts committed by the employee in the course of employment under the doctrine of *respondeat superior,* as discussed below.

PRINCIPAL'S TORTIOUS CONDUCT

A principal conducting an activity through an agent may be liable for harm resulting from the principal's own negligence or recklessness, which may include giving improper instructions; authorizing the use of improper materials, tools, or the like; establishing improper rules; or failing to prevent others' tortious conduct while they are on the principal's property or using the principal's equipment, materials, or tools. For instance, if Jack knows that Kathy cannot drive but nevertheless authorizes her to use the company truck to deliver some equipment to a customer, he will be liable for his own negligence to anyone injured by her negligent driving.

PRINCIPAL'S AUTHORIZATION OF AGENT'S TORTIOUS CONDUCT

Similarly, a principal who authorizes an agent to commit a tortious act may be liable to persons or property injured thereby, because the act is considered to be the principal's. For example, Selkow directs Warren—an agent Selkow retained to oversee the harvest of crops he bought—to cut the corn on specific acreage, which neither of them has the right to do. The harvest is therefore a trespass, and Selkow is liable to whoever owns the corn.

In the same vein, assume that Victoria instructs Guthrie, her real estate agent, to tell prospective purchasers that there is oil beneath her property, when she knows there is not. Victoria will be liable to anyone who buys the property in reliance on the statements.

MISREPRESENTATION

A principal is exposed to tort liability whenever a third person sustains a loss due to the agent's misrepresentation. The principal's liability depends on whether the agent was actually or apparently authorized to make representations and whether such representations were made within the scope of the agency.

Fraudulent Misrepresentation. Assume that Bassett is a demonstrator for Moore's products. Moore sends Bassett to a home show to demonstrate the products and to answer questions from consumers. Moore has given Bassett authority to make statements about the products. If Bassett makes only true representations, all is fine; but if he makes false claims, Moore will be liable for any injuries or damages sustained by third parties in reliance on Bassett's false representations.

An interesting series of cases has arisen on the theory that when a principal has placed an agent in a position to defraud a third party, the principal is liable for the agent's fraudulent acts. For example, Frendak is a loan officer at First Security Bank. In the ordinary course of the job, Frendak approves and services loans and has access to the credit records of all customers. Frendak falsely represents to a borrower, McMillan, that the bank feels insecure about McMillan's loan and intends to call it in unless McMillan provides additional collateral, such as stocks and bonds. McMillan gives Frendak numerous stock certificates, which Frendak keeps in her own possession and later uses to make personal investments. The bank is liable to McMillan for losses sustained on the stocks even though the bank had no direct role in or knowledge of the fraudulent scheme.

The legal theory used here is that the agent's position conveys to third persons the impression that the agent has the authority to make statements and perform acts consistent with the ordinary duties that are within the scope of the position. When an agent appears to be acting within the scope of the authority that the position of agency confers but is actually taking advantage of a third party, the principal who placed the agent in that position is liable. In the example above, if a bank teller had told McMillan that the bank required additional security for the loan, McMillan would not have been justified in relying on the person's authority to make that representation. McMillan, however, could reasonably expect that the loan officer was telling the truth.

Innocent Misrepresentation. Tort liability based on fraud requires proof that a material misstatement was made knowingly and with the intent to deceive. An agent's innocent mistakes occurring in a contract transaction or involving a warranty contained in the contract can provide grounds for the third party's rescission of the contract and the award of damages. Moreover, justice dictates that when a principal knows that an agent is not accurately advised of facts but does not correct either the agent's or the third party's impressions, the principal is directly responsible to the third party for resulting damages. The point is that the principal is always directly responsible for an agent's misrepresentation made within the scope of authority.

THE DOCTRINE OF *RESPONDEAT SUPERIOR*

Under the doctrine of ***respondeat superior***,[8] the principal-employer is liable for any harm caused to a third party by an agent-employee within the scope of employment. This doctrine imposes **vicarious liability** on the employer—that is, liability without regard to the personal fault of the employer for torts committed by an employee in the course or scope of employment.[9] Third persons injured through the negligence of an employee can sue either the employee who was negligent or the employer, if the employee's negligent conduct occurred while the employee was acting within the scope of employment.

At early common law, a servant (employee) was viewed as the master's (employer's) property. The master was deemed to have absolute control over the servant's acts and was held strictly liable for them no matter how carefully the master supervised the servant. The rationale for the doctrine of *respondeat superior* is based on the principle of social duty that requires every person to manage his or her affairs, whether accomplished by the person or through agents, so as not to injure another. Liability is imposed on employers because they are deemed to be in a better financial position to bear the loss. The superior financial position carries with it the duty to be responsible for damages.

Today the doctrine continues, but employers carry liability insurance and spread the cost of risk over the entire business enterprise. Public policy requires that an injured person be afforded effective relief, and recovery from a business enterprise provides far more effective relief than recovery from an individual employee. Liability rights exist under law because of public-policy protections of third parties. Thus, a master (employer) cannot contract with a servant (employee) to disclaim responsibilities for injuries resulting from the servant's acts, because such disclaimers are against public policy.

Liability for Employee's Negligence. For the employer to be liable for an employee's negligence, the employee's injury-causing act must have occurred within the course and scope of the employee's employment.

Scope of Employment. The *Restatement (Second) of Agency*, Section 229, indicates the following general factors that courts will consider in determining whether a particular act occurred within the course and scope of employment:

1. Whether the employee's act was authorized by the employer.
2. The time, place, and purpose of the act.
3. Whether the act was one commonly performed by employees on behalf of their employers.
4. The extent to which the employer's interest was advanced by the act.
5. The extent to which the private interests of the employee were involved.
6. Whether the employer furnished the means or instrumentality (for example, a truck or a machine) by which an injury was inflicted.
7. Whether the employer had reason to know that the employee would perform the act in question and whether the employee had done it before.
8. Whether the act involved the commission of a serious crime.

Consider an example. Mandel (the employee) is a delivery driver for Schwartz (the employer). Schwartz provides Mandel with a vehicle and instructs him to use it for making company deliveries. One day, while he is making deliveries, Mandel negligently runs into Chan, a pedestrian, causing Chan to be seriously injured. Because the negligence occurred as part of Mandel's regular duties of employment (making deliveries), Schwartz is li-

8. Pronounced ree-*spahn*-dee-uht soo-*peer*-ee-your. The doctrine of *respondeat superior* applies not only to employer-employee relationships but also to other principal-agent relationships in which the principal has the right of control over the agent.

9. The theory of *respondeat superior* is similar to the theory of strict liability covered in Chapter 6.

able to Chan for the injuries caused by Mandel's negligence.

An employee going to and from work or to and from meals is usually considered outside the scope of employment. All travel time of traveling salespersons or others whose jobs require them to travel, however, is normally considered within the scope of employment for the duration of the business trip, including the return trip home, unless there is a significant departure from the employer's business.

Departures from the Employer's Business. When an employee goes off on his or her own—that is, departs from the employer's business to take care of personal affairs—is the employer liable? The answer depends on whether the employee's activity is a minor departure from the employer's business or a substantial departure akin to an utter abandonment of the employer's business. For example, a traveling salesperson, while driving the employer's vehicle to call on a customer, decides to stop at the post office—which is one block off his route—to mail a personal letter. As the employee approaches the post office, he negligently runs into a parked vehicle owned by Inga. In this situation, because the employee's detour from the employer's business is not substantial, the employee is still within the scope of employment, and the employer is liable.

The result would be different if the employee had decided to pick up a few friends for cocktails in another city and in the process had negligently run his vehicle into Inga's. In this situation, the departure from the employer's business would be substantial, to the point of abandoning the employer's business, and the employer normally would not be liable to Inga for damages. The employee would be considered to be on a "frolic" of his own, and only the employee could be held liable to Inga.

Borrowed Servants. Employers can lend the services of their employees to other employers. Suppose that an employer leases ground-moving equipment to another employer and sends along an employee to operate the machinery. Who is liable for injuries caused by the employee's negligent actions on the job site? Liability turns on *which employer had the primary right to control* the employee at the time the injuries occurred. Generally, the employer who rents out the equipment is presumed to retain control over his or her employee. If the rental is for a relatively long period of time, however, control may be deemed to pass to the employer who is renting the equipment and presumably controlling and directing the employee.

Notice of Dangerous Conditions. The employer is charged with knowledge of any dangerous conditions discovered by an employee and pertinent to the employment situation. To illustrate: A maintenance employee in Martin's apartment building notices a lead pipe protruding from the ground in the building's courtyard. The employee neglects either to fix it or to inform the employer of the danger. John falls on the pipe and is injured. The employer is charged with knowledge of the dangerous condition regardless of whether or not the employee actually informed the employer. That knowledge is imputed to the employer by virtue of the employment relationship.

Liability for Employee's Intentional Torts.

Most intentional torts that employees commit have no relation to their employment; thus, their employers will not be held liable. Under the doctrine of *respondeat superior,* however, the employer is liable for intentional torts of the employee that are committed within the course and scope of employment, just as the employer is liable for negligence. For example, an employer is liable when an employee (such as a "bouncer" at a nightclub or a security guard at a department store) commits assault and battery or false imprisonment while acting within the scope of employment.

An employee acting at the employer's direction can be liable as a *tortfeasor* (one who commits a wrong, or tort), along with the employer, for committing the tortious act even if the employee was unaware of the wrongfulness of the act. For example, an employer directs an employee to burn out a field of crops. The employee does so, assuming that the field belongs to the employer, which it does not. Both can be found liable to the owner of the field for damages.

An employer who knows or should know that an employee has a propensity for committing tortious acts is liable for the employee's acts even if they would not ordinarily be considered within the scope of employment. For example, the Blue Moon employs Arnold Munn as a bouncer, knowing that he has a history of arrests for assault and battery. While he is working one night, and within the scope of his employment, he viciously attacks a patron who "looks at him funny." The Blue Moon will bear the responsibility for Munn's misdeeds, because it knew that he had a propensity for committing tortious acts.

An employer is also liable for permitting an employee to engage in reckless actions that can injure others. For example, an employer observes an employee smoking while filling containerized trucks with highly flammable liquids. Failure to stop the employee will cause the employer to be liable for any injuries that result if a truck explodes.

To reduce the likelihood of liability losses, employers set up stringent work rules. For example, employees who drive company vehicles may be prohibited from giving rides to other passengers. Employees who violate these rules by being careless or committing unlawful or tortious acts may be subject to discipline, including discharge. Almost without exception, employers purchase liability insurance to cover the actions of certain employees.

SECTION 4

Liability for Independent Contractor's Torts

The general rule concerning liability for the acts of independent contractors is that the employer is not liable for physical harm caused to a third person by the negligent act of an independent contractor in the performance of the contract. An employer who has no legal power to control the details of the physical performance of a contract cannot be held liable. Here again, the test is the *right to control.* Because an employer bargains with an independent contractor only for results and retains no control over the manner in which those results are achieved, the employer is generally not expected to bear the responsibility for torts committed by an independent contractor. A collection agency is a typical example of an independent contractor. The creditor is generally not liable for the acts of the collection agency, because collection is a distinct business occupation.

Generally, an exception to this doctrine prevails when unusually hazardous activities are involved. Typical examples of such activities include blasting operations, the transportation of highly volatile chemicals, and the use of poisonous gases. In these cases, an employer cannot be shielded from liability merely by using an independent contractor. Strict liability is imposed on the employer-principal as a matter of law. Also, in some states, strict liability may be imposed by statute.

See Case 32.3 at the end of this chapter. To view the full, unedited case from Westlaw,® go to this text's Web site at **http://wbl-cs.westbuslaw.com**.

SECTION 5

Liability for Agent's Crimes

Obviously, an agent is liable for his or her own crimes. A principal or employer is not liable for an agent's or employee's crime simply because the agent or employee committed the crime while otherwise acting within the scope of authority or employment, unless the principal or employer participated by conspiracy or other action. In some jurisdictions, under specific statutes, a principal may be liable for an agent's violating, in the course and scope of employment, such regulations as those governing sanitation, prices, weights, and the sale of liquor.

SECTION 6

Liability for Subagent's Acts

In three instances, an agent can hire a subagent:

1. To perform simple, definite duties.
2. When it is the business custom.
3. For unforeseen emergencies.

If an agent is authorized to hire subagents for the principal under any one of these circumstances, the principal is liable for the acts of the subagents.

The result is slightly different if the agent hires subagents for an undisclosed principal. In that situation, the agent is responsible for the subagent in contract law for such things as wages. The undisclosed principal, however, is generally held to be liable for tort injuries. An agent's unauthorized hiring of a subagent generally does not create any legal relationship between the principal and the subagent.

SECTION 7

E-Agents

Gradually, the courts have established fairly clear rules concerning the situations in which an employer may be held liable for an agent's actions. Yet do these rules apply to electronic agents? An electronic agent, or **e-agent**, is not a person but a semiautonomous computer program that is capable of executing specific tasks.[10] Examples of e-agents in e-commerce include software that can search through many databases and retrieve only relevant information for the user.

Some e-agents are used to make purchases on the Internet. Popular e-agents that search the Web and compare product prices include DealTime.com, mySimon.com, and Whenushop.com. An Internet user might employ one of the following e-agents to search the Web for a particular book: PriceScan, MX Bookfinder, or Bestbookbuys. Any one of these e-agents will scour the Web for the lowest price for that particular book title. Some shopping e-agents actually negotiate product acquisition, as well as delivery.

WHAT AGENCY LAW APPLIES?

Under traditional agency law, contracts formed by an agent normally are legally binding on the principal *if* the principal authorized the agent, either expressly or impliedly, to form the contracts. One of the controversies involving e-agents concerns the extent of an e-agent's authority to act on behalf of its principal. Consider a not-too-uncommon example.

Software that an e-agent might find for its principal will undoubtedly involve a click-on agreement. E-agents searching the Internet may run into a variety of such click-on agreements, which contain different terms and conditions. If the e-agent ignores the licensing terms and conditions outlined in the click-on agreement, is the principal bound by the agreement? Conversely, a click-on agreement may exempt a third party from liability resulting from an underlying product or service. Is the principal bound by this term? With respect to human agents, the courts occasionally have found that an agent could not agree to such a term without explicit authority.

To avoid problems created by the use of e-agents, some online merchants have blocked e-agents from accessing pricing information. Other online stores are developing click-on agreements that can be understood by a computer and that are therefore more conspicuous for e-agents.

10. The Uniform Computer Information Transactions Act (UCITA), which will be discussed shortly, defines an *e-agent* as "a computer program, electronic or other automated means used to independently initiate an action or to respond to electronic messages or performances without review by an individual" [UCITA 102(a)(28)].

See Case 32.4 at the end of this chapter. To view the full, unedited case from Westlaw,® go to this text's Web site at **http://wbl-cs.westbuslaw.com**.

E-AGENTS AND THE UCITA

As discussed in Chapter 23, in 1999 the National Conference of Commissioners on Uniform State Laws promulgated the Uniform Computer Information Transactions Act (UCITA). The act was drafted to address problems unique to electronic contracting and to the purchase and sale (licensing) of computer information, such as software. Among other things, the act specifically addresses the issue of e-agents. Section 107(d) of the UCITA provides that any individual or company that uses an e-agent "is bound by the operations of the electronic agent, even if no individual was aware of or reviewed the agent's operations or the results of the operations." The liability of individuals and companies for the acts of e-agents, however, is qualified by Section 206(a) of the UCITA, which states that "a court may grant appropriate relief if the operations resulted from fraud, electronic mistake, or the like."

SECTION 8

Termination of an Agency

Agency law is similar to contract law in that both an agency and a contract may be terminated by an act of the parties or by operation of law. Once the relationship between the principal and the agent has ended, the agent no longer has *actual* authority to bind the principal—that is, he or she lacks the principal's consent to act in the principal's behalf. Generally, if the agency is terminated by an act of the parties, the principal can still be bound by the agent's acts if the agent has acted within the scope of his or her *apparent* authority, however. To terminate the agent's apparent authority, third parties must be notified of the agency termination—as will be discussed later.

TERMINATION BY ACT OF THE PARTIES

An agency relationship may be terminated by act of the parties in a number of ways, including those discussed here.

Lapse of Time. An agency agreement may specify the time period during which the agency relationship will exist. If so, the agency ends when that time expires. For example, Akers signs an agreement of agency with Jefferson "beginning January 1, 2001, and ending December 31, 2002." The agency is automatically terminated on December 31, 2002. Of course, the parties can agree to continue the relationship, in which case the same terms will apply.

If no definite time is stated, the agency continues for a reasonable time and can be terminated at will by either party. What constitutes a reasonable time depends on the circumstances and the nature of the agency relationship. For example, Jefferson asks Akers to sell her car. If after two years Akers has not sold Jefferson's car and there has been no communication between Jefferson and Akers, it is safe to assume that the agency relationship has terminated. Akers no longer has the authority to sell Jefferson's car.

Purpose Achieved. An agent can be employed to accomplish a particular objective, such as the purchase of stock for a cattle rancher. In that situation, the agency automatically ends after the cattle have been purchased. If more than one agent is employed to accomplish the same purpose, such as the sale of real estate, the first agent to complete the sale automatically terminates the agency relationship for all the others.

Occurrence of a Specific Event. In agency can be created to terminate on the happening of a certain event. For example, Jefferson appoints Akers to handle her business affairs while she is away. When Jefferson returns, the agency automatically terminates.

Sometimes one aspect of the agent's authority terminates on the occurrence of a particular event, but the agency relationship itself does not terminate. For example, Jefferson, a banker, permits Akers, the credit manager, to grant a credit line of $5,000 to certain depositors who maintain a balance of $5,000 in a savings account. If any customer's savings account balance falls below $5,000, Akers can no longer make the credit line available to that customer. Akers, however, continues to have the right to extend credit to the other customers maintaining the minimum balance.

Mutual Agreement. Recall from basic contract law that parties can rescind (cancel) a contract by mutually agreeing to terminate the contractual relationship. The same holds true in agency law regardless of whether the agency contract is in writing or whether it is for a specific duration. For example, Jefferson no longer wishes Akers to be her agent, and Akers does not want to work for Jefferson anymore. Either party can communicate to the other the intent to terminate the relationship. Agreement to terminate effectively relieves each of the rights, duties, and powers inherent in the relationship.

Termination by One Party. As a *general* rule, either party can terminate the agency relationship. The agent's act is said to be a renunciation of authority. The principal's act is a revocation of authority. Although both parties may have the power to terminate—because agency is a consensual relationship, and thus neither party can be compelled to continue in the relationship—they may not possess the right to terminate and may therefore be liable for breach of contract. Wrongful termination can subject the canceling party to a suit for damages. For example, Akers has a one-year employment contract with Jefferson to act as Jefferson's agent for $25,000. Jefferson can discharge Akers before the contract period expires (Jefferson has the power to breach the contract); however, Jefferson will be liable to Akers for money damages, because Jefferson has no *right* to breach the contract.

Even in an agency at will (that is, an agency that either party may terminate at any time), the principal who wishes to terminate must give the agent a reasonable notice—that is, at least sufficient notice to allow the agent to recoup his or her expenses and, in some cases, to make a normal profit.

A special rule applies in an *agency coupled with an interest*. This type of agency is not an agency in the usual sense, because it is created for the agent's benefit instead of for the principal's benefit. For example, suppose that Julie borrows $5,000 from Rob, giving Rob some of her jewelry and signing a letter authorizing Rob to sell the jewelry as her agent if she fails to repay the loan. Julie, after she has received the $5,000 from Rob, then attempts to revoke Rob's authority to sell the jewelry. Julie will not succeed in this attempt, because a principal cannot revoke an agency created for the agent's benefit.

An agency coupled with an interest should not be confused with a situation in which the agent merely derives proceeds or profits from the sale of the subject matter. For example, an agent who merely receives a commission from the sale of real property does not have a beneficial interest in the property itself. Likewise, an attorney whose fee is a percentage of the recovery (a *contingency fee*—see Chapter 3) merely has an interest in the proceeds. These agency relationships are revocable by the principal, subject to any express contractual arrangements between the principal and the agent.

Notice of Termination. When an agency has been terminated by act of the parties, it is the principal's duty to inform any third parties who know of the existence of the agency that it has been terminated (although notice of the termination may be given by others).

An agent's authority continues until the agent receives some notice of termination. As previously mentioned, notice to third parties follows the general rule that an agent's *apparent authority* continues until the third person receives notice (from any source of information) that the authority has been terminated. The principal is expected to notify *directly* any third person who the principal knows has dealt with the agent. For third persons who have heard about the agency but have not dealt with the agent, *constructive notice* is sufficient.[11]

No particular form is required for notice of termination of the principal-agent relationship to be effective. The principal can actually notify the agent, or the agent can learn of the termination through some other means. For example, Manning bids on a shipment of steel, and Stone is hired as an agent to arrange transportation of the shipment. When Stone learns that Manning has lost the bid, Stone's authority to make the transportation arrangement terminates.

If the agent's authority is written, it must be revoked in writing, and the writing must be shown to all people who saw the original writing that established the agency relationship. Sometimes, a written authorization (such as a power of attorney) contains an expiration date. The passage of the expiration date is sufficient notice of termination.

Termination by Operation of Law

Certain events will terminate agency authority automatically, because their occurrence makes it impossible for the agent to perform or improbable that the principal would continue to want performance. We look at these events here. Note that when an agency terminates by operation of law, there is no duty to notify third persons—unless the agent's authority is coupled with an interest.[12]

Death or Insanity. The general rule is that the death or insanity of either the principal or the agent automatically and immediately terminates the ordinary agency relationship. Knowledge of the death is not required. For example, Jefferson sends Akers to the Far East to purchase a rare book. Before Akers makes the purchase, Jefferson dies. Akers's agent status is terminated at the moment of death, even though Akers does not know that Jefferson has died. (Some states, however, have changed the common law by statute to make knowledge of the principal's death a requirement for agency termination.)

An agent's transactions that occur after the death of the principal are not binding on the principal's estate. Assume that Akers is hired by Jefferson to collect a debt from Cochran (a third party). Jefferson dies, but Akers still collects the money from Cochran, not knowing of Jefferson's death. Cochran's payment to Akers is no longer legally sufficient to discharge Cochran's debt to Jefferson, because Akers no longer has Jefferson's authority to collect the money. If Akers absconds with the money, Cochran must pay the debt again, to Jefferson's estate.

Impossibility. When the specific subject matter of an agency is destroyed or lost, the agency terminates. For example, Jefferson employs Akers to sell Jefferson's house. Prior to any sale, the house is destroyed by fire. Akers's agency and authority to sell the house terminate. Similarly, when it is impossible for the agent to perform the agency lawfully because of war or because of a change in the law, the agency terminates.

Changed Circumstances. When an event occurs that has such an unusual effect on the subject matter of the agency that the agent can reasonably infer that the principal will not want the agency to continue,

11. With *constructive notice* of a fact, knowledge of the fact is imputed by law to a person if he or she could have discovered the fact by proper diligence. Constructive notice is often accomplished by publication in a newspaper.

12. There is an exception to this rule in banking. UCC 4–405 provides that the bank, as agent, can continue to exercise specific types of authority even after the customer's death or insanity unless it has knowledge of the death or insanity. When the bank has knowledge of the customer's death, it has authority for ten days after the death to pay checks (but not notes or drafts) drawn by the customer unless it receives a stop-payment order from someone who has an interest in the account, such as an heir.

the agency terminates. Suppose that Jefferson hires Akers to sell a tract of land for $10,000. Subsequently, Akers learns that there is oil under the land and that the land is therefore worth $1 million. The agency and Akers's authority to sell the land for $10,000 are terminated.

Bankruptcy. If either the principal or the agent petition for bankruptcy, the agency is *usually* terminated. In certain circumstances, as when the agent's financial status is irrelevant to the purpose of the agency, the agency relationship may continue. Insolvency (defined as the inability to pay debts when they become due or when liabilities exceed assets), as distinguished from bankruptcy, does not necessarily terminate the relationship.

War. When the principal's country and the agent's country are at war with each other, the agency is terminated. In this situation, the agency is automatically suspended or terminated because there is no way to enforce the legal rights and obligations of the parties.

TERMS AND CONCEPTS TO REVIEW

apparent authority 639
disclosed principal 642
e-agent 647
equal dignity rule 638
express authority 638
implied authority 639
notary public 638
partially disclosed principal 642
power of attorney 638
ratification 641
respondeat superior 644
undisclosed principal 642
vicarious liability 644

CHAPTER SUMMARY

Scope of Agent's Authority	1. *Express authority*—Can be oral or in writing. Authorization must be in writing if the agent is to execute a contract that must be in writing. 2. *Implied authority*—Authority customarily associated with the position of the agent or authority that is deemed necessary for the agent to carry out expressly authorized tasks. 3. *Apparent authority and estoppel*—Exists when the principal, by word or action, causes a third party reasonably to believe that an agent has authority to act, even though the agent has no express or implied authority. 4. *Emergency powers*—The agent has emergency powers to act for the principal when unforeseen emergencies demand action by the agent to preserve the property and rights of the principal, but the agent is unable to communicate with the principal. 5. *Ratification*—The affirmation by the principal of an agent's unauthorized action or promise. For the ratification to be effective, the principal must be aware of all material facts.
Liability in Agency Relationships	1. *Liability for contracts*—If the principal's identity is disclosed or partially disclosed at the time the agent forms a contract with a third party, the principal is liable to the third party under the contract if the agent acted within the scope of his or her authority. If the principal's identity is undisclosed at the time of contract formation, the agent is personally liable to the third party, but if the agent acted within the scope of authority, the principal is also bound by the contract. 2. *Liability for agent's torts*—Under the doctrine of respondeat superior, the principal is liable for any harm caused to another through the agent's torts if the agent was acting within the scope of his or her employment at the time the harmful act occurred. The principal is also liable for an agent's misrepresentation, whether made knowingly or by mistake. 3. *Liability for independent contractor's torts*—A principal is not liable for harm caused by an independent contractor's negligence, unless hazardous activities are involved (in which situation the principal is strictly liable for any resulting harm) or other exceptions apply. 4. *Liability for agent's crimes*—An agent is responsible for his or her own crimes, even if the crimes were committed while the agent was acting within the scope of authority or employment. A principal will be liable for an agent's crime only if the principal participated by con-

CHAPTER SUMMARY—CONTINUED

Liability in Agency Relationships—continued	spiracy or other action or (in some jurisdictions) if the agent violated certain government regulations in the course of employment. 5. *Liability for subagent's acts*—In some circumstances, a principal will be liable for the acts of a subagent (a person hired by the agent to perform certain duties).
E-Agents	An electronic agent (e-agent) is a semiautonomous computer program that is capable of executing specific tasks, such as searching through Internet databases for particular products. Traditional agency concepts have been difficult to apply to these "nonhuman" agents. The Uniform Computer Information Transactions Act (UCITA), however, filled this gap by stating that companies are bound by the operations of their e-agents, although the UCITA also allows the courts to grant relief for operations resulting from mistake.
Termination of an Agency	1. *By act of the parties*— a. Lapse of time (when a definite time for the duration of the agency was agreed on when the agency was established). b. Purpose achieved. c. Occurrence of a specific event. d. Mutual rescission (requires mutual consent of principal and agent). e. Termination by act of either the principal (revocation) or the agent (renunciation). (A principal cannot revoke an agency coupled with an interest.) f. When an agency is terminated by act of the parties, all third persons who have previously dealt with the agency must be directly notified; constructive notice will suffice for all other third parties. 2. *By operation of law*— a. Death or mental incompetence of either the principal or the agent (except in an agency coupled with an interest). b. Impossibility (when the purpose of the agency cannot be achieved because of an event beyond the parties' control). c. Changed circumstances (in which it would be inequitable to require that the agency be continued). d. Bankruptcy of the principal or the agent, or war between the principal's and agent's countries. e. When an agency is terminated by operation of law, no notice to third parties is required.

CASES FOR ANALYSIS

Westlaw. You can access the full text of each case presented below by going to the Westlaw cases on this text's Web site at http://wbl-cs.westbuslaw.com. Each Westlaw case includes the names of all plaintiffs and defendants, the dates on which the case was argued and decided, a brief summary of the issues and decisions in the case, headnotes classifying specific issues in the case according to the West Key Number System, and the court's opinion. Concurring and dissenting opinions, if any, are included as well.

CASE 32.1 IMPLIED AUTHORITY

GRAVENS v. AUTO-OWNERS INSURANCE CO.
Court of Appeals of Indiana, 1996.
666 N.E.2d 964.

ROBERTSON, Judge.

* * * *

FACTS

* * * [James] Gravens [doing business as Pappy's Sunoco Service Station] purchased an insurance policy covering his service station from [Auto-Owners Insurance Company]. This policy had a limit on the contents of the service station in the amount of $20,000.00. During the night of July 31, 1993, Gravens' service station was burgled and he suffered a substantial loss due to theft. Apparently, the loss exceeded the $20,000.00 limit of the insurance policy.

Gravens retained an attorney to assist him in pursuing a claim against the insurance company. Gravens did not discuss with this attorney the amount for which he was willing to settle nor did Gravens give his attorney the authority to settle the claim without his consent. Nevertheless, the attorney accepted the insurance company's offer to settle the claim for $18,000.00. The insurance company tendered the draft to Gravens' attorney along with a release form. Gravens immediately rejected the draft and refused to sign the form which were promptly returned to the insurance company. Gravens' attorney withdrew from representation.

Gravens obtained new counsel and filed [a suit in an Indiana state court against the insurance company]. The insurance company filed an answer and asserted the affirmative defense of accord and satisfaction—that the case had already been settled by Gravens' original attorney for $18,000.00. The insurance company obtained summary judgment on that basis and this appeal ensued.

DECISION

* * * *

Indiana law is well-settled that an attorney has, by virtue of his employment, the general implied authority to do on behalf of the client all acts in or out of court necessary or incidental to the prosecution or management of the suit or the accomplishment of the purpose for which he was retained. However, neither party has cited, nor are we aware of any Indiana authority which disposes of the precise question presented in this case, that is, whether an attorney has the implied authority to settle a case without the authorization or consent of the client.

In Indiana, the attorney-client relationship is governed by the Model Rules of Professional Conduct. * * *

Professional Conduct Rule 1.2(a) reads, in pertinent part, as follows:

> A lawyer shall abide by a client's decision concerning the objectives of representation, * * * , and shall consult with the client as to the means by which they are to be pursued. A lawyer shall abide by a client's decision whether to accept an offer of settlement of a matter.

The comments to the rule state that the client has the ultimate authority to determine the purposes to be served by the representation. * * *

* * * [U]nder Prof.Cond.R. 1.2, a client has full authority over the decision whether or not to settle his case or proceed to trial. * * * [A]ttorneys [can] enter into enforceable settlement agreements on their client's behalf if they first secure their client's consent to do so. * * *

* * * [W]e hold that the requirement that an attorney must obtain his client's authority or consent to settle a case is implicit in the client's right to exercise ultimate authority over the settlement of a case as guaranteed by Prof.Cond.R. 1.2(a). Moreover, *the rule that an attorney does not have authority to compromise an action merely by virtue of the attorney-client relationship is essentially universal.* [Emphasis added.]

In this case, as in most insurance settlements, both parties understood that there would be no settlement without a release signed by the claimant, not by his attorney. This understanding was implicit when the draft and the release were tendered together. The insurance company had no enforceable expectation that the claim had, in fact, been settled until Gravens himself had signed the release, which he declined to do.

Gravens did not authorize his original attorney to settle the case and immediately repudiated the settlement agreement purported to have been reached by that attorney. Under these circumstances, Gravens was not bound by his attorney's agreement and the trial court's entry of summary judgment on this basis was erroneous. Therefore, we must reverse and remand for trial.

Judgment reversed.

CASE 32.2 APPARENT AUTHORITY

CARGILL, INC. v. MOUNTAIN CEMENT CO.

Supreme Court of Wyoming, 1995.
891 P.2d 57.

TAYLOR, Justice.

* * * *

II. FACTS

Salt Creek Welding (Salt Creek) contracted to build a steel silo for Mountain Cement Company (Mountain Cement). The silo walls were to be built from A36 steel plate. A36 steel is an industrial grade material often used to build steel silos.

Salt Creek contacted Charlie Mandry (Mandry), a salesman for Cargill, Incorporated (Cargill), and ordered A36 steel plate for use in constructing the Mountain Cement silo. Cargill did not have the steel in stock and Mandry arranged to have the steel delivered by a Tulsa, Oklahoma supplier, Steel Deck. Several plates of steel were non-conforming carbon .33 max. alloy plates. * * * When carbon .33 max. alloy plates are welded in the same way A36 steel plates are welded, the alloy becomes very brittle. One of the brittle alloy plates in the Mountain Cement silo cracked and the silo collapsed.

Mountain Cement sued * * * Cargill [in a Wyoming state court]. * * *

The matter was tried before a jury on breach of warranty theories. The jury returned a verdict * * * against Cargill. * * * Cargill appeals the jury verdict * * * .

III. DISCUSSION

* * * *

Cargill argues that it is entitled to summary judgment or judgment as a matter of law. Specifically, Cargill argues it is not a seller [under the Uniform Commercial Code (UCC)] * * * .

* * * *

Cargill insists it is not a seller under [the UCC] because it never held title to the defective steel plate. Cargill argues that if it is not a seller, it is not liable for any breach of express or implied warranties under the * * * UCC. This argument is flawed because the question of whether Cargill held title to the defective steel plate becomes irrelevant if Mandry acted as Cargill's agent in arranging the sale of the defective plate to Salt Creek.

The proper analysis focuses on whether a reasonable jury, properly instructed, could conclude that Mandry acted as Cargill's agent. This issue is controlled by well-settled legal principles. A brief review of agency law will facilitate our analysis of this issue.

Whether an agency relationship exists and the scope of the agent's authority are questions of fact to be determined by the jury following proper instruction. *An agent may possess actual or apparent authority and either may serve to bind the principal.* [Emphasis added.]

Actual authority may be express or implied. An agent has express actual authority to bind the principal when the principal, orally or in writing, specifically grants the agent the power to bind the principal. Implied actual authority is established by the course of dealings between the parties and the circumstances surrounding the case.

Apparent authority is created when the principal holds the agent out as possessing the authority to bind the principal or when the principal allows the agent to claim such authority. To bind the principal under a theory of apparent authority, a third party must establish personal knowledge of, and reliance on, the apparent authority of the agent. * * * To recover on this theory * * * the third party must establish two facts: (1) the principal was responsible for the appearance of authority in the agent to conduct the transaction in question, and (2) the third party reasonably relied on the representations of the agent.

* * * *

We begin by noting that the jury in the appeals before us was properly instructed. Specifically, [the jury instructions] fairly and accurately apprised the jury of the law that controlled their decision regarding the nature and extent of any agency relationship between Mandry and Cargill. Since the jury was properly instructed, our review is limited. We must determine whether there was only one conclusion that a reasonable jury could have reached and, more specifically, whether the jury in this case unreasonably failed to reach that conclusion.

Mandry was hired by Cargill to work as an outside sales representative. Cargill authorized Mandry, in writing, to sell Cargill's products to Cargill's customers. To facilitate the sale of its products, Cargill provided Mandry with an office, a telephone and an expense account. Mandry was authorized by Cargill to take telephone orders for steel.

Salt Creek consistently placed verbal orders for steel with Cargill. Salt Creek bought steel from Cargill in this manner for years and many of these verbal orders were placed with Mandry. Cargill typically sold steel to customers by telephone and Mandry was authorized to do so as well.

Both the "actual authority" analysis and the "apparent authority" analysis make it clear that Mandry was Cargill's agent. It was perfectly reasonable, on these facts, for the jury to conclude that Mandry was Cargill's agent. Mandry was authorized, in writing, to sell Cargill's steel products. Further, the course of dealings between Mandry and Salt Creek established that both Mandry and Salt Creek believed that Cargill was bound by Mandry's agreement with Salt Creek. Under the express actual authority theory, or the implied actual authority theory, a reasonable jury could conclude that Mandry was Cargill's agent.

The same is true under an apparent authority theory. Cargill provided Mandry with a telephone, an expense account and office space. These facts indicate that Cargill intended to hold Mandry out as an agent who possessed the authority to bind Cargill. Further, Salt Creek reasonably relied on that apparent authority when it ordered steel from Cargill. Thus, both prongs of the apparent authority test are satisfied. Because a jury could, under either theory of agency, reasonably conclude that Mandry was Cargill's agent, Cargill was a seller under the UCC. * * *

* * * *

IV. CONCLUSION

The decision of the district court and the jury verdict are affirmed in all respects.

CASE 32.3 LIABILITY FOR INDEPENDENT CONTRACTOR'S TORTS

HAAG V. BONGERS

Supreme Court of Nebraska, 1999.
256 Neb. 170,
589 N.W.2d 318.

MILLER-LERMAN, J. [Justice]

* * * *

II. BACKGROUND

Leo Bongers died intestate [without a valid will] on October 8, 1992. Subsequently, Bongers and Kuhl, Leo Bongers' nephew and niece, were appointed as personal representatives of his estate. Upon his death, Leo Bongers left substantial real and personal property, including more than 120 antique cars, trucks, and motorcycles.

In late October 1992, Russ Moravec of Bauer-Moravec [Auctioneers and Clerks] contacted the Estate and offered his services as auctioneer. Upon doing so, Moravec learned that Bill Dolan of Dolan [Realty and Auction Company] had also contacted the Estate. On November 2 or 3, the Estate concluded that Bauer-Moravec and Dolan should conduct the auction of the vehicles jointly and split all of the expenses and commissions relating to the sale. On November 3, the Estate, Bauer-Moravec, and Dolan signed a written agreement to this effect. Therefore, in this opinion, Bauer-Moravec and Dolan will be referred to collectively as "the auctioneers."

Moravec recommended that the auction be held in May, June, or July 1993, at an airstrip in Butler County [Nebraska]. This arrangement would have allowed the parties to line up the vehicles in a row outside in good weather so that people attending the auction could go from car to car and the vehicles would not need to be moved during the auction. * * * The Estate rejected Moravec's recommendation and insisted that the sale be conducted in January 1993.

The auction was held on property owned by the Estate, a farm located * * * south of David City * * * . The Estate and the auctioneers decided that the auction would be held inside because of probable bad weather, in a building owned by the Estate that opens at both ends.

* * * The Estate specifically approved the use of assistants for the auction. One of the assistants, Doug Reznicek, had previously assisted Bauer-Moravec in preparing for other auctions. Reznicek assisted in making arrangements to move the vehicles into and out of the sale building. * * * [T]he Estate paid Reznicek, as well as all of the other assistants, except one, out of Estate funds.

Prior to the sale, the auction was heavily advertised at the Estate's insistence. As the auction approached, the parties were flooded with telephone calls regarding the sale. A joint decision was made by the Estate and the auctioneers to open both ends of the auction building and add tents on either side to accommodate more people. A joint decision was made to charge each person wishing to enter the bid barn $25 * * * .

As the auction grew closer, it became apparent that the Estate would not have many of the vehicles in running order in time for the sale. A joint decision was made to tow the vehicles into the building. The vehicles were towed with small tractors which the auctioneers borrowed from farmers in the surrounding community. In order to attach the antique vehicles to the tractors, Scot Bauer, of Bauer-Moravec, purchased * * * hitch balls * * * .

The auction took place on January 30, 1993, beginning at 9:30 A.M. * * * The bid barn was crowded, and the vehicles were towed on a path through the crowd into an area for viewing and bidding. * * *

* * * *

Approximately 1 hour into the sale, with approximately 700 to 800 people in the bid barn, an antique Studebaker truck was towed through the crowd into the building and sold. After the sale, assistants attempted to tow the Studebaker truck out of the building and experienced difficulty in doing so. As the assistants attempted to tow the vehicle, the hitch ball became detached from the drawbar, flying off the tractor and hitting [Joseph] Haag, who was standing at the back left of the tractor. Because of the accident, Haag suffered serious injuries to his head * * * .

* * * *

* * * Haag filed a [suit in a Nebraska state court] against the Estate * * * .

* * * *

Haag alleged that the hitch ball was installed in a negligent manner by one of the assistants utilized by the Estate * * * to assist in the auction. * * * Haag alleged that the negligence of this individual was imputed to the Estate * * * .

* * * *

* * * In its answer, the Estate stated that it had contracted with Bauer-Moravec and Dolan as independent contractors * * * .

* * * *

* * * [T]he trial court * * * entered judgment on the jury's verdict in the sum of $600,000 in favor of Haag and against the Estate * * * .

* * * [T]he Estate [appeals].

* * * *

IV. ANALYSIS

* * * *

Generally, the employer of an independent contractor is not liable for physical harm caused to another by the acts or omissions of the contractor or his servants. * * * The employer of an independent contractor may be vicariously liable to a third party * * * if the employer retains control over the contractor's work * * * .

There are 10 factors which are considered in determining whether a person is an employee or an independent contractor: (1) the extent of control which, by the agreement, the employer may exercise over the details of the work; (2) whether the one employed is engaged in a distinct occupation or business; (3) the kind of occupation, with reference to whether, in the locality, the work is usually done under the direction of the employer or by a specialist without supervision; (4) the skill required in the particular occupation; (5) whether the employer or the one employed supplies the instrumentalities, tools, and the place of work for the person doing the work; (6) the length of time for which the one employed is engaged; (7) the method of payment, whether by the time or by the job; (8) whether the work is part of the regular business of the employer; (9) whether the parties believe they are creating an agency relationship; and (10) whether the employer is or is not in business. The right of control is the chief factor distinguishing an employment relationship from one of an independent contractor. In examining the extent of the employer's control over the worker in this context, it is important to distinguish control over the means and methods of the assignment from control over the end product of the work to be performed.

Based on the facts of this case, we conclude that the auctioneers served as independent contractors. However, the Estate exercised sufficient control over the auction to subject it to liability, notwithstanding the participation of the auctioneers as independent contractors. The factors which demonstrate the Estate's control include, but are not limited to, the following facts: The auction was held on the Estate's property, and the Estate insisted that the auction be conducted in winter rather than in summer in a more expansive setting. The Estate was responsible for putting the vehicles in running order but failed to do so, resulting in the necessity of towing the vehicles at the auction. The Estate approved the use of tractors to tow the vehicles at the auction. The Estate approved the use of assistants. The Estate paid the assistants. The Estate insisted that the auction be heavily advertised, resulting in a shoulder-to-shoulder crowd through which the vehicles were to be towed. The Estate and the auctioneers decided to extend the bid barn and charge a $25 fee. Bongers was present at the auction at the time of the accident.

Although actual performance of the task of towing the vehicles was to be performed by the independent contractor auctioneers, the facts in this case as to the Estate's active and considerable control over the activities that led to the accident are sufficient to subject the Estate to liability. In this regard, we note that the *Restatement (Second) of Torts* [Section] 414 provides:

> One who entrusts work to an independent contractor, but who retains the control of any part of the work, is subject to liability for physical harm to others for whose safety the employer owes a duty to exercise reasonable care, which is caused by his failure to exercise his control with reasonable care.

We conclude that because the Estate retained considerable control over the relevant work, it is therefore liable for a failure to exercise reasonable care in the use of that control. Accordingly, imputing the negligence of the assistants to the Estate was justified by the facts * * * .

* * * *

V. CONCLUSION

* * * For these reasons, we affirm the orders of the [trial] court.

CASE 32.4 E-AGENTS

EBAY, INC. V. BIDDER'S EDGE, INC.

United States District Court,
Northern District of California, 2000.
100 F.Supp.2d 1058.

WHYTE, District Judge.

* * * *

I. BACKGROUND

eBay [Inc.] is an Internet-based, person-to-person trading site. eBay offers sellers the ability to list items for sale and prospective buyers the ability to search those listings and bid on items. The seller can set the terms and conditions of the auction. The item is sold to the highest bidder. The transaction is consummated directly between the buyer and seller without eBay's involvement. A potential purchaser looking for a particular item can access the eBay site and perform a key word search for relevant auctions and bidding status. eBay has also created category listings that identify items in over 2,500 categories, such as antiques, computers, and dolls. Users may browse these category listing pages to identify items of interest.

* * * *

A software robot is a computer program which operates across the Internet to perform searching, copying and retrieving functions on the web sites of others. A software robot is capable of executing thousands of instructions per minute, far in excess of what a human can accomplish. Robots consume the processing and storage resources of a system, making that portion of the system's capacity unavailable to the system owner or other users. Consumption of sufficient system resources will slow the processing of the overall system and can overload the system such that it will malfunction or ìcrash.î A severe malfunction can cause a loss of data and an interruption in services.

* * * *

[Bidder's Edge, Inc. (BE)] is a company with 22 employees that was founded in 1997. The BE web site debuted in November 1998. BE does not host auctions. BE is an auction aggregation site designed to offer on-line auction buyers the ability to search for items across numerous on-line auctions without having to search each host site individually. As of March 2000, the BE web site contained information on more than five million items being auctioned on more than one hundred auction sites. BE also provides its users with additional auction-related services and information. The information available on the BE site is contained in a database of information that BE compiles through access to various auction sites such as eBay. When a user enters a search for a particular item at BE, BE searches its database and generates a list of every item in the database responsive to the search, organized by auction closing date and time. Rather than going to each host auction site one at a time, a user who goes to BE may conduct a single search to obtain information about that item on every auction site tracked by BE. It is important to include information regarding eBay auctions on the BE site because eBay is by far the biggest consumer to consumer on-line auction site.

* * * *

In early 1998, eBay gave BE permission to include information regarding eBay-hosted auctions for Beanie Babies and Furbies in the BE database. In early 1999, BE added to the number of person-to-person auction sites it covered and started covering a broader range of items hosted by those sites, including eBay. On April 24, 1999, eBay verbally approved BE crawling the eBay web site for a period of 90 days. The parties contemplated that during this period they would reach a formal licensing agreement. They were unable to do so.

It appears that the primary dispute was over the method BE uses to search the eBay database. eBay wanted BE to conduct a search of the eBay system only when the BE system was queried by a BE user. This reduces the load on the eBay system and increases the accuracy of the BE data. BE wanted to recursively crawl the eBay system to compile its own auction database. This increases the speed of BE searches and allows BE to track the auctions generally and automatically update its users when activity occurs in particular auctions, categories of auctions, or when new items are added.

In late August or early September 1999, eBay requested by telephone that BE cease posting eBay auction listings on its site. BE agreed to do so. * * * On November 2, 1999, BE issued a press release indicating that it had resumed including eBay auction listings on its site. On November 9, 1999, eBay sent BE a letter reasserting that BE's activities were unauthorized, insisting that BE cease accessing the eBay site, alleging that BE's activities constituted a civil trespass and offering to license BE's activities. eBay and BE were again unable to agree on licensing terms. As a result, eBay attempted to block BE from accessing the eBay site * * * . BE elected to continue crawling eBay's site * * *.

* * * *

eBay [filed a suit in a federal district court against BE, alleging, among other things, trespass to personal property, and seeking] preliminary injunctive relief preventing BE from accessing the eBay computer system * * * .

* * * *

III. ANALYSIS

* * * *

If BE's activity is allowed to continue unchecked, it would encourage other auction aggregators to engage in similar recursive searching of the eBay system such that eBay would suffer irreparable harm from reduced system performance, system unavailability, or data losses. * * *

* * * *

* * * If eBay were a brick and mortar auction house with limited seating capacity, eBay would appear to be entitled to reserve those seats for potential bidders, to refuse entrance to individuals (or robots) with no intention of bidding on any of the items, and to seek preliminary injunctive relief against non-customer trespassers eBay was physically unable to exclude. The analytic difficulty is that a wrongdoer can commit an ongoing trespass of a computer system that is more akin to the traditional notion of a trespass to real property, than the traditional notion of a trespass to chattels, because even though it is ongoing, it will probably never amount to a conversion. The court concludes that under the circumstances present here, BE's ongoing violation of eBay's fundamental property right to exclude others from its computer system potentially causes sufficient irreparable harm to support a preliminary injunction.

* * * *

If eBay's irreparable harm claim were premised solely on the potential harm caused by BE's current crawling activities, evidence that eBay had licensed others to crawl the eBay site would suggest that BE's activity would not result in irreparable harm to eBay. However, the gravamen [the gist, or material part of a charge or complaint] of the alleged irreparable harm is that if BE is allowed to continue to crawl the eBay site, it may encourage frequent and unregulated crawling to the point that eBay's system will be irreparably harmed. There is no evidence that eBay has indiscriminately licensed all comers. Rather, it appears that eBay has carefully chosen to permit crawling by a limited number of aggregation sites that agree to abide by the terms of eBay's licensing agreement. The existence of such a limited license, unlike a general license offered to all comers, does not demonstrate a decision to relinquish all control over the distribution of the product in exchange for a readily computable fee. eBay's licensing activities appear directed toward limiting the amount and nature of crawling activity on the eBay site. Such licensing does not support the inference that carte blanche crawling of the eBay site would pose no threat of irreparable harm.

* * * *

BE argues that even if eBay will be irreparably harmed if a preliminary injunction is not granted, BE will suffer greater irreparable harm if an injunction is granted. According to BE, lack of access to eBay's database will result in a two-thirds decrease in the items listed on BE, and a one-eighth reduction in the value of BE, from $80 million to $70 million. * * * Barring BE from automatically querying eBay's site does not prevent BE from maintaining an aggregation site including information from eBay's site. * * *

Moreover, it appears that any harm alleged to result from being forced to cease an ongoing trespass may not be legally cognizable. In the copyright infringement context, once a plaintiff has established a strong likelihood of success on the merits, any harm to the defendant that results from the defendant being preliminarily enjoined from continuing to infringe is legally irrelevant. * * * The reasoning * * * appears to be that a defendant who builds a business model based upon a clear violation of the property rights of the plaintiff cannot defeat a preliminary injunction by claiming the business will be harmed if the defendant is forced to respect those property rights. * * *

* * * *

IV. ORDER

Bidder's Edge, its officers, agents, servants, employees, attorneys and those in active concert or participation with them who receive actual notice of this order by personal service or otherwise, are hereby enjoined [prohibited] pending the trial of this matter, from using any automated query program, robot, web crawler or other similar device, without written authorization, to access eBay's computer systems or networks, for the purpose of copying any part of eBay's auction database.

CASE PROBLEMS

32–1. The City of Delta Junction (Delta) in Alaska decided to purchase a fire tanker and sought bids from several truck dealers. The city eventually purchased a truck from Alaska Mack, Inc., a Mack truck dealer in Fairbanks. Alaska Mack modified a Mack chassis to carry a 5,000-gallon tank, but the truck exceeded the manufacturer's specified weight limits and was dangerously unbalanced and difficult to drive. When subsequent modifications failed to remedy these problems, the city brought suit for breach of warranty against Alaska Mack and against Mack Trucks, Inc., of Allentown, Pennsylvania, as principal, under the theory of apparent agency, or apparent authority. Mack Trucks, Inc., the manufacturer of Mack trucks, claimed that Alaska Mack was not its agent and that it was not responsible for any actions undertaken by Alaska Mack. Delta argued that Alaska Mack was listed in trade journals and the Fairbanks telephone directory under the heading "Mack Trucks" and that its advertisements carried the familiar Mack bulldog trademark. On the basis of these representations, both Delta's mayor and the fire chief, at the time of the purchase, believed that Alaska Mack was an agent for the manufacturer of Mack trucks. Alaska Mack's bid was accepted by the city council, even though it was the highest bid received for the truck, because of the manufacturer's reputation. The trial court granted a directed verdict for Mack Trucks, Inc. What will happen on appeal? Discuss fully. [*City of Delta Junction v. Mack Trucks, Inc.*, 670 P.2d 1128 (Alaska 1983)]

32–2. Garcia was an employee of Van Groningen & Sons, Inc., which operated an orchard, and one of Garcia's duties was to drive a tractor through the orchard while pulling machinery behind. On one occasion, Garcia invited his nephew Perez to accompany him on the job as he drove the tractor through the orchard. Perez had to sit on the toolbox, because there was only one seat on the tractor. Perez was knocked off by a tree branch and was severely injured when the tractor machinery ran over his leg. Perez sued Van Groningen & Sons under the theory of *respondeat superior.* Van Groningen testified that the company forbade anyone but the driver to ride on the tractor because of the danger and that Garcia had personally been advised of this rule. Discuss what chance Perez has of recovering under the doctrine of *respondeat superior.* [*Perez v. Van Groningen & Sons, Inc.*, 41 Cal.3d 962, 719 P.2d 676, 227 Cal.Rptr. 106 (1986)]

32–3. W. Stephen Brooks was employed as a sales representative for the Bob King Mitsubishi car dealership. Reba Stanley, age eighteen, met with Brooks to test drive a Mitsubishi pickup truck. During the test drive, Brooks assaulted Stanley "by touching and grabbing her about her arms, hands, groin area, and breasts. He also . . . exposed his genitals and placed her hand on his private parts." When they returned from the test drive, Brooks took her to the Mitsubishi service department and "again exposed himself and tried to force her to touch him." Stanley was able to free herself and left the dealership. Brooks was later convicted on charges arising out of the incident. Stanley sued both Brooks and the car dealership, claiming that she had suffered severe emotional distress as a result of the assault. The trial court granted the dealership's motion for summary judgment and entered a default judgment against Brooks. Stanley appealed, arguing that the dealership should be held liable for Brooks's torts under the doctrine of *respondeat superior.* What should the appellate court decide? Discuss. [*Stanley v. Brooks*, 436 S.E.2d 272 (N.C.App. 1993)]

32–4. The Federal Land Bank (FLB) filed an action to foreclose a mortgage on Tom and Judith Sullivan's real estate. Before the trial, FLB's attorney wrote to the Sullivans' attorney inviting settlement offers. A copy of the letter was sent to Wayne Williamson, an FLB vice president. Nine days later, on September 3, the Sullivans' attorney wrote to FLB's attorney expressing interest in settling the case. A copy of this letter was sent to Williamson. On September 11, FLB's attorney replied with an offer that "[m]y client has authorized me to extend . . . to you." The Sullivans accepted the offer. Three weeks later, FLB's attorney wrote the following to the Sullivans' attorney: "Any compromises regarding Federal Land Bank loans must be cleared through [FLB's] Omaha [office]. The proposed compromise was not approved and therefore we have been requested to proceed through the foreclosure process." The case went to trial and FLB obtained a judgment of foreclosure. The trial court found that FLB was not bound by the offer made by its attorney. The Sullivans appealed, arguing that the attorney had or appeared to have authority to settle the case. What should the appellate court decide? [*Federal Land Bank v. Sullivan*, 430 N.W.2d 700 (S.Dak. 1988)]

32–5. Red River Commodities, Inc. (RRC), entered into a contract with Kelby Eidsness under which RRC agreed to purchase 250,000 pounds of sunflower seeds. Because of a drought, Kelby was only able to deliver 75,084 pounds. The contract contained a clause stating that if Kelby could not deliver the promised 250,000 pounds because of an event unanticipated at the time the contract was formed, Kelby would be excused from performance only if he seasonably notified RRC of his inability to perform. Kelby orally notified RRC's contracting representative, Richard Frith, who Kelby assumed was RRC's agent, about his poor crop in September before the harvest. RRC insisted that Frith was not a contracting agent and had no authority to bind RRC in any way. The RRC–Kelby contract included the following statement: "The contracting representative identified below [Frith] does not have the authority to alter or vary the terms of this agreement. He is not an agent of RRC." Nevertheless, after contracts were made, Frith frequently contacted contract growers on behalf of RRC to help with their production problems. Frith talked to growers, inspected fields, and reported to RRC. RRC's manager testified that Frith was his "go-between" with growers such as Kelby. Kelby assumed that Frith was an agent of RRC and therefore that notice to Frith of the drought and Kelby's inability to perform the contract completely would suffice as notice to RRC. In RRC's suit against Kelby for breach of contract, will the court find Frith to be RRC's agent? Discuss. [*Red River Commodities, Inc. v. Eidsness*, 459 N.W.2d 805 (N.Dak. 1990)]

32–6. Richard Lanno worked for the Thermal Equipment Corp. as a project engineer. Lanno was allowed to keep a company van and tools at his home because he routinely drove to work sites directly from his home and because he was often needed for unanticipated trips during his off-hours. The arrangement had been made for the convenience of Thermal Equipment, even though Lanno's managers permitted him to make personal use of the van. Lanno was involved in a collision with Lazar while driving the van home from work. At the time of the accident, Lanno had taken a detour to stop at a store—he had intended to purchase a few items and then go home. Lazar sued Thermal Equpment, claiming that Lanno had acted while within the scope of his employment. Discuss whether Lazar was able to recover, and why. Can employees act on behalf of their employers and themselves at the same time? Explain. [*Lazar v. Thermal Equipment Corp.*, 148 Cal.App.3d 458, 195 Cal.Rptr. 890 (1983)]

32–7. Port Ship Service, Inc., a water-taxi service, ferried crew members, customs agents, supplies, and the like between ships and the shore at the Port of New Orleans. Norton, Lilly & Co. acted as an agent for various ships entering the harbor that required water taxi-services. Ships needing water-taxi services would call Norton, and Norton would communicate the names of the vessels needing such services to Port Ship. Although Norton never informed Port Ship of the names of the vessels' owners, such information was readily available to Port Ship in publications commonly used by port authorities. In addition, Norton maintained a twenty-four-hour telephone service through which Port Ship could ascertain the identities of any of the ship owners. Port Ship sought to hold Norton liable for unpaid taxi services, and the issue turned on whether the ship owners were fully disclosed principals (in which case Norton could not be held liable). The court stated that the *Restatement (Second) of Agency*, Section 4, "makes . . . clear" that "it is the agent's duty to disclose the principal's identity and not a third party's duty to ascertain that identity." Had Norton disclosed the principals' identities by giving Port Ship the names of the vessels? Discuss fully. [*Port Ship Service, Inc. v. Norton, Lilly & Co.*, 883 F.2d 23 (5th Cir. 1989)]

32–8. Lend Lease Trucks, Inc., employed Thomas Jones as an interstate truck driver. While on an assignment, Jones parked on the shoulder of U.S. Highway 301 near Kenly, North Carolina, and crossed the highway to the Dry Dock Lounge. In the lounge, Jones drank enough liquor for his blood-alcohol level to rise to dramatically above the level at which he could legally drive his truck. After a few hours, Jones left the lounge. As he started across the highway to his truck, he darted into the path of a motorcycle driven by Edward McNair. In the collision, Jones and McNair were killed. McNair's wife, Catherine, filed a suit in a North Carolina state court against Lend Lease Trucks, Inc., and others, claiming in part that Jones was acting within the scope of employment at the time of the accident. The case was removed to a federal district court. Lend Lease filed a motion to dismiss, the court granted the motion, and Catherine appealed. Was Jones acting within the scope of employment? Explain. [*McNair v. Lend Lease Trucks, Inc.*, 62 F.3d 651 (4th Cir. 1995)]

32–9. Fred Hash worked for Van Stavern Construction Co. as a field supervisor in charge of constructing a new plant facility. Hash entered into a contract with Sutton's Steel & Supply, Inc., to provide steel to the construction site in several installments. Hash gave the name of B. D. Van Stavern, the president and owner of the construction firm, instead of the firm name as the party for whom he was acting. The contract and the subsequent invoices all had B. D. Van Stavern's name on them. Several loads were delivered by Sutton. All of the invoices were signed by Van Stavern employees, and corporate checks were made out to Sutton. When Sutton Steel later sued Van Stavern personally for unpaid debts totaling $40,437, it claimed that Van Stavern had ratified the acts of his employee, Hash, by allowing payment on previous invoices. Although Van Stavern had had no knowledge of the unauthorized arrangement, had he legally ratified the agreement by his silence? Explain. [*Sutton's Steel & Supply, Inc. v. Van Stavern*, 496 So.2d 1360 (La.App. 3d Cir. 1986)]

32–10. Justin Jones suffered from genital herpes and sought treatment from Dr. Steven Baisch of Region West Pediatric Services. A nurse's assistant, Jeni Hallgren, who was a Region West employee, told her friends and some of Jones's friends about Jones's condition. This was a violation of the Region West employee handbook, which required employees to maintain the confidentiality of patients' records. Jones filed a suit in a federal district court against Region West, among others, alleging that Region West should be held liable for its employee's actions on the basis of *respondeat superior.* On what basis might the court hold that Region West was not liable for Hallgren's acts? Discuss fully. [*Jones v. Baisch, M.D.*, 40 F.3d 252 (8th Cir. 1994)]

32–11. John Dunning was the sole officer of the R. B. Dunning Co. and was responsible for the management and operation of the business. When the company rented a warehouse from Samuel and Ruth Saliba, Dunning did not say that he was acting for the firm. The parties did not have a written lease. Business faltered, and the firm stopped paying rent. Eventually, it went bankrupt and vacated the property. The Salibas filed a suit in a Maine state court against Dunning personally, seeking to recover the unpaid rent. Dunning claimed the debt belonged to the company because he had only been acting as its agent. Who is liable for the rent, and why? [*Estate of Saliba v. Dunning*, 682 A.2d 224 (Me. 1996)]

32–12. Federated Financial Reserve Corp. leases consumer and business equipment. As part of its credit approval and debt-collection practices, Federated hires credit collectors, whom it authorizes to obtain credit reports on its customers. Janice Caylor, a Federated collector, used this authority to obtain a report on Karen Jones, who was not a Federated customer but who was the former wife of Caylor's roommate, Randy Lind. When Jones discovered that Lind had her address and how he had obtained it, she filed a suit in a federal district court against Federated and others. Jones claimed in part that they had violated the Fair Credit Reporting Act, the goal of which is to protect consumers from the improper use of credit reports. Under what theory might an employer be held liable for an employee's violation of a statute? Does that theory apply in this case? Explain. [*Jones v. Federated Financial Reserve Corp.*, 144 F.3d 961 (6th Cir. 1998)]

32–13. Juanita Miller filed a complaint in an Indiana state court against Red Arrow Ventures, Ltd., Thomas Hayes, and Claudia Langman, alleging that they breached their promise to make payments on a promissory note issued to Miller. The defendants denied this allegation and asserted a counterclaim against Miller. After a trial, the judge announced that, although he would be ruling against the defendants, he had not yet determined what amount of damages would be awarded to Miller. Over the next three days, the parties' attorneys talked and agreed that the defendants would pay Miller $21,000. The attorneys exchanged correspondence acknowledging this settlement. When the defendants balked at paying this amount, the trial judge issued an order to enforce the settlement agreement. The defendants appealed to a state intermediate appellate court, arguing that they had not consented to the settlement agreement. What is the rule regarding the authority of an agent—in this case, the defendants' attorney—to agree to a settlement? How should the court apply the rule in this case? Why? [*Red Arrow Ventures, Ltd. v. Miller*, 692 N.E.2d 939 (Ind.App. 1998)]

32–14. Register.com is, among other things, a registrar of Internet domain names. Like all registrars, Register.com is required to provide free to the public an online interactive database, called the WHOIS database, containing the names and contract information of its registrants. Verio, Inc., although not a registrar of domain names, is a direct competitor of Register.com in providing other services. Verio used automated software—a spider, or robot (or bot)—to collect the WHOIS data and used the information for mass e-mail solicitations (spam) in a marketing initiative called Project Henhouse. Register.com complained to Verio, which stopped the spam but continued to collect the data with its spider. Register.com filed a suit in a federal district court against Verio, alleging, in part, trespass to chattels (personal property) and asking for an injunction. Verio responded in part that its use of a spider to collect the WHOIS data did not harm Register.com's computers. How should the court rule, and why? [*Register.com v. Verio, Inc.*, 126 F.Supp.2d 238 (S.D.N.Y. 2000)]

31–15. A Question of Ethics

Erwin Ernst was the sole shareholder and chief executive officer of Matchmaker Real Estate Sales Center, Inc., located in Chicago. During 1987 and 1988, the Leadership Council for Metropolitan Open Communities, a nonprofit corporation, conducted a series of tests to see if Matchmaker sales agents engaged in "racial steering"—that is, directing white home buyers to homes in white neighborhoods and black home buyers to homes in black or mixed neighborhoods. In each test, one white couple and one black couple, evenly matched with regard to financial qualifications and housing needs, were sent to Matchmaker and told Matchmaker that they were looking for homes in southwest Chicago. Matchmaker agents consistently directed the white couples to higher-priced homes in white neighborhoods and the black couples to lower-priced homes in black or racially mixed neighborhoods. The city of Chicago, the Leadership Council, and the individual testers (the plaintiffs) all sued Matchmaker for violations of federal laws prohibiting racial discrimination and discrimination in housing. The court found the real estate agents to be employees, not independent contractors, and both Ernst and his corporation, Matchmaker, were held liable for compensatory damages under the doctrine of *respondeat superior*. The agents were held liable for both compensatory and punitive damages. [*Chicago v. Matchmaker Real Estate Sales Center, Inc.*, 982 F.2d 1086 (7th Cir. 1992)]

1. In view of the fact that Ernst had specifically instructed his agents not to engage in discriminatory practices, is it fair to hold Ernst and Matchmaker liable for damages? Why, or why not?
2. The court concluded that Ernst and Matchmaker should not be held liable for punitive damages in this case. Do you agree with this conclusion? Why, or why not?
3. Ernst argued that the plaintiffs had no standing to sue because they had sustained no injury. The court, however, held that each of the plaintiffs had standing to bring suit. How might you justify the court's conclusion that the plaintiffs had met the injury requirement for standing to sue?

E-LINKS

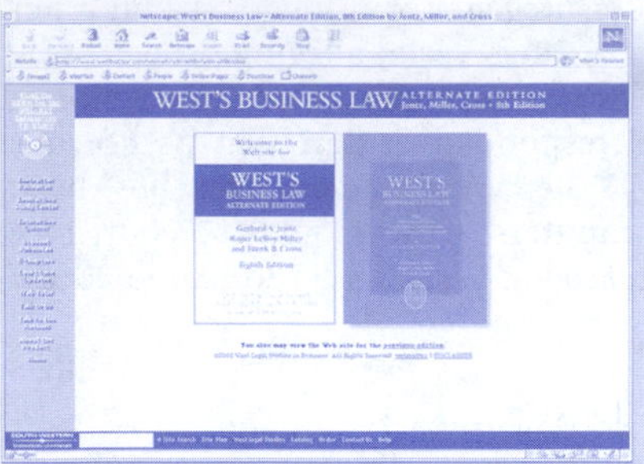

For updated links to resources available on the Web, as well as a variety of other materials, visit this text's Web site at

http://wbl-cs.westbuslaw.com

An excellent source for information on agency law, including court cases involving agency concepts, is the Legal Information Institute (LII) at Cornell University. You can access the LII's Web page on this topic at

http://www.law.cornell.edu/topics/agency.html

The 'Lectric Law Library's Lawcopedia contains a summary of agency laws at

http://www.lectlaw.com/d-a.htm

Scroll down through the A's and select the link to Agent for useful information on this area of the law.

LEGAL RESEARCH EXERCISES ON THE WEB

Go to http://wbl-cs.westbuslaw.com, the Web site that accompanies this text. Select "Interactive Study Center," and then click on "Chapter 32." There you will find the following Internet research exercise that you can perform to learn more about agency law:

Activity 32–1: Liability in Agency Relationships

Focus on Legal Reasoning

Alexander v. Brown

In this *Focus on Legal Reasoning,* we review *Alexander v. Brown,*[1] a decision that involved the application of some of the agency principles discussed in Chapters 31 and 32. The dispute in this case concerned the liability for a trespass committed by a bulldozer operator who had been hired by neighboring property owners.

Case Background

Lynell and Pamela Brown bought Lot 6 in a subdivision in Madison County, Mississippi, where they planned to build a house. Willie and Carla Alexander owned Lot 5, a vacant lot next to Lot 6. Willie Alexander told Lynell Brown that he did not want anyone on his property.

The Browns contracted for bulldozer work on their lot. One Friday, Carla Alexander saw Buddy McGowan, the bulldozer operator, trespass onto Lot 5 after being asked to stay off the property. The bulldozer had removed dirt, grass, and young trees from a 20′ by 150′ strip of Lot 5.

The Alexanders asked the Browns to pay for the alleged damage. The Browns refused and filed a suit in a Mississippi state court, seeking a declaratory judgment that no trespass had occurred. The Alexanders responded by filing an action against the Browns for damages. When the court dismissed the Alexanders' suit, they appealed to a state intermediate appellate court, which reversed the dismissal and remanded the case for a trial. The Browns appealed to the Mississippi Supreme Court.

1. 793 So.2d 601 (Miss. 2001).

Majority Opinion

MILLS, Justice, for the Court:

* * * *

* * * [T]he issue [is] whether * * * the motion to dismiss was properly granted. In deciding to reverse the [trial court's] decision, the Court of Appeals majority states:

* * * *

> The chancellor found that Mr. McGowan was an independent contractor and that therefore the Browns were not responsible for his actions. An employer is not generally liable for the torts of an independent contractor. However, the trial court cannot assume that an independent contractor relationship exists. There must be some proof of that relationship. The record is absolutely devoid of any evidence to establish that Mr. McGowan was an independent contractor. In the absence of such evidence, the [trial court] committed reversible error in holding that McGowan was an independent contractor for whom the Browns had no responsibility.

The Court of Appeals was correct in noting that there was testimony linking McGowan to the damage done on Friday. However, the issue was not whether McGowan had committed trespass, but instead whether the Browns had committed trespass, either directly or indirectly through McGowan. As noted by [the trail court] * * * , the Alexanders failed to prove that McGowan was an "employee" of the Browns. This was an element on which proof was necessary in order for the Alexanders to make a *prima facie* case of trespass. McGowan was not called to testify though he would have in all likelihood provided the link necessary to hold the Browns liable for trespass. The failure to establish employment was fatal to the Alexanders' case.

* * * *

* * * Kelly Kersh, owner and resident of Lot 7, testified that she could observe both the Alexander and the Brown lots from her kitchen window. In a fashion reminiscent of Gladys Kravitz on the television series *Bewitched,* Mrs. Kersh watched the activity on the Brown and Alexander lots with keen interest. In keeping with her Gladys Kravitz persona, Mrs. Kersh promptly reported her observations to anyone who would listen. She phoned Entergy [the local power company] and complained that the Browns were about to hook up to her electrical power box without her consent. She phoned the water treatment plant to find out where the ground water on the property was going to drain. She also phoned the building inspector because she was concerned about the slab being poured on the Brown lot, believing it to be too thin. She also kept the Alexanders updated regarding the activities occurring on the Brown property. * * *

Willie Alexander also complained that workers on the Brown property crossed his vacant lot to get to an adjoining neighbor's outdoor bathroom and that they used his property to park their vehicles. He admitted, however, that none of the workers told him that the Browns directed them to use his property in such a manner. In fact, Mr. Brown had a notice stating that no contractor was to go onto Lot 5 posted on the job site. Clearly, these acts were taken despite the Browns' directions otherwise. These acts constitute lone adventures, not joint ventures.

Mr. Alexander further admitted that he hired McGowan to do work on his own lot. He testified that he spotted McGowan bulldozing on his property. Mr. Alexander stopped McGowan and told him to "get off his property and stay off." McGowan explained that he had seen a snake in the brush nearby and was trying to clear it out. Mr. Alexander, * * * said "by all means, clear that out, but keep your bulldozer off my property." Four days later, he hired McGowan to do additional work on his own driveway. Perhaps this proof explains the Alexanders' recalcitrance to call Mr. McGowan to testify.

Mr. Alexander also testified that he spoke with Sammy Winder, a dirt contractor, on the Brown property. He had previously contracted with Winder to deliver a dump truck load of dirt. He himself went onto the Brown property to pay Winder.

A review of the testimony reveals that there was a good bit of invading of neighboring lots done by the lone adventurers in their mixed roles. Add this to the side dealings and it is difficult to know what exactly the lone adventurers were doing at any given time. Also, it is impossible to tell at whose direction, if anyone's at all, they were acting.

The case presented by the Alexanders was that the Browns committed a trespass solely through McGowan, who was not a defendant in the case, and who was not called to testify. [Under the law] *a person can be liable for trespass by causing someone else to commit the tortious act.* We do not disagree with the law. The point, however, is that no evidence was presented that the Browns caused McGowan to commit the trespass. The case fails on the facts. The only evidence linking the Browns to McGowan was that the Browns retained McGowan's services. This fact alone does not render them liable for his torts. If it did, then the Alexanders have an additional problem, since they retained his services too. * * * [Emphasis added.]

* * * It is well settled that one who contracts with an independent contractor to perform certain work or service which is not illegal, dangerous or harmful, is not liable for torts committed by him. * * * This general rule is applicable to the instant case, as there was nothing illegal, dangerous, or harmful about having this lot cleared so the Browns could build their home.

Relying on *Long v. Magnolia Hotel Co.,* 227 Miss. 625, 86 So.2d 493 (1956), the Alexanders * * * assert that the Court of Appeals properly reversed and remanded the case. * * *

The facts of the instant case are clearly not analogous to *Long,* and the law used to decide Long does not control in this case. Based upon a fair reading of the record presented before the [trial court], we find that the evidence supports the * * * finding that the Alexanders failed to make a *prima facie* case of trespass against the Browns. Consequently, we also find that the motion to dismiss was properly granted.

* * * *

For these reasons, we reverse the judgment of the Court of Appeals and reinstate the judgment of the [trial court] as it relates to the trespass action.

QUESTIONS FOR ANALYSIS

1. **Legal Analysis.** In its opinion, the court refers to *Long v. Magnolia Hotel Co.,* 227 Miss. 625, 86 So.2d 493 (1956) (see the *E-Links* feature at the end of Chapter 2 for instructions on how to access the opinions of state courts). Why did the *Alexander* court refer to the *Long* case?

2. **Legal Reasoning.** On what points did the court in the *Alexander* case just presented rely to come to its conclusions?

3. **Social Consideration.** Is the question of trespass the real issue of contention between the parties in this case? If not, what might be?

4. **Implications for the Business Employer.** Under what circumstance not discussed in this case is an employer liable for the tort of an independent contractor?

WESTLAW ONLINE RESEARCH

Go to this text's companion Web site, at http://wbl-cs.westbuslaw.com, and click on the Westlaw icon. Use your special password to access the full text of this case, including the dissenting opinion. Read through the case, and then answer the following questions.

1. Read the dissenting opinion. What is the dissent's position? How does the dissent reach this conclusion?
2. Scan the editors' summary at the beginning of this case. How is it possible to determine quickly whether there is a dissenting opinion?
3. See paragraph number 13 (omitted from the excerpt above). According to the state supreme court, how did the state intermediate appellate court "turn the [trial court's] view around"?

UNIT SEVEN
Business Organizations

CONTENTS

CHAPTER 33
Sole Proprietorships and Partnerships

A BASIC QUESTION FACING ANYONE who wishes to start up a business is which of the several forms of business organization will be most appropriate for the business endeavor. In deciding this question, the **entrepreneur** (one who initiates and assumes the financial risk of a new enterprise) needs to consider a number of factors. Four important factors are (1) ease of creation, (2) the liability of the owners, (3) tax considerations, and (4) the need for capital. In studying this unit on business organizations, keep these factors in mind as you read about the various business organizational forms available to entrepreneurs.

Traditionally, entrepreneurs have used three major forms to structure their business enterprises—the sole proprietorship, the partnership, and the corporation. In this chapter, we examine the first two of these forms. The third major traditional form—the corporation—will be discussed in detail in Chapters 34 through 37. Two relatively new forms of business enterprise—limited liability companies (LLCs) and limited liability partnerships (LLPs)—offer special advantages to businesspersons, particularly with respect to taxation and liability. We will look at these business forms, which are coming into widespread use, in Chapter 38. In Chapter 39, we will describe a number of other forms of business organization as well as private franchises.

SECTION 1

Sole Proprietorships

The simplest form of business is a **sole proprietorship.** In this form, the owner is the business; thus, anyone who does business without creating a separate business organization has a sole proprietorship. Sole proprietorships constitute over two-thirds of all American businesses. They are also usually small enterprises—about 99 percent of the sole proprietorships existing in the United States have revenues of less than $1 million per year. Sole proprietors can own and manage any type of business, ranging from an informal, home-office undertaking to a large restaurant or construction firm.

A major advantage of the sole proprietorship is that the proprietor receives all of the profits (because he or she assumes all of the risk). In addition, it is often easier and less costly to start a sole proprietorship than to start any other kind of business, as few legal forms are involved. This type of business organization also provides more flexibility than does a partnership or a corporation. The sole proprietor is free to make any decision he or she wishes to concerning the business—whom to hire, when to take a vacation, what kind of business to pursue, and so on. A sole proprietor pays only personal income taxes on the business's profits, which are reported as personal income on the proprietor's personal income tax return. Sole proprietors are also allowed to establish tax-exempt retirement accounts in the form of Keogh plans.[1]

The major disadvantage of the sole proprietorship is that, as sole owner, the proprietor alone bears the burden of any losses or liabilities incurred by the business enterprise. In other words, the sole proprietor has unlimited liability, or legal responsibility, for all obligations that arise in doing business. This

1. A *Keogh plan* is a retirement program designed for self-employed persons by which a certain percentage of their income can be contributed to the plan, and interest earnings will not be taxed until funds are withdrawn from the plan.

unlimited liability is a major factor to be considered in choosing a business form. The sole proprietorship also has the disadvantage of lacking continuity on the death of the proprietor. When the owner dies, so does the business—it is automatically dissolved. If the business is transferred to family members or other heirs, a new proprietorship is created.

Another disadvantage is that the proprietor's opportunity to raise capital is limited to personal funds and the funds of those who are willing to make loans to him or her. If the owner wishes to expand the business significantly, one way to raise more capital to finance the expansion is to join forces with another entrepreneur and establish a partnership or form a corporation.

SECTION 2

The Law Governing Partnerships

A **partnership** arises from an agreement, express or implied, between two or more persons to carry on a business for a profit. Partners are co-owners of a business and have joint control over its operation and the right to share in its profits. Note that in this chapter's discussion of partnership law and the rights and duties of partners, we are referring to ordinary partnerships, or *general partnerships*. In Chapter 38, we will examine some special forms of partnerships known as *limited partnerships* and *limited liability partnerships*, which receive different treatment under the law.

AGENCY CONCEPTS AND PARTNERSHIP LAW

When two or more persons agree to do business as partners, they enter into a special relationship with one another. To an extent, their relationship is similar to an agency relationship, because each partner is deemed the agent of the other partners and of the partnership. The agency concepts that were discussed in Chapters 31 and 32 thus apply—specifically, the imputation of knowledge of, and responsibility for, acts carried out within the scope of the partnership relationship. In their relationship to one another, partners are also bound by the fiduciary ties that bind an agent and principal under agency law.

Partnership law is distinct from agency law in one significant way, however. A partnership is based on a voluntary contract between two or more competent persons who agree to place some or all of their money or other assets, labor, and skills in a business with the understanding that profits and losses will be shared. In a nonpartnership agency relationship, the agent usually does not have an ownership interest in the business, nor is he or she obligated to bear a portion of the ordinary business losses.

THE UNIFORM PARTNERSHIP ACT

The Uniform Partnership Act (UPA) governs the operation of partnerships *in the absence of express agreement* and has done much to reduce controversies in the law relating to partnerships. The UPA has been adopted in all of the states except Louisiana, as well as in the District of Columbia. The entire text of the UPA is presented in Appendix D at the end of this text. A revised version of the UPA, known as the Revised Uniform Partnership Act (RUPA), has been adopted by several states, and others are considering its adoption. Throughout our discussion of partnership law in this chapter, we indicate in footnotes the most significant changes made by the RUPA. Appendix E contains excerpts from the RUPA.

SECTION 3

Definition of Partnership

Parties commonly find themselves in conflict over whether their business enterprise is a legal partnership, especially in the absence of a formal, written partnership agreement. The UPA defines the term *partnership* as "an association of two or more persons to carry on as co-owners a business for profit" [UPA 6(1)]. The *intent* to associate is a key element of a partnership, and one cannot join a partnership unless all other partners consent [UPA 18(g)]. In resolving disputes over whether partnership status exists, courts will usually look for the following three essential elements of partnership implicit in the UPA's definition:

1. A sharing of profits or losses.
2. A joint ownership of the business.
3. An equal right in the management of the business.

In the event that the evidence is insufficient to establish all three factors, the UPA provides a set of guidelines to be used. For example, the existence of a partnership will be inferred if profits and losses from a business are shared. No such inference is made, however, if the profits were received as payment of the following:

1. A debt by installments or interest on a loan.
2. Wages of an employee.
3. Rent to a landlord.
4. An annuity to a widow or representative of a deceased partner.
5. A sale of the goodwill of a business or property [UPA 7(4)].

To illustrate: Suppose that a debtor owes a creditor $5,000 on an unsecured debt. To repay the debt, the debtor agrees to pay (and the creditor, to accept) 10 percent of the debtor's monthly business profits until the loan with interest has been paid. Although the creditor is sharing profits from the business, the debtor and creditor are not presumed to be partners.

Joint ownership of property, obviously, does not in and of itself create a partnership. Therefore, the fact that, say, MacPherson and Bunker own real property as joint tenants or as tenants in common (a form of joint ownership) does not establish a partnership. In fact, the sharing of gross returns and even profits from such ownership is usually not enough to create a partnership [UPA 7(2), (3)]. Thus, if MacPherson and Bunker jointly owned a piece of rural property and leased the land to a farmer, the sharing of the profits from the farming operation by the farmer in lieu of set rental payments would ordinarily not make MacPherson, Bunker, and the farmer partners.

SECTION 4

The Nature of Partnerships

A partnership is sometimes called a *company* or a *firm*, terms that suggest that the partnership is an entity separate and apart from its aggregate members. Sometimes the law of partnership recognizes the independent entity for some purposes but may treat the partnership as a composite of individual partners for other purposes.

PARTNERSHIP AS AN ENTITY

At common law, a partnership was never treated as a separate legal entity. Thus, a common law suit could never be brought by or against the firm in its own name; each individual partner had to sue or be sued. Many states today provide specifically that the partnership can be treated as an entity for certain purposes. These usually include the capacity to sue or be sued, to collect judgments, and to have all accounting procedures in the name of the partnership. In addition, the UPA recognizes that partnership property may be held in the name of the partnership rather than in the names of the individual partners. Finally, federal procedural laws frequently permit the partnership to be treated as an entity in such matters as lawsuits in federal courts, bankruptcy proceedings, and the filing of federal information tax returns. These matters are discussed here in some detail.

Legal Capacity. States vary on how a partnership is viewed as a party in a legal suit. Some permit a partnership to sue and be sued in the firm name; others allow a partnership to be sued as an entity but do not allow the partnership, as a plaintiff, to sue others in its firm name (that is, the partnership must use the names of the individual partners). Federal courts recognize the partnership as an entity that can sue or be sued when a federal question is involved. Otherwise, federal courts follow the practice adopted by the state in which the federal court is located.

Judgments. When a judgment is rendered *against the firm name,* partnership liability is first paid out of partnership assets. In a general partnership, the personal assets of the individual members are subject to liability if the partnership's assets are inadequate. Even in limited partnerships, at least one of the partners—the general partner—subjects his or her personal assets to liability for the partnership's obligations. Good legal practice dictates that when state law permits a firm to be sued, the individual partners should also be sued. This ensures that a wide range of assets will be available for paying the judgment.

Marshaling Assets. The general rule is that a judgment creditor of a partnership (a creditor in whose favor a money judgment has been entered by a court) can execute the judgment against the partners either jointly or severally (joint and several liability is discussed later in this chapter). In some states, however, the judgment creditor must exhaust the remedies against partnership property before proceeding to execute against the individual property of the partners. This is in accordance with the doctrine of **marshaling assets.** Marshaling assets is a common law equitable doctrine; it is not statutory.

In marshaling assets, assets are arranged, or ranked, in a certain order toward the payment of debts outstanding. In some situations, there are two classes of assets, and some creditors can enforce their claims against both, whereas others can enforce their claims against only one. When this occurs, the creditors of the former class are compelled to exhaust the assets against which they alone have a claim before they can have recourse to other assets. This provides for the settlement of as many claims as possible.

As applied to a partnership, the doctrine of marshaling assets requires that partnership creditors have first priority to the partnership's assets and that personal creditors of the individual partners have first priority to the individual assets of those partners. When the partnership's assets are insufficient to satisfy a partnership creditor, that creditor does not have access to the assets of any individual partner until the personal creditors of that partner have been satisfied from those assets. This doctrine does not apply to partnerships that are in liquidation proceedings under Chapter 7 of the Bankruptcy Code (see Chapter 30).

Bankruptcy. In federal court, an adjudication of bankruptcy *in the firm name* applies only to the partnership entity. It does not constitute personal bankruptcy for the partners. Similarly, the personal bankruptcy of an individual partner does not bring the partnership entity or its assets into bankruptcy.

The doctrine of marshaling assets is modified when a partnership is granted an order of relief in bankruptcy. In such situations, if partnership assets are insufficient to cover debts owed to partnership creditors, each general partner becomes *personally* liable to the bankruptcy trustee for the amount of the deficiency.

Conveyance of Property. The title to real or personal property can be held in the partnership's firm name. In other words, the partnership as an entity can own property apart from that owned by its individual members [UPA 8(3)]. Thus, the property held in the firm name can be conveyed (transferred) without each of the individual partners joining in the transaction.

At common law, title to real estate could not be held in a partnership's firm name. Each partner had to join in all conveyances (transfers of rights in the real estate), because each partner was regarded as a co-owner, known in legal terminology as a *tenant in partnership*.[2] Tenancy in partnership is discussed later in this chapter. Although the modern rule of partnership property ownership does not require aggregate action (action by all the partners jointly) to convey property, there are some practical difficulties to consider.

Most states do not require that public records list the members of partnerships. Hence, in determining the validity of a conveyance in a partnership's name, it may be impossible to tell whether the person executing the deed is actually a partner and has authority to convey. Some states, however, have passed laws requiring firms to file a statement of partnership. This statement lists the members of the partnership who are authorized to execute conveyances on behalf of the firm.

AGGREGATE THEORY OF PARTNERSHIP

When the partnership is not regarded as a separate legal entity, it is treated as an *aggregate* of the individual partners. For example, for federal income tax purposes, a partnership is not a tax-paying entity. The profits or losses incurred by a partnership are "passed through" the partnership framework and attributed to the partners on their individual tax returns. The partnership as an entity has no tax liability. It is an entity only for the filing of an **information return** with the Internal Revenue Service, indicating the profit or loss that each partner will report on his or her individual tax return.

SECTION 5

Partnership Formation

As a general rule, agreements to form a partnership can be *oral*, *written*, or *implied by conduct*. Some partnership agreements, however, must be in writing to be legally enforceable within the Statute of Frauds (see Chapter 14 for details). For example, a partnership agreement that, by its terms, is to continue for more than one year or a partnership agreement that authorizes the partners to deal in transfers of real property

2. The UPA retained this concept in UPA 25(1). Although property may be held in the name of the partnership, as tenants in partnership, partners are still regarded as co-owners. The RUPA, however, discards the concept of tenancy in partnership, stating simply that "[a] partner is not a co-owner of partnership property" [RUPA 501]. Further, "[p]roperty transferred to or otherwise acquired by a partnership is property of the partnership and not of the partners individually" [RUPA 203].

must be evidenced by a sufficient writing. Generally, a partnership agreement, called **articles of partnership**, can include virtually any terms that the partners wish, unless they are illegal or contrary to public policy. A sample partnership agreement is shown in Exhibit 33–1.[3] Practically speaking, it is better if the provisions of any partnership agreement are in writing.

Duration of the Partnership

The partnership agreement can specify the duration of the partnership by designating a date or the completion of a particular project. This is called a *partnership for a term.* A dissolution of the partnership (how dissolution may occur will be discussed later in the chapter) without the consent of all the partners prior to the expiration of the partnership term constitutes a breach of the agreement, and the partner responsible for the breach can be liable for any losses resulting from it.

If no fixed duration is specified, the partnership is a *partnership at will.* Any partner can dissolve this type of partnership at any time without violating the agreement and without incurring liability for losses to other partners that result from the termination.

Capacity

Any person having the capacity to enter into a contract can become a partner. A partnership contract entered into with a minor as a partner is voidable and can be disaffirmed by the minor (see Chapter 12 for details). Lack of legal capacity due to insanity at the time of the agreement likewise allows the purported partner either to avoid the agreement or to enforce it. If a partner is adjudicated mentally incompetent during the course of the partnership, the partnership is not automatically dissolved, but dissolution can be decreed by a court on petition.

The Corporation as Partner

The Revised Model Business Corporation Act (see Appendix G) allows corporations generally to make contracts and incur liabilities. The UPA specifically permits a corporation to be a partner. By definition, "a partnership is an association of two or more persons," and the UPA defines a person as including corporations [UPA 2].

Although some states restrict the ability of corporations to become partners, such restrictions have become less common over the years. Many decisions in jurisdictions that do not permit corporate partners nevertheless validate the arrangements by characterizing them as joint ventures (see Chapter 39) rather than as partnerships.

Partnership by Estoppel

Parties who are not partners can hold themselves out as partners and make representations that third persons rely on in dealing with them. In such a situation, a court may conclude that a **partnership by estoppel** exists, in which case liability is imposed on the alleged partner or partners (although partnership *rights* are not conferred on these persons).

There are two aspects of such liability. The person representing himself or herself to be a partner in an actual or alleged partnership is liable to any third person who extends credit in good faith reliance on such representations. Similarly, a person who expressly or impliedly consents to misrepresentation of an alleged partnership relationship is also liable to third persons who extend credit in good faith reliance [UPA 16].

For example, Moreno owns a small shop. Knowing that the Midland Bank will not make a loan on his credit alone, Moreno represents that Lukas, a financially secure businessperson, is a partner in Moreno's business. Lukas knows of Moreno's misrepresentation but fails to correct the bank's information. Midland Bank, relying on the strength of Lukas's reputation and credit, extends a loan to Moreno. Moreno will be liable to the bank for the loan repayment. In many states, Lukas would also be held liable to the bank. Lukas has impliedly consented to the misrepresentation and will normally be estopped from denying that she is a partner of Moreno. She will be regarded as if she were in fact a partner in Moreno's business insofar as this loan is concerned.

When a real partnership exists and a partner represents that a nonpartner is a member of the firm, the nonpartner is regarded as an agent whose acts are binding on the partner (but normally not on the partnership). For example, Middle Earth Movers has three partners—Jansen, Mathews, and Harran. Mathews represents to the business community that

---

3. The RUPA provides for the voluntary filing of a partnership statement, containing such information as the agency authority of the partners, with the secretary of state. The statement must be executed by at least two partners, a copy must be sent to all partners, and a certified copy must be filed in the office in which transfers of real property are recorded (in most states, in the county in which the property is located).

EXHIBIT 33–1 A SAMPLE PARTNERSHIP AGREEMENT

PARTNERSHIP AGREEMENT

This agreement, made and entered into as of the ____________, by and among ____________ ________________ (hereinafter collectively sometimes referred to as "Partners").

WITNESSETH:

Whereas, the Parties hereto desire to form a General Partnership (hereinafter referred to as the "Partnership"), for the term and upon the conditions hereinafter set forth;

Now, therefore, in consideration of the mutual covenants hereinafter contained, it is agreed by and among the Parties hereto as follows:

Article I
BASIC STRUCTURE

Form. The Parties hereby form a General Partnership pursuant to the Laws of ______________ ____________.

Name. The business of the Partnership shall be conducted under the name of ______________ ____________.

Place of Business. The principal office and place of business of the Partnership shall be located at ________________, or such other place as the Partners may from time to time designate.

Term. The Partnership shall commence on _________, and shall continue for _____ years, unless earlier terminated in the following manner: (a) By the completion of the purpose intended, or (b) Pursuant to this Agreement, or (c) By applicable ____________ law, or (d) By death, insanity, bankruptcy, retirement, withdrawal, resignation, expulsion, or disability of all of the then Partners.

Purpose—General. The purpose for which the Partnership is organized is ______________ ____

Article II
FINANCIAL ARRANGEMENTS

Each Partner has contributed to the initial capital of the Partnership property in the amount and form indicated on Schedule A attached hereto and made a part hereof. Capital contributions to the Partnership shall not earn interest. An individual capital account shall be maintained for each Partner. If at any time during the existence of the Partnership it shall become necessary to increase the capital with which the said Partnership is doing business, then (upon the vote of the Managing Partner[s]): each party to this Agreement shall contribute to the capital of this Partnership within _____ days notice of such need in an amount according to his then Percentage Share of Capital as called for by the Managing Partner(s).

The Percentage Share of Profits and Capital of each Partner shall be (unless otherwise modified by the terms of this Agreement) as follows:

Names	Initial Percentage Share of Profits and Capital
____________	____________
____________	____________
____________	____________

No interest shall be paid on any contribution to the capital of the Partnership. No Partner shall have the right to demand the return of his capital contributions except as herein provided. Except as herein provided, the individual Partners shall have no right to any priority over each other as to the return of capital contributions.

Distributions to the Partners of net operating profits of the Partnership, as hereinafter defined, shall be made at ______________________________. Such distributions shall be made to the Partners simultaneously.

For the purpose of this Agreement, net operating profit for any accounting period shall mean the gross receipts of the Partnership for such period, less the sum of all cash expenses of operation of the Partnership, and such sums as may be necessary to establish a reserve for operating expenses. In determining net operating profit, deductions for depreciation, amortization, or other similar charges not requiring actual current expenditures of cash shall *not* be taken into account in accordance with generally accepted accounting principles.

EXHIBIT 33–1 A SAMPLE PARTNERSHIP AGREEMENT—CONTINUED

No Partner shall be entitled to receive any compensation from the Partnership, nor shall any Partner receive any drawing account from the Partnership.

Article III
MANAGEMENT

The Managing Partner(s) shall be ______________________.

The Managing Partner(s) shall have the right to vote as to the management and conduct of the business of the Partnership as follows:

Names	Vote
______________	______________
______________	______________
______________	______________

Article IV
DISSOLUTION

In the event that the Partnership shall hereafter be dissolved for any reason whatsoever, a full and general account of its assets, liabilities, and transactions shall at once be taken. Such assets may be sold and turned into cash as soon as possible and all debts and other amounts due the Partnership collected. The proceeds thereof shall thereupon be applied as follows:

(a) To discharge the debts and liabilities of the Partnership and the expenses of liquidation.

(b) To pay each Partner or his or her legal representative any unpaid salary, drawing account, interest, or profits to which he or she shall then be entitled and in addition, to repay to any Partner his or her capital contributions in excess of his or her original capital contribution.

(c) To divide the surplus, if any, among the Partners or their representatives as follows: (1) First (to the extent of each Partner's then capital account) in proportion to their then capital accounts. (2) Then according to each Partner's then Percentage Share of [*Capital/Income*].

No Partner shall have the right to demand and receive property in kind for his distribution.

Article V
MISCELLANEOUS

The Partnership's fiscal year shall commence on January 1st of each year and shall end on December 31st of each year. Full and accurate books of account shall be kept at such place as the Managing Partner(s) may from time to time designate, showing the condition of the business and finances of the Partnership; and each Partner shall have access to such books of account and shall be entitled to examine them at any time during ordinary business hours. At the end of each year, the Managing Partner(s) shall cause the Partnership's accountant to prepare a balance sheet setting forth the financial position of the Partnership as of the end of that year and a statement of operations (income and expenses) for that year. A copy of the balance sheet and statement of operations shall be delivered to each Partner as soon as it is available.

Each Partner shall be deemed to have waived all objections to any transaction or other facts about the operation of the Partnership disclosed in such balance sheet and/or statement of operations unless he or she shall have notified the Managing Partner(s) in writing of his or her objectives within thirty (30) days of the date on which such statement is mailed.

The Partnership shall maintain a bank account or bank accounts in the Partnership's name in a national or state bank in the State of ____________________. Checks and drafts shall be drawn on the Partnership's bank account for Partnership purposes only and shall be signed by the Managing Partner(s) or their designated agent.

Any controversy or claim arising out of or relating to this Agreement shall only be settled by arbitration in accordance with the rules of the American Arbitration Association, one Arbitrator, and shall be enforceable in any court having competent jurisdiction.

Witnesses	Partners
____________________	____________________
____________________	____________________

Dated: __________

Tully is also a partner. If Tully negotiates a contract in the name of Middle Earth Movers, the contract will be binding on Mathews but normally not on Jansen and Harran (unless, of course, Jansen and Harran knew about, and consented to, Mathews's representation about Tully). Again, partnership by estoppel requires that a third person reasonably and detrimentally rely on the representation that a person was part of the partnership.

SECTION 6

Partnership Operation

The rights and duties of partners are governed largely by the specific terms of their partnership agreement. In the absence of provisions to the contrary in the partnership agreement, the law imposes the rights and duties discussed in the following subsections. The character and nature of the partnership business generally influence the application of these rights and duties.

RIGHTS AMONG PARTNERS

The rights held by partners in a partnership relate to the following areas: management, interest in the partnership, compensation, inspection of books, accounting, and property.

Management. In a general partnership, "All partners have equal rights in the management and conduct of partnership business" [UPA 18(e)]. Unless the partners agree otherwise, each partner has one vote in management matters *regardless of the proportional size of his or her interest in the firm.* Often, in a large partnership partners will agree to delegate daily management responsibilities to a management committee made up of one or more of the partners.

The majority rule controls decisions in ordinary matters connected with partnership business, unless otherwise specified in the agreement. Unanimous consent of the partners is required, however, to bind the firm in any of the following actions, which significantly affect the nature of the partnership:

1. To alter the essential nature of the firm's business as expressed in the partnership agreement or to alter the capital structure of the partnership.
2. To admit new partners or to enter a wholly new business [UPA 18(g), (h)].
3. To assign partnership property into a trust for the benefit of creditors [UPA 9(3)(a)].
4. To dispose of the partnership's goodwill [UPA 9(3)(b)].
5. To confess judgment against the partnership or submit partnership claims to arbitration [UPA 9(3)(d), (e)]. (A **confession of judgment** is the act of a debtor in permitting a judgment to be entered against him or her by a creditor, for an agreed sum, without the institution of legal proceedings.)
6. To undertake any act that would make further conduct of partnership business impossible [UPA 9(3)(c)].
7. To amend the articles of the partnership.

Interest in the Partnership. Each partner is entitled to the proportion of business profits and losses that is designated in the partnership agreement. If the agreement does not apportion profits or losses, the UPA provides that profits are to be shared equally and losses are to be shared in the same ratio as profits [UPA 18(a)].

Compensation. Devoting time, skill, and energy to partnership business is a partner's duty and generally not a compensable service. Partners can, of course, agree otherwise. For example, the managing partner of a law firm often receives a salary in addition to his or her share of profits for performing special administrative duties in office and personnel management. UPA 18(f) provides that on the death of a partner, a surviving partner is entitled to compensation for services in winding up partnership affairs (and reimbursement for expenses incurred in the process) above and apart from his or her share in the partnership profits.

Inspection of Books. Partnership books and records must be kept accessible to all partners. Each partner has the right to receive (and the corresponding duty to produce) full and complete information concerning the conduct of all aspects of partnership business [UPA 20]. Each firm retains books in which to record and secure such information. Partners contribute the information, and a bookkeeper typically has the duty to preserve it. The books must be kept at the firm's principal business office unless the partners agree otherwise [UPA 19]. Every partner, whether active or inactive, is entitled to inspect all books and records on demand and can make copies of the materials. The personal representative of a deceased partner's estate has the same right of access to partnership books and records that the decedent would have had.

Accounting. An accounting of partnership assets or profits is done to determine the value of each partner's proportionate share in the partnership. An accounting can be called for voluntarily, or it can be compelled by the order of a court in equity.[4] Formal accounting occurs by right in connection with dissolution proceedings, but under UPA 22, a partner also has the right to a formal accounting in the following situations:

1. When the partnership agreement provides for a formal accounting.
2. When a partner is wrongfully excluded from the business, from access to the books, or from both.
3. When any partner is withholding profits or benefits belonging to the partnership in breach of the partner's fiduciary duty.
4. When circumstances render a formal accounting "just and reasonable."

Property Rights. A partner has the following three basic property rights:

1. An interest in the partnership.
2. A right in specific partnership property.
3. A right to participate in the management of the partnership, as previously discussed [UPA 24].

There is an important legal distinction between a partner's rights in specific property belonging to the firm to be used for business purposes and a partner's right to share in the firm's earned profits to the extent of his or her interest in the firm. A partner is co-owner with his or her partners of specific partnership property, holding the property as a tenant in partnership. A specific asset may constitute partnership property even when title to it is in an individual partner's name.

The rights of creditors in regard to partnerships were discussed earlier in this chapter. A judgment creditor of an individual partner has no right to execute or attach specific partnership property, but he or she can obtain the partner's share of profits. A creditor of the firm, however, can levy directly on partnership property.

Partner's Interest in the Firm. A partner's interest in the firm is a personal asset consisting of a proportionate share of the profits earned [UPA 26] and a return of capital on the partnership's termination. A partner's interest is subject to assignment or to a judgment creditor's lien. Judgment creditors can attach a partner's interest by petitioning the court that entered the judgment to grant the creditors a **charging order**. This order entitles the creditors to the profits of the partner and to any assets available to the partner on dissolution [UPA 28]. Neither an assignment nor a court's charging order entitling a creditor to receive a share of the partner's money will cause dissolution of the firm [UPA 27].

Partnership Property. UPA 8(1) provides that "all property originally brought into the partnership's stock or subsequently acquired, by purchase or otherwise, *on account of the partnership*, is partnership property" (emphasis added). Evidence that an asset was acquired with the intention that it be a partnership asset is at the heart of the phrase *on account of the partnership*. Thus, the more closely an asset is associated with the business operations of the partnership, the more likely it is to be a partnership asset.[5] Moreover, when such an asset is purchased with partnership funds, it will belong to the partnership unless a contrary intention is shown. If, for example, a piece of property is purchased with partnership funds, it is presumed to be partnership property even if title is taken in the name of one of the partners.

As mentioned, partners are tenants in partnership of all firm property [UPA 25(1)]. Tenancy in partnership has several important effects. If a partner dies, the surviving partners, not the heirs of the deceased partner, have the right of survivorship to the specific property. Although surviving partners are entitled to possession, they have a duty to account to the decedent's estate for the value of the deceased partner's interest in that property [UPA 25(2)(d), (e)].

A partner has no right to sell, assign, or in any way deal with a particular item of partnership property

4. The principal remedy of a partner against co-partners is an equity suit for dissolution, an accounting, or both. With minor exceptions, a partner cannot maintain an action against other firm members for damages until partnership affairs are settled and an accounting is done. This rule is necessary because legal disputes among partners invariably involve conflicting claims to shares in the partnership. Logically, the value of each partner's share must first be determined by an accounting.

5. Under the RUPA, property that is not acquired in the name of the partnership is nonetheless partnership property if the instrument transferring title refers to (1) the person taking title as a partner or (2) the existence of the partnership [RUPA 204(a)(2)]. If the instrument refers to neither of these, the property is still presumed to be partnership property if it is acquired with partnership funds [RUPA 204(c)]. In all other circumstances, the property is presumed to be the property of an individual partner or partners, even if it is used in the partnership business [RUPA 204(d)].

other than for partnership purposes [UPA 25(2)(a), (b)]. Nor is a partner's personal credit related to partnership property; his or her creditors cannot use partnership property to satisfy the personal debts of the partner. Partnership property is available only to satisfy partnership debts, to enhance the firm's credit, or to achieve other business purposes.

Every partner is a co-owner with all other partners of specific partnership property, such as office equipment, office supplies, and vehicles. Each partner has an equal right to possess partnership property for business purposes or in satisfaction of firm debts, but not for any other purpose without the consent of all the other partners.

DUTIES, POWERS, AND LIABILITIES OF PARTNERS

The duties and powers of partners consist of a fiduciary duty of each partner to the others and general agency powers.

Fiduciary Duties. Partners stand in a fiduciary relationship to one another just as principals and agents do (see Chapter 31). It is a relationship of extraordinary trust and loyalty. This fiduciary duty imposes a responsibility on each partner to act in utmost good faith for the benefit of the partnership. It requires that each partner subordinate his or her personal interests to the mutual welfare of the partners.[6] Thus, a partner cannot engage in any independent competitive activities without the other partners' consent.

This fiduciary duty underlies the entire body of law pertaining to partnership and to agency. From it, certain other duties are commonly implied. Thus, a partner must account to the partnership for any personal profits or benefits derived without the consent of all the partners in any partnership transactions.[7] These include transactions among partners; transactions with third parties connected with the formation, conduct, or liquidation of the partnership; and transactions involving any use of partnership property [UPA 21].

A partner's fiduciary duty requires the highest degree of good faith and fair dealing. This is particularly true when a partner makes a partnership decision that affects him or her personally, such as a division of the firm's profits. In that situation, how the profits are divided has a direct effect on the partner's own share of the profits, and thus the decision must be fair and reasonable.

General Agency Powers. Each partner is an *agent* of every other partner and acts as both a principal and an agent in any business transaction within the scope of the partnership agreement. Each partner is a general agent of the partnership in carrying out the usual business of the firm.[8] Thus, every act of a partner concerning partnership business and every contract signed in the partnership name bind the firm [UPA 9(1)].

Authority of Partners. The UPA affirms general principles of agency law that pertain to the authority of a partner to bind a partnership in contract. Under the same principles, a partner may subject a partnership to liability in tort. When a partner is apparently carrying on partnership business with third persons in the usual way, both the partner and the firm share liability. It is only when third persons know that the partner has no such authority that the partnership is not liable. For example, Patricia, a partner in the partnership of Heise, Green, and Stevens, applies for a loan on behalf of the partnership without authorization from the other partners. The bank manager knows that Patricia has no authority. If the bank manager grants the loan, Patricia will be personally bound, but the firm will not be liable.

The agency concepts relating to apparent authority, actual authority, and ratification that were discussed in Chapter 32 also apply to partnerships. The extent of *implied authority* is generally broader for partners than for ordinary agents, however.

Westlaw. See Case 33.1 at the end of this chapter. To view the full, unedited case from Westlaw,® go to this text's Web site at **http://wbl-cs.westbuslaw.com**.

The Scope of Implied Powers. The character and scope of the partnership business and the customary nature of the particular business operation determine

6. The RUPA states that partners may pursue their own interests without automatically violating their fiduciary duties [RUPA 404(e)].

7. In this sense, to *account to the partnership* means not only to divulge the information but also to determine the value of any benefits or profits derived and to hold that money or property in trust on behalf of the partnership.

8. The RUPA adds "or business of the kind carried on by the partnership" [RUPA 301(1)]. Basically, this addition gives added protection to third parties that deal with a partnership that is not familiar to them.

the implied powers of partners. For example, each partner in a trading partnership—essentially, any partnership business that has goods in inventory and makes profits buying and selling those goods—has a wide range of implied powers to borrow money in the firm name and to extend the firm's credit in issuing or indorsing instruments.

In an ordinary partnership, firm members can exercise all implied powers reasonably necessary and customary to carry on that particular business. Some customarily implied powers include the authority to make warranties on goods in the sales business, the power to convey real property in the firm name when such conveyances are part of the ordinary course of partnership business, the power to enter into contracts consistent with the firm's regular course of business, and the power to make admissions and representations concerning partnership affairs [UPA 11].

If a partner acts within the scope of authority, the partnership is bound to third parties. For example, a partner's authority to sell partnership products carries with it the implied authority to transfer title and to make usual warranties. Hence, in a partnership that operates a retail tire store, any partner negotiating a contract with a customer for the sale of a set of tires can warrant that "each tire will be warranted for normal wear for 40,000 miles."

This same partner, however, does not have the authority to sell office equipment, fixtures, or the partnership office building without the consent of all the other partners. In addition, because partnerships are formed for profit, a partner does not generally have the authority to make charitable contributions without the consent of the other partners. No such action is binding on the partnership unless it is ratified by all of the other partners.

Joint Liability. In most states, partners are subject to joint liability on partnership debts and contracts [UPA 15(b)]. **Joint liability** means that if a third party sues a partner on, for example, a partnership debt, the partner has the right to insist that the other partners be sued with him or her. In fact, if the third party does not sue all of the partners, those partners sued cannot be required to pay a judgment, and the assets of the partnership cannot be used to satisfy the judgment. (Similarly, the third party's release of one partner releases all partners.) In other words, to bring a successful claim against the partnership on a debt or contract, a plaintiff must name all the partners as defendants. To simplify this rule, some states have enacted statutes providing that a partnership may be sued in its own name, and a judgment will be binding on the partnership and the individual partners even though not all the partners are named in the complaint.[9]

If the third party is successful, he or she may collect on the judgment against the assets of one or more of the partners. In other words, each partner is liable and may be required to pay the entire amount of the judgment. When one partner pays the entire amount, the partnership is required to indemnify (reimburse) that partner [UPA 18(b)]. If the partnership cannot do so, the obligation falls on the other partners.

Joint and Several Liability. In a few states, partners are jointly and severally liable for partnership debts and contracts. In all states, partners are jointly and severally liable for torts and breaches of trust [UPA 15(a)].[10]

Joint and several liability means a third party may sue one or more of the partners separately (severally) or all of them together (jointly), at his or her option.[11] This is true even when a partner did not participate in, ratify, or know about whatever it was that gave rise to the cause of action.[12]

A judgment against one partner on his or her several (separate) liability does not extinguish the others' liability. (Similarly, a release of one partner discharges the partners' joint, but not several, liability.) Thus, those not sued in the first action may be sued subsequently. The first action, however, may have been conclusive on the question of liability. If, for example, in an action against one partner, the court held that the partnership was in no way liable, the third party cannot bring an action against another partner and succeed on the issue of the partnership's liability.

If the third party is successful, he or she may collect on the judgment only against the assets of those partners named as defendants. The partner who

9. California is such a state.

10. Under the RUPA, partners' liability is joint and several for all debts [RUPA 306].

11. The term *several* stems from the medieval English term *severall,* which meant "separately," or "severed from" one another. As used here, *several* liability means *separate* liability.

12. The RUPA prevents creditors from bringing an action to collect debts from the partners of a nonbankrupt partnership without first having attempted unsuccessfully to collect from the partnership (or having convinced a court that the attempt would be unsuccessful) [RUPA 307(d)].

committed the tort, though, is required to indemnify the partnership for any damages it pays.

Liability of Incoming Partner. A partner newly admitted to an existing partnership has limited liability for whatever debts and obligations the partnership incurred *prior* to the new partner's admission. UPA 17 provides that the new partner's liability can be satisfied only from partnership assets. This means that the new partner has no personal liability for these debts and obligations, but the new partner's capital contribution may be used to satisfy the debts and obligations.

See Case 33.2 at the end of this chapter. To view the full, unedited case from Westlaw,® go to this text's Web site at **http://wbl-cs.westbuslaw.com**.

SECTION 7

Partnership Termination

Partnerships can be terminated for a variety of reasons. The partnership may be dissolved by agreement among the parties. For example, the partners may stipulate in their partnership agreement that the partnership will end on a certain date or after a particular business objective has been achieved. Alternatively, the partners may simply agree among themselves to terminate the business. A partner's withdrawal may automatically dissolve the partnership. The partnership may also end for other reasons, such as when a partner dies or becomes incapacitated or when a court orders the partnership to be dissolved because of special circumstances.

Generally, any change in the relations of the partners that demonstrates unwillingness or inability to carry on partnership business dissolves the partnership, resulting in termination [UPA 29]. If any partner wishes to continue the business, he or she is free to reorganize into a new partnership with the remaining partners.

The termination of a partnership has two stages—dissolution and winding up. Both stages must take place before termination is complete. **Dissolution** occurs when any partner ceases to be associated with the carrying on of partnership business. **Winding up** is the actual process of collecting and distributing the partnership's assets. Dissolution terminates the right of a partnership to endure as an ongoing concern, but the partnership continues to exist long enough to wind up its affairs. When winding up is complete, the partnership's *legal* existence is terminated.

Dissolution

Dissolution, the first stage in the termination of a partnership, can be brought about by acts of the partners, by operation of law, or by judicial decree.

Dissolution by Acts of the Partners. The following acts of the partners can bring about dissolution: agreement, the withdrawal of a partner,[13] the addition of a partner, and the transfer of a partner's interest.

Dissolution by Agreement. A partnership can be dissolved when certain events stipulated in the partnership agreement occur. For example, when a partnership agreement expresses a fixed time or a particular business objective to be accomplished, the passing of the date or the accomplishment of the project dissolves the partnership. Partners do not have to abide by the stipulations in the agreement, however. They can mutually agree to dissolve the partnership early or to extend it. If they agree to continue in the partnership, they become *partners at will*—meaning that any partner can dissolve the partnership at any time by withdrawing from the firm.

Partner's Power to Withdraw. A partnership is a personal legal relationship among co-owners. No person can be compelled either to become a partner or to remain one. Implicit in a partnership is each partner's *power* to dissociate from the partnership at any time and thus dissolve the partnership. Note that although a partner always has the *power* to withdraw from the partnership, he or she may not always have the *right* to do so. In a partnership for a specified term or for a specified purpose, a partner does not have the right to withdraw until the term has lapsed or the purpose has been fulfilled. If a partner withdraws in violation of the partnership agreement, he or she will be liable to the other partners for damages resulting from wrongful dissolution of the partnership.

13. The RUPA distinguishes the withdrawal of a partner that causes a breakup of a partnership from a withdrawal that causes only the end of a partner's participation in the business (and results in a buyout of that partner's interest) [RUPA 601, 701, 801]. Dissolution results only if the partnership must be liquidated [RUPA 801].

Admission of a New Partner. A change in the composition of the partnership due to the admission of a new partner (without the consent of the other partners) results in dissolution. The new partnership carries the debts of the dissolved partnership. Creditors of the prior partnership become creditors of the partnership that is continuing the business [UPA 41].

Transfer of a Partner's Interest. The UPA provides that neither a voluntary transfer of a partner's interest[14] nor an involuntary sale of a partner's interest for the benefit of creditors [UPA 28] by itself dissolves the partnership. (A transferee—the one to whom the interest is transferred—acquires the right to the transferring partner's profits but does not become a partner; thus, a transferee has no say in the management or administration of partnership affairs and no right to inspect partnership books.) Either occurrence, however, can ultimately lead to judicial dissolution of the partnership, as will be discussed.

Dissolution by Operation of Law. A partnership is dissolved by operation of law in the event of death, bankruptcy, or illegality.

Death. A partnership is dissolved on the death of any partner, even if the partnership agreement provides for carrying on the business with the executor of the decedent's estate.[15] Any change in the composition of the partnership results in a new partnership.

Bankruptcy. The bankruptcy of a partner will dissolve a partnership. Insolvency alone will not result in dissolution. Naturally, bankruptcy of the firm itself will result in dissolution of the partnership.

Illegality. Any event that makes it unlawful for the partnership to continue its business or for any partner to carry on in the partnership will result in dissolution. If the illegality of the partnership business is a cause for dissolution, however, the partners can decide to change the nature of their business and continue in the partnership. When the illegality applies to an individual partner, the dissolution must occur. For example, suppose that the state legislature passes a law making it illegal for magistrates to engage in the practice of law. If an attorney in a law firm is appointed a magistrate, the partnership must be dissolved.

Dissolution by Judicial Decree. Dissolution of a partnership can result from judicial decree. For dissolution to occur, an application or petition must be made in an appropriate court. The court then either denies the petition or grants a decree of dissolution. Under UPA 32, a court can dissolve a partnership for the reasons discussed below or whenever circumstances render it equitable to do so.

Insanity. A partnership can obtain a judicial declaration of dissolution when a partner is adjudicated insane or is shown to be of unsound mind. This action often involves a series of complex tests and standards.

Incapacity. When it appears that a partner has become incapable of performing his or her duties under the partnership agreement, a decree of dissolution may be required. It must appear that the incapacity is permanent and will substantially affect the partner's ability to discharge his or her duties to the firm.

Business Impracticality. When it becomes obvious that the firm's business can be operated only at a loss, judicial dissolution may be ordered.

Improper Conduct. A partner's impropriety involving partnership business (for example, fraud perpetrated on the other partners) or improper behavior reflecting unfavorably on the firm (for instance, habitual drunkenness resulting in gross neglect of the partnership's business) will provide grounds for a judicial decree of dissolution.

Other Circumstances. Dissolution may also be granted in other circumstances when the court finds it equitable to do so. For example, a court might order dissolution when personal dissension between partners becomes so persistent and harmful as to undermine the confidence and cooperation necessary to carry on the firm's business.

Notice of Dissolution. A partner must communicate his or her intent to dissolve or to withdraw from a firm to each of the other partners. This notice of intent can come from the words of the partner (actual notice) or from the actions of the partner (con-

14. A single partner cannot make another person a partner in a partnership merely by transferring his or her interest to that person [UPA 27].

15. Under the RUPA, the death of a partner represents that partner's "dissociation" from the partnership, but it is not an automatic ground for the partnership's dissolution [RUPA 601].

structive notice). All partners will share liability for the acts of any partner who continues to conduct business for the firm without knowing that the partnership has been dissolved.

For example, suppose that Alzor, Jennifer, and Carla have a partnership. Alzor tells Jennifer of her intent to withdraw. Before Carla learns of Alzor's intentions, she enters into a contract with a third party. The contract is equally binding on Alzor, Jennifer, and Carla. Unless the other partners have notice, the withdrawing partner will continue to be bound as a partner to all contracts created for the firm.

To avoid liability for obligations a partner incurs after dissolution of a partnership, the firm must give notice to all affected third persons. The manner of giving notice depends on the third person's relationship to the firm. Any third person who has extended credit to the partnership must receive actual notice. For all others, a newspaper announcement or similar public notice is sufficient.

WINDING UP

Once dissolution has occurred and partners have been notified, they cannot create new obligations on behalf of the partnership. Their only authority is to complete transactions begun but not finished at the time of dissolution and to wind up the business of the partnership. Winding up includes collecting and preserving partnership assets, discharging liabilities (paying debts), and accounting to each partner for the value of his or her interest in the partnership.

When dissolution is caused by a partner's act that violates the partnership agreement, the innocent partners may have rights to damages resulting from the dissolution. Also, the innocent partners have the right to buy out the offending partner and to continue the business instead of winding up the partnership. A partner who has committed a wrongful act is barred from participating in the winding up of partnership business.

Dissolution resulting from the death of a partner vests all partnership assets in the surviving partners. The surviving partners act as fiduciaries in settling partnership affairs in a quick, practicable manner and in accounting to the estate of the deceased partner for the value of the decedent's interest in the partnership. The surviving partners are entitled to payment for their services in winding up the partnership, as well as to reimbursement for any costs incurred in the process [UPA 18(f)].

Westlaw. See Case 33.3 at the end of this chapter. To view the full, unedited case from Westlaw,® go to this text's Web site at **http://wbl-cs.westbuslaw.com**.

DISTRIBUTION OF ASSETS

Creditors of the partnership, as well as creditors of the individual partners, can make claims on the partnership's assets when the partnership is terminated. Creditors of the partnership have priority over creditors of individual partners in the distribution of partnership assets; the converse priority is followed in the distribution of individual partner assets—except under bankruptcy law, which provides that a partner's individual assets may be utilized to pay claims against a partnership involved in bankruptcy proceedings.[16] (Bankruptcy law in general was discussed in Chapter 30.)

The priorities in the distribution of a partnership's assets are as follows [UPA 40(b)]:[17]

1. Payment of third party debts.
2. Refund of advances (loans) made to or for the firm by a partner.
3. Return of capital contribution to a partner.
4. Distribution of the balance, if any, to partners in accordance with the relative proportions of their respective shares in the profits.

The distribution of partnership assets begins with the subtraction of the partnership's total liabilities from its total assets. Liabilities include amounts owed to creditors, to partners for other than capital contributions and profit, and to partners for their capital contributions. Amounts that remain after payment of the liabilities are distributed to the partners according to the profit-sharing ratio.

If the partnership's liabilities are greater than its assets, the partners bear the losses—in the absence of a contrary agreement—in the same proportion in which they shared the profits (rather than, for example, in proportion to their contributions to the partnership's capital). If the partnership is insolvent, the partners must still contribute their respective shares. If one of the partners does not contribute, the other or others must provide the additional amounts necessary to pay the liabilities; but he, she,

16. 11 U.S.C. Section 723.

17. Under the RUPA, partner creditors are included among creditors who take first priority [RUPA 808]. Capital contributions and profits or losses are then calculated together to determine the amounts that the partners receive or the amounts that they pay.

or they have a **right of contribution** against (that is, a right to be reimbursed by) whoever has not paid his or her share.[18]

Partnership Buy-Sell Agreements

Usually, when people enter into partnerships, they are getting along with one another. To prepare for the possibility that the situation may change and they may become unable to work together amicably, the partners should make express arrangements during the formation of the partnership to provide for its smooth dissolution. An agreement may be made for one or more partners to buy out the other or others, should the situation warrant. Such an agreement is called a **buy-sell agreement**, or simply a buyout agreement. To agree beforehand on who buys what, under what circumstances, and, if possible, at what price may eliminate costly negotiations or litigation later. Alternatively, it may be agreed that one or more partners will determine the value of the interest being sold, and the other or others can decide whether to buy or sell.

A similar agreement can be formed for the transfer of a partner's interest on his or her death to the surviving partners. The partners can agree that the survivors will pay the value of the deceased partner's interest in the partnership to his or her representative. To fund the payment of the value of each partner's interest on his or her death, partnership funds can be used to purchase insurance.[19]

18. If an individual partner is insolvent and for that reason cannot pay his or her share of the loss, however, the solvent partner or partners will be unable to recover their additional contributions from the insolvent partner.

19. Under the RUPA, if a partner's dissociation does not result in a dissolution of the partnership, a buyout of the partner's interest is mandatory [RUPA 701(a)]. The RUPA contains an extensive set of buyout rules. Basically, a departing partner gets the same amount through a buyout that he or she would get if the business were winding up [RUPA 701(b)].

Terms and Concepts to Review

articles of partnership 668	entrepreneur 664	partnership 665
buy-sell agreement 678	information return 667	partnership by estoppel 668
charging order 672	joint and several liability 674	right of contribution 678
confession of judgment 671	joint liability 674	sole proprietorship 664
dissolution 675	marshaling assets 666	winding up 675

Chapter Summary

Sole Proprietorships	The simplest form of business; used by anyone who does business without creating an organization. The owner is the business. The owner pays personal income taxes on all profits and is personally liable for all business debts.
Partnerships	1. Created by agreement of the parties. 2. Not treated as an entity except for limited purposes. 3. Partners have unlimited liability for partnership debts. 4. Each partner has an equal voice in management unless otherwise provided for in the partnership agreement. 5. In the absence of an agreement, partners share profits equally and share losses in the same ratio as they share profits. 6. The capital contribution of each partner is determined by agreement. 7. Each partner pays a proportionate share of income taxes on the net profits of the partnership, whether or not they are distributed; the partnership files only an information return with the Internal Revenue Service. 8. Can be terminated by agreement or dissolved by action of the partners (withdrawal), operation of law (death or bankruptcy), or court decree.

CASES FOR ANALYSIS

Westlaw. You can access the full text of each case presented below by going to the Westlaw cases on this text's Web site at http://wbl-cs.westbuslaw.com. Each Westlaw case includes the names of all plaintiffs and defendants, the dates on which the case was argued and decided, a brief summary of the issues and decisions in the case, headnotes classifying specific issues in the case according to the West Key Number System, and the court's opinion. Concurring and dissenting opinions, if any, are included as well.

CASE 33.1 AUTHORITY OF PARTNERS

HELPINSTILL V. REGIONS BANK

Texas Court of Appeals—Texarkana, 2000.
33 S.W.3d 401.

Opinion by Justice *HILL*.

Bobby Helpinstill, individually and as a general partner in MBO Computers, a Texas general partnership, appeals from a judgment in favor of Regions Bank, successor in interest to and formerly known as Longview National Bank. The Bank sued Helpinstill [in a Texas state court] to recover funds representing overdrafts that Helpinstill's partner in MBO, Mike Brown, had made when paying creditors of the partnership. Brown, while creating overdrafts on the partnership account, was shuffling funds from one bank account to another and is now in federal prison for conducting a check-kiting scheme. [*Check kiting* refers to the practice of moving funds between bank accounts for the purpose of covering account deficiencies. For example, a check drawn on an account in bank A is written to cover a deficiency in an account in bank B. Then a check drawn on an account in bank B is written to cover the deficiency in bank A—and so on.]

* * * *

Helpinstill and Brown were partners in MBO. They created a partnership banking account at Longview National Bank, each agreeing that he would be individually liable for any overdrafts created on the account. It began to be a regular procedure of the business that Brown, who was actively managing the business, would write overdrafts on the account and cover them later with deposits. Helpinstill acknowledges that Brown's activity in depositing checks to and writing checks on the partnership account and creating overdrafts on those accounts was, prior to Brown's kiting scheme, in the ordinary course of business of the partnership. * * * [Helpinstill contends] that such activity by Brown ceased to be in the ordinary course of business of the partnership when Brown initiated a check-kiting scheme by shuffling money from one account to another, all in different banks, in order to keep MBO solvent. Brown's creation of the overdrafts was in the ordinary course of business of MBO, even though the illegal check-kiting scheme was not.

* * * *

* * * [Helpinstill] suggests that the source of the overdrafts was the collapse of the kite and that the overdrafts are attributable to bank fraud. In fact, the source of the overdrafts was the fact that Brown was writing checks exceeding the actual deposits on account; the overdrafts are attributable, then, to the lack of sufficient funds to cover the checks Brown wrote. The kiting scheme, rather than creating the overdrafts, was being used to disguise them; and, while not in itself in the ordinary course of the partnership's business, the kiting scheme did not change the fact that the creation of overdrafts was in the ordinary course of the partnership's business. * * *

* * * *

* * * We * * * affirm the judgment.

CASE 33.2 LIABILITY OF INCOMING PARTNER

CITIZENS BANK OF MASSACHUSETTS V. PARHAM-WOODMAN MEDICAL ASSOCIATES

United States District Court,
Eastern District of Virginia, 1995.
874 F.Supp. 705.

PAYNE, District Judge.

* * * *

BACKGROUND

The predecessor of Citizens Bank of Massachusetts and Parham-Woodman Medical Associates, a Virginia general partnership, entered a Construction Loan Agreement and a term note dated April 30, 1985. The loan, in the principal amount of $2 million, was to fund construction of a medical office building, Parham-Woodman's principal asset. Nilda R. Ante and Larry E. King were the general partners of Parham-Woodman when the Construction Loan Agreement and the note were executed. Ante and King also executed a Guaranty in favor of Citizens Bank on April 30, 1985.

As contemplated by the documents, Citizens Bank made advances from time to time during the construction of the building. The first advance was made on April 30, 1985 in the amount of $372,482.61. From then until June 3, 1986, Citizens Bank made 24 other advances. The advances as of June 3, 1986 totalled $1,457,123.15.

Dr. Richard L. Hunley was admitted as a general partner in Parham-Woodman on June 25, 1986. Nada Tas and her husband, Joseph Tas, also became general partners then, although they contend that they did not become general partners until 1987. From July 2, 1986 through November 17, 1986, Citizens Bank made eight additional advances in the amount of $542,876.85. * * *

The medical office building was built, and the partnership made numerous payments but ultimately defaulted. On December 15, 1993, a foreclosure sale brought $912,000, which yielded net proceeds of $890,195.12 to Citizens Bank.

[Citizens obtained a deficiency judgment against Parham-Woodman in the amount of $1,218,244.98. The bank filed a suit in a federal district court against the partners to recover this amount.] The liability of Ante and King was eliminated by their respective bankruptcy discharges. * * *

DISCUSSION

The issues presented in this action [include] whether Joseph and Nada Tas * * * and Dr. Hunley * * * are personally liable for [the last] eight advances in the principal amount of $542,876.88, plus interest. * * *

* * * *

Resolution of the * * * issue * * * requires consideration of the Uniform Partnership Act and its effect on the nature and extent of the liabilities of incoming partners. This necessitates an examination of the language of the Act, the intent of the Act's drafters and the interpretation of the Act by other jurisdictions.

Section 17 of the Act makes an incoming partner liable for "all the obligations of the partnership arising before his admission," but provides that "this liability shall be satisfied only out of partnership property." Section 17 altered slightly the common law because, at common law, admission of a new partner dissolved the old partnership and created a new one. New creditors, then, were preferred over creditors of the old partnership when partnership assets were sought to cover unpaid partnership debts. To remedy this unfairness to creditors, drafters of the Act removed the preference with respect to partnership assets. "So as to preserve the present law as nearly as possible," however, and presumably to continue the common law's fair treatment of incoming partners, the drafters provided that for pre-existing debts, "liability of the incoming partner shall be satisfied only out of partnership property. It, therefore, results that existing and subsequent creditors have equal rights as against partnership property and the separate property of all the previously existing members of the partnership, while only the subsequent creditors have rights against the separate estate of the newly admitted partner." [Emphasis added.]

Decisions before and after adoption of the UPA suggest the reason why the law restricts an incoming partner's personal liability, a restriction maintained by the Act. Specifically, *where a partnership undertakes a debt before a new partner is made, the credit of the new member * * * does not enter into the consideration of the creditors of the old firm, and it would be manifestly unjust to hold the new partner liable.* These decisions and the long-standing principle which they confirm support the view that a partnership obligation arises, within the meaning of Section 17, when the creditor extends the credit to the partnership. In this instance, that occurred on April 30, 1985 and not on the occasion when the bank disbursed each advance. [Emphasis added.]

* * * *

Here the documents were executed long before Dr. Hunley and the Tases joined Parham-Woodman and, upon execution, they were binding obligations on both Citizens Bank and the partnership. That is not changed merely because the passage of part of the consideration was delayed pursuant to a schedule which also was set before Dr. Hunley and the Tases became partners.

* * * *

CONCLUSION

The interpretation of Section 17 reflected here is consistent with the language of the statute, with commercial reality as evinced by the applicable documents, and with the articulated purposes which Section 17 was enacted to achieve. This rule enables potential creditors of the partnership to know that what they see of a partnership is what they can reach, and it permits potential incoming partners to avoid surprise liabilities. Creditors, of course, can construct and administer loans to partnerships in such a fashion as to reach the personal assets of partners admitted during the disbursement of term payments. However, absent such a basis, the personal assets of an incoming partner are not available to satisfy post-admission advances under the terms of a pre-admission contract.

The court finds that all of the partners are liable for the debt owed the bank, but that the liability of * * * Richard L. Hunley, Joseph Tas, and Nada Tas may be satisfied only out of partnership assets.

* * * *

It is so ORDERED.

CASE 33.3 WINDING UP

CREEL v. LILLY

Court of Appeals of Maryland, 1999.
354 Md. 77,
729 A.2d 385.

CHASANOW, Judge.

* * * *

I. BACKGROUND

On approximately June 1, 1993, Joseph Creel began a retail business selling NASCAR racing memorabilia. His business was originally located in a section of his wife Anne's florist shop, but after about a year and a half he decided to raise capital from partners so that he could expand and move into his own space. On September 20, 1994, Mr. Creel entered into a partnership agreement—apparently prepared without the assistance of counsel—with Arnold Lilly and Roy Altizer to form a general partnership called "Joe's Racing." The partnership agreement covered such matters as the partnership's purpose, location, and operations, and stated the following regarding termination of the business:

> "7. **TERMINATION**
> (a) That, at the termination of this partnership a full and accurate inventory shall be prepared, and the assets, liabilities, and income, both in gross and net, shall be ascertained: the remaining debts or profits will be distributed according to the percentages shown above in 6(e).
> * * *
> (d) Upon the death or illness of a partner, his share will go to his estate. If his estate wishes to sell his interest, they must offer it to the remaining partners first."

The three-man partnership operated a retail store in the St. Charles Towne Center Mall in Waldorf, Maryland. For their initial investment in Joe's Racing, Mr. Lilly and Mr. Altizer each paid $6,666 in capital contributions, with Mr. Creel contributing his inventory and supplies valued at $15,000. Pursuant to the partnership agreement, Mr. Lilly and Mr. Altizer also paid $6,666 to Mr. Creel ($3,333 each) "for the use and rights to the business known as Joe's Racing Collectables." The funds were placed in a partnership bank account with First Virginia Bank-Maryland. All three partners were signatories to this account, but on May 19, 1995, unknown to Mr. Lilly and Mr. Altizer, Mr. Creel altered the account so that only he had the authority to sign checks. It was only after Mr. Creel's death that Mr. Lilly and Mr. Altizer realized they could not access the account funds, which were frozen by the bank upon Mr. Creel's passing. Moreover, on approximately February 20, 1995, Mr. Creel paid a $5,000 retainer to an attorney without his partners' knowledge. He wanted the attorney to prepare documents for the marketing of franchises for retail stores dealing in racing memorabilia.

Joe's Racing had been in existence for almost nine months when Mr. Creel died on June 14, 1995. Mrs. Creel was appointed personal representative of his estate. In this capacity, and acting without the knowledge of the surviving partners, Mrs. Creel and the store's landlord agreed to shorten the lease by one month so that it expired on August 31, 1995. June, July, and August's rent was paid by Mr. Lilly and Mr. Altizer.

* * * Joe's Racing was automatically dissolved upon Mr. Creel's death and because the partnership agreement did not expressly provide for continuation of the partnership nor did his estate consent to its continuation, the surviving partners were required under [the Uniform Partnership Act (UPA)] to wind up the business. In order to pay debts and efficiently wind up the partnership affairs, Mr. Lilly and Mr. Altizer requested that Mrs. Creel and the bank release the funds in the partnership account ($18,115.93 as of July 13, 1995). Their request was refused * * * : [T]he surviving partners, on behalf of Joe's Racing, brought an action in [a Maryland state court] against Mrs. Creel * * * .

* * * *

The court * * * found that the surviving partners sought to wind up and close out the partnership and took all reasonable steps to do so, and that there was no breach by them of any fiduciary duty to the Estate. The lease on the store premises occupied by the partnership expired on 31 August 1995, and on that date Mr. Lilly conducted an inventory of all merchandise in the store. Based on that inventory, an accountant computed the value of the partnership business; Mrs. Creel was invited to review the books and records and retain her own accountant or appraiser if she questioned Mr. Lilly or Mr. Altizer's figures. She declined to do so. After 31 August 1995, Messrs. Lilly and Altizer ceased doing business as Joe's Racing and began doing business together under the name "Good Ole Boys Racing." The court accepted the valuation prepared by Mr. Lilly and Mr. Altizer's accountant as the correct value of the partnership assets as of 31 August 1995, and found that the surviving partners fully disclosed and delivered to the Estate all records of the financial affairs of the Joe's Racing partnership up to 31 August 1995, which the court took to be the end of the winding-up period. [The court rejected] Mrs. Creel's [assertion] * * * that Mr. Lilly and Mr. Altizer were obligated to liquidate the partnership assets in order to wind up the partnership * * * .

* * * *

The Court of Special Appeals affirmed * * * . Mrs. Creel filed a petition for *certiorari* in May 1998, which we granted.

II. DISCUSSION AND ANALYSIS

* * * *

Because *a partnership is governed by any agreement between or among the partners, we must begin our analysis of the compelled liquidation issue by examining the Joe's Racing partnership agreement. We reiterate that both UPA and [the Revised Uniform Partnership Act] only apply when there is either no partnership agreement governing the partnership's affairs, the agreement is silent on a particular point, or the agreement contains provisions contrary to law.* Thus, when conflicts between partners arise, courts must first look to the partnership agreement to resolve the issue * * * . [Emphasis added.]

* * * *

Even though the partnership agreement uses the word "termination," paragraph 7(a) is really discussing the dissolution of the partnership and the attendant winding-up process that ultimately led to termination. Paragraph 7(a) requires that the assets, liabilities, and income be "ascertained," but it in no way mandates that this must be accomplished by a forced sale of the partnership assets. Indeed, a liquidation or sale of assets is not mentioned anywhere in 7(a).

In this case, the winding-up method outlined in 7(a) was followed exactly by the surviving partners: a full and accurate inventory was prepared on August 31, 1995; this information was given to an accountant, who ascertained the assets, liabilities, and income of the partnership; and finally, the remaining debt or profit was distributed according to the percentages listed in 6(e).

Mrs. Creel argues that the partnership agreement does not address the winding-up process and that we should look to UPA's default rules to fill in this gap. Her contention is incorrect. We only turn to UPA and its liquidation rule if there is no other option, and such is clearly not the case here. * * *

* * * *

Assuming *arguendo* that the Joe's Racing partnership agreement cannot be interpreted as outlining an alternative to liquidation in winding up the partnership in the event of a dissolution caused by a partner's death, we still find that a sale of all partnership assets is not required under either UPA or RUPA in order to ascertain the true value of the business. Support for this is found in Maryland's recent adoption of RUPA, which encourages businesses to continue in either their original or successor form, and also the holdings of out-of-state cases where other options besides a "fire sale" have been chosen when a partnership is dissolved under UPA.

* * * *

We find it is sound public policy to permit a partnership to continue either under the same name or as a successor partnership without all of the assets being liquidated. Liquidation can be a harmful and destructive measure, especially to a small business like Joe's Racing, and is often unnecessary to determining the true value of the partnership. * * *

* * * *

III. CONCLUSION

We hold that Maryland's UPA does not grant the estate of a deceased partner the right to demand liquidation of a partnership where the partnership agreement does not expressly provide for continuation of the partnership and where the estate does not consent to continuation. Winding up is not always synonymous with liquidation, which can be a harsh and unnecessary measure towards arriving at the true value of the business. A preferred method in a good faith winding up is the one used in this case—the payment to the deceased partner's estate of its proportionate share of the partnership. Thus, we further hold that where the surviving partners have in good faith wound up the business and the deceased partner's estate is provided with an accurate accounting allowing for payment of a proportionate share of the business, then a forced sale of all partnership assets is generally unwarranted.

CASE PROBLEMS

33–1. Two brothers, Eugene and Marlowe Mehl, operated their family farm as a partnership. Property held by the partnership consisted primarily of farming equipment and machinery. The partnership did not own any real property but leased land from the family and other people. The brothers had agreed to split all profits on an equal basis, but there had never been a written partnership agreement. In 1973, Eugene withdrew $7,200 from the partnership bank account and bought the Dagmar Bar, located in Dagmar, Montana. The warranty deed and the liquor license to the bar were held in the names of Eugene Mehl and his wife, Bonnie. In 1980, Eugene and Bonnie were divorced, and Bonnie received the bar and liquor license as part of the property settlement. In 1983, Marlowe gave written notice to Eugene that he was dissolving the partnership. Eventually a district court in Montana distributed the assets of the partnership. The court concluded that the Dagmar Bar was a partnership asset. On appeal, Eugene contended that the bar was not partnership property and entered into evidence a number of documents that tended to indicate that he was the owner of the bar. What should the appellate court decide? Discuss fully. [*Mehl v. Mehl*, 241 Mont. 310, 786 P.2d 1173 (1990)]

33–2. In 1974, Dunay, Weisglass, and Koenig formed a partnership to engage in the brokerage business. They made no capital contributions to the partnership and agreed to share all revenue and expenses on an equal basis. The partnership entered into an agreement with Ladenburg, Thalmann & Co. to manage the latter's institutional investors services. The agreement did not provide any specific time limit. Each partner was appointed vice president of Ladenburg. Later, Dunay was appointed president of Ladenburg and was promised an additional share of profits for additional work on a year-to-year basis. Dunay contributed his salary as Ladenburg president and his additional share of profits to the partnership. On April 2, 1979, Weisglass and Koenig told Dunay that they wished to dissolve the partnership and did so immediately, forming their own partnership, W.K. Associates, the same day. Dunay received from the original partnership $15,044, the amount reflected on the partnership's records as his unpaid share of partnership income. Dunay remained with Ladenburg for a short period of time, leaving when the Ladenburg board of directors removed him as president and appointed Weisglass in his place on May 10. Dunay then filed a lawsuit, alleging, among other things, that Weisglass and Koenig had breached their fiduciary duty in dissolving the partnership and forming a new partnership. As part of the suit, Dunay sought some of the profits earned by Weisglass and Koenig after the dissolution. The defendants filed a motion to dismiss Dunay's complaint. In whose favor did the court rule, and why? Discuss fully. [*Dunay v. Ladenburg, Thalmann & Co.*, 170 A.D.2d 335, 565 N.Y.S.2d 819 (1991)]

33–3. Carmen Allen and Sandy Newsome, in accordance with a written agreement dated March 11, 1987, conducted a carpet and wall-covering business under the name of Newsome Carpets and Wallcovering. The agreement provided that Allen would invest $5,000 cash in the business and that Newsome would invest carpet stock, fixtures, and equipment equal in value to $5,000. On November 4, 1987, Allen and Newsome executed a document entitled "Partnership Agreement" that established the name, place, nature, and duration of the business and outlined the operating procedures of the firm and the rights and responsibilities of the parties. The document referred to Newsome Carpets as a partnership and to Allen and Newsome as partners, each of whom received 50 percent ownership in the firm in return for her capital investment. The next day, on November 5, articles of incorporation designating Newsome and Allen as directors of Newsome Carpets, Inc., were filed in the office of the secretary of state. Evidence at trial indicated that Allen shared profits, rendered business advice, and signed documents as a general partner of Newsome Carpets. When the corporation was subsequently dissolved, one of the creditors, Orders Distributing Co., sued Allen and Newsome as partners to recover an outstanding debt. Allen (Newsome's whereabouts were unknown when the suit was brought) claimed that the business was a corporation, not a partnership, and that she therefore could not be held personally liable for the debt. Will the court hold that Newsome Carpets was a partnership and not a corporation? Discuss. [*Orders Distributing Co. v. Newsome Carpets & Wallcovering*, 418 S.E.2d 550 (S.C. 1992)]

33–4. Jebeles and Costellos were partners in "Dino's Hot Dogs," doing business on the Montgomery Highway in Alabama. From the outset, Costellos worked at the business full-time, while Jebeles involved himself only to a small extent in the actual running of the business. Jebeles was married to Costellos's sister, and when marital difficulties developed between Jebeles and his wife, Costellos barred Jebeles from the premises. Jebeles sued for an accounting of the partnership's profits and for dissolution of the partnership, claiming that the partnership was a partnership at will and the relationship between the partners made it impossible to conduct partnership business. Will the court grant the petition? Explain. [*Jebeles v. Costellos*, 391 So.2d 1024 (Ala. 1980)]

33–5. Oddo and Ries entered into a partnership agreement in March 1978 to create and publish a book describing how to restore F-100 pickup trucks. Oddo was to write the book and Ries was to provide the capital. Oddo supplied Ries with the manuscript, but Ries was dissatisfied and hired someone else to revise it. The book Ries finally published contained substantial amounts of Oddo's work. Can Oddo require Ries to formally account for the profits from the book? Explain. [*Oddo v. Ries*, 743 F.2d 630 (9th Cir. 1984)]

33–6. B. Darryl Clubb and Jeffere F. Van Liew formed a partnership to develop North Coast Park in northern San Diego County, California. The two were to share equally in the ownership and profits, and Clubb was to receive a 6 percent development fee. Later, Clubb claimed, he was forced to accept R. W. Wortham III as a partner, thereby reducing his interest to one-third. Subsequently, Wortham and Van Liew formed a new partnership called North Coast Park II, in which Clubb had no interest. Without Clubb's consent, Van Liew and Wortham transferred by sale improved North Coast property to the new partnership. Clubb sued Wortham and Van Liew, claiming—among other things—that the sale (transfer) of the North Coast property was in breach of the partnership agreement. To prove this and other information concerning the two partnerships, Clubb, during the discovery phase of the trial, moved for a court order requiring Lawrence T. Dougherty, an attorney for both partnerships, to disclose certain information. Dougherty refused, claiming attorney-client privilege. Clubb asserted that information known by one partner must be made available to all partners. Discuss whether Dougherty could be compelled to give Clubb the information. [*Wortham & Van Liew v. Superior Court (Clubb)*, 188 Cal.App.3d 927, 233 Cal.Rptr. 725 (1987)]

33–7. During June and July of 1981, Taylor Rental Center rented pumps and sandblasting equipment for use on the *M/V Courtney D,* a seagoing vessel. Apparently, the vessel was owned by Paramount Petroleum Corporation. When the request for rental was submitted, Taylor checked the authorization to rent by telephoning the number given. The phone was answered by a business calling itself "Paramount," and Taylor was instructed by phone to send invoices for the rental charges to the Houston post office box of the company. The identification of the employees picking up the equipment was also checked by Taylor. A second request to rent equipment was made by a captain claiming to represent Paramount Steamship Company, Ltd. Since the equipment was to be used on the *Courtney D,* and since the invoices were to be sent to the same address as the earlier rental, Taylor assumed the two Paramount firms were a single enterprise or a partnership. The invoices went unpaid, and Taylor learned that Paramount had apparently gone out of business. Taylor then sought payment from Paramount Petroleum, claiming that it was liable for the bill and that, if it was not the same corporation as Paramount Steamship, it was at least its partner. When the trial court held for Taylor, Paramount Petroleum appealed. Discuss whether the sharing of telephone and post office facilities by the two companies constitutes a partnership by estoppel. [*Paramount Petroleum Corp. v. Taylor Rental Center,* 712 S.W.2d 534 (Tex.Civ.App.—Houston (14th Dist.) 1986)]

33–8. Robert Lowther, Fred Riggleman, and Granville Zopp were equal partners in the Four Square Partnership. The partnership was created to acquire and develop real estate for commercial retail use. In the course of the partnership, Riggleman loaned $30,000 to the partnership, and Zopp loaned the partnership $50,000. Donald H. Lowther, Robert's brother and not a partner of the firm, loaned Four Square $80,000 and took a promissory note signed by the three partners. Four Square encountered financial difficulties shortly after the commercial venture began and eventually defaulted on payments due on a construction loan it had received from a bank. The bank foreclosed on the property securing the debt. The proceeds of the subsequent foreclosure sale satisfied the bank's interest and left a surplus of $87,783 to be returned to the partnership. In the meantime, the partnership had been dissolved and was in the process of winding up its affairs. Robert Lowther filed suit, asking the court to prevent any distribution of the firm's assets to the partners until a determination was made as to who was legally entitled to those assets. Donald Lowther intervened in the suit to establish his priority as a nonpartner creditor. Who has priority to the assets? Explain. [*Lowther v. Riggleman,* 189 W.Va. 68, 428 S.E.2d 49 (1993)]

33–9. Ian Star was a partner in the law firm of Fordham & Starrett. Under the partnership agreement, Laurence Fordham and Loyd Starrett (the founding partners) determined each partner's share of the firm's profits. The first year, the two divided the profits equally among all of the partners. Starr quit the firm on the last day of the second year. Fordham came up with a list of negative factors for determining Starr's share of the second year's profits and paid him less than half an equal share. Starr filed a suit in a Massachusetts state court against the partners, alleging, among other things, breach of fiduciary duty. The Court awarded Starr an additional share of the profits. The partners appealed this award to the state's highest court, the supreme judicial court of Massachusetts. What should the appellate court decide? Discuss. [*Starr v. Fordham,* 420 Mass. 178, 648 N.E.2d 1261 (1995)]

33–10. Attorneys Salvatore DiMasi, Ralph Donabed, and Stephen Karll shared office space, which was designated the "Law Offices of DiMasi, Donabed & Karll, A Professional Association." They also shared stationery that bore the same heading and that listed their names, along with the names of other attorneys, in the margin. Atlas Tack Corporation hired Donabed to handle a certain legal matter. All correspondence and invoices from Donabed to Atlas were on the law office's stationery, and Atlas's payment for the services was in the form of checks payable to "DiMasi, Donabed & Karll." Believing that Donabed had done something wrong in his handling of its matter, Atlas filed a suit in a Massachusetts state court against Donabed, DiMasi, and Karll. Donabed settled out of court, but Atlas maintained the suit against DiMasi and Karll, alleging that they were Donabed's partners and were thus liable for Donabed's acts. The court granted the defendants' motion for summary judgment, and Atlas appealed. What will happen on appeal? Discuss fully. [*Atlas Tack Corp. v. DiMasi,* 37 Mass.App.Ct. 66, 637 N.E.2d 230 (1994)]

33–11. Carola and Grogan were partners in a law firm. The partnership was created by an oral agreement and began doing business in 1974. On September 6, 1976, Carola withdrew from the partnership some of its files, furniture, and books, along with various other items of office equipment. The next day, Carola informed Grogan he had withdrawn from the partnership. Discuss whether Carola's actions on September 6, 1976, constituted effective notice of dissolution to Grogan. [*Carola v. Grogan,* 102 A.D.2d 934, 477 N.Y.S.2d 525 (1984)]

33–12. B&R Communications was a general partner in Amarillo CellTelco. Under the partnership agreement, each partner had the right to inspect partnership records "at reasonable times during business hours," as long as the inspection did not "unreasonably interfere with the operation of the partnership." B&R believed that the managers of the firm were using partnership money to engage in lawsuits that were too costly. B&R and other general partners filed a suit in a Texas state court against the managers. B&R wanted to inspect the firm's records to discover information about the lawsuits, but the court denied B&R's request. B&R asked a state appellate court to order the trial judge to grant the request. On what ground did the appellate court issue the order? [*B&R Communications v. Lopez,* 890 S.W.2d 224 (Tex.App.—Amarillo 1994)]

33–13. Frank Kolk was the manager of Triples American Grill, a sports bar and restaurant. Kolk and John Baines opened bank accounts in the name of the bar, each signing the account signature cards as "owner." Baines was often at the bar and had free access to its office. Baines told others that he was "an owner" and "a partner." Kolk told Steve Mager, the president of Cheesecake Factory, Inc., that Baines was a member of a partnership that owned Triples. On this basis, Cheesecake delivered its goods to Triples on credit. In fact, the bar was owned by a corporation. When the unpaid account totaled more than $20,000, Cheesecake filed a suit in a New Mexico state court against Baines to collect. On what basis might Baines be liable to Cheesecake? What does Cheesecake have to show to win its case? [*Cheesecake Factory, Inc. v. Baines*, 964 P.2d 183 (N.M.App. 1998)]

33–14. Sandra Lerner was one of the original founders of Cisco Systems. When she sold her interest in Cisco, she received a substantial amount of money, which she invested, and she became extremely wealthy. Patricia Holmes met Lerner at Holmes's horse training facility, and they became friends. One evening in Lerner's mansion, while applying nail polish, Holmes layered a raspberry color over black to produce a new color, which Lerner liked. Later, the two created other colors with names like "Bruise," "Smog," and "Oil Slick," and titled their concept "Urban Decay." Lerner and Holmes started a firm to produce and market the polishes but never discussed the sharing of profits and losses. They agreed to build the business and then sell it. Together, they did market research, experimented with colors, worked on a logo and advertising, obtained capital from an investment firm, and hired employees. Then Lerner began working to edge Holmes out of the firm. Several months later, when Holmes was told not to attend meetings of the firm's officers, she filed a suit in a California state court against Lerner, claiming, among other things, a breach of their partnership agreement. Lerner responded in part that there was no partnership agreement because there was no agreement to divide profits. Was Lerner right? Why or why not? How should the court rule? [*Holmes v. Lerner,* 74 Cal.App.4th 442, 88 Cal.Rptr.2d 130 (1 Dist. 1999)]

33–15. In August 1998, Jea Yu contacted Cameron Eppler, president of Design88, Ltd., to discuss developing a Web site to cater to investors, providing services to its members for a fee. Yu and Patrick Connelly invited Eppler and Ha Tran, another member of Design88, to a meeting to discuss the site. The parties agreed that Design88 would perform certain Web design, implementation, and maintenance functions for 10 percent of the profits from the site, which would be called "The Underground Trader." They signed a "Master Partnership Agreement," which was later amended to include Power Uptik Productions, LLC (PUP). The parties often referred to themselves as partners. From Design88's offices in Virginia, Design88 designed and hosted the site, solicited members through Internet and national print campaigns, processed member applications, provided technical support, monitored access to the site, and negotiated and formed business alliances on the site's behalf. When relations among the parties soured, PUP withdrew. Design88 filed a suit against PUP and the others in a Virginia state court. Did a partnership exist among these parties? Explain. [*Design88 Ltd. v. Power Uptik Productions, LLC,* 133 F.Supp.2d 873 (W.D.Va. 2001)]

E-LINKS

For updated links to resources available on the Web, as well as a variety of other materials, visit this text's Web site at

http://wbl-cs.westbuslaw.com

For information on the taxation of partnerships, see the article on this topic by Dennis D'Annunzio at

http://www.sunbeltnetwork.com/Journal/Current/D970804dsd.html

LEGAL RESEARCH EXERCISES ON THE WEB

Go to http://wbl-cs.westbuslaw.com, the Web site that accompanies this text. Select "Interactive Study Center," and then click on "Chapter 33." There you will find the following Internet research exercise that you can perform to learn more about partnerships:

Activity 33–1: Partnerships

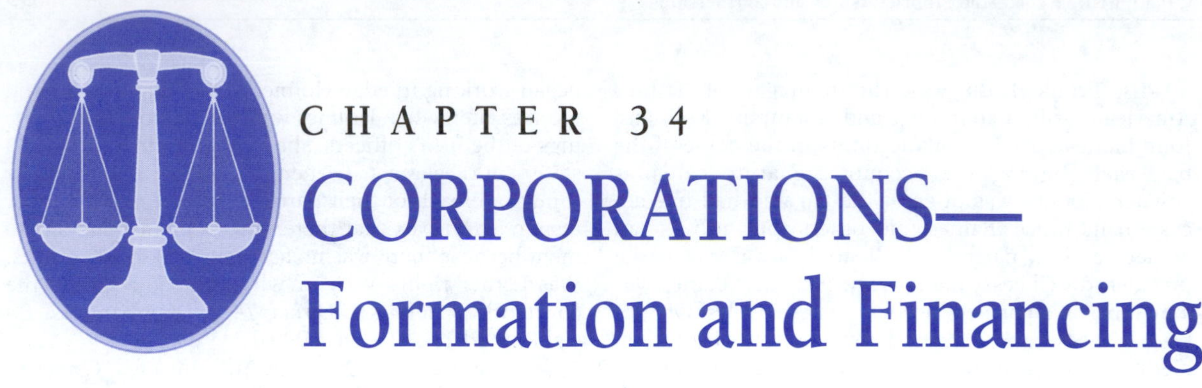

CHAPTER 34

CORPORATIONS—Formation and Financing

THE CORPORATION IS A CREATURE OF STATUTE. A corporation is an artificial being, existing in law only and neither tangible nor visible. Its existence depends generally on state law, although some corporations, especially public organizations, can be created under federal law. Each state has its own body of corporate law, and these laws are not entirely uniform.

The Model Business Corporation Act (MBCA) is a codification of modern corporation law that has been influential in the codification of state corporation statutes. Today, the majority of state statutes are guided by the most recent version of the MBCA, often referred to as the Revised Model Business Corporation Act (RMBCA). Excerpts from the latter are included in Appendix G of this text. You should keep in mind, however, that there is considerable variation among the regulations of the states that have used the MBCA or the RMBCA as a basis for their statutes, and several states do not follow either act. Because of this, individual state corporation laws should be relied on to determine corporate law rather than the MBCA or RMBCA.

In this chapter, we examine the nature of the corporate form of business enterprise and the various classifications of corporations. We then discuss the formation and financing of today's corporation.

SECTION 1

The Nature of the Corporation

A corporation can consist of one or more *natural* persons (as opposed to the artificial "person" of the corporation) identified under a common name. The corporation substitutes itself for its shareholders in conducting corporate business and in incurring liability, yet its authority to act and the liability for its actions are separate and apart from the individuals who own it. (In certain limited situations, the "corporate veil" can be pierced; that is, liability for the corporation's obligations can be extended to shareholders, a topic to be discussed later in this chapter.)

CORPORATE PERSONNEL

Responsibility for the overall management of the corporation is entrusted to a board of directors, which is elected by the shareholders. The board of directors hires corporate officers and other employees to run the daily business operations of the corporation.

When an individual purchases a share of stock in a corporation, that person becomes a shareholder and an owner of the corporation. Unlike the members in a partnership, the body of shareholders can change constantly without affecting the continued existence of the corporation. A shareholder can sue the corporation, and the corporation can sue a shareholder. Additionally, under certain circumstances, a shareholder can sue on behalf of a corporation. The rights and duties of all corporate personnel will be examined in Chapter 35.

CORPORATE TAXATION

Corporate profits are taxed by state and federal governments. Corporations can do one of two things with corporate profits—retain them or pass them on to shareholders in the form of dividends. The corporation receives no tax deduction for dividends distributed to shareholders. Dividends are again taxable (except when they represent distributions of capital) as ordinary income to the shareholder receiving them. This double-taxation feature of the corporation is one of its major disadvantages.

Profits that are not distributed are retained by the corporation. These **retained earnings,** if invested properly, will yield higher corporate profits in the future and thus cause the price of the company's stock to rise. Individual shareholders can then reap the benefits of the retained earnings in the capital gains they receive when they sell their shares.

The consequences of a failure to pay taxes can be severe. As will be discussed in Chapter 36, the state may dissolve a corporation for this reason. In the alternative, corporate status may be suspended until the taxes are paid.

See Case 34.1 at the end of this chapter. To view the full, unedited case from Westlaw,® go to this text's Web site at **http://wbl-cs.westbuslaw.com**.

CONSTITUTIONAL RIGHTS OF CORPORATIONS

A corporation is recognized under state and federal law as a "person," and it enjoys many of the same rights and privileges that natural persons who are U.S. citizens enjoy. The Bill of Rights guarantees a person, as a citizen, certain protections, and corporations are considered persons in most instances. Accordingly, a corporation has the same right of access to the courts as an entity that can sue or be sued. It also has the right of due process before denial of life, liberty, or property, as well as freedom from unreasonable searches and seizures and from double jeopardy.

Under the First Amendment, corporations are entitled to freedom of speech. As we pointed out in Chapter 4, however, commercial speech (such as advertising) and political speech (such as contributions to political causes or candidates) receive significantly less protection than noncommercial speech.

Only the corporation's individual officers and employees possess the Fifth Amendment right against self-incrimination.[1] Additionally, the privileges and immunities clause of the Constitution (Article IV, Section 2) does not protect corporations, nor does it protect an unincorporated association.[2] This clause requires each state to treat citizens of other states equally with respect to access to courts, travel rights, and so forth.

TORTS AND CRIMINAL ACTS

A corporation is liable for the torts committed by its agents or officers within the course and scope of their employment. This principle applies to a corporation exactly as it applies to the ordinary agency relationships discussed in Chapter 32. It follows the doctrine of *respondeat superior.*

Under modern criminal law a corporation may also be held liable for the criminal acts of its agents and employees, provided the punishment is one that can be applied to the corporation. Obviously, corporations cannot be imprisoned, but they can be fined. (Of course, corporate directors and officers can be imprisoned, and in recent years, many have faced criminal penalties for their own actions or for the actions of employees under their supervision. The criminal liability of corporate directors and officers was examined in Chapter 8.)

CORPORATE SENTENCING GUIDELINES

Recall from Chapter 8 that the U.S. Sentencing Commission created standardized sentencing guidelines for federal crimes. These guidelines went into effect in 1987. The commission subsequently created the Federal Organizational Corporate Sentencing Guidelines, which consist of specific sentencing guidelines for crimes committed by corporate employees (white-collar crimes). The net effect of the guidelines has been a fivefold to tenfold increase in criminal penalties for crimes committed by corporate personnel.

The corporate sentencing guidelines cover thirty-two levels of offenses. The punishment for each offense depends on such things as the seriousness of the charge, the amount of money involved, and the extent to which top company executives are involved. Under the sentencing guidelines, corporate lawbreakers face sanctions and fines that can be as high as hundreds of millions of dollars. The guidelines allow judges to ease up on penalties, however, when companies have taken substantial steps to prevent, investigate, and punish wrongdoing. Additionally, if companies cooperate with government investigators, the penalties may be less severe.

The guidelines present judges with a complicated formula for determining penalties for businesses

1. *In re Grand Jury No. 86-3 (Will Roberts Corp.)*, 816 F.2d 569 (11th Cir. 1987).

2. *W. C. M. Window Co. v. Bernardi*, 730 F.2d 486 (7th Cir. 1984).

based on the seriousness of the offense and the degree of the company's guilt. The so-called *culpability score* of a company depends on what role senior management had in the alleged wrongdoing as well as the company's history of past violations and the extent of management's cooperation with federal investigators. Additionally, the effectiveness of the company's compliance program is important. Firms can establish "credits" against potential penalties if they undertake the following measures:

1. The firm must establish and put in writing crime prevention standards and procedures for all employees and agents, and these standards must be communicated to all employees and agents in writing, training programs, or both.
2. The standards must be enforced by high-level employees.
3. When an employee has demonstrated an apparent propensity to engage in criminal activities, the company must prevent that employee from exercising discretionary authority.
4. All anticrime standards of the company must include methods of detecting as well as preventing crimes.
5. Whistleblowers must be protected from reprisals.

SECTION 2

Corporate Powers

Under modern law, except as limited by charters, statutes, or constitutions, *a corporation can engage in any act and enter into any contract available to a natural person in order to accomplish the purposes for which it was created.* When a corporation is created, the express and implied powers necessary to achieve its purpose also come into existence.

Express and Implied Powers

The express powers of a corporation are found in its **articles of incorporation** (a document containing information about the corporation, including the corporation's organization and functions), in the law of the state of incorporation, and in the state and federal constitutions. Corporate **bylaws** (rules of management adopted by the corporation at its first organizational meeting) and the resolutions of the corporation's board of directors also grant or restrict certain powers. The following order of priority is used when conflicts arise among documents involving corporations:

1. U.S. Constitution.
2. State constitutions.
3. State statutes.
4. Articles of incorporation.
5. Bylaws.
6. Resolutions of the board of directors.

Certain implied powers arise when a corporation is created. Barring express constitutional, statutory, or charter prohibitions, the corporation has the implied power to perform all acts reasonably appropriate and necessary to accomplish its corporate purposes. For this reason, a corporation has the implied power to borrow money within certain limits, to lend money, and to extend credit to those with whom it has a legal or contractual relationship.

To borrow money, the corporation acts through its board of directors to authorize the loan. Most often, the president or chief executive officer of the corporation will execute the necessary papers on behalf of the corporation. Corporate officers such as these have the implied power to bind the corporation in matters directly connected with the *ordinary* business affairs of the enterprise. A corporate officer does not have the authority to bind the corporation in matters of great significance to the corporate purpose or undertaking, such as the sale of substantial corporate assets, however.

Ultra Vires Doctrine

The term **ultra vires** means "beyond the powers." In corporate law, acts of a corporation that are beyond its express or implied powers are *ultra vires* acts. A majority of cases dealing with *ultra vires* acts have involved contracts made for unauthorized purposes. For example, it is difficult to see how a contract made by a plumbing company for the purchase of six thousand cases of brandy is reasonably related to the conduct and furtherance of the corporation's stated purpose of providing plumbing installation and services. Hence, such a contract would probably be held *ultra vires.*

In some states, when a contract is entirely executory (not yet performed by either party), a defense of *ultra vires* can be used by either party to prevent enforcement of the contract. In cases in which an *ultra vires* contract is partially or fully executed at the time of challenge, courts may enforce, or uphold, the contract if the circumstances are such that it would be inequitable to allow a party to assert the defense of *ultra vires.*

Under Section 3.04 of the RMBCA, the following remedies are available for *ultra vires* acts:

1. The shareholders may sue on behalf of the corporation to obtain an injunction (to prohibit the corporation from engaging in the *ultra vires* transactions) or to obtain damages for the harm caused by the transactions.
2. The corporation itself can sue the officers and directors who were responsible for the *ultra vires* transactions to recover damages.
3. The attorney general of the state may institute a proceeding to obtain an injunction against the *ultra vires* transactions or to institute dissolution proceedings against the corporation for *ultra vires* acts.

SECTION 3

Classification of Corporations

The classification of a corporation normally depends on its location, purpose, and ownership characteristics.

DOMESTIC, FOREIGN, AND ALIEN CORPORATIONS

A corporation is known as a **domestic corporation** in its home state (the state in which it incorporates). A corporation that is formed in one state but is doing business in another is referred to in that other state as a **foreign corporation.** A corporation formed in another country (say, Mexico) but doing business in the United States is referred to in the United States as an **alien corporation.**

A corporation does not have an automatic right to do business in a state other than its state of incorporation. A corporation normally is required to obtain a *certificate of authority* in any state in which it plans to do business. Once the certificate has been issued, the powers conferred on the corporation by its home state generally can be exercised in the other state. Should a foreign corporation do business without obtaining a certificate of authority, the state can fine the corporation; deny it the privilege of using state courts; and even hold its officers, directors, or agents personally liable for corporate obligations, including contractual obligations, incurred in that state.[3]

PUBLIC AND PRIVATE CORPORATIONS

A public corporation is one formed by the government to meet some political or governmental purpose. Cities and towns that incorporate are common examples. In addition, many federal government organizations, such as the U.S. Postal Service, the Tennessee Valley Authority, and AMTRAK, are public corporations.

Private corporations, in contrast, are created either wholly or in part for private benefit. Most corporations are private. Although they may serve a public purpose, as a public electric or gas utility does, they are owned by private persons rather than by the government.

NONPROFIT CORPORATIONS

Corporations formed for purposes other than making a profit are called *nonprofit* or *not-for-profit* corporations. Nonprofit corporations are usually (although not necessarily) private corporations. Private hospitals, educational institutions, charities, religious organizations, and the like are frequently organized as nonprofit corporations. The nonprofit corporation is a convenient form of organization that allows various groups to own property and to form contracts without the individual members' being personally exposed to liability.

CLOSE CORPORATIONS

A **close corporation** is one whose shares are held by members of a family or by relatively few persons. Close corporations are also referred to as *closely held, family,* or *privately held* corporations. Usually, the members of the small group constituting a close corporation are personally known to one another. Because the number of shareholders is so small, there is no trading market for the shares. In practice, a close corporation is often operated like a partnership. Some states recognize this similarity and have enacted special statutory provisions that cover close corporations. These provisions expressly permit close corporations to depart significantly from certain formalities required by traditional corporation law.[4]

3. *Robertson v. Levy,* 197 A.2d 443 (D.C.App. 1964).
4. For example, in some states (such as Maryland), the close corporation need not have a board of directors.

Additionally, Section 7.32 of the RMBCA—a provision added to the RMBCA in 1991 and adopted in several states—gives close corporations a substantial amount of flexibility in determining the rules by which they will operate. Under Section 7.32, if all of the shareholders of a corporation agree in writing, the corporation can operate without directors, bylaws, annual or special shareholders' or directors' meetings, stock certificates, or formal records of shareholders' or directors' decisions.[5]

Management of Close Corporations. The close corporation has a single shareholder or a closely knit group of shareholders, who usually hold the positions of directors and officers. Management of a close corporation resembles that of a sole proprietorship or a partnership. As a corporation, however, the firm must meet whatever specific legal requirements are set forth in state statutes.

To prevent a majority shareholder from dominating a close corporation, the corporation may specify that action can be taken by the board only on approval of more than a simple majority of the directors. Typically, this would not be required for ordinary business decisions but only for extraordinary actions, such as changing the amount of dividends or dismissing an employee-shareholder. Additionally, in some cases, courts have held that majority shareholders owe a fiduciary duty to minority shareholders (see Chapter 35 for a further discussion of the duties of majority shareholders).

Transfer of Shares in Close Corporations. By definition, a close corporation has a small number of shareholders. The transfer of one shareholder's shares to someone else can thus cause serious management problems. The other shareholders may find themselves required to share control with someone they do not know or like.

Consider an example. Three brothers, Terry, Damon, and Henry Johnson, are the only shareholders of Johnson's Car Wash, Inc. Henry wants to sell his shares to an unknown third person. Terry and Damon object to Henry's idea, and a dispute ensues. What could they have done to avoid this situation? The articles of incorporation could have restricted the transferability of shares to outside persons by stipulating that shareholders offer their shares to the corporation or other shareholders before selling them to an outside purchaser. In fact, a few states have statutes under which close corporation shares cannot be transferred unless certain persons—including shareholders, family members, and the corporation—are first given the opportunity to purchase the shares for the same price.

Another way that control of a close corporation can be stabilized is through the use of a shareholder agreement. A shareholder agreement can provide that when one of the original shareholders dies, his or her shares of stock in the corporation will be divided in such a way that the proportionate holdings of the survivors, and thus their proportionate control, will be maintained.

See Case 34.2 at the end of this chapter. To view the full, unedited case from Westlaw,® go to this text's Web site at **http://wbl-cs.westbuslaw.com**.

S CORPORATIONS

A close corporation that meets the qualifying requirements specified in Subchapter S of the Internal Revenue Code can operate as an **S corporation.** If a corporation has S corporation status, it can avoid the imposition of income taxes at the corporate level while retaining many of the advantages of a corporation, particularly limited liability.

Qualification Requirements for S Corporations. Among the numerous requirements for S corporation status, the following are the most important:

1. The corporation must be a domestic corporation.
2. The corporation must not be a member of an affiliated group of corporations.
3. The shareholders of the corporation must be individuals, estates, or certain trusts. Nonqualifying trusts and partnerships cannot be shareholders. Corporations can be shareholders under certain circumstances.
4. The corporation must have seventy-five or fewer shareholders.
5. The corporation must have only one class of stock, although not all shareholders need have the same voting rights.
6. No shareholder of the corporation may be a nonresident alien.

5. Shareholders cannot agree, however, to eliminate certain rights of shareholders, such as the right to inspect corporate books and records or the right to bring derivative actions (lawsuits on behalf of the corporation—see Chapter 35).

Benefits of S Corporations. At times, it is beneficial for a regular corporation to elect S corporation status. Benefits include the following:

1. When the corporation has losses, the S election allows the shareholders to use the losses to offset other income.
2. When the stockholder's tax bracket is lower than the tax bracket for regular corporations, the S election causes the corporation's entire income to be taxed in the shareholder's bracket (because it is taxed as personal income), whether or not it is distributed. This is particularly attractive when the corporation wants to accumulate earnings for some future business purpose.

Because of these tax benefits, many close corporations opted for S corporation status in the past. Today, however, the S corporation is losing some of its significance because the limited liability company and the limited liability partnership (discussed in Chapter 38) offer similar advantages plus additional benefits, including more flexibility in forming and operating the business.

PROFESSIONAL CORPORATIONS

Professional persons such as physicians, lawyers, dentists, and accountants can incorporate. Their corporations may be identified by such letters as *S.C.* (service corporation), *P.C.* (professional corporation), or *P.A.* (professional association). In general, the laws governing professional corporations are similar to those governing ordinary business corporations, but three basic areas of liability deserve brief attention.

First, a court might, for liability purposes, regard the professional corporation as a partnership in which each partner can be held liable for whatever malpractice liability is incurred by the others within the scope of the partnership. Second, a shareholder in a professional corporation is protected from the liability imposed because of torts (unrelated to malpractice) committed by other members. Third, many professional corporation statutes impose personal liability on professional persons not only for their acts but also for the professional acts performed under their supervision.

In some cases, shareholders of a professional corporation have not been shielded from personal liability by the corporate form because, in fact, they conduct the business more as a partnership than as a corporation. For example, suppose that a partnership, to obtain certain tax benefits or to limit the personal liability of partners, decides to incorporate. After incorporation, however, the members continue to conduct the business as a partnership. In a suit against the firm, a court may hold that partnership law, not corporate law, should govern the issue.

SECTION 4

Corporate Formation

Corporations generally come into existence through two steps: (1) preliminary organizational and promotional undertakings (particularly, obtaining capital for the future corporation) and (2) the legal process of incorporation.

PROMOTIONAL ACTIVITIES

Before a corporation becomes a reality, people invest in the proposed corporation as subscribers, and contracts are frequently made by promoters on behalf of the future corporation. **Promoters** are those who, for themselves or others, take the preliminary steps in organizing a corporation. One of the tasks of the promoter is to issue a **prospectus**, which is a document required by federal or state securities laws (see Chapter 37) that describes the financial operations of the corporation, thus allowing an investor to make an informed decision. The promoter also secures the corporate charter.

Promoter's Liability. A promoter may purchase or lease property with a view toward selling it to the corporation when the corporation is formed. In addition, a promoter may enter into contracts with attorneys, accountants, architects, and other professionals whose services will be needed in planning for the proposed corporation. Finally, a promoter induces people to purchase stock in the corporation.

As a general rule, a promoter is held personally liable on preincorporation contracts. Courts simply hold that promoters are not agents when a corporation has yet to come into existence. If, however, the promoter secures the contracting party's agreement to hold only the corporation (not the promoter) liable on the contract, the promoter will not be liable in the event of any breach of contract.

Once the corporation is formed (the charter issued), the promoter remains personally liable until the corporation assumes the preincorporation contract by *novation* (see Chapter 16). Novation releases the promoter and makes the corporation liable for performing the contractual obligations. In some cases, the corporation adopts the promoter's contract by undertaking to perform it. Most courts hold that adoption in and of itself does not discharge the promoter from contractual liability. A corporation normally cannot ratify a preincorporation contract, as no principal was in existence at the time the contract was made.

Subscribers and Subscriptions. Prior to the actual formation of the corporation, the promoter can contact potential individual investors, and they can agree to purchase capital stock in the future corporation. This agreement is often referred to as a *subscription agreement,* and the potential investor is called a *subscriber.* Depending on state law, subscribers become shareholders as soon as the corporation is formed or as soon as the corporation accepts the agreement. This way, if corporation X becomes insolvent, the trustee in bankruptcy (see Chapter 30) can collect the consideration for any unpaid stock from a preincorporation subscriber.

Most courts view preincorporation subscriptions as continuing offers to purchase corporate stock. On or after its formation, the corporation can choose to accept the offer to purchase stock. Many courts also treat a subscription as a contract between the subscribers, making it irrevocable except with the consent of all of the subscribers. Under the RMBCA, a subscription is irrevocable for a period of six months unless otherwise provided in the subscription agreement or unless all the subscribers agree to the revocation of the subscription [RMBCA 6.20]. In other jurisdictions, the preincorporation subscriber can revoke the offer to purchase before acceptance without liability, however.

INCORPORATION PROCEDURES

Exact procedures for incorporation differ among the states, but the basic requirements are similar.

State Chartering. The first step in the incorporation procedure is to select a state in which to incorporate. Because state incorporation laws differ, individuals have found some advantage in looking for the states that offer the most advantageous tax or incorporation provisions. Delaware has historically had the least restrictive laws. Consequently, many corporations, including a number of the largest, have incorporated there. Delaware's statutes permit firms to incorporate in Delaware and carry out business and locate operating headquarters elsewhere. (Most other states now permit this as well.) Closely held corporations, however, particularly those of a professional nature, generally incorporate in the state in which their principal stockholders live and work.

Articles of Incorporation. The primary document needed to begin the incorporation process is called the *articles of incorporation* (see Exhibit 34–1). The articles include basic information about the corporation and serve as a primary source of authority for its future organization and business functions. The person or persons who execute the articles are called *incorporators* and will be discussed shortly. Generally, the information indicated below should be included in the articles of incorporation.

Corporate Name. The choice of a corporate name is subject to state approval to ensure against duplication or deception. State statutes usually require that the secretary of state run a check on the proposed name in the state of incorporation. Some states require that the incorporators, at their own expense, run a check on the proposed name for the newly formed corporation. Once cleared, a name can be reserved for a short time, for a fee, pending the completion of the articles of incorporation. All corporate statutes require the corporation name to include the word *Corporation, Incorporated, Company,* or *Limited* or an abbreviation of one of these terms [RMBCA 4.01, 4.02].

The new corporation's name may not be the same as, or deceptively similar to, the name of an existing corporation doing business within the state. For example, if an existing corporation is named General Dynamics, Inc., the state will not allow another corporation to be called General Dynamic, Inc., because that name is deceptively similar to the first, and it would impliedly transfer a part of the goodwill established by the first corporate user to the second corporation. (See Chapter 7 for a fuller discussion of trade names.)

Nature and Purpose. The intended business activities of the corporation must be specified in the arti-

EXHIBIT 34–1 ARTICLES OF INCORPORATION

ARTICLE ONE

The name of the corporation is ____.

ARTICLE TWO

The period of its duration is __________ (may be "perpetual," a number of years, or until a certain date).

ARTICLE THREE

The purpose (or purposes) for which the corporation is organized is (are)

____

____.

ARTICLE FOUR

The aggregate number of shares that the corporation shall have authority to issue is ________ of the par value of ________ dollar(s) each (or "without par value").

ARTICLE FIVE

The corporation will not commence business until it has received for the issuance of its shares consideration of the value of _______ (can be any sum not less than $1,000).

ARTICLE SIX

The address of the corporation's registered office is ____,
and the name of its registered agent at such address is ____

____.

(Use the street or building or rural address of the registered office, not a post office box number.)

ARTICLE SEVEN

The number of initial directors is ____________________, and the names and addresses of the directors are

____

____.

ARTICLE EIGHT

The name and address of the incorporator is ____

____.

(signed) ____
Incorporator

Sworn to on ______________________ by the above-named incorporator.
(date)

____
Notary Public

(Notary Seal)

cles, and naturally, they must be lawful. Stating a general corporate purpose is usually sufficient to give rise to all of the powers necessary or convenient to the purpose of the organization. The corporate charter can state, for example, that the corporation is organized "to engage in the production and sale of agricultural products." There is a trend toward allowing corporate charters to state that the corporation is organized for "any legal business." A broadly stated purpose creates greater flexibility and avoids unnecessary future amendments to the corporate charter should the corporation change or modify its line of business [RMBCA 2.02(b)(2)(i), 3.01].

Some states prohibit the incorporation of certain professionals, such as doctors or lawyers, except pursuant to a professional incorporation statute.

Also, in some states, certain industries—such as banks, insurance companies, or public utilities—cannot be operated in the general corporate form and are governed by special incorporation statutes.

Duration. A corporation can have perpetual existence unless stated otherwise in the articles. The owners may want to prescribe a maximum duration, however, after which the corporation must formally renew its existence.

Capital Structure. The capital structure of the corporation is generally set forth in the articles. A few state statutes require a very small capital investment for ordinary business corporations but a greater capital investment for those engaged in insurance or banking. The articles must also indicate the number of shares of stock the corporation is authorized to issue and may include other information, such as the valuation of the shares and the types or classes of stock authorized for issuance [RMBCA 2.02(a)].

Internal Organization. The articles should describe the internal management structure of the corporation, although this can be included in bylaws adopted after the corporation is formed [RMBCA 2.02]. The articles of incorporation commence the corporation; the bylaws are formed after commencement by the board of directors. Bylaws are subject to, and cannot conflict with, the incorporation statute or the corporation's charter [RMBCA 2.06].

Under the RMBCA, shareholders may amend or repeal bylaws. The board of directors may also amend or repeal bylaws unless the articles of incorporation or provisions of the incorporation statute reserve that power to shareholders exclusively [RMBCA 10.20]. Typical bylaw provisions describe voting procedures and requirements for shareholders, the election of the board of directors, the methods of replacing directors, and the manner and time of scheduling shareholders' meetings and board meetings (these procedures will be discussed in Chapter 35).

Registered Office and Agent. The corporation must indicate the location and address of its registered office within the state [RMBCA 2.02(a)(3)]. Usually, the registered office is also the principal office of the corporation. The corporation must give the name and address of a specific person who has been designated as an agent and who can receive legal documents on behalf of the corporation. These legal documents include service of process (the delivery of a court order requiring an appearance in court).

Incorporators. Each incorporator must be listed by name and must also indicate an address [RMBCA 2.02(a)(4)]. An incorporator is a person—often, the corporate promoter—who applies to the state on behalf of the corporation to obtain its corporate charter. The incorporator need not be a subscriber and need not have any interest at all in the corporation. Many states do not impose residency or age requirements for incorporators. States vary as to the required number of incorporators; it can be as few as one or as many as three. Incorporators are required to sign the articles of incorporation when they are submitted to the state; often, this is their only duty. In some states, they participate at the first organizational meeting of the corporation.

Certificate of Incorporation.

Once the articles of incorporation have been prepared, signed, and authenticated by the incorporators, they are sent to the appropriate state official, usually the secretary of state, along with the appropriate filing fee. In many states, the secretary of state will then issue a **certificate of incorporation** representing the state's authorization for the corporation to conduct business. (This may be called the **corporate charter.**) The certificate and a copy of the articles are returned to the incorporators. The incorporators then hold the initial organizational meeting, which completes the details of incorporation [RMBCA 2.03].

First Organizational Meeting.

The first organizational meeting is often provided for in the articles of incorporation but is held after the charter is actually granted. At this meeting, the incorporators elect the first board of directors and complete the routine business of incorporation (pass bylaws, issue stock, and so forth). Sometimes, the meeting is held after the election of the board of directors, and the business to be transacted depends on the requirements of the state's incorporation statute, the nature of the business, the provisions made in the articles, and the desires of the promoters [RMBCA 2.05].

Adoption of bylaws—the internal rules of management for the corporation—is probably the most important function of the first organizational meeting. The shareholders, directors, and officers must abide by the bylaws in conducting corporate business.

Corporate employees and third persons dealing with the corporation are not bound by them, however, unless they have reason to be familiar with them.

SECTION 5

Improper Incorporation

The procedures for incorporation are very specific. If they are not followed precisely, others may be able to challenge the existence of the corporation.

Errors in incorporation procedures can become important when, for example, a third person who is attempting to enforce a contract or bring suit for a tort injury fortuitously learns of them. On the basis of improper incorporation, the plaintiff could seek to make the would-be shareholders personally liable. Also, when the corporation attempts to enforce a contract against a defaulting party, if the defaulting party learns of a defect in the incorporation procedures, he or she may be able to avoid liability on that ground.

To prevent injustice, courts will sometimes attribute corporate existence to an improperly formed corporation by holding it to be a *de jure* corporation or a *de facto* corporation, as discussed below. In some cases, corporation by estoppel may also occur.

DE JURE AND *DE FACTO* CORPORATIONS

In the event of substantial compliance with all conditions precedent to incorporation, a corporation is said to have *de jure* existence in law. In most states and under RMBCA 2.03(b), the certificate of incorporation is viewed as conclusive evidence that all mandatory statutory provisions have been met. This means that the corporation is properly formed, and only the state, not a third party, can attack its existence. If, for example, an incorporator's address was incorrectly listed, this would mean that the corporation was improperly formed. The law, however, does not regard such inconsequential procedural defects as detracting from substantial compliance, and courts will uphold the *de jure* status of the corporate entity.

Sometimes there is a defect in complying with statutory mandates—for example, the corporation charter may have expired. Under these circumstances, the corporation may have *de facto* status, meaning that its existence cannot be challenged by third parties except the state. The following elements are required for *de facto* status:

1. There must be a state statute under which the corporation can be validly incorporated.
2. The parties must have made a good faith attempt to comply with the statute.
3. The enterprise must already have undertaken to do business as a corporation.

CORPORATION BY ESTOPPEL

If an association that is neither an actual corporation nor a *de facto* or *de jure* corporation holds itself out as being a corporation, it will be estopped from denying corporate status in a lawsuit by a third party. This usually occurs when a third party contracts with an association that claims to be a corporation but does not hold a certificate of incorporation. When the third party brings suit naming the so-called corporation as the defendant, the association may not escape from liability on the ground that no corporation exists. When justice requires, the courts treat an alleged corporation as if it were an actual corporation for the purpose of determining the rights and liabilities involved in a particular situation. Corporation by estoppel is thus determined by the circumstances. It does not extend recognition of corporate status beyond the resolution of the problem at hand.

SECTION 6

Disregarding the Corporate Entity

In some unusual situations, a corporate entity is used by its owners to perpetrate a fraud, circumvent the law, or in some other way accomplish an illegitimate objective. In these cases, the court will ignore the corporate structure by "piercing the corporate veil," exposing the shareholders to personal liability [RMBCA 2.04].

The following are some of the factors that may cause the courts to pierce the corporate veil:

1. A party is tricked or misled into dealing with the corporation rather than the individual.
2. The corporation is set up never to make a profit or always to be insolvent, or it is too "thinly" capitalized—that is, it has insufficient capital at the time it is formed to meet its prospective debts or potential liabilities.
3. Statutory corporate formalities, such as holding required corporation meetings, are not followed.

4. Personal and corporate interests are mixed together, or **commingled**, to the extent that the corporation has no separate identity.

To elaborate on the fourth factor in the preceding list, consider a close corporation that is formed according to law by a single person or by a few family members. In such a situation, the corporate entity and the sole stockholder (or family-member stockholders) must carefully preserve the separate status of the corporation and its owners. Certain practices invite trouble for the one-person or family-owned corporation: the commingling of corporate and personal funds; the failure to remit taxes, including payroll and sales taxes; and the shareholders' continuous personal use of corporate property (for example, vehicles).

Corporation laws usually do not specifically prohibit a stockholder from lawfully lending money to his or her corporation. When an officer, director, or majority shareholder lends the corporation money and takes back security in the form of corporate assets, however, the courts will scrutinize the transaction closely. Any such transaction must be made in good faith and for fair value.

When the corporate privilege is abused for personal benefit and the corporate business is treated in such a careless manner that the corporation and the shareholder in control are no longer separate entities, the court usually will require the shareholder to assume personal liability to creditors for the corporation's debts. In short, when the facts show that great injustice would result from the use of a corporation to avoid individual responsibility, a court of equity will look behind the corporate structure to the individual stockholder.

See Case 34.3 at the end of this chapter. To view the full, unedited case from Westlaw,® go to this text's Web site at **http://wbl-cs.westbuslaw.com**.

SECTION 7

Corporate Financing

Corporations are financed by the issuance and sale of corporate securities—that is, bonds and stock. **Securities** evidence the obligation to pay money or the right to participate in earnings and the distribution of corporate assets. **Stocks**, or *equity securities,* represent the purchase of ownership in the business firm. **Bonds** (debentures), or *debt securities,* represent the borrowing of money by firms (and governments). Of course, not all debt is in the form of debt securities. For example, some debt is in the form of accounts payable and notes payable. Accounts and notes payable are typically short-term debts. Bonds are simply a way for a corporation to split up its long-term debt so that it can market the debt more easily.

BONDS

Bonds are issued by business firms and by governments at all levels as evidence of the funds they are borrowing from investors. Bonds almost always have a designated *maturity date*—the date when the principal, or face amount, of the bond (or loan) is returned to the investor—and are sometimes referred to as *fixed-income securities,* because their owners receive fixed-dollar interest payments during the period of time prior to maturity.

The characteristics of corporate bonds vary widely, in part because corporations differ in their ability to generate the earnings and cash flow necessary to make interest payments and to repay the principal amount of the bonds at maturity. Furthermore, corporate bonds are only a part of the total debt and the overall financial structure of corporate business. The various types of corporate bonds are described in Exhibit 34–2.

EXHIBIT 34–2 TYPES OF CORPORATE BONDS

TYPE	DEFINITION
Debenture Bonds	Bonds for which no specific assets of the corporation are pledged as backing. Rather, they are backed by the general credit rating of the corporation, plus any assets that can be seized if the corporation allows the debentures to go into default.
Mortgage Bonds	Bonds that pledge specific property. If the corporation defaults on the bonds, the bondholders can foreclose on the property.
Convertible Bonds	Bonds that can be exchanged for a specified number of shares of stock under certain conditions.
Callable Bonds	Bonds that may be called in and the principal repaid at specified times or under conditions stipulated in the bond when it is issued.

EXHIBIT 34–3 HOW DO STOCKS AND BONDS DIFFER?

STOCKS	BONDS
1. Stocks represent ownership.	1. Bonds represent debt.
2. Stocks (common) do not have a fixed dividend rate.	2. Interest on bonds must always be paid, whether or not any profit is earned.
3. Stockholders can elect a board of directors, which controls the corporation.	3. Bondholders usually have no voice in or control over management of the corporation.
4. Stocks do not have a maturity date; the corporation does not usually repay the stockholder.	4. Bonds have a maturity date, when the corporation is to repay the bondholder the face value of the bond.
5. All corporations issue or offer to sell stocks. This is the usual definition of a corporation.	5. Corporations do not necessarily issue bonds.
6. Stockholders have a claim against the property and income of a corporation after all creditors' claims have been met.	6. Bondholders have a claim against the property and income of a corporation that must be met before the claims of stockholders.

STOCKS

Issuing stocks is another way for corporations to obtain financing [RMBCA 6.01]. The ways in which stocks differ from bonds are summarized in Exhibit 34–3. Basically, stocks represent ownership in a business firm, whereas bonds represent borrowing by the firm.

Exhibit 34–4 offers a summary of the types of stocks issued by corporations. The two major types are *common stock* and *preferred stock*.

Common Stock. **Common stock** represents the true ownership of a corporation. It provides a proportionate interest in the corporation with regard to (1) control, (2) earnings, and (3) net assets. A shareholder's interest is generally in proportion to the number of shares owned out of the total number of shares issued.

Any person who purchases shares acquires voting rights—one vote per share held. Voting rights in a corporation apply to the election of the firm's board

EXHIBIT 34–4 TYPES OF STOCKS

TYPE	DEFINITION
Common Stock	Voting shares that represent ownership interest in a corporation. Common stock has the lowest priority with respect to payment of dividends and distribution of assets on me corporation's dissolution.
Preferred Stock	Shares of stock that have priority over common-stock shares as to payment of dividends and distribution of assets on dissolution. Dividend payments are usually a fixed percentage of the face value of the share. Preferred shares may or may not be nonvoting shares.
Cumulative Preferred Stock	Preferred shares for which required dividends not paid in a given year must be paid in a subsequent year before any common-stock dividends can be paid.
Participating Preferred Stock	Preferred shares entitling the owner to receive (1) the preferred-stock dividend and (2) additional dividends after the corporation has paid dividends on common stock.
Convertible Preferred Stock	Preferred shares entitling the owner to convert his or her shares into a specified number of common shares either in the issuing corporation or, sometimes, in another corporation.
Redeemable, or Callable, Preferred Stock	Preferred shares issued with the express condition that the issuing corporation has the right to repurchase the shares as specified.

Exhibit 34–5 Cumulative Convertible Preferred-Stock Certificate

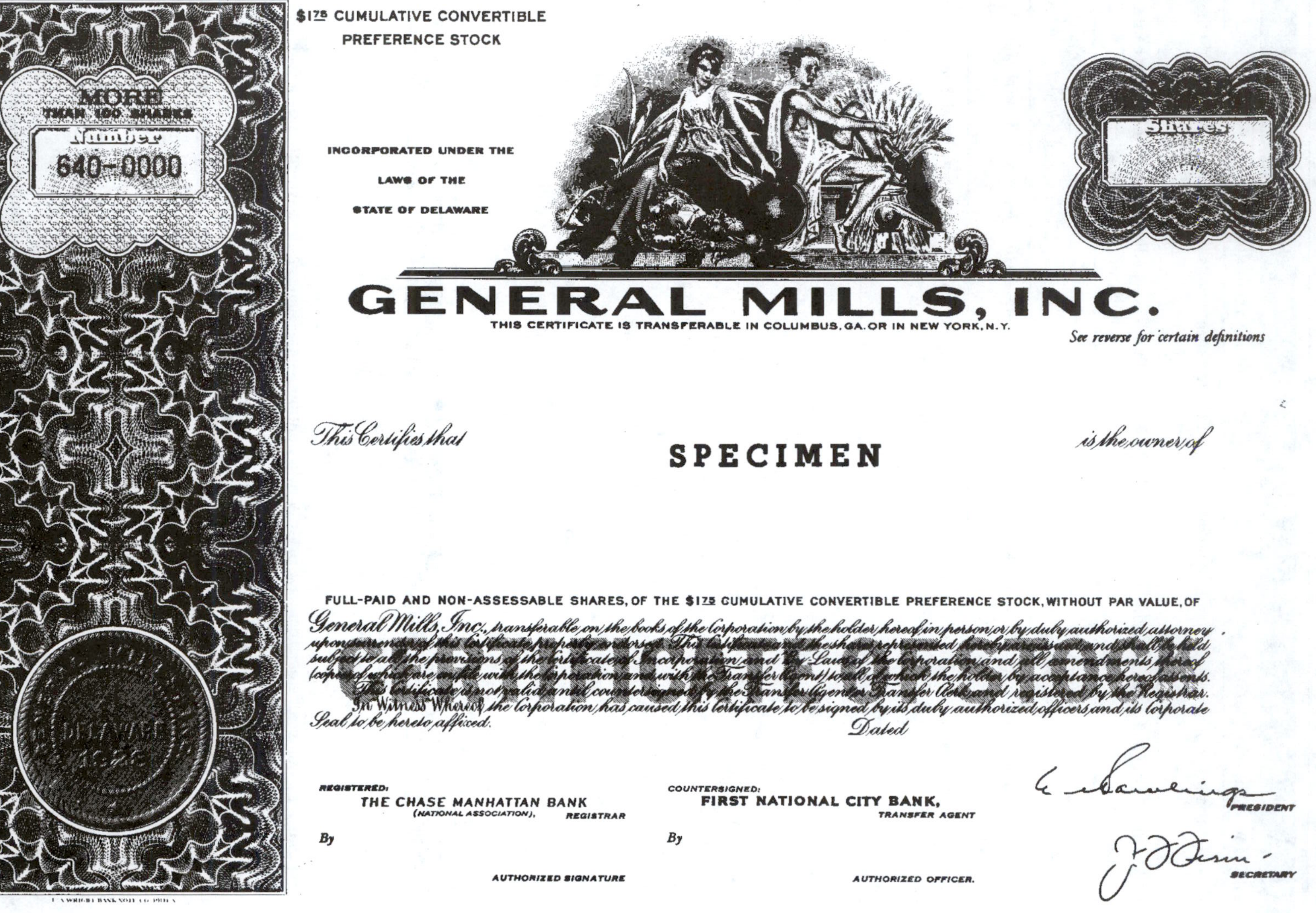

of directors and to any proposed changes in the ownership structure of the firm.[6] For example, a holder of common stock generally has the right to vote in a decision on a proposed merger, as mergers can change the proportion of ownership.

Holders of common stock are a group of investors who assume a *residual* position in the overall financial structure of a business. In terms of receiving returns on their investments, they are last in line. Their earnings depend on the corporation's paying all the other groups—suppliers, employees, managers, bankers, governments, bondholders, and holders of preferred stock—what is due them first. Once those groups are paid, the owners of common stock may be entitled to *all* the remaining earnings. But the board of directors normally is not under any duty to declare the remaining earnings as dividends.

Preferred Stock. **Preferred stock** is stock with *preferences*. Usually, this means that holders of preferred stock have priority over holders of common stock as to dividends and to payment on dissolution of the corporation. Preferred stockholders may or may not have the right to vote (the trend is toward giving preferred stockholders the right to vote).

From an investment standpoint, preferred stock is more similar to bonds than to common stock. Preferred shareholders receive periodic dividend payments, usually established as a fixed percentage of the face amount of each preferred share. A share of 6 percent preferred stock with a face amount of $100 per share would pay its owner a $6 dividend each year. Payment of these dividends is not a legal obligation on the part of the firm. Preferred stock is not included among the liabilities of a business, because it is technically equity. Like other equity securities, preferred shares have no fixed maturity date on which they must be retired by the firm. Although occasionally firms retire preferred stock, they are not legally obligated to do so. A sample cumulative convertible preferred-stock certificate is shown in Exhibit 34–5 on the facing page.

6. State corporation law specifies the types of actions for which shareholder approval must be obtained.

Terms and Concepts to Review

alien corporation 689	common stock 697	retained earnings 687
articles of incorporation 688	corporate charter 694	S corporation 690
bond 696	domestic corporation 689	securities 696
bylaw 688	foreign corporation 689	stock 696
certificate of incorporation 694	preferred stock 699	*ultra vires* 688
close corporation 689	promoter 691	
commingle 696	prospectus 691	

Chapter Summary

The Nature of the Corporation	A corporation is a legal entity distinct from its owners. Formal statutory requirements, which vary somewhat from state to state, must be followed in forming a corporation. The corporation can have perpetual existence or be chartered for a specific period of time. **1.** *Corporate parties*—The shareholders own the corporation. They elect a board of directors to govern the corporation. The board of directors hires corporate officers and other employees to run the daily business of the firm. **2.** *Corporate taxation*—The corporation pays income tax on net profits; shareholders pay income tax on the disbursed dividends that they receive from the corporation (double-taxation feature). **3.** *Torts and criminal acts*—The corporation is liable for the torts committed by its agents or officers within the course and scope of their employment (under the doctrine of

CHAPTER SUMMARY—CONTINUED

The Nature of the Corporation—continued	*respondeat superior*). In some circumstances, a corporation can be held liable (and be fined) for the criminal acts of its agents and employees. In certain situations, corporate officers may be held personally liable for corporate crimes.
Corporate Powers	1. *Express powers*—The express powers of a corporation are granted by the following laws and documents (listed according to their priority): federal constitution, state constitutions, state statutes, articles of incorporation, bylaws, and resolutions of the board of directors. 2. *Implied powers*—Barring express constitutional, statutory, or other prohibitions, the corporation has the implied power to do all acts reasonably appropriate and necessary to accomplish its corporate purposes. 3. Ultra vires *doctrine*—Any act of a corporation that is beyond its express or implied powers to undertake is an *ultra vires* act. a. *Ultra vires* contracts may or may not be enforced by the courts, depending on the circumstances. b. The corporation (or shareholders on behalf of the corporation) may sue to enjoin or recover damages for *ultra vires* acts of corporate officers or directors. In addition, the state attorney general may bring an action either to institute an injunction against the transaction or to institute dissolution proceedings against the corporation for *ultra vires* acts.
Classification of Corporations	1. *Domestic, foreign, and alien corporations*—A corporation is referred to as a *domestic corporation* within its home state (the state in which it incorporates). A corporation is referred to as a *foreign corporation* by any state that is not its home state. A corporation is referred to as an alien *corporation* if it originates in another country but does business in the United States. 2. *Public and private corporations*—A public corporation is one formed by government (for example, cities, towns, and public projects). A private corporation is one formed wholly or in part for private benefit. Most corporations are private corporations. 3. *Nonprofit corporations*—Corporations formed without a profit-making purpose (for example, charitable, educational, and religious organizations and hospitals). 4. *Close corporations*—Corporations owned by a family or a relatively small number of individuals; transfer of shares is usually restricted, and the corporation cannot make a public offering of its securities. 5. *S corporations*—Small domestic corporations (must have seventy-five or fewer shareholders as members) that, under Subchapter S of the Internal Revenue Code, are given special tax treatment. These corporations allow shareholders to enjoy the limited legal liability of the corporate form but avoid its double-taxation feature (taxes are paid by shareholders as personal income, and the S corporation is not taxed separately). 6. *Professional corporations*—Corporations formed by professionals (for example, doctors and lawyers) to obtain the benefits of incorporation (such as tax benefits and limited liability). In most situations, the professional corporation is treated as other corporations, but sometimes the courts will disregard the corporate form and treat the shareholders as partners.
Corporate Formation	1. *Promotional activities*—A corporate promoter is one who takes the preliminary steps in organizing a corporation (issues a prospectus, secures the charter, interests investors in the purchase of corporate stock, forms subscription agreements, makes contracts with third parties so that the corporation can immediately begin doing business, and so on). 2. *Incorporation procedures*— a. A state in which to incorporate is selected. b. The articles of incorporation are prepared and filed. The articles generally should include the corporate name, duration, nature and purpose, capital structure, internal organization, registered office and agent, and incorporators. c. The certificate of incorporation (or charter), which authorizes the corporation to conduct business, is received from the appropriate state office (usually the secretary of state) after the articles of incorporation have been filed.

CHAPTER SUMMARY—CONTINUED

Corporate Formation—continued	**d.** The first organizational meeting is held after the charter is granted. The board of directors is elected and other business completed (bylaws passed, stock issued, and so on).
Improper Incorporation	**1.** De jure *or* de facto *corporation*—If a corporation has been improperly incorporated, courts will sometimes impute corporate status to the firm by holding that the firm is a *de jure* corporation (cannot be challenged by the state or third persons) or a *de facto* corporation (can be challenged by the state but not by third persons). **2.** *Corporation by estoppel*—If a firm is neither a *de jure* nor a *de facto* corporation but represents itself to be a corporation and is sued as such by a third party, it may be held to be a corporation by estoppel.
Disregarding the Corporate Entity	To avoid injustice, courts may "pierce the corporate veil" and hold a shareholder or shareholders personally liable for a judgment against the corporation. This usually occurs only when the corporation was established to circumvent the law, when the corporate form is used for an illegitimate or fraudulent purpose, or when the controlling shareholder commingles his or her own interests with those of the corporation to such an extent that the corporation no longer has a separate identity.
Corporate Financing—Bonds	Corporate bonds are securities representing *corporate debt*—money borrowed by a corporation. See Exhibit 34–2 for a list describing the various types of corporate bonds.
Corporate Financing—Stocks	Stocks (see Exhibit 34–4) are equity securities issued by a corporation that represent the purchase of ownership in the business firm. Types of stock include— **1.** *Common stock*—Represents the true ownership of the firm. Holders of common stock share in the control, earning capacity, and net assets of the corporation. Common stockholders carry more risk than preferred stockholders but, if the corporation is successful, are compensated for this risk by greater returns on their investments. **2.** *Preferred stock*—Stock the holders of which have a preferred status. Preferred stockholders have a stronger position than common shareholders with respect to dividends and claims on assets, but as a result, they will not share in the full prosperity of the firm if it grows successfully over time. The return and risk for preferred stock lie somewhere between those for bonds and those for common stock.

CASES FOR ANALYSIS

Westlaw. You can access the full text of each case presented below by going to the Westlaw cases on this text's Web site at http://wbl-cs.westbuslaw.com. Each Westlaw case includes the names of all plaintiffs and defendants, the dates on which the case was argued and decided, a brief summary of the issues and decisions in the case, headnotes classifying specific issues in the case according to the West Key Number System and the court's opinion. Concurring and dissenting opinions, if any, are included as well.

CASE 34.1 CORPORATE TAXATION

BULLINGTON V. PALANGIO

Arkansas Supreme Court, 2001.
345 Ark. 320,
45 S.W.3d 834.

RAY THORNTON, Justice.

Appellant, Jerry Bullington, doing business as Bullington Builders, Inc., appeals the January 27, 2000, judgment of [an Arkansas state court], finding him individually liable to appellee, Helen Palangio, and awarding damages to appellee in the amount of $19,000.00. Appellant [argues that] the trial court erred in allowing the jury to impose personal liability upon appellant * * * . We find no reversible error and affirm.

On July 9, 1994, the parties entered into a contract for the construction of appellee's new residence in Damascus [Arkansas]. The contract was signed on July 11, 1994, and is entitled "Bullington Builders, Inc." at the top of the contract, but is entitled "Jerry Bullington" at the upper right-hand corner. The language of the contract provides that the contract is between "Jerry Bullington, d/b/a Bullington Builders, Inc." and "Helen Palangio." The contract was executed by Jerry Bullington, d/b/a Bullington Builders, Inc., and does not indicate any official capacity as a corporate officer.

Bullington Builders, Inc. ("Corporation"), was incorporated on December 29, 1993. The Corporation's only stockholders were appellant, who managed the business, and appellant's wife. The Corporation failed to pay its franchise taxes, and its charter was revoked approximately one and one-half months before the completion of construction on appellee's home. The Corporation's charter was not reinstated.

The contract provides for a one-year express warranty for workmanship and materials beyond normal wear and tear. The contract further states that the "[c]ontractor will expedite work in a timely manner without sacrificing quality. *Quality will not be sacrificed under any circumstances.*" The contract is silent with regard to implied warranties of habitability and proper construction.

Following completion of the residence, appellant sought to remedy appellee's complaints about the construction, but she was not satisfied. After more than one year had passed, appellee contracted with another builder to remedy the defects she alleged.

On October 15, 1997, following the completion of these repairs, appellee brought this action against Jerry Bullington, d/b/a Bullington Builders, Inc., alleging negligence, breach of implied warranty, and breach of contract. Specifically, appellee alleged various acts of negligent construction, including negligent construction of steps from the garage into the house, negligent construction of the concrete driveway, negligent construction of the attic, negligent construction of support piers, and various instances of negligence pertaining to cosmetic features of the house. On December 10, 1998, the complaint was amended to include Bullington personally as a defendant, asserting that the corporate entity did not shield him from personal liability for negligence, breach of implied warranties, and breach of contract, and asking the court to hold him and the Corporation jointly and severally liable for appellee's damages. The complaint was further amended to allege that appellant failed to follow the plan provided by appellee as set out in the contract between the parties, amounting to breach of contract.

At the conclusion of the trial, the jury returned a general verdict, finding appellant individually liable to appellee and awarding damages of $19,000.00 to her. The jury found no liability with regard to the Corporation. The trial court entered judgment in accordance with the jury verdict, and appellant brings this appeal.

* * * *

* * * [Arkansas Code Annotated Section] 26-54-104(a) provides, in relevant part: "(a) Every corporation shall file an annual franchise tax report and pay an annual franchise tax, unless exempted under [Section] 26-54-105 * * * ." Additionally, Ark.Code Ann. [Section] 26-54-111(a) provides:

> (a) On or before January 1 of each year, the Secretary of State shall issue a proclamation proclaiming as forfeited the corporate charters or authorities, as the case may be, of all corporations, both domestic and foreign which, according to his records, are delinquent in the payment of the annual franchise tax for any prior year.

Finally, Ark.Code Ann. [Section] 4-27-1420 provides:

> The Secretary of State may commence a proceeding under [Section] 4-27-1421 to administratively dissolve a corporation if:
> 1. The corporation does not pay within sixty (60) days after they are due any franchise taxes or penalties imposed by this chapter or other law. * * *

Reading these statutory provisions together, *it is clear that our statutory law imposes an affirmative duty on the corporation to file franchise tax forms and pay the corresponding fees in order to maintain its corporate status.* [Emphasis added.]

In addition to our statutory law, we have well-established case law regarding the issue of whether personal liability attaches [arises] for liabilities that arise if a corporate charter is not perfected or is revoked. * * * [T]o exempt any association of persons from personal liability for the debts of a proposed corporation, they must comply fully with the act under which the corporation is created and that partial compliance with the act is not sufficient.

* * * [T]he reasoning behind cases holding officers and stockholders individually liable for obligations that arise during the operation of a corporation when the corporate charter has been revoked for nonpayment of franchise taxes is that they ought not be allowed to avoid personal liability because of their nonfeasance.

* * * *

In the instant case, it is undisputed that the corporate charter of Bullington Builders, Inc., was revoked for failure to pay franchise taxes approximately one and one-half months prior to the completion of construction, and the charter was not reinstated. After the corporate charter was revoked, appellant individually assumed the performance of the contract. * * * [W]e hold that appellant was personally liable for any liabilities that resulted from faulty or incomplete performance of the contract, including those arising as breaches of express or implied warranties.

CASE 34.2 TRANSFER OF SHARES IN CLOSE CORPORATIONS

CROWDER CONSTRUCTION CO. V. KISER

Court of Appeals of North Carolina, 1999.
134 N.C.App. 190,
517 S.E.2d 178.

HORTON, Judge.

* * * *

Crowder Construction Company was founded in the 1940's by O. P. and W. T. Crowder, Sr., and was incorporated as a North Carolina corporation on 28 May 1953. Stock in the Company has always been closely held by members of the Crowder family and by certain key employees. Since at least 1955, a shareholders' restriction agreement has provided that shareholders who wish to sell their shares of stock in the Company must first offer the shares to the Company at a price based on the book value of the shares. The various shareholders' agreements have also included a "buy-out" provision requiring that the Company purchase the shares of stock at book value * * * . [Eugene] Kiser is a certified public accountant (CPA) who was hired by Crowder in 1981 as its corporate Controller. Kiser was elected Vice-President of Finance (later, Chief Financial Officer) and Corporate Secretary in or about 1985, and served in those capacities until his discharge in 1995.

In 1986, the Company developed a stock option plan for key employees. Those employees, including Kiser, were allowed to purchase Crowder stock at $7.00 per share, a substantial discount from the then book value of $31.83 per share. Kiser purchased 2,000 shares under the 1986 plan, an investment of $14,000.00. In 1988, a second stock option plan was adopted. Again, Kiser and other key employees were allowed to purchase Crowder stock at $7.00 per share, again a substantial discount from the book value of $44.83 per share. Kiser purchased 4,750 shares of Company stock at $7.00 per share, for a total investment of $33,250.00. * * *

* * * *

Both plans also provided * * * that in order for an employee to receive full book value for his shares, the employee must have maintained an employment relationship with the corporation for at least seven years since the issuance of the stock to the employee pursuant to the stock option plans. * * * In 1991, all shareholders, including Kiser, executed a Revised and Restated Stock Restriction and Purchase Agreement (the 1991 Agreement), superseding all previous agreements. The 1991 Agreement provided in pertinent part that a terminated Company shareholder must offer his shares of stock to the Company, and the Company must purchase the shares at a price [based on the "adjusted book value"] determined by use of a formula set out in the agreement. * * *

* * * *

In the case of shares issued pursuant to the 1988 option agreement, and held by an employee less than seven years at the time of termination of the employee's employment with the Company, the [price was less].

* * * *

By the end of 1994, working relations between Kiser and Otis Crowder had become very bad. Otis Crowder and his brother owned about 70% of the outstanding shares of Company stock. In early 1995, the Company decided to terminate Kiser's employment effective 23 January 1995. Kiser's employment was in fact terminated on that date, and he was formally removed as Vice-President and Secretary by the Company's Board of Directors on 3 February 1995.

When he was terminated, the shares of stock issued to Kiser pursuant to the exercise of his 1988 stock options had not fully vested, but his shares issued pursuant to the 1986 stock option plan had been issued more than seven years and had fully vested. On the 1986 shares, Kiser was entitled to receive the full adjusted book value of $56.42 per share, for a total of $112,840.00, a substantial gain over his original investment of $14,000.00. Because the 1988 shares were not fully vested, however, Kiser was only entitled under the terms of the 1991 Agreement to receive $18.59 per share for a total of $88,302.50, an increase of $55,052.50 over his initial investment. However, had Kiser remained an employee of the corporation an additional seven months, he would have been fully vested in the shares issued to him in 1988, and entitled to receive the full adjusted book value for those shares, an additional $180,000.00. The Company tendered payment, but Kiser refused to sell his stock to the Company in accordance with the 1991 Agreement. The Company then instituted this action [in a North Carolina state court against Kiser] to force defendant's specific compliance with the 1991 Agreement. Kiser contested the action, contending that [among other things] enforcement of the 1991 Agreement would be unconscionable * * * . On 10 March 1998, the trial court granted the plaintiff Company's motion for summary judgment, and Kiser appealed.

* * * *

* * * In family owned corporations, or other corporations in which all shares of stock are held by a relatively small number of shareholders, it is not unusual for all shareholders to agree that the corporation, or the other shareholders, will be given the first opportunity to purchase the shares of a terminated or retiring shareholder. This agreement is valid under the North Carolina Corporations Act provided it is "reasonable" and is not "unconscionable under the circumstances." These restrictions allow shareholders to choose their business associates, to restrict ownership to family members, and to ensure congenial and knowledgeable associates. Present or potential business competitors are prevented from purchasing shares and thereby becoming familiar with the corporation's financial condition and future plans. There are also important tax planning reasons for the restrictions * * * .

Since such restrictions make it even more difficult to dispose of minority stock interests in a closely held corporation, these agreements often contain some version of mandatory "buy-out" provisions to ensure shareholders a ready market for their shares where there otherwise might not be one. * * * For that reason, the buy-out agreement will usually set out a simple formula for determining the price to be paid for the employee's shares in order to ensure a prompt, inexpensive resolution of the question of price. Thus, agreements often set out a formula tied to the "book value" of the corporation because that figure is easily ascertained from the corporation's balance sheet. The "book value" of a corporation is generally understood to mean the value of the corporation's total assets less its total liabilities. The net value realized by the computation is equivalent to the total shareholders' equity in the corporation. The net book value per share of common stock is then obtained by dividing the shareholders' equity by the total number of shares of stock outstanding. The 1991 Agreement provided for a determination of the purchase price per share by providing that the firm of certified public accountants providing accounting services to the corporation would adjust the book value per share to account for several possible contingencies related to the Company's bookkeeping practices. * * *

* * * *

Defendant was terminated some seven months before his 1988 stock options would have fully vested. Defendant contends that by prematurely terminating him, plaintiff saved $180,000.00 which defendant would have been due, and that defendant's termination only seven months before he would have been fully vested raises a reasonable inference—and thus a triable issue of fact—that the termination was motivated by plaintiff's desire to avoid paying defendant full value for his shares of stock. We disagree.

Plaintiff met its burden by forecasting evidence to show a reasonable business purpose in terminating defendant. Plaintiff's evidence tends to show that defendant was discharged for openly questioning the ability and competence of Company management to guide the affairs of the Company, resulting in an adversarial relationship between Kiser and other members of management. * * *

Defendant was at all times an employee at will of plaintiff. Nothing in his employment contract, the 1991 Agreement, or 1986 and 1988 stock option agreements guaranteed defendant continued employment with plaintiff. Even assuming, for the sake of argument, that enforcement of the stock purchase agreement would be inequitable if plaintiff had terminated defendant's employment solely to prevent his stock options from fully vesting, defendant comes forward with no evidence to support his bare assertion that he was discharged for an improper purpose. If we were to adopt defendant's position, every employee holding restricted stock subject to a buy-out agreement who is discharged by his or her company prior to the date the shares are fully vested, would, without further proof of improper motive on the part of that company, have raised an issue of material fact which would have to be submitted to a trier of fact for decision. Other than defendant's argument that an inference of wrongful purpose arises from his termination, defendant does not offer any evidence to show there is a genuine question for trial on the issue of his early termination. Plaintiff having offered competent evidence of a justifiable business purpose motivating defendant's termination, and defendant having failed to offer evidence on this issue in opposition to the motion for summary judgment, the trial court properly entered summary judgment on this issue.

* * * *

Affirmed.

CASE 34.3 DISREGARDING THE CORPORATE ENTITY

HOSKINS CHEVROLET, INC. V. HOCHBERG

Appellate Court of Illinois,
First District,
First Division, 1998.
294 Ill.App.3d 550,
691 N.E.2d 28,
229 Ill.Dec. 92.

Presiding Justice *BUCKLEY* delivered the opinion of the court:

* * * *

[Hoskins Chevrolet, Inc.], an Illinois corporation engaged in the sale of automobiles and automobile parts, filed a complaint [in an Illinois state court] for breach of contract * * * against [Ronald Hochberg] alleging that he ordered and received from plaintiff automobile parts valued at $40,198.16 for which he never paid. Defendant filed a motion to dismiss asserting that at all times relevant to plaintiff's complaint he was the president of Diamond Auto Body & Repair, Inc., an Illinois corporation, and that at no time did he conduct business with plaintiff in any capacity other than as the president of the corporation. Plaintiff filed a response, stating that the invoices it sent for the automobile parts were in the name of Diamond Auto Construction and that payment was always made to plaintiff with checks drawn on the bank account of Diamond Auto Construction. Defendant's motion to dismiss was denied.

Defendant filed an answer in which he admitted that he received all of the automobile parts at issue, but only as president of a corporation and not individually or doing business as Diamond Auto Construction. * * * His answer asserted as an affirmative defense that Diamond Auto Construction was at all times material to plaintiff's complaint the "operating name" of the corporation and that he was the president of the corporation.

Plaintiff filed a motion for summary judgment asserting that at all pertinent times, it had done business with defendant and Diamond Auto Construction, and Diamond Auto Construction was not a corporation nor had it ever been registered with the Illinois Secretary of State as the assumed name of a corporation * * * . In support of its motion, plaintiff noted that defendant admitted in his answer that parts were purchased under the name Diamond Auto Construction and that the invoices attached to the complaint were true and correct copies of Diamond Auto Construction's account. Plaintiff also noted that because defendant failed to respond to plaintiff's request for admission of facts, defendant was deemed to have admitted that Diamond Auto Construction was neither incorporated nor registered as an assumed name of a corporation. Plaintiff asserted that because the amount owing was undisputed, the only issue before the court was whether defendant, as the principal of Diamond Auto Construction, was individually liable for the debt. Plaintiff attached copies of checks written to plaintiff from the checking account of Diamond Auto Construction and invoices sent by plaintiff to Diamond Auto Construction.

Defendant filed a response asserting that Illinois law provides that a corporation's use of an unauthorized name does not impose vicarious [indirect] liability upon the corporation's shareholders or officers. He stated that plaintiff knew from the beginning that he represented a corporation and, therefore, was estopped from pursuing him individually on the debt. In support of his assertion, he noted plaintiff's admission in its answer to defendant's request to admit that defendant had applied for credit with plaintiff as president of Diamond Auto Construction and in the application had described Diamond Auto Construction as a corporation. * * *

Plaintiff filed a reply, asserting that it was not its knowledge or belief that determined whether Diamond Auto Construction was a corporation, but Illinois law. Plaintiff claimed that according to defendant's argument, no individual would ever have to incorporate in order to receive the benefits of limited liability because, as long as he represented to others that he was a corporation, others would be estopped from treating him otherwise.

After a hearing, the trial court granted plaintiff's motion for summary judgment and found that defendant owed plaintiff the amount of $28,198.16 plus costs. [Hochberg appealed to a state intermediate appellate court.]

* * * *

The [Illinois] Business Corporations Act (the Act) permits a corporation to elect to adopt an assumed name provided that certain procedures are followed. Where those procedures are not followed, the corporation is required to conduct business under its corporate name. However, the Act provides that a corporation may use the "name of a division, not separately incorporated * * * provided the corporation also clearly discloses its corporate name." The use of an assumed name without complying with the Act or disclosing the corporate name neither creates a legal entity nor does it inform creditors of the existence of the "parent" corporation.

In the case at bar, defendant admitted that Diamond Auto Body & Repair, Inc., used the assumed name of Diamond Auto Construction without complying with the filing requirements of the Act. Further, the record contains no evidence that while using the assumed name in his dealings with plaintiff, defendant also disclosed the corporate name as required by * * * the Act. Accordingly, we find no error in the trial court's determination that under the Act, Diamond Auto Construction was neither a corporation nor the assumed name of a corporation for purposes of establishing contract liability in anyone other than defendant.

* * * *

* * * An organization which is not technically a corporation because of the failure to meet some statutory requirement will be recognized as a *de facto* corporation if there is a valid law under which it may be organized, a good-faith effort to organize under the law, * * * [an] apparent compliance with the law, and if the organization is a user of corporate powers. A person who contracts with an entity while the entity is acting as a *de facto* corporation, and who contracts with it as an organized corporation, is estopped from denying its corporate status at the time the parties entered into the agreement. If the organization was not a *de facto* corporation, however, there is no estoppel to deny its corporate existence.

Here, * * * we find that defendant presented no evidence of a good-faith effort to comply with the statutory formalities of the Act for either creating a corporation or operating under an assumed name. Accordingly, Diamond Auto Construction was not a *de facto* corporation and plaintiff was not estopped to deny its corporate existence.

For these reasons, the order of the [trial] court * * * granting summary judgment in favor of plaintiff is affirmed.

Affirmed.

Case Problems

34–1. The defendant, Cohen, Stracher & Bloom, P.C., a law firm organized as a professional corporation under New York law, entered into an agreement with the plaintiff, We're Associates Co., for the lease of office space located in Lake Success, New York. The lease was signed for We're Associates by one of the partners of the plaintiff's company and for the defendant professional corporation by Paul J. Bloom, as vice president. Bloom and the other two defendants, Cohen and Stracher, were the sole officers, directors, and shareholders of the professional corporation. The corporation became delinquent in paying its rent, and the plaintiff brought an action to recover rents and other charges of approximately $9,000 alleged to be due and owing under the lease. The complaint was filed against the professional corporation and each individual shareholder of the corporation. The shareholders moved to dismiss the action against them individually. Will the court grant their motion? Discuss. [*We're Associates Co. v. Cohen, Stracher & Bloom, P.C.*, 103 A.D.2d 130, 478 N.Y.S.2d 670 (1984)]

34–2. Pat Daniels, John Daniels, and Bill Mandell (the defendants) planned to purchase a tavern and restaurant business in St. Charles, Illinois, and to organize their business in the form of a corporation under the name D&M, Inc. The defendants negotiated with Howard Realty Group to lease the premises on which the tavern and restaurant were located. While the sale of the business and the negotiation of the lease were proceeding, neither the seller of the business nor Howard contemplated personal guaranties from the defendants. On January 18, 1987, although D&M had not yet been incorporated, the lease was signed in the name of D&M, Inc., by Pat Daniels and Bill Mandell, in their capacity as president and secretary, respectively, of the future corporation. On February 11, 1987, the defendants filed the articles of incorporation for D&M with the secretary of state. The articles were returned by the secretary of state's office because the name "D&M, Inc." was already in use by another Illinois corporation. The defendants then decided to file the articles of incorporation under the name The Lodge at Tin Cup Pass, Inc. (the Lodge). They first checked with the landlord to see if they could use that name, because it was similar to the name of the property, Tin Cup Pass. The Lodge was duly incorporated on March 5, 1987. In late 1988, when the Lodge defaulted on its lease payments, Tin Cup Pass Limited Partnership, to whom Howard had assigned the lease, sued the defendants personally to recover the lease payments due, alleging that the defendants should be held liable as corporate promoters for D&M, Inc., a corporation that was never formed. What will result in court? Discuss fully. [*Tin Cup Pass Limited Partnership v. Daniels,* 195 Ill.App.3d 847, 553 N.E.2d 82, 142 Ill.Dec. 732 (1990)]

34–3. In the early 1950s, Mary Emmons opened an account at M & M Wholesale Florist, Inc., to purchase flowers and florist supplies for her flower shop, called Bay Minette Flower Shop, which she operated as a sole proprietorship. In 1973, the flower shop was incorporated as Bay Minette Flower Shop, Inc. Emmons continued to order supplies from M & M, as did her son when he began to manage the day-to-day operations of the shop during the 1980s. M & M, which had no knowledge that Bay Minette was now a corporation, sued Emmons and her son personally to recover a balance owing on the Bay Minette account (for purchases made after Bay Minette had incorporated). Is the fact that M & M was never informed of the subsequent incorporation of the Bay Minette Flower Shop a sufficient ground for piercing the corporate veil and holding Emmons and her son personally liable for the debt? Explain. [*M & M Wholesale Florist, Inc. v. Emmons,* 600 So.2d 998 (Ala. 1992)]

34–4. Joe Alexander contracted with Robert Harris for the sale of Harris's business on February 1, 1988. Alexander purported to act on behalf of J & R Construction (J & R), a newly formed corporation. As the incorporators, Joe and Rita Alexander and Avanell Looney signed the articles of incorporation for J & R on the same day that Joe contracted with Harris. The articles were not filed with the secretary of state, however, until February 3. When J & R defaulted on its payments due under the contract with Harris in 1991, Harris sued the Alexanders and Looney personally for the $49,696.21 still owed. The trial court held Joe Alexander personally liable for the debt (because he had signed the contract with Harris) but not Rita Alexander or Avanell Looney. The relevant state statute imposes joint and several liability on those purporting to act as, or on behalf of, a corporation while knowing that the corporation has not yet come into existence. On appeal, Harris argued that because the Alexanders and Looney acted on behalf of J & R while knowing that no corporation existed, all three incorporators should be held jointly and severally liable as partners. Did Rita Alexander and Avanell Looney also "act as, or on behalf of," the corporation? On appeal, how should the court decide? [*Harris v. Looney,* 43 Ark.App. 127, 862 S.W.2d 282 (1993)]

34–5. Leslie R. Barth was the president of five corporations. During the course of an investigation for failure to file corporate and personal income tax returns, the Internal Revenue Service (IRS) served an administrative summons for Barth to turn over prescribed corporate records. Barth only partially complied, and the IRS took him to court. The court ordered the corporations to furnish the requested information and to designate an agent to testify for the corporations "without revoking their personal privileges against self-incrimination." Barth appealed the order, claiming that such an order violated the "agent's" (his) constitutional right against self-incrimination and that Fifth Amendment protection against self-incrimination extended to the corporations. Discuss whether the corporations did possess Fifth Amendment privileges against self-incrimination and whether Barth's such privilege as an individual officer, was denied by the district court's order. [*United States v. Barth,* 745 F.2d 184 (2d Cir. 1984)]

34–6. Charles Wolfe was the sole shareholder and president of Wolfe & Co., a firm that leased tractor-trailers. The corporation had no separate bank account. Banking transactions were conducted through Wolfe's personal accounts, and employees were paid from them. Wolfe never consulted with any other corporate directors. During the tax years 1974–1976, the corporation incurred $114,472.91 in federal tax liabilities. The government held Wolfe personally liable for the taxes. Wolfe paid the tax bill and then brought an action against the government for disregarding his corporate entity. Discuss whether the government can "pierce the corporate veil" in Wolfe's case and hold Wolfe personally liable for corporate taxes. [*Wolfe v. United States,* 798 F.2d 124 (9th Cir. 1961)]

34–7. Hamfab Credit Union (HCU) borrowed from the Ohio Central Credit Union, Inc. (OCCU), in a series of loans, a total of $550,000. This amount exceeded 25 percent of HCU's capital and surplus, which was in violation of Ohio state law. The statute in question provided that "[a] credit union may not borrow money in excess of twenty-five per cent of its unimpaired capital and surplus, without prior specific authorization by the supervisor." HCU had not received any such authorization. When HCU became insolvent, Wagner was appointed as the liquidator (a person who winds up the financial affairs of a dissolved corporation). Wagner refused to pay the full amount of the debt owed to OCCU, claiming that some of the loans had been made in violation of state law and therefore OCCU had acted *ultra vires* in making the loans. Did Wagner succeed in this defense? Explain. [*Ohio Central Credit Union, Inc. v. Wagner,* 67 Ohio App.2d 138, 426 N.E.2d 198 (1980)]

34–8. Skandinavia, Inc., manufactured and sold polypropylene underwear. Following two years of poor sales, Skandinavia entered into negotiations to sell the business to Odilon Cormier, an experienced textile manufacturer. Skandinavia and Cormier agreed that Cormier would take Skandinavia's underwear inventory and use it in a new corporation, which would be called Polypro, Inc. In return, Skandinavia would receive a commission on future sales from Polypro. Polypro was subsequently established and began selling the underwear. Skandinavia, however, never received any commissions from the sales. It therefore brought suit against Polypro and Cormier to recover its promised commissions. The claim against Polypro was dismissed by the trial court, but the court found Cormier to be personally liable for the commissions owed. Cormier appealed to the Supreme Court of New Hampshire. Is Cormier personally liable for the contract he signed in the course of setting up a new corporation? Discuss. [*Skandinavia, Inc. v. Cormier,* 128 N.H. 215, 214 A.2d 1250 (1986)]

34–9. The Midtown Club, Inc., was a nonprofit corporation; its certificate of incorporation stated that the sole purpose of the club was "to provide facilities for the serving of luncheon or other meals to members." Samuel Cross, a member of the club, brought a female guest to lunch at the club, but he and his friend were both refused seating. On several occasions, Cross made applications on behalf of females for their admission to the club, but the club either ignored or rejected them. Cross brought an action against the club, alleging that the club's actions were *ultra vires.* Did he succeed? Explain. [*Cross v. Midtown Club, Inc.,* 33 Conn.Supp. 150, 365 A.2d 127 (1976)]

34–10. Moseley Group Management Co. (MGM) provided management services to apartment complexes. MGM's only assets were equipment worth $500 and a bank account with an average balance of $1,500. Richard Moseley ran the company and owned half of the stock. MGM contracted with Property Tax Research

Co. (PTR) to obtain a lower property tax assessment on one of its complexes. PTR performed, but MGM refused to pay and transferred its assets and employees to Terrace Management, Inc., a corporation controlled by Moseley. PTR filed a suit in a Missouri state court against Moseley and others to recover the unpaid fees. Should the court pierce the corporate veil and hold Moseley personally liable for the debt? If so, on what basis? [*Sansone v. Moseley,* 912 S.W.2d 666 (Mo.App.W.D. 1995)]

34–11. Soda Dispensing Systems, Inc., was owned by two shareholders, each of whom owned half of the stock. One shareholder was president of the corporation, and the other was vice president. Their shareholder agreement stated that neither shareholder could "encumber any corporate property . . . without the written consent of the other." When Soda Dispensing went out of business, the two shareholders agreed to sell the assets, split the proceeds, and pay $9,900 to their accountants, Cooper, Selvin & Strassberg. Later, the president committed Soda Dispensing to pay Cooper, Selvin more than $24,000, claiming that he had the authority, as president, to make that commitment. When the accountants tried to collect, the vice president objected, asserting that the president had exceeded his authority. Will the court order Soda Dispensing to pay? Explain. [*Cooper, Selvin & Strassberg v. Soda Dispensing Systems, Inc.,* 212 A.D.2d 498, 622 N.Y.S.2d 312 (1995)]

34–12. Cecil Hill was in the construction trade. He did business as "C&M Builders, Inc.," although there was no such corporation. County Concrete Co. supplied "C&M Builders, Inc." with over $50,000 worth of concrete for which it was not paid. The supplier filed a suit in a Maryland state court against Hill personally. Hill argued that because the supplier thought it was doing business with a corporate entity, C&M was a *de facto* corporation, and thus Hill was not personally liable. Should Hill be allowed to avoid liability on this basis? Why, or why not? [*Hill v. County Concrete Co.,* 108 Md.App. 527, 672 A.2d 667 (1996)]

34–13. Steven and Janis Gimbert leased a warehouse to a manufacturing business owned by Manzar Zuberi. Zuberi signed the lease as the purported representative of "ATM Manufacturing, Inc.," which was a nonexistent corporation. Zuberi was actually the president of two existing corporations, ATM Enterprises, Inc., and Ameri-Pak International. Under the Ameri-Pak name, Zuberi manufactured a household cleaning product in the Gimberts' warehouse. The use of hydrochloric acid in the operations severely damaged the premises, and the Gimberts filed a suit in a Georgia state court against Zuberi personally to collect for the damage. On what basis might Zuberi be held personally liable? Discuss fully. [*Zuberi v. Gimbert,* 230 Ga.App. 471, 496 S.E.2d 741 (1998)]

34–14. James, Randolph, and Judith Agley, and Michael and Nancy Timmis were shareholders in F & M Distributors, Inc., Venture Packaging, Inc., and Diamond Automations, Inc. James Agley was also a shareholder in Middletown Aerospace. All of the firms were S corporations organized and located in Michigan and doing business in Ohio. None of the shareholders was a resident of Ohio, and none of them personally did business in Ohio. Between 1988 and 1992, the Agleys and the Timmises included their prorated share of the S corporations' income on Ohio personal income tax returns. They believed, however, that an out-of-state shareholder should not be taxed in Ohio on the income that he or she receives from an S corporation doing business in Ohio. They contended it is the S corporation that earns the income, not the shareholder. They also emphasized that none of them personally did business in the state. Finally, they asked the Ohio Tax Commissioner for refunds for those years. Should the state grant their request? Why or why not? [*Agley v. Tracy,* 87 Ohio St.3d 265, 719 N.E.2d 951 (1999)]

34–15. William Soerries was the sole shareholder of Chickasaw Club, Inc., which operated a popular nightclub of the same name in Columbus, Georgia. Soerries maintained corporate checking accounts, but he paid his employees, suppliers, and entertainers in cash out of the club's proceeds. He owned the property on which the club was located and rented it to the club, but also made the mortgage payments out of the club's proceeds. Soerries often paid corporate expenses out of his personal funds. At 11:45 P.M. on July 31, 1996, eighteen-year-old Aubrey Lynn Pursley, who was already intoxicated, entered the Chickasaw Club. A city ordinance prohibited individuals under the age of twenty-one from entering nightclubs, but Chickasaw employees did not check Pursley's identification. Pursley drank more alcohol and was visibly intoxicated when she left the club at 3:00 A.M. with a beer in her hand. Shortly afterward, Pursley was killed when she lost control of her car and struck a tree. Joseph Dancause, Pursley's stepfather, filed a suit in a Georgia state court against Chickasaw Club, Inc., and Soerries for damages. Can Soerries be held personally liable? If so, on what basis? Explain. [*Soerries v. Dancause,* 546 S.E.2d 356 (Ga.App. 2001)]

E-LINKS

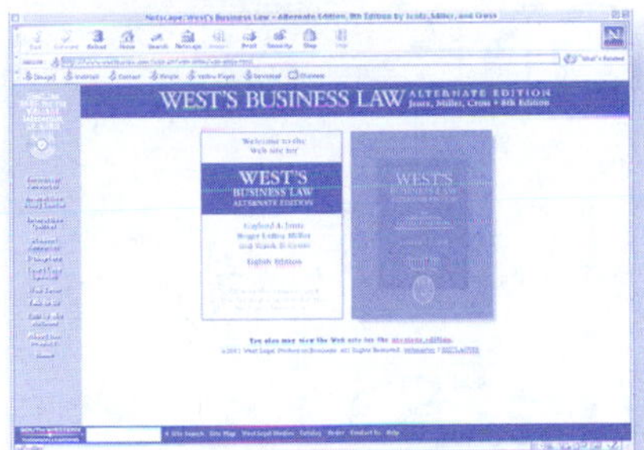

For updated links to resources available on the Web, as well as a variety of other materials, visit this text's Web site at

http://wbl-cs.westbuslaw.com

Cornell University's Legal Information Institute has links to state corporation statutes at

http://fatty.law.cornell.edu/topics/state_statutes.html

For an example of one state's (Florida's) statute governing corporations, go to

http://www.ilrg.com/whatsnews/statute.html

and scroll down the page to "Corporations."

The Center for Corporate Law at the University of Cincinnati College of Law is a good source of information on corporate law. Go to

http://www.law.uc.edu/CCL

For information on incorporation, including a list of "frequently asked questions" on this topic, go to

http://www.bizfilings.com

LEGAL RESEARCH EXERCISES ON THE WEB

Go to http://wbl-cs.westbuslaw.com, the Web site that accompanies this text. Select "Interactive Study Center," and then click on "Chapter 34." There you will find the following Internet research exercise that you can perform to learn more about the law governing corporations:

Activity 34–1: Corporate Law

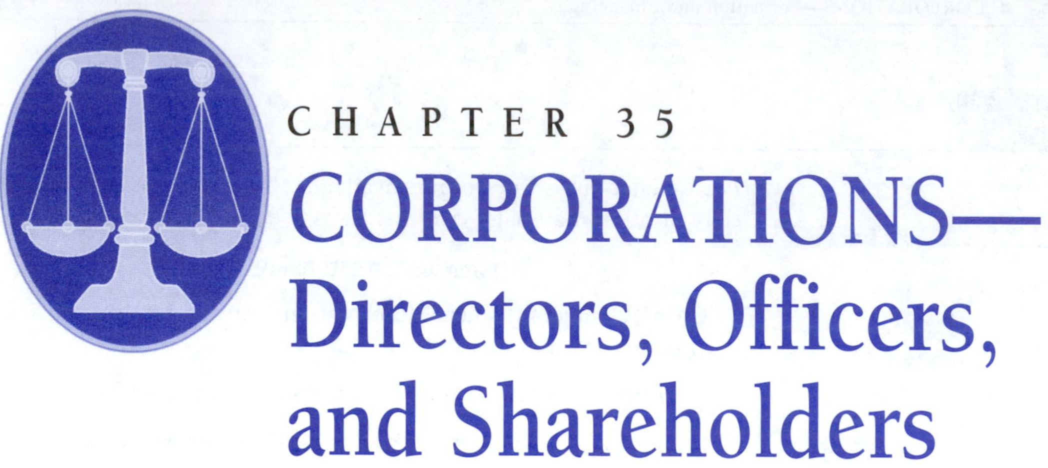

CHAPTER 35 CORPORATIONS—Directors, Officers, and Shareholders

CORPORATE DIRECTORS, OFFICERS, and shareholders all play different roles within the corporate entity. Sometimes, actions that may benefit the corporation as a whole do not coincide with the separate interests of the individuals making up the corporation. In such situations, it is important to know the rights and duties of all participants in the corporate enterprise. This chapter focuses on these rights and duties and the ways in which conflicts among corporate participants are resolved.

SECTION 1

Role of Directors

Every corporation is governed by a board of directors. A director occupies a position of responsibility unlike that of other corporate personnel. Directors are sometimes inappropriately characterized as *agents* because they act on behalf of the corporation. No individual director, however, can act as an agent to bind the corporation; and as a group, directors collectively control the corporation in a way that no agent is able to control a principal. Directors are sometimes incorrectly characterized as *trustees* because they occupy positions of trust and control over the corporation. Unlike trustees, however, they do not own or hold title to property for the use and benefit of others.

Few legal requirements exist concerning directors' qualifications. Only a handful of states impose minimum age and residency requirements. A director is sometimes a shareholder, but this is not a necessary qualification—unless, of course, statutory provisions or corporate articles or bylaws require ownership.

ELECTION OF DIRECTORS

Subject to statutory limitations, the number of directors is set forth in the corporation's articles or bylaws. Historically, the minimum number of directors has been three, but today many states permit fewer. Indeed, the Revised Model Business Corporation Act (RMBCA), in Section 8.01, permits corporations with fewer than fifty shareholders to eliminate the board of directors.

The first board of directors is normally appointed by the incorporators on the creation of the corporation, or directors are named by the corporation itself in the articles. The initial board serves until the first annual shareholders' meeting. Subsequent directors are elected by a majority vote of the shareholders.

The term of office for a director is usually one year—from annual meeting to annual meeting. Longer and staggered terms are permissible under most state statutes. A common practice is to elect one-third of the board members each year for a three-year term. In this way, there is greater management continuity.

A director can be removed *for cause* (that is, for failing to perform a required duty), either as specified in the articles or bylaws or by shareholder action. Even the board of directors itself may be given power to remove a director for cause, subject to shareholder review. In most states, unless the shareholders have reserved the right at the time of election, a director cannot be removed without cause.

Vacancies can occur on the board of directors because of death or resignation or when a new position is created through amendment of the articles or bylaws. In these situations, either the shareholders or the board itself can fill the position, depending on state law or on the provisions of the bylaws.

BOARD OF DIRECTORS' MEETINGS

The board of directors conducts business by holding formal meetings with recorded minutes. The date on which regular meetings are held is usually established in the articles or bylaws or by board resolution, and no further notice is customarily required. Special meetings can be called, with notice sent to all directors.

Quorum requirements can vary among jurisdictions. (A **quorum** is the minimum number of members of a body of officials or other group that must be present in order for business to be validly transacted.) Many states leave the decision as to quorum requirements to the corporate articles or bylaws. In the absence of specific state statutes, most states provide that a quorum is a majority of the number of directors authorized in the articles or bylaws. Voting is done in person (unlike voting at shareholders' meetings, which can be done by proxy, as discussed later in this chapter).[1] The rule is one vote per director. Ordinary matters generally require a simple majority vote; certain extraordinary issues may require a greater-than-majority vote.

RIGHTS OF DIRECTORS

A director of a corporation has a number of rights, including the rights of participation, inspection, compensation, and indemnification.

Participation and Inspection. A corporate director must have certain rights to function properly in that position. The main right is one of participation—meaning that the director must be notified of board of directors' meetings so as to participate in them. As pointed out earlier in this chapter, regular board meetings are usually established by the bylaws or by board resolution, and no notice of these meetings is required. If special meetings are called, however, notice is required unless waived by the director.

A director must have access to all of the corporate books and records to make decisions and to exercise the necessary supervision over corporate officers and employees. This right of inspection is virtually absolute and cannot be restricted.

Compensation and Indemnification. Nominal sums are often paid as honorariums to directors. In many corporations, directors are also chief corporate officers (president or chief executive officer, for example) and receive compensation in their managerial positions. Most directors also gain through indirect benefits, such as business contacts, prestige, and other rewards. There is a trend toward providing more than nominal compensation for directors, especially in large corporations in which directorships can be burdensome in terms of time, work, effort, and risk. Many states permit the corporate articles or bylaws to authorize compensation for directors, and in some cases the board can set its own compensation unless the articles or bylaws provide otherwise.

Corporate directors may become involved in lawsuits by virtue of their positions and their actions as directors. Most states (and RMBCA 8.51) permit a corporation to indemnify (guarantee reimbursement to) a director for legal costs, fees, and judgments involved in defending corporation-related suits. Many states specifically permit a corporation to purchase liability insurance for the directors and officers to cover indemnification. When the statutes are silent on this matter, the authority to purchase such insurance is usually considered to be part of the corporation's implied power.

DIRECTORS' MANAGEMENT RESPONSIBILITIES

Directors have responsibility for all policymaking decisions necessary to the management of all corporate affairs. Just as shareholders cannot act individually to bind the corporation, the directors must act as a body in carrying out routine corporate business. One director has one vote, and customarily the majority rules. The general areas of responsibility of the board of directors include the following:

1. Except in Louisiana, which allows a director to vote by proxy under certain circumstances. Most states, including California, Delaware, and New York, expressly permit companies to hold board meetings by conference call or similar means, as long as all participants can hear one another. To date, only one state—California—permits a board of directors to conduct meetings via electronic video screens.

1. Authorization for major corporate policy decisions—for example, the initiation of proceedings for the sale or lease of corporate assets outside the regular course of business, the determination of new product lines, and the overseeing of major contract negotiations and major management-labor negotiations.
2. Appointment, supervision, and removal of corporate officers and other managerial employees and determination of their compensation.
3. Financial decisions, such as the declaration and payment of dividends to shareholders and the issuance of authorized shares and bonds.

Most states permit the board of directors to elect an executive committee from among the directors to handle the interim management decisions between board of directors' meetings, as provided in the bylaws. The executive committee is limited to making management decisions about ordinary business matters.

The board of directors can delegate some of its functions to an executive committee or to corporate officers. In doing so, the board is not relieved of its overall responsibility for directing the affairs of the corporation, but corporate officers and managerial personnel are empowered to make decisions relating to ordinary, daily corporate affairs within well-defined guidelines.

SECTION 2

Role of Corporate Officers and Executives

Officers and other executive employees are hired by the board of directors or, in rare instances, by the shareholders. In addition to carrying out the duties articulated in the bylaws, corporate and managerial officers act as agents of the corporation, and the ordinary rules of agency (discussed in Chapters 31 and 32) normally apply to their employment. The qualifications required of officers and executive employees are determined at the discretion of the corporation and are included in the articles or bylaws. In most states, a person can hold more than one office and can be both an officer and a director of the corporation.

The rights of corporate officers and other high-level managers are defined by employment contracts, because these persons are employees of the company. Corporate officers, though, can normally be removed by the board of directors at any time with or without cause and regardless of the terms of the employment contracts—although in so doing, the corporation may be liable for breach of contract. The duties of corporate officers are the same as those of directors, because both groups are involved in decision making and are in similar positions of control. Hence, officers and directors are viewed as having the same fiduciary duties of care and loyalty in their conduct of corporate affairs, a subject to which we now turn.

SECTION 3

Fiduciary Duties of Directors and Officers

Directors and officers are deemed fiduciaries of the corporation, because their relationship with the corporation and its shareholders is one of trust and confidence. As fiduciaries, directors and officers owe ethical—and legal—duties to the corporation and the shareholders. These fiduciary duties include the duty of care and the duty of loyalty.

DUTY OF CARE

Directors and officers must exercise due care in performing their duties. The standard of *due care* has been variously described in judicial decisions and codified in many corporation codes. Generally, a director or officer is expected to act in good faith, to exercise the care that an ordinarily prudent person would exercise in similar circumstances, and to act in what he or she considers to be the best interests of the corporation [RMBCA 8.30(a)]. Directors and officers who have not exercised the required duty of care can be held liable for the harms suffered by the corporation as a result of their negligence.

Duty to Make Informed and Reasonable Decisions. Directors and officers are expected to be informed on corporate matters. To be informed, a director or officer must do what is necessary to become informed: attend presentations, ask for information from those who have it, read reports, review other written materials such as contracts—in other words, carefully study a situation and its alternatives. Depending on the nature of the business, directors and officers are often expected to act in accordance with their own knowledge and training. Most states and Section 8.30(b) of the RMBCA, however, allow a director to make decisions in reliance on information furnished by competent officers or employees, professionals such as attorneys and accountants, or even an executive committee of the board without being accused of acting in bad faith or failing to exercise due care if such information turns out to be faulty.

Directors are also expected to make reasonable decisions. For example, a director should not accept a tender offer (an offer to purchase shares in the company that is made by another company directly to the shareholders) with only a moment's consideration based solely on the price per share offered by the group making the tender offer.

Duty to Exercise Reasonable Supervision. Directors are also expected to exercise a reasonable amount of supervision when they delegate work to corporate officers and employees. For example, suppose that a corporate bank director fails to attend any board of directors' meetings for five years, never inspects any of the corporate books or records, and generally neglects to supervise the efforts of the bank president and the loan committee. Meanwhile, a corporate officer, the bank president, makes various improper loans and permits large overdrafts. In this situation, the corporate director may be held liable to the corporation for losses resulting from the unsupervised actions of the bank president and the loan committee.

Dissenting Directors. Directors are expected to attend board of directors' meetings, and their votes should be entered into the minutes of corporate meetings. Unless a dissent is entered, the director is presumed to have assented. Directors who dissent are rarely held individually liable for mismanagement of the corporation. For this reason, a director who is absent from a given meeting sometimes registers with the secretary of the board a dissent to actions taken at the meeting.

Duty of Loyalty

Loyalty can be defined as faithfulness to one's obligations and duties. In the corporate context, the duty of loyalty requires directors and officers to subordinate their personal interests to the welfare of the corporation.

For example, directors may not use corporate funds or confidential corporate information for personal advantage. Similarly, they must refrain from putting their personal interests above those of the corporation. For instance, a director should not oppose a transaction that is in the corporation's best interest simply because its acceptance may cost the director her or his position. Cases dealing with fiduciary duty typically involve one or more of the following:

1. Competing with the corporation.
2. Usurping (taking personal advantage of) a corporate opportunity.
3. Having an interest that conflicts with the interest of the corporation.
4. Engaging in insider trading (using information that is not public to make a profit trading securities, as discussed in Chapter 37).
5. Authorizing a corporate transaction that is detrimental to minority shareholders.
6. Selling control over the corporation.

See Case 35.1 at the end of this chapter. To view the full, unedited case from Westlaw,® go to this text's Web site at **http://wbl-cs.westbuslaw.com**.

Conflicts of Interest

Corporate directors often have many business affiliations, and a director can sit on the board of more than one corporation. Of course, directors are precluded from entering into or supporting businesses that operate in direct competition with corporations on whose boards they serve. Their fiduciary duty requires them to make a full disclosure of any potential conflicts of interest that might arise in any corporate transaction [RMBCA 8.60].

Sometimes a corporation enters into a contract or engages in a transaction in which an officer or director has a personal interest. The director or officer must make a *full disclosure* of that interest and must abstain from voting on the proposed transaction. For example, Ballo Corporation needs office space. Stephan Colson, one of its five directors, owns the building adjoining the corporation's headquarters. He negotiates a lease with Ballo for the space, making a full disclosure to Ballo and the other four board directors. The lease arrangement is fair and reasonable, and it is unanimously approved by the other members of the corporation's board of directors. In such a case, the contract is valid. The rule is one of reason; otherwise, directors would be prevented from ever giving financial assistance to the corporations they serve.

State statutes contain different standards, but a contract will generally not be voidable if it was fair and reasonable to the corporation at the time it was made, if there was a full disclosure of the interest of the officers or directors involved in the transaction, and if the contract was approved by a majority of the disinterested directors or shareholders [RMBCA 8.62].

Often, contracts are negotiated between corporations having one or more directors who are members of both boards. Such transactions require great care, as they are closely scrutinized by the courts. (As will be discussed in Chapter 45, in certain circumstances—if two large corporations are competing with each other, for example—it may constitute a violation of antitrust laws for a director to sit on the boards of both companies.)

SECTION 4

Liability of Directors and Officers

Directors and officers are exposed to liability on many fronts. Corporate directors and officers may be held liable for the crimes and torts committed by themselves or by corporate employees under their supervision, as discussed in Chapters 8 and 34. Additionally, shareholders may perceive that the corporate directors are not acting in the best interests of the corporation and may sue the directors, in what is called a *shareholder's derivative suit,* on behalf of the corporation. (This type of action is discussed later in this chapter, in the context of shareholders' rights.) Directors and officers are expected to exercise due care and to use their best judgment in guiding corporate management; if they do not, they may be held liable to the corporation for any resulting damages.

Under the so-called **business judgment rule**, however, a corporate director or officer may be able to avoid liability to the corporation or to its shareholders for exercising poor business judgment. After all, directors and officers are not insurers of business success, and honest mistakes of judgment and poor business decisions on their part do not automatically make them liable to the corporation. The business judgment rule generally immunizes directors and officers from liability for the consequences of a decision that is within managerial authority, as long as the decision complies with management's fiduciary duties and as long as acting on the decision is within the powers of the corporation. Consequently, if there is a reasonable basis for a business decision, it is unlikely that the court will interfere with that decision, even if the corporation suffers as a result.

To benefit from the rule, directors and officers must act in good faith, in what they consider to be the best interests of the corporation, and with the care that an ordinarily prudent person in a similar position would exercise in like circumstances. This requires an informed decision, with a rational basis, and with no conflict between the decision maker's personal interest and the interest of the corporation.

See Case 35.2 at the end of this chapter. To view the full, unedited case from Westlaw,® go to this text's Web site at **http://wbl-cs.westbuslaw.com**.

SECTION 5

Role of Shareholders

The acquisition of a share of stock makes a person an owner and shareholder in a corporation. Shareholders thus own the corporation. Although they have no legal title to corporate property vested in the corporation, such as buildings and equipment, they do have an *equitable* (ownership) interest in the firm.

As a general rule, shareholders have no responsibility for the daily management of the corporation, although they are ultimately responsible for choosing the board of directors, which does have such control. Ordinarily, corporate officers and other employees owe no direct duty to individual stockholders. Their duty is to the corporation as a whole. A director, however, is in a fiduciary relationship to the corporation and therefore serves the interests of the shareholders in general. Ordinarily, there is no legal relationship between shareholders and creditors of the corporation. Shareholders can, in fact, be creditors of the corporation and have the same rights of recovery against the corporation as any other creditor.

In this section, we look at the powers, rights, and liabilities of shareholders, which may be established in the articles of incorporation and under the state's general incorporation law.

SHAREHOLDERS' POWERS

Shareholders must approve fundamental changes affecting the corporation before the changes can be implemented. Hence, shareholders are empowered to amend the articles of incorporation (charter) and bylaws, approve a merger or the dissolution of the corporation, and approve the sale of all or substantially all of the corporation's assets. Some of these powers are subject to prior board approval.

Election and removal of the board of directors are accomplished by a vote of the shareholders. The first board of directors is either named in the articles of incorporation or chosen by the incorporators to serve until the first shareholders' meeting. From that time on, selection and retention of directors are exclusively shareholder functions.

Directors usually serve their full terms; if they are not satisfactory, they are simply not reelected. Shareholders have the inherent power, however, to remove a director from office *for cause* (breach of duty or misconduct) by a majority vote.[2] Some state statutes even permit removal of directors without cause by the vote of a majority of the holders of outstanding shares entitled to vote.[3] Some corporate charters also expressly provide that shareholders, by majority vote, can remove a director at any time without cause.

SHAREHOLDERS' MEETINGS

Shareholders' meetings must occur at least annually, and in addition, special meetings can be called to handle urgent matters.

Notice of Meetings. Shareholders are notified of the date and hour of a shareholders' meeting in a written announcement that is sent a reasonable length of time prior to the date of the meeting.[4] Notices of special meetings must include a statement of the purpose of the meeting; business transacted at a special meeting is limited to that purpose.

Proxies. Because it usually is not practical for owners of only a few shares of stock of publicly traded corporations to attend a shareholders' meeting, such shareholders normally give third parties written authorization to vote their shares at the meeting. This authorization is called a **proxy** (from the Latin *procurare,* "to manage, take care of"). Proxies are often solicited by management, but any person can solicit proxies to concentrate voting power. Proxies have been used by a group of shareholders as a device for taking over a corporation (corporate takeovers are discussed in Chapter 36). Proxies are normally revocable (that is, they can be withdrawn), unless they are specifically designated as irrevocable. Under RMBCA 7.22(c), proxies last for eleven months.

Proxy Materials and Shareholder Proposals. When shareholders want to change a company policy, they can put their ideas up for a shareholder vote. They can do this by submitting a shareholder proposal to the board of directors and asking the board to include the proposal in the proxy materials that are sent to all shareholders before meetings.

The Securities and Exchange Commission (SEC), which regulates the purchase and sale of securities (see Chapter 37), has special provisions relating to proxies and shareholder proposals. SEC Rule 14a-8 requires that when a company sends proxy materials to its shareholders, the company must also include whatever proposals will be considered at the meeting and provide shareholders with the opportunity to vote on the proposals by marking and returning their proxy cards. SEC Rule 14a-8 provides that all shareholders who own stock worth at least $1,000 are eligible to submit proposals for inclusion in corporate proxy materials.

A corporation is not required to include in proxy materials proposals that relate to "ordinary business operations." Normally, only those proposals that relate to significant policy considerations must be included. Often, however, it is difficult to determine whether a proposal relates to ordinary business activities or significant policy issues. For example, in a 1976 ruling, the SEC stated that shareholder proposals concerning equal opportunity and affirmative action relate to significant policy issues on which shareholders should be allowed to vote.[5] In 1992, however, the SEC reversed its position and ruled that all

2. A director can often demand court review of removal for cause.

3. Most states allow *cumulative voting* (which will be discussed shortly) for directors. If cumulative voting is authorized, a director may not be removed if the number of votes sufficient to elect him or her under cumulative voting is voted against his or her removal. See, for example, California Corporate Code Section 303A. Also see Section 8.08(c) of the RMBCA.

4. The shareholder can waive the requirement of written notice by signing a waiver form [RMBCA 7.06]. A shareholder who does not receive written notice but who learns of the meeting and attends without protesting the lack of notice is said to have waived notice by such conduct. State statutes and corporate bylaws typically set forth the time within which notice must be sent, what methods can be used, and what the notice must contain.

5. *Adoption of Amendments Relating to Proposals by Security Holders,* Exchange Act Release No. 12999, 41 Fed.Reg. 52,994 (December 3, 1976).

employment-related shareholder proposals would be automatically omittable under the "ordinary business" exclusion, even if they raised social policy concerns. In the wake of substantial criticism of its 1992 rule, the SEC again changed its stance. In 1998, the SEC issued a rule that essentially allows such decisions to be made on a case-by-case basis.

SHAREHOLDER VOTING

Shareholders exercise ownership control through the power of their votes. Each common shareholder is entitled to one vote per share, although the voting techniques discussed below all enhance the power of the shareholder's vote. The articles of incorporation can exclude or limit voting rights, particularly to certain classes of shares. For example, owners of preferred shares are usually denied the right to vote [RMBCA 7.21].

Quorum Requirements. For shareholders to act during a meeting, a quorum must be present. Generally, this condition is met when shareholders holding more than 50 percent of the outstanding shares are present. Corporate business matters are presented in the form of resolutions, which shareholders vote to approve or disapprove. If a state statute sets forth specific voting requirements, the corporation's articles or bylaws must be consistent with these statutory limitations. Some states provide that obtaining the unanimous written consent of shareholders is a permissible alternative to holding a shareholders' meeting [RMBCA 7.25].

Once a quorum is present, voting can proceed. A majority vote of the shares represented at the meeting is usually required to pass resolutions. Assume that Novo Pictures, Inc., has 10,000 outstanding shares of voting stock. Its articles of incorporation set the quorum at more than 50 percent of outstanding shares and provide that a majority vote of the shares present is necessary to pass on ordinary matters. Therefore, for this firm, at the shareholders' meeting, a quorum of stockholders representing 5,000 outstanding shares must be present to conduct business, and a vote of at least 2,501 of those shares is needed to pass ordinary resolutions. If 6,000 shares are represented, a vote of 3,001 will be necessary, and so on.

At times, more than a simple majority vote will be required either by a state statute or by the corporate charter. Extraordinary corporate matters, such as a merger, a consolidation, or the dissolution of the corporation (see Chapter 36), require approval by a higher percentage of the representatives of all corporate shares entitled to vote, not just a majority of those present at that particular meeting [RMBCA 7.27].

Voting Lists. A voting list is prepared by the corporation prior to each shareholders' meeting. Persons whose names appear on the corporation's stockholder records as owners are the ones ordinarily entitled to vote.[6] The voting list contains the name and address of each shareholder as shown on the corporate records on a given cutoff date, or record date. (Under RMBCA 7.07, the record date may be as much as seventy days before the meeting.) The voting list also includes the number of voting shares held by each owner. The list is usually kept at the corporate headquarters and is available for shareholder inspection [RMBCA 7.20].

Cumulative Voting. Most states permit or require shareholders to elect directors by *cumulative voting,* a method of voting designed to allow minority shareholders representation on the board of directors.[7] When cumulative voting is allowed or required, the number of members of the board to be elected is multiplied by the total number of voting shares. The result equals the number of votes a shareholder has, and this total can be cast for one or more nominees for director. All nominees stand for election at the same time. When cumulative voting is not required either by statute or under the articles, the entire board can be elected by a majority of shares at a shareholders' meeting.

Suppose, for example, that a corporation has 10,000 shares issued and outstanding. The minority shareholders hold only 3,000 shares, and the majority shareholders hold the other 7,000 shares. Three members of the board are to be elected. The majority shareholders' nominees are Alomon, Beasley, and Caravel. The minority shareholders' nominee is Dovrik. Can Dovrik be elected to the board by the minority shareholders?

---

6. When the legal owner is deceased, bankrupt, incompetent, or in some other way under a legal disability, his or her vote can be cast by a person designated by law to control and manage the owner's property.

7. See, for example, California Corporate Code Section 708. Under RMBCA 7.28, however, no cumulative voting rights exist unless the articles of incorporation so provide.

If cumulative voting is allowed, the answer is yes. The minority shareholders have 9,000 votes among them (the number of directors to be elected times the number of shares equals 3 times 3,000, which equals 9,000 votes). All of these votes can be cast to elect Dovrik. The majority shareholders have 21,000 votes (3 times 7,000 equals 21,000 votes), but these votes have to be distributed among their three nominees. The principle of cumulative voting is that no matter how the majority shareholders cast their 21,000 votes, they will not be able to elect all three directors if the minority shareholders cast all of their 9,000 votes for Dovrik, as illustrated in Exhibit 35–1.

Other Voting Techniques. A group of shareholders can agree in writing prior to a shareholders' meeting, in a *shareholder voting agreement,* to vote their shares together in a specified manner. Such agreements usually are held to be valid and enforceable. A shareholder can also appoint a voting agent and vote by proxy. As mentioned previously, a proxy is a written authorization to cast the shareholder's vote, and a person can solicit proxies from a number of shareholders in an attempt to concentrate voting power [RMBCA 7.22, 7.31].

Another technique is for shareholders to enter into a **voting trust**, which is an agreement (a trust contract) under which legal title (recorded ownership on the corporate books) is transferred to a trustee who is responsible for voting the shares. The agreement can specify how the trustee is to vote, or it can allow the trustee to use his or her discretion. The trustee takes physical possession of the stock certificate and in return gives the shareholder a *voting trust certificate.* The shareholder retains all of the rights of ownership (for example, the right to receive dividend payments) except for the power to vote the shares [RMBCA 7.30].

SECTION 6

Rights of Shareholders

Shareholders possess numerous rights. A significant right—the right to vote their shares—has already been discussed. In addition to voting rights, a shareholder has the rights, based on ownership of stock, to receive stock certificates (depending on the jurisdiction), to purchase newly issued stock, to receive dividends, to inspect corporate records, to transfer shares (with some exceptions), to receive a proportionate share of corporate assets on corporate dissolution, and to file suit on behalf of the corporation. These rights are discussed in the following subsections.

Stock Certificates

A **stock certificate** is a certificate issued by a corporation that evidences ownership of a specified number of shares in the corporation. In jurisdictions that require the issuance of stock certificates, shareholders have the right to demand that the corporation issue certificates and record their names and addresses in the corporate stock record books. In most states (and under RMBCA 6.26), boards of directors may provide that shares of stock be uncertificated (that is, that no actual, physical stock certificates need be issued). In that circumstance, the corporation may be required to send the holders of uncertificated shares letters or some other form of notice containing the same information required to be included on the face of stock certificates.

Stock is intangible personal property, and the ownership right exists independently of the certificate itself. A stock certificate may be lost or destroyed, but ownership is not destroyed with it. A new certificate can be issued to replace one that has

EXHIBIT 35–1 RESULTS OF CUMULATIVE VOTING

Ballot	Majority Shareholder Votes			Minority Shareholder Votes	Directors Elected
	Alomon	*Beasley*	*Caravel*	*Dovrik*	
1	10,000	10,000	1,000	9,000	Alomon, Beasley, Dovrik
2	9,001	9,000	2,999	9,000	Alomon, Beasley, Dovrik
3	6,000	7,000	8,000	9,000	Beasley, Caravel, Dovrik

been lost or destroyed.[8] Notice of shareholders' meetings, dividends, and operational and financial reports are all distributed according to the recorded ownership listed in the corporation's books, not on the basis of possession of the certificate.

Preemptive Rights

A **preemptive right** is a common law concept under which a preference is given to a shareholder over all other purchasers to subscribe to or purchase a prorated share of a new issue of stock. This right does not apply to **treasury shares**—shares that are authorized but that have not been issued. This allows the shareholder to maintain his or her portion of control, voting power, or financial interest in the corporation. Most statutes either (1) grant preemptive rights but allow them to be negated in the corporation's articles or (2) deny preemptive rights except to the extent that they are granted in the articles [RMBCA 6.30]. The result is that the articles of incorporation determine the existence and scope of preemptive rights. Generally, preemptive rights apply only to additional, newly issued stock sold for cash and must be exercised within a specified time period (such as thirty days).

For example, Tron Corporation authorizes and issues 1,000 shares of stock, and Omar Loren purchases 100 shares, making him the owner of 10 percent of the company's stock. Subsequently, Tron, by vote of its shareholders, authorizes the issuance of another 1,000 shares (amending the articles of incorporation). This increases its capital stock to a total of 2,000 shares. If preemptive rights have been provided, Loren can purchase one additional share of the new stock being issued for each share currently owned—or 100 additional shares. Thus, he can own 200 of the 2,000 shares outstanding, and his relative position as a shareholder will be maintained. If preemptive rights are not reserved, his proportionate control and voting power will be diluted from that of a 10 percent shareholder to that of a 5 percent shareholder because of the issuance of the additional 1,000 shares.

Preemptive rights can be very important for shareholders in close corporations. This is because of the relatively small number of shares and the substantial interest that each shareholder controls in a close corporation. Without preemptive rights, it would be possible for a shareholder to lose his or her proportionate control over the firm.

Stock Warrants

Usually, when preemptive rights exist and a corporation is issuing additional shares, each shareholder is given **stock warrants**, which are transferable options to acquire a given number of shares from the corporation at a stated price. Warrants are often publicly traded on securities exchanges. When the warrant option is for a short period of time, the stock warrants are usually referred to as *rights*.

Dividends

A **dividend** is a distribution of corporate profits or income *ordered by the directors* and paid to the shareholders in proportion to their respective shares in the corporation. Dividends can be paid in cash, property, stock of the corporation that is paying the dividends, or stock of other corporations.[9]

State laws vary, but every state determines the general circumstances and legal requirements under which dividends are paid. State laws also control the sources of revenue to be used; only certain funds are legally available for paying dividends. Once declared, a cash dividend becomes a corporate debt enforceable at law like any other debt. Depending on state law, dividends may be paid from the following sources:

1. *Retained earnings.* All state statutes allow dividends to be paid from the undistributed net profits earned by the corporation, including capital gains from the sale of fixed assets. The undistributed net profits are called retained earnings.
2. *Net profits.* A few state statutes allow dividends to be issued from current net profits without regard to deficits in prior years.
3. *Surplus.* A number of state statutes allow dividends to be paid out of any kind of surplus.

Illegal Dividends. Sometimes dividends are improperly paid from an unauthorized account, or their payment causes the corporation to become insolvent.

8. For a lost or destroyed certificate to be reissued, a shareholder normally must furnish an indemnity bond (a guaranty of payment) to protect the corporation against potential loss should the original certificate reappear at some future time in the hands of a bona fide purchaser [UCC 8–302, 8–405(2)].

9. Technically, dividends paid in stock are not dividends. They maintain each shareholder's proportional interest in the corporation. On one occasion, a distillery declared and paid a "dividend" in bonded whiskey.

Generally, in such cases, shareholders must return illegal dividends only if they knew that the dividends were illegal when they received them. A dividend paid while the corporation is insolvent is automatically an illegal dividend, and shareholders may be liable for returning the payment to the corporation or its creditors. In all cases of illegal and improper dividends, the board of directors can be held personally liable for the amount of the payment. When directors can show that a shareholder knew a dividend was illegal when it was received, however, the directors are entitled to reimbursement from the shareholder.

Directors' Failure to Declare a Dividend. When directors fail to declare a dividend, shareholders can ask a court of equity for an injunction to compel the directors to meet and to declare a dividend. For the injunction to be granted, it must be shown that the directors have acted so unreasonably in withholding the dividend that their conduct is an abuse of their discretion.

Often, large money reserves are accumulated for a bona fide purpose, such as expansion, research, or some other legitimate corporate use. The mere fact that sufficient corporate earnings or surplus is available to pay a dividend is not enough to compel directors to distribute funds that, in the board's opinion, should not be distributed.[10] The courts are hesitant to interfere with corporate operations and will not compel directors to declare dividends unless abuse of discretion is clearly shown.

INSPECTION RIGHTS

Shareholders in a corporation enjoy both common law and statutory inspection rights. The shareholder's right of inspection is limited, however, to the inspection and copying of corporate books and records *for a proper purpose,* provided the request is made in advance. Either the shareholder can inspect in person, or an attorney, accountant, or other type of assistant can do so as the shareholder's agent. The RMBCA requires the corporation to maintain an alphabetical voting list of shareholders with addresses and number of shares owned; this list must be kept open at the annual meeting for inspection by any shareholder of record [RMBCA 7.20].

The power of inspection is fraught with potential abuses, and the corporation is allowed to protect itself from them. For example, a shareholder can properly be denied access to corporate records to prevent harassment or to protect trade secrets or other confidential corporate information. Some states require that a shareholder must have held his or her shares for a minimum period of time immediately preceding the demand to inspect or must hold a minimum number of outstanding shares. The RMBCA provides that every shareholder is entitled to examine specified corporate records [RMBCA 16.02]. A shareholder who is denied the right of inspection can seek a court order to compel the inspection.

TRANSFER OF SHARES

Corporate stock represents an ownership right in intangible personal property. The law generally recognizes the right of an owner to transfer property to another person unless there are valid restrictions on its transferability. Although stock certificates are negotiable and freely transferable by indorsement and delivery, transfer of stock in closely held corporations is generally restricted by the bylaws, by a restriction stamped on the stock certificate, or by a shareholder agreement (see Chapter 34). The existence of any restrictions on transferability must always be noted on the face of the stock certificate, and these restrictions must be reasonable.

Sometimes, corporations or their shareholders restrict transferability by reserving the option to purchase any shares offered for resale by a shareholder. This **right of first refusal** remains with the corporation or the shareholders for only a specified time or a reasonable period of time. Variations on the purchase option are possible. For example, a shareholder might be required to offer the shares to other shareholders or to the corporation first.

When shares are transferred, a new entry is made in the corporate stock book to indicate the new owner. Until the corporation is notified and the entry is complete, voting rights, notice of shareholders' meetings, dividend distribution, and so forth are all held by the current owner of record.

RIGHTS ON DISSOLUTION

When a corporation is dissolved and its outstanding debts and the claims of its creditors have been

10. A striking exception to this rule was made in *Dodge v. Ford Motor Co.,* 204 Mich. 459, 170 N.W. 668 (1919), when Henry Ford, the president and major stockholder of Ford Motor Company, refused to declare a dividend notwithstanding the firm's large capital surplus. The court, holding that Ford had abused his discretion, ordered the company to declare a dividend.

satisfied, the remaining assets are distributed on a pro rata basis among the shareholders. If no preferences in distribution of assets on liquidation are given to any class of stock, then all of the stockholders share the remaining assets.

Shareholders also have the right to petition the court to dissolve the corporation. Suppose that a minority shareholder knows that the board of directors is mishandling corporate assets or is permitting a deadlock to threaten or irreparably injure the corporation's finances. The minority shareholder is not powerless to intervene. He or she can petition a court to appoint a receiver and to liquidate the business assets of the corporation.

The RMBCA permits any shareholder to initiate such an action in any of the following circumstances [RMBCA 14.30]:

1. The directors are deadlocked in the management of corporate affairs, shareholders are unable to break that deadlock, and irreparable injury to the corporation is being suffered or threatened.
2. The acts of the directors or those in control of the corporation are illegal, oppressive, or fraudulent.
3. Corporate assets are being misapplied or wasted.
4. The shareholders are deadlocked in voting power and have failed, for a specified period (usually two annual meetings), to elect successors to directors whose terms have expired or would have expired with the election of successors.

THE SHAREHOLDER'S DERIVATIVE SUIT

When those in control of a corporation—the corporate directors—fail to sue in the corporate name to redress a wrong suffered by the corporation, shareholders are permitted to do so "derivatively" in what is known as a **shareholder's derivative suit.** Some wrong must have been done to the corporation, and before a derivative suit can be brought, the shareholders must first state their complaint to the board of directors. Only if the directors fail to solve the problem or to take appropriate action can the derivative suit go forward.

The right of shareholders to bring a derivative action is especially important when the wrong suffered by the corporation results from the actions of corporate directors. This is because the directors and officers would probably be unwilling to take any action against themselves.[11]

11. See RMBCA 7.40–7.47.

The shareholder's derivative suit is unusual in that those suing are not pursuing rights or benefits for themselves personally but are acting as guardians of the corporate entity. Therefore, any damages recovered by the suit normally go into the corporation's treasury, not to the shareholders personally.

SECTION 7

Liability of Shareholders

One of the hallmarks of the corporate organization is that shareholders are not personally liable for the debts of the corporation. If the corporation fails, shareholders can lose their investments, but that is generally the limit of their liability. As discussed in Chapter 34, in certain instances of fraud, undercapitalization, or careless observance of corporate formalities, a court will pierce the corporate veil (disregard the corporate entity) and hold the shareholders individually liable. But these situations are the exception, not the rule.

Although rare, there are certain other instances in which a shareholder can be personally liable. One relates to illegal dividends, which were discussed previously. Two others relate to *stock subscriptions* and *watered stock*.

STOCK-SUBSCRIPTION AGREEMENTS

Sometimes, stock-subscription agreements—written contracts by which one agrees to buy capital stock of a corporation—exist prior to incorporation. Normally, these agreements are treated as continuing offers and are irrevocable (for up to six months under RMBCA 6.20). Once the corporation has been formed, it can sell shares to investors. In either case, once the subscription agreement or stock offer is accepted, a binding contract is formed. Any refusal to pay constitutes a breach resulting in the personal liability of the shareholder.

WATERED STOCK

Shares of stock can be paid for with property or services rendered instead of cash. (Shares cannot be purchased with promissory notes, however.) The general rule is that for **par-value shares** (that is, shares that have a specific face value, or formal cash-in value, written on them, such as one penny or one dollar), the corporation must receive a value at least equal to the par-value amount. For **no-par shares** (that is, shares without a par value), the corporation must receive the value of the shares as determined by the board or the shareholders.

For either par-value or no-par shares, the setting of the value is based on the same factors: tax rates, whether the corporation needs capital surplus, and what the corporation will receive for the shares (money, property, or services). When shares are issued by the corporation for less than these stated values, the shares are referred to as **watered stock.**[12] In most cases, the shareholder who receives watered stock must pay the difference to the corporation (the shareholder is personally liable). In some states, the shareholder who receives watered stock may be liable to creditors of the corporation for unpaid corporate debts.

To illustrate the concept of watered stock: Suppose that during the formation of a corporation, Gomez, as one of the incorporators, transfers his property, Sunset Beach, to the corporation for 10,000 shares of stock at a par value of $100 per share for a total price of $1 million. After the property is transferred and the shares are issued, Sunset Beach is carried on the corporate books at a value of $1 million. On appraisal, it is discovered that the market value of the property at the time of transfer was only $500,000. The shares issued to Gomez are therefore watered stock, and he is liable to the corporation for the difference between the value of the shares and the value of the property.

12. The phrase *watered stock* was originally used to describe cattle that—kept thirsty during a long drive—were allowed to drink large quantities of water just prior to their sale. The increased weight of the "watered stock" allowed the seller to reap a higher profit.

SECTION 8

Duties of Majority Shareholders

In some cases, a majority shareholder is regarded as having a fiduciary duty to the corporation and to the minority shareholders. This occurs when a single shareholder (or a few shareholders acting in concert) owns a sufficient number of shares to exercise *de facto* (actual) control over the corporation. In these situations, majority shareholders owe a fiduciary duty to minority shareholders.

Consider an example. Three brothers, Alfred, Carl, and Eugene, each own a one-third interest in a corporation and had worked for the corporation for most of their adult lives. When a dispute arose concerning discrepancies in the corporation's accounting records, Carl and Eugene fired Alfred and told the company's employees that Alfred had had a nervous breakdown, which was not true. Alfred sued Carl and Eugene, alleging, among other things, that they had breached their fiduciary duties. The brothers argued that because there was no diminution in the value of the corporation or the value of Alfred's shares in the company, they had not breached their fiduciary duties. The court, however, held that the brothers' conduct, which was unfairly prejudicial toward Alfred, supported a finding of breach of fiduciary duty.[13]

13. *Pedro v. Pedro,* 489 N.W.2d 798 (Minn.App. 1992).

See Case 35.3 at the end of this chapter. To view the full, unedited case from Westlaw,® go to this text's Web site at **http://wbl-cs.westbuslaw.com**.

Terms and Concepts to Review

business judgment rule 714
dividend 718
no-par share 721
par-value share 720
preemptive rights 718
proxy 715
quorum 711
right of first refusal 719
shareholder's derivative suit 720
stock certificate 717
stock warrant 718
treasury share 718
voting trust 717
watered stock 721

Chapter Summary

Role of Directors	1. *Election of directors*—The first board of directors is usually appointed by the incorporators; thereafter, directors are elected by the shareholders. Directors usually serve a one-year term, although the term can be longer and staggered terms are permitted under most state statutes. 2. *Directors' qualifications and compensation*—Few qualifications are required; a director can be a shareholder but is not required to be. Compensation is usually specified in the corporate articles or bylaws. 3. *Board of directors' meetings*—The board of directors conducts business by holding formal meetings with recorded minutes. The date of regular meetings is usually established in the corporate articles or bylaws; special meetings can be called, with notice sent to all directors. Quorum requirements vary from state to state; usually, a quorum is a majority of the corporate directors. Voting must usually be done in person, and in ordinary matters only a majority vote is required. 4. *Rights of directors*—Directors' rights include the rights of participation, inspection, compensation, and indemnification. 5. *Directors' management responsibilities*—Directors are responsible for declaring and paying corporate dividends to shareholders; authorizing major corporate decisions; appointing, supervising, and removing corporate officers and other managerial employees; determining employees' compensation; making financial decisions necessary to the management of corporate affairs; and issuing authorized shares and bonds. Directors may delegate some of their responsibilities to executive committees and corporate officers and executives.
Role of Corporate Officers and Executives	Corporate officers and other executive employees are normally hired by the board of directors. In most states, a person can hold more than one office and can be both an officer and a director of a corporation. The rights of corporate officers and executives are defined by employment contracts. The duties of corporate officers are the same as those of directors.
Fiduciary Duties of Directors and Officers	1. *Duty of care*—Directors are obligated to act in good faith, to use prudent business judgment in the conduct of corporate affairs, and to act in the corporation's best interests. If a director fails to exercise this duty of care, he or she can be answerable to the corporation and to the shareholders for breaching the duty. 2. *Duty of loyalty*—Directors have a fiduciary duty to subordinate their own interests to those of the corporation in matters relating to the corporation. 3. *Conflicts of interest*—To fulfill their duty of loyalty, directors and officers must make a full disclosure of any potential conflicts of interest between their personal interests and those of the corporation.
Liability of Directors and Officers	Corporate directors and officers are personally liable for their own torts and crimes; additionally, they may be held personally liable for the torts and crimes committed by corporate personnel under their direct supervision (see Chapters 8 and 34). The *business judgment rule* immunizes a director from liability for a corporate decision as long as the decision was within the powers of the corporation and the authority of the director to make and was an informed, reasonable, and loyal decision.
Role of Shareholders	1. *Shareholders' powers*—Shareholders' powers include the approval of all fundamental changes affecting the corporation and the election of the board of directors. 2. *Shareholders' meetings*—Shareholders' meetings must occur at least annually; special meetings can be called when necessary. Notice of the date, time, and place of the meeting (and its purpose, if it is specially called) must be sent to shareholders. Shareholders may vote by proxy (authorizing someone else to vote their shares) and may submit proposals to be included in the company's proxy materials sent to shareholders before meetings. 3. *Shareholder voting*—Shareholder voting requirements and procedures are as follows: a. A minimum number of shareholders (a quorum—generally, more than 50 percent of shares held) must be present at a meeting for business to be conducted; resolutions are passed (usually) by simple majority vote.

Chapter Summary—Continued

Role of Shareholders—continued	b. The corporation must prepare voting lists of shareholders of record prior to each shareholders' meeting. c. Cumulative voting may or may not be required or permitted. Cumulative voting gives minority shareholders a greater chance of representation on the board of directors. d. A shareholder voting agreement (an agreement of shareholders to vote their shares together) is usually held to be valid and enforceable. e. A shareholder may appoint a proxy (substitute) to vote his or her shares. f. A shareholder may enter into a voting trust agreement by which title (record ownership) of his or her shares is given to a trustee, and the trustee votes the shares in accordance with the trust agreement.
Rights of Shareholders	Shareholders have numerous rights, which may include the following: 1. The right to a stock certificate, preemptive rights, and the right to stock warrants (depending on the corporate charter). 2. The right to obtain a dividend (at the discretion of the directors). 3. Voting rights. 4. The right to inspect the corporate records. 5. The right to transfer shares (this right may be restricted in close corporations). 6. The right to a share of corporate assets when the corporation is dissolved. 7. The right to sue on behalf of the corporation (bring a shareholder's derivative suit) when the directors fail to do so.
Liability of Shareholders	Shareholders may be liable for the retention of illegal dividends, for breach of a stock-subscription agreement, and for the value of watered stock.
Duties of Majority Shareholders	In certain situations, majority shareholders may be regarded as having a fiduciary duty to minority shareholders and will be liable if that duty is breached.

Cases for Analysis

Westlaw. You can access the full text of each case presented below by going to the Westlaw cases on this text's Web site at http://wbl-cs.westbuslaw.com. Each Westlaw case includes the names of all plaintiffs and defendants, the dates on which the case was argued and decided, a brief summary of the issues and decisions in the case, headnotes classifying specific issues in the case according to the West Key Number System, and the court's opinion. Concurring and dissenting opinions, if any, are included as well.

Case 35.1 Duty of Loyalty

Stokes v. Bruno
Court of Appeal of Louisiana,
Third Circuit, 1998.
720 So.2d 388.

DECUIR, Judge.

* * * *

Point Cotile Parks Association, Inc. is a nonprofit, nonstock corporation established by developers of the Point Cotile Subdivision in Rapides Parish [Louisiana]. The corporation's membership is limited to owners of a lot or building site. On February 13, 1990, according to minutes of the meeting [of the board of directors] on that date, a resolution was adopted designating [Gerald] Bruno and Michael Wright, two members of the board of directors of the corporation, as "legal signers" for the corporation. Furthermore, the minutes of the meeting of that date indicate that the board of directors voted to accept the recommendation of the Common Grounds Committee to adopt resolutions to authorize the sale of "common ground" property * * *. [P]roperty values for the various tracts were established through comparative values and consultation with a realtor. * * *

* * * *

Bruno contend[ed] that the purpose of the minutes of the February 1990 board meeting was to grant him and

Wright authority to act on behalf of the corporation in all sales transactions * * * to "anyone," including himself and Wright, if fair. * * * [In February 1996, Bruno and Wright sold to themselves and Bruno's wife 5.45 acres of the "common ground," including lots with timber, for a price lower than the board had set for the individual lots.] Upon learning of this sale, [Craig Stokes and other Association members] filed suit [in a Louisiana state court against Bruno and Wright, asking that the sale be declared void. The court ordered a rescission of the sale. Bruno and Wright appealed to a state intermediate appellate court.]

The trial court found there was no valid formal resolution authorizing the sale of the property at issue. The record clearly supports such a finding. *The authority to alienate [transfer to another] immovable property must be in writing and given expressly*. * * * There was never a resolution accepted by the Corporation authorizing Mr. Bruno and/or Mr. Wright authority to negotiate and execute the sale in question. * * * [Emphasis added.]

Likewise, we find defendant's contention that the trial court erred in finding that he had breached his fiduciary duty to the corporation to be without merit. * * * No formal process for setting the sales price of this property was followed. Apparently Mr. Bruno just decided a value for the property that was less than the values set [by the board]. He did his own form of appraisal, set a value without any consultation of the common grounds committee and apparently worked under a perceived apparent authority he could set values and complete sales on his own. * * *

This brings us to the issue of fair dealing and fiduciary duty to the Association. This apparently was a clear case of self-dealing. * * * [Bruno had] a duty to disclose to the Corporation several items. First that the sale consummated was the whole tract, not just the first lots as had been offered in prior sales. The valuations placed on the property, including the back acreage, was significantly less than the original proposal for just the lots. Next he had a duty to disclose to the Corporation the potential for sales of timber, as well as the fact that the revised values he was negotiating with himself on behalf of the Corporation were based on his own determinations and no outside source. Once he took the position of evaluator of the land, he would be barred by fiduciary duty from consummating the sale without disclosing the reduction in price, offering an opportunity for other Association members to purchase, or make an effort to market the entire tract of land, as opposed to just the front lots. * * * Mr. Bruno and Mr. Wright owed a fiduciary duty to the Corporation to maximize the return and the mere fact that a portion of the property had not sold at the original requested prices did not give him the unilateral authorization to add more land, reduce the price and then purchase themselves without disclosure. * * * The sale was not properly authorized by the Corporation and the sale constituted breach of the fiduciary duty Mr. Bruno owed to the Corporation. * * *

* * * *

The judgment of the trial court is affirmed. Costs of appeal are assessed to defendant-appellant.

AFFIRMED.

CASE 35.2 LIABILITY OF DIRECTORS

FEDERAL DEPOSIT INSURANCE CORP. v. CASTETTER

United States Court of Appeals,
Ninth Circuit, 1999.
184 F.3d 1040.

THOMAS, Circuit Judge:

* * * *

I

This case arises from the failure of the Balboa National Bank ("the bank"), a federally-insured national bank located in National City, California. Edward Peterson, a banker with twenty-six years of experience, including a tenure as a senior banking examiner for the state of California, obtained a federal charter for the bank and opened it in February 1983. Peterson was President, Chief Executive Officer ("CEO"), and the only inside member of the board of directors. Peterson solicited individuals [including Robert Castetter] to serve as outside directors on the bank's board * * *. Although some of the outside directors had served on boards of directors in the past, none had any significant banking experience and all were engaged in other professions. * * *

Peterson placed much of the bank's loan portfolio into automobile lending. * * * Peterson hired Frances Cragen, an experienced and high-level employee in Bank of America's auto loan department, to work for Balboa's auto loan department. A January 1984 Office of the Comptroller of the Currency ("OCC") report contained no criticisms of Balboa. * * *

Peterson died unexpectedly after a heart attack in May 1984. * * * [T]he board engaged Jerry Findley, an outside bank consultant, to make recommendations for the President/CEO position and to assess the bank's condition. Findley recommended Michael Jones for the position, but also identified many serious problems with the bank, including a too-rapid growth rate, unreliable sources of funding, liquidity problems, and insufficient equity capital.

A few weeks after Jones became President and CEO, federal regulators examined the bank. They reported many problems that Findley had predicted * * *.

In response to Findley's and the regulators' reports, the board requested that Jones develop and implement a "Credit Quality Action Plan." This included implementing better procedures for billing, reporting delinquency data, and tracking the performances of loan officers. The board retained an outside consultant to improve the bank's loan guidelines. The board also hired consultants to audit the auto loan underwriting files * * *. [T]he directors regularly attended board meetings and committees of the board were active.

* * * *

The bank continued to experience serious difficulty throughout 1986 and 1987. In 1987, the board learned that the reports of the national accounting firm, which had stated that the bank's loan loss reserves were adequate, were invalid. In July 1987, the OCC * * * called the board's supervision of the bank "inexcusable," explaining that the bank's condition was critical * * *. To address the [bank's] lack of capital, board members personally contributed over $2.8 million in an attempt to save the bank.

In early 1988, the OCC determined that the bank was insolvent and ordered it closed. The Federal Deposit Insurance Corporation ("FDIC") eventually seized the bank, was appointed receiver, and instituted this lawsuit [in a federal district court] against the directors. The FDIC contended that the directors were negligent in the performance of their directorial duties and should be personally liable for the losses in the bank's portfolio.

* * * [T]he district court granted the directors' motion for summary judgment. The FDIC timely appeals.

II

* * * *

Although the defendants are directors of a federally-insured national bank, their liability is determined by California state law. * * *

* * * *

* * * The California business judgment rule is intended to protect a director from liability for a mistake in business judgment which is made in good faith and in what he or she believes to be the best interest of the corporation, where no conflict of interest exists. It requires directors to act in good faith and with the prudence that an ordinary person would under like circumstances. However, it also entitles a director to rely on information supplied by others. *If directors meet the requirements of the business judgment rule, they are entitled to immunity from personal liability for acts of ordinary negligence under California law.* [Emphasis added.]

* * * *

* * * Under California law, a *prima facie* showing of good faith and reasonable investigation is established when a majority of the board is comprised of outside directors and the board has received the advice of independent consultants.

* * * *

Here, the defendant directors established a *prima facie* showing of a reasonable investigation. A majority of the board consisted of outside directors and it is undisputed that the board sought and obtained the advice of a number of outside expert consultants.

* * * *

This is not to say that directors of California corporations may immunize themselves simply by acquiring information. It is clear that the rule does not protect a director in certain situations, such as where there is a conflict of interest, fraud, oppression, or corruption. Neither does the business judgment rule protect a director who has wholly abdicated [renounced; as used here, ignored] his corporate responsibility, closing his or her eyes to corporate affairs. But the rule does protect well-meaning directors who are misinformed, misguided, and honestly mistaken. * * * [California law] does not impose on directors a duty of possessing specialized knowledge. Rather, directors are charged with a duty of good faith and conducting business in a manner such director believes to be in the best interests of the corporation and its shareholders.

* * * *

In this case, there is no dispute that the directors acted in good faith and with the belief that their actions were in the best interests of the corporation. The directors were initially misguided by the analysis of former President Peterson, who had over a quarter century of experience as a bank regulator. They were further misguided by an analysis of a national accounting firm. They attempted to follow the advice of several consultants, and invested—and lost—substantial sums of their own money. Despite these efforts, they were unable to avert the bank's collapse. The undisputed record indicates that the directors were entitled to the protection of the business judgment rule. Accordingly, the defendant directors cannot, as a matter of law, be held liable for solely negligent acts. The district court properly granted summary judgment.

CASE 35.3 DUTY OF MAJORITY SHAREHOLDERS

HAYES v. OLMSTED & ASSOCIATES, INC.

Oregon Court of Appeals, 2001.
173 Or.App 259,
21 P.3d 178.

BREWER, J. [Judge]

* * * *

* * * Oppression of minority shareholders in closely held corporations is frequently linked to breaches of fiduciary duty. As is the case among partners, those in control of the affairs of a closely held corporation have fiduciary duties of good faith, fair dealing, and full disclosure toward minority shareholders. * * * [A] breach of fiduciary duty occurs when the majority shareholders of a closely held corporation use their control over the corporation to

their own advantage and exclude the minority from the benefits of participating in the corporation, [in the absence of] a legitimate business purpose * * * . A breach of fiduciary duty by those who control a closely held corporation normally constitutes oppression.

The lack of marketability of the shares of a closely held corporation means that minority shareholders are especially vulnerable to the loss of their investments. The "squeeze-out" tactics of majority shareholders often deprive minority shareholders of management participation, employment income or other advantages that they reasonably have come to expect, and which are the essential benefits of their investment. Nonetheless, * * * [a] court must defer to the business decisions made by the majority shareholders of a close corporation, as long as they are genuine. Moreover, the existence of one or more badges of oppression in isolation does not necessarily justify relief. Instead, we examine the pattern of conduct of those in control and the effect of that conduct on the minority to determine whether, in sum, they show oppression.

With the foregoing principles in mind, we turn to the evidence in this case. [Olmsted & Associates, Inc. (O & A)] was formed in 1978 as a partnership * * * . [Dan Hayes] joined the firm as a partner in 1979, and in 1981 the partners decided to incorporate. The voting shareholders of the corporation [included Hayes and Arthur] Olmstead * * * . The voting shareholders were also the officers and the managers of the corporation. Olmstead was the president and general manager, and [Hayes] served over the years as vice-president, treasurer and secretary. At the time of corporate formation, he acquired approximately 14 percent of O & A's outstanding shares.

The corporation's lawyer prepared the Stock Purchase Agreement (SPA) among the corporation and its shareholders. The SPA directed that "[t]he parties to this Agreement shall, at least annually, and more frequently as may be determined by the parties, set the per share value of stock of the Corporation for the purposes of this Agreement." It also required any terminated employee to offer his or her stock to O & A. However, O & A was not required to accept the offer. In addition, O & A could "accept" the offer at the price per share established under the SPA, if the shareholder's offering price was higher.

Originally, Olmstead held 51 percent of the voting shares. In 1991, [Hayes] and other shareholders became concerned about Olmstead's dominance of corporate affairs to the exclusion of other shareholders and directors. Under pressure, Olmstead transferred 5 voting and 540 nonvoting shares to [David] Arbanas, who had joined the company in 1988, for approximately $40 per share. Management of the business also shifted from Olmstead to a "management team," which consisted of the voting shareholders and directors * * * .

* * * [I]n June 1994, the shareholders set the SPA share value at $64 * * * . Arbanas became president and general manager of O & A.

Until June 1995, the annual salaries of the voting shareholders were relatively comparable, ranging from $100,000 to $130,000. Until that time, the voting shareholders had annually distributed approximately equal cash bonuses among themselves. In June 1995, the management team agreed to implement a more achievement-oriented bonus plan. * * * The Board of Directors approved a bonus for Arbanas of either $10,000 in cash or 60 shares of voting stock. Arbanas initially decided to accept cash. * * *

The food brokerage industry changed in the mid-1990s as clients became more interested in working with regional brokerages. In early 1996, in an effort to retain a key client, Pillsbury Foods, O & A acquired Performance Northwest, another food brokerage firm. O & A doubled its revenues as a result of the acquisition. * * *

The Performance Northwest transaction resulted in a significant restructuring of O & A. * * * [M]anagement control shifted to an "*ad hoc* management group" consisting of Olmstead, Arbanas, and [two non-shareholders], which became known as the Executive Committee. * * * After the Executive Committee assumed control over O & A's affairs, there were no further meetings of the Board of Directors. * * *

* * * *

* * * [I]n June 1996, Olmstead urged Arbanas to take voting shares as his 1995 bonus in lieu of the cash that he had already received; Arbanas agreed and issued a stock certificate for the shares, signing both as president and secretary of O & A. Arbanas executed a promissory note to repay the cash bonus that he previously had received * * * . With the issuance of the additional 60 shares to Arbanas, shareholder voting control shifted to Arbanas and Olmstead * * * . The other shareholders, including plaintiff, were not informed that Arbanas had received the shares.

* * * In December 1996, after paying all other bonuses, the members of the Executive Committee met separately and secretly to fix their own bonuses for the fiscal year ending June 30, 1996. Although bonuses paid to other shareholders and managers for 1996 ranged from $10,000 to $30,000 each, the Executive Committee members each received bonuses that year exceeding $100,000. * * * [T]he Executive Committee did not disclose any information concerning the bonuses paid to its members to the other voting shareholders. In late 1996, [Hayes] requested information about bonus payments made that year, but his request was refused. * * *

In late 1996 and early 1997, [Hayes] complained about his exclusion from top level management decisions. He attempted to obtain financial records from [O & A's comptroller], who told [Hayes] that the records were not available to him and that he should talk to the corporation's attorney. * * *

* * * [O]n April 17, [Hayes] was told that his position would be eliminated as of May 31. * * *

* * * *

* * * The company then offered to purchase [Hayes'] stock for $67 per share. [Hayes] rejected that offer. In the fall of 1997, [Hayes] was removed from the Board of Directors. [He filed a suit in an Oregon state court against Olmsted, Arbanas, and O & A, alleging, among other things, breach of fiduciary duty. Before the trial, Hayes agreed to sell his stock to O & A. The court declared the price to be $67 per share. Hayes appealed to a state intermediate appellate court, asserting that the price should be higher, in part because Olmsted and Arbanas had engaged in oppressive conduct.]

* * * *

The trial court found that plaintiff was the victim of oppression "because minority shareholders were not given the formal and required opportunities to participate in or comment upon major changes in direction of [O & A]." We agree. Because they believed that they were most fit to govern corporate affairs, Olmstead and Arbanas assumed control of O & A by creating a *de facto* Executive Committee in violation of the bylaws. From 1995 to 1997, when plaintiff was fired, the Executive Committee did not observe corporate formalities and failed to hold regular meetings of the corporation's Board of Directors and shareholders. Executive Committee members paid themselves bonuses that were not authorized by or reported to the Board of Directors, also in violation of the bylaws. They kept their bonuses secret from the other shareholders and board members, despite plaintiff's requests for the bonus information, again in violation of the bylaws. In short, the Executive Committee, led by Olmstead and Arbanas, systematically disregarded the formalities and substance of O & A's organic governing documents.

When plaintiff complained about his exclusion from corporate decisions and information, the Executive Committee fired him * * * .

* * * *

* * * [W]e find that the conduct of the Executive Committee, spearheaded by Olmstead and Arbanas, was oppressive toward plaintiff.

* * * *

Remanded for entry of modified judgment for plaintiff reflecting a [higher] price * * * for plaintiff's stock in O & A; otherwise affirmed.

CASE PROBLEMS

35–1. Frederick Valerino and his family owned 50 percent of the stock in EMA (Electrical-Mechanical of America, Inc.), and the remaining 50 percent was owned by Charles Little. Both Valerino and Little participated actively in operating the corporation until 1979, when a dispute arose, resulting in a stalemate. For two years no shareholders' meeting was held and no board of directors could be elected. Little held a shareholders' meeting in 1981 and sent a telegram to Valerino stating that the purpose of the meeting was "[f]or the sale and purchase of the Capital Stock of EMA." Valerino did not attend and sent a reply letter indicating that he did not wish to sell any of his stock. Actually, Little held the meeting with the intention of issuing more stock to himself and his family, thus reducing Valerino's ownership to 25 percent. Valerino sued to enforce his preemptive rights in the corporation and to set aside the new stock issuance because of fraud. Discuss whether Valerino should succeed in his claim. [*Valerino v. Little,* 62 Md.App. 588, 490 A.2d 756 (1985)]

35–2. Abe Schultz, Sol Schultz, and Lawrence Newfeld were the managing directors and officers of Chemical Dynamics, Inc., a close corporation. In 1967, the corporation leased a building in which to house its offices and operations. Included in the lease agreement was a provision giving Chemical Dynamics an option to purchase the property for $300,000. In 1970, because the corporation was experiencing financial problems and could not pay its rent, it assigned the lease and the purchase option to Newfeld in return for Newfeld's loan to the corporation of approximately $21,500. In 1973, Newfeld purchased the property. Eventually, when the corporation's financial situation had improved and its debts were paid, Abe Schultz sued Newfeld on behalf of the corporation, claiming that Newfeld had breached his fiduciary duty by usurping a corporate opportunity to purchase the property. Evaluate Schultz's claim. [*Chemical Dynamics, Inc. v. Newfeld,* 728 S.W.2d 590 (Mo.App. 1987)]

35–3. A group of stockholders of Ono Development Co. and Ono East, Inc., brought suit, on behalf of themselves and the other stockholders of the corporations, and derivatively, on behalf of the corporations, against Pannell Kerr Forster, an accounting firm, and two of its employees (the defendants) to recover damages for breach of contract and fraud. The stockholders alleged that the defendants had failed to disclose in annual audits of the corporations' books that certain commissions were being improperly paid to and by three of the corporation's principal officers and directors. As a result, the corporations had been deprived of the use of large sums of money over an approximate ten-year period. While the action was pending, the plaintiff stockholders all sold their stock back to the corporations. The defendants argued that the stockholders lacked standing to sue the corporations either on their own behalf or on behalf of the corporations. What should the court decide, and why? [*McLaughlin v. Pannell Kerr Forster,* 589 So.2d 143 (Ala. 1991)]

35–4. Ohio Edison Co. is a public utility. Ohio Edison's articles of incorporation vest the authority to make capital expenditures solely in the board of directors. Since 1982, the company's capital expenditures have averaged $595 million per year. C. L. Grimes, a shareholder in Ohio Edison, proposed that the company amend its articles of incorporation to require shareholder approval of certain capital expenditures in excess of $300 million. In other words, under Grimes's proposal, once the spending threshold of $300 million was reached, each expenditure, including such routine expenditures as the purchase of a typewriter or a new desk, would require shareholder approval. On October 23, 1990, Grimes asked Ohio Edison to enclose his proposal in the proxy materials for the next shareholders' meeting. Ohio Edison submitted the proposal to the Securities and Exchange Commission (SEC) for an opinion as to whether it needed to be included with the proxy materials. The SEC ruled that the proposal could be omitted, because it concerned ordinary business operations. When Ohio Edison distributed proxy materials for the meeting without mentioning Grimes's proposal, Grimes filed suit. Grimes contended that Ohio Edison violated SEC rules by failing to include his proposal in its proxy materials and by failing to inform its shareholders that he would offer his proposal at the meeting (which, Grimes argued, made the proxy materials "false and misleading"). Ohio Edison responded with a motion to dismiss the complaint. The court granted the motion. Grimes appealed. How will the appellate court rule? Discuss fully. [*Grimes v. Ohio Edison Co.*, 992 F.2d 455 (2d Cir. 1993)]

35–5. J. R. Mullins, the sole director and shareholder of the Food Stores of South Carolina, Inc. (FSSC), opened two Sav-A-Lot grocery stores in Myrtle Beach. He then established another corporation, Food Stores of Greenville (FSG), and opened a Sav-A-Lot store in the Greenville community. Mullins was also FSG's sole shareholder and director. He instructed FSG's vice president to place Sav-A-Lot advertisements with the Greenville News-Piedmont, which was owned by Multimedia Publishing of South Carolina, Inc. The two Myrtle Beach stores were later closed and their inventory transferred to the Greenville store. FSG then transferred $144,000 to Mullins and other of his corporations—purportedly to repay debts owed by FSG. When the Greenville Sav-A-Lot closed following this transfer, Multimedia was left unpaid for the advertising services that it had provided to FSG. Mullins claimed that he had relinquished management of FSG to others and did not know that Multimedia had not been paid. Can Mullins, as corporate director and sole shareholder of FSG, avoid liability for the debts of the FSG corporation when he was on notice that the advertising had been ordered from Multimedia? Is Mullins's statement that he did not know of the debt tantamount to negligence and a breach of his duties as a director? Should Mullins have inquired into whether the Multimedia account had been paid? Discuss these issues and whether Mullins should escape liability for the Multimedia debt. [*Multimedia Publishing of South Carolina, Inc. v. Mullins*, 431 S.E.2d 569 (S.C. 1993)]

35–6. Air Engineered Systems and Services, Inc., a Louisiana corporation, had three shareholders: Naquin, Dubois, and Hoffpauir. Each of the shareholders owned one-third of the corporation's outstanding shares. Naquin was fired after he had worked six years as an employee of the firm, but he retained his shares in the corporation. He then formed a competing business, hired away one of Air Engineered's employees, tried to hire another, and obtained a job for his own business that he had originally solicited for Air Engineered. Under Louisiana law, any shareholder who is also a business competitor is entitled to inspect the corporate records if she or he owns 25 percent of the outstanding shares for six months prior to the demand. When Naquin requested that Air Engineered allow him to inspect the corporate records, however, Air Engineered denied his request because Naquin refused to sign an indemnity agreement protecting Air Engineered from any damages it might suffer as a result of Naquin's use of the information contained in the corporate records. Shortly thereafter, Dubois and Hoffpauir voted to increase the capital stock of the corporation; then they each purchased additional shares. This had the effect of reducing Naquin's percentage to less than 25 percent—which meant that Naquin was not entitled under Louisiana law to inspect Air Engineered's records. Naquin filed suit to require the corporation to permit him to inspect the books, because at the time his request was made, he owned more than 25 percent of the outstanding shares of Air Engineered. What was the result? [*Naquin v. Air Engineered Systems and Services, Inc.*, 463 So.2d 992 (La.App. 1985)]

35–7. Klinicki and Lundgren formed Berlinair, a closely held Oregon corporation, to provide air transportation out of West Germany. Klinicki, who owned 33 percent of the company stock, was the vice president and a director. Lundgren, who also owned 33 percent of the stock, was the president and a director. Lelco, Inc., a corporation owned by Lundgren and his family, owned 33 percent of Berlinair, and Berlinair's attorney owned the last 1 percent of stock. One of the goals of Berlinair was to obtain a contract with BFR, a West German consortium of travel agents, to provide BFR with air charter service. Later, Lundgren learned that the BFR contract might become available. Lundgren then incorporated Air Berlin Charter Co., of which he was the sole owner, and bid for the BFR contract. Lundgren won the BFR contract for Air Berlin while using Berlinair working time, staff, money, and facilities without the knowledge of Klinicki. When Klinicki learned of the BFR contract, he filed a derivative suit, as a minority stockholder, against Air Berlin for usurping a corporate opportunity. Did Klinicki recover against Air Berlin? If so, what was Klinicki awarded as damages? [*Klinicki v. Lundgren*, 67 Or.App. 160, 678 P.2d 1250 (1984)]

35–8. Dighton Grain, Inc., was a newly formed corporation operating a grain elevator business. Walter Gormley, the manager of the corporation, wrote $87,000 in corporate checks to himself during the first year of the firm's operation, kept inadequate records concerning grain shipments, and maintained an inadequate inventory of grain. An auditor's report recommended that the directors hold more frequent meetings, that Gormley discontinue his unauthorized use of the corporation's funds, and that new procedures be instituted by the corporation, such as requiring two signatures on corporate checks. None of these recommendations was followed, and Gormley continued to make personal use of corporate funds. After it had been in operation for two years, the firm went out of business, owing $400,000 to unsecured creditors. Gormley was convicted for misappropriating the firm's funds. One of the firm's creditors, Speer, brought a suit against the directors and officers of the corporation, alleging that they had been negligent in their duties and were thus personally liable for the debt to Speer. Did Speer succeed? [*Speer v. Dighton Grain, Inc.*, 229 Kan. 272, 624 P.2d 952 (1981)]

35–9. Melissa and Gary Callicoat each owned 50 percent of Callicoat, Inc. They were also Callicoat's only directors. They could not agree on the day-to-day management of the firm; neither could they agree on whether a debt owed to Arthur Baz was a personal or a corporate debt. Melissa suggested that they dissolve the corporation. Gary refused and excluded her from the operations of the firm. Melissa filed a petition in an Ohio state court against Gary and Callicoat, asking the court to dissolve the corporation. On what basis might the court order the dissolution? [*Callicoat v. Callicoat*, 73 Ohio Misc.2d 38, 657 N.E.2d 874 (1994)]

35–10. William Bear was the president of the William R. Bear Agency, Inc. (Bear Agency). Timothy Schirmer was a shareholder. In 1990, the YMCA was an important client of Bear Agency, and Bear spent company funds for family memberships in the YMCA. The same year, Bear put his wife on the payroll because, at the time, she was the only one in the office with computer experience. He decided not to declare a bonus for the employees in 1990, in part to invest the money in computers for the firm. The next April, Bear bought a BMW with company funds to use as a company car. Disapproving these actions, Schirmer filed a suit against Bear, Bear Agency, and others in an Illinois state court, asking the court to dissolve the corporation, among other things. Discuss how the decision not to dissolve Bear Agency might be supported by the business judgment rule. [*Schirmer v. Bear*, 271 Ill.App.3d 778, 648 N.E.2d 1131, 208 Ill.Dec. 209 (1994)]

35–11. Jacob Schachter and Herbert Kulik, the founders of Ketek Electric Corp., each owned 50 percent of the corporation's shares, and they served as the corporation's only officers. Arnold Glenn, as trustee, and Kulik brought a shareholder's derivative suit in a New York state court against Schachter, alleging that Schachter had diverted Ketek assets and opportunities to Hoteltron Systems, Inc., a corporation wholly owned by Schachter. The trial court held for Glenn and Kulik, and it awarded damages to Kulik, not to Ketek. On appeal, the appellate court ruled that the damages should be awarded to the injured corporation, Ketek, rather than to the innocent shareholder, Kulik. Kulik appealed to the state supreme court, arguing that awarding damages to the corporation was inequitable because Schachter, as a shareholder of Ketek, would ultimately share in the proceeds of the award. How should the state supreme court rule, and why? [*Glenn v. Hoteltron Systems, Inc.*, 74 N.Y.2d 386, 547 N.E.2d 71, 547 N.Y.S.2d 816 (1989)]

35–12. Mackinac Cellular Corp. offered to sell Robert Broz a license to operate a cellular phone system in Michigan. Broz was a director of Cellular Information Systems, Inc. (CIS). CIS, as a result of bankruptcy proceedings, was in the process of selling its cellular holdings. Broz did not formally present the opportunity to the CIS board, but he told some of the firm's officers and directors, who replied that CIS was not interested. At the time, PriCellular, Inc., a firm that wanted the Michigan license, was attempting to buy CIS. Without telling PriCellular, Broz bought the license himself. After PriCellular took over CIS, the company sued Broz, alleging that he had usurped a corporate opportunity. Has Broz done anything wrong? Discuss. [*Broz v. Cellular Information Systems, Inc.*, 673 A.2d 148 (Del. 1996)]

35–13. The board of directors of Baltimore Gas and Electric Company (BGE) recommended a merger with Potomac Electric Power Company (PEPCO). After full disclosure, the BGE shareholders approved the merger. On the ground that each BGE director stood a chance of being named to the new company's board, Janice Wittman, a BGE shareholder, sued the directors, alleging, among other things, that they were prohibited from deciding whether to recommend the merger. Did the directors breach their duty of care by voting in favor of the merger? Discuss. [*Wittman v. Crooke*, 120 Md.App. 369, 707 A.2d 422 (1998)]

35–14. Charles Pace and Maria Fuentez were shareholders of Houston Industries, Inc. (HII), and employees of Houston Lighting & Power, a subsidiary of HII, when they lost their jobs because of a company-wide reduction in its work force. Pace, as a shareholder, three times wrote to HII, demanding that the board of directors terminate certain HII directors and officers, and file a suit to recover damages for breach of fiduciary duty. Three times, the directors referred the charges to board committees and an outside law firm, which found that the facts did not support the charges. The board also received input from federal regulatory authorities about the facts behind some of the charges. The board notified Pace that it would refuse his demands. In response, Pace and Fuentez filed a shareholder's derivative suit against Don Jordan and the other HII directors, contending that the board's investigation was inadequate. The defendants moved for summary judgment, arguing that the suit was barred by the business judgment rule. How should the court rule? Why? [*Pace v. Jordan,* 999 S.W.2d 615 (Tex.App.—Houston [1 Dist.] 1999)]

35–15. Atlas Food Systems & Services, Inc., based in South Carolina, was a food vending service that provided refreshments to factories and other businesses. Atlas was a closely held corporation. John Kiriakides was an Atlas minority shareholder. Alex Kiriakides was the majority shareholder. Throughout most of Atlas's history, Alex was the chairman of the board, which included John as a director. In 1995, while John was the president of the firm, the board and shareholders decided to convert Atlas to an S corporation. A few months later, however, Alex, without calling a vote, decided that the firm would not convert. In 1996, a dispute arose over Atlas's contract to buy certain property. John and others decided not to buy it. Without consulting anyone, Alex elected to go through with the sale. Within a few days, Alex refused to allow John to stay on as president. Two months later, Atlas offered to buy John's interest in the firm for almost $2 million. John refused, believing the offer too low. John filed a suit in a South Carolina state court against Atlas and Alex, seeking, among other things, to force a buyout of John's shares. On what basis might the court grant John's request? Discuss. [*Kiriakides v. Atlas Food Systems & Services, Inc.,* 541 S.E.2d 257 (S.C. 2001)]

E-LINKS

For updated links to resources available on the Web, as well as a variety of other materials, visit this text's Web site at

http://wbl-cs.westbuslaw.com

One of the best sources on the Web for information on corporations, including their directors, is the EDGAR database of the Securities and Exchange Commission (SEC) at

http://www.sec.gov/edgarhp.shtml

Legal Research Exercises on the Web

Go to http://wbl-cs.westbuslaw.com, the Web site that accompanies this text. Select "Interactive Study Center," and then click on "Chapter 35." There you will find the following Internet research exercise that you can perform to learn more about the liability of corporate directors and officers:

Activity 35–1: Liability of Directors and Officers

CHAPTER 36

CORPORATIONS—Merger, Consolidation, and Termination

A CORPORATION TYPICALLY EXTENDS its operations by combining with another corporation through a merger, a consolidation, a purchase of assets, or a purchase of a controlling interest in the other corporation. This chapter examines these four types of corporate expansion. *Dissolution* and *liquidation* are the combined processes by which a corporation terminates its existence. The last part of this chapter discusses some of the typical reasons for terminating a corporation's existence and the methods used in the termination process.

SECTION 1

Merger and Consolidation

The terms *merger* and *consolidation* are often used interchangeably, but they refer to two legally distinct proceedings. Whether a combination is in fact a merger or a consolidation, however, the rights and liabilities of shareholders, the corporation, and the corporation's creditors are the same.

MERGER

A **merger** involves the legal combination of two or more corporations. After a merger, only one of the corporations continues to exist. For example, Corporation A and Corporation B decide to merge. It is agreed that A will absorb B; so on merger, B ceases to exist as a separate entity, and A continues as the **surviving corporation**. This process is illustrated in Exhibit 36–1 on the next page.

After the merger, A is recognized as a single corporation possessing all the rights, privileges, and powers of itself and B. A automatically acquires all of B's property and assets without the necessity of formal transfer. A becomes liable for all of B's debts and obligations.[1] Finally, A's articles of incorporation are deemed amended to include any changes that are stated in the *articles of merger.*

In a merger, the surviving corporation is vested with the disappearing corporation's preexisting legal rights and obligations. For example, if the disappearing corporation had a right of action against a third party, the surviving corporation could bring suit after the merger to recover the disappearing corporation's damages.

CONSOLIDATION

In a **consolidation**, two or more corporations combine so that each corporation ceases to exist and a new one emerges. Corporation A and Corporation B consolidate to form an entirely new organization, Corporation C. A and B both terminate, and C comes into existence as an entirely new entity. This process is illustrated in Exhibit 36–2 on page 732.

The results of a consolidation are essentially the same as the results of a merger. C is recognized as

1. A corporation that is subject to suit in some jurisdictions cannot avoid liability by merging with a corporation that could not otherwise have been sued in those jurisdictions. See, for example, *In re Silicone Gel Breast Implants Product Liability Litigation*, 837 F.Supp. 1123 (N.D. Ala. 1993).

EXHIBIT 36–1 MERGER

In this illustration, Corporations A and B decide to merge. They agree that A will absorb B; so on merging, B ceases to exist as a separate entity, and A continues as the surviving corporation.

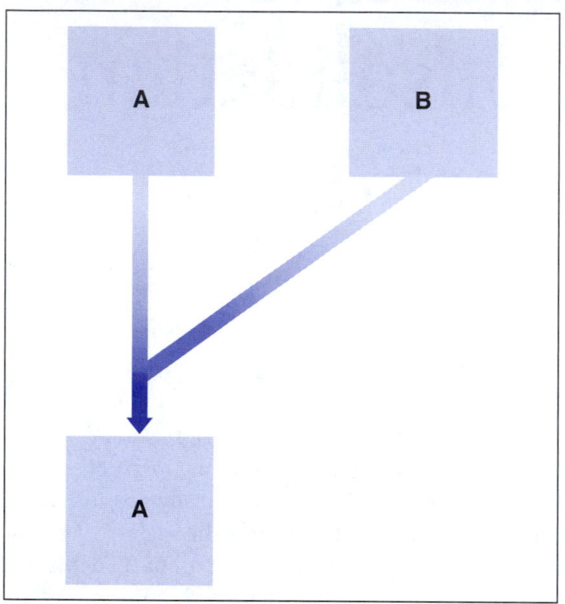

EXHIBIT 36–2 CONSOLIDATION

In this illustration, Corporations A and B consolidate to form an entirely new organization, Corporation C. In the process, A and B terminate, and C comes into existence as an entirely new entity.

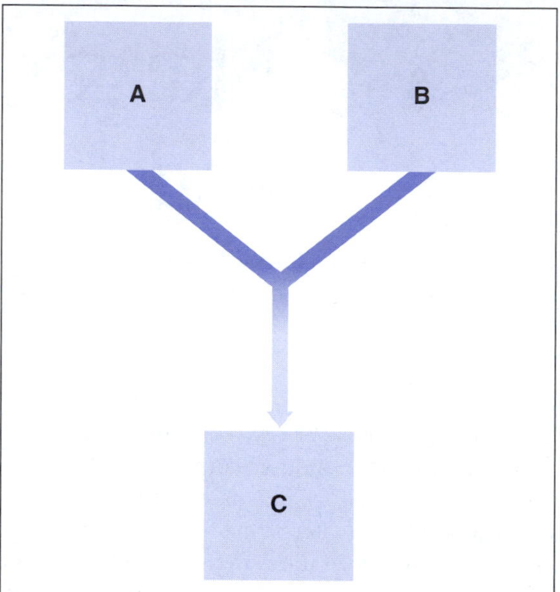

a new corporation and a single entity; A and B cease to exist. C accedes to all the rights, privileges, and powers previously held by A and B. Title to any property and assets owned by A and B passes to C without formal transfer. C assumes liability for all debts and obligations owed by A and B. The *articles of consolidation* take the place of A's and B's original corporate articles and are thereafter regarded as C's corporate articles.

When a merger or a consolidation takes place, the surviving corporation or newly formed corporation will issue shares or pay some fair consideration to the shareholders of the corporation that ceases to exist.

MERGER AND CONSOLIDATION PROCEDURES

All states have statutes authorizing mergers and consolidations for domestic (in-state) corporations, and most states allow the combination of domestic and foreign (out-of-state) corporations. Although the procedures vary somewhat among jurisdictions, the basic requirements are as outlined below [RMBCA 11.01–11.07].

1. The board of directors of *each* corporation involved must approve a merger or consolidation plan.[2]
2. The shareholders of *each* corporation must vote approval of the plan at a shareholders' meeting. Most state statutes require the approval of two-thirds of the outstanding shares of voting stock, although some states require only a simple majority, and others require a four-fifths vote. Frequently, statutes require that each class of stock approve the merger; thus, the holders of nonvoting stock must also approve. A corporation's bylaws can dictate a stricter requirement.
3. Once approved by the directors and the shareholders of both corporations, the plan (articles of merger or consolidation) is filed, usually with the secretary of state.

2. When a corporation undertakes a transaction that will cause a change in corporate control or that will break up the corporate entity, the directors have an obligation "to seek the best value reasonably available to the stockholders." See, for example, *Paramount Communications, Inc., v. QVC Network, Inc.*, 637 A.2d 34 (Del. 1994).

4. When state formalities are satisfied, the state issues a certificate of merger to the surviving corporation or a certificate of consolidation to the newly consolidated corporation.

Short-Form Mergers. RMBCA 11.04 provides a simplified procedure for the merger of a substantially owned subsidiary corporation into its parent corporation. Under these provisions, a **short-form merger**—also referred to as a **parent-subsidiary merger**—can be accomplished *without* the approval of the shareholders of either corporation. The short-form merger can be used only when the parent corporation owns at least 90 percent of the outstanding shares of each class of stock of the subsidiary corporation. The simplified procedure requires that a plan for the merger be approved by the board of directors of the parent corporation before it is filed with the state. A copy of the merger plan must be sent to each shareholder of record of the subsidiary corporation.

Appraisal Rights. What if a shareholder disapproves of a merger or a consolidation but is outvoted by the other shareholders? The law recognizes that a dissenting shareholder should not be forced to become an unwilling shareholder in a corporation that is new or different from the one in which the shareholder originally invested. The shareholder has the right to dissent and may be entitled to be paid the fair value for the number of shares held on the date of the merger or consolidation. This right is referred to as the shareholder's **appraisal right.** If a shareholder is dissatisfied with the price received for the stock, he or she cannot sue the corporation on the ground of fraud or other illegal conduct; appraisal rights are the exclusive remedy.

Appraisal rights are available only when a state statute specifically provides for them. Appraisal rights normally extend to regular mergers, consolidations, short-form mergers, and sales of substantially all of the corporate assets not in the ordinary course of business.

Shareholders may lose their appraisal rights if they do not follow precisely the elaborate procedures prescribed by statute. When they lose the right to an appraisal, dissenting shareholders must go along with the transaction despite their objections. One of the usual requirements is that the dissenting shareholders file a written notice of dissent prior to the shareholders' vote on the proposed transaction. This notice of dissent is also basically a notice to all shareholders of the costs that dissenting shareholders may impose should the merger or consolidation be approved. In addition, after approval, the dissenting shareholders must make a written demand for payment and for the fair value of their shares.

Appraisal Rights and Shareholder Status. Once a dissenting shareholder elects appraisal rights under a statute, in some jurisdictions the shareholder loses his or her shareholder status. Without that status, a shareholder cannot vote, receive dividends, or sue to enjoin whatever action prompted the dissent. In some of those jurisdictions, statutes provide or courts have held that shareholder status may be reinstated during the appraisal process (for example, if the shareholder decides to withdraw from the process and the corporation approves). In other jurisdictions, shareholder status may not be reinstated until the appraisal is concluded. Even if an individual loses his or her shareholder status, courts may allow the individual to sue on the ground of fraud or other illegal conduct associated with the merger.

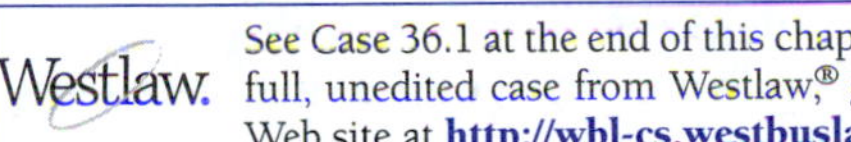

See Case 36.1 at the end of this chapter. To view the full, unedited case from Westlaw,® go to this text's Web site at **http://wbl-cs.westbuslaw.com**.

Valuation of Shares. Valuation of shares is often a point of contention between the dissenting shareholder and the corporation. RMBCA 13.01 provides that the "fair value of shares" normally is the value on the day prior to the date on which the vote was taken. The corporation must make a written offer to purchase a dissenting shareholder's stock, accompanying the offer with a current balance sheet and income statement for the corporation. If the shareholder and the corporation do not agree on the fair value, a court will determine it.

SECTION 2

Purchase of Assets

When a corporation acquires all or substantially all of the assets of another corporation by direct purchase, the corporation purchasing the assets, or *acquiring corporation,* simply extends its ownership and control over more physical assets. Because no change in the legal entity occurs, the acquiring corporation is not required to obtain shareholder approval for the purchase.[3]

Although the acquiring corporation may not be required to obtain the shareholders' approval, the U.S. Department of Justice has issued guidelines that significantly constrain and often prohibit mergers that could result from a purchase of assets. These guidelines are part of the federal antitrust laws to enforce Section 7 of the Clayton Act (discussed in Chapter 45).

Note that the corporation that is *selling* all its assets is substantially changing its business position and perhaps its ability to carry out its corporate purposes. For that reason, the corporation the assets of which are *acquired* must obtain approval from both its board of directors and its shareholders. In most states and under the RMBCA, a dissenting shareholder of the selling corporation can demand appraisal rights.

Generally, a corporation that purchases the assets of another corporation is not responsible for the liabilities of the selling corporation. Exceptions to this rule are made in the following circumstances:

1. When the purchasing corporation impliedly or expressly assumes the seller's liabilities.
2. When the sale amounts to what in fact is a merger or a consolidation.
3. When the purchaser continues the seller's business and retains the same personnel (same shareholders, directors, and officers).
4. When the sale is fraudulently executed to escape liability.

In any of these situations, the acquiring corporation will be held to have assumed both the assets and the liabilities of the selling corporation.

Westlaw. See Case 36.2 at the end of this chapter. To view the full, unedited case from Westlaw,® go to this text's Web site at **http://wbl-cs.westbuslaw.com**.

3. If the acquiring corporation plans to pay for the assets with its own corporate stock and not enough authorized unissued shares are available, the shareholders must vote to approve issuance of additional shares by amendment of the corporate articles. Also, acquiring corporations the stock of which is traded on a national stock exchange can be required to obtain their own shareholders' approval if they plan to issue a significant number of shares, such as a number equal to 20 percent or more of the outstanding shares.

SECTION 3

Purchase of Stock

An alternative to the purchase of another corporation's assets is the purchase of a substantial number of the voting shares of its stock. This enables the acquiring corporation to control the acquired corporation, or **target corporation.** The process of acquiring control over a corporation in this way is commonly referred to as a corporate **takeover.** The acquiring corporation deals directly with the shareholders in seeking to purchase the shares they hold.

When the acquiring corporation makes a public offer to all shareholders of the target corporation, it is called a **tender offer.** The price offered is generally higher than the market price of the target stock prior to the announcement of the tender offer. The higher price induces shareholders to tender (offer to sell) their shares to the acquiring firm. The tender offer can be conditioned on the receipt of a specified number of outstanding shares by a certain date. The offering corporation can make an *exchange* tender offer in which it offers target stockholders its own securities in exchange for their target stock. In a cash tender offer, the offering corporation offers cash in exchange for the target stock.

Federal securities laws strictly control the terms, duration, and circumstances under which most tender offers are made. In addition, a majority of states have passed takeover statutes that impose additional regulations on tender offers.

A firm may respond to a tender offer in numerous ways. Sometimes, a target firm's board of directors will see a tender offer as favorable and will recommend to the shareholders that they accept it. In contrast, to resist a takeover, a target company may make a *self-tender,* which is an offer to acquire stock from its own shareholders and thereby retain corporate control. Alternatively, a target corporation might resort to one of several other tactics to resist a takeover. One commonly used tactic is known as the "poison pill"—a target company gives its shareholders rights to purchase additional shares at low prices when there is a takeover attempt. The use of poison pills prevents takeovers by making them prohibitively expensive.

SECTION 4

Termination

Termination of a corporate life, like termination of a partnership, has two phases—dissolution and liquidation. **Dissolution** is the legal death of the artificial "person" of the corporation. **Liquidation** is the process by which corporate assets are converted into cash and distributed among creditors and shareholders according to specific rules of preference.[4]

DISSOLUTION

Dissolution can be brought about voluntarily by the directors and shareholders or involuntarily by the state or through a court's order. Once a corporation is dissolved, either voluntarily or involuntarily, its corporate existence is ended except for the process of winding up corporate affairs and distributing corporate assets.

Voluntary Dissolution. There are basically two ways in which a corporation can be voluntarily dissolved once it has issued shares and commenced business operations.[5] First, the shareholders can initiate corporate dissolution proceedings by a unanimous vote to dissolve the corporation.[6] Second, the directors can propose that the corporation be dissolved and submit the proposal to the shareholders for a vote at a shareholders' annual meeting or a specially called shareholders' meeting.

Under RMBCA 14.03, once a decision is reached to dissolve the corporation, the corporation must file *articles of dissolution* with the secretary of state. These articles must include the name of the corporation, the date on which the dissolution was authorized, and how the dissolution was authorized. The effective date of dissolution will be the date of the articles of dissolution. The corporation must also notify the creditors of the dissolution and establish a date (at least 120 days following the date of dissolution) by which all claims against the corporation must be received [RMBCA 14.06].

Involuntary Dissolution. Corporations are creatures of statute, as stated earlier. Just as the state can allow a corporation to come into existence, so can it end that existence. The state, in an action brought by the secretary of state or the state attorney general, can dissolve a corporation for any of the following reasons [RMBCA 14.20]:

1. Failure of the corporation to comply with administrative requirements (such as failure to pay annual taxes, submit an annual report, or have a designated registered agent).
2. Procurement of a corporate charter through fraud or misrepresentation on the state.
3. Abuse of corporate powers (*ultra vires* acts).
4. Violation of the state criminal code after a demand to discontinue the violation has been made by the secretary of state.
5. Failure to commence business operations.
6. Abandonment of operations before starting up.

Corporate statutory provisions in some states provide that the articles of incorporation of a close corporation can empower any shareholder to dissolve the corporation at will or on the occurrence of a specified event—such as the death of another shareholder. This provides a shareholder in a close corporation with the same power to dissolve his or her business organization as a partner in a partnership.

Sometimes, an involuntary dissolution of a corporation is necessary—for example, when a board of directors is deadlocked. Courts hesitate to order involuntary dissolution in such circumstances unless there is specific statutory authorization to do so, but if the deadlock cannot be resolved by the shareholders and if it will irreparably injure the corporation, the court will proceed with an involuntary dissolution. Courts can also dissolve a corporation for mismanagement [RMBCA 14.30].

See Case 36.3 at the end of this chapter. To view the full, unedited case from Westlaw,® go to this text's Web site at http://wbl-cs.westbuslaw.com.

LIQUIDATION

When dissolution takes place by voluntary action, the members of the board of directors act as trustees of the corporate assets. As trustees, they are responsible for winding up the affairs of the corporation for the benefit of corporate creditors and shareholders. This makes the board members personally liable for any breach of their fiduciary trustee duties.

4. On dissolution, the liquidated assets are first used to pay creditors. Any remaining assets are distributed to shareholders according to their respective stock rights; preferred stock has priority over common stock, generally by charter.

5. If the corporation was formed but has not yet undertaken any business or issued any shares, a majority of the incorporators can dissolve the corporation relatively simply—by filing articles of dissolution with the secretary of state's office, which will then issue a certificate of dissolution.

6. Delaware Code Section 275(c).

Liquidation can be accomplished without court supervision unless the members of the board do not wish to act in this capacity or unless shareholders or creditors can show cause to the court why the board should not be permitted to assume the trustee function. In either case, the court will appoint a **receiver** to wind up the corporate affairs and liquidate corporate assets. A receiver is always appointed by the court if the dissolution is involuntary.

TERMS AND CONCEPTS TO REVIEW

appraisal right 733	merger 731	surviving corporation 731
consolidation 731	parent-subsidiary merger 733	takeover 734
dissolution 735	receiver 736	target corporation 734
liquidation 735	short-form merger 733	tender offer 734

CHAPTER SUMMARY

Merger and Consolidation

1. *Merger*—The legal combination of two or more corporations, the result of which is that the surviving corporation acquires all the assets and obligations of the other corporation, which then ceases to exist.
2. *Consolidation*—The legal combination of two or more corporations, the result of which is that each corporation ceases to exist and a new one emerges. The new corporation assumes all the assets and obligations of the former corporations.
3. *Procedure*—Determined by state statutes. Basic requirements are the following:
   a. The board of directors of each corporation involved must approve the merger or consolidation plan.
   b. The shareholders of each corporation must approve the merger or consolidation plan at a shareholders' meeting.
   c. Articles of merger or consolidation (the plan) must be filed, usually with the secretary of state.
   d. The state issues a certificate of merger (or consolidation) to the surviving (or newly consolidated) corporation.
4. *Short-form merger (parent-subsidiary merger)*—Possible when the parent corporation owns at least 90 percent of the outstanding shares of each class of stock of the subsidiary corporation.
   a. Shareholder approval is not required.
   b. The merger must be approved only by the board of directors of the parent corporation.
   c. A copy of the merger plan must be sent to each shareholder of record.
   d. The merger plan must be filed with the state.
5. *Appraisal rights*—Rights of dissenting shareholders (given by state statute) to receive the *fair value* for their shares when a merger or consolidation takes place. If the shareholder and the corporation do not agree on the fair value, a court will determine it.

Purchase of Assets

A purchase of assets occurs when one corporation acquires all or substantially all of the assets of another corporation.

1. *Acquiring corporation*—The acquiring (purchasing) corporation is not required to obtain shareholder approval; the corporation is merely increasing its assets, and no fundamental business change occurs.
2. *Acquired corporation*—The acquired (purchased) corporation is required to obtain the approval of both its directors and its shareholders for the sale of its assets, because this creates a substantial change in the corporation's business position.

CHAPTER SUMMARY—CONTINUED

Purchase of Stock	A purchase of stock occurs when one corporation acquires a substantial number of the voting shares of the stock of another (target) corporation. 1. *Tender offer*—A public offer to all shareholders of the target corporation to purchase its stock at a price generally higher than the market price of the target stock prior to the announcement of the tender offer. Federal and state securities laws strictly control the terms, duration, and circumstances under which most tender offers are made. 2. *Target responses*—Ways in which target corporations respond to takeover bids. These include self-tender (the target firm's offer to acquire its own shareholders' stock), poison pills, and other strategies.
Termination	The termination of a corporation involves the following two phases: 1. *Dissolution*—The legal death of the artificial "person" of the corporation. Dissolution can be brought about in any of the following ways: a. An act of a legislature in the state of incorporation. b. Expiration of the time provided in the corporate charter. c. Voluntary approval of the shareholders and the board of directors. d. Unanimous action by all shareholders. e. Court decree. 2. *Liquidation*—The process by which corporate assets are converted into cash and distributed to creditors and shareholders according to specified rules of preference. May be supervised by members of the board of directors (when dissolution is voluntary) or by a receiver appointed by the court to wind up corporate affairs.

CASES FOR ANALYSIS

Westlaw. You can access the full text of each case presented below by going to the Westlaw cases on this text's Web site at http://wbl-cs.westbuslaw.com. Each Westlaw case includes the names of all plaintiffs and defendants, the dates on which the case was argued and decided, a brief summary of the issues and decisions in the case, headnotes classifying specific issues in the case according to the West Key Number System, and the court's opinion. Concurring and dissenting opinions, if any, are included as well.

CASE 36.1 APPRAISAL RIGHTS

GLASSMAN v. UNOCAL EXPLORATION CORP.
Delaware Supreme Court, 2001.
777 A.2d 242.

BERGER, Justice.

* * * *

I. Factual and Procedural Background

Unocal Corporation is an earth resources company primarily engaged in the exploration for and production of crude oil and natural gas. At the time of the merger at issue, Unocal owned approximately 96% of the stock of Unocal Exploration Corporation ("UXC"), an oil and gas company operating in and around the Gulf of Mexico. In 1991, low natural gas prices caused a drop in both companies' revenues and earnings. Unocal investigated areas of possible cost savings and decided that, by eliminating the UXC minority, it would reduce taxes and overhead expenses.

In December 1991 the boards of Unocal and UXC appointed special committees to consider a possible merger. The UXC committee consisted of three directors who, although also directors of Unocal, were not officers or employees of the parent company. The UXC committee retained financial and legal advisors and met four times before agreeing to a merger exchange ratio of .54 shares of Unocal stock for each share of UXC. Unocal and UXC announced the merger on February 24, 1992, and it was effected, pursuant to 8 [Delaware Code Section] 253, on May 2, 1992. The Notice of Merger and Prospectus stated the terms of the merger and advised the former UXC stockholders of their appraisal rights.

Plaintiffs filed this * * * action [in a Delaware state court], on behalf of UXC's minority stockholders, on the day the merger was announced. They asserted, among other claims, that Unocal and its directors breached their fiduciary duties of entire fairness and full disclosure. The Court * * * held that: (i) the Prospectus did not contain any material misstatements or omissions; (ii) the entire fairness standard does not control in a short-form merger; and (iii) plaintiffs' exclusive remedy in this case was appraisal. * * *

II. Discussion

* * * In its current form, * * * 8 Del. C. [Section] 253 provides in relevant part:

> (a) In any case in which at least 90 percent of the outstanding shares of each class of the stock of a corporation * * * is owned by another corporation * * * , the corporation having such stock ownership may * * * merge the other corporation * * * into itself * * * by executing, acknowledging and filing * * * a certificate of such ownership and merger setting forth a copy of the resolution of its board of directors to so merge and the date of the adoption; provided, however, that in case the parent corporation shall not own all the outstanding stock of * * * the subsidiary corporation[ ], * * * the resolution * * * shall state the terms and conditions of the merger, including the securities, cash, property or rights to be issued, paid delivered or granted by the surviving corporation upon surrender of each share of the subsidiary corporation * * * .
>
> * * * *
>
> (d) In the event that all of the stock of a subsidiary Delaware corporation * * * is not owned by the parent corporation immediately prior to the merger, the stockholders of the subsidiary Delaware corporation party to the merger shall have appraisal rights * * * .
>
> * * * *

* * * [W]e must decide whether a minority stockholder may challenge a short-form merger by seeking equitable relief through an entire fairness claim. Under settled principles, a parent corporation and its directors undertaking a short-form merger are self-dealing fiduciaries who should be required to establish entire fairness, including fair dealing and fair price. The problem is that [Section] 253 authorizes a summary procedure that is inconsistent with any reasonable notion of fair dealing. In a short-form merger, there is no agreement of merger negotiated by two companies; there is only a unilateral act—a decision by the parent company that its 90% owned subsidiary shall no longer exist as a separate entity. The minority stockholders receive no advance notice of the merger; their directors do not consider or approve it; and there is no vote. Those who object are given the right to obtain fair value for their shares through appraisal.

The equitable claim plainly conflicts with the statute. If a corporate fiduciary follows the truncated process authorized by [Section] 253, it will not be able to establish the fair dealing prong of entire fairness. If, instead, the corporate fiduciary sets up negotiating committees, hires independent financial and legal experts, etc., then it will have lost the very benefit provided by the statute—a simple, fast and inexpensive process for accomplishing a merger. * * * In order to serve its purpose, [Section] 253 must be construed to obviate the requirement to establish entire fairness.

Thus, we * * * hold that, absent fraud or illegality, appraisal is the exclusive remedy available to a minority stockholder who objects to a short-form merger. * * * The determination of fair value must be based on *all* relevant factors, including damages and elements of future value, where appropriate. So, for example, if the merger was timed to take advantage of a depressed market, or a low point in the company's cyclical earnings, or to precede an anticipated positive development, the appraised value may be adjusted to account for those factors. * * *

Although fiduciaries are not required to establish entire fairness in a short-form merger, the duty of full disclosure remains, in the context of this request for stockholder action. Where the only choice for the minority stockholders is whether to accept the merger consideration or seek appraisal, they must be given all the factual information that is material to that decision. * * *

III. Conclusion

Based on the foregoing, we affirm the [lower] Court * * * and hold that plaintiffs' only remedy in connection with the short-form merger of UXC into Unocal was appraisal.

CASE 36.2 PURCHASE OF ASSETS

EAGLE PACIFIC INSURANCE CO. v. CHRISTENSEN MOTOR YACHT CORP.

Washington Supreme Court, 1998.
135 Wash.2d 894,
959 P.2d 1052.

DOLLIVER, Justice.

* * * *

David H. Christensen organized [Christensen Group, Inc. (CGI)] in 1962 to do construction and leasing. In 1985 Christensen and another person organized [Christensen Motor Yacht Corporation (CMYC)] to build luxury yachts in Vancouver, Washington. [Christensen Shipyards, Limited (CSL)] is a third corporation created by Christensen in 1993 or 1994. Christensen is the chief executive officer and sole shareholder of CMYC, CGI, and CSL. * * *

Eagle Pacific [Insurance Company] issued two workers' compensation insurance policies to CMYC in 1990 and 1991. These policies were canceled in December 1991 because CMYC failed to pay the premiums. * * * CMYC's debt to Eagle Pacific was $268,443 as of August 9, 1993. * * *

* * * *

In 1993, CMYC was building three boats, referred to as the Lastebro, Armstrong, and L & L boats. The buyers of the Armstrong and L & L boats paid CMYC in installments as construction progressed. The Lastebro boat was financed by KHD Deutz of America Corporation (KHD Deutz). * * *

* * * *

Christensen personally guaranteed completion of the three boats to the buyers, and Christensen and CGI had also guaranteed payment of the loans made by KHD Deutz. Because of these personal guarantees, Christensen had a strong incentive to see that the boats were completed and delivered to the buyers.

Christensen admits CMYC was, or became, insolvent in 1993. The buyers' payments on the boats were not covering all costs. * * *

* * * Christensen then created [CSL] to complete the boats. CSL, being unburdened by any of CMYC's debts, was able to obtain a line of credit from U.S. National Bank. CSL subcontracted with CMYC to finish construction of the three yachts. CSL paid nothing to take over the yacht contracts, but if the contracts ultimately yielded a profit, the subcontract agreement contained a formula whereby CSL was to pay a percentage of the profits to CMYC. CSL paid $70,000 to CMYC for supplies inventory, and CSL agreed to pay CMYC $5,500 per month to lease CMYC's machinery and equipment to be used in the construction of the boats.

CMYC did not own the facilities where the yachts were constructed. * * * CMYC was subleasing the space from CGI. After CSL took over the yacht contracts, CMYC forfeited its lease of the building to CGI, and CSL began renting the same space. In the end, CSL, with the same employees and in the same facilities, continued construction of the same three yachts. * * *

[After attempting, and failing, to collect the amount of the unpaid insurance premiums from CMYC, Eagle Pacific filed a suit in a Washington state court against CMYC and obtained a judgment for $268,443. Because CMYC was insolvent, Eagle Pacific sought to recover the debt from CSL.] Eagle Pacific claimed CSL was liable because it was a "[m]ere continuation" of CMYC. * * * The trial court granted partial summary judgment to Eagle Pacific * * *, and the [state intermediate] Court of Appeals affirmed. * * *

* * * *

Normally, when a corporation sells its assets to another corporation, the purchasing corporation does not become liable for the debts of the selling corporation. The rationale for this rule is a bona fide purchaser who gives adequate consideration and who lacks notice of prior claims against the property acquires no liability for those claims. Four exceptions to this rule of non-liability exist. Successor liability is imposed if: (1) the purchaser expressly or impliedly agrees to assume liability; (2) the purchase is a *de facto* merger or consolidation; (3) the purchaser is a mere continuation of the seller; or (4) the transfer of assets is for the fraudulent purpose of escaping liability. Liability may be imposed regardless of the exact form of transfer of assets between the corporations. [Emphasis added.]

* * * *

[CSL] asserts a transfer of assets between corporations can never be fraudulent absent a showing of insufficient consideration: Eagle Pacific failed to prove CMYC's transfer of assets to CSL lacked consideration, so the transfer cannot be fraudulent. CSL's argument oversimplifies the fraudulent transfer ground for imposing successor liability.

* * * Adequate consideration for a transfer of assets between a buying and selling corporation is an important element when determining whether to impose successor liability. If the buying corporation pays sufficient consideration for the seller's assets, the selling corporation's creditors can then seek to satisfy their judgments from the sale proceeds. *If the sale proceeds are equivalent in value to the transferred assets, then, assumedly, but not necessarily, no harm has been done to the creditors of the selling corporation.* [Emphasis added.]

In some situations, however, the selling corporation has intangible assets on which it is difficult to place a value. CSL paid nothing to CMYC for CSL's assumption of the yacht contracts. The only benefit CMYC received for transferring the yacht contracts was a contractual promise by CSL to share a percentage of profits, if any, resulting from CSL's completion of the yachts. CSL argues the yacht contracts had no market value since any potential profit from completing the contracts was too speculative.

Eagle Pacific was unable to prove that these yacht contracts had a current market value; but this does not diminish the harm resulting to Eagle Pacific when CSL took over the yacht contracts. By taking over the contracts, CSL thereby became entitled to future installment payments on the construction of the boats—payments from which Eagle Pacific could have satisfied its debts had CMYC continued the contracts. Indeed, as a result of CSL's taking over the contracts, Eagle Pacific lost the right to recover any of the future payments and potential future profits deriving from the construction of the three boats. CMYC used Eagle Pacific's insurance services without fully paying for those services; and, by CSL's taking over CMYC's operations, CSL ultimately yields the profits from CMYC's operations while cutting off Eagle Pacific's ability to recover its debts.

Eagle Pacific's inability to establish inadequate consideration does not preclude a court from finding the transfer of assets was fraudulent. * * * [I]nsufficient consideration is [not] a *necessary* element for a finding of fraud. Rather, insufficient consideration is merely a sufficient element.

* * * [F]raud can be present despite the payment of adequate consideration. * * *

* * * *

* * * CMYC's principal business purpose was the construction of yachts. In the course of the construction of the three yachts, CMYC incurred debts which it could not pay. With the transfer of the three yacht contracts to CSL, and CMYC's surrender of its employees and facilities to CSL, CMYC was stripped of its main potential source for future revenues. Christensen admits the yacht contracts were transferred to CSL to allow the continuation of construction on the yachts unhampered by creditors' efforts to collect unpaid bills.

Christensen's admitted reason for the transfer of assets from CMYC to CSL fits the definition of a fraudulent transfer. Eagle Pacific's inability to prove CSL paid insufficient consideration for the transferred assets does not automatically purge the transaction of fraud. The intent behind the transfer of assets can render the transaction fraudulent * * *.

* * * *

* * * [T]ransferring corporate assets for the purpose, or with the intention, of escaping liability is, by definition, a transfer of assets with fraudulent purpose.

* * * *

* * * Transferring assets to another corporation to hinder or delay creditors is by definition a fraudulent transfer. * * * In the course of conducting business and building yachts, CMYC incurred debts which Christensen sought to avoid by transferring the business to CSL. Because the assets were transferred to CSL to avoid the reach of the creditors, the transaction is fraudulent and successor liability attaches to CSL. The fact that the transaction was designed to "save the business" does not defeat imposition of successor liability. We affirm the Court of Appeals as to CSL's liability.

CASE 36.3 INVOLUNTARY DISSOLUTION

CHANCE v. NORWALK FAST OIL, INC.

Appellate Court of Connecticut, 1999.
55 Conn.App. 272,
739 A.2d 1275.

LAVERY, J. [Judge]

The individual defendants appeal from the judgment of the [Connecticut state] trial court dissolving the corporate defendant Norwalk Fast Oil, Inc. (corporation). On appeal, the defendants claim that the trial court improperly (1) ordered the dissolution and winding-up of the corporation and (2) denied their motion to dismiss the cause of action. * * *

The following facts are relevant to this appeal. The plaintiff, Albert Chance, commenced this action to dissolve the corporation by summons and complaint dated May 9, 1997. The complaint alleges, in part, that the shareholders are deadlocked in voting power for the election of directors and have been unable to elect successor directors. The complaint prayed that the trial court dissolve the corporation, declare the date of dissolution and order the winding-up of the corporation. In response, the defendants asserted as a special defense paragraph six of the shareholders agreement (stalemate provision), which provides that "in the event that a stalemate is reached after tallying the votes on any substantive issue affecting the Corporation, then it is hereby agreed that the stalemate shall be broken by Chance and [Richard] Kosminoff each selecting the same third person to whom the proposed question shall be submitted, and his decision on the matter shall be binding upon the Corporation and all of its shareholders." After trial, the defendants filed a motion to dismiss the case claiming that the trial court lacked subject matter jurisdiction because Chance failed to comply with the stalemate provision.

The trial court issued a memorandum of decision dated March 23, 1998, finding the following facts and rendering judgment in Chance's favor. The corporation is incorporated under the laws of this state and its principal place of business is in Norwalk. Chance is a 40 percent shareholder who holds 50 percent of the voting rights in the corporation. Kosminoff is also a 40 percent shareholder who holds 50 percent of the voting rights in the corporation. Seymour Epstein and Morris Epstein each own 10 percent of the stock in the corporation but ceded their voting rights to Chance and Kosminoff in equal shares.

* * * [I]n 1990 * * * corporate minutes and waivers * * * were sent to the shareholders for their signatures. Only Chance signed the documents. Similar events occurred in 1991. The parties attempted to resolve their disputes and to close the business in 1994, but the closing never took place. Chance is involved in other litigation with the defendants and no longer is on speaking terms with them.

On April 22, 1997, Chance, as president of the corporation, called a special meeting of the shareholders to be held on May 1, 1997, at 11 a.m. The purpose of the meeting was to elect directors. The slate presented by Chance was defeated, as was the slate presented by Kosminoff. Thereafter, Chance suggested, pursuant to the stalemate provision, that Howard M. Rosenkrantz be appointed to break the stalemate regarding the appointment of directors. Kosminoff rejected the suggestion and sometime later recommended that Nicholas Cioffi be appointed, which recommendation was not accepted. The trial court concluded that the shareholders are deadlocked in voting power for the election of directors and, for that reason, have been unable to elect successors to directors whose terms normally would have expired upon election of successors * * * .

The trial court also found that the defendants did not prove by a fair preponderance of the evidence that Chance is estopped or has waived his rights to seek a dissolution of the corporation as alleged in the defendants' special defenses. The trial court concluded that the stalemate provision is not a condition precedent to a court-ordered dissolution and is not an unequivocal waiver of Chance's rights * * * . The trial court declared * * * that the corporation be dissolved as of April 15, 1998, and ordered that the winding-up and liquidation of the corporation's affairs be done * * * . This appeal followed.

I

The defendants claim first that the trial court improperly dissolved the corporation and ordered its winding-up. We are not persuaded.

* * * *

The parties conceded before us that they have not been able to elect successor directors since the early 1990s. Only Chance signed the corporate minutes and waivers at that time; the defendants did not. The trial court found that the parties were deadlocked with respect to electing successor directors of the corporation. General Statutes [Section] 33-896(b)(2)(B) provides that [a Connecticut state] Court may dissolve a corporation when "the shareholders are deadlocked in voting power for the election of directors and for that reason have been unable at the next * * * annual meeting to elect successors to directors whose term would normally have expired * * * ."

The basis of the defendants' argument is that the statute requires that the shareholders not reach agreement at the next * * * *annual* meeting. They claim that because Chance called a "special" meeting to be held on May 1, 1997, for the purpose of electing directors, the requirements of the statute have not been met. The defendants rely on the fact that Chance called a "special" meeting to elect directors and overlook the fact that Chance and Kosminoff were not able to elect directors at the next * * * annual meeting, i.e., the trial court specifically found that the defendants did not sign the minutes and waivers of the corporation in 1990 and 1991, which included the election of successor directors. At the time of trial, the parties had not been able to elect successor directors for more than five years.

* * * *

* * * It is generally true that disagreement and dissension among stockholders is not in itself sufficient ground for a corporate receivership * * * . Nevertheless, the statute is broad in its purpose and intent * * * . It confers extensive equitable powers. It gives considerable latitude to the exercise of judicial discretion and does not hold the court to the stark letter of the law. * * * [That] the parties failed to hold annual meetings as required by statute and the corporation's bylaws * * * in and of itself is a violation of the law that necessitates corporate dissolution.

It is fundamental to the concept of a corporation that its affairs are to be controlled by a board of directors elected by a majority of the stockholders * * * . In the instant case, there is no such board and no such board can be elected. Consequently, there has not been and cannot be any deliberative control of the company by a board of directors. The corporation is a mere shell inhabited by a business * * * . A receiver is properly appointed when there are such dissensions in the governing body of a corporation, or between sets of stockholders, each owning an equal amount of stock, that the corporation ceases to function in the manner provided for by its own by-laws and in accordance with the statutes relating to corporations. * * * For more than five years since the last annual meeting, the parties have failed to hold an annual meeting and to elect successor directors. Chance's effort to hold a special meeting of the corporation to elect successor directors is irrelevant. Furthermore, the parties created the stalemate themselves when they invited its possibility by entering into an agreement whereby control of the corporation was divided equally among them.

The trial court, therefore, properly concluded that there is no more chance of breaking the deadlock between the parties in the future than there has been in the past and ordered the winding-up of the corporation.

II

The defendants' second claim is that the trial court improperly denied their motion to dismiss Chance's cause of action because it was barred by the stalemate provision of the shareholder agreement. We do not agree.

* * * *

The language of the stalemate provision clearly states that any stalemate shall be broken by Chance's and Kosminoff's each selecting the same third person to whom the proposed question shall be submitted. Given the five years of litigation among and between the parties, their failure to speak or to hold an annual meeting of the corporation and the equal voting power created by the parties, it is likely that the parties will never be able to break their deadlock. The trial court properly found the interaction between Chance and Kosminoff to be a perpetual power struggle with little or no regard for the shareholder agreement or statutory requirements. The conflict was the result of the parties' own making and the trial court properly stepped in to break the stalemate by dissolving the corporation.

* * * *

The judgment is affirmed.

Case Problems

36–1. Burack, Inc., was a family-operated close corporation that sold plumbing supplies in New York. The founder and president, Israel Burack, transferred his shares in the corporation to other family members; when Israel died in 1974, the position of president passed to his son, Robert Burack. Robert held a one-third interest in the company, and the remainder was divided among Israel's other children and grandchildren. All shareholders participated in the corporation as employees or officers and thus relied on salaries and bonuses, rather than dividends, for distribution of the corporation's earnings. In 1976, several of the family-member employees requested a salary increase from Robert, who claimed that company earnings were not sufficient to warrant any employee salary increases. Shortly thereafter, a shareholders' meeting was held (the first in the company's fifty-year history), and Robert was removed from his position as president and denied the right to participate in any way in the corporation. Robert sued to have the company dissolved because he had been frozen out. Discuss whether Robert should would succeed in his suit or whether the court should choose another alternative. [*Burack v. I. Burack, Inc.*, 137 A.D.2d 523, 524 N.Y.S.2d 457 (1988)]

36–2. On March 6, 1981, Carolyn Hamaker lost three fingers from her left hand while operating a notcher machine (lathe) at her place of employment in South Dakota, Pallets and Wood Products. The notching machine had been manufactured by Kenwel Machine Co. On December 31, 1975, Kenwel sold its assets to John and Rosemary Jackson, who created a new company called Kenwel-Jackson Machine Co. Kenwel Machine Co. terminated its existence in August 1977. Kenwel-Jackson Machine Co. continued to manufacture notchers, but it made several design changes and was in fact producing a different machine from the one that injured Carolyn Hamaker. As a result of her injuries, Hamaker brought a suit for damages against Kenwel-Jackson, because Kenwel Machine Co. no longer existed. Discuss whether Kenwel-Jackson is liable for injuries caused by a machine manufactured by a company it purchased. [*Hamaker v. Kenwel-Jackson Machine Co.*, 387 N.W.2d 515 (S.D. 1986)]

36–3. Two brothers, Albert and Raymond Martin, each owned 50 percent of the stock in Martin's News Service, Inc. Albert and Raymond had difficulty working together and communicated only through their accountant. For ten years, there were no corporate meetings, elections to the board of directors, or other corporate formalities. During that time, Raymond operated the business much as a sole proprietorship, failing to consult Albert on any matter and making all of the decisions himself. The corporation, however, was a viable concern that had grown successfully through the years. Albert sued to have the corporation dissolved. Should he succeed? Discuss. [*Martin v. Martin's News Service, Inc.*, 9 Conn.App. 304, 518 A.2d 951 (1986)]

36–4. Lori Ann Nilsson, in the course of her employment as a machine operator, was injured by a pipe and tube cutoff machine that had been manufactured and sold by Continental Machine Co. prior to 1978. In 1986, Fredor Corp. purchased all of the production assets of Continental, including the pipe and tube machine product line, and formed Continental Machine Manufacturing Co. (CMM). The assets purchased from Continental were transferred to CMM. CMM continued to manufacture the same product lines as Continental had. The shareholders of Continental did not become shareholders, officers, or employees of Fredor or CMM. Most of the employees of Continental became employees of CMM, however. There was no evidence that the transaction was undertaken for a fraudulent purpose, nor did Fredor or CMM agree to assume Continental's liabilities. After the sale of assets, Continental continued to exist, but it had no productive assets. Continental continued to own the building in which the assets had been located, however, and leased the building to CMM. Nilsson brought a product liability suit against CMM. Will the court hold CMM liable for injuries caused by a machine manufactured by Continental? What factors will the court consider in reaching its decision? Discuss fully. [*Nilsson v. Continental Machine Manufacturing Co.*, 251 Ill.App.3d 415, 621 N.E.2d 1032, 190 Ill.Dec. 579 (1993)]

36–5. Mike and Peter Schwadel were major shareholders in HJU Sales & Investments, Inc. Over several years the assets of the corporation had been sold off until only one asset remained—a restaurant called "The Place for Steak." The Schwadels sued the president and third major shareholder of the corporation, Hy Uchitel, when he entered into a contract to sell this remaining asset. Florida state law prohibits the sale of all or substantially all of a corporation's assets without shareholder approval. The Schwadels sought an injunction to prevent the sale of the restaurant. Will the court grant the injunction? Discuss. [*Schwadel v. Uchitel*, 455 So.2d 401 (Fla.App. 1984)]

36–6. In January 1981, Frederick Brandt purchased a Tredex treadmill from Atlantic Fitness Products. The treadmill was manufactured by American Tredex Corporation. In July 1981, Nissen Corp. purchased all of the assets of American Tredex, as well as its goodwill and the name American Tredex. The contract for the purchase of assets expressly excluded assumption of liability for injuries arising from any product previously sold by American Tredex. Although Nissen did not continue to manufacture and sell the treadmills, it did continue to sell replacement parts for equipment that had been sold by American Tredex before the sale of its assets. After Nissen's purchase of American Tredex's assets, Brandt obtained replacement parts for his treadmill from Nissen. In the fall of 1986, Brandt was injured when he caught one of his fingers in the treadmill's operating mechanism while adjusting the treadmill. Brandt and his wife sued Nissen and Atlantic Fitness to recover damages, alleging, among other things, negligence and breach of warranty. Nissen moved for summary judgment, contending that it was not responsible for any injuries involving equipment sold or manufactured by American Tredex prior to the date of the asset purchase agreement (July 1981). Should the court grant Nissen's motion? Why, or why not? [*Nissen Corp. v. Miller,* 323 Md. 613, 594 A.2d 564 (1991)]

36–7. In 1987, William Myers sustained injuries to his hand while operating a cement pump manufactured by Thomsen Equipment Co. Myers alleged that the pump was unreasonably dangerous because it had an "unguarded nip point in a flapper valve." Putzmeister, Inc., had purchased Thomsen's assets in 1982. If Myers has a valid product liability claim, what factors will the court consider in determining whether Putzmeister can be held liable for injuries caused by Thomsen's product? [*Myers v. Putzmeister, Inc.*, 232 Ill.App.3d 419, 596 N.E.2d 754, 173 Ill.Dec. 130 (1992)]

36–8. Edward Antar and William Markowitz were the sole stockholders and directors of E.B.M., Inc., a corporation formed for the purpose of buying and managing real estate. Antar and Markowitz were also the controlling shareholders and directors of Acousti-Phase, Inc., a corporation that manufactured and sold stereo speakers. In 1982, Acousti-Phase was effectively shut down when a fire destroyed the manufacturing and storage facility that it was renting from E.B.M. Shortly after the fire, E.B.M. contracted with a New York firm to assemble the speakers, affix the Acousti-Phase name, and sell the final product, primarily to former customers of Acousti-Phase. At the time of the fire, Acousti-Phase owed $26,470 to Cab-Tek, Inc., a corporation that supplied it with cabinet housings for its stereo speakers. In 1985, Cab-Tek sued E.B.M. to recover the debt owed by Acousti-Phase. Discuss fully whether E.B.M. can be held liable for Acousti-Phase's debt. [*Cab-Tek, Inc. v. E.B.M., Inc.*, 153 Vt. 432, 571 A.2d 671 (1990)]

36–9. Ernie Gross and his brother started Sealomatic Electronics Corp. in the 1940s, later changing the name to Solidyne Corp. Sealomatic became a division of Solidyne, which continued to make heat-sealing machines under the brand name Sealomatic. Gross bought other heat-sealing equipment makers, including Thermex and Thermatron, which became other divisions of Solidyne. After the brothers died in 1981, Solidyne was sold and its heat-sealing equipment divisions were consolidated into a single division, Thermex-Thermatron. The new division, with its assets and liabilities, was resold to TTI Acquisitions, which merged to become Thermex-Thermatron, Inc. Thermex-Thermatron continued to use Solidyne customer lists. The names of former Solidyne divisions were on the window of Thermex-Thermatron's public sales office. Listings in phone directories maintained and paid for by Thermex-Thermatron continued to use the names of Solidyne and its former divisions. Meanwhile, Solidyne was completely dissolved. Juanita Rosales, an employee of Perfect Plastics Products, was using a Solidyne Sealomatic machine made in 1969 when it collapsed on her hand. She was seriously injured. She filed a suit in a California state court against Thermex-Thermatron and others. Is Thermex-Thermatron liable for her injury? If so, on what basis? If not, why not? How should the court rule? Explain. [*Rosales v. Thermex-Thermatron, Inc.*, 67 Cal.App.4th 187, 78 Cal.Rptr.2d 861 (1998)]

36–10. The management of First National Supermarket, Inc., wanted to buy the company and offered the shareholders $24.45 per share. A majority of the shareholders voted to accept the offer, but Jeffrey Chokel voted against it. Chokel later filed a suit in a Massachusetts state court to obtain an appraisal of his shares. The judge appraised the value at $29.78 per share, based in part on a price-earnings ratio (calculated by dividing the stock's market price per share by its annual income per share) of twenty. First National appealed to the Supreme Judicial Court of Massachusetts, the state's highest court, arguing in part that the price-earnings ratio was too high. What will happen on appeal? Discuss. [*Chokel v. First National Supermarkets, Inc.*, 421 Mass. 631, 660 N.E.2d 644 (1996)]

36–11. MRS Manufacturing, Inc., manufactured tractors, which it sold to Glades Equipment, Inc. Glades Equipment sold one of the tractors to the U.S. Sugar Corp. Later, Glade and Grove Supply, Inc., bought the Glades Equipment dealership under a contract that stated the sale covered only such property "as [Glades Equipment] has on hand at the time of the . . . sale." Daniel Brown, an employee of the U.S. Sugar Corp., was operating an MRS tractor when it rolled over and killed him. His wife, Patricia, filed a product liability suit against Glade and Grove, among others. What factors will the court consider in determining whether Glade and Grove is liable? [*Brown v. Glade and Grove Supply, Inc.*, 647 So.2d 1033 (Fla.App. 1994)]

36–12. Travelers Corp. announced that it would merge with Primerica Corp. At a special shareholders' meeting, a vote of the Travelers shareholders revealed that 95 percent approved of the merger. Robert Brandt and other shareholders who did not approve of the merger sued Travelers and others, complaining that the defendants had not obtained "the highest possible price for shareholders." Travelers asked the court to dismiss the suit, contending that Brandt and the others had, as a remedy for their complaint, their statutory appraisal rights. On what basis might the court dismiss the suit? Discuss. [*Brandt v. Travelers Corp.*, 44 Conn.Supp. 12, 665 A.2d 616 (1995)]

36–13. Jerry Yarmouth incorporated J&R Interiors, Inc., and was its president, secretary, and sole shareholder. J&R failed to file annual reports and pay annual fees, however, and was involuntarily dissolved by the state. More than a year later, Yarmouth bought a workbench in J&R's name from Equipto Division of Aurora Equipment Co. When the price was not paid, Equipto filed a suit in a Washington state court against Yarmouth, claiming that he was personally liable for payment. Yarmouth argued that he was not personally liable because he had acted as an agent for J&R. Does a corporation continue to exist after it is dissolved? If so, can it continue to conduct business? In whose favor should the court rule in this case, and why? [*Equipto Division Aurora Equipment Co. v. Yarmouth,* 83 Wash.App. 817, 924 P.2d 405 (1996)]

36–14. In 1988, Farad Mohammed and Syed Parveen formed Hina Pharmacy, Health & Beauty Aids, Inc., to operate a pharmacy in New York. Syed, an experienced pharmacist, contributed his expertise and $7,000. Farad contributed $120,000. Each took 50 percent of the Hina stock. Farad assigned his shares to his brother Azam, and Syed assigned his to his wife Aisha. A dispute soon arose over the disparity in capital contributions. The parties held only one shareholders' meeting, and they never attempted to elect directors. Syed later claimed that Azam, who exercised sole control over the daily management of Hina, kept 80 percent of the profits. Azam argued that Syed had agreed to work for 20 percent of the profits plus a salary. Syed stopped working at the pharmacy in 1994. Aisha filed a petition in a New York state court to dissolve Hina. Should the court grant the petition? If so, on what basis? If not, why not? [*In re Parveen,* 259 A.D.2d 389, 687 N.Y.S.2d 90 (1 Dept. 1999)]

36–15. In 1996, Robert McClellan, a licensed contractor doing business as McClellan Design and Construction, entered into a contract with Peppertree North Condominium Association, Inc., to do earthquake repair work on Peppertree's condominium complex consisting of seventy-six units in Northridge, California. McClellan completed the work, but Peppertree failed to pay. In an arbitration proceeding against Peppertree to collect the amount due, McClellan was awarded $141,000, plus 10 percent interest, attorneys' fees, and costs. McClellan filed a suit in a California state court against Peppertree to confirm the award. Meanwhile, the Peppertree board of directors filed articles of incorporation for Northridge Park Townhome Owners Association, Inc., and immediately transferred Peppertree's authority, responsibilities, and assets to the new association. Two weeks later, the court issued a judgment against Peppertree. When McClellan learned about the new association, he filed a motion asking the court to add Northridge as a debtor to the judgment. Should the court grant the motion? Why, or why not? [*McClellan v. Northridge Park Townhome Owners Association, Inc.,* 89 Cal.App.4th 746, 107 Cal.Rptr.2d 702 (2 Dist. 2001)]

E-LINKS

For updated links to resources available on the Web, as well as a variety of other materials, visit this text's Web site at

http://wbl-cs.westbuslaw.com

You may be able to find your state's statutory requirements for merger and consolidation procedures at

http://wwwsecure.law.cornell.edu/topics/state_statutes.html

The court opinions of Delaware's Court of Chancery, which is widely considered to be the nation's premier trial court for corporate law, are now available on the Web in a searchable database offered by the Delaware Corporate Law Clearinghouse. The site also offers valuable links to other sites dealing with corporate law and litigation. Go to

http://corporate-law.widener.edu

LEGAL RESEARCH EXERCISES ON THE WEB

Go to http://wbl-cs.westbuslaw.com, the Web site that accompanies this text. Select "Interactive Study Center," and then click on "Chapter 36." There you will find the following Internet research exercise that you can perform to learn more about mergers:

Activity 36–1: Mergers

CHAPTER 37

CORPORATIONS—Investor Protection and Online Securities Offerings

THE STOCK MARKET CRASH OF OCTOBER 29, 1929, and the ensuing economic depression caused the public to focus on the importance of securities markets for the economic well-being of the nation. Congress was pressured to regulate securities trading, and the result was the Securities Act of 1933[1] and the Securities Exchange Act of 1934.[2] Both acts were designed to provide investors with more information to help them make buying and selling decisions about securities—generally defined as any documents evidencing corporate ownership (stock) or debts (bonds)—and to prohibit deceptive, unfair, and manipulative practices in the purchase and sale of securities. Basically, the 1933 act regulates the initial sales of corporate securities by businesses, and the 1934 act regulates subsequent purchases and sales of securities once they have been issued.

This chapter discusses the nature of federal securities regulation and its effect on the business world. We begin by looking at the federal administrative agency that regulates securities transactions, the Securities and Exchange Commission. The liability of accountants and attorneys for violations of the securities laws is discussed in more detail in Chapter 51.

SECTION 1

The Securities and Exchange Commission

The 1934 act created the Securities and Exchange Commission (SEC) as an independent regulatory agency whose function was to administer the 1933 and 1934 acts. The SEC plays a key role in interpreting the provisions of these acts (and their amendments) and in creating regulations governing the purchase and sale of securities.

1. 15 U.S.C. Sections 77a–77aa.
2. 15 U.S.C. Sections 78a–78mm.

THE BASIC FUNCTIONS OF THE SEC

The SEC regulates the securities industry by undertaking the following activities:

1. Requiring disclosure of facts concerning offerings of securities listed on national securities exchanges and offerings of certain securities traded over the counter (OTC).
2. Regulating the trade in securities on the national and regional securities exchanges and in the OTC markets.
3. Investigating securities fraud.
4. Requiring the registration of securities brokers, dealers, and investment advisers and regulating their activities.
5. Supervising activities conducted by mutual funds companies.
6. Recommending administrative sanctions, injunctive remedies, and criminal prosecution in cases involving violations of securities laws. (The Fraud Section of the Criminal Division of the Department of Justice prosecutes violations of federal securities laws.)

THE REGULATORY POWERS OF THE SEC

From the time of its creation until the present, the SEC's regulatory functions have gradually been increased by legislation granting it authority in different areas. During the 1990s, for example, Congress passed several acts that have significantly expanded the SEC's powers.

To further curb securities fraud, the Securities Enforcement Remedies and Penny Stock Reform Act of 1990[3] amended existing securities laws to expand greatly the types of securities violation cases that SEC administrative law judges can hear and the SEC's enforcement options. The act also provides that courts can bar persons who have engaged in securities fraud from serving as officers and directors of publicly held corporations.

The Securities Acts Amendments of 1990 authorized the SEC to seek sanctions against those who violate foreign securities laws.[4] These amendments increase the ability of the SEC to cooperate in international enforcement of securities laws. Under the Market Reform Act of 1990, the SEC can suspend trading in securities in the event that prices rise and fall excessively in a short period of time.[5]

The National Securities Markets Improvement Act of 1996 expanded the power of the SEC to exempt persons, securities, and transactions from the requirements of the securities laws.[6] (This part of the act is also known as the Capital Markets Efficiency Act.) The act also limited the authority of the states to regulate certain securities transactions, as well as particular investment advisory firms.[7]

Over the years, as more and more SEC rules were issued, the body of regulations governing securities transactions became increasingly cumbersome and complex. Congress and the SEC are now in the process of eliminating some rules, revising others, and generally attempting to streamline the regulatory process to make it more efficient and more relevant to today's securities trading practices.

SECTION 2

The Securities Act of 1933

As mentioned, the Securities Act of 1933 governs initial sales of stock by businesses. The act was designed to prohibit various forms of fraud and to stabilize the securities industry by requiring that all essential information concerning the issuance of securities be made available to the investing public.

Basically, the courts have interpreted the act's definition of what constitutes a security[8] to mean that a security exists in any transaction in which a person (1) invests (2) in a common enterprise (3) reasonably expecting profits (4) derived *primarily* or *substantially* from others' managerial or entrepreneurial efforts.[9]

For our purposes, it is probably most convenient to think of securities in their most common form—stocks and bonds issued by corporations. Bear in mind, though, that securities can take many forms and have been held to include whiskey, cosmetics, worms, beavers, boats, vacuum cleaners, muskrats, and cemetery lots, as well as investment contracts in condominiums, franchises, limited partnerships, oil or gas or other mineral rights, and farm animals accompanied by care agreements.

REGISTRATION STATEMENT

Section 5 of the Securities Act of 1933 broadly provides that if a security does not qualify for an exemption, that security must be *registered* before it is offered to the public either through the mails or through any facility of interstate commerce, including securities exchanges. Issuing corporations must file a *registration statement* with the SEC. Investors must be provided with a prospectus that describes the security being sold, the issuing corporation, and the risk attaching to the security. In principle, the registration statement and the prospectus supply sufficient information to enable unsophisticated investors to evaluate the financial risk involved.

Contents of the Registration Statement. The registration statement must include the following:

1. A description of the significant provisions of the security offered for sale, including the relationship between that security and the other capital securities of the registrant. Also, the corporation must disclose how it intends to use the proceeds of the sale.
2. A description of the registrant's properties and business.

3. 15 U.S.C. Section 77g.
4. See, for example, 15 U.S.C. Section 78o(b)(4)(B).
5. 15 U.S.C. Section 78i(h).
6. 15 U.S.C. Sections 77z-3, 78mm.
7. 15 U.S.C. Section 80b-3a.
8. See 15 U.S.C. Section 77b(a)(1).
9. *SEC v. W. J. Howey Co.*, 328 U.S. 293, 66 S.Ct. 1100, 90 L.Ed. 1244 (1946).

3. A description of the management of the registrant; its security holdings; and its remuneration and other benefits, including pensions and stock options. Any interests of directors or officers in any material transactions with the corporation must be disclosed.
4. A financial statement certified by an independent public accounting firm.
5. A description of pending lawsuits.

Other Requirements. Before filing the registration statement and the prospectus with the SEC, the corporation is allowed to obtain an underwriter who will monitor the distribution of the new issue. There is a twenty-day waiting period (which can be accelerated by the SEC) after registration before the sale can take place. During this period, oral offers between interested investors and the issuing corporation concerning the purchase and sale of the proposed securities may take place, and very limited written advertising is allowed. At this time, what is known as a **red herring** prospectus may be distributed. It gets its name from the red legend printed across it stating that the registration has been filed but has not yet become effective.

After the waiting period, the registered securities can be legally bought and sold. Written advertising is allowed in the form of a so-called **tombstone ad**, so named because historically the format resembled a tombstone. Such ads simply tell the investor where and how to obtain a prospectus. Normally, any other type of advertising is prohibited.

Exempt Securities

A number of specific securities are exempt from the registration requirements of the Securities Act of 1933. These securities—which can also generally be resold without being registered—include the following:[10]

1. All bank securities sold prior to July 27, 1933.
2. Commercial paper, if the maturity date does not exceed nine months.
3. Securities of charitable organizations.
4. Securities resulting from a corporate reorganization issued for exchange with the issuer's existing security holders and certificates issued by trustees, receivers, or debtors in possession under the bankruptcy laws (bankruptcy was discussed in Chapter 30).
5. Securities issued exclusively for exchange with the issuer's existing security holders, provided no commission is paid (for example, stock dividends and stock splits).
6. Securities issued to finance the acquisition of railroad equipment.
7. Any insurance, endowment, or annuity contract issued by a state-regulated insurance company.
8. Government-issued securities.
9. Securities issued by banks, savings and loan associations, farmers' cooperatives, and similar institutions subject to supervision by governmental authorities.
10. In consideration of the "small amount involved,"[11] an issuer's offer of up to $5 million in securities in any twelve-month period.

For the last exemption, under Regulation A,[12] the issuer must file with the SEC a notice of the issue and an offering circular, which must also be provided to investors before the sale. This is a much simpler and less expensive process than the procedures associated with full registration. Companies are allowed to "test the waters" for potential interest before preparing the offering circular. (To *test the waters* means to determine potential interest without actually selling any securities or requiring any commitment on the part of those who are interested.) Small-business issuers (companies with less than $25 million in annual revenues and less than $25 million in outstanding voting stock) can also utilize an integrated registration and reporting system that uses simpler forms than the full registration system.

Exhibit 37–1 on page 748 summarizes the securities and transactions (discussed next) that are exempt from the registration requirements under the Securities Act of 1933 and SEC regulations.

Exempt Transactions

An issuer of securities that are not exempt under any of the categories listed above can avoid the high cost and complicated procedures associated with registration by taking advantage of certain *exempt transactions*. These exemptions are very broad, and thus many sales occur without registration. Because there is some overlap in the coverage of the exemptions, an offering may qualify for more than one.

10. 15 U.S.C. Section 77c.

11. 15 U.S.C. Section 77c(b).
12. 17 C.F.R. Sections 230.251–230.263.

EXHIBIT 37–1 EXEMPTIONS UNDER THE 1933 ACT FOR SECURITIES OFFERINGS BY BUSINESSES

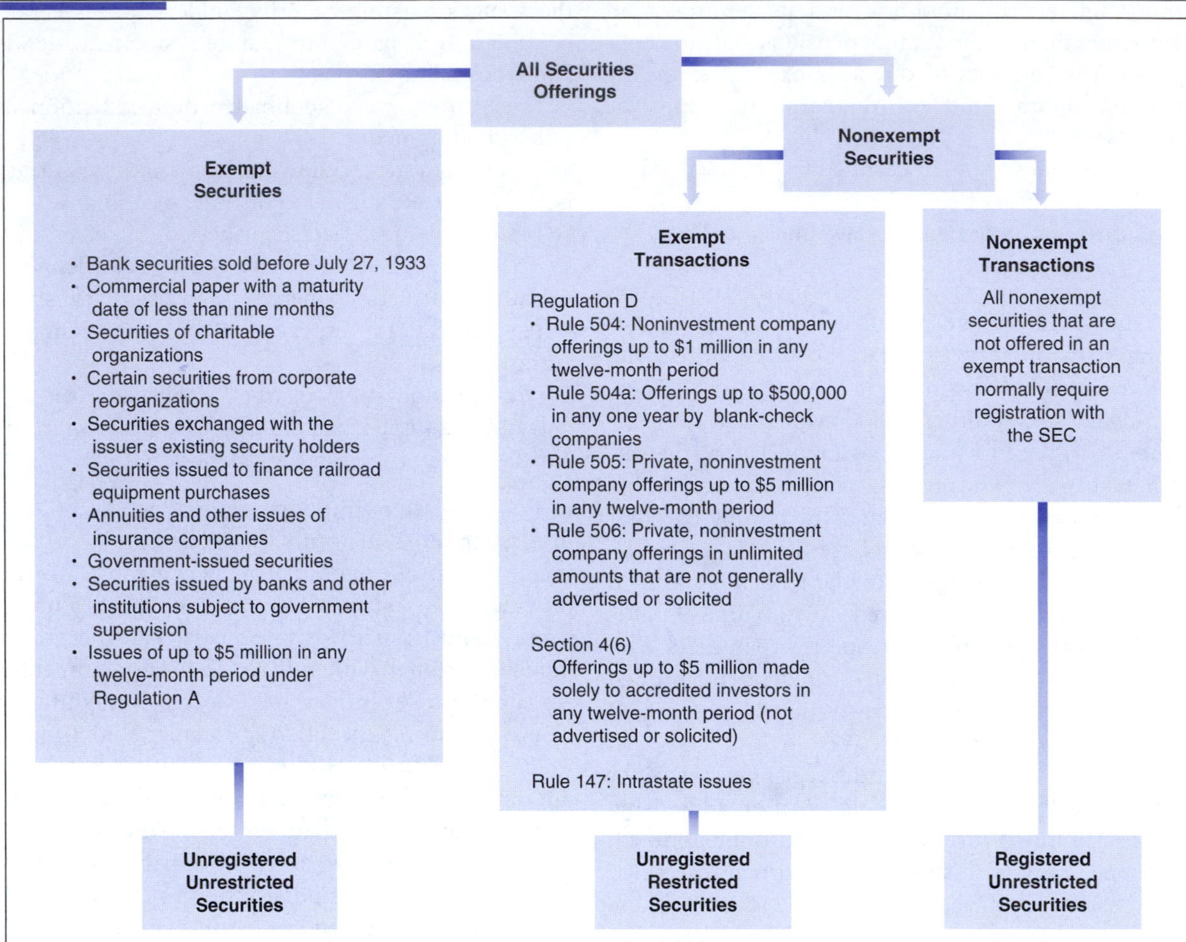

Small Offerings—Regulation D. The SEC's Regulation D contains four separate exemptions from registration requirements for limited offers (offers that either involve a small amount of money or are made in a limited manner). Regulation D provides that any of these offerings made during any twelve-month period are exempt from the registration requirements.

Rule 504. Noninvestment company offerings up to $1 million in any twelve-month period are exempt.[13] In contrast to investment companies (discussed later in this chapter), noninvestment companies are firms that are not engaged primarily in the business of investing or trading in securities.

Rule 504a. Offerings up to $500,000 in any one year by so-called blank-check companies—companies with no specific business plans except to locate and acquire presently unknown businesses or opportunities—are exempt if no general solicitation or advertising is used; the SEC is notified of the sales; and precaution is taken against nonexempt, unregistered resales.[14] The limits on advertising and unregistered resales do not apply if the offering is made

13. 17 C.F.R. Section 230.504. Rule 504 is the exemption used by most small businesses, but that could change under new SEC Rule 1001. This rule permits, under certain circumstances, "testing the waters" for offerings of up to $5 million *per transaction*. These offerings, however, can be made only to "qualified purchasers" (knowledgeable, sophisticated investors).

14. Precautions to be taken against nonexempt, unregistered resales include asking the investor whether he or she is buying the securities for others; before the sale, disclosing to each purchaser in writing that the securities are unregistered and thus cannot be resold, except in an exempt transaction, without first being registered; and indicating on the certificates that the securities are unregistered and restricted.

solely in states that provide for registration and disclosure and the securities are sold in compliance with those provisions.[15]

Rule 505. Private, noninvestment company offerings up to $5 million in any twelve-month period are exempt, regardless of the number of **accredited investors** (banks, insurance companies, investment companies, the issuer's executive officers and directors, and persons whose income or net worth exceeds certain limits), so long as there are no more than thirty-five unaccredited investors; no general solicitation or advertising is used; the SEC is notified of the sales; and precaution is taken against nonexempt, unregistered resales. If the sale involves *any* unaccredited investors, *all* investors must be given material information about the offering company, its business, and the securities before the sale. Unlike Rule 506 (discussed next), Rule 505 includes no requirement that the issuer believe each unaccredited investor "has such knowledge and experience in financial and business matters that he is capable of evaluating the merits and the risks of the prospective investment."[16]

Rule 506. Private offerings in unlimited amounts that are not generally solicited or advertised are exempt if the SEC is notified of the sales; precaution is taken against nonexempt, unregistered resales; and the issuer believes that each unaccredited investor has sufficient knowledge or experience in financial matters to be capable of evaluating the investment's merits and risks. There may be no more than thirty-five unaccredited investors, although there may be an unlimited number of accredited investors. If there are any unaccredited investors, the issuer must provide to all purchasers material information about itself, its business, and the securities before the sale.[17]

This exemption is perhaps most important to those firms that want to raise funds through the sale of securities without registering them. It is often referred to as the *private placement* exemption, because it exempts "transactions not involving any public offering."[18] This provision applies to private offerings to a limited number of persons who are sufficiently sophisticated and in a sufficiently strong bargaining position to be able to assume the risk of the investment (and who thus have no need for federal registration protection), as well as to private offerings to similarly situated institutional investors.

Small Offerings—Section 4(6). Under Section 4(6) of the Securities Act of 1933, an offer made *solely* to accredited investors is exempt if its amount is not more than $5 million. Any number of accredited investors may participate, but no unaccredited investors may do so. No general solicitation or advertising may be used; the SEC must be notified of all sales; and precaution must be taken against nonexempt, unregistered resales. Precaution is necessary because these are *restricted* securities and may be resold only by registration or in an exempt transaction.[19] (The securities purchased and sold by most people who deal in stock are called, in contrast, *unrestricted* securities.)

Intrastate Issues—Rule 147. Also exempt are intrastate transactions involving purely local offerings.[20] This exemption applies to most offerings that are restricted to residents of the state in which the issuing company is organized and doing business. For nine months after the last sale, virtually no resales may be made to nonresidents, and precautions must be taken against this possibility. These offerings remain subject to applicable laws in the state of issue.

Resales. Most securities can be resold without registration (although some resales may be subject to restrictions, which are discussed above in connection with specific exemptions). The Securities Act of 1933 provides exemptions for resales by most persons other than issuers or underwriters. The average investor who sells shares of stock does not have to file a registration statement with the SEC. Resales of restricted securities acquired under Rule 504a, Rule 505, Rule 506, or Section 4(6), however, trigger the registration requirements unless the party selling them complies with Rule 144 or Rule 144A. These rules are sometimes referred to as "safe harbors."

Rule 144. Rule 144 exempts restricted securities from registration on resale if there is adequate current public information about the issuer, the person selling the

15. 17 C.F.R. Section 230.504a.
16. 17 C.F.R. Section 230.505.
17. 17 C.F.R. Section 230.506.
18. 15 U.S.C. Section 77d(2).
19. 15 U.S.C. Section 77d(6).
20. 15 U.S.C. Section 77c(a)(11); 17 C.F.R. Section 230.147.

securities has owned them for at least one year, they are sold in certain limited amounts in unsolicited brokers' transactions, and the SEC is given notice of the resale.[21] "Adequate current public information" consists of the reports that certain companies are required to file under the Securities Exchange Act of 1934. A person who has owned the securities for at least two years is subject to none of these requirements, unless the person is an affiliate. An *affiliate* is one who controls, is controlled by, or is in common control with the issuer. Sales of *nonrestricted* securities by an affiliate are also subject to the requirements for an exemption under Rule 144 (except that the affiliate need not have owned the securities for at least two years).

Rule 144A. Securities that at the time of issue are not of the same class as securities listed on a national securities exchange or quoted in a U.S. automated interdealer quotation system may be resold under Rule 144A.[22] They may be sold only to a qualified institutional buyer (an institution, such as an insurance company, an investment company, or a bank, that owns and invests at least $100 million in securities). The seller must take reasonable steps to ensure that the buyer knows that the seller is relying on the exemption under Rule 144A. A sample restricted stock certificate is shown in Exhibit 37–2.

Violations of the 1933 Act

It is a violation of the Securities Act of 1933 to intentionally defraud investors by misrepresenting or omitting facts in a registration statement or prospectus. Liability is also imposed on those who are negligent for not discovering the fraud. Selling securities before the effective date of the registration statement or under an exemption for which the securities do not qualify results in liability.

Defenses. There are three basic defenses to charges of violations under the 1933 act. A defendant can avoid liability if he or she can prove that, even if a statement was not true or a fact was left out, the statement or omission was not material. A defendant can also avoid liability by proving that the plaintiff knew about the misrepresentation and bought the stock anyway.

Any defendant, except the issuer of the stock, can also assert what is called the *due diligence* defense. To make this defense, a person must prove that he or she reasonably believed, at the time the registration statement became effective, that the statements in it were true and there were no omissions of material facts. (This defense is discussed in further detail in Chapter 51, in the context of the liability of accountants.)

Criminal Penalties. The U.S. Department of Justice brings criminal actions against those who willfully violate the 1933 act. Violators may be penalized by fines up to $10,000, imprisonment up to five years, or both.

Civil Sanctions. The SEC is authorized to seek, against those who willfully violate the 1933 act, an injunction against further sales of the securities involved. The SEC can also ask the court to grant other relief, such as an order to a violator to refund profits.

Those who purchase the securities and suffer harm as a result of the false or omitted statements, or other violation, may bring a suit in a federal court to recover their losses and other damages. If a registration statement or a prospectus contains material false statements or material omissions, for example, damages may be imposed on those who signed the statement or those who provided information used in preparing the statement (such as accountants and other experts—see Chapter 51).

SECTION 3

The Securities Exchange Act of 1934

The Securities Exchange Act of 1934 provides for the regulation and registration of securities exchanges, brokers, dealers, and national securities associations, such as the National Association of Securities Dealers (NASD). The SEC regulates the markets in which securities are traded by maintaining a continuous disclosure system for all corporations with securities on the securities exchanges and for those companies that have assets in excess of $10 million and five hundred or more shareholders. These corporations are referred to as Section 12 companies, as they are required to register their securities under Section 12 of the 1934 act.

The act regulates proxy solicitation for voting (see Chapter 35), and it allows the SEC to engage in market surveillance to regulate undesirable market practices such as fraud, market manipulation, misrepresentation, and stabilization. (*Stabilization* is a

21. 17 C.F.R. Section 230.144.

22. 17 C.F.R. Section 230.144A.

EXHIBIT 37–2 A SAMPLE RESTRICTED STOCK CERTIFICATE

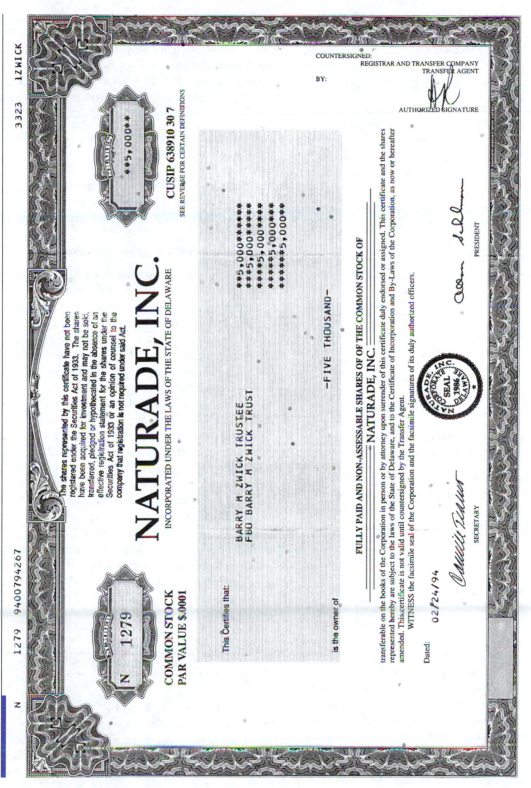

N 1279 9400794267 3323 1ZWICK

N 1279

5,000

COMMON STOCK
PAR VALUE $.0001

The shares represented by this certificate have not been registered under the Securities Act of 1933. The shares have been acquired for investment and may not be sold, transferred, pledged or hypothecated in the absence of an effective registration statement for the shares under the Securities Act of 1933 or an opinion of counsel to the company that registration is not required under said Act.

NATURADE, INC.

INCORPORATED UNDER THE LAWS OF THE STATE OF DELAWARE

CUSIP 638910 30 7
SEE REVERSE FOR CERTAIN DEFINITIONS

This Certifies that:

BARRY M ZWICK TRUSTEE
FBO BARRY M ZWICK TRUST

5,000****
5,000**
****5,000****
*****5,000***
******5,000**

is the owner of

–FIVE THOUSAND–

FULLY PAID AND NON-ASSESSABLE SHARES OF OF THE COMMON STOCK OF

NATURADE, INC.

transferable on the books of the Corporation in person or by attorney upon surrender of this certificate duly endorsed or assigned. This certificate and the shares represented hereby are subject to the laws of the State of Delaware, and to the Certificate of Incorporation and By-Laws of the Corporation, as now or hereafter amended. This certificate is not valid until countersigned by the Transfer Agent.

WITNESS the facsimile seal of the Corporation and the facsimile signatures of its duly authorized officers.

Dated: 02/24/94

SECRETARY

NATURADE, INC. CORPORATE SEAL 1986 DELAWARE

PRESIDENT

COUNTERSIGNED:
REGISTRAR AND TRANSFER COMPANY
TRANSFER AGENT

BY:

AUTHORIZED SIGNATURE

market-manipulating technique by which securities underwriters bid for securities to stabilize their prices during their issuance.)

SECTION 10(b) AND SEC RULE 10b-5

Section 10(b) is one of the most important sections of the Securities Exchange Act of 1934. This section prohibits the use of any manipulative or deceptive device in violation of SEC rules and regulations. Among the rules that the SEC has prescribed is **SEC Rule 10b-5**, which prohibits the commission of fraud in connection with the purchase or sale of any security. Rule 10b-5 states as follows:

> It shall be unlawful for any person, directly or indirectly, by the use of any means or instrumentality of interstate commerce, or of the mails or of any facility of any national securities exchange,
>
> (a) To employ any device, scheme, or artifice to defraud,
>
> (b) To make any untrue statement of a material fact or to omit to state a material fact necessary in order to make the statements made, in the light of the circumstances under which they were made, not misleading, or
>
> (c) To engage in any act, practice, or course of business which operates or would operate as a fraud or deceit upon any person, in connection with the purchase or sale of any security.[23]

One of the most important purposes of Section 10(b) and SEC Rule 10b-5 relates to what is called **insider trading**. Because of their positions, corporate directors and officers often obtain advance inside information that can affect the future market value of the corporate stock. Obviously, their positions can give them a trading advantage over the general public and shareholders. The 1934 Securities Exchange Act defines inside information and extends liability to officers and directors in their personal transactions for taking advantage of such information when they know that it is unavailable to the person with whom they are dealing.

Section 10(b) of the 1934 act and SEC Rule 10b-5 cover not only corporate officers, directors, and majority shareholders but also any persons having access to or receiving information of a nonpublic nature on which trading is based.

Disclosure Requirements under SEC Rule 10b-5. Any material omission or misrepresentation of material facts in connection with the purchase or sale of a security may violate Section 10(b) and SEC Rule 10b-5. The key to liability (which can be civil or criminal) under this rule is whether the insider's information is *material*. The following are some examples of material facts calling for disclosure under the rule:

1. Fraudulent trading in the company stock by a broker-dealer.
2. A dividend change (whether up or down).
3. A contract for the sale of corporate assets.
4. A new discovery, a new process, or a new product.
5. A significant change in the financial condition of the firm.
6. Potential litigation against the company.

Ironically, one of the effects of SEC Rule 10b-5 was to deter disclosure. To understand why, consider an example. A company announces that its projected earnings in a certain time period will be X amount. It turns out that the forecast is wrong. The earnings are in fact much lower, and the price of the company's stock is affected—negatively. The shareholders then bring a class-action suit against the company, alleging that the directors violated SEC Rule 10b-5 by disclosing misleading financial information.

In an attempt to rectify this problem and promote disclosure, Congress passed the Private Securities Litigation Reform Act of 1995. Among other things, the act provides a "safe harbor" for publicly held companies that make forward-looking statements, such as financial forecasts. Those who make such statements are protected against federal liability for securities fraud as long as the statements are accompanied by "meaningful cautionary statements identifying important factors that could cause actual results to differ materially from those in the forward-looking statement."[24]

See Case 37.1 at the end of this chapter. To view the full, unedited case from Westlaw,® go to this text's Web site at **http://wbl-cs.westbuslaw.com**.

Applicability of SEC Rule 10b-5. SEC Rule 10b-5 applies in virtually all cases concerning the trading of securities, whether on organized exchanges, in over-the-counter markets, or in private transactions. The rule covers, among other things, notes,

23. 17 C.F.R. Section 240.10b-5.

24. 15 U.S.C. Sections 77z-2, 78u-5.

bonds, agreements to form a corporation, and joint-venture agreements. Generally, the rule covers just about any form of security. It is immaterial whether a firm has securities registered under the 1933 act for the 1934 act to apply.

SEC Rule 10b-5 is applicable only when the requisites of federal jurisdiction (such as the use of the mails, of stock exchange facilities, or of any instrumentality of interstate commerce) are present. Virtually no commercial transaction, however, can be completed without such contact. In addition, the states have corporate securities laws, many of which include provisions similar to SEC Rule 10b-5.

SEC Rule 10b-5 and state securities laws also apply to online securities offerings and disclosures.

Outsiders and SEC Rule 10b-5. The traditional insider-trading case involves true insiders—corporate officers, directors, and majority shareholders who have access to (and trade on) inside information. Increasingly, liability under Section 10(b) of the 1934 act and SEC Rule 10b-5 has been extended to include certain "outsiders"—those who trade on inside information acquired indirectly. Two theories have been developed under which outsiders may be held liable for insider trading: the *tipper/tippee theory* and the *misappropriation theory*.

Tipper/Tippee Theory. Anyone who acquires inside information as a result of a corporate insider's breach of his or her fiduciary duty can be liable under SEC Rule 10b-5. This liability extends to **tippees** (those who receive "tips" from insiders) and even remote tippees (tippees of tippees).

The key to liability under this theory is that the inside information be obtained as a result of someone's breach of a fiduciary duty to the corporation the shares of which are involved in the trading. Unless there is a breach of a duty not to disclose inside information, the disclosure is made in exchange for personal benefit, and the tippee knows of this breach (or should know of it) and benefits from it, there is no liability under this theory.[25]

Westlaw. See Case 37.2 at the end of this chapter. To view the full, unedited case from Westlaw,® go to this text's Web site at **http://wbl-cs.westbuslaw.com**.

Misappropriation Theory. Liability for insider trading may also be established under the misappropriation theory. This theory holds that if an individual wrongfully obtains (misappropriates) inside information and trades on it for his or her personal gain, the individual should be held liable because, in essence, the individual stole information rightfully belonging to another.

The misappropriation theory has been controversial because it significantly extends the reach of SEC Rule 10b-5 to outsiders who would not ordinarily be deemed fiduciaries of the corporations in the stock of which they trade.

See Case 37.3 at the end of this chapter. To view the full, unedited case from Westlaw,® go to this text's Web site at **http://wbl-cs.westbuslaw.com**.

INSIDER REPORTING AND TRADING—SECTION 16(b)

Officers, directors, and certain large stockholders[26] of Section 12 corporations are required to file reports with the SEC concerning their ownership and trading of the corporation's securities.[27] Section 16(b) of the 1934 act provides for the recapture by the corporation of all profits realized by the insider on any purchase and sale or sale and purchase of the corporation's stock within any six-month period. It is irrelevant whether the insider actually uses inside information; *all such short-swing profits must be returned to the corporation.*

Section 16(b) applies not only to stock but to warrants, options, and securities convertible into stock. In addition, the courts have fashioned complex rules for determining profits. The SEC exempts a number of transactions under Rule 16b-3.[28] For all of these reasons, corporate insiders are wise to seek competent counsel prior to trading in the corporation's stock. Exhibit 37–3 on the following page compares the effects of SEC Rule 10b-5 and Section 16(b). Shareholders owning 10 percent or more of the stock of a Section 12 corporation may be held liable under Section 16(b).

Westlaw. See Case 37.4 at the end of this chapter. To view the full, unedited case from Westlaw,® go to this text's Web site at **http://wbl-cs.westbuslaw.com**.

25. See, for example, *Chiarella v. United States,* 445 U.S. 222, 100 S.Ct. 1108, 63 L.Ed.2d 348 (1980); and *Dirks v. SEC,* 463 U.S. 646, 103 S.Ct. 3255, 77 L.Ed.2d 911 (1983).

26. Those stockholders owning 10 percent of the class of equity securities registered under Section 12 of the 1934 act.

27. 15 U.S.C. Section 78*l*.

28. 17 C.F.R. Section 240.16b-3.

PROXY STATEMENTS

Section 14(a) of the Securities Exchange Act of 1934 regulates the solicitation of proxies (see Chapter 35) from shareholders of Section 12 companies. The SEC regulates the content of proxy statements, which are statements sent to shareholders by corporate managers who are requesting authority to vote on behalf of the shareholders in a particular election on specified issues. Whoever solicits a proxy must fully and accurately disclose in the proxy statement all of the facts that are pertinent to the matter on which the shareholders are to vote. SEC Rule 14a-9 is similar to the antifraud provisions of SEC Rule 10b-5. Remedies for violations are extensive, ranging from injunctions to prevent a vote from being taken to monetary damages.

VIOLATIONS OF THE 1934 ACT

Violations of Section 10(b) and Rule 10b-5 of the Securities Exchange Act of 1934 include insider trading. This is a criminal offense, with criminal penalties. Violators of these laws may also be subject to civil liability. For any sanctions to be imposed, however, there must be *scienter*—the violator must have had an intent to defraud or knowledge of his or her misconduct (see Chapter 13). *Scienter* can be proved by showing a defendant made false statements or wrongfully failed to disclose material facts.

Violations of Section 16(b) include the sale by insiders of stock acquired less than six months before the sale. These violations are subject to civil sanctions. Liability under Section 16(b) is strict liability. *Scienter* is not required.

See Case 37.5 at the end of this chapter. To view the full, unedited case from Westlaw,® go to this text's Web site at http://wbl-cs.westbuslaw.com.

Criminal Penalties. For violations of Section 10(b) and Rule 10b-5, an individual may be fined up to $1 million, imprisoned up to ten years, or both. A partnership or a corporation may be fined up to $2.5 million.

EXHIBIT 37–3 COMPARISON OF COVERAGE, APPLICATION, AND LIABILITY UNDER SEC RULE 10b-5 AND SECTION 16(b)

	RULE 10b-5	SECTION 16(b)
Subject matter of transaction	Any security (does not have to be registered).	Any security (does not have to be registered).
Transactions covered	Purchase or sale.	Short-swing purchase and sale or short-swing sale and purchase.
Who is subject to liability?	Virtually anyone with inside information under a duty to disclose—including officers, directors, controlling stockholders, and tippees.	Officers, directors, and certain holders of large amounts of stock.
Is omission or misrepresentation necessary for liability?	Yes.	No.
Any exempt transactions?	No.	Yes, a variety of exemptions.
Is direct dealing with the party necessary?	No.	No.
Who may bring an action?	A person transacting with an insider, the SEC, or a purchaser or seller damaged by a wrongful act.	Corporation and shareholder by derivative action.

Civil Sanctions. Both the SEC and private parties can bring actions to seek civil sanctions against violators of the 1934 act.

The Insider Trading Sanctions Act of 1984 permits the SEC to bring suit in a federal district court against anyone violating or aiding in a violation of the 1934 act or SEC rules by purchasing or selling a security while in the possession of material nonpublic information.[29] The violation must occur on or through the facilities of a national securities exchange or from or through a broker or dealer. Transactions pursuant to a public offering by an issuer of securities are excepted. The court may assess as a penalty as much as triple the profits gained or the loss avoided by the guilty party. Profit or loss is defined as "the difference between the purchase or sale price of the security and the value of that security as measured by the trading price of the security at a reasonable period of time after public dissemination of the nonpublic information."[30]

The Insider Trading and Securities Fraud Enforcement Act of 1988 enlarged the class of persons who may be subject to civil liability for insider-trading violations. This act also gave the SEC authority to award **bounty payments** (rewards given by government officials for acts beneficial to the state) to persons providing information leading to the prosecution of insider-trading violations.[31]

Private parties may also sue violators of Section 10(b) and Rule 10b-5. A private party may obtain rescission of a contract to buy securities or damages to the extent of the violator's illegal profits. Those found liable have a right to seek contribution from those who share responsibility for the violations, including accountants, attorneys, and corporations.[32] (The liability of accountants and attorneys for violations of the securities laws is discussed in more detail in Chapter 51.) For violations of Section 16(b), a corporation can bring an action to recover the short-swing profits.

29. 15 U.S.C. Section 78u(d)(2)(A).

30. 15 U.S.C. Section 78u(d)(2)(C).

31. 15 U.S.C. Section 78u-1.

32. Note that a private cause of action under Section 10(b) and SEC Rule 10b-5 cannot be brought against accountants, attorneys, and others who "aid and abet" violations of the act. Only the SEC can bring actions against so-called aiders and abettors. See *SEC v. Fehn*, 97 F.3d 1276 (9th Cir. 1996).

SECTION 4

Regulation of Investment Companies

Investment companies, and mutual funds in particular, grew rapidly after World War II. **Investment companies** act on behalf of many smaller shareholders/owners by buying a large portfolio of securities and managing that portfolio professionally. A **mutual fund** is a specific type of investment company that continually buys or sells to investors shares of ownership in a portfolio. Such companies are regulated by the Investment Company Act of 1940,[33] which provides for SEC regulation of their activities. The 1940 act was expanded by the Investment Company Act Amendments of 1970. Further minor changes were made in the Securities Acts Amendments of 1975. The National Securities Markets Improvement Act of 1996 increased the SEC's authority to regulate investment companies by limiting virtually all of the authority of the states to regulate these enterprises.

The 1940 act requires that every investment company register with the SEC and imposes restrictions on the activities of such companies and persons connected with them. For the purposes of the act, an investment company is defined as any entity that (1) "is . . . engaged primarily . . . in the business of investing, reinvesting, or trading in securities" or (2) is engaged in such business and more than 40 percent of the company's assets consist of investment securities. Excluded from coverage by the act are banks, insurance companies, savings and loan associations, finance companies, oil and gas drilling firms, charitable foundations, tax-exempt pension funds, and other special types of institutions, such as closely held corporations.

All investment companies must register with the SEC by filing a notification of registration. Each year, registered investment companies must file reports with the SEC. To safeguard company assets, all securities must be held in the custody of a bank or stock exchange member, and that bank or stock exchange member must follow strict procedures established by the SEC.

No dividends may be paid from any source other than accumulated, undistributed net income. Furthermore, there are some restrictions on investment activities. For example, investment companies are not allowed to purchase securities on the margin (pay only part of the total price, borrowing the rest),

33. 15 U.S.C. Sections 80a-1 to 80a-64.

sell short (sell shares not yet owned), or participate in joint trading accounts.

SECTION 5

State Securities Laws

Today, all states have their own corporate securities laws, or **blue sky laws**, that regulate the offer and sale of securities within individual state borders. (The phrase *blue sky laws* dates to a 1917 United States Supreme Court decision in which the Court declared that the purpose of such laws was to prevent "speculative schemes which have no more basis than so many feet of 'blue sky.'"[34]) Article 8 of the Uniform Commercial Code, which has been adopted by all of the states, also imposes various requirements relating to the purchase and sale of securities. State securities laws apply only to intrastate transactions. Since the adoption of the 1933 and 1934 federal securities acts, the state and federal governments have regulated securities concurrently. Issuers must comply with both federal and state securities laws, and exemptions from federal law are not exemptions from state laws.

There are differences in philosophy among state statutes, but certain features are common to all state blue sky laws. Typically, state laws have disclosure requirements and antifraud provisions, many of which are patterned after Section 10(b) of the Securities Exchange Act of 1934 and SEC Rule 10b-5. State laws also provide for the registration or qualification of securities offered or issued for sale within the state and impose disclosure requirements. Unless an applicable exemption from registration is found, issuers must register or qualify their stock with the appropriate state official, often called a *corporations commissioner.* Additionally, most state securities laws regulate securities brokers and dealers. The Uniform Securities Act, which has been adopted in part by several states, was drafted to be acceptable to states with differing regulatory philosophies.

The dual federal and state system has not always worked well, particularly during the early 1990s, when there was considerable expansion of the securities markets. The National Securities Markets Improvement Act of 1996 eliminated some of the duplicate regulations. While the states still regulate local and regional matters, the SEC exclusively regulates most of the national securities activities.

34. *Hall v. Geiger-Jones Co.,* 242 U.S. 539, 37 S.Ct. 217, 61 L.Ed. 480 (1917).

SECTION 6

Online Securities Offerings and Disclosures

The Spring Street Brewing Company, headquartered in New York, made history when it became the first company to attempt to sell securities via the Internet. Through its online initial public offering (IPO), which ended in early 1996, Spring Street raised about $1.6 million. No commissions were paid to any brokers or any underwriters. The offering was made pursuant to Regulation A, which, as mentioned earlier in this chapter, allows small-business issuers to employ a simplified registration procedure.

Any company wishing to make a traditional IPO has to comply with filing requirements dictated by federal and state law. Because such filings are costly and time consuming, online IPOs are particularly attractive to small companies and start-up ventures that may find it difficult to raise capital from institutional investors or through underwriters.

Regulations Governing Online Securities Offerings

One of the early questions posed by online offerings was whether the delivery of securities *information* via the Internet met the requirements of the Securities Act, which traditionally were applied to the delivery of paper documents. The SEC addressed this issue in its October 1995 interpretive release titled *Use of Electronic Media for Delivery Purposes.*[35] In this release, the SEC stated that "[t]he use of electronic media should be at least an equal alternative to the use of paper-based media" and that anything that can be delivered in paper form under the current securities laws might also be delivered in electronic form.

A law firm specializing in securities regulation then asked the SEC to comment on whether a prospectus in downloadable form would meet SEC requirements. In essence, the SEC concluded that it did. There was no change in the substantive law of disclosure; only the delivery vehicle has changed.

Basically, then, when the Internet is used for the delivery of a prospectus, the same rules apply as for

35. Securities Act Release No. 33-7233 (October 6, 1995). The rules governing the use of electronic transmissions for delivery purposes were subsequently confirmed in Securities Act Release No. 33-7289 (May 9, 1996) and expanded in Securities Act Release No. 33-7856 (April 28, 2000).

the delivery of a paper prospectus. These rules are as follows:

1. *Timely and adequate notice of the delivery of information.* Hosting a prospectus on a Web site does not constitute adequate notice, but separate e-mails or even postcards will satisfy the SEC's notice requirements.
2. *The online communication system must be easily accessible.* This is very simple to do today because virtually anyone interested in purchasing securities has access to the Web.
3. *Some evidence of delivery must be created.* This is a complicated issue with respect to the delivery of prospectuses via the Web. Today, though, this requirement is relatively easy to satisfy. Those making online offerings can require an e-mail return receipt verification of any materials sent electronically.

Once the three requirements above have been satisfied, successful delivery of the prospectus has occurred.

Potential Liability Created by Online Offering Materials

All printed prospectuses indicate that only the information given in the prospectuses can be used in conjunction with making an investment decision in the securities offered. The same wording, of course, appears on Web-based offerings. Those who create such Web-based offerings may be tempted, however, to go one step further. They may include hyperlinks to other sites that might have analyzed the future prospects of the company, the products and services sold by the firm, or the offering itself. To avoid potential liability, however, online offerors (the entities making the offerings) need to exercise caution when including such hyperlinks.

For example, suppose that a hyperlink goes to an analyst's Web page in which the company making the offering is heavily touted. Further suppose that after the IPO, the stock price falls. By placing the hyperlink on the Web site of the offering company, that company is impliedly supporting the information presented on the linked page. In such a situation, the company may be liable under federal securities laws.[36]

Remember also that for Regulation D offerings, only accredited investors may participate in such private placements. If the offeror places the offering circular on its Web site for general consumption by anybody on the Internet, potential problems may occur. General solicitation is restricted, obviously, because Regulation D offerings are private placements. If anyone can have access to the offering circular on the Web, the Regulation D exemption may be disqualified.

Online Securities Offerings by Foreign Companies

One of the questions raised by Internet transactions has to do with securities offerings by foreign companies. Traditionally, foreign companies have not been able to offer new shares to the U.S. public without first registering them with the SEC. Today, however, anybody in the world can offer shares of stock worldwide via the Web.

The SEC asks that foreign issuers on the Internet implement measures to warn U.S. investors. For example, a foreign company offering shares of stock on the Internet must add a disclaimer on its Web site stating that it has not gone through the registration procedure in the United States. If the SEC believes that a Web site's offering of foreign securities has been targeted at U.S. residents, it will pursue that company in an attempt to require it to register in the United States.[37]

SECTION 7

Online Securities Fraud

A major problem facing the SEC today is how to enforce the antifraud provisions of the securities laws in the online environment. An ongoing concern is how to curb online investment scams. One fraudulent investment scheme involved twenty thousand investors, who lost, in all, more than $3 million. Some cases have involved false claims about the earnings potential of home-business programs, such as the claim that one could "earn $4,000 or more each month." Others have concerned claims for "guaranteed credit repair."

Here we look at some other significant Internet-related issues concerning securities fraud, including the use and abuse of Internet chat rooms to praise or criticize certain securities. Today, there are tens of thousands of online chat rooms devoted to the buying and selling of securities. None of these is an official site of any company, securities dealer, or other professional group. The increasing abuse of these

36. See, for example, *In re Syntec Corp.*, 95 F.3d. 92 (9th Cir. 1966).

37. International Series Release No. 1125, March 23, 1998.

online chat forums for private gain in securities trading has become almost rampant, yet what can the SEC do to curb such speech? Clearly, the chat rooms cannot be shut down. After all, the First Amendment to the U.S. Constitution guarantees freedom of speech. Yet where does one draw the line between free speech and statements made to manipulate stock prices? Other issues relate to fictitious press releases and illegal offerings of securities.

Using Chat Rooms to Manipulate Stock Prices

"Pumping and dumping" occurs when a person who has purchased a particular stock heavily promotes ("pumps up") that stock—thereby creating a great demand for it and driving up its price—and then sells ("dumps") it. The concept of pumping up a stock and then dumping it is quite old. In the online world, however, the process can occur much more quickly and efficiently than before.

The most famous case in this area involved Jonathan Lebed, a fifteen-year-old stock trader and Internet user from New Jersey. While Lebed was the first minor that the SEC charged with securities fraud, he certainly will not be the last. The SEC charged that Lebed bought thinly traded stocks; then, after the purchases, he flooded stock-related chat rooms, particularly at Yahoo's finance boards, with messages touting those stocks' virtues. He used numerous false names so that no one would know that a single person was posting the messages. He said that the stock was the most "undervalued stock in history" and that its price would jump by 1,000 percent "very soon." When other investors would then buy the stock, the price would go up quickly, and Lebed would sell out. The SEC forced the teenager to repay almost $300,000 in gains plus interest. He was allowed, however, to keep about $500,000 of the profits he made trading small-company stocks that he also touted on the Internet.

The SEC has been bringing an increasing number of cases against those who manipulate stock prices in this way. Consider that in 1995, such fraud resulted in only six SEC cases. By 2001, the SEC had brought an estimated one hundred actions against online perpetrators of fraudulent stock-price manipulation.

Illegal Securities Offerings

In the first case of its kind, the SEC filed suit against three individuals for illegally offering securities on an Internet auction site.[38] In essence, all three indicated that their companies would go public soon. They attempted to sell unregistered securities via the Web auction sites. All of these actions were in violation of Section 5, 17(a)(1) and 17(a)(3) of the 1933 Securities Act.

In 2001, the SEC brought a variety of Internet-related fraud cases, many of them related to the initial three cases just mentioned. For example, in March 2001, the SEC filed twelve separate actions in cases involving solicitations to invest in private companies that purportedly were going to go public (through an IPO).

38. *In re Davis*, SEC Administrative File No. 3-10080, 10/20/99; *In re Haas*, SEC Administrative File No. 3-10081, 10/20/99; and *In re Sitaras*, SEC Administrative File No. 3-10082, 10/20/99.

Terms and Concepts to Review

accredited investor 749	investment company 755	tippee 753
blue sky law 756	mutual fund 755	tombstone ad 747
bounty payment 755	red herring 747	
insider trading 752	SEC Rule 10b-5 752	

CHAPTER SUMMARY

The Securities Act of 1933	Prohibits fraud and stabilizes the securities industry by requiring disclosure of all essential information relating to the issuance of stocks to the investing public. 1. *Registration requirements*—Securities, unless exempt, must be registered with the SEC before being offered to the public through the mails or any facility of interstate commerce (including securities exchanges). The *registration statement* must include detailed financial information about the issuing corporation; the intended use of the proceeds of the securities being issued; and certain disclosures, such as interests of directors or officers and pending lawsuits. 2. *Prospectus*—A *prospectus* must be provided to investors, describing the security being sold, the issuing corporation, and the risk attaching to the security. 3. *Exemptions*—The SEC has exempted certain offerings from the requirements of the Securities Act of 1933. Exemptions may be determined on the basis of the size of the issue, whether the offering is private or public, and whether advertising is involved. Exemptions are summarized in Exhibit 37–1.
The Securities Exchange Act of 1934	Provides for the regulation and registration of securities exchanges, brokers, dealers, and national securities associations (such as the NASD). Maintains a continuous disclosure system for all corporations with securities on the securities exchanges and for those companies that have assets in excess of $5 million and five hundred or more shareholders (Section 12 companies). 1. *SEC Rule 10b-5 [under Section 10(b) of the 1934 act]*— a. Applies to insider trading by corporate officers, directors, majority shareholders, and any persons receiving information not available to the public who base their trading on this information. b. Liability for violation can be civil or criminal. c. May be violated by failing to disclose "material facts" that must be disclosed under this rule. d. Applies in virtually all cases concerning the trading of securities—a firm does not have to have its securities registered under the 1933 act for the 1934 act to apply. e. Liability may be based on the tipper-tippee or the misappropriation theory. f. Applies only when the requisites of federal jurisdiction (such as use of the mails, stock exchange facilities, or any facility of interstate commerce) are present. 2. *Insider trading [under Section 16(b) of the 1934 act]*—To prevent corporate officers and directors from taking advantage of inside information (information not available to the investing public), the 1934 act requires officers, directors, and shareholders owning 10 percent or more of the issued stock of a corporation to turn over to the corporation all short-term profits (called *short-swing profits*) realized from the purchase and sale or sale and purchase of corporate stock within any six-month period. 3. *Proxies [under Section 14(a) of the 1934 act]*—The SEC regulates the content of proxy statements sent to shareholders by corporate managers of Section 12 companies who are requesting authority to vote on behalf of the shareholders in a particular election on specified issues. Section 14(a) is essentially a disclosure law, with provisions similar to the antifraud provisions of SEC Rule 10b-5.
Regulation of Investment Companies	The Investment Company Act of 1940 provides for SEC regulation of investment company activities. It was altered and expanded by the amendments of 1970 and 1975.
State Securities Laws	All states have corporate securities laws *(blue sky laws)* that regulate the offer and sale of securities within state borders; designed to prevent "speculative schemes which have no more basis than so many feet of 'blue sky.' " States regulate securities concurrently with the federal government.

CHAPTER SUMMARY—CONTINUED

Online Securities Offerings and Disclosures	In 1995, the SEC announced that anything that can be delivered via paper documents under current securities laws may also be delivered in electronic form. Generally, when the Internet is used for the delivery of a prospectus, the same rules apply as for the delivery of a paper prospectus. When securities offerings are made online, the offerors should be careful that any hyperlinked materials do not mislead investors. Caution should also be used when making Regulation D offerings (private placements), because general solicitation is restricted with these offerings.
Online Securities Fraud	A major problem facing the SEC today is how to enforce the antifraud provisions of the securities laws in the online environment. Internet-related forms of securities fraud include the manipulation of stock prices in online chat rooms and illegal securities offerings.

CASES FOR ANALYSIS

Westlaw. You can access the full text of each case presented below by going to the Westlaw cases on this text's Web site at http://wbl-cs.westbuslaw.com. Each Westlaw case includes the names of all plaintiffs and defendants, the dates on which the case was argued and decided, a brief summary of the issues and decisions in the case, headnotes classifiying specific issues in the case according to the West Key Number System, and the court's opinion. Concurring and dissenting opinions, if any, are included as well.

CASE 37.1 DISCLOSURE REQUIREMENTS UNDER SEC RULE 10b-5

SECURITIES AND EXCHANGE COMMISSION v. TEXAS GULF SULPHUR CO.
United States Court of Appeals,
Second Circuit, 1968.
401 F.2d 833.

WATERMAN, Circuit Judge:

This action was commenced in the United States District Court for the Southern District of New York by the Securities and Exchange Commission (the SEC) * * * against Texas Gulf Sulphur Company (TGS) and several of its officers, directors and employees, to enjoin certain conduct by TGS and the individual defendants said to violate Section 10(b) of the [Securities Exchange] Act and [SEC] Rule 10b-5 * * * and to compel the rescission by the individual defendants of securities transactions assertedly conducted contrary to law. The complaint alleged (1) that defendants * * * had either personally or through agents purchased TGS stock or calls thereon from November 12, 1963 through April 16, 1964 on the basis of material inside information concerning the results of TGS drilling in Timmins, Ontario, while such information remained undisclosed to the investing public generally or to the particular sellers; (2) that defendants * * * had divulged such information to others for use in purchasing TGS stock or calls or recommended its purchase while the information was undisclosed to the public or to the sellers; (3) that defendants * * * had accepted options to purchase TGS stock on Feb. 20, 1964 without disclosing the material information as to the drilling progress to * * * TGS * * *; and (4) that TGS issued a deceptive press release on April 12, 1964. [The court held that most of the defendants had not violated Section 10(b) or Rule 10b-5. The SEC appealed to the U.S. Court of Appeals for the Second Circuit.]

* * * *

This action derives from the exploratory activities of TGS begun in 1957 on the Canadian Shield in eastern Canada. In March of 1959, aerial geophysical surveys were conducted over more than 15,000 square miles of this area * * *. These operations resulted in the detection of numerous anomalies, i.e., extraordinary variations in the conductivity of rocks, one of which was on the Kidd 55 segment of land located near Timmins, Ontario.

* * * Drilling of the initial hole * * * at the strongest part of the anomaly was commenced on November 8 [1963] and terminated on November 12 at a depth of 655 feet. Visual estimates * * * of the core * * * indicated an average copper content of 1.15% and an average zinc content of 8.64% over a length of 599 feet. This visual estimate convinced TGS that it was desirable to acquire the remainder of the Kidd 55 segment, and in order to facilitate this acquisition TGS President Stephens instructed the exploration group to keep the results of [the initial drilling] confidential and undisclosed even as to other officers, directors, and employees of TGS. * * * By March

27, 1964, TGS decided that the land acquisition program had advanced to such a point that the company might well resume drilling, and drilling was resumed on March 31.

During this period, from November 12, 1963 * * * to March 31, 1964 * * * , [TGS officers and employees] and persons * * * said to have received "tips" from them, purchased TGS stock or calls thereon. * * *

On February 20, 1964, also during this period, TGS issued stock options to 26 of its officers and employees * * * [who] knew that a hole containing favorable bodies of copper and zinc ore had been drilled in Timmins. At this time, neither the TGS Stock Option Committee nor its Board of Directors had been informed of the results of [the initial drilling], presumably because of the pending land acquisition program which required confidentiality. All of the foregoing [persons] accepted the options granted them.

* * * *

Meanwhile, rumors that a major ore strike was in the making had been circulating throughout Canada. * * * [TGS] drafted a press release designed to quell the rumors, which release * * * was issued at 3:00 P.M. on Sunday, April 12, and which appeared in the morning newspapers of general circulation on Monday, April 13. * * *

* * * *

While drilling activity ensued to completion, TGS officials were taking steps toward ultimate disclosure of the discovery. * * * An official detailed statement, announcing a strike of at least 25 million tons of ore, * * * was read to representatives of American financial media from 10:00 A.M. to 10:10 or 10:15 A.M. on April 16, and appeared over Merrill Lynch's private wire at 10:29 a.m. and, somewhat later than expected, over the Dow Jones ticker tape at 10:54 A.M.

* * * *

During the period of drilling in Timmins, the market price of TGS stock fluctuated but steadily gained overall. On Friday, November 8, when the drilling began, the stock closed at 17⅜; on Friday, November 15, after [the initial drilling] had been completed, it closed at 18. After a slight decline to 16⅜ by Friday, November 22, the price rose to 20⅞ by December 13, when the chemical assay results of [the initial drilling] were received, and closed at a high of 24⅛ on February 21, the day after the stock options had been issued. It had reached a price of 26 by March 31, after the land acquisition program had been completed and drilling had been resumed, and continued to ascend to 30⅛ by the close of trading on April 10, at which time the drilling progress up to then was evaluated for the April 12th press release. On April 13, the day on which the April 12 release was disseminated, TGS opened at 30⅛, rose immediately to a high of 32 and gradually tapered off to close at 30⅞. It closed at 30¼ the next day, and at 29⅜ on April 15. On April 16, the day of the official announcement of the Timmins discovery, the price climbed to a high of 37 and closed at 36⅜. By May 15, TGS stock was selling at 58¼.

* * * *

* * * [W]hether facts are material within Rule 10b-5 when the facts relate to a particular event and are undisclosed by those persons who are knowledgeable thereof will depend at any given time upon a balancing of both the indicated probability that the event will occur and the anticipated magnitude of the event in light of the totality of the company activity. Here, * * * knowledge of the possibility, which surely was more than marginal, of the existence of a mine of the vast magnitude indicated by the remarkably rich drill core located rather close to the surface (suggesting mineability by the less expensive openpit method) within the confines of a large anomaly (suggesting an extensive region of mineralization) might well have affected the price of TGS stock and would certainly have been an important fact to a reasonable, if speculative, investor in deciding whether he should buy, sell, or hold. * * *

* * * *

Finally, a major factor in determining whether the * * * discovery was a material fact is the importance attached to the drilling results by those who knew about it. In view of other unrelated recent developments favorably affecting TGS, participation by an informed person in a regular stock-purchase program, or even sporadic trading by an informed person, might lend only nominal support to the inference of the materiality of the * * * discovery; nevertheless, the timing by those who knew of it of their stock purchases and their purchases of short-term calls—purchases in some cases by individuals who had never before purchased calls or even TGS stock—virtually compels the inference that the insiders were influenced by the drilling results. * * *

* * * *

We hold, therefore, that all transactions in TGS stock or calls by individuals apprised of the drilling results * * * were made in violation of Rule 10b-5. Inasmuch as the visual evaluation of that drill core (a generally reliable estimate though less accurate than a chemical assay) constituted material information, those advised of the results of the visual evaluation as well as those informed of the chemical assay traded in violation of law. * * *

* * * *

MOORE, Circuit Judge (dissenting) * * * :

* * * *

* * * [T]he most disturbing aspect of the majority opinion is its utterly unrealistic approach to the problem of the corporate press release. * * * When and how are promising results to be disclosed: if they are not disclosed, the corporation is concealing information; if disclosed and hoped-for results do not materialize, there will always be those with the advantage of hindsight to brand them as false or misleading. * * * And finally there is the sardonic anomaly [bitter and irregular result] that the very members of society which Congress has charged the SEC with

protecting, i.e., the stockholders, will be the real victims of its misdirected zeal. May the Future, the Congress or possibly the SEC itself be able to bring some semblance of order by means of workable rules and regulations in this field so that the corporations and their stockholders may not be subjected to countless lawsuits at the whim of every purchaser, seller or potential purchaser who may claim he would have acted or refrained from acting had a news release been more comprehensive, less comprehensive or had it been adequately published in the news media of the 50 States.

CASE 37.2 OUTSIDERS AND SEC RULE 10b-5

SECURITIES EXCHANGE COMMISSION V. WARDE

United States Court of Appeals,
Second Circuit, 1998.
151 F.3d 42.

LEVAL, Circuit Judge:

* * * *

Background

* * * [Thomas] Warde was a good friend of Edward Downe. Both were active stock market investors. Downe in turn was a close friend of Fred Sullivan, Chairman of Kidde, Inc. ("Kidde"). Kidde is a conglomerate valued at over $1.5 billion. * * * At Sullivan's request, Downe had become a director of Kidde in 1986. Sullivan kept the Kidde directors regularly informed of developments at Kidde.

Throughout the spring of 1987, reports and rumors in the financial community suggested that [Kidde was] a likely takeover target. On June 3, the Kidde board met. The next day, Sullivan retained the investment banking firm of Bear, Stearns & Co. to discuss * * * [defenses] against a takeover. * * *

By Monday, June 22, Sullivan had learned that an undisclosed British buyer was accumulating Kidde shares. * * * On Sunday morning, June 28, Sullivan met with investment bankers at his house on Long Island to respond to takeover developments. Visibly depressed, Sullivan visited Downe at Downe's house later that afternoon.

On Monday, June 29, Sullivan learned from his lawyers that the accumulating buyer was Hanson Trust PLC ("Hanson"), a large British conglomerate. * * * On July 6, Sullivan met with the CEO of Hanson; the next day, the Kidde board convened to discuss the Hanson initiative as well as a buyout inquiry from Kohlberg Kravis Roberts ("KKR"), and the possibility of a leveraged buyout by management. * * * On July 7, Kidde issued a press release announcing that it * * * was actively engaged with two companies in discussions regarding a possible sale of all or a substantial portion of Kidde. * * *

* * * The Kidde board voted to accept the Hanson offer on August 3. * * * As the result of these events, Kidde stock rose from $34 at the beginning of June to about $66 on August 5. Warrants priced at $1 on June 5 and at $7.50–$9.25 on June 29 went to $26.50 on August 5.

While these events were unfolding, * * * Warde * * * made substantial purchases of warrants to buy Kidde stock and earned very large profits. * * *

* * * After talking with Downe by telephone, Warde invested $350,000 in Kidde warrants on June 29 and 30.

Downe and Warde spoke together the following weekend about Kidde. The following Monday, July 6, * * * Warde added approximately $460,000 to his investment. Warde's investments appreciated by $866,000 that day * * *.

On July 20, * * * [Downe] spoke by telephone with Warde. That day Warde invested an additional $200,000 to purchase warrants at about $22. * * * Warde * * * ultimately earned profits of about $33,000 * * * on this final wave of purchases.

In 1992, the Securities and Exchange Commission ("SEC" or "the Commission") filed a complaint [in a federal district court] against Warde * * *, among others, alleging insider trading in violation of [Section] 10(b) * * * of the [Securities Exchange Act of 1934]. * * *

The Commission contended that Warde's investments in Kidde warrants were made with the benefit of Kidde's nonpublic information about competing bids to acquire the company—information that Downe had obtained as a Kidde director and passed on to Warde. Warde denied possession of any nonpublic information. He * * * testified that [his] purchases were based on market savvy, rumor and public information alone. * * *

* * * [T]he jury found Warde liable. The final judgment permanently enjoined Warde from securities trading violations and ordered him to disgorge some $872,000 in profits, pay a civil penalty in the same amount, and disgorge $1.26 million in prejudgment interest. [Warde appealed to the U.S. Court of Appeals for the Second Circuit.]

Discussion

1. *Sufficiency of the Evidence.* Warde's principal challenge on appeal is to the sufficiency of the Commission's evidence. He contends the Commission's case was based entirely on guilt by association and "thin pieces of circumstantial evidence," which, in the aggregate, were insufficient to support the jury's finding of liability * * *.

To affirm Warde's liability as a tippee under [Section] 10(b), we must find sufficient evidence to permit a reasonable finding that (1) Downe possessed material, nonpublic information regarding Kidde; (2) Downe disclosed this information to Warde; (3) Warde traded in Kidde warrants while in possession of that nonpublic information provided by Downe; (4) Warde knew or should have known that Downe violated a relationship of trust by relaying Kidde information; and (5) Downe benefitted by the disclosure to Warde. * * *

a. *Downe's Possession of Nonpublic Information.* There was ample evidence that Downe possessed nonpublic information regarding the threat of a takeover of Kidde. Downe was a director of Kidde. His friend Sullivan, the CEO of Kidde, kept the directors informed on the takeover developments, and Downe attended meetings of the board in which the developing situation and Kidde's strategy were discussed.

* * * *

b. *Materiality.* The materiality of Downe's information is also not open to doubt. Information is material if there is a substantial likelihood that a reasonable investor would consider it important in deciding how to invest. The facts that Hanson was accumulating Kidde stock and contemplating a tender offer, that KKR was also interested in bidding for Kidde, and that management was contemplating a leveraged buyout to fend off the unwelcome bids had a very high likelihood of affecting the price of Kidde's stock, as confirmed by the fact that the stock price jumped when this information was made public. * * *

c. *Disclosure of the Information to Warde.* Warde also challenges the Commission's evidence that Downe transferred to him any nonpublic information, material or otherwise. While Warde acknowledges that the two men discussed Kidde's prospects, he maintains that the conversations were limited to public information, especially the views of other investors.

The Commission presented ample circumstantial evidence to support the jury finding to the contrary. The Commission's evidence demonstrated a pattern in which Downe received nonpublic information, then communicated with Warde, and then * * * Warde * * * purchased Kidde warrants. * * *

* * * Warde engaged in uncharacteristic, substantial and exceedingly risky investments in Kidde warrants shortly after speaking with [Downe], suggesting that they discussed not only the inside information, but also the best way to profit from it. * * *

* * * *

d. *Warde's Knowledge of Violation of Trust.* Warde next disputes the sufficiency of the evidence to sustain the jury's finding that Warde knew or should have known that Downe was a Kidde director and thus violated a trust by relaying inside information.

The claim is meritless. The SEC showed that Downe and Warde were good friends who often discussed their business and investing interests, and that Warde habitually discovered who was on the board of directors of a company before investing in it. While this evidence does not compel the conclusion that Warde knew Downe was a Kidde director, it certainly allows that inference. * * *

e. *Benefit to Tipper.* Warde also claims that the SEC provided no evidence that Downe benefitted from Warde's trades, precluding liability under [Section] 10(b) * * * . However, * * * to prove a [Section] 10(b) violation, the SEC need not show that the tipper expected or received a specific or tangible benefit in exchange for the tip. Rather, the "benefit" element of [Section] 10(b) is satisfied when the tipper intends to benefit the * * * recipient or makes a gift of confidential information to a trading relative or friend.

Under this standard, Downe clearly benefitted from Warde's inside trades. Warde's trades resembled trading by the insider himself followed by a gift of the profits to the recipient. The close friendship between Downe and Warde suggests that Downe's tip was intended to benefit Warde, and therefore allows a jury finding that Downe's tip breached a duty under [Section] 10(b).

* * * *

Conclusion

The judgment of the district court is affirmed.

CASE 37.3 OUTSIDERS AND SEC RULE 10b-5

UNITED STATES v. O'HAGAN

Supreme Court of the United States, 1997.
521 U.S. 642,
117 S.Ct. 2199,
138 L.Ed.2d 724.

Justice *GINSBURG* delivered the opinion of the Court.

* * * *

I

Respondent James Herman O'Hagan was a partner in the law firm of Dorsey & Whitney in Minneapolis, Minnesota. In July 1988, Grand Metropolitan PLC (Grand Met), a company based in London, England, retained Dorsey & Whitney as local counsel to represent Grand Met regarding a potential tender offer for the common stock of the Pillsbury Company, headquartered in Minneapolis. Both Grand Met and Dorsey & Whitney took precautions to protect the confidentiality of Grand Met's tender offer plans. O'Hagan did no work on the Grand Met representation. Dorsey & Whitney withdrew from representing Grand Met on September 9, 1988. Less than a month later, on October 4, 1988, Grand Met publicly announced its tender offer for Pillsbury stock.

On August 18, 1988, while Dorsey & Whitney was still representing Grand Met, O'Hagan began purchasing call options for Pillsbury stock. Each option gave him the right to purchase 100 shares of Pillsbury stock by a specified date in September 1988. Later in August and in September, O'Hagan made additional purchases of Pillsbury call options. By the end of September, he owned 2,500 unexpired Pillsbury options, apparently more than any other individual investor. O'Hagan also purchased, in September 1988, some 5,000 shares of Pillsbury common stock, at a price just under $39 per share. When Grand Met announced its tender offer in October, the price of Pillsbury stock rose to nearly $60 per share. O'Hagan then sold his Pillsbury call options and common stock, making a profit of more than $4.3 million.

The Securities and Exchange Commission (SEC or Commission) initiated an investigation into O'Hagan's transactions * * * . O'Hagan was charged with * * * securities fraud, in violation of [Section] 10(b) of the Securities Exchange Act of 1934 (Exchange Act) [and other crimes]. A jury convicted O'Hagan * * * .

A divided panel of the [U.S.] Court of Appeals for the Eighth Circuit reversed all of O'Hagan's convictions. * * *

* * * We granted *certiorari* * * * .

II

* * * [T]he Eighth Circuit rejected the misappropriation theory as a basis for [Section] 10(b) liability. * * *

A

* * * *

[Section 10(b)] proscribes (1) using any deceptive device (2) in connection with the purchase or sale of securities, in contravention of rules prescribed by the Commission. The provision, as written, does not confine its coverage to deception of a purchaser or seller of securities, rather, the statute reaches any deceptive device used "in connection with the purchase or sale of any security."

* * * *

The "misappropriation theory" holds that a person commits fraud "in connection with" a securities transaction, and thereby violates [Section] 10(b) * * * , when he misappropriates confidential information for securities trading purposes, in breach of a duty owed to the source of the information. Under this theory, a fiduciary's undisclosed, self-serving use of a principal's information to purchase or sell securities, in breach of a duty of loyalty and confidentiality, defrauds the principal of the exclusive use of that information. *In lieu of premising liability on a fiduciary relationship between company insider and purchaser or seller of the company's stock, the misappropriation theory premises liability on a fiduciary-turned-trader's deception of those who entrusted him with access to confidential information.* [Emphasis added.]

* * * [T]he misappropriation theory outlaws trading on the basis of nonpublic information by a corporate "outsider" in breach of a duty owed not to a trading party, but to the source of the information. The misappropriation theory is thus designed to protect the integrity of the securities markets against abuses by "outsiders" to a corporation who have access to confidential information that will affect the corporation's security price when revealed, but who owe no fiduciary or other duty to that corporation's shareholders.

In this case, the indictment alleged that O'Hagan, in breach of a duty of trust and confidence he owed to his law firm, Dorsey & Whitney, and to its client, Grand Met, traded on the basis of nonpublic information regarding Grand Met's planned tender offer for Pillsbury common stock. This conduct, the Government charged, constituted a fraudulent device in connection with the purchase and sale of securities.

B

We agree with the Government that misappropriation, as just defined, satisfies [Section] 10(b)'s requirement that chargeable conduct involve a "deceptive device or contrivance" used "in connection with" the purchase or sale of securities. We observe, first, that misappropriators, as the Government describes them, deal in deception. A fiduciary who pretends loyalty to the principal while secretly converting the principal's information for personal gain "dupes" or defrauds the principal.

* * * *

* * * Because the deception essential to the misappropriation theory involves feigning fidelity to the source of information, if the fiduciary discloses to the source that he plans to trade on the nonpublic information, there is no "deceptive device" and thus no [Section] 10(b) violation * * * .

We turn next to the [Section] 10(b) requirement that the misappropriator's deceptive use of information be "in connection with the purchase or sale of [a] security." This element is satisfied because the fiduciary's fraud is consummated, not when the fiduciary gains the confidential information, but when, without disclosure to his principal, he uses the information to purchase or sell securities. The securities transaction and the breach of duty thus coincide. This is so even though the person or entity defrauded is not the other party to the trade, but is, instead, the source of the nonpublic information. A misappropriator who trades on the basis of material, nonpublic information, in short, gains his advantageous market position through deception; he deceives the source of the information and simultaneously harms members of the investing public.

* * * *

* * * The [misappropriation] theory is also well tuned to an animating purpose of the Exchange Act: to insure honest securities markets and thereby promote investor confidence. Although informational disparity is inevitable in the securities markets, investors likely would hesitate to venture their capital in a market where trading based on misappropriated nonpublic information is unchecked by law. An investor's informational disadvan-

tage vis-à-vis a misappropriator with material, nonpublic information stems from contrivance, not luck; it is a disadvantage that cannot be overcome with research or skill.

* * * *

The judgment of the Court of Appeals for the Eighth Circuit is reversed, and the case is remanded for further proceedings consistent with this opinion.

It is so ordered.

Justice *THOMAS* * * * dissenting * * * .

* * * Central to the majority's holding is the need to interpret [Section] 10(b)'s requirement that a deceptive device be "use[d] or employ[ed], in connection with the purchase or sale of any security." Because the Commission's misappropriation theory fails to provide a coherent and consistent interpretation of this essential requirement for liability under [Section] 10(b), I dissent.

* * * *

* * * [For example, if] the relevant test under the "in connection with" language is whether the fraudulent act is *necessarily* tied to a securities transaction [as the government seems to argue and the majority seems to accept], then the misappropriation of confidential information used to trade no more violates [Section] 10(b) than does the misappropriation of funds used to trade. * * *

* * * *

* * * [T]he majority also points to various policy considerations underlying the securities laws, such as maintaining fair and honest markets, promoting investor confidence, and protecting the integrity of the securities markets. But the repeated reliance on such broad-sweeping legislative purposes reaches too far and is misleading in the context of the misappropriation theory. It reaches too far in that, regardless of the overarching purpose of the securities laws, it is not illegal to run afoul of the "purpose" of a statute, only its letter. The majority's approach is misleading in this case because it glosses over the fact that the supposed threat to fair and honest markets, investor confidence, and market integrity comes not from the supposed fraud in this case, but from the mere fact that the information used by O'Hagan was nonpublic.

CASE 37.4 INSIDER REPORTING AND TRADING

MEDTOX SCIENTIFIC, INC. V. MORGAN CAPITAL L.L.C.

United States District Court,
District of Minnesota, 1999.
50 F.Supp.2d 896.

MONTGOMERY, District Judge.

* * * *

* * * Medtox Scientific, Inc. ("Medtox"), f/k/a Editek, Inc. ("Editek"), filed this action on January 31, 1997, to recover alleged short-swing insider profits realized by * * * Morgan Capital L.L.C. ("Morgan Capital") and its alleged control persons, * * * Alex and David Bistricer ("Bistricers"), on a series of 1996 transactions involving Editek stock. * * * The matter is currently before the Court on * * * Plaintiff's Motion for Partial Summary Judgment. * * *

* * * *

On or about February 1, 1996, Editek, a Delaware corporation with its principal place of business in Minnesota, issued shares of Convertible Preferred Stock ("Preferred Stock") in an offering conducted under * * * the Securities Act of 1933 ("the Offering"). At the option of the holder, each share of Preferred Stock was convertible to Editek common stock ("Common Stock") at a price equal to the average closing price of the shares of Common Stock for the five trading day period preceding the date notice of conversion was given to Editek by such holder. Consequently, the number of shares of Common Stock that the Preferred Stock would buy floated with the average trading price of the Common Stock. As the trading price of the Common Stock declined, the number of shares of Common Stock that the Preferred Stock would buy increased, and vice-versa. The right to convert the Preferred Stock was not exercisable until 60 days after issuance of the shares.

Morgan Capital, a limited liability corporation with offices in Brooklyn, New York, purchased Preferred Stock from Editek in the Offering. At the time of its purchase, the number of shares of Common Stock that Morgan Capital would have received upon conversion of its Preferred Stock (were it allowed to immediately convert the stock) would have been less than ten percent of the outstanding shares of Editek's Common Stock.

On March 28, 1996, as a result of a decline in the price of the Common Stock, the amount of shares of Common Stock that Morgan Capital would have received upon conversion of its Preferred Stock (again, were it allowed to convert the stock at such time) would have been greater than ten percent of the outstanding shares of Editek's Common Stock. March 30, 1996, marked the first day upon which Morgan Capital was eligible to convert its Preferred Stock into Common Stock.

On May 1, 1996, Morgan Capital converted all of its Preferred Stock into Common Stock. The Common Stock that Morgan Capital received in the conversion amounted to greater than ten percent of the outstanding shares of Editek's Common Stock. Morgan Capital then sold a portion of its shares of Common Stock on five separate occasions in May and June 1996, realizing a profit of at least $500,000.

* * * *

In its sole claim for relief, Editek alleges that Morgan Capital's conduct violated Section 16(b) of the Securities Exchange Act of 1934. Section 16(b) was enacted to prevent corporate "insiders" from abusing their fiduciary positions by using confidential corporate information to aid their personal market activities. The statute provides in relevant part as follows:

> For the purpose of preventing the unfair use of information which may have been obtained by [a] beneficial owner, director, or officer by reason of his relationship to the issuer, any profit realized by him from any purchase and sale, or any sale and purchase, of any equity security of such issuer (other than an exempted security) within any period of less than six months, unless such security was acquired in good faith in connection with a debt previously contracted, shall inure to and be recoverable by the issuer, irrespective of any intention on the part of such beneficial owner, director, or officer in entering into such transaction of holding the security purchased or of not repurchasing the security sold for a period exceeding six months * * * .

The term "beneficial owner" is defined in Section 16(a) as "[e]very person who is directly or indirectly the beneficial owner of more than 10 per centum of any class of any equity security (other than an exempted security) which is registered pursuant to section 78*l*" of the Act. *The so-called "ten percent beneficial owners" are considered insiders, and therefore included within the statute's reach, because the size of their holdings affords the potential for access to corporate information.* [Emphasis added.]

Determining who qualifies as a ten percent beneficial owner under Section 16(b) is no simple task. Rule 16a-1 of the governing regulations states the following:

> Solely for purposes of determining whether a person is a beneficial owner of more than ten percent of any class of equity securities registered pursuant to section 12 of the [1934] Act, the term "beneficial owner" shall mean any person deemed a beneficial owner pursuant to section 13(d) of the Act * * * .

Under Section 13(d), a beneficial owner of a security includes any person who has voting power or investment power in relation to the security. Furthermore, "[a] person shall be deemed to be the beneficial owner of a security if that person has the right to acquire beneficial ownership of such security, as defined in Rule 13d-3(a) within sixty days * * * [t]hrough the conversion of a security." In other words, persons who have the right to acquire voting power or investment power in relation to a security within sixty days are deemed "beneficial owners" of that security for purposes of determining ten percent beneficial ownership.

Finally, to be liable under Section 16(b), a ten percent beneficial owner must have been such both at the time of the purchase and sale, or the sale and purchase, of the security involved. Since owners below the ten percent threshold presumptively lack access to inside information, the acquisition that takes a buyer above ten percent beneficial ownership does not count as a purchase matchable against a later sale for Section 16(b) purposes.

* * * *

* * * After March 30, 1996, if Morgan Capital could have converted its Preferred Stock into more than ten percent of the outstanding shares of Editek's Common Stock on any given day, then the presumption arises under Section 16(b) that Morgan Capital's holdings afforded it the potential for access to corporate information not available to a smaller shareholder on that day. At the same time, however, due to the floating conversion rate of the Preferred Stock, Morgan Capital's standing as a "ten percent beneficial owner" was potentially subject to change daily. Thus, to establish liability under Section 16(b), Plaintiff will not simply have to show that Morgan Capital could have obtained more than ten percent of Editek's Common Stock on any given day prior to May 1, 1996, but that Morgan Capital could have obtained more than ten percent of Editek's Common Stock on the day before it actually made the illicit purchase—April 30, 1996. Otherwise, Morgan Capital presumably would not have had access to inside information when it actually purchased Editek Common Stock and, therefore, would not be subject to the strictures of Section 16(b).

* * * *

The price of Editek's Common Stock steadily declined throughout March and April 1996. As a result, on any day between April 9 and April 30, 1996, the price was sufficiently low that had Morgan Capital elected to convert its Preferred Stock, it would have received more than ten percent of the outstanding shares of Editek's Common Stock. During this time interval, Defendants David and Alex Bistricer, officers and controlling principals of Morgan Capital's day-to-day business affairs, had weekly telephone conversations with Editek management. Approximately one-half of these calls were placed by Alex Bistricer to Editek's Minnesota office. The topics discussed included Editek's declining stock price and its implications for Morgan Capital's conversion rights. * * *

On May 1, 1996, Morgan Capital converted its Preferred Stock into 4,584,795 shares of Common Stock. At the time of conversion, the shares received represented more than ten percent of the outstanding shares of Editek Common Stock. Following the conversion, the Bistricers' weekly telephone conversations with Editek continued throughout May 1996. In several trades during May and June 1996, Morgan Capital sold 688,272 shares of Editek Common Stock for a total of $919,269.39. Morgan

Capital's basis in the shares it sold was $367,812.55. As a result of these transactions, Morgan Capital realized total profits of $551,456.84.

* * * *

Morgan Capital became a "ten percent beneficial owner" of Editek Common Stock on April 9, 1996, and remained such through at least June 30, 1996. By exercising the option to convert its Preferred Stock into Common Stock on May 1, 1996, Morgan Capital fixed the conversion price and thereby engaged in a matchable purchase of Editek's Common Stock for Section 16(b) liability purposes. Over the next two months, Morgan Capital sold a portion of the stock it purchased on May 1, 1996, for a total profit of $551,456.84. Because these transactions constitute "short-swing" insider trading in violation of Section 16(b), Editek is entitled to recover the full profit realized by Morgan Capital. Plaintiff's motion is therefore granted.

CASE 37.5 SECTION 10(b) AND SEC RULE 10b-5

IN RE MCI WORLDCOM, INC. SECURITIES LITIGATION

United States District Court,
Eastern District of New York, 2001.
93 F.Supp.2d 276.

GLASSER, District Judge.

This is an action against MCI Worldcom, Inc. ("MCI") brought by plaintiffs on their own behalf and on behalf of a class consisting of all persons who sold securities of SkyTel Communications, Inc. ("SkyTel") on the open market during the period of May 25, 1999 through May 28, 1999. Plaintiffs assert securities fraud claims against MCI pursuant to Section 10(b) of the Securities Exchange Act of 1934 and SEC Rule 10b-5. Plaintiffs contend that misleading statements by MCI artificially deflated the share price of SkyTel, which MCI acquired soon after those statements were made. * * *

* * * *

Defendant MCI moves to dismiss the Complaint pursuant to * * * the Private Securities Litigation Reform Act ("PSLRA"). * * *

FACTS AS ALLEGED IN THE COMPLAINT

* * * *

In early 1999, SkyTel, then a leading provider of wireless messaging services in the United States, had been the subject of takeover rumors for several months. When SkyTel announced its first quarter 1999 results on April 20, 1999, it also announced that subscriber growth was significantly below expectations and that the investment bank Warburg Dillion Read LLC had been retained to assist the company in evaluating its strategic alternatives. This caused more takeover speculation, as an announcement of this type often signals that a company is seeking to be acquired. * * * [T]he price of SkyTel shares rose 12% due to these rumors. * * *

* * * [D]uring the morning of May 25, 1999, an Internet news service, the Company Sleuth, reported that MCI had registered "skytelworldcom.com" as an Internet domain name. It has become common practice for corporations to register domain names prior to their actual use in order to protect companies from "cyber-squatters," individuals who register domain names perceived to have value in order to sell the names at high prices to companies for whom the names are valuable.

On May 25, 1999, shares in SkyTel opened at $18.875. When news of the new Internet address was reported sometime that morning, takeover rumors again flourished, sending SkyTel shares to as high as $21.875 around noontime, a gain of 16% from its close the previous day.

* * * [S]hortly after noon, MCI sent Barbara Gibson to address reporters. At that time, Ms. Gibson was an official MCI corporate spokesperson and Senior Manager of Corporate Communication. When asked about the significance of the registration of the "skytelworldcom.com" name, she responded:

> From time to time, MCI Worldcom employees, sometimes acting on their own initiatives, register domain names they believe may be potential targets of domain-name squatters. In this case, the action is not an indication of official company intention.

* * *

The market interpreted MCI's statements as a denial that it had any interest in acquiring SkyTel and immediately following Ms. Gibson's statement, SkyTel's stock price fell below the previous day's close to as low as $18.6875. Shares of SkyTel closed on May 25, 1999 at $20.125 per share on volume of 7.5 million shares, three times the stock's recent average daily volume.

Plaintiffs allege that MCI's statements were materially misleading because SkyTel and MCI had in fact been negotiating a merger since early February 1999. During the last three weeks of April 1999, SkyTel, MCI and their advisors were negotiating specific terms for the merger and conducting further due diligence. By May 25, 1999, nearly all the significant terms of the agreement had been negotiated, including the exchange price ratio for the stock. At that time, the agreement was awaiting finalization of the last details and final approval by the companies' boards of directors.

On May 28, 1999, MCI announced an agreement to buy SkyTel for $1.3 billion in stock, or approximately $21.50 per SkyTel share. The agreement provided that

SkyTel shareholders were to receive .25 shares of MCI stock for each share of SkyTel stock they owned. The merger was completed October 1, 1999. * * *

According to plaintiffs, MCI's motive for the false denial on May 25, 1999 of its intention to takeover SkyTel was to deflate SkyTel's share price and to avoid having to pay more if SkyTel's stock price rose prior to the announcement of the merger.

ARGUMENT

* * * *

In 1995, Congress enacted the PSLRA [Private Securities Litigation Reform Act] which provides that plaintiffs must, "with respect to each act or omission alleged to violate this chapter, state with particularity facts giving rise to a strong inference that the defendant acted with the required state of mind." The "required state of mind" for a Section 10(b) or Rule 10b-5 violation is *scienter*, an intent to deceive, manipulate or defraud.

* * * [A] plaintiff can plead fraudulent intent in one of two ways: (1) by identifying circumstances indicating conscious or reckless behavior by the defendant, or (2) by alleging facts showing a motive to commit fraud and a clear opportunity to do so. * * *

* * * *

To show motive, plaintiffs must show concrete benefits to a defendant that could be realized by one or more of the false statements and wrongful nondisclosures alleged. * * * Plaintiffs assert that MCI was motivated to artificially deflate the price of SkyTel stock in order to help ensure that the acquisition price would not have to be increased. It also did so to make the intended takeover more attractive and at a higher premium than if SkyTel's stock price had remained higher because of the merger rumors reignited by the news stories reporting on the registration of the skytelworldcom.com domain name.

* * * *

In response, defendant asserts that plaintiffs fail to allege that Gibson had any knowledge of the confidential merger negotiations, and that such knowledge cannot be assumed or conclusorily asserted. MCI argues that if Gibson is not alleged to have had any knowledge of the confidential merger negotiations, opportunity has not been sufficiently alleged. Gibson's knowledge of the merger is a matter of factual dispute for discovery. At this stage, the Court finds that it is reasonable to assume the official MCI spokesperson, the Senior Manager of Corporation Communications at MCI, did know of an impending merger which was announced three days later.

* * * *

* * * Defendant argues that its alleged motive is insufficient as a matter of law because the alleged fraud did not entail any "concrete" economic benefit to MCI and, therefore, it was not in MCI's economic interests to deflate the price of SkyTel shares.

* * * [B]eing able to acquire a company for a significantly reduced price is a sufficient economic benefit to satisfy the motive requirement for *scienter.* * * * Defendant argues that it had no incentive to deflate the value of SkyTel's stock. The price for the acquisition had already been set at the time of the May 25, 1999 press conference, and therefore MCI was without a motive to defraud. This assertion is not persuasive * * * .

MCI was acquiring SkyTel for stock. The purchase price was determined by the number of MCI shares to be exchanged for each SkyTel share, which was set by the "exchange ratio." That ratio depended on the value of MCI's stock as measured by an objective formula. However, although * * * the exchange ratio had been negotiated by May 25, * * * it had [not] been finalized. In fact, the exchange ratio had not been precisely fixed at the time of MCI's public statement. On May 25, 1999, MCI proposed, among other things, adjusting the exchange ratio upward in the event that trading prices for MCI shares declined.

* * * *

Plaintiffs have also alleged facts that constitute strong circumstantial evidence of conscious misbehavior or recklessness by MCI. * * * [T]hree days prior to the announcement of the merger, MCI's official corporate spokesperson falsely denied any "official company intention" regarding the registration of a domain name that was an obvious combination of MCI's and SkyTel's names. The market understood the denial to mean there would be no takeover, as evidenced by the drop in SkyTel's price. * * * [I]t was MCI itself that registered the domain name, and not, as Ms. Gibson suggested, an MCI employee acting alone. These facts demonstrate conscious misbehavior or recklessness on the part of MCI sufficient to plead *scienter.*

* * * *

CONCLUSION

For the foregoing reasons, this Court denies defendant's motion to dismiss.

CASE PROBLEMS

37–1. Leston Nay owned 90 percent of the stock of First Securities Co. Between the years 1942 and 1966, Hochfelder sent large sums of money to Nay to be invested in escrow accounts—accounts belonging to one entity but held by another entity—of First Securities. The whole investment scheme was a fraud, and Nay converted the money sent by Hochfelder to his own use. When Hochfelder discovered the fraud, he sued Ernst & Ernst, the auditor of First Securities, for failing to use proper auditing procedures and thus negligently failing to discover the fraudulent scheme. Was the firm of Ernst & Ernst found guilty of violating Section 10(b) of the 1934 Securities Exchange Act and the Securities and Exchange Commission Rule 10b-5? Explain. [*Ernst & Ernst v. Hochfelder,* 425 U.S. 185, 96 S.Ct. 1375, 47 L.Ed.2d 668 (1976)]

37–2. Energy Resource Group, Inc. (ERG), entered into a written agreement with Ivan West for West to find an investor willing to purchase ERG stock. West later formed a partnership, called Investment Management Group (IMG), with Don Peters and another person. According to the terms of the partnership agreement, West's consulting work for ERG was excluded from the work of the IMG partnership. West learned through his consulting position with ERG that ERG was to be acquired by another corporation for $6.00 per share. At the time West learned of the acquisition, ERG stock was trading at $3.50 per share. Apparently, Peters learned of the acquisition from papers on West's desk in the IMG office and then shared the information with Ken Mick, his stockbroker. Mick then encouraged several clients to buy ERG stock prior to the public announcement of the acquisition. Mick, in return for leaking this inside information to clients, received a special premium from the enriched investors. Mick then paid a portion of the premium to Peters. The Securities and Exchange Commission brought an action against Peters for violating Rule 10b-5. Under what theory might Peters be held liable for insider trading in violation of Rule 10b-5? Discuss fully. [*SEC v. Peters,* 735 F.Supp. 1505 (D.Kans. 1990)]

37–3. William Gotchey owned 50 percent of the shares of First American Financial Consultants, Inc. (FAFC), an investment company registered with the Securities and Exchange Commission. In the fall of 1987, Paul Hatfield, a client of FAFC, spoke with Gotchey about investing. In December, Hatfield told Gotchey that he wished to invest $15,000 in a secure investment. Gotchey told Hatfield that he would be placing the $15,000 in mortgage-backed securities to be invested through a mortgage company. Hatfield received interest payments from FAFC purportedly from the alleged investment. He also received statements confirming that the investment had been made. In fact, Gotchey had deposited the entire amount into an FAFC bank account. When Hatfield did not receive his interest payment due at the beginning of July 1988, he confronted Gotchey. Gotchey responded by asking Hatfield to sign an agreement whereby FAFC would repay the $15,000 in monthly installments over ten years. Hatfield refused. To date, Gotchey has not accounted for the $15,000, nor has Hatfield received any interest payments since June 1988. Has Gotchey violated Section 10b-5 of the Securities Exchange Act? Why, or why not? [*SEC v. Gotchey,* 981 F.2d 1251 (4th Cir. 1992)]

37–4. Campbell was a financial columnist for a Los Angeles newspaper owned by Hearst Corp. He often bought shares in companies on which he was about to give a favorable report and then sold the shares at a profit after the columns appeared. In June of 1969, Campbell interviewed the officers of American Systems, Inc. (ASI). The ASI officers did not disclose to Campbell adverse information concerning the company's financial condition. Campbell relied on the officers' presentation of ASI's financial status, however, and made no independent investigation. Planning to write a favorable report, Campbell purchased 5,000 shares of ASI stock for $2 per share. Following the publication of Campbell's favorable, and misleading, article, ASI's stock rose rapidly in price, and on June 5 Campbell sold 2,000 of his shares at $5 per share. Earlier, in February of 1969, ASI had made an agreement with another corporation, RGC, under which RGC would merge with ASI and ASI would pay RGC stockholders enough ASI stock to equal a market value of $1.8 million on the closing date of June 10, 1969. Zweig and Bruno, each of whom owned one-third of RGC shares, brought suit against Hearst Corp., alleging that because of the artificial rise in ASI stock caused by Campbell's column, they ended up with a smaller percentage of the total outstanding shares of ASI than they would have received otherwise. Explain whether Hearst is liable under Rule 10b-5. [*Zweig v. Hearst Corp.,* 594 F.2d 1261 (9th Cir. 1979)]

37–5. Ronald Rodeo's investment group purchased limited partnership interests in certain Illinois apartment buildings. Separately, by contract, it acquired an option to buy out the remaining interests of the general partners. According to the arrangement, the general partners would operate the apartments, and the limited partners would provide essential capital while retaining their limited liability. Rodeo could not actively intervene in the business without losing his limited liability. He therefore had to rely solely on the general partners for the partnership's profitability. Two years later, Rodeo became disenchanted with the partnership's operation and sued R. Dean Gillman and the other general partners under the Illinois blue sky act. In his claim, Rodeo stated that material misrepresentations and omissions had been made during the negotiation of the limited partnership contracts in violation of the state securities act. The general partners responded that no securities were involved and that, because of the buyout option, the limited partners actually had ultimate control over the management of the apartments. Discuss the definition of a security and whether the limited partnership contracts meet this definition. [*Rodeo v. Gillman,* 787 F.2d 1175 (7th Cir. 1986)]

37–6. Emerson Electric Co. purchased 13.2 percent of Dodge Manufacturing Co.'s stock in an unsuccessful takeover attempt in June 1967. Later, when Dodge merged with Reliance Electric Co., Emerson decided to sell its shares. To avoid being subject to the restrictions of Section 16 of the Securities Exchange Act of 1934, which pertain to any purchase and sale by any owner of 10 percent or more of a corporation's stock, Emerson decided on a two-step selling plan. First, it sold off sufficient shares to reduce its holdings to 9.96 percent, and then it sold the remaining stock—all within a six-month period. Because under Section 16(b) of the act, the owner must be a 10 percent owner "both at the time of the purchase and sale . . . of the security involved," Emerson thought it had succeeded in avoiding potential liability under Section 16(b). Reliance demanded that Emerson return the profits made on both sales. Emerson sought a declaratory judgment from the court that it was not liable, arguing that because at the time of the second sale it had not owned 10 percent of Dodge stock, Section 16 did not apply. Does Section 16 of the Securities Exchange Act of 1934 apply to Emerson's transactions, and is Emerson liable to Reliance for its profits? [*Reliance Electric Co. v. Emerson Electric Co.,* 404 U.S. 418, 92 S.Ct. 596, 30 L.Ed.2d 575 (1972)]

37–7. Danny Cherif was employed by the First National Bank of Chicago in its International Financial Institutions Department from 1979 until 1987, when Cherif's position was eliminated because of an internal reorganization. Cherif, using a forged memo to the bank's security department, caused his magnetic identification (ID) card—which he had received as an employee to allow him to enter the bank building—to remain activated after his employment was terminated. Cherif used his ID card to enter the building at night to obtain confidential financial information from the bank's Specialized Finance Department regarding extraordinary business transactions, such as tender offers. During 1988 and 1989, Cherif made substantial profits through securities trading based on this information. Eventually, Cherif's activities were investigated by the Securities and Exchange Commission (SEC), and Cherif was charged with violating Section 10(b) and SEC Rule 10b-5 by misappropriating and trading on inside information in violation of his fiduciary duties to his former employer. Cherif argued that the SEC had wrongfully applied the misappropriation theory to his activities, because as a former employee, he no longer had a fiduciary duty to the bank. Explain whether Cherif is liable under SEC Rule 10b-5. [*SEC v. Cherif,* 933 F.2d 403 (7th Cir. 1991)]

37–8. Susan Waldbaum was a niece of the president and controlling shareholder of Waldbaum, Inc. Susan's mother (the president's sister) told Susan that the company was going to be sold at a favorable price and that a tender offer was soon to be made. She told Susan not to tell anyone except her husband, Keith Loeb, about the sale. The next day, Susan told her husband of the sale and cautioned him not to tell anyone, because "it could possibly ruin the sale." The day after he learned of the sale, Loeb called Robert Chestman, his broker, and told him that he "had some accurate information" that the company was about to be sold at a price "substantially higher" than the market value of its stock. That day, Chestman purchased shares of the company for himself, as well as for Loeb. Chestman was later convicted by a jury of, among other things, trading on misappropriated inside information in violation of SEC Rule 10b-5. On appeal, the central question in regard to liability under the misappropriation theory was whether Chestman had acquired the inside information about the Waldbaum company as a result of an insider's breach of a fiduciary duty. Essentially, the inquiry focused on whether Loeb owed a fiduciary duty to his wife's family or to his wife to keep the information confidential. How should the court rule? [*United States v. Chestman,* 947 F.2d 551 (2d Cir. 1991)]

37–9. U.S. News & World Report, Inc., set up a profit-sharing plan in 1962 that allotted to certain employees specially issued stock known as bonus or anniversary stock. The stock was given to the employees for past services and could not be traded or sold to anyone other than the corporate issuer, U.S. News. This special stock was issued only to employees and for no other purpose than as bonuses. Because there was no market for the stock, U.S. News hired an independent appraiser to estimate the fair value of the stock so that the employees could redeem the shares. Charles Foltz and several other employees held stock through this plan and sought to redeem the shares with U.S. News, but Foltz disputed the value set by the appraisers. Foltz sued U.S. News for violation of securities regulations. What defense would allow U.S. News to resist Foltz's claim successfully? [*Foltz v. U.S. News & World Report, Inc.,* 627 F.Supp. 1143 (D.D.C. 1986)]

37–10. Louis Ferraro was the chairman and president of Anacomp, Inc. In June 1988, Ferraro told his good friend Michael Maio that Anacomp was negotiating a tender offer for stock in Xidex Corp. Maio passed on the information to Patricia Ladavac, a friend of both Ferraro and Maio. Maio and Ladavac immediately purchased shares in Xidex stock. On the day that the tender offer was announced—an announcement that caused the price of Xidex shares to increase—Maio and Ladavac sold their Xidex stock and made substantial profits (Maio made $211,000 from the transactions, and Ladavac gained $78,750). The SEC brought an action against the three individuals, alleging that they had violated, among other laws, SEC Rule 10b-5. Maio and Ladavac claimed that they had done nothing illegal. They argued that they had no fiduciary duty either to Anacomp or to Xidex, and therefore they had no duty to disclose or abstain from trading in the stock of those corporations. Had Maio and Ladavac violated SEC Rule 10b-5? Discuss fully. [*SEC v. Maio,* 51 F.3d 623 (7th Cir. 1995)]

37–11. Joseph Jett worked for Kidder, Peabody & Co., a financial services firm owned by General Electric Co. (GE). Over a three-year period, Jett allegedly engaged in a scheme to generate false profits at Kidder, Peabody to increase his performance-based bonuses. When the scheme was discovered, Daniel Chill and other GE shareholders who had bought stock in the previous year filed a suit in a federal district court against GE. The shareholders alleged that GE had engaged in securities fraud in violation of Section 10(b). They claimed that GE's interest in justifying its investment in Kidder, Peabody gave GE "a motive to willfully blind itself to facts casting doubt on Kidder's purported profitability." On what basis might the court dismiss the shareholders' complaint? Discuss fully. [*Chill v. General Electric Co.,* 101 F.3d 263 (2d Cir. 1996)]

37–12. Grand Metropolitan PLC (Grand Met) planned to make a tender offer as part of an attempted takeover of the Pillsbury Company. Grand Met hired Robert Falbo, an independent contractor, to complete electrical work as part of security renovations to its offices to prevent leaks of information concerning the planned tender offer. Falbo was given a master key to access the executive offices. When an executive secretary told Falbo that a takeover was brewing, he used his key to access the offices and eavesdrop on conversations to learn that Pillsbury was the target. Falbo bought thousands of shares of Pillsbury stock for less than $40 per share. Within two months, Grand Met made an offer for all outstanding Pillsbury stock at $60 per share and ultimately paid up to $66 per share. Falbo made over $165,000 in profits. The Securities and Exchange Commission (SEC) filed a suit in a federal district court against Falbo and others for alleged violations of, among other things, SEC Rule 10b-5. Under what theory might Falbo be liable? Do the circumstances of this case meet all of the requirements for liability under that theory? Explain. [*SEC v. Falbo,* 14 F.Supp.2d 508 (S.D.N.Y. 1998)]

37–13. In 1997, Scott and Sabrina Levine formed Friendly Power Co. (FPC) and Friendly Power Franchise Co. (FPC-Franchise). FPC obtained a license to operate as a utility company in California. FPC granted FPC-Franchise the right to pay commissions to "operators" who converted residential customers to FPC. Each operator paid for a "franchise"—a geographic area, determined by such factors as the number of households and competition from other utilities. In exchange for 50 percent of FPC's net profits on sales to residential customers in its territory, each franchise was required to maintain a 5 percent market share of power customers in that territory. Franchises were sold to telemarketing firms, which solicited customers. The telemarketers sold interests in each franchise to between fifty and ninety-four "partners," each of whom invested money. FPC began supplying electricity to its customers in May 1998. Less than three months later, the Securities and Exchange Commission (SEC) filed a suit in a federal district court against the Levines and others, alleging that the "franchises" were unregistered securities offered for sale to the public in violation of the Securities Act of 1933. What is the definition of a security? Should the court rule in favor of the SEC? Why, or why not? [*SEC v. Friendly Power Co., LLC,* 49 F.Supp.2d 1363 (S.D.Fla. 1999)]

37–14. 2TheMart.com, Inc., was conceived in January 1999 to launch an auction Web site to compete with eBay, Inc. On January 19, 2TheMart announced that its Web site was in its "final development" stages and expected to be active by the end of July as a "preeminent" auction site, and that the company had "retained the services of leading Web site design and architecture consultants to design and construct" the site. Based on the announcement, investors rushed to buy 2TheMart's stock, causing a rapid increase in the price. On February 3, 2TheMart entered into an agreement with IBM to take preliminary steps to plan the site. Three weeks later, 2TheMart announced that the site was "currently in final development." On June 1, 2TheMart signed a contract with IBM to design, build, and test the site, with a target delivery date of October 8. When 2TheMart's site did not debut as announced, Mary Harrington and others who had bought the stock filed a suit in a federal district court against the firm's officers, alleging violations of the Securities Exchange Act of 1934. The defendants responded, in part, that any alleged misrepresentations were not material and asked the court to dismiss the suit. How should the court rule, and why? [*In re 2TheMart.com, Inc. Securities Litigation,* 114 F.Supp.2d 955 (C.D.Ca. 2000)]

37–15. A Question of Ethics

Between 1970 and 1981, Sanford Weill served as the chief executive officer (CEO) of Shearson Loeb Rhodes and several of its predecessor entities (collectively, "Shearson"). In 1981, Weill sold his controlling interest in Shearson to the American Express Co., and between 1981 and 1985, he served as president of that firm. In 1985, Weill developed an interest in becoming CEO for BankAmerica and secured a commitment from Shearson to invest $1 billion in BankAmerica if he was successful in his negotiations with that firm. In early 1986, Weill met with BankAmerica directors several times, but these contacts were not disclosed publicly until February 20, 1986, when BankAmerica announced that Weill had sought to become its CEO but that BankAmerica was not interested in his offer. The day after the announcement, BankAmerica stock traded at prices higher than the prices at which it had traded during the five weeks preceding the announcement. Weill had discussed his efforts to become CEO of BankAmerica with his wife, who had discussed the information with her psychiatrist, Dr. Willis, prior to BankAmerica's public announcement of February 20. She had also told Dr. Willis about Shearson's decision to invest in BankAmerica if Weill succeeded in becoming its CEO. Willis disclosed to his broker this material, confidential information and purchased BankAmerica common stock. After BankAmerica's public announcement and the subsequent increase in the price of its stock, Willis sold his shares and realized a profit of approximately $27,500. The court held that Willis was liable for insider trading under the misappropriation theory. [*United States v. Willis,* 737 F.Supp. 269 (S.D.N.Y. 1990)]

1. The court stated in its opinion in this case that "[i]t is difficult to imagine a relationship that requires a higher degree of trust and confidence than the traditional relationship of physician and patient." It then quoted the concluding words of the Hippocratic oath: "Whatsoever things I see or hear concerning the life of men, in my attendance on the sick or even apart therefrom, which ought not be noised abroad, I will keep silence thereon, counting such things to be as sacred secrets." The court held that Willis had violated his fiduciary duty to Mrs. Weill, his patient, by investing in BankAmerica stock. Do you agree that Willis's private investments, which were based on information learned through his sessions with Mrs. Weill, constituted a violation of his duty to his patient? After all, Willis had not "noised abroad" Mrs. Weill's secrets—that is, he had not told others (except for his stockbroker) about the information. If you had been in Willis's position, would you have felt ethically restrained from trading on the information?
2. Can you think of any ways in which Willis's trading could have been harmful to Mrs. Weill's interests? Does your answer to this question have a bearing on how you answered Question 1?
3. Do you think that the misappropriation theory of liability imposes too great a burden on outsiders, such as Willis? Why, or why not? How might you justify, from an ethical point of view, the application of the misappropriation theory to "outsider trading"?

E-LINKS

For updated links to resources available on the Web, as well as a variety of other materials, visit this text's Web site at

http://wbl-cs.westbuslaw.com

To access the SEC's EDGAR database, go to

http://www.sec.gov/edgarhp.shtml

The Center for Corporate Law at the University of Cincinnati College of Law examines all of the acts discussed in this chapter. Go to

http://www.law.uc.edu/CCL

To find the Securities Act of 1933, go to

http://www.law.uc.edu/CCL/33Act/index.html

To examine the Securities Exchange Act of 1934, go to

http://www.law.uc.edu/CCL/34Act/index.html

For information on investor protection and securities fraud, including answers to frequently asked questions on the topic of securities fraud, go to

http://www.securitieslaw.com

LEGAL RESEARCH EXERCISES ON THE WEB

Go to http://wbl-cs.westbuslaw.com, the Web site that accompanies this text. Select "Interactive Study Center," and then click on "Chapter 37." There you will find the following Internet research exercise that you can perform to learn more about the SEC:

Activity 37–1: The SEC's Role

CHAPTER 38

Limited Liability Companies and Limited Partnerships

THE TWO MOST COMMON FORMS of business organization selected by two or more persons entering into business together are the partnership and the corporation. As explained in previous chapters, each form has distinct advantages and disadvantages. For partnerships, the advantage is that partnership income is taxed only once (all income is "passed through" the partnership entity to the partners themselves, who are taxed only as individuals); the disadvantage is the personal liability of the partners. For corporations, the advantage is the limited liability of shareholders; the disadvantage is the double taxation of corporate income. For many entrepreneurs and investors, the ideal business form would combine the tax advantages of the partnership form of business with the limited liability of the corporate enterprise.

A relatively new form of business organization called the **limited liability company (LLC)** is a hybrid form of business enterprise that meets these needs by offering the limited liability of the corporation and the tax advantages of a partnership. Increasingly, LLCs are becoming an organizational form of choice among businesspersons, a trend encouraged by state statutes permitting their use.

In this chapter, we begin by examining the LLC. We then look at a similar type of entity that is also relatively new—the limited liability partnership (LLP). The chapter concludes with a discussion of the limited partnership, a special type of partnership in which some of the partners have limited liability, and the limited liability limited partnership (LLLP).

SECTION 1

Limited Liability Companies

In 1977, Wyoming became the first state to pass legislation authorizing the creation of a limited liability company (LLC). Although LLCs emerged in the United States only in 1977, they have been in existence for over a century in other areas, including several European and South American nations. For example, the South American *limitada* is a form of business organization that operates more or less as a partnership but provides limited liability for the owners.

In the United States, after Wyoming's adoption of an LLC statute, it still was not known how the Internal Revenue Service (IRS) would treat the LLC for tax purposes. In 1988, however, the IRS ruled that Wyoming LLCs would be taxed as partnerships instead of as corporations, providing that certain requirements were met. Prior to this ruling, only one other state—Florida, in 1982—had authorized LLCs. The 1988 ruling encouraged other states to enact LLC statutes, and in less than a decade, all states had done so.

IRS rules that went into effect on January 1, 1997, encouraged even more widespread use of LLCs in the business world. These rules provide that any unincorporated business will automatically be taxed as a partnership unless it indicates otherwise on the tax form. The exceptions involve publicly traded companies, companies formed under a state incorporation statute, and certain foreign-owned companies. If a business chooses to be taxed as a corporation, it can indicate this choice by checking a box on the IRS form.

Part of the impetus behind creating LLCs in this country is that foreign investors are allowed to become LLC members. Generally, in an era increasingly characterized by global business efforts and investments, the LLC offers U.S. firms and potential investors from other countries flexibility and opportunities greater than those available through partnerships or corporations.

LLC Formation

Like the corporation, an LLC must be formed and operated in compliance with state law. About one-fourth of the states specifically require LLCs to have at least two owners, called **members.** In the rest of the states, although some LLC statutes are silent on this issue, one-member LLCs are usually permitted.

To form an LLC, **articles of organization** must be filed with a central state agency—usually the secretary of state's office. Typically, the articles are required to set forth such information as the name of the business, its principal address, the name and address of a registered agent, the names of the owners, and information on how the LLC will be managed. The business's name must include the words "Limited Liability Company" or the initials "LLC." In addition to filing the articles of organization, a few states require that a notice of the intention to form an LLC be published in a local newspaper.

Note that although the LLC, like the corporation, is a legal entity apart from its owners, for federal jurisdictional purposes an LLC is treated differently than a corporation. The federal jurisdiction statute provides that a corporation is deemed to be a citizen of the state in which it is incorporated and in which it maintains its principal place of business. The statute does not mention the citizenship of partnerships and other unincorporated associations, but courts have tended to regard these entities as citizens of every state in which their members are citizens.

The citizenship of LLCs may come into play when a party sues an LLC based on diversity of citizenship. Remember from Chapter 2 that in some circumstances, such as when parties to a lawsuit are from different states, a federal court can exercise diversity jurisdiction in cases in which the amount in controversy exceeds $75,000. *Complete* diversity of citizenship must exist, however. For example, a citizen of New York will not be able to bring a suit in federal court—on the basis of diversity jurisdiction—against multiple defendants if one of the defendants is also a citizen of New York.

See Case 38.1 at the end of this chapter. To view the full, unedited case from Westlaw,® go to this text's Web site at **http://wbl-cs.westbuslaw.com**.

Advantages and Disadvantages of LLCs

A key advantage of the LLC is that the liability of members is limited to the amount of their investments. Another significant advantage is that an LLC with two or more members can choose whether to be taxed as a partnership or a corporation.

LLCs that want to distribute profits to the members may prefer to be taxed as a partnership, to avoid the "double taxation" characteristic of the corporate entity. Remember that in the corporate form of business, the corporation as an entity pays income taxes on its profits, and the shareholders pay personal income taxes on profits distributed as dividends. Unless the LLC indicates that it wishes to be taxed as a corporation, it is automatically taxed as a partnership by the IRS. This means that the LLC as an entity pays no taxes; rather, as in a partnership, profits are "passed through" the LLC and paid personally by the members. If LLC members want to reinvest profits in the business, however, rather than distribute the profits to members, they may prefer to be taxed as a corporation if corporate income tax rates are lower than personal tax rates. Part of the attractiveness of the LLC for businesspersons is this flexibility with respect to taxation options.

For federal income tax purposes, one-member LLCs are automatically taxed as sole proprietorships unless they indicate that they wish to be taxed as corporations. With respect to state taxes, most states follow the IRS rules. Still another advantage of the LLC for businesspersons is the flexibility it offers in terms of business operations and management—as will be discussed shortly.

The disadvantages of the LLC are relatively few. Some of the initial disadvantages with respect to uncertainties over how LLCs would be taxed no longer exist. The only remaining disadvantage of the LLC is that state statutes are not yet uniform. In an attempt to promote some uniformity among the states in respect to LLC statutes, the National Conference of Commissioners on Uniform State Laws drafted a

Uniform Limited Liability Company Act for submission to the states to consider for adoption. Until all of the states have adopted the uniform law, however, an LLC in one state will have to check the rules in the other states in which the firm does business to ensure that it retains its limited liability.

The LLC Operating Agreement

In an LLC, the members themselves can decide how to operate the various aspects of the business by forming an **operating agreement**. Operating agreements typically contain provisions relating to management, how profits will be divided, the transfer of membership interests, whether the LLC will be dissolved on the death or departure of a member, and other important issues.

Operating agreements need not be in writing, and indeed they need not even be formed for an LLC to exist. Generally, though, LLC members should protect their interests by forming a written operating agreement.[1] As with any business arrangement, disputes may arise over any number of issues. If there is no agreement covering the topic being disputed, such as how profits will be divided, the state LLC statute will govern the outcome. For example, most LLC statutes provide that if the members have not specified how profits will be divided among the members, they will be divided equally.

Generally, with respect to issues not covered by an operating agreement or by an LLC statute, the principles of partnership law are applied.

See Case 38.2 at the end of this chapter. To view the full, unedited case from Westlaw,® go to this text's Web site at **http://wbl-cs.westbuslaw.com**.

LLC Management

Basically, there are two options with respect to the management of an LLC. The members may decide in their operating agreement to be either a "member-managed" or a "manager-managed" LLC.

In a *member-managed* LLC, all of the members participate in management. In a *manager-managed* LLC, the members designate a group of persons to manage the firm. The management group may consist of only members, both members and nonmembers, or only nonmembers. Most LLC statutes provide that unless the members agree otherwise, all members of the LLC will participate in management.

The members of an LLC can also set forth in their operating agreement provisions governing decision-making procedures. For example, the agreement can indicate what procedures are to be followed for choosing or removing managers, an issue on which most LLC statutes are silent. The members are also free to include in the agreement provisions designating when and for what purposes formal members' meetings will be held. In contrast to state laws governing corporations, LLC statutes in most states have no provisions regarding members' meetings. Members may also specify in their agreement how voting rights will be apportioned. If they do not, LLC statutes in most states provide that voting rights are apportioned according to the capital contributions made by each member. Some states provide that, in the absence of an agreement to the contrary, each member has one vote.

SECTION 2

Limited Liability Partnerships

The **limited liability partnership (LLP)** is similar to the LLC. The difference between an LLP and an LLC is that the LLP is designed more for professionals who normally do business as partners in a partnership. The major advantage of the LLP is that it allows a partnership to continue as a pass-through entity for tax purposes but limits the personal liability of the partners.

The first state to enact an LLP statute was Texas, in 1991. Other states quickly followed suit, and by 1997, virtually all of the states had enacted LLP statutes. Like LLCs, LLPs must be formed and operated in compliance with state statutes. The appropriate form must be filed with a central state agency, usually the secretary of state's office, and the business's name must include either "Limited Liability Partnership" or "LLP."

In most states, it is relatively easy to convert a traditional partnership into an LLP because the firm's basic organizational structure remains the same. Additionally, all of the statutory and common law rules governing partnerships still apply (apart from those modified by the LLP statute). Normally, LLP

1. Some experts suggest that even a one-member LLC should have an operating agreement. An operating agreement provides evidence that the LLC is a separate entity and thus strengthens the member-owner's protection against being held personally liable for a business obligation.

statutes are simply amendments to a state's already existing partnership law.

The LLP is especially attractive for two categories of businesses: professional services and family businesses. Professional service companies include law firms and accounting firms. Family limited liability partnerships are basically business organizations in which all of the partners are related (see the discussion later in this chapter).

LIABILITY IN AN LLP

Many professionals, such as attorneys and accountants, work together using the business form of the partnership. Remember from Chapter 33 that a major disadvantage of the partnership is the unlimited personal liability of its owner-partners. Partners are also subject to joint and several (individual) liability for partnership obligations. For example, suppose that a group of lawyers is operating as a partnership. A client sues one of the attorneys for malpractice and wins a large judgment, and the firm's malpractice insurance is insufficient to cover the obligation. When the attorney's personal assets are exhausted, the personal assets of the other, innocent partners can be used to satisfy the judgment.

The LLP allows professionals to avoid personal liability for the malpractice of other partners. Although LLP statutes vary from state to state, generally each state statute limits in some way the liability of partners. For example, Delaware law protects each innocent partner from the "debts and obligations of the partnership arising from negligence, wrongful acts, or misconduct." In North Carolina, Texas, and Washington, D.C., the statutes protect innocent partners from obligations arising from "errors, omissions, negligence, incompetence, or malfeasance." Although the language of these statutes may seem to apply specifically to attorneys, virtually any group of professionals can use the LLP.

Questions remain, however, regarding the exact limits of this exemption from liability. One question concerns limits on liability outside the state in which the LLP was formed. Another question involves whether liability should be imposed to some extent on a negligent partner's supervising partner.

Liability outside the State of Formation. Because state LLP statutes are not uniform, a question arises when an LLP formed in one state does business in another state. If the LLP statutes in the two states provide different liability protection, which law applies? Most states apply the law of the state in which the LLP was formed, even when the firm does business in another state. Some states, though, do not expressly recognize foreign LLPs (that is, LLPs formed in another state), and others do not require foreign LLPs to register before doing business.[2]

Supervising Partner's Liability. A partner who commits a wrongful act, such as negligence, is liable for the results of the act. Also liable is the partner who supervises the party who commits a wrongful act. This is generally true for all types of partners and partnerships, including LLPs.

When the partners are members of an LLP and more than one member is negligent, there is a question as to how liability is to be shared. Is each partner jointly and severally liable for the entire result, as a general partner would be in most states? Some states provide for proportionate liability—that is, for separate determinations of the negligence of the partners.[3]

For example, suppose that accountants Don and Jane are partners in an LLP, with Don supervising Jane. Jane negligently fails to file tax returns for their client, Centaur Tools. Centaur files a suit against Don and Jane. In a state that does not allow for proportionate liability, Don can be held liable for the entire loss. Under a proportionate liability statute, Don will be liable for no more than his portion of the responsibility for the missed tax deadline. (Even if Jane settles the case quickly, Don will still be liable for his portion.)

FAMILY LIMITED LIABILITY PARTNERSHIPS

A **family limited liability partnership (FLLP)** is a limited liability partnership in which the majority of the partners are persons related to each other, essentially as spouses, parents, grandparents, siblings, cousins, nephews, or nieces. A person acting in a fiduciary capacity for persons so related can also be a

2. See, for example, 6 Delaware Code Section 15-1101.

3. See, for example, Colorado Revised Statutes Annotated Section 13-21-111.5(1) and Utah Code Annotated Section 78-27-39. The American Institute of Certified Public Accountants also supports the enactment of proportionate liability statutes.

partner. All of the partners must be natural persons or persons acting in a fiduciary capacity for the benefit of natural persons.

Probably the most significant use of the FLLP form of business organization is in agriculture. Family-owned farms sometimes find this form to their benefit. The FLLP has the same advantages as other LLPs with some additional advantages, such as, in Iowa, an exemption from real estate transfer taxes when partnership real estate is transferred among partners.[4]

SECTION 3

Limited Partnerships

To this point, we have been discussing relatively new forms of limited liability business organizations. We now look at a far older business organizational form that limits the liability of some of its owners—the **limited partnership.** Limited partnerships originated in medieval Europe and have been existence in the United States since the early 1800s. In many ways, limited partnerships are like the general partnerships discussed in Chapter 33, but they also differ from general partnerships in several ways. Because of this, they are sometimes referred to as *special partnerships*.

Limited partnerships consist of at least one **general partner** and one or more **limited partners.** A general partner assumes management responsibility for the partnership and so has full responsibility for the partnership and for all debts of the partnership. A limited partner contributes cash or other property and owns an interest in the firm but does not undertake any management duties and is not personally liable for partnership debts beyond the amount of his or her investment. A limited partner can forfeit limited liability by taking part in the management of the business. A comparison of the basic characteristics of general partnerships and limited partnerships appears in Exhibit 38–1 on the next page.[5]

4. Iowa Statutes Section 428A.2.

5. Under the Revised Uniform Partnership Act (RUPA), which was discussed in Chapter 33, a general partnership can be converted into a limited partnership and vice versa [RUPA 902, 903]. The RUPA also provides for the merger of a general partnership with one or more general or limited partnerships under rules that are similar to those governing corporate mergers [RUPA 905].

Until 1976, the law governing limited partnerships in all states except Louisiana was the Uniform Limited Partnership Act (ULPA). Since 1976, most states and the District of Columbia have adopted the revised version of the ULPA, known as the Revised Uniform Limited Partnership Act (RULPA). Because the RULPA is the dominant law governing limited partnerships in the United States, we will refer to the RULPA in the following discussion of limited partnerships.

FORMATION OF A LIMITED PARTNERSHIP

Compared with the informal, private, and voluntary agreement that usually suffices for a general partnership (see Chapter 33), the formation of a limited partnership is a public and formal proceeding that must follow statutory requirements. A limited partnership must have at least one general partner and one limited partner, as mentioned previously. Additionally, the partners must sign a **certificate of limited partnership**, which requires information similar to that found in a corporate charter (see Chapter 34). The certificate must be filed with the designated state official—under the RULPA, the secretary of state. The certificate is usually open to public inspection.

Westlaw. See Case 38.3 at the end of this chapter. To view the full, unedited case from Westlaw,® go to this text's Web site at **http://wbl-cs.westbuslaw.com**.

RIGHTS AND LIABILITIES OF PARTNERS

General partners, unlike limited partners, are personally liable to the partnership's creditors; thus, at least one general partner is necessary in a limited partnership so that someone has personal liability. This policy can be circumvented in states that allow a corporation to be the general partner in a partnership. Because the corporation has limited liability by virtue of corporate laws, if a corporation is the general partner, no one in the limited partnership has personal liability.

Rights of Limited Partners. Subject to the limitations that will be discussed here, limited partners have essentially the same rights as general partners, including the right of access to partnership books and the right to other information regarding partnership business. On dissolution of the partnership, limited partners are entitled to a return of their contributions in accordance with the partnership certificate

EXHIBIT 38–1 A COMPARISON OF GENERAL PARTNERSHIPS AND LIMITED PARTNERSHIPS

CHARACTERISTIC	GENERAL PARTNERSHIP (UPA)	LIMITED PARTNERSHIP (RULPA)
Creation	By agreement of two or more persons to carry on a business as co-owners for profit.	By agreement of two or more persons to carry on a business as co-owners for profit. Must include one or more general partners and one or more limited partners. Filing of a certificate with the secretary of state is required.
Sharing of Profits and Losses	By agreement; or, in the absence of agreement, profits are shared equally by the partners, and losses are shared in the same ratio as profits.	Profits are shared as required in the certificate agreement, and losses are shared likewise, up to the amount of the limited partners' capital contributions. In the absence of a provision in the certificate agreement, profits and losses are shared on the basis of percentages of capital contributions.
Liability	Unlimited personal liability of all partners.	Unlimited personal liability of all general partners; limited partners liable only to the extent of their capital contributions.
Capital Contribution	No minimum or mandatory amount; set by agreement.	Set by agreement.
Management	By agreement, or in the absence of agreement, all partners have an equal voice.	General partners by agreement, or else each has an equal voice. Limited partners have no voice or else are subject to liability as general partners (but only if a third party has reason to believe that the limited partner is a general partner). A limited partner may act as an agent or employee of the partnership and vote on amending the certificate or on the sale or dissolution of the partnership.
Duration	By agreement, or can be dissolved by action of the partners (withdrawal), operation of law (death or bankruptcy), or court decree.	By agreement in the certificate or by withdrawal, death, or mental incompetence of a general partner in the absence of the right of the other general partners to continue the partnership. Death of a limited partner, unless he or she is the only remaining limited partner, does not terminate the partnership.
Distribution of Assets on Liquidation—Order of Priorities	1. Outside creditors. 2. Partner creditors. 3. Partners, according to capital contributions. 4. Partners, according to profits.	1. Outside creditors and partner creditors. 2. Partners and former partners entitled to distributions before withdrawal under the agreement or the RULPA. 3. Partners, according to capital contributions. 4. Partners, according to profits.

[RULPA 201(a)(10)]. They can also assign their interests subject to the certificate [RULPA 702, 704].

The RULPA provides a limited partner with the right to sue an outside party on behalf of the firm if the general partners with authority to do so have refused to file suit [RULPA 1001]. In addition, investor protection legislation, such as securities laws (discussed in Chapter 37), may give some protection to limited partners.

Liabilities of Limited Partners. In contrast to the personal liability of general partners, the liability of a limited partner is limited to the capital that he or she contributes or agrees to contribute to the partnership [RULPA 502].

A limited partnership is formed by good faith compliance with the requirements for signing and filing the certificate, even if it is incomplete or defective. When a limited partner discovers a defect in the formation of the limited partnership, he or she can avoid future liability by causing an appropriate amendment or certificate to be filed or by renouncing an interest in the profits of the partnership [RULPA 304]. If the limited partner takes neither of these actions on the discovery of the defect, however, the partner can be held personally liable by the firm's creditors. Liability for false statements in a partnership certificate runs in favor of persons relying on the false statements and against members who know of the falsity but still sign the certificate [RULPA 207].

Limited Partners and Management. Limited partners enjoy limited liability so long as they do not participate in management [RULPA 303]. A limited partner who participates in management will be just as liable as a general partner to any creditor who transacts business with the limited partnership and believes, based on a limited partner's conduct, that the limited partner is a general partner [RULPA 303]. How much actual review and advisement a limited partner can engage in before being exposed to liability is an unsettled question.[6] A limited partner who knowingly permits his or her name to be used in the name of the limited partnership is liable to creditors who extend credit to the limited partnership without knowledge that the limited partner is not a general partner [RULPA 102, 303(d)].

Although limited partners cannot participate in management, this does not mean that the general partners are totally free of restrictions in running the business. The general partners in a limited partnership have fiduciary obligations to the partnership and to the limited partners.

Westlaw. See Case 38.4 at the end of this chapter. To view the full, unedited case from Westlaw,® go to this text's Web site at **http://wbl-cs.westbuslaw.com**.

DISSOLUTION OF THE LIMITED PARTNERSHIP

A limited partnership is dissolved in much the same way as an ordinary partnership (see Chapter 33). The retirement, death, or mental incompetence of a general partner can dissolve the partnership, but not if the business can be continued by one or more of the other general partners in accordance with their certificate or by the consent of all of the members [RULPA 801]. The death or assignment of interest of a limited partner does not dissolve the limited partnership [RULPA 702, 704, 705]. A limited partnership can be dissolved by court decree [RULPA 802].

Bankruptcy or the withdrawal of a general partner dissolves a limited partnership. Bankruptcy of a limited partner, however, does not dissolve the partnership unless it causes the bankruptcy of the limited partnership. The retirement of a general partner causes a dissolution unless the members consent to a continuation by the remaining general partners or unless this contingency is provided for in the certificate.

On dissolution, creditors' rights, including those of partners who are creditors, take first priority. Then partners and former partners receive unpaid distributions of partnership assets and, except as otherwise agreed, amounts representing returns on their contributions and amounts proportionate to their shares of the distributions [RULPA 804].

SECTION 4

Limited Liability Limited Partnerships

A **limited liability limited partnership (LLLP)** is similar to a limited partnership, except that the liability of a general partner in an LLLP is the same as the liability of a limited partner. That is, the liability of all partners is limited to the amount of their investments in the firm.

A few states provide expressly for LLLPs.[7] In states that do not provide for LLLPs but do allow for limited partnerships and limited liability partnerships, a limited partnership should probably still be able to register with the state as an LLLP.

SECTION 5

Major Business Forms Compared

Exhibit 38–2 on the next two pages summarizes the essential advantages and disadvantages of each of the forms of business organization discussed in Chapters 33 through 37, as well as in this chapter.

6. It is an unsettled question partly because there are differences among the laws in different states. Factors to be considered under the RULPA are listed in RULPA 303(b), (c).

7. States that provide expressly for limited liability limited partnerships include Colorado, Delaware, Florida, Missouri, Pennsylvania, Texas, and Virginia.

Exhibit 38–2 Major Forms of Business Compared

Characteristic	Sole Proprietorship	Partnership	Corporation
Method of Creation	Created at will by owner.	Created by agreement of the parties.	Charter issued by state—created by statutory authorization.
Legal Position	Not a separate entity; owner is the business.	Not a separate legal entity in many states.	Always a legal entity separate and distinct from its owners—a legal fiction for the purposes of owning property and being a party to litigation.
Liability	Unlimited liability.	Unlimited liability.	Limited liability of shareholders—shareholders are not liable for the debts of the corporation.
Duration	Determined by owner; automatically dissolved on owner's death.	Terminated by agreement of the partners, by the death of one or more of the partners, by withdrawal of a partner, by bankruptcy, and so on.	Can have perpetual existence.
Transferability of Interest	Interest can be transferred, but individual's proprietorship then ends.	Although partnership interest can be assigned, assignee does not have full rights of a partner.	Shares of stock can be transferred.
Management	Completely at owner's discretion.	Each general partner has a direct and equal voice in management unless expressly agreed otherwise in the partnership agreement.	Shareholders elect directors, who set policy and appoint officers.
Taxation	Owner pays personal taxes on business income.	Each partner pays pro rata share of income taxes on net profits, whether or not they are distributed.	Double taxation—corporation pays income tax on net profits, with no deduction for dividends, and shareholders pay income tax on disbursed dividends they receive.
Organizational Fees, Annual License Fees, and Annual Reports	None.	None.	All required.
Transaction of Business in Other States	Generally no limitation.	Generally no limitation.[a]	Normally must qualify to do business and obtain certificate of authority.

a. A few states have enacted statutes requiring that foreign partnerships qualify to do business there.

EXHIBIT 38–2 MAJOR FORMS OF BUSINESS COMPARED (CONTINUED)

CHARACTERISTIC	LIMITED PARTNERSHIP	LIMITED LIABILITY COMPANY	LIMITED LIABILITY PARTNERSHIP
Method of Creation	Created by agreement to carry on a business for a profit. At least one party must be a general partner and the other(s) limited partner(s). Certificate of limited partnership is filed. Charter must be issued by the state.	Created by an agreement of the owner-members of the company. Articles of organization are filed. Charter must be issued by the state.	Created by agreement of the partners. Certificate of a limited liability partnership is filed. Charter must be issued by state.
Legal Position	Treated as a legal entity.	Treated as a legal entity.	Generally, treated same as a general partnership.
Liability	Unlimited liability of all general partners; limited partners are liable only to the extent of capital contributions.	Member-owners' liability is limited to the amount of capital contributions or investments.	Varies from state to state but usually limits liability of a partner for certain acts committed by other partners.
Duration	By agreement in certificate, or by termination of the last general partner (withdrawal, death, and so on) or last limited partner.	Unless a single-member LLC, can have perpetual existence (same as a corporation).	Terminated by agreement of partners, by death or withdrawal of a partner, or by law (such as bankruptcy).
Transferability of Interest	Interest can be assigned (same as general partnership), but if assignee becomes a member with consent of other partners, certificate must be amended.	Member interests are freely transferable.	Interest can be assigned same as in a general partnership.
Management	General partners have equal voice or by agreement. Limited partners may not retain limited liability if they actively participate in management.	Member-owners can fully participate in management, or member-owners can select managers to manage the firm on behalf of the members.	Same as a general partnership.
Taxation	Generally taxed as a partnership.	LLC is not taxed, and members are taxed personally on profits "passed through" the LLC.	Same as a general partnership.
Organizational Fees, Annual License Fees, and Annual Reports	Organizational fee required; usually not others.	Organizational fee required; others vary with states.	Organizational fee required (such as a set amount per partner); usually not others.
Transaction of Business in Other States	Generally, no limitation.	Generally, no limitation but may vary depending on state.	Generally, no limitation, but state laws vary as to formation and limitation of liability.

When deciding which form of business organization would be most appropriate, businesspersons normally take several factors into consideration. As mentioned earlier, these factors include ease of creation, the liability of the owners, tax considerations, and the need for capital. Each major form of business organization offers distinct advantages and disadvantages with respect to these and other factors.

For example, the sole proprietorship has the advantage of being easily and inexpensively established, but the owner faces personal liability for business obligations as well as restrictions on obtaining capital for additional financing. The partnership is relatively easy to establish and provides a way for the business to obtain capital (from partners' contributions). It enjoys tax benefits as well. The partnership also has a major disadvantage: the personal liability of the partners. One of the advantages of the corporate form is that capital for expansion can be obtained by the issuance of shares of stock. Another advantage is the limited liability of the shareholder-owners. The limited liability company and the limited liability partnership increasingly are becoming forms of choice because of the many advantages they offer with respect to both the liability of the owners and taxation.

Terms and Concepts to Review

articles of organization 774
certificate of limited partnership 777
family limited liability partnership (FLLP) 776
general partner 777
limited liability company (LLC) 773
limited liability limited partnership (LLLP) 779
limited liability partnership (LLP) 775
limited partner 777
limited partnership 777
member 774
operating agreement 775

Chapter Summary

Limited Liability Company (LLC)	1. *Formation*—Articles of organization must be filed with the appropriate state office—usually the office of the secretary of state—setting forth the name of the business, its principal address, the names of the owners (called *members*), and other relevant information. 2. *Advantages and disadvantages of the LLC*—Advantages of the LLC include limited liability, the option to be taxed as a partnership or as a corporation, and flexibility in deciding how the business will be managed and operated. 3. *Operating agreement*—When an LLC is formed, the members decide, in an operating agreement, how the business will be managed and what rules will apply to the organization. 4. *Management*—An LLC may be managed by members only, by some members and some nonmembers, or by nonmembers only.
Limited Liability Partnership (LLP)	1. *Formation*—Articles must be filed with the appropriate state agency, usually the secretary of state's office. Typically, an LLP is formed by professionals who work together as partners in a partnership. Under most state LLP statutes, it is relatively easy to convert a traditional partnership into an LLP. 2. *Liability of partners*—LLP statutes vary, but generally they allow professionals to avoid personal liability for the malpractice of other partners. The extent to which partners' limited liability will be recognized when the partnership does business in another state depends on the other state's laws. Partners in an LLP continue to be liable for their own wrongful acts and for the wrongful acts of those whom they supervise. 3. *Family limited liability partnership (FLLP)*—A form of LLP in which all of the partners are family members or fiduciaries of family members; the most significant use of the FLLP is by families engaged in agricultural enterprises.

CHAPTER SUMMARY—CONTINUED

Limited Partnership	1. *Formation*—A certificate of limited partnership must be filed with the secretary of state's office or other designated state official. The certificate must include information about the business, similar to the information included in a corporate charter. The partnership consists of one or more general partners and one or more limited partners. 2. *Rights and liabilities of partners*—With some exceptions, the rights of partners are the same as the rights of partners in a general partnership. General partners have unlimited liability for partnership obligations; limited partners are liable only to the extent of their contributions. 3. *Limited partners and management*—Only general partners can participate in management. Limited partners have no voice in management; if they do participate in management activities, they risk having general-partner liability. 4. *Dissolution*—Generally, a limited partnership can be dissolved in much the same way as an ordinary partnership. The death or assignment of interest of a limited partner does not dissolve the partnership; bankruptcy of a limited partner will also not dissolve the partnership unless it causes the bankruptcy of the firm.
Limited Liability Limited Partnership (LLLP)	A special type of limited partnership in which the liability of all partners, including general partners, is limited to the amount of their investments.

CASES FOR ANALYSIS

Westlaw. You can access the full text of each case presented below by going to the Westlaw cases on this text's Web site at http://wbl-cs.westbuslaw.com. Each Westlaw case includes the names of all plaintiffs and defendants, the dates on which the case was argued and decided, a brief summary of the issues and decisions in the case, headnotes classifying specific issues in the case according to the West Key Number System, and the court's opinion. Concurring and dissenting opinions, if any, are included as well.

CASE 38.1 LIMITED LIABILITY COMPANY FORMATION

SKYWIZARD.COM, LLC v. COMPUTER PERSONALITIES SYSTEMS, INC.

United States District Court,
District of Maine, 2000.
__ F.Supp.2d __.

COHEN, Magistrate J. [Judge]

* * * *

I. Findings of Fact

1. In early 1998 Gary Cubeta and his sister Gail Ejdys founded [Skywizard.com, LLC], a Maine limited liability company with its principal place of business in York, Maine, for the purpose of entering the internet service provider ("ISP") market. Cubeta is president and Ejdys is vice-president of Skywizard.

2. The highly competitive ISP business comprises approximately 5,000 providers nationwide, including America On Line ("AOL"), CompuServe and Prodigy.

3. To break into the ISP business, Cubeta and Edjys determined that they would form a strategic alliance with either a manufacturer or reseller of computer hardware in which the manufacturer or reseller would promote Skywizard's service. They elected to enter into such an agreement with [Computer Personalities Systems, Inc. ("CPSI")], a Pennsylvania-based retailer of computer hardware and software whose principal, George Cappell, markets products through so-called "infomercials" aired both on national cable channels and on "Direct 2 U," an infomercial channel owned or controlled by CPSI.

4. On or about May 13, 1999 Skywizard and CPSI entered into an agreement (the "Contract") that provides, in relevant part:

> 4. *Exclusive Promotion.* During the Term of this Agreement, CPSI shall promote Skywizard.com's internet access services, to the exclusion of any other internet access services (including, without limitation, America On-Line, Compuserve, Prodigy, Mindspring, Earthlink, AT & T Worldnet, etc.), in the following

manner: (a) CPSI shall add Skywizard.com's internet access software, to the exclusion of any other internet access software, on each and every computer unit sold by CPSI or any agent thereof * * * .

* * * *

7. *Special Promotion Program.* On September 1 of each calendar year during the Term of this Agreement (each, a "Start Date") and continuing thereafter for a period of twelve (12) months from each such Start Date (each, a "Promotion Year") during the Term of this Agreement, the parties shall conduct a special promotion program (the "Program"), pursuant to which CPSI shall include twelve (12) months of prepaid Skywizard.com-brand internet access service as part of each customer's Promotion Unit * * * . Such services shall be provided by Skywizard.com to customers under Skywizard.com's normal terms and conditions. The parties acknowledge and agree that the Program shall commence as of September 1, 1999 (the "Program Start Date").

* * * *

(c) *Promotion Fees.* * * * Within seven (7) days following the end of each calendar month during which a Special Promotion is completed, CPSI shall remit to Skywizard.com * * * an internet access service fee (each, a "Promotion Fee") equal to the Wholesale Cost (as defined below) multiplied by the number of Promotion Units shipped by CPSI to customers during such month pursuant to a Special Promotion hereunder * * * . For purposes of this paragraph, the term "Wholesale Cost" shall mean the sum of seventy-nine dollars ($79.00). * * *

* * * *

5. Cubeta considers the Contract Skywizard's "lifeblood." The vast majority, if not all, of Skywizard's subscribers are people who bought computers through CPSI. Skywizard has two types of subscribers: paying and "prepaid." Paying subscribers are charged between $16.39 and $21.95 per month. Prepaid subscribers consist of those who signed up with Skywizard after purchasing computers during CPSI's Special Promotions, in which they are offered one year's free internet access through Skywizard.

6. As of the time of trial Skywizard had about 6,200 subscribers, of whom approximately 2,200 (roughly one-third) were prepaid. * * *

7. CPSI pays Skywizard $79 per computer shipped as a result of a Special Promotion, in consideration for the offer to CPSI's customers of one year of free internet access. Approximately 2,200 CPSI customers have elected to take advantage of the year's free access by signing up with Skywizard—representing about one-third of the total of 6,677 Special Promotion customers to whom computers had been shipped through March 2000. Skywizard has not to date imposed a deadline by which the offer must be accepted. However, Skywizard does not contact CPSI Special Promotion customers to inquire why they have not signed up or to encourage them to do so.

8. Skywizard incurs an average wholesale cost of $10.25 per subscriber per month for phone connections to the internet. In the case of Special Promotion customers, this cost is not incurred unless and until the customer subscribes for the year's free internet service. For each of those Special Promotion subscribers, Skywizard incurs a loss of approximately $3.67 per month (or $44.04 per year), representing the average wholesale cost of $10.25 per month minus the CPSI Special Promotion fee, equal to $6.58 per month. Skywizard also has overhead costs that include payroll for its twenty-six employees and the cost of leasing office space.

9. Many variables factor into a consumer's choice of ISP, including (i) name-brand recognition, (ii) availability of technical support (Skywizard offers technical support from 9 A.M. to 11 P.M. Eastern Standard Time; AOL offers it twenty-four hours a day), (iii) ease of connection to the service (one must dial an 800 number to access Skywizard's service); (iv) price (some advertiser-supported ISPs offer free service), (v) availability of a local access number, thus avoiding toll charges to connect to the internet (Skywizard has not been able to provide local access numbers to all interested in subscribing) and (vi) availability of a high-speed cable connection (which Skywizard does not offer).

* * * *

16. CPSI failed to run a Special Promotion in September 1999. For this claimed breach [of contract] Skywizard sought two components of damages: (i) the lost fee of $79 per computer shipped and (ii) lost profits of $135 per subscriber. Cubeta estimated, based on actual sales figures and promises made by Cappell, that 1,500 units would have been shipped as a result of a September 1999 Special Promotion, for lost fees totalling $118,500. He further calculated that, of those 1,500, one-third would have subscribed to Skywizard, representing lost profits of $67,500 (500 × $135 per subscriber).

17. Skywizard has not to date made a profit.

II. Conclusions of Law

* * * *

[7.] Regardless of the number of computers that CPSI may have shipped to customers had a September 1999 Special Promotion aired, the evidence is insufficient to substantiate the amount of Skywizard's damages based on loss of the $79 fee with reasonable probability. As counsel for the defendant pointed out at trial, were all of CPSI's Special Promotion customers to take advantage of the offer of one year's free internet service (as they theoretically could), the $79 per customer fee would be more than offset by the cost to Skywizard to service all of the new subscribers. Skywizard adduced evidence that as of March 2000 only one-third of CPSI's Special Promotion customers were Skywizard subscribers. If I could conclude with confidence that, had the September 1999 Special Promotion aired, only one-third of the resultant customers would have become Skywizard subscribers,

Skywizard would have demonstrated that, by avoiding the cost of servicing the remaining two-thirds of the Special Promotion customers, it lost monies that would have been generated by the $79 fee. However, in view of the newness of the Skywizard enterprise, the fact that Skywizard imposed no deadline within which customers were obliged to accept the offer of one year's free internet service and the fact that Skywizard's evidence at most amounted to a snapshot of its customer base as of one point in time, I am constrained to conclude that the record is barren of sufficient historic company data from which a reliable projection of the composition of the customer base can be made. In view of the clear breach of contract, an award of nominal damages nonetheless is appropriate.

* * * *

[11.] * * * In light of the foregoing, judgment shall enter in favor of Skywizard and against CPSI in the amount of $100.00.

* * * *

So ordered.

CASE 38.2 LIMITED LIABILITY COMPANY OPERATING AGREEMENT

HURWITZ V. PADDEN

Court of Appeals of Minnesota, 1998.
581 N.W.2d 359.

SHORT, Judge.

* * * *

FACTS

In September 1991, Thomas R. Hurwitz and Michael B. Padden formed a two-person law firm, Hurwitz & Padden, PLC ("firm"), but failed to enter into a written partnership agreement. The partners shared all firm proceeds on a 50-50 basis, and reported all income as partnership income. In January 1993, Hurwitz filed articles of organization, which established the firm as a limited liability company with the Secretary of State. * * *

On February 15, 1996, Padden notified Hurwitz that he wanted to dissolve their professional relationship as of March 1, 1996. The parties successfully resolved all business issues involving their relationship, except for the division of attorney fees from several of the firm's contingency fee cases. In August 1996, Hurwitz filed this declaratory judgment action [in a Minnesota state court] against Padden seeking a formal dissolution, a post-dissolution distribution of attorney fees on a 50-50 basis, and injunctive relief. By counterclaim, Padden requested a full accounting and an award of defense costs and fees. Both parties filed cross-motions for partial summary judgment. The trial court found in favor of Hurwitz, deciding the contingency fees should be divided equally, and submitted all accounting matters to a referee. After adopting the referee's findings, the trial court entered judgment in favor of Hurwitz for $101,750.

ISSUE

Did the trial court err in dividing contingency fees equally between former law partners where there was no written fee allocation agreement?

ANALYSIS

A partnership is based on mutual trust and confidence. In their dealings with one another, partners are subject to the highest standards of good faith and integrity. Without an agreement to the contrary, a partnership is dissolved under the Uniform Partnership Act (UPA).

We are asked to determine whether, in the absence of a contrary agreement, pre-dissolution contingency fee files remain assets of a law firm following its dissolution. * * *

Dissolution of a partnership triggers an end to the relationship, but it does not end the partnership itself. *Despite a dissolution, a partnership relationship continues to exist until all issues involving the business of the partnership entity are resolved. When the partnership's business is completely resolved, only then are the entity and the partnership relationship finally terminated.* [Emphasis added.]

As a partnership moves toward termination, it conducts a "winding up" of its affairs. When a partnership is in this "winding up" stage, the UPA confers no right of compensation for services rendered by the partners in furtherance of the partnership business. * * *

During the period between dissolution and termination, partnership distributions continue to be made according to pre-dissolution rules.

In addition, prior to the termination of the partnership, the partners' fiduciary duties continue to flow from the underlying partnership relationship. Pending contingency files are uncompleted transactions of the partnership, and the fees obtained from such cases are assets of the firm subject to distribution under the UPA. Thus, in the absence of a contrary agreement, the partners' fiduciary duties extend to pre-dissolution contingency fee files.

Padden argues the trial court erred in applying partnership principles to the dissolution of a limited liability company. However, the Minnesota Limited Liability Company Act specifically incorporates the definition and use of the term "dissolution" from the Uniform Partnership Act. Under both statutes, the entity is not terminated upon dissolution, but continues until all business issues are resolved. Thus, the UPA provides guidance when examining the end stages of either entity's life. Moreover, the mere fact that the parties filed a limited liability company document with the state does not foreclose an examination of partnership law.

It is undisputed: (1) the firm had no written or oral agreement regarding the division of contingency fees upon dissolution; (2) the firm existed for approximately five-and-a-half years before Padden requested dissolution; (3) a little over five months elapsed between the date of dissolution and the date the parties cross-claimed to settle the firm's remaining issues; (4) the firm's contingency fee cases were acquired before the firm's dissolution; (5) prior to its dissolution, the firm divided fees equally between the parties; and (6) at the time the parties filed suit, the firm was in a winding-up phase. Under these circumstances, partnership principles, including the "no-compensation rule," govern the division of fees obtained from pre-dissolution contingency fee files. Thus, the contingency fees obtained from pre-dissolution case files must be divided equally between the parties, which is consistent with the pre- dissolution method of allocation. * * *

* * * *

DECISION

Contingency fee cases are partnership assets. In the absence of an agreement to the contrary, those fees are allocated, upon dissolution, according to partnership principles. * * *

Affirmed.

CASE 38.3 FORMATION OF A LIMITED PARTNERSHIP

MILLER V. DEPARTMENT OF REVENUE, STATE OF OREGON

Supreme Court of Oregon, 1998.
327 Or. 129,
958 P.2d 833.

LEESON, Justice.

* * * *

FACTUAL BACKGROUND

The [Oregon] Tax Court made the following findings of fact, none of which the parties challenge:

"In 1984, Robert Loverin and Paul Miller, who are brothers-in-law, were employed by Rockwood Development Corporation (Rockwood), an Oregon Corporation. Rockwood was owned by Miller's parents and other family members. Rockwood engaged in creating, purchasing, and managing low-income housing projects, most of which were owned by limited partnerships. * * *

"In 1984, Loverin and Miller decided to start their own business because Rockwood was having financial difficulties. They formed BP Corporation to engage in the same kind of business as Rockwood. Knowing they did not have the level of management experience in low-income housing required by the U.S. Department of Housing and Urban Development (HUD), they obtained the extensive experience of Rockwood through a series of management agreements.

"It was through Rockwood that Loverin and Miller became aware of Edward and Fern Fischer, owners of four low-income housing projects commonly know as Fischer Court I, Fischer Court II, East Ninth Street (Maple Court), and Southfair. * * * In September 1984, BP Corporation made an offer [to buy the projects] which the Fischers accepted. The offering price was $3,500,000, with $650,000 down and the balance of $2,850,000 in the form of a 15-year * * * note bearing nine percent simple interest. * * *

"The principals of BP Corporation, Loverin and Miller, * * * formed a limited partnership for each property and thereafter sought investors for the partnerships. Money invested by the limited partners would be used to make the down payments on the apartment projects.

* * * *

"* * * [O]n their income tax returns, the general partners allocated 99.9 percent of the losses to themselves up to the time the investing limited partners were admitted. The [state tax] auditor reallocated these losses according to the provisions in the limited partnership agreement, allocating two percent to general partners and 98 percent to limited partners."

Taxpayers appealed the notices of assessment that were issued pursuant to the audit. After the administrative hearing, the [Oregon] Department of Revenue (Department) * * * sustained the auditor's adjustments * * * regarding allocation of profits and losses to the general and limited partners. Taxpayers appealed to the Tax Court.

* * * The court concluded that * * * the limited partnership agreement did not provide for allocation of 99.9 percent of the profits and losses to the general partners. * * *

* * * *

ALLOCATION OF PROFITS AND LOSSES

* * * [T]axpayers contend that the Tax Court erred in holding that, as to their 1985 tax returns, they were not entitled to allocate 99.9 percent of their losses to the general partners and one-tenth of one percent of their losses to the initial limited partner. The Tax Court held that the only written agreements regarding allocations of profits and losses unambiguously prevent such an allocation. Taxpayers contend that Section 8.1 of the Amended and Restated Articles of Limited Partnership (amended articles) authorizes them to allocate profits and losses among the general and original or substituted limited partners as they "may agree" before admission of the investor limited partners. According to taxpayers, they and the substitute limited partner agreed to the 1985 allocation. The Department responds that, under Section 1.5.1 A of the Articles of Limited Partnership (articles) and amended articles, taxpayers were entitled to claim only two percent of the profits and losses on the 1985 tax returns. * * *

The articles, adopted on September 10, 1984, stated that taxpayers were general partners and that Rockwood Development Corporation (Rockwood) was the initial limited partner. Section 1.5.1 A of the articles allocated two percent of the net operating profits and losses to the general partners and 98 percent of the profits and losses to the limited partners. * * * A statement next to the signatures of the general partners declared that the general partnership held 100 percent of the partnership interests. A statement next to signature of the initial limited partner declared that the limited partnership held one-tenth of one percent of the limited partnership interests. American Properties Corporation (APC) subsequently was substituted as a limited partner for Rockwood. Thereafter, taxpayers and APC signed the amended articles, under which APC withdrew as a limited partner. Section 1.5.1 A of the amended articles allocates one percent of the net operating profits and losses to the general partners and 99 percent of the profits and losses to the limited partners. Section 8.1 of the amended articles provides:

> "Prior to the admission of the Investor Limited Partners pursuant to Section 6.3, Operating Profits and Losses shall be allocated among the General Partners and the Original Limited Partner as they may agree."

Statements identical to those appearing next to the signatures of the general and limited partners in the articles appeared next to the signatures of the general and limited partners in the amended articles. "Schedule A," which was appended to the amended articles, contained a list of the names of 21 new limited partners.

Relying on the wording in Section 8.1 of the amended articles, taxpayers and APC agreed to allocate profits and losses for the 1985 tax year based on the statements of ownership that appeared next to the signature lines of the general and limited partners. In analyzing taxpayers' claim that Section 8.1 of the amended articles authorized them to allocate profits and losses as they and the limited partner "may agree" before admission of the investor limited partners, the Tax Court noted that the amended articles contained "no signatures for the 21 limited partners." The absence of the signatures of the new limited partners is not without legal significance.

The formation and amendment of a limited partnership is governed by statute. [Oregon Revised Statutes (ORS)] 69.180(1) describes the procedure required for forming a limited partnership that was in effect when taxpayers' limited partnership was formed and amended. It provides, in part, that when two or more persons desire to form a limited partnership they shall "[s]ign and verify a certificate" and shall "[f]ile one copy of such certificate in the office of the Corporation Commissioner." Taxpayers followed that procedure with respect to the articles, evidence of which was introduced to the Tax Court as an exhibit. ORS 69.410(1) describes the procedure required to amend a certificate of limited partnership to change a limited partnership's composition. That statute provides that the writing to amend a certificate of limited partnership shall:

> "Be signed and verified by all partners. An amendment substituting a limited partner or adding a limited or general partner shall be signed also by the partners to be substituted or added. When a limited partner is to be substituted, the amendment shall also be signed by the assigning limited partner."

The only evidence regarding the amended articles that taxpayers submitted to the Tax Court was a document signed by taxpayers and the president of APC. There is no evidence in this record that the amended articles were signed by the 21 new limited partners, as required by statute, or that the general partners exercised a power of attorney to sign on behalf of the investor limited partners. Thus, the amended articles were not properly executed. Consequently, taxpayers were not entitled to rely on Section 8.1 of the amended articles for the purposes of allocating profits and losses on their 1985 tax returns. The only document that conforms to the statutory requirements and that is binding is the articles. Section 1.5.1 A of the articles unambiguously allocates two percent of the losses to the general partners and 98 percent of the losses to the limited partners. The Tax Court did not err in holding that, with respect to their 1985 tax returns, taxpayers were not entitled to allocate 99.9 percent of their losses to the general partners and one-tenth of one percent of their losses to the initial limited partner.

The judgment of the Tax Court is affirmed.

CASE 38.4 LIMITED PARTNERS AND MANAGEMENT

BT-I v. EQUITABLE LIFE ASSURANCE SOCIETY OF THE UNITED STATES

California Court of Appeal,
Fourth District, 1999.
75 Cal.App.4th 1406,
89 Cal.Rptr.2d 811.

BEDSWORTH, J. [Judge]

This is an appeal by a limited partner that was squeezed out of the partnership when the general partner purchased and foreclosed a deed of trust on the partnership's sole asset, an office building.

* * * *

In 1985, BT-I (a California general partnership) entered into a general partnership with [The Equitable Life Assurance Society of the United States] named Brin-Mar I, to develop and operate a commercial office building and retail complex in Orange County [California]. Two phases were planned, first an office building and then a retail complex. Banque Paribas provided a $62.5 million loan secured by a trust deed on the project.

In 1991, BT-I and Equitable canceled their 1985 general partnership and entered into the present limited partnership, Brin-Mar I, L.P., with Equitable the general partner and BT-I the limited partner. Equitable had a 70 percent interest and BT-I had a 30 percent interest. Under an accompanying loan modification agreement, Banque Paribas agreed to the change, advanced additional funds secured by a second trust deed, and extended the maturity date of the first loan so that both were due on August 31, 1995. Equitable put up $6 million in additional capital and received in return sole title to the retail complex, along with extensive powers giving it the sole right to manage and control the partnership and its assets. * * *

Paragraph 5.1(c) of the limited partnership agreement gave Equitable broad powers to refinance and restructure the partnership debt, "provided, however, that in no event shall the General Partner amend, modify, cancel or rescind the terms of the Existing Paribas Loan * * * on or prior to August 31, 1995; and provided further, that in no event shall the General Partner be required to take any action (including, without limitation, contributing additional sums to the Partnership or otherwise expending any of its own funds) to prevent Banque Paribas or any other lender from exercising any remedies in connection with any loan made to the Partnership or otherwise related thereto."

As the due date of the Paribas loans approached, Equitable no longer wanted BT-I as a partner and maneuvered to oust it. Equitable learned the bank was interested in selling the loans at a steep discount, notified BT-I that the bank was soliciting bids, and suggested [that] an offer of $35 million would succeed. Unknown to BT-I or other bidders, the bank had already agreed to sell the loans to Equitable if it matched the high bid, and further agreed not to deal directly with BT-I. BT-I alleged Equitable's proffer of the opportunity was a charade, since neither the partnership nor BT-I had the necessary funds.

Equitable bought the loans on August 21, 1995 for $38.5 million. On September 1, 1995, the day after the loans were due, Equitable demanded full payment of approximately $65 million within 10 days. On the 11th day, no payment having been received, Equitable recorded notices of default.

In October 1995, Equitable offered to sell the loan to the partnership at its own cost. The offer was not accepted. BT-I asked Equitable to attempt to refinance the project, but the general partner refused. It made no attempt to sell the building, nor did it consider filing for bankruptcy protection. BT-I's own attempts to locate a new lender came to naught, because Equitable refused to provide partnership balance sheets and other financial information when requested, and refused to give BT-I access to the partnership books and records. A foreclosure sale was scheduled for March 1996. Three days before the sale, BT-I made a $39 million cash offer for the project but Equitable turned it down, both as lender and on behalf of the partnership. Equitable then acquired the building at the foreclosure sale.

[BT-I filed a suit in a California state court against Equitable, alleging in part breach of fiduciary duty. The court entered a judgment in Equitable's favor. BT-I appealed to a state intermediate appellate court.]

* * * *

I

BT-I contends the partnership agreement did not expressly authorize Equitable's purchase and forclosure of partnership debt, and we should not interpret it to allow such conduct because *the fiduciary duties of loyalty and good faith cannot be waived.* We agree. [Emphasis added.]

Partnership is a fiduciary relationship, and partners are held to the standards and duties of a trustee in their dealings with each other. *Partners are trustees for each other, and in all proceedings connected with the conduct of the partnership every partner is bound to act in the highest good faith to his copartner and may not obtain any advantage over him in the partnership affairs by the slightest misrepresentation, concealment, threat or adverse pressure of any kind.* Moreover, this duty extends to all aspects of the relationship and all transactions between the partners. Each partner occupies the position of a trustee to the other with regard to all the partnership transactions, including the transactions contemplated by the firm and constituting the object or purpose for which the partnership was formed. [Emphasis added.]

In general, under the California Revised Limited Partnership Act, partners may determine by agreement many aspects of their relationship. But there are limitations. A general partner of a limited partnership is subject to the same restrictions, and has the same liabilities to the partnership and other partners, as in a general partnership. One of these is the duty to account to the partnership for any benefit, and hold as trustee for it any profits, derived * * * without the consent of the other partners from any transaction connected with the * * * conduct * * * of the partnership * * * .

* * * [T]he acquisition of partnership debt by a general partner * * * is a breach of fiduciary duty. A general partner that acquires a partnership obligation cannot foreclose on partnership assets.

The question then becomes whether the fiduciary duty not to purchase partnership debt and foreclose out one's partner can be contracted away in the partnership agreement. We hold it cannot. * * *

* * * [A] limited partnership agreement cannot relieve the general partner of its fiduciary duties in matters fundamentally related to the partnership business. Exactly where the line resides between those matters upon which

partners may and may not reduce or eliminate their fiduciary duties is a question we need not decide, because Equitable's transgression is beyond all doubt on the wrong side of the line.

* * * *

We do not believe the partnership agreement can be read as permitting Equitable to purchase the loans for its own account and then foreclosure. Certainly, it does not expressly allow such conduct. Even if the language were broad enough to justify such an interpretation, we hold a partnership agreement cannot relieve a general partner of its fiduciary duties to a limited partner and the partnership where the purchase and foreclosure of partnership debt is involved.

Paragraph 5.1(c) provides Equitable did not have to contribute any more money to the partnership or otherwise take any action to prevent foreclosure by any lender. Fairly read, this absolves Equitable of the duty to act affirmatively to bail out the partnership from the consequences of default. But Equitable's conduct in buying and foreclosing the loans went far beyond whatever safe harbor might be found in the partnership agreement. It is one thing simply to do nothing and suffer the consequences equally with all other partners. It is another to step out of the role of partner and into that of an aggressive (and apparently greedy) lender in the marketplace. Equitable admits no less with the argument that "[a] lender other than Equitable certainly would not have offered BT-I these accommodations [offering the loan to BT-I at its cost] and would have proceeded straight to foreclosure." Equitable was BT-I's partner, not its lender, and it lost sight of this most basic distinction in its haste to pounce upon the loan.

Nor can we agree with Equitable that the Revised Uniform Limited Partnership Act or other provisions in the partnership agreement justify what it did. It is true the act permits the parties to vary its effect * * *. But the fact that the act allows the parties to structure many aspects of their relationship is not a license to freely engage in self-dealing—it remains our responsibility to delimit the outer boundaries of permissible conduct by a fiduciary. In view of the rule against waiving fundamental fiduciary duties, we cannot stretch these general provisions to include giving Equitable a free hand to act for its own self-interest. Equitable was still a fiduciary, and its conduct must be measured by fiduciary standards.

* * * *

The judgment is reversed.

CASE PROBLEMS

38–1. Fidelity Lease Limited, a limited partnership, had over twenty limited partners and one general partner. The general partner was a corporation, Interlease Corporation, and was managed by Sanders, Kahn, and Crombie, all three of whom happened to be limited partners of Fidelity Lease Limited. Assuming that in Texas, where this partnership was established, corporations are allowed to be partners in a limited partnership, what will the liability of Sanders, Kahn, and Crombie be in a suit against Fidelity Lease Limited? Will their liability be limited? [*Delaney v. Fidelity Lease Limited,* 517 S.W.2d 420 (Tex.Civ.App.1974)]

38–2. Columbia-Heather was a limited partnership engaged in the construction of an apartment complex in Toledo, Ohio. Partnership Equities, Inc., the plaintiff, was one of the general partners, and Amin Khoury and James Marten, the defendants, were two of the limited partners. In becoming limited partners, the defendants had agreed to make contributions over a four-year period. The defendants refused to make contributions for the last two years. They claimed that the general partners had breached the partnership agreement and therefore the limited partners were not obligated to make continued contributions to the limited partnership. The general partners sued for the unpaid contributions under Section 17 of the Uniform Limited Partnership Act (Section 502 of the Revised Uniform Limited Partnership Act). Discuss who will prevail. [*Partnership Equities, Inc. v. Marten,* 15 Mass.App. 42, 443 N.E.2d 134 (1982)]

38–3. The Sports Factory, Inc., executed a lease with Ridley Park Associates, a limited partnership, to operate a health and racquetball club. William Chanoff was the general partner of Ridley Park Associates. Over several months, Ridley Park failed to meet the original agreement with Sports Factory, Inc., in several respects, including altering architectural plans for the racquetball courts and failing to acquire the zoning changes needed for operation of a health spa. If Sports Factory brought a cause of action for breach of its agreement with Ridley Park, who would be found liable? [*Sports Factory, Inc. v. Chanoff,* 586 F.Supp. 342 (E.D.Pa. 1984)]

38–4. In a limited partnership having one general partner, the general partner loaned over $1 million to the partnership and executed notes payable to herself. The limited partner knew that these notes were carried as outstanding debts on the partnership books for seven years. When the general partner died, the limited partner maintained that the partnership agreement did not authorize the general partner to borrow money and that the amount constituted a contribution to capital rather than loans. How did the court treat the money? [*Park Cities Corp. v. Byrd,* 522 S.W.2d 572 (Tex.Civ.App. 1975)]

38–5. Caton Avenue Associates was a limited partnership that owned rental property. Caton paid Theodore Dalmazio, one of the general partners, a management fee to manage the property. Dalmazio paid his employees with Caton's money. Dalmazio billed Caton for services that are normally performed by property management firms at no cost and also billed Caton at an hourly rate for work that is normally billed per rental unit. Alfred Friedman and the other limited partners filed a suit on Caton's behalf in a New York state court against Dalmazio and the other general partner to recover damages. On what basis might the court rule in favor of the limited partners? Explain. [*Friedman v. Dalmazio,* 644 N.Y.S.2d 548 (App.Div. 1996)]

38–6. Elfon Realty Co. was a limited partnership in which Harry Macklowe was the sole general partner and 42nd Street Development Corp. was the sole limited partner. The limited partner assigned its right to receive partnership distributions to a third party, in violation of the express conditions of the partnership agreement. In the litigation that followed, a central issue was whether 42nd Street Development Corp. should be entitled to an accounting in view of the fact that it had breached the partnership agreement. Discuss fully whether 42nd Street's assignment was sufficient misconduct to bar it from an accounting of partnership assets and profits. [*Macklowe v. 42nd Street Development Corp.,* 157 A.D.2d 566, 550 N.Y.S.2d 309 (1990)]

38–7. Mige Associates II was a limited partnership. Mige owned an apartment building that could have been converted into a cooperative (a housing complex jointly owned by the residents) at a substantial profit. The conversion required, under the voting provisions of the partnership agreement, the consent of Jon Meadow, one of the general partners. Before consenting, Meadow demanded that he receive more money than the other general partners. When his demand was rejected, he blocked the conversion. Ronald Drucker and Ronald Schaffer, two of the limited partners, filed a suit in a New York state court against Meadow, contending that Meadow had breached a fiduciary duty to the other partners. The court ruled in Meadow's favor. Drucker and Schaffer appealed. What will the appellate court decide? [*Drucker v. Mige Associates II,* 639 N.Y.S.2d 365 (1996)]

38–8. Robert Pitman was one of two limited partners in Ramsey Homebuilders, a limited partnership that engaged in the business of residential construction. Michael Ramsey was the sole general partner in the partnership. Because Ramsey had a poor credit history, he was unable to borrow the money or obtain the credit needed to sustain the partnership's business. Pitman, who had a personal account with Flanagan Lumber Co., contacted Flanagan's credit manager and secured an account in the partnership's name. After the partnership failed to pay the account, Flanagan sued Pitman, alleging that although Pitman was a limited partner in Ramsey Homebuilders, he was responsible for the partnership's debt under RULPA 303. Pitman argued that, if anything, he was operating within the waters of the "safe harbor" provided by RULPA 303(b)(3), which states that a limited partner does not participate in the control of the partnership solely by acting as a surety or guarantor for any liabilities incurred by the partnership. Can Pitman be held liable for the partnership's debt to Flanagan? [*Pitman v. Flanagan Lumber Co.,* 567 So.2d 1335 (Ala. 1990)]

38–9. Combat Associates was formed as a limited partnership to promote an exhibition boxing match between Lyle Alzado (a professional football player) and Muhammad Ali. Alzado and others had formed Combat Promotions; this organization was to be the general partner and Blinder, Robinson & Co. (Blinder), the limited partner in Combat Associates. The general partner's contribution consisted of assigning all contracts pertaining to the match, and the limited partner's contribution was a $250,000 letter of credit to ensure Ali's compensation. Alzado personally guaranteed to repay Blinder for any amount of loss if the proceeds of the match were less than $250,000. In preparation for the match, at Alzado's request, Blinder's president participated in interviews and a promotional rally, and the company sponsored parties and allowed its local office to be used as a ticket sales outlet. The proceeds of the match were insufficient, and Blinder sued Alzado on his guaranty. Alzado counterclaimed by asserting that Blinder had taken an active role in the control and management of Combat Associates and should be held liable as a general partner. How did the court rule on Alzado's counterclaim? Discuss. [*Blinder, Robinson & Co. v. Alzado,* 713 P.2d 1314 (Colo.App. 1985)]

38–10. Val Somers, Pat McGowan, and Brent Roberson were general partners in Vermont Place, a limited partnership formed to construct duplexes on a tract of land in Fort Smith, Arkansas. In 1984, the partnership mortgaged the property so that it could build there. McGowan owned a separate company, Advance Development Corp., which was hired by the partnership to develop the project. On September 3, 1984, Somers and Roberson discovered that McGowan had not been paying the suppliers to the project, including National Lumber Co., and had not been making the mortgage payments. The suppliers and the bank sued the partnership and the general partners individually. Discuss whether Somers and Roberson could be held individually liable for the debts incurred by McGowan. [*National Lumber Co. v. Advance Development Corp.,* 293 Ark. 1, 732 S.W.2d 840 (1987)]

38–11. Page, Scrantom, Sprouse, Tucker & Ford, a Georgia law firm, entered into a lease of office equipment in Georgia. The lessor assigned the lease to Danka Funding Co. (DFC), a New York limited liability company (LLC) with its principal place of business in New Jersey. DFC was registered as a foreign LLC in New Jersey for almost two years before the registration lapsed or was withdrawn. Under the applicable statute, a foreign LLC "may not maintain any action . . . in this State until it has registered." When Page defaulted on the lease, DFC filed a complaint in a New Jersey state court against Page for more than $100,000. In its response, Page pointed out that DFC was not registered as a foreign LLC. DFC reregistered. Asserting that DFC had not been registered when it filed its suit, Page asked a federal district court to dismiss it. Should the court grant this request? Why, or why not? [*Danka Funding, L.L.C. v. Page, Scrantom, Sprouse, Tucker & Ford, P.C.*, 21 F.Supp.2d 465 (D.N.J. 1998)]

38–12. Mudge Rose Guthrie Alexander & Ferdon, a law firm, was organized as a general partnership but converted into a limited liability partnership (LLP). Mudge's principal place of business was New York, where it was organized, but some of its members were citizens of Maryland. The firm filed a suit in a federal district court to recover unpaid legal fees from Robert Pickett and other citizens of Maryland. The defendants filed a motion to dismiss on the ground that there was not complete diversity of citizenship, because some of the LLC members were Maryland citizens also. Mudge argued that an LLP was like a corporation, and therefore the citizenship of the firm's members was irrelevant. How should the court rule? Explain. [*Mudge Rose Guthrie Alexander & Ferdon v. Pickett,* 11 F.Supp.2d 449 (S.D.N.Y. 1998)]

38–13. Gloria Duchin, a Rhode Island resident, was the sole shareholder and chief executive officer of Gloria Duchin, Inc. (Duchin, Inc.), which manufactured metallic Christmas ornaments and other novelty items. The firm was incorporated in Rhode Island. Duchin Realty, Inc., also incorporated in Rhode Island, leased real estate to Duchin, Inc. The Duchin entities hired Gottesman Co. to sell Duchin, Inc., and to sign with the buyer a consulting agreement for Gloria Duchin and a lease for Duchin Realty's property. Gottesman negotiated a sale, a consulting agreement, and a lease with Somerset Capital Corp. James Mitchell, a resident of Massachusetts, was the chairman and president of Somerset, and Mary Mitchell, also a resident of Massachusetts, was the senior vice president. The parties agreed that to buy Duchin, Inc., Somerset would create a new limited liability company, JMTR Enterprises, LLC, in Rhode Island, with the Mitchells as its members. When the deal fell apart, JMTR filed a suit in a Massachusetts state court against the Duchin entities, alleging, among other things, breach of contract. When the defendants tried to remove the case to a federal district court, JMTR argued that the court did not have jurisdiction because there was no diversity of citizenship between the parties: all of the plaintiffs and defendants were citizens of Rhode Island. Is JMTR correct? Why, or why not? [*JMTR Enterprises, LLC v. Duchin,* 42 F.Supp.2d 87 (D.Mass. 1999)]

38–14. Walter Matjasich and Cary Hanson organized Capital Care, LLC, in Utah. Capital Care operated, and Matjasich and Hanson managed, Heartland Care Center in Topeka, Kansas. LTC Properties, Inc., held a mortgage on the Heartland facilities. When Heartland failed as a business, its residents were transferred to other facilities. Heartland employees who provided care to the residents for five days during the transfers were not paid wages. The employees filed claims with the Kansas Department of Human Resources for the unpaid wages. Kansas state law provides that a *corporate* officer or manager may be liable for a firm's unpaid wages, but protects LLC members from personal liability generally and states that an LLC cannot be construed as a corporation. Under Utah state law, the members of an LLC can be personally liable for wages due the LLC's employees. Should Matjasich and Hanson be held personally liable for the unpaid wages? Explain. [*Matjasich v. State Department of Human Resources,* 21 P.3d 985 (Kan. 2001)]

38–15. A QUESTION OF ETHICS

Mt. Hood Meadows Oregon, Ltd., was a limited partnership established to carry on the business of constructing and operating a winter sports development in the Hood River area of Oregon. Elizabeth Brooke and two of the other limited partners were dissatisfied because, for all the years in which profits were earned after 1974, the general partner distributed only 50 percent of the limited partners' taxable profits. The remaining profits were retained and reinvested in the business. Each of the limited partners was taxed on his or her distributable share of the profits, however, regardless of whether the cash was actually distributed. Brooke and the others brought an action to compel the general partner to distribute all of the limited partnership's profits. The court held that, in the absence of a limited partnership agreement concerning the distribution of profits, the decision to reinvest profits was strictly a managerial one. Unless the limited partners could prove that the general partner's conduct was inappropriate or violated a fiduciary duty, the decision of the general partner was binding on the limited partners. [*Brooke v. Mt. Hood Meadows Oregon, Ltd.*, 81 Or.App. 387, 725 P.2d 925 (1986)]

1. The major attraction of limited partnerships is that the investors, as limited partners, are not liable for partnership obligations beyond the amount that they have invested. The "price" paid for this limited liability, however, is that limited partners have no say in management—as is well illustrated by the case described here. What ethical considerations are expressed in the rule that limited partners cannot participate in management? Do you think such a rule is fair?
2. This case also illustrates how relatively helpless the limited partners are when faced with a general partner whose actions do not correspond to the limited partners' wishes. Apart from selling their partnership shares to others (and at times, buyers are hard to find) or participating in management (and losing their limited liability as a result), limited partners have little recourse against

the decisions of general partners so long as the general partners have not violated their fiduciary duties or the partnership agreement. Do you think that, because limited partners cannot participate in management, general partners have ethical duties to limited partners that go beyond those prescribed by law? If not, why not? If so, how would you describe or define such duties?

E-Links

For updated links to resources available on the Web, as well as a variety of other materials, visit this text's Web site at

http://wbl-cs.westbuslaw.com

You can find information on how to form an LLC, including the fees charged in each state for filing LLC articles of organization, at the Web site of BIZCORP International, Inc. Go to

http://www.bizcorp.com

For an example of a state law (that of Florida) governing LLPs, go to the Internet Legal Resource Guide's Web page at

http://www.ilrg.com/whatsnews/statute.html

and scroll down the page to "Registered Limited Liability Partnerships."

The law firm of Wordes, Wilshin, Goren & Conner offers a comparison of the advantages and disadvantages of major business forms with respect to various factors, including ease of formation, management, and ability to raise capital. The firm's Web site can be accessed at

http://www.wwgc.com/wwgc-be1.htm

Legal Research Exercises on the Web

Go to http://wbl-cs.westbuslaw.com, the Web site that accompanies this text. Select "Interactive Study Center," and then click on "Chapter 38." There you will find the following Internet research exercise that you can perform to learn more about limited liability companies:

Activity 38–1: Limited Liability Companies

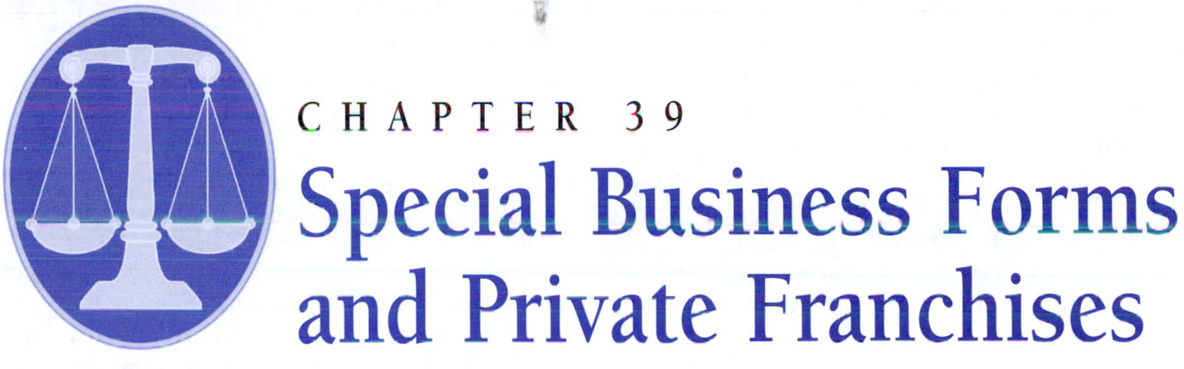

CHAPTER 39
Special Business Forms and Private Franchises

WE HAVE EXAMINED IN THE preceding chapters some of the most significant business forms—including sole proprietorships, partnerships, corporations, and limited liability companies and partnerships. In this chapter, after first describing a number of forms that can be used for special types of business ventures, we look in detail at private franchises. Although the franchise is not really a business organizational form, the franchising arrangement is widely used today by those seeking to make profits.

SECTION 1
Special Business Forms

Besides the business forms already discussed, several other forms can be used to organize a business. For the most part, these other business forms are hybrid organizations—that is, they have characteristics similar to those of partnerships or corporations, or combine features of both.

JOINT VENTURE

A **joint venture**, which is sometimes referred to as a *joint adventure,* is a relationship in which two or more persons or business entities combine their efforts or their property for a single transaction or project or a related series of transactions or projects. Unless otherwise agreed, joint venturers share profits and losses equally. For example, when several contractors combine their resources to build and sell houses in a single development, their relationship is a joint venture.

Joint ventures range in size from very small activities to huge, multimillion-dollar joint actions undertaken by some of the world's largest corporations. Large organizations often investigate new markets or new ideas by forming joint ventures with other enterprises. For instance, General Motors Corporation and Volvo Truck Corporation were involved in a joint venture—Volvo GM—to manufacture heavy-duty trucks and market them in the United States.

Characteristics of Joint Ventures. A joint venture resembles a partnership and is taxed like a partnership. The essential difference is that a joint venture typically involves the pursuit of a single project or series of transactions, and a partnership usually concerns an ongoing business. Of course, a partnership may be created to conduct a single transaction. For this reason, most courts apply the same principles to joint ventures as they apply to partnerships. Exceptions include the following:

1. The members of a joint venture have less implied and apparent authority than the partners in a partnership (under partnership law, each partner is an agent of the other partners), because the activities of a joint venture are more limited than the business of a partnership.
2. Although the death of a partner terminates a partnership, the death of a joint venturer ordinarily does not terminate a joint venture.

Duration. The members of a joint venture can specify its duration. If the members do not stipulate a duration, a joint venture normally terminates when the project or the transaction for which it was formed has been completed. Thus, the joint venture to build and sell houses in a single development would terminate once all the houses had been built and sold. If the members of a joint venture do not specify a particular duration and the joint venture does not clearly relate to the achievement of a certain goal, the joint venture is terminable at the will of any of its members.

Duties, Rights, and Liabilities among Joint Venturers. The duties that joint venturers owe to each other are the same as the duties that partners owe to each other (discussed in Chapter 33). Thus, joint venturers owe each other fiduciary duties, including a duty of loyalty. If one of the venturers secretly buys land that was to be acquired by the joint venture, the other joint venturers may be awarded damages for the breach of loyalty.

When the members of a joint venture are separately engaged in business operations that are similar to the activity of the joint venture, conflicts may develop in two areas of the law. First, when the members of a joint venture are competitors, each member may face a choice between disclosing trade secrets to a competitor and breaching the duty to disclose. Second, in those circumstances, there is also a potential for a violation of the antitrust laws (see Chapter 45). For both reasons, joint venturers should specify exactly the information that each will be required to disclose.

The joint venturers have equal rights to manage the activities of the enterprise. Control of the operation may be given to one of the members, however, without affecting the status of the relationship. Each joint venturer is liable to third parties for the actions of the other members of the joint venture in pursuit of the enterprise's goal.

Westlaw. See Case 39.1 at the end of this chapter. To view the full, unedited case from Westlaw,® go to this text's Web site at **http://wbl-cs.westbuslaw.com**.

Syndicate

A group of individuals getting together to finance a particular project, such as the building of a shopping center or the purchase of a professional basketball franchise, is called a **syndicate**, or an *investment group*. The form of such groups varies considerably. A syndicate may exist as a corporation or as a general or limited partnership. In some cases, the members merely own property jointly and have no legally recognized business arrangement.

Joint Stock Company

A **joint stock company** is a true hybrid of a partnership and a corporation. It has many characteristics of a corporation in that (1) its ownership is represented by transferable shares of stock, (2) it is usually managed by directors and officers of the company or association, and (3) it can have a perpetual existence. Most of its other features, however, are more characteristic of a partnership, and it is usually treated like a partnership. As with a partnership, it is formed by agreement (not statute), property is usually held in the names of the members, shareholders have personal liability, and generally the company is not treated as a legal entity for purposes of a lawsuit. In a joint stock company, however, shareholders are not considered to be agents of each other, as would be the case if the company were a true partnership (see Chapter 33).

Business Trust

A **business trust** is created by a written trust agreement that sets forth the interests of the beneficiaries and the obligations and powers of the trustees. With a business trust, legal ownership and management of the property of the business stay with one or more of the trustees, and the profits are distributed to the beneficiaries.

The business trust was started in Massachusetts in an attempt to obtain the limited liability advantage of corporate status while avoiding certain restrictions on a corporation's ownership and development of real property. The business trust resembles a corporation in many respects. For example, beneficiaries of the trust are not personally responsible for the trust's debts or obligations. In fact, in a number of states, business trusts must pay corporate taxes.

Cooperative

A **cooperative** is an association, which may or may not be incorporated, that is organized to provide an economic service to its members (or shareholders). Most cooperatives are incorporated under either state statutes for cooperatives, general business incorporation statutes, or limited liability company (LLC) statutes. Generally, an incorporated cooperative will distribute dividends, or profits, to its owners on the basis of their transactions with the cooperative rather than on the basis of the amount of capital they contributed. Members of incorporated cooperatives have limited liability, as do shareholders of corporations or members of LLCs. Cooperatives that are unincorporated are often treated like partnerships. The members have joint liability for the cooperative's acts.

This form of business is generally adopted by groups of individuals who wish to pool their resources to gain some advantage in the marketplace. Consumer purchasing co-ops are formed to obtain lower prices through quantity discounts. Seller marketing co-ops are formed to control the market and thereby obtain higher sales prices from consumers. Co-ops range in size from small, local, consumer cooperatives to national businesses such as Ace Hardware and Land 'O Lakes, the well-known producer of dairy products.

SECTION 2

Private Franchises

A **franchise** is defined as any arrangement in which the owner of a trademark, a trade name, or a copyright licenses others to use the trademark, trade name, or copyright in the selling of goods or services. A **franchisee** (a purchaser of a franchise) is generally legally independent of the **franchisor** (the seller of the franchise). At the same time, the franchise is economically dependent on the franchisor's integrated business system. In other words, a franchisee can operate as an independent businessperson but still obtain the advantages of a regional or national organization. Well-known franchises include McDonald's, KFC, and Burger King.

TYPES OF FRANCHISES

Because the franchising industry is so extensive and so many different types of businesses sell franchises, it is difficult to summarize the many types of franchises that now exist. Generally, though, franchises fall into one of the following three classifications: distributorships, chain-style business operations, and manufacturing or processing-plant arrangements.

Distributorship. A *distributorship* arises when a manufacturing concern (franchisor) licenses a dealer (franchisee) to sell its product. Often, a distributorship covers an exclusive territory. An example is an automobile dealership.

Chain-Style Business Operation. A *chain-style business operation* exists when a franchise operates under a franchisor's trade name and is identified as a member of a select group of dealers that engage in the franchisor's business. The franchisee is generally required to follow standardized or prescribed methods of operation. Often, the franchisor demands that the franchisee maintain certain standards of operation. In addition, sometimes the franchisee is obligated to deal exclusively with the franchisor to obtain materials and supplies. Examples of this type of franchise are McDonald's and most other fast-food chains.

Manufacturing or Processing-Plant Arrangement. A *manufacturing* or *processing-plant arrangement* exists when the franchisor transmits to the franchisee the essential ingredients or formula to make a particular product. The franchisee then markets it either at wholesale or at retail in accordance with the franchisor's standards. Examples of this type of franchise are Coca-Cola and other soft-drink bottling companies.

LAWS GOVERNING FRANCHISING

Because a franchise relationship is primarily a contractual relationship, it is governed by contract law. If the franchise exists primarily for the sale of products manufactured by the franchisor, the law governing sales contracts as expressed in Article 2 of the Uniform Commercial Code applies (see Chapters 18 through 23). Additionally, the federal government and most states have enacted laws governing certain aspects of franchising. Generally, these laws are designed to protect prospective franchisees from dishonest franchisors and to prohibit franchisors from terminating franchises without good cause.

Federal Protection for Franchisees. Automobile dealership franchisees are protected from automobile manufacturers' bad faith termination of their franchises by the Automobile Dealers' Franchise Act[1]—also known as the Automobile Dealers' Day in Court Act—of 1965. If a manufacturer-franchisor terminates a franchise because of a dealer-franchisee's failure to comply with unreasonable demands (for example, failure to attain an unrealistically high sales quota), the manufacturer may be liable for damages.

1. 15 U.S.C. Sections 1221 *et seq.*

Another federal statute is the Petroleum Marketing Practices Act (PMPA)[2] of 1979, which prescribes the grounds and conditions under which a franchisor may terminate or decline to renew a gasoline station franchise. Federal antitrust laws (discussed in Chapter 45), which prohibit certain types of anticompetitive agreements, may also apply in certain circumstances.

Additionally, the Federal Trade Commission (FTC) has issued regulations that require franchisors to disclose material facts necessary to a prospective franchisee's making an informed decision concerning the purchase of a franchise.

State Protection for Franchisees. State legislation tends to be similar to federal statutes and the FTC regulations. For example, to protect franchisees, a state law might require the disclosure of information that is material to making an informed decision regarding the purchase of a franchise. This could include such information as the actual costs of operation, recurring expenses, and profits earned, along with facts substantiating these figures. State deceptive trade practices acts may also prohibit certain types of actions on the part of franchisors.

In response to the need for a uniform franchise law, the National Conference of Commissioners on Uniform State Laws drafted a model law that standardizes the various state franchise regulations. Because the uniform law represents a compromise of so many diverse interests, it has met with little success in being adopted as law by the various states.

The Franchise Contract

The franchise relationship is defined by a contract between the franchisor and the franchisee. The franchise contract specifies the terms and conditions of the franchise and spells out the rights and duties of the franchisor and the franchisee. If either party fails to perform its contractual duties, that party may be subject to a lawsuit for breach of contract. Furthermore, if a franchisee is induced to enter into a franchise contract by the franchisor's fraudulent misrepresentation, the franchisor may be liable for damages. Generally, the statutory and case law governing franchising tend to emphasize the importance of good faith and fair dealing in franchise relationships.

2. 15 U.S.C. Sections 2801 *et seq.*

Because each type of franchise relationship has its own characteristics, it is difficult to describe the broad range of details a franchising contract may include. In the remaining pages of this chapter, we look at some of the major issues that typically are addressed in a franchise contract.

Payment for the Franchise. The franchisee ordinarily pays an initial fee or lump-sum price for the franchise license (the privilege of being granted a franchise). This fee is separate from the various products that the franchisee purchases from or through the franchisor. In some industries, the franchisor relies heavily on the initial sale of the franchise for realizing a profit. In other industries, the continued dealing between the parties brings profit to both. In most situations, the franchisor will receive a stated percentage of the annual sales or annual volume of business done by the franchisee. The franchise agreement may also require the franchisee to pay a percentage of the franchisor's advertising costs and certain administrative expenses.

Business Premises. The franchise agreement may specify whether the premises for the business must be leased or purchased outright. In some cases, construction of a building is necessary to meet the terms of the agreement. Certainly, the agreement will specify whether the franchisor supplies equipment and furnishings for the premises or whether this is the responsibility of the franchisee.

Location of the Franchise. Typically, the franchisor will determine the territory to be served. Some franchise contracts will give the franchisee exclusive rights, or "territorial rights," to a certain geographic area. Other franchise contracts, while they define the territory allotted to a particular franchise, either specifically state that the franchise is nonexclusive or are silent on the issue of territorial rights.

Many franchise lawsuits involve disputes over territorial rights, and this is one area of franchising in which the implied covenant of good faith and fair dealing often comes into play. For example, suppose that a franchisee is not given exclusive territorial rights in the franchise contract, or the contract is silent on the issue. If the franchisor allows a competing franchise to be established nearby, the franchisee may suffer a significant loss in profits. In this situation, a court may hold that the franchisor's actions breached an implied covenant of good faith and fair dealing.

Business Organization. The business organization of the franchisee is of great concern to the franchisor. Depending on the terms of the franchise agreement, the franchisor may specify particular requirements for the form and capital structure of the business. The franchise agreement may also provide that standards of operation—relating to such aspects of the business as sales quotas, quality, and record keeping—be met by the franchisee. Furthermore, a franchisor may wish to retain stringent control over the training of personnel involved in the operation and over administrative aspects of the business.

Quality Control. Although the day-to-day operation of the franchise business is normally left up to the franchisee, the franchise agreement may provide for the amount of supervision and control agreed on by the parties. When the franchise is a service operation, such as a motel, the contract often provides that the franchisor will establish certain standards for the facility in order to protect the franchise's name and reputation. Typically, the contract will state that the franchisor is permitted to make periodic inspections to ensure that the standards are being maintained.

As a general rule, the validity of a provision permitting the franchisor to establish and enforce certain quality standards is unquestioned. Because the franchisor has a legitimate interest in maintaining the quality of the product or service to protect its name and reputation, it can exercise greater control in this area than would otherwise be tolerated. Increasingly, however, franchisors are finding that if they exercise too much control over the operations of their franchisees, they may incur liability under agency theory for the acts of their franchisees' employees. (A court may also find that a franchisee is, in fact, an employee, if the franchisor exercises a significant degree of control over the franchisee's work schedule and activities.)[3]

Westlaw. See Case 39.2 at the end of this chapter. To view the full, unedited case from Westlaw,® go to this text's Web site at **http://wbl-cs.westbuslaw.com**.

Pricing Arrangements. Franchises provide the franchisor with an outlet for the firm's goods and services. Depending on the nature of the business, the franchisor may require the franchisee to purchase certain supplies from the franchisor at an established price.[4] A franchisor cannot, however, set the prices at which the franchisee will resell the goods, because this may be a violation of state or federal antitrust laws, or both. A franchisor can suggest retail prices but cannot mandate them.

Termination of the Franchise. The duration of the franchise is a matter to be determined between the parties. Generally, a franchise relationship starts with a short trial period, such as a year, so that the franchisee and the franchisor can determine whether they want to stay in business with one another. Usually, the franchise agreement specifies that termination must be "for cause," such as death or disability of the franchisee, insolvency of the franchisee, breach of the franchise agreement, or failure to meet specified sales quotas. Most franchise contracts provide that notice of termination must be given. If no set time for termination is specified, then a reasonable time, with notice, is implied. A franchisee must be given reasonable time to wind up the business—that is, to do the accounting and return the copyright or trademark or any other property of the franchisor.

Because a franchisor's termination of a franchise often has adverse consequences for the franchisee, much franchise litigation involves claims of wrongful termination. Generally, the termination provisions of contracts are more favorable to the franchisor than the franchisee. This means that the franchisee, who normally invests a substantial amount of time and money in the franchise operation to make it successful, may receive little or nothing for the business on termination. The franchisor owns the trademark and hence the business.

It is in this area that statutory and case law become important. The federal and state laws discussed earlier attempt, among other things, to protect franchisees from the arbitrary or unfair termination of their franchises by the franchisors. Generally, both statutory and case law emphasize the importance of good faith and fair dealing in terminating a franchise relationship.

3. See, for example, *West Sanitation Services, Inc. v. Francis*, 1998 WL 11023 (N.Y.Sup.Ct.App.Div. 1998).

4. Although a franchisor can require franchisees to purchase supplies from it, requiring a franchisee to purchase exclusively from the franchisor may violate federal antitrust laws (see Chapter 45). For two landmark cases in these areas, see *United States v. Arnold, Schwinn & Co.*, 388 U.S. 365, 87 S.Ct. 1956, 18 L.Ed.2d 1249 (1967), and *Fortner Enterprises, Inc. v. U.S. Steel Corp.*, 394 U.S. 495, 89 S.Ct. 1252, 22 L.Ed.2d 495 (1969).

In determining whether a franchisor has acted in good faith when terminating a franchise agreement, the courts generally try to balance the rights of both parties. If a court perceives that a franchisor has arbitrarily or unfairly terminated a franchise, the franchisee will be provided with a remedy for wrongful termination. If a franchisor's decision to terminate a franchise was made in the normal course of the franchisor's business operations, however, and reasonable notice of termination was given to the franchisee, normally a court would not consider the termination wrongful.

See Case 39.3 at the end of this chapter. To view the full, unedited case from Westlaw,® go to this text's Web site at **http://wbl-cs.westbuslaw.com**.

TERMS AND CONCEPTS TO REVIEW

business trust 794	franchisee 795	joint venture 793
cooperative 794	franchisor 795	syndicate 794
franchise 795	joint stock company 794	

CHAPTER SUMMARY

Special Business Forms

1. *Joint venture*—An organization created by two or more persons in contemplation of a limited activity or a single transaction; otherwise, similar to a partnership.
2. *Syndicate*—An investment group that undertakes to finance a particular project; may exist as a corporation or as a general or limited partnership.
3. *Joint stock company*—A business form similar to a corporation in some respects (transferable shares of stock, management by directors and officers, perpetual existence) but otherwise resembling a partnership.
4. *Business trust*—Created by a written trust agreement that sets forth the interests of the beneficiaries and obligations and powers of the trustee(s). Similar to a corporation in many respects. Beneficiaries are not personally liable for the debts or obligations of the business trust.
5. *Cooperative*—An association organized to provide an economic service to its members. May be incorporated or unincorporated.

Private Franchises

1. *Types of franchises*—
   a. Distributorship (for example, automobile dealerships).
   b. Chain-style operation (for example, fast-food chains).
   c. Manufacturing/processing-plant arrangement (for example, soft-drink bottling companies, such as Coca-Cola).
2. *Laws governing franchising*—
   a. Franchises are governed by contract law.
   b. Franchises are also governed by federal and state statutory and regulatory laws, as well as agency law.
3. *The franchise contract*—
   a. Ordinarily requires the franchisee (purchaser) to pay a price for the franchise license.
   b. Specifies the territory to be served by the franchisee's firm.
   c. May require the franchisee to purchase certain supplies from the franchisor at an established price.
   d. May require the franchisee to abide by certain standards of quality relating to the product or service offered but cannot set retail resale prices.
   e. Usually provides for the date and/or conditions of termination of the franchise arrangement. Both federal and state statutes attempt to protect certain franchisees from franchisors who unfairly or arbitrarily terminate franchises.

CASES FOR ANALYSIS

Westlaw. You can access the full text of each case presented below by going to the Westlaw cases on this text's Web site at http://wbl-cs.westbuslaw.com. Each Westlaw case includes the names of all plaintiffs and defendants, the dates on which the case was argued and decided, a brief summary of the issues and decisions in the case, headnotes classifying specific issues in the case according to the West Key Number System, and the court's opinion. Concurring and dissenting opinions, if any, are included as well.

CASE 39.1 JOINT VENTURE

ULTRALITE CONTAINER CORP. V. AMERICAN PRESIDENT LINES, LTD.

United States Court of Appeals,
Seventh Circuit, 1999.
170 F.3d 784.

EASTERBROOK, Circuit Judge.

American President Lines (APL) and Stoughton Composites formed a joint venture, Ultralite Container, to manufacture shipping containers. The containers were to be made of composites (combinations of resin and fiberglass), with thin walls, meeting International Standards Organization requirements for intermodal shipping. ("Intermodal" containers can be hauled by ship, rail, or truck, and commonly use a combination of these to reach their destination.) A composite intermodal shipping container would be lighter than the standard ISO container—especially if built with very thin walls—and the parties anticipated that it would require less maintenance. APL contributed to the joint venture its knowledge of shipping requirements, plus about $3.8 million; Stoughton contributed its expertise in the design and manufacture of composite containers, plus its manufacturing facilities. Stoughton was to design and manufacture the containers. APL undertook to purchase * * * 2,000 refrigerated containers * * * . APL also negotiated a side agreement with Transamerica Leasing to take 1,000 of these containers.

* * * When Ultralite finished its first refrigerated containers in 1995, APL was not happy. It asserted that the containers were prone to "delamination" (that is, separation of the foam insulation from the wall). By the time APL registered this protest, Ultralite had made 127 refrigerated containers. APL and Stoughton renegotiated their agreement to provide that APL would pay $1,076,766.40 for 62 of these containers and Transamerica would take the rest * * * . Ultralite delivered 62 containers to APL, which * * * sent them back as defective and refused to pay. [Stoughton and Ultralite filed a suit in a federal district court against APL, alleging breach of contract. APL counterclaimed, asking the court to order Stoughton not to use what APL argued was confidential information—the know-how to produce thin-walled shipping containers. The jury] concluded that the containers were not defective and ordered APL to pay the whole purchase price. Acting on APL's counterclaim, the district judge enjoined Stoughton from making for the trucking industry any container with a wall less than 0.09 inches thick. The judge thought that the know-how to produce thin walls came in part from work Stoughton performed on the Ultralite project. Stoughton represents (without contradiction from APL) that this injunction has essentially put it out of business, because it needs to make thin-walled trailers in order to compete. Both sides have appealed.

* * * *

Although the parties have locked horns on many additional issues, the cornerstone to all of them is two confidentiality agreements that the parties signed. * * *

The first confidentiality agreement, signed in May 1993, committed both APL and Stoughton "to keep in confidence, *and not use for its own commercial benefit* and prevent the disclosure * * * [of] all Proprietary Information designated by the disclosing party" [emphasis added]. This agreement goes on to say that information is restricted only if so "designated by the disclosing party in writing or by an appropriate stamp or legend to be Proprietary Information which is received by the other pursuant to this Agreement." Information Stoughton used to make its over-the-road trailers was developed by Stoughton itself; so Stoughton was the "disclosing" rather than the "receiving" party for this information, and it did not tell itself to keep the knowledge confidential from itself. So far, then, no contractual problems. The May 1993 agreement means that APL can't use information Stoughton discloses to it, and Stoughton can't use information APL discloses to it, not that Stoughton can't use internally-developed information in its own business.

According to APL, everything changed in 1995, when the parties signed a second agreement containing confidentiality provisions. This provides in part that information

> generated or otherwise produced in connection with the design, research, development and testing of the Prototype Refrigerated Containers shall (i) be considered Proprietary Information *disclosed by each of SCI [Stoughton] and APL to the other* and to Ultralite for

> purposes of that certain Proprietary Information Disclosure Agreement dated as of May 21, 1993, by and between APL and SCI, (ii) *remain the joint property of APL and SCI exclusively and (iii) be considered information and technology jointly licensed by APL and SCI to Ultralite * * * . APL and SCI each hereby agrees not to license (other than to Ultralite as contemplated herein), pledge, sell or otherwise transfer any Proprietary Information, which is the subject to [sic] such Proprietary Information Disclosure Agreement referred to in the immediately preceding sentence, without the prior written consent of the other.* [Emphasis added.]

Under the 1995 agreement any information Stoughton creates in connection with the project is treated as information disclosed by "each" party to the other, and therefore as information disclosed by APL to Stoughton. Under the 1993 agreement Stoughton may not "use for its own commercial benefit" any information disclosed to it by APL, which wants us to stop reading here. But why should we? If the information is treated as disclosed by APL to Stoughton, it is also treated as disclosed by Stoughton to APL—and there can be no doubt that Stoughton is free under the 1993 agreement to use for its own purposes the information it discloses to APL, for the 1993 agreement imposes obligations only on the "receiving party." This implies that the real restrictions on a party's use of its own information come in the following clauses, which provide that the information is the "joint property of APL and SCI" and must not be licensed or transferred without the other's consent; this language would be pointless if "joint property" were subject to an absolute prohibition on use or disclosure. To say that it must not be licensed or transferred without consent is to imply that it may be used internally without the other's consent, just as Stoughton did.

* * * *

* * * Having put up development capital, APL wants to control (or profit from) all uses of the technology. Why would it finance Stoughton's engineering for a separate business, APL asks? But things are not so simple—and not only because APL agreed by contract that the intellectual property of the joint venture was the "joint property" of APL, Ultralite, and Stoughton. Stoughton invested too, contributing its personnel and manufacturing facilities. Stoughton's total outlay exceeded APL's. Ultralite was more likely to make progress if Stoughton committed the engineers most familiar with composite technology. If the contracts mean what APL says they mean, however, by putting its staff to work on the Ultralite project even for a day Stoughton disabled everyone, perhaps forever, from working on the over-the-road part of its business. It would have had to erect a Chinese Wall to separate the knowledge, and the only practical way to do this would have been to have separate staffs for intermodal containers and over-the-road containers. That would have forfeited any economies of scope from investigating thin composite technology that has applications to different kinds of containers—in other words, it would have required Stoughton to perform the same work twice, perhaps by sending Ultralite a cadre of inexperienced engineers, so that it would not poison the well for its core business.

Sometimes partners to a joint venture agree to a Chinese Wall around the information. Such agreements are most common when the parties otherwise are competitors, for neither wants to give the other a leg up, but APL and Stoughton are not rivals. Their businesses are complementary. (APL has conceded that Stoughton's over-the-road containers do not compete with it, and that it had no lost profits.) This joint venture was designed to jump off from intellectual property Stoughton already possessed; that could not be achieved if Stoughton had to segregate the bodies of knowledge rigidly, on pain of forfeiting the opportunity to make any technical advances in its original product base. Nothing in the 1993 or 1995 agreements demonstrates that the parties were this self-destructive. A firm in APL's position might think that the no-outside-disclosure and no-competition clauses gave it quite enough protection, and that to strive for more would undercut the economies that the joint venture sought to achieve. Thus we conclude that the contracts permit Stoughton to use information from the Ultralite project in Stoughton's original business.

The judgment on the jury verdict in Stoughton's favor is affirmed. The equitable relief in APL's favor is reversed.

CASE 39.2 FRANCHISOR'S LIABILITY

MILLER v. D. F. ZEE'S, INC.

United States District Court,
District of Oregon, 1998.
31 F.Supp.2d 792.

AIKEN, District Judge.

On August 16, 1996, * * * female employees of a Denny's restaurant located in Tualatin, Oregon, filed suit against defendants D. F. Zee's, Inc., * * * Denny's, Inc. ("Denny's"), [and others] for sex discrimination, harassment, retaliation, and constructive discharge under the Civil Rights Act of 1964; and stating common law claims for wrongful discharge and the intentional infliction of emotional distress. Plaintiffs allege that Stanley Templeton, the General Manager of the Tualatin Denny's, and other employees created a hostile work place through sexually inappropriate comments and conduct.

The Tualatin Denny's restaurant is owned and managed by a partnership entitled D. F. Zee's/Denny's Tualatin. * * *

* * * *

* * * Each of the plaintiffs believed they were "Denny's" employees. Servers wore Denny's uniforms. Denny's signs and logos were prominently displayed throughout the restaurant. There was no observable indication in the restaurant that the Tualatin Denny's was a franchise restaurant and there was no indication who its owners were, other than "Denny's."

* * * *

DISCUSSION

* * * *

Denny's moves for summary judgment arguing that franchisors cannot be liable for harassment or discrimination alleged by franchise employees. * * *

* * * *

Here, Denny's is responsible for acts of harassment by employees at the Tualatin Denny's because employees of the Tualatin Denny's are agents of * * * Denny's * * *.

* * * [A]n agency results from the manifestation of consent by one person to another so that the other will act on his or her behalf and "subject" to his or her control, and consent by the other to so act. *An agency relationship may be evidenced by an express agreement between the parties, or it may be implied from the circumstances and conduct of the parties.* The principal's consent and "right to control" are the essential elements of an agency relationship. It does not matter whether the putative [supposed] principal actually exercises control; what is important is that it has the right to do so. * * * [Emphasis added.]

* * * *

Here, * * * the franchise agreement requires adherence to comprehensive, detailed manuals for the operation of the restaurant. The Franchise Agreement between Denny's and Zee's provides, in part:

> Franchisee acknowledged and agrees that strict and continued adherence by the franchisee to the company's standards, policies, procedures and requirements * * * is expressly made a condition of this agreement, so that failure on the part of franchisee to so perform will be grounds for termination of this agreement * * *. The company has prepared an operations manual and a food service standards manual. Franchisee understands that the company has entered into this agreement in reliance upon franchisee's representation that it will strictly comply with all provisions of the manuals.

Here, * * * defendants enforce the use of these methods by regularly sending inspectors into the restaurant to assess compliance and by its retained power to cancel the agreement.

Further, the Franchise Operations Manual provides that the defendants had the right to control their franchisees in the precise parts of the franchisee's business that allegedly resulted in plaintiffs' injuries—training and discipline of employees. Under the Agreement, the franchisee agrees to "hire, train and supervise restaurant employees in accordance with the applicable provisions of the operations manual." The Franchise Agreement specifically authorizes the franchisor to terminate the agreement in the event that Franchisee employees do not comply with the Operations Manual.

Further, the agreement requires that the franchisee submit its own managers to training from the company and that all managers subsequently employed submit to such training as the company requires. Denny's undertakes to train franchise employees in diversity and nondiscrimination. Further, Denny's Franchise Operations Manual involves the Denny's defendants directly in complaints, investigation, and discipline of franchise employees for discrimination. Denny's Franchise Operations Manual reserves the right to decide the amount of discipline assessed against franchise employees, decides the level of discipline that should be administered, and sets mandatory levels of discipline.

* * * *

Defendants argue that the Franchise Agreement specifically provides that employees of franchisee's are not to be considered employees of Denny's. * * * Here, * * * plaintiffs' evidence that defendants reserved the right to train and discipline franchise employees is significant.

However, even if this court determined that plaintiffs' evidence of "actual authority" was insufficient to create an issue of fact, I find there is sufficient evidence to create a material issue of fact that employees of franchisees had apparent authority to act on behalf of Denny's * * *.

Here, * * * there was no indication in the restaurant that the restaurant was owned by a franchisee. Prior to April 1996, there were no signs in the Tualatin Denny's indicating who the owners were. The Denny's trademark was prominently displayed throughout the restaurant on the servers' uniforms, signs at the entrance of the restaurant, and on menus. None of the plaintiffs realized that the restaurant was owned by Zee's. Each of the plaintiffs believed they were "Denny's" employees. Servers were told they were Denny's employees.

Further, * * * the franchisee pays a 4% royalty fee for use of the Denny's trademark, and the availability of company supplied supervisory training and other professional personnel. The franchisee also pays a 2% royalty fee for institutional advertising, public relations, and promotion of the Denny's product. The franchisee is prohibited from engaging in its own institutional advertising activities.

* * * *

CONCLUSION

* * * Denny's * * * [motion] for summary judgment * * * [is] denied.

IT IS SO ORDERED.

CASE 39.3 FRANCHISE TERMINATION

GENERAL MOTORS CORP. V. MONTE ZINN CHEVROLET CO.

Ohio Court of Appeals,
Tenth District, 2000.
136 Ohio App.3d 157,
736 N.E.2d 62.

BOWMAN, Judge.

Appellants, Monte Zinn Chevrolet Company and Monte Zinn Motor Company ("Monte Zinn"), appeal a judgment of the [Ohio state trial court] reversing an order of the Ohio Motor Vehicle Dealers Board ("board") that appellees, General Motors Corporation, Chrysler Corporation, and Toyota Motor Sales, U.S.A., Inc., could not terminate their respective automobile dealer franchises with appellants because appellees had not established good cause. * * *

In 1995, Monte Zinn pleaded guilty to [committing] a federal felony involving fraud, and a federal felony involving conspiracy to commit fraud. In January 1996, Zinn was sentenced to two years' probation and ordered to pay a fine and a special assessment.

Zinn had separate franchise agreements with each of appellees, the franchisors. Each agreement contained a provision to the effect that the franchisor could terminate the dealership if the dealer was convicted of a felony. Between August 1995 and January 1996, appellees individually served notice of their intent to terminate appellants' respective agreements with them.

Under Ohio law, * * * a franchisor cannot terminate a franchise without "good cause." In turn, a franchisor who wants to terminate a franchise must send written notice to the franchisee, who may then file a protest with the board. When a timely protest is filed, the franchisee is entitled to a hearing, and the franchisor cannot terminate the franchise until and unless the board determines that good cause exists. It is the franchisor's burden to establish good cause.

* * * *

Separate hearings on each of the protests were held before a board hearing examiner. As to each protest, the hearing examiner found that good cause had been shown and recommended that the protest be denied. Appellants appealed the recommendations to the board, which remanded the matters with instructions that the hearing examiner make factual findings * * * . The hearing examiner filed amended recommendations, again recommending termination of appellants' franchises.

Although the hearing examiner's amended recommendations for the General Motors and Toyota protests are not identical, the fundamental conclusions are the same. * * * Specifically, the hearing examiner found a felony conviction constitutes a material breach of the dealer agreements and, thus, establishes good cause to terminate. The hearing examiner concluded that Zinn's felony conviction on charges of fraud and conspiracy to commit fraud, and the circumstances surrounding General Motors and Toyota's decisions to terminate appellants' franchises satisfied the good-cause requirement.

* * * *

[T]he board did not adopt the hearing examiner's conclusions of law that appellees had established that Zinn's felony conviction constituted a material breach of the franchise agreements * * * and that Zinn's felony conviction and the circumstances surrounding the decisions to terminate the franchises satisfied the good cause requirement * * * . The board stated that it would "look to other factors to determine if there was good cause to terminate. The board concludes there were no other factors presented * * * that either combined with the conviction or on their own constituted good cause." Thus, the board determined that appellees had not established good cause. * * *

* * * [A]ppellees appealed the board's orders to [an Ohio state court] * * * .

The trial court found that Zinn's fraud conviction, which was also a crime that involved moral turpitude as well as an employee of his dealership, constituted, without question, good cause to terminate a dealership. * * *

* * * *

On appeal, appellants contend that the trial court improperly [applied the law].

* * * *

* * * [A] felony conviction for fraud committed by a dealer/operator undermines the trust between the manufacturer and the dealer, and between the public and the dealer. * * * [F]rom 1991 to 1995, appellants' overall sales effectiveness had been in the bottom half of Chevrolet dealers in their service area and consistently ranked in the bottom twenty percent of all dealers in customer service and satisfaction. * * * [A]ppellants, the dealerships, as corporate entities, had made few investments into the dealership and * * * the property and facilities were personally owned by Zinn. These findings of fact all weigh in favor of finding good cause to terminate the franchise. The board's conclusion that General Motors had not met its burden of demonstrating good cause is not supported by the facts as found by the hearing examiner and accepted by the board.

Similarly, under the Chrysler protest, the hearing examiner made findings of fact that appellants had been sizably undercapitalized every year from 1991; that between 1992 and 1996, their new vehicle sales volume increased at less than half the rate as the zone level and actually decreased between 1995 and 1996; and that appellants performed poorly in service-related areas compared to the zone average and that their scores on owner loyalty were below both zone and national averages. * * * Thus, in light of the board's acceptance of the hearing examiner's findings of fact, which weigh heavily in favor of termination, the board's order to the contrary is not supported by reliable, probative, and substantial evidence, and is error as a matter of law.

Finally, as to the Toyota protest, in addition to the circumstances underlying the conviction, the hearing examiner found that Toyota's felony-termination clause was very important to Toyota, that it uniformly terminated dealerships following felony convictions, that Zinn personally owned the dealership facilities and would continue to retain them after termination of the franchise, and that other Toyota dealers could provide adequate service if appellants' franchises were terminated. In light of the absence of other findings of fact that weigh against finding good cause, the board's order is not supported by reliable, probative, and substantial evidence.

For the above reasons, * * * the judgment of the [lower court] is affirmed.

CASE PROBLEMS

39–1. H. C. Blackwell Co. was a truck dealership owned by the Blackwell family. In 1961 the Blackwells purchased a franchise from Kenworth Truck Co. to sell Kenworth trucks. The franchise agreement had been renewed several times. In November 1975 the family began negotiations with Kenworth to renew the recently expired franchise, and disagreements arose concerning the franchise. On February 4, 1976, Kenworth wrote to Blackwell that the franchise would be terminated in ninety days unless Blackwell met twelve specific demands made by Kenworth. In trying to meet these demands—which included increased sales, a better method of keeping business records, and capital improvements at its dealership—Blackwell spent approximately $90,000. By the end of the ninety-day period, however, the demands had not been met, so Kenworth terminated the franchise. Blackwell sued Kenworth for damages on the grounds that Kenworth had wrongfully terminated the franchise agreement and, in so doing, had violated the Automobile Dealers' Franchise Act. During the trial, Kenworth's own regional sales manager stated that the demands imposed by Kenworth on Blackwell would have taken at least a year to meet. Has Kenworth wrongfully terminated the franchise under the Automobile Dealers' Franchise Act? Discuss fully. [*H. C. Blackwell Co. v. Kenworth Truck Co.*, 620 F.2d 104 (5th Cir. 1980)]

39–2. Gustave Peterson contacted his family doctor, Leland Reichelt, complaining of abdominal pain. The doctor recommended gallbladder surgery. Dr. George Fortier performed the surgery, and Reichelt assisted. It was Reichelt's normal practice to refer patients to Fortier for surgery, and each doctor charged the patient separately for his services. During the operation, a metal clip was inadvertently left inside Peterson's abdominal cavity. It eventually formed a stone, which later caused Peterson chest and gastric pain. Peterson repeatedly complained to Reichelt, who diagnosed the problem as being related to either a hernia or stress. Peterson finally sought the advice of another physician, who, on performing surgery, discovered the metal clip. Peterson filed suit against both Reichelt and Fortier for malpractice under the theory that Fortier and Reichelt were engaged in a joint enterprise (joint venture). Discuss fully whether the two doctors were joint venturers. [*Peterson v. Fortier*, 406 N.W.2d 563 (Minn.App. 1987)]

39–3. Ernst and Barbara Larese entered into a ten-year franchise agreement with Creamland Dairies, Inc., in 1974. The agreement provided that the franchisee "shall not assign, transfer or sublet this franchise, or any of [the] rights under this agreement, without the prior written consent of Area Franchisor [Creamland] and Baskin Robbins, any such authorized assignment, transfer or subletting being null and without effect." The Lareses attempted to sell their franchise rights in February and August 1979, but Creamland refused to consent to the sales. The Lareses brought suit, alleging that Creamland had interfered with their contractual relations with the prospective buyers by unreasonably withholding its consent; they held that Creamland had a duty to act in good faith and in a commercially reasonable manner when a franchisee sought to transfer its rights under the franchise agreement. Creamland contended that the contract gave it an unqualified right to refuse to consent to proposed sales of the franchise rights. Which party prevailed? Explain. [*Larese v. Creamland Dairies, Inc.*, 767 F.2d 716 (10th Cir. 1985)]

39–4. AB & B, Inc., sold wines produced by Banfi Products, Inc., under a distributorship agreement. In 1986, AB & B experienced a severe decline in the demand for one of Banfi's wines, Riunite, mostly as a result of a recall of that wine resulting from contamination problems in the fall of 1985. Because of decreasing sales, Banfi sent a letter to AB & B, which stated as follows: "You are aware that Banfi's corporate policy requires our distributors to maintain no less than a 60-day inventory of products. Not only are you out of stock on most items in our line, but our records indicate that the last activity on your account was a credit in January of 1986, and your last purchase was in April of 1985. Your lack of interest in and support of the Banfi line leaves us no alternative but to terminate our distributorship relationship with you, effective sixty (60) days from your receipt of this notice." In fact, AB & B held, on average, a ninety-six-day inventory of Banfi wines. In support of its allegation that AB & B showed a "lack of interest in and support of the Banfi line," Banfi had indicated that AB & B routinely failed to send a representative to Banfi's sales meetings. Yet there was no evidence that those meetings were mandatory, and AB & B always received notebooks from Banfi containing the information from those meetings. Although AB & B requested a meeting with Banfi to discuss these issues, Banfi terminated the franchise relationship without responding to AB & B's request. In AB & B's lawsuit against Banfi for wrongful termination of the franchise relationship, what should the court decide? Discuss. [*AB & B, Inc. v. Banfi Products, Inc.*, 71 Ohio App.3d 650, 594 N.E.2d 1151 (1991)]

39–5. Windy City Balloon Port, Ltd., operated a balloon launching facility near Barrington Hills, Illinois, offering public commercial sightseeing flights in hot-air and helium balloons owned by third parties. Windy City sold tickets for the balloon rides for $100 to $150 per person per ride. The pilot of the balloon would receive $60 to $70 directly from Windy City for each ticket sold but otherwise received no consideration from Windy City. Although Windy City provided refueling and repair facilities for the balloons and canceled balloon flights when the weather conditions were unsafe, Windy City had no control over the balloons after they departed from the balloon launch. On August 15, 1981, a hot-air balloon piloted by James Bickett departed from a launching site at Windy City. It was carrying five passengers—Kenneth Coleman, Jr., Terry Ritter, Brian Baker, William Keating, and Harry Evans. Shortly after takeoff, the balloon struck power lines and crashed to the ground, killing Bickett, Coleman, Ritter, Baker, and Keating. Evans survived, but sustained severe burns and injuries. In a lawsuit filed by representatives of the deceased passengers and others, one of the issues was whether Windy City and Bickett were involved in a joint venture. How did the court rule? Discuss fully. [*Coleman v. Charlesworth*, 157 Ill.2d 257, 623 N.E.2d 1366, 191 Ill.Dec. 480 (1993)]

39–6. In 1981 the Huangs entered into a franchise agreement with Holiday Inns, Inc., under which the Huangs agreed to adhere to the quality standards established by Holiday Inns and to comply in every respect with the Holiday Inns Standards Manual. In November 1983, the district director of Holiday Inns made a courtesy inspection that revealed cracked windows, damaged and discolored walls, inoperative smoke detectors, and numerous other indications that the Huangs were not maintaining the established Holiday Inn quality standards in accordance with the franchise agreement. A formal inspection in February 1984 revealed no significant improvement in quality standards, and the hotel was given an official rating of "unacceptable." The Huangs, who had been given detailed reports concerning the findings of both inspections, were advised that if the noted deficiencies were not remedied within sixty days, Holiday Inns would have grounds to terminate the franchise. When an inspection in April 1984 revealed that the deficiencies had not been cured, Holiday Inns notified the Huangs that the franchise would be terminated on July 30 unless the deficiencies were remedied by June 28. The Huangs, who in May had begun renovations on the hotel costing $55,000, requested a ninety-day extension to the June 28 deadline, which Holiday Inns refused to grant. The Huangs then petitioned the court for a preliminary injunction against Holiday Inns' termination of the franchise, claiming that Holiday Inns had acted "capriciously and arbitrarily" by (1) not stating precisely the nature of the deficiencies and what was required to make repairs and improvements and (2) not giving the Huangs a reasonable time in which to remedy the deficiencies. Discuss fully whether Holiday Inns should be enjoined from terminating the franchise, given these circumstances. [*Huang v. Holiday Inns, Inc.*, 594 F.Supp. 352 (C.D.Cal.1984)]

39–7. Kubis & Perszyk Associates, Inc., was in business as Entre Computer. As a franchise, Entre sold, among other products, computer systems marketed by Sun Microsystems, Inc. Entre's agreement with Sun included a forum-selection clause that provided that any suit between the parties had to be filed in a California court. When Sun terminated its relationship with Entre, Entre filed a suit in a New Jersey state court. Sun asked the court to dismiss the suit on the basis of the forum-selection clause. Entre argued that the clause violated state franchise law, which invalidated such clauses in auto dealership franchises. On what basis might the court extend this law to cover Entre's franchise? Discuss. [*Kubis & Perszyk Associates, Inc. v. Sun Microsystems, Inc.*, 146 N.J. 176, 680 A.2d 618 (1996)]

39–8. In 1953, Atlantic Richfield Co. (Arco) and Razumic signed a printed form titled a "Dealer Lease." The agreement referred to the parties as lessor and lessee. It authorized Razumic to operate an Arco service station and provided, among other things, for Arco's signs and trade name to be prominently displayed at the service station and for gasoline and other related products to be sold. The agreement detailed other aspects of the parties' business relationship, including Razumic's obligation to operate the service station in such a manner as to reflect favorably on Arco's goodwill. These basic terms were in all renewal agreements made by the parties over the years. In 1973, Arco notified Razumic that the agreement was being terminated and gave him thirty days to vacate the premises. Razumic refused, and Arco filed suit to force termination of the agreement. Did the "Dealer Lease" constitute a franchise agreement? If so—in view of the fact that the Petroleum Marketing Practices Act had not yet been passed when this case was decided—on what grounds might the court hold that Arco could not terminate the franchise at will? Discuss. [*Atlantic Richfield Co. v. Razumic*, 480 Pa. 366, 390 A.2d 736 (1978)]

39–9. Frank Hartman, Jr., and Robert Wiesner visited the site of a derailment of a Burlington Northern (BN) train to bid on lumber carried on the train. Hartman was to provide the salvage expertise, and Wiesner was to provide the expertise to sell the lumber. They submitted a bid of $113,663, which BN accepted. To make the payment, Hartman and Wiesner contacted Dave Anderson, who contacted Doug Feller, the managing partner of BBD Partnership. Hartman, Wiesner, Anderson, and Feller agreed to share profits from the sale of the lumber. BBD then borrowed the money to pay BN. BBD, through Feller, had promised to get involved only if it could own the lumber, however. Thus, on the bill of sale, BN entered the names "Hartman Construction" and "Feller Associates," a sole proprietorship owned by Feller. BBD later sold its interest in the deal to another party. Two years later, Hartman, Wiesner, BBD, and Feller became involved in a lawsuit over the funds that BBD had borrowed. Was the deal between the parties a joint venture or simply a loan from BBD to Hartman and the others? Discuss fully. [*Wiesner v. BBD Partnership*, 845 P.2d 120 (Mont. 1993)]

39–10. Ormsby Motors, Inc. (OMI), was a General Motors Corp. (GM) dealership. Their agreement provided for termination if OMI submitted "false . . . claims for any payment." Larry Kain was in charge of OMI's warranty claims. After several years of excessive claims, GM complained to OMI. When nothing changed, GM conducted a dealer audit. The audit uncovered, among other things, over eighty claims in one ten-day period for paint repair work that was never done. OMI denied knowledge of Kain's activities. GM terminated its dealership agreement with OMI. OMI asked a federal district court to stop the termination, arguing in part that GM did not have good cause. Did GM have good cause? Explain. [*Ormsby Motors, Inc. v. General Motors Corp.*, 842 F.Supp. 344 (N.D.Ill. 1994)]

39–11. Barn-Chestnut, Inc. (BCI), entered into a franchise agreement with Grocers Development Corp. (GDC) for a Convenient Food Mart "for as long as [BCI] . . . shall have a good and valid lease" to the property. GDC sold its interest in the franchise and the property to CFM Development Corp. When the lease was about to expire, CFM offered to enter into a new lease and franchise agreement with BCI at a significantly higher price. BCI declined. When CFM refused to make another deal, BCI filed a suit against CFM in a West Virginia state court on the ground that CFM had to offer BCI a lease because the franchise was contingent on a lease. The court did not agree. BCI then argued that the implied obligation of good faith required CFM to offer to renew the lease. Essentially, the question on appeal was whether the franchisor had an obligation to renew the franchise even though there was no clause in the contract requiring that the lease /franchise be renewed. Was BCI correct in contending that the franchisor did have such an obligation? Explain. [*Barn-Chestnut, Inc. v. CFM Development Corp.*, 193 W.Va. 565, 457 S.E.2d 502 (1995)]

39–12. C. B. Management Co. operated McDonald's restaurants in Cleveland, Ohio, under a franchise agreement with McDonald's Corp. The agreement required C. B. to make monthly payments of, among other things, certain percentages of the gross sales to McDonald's. If any payment was more than thirty days late, McDonald's had the right to terminate the franchise. The agreement stated, "No waiver by [McDonald's] of any breach . . . shall constitute a waiver of any subsequent breach." McDonald's sometimes accepted C. B.'s late payments, but when C. B. defaulted on the payments in July 1997 McDonald's gave notice of thirty days to comply or surrender possession of the restaurants. C. B. missed the deadline. McDonald's demanded that C. B. vacate the restaurants. C. B. refused. McDonald's filed a suit in a federal district court against C. B., alleging violations of the franchise agreement. C. B. counterclaimed in part that McDonald's had breached the implied covenant of good faith and fair dealing. McDonald's filed a motion to dismiss C. B.'s counterclaim. On what did C. B. base its claim? Will the court agree? Why, or why not? [*McDonald's Corp. v. C. B. Management Co.*, 13 F.Supp.2d 705 (N.D.Ill. 1998)]

39–13. Heating & Air Specialists, Inc., doing business as A/C Service Co., marketed heating and air conditioning products. A/C contracted with Lennox Industries, Inc., to be a franchised dealer of Lennox products. The parties signed a standard franchise contract drafted by Lennox. The contract provided that either party could terminate the agreement with or without cause on thirty days' notice and that the agreement would terminate immediately if A/Copened another facility at a different location. At the time, A/C operated only one location in Arkansas. A few months later, A/C opened a second location in Tulsa, Oklahoma. Lennox's district sales manager gave A/C oral authorization to sell Lennox products in Tulsa, at least on a temporary basis, but nothing was put in writing. Several of Lennox's other dealers in Tulsa complained to Lennox about A/C's presence. Lennox gave A/C notice that it was terminating A/C's Tulsa franchise. Meanwhile, A/C had failed to keep its Lennox account current and owed the franchisor more than $200,000. Citing this delinquency, Lennox notified A/C that unless it paid its account within ten days, Lennox would terminate both franchises. A/C did not pay. Lennox terminated the franchises. A/C filed a suit in a federal district court against Lennox, alleging in part breach of the franchise agreement for terminating the Tulsa franchise. Is A/C correct? Explain. [*Heating & Air Specialists, Inc. v. Jones*, 180 F.3d 923 (8th Cir. 1999)]

39–14. In 1985, Bruce Byrne, with his sons Scott and Gordon, opened Lone Star R.V. Sales, Inc., a motor home dealership in Houston, Texas. In 1994, Lone Star became a franchised dealer for Winnebago Industries, Inc., a manufacturer of recreational vehicles. The parties renewed the franchise in 1995, but beginning the next year, their relationship began to deteriorate. Lone Star did not maintain a current inventory, its sales did not meet goals agreed to between the parties, and Lone Star disparaged

Winnebago products to consumers and otherwise failed to actively promote them. Several times, the Byrnes subjected Winnebago employees to verbal abuse. During one phone conversation, Bruce threatened to throw a certain Winnebago sales manager off Lone Star's lot if he appeared at the dealership. Bruce was, however, physically incapable of carrying out the threat. In 1998, Winnebago terminated the franchise, claiming, among many other things, that it was concerned for the safety of its employees. Lone Star filed a protest with the Texas Motor Vehicle Board. Did Winnebago have good cause to terminate Lone Star's franchise? Discuss. [*Lone Star R.V. Sales, Inc. v. Motor Vehicle Board of the Texas Department of Transportation*, 49 S.W.3d 492 (Tex.App.—Austin, 2001)]

39–15. A Question of Ethics

Graham Oil Co. (Graham) had been a distributor of ARCO gasoline in Coos Bay, Oregon, for nearly forty years under successive distributorship agreements. ARCO notified Graham that it intended to terminate the franchise because Graham had not been purchasing the minimum amount of gasoline required under their most recent agreement. Graham sought a preliminary injunction against ARCO, arguing that ARCO had violated the Petroleum Marketing Practices Act (PMPA) by deliberately raising its prices so that Graham would be unable to meet the minimum gasoline requirements; thus, ARCO should not be allowed to terminate the agreement. The court ordered Graham to submit the claim to arbitration, in accordance with an arbitration clause in the distributorship agreement. Graham refused to do so, and the court granted summary judgment for ARCO. On appeal, Graham claimed that the arbitration clause was invalid because it forced him to forfeit rights given to franchisees under the PMPA, including the right to punitive damages and attorneys' fees. The appellate court agreed with Graham and remanded the case for trial. In view of these facts, answer the following questions. [*Graham Oil Co. v. Arco Products Co., A Division of Atlantic Richfield Co.*, 43 F.3d 1244 (9th Cir. 1994)]

1. Do you agree with Graham and the appellate court that statutory rights cannot be forfeited contractually, through an arbitration clause?
2. Review the discussion of arbitration in Chapter 2. Does the decision in the above case conflict with any established public policy concerning arbitration? Is the decision in the case consistent with other court decisions on arbitration discussed in Chapter 2, including decisions of the United States Supreme Court?

E-Links

For updated links to resources available on the Web, as well as a variety of other materials, visit this text's Web site at

http://wbl-cs.westbuslaw.com

The Web site of the law firm of Reinhart et al. provides extensive information about business organizations. The URL for this site is

http://www.rbvdnr.com

To learn how the U.S. Small Business Administration assists in forming, financing, and operating businesses, go to

http://www.sbaonline.sba.gov

For information on the FTC regulations on franchising, as well as state laws regulating franchising, go to

http://www.ftc.gov/bcp/franchise/netfran.htm

A good source of information on the purchase and sale of franchises is Franchising.org, which is online at

http://www.franchising.org

Legal Research Exercises on the Web

Go to http://wbl-cs.westbuslaw.com, the Web site that accompanies this text. Select "Interactive Study Center," and then click on "Chapter 39." There you will find the following Internet research exercise that you can perform to learn more about franchises:

Activity 39–1: Franchises

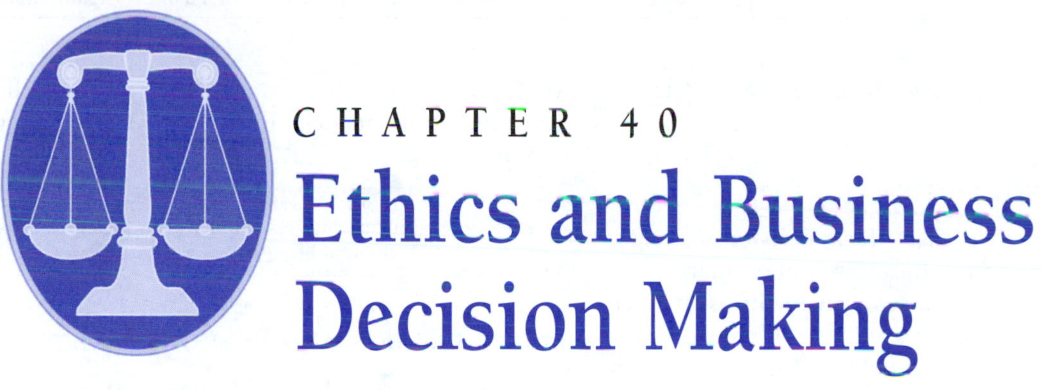

CHAPTER 40 Ethics and Business Decision Making

THE PURPOSE OF ORGANIZING a business, no matter what business form is chosen for the enterprise, normally is to make a profit. Generally, profit-making activities are encouraged by the laws, because the flourishing of trade and commerce confers benefits on society as a whole. At the same time, businesspersons should not let their profit-making activities exceed the ethical boundaries established by society. In the past, these boundaries were often regarded as being coterminous with the law—that is, if something was legal, it was ethical. In today's rights-conscious world, however, a business firm that decides it has no duties other than those prescribed by law may find it difficult to survive. If a firm's behavior is perceived as unethical—even though it may be legal—that firm may suffer negative publicity, lost profits, and even government sanctions.

In this chapter, we first examine the nature of business ethics and some commonly used approaches to ethical reasoning. We then look at the ethical component of business decision making in some detail. Throughout the chapter, we include specific examples of ethical issues that commonly arise in the business world.

SECTION 1

The Nature of Business Ethics

Before we examine the nature of business ethics, we need to discuss what is meant by ethics generally. **Ethics** can be defined as the study of what constitutes right or wrong behavior. It is the branch of philosophy that focuses on morality and the way in which moral principles are derived or the way in which a given set of moral principles applies to one's conduct in daily life. Ethics has to do with questions relating to the fairness, justness, rightness, or wrongness of an action. What is fair? What is just? What is the right thing to do in this situation? These are essentially ethical questions.

Often, moral principles serve as the guiding force in an individual's personal ethical system. Although the terms *ethical* and *moral* often are used interchangeably, these terms refer to slightly different concepts. Whereas ethics has to do with the philosophical, rational basis for conduct, morals are often defined as *universal* rules or guidelines (such as those rooted in religious precepts) that determine our actions and character. Morals generally are "revealed" truths—that is, they are revealed to us by our family, influential mentors, or religious sources, such as the Bible (for Christians) or the Koran (for Muslims). Ethics, in contrast, is a reasoned set of principles of conduct. These principles may be based either on moral truths or on premises derived through logic and reasoning.

DEFINING BUSINESS ETHICS

Business ethics focuses on what constitutes right or wrong behavior in the business world and on how moral and ethical principles are applied by businesspersons to situations that arise in their daily activities in the workplace. Note that business ethics is not a separate *kind* of ethics. The ethical standards that guide our behavior as, say, mothers, fathers, or students apply equally well to our activities as businesspersons. Business decision makers, though, often must address more complex ethical issues and conflicts in the workplace than they do in their personal lives.

Conflicting Duties

One of the reasons that ethical decision making is more complex in the business context than in our personal lives is because business firms are perceived to owe duties to a number of groups. These groups include the firm's owners (in a corporation, the shareholders), its employees, its suppliers, those who use its products or services (consumers), the community in which it operates, and, according to many, society at large. When these duties come into conflict, difficult choices must be made.

For example, suppose that Jemico, Inc., decides to reduce its costs by downsizing and restructuring its operations. Among other things, this would allow the company to cut back on its overhead by consolidating various supervisory and managerial positions. The question for Jemico is, which employees should be retained and which should be let go? Should the firm retain highly paid employees who have worked for—and received annual raises from—the firm for years? Alternatively, in the interests of cutting costs, should it retain (or hire) younger, less experienced persons at lower salaries?

Jemico would not necessarily be acting illegally if it pursued the second option. Unless a fired employee can prove that the employer has breached an employment contract or violated the Age Discrimination in Employment Act (ADEA) of 1967, he or she will not have a cause of action against the employer. As you will learn in Chapter 42, the ADEA prohibits discrimination against workers forty years of age and older on the basis of their age.

In deciding this issue, remember that Jemico must keep its eye on its profit margin. If it does not, the firm may fail, and the shareholders will lose their investments. Furthermore, why should the firm retain highly paid employees if it can obtain essentially the same work output for a lower cost from lower–paid employees? Does Jemico owe an ethical duty to employees who have served the firm loyally over a long period of time? Most people would say yes. Should this duty take precedence over Jemico's duty to the firm's owners to maintain or increase the profitability of the firm? What if the firm faced imminent bankruptcy if it could not lower its operational costs? What if longtime employees were willing to take a slight reduction in pay to help the firm through its financial difficulties? What if they were not?

See Case 40.1 at the end of this chapter. To view the full, unedited case from Westlaw,® go to this text's Web site at **http://wbl-cs.westbuslaw.com**.

Public Opinion and Business Ethics

Another factor complicating business ethics is the increasingly important role played by public opinion in determining what is or is not ethical business behavior. In the last two decades, and particularly since the advent of the Internet, the actions of business firms have been much more closely scrutinized by the media and various interest groups (groups supporting human rights, animal rights, the environment, consumers, employees, and so on) than they ever were in the past. What this means is that if a corporation undertakes or continues an action deemed to be unethical by one or more of these groups, the firm's "unethical" behavior will probably become widely known. In the interests of preserving their good reputations, business firms thus pay attention to public opinion. If they do not, they may lose customers, be boycotted by investors concerned about ethical issues, and, ultimately, lose profits.

Business ethics thus has a practical element. As a manager, you might personally be convinced that there is nothing unethical about a certain business action. If a highly vocal interest group believes otherwise, though, you might want to reassess your decision with a view toward preserving the firm's goodwill and reputation in the community. If you decide to pursue the action regardless of public opinion, you may violate your ethical (and legal) duty to act in the firm's best interests. You should keep this practical concern with public opinion in mind as you read through the remaining pages in this chapter.

Section 2

Approaches to Ethical Reasoning

Each individual, when faced with a particular ethical dilemma, engages in **ethical reasoning**—that is, a reasoning process in which the individual links his or her moral convictions or ethical standards to the particular situation at hand. Businesspersons do likewise when making decisions with ethical implications.

How do business decision makers decide whether a given action is the "right" one for their firms? What ethical standards should be applied? Broadly speaking, ethical reasoning relating to business traditionally has been characterized by two fundamental approaches. One approach defines ethical behavior in terms of duty, which also implies certain rights. The other approach determines what is ethical in terms of the consequences, or outcome, of any given action. We examine each of these approaches here.

Duty-Based Ethics

Duty-based ethical standards often are derived from revealed truths, such as religious precepts. They can also be derived through philosophical reasoning.

Religious Ethical Standards. In the Judeo-Christian tradition, which is the dominant religious tradition in the United States, the Ten Commandments of the Old Testament establish fundamental rules for moral action. Other religions have their own sources of revealed truth. Religious rules generally are absolute with respect to the behavior of their adherents. For example, the commandment "Thou shalt not steal" is an absolute mandate for a person, such as a Jew or a Christian, who believes that the Ten Commandments reflect revealed truth. Even a benevolent motive for stealing (such as Robin Hood's) cannot justify the act, because the act itself is inherently immoral and thus wrong.

Ethical standards based on religious teachings also involve an element of *compassion*. Therefore, for example, even though it might be profitable for a firm to lay off a less productive employee, if that employee would find it difficult to find employment elsewhere and his or her family would suffer as a result, this potential suffering would be given substantial weight by the decision makers. Compassionate treatment of others is also mandated—to a certain extent, at least—by the Golden Rule of the ancients ("Do unto others as you would have them do unto you"), which has been adopted by most religions.

Kantian Ethics. Duty-based ethical standards may also be derived solely from philosophical reasoning. The German philosopher Immanuel Kant (1724–1804), for example, identified some general guiding principles for moral behavior based on what he believed to be the fundamental nature of human beings. Kant held that it is rational to assume that human beings are qualitatively different from other physical objects occupying space. Persons are endowed with moral integrity and the capacity to reason and conduct their affairs rationally. Therefore, their thoughts and actions should be respected. When human beings are treated merely as a means to an end, they are being treated as the equivalent of objects and are being denied their basic humanity.

A central postulate in Kantian ethics is that individuals should evaluate their actions in light of the consequences that would follow if *everyone* in society acted in the same way. This **categorical imperative** can be applied to any action. For example, say that you are deciding whether to cheat on an examination. If you have adopted Kant's categorical imperative, you will decide not to cheat, because if everyone cheated, the examination would be meaningless.

The Principle of Rights. Duty-based ethical standards imply that human beings have basic rights, because a duty cannot exist without a corresponding right. For example, the commandment "Thou shalt not kill" implies that individuals have a right to live. Additionally, religious ethics may involve a rights component because of the belief—characteristic of many religions—that an individual is "made in the image of God" or "Allah." This belief confers on the individual great dignity as a person. For one who holds this belief, not to respect that dignity—and the rights and status that flow from it—would be morally wrong. Kantian ethics also implies fundamental rights based on the personal dignity of each individual. Just as individuals have a duty not to treat others as means to an end, so individuals have a right to have their status and moral integrity as human beings treated with respect.

The principle that human beings have certain fundamental rights (to life, freedom, and the pursuit of happiness, for example) is deeply embedded in Western culture. As discussed in Chapter 1, the natural law tradition embraces the concept that certain actions (such as killing another person) are morally wrong because they are contrary to nature (the natural desire to continue living). Those who adhere to this **principle of rights**, or "rights theory," believe that a key factor in determining whether a business decision is ethical is how that decision affects the rights of various groups. These groups include the firm's owners, its employees, the consumers of its products or services, its suppliers, the community in which it does business, and society as a whole.

OUTCOME-BASED ETHICS: UTILITARIANISM

"Thou shalt act so as to generate the greatest good for the greatest number." This is a paraphrase of the major premise of the utilitarian approach to ethics. **Utilitarianism** is a philosophical theory developed by Jeremy Bentham (1748–1832) and then advanced, with some modifications, by John Stuart Mill (1806–1873)—both British philosophers. In contrast to duty-based ethics, utilitarianism is outcome oriented. It focuses on the consequences of an action, not on the nature of the action itself or on any set of preestablished moral values or religious beliefs.

Under a utilitarian model of ethics, an action is morally correct, or "right," when, among the people it affects, it produces the greatest amount of good for the greatest number. When an action affects the majority adversely, it is morally wrong. Applying the utilitarian theory thus requires (1) a determination of which individuals will be affected by the action in question; (2) a **cost-benefit analysis**—an assessment of the negative and positive effects of alternative actions on these individuals; and (3) a choice among alternative actions that will produce maximum societal utility (the greatest positive net benefits for the greatest number of individuals).

The utilitarian approach to decision making commonly is employed by businesses, as well as by individuals. Weighing the consequences of a decision in terms of its costs and benefits for everyone affected by it is a useful analytical tool in the decision-making process. At the same time, utilitarianism is often criticized because its objective, calculated approach to problems tends to reduce the welfare of human beings to plus and minus signs on a cost-benefit worksheet and to "justify" human costs that many find totally unacceptable.

For example, from a utilitarian standpoint it might be ethically acceptable to test drugs or medicines on human beings because presumably a majority of the population would benefit from the experiments. If, however, one accepts the principle that each individual has basic human rights, an action that deprives an individual or group of individuals of these rights—even for the greater good of society—is ethically unacceptable.

SECTION 3

Ethical Decision Making

Most major companies today ask three questions about any action before it is undertaken: Is the action profitable? Is it legal? Is it ethical? The first prong of this test for business decision making—determining whether a given course of action will be profitable—is foremost. After all, for-profit firms remain in business only if they make a profit. If the action would not be profitable, it probably will not be undertaken. If the action would be profitable, then the decision makers need to evaluate whether it also would be legal and ethical.

IS THE CONTEMPLATED ACTION LEGAL?

In today's business world, legal compliance usually is regarded as the **moral minimum.** In other words, the minimal acceptable standard for ethical business behavior is compliance with the law.

It may seem that answering a question concerning the legality of a given action should be simple. Either something is legal or it is not. In fact, one of the major challenges businesspersons face is that the legality of a particular action is not always clear. In part, this is because there are so many laws regulating business that it is possible to violate one of them without realizing it. There are also numerous "gray areas" in the law, making it difficult to predict with certainty how a court may apply a given law to a particular action.

Laws Regulating Business. Today's business firms are subject to extensive government regulation. As mentioned in Chapter 1, virtually every action a firm undertakes—from the initial act of going into business to hiring and firing personnel to selling products in the marketplace—is subject to statutory law and to numerous rules and regulations issued by administrative agencies. Furthermore, these rules and regulations are changed or supplemented frequently.

Determining whether a planned action is legal thus requires the decision makers to keep abreast of the law. Normally, large business firms have attorneys on their staffs to assist them in making key decisions. Small firms must also seek legal advice before making important business decisions—because the consequences of just one violation of a regulatory rule may be costly.

Ignorance of the law will not excuse a business owner or manager from liability for violating a statute or regulation. Recall from Chapter 8 that in one case, the court imposed criminal fines, as well as imprisonment, on a company's supervisory employee for violating a federal environmental act—even though the employee was totally unaware of what was required under the provisions of that act.[1]

Westlaw. See Case 40.2 at the end of this chapter. To view the full, unedited case from Westlaw,® go to this text's Web site at **http://wbl-cs.westbuslaw.com.**

"Gray Areas" in the Law. In many situations, business firms can predict with a fair amount of certainty whether a given action would be legal. For example, firing an employee solely because of that person's race or gender would clearly violate federal laws prohibiting employment discrimination. In some situations, though, the legality of a particular action may be less clear.

For example, suppose that a firm decides to launch a new advertising campaign. How far can the firm go in making claims for its product or services? Federal and state laws prohibit firms from engaging in "deceptive advertising." At the federal level, the test for deceptive advertising normally used by the Federal Trade Commission is whether an advertising claim would deceive a "reasonable consumer."[2] At what point, though, would a reasonable consumer be deceived by a particular ad?

Another gray area in the law has to do with product misuse. Recall from Chapter 6 that product liability laws require manufacturers and sellers to warn consumers of the kinds of injuries that might result from the foreseeable misuse of their products. An exception to this rule is made when a risk associated with a product is "open and obvious." Sharp knives, for example, can obviously injure their users. Sometimes, a business has no way of predicting how a court might rule in deciding whether a particular risk is open and obvious or whether consumers should be warned of the risk.

In short, whether a given action will be deemed legal or illegal often depends on how an administrative agency or a court in a particular jurisdiction decides to interpret and apply the law to the facts and issues of a particular case. Business decision makers thus need to proceed with caution and evaluate the action and its consequences from an ethical perspective. Generally, if a company can demonstrate that it acted in good faith and responsibly in the circumstances, it has a better chance of successfully defending its action in court or before an administrative law judge.

Uncertainties concerning how particular laws may apply to specific factual situations have been compounded in the cyber age. As noted in earlier chapters, the widespread use of the Internet has given rise to situations never before faced by the courts.

See Case 40.3 at the end of this chapter. To view the full, unedited case from Westlaw,® go to this text's Web site at **http://wbl-cs.westbuslaw.com.**

Is the Contemplated Action Ethical?

Even if a company is certain of the legality of a particular action, that does not necessarily mean that the action is ethical. For example, suppose that a corporation that markets baby formula in developing countries has learned that mothers in those countries often mix the formula with impure water, to make the formula go further. As a result, babies there are suffering from malnutrition, diarrhea, and even death. Although the corporation is not violating any law, many would contend that it should suspend sales of the formula in those countries.[3]

Typically, in deciding whether a given action would be ethical, a firm's decision makers are guided not only by their own ethical principles and reasoning processes but also by their company's ethical policies and code of conduct.

Ethical Codes and Corporate Compliance Programs. Virtually all large corporations today have established ethical policies or codes of conduct to help guide their executives and managers (and all company personnel) in making decisions. Typically, an ethical code, or code of conduct, will indicate the company's commitment to legal compliance, as well as to the welfare of its

1. *United States v. Hanousek,* 176 F.3d 1116 (9th Cir. 1999). This case was presented as Case 8.1 in Chapter 8.

2. See Chapter 44 for a discussion of the Federal Trade Commission's role in regulating deceptive trade practices, including misleading advertising.

3. This situation faced the Nestlé Company in the 1970s. That company had concluded, on the basis of a cost-benefit analysis, that it was ethically justified in continuing to market its baby formula in developing countries. Nestlé was severely criticized for its behavior.

employees, suppliers, consumers, and others who may be affected by the company's decisions and practices.

In a large corporation, an ethical code usually is just one part of a comprehensive corporate compliance program. Other components of such a program may include a corporate ethics committee, ethical training programs, and internal audits (to monitor compliance with applicable laws and the company's standards of conduct). Some companies also have a special office to which employees can report—in person or perhaps anonymously via an 800 number—suspected improper conduct, including any legal, ethical, or policy violations that may occur.

By making ethical and legal conduct a top priority, ethical codes and compliance programs help business managers to conduct their firms' affairs responsibly. Still, questions often arise for which there are no clear-cut answers, particularly when they involve conflicting goals. For example, suppose that a company's employees are pressuring management for a wage increase. If the company agrees to increase employees' wages, this will cut into the firm's profits and thus adversely affect the shareholder-owners' interests. The decision to be made here involves not a choice between an ethical and an unethical action but rather a choice between two conflicting goals.

Determining Ethical Priorities. An ethical issue involving conflicting duties can only be resolved by establishing which duties should take priority over others. For example, suppose that the Wellsen Company, a glue-manufacturing firm, learns that thousands of children in several Latin American countries have been inhaling its glue. As a result, many of the children may suffer severe health consequences in the future, including kidney disease and brain damage. Consumer activists have launched a media campaign against Wellsen, accusing it of being unethical by marketing its glue in those countries. What is the right thing to do in this situation? Should Wellsen cease selling its glue in the countries in question even though selling it is legal and profitable?

Assume that Wellsen decides to pull out of those markets. Whose interests would be adversely affected? First of all, the interests of the company's shareholder-owners would be—because the decision probably would result in lower profits. The interests of employees, particularly those with jobs at stake, would also be adversely affected by the decision. Additionally, those firms that supply Wellsen with the materials it needs in the glue-manufacturing process would see decreased profits, at least temporarily, because Wellsen would need fewer materials. Finally, what about the interests of the majority of the consumers in the Latin American countries, who do not misuse the glue? These consumers would also be adversely affected, because they could no longer purchase the glue for home or business purposes.

Clearly, if equal ethical weight were attached to the interests of each group, the right decision would be to continue marketing the product in Latin American countries. Indeed, from a utilitarian perspective, this action might be deemed the most ethical, because the action would benefit the majority of those affected by the decision. From a duty-based (or rights-based) perspective, however, it would be difficult to justify a decision to continue selling a product that was harming some human beings, regardless of the fact that the harm was caused by product misuse.

SECTION 4

Maximum versus Optimum Profits

Today's corporate decision makers are, in a sense, poised on a fulcrum between profitability and ethical responsibility. If they emphasize profits at the expense of perceived ethical responsibilities to other groups, they may become the target of negative media exposure and even lawsuits. If they go too far in the other direction (keep an unprofitable plant open so that the employees do not lose their jobs, invest too heavily in charitable works or social causes, and so on), their profits will suffer and they may have to go out of business.

Striking the right balance on this fulcrum is difficult, and usually some profits must be sacrificed in the process. Instead of maximum profits, many firms today aim for **optimum profits**—the maximum profits a firm can realize while staying within legal *and* ethical limits. In the Wellsen Company's situation, if the decision makers base their reasoning on duty/rights-based ethical standards, they may conclude that they have an ethical duty to pull out of the Latin American markets. In other words, they may decide to settle for optimum profits rather than maximum profits.

Even from a utilitarian perspective, it might be wise to discontinue sales in the Latin American countries in question. Although utilitarian reasoning may lead to the conclusion that there is nothing unethical about continuing sales in those areas—because it would benefit the majority of persons affected by such a decision—Wellsen's reputation could suffer irreparable damage if it did so. In the long run, a decision to continue the sales thus could be an unprofitable one.

Note that in a utilitarian cost-benefit analysis of the ethical issue facing the Wellsen Company, the "cost" of potentially decreased profits in the long run was acknowledged primarily because of the media campaign against Wellsen. In other words, if consumer activists had not created widespread public awareness of Wellsen's actions, the outcome of the utilitarian analysis of the issue would probably be a decision to continue marketing the glue in the Latin American countries.

SECTION 5

The Ever-Changing Ethical Landscape

Society's determination of what constitutes ethical business behavior changes over time. Consider the ethical landscape of business as it existed seventy-five years ago. At that time, a corporation was perceived to have one major duty: to serve the interests of its shareholders (basically, make profitable decisions) and to act within legal limits when doing so. In other words, in the corporate decision-making process, only two questions normally were asked: Is it profitable? Is it legal? The third question (Is it ethical?) was largely answered by the first two.

Indeed, most of the ethical and social issues discussed in this chapter and elsewhere in this text either did not exist or were of little public concern at that time. Technological innovations, the communications revolution, pressing environmental problems, and social movements resulting in greater rights for minorities, women, and consumers have all dramatically changed the society in which we live and, consequently, the business and ethical landscape of the United States. Today, society expects business leaders to acknowledge and fulfill ethical duties to all persons and groups that are affected by the decisions and activities of their firms.

Moreover, the global dimension of business activity today has led to ethical issues that were of little concern to American firms—or to the American public—in the past. We look next at some of these issues.

MONITORING THE EMPLOYMENT PRACTICES OF FOREIGN SUPPLIERS

Many U.S. businesses now contract with companies in developing nations to produce goods, such as shoes and clothing, because the wage rates in those nations are significantly lower than in the United States. Yet what if a foreign company exploits its workers—by hiring women and children at rates below the minimum wage, for example, or by requiring its employees to work long hours in a workplace replete with health hazards? What if the company's supervisors routinely engage in workplace conduct that is offensive to women?

Given today's global communications network, few companies can assume that their actions in other nations will go unnoticed by "corporate watch" groups that discover and publicize unethical corporate behavior. As a result, American businesses today usually take steps to avoid such adverse publicity—either by refusing to deal with certain suppliers or by making arrangements to monitor their suppliers' workplaces to make sure that the workers are not being mistreated.

THE FOREIGN CORRUPT PRACTICES ACT

Another ethical problem in international business dealings has to do with the legitimacy of certain side payments to government officials. In the United States, the majority of contracts are formed within the private sector. In many foreign countries, however, decisions on most major construction and manufacturing contracts are made by government officials because of extensive government regulation and control over trade and industry. Side payments to government officials in exchange for favorable business contracts are not unusual in such countries, nor are they considered to be unethical. In the past, U.S. corporations doing business in developing countries largely followed the dictum, "When in Rome, do as the Romans do."

In the 1970s, however, the U.S. press, and government officials as well, uncovered a number of business scandals involving large side payments by U.S. corporations—such as Lockheed Aircraft—to foreign representatives for the purpose of securing advantageous international trade contracts. In response to this unethical behavior, in 1977 Congress passed the Foreign Corrupt Practices Act (FCPA), which prohibits U.S. businesspersons from bribing foreign officials to secure advantageous contracts.

Prohibition against the Bribery of Foreign Officials. The first part of the FCPA applies to all U.S. companies and their directors, officers, shareholders, employees, and agents. This part prohibits the bribery of most officials of foreign governments if the purpose of the payment is to get the official to act in his or her official capacity to provide business opportunities.

The FCPA does not prohibit payment of substantial sums to minor officials whose duties are ministerial. These payments are often referred to as "grease," or facilitating payments. They are meant to ensure that administrative services that might otherwise be performed at a slow pace are sped up. Thus, for example, if a firm makes a payment to a minor official to speed up an import licensing process, the firm has not violated the FCPA. Generally, the act, as amended, permits payments to foreign officials if such payments are lawful within the foreign country. The act also does not prohibit payments to private foreign companies or other third parties unless the U.S. firm knows that the payments will be passed on to a foreign government in violation of the FCPA.

Accounting Requirements. The second part of the FCPA is directed toward accountants, because in the past bribes were often concealed in corporate financial records. All companies must keep detailed records that "accurately and fairly" reflect the company's financial activities. In addition, all companies must have an accounting system that provides "reasonable assurance" that all transactions entered into by the company are accounted for and legal. These requirements assist in detecting illegal bribes. The FCPA further prohibits any person from making false statements to accountants or false entries in any record or account.

Penalties for Violations. In 1988, the FCPA was amended to provide that business firms that violate the act may be fined up to $2 million. Individual officers or directors who violate the FCPA may be fined up to $100,000 (the fine cannot be paid by the company) and may be imprisoned for up to five years.

Other Nations Denounce Bribery

For twenty years, the FCPA was the only law of its kind in the world, despite attempts by U.S. political leaders to convince other nations to pass similar legislation. That situation is now changing. In 1997, the Organization for Economic Cooperation and Development, to which twenty-six of the world's leading industrialized nations belong, signed a convention (treaty) that made the bribery of foreign public officials a serious crime. Each signatory is obligated to enact legislation within its nation in accordance with the treaty. The agreement will not only improve the ethical climate in international trade but also level the playing field for U.S businesspersons.

Terms and Concepts to Review

business ethics 807	ethical reasoning 808	optimum profits 812
categorical imperative 809	ethics 807	principle of rights 809
cost-benefit analysis 810	moral minimum 810	utilitarianism 810

Chapter Summary

The Nature of Business Ethics	Ethics can be defined as the study of what constitutes right or wrong behavior. Business ethics focuses on how moral and ethical principles are applied in the business context. Business ethics is complicated by the fact that corporations owe ethical (and legal) duties to a number of groups; when these duties come into conflict, difficult choices must be made. The law reflects society's convictions on what constitutes right or wrong behavior. The law has its limits, though, and some actions may be legal yet not be ethical.
Approaches to Ethical Reasoning	1. *Duty-based ethics*—Ethics based on religious beliefs; philosophical reasoning, such as that of Immanuel Kant; and the basic rights of human beings (the principle of rights).

CHAPTER SUMMARY—CONTINUED

Approaches to Ethical Reasoning—continued	2. *Outcome-based ethics (utilitarianism)*–Ethics based on philosophical reasoning, such as that of John Stuart Mill, that focuses on the consequences of an action.
Ethical Decision Making	When deciding whether to undertake a given action, an ethical business firm will typically consider the following questions (if the answer to any question is no, the action should not be undertaken): 1. *Is it profitable?*—If it is not, the action likely will not be undertaken. 2. *Is it legal?*—This may be difficult to predict with certainty given the numerous and frequently changing laws regulating business and the "gray areas" in the law. 3. *Is it ethical?*—Most large firms have ethical codes or policies and corporate compliance programs that guide their determinations of whether certain actions are ethical. Public opinion may also play a role in making such determinations.
Maximum versus Optimum Profits	Corporate decision makers often choose to sacrifice some profits in order to operate ethically in the marketplace. Many firms today aim for *optimum profits*—the maximum profits a firm can realize while staying within legal and ethical limits.
The Ever-Changing Ethical Landscape	What is considered ethical business behavior changes over time. The global dimension of business activity today has led to ethical issues that were of little concern to American firms—and to American society generally—in the past. Two general areas of concern when doing business internationally involve the employment practices of foreign suppliers and the practice of giving side payments to foreign officials to secure favorable contracts.

CASES FOR ANALYSIS

Westlaw. You can access the full text of each case presented below by going to the Westlaw cases on this text's Web site at http://wbl-cs.westbuslaw.com. Each Westlaw case includes the names of all plaintiffs and defendants, the dates on which the case was argued and decided, a brief summary of the issues and decisions in the case, headnotes classifying specific issues in the case according to the West Key Number System, and the court's opinion. Concurring and dissenting opinions, if any, are included as well.

CASE 40.1 CONFLICTING DUTIES

VARITY CORP. V. HOWE

Supreme Court of the United States, 1996.
516 U.S. 489,
116 S.Ct. 1065,
134 L.Ed.2d 130.

Justice *BREYER* delivered the opinion of the Court.

* * * *

I

The key facts, as found by the [federal] District Court after trial, include the following: Charles Howe, and the other respondents, used to work for Massey-Ferguson, Inc., a farm equipment manufacturer, and a wholly owned subsidiary of the petitioner, Varity Corporation. (Since the lower courts found that Varity and Massey-Ferguson were "alter egos," we shall refer to them interchangeably.) These employees all were participants in, and beneficiaries of, Massey-Ferguson's self-funded employee welfare benefit plan—an ERISA [Employee Retirement Income Security Act of 1974] protected plan that Massey-Ferguson itself administered. In the mid-1980's, Varity became concerned that some of Massey-Ferguson's divisions were losing too much money and developed a business plan to deal with the problem.

The business plan—which Varity called "Project Sunshine"—amounted to placing many of Varity's money-losing eggs in one financially rickety basket. It called for a transfer of Massey-Ferguson's money-losing divisions, along with various other debts, to a newly created, separately incorporated subsidiary called Massey Combines. The plan foresaw the possibility that Massey Combines would fail. But it viewed such a failure, from Varity's business perspective, as closer to a victory than to a defeat. That is because Massey Combine's failure would not only eliminate several of Varity's poorly performing divisions, but it would also eradicate various debts that Varity would transfer to Massey Combines, and which, in the absence of the reorganization, Varity's more profitable subsidiaries or divisions might have to pay.

Among the obligations that Varity hoped the reorganization would eliminate were those arising from the Massey-Ferguson benefit plan's promises to pay medical and other nonpension benefits to employees of Massey-Ferguson's money-losing divisions. Rather than terminate those benefits directly (as it had retained the right to do), Varity attempted to avoid the undesirable fallout that could have accompanied cancellation by inducing the failing divisions' employees to switch employers and thereby voluntarily release Massey-Ferguson from its obligation to provide them benefits (effectively substituting the new, self-funded Massey Combines benefit plan for the former Massey-Ferguson plan). Insofar as Massey-Ferguson's employees did so, a subsequent Massey Combines failure would eliminate—simply and automatically, without distressing the remaining Massey-Ferguson employees—what would otherwise have been Massey-Ferguson's obligation to pay those employees their benefits.

To persuade the employees of the failing divisions to accept the change of employer and benefit plan, Varity called them together at a special meeting and talked to them about Massey Combines' future business outlook, its likely financial viability, and the security of their employee benefits. The thrust of Varity's remarks * * * was that the employees' benefits would remain secure if they voluntarily transferred to Massey Combines. As Varity knew, however, the reality was very different. Indeed, the District Court found that Massey Combines was insolvent from the day of its creation and that it hid a $46 million negative net worth by overvaluing its assets and underestimating its liabilities.

After the presentation, about 1,500 Massey-Ferguson employees accepted Varity's assurances and voluntarily agreed to the transfer. (Varity also unilaterally assigned to Massey Combines the benefit obligations it owed to some 4,000 workers who had retired from Massey-Ferguson prior to this reorganization, without requesting permission or informing them of the assignment.) Unfortunately for these employees, Massey Combines ended its first year with a loss of $88 million, and ended its second year in a receivership, under which its employees lost their nonpension benefits. Many of those employees (along with several retirees whose benefit obligations Varity had assigned to Massey Combines and others * * *) brought this lawsuit, seeking the benefits they would have been owed under their old, Massey-Ferguson plan, had they not transferred to Massey Combines.

After trial, the District Court found, among other things, that Varity and Massey-Ferguson, acting as ERISA fiduciaries, had harmed the plan's beneficiaries through deliberate deception. * * * The [U.S.] Court of Appeals [for the Eighth Circuit] later affirmed the District Court's determinations * * * .

We granted *certiorari* * * * .

* * * *

II

ERISA protects employee pensions and other benefits by providing insurance * * * , specifying certain plan characteristics in detail (such as when and how pensions vest), and by setting forth certain general fiduciary duties applicable to the management of both pension and nonpension benefit plans. * * *

* * * *

The * * * question—whether Varity's deception violated ERISA-imposed fiduciary obligations—calls for a brief, affirmative answer. ERISA requires a "fiduciary" to "discharge his duties with respect to a plan solely in the interest of the participants and beneficiaries." To participate knowingly and significantly in deceiving a plan's beneficiaries in order to save the employer money at the beneficiaries' expense is not to act "solely in the interest of the participants and beneficiaries." As other courts have held, "[l]ying is inconsistent with the duty of loyalty owed by all fiduciaries and codified in section 404(a)(1) of ERISA." Because the breach of this duty is sufficient to uphold the decision below, we need not reach the question whether ERISA fiduciaries have any fiduciary duty to disclose truthful information on their own initiative, or in response to employee inquiries.

* * * [W]e can find no adequate basis here, in the statute or otherwise, for any special interpretation that might insulate Varity, acting as a fiduciary, from the legal consequences of the kind of conduct (intentional misrepresentation) that often creates liability even among strangers.

* * * *

For these reasons, the judgment of the Court of Appeals is

Affirmed.

Justice *THOMAS* * * * dissenting.

* * * *

* * * [T]he majority's conclusion that a fiduciary duty was breached is based upon an inaccurate assessment of the record in this case. It is true that Varity expressed falsely optimistic forecasts about its new

venture's prospects for success in an effort to entice employees to transfer to the new company. But the majority, I believe, tells only part of the story * * * . As I read the record, the message Varity conveyed was that the security of jobs and benefits would be contingent upon the success of the new company. Varity repeatedly informed its employees that "[e]mployment conditions in the future will depend on our ability to make Massey Combines Corporation a success and *if changes are considered necessary or appropriate, they will be made.*" ([E]mphasis added). The majority also fails to note that the plan documents expressly reserved to Varity the right "[t]o Terminate, Suspend, Withdraw, Amend or Modify the Plan in Whole or in Part." The Court thus holds today that an employer breaches a fiduciary obligation to participants in an ERISA plan when it makes optimistic statements about the company's financial condition and thereby implies that unvested welfare benefits will be secure, even though the employer simultaneously informs plan participants that changes will be made if economic conditions so require and the plan documents expressly authorize the employer to terminate the unvested welfare benefits at any time. I cannot agree with this result.

* * * *

I respectfully dissent.

CASE 40.2 ETHICAL DECISION MAKING

NEW YORK STATE SOCIETY OF CERTIFIED PUBLIC ACCOUNTANTS v. ERIC LOUIS ASSOCIATES, INC.

United States District Court,
Southern District of New York, 1999.
79 F.Supp.2d 331.

SAND, District Judge.

* * * *

Findings of Fact

Founded in 1897, the [New York State Society of Certified Public Accountants] is a not-for-profit corporation organized and existing under the laws of New York. It has eleven local chapters—each representing a portion of New York State—and a total membership in excess of 30,000. The Society seeks to cultivate, promote, and disseminate information concerning certified public accountants, establish and maintain high standards of integrity, honor, and character among certified public accountants, furnish information regarding accountancy and the practice and methods thereof to its members and the general public, and protect the interests of its members and the general public with respect to the practice of accountancy.

Since 1984, the Society has been using the common-law servicemark "NYSSCPA" to identify itself in connection with services and goods it offers to its professional membership and to the public at large. * * *

* * * [T]he Society uses the NYSSCPA mark on its promotional material, e.g., business cards, mailing envelops, press releases, and letterhead. Furthermore, the Society receives a good deal of unsolicited media coverage, most of which refers to the society as the NYSSCPA.

On November 18, 1994, the Society registered the domain name "nysscpa.org.", and, since March 1997, the Society has operated a web site at this internet address. The web site provides information about the Society, certified public accounting, and accounting in general, including news stories and press releases concerning topics and activities that are of interest to the Society's members. The web site also provides information about Society publications, member services, conferences and social events, the New York State CPA licensing requirements, and CPA societies in other states. Finally, the web site includes a classifieds page, a member directory, and tax forms.

Incorporated in 1996, [Eric Louis Associates (ELA)] is a small firm specializing in * * * placement of financial, accounting, brokerage and support professionals at all levels throughout the New York, New Jersey, [and] Connecticut area. As of April 1999, ELA had two employees and assets of approximately $23,000. On December 9, 1998, ELA registered the domain name "eric-louis.com". On January 8, 1999, ELA registered the domain name "ericlouis.com". On January 9, 1999, ELA registered the domain name "nysscpa.com". Shortly thereafter, ELA began operating identical web sites at each of these three internet addresses. The home page of each site clearly indicated that the site belonged to ELA, stated that the "site is not affiliated with" the Society, and provided a hyperlink to the Society's web site at "www.nysscpa.org". Upon clicking on this hyperlink, the Society's web site would appear "framed" within ELA's site. * * * Furthermore, each of the three sites used "NYSSCPA" as a "meta-tag" [key word] within its HTML code, such that an internet search for NYSSCPA would lead to each of the three sites.

Upon learning of Defendant's use of its NYSSCPA mark, the Society, in a letter dated March 25, 1999, demanded that ELA cease and desist its continued use of the "nysscpa.com" domain name and its hyperlinking to and framing of the Society's web site. In a letter dated March 26, 1999, ELA responded that it would agree to the Society's demands on the condition that the Society paid it $20,000 or provided it, free of charge, an exhibitor's booth at the annual NYSSCPA conference for the next five years. In a memorandum dated April 6, 1999, ELA informed the Society that two local CPA firms had expressed interest in purchasing the "nysscpa.com" domain name. In a letter dated April 6, 1999, the Society rejected ELA's March 26 offer, and reiterated its cease and desist demand. The Society then began preparing a legal action against Defendant, and, in view of Defendant's failure to cease and desist, commenced this action on April 27, 1999. [The allegations included trademark infringement. On May 24, ELA agreed to a permanent injunction. The Society applied for an award of attorney fees.]

Conclusions of Law

* * * *

* * * Defendant's use of the "nysscpa.com" domain name and the "NYSSCPA" meta-tag is clear evidence of an attempt to plagiarize the Society's mark. According to Defendant's web site, Defendant's partners are members of the Society, and thus there is little chance that they were unaware that the Society uses the NYSSCPA mark to identify itself. Furthermore, the name "nysscpa" neither appears to be related to any characteristic of Defendant's business, nor has Defendant asserted any such relation. Therefore, it is highly likely that Defendant adopted the "nysscpa.com" domain name and employed the "NYSSCPA" meta-tag with a clear intent to copy the Society's NYSSCPA mark.

* * * *

Section 35(a) of the Lanham Act provides in relevant part that a court "in exceptional cases may award attorney fees to the prevailing party," in a suit alleging violation of trademark rights * * * . Such fees should be awarded only on evidence of fraud or bad faith. * * *

* * * *

Our earlier determination that Defendant intentionally copied Plaintiff's mark takes us a considerable way toward determining that this copying was tinged with bad faith. * * * Defendant's partners were clearly aware of the Society's mark, and, unlike ELA's other two domain names—"ericlouis.com" and "eric-louis.com"—the "nysscpa.com" domain name clearly was not selected because it reflected some characteristic of ELA. Rather, it appears that ELA adopted * * * it with the intention of capitalizing on plaintiff's reputation and goodwill * * * . As Mr. Elias [testified], ELA was a small, young company in the business of placing CPA's and other financial professionals. It was thus presented with the challenge of making such professionals aware of its services. The web site was presumably created for this purpose. What better way to attract CPA's to this site than to give it the "nysscpa.com" domain name, and embed the "NYSSCPA" meta-tag in the site's HTML code. After all, not only does the Society have upwards of 30,000 members, but its web site includes classified employment advertisements. Hence, any CPA interested in accessing the Society's on-line classifieds, but who was unaware of the Society's exact internet address—and thus tried to access the Society's site by means of "nysscpa.com" or "NYSSCPA"—would find himself at ELA's web site. As the Society succinctly puts the point, "[s]ince, by [Mr. Elias's] own admission, defendant had not developed a reputation to speak of, it simply helped itself to that of the plaintiff."

* * * *

This brings us, finally, to the question of whether Defendant has offered a credible innocent explanation of its adoption of Plaintiff's mark. * * *

* * * *

Consider first Mr. Elias's response to the Society's March 25th cease and desist demand. Even if Mr. Elias genuinely believed that ELA had done nothing wrong prior to this date, this demand put him on notice that ELA's use of the "nysscpa.com" domain name and the "NYSSCPA" meta-tag was potentially illegal. If Mr. Elias had then consulted an attorney and been advised that ELA's actions were arguably legal, ELA could plausibly maintain that its continued infringement * * * of the Society's mark subsequent to the cease and desist demand was not willful. But Mr. Elias chose a quite different course of conduct. Not only did he fail to seek the advice of counsel, but he proceeded to act on his uninformed belief that registration of the "nysscpa.com" domain name had given him certain rights by attempting to sell the name to the Society.

* * * *

Even if we assume, however, that Mr. Elias had not crossed this line on March 26, with his offer to sell the domain name to Plaintiff, he surely crossed it by April 6, 1999: the date Defendant received Plaintiff's second cease and desist demand. * * * Defendant responded to this second cease and desist demand by continuing its two-pronged strategy of neither ceasing and desisting nor seeking the advice of counsel. On this date, therefore—at the latest—Mr. Elias's belief that ELA's actions were not violative of Plaintiff's trademark rights ceased being reasonable. As such, on this date—at the latest—Defendant's conduct commenced being willful and tinged with bad faith.

The Court finds, therefore, that ELA's infringing and diluting conduct subsequent to April 6, 1999 was willful and in bad faith. As such, Defendant's violation of Plaintiff's trademark rights is "exceptional," and the reasonable attorney fees incurred by Plaintiff in protecting these rights should be shifted to Defendant.

* * * *

Conclusion

For the reasons stated above, Plaintiff's application for an award of attorney fees is granted * * * .

CASE 40.3 ETHICAL DECISION MAKING

BLAKEY V. CONTINENTAL AIRLINES, INC.
Supreme Court of New Jersey, 2000.
164 N.J. 38,
751 A.2d 538.

O'HERN, J. [Justice]
* * * *

I.
* * * *

* * * Tammy S. Blakey, a pilot for Continental Airlines since 1984, appears from the record to be a highly qualified commercial airline pilot. In December 1989, Blakey became that airline's first female captain to fly an Airbus or A300 aircraft (A300). * * * Plaintiff was one of five qualified A300 pilots in the service of Continental Airlines. Shortly after qualifying to be a captain on the A300, Blakey complained of sexual harassment and a hostile working environment based on conduct and comments directed at her by male co-employees. From 1990 to 1993, Blakey was based in Newark, New Jersey, * * * . According to Blakey, in February 1991, she began to file systematic complaints with various representatives of Continental about the conduct of her male co-employees. Specifically, Blakey complained to Continental's management concerning pornographic photographs and vulgar gender-based comments directed at her that appeared in the workplace, specifically in her plane's cockpit and other work areas.

In February 1993, Blakey filed a charge of sexual discrimination and retaliation in violation of Title VII of the Civil Rights Act of 1964 and the Civil Rights Act of 1991 against Continental with the Equal Employment Opportunity Commission in Seattle, Washington, her home state. She simultaneously filed a complaint in [a federal district court]. * * * At her own request, Blakey transferred to Houston in May 1993. To be relieved of the continuing stress that she had experienced in Newark, Blakey assumed a voluntary unpaid leave of absence beginning in August 1993.
* * * *

In the midst of that federal litigation, her fellow pilots continued to publish a series of what plaintiff views as harassing gender-based messages, some of which she alleges are false and defamatory. From February to July 1995, a number of Continental's male pilots posted derogatory and insulting remarks about Blakey on the pilots on-line computer bulletin board called the Crew Members Forum ("Forum"). The Forum is accessible to all Continental pilots and crew member personnel through the Internet [service] provider [ISP], CompuServe. * * *

* * * CompuServe is the ISP approved by Continental to provide pilot and crew access to [Continental's information system, which includes flight schedules]. * * * Continental personnel simply need a personal computer, a modem (a device that connects the computer to a phone line), and a phone line. CompuServe provides "membership kits," containing customized computer software to all Continental personnel who may wish to connect to [Continental's information system] in this manner. The CompuServe software provides access * * * to any individual with a Continental employee identification number that identifies that individual as a pilot or crew member. As part of the package provided to pilots and crew personnel, CompuServe made the Crew Members Forum available for crew members to exchange ideas and information. * * *
* * * *

* * * The Forum is like a bulletin board where employees can post messages or "threads" for each other. * * * System operators, or SYSOPS as they are called, provide technical assistance for the Forum. SYSOPS were Continental crew members who volunteered with CompuServe for the position and received no compensation from Continental for that work. Although it was said that Continental management was not permitted to post messages or reply to any messages on the Forum, its chief pilots and assistant chief pilots had access to the Forum if they signed up with CompuServe * * * . [P]laintiff asserts that chief pilots are considered management within Continental. Although Continental may have no duty to monitor the Forum, it is possible that a jury could find that Continental had knowledge, either direct or vicarious through managerial employees, of the content of certain messages posted on the Forum.
* * * *

In August 1995, Blakey sought to amend her federal complaint against Continental to add these allegedly defamatory remarks as the basis for an additional cause of action and as further support for her claim of a hostile environment. The federal court denied leave to amend because "[p]laintiff [had] other judicial recourse available to pursue her claims." In December 1995, Blakey filed this complaint in [a New Jersey state court] seeking "other judicial recourse" against Continental and the pilots alleging [in part] * * * sexual harassment/hostile work environment * * * .

In December 1997, Continental filed a motion for summary judgment * * * , which was subsequently granted in April 1998.

Meanwhile, the federal litigation proceeded to conclusion. In October 1997, a jury in the United States District Court for the District of New Jersey found in favor of Blakey on the claim of sexual harassment, awarding her $480,000 in back pay, $15,000 in front pay, and $500,000 for emotional distress, pain and suffering, but did not award any punitive damages. The jury also found that Blakey had failed to mitigate damages, and subtracted $120,000 from her back pay award of $480,000. The $500,000 award for emotional distress, pain and suffering was subsequently halved.

Returning our attention to these State proceedings, we find that on plaintiff's appeal the [state intermediate appellate court upheld the summary judgment] * * * .

* * * *

We granted plaintiff's petition for certification.

II.

* * * *

* * * *When an employer knows or should know of the harassment and fails to take effective measures to stop it, the employer has joined with the harasser in making the working environment hostile.* The employer, by failing to take action, sends the harassed employee the message that the harassment is acceptable and that the management supports the harasser. "Effective" remedial measures are those reasonably calculated to end the harassment. * * * [Emphasis added.]

* * * *

* * * Continental's liability * * * depend[s] on whether the Crew Members Forum was such an integral part of the workplace that harassment on the Crew Members Forum should be regarded as a continuation or extension of the pattern of harassment that existed in the Continental workplace.

Our common experience tells us how important are the extensions of the workplace where the relations among employees are cemented or sometimes sundered. If an "old boys' network" continued, in an after-hours setting, the belittling conduct that edges over into harassment, what exactly is the outsider (whether black, Latino, or woman) to do? Keep swallowing the abuse or give up the chance to make the team? We believe that severe or pervasive harassment in a work-related setting that continues a pattern of harassment on the job is sufficiently related to the workplace that an informed employer who takes no effective measures to stop it, sends the harassed employee the message that the harassment is acceptable and that the management supports the harasser. * * *

* * * *

CompuServe's role may * * * be analogized to that of a company that builds an old-fashioned bulletin board. If the maker of an old-fashioned bulletin board provided a better bulletin board by setting aside space on it for employees to post messages, we would have little doubt that messages on the company bulletin board would be part of the workplace setting. Here, the Crew Members Forum is an added feature to the company bulletin board.

* * * *

IV.

* * * *

[On remand, the] first step is to sort out those statements that cannot be regarded as harassing or defamatory. Concerning those that may be viewed as harassing, the court must determine if triable issues of fact are presented concerning whether (1) the Crew Members Forum was sufficiently integrated with Continental's operations so as to provide a benefit to it; (2) the employer had notice of the conduct; and (3) the conduct complained of was severe or pervasive enough to make a * * * reasonable person believe that * * * the conditions of employment are altered and the working environment is hostile or abusive. * * * A demonstrated promptness to correct harassment on Continental's part may leave no triable issue of fact on its liability.

* * * *

The judgment of the [state intermediate appellate court] is reversed. The matter is remanded * * * for further proceedings in accordance with this opinion.

CASE PROBLEMS

40–1. George Geary was employed by the United States Steel Corp. to sell tubular products to the oil and gas industry. Geary believed that one of the company's new products, a tubular casing, had not been adequately tested and constituted a serious danger to anyone who used it. Even though Geary at all times performed his duties to the best of his ability, he continued to express his reservations with respect to the company's new product. Geary alleged that because of his complaints, he was summarily discharged without notice. Given these particulars, and in view of the fact that Geary was not a safety expert and had bypassed ordinary company procedures in his complaints, address the following questions. [*Geary v. United States Steel Corp.*, 456 Pa. 171, 319 A.2d 174 (1974)]

(a) Did the employer act wrongfully in discharging Geary?

(b) Did Geary have an ethical duty to complain about the company's product?

(c) Did the employer's need to maintain internal administrative order and harmony in the company outweigh its duty to do all it could to ensure product safety? Suppose that you were a manager and Geary raised the matter with you. How would you act, and what ethical factors would influence your decision?

40–2. In 1984, the General Telephone Co. of Illinois, Inc. (GTE), for reasons of efficiency, decided to consolidate its nationwide operations and eliminate unnecessary job positions. One of the positions eliminated was held by John Burnell, a fifty-two-year-old employee who had worked for GTE for thirty-four years and had always received above-average performance ratings. GTE offered Burnell the choice of either accepting another position within the firm at the same salary or accepting early retirement with a salary continuation for a certain period of time. Burnell did not want to retire, but he was afraid that if he did accept the other position and if the other position was later eliminated, he might not then have the choice of early retirement with the same separation benefit. Because he received no assurances that the other job would be secure in the future, he accepted the early-retirement alternative. Burnell later alleged that he had been "constructively discharged" (forced to resign) because GTE had made his working conditions so intolerable that he was forced to resign. Had GTE constructively discharged Burnell? Can GTE's actions toward Burnell be justified from an ethical standpoint? Discuss. [*Burnell v. General Telephone Co. of Illinois, Inc.*, 181 Ill.App.3d 533, 536 N.E.2d 1387, 130 Ill.Dec. 176 (1989)]

40–3. Beverly Landrine's infant daughter died after the baby swallowed a balloon while playing with a doll known as "Bubble Yum Baby." When a balloon was inserted into the doll's mouth and the doll's arm was pumped, thereby inflating the balloon, the doll simulated the blowing of a bubble gum bubble. The balloon was made by Perfect Product Co. and distributed by Mego Corp. Landrine brought a suit against the manufacturer and distributor, alleging that the balloon was defectively made or inherently unsafe when used by children and that Perfect had failed to warn of the danger associated with the balloon's use. Discuss whether the producer and distributor of the balloon should be held liable for the harm caused by this product. [*Landrine v. Mego Corp.*, 95 A.D.2d 759, 464 N.Y.S.2d 516 (1983)]

40–4. The father of an eleven-year-old child sued the manufacturer of a jungle gym because the manufacturer had failed to warn users of the equipment that they might fall off the gym and get hurt, as the boy did in this case. The father also claimed that the jungle gym was "unreasonably dangerous" (a ground, or basis, for liability under product liability laws) because, as his son began to fall and reached frantically for a bar to grasp, there was no bar within reach. The father based his argument in part on a previous case involving a plaintiff who was injured as a result of somersaulting off a trampoline. In that case [*Pell v. Victor J. Andrew High School*, 123 Ill.App.3d 423, 462 N.E.2d 858, 78 Ill.Dec. 739 (1984)], the court had held that the trampoline's manufacturer was liable for the plaintiff's injuries because it had failed to warn of the trampoline's propensity to cause severe spinal cord damage if it was used for somersaulting. Should the court be convinced by the father's arguments? Why, or why not? [*Cozzi v. North Palos Elementary School District No. 117*, 232 Ill.App.3d 379, 597 N.E.2d 683, 173 Ill.Dec. 70 (1992)]

40–5. Terry Campbell, a six-year-old boy, placed a cigarette lighter under his shirt and lit the lighter. His shirt caught on fire, causing him to suffer severe burns. Terry's mother, Mary Campbell, sued BIC Corp., the manufacturer of the lighter, for damages. Mrs. Campbell contended that the corporation had the capacity to produce cigarette lighters with child-resistant qualities and that its failure to do so was a design defect that made its lighters unreasonably dangerous. (Under strict product liability laws, if a design defect makes a product unreasonably dangerous, the manufacturer and seller of the product may be held liable for any resulting injuries.) BIC sought to dismiss the complaint, claiming that it did not have a duty to design and manufacture child-resistant lighters because the lighters it manufactured were intended only for adult use. BIC cited the *Restatement (Second) of Torts*, which holds that manufacturers are subject to liability for physical harm caused to consumers by the manufacturers' products only when the products are being used "for the purposes and in the manner normally intended." BIC further argued that the risks associated with a lighter are open and obvious and that the corporation therefore should not be held liable. Should BIC be held liable for Terry Campbell's injuries, even though the lighter was not being used as intended? Discuss fully. [*Campbell v. BIC Corp.*, 586 N.Y.S.2d 871 (Sup.Ct., Fulton City, 1992)]

40–6. Two eight-year-old boys, Douglas Bratz and Bradley Baughn, were injured while riding a mini–trail bike manufactured by Honda Motor Co. Bratz, who was driving the bike while Baughn rode as a passenger behind him, ran three stop signs and then collided with a truck. Bratz's helmet flew off on impact because it was unfastened. Baughn was not wearing a helmet. Both the owner's manual for the mini–trail bike and a label on the bike itself prominently stated that the bike was intended for off-the-road use, that the bike should not be used on public streets or highways, and that users should "Always Wear a Helmet." Bratz's father had repeatedly told the boy not to ride the bike in the street. The parents of the boys sued Honda for damages. Honda claimed it had sufficiently warned consumers of the potential dangers that could result if the bike was not used as directed. Should Honda be held responsible for the boys' injuries? Why, or why not? [*Baughn v. Honda Motor Co.*, 107 Wash.2d 127, 727 P.2d 655 (1986)]

40–7. The Seven-Up Co., as part of a marketing scheme, placed two glass bottles of "Like" cola at the front entrance of the Gruenemeier residence. Russell

Gruenemeier, a nine-year-old boy, began playing while holding one of the bottles. He tripped and fell, and the bottle broke, severely cutting his right eye and causing him to eventually lose the eye. Russell's mother brought an action against the Seven-Up Co. for damages, claiming that the cause of Russell's injury was Seven-Up's negligence. She claimed that the company had been negligent in placing potentially dangerous instrumentalities—glass bottles—within the reach of small children and that the firm should have used unbreakable bottles for its marketing scheme. Are glass bottles so potentially dangerous that the Seven-Up Co. should be held liable for the boy's harm? If you were the judge, how would you decide the issue? [*Gruenemeier v. Seven-Up Co.*, 229 Neb. 267, 426 N.W.2d 510 (1988)]

40–8. In 1982, after learning that when pregnant women are exposed to high lead levels their fetuses may be harmed, Johnson Controls, Inc., adopted a "fetal protection policy." The policy prohibited women of childbearing age from working in the company's Battery Division. Employees and their union, United Automobile Workers, brought a suit in a federal court against Johnson, claiming that the policy violated federal law prohibiting employment discrimination on the basis of gender and pregnancy. The relevant statutory provision states that unless pregnant employees differ from others "in their ability or inability to work," they must be "treated the same" as other employees "for all employment related purposes." Does this mean that Johnson's fetal protection policy is illegal? If you were the judge, how would you decide the issue, and why? [*United Automobile Workers v. Johnson Controls, Inc.*, 499 U.S. 187, 111 S.Ct. 1196, 113 L.Ed.2d 158 (1991)]

40–9. Matt Theurer, an eighteen-year-old high school senior, worked part-time at a McDonald's restaurant in Oregon. Theurer volunteered to work an extra shift one day, in addition to his regular shifts (one preceding and one following the extra shift). After working about twelve hours during a twenty-four-hour period, Theurer told the manager that he was tired and asked to be excused from his next regularly scheduled shift so that he could rest. The manager agreed. While driving home from work, Theurer fell asleep at the wheel and crashed into a van driven by Frederic Faverty. Theurer died, and Faverty was severely injured. Faverty sued McDonald's, alleging, among other things, that McDonald's had been negligent in permitting Theurer to drive a car when it should have known that he was too tired to drive safely. Do employers have a duty to prevent fatigued employees from driving home from work? Should such a duty be imposed on them? How should the court decide this issue? How would you decide the issue if you were the judge? [*Faverty v. McDonald's Restaurants of Oregon, Inc.*, 133 Or.App. 514, 892 P.2d 703 (1994)]

40–10. Valdak Corp. operated a car wash that used an industrial dryer to spin-dry towels. The dryer was equipped with a device that was supposed to keep it locked while it spun, but the device often did not work. An employee reached into the dryer while it was spinning, and his arm was cut off above the elbow. The Occupational Safety and Health Administration (OSHA) cited Valdak for, among other things, a willful violation of a machine-guarding regulation and assessed a $28,000 penalty. Valdak appealed the decision, and ultimately the case was reviewed by a federal appellate court. On appeal, Valdak argued, in part, that it did not know about the specific regulation and thus could not be cited for a "willful" violation of it. What will the court decide, and why? [*Valdak Corp. v. Occupational Safety and Health Review Commission*, 73 F.3d 1466 (8th Cir. 1966)]

40–11. Isuzu Motors America, Inc., does not warn its customers of the danger of riding unrestrained in the cargo beds of its pickup trucks. Seventeen-year-old Donald Josue was riding unrestrained in the bed of an Isuzu truck driven by Iaone Frias. When Frias lost control of the truck, it struck a concrete center divider. Josue was ejected, and his consequent injuries rendered him a paraplegic. Josue filed a suit in a Hawaii state court against Isuzu, asserting a variety of legal claims based on its failure to warn of the danger of riding in the bed of the truck. Should Isuzu be held liable for Josue's injuries? Why, or why not? [*Josue v. Isuzu Motors America, Inc.*, 87 Haw. 413, 958 P.2d 535 (1998)]

40–12. Richard and Suzanne Weinstein owned Elm City Cheese Co. Elm City sold its products to three major customers that used the cheese as a "filler" to blend into their cheeses. In 1982, Mark Federico, a certified public accountant, became Elm City's accountant and the Weinsteins' personal accountant. The Weinsteins had known Federico since he was seven years old, and even before he became their accountant he knew the details of Elm City's business. Federico's duties went beyond typical accounting work, and when the Weinsteins were absent, Federico was put in charge of operations. In 1992, Federico was made a vice president of the company, and a year later he was placed in charge of day-to-day operations. He also continued to serve as Elm City's accountant. The relationship between Federico and the Weinsteins deteriorated, and in 1995, he resigned as Elm City's employee and as its accountant. Less than two years later, Federico opened Lomar Foods, Inc., to make the same products as Elm City by the same process and to sell the products to the same customers. Federico located Lomar closer to Elm City's suppliers. Elm City filed a suit in a Connecticut state court against Federico and Lomar, alleging, among other things, misappropriation of trade secrets. Elm City argued that it was entitled to punitive damages because Federico's conduct was "willful and malicious." Federico responded in part that he did not act willfully and maliciously because he did not know that Elm City's business details were trade secrets. Were Federico's actions "willful and malicious"? Were they ethical? Explain. [*Elm City Cheese Co. v. Federico,* 251 Conn. 59, 752 A.2d 1037 (1999)]

40–13. Lockheed Corp. has used the name "Lockheed" since the 1930s. In 1995, Lockheed merged with Martin Marietta Corp., another large company with an international reputation, to form Lockheed Martin Corp. Lockheed Martin, one of the world's largest and best-known aerospace, electronics, and advanced materials manufacturers, continued to use the Lockheed name. In 1998, Dan Parisi registered the domain names "lockheedsucks.com" and "lockheedmartinsucks.com." Parisi used the names to point to a Web site that offered visitors an opportunity to vent their views on Lockheed and other companies. Lockheed demanded that Parisi transfer the names to it. Parisi refused. Lockheed filed a complaint with a provider of arbitration services—the World Intellectual Property Organization Arbitration and Mediation Center (WIPO Center)—asking it to transfer the names. Lockheed contended in part that the names were "confusingly similar" to Lockheed's trademarks. Parisi responded that "no one would reasonably believe [Lockheed] operates a website that appends the word 'sucks' to its name and then uses it to criticize corporate America." In whose favor should the WIPO Center rule, and why? [*Lockheed Martin Corp. v. Parisi,* WIPO Case No. D2000-1015 (2000)]

40–14. Richard Fraser was an "exclusive career insurance agent" under a contract with Nationwide Mutual Insurance Co. Fraser leased computer hardware and software from Nationwide for his business. During a dispute between Nationwide and the Nationwide Insurance Independent Contractors Association, an organization representing Fraser and other exclusive career agents, Fraser prepared a letter to Nationwide's competitors asking whether they were interested in acquiring the represented agents' policyholders. Nationwide obtained a copy of the letter and searched its electronic file server for e-mail indicating that the letter had been sent. It found a stored e-mail that Fraser had sent to a co-worker indicating that the letter had been sent to at least one competitor. The e-mail was retrieved from the co-worker's file of already received and discarded messages stored on the computer. When Nationwide canceled its contract with Fraser, he filed a suit in a federal district court against the firm, alleging, among other things, violations of various federal laws that prohibit the interception of electronic communications during transmission. In whose favor should the court rule, and why? In any case, did Nationwide act ethically in retrieving the e-mail? [*Fraser v. Nationwide Mutual Insurance Co.,* 135 F.Supp.2d 623 (E.D.Pa. 2001)]

40–15. A Question of Ethics

Three-year-old Randy Welch climbed up to a shelf and picked up a disposable butane cigarette lighter. Randy then used the lighter to ignite a flame, which set fire to his pajama top. Welch and his parents brought a product liability suit against the lighter's manufacturer, Scripto-Tokai Corp., for damages. One of the questions raised in this case was whether the risks attending the lighter were sufficiently "open and obvious" that the manufacturer did not need to warn of those risks. [*Welch v. Scripto-Tokai Corp.,* 651 N.E.2d 810 (Ind.App. 1995)]

1. If you were the judge, how would you decide this issue? Explain your reasoning.
2. Generally, how can a court decide what kinds of risks should be open and obvious for the ordinary consumer? How can a business decision maker decide such questions?

For updated links to resources available on the Web, as well as a variety of other materials, visit this text's Web site at

http://wbl-cs.westbuslaw.com

The Web site of DePaul University's Institute for Business and Professional Ethics includes several examples of the types of ethical issues that can arise in the business context. Go to

http://condor.depaul.edu/ethics/biz17.html

You can find articles on issues relating to shareholders and corporate accountability at the Corporate Governance Web site. Go to

http://www.corpgov.net

Numerous online groups focus on the activities of various corporations from an ethical perspective. A good starting point for locating these kinds of Web sites is Baobab's Corporate Power Information Center at

http://www.baobabcomputing.com/corporatepower

Legal Research Exercises on the Web

Go to http://wbl-cs.westbuslaw.com, the Web site that accompanies this text. Select "Interactive Study Center," and then click on "Chapter 40." There you will find the following Internet research exercises that you can perform to learn more about ethics and business decision making:

Activity 40–1: Ethics in Business

Activity 40–2: Environmental Self-Audits

FOCUS ON LEGAL REASONING

Tschetter v. Berven

The elements of the definition of a *security,* in the context of the securities laws, are listed in Chapter 37. The ownership of a limited liability company (LLC) is reviewed in Chapter 38. In this *Focus on Legal Reasoning,* we examine *Tschetter v. Breven,*[1] a decision that considers whether an "investment unit" in an LLC falls within the definition of a security.

CASE BACKGROUND

In 1994, Venerts Investment, Inc., entered into an agreement with Country Hospitality Corporation to build and run several Country Kitchen restaurants. Venerts formed Huron Kitchen LLC, a limited liability company, to construct and own one of the restaurants in Huron, South Dakota. An operating agreement was entered into in April 1995. In July, Venerts entered into a fifteen-year management contract with Country Kitchen International (CKI), which agreed to run Huron LLC's restaurant.

Venerts contacted Marvie, Kim, Clarence, and Goldie Tschetter, who bought "investment units" in Huron LLC in September. The restaurant opened that fall. Within months, financial problems led the Tschetters, and others, to personally guarantee bank loans to Huron LLC. After the restaurant closed in November 1996, the bank filed a suit in a South Dakota state court against the guarantors to recover the amount of the loans.

The Tschetters filed claims with the court against Venerts's owners, including James Berven. The Tschetters filed a motion for summary judgment, asserting in part that the Huron units were "securities" and that Venerts's owners had breached South Dakota securities law by failing to advise the Tschetters of the risks attending their investments. The court denied the motion and dismissed the Tschetters' claims. The Tschetters appealed to the South Dakota Supreme Court.

1. 2001 SD 11, 621 N.W.2d 372 (2001).

MAJORITY OPINION

SABERS, Justice.

* * * *

We must * * * begin where all analyses of investment contracts start, with *Securities & Exchange Commission v. W. J. Howey Co.,* 328 U.S. 293, 66 S.Ct. 1100, 90 L.Ed. 1244 (1946). LLC membership interests constitute "securities" if they fulfill the criteria established by the United States Supreme Court in Howey. The United States Supreme Court has stated that an "investment contract" is a "security" when a person 1.) invests money 2.) in a common enterprise and 3.) is led to expect profits solely from the efforts of the promotor or a third party.

The critical inquiry is the third prong of the *Howey* test—whether Tschetters were led to expect profits solely from the efforts of the promotor or a third party. We acknowledge, as other courts have done, that the use of the term "solely" is not to be taken literally. Rather, the third prong is satisfied if the efforts made by those other than the investor are the undeniably significant ones, those essential managerial efforts which effect the failure or success of the enterprise. The United States Supreme Court has also noted *the definition of a security "embodies a flexible rather than a static principle, one that is capable of adaptation to meet the countless and variable schemes devised by those who seek the use of the money of others in the promise of profits."* [Emphasis added.]

The leading case interpreting the third prong of the *Howey* test is *Williamson v. Tucker,* 645 F.2d 404 (5th Cir.1981). * * * The *Williamson* court set forth three factors to aid in this determination:

> 1. an agreement among the parties leaves so little power in the hands of the partner or venturer that the arrangement in fact distributes power as would a limited partnership; or
>
> 2. the partner or venturer is so inexperienced and unknowledgeable in business affairs that he is incapable of intelligently exercising his partnership or venture powers; or
>
> 3. the partner or venturer is so dependent on some unique entrepreneurial or managerial ability of the promoter or manager that he cannot replace the manager or the enterprise or otherwise exercise meaningful partnership or venture powers.

* * *

* * * Tschetters had substantial rights and powers. South Dakota law vests the members of an LLC with management powers in proportion to their contribution of capital. The members have the power to elect the managers of the LLC and set their responsibilities.

In addition, the Operating Agreement vested management powers of the Huron LLC in its members, which included Tschetters. These members were given notice of meetings and any member could call a meeting. The day-to-day decisions were made by two managers who were required to be members of the Huron LLC, and selected by the other members. The Huron LLC maintained and provided access to all records of actions taken by its members. Members could authorize loans on behalf of the company by agreement. The members had the authority to select an attorney to review the legal affairs of the Huron LLC. The members had the right to receive profits and distributions when warranted. The members could authorize incidental expenses within an aggregate of $12,500. The members were empowered to make any other routine actions incidental to the day-to-day activity of Huron LLC. The members were allowed to select officers for the Huron LLC and could remove the accountant with or without cause.

Focus on Legal Reasoning

The Huron LLC's operating agreement establishes that substantial power and responsibility was vested in its members. * * * The minutes kept by the Huron LLC show that Tschetters were informed and active in this entity. Tschetters' actions on behalf of Huron LLC after the restaurant began to fail shows they were aware of and capable of exercising the powers which they held as members.

Tschetters stress the fact that Huron LLC entered into a management agreement with [CKI] to establish their dependence on the efforts of others. However, our inquiry is the Tschetters role in the Huron LLC. The fact that Huron LLC acquiesced in management powers to [CKI] is not determinative. The Huron LLC retained the ability to terminate the management contract if the manager failed to perform "any material covenant, agreement, term or provision * * * for a period of thirty days." Apparently, here, the failure to perform exceeded a period of thirty days several times over. The management agreement required [CKI] to "direct, supervise, manage, and operate the [r]estaurant in an efficient and economical manner," "execute a marketing plan to attract guests," "determine and arrange to contract for all advertising and promotion * * * deem[ed] necessary and appropriate for the operation of the [r]estaurant." Apparently, the failure to perform as required caused [CKI's] termination. The management agreement does not divest all power from Huron LLC but, instead, provides Tschetters and other members of Huron LLC substantial power and ability to conduct the necessary oversight of the restaurant's operation.

The record fails to establish that this was a situation where the managers were so dominant that the members would be lost without them. The mere choice by a [member] to remain passive is not sufficient to create a security interest. This determination does not and should not hinge on the particular degree of responsibility assumed within the firm, nor does the delegation of membership responsibilities, or the failure to exercise membership powers, diminish the investor's legal right to a voice in partnership or company matters. We acknowledge that the investor asserting that an "investment contract" constitutes a "security" has a difficult burden to overcome.

Tschetters have the burden of establishing that their expectation of profits was based on the entrepreneurial efforts of others to establish an "investment contract." * * * [O]nly in unusual circumstances would a member-managed LLC be able to argue that they must rely on the entrepreneurial efforts of others rather than on their own management skills. This may be especially true when, as here, the investment related to a restaurant * * * . In such an entity, the members retain substantial power over the LLC. The general framework is essentially antithetical to the notion of member passivity.

We hold that the third prong of the *Howey* test * * * has not been met. * * *

If an interest in a limited liability company constitutes a "security," then that entity must comply with our securities law or exempt themselves from the application of those laws. This question can only be addressed on a case-by-case basis. Here, Tschetters did not sustain their burden. These "units" were not "securities" under this law * * * .

* * * *

We conclude that the trial court correctly granted summary judgment in favor of Venerts.

Questions for Analysis

1. **Legal Analysis.** In the *Tschetter* case, the court cites *Securities & Exchange Commission v. W. J. Howey Co.*, 328 U.S. 293, 66 S.Ct. 1100, 90 L.Ed. 1244 (1946), and *Williamson v. Tucker,* 645 F.2d 404 (5th Cir. 1981) (see the *E-Links* feature at the end of Chapter 2 for instructions on how to access the opinions of the federal courts). For what purpose did the *Tschetter* court cite these cases? How did these courts commonly approach the issue of what constitutes a "security"?

2. **Legal Reasoning.** From a reading of the Tschetter opinion, what was the plaintiffs' likely argument regarding control of the LLC? What did the majority conclude on this issue, and why?

3. **Political Dimensions.** Should there be any effect on the liability of investors in a limited liability entity if the investors have the power to control the enterprise but choose to remain passive?

4. **Implications for the Business Investor.** Does the holding in the *Tschetter* case indicate any legal steps that an investor might take when considering a particular investment?

Westlaw Online Research

Westlaw. Go to this text's companion Web site, at http://wbl-cs.westbuslaw.com, and click on the Westlaw icon. Use your special password to access the full text of this case, including the dissenting opinions. Read through the case, and then answer the following questions.

1. Read the dissenting opinion. What was the dissent's major point concerning the "control" issue? What was the dissent's reasoning on this point?
2. Check the majority's outline of its opinion. What main questions, other than the issue in the excerpt in this *Focus on Legal Reasoning* feature, were directed to the court?
3. As stated by the court, on what basis might the investors have maintained an action against CKI?

Unit Eight
Labor and Employment Relations

CONTENTS

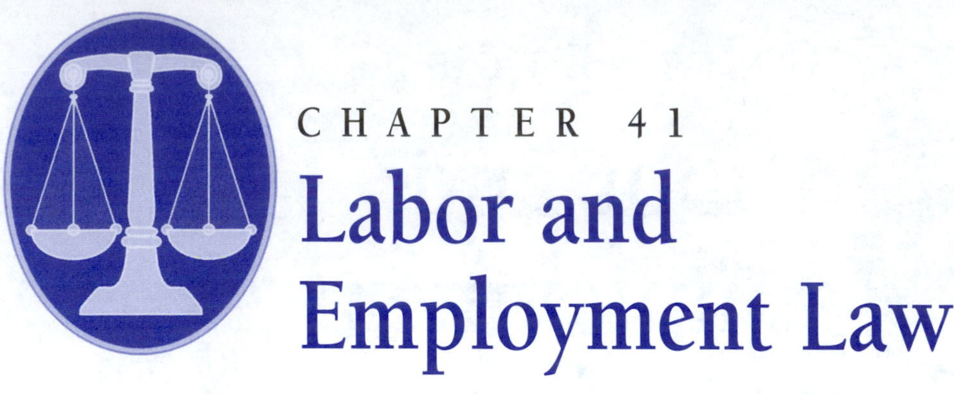

CHAPTER 41 Labor and Employment Law

At one time in the United States, employment relationships were governed primarily by the common law. Under the common law doctrine of **employment at will,** normally either party can terminate the employment relationship at any time and for any reason, unless an employment contract provides to the contrary. Other common law concepts governing employment relationships include those of contract, agency, and tort law.

Today, in contrast, the workplace is regulated extensively by federal and state statutes. Recall from Chapter 1 that common law doctrines only apply to areas *not* covered by statutory law. The common law employment-at-will doctrine has thus been displaced to a significant extent by statutory law. Additionally, even when the at-will doctrine is applicable, courts make a number of exceptions to the doctrine—as you will read later in this chapter.

In this chapter, we look at the most significant laws regulating employment relationships. We examine other important laws regulating the workplace—those prohibiting employment discrimination—in the next chapter.

Section 1

Wage-Hour Laws

In the 1930s, to protect employees against some of the adverse effects of the employment-at-will doctrine, Congress enacted several laws regulating the wages and working hours of employees. In 1931, Congress passed the Davis-Bacon Act,[1] which requires the payment of "prevailing wages" to employees of contractors and subcontractors working on government construction projects. In 1936, the Walsh-Healey Act[2] was passed. This act requires that a minimum wage, as well as overtime pay of time and a half, be paid to employees of manufacturers or suppliers entering into contracts with agencies of the federal government.

In 1938, with the passage of the Fair Labor Standards Act[3] (FLSA), Congress extended wage-hour requirements to cover all employers engaged in interstate commerce or engaged in the production of goods for interstate commerce. We examine here the FLSA's provisions in regard to child labor, maximum hours, and minimum wages.

Child Labor

The FLSA prohibits oppressive child labor. Children under fourteen years of age are allowed to do certain types of work, such as deliver newspapers, work for their parents, and be employed in the entertainment and (with some exceptions) agricultural areas. Children who are fourteen or fifteen years of age are allowed to work, but not in hazardous occupations. There are also numerous restrictions on how many hours per day and per week they can work. For example, they cannot work during school hours, for more than three hours on a school day (or eight hours on a nonschool day), for more than eighteen hours during a school week (or forty hours during a nonschool week), or before 7 A.M. or after 7 P.M. (9 P.M. during the summer). Most states require persons under sixteen years of age to obtain work permits.

1. 40 U.S.C. Sections 276a–276a-5.

2. 41 U.S.C. Sections 35–45.

3. 29 U.S.C. Sections 201–260.

Persons between the ages of sixteen and eighteen do not face such restrictions on working times and hours, but they cannot be employed in hazardous jobs or in jobs detrimental to their health and well-being. Persons over the age of eighteen are not affected by any of the above-mentioned restrictions.

HOURS AND WAGES

Under the FLSA, any employee who agrees to work more than forty hours per week must be paid no less than one and a half times his or her regular pay for all hours over forty. Certain employees are exempt from the overtime provisions of the act. Exempt employees fall into four categories: executives, administrative employees, professional employees, and outside salespersons. Generally, to fall into one of these categories, an employee must earn more than a specified amount of income per week and devote a certain percentage of work time to the performance of specific types of duties, as determined by the FLSA. To qualify as an outside salesperson, the employee must regularly engage in sales work away from the office and spend no more than 20 percent of work time per week performing duties other than sales.

The FLSA provides that a **minimum wage** of a specified amount (currently, $5.15 per hour) must be paid to employees in covered industries. Congress periodically revises the amount of the minimum wage. Under the FLSA, the term *wages* includes the reasonable costs of the employer in furnishing employees with board, lodging, and other facilities if they are customarily furnished by that employer.

SECTION 2

Labor Unions

In the 1930s, in addition to wage-hour laws, the government enacted several other laws. These laws protect employees' rights to join labor unions, to bargain with management over the terms and conditions of employment, and to conduct strikes.

FEDERAL LABOR LAWS

Federal labor laws governing union-employer relations have developed considerably since the first law was enacted in 1932. Initially, the laws were concerned with protecting the rights and interests of workers. Subsequent legislation placed some restraints on unions and granted rights to employers. We look here at four major federal statutes regulating union-employer relations.

Norris-LaGuardia Act. Congress protected peaceful strikes, picketing, and boycotts in 1932 in the Norris-LaGuardia Act.[4] The statute restricted the power of federal courts to issue injunctions against unions engaged in peaceful strikes. In effect, this act declared a national policy permitting employees to organize.

National Labor Relations Act. One of the foremost statutes regulating labor is the National Labor Relations Act (NLRA) of 1935.[5] This act established the rights of employees to engage in collective bargaining and to strike. The act also specifically defined a number of employer practices as unfair to labor:

1. Interference with the efforts of employees to form, join, or assist labor organizations or to engage in concerted activities for their mutual aid or protection.
2. An employer's domination of a labor organization or contribution of financial or other support to it.
3. Discrimination in the hiring of or the awarding of tenure to employees for reason of union affiliation.
4. Discrimination against employees for filing charges under the act or giving testimony under the act.
5. Refusal to bargain collectively with the duly designated representative of the employees.

The act also created the National Labor Relations Board (NLRB) to oversee union elections and to prevent employers from engaging in unfair and illegal union-related activities and unfair labor practices. The purpose of the NLRA was to secure for employees the rights to organize; to bargain collectively through representatives of their own choosing; and to engage in concerted activities for organizing, collective bargaining, and other purposes.

The NLRB has the authority to investigate employees' charges of unfair labor practices and to serve complaints against employers in response to these charges. The NLRB may also issue **cease-and-desist orders**—orders compelling employers to

4. 29 U.S.C. Sections 101–110, 113–115.

5. 20 U.S.C. Sections 151–169.

cease engaging in the unfair practices—when violations are found. Cease-and-desist orders can be enforced by a circuit court of appeals if necessary. Arguments over alleged unfair labor practices are first decided by the NLRB and may then be appealed to a federal court.

Labor-Management Relations Act. The Labor-Management Relations Act (LMRA) of 1947[6] was passed to proscribe certain unfair union practices, such as the *closed shop*. A **closed shop** is a firm that requires union membership of its workers as a condition of employment. Although the act made the closed shop illegal, it preserved the legality of the union shop. A **union shop** does not require membership as a prerequisite for employment but can, and usually does, require that workers join the union after a specified amount of time on the job.

The act also prohibited unions from refusing to bargain with employers, engaging in certain types of picketing, and featherbedding (causing employers to hire more employees than necessary). In addition, the act allowed individual states to pass their own **right-to-work laws**—laws making it illegal for union membership to be required for *continued* employment in any establishment. Thus, union shops are technically illegal in states with right-to-work laws.

Labor-Management Reporting and Disclosure Act. The Labor-Management Reporting and Disclosure Act (LMRDA) of 1959[7] established an employee bill of rights and reporting requirements for union activities. The act strictly regulates internal union business procedures. Union elections, for example, are regulated by the LMRDA, which requires that regularly scheduled elections of officers occur and that secret ballots be used. Former convicts and Communists are prohibited from holding union office. Moreover, union officials are accountable for union property and funds. Members have the right to attend and to participate in union meetings, to nominate officers, and to vote in most union proceedings.

The act also outlawed **hot-cargo agreements**—agreements in which employers voluntarily agree with unions not to handle, use, or deal in goods of other employers produced by nonunion employees. The act made all such boycotts (called **secondary boycotts**) illegal.

6. 29 U.S.C. Sections 141 *et seq.*

7. 29 U.S.C. Sections 401 *et seq.*

Union Organization

Suppose that the workers of a particular firm want to join a union. How is a union formed? Typically, the first step in the process is to have the workers sign authorization cards. An authorization card usually states that the worker desires to have a certain union, such as the American Federation of Labor and Congress of Industrial Organizations (AFL–CIO), represent the work force. If those in favor of the union can obtain authorization cards from a majority of the workers, they may present the cards to the employer and ask the employer to recognize the union formally. If the employer refuses to do so, the unionizers can petition the NLRB for an election.

Union Elections. For an election to be held, the unionizers must demonstrate that at least 30 percent of the workers to be represented support a union or an election on unionization. The NLRB supervises the election and ensures that the voting is secret and that the voters are eligible. If the election is a fair one and if the proposed union receives majority support, the NLRB certifies the union as the bargaining representative for the employees.

Union Election Campaigns. Many disputes between labor and management arise during union election campaigns. Generally, the employer has control over unionizing activities that take place on company property and during working hours. Employers may thus limit the campaign activities of union supporters. For example, an employer may prohibit all solicitations and pamphlets on company property as long as the employer has a legitimate business reason for doing so. Suppose that a union sought to organize clerks at a department store. Courts have found that an employer can prohibit all solicitation in areas of the store open to the public. Union campaign activities in these circumstances could seriously interfere with the store's business. The employer may not, however, discriminate in its prohibition against solicitation in the workplace. For example, the employer could not prohibit union solicitation but allow solicitation for charitable causes.

An employer may also campaign among its workers against the union, but the NLRB carefully monitors and regulates the campaign tactics of management. Otherwise, management might use its economic power to coerce the workers to vote not to unionize. For example, an employer might tell its workers, "If the union wins, you'll all be fired." The NLRB prohibits employers from making such threats. If the employer issues threats or engages in other unfair labor practices, the NLRB may certify the union even though it lost the election. Alternatively, the NLRB may ask a court to order a new election.

COLLECTIVE BARGAINING

If a fair election is held and the union wins, the NLRB will certify the union as the *exclusive bargaining representative* of the workers. The central legal right of a union is to engage in collective bargaining on the members' behalf. **Collective bargaining** can be defined as the process by which labor and management negotiate the terms and conditions of employment, including wages, benefits, working conditions, and other matters. Through collective bargaining, union representatives elected by union members speak on behalf of the members at the bargaining table.

When a union is officially recognized, it may demand to bargain with the employer and negotiate new terms or conditions of employment. In collective bargaining, as in most other business negotiations, each side uses its economic power to pressure or persuade the other side to grant concessions.

Bargaining is a somewhat vague term. Bargaining does not mean that one side must give in to the other or that compromises must be made. It does mean that a demand to bargain with the employer must be taken seriously and that both sides must bargain in "good faith." Good faith bargaining requires that management, for example, must be willing to meet with union representatives and consider the union's wishes when negotiating a contract. Examples of bad faith bargaining on the part of management include engaging in a campaign among workers to undermine the union, constantly shifting positions on disputed contract terms, and sending bargainers who lack authority to commit the company to a contract. If an employer (or a union) refuses to bargain in good faith without justification, it has committed an unfair labor practice, and the other party may petition the NLRB for an order requiring good faith bargaining.

STRIKES

Even when labor and management have bargained in good faith, they may be unable to reach a final agreement. When extensive collective bargaining has been conducted and an impasse results, the union may call a strike against the employer to pressure it into making concessions. A **strike** occurs when the unionized employees leave their jobs and refuse to work. The workers also typically picket the plant, standing outside the facility with signs that complain of management's unfairness.

A strike is an extreme action. Striking workers lose their right to be paid, and management loses production and may lose customers, whose orders cannot be filled. Labor law regulates the circumstances and conduct of strikes. Most strikes are "economic strikes," which are initiated because the union wants a better contract. A union may also strike when the employer has engaged in unfair labor practices.

The right to strike is guaranteed by the NLRA, within limits, and strike activities, such as picketing, are protected by the free speech guarantee of the First Amendment to the Constitution. Nonworkers have a right to participate in picketing an employer. The NLRA also gives workers the right to refuse to cross a picket line of fellow workers who are engaged in a lawful strike. Employers are permitted to hire replacement workers to substitute for the workers who are on strike.

An important issue concerns the rights of strikers after a strike ends. In a typical economic strike over working conditions, the strikers have no right to return to their jobs. If satisfactory replacement workers have been found, the strikers may find themselves out of work. The law does prohibit the employer from discriminating against former strikers, however. Employers must give former strikers preferential rights to any new vacancies that arise and also allow them to retain their seniority rights. Different rules apply when a union strikes because the employer has engaged in unfair labor practices. In this situation, the employer may still hire replacements but must give the strikers back their jobs once the strike is over.

SECTION 3

Worker Health and Safety

Under the common law, employees injured on the job had to rely on tort law or contract law theories in suits they brought against their employers. Additionally, workers had some recourse under the common law governing agency relationships (discussed in Chapters

31 and 32), which imposes a duty on a principal-employer to provide a safe workplace for his or her agent-employee. Today, numerous state and federal statutes protect employees from the risk of accidental injury, death, or disease resulting from their employment. This section discusses the primary federal statute governing health and safety in the workplace, along with state workers' compensation acts.

The Occupational Safety and Health Act

At the federal level, the primary legislation for employee health and safety protection is the Occupational Safety and Health Act of 1970.[8] Congress passed this act in an attempt to ensure safe and healthful working conditions for practically every employee in the country. The act provides for specific standards that employers must meet, plus a general duty to keep workplaces safe.

Enforcement Agencies. Three federal agencies develop and enforce the standards set by the Occupational Safety and Health Act. The Occupational Safety and Health Administration (OSHA) is part of the Department of Labor and has the authority to promulgate standards, make inspections, and enforce the act. OSHA has safety standards governing many workplace details, such as the structural stability of ladders and the requirements for railings. OSHA also establishes standards that protect employees against exposure to substances that may be harmful to their health.

The National Institute for Occupational Safety and Health is part of the Department of Health and Human Services. Its main duty is to conduct research on safety and health problems and to recommend standards to OSHA for adoption. Finally, the Occupational Safety and Health Review Commission is an independent agency set up to handle appeals from actions taken by OSHA administrators.

Procedures and Violations. OSHA compliance officers may enter and inspect facilities of any establishment covered by the Occupational Safety and Health Act.[9] Employees may also file complaints of violations. Under the act, an employer cannot discharge an employee who files a complaint or who, in good faith, refuses to work in a high-risk area if bodily harm or death might result.

Employers with eleven or more employees are required to keep occupational injury and illness records for each employee. Each record must be made available for inspection when requested by an OSHA inspector. Whenever a work-related injury or disease occurs, employers must make reports directly to OSHA. Whenever an employee is killed in a work-related accident or when five or more employees are hospitalized in one accident, the employer must notify the Department of Labor within forty-eight hours. If the company fails to do so, it will be fined. Following the accident, a complete inspection of the premises is mandatory.

Criminal penalties for willful violation of the Occupational Safety and Health Act are limited. Employers may be prosecuted under state laws, however. In other words, the act does not preempt state and local criminal laws.[10]

State Workers' Compensation Laws

State **workers' compensation laws** establish an administrative procedure for compensating workers injured on the job. Instead of suing, an injured worker files a claim with the administrative agency or board that administers the local workers' compensation claims.

Most workers' compensation statutes are similar. No state covers all employees. Typically excluded are domestic workers, agricultural workers, temporary employees, and employees of common carriers (companies that provide transportation services to the public). Generally, the statutes cover minors. Usually, the statutes allow employers to purchase insurance from a private insurer or a state fund to pay workers' compensation benefits in the event of a claim. Most states also allow employers to be *self-insured*—that is, employers who show an ability to pay claims do not need to buy insurance.

In general, the right to recover benefits is predicated wholly on the existence of an employment relationship and the fact that the worker's injury was *accidental* and *occurred on the job or in the course of employment,* regardless of fault. Intentionally in-

8. 29 U.S.C. Sections 553, 651–678.

9. In the past, warrantless inspections were conducted. In 1978, however, the United States Supreme Court held that warrantless inspections violated the warrant clause of the Fourth Amendment to the Constitution. See *Marshall v. Barlow's, Inc.*, 436 U.S. 307, 98 S.Ct. 1816, 56 L.Ed.2d 305 (1978).

10. *Pedraza v. Shell Oil Co.*, 942 F.2d 48 (1st Cir. 1991); *cert. denied, Shell Oil Co. v. Pedraza,* 502 U.S. 1082, 112 S.Ct. 993, 117 L.Ed.2d 154 (1992).

flicted self-injury, for example, would not be considered accidental and hence would not be covered. If an injury occurred while an employee was commuting to or from work, it usually would not be considered to have occurred on the job or in the course of employment and hence would not be covered.

An employee must notify his or her employer of an injury promptly (usually within thirty days of the injury's occurrence). Generally, an employee also must file a workers' compensation claim with the appropriate state agency or board within a certain period (sixty days to two years) from the time the injury is first noticed, rather than from the time of the accident.

An employee's acceptance of workers' compensation benefits bars the employee from suing for injuries caused by the employer's negligence. By barring lawsuits for negligence, workers' compensation laws also bar employers from raising common law defenses to negligence, such as contributory negligence. For example, an employer can no longer raise such defenses as contributory negligence or assumption of risk to avoid liability for negligence. A worker may sue an employer who *intentionally* injures the worker, however.

Westlaw. See Case 41.1 at the end of this chapter. To view the full, unedited case from Westlaw,® go to this text's Web site at **http://wbl-cs.westbuslaw.com**.

SECTION 4

Income Security

Federal and state governments participate in insurance programs designed to protect employees and their families by covering the financial impact of retirement, disability, death, hospitalization, and unemployment. The key federal law on this subject is the Social Security Act of 1935.[11]

Social Security and Medicare

The Social Security Act of 1935 provides for old-age (retirement), survivors, and disability insurance. The act is therefore often referred to as OASDI. Both employers and employees must "contribute" under the Federal Insurance Contributions Act (FICA)[12] to help pay for the employees' loss of income on retirement. The basis for the employee's and the employer's contribution is the employee's annual wage base—the maximum amount of the employee's wages that are subject to the tax. The employer withholds the employee's FICA contribution from the employee's wages and then matches this contribution. (In 2002, employers were required to withhold 6.2 percent of each employee's wages, up to a maximum amount of $84,900, and to match this contribution.)

Retired workers are eligible to receive monthly payments from the Social Security Administration, which administers the Social Security Act. Social Security benefits are fixed by statute but increase automatically with increases in the cost of living.

Medicare, a health-insurance program, is administered by the Social Security Administration for people sixty-five years of age and older and for some under age sixty-five who are disabled. It has two parts, one pertaining to hospital costs and the other to nonhospital medical costs, such as visits to doctors' offices. People who have Medicare hospital insurance can obtain additional federal medical insurance if they pay small monthly premiums, which increase as the cost of medical care increases. As with Social Security contributions, both the employer and the employee contribute to Medicare. Currently, 1.45 percent of the amount of all wages and salaries paid to employees, plus a matching amount paid by the employer, go toward financing Medicare. There is no cap on the amount of wages subject to the Medicare tax.

Westlaw. See Case 41.2 at the end of this chapter. To view the full, unedited case from Westlaw,® go to this text's Web site at **http://wbl-cs.westbuslaw.com**.

Private Pension Plans

There has been significant legislation to regulate employee retirement plans set up by employers to supplement Social Security benefits. The major federal act covering these retirement plans is the Employee Retirement Income Security Act (ERISA) of 1974.[13] This statute empowers the Labor Management Services Administration of the Department of Labor to enforce its provisions governing employers who have private pension funds for their employees. ERISA does not require an employer to establish a

11. 42 U.S.C. Sections 301–1397e.

12. 26 U.S.C. Sections 3101–3125.

13. 29 U.S.C. Sections 1001 *et seq.*

pension plan. When a plan exists, however, ERISA establishes standards for its management.

A key provision of ERISA concerns vesting. **Vesting** gives an employee a legal right to receive pension benefits at some future date when he or she stops working. Before ERISA was enacted, some employees who had worked for companies for as long as thirty years received no pension benefits when their employment terminated, because those benefits had not vested. ERISA establishes complex vesting rules. Generally, however, all employee contributions to pension plans vest immediately, and employee rights to employer pension-plan contributions vest after five years of employment.

In an attempt to prevent mismanagement of pension funds, ERISA has established rules on how they must be invested. Pension managers must be cautious in their investments and refrain from investing more than 10 percent of the fund in securities of the employer. ERISA also contains detailed record-keeping and reporting requirements.

Unemployment Compensation

The United States has a system of unemployment insurance in which employers pay into a fund, the proceeds of which are paid out to qualified unemployed workers. The Federal Unemployment Tax Act of 1935[14] created a state-administered system that provides unemployment compensation to eligible individuals. The FUTA and state laws require employers that fall under the provisions of the act to pay unemployment taxes at regular intervals.

Section 5

COBRA

Federal legislation also addresses the issue of health insurance for workers whose jobs have been terminated and who are thus no longer eligible for group health-insurance plans. The Consolidated Omnibus Budget Reconciliation Act (COBRA) of 1985[15] prohibits the elimination of a worker's medical, optical, or dental insurance coverage on the voluntary or involuntary termination of the worker's employment. The act applies to most workers who have either lost their jobs or had their hours decreased so that they are no longer eligible for coverage under the employer's health plan. Only workers fired for gross misconduct are excluded from protection.

Application of COBRA

The worker has sixty days (beginning with the date that the group coverage would stop) to decide whether to continue with the employer's group insurance plan. If the worker chooses to discontinue the coverage, the employer has no further obligation. If the worker chooses to continue coverage, however, the employer is obligated to keep the policy active for up to eighteen months. If the worker is disabled, the employer must extend coverage up to twenty-nine months. The coverage provided must be the same as that enjoyed by the worker prior to the termination or reduction of employment. If family members were originally included, for example, COBRA would prohibit their exclusion. This is not a free ride for the worker, however. To receive continued benefits, he or she may be required to pay all of the premium, as well as a 2 percent administrative charge.

Employers' Obligations under COBRA

Employers, with some exceptions, must comply with COBRA if they employ twenty or more workers and provide a benefit plan to those workers. An employer must inform an employee of COBRA's provisions when that worker faces termination or a reduction of hours that would affect his or her eligibility for coverage under the plan.

An employer is relieved of the responsibility to provide benefit coverage if it completely eliminates its group benefit plan. An employer is also relieved of responsibility when the worker becomes eligible for Medicare, falls under a spouse's health plan, becomes insured under a different plan (with a new employer, for example), or fails to pay the premium.

An employer that fails to comply with COBRA risks substantial penalties. These penalties include a tax of up to 10 percent of the annual cost of the group plan or $500,000, whichever is less.

Section 6

Family and Medical Leave

In 1993, Congress passed the Family and Medical Leave Act (FMLA)[16] to protect employees who need

14. 26 U.S.C. Sections 3301–3310.

15. 29 U.S.C. Sections 1161–1169.

16. 29 U.S.C. Sections 2601, 2611–2619, and 2651–2654.

time off work for family or medical reasons. A majority of the states also have legislation allowing for a leave from employment for family or medical reasons, and many employers maintain private family-leave plans for their workers.

COVERAGE AND APPLICATION OF THE FMLA

The FMLA requires employers who have fifty or more employees to provide employees with up to twelve weeks of family or medical leave during any twelve-month period. During the employee's leave, the employer must continue the worker's health-care coverage and guarantee employment in the same or a comparable position when the employee returns to work. An important exception to the FMLA, however, allows the employer to avoid reinstatement of a *key employee*—defined as an employee whose pay falls within the top 10 percent of the firm's work force. Additionally, the act does not apply to employees who have worked less than one year or less than twenty-five hours a week during the previous twelve months.

Generally, an employee may take family leave when he or she wishes to care for a newborn baby, a newly adopted child, or a foster child just placed in the employee's care.[17] An employee may take medical leave when the employee or the employee's spouse, child, or parent has a "serious health condition" requiring care. For most absences, the employee must demonstrate that the health condition requires continued treatment by a health-care provider and includes a period of incapacity of more than three days.

Under regulations issued by the Department of Labor (DOL) in 1995, employees suffering from certain chronic health conditions may take FMLA leave for their own incapacities that require absences of less than three days. For example, an employee who has asthma or diabetes may have periodic occurrences of illness, rather than episodes continuing over an extended period of time. Similarly, pregnancy may involve periodic visits to a health-care provider and bouts of morning sickness. According to the DOL's regulations, employees with such conditions are covered by the FMLA.

17. The foster care must be state sanctioned for such an arrangement to fall within the coverage of the FMLA.

REMEDIES FOR VIOLATIONS OF THE FMLA

Remedies for violations of the FMLA include (1) damages for unpaid wages (or salary), lost benefits, denied compensation, and actual monetary losses (such as the cost of providing for care) up to an amount equivalent to the employee's wages for twelve weeks; (2) job reinstatement; and (3) promotion. The successful plaintiff is entitled to court costs, attorneys' fees, and—in cases involving bad faith on the part of the employer—double damages.

SECTION 7

Employee Privacy Rights

In the last two decades, concerns about the privacy rights of employees have arisen in response to the sometimes invasive tactics used by employers in their efforts to monitor and screen workers. Perhaps the greatest privacy concern in today's employment arena has to do with electronic performance monitoring. Clearly, employers need to protect themselves from liability for their employees' online activities. They also have a legitimate concern with monitoring the productivity of their workers. At the same time, employees expect to have a certain zone of privacy in the workplace. Indeed, many lawsuits have involved allegations that employers' intrusive monitoring practices violate employees' privacy rights.

ELECTRONIC MONITORING

According to a recent survey by the American Management Association, more than two-thirds of employers engage in some form of surveillance of their employees.[18] Tracking employees' Internet use is made easy by a variety of specially designed software products. For example, software is now available that allows employers to track virtually every move made by a worker using the Internet, including the specific Web sites visited and the time spent surfing the Web. Often, employer security measures involve the use of filtering software as well. As discussed in Chapter 4, this software prevents access to specified Web sites, such as sites containing pornographic or sexually explicit images. Other

18. For a discussion of this survey and its results, see Allison R. Michael and Scott M. Lidman, "Monitoring of Employees Still Growing," *The National Law Journal*, January 29, 2001, p. B9.

filtering software may be used to screen incoming e-mail and block mail that consists of spam or that may contain a virus.

The use of filtering software by public employers (government agencies) has led to charges that blocking access to Web sites violates employees' rights to free speech, which are guaranteed by the First Amendment to the Constitution. Although the use of filtering software by government institutions has been controversial, this is not an issue in the context of private businesses. This is because the First Amendment's protection of free speech applies to *government* restraints on speech, not restraints imposed in the private sector.

Laws Protecting Employee Privacy Rights. Recall from Chapter 4 that there is no provision in the U.S. Constitution that guarantees a right to privacy. A personal right to privacy, however, has been inferred from other constitutional guarantees provided by the First, Third, Fourth, Fifth, and Ninth Amendments to the Constitution. Tort law (see Chapter 5), state constitutions, and a number of state and federal statutes also provide for privacy rights.

The major statute with which employers must comply is the Electronic Communications Privacy Act (ECPA) of 1986.[19] This act amended existing federal wiretapping law to cover electronic forms of communications, such as communications via cellular telephones or e-mail. The ECPA prohibits the intentional interception of any wire or electronic communication or the intentional disclosure or use of the information obtained by the interception. The act excludes from coverage, however, any electronic communications through devices that are "furnished to the subscriber or user by a provider of wire or electronic communication service" and that are being used by the subscriber or user, or by the provider of the service, "in the ordinary course of its business."

This "business-extension exception" to the ECPA permits employers to monitor employee electronic communications in the ordinary course of their businesses. It does not, however, permit employers to monitor employees' personal communications. Under another exception to the ECPA, however, employers may avoid liability under the act if the employees consent to having their electronic communications intercepted by the employer. Thus, an employer may be able to avoid liability under the ECPA by simply requiring employees to sign forms indicating that they consent to such monitoring.

Factors Considered by the Courts in Employee Privacy Cases. When determining whether an employer should be held liable for violating an employee's privacy rights, the courts generally weigh the employer's interests against the employee's reasonable expectation of privacy. Generally, if employees are told that their communications are being monitored, they cannot reasonably expect those communications to be private. If employees are *not* told that certain communications are being monitored, however, the employer may be held liable for invading their privacy.

For example, in one case an employer secretly recorded conversations among his four employees by placing a tape recorder in their common office. The conversations were of a highly personal nature and included harsh criticisms of the employer. The employer immediately fired two of the employees, informing them that their termination was due to their comments on the tape. In the suit that followed, one of the issues was whether the employees, in these circumstances, had a reasonable expectation of privacy. The court held that they did and granted summary judgment in their favor. The employees clearly would not criticize their boss if they did not assume their conversations were private. Furthermore, the office was small, and the employees were careful that no third parties ever overheard their comments.[20]

Privacy Expectations and E-Mail Systems. With respect to e-mail monitoring, the courts have tended to hold for employers in cases brought by employees alleging that their privacy has been invaded. This is true even when employees were not informed that their e-mail would be monitored.

In a leading case on this issue, the Pillsbury Company promised its employees that it would not read their e-mail, or terminate or discipline them based on the content of their e-mail. Despite this promise, Pillsbury intercepted employee Michael Smyth's e-mail, decided that it was unprofessional and inappropriate, and fired him. In Pennsylvania, where the discharge occurred, it is against public policy for an employer to fire an employee based on a violation of the employee's right to privacy. In Smyth's suit against the company, he claimed that his termination was a violation of this policy. The court, however,

19. 18 U.S.C. Sections 2510–2521.

20. *Dorris v. Abscher*, 179 F.3d 420 (6th Cir. 1999).

found no "reasonable expectation of privacy in e-mail communications voluntarily made by an employee to his supervisor over the company e-mail system."[21]

Other Types of Monitoring

Other types of monitoring or allegedly intrusive practices include lie-detector tests, drug testing, AIDS testing, and preemployment screening procedures.

Lie-Detector Tests. At one time, many employers required employees or job applicants to take polygraph examinations (lie-detector tests) in connection with their employment. To protect the privacy interests of employees and job applicants, in 1988 Congress passed the Employee Polygraph Protection Act.[22] The statute prohibits employers from (1) requiring or causing employees or job applicants to take lie-detector tests or suggesting or requesting that they do so; (2) using, accepting, referring to, or asking about the results of lie-detector tests taken by employees or applicants; and (3) taking or threatening negative employment-related action against employees or applicants based on results of lie-detector tests or on their refusal to take the tests.

Employers excepted from these prohibitions include federal, state, and local government employers; certain security service firms; and companies manufacturing and distributing controlled substances. Other employers may use polygraph tests when investigating losses attributable to theft, including embezzlement and the theft of trade secrets.

Drug Testing. In the interests of public safety and to reduce unnecessary costs, many of today's employers, including the government, require their employees to submit to drug testing. Laws relating to the privacy rights of private-sector employees vary from state to state. Some state constitutions prohibit private employers from testing for drugs, and state statutes may restrict drug testing by private employers in any number of ways. A collective bargaining agreement may also provide protection against drug testing. In some instances, employees have brought actions against their employers for the tort of invasion of privacy.

Constitutional limitations apply to the testing of government employees. The Fourth Amendment provides that individuals have the right to be "secure in their persons" against "unreasonable searches and seizures" conducted by government agents. Drug tests have been held to be constitutional, however, when there was a reasonable basis for suspecting government employees of using drugs. Additionally, when drug use in a particular government job could threaten public safety, testing has been upheld. For example, a U.S. Department of Transportation rule that requires employees engaged in oil and gas pipeline operations to submit to random drug testing was upheld, even though the rule did not require that before being tested the individual must have been suspected of drug use.[23] The court held that the government's interest in promoting public safety in the pipeline industry outweighed the employees' privacy interests.

An ongoing problem with respect to drug testing is that such tests are not foolproof. Suppose that a job applicant is not hired because of a positive drug test. If the results of the test are false, does the applicant have any legal recourse? In one case, for example, after a drug-testing laboratory mistakenly reported to an employer that a job applicant had failed a drug test, the applicant filed a suit against the laboratory. The court granted the employer's request for summary judgment, holding—as have a number of other courts—that while a laboratory may owe a duty of care to the employer for whom it conducts the drug tests, it owes no such duty to the employee being tested.[24]

In another case, a worker who had been fired because of a positive drug test sued the employer, alleging that the real reason he had been fired was racial hostility. The fired employee claimed that his job had been classified as a "safety-sensitive position" even though it should not have been and that he had not ingested any drugs that would account for the positive drug-testing results. In short, claimed the worker, he had been "set up" by the employer. The court, however, granted summary judgment for the employer, largely because the employee did not follow the proper procedures for contesting drug-test results. (The procedures require the employee to mail a request in writing, along with $125, to the laboratory that performed the test. Moreover, the request had to arrive within twenty-four hours, and the laboratory would only re-test the same sample, not a new one.)[25]

21. *Smyth v. Pillsbury Co.*, 914 F.Supp. 97 (E.D.Pa. 1996).

22. 29 U.S.C. Sections 2001 *et seq.*

23. *Electrical Workers Local 1245 v. Skinner*, 913 F.2d 1454 (9th Cir. 1990).

24. *Ney v. Axelrod*, 723 A.2d 719 (Pa.Super. 1999).

25. *Brown v. Allied Printing Ink Co.*, 241 Ga.App. 310, 526 S.E.2d 626 (1999).

AIDS Testing. An increasing number of employers are testing their workers for acquired immune deficiency syndrome (AIDS). Few public issues involve more controversy than this practice. Some state laws restrict AIDS testing, and federal statutes offer some protection to employees and job applicants who have AIDS or have tested positive for the AIDS virus. The federal Americans with Disabilities Act of 1990[26] (discussed in Chapter 42), for example, prohibits discrimination against individuals with disabilities, and the term *disability* has been broadly defined to include those individuals with diseases such as AIDS. The law also requires employers to reasonably accommodate the needs of persons with disabilities. Generally, although the law may not prohibit AIDS testing, it may prohibit the discharge of employees based on the results of those tests.

Preemployment Screening Procedures. An area of concern to potential employees has to do with preemployment screening procedures. What kinds of questions on an employment application or a preemployment test are permissible? What kinds of questions go too far in terms of invading the potential employee's privacy? Is it an invasion of the potential employee's privacy, for example, to ask questions about his or her sexual orientation or religious convictions? Although an employer may believe that such information is relevant to the job for which the individual has applied, the applicant may feel differently about the matter. Generally, questions on an employment application must have a reasonable nexus, or connection, with the job for which an applicant is applying.

SECTION 8

Employment-Related Immigration Laws

The most important immigration laws governing employment relationships are the Immigration Reform and Control Act (IRCA) of 1986[27] and the Immigration Act of 1990.[28] The IRCA, which is administered by the U.S. Immigration and Naturalization Service (INS), prohibits employers from hiring illegal immigrants. Employers must complete a special form—called INS Form I-9—for each employee and indicate on it that the employer has verified that the employee is either a U.S. citizen or is otherwise entitled to work in this country.

The Immigration Act of 1990 limits the number of legal immigrants entering the United States by capping the number of visas (entry permits) that are issued each year. Under the act, employers recruiting employees from other countries must complete a certification process and satisfy the Department of Labor that there is a shortage of qualified U.S. workers capable of performing the work. The employer must also establish that bringing immigrants into this country will not adversely affect the existing labor market in that particular area. In this way, the act attempts to serve two purposes: encouraging skilled workers to enter this country and at the same time restricting competition for American jobs.

SECTION 9

Wrongful Discharge

Whenever an employer discharges an employee in violation of an employment contract or a statutory law protecting employees, the employee may bring an action for **wrongful discharge**. If an employer's actions do not violate any express employment contract or statute, then the question is whether the employer has violated a common law doctrine. Because of the harsh effects of the employment-at-will doctrine for employees, courts have carved out various exceptions to the doctrine. These exceptions are based on contract theory, tort theory, and public policy.

Exceptions Based on Contract Theory

Some courts have held that an *implied* employment contract exists between the employer and the employee. If the employee is fired outside the terms of the implied contract, he or she may succeed in an action for breach of contract even though no written employment contract exists.

For example, an employer's manual or personnel bulletin may state that, as a matter of policy, workers will be dismissed only for good cause. If the employee is aware of this policy and continues to work for the employer, a court may find that there is an implied contract based on the terms stated in the

26. 42 U.S.C. Sections 12102–12118.
27. 29 U.S.C. Section 1802.
28. This act amended various provisions of the Immigration and Nationality Act of 1952, 8 U.S.C. Sections 1101 *et seq.*

manual or bulletin. Promises that an employer makes to employees regarding discharge policy may also be considered part of an implied contract. If the employer fires a worker in a manner contrary to the procedure promised, a court may hold that the employer has violated the implied contract and is liable for damages. Most state courts will consider this claim and judge it by traditional contract standards.

A few states have gone further and held that all employment contracts contain an implied covenant of good faith. This means that both sides promise to abide by the contract in good faith. If an employer fires an employee for an arbitrary or unjustified reason, the employee can claim that the covenant of good faith was breached and the contract violated.

EXCEPTIONS BASED ON TORT THEORY

In a few cases, the discharge of an employee may give rise to an action for wrongful discharge under tort theories. Abusive discharge procedures may result in intentional infliction of emotional distress or defamation. In one case, a restaurant had suffered some thefts of supplies, and the manager announced that he would start firing waitresses alphabetically until the thief was identified. The first waitress fired said that she suffered great emotional distress as a result. The state's highest court upheld her claim as stating a valid cause of action.[29]

Some courts have permitted workers to sue their employers under the tort theory of fraud. Under this theory, an employer may be held liable for making false promises to a prospective employee if the employee detrimentally relies on the employer's representations by taking the job. For example, suppose that an employer induces a prospective employee to leave a lucrative job and move to another state by offering "a long-term job with a thriving business." In fact, the employer is having significant financial problems. Furthermore, the employer is planning a merger that will involve the elimination of the position offered to the prospective employee. If the employee takes the job in reliance on the employer's representations and is fired shortly thereafter, the employee may be able to bring an action against the employer for fraud.[30]

EXCEPTIONS BASED ON PUBLIC POLICY

The most widespread common law exception to the employment-at-will doctrine is an exception made on the basis of public policy. Courts may apply this exception when an employer fires a worker for reasons that violate a fundamental public policy of the jurisdiction.

Generally, the courts require that the public policy involved must be expressed clearly in the statutory law governing the jurisdiction. The public policy against employment discrimination, for example, is expressed clearly in federal and state statutes. Thus, if a worker is fired for discriminatory reasons but has no cause of action under statutory law (for example, if the workplace has too few employees to be covered by the statute), that worker may succeed in a suit against the employer for wrongful discharge in violation of public policy.[31]

Sometimes, an employer will direct an employee to perform an illegal act. If the employee refuses to perform the act, the employer may decide to fire the worker. Similarly, employees who "blow the whistle" on the wrongdoing of their employers often find themselves disciplined or even out of a job. **Whistleblowing** occurs when an employee tells a government official, upper-management authorities, or the press that his or her employer is engaged in some unsafe or illegal activity. Whistleblowers on occasion have been protected from wrongful discharge for reasons of public policy. For example, a bank was held to have wrongfully discharged an employee who pressured the employer to comply with state and federal consumer credit laws.[32]

Westlaw. See Case 41.3 at the end of this chapter. To view the full, unedited case from Westlaw,® go to this text's Web site at **http://wbl-cs.westbuslaw.com**.

SECTION 10

Statutory Protection for Whistleblowers

To encourage workers to report employers' wrongdoing, such as fraud, most states have enacted so-called whistleblower statutes. These statutes protect whistleblowers from subsequent retaliation on the

29. *Agis v. Howard Johnson Co.*, 371 Mass. 140, 355 N.E.2d 315 (1976).

30. See, for example, *Lazar v. Superior Court of Los Angeles Co.*, 12 Cal.4th 631, 909 P.2d 981, 49 Cal.Rptr.2d 377 (1996).

31. See, for example, *Molesworth v. Brandon*, 341 Md. 621, 672 A.2d 608 (1996).

32. *Harless v. First National Bank in Fairmont*, 162 W.Va. 116, 246 S.E.2d 270 (1978).

part of employers. On the federal level, the Whistleblower Protection Act of 1989[33] protects federal employees who blow the whistle on their employers from their employers' retaliatory actions. Whistleblower statutes may also provide an incentive to disclose information by providing the whistleblower with a monetary reward. For example, the federal False Claims Reform Act of 1986[34] requires that a whistleblower who has disclosed information relating to a fraud perpetrated against the U.S. government receive between 15 and 25 percent of the proceeds if the government brings suit against the wrongdoer.

33. 5 U.S.C. Section 1201.

34. 31 U.S.C. Sections 3729–3733. This act amended the False Claims Act of 1863.

Terms and Concepts to Review

cease-and-desist order 829	minimum wage 829	vesting 834
closed shop 830	right-to-work law 830	whistleblowing 839
collective bargaining 831	secondary boycott 830	workers' compensation laws 832
employment at will 828	strike 831	wrongful discharge 838
hot-cargo agreement 830	union shop 830	

Chapter Summary

Wage-Hour Laws	**1.** *Davis-Bacon Act (1931)*—Requires the payment of "prevailing wages" to employees of contractors and subcontractors working on federal government construction projects. **2.** *Walsh-Healey Act (1936)*—Requires that a minimum wage and overtime pay be paid to employees of firms that contract with federal agencies. **3.** *Fair Labor Standards Act (1938)*—Extended wage-hour requirements to cover all employers whose activities affect interstate commerce plus certain businesses. The act has specific requirements in regard to child labor, maximum hours, and minimum wages.
Labor Unions	**1.** *Federal labor laws*— **a.** Norris-LaGuardia Act (1932)—Protects peaceful strikes, picketing, and primary boycotts. **b.** National Labor Relations Act (1935)—Established the rights of employees to engage in collective bargaining and to strike; also defined specific employer practices as unfair to labor. The National Labor Relations Board (NLRB) was created to administer and enforce the act. **c.** Labor-Management Relations Act (1947)—Proscribes certain unfair union practices, such as the closed shop. **d.** Labor-Management Reporting and Disclosure Act (1959)—Established an employee bill of rights and reporting requirements for union activities. **2.** *Union organization*—Union campaign activities and elections must comply with the requirements established by federal labor laws and the NLRB. **3.** *Collective bargaining*—The process by which labor and management negotiate the terms and conditions of employment (wages, benefits, working conditions, and so on). The central legal right of a labor union is to engage in collective bargaining on the members' behalf. **4.** *Strikes*—When collective bargaining reaches an impasse, union members may use their ultimate weapon in labor-management struggles—the strike. A strike occurs when unionized workers leave their jobs and refuse to work.

CHAPTER SUMMARY—CONTINUED

Worker Health and Safety	1. *Occupational Safety and Health Act of 1970*—Requires employers to meet specific safety and health standards that are established and enforced by the Occupational Safety and Health Administration (OSHA). 2. *State workers' compensation laws*—Establish an administrative procedure for compensating workers who are injured in accidents that occur on the job, regardless of fault.
Income Security	1. *Social Security and Medicare*—The Social Security Act of 1935 provides for old-age (retirement), survivors, and disability insurance. Both employers and employees must make contributions under the Federal Insurance Contributions Act (FICA) to help pay for the employees' loss of income on retirement. The Social Security Administration administers Medicare, a health-insurance program for older or disabled persons. 2. *Private pension plans*—The federal Employee Retirement Income Security Act (ERISA) of 1974 establishes standards for the management of employer-provided pension plans. 3. *Unemployment insurance*—The Federal Unemployment Tax Act of 1935 created a system that provides unemployment compensation to eligible individuals. Covered employers are taxed to help defray the costs of unemployment compensation.
COBRA	The Consolidated Omnibus Budget Reconciliation Act (COBRA) of 1985 requires employers to give employees, on termination of employment, the option of continuing their medical, optical, or dental insurance coverage for a certain period.
Family and Medical Leave	The Family and Medical Leave Act (FMLA) of 1993 requires employers with fifty or more employees to provide their employees (except for key employees) with up to twelve weeks of unpaid family or medical leave during any twelve-month period for the following reasons: 1. *Family leave*—May be taken to care for a newborn baby, an adopted child, or a foster child. 2. *Medical leave*—May be taken when the employee or the employee's spouse, child, or parent has a serious health condition requiring care.
Employee Privacy	A right to privacy has been inferred from guarantees provided by the First, Third, Fourth, Fifth, and Ninth Amendments to the U.S. Constitution. State laws may also provide for privacy rights. Employer practices that are often challenged by employees as invasive of their privacy rights include electronic performance monitoring, lie-detector tests, drug testing, AIDS testing, and preemployment screening procedures.
Employment-Related Immigration Laws	1. *Immigration Reform and Control Act (1986)*—Prohibits employers from hiring illegal immigrants; administered by the U.S. Immigration and Naturalization Service. 2. *Immigration Act (1990)*—Limits the number of legal immigrants entering the United States by capping the number of visas (entry permits) that are issued each year.
Wrongful Discharge	Wrongful discharge occurs whenever an employer discharges an employee in violation of the law or of an employment contract. To protect employees from some of the harsh results of the common law employment-at-will doctrine (under which employers may hire or fire employees "at will" unless a contract indicates the contrary), courts have made exceptions to the doctrine on the basis of contract theory, tort theory, and public policy.
Statutory Protection for Whistleblowers	Most states have passed whistleblower statutes specifically to protect employees who "blow the whistle" on their employers from subsequent retaliation by those employers. The federal Whistleblower Protection Act of 1989 protects federal employees who report their employers' wrongdoing. The federal False Claims Reform Act of 1986 provides monetary rewards for whistleblowers who disclose information relating to fraud perpetrated against the U.S. government.

CASES FOR ANALYSIS

Westlaw. You can access the full text of each case presented below by going to the Westlaw cases on this text's Web site at http://wbl-cs.westbuslaw.com. Each Westlaw case includes the names of all plaintiffs and defendants, the dates on which the case was argued and decided, a brief summary of the issues and decisions in the case, headnotes classifying specific issues in the case according to the West Key Number System, and the court's opinion. Concurring and dissenting opinions, if any, are included as well.

CASE 41.1 WORKERS' COMPENSATION

ROGERS V. PACESETTER CORP.
Missouri Court of Appeals,
Eastern District,
Division 4, 1998.
972 S.W.2d 540.

ROBERT G. DOWD, Jr., Presiding Judge.

Claimant, Sean Rogers, appeals from a Final Award issued by the [Missouri] Labor and Industrial Relations Commission ("Commission") denying him compensation benefits. Claimant was injured in an automobile accident while traveling on his way home after a meeting with his employer at the River Port Club, a bar/club. [A state] Administrative Law Judge (ALJ) awarded Claimant compensation benefits. The Commission reversed the award in a two-to-one decision finding that Claimant's injuries did not arise out of and in the course of employment. * * *

The Commission found the following:

On or about April 7, 1992, employee was employed by Pacesetter Corporation in a managerial capacity. His duties included supervision and evaluation of telemarketing sales representatives. Employee regularly worked at his employer's Earth City [Missouri] offices from approximately 9:00 A.M. to 9:00 P.M., Monday through Friday and from 10:00 A.M. to 4:00 P.M. on Saturdays. He routinely performed work at home, drafting ads and conducting performance reviews. He testified that these duties were performed at home because there was insufficient time to perform them during the regular office hours and that the work done at home was an integral part of the conduct of his employer's business.

On April 6, 1992, employee was invited by his supervisor, Mr. Lewis, to meet him at the River Port Club after office hours. Employee felt it was necessary for him to meet with Mr. Lewis, in order to safeguard his position with the company and to discuss a promotion. He was advised by Mr. Lewis that evening that he would be promoted and that company officials would be arriving at the office the next day to finalize these arrangements. Employee admitted that he consumed about four beers and three shots of tequila while at the club. There were other employees of Pacesetter who were also at Club River Port that evening. Employee acknowledged that Mr. Lewis left the Club River Port at approximately 10:21 P.M. After Mr. Lewis left, employee testified he stayed about another 20 minutes or so at the club. He may have bought one more beer after Mr. Lewis left. After he left Club River Port, he went out to the parking lot and had a conversation with a Mr. Wagner. Employee admitted that he left the parking lot somewhere between 11:15–11:30 P.M. Employee testified that it was his intention after leaving the River Port Club and going [sic] home to do performance reviews before coming to work the next day. He admitted he felt the affects [sic] of the alcohol when he left the Club.

Employee testified that when he left the River Port Club he was in a hurry to get home and driving a little faster than he should. There was a slight drizzle when claimant left. Employee had to drive through highway construction sites on the way home. His pickup truck dipped down into a 12" drop off and employee tried to correct his steering. It caused the truck to spin around and slide over to the other side of the highway to the median where it stopped. When he initially wrecked, several people stopped and offered to call a tow truck. Employee flagged them on. The truck was old and had a bad starter in it. Employee decided to try to make the starter kick again. He got out of the truck, opened the hood and started to hit on the "bendix" to make it start. He testified "someone obviously did not see my bright lights and my hazard lights and hit me head on and mashed me between my truck and their car."

Claimant filed a claim for compensation with the [Missouri] Division of Workers' Compensation. After a hearing, the ALJ found Claimant's accident arose out of and in the course of his employment. The ALJ awarded Claimant $333.33 per week for permanent partial disability from the date of the injury to November 1, 1995, less 12 weeks during which Claimant actually worked, and 400 weeks of permanent partial disability at a rate of $213.57 per week. Employer, Pacesetter Corporation, filed its appeal from the ALJ's decision with the

Commission. The Commission reversed the ALJ's award and denied Claimant compensation benefits finding that the injury did not arise out of and in the course of his employment.

* * * *

The purpose of Workers' Compensation Law is to place upon industry the losses sustained by employees resulting from injuries arising out of and in the course of employment and, consequently, the law should be liberally construed so as to effectuate its purpose and humane design. The law is intended to extend its benefits to the largest possible class. Therefore, *any question as to the right of an employee to compensation must be resolved in favor of the injured employee.* [Emphasis added.]

An employee's injuries arise out of his employment if they are a natural and reasonable incident thereof, and they are in the course of employment if the accident occurs within the period of employment at a place where the employee may reasonably be fulfilling the duties of employment. * * *

In general, an employee does not suffer injury arising out of and in the course of employment if the employee is injured while going or journeying to or returning from the place of employment. This is true because in most circumstances, a trip to or from one's place of work is merely an inevitable circumstance with which every employee is confronted and which ordinarily bears no immediate relation to the actual services to be performed. However, there are exceptions to this general rule. One exception is the "dual purpose" doctrine which states: *If the work of the employee creates the necessity for travel, he is in the course of his employment, though he is serving at the same time some purpose of his own.* The rationale of the dual purpose doctrine is that if the exposure to the perils of the highway is related to the employment even though the employment is not the sole cause of such exposure to such risks but is combined with or is a concurrent personal cause, the benefit of compensation is not to be withdrawn. * * * [Emphasis added.]

In his sole point on appeal, Claimant asserts the Commission erred in finding that his injuries did not arise out of and in the course of his employment because:

> The employee/Appellant herein was injured while transporting documents to his home necessary to perform specific employment duties which were due to be completed prior to the start of work the next day and which were customarily performed at home for business reasons and not merely for the convenience of the employee.

* * * *

* * * [C]ompensation for injuries while traveling home may be proper under the dual purpose doctrine when it can genuinely and not fictionally be said that the home has become part of the employment premises. In those circumstances, an employee fulfills a dual purpose by traveling home: the personal purpose of making a normal trip home, and the business purpose of reaching a second employment situs. * * * [A]n employee demonstrates this by showing a clear business use of the home at the end of the specific journey during which the accident occurred.

* * * [R]ecovery [is] limited to those exceptional circumstances in which the employee's home is truly a second employment location in that more than occasional employment services are required to be rendered there.

Upon review of the record before us, and bearing in mind the above principles, we find the denial of benefits was unsupported by the facts as found by the Commission. * * * Here, Claimant regularly worked twelve hours, Monday through Friday, and six hours each Saturday. Claimant also regularly did work for his employer at home, including writing advertisements and conducting performance reviews. The night of the accident was a Monday and it was Claimant's practice to do performance reviews of the week before on the telemarketers on Monday evenings in order that on Tuesday mornings he could discuss their performance with them. Claimant testified it was necessary to conduct these performance reviews at home because, as the Commission found, "there was insufficient time to perform [his duties] during regular office hours." Moreover, the Commission found that the work performed at home by Claimant "was an integral part of the conduct of his employer's business," and not only a convenience to Claimant. Clearly a benefit accrued to employer by Claimant conducting these performance reviews at home. We conclude that under the facts as found by the Commission, Claimant demonstrated that the demands of his employment created the expectation that work needed to be done at home for the benefit of his employer.

Furthermore, we note that the fact Claimant was traveling to his home from a meeting with his employer at a club does not change our analysis. * * * Claimant was conducting business at the club with his employer. Specifically, employer discussed with Claimant his position in employer's company and Claimant's impending promotion.

Accordingly, the Commission's order denying compensation is reversed and the cause is remanded for entry of an appropriate award of compensation.

CASE 41.2 SOCIAL SECURITY AND MEDICARE

UNITED STATES V. CLEVELAND INDIANS BASEBALL CO.

Supreme Court of the United States, 2001.
532 U.S. 200,
121 S.Ct. 1433,
149 L.Ed.2d 401.

Justice *GINSBURG* delivered the opinion of the Court.

The Federal Insurance Contributions Act (FICA) and the Federal Unemployment Tax Act (FUTA) impose excise taxes on employee wages to fund Social Security, Medicare, and unemployment compensation programs. This case concerns the application of FICA and FUTA taxes to payments of back wages. The Internal Revenue Service has consistently maintained that, for tax purposes, backpay awards should be attributed to the year the award is actually paid. Respondent Cleveland Indians Baseball Company (Company) urges, and the [United States] Court of Appeals for the Sixth Circuit held, that such awards must be allocated, as they are for purposes of Social Security benefits eligibility, to the periods in which the wages should have been paid. According due respect to the Service's reasonable, longstanding construction of the governing statutes and its own regulations, we hold that back wages are subject to FICA and FUTA taxes by reference to the year the wages are in fact paid.

I

Pursuant to a settlement of grievances asserted by the Major League Baseball Players Association concerning players' free agency rights, several Major League Baseball clubs agreed to pay $280 million to players with valid claims for salary damages. Under the agreement, the Company owed 8 players a total of $610,000 in salary damages for 1986, and it owed 14 players a total of $1,457,848 in salary damages for 1987. The Company paid the awards in 1994. No award recipient was a Company employee in that year.

This case concerns the proper FICA and FUTA tax treatment of the 1994 payments. Under FICA, both employees and employers must pay tax on wages to fund Social Security and Medicare; under FUTA, employers (but not employees) must pay tax on wages to fund unemployment benefits. For purposes of this litigation, the Government and the Company stipulated that the settlement payments awarded to the players qualify as "wages" within the meaning of FICA and FUTA. The question presented is whether those payments, characterized as back wages, should be taxed by reference to the year they were actually paid (1994), as the Government urges, or by reference to the years they should have been paid (1986 and 1987), as the Company and * * * the Major League Baseball Players Association, contend.

In any given year, the amount of FICA and FUTA tax owed depends on two determinants. The first is the tax rate. The second is the statutory ceiling on taxable wages (also called the wage base), which limits the amount of annual wages subject to tax. Both determinants have increased over time. In 1986, the Social Security tax on employees and employers was 5.7 percent on wages up to $42,000; in 1987, it was 5.7 percent on wages up to $43,800; and in 1994, 6.2 percent on wages up to $60,600. Although the Medicare tax on employees and employers remained constant at 1.45 percent from 1986 to 1994, the taxable wage base rose from $42,000 in 1986 to $43,800 in 1987, and by 1994, Congress had abolished the wage ceiling, thereby subjecting all wages to the Medicare tax. In 1986 and 1987, the FUTA tax was 6.0 percent on wages up to $7,000; in 1994, it was 6.2 percent on wages up to $7,000.

In this case, allocating the 1994 payments back to 1986 and 1987 works to the advantage of the Company and its former employees. The reason is that all but one of the employees who received back wages in 1994 had already collected wages from the Company exceeding the taxable maximum in 1986 and 1987. Because those employees as well as the Company paid the maximum amount of employment taxes chargeable in 1986 and 1987, allocating the 1994 payments back to those years would generate no additional FICA or FUTA tax liability. By contrast, treating the back wages as taxable in 1994 would subject both the Company and its former employees to significant tax liability. The Company paid none of the employees any other wages in 1994, and FICA and FUTA taxes attributable to that year would be calculated according to tax rates and wage bases higher than their levels in 1986 and 1987.

Uncertain about the proper rule of taxation, the Company paid its share of employment taxes on the back wages according to 1994 tax rates and wage bases. Its FICA payment totaled $99,382, and its FUTA payment totaled $1,008. After the Internal Revenue Service denied its claims for a refund of those payments, the Company initiated this action in [a federal] District Court * * * . The District Court * * * entered judgment for the Company and ordered the Government to refund $97,202 in FICA and FUTA taxes.

* * * The Court of Appeals for the Sixth Circuit * * * affirmed * * * .

We granted *certiorari* * * * .

II

* * * *

The Internal Revenue Service has long maintained regulations interpreting the FICA and FUTA tax provisions. In their current form, the regulations specify that the employer tax "attaches *at the time that the wages are paid* by the employer" and "is computed by applying to the wages paid by the employer the rate in effect *at the time such wages are paid.*" [Emphasis added.] Echoing the language in [FICA] and [FUTA], these regulations have continued unchanged in their basic substance since 1940.

Although the regulations, like the statute, do not specifically address backpay, the Internal Revenue Service has consistently interpreted them to require taxation of back wages according to the year the wages are actually paid, regardless of when those wages were earned or should have been paid. We need not decide whether the Revenue Rulings themselves are entitled to deference. In this case, the Rulings simply reflect the agency's long-standing interpretation of its own regulations. Because that interpretation is reasonable, it attracts substantial judicial deference. We do not resist according such deference in reviewing an agency's steady interpretation of its own 61-year-old regulation implementing a 62-year-old statute. Treasury regulations and interpretations long continued without substantial change, applying to unamended or substantially reenacted statutes, are deemed to have received congressional approval and have the effect of law.

* * * *

In line with the text and administrative history of the relevant taxation provisions, we hold that, for FICA and FUTA tax purposes, back wages should be attributed to the year in which they are actually paid. Accordingly, the judgment of the United States Court of Appeals for the Sixth Circuit is reversed.

It is so ordered.

CASE 41.3 WRONGFUL DISCHARGE

LINS V. CHILDREN'S DISCOVERY CENTERS OF AMERICA, INC.

Court of Appeals of Washington,
Division 2, 1999.
95 Wash.App. 486,
976 P.2d 168.

MORGAN, J. [Judge]

* * * *

Children's Discovery Centers of America, Inc. [CDC], operates a number of childcare centers. In March 1995, it employed Pam French as its operations director for the West Coast. One of French's subordinates was Diane Lins, a regional director in charge of six childcare centers in the Portland/Vancouver [Washington] area. French had authority to direct, evaluate, and fire Lins.

Before the events in issue here, CDC promoted Lins and gave her good performance ratings. It did not put her on probation or assert that she was performing deficiently.

On March 8, 1995, Lins and five other CDC employees were injured in an auto accident that occurred in the course and scope of their employment for CDC. Lins later referred to the other five as "directors" because each of the five was the director of a particular childcare center. Each of those injured, including Lins, filed a workers' compensation claim with the Washington Department of Labor and Industries.

A week or two after the accident, French ordered Lins to fire the other five employees no later than May 1, 1995. French had heard that two of them were consulting attorneys and "contemplating suing CDC"; she "didn't trust either of them not to sue the company, and she was not going to allow that to happen." She harbored similar feelings about the remaining three, even though they had not yet seen attorneys. * * *

Lins could not lawfully have carried out French's order. [Revised Code of Washington (RCW) Section] 51.48.025 declares, "No employer may discharge or in any manner discriminate against any employee because such employee has filed or communicated to the employer an intent to file a claim for compensation or exercises any rights provided under [Title 51 RCW]."

Realizing she could not lawfully perform French's order, Lins refused to do so. * * *

On May 5, 1995, French gave Lins her first poor performance review and put her on probation. Effective June 22, 1995, French fired Lins for "Neglect of Duties/Poor Performance." French did not fire the other five employees, but four of them later left CDC.

On December 11, 1996, Lins sued CDC [in a Washington state court]. She alleged that she had been wrongfully discharged "in violation of the public policy of the state of Washington which mandates that an employee may not be terminated for refusing to perform an illegal act." She further alleged that CDC knew or should have known about French's actions.

Six months later, CDC moved for summary judgment. It correctly pointed out that Lins was not claiming she had been fired for filing her own worker's compensation claim; rather, she was claiming that she had been fired for refusing to obey French's unlawful order. Although conceding that it could not lawfully fire an employee for filing a worker's compensation claim, it argued that it could lawfully fire an employee for refusing to obey an unlawful order to fire other employees because the others had filed such claims. The trial court granted the motion and dismissed the case.

The issue on appeal is whether public policy prevents an employer from retaliating for an employee's refusal to carry out the employer's clearly unlawful order. * * *

Subject to many exceptions, an employer may discharge an employee at will. The exceptions pertinent here arise from public policy.

Public policy prohibits an employer from considering certain characteristics when deciding whether to discharge an employee. Thus, it is unlawful for an employer to discharge an employee because of age, sex, marital status, race, creed, color, national origin, or the presence of any sensory, mental, or physical disability * * * . It is also unlawful for an employer to discharge because an employee has tested positive for HIV unless the absence of HIV infection is a bona fide occupational qualification for the job in question.

Public policy also prohibits an employer from considering certain activities when deciding whether to discharge an employee. Thus, it is unlawful for an employer to discharge an employee because the employee refuses to do an illegal act, or performs a public duty or obligation such as serving on a jury or saving another citizen's life. It is unlawful for an employer to discharge an employee because the employee exercises a legal right or privilege, such as filing a worker's compensation complaint * * * ; filing a discrimination complaint * * * ; filing a whistleblower complaint * * * ; filing a complaint under the Washington Industrial Safety and Health Act (WISHA); filing a community-right-to-know complaint * * * ; reporting nursing home abuse * * * ; filing a farm-labor claim * * * ; filing a minimum wage claim * * * ; filing a family-leave claim * * * ; or engaging in collective bargaining activities * * * . It is unlawful for an employer to discharge an employee because of certain garnishments and wage assignments. These and similar provisions are often summarized by saying that it is unlawful for an employer to "retaliate" against an employee for "protected activity."

The problem, of course, is defining the "activity" that public policy "protects." Either the legislature or the judiciary may address that problem, the legislature through statutes and the judiciary through decisional law. When the judiciary addresses the problem, it inquires (1) whether a clear public policy exists; (2) whether that policy will be jeopardized unless the activity in issue is protected; (3) whether employers in general have "overriding justification" for wanting to use the activity in issue as a factor affecting the decision to discharge; and (4) whether the particular employee's activity in the case at bar was a substantial factor in (i.e., a cause of) the particular employer's decision to discharge. Always, however, the judiciary should be slow to protect activity not previously protected * * * .

Turning to the first of the four elements just identified, we hold that Washington has a clear public policy against firing an employee because he or she has filed a worker's compensation claim. As already seen, the legislature declared in RCW [Section] 51.48.025 that "no employer may discharge or in any manner discriminate against any employee because such employee has filed or communicated to the employer an intent to file a claim for compensation or exercises any rights provided under [Title 51 RCW]." * * *

Turning to the second element, we hold that the policy just described will be jeopardized if, without incurring liability, an employer can fire an employee for refusing to carry out a clearly unlawful order. If the employee's refusal is not protected from retaliation, the employee will likely perform the order to save his or her job; the employer will have a readily available means by which to implement its unlawful order; and the policy * * * will be impaired or destroyed. But if the employee's refusal is protected, the employee will be likely to refuse the order; the employer will be denied a readily available means by which to implement the order; and the policy * * * will be served.

Turning to the third element, we hold that employers do not have any "overriding justification" for wanting to consider an employee's refusal to perform an unlawful order when deciding whether to fire the employee. By virtue of the order being unlawful in the first instance, the employer should not have given it, and the employer has no legitimate interest in having it carried out.

Finally, on the fourth element, a jury could reasonably infer from the evidence in this record that Lins' refusal to carry out French's unlawful order was a substantial factor in Lins' being fired. We conclude that Lins' refusal to carry out French's order was conduct protected by public policy, that French's retaliation was unlawful, and that Lins has presented evidence sufficient to go to a jury.

* * * *

Reversed and remanded for further proceedings.

CASE PROBLEMS

41–1. Richard Winters was an at-will employee for the *Houston Chronicle* from April 1977 to June 1986. Beginning in 1980, he became aware of alleged illegal activities carried out by other employees. He claimed that the *Chronicle* was falsely reporting an inflated number of paid subscribers, that several employees were engaged in inventory theft, and that his supervisor had offered him an opportunity to participate in a kickback scheme with the manufacturers of plastic bags. Winters reported all these activities to upper-level management in January 1986 but made no report to law enforcement agencies. He was fired six months later. He sued the *Chronicle* for wrongful termination. What should the court decide? Discuss fully. [*Winters v. Houston Chronicle Publishing,* 795 S.W.2d 723 (Tex. 1990)]

41–2. Debra Roxberry supervised the dry-cleaning department for Robertson and Penn, Inc. (R&P), a private contractor to the U.S. government for laundry and dry-cleaning services at Fort Riley, Kansas. Willie Dawson was an employee of another private contractor to the U.S. government, which operated the Central Issue Facility at Fort Riley. On one occasion, when Dawson was picking up some shirts from R&P, Roxberry informed him that the shirts had been washed instead of dry-cleaned, the process for which they had been delivered and that R&P was contractually obligated to perform. Roxberry was fired a short time later, and she sued R&P for wrongful discharge, alleging that she had been fired for "blowing the whistle" on her employer's violation of its contract with the government. Under the relevant state law, at-will employees have a cause of action against an employer for discharge in retaliation for whistleblowing. R&P contended, among other things, that Roxberry was not a whistleblower because she did not report the incident to the proper authorities but only to an employee of a private company. Will the court agree with R&P's conclusion that Roxberry was not a whistleblower? Discuss. [*Roxberry v. Robertson and Penn, Inc.*, 963 F.2d 382 (10th Cir. 1992)]

41–3. Earl Angus, as a condition of his employment, lived in a mobile home owned by his employer, Deffenbaugh Industries. The mobile home was located on the grounds of Deffenbaugh's plant and was purchased by Deffenbaugh to house the Angus family because it wanted Angus to "maintain a constant presence on the premises." Although Angus ordinarily worked out of an office located in a different building, the mobile home had a telephone, so Angus would be able to contact company drivers and customers as needed. One day, Angus returned to the mobile home and awaited the arrival of a truck on company business. About fifteen minutes after Angus had arrived at the mobile home, and while the family was eating dinner, a tornado struck. The tornado left Angus's wife dead and Angus and his daughter severely injured. Angus filed a workers' compensation claim against Deffenbaugh, alleging that his injuries "arose out of his employment." Among other things, Deffenbaugh argued that the injury did not occur within the course of employment, because Angus was not working but eating dinner with his family when the tornado struck. How should the court decide this case? [*Deffenbaugh Industries v. Angus*, 313 Ark. 100, 852 S.W.2d 804 (1993)]

41–4. In June 1979, Castaways Management, Inc., purchased the Castaways Motel in Miami Beach, Florida. The general manager of Castaways actively supported one of the two union locals that sought to represent the motel's employees. Employees were told that voting for the other union could result in demotions, transfers, and pay reductions, and a number of employees who supported the other union were fired for reasons asserted to be unrelated to the union activities prior to a union election. Both unions eventually filed unfair labor practice charges against Castaways, and the National Labor Relations Board (NLRB) found that Castaways had violated federal labor provisions by discharging employees for supporting union activity. Castaways was ordered to reinstate the discharged employees, award them back pay with interest, conduct a new election, and post notice of its violations on motel premises. By the time the initial order was affirmed by an NLRB panel in 1987, the motel had been demolished—although Castaways still existed as a business entity. On appeal, Castaways argued, among other things, that the NLRB's order was rendered moot (of no legal significance) because the motel no longer existed. Under these circumstances, is the NLRB's order unenforceable? Discuss. [*NLRB v. Castaways Management, Inc.*, 870 F.2d 1539 (11th Cir. 1989)]

41–5. Dayton Hudson Corp. owns and operates Target Stores. Target hires store security officers (SSOs) to observe, apprehend, and arrest suspected shoplifters. SSOs are not armed, but they carry handcuffs and may use force, in self-defense, against suspected shoplifters. Target views good judgment and emotional stability as important SSO job skills. To determine whether applicants for SSO positions possess these qualities, Target uses a psychological test that it calls the Psychscreen. All job applicants must take the test as a condition of employment. A number of the questions included in the Psychscreen test are highly personal and intimate. Some of the questions relate to the applicant's religious beliefs ("I believe in the second coming of Christ" and "I believe my sins are unpardonable"); other questions concern the job candidate's sexual orientation ("I have often wished that I were a girl" and "Many of my dreams are about sex matters"). Sibi Soroka and two other applicants (the plaintiffs) found the test objectionable and brought a class-action suit against Dayton Hudson, challenging the test as violating their privacy rights. Did Target's use of the Psychscreen violate the job applicants' right to privacy? Why, or why not? [*Soroka v. Dayton Hudson Corp.*, 7 Cal.App.4th 203, 1 Cal.Rptr.2d 77 (1 Dist. 1991)]

41–6. At an REA Express, Inc., shipping terminal, a conveyor belt was inoperative because an electrical circuit had shorted out. The manager called a licensed electrical contractor. When the contractor arrived, REA's maintenance supervisor was in the circuit breaker room. The floor was wet, and the maintenance supervisor was using sawdust to try to soak up the water. While the licensed electrical contractor was standing on the wet floor and attempting to fix the short circuit, he was electrocuted. Simultaneously, REA's maintenance supervisor, who was standing on a wooden platform, was burned and knocked unconscious. The Occupational Safety and Health Administration (OSHA) sought to fine REA Express $1,000 for failure to furnish a place of employment free from recognized hazards. Will the court uphold OSHA's decision? Discuss fully. [*REA Express, Inc. v. Brennan*, 495 F.2d 822 (2d Cir. 1974)]

41–7. Barbara Kraus was vice president of nursing at the New Rochelle Hospital Medical Center. She learned that a certain doctor had written on the charts of some patients that he had performed procedures for them that he had not performed, and in fact, he had not obtained consent forms from the patients to perform those procedures. She reported this to the doctor's superiors, who took little action against the doctor. Some time later, Kraus was terminated. She filed a suit in a New York state court against the hospital in order to recover damages for wrongful termination. What is required for the court to rule in Kraus's favor? [*Kraus v. New Rochelle Hospital Medical Center,* 628 N.Y.S.2d 360 (1995)]

41–8. The city of Los Angeles requires a polygraph examination for police officers who ask to be promoted or transferred into a few specialized divisions in which the work is unusually sensitive and requires a high level of integrity. Generally, those who fail the test are not promoted or transferred, but neither are they demoted or otherwise penalized. The Los Angeles Protective League filed a suit against the city in a California state court, asking the court, among other things, to order the city to stop the testing. On what basis might the court grant the league's request? On what basis might it refuse to do so? [*Los Angeles Protective League v. City of Los Angeles,* 35 Cal.App.4th 1535, 42 Cal.Rptr.2d 23 (1995)]

41–9. Robert Adams worked as a delivery truck driver for George W. Cochran & Co. Adams persistently refused to drive a truck that lacked a required inspection sticker and was subsequently fired as a result of his refusal. Adams was an at-will employee, and Cochran contended that because there was no written employment contract stating otherwise, Cochran was entitled to discharge Adams at will—that is, for cause or no cause. Adams sought to recover $7,094 in lost wages and $200,000 in damages for the "humiliation, mental anguish and emotional distress" that he had suffered as a result of being fired from his job. Under what legal doctrines discussed in this chapter—or exceptions to those doctrines—might Adams be able to recover damages from Cochran? Discuss fully. [*Adams v. George W. Cochran & Co.,* 597 A.2d 28 (D.C.App. 1991)]

41–10. Linda Burnett Kidwell, employed as a state traffic officer by the California Highway Patrol (CHP), suffered an injury at home, off duty, while practicing the standing long jump. The jump is a required component of the CHP's annual physical performance program fitness test. Kidwell filed a claim for workers' compensation benefits. The CHP and the California workers' compensation appeals board denied her claim. Kidwell appealed to a state appellate court. What is the requirement for granting a workers' compensation claim? Should Kidwell's claim be granted? [*Kidwell v. Workers' Compensation Appeals Board,* 33 Cal.App.4th 1130, 39 Cal.Rptr.2d 540 (1995)]

41–11. Gabor Nagy was a car salesperson for Whittlesey Automotive Group. Whittlesey asked Nagy to allow some of his phone conversations with "customers" to be recorded. The "customers" were actually employees of a company Whittlesey had hired to conduct a sales training program. Nagy refused to consent. He was eventually fired for his "negative attitude." Nagy filed a suit in a California state court against Whittlesey. He cited a state statute that makes eavesdropping a crime and alleged in part that he was wrongfully terminated in violation of public policy. Will the court agree? Discuss fully. [*Nagy v. Whittlesey Automotive Group,* 40 Cal.App.4th 1328, 47 Cal.Rptr.2d 395 (1995)]

41–12. Stephen Fredrick, a pilot for Simmons Airlines, Inc., criticized the safety of the aircraft that Simmons used on many of its flights and warned the airline about possible safety problems. Simmons took no action. After one of the planes crashed, Fredrick appeared on the television program *Good Morning America* to discuss his safety concerns. The same day, Fredrick refused to allow employees of Simmons to search his personal bags before a flight that he was scheduled to work. Claiming insubordination, the airline terminated Fredrick. Fredrick filed a suit in a federal district court against Simmons, claiming, among other things, retaliatory discharge for his public criticism of the safety of Simmons's aircraft and that this discharge violated the public policy of providing for safe air travel. Simmons responded that an employee who "goes public" with his or her concerns should not be protected by the law. Will the court agree with Simmons? Explain. [*Fredrick v. Simmons Airlines Corp.,* 144 F.3d 500 (7th Cir. 1998)]

41–13. Richard Ackerman was an advance sales representative and account manager for Coca-Cola Enterprises, Inc. His primary responsibility was to sell Coca-Cola products to grocery stores, convenience stores, and other sales outlets. Coca-Cola also employed merchandisers, who did not sell Coca-Cola products but performed tasks associated with their distribution and promotion, including restocking shelves, filling vending machines, and setting up displays. The account managers, who serviced the smaller accounts themselves, regularly worked between fifty-five and seventy-two hours each week. Coca-Cola paid them a salary, bonuses, and commissions, but it did not pay them—unlike the merchandisers—additional compensation for the overtime. Ackerman and the other account managers filed a suit in a federal district court against Coca-Cola, alleging that they were entitled to overtime compensation. Coca-Cola responded that because of an exemption under the Fair Labor Standards Act, it was not required to pay them overtime. Is Coca-Cola correct? Explain. [*Ackerman v. Coca-Cola Enterprises, Inc.,* 179 F.3d 1260 (10th Cir. 1999)]

41–14. Patience Oyoyo was a claims analyst in the claims management department of Baylor Healthcare Network, Inc. When questions arose about Oyoyo's performance on several occasions, department manager Debbie Outlaw met with Oyoyo to discuss, among other things, Oyoyo's personal use of a business phone. Outlaw reminded Oyoyo that company policy prohibited excessive personal calls and that these would result in the termination of her employment. Outlaw began to monitor Oyoyo's phone usage, noting lengthy outgoing calls on several occasions, including some long-distance calls. Eventually, Outlaw terminated Oyoyo's employment, and Oyoyo filed a suit in a federal district court against Baylor. Oyoyo asserted in part that in monitoring her phone calls, the employer had invaded her privacy. Baylor asked the court to dismiss this claim. In whose favor should the court rule, and why? [*Oyoyo v. Baylor Healthcare Network, Inc.*, ___ F.Supp.2d ___ (N.D.Tex. 2000)]

41–15. A Question of Ethics

Keith Cline worked for Wal-Mart Stores, Inc., as a night maintenance supervisor. When he suffered a recurrence of a brain tumor, he took a leave from work, which was covered by the Family Medical and Leave Act (FMLA) of 1993 and authorized by his employer. When he returned to work, his employer refused to allow him to continue his supervisory job and demoted him to the status of a regular maintenance worker. A few weeks later, the company fired him, ostensibly because he "stole" company time by clocking in thirteen minutes early for a company meeting. Cline sued Wal-Mart, alleging, among other things, that Wal-Mart had violated the FMLA by refusing to return him to his prior position when he returned to work. In view of these facts, answer the following questions. [*Cline v. Wal-Mart Stores, Inc.*, 144 F.3d 294 (4th Cir. 1998)]

1. Did Wal-Mart violate the FMLA by refusing to return Cline to his prior position when he returned to work?
2. From an ethical perspective, the FMLA has been viewed as a choice on the part of society to shift to the employer family burdens caused by changing economic and social needs. What "changing" needs does the act meet? In other words, why did Congress feel that workers should have the right to family and medical leave in 1993, but not in 1983, or 1973, or earlier?
3. "Congress should amend the FMLA, which currently applies to employers with fifty or more employees, so that it applies to employers with twenty-five or more employees." Do you agree with this statement? Why, or why not?

E-Links

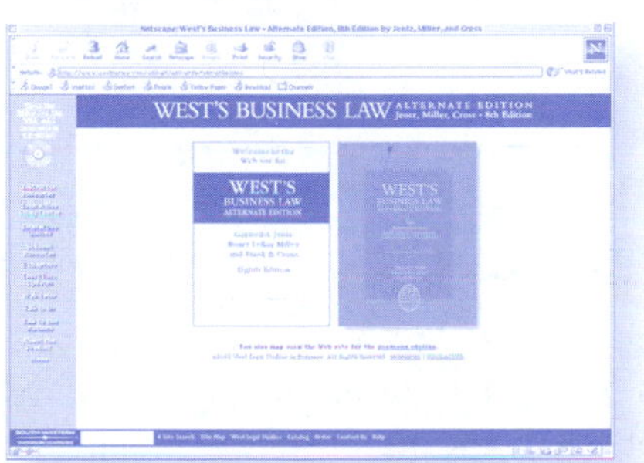

For updated links to resources available on the Web, as well as a variety of other materials, visit this text's Web site at

http://wbl-cs.westbuslaw.com

An excellent Web site for information on employee benefits, including the full text of the FMLA, COBRA, other relevant statutes and case law, and current articles, is BenefitsLink. Go to

http://www.benefitslink.com/columns.shtml

The American Federation of Labor–Congress of Industrial Organizations (AFL–CIO) provides links to a broad variety of labor-related resources at

http://www.aflcio.org/home.htm

The Occupational Safety and Health Administration (OSHA) offers information related to workplace health and safety at

http://www.osha.gov

The Bureau of Labor Statistics provides a wide variety of data on employment, including data on employment compensation, working conditions, and productivity. Go to

http://www.bls.gov

The National Labor Relations Board is online at the following URL:

http://www.nlrb.gov

Legal Research Exercises on the Web

Go to http://wbl-cs.westbuslaw.com, the Web site that accompanies this text. Select "Interactive Study Center," and then click on "Chapter 41." There you will find the following Internet research exercises that you can perform to learn more about employment laws and issues:

Activity 41–1: Workers' Compensation

Activity 41–2: Workplace Monitoring and Surveillance

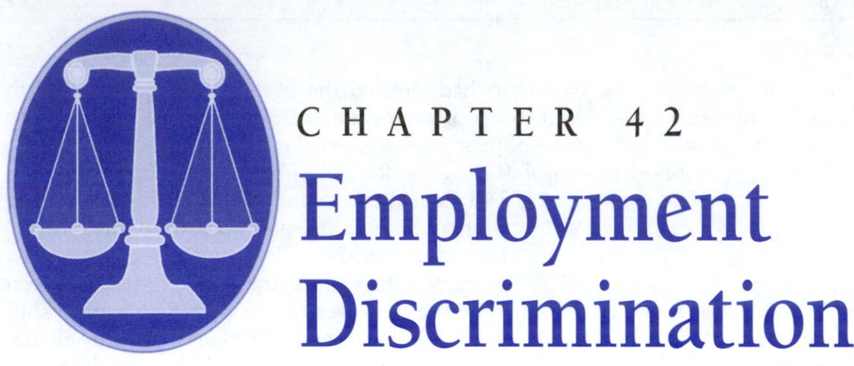

CHAPTER 42 Employment Discrimination

OUT OF THE 1960s CIVIL RIGHTS movement to end racial and other forms of discrimination grew a body of law protecting employees against discrimination in the workplace. This protective legislation further eroded the employment-at-will doctrine, which was discussed in Chapter 41. In the past several decades, judicial decisions, administrative agency actions, and legislation have restricted the ability of employers, as well as unions, to discriminate against workers on the basis of race, color, religion, national origin, gender, age, or disability. A class of persons defined by one or more of these criteria is known as a **protected class.**

Several federal statutes prohibit **employment discrimination** against members of protected classes. The most important statute is Title VII of the Civil Rights Act of 1964.[1] Title VII prohibits employment discrimination on the basis of race, color, religion, national origin, and gender. Discrimination on the basis of age and disability are prohibited by the Age Discrimination in Employment Act of 1967[2] and the Americans with Disabilities Act of 1990,[3] respectively. The protections afforded under these laws extend to U.S. citizens who are working abroad for U.S. firms or for companies that are controlled by U.S. firms—*unless* to do so would violate the laws of the countries in which their workplaces are located. This "foreign laws exception" allows employers to avoid being subjected to conflicting laws.

This chapter focuses on the kinds of discrimination prohibited by these federal statutes. Note, however, that discrimination against employees on the basis of any of the above-mentioned criteria may also violate state human rights statutes or other state laws prohibiting discrimination.

1. 42 U.S.C. Sections 2000e–2000e-17.
2. 29 U.S.C. Sections 621–634.
3. 42 U.S.C. Sections 12102–12118.

SECTION 1

Title VII of the Civil Rights Act of 1964

Title VII of the Civil Rights Act of 1964 and its amendments prohibit job discrimination against employees, applicants, and union members on the basis of race, color, national origin, religion, and gender at any stage of employment. Title VII applies to employers affecting interstate commerce with fifteen or more employees, labor unions with fifteen or more members, labor unions that operate hiring halls (to which members go regularly to be rationed jobs as they become available), employment agencies, and state and local governing units or agencies. A special section of the act prohibits discrimination in most federal government employment.

Title VII applies to any employer that "has fifteen or more employees for each working day in each of twenty or more calendar weeks in the current or preceding calendar year." One of the problems that courts have faced in applying Title VII is how to interpret the phrase "has fifteen or more employees." Does an employer "have" an employee on any working day on which the employer maintains an employment relationship with the employee, or only on working days on which the employee is actually receiving compensation from the employer?

In 1997, the United States Supreme Court resolved this issue by holding that the test for when an employer "has" an employee is whether the employer has an employment relationship with the individual on the day in question. This test is generally called the "payroll method," because the employment relationship is most readily demonstrated by the individual's appearance on the employer's payroll as a full-time or part-time worker.[4]

PROCEDURES UNDER TITLE VII

Compliance with Title VII is monitored by the Equal Employment Opportunity Commission (EEOC). A victim of alleged discrimination, before bringing a suit against the employer, must first file a claim with the EEOC. The EEOC may investigate the dispute and attempt to obtain the parties' voluntary consent to an out-of-court settlement. If voluntary agreement cannot be reached, the EEOC may then file a suit against the employer on the employee's behalf. If the EEOC decides not to investigate the claim, the victim may bring his or her own lawsuit against the employer.

The EEOC does not investigate every claim of employment discrimination; rather, it investigates only "priority cases." Generally, priority cases are cases that affect many workers, cases involving retaliatory discharge (firing an employee in retaliation for submitting a claim with the EEOC), and cases involving types of discrimination that are of particular concern to the EEOC.

INTENTIONAL AND UNINTENTIONAL DISCRIMINATION

Title VII of the Civil Rights Act of 1964 prohibits both intentional and unintentional discrimination.

Intentional Discrimination. Intentional discrimination by an employer against an employee is known as **disparate-treatment discrimination.** Because intent may sometimes be difficult to prove, courts have established certain procedures for resolving disparate-treatment cases. Suppose that a woman applies for employment with a construction firm and is rejected. If she sues on the basis of disparate-treatment discrimination in hiring, she must show that (1) she is a member of a protected class, (2) she applied and was qualified for the job in question, (3) she was rejected by the employer, and (4) the employer continued to seek applicants for the position or filled the position with a person not in a protected class.

If the woman can meet these relatively easy requirements, she makes out a ***prima facie* case** of illegal discrimination. Making out a *prima facie* case of discrimination means that the plaintiff has met her initial burden of proof and will win in the absence of a legally acceptable employer defense (defenses to claims of employment discrimination will be discussed later in this chapter). The burden then shifts to the employer-defendant, who must articulate a legal reason for not hiring the plaintiff. For example, the employer might say that the plaintiff was not hired because she lacked sufficient experience or training. To prevail, the plaintiff must then show that the employer's reason is a *pretext* (not the true reason) and that discriminatory intent actually motivated the employer's decision.

Disparate-Impact Discrimination. Employers often find it necessary to use interviews and testing procedures to choose from among a large number of applicants for job openings. Minimum educational requirements are also common. Employer practices, such as those involving educational requirements, may have an unintended discriminatory impact on a protected class. **Disparate-impact discrimination** occurs when, as a result of educational or other job requirements or hiring procedures, an employer's work force does not reflect the percentage of nonwhites, women, or members of other protected classes that characterizes the pool of qualified individuals in the local labor market. If a person challenging an employment practice having a discriminatory effect can show a connection between the practice and the disparity, he or she makes out a *prima facie* case, and no evidence of discriminatory intent needs to be shown.

Disparate-impact discrimination can also occur when an educational or other job requirement or hiring procedure excludes members of a protected class from an employer's work force at a substantially higher rate than nonmembers, regardless of the racial balance in the employer's work force. The EEOC has devised a test, called the "four-fifths rule," to determine whether an employment examination is discriminatory on its face. Under this rule, a selection rate for protected classes that is less than four-fifths, or 80 percent, of the rate for the group with the highest

4. *Walters v. Metropolitan Educational Enterprises, Inc.*, 519 U.S. 202, 117 S.Ct. 660, 136 L.Ed.2d 644 (1997).

rate will generally be regarded as evidence of disparate impact. To illustrate: One hundred majority applicants take an employment test, and fifty pass the test and are hired. One hundred minority applicants take the test, and twenty pass the test and are hired. Because twenty is less than four-fifths (80 percent) of fifty, the test would be considered discriminatory under the EEOC guidelines.

Discrimination Based on Race, Color, and National Origin

Title VII prohibits employers from discriminating against employees or job applicants on the basis of race, color, or national origin. This prohibition extends to both intentional (disparate-treatment) and unintentional (disparate-impact) discrimination. If a company's standards or policies for selecting or promoting employees have the effect of discriminating against employees or job applicants on the basis of race, color, or national origin, they are illegal—unless (except for race) they have a substantial, demonstrable relationship to realistic qualifications for the job in question. Discrimination against these protected classes in regard to employment conditions and benefits is also illegal.

Note that victims of racial or ethnic discrimination also may have a cause of action under 42 U.S.C. Section 1981. This section, which was enacted as part of the Civil Rights Act of 1866, prohibits discrimination on the basis of race or ethnicity in the formation or enforcement of contracts. Although Section 1981 remained a "dead letter" on the books for over a century, since the 1970s many plaintiffs have succeeded in Section 1981 cases against their employers. Unlike Title VII, Section 1981 does not place a cap on damages (see the discussion of Title VII remedies later in this chapter). Thus, if an employee can prove that he or she was discriminated against in the formation or enforcement of a contract, the employee may be able to obtain a greater amount in damages under Section 1981 than under Title VII.

Discrimination Based on Religion

Title VII of the Civil Rights Act of 1964 also prohibits government employers, private employers, and unions from discriminating against persons because of their religion. An employer must "reasonably accommodate" the religious practices of its employees, unless to do so would cause undue hardship to the employer's business. For example, if an employee's religion prohibits him or her from working on a certain day of the week or at a certain type of job, the employer must make a reasonable attempt to accommodate these religious requirements. Employers must reasonably accommodate an employee's religious belief even if the belief is not based on the tenets or dogma of a particular church, sect, or denomination. The only requirement is that the belief be sincerely held by the employee.[5]

Discrimination Based on Gender

Under Title VII, as well as other federal acts, employers are forbidden to discriminate against employees on the basis of gender. Employers are prohibited from classifying jobs as male or female and from advertising in help-wanted columns that are designated male or female unless the employer can prove that the gender of the applicant is essential to the job. Furthermore, employers cannot have separate male and female seniority lists. Generally, to succeed in a suit for gender discrimination, a plaintiff must demonstrate that gender was a determining factor in the employer's decision to hire, fire, or promote him or her. Typically, this involves looking at all of the surrounding circumstances.

The Pregnancy Discrimination Act of 1978,[6] which amended Title VII, expanded the definition of gender discrimination to include discrimination based on pregnancy. Women affected by pregnancy, childbirth, or related medical conditions must be treated—for all employment-related purposes, including the conferring of benefits under employee benefit programs—the same as other persons not so affected but similar in ability to work.

Westlaw. See Case 42.1 at the end of this chapter. To view the full, unedited case from Westlaw,® go to this text's Web site at **http://wbl-cs.westbuslaw.com**.

Sexual Harassment

Title VII also protects employees against **sexual harassment** in the workplace. Sexual harassment can take two forms: *quid pro quo* harassment and hostile-environment harassment. *Quid pro quo* is a Latin

5. *Frazee v. Illinois Department of Employment Security,* 489 U.S. 829, 109 S.Ct. 1514, 103 L.Ed.2d 914 (1989).

6. 42 U.S.C. Section 2000e(k).

phrase that is often translated to mean "something in exchange for something else." *Quid pro quo* harassment occurs when job opportunities, promotions, salary increases, and so on are given in return for sexual favors. According to the United States Supreme Court, hostile-environment harassment occurs when "the workplace is permeated with discriminatory intimidation, ridicule, and insult, that is sufficiently severe or pervasive to alter the conditions of the victim's employment and create an abusive working environment."[7]

Generally, the courts apply this Supreme Court guideline on a case-by-case basis. Some courts have held that just one incident of sexually offensive conduct—such as a sexist remark by a co-worker or a photo on an employer's desk of his bikini-clad wife—can create a hostile environment.[8] At least one court has held that a worker may recover damages under Title VII because *other* persons were harassed sexually in the workplace.[9] According to some employment specialists, employers should assume that hostile-environment harassment has occurred if an employee claims that it has.

Harassment by Supervisors. What if an employee is harassed by a manager or supervisor of a large firm, and the firm itself (the "employer") is not aware of the harassment? Should the employer be held liable for the harassment nonetheless? For some time, the courts were in disagreement on this issue. Typically, employers were held liable for Title VII violations by the firm's managerial or supervisory personnel in *quid pro quo* harassment cases regardless of whether the employer knew about the harassment. In hostile-environment cases, in contrast, the majority of courts tended to hold employers liable only if the employer knew or should have known of the harassment and failed to take prompt remedial action.

In 1998, in two separate cases, the United States Supreme Court issued some significant guidelines relating to the liability of employers for their supervisors' harassment of employees in the workplace. In *Faragher v. City of Boca Raton*,[10] the Court held that an employer (a city) could be held liable for a supervisor's harassment of employees even though the employer was unaware of the behavior. The Court reached this conclusion primarily because, although the city had a written policy against sexual harassment, the policy had not been distributed to city employees. Additionally, the city had not established any procedures that could be followed by employees who felt that they were victims of sexual harassment. In *Burlington Industries, Inc. v. Ellerth*,[11] the Court ruled that a company could be held liable for the harassment of an employee by one of its vice presidents even though the employee suffered no adverse job consequences.

In these two cases, the Court set forth some common-sense guidelines on liability for harassment in the workplace that will be helpful to employers and employees alike. On the one hand, employees benefit by the ruling that employers may be held liable for their supervisors' harassment even though they were unaware of the actions and even though the employees suffered no adverse job consequences. On the other hand, the Court made it clear in both decisions that employers have an affirmative defense against liability for their supervisors' harassment of employees if they can show that (1) they have taken "reasonable care to prevent and correct promptly any sexually harassing behavior" (by establishing effective harassment policies and complaint procedures, for example), and (2) the employee suing for harassment failed to follow these policies and procedures.

Harassment by Co-Workers and Nonemployees. Often, employees alleging harassment complain that the actions of co-workers, not supervisors, are responsible for creating a hostile working environment. In such cases, the employee still has a cause of action against the employer. Generally, though, the employer will be held liable only if it knew or should have known about the harassment and failed to take immediate remedial action.

Employers may also be liable for harassment by *nonemployees* under certain conditions. For example, if a restaurant owner or manager knows that a certain customer repeatedly harasses a waitress and permits the harassment to continue, the restaurant owner may be liable under Title VII even though the customer is not an employee of the restaurant. The issue turns on the control that the employer exerts

7. *Harris v. Forklift Systems*, 510 U.S. 17, 114 S.Ct. 367, 126 L.Ed.2d 295 (1993).

8. For other examples, see *Radtke v. Everett*, 442 Mich. 368, 501 N.W.2d 155 (1993); and *Nadeau v. Rainbow Rugs, Inc.*, 675 A.2d 973 (Me. 1996).

9. *Leibovitz v. New York City Transit Authority*, 4 F.Supp.2d 144 (E.D.N.Y. 1998).

10. 524 U.S. 725, 118 S.Ct. 2275, 141 L.Ed.2d 662 (1998).

11. 524 U.S. 742, 118 S.Ct. 2257, 141 L.Ed.2d 633 (1998).

over a nonemployee. In one case, the owner of a Pizza Hut franchise was held liable for the harassment of a waitress by two male customers because no steps were taken to prevent the harassment.[12]

Same-Gender Harassment. The courts have also had to address the issue of whether men who are harassed by other men, or women who are harassed by other women, are also protected by laws that prohibit gender-based discrimination in the workplace. For example, what if the male president of a firm demands sexual favors from a male employee? Does this action qualify as sexual harassment? For some time, the courts were widely split on this question. In 1998, in *Oncale v. Sundowner Offshore Services, Inc.*,[13] the Supreme Court resolved the issue by holding that Title VII protection extends to situations in which individuals are harassed by members of the same gender.

Remedies under Title VII

Employer liability under Title VII may be extensive. If the plaintiff successfully proves that unlawful discrimination occurred, he or she may be awarded reinstatement, back pay, retroactive promotions, and damages.[14] Compensatory damages are available only in cases of intentional discrimination. Punitive damages may be recovered against a private employer only if the employer acted with malice or reckless indifference to an individual's rights. The sum of the amount of compensatory and punitive damages is limited by the statute to specific amounts against specific employers—ranging from $50,000 against employers with one hundred or fewer employees to $300,000 against employers with more than five hundred employees.

Section 2

Equal Pay Act of 1963

The Equal Pay Act of 1963 was enacted as an amendment to the Fair Labor Standards Act of 1938. Basically, the act prohibits gender-based discrimination in the wages paid for similar work. For the equal pay requirements to apply, the male and female employees must be employed at the same establishment.

A person alleging wage discrimination in violation of the Equal Pay Act may sue his or her employer. To determine whether the act has been violated, a court will look to the primary duties of the two jobs—it is job content rather than job description that controls in all cases. The jobs of a barber and a beautician, for example, are considered essentially equal. So, too, are those of a tailor and a seamstress. Small differences in job content do not justify higher pay for one gender. An employer will not be found liable for violating the act if it can be shown that the wage differential for equal work was based on (1) a seniority system, (2) a merit system, (3) a system that pays according to quality or quantity of production, or (4) any factor other than gender.

Section 3

Discrimination Based on Age

Age discrimination is potentially the most widespread form of discrimination, because anyone—regardless of race, color, national origin, or gender—could be a victim at some point in life. The Age Discrimination in Employment Act (ADEA) of 1967, as amended, prohibits employment discrimination on the basis of age against individuals forty years of age or older. The act also prohibits mandatory retirement for nonmanagerial workers. For the act to apply, an employer must have twenty or more employees, and the employer's business activities must affect interstate commerce. The EEOC administers the ADEA, but the act also permits private causes of action against employers for age discrimination.

Procedures under the ADEA

The burden-shifting procedure under the ADEA is similar to that under Title VII. If a plaintiff can establish that he or she (1) was a member of the protected age group, (2) was qualified for the position from which he or she was discharged, and (3) was discharged under circumstances that give rise to an inference of discrimination, the plaintiff has established a *prima facie* case of unlawful age discrimination. The burden then shifts to the employer, who must articulate a legitimate reason for the discrimination. If the plaintiff can prove that the employer's reason is only a pretext and that the plaintiff's age

12. *Lockard v. Pizza Hut, Inc.*, 162 F.3d 1062 (10th Cir. 1998).
13. 523 U.S. 75, 118 S.Ct. 998, 140 L.Ed.2d 207 (1998).
14. Damages were not available under Title VII until 1991. The Civil Rights Act of that year amended Title VII to provide for both compensatory and punitive damages, as well as jury trials.

was a determining factor in the employer's decision, the employer will be held liable under the ADEA.

Numerous cases of alleged age discrimination have been brought against employers who, to cut costs, replaced older, higher-salaried employees with younger, lower-salaried workers. Whether a firing is discriminatory or simply part of a rational business decision to prune the company's ranks is not always clear. Companies generally defend a decision to discharge a worker by asserting that the worker could no longer perform his or her duties or that the worker's skills were no longer needed. The employee must prove that the discharge was motivated, at least in part, by age bias. Proof that qualified older employees are generally discharged before employees who are younger or that co-workers continually made unflattering age-related comments about the discharged worker may be enough.

In the past, courts sometimes held that to establish a *prima facie* case of age discrimination, the plaintiff had to prove that he or she had been replaced by a person outside the protected class—that is, by a person under the age of forty years. In 1996, however, in *O'Connor v. Consolidated Coin Caterers Corp.*,[15] the United States Supreme Court held that a cause of action for age discrimination under the ADEA does not require the replacement worker to be outside the protected class. Rather, the issue in all ADEA cases turns on whether age discrimination has in fact occurred, regardless of the age of the replacement worker.

A Special Case—State Employees

Under the Eleventh Amendment to the Constitution, as that amendment has been interpreted by the Supreme Court, states are immune from lawsuits brought by private individuals in federal court, unless a state consents to the suit. In a number of age-discrimination cases brought in the late 1990s, state agencies that were sued by state employees for age discrimination sought to have the suits dismissed on this ground.

For example, in two Florida cases, professors and librarians contended that their employers—two Florida state universities—denied them salary increases and other benefits because they were getting old and their successors could be hired at lower cost. The universities claimed that as agencies of a sovereign state, they could not be sued without the state's consent. Because the courts were rendering conflicting opinions in these cases, the United States Supreme Court agreed to address the issue. In *Kimel v. Florida Board of Regents*,[16] decided in early 2000, the Court held that the sovereign immunity granted the states by the Eleventh Amendment precluded suits against them in federal court by private parties alleging violations of the ADEA. According to the Court, Congress had exceeded its constitutional authority when it included in the ADEA a provision stating that "all employers," including state employers, were subject to the act.

Section 4

Discrimination Based on Disability

The Americans with Disabilities Act (ADA) of 1990 is designed to eliminate discriminatory employment practices that prevent otherwise qualified workers with disabilities from fully participating in the national labor force. Prior to 1990, the major federal law providing protection to those with disabilities was the Rehabilitation Act of 1973. That act covered only federal government employees and those employed under federally funded programs. The ADA extends federal protection against disability-based discrimination to all workplaces with fifteen or more workers. Basically, the ADA requires that employers "reasonably accommodate" the needs of persons with disabilities unless to do so would cause the employer to suffer an "undue hardship." Note, though, that the United States Supreme Court has held, as it did with respect to the ADEA, that lawsuits under the ADA cannot be brought against state government employers.[17]

To prevail on a claim under the ADA, a plaintiff must show that he or she (1) has a disability, (2) is otherwise qualified for the employment in question, and (3) was excluded from the employment solely because of the disability. As in Title VII cases, a claim alleging violation of the ADA may be commenced only after the plaintiff has pursued the claim through the EEOC, which administers the provisions of the act relating to disability-based discrimination in the employment context. Plaintiffs may sue for many of the same remedies available under Title VII. They

15. 517 U.S. 308, 116 S.Ct. 1307, 134 L.Ed.2d 433 (1996).

16. 528 U.S. 62, 120 S.Ct. 631, 145 L.Ed.2d 522 (2000).

17. *Board of Trustees of the University of Alabama v. Garrett*, 531 U.S. 356, 121 S.Ct. 955, 148 L.Ed.2d 866 (2001).

may seek reinstatement, back pay, a limited amount of compensatory and punitive damages (for intentional discrimination), and certain other forms of relief. Repeat violators may be ordered to pay fines of up to $100,000.

What Is a Disability?

The ADA is broadly drafted to define persons with disabilities as persons with physical or mental impairments that "substantially limit" their everyday activities. More specifically, the ADA defines *disability* as "(1) a physical or mental impairment that substantially limits one or more of the major life activities of such individuals; (2) a record of such impairment; or (3) being regarded as having such an impairment."

Generally, the determination of whether an individual has a disability as defined by the ADA is made on a case-by-case basis. Unlike plaintiffs in cases brought under Title VII or the ADEA, who clearly are or are not members of the classes protected by those acts, a plaintiff suing under the ADA must *prove* that he or she has a disability and thus falls under the protection of the ADA. Meeting this first requirement for a case of disability-based discrimination may be difficult.

Health conditions that have been considered disabilities under federal law include blindness, alcoholism, heart disease, cancer, muscular dystrophy, cerebral palsy, paraplegia, diabetes, acquired immune deficiency syndrome (AIDS), the human immunodeficiency virus (HIV), and morbid obesity (defined as existing when an individual's weight is two times that of a normal person).[18] The ADA excludes from coverage certain conditions, such as kleptomania.

For some time, the courts were divided on the issue of whether carpal tunnel syndrome (or other repetitive-stress injury) constituted a disability under the ADA. In 2002, in a case involving this issue, the Supreme Court unanimously held that it did not. The Court concluded that although an employee with carpal tunnel syndrome could not perform the manual tasks associated with her job, the injury did not "substantially limit the major life activity of performing manual tasks."[19]

Westlaw. See Case 42.2 at the end of this chapter. To view the full, unedited case from Westlaw,® go to this text's Web site at **http://wbl-cs.westbuslaw.com**.

Reasonable Accommodation

If a job applicant or an employee with a disability can perform essential job functions with reasonable accommodation, the employer must make the accommodation. Required modifications may include installing ramps for a wheelchair, establishing flexible working hours, creating or modifying job assignments, and creating or improving training materials and procedures.

Generally, employers should give primary consideration to employees' preferences in deciding what accommodations should be made. If an applicant or employee fails to let the employer know how his or her disability can be accommodated, the employer may avoid liability for failing to hire or retain the individual on the ground that the individual has failed to meet the "otherwise qualified" requirement.[20] Employers should be cautious in making this assumption in cases involving mental illness, though. For example, in one case, an employee was held to have a cause of action against his employer under the ADA even though the employee never explicitly told the employer how his disability could be accommodated.[21]

Employers who do not accommodate the needs of persons with disabilities must demonstrate that the accommodations would cause *undue hardship*. Generally, the law offers no uniform standards for identifying what is an undue hardship other than the imposition of a "significant difficulty or expense" on the employer.

Usually, the courts decide whether an accommodation constitutes an undue hardship on a case-by-case basis. In one case, the court decided that paying for a parking space near the office for an employee with a disability was not an undue hardship.[22] In another case, the court held that accommodating the request of an employee with diabetes for indefinite leave until his disease was under control would create an undue hardship for the employer, because the employer would not know when the employee was returning to work. The court stated that reasonable accommodation under the ADA means accommodation so that the employee can perform the job now

18. *Cook v. Rhode Island Department of Mental Health*, 10 F.3d 17 (1st Cir. 1993).

19. *Toyota Motor Manufacturing, Kentucky, Inc. v. Williams*, ____ U.S. ____, ____ S.Ct. ____, ____ L.Ed.2d ____ (2002).

20. See, for example, *Beck v. University of Wisconsin Board of Regents*, 75 F.3d 1130 (7th Cir. 1996); and *White v. York International Corp.*, 45 F.3d 357 (10th Cir. 1995).

21. *Bultemeyer v. Fort Wayne Community Schools*, 100 F.3d 1281 (7th Cir. 1996).

22. See *Lyons v. Legal Aid Society*, 68 F.3d 1512 (2d Cir. 1995).

or "in the immediate future" rather than at some unspecified distant time.[23]

Job Applications and Preemployment Physical Exams. Employers must modify their job-application process so that those with disabilities can compete for jobs with those who do not have disabilities. A job announcement that has only a phone number, for example, would discriminate against potential job applicants with hearing impairments. Thus, the job announcement must also provide an address.

Employers are restricted in the kinds of questions they may ask on job-application forms and during preemployment interviews. Furthermore, employers cannot require persons with disabilities to submit to preemployment physicals unless such exams are required of all other applicants. Employers can condition an offer of employment on the employee's successfully passing a medical examination, but disqualifications must result from the discovery of problems that render the applicant unable to perform the job for which he or she is to be hired.

Dangerous Workers. Employers are not required to hire or retain workers who, because of their disabilities, pose a "direct threat to the health or safety" of their co-workers. In the wake of the AIDS epidemic, many employers are concerned about hiring or continuing to employ a worker who has AIDS under the assumption that he or she might pose a direct threat to the health or safety of others in the workplace. Courts have generally held, however, that AIDS is not so contagious as to disqualify employees from most jobs. Therefore, employers must reasonably accommodate job applicants or employees who have AIDS or who test positive for HIV, the virus that causes AIDS.

The ADA prohibits employers from refusing to hire or retain persons with disabilities who are otherwise qualified for a particular position. The ADA does not require that *unqualified* disabled applicants be hired or retained, however.

Substance Abusers. Drug addiction is a disability under the ADA, because drug addiction is a substantially limiting impairment. Those who are currently using illegal drugs are not protected by the act. The ADA only protects persons with *former* drug addictions—those who have completed a supervised drug-rehabilitation program or who are currently in a supervised rehabilitation program. Individuals who have used drugs casually in the past are not protected under the act. They are not considered addicts and therefore do not have a disability (addiction).

People suffering from alcoholism are protected by the ADA. Employers cannot legally discriminate against employees simply because they are living with alcoholism and must treat them in the same way as they treat other employees. For example, an employee with alcoholism who comes to work late because he or she was drinking the night before cannot be disciplined any differently than an employee who comes to work late for another reason. Of course, employers have the right to prohibit the use of alcohol in the workplace and can require that employees not be under the influence of alcohol while working. Employers can also fire or refuse to hire a person with alcoholism if he or she poses a substantial risk of harm either to himself or herself or to others and the risk cannot be reduced by reasonable accommodation.

Health-Insurance Plans. Workers with disabilities must be given equal access to any health insurance provided to other employees. Employers can exclude from coverage preexisting health conditions and certain types of diagnostic or surgical procedures, however. An employer can also put a limit, or cap, on health-care payments in its particular group-health policy—as long as such caps are "applied equally to all insured employees" and do not "discriminate on the basis of disability." Whenever a group health-care plan makes a disability-based distinction in its benefits, the plan violates the ADA. The employer must then be able to justify the distinction by proving one of the following:

1. That limiting coverage of certain ailments is required to keep the plan financially sound.
2. That coverage of certain ailments would cause a significant increase in premium payments or their equivalent, making the plan unappealing to a significant number of employees.
3. That the disparate treatment is justified by the risks and costs associated with a particular disability.

Hostile-Environment Claims under the ADA

As discussed earlier in this chapter, under Title VII of the Civil Rights Act of 1964, an employee may

23. *Myers v. Hase*, 50 F.3d 278 (4th Cir. 1995).

base causes of action for certain types of employment discrimination on a hostile-environment theory. Using this theory, a worker may successfully sue his or her employer, even if the worker was not fired or did not otherwise experience discrimination.

Can a worker file a suit under the ADA founded on a hostile-environment claim? The ADA does not expressly provide for such suits, but some courts have allowed them. Others have assumed that the claim was possible, without deciding whether the ADA allowed it.[24] Acts that might form the basis for such a claim would likely consist of conduct that a reasonable person would find so offensive that it would change the conditions of the person's employment.

Westlaw. See Case 42.3 at the end of this chapter. To view the full, unedited case from Westlaw,® go to this text's Web site at **http://wbl-cs.westbuslaw.com**.

SECTION 5

Defenses to Employment Discrimination

The first line of defense for an employer charged with employment discrimination is, of course, to assert that the plaintiff has failed to meet his or her initial burden of proof—proving that discrimination in fact occurred. As noted, plaintiffs bringing cases under the ADA may find it difficult to meet this initial burden, because they must prove that their alleged disabilities are disabilities covered by the ADA. Furthermore, plaintiffs in ADA cases must prove that they were otherwise qualified for the job.

Once a plaintiff succeeds in proving that discrimination occurred, the burden shifts to the employer to justify the discriminatory practice. Often, employers attempt to justify the discrimination by claiming that it was the result of a business necessity, a bona fide occupational qualification, a seniority system, or employee misconduct.

Business Necessity

An employer may defend against a claim of discrimination by asserting that a practice that has a discriminatory effect is a **business necessity**. If requiring a high school diploma, for example, is shown to have a discriminatory effect, an employer might argue that a high school education is required for workers to perform the job at a required level of competence. If the employer can demonstrate to the court's satisfaction that a definite connection exists between a high school education and job performance, the employer will succeed in this business necessity defense.

Bona Fide Occupational Qualification

Another defense applies when discrimination against a protected class is essential to a job—that is, when a particular trait is a **bona fide occupational qualification (BFOQ)**. For example, a women's clothing boutique might legitimately hire only female attendants if part of an attendant's job involves assisting clients in the boutique's dressing rooms. Similarly, the Federal Aviation Administration can legitimately impose age limits for airline pilots. Race, however, can never be a BFOQ. Generally, courts have restricted the BFOQ defense to instances in which the employee's gender or religion is essential to the job.

Seniority Systems

An employer with a history of discrimination may have no members of protected classes in upper-level positions. Even if the employer now seeks to be unbiased, it may face a lawsuit seeking an order that minorities be promoted ahead of schedule to compensate for past discrimination. If no present intent to discriminate is shown, however, and if promotions or other job benefits are distributed according to a fair **seniority system** (in which workers with more years of service are promoted first or laid off last), the employer has a good defense against the suit.

After-Acquired Evidence of Employee Misconduct

In some situations, employers have attempted to avoid liability for employment discrimination on the basis of "after-acquired evidence" of an employee's misconduct. For example, suppose that an employer fires a worker, and the employee sues the employer for employment discrimination. During pretrial investigation, the employer learns that the

24. See, for example, *Steele v. Thiokol Corp.*, 241 F.3d 1248 (10th Cir. 2001).

employee made material misrepresentations on his or her employment application—misrepresentations that, had the employer known about them, would have served as a ground to fire the individual. Can this after-acquired evidence be used as a defense?

According to the United States Supreme Court, after-acquired evidence of wrongdoing should not operate, "in every instance, to bar all relief for an earlier violation" of a federal law prohibiting discrimination.[25] Since this decision, the courts have generally held that after-acquired evidence, at best, can only serve to limit liability. While such evidence cannot be used to shield an employer entirely from liability for employment discrimination, it may be used to limit the amount of damages for which the employer is liable.

SECTION 6

Affirmative Action

Federal statutes and regulations providing for equal opportunity in the workplace were designed to reduce or eliminate discriminatory practices with respect to hiring, retaining, and promoting employees. **Affirmative action** programs go a step further and attempt to "make up" for past patterns of discrimination by giving members of protected classes preferential treatment in hiring or promotion.

Affirmative action programs have caused much controversy, particularly when they result in what is frequently called "reverse discrimination"—discrimination against "majority" workers, such as white males (or discrimination against other minority groups that are not given preferential treatment under a particular affirmative action program). At issue is whether affirmative action programs, because of their inherently discriminatory nature, violate the equal protection clause of the Fourteenth Amendment to the Constitution.

THE *BAKKE* CASE

An early case addressing this issue, although not related to employment, was *Regents of the University of California v. Bakke.*[26] That case involved an affirmative action program implemented by the University of California at Davis. Allan Bakke, who had been turned down for medical school at the Davis campus, sued the university for reverse discrimination after he discovered that his academic record was better than those of some of the minority applicants who had been admitted to the program.

The United States Supreme Court held that affirmative action programs were subject to intermediate scrutiny. Recall from the discussion of the equal protection clause in Chapter 4 that any law or action evaluated under a standard of intermediate scrutiny, to be constitutionally valid, must be substantially related to important government objectives. Applying this standard, the Court held that the university could give favorable weight to minority applicants as part of a plan to increase minority enrollment so as to achieve a more culturally diverse student body. The Court stated, however, that the use of a quota system, in which a certain number of places are explicitly reserved for minority applicants, violated the equal protection clause of the Fourteenth Amendment.

THE *ADARAND* CASE AND SUBSEQUENT DEVELOPMENTS

Although the *Bakke* case and later court decisions alleviated the harshness of the quota system, today's courts are going even further in questioning the constitutional validity of affirmative action programs. In 1995, in its landmark decision in *Adarand Constructors, Inc. v. Peña,*[27] the United States Supreme Court held that any federal, state, or local affirmative action program that uses racial or ethnic classifications as the basis for making decisions is subject to strict scrutiny by the courts.

In effect, the Court's opinion in *Adarand* means that an affirmative action program is constitutional only if it attempts to remedy past discrimination and does not make use of quotas or preferences. Furthermore, once such a program has succeeded in the goal of remedying past discrimination, it must be changed or dropped. Since then, other federal courts have followed the Supreme Court's lead by declaring affirmative action programs invalid unless they attempt to remedy past or current discrimination.[28]

The Court of Appeals for the Fifth Circuit went even further than the Supreme Court in its 1996

25. *McKennon v. Nashville Banner Publishing Co.,* 513 U.S. 352, 115 S.Ct. 879, 130 L.Ed.2d 852 (1995).

26. 438 U.S. 265, 98 S.Ct. 2733, 57 L.Ed.2d 750 (1978).

27. 575 U.S. 200, 115 S.Ct. 2097, 132 L.Ed.2d 158 (1995).

28. See, for example, *Taxman v. Board of Education of the Township of Piscataway,* 91 F.3d 1547 (3d Cir. 1996); and *Schurr v. Resorts International Hotel, Inc.,* 196 F.3d 486 (3d Cir. 1999).

decision in *Hopwood v. State of Texas.*[29] In that case, two white law school applicants sued the University of Texas School of Law in Austin, alleging that they were denied admission because of the school's affirmative action program. The program allowed admitting officials to take racial and other factors into consideration when determining which students would be admitted. The Court of Appeals for the Fifth Circuit held that the program violated the equal protection clause because it discriminated in favor of minority applicants. In its decision, the court directly challenged the *Bakke* ruling by stating that the use of race even as a means of achieving diversity on college campuses "undercuts the Fourteenth Amendment." The United States Supreme Court declined to hear the case, thus letting the lower court's decision stand.

Additionally, California and Washington, by voter initiatives in 1996 and 1998, respectively, ended state-sponsored affirmative action in those states. Similar movements are currently under way in other states as well.

29. 84 F.3d 720 (5th Cir. 1996).

SECTION 7

State Laws Prohibiting Discrimination

Although the focus of this chapter is on federal legislation, most states also have statutes that prohibit employment discrimination. Generally, the kinds of discrimination prohibited under federal legislation are also prohibited by state laws. In addition, state statutes often provide protection for certain individuals who are not protected under federal laws. For example, a New Jersey appellate court has held that anyone over the age of eighteen was entitled to sue for age discrimination under the state law, which specified no threshold age limit.[30] Furthermore, state laws prohibiting discrimination may apply to firms with fewer employees than the threshold number required under federal statutes, thus offering protection to a greater number of workers. Finally, state laws may provide for additional damages, such as damages for emotional distress, that are not provided for under federal statutes.

30. *Bergen Commercial Bank v. Sisler,* 307 N.J.Super. 333, 704 A.2d 1017 (1998).

TERMS AND CONCEPTS TO REVIEW

affirmative action 859

bona fide occupational qualification (BFOQ) 858

business necessity 858

disparate-impact discrimination 851

disparate-treatment discrimination 851

employment discrimination 850

prima facie case 851

protected class 850

seniority system 858

sexual harassment 852

CHAPTER SUMMARY

Title VII of the Civil Rights Act of 1964

Title VII prohibits employment discrimination based on race, color, national origin, religion, or gender.

1. *Procedures*—Employees must file a claim with the Equal Employment Opportunity Commission (EEOC). The EEOC may sue the employer on the employee's behalf; if not, the employee may sue the employer directly.
2. *Types of discrimination*—Title VII prohibits both intentional (disparate-treatment) and unintentional (disparate-impact) discrimination. Disparate-impact discrimination occurs when an employer's practice, such as hiring only persons with a certain level of education, has the effect of discriminating against a class of persons protected by Title VII. Title VII also extends to discriminatory practices, such as various forms of harassment, in the online environment.
3. *Remedies for discrimination under Title VII*—If a plaintiff proves that unlawful discrimination occurred, he or she may be awarded reinstatement, back pay, and retroactive promotions. Damages (both compensatory and punitive) may be awarded for intentional discrimination.

CHAPTER SUMMARY—CONTINUED

Equal Pay Act of 1963	The Equal pay Act of 1963 prohibits gender-based discrimination in the wages paid for equal work on jobs when their performance requires equal skill, effort, and responsibility under similar conditions.
Discrimination Based on Age	The Age Discrimination in Employment Act (ADEA) of 1967 prohibits employment discrimination on the basis of age against individuals forty years of age or older. Procedures for bringing a case under the ADEA are similar to those for bringing a case under Title VII.
Discrimination Based on Disability	The Americans with Disabilities Act (ADA) of 1990 prohibits employment discrimination against persons with disabilities who are otherwise qualified to perform the essential functions of the jobs for which they apply. 1. *Procedures and remedies*—To prevail on a claim under the ADA, the plaintiff must show that he or she has a disability, is otherwise qualified for the employment in question, and was excluded from the employment solely because of the disability. Procedures under the ADA are similar to those required in Title VII cases; remedies are also similar to those under Title VII. 2. *Definition of disability*—The ADA defines the term disability as a physical or mental impairment that substantially limits one or more major life activities; a record of such impairment; or being regarded as having such an impairment. 3. *Reasonable accommodation*—Employers are required to reasonably accommodate the needs of persons with disabilities. Reasonable accommodations may include altering job-application procedures, modifying the physical work environment, and permitting flexible work schedules. Employers are not required to accommodate the needs of all workers with disabilities. For example, employers need not accommodate workers who pose a definite threat to health and safety in the workplace or those who are not otherwise qualified for their jobs.
Defenses to Employment Discrimination	If a plaintiff proves that employment discrimination occurred, employers may avoid liability by successfully asserting certain defenses. Employers may assert that the discrimination was required for reasons of business necessity, to meet a bona fide occupational qualification, or to maintain a legitimate seniority system. Evidence of prior employee misconduct acquired after the employee has been fired is not a defense to discrimination.
Affirmative Action	Affirmative action programs attempt to "make up" for past patterns of discrimination by giving members of protected classes preferential treatment in hiring or promotion. Increasingly, such programs are being strictly scrutinized by the courts, and state-sponsored affirmative action has been banned in California and Washington.
State Laws Prohibiting Discrimination	Generally, the kinds of discrimination prohibited by federal statutes are also prohibited by state laws. State laws may provide for more extensive protection and remedies than federal laws.

CASES FOR ANALYSIS

Westlaw. You can access the full text of each case presented below by going to the Westlaw cases on this text's Web site at http://wbl-cs.westbuslaw.com. Each Westlaw case includes the names of all plaintiffs and defendants, the dates on which the case was argued and decided, a brief summary of the issues and decisions in the case, headnotes classifiying specific issues in the case according to the West Key Number System, and the court's opinion. Concurring and dissenting opinions, if any, are included as well.

CASE 42.1 DISCRIMINATION BASED ON GENDER

CAREY v. MOUNT DESERT ISLAND HOSPITAL

United States Court of Appeals,
First Circuit, 1998.
156 F.3d 31.

COFFIN, Senior Circuit Judge.

Michael D. Carey brought this suit [in a federal district court] against Mt. Desert Island Hospital ("MDI") for gender discrimination in violation of Title VII of the Civil Rights Act of 1964 and the Maine Human Rights Act. He alleged that he was discharged from his position as Vice-President of Finance because he was male.

After a seven-day trial, a jury returned a verdict in Carey's favor, awarding compensatory and punitive damages of $210,000 and $400,000, respectively. The district court reduced the $610,000 total to $200,000 to conform with the statutory cap for awards of compensatory and punitive damages under Title VII. The court declined to award front pay, reasoning that it was included under the statutory cap, and was inappropriate under the circumstances of the case. The court awarded back pay in the amount of $110,070, making the total amount of recovery $310,070.

* * * MDI appeals * * * .

Our review of the record reveals that this was a case with much to say on either side, involving the always difficult question of probing the wellsprings of human motivation. Moreover, it was in our minds an exceptionally hard fought trial. * * *

* * * *

MDI is a thirty-nine-bed community hospital in Bar Harbor, Maine, with approximately 200 employees. In 1983, James Mroch, the Hospital's CEO, hired Carey as Comptroller. In 1991, Carey was promoted to Vice-President of Finance. His responsibilities included preparation of budgets and financial reports, working with outside auditors, service on various committees, including the Management Committee, and supervision of the Hospital's accounting and business offices.

The critical period in this case begins in January 1993 and extends to June 1994. In January 1993, MDI's Board of Trustees discharged Mroch, and Dan Hobbs carried out the duties of CEO until September of that year. In the meantime, Lynda Tyson, who had become a Board member in 1989 and chairperson in 1993, engaged a professional recruiter, Anna Phillips, to find a permanent replacement for Mroch. Carey applied for the position but in June was told he would not be considered further. In July 1993, after its first choice, David Pagniucci, declined the offer, the Board offered the job to Leslie Hawkins. She accepted and commenced employment in mid-September 1993.

In the interim, on April 30, 1993, MDI's new outside auditors, Berry, Dunn, McNeil & Parker ("Berry, Dunn") prepared a "1993 Management Letter" reporting conditions observed during its end of the fiscal year audit of MDI. * * *

Shortly after Hawkins commenced her duties, in September 1993, Tyson arranged a meeting with Hawkins, the Board, and the Berry, Dunn auditors to discuss the Management Letter. Carey was not invited. The auditors said that while the items in the letter were serious and needed to be addressed, the finance department, with some assistance, should be able to rectify them before the next audit.

In April 1994, Hawkins asked Carey to present a proposed fiscal 1995 budget to the Board before April 30. Realizing one week before the deadline that he could not complete the assignment in time, Carey asked for and was granted a one-month extension. In May, he submitted a budget, which projected large deficits and some high expenses. Hawkins and MDI's finance committee found the proposal unacceptable and sent the budget back for reworking.

* * * On June 23, Hawkins terminated Carey, followed soon by his female assistant, Robinson. She gave as reasons the uncorrected problems noted in the 1993 Management Letter, lack of a budget, and lack of confidence in Carey and Robinson. Hawkins advised Lynda Tyson, the Executive Committee, and the full Board; all supported her action.

* * * *

The series of events and concerns described above indicates a very legitimate, non-discriminatory justification for discharging Carey. More than speculation or random evidence of satisfactory performance is required to constitute a sufficient basis for a jury finding that incompetency and mismanagement were not the real reason for the discharge. We therefore distill all the evidence that points to [MDI's reasons as] pretext [for discrimination].

* * * *

* * * [G]ermane is Hobbs' recommendation to the CEO Search Committee in June 1993 that Carey be considered for the position of CEO * * * .

Then there is the key 1993 Management Letter itself. What sounds like a massive indictment could have been read by a skeptical jury as a list of technical accounting recommendations to be expected from a firm making its first impression on a client. * * *

A jury could reasonably conclude that nothing in this suggested an alarming hazard or a smoking gun, such as that portrayed by Hawkins. Indeed, at least five of the recommendations ended with the observation that the finance staff was already attacking the problem. * * *

* * * *

Finally, the jury might have doubted the facial [apparent] justifications advanced by Hawkins concerning the relative infrequency of meetings between Hawkins and Carey, whose offices were in close proximity. And they may have suspected that she thwarted his ability to succeed based on evidence that she refused to allow Carey to fill all the budgeted positions allotted him, did not give him any advance warnings of serious trouble despite earlier assurance that she would inform him if she had problems with his job performance, and the absence of any effort to institute "progressive discipline" or corrective action, as was general practice, before dismissal.

We therefore cannot say that disbelief of the reasons proffered by MDI would be unsupported or unfounded.

* * * *

This conclusion, however, would not be enough to support the verdict. It may very well be that Hawkins, Tyson, and the entire Board had come to the point where they did not like Carey's style, finding him too openly critical of others and insensitive in his public utterances. If such were the real motivation for his discharge, it might or might not be fair but certainly would not be discrimination prohibited by law. It therefore was incumbent on Carey to introduce sufficient evidence to enable a reasonable jury to find that the justifications advanced by MDI for his discharge were a cover for an underlying anti-male animus.

In a case such as this, where a plaintiff must rely on circumstantial as opposed to direct evidence of gender discrimination, the evidence will necessarily be composed of bits and pieces, which may or may not point to an atmosphere of gender discrimination. While an employer should not find itself in jeopardy by reason of occasional stray remarks by ordinary employees, circumstantial evidence of a discriminatory atmosphere at a plaintiff's place of employment is relevant to the question of motive in considering a discrimination claim * * * . *Evidence of a corporate state-of-mind or a discriminatory atmosphere is not rendered irrelevant by its failure to coincide precisely with the particular actors or timeframe involved in the specific events that generated a claim of discriminatory treatment.* [Emphasis added.]

The record reveals * * * evidence in support of [Carey's] claim of sex-based discriminatory *animus:*

* * * *

—In the spring of 1993, a management committee member, Brian McCarthy, complained to Evans about another employee's having thrown water in his face. He testified that Evans was not receptive to his complaint, telling him not to worry about it. When he asked what she would do in the event water was thrown at a female employee, Evans said the person would probably be fired. She explained, "we have different standards for men and women."

—Tyson, then Vice-Chair of the Board, helped secure the discharge of Mroch as President and CEO. Upon his termination in early 1993, she hired an executive search firm, placing Anna Phillips in charge of identifying a prospective CEO for MDI. In the summer of 1993, Gordon, Brian McCarthy, David Frongillo, Director of the MDI Pharmacy, and Hawkins, who was then a candidate, met with Phillips. Frongillo asked if there was a selection criterion involving gender, to which Gordon responded, "it's about time that we get a woman for this position," and Phillips said that "they would very much like to put a woman in that position." * * *

* * * *

* * * We * * * hold that there was sufficient evidence to support a finding that deficiencies in Carey's handling of financial controls were not the real reason for his discharge but instead covered an action stemming from gender discrimination.

* * * *

V. *Conclusion*

We therefore affirm the district court * * * .

CASE 42.2 DISCRIMINATION BASED ON DISABILITY

SUTTON V. UNITED AIRLINES, INC.

Supreme Court of the United States, 1999.
527 U.S. 471,
119 S.Ct. 2139,
144 L.Ed.2d 450.

Justice *O'CONNOR* delivered the opinion of the Court.

* * * *

Petitioners [Karen and Kimberly Sutton] are twin sisters, both of whom have severe myopia. Each petitioner's uncorrected visual acuity is 20/200 or worse in her right eye and 20/400 or worse in her left eye, but with the use of corrective lenses, each * * * has vision that is 20/20 or better. Consequently, without corrective lenses, each effectively cannot see to conduct numerous activities such as driving a vehicle, watching television or shopping in public stores, but with corrective measures, such as glasses or contact lenses, both function identically to individuals without a similar impairment.

In 1992, petitioners applied to respondent [United Airlines, Inc.] for employment as commercial airline pilots. They met respondent's basic age, education, experience, and Federal Aviation Administration certification qualifications. After submitting their applications for employment, both petitioners were invited by respondent to an interview and to flight simulator tests. Both were told during their interviews, however, that a mistake had been made in inviting them to interview because petitioners did not meet respondent's minimum vision requirement, which was uncorrected visual acuity of 20/100 or better. Due to their failure to meet this requirement, petitioners' interviews were terminated, and neither was offered a pilot position.

In light of respondent's proffered reason for rejecting them, petitioners filed a charge of disability discrimination under the [Americans with Disabilities Act of 1990 (ADA)] with the Equal Employment Opportunity Commission (EEOC). After receiving a right to sue letter, petitioners filed suit in the United States District Court for the District of Colorado, alleging that respondent had discriminated against them "on the basis of their disability, or because [respondent] regarded [petitioners] as having a disability" in violation of the ADA. Specifically, petitioners alleged that due to their severe myopia they actually have a substantially limiting impairment or are regarded as having such an impairment and are thus disabled under the Act.

The District Court dismissed petitioners' complaint for failure to state a claim upon which relief could be granted. * * * [T]he Court of Appeals for the Tenth Circuit affirmed the District Court's judgment. * * * We granted *certiorari* * * * .

* * * *

* * * The Act defines a "disability" as "a physical or mental impairment that *substantially limits* one or more of the major life activities" of an individual. [Emphasis added.] Because the phrase "substantially limits" appears in the Act in the present indicative verb form, we think the language is properly read as requiring that a person be presently—not potentially or hypothetically—substantially limited in order to demonstrate a disability. A "disability" exists only where an impairment "substantially limits" a major life activity, not where it "might," "could," or "would" be substantially limiting if mitigating measures were not taken. A person whose physical or mental impairment is corrected by medication or other measures does not have an impairment that presently "substantially limits" a major life activity. To be sure, *a person whose physical or mental impairment is corrected by mitigating measures still has an impairment, but if the impairment is corrected it does not "substantially limi[t]" a major life activity.* [Emphasis added.]

* * * *

* * * The use of a corrective device does not, by itself, relieve one's disability. Rather, one has a disability under [the ADA] if, notwithstanding the use of a corrective device, that individual is substantially limited in a major life activity. For example, individuals who use prosthetic limbs or wheelchairs may be mobile and capable of functioning in society but still be disabled because of a substantial limitation on their ability to walk or run. The same may be true of individuals who take medicine to lessen the symptoms of an impairment so that they can function but nevertheless remain substantially limited. Alternatively, one whose high blood pressure is "cured" by medication may be regarded as disabled by a covered entity, and thus disabled under [the ADA]. The use or nonuse of a corrective device does not determine whether an individual is disabled; that determination depends on whether the limitations an individual with an impairment *actually* faces are in fact substantially limiting.

Applying this reading of the Act to the case at hand, we conclude that the Court of Appeals correctly resolved the issue of disability in respondent's favor. As noted above, petitioners allege that with corrective measures, their visual acuity is 20/20 and that they "function identically to individuals without a similar impairment." In addition, petitioners concede that they "do not argue that the use of corrective lenses in itself demonstrates a substantially limiting impairment." Accordingly, because we decide that disability under the Act is to be determined with reference to corrective measures, we agree with the [lower] courts * * * that petitioners have not stated a claim that they are substantially limited in any major life activity.

* * * *

Our conclusion that petitioners have failed to state a claim that they are actually disabled under [the ADA's] disability definition does not end our inquiry. * * * [The ADA] provides that having a disability includes "being regarded as having a physical or mental impairment that substantially limits one or more of the major life activities of such individual." There are two apparent ways in which individuals may fall within this statutory definition: (1) a covered entity mistakenly believes that a person has a physical impairment that substantially limits one or more major life activities, or (2) a covered entity mistakenly believes that an actual, nonlimiting impairment substantially limits one or more major life activities. In both cases, it is necessary that a covered entity entertain misperceptions about the individual—it must believe either that one has a substantially limiting impairment that one does not have or that one has a substantially limiting impairment when, in fact, the impairment is not so limiting. These misperceptions often result from stereotypic assumptions not truly indicative of * * * individual ability.

* * * *

* * * By its terms, the ADA allows employers to prefer some physical attributes over others and to establish physical criteria. *An employer runs afoul of the ADA when it makes an employment decision based on a physical or mental impairment, real or imagined, that is regarded as substantially limiting a major life activity.* * * * [Emphasis added.]

* * * The EEOC has codified regulations interpreting the term "substantially limits" * * * to mean "[u]nable to perform" or "[s]ignificantly restricted." When the major life activity under consideration is that of working, the statutory phrase "substantially limits" requires, at a minimum, that plaintiffs allege they are unable to work in a broad class of jobs. * * * The inability to perform a single, particular job does not constitute a substantial limitation in the major life activity of working.

* * * *

* * * [P]etitioners have failed to allege adequately that their poor eyesight is regarded as an impairment that substantially limits them in the major life activity of working. They allege only that respondent regards their poor vision as precluding them from holding positions as a "global airline pilot." Because the position of global airline pilot is a single job, this allegation does not support the claim that respondent regards petitioners as having a *substantially limiting* impairment. Indeed, there are a number of other positions utilizing petitioners' skills, such as regional pilot and pilot instructor to name a few, that are available to them. * * *

* * * *

For these reasons, the judgment of the Court of Appeals for the Tenth Circuit is affirmed.

It is so ordered.

Justice *STEVENS* * * * dissenting.

* * * [I]f we apply customary tools of statutory construction, it is quite clear that the threshold question whether an individual is "disabled" within the meaning of the Act * * * focuses on her past or present physical condition without regard to mitigation that has resulted from rehabilitation, self-improvement, prosthetic devices, or medication. One might reasonably argue that the general rule should not apply to an impairment that merely requires a nearsighted person to wear glasses. * * *

* * * *

Accordingly, * * * I am persuaded that [the petitioners] have a disability covered by the ADA. I therefore respectfully dissent.

CASE 42.3 DISCRIMINATION BASED ON DISABILITY

FLOWERS v. SOUTHERN REGIONAL PHYSICIAN SERVICES, INC.

United States Court of Appeals,
Fifth Circuit, 2001.
247 F.3d 229.

KING, Chief Judge:

* * * *

I. FACTUAL AND PROCEDURAL BACKGROUND

Plaintiff-Appellee Sandra Spragis Flowers was employed by Defendant-Appellant Southern Regional Physician Services, Inc. ("Southern Regional") from September 1, 1993 to November 13, 1995. Flowers worked primarily as a medical assistant for Dr. James Osterberger, a physician at Southern Regional. In early March 1995, Margaret Hallmark, Flowers's immediate supervisor, discovered that Flowers was infected with the Human Immunodeficiency Virus ("HIV"). Flowers was terminated from Southern Regional in November 1995.

On October 6, 1996, Flowers filed a charge of discrimination with the Equal Employment Opportunity Commission ("EEOC"), alleging that Southern Regional had engaged in unlawful discrimination because of Flowers's status as a disabled person. After receiving the requisite Right to Sue Letter from the EEOC, Flowers filed suit in [a] federal [district] court asserting a violation of the Americans with Disabilities Act ("ADA"). Flowers claimed both that she was terminated because of her disability and also that she was subjected to "harassing conduct" designed to "force [her] from her position or cast her in a false light for the purpose of terminating her because of her HIV status."

Flowers's claims proceeded to trial by jury on December 8, 1998. * * * After deliberation, the jury determined * * * that Flowers was subjected to disability-based harassment that created a hostile work environment. As a result of its finding of a hostile work environment, the jury awarded Flowers $350,000. The district court reduced the amount to $100,000 * * *. The district court then entered final judgment in her favor on July 21, 1999. * * *

Southern Regional timely appealed.

II. AVAILABILITY OF A CAUSE OF ACTION UNDER THE ADA FOR DISABILITY-BASED HARASSMENT

* * * [T]he district court concluded that the ADA encompasses a cause of action for disability-based

harassment. Southern Regional contends, however, that no cause of action under the ADA exists * * * .

* * * *

The ADA provides that no employer covered by the Act "shall discriminate against a qualified individual with a disability because of the disability of such individual in regard to * * * *terms, conditions, and privileges of employment.*" In almost identical fashion, Title VII provides that it is unlawful for an employer "to fail or refuse to hire or to discharge any individual, or otherwise to discriminate against any individual with respect to his compensation, *terms, conditions, or privileges of employment,* because of such individual's race, color, religion, sex, or national origin[.]" [Emphasis added.]

It is evident, after a review of the ADA's language, purpose, and remedial framework, that Congress's intent in enacting the ADA was, *inter alia,* to eradicate disability-based harassment in the workplace. First, as a matter of statutory interpretation, * * * the [United States] Supreme Court interpreted Title VII, which contains language similar to that in the ADA, to provide a cause of action for harassment which is sufficiently severe or pervasive to alter the conditions of the victim's employment and create an abusive working environment * * * because it affects a term, condition, or privilege of employment. We conclude that the language of Title VII and the ADA dictates a consistent reading of the two statutes. Therefore, following the Supreme Court's interpretation of the language contained in Title VII, we interpret the phrase "terms, conditions, and privileges of employment," as it is used in the ADA, to strike at harassment in the workplace.

Not only are Title VII and the ADA similar in their language, they are also alike in their purposes and remedial structures. Both Title VII and the ADA are aimed at the same evil—employment discrimination against individuals of certain classes. Moreover, this court has recognized that the ADA is part of the same broad remedial framework as * * * Title VII, and that all the anti-discrimination acts have been subjected to similar analysis. Furthermore, other courts of appeals have noted the correlation between the two statutes. We conclude, therefore, that the purposes and remedial frameworks of the two statutes also command our conclusion that the ADA provides a cause of action for disability-based harassment.

* * * *

IV. ANY EVIDENCE OF INJURY

Finally, Southern Regional argues that Flowers failed to offer any evidence at trial relating to damages sustained as a result of the harassment. * * *

To recover more than nominal damages for emotional harm, a plaintiff must provide proof of actual injury resulting from the harassment. Furthermore, *emotional harm will not be presumed simply because the plaintiff is a victim of discrimination. To demonstrate an actual, or specific discernable, injury, the existence, nature, and severity of emotional harm must be proved.* [Emphasis added.]

* * * The only evidence of injury adduced by Flowers was of events that occurred after she was terminated from Southern Regional, evidence that is irrelevant to the question of actual injury stemming from the harassment.

Flowers asserts that because she testified at trial that the harassment and subsequent discharge "took away [her] self-respect and [her] dignity," she has demonstrated "some evidence" of damage. However, we conclude that this testimony, by itself, cannot support an award greater than nominal damages. Not only is the totality of the evidence solely Flowers's own testimony, it fails to demonstrate the nature or severity of the alleged emotional harm.

* * * [D]aily harassment towards an HIV-positive individual such as Flowers may not only affect that individual emotionally, but may also cause a decline in the health of that individual, resulting in a particularized physical consequence. Dr. Osterberger, Flowers's personal physician at the time of her employment with Southern Regional, provided general testimony regarding the effects of stress on a person with HIV and stated that such stress "can" aggravate HIV; however, this general testimony did not connect the possible effects of such stress with a particular injury to Flowers. Dr. Osterberger did not testify that Flowers suffered injury, but only stated that it was possible for HIV-positive individuals to suffer injury. Moreover, there is no testimony that Flowers's health deteriorated during the period of time between Hallmark's discovery of Flowers's HIV-positive condition and Flowers's termination from Southern Regional.

Because there is no evidence in the record focusing on the existence of actual injury during the time period before Flowers was discharged, we must vacate the jury's award of damages.

V. CONCLUSION

For the foregoing reasons, we AFFIRM the final judgment entered on the jury verdict as to Southern Regional's liability for disability-based harassment. However, we VACATE the jury's damages award and REMAND the case for the entry of an award of nominal damages.

CASE PROBLEMS

42–1. Wise, a female employee of Mead Corp., became involved in a dispute in the lunchroom of her place of employment with another employee, Pruitt. A fight ensued, and Wise kicked and scratched Pruitt and used "abusive and uncivil" language. Because of this behavior, Wise's employment at Mead was terminated by her employer. Wise brought suit, alleging gender discrimination on the part of Mead Corp. in violation of Title VII of the Civil Rights Act of 1964, on the ground that at least four other fights at Mead had occurred under similar circumstances and none of the participants had been fired. None of the other fights had involved a female. Did Wise's employment termination constitute gender discrimination by Mead Corp.? Discuss. [*Wise v. Mead Corp.*, 614 F.Supp. 1131 (M.D.Ga. 1985)]

42–2. Fleming Tullis was hired as a bus driver by a private school in Dade County, Florida, in September 1982. Tullis turned sixty-five on January 1, 1986. Because the insurance company would no longer insure drivers over the age of sixty-five, Tullis's employment was terminated. Tullis sued the school, alleging age discrimination in violation of the Age Discrimination in Employment Act (ADEA). Can the school successfully defend against the age-discrimination charge by stating that an age of sixty-four years or younger was a bona fide occupational qualification? Is the increased cost of insurance a factor that would exempt the school from compliance with the ADEA? Discuss fully. [*Tullis v. Lear School, Inc.*, 874 F.2d 1489 (11th Cir. 1989)]

42–3. Beginning in June 1966, Corning Glass Works started to make available jobs on the night shift to women. The previously separate male and female seniority lists were consolidated, and the women became eligible to exercise their seniority on the same basis as men and to bid for higher-paid night inspection jobs as vacancies occurred. On January 20, 1969, however, a new collective bargaining agreement went into effect; it established a new job-evaluation system for setting wage rates. This agreement abolished (for the future) separate base wages for night- and day-shift inspectors and imposed a uniform base wage for inspectors that exceeded the wage rate previously in effect for the night shift. The agreement, however, did allow for a higher "red circle" rate for employees hired prior to January 20, 1969, when they were working as inspectors on the night shift. This "red circle" wage served essentially to perpetuate the differential in base wages between day and night inspectors. Had Corning violated Title VII of the Civil Rights Act of 1964? Discuss. [*Corning Glass Works v. Brennan*, 417 U.S. 188, 94 S.Ct. 2223, 41 L.Ed.2d 1 (1974)]

42–4. Patricia Jackson, a black female and an experienced food server, applied for a job as a part-time waitress at a restaurant owned by Jackie McCleod in Foley, Alabama. An interview was arranged for the afternoon of June 2, 1989, which was a Friday. During the course of the interview, Jackson and McCleod entered into a verbal contract for Jackson to be hired as a part-time waitress, beginning Monday, June 5. Jackson was to work her first two days in the kitchen and following that orientation period would start working as a waitress. On Sunday, June 4, McCleod made up the work schedule for the period June 5 through June 11. Jackson was scheduled to work four days during the week and on each of those days would be doing kitchen work. Jackson appeared for work on Monday, June 5, as agreed. When she discovered that she had been scheduled to work in the kitchen for four days, as opposed to the two-day orientation period she expected, she confronted McCleod and asked to be put on the floor as a waitress. When her request was denied, Jackson left the restaurant. On that same day, McCleod hired a white female for the position of waitress. Jackson sued McCleod for discrimination on the basis of race in McCleod's hiring procedures, and the issue turned on whether any discrimination occurred during the "hiring" of Jackson. Will Jackson prevail in court? Discuss fully. [*Jackson v. McCleod*, 748 F.Supp. 831 (S.C.Ala. 1990)]

42–5. Duke Power Co. was sued by a number of its black employees for practicing racial discrimination in the hiring and assigning of employees at its Dan River plant. The plant was organized into five operating departments: (1) labor, (2) coal handling, (3) operations, (4) maintenance, and (5) laboratory testing. Blacks were employed only in the labor department, in which the highest-paying jobs paid less than the lowest-paying jobs in the other four departments (which employed only whites). Promotions were normally made within each department on the basis of seniority. Transferees into a department usually began in the lowest position. In 1955, the company began to require a high school education for an initial assignment into any department except the labor department. In addition, it required a high school education for any transfer from the coal-handling department to any inside department (operations, maintenance, or laboratory). For ten years, this company-wide policy was enforced. In 1965, when the company abandoned its policy of restricting blacks to the labor department, a high school diploma or equivalency test was nevertheless made a prerequisite to transfer from the labor department into any other department. This requirement rendered a markedly disproportionate number of blacks ineligible for employment advancement in the company. Did these employer practices violate Title VII of the Civil Rights Act? Discuss fully. [*Griggs v. Duke Power Co.*, 401 U.S. 424, 91 S.Ct. 849, 28 L.Ed.2d 158 (1971)]

42–6. Melvin Hicks was a black shift supervisor at the St. Mary's Honor Center, a halfway house operated by the Missouri Department of Corrections and Human Resources. Prior to the replacement of his immediate supervisor (the shift commander) and the appointment of a new superintendent, Hicks had always had a satisfactory employment record. After the change in personnel, however, Hicks was disciplined repeatedly and with increasing severity until he was eventually fired. He then brought an action under Title VII, alleging racial discrimination. Hicks successfully presented a *prima facie* case: he was black, he was qualified for the job of shift commander, he was demoted and then discharged, and the position he vacated was filled by a white man. The burden then shifted to St. Mary's Honor Center to prove that it had acted for legitimate, nondiscriminatory reasons. The center asserted that Hicks had violated procedures and threatened his supervisor. The district court found the claims to be a mere pretext (a fabricated reason for dismissing Hicks). The court nonetheless held for the center because Hicks had failed to prove that the center's actions were motivated by any racial bias—in other words, Hicks had not been discriminated against on the basis of race, as he had contended. The appellate court reversed, holding that once the district court had found that the center's reasons were pretextual, Hicks was entitled to judgment as a matter of law. The case was appealed to the United States Supreme Court. Discuss how the Supreme Court should decide this case, and why. [*St. Mary's Honor Center v. Hicks*, 509 U.S. 502, 113 S.Ct. 2742, 125 L.Ed.2d 407 (1993)]

42–7. Dorothea O'Driscoll had worked as a quality control inspector for Hercules, Inc., for six years when her employment was terminated in 1986. O'Driscoll, who was over forty years of age, sued Hercules for age discrimination in violation of the Age Discrimination in Employment Act of 1967. While preparing for trial, Hercules learned that O'Driscoll had made several misrepresentations when she applied for the job. Among other things, she misrepresented her age, did not disclose a previous employer, falsely represented that she had never applied for work with Hercules before, and untruthfully stated that she had completed two quarters of study at a technical college. Additionally, on her application for group insurance coverage, she misrepresented the age of her son, who would otherwise have been ineligible for coverage as her dependent. Hercules defended against O'Driscoll's claim of age discrimination by stating that had it known of this misconduct, it would have terminated her employment anyway. What should the court decide? Discuss fully. [*O'Driscoll v. Hercules, Inc.*, 12 F.3d 176 (10th Cir. 1994)]

42–8. Phanna Xieng was sent by the Cambodian government to the United States in 1974 for "advanced military training." When the Cambodian government fell in 1975, Xieng remained in the United States and in 1979 was employed by Peoples National Bank of Washington. In performance appraisals from 1980 through 1985, Xieng was rated by his supervisors as "capable of dealing effectively with customers" and qualified for promotion, although in each appraisal it was noted that Xieng might improve his communication skills to maximize his possibilities for future advancement. Xieng sought job promotions on numerous occasions but was never promoted. In 1986, he filed a complaint against the bank, alleging employment discrimination based on national origin. The employer argued that its refusal to promote Xieng because of his accent or communication skills did not amount to discrimination based on national origin. Is it possible to separate discrimination based on an employee's accent and communication skills from discrimination based on national origin? How should the court rule on this issue? [*Xieng v. Peoples National Bank of Washington*, 120 Wash.2d 512, 844 P.2d 389 (1993)]

42–9. When the University of Maryland Medical System Corp. learned that one of its surgeons was HIV positive, the university offered him transfers to positions that did not involve surgery. The surgeon refused, and the university terminated him. The surgeon filed a suit in a federal district court against the university, alleging in part a violation of the Americans with Disabilities Act. The surgeon claimed that he was "otherwise qualified" for his former position. What does he have to prove to win his case? Should he be reinstated? [*Doe v. University of Maryland Medical System Corp.*, 50 F.3d 1261 (4th Cir. 1995)]

42–10. Theodore Rosenblatt, a white attorney, worked for the law firm of Bivona & Cohen, P.C. When Bivona & Cohen terminated Rosenblatt's employment, he filed a suit in a federal district court against the firm. Rosenblatt claimed that he had been discharged because he was married to an African American and that a discharge for such a reason violated Title VII and other laws. The firm filed a motion for summary judgment, arguing that he was alleging discrimination against his wife, not himself, and thus did not have standing to sue under Title VII for racial discrimination. Should the court grant or deny the motion? Explain. [*Rosenblatt v. Bivona & Cohen, P.C.*, 946 F.Supp. 298 (S.D.N.Y. 1996)]

42–11. Mary Tiano, a devout Roman Catholic, worked for Dillard Department Stores, Inc. (Dillard's), in Phoenix, Arizona. Dillard's considered Tiano a productive employee because her sales exceeded $200,000 a year. At the time, the store gave its managers the discretion to grant unpaid leave to employees but prohibited vacations or leave during the holiday season—October through December. Tiano felt that she had a "calling" to go on a "pilgrimage" in October 1988 to Medjugorje, Yugoslavia, where some persons claimed to have had visions of the Virgin Mary. The Catholic Church had not designated the site an official pilgrimage site, the visions were not expected to be stronger in October, and tours were available at other times. The store managers denied Tiano's request for leave, but she had a nonrefundable ticket and left anyway. Dillard's terminated her employment. For a year, Tiano searched for a new job and did not attain the level of her Dillard's salary for four years. She filed a suit in a federal district court against Dillard's, alleging religious discrimination in violation of Title VII. Can Tiano establish a *prima facie* case of religious discrimination? Explain. [*Tiano v. Dillard Department Stores, Inc.*, 139 F.3d 679 (9th Cir. 1998)]

42–12. Vaughn Murphy was first diagnosed with hypertension (high blood pressure) when he was ten years old. Unmedicated, his blood pressure is approximately 250/160. With medication, however, he can function normally and engage in the same activities as anyone else. In 1994, United Parcel Service, Inc. (UPS), hired Murphy to be a mechanic, a position that required him to drive commercial motor vehicles. To get the job, Murphy had to meet a U.S. Department of Transportation (DOT) regulation that a driver have "no current clinical diagnosis of high blood pressure likely to interfere with his/her ability to operate a commercial vehicle safely." At the time, Murphy's blood pressure was measured at 186/124, but he was erroneously certified and started work. Within a month, the error was discovered and he was fired. Murphy obtained another mechanic's job—one that did not require DOT certification—and filed a suit in a federal district court against UPS, claiming discrimination under the Americans with Disabilities Act. UPS filed a motion for summary judgment. Should the court grant UPS's motion? Explain. [*Murphy v. United Parcel Service, Inc.*, 527 U.S. 516, 119 S.Ct. 2133, 144 L.Ed.2d 484 (1999)]

42–13. Local 1066 of the Steamship Clerks Union accepted only new members who were sponsored by existing members. All of the existing members were white. During a six-year period, the local admitted thirty new members, all of whom were relatives of present members and also white. The Equal Employment Opportunity Commission filed a suit in a federal district court against the union, alleging that this practice constituted disparate-impact discrimination under Title VII. The union argued that it was only continuing a family tradition. What does each party have to prove to win its case? Should the union be required to change its practice? [*EEOC v. Steamship Clerks Union, Local 1066*, 48 F.3d 594 (1st Cir. 1995)]

42–14. PGA Tour, Inc., sponsors professional golf tournaments. A player may enter in several ways, but it is most common to successfully compete in a three-stage qualifying tournament known as the "Q-School." Anyone may enter the Q-School by submitting two letters of recommendation and paying $3,000 to cover greens fees and the cost of a golf cart, the use of which is permitted during the first two stages, but prohibited during the third stage. The rules governing the events include the "Rules of Golf," which apply at all levels of amateur and professional golf and do not prohibit the use of golf carts, and the "hard card," which applies specifically to PGA tours and requires the players to walk the course during most of a tournament. Casey Martin is a talented golfer with a degenerative circulatory disorder that prevents him from walking golf courses. Martin entered the Q-School, and asked for permission to use a cart during the third stage. PGA refused. Martin filed a suit in a federal district court against PGA, alleging a violation of the Americans with Disabilities Act. Is a golf cart in these circumstances a "reasonable accommodation" under the ADA? Why, or why not? [*PGA Tour, Inc. v. Martin*, 531 U.S. 1049, 121 S.Ct. 1879, 149 L.Ed.2d 904 (2001)]

42–15. A QUESTION OF ETHICS

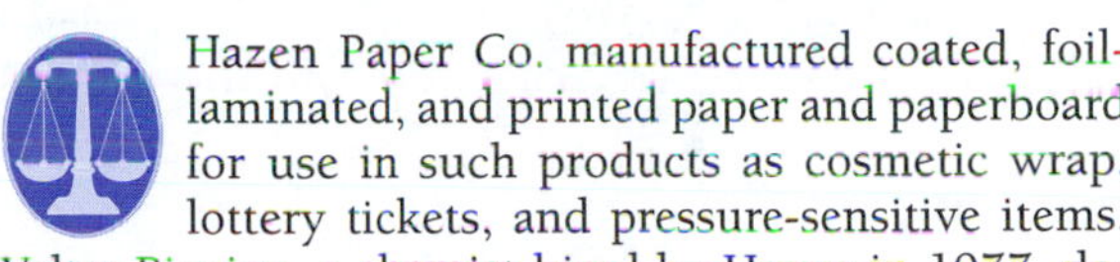

Hazen Paper Co. manufactured coated, foil-laminated, and printed paper and paperboard for use in such products as cosmetic wrap, lottery tickets, and pressure-sensitive items. Walter Biggins, a chemist hired by Hazen in 1977, developed a water-based paper coating that was both environmentally safe and of superior quality. By the mid-1980s, the company's sales had increased dramatically as a result of its extensive use of "Biggins Acrylic." Because of this, Biggins thought he deserved a substantial raise in salary, and from 1984 to 1986, Biggins's persistent requests for a raise became a bone of contention between him and his employers. Biggins ran a business on the side cleaning up hazardous wastes for various companies. Hazen told Biggins that unless he signed a "confidentiality agreement" promising to restrict his outside activities during the time he was employed by Hazen and for a limited time afterward, he would be fired. Biggins said he would sign the agreement only if Hazen raised his salary to $100,000. Hazen refused to do so, fired Biggins, and hired a younger man to replace him. At the time of his discharge in 1986, Biggins was sixty-two years old, had worked for the company nearly ten years, and was just a few weeks away from being entitled to pension rights worth about $93,000. In view of these circumstances, evaluate and answer the following questions. [*Hazen Paper Co. v. Biggins*, 507 U.S. 604, 113 S.Ct.1701, 123 L.Ed.2d 338 (1993)]

1. Biggins sued Hazen for age discrimination in violation of the Age Discrimination in Employment Act of 1967. If you were the judge, would you hold for Biggins or Hazen? Discuss fully.
2. Did the company owe an ethical duty to Biggins to increase his salary, given the fact that its sales increased dramatically as a result of Biggins's efforts and ingenuity in developing the coating? If you were one of the company's owners, would you have raised Biggins's salary? Why, or why not?
3. Generally, what public policies come into conflict in cases involving employers who, for reasons of cost and efficiency of operations, fire older, higher-paid workers and replace them with younger, lower-paid workers? What would you do, and on what ethical premises would you justify your decision, if you were an employer facing the need to cut back on personnel to save costs?

E-LINKS

For updated links to resources available on the Web, as well as a variety of other materials, visit this text's Web site at

http://wbl-cs.westbuslaw.com

The law firm of Arent Fox posts articles on current issues in the area of employment law, including sexual harassment, on its Web site at

http://www.arentfox.com/home.html

An abundance of helpful information on disability-based discrimination, including the text of the Americans with Disabilities Act of 1990, can be found at the following Web site:

http://janweb.icdi.wvu.edu/kinder

An excellent source for information on various forms of employment discrimination is the Equal Employment Opportunity Commission's Web site at

http://www.eeoc.gov

LEGAL RESEARCH EXERCISES ON THE WEB

Go to http://wbl-cs.westbuslaw.com, the Web site that accompanies this text. Select "Interactive Study Center," and then click on "Chapter 42." There you will find the following Internet research exercises that you can perform to learn more about laws prohibiting employment discrimination:

Activity 42–1: Americans with Disabilities

Activity 42–2: Equal Employment Opportunity

Focus on Legal Reasoning

National Labor Relations Board v. Kentucky River Community Care, Inc.

The National Labor Relations Act (NLRA) of 1935 is discussed in Chapter 41. The NLRA protects *employees* from employers' unfair labor practices. Workers are not protected, however, if they are deemed to be *supervisors*—employees who exercise "independent judgment" in "responsibly . . . direct[ing]" other employees "in the interest of the employer."[1] In this *Focus on Legal Reasoning,* we examine *National Labor Relations Board v. Kentucky River Community Care, Inc.,*[2] a decision that applied this definition to a group of nurses.

1. 29 U.S.C. Section 152(11).
2. 532 U.S. 706, 121 S.Ct. 1861, 149 L.Ed.2d 939 (2001).

Case Background

In Pippa Passes, Kentucky, Kentucky River Community Care, Inc., operates the Caney Creek Developmental Complex, a care facility for residents who suffer from mental retardation and mental illness. Caney Creek employs approximately 110 professional and nonprofessional employees, and a dozen managers and supervisors. In 1997, the Kentucky State District Council of Carpenters (a labor union) petitioned the National Labor Relations Board (NLRB) to represent as a single unit all 110 employees at Caney Creek.

Kentucky River objected to the inclusion of Caney Creek's six registered nurses in the bargaining unit, arguing that they were supervisors. The nurses directed some of the patient care performed by the nurses' aides and, on some shifts, were responsible for maintaining adequate staffing levels. They could only ask—not force—employees to work, however. The NLRB included the nurses, directed an election, and certified the winning union as the employees' representative.

Kentucky River refused to bargain with the union. On an unfair labor practice complaint, the NLRB issued a bargaining order against the employer, who appealed to the U.S. Court of Appeals for the Sixth Circuit. The court refused to enforce the order. The NLRB appealed to the United States Supreme Court.

Majority Opinion

Justice *SCALIA* delivered the opinion of the Court.

* * * *

* * * The only basis asserted by the Board [NLRB] * * * for rejecting respondent's [Kentucky River's] proof of [the nurses'] supervisory status with respect to directing patient care was the Board's interpretation * * * that employees do not use "independent judgment" when they exercise "ordinary professional or technical judgment in directing less-skilled employees to deliver services in accordance with employer-specified standards." * * *

Two aspects of the Board's interpretation are reasonable * * * . First, it is certainly true that the statutory term "independent judgment" is ambiguous with respect to the *degree* of discretion required for supervisory status. Many nominally supervisory functions may be performed without the exercise of such a degree of * * * judgment or discretion * * * as would warrant a finding of supervisory status under the Act [NLRA]. It falls clearly within the Board's discretion to determine, within reason, what scope of discretion qualifies. Second, * * * it is also undoubtedly true that the degree of judgment that might ordinarily be required to conduct a particular task may be reduced below the statutory threshold by detailed orders and regulations issued by the employer. * * *

The Board, however, argues further that the judgment even of employees who are permitted by their employer to exercise a sufficient *degree* of discretion is not "independent judgment" if it is a particular *kind* of judgment, namely, "ordinary professional or technical judgment in directing less-skilled employees to deliver services." The first five words of this interpretation insert a startling categorical exclusion into statutory text that does not suggest its existence. The text, by focusing on the "clerical" or "routine" (as opposed to "independent") nature of the judgment, introduces the question of degree of judgment that we have agreed falls within the reasonable discretion of the Board to resolve. But the Board's categorical exclusion turns on factors that have nothing to do with the degree of discretion an employee exercises. Let the judgment be significant and only loosely constrained by the employer; if it is "professional or technical" it will nonetheless not be independent. The breadth of this exclusion is made all the more startling by virtue of the Board's extension of it to judgment based on greater "experience" as well as formal training. What supervisory judgment worth exercising, one must wonder, does not rest on "professional or technical skill or experience"? If the Board applied this aspect of its test to every exercise of a supervisory function, it would virtually eliminate "supervisors" from the Act.

As it happens, though, only one class of supervisors would be eliminated in practice, because the Board limits its categorical exclusion with a qualifier: Only professional judgment that is applied "in directing less-skilled employees to deliver services" is excluded from the statutory category of "independent judgment." This second rule is no less striking than the first, and is directly contrary to the text of the statute. *Every* supervisory function listed by the Act is accompanied by the statutory requirement that its exercise requires the use of independent judgment before supervisory status will obtain, but the Board would apply its restriction upon "independent judgment" to just 1 of the 12 listed functions: "responsibly to direct." There is no apparent textual justification for this asymmetrical limitation, and the Board has offered none. Surely no conceptual justification can be found in the proposition that supervisors exercise professional, technical, or experienced judgment only when they direct other employees. Decisions to hire, * * * suspend, lay off, recall, promote, discharge, * * * or discipline other employees, must often depend upon that same judgment, which enables assessment of the employee's proficiency in performing his job. * * *

The Board's refusal to apply its limiting interpretation of "independent judgment" to any supervisory function other than responsibly directing other employees is particularly troubling because just seven years ago we rejected the Board's interpretation of part three of the supervisory test that similarly was applied only to the same supervisory function. See *NLRB v. Health Care & Retirement Corp. of America,* 511 U.S. 571, 114 S.Ct. 1778, 128 L.Ed.2d 586 (1994).

* * * *

* * * [T]he Board contends that its interpretation is necessary to preserve the inclusion of "professional employees" within the coverage of the Act. Professional employees by definition engage in work "involving the consistent exercise of discretion and judgment." Therefore, the Board argues, if judgment of that sort makes one a supervisor * * * , then Congress's intent to include professionals in the Act will be frustrated, because "many professional employees (such as lawyers, doctors, and nurses) customarily give judgment-based direction to the less-skilled employees with whom they work." The problem with the argument is not the soundness of its labor policy (the Board is entitled to judge that without our constant second-guessing). It is that the policy cannot be given effect through this statutory text. Perhaps the Board could offer a limiting interpretation of the supervisory function of responsible direction by distinguishing employees who direct the manner of others' performance of discrete *tasks* from employees who direct other *employees* * * * . Certain of the Board's decisions appear to have drawn that distinction in the past. We have no occasion to consider it here, however, because the Board has carefully insisted that the proper interpretation of "responsibly to direct" is not at issue in this case.

What is at issue is the Board's contention that the policy of covering professional employees under the Act justifies the categorical exclusion of professional judgments from a term, "independent judgment," that naturally includes them. And further, that it justifies limiting this categorical exclusion to the supervisory function of responsibly directing other employees. These contentions contradict both the text and structure of the statute and they contradict as well the rule * * * that the test for supervisory status applies no differently to professionals than to other employees. We therefore find the Board's interpretation unlawful.

* * * *

* * * [T]he Board's error in interpreting "independent judgment" precludes us from enforcing its order. * * * The judgment of the Court of Appeals is affirmed.

It is so ordered.

QUESTIONS FOR ANALYSIS

1. **Legal Analysis.** In the *Kentucky River* case, the Supreme Court cites one of its own decisions, *NLRB v. Health Care & Retirement Corp. of America,* 511 U.S. 571, 114 S.Ct. 1778, 128 L.Ed.2d 586 (1994) (see the *E-Links* feature at the end of Chapter 2 for instructions on how to access the opinions of the federal courts). Why did the Court cite this case? How were the holdings of the Court in the *Kentucky River* and *Health Care* cases consistent?
2. **Legal Reasoning.** What did the majority conclude on the central issue in the *Kentucky River* case, and what support did it provide for that conclusion?
3. **Political Dimensions.** As highlighted by a reading of the opinion in this case, what is the source of the opposing parties' contentions?
4. **Implications for the Business Employer.** Does the holding in this case indicate what an employer might do to exempt certain employees from the protection of federal labor laws?

WESTLAW ONLINE RESEARCH

Go to this text's companion Web site, at http://wbl-cs.westbuslaw.com, and click on the Westlaw icon. Use your special password to access the full text of this case, including the dissenting opinions. Read through the case, and then answer the following questions.

1. Consider the majority's reasoning in the *Kentucky River* case. In this and similar cases, who should have the burden of proving that an employee is, or is not, a supervisor, and why?
2. Scan the Court's *Syllabus*. What purpose does this brief review of the case serve?
3. With the circumstances of the *Kentucky River* case in mind, which employees does the decision in the case affect most, and what is one of the ultimate results of that decision?

UNIT NINE
Government Regulation

CONTENTS

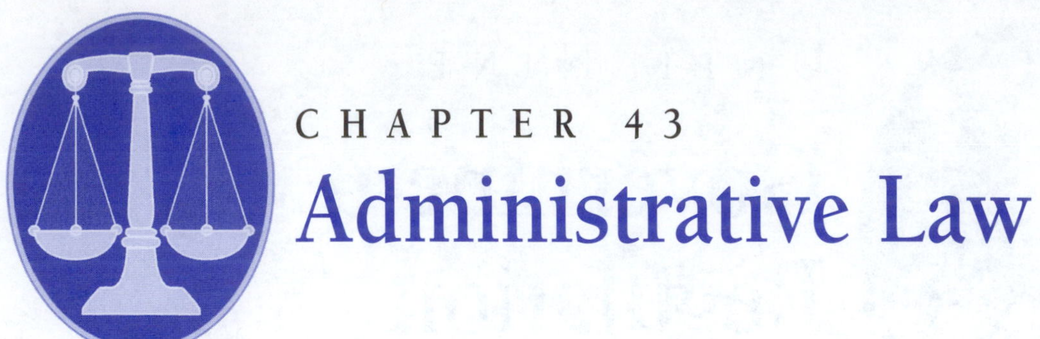

CHAPTER 43
Administrative Law

GOVERNMENT AGENCIES ESTABLISHED to administer the law have a tremendous impact on the day-to-day operation of the government and the economy. In the early years of our nation, the United States had a relatively simple, nonindustrial economy that required little regulation. Because often the purpose of administrative agencies is to create and enforce such regulations, there were relatively few such agencies. Today, however, there are rules covering virtually every aspect of a business's operation. Consequently, agencies have multiplied.

At the federal level, the Securities and Exchange Commission regulates the firm's capital structure and financing, as well as its financial reporting. The National Labor Relations Board oversees relations between the firm and any unions with which it may deal. The Equal Employment Opportunity Commission also regulates employer-employee relationships. The Environmental Protection Agency and the Occupational Safety and Health Administration affect the way the firm manufactures its products. The Federal Trade Commission influences the way it markets these products.

Added to this layer of federal regulation is a second layer of state regulation that, when not preempted by federal legislation, may cover many of the same activities or regulate independently those activities not covered by federal regulation. Finally, agency regulations at the county or municipal level also affect certain types of business activities.

Administrative agencies issue rules, orders, and decisions. These regulations make up the body of *administrative law.* You were introduced briefly to some of the main principles of administrative law in Chapter 1. In the following pages, we look at these principles in much greater detail.

SECTION 1

Agency Creation and Powers

Because Congress cannot possibly oversee the actual implementation of all the laws it enacts, it must delegate such tasks to others, particularly when the issues relate to highly technical areas, such as air and water pollution. By delegating some of its authority to make and implement laws to administrative agencies, Congress can monitor indirectly a particular area in which it has passed legislation without becoming bogged down in the details relating to enforcement—details that are often best left to specialists.

ENABLING LEGISLATION

To create an administrative agency, Congress passes **enabling legislation**, which specifies the name, purposes, functions, and powers of the agency being created. The enabling legislation for the Federal Trade Commission (FTC), for example, is the Federal Trade Commission Act of 1914.[1] The act prohibits unfair methods of competition and deceptive trade practices. It also describes the procedures that the FTC must follow to charge persons or organizations with violations of the act, and it provides for judicial review of agency orders. The act grants the FTC the power to do the following:

1. Create "rules and regulations for the purpose of carrying out the Act."
2. Conduct investigations of business practices.

1. 15 U.S.C. Sections 41–58.

3. Obtain reports from interstate corporations concerning their business practices.
4. Investigate possible violations of federal antitrust statutes.[2]
5. Publish findings of its investigations.
6. Recommend new legislation.
7. Hold trial-like hearings to resolve certain kinds of trade disputes that involve FTC regulations or federal antitrust laws.

The commission that heads the FTC is composed of five members, each of whom the president appoints, with the advice and consent of the Senate, for a term of seven years. The president designates one of the commissioners to be chairperson. Various offices and bureaus within the FTC undertake different administrative activities for the agency. Exhibit 43–1 illustrates the organization of the FTC.

Federal administrative agencies may exercise only those powers that Congress has delegated to them in enabling legislation. Through similar enabling acts, state legislatures create state administrative agencies.

TYPES OF AGENCIES

As discussed in Chapter 1, there are two basic types of administrative agencies: executive agencies and independent regulatory agencies. Federal *executive agencies* include the cabinet departments of the executive branch, which were formed to assist the president in carrying out executive functions, and the subagencies within the cabinet departments. The Occupational Safety and Health Administration, for example, is a subagency within the Department of Labor. Exhibit 43–2 on page 876 lists the cabinet departments and their most important subagencies.

All administrative agencies are part of the executive branch of government, but *independent regulatory agencies* are outside the major executive departments. The Federal Trade Commission and the Securities and Exchange Commission are examples of independent regulatory agencies. Selected independent regulatory agencies, as well as their principal functions, are listed in Exhibit 43–3 on page 877.

The significant difference between the two types of agencies lies in the accountability of the regulators. Agencies that are considered part of the executive branch are subject to the authority of the president, who has the power to appoint and remove federal officers. In theory, this power is less pronounced in regard to independent agencies, the officers of which serve for fixed terms and cannot be removed without just cause. In practice, however, the president's ability to exert influence over independent agencies is often considerable.

AGENCY POWERS AND THE CONSTITUTION

Administrative agencies occupy an unusual niche in the American legal scheme, because they exercise powers that are normally divided among the three branches of government. Notice that in the FTC's

2. The FTC shares enforcement of the Clayton Act with the Antitrust Division of the U.S. Department of Justice.

EXHIBIT 43–1 ORGANIZATION OF THE FEDERAL TRADE COMMISSION

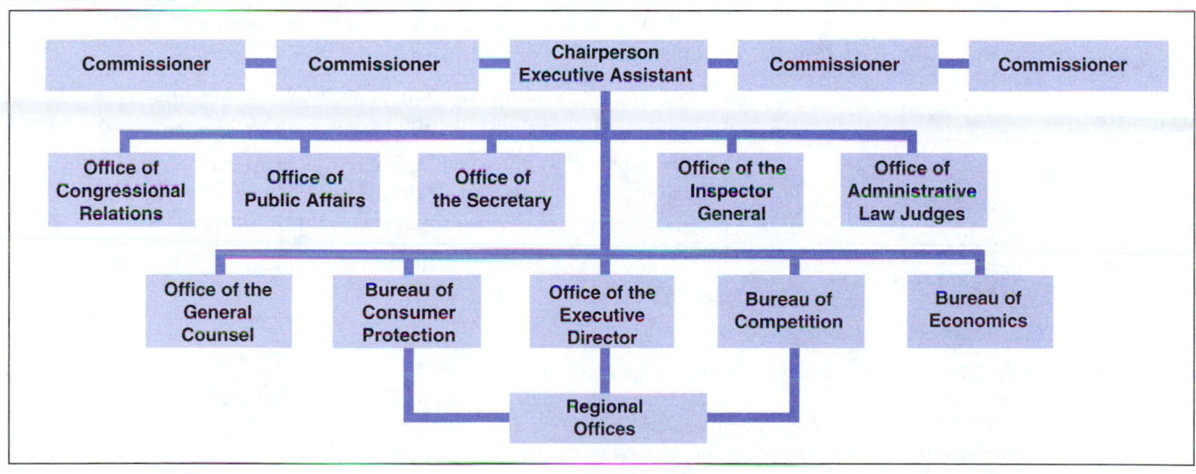

EXHIBIT 43–2 EXECUTIVE DEPARTMENTS AND IMPORTANT SUBAGENCIES

DEPARTMENT	DATE FORMED	IMPORTANT SUBAGENCIES
State	1789	Passport Office; Bureau of Diplomatic Security; Foreign Service; Bureau of Human Rights and Humanitarian Affairs; Bureau of Consular Affairs; Bureau of Intelligence and Research
Treasury	1789	Internal Revenue Service; Bureau of Alcohol, Tobacco, and Firearms; U.S. Secret Service; U.S. Mint; Customs Service
Interior	1849	U.S. Fish and Wildlife Service; National Park Service; Bureau of Indian Affairs; Bureau of Land Management
Justice	1870[a]	Federal Bureau of Investigation; Drug Enforcement Administration; Bureau of Prisons; U.S. Marshals Service; Immigration and Naturalization Service
Agriculture	1889	Soil Conservation Service; Agricultural Research Service; Food Safety and Inspection Service; Federal Crop Insurance Corporation; Farmers Home Administration
Commerce	1913[b]	Bureau of the Census; Bureau of Economic Analysis; Minority Business Development Agency; Patent and Trademark Office; National Oceanic and Atmospheric Administration; U.S. Travel and Tourism Administration
Labor	1913[b]	Occupational Safety and Health Administration; Bureau of Labor Statistics; Employment Standards Administration; Office of Labor-Management Standards; Employment and Training Administration
Defense	1949[c]	National Guard; Defense Investigative Service; National Security Agency; Joint Chiefs of Staff; Departments of the Air Force, Navy, Army
Housing and Urban Development	1965	Assistant Secretary for Community Planning and Development; Government National Mortgage Association; Assistant Secretary for Housing—Federal Housing Commissioner; Assistant Secretary for Fair Housing and Equal Opportunity
Transportation	1967	Federal Aviation Administration; Federal Highway Administration; National Highway Traffic Safety Administration; U.S. Coast Guard; Federal Transit Administration
Energy	1977	Office of Civilian Radioactive Waste Management; Bonneville Power Administration; Office of Nuclear Energy; Energy Information Administration; Office of Conservation and Renewable Energy
Health and Human Services	1980[d]	Food and Drug Administration; Health Care Financing Administration; Public Health Service
Education	1980[e]	Office of Special Education and Rehabilitation Services; Office of Elementary and Secondary Education; Office of Postsecondary Education; Office of Vocational and Adult Education
Veterans' Affairs	1989	Veterans Health Administration; Veterans Benefits Administration; National Cemetery System

a. Formed from the Office of the Attorney General (created in 1789).
b. Formed from the Department of Commerce and Labor (created in 1903).
c. Formed from the Department of War (created in 1789) and the Department of the Navy (created in 1798).
d. Formed from the Department of Health, Education, and Welfare (created in 1953).
e. Formed from the Department of Health, Education, and Welfare (created in 1953).

EXHIBIT 43–3 SELECTED INDEPENDENT REGULATORY AGENCIES

NAME	DATE FORMED	PRINCIPAL DUTIES
Federal Reserve System Board of Governors (Fed)	1913	Determines policy with respect to interest rates, credit availability, and the money supply.
Federal Trade Commission (FTC)	1914	Prevents businesses from engaging in unfair trade practices; stops the formation of monopolies in the business sector; protects consumer rights.
Securities and Exchange Commission (SEC)	1934	Regulates the nation's stock exchanges, in which shares of stock are bought and sold; enforces the securities laws, which require full disclosure of the financial profiles of companies that wish to sell stock and bonds to the public.
Federal Communications Commission (FCC)	1934	Regulates all communications by telegraph, cable, telephone, radio, satellite, and television.
National Labor Relations Board (NLRB)	1935	Protects employees' rights to join unions and bargain collectively with employers; attempts to prevent unfair labor practices by both employers and unions.
Equal Employment Opportunity Commission (EEOC)	1964	Works to eliminate discrimination in employment based on religion, gender, race, color, disability, national origin, or age; investigates claims of discrimination.
Environmental Protection Agency (EPA)	1970	Undertakes programs aimed at reducing air and water pollution; works with state and local agencies to help fight environmental hazards. (It has been suggested recently that its status be elevated to that of a department.)
Nuclear Regulatory Commission (NRC)	1975	Ensures that electricity-generating nuclear reactors in the United States are built and operated safely; regularly inspects operations of such reactors.

enabling legislation, discussed above, the FTC's grant of power incorporates functions associated with the legislative branch (rulemaking), the executive branch (enforcement of the rules), and the courts (**adjudication**, or the formal resolution of disputes).

The constitutional principle of checks and balances allows each branch of government to act as a check on the actions of the other two branches. Furthermore, the Constitution authorizes only the legislative branch to create laws. Yet administrative agencies, to which the Constitution does not specifically refer, make **legislative rules**, or *substantive rules*, that are as legally binding as laws that Congress passes.

Courts generally hold that Article I of the U.S. Constitution authorizes delegating such powers to administrative agencies. In fact, courts generally hold that Article I is the basis for all administrative law. Section 1 of that article grants all legislative powers to Congress and requires Congress to oversee the implementation of all laws. Article I, Section 8, gives Congress the power to make all laws necessary for executing its specified powers. The courts interpret these passages, under what is referred to as the **delegation doctrine**, as granting Congress the power to establish administrative agencies that can create rules for implementing those laws.

The three branches of government exercise certain controls over agency powers and functions, as will be discussed later in this chapter, but in many ways administrative agencies function independently. For this reason, administrative agencies, which constitute the **bureaucracy**, are sometimes referred to as the "fourth branch" of the U.S. government.

SECTION 2

Administrative Process

The three functions mentioned previously—rulemaking, enforcement, and adjudication—make up what is known as the **administrative process**. Administrative process involves the administration of law by administrative agencies, in contrast to **judicial process**, which comprises the administration of law by the courts.

All federal agencies must follow specific procedural requirements in their rulemaking, adjudication, and other functions. Sometimes, Congress specifies certain procedural requirements in an agency's enabling legislation. In the absence of any directives from Congress concerning a particular agency procedure, the Administrative Procedure Act (APA) of 1946[3] applies. The APA is such an integral part of the administrative process that its application will be examined as we go through the basic functions carried out by administrative agencies. In addition, agency procedures are guided indirectly by the courts' interpretation of APA requirements.

RULEMAKING

A major function of an administrative agency is **rulemaking**—the formulation of new regulations. In an agency's enabling legislation, Congress confers the agency's power to make rules. For example, the Occupational Safety and Health Act of 1970 authorized the Occupational Safety and Health Administration (OSHA) to develop and issue rules governing safety in the workplace. In formulating any new legislative rule, OSHA has to follow specific rulemaking procedures required under the APA.

Note that administrative agencies also make *interpretive rules*. These rules are not legally binding on the public but simply indicate how an agency plans to interpret and enforce its statutory authority. For example, the Equal Employment Opportunity Commission periodically issues interpretive rules, usually referred to as enforcement guidelines, indicating how it plans to interpret and apply a provision of a certain statute, such as the Americans with Disabilities Act. When making interpretive rules, an agency need not follow the requirements of the APA.

The most commonly used rulemaking procedure is called **notice-and-comment rulemaking.** This procedure involves three basic steps: notice of the proposed rulemaking, a comment period, and the final rule.

Notice of the Proposed Rulemaking. When a federal agency decides to create a new rule, the agency publishes a notice of the proposed rulemaking proceedings in the *Federal Register*, a daily publication of the executive branch that prints government orders, rules, and regulations. The notice states where and when the proceedings will be held, the agency's legal authority for making the rule (usually its enabling legislation), and the terms or subject matter of the proposed rule.

Comment Period. Following the publication of the notice of the proposed rulemaking proceedings, the agency must allow ample time for persons to comment in writing on the proposed rule. The purpose of this comment period is to give interested parties the opportunity to express their views on the proposed rule in an effort to influence agency policy. The comments may be in writing or, if a hearing is held, may be given orally. The agency need not respond to all comments, but it must respond to any significant comments that bear directly on the proposed rule. The agency responds by either modifying its final rule or explaining, in a statement accompanying the final rule, why it did not make any changes. In some circumstances, particularly when the procedure being used in a specific instance is less formal, an agency may accept comments after the comment period is closed. The agency should summarize these *ex parte* (private, "off-the-record") comments in the record for possible review.

The Final Rule. After the agency reviews the comments, it drafts the final rule and publishes it in the *Federal Register.* The final rule is later compiled with the rules and regulations of other federal administrative agencies in the *Code of Federal Regulations* (C.F.R.). Final rules have binding legal effect unless the courts later overturn them.

Westlaw. See Case 43.1 at the end of this chapter. To view the full, unedited case from Westlaw,® go to this text's Web site at **http://wbl-cs.westbuslaw.com**.

INVESTIGATION

Administrative agencies conduct investigations of the entities that they regulate. One type of agency investigation occurs during the rulemaking process to obtain information about a certain individual, firm, or industry. The purpose of such an investigation is to ensure that the rule issued is based on a consideration of relevant factors rather than being arbitrary and capricious. After final rules are issued,

3. 5 U.S.C. Sections 551–706.

agencies conduct investigations to monitor compliance with those rules. A typical agency investigation of this kind might begin when a citizen reports a possible violation.

Inspections. Many agencies gather information through on-site inspections. Sometimes, inspecting an office, a factory, or some other business facility is the only way to obtain the evidence needed to prove a regulatory violation. Administrative inspections and tests cover a wide range of activities, including safety inspections of underground coal mines, safety tests of commercial equipment and automobiles, and environmental monitoring of factory emissions. An agency may also ask a firm or individual to submit certain documents or records to the agency for examination.

Normally, business firms comply with agency requests to inspect facilities or business records, because it is in any firm's interest to maintain a good relationship with regulatory bodies. In some instances, however, such as when a firm thinks an agency's request is unreasonable and may be detrimental to the firm's interest, the firm may refuse to comply with the request. In such situations, an agency may resort to the use of a subpoena or a search warrant.

Subpoenas. There are two basic types of subpoenas. The subpoena *ad testificandum* ("to testify") is an ordinary subpoena. It is a writ, or order, compelling a witness to appear at an agency hearing. The subpoena *duces tecum*[4] ("bring it with you") compels an individual or organization to hand over books, papers, records, or documents to the agency. An administrative agency may use either type of subpoena to obtain testimony or documents.

There are limits on what an agency can demand. To determine whether an agency is abusing its discretion in its pursuit of information as part of an investigation, a court may consider such factors as the following:

1. The purpose of the investigation. An investigation must have a legitimate purpose. An improper purpose is, for example, harassment.
2. The relevance of the information being sought. Information is relevant if it reveals that the law is being violated or if it assures the agency that the law is not being violated.
3. The specificity of the demand for testimony or documents. A subpoena must, for example, adequately describe the material being sought.
4. The burden of the demand on the party from whom the information is sought. In responding to a request for information, a party must bear the costs of, for example, copying the documents that must be handed over; a business is generally protected from revealing such information as trade secrets, however.

See Case 43.2 at the end of this chapter. To view the full, unedited case from Westlaw,® go to this text's Web site at **http://wbl-cs.westbuslaw.com**.

Search Warrants. The Fourth Amendment protects against unreasonable searches and seizures by requiring that in most instances a physical search for evidence must be conducted under the authority of a search warrant. An agency's search warrant is an order directing law enforcement officials to search a specific place for a specific item and present it to the agency. Although it was once thought that administrative inspections were exempt from the warrant requirement, the United States Supreme Court held in *Marshall v. Barlow's, Inc.*[5] that the requirement does apply to the administrative process.

Agencies can conduct warrantless searches in several situations. Warrants are not required to conduct searches in highly regulated industries. Firms that sell firearms or liquor, for example, are automatically subject to inspections without warrants. Sometimes, a statute permits warrantless searches of certain types of hazardous operations, such as coal mines. Also, a warrantless inspection in an emergency situation is normally considered reasonable.

ADJUDICATION

After conducting an investigation of a suspected rule violation, an agency may begin to take administrative action against an individual or organization. Most administrative actions are resolved through negotiated settlements at their initial stages, without the need for formal adjudication.

Negotiated Settlements. Depending on the agency, negotiations may take the form of a simple conversation or a series of informal conferences. Whatever form the negotiations take, their purpose is to rectify

4. Pronounced *doo*-cheez *tee*-kum.

5. 436 U.S. 307, 98 S.Ct. 1816, 56 L.Ed.2d 305 (1978).

the problem to the agency's satisfaction and eliminate the need for additional proceedings.

Settlement is an appealing option to firms for two reasons: to avoid appearing uncooperative and to avoid the expense involved in formal adjudication proceedings and in possible later appeals. Settlement is also an attractive option for agencies. To conserve their own resources and avoid formal actions, administrative agencies devote a great deal of effort to giving advice and negotiating solutions to problems.

Formal Complaints. If a settlement cannot be reached, the agency may issue a formal complaint against the suspected violator. If the Environmental Protection Agency (EPA), for example, finds that a factory is polluting groundwater in violation of federal pollution laws, the EPA will issue a complaint against the violator in an effort to bring the plant into compliance with federal regulations. This complaint is a public document, and a press release may accompany it. The factory charged in the complaint will respond by filing an answer to the EPA's allegations. If the factory and the EPA cannot agree on a settlement, the case is heard in a trial-like setting before an **administrative law judge (ALJ).** The adjudication process is described in the following subsections and illustrated graphically in Exhibit 43–4.

EXHIBIT 43–4 THE PROCESS OF FORMAL ADMINISTRATIVE ADJUDICATION

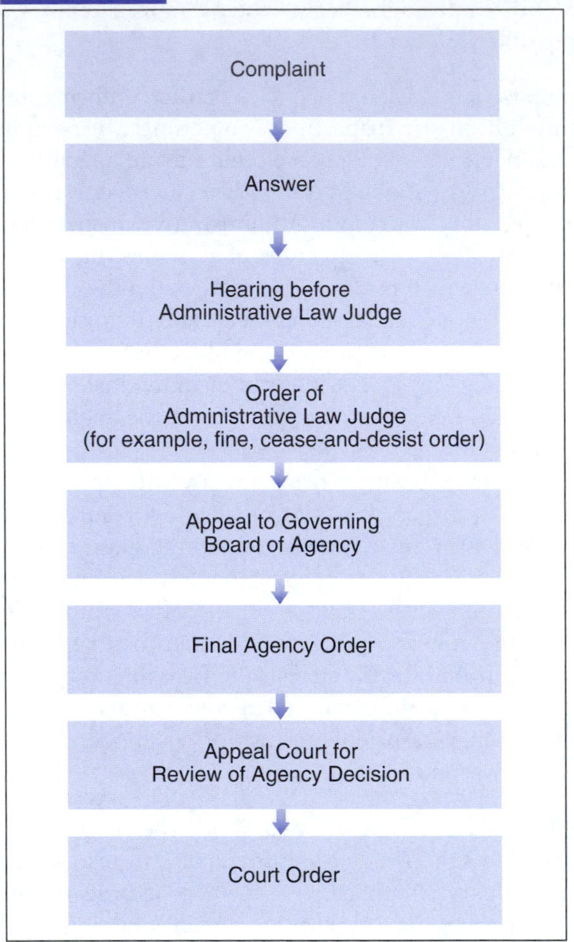

The Role of the Administrative Law Judge. The ALJ presides over the hearing and has the power to administer oaths, take testimony, rule on questions of evidence, and make determinations of fact. Although formally, the ALJ works for the agency prosecuting the case (in our example, the EPA), the law requires an ALJ to be an unbiased adjudicator (judge).

Certain safeguards prevent bias on the part of the ALJ and promote fairness in the proceedings. For example, the APA requires that the ALJ be separate from an agency's investigative and prosecutorial staff. The APA also prohibits *ex parte* (private) communications between the ALJ and any party to an agency proceeding, such as the EPA or the factory. Finally, provisions of the APA protect the ALJ from agency disciplinary actions unless the agency can show good cause for such an action.

Hearing Procedures. Hearing procedures vary widely from agency to agency. Administrative agencies generally exercise substantial discretion over the type of hearing procedure that will be used. Frequently, disputes are resolved through informal adjudication proceedings. For example, the parties, their counsel, and the ALJ may simply meet at a table in a conference room for the dispute-settlement proceedings.

A formal adjudicatory hearing, in contrast, resembles a trial in many respects. Prior to the hearing, the parties are permitted to undertake extensive discovery (involving depositions, interrogatories, and requests for documents or other information, as described in Chapter 3). During the hearing, the parties may give testimony, present other evidence, and cross-examine adverse witnesses. A significant difference between a trial and an administrative agency hearing, though, is that normally much more information, including hearsay (secondhand information) can be introduced as evidence during an administrative hearing.

Agency Orders. Following a hearing, the ALJ renders an **initial order**, or decision, on the case. Either party can appeal the ALJ's decision to the board or commission that governs the agency. If the factory is dissatisfied with the ALJ's decision, for example, it can appeal the decision to the commission that governs the EPA. If the factory is dissatisfied with the commission's decision, it can appeal the decision to a federal court of appeals. If no party appeals the case, the ALJ's decision becomes the **final order** of the agency. The ALJ's decision also becomes final if a party appeals and the commission and the court decline to review the case. If a party appeals the case and the case is reviewed, the final order comes from the commission's decision or (if that decision is appealed to a federal appellate court) that of the court.

Westlaw. See Case 43.3 at the end of this chapter. To view the full, unedited case from Westlaw,® go to this text's Web site at **http://wbl-cs.westbuslaw.com**.

SECTION 3

Limitations on Agency Powers

Combining the functions normally divided among the three branches of government into an administrative agency concentrates considerable power in a single organization. Because of this concentration of authority, one of the major policy objectives of the government is to control the risks of arbitrariness and overreaching by administrative agencies without hindering the effective use of agency power to deal with particular problem areas, as Congress intends.

The judicial branch of the government exercises control over agency powers through the courts' review of agency actions. The executive and legislative branches of government also exercise control over agency authority.

JUDICIAL CONTROLS

The APA provides for judicial review of most agency decisions, as described above. Agency actions are not automatically subject to judicial review, however. Parties seeking review must demonstrate that they meet certain requirements. The party bringing the action must have *standing to sue* the agency (the party must have a direct stake in the outcome of the judicial proceeding), and there must be an *actual controversy* at issue. These are basic judicial requirements that must be met before a court will hear a case, as discussed in Chapter 2. Furthermore, the party must have *exhausted all possible administrative remedies*. Each agency has its "chain of review," and the party must follow agency appeal procedures before a court will deem that administrative remedies have been exhausted.

Recall from Chapter 2 that appellate courts normally defer to the decisions of trial courts on questions of fact. In reviewing administrative actions, the courts are similarly reluctant to question the factual findings of agencies. In reviewing an administrative agency's decision, a court normally will consider the following types of issues:

1. Whether the agency has exceeded its authority under its enabling legislation.
2. Whether the agency has properly interpreted laws applicable to the agency action under review.
3. Whether the agency has violated any constitutional provisions.
4. Whether the agency has acted in accordance with procedural requirements of the law.
5. Whether the agency's actions were arbitrary, capricious, or an abuse of discretion.
6. Whether any conclusions drawn by the agency are not supported by substantial evidence.

EXECUTIVE CONTROLS

The executive branch of government exercises control over agencies both through the president's power to appoint federal officers and through the president's veto power. The president may veto enabling legislation presented by Congress or congressional attempts to modify an existing agency's authority.

LEGISLATIVE CONTROLS

Congress also exercises authority over agency powers. Through enabling legislation, Congress gives power to an agency. Of course, an agency may not exceed the power that Congress has delegated to it. Through subsequent legislation, Congress can take away that power or even abolish an agency altogether. Legislative authority is required to fund an agency, and enabling legislation usually sets certain time and monetary limits on the funding of particular programs. Congress can always revise these limits.

In addition to its power to create and fund agencies, Congress has the authority to investigate the implementation of its laws and the agencies that it has created. Individual legislators may also affect agency policy through their "casework" activities, which involve attempts to help their constituents deal with agencies.

Congress also has the power to "freeze" the enforcement of most federal regulations before the regulations take effect. Under the Small Business Regulatory Enforcement Fairness Act of 1996,[6] all federal agencies must submit final rules to Congress before the rules become effective. If, within sixty days, Congress passes a joint resolution of disapproval concerning a rule, enforcement of the regulation is frozen while the rule is reviewed by congressional committees.

Another legislative check on agency actions is the Administrative Procedure Act, discussed earlier in this chapter. Additionally, the laws discussed in the next section provide certain checks on the actions of administrative agencies.

SECTION 4

Public Accountability

As a result of growing public concern over the powers exercised by administrative agencies, Congress passed several laws to make agencies more accountable through public scrutiny. We discuss here the most significant of these laws.

FREEDOM OF INFORMATION ACT

Enacted in 1966, the Freedom of Information Act (FOIA)[7] requires the federal government to disclose certain "records" to "any person" on request, even if no reason is given for the request. The FOIA exempts certain types of records. For other records, though, a request that complies with the FOIA procedures need only contain a reasonable description of the information sought (see Exhibit 43–5). An agency's failure to comply with a request may be challenged in a federal district court. The media, industry trade associations, public-interest groups, and even companies seeking information about competitors rely on these FOIA provisions to obtain information from government agencies.

Under a 1996 amendment to the FOIA, all federal government agencies now have to make their records available electronically—on the Internet, on computer disks, and in other electronic formats. As of November 1, 1996, any document created by an agency must be available on computer within a year after its creation. Agencies must also provide a clear index to all of their documents.

GOVERNMENT-IN-THE-SUNSHINE ACT

Congress passed the Government-in-the-Sunshine Act,[8] or open meeting law, in 1976. It requires that "every portion of every meeting of an agency" be open to "public observation." The act also requires the establishment of procedures to ensure that the public is provided with adequate advance notice of scheduled meetings and agendas. Like the FOIA, the sunshine act contains certain exceptions. Closed meetings are permitted when (1) the subject of the meeting concerns accusing any person of a crime, (2) an open meeting would frustrate implementation of agency actions, or (3) the subject of the meeting involves matters relating to future litigation or rulemaking. Courts interpret these exceptions to allow open access whenever possible.

REGULATORY FLEXIBILITY ACT

Concern over the effects of regulation on the efficiency of businesses, particularly smaller ones, led Congress to pass the Regulatory Flexibility Act in 1980.[9] Under this act, whenever a new regulation will have a "significant impact upon a substantial number of small entities," the agency must conduct a regulatory flexibility analysis. The analysis must measure the cost that the rule would impose on small businesses and must consider less burdensome alternatives. The act also contains provisions to alert small businesses—through advertising in trade journals, for example—about forthcoming regulations. The act reduces some record-keeping burdens for small businesses, especially with regard to hazardous waste management.

SMALL BUSINESS REGULATORY ENFORCEMENT FAIRNESS ACT

As mentioned above, the Small Business Regulatory Enforcement Fairness Act (SBREFA) of 1996 allows

6. 5 U.S.C. Sections 801–808.
7. 5 U.S.C. Section 552.
8. 5 U.S.C. Section 552b.
9. 5 U.S.C. Sections 601–612.

EXHIBIT 43–5 SAMPLE LETTER REQUESTING INFORMATION FROM AN EXECUTIVE DEPARTMENT OR AGENCY

Date

Agency Head or FOIA Officer
Title
Name of Agency
Address of Agency
City, State, Zip

Re: Freedom of Information Act Request.

Dear _______________ :

Under the provisions of the Freedom of Information Act, 5 U.S.C. Section 552, I am requesting access to ____ [identify the records as clearly as possible].

[Optional] I am requesting this information because ____ [state the reason for your request if you think it will assist you in obtaining the information].

If there are any fees for searching for, or copying, the records I have requested, please inform me before you fill the request [or:] please supply the records without informing me if the fees do not exceed $ __________.

[or:] As you know, the act permits you to reduce or waive fees when the release of the information is considered as "primarily benefiting the public." I believe that this request fits that category, and I therefore ask that you waive any fees.

If all or any part of this request is denied, please cite the specific exemption(s) that you think justifies your refusal to release the information, and inform me of the appeal procedures available to me under the law.

I would appreciate your handling this request as quickly as possible, and I look forward to hearing from you within 10 days, as the law stipulates.

Sincerely,
[Signature]
Name
Address
City, State, Zip

SOURCE: U.S. Congress, House Committee on Government Operations, *A Citizen's Guide on How to Use the Freedom of Information Act and the Privacy Act Requesting Government Documents,* 95th Congress, 1st session, 1977.

Congress to review new federal regulations for at least sixty days before they take effect. This period gives opponents of the rules time to present their arguments to Congress.

The SBREFA also authorizes the courts to enforce the Regulatory Flexibility Act. This helps to ensure that federal agencies, such as the Internal Revenue Service, will consider ways to reduce the economic impact of new regulations on small businesses. Federal agencies are required to prepare guides that explain in "plain English" how small businesses can comply with federal regulations.

At the Small Business Administration, the SBREFA set up the National Enforcement Ombudsman to receive comments from small businesses about their dealings with federal agencies. Based on these comments, Regional Small Business Fairness Boards rate the agencies and publicize their findings.

Finally, the SBREFA allows small businesses to recover their expenses and legal fees from the government when an agency makes demands for fines or penalties that a court considers excessive.

SECTION 5

State Administrative Agencies

Although most of this chapter deals with federal administrative agencies, state agencies play a significant role in regulating activities within the states. Many of the factors that encouraged the proliferation of federal agencies also fostered the expanding presence of state agencies. For example, one reason for the growth of administrative agencies at all levels of government is the inability of Congress and state legislatures to oversee the implementation of their laws. Another is the greater technical competence of the agencies.

PARALLEL AGENCIES

Commonly, a state creates an agency as a parallel to a federal agency to provide similar services on a more localized basis. Such parallel agencies include the federal Social Security Administration and the state welfare agency, the Internal Revenue Service and the state revenue department, and the Environmental Protection Agency and the state pollution-control agency. Not all federal agencies have parallel state agencies, however. For example, the Federal Bureau of Investigation and the Nuclear Regulatory Commission have no parallel agencies at the state level.

CONFLICTS BETWEEN PARALLEL AGENCIES

If the actions of parallel state and federal agencies conflict, the actions of the federal agency will prevail. For example, if the Federal Aviation Administration specifies the hours during which airplanes may land at and depart from airports, a state or local government cannot issue inconsistent laws or regulations governing the same activities. The priority of federal laws over conflicting state laws is based on the supremacy clause of the U.S. Constitution. Remember from Chapter 4 that this clause, which is found in Article VI of the Constitution, states that the Constitution and "the Laws of the United States which shall be made in Pursuance thereof . . . shall be the supreme Law of the Land."

TERMS AND CONCEPTS TO REVIEW

adjudication 877
administrative law judge (ALJ) 880
administrative process 877
bureaucracy 877
delegation doctrine 877
enabling legislation 874
final order 881
initial order 881
judicial process 878
legislative rule 877
notice-and-comment rulemaking 878
rulemaking 878

CHAPTER SUMMARY

Creation and Powers of Administrative Agencies	**1.** Under the U.S. Constitution, Congress may delegate the task of implementing its laws to government agencies. By delegating the task, Congress may indirectly monitor an area in which it has passed legislation without becoming bogged down in the details relating to enforcement of the legislation. **2.** Administrative agencies are created by enabling legislation, which usually specifies the name, composition, and powers of the agency. **3.** Administrative agencies exercise enforcement, rulemaking, and adjudicatory powers.
Administrative Process—Rulemaking	**1.** Agencies are authorized to create new regulations—their rulemaking function. This power is conferred on an agency in the enabling legislation. **2.** Agencies may create legislative rules, which are as important as formal acts of Congress. **3.** Notice-and-comment rulemaking, the most common rulemaking procedure, begins with the publication of the proposed regulation in the *Federal Register.* Publication of the notice is followed by a comment period to allow private parties to comment on the proposed rule.
Administrative Process—Investigation	**1.** Administrative agencies investigate the entities that they regulate. Investigations are conducted during the rulemaking process to obtain information and after rules are issued to monitor compliance.

CHAPTER SUMMARY—CONTINUED

Administrative Process—Investigation—continued	**2.** The most important investigative tools available to an agency are the following: **a.** Inspections and tests—Used to gather information and to correct or prevent undesirable conditions. **b.** Subpoenas—Orders that direct individuals to appear at a hearing or to hand over specified documents. **3.** Limits on administrative investigations include the following: **a.** The investigation must be for a legitimate purpose. **b.** The information sought must be relevant, and the investigative demands must be specific and not unreasonably burdensome. **c.** The Fourth Amendment protects companies and individuals from unreasonable searches and seizures by requiring search warrants in most instances.
Administrative Process—Adjudication	**1.** After a preliminary investigation, an agency may initiate an administrative action against an individual or organization by filing a complaint. Most such actions are resolved at this stage before they go through the formal adjudicatory process. **2.** If there is no settlement, the case is presented to an administrative law judge (ALJ) in a proceeding similar to a trial. **3.** After a case is concluded, the ALJ renders an initial order that may be appealed by either party in federal appeals court. If no appeal is taken or the case is not reviewed, the order becomes the final order of the agency. It may order the charged party to pay damages, or it may forbid the party from carrying on some specified activity.
Limitations on Agency Powers	**1.** *Judicial controls*—Administrative agencies are subject to the judicial review of the courts. A court may review whether— **a.** An agency has exceeded the scope of its enabling legislation. **b.** An agency has properly interpreted the laws. **c.** An agency has violated the U.S. Constitution. **d.** An agency has complied with all applicable procedural requirements. **e.** An agency's actions are arbitrary or capricious, or an abuse of discretion. **f.** An agency's conclusions are not supported by substantial evidence. **2.** *Executive controls*—The president can control administrative agencies through appointments of federal officers and through vetoes of legislation creating or affecting agency powers. **3.** *Legislative controls*—Congress can give power to an agency, take it away, increase or decrease the agency's finances, or abolish the agency. The Administrative Procedure Act of 1946 also limits the actions of agencies.
Public Accountability	**1.** *Freedom of Information Act of 1966*—Requires the government to disclose records to "any person" on request. **2.** *Government-in-the-Sunshine Act of 1976*—Requires the following: **a.** "[E]very portion of every meeting of an agency" must be open to "public observation." **b.** Procedures must be implemented to ensure that the public is provided with adequate advance notice of an agency's scheduled meeting and agenda. **3.** *Small Business Regulatory Enforcement Fairness Act of 1996*—Allows Congress to review new federal regulations. Requires federal agencies to explain in "plain English" how to comply with regulations. Established Regional Small Business Fairness Boards to rate agencies from a small-business perspective. Provides for the recovery of expenses and fees when an agency imposes an excessive penalty. **4.** *Regulatory Flexibility Act of 1980*—Requires a regulatory flexibility analysis whenever a new regulation will have a "significant impact upon a substantial number of small entities."
State Administrative Agencies	**1.** States create agencies that parallel federal agencies to provide similar services on a more localized basis. **2.** If the actions of parallel state and federal agencies conflict, the actions of the federal agency will prevail.

CASES FOR ANALYSIS

Westlaw. You can access the full text of each case presented below by going to the Westlaw cases on this text's Web site at http://wbl-cs.westbuslaw.com. Each Westlaw case includes the names of all plaintiffs and defendants, the dates on which the case was argued and decided, a brief summary of the issues and decisions in the case, headnotes classifiying specific issues in the case according to the West Key Number System, and the court's opinion. Concurring and dissenting opinions, if any, are included as well.

CASE 43.1 RULEMAKING

AT&T CORP. V. IOWA UTILITIES BOARD

Supreme Court of the United States, 1999.
525 U.S. 366,
119 S.Ct. 721,
142 L.Ed.2d 835.

Justice *SCALIA* delivered the opinion of the Court.

* * * *

I

Until the 1990's, local phone service was thought to be a natural monopoly. States typically granted an exclusive franchise in each local service area to a local exchange carrier (LEC), which owned, among other things, the local loops (wires connecting telephones to switches), the switches (equipment directing calls to their destinations), and the transport trunks (wires carrying calls between switches) that constitute a local exchange network. Technological advances, however, have made competition among multiple providers of local service seem possible, and Congress recently ended the longstanding regime of state-sanctioned monopolies.

The Telecommunications Act of 1996 (1996 Act or Act) fundamentally restructures local telephone markets. * * * [I]ncumbent LECs are subject to a host of duties intended to facilitate market entry. Foremost among these duties is the LEC's obligation * * * to share its network with competitors. * * *

Six months after the 1996 Act was passed, the FCC issued its [rules, referred to as *First Report and Order*] implementing the local-competition provisions. The numerous challenges to this rulemaking, filed across the country by incumbent LECs and [others], were consolidated in the United States Court of Appeals for the Eighth Circuit.

* * * *

* * * [47 C.F.R. Section 51.319 (Rule 319)] * * * sets forth a minimum number of network elements that incumbents must make available to requesting carriers. The LECs complained that, in compiling this list, the FCC had virtually ignored the 1996 Act's requirement that it consider whether access to proprietary elements was "necessary" and whether lack of access to nonproprietary elements would "impair" an entrant's ability to provide local service. * * * The Eighth Circuit * * * [held] that the Commission's interpretations of the "necessary and impair" standard * * * [was] reasonable and hence lawful * * * .

* * * *

* * * [T]he incumbent LECs [petitioned] for review * * * .

* * * *

III

* * * *

B

* * * [Rule 319] requires an incumbent to provide requesting carriers with access to a minimum of seven network elements: the local loop, the network interface device, switching capability, interoffice transmission facilities, signaling networks and call-related data bases, operations support systems functions, and operator services and directory assistance. If a requesting carrier wants access to additional elements, it may petition the state commission, which can make other elements available on a case-by-case basis.

Section 251(d)(2) of the Act provides:

> "In determining what network elements should be made available for purposes of subsection (c)(3) of this section, the Commission shall consider, at a minimum, whether—
> "(A) access to such network elements as are proprietary in nature is necessary; and
> "(B) the failure to provide access to such network elements would impair the ability of the telecommunications carrier seeking access to provide the services that it seeks to offer."

* * * [W]e * * * agree with the incumbents that the Act requires the FCC to apply *some* limiting standard, rationally related to the goals of the Act, which it has simply failed to do. In the general statement of

its methodology set forth in the *First Report and Order*, the Commission announced that it would regard the "necessary" standard as having been met regardless of whether "requesting carriers can obtain the requested proprietary element from a source other than the incumbent," since "[r]equiring new entrants to duplicate unnecessarily even a part of the incumbent's network could generate delay and higher costs for new entrants, and thereby impede entry by competing local providers and delay competition, contrary to the goals of the 1996 Act." And it announced that it would regard the "impairment" standard as having been met if "the failure of an incumbent to provide access to a network element would decrease the quality, or increase the financial or administrative cost of the service a requesting carrier seeks to offer, compared with providing that service *over other unbundled elements in the incumbent LEC's network*"—which means that comparison with self-provision, or with purchasing from another provider, is excluded. Since any entrant will request the most efficient network element that the incumbent has to offer, it is hard to imagine when the incumbent's failure to give access to the element would not constitute an "impairment" under this standard. * * * [This] allows entrants, rather than the Commission, to determine whether access to proprietary elements is necessary, and whether the failure to obtain access to nonproprietary elements would impair the ability to provide services. The Commission cannot, consistent with the statute, blind itself to the availability of elements outside the incumbent's network. That failing alone would require the Commission's rule to be set aside. In addition, however, the Commission's assumption that any increase in cost (or decrease in quality) imposed by denial of a network element renders access to that element "necessary," and causes the failure to provide that element to "impair" the entrant's ability to furnish its desired services, is simply not in accord with the ordinary and fair meaning of those terms. An entrant whose anticipated annual profits from the proposed service are reduced from 100% of investment to 99% of investment has perhaps been "impaired" in its ability to amass earnings, but has not *ipso facto* been "impair[ed] * * * in its ability to provide the services it seeks to offer"; and it cannot realistically be said that the network element enabling it to raise its profits to 100% is "necessary." In a world of perfect competition, in which all carriers are providing their service at marginal cost, the Commission's total equating of increased cost (or decreased quality) with "necessity" and "impairment" might be reasonable; but it has not established the existence of such an ideal world. * * *

* * * *

* * * Because the Commission has not interpreted the terms of the statute in a reasonable fashion, we must vacate [Rule 319].

* * * *

For the reasons stated, the * * * judgment of the Court of Appeals is reversed in part * * * and the cases are remanded for proceedings consistent with this opinion.

* * * *

Justice *SOUTER*, * * * dissenting * * * .

* * * I disagree with the Court's holding that the Commission was unreasonable in its interpretation of [Section 251(d)(2).] Because I think that * * * the Commission reasonably interpreted its duty to consider necessity and impairment, I respectfully dissent from Part III-B of the Court's opinion.

* * * *

* * * [In adopting] Rule 319 * * * , the Commission explicitly addressed the consequences that would follow from requiring an entrant to satisfy the necessity and impairment criteria by showing that alternative facilities were unavailable at reasonable cost from anyone except the incumbent LEC. To require that kind of a showing, the Commission said, would encourage duplication of facilities and personnel, with obvious systemic costs. The Commission, in other words, was approaching the task of giving reasonable interpretations to "necessary" and "impair" by asking whether Congress would have mandated economic inefficiency as a limit on the objective of encouraging competition through ease of market entry. The Commission concluded, without any apparent implausibility, that the answer was no, and proceeded to implement the necessity and impairment provisions in accordance with that answer.

Before we conclude that the Commission's reading of the statute was unreasonable, * * * [w]e have to ask whether the Commission's * * * question is an irrelevant one, and (if it is not), whether the Commission's answer is reasonably defensible. If the question is sensible and the answer fair, * * * [we must] respect the Commission's conclusion. * * * This, indeed, is surely a classic case for * * * deference [to an administrative agency], the statute here being infected not only with "ambiguity" but even "self-contradiction." I would accordingly respect the Commission's choice to give primacy to the question it chose.

CASE 43.2 INVESTIGATION

FEDERAL DEPOSIT INSURANCE CORP. V. WENTZ

United States Court of Appeals,
Third Circuit, 1995.
55 F.3d 905.

WEIS, Circuit Judge.

* * * *

Natalie I. Koether and Sidney F. Wentz were directors of The Howard Savings Bank of Livingston, New Jersey, which was declared insolvent on October 2, 1992. On that same day, the [Federal Deposit Insurance Corporation (FDIC)] was appointed receiver.

In April 1993, the FDIC issued an "Order of Investigation" * * * , targeting former officers and directors of the bank. Four purposes were cited in the order: (1) determining whether the individuals may be liable as a result of any action or inaction that could have affected the bank; (2) assessing whether the pursuit of litigation would be cost-effective by considering the ability of the individuals to satisfy a judgment; (3) establishing whether the FDIC should seek to avoid transfers of interests or incurrences of obligations; and (4) ascertaining whether the FDIC should seek attachments of assets. The order authorized FDIC representatives to issue subpoenas *duces tecum*.

The directors, together with other bank principals, were served with notices to appear for depositions and ordered to produce documents in some twenty-eight different categories covering the six-year period preceding October 1992. Included were records in their possession pertaining to bank operations. In addition, the subpoena demanded production of such documents as financial statements and credit applications of the directors * * * ; records of any bank accounts of the directors * * * , including canceled checks and bank statements; tax returns; title and registration papers for motor vehicles, boats, and airplanes; pension and profit-sharing plans in which the directors * * * had an interest; insurance policies; and records of inheritance, and other such gifts received by the directors * * * .

The directors timely complied with the requests for documents having any connection with their activities as officials of the bank, but refused to produce their personal records * * * .

In seeking enforcement of the subpoena in [a federal] district court, the FDIC * * * stated that the documents were necessary to enable the FDIC to determine the nature and extent of any losses sustained by the bank because of negligence or breach of fiduciary duty by the directors, and to establish whether it would be cost-effective to pursue any such claims. * * *

The district court * * * ordered the directors to produce all records that demonstrated increases or depletions in, or transfers of, their assets. * * *

* * * *

The directors now contend that * * * the FDIC's statutory powers do not permit an unwarranted intrusion into their personal affairs * * * .

* * * *

To obtain enforcement of an administrative subpoena, the agency must show that the investigation will be conducted pursuant to a legitimate purpose, that the inquiry is relevant, that the information demanded is not already within the agency's possession, and that the administrative steps required by the statute have been followed. The demand for information must not be unreasonably broad or burdensome.

* * * *

When personal documents of individuals, as contrasted with business records of corporations, are the subject of an administrative subpoena, privacy concerns must be considered. * * * [R]elevant factors [include] such matters as the type of record requested, the information that it might contain, the potential for harm and subsequent nonconsensual disclosure, the adequacy of safeguards to prevent unauthorized disclosure, the degree of need for access, the specificity of the agency's statutory mandate, and the presence of recognizable public interests justifying access.

12 U.S.C. Section 1818(n) supplies the FDIC with the power to issue subpoenas *duces tecum*. The permissible purposes are * * * "carrying out any power, authority, or duty with respect to an insured depository institution (including determining any claim against the institution and determining and realizing upon any asset of any person in the course of collecting money due the institution)." The FDIC is empowered to avoid fraudulent asset transfers, assert claims against directors and officers, and seek court orders attaching assets.

* * * *

* * * [W]e observe at the outset that there is a significant public interest in promptly resolving the affairs of insolvent banks on behalf of their creditors and depositors, many of whom have lost significant sums of money and are often left with little hope for recovery. * * *

The FDIC has shown a reasonable need for gaining access to the directors' records in order to determine whether they reveal breaches of fiduciary duties through the improper channeling of bank funds for personal benefit. Moreover, the directors have not produced any evidence to show that the information contained in their personal financial records is of such a high degree of sensitivity that the intrusion could be considered severe or that the directors are likely to suffer any adverse effects from disclosure to FDIC personnel. Finally, we observe that regulatory provisions have been promulgated to guard against subsequent unauthorized disclosure of the subpoenaed information.

Accordingly, we conclude that the strong public interest in safeguarding the FDIC's legislative mandate outweighs the minimal intrusion into the privacy that surrounds the directors' personal financial records and any accompanying burdens of production.

* * * *

The order of the district court will be affirmed.

CASE 43.3 ADJUDICATION

BUCK CREEK COAL, INC. V. FEDERAL MINE SAFETY AND HEALTH ADMINISTRATION

United States Court of Appeals,
Seventh Circuit, 1995.
52 F.3d 133.

ILANA DIAMOND ROVNER, Circuit Judge.

* * * *

I.

Buck Creek owns and operates a coal mine located in Sullivan County, Indiana. When [Mine Safety and Health Administration (MSHA)] inspector James Holland inspected the mine on March 31, 1993, he noted an accumulation of loose coal and coal dust in the "feeder" area, where mined coal is transferred from shuttle cars to conveyor belts. Pursuant to * * * the Federal Mine Safety and Health Act of 1977, he issued a citation, which contained these charges:

> Accumulation of loose fine coal and float coal dust, black in color was permitted to accumulate underneath the belt conveyor, tail roller, and feeder from the check curtain behind the feeder and extended in by [sic] the feeder and including all three dumping points, a distance of 116 feet. The accumulations ranged from 2 inches to 3½ feet in depth and 18 feet in width.

According to the citation, the accumulation violated 30 C.F.R. Section 75.400, which provides:

> Coal dust, including float coal dust deposited on rock-dusted surfaces, loose coal, and other combustible materials, shall be cleaned up and not be permitted to accumulate in active workings, or on electric equipment therein.

The inspector further found that the violation was both "significant and substantial" and "unwarrantable," as defined in 30 U.S.C. Section 814(d)(1), which provides:

> If, upon any inspection of a coal or other mine, an authorized representative of the Secretary finds that there has been a violation of any mandatory health or safety standard, and if he also finds that, while the conditions created by such violation do not cause imminent danger, such violation is of a nature as could significantly and substantially contribute to the cause and effect of a coal or other mine safety or health hazard, and if he finds such violation to be caused by an unwarrantable failure of such operator to comply with such mandatory health or safety standards, he shall include such finding in any citation given to the operator * * *.

* * * [A] $2,000 civil penalty for the violation was proposed. After an evidentiary hearing, the administrative law judge ("ALJ") found that each of the inspector's conclusions was supported by the evidence and affirmed the citation and penalty. Not contesting the propriety of either the citation or the penalty, Buck Creek now contests only the ALJ's conclusions, which became those of the [U.S] Secretary [of the Interior] after the [Federal Mine Safety and Health] Review Commission declined review, that the violation was both "significant and substantial" and "unwarrantable." * * *

II.

* * * *

As for the finding that a violation is "significant and substantial," * * * four conditions must be met:

> (1) the underlying violation of a mandatory safety standard; (2) a discrete safety hazard—that is, a measure of danger to safety—contributed to by the violation; (3) a reasonable likelihood that the hazard contributed to will result in an injury; and (4) a reasonable likelihood that the injury in question will be of a reasonably serious nature.

Here, Buck Creek contends that the ALJ's determination as to the third and fourth of those conditions * * * were not supported by substantial evidence. * * *

* * * [T]he ALJ's conclusions as to the third and fourth factors were admittedly sparse, consisting only of this sentence:

> * * * Inspector Holland credibly testified and I accept his opinion, that in the event of a fire, smoke and gas inhalation by miners in the area would cause a reasonably serious injury requiring medical attention.

But contrary to Buck Creek's contention, no further evidence was necessary to support the ALJ's conclusion. First, credibility determinations reside in the province of the ALJ and the ALJ certainly did not abuse his discretion here in crediting the opinion of Inspector Holland, a federal mine inspector with 32 years of mining experience who specializes in mine ventilation. Nor was anything more than Inspector Holland's opinion necessary to support the common sense conclusion that a fire burning in an underground coal mine would present a serious risk of smoke and gas inhalation to miners who are present. Indeed, a brief review of the legislative history of the 1977 Act makes clear that fire is one of the primary safety concerns that has motivated federal regulation of the coal mining industry.

Nor has Buck Creek identified any evidence that tends to undermine the ALJ's conclusion. In attempting to do so, Buck Creek has relied mainly on the testimony of H. Michael McDowell, its vice president of human resources * * * . But the only testimony of McDowell that actually bears on the question of whether a fire would be likely to result in serious injury pertained to Buck Creek's fire safety systems. * * * The fact that Buck Creek has safety measures in place to deal with a fire does not mean that fires do not pose a serious safety risk to miners. Indeed, the precautions are presumably in place (as MSHA regulations require them to be) precisely because of the significant dangers associated with coal mine fires.

III. Unwarrantability

Buck Creek also argues that the ALJ's finding of unwarrantability was not supported by substantial evidence. An "unwarrantable failure" * * * may be established by showing that a violative condition or practice was not corrected prior to the issuance of a citation or order because of indifference, willful intent or serious lack of reasonable care. * * *

Here, the ALJ's conclusion that Buck Creek's violation * * * was unwarrantable was based in large part on the mere extent of the accumulation, which Inspector Holland believed to reflect at least three shifts of buildup and which the ALJ more conservatively found must have been present since at least the previous shift. * * * [The ALJ] also noted * * * that a pre-shift examination had already been conducted and that the section foreman had been on duty for one and one half hours, but that still nothing was being done upon Inspector Holland's arrival to remove the extensive accumulation. And even more significant in our view, the ALJ found Buck Creek's failure to remedy the situation to be particularly egregious in light of the fact that the company had already received repeated warnings regarding this very problem. In March 1993 alone, Buck Creek had received nine citations for violations of the same regulation, one of which pertained to the same area in which the accumulation now at issue was located. The ALJ's conclusion that the violation was in this instance "unwarrantable" was therefore clearly supported by substantial evidence. * * *

IV.

The ALJ's conclusions were both well-reasoned and supported by the evidence. Buck Creek's petition for review is DENIED.

CASE PROBLEMS

43–1. Congress passed legislation in 1966 that required the National Highway Traffic Safety Administration (NHTSA) to adopt automobile safety standards. Among the standards required by Section 203 of the act are rules for grading the quality of automobile tires. In 1975, the NHTSA adopted tread-wear regulations based on certain road-testing procedures. In 1983, as part of the Reagan administration's program of deregulation, the NHTSA indefinitely suspended the tire-quality regulations. The NHTSA contended that the standards were too costly for the economically troubled U.S. automobile industry and that the test procedures were not sufficiently reliable. Public Citizen, a public-interest group, sued the NHTSA, claiming that the suspension of the tire-quality standards was arbitrary and capricious. Will the court agree? Discuss. [*Public Citizen v. Steed*, 733 F.2d 93 (D.C.Cir. 1984)]

43–2. The Federal Home Loan Bank Board (FHLBB) operated the Federal Savings and Loan Insurance Corporation (FSLIC). The FHLBB's duties included examining all FSLIC–insured institutions to determine whether they were being operated properly under applicable laws and regulations. As part of an investigation of Texas-based Vision Banc Savings and Loan, the FHLBB became suspicious of a large loan made to Sandsend Financial Consultants, Ltd. Hoping to trace the proceeds of the loan, the FHLBB subpoenaed Sandsend's financial records from a second bank, West Belt. Sandsend requested a federal district court to void the subpoena. Should the court grant this request? Explain fully. [*Sandsend Financial Consultants, Ltd. v. Federal Home Loan Bank Board*, 878 F.2d 875 (5th Cir. 1989)]

43–3. In October 1985, four nonprofit organizations sued the Army Corps of Engineers, claiming that the corps had violated the National Environmental Policy Act of 1969. The organizations asserted that the corps had failed to prepare a supplemental environmental impact statement (EIS) based on information contained in two studies—an Oregon Department of Fish and Wildlife memorandum and a U.S. Soil Conservation

Service survey—suggesting that construction of a third dam on the Rogue River would increase the temperature and turgidity of the river. The corps contended that the EIS was unnecessary, because on the basis of its own analysis, as well as that of independent research commissioned by the corps, the two studies were not indisputable and in any event were of exaggerated importance in assessing the project. Should the court order that the project be stopped? Discuss. [*Marsh v. Oregon Natural Resources Council,* 490 U.S. 360, 109 S.Ct. 1851, 104 L.Ed.2d 377 (1989)]

43–4. The Food and Drug Administration has authority to protect the public health from misbranded or dangerous food products. After the FDA found that a company was marketing a product, "Nutrilite Food Supplement," that was mislabeled, the FDA seized all inventory from the company's warehouse. The FDA did so without granting the company a hearing. The company sued, arguing that this action was destroying its business. Should the court uphold the FDA's decision? [*Ewing v. Mytinger & Casselberry, Inc.*, 339 U.S. 594, 70 S.Ct 870, 94 L.Ed. 1088 (1950)]

43–5. A state statute required vehicle dismantlers—persons whose business includes dismantling automobiles and selling the parts—to be licensed and to keep records regarding the vehicles and parts in their possession. The statute also authorized warrantless administrative inspections; that is, without first obtaining a warrant, agents of the state department of motor vehicles or police officers could inspect a vehicle dismantler's license and records, as well as vehicles on the premises. Pursuant to this statute, police officers entered an automobile junkyard and asked to see the owner's license and records. The owner replied that he did not have the documents. The officers inspected the premises and discovered stolen vehicles and parts. Charged with possession of stolen property and unregistered operation as a vehicle dismantler, the junkyard owner argued that the warrantless inspection statute was unconstitutional under the Fourth Amendment. The trial court disagreed, reasoning that the junkyard business was a highly regulated industry. On appeal, the highest state court concluded that the statute had no truly administrative purpose and impermissibly authorized searches only to discover stolen property. The state appealed to the United States Supreme Court. Should the Court uphold the statute? Discuss. [*New York v. Burger,* 482 U.S. 691, 107 S.Ct. 2636, 96 L.Ed.2d 601 (1987)]

43–6. In 1976, the Environmental Protection Agency (EPA) proposed a rule establishing new pollution-control standards for coal-fired steam generators. The agency gave notice and received comments in the manner prescribed by the Administrative Procedure Act. After the public comments had been received, the EPA accepted informal suggestions from members of Congress and other federal officials. In 1979, the EPA published its final standards. Several environmental groups protested these standards, arguing that they were too lax. As part of this protest, the groups complained that political influence from Congress and other federal officials had encouraged the EPA to relax the proposed standards. The groups went on to argue that these *ex parte* comments were themselves illegal or that such comments at least should have been summarized in the record. What will the court decide? Discuss fully. [*Sierra Club v. Costle,* 657 F.2d 298 (D.C.Cir. 1981)]

43–7. The U.S. Forest Service issued a plan for cutting timber from the Wayne National Forest. Most of the cutting was to be done by a technique known as even-aged management, which requires clearcutting. Clearcutting involves the removal of all trees within areas ranging in size from fifteen to thirty acres. The Sierra Club challenged the plan in an appeal to Jack Ward Thomas, chief of the Forest Service. When Thomas affirmed the plan, the Sierra Club and others filed a suit in a federal district court against Thomas and others, arguing that the plan was arbitrary and capricious because, in making it, the Forest Service had not complied with the National Forest Management Act. The court granted the Forest Service's motion for summary judgment, and the Sierra Club appealed. What will happen on appeal? Discuss. [*Sierra Club v. Thomas,* 105 F.3d 248 (6th Cir. 1997)]

43–8. In 1991, the Occupational Safety and Health Administration (OSHA) promulgated a rule to protect health-care workers from viruses that can be transmitted in the blood of patients. The rule requires employers in the health-care industry to take certain precautions relating to the handling of contaminated instruments (such as needles), the disposal of contaminated waste, and the use of protective clothing (such as gloves, masks, and gowns). The rule also requires employers to provide vaccinations for hepatitis B for their employees and confidential blood testing of workers following accidental exposures (such as being stuck with a contaminated needle). The American Dental Association (ADA) and two other groups asked a federal court to review the rule. The ADA argued, among other things, that OSHA had failed to establish that dental workers were sufficiently at risk to benefit from the rule. Furthermore, the rule would unnecessarily burden consumers with increased medical costs and, hence, diminished care. What should the appellate court decide? Discuss fully. [*American Dental Association v. Martin,* 984 F.2d 823 (7th Cir. 1993)]

43–9. The Department of Commerce issued a flammability standard that required all mattresses, including crib mattresses, to pass a test that involved contact with a burning cigarette. The manufacturers of crib mattresses petitioned the department to exempt their product from the test procedure, but the department refused to do so. The crib manufacturers sued the department and argued that applying such a rule to crib mattresses was arbitrary and capricious because infants do not smoke. On what basis might the court hold that the rule is not arbitrary and capricious? [*Bunny Bear, Inc. v. Peterson,* 473 F.2d 1002 (1st Cir. 1973)]

43–10. The Atomic Energy Commission (AEC) was engaged in rulemaking proceedings for nuclear reactor safety. An environmental group sued the commission, arguing that its proceedings were inadequate. The commission had carefully complied with all requirements of the Administrative Procedure Act. The environmentalists argued, however, that the very hazardous and technical nature of the reactor safety issue required elaborate procedures above and beyond those set forth in the act. A federal court of appeals agreed and overturned the AEC rules. The commission appealed the case to the United States Supreme Court. How should the Court rule? Discuss. [*Vermont Yankee Nuclear Power Corp. v. Natural Resources Defense Council, Inc.,* 435 U.S. 519, 98 S.Ct. 1197, 55 L.Ed.2d 460 (1978)]

43–11. In 1982, the president of the United States appointed Matthew Chabal, Jr., to the position of U.S. marshal. U.S. marshals are assigned to the federal courts. In the fall of 1985, Chabal received an unsatisfactory annual performance rating, and he was fired shortly thereafter by the president. Given that U.S. marshals are assigned to the federal courts, are these appointees members of the executive branch? Did the president have the right to fire Chabal without consulting Congress about the decision? [*Chabal v. Reagan,* 841 F.2d 1216 (3d Cir. 1988)]

43–12. In 1977, the Department of Transportation (DOT) adopted a passive-restraint standard (known as Standard 208) that required new cars to have either air bags or automatic seat belts. By 1981, it had become clear that all of the major auto manufacturers would install automatic seat belts to comply with this rule. The DOT determined that most purchasers of cars would detach their automatic seat belts, thus making them ineffective. Consequently, the department repealed the regulation. State Farm Mutual Automobile Insurance Co. and other insurance companies sued in the District of Columbia Circuit Court of Appeals for a review of the DOT's repeal of the regulation. That court held that the repeal was arbitrary and capricious because the DOT had reversed its rule without sufficient support. The motor vehicle manufacturers, who initially had wanted to avoid the costs associated with implementing Standard 208, then appealed this decision to the United States Supreme Court. What will result? Discuss fully. [*Motor Vehicle Manufacturers Association v. State Farm Mutual Automobile Insurance Co.,* 463 U.S. 29, 103 S.Ct. 2856, 77 L.Ed.2d 443 (1983)]

43–13. American Message Centers (AMC) provides answering services to retailers. Calls to a retailer are automatically forwarded to AMC, which pays for the calls. AMC obtains telephone service at a discount from major carriers, including Sprint. Sprint's tariff (a public document setting out rates and rules relating to Sprint's services) states that the "subscriber shall be responsible for the payment of all charges for service." When AMC learned that computer hackers had obtained the access code for AMC's lines and had made nearly $160,000 in long-distance calls, it asked Sprint to absorb the cost. Sprint refused. AMC filed a complaint with the Federal Communications Commission (FCC), claiming in part that Sprint's tariff was vague and ambiguous, in violation of the Communications Act of 1934 and FCC rules. These laws require that a carrier's tariff "clearly and definitely" specify any "exceptions or conditions which in any way affect the rates named in the tariff." The FCC rejected AMC's complaint. AMC appealed the FCC's decision to a federal appellate court, claiming that the FCC's decision to reject AMC's complaint was arbitrary and capricious. What should the court decide? Discuss fully. [*American Message Centers v. Federal Communications Commission,* 50 F.3d 35 (D.C.Cir. 1995)]

43–14. The Occupational Safety and Health Administration (OSHA) is part of the U.S. Department of Labor. OSHA issued a "Directive" under which each employer in selected industries was to be inspected unless it adopted a "Comprehensive Compliance Program (CCP)"—a safety and health program designed to meet standards that in some respects exceeded those otherwise required by law. The Chamber of Commerce of the United States objected to the Directive and filed a petition for review with the U.S. Court of Appeals for the District of Columbia Circuit. The Chamber claimed, in part, that OSHA did not use proper rulemaking procedures in issuing the Directive. OSHA argued that it was not required to follow those procedures because the Directive itself was a "rule of procedure." OSHA claimed that the rule did not "alter the rights or interests of parties, although it may alter the manner in which the parties present themselves or their viewpoints to the agency." What are the steps of the most commonly used rulemaking procedure? Which steps are missing in this case? In whose favor should the court rule? Why? [*Chamber of Commerce of the United States v. U.S. Department of Labor,* 74 F.3d 206 (D.C.Cir. 1999)]

43–15. A QUESTION OF ETHICS

The Marine Mammal Protection Act was enacted in 1972 to reduce incidental killing and injury of marine mammals during commercial fishing operations. Under the act, commercial fishing vessels are required to allow an employee of the National Oceanic and Atmospheric Administration (NOAA) to accompany the vessels to conduct research and observe operations. In December 1986, after NOAA had adopted a new policy of recruiting female as well as male observers, NOAA notified Caribbean Marine Services Co. that female observers would be assigned to accompany two of the firm's fishing vessels on their next voyages. The owners and crew members of the ships (the plaintiffs) moved for an injunction against the implementation of the NOAA directive. The plaintiffs contended that the presence of a female on board a fishing vessel would be very awkward, because the female would have to share the crew's quarters, and crew members enjoyed little or no privacy with respect to bodily functions. Further, they alleged that the presence of a female would be disruptive to fishing operations, because some of the crew members were "crude" men with little formal education who might harass or sexually assault a female observer, and the officers would therefore have to devote time to protecting the female from the crew. Finally, the plaintiffs argued that the presence of a female observer could destroy morale and distract the crew, thus affecting the crew's efficiency and decreasing the vessel's profits. [*Caribbean Marine Services Co. v. Baldrige*, 844 F.2d 668 (9th Cir. 1988)]

1. In general, do you think that the public policy of promoting equal employment opportunity should override the concerns of the vessel owners and crew? If you were the judge, would you grant the injunction? Why, or why not?
2. The plaintiffs pointed out that fishing voyages could last three months or longer. Would the length of a particular voyage affect your answer to the preceding question?
3. The plaintiffs contended that even if the indignity of sharing bunk rooms and toilet facilities with a female observer could be overcome, the observer's very presence in the common areas of the vessel, such as the dining area, would unconstitutionally infringe on the crew members' right to privacy in these areas. Evaluate this claim.

E-LINKS

For updated links to resources available on the Web, as well as a variety of other materials, visit this text's Web site at

http://wbl-cs.westbuslaw.com

The Federal Web Locator permits searches for the names of federal administrative agencies and provides links to agency-related information. Go to

http://www.infoctr.edu/fwl

The Web site of the U.S. Government Printing Office, called GPO Access, offers free online access to the *Federal Register,* at

http://www.access.gpo.gov/su_docs

LEGAL RESEARCH EXERCISES ON THE WEB

Go to http://wbl-cs.westbuslaw.com, the Web site that accompanies this text. Select "Interactive Study Center," and then click on "Chapter 43." There you will find the following Internet research exercise that you can perform to learn more about how to obtain information from government agencies:

Activity 43–1: The Freedom of Information Act

CHAPTER 44
Consumer and Environmental Law

ALL STATUTES, AGENCY RULES, AND COMMON law judicial decisions that serve to protect the interests of consumers are classified as **consumer law**. Traditionally, in disputes involving consumers, it was assumed that the freedom to contract carried with it the obligation to live by the deal made. Over time, this attitude has changed considerably. Today, myriad federal and state laws protect consumers from unfair trade practices, unsafe products, discriminatory or unreasonable credit requirements, and other problems related to consumer transactions. Nearly every agency and department of the federal government has an office of consumer affairs, and most states have one or more such offices to help consumers. Also, typically the attorney general's office assists consumers at the state level.

In the first part of this chapter, we examine some of the major laws and regulations protecting consumers. We then turn to a discussion of **environmental law**—which consists of all of the laws and regulations designed to protect and preserve our environmental resources.

SECTION 1

Consumer Law

Consumer transactions take a variety of forms, but they generally include those that involve an exchange of value for the purpose of acquiring goods, services, land, or credit for personal or family use. Because of the wide variation among state consumer protection laws, our primary focus in this chapter is on federal legislation. Exhibit 44–1 indicates some of the types of consumer transactions that are regulated by federal laws.

DECEPTIVE ADVERTISING

One of the earliest federal consumer protection laws—and still one of the most important—was the Federal Trade Commission Act of 1914.[1] As mentioned in the preceding chapter, the act created the Federal Trade Commission (FTC) to carry out the broadly stated goal of preventing unfair and deceptive trade practices, including deceptive advertising.[2]

Deceptive Advertising Defined. Advertising will be deemed deceptive if a consumer would be misled by the advertising claim. Vague generalities and obvious exaggerations are permissible. These claims are known as *puffing*. When a claim takes on the appearance of literal authenticity, however, it may create problems. Advertising that *appears* to be based on factual evidence but that in fact is not will be deemed deceptive. A classic example is provided by a 1944 case in which the claim that a skin cream would restore youthful qualities to aged skin was deemed deceptive.[3]

Some advertisements contain "half-truths," meaning that the presented information is true but incomplete, and it leads consumers to a false conclusion. For example, the makers of Campbell's soups advertised that "most" Campbell's soups were low in fat and cholesterol and thus were helpful in fighting heart disease. What the ad did not say was that Campbell's soups are high in sodium, and high-sodium diets may increase the risk of heart disease.

1. 15 U.S.C. Sections 41–58.
2. 15 U.S.C. Section 45.
3. *Charles of the Ritz Distributing Corp. v. Federal Trade Commission*, 143 F.2d 676 (2d Cir. 1944).

EXHIBIT 44–1 AREAS OF CONSUMER LAW REGULATED BY STATUTES

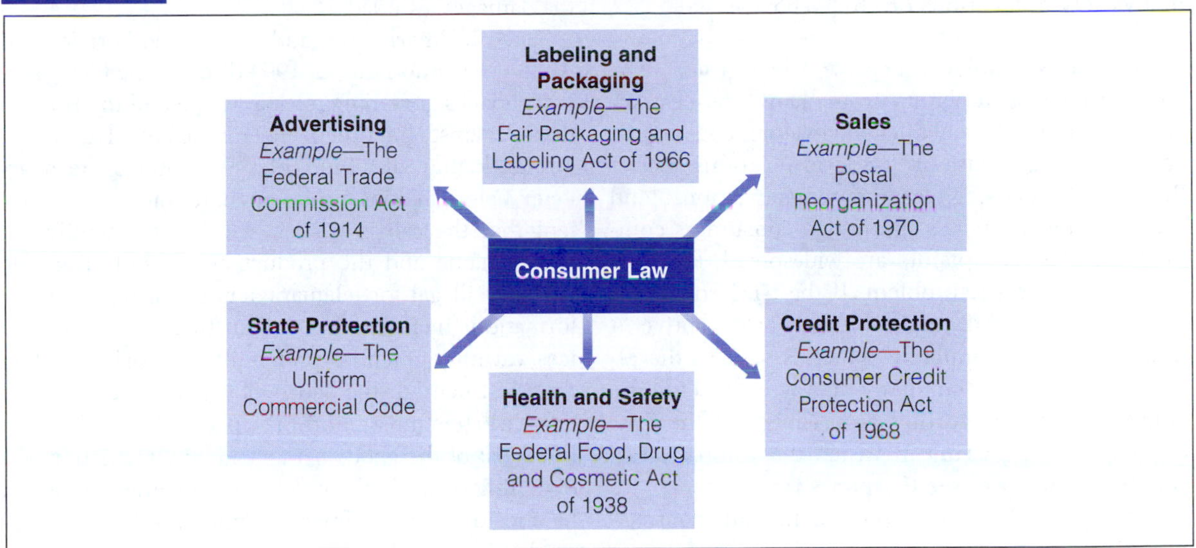

The FTC ruled that Campbell's claims were thus deceptive. Advertising that contains an endorsement by a celebrity may be deemed deceptive if the celebrity actually makes no use of the product.

Bait-and-Switch Advertising. The FTC has promulgated specific rules to govern advertising techniques. One of the most important rules is contained in the FTC's "Guides Against Bait Advertising,"[4] issued in 1968. The rule seeks to prevent **bait-and-switch advertising**—that is, advertising a very low price for a particular item that will likely be unavailable to the consumer, who will then be encouraged to purchase a more expensive item. The low price is the "bait" to lure the consumer into the store. The salesperson is instructed to "switch" the consumer to a different, more expensive item. Under the FTC guidelines, bait-and-switch advertising occurs if the seller refuses to show the advertised item, fails to have in stock a reasonable quantity of the item, fails to promise to deliver the advertised item within a reasonable time, or discourages employees from selling the item.

Online Deceptive Advertising. Deceptive advertising may occur in the online environment, as well. For several years, the FTC has been quite active in monitoring online advertising and has identified hundreds of Web sites that have made false or deceptive advertising claims concerning products ranging from medical treatments for various diseases to exercise equipment and weight loss products.

In September 2000, to help businesses comply with existing laws prohibiting deceptive advertising, the FTC issued new guidelines.[5] The guidelines do not set forth new rules but rather describe how existing laws apply to online advertising. Generally, the rules emphasize that any ads—online or offline—must be truthful and not misleading, and that any claims made in any ads must be substantiated. Additionally, ads cannot be unfair, defined in the guidelines as "caus[ing] or . . . likely to cause substantial consumer injury that consumers could not reasonably avoid and that is not outweighed by the benefit to consumers or competition."

The guidelines also call for "clear and conspicuous" disclosure of any qualifying or limiting information. The FTC suggests that advertisers should assume that consumers will not read an entire Web page. Therefore, to satisfy the "clear and conspicuous" requirement, advertisers should place the disclosure as close as possible to the claim being qualified, or include the disclosure within the claim itself. If such placement is not feasible, the next-best placement would be a section of the page to which a consumer could easily scroll. Generally, hyperlinks to a disclosure are recommended only for lengthy

4. 16 C.F.R. Part 238.

5. *Advertising and Marketing on the Internet: Rules of the Road,* September 2000.

disclosures or for disclosures that must be repeated in a variety of locations on the Web page.

FTC Actions against Deceptive Advertising. The FTC receives complaints from many sources, including competitors of alleged violators, consumers, consumer organizations, trade associations, Better Business Bureaus, government organizations, and state and local officials. If enough consumers complain and the complaints are widespread, the FTC will investigate the problem. If the FTC concludes that a given advertisement is unfair or deceptive, it drafts a formal complaint, which is sent to the alleged offender. The company may agree to settle the complaint without further proceedings, or the FTC can conduct a hearing in which the company can present its defense (see Chapter 43).

If the FTC succeeds in proving that an advertisement is unfair or deceptive, it usually issues a **cease-and-desist order** requiring that the challenged advertising be stopped. It might also impose a sanction known as **counteradvertising** by requiring the company to advertise anew—in print, on radio, and on television—to inform the public about the earlier misinformation. The FTC may institute **multiple product orders**, which require a firm to cease and desist from false advertising not only in regard to the product that was the subject of the action but also in regard to all of the firm's other products.

Telemarketing and Electronic Advertising. The pervasive use of the telephone to market goods and services to homes and businesses led to the passage in 1991 of the Telephone Consumer Protection Act (TCPA).[6] The act prohibits telephone solicitation using an automatic telephone dialing system or a prerecorded voice. Most states also have laws regulating telephone solicitation. The TCPA also makes it illegal to transmit ads via fax without first obtaining the recipient's permission. (Similar issues have arisen with respect to junk e-mail, called "spam"—see Chapter 5 for a discussion of this topic.)

The act is enforced by the Federal Communications Commission and also provides for a private right of action. Consumers can recover any actual monetary loss resulting from a violation of the act or receive $500 in damages for each violation, whichever is greater. If a court finds that a defendant willfully or knowingly violated the act, the court has the discretion to treble the damages awarded.

The Telemarketing and Consumer Fraud and Abuse Prevention Act[7] of 1994 directed the FTC to establish rules governing telemarketing and to bring actions against fraudulent telemarketers. The FTC's Telemarketing Sales Rule[8] of 1995 requires a telemarketer, before making a sales pitch, to inform the recipient that the call is a sales call and to identify the seller's name and the product being sold. The rule makes it illegal for telemarketers to misrepresent information (including facts about their goods or services, earnings potential, profitability, the risk attending an investment, or the nature of a prize). Additionally, telemarketers must inform the people they call of the total cost of the goods being sold, any restrictions on obtaining or using the goods, and whether a sale will be considered to be final and nonrefundable. A telemarketer must also remove a consumer's name from its list of potential contacts if the customer so requests.

See Case 44.1 at the end of this chapter. To view the full, unedited case from Westlaw,® go to this text's Web site at http://wbl-cs.westbuslaw.com.

LABELING AND PACKAGING LAWS

A number of federal and state laws deal specifically with the information given on labels and packages. In general, labels must be accurate, and they must use words that are easily understood by the ordinary consumer. For example, a box of cereal cannot be labeled "giant" if that would exaggerate the amount of cereal contained in the box. In some instances, labels must specify the raw materials used in the product, such as the percentage of cotton, nylon, or other fiber used in a garment. In other instances, the product must carry a warning. Cigarette packages and advertising, for example, must include one of several warnings about the health hazards associated with smoking.[9]

Federal laws regulating the labeling and packaging of products include the Wool Products Labeling Act of 1939,[10] the Fur Products Labeling Act of 1951,[11] the Flammable Fabrics Act of 1953,[12] the

6. 47 U.S.C. Sections 227 *et seq.*

7. 15 U.S.C. Sections 6101–6108.
8. 16 C.F.R. Sections 310.1–310.8.
9. 15 U.S.C. Sections 1331–1341.
10. 15 U.S.C. Section 68.
11. 15 U.S.C. Section 69.
12. 15 U.S.C. Section 1191.

Fair Packaging and Labeling Act of 1966,[13] the Comprehensive Smokeless Tobacco Health Education Act of 1986,[14] and the Nutrition Labeling and Education Act of 1990.[15] The Comprehensive Smokeless Tobacco Health Education Act, for example, requires that producers, packagers, and importers of smokeless tobacco label their product with one of several warnings about the health hazards associated with the use of smokeless tobacco; the warnings are similar to those contained on other tobacco product packages.

The Fair Packaging and Labeling Act requires that products carry labels that identify the product; the net quantity of the contents, as well as the quantity of servings, if the number of servings is stated; the manufacturer; and the packager or distributor. The act also authorizes requirements concerning words used to describe packages, terms that are associated with savings claims, information disclosures for ingredients in nonfood products, and standards for the partial filling of packages. Food products must bear labels detailing nutritional content, including how much fat the food contains and what kind of fat it is. These restrictions are enforced by the Department of Health and Human Services, as well as the FTC. The Nutrition Labeling and Education Act of 1990 requires standard nutrition facts (including fat content) on food labels; regulates the use of such terms as *fresh* and *low fat;* and, subject to the federal Food and Drug Administration's approval, authorizes certain health claims.

SALES

Many of the laws that protect consumers concern the disclosure of certain terms in sales transactions and provide rules governing the various forms of sales, such as door-to-door sales, mail-order sales, referral sales, and the unsolicited receipt of merchandise. Much of the federal regulation of sales is conducted by the FTC under its regulatory authority to curb unfair trade practices. Other federal agencies, however, are involved to various degrees. For example, the Federal Reserve Board of Governors has issued **Regulation Z**,[16] which governs credit provisions associated with sales contracts. Many states have also enacted laws governing consumer sales transactions. Moreover, states have provided a number of consumer protection provisions through the adoption of the Uniform Commercial Code and, in those states that have adopted it, the Uniform Consumer Credit Code.

Door-to-Door Sales. Door-to-door sales are singled out for special treatment in the laws of most states, in part because of the nature of the sales transaction. Repeat purchases are not as likely as they are in stores, and thus the seller has less incentive to cultivate the goodwill of the purchaser. Furthermore, the seller is unlikely to present alternative products and their prices. Thus, a number of states have passed "cooling-off" laws that permit the buyers of goods sold door-to-door to cancel their contracts within a specified period of time, usually two to three days after the sale.

An FTC regulation also requires sellers to give consumers three days to cancel any door-to-door sale. Because this rule applies in addition to the relevant state statutes, consumers are given the most favorable benefits of the FTC rule and their own state statutes. In addition, the FTC rule requires that consumers be notified in Spanish of this right if the oral negotiations for the sale were in that language.

Telephone and Mail-Order Sales. Sales made by either telephone or mail order are the greatest source of complaints to the nation's Better Business Bureaus. Many mail-order firms are far removed from most of their buyers, thus making it burdensome for buyers to bring complaints against them. To a certain extent, consumers are protected under federal laws prohibiting mail fraud, which were discussed in Chapter 8, and under state consumer protection laws that parallel and supplement the federal laws.

The FTC Mail or Telephone Order Merchandise Rule of 1993, which amended the FTC Mail-Order Rule of 1975,[17] provides specific protections for consumers who purchase goods via phone lines or through the mails. The 1993 rule extended the 1975 rule to include sales in which orders are transmitted by computer, fax machine, or some similar means involving telephone lines. Among other things, the rule requires mail-order merchants to ship orders within the time promised in their catalogues or advertisements, to notify consumers when orders cannot be shipped on time, and to issue a refund within a specified period of time when a consumer cancels an order.

13. 15 U.S.C. Sections 1451 *et seq.*
14. 15 U.S.C. Sections 4401–4408.
15. 21 U.S.C. Section 343-1.
16. 12 C.F.R. Sections 226.1–226.30.
17. 16 C.F.R. Sections 435.1–435.2.

In addition, the Postal Reorganization Act of 1970[18] provides that *unsolicited* merchandise sent by U.S. mail may be retained, used, discarded, or disposed of in any manner deemed appropriate, without the recipient's incurring any obligation to the sender.

Online Sales. In recent years, the Internet has become a vehicle for a wide variety of business-to-consumer (B2C) sales transactions. Most mail-order houses now have a Web presence, and consumers can purchase from other Web sites an increasing array of goods, ranging from airline tickets to books to xylophones. Protecting consumers from fraudulent and deceptive sales practices conducted via the Internet has proved to be a challenging task. Nonetheless, the FTC and other federal agencies have brought a number of enforcement actions against those who perpetrate online fraud. Additionally, the laws mentioned earlier, such as the federal statute prohibiting wire fraud, apply to online transactions.

Some states have amended their consumer protection statutes to cover Internet transactions as well. For example, the California legislature revised its Business and Professional Code to include transactions conducted over the Internet or by "any other electronic means of communication." Previously, that code only covered telephone, mail-order catalogue, radio, and television sales. Now any entity selling over the Internet in California must explicitly create an on-screen notice indicating its refund and return policies, where its business is physically located, its legal name, and a number of other details. Various states are also setting up information sites to help consumers protect themselves.

Credit Protection

Because of the extensive use of credit by American consumers, credit protection has become an especially important area regulated by consumer protection legislation. One of the most significant statutes regulating the credit and credit-card industry is Title I of the Consumer Credit Protection Act (CCPA),[19] which was passed by Congress in 1968 and is commonly referred to as the Truth-in-Lending Act (TILA).

The Truth-in-Lending Act. The TILA is basically a *disclosure law.* It is administered by the Federal Reserve Board and requires sellers and lenders to disclose credit terms or loan terms so that individuals can shop around for the best financing arrangements. TILA requirements apply only to persons who, in the ordinary course of business, lend money, sell on credit, or arrange for the extension of credit. Thus, sales or loans made between two consumers do not come under the protection of the act. Additionally, only debtors who are natural persons (as opposed to the artificial "person" of the corporation) are protected by this law; other legal entities are not.

The disclosure requirements are contained in Regulation Z, which, as already mentioned, was promulgated by the Federal Reserve Board. If the contracting parties are subject to the TILA, the requirements of Regulation Z apply to any transaction involving an installment sales contract in which payment is to be made in more than four installments. Transactions subject to Regulation Z typically include installment loans, retail and installment sales, car loans, home-improvement loans, and certain real estate loans if the amount of financing is less than $25,000.

Under the provisions of the TILA, all of the terms of a credit instrument must be clearly and conspicuously disclosed. The TILA provides for contract rescission (cancellation) if a creditor fails to follow *exactly* the procedures required by the act.[20] TILA requirements are strictly enforced.

Equal Credit Opportunity. In 1974, the Equal Credit Opportunity Act (ECOA)[21] was enacted as an amendment to the TILA. The ECOA prohibits the denial of credit solely on the basis of race, religion, national origin, color, gender, marital status, or age. The act also prohibits credit discrimination on the basis of whether an individual receives certain forms of income, such as public-assistance benefits. Under the ECOA, a creditor may not require the signature of an applicant's spouse, other than as a joint applicant, on a credit instrument if the applicant qualifies

18. 39 U.S.C. Section 3009.

19. 15 U.S.C. Sections 1601–1693r.

20. Note, however, that amendments to the TILA enacted in 1995 prevent borrowers from rescinding loans for minor clerical errors in closing documents [15 U.S.C. Sections 1605, 1631, 1635, 1640, and 1641].

21. 15 U.S.C. Sections 1691–1691f.

under the creditor's standards of creditworthiness for the amount and terms of the credit request. Creditors are permitted to ask for any information from a credit applicant except that which could be used for the type of discrimination covered in the act or its amendments.

Credit-Card Rules. The TILA also contains provisions regarding credit cards. One provision limits the liability of a cardholder to $50 per card for unauthorized charges made before the creditor is notified that the card has been lost. Another provision prohibits a credit-card company from billing a consumer for any unauthorized charges if the credit card was improperly issued by the company; for example, if a consumer receives an unsolicited credit card in the mail and the card is later stolen and used by the thief to make purchases, the consumer to whom the card was sent will not be liable for the unauthorized charges.

Further provisions of the act concern billing disputes related to credit-card purchases. If a debtor thinks that an error has occurred in billing or wishes to withhold payment for a faulty product purchased by credit card, the act outlines specific procedures for both the consumer and the credit-card company to follow in settling the dispute.

Consumer Leases. The Consumer Leasing Act (CLA) of 1988[22] amended the TILA to provide protection for consumers who lease automobiles and other goods. The CLA applies to those who lease or arrange to lease consumer goods in the ordinary course of their business. The act applies only if the goods are priced at $25,000 or less and if the lease term exceeds four months. The CLA and its implementing regulation, Regulation M,[23] require lessors to disclose in writing all of the material terms of the lease.

The Fair Credit Reporting Act. In 1970, to protect consumers against inaccurate credit reporting, Congress enacted the Fair Credit Reporting Act (FCRA).[24] The act provides that consumer credit reporting agencies may issue credit reports to users only for specified purposes, including the extension of credit, the issuance of insurance policies, compliance with a court order, and in response to a consumer's request for a copy of his or her own credit report. The act further provides that any time a consumer is denied credit or insurance on the basis of the consumer's credit report, or is charged more than others ordinarily would be for credit or insurance, the consumer must be notified of that fact and of the name and address of the credit reporting agency that issued the credit report.

Under the act, consumers may request the source of any information being given out by a credit agency, as well as the identity of anyone who has received an agency's report. Consumers are also permitted to have access to the information contained about them in a credit reporting agency's files. If a consumer discovers that a credit reporting agency's files contain inaccurate information about the consumer's credit standing, the agency, on the consumer's written request, must investigate the matter and delete any unverifiable or erroneous information within a reasonable period of time.

An agency that fails to comply with the act is liable for actual damages, plus additional damages not to exceed $1,000 and attorneys' fees.[25] Damages are also available against anyone who uses a credit report for an improper purpose, as well as banks, credit-card companies, and other businesses that report information to credit agencies and do not respond adequately to customer complaints.

The Fair Debt Collection Practices Act. In 1977, Congress enacted the Fair Debt Collection Practices Act (FDCPA)[26] in an attempt to curb what were perceived to be abuses by collection agencies. The act applies only to specialized debt-collection agencies that regularly attempt to collect debts on behalf of someone else, usually for a percentage of the amount owed. Creditors attempting to collect debts are not covered by the act unless, by misrepresenting themselves, they cause debtors to believe they are collection agencies. The act explicitly prohibits a collection agency from using any of the following tactics:

1. Contacting the debtor at the debtor's place of employment if the debtor's employer objects.
2. Contacting the debtor during inconvenient or unusual times (for example, calling the debtor at three o'clock in the morning) or at any time if the debtor is being represented by an attorney.

22. 15 U.S.C. Sections 1667–1667e.
23. 12 C.F.R. Part 213.
24. 15 U.S.C. Sections 1681–1681t.
25. 15 U.S.C. Section 1681n.
26. 15 U.S.C. Section 1692.

3. Contacting third parties other than the debtor's parents, spouse, or financial adviser about payment of a debt unless a court authorizes such action.
4. Using harassment or intimidation (for example, using abusive language or threatening violence) or employing false or misleading information (for example, posing as a police officer).
5. Communicating with the debtor at any time after receiving notice that the debtor is refusing to pay the debt, except to advise the debtor of further action to be taken by the collection agency.

The FDCPA also requires a collection agency to include a **validation notice** whenever it initially contacts a debtor for payment of a debt or within five days of that initial contact. The notice must state that the debtor has thirty days within which to dispute the debt and to request a written verification of the debt from the collection agency. The debtor's request for debt validation must be in writing.

The enforcement of the FDCPA is primarily the responsibility of the Federal Trade Commission. The act provides that a debt collector that fails to comply with the act is liable for actual damages, plus additional damages not to exceed $1,000[27] and attorneys' fees.

Cases brought under the FDCPA often raise questions as to who qualifies as a debt collector or debt-collection agency subject to the act. For example, for several years it was not clear whether attorneys who attempted to collect debts owed to their clients were subject to the FDCPA's provisions. In 1995, the United States Supreme Court addressed this issue to resolve conflicting opinions in the lower courts. The Court held that an attorney who regularly tries to obtain payment of consumer debts through legal proceedings meets the FDCPA's definition of "debt collector."[28]

Westlaw. See Case 44.2 at the end of this chapter. To view the full, unedited case from Westlaw,® go to this text's Web site at **http://wbl-cs.westbuslaw.com**.

Garnishment of Wages. Despite the increasing number of protections afforded debtors, creditors are not without means of securing payment on debts. One of these is the right to garnish a debtor's wages after the debt has gone uncollected for a prolonged period. Recall from Chapter 29 that *garnishment* is the legal procedure by which a creditor may collect on a debt by directly attaching, or seizing, a portion of the debtor's assets (such as wages) that are in the possession of a third party (such as an employer).

State law provides the basis for a process of garnishment, but the law varies among the states as to how easily garnishment can be obtained. Indeed, a few states, such as Texas, prohibit garnishment of wages altogether except for child support. In addition, constitutional due process and federal legislation under the TILA provide further protections against abuse.[29] In general, the debtor is entitled to notice and an opportunity to be heard in a process of garnishment. Moreover, wages cannot be garnished beyond 25 percent of the debtor's after-tax earnings, and the garnishment must leave the debtor with at least a specified minimum income.

Consumer Health and Safety

Laws discussed earlier regarding the labeling and packaging of products go a long way toward promoting consumer health and safety. But there is a significant distinction between regulating the information dispensed about a product and regulating the content of the product. The classic example is tobacco products. Tobacco products have not been altered by regulation or banned outright despite their obvious hazards. What has been regulated are the warnings that producers are required to give consumers about the hazards of tobacco.[30] This section focuses on laws that regulate the actual products made available to consumers.

The Federal Food, Drug and Cosmetic Act. The first federal legislation regulating food and drugs was enacted in 1906 as the Pure Food and Drugs Act. That law, as amended in 1938, exists presently as the Federal Food, Drug and Cosmetic Act (FFDCA).[31] The act protects consumers against adulterated and misbranded foods and drugs. More recent amendments have added substantive and procedural requirements to the act. In its present form,

27. According to the U.S. Court of Appeals for the Sixth Circuit, the $1,000 limit on damages applies to each lawsuit, not to each violation. See *Wright v. Finance Service of Norwalk, Inc.*, 22 F.3d 647 (6th Cir. 1994).

28. *Heintz v. Jenkins*, 514 U.S. 291, 115 S.Ct. 1489, 131 L.Ed.2d 395 (1995).

29. 15 U.S.C. Sections 1671–1677.

30. In 1996, the Food and Drug Administration attempted to regulate the sale of tobacco products by stating that nicotine is a drug. The United States Supreme Court, however, invalidated the rule, holding that the Federal Food, Drug and Cosmetic Act of 1938 did not define nicotine as a drug. See *Food and Drug Administration v. Brown S. Williamson Tobacco Corp.*, 529 U.S. 120 S.Ct. 1291, 146 L.Ed.2d 121 (2000).

31. 21 U.S.C. Sections 301–393.

the act establishes food standards, specifies safe levels of potentially hazardous food additives, and sets classifications of food and food advertising.

Most of these statutory requirements are monitored and enforced by the Food and Drug Administration (FDA). Under an extensive set of procedures established by the FDA, drugs must be shown to be effective as well as safe before they may be marketed to the public, and the use of some food additives suspected of being carcinogenic is prohibited. A 1976 amendment to the FFDCA[32] authorizes the FDA to regulate medical devices, such as pacemakers and other health devices and equipment, and to withdraw from the market any such device that is mislabeled.

The Consumer Product Safety Act. Consumer product safety legislation began in 1953 with the passage of the Flammable Fabrics Act, which prohibits the sale of highly flammable clothing or materials. Over the next two decades, Congress enacted legislation regarding the design or composition of specific classes of products. Then, in 1972, Congress, by enacting the Consumer Product Safety Act,[33] created a comprehensive scheme of regulation over matters of consumer safety. The act also established far-reaching authority over consumer safety under the Consumer Product Safety Commission (CPSC).

The CPSC conducts research on the safety of individual products, and it maintains a clearinghouse of information on the risks associated with various consumer products. The Consumer Product Safety Act authorizes the CPSC to set standards for consumer products and to ban the manufacture and sale of any product that it deems to be potentially hazardous to consumers. The CPSC also has authority to remove from the market any products it believes to be imminently hazardous and to require manufacturers to report on any products already sold or intended for sale if the products have proved to be dangerous. The CPSC also has authority to administer other product safety legislation, such as the Child Protection and Toy Safety Act of 1969[34] and the Federal Hazardous Substances Act of 1960.[35]

The CPSC's authority is sufficiently broad to allow it to ban any product that it believes poses an "unreasonable risk" to consumers. Some of the products that the CPSC has banned include various types of fireworks, cribs, and toys, as well as many products containing asbestos or vinyl chloride.

STATE CONSUMER PROTECTION LAWS

Thus far, our primary focus has been on federal legislation. State laws, however, often provide more sweeping and significant protections for the consumer than do federal laws. The warranty and unconscionability provisions of the Uniform Commercial Code, or UCC (the UCC was discussed in Chapters 18 through 23) offer important protections for consumers against unfair practices on the part of sellers and lessors. The Magnuson-Moss Warranty Act, which was discussed in Chapter 22, supplements the UCC provisions in cases involving both a consumer transaction of at least $10 and an express written warranty.

Far less widely adopted than the UCC is the Uniform Consumer Credit Code (UCCC). The UCCC has provisions concerning truth in lending, maximum credit ceilings, door-to-door sales, fine-print clauses, and other practices affecting consumer transactions.

Virtually all states have specific consumer protection acts, often titled "deceptive trade practices acts." Although state consumer protection statutes vary widely in their provisions, a common thread runs through most of them. Typically, state consumer protection laws are directed at deceptive trade practices, such as a seller's providing false or misleading information to consumers. As just mentioned, some of the legislation provides broad protection for consumers. A prime example is the Texas Deceptive Trade Practices Act of 1973, which forbids a seller from selling to a buyer anything that the buyer does not need or cannot afford.

SECTION 2

Environmental Law

We now turn to a discussion of the various ways in which businesses are regulated by the government in the interest of protecting the environment. To a great extent, environmental law consists of statutes passed by federal, state, or local governments and regulations

---

32. 21 U.S.C. Sections 352(o), 360(j), 360(k), and 360c–360k.

33. 15 U.S.C. Sections 2051–2083.

34. This act consists of amendments to 15 U.S.C. Sections 1261, 1262, and 1274.

35. 15 U.S.C. Sections 1261–1277.

issued by administrative agencies. Before examining statutory and regulatory environmental laws, however, we look at the remedies against environmental pollution available under the common law.

Common Law Actions

Common law remedies against environmental pollution originated centuries ago in England. Those responsible for operations that created dirt, smoke, noxious odors, noise, or toxic substances were sometimes held liable under common law theories of nuisance or negligence. Today, injured individuals continue to rely on the common law to obtain damages and injunctions against business polluters. (Statutory remedies are also available, a topic that we treat later.)

Nuisance. Under the common law doctrine of **nuisance**, persons may be held liable if they use their property in a manner that unreasonably interferes with others' rights to use or enjoy their own property. In these situations, it is common for courts to balance the equities between the harm caused by the pollution and the costs of stopping it.

Courts have often denied injunctive relief on the ground that the hardships to be imposed on the polluter and on the community are greater than the hardships to be suffered by the plaintiff. For example, a factory that causes neighboring landowners to suffer from smoke, dirt, and vibrations may be left in operation if it is the core of a local economy. The injured parties may be awarded only money damages. These damages may include compensation for the decreased value of their property that results from the factory's operation.

A property owner may be given relief from pollution in situations in which he or she can identify a distinct harm separate from that affecting the general public. This harm is referred to as a "private" nuisance. Under the common law, citizens were denied standing (access to the courts—see Chapter 2) unless they suffered a harm distinct from the harm suffered by the public at large. Some states still require this. Therefore, a group of citizens who wished to stop a new development that would cause significant water pollution was denied access to the courts on the ground that the harm to them did not differ from the harm to the general public.[36] A public authority (such as a state's attorney general) can sue to abate a "public" nuisance.

Negligence and Strict Liability. An injured party may sue a business polluter in tort under the negligence and strict liability theories discussed in Chapters 5 and 6. The basis for a negligence action is a business's alleged failure to use reasonable care toward a party whose injury was foreseeable and, of course, caused by the lack of reasonable care. For example, employees might sue an employer whose failure to use proper pollution controls contaminated the air, causing the employees to suffer respiratory illnesses. A developing area of tort law involves **toxic torts**—actions against toxic polluters.

Businesses that engage in ultrahazardous activities—such as the transportation of radioactive materials—are strictly liable for whatever injuries the activities cause. In a strict liability action, the injured party does not need to prove that the business failed to exercise reasonable care.

State and Local Regulation

Many states regulate the degree to which the environment may be polluted. Thus, for example, even when state zoning laws permit a business's proposed development, the proposal may have to be altered to change the development's impact on the environment. State laws may restrict a business's discharge of chemicals into the air or water or regulate its disposal of toxic wastes. States may also regulate the disposal or recycling of other wastes, including glass, metal, and plastic containers and paper. Additionally, states may restrict the emissions from motor vehicles.

City, county, and other local governments control some aspects of the environment. For instance, local zoning laws control some land use. These laws may be designed to inhibit or direct the growth of cities and suburbs or to protect the natural environment. Other aspects of the environment may be subject to local regulation for other reasons. Methods of waste and garbage removal and disposal, for example, can have a substantial impact on a community. The appearance of buildings and other structures, including advertising signs and billboards, may affect traffic safety, property values, or local aesthetics. Noise generated by a business or its customers may be annoying, disruptive, or damaging to its neighbors. The location and condition of parks, streets, and other

36. *Save the Bay Committee, Inc. v. Mayor of City of Savannah*, 227 Ga. 436, 181 S.E.2d 351 (1971).

public uses of land subject to local control affect the environment and can also affect business.

In recent years, several state and local governments have passed what are referred to as *brownfields redevelopment laws.* These laws are designed to provide incentives to buyers to purchase and clean up contaminated land ("brownfields") or older buildings containing asbestos. Incentives may be in the form of tax credits, government grants, or other assistance. Currently, Congress is considering a bill that would provide such incentives to communities throughout the nation.

FEDERAL REGULATION

Congress has enacted a number of statutes to control the impact of human activities on the environment. Exhibit 44–2 on the next page lists and summarizes the major federal environmental statutes discussed in this chapter. Some of these statutes were passed in an attempt to improve air and water quality. Others specifically regulate toxic chemicals—including pesticides, herbicides, and hazardous wastes.

The most well known of the agencies regulating environmental law is the Environmental Protection Agency (EPA), which was created in 1970 to coordinate federal environmental responsibilities. Other federal agencies with authority for regulating specific environmental matters include the Department of the Interior, the Department of Defense, the Department of Labor, the Food and Drug Administration, and the Nuclear Regulatory Commission. These regulatory agencies—and all other agencies of the federal government—must take environmental factors into consideration when making significant decisions.

The National Environmental Policy Act (NEPA) of 1969[37] requires that for every major federal action that significantly affects the quality of the environment, an **environmental impact statement (EIS)** must be prepared. An EIS must analyze (1) the impact on the environment that the action will have, (2) any adverse effects on the environment and alternative actions that might be taken, and (3) irreversible effects the action might generate. EISs have become instruments for private citizens, consumer interest groups, businesses, and others to challenge federal agency actions on the basis that the actions improperly threaten the environment.

37. 42 U.S.C. Sections 4321–4370d.

Other federal laws also require that environmental values be considered in agency decision making. Among the most important of these laws are those that have been enacted to protect fish and wildlife. Under the Fish and Wildlife Coordination Act of 1958,[38] federal agencies proposing to approve the impounding or diversion of a stream's waters must consult with the Fish and Wildlife Service with a view to preventing the loss of fish and wildlife resources. Also important is the Endangered Species Act of 1973.[39] Under this act, all federal agencies are required to take steps to ensure that their actions "do not jeopardize the continued existence of endangered species" or the habitat of an endangered species. An action may jeopardize the continued existence of a species if it sets in motion a chain of events that reduces the chances that the species will survive.

AIR POLLUTION

Federal involvement with air pollution goes back to the 1950s, when Congress authorized funds for air-pollution research. In 1963, the federal government passed the Clean Air Act,[40] which focused on multistate air pollution and provided assistance to states. Various amendments, particularly in 1970, 1977, and 1990, strengthened the government's authority to regulate air quality. These laws provide the basis for issuing regulations to control pollution coming primarily from mobile sources (such as automobiles) and stationary sources (such as electric utilities and industrial plants).

Mobile Sources. Regulations governing air pollution from automobiles and other mobile sources specify pollution standards and time schedules for meeting these standards. For example, under the 1990 amendments to the Clean Air Act, automobile manufacturers must cut new automobiles' exhaust emission of nitrogen oxide by 60 percent and emission of other pollutants by 35 percent. By 1998, all new automobiles had to meet this standard. Regulations that will go into effect beginning with 2004 model cars call for cutting nitrogen oxide tailpipe emissions by nearly 10 percent by 2007. For the first time, sport utility vehicles and light trucks

38. 16 U.S.C. Sections 661–666c.
39. 16 U.S.C. Sections 1531–1544.
40. 42 U.S.C. Sections 7401–7671q.

EXHIBIT 44–2 FEDERAL ENVIRONMENTAL STATUTES

POPULAR NAME	PURPOSE	STATUTE REFERENCE
Rivers and Harbors Appropriations Act (1899)	To prohibit ships and manufacturers from discharging and depositing refuse in navigable waterways.	33 U.S.C. Sections 401–418.
Federal Insecticide, Fungicide, and Rodenticide Act (FIFRA) (1947)	To control the use of pesticides and herbicides.	7 U.S.C. Sections 136–136y.
Federal Water Pollution Control Act (FWPCA) (1948)	To eliminate the discharge of pollutants from major sources into navigable waters.	33 U.S.C. Sections 1251–1387.
Atomic Energy Act (1954)	To limit environmental harm from the private nuclear industry.	42 U.S.C. Sections 2011 to 2297g-4.
Clean Air Act (1963)	To control air pollution from mobile and stationary sources.	42 U.S.C. Sections 7401–7671q.
National Environmental Policy Act (NEPA) (1969)	To limit environmental harm from federal government activities.	42 U.S.C. Sections 4321–4370d.
Marine Protection, Research, and Sanctuaries Act (Ocean Dumping Act) of 1972	To regulate the transporting and dumping of material into ocean waters.	16 U.S.C. Sections 1401–1445.
Noise Control Act (1972)	To regulate noise pollution from transportation and nontransportation sources.	42 U.S.C. Sections 4901–4918.
Endangered Species Act (1973)	To protect species that are threatened with extinction.	16 U.S.C. Sections 1531–1544.
Safe Drinking Water Act (1974)	To regulate pollutants in public drinking water systems.	42 U.S.C. Sections 300f to 300j-25.
Resource Conservation and Recovery Act (RCRA) (1976)	To establish standards for hazardous waste disposal.	42 U.S.C. Sections 6901–6986.
Toxic Substances Control Act (1976)	To regulate toxic chemicals and chemical compounds.	15 U.S.C. Sections 2601–2692.
Comprehensive Environmental Response, Compensation, and Liability Act (CERCLA) (Superfund) (1980)	To regulate the clean-up of hazardous waste-disposal sites.	42 U.S.C. Sections 9601–9675.
Low Level Radioactive Waste Policy Act (1980)	To assign to the states responsibility for nuclear power plants' low-level radioactive waste.	42 U.S.C. Sections 2021b–2021j.
Nuclear Waste Policy Act (1982)	To provide for the designation of a permanent radioactive waste-disposal site.	42 U.S.C. Sections 10101–10270.
Oil Pollution Act (1990)	To establish liability for the clean-up of navigable waters after oil-spill disasters.	33 U.S.C. Sections 2701–2761.

were also required to meet the same emission standards as automobiles.

Service stations are also subject to environmental regulations. The 1990 amendments require service stations to sell gasoline with a higher oxygen content in forty-one cities that experience carbon monoxide pollution in the winter. Service stations are required to sell even cleaner burning gasoline in

Los Angeles and another eight of the most polluted urban areas.

The EPA attempts to update pollution-control standards when new scientific information becomes available. In light of evidence that very small particles (2.5 microns, or millionths of a meter) of soot affect our health as significantly as larger particles, the EPA issued new particulate standards for motor vehicle exhaust systems and other sources of pollution. The EPA also increased the acceptable standard for ozone, which is formed when sunlight combines with pollutants from cars and other sources. Ozone is the basic ingredient of smog.

The EPA's particulate standards and the acceptable standard for ozone were challenged in the courts by business groups that claimed that the EPA had exceeded its authority under the Clean Air Act by issuing the regulations. The groups also claimed that the EPA had to take economic costs into account when developing new regulations. In 2000, however, the United States Supreme Court held that the EPA had not exceeded its authority under the Clean Air Act by issuing the new standards and confirmed that the EPA need not take economic costs into account when creating new rules.[41]

Stationary Sources. The Clean Air Act authorizes the EPA to establish air-quality standards for stationary sources (such as manufacturing plants) but recognizes that the primary responsibility for preventing and controlling air pollution rests with state and local governments. The EPA sets primary and secondary levels of ambient standards—that is, the maximum levels of certain pollutants—and the states formulate plans to achieve those standards. The plans are to provide for the attainment of primary standards within three years and secondary standards within a reasonable time. For economic, political, and technological reasons, however, the deadlines are often subject to change.

Different standards apply to sources of pollution in clean areas and those in polluted areas. Different standards also apply to existing sources of pollution and major new sources. Major new sources include existing sources modified by a change in a method of operation that increases emissions. Performance standards for major sources require use of the *maximum achievable control technology*, or MACT, to reduce emissions from the combustion of fossil fuels (coal and oil). As mentioned, the EPA issues guidelines as to what equipment meets this standard.

Under the 1990 amendments to the Clean Air Act, 110 of the oldest coal-burning power plants in the United States had to cut their emissions by 40 percent by the year 2001 to reduce acid rain. Utilities were granted "credits" to emit certain amounts of sulfur dioxide, and those that emit less than the allowed amounts can sell their credits to other polluters. Controls on other factories and businesses are intended to reduce ground-level ozone pollution in ninety-six cities to healthful levels by 2005 (except Los Angeles, which has until 2010). Industrial emissions of 189 hazardous air pollutants had to be reduced by 90 percent by 2000. By 2002, the production of chlorofluorocarbons (such as Freon), carbon tetrachloride, and methyl chloroform—used in air conditioning, refrigeration, and insulation and linked to depletion of the ozone layer—had to cease.

Hazardous Air Pollutants. Hazardous air pollutants are those likely to cause death or serious irreversible or incapacitating illness. As noted, there are 189 of these pollutants, including asbestos, benzene, beryllium, cadmium, mercury, and vinyl chloride. These pollutants may cause cancer as well as neurological and reproductive damage. They are emitted from stationary sources by a variety of business activities, including smelting, dry cleaning, house painting, and commercial baking. Instead of establishing specific emissions standards for each hazardous air pollutant, the 1990 amendments to the Clean Air Act require industry to use pollution-control equipment that represents the maximum achievable control technology, or MACT, to limit emissions. As mentioned, the EPA issues guidelines as to what equipment meets this standard.

In 1996, the EPA issued a rule to regulate hazardous air pollutants emitted by landfills. The rule requires landfills constructed after May 30, 1991, that emit more than a specified amount of pollutants to install landfill gas collection and control systems. The rule also requires the states to impose the same requirements on landfills constructed before May 30, 1991, if they accepted waste after November 8, 1987.[42]

Violations of the Clean Air Act. For violations of emission limits under the Clean Air Act, the EPA can assess civil penalties of up to $25,000 per day.

41. *Whitman v. American Trucking Associations*, 531 U.S. 457, 121 S.Ct. 903, 149 L.Ed.2d 1 (2000).

42. 40 C.F.R. Sections 60.750–759.

Additional fines of up to $5,000 per day can be assessed for other violations, such as failing to maintain the required records. To penalize those for whom it is more cost effective to violate the act than to comply with it, the EPA is authorized to obtain a penalty equal to the violator's economic benefits from noncompliance. Persons who provide information about violators may be paid up to $10,000. Private citizens can also sue violators.

Those who knowingly violate the act may be subject to criminal penalties, including fines of up to $1 million and imprisonment for up to two years (for false statements or failures to report violations). Corporate officers are among those who may be subject to these penalties.

WATER POLLUTION

Federal regulations governing water pollution can be traced back to the Rivers and Harbors Appropriations Act of 1899.[43] These regulations prohibited ships and manufacturers from discharging or depositing refuse in navigable waterways.

Navigable Waters. Once limited to waters actually used for navigation, the term *navigable waters* is today interpreted to include intrastate lakes and streams used by interstate travelers and industries, as well as coastal and freshwater wetlands (wetlands will be discussed shortly). In 1948, Congress passed the Federal Water Pollution Control Act (FWPCA),[44] but its regulatory system and enforcement proved inadequate. In 1972, amendments to the FWPCA—known as the Clean Water Act—established the following goals: (1) make waters safe for swimming, (2) protect fish and wildlife, and (3) eliminate the discharge of pollutants into the water. The amendments required that municipal and industrial polluters apply for permits before discharging wastes into navigable waters.

They also set forth specific time schedules, which were extended by amendment in 1977 and by the Water Quality Act of 1987.[45] Under these schedules, the EPA establishes limitations for discharges of types of pollutants based on the technology available for controlling them. Regulations, for the most part, specify that the *best available control technology,* or BACT, be installed. The EPA issues guidelines as to what equipment meets this standard, which essentially requires the most effective pollution-control equipment available. New sources must install BACT equipment before beginning operations. Existing sources are subject to timetables for installation of BACT equipment. These sources must immediately install equipment that utilizes the *best practical control technology,* or BPCT. The EPA also issues guidelines as to what equipment meets this standard.

Under the Clean Water Act, violators are subject to a variety of civil and criminal penalties. Depending on the violation, civil penalties range from a maximum of $10,000 per day, and not more than $25,000 per violation, to as much as $25,000 per day. Criminal penalties range from a fine of $2,500 per day and imprisonment for up to one year to a fine of $1 million and fifteen years' imprisonment. Injunctive relief and damages can also be imposed. The polluting party can be required to clean up the pollution or pay for the cost of doing so. Criminal penalties apply only if a violation was intentional.

Wetlands. The Clean Water Act prohibits the filling or dredging of **wetlands** unless a permit is obtained from the Army Corps of Engineers. The EPA defines *wetlands* as "those areas that are inundated or saturated by surface or ground water at a frequency and duration sufficient to support, and that under normal circumstances do support, a prevalence of vegetation typically adapted for life in saturated soil conditions." In recent years, federal regulatory policy in regard to wetlands has elicited substantial controversy because of the broad interpretation of what constitutes a wetland subject to the regulatory authority of the federal government.

Perhaps one of the most controversial regulations was that issued by the Army Corps of Engineers, which became known as the "migratory-bird rule." Under this rule, any body of water that could affect interstate commerce, including seasonal ponds or waters "used or suitable for use by migratory birds" that fly over state borders, were "navigable waters" subject to federal regulation under the Clean Water Act as a wetland.

In 2001, after years of controversy, the United States Supreme Court struck down the rule. The case involved a group of communities in the Chicago suburbs that wanted to build a landfill in a tract of land northwest of Chicago that had once been used as a

43. 33 U.S.C. Sections 401–418.

44. 33 U.S.C. Sections 1251–1387.

45. This act amended 33 U.S.C. Section 1251.

strip mine. Over time, areas that were once pits in the mine became ponds used by a variety of migratory birds. State and local agencies approved the project, but the Army Corps of Engineers, claiming that the shallow ponds formed a habitat for migratory birds, refused to grant a permit to create the landfill. A lawsuit followed, and when the case reached the Supreme Court, the Court held that the Army Corps of Engineers had exceeded its authority under the Clean Water Act. The Court stated that it was not prepared to hold that isolated and seasonal ponds, puddles, and "prairie potholes" become "navigable waters of the United States" simply because they serve as a habitat for migratory birds.[46]

Drinking Water. Another statute governing water pollution is the Safe Drinking Water Act.[47] Passed in 1974, this act requires the EPA to set maximum levels for pollutants in public water systems. Operators of public water supply systems must come as close as possible to meeting the EPA's standards by using the best available technology that is economically and technologically feasible. The EPA is particularly concerned with contamination from underground sources. Pesticides and wastes leaked from landfills or disposed of in underground injection wells are among the more than two hundred pollutants known to exist in groundwater used for drinking in at least thirty-four states. Many of these substances are associated with cancer and damage to the central nervous system, liver, and kidneys.

The act was amended in 1996 to give the EPA greater flexibility in setting regulatory standards governing drinking water. Prior to the 1996 amendments, the EPA had to set standards for twenty-five different drinking water contaminants every three years, which it had largely failed to do. Under the 1996 amendments, the EPA can move at whatever rate it deems necessary to control contaminants that are of greatest concern to the public health. The 1996 amendments also imposed new requirements on suppliers of drinking water. Each supplier must send to every household it supplies with water an annual statement describing the source of its water, the level of any contaminants contained in the water, and any possible health concerns associated with the contaminants.

46. *Solid Waste Agency of Northern Cook County v. U.S. Army Corps of Engineers*, 531 U.S. 159, 121 S.Ct. 675, 148 L.Ed.2d 576 (2001).

47. 42 U.S.C. Sections 300f to 300j-25.

Ocean Dumping. The Marine Protection, Research, and Sanctuaries Act of 1972[48] (known popularly as the Ocean Dumping Act) regulates the transportation and dumping of material into ocean waters. (The term *material* is synonymous with the term *pollutant* as used in the Federal Water Pollution Control Act.) The Ocean Dumping Act prohibits entirely the ocean-dumping of radiological, chemical, and biological warfare agents and high-level radioactive waste. The act establishes a permit program for transporting and dumping other materials. There are specific exemptions—materials subject to the permit provisions of other pollution legislation, wastes from structures regulated by other laws (for example, offshore oil exploration and drilling platforms), sewage, and other wastes. The Ocean Dumping Act also authorizes the designation of marine sanctuaries for "preserving or restoring such areas for their conservation, recreational, ecological, or esthetic values."

Each violation of any provision or permit may result in a civil penalty of not more than $50,000 or revocation or suspension of the permit. A knowing violation is a criminal offense that may result in a $50,000 fine, imprisonment for not more than a year, or both. An injunction may also be imposed.

Oil Pollution. The Oil Pollution Act of 1990[49] provides that any onshore or offshore oil facility, oil shipper, vessel owner, or vessel operator that discharges oil into navigable waters or onto an adjoining shore may be liable for clean-up costs, as well as damages. The act created a $1 billion oil clean-up and economic compensation fund and decreed that by the year 2011, oil tankers using U.S. ports must be double hulled to limit the severity of accidental spills.

Under the act, damage to natural resources, private property, and the local economy, including the increased cost of providing public services, is compensable. The act provides for civil penalties of $1,000 per barrel spilled or $25,000 for each day of the violation. The party held responsible for the clean-up costs can bring a civil suit for contribution from other potentially liable parties.

Noise Pollution

Regulations concerning noise pollution include the Noise Control Act of 1972.[50] This act requires the

48. 16 U.S.C. Sections 1401–1445.

49. 33 U.S.C. Sections 2701–2761.

50. 42 U.S.C. Sections 4901–4918.

EPA to establish noise emission standards (maximum noise levels below which no harmful effects occur from interference with speech or other activity)—for example, for railroad noise emissions. The standards must be achievable by the best available technology, and they must be economically within reason.

The act prohibits, among other things, distributing products manufactured in violation of the noise emission standards and tampering with noise control devices. Either of these activities can result in an injunction or whatever other remedy "is necessary to protect the public health and welfare." Illegal product distribution can also result in a fine and imprisonment. Violations of provisions of the Noise Control Act can result in penalties of not more than $50,000 per day and imprisonment for not more than two years.

Toxic Chemicals

Originally, most environmental clean-up efforts were directed toward reducing smog and making water safe for fishing and swimming. Over time, however, control of toxic chemicals has become an important part of environmental law.

Pesticides and Herbicides. The federal statute regulating pesticides and herbicides is the Federal Insecticide, Fungicide, and Rodenticide Act (FIFRA) of 1947.[51] Under FIFRA, pesticides and herbicides must be (1) registered before they can be sold, (2) certified and used only for approved applications, and (3) used in limited quantities when applied to food crops. If a substance is identified as harmful, the EPA can cancel its registration after a hearing. If the harm is imminent, the EPA can suspend registration pending the hearing. The EPA, or state officers or employees, may also inspect factories in which these chemicals are manufactured.

Under 1996 amendments to the Federal Food, Drug and Cosmetic Act, for a pesticide to remain on the market, there must be a "reasonable certainty of no harm" to people from exposure to the pesticide.[52] This means that there must be no more than a one-in-a-million risk to people of developing cancer from exposure in any way, including eating food that contains residues from the pesticide. Pesticide residues are in nearly all fruits and vegetables and processed foods. Under the 1996 amendments, the EPA must distribute to grocery stores brochures on high-risk pesticides that are in food, and the stores must display these brochures for consumers.

It is a violation of FIFRA to sell a pesticide or herbicide that is unregistered, a pesticide or herbicide with a registration that has been canceled or suspended, or a pesticide or herbicide with a false or misleading label. For example, it is an offense to sell a substance that is adulterated (that has a chemical strength different from the concentration declared on the label). It is also an offense to destroy or deface any labeling required under the act. The act's labeling requirements include directions for the use of the pesticide or herbicide, warnings to protect human health and the environment, a statement of treatment in the case of poisoning, and a list of the ingredients.

A private party can petition the EPA to suspend or cancel the registration of a pesticide or herbicide. If the EPA fails to act, the private party can petition a federal court to review the EPA's failure. Penalties for registrants and producers for violating FIFRA include imprisonment for up to one year and a fine of no more than $50,000. Penalties for commercial dealers include imprisonment for up to one year and a fine of no more than $25,000. Farmers and other private users of pesticides or herbicides who violate the act are subject to a $1,000 fine and imprisonment for up to thirty days.

Toxic Substances. The first comprehensive law covering toxic substances was the Toxic Substances Control Act of 1976.[53] The act was passed to regulate chemicals and chemical compounds that are known to be toxic—such as asbestos and polychlorinated biphenyls, popularly known as PCBs—and to institute investigation of any possible harmful effects from new chemical compounds. The regulations authorize the EPA to require that manufacturers, processors, and other organizations planning to use chemicals first determine their effects on human health and the environment. The EPA can regulate substances that may pose an imminent hazard or an unreasonable risk of injury to health or the environment. The EPA may require special labeling, limit the use of a substance, set production quotas, or prohibit the use of a substance altogether.

Hazardous Wastes

Some industrial, agricultural, and household wastes pose more serious threats than others. If not prop-

51. 7 U.S.C. Sections 136–136y.
52. 21 U.S.C. Section 346a.
53. 15 U.S.C. Sections 2601–2692.

erly disposed of, these toxic chemicals may present a substantial danger to human health and the environment. If released into the environment, they may contaminate public drinking water resources.

Resource Conservation and Recovery Act. In 1976, Congress passed the Resource Conservation and Recovery Act (RCRA)[54] in reaction to an ever-increasing concern with the effects of hazardous waste materials on the environment. The RCRA required the EPA to establish regulations to monitor and control hazardous waste disposal and to determine which forms of solid waste should be considered hazardous and thus subject to regulation. The act authorized the EPA to promulgate various technical requirements for some types of facilities for storage and treatment of hazardous waste. The act also requires all producers of hazardous waste materials to label and package properly any hazardous waste to be transported.

The RCRA was amended in 1984 and 1986 to decrease the use of land containment in the disposal of hazardous waste and to require compliance with the act by some generators of hazardous waste—such as those generating less than 1,000 kilograms (2,200 pounds) a month—that had previously been excluded from regulation under the RCRA.

Under the RCRA, a company may be assessed a civil penalty based on the seriousness of the violation, the probability of harm, and the extent to which the violation deviates from RCRA requirements. The assessment may be up to $25,000 for each violation. Criminal penalties include fines up to $50,000 for each day of violation, imprisonment for up to two years (in most instances), or both. Criminal fines and the time of imprisonment can be doubled for certain repeat offenders.

Superfund. In 1980, the U.S. Congress passed the Comprehensive Environmental Response, Compensation, and Liability Act (CERCLA),[55] commonly known as Superfund. The basic purpose of Superfund is to regulate the clean-up of disposal sites in which hazardous waste is leaking into the environment. A special federal fund was created for that purpose.

Superfund provides that when a release or a threatened release of hazardous chemicals from a site occurs, the EPA can clean up the site and recover the cost of the clean-up from the following persons: (1) the person who generated the wastes disposed of at the site, (2) the person who transported the wastes to the site, (3) the person who owned or operated the site at the time of the disposal, or (4) the current owner or operator. A person falling within one of these categories is referred to as a **potentially responsible party (PRP).**

Liability under Superfund is usually joint and several—that is, a PRP who generated *only a fraction* of the hazardous waste disposed of at the site may nevertheless be liable for *all* of the clean-up costs. CERCLA authorizes a party who has incurred clean-up costs to bring a "contribution action" against any other person who is liable or potentially liable for a percentage of the costs.

See Case 44.3 at the end of this chapter. To view the full, unedited case from Westlaw,® go to this text's Web site at **http://wbl-cs.westbuslaw.com**.

54. 42 U.S.C. Sections 6901–6986.

55. 42 U.S.C. Sections 9601–9675.

TERMS AND CONCEPTS TO REVIEW

bait-and-switch advertising 895
cease-and-desist order 896
consumer law 894
counteradvertising 896
environmental impact statement (EIS) 903
environmental law 894
multiple product orders 896
nuisance 902
potentially responsible party (PRP) 909
Regulation Z 897
toxic tort 902
validation notice 900
wetland 906

CHAPTER SUMMARY

CONSUMER LAW

Deceptive Advertising	**1.** *Definition of deceptive advertising*—Generally, an advertising claim will be deemed deceptive if it would mislead a reasonable consumer. **2.** *Bait-and-switch advertising*—Advertising a lower-priced product (the "bait") when the intention is not to sell the advertised product but to lure consumers into the store and convince them to buy a higher-priced product (the "switch") is prohibited by the FTC. **3.** *Online deceptive advertising*—The FTC has issued guidelines to help online businesses comply with existing laws prohibiting deceptive advertising. The guidelines do not set forth new rules but rather describe how existing laws apply to online advertising. **4.** *FTC actions against deceptive advertising*— **a.** Cease-and-desist orders—Requiring the advertiser to stop the challenged advertising. **b.** Counteradvertising—Requiring the advertiser to advertise to correct the earlier misinformation. **5.** *Telemarketing and electronic advertising*—The Telephone Consumer Protection Act of 1991 prohibits telephone solicitation using an automatic telephone dialing system or a prerecorded voice, as well as the transmission of advertising materials via fax without first obtaining the recipient's permission to do so.
Labeling and Packaging	Manufacturers must comply with labeling or packaging requirements for their specific products. In general, all labels must be accurate and not misleading.
Sales	**1.** *Door-to-door sales*—The FTC requires all door-to-door sellers to give consumers three days (a "cooling-off" period) to cancel any sale. States also provide for similar protection. **2.** *Telephone and mail-order sales*—Federal and state statutes and regulations govern certain practices of sellers who solicit over the telephone or through the mails and prohibit the use of the mails to defraud individuals. **3.** *Online sales*—Increasingly, the Internet is being used to conduct business-to-consumer (B2C) transactions. Consumers are protected to some extent under both state and federal laws against fraudulent and deceptive online sales practices.
Credit Protection	**1.** *Consumer Credit Protection Act, Title I (Truth-in-Lending Act, or TILA)*—A disclosure law that requires sellers and lenders to disclose credit terms or loan terms in certain transactions, including retail and installment sales and loans, car loans, home-improvement loans, and certain real estate loans. Additionally, the TILA provides for the following: **a.** Equal credit opportunity—Creditors are prohibited from discriminating on the basis of race, religion, marital status, gender, and so on. **b.** Credit-card protection—Credit-card users may withhold payment for a faulty product sold, or for an error in billing, until the dispute is resolved; liability of cardholders for unauthorized charges is limited to $50, providing notice requirements are met; consumers are not liable for unauthorized charges made on unsolicited credit cards. **c.** Consumer leases—The Consumer Leasing Act (CLA) of 1988 protects consumers who lease automobiles and other goods priced at $25,000 or less if the lease term exceeds four months. **2.** *Fair Credit Reporting Act*—Entitles consumers to request verification of the accuracy of a credit report and to have unverified or false information removed from their files. **3.** *Fair Debt Collection Practices Act*—Prohibits debt collectors from using unfair debt-collection practices, such as contacting the debtor at his or her place of employment if the employer objects or at unreasonable times, contacting third parties about the debt, harassing the debtor, and so on.
Health and Safety Protection	**1.** *Food and drugs*—The Federal Food, Drug and Cosmetic Act of 1938, as amended, protects consumers against adulterated and misbranded foods and drugs. The act establishes

CHAPTER SUMMARY—CONTINUED

Health and Safety Protection—continued	food standards, specifies safe levels of potentially hazardous food additives, and sets classifications of food and food advertising. **2.** *Consumer product safety*—The Consumer Product Safety Act of 1972 seeks to protect consumers from risk of injury from hazardous products. The Consumer Product Safety Commission has the power to remove products that are deemed imminently hazardous from the market and to ban the manufacture and sale of hazardous products.
State Consumer Protection Laws	State laws often provide for greater consumer protection against deceptive trade practices than do federal laws. In addition, the warranty and unconscionability provisions of the Uniform Commercial Code protect consumers against sellers' deceptive practices. The Uniform Consumer Credit Code, which has not been widely adopted by the states, provides credit protection for consumers.
	ENVIRONMENTAL LAW
Common Law Actions	**1.** *Nuisance*—A common law doctrine under which actions against pollution-causing activities may be brought. An action is permissible only if an individual suffers a harm separate and distinct from that of the general public. **2.** *Negligence and strict liability*—Parties may recover damages for injuries sustained as a result of a firm's pollution-causing activities if it can be demonstrated that the harm was a foreseeable result of the firm's failure to exercise reasonable care (negligence); businesses engaging in ultrahazardous activities are liable for whatever injuries the activities cause, regardless of whether the firms exercise reasonable care.
State and Local Regulation	Activities affecting the environment are controlled at the local and state levels through regulations relating to land use, the disposal and recycling of garbage and waste, and pollution-causing activities in general.
Federal Regulation	**1.** *Environmental protection agencies*—The most well known of the agencies regulating environmental law is the federal Environmental Protection Agency (EPA), which was created in 1970 to coordinate federal environmental programs. The EPA administers most federal environmental policies and statutes. **2.** *Assessing environmental impact*—The National Environmental Policy Act of 1969 imposes environmental responsibilities on all federal agencies and requires for every major federal action the preparation of an environmental impact statement (EIS). An EIS must analyze the action's impact on the environment, its adverse effects and possible alternatives, and its irreversible effects on environmental quality. **3.** *Important areas regulated by the federal government*—In addition to fish and wildlife (regulated by the Fish and Wildlife Coordination Act of 1958) and endangered species (regulated under the Endangered Species Act of 1973), important areas regulated by the federal government include the following: **a.** Air pollution—Regulated under the authority of the Clean Air Act of 1963 and its amendments, particularly those of 1970, 1977, and 1990. **b.** Water pollution—Regulated under the authority of the Rivers and Harbors Appropriation Act of 1899, as amended, and the Federal Water Pollution Control Act of 1948, as amended by the Clean Water Act of 1972. **c.** Noise pollution—Regulated by the Noise Control Act of 1972. **d.** Toxic chemicals and hazardous waste—Pesticides and herbicides, toxic substances, and hazardous waste are regulated under the authority of the Federal Insecticide, Fungicide, and Rodenticide Act of 1947, the Toxic Substances Control Act of 1976, and the Resource Conservation and Recovery Act of 1976, respectively. The Comprehensive Environmental Response, Compensation, and Liability Act (CERCLA) of 1980, as amended, regulates the clean-up of hazardous waste disposal sites.

CASES FOR ANALYSIS

Westlaw. You can access the full text of each case presented below by going to the Westlaw cases on this text's Web site at http://wbl-cs.westbuslaw.com. Each Westlaw case includes the names of all plaintiffs and defendants, the dates on which the case was argued and decided, a brief summary of the issues and decisions in the case, headnotes classifying specific issues in the case according to the West Key Number System, and the court's opinion. Concurring and dissenting opinions, if any, are included as well.

CASE 44.1 DECEPTIVE TELEMARKETING

FEDERAL TRADE COMMISSION V. GROWTH PLUS INTERNATIONAL MARKETING, INC.
United States District Court,
Northern District of Illinois, 2001.
__ F.Supp.3d __.

ASPEN, Chief District J. [Judge]

On December 18, 2000, the Federal Trade Commission ("Commission") initiated this action for injunctive and other relief pursuant to * * * the Federal Trade Commission Act ("FTC Act") and the Telemarketing and Consumer Fraud and Abuse Prevention Act ("Telemarketing Act"). The defendants are a group of Canadian corporations and individuals: Growth Plus International Marketing, Inc., also doing business as Growth Potential International, GPI, and GPIM ("Growth"); Gains International Marketing, Inc., also doing business as Gains Wealth International ("Gains"); Ploto Computer Services, Inc. ("Ploto"); Victor Thiruchelvam; Jessie Nadarajah, Kandan Nadarajah, Arudchelvam Nagamuthu; and Julie Turgeon. The Commission charges that defendants have engaged in a telemarketing enterprise to deceptively sell Canadian lottery packages to consumers in the United States without disclosing that those sales are illegal. To the contrary, the Commission alleges that defendants have affirmatively misrepresented that they are authorized under Canadian law to make the sales and that the sales are legal. The Commission further alleges that these defendants have misrepresented to consumers the chances of their success in playing these lotteries, and have engaged in high-pressure tactics to persuade customers to participate in the lotteries.

* * * The matter is now before this Court * * * for a report and recommendation on the issuance of a preliminary injunction.

* * * *

* * * The findings and conclusions [of the court] are set forth below:

* * * *

2. * * * [T]he FTC Act authorizes the FTC to seek preliminary injunctive relief in a proper case. Cases that involve allegations of routine fraud establish the kind of proper case in which the Commission is empowered to seek immediate injunctive relief. The allegations in this case—that the defendants engaged in a scheme involving both concealment of material information and affirmative misrepresentations—constitute the kind of routine fraud for which the Commission is authorized to seek preliminary injunctive relief.

3. When the Commission seeks an injunction, the "public interest" test applies, which involves two factors: (a) the likelihood that the Commission will ultimately succeed on the merits, and (b) the balance of the equities [fairness]. In considering those two factors, the Court employs a sliding scale so that the greater the plaintiff's success on the merits, the less harm she must show in relation to the harm defendant will suffer if the preliminary injunction is granted.

4. The evidence before the Court at this time demonstrates a strong likelihood that the Commission will prevail on the merits of its claims. * * * [T]he FTC Act provides that "[u]nfair methods of competition in or affecting commerce, and unfair or deceptive acts or practices in or affecting commerce, are hereby declared unlawful." Under this standard, misrepresentations of material facts made for the purpose of inducing consumers to purchase services constitute unfair or deceptive acts or practices * * * . In addition, the omission of material information, even without affirmative falsehood, may lead to a violation * * * . At bottom, what the Commission must establish is that the representations, omissions, or practices likely would mislead consumers, acting reasonably, to their detriment.

5. The evidentiary materials at this point establish a strong case that the defendants were guilty of numerous misrepresentations or omissions. For example, (a) the defendants told customers that it was legal for them to sell the lottery tickets in the United States, when it was not; (b) the defendants told customers that they were authorized by the Canadian government to sell lottery tickets, when in fact they were not; (c) the defendants represented to consumers that they had a good chance of winning the lottery because they would be playing with a large pool of people, without disclosing that the odds of winning were roughly 1 in 14 mil-

lion. This information that was misrepresented or concealed plainly was material to the consumers' decisions to purchase the tickets: The knowledge that the sale of the tickets was illegal under federal law and that the "good chance" of winning was in fact a 1 in 14 million shot certainly are the types of information that would likely affect the decision of whether to participate in the lottery. And, in fact, the Commission has provided sworn statements from several consumers indicating that they would not have purchased the lottery tickets had they known that the sales of tickets were illegal.

6. For these same reasons, the Commission has made a strong case that it will likely prevail on the merits of its claim that defendants have violated the Telemarketing Sales Rule, which prohibits sellers and telemarketers from making false or misleading statements to induce persons to acquire goods or services.

7. Turning to the balance of the equities, the Court notes that although private equities may be considered, public equities receive far greater weight. In this case, the balance of equities weighs heavily in favor of the issuance of preliminary injunctive relief. There is a strong public interest in an immediate halt to illegal sale of lottery tickets accomplished through the use of misleading devices. By contrast, the Court perceives very little private interest in the continuance of such sales pending further proceedings in the case, especially given the unrebutted evidence to date that the defendants are not even authorized within Canada to sell lottery tickets. Taken together, the great weight that is accorded to the public interest in this balancing test and the strong showing that the Commission has made of a likelihood of success lead the Court to conclude that the balancing of equities strongly favors the issuance of the preliminary injunction.

* * * *

11. In addition to a preliminary injunction prohibiting the alleged fraudulent activity, the Court finds that the Commission has established entitlement to an asset freeze. If the Commission prevails in this case, restitution would be an appropriate remedy. Thus, the Court has a duty to ensure that the assets of the corporate defendants are available to make restitution to the injured customers. * * *

For the foregoing reasons, the Court respectfully recommends that the Commission's motion for a preliminary injunction with asset freeze and other relief be granted as against the defendants * * * .

CASE 44.2 FAIR DEBT COLLECTION PRACTICES ACT

SNOW V. JESSE L. RIDDLE, P.C.

United States Court of Appeals,
Tenth Circuit, 1998.
143 F.3d 1350.

MCWILLIAMS, Senior Circuit Judge.

Background

On September 23, 1994, Alan Snow purchased consumer goods from a Circle-K Store and paid for the merchandise with his personal check in the amount of $23.12. Circle-K deposited the check with its bank, but the check was dishonored because of insufficient funds. Circle-K then forwarded the returned check to its attorney, Jesse L. Riddle, P.C., to pursue collection.

On May 10, 1996, Riddle sent the following letter to Snow:

> * * *
>
> Dear Mr. Snow:
>
> The check written by you to Circle-K on or about September 23, 1994 for $23.12 was dishonored. Pursuant to [Utah Code Annotated (UCA) Section] 7-15-1, the check amount, along with a service fee of $15, must be paid within seven (7) days of this notice. If it is not paid, that statute provides for suit to be filed and for the court to award attorney fees, collection costs and other costs associated with the suit.
>
> In addition, the criminal code provides in UCA [Section] 76-6-505 that any person who issues a bad check knowing that it will not be honored is guilty of a crime. That statute also presumes criminal intent if the check is not paid within fourteen (14) days of actual notice.
>
> My client did not offer or extend credit to you. More than fourteen days has elapsed since you received actual notice, thus making UCA [Section] 76-6-505 applicable. Please pay the amount prescribed by statute.
>
> Sincerely,
> /s/ Jesse L. Riddle
> Jesse L. Riddle, P.C.

In response to Riddle's letter of May 10, 1996, Snow paid the face amount of the check, i.e., $23.12, but refused to pay the $15.00 service charge. Instead, Snow brought the present action against Riddle.

Proceedings in the District Court

On May 19, 1996, Alan Snow filed a complaint in the United States District Court for the District of Utah against Jesse L. Riddle, P.C. based on that part of the Consumer Credit Protection Act known as the Fair Debt

Collections Practices Act ("Act"). Riddle responded thereto by filing a motion to dismiss. After hearing, the district court granted Riddle's motion to dismiss and dismissed Snow's action. Snow appeals. * * *

More specifically, in his complaint Snow alleged that his action was based on that part of the Act "which prohibits debt collectors from engaging in abusive, deceptive and unfair practices." Continuing, Snow alleged that Riddle, an attorney who engaged in debt collection, sent him a letter on May 10, 1996 demanding payment of a dishonored check which Snow had given Circle-K Stores. According to the complaint, Riddle's letter violated the Act because it did not include a so-called "validation notice" alerting him to his legal rights under the Act. As a result of Riddle's violation of the Act, Snow claimed that he had suffered actual damages in an unspecified amount, which included his emotional distress over the letter, and, in addition, he asked for statutory damages in the amount of $1,000.00.

In his motion to dismiss, which was filed on November 19, 1996, Riddle stated that the complaint failed to state a claim upon which relief could be granted because the Act "does not cover the collection of dishonored checks, but rather is limited to the collection of debts resulting from transactions in which there is an offer or extension of credit * * * ."

* * * *

Discussion

[The Act] provides as follows:

[Section] 1692. Congressional findings and declaration of purpose

(a) **Abusive practices**

There is abundant evidence of the use of abusive, deceptive, and unfair debt collection practices by many debt collectors. Abusive debt collection practices contribute to the number of personal bankruptcies, to marital instability, to the loss of jobs, and to invasions of individual privacy.

(b) **Inadequacy of laws**

Existing laws and procedures for redressing these injuries are inadequate to protect consumers.

(c) **Available non-abusive collection methods**

Means other than misrepresentation or other abusive debt collection practices are available for the effective collection of debts.

(d) **Interstate commerce**

Abusive debt collection practices are carried on to a substantial extent in interstate commerce and through means and instrumentalities of such commerce. Even where abusive debt collection practices are purely intrastate in character, they nevertheless directly affect interstate commerce.

(e) **Purposes**

It is the purpose of this subchapter to eliminate abusive debt collection practices by debt collectors, to insure that those debt collectors who refrain from using abusive debt collection practices are not competitively disadvantaged, and to promote consistent State action to protect consumers against debt collection abuses.

* * * *

* * * [A] payment obligation arising from a dishonored check create[s] a "debt" triggering the protections of the Act. * * * [A]n offer or extension of credit is not required for a payment obligation to constitute a "debt" under the Act. * * *

* * * Under the "plain meaning" test, it would seem to us that a "debt" is created where one obtain goods and gives a dishonored check in return therefor.

Conclusion

We reverse the judgment of the district court holding that a dishonored check, under the circumstances of the present case, does not constitute a "debt" within the purview of the Act. * * * Case remanded for further proceedings consonant with the views herein expressed.

CASE 44.3 SUPERFUND

BROWNING-FERRIS INDUSTRIES OF ILLINOIS, INC. v. TER MAAT

United States Court of Appeals,
Seventh Circuit, 1999.
195 F.3d 953.

POSNER, Chief Judge.

Browning-Ferris [Industries of Illinois, Inc.] and several other companies have brought a suit for contribution under the Comprehensive Environmental Response, Compensation, and Liability Act (CERCLA—the Superfund statute). The suit is against Richard Ter Maat and two corporations of which he is (or was—one of the corporations has been sold) the president and principal shareholder; they are M.I.G. Investments, Inc. and AAA Disposal Systems, Inc.

Back in 1971 the owners of a landfill had leased it to a predecessor of Browning-Ferris, which operated it until the fall of 1975. Between then and 1988 it was operated by M.I.G. and AAA. In June of that year, after

AAA was sold and Ter Maat moved to Florida, M.I.G. abandoned the landfill without covering it properly. For tax reasons, M.I.G. had been operated with very little capital, and it lacked funds for a proper cover. Two years after the abandonment, the EPA placed the site on the National Priorities List, the list of the toxic waste sites that the Superfund statute requires be cleaned up, and shortly afterward Browning-Ferris and the other plaintiffs, which shared responsibility for some of the pollution at the site, agreed to clean it up.

Section 113(f)(1) of the Superfund law authorizes any person who incurs costs in cleaning up a toxic waste site to "seek contribution from any other person who is liable or potentially liable under [S]ection 9607(a) of this title * * * . *In resolving contribution claims, the court may allocate response costs among liable parties using such equitable factors as the court determines are appropriate.*" Section [9607](a)(1) * * * includes in the set of potentially liable persons anyone who owned or operated a landfill when a hazardous substance was deposited in it, and this set is conceded to include both M.I.G. and AAA. The district judge held, however, that Ter Maat was not himself a potentially liable person, because he had done nothing that would subject him to liability on a "piercing the corporate veil" theory for the actions of the two corporations. So far as corporate liability for clean-up costs was concerned, the judge ruled that of the 55 percent of those costs that he deemed allocable to transporters and operators (the other 45 percent he allocated to the owners of the landfill and the generators of the toxic wastes dumped in it), 40 percent was the responsibility of Browning-Ferris and the other 60 percent the responsibility of M.I.G. and AAA. As between those two, the judge allocated responsibility equally, holding that, although the two corporations had operated the landfill jointly, the statute required him to allocate liability severally rather than jointly. [Emphasis added.]

* * * [On appeal] Browning-Ferris argues that the district court allocated too much of the liability for the pollution at the site to it relative to M.I.G. and AAA.

* * * *

* * * The judge allocated as large a share as he did to Browning-Ferris because he found that it had operated the landfill poorly and had dumped particularly toxic wastes from a nearby Chrysler plant in violation of its operating permit, and the liquid character of the wastes had hastened their absorption into groundwater. Browning-Ferris argues both that these findings are erroneous and that, in any event, there is no evidence that the wastes from the Chrysler plant increased the cost of cleaning up the site and anyway the amount dumped in the landfill was not as great as the district judge found. From evidence that a considerable portion of the Chrysler wastes were dumped elsewhere, Browning-Ferris argues that defendants' expert had exaggerated the amount deposited in the landfill. Browning-Ferris may be correct on all these factual points, but we cannot say that the district court committed any clear errors in finding as it did, and that of course is our criterion.

The trickier question, which returns us to the issue of the district court's equitable discretion in allocating liability among polluters, is whether the court must find a causal relation between a party's pollution and the actual cost of cleaning up the site. To answer this question we have to distinguish between a necessary condition (or "but-for cause") and a sufficient condition. If event A is a necessary condition of event B, this means that, without A, B will not occur. If A is a sufficient condition of B, this means that, if A occurs, B will occur. If A is that the murder weapon was loaded and B is the murder, then A is a necessary condition. If A is shooting a person through the heart and B is the death of the shooting victim, then A is a sufficient condition of B but not a necessary condition, because a wound to another part of the victim's body might have been fatal as well.

This distinction may sometimes be important in the pollution context. It is easy to imagine a case in which, had X not polluted a site, no clean-up costs would have been incurred; X's pollution would be a necessary condition of those costs and it would be natural to think that he should pay at least a part of them. But suppose that even if X had not polluted the site, it would have to be cleaned up—and at the same cost—because of the amount of pollution by Y. (That would be a case, perhaps rare, in which the clean-up costs were sensitive neither to the amount of pollution nor to any synergistic interaction between the different pollutants.) Then X's pollution would not be a necessary condition of the clean up, or of any of the costs incurred in the clean up. But that should not necessarily let X off the hook. For suppose that though if X had not polluted the site at all there still would have been enough pollution from Y to require a clean up, if Y had not polluted the site X's pollution would have been sufficient to require the clean up. In that case, the conduct of X and the conduct of Y would each be a sufficient but not a necessary condition of the clean up, and it would be entirely arbitrary to let either (or, even worse, both) off the hook on this basis. So far as appears, this is such a case; Browning-Ferris's pollution was serious enough (if indeed it dumped a large quantity of Chrysler's particularly toxic wastes) to require that the site be cleaned up, but the other pollution at the site was also enough. If Browning-Ferris's conduct was thus a sufficient though not a necessary condition of the clean up, it is not inequitable to make it contribute substantially to the cost.

We do not suggest that this is one of the presumably rare cases in which the total costs of clean up are unaffected by the number of polluters or the specific amounts or types of pollution contributed by each. Browning-Ferris's pollution was not, so far as appears, so serious all by itself as to have required the incurring of *all* the clean-up costs that were incurred. Even so, no principle of law, logic, or common sense required the court to allocate those total costs among the polluters on the basis of the volume of wastes alone. Not only do wastes differ in their toxicity, harm to the environment, and costs of cleaning up, and so relative volume is not a reliable guide to the marginal costs imposed by each polluter; but polluters differ in the blameworthiness of the decisions or omissions that led to the pollution, and blameworthiness is relevant to an equitable allocation of joint costs. (Presumably it would not entitle the judge to make one polluter pay for separable costs wholly imposed by other polluters.) The district judge did not abuse his discretion in deciding that all these factors warranted making Browning-Ferris bear more than its proportional volumetric share of the pollution.

* * * *

AFFIRMED * * * . [The court remanded the case for consideration of other issues.]

CASE PROBLEMS

44–1. Sears, Roebuck & Co. adopted a new advertising program to boost sales of its Lady Kenmore dishwashers. The new ads claimed that these dishwashers "completely eliminated" the need for rinsing dishes before placing them in the dishwasher. The owner's manuals accompanying the machines, however, recommended prerinsing. Interviews with consumers indicated that prerinsing was still required for truly clean dishes. In an action against Sears, the Federal Trade Commission (FTC) held that the advertising was misleading. The FTC's remedial order required that Sears keep records to support all future advertising claims for all "major home appliances" and submit them to the FTC. Sears conceded that its dishwasher advertising was misleading but argued that the remedial order, which covered other appliances as well as Lady Kenmore dishwashers, was overly broad and unfair. Discuss fully whether the FTC's broad order is legal. [*Sears, Roebuck & Co. v. FTC*, 676 F.2d 385 (9th Cir. 1982)]

44–2. Swanson owed $262.20 to a hospital in southern Oregon for medical services he had received. When Swanson failed to pay the debt, the hospital turned the account over to a local collection agency, which sent Swanson a letter requesting payment of the bill. Swanson alleged that the letter violated Section 809(a) of the Fair Debt Collection Practices Act (FDCPA), which mandates that any debt collector or agency subject to the act must notify the consumer early in the collection process that the consumer has thirty days within which to request validation of the debt. In the meantime, the consumer may withhold payment on the debt until assured that she or he actually owes the money. The letter did contain notice that the consumer had thirty days in which to demand verification of the debt, but the notice was, according to Swanson, overshadowed and effectively negated by the following statement—which was printed in boldface, underlined, and set in a larger-than-standard typeface: IF THIS ACCOUNT IS PAID WITHIN THE NEXT 10 DAYS IT WILL NOT BE RECORDED IN OUR MASTER FILE AS AN UNPAID COLLECTION ITEM. A GOOD CREDIT RATING IS YOUR MOST VALUABLE ASSET. Had the collection agency violated Section 809(a) of the FDCPA? Explain. [*Swanson v. Southern Oregon Credit Service, Inc.*, 869 F.2d 1222 (9th Cir. 1989)]

44–3. Sebastian and Maria Shaumyan entered into a home-improvement contract with Sidetex Co. Sidetex agreed to install siding, replace windows, and perform other related work at the Shaumyans' home, and the Shaumyans agreed to pay Sidetex a total of $14,800 according to the following schedule: $3,000 as a deposit; $4,000 when Sidetex began the work; $3,900 when the work was half completed; $1,950 on completion of the installation of the siding; and $1,950 on completion of the work on the storm doors and shutters. Although a clause in the agreement referred to the contract as a "consumer credit contract," the Shaumyans' payments were not subject to any finance charges. Sidetex commenced work under the contract, and the Shaumyans made the scheduled payments of $3,000, $4,000, and $3,900. Performance was not completed, however, because a dispute arose concerning the quality of the windows that Sidetex was to install. The Shaumyans brought an action against Sidetex to recover damages, claiming that Sidetex had violated the antidiscrimination provision of the Equal Credit Opportunity Act (ECOA) by requiring the signature of Mrs. Shaumyan on the home-improvement contract. The central issue before the court was whether the home improvement contract, which provided for progressive payments by the Shaumyans, constituted a "credit transaction" subject to the antidiscrimination provisions of the ECOA. How should the court rule? Discuss fully. [*Shaumyan v. Sidetex Co.*, 900 F.2d 16 (1990)]

44–4. Kraft, Inc., produces individually wrapped cheese slices, or "Singles Slices," made from real cheese, which cost more than the imitation cheese slices on the market. In the early 1980s, Kraft began losing its market share to an increasing number of producers of imitation cheese slices. Kraft responded with a series of advertisements, collectively known as the "Five Ounces of Milk" campaign. The ads claimed that Kraft Singles cost more than imitation slices because they were made from five ounces of milk rather than less expensive ingredients. The ads also implied that because each slice contained five ounces of milk, Kraft Singles contained a higher calcium content than imitation cheese slices. The Federal Trade Commission (FTC) filed a complaint against Kraft, charging that Kraft had materially misrepresented the calcium content and relative calcium benefit of Kraft Singles. Was Kraft's advertising campaign deceptive and likely to mislead consumers? [*Kraft, Inc. v. FTC*, 970 F.2d 311 (7th Cir. 1992)]

44–5. Asarco, Inc., had a copper smelter at Ruston, Washington. As part of its operations, Asarco produced a by-product called "slag," a hard, rocklike substance. Industrial Mineral Products (IMP) sold the slag for Asarco to Louisiana-Pacific Corp. and other businesses, which used the slag as ballast to stabilize the ground at log-sorting yards in the Tacoma, Washington, area. About nine months after IMP stopped selling the slag, it sold substantially all of its assets to L-Bar Products, Inc. Government agencies later discovered that the slag reacted with the acidic wood waste in the log-sorting yards, causing heavy metals from the slag to leach into the groundwater and soil. Louisiana-Pacific and the Port of Tacoma sued Asarco under the Comprehensive Environmental Response, Compensation, and Liability Act (CERCLA), claiming that Asarco was liable for clean-up costs. Asarco brought a third party claim against L-Bar as corporate successor to IMP. L-Bar moved for summary judgment, claiming that it was not the successor to IMP and could not be liable under CERCLA for IMP's actions. Will the court agree with L-Bar? Discuss fully. [*Louisiana-Pacific Corp. v. Asarco, Inc.*, 909 F.2d 1260 (9th Cir. 1990)]

44–6. The Resource Conservation and Recovery Act gives the Environmental Protection Agency (EPA) authority to require a company to clean up a hazardous waste site that presents an "imminent and substantial endangerment" to public health or to the environment. A company disposed of dioxin by discharging it into a pond located on its property. The EPA ordered that the company stop the disposal and clean up the site. The company argued that the EPA had no evidence of any actual harm to the health of nearby residents. Should the company be compelled to clean up the dioxin even in the absence of evidence of actual harm? Discuss. [*United States v. Vertac Chemical Corp.*, 489 F.Supp. 870 (E.D.Ark. 1980)]

44–7. Cities Service Co. operated a phosphate rock mine that included large settling ponds for the extraction of phosphate. A dam outside of one of these ponds broke, sending a billion gallons of phosphate slime into the nearby Peace River. This killed fish and caused other damage. The state of Florida sued Cities Service under a theory of strict liability for damages. Given these facts, should Cities Service be liable? [*Cities Service Co. v. State*, 312 So.2d 799 (Fla.App. 1975)]

44–8. Portland General Electric Co. maintained a turbine facility. Nearby residents complained that the facility emitted low-frequency sound waves that caused them to suffer loss of sleep, emotional distress, and mental strain. Consequently, these residents sued the company, claiming that it was creating a nuisance. The defendant contended that the plaintiffs had suffered no special harm. The district court dismissed the plaintiffs' complaint, and the plaintiffs appealed the decision. Should the appellate court affirm the dismissal? Explain. [*Frady v. Portland General Electric Co.*, 55 Or.App. 344, 637 P.2d 1345 (1981)]

44–9. Thompson Medical Co. marketed a new cream called Aspercreme that was supposed to help arthritis victims and others suffering from minor aches. Aspercreme contained no aspirin. Thompson's television advertisements stated that the product provided "the strong relief of aspirin right where you hurt" and showed the announcer holding up aspirin tablets as well as a tube of Aspercreme. The Federal Trade Commission held that the advertisements were misleading because they led consumers to believe that Aspercreme contained aspirin. Thompson Medical Co. appealed this decision and argued that the advertisements never actually stated that the product contained aspirin. How should the court rule? Discuss. [*Thompson Medical Co. v. Federal Trade Commission*, 791 F.2d 189 (D.C.Cir. 1986)]

44–10. Renee Purtle bought a 1986 Chevrolet Blazer from Eldridge Auto Sales, Inc. To finance the purchase through Eldridge, Purtle filled out a credit application on which she misrepresented her employment status. Based on the misrepresentation, Eldridge extended credit. In the credit contract, Eldridge did not disclose the finance charge, the annual percentage rate, or the total sales price or use the term "amount financed," as the Truth-in-Lending Act (TILA) and its regulations require. Purtle defaulted on the loan, and Eldridge repossessed the vehicle. Purtle filed a suit in a federal district court against Eldridge, alleging violations of the TILA. The court awarded Purtle $1,000 in damages, plus attorneys' fees and costs. Eldridge appealed, arguing in part that Purtle was not entitled to damages because she had committed fraud on her credit application. What will the court decide on appeal? Why? [*Purtle v. Eldridge Auto Sales, Inc.*, 91 F.3d 797 (6th Cir. 1996)]

44–11. Attique Ahmad owned the Spin-N-Market, a convenience store and gas station. The gas pumps were fed by underground tanks, one of which had a leak at its top that allowed water to enter. Ahmad emptied the tank by pumping its contents into a storm drain and a sewer system. Through the storm drain, gasoline flowed into a creek, forcing the city to clean the water. Through the sewer system, gasoline flowed into a sewage treatment plant, forcing the city to evacuate the plant and two nearby schools. Ahmad was charged with discharging a pollutant without a permit, which is a criminal violation of the Clean Water Act. The act provides that a person who "knowingly violates" the act commits a felony. Ahmad claimed that he had believed he was discharging only water. Did Ahmad commit a felony? Why, or why not? Discuss fully. [*U.S. v. Ahmad,* 101 F.3d 386 (5th Cir. 1996)]

44–12. A condominium association, Rancho Santa Margarita Recreation and Landscape Corp., attempted unsuccessfully to collect an assessment fee from Andrew Ladick. The association referred the matter to the Law Offices of Gerald J. Van Gemert. Van Gemert sent Ladick a letter demanding payment of the fee. The letter did not include a "validation notice," as required by the Fair Debt Collection Practices Act (FDCPA), nor did it disclose that Van Gemert was attempting to collect a debt and that any information obtained would be used for that purpose. Ladick filed a suit in a federal district court against Van Gemert and his office, alleging violations of the FDCPA. Van Gemert filed a motion for summary judgment on the ground that the assessment was not a "debt," as defined by the FDCPA, in part because there was no "transaction," as required by the FDCPA definition, out of which Ladick's obligation arose. Will the court agree with Van Gemert? Why, or why not? [*Ladick v. Van Gemert,* 146 F.3d 1205 (10th Cir. 1998)]

44–13. Gloria Mahon incurred a bill of $279.70 for medical services rendered by Dr. Larry Bowen. For more than two years, Bowen sent monthly billing statements to the Mahons at their home address (where they had lived for forty-five years). Getting no response, Bowen assigned the collection of their account to Credit Bureau of Placer County, Inc. Credit Bureau uses computerized collection tracking and filing software, known as Columbia Ultimate Business Systems (CUBS). CUBS automatically generates standardized collection notices and acts as an electronic filing system for each account, recording all collection activities, including which notices are sent to whom and on what date. Credit Bureau employees monitor the activity, routinely noting whether an envelope is returned undelivered. Credit Bureau mailed three CUBS–generated notices to the Mahons. According to Credit Bureau's records, the notices were not returned and the Mahons did not respond. Credit Bureau reported the Mahons' account as delinquent. The Mahons filed a suit in a federal district court against Credit Bureau, alleging in part that the agency had failed to send a validation notice, as required by the Fair Debt Collection Practices Act. Credit Bureau filed a motion for summary judgment. Should a notice be considered sent only if a debtor acknowledges its receipt? Why, or why not? [*Mahon v. Credit Bureau of Placer County, Inc.,* 171 F.3d 1197 (9th Cir. 1999)]

44–14. Equifax A.R.S., a debt-collection agency, sent Donna Russell a notice about one of her debts. The front of the notice stated that "[i]f you do not dispute this claim (see reverse side) and wish to pay it within the next 10 days we will not post this collection to your file." The reverse side set out Russell's rights under the Fair Debt Collection Practices Act (FDCPA), including that she had thirty days to decide whether to contest the claim. Russell filed a suit in a federal district court against Equifax. The court ruled against Russell, who appealed. On what basis might Russell argue that Equifax violated the FDCPA? [*Russell v. Equifax A.R.S.,* 74 F.3d 30 (2d Cir. 1996)]

44–15. CrossCheck, Inc., is in the business of providing check-authorization services to retail merchants. When a customer presents a check, the merchant contacts CrossCheck, which estimates the probability that the check will clear the bank. If the check is within an acceptable statistical range, CrossCheck notifies the merchant. If the check is dishonored, the merchant sends it to CrossCheck, which pays it. CrossCheck then attempts to redeposit it. If this fails, CrossCheck takes further steps to collect the amount. CrossCheck attempts to collect on more than two thousand checks per year and spends $2 million on these efforts, which involve about 7 percent of its employees and 6 percent of its total expenses. William Winterstein took his truck to C&P Auto Service Center, Inc., for a tune-up and paid for the service with a check. C&P contacted CrossCheck and, on its recommendation, accepted the check. When the check was dishonored, C&P mailed it to CrossCheck, which reimbursed C&P and sent a letter to Winterstein, requesting payment. Winterstein filed a suit in a federal district court against CrossCheck, asserting that the letter violated the FDCPA. CrossCheck filed a motion for summary judgment. On what ground might the court grant the motion? Explain. [*Winterstein v. CrossCheck, Inc.,* 149 F.Supp.2d 466 (N.D.Ill. 2001)]

E-LINKS

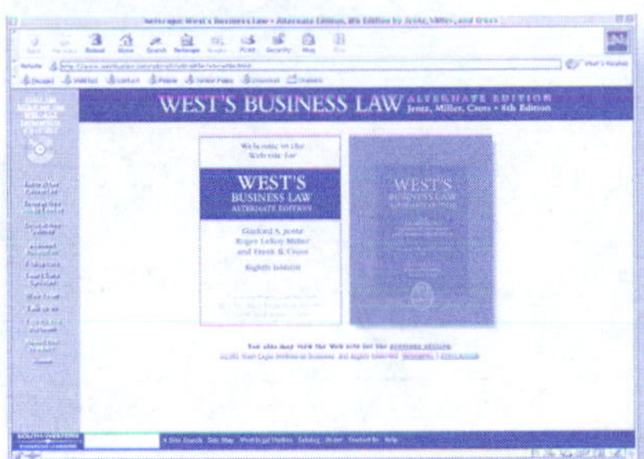

For updated links to resources available on the Web, as well as a variety of other materials, visit this text's Web site at

http://wbl-cs.westbuslaw.com

For current articles concerning consumer issues, go to the Alexander Law Firm's "Consumer Law Page," which is online at

http://consumerlawpage.com/intro.html

The law firm of Arent Fox offers extensive information relating to advertising law at

http://www.advertisinglaw.com

The Virtual Law Library of the Indiana University School of Law provides numerous links to online environmental law sources. Go to

http://www.law.indiana.edu

LEGAL RESEARCH EXERCISES ON THE WEB

Go to http://wbl-cs.westbuslaw.com, the Web site that accompanies this text. Select "Interactive Study Center," and then click on "Chapter 44." There you will find the following Internet research exercises that you can perform to learn more about consumer and environmental law:

Activity 44–1: Consumer Law

Activity 44–2: Nuisance Law

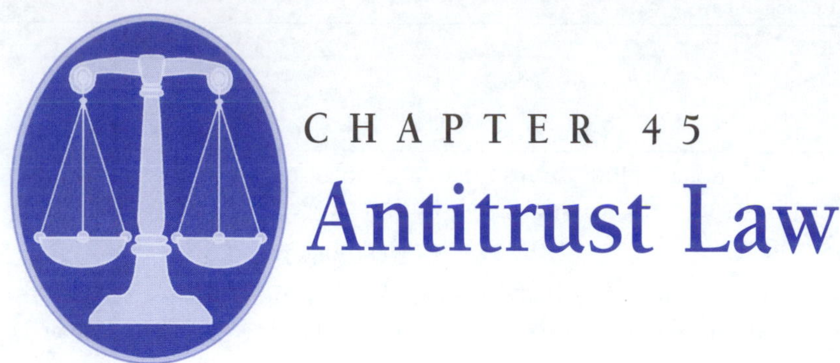

CHAPTER 45
Antitrust Law

TODAY'S ANTITRUST LAWS ARE the direct descendants of common law actions intended to limit **restraints on trade** (agreements between firms that have the effect of reducing competition in the marketplace). Concern over monopolistic practices arose following the Civil War with the growth of large corporate enterprises and their attempts to reduce or eliminate competition. They did this by legally tying themselves together in a *business trust,* a type of business entity described in Chapter 39. The participants in the most famous trust—the Standard Oil trust in the late 1800s—transferred their stock to a trustee and received trust certificates in exchange. The trustee then made decisions fixing prices, controlling production, and determining the control of exclusive geographic markets for all of the oil companies that were in the Standard Oil trust. It became apparent that the trust wielded so much economic power that corporations outside the trust could not compete effectively.

Many states attempted to control such monopolistic behavior by enacting statutes outlawing the use of trusts. That is why all of the laws that regulate economic competition today are referred to as **antitrust laws.** At the national level, the government recognized the problem in 1887 and passed the Interstate Commerce Act,[1] followed by the Sherman Antitrust Act in 1890.[2] In 1914, Congress passed the Clayton Act[3] and the Federal Trade Commission Act[4] to further curb anticompetitive or unfair business practices. Since their passage, the 1914 acts have been amended by Congress to broaden and strengthen their coverage, and they continue to be an important element in the legal environment in which businesses operate.

This chapter examines these major antitrust statutes, focusing particularly on the Sherman Act and the Clayton Act, as amended, and the types of activities prohibited by those acts. Remember in reading this chapter that the basis of antitrust legislation is the desire to foster competition. Antitrust legislation was initially created—and continues to be enforced—because of our belief that competition leads to lower prices, more product information, and a better distribution of wealth between consumers and producers.

SECTION 1

The Sherman Antitrust Act

The author of the Sherman Antitrust Act of 1890, Senator John Sherman, was the brother of the famed Civil War general and a recognized financial authority. He had been concerned for years about the diminishing competition within American industry. He told Congress that the Sherman Act "does not announce a new principle of law, but applies old and well-recognized principles of the common law."[5]

The common law regarding trade regulation was not always consistent. Certainly, it was not very familiar to the legislators of the Fifty-first Congress of the United States in 1890. The public concern over large business integrations and trusts was familiar, however, and in 1890 Congress passed "An Act to

1. 49 U.S.C. Sections 501–526.
2. 15 U.S.C. Sections 1–7.
3. 15 U.S.C. Sections 12–26a.
4. 15 U.S.C. Sections 45–48.

5. 21 Congressional Record 2456 (1890).

Protect Trade and Commerce against Unlawful Restraints and Monopolies"—more commonly referred to as the Sherman Antitrust Act, or simply the Sherman Act.

MAJOR PROVISIONS OF THE SHERMAN ACT

Sections 1 and 2 contain the main provisions of the Sherman Act:

> 1: Every contract, combination in the form of trust or otherwise, or conspiracy, in restraint of trade or commerce among the several States, or with foreign nations, is hereby declared to be illegal [and is a felony punishable by fine and/or imprisonment].
> 2: Every person who shall monopolize, or attempt to monopolize, or combine or conspire with any other person or persons, to monopolize any part of the trade or commerce among the several States, or with foreign nations, shall be deemed guilty of a felony [and is similarly punishable].

These two sections of the Sherman Act are quite different. Section 1 requires two or more persons, as a person cannot contract, combine, or conspire alone. Thus, the essence of the illegal activity is *the act of joining together.* Section 2 applies both to an individual person and to several people, because it refers to "[e]very person." Thus, unilateral conduct can result in a violation of Section 2.

The cases brought to the courts under Section 1 of the Sherman Act differ from those brought under Section 2. Section 1 cases are often concerned with finding an agreement (written or oral) that leads to a restraint of trade. Section 2 cases deal with the structure of a **monopoly** that exists in the marketplace. The term *monopoly* is generally used to describe a market in which there is a single seller. Whereas Section 1 focuses on agreements that are restrictive—that is, agreements that have a wrongful purpose—Section 2 looks at the so-called misuse of **monopoly power** in the marketplace. Monopoly power exists when a firm has an extreme amount of **market power**—the power to affect the market price of its product. Both Section 1 and Section 2 seek to curtail market industrial practices that result in undesired monopoly pricing and output behavior. Any case brought under Section 2, however, must be one in which the "threshold" or "necessary" amount of monopoly power already exists. We will return to a discussion of these two sections of the Sherman Act after we look at the act's jurisdictional requirements.

JURISDICTIONAL REQUIREMENTS

The Sherman Act applies only to restraints that have a significant impact on interstate commerce. As will be discussed later in this chapter, the Sherman Act also extends to U.S. nationals abroad who are engaged in activities that have an effect on U.S. foreign commerce. State regulation of anticompetitive practices addresses purely local restraints on competition. Courts have generally held that any activity that substantially affects interstate commerce falls within the ambit of the Sherman Act. As discussed in Chapter 4, courts have construed the meaning of *interstate commerce* more and more broadly over the years, bringing even local activities within the regulatory power of the national government.

SECTION 2

Section 1 of the Sherman Act

The underlying assumption of Section 1 of the Sherman Act is that society's welfare is harmed if rival firms are permitted to join in an agreement that consolidates their market power or otherwise restrains competition. Not all agreements between rivals, however, result in enhanced market power or *unreasonably* restrain trade. Under what is called the **rule of reason**, anticompetitive agreements that allegedly violate Section 1 of the Sherman Act are analyzed with the view that they may, in fact, constitute reasonable restraints on trade. When applying this rule, the court considers the purpose of the arrangement, the powers of the parties, and the effect of their actions in restraining trade. If the court deems that legitimate competitive benefits outweigh the anticompetitive effects of the agreement, it will be held lawful.

The need for a rule-of-reason analysis of some agreements in restraint of trade is obvious—if the rule of reason had not been developed, virtually any business agreement could conceivably violate the Sherman Act. Justice Louis D. Brandeis effectively phrased this sentiment in *Chicago Board of Trade v. United States*,[6] a case decided in 1918:

> Every agreement concerning trade, every regulation of trade, restrains. To bind, to restrain, is of their very essence. The true test of legality is whether the restraint imposed is such as merely regulates and

6. 246 U.S. 231, 38 S.Ct. 242, 62 L.Ed. 683 (1918).

perhaps thereby promotes competition or whether it is such as may suppress or even destroy competition.

When analyzing an alleged Section 1 violation under the rule of reason, a court will consider several factors, including the purpose of the agreement, the parties' power to implement the agreement to achieve that purpose, and the effect or potential effect of the agreement on competition. Another factor that might be considered is whether the parties could have relied on less restrictive means to achieve their purpose.

Some agreements, however, are so blatantly and substantially anticompetitive that they are deemed illegal *per se* (on their faces, or inherently) under Section 1. If an agreement is found to be of a type that is deemed a ***per se* violation**, a court is precluded from determining whether the agreement's benefits outweigh its anticompetitive effects.

The dividing line between agreements that constitute *per se* violations and agreements that should be judged under a rule of reason is seldom clear. Moreover, in some cases, the United States Supreme Court has stated that it is applying a *per se* rule, and yet a careful reading of the Court's analysis suggests that the Court is weighing benefits against harms under a rule of reason. Perhaps the most that can be said with certainty is that although the distinction between the two rules seems clear in theory, in the actual application of antitrust laws, the distinction has not always been so obvious.

We turn now to the types of trade restraints prohibited by Section 1 of the Sherman Act. Generally, these restraints fall into two broad categories: *horizontal restraints* and *vertical restraints*. Some restraints are *per se* violations of Section 1, but others may be permissible; those that are not *per se* violations are tested under the rule of reason.

Horizontal Restraints

The term **horizontal restraint** is encountered frequently in antitrust law. A horizontal restraint is any agreement that in some way restrains competition between rival firms competing in the same market.

Price Fixing. Any agreement among competitors to fix prices, or **price-fixing agreement**, constitutes a *per se* violation of Section 1 of the Sherman Act. Perhaps the definitive case regarding price-fixing agreements remains the 1940 case of *United States v. Socony-Vacuum Oil Co.*[7] In that case, a group of independent oil producers in Texas and Louisiana were caught between falling demand due to the Great Depression of the 1930s and increasing supply from newly discovered oil fields in the region. In response to these conditions, a group of the major refining companies agreed to buy "distress" gasoline (excess supplies) from the independents so as to dispose of it in an "orderly manner."

Although there was no explicit agreement as to price, it was clear that the purpose of the agreement was to limit the supply of gasoline on the market and thereby raise prices. There may have been good reasons for the agreement. Nonetheless, the United States Supreme Court recognized the dangerous effects that such an agreement could have on open and free competition. The Court held that the reasonableness of a price-fixing agreement is never a defense; any agreement that restricts output or artificially fixes price is a *per se* violation of Section 1. The rationale of the *per se* rule was best stated in what is now the most famous portion of the Court's opinion. In footnote 59, Justice William O. Douglas compared a freely functioning price system to a body's central nervous system, condemning price-fixing agreements as threats to "the central nervous system of the economy."

Group Boycotts. A **group boycott** is an agreement by two or more sellers to refuse to deal with (boycott) a particular person or firm. Such group boycotts have been held to constitute *per se* violations of Section 1 of the Sherman Act. Section 1 has been violated if it can be demonstrated that the boycott or joint refusal to deal was undertaken with the intention of eliminating competition or preventing entry into a given market. Some boycotts, such as group boycotts against a supplier for political reasons, may be protected under the First Amendment right to freedom of expression.

Horizontal Market Division. It is a *per se* violation of Section 1 of the Sherman Act for competitors to divide up territories or customers. For example, manufacturers A, B, and C compete against one another in the states of Kansas, Nebraska, and Iowa. By agreement, A sells products only in Kansas; B sells only in Nebraska; and C sells only in Iowa. This concerted action reduces costs and allows each of the three (assuming there is no other competition)

7. 310 U.S. 150, 60 S.Ct. 811, 84 L.Ed.2d 1129 (1940).

to raise the price of the goods sold in its own state. The same violation would take place if A, B, and C simply agreed that A would sell only to institutional purchasers (school districts, universities, state agencies and departments, cities, and so on) in the three states, B only to wholesalers, and C only to retailers.

Trade Associations. Businesses in the same general industry or profession frequently organize trade associations to pursue common interests. Their joint activities may provide for exchanges of information, representation of the members' business interests before governmental bodies, advertising campaigns, and the setting of regulatory standards to govern their industry or profession. Generally, the rule of reason is applied to many of these horizontal actions. For example, if a court finds that a trade association practice or agreement that restrains trade is nonetheless sufficiently beneficial both to the association and to the public, it may deem the restraint reasonable.

Other trade association agreements may have such substantially anticompetitive effects that the court will consider them to be in violation of Section 1 of the Sherman Act. In *National Society of Professional Engineers v. United States,*[8] for example, it was held that the society's code of ethics—which prohibited discussion of prices with a potential customer until after the customer had chosen an engineer—was a Section 1 violation. The United States Supreme Court found that this ban on competitive bidding was "nothing less than a frontal assault on the basic policy of the Sherman Act."

Joint Ventures. Joint ventures undertaken by competitors are also subject to antitrust laws. As discussed in Chapter 39, a *joint venture* is an undertaking by two or more individuals or firms for a specific purpose. If a joint venture does not involve price fixing or market divisions, the agreement will be analyzed under the rule of reason. Whether the venture will then be upheld under Section 1 depends on an overall assessment of the purposes of the venture, a strict analysis of the potential benefits relative to the likely harms, and in some cases, an assessment of whether there are less restrictive alternatives for achieving the same goals.[9]

VERTICAL RESTRAINTS

A **vertical restraint** of trade is one that results from an agreement between firms at different levels in the manufacturing and distribution process. In contrast to horizontal relationships, which occur at the same level of operation, vertical relationships encompass the entire chain of production: the purchase of inputs, basic manufacturing, distribution to wholesalers, and eventual sale of a product at the retail level. For some products, these distinct phases are carried on by different firms. In other instances, a single firm carries out two or more of the separate functional phases. Such enterprises are considered to be **vertically integrated firms**.

Even though firms operating at different functional levels are not in direct competition with one another, they are in competition with other firms operating at their own respective levels of operation. Thus, agreements between firms standing in a vertical relationship do significantly affect competition. Some vertical restraints are *per se* violations of Section 1; others are judged under the rule of reason.

Territorial or Customer Restrictions. In arranging for the distribution of its products, a manufacturer often wishes to insulate dealers from direct competition with other dealers selling its products. In this endeavor, the manufacturer may institute territorial restrictions or may attempt to prohibit wholesalers or retailers from reselling the products to certain classes of buyers, such as competing retailers. There may be legitimate, procompetitive reasons for imposing such territorial or customer restrictions. For example, a manufacturer may wish to prevent a dealer from reducing costs and undercutting rivals by providing the product without promotion or customer service, while relying on a nearby dealer to provide these services. In this situation, the cost-cutting dealer reaps the benefits (sales of the product) paid for by other dealers who undertake promotion and arrange for customer service. This is an example of the "free rider" problem.[10] The cost-cutting dealer, by not providing customer service, may also harm the manufacturer's reputation.

Westlaw. See Case 45.1 at the end of this chapter. To view the full, unedited case from Westlaw,® go to this text's Web site at **http://wbl-cs.westbuslaw.com**.

8. 453 U.S. 679, 98 S.Ct. 1355, 55 L.Ed.2d 637 (1978).

9. See, for example, *United States v. Morgan,* 118 F.Supp. 621 (S.D.N.Y. 1953). This case is often cited as a classic example of how to judge joint ventures under the rule of reason.

10. For a discussion of the free rider problem in the context of sports telecasting, see *Chicago Professional Sports Limited Partnership v. National Basketball Association,* 961 F.2d 667 (7th Cir. 1993).

Resale Price Maintenance Agreements. An agreement between a manufacturer and a distributor or retailer in which the manufacturer specifies what the retail prices of its products must be is known as a **resale price maintenance agreement.** This type of agreement may violate Section 1 of the Sherman Act.

In a 1968 case, *Albrecht v. Herald Co.*,[11] the United States Supreme Court held that these vertical price-fixing agreements constituted *per se* violations of Section 1 of the Sherman Act. In *State Oil Co. v. Khen*, which is presented as Case 45.2 at the end of this chapter and which involved an agreement that set a maximum price for the resale of products supplied by a wholesaler to a dealer, the Supreme Court reevaluated its approach in *Albrecht*.

Westlaw. See Case 45.2 at the end of this chapter. To view the full, unedited case from Westlaw,® go to this text's Web site at **http://wbl-cs.westbuslaw.com**

Refusals to Deal. As discussed previously, joint refusals to deal (group boycotts) are subject to close scrutiny under Section 1 of the Sherman Act. A single manufacturer acting unilaterally, however, is generally free to deal, or not to deal, with whomever it wishes. In vertical arrangements, however, a manufacturer can refuse to deal with retailers or dealers that cut prices to levels substantially below the manufacturer's suggested retail prices. In *United States v. Colgate & Co.*,[12] for example, the United States Supreme Court held that a manufacturer's advance announcement that it would not sell to price cutters was not a violation of the Sherman Act.

There are instances, however, in which a unilateral refusal to deal violates antitrust laws. These instances involve offenses proscribed under Section 2 of the Sherman Act and occur only if (1) the firm refusing to deal has—or is likely to acquire—monopoly power and (2) the refusal is likely to have an anticompetitive effect on a particular market.

SECTION 3

Section 2 of the Sherman Act

Section 1 of the Sherman Act proscribes certain concerted, or joint, activities that restrain trade. In contrast, Section 2 condemns "every person who shall monopolize, or attempt to monopolize." Thus, two distinct types of behavior are subject to sanction under Section 2: *monopolization* and *attempts to monopolize*. A tactic that may be involved in either offense is **predatory pricing.** Predatory pricing involves an attempt by one firm to drive its competitors from the market by selling its product at prices substantially *below* the normal costs of production; once the competitors are eliminated, the firm will attempt to recapture its losses and go on to earn higher profits by driving prices up far above their competitive levels.

MONOPOLIZATION

In *United States v. Grinnell Corp.*,[13] the United States Supreme Court defined **monopolization** as involving the following two elements: "(1) the possession of monopoly power in the relevant market and (2) the willful acquisition or maintenance of the power as distinguished from growth or development as a consequence of a superior product, business acumen, or historic accident." A violation of Section 2 requires that both these elements—monopoly power and an intent to monopolize—be established.

Monopoly Power. The Sherman Act does not define *monopoly*. In economic parlance, monopoly refers to control by a single entity. It is well established in antitrust law, however, that a firm may be a monopolist even though it is not the sole seller in a market. Additionally, size alone does not determine whether a firm is a monopoly. For example, a "mom and pop" grocery located in an isolated desert town is a monopolist if it is the only grocery serving that particular market. Size in relation to the market is what matters, because monopoly involves the power to affect prices and output. *Monopoly power*, as mentioned earlier in this chapter, exists when a firm has sufficient market power to control prices and exclude competition.

As difficult as it is to define market power precisely, it is even more difficult to measure it. Courts often use the so-called **market-share test**[14]—a firm's percentage share of the "relevant market"—in determining the extent of the firm's market power. A firm generally is considered to have monopoly power if its share of the relevant market is 70 percent or

11. 390 U.S. 145, 88 S.Ct. 869, 19 L.Ed.2d 998 (1968).

12. 250 U.S. 300, 39 S.Ct. 465, 63 L.Ed. 992 (1919).

13. 384 U.S. 563, 86 S.Ct. 1698, 16 L.Ed.2d 778 (1966).

14. Other measures of market power have been devised, but the market-share test is the most widely used.

more. This is merely a rule of thumb, however; it is not a binding principle of law. In some cases, a smaller share may be held to constitute monopoly power.[15]

The relevant market consists of two elements: (1) a relevant product market and (2) a relevant geographic market. What should the relevant product market include? No doubt, it must include all products that, although produced by different firms, have identical attributes, such as sugar. Products that are not identical, however, may sometimes be substituted for one another. Coffee may be substituted for tea, for example. In defining the relevant product market, the key issue is the degree of interchangeability between products. If one product is a sufficient substitute for another, the two products are considered to be part of the same product market.

The second component of the relevant market is the geographic boundaries of the market. For products that are sold nationwide, the geographic boundaries of the market encompass the entire United States. If a producer and its competitors sell in only a limited area (one in which customers have no access to other sources of the product), the geographic market is limited to that area. A national firm may thus compete in several distinct areas and have monopoly power in one area but not in another.

The Intent Requirement. Monopoly power, in and of itself, does not constitute the offense of monopolization under Section 2 of the Sherman Act. The offense also requires an *intent* to monopolize. A dominant market share may be the result of business acumen or the development of a superior product. It may simply be the result of historic accident. In these situations, the acquisition of monopoly power is not an antitrust violation. Indeed, it would be counter to society's interest to condemn every firm that acquired a position of power because it was well managed, was efficient, and marketed a product desired by consumers. If, however, a firm possesses market power as a result of carrying out some purposeful act to acquire or maintain that power through anticompetitive means, it is in violation of Section 2. In most monopolization cases, intent may be inferred from evidence that the firm had monopoly power and engaged in anticompetitive behavior.

See Case 45.3 at the end of this chapter. To view the full, unedited case from Westlaw,® go to this text's Web site at **http://wbl-cs.westbuslaw.com**.

ATTEMPTS TO MONOPOLIZE

Section 2 also prohibits **attempted monopolization** of a market. Any action challenged as an attempt to monopolize must have been specifically intended to exclude competitors and garner monopoly power. In addition, the attempt must have had a "dangerous" probability of success—only *serious* threats of monopolization are condemned as violations. The probability cannot be dangerous unless the alleged offender possesses some degree of market power.

SECTION 4

The Clayton Act

In 1914, Congress attempted to strengthen federal antitrust laws by enacting the Clayton Act. The Clayton Act was aimed at specific anticompetitive or monopolistic practices that the Sherman Act did not cover. The substantive provisions of the act deal with four distinct forms of business behavior, which are declared illegal but not criminal. With regard to each of the four provisions, the act's prohibitions are qualified by the general condition that the behavior is illegal only if it tends to substantially lessen competition or to create monopoly power. The major offenses under the Clayton Act are set out in Sections 2, 3, 7, and 8 of the act.

PRICE DISCRIMINATION

Price discrimination, which occurs when a seller charges different prices to competing buyers for identical goods, is prohibited by Section 2 of the Clayton Act. Because businesses frequently circumvented Section 2 of the act, Congress strengthened this section by amending it with the passage of the Robinson-Patman Act in 1936.

As amended, Section 2 prohibits price discrimination that cannot be justified by differences in production costs, transportation costs, or cost differences due to other reasons. To violate Section 2, the seller must be engaged in interstate commerce, and the effect of

15. This standard was first articulated by Judge Learned Hand in *United States v. Aluminum Co. of America*, 148 F.2d 416 (2d Cir. 1945). A 90 percent share was held to be clear evidence of monopoly power. Anything less than 64 percent, said Judge Hand, made monopoly power doubtful, and anything less than 30 percent was clearly not monopoly power.

the price discrimination must be to substantially lessen competition or create a competitive injury.

In other words, a seller is prohibited from reducing a price to one buyer below the price charged to that buyer's competitor. An exception is made if the seller can justify the price reduction by demonstrating (1) that he or she charged the lower price temporarily and in good faith to meet another seller's equally low price to the buyer's competitor or (2) that a particular buyer's purchases saved the seller costs in producing and selling the goods (called *cost justification*). To violate the Clayton Act, a seller's pricing policies must also include a reasonable prospect of the seller's recouping its losses.[16]

EXCLUSIONARY PRACTICES

Under Section 3 of the Clayton Act, sellers or lessors cannot sell or lease goods "on the condition, agreement or understanding that the . . . purchaser or lessee thereof shall not use or deal in the goods . . . of a competitor or competitors of the seller." In effect, this section prohibits two types of vertical agreements involving exclusionary practices—exclusive-dealing contracts and tying arrangements.

Exclusive-Dealing Contracts. A contract under which a seller forbids a buyer to purchase products from the seller's competitors is called an **exclusive-dealing contract.** A seller is prohibited from making an exclusive-dealing contract under Section 3 if the effect of the contract is "to substantially lessen competition or tend to create a monopoly."

The leading exclusive-dealing decision was made by the Supreme Court in the case of *Standard Oil Co. of California v. United States.*[17] In this case, the then-largest gasoline seller in the nation made exclusive-dealing contracts with independent stations in seven western states. The contracts involved 16 percent of all retail outlets, the sales of which were approximately 7 percent of all retail sales in that market. The Court noted that the market was substantially concentrated because the seven largest gasoline suppliers all used exclusive-dealing contracts with their independent retailers and together controlled 65 percent of the market. Looking at market conditions after the arrangements were instituted, the Court found that market shares were extremely stable, and entry into the market was apparently restricted. Thus, the Court held that Section 3 of the Clayton Act had been violated, because competition was "foreclosed in a substantial share" of the relevant market.

Tying Arrangements. When a seller conditions the sale of a product (the tying product) on the buyer's agreement to purchase another product (the tied product) produced or distributed by the same seller, a **tying arrangement**, or *tie-in sales agreement,* results. The legality of a tie-in agreement depends on many factors, particularly the purpose of the agreement and the agreement's likely effect on competition in the relevant markets (the market for the tying product and the market for the tied product). In 1936, for example, the United States Supreme Court held that International Business Machines and Remington Rand had violated Section 3 of the Clayton Act by requiring the purchase of their own machine cards (the tied product) as a condition to the leasing of their tabulation machines (the tying product). Because only these two firms sold completely automated tabulation machines, the Court concluded that each possessed market power sufficient to "substantially lessen competition" through the tying arrangements.[18]

Section 3 of the Clayton Act has been held to apply only to commodities, not to services. Tying arrangements, however, also can be considered agreements that restrain trade in violation of Section 1 of the Sherman Act. Thus, cases involving tying arrangements of services have been brought under Section 1 of the Sherman Act. Traditionally, the courts have held tying arrangements brought under the Sherman Act to be illegal *per se.* In recent years, however, courts have shown a willingness to look at factors that are important in a rule-of-reason analysis.

MERGERS

Under Section 7 of the Clayton Act, a person or business organization cannot hold stock or assets in more than one business where "the effect . . . may be to substantially lessen competition." Section 7 is the statutory authority for preventing mergers that could result in monopoly power or a substantial lessening

16. See, for example, *Brooke Group, Ltd. v. Brown & Williamson Tobacco Corp.,* 509 U.S. 209, 113 S.Ct. 2578, 125 L.Ed.2d 168 (1993), in which the Supreme Court held that a seller's price-cutting policies could not be predatory "[g]iven the market's realities"—the size of the seller's market share, expanding output by other sellers, and other factors.

17. 37 U.S. 293, 69 S.Ct. 1051, 93 L.Ed. 1371 (1949).

18. *International Business Machines Corp. v. United States,* 298 U.S. 131, 56 S.Ct. 701, 80 L.Ed. 1085 (1936).

of competition in the marketplace. Section 7 applies to three types of mergers: horizontal mergers, vertical mergers, and conglomerate mergers. We discuss each type of merger in the following subsections.

A crucial consideration in most merger cases is **market concentration.** Determining market concentration involves allocating percentage market shares among the various companies in the relevant market. When a small number of companies share a large part of the market, the market is concentrated. For example, if the four largest grocery stores in Chicago accounted for 80 percent of all retail food sales, the market clearly would be concentrated in those four firms. Competition, however, is not necessarily diminished solely as a result of market concentration, and other factors must be considered in determining whether a merger will violate Section 7. Another concept of particular importance in evaluating the effects of a merger is whether the merger will make it more difficult for potential competitors to enter the relevant market.

Horizontal Mergers. Mergers between firms that compete with each other in the same market are called **horizontal mergers.** If a horizontal merger creates an entity with anything other than a small-percentage market share, the merger will be presumed illegal. This is because of the United States Supreme Court's interpretation that Congress, in amending Section 7 of the Clayton Act in 1950, intended to prevent mergers that increase market concentration.[19] Three other factors that the courts also consider in analyzing the legality of a horizontal merger are the overall concentration of the relevant market, the relevant market's history of tending toward concentration, and whether the merger is apparently designed to establish market power or restrict competition.

The Federal Trade Commission (FTC) and the U.S. Department of Justice (DOJ) have established guidelines indicating which mergers will be challenged. Under the guidelines, the first factor to be considered in determining whether a merger will be challenged is the degree of concentration in the relevant market. This is done by comparing the premerger market concentration with the anticipated postmerger market concentration.

In determining market concentration, the FTC and the DOJ employ what is known as the **Herfindahl-Hirschman Index (HHI).** The HHI is computed by summing the squares of each of the percentage market shares of firms in the relevant market. For example, if there are four firms with shares of 30 percent, 30 percent, 20 percent, and 20 percent, respectively, then the premerger HHI equals 2,600 ($30^2 + 30^2 + 20^2 + 20^2 = 2{,}600$).

If the premerger HHI is less than 1,000, the market is unconcentrated, and the merger will not likely be challenged. If the premerger HHI is between 1,000 and 1,800, the industry is moderately concentrated, and the merger will be challenged only if it increases the HHI by 100 points or more. If the premerger HHI is greater than 1,800, the market is highly concentrated. In a highly concentrated market, a merger that produces an increase in the HHI between 50 and 100 points raises significant competitive concerns. Mergers that produce an increase in the HHI of more than 100 points in a highly concentrated market are deemed likely to enhance market power.

The guidelines stress that the determination of market share and market concentration is only the starting point in analyzing the potential anticompetitive effects of a merger. Before deciding to challenge a merger, the FTC and the DOJ will look at a number of other factors, including the ease of entry into the relevant market, economic efficiency, the financial condition of the merging firms, the nature and price of the product or products involved, and so on. In the case of a leading firm—one having a market share that is at least 35 percent and is twice that of the next leading firm—any merger with a firm having as little as a 1 percent share will be challenged.

Vertical Mergers. A **vertical merger** occurs when a company at one stage of production acquires a company at a higher or lower stage of production. An example of a vertical merger is a company merging with one of its suppliers or retailers. Courts in the past have almost exclusively focused on "foreclosure" in assessing vertical mergers. Foreclosure occurs when competitors of the merging firms lose opportunities either to sell products to or buy products from the merging firms.

For example, in *United States v. E. I. du Pont de Nemours & Co.*,[20] du Pont was challenged for acquiring a considerable amount of General Motors (GM) stock. In holding that the transaction was illegal, the United States Supreme Court noted that stock acquisition would enable du Pont to foreclose other sellers

19. *Brown Shoe v. United States*, 370 U.S. 294, 82 S.Ct. 1502, 8 L.Ed.2d 510 (1962).

20. 353 U.S. 586, 77 S.Ct. 872, 1 L.Ed.2d 1057 (1957).

of fabrics and finishes from selling to GM, which then accounted for 50 percent of all auto fabric and finishes purchases.

Today, whether a vertical merger will be deemed illegal generally depends on several factors, including market concentration, barriers to entry into the market, and the apparent intent of the merging parties. Mergers that do not prevent competitors of either of the merging firms from competing in a segment of the market will not be condemned as foreclosing competition and are legal.

Conglomerate Mergers. There are three general types of **conglomerate mergers:** market-extension, product-extension, and diversification mergers. A market-extension merger occurs when a firm seeks to sell its product in a new market by merging with a firm already established in that market. A product-extension merger occurs when a firm seeks to add a closely related product to its existing line by merging with a firm already producing that product. For example, a manufacturer might seek to extend its line of household products to include floor wax by acquiring a leading manufacturer of floor wax. Diversification occurs when a firm merges with another firm that offers a product or service wholly unrelated to the first firm's existing activities. An example of a diversification merger is an automobile manufacturer's acquisition of a motel chain.

INTERLOCKING DIRECTORATES

Section 8 of the Clayton Act deals with *interlocking directorates*—that is, the practice of having individuals serve as directors on the boards of two or more competing companies simultaneously. Specifically, no person may be a director in two or more competing corporations at the same time if either of the corporations has capital, surplus, or undivided profits aggregating more than $18,142,000 or competitive sales of $1,814,200 or more. The threshold amounts are adjusted each year by the Federal Trade Commission (FTC). (The amounts given here are those announced by the FTC in 2001.)

SECTION 5

The Federal Trade Commission Act

The Federal Trade Commission Act was enacted in 1914, the same year the Clayton Act was written into law. Section 5 is the sole substantive provision of the act. It provides, in part, as follows: "Unfair methods of competition in or affecting commerce, and unfair or deceptive acts or practices in or affecting commerce are hereby declared illegal." Section 5 condemns all forms of anticompetitive behavior that are not covered under other federal antitrust laws. The act also created the Federal Trade Commission to implement the act's provisions.

SECTION 6

Enforcement of Antitrust Laws

The federal agencies that enforce the federal antitrust laws are the U.S. Department of Justice (DOJ) and the Federal Trade Commission (FTC). Only the DOJ can prosecute violations of the Sherman Act as either criminal or civil violations. Violations of the Clayton Act are not crimes, and the DOJ or the FTC can enforce that statute through civil proceedings. The various remedies that the DOJ or the FTC has asked the courts to impose include **divestiture** (making a company give up one or more of its operating functions) and dissolution. The DOJ or the FTC might force a group of meat packers, for example, to divest itself of control or ownership of butcher shops.

The FTC has sole authority to enforce violations of Section 5 of the Federal Trade Commission Act. FTC actions are effected through administrative orders, but if a firm violates an FTC order, the FTC can seek court sanctions for the violation.

A private party can sue for treble (triple) damages and attorneys' fees if the party is injured as a result of a violation of the Sherman Act or the Clayton Act. In some instances, private parties may also seek injunctive relief to prevent antitrust violations. The courts have determined that the ability to sue depends on the directness of the injury suffered by the would-be plaintiff. Thus, a person wishing to sue under the Sherman Act must prove (1) that the antitrust violation either caused or was a substantial factor in causing the injury that was suffered and (2) that the unlawful actions of the accused party affected business activities of the plaintiff that were protected by the antitrust laws.

In recent years, more than 90 percent of all antitrust actions have been brought by private plaintiffs. One reason for this is, of course, that successful plaintiffs may recover three times the damages that they have suffered as a result of the violation. Such recoveries by private plaintiffs for antitrust violations have been rationalized as encouraging people to act as "private attorneys general" who will vigorously pursue antitrust violators on their own initiative.

SECTION 7

U.S. Antitrust Laws in the Global Context

U.S. antitrust laws have a broad application. They may subject persons in foreign nations to their provisions as well as protect foreign consumers and competitors from violations committed by U.S. business firms. Consequently, *foreign persons,* a term that by definition includes foreign governments, may sue under U.S. antitrust laws in U.S. courts.

Section 1 of the Sherman Act of 1890 provides for the extraterritorial effect of the U.S. antitrust laws. The United States is a major proponent of free competition in the global economy, and thus any conspiracy that has a substantial effect on U.S. commerce is within the reach of the Sherman Act. The violation may even occur outside the United States, and foreign governments as well as persons can be sued for violation of U.S. antitrust laws. Before U.S. courts will exercise jurisdiction and apply antitrust laws, it must be shown that the alleged violation had a *substantial effect* on U.S. commerce. U.S. jurisdiction is automatically invoked, however, when a *per se* violation occurs.

If a domestic firm, for example, joins a foreign cartel to control the production, price, or distribution of goods, and this cartel has a *substantial effect* on U.S. commerce, a *per se* violation may exist. Hence, both the domestic firm and the foreign cartel could be sued for violation of the U.S. antitrust laws. Likewise, if a foreign firm doing business in the United States enters into a price-fixing or other anticompetitive agreement to control a portion of U.S. markets, a *per se* violation may exist.

In 1982, Congress amended the Sherman Act and the Federal Trade Commission Act of 1914 to limit their application when unfair methods of competition are involved in U.S. export trade or commerce with foreign nations. The acts are not limited, however, when there is a "direct, substantial, and reasonably foreseeable effect" on U.S. domestic commerce that results in a claim for damages.

SECTION 8

Exemptions from Antitrust Law

There are many legislative and constitutional limitations on antitrust enforcement. Most statutory and judicially created exemptions to the antitrust laws apply to the following areas or activities:

1. *Labor.* Section 6 of the Clayton Act generally permits labor unions to organize and bargain without violating antitrust laws. Section 20 of the Clayton Act specifies that strikes and other labor activities are not violations of any law of the United States. A union can lose its exemption, however, if it combines with a nonlabor group rather than acting simply in its own self-interest.
2. *Agricultural associations and fisheries.* Section 6 of the Clayton Act (along with the Cooperative Marketing Associations Act of 1922[21]) exempts agricultural cooperatives from the antitrust laws. The Fisheries Cooperative Marketing Act of 1976 exempts from antitrust legislation individuals in the fishing industry who collectively catch, produce, and prepare their products for market. Both exemptions allow members of such co-ops to combine and set prices for a particular product, but they do not allow them to engage in exclusionary practices or restraints of trade directed at competitors.
3. *Insurance.* The McCarran-Ferguson Act[22] of 1945 exempts the insurance business from the antitrust laws whenever state regulation exists. This exemption does not cover boycotts, coercion, or intimidation on the part of insurance companies.
4. *Foreign trade.* Under the provisions of the 1918 Webb-Pomerene Act,[23] American exporters may engage in cooperative activity to compete with similar foreign associations. This type of cooperative activity may not, however, restrain trade within the United States or injure other American exporters. The Export Trading Company Act[24] of 1982 broadened the Webb-Pomerene Act by permitting the Department of Justice to certify properly qualified export trading companies. Any activity within the scope described by the certificate is exempt from public prosecution under the antitrust laws.

21. 7 U.S.C. Sections 291–292.
22. 15 U.S.C. Sections 1011–1015.
23. 15 U.S.C. Sections 61–66.
24. 15 U.S.C. Sections 4001–4003.

5. *Professional baseball.* In 1922, the United States Supreme Court held that professional baseball was not within the reach of federal antitrust laws because it did not involve "interstate commerce."[25] Some of the effects of this decision, however, were modified by the Curt Flood Act of 1998. Essentially, the act allows players the option of suing team owners for anticompetitive practices if, for example, the owners collude to "blacklist" players, hold down players' salaries, or force players to play for specific teams.

6. *Oil marketing.* The 1935 Interstate Oil Compact allows states to determine quotas on oil that will be marketed in interstate commerce.

7. *Cooperative research and production.* Cooperative research among small business firms is exempt under the Small Business Act[26] of 1958. Research or production of a product, process, or service by joint ventures consisting of competitors is exempt under special federal legislation, including the National Cooperative Research Act[27] of 1984, as amended by the National Cooperative Research and Production Act of 1993.

8. *Joint efforts by businesspersons to obtain legislative or executive action.* This is often referred to as the *Noerr-Pennington* doctrine.[28] For example, video producers might jointly lobby Congress to change the copyright laws without being held liable for attempting to restrain trade. Though selfish rather than purely public-minded conduct is permitted, there is an exception: an action will not be protected if it is clear that the action is "objectively baseless in the sense that no reasonable [person] could reasonably expect success on the merits" and it is an attempt to make anticompetitive use of government processes.[29]

9. *Other exemptions.* Other activities exempt from antitrust laws include activities approved by the president in furtherance of the defense of our nation (under the Defense Production Act[30] of 1950); state actions, when the state policy is clearly articulated and the policy is actively supervised by the state;[31] and activities of regulated industries (such as the transportation, communication, and banking industries) when federal agencies (such as the Federal Communications Commission) have primary regulatory authority.

25. *Federal Baseball Club of Baltimore, Inc. v. National League of Professional Baseball Clubs,* 259 U.S. 200, 42 S.Ct. 465, 66 L.Ed. 898 (1922).

26. 15 U.S.C. Sections 631–657.

27. 15 U.S.C. Sections 4301–4306.

28. See *United Mine Workers of America v. Pennington,* 381 U.S. 657, 89 S.Ct. 1585, 14 L.Ed.2d 626 (1965); and *Eastern Railroad Presidents Conference v. Noerr Motor Freight, Inc.,* 365 U.S. 127, 81 S.Ct. 523, 5 L.Ed.2d 464 (1961).

29. *Professional Real Estate Investors, Inc. v. Columbia Pictures Industries, Inc.,* 508 U.S. 49, 113 S.Ct. 1920, 123 L.Ed.2d 611 (1993).

30. 50 App.U.S.C. 2061–2171.

31. See *Parker v. Brown,* 347 U.S. 341, 63 S.Ct. 307, 87 L.Ed. 315 (1943).

Terms and Concepts to Review

antitrust law 920
attempted monopolization 925
conglomerate merger 928
divestiture 928
exclusive-dealing contract 926
group boycott 922
Herfindahl-Hirschman Index (HHI) 927
horizontal merger 927
horizontal restraint 922
market concentration 927
market power 921
market-share test 924
monopolization 924
monopoly 921
monopoly power 921
per se violation 922
predatory pricing 924
price discrimination 925
price-fixing agreement 922
resale price maintenance agreement 924
restraint on trade 920
rule of reason 921
tying arrangement 926
vertical merger 927
vertical restraint 923
vertically integrated firm 923

CHAPTER SUMMARY

The Sherman Antitrust Act (1890)	1. *Major provisions*— a. Section 1—Prohibits contracts, combinations, and conspiracies in restraint of trade. (1) Horizontal restraints subject to Section 1 include price-fixing agreements, group boycotts (joint refusals to deal), horizontal market division, trade association agreements, and joint ventures. (2) Vertical restraints subject to Section 1 include resale price maintenance agreements, territorial or customer restrictions, and refusals to deal. b. Section 2—Prohibits monopolies and attempts to monopolize. 2. *Jurisdictional requirements*—The Sherman Act applies only to activities that have a significant impact on interstate commerce. 3. *Interpretative rules*— a. *Per se* rule—Applied to restraints on trade that are so inherently anticompetitive that they cannot be justified and are deemed illegal as a matter of law. b. Rule of reason—Applied when an anticompetitive agreement may be justified by legitimate benefits. Under the rule of reason, the lawfulness of a trade restraint will be determined by the purpose and effects of the restraint.
The Clayton Act (1914)	The major provisions are as follows: 1. *Section 2*—As amended in 1936 by the Robinson-Patman Act, prohibits price discrimination that substantially lessens competition and prohibits a seller engaged in interstate commerce from selling to two or more buyers goods of similar grade and quality at different prices when the result is a substantial lessening of competition or the creation of a competitive injury. 2. *Section 3*—Prohibits exclusionary practices, such as exclusive-dealing contracts and tying arrangements, when the effect may be to substantially lessen competition. 3. *Section 7*—Prohibits mergers when the effect may be to substantially lessen competition or to tend to create a monopoly. a. Horizontal mergers—The acquisition by merger or consolidation of a competing firm engaged in the same relevant market. Will be unlawful only if a merger results in the merging firms' holding a disproportionate share of the market, resulting in a substantial lessening of competition, and if the merger does not enhance consumer welfare by increasing efficiency of production or marketing. b. Vertical mergers—The acquisition by a seller of one of its buyers or vice versa. Will be unlawful if the merger prevents competitors of either merging firm from competing in a segment of the market that otherwise would be open to them, resulting in a substantial lessening of competition. c. Conglomerate mergers—The acquisition of a noncompeting business. 4. *Section 8*—Prohibits interlocking directorates.
The Federal Trade Commission Act (1914)	Prohibits unfair methods of competition; established and defined the powers of the Federal Trade Commission.
Enforcement of Antitrust Laws	Antitrust laws are enforced by the Department of Justice, by the Federal Trade Commission, and in some cases by private parties, who may be awarded treble damages and attorneys' fees.
Exemptions from Antitrust Laws	1. Labor unions (under Section 6 of the Clayton Act of 1914). 2. Agricultural associations and fisheries (under Section 6 of the Clayton Act of 1914, the Capper-Volstead Act of 1922, and the Fisheries Cooperative Marketing Act of 1976). 3. Insurance—when state regulation exists (under the McCarran-Ferguson Act of 1945). 4. Export trading companies (under the Webb-Pomerene Act of 1918 and the Export Trading Company Act of 1982).

CHAPTER SUMMARY—CONTINUED

Exemptions from Antitrust Laws—continued	5. Professional baseball (by a 1922 judicial decision), although modified by a 1998 federal statute. 6. Oil marketing (under the Interstate Oil Compact of 1935). 7. Cooperative research and production (under various acts, including the Small Business Administration Act of 1958, as amended, the National Cooperative Research Act of 1984, and the National Cooperative Production Amendments of 1993). 8. Joint efforts by businesspersons to obtain legislative or executive action (under the *Noerr-Pennington* doctrine). 9. Other activities, including certain national defense actions, state actions, and actions of certain regulated industries.

CASES FOR ANALYSIS

Westlaw. You can access the full text of each case presented below by going to the Westlaw cases on this text's Web site at http://wbl-cs.westbuslaw.com. Each Westlaw case includes the names of all plaintiffs and defendants, the dates on which the case was argued and decided, a brief summary of the issues and decisions in the case, headnotes classifying specific issues in the case according to the West Key Number System, and the court's opinion. Concurring and dissenting opinions, if any, are included as well.

CASE 45.1 VERTICAL RESTRAINTS

CONTINENTAL T.V., INC. v. GTE SYLVANIA, INC.

Supreme Court of the United States, 1997.
433 U.S. 36,
97 S.Ct. 2549,
53 L.Ed.2d 568.

Mr. Justice *POWELL* delivered the opinion of the Court.

Franchise agreements between manufacturers and retailers frequently include provisions barring the retailers from selling franchised products from locations other than those specified in the agreements. This case presents important questions concerning the appropriate antitrust analysis of these restrictions under [Section] 1 of the Sherman Act * * * .

* * * *

Respondent GTE Sylvania, Inc. (Sylvania) manufactures and sells television sets through its Home Entertainment Products Division. Prior to 1962, like most other television manufacturers, Sylvania sold its televisions to independent or company-owned distributors who in turn resold to a large and diverse group of retailers. Prompted by a decline in its market share to a relatively insignificant 1% to 2% of national television sales, Sylvania conducted an intensive reassessment of its marketing strategy, and in 1962 adopted the franchise plan challenged here. Sylvania phased out its wholesale distributors and began to sell its televisions directly to a smaller and more select group of franchised retailers. An acknowledged purpose of the change was to decrease the number of competing Sylvania retailers in the hope of attracting the more aggressive and competent retailers thought necessary to the improvement of the company's market position. To this end, Sylvania limited the number of franchises granted for any given area and required each franchisee to sell his Sylvania products only from the location or locations at which he was franchised. A franchise did not constitute an exclusive territory, and Sylvania retained sole discretion to increase the number of retailers in an area in light of the success or failure of existing retailers in developing their market. The revised marketing strategy appears to have been successful during the period at issue here, for by 1965 Sylvania's share of national television sales had increased to approximately 5%, and the company ranked as the Nation's eighth largest manufacturer of color television sets.

* * * Dissatisfied with its sales in the city of San Francisco, Sylvania decided in the spring of 1965 to franchise Young Brothers, an established San Francisco retailer of televisions, as an additional San Francisco retailer. The proposed location of the new franchise was approximately a mile from a retail outlet operated by petitioner Continental T.V., Inc. (Continental), one of

the most successful Sylvania franchisees. Continental protested that the location of the new franchise violated Sylvania's marketing policy, but Sylvania persisted in its plans. Continental then canceled a large Sylvania order and placed a large order with Phillips, one of Sylvania's competitors.

During this same period, Continental expressed a desire to open a store in Sacramento, Cal., a desire Sylvania attributed at least in part to Continental's displeasure over the Young Brothers decision. Sylvania believed that the Sacramento market was adequately served by the existing Sylvania retailers and denied the request. In the face of this denial, Continental advised Sylvania in early September 1965, that it was in the process of moving Sylvania merchandise from its San Jose, Cal., warehouse to a new retail location that it had leased in Sacramento. Two weeks later, allegedly for unrelated reasons, Sylvania's credit department reduced Continental's credit line from $300,000 to $50,000. In response to the reduction in credit and the generally deteriorating relations with Sylvania, Continental withheld all payments owed to John P. Maguire & Co., Inc. (Maguire), the finance company that handled the credit arrangements between Sylvania and its retailers. Shortly thereafter, Sylvania terminated Continental's franchises, and Maguire filed this * * * action in the United States District Court for the Northern District of California seeking recovery of money owed and of secured merchandise held by Continental.

The antitrust issues before us originated in cross-claims brought by Continental against Sylvania and Maguire. Most important for our purposes was the claim that Sylvania had violated [Section] 1 of the Sherman Act by entering into and enforcing franchise agreements that prohibited the sale of Sylvania products other than from specified locations. * * *

* * * [T]he jury found that Sylvania had engaged "in a contract, combination or conspiracy in restraint of trade in violation of the antitrust laws with respect to location restrictions alone," and assessed Continental's damages at $591,505, which was trebled * * * to * * * $1,774,515.

On appeal, the [U.S.] Court of Appeals for the Ninth Circuit * * * reversed * * * . [T]he court concluded that Sylvania's location restriction * * * should be judged under the "rule of reason" rather than the *per se* rule * * * .

We granted Continental's petition for *certiorari* to resolve this important question of antitrust law.

* * * *

The traditional framework of analysis under [Section] 1 of the Sherman Act is familiar and does not require extended discussion. Section 1 prohibits "[e]very contract, combination * * * , or conspiracy, in restraint of trade or commerce." Since the early years of this century a judicial gloss on this statutory language has established the "rule of reason" as the prevailing standard of analysis. Under this rule, the factfinder weighs all of the circumstances of a case in deciding whether a restrictive practice should be prohibited as imposing an unreasonable restraint on competition. *Per se* rules of illegality are appropriate only when they relate to conduct that is manifestly anticompetitive. * * * [T]here are certain agreements or practices which because of their pernicious effect on competition and lack of any redeeming virtue are conclusively presumed to be unreasonable and therefore illegal without elaborate inquiry as to the precise harm they have caused or the business excuse for their use.

In essence, the issue before us is whether * * * vertical restrictions satisf[y] those standards. * * *

The market impact of vertical restrictions is complex because of their potential for a simultaneous reduction of intrabrand competition [competition between those who sell the same product brand] and stimulation of interbrand competition [competition between those who sell different product brands]. * * *

* * * *

Vertical restrictions reduce intrabrand competition by limiting the number of sellers of a particular product competing for the business of a given group of buyers. Location restrictions have this effect because of practical constraints on the effective marketing area of retail outlets. Although intrabrand competition may be reduced, the ability of retailers to exploit the resulting market may be limited both by the ability of consumers to travel to other franchised locations and, perhaps more importantly, to purchase the competing products of other manufacturers. None of these key variables, however, is affected by the form of the transaction by which a manufacturer conveys his products to the retailers.

Vertical restrictions promote interbrand competition by allowing the manufacturer to achieve certain efficiencies in the distribution of his products. These "redeeming virtues" are implicit in every decision sustaining vertical restrictions under the rule of reason. Economists have identified a number of ways in which manufacturers can use such restrictions to compete more effectively against other manufacturers. For example, new manufacturers and manufacturers entering new markets can use the restrictions in order to induce competent and aggressive retailers to make the kind of investment of capital and labor that is often required in the distribution of products unknown to the consumer. Established manufacturers can use them to induce retailers to engage in promotional activities or to provide service and repair facilities necessary to the efficient marketing of their products. Service and repair are vital for many products, such as automobiles and major household appliances. The availability and quality of such services affect a manufacturer's goodwill and the competitiveness of his product. Because of market imperfections such as the so-called "free rider" effect, these services might not be provided by retailers in a purely competitive situation, despite the fact that each retailer's benefit would be greater if all provided the services than if none did.

* * * *

In sum, we conclude that the appropriate decision is to [apply] the rule of reason * * * [to] vertical restrictions * * * . When anticompetitive effects are shown to result from particular vertical restrictions they can be adequately policed under the rule of reason, the standard traditionally applied for the majority of anticompetitive practices challenged under [Section] 1 of the Act. Accordingly, the decision of the Court of Appeals is Affirmed.

CASE 45.2 VERTICAL RESTRAINTS

STATE OIL CO. V. KHAN

Supreme Court of the United States, 1997.
522 U.S. 3,
118 S.Ct. 275,
139 L.Ed.2d 199.

Justice *O'CONNOR* delivered the opinion of the Court.

* * * *

I

Respondents, Barkat U. Khan and his corporation, entered into an agreement with petitioner, State Oil Company, to lease and operate a gas station and convenience store owned by State Oil. The agreement provided that respondents would obtain the station's gasoline supply from State Oil at a price equal to a suggested retail price set by State Oil, less a margin of 3.25 cents per gallon. Under the agreement, respondents could charge any amount for gasoline sold to the station's customers, but if the price charged was higher than State Oil's suggested retail price, the excess was to be rebated to State Oil. Respondents could sell gasoline for less than State Oil's suggested retail price, but any such decrease would reduce their 3.25 cents-per-gallon margin.

About a year after respondents began operating the gas station, they fell behind in lease payments. State Oil then gave notice of its intent to terminate the agreement and commenced [an Illinois] state court proceeding to evict respondents. * * *

Respondents sued State Oil in the United States District Court for the Northern District of Illinois, alleging in part that State Oil had engaged in price fixing in violation of [Section] 1 of the Sherman Act by preventing respondents from raising or lowering retail gas prices. According to the complaint, but for the agreement with State Oil, respondents could have charged different prices based on the grades of gasoline, * * * thereby achieving increased sales and profits. State Oil responded that the agreement did not actually prevent respondents from setting gasoline prices, and that, in substance, respondents did not allege a violation of antitrust laws by their claim that State Oil's suggested retail price was not optimal.

The District Court found that the allegations in the complaint did not state a *per se* violation of the Sherman Act * * * . Accordingly, the District Court entered summary judgment for State Oil on respondents' Sherman Act claim.

The [U.S.] Court of Appeals for the Seventh Circuit reversed. The court first noted that the agreement between respondents and State Oil did indeed fix maximum gasoline prices by making it "worthless" for respondents to exceed the suggested retail prices. After reviewing legal and economic aspects of price fixing, the court concluded that State Oil's pricing scheme was a per se antitrust violation * * * . [T]he court found that respondents could have suffered antitrust injury from not being able to adjust gasoline prices.

We granted *certiorari* to consider two questions, whether State Oil's conduct constitutes a *per se* violation of the Sherman Act and whether respondents are entitled to recover damages based on that conduct.

II

* * * *

Although the Sherman Act, by its terms, prohibits every agreement "in restraint of trade," this Court has long recognized that Congress intended to outlaw only unreasonable restraints. As a consequence, most antitrust claims are analyzed under a "rule of reason," according to which the finder of fact must decide whether the questioned practice imposes an unreasonable restraint on competition, taking into account a variety of factors, including specific information about the relevant business, its condition before and after the restraint was imposed, and the restraint's history, nature, and effect.

Some types of restraints, however, have such predictable and pernicious [harmful] anticompetitive effect, and such limited potential for procompetitive benefit, that they are deemed unlawful *per se*. *Per se* treatment is appropriate once experience with a particular kind of restraint enables the Court to predict with confidence that the rule of reason will condemn it. Thus, we have expressed reluctance to adopt *per se* rules with regard to restraints imposed in the context of business relationships where the economic impact of certain practices is not immediately obvious.

* * * *

* * * Our analysis is * * * guided by our general view that the primary purpose of the antitrust laws is to protect interbrand competition. Low prices * * * benefit consumers regardless of how those prices are set, and so long as they are above predatory levels, they do not threaten competition. Our interpretation of the Sherman Act also incorporates the notion that condemnation of practices resulting in lower prices to consumers is especially costly because cutting prices in order to increase business often is the very essence of competition.

So informed, we find it difficult to maintain that vertically imposed maximum prices could harm consumers or competition to the extent necessary to justify their *per se* invalidation. As * * * the Court of Appeals [stated] in this case:

> "As for maximum resale price fixing, unless the supplier is a monopsonist he cannot squeeze his dealers' margins below a competitive level; the attempt to do so would just drive the dealers into the arms of a competing supplier. A supplier might, however, fix a maximum resale price in order to prevent his dealers from exploiting a monopoly position. * * * [S]uppose that State Oil, perhaps to encourage * * * dealer services * * * has spaced its dealers sufficiently far apart to limit competition among them (or even given each of them an exclusive territory); and suppose further that Union 76 is a sufficiently distinctive and popular brand to give the dealers in it at least a modicum of monopoly power. Then State Oil might want to place a ceiling on the dealers' resale prices in order to prevent them from exploiting that monopoly power fully. It would do this not out of disinterested malice, but in its commercial self-interest. The higher the price at which gasoline is resold, the smaller the volume sold, and so the lower the profit to the supplier if the higher profit per gallon at the higher price is being snared by the dealer."

We recognize that * * * [there are] a number of theoretical justifications for a *per se* rule against vertical maximum price fixing. But criticism of those premises abounds. * * * [There is] the fear that maximum price fixing by suppliers could interfere with dealer freedom. [But] * * * the ban on maximum resale price limitations declared * * * in the name of "dealer freedom" has actually prompted many suppliers to integrate forward into distribution, thus eliminating the * * * independent trader * * * .

* * * [There is] the concern that maximum prices may be set too low for dealers to offer consumers essential or desired services. But such conduct, by driving away customers, would seem likely to harm manufacturers as well as dealers and consumers, making it unlikely that a supplier would set such a price as a matter of business judgment. In addition, * * * vertical maximum price fixing could effectively channel distribution through large or specially advantaged dealers. It is unclear, however, that a supplier would profit from limiting its market by excluding potential dealers. Further, *although vertical maximum price fixing might limit the viability of inefficient dealers, that consequence is not necessarily harmful to competition and consumers.* [Emphasis added.]

Finally, * * * [there is the] fear that maximum price fixing could be used to disguise arrangements to fix minimum prices, which remain illegal *per se*. Although we have acknowledged the possibility that maximum pricing might mask minimum pricing, we believe that such conduct * * * can be appropriately recognized and punished under the rule of reason.

Not only are the potential injuries * * * less serious than * * * imagined, the *per se* rule * * * could in fact exacerbate problems related to the unrestrained exercise of market power by monopolist-dealers. Indeed, * * * [the application of the *per se*] rule may actually harm consumers and manufacturers. * * *

* * * [W]e conclude that there is insufficient economic justification for *per se* invalidation of vertical maximum price fixing. * * *

* * * *

* * * [W]e of course do not hold that all vertical maximum price fixing is *per se* lawful. Instead, vertical maximum price fixing, like the majority of commercial arrangements subject to the antitrust laws, should be evaluated under the rule of reason. In our view, rule-of-reason analysis will effectively identify those situations in which vertical maximum price fixing amounts to anticompetitive conduct.

There remains the question whether respondents are entitled to recover damages based on State Oil's conduct. Although the Court of Appeals noted that "the district judge was right to conclude that if the rule of reason is applicable, Khan loses," its consideration of this case was necessarily premised on [the application of the] *per se* rule. Under the circumstances, the matter should be reviewed by the Court of Appeals in the first instance. We therefore vacate the judgment of the Court of Appeals and remand the case for further proceedings consistent with this opinion.

It is so ordered.

CASE 45.3 MONOPOLIZATION

UNITED STATES v. MICROSOFT CORP.
United States Court of Appeals,
District of Columbia Circuit, 2001.
253 F.3d 34.

PER CURIAM:

Microsoft Corporation appeals from judgments of [a federal] District Court finding the company in violation of * * * [Section] 2 of the Sherman Act and ordering various remedies.

The action against Microsoft arose pursuant to a complaint filed by the United States [Department of Justice (DOJ)] and separate complaints filed by individual States. The District Court determined [in part] that Microsoft had maintained a monopoly in the market for Intel-compatible PC operating systems in violation of [Section] 2 * * * .

* * * *

II. MONOPOLIZATION

Section 2 of the Sherman Act makes it unlawful for a firm to "monopolize." The offense of monopolization has two elements: "(1) the possession of monopoly power in the relevant market and (2) the willful acquisition or maintenance of that power as distinguished from growth or development as a consequence of a superior product, business acumen, or historic accident." The District Court applied this test and found that Microsoft possesses monopoly power in the market for Intel-compatible PC operating systems. Focusing primarily on Microsoft's efforts to suppress Netscape Navigator's threat to its operating system monopoly, the court also found that Microsoft maintained its power not through competition on the merits, but through unlawful means. * * *

* * * *

A. Monopoly Power

* * * [M]onopoly power [is] the power to control prices or exclude competition. * * * [M]onopoly power may be inferred from a firm's possession of a dominant share of a relevant market that is protected by entry barriers. * * *

* * * *

1. Market Structure

* * * *

* * * In this case, the District Court defined the market as "the licensing of all Intel-compatible PC operating systems worldwide," finding that there are "currently no products—and * * * there are not likely to be any in the near future—that a significant percentage of computer users worldwide could substitute for [these operating systems] without incurring substantial costs." * * *

* * * *

Having thus * * * defined the relevant market, the District Court found that Windows accounts for a greater than 95% share. * * *

* * * [T]he structural barrier that protects the company's future position * * * stems from two characteristics of the software market: (1) most consumers prefer operating systems for which a large number of applications have already been written; and (2) most developers prefer to write for operating systems that already have a substantial consumer base. This "chicken-and-egg" situation ensures that applications will continue to be written for the already dominant Windows, which in turn ensures that consumers will continue to prefer it over other operating systems.

* * * *

2. Direct Proof

Having sustained the District Court's conclusion that * * * Microsoft possesses monopoly power, we turn to Microsoft's * * * argument that it does not behave like a monopolist. Claiming that software competition is uniquely "dynamic," the company suggests * * * that monopoly power in the software industry should be proven directly, that is, by examining a company's actual behavior to determine if it reveals the existence of monopoly power. * * *

Microsoft's argument fails because, even assuming that the software market is uniquely dynamic in the long term, * * * the company faces [no] competition in the short term. * * * The District Court expressly considered and rejected Microsoft's claims that innovations such as handheld devices and portal websites would soon expand the relevant market beyond Intel-compatible PC operating systems. * * *

* * * *

* * * The District Court also found that Microsoft's pattern of exclusionary conduct could only be rational "if the firm knew that it possessed monopoly power." It is to that conduct that we now turn.

B. Anticompetitive Conduct

* * * *

1. Licenses Issued to Original Equipment Manufacturers [OEMs]

The District Court condemned a number of provisions in Microsoft's agreements licensing Windows to OEMs, because it found that Microsoft's imposition of those provisions * * * serves to reduce usage share of Netscape's browser and, hence, protect Microsoft's operating system monopoly. * * *

Browser usage share is important because a browser * * * must have a critical mass of users in order to attract software developers to write applications relying upon the [Application Programming Interfaces (APIs)] it exposes * * * . Applications written to a particular browser's APIs * * * would run on any computer with that browser, regardless of the underlying operating system. * * *

Therefore, Microsoft's efforts to gain market share in one market (browsers) served to meet the threat to Microsoft's monopoly in another market (operating systems) by keeping rival browsers from gaining the critical mass of users necessary to attract developer attention away from Windows as the platform for software development. * * *

* * * *

* * * [T]he District Court condemned the license provisions prohibiting the OEMs from: (1) removing any desktop icons, folders, or "Start" menu entries; [and] (2) altering the initial boot sequence * * * .

* * * *

* * * By preventing OEMs from removing visible means of user access to [Microsoft's browser, Internet Explorer (IE)], the license restriction prevents many OEMs from pre-installing a rival browser and, therefore, protects Microsoft's monopoly from the competition * * * .

* * * [Prohibiting] OEMs from modifying the initial boot sequence—the process that occurs the first time a consumer turns on the computer— * * * has the effect of decreasing competition against IE by preventing OEMs from promoting rivals' browsers. Because this prohibition has a substantial effect in protecting Microsoft's market power, and does so through a means other than competition on the merits, it is anticompetitive. * * *

* * * *

2. Integration of IE and Windows

* * * *

Technologically binding IE to Windows, the District Court found, both prevented OEMs from pre-installing other browsers and deterred consumers from using them. * * *

* * * *

* * * Because Microsoft's conduct, through something other than competition on the merits, has the effect of significantly reducing usage of rivals' products and hence protecting its own operating system monopoly, it is anticompetitive * * * .

* * * *

3. Agreements with Internet Access Providers [IAPs]

The District Court also condemned as exclusionary Microsoft's agreements with various IAPs. The IAPs include both Internet Service Providers, which offer consumers internet access, and Online Services ("OLSs") such as America Online ("AOL"), which offer proprietary content in addition to internet access and other services. * * *

* * * *

* * * The IAPs constitute one of the two major channels by which browsers can be distributed. Microsoft has exclusive deals with "fourteen of the top fifteen access providers in North America [which] account for a large majority of all Internet access subscriptions in this part of the world." By ensuring that the "majority" of all IAP subscribers are offered IE either as the default browser or as the only browser, Microsoft's deals with the IAPs clearly have a significant effect in preserving its monopoly * * * .

* * * *

VII. CONCLUSION

The judgment of the District Court is affirmed in part * * * . [For other reasons, we] vacate in full the Final Judgment embodying the remedial order, and remand the case to the District Court * * * for further proceedings consistent with this opinion.

CASE PROBLEMS

45–1. In contracts with television networks for the 1982–1985 football seasons, the National Collegiate Athletic Association (NCAA), a nonprofit organization, gave the ABC, CBS, and Turner broadcasting networks exclusive rights to negotiate with NCAA colleges to televise games. The contracts limited the number of games that could be televised by the networks, the number of appearances that any one team could make on television, and the amount of money a school could receive for televising its games. The NCAA plan also required that a certain number of games between small colleges be televised, and it prohibited any individual institution from contracting separately for television coverage of its games. Not surprisingly, the NCAA plan drew criticism from major college teams, which felt that they deserved more network appearances and more money than teams from smaller schools. Their efforts to gain a greater voice in the NCAA television policy, though supported by the College Football Association, proved unsuccessful. As a result, the University of Oklahoma and the University of Georgia brought an action against the NCAA, alleging that its contracts with the television networks violated Sections 1 and 2 of the Sherman Act. Specifically, the NCAA was charged with price fixing, horizontal limitations on production, group boycott, and monopolization. The NCAA argued, among other things, that as a nonprofit organization with "noneconomic" motives, it should not be subject to antitrust laws. How should the United States Supreme Court rule? [*NCAA v. Board of Regents of the University of Oklahoma,* 468 U.S. 85, 104 S.Ct. 2948, 82 L.Ed.2d 70 (1984)]

45–2. American Academic Suppliers, Inc., and Beckley-Cardy, Inc., were wholesalers engaged in the sale of school supplies. American's major markets were largely concentrated in the Midwest; Beckley's markets were on a more national scale. American had been started by Beckley's former president on a small initial investment of less than $500,000. American had also hired a number of salespersons away from Beckley. Initially, American had experienced fairly rapid expansion in the markets in which it competed with Beckley. Beckley responded by giving steep discounts on the prices of some of its products and, according to American, by making disparaging remarks and starting rumors about American's business operations. American sued Beckley, alleging, among other things, that Beckley had violated Section 2 of the Sherman Act by attempting to monopolize the school-supply market. Did Beckley's actions constitute an attempt to monopolize the school-supply market in violation of Section 2 of the Sherman Act? Discuss fully. [*American Academic Suppliers, Inc. v. Beckley-Cardy, Inc.*, 922 F.2d 1317 (7th Cir. 1991)]

45–3. To offer a competitive alternative to health-maintenance organizations and to promote fee-for-service medicine, members of the Maricopa County Medical Society and another medical society established a fee schedule that prescribed the maximum fees that the physicians could charge patients who were insured under specified health-insurance plans. The state of Arizona filed a complaint against the medical societies, alleging that the fee schedule constituted a horizontal price-fixing conspiracy and a *per se* violation of Section 1 of the Sherman Act. The medical societies claimed that the *per se* rule should not apply because (1) the medical societies were professional organizations; (2) the agreement fixed maximum prices, not minimum or uniform prices; (3) the judiciary had insufficient experience in the medical industry to justify applying the *per se* rule; and (4) the fee schedule was justified by its procompetitive effects. The district and appellate courts both agreed with the medical societies that the case should not be judged under the *per se* rule. What will the United States Supreme Court decide? [*Arizona v. Maricopa County Medical Society,* 457 U.S. 332, 102 S.Ct. 2466, 73 L.Ed.2d 48 (1982)]

45–4. Dr. Beard, an osteopathic physician specializing in radiology, worked for G. S. Bucholz, Inc. Bucholz is the exclusive provider of radiological services to Parkview Hospital. When Beard resigned from his position at Bucholz, he had every intention of providing radiological services himself to the patients at Parkview, but the Parkview administration informed him that the hospital had an exclusive contract with Bucholz for the provision of radiological services and that Beard would no longer be permitted to work in Parkview's radiology department. Beard sued Parkview, alleging that the exclusive contract between the hospital and Bucholz was a tying arrangement in violation of Section 1 of the Sherman Act. Parkview claimed that its arrangement with Bucholz ensured responsibility and accountability for the radiology department and guaranteed the availability of services when needed. Under the terms of the agreement between Bucholz and Parkview, Bucholz bills patients directly for the services it provides; Parkview does not get a portion of any fees charged by Bucholz. Does the exclusive contract between Parkview and Bucholz violate Section 1 of the Sherman Act? Discuss fully. [*Beard v. Parkview Hospital,* 912 F.2d 138 (6th Cir. 1990)]

45–5. In an attempt to control costs, dental health insurers adopted a policy that required dentists to submit diagnostic dental X-rays to the insurance company for review before the company would approve payment for treatment. The Indiana Federation of Dentists objected to this policy and adopted a resolution not to submit X-rays as requested by the insurers. Most dentists complied with this resolution and refused to submit X-rays. In 1978, the Federal Trade Commission (FTC) issued a complaint against the federation and found that the joint refusal to submit X-rays was a violation of antitrust laws. According to the FTC, the policy of not submitting X-rays had the effect of encouraging unnecessary dental procedures and raising costs. The federation appealed this finding, and the court of appeals overturned the FTC's ruling. The appellate court contended that the FTC had not shown that the federation's policy had an anticompetitive effect. The FTC then appealed to the United States Supreme Court. How should the Supreme Court rule? Discuss fully. [*FTC v. Indiana Federation of Dentists,* 476 U.S. 447, 106 S.Ct. 2009, 90 L.Ed.2d 445 (1986)]

45–6. Radial keratotomy is a surgical procedure to correct myopia (nearsightedness). In 1980, at the recommendation of the National Eye Institute, the American Academy of Ophthalmology, Inc., issued a press release urging "patients, ophthalmologists and hospitals to approach [radial keratotomy] with caution until additional research is completed." Schachar and several other ophthalmologists who specialized in radial keratotomy claimed that the demand for their services declined following the press release. They brought an action against the academy, contending that the press release constituted an illegal horizontal trade restraint. The district court held that the academy had not violated any antitrust law. What will result on appeal? [*Schachar v. American Academy of Ophthalmology, Inc.*, 870 F.2d 397 (7th Cir. 1989)]

45–7. Hartwell and Business Electronics Corp. were both authorized by Sharp Electronics to sell Sharp electronic products in the Houston, Texas, area. Business Electronics continuously sold Sharp products at below suggested retail prices. Hartwell complained to Sharp Electronics about its rival's price-cutting tactics, and Sharp Electronics eventually terminated Business Electronics's dealership. Business Electronics brought an action, claiming that Sharp and Hartwell had conspired together to create a vertical restraint of trade that was illegal *per se* under Section 1 of the Sherman Act. Does Sharp's termination of Business Electronics's dealership constitute a *per se* violation of Section 1, or should the rule of reason apply? Discuss fully. [*Business Electronics Corp. v. Sharp Electronics Corp.*, 485 U.S. 717, 108 S.Ct. 1515, 99 L.Ed.2d 806 (1988)]

45–8. Harcourt Brace Jovanovich Legal and Professional Publications (HBJ), the nation's largest provider of bar review materials and lecture services, began offering a Georgia bar review course in 1976. It was in direct, and often intense, competition with BRG of Georgia, Inc., the other main provider of bar review courses in Georgia, from 1977 to 1979. In early 1980, HBJ and BRG entered into an agreement that gave BRG the exclusive right to market HBJ's materials in Georgia and to use its trade name, Bar/Bri. The parties agreed that HBJ would not compete with BRG in Georgia and that BRG would not compete with HBJ outside of Georgia. Immediately after the 1980 agreement, the price of BRG's course was increased from $150 to over $400. Jay Palmer, a former law student, brought an action against the two firms, alleging that the 1980 agreement violated Section 1 of the Sherman Act. What will the court decide? Discuss fully. [*Palmer v. BRG of Georgia, Inc.*, 498 U.S. 46, 111 S.Ct. 401, 112 L.Ed.2d 349 (1990)]

45–9. Eastman Kodak Co. has about a 20 percent share of the highly competitive market for high-volume photocopiers and microfilm equipment and controls nearly the entire market for replacement parts for its equipment (which are not interchangeable with parts for other manufacturers' equipment). Prior to 1985, Kodak sold replacement parts for its equipment without significant restrictions. As a result, a number of independent service organizations (ISOs) purchased Kodak parts to use when repairing and servicing Kodak copiers. In 1985, Kodak changed its policy to prevent the ISOs from competing with Kodak's own service organizations. It ceased selling parts to ISOs and refused to sell replacement parts to its customers unless they agreed not to have their equipment serviced by ISOs. In 1987, Image Technical Services, Inc., and seventeen other ISOs sued Kodak, alleging that Kodak's policy was a tying arrangement in violation of Section 1 of the Sherman Act. Assuming that Kodak does not have market power in the market for photocopying and microfilm equipment, does Kodak's restrictive policy constitute an illegal tying arrangement? Does it violate antitrust laws in any way? Discuss fully. [*Eastman Kodak Co. v. Image Technical Services, Inc.*, 504 U.S. 451, 112 S.Ct. 2072, 119 L.Ed.2d 265 (1992)]

45–10. Stelwagon Manufacturing Co. agreed with Tarmac Roofing Systems, Inc., to promote and develop a market for Tarmac's products in the Philadelphia area. In return, Tarmac promised not to sell its products to other area distributors. In 1991, Stelwagon learned that Tarmac had been selling its products to Stelwagon's competitors—the Standard Roofing Co. and the Celotex Corp.—at substantially lower prices. Stelwagon filed a suit against Tarmac in a federal district court. What is the principal factor in determining whether Tarmac violated the Robinson-Patman Act? Did Tarmac violate the act? [*Stelwagon Manufacturing Co. v. Tarmac Roofing Systems, Inc.*, 63 F.3d 1267 (3d Cir. 1995)]

45–11. Great Western Directories, Inc. (GW), is an independent publisher of telephone directory Yellow Pages. GW buys information for its listings from Southwestern Bell Telephone Co. (SBT). Southwestern Bell Corp. owns SBT, as well as Southwestern Bell Yellow Pages (SBYP), which publishes a directory in competition with GW. In June 1988, in some markets, SBT raised the price for its listing information, and SBYP lowered the price for advertising in its Yellow Pages. GW feared that these companies would do the same thing in other local markets, and it would then be too expensive to compete in those markets. Because of this fear, GW left one market and declined to compete in another. Consequently, SBYP had a monopoly in those markets. GW and another independent publisher filed a suit in a federal district court against Southwestern Bell Corp. What antitrust law, if any, did Southwestern Bell Corp. violate? Should the independent companies be entitled to damages? [*Great Western Directories, Inc. v. Southwestern Bell Telephone Co.*, 74 F.3d 613 (5th Cir. 1996)]

45–12. The National Collegiate Athletic Association (NCAA) coordinates the intercollegiate athletic programs of its members by issuing rules and setting standards governing, among other things, the coaching staffs. The NCAA set up a "Cost Reduction Committee" to consider ways to cut the costs of intercollegiate athletics while maintaining competition. The committee included financial aid personnel, intercollegiate athletic administrators, college presidents, university faculty members, and a university chancellor. It was felt that "only a collaborative effort could reduce costs while maintaining a level playing field." The committee proposed a rule to restrict the annual compensation of certain coaches to $16,000. The NCAA adopted the rule. Basketball coaches affected by the rule filed a suit in a federal district court against the NCAA, alleging a violation of Section 1 of the Sherman Antitrust Act. Is the rule a *per se* violation of the Sherman Act, or should it be evaluated under the rule of reason? If it is subject to the rule of reason, is it an illegal restraint of trade? Discuss fully. [*Law v. National Collegiate Athletic Association,* 134 F.3d 1010 (10th Cir. 1998)]

45–13. Public Interest Corp. (PIC) owned and operated television station WTMV-TV in Lakeland, Florida. MCA Television, Ltd., owns and licenses syndicated television programs. The parties entered into a licensing contract with respect to several television shows. MCA conditioned the license on PIC's agreeing to take another show, *Harry and the Hendersons.* PIC agreed to this arrangement, although it would not have chosen to license *Harry* if it did not have to do so to secure the licenses for the other shows. More than two years into the contract, a dispute arose over PIC's payments, and negotiations failed to resolve the dispute. In a letter, MCA suspended PIC's broadcast rights for all of its shows and stated that "[a]ny telecasts of MCA programming by WTMV-TV . . . will be deemed unauthorized and shall constitute an infringement of MCA's copyrights." PIC nonetheless continued broadcasting MCA's programs, with the exception of *Harry.* MCA filed a suit in a federal district court against PIC, alleging breach of contract and copyright infringement. PIC filed a counterclaim, contending in part that MCA's deal was an illegal tying arrangement. Is PIC correct? Explain. [*MCA Television, Ltd. v. Public Interest Corp.,* 171 F.3d 1265 (11th Cir. 1999)]

45–14. To make personal computers (PCs) easier to use, Intel Corporation and other companies developed in 1995 a standard to enable the easy attachment of peripherals (printers and other hardware) to PCs called the Universal Serial Bus (USB) specification. Intel and others formed the Universal Serial Bus Implementers Forum (USB-IF) to promote USB technology and products. Intel, however, makes relatively few USB products and does not make any USB interconnect devices. Multivideo Labs, Inc. (MVL), designed and distributed Active Extension Cables (AECs) to connect peripheral devices to each other or to a PC. The AECs were not USB compliant, a fact that Intel employees told other USB-IF members. Asserting that this caused a "general cooling of the market" for AECs, MVL filed a suit in a federal district court against Intel, claiming in part attempted monopolization in violation of the Sherman Act. Intel filed a motion for summary judgment. How should the court rule, and why? [*Multivideo Labs, Inc. v. Intel Corp.,* __ F.Supp.2d __ (S.D.N.Y. 2000)]

45–15. A Question of Ethics

A group of lawyers in the District of Columbia regularly acted as court-appointed attorneys for indigent defendants in District of Columbia criminal cases. At a meeting of the Superior Court Trial Lawyers Association (SCTLA), the attorneys agreed to stop providing this representation until the district increased their compensation. Their subsequent boycott had a severe impact on the district's criminal justice system, and the District of Columbia gave in to the lawyers' demands for higher pay. After the lawyers had returned to work, the Federal Trade Commission filed a complaint against the SCTLA and four of its officers and, after an investigation, ruled that the SCTLA's activities constituted an illegal group boycott in violation of antitrust laws. [*Federal Trade Commission v. Superior Court Trial Lawyers Association,* 493 U.S. 411, 110 S.Ct. 768, 107 L.Ed.2d 851 (1990)]

1. The SCTLA obviously was aware of the negative impact its decision would have on the district's criminal justice system. Given this fact, do you think the lawyers behaved ethically?
2. On appeal, the SCTLA claimed that its boycott was undertaken to publicize the fact that the attorneys were underpaid and that the boycott thus constituted an expression protected by the First Amendment. Do you agree with this argument?
3. Labor unions have the right to strike when negotiations between labor and management fail. The SCTLA is prohibited from striking. Is it fair to prohibit members of the SCTLA from "striking" against their employer, the District of Columbia, simply because the SCTLA is a professional organization and not a labor union?

E-LINKS

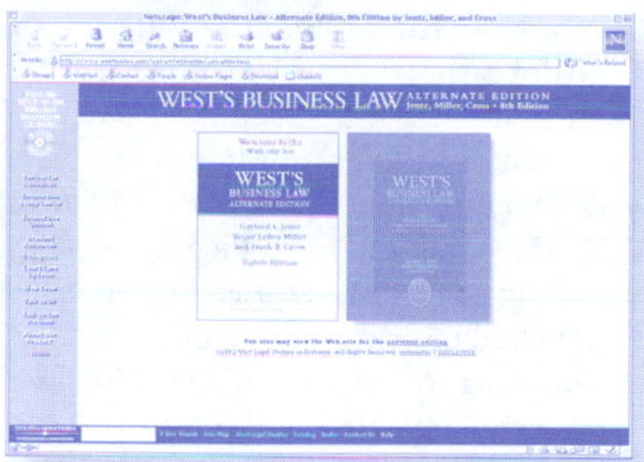

For updated links to resources available on the Web, as well as a variety of other materials, visit this text's Web site at

http://wbl-cs.westbuslaw.com

You can access the Antitrust Division of the U.S. Department of Justice online at

http://www.usdoj.gov

To see the American Bar Association's Web page on antitrust law, go to

http://www.abanet.org/antitrust

The Federal Trade Commission offers an abundance of information on antitrust law, including "A Plain English Guide to Antitrust Laws," at

http://www.ftc.gov/ftc/antitrust.htm

LEGAL RESEARCH EXERCISES ON THE WEB

Go to http://wbl-cs.westbuslaw.com, the Web site that accompanies this text. Select "Interactive Study Center," and then click on "Chapter 45." There you will find the following Internet research exercises that you can perform to learn more about the application of antitrust laws to vertical restraints and monopolization:

Activity 45–1: Vertical Restraints and the Rule of Reason

Activity 45–2: Microsoft and Monopolization

Focus on Legal Reasoning

Milford Lumber, Inc. v. RCB Realty,Inc.

State consumer protection statutes, which are discussed in Chapter 44, are typically focused on protecting consumers from deceptive trade practices on the part of business sellers. In this *Focus on Legal Reasoning,* we examine *Milford Lumber Co. v. RCB Realty, Inc.,*[1] a decision that considered whether such a statute could be applied to afford a right of action to a business *seller* against a deceptive business *buyer.*

Case Background

RCB Realty, Inc., Century 21 Team Berube, and Richard Berube were involved in a joint venture with John Howe to develop property in Windsor Heights in Londonderry, New Hampshire. At Howe's request, Milford Lumber, Inc., agreed to supply building materials to RCB and the others, beginning in November 1995. Milford billed the buyers through an account that Howe had established for his business, Welcome Home.

Through the summer of 1996, Milford continued to supply lumber, but its invoices went unpaid. Berube assured Milford that he was in control of the funds and would arrange for full payment. That never happened. Eventually, Berube asserted that he was not responsible for payment and that Milford should ask Howe for the money.

Milford filed a suit in a New Hampshire state court against RCB, Berube, and Century, alleging, among other things, a violation of the state consumer protection act. The court ruled for Milford. The defendants appealed to the New Hampshire Supreme Court, arguing that the statute's protection applied only to "consumers," not "sellers" such as Milford.

1. 780 A.2d 1259 (N.H. 2001).

Majority Opinion

NADEAU, J. [Justice]

* * * *

On questions of statutory interpretation, this court is the final arbiter of the intent of the legislature as expressed in the words of a statute considered as a whole. We begin by considering the plain meaning of the words of the statute. In conducting our analysis we will focus on the statute as a whole, not on isolated words or phrases. We will not consider what the legislature might have said or add words that the legislature did not include.

The [state Consumer Protection] Act provides that "[i]t shall be unlawful for *any* person to use any unfair method of competition or *any* unfair or deceptive act or practice in the conduct of *any* trade or commerce within this state." The Act broadly defines who may bring a private action as "*[a]ny* person injured by another's use of any method, act or practice declared unlawful under this chapter." "Person" also is defined broadly to include "natural persons, corporations, trusts, partnerships, incorporated or unincorporated associations, and any other legal entity." Thus, the defendants' suggestion that the statute forecloses a seller from a private cause of action is unsupported by a plain reading of the statute's language.

The structure of the statute also militates against the defendants' assertion that the protection provided by the statute is limited to buyers. Although the legislature listed a number of possible violations, it specifically indicated that the list was non-exhaustive. Furthermore, while the legislature exempted certain types of transactions from the provisions of the chapter, it did not exempt private causes of action brought by sellers against deceptive buyers.

In the past, we have noted the difficulty in determining which commercial actions are covered by the Act. Looking to the Massachusetts courts for guidance, we have found the following test helpful: *The objectionable conduct must attain a level of rascality [mischievousness or unscrupulousness] that would raise an eyebrow of someone inured to the rough and tumble of the world of commerce.* [Emphasis added.]

In *Levings v. Forbes & Wallace, Inc.,* 8 Mass.App.Ct. 498, 396 N.E.2d 149 (1979), the court examined the similarly worded Massachusetts consumer protection statute and explicitly rejected the argument that "only buyers, not sellers, may avail themselves * * * " of that statute. Although * * * the Massachusetts statute covers business-to-business transactions, the New Hampshire statute has no separate section for such transactions. It does, however, contain broad language similar to that in [the Massachusetts statute]: "Any person who engages in the conduct of any trade or commerce and who suffers any loss of money or property * * * may * * * bring an action in [state] court * * * ."

The *Levings* court also noted that an abandoned restriction in the original version of the Massachusetts statute specifically limited those who could avail themselves of the statute's protection to "purchasers and lessees." Though the New Hampshire statute is similar in many respects to the Massachusetts statute, our legislature never restricted who could bring suit under the Act to buyers.

Accordingly, we hold that [the New Hampshire statute] does not bar sellers from availing themselves of its protection. We are cognizant that our reading according to the plain meaning of the Act is very broad, and may permit suits beyond what the legislature intended when it promulgated the Act. For instance, when [state] Senator Jacobson commented on the breadth of [the Act], which defines what acts would be unlawful, he said "It was the feeling of the Committee [that the statute] was too broad an authority and did not specify clearly what unfair methods of competition were or what were unfair or deceptive acts or practices in the conduct of any business." Accordingly, the body adopted the non-exhaustive list of examples as to what would be unlawful. The parties offer, and we can find, no additional legislative history that indicates any intention to limit who may bring suit under the Act.

Today's holding, however is narrowed by our decision in Chase v. Dorais, 122 N.H. 600, 601, 448 A.2d 390 (1982). While a seller may bring suit under the Act against a deceptive buyer, the relevant transaction must "take place in a trade or business context."

In order to have prevailed on its Consumer Protection Act claim, the plaintiff must have demonstrated that the buyer defendant's actions are among the unlawful acts proscribed [prohibited] by [the statute]. * * * In this case, the trial court noted that "the multifaceted business relationships presented by the facts of this case trigger the language of this comprehensive" Act. While the court noted that the defendants' actions fell within two particularized types of transactions * * * , its order makes clear that it considered the acts unlawful under the broader definition of unlawful acts provided in [the statute's] introductory paragraph. Specifically, the trial court was concerned that the defendants "kept [their] relationship with Howe intentionally vague and then when it came time to make payment for materials provided by Milford, RCB capitalized upon that vagueness in an attempt to improperly shield itself from liability."

In determining what acts are unlawful under [the New Hampshire statute] we look to the federal courts' interpretation of the Federal Trade Commission Act for guidance. The Federal Trade Commission determines if actions are unfair or deceptive by inquiring:

> (1) whether the practice, without necessarily having been previously considered unlawful, offends public policy as it has been established by statutes, the common law, or otherwise—whether, in other words, it is within at least the penumbra of some common-law statutory or other established concept of unfairness; (2) whether it is immoral, unethical, oppressive, or unscrupulous; (3) whether it causes substantial injury to consumers (or competitors or other businessmen).

The trial court properly used this standard to conclude that the defendants' actions violated the Act.

We have held that an ordinary breach of contract claim does not present an occasion for the remedies under the Consumer Protection Act. The defendants, however, did not simply fail to pay invoices. Rather, they made intentionally vague representations regarding their relationship with Howe to facilitate the use of Howe's account with the plaintiff to procure lumber for the Windsor Heights project. Then, the defendants used those same misrepresentations as a basis for completely disclaiming liability for the goods. It would be harmful for commerce in New Hampshire to allow such unethical and unscrupulous activity to occur. The legislature promulgated the Act to protect citizens engaged in commerce from this type of activity. Accordingly, we affirm the trial court's application of the Act to the facts of this case.

* * * *

The unique facts of this case place the plaintiff squarely within the legislatively prohibited conduct because during a continuing commercial relationship it was subjected to a course of deceptive acts and practices by the defendants.

* * * *

Affirmed.

QUESTIONS FOR ANALYSIS

1. **Legal Analysis.** In the *Milford* case that you have just read, the New Hampshire Supreme Court cites one of its decisions, *Chase v. Dorais*, 122 N.H. 600, 601, 448 A.2d 390 (1982); and a decision of a Massachusetts state intermediate appellate court, *Levings v. Forbes & Wallace, Inc.*, 8 Mass.App.Ct. 498, 396 N.E.2d 149 (1979) (see the *E-Links* feature at the end of Chapter 2 for instructions on how to access the opinions of the state courts). Why did the court in the *Milford* case cite these cases?

2. **Legal Reasoning.** What did the majority in the *Milford* case conclude, and how did the majority interpret the applicable state statute to come to that conclusion?

3. **Ethical Dimensions.** What did the defendants in the *Milford* case do that was "unethical and unscrupulous"?

4. **Implications for the Business Seller.** How does the holding in this case protect business sellers in their dealings with business buyers?

Focus on Legal Reasoning

Westlaw Online Research

Westlaw. Go to this text's companion Web site, at http://wbl-cs.westbuslaw.com, and click on the Westlaw icon. Use your special password to access the full text of this case, including the dissenting opinions. Read through the case, and then answer the following questions.

1. Consider the dissent's position and reasoning in the *Milford* case. What did the dissent conclude, and why?
2. Note the lines immediately preceding the majority's opinion. Who was the attorney for the plaintiff "on the brief and orally"?
3. As suggested in the dissent's statement of the facts in the *Milford* case, why did this plaintiff charge these defendants with violations of the state consumer protection act?

UNIT TEN

Property

CONTENTS

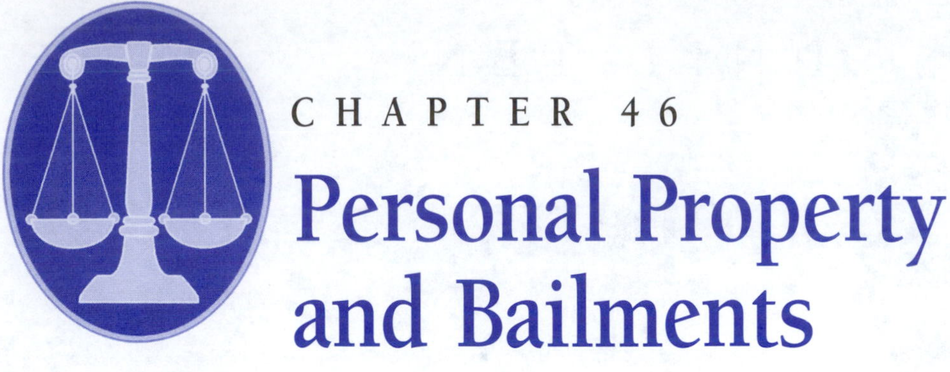

CHAPTER 46
Personal Property and Bailments

PROPERTY CONSISTS OF THE LEGALLY protected rights and interests a person has in anything with an ascertainable value that is subject to ownership. Property would have little value if the law did not define the right to use it, to sell or dispose of it, and to prevent trespassing on it.

In the beginning of this chapter, we examine the basic attributes of personal and real property, the ways in which ownership rights in both of these forms of property can be held, and issues relating to various types of property. The remainder of the chapter focuses on bailment relationships. A *bailment* is created when property is temporarily delivered into the care of another without a transfer of title. This is the distinguishing characteristic of a bailment compared with a sale or a gift—there is no passage of title and no intent to transfer title.

SECTION 1
Property Classification

Property may be divided into real property and personal property. **Real property** (sometimes called *realty* or *real estate*) means the land and everything permanently attached to it. When structures are permanently attached to the land, then everything attached permanently to the structures is also realty. Everything else is **personal property**, or *personalty*. Attorneys sometimes refer to personal property as **chattel**, a term used under the common law to denote all forms of personal property.

Personal property can be tangible or intangible. *Tangible* personal property, such as a television set, heavy construction equipment, or a car, has physical substance. *Intangible* personal property represents some set of rights and interests, but it has no real physical existence. Stocks and bonds are intangible personal property. So, too, are patents, trademarks, and copyrights, as discussed in Chapter 7.

SECTION 2
Fixtures

Certain personal property can become so closely associated with the real property to which it is attached that the law views it as real property. Such property is known as a **fixture**—a thing affixed to realty. A thing is affixed to realty when it is attached to it by roots; embedded in it; or permanently attached by means of cement, plaster, bolts, nails, or screws. The fixture can be physically attached to real property, or attached to another fixture; it can even be an item, such as a statue, that is not physically attached to the land, as long as the owner *intends* the property to be a fixture.

Fixtures are included in the sale of land if the sales contract does not provide otherwise. The sale of a house includes the land and the house and garage on it, as well as the cabinets, plumbing, and windows. Because these are permanently affixed to the property, they are considered to be a part of it. Unless otherwise agreed, however, the curtains and throw rugs are not included. Items such as drapes and window-unit air conditioners are difficult to classify. Thus, a contract for the sale of a house or commercial property should indicate which items of this sort are included in the sale.

THE ROLE OF INTENT

To determine whether a certain item is a fixture, the *intention* of the party who placed the object must be examined. If the facts indicate that the person intended the item to be a fixture, it will be a fixture. When the intent of the party who placed the fixture on the realty is in dispute, the courts usually determine the intent based on either or both of the following factors:

1. If the property attached cannot be removed without causing substantial damage to the remaining realty, it is usually deemed a fixture.
2. If the property attached is so adapted to the rest of the realty as to become a part of it, the property is usually deemed a fixture.

Certain items can only be attached to property permanently; such items are fixtures. It is assumed that the owner intended them to be fixtures, because they had to be permanently attached to the property. A tile floor, cabinets, and carpeting are examples. Also, when an item of property is custom-made for installation on real property, as storm windows are, the item is usually classified as a fixture. The courts assume that owners, in making such installations, intend the objects to become part of their real property.

See Case 46.1 at the end of this chapter. To view the full, unedited case from Westlaw,® go to this text's Web site at **http://wbl-cs.westbuslaw.com**.

Trade Fixtures

An exception to the rule that fixtures are a part of the real property involves **trade fixtures.** A trade fixture is personal property that is installed for a commercial purpose by the tenant (one who rents real property from the owner, or landlord). Trade fixtures remain the property of the tenant, unless removal would irreparably damage the building or realty. A walk-in cooler, for example, purchased and installed by a tenant who uses the premises for a restaurant, is a trade fixture. The tenant can remove the cooler from the premises when the lease terminates but ordinarily must repair any damage that the removal causes or compensate the landlord for the damage.

SECTION 3

Property Ownership

Property ownership can be viewed as a bundle of rights. These rights include the right to possess the property and the right to dispose of the property—by sale, gift, rental, lease, and so on.

Fee Simple

A person who holds the entire bundle of rights is said to be the owner in **fee simple.** The owner in fee simple is entitled to use, possess, and dispose of the property as he or she chooses during his or her lifetime; and on death, the owner's interest in the property descends to his or her heirs. We will look further at ownership in fee simple in Chapter 47, in the context of real property ownership.

Concurrent Ownership

Persons who share ownership rights simultaneously in particular property are said to be concurrent owners. There are two principal types of **concurrent ownership:** *tenancy in common* and *joint tenancy.* Concurrent ownership rights can also be held in a *tenancy by the entirety* or as *community property,* although these latter two types of concurrent ownership are less common.

Tenancy in Common. The term **tenancy in common** refers to a form of co-ownership in which each of two or more persons owns an undivided interest in the property. The interest is undivided because each tenant has rights in the *whole* property. For example, Rosa and Chad own a rare stamp collection as tenants in common. This does not mean that Rosa owns some particular stamps and Chad others. Rather, it means that Rosa and Chad each have rights in the entire collection. (If each person had rights in specific items of property, the interest would be divided.)

On the death of a tenant in common, that tenant's interest in the property passes to his or her heirs. For example, should Rosa die before Chad, a one-half interest in the stamp collection would become the property of Rosa's heirs. If Rosa sold her interest to Fred before she died, Fred and Chad would be co-owners as tenants in common. If Fred died, his interest in the personal property would pass to his heirs, and they in turn would own the property with Chad as tenants in common.

Joint Tenancy. In a **joint tenancy,** each of two or more persons owns an undivided interest in the property, and a deceased joint tenant's interest passes to the surviving joint tenant or tenants. The rights of a surviving joint tenant to inherit a deceased joint tenant's ownership interest, which are referred to as *survivorship rights*, distinguish the joint tenancy from the tenancy in common. A joint tenancy can be terminated before a joint tenant's death by gift or by sale, in which situation the person who receives the property as a gift or who purchases the property becomes a tenant in common, not a joint tenant.

To illustrate: In the preceding example, if Rosa and Chad held their stamp collection in a joint tenancy and if Rosa died before Chad, the entire collection would become Chad's property; Rosa's heirs would receive absolutely no interest in the collection. If Rosa, while living, sold her interest to Fred, however, the sale would terminate the joint tenancy, and Fred and Chad would become owners as tenants in common.

Additionally, a joint tenancy can be transferred by *partition;* that is, the tenants can physically divide the property into equal parts. Because a joint tenant's interest is capable of being conveyed without the consent of the other joint tenants, it can be levied against (seized by court order) to satisfy the tenant's judgment creditors. This characteristic is also a feature of the tenancy in common.

Generally, it is presumed that a co-tenancy is a tenancy in common unless there is a clear intention to establish a joint tenancy. Thus, language such as "to Jerrold and Eva as joint tenants with right of survivorship, and not as tenants in common" would be necessary to create a joint tenancy.

Tenancy by the Entirety. A **tenancy by the entirety** typically is created by a conveyance (transfer) of real property to a husband and wife. It is distinguished from a joint tenancy by the inability of either spouse to transfer separately his or her interest during his or her lifetime without the consent of the other spouse. In some states where statutes give the wife the right to convey her property, this form of concurrent ownership has been effectively abolished. A divorce, either spouse's death, or mutual agreement will terminate a tenancy by the entirety. A tenancy by the entirety is less common today than it once was.

Community Property. Only a limited number of states[1] allow property to be owned by a married couple as **community property.** If property is held as community property, each spouse technically owns an undivided one-half interest in the property. This type of ownership applies to most property acquired by the husband or the wife during the course of the marriage. It generally does not apply to property acquired prior to the marriage or to property acquired by gift or inheritance during the marriage. After a divorce, community property is divided equally in some states and according to the discretion of the court in other states.

1. These states include Alaska, Arizona, California, Idaho, Louisiana, Nevada, New Mexico, Texas, Washington, and Wisconsin. Puerto Rico allows property to be owned as community property as well.

SECTION 4

Acquiring Ownership of Personal Property

Ownership of personal property can be acquired through purchase, possession, production, gift, will or inheritance, accession, and confusion. Purchasing personal property, which was discussed in Chapters 18 through 23, is one of the most common ways of acquiring or transferring personalty. The other forms of acquisition are discussed below.

POSSESSION

One example of acquiring ownership through possession is the capture of wild animals. Wild animals belong to no one in their natural state, and the first person to take possession of a wild animal normally owns it. The killing of a wild animal amounts to assuming ownership of it. Merely being in hot pursuit does not give title, however. There are two exceptions to this basic rule. First, any wild animals captured by a trespasser are the property of the landowner, not the trespasser. The fish in a pond on a farmer's land, for example, are the farmer's property, not the property of a trespasser who fishes for and catches them. Second, if wild animals are captured or killed in violation of wild game statutes, the capturer does not obtain title to the animals; rather, the state does.

Those who find lost or abandoned property also can acquire ownership rights through mere possession of the property, as will be discussed later in this chapter. (Real property can also be acquired through possession—see the discussion of adverse possession in the next chapter.)

PRODUCTION

Production is another means of acquiring ownership of personal property. As discussed in Chapter 7, writers, inventors, manufacturers, and others who produce personal property may thereby acquire title to it. (In some situations, though, as when a researcher is hired to invent a new product or technique, the researcher may not own what is produced—see Chapter 31.)

GIFT

A **gift** is another fairly common means of acquiring or transferring ownership of property. A gift is essentially a *voluntary* transfer of property ownership. It is not supported by legally sufficient consideration (see Chapter 11), because the very essence of a gift is giving without consideration. Gifts can be made during a person's lifetime, or they can be made in a last will and testament. A gift made by will is called a *testamentary* gift.

There are three requirements for an effective gift—delivery, donative intent on the part of the *donor* (the one giving the gift), and acceptance by the *donee* (the one receiving the gift). Each of these requirements is discussed below. Until these three requirements are met, no effective gift has been made. For example, suppose that your aunt tells you that she is going to give you a new Mercedes-Benz for your next birthday. This is simply a promise to make a gift. It is not considered a gift until the Mercedes-Benz is delivered.

Delivery. Delivery is obvious in most cases, but some objects cannot be relinquished physically. Then the question of delivery depends on the surrounding circumstances. When the physical object itself cannot be delivered, a symbolic delivery, or **constructive delivery**, will be sufficient.

Constructive delivery does not confer actual possession of the object in question. It is a general term for all those acts that the law holds to be equivalent to acts of real delivery. Suppose that you want to make a gift of various old rare coins that you have stored in a safe-deposit box at your bank. You certainly cannot deliver the box itself to the donee, and you do not want to take the coins out of the bank. Instead, you can simply deliver the key to the box to the donee and authorize the donee's access to the box and its contents. This constitutes symbolic, or constructive, delivery of the contents of the box. Delivery of intangible personal property, such as stock-ownership rights, must be accomplished by symbolic or constructive delivery, such as by the delivery of a stock certificate.

An effective delivery also requires giving up *complete dominion*[2] *and control* over the subject matter of the gift. The outcome of disputes often turns on the retaining or relinquishing of control. The Internal Revenue Service scrutinizes transactions between relatives when one has given income-producing property to the other. A relative who does not relinquish complete control over a piece of property will have to pay taxes on the income from that property.

Delivery can be accomplished by means of a third person. The third person may be the agent of the donor or of the donee. If the person is the agent of the donor, the gift is effective when the agent delivers the property to the donee. If, in contrast, the third person is the agent of the donee, the gift is effective when the donor delivers the property to the donee's agent.[3] When there is doubt as to whose agent the third party is, he or she is generally presumed to be the agent of the donor. Naturally, no delivery is necessary if the gift is already in the hands of the donee. All that is necessary to complete the gift in such a case is the required intent and acceptance by the donee.

Donative Intent. Donative intent (the intent to make a gift) is determined from the language of the donor and the surrounding circumstances. When a gift is challenged in court, for example, the court may look at the relationship between the parties and the size of the gift in relation to the donor's other assets. Donative intent might be questioned by a court if the gift was made to an archenemy. Similarly, when a person has given away a large portion of his or her assets, the court will scrutinize the transactions to determine whether the donor was mentally competent or whether fraud or duress was involved.

Westlaw. See Case 46.2 at the end of this chapter. To view the full, unedited case from Westlaw,® go to this text's Web site at **http://wbl-cs.westbuslaw.com**.

Acceptance. The final requirement of a valid gift is acceptance by the donee. This rarely presents any problems, because most donees readily accept their gifts. The courts generally assume acceptance unless shown otherwise.

2. The term *dominion* in this sense refers to absolute ownership rights in, and control over, property. One who has dominion over property both possesses and has title to the property.

3. *Bickford v. Mattocks*, 95 Me. 547, 50 A.894 (1901).

Gifts *Inter Vivos* and Gifts *Causa Mortis.* A gift made during the donor's lifetime is called a **gift *inter vivos.*** A **gift *causa mortis*** is made in contemplation of imminent death. To be effective, a gift *causa mortis* must meet the three requirements of delivery, intent, and acceptance. Gifts *causa mortis* do not become absolute until the donor dies from the contemplated illness or disease. A gift *causa mortis* is revocable at any time up to the death of the donor and is automatically revoked if the donor recovers.

Suppose that Steck is to be operated on for a cancerous tumor. Before the operation, he delivers an envelope to a close business associate. The envelope contains a letter saying, "I realize my days are numbered, and I want to give you this check for $1 million in the event of my death from this operation." The business associate cashes the check. The surgeon performs the operation and removes the tumor. Steck recovers fully. Several months later, Steck dies from a heart attack that is totally unrelated to the operation. If Steck's personal representative (the party charged with administering Steck's estate) tries to recover the $1 million, normally she will succeed. The gift *causa mortis* is automatically revoked if the donor recovers. The *specific event* that was contemplated in making the gift was death from a particular operation. Because Steck's death was not the result of this event, the gift is revoked, and the $1 million passes to Steck's estate.[4]

Will or Inheritance

Ownership of property may be transferred by will or by inheritance under state statutes. These types of transfers will be dealt with at length in Chapter 50.

Accession

Accession means "something added." It occurs when someone adds value to a piece of personal property by use of either labor or materials. Generally, there is no dispute about who owns the property after accession has occurred, especially when the accession is accomplished with the owner's consent. For example, a Corvette-customizing specialist comes to Hoshi's house. Hoshi has all the materials necessary. The customizing specialist uses them to add a unique bumper to Hoshi's Corvette. Hoshi simply pays the customizer for the value of the labor, obviously retaining title to the property.

Ownership can be at issue after the occurrence of an accession if (1) a party has wrongfully caused the accession or (2) the materials added or labor expended greatly increases the value of the property or changes the identity of the property. Some general rules can be applied in these situations.

When accession occurs without the owner's consent, the courts will tend to favor the owner over the improver—the one who improves the property—provided the accession is done in bad faith. This is true even if the value of the property is increased substantially. In addition, many courts will deny the improver (wrongdoer) any compensation for the value added; for example, a car thief who puts new tires on the stolen car will obviously not be compensated for the value of the new tires when the rightful owner recovers the car.

If the accession is performed in good faith, however, even without the owner's consent, ownership of the improved item most often depends on whether the accession has increased the value of the property or changed its identity. The greater the increase, the more likely that ownership will pass to the improver. Obviously, when this occurs, the improver must compensate the original owner for the value the property had prior to the accession. If the increase in value is not sufficient for ownership to be passed to the improver, most courts require the owner to compensate the improver for the value added.

Confusion

Confusion is defined as the commingling of goods so that one person's personal property cannot be distinguished from another's. It frequently involves goods that are fungible.[5] *Fungible goods* are goods consisting of identical particles, such as grain or oil. For example, if two farmers put their number 2 grade winter wheat into the same silo, confusion will occur. When goods are confused due to a wrongful and willful act and the wrongdoer is unable to prove what percentage of the confused goods belongs to him or her, the innocent party ordinarily acquires title to the whole.

This rule does not apply when confusion occurs by agreement, honest mistake, or the act of some third party. When any of these three events occurs, the owners all share ownership as tenants in common. Suppose that you enter into a cooperative arrangement with five other farmers in your local

4. *Brind v. International Trust Co.*, 66 Colo. 60, 179 P. 148 (1919).

5. Fungible goods are defined in UCC 1–201(17).

community of Midway, Iowa. Each fall, everyone harvests the same amount of number 2 yellow corn. The corn is stored in silos that are held by the cooperative. Each of you owns one-sixth of the total corn in the silos. If anything happens to the corn, you will bear the loss in equal proportions of one-sixth.

Now suppose you share ownership in some other proportion. Often, owners do not have equal interests. In such cases, the owners must keep careful records of their respective proportions. If a dispute over ownership or loss arises, the courts will presume that everyone has an equal interest in the goods. Therefore, you must be prepared to prove that you own more or less than an equal part.

Suppose that you own two-thirds of the corn in the Midway co-op silos. Further assume that the silos are damaged by a tornado and thunderstorm. How much have you lost if one-half of the corn is blown away by the storm? You have lost one-half of your two-thirds, or one-third of the total. When corn is stored by several owners, each owning a different proportion of the total, loss is shared proportionally.

SECTION 5

Mislaid, Lost, or Abandoned Property

As already noted, one of the methods of acquiring ownership of property is to possess it. Simply finding something and holding onto it, however, does not *necessarily* entitle the finder to it. Different rules apply, depending on whether the property was mislaid, lost, or abandoned.

Mislaid Property

Property that has been voluntarily placed somewhere by the owner and then inadvertently forgotten is **mislaid property.** Suppose that you go to the theater and leave your opera glasses at the concession stand. The glasses are mislaid property, and the theater owner is entrusted with the duty of reasonable care for the goods. When mislaid property is found, the finder does not obtain title to the goods.[6] Instead, the owner of the place where the property was mislaid becomes the caretaker of the property, because it is highly likely that the true owner will return.[7]

Lost Property

Property that is *involuntarily* left is **lost property.** A finder of lost property can claim title to the property against the whole world, *except the true owner.* If the true owner demands that the lost property be returned, the finder must return it. If a third party attempts to take possession of lost property from a finder, the third party cannot assert a better title than the finder.

When a finder knows who the true owner of property is and fails to return the property to that person, the finder is guilty of a tort known as *conversion* (see Chapter 5). Finally, many states require the finder to make a reasonably diligent search to locate the true owner of lost property.

Suppose Kamal works in a large library at night. After work, as he is walking through the courtyard of the library, he finds a piece of gold jewelry that contains several apparently precious stones. Kamal decides to take it to a jewelry store to have it appraised. While pretending to weigh the jewelry, an employee of the jeweler removes several of the stones. If Kamal brings an action to recover the stones from the jeweler, he will win, because he found lost property and holds valid title against everyone except the true owner. Because the property was lost and not mislaid, the owner of the library is not the caretaker of the jewelry. Instead, Kamal acquires title good against the whole world (except the true owner).[8]

Many states have **estray statutes** to encourage and facilitate the return of property to its true owner and to reward the finder for honesty if the property remains unclaimed. Such statutes provide an incentive for finders to report their discoveries by making it possible for them, after passage of a specified period of time, to acquire legal title to the property they have found if the property remains unclaimed. The statutes usually require the county clerk to advertise the property in an attempt to help the owner recover what has been lost. Some preliminary questions must always be resolved before the estray statute can be employed. The item must be lost property, not mislaid or abandoned property. When the situation indicates that the property was

6. The finder is an involuntary bailee—see the discussion of bailments later in this chapter.

7. The owner of the place where property is mislaid is a bailee with right of possession against all except the true owner.

8. See *Armory v. Delamirie*, 93 Eng. Rep. 664 (K.B. [King's Bench] 1722). If Kamal had found the jewelry during the course of his employment, however, his employer would be the involuntary bailee. Further, many courts now say that when lost property is recovered in a private place, the owner of the place, not the finder, becomes the bailee (even if the finder is not a trespasser).

probably lost and not mislaid or abandoned, as a matter of public policy, loss is presumed, and the estray statute applies.

ABANDONED PROPERTY

Property that has been *discarded* by the true owner, who has *no intention* of claiming title to it, is referred to as abandoned property. Someone who finds **abandoned property** acquires title to it, and such title is good against the whole world, *including the original owner.* The owner of lost property who eventually gives up any further attempt to find it is frequently held to have abandoned the property.

For example, assume that Aleka is driving with the windows down in her car. Somewhere along her route, a valuable scarf blows out the window. She retraces her route and searches for the scarf but cannot find it. She finally decides that further search is futile and proceeds to her destination five hundred miles away. Six months later, Frye, a hitchhiker, finds the scarf. Frye has acquired title, which is good even against Aleka. By completely giving up her search, Aleka abandoned the scarf just as effectively as if she had intentionally discarded it.

A trespasser who finds an item of abandoned personal property does not acquire title to it, however. The owner of the real property on which it was found does. The same rule applies if the property was lost. Similarly, if a landowner employs a crew to install an underground septic tank, for example, and the crew digs up a cache of pioneer relics, the landowner has first claim to the relics, because they were buried in his or her ground.

In contrast, if the crew unearths money, gold, silver, or bullion (instead of pewter dishes, tin cups, brass buttons, and old muskets), the find may be classified as **treasure trove** (treasure that is found), and the crew may be able to keep it. In the United States, in the absence of a statute, a finder has title to treasure trove against all but the true owner. (In Great Britain, the Crown gets it.) Generally, to constitute treasure trove, property need not have been buried—it can have been hidden in some other private place, such as behind loose bricks in an old chimney—but its owner must be unknown, and its finders must not have been trespassing.

See Case 46.3 at the end of this chapter. To view the full, unedited case from Westlaw,® go to this text's Web site at **http://wbl-cs.westbuslaw.com**.

SECTION 6

Bailments

A **bailment** is formed by the delivery of personal property, without transfer of title, by one person (called a **bailor**) to another (called a **bailee**), usually under an agreement for a particular purpose—for example, to loan, store, repair, or transport the property. On completion of the purpose, the bailee is obligated to return the bailed property in the same or better condition to the bailor or a third person or to dispose of it as directed.

Most bailments are created by agreement, but not necessarily by contract, because in many bailments not all of the elements of a contract (such as mutual assent and consideration) are present. For example, if you loan your business law text to a friend, a bailment is created, but not by contract, because there is no consideration. Most commercial bailments, such as the delivery of your suit to the cleaners for dry cleaning, are based on contract, however. A bailment is distinguished from a sale or a gift in that possession is transferred without passage of title or intent to transfer title. In a sale or a gift, title is transferred from the seller or donor to the buyer or donee.

The law of bailments applies to many routine personal and business transactions. When individuals deal with bailments, whether they realize it or not, they are subject to the obligations and duties that arise from the bailment relationship. The number, scope, and importance of bailments created daily in the business community and in everyday life make it desirable to understand the elements necessary for the creation of a bailment and to know what rights, duties, and liabilities flow from bailments.

ELEMENTS OF A BAILMENT

Not all transactions involving the delivery of property from one person to another create a bailment. For such a transfer to become a bailment, the following three elements must be present:

1. Personal property.
2. Delivery of possession (without title).
3. Agreement that the property be returned to the bailor or otherwise disposed of according to its owner's directions.

Personal Property Requirement. Only personal property is bailable; there can be no bailment of persons. Although a bailment of your luggage is created when it is transported by an airline, as a passenger you are not the subject of a bailment. Also, you cannot bail realty; thus, leasing your house to a tenant is not a bailment. Bailments commonly involve *tangible* items—jewelry, cattle, automobiles, and the like. *Intangible* personal property, such as promissory notes and shares of corporate stock, may also be bailed.

Delivery of Possession. *Delivery of possession* means transfer of possession of property to the bailee. Two requirements must be met for delivery of possession to occur:

1. The bailee must be given exclusive possession and control over the property.
2. The bailee must *knowingly* accept the personal property.[9] In other words, the bailee must *intend* to exercise control over it.

If either delivery of possession or knowing acceptance is lacking, there is no bailment relationship. For example, suppose that Sudi is in a hurry to catch his plane. He has a package he wants to check at the airport. He arrives at the airport check-in station, but the person in charge has gone on a coffee break. Sudi decides to leave the package on the counter. Even though there has clearly been physical transfer of the package, the person in charge of the check-in station has not knowingly accepted the personal property. Therefore, there has been no effective delivery. The result is the same in the following example: Delacroix checks her coat at a restaurant. In the coat pocket is a $20,000 diamond necklace. In accepting the coat, the bailee does not *knowingly* also accept the necklace.

Two types of delivery—*physical* and *constructive*—will result in the bailee's exclusive possession of and control over the property. Physical delivery, as the phrase implies, occurs when the property is actually, physically transferred to the bailee. For example, if a restaurant patron checks a coat with an attendant, the property has been physically delivered to the bailee. As discussed earlier, in the context of gifts, constructive delivery is a substitute, or symbolic, delivery. What is delivered to the bailee is not the actual property bailed (such as a car) but something so related to the property (such as the car keys) that the requirement of delivery is satisfied.

In certain unique situations, a bailment is found despite the apparent lack of the requisite elements of control and knowledge. One example of such a situation occurs when the bailee acquires the property accidentally or by mistake—as in finding someone else's lost or mislaid property. A bailment is created even though the bailor did not voluntarily deliver the property to the bailee. Such bailments are referred to as *constructive* or *involuntary* bailments.

THE BAILMENT AGREEMENT

A bailment agreement can be *express* or *implied*. Although no written agreement is required for bailments of less than one year (that is, the Statute of Frauds does not apply—see Chapter 14), it is a good idea to have a written agreement, especially when valuable property is involved.

The bailment agreement expressly or impliedly provides for the return of the bailed property to the bailor or to a third person, or provides for disposal by the bailee. The agreement presupposes that the bailee will return the identical goods originally given by the bailor. In certain types of bailments, however, such as bailments of fungible goods,[10] only equivalent property must be returned. For example, if Hobson stores his grain (fungible goods) in Kwam's grain elevator, a bailment is created. But at the end of the storage period, the grain elevator company is not obligated to return to Hobson exactly the same grain that was stored. As long as the company returns goods of the same type, grade, and quantity, the company—the bailee—has performed its obligation.

SECTION 7

Ordinary Bailments

Bailments are either *ordinary* or *special (extraordinary)*. There are three types of ordinary bailments. The

9. We are dealing here with *voluntary bailments*. Under some circumstances, regardless of whether a person intentionally accepts possession of someone else's personal property, the law imposes on him or her the obligation to redeliver it. For example, if property is accidentally left in another's possession without negligence on the part of its owner, the person in whose possession it has been left may be responsible for its return. This is referred to as an *involuntary bailment*.

10. As mentioned earlier, *fungible goods* are goods that consist of identical particles, such as wheat. See UCC 1–201(17).

distinguishing feature among them is which party receives a benefit from the bailment. Ultimately, the courts may use this factor to determine the standard of care required of the bailee while in possession of the personal property, and this factor will dictate the rights and liabilities of the parties. The three types of ordinary bailments are as follows:

1. *Bailment for the sole benefit of the bailor.* This is a type of gratuitous bailment (one that involves no consideration) for the convenience and benefit of the bailor. The bailee is liable only for gross negligence. (Negligence is discussed in Chapter 5.)
2. *Bailment for the sole benefit of the bailee.* This is typically a loan of an article to a person (the bailee) solely for that person's convenience and benefit. The bailee is liable for even slight negligence.
3. *Bailment for the mutual benefit of the bailee and the bailor.* This is the most common kind of bailment and involves some form of compensation for storing items or holding property. It is a contractual bailment and is often referred to as a bailment for hire. The bailee is liable for ordinary negligence, or the failure to observe ordinary care, which is the care that a reasonably prudent person would use under the circumstances.

RIGHTS OF THE BAILEE

In a bailment situation, both the bailee and the bailor have rights and duties. Implicit in the bailment agreement is the right of the bailee to take possession, to utilize the property for accomplishing the purpose of the bailment, to receive some form of compensation (unless the bailment is intended to be gratuitous), and to limit his or her liability for the bailed goods. Depending on the nature of the bailment and the terms of the bailment agreement, these rights of the bailee are present (with some limitations) in varying degrees in all bailment transactions.

Rights of Possession. A hallmark of the bailment agreement is that the bailee acquires the *right to control and possess the property temporarily.* The meaning of *temporary* depends on the terms of the bailment agreement. If a specified period is expressed in the bailment agreement, the bailment is continuous for that time period. Earlier termination by the bailor is a breach of contract (if the bailment involves consideration), and the bailee can recover damages from the bailor. If no duration is specified, the bailment ends when either the bailor or the bailee so demands and possession of the bailed property is returned to the bailor.

A bailee's right of possession, even though temporary, permits the bailee to recover damages from any third persons for damage or loss to the property. For example, No-Spot Dry Cleaners sends all suede leather garments to Cleanall Company for special processing. If Cleanall loses or damages any leather goods, No-Spot has the right to recover against Cleanall.

If the personal property is stolen from the bailee during the bailment, the bailee has a legal right to regain possession of (to recapture) the goods or to obtain damages from any third person who has wrongfully interfered with the bailee's possessory rights.

Right to Use Bailed Property. Naturally, the extent to which bailees can use the personal property entrusted to them depends on the terms of the bailment contract. When no provision is made, the extent of use depends on how necessary it is for the goods to be at the bailee's disposal for the ordinary purpose of the bailment to be carried out. When leasing drilling machinery, for example, the bailee is expected to use the equipment to drill. In contrast, when providing long-term storage for a car, the bailee is not expected to use the car, because the ordinary purpose of a storage bailment does not include use of the property (unless an emergency dictates such use to protect the car).

Right of Compensation. A bailee has a right to be compensated as provided for in the bailment agreement, to be reimbursed for costs and services rendered in the keeping of the bailed property, or both. In mutual-benefit bailments, the amount of compensation is often expressed in the bailment contract. For example, in the rental (bailment) of a car, the contract provides for charges on the basis of time, mileage, or a combination of the two, plus other possible charges. In nonrental bailments, such as when a car is left at a service station for an oil change, the bailee makes a service charge for the work performed.

Even in a gratuitous bailment, a bailee has a right to be reimbursed or compensated for costs incurred in the keeping of the bailed property. For example, Hetta loses her pet dog, which is found by Jesse. Jesse takes Hetta's dog to his home and feeds it. Even though he takes good care of the dog, it becomes ill, and a veterinarian is called. Jesse pays the bill for the veterinarian's services and the medicine. He is normally entitled to be reimbursed by Hetta for these reasonable costs incurred in the keeping of her dog.

To enforce the right of compensation, the bailee has a right to place a *possessory* lien (claim) on the specific bailed property until he or she has been fully compensated. This lien on specific bailed property is sometimes referred to as a **bailee's lien,** or artisan's lien. The lien is effective only so long as the bailee has not agreed to extend credit to the bailor and the bailee retains possession over the bailed property.

If the bailor refuses to pay or cannot pay the charges (compensation), the bailee is entitled in most states to foreclose on the lien. This means that the bailee can sell the property and be paid out of the proceeds for the amount owed from the bailment, returning any excess to the bailor.

For example, Sarito takes his car to the garage and enters into an agreement for repairs. The repairs are to be paid for in cash. On completion of the repairs, the garage tenders Sarito his car, but because of unexpected bills, he cannot pay the garage. The garage has a right to retain possession of Sarito's car, exercising a bailee's lien. Unless Sarito can make arrangements for payment, the garage will normally be entitled to sell the car to be compensated for the repairs.

Right to Limit Liability. In ordinary bailments, bailees have the right to limit their liability by type of risk, by monetary amount, or both, as long as (1) the limitations are called to the attention of the bailor and (2) the limitations are not against public policy.

Any enforceable limitation on liability imposed by the ordinary bailee must be brought to the bailor's attention. Although the bailee is not required to read orally or interpret the limitation for the bailor, the bailor must in some way know of the limitation. Thus, a sign in Nikolai's garage stating that Nikolai will not be responsible "for loss due to theft, fire, or vandalism" may or may not be held to be notice to the bailor. Whether the notice will be effective will depend on the size of the sign, its location, and any other circumstances affecting the likelihood of its being noticed by Nikolai's patrons. The same holds true with limitations placed on the back of identification receipts (stubs) for parked cars, checked coats, or stored bailed goods. Most courts require additional notice, because the bailor rarely reads the receipt and usually treats it merely as an identification number to be used when reclaiming the bailed goods.

Even if the bailor has received notice, certain types of disclaimers of liability are considered to be against public policy and therefore illegal. Clauses that limit a person's liability for his or her own wrongful acts, called *exculpatory clauses,* are carefully scrutinized by the courts, and in bailments they are often held to be illegal. The classic illustration of an exculpatory clause is found on parking receipts: "We assume no risk for damage to or loss of automobile or its contents regardless of cause. It is agreed that the vehicle owner assumes all such risks." Even though the language may vary, if the bailee attempts to exclude liability for the bailee's own negligence, the result is the same—the clause is unenforceable because it is against public policy. This is especially true in the case of bailees providing quasi-public services, such as warehousers (discussed later in this chapter).

DUTIES OF THE BAILEE

The bailee has two basic responsibilities: (1) to take appropriate care of the property and (2) to surrender or dispose of the property at the end of the bailment. The bailee's duties are based on a mixture of tort law and contract law.

The Duty of Care. The bailee must exercise reasonable care in preserving the bailed property. The duty of care involves the standards and principles of tort law discussed in Chapter 5. What constitutes reasonable care in a bailment situation normally depends on the nature and specific circumstances of the bailment. Traditionally, courts have determined the appropriate standard of care on the basis of the type of bailments involved. In a bailment for the sole benefit of the bailor, for example, the bailee need exercise only a slight degree of care. In a bailment for the sole benefit of the bailee, however, the bailee must exercise great care. In a mutual-benefit bailment, courts normally will impose a reasonable standard of care—that is, the bailee must exercise the degree of care that a reasonable and prudent person would exercise in the same circumstances. Exhibit 46–1 on the next page illustrates these concepts.

Determining whether a bailee exercised an appropriate degree of care is usually a question of fact. This means that the trier of fact (a judge or a jury) weighs the facts of a particular situation and concludes that the bailee did or did not exercise the requisite degree of care at the time the loss or damage occurred. A bailee's failure to exercise appropriate care in handling the bailor's property results in tort liability.

EXHIBIT 46–1 DEGREE OF CARE REQUIRED OF A BAILEE

Bailment for the Sole Benefit of the Bailor	Mutual-Benefit Bailment	Bailment for the Sole Benefit of the Bailee
DEGREE OF CARE →		
SLIGHT	REASONABLE	GREAT

Duty to Return Bailed Property. At the end of the bailment, the bailee normally must relinquish the identical undamaged property (unless it is fungible) to either the bailor or someone the bailor designates or must otherwise dispose of it as directed. This is usually a *contractual* duty arising from the bailment agreement (contract). Failure to give up possession at the time the bailment ends is a breach of contract and could result in the tort of conversion.

Generally, the bailee has a duty to return the bailed goods to the bailor. A bailee may be liable if the goods being held or delivered are given to the wrong person. Hence, a bailee must be satisfied that a person (other than the bailor) to whom the goods are being delivered is the actual owner or has authority from the owner to take possession of the goods. Should the bailee deliver in error, then the bailee may be liable for conversion or misdelivery.

Presumption of Negligence. Sometimes, the duty of care and the duty to return bailed property are combined to determine the bailee's liability. At the end of the bailment, a bailee has the duty to return the bailor's property in the condition in which it was received (allowing for ordinary wear and aging). In some cases, the bailor can sue the bailee in tort for damage to or loss of goods on the theory of negligence or conversion. There are times, though, when it is not possible for the bailor to discover and prove what specific acts of negligence or conversion committed by the bailee caused damage or loss to the property.[11] Thus, the law of bailments recognizes a rule whereby a *presumption* that the bailee is guilty of negligence or conversion will be made if the bailee fails to return the property or dispose of it in accordance with the bailor's instructions or if the bailee returns the property in a damaged condition. Once this is shown, the bailee must prove that he or she was not at fault. A bailee who is able to *rebut* (contradict) the presumption is not liable to the bailor.

When damage to goods is of the type that normally results only from someone's negligence, and when the bailee had full control of the goods, it is more likely than not that the damage was caused by the bailee's negligence. Therefore, the bailee's negligence is presumed.

See Case 46.4 at the end of this chapter. To view the full, unedited case from Westlaw,® go to this text's Web site at **http://wbl-cs.westbuslaw.com**.

RIGHTS AND DUTIES OF THE BAILOR

A bailee's duties and a bailor's rights are complementary. In other words, the rights of the bailor are essentially the same as the duties of a bailee, and vice versa.

Rights of the Bailor. A bailor has the right to expect the following:

1. The property will be protected with reasonable care while in the possession of the bailee.
2. The bailee will utilize the property as agreed in the bailment agreement (or not at all).
3. The property will be relinquished at the conclusion of the bailment according to directions given by the bailor.
4. The bailee will not convert (alter) the goods except as agreed.
5. The bailor will not be bound by any limitations on the bailee's liability unless these limitations are known and are enforceable by law.
6. Repairs or service on the property will be completed without defective workmanship.

11. The basic formula for finding negligence requires proof that (1) a duty exists, (2) a breach of that duty occurred, (3) the breach is the proximate cause of damage or loss, and (4) actual loss or damage resulted.

Duties of the Bailor. Obviously, a bailor has a duty to compensate the bailee either as agreed or as reimbursement for costs incurred by the bailee in keeping the bailed property. A bailor also has an all-encompassing duty to provide the bailee with goods or chattel that are free from hidden defects that could injure the bailee. This duty translates into two rules:

1. In a *mutual-benefit bailment,* the bailor must notify the bailee of all known defects and any hidden defects that the bailor knew of or could have discovered with reasonable diligence and proper inspection.
2. In a *bailment for the sole benefit of the bailee,* the bailor must notify the bailee of any known defects.

The bailor's duty to reveal defects is based on a negligence theory of tort law. A bailor who fails to give the appropriate notice is liable to the bailee and to any other person who might reasonably be expected to come into contact with the defective article.

For example, assume that Rentco (the bailor) leases four tractors to Hal Iverson. Unknown to Rentco (but discoverable by reasonable inspection), the brake mechanism on one of the tractors is defective at the time the bailment is made. Iverson uses the defective tractor without knowledge of the brake problem and is injured along with two other field workers when the tractor rolls out of control. Rentco is liable on a negligence theory for injuries sustained by Iverson and the two others.

This is the analysis: Rentco has a mutual-benefit bailment and a *duty* to notify Iverson of the discoverable brake defect. Rentco's failure to notify is the *proximate cause* of injuries to farm workers who might be expected to use, or have contact with, the tractor. Therefore, Rentco is liable for the resulting injuries.

A bailor can also incur warranty liability based on contract law (see Chapter 22) for injuries resulting from bailment of defective articles. Property leased by a bailor must be *fit for the intended purpose of the bailment.* The bailor's knowledge of or ability to discover any defects is immaterial. Warranties of fitness arise by law in sales contracts and have been applied by judicial interpretation in cases involving bailments "for hire." Article 2A of the UCC extends implied warranties of merchantability and fitness for a particular purpose to bailments whenever those bailments include rights to use the bailed goods.[12]

12. UCC 2A–212, 2A–213.

TERMINATION OF BAILMENTS

Bailments for a specific term end when the stated period lapses. When no duration is specified, the bailment can be terminated at any time by the following events:

1. The mutual agreement of both parties.
2. A demand by either party.
3. The completion of the purpose of the bailment.
4. An act by the bailee that is inconsistent with the terms of the bailment.
5. The operation of law.

SECTION 8

Special Types of Bailments

Most of this discussion of bailments has concerned ordinary bailments, or bailments in which bailees are expected to exercise ordinary care in the handling of bailed property. Some bailment transactions warrant special consideration. These include bailments in which the bailee's duty of care is extraordinary—that is, his or her liability for loss or damage to the property is absolute—as is generally true in cases involving common carriers and innkeepers. Warehouse companies have the same duty of care as ordinary bailees; but like carriers, they are subject to extensive coverage of federal and state laws, including the Article 7 of the Uniform Commercial Code (UCC).

DOCUMENTS OF TITLE AND ARTICLE 7

A shipment or storage of goods may be covered by a *bill of lading,* a *warehouse receipt,* or a *delivery order.* These documents of title are subject to Article 7 of the UCC.[13] To be a **document of title,** a document "must purport to be issued by or addressed to a bailee and purport to cover goods in the bailee's possession which are either identified or are fungible portions of an identified mass."[14]

13. Of course, when applicable, federal law takes priority [see UCC 7–103]. For example, the Federal Bills of Lading Act [49 U.S.C. Sections 81–124], enacted in 1916, applies to bills of lading issued by common carriers for goods shipped in interstate or foreign commerce, and the United States Warehouse Act [7 U.S.C. Sections 241–243], also enacted in 1916, applies to receipts covering agricultural products stored for interstate or foreign commerce.

14. UCC 1–201(15) and 7–102(1)(e); see also UCC 7–401.

A **bill of lading** is a document verifying the receipt of goods for shipment issued by a person engaged in the business of transporting or forwarding goods.[15] A **warehouse receipt** is a receipt issued by a person engaged in the business of storing goods for hire.[16] A **delivery order** is a written order to deliver goods directed to a warehouser, carrier, or other person who, in the ordinary course of business, issues warehouse receipts or bills of lading.[17]

Simply put, a document of title is a receipt for goods in the charge of a bailee-carrier or a bailee-warehouser and a contract for the shipment or storage of identified goods.

Negotiability of Documents of Title

Negotiability is a concept that applies to documents of title when they contain the words "bearer" or "to the order of."[18] If a document of title is negotiable—that is, if it specifies that the goods are to be delivered to bearer or to the order of a named person—the following are also possible:

1. The possessor of the document of title is entitled to receive, hold, and dispose of the document and the goods it covers.
2. A good faith purchaser of the document may acquire greater rights to the document and the goods it covers than the transferor had or had the authority to convey (that is, a good faith purchaser may take free of the claims and defenses of prior parties).

If a document of title is nonnegotiable—that is, if it is not made payable to the order of any named person or to bearer—it may be transferred by assignment but not negotiation.[19]

The concept of negotiability under Articles 3 and 7 of the UCC are similar. There are important distinctions between them, however. For example, Article 7 refers to the negotiation process as due negotiation. **Due negotiation** requires that the purchaser of a document of title take it in good faith, for value, without notice of a defense against or a claim to it, in the regular course of business or financing, and not in the settlement or payment of a money obligation.[20] In other words, even if all other requirements are met, transfer of a negotiable document of title to a nonbusinessperson is not due negotiation. In such situations, the transferee acquires only those rights the transferor had or had the authority to convey.[21]

On due negotiation, however, a transferee can acquire greater rights in a document of title than the transferor had. The transferee obtains title to the document and to the goods, including rights to goods delivered to the bailee after the document was issued, and takes free of all prior claims and defenses of which he or she had no notice. The document's issuer remains obligated to store or deliver the goods according to the document's terms.[22] Under this provision, businesspersons can extend credit on documents of title without concern for adverse claims of third parties.

To prevent a thief or a finder of goods from defeating the rights of the true owner (by, for example, taking them to a warehouse and subsequently negotiating the warehouse receipt to a third party who would otherwise take the goods free of the claims of others), the goods must be delivered to the issuer of the document of title by their owner or the owner's agent.[23] Otherwise, the document does not represent title to the goods. Even if the document does not represent title, however, the bailee will not be liable if he or she acts in good faith and observes reasonable commercial standards in receiving and delivering the goods.[24]

In other words, a carrier or warehouser who receives goods from a thief or finder and delivers them according to that individual's instructions is not liable to the goods' true owner. The reason for this rule is that carriers and warehousers are not links in the chain of title and do not represent the owner in transactions affecting title but simply furnish a service necessary to trade and commerce.

15. UCC 1–201(6).
16. UCC 1–201(45); see also UCC 7–201 and 7–202. UCC 7–102(h) defines the person engaged in the storing of goods for hire as a *warehouseman*.
17. UCC 7–102(1)(d).
18. UCC 7–104(1). Negotiability is a concept that also applies in situations involving negotiable instruments.
19. UCC 7–104(2).
20. UCC 7–501(4).
21. UCC 7–504. Until the bailee is notified of the transfer, the transferee's rights may be defeated by certain creditors of the transferor; by a buyer from the transferor in the ordinary course of business, if the bailee has delivered the goods to the buyer; or by the bailee who has dealt with the transferor in good faith.
22. UCC 7–502.
23. UCC 7–503(1).
24. UCC 7–404.

COMMON CARRIERS

Common carriers are publicly licensed to provide transportation services to the general public. They are distinguished from private carriers, which operate transportation facilities for a select clientele. A private carrier is not bound to provide service to every person or company making a request. The common carrier, however, must arrange carriage for all who apply, within certain limitations.[25]

The common-carrier contract of transportation creates a *mutual-benefit bailment*. Unlike the bailee in ordinary mutual-benefit bailments, however, the common carrier is held to a standard of care based on *strict liability,* rather than a standard of reasonable care, in protecting the bailed personal property. This means that the common carrier is absolutely liable, regardless of negligence, for all loss or damage to goods except loss or damage caused by one of the five common law exceptions:

1. An act of God.
2. An act of a public enemy.
3. An order of a public authority.
4. An act of the shipper.
5. The inherent nature of the goods.

The UCC retained the common law liability of common carriers in UCC 7–309. Common carriers are treated as if they were absolute insurers for the safe delivery of goods to the destination, even though they are not. They cannot contract away this liability for damaged goods; subject to government regulations, however, they are permitted to limit their dollar liability to an amount stated on the shipment contract.[26]

Except for the five exceptions mentioned, the common carrier is liable for any damage to goods in shipment, even that caused by the willful acts of third persons or by sheer accident. Thus, a common-carrier trucking company moving cargo is liable for acts of vandalism, mechanical defects in refrigeration units, or a dam bursting, if any of these acts results in damage to the cargo. But damage caused by acts of God—an earthquake or lightning, for example—is the shipper's loss.

Shipper's Loss. The shipper bears any loss occurring through its own faulty or improper crating or packaging procedures. For example, if a bird dies because its crate was poorly ventilated, the shipper, not the carrier, bears the loss.

Connecting Carriers. A bill of lading that specifies one or more connecting carriers is called a *through bill of lading*. When connecting carriers are involved in transporting goods under a through bill of lading, the shipper can recover from the original carrier or any connecting carrier.[27] Normally, the *last* carrier is presumed to have received the goods in satisfactory condition.

WAREHOUSE COMPANIES

Warehousing is the business of providing storage of property for compensation. Like ordinary bailees, warehouse companies are liable for loss or damage to property resulting from *negligence*. A warehouser must "exercise such care . . . as a reasonably careful [person] would exercise under like circumstances but unless otherwise agreed he is not liable for damages which could not have been avoided by the exercise of such care."[28] A warehouse company can limit the dollar amount of liability, but the bailor must be given the option of paying an increased storage rate for an increase in the liability limit.[29]

INNKEEPERS

At common law, innkeepers, hotel owners, and similar operators were held to the same strict liability as common carriers with respect to property brought into the rooms by guests. Today, only those who provide lodging to the public for compensation as *regular* business are covered under this rule of strict liability. Moreover, the rule applies only to those who are *guests*, as opposed to *lodgers*. A lodger is a permanent resident of the hotel or inn, whereas a guest is a traveler.

In many states, innkeepers can avoid strict liability for loss of guests' valuables and money by providing a safe in which to keep them. Each guest must be

25. A common carrier is not required to take any and all property anywhere in all instances. Public regulatory agencies govern common carriers, and carriers may be restricted to geographic areas. They may also be limited to carrying certain kinds of goods or to providing only special types of transportation equipment.

26. Federal laws require common carriers to offer shippers the opportunity to obtain higher dollar limits for loss by paying a higher fee for the transport.

27. UCC 7–302.

28. UCC 7–204(1).

29. UCC 7–204(2).

clearly notified of the availability of such a safe. Statutes often limit the liability of innkeepers with regard to articles that are not kept in the safe or that are of such a nature that they are not ordinarily kept in a safe. These statutes may limit the amount of monetary damages or even provide that the innkeeper incurs no liability in the absence of negligence. Commonly, hotels notify guests of the state laws governing the liability of innkeepers by posting a notice on the inside of the door of the hotel room or in some other prominent place within the room.

Normally, the innkeeper assumes no responsibility for the safety of a guest's automobile, because the guest usually retains possession and control. If, however, the innkeeper provides parking facilities, and the guest's car is entrusted to the innkeeper or to an employee, the rules governing ordinary bailments will apply.

Terms and Concepts to Review

abandoned property 952	constructive delivery 949	lost property 951
accession 950	delivery order 958	mislaid property 951
bailee 952	document of title 957	personal property 946
bailee's lien 955	due negotiation 958	property 946
bailment 952	estray statute 951	real property 946
bailor 952	fee simple 947	tenancy by the entirety 948
bill of lading 958	fixture 946	tenancy in common 947
chattel 946	gift 949	trade fixture 947
community property 948	gift *causa mortis* 950	treasure trove 952
concurrent ownership 947	gift *inter vivos* 950	warehouse receipt 958
confusion 950	joint tenancy 947	

Chapter Summary

PERSONAL PROPERTY

Property Classification	Property is divided into real property and personal property. **1.** *Real property (realty, or real estate)*—Includes the land and everything permanently attached to the land. **2.** *Personal property (personalty)*—Includes all property not classified as real property. Personal property can be tangible (such as a TV set or a car) or intangible (such as stocks or bonds). Personal property may be referred to legally as *chattel*—a term used under the common law to denote all forms of personal property.
Fixtures	Fixtures are items of personal property that are so closely associated with the real property to which they are attached that the law views them as real property. A fixture may be physically attached to real property, or attached to another fixture. Generally, if the owner intends certain personal property to be a fixture, it is considered a fixture.
Property Ownership	**1.** *Fee simple*—Exists when individuals have the right to use, possess, or dispose of the property as they choose during their lifetimes and to pass on the property to their heirs at death. **2.** *Concurrent ownership*— **a.** Tenancy in common—Co-ownership in which two or more persons own an undivided interest in the property; on one tenant's death, the property interest passes to his or her heirs.

CHAPTER SUMMARY—CONTINUED

Property Ownership—continued

b. Joint tenancy—Exists when two or more persons own an undivided interest in property; on the death of a joint tenant, the property interest transfers to the remaining tenant(s), not to the heirs of the deceased.
c. Tenancy by the entirety—A form of co-ownership between a husband and wife that is similar to a joint tenancy, except that a spouse cannot transfer separately his or her interest during his or her lifetime without the consent of the other spouse.
d. Community property—A form of co-ownership in which each spouse technically owns an undivided one-half interest in property acquired during the marriage. This type of ownership occurs in only a few states.

Acquiring Ownership of Personal Property

The most common means of acquiring ownership in personal property is by purchasing it (see Chapters 18 through 23). Another way in which personal property is often acquired is by will or inheritance (see Chapter 50). The following are additional methods of acquiring personal property:

1. *Possession*—Ownership may be acquired by possession if no other person has ownership title (for example, capturing wild animals or finding abandoned property).
2. *Production*—Any product or item produced by an individual (with minor exceptions) becomes the property of that individual.
3. *Gift*—An effective gift is made when the following conditions exist:
   a. There is evidence of *intent* to make a gift of the property in question.
   b. The gift is *delivered* (physically or constructively) to the donee or the donee's agent.
   c. The gift is *accepted* by the donee or the donee's agent.
4. *Accession*—When someone adds value to an item of personal property by labor or materials, the added value generally becomes the property of the owner of the original property (includes accessions made in bad faith or wrongfully). Good faith accessions that substantially increase the property's value or change the identity of the property may cause title to pass to the improver.
5. *Confusion*—In the case of fungible goods, if a person wrongfully and willfully commingles goods with those of another in order to render them indistinguishable, the innocent party acquires title to the whole. Otherwise, the owners become tenants in common of the commingled goods.

Mislaid, Lost, and Abandoned Property

1. *Mislaid property*—Property that is placed somewhere voluntarily by the owner and then inadvertently forgotten. A finder of mislaid property will not acquire title to the goods, and the owner of the place where the property was mislaid becomes a caretaker of the mislaid property.
2. *Lost property*—Property that is involuntarily left and forgotten. A finder of lost property can claim title to the property against the whole world *except the true owner.*
3. *Abandoned property*—Property that has been discarded by the true owner, who has no intention of claiming title to the property in the future. A finder of abandoned property can claim title to it against the whole world, *including the original owner.*

BAILMENTS

Elements of a Bailment

1. *Personal property*—Bailments involve only personal property.
2. *Delivery of possession*—For an effective bailment to exist, the bailee (the one receiving the property) must be given exclusive possession and control over the property, and in a voluntary bailment, the bailee must knowingly accept the personal property.
3. *The bailment agreement*—Expressly or impliedly provides for the return of the bailed property to the bailor or a third party, or for the disposal of the bailed property by the bailee.

Ordinary Bailments

1. *Types of bailments*—
   a. Bailment for the sole benefit of the bailor—A gratuitous bailment undertaken for the sole benefit of the bailor (for example, as a favor to the bailor).

Chapter Summary—continued

Ordinary Bailments—continued	**b.** Bailment for the sole benefit of the bailee—A gratuitous loan of an article to a person (the bailee) solely for the bailee's benefit. **c.** Mutual-benefit (contractual) bailment—The most common kind of bailment; involves compensation between the bailee and bailor for the service provided. **2.** *Rights of a bailee (duties of a bailor)*— **a.** The right of possession—Allows actions against third persons who damage or convert the bailed property and allows actions against the bailor for wrongful breach of the bailment. **b.** The right to be compensated and reimbursed for expenses—In the event of nonpayment, the bailee has the right to place a possessory (bailee's) lien on the bailed property. **c.** The right to limit liability—An ordinary bailee can limit his or her liability for loss or damage, provided proper notice is given and the limitation is not against public policy. In special bailments, limitations on liability for negligence or on types of losses are usually not allowed, but limitations on the monetary amount of liability are permitted. **3.** *Duties of a bailee (rights of a bailor)*— **a.** A bailee must exercise appropriate care over property entrusted to him or her. What constitutes appropriate care normally depends on the nature and circumstances of the bailment. **b.** Bailed goods in a bailee's possession must be either returned to the bailor or disposed of according to the bailor's directions. A bailee's failure to return the bailed property creates a presumption and constitutes a breach of contract or the tort of conversion of goods.
Special Types of Bailments	**1.** *Common carriers*—Carriers that are publicly licensed to provide transportation services to the general public. The common carrier is held to a standard of care based on *strict liability* unless the bailed property is lost or destroyed due to (a) an act of God, (b) an act of a public enemy, (c) an order of a public authority, (d) an act of a shipper, or (e) the inherent nature of the goods. **2.** *Warehouse companies*—Professional bailees that differ from ordinary bailees because they (a) can issue documents of title (warehouse receipts) and (b) are subject to state and federal statutes, including Article 7 of the UCC (as are common carriers). They must exercise a high degree of care over the bailed property and are liable for loss or damage of property if they fail to do so. **3.** *Innkeepers (hotel operators)*—Those who provide lodging to the public for compensation as a *regular* business. The common law strict liability standard to which innkeepers were once held is limited today by state statutes, which vary from state to state.

Cases for Analysis

Westlaw. You can access the full text of each case presented below by going to the Westlaw cases on this text's Web site at http://wbl-cs.westbuslaw.com. Each Westlaw case includes the names of all plaintiffs and defendants, the dates on which the case was argued and decided, a brief summary of the issues and decisions in the case, headnotes classifying specific issues in the case according to the West Key Number System, and the court's opinion. Concurring and dissenting opinions, if any, are included as well.

Case 46.1 FIXTURES

In re Sand & Sage Farm & Ranch, Inc.
United States Bankruptcy Court,
District of Kansas, 2001.
266 Bankr. 507.

ROBERT E. NUGENT, Bankruptcy Judge.

* * * Randolf and Sandra Ardery, owners of Sand & Sage [Farm & Ranch, Inc.], filed [bankruptcy] petitions on June 13, 2000. * * * [As part of the proceedings the] Arderys seek to sell real and personal property located in Edwards County, Kansas, to Bohn Enterprises, L.P. ("Bohn") for $100,000.00. Ag Services of America ("Ag Services") objected to the proposed

sale asserting a first and prior lien over Offerle National Bank, formerly Farmer's State Bank ("the Bank") in the irrigation system * * * .

* * * *

FINDINGS OF FACT

* * * In 1988, Mr. Ardery bought an eighty-acre tract in Edwards County * * * . Ardery purchased the property from Kinsley Bank. In order to secure a purchase money loan to acquire the land, the Arderys granted a mortgage to Farmers State Bank which covered both the real estate as well as improvements and fixtures. By its terms, the mortgage conveyed a lien to Farmer's State Bank in the * * * real property,

> "together with all the right, title and interest of the Mortgagor in said property now owned or hereafter acquired *and all buildings, improvements, and fixtures of any type now or hereafter placed on said property* * * * ." [Emphasis added.]

* * * Farmers State Bank recorded the mortgage in the office of the Register of Deeds of Edwards County on June 2, 1988. Offerle National Bank is the successor to Farmers State Bank and the current holder of the mortgage.

Eight years later, on January 4, 1996, the Arderys and Sand & Sage executed a security agreement granting Ag Services a security interest in their equipment as well as other farm-related assets. Ag Services filed a financing statement with the Kansas Secretary of State on January 17, 1996. Neither the security agreement nor the financing statement refers to fixtures.

* * * [A]n eight-tower Zinmatic center pivot [irrigation] system * * * was attached to the land when Ardery purchased it in 1988. The irrigation system is comprised of an underground well and pump which is connected to a pipe which runs from the pump to the pivot where the water line is attached to a further system of pipes and sprinklers which are suspended from the towers, extending out over the crops in a circular fashion transmitting water for irrigation. Integral parts of the system are the engine and gearhead which are bolted aboveground to a concrete slab directly above the pump and well and are attached to the irrigation pipe. The irrigation system is neither easily removed from its present location nor easily transportable to another. Unlike some pivot systems, the towers of this system are not towable, meaning that they must be partially disassembled and transported one tower at a time because their tires are not positioned in a manner which would allow them to be towed on the road. Removal of the system would also require disassembly of the engine and removal of the gearhead.

Extraction of the down-hole pump which sits 120–130 feet below the ground would be expensive and would require the services of an oil service company or some other person owning pulling equipment. Mr. Ardery estimated that it would take two experienced men a full day to disassemble and move the entire irrigation system including the pipes, engine, pump and gearhead at a cost of approximately $2,500–3,000. The irrigation pipes are valued at $5,000, the engine at $1,000–1,200, the pump at $2,500, and the gearhead at $700–800, equaling a total maximum value of approximately $10,000. * * *

Ardery testified that he intended to purchase the irrigation system when he purchased the land from the Kinsley Bank. Both he and [Gary] Bartlett, the Bank's president, testified that they intended the sprinkler system to be a part of what was encumbered [burdened] by the Bank's mortgage. Ardery also intended to sell the irrigation system to Bohn. * * *

Mr. Bartlett, an experienced banker who has worked in Edwards County for a number of years and is familiar with irrigated land and with the Zinmatic system in question, also estimated the value of the irrigation system to be approximately $10,000. * * * While Bartlett agreed with Ardery's values with respect to the entire irrigation system, he contended that the moving costs might be as high as $4,500, thus resulting in a net value of $4,000–6,000.

* * * *

Bartlett agreed with Ardery that, without irrigation, the value of the eighty acres would be substantially lower.

* * * *

DISCUSSION

* * * To be determined * * * is the nature of the irrigation system * * * : is it a "fixture" * * * , or is it simply "equipment?" * * *

* * * [There is] a three-step judicial test for determining whether personalty [personal property] attached to real estate is legally a fixture. Paraphrased, the steps are:

> (i) how firmly the goods are attached or the ease of their removal (annexation);
> (ii) the relationship of the parties involved (intent); and
> (iii) how operation of the goods is related to the use of the land (adaptation).

Of the three factors, intent is the controlling factor and is deduced largely from the property-owner's acts and the surrounding circumstances.

* * * *

* * * [T]he Court concludes that the irrigation system is a fixture. It is firmly attached to the realty. The irrigation pipes are connected to the center pivot which is bolted to a cement slab in the center of the irrigation property and connected to the underground well and pump by wires and pipes. Further, the system is not

easily removable. The towers must be disassembled in sections and transported separately, and disassembly and removal of the engine, gearhead and pump would be time-consuming and require the assistance of experienced people. It would also be expensive, particularly in view of the fact that the system's likely value is not more than $10,000, and the cost of removal could reach $6,000.

The relationships between the parties involved in each transaction also suggest the shared intent that the irrigation system be a fixture. In 1988, the Kinsley Bank sold the land to Ardery with the irrigation system included. Ardery, in turn, mortgaged the land, and the fixtures, to the Bank. Banker Bartlett testified that he considered the conveyance of the mortgage to include the system as that was the Bank's custom and practice in Edwards County. Ardery and Bohn clearly intend the system to pass with the land in the sale now before the Court. Finally, Ag Service's security agreement contains a specific reference to an irrigation system other than that which is at issue here, but contains no reference whatever to this system. The debtor, his grantor, his lender, and his grantee, all share the intent that the system in question should pass with the land.

The irrigation system is suitably adapted to the land. There can be little dispute concerning the need for pivot irrigation in the semi-arid conditions of southwestern Kansas. All witnesses agreed, and it is well within this Court's common experience, that irrigated units of land are substantially more productive of crops than dryland acres. This alone demonstrates the relation between the operation of the goods and use of the land.

Finally, as suggested above, it is apparently not unreasonable for a western Kansas buyer to expect a center pivot system to be sold as part of a transaction involving arable ground. Both Ardery and Bartlett testified to as much and Ag Services offered no rebuttal testimony on that point.

Based on the foregoing, this Court concludes that the center pivot system is indeed a "fixture" * * * .

* * * *

Because the Bank has a valid and perfected encumbrance on the Arderys' fixtures by virtue of its mortgage, * * * the Court finds the Bank's interest in the center pivot irrigation system to be first and prior.

* * * *

The Court directs that * * * $10,000.00 * * * representing [the value of the irrigation system in the] proceeds from the real estate sale be turned over to Offerle National Bank forthwith.

* * * *

IT IS SO ORDERED.

CASE 46.2 GIFTS

IN RE ESTATE OF PIPER

Missouri Court of Appeals,
Southern District, 1984.
676 S.W.2d 897.

GREENE, Judge.

Gladys Piper, the widow of Andy Piper, died intestate in St. Clair County, Missouri, on November 15, 1982. Her heirs, consisting of nieces and nephews, all lived out of state. At the request of a majority of the heirs, Morran D. Harris, a local attorney, was appointed administrator of the estate of Gladys.

Personal property consisting of household goods, two old automobiles, farm machinery and "miscellaneous," a total appraised value of $5,150, was inventoried in the estate. "Miscellaneous" did not include jewelry or cash. At the time of her death, Gladys Piper owned two diamond rings, known as the "Andy Piper" rings and $206.57 in cash. The rings and cash were in Gladys' purse when she died. Gladys' niece, Wanda Brown who lived in Reno, Nevada, took possession of the rings and the cash after the funeral, allegedly to preserve those items for the estate.

Clara E. Kauffman, a friend of Gladys Piper, filed a claim [in a Missouri state court] against the estate in the sum of $4,800, contending that from October of 1974 until the date of death of Gladys, Clara took Gladys to the doctor, beauty shop and grocery store, wrote her checks to pay her bills and assisted her in the care of her home by reason of the promise of Gladys to pay Clara in cash or diamond rings at her death "all to reasonable value of $50 per month for eight years." The claim was heard by the trial court, after which the claim was denied for the reason that the services performed by Clara for Gladys were done as a volunteer. No appeal was taken from the denial of the claim.

Clara Kauffman then filed a petition [in a Missouri state court] for delivery of personal property. Named defendants were the administrator of the estate as well as the nieces and nephews, including Wanda Brown, of Gladys Piper. The petition * * * alleged that the "Andy Piper" rings, of the appraised value of $2,500, were in the possession of Wanda Brown, having never been surrendered to the estate's administrator, and that the rings were the property of Clara, "having been a consummated [completed, fulfilled] gift long prior to the death of Gladys Piper." Clara requested an order from the trial court directing Wanda Brown to deliver the rings to

Clara and, if Wanda did not comply, that Clara have judgment "against the defendants in the sum of $2,500."

* * * *

After hearing evidence, the trial court entered judgment directing Wanda Brown to deliver the rings and the cash to the administrator of the estate. The judgment further found that the value of the rings was $2,500, that they were the property of Clara Kauffman, and that Clara was entitled to possession of them. The judgment concluded by saying that if the rings were not delivered to Clara that she was entitled to a judgment of $2,500 against the estate. All defendants appealed from the judgment.

We first observe that there is no evidence in this case that gives Wanda Brown the legal right to retain in her possession the "Andy Piper" rings, or the $206.57 cash which were in Gladys Piper's purse when she died. Those items should have been delivered to the administrator as soon as the estate was opened so that they could be inventoried and preserved as assets of the estate. We find no quarrel with those portions of the judgment ordering Wanda Brown to turn the rings and cash over to the administrator.

We direct our attention to that portion of the judgment declaring that the rings were the property of Clara Kauffman. Clara's petition claimed the rings belonged to her by reason of "a consummated gift long prior to the death of Gladys Piper." The only evidence on the gift issue came from two witnesses. James Naylor, who had known Gladys for over 20 years, testified that when he saw Gladys "[b]etween the time of her last admission to the hospital and the date of her death," Gladys told him, after Naylor had complimented her on her rings, that "these are Clara's, but I am wearing them until I am finished with them, or until I am dead or whatever she may have said," and "[b]ut she made the comment that these are Clara's but I am going to wear them until I am done with them." Beverly Marcus testified that Gladys told her "when she was through with those rings, they were to be Clara's."

There was no evidence of any actual delivery to Clara, at any time, of the rings. A person claiming an *inter vivos* gift of personal property has the burden of proving it by clear and convincing evidence. The essentials of such a gift are 1) a present intention to make a gift on the part of the donor, 2) a delivery of the property by donor to donee, and 3) an acceptance by donee, whose ownership takes effect immediately and absolutely.

While no particular form is necessary to effect a delivery, and while the delivery may be actual, constructive, or symbolical, there must be some evidence to support a delivery theory. What we have here, at best, through the testimony of James Naylor and Beverly Marcus, was an intention on the part of Gladys, at some future time, to make a gift of the rings to Clara. Such an intention, no matter how clearly expressed, which has not been carried into effect, confers no ownership rights in the property in the intended donee. *Language written or spoken, expressing an intention to give, does not constitute a gift, unless the intention is executed by a complete and unconditional delivery of the subject matter, or delivery of a proper written instrument evidencing the gift.* There is no evidence in this case to prove delivery, and, for such reason, the trial court's judgment is erroneous. [Emphasis added.]

The judgment of the trial court is reversed, and the cause is remanded to the trial court with directions to enter a new judgment consistent with this opinion.

CASE 46.3 MISLAID, LOST, OR ABANDONED PROPERTY

SEA HUNT, INC. V. UNIDENTIFIED SHIPWRECKED VESSEL OR VESSELS

United States Court of Appeals,
Fourth Circuit, 2000.
221 F.3d 634.

WILKINSON, Chief Judge:

* * * *

I.

LA GALGA ("The Greyhound") was a fifty-gun frigate commissioned into the Spanish Navy in 1732. LA GALGA left Havana on its last voyage on August 18, 1750, in order to escort a convoy of merchant ships to Spain. * * * On August 25, 1750, the convoy encountered a hurricane near Bermuda that scattered the ships and forced them westward toward the American coast. LA GALGA eventually sank off the coast of the Maryland/Virginia border. * * *

The JUNO, a thirty-four gun frigate, entered the service of the Spanish Navy in 1790. On January 15, 1802, JUNO set sail from Veracruz bound for Spain. * * * . The JUNO was beset by a ferocious storm and [sank off the coast of Virginia]. * * *

The Commonwealth of Virginia has asserted ownership over LA GALGA and JUNO pursuant to the Abandoned Shipwreck Act of 1987 (ASA). The ASA gives states title to shipwrecks that are abandoned and are embedded in the submerged lands of a state. Sea Hunt [Inc.] is a maritime salvage company based in the Eastern Shore of Virginia. The Virginia Marine Resources Commission granted Sea Hunt permits to explore for shipwrecks off the Virginia coast and conduct salvage operations. Sea Hunt began to explore for shipwrecks within its permit areas and has spent about a million dollars in conducting remote sensing, survey, diving, and identification operations. Sea Hunt claims that its efforts have resulted in finding the remains of LA GALGA and JUNO.

To avoid interference with its operations, Sea Hunt initiated an * * * action [in a federal district court] against the two wrecks on March 11, 1998. Sea Hunt sought a declaratory judgment * * * that "the Commonwealth of Virginia be adjudged the true, sole and exclusive owner of the Shipwrecked Vessel(s)," and that any items salvaged therefrom by Sea Hunt be distributed pursuant to the permits issued by Virginia. In the alternative, Sea Hunt sought a liberal salvage award for its efforts. On March 12, 1998, the district court issued an order directing the arrest of the shipwrecked vessels and granting Sea Hunt exclusive rights of salvage until further notice. The court also directed Sea Hunt to send specific notice of the action to both the United States and to Spain.

* * * Spain's [response] stated that the Kingdom of Spain "was and still is the true and bona fide owner of the vessels JUNO and LA GALGA * * * and that title and ownership interest in said vessels has never been abandoned or relinquished or transferred by the Kingdom of Spain." Spain put forth affidavits and exhibits showing that at the time of their sinking both ships were serving as vessels of the Royal Navy, that both vessels are currently on the register of the Spanish Navy, and that transfer or abandonment of the vessels would require formal authorization by the government of Spain.

On April 27, 1999, the district court found that the express abandonment standard applied to these shipwrecks and that Spain had abandoned its claim to LA GALGA * * * . It further found that Spain did not expressly abandon JUNO * * * . In a later decision the district court held that Sea Hunt could not rightfully claim a salvage award * * * . The Kingdom of Spain now appeals the judgment concerning LA GALGA. The Commonwealth and Sea Hunt note a cross-appeal with regard to JUNO and the denial of a salvage award.

II.

In order for Virginia to acquire title to the shipwrecks and to issue salvage permits to Sea Hunt, these vessels must have been abandoned by Spain. Sea Hunt and the Commonwealth argue that the Abandoned Shipwreck Act requires application of an implied abandonment standard for shipwrecks in coastal waters, and that Spain has abandoned LA GALGA and JUNO. * * *

* * * *

Under the ASA, the United States asserts title to any abandoned shipwreck that is on or embedded in the submerged lands of a State. Title is then automatically transferred to the State in whose submerged lands the shipwreck is located. "Submerged lands" for the purposes of the ASA includes coastal waters three miles from shore. For a state to acquire title to a shipwreck it must be (1) abandoned and (2) on or embedded in the submerged lands of a state. It is undisputed that LA GALGA and JUNO are within Virginia's submerged lands. That, however, is not enough. We must address whether these frigates were abandoned by Spain. If the shipwrecks were abandoned, then Sea Hunt would have control over them in accordance with its state-issued permits. [Emphasis added.]

The ASA does not define the critical term "abandoned." Nothing in the Act indicates, however, that implied abandonment should be the standard in a case such as this where a sovereign asserts ownership to its vessels. The Act states * * * that "abandoned shipwrecks" are those "to which the owner has relinquished ownership rights with no retention." *The statute thus provides that a shipwreck is abandoned only where the owner has relinquished ownership rights.* When an owner comes before the court to assert his rights, relinquishment would be hard, if not impossible, to show. Requiring express abandonment where an owner makes a claim thus accords with the statutory text. Further, although * * * abandonment may be implied, it may be implied as by an owner never asserting any control over or otherwise indicating his claim of possession. An owner who comes forward has definitely indicated his claim of possession, and in such a case abandonment cannot be implied. [Emphasis added.]

* * * *

Finally, the express abandonment standard is required by * * * the 1902 Treaty of Friendship and General Relations between the United States and Spain. * * *

* * * *

Under the terms of the 1902 Treaty, Spanish vessels can * * * be abandoned only by express renunciation. Both Spain and the United States agree that this treaty provision requires that in our territorial waters Spanish ships are to be accorded the same immunity as United States ships. They also agree that such immunity requires application of the express abandonment standard. When the parties to a treaty both agree as to the meaning of a treaty provision, and that interpretation follows from the clear treaty language, we must, absent extraordinarily strong contrary evidence, defer to that interpretation. We cannot therefore adopt an implied abandonment standard in the face of treaties and mutual understandings requiring express abandonment. Such a standard would supplant the textual framework of negotiated treaties with an unpredictable judicial exercise in weighing equities.

* * * *

III.

* * * *

Although we believe the standard of express abandonment controls in the circumstances of this case, it would be difficult under any test to conclude that LA GALGA was abandoned. The mere passage of time since a shipwreck is not enough to constitute abandonment. Spain attempted salvage after LA GALGA sank, maintained LA GALGA on its naval registry, and asserted a claim after Sea Hunt brought its admiralty action. * * * In other cases where abandonment was found for Spanish wrecks, Spain made no claim of ownership. By contrast, Spain has vigorously asserted its interest in the wreck of LA GALGA and wishes to maintain it as a sacred military gravesite. In light of these circumstances, even a finding of implied abandonment would be improper.

* * * *

IV.

We reverse the judgment of the district court that the Kingdom of Spain abandoned the vessel LA GALGA. We affirm the judgment of the district court as to JUNO. Both vessels remain the property of Spain. The judgment of the district court is accordingly

AFFIRMED IN PART AND REVERSED IN PART.

CASE 46.4 DUTIES OF THE BAILEE

LEMBAGA ENTERPRISES, INC. v. CACE TRUCKING & WAREHOUSE, INC.

Superior Court of New Jersey,
Appellate Division, 1999.
320 N.J.Super. 501,
727 A.2d 1026.

RODRIGUEZ, A.A., J.A.D. [Judge, Appellate Division]

* * * *

These are the pertinent facts. Lembaga [Enterprises, Inc.] is an importer and distributor of toiletries and cosmetics. Cace [Trucking & Warehouse, Inc.] is a common carrier of goods and warehouser for hire. Lembaga and Cace have had a business relationship for several years. Cace would pick up shipment containers from Port Elizabeth [New Jersey], store them in its warehouse and deliver them for Lembaga. Cace employees were not allowed to unload Lembaga's containers. Unlike Cace's other clients, Lembaga opened its own containers and logged its own inventory. To coordinate this procedure, Lembaga leased a small office space within Cace's warehouse. Cace's warehouse was bordered by an eight-foot high, barbed-wire fence. Two gates were left open in the daytime, but locked at night. There were no security guards posted at the gates or at any other location in the warehouse. The trailers, however, were locked at all times with pin locks. The interior of the warehouse was alarmed.

On June 22, 1997, a Cace driver picked up two containers of perfume for Lembaga at the port. The driver noted that the security seals on the two trailers were intact. According to Cace's President, Kevin Erem, and Vice President of Operations, George "Skip" Cunningham, the two containers arrived at the warehouse in the afternoon. Cunningham telephoned Lembaga's president, Nathan Kumar, and informed him of the delivery. Kumar told Cunningham not to unload the containers until he arrived the next day. The containers were brought out to the yard. Cunningham neither placed nor observed anyone else place a pin lock on either container.

The next day, Cunningham arrived at the warehouse at 7:00 A.M. and inspected the two containers in the yard. He does not recall whether he observed pin locks on the containers. When Kumar arrived at the warehouse, the first container was brought into the warehouse and unloaded. When a driver went to retrieve the second container, it had disappeared. Cunningham and Erem went to the yard to investigate. They found part of a broken pin lock on the ground where the container had been.

Lembaga sued Cace [in a New Jersey state court] for the loss of its cargo. The complaint alleged breach of contract, negligence and conversion causes of action. * * *

This action was tried to a jury. * * * The parties stipulated that Lembaga sustained $366,879.53 in damages.

John Tichenor, a marine cargo surveyor, testified as an expert on behalf of Lembaga. Tichenor conducted an investigation. No one informed him that a pin lock was used on the container. He also noted that the police report did not refer to a broken pin lock being found at the scene. There were no pin locks on any of the trailers when he inspected the warehouse. Accordingly, he opined that Cace's warehouse did not meet the industry standard for security. Specifically, Cace failed to control access to cargo, pin lock all containers, install physical barriers, hire a gate guard or use close circuit television monitoring.

Francis R. Murphy, a self-employed security consultant and president of Murphy Protective Investigative Resources, testified for Cace. Murphy could not inspect the warehouse because it had burned down by the time he was retained. However, he reviewed the discovery materials in this case. He opined that Cace had adequate security. This was based on the fact that there were no prior thefts from the warehouse. Lembaga did not ask for additional security. Cace's yard was fenced-in. He further opined that the measures proposed by Lembaga—such as television monitors and gate guards—were extraordinary security measures for a small warehouse like Cace.

At the close of Cace's defense, Lembaga moved for a directed verdict, arguing that Cace is presumed to have converted the container because it disappeared mysteriously from its warehouse. * * * Lembaga argued that Cace is presumed negligent and this presumption cannot be overcome by mere evidence that Cace was not negligent. Cace must prove exactly what happened to the goods. Because it was undisputed that no one knows exactly what happened to the goods, there is no factual dispute on this issue for the jury to decide. Lembaga argued that it is entitled to judgment as a matter of law on the conversion claim.

The judge disagreed with Lembaga's argument, finding that conversion "was never asserted here * * * . The only facts before this Court deal * * * with a theft." Therefore, the judge did not instruct the jury on the conversion cause of action. The matter was submitted to the jury solely on a negligence cause of action. The jury found that Cace was not negligent. Lembaga moved for judgment notwithstanding the verdict and for a new trial. The motions were denied.

On appeal, Lembaga contends that * * * it was error to dismiss the conversion cause of action before it was submitted to the jury * * * .

The crux of Lembaga's argument is that Cace failed to meet its burden of proving that the container was not converted. * * * Lembaga contends that Cace did not rebut the presumption of conversion.

It is helpful to review the law of bailment as it exists in New Jersey. A bailor may sue a bailee in conversion and/or negligence. * * * [I]ntentional or negligent acts can give rise to a conversion cause of action. The tort arises from the bailee's commission of an unauthorized act of dominion over the bailor's property inconsistent with its rights in that property. *The good faith or intent of the bailee do not play a part in an action for conversion.* For example, a bailee who mistakenly destroys or disposes of the goods is liable in conversion although there is no intent to steal or destroy the goods. [Emphasis added.]

Therefore, in a conversion action, the bailor has the burden to prove that the bailee has unlawfully converted the goods. When goods are delivered to a bailee in good condition and then are lost or damaged, the law presumes a conversion and casts upon the bailee the burden of going forward with the evidence to show that the loss did not occur through his negligence or if he cannot affirmatively do this, that he exercised a degree of care sufficient to rebut the presumption of it. * * *

* * * *

Here, the thrust of Cace's defense was that it had adequate security to prevent a theft of the container by third parties. It did not present evidence to rebut the presumption that Cace, its agents or employees had converted the container. Thus, a jury question was presented on the conversion cause of action. * * * [C]onversion is a broader concept than theft. A conversion can occur even when a bailee has not stolen the merchandise but has acted negligently in permitting the loss of the merchandise from its premises.

Therefore, here, the judge should have instructed the jury that if Lembaga established that the container had disappeared while in the care of Cace, there is a rebuttable [refutable] presumption of conversion based either on Cace's negligent conduct in permitting third parties to steal the container, or by the negligent or intentional conduct of Cace's employees or agents. The burden to prove conversion, however, rests at all times with Lembaga.

Accordingly, we reverse and remand to the [lower court] for a new trial. At that trial, the judge should instruct the jury that if Lembaga establishes that the container disappeared while in Cace's care, there is a rebuttable presumption that Cace is liable for the loss. In that instance, Cace has the burden of rebutting the presumption. The jury should then be asked to determine whether Lembaga met its burden to prove that the loss was caused by: (a) the intentioned conversion of the goods by Cace; or (b) negligent conversion by Cace or theft by third parties.

Case Problems

46–1. For some time before she died, Merle Zimmerman allowed her good friend, Joan Robertson, to assist her with her financial affairs. Robertson was given access to Zimmerman's funds, through joint bank accounts, and to Zimmerman's safe-deposit box. At one point, Zimmerman gave Robertson a number of municipal bonds to "put . . . in safekeeping." Robertson noticed that the bonds had been placed in a series of Manila envelopes, and each envelope contained a piece of paper on which was written the name of one of Zimmerman's relatives. One envelope, which contained bonds with a face value of $22,000, had Robertson's name in it. When Zimmerman died, Robertson distributed the bonds to the people whose names were in the envelopes and retained the bonds in the envelope with her own name in it. Zimmerman's estate claimed ownership of the bonds. Robertson asserted that Zimmerman had made a gift to her of the bonds. Discuss whether an effective gift had been made. [*Robertson v. Estate of Zimmerman,* 778 S.W.2d 805 (Mo.App. 1989)]

46–2. Leonard Charrier, an amateur archaeologist in Louisiana, uncovered artifacts from an Native American burial ground that was several hundred years old. The artifacts had been made by the ancestors of the present-day Tunica Indian tribe of Louisiana. The Tunica tribe asked the court to award it custody of the property, which included burial pots, ornaments, and pottery. Charrier claimed that the property had been abandoned and that he had the right to title because he had taken possession of the property. Discuss whether the Tunica tribe, as heirs to the former owners of the property, should succeed in their claim to the artifacts, or whether the property was indeed abandoned. [*Charrier v. Bell,* 496 So.2d 601 (La.App.1st Cir. 1986)]

46–3. Before her death, Melanie McCarthy had written and sent or otherwise delivered nine $3,000 checks intended as gifts to various relatives. None of the checks had been cashed prior to Melanie's death. Melanie's son, Daniel, who was one of the administrators of her estate, claimed that the Internal Revenue Service (IRS) should not levy estate taxes on the $27,000 still in Melanie's bank account to cover these checks, because the checks were completed gifts. The IRS contended that the gifts had not been effectively delivered prior to Melanie's death, because Melanie could have ordered the bank to stop payment on the uncashed checks and therefore had not relinquished complete dominion and control over the checks sufficient to establish a completed gift. What should the court decide? Discuss. [*McCarthy v. United States,* 806 F.2d 129 (7th Cir. 1986)]

46–4. Before her marriage to Herman Blettell in 1951, Mary Blettell owned a residence. Darlene Snider was Mary's daughter by a previous marriage. In 1965, Herman and Mary moved into the residence. Herman's name was never added to the title. In 1974, Mary executed a deed to the property to Darlene but did not deliver or record it. In 1978, Mary informed Darlene about the deed and told her that it was located in Mary and Darlene's joint safe-deposit box. In August 1987, Mary's health was declining, and she told Darlene to get the deed from their safe-deposit box, rent a safe-deposit box in Darlene's name only, and put the deed in it so "nobody can get [it] but you." Darlene removed the deed from the joint safe-deposit box and placed it in her own box. Herman was not aware of these events until shortly before Mary's death in 1989. On the day after Mary died, Darlene recorded the deed. Herman, as Mary's personal representative (the person appointed in Mary's will to look after her affairs after her death), contended that Mary's transfer of the deed to Darlene was not a valid gift *inter vivos* because the deed was never effectively delivered to Darlene. Darlene argued that there was a valid delivery in 1987, when Mary instructed Darlene to place the deed in her own safe-deposit box. What should the court decide? Explain. [*Estate of Blettell v. Snider,* 114 Or.App. 162, 834 P.2d 505 (1992)]

46–5. James Wilson learned that he had terminal cancer in 1983 or 1984. At about that time, he arranged for a friend, Harold Buell, to have joint access to Wilson's safe-deposit box. Wilson gave Buell a key. The box contained, among other things, a copy of a promissory note for $65,000 from Michael Cronan. Wilson told Buell that the debt represented by the note was to be forgiven when he died and that on Wilson's death, Buell was to deliver the copy of the note to Cronan. In 1984, Cronan learned of Wilson's illness, and Wilson told Cronan on at least two occasions that Cronan's debt was to be forgiven on Wilson's death. In the meantime, Cronan continued to make payments on the note. Wilson died in July 1987. On the day after Wilson died, Buell delivered the copy of the note to Cronan, as directed. Wilson's personal representative (a person appointed to look after the deceased's affairs), Carol Kesterson, sought to recover from Cronan the balance owing on the $65,000 note, the original of which was found among Wilson's personal effects after his death. Cronan claimed that the debt had been forgiven, as a gift to Cronan. Were the requirements of a gift satisfied? How should this case be resolved? Discuss fully. [*Kesterson v. Cronan,* 105 Or.App. 551, 806 P.2d 134 (1991)]

46–6. K-2 Petroleum, Inc., and El Dorado Oil and Gas, Inc., were engaged in a joint-venture drilling project. They operated under an agreement whereby El Dorado provided an operational electric generator for K-2's working interest in the well. The generator became nonfunctional, and K-2 sought to have El Dorado replace or repair it. El Dorado refused. K-2 subsequently contracted with Stewart & Stevenson Services, Inc. (S & S), for the repair of the generator. Shortly after receiving the generator for repair, S & S was notified by El Dorado that it was the true owner of the generator. El Dorado identified it by model and serial number and demanded its return on completion of repairs. Because S & S knew of the common practice among oil-field companies of switching, loaning, and borrowing equipment among themselves, it allowed El Dorado to take possession of the generator after El Dorado had paid for the repair. Before K-2 received any notice of S & S's delivery to El Dorado, K-2 and El Dorado terminated their joint venture and agreed that all salvageable equipment and supplies from the project were the property of K-2. K-2 later filed suit against S & S, claiming that S & S's failure to return the generator to K-2 and its delivery of the generator to El Dorado constituted the tort of conversion. Discuss K-2's claim. [*Stewart & Stevenson Services, Inc. v. Kratochvil,* 737 S.W.2d 65 (Tex.App.—San Antonio 1987)]

46–7. Several individuals placed personal property in a storage facility offered by the Winnebago County Fair Association, Inc. All who stored property in the building were required by the Winnebago County Fair

Association to sign a storage agreement that included the following provision: "No liability exists for damage or loss to the stored equipment from the perils of fire." The storage building burned down, and all the property within it was destroyed. A number of the people who had stored their property in the building brought suit against the fair association, claiming that the fire resulted from its negligence. Allstate Insurance Co., which had paid a number of claims for losses incurred due to the fire, joined the plaintiffs in the lawsuit. The Winnebago County Fair Association claimed that the exculpatory clause in its contract relieved it from any and all liability. The issue before the court was whether the bailee (the fair association) could validly contract away *all* liability for fire damage. What was the result? [*Allstate Insurance Co. v. Winnebago County Fair Association, Inc.*, 131 Ill.App.3d 225, 475 N.E.2d 230, 86 Ill.Dec. 233 (1985)]

46–8. Wanda Perry, who had an account with Farmers Bank of Greenwood, wanted to rent a safe-deposit box from the bank. The boxes were available only to bank customers, and no rent was charged. When renting the box, Wanda was asked to sign a signature card that stated the following: "The undersigned customer holds the Farmers Bank harmless for loss of currency or coin left in the box." A little over four years later, the bank was burglarized, and most of the safe-deposit boxes were broken into. Wanda's box was among those burglarized, and she lost all the currency and coins contained in it. At trial, evidence showed that the bank had been negligent in failing to restore a burglar alarm system that had been inoperative for more than a week prior to (and including) the day the bank was burglarized. Wanda sued the bank to recover the currency and coins, alleging negligence on the part of the bank. Discuss fully whether the bank should be held liable for the loss. [*Farmers Bank of Greenwood v. Perry*, 301 Ark. 547, 787 S.W.2d 645 (1990)]

46–9. Augustine attended a dental seminar held at a Marriott Hotel. The sponsor of the seminar had rented the banquet room in which the seminar was held and had requested the hotel to place a movable coat rack outside the room, in the public lobby. Augustine placed his coat on the rack before entering the seminar room. When he tried to find the coat at the noon recess, however, he noted that the rack had been moved a distance down the lobby and around a corner, near an exit. To his dismay, his cashmere coat was missing. Claiming that the hotel was liable for the loss, Augustine brought an action against it. Was the hotel a bailee of the coat and thus liable to its owner for the loss? Explain fully. [*Augustine v. Marriott Hotel*, 132 Misc.2d 180, 503 N.Y.S.2d 498 (Amherst Twn.Ct., Erie Cty. 1986)]

46–10. Mabel Meredith gave Jeanette Taylor and Ann Dumler each a $25,000 check. Although Meredith owned property worth more than $2 million, she did not have enough in her checking account to cover the checks. Meredith died six years later, and Taylor and Dumler filed claims in a Maryland state court against her estate, represented by William Dulany, to recover the amounts of the checks. Does the receipt of a check represent a completed gift? Should Taylor and Dumler be awarded $25,000 each? [*Dulany v. Taylor*, 105 Md.App. 619, 660 A.2d 1046 (1995)]

46–11. Gerald Stavely entrusted a valuable painting to the care of Patricia Bolger. Bolger put the painting in the trunk of her husband's Cadillac. Her husband left the car at his country club in the care of a parking attendant who worked for Jack Boles Services, Inc. The car and painting were stolen. Bolger's car was eventually returned to him, but the painting was missing. Stavely filed a suit in a Texas state court against Boles, arguing that the bailee was responsible for the theft. The court agreed. Boles appealed. What will the appellate court decide? Why? [*Jack Boles Services, Inc. v. Stavely*, 906 S.W.2d 185 (Tex.App.—Austin 1995)]

46–12. Using a metal detector, Billy Ray Shivers found metal tokens at the site of an abandoned sawmill that once belonged to Aldridge Lumber Company. The tokens were used fifty to a hundred years ago by the mill as payment for its workers. Because the site was in Angelina National Forest, the federal government claimed ownership of the tokens and seized them. Shivers filed a motion in a federal district court against the government, seeking to have the tokens returned. Should the court grant the motion? Why, or why not? [*United States v. Shivers*, 96 F.3d 120 (5th Cir. 1996)]

46–13. Hugh Chalmers issued a promissory note to his father in the amount of $50,000, plus interest. The note was secured by a deed of trust on certain real estate and was payable on demand or within sixty days of the father's death. More than seventeen years later, the father assigned the deed of trust to his wife, Nina. The existence of the note was mentioned in the assignment, which was recorded in the appropriate state office with the deed of trust. After the father died, Nina found the note in a safe-deposit box. On the back of the note, the father had indorsed the note to Nina. When Chalmers refused to pay the amount due, Nina filed a lawsuit in an Arkansas state court against him. Chalmers argued that the note had not been effectively delivered. What should the court hold? Discuss. [*Chalmers v. Chalmers*, 937 S.W.2d 171 (Ark. 1997)]

46–14. Thomas Stafford owned four promissory notes. Payments on the notes were deposited into a bank account in the names of Stafford and his daughter, June Zink, "as joint tenants with right of survivorship." Stafford kept control of the notes and would not allow Zink to spend any of the proceeds. He also kept the interest on the account. On one note, Stafford endorsed "Pay to the order of Thomas J. Stafford or June S. Zink, or the survivor." The payee on each of the other notes was "Thomas J. Stafford and June S. Zink, or the survivor." When Stafford died, Zink took possession of the notes, claiming that she had been a joint tenant of the notes with her father. Stafford's son, also Thomas, filed a suit in a Virginia state court against Zink, claiming that the notes were partly his. Thomas argued that their father had not made a valid gift *inter vivos* of the notes to Zink. In whose favor will the court rule? Why? [*Zink v. Stafford,* 509 S.E.2d 833 (Va. 1999)]

46–15. A. D. Lock owned Lock Hospitality, Inc., which in turn owned the Best Western motel in Conway, Arkansas. Joe Terry and David Stocks were preparing the motel for renovation. As they were removing the ceiling tiles in room 118, with Lock present in the room, a dusty cardboard box was noticed near the heating and air supply vent where it had apparently been concealed. Terry climbed a ladder to reach the box, opened it, and handed it to Stocks. The box was filled with more than $38,000 in old currency. Lock took possession of the the box and its contents. Terry and Stocks filed a suit in an Arkansas state court against Lock and his corporation to obtain the money. Should the money be characterized as lost, mislaid, or abandoned property? To whom should the court award it? Explain. [*Terry v. Lock,* 37 S.W.3d 202 (Ark. 2001)]

E-LINKS

For updated links to resources available on the Web, as well as a variety of other materials, visit this text's Web site at

http://wbl-cs.westbuslaw.com

To learn about whether a married person has ownership rights in a gift received by his or her spouse, go to Scott Law Firm's Web page at

http://www.scottlawfirm.com/property.htm

For a discussion of the origins of the term bailment and how bailment relationships have been defined, go to

http://www.lectlaw.com/def/b005.htm

LEGAL RESEARCH EXERCISES ON THE WEB

Go to http://wbl-cs.westbuslaw.com, the Web site that accompanies this text. Select "Interactive Study Center," and then click on "Chapter 46." There you will find the following Internet research exercise that you can perform to learn more about bailment relationships:

Activity 46–1: Bailments

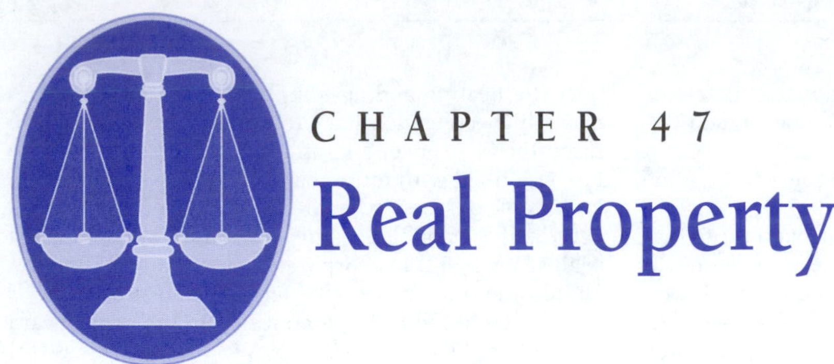

CHAPTER 47

Real Property

FROM THE EARLIEST TIMES, PROPERTY has provided a means for survival. Primitive peoples lived off the fruits of the land, eating the vegetation and wildlife. Later, as the wildlife was domesticated and the vegetation cultivated, property provided pasturage and farmland. In the twelfth and thirteenth centuries, the power of feudal lords was exemplified by the amount of land that they held. After the age of feudalism passed, property continued to be an indicator of family wealth and social position. In the Western world, the protection of an individual's right to his or her property has become one of the most important features of citizenship.

In this chapter, we first look at the nature of ownership rights in real property. We then examine the legal requirements involved in the transfer of real property, including the kinds of rights that are transferred by various types of deeds; the procedures used in the sale of real estate; and a way in which real property can, under certain conditions, be transferred merely by possession.

Realize that real property rights are never absolute. There is a higher right—that of the government to take, for compensation, private land for public use. The concluding section in this chapter discusses this right, called *eminent domain,* as well as zoning laws and other restrictions on the ownership of property.

SECTION 1

The Nature of Real Property

As discussed in Chapter 46, *real property* consists of land and the buildings, plants, and trees that it contains. Personal property is movable; real property is immovable. Real property usually means land, but it also includes subsurface and air rights, plant life and vegetation, and fixtures.

LAND

Land includes the soil on the surface of the earth and the natural products or artificial structures that are attached to it. Land further includes all the waters contained on or under its surface and the air space above it (subject, of course, to the legal use by pilots). In other words, unless a statute or case law holds otherwise, a landowner has the right to everything existing permanently below the surface of his or her property to the center of the earth and above it to the heavens.

AIR SPACE AND SUBSURFACE RIGHTS

The owner of real property has relatively exclusive rights to the air space above the land as well as the soil and minerals underneath it. Significant limitations on either air rights or subsurface rights normally have to be indicated on the document transferring title at the time of purchase. When no such limitations, or *encumbrances,* are noted, a purchaser can expect to have an unfettered right to possession of the property. The ways in which ownership rights in real property can be limited are examined in detail later in this chapter.

Air Rights. Until seventy-five years ago, the right to use the air space over an owner's property was not too significant. Early cases involving air rights dealt with matters such as whether a telephone wire could be run across a person's property when the wire did not touch any of the property[1] and whether a bullet shot over a person's land constituted trespass.[2]

Today, cases involving air rights present questions such as the right of commercial and private planes to fly over property and the right of individuals and governments to seed clouds and produce artificial rain. Flights over private land normally do not violate the property owners' rights unless the flights are low and frequent, causing a direct interference with the enjoyment and use of the land.[3]

Subsurface Rights. Ownership of the surface of land can be separated from ownership of its subsurface. Subsurface rights can be extremely valuable when minerals, oil, or natural gas is located beneath the surface. But a subsurface owner's rights would be of little value if he or she could not use the surface to exercise those rights. Hence, a subsurface owner will have a right (called a *profit,* discussed later in this chapter) to go onto the surface of the land to, for example, find and remove minerals.

Of course, conflicts may arise between surface and subsurface owners when attempts are made to excavate below the surface. At common law, a landowner has the right to have the land supported in its natural condition by the owners of the interests under the surface. If the owners of the subsurface rights excavate, they are absolutely liable if their excavation causes the surface to collapse. Depending on the circumstances, the excavators may also be liable for any damage to structures on the land. Many states have statutes that extend excavators' liability to include damage to structures on the property. Typically, these statutes provide exact guidelines as to the requirements for excavations of various depths.

Plant Life and Vegetation

Plant life, both natural and cultivated, is also considered to be real property. In many instances, natural vegetation, such as trees, adds greatly to the value of realty. When a parcel of land is sold and the land has growing crops on it, the sale includes the crops, unless otherwise specified in the sales contract. When crops are sold by themselves, however, they are considered to be personal property or goods. Consequently, the sale of crops is a sale of goods, and it is governed by the Uniform Commercial Code rather than by real property law.[4]

1. *Butler v. Frontier Telephone Co.,* 186 N.Y. 486, 79 N.E. 716 (1906). Stringing a wire across someone's property violates the air rights of that person. Leaning walls and projecting eave spouts and roofs also violate the air rights of the property owner.

2. *Herrin v. Sutherland,* 74 Mont. 587, 241 P. 328 (1925). Shooting over a person's land normally constitutes trespass.

3. *United States v. Causby,* 328 U.S. 256, 66 S.Ct. 1062, 90 L.Ed. 1206 (1946).

4. See UCC 2–107(2).

Section 2

Ownership Interests in Real Property

Ownership of property is an abstract concept that cannot exist independently of the legal system. No one can actually possess, or *hold,* a piece of land, the air above, the earth below, and all the water contained on it. One can only possess *rights* in real property. Numerous rights are involved in real property ownership. As discussed in Chapter 46, one who holds the entire bundle of rights owns the property in *fee simple.* Here we look first at the fee simple and then at some common examples of how an owner in fee simple can part with some, but not all, of his or her rights in real property.

Fee Simple

In a **fee simple absolute,** the owner has the greatest aggregation of rights, privileges, and power possible. The owner can give the property away, sell the property for a price, or transfer the property by will to another. The fee simple absolute is limited to a person and his or her heirs and is assigned forever without limitation or condition. The rights that accompany a fee simple absolute include the right to use the land for whatever purpose the owner sees fit, subject to laws that prevent the owner from unreasonably interfering with another person's land and subject to applicable zoning laws. Furthermore, the owner has the right of *exclusive* possession of the property. A fee simple is potentially infinite in duration and can be disposed of by deed or by will (by selling or giving it to another). When there is no will, the fee simple passes to the owner's legal heirs.

Life Estates

A **life estate** is an estate that lasts for the life of some specified individual. A **conveyance,** or transfer of real property, "to A for his life" creates a life estate.[5] In a life estate, the life tenant's ownership rights cease to exist on the life tenant's death. The life tenant has the right to use the land, provided no waste (injury to the land) is committed. In other words, the life tenant cannot injure the land in a manner that would adversely affect its value. The life tenant can use the land to harvest crops or, if mines and oil wells are already on the land, can extract minerals and oil from it, but the life tenant cannot exploit the land by creating new wells or mines.

The life tenant has the right to mortgage the life estate and create liens, easements, and leases; but none can extend beyond the life of the tenant. In addition, with few exceptions, the owner of a life estate has an exclusive right to possession during his or her lifetime.

Along with these rights, the life tenant also has some duties—to keep the property in repair and to pay property taxes. In sum, the owner of the life estate has the same rights as a fee simple owner except that he or she must maintain the value of the property during his or her tenancy, less the decrease in value resulting from the normal use of the property allowed by the life tenancy.

LEASEHOLD ESTATES

A **leasehold estate** is created when a real property owner or lessor (landlord) agrees to convey the right to possess and use the property to a lessee (tenant) for a certain period of time. In every leasehold estate, the tenant has a *qualified* right to exclusive possession (qualified by the right of the landlord to enter on the premises to assure that waste is not being committed). The tenant can use the land—for example, by harvesting crops—but cannot injure the land by such activities as cutting down timber for sale or extracting oil. The respective rights and duties of the landlord and tenant that arise under a lease agreement will be discussed in greater detail in Chapter 48. Here, we look at the types of leasehold estates, or tenancies, that can be created when real property is leased.

Tenancy for Years. A **tenancy for years** is created by an express contract (which can sometimes be oral) by which property is leased for a specified period of time, such as a month, a year, or a period of years. For example, signing a one-year lease to occupy an apartment creates a tenancy for years. At the end of the period specified in the lease, the lease ends (without notice), and possession of the apartment returns to the lessor. If the tenant dies during the period of the lease, the lease interest passes to the tenant's heirs as personal property. Often, leases include renewal or extension provisions.

Periodic Tenancy. A **periodic tenancy** is created by a lease that does not specify how long it is to last but does specify that rent is to be paid at certain intervals. This type of tenancy is automatically renewed for another rental period unless properly terminated. For example, a periodic tenancy is created by a lease that states, "Rent is due on the tenth day of every month." This provision creates a tenancy from month to month. A week-to-week or year-to-year tenancy can also be created. A periodic tenancy sometimes arises when a landlord allows a tenant under a tenancy for years to hold over (retain possession after the lease term ends) and continue paying monthly or weekly rent.

At common law, to terminate a periodic tenancy, the landlord or tenant must give one period's notice to the other party. If the tenancy is month to month, for example, one month's notice must be given. State statutes often require a different period for notice of termination in a periodic tenancy, however.

Tenancy at Will. Suppose that a landlord rents an apartment to a tenant "for as long as both agree." In such a case, the tenant receives a leasehold estate known as a **tenancy at will.** At common law, either party can terminate the tenancy without notice (that is, "at will"). This type of estate usually arises when a tenant who has been under a tenancy for years retains possession after the termination date of that tenancy with the landlord's consent. Before the tenancy has been converted into a periodic tenancy (by the periodic payment of rent), it is a tenancy at will, terminable by either party without notice. Once the tenancy is treated as a periodic tenancy, termination notice must conform to the requirements already discussed. The death of either party or the voluntary commission of waste by the tenant will terminate a tenancy at will.

Tenancy at Sufferance. The possession of land without right is called a **tenancy at sufferance.** A

5. A less common type of life estate is created by the conveyance "to A for the life of B." This is known as an estate *pur autre vie,* or an estate for the duration of the life of another.

tenancy at sufferance is created when a tenant *wrongfully* retains possession of property. It is not a true tenancy for that reason. For example, when a tenancy for years or a periodic tenancy ends and the tenant continues to retain possession of the premises without the owner's permission, a tenancy at sufferance is created.

NONPOSSESSORY INTERESTS

Some interests in land do not include any rights of possession. These interests, known as nonpossessory interests, include *easements, profits,* and *licenses.* Because easements and profits are similar, and the same rules apply to both, we discuss them together.

Easements and Profits. An **easement** is the right of a person to make limited use of another person's real property without taking anything from the property. An easement, for example, can be the right to walk across another's property. In contrast, a **profit** is the right to go onto land in possession of another and take away some part of the land itself or some product of the land. For example, Mack, the owner of Sandy View, gives Ann the right to go there and remove all the sand and gravel that she needs for her cement business. Ann has a profit. Easements and profits can be classified as either appurtenant or in gross.

An easement or profit *appurtenant* arises when the owner of one piece of land has a right to go onto (or remove things from) an adjacent piece of land owned by another. Suppose Owen has a right to drive his car across Green's land, which is adjacent to Owen's property. This right-of-way over Green's property is an easement appurtenant to Owen's land and can be used only by Owen. Owen can convey the easement when he conveys his property.

With an easement or profit *in gross,* the right to use or take things from another's land does not depend on the owner of the easement or profit's owning an adjacent tract of land. When a utility company is granted an easement to run its power lines across another's property, it obtains an easement in gross. An easement or profit in gross requires the existence of only one parcel of land, which must be owned by someone other than the owner of the easement or profit in gross.

Creation of an Easement or Profit. Profits and easements can be created by deed or by will, contract, implication, necessity, or prescription. Creation by deed or will simply involves the delivery of a *deed* or a transfer by *will* by the owner of an easement stating that the grantee (the person receiving the profit or easement) is granted the rights that the grantor had in the easement or profit. Easements or profits can also be created by *contract,* with the contract terms defining the extent and length of time of use.

An easement or profit may arise by *implication* when the circumstances surrounding the division of a parcel of property imply its creation. If Barrow divides a parcel of land that has only one well for drinking water and conveys the half without a well to Dan, a profit by implication arises, because Dan needs drinking water.

An easement may also be created by necessity. An easement by *necessity* does not require division of property for its existence. A person who rents an apartment, for example, has an easement by necessity in the private road leading up to the dwelling.

An easement arises by *prescription* when one person exercises an easement, such as a right-of-way, on another person's land without the landowner's consent, and the use is apparent and continues for a period of time equal to the applicable statute of limitations. In much the same way, title to property may be obtained by adverse possession, discussed later in this chapter.

Effect of a Sale of Property. When a parcel of land that is *benefited* by an easement or profit appurtenant is sold, the property carries the easement or profit along with it. Thus, if Owen sells his property to Thomas and includes the appurtenant right-of-way across Green's property in the deed to Thomas, Thomas will own both the property and the easement that benefits it.

When a parcel of land that has the *burden* of an easement or profit appurtenant is sold, the new owner must recognize its existence only if he or she knew or should have known of it or if it was recorded in the appropriate office of the county. Thus, if Owen records his easement across Green's property in the appropriate county office before Green conveys the land, the new owner of Green's property will have to allow Owen, or any subsequent owner of Owen's property, to continue to use the path across the land formerly owned by Green.

Termination of an Easement or Profit. An easement or profit can be terminated or extinguished in several ways. The simplest way is to deed it back to the owner of the land that is burdened by it. Also, if the owner of an easement or profit becomes the owner of the property burdened by it, it is merged into the property. Another way is to abandon it with the intent to relinquish the right to use it.

Licenses. A **license** is the revocable right of a person to come onto another person's land. It is a personal privilege that arises from the consent of the owner of the land and that can be revoked by the owner. A ticket to attend a movie at a theater is an example of a license. Assume that a Broadway theater owner issues to Roxanna a ticket to see a play. If Roxanna is refused entry into the theater because she is improperly dressed, she has no right to force her way into the theater. The ticket is only a revocable license, not a conveyance of an interest in property.

SECTION 3

Transfer of Ownership

Ownership of real property can pass from one person to another in a number of ways. Ownership rights in real property are commonly transferred through sale of the property or by will or inheritance. Real property ownership can also be transferred by gift, by possession, or (as will be discussed later in the chapter) by eminent domain. When ownership rights in real property are transferred, the type of interest being transferred and the conditions of the transfer normally are set forth in a *deed* executed by the one who is conveying the property.

DEEDS

Possession and title to land are passed from person to person by means of a **deed**—the instrument of conveyance of real property. A deed is a writing signed by an owner of real property by which title to it is transferred to another. Deeds must meet certain requirements. Unlike a contract, a deed does not have to be supported by legally sufficient consideration. Gifts of real property are common, and they require deeds even though there is no consideration for the gift. The necessary components of a valid deed are the following:

1. The names of the *grantor* (the giver or seller) and the *grantee* (the donee or buyer).
2. Words evidencing an intent to convey (for example, "I hereby bargain," "I hereby sell," "I hereby grant," or "I hereby give").
3. A legally sufficient description of the land.
4. The grantor's (and usually his or her spouse's) signature.
5. Delivery of the deed.

Warranty Deed. The **warranty deed** makes the greatest number of warranties and thus provides the most extensive protection against defects of title. A sample warranty deed is illustrated in Exhibit 47–1. In most states, special language is required to make a warranty deed. If a contract calls for a "warranty deed" without specifying the covenants to be included in the deed, or if a deed states that the seller is providing the "usual covenants," most courts will infer from this language that the following covenants are being made: a covenant that the grantor has the title to, and the power to convey, the property; a covenant that the buyer will not be disturbed in his or her possession of the land; and a covenant that transfer of the property is made without knowledge of adverse claims of third parties.

Special Warranty Deed. In contrast to the warranty deed, the **special warranty deed** warrants only that the grantor or seller has not previously done anything to lessen the value of the real estate. If the special warranty deed discloses all liens or other encumbrances, the seller will not be liable to the buyer if a third person subsequently interferes with the buyer's ownership. If the third person's claim arises out of, or is related to, some act of the seller, however, the seller will be liable to the buyer for damages.

Quitclaim Deed. A **quitclaim deed** warrants less than any other deed. Essentially, it simply conveys to the grantee whatever interest the grantor had. In other words, if the grantor had nothing, then the grantee receives nothing. Naturally, if the grantor had a defective title or no title at all, a conveyance by warranty deed or special warranty deed would not cure the defects. Such deeds, however, will give the buyer a cause of action to sue the seller.

A quitclaim deed can and often does serve as a release of the grantor's interest in a particular parcel of property. For instance, suppose Sandor owns a strip of waterfront property on which he wants to build condominiums. Lanz has an interest in a section of the property, which he might assert either to

EXHIBIT 47–1 A SAMPLE WARRANTY DEED

Date: May 31, 2003

Grantor: GAYLORD A. JENTZ AND WIFE, JOANN H. JENTZ

Grantor's Mailing Address (including county):
4106 North Loop Drive
Austin, Travis County, Texas

Grantee: DAVID F. FRIEND AND WIFE, JOAN E. FRIEND AS JOINT TENANTS WITH RIGHT OF SURVIVORSHIP

Grantee's Mailing Address (including county):
5929 Fuller Drive
Austin, Travis County, Texas

Consideration:
For and in consideration of the sum of Ten and No/100 Dollars ($10.00) and other valuable consideration to the undersigned paid by the grantees herein named, the receipt of which is hereby acknowledged, and for which no lien is retained, either express or implied.

Property (including any improvements):
Lot 23, Block "A", Northwest Hills, Green Acres Addition, Phase 4, Travis County, Texas, according to the map or plat of record in volume 22, pages 331-336 of the Plat Records of Travis County, Texas.

Reservations from and Exceptions to Conveyance and Warranty:

This conveyance with its warranty is expressly made subject to the following:

Easements and restrictions of record in Volume 7863, Page 53, Volume 8430, Page 35, Volume 8133, Page 152 of the Real Property Record of Travis County, Texas, Volume 22, Pages 335-339, of the Plat Records of Travis County, Texas; and to any other restrictions and easements affecting said property which are of record in Travis County, Texas.

Grantor, for the consideration and subject to the reservations from and exceptions to conveyance and warranty, grants, sells, and conveys to Grantee the property, together with all and singular the rights and appurtenances thereto in any wise belonging, to have and hold it to Grantee, Grantee's heirs, executors, administrators, successors, or assigns forever. Grantor binds Grantor and Grantor's heirs, executors, administrators, and successors to warrant and forever defend all and singular the property to Grantee and Grantee's heirs, executors, administrators, successors, and assigns against every person whomsoever lawfully claiming or to claim the same or any part thereof, except as to the reservations from and exceptions to conveyance and warranty.

When the context requires, singular nouns and pronouns include the plural.

BY: *Gaylord A. Jentz*
Gaylord A. Jentz

BY: *JoAnn H. Jentz*
JoAnn H. Jentz

(Acknowledgment)

STATE OF TEXAS
COUNTY OF TRAVIS

This instrument was acknowledged before me on the 31st day of May , 2003
by Gaylord A. and JoAnn H. Jentz

Rosemary Potter
Notary Public, State of Texas
Notary's name (printed): Rosemary Potter

Notary Seal

Notary's commission expires: **1/31/2007**

prevent the development or to insist on a share of its earnings. Sandor can negotiate with Lanz for a release of the claim. Lanz's signing of a quitclaim deed would constitute such a release.

Grant Deed. With a **grant deed**, the grantor simply states, "I grant the property to you" or "I convey, or bargain and sell, the property to you." By state statute, grant deeds may carry with them an implied warranty that the grantor owns the property being transferred and has not previously encumbered it or conveyed it to someone else.

Sheriff's Deed. A **sheriff's deed** is a document giving ownership rights to a buyer at a sheriff's sale, which is a sale held by a sheriff to pay a court judgment against the owner of the property. Typically, the property was subject to a mortgage or tax payments and the owner defaulted on the payments. A deed is given to the buyer at the sale as part of the foreclosure process on the mortgage or tax lien. The giving of the deed begins the running of the period of time during which the defaulting owner can redeem the property (see Chapter 29).

Recording Statutes. Every jurisdiction has **recording statutes,** which allow deeds to be recorded. Recording a deed gives notice to the public that a certain person is now the owner of a particular parcel of real estate. Thus, prospective buyers can check the public records for transactions creating interests or rights in specific parcels of real property. Placing everyone on notice as to the true owner is intended to prevent the previous owners from fraudulently conveying the land to other purchasers. Deeds are generally recorded in the county in which the property is located. Many state statutes require that the grantor sign the deed in the presence of two witnesses before it can be recorded. There are three basic types of recording statutes:

1. A *race statute* provides that the first purchaser to record a deed has superior rights to the property, regardless of whether he or she knew that someone else had already bought the property but had failed to record the deed.[6] Under these statutes, recording is a "race," and whoever files first "wins."
2. A *pure notice statute* provides that, regardless of who files first, a person who knows that someone else has already bought the property cannot claim priority. In contrast, a subsequent good faith purchaser who, at the time he or she acquires a deed, has no notice of a previous deed—because, for example, it has not been recorded—may successfully assert a superior claim to the property. (A *good faith purchaser* is one who purchases for value, in good faith, and without notice.)
3. A *notice-race statute* protects a purchaser who does not know that someone else has already bought the property and who records his or her deed first.

Recording a deed involves a fee. The grantee typically pays this fee, because he or she is the one who will be protected by recording the deed.

Contracts for the Sale of Real Estate

Transfers of ownership interests in real property are frequently accomplished by means of a sale. The sale of real estate is similar to the sale of goods, because it involves a transfer of ownership, often with specific warranties. In the sale of real estate, however, certain formalities are observed that are not required in the sale of goods. For example, to meet the requirements of law, a deed must be signed and delivered.[7]

Exhibit 47–2 lists the steps involved in any sale of real property. The first step is the formation of the land sales contract. A title search (to verify that the seller has good title to the property and that no other claims to the property exist) follows, along with, usually, negotiations to obtain financing for the purchase. The final step is the closing. We examine some of the legal considerations involved in these steps below, as well as other requirements relating to the sale of real property. First, however, we look at the important role played by real estate agents, or brokers, in the sale of real property.

Brokers. Buyers and sellers of real property frequently enlist the services of a *real estate agent,* or broker. Real estate agents are information brokers. They provide buyers and sellers of real estate with information and specialize in matching the wants of

6. Only two states (Delaware and North Carolina) use race statutes. Usage in the rest of the states is split about evenly between the pure notice statute and the notice-race statute.

7. The phrase *signed, sealed, and delivered* once referred to the requirements for transferring title to real property by deed. The seal has fallen from use, but signature and delivery are still required.

EXHIBIT 47–2 STEPS INVOLVED IN THE SALE OF REAL ESTATE

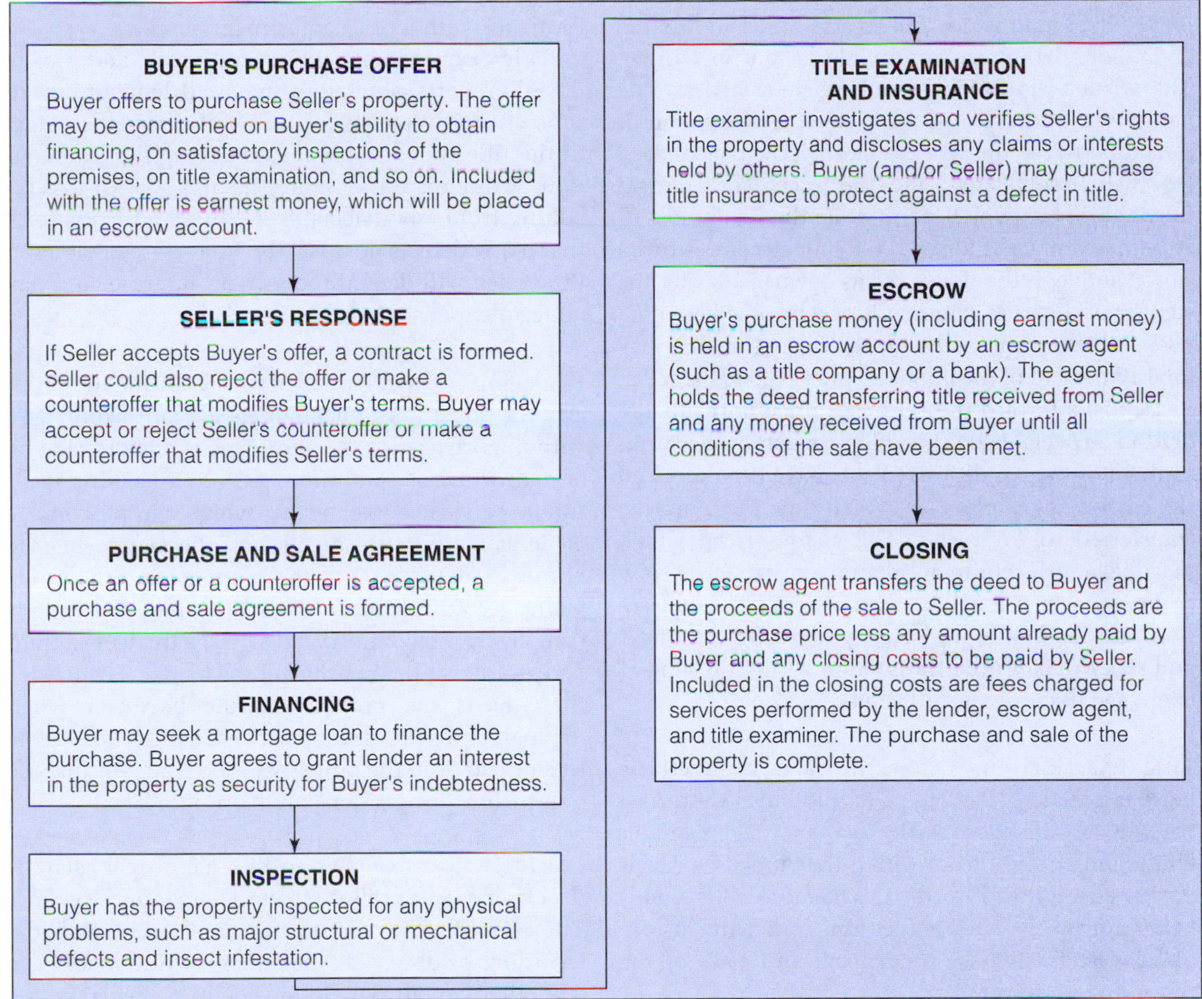

buyers with the property being offered for sale by sellers.

Normally, the broker is retained by the seller and acts as the seller's agent in the sale of the property. In compensation for their services, brokers usually receive a commission (which can range from 1 to 10 percent of the purchase price) from the seller when the sale is concluded. A broker can also act as an agent of the buyer, in which case a dual agency exists. Generally, a broker may not act as an agent for more than one party without the consent of all parties involved, and state laws often place further restrictions on dual agencies. Most states require real estate brokers to be licensed, and in some states, brokers may be required to meet continuing-education or other requirements.

Formation of the Sales Contract. If someone decides to purchase real estate, normally he or she makes a written offer to purchase the property and puts up *earnest money* to show that an earnest, or serious, offer is being made. (If the buyer decides to withdraw the offer, the earnest money will often be forfeited, as liquidated damages, to the seller.) The offer states in some detail the exact offering price for the property and lists any other conditions that may be appropriate. The offer may be conditioned on the offeror's ability to obtain financing, for example. Within a specified time period, the seller of the property either accepts or rejects the offer—or, as is often the case, makes a counteroffer. The seller then becomes the offeror and the buyer the offeree.

Once the offer (or counteroffer) is accepted, a contract of sale is drawn up. Because an oral agreement for a sale of land is not enforceable under the Statute of Frauds, the agreement should be put in writing. The written agreement should include at least the names and addresses of the parties, a description of the property, the time for the closing, the type of deed that will be delivered, and the price. The contract might also state which party bears the risk of loss if, after the contract is formed, the property is destroyed (for example, if the house burns down).[8] Usually, the signing of the sales contract is accompanied by a deposit, which, combined with the earnest money, may total 10 percent of the purchase price paid to the seller.

Deposits toward the purchase price normally are held in a special account, called an **escrow account**, until all of the conditions of sale have been met and the closing takes place, at which time the money is transferred to the seller. The *escrow agent*, which may be a title company, bank, or special escrow company, acts as a neutral party in the sales transaction and facilitates the sale by allowing the buyer and seller to close the transaction without having to exchange documents and funds.

Title Examination. After the sales contract has been negotiated, the buyer or the buyer's attorney (or the escrow agent, title insurance company, or lending institution from which the purchase price is borrowed) performs a *title examination*. This entails examining at the county recording office the history of all past transfers of, liens on, and sales of the property in question.

A contract for the sale of land includes the seller's implied obligation to transfer marketable title. **Marketable title** is title that is free from encumbrances (such as mortgages and restrictive covenants, both of which are discussed below), defects in the chain of title (such as a previous sale of the property by the seller), and other events that affect title (such as adverse possession and eminent domain, both of which are discussed below). Title is considered marketable even if the property is subject to zoning restrictions or public easements, such as sidewalks and sewers. If a title examination uncovers a material defect that has not been disclosed in the contract, the seller is considered to have breached the contract, and the buyer may seek any appropriate remedies (damages, rescission, or specific performance with a price adjustment).

Title examinations are not foolproof, and buyers of real property generally purchase **title insurance** to protect their interests in the event that some defect in the title was not discovered during the examination. A title insurance policy insures against loss resulting from any defects in the title and guarantees that if any defects do arise, the title company issuing the policy will defend the owner's interests and pay all legal expenses involved.

Financing. Unless a buyer pays cash for the property, the buyer must obtain financing for the purchase with a mortgage loan. A **mortgage** is a loan made by an individual or institution, such as a banking institution or trust company, for which the property is given as security. In some states, the *mortgagor* (the borrower) holds title to the property; in others, the *mortgagee* (the lender) holds title until the loan is completely repaid. In several states, a trustee—a third party—holds title on behalf of the lender. The trustee then deeds the property to the borrower when the loan is repaid. If the payments are not made, the trustee can deed the property to the lender or dispose of it by foreclosure, depending on state law.

Closing. The final step in the sale of real estate is the **closing**—also called *settlement* or *closing of escrow*. The escrow agent coordinates the closing with the recording of deeds, the obtaining of title insurance, and other concurrent closing activities. Several costs must be paid, in cash, at the time of closing. These costs include fees for services, including those performed by the lender, escrow agent, and title company, and they can range from several hundred to several thousand dollars, depending on the amount of the mortgage loan and other conditions of sale. The 1976 amendments to the Real Estate Settlement Procedures Act of 1974[9] require lending institutions to notify—within a specified time period—each applicant for a mortgage loan of the specific costs that must be paid at the closing.

Warranty of Habitability. The common law rule of *caveat emptor* ("let the buyer beware") held that the seller of a home made no warranties with respect to its soundness or fitness unless such a warranty was

8. Unless the contract states otherwise, the buyer will suffer any loss (assuming that the loss is not the seller's fault). Either party can take out an insurance policy against the risk, however.

9. 12 U.S.C. Sections 2601–2617.

specifically included in the deed or contract of sale. There is currently a strong trend against this rule and in favor of an **implied warranty of habitability.** Under this approach, which is the law in the majority of states, the seller of a new house warrants that it will be fit for human habitation regardless of whether any such warranty is included in the deed or contract of sale. This warranty is similar to the UCC's implied warranty of merchantability for sales of personal property.

Essentially, under an implied warranty of habitability, the seller warrants that the house is in reasonable working order and is of reasonably sound construction. To recover damages for breach of the implied warranty of habitability, the purchaser is required to prove only that the home he or she purchased was somehow defective and to prove that the damages were caused by the defect. Thus, under the warranty of habitability theory, the seller of a new home is in effect a guarantor of the home's fitness. In some states, the warranty protects not only the first purchaser but any subsequent purchaser as well.

Seller's Duty to Disclose. Traditionally, under the rule of *caveat emptor,* a seller had no duty to disclose to the buyer defects in the property, even if the seller knew about the defects and the buyer had no reasonable way to discover them. Currently, in most jurisdictions, courts have placed on sellers a duty to disclose any known defect that materially affects the value of the property and that the buyer could not reasonably discover. Under these circumstances, nondisclosure is similar to representing that the defect does not exist, and the buyer may have grounds for a successful lawsuit based on fraud or misrepresentation.

For example, Nick sells Nora a five-year-old house that he knows has roof problems. Nick does not tell Nora about these problems. During the first rain after the sale, water gushes from the house's ceilings and light fixtures. Nora contacts a roofing contractor, who tells her that repair would be a temporary solution and only a new roof would be watertight. Nora might sue Nick for breach of contract, fraud, and misrepresentation, seeking rescission of their contract and a return of whatever amount she paid Nick toward the purchase price of the house.

Westlaw. See Case 47.1 at the end of this chapter. To view the full, unedited case from Westlaw,® go to this text's Web site at **http://wbl-cs.westbuslaw.com**.

Transfer by Inheritance

Property that is transferred on an owner's death is passed either by will or by inheritance laws. If the owner of land dies with a will, that land passes according to the terms of the will. If the owner dies without a will, state statutes prescribe how and to whom the property will pass. The transfer of property by inheritance will be discussed in Chapter 50.

Adverse Possession

Adverse possession is a means of obtaining title to land without delivery of a deed. Essentially, when one person possesses the property of another for a certain statutory period of time (three to thirty years, with ten years being most common), that person, called the adverse possessor, acquires title to the land and cannot be removed from it by the original owner. The adverse possessor may ultimately be vested with good title just as if there had been a conveyance by deed.

For property to be held adversely, four elements must be satisfied:

1. Possession must be actual and exclusive; that is, the possessor must take sole physical occupancy of the property.
2. The possession must be open, visible, and notorious, not secret or clandestine. The possessor must occupy the land for all the world to see.
3. Possession must be continuous and peaceable for the required period of time. This requirement means that the possessor must not be interrupted in the occupancy by the true owner or by the courts.
4. Possession must be hostile and adverse. In other words, the possessor must claim the property as against the whole world. He or she cannot be living on the property with the permission of the owner.

There are a number of public-policy reasons for the adverse possession doctrine. These include society's interest in resolving boundary disputes, in quieting (determining) title when title to property is in question, and in assuring that real property remains in the stream of commerce. More fundamentally, policies behind the doctrine include punishing owners who sit on their rights too long and rewarding possessors for putting land to productive use.

See Case 47.2 at the end of this chapter. To view the full, unedited case from Westlaw,® go to this text's Web site at **http://wbl-cs.westbuslaw.com**.

SECTION 4

Limitations on the Rights of Property Owners

No ownership rights in real property can ever really be absolute. That is, an owner of real property cannot always do whatever he or she wishes on or with the property. Nuisance and environmental laws, for example, restrict certain types of activities. Holding the property is also conditional on the payment of property taxes. If these taxes are not paid, ownership of the property will be forfeited to the state. In addition, if a property owner fails to pay debts, the property may be seized to satisfy judgment creditors. In short, the rights of every property owner are subject to certain conditions and limitations. In this final section of the chapter, we look at some of the important ways in which owners' rights in real property can be limited.

EMINENT DOMAIN

Even if ownership in real property is in fee simple absolute, there is still a superior ownership that limits the fee simple absolute. Just as the king was the ultimate landowner in medieval England, so in the United States, the government has ultimate ownership rights in all land. This right is called **eminent domain**, and it is sometimes referred to as the *condemnation power* of the government to take land for public use. It gives a right to the government to acquire possession of real property in the manner directed by the Constitution and the laws of the state whenever the public interest requires it. Property may not be taken for private benefit, but only for public use.

For example, when a new public highway is to be built, the government must decide where to build it and how much land to condemn. The power of eminent domain is generally invoked through condemnation proceedings. After the government determines that a particular parcel of land is necessary for public use, it brings a judicial proceeding to obtain title to the land. Then, in another proceeding, the court determines the *fair value* of the land, which is usually approximately equal to its market value. When the government takes land owned by a private party for public use, it is referred to as a **taking**, and the government must compensate the private party. Under the so-called *takings clause* of the Fifth Amendment, the government may not take private property for public use without "just compensation." State constitutions contain similar provisions.

See Case 47.3 at the end of this chapter. To view the full, unedited case from Westlaw,® go to this text's Web site at **http://wbl-cs.westbuslaw.com**.

ZONING

The state's power to control the use of land through legislation is derived from two sources: eminent domain and police power. Through eminent domain, the government can take land for public use, but it must pay just compensation. Consequently, eminent domain is an expensive method of land-use control. Under its police power, however, the state can pass laws aimed at protecting public health, safety, morals, and general welfare. These laws include *zoning laws,* by which the state can regulate uses of land without having to compensate the landowner. If, however, a state law restricts a landowner's property rights too much, the state's regulation will be deemed a *confiscation,* or a taking, and may be subject to the eminent domain requirement that just compensation be paid.

Suppose that Perez owns a large tract of land, which she purchased with the intent to subdivide it and develop it into residential properties. At the time of the purchase, there were no zoning regulations restricting use of the land. If the government attempts to zone Perez's entire tract of land as "public parkland only" and thus to prohibit her from developing any part of it, the action will be deemed confiscatory; this is because the government will be denying her the ability to use her property for any reasonable income-producing or private purpose for which it is suited and because she had reasonable, investment-backed expectations in her development plans. The zoning regulation normally will be held unconstitutional and void, or the government will have to compensate Perez, because it has effectively confiscated her land.

The state's power to regulate the use of land is limited in two other ways, both of which arise from the Fourteenth Amendment. First, the state cannot regulate the use of land arbitrarily or unreasonably, because this would be taking property without due process. There must be a *rational basis* for the classifications that the state imposes on property. Any act that is reasonably related to the health or general welfare of the public is deemed to have a rational basis. Second, a state's regulation of land use cannot be discriminatory. A zoning ordinance is considered discriminatory if it affects one parcel of land in a way in which it does not affect surrounding parcels and if there is no rational basis for the difference.

Variances. A landowner whose land has been limited by a zoning ordinance to a particular use cannot make an alternative use of the land unless he or she first obtains a zoning variance. A landowner must meet three criteria to be entitled to a variance:

1. The landowner must find it impossible to realize a reasonable return on the land as zoned.
2. The zoning ordinance must have an adverse effect that is particular to the person seeking the variance rather than being similar for all the landowners within the same zone.
3. Granting of the variance must not substantially alter the essential character of the zoned area.

Courts tend to be rather lenient about the first two requirements. By far the most important criterion in granting a variance is whether it will substantially alter the character of the neighborhood.

Building Permits. As part of its power to control the use of land through legislation, the state can regulate such things as the overall appearance of a community. For example, local ordinances may prohibit a property owner's tearing down or remodeling a historic landmark. The state may also require property owners to make concessions for such public needs as transportation. Typically, these goals are accomplished in part by requiring that an owner obtain a building permit from a local review board before undertaking a building project. In issuing a permit, the board may impose certain restrictions. Builder-developers are routinely required, for example, to include sidewalks and access roads in their developments.

The United States Supreme Court has held that such restrictions do not constitute a taking of an owner's property if they "substantially advance legitimate state interests" and do not "den[y] an owner economically viable use of his land."[10] It is not clear, however, exactly what constitutes a "legitimate state interest" or when particular restrictions "substantially advance" that interest. Furthermore, the phrase "economically viable use" is not yet clearly defined.

10. *Agins v. Tiburon*, 447 U.S. 255, 100 S.Ct. 2138, 65 L.Ed.2d 106 (1980).

RESTRICTIVE COVENANTS

A private restriction on the use of land is known as a **restrictive covenant.** If the restriction is binding on the party who purchases the property originally and on subsequent purchasers as well—in other words, if its benefit or obligation passes with the land's ownership—it is said to "run with the land."

Covenants Running with the Land. A restrictive covenant that runs with the land goes with the land and cannot be separated from it. Consider an example. Owen is the owner of Grasslands, a twenty-acre estate the northern half of which contains a small reservoir. Owen wishes to convey the northern half to Arid City, but before he does, he digs an irrigation ditch connecting the reservoir with the lower ten acres, which he uses as farmland. When Owen conveys the northern ten acres to Arid City, he enters into an agreement with the city. The agreement, which is contained in the deed, states, "Arid City, its heirs and assigns, promises not to remove more than five thousand gallons of water per day from the Grasslands reservoir." Owen has created a restrictive covenant running with the land. Under this covenant, Arid City and all future owners of the northern ten acres of Grasslands are limited as to the amount of water they can draw from its reservoir.

Four requirements must be met for a covenant running with the land to be enforceable. If they are not met, the covenant will apply to the two original parties to a contract only and will not run with the land to future owners. The requirements are as follows:

1. The covenant running with the land must be created in a written agreement (covenant). It is usually contained in the document that conveys the land.
2. The parties must intend that the covenant run with the land. In other words, the instrument that contains the covenant must state not only that the promisor is bound by the terms of the covenant but that all the promisor's "successors, heirs, or assigns" will be bound.
3. The covenant must *touch and concern* the land. That is, the limitations on the activities of the owner of the burdened land must have some connection with the land. For example, a purchaser of land cannot be bound by a covenant requiring him or her to drive only Ford pickups, because such a restriction has no relation to the land purchased.
4. The successors to the original parties to the covenant must have notice of the covenant.

To satisfy the last requirement, the notice may be actual or constructive. For example, in the course of developing a fifty-lot suburban subdivision, Levitt records a declaration of restrictions that effectively limits construction on each lot to one single-family house. In each lot's deed is a reference to the declaration with a provision that the purchaser and his or her successors are bound to those restrictions. Thus, each purchaser assumes ownership with notice of the restrictions. If an owner attempts to build a duplex (or any structure that does not comply with the restrictions) on a lot, the other owners may obtain a court order enjoining the construction.

In fact, Levitt might simply have included the restrictions on the subdivision's map, filed the map in the appropriate public office, and included a reference to the map in each deed. In this way, each owner would also have been held to have constructive notice of the restrictions.

Illegal Restrictive Covenants. Restrictive covenants have sometimes been used to perpetuate neighborhood segregation, and in these cases they have been invalidated by the courts. In the United States Supreme Court case of *Shelley v. Kraemer,*[11] restrictive covenants proscribing resale to members of minority groups were declared unconstitutional. In addition, the Civil Rights Act of 1968 (also known as the Fair Housing Act) prohibits all discrimination based on race, color, religion, or national origin in the sale and leasing of housing.

11. 334 U.S. 1, 68 S.Ct. 836, 92 L.Ed. 1161 (1948).

Terms and Concepts to Review

adverse possession 981
closing 980
conveyance 973
deed 976
easement 975
eminent domain 982
escrow account 980
fee simple absolute 973
grant deed 978
implied warranty of habitability 981
leasehold estate 974
license 976
life estate 973
marketable title 980
mortgage 980
periodic tenancy 974
profit 975
quitclaim deed 976
recording statute 978
restrictive covenant 983
sheriff's deed 978
special warranty deed 976
taking 982
tenancy at sufferance 974
tenancy at will 974
tenancy for years 974
title insurance 980
warranty deed 976

Chapter Summary

The Nature of Real Property	Real property (also called real estate, or realty) is immovable. It includes land, subsurface and air rights, plant life and vegetation, and fixtures.
Ownership Interests in Real Property	**1.** *Fee simple absolute*—The most complete form of ownership. **2.** *Fee simple defeasible*—Ownership in fee simple that can end if a specified event or condition occurs. **3.** *Life estate*—An estate that lasts for the life of a specified individual, during which time the individual is entitled to possess, use, and benefit from the estate; ownership rights in a life estate are subject to the rights of the future-interest holder. **4.** *Leasehold estate*—An interest in real property that is held only for a limited period of time, as specified in the lease agreement. **5.** *Nonpossessory interest*—An interest that involves the right to use real property but not to possess it. Easements, profits, and licenses are nonpossessory interests.

CHAPTER SUMMARY—CONTINUED

Transfer of Ownership	1. *By deed*—When real property is sold or transferred as a gift, title to the property is conveyed by means of a deed. A deed must meet specific legal requirements. A *warranty deed* warrants the most extensive protection against defects of title. A *quitclaim deed* conveys to the grantee only whatever interest the grantor had in the property. A deed may be recorded in the manner prescribed by *recording statutes* in the appropriate jurisdiction to give third parties notice of the owner's interest. 2. *By sale*—Ownership rights in real property are frequently transferred by sale, by means of a sales contract between the seller and buyer of the property. A sale of real property typically involves a title examination, financing arrangements, and the "closing" of the transaction. 3. *By will or inheritance*—If the owner dies after having made a valid will, the land passes as specified in the will. If the owner dies without having made a will, the heirs inherit according to state inheritance statutes. 4. *By adverse possession*—When a person possesses the property of another for a statutory period of time (three to thirty years, with ten years being the most common), that person acquires title to the property, provided the possession is actual and exclusive, open and visible, continuous and peaceable, and hostile and adverse (without the permission of the owner). 5. *By eminent domain*—The government can take land for public use, with just compensation, when the public interest requires the taking.
Limitations on the Rights of Property Owners	The rights of owners of real property can be limited in three ways: 1. *By eminent domain*—The government's power to take land for public use, with just compensation, when the public interest requires the taking. 2. *By zoning laws*—State and local government regulations that impose certain restrictions on land use in specific areas. 3. *By restrictive covenants*—Private restrictions created by contract, including "covenants running with the land," that limit the use of the land.

CASES FOR ANALYSIS

Westlaw. You can access the full text of each case presented below by going to the Westlaw cases on this text's Web site at http://wbl-cs.westbuslaw.com. Each Westlaw case includes the names of all plaintiffs and defendants, the dates on which the case was argued and decided, a brief summary of the issues and decisions in the case, headnotes classifying specific issues in the case according to the West Key Number System, and the court's opinion. Concurring and dissenting opinions, if any, are included as well.

CASE 47.1 SELLER'S DUTY TO DISCLOSE

SMITH V. LEVINE

Court of Appeals of Texas—San Antonio, 1995.
911 S.W.2d 427.

DUNCAN, Justice.

* * * *

FACTS

This case arises out of the sale of a house by [Donald and Pat Smith] to [Ronald and Serena Levine] in 1991. The house, which was next door to the Smiths' home, was occupied by Mrs. Smith's mother from 1981 until 1988; thereafter, the house was completely remodeled and then leased to Monte Grissom. In 1989, when Grissom was considering purchasing the house, he hired Jim Bradley of American Engineering to do a mechanical and foundation analysis. On January 23, 1989, in his written report to the Grissoms, Bradley stated, in relevant part, that the foundation of the house "has deflected to the extent that it has damaged the superstructure and therefore the foundation is defective." Grissom discussed the report with Mr. Smith and even offered to give him a copy of Bradley's report in exchange for Mr. Smith paying one-half of Bradley's fee. Mr. Smith declined, stating that "[t]he foundation report that you mention would have no value to us as we do not plan to put any additional money into the house prior to selling it." Because of the defective foundation, the Grissoms decided against buying the house.

Thereafter, the Smiths listed the house with a real estate agent. They did not, however, mention the defective foundation on the agent's questionnaire. When the agent failed to produce a purchaser, the Smiths put the house on the market themselves—running newspaper advertisements and distributing brochures describing the house as being in "excellent" condition. In response to one of these newspaper advertisements, the Levines became interested in the house. Although the Levines observed minor cracks and a slight slope to the floor in one area of the house, Mr. Smith assured them that the cracks were superficial and routine for a house in that area. At no time did the Smiths inform the Levines that Bradley had determined that the foundation was defective. Nor was the defective foundation picked up by Henri Leonidov, an engineer hired by the Levines to do a "walk through" inspection. Instead Leonidov's report stated that the cracks were minor and superficial. The Levines ultimately purchased the house for the Smiths' full asking price, paying $25,000 at closing and giving the Smiths a promissory note, secured by the house, for the balance.

In late 1992, the Levines had financial difficulties and decided to sell the house to pay off their debts. They obtained a second report from Leonidov, which was similar to the first, and listed the house with a realtor. The Levines disclosed to the realtor the existence of what they thought were nonstructural cracks. In early 1993, the Levines contracted to sell the house to David Holmes. Although they gave Holmes copies of both of Leonidov's reports, Holmes decided to hire his own inspector. By coincidence, Holmes hired Bradley. Upon learning that Bradley had earlier determined that the foundation was defective, Holmes demanded the return of his earnest money and termination of the contract. The Levines immediately complied.

Upon reviewing Bradley's report, the Levines hired an attorney and made demand on the Smiths. The Smiths responded by hiring their own attorney, who accelerated the balance due on the promissory note and attempted to foreclose on the house. A restraining order and later a temporary injunction prevented the Smiths' attempt to foreclose on the Levines' home pending trial [in a Texas state court].

The jury found that the Smiths knowingly engaged in a false, misleading or deceptive act or practice * * * [that was] a producing cause of damages to the Levines. The jury found the difference in value of the house as represented and received to be $33,800 and that the Levines should receive $14,400 each for their mental anguish. Finally, the jury assessed punitive damages in the amount of $65,000 against Mr. Smith and $32,750 against Mrs. Smith and found the attorney's fees reasonably incurred by the Smiths and the Levines as dollar amounts and, as to the Levines, as a percentage of their recovery.

* * * The net recovery to the Levines was $81,792.62, together with postjudgment interest and costs. The Smiths appeal, seeking either * * * [a] judgment in their favor or, alternatively, a new trial. * * *

DECEPTIVE TRADE PRACTICE

* * * [T]he Smiths contend that there is legally and factually insufficient evidence to support the jury's findings that the Smiths knowingly committed a deceptive trade practice that was a producing cause of damage to the Levines. * * *

* * * *

* * * [T]he Smiths argue * * * that they cannot be held liable for knowingly failing to disclose information of which the Levines were or should have been equally aware. We cannot agree that the record supports the Smiths' factual premise.

By virtue of their awareness of Bradley's report, and Grissom's resulting refusal to purchase, the jury was entitled to find that the Smiths knew the foundation was defective by the time of the Smith-Levine transaction. This foundation problem was not simply a matter of "superficial" and "routine" cracks in interior walls or the slope in the floor—defects of which the Levines were made aware by their own visual inspection, as well as by Leonidov's report. Rather, the foundation problem arose out of a perimeter grade beam that had become so deflected as to damage the superstructure of the house. That is the information contained in Bradley's report, and that is the information the jury could reasonably have found the Smiths should have but did not disclose to the Levines. * * *

* * * *

* * * [T]he judgment is affirmed.

CASE 47.2 ADVERSE POSSESSION

KLOS v. MOLENDA

Superior Court of Pennsylvania, 1986.
355 Pa.Super. 399,
513 A.2d 490.

WIEAND, Judge:

* * * *

* * * On September 20, 1950, Michael and Albina Klos, the appellees, purchased a tract of land, measuring fifty (50) feet in width and one hundred thirty-five (135) feet in depth, from a larger tract owned by John and Anne Molenda on Greenwood Avenue in Scranton [Pennsylvania]. In lieu of a survey, John Molenda and Michael Klos paced off the lot and placed stakes in the ground to mark the boundary between the lot pur-

chased by Klos and the land retained by Molenda. Michael and Albina Klos built a residence on their lot and, in 1952, poured a concrete sidewalk along the front of the property which extended to the property line designated by the stakes previously placed by the parties. The Kloses also installed a concrete driveway on their property, the edge of which was thirty (30) inches from the line designated by the stakes. In the intervening thirty-inch strip, they placed top soil and planted grass, which they maintained continuously until the events which led to the instant litigation [the litigation now before the court]. In either 1956 of 1957, the Molendas also planted hedge along the staked property line. This hedge line remained in place until 1981 or 1982, when it was partially removed. The remaining hedge plants were removed in 1984.

John Molenda died in 1983. His widow employed a surveyor to survey the land which she owned. The surveyor located the property line separating the Klos and Molenda lands along the edge of the Klos driveway. Thereafter, Anne Molenda, the appellant herein, caused a fence to be constructed along the edge of the Klos driveway. This prompted Michael and Albina Klos to commence an action in [a Pennsylvania state court] to establish their ownership of the thirty (30) inch strip and to enjoin Anne Molenda's interference therewith. [The court held that the Kloses had title to the land. Mrs. Molenda appealed to a state intermediate appellate court.]

It is well settled that he who asserts title by adverse possession must prove it affirmatively. *One who claims title by adverse possession must prove that he had actual, continuous, exclusive, visible, notorious, distinct, and hostile possession of the land for twenty-one years* * * * . Each of these elements must exist, otherwise the possession will not confer title. An adverse possessor must intend to hold the land for himself, and that intention must be made manifest by his acts * * * . He must keep his flag flying and present a hostile front to all adverse pretensions. [Emphasis added.]

On appeal, Mrs. Molenda's principal contentions are that the Klos possession was (1) sporadic rather than continuous, and (2) permissive and neither hostile nor adverse. We reject these arguments. The evidence disclosed that appellees had continuously maintained the strip of land in lawn between 1952 and 1984, when their maintenance of the lawn was prevented by the fence which Anne Molenda had erected. The use of land for lawn purposes and the continuous maintenance thereof in connection with a residence, it has been held, are sufficient to establish adverse possession.

The hostile nature of the Klos possession was not destroyed because the stake line may have been placed along a property line mistakenly located by the adjoining landowners. This fact did not render Klos' possession permissive. The parties intended that the Kloses should have title to that line, and thereafter the Kloses kept their flag flying continuously on the thirty (30) inch strip of land. Their possession, open, notorious and exclusive for more than twenty-one years, presented a hostile front to any person or persons intending to make a conflicting pretension of ownership.

[The trial court's judgment is affirmed.]

CASE 47.3 EMINENT DOMAIN

PURDIE V. ATTORNEY GENERAL

Supreme Court of New Hampshire, 1999.
143 N.H. 661,
732 A.2d 442.

BRODERICK, J. [Justice]

* * * *

I

In 1995, the [New Hampshire] legislature enacted [Revised Statutes Annotated (RSA) Chapter] 483-C, which recognizes the State's public trust rights in "all shorelands subject to the ebb and flow of the tide to the high water mark and subject to those littoral rights recognized at common law." The statute defines "high water mark" * * * "the furthest landward limit reached by the highest tidal flow" over the nineteen-year tidal cycle, excluding "abnormal" storms. Soon after the statute was enacted, [William Purdie and forty other beach-front property owners] brought an action [in a New Hampshire state court against the state] asserting that the statute effected a taking of their property without just compensation in violation of * * * the New Hampshire Constitution and the Fifth Amendment of the United States Constitution.

* * * [T]he parties * * * file[d] cross-motions for summary judgment. In ruling for the plaintiffs, the trial court concluded that "settled" common law defines the term "high water mark" as the " mean high tide line," and therefore, the legislature's action in setting the boundary line at the highest elevation of tidal action was an unconstitutional extension of public property rights and a taking of the plaintiffs' property. The State's motion for reconsideration was denied, and this appeal followed.

II

* * * [The state argues] that the trial court erred in denying its motion for summary judgment because the legislature acted within its authority in establishing the "high water mark" as the boundary for public trust

rights in coastal shorelands at the highest elevation of tidal action. * * *

* * * *

After an extensive review, we conclude that New Hampshire common law establishes the high water mark at the level of mean high tide. In 1862, this court referred to the public-private shoreland boundary line as the "*ordinary* high water mark." [In 1969, in *Sibson v. State*] we held that public "[t]idewaters are those in which the tide *ordinarily* ebbs and flows."

The context of the *Sibson* case makes clear that the common law public-private boundary line or "ordinary high water mark" was at the level of mean high tide. * * * [T]he United States Supreme Court [has] held that the shoreland boundary for purposes of federal grants was the "ordinary high water mark," which it defined as the "mean high tide line," that is, "the average height of all the high waters" over a complete tidal cycle. * * *

Further, the definition of the term "ordinary" * * * and the definition of the term "ordinarily" * * * lend support to the interpretation of the common law public-private shoreland boundary or high water mark as the mean high tide line. The word "ordinary" is defined [in *Webster's Third New International Dictionary*] as "occurring or encountered in the usual course of events: not uncommon or exceptional: not remarkable: routine, normal." Similarly, the word "ordinarily" is defined as "in the ordinary course of events" and "to the usual extent." The term "ordinary," therefore, is synonymous with the term "mean." In fact, one of the definitions of the word "mean" is "ordinary."

Finally, New Hampshire common law regarding other public waters indicates that the mean high tide mark was intended as the public-private shoreland boundary. [In other cases, we] have held that large ponds are owned by the State in trust for public use up to their "natural mean high water mark." Moreover, we have noted that "[t]he law of public waters is presumably uniform, and on many questions it is not material whether an authority relates to tide-water or to large ponds." Accordingly, we conclude that the mean high tide is the high water mark or common law coastal boundary between public and private shorelands.

Our holding today is consistent with the law in most of the other coastal States. The few States that reject the mean high tide mark as the public-private shoreland boundary do so on distinct histories not applicable to our State.

Having determined that New Hampshire common law limits public ownership of the shorelands to the mean high water mark, we conclude that the legislature went beyond these common law limits by extending public trust rights to the highest high water mark. *Although the legislature has the power to change or redefine the common law to conform to current standards and public needs, property rights created by the common law may not be taken away legislatively without due process of law.* Because RSA chapter 483-C unilaterally authorizes the taking of private shoreland for public use and provides no compensation for landowners whose property has been appropriated, it violates the prohibition in * * * the State Constitution and the Fifth Amendment of the Federal Constitution against the taking of property for public use without just compensation. Although it may be desirable for the State to expand public beaches to cope with increasing crowds, the State may not do so without compensating the affected landowners. Accordingly, we conclude that RSA chapter 483-C is unconstitutional because it constitutes a taking of private property without just compensation, and therefore, the trial court's denial of the State's motion for summary judgment was proper. [Emphasis added.]

III

* * * *

Because the actual location of the mean high water mark still needs to be decided to determine which, if any, of the plaintiffs have a claim for damages, we remand this case to the trial court for further proceedings consistent with this opinion.

Affirmed and remanded.

Case Problems

47–1. As the result of a survey in 1976, the Nolans discovered that their neighbor's garage extended more than a foot onto their property. As a result, Nolan requested that his neighbor, Naab, tear down the garage. The Naabs refused to do this, stating that the garage had been built in 1952 and had been on the property when the Naabs purchased it in 1973. In West Virginia, where these properties were located, there is a ten-year statute of limitations covering adverse possession of property. Were the Naabs able to claim title to the land on which the garage was situated by adverse possession? Explain. [*Naab v. Nolan*, 327 S.E.2d 151 (W.Va.1985)]

47–2. Dixie Gardens, Inc., was a developer in Pasco County, Florida. Henry Sloane purchased a lot and residence in a Dixie Gardens development. The deed read in part as follows: "If the developer or the Crestridge Utilities Corporation causes garbage collection service bi-weekly to be made available, the owner of each lot shall pay the developer or its assigns, the sum of $1.75 per month therefor." Sloane wished to employ another contractor for garbage collection, but Dixie Gardens argued that Sloane was bound by the provision in the deed, which amounted to a covenant running with the land. Is Dixie Gardens correct? Explain. [*Sloane v. Dixie Gardens, Inc.*, 278 So.2d 309 (Fla.App. 2d Dist. 1973)]

47–3. Donald Kirsch and Martha Kaye Dunn owned residential property in Prince George's County, Maryland. Kirsch and Dunn wished to rent their property to students. Stephanie Stockman and Daniel Cones were students at the University of Maryland living off-campus in Prince George's County. In 1989, the county council enacted a "mini-dorm" zoning ordinance. The ordinance regulated the rental of residential property to persons "who are registered full-time or part-time students at an institution of higher learning." The ordinance imposed restrictions that were intended to address complaints about the noise, litter, and parking of mini-dorm residents from other residents of College Park, the site of the principal campus of the University of Maryland. The ordinance took effect on July 1, 1990. On July 3, Kirsch, Dunn, Stockman, and Cones filed a lawsuit against the county, seeking a declaration that the ordinance was invalid. The plaintiffs argued in part that the ordinance discriminated against students as a classification in violation of the Fourteenth Amendment. How should the court rule? Discuss fully. [*Kirsch v. Prince George's County*, 331 Md. 89, 626 A.2d 372 (1993)]

47–4. James and Marilyn Nollan sought a building permit from the California Coastal Commission (CCC) to replace a single-story house on the Nollans' beachfront property with a two-story structure approximately three times larger. The CCC concluded that the new house would obstruct the public's view of the ocean, increase private use of the beach, and create a "psychological barrier" to access to the public beaches that were on both sides of the Nollans' property. The CCC agreed to issue the permit if the Nollans would dedicate a strip of their land for public use. The strip, which ran next to the water's edge along the beach, would connect the public beaches. The Nollans appealed to a court, contending that the CCC's condition was a taking of private property for public use without compensation. Is the CCC's condition a taking? Discuss fully. [*Nollan v. California Coastal Commission*, 483 U.S. 825, 107 S.Ct. 3141, 97 L.Ed.2d 677 (1987)]

47–5. Paul and Barbara Sue Flanagan owned property in Alma, Arkansas, which was being purchased by the Smiths under an installment land contract. It had been assumed by all owners of the property since 1946 that a fence located at the southern end of the property was the southern boundary of the property. Over the years, all owners had maintained and generally exercised dominion over the property up to the fence. In 1985, when Jerry and Mildred Hicks purchased a lot bordering the southern side of the Flanagan property, a survey showed that the true boundary was approximately eleven feet north of the existing fence. The Hickses asked the Smiths to remove the fence, but they refused to do so. The Hickses then brought an action to compel their neighbors to remove the fence. What will the court decide? Discuss fully. [*Hicks v. Flanagan*, 30 Ark.App. 53, 782 S.W.2d 587 (1990)]

47–6. Merton Peterson owned a golf course, a supper club, and the parking lot between them. Both golfers and club patrons always parked in the lot. Peterson sold the club and the lot to the American Legion, which sold them to VBC, Inc. (owned by Richard Beck and others). When VBC demanded rent from Peterson for use of the lot, Peterson filed a suit in a South Dakota state court to determine title. On what basis might the court hold that Peterson has an easement for the use of the lot? Does Peterson have an easement? [*Peterson v. Beck*, 537 N.W.2d 375 (S.Dak. 1995)]

47–7. Claudia Churchill installed a satellite dish in the backyard of her home, which was located in a residential subdivision called the Piedmont Subdivision. The Piedmont Subdivision was subject to a restrictive covenant that provided in part as follows: "No outside radio, television, ham broadcasting, or other electronic antenna or aerial shall be erected or placed on any structure or on any lot. If used, any such antenna or aerial shall be placed in the attic of the house or in any other place in the house where it will be concealed from public view from any side of the house." Roy Breeling and a number of other homeowners in the subdivision filed an action in a Nebraska state court, asking that Churchill be required to remove the satellite dish. The trial court held that the covenant applied to the satellite dish, even though such dishes were not in use in the early 1970s when the covenant was drafted. The court therefore granted the homeowners' request and ordered Churchill to remove the dish from her property. Churchill appealed. What will happen on appeal? Discuss. [*Breeling v. Churchill*, 228 Neb. 596, 423 N.W.2d 469 (1988)]

47–8. In 1948, Cecil and Edna Wood conveyed land in Riverton, Wyoming, to Fremont County. The deed stated that the land was conveyed "for the purpose of constructing and maintaining thereon a County Hospital in memorial to the gallant men of the Armed Forces of the United States of America from Fremont County, Wyoming." The county built a hospital on the land and operated it until November 1983, when the property was sold to a private company. The buyer operated the hospital until September 1984, when it moved the hospital to new facilities and put the Wood property up for sale. The Woods appealed, contending in part that the language in the deed created a fee simple defeasible. What should the appellate court decide? Discuss fully. [*Wood v. Board of County Commissioners of Fremont County*, 759 P.2d 1250 (Wyo. 1988)]

47–9. The Minneapolis Police Department, in trying to apprehend a suspect who had entered and hidden himself in Harriet Wegner's house, severely damaged the house. The police and a SWAT team called in to assist the police were unable to persuade the suspect to come out, so they fired twenty-five rounds of tear gas into the house, as well as three concussion ("flash-bang") grenades. The police finally apprehended the suspect as he crawled out of a basement window. Wegner alleged that these events caused damages of $71,000 to her home. Her insurance carrier, Milwaukee Mutual Insurance Company, paid her about $28,000 but refused to pay for the rest of the damage. Wegner and Milwaukee Mutual both sued the city of Minneapolis, alleging that the police department's actions constituted a compensable taking under the Minnesota constitution. (The insurance company sought reimbursement for the money it had paid to Wegner and for possible future liability on her claim.) The trial court granted summary judgment for the city on the taking issue, holding that "[e]minent domain is not intended as a limitation on [the] police power" of the state. The appellate court affirmed. Wegner and the insurance company appealed to the Minnesota Supreme Court. How should the court rule? Explain. [*Wegner v. Milwaukee Mutual Insurance Co.*, 479 N.W.2d 38 (Minn. 1991)]

47–10. In 1961, Mary Schaefers divided her real property and conveyed it to her children, William, Elfreda, Julienne, and Rosemary. The deed from Mary Schaefers to her daughter Rosemary contained the following language: "It is further mutually agreed by and between the grantor and the grantee that as part of the consideration set out above, the grantee agrees to provide a permanent home for my daughter, Elfreda, should she desire or request one, and for my son, William Schaefers, should he desire or request one. Failure to perform the above will be considered a material breach of the consideration set out herein." In 1974, Rosemary conveyed her portion of her mother's property to Edward and Arthur Apel. Subsequently, William Schaefers attempted to prevent the sale to the Apels from taking place by telling them that the house was encumbered by a covenant running with the land and that if they purchased the house, they would be bound to provide a home for William and Elfreda Schaefers. Is Rosemary's promise to provide a home for William and Elfreda (should they demand one) a covenant running with the land? Explain. [*Schaefers v. Apel*, 295 Ala. 277, 328 So.2d 274 (1976)]

47–11. Moses Webster owned a parcel of land that extended down to the Atlantic Ocean. He conveyed the strip of the property fronting the ocean to another party. The deed included the following statement: "Reserve being had for said Moses Webster the right of way by land or water." The strip of property is now owned by Margaret Williams, and the portion retained by Webster now belongs to Thomas O'Neill. Williams is denying O'Neill access to the ocean. O'Neill has brought an action to establish his title to an easement over Williams's property. What should the court decide? Discuss fully. [*O'Neill v. Williams*, 527 A.2d 322 (Me. 1987)]

47–12. Florence Dolan owned the A-Boy West Hardware store in downtown Tigard, Oregon. Wanting to expand the store and its parking lot, Dolan applied to the city for a permit. Under the Tigard Community Development Code (the local zoning regulations), the city could attach conditions to downtown development to provide for projected transportation and public-facility needs. The city told Dolan that she could expand if she would dedicate a portion of her property for the improvement of a storm drainage system, including a public greenway along a creek, and dedicate an additional strip of land as a pedestrian/bicycle pathway. The dedication would represent about 10 percent of Dolan's property. Dolan sought a variance, which the city denied, and Dolan appealed. The city claimed that there was a sufficient connection between the expansion of the store and the dedication requirements, because the expansion would increase traffic to the area and would also increase storm runoff. Dolan conceded that there would be increases but contended that the increases would not be enough to justify taking 10 percent of her property. Dolan claimed that the city's restriction was an uncompensated taking of her property in violation of the Fifth Amendment. How should the court rule? Discuss fully. [*Dolan v. City of Tigard*, 512 U.S. 374, 114 S.Ct. 2309, 129 L.Ed.2d 304 (1994)]

47–13. Richard and Jaquelyn Jackson owned property in a residential subdivision near an airport operated by the Metropolitan Knoxville Airport Authority in Blount County, Tennessee. The Airport Authority considered extending a runway near the subdivision and undertook a study that found that the noise, vibration, and pollution from aircraft using the extension would render the Jacksons' property incompatible with residential use. The airport built the extension, bringing about the predicted results, and the Jacksons filed a suit against the Airport Authority, alleging a taking of their property. The Airport Authority responded that there was no taking because there were no direct flights over the Jacksons' property. In whose favor will the court rule, and why? [*Jackson v. Metropolitan Knoxville Airport Authority*, 922 S.W.2d 860 (Tenn. 1996)]

47–14. In 1972, Ted Pafundi bought a quarry in West Pawlet, Vermont, from his neighbor, Marguerite Scott. The deed vaguely described the eastern boundary of the quarry as "the westerly boundary of the lands of" the neighboring property owners. Pafundi quarried green slate from the west wall until his death in 1979, when his son Gary began to work the east wall until *his* death in 1989. Gary's daughter Connie took over operations. All of the Pafundis used the floor of the quarry as their base of operations. In 1992, N.A.S. Holdings, Inc., bought the neighboring property. A survey revealed that virtually the entire quarry was within the boundaries of N.A.S.'s property and that twenty years earlier, Ted had actually bought only a small strip of land on the west side. When N.A.S. attempted to begin quarrying, Connie blocked the access. N.A.S. filed a suit in a Vermont state court against Connie, seeking to establish title. Connie argued that she had title to the quarry through adverse possession under a state statute with a possessory period of fifteen years. What are the elements necessary to acquire title by adverse possession? Are they satisfied in this case? In whose favor should the court rule, and why? [*N.A.S. Holdings, Inc. v. Pafundi*, 736 A.2d 280 (Vt. 1999)]

47–15. A QUESTION OF ETHICS

The Stanards have owned lakeshore property since 1963. In 1969, the Urbans purchased lakeshore property adjoining the Stanards' lot and used the property for a summer cabin from 1969 through 1974. In 1975, the Urbans converted the summer cabin into a year-round home and moved there permanently. Since 1969, the Urbans have used a grassy area of land—part of which belonged to the Stanards—up to a wooded area between the two houses. Between 1969 and 1988, the Urbans mowed the grassy area up to the woods line and kept the weeds down, let their children and grandchildren play in the grassy area, and stored their boat dock on the grassy area each winter. In 1981, the Urbans constructed a white tin storage shed—mounted on a concrete slab—on the grassy area. Most of the shed was located on the Stanards' property. In 1988, the Stanards brought a lawsuit against the Urbans for trespass and sought removal of the white shed. The Urbans claimed that they acquired ownership of the property by adverse possession because they had used the property since 1969 (the state's statutory requirement for adverse possession was fifteen years). The Stanards claimed that the measurement of the statutory period should begin in 1981, when the permanent storage shed was constructed. Given these circumstances, consider the following questions. [*Stanard v. Urban,* 453 N.W.2d 733 (Minn.App. 1990)]

1. Do you think that the Urbans' use of the Stanards' property prior to 1981 (when the shed was built) met the requirements for adverse possession? That is, was the use actual, open, hostile, continuous, and exclusive during those years? Or is this situation similar to many others in which there are no fences between neighboring lots and the respective owners and their families occasionally trespass on the others' property?
2. Would it affect your answer to the preceding question if you knew that the Urbans, sometime between 1980 and 1982, offered to purchase the parcel of property in question from the Stanards?
3. At what point should trespass on another's property constitute adverse possession? For example, if your neighbors customarily store their boat partially on your property, and you do not object, should this circumstance trigger a statutory period for adverse possession? What if your neighbors' children also customarily play on your side of the boundary line between your property and your neighbors' property?
4. Why do you think that state statutes permit people to acquire title to property by adverse possession? What public policy is reflected in these statutes?

E-LINKS

For updated links to resources available on the Web, as well as a variety of other materials, visit this text's Web site at

http://wbl-cs.westbuslaw.com

Homes and Communities is a Web site offered by the U.S. Department of Housing and Urban Development. Information of interest to both consumers and businesses is available at this site, which can be accessed at

http://www.hud.gov

You can find answers to frequently asked questions on Veterans Administration home loans by going to

http://www.homeloans.va.gov

LEGAL RESEARCH EXERCISES ON THE WEB

Go to http://wbl-cs.westbuslaw.com, the Web site that accompanies this text. Select "Interactive Study Center," and then click on "Chapter 47." There you will find the following Internet research exercises that you can perform to learn more about laws governing real property:

Activity 47–1: Real Estate Law

Activity 47–2: Fair Housing

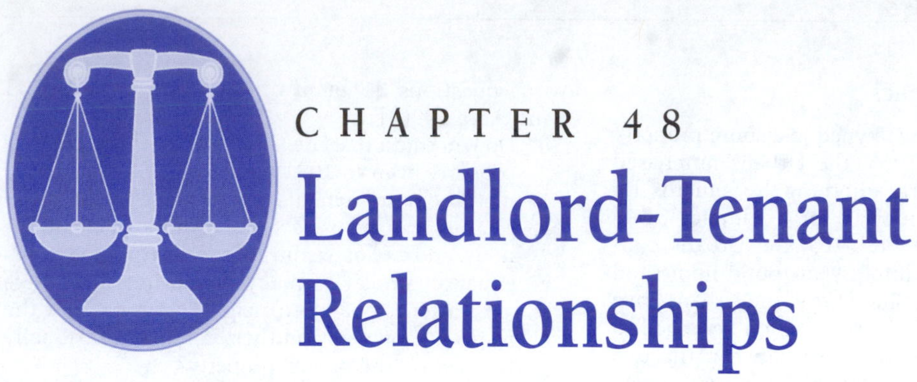

CHAPTER 48

Landlord-Tenant Relationships

Anyone who rents housing or rents space for commercial purposes becomes subject to the laws governing landlord-tenant relationships. The owner of the property is the landlord, or **lessor**; the party assuming temporary possession is the tenant, or **lessee**; and their rental agreement is the lease contract, or, more simply, the **lease.** The property interest involved in a landlord-tenant relationship is known as a *leasehold estate,* as discussed in chapter 47. The *temporary* nature of possession, under a lease, is what distinguishes a tenant from a purchaser, who acquires title to the property. The *exclusivity* of possession distinguishes a tenant from a licensee, who acquires the temporary right to a *nonexclusive* use, such as sitting in a theater seat.

In the past century—and particularly in the past three decades—landlord-tenant relationships have become much more complex than they once were, as have the laws governing them. Generally, the law has come to apply contract doctrines, such as those providing for implied warranties and unconscionability, to the landlord-tenant relationship. Increasingly, landlord-tenant relationships have become subject to specific state and local statutes and ordinances as well. In 1972, in an effort to create more uniformity in the law governing landlord-tenant relationships, the National Conference of Commissioners on Uniform State Laws approved the Uniform Residential Landlord and Tenant Act (URLTA) for adoption by the states. Over one-fourth of the states have adopted variations of the URLTA.

SECTION 1

Creation of the Landlord-Tenant Relationship

A landlord-tenant relationship is established by a lease contract, which may be oral or written. As is the case with most oral agreements, however, a party who seeks to enforce an oral lease may have difficulty proving its existence. In all states, statutes mandate that leases be in writing for some tenancies (such as those exceeding one year).

Form of the Lease

To create a landlord-tenant relationship, a contract must do the following:

1. Express an intent to establish the relationship.
2. Provide for transfer of the property's possession to the tenant at the beginning of the term.
3. Provide for the landlord's *reversionary* (future) interest, which entitles the property owner to retake possession at the end of the term.
4. Describe the property—for example, give its street address.
5. Indicate the length of the term, the amount of the rent, and how and when it is to be paid.

In the drafting of commercial leases, sound business practice dictates that the leases be written carefully and that the parties' rights and obligations be clearly defined in the lease agreements.

ILLEGALITY

State or local law often dictates permissible lease terms. The URLTA, for example, prohibits the inclusion in a lease agreement of a clause under which the tenant agrees to pay the landlord's attorneys' fees in a suit to enforce the lease. A statute or ordinance may prohibit leasing a structure that is in disrepair or is not in compliance with local building codes. Similarly, a statute may prohibit the leasing of property for a particular purpose, such as gambling. In this case, if a landlord and tenant intend that the leased premises be used only to house an illegal betting operation, their lease is unenforceable.

A property owner cannot legally discriminate against prospective tenants on the basis of race, color, religion, national origin, or gender. Similarly, a tenant cannot legally promise to do something counter to laws prohibiting discrimination. A tenant, for example, cannot legally promise to do business only with members of a particular race. The public policy underlying these prohibitions is to treat all people equally.

UNCONSCIONABILITY

The unconscionability concept is one of the most important of the contract doctrines applied to leases. Basically, in some jurisdictions (and under URLTA 1.303), the concept follows the provision of Section 2–302 of the Uniform Commercial Code. As discussed in Chapter 18, under this provision, a court may declare an entire contract or any of its clauses unconscionable and thus illegal, depending on the circumstances surrounding the transaction and the parties' relative bargaining positions. In a residential lease, for example, a clause claiming to absolve a landlord from responsibility for interruptions in such essential services as central heating and air conditioning will not shield a landlord from liability if the systems break down when they are needed the most.

SECTION 2

Parties' Rights and Duties

At common law, the parties to a lease had relative freedom to include whatever terms they chose in the lease. Currently, the trend is to base the rights and duties of the parties on the principles of real estate law and contract law. These rights and duties generally pertain to the four broad areas of concern for landlords and tenants—the possession, use, maintenance, and, of course, rent of the leased property.

POSSESSION

A landlord is obligated to give a tenant possession of the property that the tenant has agreed to lease. The "English" rule, followed in many states and by the URLTA, requires the landlord to provide actual *physical possession* to the tenant—unless the parties agree otherwise. If, for example, a previous tenant is still living on the premises on the date the new tenant is entitled to possession, the landlord must remove the previous tenant or breach the obligation to the new tenant. The "American" rule, followed in other states, requires the landlord to transfer only the legal right to possession. Under this rule, the new tenant in the preceding example would have been responsible for removing the previous tenant, who no longer had the *legal right to possession.*

After obtaining possession, the tenant retains it exclusively until the lease expires, unless the lease provides otherwise or the tenant defaults under the terms of the lease. Most leases expressly give the landlord the right to come onto the property for the purpose of inspecting it, making necessary repairs, or showing the property to prospective purchasers or (toward the end of an expiring term) to possible future tenants.

COVENANT OF QUIET ENJOYMENT

Under the *covenant of quiet enjoyment,* the landlord promises that during the lease term neither the landlord nor anyone having a superior title to the property will disturb the tenant's use and enjoyment of the property. This covenant forms the essence of the landlord-tenant relationship. If the covenant is breached, the tenant can terminate the lease and sue for damages.

EVICTION

If the landlord deprives the tenant of the tenant's possession of the leased property or interferes with his or her use or enjoyment of the property, an **eviction** occurs. This is the case, for example, when the landlord changes the lock and refuses to give the tenant a new key. A *partial eviction* occurs if the landlord deprives the tenant of the use of a part—one room, for example—of the leased premises. Assuming that the tenant has a legal right to possession of the property, he or she may either (1) sue for damages or possession or (2) consider the eviction a breach of the lease contract and cease paying rent or terminate the lease.

Constructive eviction occurs whenever the landlord wrongfully performs, or fails to perform, any of the duties the lease requires, thereby making the tenant's further use and enjoyment of the property exceedingly difficult or virtually impossible. Examples of constructive eviction include a landlord's failure to provide heat in the winter, light, or other essential utilities. To claim that a constructive eviction has occurred, the tenant must first notify the landlord of the problem. If the landlord fails to remedy the situation within a reasonable period of time, the tenant must then abandon the premises. On vacating the premises, the tenant's obligation to pay further rent ceases. As in cases of wrongful eviction, the tenant may sue to move back onto the property or terminate the lease and seek damages.

When a landlord evicts a tenant for complaining to a government agency about the improper condition of the leased premises, it is termed a **retaliatory eviction.** Under some statutes, a retaliatory motive is presumed when eviction proceedings are begun within a certain time after a tenant has complained. Regardless of the time elapsed, if a tenant can prove that a landlord's primary purpose in evicting or attempting to evict the tenant is retaliation for reporting violations—of a housing or sanitation code, for example—the tenant may be entitled to stop the eviction proceedings or collect damages.

USE OF THE PREMISES

If the parties do not limit by agreement the uses to which the property may be put, the tenant may make any use of it, so long as the use is legal, reasonably relates to the purpose for which the property is adapted or ordinarily used, and does not injure the landlord's interest.

Also, the tenant is not entitled to create a *nuisance* by substantially interfering with others' quiet enjoyment of their property rights. To constitute a nuisance, conduct must be more than simply aggravating. Arguing with the neighbors may be annoying behavior, for example, but it would probably not qualify as a nuisance, unless it constituted harassment. Consistently playing drums in the middle of the night in an apartment complex, however, probably would be considered a nuisance.

Tenant's Duty Not to Commit Waste. The tenant has no right to remove or otherwise damage leased property without the landlord's consent. The duty of a tenant not to damage the premises is a duty not to commit **waste**, which is the abuse or destructive use of property by one in rightful possession. A tenant cannot knock out an inside wall in a leased house to enlarge a living room, for example, or remove a fence or a grove of trees to accommodate grazing livestock unless he or she first obtains the landlord's permission to do so.

The tenant is responsible for all damage he or she causes, intentionally or negligently, and the tenant may be held liable for the cost of returning the property to the physical condition it was in at the lease's inception. Unless the parties have agreed otherwise, however, the tenant is not responsible for ordinary wear and tear and the property's consequent depreciation in value.

If, at some time during the lease term, the tenant decides to stop using the property but to continue paying the rent, the lease may require the tenant to give the landlord notice of the nonuse. There is always a greater chance of vandalism, fire, or some other cause of damage to property when it is not being used, and the nonuse may affect insurance coverage.

Altering the Premises. In most states, the tenant may make no alterations to the leased premises without the landlord's consent. In other jurisdictions, the tenant may make alterations, without being liable for the expense of their removal, if they were necessary for the tenant's use of the property and did not reduce its value. **Alterations** include improvements or changes that materially affect the condition of the property. Thus, for example, erecting additional structures probably would be considered making alterations, whereas painting interior walls would not. Unless the parties have agreed otherwise, neither the landlord nor the tenant is required to make specific alterations or otherwise improve the property.

Once a residential tenant affixes an item of personal property—such as a storage cabinet—to real property, it becomes a *fixture* (see Chapter 46). In some jurisdictions, fixtures become the landlord's property and may not be removed at the end of the lease term. In other jurisdictions, fixtures can be removed at the end of the lease period if they can be taken without damage to the landlord's property.

MAINTAINING THE PREMISES

At common law, a tenant took the property "as is." Today, this common law rule has generally been replaced with statutes requiring landowners to comply with certain safety, health, and fire-protection standards. Also, in most states, statutes or judicial decisions impose a duty on a landlord who leases residential property to furnish premises that are *habitable*—that is, in a condition fit for human occupancy—and to make repairs for damages not caused by the tenant's actions. Nevertheless, under a long-term commercial lease, a tenant may still assume the responsibility of making all necessary repairs, including, for example, rebuilding a structure after its destruction in a fire.

Statutory Requirements. Usually, the landlord must comply with state statutes and city ordinances that delineate specific standards for the construction and maintenance of buildings. Typically, these codes contain structural requirements common to the construction, wiring, and plumbing of residential and commercial buildings. In some jurisdictions, landlords of residential property are required by statute to maintain the premises in good repair.

The landlord is also responsible for maintaining **common areas**—areas such as halls, stairways, elevators, and so on that are used by all tenants. This duty relates not only to defects of which the landlord has actual knowledge but also to those about which the landlord should reasonably know. A landlord, for example, cannot avoid responsibility for repairing a dilapidated but little-used back stairway by asserting that he or she never used it and did not know it needed to be fixed.

Obligations under the Lease. In a long-term lease for the use of commercial property, the parties may choose to designate in the lease which of them has the responsibility to maintain the leased premises and to what extent. Generally, an express promise to repair is legally binding.

Under most circumstances, a residential tenant is not required to make major repairs, such as replacing an old roof or laying a new foundation. Additionally, without a lease provision under which the tenant assumes a duty to maintain the leased property, the tenant is under no obligation to do so. The tenant is liable for repairs required as a result of his or her intentional or negligent actions, however.

See Case 48.1 at the end of this chapter. To view the full, unedited case from Westlaw,® go to this text's Web site at http://wbl-cs.westbuslaw.com.

Implied Warranty of Habitability. The implied warranty of habitability requires that a landlord who leases residential property furnish the premises in a habitable condition at the beginning of a lease term and maintain them in that condition for the lease's duration. Some state legislatures have enacted this warranty into law. In other jurisdictions, courts have based this warranty on the existence of a landlord's statutory duty to repair or simply have applied it as a matter of public policy.

Generally, this warranty applies only to major—or substantial—physical defects that the landlord knows or should know about and has had a reasonable time to repair (for example, a big hole in the roof). In deciding whether a defect is sufficiently substantial to be in violation of the warranty, courts may consider the following factors:

1. Whether the tenant caused the defect or is otherwise responsible for it.
2. How long the defect has existed.
3. The age of the building, because a newer dwelling is expected to have fewer problems.
4. The defect's impact—potential or real—on the tenant's health, safety, and activities such as sleeping and eating.
5. Whether the defect contravenes applicable housing, building, or sanitation statutes.

An unattractive or annoying feature, such as a crack in the wall, may be unpleasant, but unless the crack is evidence of a structural defect or affects the residence's capacity to be heated, it is probably not sufficiently substantial to make the structure uninhabitable. A leak that causes the carpet in a portion of the leased structure to become soaked periodically, however, may be enough to make the premises uninhabitable. A malfunctioning air conditioner, the presence of rodents and pests on the premises, and the periodic lack of hot water and electricity—if the landlord promised to maintain the premises and provide utilities—is enough to render the premises uninhabitable.

Westlaw. See Case 48.2 at the end of this chapter. To view the full, unedited case from Westlaw,® go to this text's Web site at **http://wbl-cs.westbuslaw.com**.

Remedies for Landlord's Failure to Maintain Leased Property. The tenant's remedies for the landlord's failure to maintain the leased premises vary with the circumstances and with state laws.

Withholding Rent. Rent withholding is a remedy that is generally associated with the landlord's breach of the warranty of habitability. When rent withholding is authorized under a statute (sometimes referred to as a "rent strike" statute), the tenant must usually put the amount withheld into an *escrow account*. This account is held in the name of the depositor (in this case, the tenant) and an *escrow agent* (in this case, usually the court or a government agency), and the funds are returnable to the depositor if the third person (in this case, the landlord) fails to fulfill the escrow condition.

Generally, the tenant may withhold an amount equal to the amount by which the defect rendering the premises unlivable reduces the property's rental value. How much that is may be determined in different ways, and the tenant who withholds more than is legally permissible is liable to the landlord for the excessive amount withheld.

Repairing and Deducting. Under **repair-and-deduct statutes** or judicial recognition of a right to repair and deduct, the tenant pays for the repairs and deducts their cost from the rent. As in the case of rent withholding, this remedy is usually associated with the landlord's breach of the warranty of habitability.

Before a tenant can use this remedy, the problem—which in some states must concern a basic service, such as heat or water—must be the landlord's responsibility, and the landlord must be notified and fail to do anything about the situation within a reasonable time. Under some statutes, the deductible amount is restricted to a month's rent or some other fixed sum.

Canceling the Lease. Terminating the lease is a remedy normally available to the tenant only when the landlord's failure to repair constitutes either constructive eviction or a breach of the warranty of habitability.

Suing for Damages. Although a lawsuit for damages is always a possible course of action, it is not necessarily economical. The amount a tenant can negotiate or be awarded may be based on the cost of a defect's repair or on the difference between the rental values of the defective property and the repaired property.

Rent

Rent is the tenant's payment to the landlord for the tenant's occupancy or use of the landlord's real property. Generally, the tenant must pay the rent even if he or she refuses to occupy the property or moves out, as long as the refusal or the move is unjustifiable and the lease is in force. Rent is payable according to an applicable statute, custom, or what the parties decide. The amount may be subject to a legislated ceiling—as in New York City—or it may be as much or as little as the market will bear. Usually, rent is payable in advance or periodically throughout the lease term, but rent payable in crops may not be due until the end of a term.

Some states provide that the landlord must wait for as many as ten days after the rent's due date before initiating proceedings to terminate the lease for failure on the part of the tenant to pay rent. Notice may be required before a suit can be filed. Also, the landlord may impliedly waive the right to prompt payment if in the past he or she has accepted late payments.

Security Deposits. At the lease's inception, the landlord may require a deposit to secure the tenant's obligation to fulfill the lease. If the tenant fails to pay the rent or damages the property, the landlord may retain the deposit.

Under the URLTA (for residential leases only), the amount of the deposit is limited to one month's rent. After the end of the lease term, the deposit must be returned—less any amounts owed for damages or unpaid rent—within fourteen days of the tenant's request for its return. Some states permit larger deposits and longer periods before their return. Under the URLTA and some state laws, if the landlord withholds any amount from the deposit to cover damages, the tenant must be given an itemized list of the damages. In some states, the landlord must also pay interest on the deposit, less an appropriate sum as compensation for the effort involved in meeting this obligation. If the landlord fails to comply with these requirements, the tenant may recover at least the amount due. In some states, the tenant may recover triple the amount due and attorneys' fees.

Late Charges. Legally, late charges can be imposed if a tenant does not pay rent when it is due. In general, the amount of a late charge may not be excessive, and it must bear some logical relation to the amount of the rent or to how long the payment has been overdue.

Rent Escalation. Unless there is a clause in the lease providing otherwise, the amount of the rent cannot be increased during the lease term. If there is a clause allowing for the rent to be increased in the future—a **rent escalation clause**—the amount may be linked to the landlord's operating costs, indexed to increases in the cost of living or increases in property taxes, or subject to a real or anticipated increase in a commercial tenant's business activity.

Property Taxes. In most jurisdictions, the tenant is not obligated to pay assessments and taxes on leased property. The responsibility for paying those charges may be transferred from the landlord to the tenant in the lease, however, or the lease may provide that the rent will be raised if the taxes increase. The tenant may be liable for the amount of the increase if it is due to improvements (such as the installation of trade fixtures in commercial premises) made by the tenant.

Landlord's Remedies for Tenant's Failure to Pay Rent. Depending on the jurisdiction, if a tenant fails to pay rent or refuses to give up possession of leased property, the landlord can resort to one of three actions: a landlord's lien, a lawsuit, or recovery of possession.

Landlord's Lien. At common law, when a tenant did not pay the rent, the landlord could simply take and keep or sell whatever of the defaulting tenant's personal property was on the leased premises. Today, the landlord does not have this alternative unless the parties have contracted for it or it is permitted under a statute.

Among states that by statute preserve this remedy, known as a **landlord's lien**, some states grant the landlord a lien on all of the tenant's personal property but require the landlord to initiate court proceedings to exercise the lien. Typically, the court will authorize a sheriff to seize the tenant's property. Other states allow the landlord to seize specific items of the tenant's property and hold them as *security* for unpaid rent (that is, as protection or assurance that the landlord will recoup something on the tenant's obligation), but the landlord must obtain a court order to sell the tenant's property.

Lawsuit. Just as the landlord may sue a tenant responsible for damaging leased property, so the landlord may sue a defaulting tenant to collect unpaid rent.

Recovery of Possession. At common law, on the tenant's breach of the lease, the landlord could—with force, if necessary—evict the tenant and recover possession of the leased property without legal proceedings. Today, the landlord must use legal process, even if the parties have stipulated in the lease that the landlord has, and may exercise without legal proceedings, a **right of entry** (a right to retake possession peaceably).

There are two procedures to which the landlord may resort to evict the tenant. One is the common law remedy of **ejectment**, which requires the landlord to appear in court and show that the defaulting tenant is in wrongful possession. An action in ejectment does not take priority over other proceedings and, consequently, may be delayed for a long time. During the delay, the tenant can remain in possession. Thus, this action is used infrequently.

The remedy of ejectment has been modified under statutes that provide for a summary judicial procedure, generally referred to as an **unlawful detainer.** During the unlawful detainer proceeding, the landlord attempts to prove that the tenant breached the lease or that the lease expired and the tenant refused to leave. The court makes its decision quickly, or summarily. If the landlord prevails, the court orders the sheriff to remove the tenant.

Landlord's Duty to Mitigate Damages. At common law and in many states, when a tenant vacates leased property unjustifiably (not as a result of constructive eviction or the landlord's breach of the warranty of habitability), the tenant remains obligated to pay the rent for the remainder of the lease term—however long that might be. The landlord may refuse to lease the premises to an acceptable new tenant and let the property stand vacant.

In a growing number of jurisdictions, however, the landlord is required to *mitigate* his or her damages—that is, the landlord is required to make a reasonable attempt to lease the property to another party. In those jurisdictions, the tenant's liability for unpaid rent is restricted to the period of time that it would reasonably take for the landlord to lease the property to another tenant. Damages may also be allowed for the landlord's costs in reletting the property.[1]

What is considered a reasonable period of time with respect to reletting the property varies with the type of lease and the location of the leased premises. Under a long-term residential lease, for example, this period might be three months. In some jurisdictions, if reasonable—but unsuccessful—attempts are made to relet, the tenant remains liable for the rent for the remainder of the lease.

SECTION 3

Liability for Injuries on the Premises

At common law, whether a party in possession of property was liable to an individual who was injured on the property depended in part on that individual's classification as an invitee, a licensee, or a trespasser. Recall from Chapter 5 that an invitee is one whom the party in possession invites onto the premises for the possessing party's benefit, such as a business customer or a dinner-party guest. A *licensee* is one whom the party in possession invites or allows onto the premises for the licensee's benefit, such as a salesperson. A *trespasser* is one whom the party in possession does not invite and who has no other right to be on the premises. Each classification might require a different standard of care on the part of the person in possession of the property. Under certain circumstances—if the injured trespasser was a very young child, who might be expected to be attracted to a dangerous condition on the property, such as an unfenced swimming pool—the **attractive nuisance doctrine** could apply, requiring yet a different standard of care.

These distinctions are still made. Today, however, liability is more likely to depend on who controls the area where the injury occurred, and the governing standard is one of *reasonable care* under all circumstances. Applying the standard of reasonable care requires taking into consideration the predictability of a particular event (that is, applying the principle of *foreseeable risk*). The person who has responsibility for a particular part of the premises must take the same precautions regarding the area's safety as would a person of ordinary prudence in the same circumstances.[2]

LANDLORD'S LIABILITY

Traditionally, when the landlord surrendered possession of his or her property to the tenant, the landlord also relinquished responsibility for injuries occurring on the property. This was true regardless of whether the injury was caused by a condition that existed at the time the property was leased or a condition that developed later. Today, however, in recognition of the policies underlying the warranty of habitability, the landlord bears greater responsibility for the conditions of the premises and for injuries resulting from those conditions.

Currently, the landlord is generally liable for injuries occurring on the part of the property within the landlord's control—that is, common areas such as basements, hallways, and elevators. Also, when the landlord assumes an obligation to repair, the landlord's liability may extend to injuries attributable either to failure to make repairs or to negligently made repairs. Thus, the landlord may be responsible for injuries that occur on the part of the premises subject to the tenant's control—that is, the apartment, the house, or the store that the tenant leased from the landlord—when that responsibility is based on the landlord's duty to repair.

Injuries Caused by Defects on the Premises. The landlord's liability extends to injuries resulting from a dangerous condition about which the landlord knew or should have known, when the landlord fails to tell the tenant about it or actually conceals it. The landlord need not believe that the condition is unsafe; the situation need only be one that would lead a reasonable person to conclude that there is an unreasonable risk of harm. The landlord may be liable if he or she knows that the mortar is very loose in a

1. For a fuller discussion of mitigation of damages, see Chapter 17.

2. Essentially, this standard of care is the same as that applied in cases of negligence (discussed in Chapter 5).

brick wall, for example, and a brick subsequently falls and injures a tenant.

In most states, the landlord is not under a duty to inspect residential premises before leasing them, unless there is reason to suspect that a potentially harmful defect exists. Also, the landlord is under no obligation to disclose to the tenant conditions about which the tenant knows when he or she signs the lease or conditions that are obvious, such as a lumpy carpet in the hall.

Commercial Property. When property is leased for public purposes, including commercial activities, the landlord does have an obligation to inspect the property and make repairs before the tenant takes possession. This obligation is imposed to protect the public from unreasonable risks. Unreasonable risks do not include obvious conditions, which people can be expected to avoid.

The landlord's liability covers only that part of the leased premises that is open to the public. If, for example, a customer disregards a sign reading "Employees Only," goes through the door, and is somehow injured on the other side, the landlord normally will not be held liable. Similarly, the landlord is normally not liable for the tenant's negligence in maintaining the premises, assuming that they were in good condition when the tenant moved in.

See Case 48.3 at the end of this chapter. To view the full, unedited case from Westlaw®, go to this text's Web site at **http://wbl-cs.westbuslaw.com**.

Common Areas. The landlord is responsible for—and liable for any injuries resulting from—the condition of common areas, as long as the areas are under his or her control. This responsibility includes a duty to inspect and repair such conditions as peeling lead-based paint, rotting stair railings, burned-out or dim lighting, and defective water heaters. It also includes a duty to correct such conditions as wet steps or a loose mat placed over the slippery surface of a polished floor.

When the landlord retains control over part of the premises leased to the tenant—for example, an apartment's walls—the landlord may be liable for injuries caused by that part's disrepair. The landlord is not, however, liable for injuries occurring on parts of his or her residential property where people could not be reasonably expected to go—for example, a roof or a closed basement.

Repairs. In many jurisdictions, under building, housing, or sanitation codes or the warranty of habitability, the landlord is required to put or keep premises for lease in good repair. Breach of this duty may constitute negligence and establish the landlord's liability for any injuries caused by this negligence.

The landlord's express agreement to repair may be a basis for the landlord's liability if an injury is caused by the landlord's failure to fulfill the agreement. Ordinarily, the landlord has a reasonable time, after discovering or being told that a condition requires repair, within which to do the repair work or see that it is done. Regardless of whether the landlord has agreed to make repairs, once the landlord undertakes them, he or she is liable for injuries attributable to negligence in the repair work.

Injuries Caused by Crimes of Third Persons. The landlord normally is not required to set up an elaborate security system to protect tenants from criminals. But when crimes are reasonably foreseeable and the landlord takes no steps to prevent them, he or she may be liable for negligence—failure to provide adequate security—if an injury results.

Courts consider several factors in determining whether a crime is foreseeable and preventable. It is logical to assume that some prior criminal activity in the geographic area in which the property is located is required to make future crimes reasonably predictable. Similarly, it is reasonable to base an expectation of future crime on how recently the previous crime occurred.

Also, courts may consider the type of crime that occurred previously. In this area, the courts are divided. Some follow the *prior similar incidents* rule, under which establishing foreseeability requires showing the existence of earlier, similar crimes. Others follow what is known as the *totality of the circumstances* rule. Under the latter rule, foreseeability is determined in light of all of the circumstances, and what must be foreseeable is the general character of the event or harm, not its precise nature or manner of occurrence.

Exculpatory Clauses. A lease may contain a clause that claims to relieve the landlord from any liability for injuries or other damages, including those caused by the landlord's own negligence. Known as *exculpatory clauses* (see Chapter 12), these provisions are unenforceable if injury or damage results from the landlord's failure to fulfill a statutory duty, such as compliance with a state's building code. When included in a lease for residential property, an exculpatory clause releasing a landlord from liability for his or her negligence is unenforceable.

Tenant's Liability

A tenant has a duty to maintain in a reasonably safe condition those areas under his or her control. When commercial property is involved, this duty extends to all parts of the premises onto which a customer or other member of the public might be expected to go—such as the aisles in a grocery store. The grocer's duty includes using care in displaying his or her wares so that they present no threat to customers' safety. The goods should not be stacked, for example, so as to block an aisle or to fall onto a customer taking an item for purchase. Similarly, the grocer may be liable if a customer slips on the spilled contents of a broken jar and is injured.

In some situations—particularly when property is leased for commercial purposes—the tenant's duty may coincide with the landlord's duty. When this happens, both the landlord and the tenant may be liable for a third party's injuries.

SECTION 4

Transferring Rights to Leased Property

Either the landlord or the tenant may wish to transfer his or her rights to the leased property during the term of the lease.

Transferring the Landlord's Interest

Just as any other real property owner can sell, give away, or otherwise transfer his or her real property (see Chapter 47), so can a landlord—who is, of course, the leased property's owner. Furthermore, the landlord may make a deal involving only the lease, only the landlord's interest in the property after the lease has been terminated, only the rent accruable under the lease, or any of these property rights in combination.

If complete title—that is, the landlord's reversionary interest—to the leased property is transferred, the tenant becomes the tenant of the new owner. The new owner may collect subsequent rent but must then abide by the terms of the existing lease agreement.

Transferring the Tenant's Interest

The tenant's transfer of his or her entire interest in the leased property to a third person is an *assignment* of the lease. The tenant's transfer of all or part of the premises for a period shorter than the lease term is a **sublease.** Under neither an assignment nor a sublease can the assignee's or sublessee's rights against the landlord be *greater* than those of the original tenant.

Assignments. A controlling statute or a clause in the lease may require the landlord's consent to the tenant's assignment of his or her interest in the lease. It may also require that the landlord not unreasonably withhold such consent, however. If the statute does not contain the latter condition, some courts will impose it nonetheless. Typically, clauses that require the landlord's consent to assignment are written as *forfeiture restraints*—that is, they provide that the landlord may terminate the tenancy if the tenant attempts to assign the lease without consent. This restriction is meant to protect the landlord from an assignee-tenant who might damage the property, fail to pay the rent, or otherwise be irresponsible. The landlord's knowing acceptance of rent from an assignee, however, may constitute a waiver of the consent requirement.

When an assignment is valid, the assignee acquires all of the tenant's rights under the lease. But an assignment does not release the assigning tenant from the obligation to pay rent should the assignee default. Also, if the assignee exercises an option under the original lease to extend the term, the assigning tenant remains liable for the rent during the extension, unless the landlord agrees otherwise.

Subleases. The restrictions that apply to an assignment of the tenant's interest in the leased premises also apply to a sublease. For example, if the landlord's consent is required, a sublease without such permission is ineffective. Also, a sublease does not release the tenant from his or her obligations under the lease any more than an assignment does.

To illustrate: A student, Adya, leases an apartment for a two-year period. Adya has been planning to attend summer school, but she is offered a job in Europe for the summer months, and she accepts. To avoid paying three months' rent for an unoccupied apartment, she can sublease the apartment to another student. (Adya may have to obtain her landlord's consent for this sublease if the lease requires it.) The sublessee will take the apartment under the same lease terms as Adya. The landlord can hold Adya liable should the sublessee violate those terms.

SECTION 5

Termination or Renewal of the Lease

Usually, a lease terminates when its term ends. The tenant surrenders the property to the landlord, who retakes possession. If the lease does not contain an option for renewal and the parties have not agreed that the tenant may stay on, the tenant has no right to remain. If the lease is renewable and the tenant decides to exercise the option, the tenant must comply with any conditions requiring notice to the landlord of the tenant's decision.

TERMINATION

In addition to the expiration of the lease term, a lease can be terminated in several other ways.

Termination by Notice. If the lease states the time it will end, the landlord is not required to give the tenant notice—that is, to remind the tenant that the lease is going to expire—even as the time approaches. The lease terminates automatically. The lease may require that notice be given, however, or notice may be required under a statute. The procedures and time periods vary, but usually one or two months' notice is enough to end a tenancy for a year, and a week will suffice to end a tenancy for a shorter period.

In contrast, a *periodic tenancy* will renew automatically unless one of the parties gives timely notice (usually, one rental period) of termination. A periodic tenancy is a tenancy from week to week, month to month, or year to year. (Periodic tenancies were discussed in Chapter 47.)

Release and Merger. A lease may also give the tenant the opportunity to purchase the leased property during the term or at its end. Regardless of whether the lease provides this option, the landlord can convey his or her interest in the property to the tenant. This transfer is a **release**, and the tenant's interest in the property merges into the title to the property, which he or she now holds. Of course, a release effectively relieves the tenant of his or her obligations under the lease while bestowing on him or her title to the property, as well as all of the former landlord's responsibilities regarding the property. Because a release is a transfer of real property, it is subject to the Statute of Frauds (discussed in Chapter 14) and thus must be in writing.

Surrender by Agreement. The parties may agree to end a tenancy before it would otherwise terminate. If the lease was subject to the Statute of Frauds, surrender of the property by agreement must be in writing, because technically, the tenant is conveying his or her possessory interest in the property to the landlord. Surrender of the property by operation of law, however, does not require a writing. A surrender by operation of law is sometimes held to occur when the tenant abandons the property (as discussed below).

Abandonment. A landlord may treat a tenant's **abandonment** of the property—that is, the tenant's moving off the premises completely with no intention of returning—before the end of the term as an offer of surrender. The landlord's retaking of possession of the property will relieve the tenant of the obligation to pay rent. Sometimes, actions that the landlord takes to mitigate his or her damages—for example, refinishing an abandoned apartment's floors when preparing to lease it to another party—may be interpreted as accepting the tenant's offer of surrender, thereby absolving the tenant of responsibility for future rent payment.

Forfeiture. The termination of a lease, according to its terms or the terms of a statute, when one of the parties fails to fulfill a condition under the lease and thereby breaches it, is referred to as a **forfeiture**. If, for instance, the lease provides that the tenant will forfeit his or her interest in the leased property on failing to pay rent when it is due, the tenant's late payment of rent could prompt forfeiture. Generally, the courts do not favor forfeiture, and when neither the lease nor a statute provides for it, the landlord may only claim damages.

Destruction of the Property. Under statutes in most states, destruction of the leased property brought about by a fire, flood, or other cause beyond the landlord's control can terminate a residential lease. Usually, the landlord is under no obligation to restore the premises.

Similarly, the destruction of an entire building leased for business purposes may release the commercial tenant from any responsibility for continued payment of rent. (Terms vary among leases. If there is, for example, a fire, a commercial tenant's rent may only be reduced proportionally, according to how much property has been destroyed. The responsibility for restoring the property may rest on the tenant.)

RENEWAL

The lease may provide for renewal, or the landlord and the tenant may simply agree to renew it. When the lease includes an option to renew, it typically also includes a requirement that the tenant notify the landlord within a specific period of time—usually days or months—before the lease expires as to whether the tenant will exercise the option. The tenant must comply with any particulars regarding the notice's form (for example, that it be in writing), or the renewal will be invalid, even if the tenant stays on the property. The tenant's attempt to alter other terms to which the renewal is subject can be interpreted as a choice not to exercise the option to renew.

If a tenant neither renews a lease in accordance with its terms nor moves off the leased premises, but stays on without the landlord's consent, he or she can be treated as a trespasser. The tenant may be held liable to the landlord for damages.

TERMS AND CONCEPTS TO REVIEW

CHAPTER SUMMARY

Creation of the Landlord-Tenant Relationship	The landlord-tenant relationship is created by a lease agreement. State or local laws may dictate whether the lease must be in writing and what lease terms are permissible.
Parties' Rights and Duties	The rights and duties that arise under a lease agreement generally pertain to the following areas: 1. *Possession*—The tenant has an exclusive right to possess the leased premises, which must be available to the tenant at the agreed-on time. 2. *Covenant of quiet enjoyment*—The landlord promises that during the lease term neither the landlord nor anyone having a superior title to the property will disturb the tenant's use and enjoyment of the property. 3. *Eviction*—An eviction occurs whenever a landlord deprives the tenant of the tenant's possession of the leased property or interferes with his or her use or enjoyment of the property. A constructive eviction occurs whenever the landlord wrongfully performs, or fails to perform, any of the duties required under the lease, thereby making the tenant's further use and enjoyment of the property exceedingly difficult or virtually impossible. 4. *Use of the premises*—Unless the parties agree otherwise, the tenant may make any legal use of the property. The tenant is responsible for any damage that he or she causes. The landlord must comply with laws that set specific standards for the maintenance of real property.

CHAPTER SUMMARY—CONTINUED

Parties' Rights and Duties—continued	5. *Maintenance of the premises*—The landlord must comply with state and local legal standards for the construction and maintenance of buildings. The landlord is responsible for maintaining the common areas (areas such as halls or stairways) of leased property. The implied warranty of habitability requires that a landlord furnish and maintain residential premises in a habitable condition (that is, in a condition safe and suitable for human life). 6. *Rent*—The tenant must pay the rent as long as the lease is in force, unless the tenant justifiably refuses to occupy the property or withholds the rent because of the landlord's failure to maintain the premises properly.
Liability for Injuries on the Premises	1. *Landlord's liability*—Generally, the landlord is liable for injuries occurring in common areas—areas within the landlord's control. Also, when the landlord assumes an obligation to repair, the landlord's liability may extend to injuries caused by the failure to make repairs or by negligently made repairs. 2. *Tenant's liability*—The tenant has a duty to maintain in a reasonably safe condition those areas under his or her control. When commercial property is involved, this duty extends to all parts of the premises onto which a customer or other member of the public might be expected to go.
Transferring Rights to Leased Premises	1. *Transferring the landlord's interest*—If the landlord transfers complete title to the leased property, the tenant becomes the tenant of the new owner. The new owner may then collect the rent but must abide by the existing lease. 2. *Transferring the tenant's interest*—Generally, in the absence of an agreement to the contrary, tenants may assign their rights (but not their duties) under a lease contract to a third person. Tenants may also sublease leased property to a third person, but the original tenant is not relieved of any obligations to the landlord under the lease. In either case, the landlord's consent may be required.
Termination or Renewal of the Lease	A lease usually terminates when its term ends. If the lease states when it will end, the landlord is not required to give notice to the tenant—unless the lease (or a governing statute) requires that notice be given. A lease may also terminate in other ways—if the tenant purchases the property, for example, or if the parties agree to terminate the lease before its termination date. The lease may provide for renewal of the lease, or the landlord and tenant may agree to renew it.

CASES FOR ANALYSIS

Westlaw. You can access the full text of each case presented below by going to the Westlaw cases on this text's Web site at http://wbl-cs.westbuslaw.com. Each Westlaw case includes the names of all plaintiffs and defendants, the dates on which the case was argued and decided, a brief summary of the issues and decisions in the case, headnotes classifying specific issues in the case according to the West Key Number System, and the court's opinion. Concurring and dissenting opinions, if any, are included as well.

CASE 48.1 LANDLORD'S OBLIGATIONS UNDER THE LEASE

DECADE 80-I, LTD. v. PDQ FOOD STORES, INC., OF MADISON

Court of Appeals of Wisconsin, 1999.
226 Wis.2d 42,
593 N.W.2d 94.

BROWN, J. [Judge]

This case is about a retail store tenant's rights when its landlord fails to repair potholes in the parking lot and the lease contains a provision requiring the landlord to maintain the parking area. When the landlord did not repair the potholes after the tenant notified the landlord that the potholes were a problem, the tenant quit paying rent and vacated. The landlord sued for the rent. The tenant claimed the landlord had breached the lease, entitling it to terminate the relationship. We deem the main question on this appeal to be whether the tenant must prove considerable damages to the business in order to show that a breach of the lease was "substantial" enough to allow rescission. * * *

This is the second time this case comes to us. The first time, PDQ Food Stores, Inc. of Madison and Nash-Finch Company (PDQ), the tenant, appealed from a summary judgment entered [by a Wisconsin state court] in favor of Decade 80-I, Ltd. (Decade), the landlord. We held that summary judgment was inappropriate as material facts were still in dispute. On remand, we asked the trial court to resolve what we considered to be two factual questions: (1) did the existence of potholes constitute a breach of the lease? and (2) did the construction of other establishments on outlots reduce the size of PDQ's parking lot in violation of the lease? The trial court found that the potholes did constitute a breach of the lease, but that the construction on the outlots had not reduced the parking area in violation of the lease. Decade appeals the first result.

The relevant facts are as follows. The lease between PDQ and Decade was entered into by their predecessors-in-interest in October 1978. In an October 28, 1992 letter, PDQ provided notice of default to Decade that "the driveways, walkways and parking lots of the Shopping Center have not been maintained and at present contain numerous potholes." The letter further warned Decade that PDQ would "declare the lease terminated and void and * * * vacate the * * * premises" if the "defaults [were] not cured within 30 days." On November 23, Decade responded to PDQ in a letter stating that it would repair the potholes when construction of a nearby McDonald's was complete. On December 2, PDQ notified Decade that since "[t]he defaults * * * ha[d] not been cured within the allotted notice period," it "declare[d] the Lease terminated and void" and would vacate within thirty days. PDQ moved out later that month.

We first document the language from the relevant portions of the lease. Under one provision, "[a]s *additional rental,* Tenant shall pay to Landlord * * * [a] sum * * * to be applied toward the estimated reasonable cost of * * * maintaining, repairing * * * the parking areas." [Emphasis added.] Under a paragraph entitled REPAIRS AND MAINTENANCE, the "Landlord shall repair, replace and maintain the common areas of the Shopping Center, including sidewalk, parking areas and driveways." It is important to underscore the language used by the parties here. They agreed that PDQ would pay an additional sum over and above the rent of the premises in return for a well-maintained parking lot. Finally, there were default provisions, one of which reads as follows:

> *DEFAULT BY LANDLORD.* Tenant shall give Landlord written notice of any default by Landlord in the performance of any covenant or obligation to be kept or performed hereunder, and if such default continues for a period of thirty (30) days after receipt by Landlord of a written notice from Tenant specifying such default, then and in such event, Tenant at its election may declare this Lease terminated and void and vacate demised premises within an additional period of thirty (30) days, paying rent only to the day of said vacating.

* * * Decade claims that "PDQ failed to prove that the potholes constituted a default that would justify terminating the lease" because it did not show that the potholes "deprived it of the use of its property for a material period of time." * * *

* * * *

* * * [W]as it necessary for PDQ, in some concrete way, to show substantial damages to its business in order to establish a breach that justified terminating the lease? Decade argues that PDQ had to prove more than a mere breach. According to Decade, PDQ had to provide proof of damages resulting from the breach and it failed to meet this burden. Decade maintains that PDQ had to show the existence of one or more of the following: lost profits, loss of use of the building for a substantial period of time, an inability of suppliers or customers to get to the store, or a loss of goodwill. * * *

* * * *

* * * PDQ claims that Decade made an agreement to do something, to do it within a certain time period, and then did not do it. * * *

The covenant at issue in this case is a specific provision requiring maintenance of the parking lot * * * . It makes sense that a commercial retail lease would contain a specific covenant for parking lot maintenance for aesthetics and the convenience of customers, if nothing else. For these reasons, a well-maintained parking lot is very important to a retailer, as the testimony in this case and common sense show. The inclusion of the maintenance provision in the lease was part of the bargain struck between PDQ and Decade just as much as the rent was. PDQ is entitled to the benefit of that bargain. Nothing in the covenant envisions that the tenant must prove the infliction of actual economic loss before invoking the remedies provided. Furthermore, to read in such a requirement would be an unfaithful interpretation of the lease. In construing the lease, we must apply its unambiguous language—here, a specific promise to maintain a parking lot. * * * [T]he language of the lease itself, the embodiment of the parties' bargain, controls.

To rule otherwise would render largely illusory any specific agreement that the owner of commercial property keep the parking lot well maintained. *In a commercial setting, it will almost always be difficult for a tenant to prove a connection between large potholes in a parking lot and loss of profits.* Knowing this, the landlord could simply ignore its agreement to maintain the parking lot, understanding that its failure to act would rarely result in any significant consequences. We refuse to offer a free pass to landlords to ignore contractual agreements. If the owner of commercial property agrees to keep a parking lot maintained, and rent is paid partly in consideration for that promise, then a breach of that promise is grounds for terminating the lease, whether the breach causes lost profits or not. The tenant, after all, is paying for parking lot maintenance and expects the lot to be kept in good condition. The tenant should be allowed to obtain the full measure of its expectations without having to prove a dent in profits. [Emphasis added.]

In addition to the clear promise to maintain the parking area, this lease also dictated the available time for curing a default and the tenant's remedy when a default was not cured. The landlord had thirty days to repair, which it did not do in this case. The tenant, then, had the option to "declare this Lease terminated and void and vacate demised premises within an additional period of thirty (30) days, paying rent only to the day of said vacating." Here, PDQ had the right under the lease to avail itself of that remedy. Thus, the trial court's judgment is affirmed.

CASE 48.2 IMPLIED WARRANTY OF HABITABILITY

SCHIERNBECK V. DAVIS

United States Court of Appeals,
Eighth Circuit, 1998.
143 F.3d 434.

WATERS, District Judge.

* * * *

I. BACKGROUND

This action was brought [in a federal district court] by Linda Schiernbeck ("Schiernbeck") against her former landlords, Clark and Rosa Davis (the "Davises"). In October of 1991, Schiernbeck and her now ex-husband, Merlin Schiernbeck, began leasing a house [in South Dakota] from the Davises. The Schiernbecks did not have a written lease with the Davises. The parties orally agreed that the Schiernbecks would pay $150 per month. They also orally agreed that the Davises would make certain "functional" repairs to the house, *e.g.*, the Davises replaced the wood burning stove with a propane furnace. In addition, the Davises agreed to allow the Schiernbecks to do some redecorating of the house, *e.g.*, repainting.

Schiernbeck asserts that approximately one month after she moved into the house, she noticed a discolored circular area on one of the walls with a screw inserted in the middle. Schiernbeck determined that a smoke detector had previously been attached to the wall, however, there was no smoke detector present when she moved into the house. Schiernbeck contends that she approached Clark Davis and told him about the missing detector and requested that he provide her with a new one. Schiernbeck further contends that Clark Davis agreed to furnish her with a new smoke detector.

The Davises refute Schiernbeck's assertions and claim that no agreement was ever made with Schiernbeck that the Davises would equip the house with a smoke detector. Clark Davis denies that Schiernbeck ever asked him to purchase a detector for the house. He does admit that in June of 1992, he purchased a smoke detector for the house and gave it to Schiernbeck. He claims, however, that he did not know at the time that he purchased the detector, that the old one was missing. Schiernbeck contends that Clark Davis never provided her with a smoke detector for the house.

* * * *

On February 10, 1993, a fire broke out in the house that severely injured Schiernbeck and her daughter. On February 2, 1996, Schiernbeck filed suit against the Davises alleging negligence and breach of contract for failing to provide her with a smoke detector. The Davises moved for summary judgment on the basis that there is no common law or statutory duty owed by a landlord to install a smoke detector in a rental house. On August 1, 1997, the district court granted the Davises' motion for summary judgment. Schiernbeck appeals the district court's decision.

II. DISCUSSION

* * * *

A. IS THERE A COMMON LAW DUTY?

* * * *

* * * Schiernbeck states that she asked the Davises to make various functional repairs in the house, and the Davises made such repairs. Thus, Schiernbeck contends that she reasonably believed that when she asked Clark Davis to provide her with a smoke detector, and he agreed, there was an agreement between the parties that the Davises would replace the smoke detector. Schiernbeck asserts that replacing a smoke detector constitutes a "repair" * * * .

* * * The Davises assert that, even if the replacement of a smoke detector constitutes a "repair," * * * there was no contract to repair. The Davises contend that there was no agreement, formal or informal, between the parties to replace the smoke detector.

We agree. Even if replacing a smoke detector constituted a "repair," *the Davises had no common law duty to provide Schiernbeck with a smoke detector* * * * *because there was no contract to repair.* [Emphasis added.]

* * * *

There is no evidence that the Davises ever promised to provide Schiernbeck with a smoke detector. The only evidence that plaintiff has offered in support of her case is her own affidavit, which conflicts with her earlier deposition testimony, and thus, is unreliable * * * .

* * * *

* * * [O]ur decision is in agreement with a majority of the state courts that have held that no common law duty exists on behalf of a landlord to provide a smoke detector to his or her tenant.

* * * *

B. IS THERE A STATUTORY DUTY?

Schiernbeck asserts that South Dakota Codified Law [Section] 43-32-8 * * * imposes an affirmative duty upon landlords to provide their tenants with fit, habitable and safe places to live, and the failure to do so results in liability to the landlords. Schiernbeck contends that the Davises' failure to replace her smoke detector is a violation of [Section] 43-32-8.

The Davises assert that Schiernbeck is asking the court to create a duty where none exists * * * .

* * * *

[Section] 43-32-8 requires that the lessor keep the leased premises "in reasonable repair and fit for human habitation and in good and safe working order during the term of the lease * * * ." We do not believe that equipping the leased premises with a smoke detector constitutes keeping the premises in "reasonable repair." * * * [T]here are some varying shades of difference in the general definition of the term "repair." But there is none more apt and comprehensible than the accepted [*Black's Law Dictionary*] definition: "To restore to a sound or good state after decay, injury, dilapidation, or partial destruction." Schiernbeck cites an additional part of the dictionary's definition which states: "[t]he word 'repair' contemplates an existing structure or thing which has become imperfect, and means to supply in the original existing structure that which is lost or destroyed, and thereby restore it to the condition in which it originally existed, as near as may be." Schiernbeck relies on the phrase in the definition "to supply * * * that which is lost or destroyed" to include replacing a missing smoke detector in the definition of repair. We conclude, however, that when reading the entire definition, the term "repair" does not encompass replacing a missing smoke detector.

* * * *

In addition, we do not believe that the Davises were required to replace the smoke detector in order to make the rental house "fit for human habitation." * * * [A] lessor could be liable for failure to make the necessary repairs to keep the premises in a "fit and habitable" condition [if, for example, the] uninhabitable condition * * * was collapsing and dilapidated staircases. Clearly, unstable stairs create a place that is unfit for human habitation, as does a lack of running water, heat, or electricity. We do not believe, however, that a lessor, under the language of [Section] 43-32-8, is required to equip his or her residential premises with smoke detectors, fire extinguishers, carbon monoxide detectors, etc. in order to make the leased premises "fit for human habitation."

Furthermore, we do not believe that a lessor is required to provide such items to keep the premises in "good and safe working order." Schiernbeck urges this court to read the statute to require that a lessor "keep the premises safe." Schiernbeck asserts that clearly a residence is not "safe" without a smoke detector. We disagree with Schiernbeck's reading of the statute. The statute, when read carefully, does not state that the leased premises must be kept safe. On the contrary, the statute says that the lessor must keep the residential premises "in good and safe working order." There is a notable difference between the two statements. A lessor is not required under the statute to keep the premises safe * * * .

In addition, the statute also states that, "[t]he lessor shall maintain in good and safe working order and condition all electrical, plumbing or heating systems of the premises * * * ." A smoke detector is not a part or function of either the electrical, plumbing or heating systems of a house.

Therefore, we conclude, that [Section] 43-32-8 does not impose a statutory duty upon a lessor to install a smoke detector in his or her residential premises. * * *

* * * *

III. CONCLUSION

The Davises owed Schiernbeck no common law and/or statutory duty to install a smoke detector. We affirm the district court's decision.

CASE 48.3 LANDLORD'S LIABILITY—COMMERCIAL PROPERTY

JOHNSON COUNTY SHERIFF'S POSSE, INC. V. ENDSLEY

Supreme Court of Texas, 1996.
926 S.W.2d 284.

Justice *GONZALEZ* delivered the opinion for a unanimous Court.

* * * *

The Johnson County Sheriff's Posse owns an enclosed arena that it rents to sponsors of functions such as barrel races, roping contests, dog shows, and 4-H events. For $225, the Posse orally agreed to rent the arena to Teresa McClendon and Cynthia Skinner for a single-day barrel racing competition. Ms. McClendon had leased the arena for barrel racing events on five or six other occasions. During the competition, Tim Endsley was watching the event from the bleachers. He suffered a serious eye injury when he was struck by an unknown object, presumably a rock, that was apparently kicked into the air by a horse. Endsley then sued the Posse [in a Texas state court] alleging negligence and gross negligence, and he prayed [asked] for one million dollars in damages. Endsley alleged that his injury resulted from the Posse's negligence in failing to maintain the dirt floor of the arena free of rocks. Endsley also alleged that the existence of rocks on the arena floor created an unreasonably dangerous condition. The Posse moved for summary judgment on the basis that, as lessor of the premises, it owed no duty to its lessees' invitees. The trial court granted the motion, and Endsley appealed [to a state intermediate appellate court]. The court of appeals reversed. [The Posse appealed to the Texas Supreme Court.]

* * * The Posse contends that the trial court properly rendered summary judgment because its summary judgment proof negated an essential element of Endsley's cause of action, the existence of any duty owed by the Posse. * * *

A lessor generally has no duty to tenants or their invitees for dangerous conditions on the leased premises. This general rule stems from the notion that a lessor relinquishes possession or occupancy of the premises to the lessee. We have, however, recognized several exceptions to the general rule. For example, a lessor who makes repairs may be liable for injuries resulting from the lessor's negligence in making the repairs. A lessor who conceals defects on the leased premises of which the lessor is aware may also be liable. In addition, a lessor may be liable for injuries caused by a defect on a portion of premises that remain under the lessor's control.

The Posse presented summary judgment proof that it leased the premises to the lessees without a right of re-entry, and that the lessees were in possession of the arena at the time of the accident. Thus, unless contradicted by Endsley's response to the Posse's motion for summary judgment, the Posse's proof brings the case within the general rule of non-liability * * * . Endsley responded that the Posse had retained the right of control over the composition of the dirt in the arena.

Concerning the right of control, the parties relied on affidavits and deposition excerpts from a member of the Posse, Tom Frank Jones, and one of the tenants, McClendon. The uncontradicted evidence shows that the Posse had a policy requiring the tenants to maintain and prepare the arena grounds for their particular event. The Posse had a water truck, a tractor, a harrow, and other equipment available, but did not instruct the tenants on the preparation of the arena grounds. On occasion, a Posse member helped with the water truck or helped start the tractor, but did not otherwise help with the preparation of the arena. Jones testified that the same dirt was in the arena as when it was built several years before. * * *

* * * No witness testified that there was any limitation on the tenant's control of the arena. Resolving every reasonable inference in favor of Endsley, there is no evidence raising an issue of fact that the Posse retained a right of control over any part of the premises during the period of the tenancy. The Posse yielded control of the premises to the lessees, and it was up to them to prepare the arena to fit their needs. * * *

* * * *

* * * Endsley presented the affidavit of Clem McSpadden, a general manager, producer, and announcer for rodeos, who testified that anyone furnishing a rodeo arena with any rocks in the dirt is "derelict in his duty" because a rock can be propelled at great speed, causing injury to contestants, animals, and spectators. Endsley testified that he was "pretty certain" he was hit by a rock, and saw some rocks underneath the bleachers where he was sitting. Posse member Jones testified that he had seen rocks in the arena dirt "thumbnail" size or smaller.

* * * Endsley's theory is that the Posse should have made the dirt "rock free," or in other words, safer than ordinary dirt. The natural state of dirt, that it may be slippery when wet or may contain small rocks, can present a hazard under the right conditions, but not unreasonably so. Otherwise, a landlord would be an insurer against all injury to a tenant's lessees. Under the facts of this case, dirt containing small rocks is not an unreasonably dangerous condition for which a landlord may be held liable as a matter of law.

Upon consideration of the summary judgment evidence, we conclude that there is no basis for holding the lessor liable under the undisputed facts of this case. We reverse the judgment of the court of appeals and render judgment that Endsley take nothing from the Posse.

CASE PROBLEMS

48–1. Spirn, a shopping-mall tenant, sustained injuries when he fell while on the property of Joseph, the mall's owner. At the time of the injury, Spirn was on his way to a furnace room in the mall to check the furnace, which seemed to be malfunctioning. The furnace room was only accessible through an outside door, approximately twelve feet from the street. There was no paved walkway leading to the door, but a "trodden path" had been created in the snow by persons who had been called earlier by Joseph to repair the furnace. The repairpersons' footprints had made depressions in the snow, which had subsequently been iced over. Spirn slipped and injured himself. He filed suit against Joseph, alleging that the path was an unnatural (or aggravated natural) condition of the premises created by agents of Joseph and that Joseph had a duty to maintain safe premises. Joseph had therefore been negligent in failing to warn Spirn of the path's condition. Discuss whether Spirn was successful. [*Spirn v. Joseph,* 144 Ill.App.3d 127, 493 N.E.2d 1197, 98 Ill.Dec. 176 (1986)]

48–2. Tachtronic Instruments, Inc., leased office and warehouse space in a building owned by Provident Mutual Life Insurance Co. The three-year lease ran until October 31, 1985, and specified monthly payments to Provident in the amount of $2,463. Within the first year of the lease term, Tachtronic defaulted on its payments. When Provident brought an action to evict Tachtronic, the small firm paid a portion of the rent due, and the action was dismissed. By February 1984, Tachtronic had largely vacated the premises. On March 1, 1984, Tachtronic met with representatives of Provident at the "leased" premises. The premises were inspected by Provident, and Tachtronic removed its remaining possessions, swept the floor with a broom, and turned over the keys to Provident. Immediately thereafter, Provident sought a new tenant for the premises. A new tenant was found, and a more lucrative lease beginning November 1, 1984, was created between Provident and the new tenant. In June 1984, Provident commenced an action to recover the rent due from Tachtronic prior to its departure from the leased premises and also the rent due and payable for the remainder of the lease. Discuss whether Provident could collect. [*Provident Mutual Life Insurance Co. v. Tachtronic Instruments, Inc.,* 394 N.W.2d 161 (Minn.App. 1986)]

48–3. The landlord of an apartment leased a building he owned nearby for use as a cocktail lounge. The residential tenants complained to the landlord about the late-evening and early-morning music and disturbances coming from the lounge. Although the lease for the lounge provided that entertainment had to be conducted so that it could not be heard outside the building and would not disturb the apartment tenants, the landlord was unable to remedy the problem. The tenants vacated their apartments. Was the landlord successful in his suit to collect rent from the tenants who vacated? Discuss. [*Blackett v. Olanoff,* 371 Mass. 714, 358 N.E.2d 817 (1977)]

48–4. ARG Enterprises, Inc., operated a Black Angus restaurant on premises leased from SDR Associates. The lease included a provision that required ARG to return the premises in the condition in which it had received them. In return for ARG's agreeing to maintain the premises, SDR charged lower rent payments than it otherwise would have. About six months before the lease was due to expire, SDR notified ARG of the need to restore the premises to good condition if the lease was not renewed. When the lease expired, however, the premises were in disrepair. Extensive repairs were required for the roof as well as for the air-conditioning unit, the exhaust fans, and the parking lot. These problems prevented SDR from renting the premises to anyone else. Before the lease expired, SDR had been negotiating with Toys "Я" Us, Inc., about the possibility of demolishing the building and selling just the land; but SDR's preference was to relet the building as a restaurant. At the time of trial, the structure had not been destroyed. SDR sued ARG, alleging that ARG had breached the lease agreement by failing to return the premises to SDR in good condition. Among other things, SDR sought damages in the amount of $200,000 as the cost for restoring the premises to good condition. Given the fact that SDR was contemplating the demolition of the building, should the court require ARG to pay the $200,000 in damages to restore the premises to their earlier condition? Explain. [*SDR Associates v. ARG Enterprises, Inc.,* 170 Ariz. 1, 821 P.2d 268 (App. Div. 2 1991)]

48–5. Jeanne Koferl, a single woman with an eight-year-old son, was a tenant of Highview Associates under a written lease that was to expire on May 26, 1983. Her apartment complex had become the target of burglars and thieves, and break-ins and thefts were frequent. Prior to January 1983, she had suffered the traumatic experience of having a peeping Tom peek through her window. This event was reported to the management. At the end of January 1983, two men attempted to burglarize her apartment at 3:00 A.M. She fled with her child to her mother's home and never returned to the apartment. The landlord was able to rent the apartment to another tenant before May 1983. The landlord sued Koferl for unpaid rent for the months of February and March and for rerenting expenses. Was the tenant liable for the costs of rerenting her apartment prior to the end of the lease term? How did the court rule on this issue? [*Highview Associates v. Koferl,* 124 Misc.2d 797, 477 N.Y.S.2d 585 (Dist.Ct. 1984)]

48–6. James and Bernadine Winn rented a house from Rick and Cynthia McGeehan. Each month, the rent was either late or underpaid. When the McGeehans told the Winns that no further late payments would be accepted, the Winns complained of a number of habitability problems. The McGeehans made repairs. The Winns again failed to pay the rent on time. The McGeehans filed a suit in an Oregon state court to regain possession of the house. While the suit was pending, the Winns paid the rent to the court. The court held that the McGeehans were entitled to possession. The Winns appealed, claiming that they were entitled to possession. Who should have possession of the house, and why? [*Winn v. McGeehan*, 142 Or.App. 390, 921 P.2d 1337 (1996)]

48–7. Inwood North Professional Group—Phase I leased medical office space to Joseph Davidow, a physician. The terms of the five-year lease specified that Inwood would provide electricity, hot water, air conditioning, janitorial and maintenance services, light fixtures, and security services. During his tenancy, Davidow encountered a number of problems. The roof leaked, and the air conditioning did not function properly. The premises were not cleaned and maintained by Inwood as promised in the lease agreement, and as a consequence, rodents and pests infested the premises, and trash littered the parking area. There was frequently no hot water, and at one point Davidow was without electricity for several days because Inwood had not paid the bill. About a year prior to the lease's expiration, Davidow moved to another office building and refused to pay the remaining rent due under the lease. Inwood sued for the unpaid rent. Must Davidow pay the remaining rent due under the lease? Discuss. [*Davidow v. Inwood North Professional Group—Phase I*, 747 S.W.2d 373 (Tex. 1988)]

48–8. Christine Callis formed a lease agreement with Colonial Properties, Inc., to lease property in a shopping center in Montgomery, Alabama. Callis later alleged that before signing the lease agreement, she had told a representative of Colonial that she wanted a location in a shopping center that would attract a wealthy clientele, and the representative had assured her that no discount stores would be allowed to lease space in the shopping center. The written lease agreement, which Callis signed, contained a clause stating that "[n]o representation, inducement, understanding or anything of any nature whatsoever made, stated or represented on Landlord's behalf, either orally or in writing (except this Lease), has induced Tenant to enter into this lease." The lease also stipulated that Callis would not conduct any type of business commonly called a discount store, surplus store, or other similar business. Later, Colonial did, in fact, lease space to discount stores, and Callis sued Colonial for breach of the lease contract. Will Callis succeed in her claim? Discuss fully. [*Callis v. Colonial Properties, Inc.*, 597 So.2d 660 (Ala. 1991)]

48–9. Kristi Kellogg, her daughter Mindy, and her boyfriend James Greene attempted to lease half of a house. The house was owned by Keith Osborn and Pam Lyman, and managed, as rental property, by Keith's mother, Barbara Osborn. Kellogg was white; Greene was African American. The owners refused to rent to them, claiming, among other things, that three people were too many, Greene's income was too low, and Greene had not provided credit references. The owners later rented half of the house to the Li family, which had five members, and the other half to the Suggett family, which numbered three. Both the Li family and the Suggett family had less income than Kellogg and Greene. Kellogg had provided extensive credit references, but the Lis and the Suggetts had provided none. Kellogg filed a complaint with the Nebraska Equal Opportunity Commission (NEOC) against the Osborns and Lyman. The NEOC concluded that the defendants had discriminated against Kellogg in violation of state fair housing laws. A Nebraska state trial court adopted the NEOC's conclusion. The defendants appealed to an intermediate state appellate court. What will happen on appeal? Discuss. [*Osborn v. Kellogg*, 4 Neb.App. 594, 547 N.W.2d 504 (1996)]

48–10. Don Weingarden notified his landlord, Eagle Ridge Condominiums, that his apartment basement leaked when it rained or when snow melted. The water soaked the carpeting and caused the growth of mildew; this rendered the basement—which was one-third of the apartment—useless and spread odor throughout the apartment. For these and other reasons, Weingarden vacated the premises before the end of the lease term. When his security deposit was not returned, Weingarden filed a suit in an Ohio state court against Eagle Ridge. In whose favor will the court decide? Why? [*Weingarden v. Eagle Ridge Condominiums*, 71 Ohio Misc.2d 7, 653 N.E.2d 759 (1995)]

48–11. MCM Ventures, II, Inc., leased premises from Rushing Construction Co. on which to operate a restaurant. The lease term was for two years: January 1, 1987, to December 31, 1988. The lease agreement stated in part that MCM "shall have a continuing option for a period of eight (8) consecutive years to renew this lease." MCM did nothing to renew the lease before it expired but, after it expired on December 31, 1988, made monthly rent payments in the same amount as before in January and February 1989. Then, on February 28, 1989, MCM notified Rushing by mail that it wanted to exercise its option to renew the lease. Rushing refused to renew the lease, contending that MCM had forfeited the option by not exercising it prior to the expiration of the lease agreement in which the option had been given. Discuss fully whether MCM still had a right to exercise the lease renewal option as late as February 28, 1989. [*Rushing Construction Co. v. MCM Ventures, II, Inc.*, 100 N.C.App. 259, 395 S.E.2d 130 (1990)]

48–12. Commerce Properties, Inc. (CPI), owned an apartment complex in which Jonathan Linthicum, who was four years old, and his parents lived as tenants. There were no warning signs in the parking area adjacent to the rental units to notify automobile drivers that they should reduce driving speed because children might be playing there. There were no speed bumps to slow the automobile traffic, nor was any other traffic warning or safety device in place. Jonathan was playing in the parking lot when he was struck by a car driven by a neighbor and seriously injured. Jonathan sued CPI for negligent maintenance of the parking lot. How should the court decide this case? If Jonathan's parents knew or should have known of the risk, will CPI escape liability? Discuss fully. [*Commerce Properties, Inc. v. Linthicum,* 209 Ga.App. 853, 434 S.E.2d 769 (1993)]

48–13. Three-year-old Nkenge Lynch fell from the window of her third-floor apartment and suffered serious and permanent injuries. There were no window stops or guards on the window. The use of window stops, even if installed, is at the tenant's option. Stanley James owned the apartment building. Zsa Zsa Kinsey, Nkenge's mother, filed a suit on Nkenge's behalf in a Massachusetts state court against James, alleging in part a breach of an implied warranty of habitability. The plaintiff did not argue that the absence of stops or guards made the apartment unfit for human habitation but that their absence "endangered and materially impaired her health and safety," and therefore the failure to install them was a breach of warranty. Should the court rule that the absence of window stops breached a warranty of habitability? Should the court mandate that landlords provide window guards? Why, or why not? [*Lynch v. James,* 44 Mass.App.Ct. 448, 692 N.E.2d 81 (1998)]

48–14. Jennifer Tribble leased an apartment from Spring Isle II, a limited partnership. The written lease agreement provided that if Tribble was forced to move because of a job transfer or because she accepted a new job, she could vacate on sixty days' notice and owe only an extra two months' rent plus no more than a $650 rerenting fee. The initial term was for one year, and the parties renewed the lease for a second one-year term. The security deposit was $900. State law allowed a landlord to withhold a security deposit for the nonpayment of rent but required timely notice stating valid reasons for the withholding or the tenant would be entitled to twice the amount of the deposit as damages. One month into the second term, Tribble notified Spring Isle in writing that she had accepted a new job and would move out within a week. She paid the extra rent required by the lease, but not the rerental fee, and vacated the apartment. Spring Isle wrote her a letter, stating that it was keeping the entire security deposit until the apartment was rerented or the lease term ended, whichever came first. Spring Isle later filed a suit in a Wisconsin state court against Tribble, claiming that she owed, among other things, the rest of the rent until the apartment had been rerented and the costs of rerenting. Tribble responded that withholding the security deposit was improper, and she was entitled to "any penalties." Does Tribble owe Spring Isle anything? Does Spring Isle owe Tribble anything? Explain. [*Spring Isle II v. Tribble,* 610 N.W.2d 229, 2000 WL 38918 (Wis.App. 2000)]

48–15. A Question of Ethics

John and Terry Hoffius own property in Jackson, Michigan, which they offered to rent. Kristal McCready and Keith Kerr responded to the Hoffiuses' ad about the property. The Hoffiuses refused to rent to McCready and Kerr, however, when they learned that the two were single and intended to live together. John Hoffius told all prospective tenants that unmarried cohabitation violated his religious beliefs. McCready and others filed a suit in a Michigan state court against the Hoffiuses. They alleged in part that the Hoffiuses' actions violated the plaintiffs' civil rights under a state law that prohibits discrimination on the basis of "marital status." The Hoffiuses responded in part that forcing them to rent to unmarried couples in violation of the Hoffiuses' religious beliefs would be unconstitutional. [*McCready v. Hoffius,* 586 N.W.2d 723 (Mich. 1998)]

1. Was it the plaintiffs' "marital status" or their conduct to which the defendants objected? Did the defendants violate the plaintiffs' civil rights? Explain.
2. Should a court, in the interest of preventing discrimination in housing, compel a landlord to violate his or her conscience? In other words, whose rights should prevail in this case? Why?
3. Is there an objective rule that determines when civil rights or religious freedom, or any two similarly important principles, should prevail? If so, what is it? If not, should there be?

E-LINKS

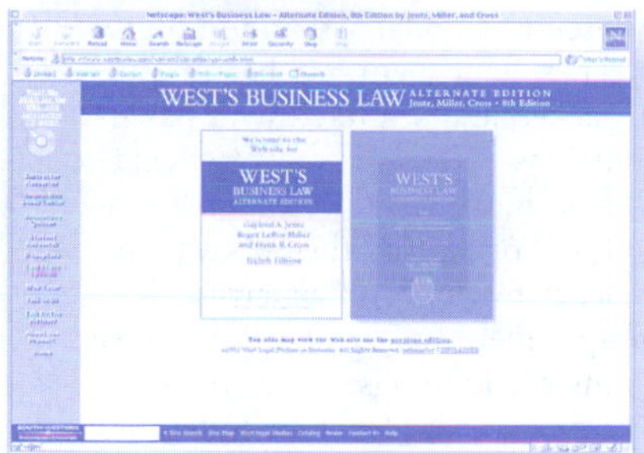

For updated links to resources available on the Web, as well as a variety of other materials, visit this text's Web site at

http://wbl-cs.westbuslaw.com

You can find online links to most uniform laws, including the URLTA, at

http://www.lawsource.com/also

Many Web sites now provide information on laws and other information relating to landlord-tenant relaionships. One of them is TenantNet at

http://tenant.net

LEGAL RESEARCH EXERCISES ON THE WEB

Go to http://wbl-cs.westbuslaw.com, the Web site that accompanies this text. Select "Interactive Study Center," and then click on "Chapter 48." There you will find the following Internet research exercise that you can perform to learn more about landlord-tenant relationships:

Activity 48–1: The Rights of Tenants

Focus on Legal Reasoning

Stewart v. Johnson

Chapter 48 discussed the different types of leasehold estates and the law governing landlord-tenant relationships. One type of tenancy is a periodic tenancy. Termination of a periodic tenancy requires that either the landlord or the tenant give at least one period's notice to the other party. Without this notice, an attempt to terminate the relationship may be construed as a wrongful eviction. In this *Focus on Legal Reasoning*, we examine *Stewart v. Johnson,*[1] a decision that involved these principles.

Case Background

In October 1998, in Huntington, West Virginia, Ron and Vera Stewart entered into an oral agreement with Dennis Johnson. Ron Stewart agreed to perform maintenance work on Johnson's properties, which included more than $3 million in rental real estate. Johnson agreed to let the Stewarts live in one of his apartments without directly paying rent. Johnson also agreed to pay Stewart if the labor cost of his work, according to a specific hourly wage, exceeded $350 in a single month.

Stewart worked for Johnson from seven to twelve hours a day, seven days a week. Despite Stewart's repeated requests, however, Johnson never paid him. In December and January, needing food, Stewart pawned two of Johnson's tools. He retrieved and returned one, but Johnson was upset when he learned what had happened.

On February 3, Stewart finished remodeling work on Johnson's own home. Returning home the next evening, the Stewarts found on their door a note: "I got a warrant for your arrest for selling & pawning my tools. You need to vacate my premises no later than tomorrow."[2] Their apartment had been ransacked and scattered with pawn tickets. A TV set was missing. The next morning, Johnson's associate, Lou Porter, told the Stewarts to leave by noon. The Stewarts left the apartment to get a truck to move their belongings. When they returned, everything, including their pets, was gone.

The Stewarts filed a suit in a West Virginia state court against Johnson, seeking damages for wrongful eviction. The court granted judgment as a matter of law to Johnson. The Stewarts appealed to the West Virginia Supreme Court of Appeals (West Virginia's highest court).

1. 209 W.Va. 476, 549 S.E.2d 670 (2001).

2. Although there was not yet a warrant for Stewart's arrest, he later pled guilty to a misdemeanor charge involving stolen property.

Majority Opinion

PER CURIAM.

* * * *

DISCUSSION

A. Judgment as a Matter of Law

The Stewarts presented evidence at trial to show that they had a month-to-month tenancy with Mr. Johnson and that he failed to provide to them proper notice before terminating the tenancy. Granting judgment as a matter of law, the [trial] court ruled that the statute of frauds precluded the action; that the tenancy agreement between the parties was not in writing; and that it was indefinite in duration. In making these findings, the [trial] court relied upon our general statute of frauds and the statute of frauds concerning the sale or lease of land.[3] The trial court stated on the record:

> * * * [W]e have statutes that deal with real property and if there is an oral agreement regarding [real property] that's not reduced to writing, if that oral agreement can last for a year or more * * * it has to be in writing[.]
>
> * * * *
>
> * * * [There is also the] agreement that Mr. Stewart allegedly had with Mr. Johnson relative to working for him. There was no time specified for that and the law in West Virginia [is], if an agreement for personal services cannot be performed within one year it has to be reduced to writing * * *.
>
> There was never any testimony that they intended to be there six months or nine months or anything else, so it was an oral agreement about a work situation that would exceed one year in duration.

Based upon the evidence developed at trial, it was error for the trial court to hold, as a matter of law, that such evidence established a violation of the statute of frauds concerning the sale or lease of land. The evidence presented by the Stewarts clearly established a *prima facie* case that a month-to-month tenancy existed between the parties. The statute of frauds concerning the sale or lease of land, however, does not require that month-to-month tenancy agreements be reduced to writing.

Where, as here, there exists a month-to-month tenancy, West Virginia Code Section 37-6-5 requires a landlord provide notice equal to a full period of the tenancy. Through the testimony of the Stewarts and Mr. Johnson, it was shown that the oral tenancy agreement between the parties was indefinite in duration. We have held that

3. The Statute of Frauds requires that certain contracts, including contracts relating to interests in land, be in writing to be enforceable. This statute and its exceptions are explained fully in Chapter 14.

the length of a tenancy indefinite in duration may be determined by the terms of the rent payment. See *Hans Watts Realty Co. v. Nash Huntington Sales Co.,* 107 W.Va. 80, 147 S.E. 282 (1929) * * * . The evidence presented by the Stewarts established that they paid Mr. Johnson $350 a month for rent, through work performed by Mr. Stewart for Mr. Johnson. It was further shown that Mr. Johnson did not provide the Stewarts with notice equal to a full period of the tenancy (one month) before evicting them. To the extent that the Stewarts presented evidence showing that a month-to-month tenancy existed with Mr. Johnson, and that Mr. Johnson evicted them without providing notice equal to a full period of the tenancy, it was incumbent upon Mr. Johnson to put on evidence to refute the Stewarts' contentions. * * *

In the instant case, the trial court halted further proceedings at the close of the Stewarts' case. This was error. *Only when the plaintiff's evidence, considered in the light most favorable to him, fails to establish a* prima facie *right to recovery, should the trial court * * * grant judgment as a matter of law in favor of the defendant. In this regard, every reasonable and legitimate inference fairly arising from the testimony, when considered in its entirety, must be indulged in favorably to plaintiff; and the court must assume as true those facts which the jury may properly find under the evidence. The trial court failed to apply the above standards in this matter. Therefore, we must reverse and remand the case for further proceedings.* [Emphasis added.]

B. Evidentiary Rulings

The Stewarts also * * * contend the trial court improperly excluded evidence of other prior evictions by Mr. Johnson. * * *

* * * During the trial, Mr. Johnson stated * * * that he had never unlawfully evicted anyone. The Stewarts sought to present evidence of alleged prior unlawful evictions by Mr. Johnson but the trial court ruled that such evidence was character evidence and therefore inadmissible under Rule 404(b) of the *West Virginia Rules of Evidence.* Rule 404(b) provides, in relevant part, that "[e]vidence of other crimes, wrongs, or acts is not admissible to prove the character of a person in order to show that he or she acted in conformity therewith." * * * [T]he Stewarts wanted to present evidence to illustrate why they were afraid of Mr. Johnson and to show a pattern of unlawful eviction as a normal business practice by Mr. Johnson.

The record indicates that the trial court failed to perform the balancing test required for Rule 404(b) evidence. In * * * *State v. McGinnis,* 193 W.Va. 147, 455 S.E.2d 516 (1994), we addressed the role of the trial court in assessing Rule 404(b) evidence:

> Where an offer of evidence is made under Rule 404(b), the trial court * * * is to determine its admissibility. * * * [T]he trial court must be satisfied by a preponderance of the evidence that the acts or conduct occurred and that the defendant committed the acts. If the trial court does not find by a preponderance of the evidence that the acts or conduct was committed or that the defendant was the actor, the evidence should be excluded * * * . If a sufficient showing has been made, the trial court must then determine the relevancy of the evidence under Rules 401 and 402 and conduct the balancing required under Rule 403. If the trial court is then satisfied that the evidence is admissible, it should instruct the jury on the limited purpose for which such evidence has been admitted. * * *

We will not determine in this appeal whether evidence of prior evictions by Mr. Johnson should be admitted. However, should the Stewarts again attempt to present evidence of other evictions by Mr. Johnson, the trial court must perform the balancing test required for [the] evidence when making its determination on the admissibility of such evidence.

* * * *

CONCLUSION

For the foregoing reasons, the trial court's award of judgment as a matter of law to Mr. Johnson is reversed, and this case remanded for further proceedings consistent with this opinion.

Reversed and Remanded.

Questions for Analysis

1. **Legal Reasoning.** In the *Stewart* case, the West Virginia Supreme Court of Appeals cites two of its decisions: *Hans Watts Realty Co. v. Nash Huntington Sales Co.*, 107 W.Va. 80, 147 S.E. 282 (1929); and *State v. McGinnis,* 193 W.Va. 147, 455 S.E.2d 516 (1994) (see the *E-Links* feature at the end of Chapter 2 for instructions on how to access the opinions of state courts). Considering the purposes for which the court referred to these cases, is it significant that those cases may not be on "all fours" (precisely alike in all important respects) with *Stewart?*

2. **Legal Analysis.** If Johnson were to file a suit against the party who pawned the tool from Stewart, what would be the likely result?

3. **Economic Consideration.** Considering that the plaintiffs did not have much income, what is noteworthy about this case?

4. **Implications for the Landlord.** Besides the eviction attempted in this case, what might a landlord do in similar circumstances to obtain relief from an employee?

FOCUS ON LEGAL REASONING

WESTLAW ONLINE RESEARCH

Westlaw. Go to this text's companion Web site, at http://wbl-cs.westbuslaw.com, and click on the Westlaw icon. Use your special password to access the full text of this case, including the dissenting opinions. Read through the case, and then answer the following questions.

1. Contrast the dissenting and the concurring opinions in the *Stewart* case. (Note, too, the dates of these two opinions.) What is the basic difference between these two justices' views?
2. Consider the role of appellate courts. Should the majority have taken the opportunity presented by this appeal to rule on the evidence?
3. As suggested by the majority opinion in *Stewart* in a case involving an oral lease, who has the burden of proving its terms? Is this fair?

UNIT ELEVEN

Special Topics

CONTENTS

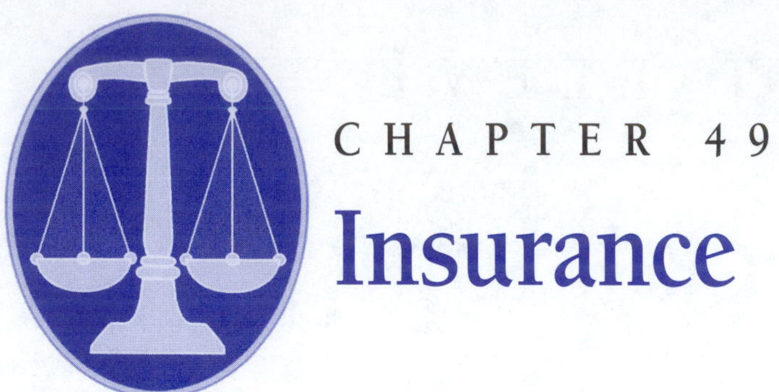

CHAPTER 49

Insurance

MANY PRECAUTIONS CAN BE TAKEN to protect against the hazards of life. For example, an individual can wear a seat belt to protect against automobile injuries or install smoke detectors to guard against the risk of injury from fire. Of course, no one can predict whether an accident or a fire will ever occur, but individuals and businesses must establish plans to protect their personal and financial interests should some event threaten to undermine their security.

Insurance is a contract by which the insurance company (the insurer) promises to pay a sum of money or give something of value to another (either the insured or the beneficiary) to compensate the other for a particular, stated loss. Insurance protection may provide for compensation for the injury or death of the insured or another, for damage to the insured's property, or for other types of losses, such as those resulting from lawsuits. Basically, insurance is an arrangement for *transferring and allocating risk*. In many cases, **risk** can be described as a prediction concerning potential loss based on known and unknown factors. Insurance, however, involves much more than a game of chance.

Risk management normally involves the transfer of certain risks from the individual to the insurance company by a contractual agreement. We examine the insurance contract and its provisions in this chapter. First, however, we look at some basic insurance terminology and concepts.

SECTION 1

Insurance Terminology and Concepts

Like other areas of law, insurance has its own special concepts and terminology, a knowledge of which is essential to an understanding of insurance law.

INSURANCE TERMINOLOGY

An insurance contract is called a **policy**; the consideration paid to the insurer is called a **premium**; and the insurance company is sometimes called an **underwriter.** The parties to an insurance policy are the *insurer* (the insurance company) and the *insured* (the person covered by its provisions).

Insurance contracts are generally obtained through an *agent*, who usually works for the insurance company, or through a *broker,* who is most often an independent contractor. When a broker deals with an applicant for insurance, the broker is, in effect, the applicant's agent. In contrast, an insurance agent is an agent of the insurance company, not an agent of the applicant. As a general rule, the insurance company is bound by the acts of its agents when they act within the scope of the agency relationship (see Chapters 31 and 32). In most situations, state law determines the status of all parties writing or obtaining insurance.

THE CONCEPT OF RISK POOLING

All types of insurance companies use the principle of risk pooling; that is, they spread the risk among a large number of people—the pool—to make the premiums small compared with the coverage offered. Life insurance companies, for example, know that only a small proportion of the individuals in any particular age group will die in any one year. If a large percentage of people in this age group pay premiums to the company in exchange for a benefit payment in the event of death, there will be a sufficient amount of money to pay the beneficiaries of the policyholders who die. Through the extensive correlation of data over a period of time, insurers can estimate fairly accurately the total amount they will have to pay if they insure a particular group, as well as the rates that they will have to charge each member of the group so they can make the necessary payments and still show a profit.

CLASSIFICATIONS OF INSURANCE

Insurance is classified according to the nature of the risk involved. For example, fire insurance, casualty insurance, life insurance, and title insurance apply to different types of risk. Furthermore, policies of these types differ in the persons and interests that they protect. This is reasonable because the types of losses that are expected and the types that are foreseeable or unforeseeable vary with the nature of the activity. See Exhibit 49–1 for a list of various insurance classifications.

INSURABLE INTEREST

A person can insure anything in which he or she has an **insurable interest.** Without this insurable interest, there is no enforceable contract, and a transaction to purchase insurance coverage would have to be treated as a wager. The existence of an insurable interest is a primary concern in determining liability under an insurance policy.

Life Insurance. In regard to life insurance, one must have a reasonable expectation of benefit from the continued life of another to have an insurable interest in that person's life. The insurable interest must exist *at the time the policy is obtained.* The benefit may be pecuniary (related to money), or it may be founded on the relationship between the parties (by blood or affinity). Close family relationships give a person an insurable interest in the life of another. Generally, blood or marital relationships fit this category. A husband can take out an insurance policy on his wife and vice versa; parents can take out life insurance policies on their children; brothers and sisters, on each other; and grandparents, on grandchildren—as all these are close family relationships. A policy that a person takes out on his or her spouse remains valid even if they divorce, unless a specific provision in the policy calls for its termination on divorce.

Key-person insurance is insurance obtained by an organization on the life of a person who is important to that organization. Because the organization expects to receive some pecuniary gain from the continuation of the key person's life or some financial loss from the key person's death, the organization has an insurable interest. Typically, a partnership will insure the life of each partner, because the death of any one partner will cause some degree of loss to the partnership. Similarly, a corporation has an insurable interest in the life expectancy of a key executive whose death would result in financial loss to the company. If a firm insures a key person's life and then that person leaves the firm and afterwards dies, the firm can collect on the insurance policy, provided it continued to pay premiums.

Property Insurance. In regard to real and personal property, an insurable interest exists when the insured derives a pecuniary benefit from the preservation and

EXHIBIT 49–1 INSURANCE CLASSIFICATIONS

TYPE OF INSURANCE	COVERAGE
Accident	Covers expenses, losses, and suffering incurred by the insured because of accidents causing physical injury and any consequent disability; sometimes includes a specified payment to heirs of the insured if death results from an accident.
All-risk	Covers all losses that the insured may incur except those resulting from fraud on the part of the insured.
Automobile	May cover damage to automobiles resulting from specified hazards or occurrences (such as fire, vandalism, theft, or collision); normally provides protection against liability for personal injuries and property damage resulting from the operation of the vehicle.
Casualty	Protects against losses that may be incurred by the insured as a result of being held liable for personal injuries or property damage sustained by others.

EXHIBIT 49–1 INSURANCE CLASSIFICATIONS (CONTINUED)

TYPE OF INSURANCE	COVERAGE
Credit	Pays to a creditor the balance of a debt on the disability, death, insolvency, or bankruptcy of the debtor; often offered by lending institutions.
Decreasing-term life	Provides life insurance; requires uniform payments over the life (term) of the policy, but with a decreasing face value (amount of coverage).
Employer's liability	Insures employers against liability for injuries or losses sustained by employees during the course of their employment; covers claims not covered under workers' compensation insurance.
Fidelity or guaranty	Provides indemnity against losses in trade or losses caused by the dishonesty of employees, the insolvency of debtors, or breaches of contract.
Fire	Covers losses to the insured caused by fire.
Floater	Covers movable property, as long as the property is within the territorial boundaries specified in the contract.
Group	Provides individual life, medical, or disability insurance coverage but is obtainable through a group of persons, usually employees; the policy premium is paid either entirely by the employer or partially by the employer and partially by the employee.
Health	Covers expenses incurred by the insured resulting from physical injury or illness and other expenses relating to health and life maintenance.
Homeowners'	Protects homeowners against some or all risks of loss to their residences and the residences' contents or liability arising from the use of the property.
Key-person	Protects a business in the event of the death or disability of a key employee.
Liability	Protects against liability imposed on the insured resulting from injuries to the person or property of another.
Life	Covers the death of the policyholder. On the death of the insured, an amount specified in the policy is paid by the insurer to the insured's beneficiary.
Major medical	Protects the insured against major hospital, medical, or surgical expenses.
Malpractice	Protects professionals (doctors, lawyers, and others) against malpractice claims brought against them by their patients or clients; a form of liability insurance.
Marine	Covers movable property (including ships, freight, and cargo) against certain perils or navigation risks during a specific voyage or time period.
Mortgage	Covers a mortgage loan; the insurer pays the balance of the mortgage to the creditor on the death or disability of the debtor.
No-fault auto	Covers personal injury and (sometimes) property damage resulting from automobile accidents. The insured submits his or her claims to his or her own insurance company, regardless of who was at fault. A person may sue the party at fault or that party's insurer only in cases involving serious medical injury and consequent high medical costs. Governed by state "no-fault" statutes.
Term life	Provides life insurance for a specified period of time (term) with no cash surrender value; usually renewable.
Title	Protects against any defects in title to real property and any losses incurred as a result of existing claims against or liens on the property at the time of purchase.

continued existence of the property. That is, one has an insurable interest in property when one would sustain a pecuniary loss from its destruction. Both a mortgagor and a mortgagee, for example, have an insurable interest in the mortgaged property. So do a landlord and a tenant in leased property, a secured party in the property in which he or she has a security interest, a partner in partnership property, and a stockholder in corporate property. John or Jane Doe, however, cannot obtain fire insurance on the White House.

Westlaw. See Case 49.1 at the end of this chapter. To view the full, unedited case from Westlaw,® go to this text's Web site at **http://wbl-cs.westbuslaw.com**.

SECTION 2

The Insurance Contract

An insurance contract is governed by the general principles of contract law, although the insurance industry is heavily regulated by the states.[1] Customarily, a party offers to purchase insurance by submitting an insurance application to the insurance company. The company can either accept or reject the offer. Sometimes, the insurance company's acceptance is conditional—on the results of a life insurance applicant's medical examination, for example. For the insurance contract to be binding, consideration (in the form of a premium) must be given, and the parties forming the contract must have the required contractual capacity to do so.

Application for Insurance

The filled-in application form for insurance is usually attached to the policy and made a part of the insurance contract. Thus, an insurance applicant is bound by any false statements that appear in the application (subject to certain exceptions). Because the insurance company evaluates the risk factors based on the information included in the insurance application, misstatements or misrepresentations can void a policy, especially if the insurance company can show that it would not have extended insurance if it had known the facts.

1. The states were given authority to regulate the insurance industry by the McCarran-Ferguson Act of 1945, 15 U.S.C. Sections 1011–1015.

Effective Date

The effective date of an insurance contract—that is, the date on which the insurance coverage begins—is important. In some instances, the insurance applicant is not protected until a formal written policy is issued. In other situations, the applicant is protected between the time the application is received and the time the insurance company either accepts or rejects it. Four facts should be kept in mind:

1. A broker is the agent of an applicant. Therefore, if the broker fails to procure a policy, the applicant normally is not insured. According to general principles of agency law, if the broker fails to obtain policy coverage and the applicant is damaged as a result, the broker is liable to the damaged applicant-principal for the loss.
2. A person who seeks insurance from an insurance company's agent is usually protected from the moment the application is made, provided—in the case of life insurance—that some form of premium has been paid. Between the time the application is received and the time it is either rejected or accepted, the applicant is covered (possibly subject to certain conditions, such as passing a physical examination). Usually, the agent will write a memorandum, or **binder**, indicating that a policy is pending and stating its essential terms.
3. If the parties agree that the policy will be issued and delivered at a later time, the contract is not effective until the policy is issued and delivered or sent to the applicant, depending on the agreement. Thus, any loss sustained between the time of application and the delivery of the policy is not covered.
4. Parties may agree that a life insurance policy will be binding at the time the insured pays the first premium, or the policy may be expressly contingent on the applicant's passing a physical examination. If the applicant pays the premium and passes the examination, the policy coverage is continuously in effect. If the applicant pays the premium but dies before having the physical examination, then in order to collect, the applicant's estate normally must show that the applicant *would have passed* the examination had he or she not died. An insurance contract may also include a clause stating that the applicant must be "still insurable" on the effective date of the policy.

In sum, coverage on an insurance policy can begin when a binder is written; when the policy is issued; or, depending on the terms of the contract, after a certain period of time has elapsed.

Provisions and Clauses

Some of the important provisions and clauses contained in insurance contracts are defined and discussed in the following subsections.

Provisions Mandated by Statute. If a statute mandates that a certain provision be included in insurance contracts, a court will deem that an insurance policy contains the provision regardless of whether the parties actually included it in the language of their contract. If a statute requires that any limitations regarding coverage be stated in the contract, a court will not allow an insurer to avoid liability for a claim through reliance on an unexpressed restriction.

Incontestability Clauses. Statutes commonly require that a life or health insurance policy provide that after the policy has been in force for a specified length of time—often two or three years—the insurer cannot contest statements made in the application. This is known as an *incontestability clause.* Once a policy becomes incontestable, the insurer cannot later avoid a claim on the basis of, for example, fraud on the part of the insured, unless the clause provides an exception for that circumstance. The clause does not prohibit an insurer's refusal or reduction of payment for a claim due to nonpayment of premiums, failure to file proof of death within a certain period, or lack of an insurable interest.

Coinsurance Clauses. Often, when taking out fire insurance policies, property owners insure their property for less than full value. Part of the reason for this is that most fires do not result in a total loss. To encourage owners to insure their property for an amount as close to full value as possible, a standard provision of fire insurance policies is a coinsurance clause. Typically, a *coinsurance clause* provides that if the owner insures the property up to a specified percentage—usually 80 percent—of its value, he or she will recover any loss up to the face amount of the policy. If the insurance is for less than the fixed percentage, the owner is responsible for a proportionate share of the loss.

Coinsurance applies only in instances of partial loss. For example, if the owner of property valued at $100,000 took out a policy in the amount of $40,000 and suffered a loss of $30,000, the recovery would be $15,000. The formula for calculating the recovery amount is as follows:

$$\frac{\text{amount of insurance}\ (\$40{,}000)}{\text{coinsurance percentage}\ (80\%) \times \text{property value}\ (\$100{,}000)} = \text{recovery percentage}\ (50\%)$$

recovery percentage (50%) × amount of loss ($30,000) = recovery amount ($15,000)

If the owner had taken out a policy in the amount of $80,000, then according to the same formula, the full loss would have been recovered.

Appraisal and Arbitration Clauses. Most fire insurance policies provide that if the parties cannot agree on the amount of a loss covered under the policy or on the value of the property lost, an *appraisal* can be demanded. An appraisal is an estimate of the property's value determined by suitably qualified individuals who have no interest in the property. Typically, two appraisers are used, one being appointed by each party. A third party, or umpire, may be called on to resolve differences. Other types of insurance policies also contain provisions for appraisal and arbitration when the insured and insurer disagree as to the value of a loss.

Multiple Insurance Coverage. If an insured has *multiple insurance coverage*—that is, policies with several companies covering the same insurance interest—and the amount of coverage exceeds the loss, the insured can collect from each insurer only the company's proportionate share of the liability, relative to the total amount of insurance. Many fire insurance policies include a pro rata clause, which requires that any loss be shared proportionately by all carriers. For example, say that Grumbling insured $50,000 worth of property with two companies, and each policy had a liability limit of $40,000. On the property's total destruction, Grumbling could collect only $25,000 from each insurer.

Antilapse Clauses. A life insurance policy may provide, or a statute may require a policy to provide, that it will not automatically lapse if no payment is made on the date due. Ordinarily, under an *antilapse provision,* the insured has a *grace period* of thirty or thirty-one days within which to pay an overdue premium. If the insured fails to pay a premium altogether, there are alternatives to cancellation:

1. The insurer may be required to extend the insurance for a period of time.
2. The insurer may issue a policy with less coverage to reflect the amount of the payments made.
3. The insurer may pay to the insured the policy's **cash surrender value**—the amount the insurer has agreed to pay on the policy's cancellation before the insured's death. (In determining this value, the following factors are considered: the period that the policy has already run, the amount of the premium, the insured's age and life expectancy, and amounts to be repaid on any outstanding loans taken out against the policy.)

When the insurance contract states that the insurer cannot cancel the policy, these alternatives are important.

Interpreting Provisions of an Insurance Contract

The courts are increasingly cognizant of the fact that most people do not have the special training necessary to understand the intricate terminology used in insurance policies. The words used in an insurance contract have their ordinary meanings and are interpreted by courts in light of the nature of the coverage involved. When there is an ambiguity in the policy, the provision is interpreted against the insurance company. When it is unclear whether an insurance contract actually exists because the written policy has not been delivered, the uncertainty is resolved against the insurance company. The court presumes that the policy is in effect unless the company can show otherwise. Similarly, an insurer must take care to make sure that the insured is adequately notified of any change in coverage under an existing policy.

See Case 49.2 at the end of this chapter. To view the full, unedited case from Westlaw®, go to this text's Web site at **http://wbl-cs.westbuslaw.com**.

Cancellation

The insured can cancel a policy at any time, and the insurer can cancel under certain circumstances. When an insurance company can cancel its insurance contract, the policy or a state statute usually requires that the insurer give advance written notice of the cancellation. Any premium paid in advance and not yet earned may be refundable. The insured may also be entitled to a life insurance policy's cash surrender value.

The insurer may cancel an insurance policy for various reasons, depending on the type of insurance. For example, automobile insurance can be canceled for nonpayment of premiums or suspension of the insured's driver's license. Property insurance can be canceled for nonpayment of premiums or for other reasons, including the insured's fraud or misrepresentation, gross negligence, or conviction for a crime that increases the hazard insured against. Life and health policies can be canceled because of false statements made by the insured in the application, but cancellation can only take place before the effective date of an incontestability clause. An insurer cannot cancel—or refuse to renew—a policy because of the national origin or race of an applicant or because the insured has appeared as a witness in a case brought against the company.

State laws normally impose a requirement that an insured must be notified in writing of an insurance policy cancellation.[2] The same requirement applies when only part of a policy is canceled.

Basic Duties and Rights

Essentially, the parties to an insurance contract are responsible for the obligations the contract imposes. These include the basic contractual duties discussed in Chapters 9 through 17 of this text, which cover contract law.

In applying for insurance, for example, the obligation to act in good faith means that a party must reveal everything necessary for the insurer to evaluate the risk. In other words, the applicant must disclose all material facts. These include all facts that would influence an insurer in determining whether to charge a higher premium or to refuse to issue a policy altogether.

Once the insurer has accepted the risk, and on the occurrence of an event giving rise to a claim, the insurer has a duty to investigate to determine the facts. When a policy provides insurance against third party claims, the insurer is obligated to make reasonable efforts to settle such a claim. If a settlement cannot be reached, then regardless of the claim's merit, the

2. Notification of cancellation included on a diskette sent to an insured may constitute "written notice" of cancellation.

insurer must defend any suit against the insured. Usually, a policy provides that in this situation the insured must cooperate. A policy provision may expressly require the insured to attend hearings and trials, to help in obtaining evidence and witnesses, and to assist in reaching a settlement.

DEFENSES AGAINST PAYMENT

An insurance company can raise any of the defenses that would be valid in any ordinary action on a contract, as well as some defenses that do not apply in ordinary contract actions. If the insurance company can show that the policy was procured through fraud or misrepresentation, for example, it may have a valid defense for not paying on a claim. (The insurance company may also have the right to disaffirm or rescind an insurance contract.) An absolute defense exists if the insurer can show that the insured lacked an insurable interest—thus rendering the policy void from the beginning. Improper actions, such as those that are against public policy or that are otherwise illegal, can also give the insurance company a defense against the payment of a claim or allow it to rescind the contract.

The insurance company can be prevented, or estopped, from asserting some defenses that are normally available. For example, if a company tells an insured that information requested on a form is optional and the insured provides it anyway, the company cannot use the information to avoid its contractual obligation under the insurance contract. Similarly, incorrect statements as to the age of the insured normally do not provide the insurance company with a way to escape payment on the death of the insured. Also, incontestability clauses prevent the insurer from asserting certain defenses. Some states follow the *concurrent causation doctrine,* which requires that the insurer pay on a claim when the accident was due to more than one cause, at least one of which was covered under the policy.[3]

See Case 49.3 at the end of this chapter. To view the full, unedited case from Westlaw,® go to this text's Web site at **http://wbl-cs.westbuslaw.com**.

3. This doctrine was enunciated by the California Supreme Court in *State Farm Mutual Automobile Insurance Co. v. Partridge,* 10 Cal.3d 94, 514 P.2d 123, 109 Cal.Rptr. 811 (1973). Subsequently, a number of other states, particularly in the Midwest, adopted the doctrine. But see *Vanguard Insurance Co. v. Clarke,* 438 Mich. 463, 475 N.W.2d 48 (1991), in which the Michigan Supreme Court rejected the doctrine.

SECTION 3

Types of Insurance

There are four general types of insurance coverage: life insurance, fire and homeowners' insurance, automobile insurance, and business liability insurance. We now examine briefly the coverage available under each of these types of insurance. In the course of our discussion, we point out certain features and provisions as they relate to the law, with special emphasis on life and fire insurance policies.

LIFE INSURANCE

There are five basic types of life insurance:

1. **Whole life** is sometimes referred to as straight life, ordinary life, or cash-value insurance. This type of insurance provides protection with a cumulated cash surrender value that can be used as collateral for a loan. Premiums are paid by the insured during the insured's entire lifetime, with a fixed payment to the beneficiary on death.
2. **Limited-payment life** might be a twenty-payment life policy. Premiums are paid for a stated number of years, after which the policy is paid up and fully effective during the insured's life. Naturally, premiums are higher than for whole life. This insurance has a cash surrender value.
3. **Term insurance** is a type of policy for which premiums are paid for a specified term. Payment on the policy is due only if death occurs within the term period. Premiums are less expensive than for whole life or limited-payment life, and there is usually no cash surrender value. Frequently, this type of insurance can be converted to another type of life insurance.
4. **Endowment insurance** involves fixed premium payments that are made for a definite term. At the end of the term, a fixed amount is to be paid to the insured or, on the death of the insured during the specified period, to a beneficiary. Thus, this type of insurance represents both term insurance and a form of **annuity** (the right to receive fixed, periodic payments for life or—as in this case—for a term of years). Endowment insurance has a rapidly increasing cash surrender value, but premiums are high, as payment is required at the end of the term even if the insured is still living.
5. **Universal life** is a type of insurance that combines some aspects of term insurance and some of whole life insurance. Every payment, usually called

a "contribution," involves two deductions made by the issuing life insurance company. The first one is a charge for term insurance protection; the second is for company expenses and profit. The money that remains after these deductions earns interest for the policyholder at a rate determined by the company. The interest-earning money in the policy is called the policy's cash value, but that term does not mean the same thing as it does for a traditional whole life insurance policy. With a universal life policy, the cash value grows at a variable interest rate rather than at a predetermined rate.

The rights and liabilities of the parties in life insurance are basically dependent on the insurance contract. A few features deserve special attention.

Liability. The life insurance contract determines not only the extent of the insurer's liability but, generally, whether the insurer is liable on the death of the insured. Most life insurance contracts exclude liability for death caused by suicide, military action during war, execution by a state or federal government, and even a mishap that occurs while the insured is a passenger in a commercial vehicle. In the absence of exclusion, most courts today construe any cause of death to be one of the insurer's risks.

Adjustment Due to Misstatement of Age. The insurance policy constitutes the agreement between the parties. The application for insurance is part of the policy and is usually attached to the policy. When the insured misstates his or her age in the application, an error is introduced, particularly as to the amount of premiums paid. Misstatement of age is not a material error sufficient to allow the insurer to void the policy. Instead, on discovery of the error, the insurer will adjust the premium payments and/or benefits accordingly.

Assignment. Most life insurance policies permit the insured to change beneficiaries. When this is the case, in the absence of any prohibition or notice requirement, the insured can assign the rights to the policy (for example, as security for a loan) without the consent of the insurer or the beneficiary. If the beneficiary's right is *vested*—that is, has become absolute, entitling the beneficiary to payment of the proceeds—the policy cannot be assigned without the consent of the beneficiary. For the most part, life insurance contracts permit assignment and require notice only to the insurer to be effective.

Creditors' Rights. Unless insurance proceeds are exempt under state law, the insured's interest in life insurance is an asset that is subject to the rights of judgment creditors. These creditors generally can reach insurance proceeds payable to the insured's estate, proceeds payable to anyone if the payment of premiums constituted a fraud on creditors, and proceeds payable to a named beneficiary unless the beneficiary's rights have vested. Creditors, however, cannot compel the insured to make available the cash surrender value of the policy or to change the named beneficiary to that of the creditor. Almost all states exempt at least a part of the proceeds of life insurance from creditors' claims.

Termination. Although the insured can cancel and terminate the policy, the insurer generally cannot do so. Therefore, termination usually takes place only on the occurrence of the following:

1. Default in premium payments that causes the policy to lapse.
2. Death and payment of benefits.
3. Expiration of the term of the policy.
4. Cancellation by the insured.

Fire and Homeowners' Insurance

There are basically two types of insurance policies for a home—standard fire insurance policies and homeowners' policies.

Standard Fire Insurance Policies. The standard fire insurance policy protects the homeowner against fire and lightning, as well as damage from smoke and water caused by the fire or the fire department. Most fire insurance policies are classified according to the type of property covered and the extent (amount) of the issuer's liability. Exhibit 49–2 on page 1024 lists typical fire insurance policies.

As with life insurance, certain features and provisions of fire insurance deserve special mention. In reading the following, it is important to note some basic differences in the treatment of life and fire policies.

Liability. The insurer's liability is determined from the terms of the policy. Most policies, however, limit recovery to losses resulting from *hostile* fires—basically, those that break out or begin in places where no fire was intended to burn. A *friendly* fire—one burning in a place where it was intended to burn—is not covered. Therefore, smoke from a fireplace is not

EXHIBIT 49–2 TYPICAL FIRE INSURANCE POLICIES

TYPE OF POLICY	COVERAGE
Blanket	Covers a class of property rather than specific property, because the property is expected to shift or vary in nature. A policy covering the inventory of a business is an example.
Floater	Usually supplements a specific policy. It is intended to cover property that may change in either location or quantity. To illustrate, if the painting mentioned below under "specific policy" were to be exhibited during the year at numerous locations throughout the state, a floater policy would be desirable.
Open	A policy in which the value of the property insured is not agreed on. The policy usually provides for a maximum liability of the insurer, but payment for loss is restricted to the fair market value of the property at the time of loss or to the insurer's limit, whichever is less.
Specific	Covers a specific item of property at a specific location. An example is a particular painting located in a residence or a piece of machinery located in a factory or business.
Valued	A policy in which, by agreement, a specific value is placed on the subject to be insured to cover the eventuality of its total loss.

covered, but smoke from a fire caused by a defective electrical outlet is covered. Sometimes, owners add "extended coverage" to the fire policy to cover losses from "friendly" fires.

If the policy is a *valued* policy (see Exhibit 49–2) and the subject matter is completely destroyed, the insurer is liable for the amount specified in the policy. If it is an *open* policy, the extent of actual loss must be determined, and the insurer is liable only for the amount of the loss or for the maximum amount specified in the policy, whichever is less. For partial losses, actual loss must always be determined, and the insurer's liability is limited to that amount. Most insurance policies permit the insurer either to restore or replace the property destroyed or to pay for the loss.

Proof of Loss. Fire insurance policies require the insured to file with the insurer, within a specified period or immediately (within a reasonable time), a proof of loss as a condition for recovery. Failure to comply *could* allow the insurance carrier to avoid liability. Courts vary somewhat on the enforcement of such clauses.

Occupancy Clause. Most standard policies require that the premises be occupied at the time of loss. The relevant clause states that if the premises become vacant or unoccupied for a given period, unless consent by the insurer is given, the coverage is suspended until the premises are reoccupied. Persons going on extended vacations should check their policies regarding this point.

Assignment. Before a loss has occurred, a fire insurance policy is not assignable without the consent of the insurer. The theory is that the fire insurance policy is a personal contract between the insured and the insurer. The nonassignability of the policy is extremely important in the purchase of a house. The purchaser must procure his or her own insurance. If the purchaser wishes to assume the remaining insurance coverage period of the seller, consent of the insurer is essential.

To illustrate: Ann is selling her home and lot to Jeff. Ann has a one-year fire policy with Ajax Insurance Company, with six months of coverage remaining at the date on which the sale is to close. Ann agrees to assign the balance of her policy, but Ajax has not given its consent. One day after passage of the deed, a fire totally destroys the house. Can Jeff recover from Ajax?

The answer is no, as the policy is actually voided on the closing of the transaction and the deeding of the property. The reason the policy is voided is that Ann no longer has an insurable interest at the time of loss, and Jeff has no rights in a nonassignable policy.

Homeowners' Policies. A homeowners' policy provides protection against a number of risks under a single policy, allowing the policyholder to avoid the cost of buying each protection separately. There are two basic types of homeowners' coverage:

1. *Property coverage* includes the garage, house, and other private buildings on the policyholder's lot. It

also includes the personal possessions and property of the policyholder at home, in travel, or at work. It pays additional expenses for living away from home because of a fire or some other covered peril.
2. *Liability coverage* is for personal liability in case someone is injured on the insured's property, the insured damages someone else's property, or the insured injures someone else who is not in an automobile.

Perils insured under property coverage often include fire, lightning, wind, hail, vandalism, and theft (of personal property). Personal property that is typically not included under property coverage, in the absence of a specific provision, includes such items as motor vehicles, farm equipment, airplanes, and boats. Coverage for other property, such as jewelry and securities, is usually limited to a specified dollar amount.

Liability coverage under a homeowners' policy applies when others are injured or property is damaged because of the unsafe condition of the policyholder's premises. It also applies when the policyholder is negligent. It does not normally apply, however, if the liability arises from business or professional activities or from the operation of a motor vehicle. These are subjects for separate policies. Also excluded is liability arising from intentional misconduct. Similar to liability coverage is coverage for the medical payments of others who are injured on the policyholder's property and coverage for property of others that is damaged by a member of the policyholder's family.

Renters, too, take out insurance policies to protect against losses to personal property. Renters' insurance covers personal possessions against various perils and includes coverage for additional living expenses and liability.

Automobile Insurance

There are two basic kinds of automobile insurance: liability insurance and collision and comprehensive insurance.

Liability Insurance. Automobile liability insurance covers bodily injury and property damage liability. Liability limits are usually described by a series of three numbers, such as 100/300/50. This means that the policy, for one accident, will pay a maximum of $100,000 for bodily injury to one person, a maximum of $300,000 for bodily injury to more than one person, and a maximum of $50,000 for property damage. Many insurance companies offer liability up to $500,000 and sometimes higher.

Individuals who are dissatisfied with the maximum liability limits offered by regular automobile insurance coverage can purchase separate coverage under an *umbrella policy.* Umbrella limits sometimes go as high as $5 million. Umbrella policies also cover personal liability in excess of the liability limits of a homeowners' policy.

Collision and Comprehensive Insurance. Collision insurance covers damage to the insured's car in any type of collision. Usually, it is not advisable to purchase full collision coverage (otherwise known as zero deductible). The price per year is relatively high, because it is likely that some small repair jobs will be required each year. Most people prefer to take out coverage with a deductible of $100, $250, or $500, which costs substantially less than zero-deductible coverage.

Comprehensive insurance covers loss, damage, and destruction due to fire, hurricane, hail, vandalism, and theft. It can be obtained separately from collision insurance.

Other Automobile Insurance. Other types of automobile insurance coverage include the following:

1. *Uninsured motorist coverage.* Uninsured motorist coverage insures the driver and passengers against injury caused by any driver without insurance or by a hit-and-run driver. Certain states require that it be included in all insurance policies sold to drivers.
2. *Accidental death benefits.* Sometimes referred to as *double indemnity,* accidental death benefits provide a lump sum to named beneficiaries if the policyholder dies in an automobile accident. This coverage generally costs very little, but it may not be necessary if the insured has a sufficient amount of life insurance.
3. *Medical payment coverage.* Medical payment coverage provided by an auto insurance policy pays hospital and other medical bills and sometimes funeral expenses. This type of insurance protects all the passengers in the insured's car when the insured is driving.
4. *Other-driver coverage.* An **omnibus clause,** or an *other-driver clause,* protects the vehicle owner who has taken out the insurance and anyone who drives the vehicle with the owner's permission. This coverage may be held to extend to a third party who drives the vehicle with the permission of the person to whom the owner gave permission.

5. *No-fault insurance.* Under no-fault statutes, claims arising from an accident are made against the claimant's own insurer, regardless of who caused the accident. In some cases—for example, when injuries involve expensive medical treatment—an injured party may seek recovery from another party or insurer. In those instances, the injured party may collect the maximum amount of no-fault insurance and still sue for total damages from the party at fault, although usually, on winning an award, the injured party must reimburse the insurer for its no-fault payments.

BUSINESS LIABILITY INSURANCE

A business may be vulnerable to all sorts of risks. A key employee may die or become disabled; a customer may be injured when using a manufacturer's product; the patron of an establishment selling liquor may leave the premises and injure a third party in an automobile accident; or a professional may overlook some important detail, causing liability for malpractice. Should the first situation arise (for instance, if the company president dies), the firm may have some protection under a key-person insurance policy, discussed previously. In the other circumstances, other types of insurance may apply.

General Liability. Comprehensive general liability insurance can cover virtually as many risks as the insurer agrees to cover. For example, among the types of coverage that a business might wish to acquire is protection from liability for injuries arising from on-premises events not otherwise covered, such as company social functions. Some specialized establishments, such as taverns, may be subject to liability in individualized circumstances, and policies can be drafted to meet their needs. In many jurisdictions, for example, statutes impose liability on a seller of liquor when a buyer of the liquor, intoxicated as a result of the sale, injures a third party. Legal protection may extend not only to immediately consequent injuries, such as quadriplegia resulting from an automobile accident, but also to the loss of financial support suffered by a family because of the injuries. Insurance can provide coverage for these injuries and financial losses.

Product Liability. Manufacturers may be subject to liability for injuries that their products cause, and product liability insurance can be written to match specific products' risks. Coverage can be procured under a comprehensive general liability policy or under a separate policy. The coverage may include payment for expenses involved in recalling and replacing a product that has proved to be defective. (For a comprehensive discussion of product liability, see Chapter 6.)

Professional Malpractice. In recent years, professionals—attorneys, physicians, architects, and engineers, for example—have increasingly become the targets of negligence suits. Professionals may purchase malpractice insurance to protect themselves against such claims. The large judgments in some malpractice suits have received considerable publicity and are sometimes cited in what has been termed "the insurance crisis," because they have contributed to a significant increase in malpractice insurance premiums.

Workers' Compensation. Workers' compensation insurance covers payments to employees who are injured in accidents arising out of and in the course of employment (that is, on the job). Workers' compensation, which was discussed in detail in Chapter 41, is governed by state statutes.

TERMS AND CONCEPTS TO REVIEW

annuity 1022	limited-payment life 1022	term insurance 1022
binder 1019	omnibus clause 1025	underwriter 1016
cash surrender value 1021	policy 1016	universal life 1022
endowment insurance 1022	premium 1016	whole life 1022
insurable interest 1017	risk 1016	
insurance 1016	risk management 1016	

CHAPTER SUMMARY

Insurance Terminology	1. *Policy*—The insurance contract. 2. *Premium*—The consideration paid to the insurer for a policy. 3. *Underwriter*—The insurance company. 4. *Parties*—Include the insurer (the insurance company), the insured (the person covered by insurance), an agent (a representative of the insurance company) or a broker (ordinarily an independent contractor), and a beneficiary (a person to receive proceeds under the policy).
Classifications of Insurance	See Exhibit 49–1.
Insurable Interest	An insurable interest exists whenever an individual or entity benefits from the preservation of the health or life of the insured or the property to be insured. For life insurance, an insurable interest must exist at the time the policy is issued. For property insurance, an insurable interest must exist at the time of the loss.
The Insurance Contract	1. *Laws governing*—The general principles of contract law are applied; the insurance industry is also heavily regulated by the states. 2. *Application for insurance*—An insurance applicant is bound by any false statements that appear in the application (subject to certain exceptions), which is part of the insurance contract. Misstatements or misrepresentations may be grounds for voiding the policy. 3. *Effective date*—Coverage on an insurance policy can begin when the binder (a written memorandum indicating that a formal policy is pending and stating its essential terms) is written; when the policy is issued; at the time of contract formation; or, depending on the terms of the contract, when certain conditions are met. 4. *Provisions and clauses*—Important provisions and clauses in insurance contracts include provisions mandated by statute, incontestability clauses, coinsurance clauses, appraisal and arbitration clauses, clauses relating to multiple insurance coverage, cancellation clauses, and antilapse clauses. 5. *Interpreting provisions of an insurance contract*—Words will be given their ordinary meanings, and any ambiguity in the policy will be interpreted against the insurance company. When the written policy has not been delivered and it is unclear whether an insurance contract actually exists, the uncertainty will be determined against the insurance company. The court will presume that the policy is in effect unless the company can show otherwise. 6. *Defenses against payment to the insured*—Defenses include misrepresentation, fraud, or violation of warranties by the applicant.
Types of Insurance	Types of insurance include various forms of life insurance, fire and homeowners' insurance, automobile insurance, and business liability insurance.

CASES FOR ANALYSIS

Westlaw. You can access the full text of each case presented below by going to the Westlaw cases on this text's Web site at http://wbl-cs.westbuslaw.com. Each Westlaw case includes the names of all plaintiffs and defendants, the dates on which the case was argued and decided, a brief summary of the issues and decisions in the case, headnotes classifying specific issues in the case according to the West Key Number System, and the court's opinion. Concurring and dissenting opinions, if any, are included as well.

CASE 49.1 INSURABLE INTEREST

SOTELO v. WASHINGTON MUTUAL INSURANCE CO.

Superior Court of Pennsylvania, 1999.
734 A.2d 421.

TAMILIA, J. [Judge]:

This action involves cross-appeals from [a Pennsylvania state court] judgment entered on July 20, 1998. Appellee/appellant, Carol Sotelo, held two mortgages on property insured by appellants/appellees, Washington Mutual Insurance Company and Everett Cash Mutual Insurance Company (hereinafter appellants). When the property burned down, Sotelo sought to recover under the policy issued by appellants, and the parties now dispute the extent of Sotelo's insurable interest and the amount due under the policy. Appellants claim the trial court erred by accepting *in toto* the valuation of the above property by Sotelo's expert and in awarding Sotelo a recovery (1) in excess of the property's value, (2) in excess of the mortgage debt on the date of the loss and (3) in excess of the applicable policy limit for loss to building items. In her cross-appeal, Sotelo claims the trial court erred by allowing appellants credit for a payment they made to North East Township.

On October 27, 1992, a fire destroyed the Delhurst Country Inn at 10120 West Main Road, North East Township, Erie County, Pennsylvania. At the time, Randco, Inc. (hereinafter Randco), owned the property, and it owed Sotelo a total of $395,545.37, which included substantial late payment penalties. Sotelo held two mortgages on the property in the combined amount of $389,000, and Washington Mutual Insurance Company insured the building under a policy with a $432,000 limit.

Following the fire, Washington Mutual denied the insurance claims of both Randco and Sotelo. Washington Mutual defended against Randco's claim on the basis of arson, and Randco and Washington Mutual eventually reached a settlement. Sotelo was not implicated in any wrongdoing, but Washington Mutual nevertheless failed to pay Sotelo the policy proceeds until June 28, 1993, some eight months after the fire. On that date, Washington Mutual sent Sotelo a check for $220,576.17 * * * . Washington Mutual also paid North East Township $9,020.83 * * * .

On July 26, 1993, Sotelo initiated the instant action against appellants, asserting a breach of contract. Subsequently, appellants filed a motion for partial judgment on the pleadings and Sotelo responded with her own motion for judgment on the pleadings/motion for summary judgment. On June 7, 1994, the trial court denied Sotelo's motion and granted partial judgment on the pleadings in favor of appellants. The court found that, "by the express terms of the policy, [Sotelo] is only entitled to actual cash value and not replacement cost as the property was not rebuilt." The trial court also held that appellants' "payment of $9,020.83 to North East Township * * * was properly made * * * , and that the amount of this payment should be deducted from [Sotelo's] recovery in this case."

Following the above decision, the case proceeded. * * * After a nonjury trial on April 27, 1998, the trial court found in favor of Sotelo and awarded her two hundred and fifty-five thousand, four hundred and three dollars ($255,403). In doing so, the court accepted the opinion of Sotelo's expert that the actual cash value of the property was $485,000. It then deducted appellants' previous payments of $220,576.17 to Sotelo and $9,020.83 to North East Township. Appellants and Sotelo both filed post-trial motions, which were denied. The parties then filed notices of these appeals.

On appeal, the parties primarily dispute the amount of Sotelo's insurable interest and the limits it imposes on Sotelo's recovery as a mortgagee. In order to have an insurable interest in property, a person must derive pecuniary advantage from the continued existence of the property or suffer pecuniary loss from its destruction. The mortgagee's insurable interest is prima facie the value mortgaged, and extends only to the amount of the debt, not exceeding the value of the mortgaged property. Generally, the mortgagee's insurable interest is the amount of the mortgage debt since the debt represents its personal interest in the property. The mortgagee's insurable interest is initially presumed to be the value mortgaged, however, and a mortgagee's insurable interest cannot exceed the value of the property subject to the mortgage. Consequently, a mortgagee's ability to recover is limited to the extent of the debt secured by the property.

* * * *

Having accepted the trial court's determination that the property's ACV was $485,000, we nevertheless conclude the trial court erred by basing its award on the property's ACV, instead of the mortgage amount. As previously stated, a mortgagee's insurable interest cannot exceed the value of the property subject to the mortgage. If the mortgage amount exceeds the property's ACV, then the value of the property "subject to the mortgage" would obviously include the entire ACV of the property. However, in this case, the property's ACV exceeded the mortgage amount.

A mortgagee's insured interest is limited to the outstanding mortgage debt, to the extent it is secured by the property. There is no dispute that the principal balance owed on the mortgages on October 27, 1992, the date of the loss, was $382,781.75. As previously noted, however, Randco also owed an additional $12,763.62 incurred as late payment penalties. This part of the debt was secured by both mortgage agreements. Thus, appellee's insurable interest was $395,545.37 or the total of the outstanding mortgage debt. * * *

* * * *

On cross-appeal, Sotelo contends the trial court erred by crediting appellants for their $9,020.83 payment to North East Township. We agree. Under the relevant [state] statute, a *named insured* may not be paid for fire damage to a structure until the insurance company satisfies the municipality's claims for delinquent taxes and assessments. By its terms, the statute does not apply to the claim of a mortgagee, such as Sotelo. Moreover, the statute requires the payment of obligations which are not the responsibility of a mortgagee. Finally, we fail to understand how Sotelo could benefit from appellants' payment to the township. Since the municipality's claims accrued after Sotelo's validly recorded mortgages, Sotelo could foreclose on the property, have her mortgages satisfied and never pay the municipality's claims.

For the aforesaid reasons, the judgment of the trial court is vacated. On remand, Sotelo's recovery will be based on her insurable interest in the amount of $395,545.37. Appellants will be given credit for their partial payment to Sotelo of $220,576.17, but they will not receive credit for their $9,020.83 payment to North East Township. Finally, the trial court will award Sotelo pre- and post-judgment interest at the legal rate of six percent per annum.

Judgment vacated and case remanded for proceedings in accordance with this Opinion.

CASE 49.2 INTERPRETING PROVISIONS OF AN INSURANCE CONTRACT

AMERICAN GUARANTEE & LIABILITY INSURANCE CO. v. INGRAM MICRO, INC.

United States District Court,
District of Arizona, 2000.
__ F.Supp.2d __.

MARQUEZ, Senior District J. [Judge]

This case presents an insurance coverage dispute between * * * American Guarantee & Liability Insurance Company ("American") and * * * Ingram Micro, Inc. ("Ingram"). American issued Ingram a property damage policy which insured against certain business interruption and service interruption losses. As a result of a power outage, Ingram's computer systems were rendered inoperable. Ingram made a claim under its policy to American and American denied the claim. Thereafter, American filed a Complaint for declaratory relief against Ingram and Ingram filed a Counterclaim for breach of contract.

Pending before the Court are cross-motions for partial summary judgment on the issue of whether a 1998 power outage caused "direct physical loss or damage from any cause, howsoever or wheresoever occurring" to Ingram's computer system.

* * * *

I. Relevant Undisputed Facts

Ingram is a wholesale distributor of microcomputer products. The company uses a worldwide computer network (the Impulse System) to track its customers, products, and daily transactions. Ingram receives orders from its customers both electronically and through telesales representatives. All of Ingram's orders are processed through Impulse and Ingram's entire business operation depends upon the proper functioning of Impulse.

In October of 1998, Ingram procured an insurance policy from American which insured Ingram's "[r]eal, and personal property, business income and operations in the world wherever situated except for U.S. Embargo Countries." The policy insured against "All Risks of direct physical loss or damage from any cause, howsoever or wheresoever occurring, including general average, salvage charges or other charges, expenses and freight." Ingram's computers, including Impulse, are insured under the Policy.

Ingram's data processing and data base maintenance operations are performed primarily at Ingram's Tucson Data Center. At approximately 8:00 A.M. on the morning of December 22, 1998, the Data Center experienced a power outage which was apparently caused by a ground fault in the fire alarm panel. While electrical power service to the building itself was not disrupted, all of the electronic equipment at the Data Center, including the computers and telephones, stopped working.

Power was restored to the Data Center within a half hour. Ingram employees reset all of the circuit breakers that had been tripped by the power outage. Some of Ingram's equipment, such as the printers, were fully operational as soon as power was restored. The three mainframe computers, however, lost all of the programming information that had been stored in their random access memory and Ingram employees had to reload the lost programming information. One and one half hours after the power outage, the Data Center was up and running at the mainframe level.

The return of the mainframes to operation did not restore to action the computers and other equipment that connect the Data Center to the rest of the Impulse System. Connections between Tucson and six Impulse locations in the U.S. and Europe were interrupted and Ingram could not conduct business. After working for hours to determine the source of the problem, Ingram employees finally brought the network back up to operation by means of bypassing a malfunctioning matrix switch. Impulse was restored to full operation by 4:00 P.M., approximately eight hours after the shutdown.

In the days following the power outage, Ingram employees determined that when the power outage occurred, all of the programming information disappeared from the random access memory. The custom configurations that existed prior to the outage were different than the default settings after the outage. So when power was restored to the matrix switch, the custom configurations remained lost. The matrix switch had to be reprogrammed with the necessary custom configurations before communications with the six Impulse locations could be restored.

II. Discussion

American and its expert witnesses admit that Ingram's mainframe computers and the matrix switch did not function as before the power outage and that certain data entry and reconfiguration processes were necessary to make Impulse operate as it had before the power outage. American argues however, that the computer system and the matrix switch were not "physically damaged" because their capability to perform their intended functions remained intact. The power outage did not adversely affect the equipment's inherent ability to accept and process data and configuration settings when they were subsequently reentered into the computer system.

Ingram argues that the fact that the mainframe computers and the matrix switch retained the ability to accept the restored information and eventually operate as before, does not mean that they did not undergo "physical damage." Ingram offers a broader definition of this term and contends that "physical damage" includes loss of use and functionality.

At a time when computer technology dominates our professional as well as personal lives, the Court must side with Ingram's broader definition of "physical damage." The Court finds that "physical damage" is not restricted to the physical destruction or harm of computer circuitry but includes loss of access, loss of use, and loss of functionality.

The Court is not alone in this interpretation. [For example, the] federal [Computer Fraud and Abuse Act], which makes it an offense to cause damage to a protected computer, defines damage as "any impairment to the integrity or availability of data, a program, a system, or information." * * * In Missouri, [under a certain statute] damage to a computer is defined as "any alteration, deletion, or destruction of any part of a computer system or network." In New York, [under a certain statute] a person is guilty of computer tampering in the fourth degree when he "intentionally alters in any manner or destroys computer data or a computer program of another person."

The Court is mindful that these definitions appear not in insurance coverage cases, but in the penal codes of various states. Their relevance however, is significant. Lawmakers around the country have determined that when a computer's data is unavailable, there is damage; when a computer's services are interrupted, there is damage; and when a computer's software or network is altered, there is damage. Restricting the Policy's language to that proposed by American would be archaic.

* * * *

In this case, Ingram does allege property damage—that as a result of the power outage, Ingram's computer system and worldwide computer network physically lost the programming information and custom configurations necessary for them to function. * * * It wasn't until Ingram employees manually reloaded the lost programming information that the mainframes were "repaired." Impulse was "physically damaged" for eight hours. Ingram employees "repaired" Impulse by physically bypassing a malfunctioning matrix switch. Until this restorative work was conducted, Ingram's mainframes and Impulse were inoperable.

* * * *

IT IS ORDERED that Ingram's Motion for Partial Summary Judgment is GRANTED.

IT IS FURTHER ORDERED that American's Cross-Motion for Summary Judgment * * * is DENIED.

CASE 49.3 DEFENSES AGAINST PAYMENT

PAUL REVERE LIFE INSURANCE CO. V. FIMA

United States Court of Appeals,
Ninth Circuit, 1997.
105 F.3d 490.

BRUNETTI, Circuit Judge:

* * * *

I.

[A] disability insurance policy * * * was issued by [Paul Revere Life Insurance Company (Revere)] to [Raoul] Fima on January 8, 1988. The policy contained an incontestability clause which stated:

> After your policy has been in force for two years, excluding any time that you are disabled, we cannot contest the statements in the application.

* * * *

In the application for disability insurance, Fima stated that his income for 1986 was $105,000, for 1987 was $85,000, and projected an income of $80,000 for 1988. At trial, the jury found that Fima's actual income for 1986 was $21,603, and that his actual income for 1987 was $6,320. On May 13, 1990, Fima submitted a Notice of Claim to Revere stating that he became disabled from his regular occupation on March 30, 1990. Revere then investigated Fima's Claim and determined that Fima's statements on the application concerning his income were overstated and bore no relation to his true income.

On April 10, 1991, Revere filed its Complaint against Fima in [a federal] district court seeking declaratory relief.

Revere requested a declaration that Fima's 1988 policy was void *ab initio* [from the beginning] because Fima lacked an insurable interest. On May 24, 1994, the district court filed an Order and Judgment against Revere on Revere's declaratory relief claim. Relying on the California Insurance Code, the district court concluded that Fima had an unlimited insurable interest in his life and health.

II.

* * * *

California public policy gives effect to incontestability clauses, which all disability insurance policies are required by law to contain. *Where the incontestability period has run, incontestability clauses prevent lawsuits to rescind disability insurance policies based upon claims of fraud or misrepresentation in the procurement of the policy.* * * * When an insurance policy by its provisions is made incontestable after a specified period, the intent of the parties is to fix a limited time within which the insurer must discover and assert any grounds it might have to justify a rescission of the contract. [Emphasis added.]

However, California law provides that a policy which is void *ab initio* may be contested at any time, even after the incontestability period has expired. An insurance policy is void *ab initio* where the insured lacks an insurable interest. Thus, where, as in the present case, an incontestability clause is in effect, an insurance policy may be challenged only on the ground that it is void *ab initio* for lack of an insurable interest.

Fima had an insurable interest under California Insurance Code [S]ection 10110 as a matter of law. Section 10110 * * * states that "[e]very person has an insurable interest in the life and health of * * * [h]imself." Because Fima had an insurable interest under [S]ection 10110, his disability insurance policy was not void *ab initio*.

* * * *

Revere argues that the measure of Fima's insurable interest should be governed by those sections of the California Insurance Code that govern insurance in property. This argument requires the court to reject the clear statutory language providing that the extent of an insured's insurable interest in a life and disability insurance policy is determined by the terms of the insurance contract itself. Fima had an insurable interest to the extent provided by the 1988 policy. Because that policy is not void *ab initio* and because the period for contesting the policy has passed under the incontestability clause, Revere may not now challenge the terms of the policy or the extent of Fima's insurable interest.

* * * *

The district court's judgment is AFFIRMED.

CASE PROBLEMS

49–1. James and Hazel Gray signed a joint application for health-insurance coverage with Great American Reserve Insurance Co. The application was taken by John L. Sides, who at the time was not an agent for Great American but an independent insurance broker. On signing the application, the Grays gave Sides $188.50, the first month's premium, and later alleged that Sides had told them the policy would become effective when the first payment was made. Sides then sent the application to Great American, along with his own application to become a salesperson for Great American. Sides subsequently was allowed to sell Great American insurance policies. After several initial difficulties, Great American received the Grays' policy application two and a half months after they had signed it, and only then did the company begin to process the application. Two days before Great American received the policy application, James Gray was thrown from a horse and was injured. Hazel Gray notified Sides of the injury, but Sides learned from Great American that the Grays were not covered as of the date of the injury. James Gray then brought suit against Great American and Sides for breach of an insurance contract. Did the Grays have a valid insurance policy with Great American on the date of James Gray's injury? Explain. [*Gray v. Great American Reserve Insurance Co.*, 495 So.2d 602 (Ala. 1986)]

49–2. Martha Frances purchased insurance coverage from Nationwide Mutual Insurance Co. prior to going on a cruise. The policy covered "accidental bodily injury occurring anywhere in the world which arises solely from accident" and "is not contributed to by sickness, disease or bodily or mental infirmity." The policy also stated that if the injury resulted in the loss of life "within 180 days after the date of the accident," the company would pay the beneficiary $75,000. While on the cruise, Frances fell and broke her hip. She was immediately taken to a Florida hospital for surgery, during which she had a fatal heart attack. The death certificate described the cause of death as "terminal cardiac arrest due to or as a consequence of arteriosclerotic cardiovascular disease due to or as a consequence of previous [heart problems]." Audrey Allison, Frances's beneficiary, sought payment under the policy, but Nationwide refused to pay because Frances's death was caused in part by her preexisting heart condition. Allison then sued Nationwide to collect the death benefit. Assuming that Frances would not have died (at least, at that time) from her heart problems had it not been for the surgery, how should the court decide? Discuss fully. [*Allison v. Nationwide Mutual Insurance Co.*, 964 F.2d 291 (3d Cir. 1992)]

49–3. Martin A. Gurrentz applied for life insurance from Federal Kemper Life Assurance Co. through an insurance agent named Alfrey. In September 1982, Gurrentz filled out an application but paid no premiums. Between the submission of the application and the delivery of the policy, Gurrentz sought medical advice from a physician about an ear problem. On examination, a throat lesion was noted. A biopsy was done, and Gurrentz was advised that he had a throat malignancy, for which he subsequently received radiation treatments. On delivery of the policies, Gurrentz signed a statement stating that there had been no changes in his health status and that he had not seen a doctor since filing the application for insurance. In April 1983, Federal learned of Gurrentz's throat problem when he filed a claim under a separate medical health policy. After an investigation, Federal notified Gurrentz in February 1984 that it was canceling the life insurance policy and refunding all premiums paid. Was Federal able to rescind Gurrentz's life insurance policy? Explain. [*Gurrentz v. Federal Kemper Life Assurance Co.*, 513 So.2d 241 (Fla.Dist.App. 1987)]

49–4. Claude and Mildred O'Donnell owned their home in Lexington and had a fire insurance policy on it. Claude and Mildred contracted with Benjamin to build a new home for them in exchange for cash and transfer of their present home. After conveying the home to Benjamin, Claude and Mildred continued living there and paid both rent and the insurance premium. The fire insurance policy was never assigned to Benjamin. While Claude and Mildred were still living in their old home, a fire damaged it. The insurance company would not pay, claiming that Claude and Mildred had no insurable interest in the property at the time of the loss. Discuss fully how a court will rule. [*O'Donnell v. MFA Insurance Co.*, 671 S.W.2d 302 (Mo.App. 1984)]

49–5. The insured brought an action to recover losses in excess of $100,000 sustained because of employee theft. The thefts occurred during the terms of two different policies but were not discovered until the second policy had replaced the first. Each policy limited recovery to $50,000 for employee dishonesty and provided that for a loss "which occurs partly during the Effective Period of this endorsement and partly during the period of other policies, the total liability of the Company shall not exceed in the aggregate the amount of this endorsement." The insured maintained that he was entitled to recover $50,000 on each policy. What should the court decide? Discuss fully. [*Davenport Peters Co. v. Royal Globe Insurance Co.*, 490 F.Supp. 286 (Mass. 1980)]

49–6. RLI Insurance Co. issued an insurance policy to Richard Brown to cover his aircraft. One provision of the policy excluded coverage for a "resident spouse." A different provision included coverage for "any passenger." Richard was piloting the aircraft, with his wife, Janet, as a passenger, when it crashed. Richard was killed, and Janet was injured. At the time, Janet and Richard had been living together. Janet filed a suit in a federal district court to collect under the policy for her injuries. RLI claimed that the policy clearly excluded Janet. Janet argued that the policy was ambiguous. What will the court decide? Why? [*RLI Insurance Co. v. Drollinger*, 97 F.3d 230 (8th Cir. 1996)]

49–7. On April 16, 1982, Frances and Michael Berthiaume made a written application for life insurance with the Minnesota Mutual Life Insurance Co. The policy sought was to provide $44,308.37 in insurance to cover the Berthiaumes' loan balance on the mortgage for their house, for a monthly premium of $12.42. Mr. Berthiaume did not take a physical examination for the policy, but in filling out the application, he answered no to a question asking whether he had ever been treated for, or had ever been advised that he had, high blood pressure. The answer Mr. Berthiaume gave was incorrect; in fact, he had been diagnosed as having hypertension four months before the application was made. In October 1982, Mr. Berthiaume became ill, and he died two months later. When his widow submitted a claim for the mortgage insurance, the insurance company denied payment, citing Mr. Berthiaume's inaccurate answer on the application. Minnesota Mutual sought summary judgment, which was granted by the trial court. Mrs. Berthiaume appealed. Discuss whether Mr. Berthiaume's inaccurate answer on the insurance policy application voided Minnesota Mutual's obligation to pay on the policy. [*Berthiaume v. Minnesota Mutual Life Insurance Co.*, 388 N.W.2d 15 (Minn.App. 1986)]

49–8. Valley Furniture & Interiors, Inc., bought an insurance policy from Transportation Insurance Co. (TIC). The policy provided coverage of $50,000 for each occurrence of property loss caused by employee dishonesty. An "occurrence" was defined as "a single act or series of related acts." Valley allowed its employees to take pay advances and to buy discounted merchandise, with the advances and the cost of the merchandise deducted from their paychecks. The payroll manager was to notify the payroll company to make the deductions. Over a period of six years, without notifying the payroll company, the payroll manager issued advances to other employees and herself, and bought merchandise for herself, in amounts totaling more than $200,000. Valley filed claims with TIC for three "occurrences" of employee theft. TIC considered the acts a "series of related acts" and paid only $50,000. Valley filed a suit in a Washington state court against TIC, alleging, in part, breach of contract. What is the standard for interpreting an insurance clause? How should this court define "series of related acts"? Why? [*Valley Furniture & Interiors, Inc. v. Transportation Insurance Co.*, 107 Wash.App. 104, 26 P.3d 952 (Div. 1 2001)]

49–9. When William Clyburn's house burned to the ground, two years had passed since he had paid a premium on his policy with the Allstate Insurance Company. Allstate refused to cover the loss of the house, and Clyburn brought suit against the insurer, claiming that the policy had not been legally canceled and that the insurer had therefore improperly denied coverage. Specifically, Clyburn argued that Allstate had not followed the state's statutory requirements governing policy cancellation. The relevant state statute required an insurer to send written notice to both the insured and the insurer's "agent of record"—the insurance agent who had issued the policy to the insured.

Allstate argued that it had properly notified Clyburn in writing of the cancellation and that it had also sent its agent of record, Thomas Young, a computer diskette containing the cancellation notice. The jury found in Clyburn's favor, concluding that Allstate had sent written notice to Clyburn but not to Allstate's agent of record. Allstate made a motion for either a new trial or a judgment notwithstanding the verdict (judgment *n.o.v.*). The key issue before the court was whether notice sent via a computer diskette constituted "written" notice. How should the court decide this issue? Discuss fully. [*Clyburn v. Allstate Insurance Co.*, 826 F.Supp. 955 (D.S.C. 1993)]

49–10. Waldemar Cichowlas applied to the Life Insurance Company of North America (LINA) for insurance, naming his wife, Ewa, as beneficiary. The application asked if he had been hospitalized during the past five years and if he had ever been treated for lung disease. A yes answer would have affected his insurability. Waldemar truthfully answered no. The policy required that an applicant be "still insurable" on the effective date of the policy. Three weeks before the policy took effect, Waldemar was hospitalized with a lung disease. He did not tell LINA. When he died of other causes, LINA refused to pay Ewa. She filed a suit in a Florida state court against the insurer. The court ordered LINA to pay. The insurer appealed. Explain what will happen on appeal. [*Life Insurance Co. of North America v. Cichowlas*, 659 So.2d 1333 (Fla.App.—4th Dist. 1995)]

49–11. Robert Gladney applied for disability insurance from Paul Revere Life Insurance Co., enclosing with the application a check for $3,100, which represented the first semiannual premium. The issuance of the policy was conditional on the insurance company's receipt of a medical form that was to be completed by Gladney's doctor following a physical examination. Gladney was a busy man and kept putting off the physical examination. Over a month later, Gladney submitted a second application, because the first one was too old. The insurance agent advised Gladney to leave the application undated so that if Gladney failed to have the physical examination within a month, he would not have to submit yet a third application. Gladney told the agent that he would notify him when the examination was completed. Soon thereafter, Gladney fell ill. His doctor examined him but did not conduct all the tests normally required by Paul Revere for disability insurance. A month later, Gladney was hospitalized and underwent heart surgery. Gladney never told the insurance agent about his visit to the doctor and the fact that the doctor had examined him. Gladney now claims that he is entitled to disability benefits under the policy because he paid the premium and would have been approved for insurance had he notified the insurance company of his examination. Will the court agree? Discuss fully. [*Gladney v. Paul Revere Life Insurance Co.*, 895 F.2d 238 (5th Cir. 1990)]

49–12. Kirk Johnson applied for life insurance with New York Life Insurance Co. on October 7, 1986. In answer to a question about smoking habits, Johnson stated that he had not smoked in the past twelve months and that he had never smoked cigarettes. In fact, Johnson had smoked for thirteen years, and during the month prior to the insurance application, he was smoking approximately ten cigarettes per day. Johnson died on July 17, 1988, for reasons unrelated to smoking. Johnson's father, Lawrence Johnson, who was the beneficiary of the policy, filed a claim for the insurance proceeds. While investigating the claim, New York Life discovered Kirk Johnson's misrepresentation and denied the claim. The company canceled the policy and sent Lawrence Johnson a check for the premiums that had been paid. Lawrence Johnson refused to accept the check, and New York Life brought an action for a declaratory judgment (a court determination of a plaintiff's rights). What should the court decide? Discuss fully. [*New York Life Insurance Co. v. Johnson*, 923 F.2d 279 (3d Cir. 1991)]

49–13. Jeffrey Duke purchased a life insurance policy on his own life from New England Mutual Life Insurance Co. Duke listed as his beneficiary his lover and business adviser, William Remmelink. On his insurance application, however, Duke described his beneficiary as merely his business partner. After Duke died of acquired immune deficiency syndrome (AIDS), New England Mutual brought an action against William Johnson, the executor of Duke's estate, to rescind (cancel) the insurance contract on the ground that Duke had "materially misrepresented his relationship with his beneficiary." Johnson claimed that New England Mutual's attempt to rescind the contract was in bad faith and asked for both punitive damages and attorneys' fees. During the trial, an underwriter with twenty-four years of experience testified that New England Mutual had never before rescinded a policy because of a misrepresentation regarding the relationship between the beneficiary and the insured. Did Duke mischaracterize his relationship with his beneficiary? If so, was such a misrepresentation material? How should the court decide? [*New England Mutual Life Insurance Co. v. Johnson*, 155 Misc.2d 680, 589 N.Y.S.2d 736 (1992)]

49–14. The City of Worcester, Massachusetts, adopted an ordinance in 1990 that required rooming houses to be equipped with automatic sprinkler systems no later than September 25, 1995. In Worcester, James and Mark Duffy owned a forty-eight–room lodging house with two retail stores on the first floor. In 1994, the Duffys applied with General Star Indemnity Co. for an insurance policy to cover the premises. The application indicated that the premises had sprinkler systems. General issued a policy that required, among other safety features, a sprinkler system. Within a month, the premises were inspected on behalf of General. On the inspection form forwarded to the insurer, in the list of safety systems, next to the word "sprinkler" the inspector had inserted only a hyphen. In July 1995, when the premises sustained over $100,000 in fire damage, General learned that there was no sprinkler system. The insurer filed a suit in a federal district court against the Duffys to rescind the policy, alleging misrepresentation in their insurance application about the presence of sprinklers. How should the court rule, and why? [*General Star Indemnity Co. v. Duffy,* 191 F.3d 55 (1st Cir. 1999)]

49–15. A Question of Ethics

Alma McMillan worked as a sales and reservations supervisor in a Trans World Airlines, Inc. (TWA), office located in Philadelphia. At 10:00 P.M. one evening, after she had completed her work shift, McMillan left her office and exited the building onto a covered walkway. While she stood on this walkway, her estranged husband fatally stabbed her. As a TWA employee, McMillan was covered by a group life insurance policy issued by State Mutual Life Assurance Co. of America. A provision of the policy, marked "Hazard F," provided for a payment of $100,000 to the insured's beneficiaries in the event of death resulting from "a felonious assault while on authorized business of [TWA]." The term *felonious assault* was defined to include murder. State Mutual refused to pay the proceeds of the policy to McMillan's beneficiaries (her children) on the grounds that McMillan had not been "on authorized business" at the time of her death. The beneficiaries then sued State Mutual to recover the proceeds. [*McMillan v. State Mutual Life Assurance Co. of America,* 922 F.2d 1073 (3d Cir. 1990)]

1. One of the questions posed by this case was the following: At what instant following the conclusion of an employee's work shift should separation from the employer's authorized business be complete? The trial court held that this instant occurred when McMillan left the employer's premises. Although she had left the building in which she worked, she was still on her employer's premises at the time of the fatal stabbing. The appellate court agreed. One appellate court judge dissented, however, concluding that at the time of the tragedy, McMillan was on her own business, not on the business of her employer. Argue the merits of each conclusion. Which one do you think is the fairer one? Why?
2. Is the phrase *on authorized business* sufficiently ambiguous for the court to construe the phrase against the insurer, State Mutual? Do you discern any ethical principle underlying the rule that ambiguous terms and phrases will be construed *against* the insurance company? Given the fact that both parties to an insurance contract must agree to the terms contained therein or no contract will be formed, do you think that it is fair to hold just one of the parties responsible for ambiguous terms or phrases?

E-LINKS

For updated links to resources available on the Web, as well as a variety of other materials, visit this text's Web site at

http://wbl-cs.westbuslaw.com

For a summary of the law governing insurance contracts in the United States, including rules of interpretation, go to

http://www.consumerlawpage.com/article/insureds.shtml

The law firm of Anderson Kill & Olick includes information and links relating to insurance on its Web site. Go to:

http://www.andersonkill.com

To learn more about business insurance, go to

http://www.insure.com/business

Legal Research Exercises on the Web

Go to http://wbl-cs.westbuslaw.com, the Web site that accompanies this text. Select "Interactive Study Center," and then click on "Chapter 49." There you will find the following Internet research exercises that you can perform to learn more about new types of insurance coverage and some of the consequences of settlements in insurance cases:

Activity 49–1: Technoinsurance

Activity 49–2: Disappearing Decisions

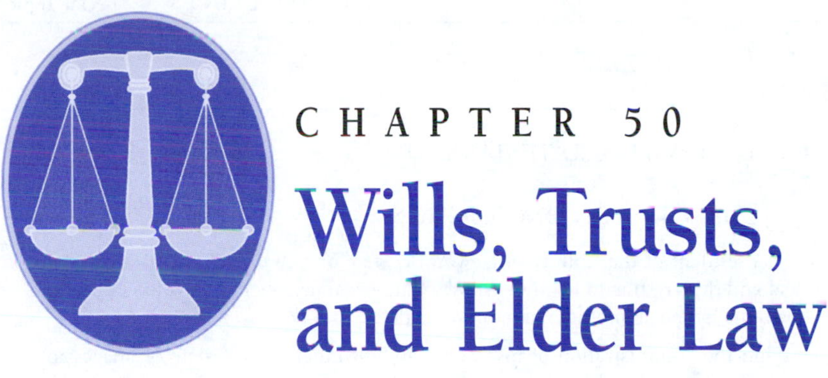

CHAPTER 50

Wills, Trusts, and Elder Law

As the old adage states, "You can't take it with you." All of the real and personal property that you own will be transferred on your death to others. A person can direct the passage of his or her property after death by *will*, subject to certain limitations imposed by the state. If no valid will has been executed, the decedent is said to have died **intestate**, and state **intestacy laws** prescribe the distribution of the property among heirs or next of kin. If no heirs or kin can be found, the property will **escheat**[1] (title will be transferred to the state). In addition, a person can transfer property through a *trust*. In a trust arrangement, the owner (who may be called the *grantor* or the *settlor*) of the property transfers legal title to a trustee, who has a duty imposed by law to hold the property for the use or benefit of another (the beneficiary).

Wills and trusts are two basic devices used in the process of **estate planning**—planning in advance how one's property and obligations should be transferred on death. In this chapter, we examine wills and trusts in some detail. Other estate-planning devices include life insurance (discussed in Chapter 49) and joint-tenancy arrangements (described in Chapter 46). Typically, estate planning involves consultations with professionals, including attorneys, accountants, and financial planners.

For many people, a major estate-planning consideration is the possibility of becoming incapacitated, through accident or illness, at some future time or of needing long-term health care. In the final section of this chapter, we look at a relatively new legal specialty, *elder law*, which addresses these and other needs of older persons.

1. Pronounced ush-*cheet*.

SECTION 1

Wills

A **will** is the final declaration of how a person desires to have his or her property disposed of after death. One who makes a will is known as a **testator** (from the Latin *testari*, "to make a will"). A will is referred to as a *testamentary disposition* of property, and one who dies after having made a valid will is said to have died **testate.**

A will can serve other purposes besides the distribution of property. It can appoint a guardian for minor children or incapacitated adults. It can also appoint a personal representative to settle the affairs of the deceased. An **executor** is a personal representative named in a will. An **administrator** is a personal representative appointed by the court for a decedent who dies without a will, who fails to name an executor in the will, who names an executor lacking the capacity to serve, or who writes a will that the court refuses to admit to probate. Exhibit 50–1 on page 1036 presents a copy of the will written by John Lennon, the musician and former member of the "Beatles" musical group.

Laws Governing Wills

Laws governing wills come into play when a will is probated. To **probate** (prove) a will means to establish its validity and carry the administration of the estate through a process supervised by a probate court. Probate laws vary from state to state. In 1969, however, the American Bar Association and the National Conference of Commissioners on Uniform State Laws approved the Uniform Probate Code (UPC).

EXHIBIT 50–1 A SAMPLE WILL

LAST WILL AND TESTAMENT
OF
JOHN WINSTON ONO LENNON

I, JOHN WINSTON ONO LENNON, a resident of the County of New York, State of New York, which I declare to be my domicile do hereby make, publish and declare this to be my Last Will and Testament, hereby revoking all other Wills, Codicils and Testamentary dispositions by me at any time heretofore made.

FIRST: The expenses of my funeral and the administration of my estate, and all inheritance, estate or succession taxes, including interest and penalties, payable by reason of my death shall be paid out of and charged generally against the principal of my residuary estate without apportionment or proration. My Executor shall not seek contribution or reimbursement for any such payments.

SECOND: Should my wife survive me, I give, devise and bequeath to her absolutely, an amount equal to that portion of my residuary estate, the numerator and denominator of which shall be determined as follows:

1. The numerator shall be an amount equal to one-half (½) of my adjusted gross estate less the value of all other property included in my gross estate for Federal Estate Tax purposes and which pass or shall have passed to my wife either under any other provision of this Will or in any manner outside of this Will in such manner as to qualify for and be allowed as a marital deduction. The words “pass,” “have passed,” “marital deduction” and “adjusted gross estate” shall have the same meaning as said words have under those provisions of the United States Internal Revenue Code applicable to my estate.

2. The denominator shall be an amount representing the value of my residuary estate.

THIRD: I give, devise and bequeath all the rest, residue and remainder of my estate, wheresoever situated, to the Trustees under a Trust Agreement dated November 12, 1979, which I signed with my wife YOKO ONO, and ELI GARBER as Trustees, to be added to the trust property and held and distributed in accordance with the terms of that agreement and any amendments made pursuant to its terms before my death.

FOURTH: In the event that my wife and I die under such circumstances that there is not sufficient evidence to determine which of us has predeceased the other, I hereby declare it to be my will that it shall be deemed that I shall have predeceased her and that this, my Will, and any and all of its provisions shall be construed based upon that assumption.

FIFTH: I hereby nominate, constitute and appoint my beloved wife, YOKO ONO, to act as the Executor of this my Last Will and Testament. In the event that my beloved wife YOKO ONO shall predecease me or chooses not to act for any reason, I nominate and appoint ELI GARBER, DAVID WARMFLASH and CHARLES PETTIT, in the order named, to act in her place and stead.

SIXTH: I nominate, constitute and appoint my wife YOKO ONO, as the Guardian of the person and property of any children of the marriage who may survive me. In the event that she predeceases me, or for any reason she chooses not to act in that capacity, I nominate, constitute and appoint SAM GREEN to act in her place and stead.

SEVENTH: No person named herein to serve in any fiduciary capacity shall be required to file or post any bond for the faithful performance of his or her duties, in that capacity in this or in any other jurisdiction, any law to the contrary notwithstanding.

EIGHTH: If any legatee or beneficiary under this will or the trust agreement between myself as Grantor and YOKO ONO LENNON and ELI GARBER as Trustees, dated November 12, 1979 shall interpose objections to the probate of this Will, or institute or prosecute or be in any way interested or instrumental in the institution or prosecution of any action or proceeding for the purpose of setting aside or invalidating this Will, then and in each such case, I direct that such legatee or beneficiary shall receive nothing whatsoever under this Will or the aforementioned Trust.

IN WITNESS WHEREOF, I have subscribed and sealed and do publish and declare these presents as and for my Last Will and Testament, this 12th day of November, 1979.

/s/

John Winston Ono Lennon

THE FOREGOING INSTRUMENT consisting of four (4) typewritten pages, including this page, was on the 12th day of November, 1979, signed, sealed, published and declared by JOHN WINSTON ONO LENNON, the Testator therein named as and for his Last Will and Testament, in the presence of us, who at his request, and in his presence, and in the presence of each other, have hereunto set our names as witnesses.

(The names of the three witnesses are illegible.)

The UPC, which was significantly revised in 1990, codifies general principles and procedures for the resolution of conflicts in settling estates and relaxes some of the requirements for a valid will contained in earlier state laws. Nearly all of the states have enacted some part of the UPC and incorporated it into their own probate codes. For this reason, references to its provisions will be included in this chapter. Nonetheless, succession and inheritance laws vary widely among states, and one should always check the particular laws of the state involved.[2]

GIFTS BY WILL

A gift of real estate by will is generally called a **devise**, and a gift of personal property under a will is called a **bequest**, or **legacy**. The recipient of a gift by will is a *devisee* or a *legatee*, depending on whether the gift was a devise or a legacy.

Types of Gifts.

Gifts by will can be specific, general, or residuary. A *specific* devise or bequest (legacy) describes particular property (such as "Eastwood Estate" or "my gold pocket watch") that can be distinguished from the rest of the testator's property. A *general* devise or bequest (legacy) uses less restrictive terminology. For example, "I devise all my lands" is a general devise. A general bequest often specifies a sum of money instead of a particular item of property, such as a watch or an automobile. For example, "I give to my nephew, Carleton, $30,000" is a general bequest.

Sometimes a will provides that any assets remaining after specific gifts have been made and debts have been paid—called the *residuary* (or *residuum*) of the estate—are to be given to the testator's spouse, distributed to the testator's descendants, or disposed of in some other way. If the testator has not indicated what party or parties should receive the residuary of the estate, the residuary passes according to state laws of intestacy.

Abatement.

If the assets of an estate are insufficient to pay in full all general bequests provided for in the will, an *abatement* takes place, meaning that the legatees receive reduced benefits. For example, Julie's will leaves "$15,000 each to my children, Tamara and Lynn." On Julie's death, only $10,000 is available to honor these bequests. By abatement, each child will receive $5,000. If bequests are more complicated, abatement may be more complex. The testator's intent, as expressed in the will, controls.

Lapsed Legacies.

If a legatee dies prior to the death of the testator or before the legacy is payable, a lapsed legacy results. At common law, the legacy failed. Today, the legacy may not lapse if the legatee is in a certain blood relationship to the testator (such as a child, grandchild, brother, or sister) and has left a child or other surviving descendant.

REQUIREMENTS FOR A VALID WILL

A will must comply with statutory formalities designed to ensure that the testator understood his or her actions at the time the will was made. These formalities are intended to help prevent fraud. Unless they are followed, the will is declared void, and the decedent's property is distributed according to the laws of intestacy of that state. The requirements are not uniform among the jurisdictions. Most states, however, uphold certain basic requirements for executing a will. We now look at these requirements.

Testamentary Capacity and Intent.

For a will to be valid, the testator must have testamentary capacity—that is, the testator must be of legal age and sound mind *at the time the will is made*. The legal age for executing a will varies, but in most states and under the UPC the minimum age is eighteen years [UPC 2–501]. Thus, the will of a twenty-one-year-old decedent written when the person was sixteen is invalid if, under state law, the legal age for executing a will is eighteen.

The concept of "being of sound mind" refers to the testator's ability to formulate and to comprehend a personal plan for the disposition of property. Generally, a testator must (1) intend the document to be his or her last will and testament, (2) comprehend the kind and character of the property being distributed, and (3) comprehend and remember the "natural objects of his or her bounty" (usually, family members and persons for whom the testator has affection).

A valid will is one that represents the maker's intention to transfer and distribute his or her property. When it can be shown that the decedent's plan of distribution was the result of fraud or of undue influence, the will is declared invalid. Undue influence may be inferred by the court if the testator ignored blood relatives and named as beneficiary a nonrelative who was

2. For example, California law differs substantially from the UPC.

in constant close contact with the testator and in a position to influence the making of the will. For example, if a nurse or friend caring for the testator at the time of death was named as beneficiary to the exclusion of all family members, the validity of the will might well be challenged on the basis of undue influence.

Westlaw. See Case 50.1 at the end of this chapter. To view the full, unedited case from Westlaw,® go to this text's Web site at **http://wbl-cs.westbuslaw.com**.

Writing Requirements. Generally, a will must be in writing. The writing itself can be informal as long as it substantially complies with the statutory requirements. In some states, a will can be handwritten in crayon or ink. It can be written on a sheet or scrap of paper, on a paper bag, or on a piece of cloth. A will that is completely in the handwriting of the testator is called a **holographic will** (sometimes referred to as an *olographic will*).

A **nuncupative will** is an oral will made before witnesses. It is not permitted in most states. Where authorized by statute, such wills are generally valid only if made during the last illness of the testator and are therefore sometimes referred to as *deathbed wills*. Normally, only personal property can be transferred by a nuncupative will. Statutes frequently permit soldiers and sailors to make nuncupative wills when on active duty.

Signature Requirements. A fundamental requirement for a valid will is that the testator's signature appear on the will, generally at the end of the document. Each jurisdiction dictates by statute and court decision what constitutes a signature. Initials, an X or other mark, and words such as "Mom" have all been upheld as valid when it was shown that the testators *intended* them to be signatures.

Witness Requirements. A will normally must be attested (sworn to) by two, and sometimes three, witnesses. The number of witnesses, their qualifications, and the manner in which the witnessing must be done are generally set out in a statute. A witness may be required to be disinterested—that is, not a beneficiary under the will. The UPC, however, provides that a will is valid even if it is attested by an interested witness [UPC 2–505]. There are no age requirements for witnesses, but witnesses must be mentally competent.

The purpose of witnesses is to verify that the testator actually executed (signed) the will and had the requisite intent and capacity at the time. A witness does not have to read the contents of the will. Usually, the testator and all witnesses must sign in the sight or the presence of one another, but the UPC deems it sufficient if the testator acknowledges his or her signature to the witnesses [UPC 2–502]. The UPC does not require all parties to sign in the presence of one another.

Publication Requirements. The maker of a will *publishes* the will by orally declaring to the witnesses that the document they are about to sign is his or her "last will and testament." Publication is becoming an unnecessary formality in most states, and it is not required under the UPC.

Revocation of Wills

An executed will is revocable by the maker at any time during the maker's lifetime. The maker may revoke a will by a physical act, such as tearing up the will, or by a subsequent writing. Wills can also be revoked by operation of law. Revocation can be partial or complete, and it must follow certain strict formalities.

Revocation by a Physical Act of the Maker. The testator may revoke a will by intentionally burning, tearing, canceling, obliterating, or destroying it or by having someone else do so in the presence of the maker and at the maker's direction.[3] In some states, partial revocation by physical act of the maker is recognized. Thus, those portions of a will lined out or torn away are dropped, and the remaining parts of the will are valid. In no case, however, can a provision be crossed out and an additional or substitute provision written in. Such altered portions require reexecution (re-signing) and reattestation (rewitnessing).

To revoke a will by physical act, it is necessary to follow the mandates of a state statute exactly. When a state statute prescribes the specific methods for revoking a will by physical act, those are the only methods that will revoke the will.

3. The destruction cannot be inadvertent. The maker's intent to revoke must be shown. When a will has been burned or torn accidentally, it is normally recommended that the maker have a new document created so that it will not falsely appear that the maker intended to revoke the will.

Revocation by a Subsequent Writing. A will may also be wholly or partially revoked by a **codicil**, a written instrument separate from the will that amends or revokes provisions in the will. A codicil eliminates the necessity of redrafting an entire will merely to add to it or amend it. It can also be used to revoke an entire will. The codicil must be executed with the same formalities required for a will, and it must refer expressly to the will. In effect, it updates a will, because the will is "incorporated by reference" into the codicil.

A new will (second will) can be executed that may or may not revoke the first or a prior will, depending on the language used. To revoke a prior will, the second will must use language specifically revoking other wills, such as, "This will hereby revokes all prior wills." If the second will is otherwise valid and properly executed, it will revoke all prior wills. If the express *declaration of revocation* is missing, both wills are read together. If any of the dispositions made in the second will are inconsistent with the prior will, the second will controls.

Revocation by Operation of Law. Revocation by operation of law occurs when marriage, divorce or annulment, or the birth of a child takes place after a will has been executed. In most states, when a testator marries after executing a will that does not include the new spouse, on the testator's death the spouse can still receive the amount he or she would have taken had the testator died intestate (how an intestate's property is distributed under state laws will be discussed shortly). In effect, this revokes the will to the point of providing the spouse with an intestate share. The rest of the estate is passed under the will [UPC 2–301, 2–508]. If, however, the new spouse is otherwise provided for in the will (or by transfer of property outside the will), the new spouse will not be given an intestate amount.

At common law and under the UPC, divorce does not necessarily revoke the entire will. A divorce or an annulment occurring after a will has been executed will revoke those dispositions of property made under the will to the former spouse [UPC 2–508].

If a child is born after a will has been executed and if it appears that the deceased parent would have made a provision for the child, the child is entitled to receive whatever portion of the estate he or she is allowed under state laws providing for the distribution of an intestate's property. Most state laws allow a child to receive some portion of a parent's estate if no provision is made in the parent's will, unless it appears from the terms of the will that the testator intended to disinherit the child. Under the UPC, the rule is the same.

RIGHTS UNDER A WILL

The law imposes certain limitations on the way a person can dispose of property in a will. For example, a married person who makes a will generally cannot avoid leaving a certain portion of the estate to the surviving spouse. In most states, this is called an elective share, a forced share, or a widow's (or widower's) share, and it is often one-third of the estate or an amount equal to a spouse's share under intestacy laws.

Beneficiaries under a will have rights as well. A beneficiary can renounce (disclaim) his or her share of the property given under a will. Further, a surviving spouse can renounce the amount given under a will and elect to take the forced share when the forced share is larger than the amount of the gift—this is the widow's (or widower's) election, or right of election. State statutes provide the methods by which a surviving spouse accomplishes renunciation. The purpose of these statutes is to allow the spouse to obtain whichever distribution would be most advantageous. The revised UPC gives the surviving spouse an elective right to take a percentage of the total estate determined by the length of time that the spouse and the decedent were married to each other [UPC 2–201].

PROBATE PROCEDURES

Typically, probate procedures vary, depending on the size of the decedent's estate.

Informal Probate Proceedings. For smaller estates, most state statutes provide for the distribution of assets without formal probate proceedings. Faster and less expensive methods are then used. For example, property can be transferred by affidavit (a written statement taken in the presence of a person who has authority to affirm it), and problems or questions can be handled during an administrative hearing. In addition, some state statutes provide that title to cars, savings and checking accounts, and certain other property can be passed merely by filling out forms.

A majority of states also provide for family settlement agreements, which are private agreements among the beneficiaries. Once a will is admitted to probate, the family members can agree to settle among themselves the distribution of the decedent's assets. Although a family settlement agreement speeds the settlement process, a court order is still needed to protect the estate from future creditors and to clear title to the assets involved. The use of these and other types of summary procedures in estate administration can save time and money.

Formal Probate Proceedings. For larger estates, formal probate proceedings are normally undertaken, and the probate court supervises every aspect of the settlement of the decedent's estate. Additionally, in some situations—such as when a guardian for minor children or for an incompetent person must be appointed and a trust has been created to protect the minor or the incompetent person—more formal probate procedures cannot be avoided. Formal probate proceedings may take several months to complete, and as a result, a sizable portion of the decedent's assets (up to perhaps 10 percent) may have to go toward payment of fees charged by attorneys and personal representatives, as well as court costs.

Property Transfers outside the Probate Process

Commonly, beneficiaries under a will must wait until the probate process is complete—which can take several months if formal probate proceedings are undertaken—to have access to money or other assets received under the will. For this and other reasons, some persons arrange to have property transferred in ways other than by will and outside the probate process.

One method of accomplishing this is by establishing a living trust, as discussed later in this chapter. Another method is through the joint ownership of property. For example, a person can arrange to hold title to certain real or personal property as a joint tenant with a spouse or other person. Recall from Chapter 46 that in a joint tenancy, when one joint tenant dies, the other joint tenant or tenants automatically inherit the deceased tenant's share of the property. This is true even if the deceased tenant has provided otherwise in his or her will.

Yet another way of transferring property outside the probate process is by making gifts to children or others while one is still living. Additionally, to make sure that a spouse, children, or some other dependent is provided for, many people take out life insurance policies. On the death of the policyholder, the proceeds of the policy go directly to the beneficiary and are not involved in the probate process. The balance in an Individual Retirement Account (IRA) may also pass to a named beneficiary without being involved in the probate process.

In all of these situations, the person who sets up the living trust, arranges for the joint tenancy, takes out the insurance policy, or names a beneficiary for an IRA should pay careful attention regarding whom the arrangement benefits.

See Case 50.2 at the end of this chapter. To view the full, unedited case from Westlaw,® go to this text's Web site at **http://wbl-cs.westbuslaw.com**.

SECTION 2

Intestacy Laws

Each state regulates by statute how property will be distributed when a person dies intestate (without a valid will). These statutes are called statutes of descent and distribution—or, more simply, intestacy laws, as mentioned in this chapter's introduction. Intestacy laws attempt to carry out the likely intent and wishes of the decedent. These laws assume that deceased persons would have intended that their natural heirs (spouses, children, grandchildren, or other family members) inherit their property. Therefore, intestacy statutes set out rules and priorities under which these heirs inherit the property. If no heirs exist, the state will assume ownership of the property.

The rules of descent vary widely from state to state. It is thus extremely important to refer to the exact terms of the applicable state statutes when addressing any problem of intestacy distribution.

Surviving Spouse and Children

Usually, state statutes provide for the rights of the surviving spouse and children. In addition, the law provides that first the debts of the decedent must be satisfied out of his or her estate, and then the remaining assets can pass to the surviving spouse and the children. A surviving spouse usually receives only a share of the estate—one-half if there is also a surviving child and one-third if there are two or more children. Only if no children or grandchildren survive the decedent will a surviving spouse receive the entire estate.

Assume that Allen dies intestate and is survived by his wife, Della, and his children, Duane and Tara. Allen's property passes according to intestacy laws. After Allen's outstanding debts are paid, Della will receive the homestead (either in fee simple or as a life estate) and ordinarily a one-third to one-half interest in all other property. The remaining real and personal property will pass to Duane and Tara in equal portions. Under most state intestacy laws and under the UPC, in-laws do not share in an estate. If a child dies before his or her parents, the child's spouse will not receive an inheritance on the parents' death. For example, if Duane died before his father (Allen), Duane's spouse would not inherit Duane's share of Allen's estate.

When there is no surviving spouse or child, the order of inheritance is grandchildren, then parents of the decedent. These relatives are usually called *lineal descendants*. If there are no lineal descendants, *collateral heirs*—brothers, sisters, nieces, nephews, aunts, and uncles of the decedent—make up the next group to share. If there are no survivors in any of these groups, most statutes provide for the property to be distributed among the next of kin of the collateral heirs.

Stepchildren, Adopted Children, and Illegitimate Children

Under intestacy laws, stepchildren are not considered kin. Legally adopted children, however, are recognized as lawful heirs of their adoptive parents. Whether an illegitimate child inherits depends on state statutes. In some states, intestate succession between the father and the child can occur only when the child has been "legitimized" by ceremony or "acknowledged" by the father. Under the revised UPC, the same rule applies to intestate succession between the child and the mother [UPC 2–114]. The United States Supreme Court has allowed state illegitimacy statutes to stand, concluding that they serve legitimate state purposes.[4]

Distribution to Grandchildren

When a person who dies is survived by descendants of deceased children, a question arises as to what share the grandchildren of the decedent will receive. ***Per stirpes*** is a method of dividing an intestate share by which a class or group of distributees (for example, grandchildren) take the share that their deceased parent would have been entitled to inherit had that parent lived.

Assume that Moss, a widower, has two children, Scott and Jules. Scott has two children (Bonita and Holly), and Jules has one child (Paul). At the time of Moss's death, Scott and Jules have already died. If Moss's estate is distributed *per stirpes,* the following distribution will take place:

1. Bonita and Holly: one-fourth each, taking Scott's share.
2. Paul: one-half, taking Jules's share.

Exhibit 50–2 on the next page illustrates the *per stirpes* method of distribution.

An estate may also be distributed on a ***per capita*** basis. This means that each person takes an equal share of the estate. If Moss's estate is distributed *per capita,* Bonita, Holly, and Paul will each receive a one-third share. Exhibit 50–3 on page 1043 illustrates the *per capita* method of distribution.

SECTION 3

Trusts

A **trust** involves any arrangement by which legal title to property is transferred from one person to be administered by a trustee for another's benefit. It can also be defined as a right of property (real or personal) held by one party for the benefit of another. A trust can be created for any purpose that is not illegal or against public policy. As mentioned, trusts are important estate-planning devices for several reasons. These reasons will become clear as you read through this section.

Essential Elements of a Trust

The essential elements of a trust are as follows:

1. A designated beneficiary.
2. A designated trustee.
3. A fund sufficiently identified to enable title to pass to the trustee.
4. Actual delivery to the trustee with the intention of passing title.

If Shanahan conveys his farm to First Bank of Minnesota to be held for the benefit of his daughters,

4. *Labine v. Vincent,* 401 U.S. 532, 91 S.Ct. 1017, 28 L.Ed.2d 288 (1971). In *Trimble v. Gordon,* 430 U.S. 762, 97 S.Ct. 1459, 52 L.Ed.2d 31 (1977), however, the United States Supreme Court ruled that an Illinois illegitimacy statute was unconstitutional because it did not bear a rational relationship to a legitimate state purpose.

EXHIBIT 50–2 *PER STIRPES* DISTRIBUTION

Under this method of distribution, an heir takes the share that his or her deceased parent would have been entitled to inherit, had the parent lived. This may mean that a class of distributees—the grandchildren, in this example—will not inherit in equal portions. (Note that Bonita and Holly receive only one-fourth of Moss's estate, whereas Paul inherits one-half.)

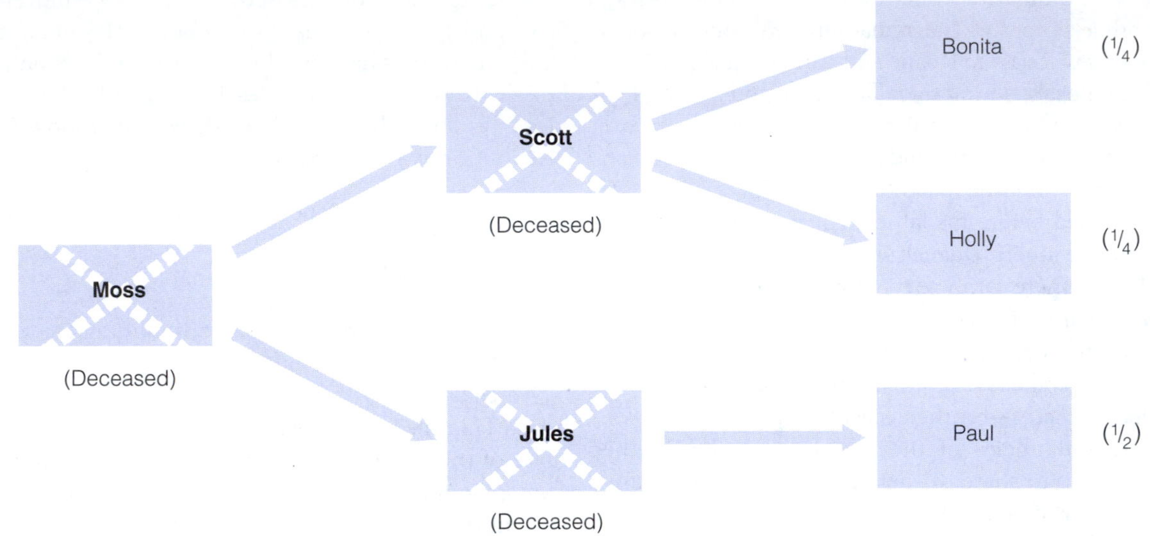

Shanahan has created a trust. Shanahan is the settlor, or grantor (the one creating the trust), First Bank of Minnesota is the trustee, and Shanahan's daughters are the beneficiaries. This arrangement is illustrated in Exhibit 50–4.

EXPRESS TRUSTS

An *express trust* is one that is created or declared in explicit terms, usually in writing. There are numerous types of express trusts, each with its own special characteristics.

Living Trust. A living trust—or ***inter vivos* trust** (*inter vivos* is Latin for "between or among the living")—is a trust executed by a grantor during his or her lifetime. A living trust may be an attractive estate-planning option because living trusts are not included in the property of a decedent's estate that is probated.

Living trusts can be irrevocable or revocable. The distinction between these two types of trusts is an important one for estate planners. In an *irrevocable* living trust, the grantor permanently gives up control over the property. In a *revocable* living trust, in contrast, the grantor retains control over the trust property during his or her lifetime.

To establish an irrevocable living trust, the grantor executes a trust deed, and legal title to the trust property passes to the named trustee. The trustee has a duty to administer the property as directed by the grantor for the benefit and in the interest of the beneficiaries. The trustee must preserve the trust property; make it productive; and, if required by the terms of the trust agreement, pay income to the beneficiaries, all in accordance with the terms of the trust. Once an irrevocable *inter vivos* trust has been created, the grantor has, in effect, given over the property for the benefit of the beneficiaries.

To establish a revocable living trust, the grantor deeds the property to the trust but retains the power to amend, alter, or revoke the trust during his or her lifetime. The grantor may also arrange to receive income earned by the trust assets during his or her lifetime. Unless the trust is revoked, the principal of the trust is transferred to the trust beneficiary on the grantor's death.

Testamentary Trusts. A trust created by will to come into existence on the settlor's death is called a **testamentary trust.** Although a testamentary trust has a trustee who maintains legal title to the trust property, actions of the trustee are subject to judicial

EXHIBIT 50–3 *PER CAPITA* DISTRIBUTION

Under this method of distribution, all heirs in a certain class—in this case, the grandchildren—inherit equally. Note that Bonita and Holly in this situation each inherit one-third of Moss's estate (not one-fourth, as they do under the *per stirpes* method of distribution).

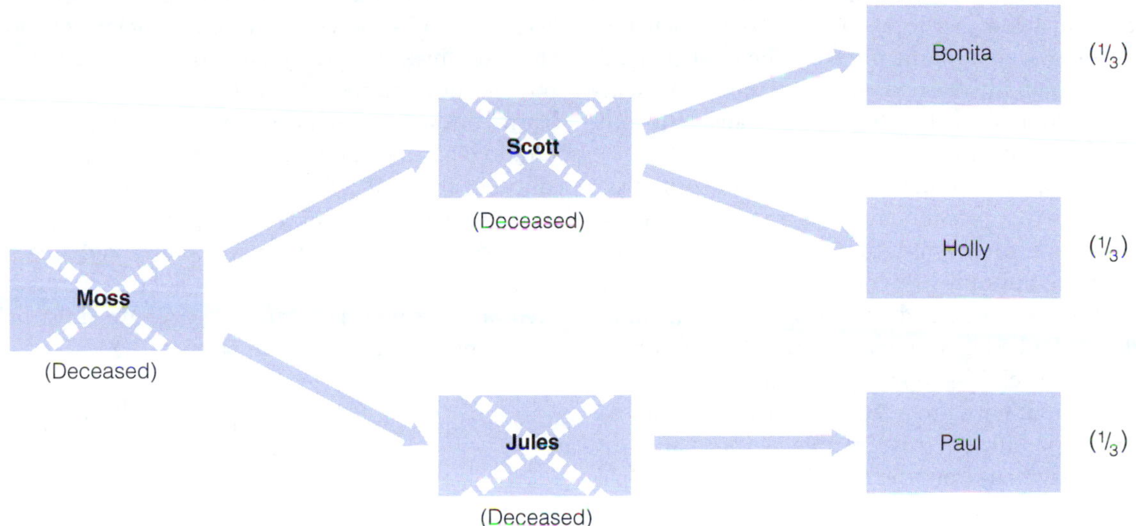

approval. This trustee can be named in the will or appointed by the court. Thus, a testamentary trust does not fail because a trustee has not been named in the will. The legal responsibilities of the trustee are the same as in an *inter vivos* trust.

If the will setting up a testamentary trust is invalid, the trust will also be invalid. The property that was supposed to be in the trust will then pass according to intestacy laws, not according to the terms of the trust.

Charitable Trusts. A trust designed for the benefit of a segment of the public or the public in general is a **charitable trust**. It differs from other types of trusts in that the identities of the beneficiaries are uncertain. Usually, to be deemed a charitable trust, a trust must be created for charitable, educational, religious, or scientific purposes.

Spendthrift Trusts. As a general rule, a trust beneficiary may assign his or her rights to receive the

EXHIBIT 50–4 TRUST ARRANGEMENT

In a trust, there is a separation of interests in the trust property. The trustee takes legal title, which appears to be complete ownership and possession but which does not include the right to receive any benefits from the property. The beneficiary takes *equitable title,* which is the right to receive all benefits from the property.

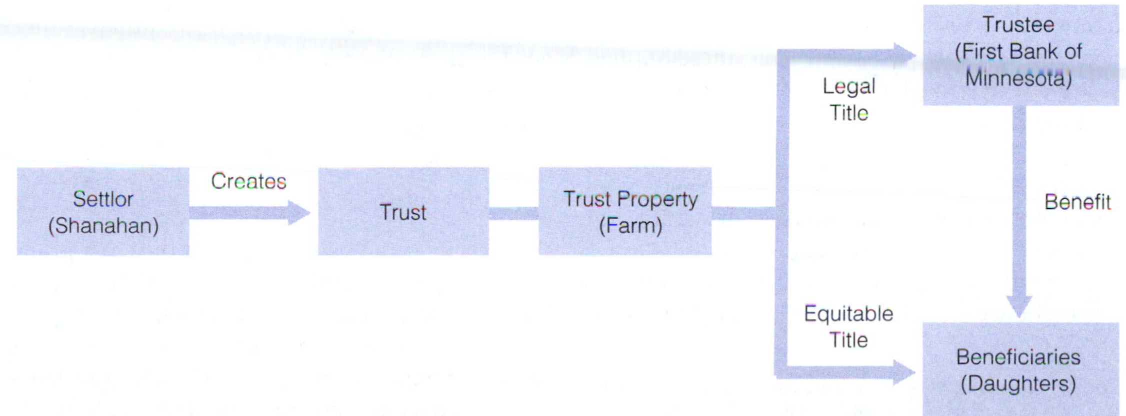

principal or income of a trust to a third party (assignments are discussed in Chapter 15). Additionally, distributions of trust funds to beneficiaries normally are subject to creditors' claims. In a **spendthrift trust**, however, the beneficiary is not permitted to transfer his or her right to the trust's principal or to future payments of income from the trust. To qualify as a spendthrift trust, the trust must explicitly place restraints on the alienation—transfer to others—of the trust funds.

The majority of states enforce spendthrift trust provisions that prohibit creditors from attaching the beneficiary's interest in future distributions from the trust. State laws provide for some exceptions, however. For example, a divorced spouse or a minor child of the beneficiary may be permitted to obtain alimony or child-support payments. Additionally, creditors that have provided *necessaries* (see Chapter 12) to spendthrift trust recipients normally can compel payment from the trust income or principal.

Totten Trusts. A special type of trust created when one person deposits money in his or her own name as a trustee for another is a **Totten trust**,[5] or tentative trust. This trust is tentative in that it is revocable at will until the depositor dies or completes the gift in his or her lifetime by some unequivocal act or declaration (for example, delivery of the funds to the intended beneficiary). If the depositor dies before the beneficiary dies and if the depositor has not revoked the trust expressly or impliedly, a presumption arises that an absolute (a binding, irrevocable) trust has been created for the benefit of the beneficiary. At the death of the depositor, the beneficiary obtains property rights to the balance on hand.

Implied Trusts

Sometimes a trust is imposed by law, even in the absence of an express trust. Customarily, these implied trusts are characterized as either constructive trusts or resulting trusts.

Constructive Trusts. A **constructive trust** arises by operation of law in the interests of equity and fairness. A constructive trust enables plaintiffs to recover property (and sometimes damages) from defendants who would otherwise be unjustly enriched. In a constructive trust, the legal owner is declared to be a trustee for the parties who are, in equity, actually entitled to the beneficial enjoyment that flows from the trust.

One source of a constructive trust is a wrongful action, such as the violation of a fiduciary relationship. To illustrate: Arturo and Spring are partners in buying, developing, and selling real estate. Arturo learns through the staff of the partnership that two hundred acres of land will soon come on the market and that the staff will recommend that the partnership purchase the land. Arturo purchases the property secretly in his own name, thus violating his fiduciary relationship. When these facts are discovered, a court will determine that Arturo must hold the property in trust for the partnership.

See Case 50.3 at the end of this chapter. To view the full, unedited case from Westlaw,® go to this text's Web site at **http://wbl-cs.westbuslaw.com**.

Resulting Trusts. A **resulting trust** arises from the conduct of the parties. Here, the trust results, or is created, when circumstances raise an inference that the party holding legal title to the property does so for the benefit of another, unless the inference is refuted or the beneficial interest is otherwise disposed of.

To illustrate: Glenda wants to put one acre of land she owns on the market for sale. Because she is going out of the country for two years and will not be available to deed the property to a buyer during that period, she conveys the property to her good friend Oscar. Oscar can then sell and deed the property, with the proceeds to be turned over to Glenda. Because Glenda's intent in deeding the property to Oscar is neither a sale nor a gift, the property will be held in a resulting trust by Oscar (as trustee) for the benefit of Glenda. Therefore, on Glenda's return, Oscar will be required either to deed back the property to Glenda or, if the property has been sold, to turn over the proceeds (held in trust) to her.

The Trustee

The trustee is the person holding the trust property. Anyone legally capable of holding title to, and dealing in, property can be a trustee. If the settlor of a trust fails to name a trustee, or if a named trustee cannot or will not serve, the trust does not fail—an appropriate court can appoint a trustee.

5. This type of trust derives its unusual name from *In the Matter of Totten,* 179 N.Y. 112, 71 N.E. 748 (1904).

Trustee's Duties. A trustee must act with honesty, good faith, and prudence in administering the trust and must exercise a high degree of loyalty toward the trust beneficiary. The general standard of care is the degree of care a prudent person would exercise in his or her personal affairs.[6] The duty of loyalty requires that the trustee act in the exclusive interest of the beneficiary.

Among specific duties, a trustee must keep clear and accurate accounts of the trust's administration and furnish complete and correct information to the beneficiary. A trustee must keep trust assets separate from his or her own assets. A trustee has a duty to pay to an income beneficiary the net income of the trust assets at reasonable intervals. A trustee has a duty to distribute the risk of loss from investments by reasonable diversification and a duty to dispose of assets that do not represent prudent investments. Investments in federal, state, or municipal bonds; corporate bonds; and shares of preferred or common stock may be prudent investments under particular circumstances.

Trustee's Powers. When a settlor creates a trust, he or she may prescribe the trustee's powers and performance. Generally, state law[7] applies in the absence of specific terms in the trust.[8] When state law does apply, it is most likely to restrict the trustee's investment of trust funds. Typically, statutes confine trustees to investments in conservative debt securities such as government, utility, and railroad bonds and first-mortgage loans on realty. It is common, however, for a settlor to grant a trustee discretionary investment power. In that circumstance, any statute may be considered only advisory, with the trustee's decisions subject in most states to the prudent person rule.

A difficult question concerns the extent of a trustee's discretion to "invade" the principal and distribute it to an income beneficiary, if the income is found to be insufficient to provide for the beneficiary in an appropriate manner. A similar question concerns the extent of a trustee's discretion to retain trust income and add it to the principal, if the income is found to be more than sufficient to provide for the beneficiary in an appropriate manner. Generally, the answer to both questions is that the income beneficiary should be provided with a somewhat predictable annual income, but with a view to the safety of the principal. Thus, a trustee may make individualized adjustments in annual distributions.

Of course, a trustee is responsible for carrying out the purposes of the trust. If the trustee fails to comply with the terms of the trust or the controlling statute, he or she is personally liable for any loss.

Allocations between Principal and Income. Frequently, a settlor will provide one beneficiary with a life estate and another beneficiary with the remainder interest in a trust. A farmer, for example, may create a testamentary trust providing that the farm's income be paid to his or her surviving spouse and that on the surviving spouse's death, the farm be given to their children. Among the income and principal beneficiaries, questions may arise concerning the apportionment of receipts and expenses for the farm's management, as well as the trust's administration, between income and principal. Even when income and principal beneficiaries are the same, these questions may arise.

To the extent that a trust instrument does not provide instructions, a trustee must refer to applicable state law. The general rule is that ordinary receipts and expenses are chargeable to the income beneficiary, whereas extraordinary receipts and expenses are allocated to the principal beneficiaries.[9] To illustrate: The receipt of rent from trust realty would be ordinary, as would the expense of paying the property's taxes. The cost of long-term improvements and proceeds from the property's sale, however, would be extraordinary.

TRUST TERMINATION

The terms of a trust should expressly state the event on which the settlor wishes it to terminate—for example, the beneficiary's or the trustee's death. If the trust instrument does not provide for termination on the beneficiary's death, the beneficiary's death

6. Revised Uniform Principal and Income Act Section 2(a)(3); *Restatement (Third) of Trusts*, Section 227. This rule is in force in the majority of states by statute and in a small number of states under the common law. See also *O'Neill v. Commissioner of Internal Revenue*, 994 F.2d 302 (6th Cir. 1993).

7. In eight states, the law consists, in part, of the Uniform Principal and Income Act, published in 1931. The Revised Uniform Principal and Income Act, issued in 1962, has been adopted in thirty-four states. There are other uniform acts that may apply—for instance, about a third of the states have enacted the Uniform Trustees' Powers Act, promulgated in 1964. In addition, most states have their own statutes covering particular procedures and practices.

8. Revised Uniform Principal and Income Act Section 2(a)(1); *Restatement (Second) of Trusts*, Section 164.

9. Revised Uniform Principal and Income Act, Sections 3, 6, 8, 13; *Restatement (Second) of Trusts*, Section 233.

will not end it. Similarly, without an express provision, a trust will not terminate on the trustee's death.

Typically, a trust instrument specifies a termination date. For example, a trust created to educate the settlor's child may provide that the trust ends when the beneficiary reaches the age of twenty-five. If the trust's purpose is fulfilled before that date, a court may order the trust's termination. If no date is specified, a trust will terminate when its purpose has been fulfilled. Of course, if a trust's purpose becomes impossible or illegal, the trust will terminate.

SECTION 4

Estate Administration

The orderly procedure used to collect assets, settle debts, and distribute the remaining assets when a person dies is the subject matter of estate administration. The rules and procedures for managing the estate of a deceased are controlled by statute. Thus, they vary from state to state. In every state, there is a special court, often called a probate court, that oversees the management of estates of decedents.

LOCATING THE WILL

The first step after a person dies is usually to determine whether the decedent left a will. In most cases, the decedent's attorney will have that information. If there is uncertainty as to whether a valid will exists, the personal papers of the deceased must be reviewed. If a will exists, it probably names a personal representative (executor) to administer the estate. If there is no will, or if the will fails to name a personal representative, the court must appoint an administrator. Under the UPC, the term *personal representative* refers to either an executor (a person named in the will) or an administrator (a person appointed by the court) [UPC 1–201(30)].

DUTIES OF THE PERSONAL REPRESENTATIVE

The personal representative has a number of duties. The first is to inventory and collect the assets of the decedent. If necessary, the assets are appraised to determine their value. Both the rights of creditors and the rights of beneficiaries must be protected during the estate-administration proceedings. In addition, the personal representative is responsible for managing the assets of the estate during the administration period and for preventing them from being wasted or unnecessarily depleted.

The personal representative receives and pays valid claims of creditors and arranges for the estate to pay federal and state income taxes and estate taxes (or inheritance taxes, depending on the state). A personal representative is required to post a bond to ensure honest and faithful performance. Usually, the bond exceeds the estimated value of the personal estate of the decedent. Under most state statutes, the will can specify that the personal representative need not post a bond.

ESTATE AND INHERITANCE TAXES

The death of an individual may result in tax liabilities at both the federal and state levels. At the federal level, a tax is levied on the total value of the estate after debts and expenses for administration have been deducted and after various exemptions have been allowed. The tax is on the estate itself rather than on the beneficiaries.

The majority of states assess a death tax in the form of an inheritance tax imposed on the recipient of a bequest rather than the estate. Some states also have a state estate tax similar to the federal estate tax. In general, inheritance tax rates are graduated according to the type of relationship between the beneficiary and the decedent. The lowest rates and largest exemptions are applied to a surviving spouse and the children of the decedent.

DISTRIBUTION OF ASSETS

When the ultimate distribution of assets to the beneficiaries is determined, the personal representative is responsible for distributing the estate pursuant to the court order. Once the assets have been distributed, an accounting is rendered to the court, the estate is closed, and the personal representative is relieved of any further responsibility or liability for the estate.

SECTION 5

Elder Law

In the past, elderly people sought legal assistance primarily for estate-planning purposes, in preparation for their deaths. Today, an increasing percentage of

Americans are reaching retirement age, and elderly persons are facing the need to prepare for other possibilities—that they will become incapacitated, for example, or will have to depend on others for their health care and basic needs.

The aging of the U.S. population, a trend that will continue for decades to come, has led to a new legal specialty—elder law. Basically, **elder law** is a legal practice area in which attorneys assist older persons in dealing with such problems as disability, long-term health care, age discrimination, grandparents' visitation rights, and other problems relating to age. Here we look at just two aspects of elder law—planning for disability and Medicaid planning.

PLANNING FOR DISABILITY

With an increasing number of individuals living into their eighties and nineties, one important issue in elder law relates to power of attorney. Adult children need to seek power of attorney from their aging parents, particularly if the parents are becoming mentally incompetent or afflicted by Alzheimer's disease. An elder law attorney might help in arranging for the aging parent to sign a power of attorney and other documents, such as a durable power of attorney or a living will, that will enable the adult children to take over the parent's affairs if the parent becomes mentally and perhaps physically incapacitated.

Durable Power of Attorney. One method that is often used to provide for future disability involves the durable power of attorney. A **durable power of attorney** authorizes a person to act on behalf of an incompetent person—write checks, collect insurance proceeds, and otherwise manage the disabled person's affairs, including health care—when he or she becomes incapacitated. A person of advanced age may give such a power of attorney to an adult child. Although becoming incapacitated is of particular concern to older persons, younger spouses often give each other durable power of attorney as well—in the event they are incapacitated due to an accident, for example.

Health-Care Power of Attorney. A **health-care power of attorney** designates a person who will have the power to choose what type of and how much medical treatment a person who is unable to make such a choice will receive. The health-care power of attorney is growing in importance as medical technology allows doctors and hospitals to keep people technically alive but in a so-called vegetative state for ever-increasing periods of time.

Living Will. A similar power is created by what is referred to as a **living will.** A living will is not a will in the usual sense—that is, it does not appoint an estate representative, dispose of property, establish trusts, and so on. Rather, it allows a person to control what medical treatment may be used after a serious accident or illness. Through a living will, a person can designate whether he or she wants certain lifesaving procedures to be undertaken in situations in which the treatment will not result in a reasonable quality of life. Most states have enacted statutes permitting living wills, and it is important that the requirements of state law be followed exactly in creating such wills. Typically, under state statutes, physicians are obligated to abide by the terms of living wills, and living wills often are included with a patient's medical records.

MEDICAID PLANNING

A serious problem facing older persons is the cost of long-term care—in a nursing home, for example. Suppose that a person can no longer look after his or her own needs and either cannot or does not wish to rely on family or friends to provide full-time care. In all likelihood, this person will end up in an assisted-living facility or a nursing home, and such arrangements are costly. Even those who can afford to spend $60,000 or more per year for nursing-home care might prefer to transfer their assets to others, such as their children, and "go on Medicaid" so that the government will pay for the care. One area of elder law addresses Medicaid planning.

Medicaid versus Medicare. Medicaid is not the same as Medicare. As you read in Chapter 41, Medicare is a federal program that is financed through the Social Security system and primarily addresses the needs of the elderly. Medicaid, in contrast, is a cooperative federal-state program that provides health-care services to the poor of all ages. Because the program is administered by state agencies, regulations governing Medicaid vary from state to state. At the federal level, Medicaid is administered by the Health Care Financing Administration.

Medicaid Planning. When Medicaid pays for long-term care, all of the person's income must be paid to the state. There are exceptions, though, and this is where Medicaid planning becomes important. One home, one automobile, and other assets up to a total value of $75,000 are exempt from Medicaid accounting. Thus, one strategy is for the elderly person to bring down the total value of all of his or her other assets to less than $75,000 by spending assets in excess of that amount to fix up his or her house or to buy an expensive new car.

Assets might also be transferred to others, such as children and friends, prior to applying for Medicaid. A person who makes uncompensated transfers within three years (or five years, if a trust transfer is involved) prior to applying for Medicaid, however, faces a "penalty period" during which he or she will not qualify for Medicaid.[10] This waiting period is derived by dividing the value of uncompensated transfers made during the "look back" period of three (or five) years by the average monthly cost of nursing-home care in the region. For example, suppose that Joanne transfers stock worth $60,000 to her daughter so as to reduce her assets to a value of less than $75,000. A year later, Joanne applies for Medicaid to cover nursing-home costs. If the average nursing home in her area charges $6,000, Joanne will not be eligible to receive Medicaid for ten months ($60,000 divided by $6,000).

Criminalizing Medicaid Planning. In 1996, Congress passed a law[11] that made it a crime for elderly Americans to transfer their assets to others, including trusts, before going into a nursing home if state Medicaid officials concluded that the transfer triggered a "penalty period." A person who violated the act was subject to a fine of up to $25,000, imprisonment for up to five years, or both. The law, which became effective on January 1, 1997, outraged elder-care professionals and others and was immediately dubbed the "Granny Goes to Jail" law.

The law was short lived. In August 1997, Congress amended the law to strike the language in Section 217 and add a provision making it a crime for attorneys to advise elderly clients to give away assets to get Medicaid coverage of nursing-home costs.[12] Attorneys who violated the act were subject to a fine of up to $10,000, imprisonment for up to one year, or both. This provision, popularly called the "Granny's Lawyer Goes to Jail" law, has also been under attack. Attorneys claim that it poses an ethical dilemma for them because it forces them to choose between committing a crime by giving advice and committing malpractice by not doing so. In 1998, U.S. attorney general Janet Reno stated that the Justice Department would not defend the constitutionality of the act, and a federal district court granted a preliminary injunction against the law's enforcement on constitutional grounds.[13] Until the law is repealed by Congress, though, attorneys have no guarantees that the Justice Department will continue its policy of nonenforcement.

10. 42 U.S.C. Section 1396p(c)(1)(B).
11. Section 217 of the Health Insurance Portability and Accountability Act of 1996 [42 U.S.C. Section 1320a-7b(a)].
12. Section 4734 of the Balanced Budget Act of 1997 [42 U.S.C. Section 1320a-7b(a)].
13. *New York State Bar Association v. Reno*, 999 F.Supp. 710 (N.D.N.Y. 1998).

Terms and Concepts to Review

CHAPTER SUMMARY

WILLS

Wills—Terminology	1. *Intestate*—One who dies without a valid will. 2. *Testator*—A person who makes a will. 3. *Personal representative*—A person appointed in a will or by a court to settle the affairs of a decedent. A personal representative named in the will is an *executor*; a personal representative appointed by the court for an intestate decedent is an *administrator.*
Laws Governing Wills	Laws governing wills come into play when a will is probated. To *probate* a will means to establish its validity and to carry the administration of the estate through a court process. Probate laws vary from state to state. Probate procedures may be informal or formal, depending on the size of the estate and other factors, such as whether a guardian for minor children must be appointed.
Gifts by Will	1. *Specific devise*—A specific devise or bequest (legacy) describes particular property that can be distinguished from the rest of the testator's property. 2. *General devise*—A general devise or bequest (legacy) uses less restrictive terminology. 3. *Residuary of the estate*—The residuary of the estate (any assets that remain after all specific gifts have been made and all debts have been paid) may be given to the testator's spouse, distributed to the testator's descendants, or disposed of in some other way. If the testator does not indicate what party or parties should receive the residuary of the estate, the residuary passes according to the laws of intestacy.
Requirements for a Valid Will	1. The testator must have testamentary capacity (be of legal age and sound mind at the time the will is made). 2. A will must be in writing (except for nuncupative wills). A holographic will is completely in the handwriting of the testator. 3. A will must be signed by the testator; what constitutes a signature varies from jurisdiction to jurisdiction. 4. A nonholographic will (an attested will) must be witnessed in the manner prescribed by state statute. 5. A will may have to be *published*—that is, the testator may be required to announce to witnesses that this is his or her "last will and testament"; not required under the UPC.
Revocation of Wills	1. *By physical act of the maker*—Tearing up, canceling, obliterating, or deliberately destroying part or all of a will. 2. *By subsequent writing*— a. Codicil—A formal, separate document to amend or revoke an existing will. b. Second will or new will—A new, properly executed will expressly revoking the existing will. 3. *By operation of law*— a. Marriage—Generally revokes part of a will written before the marriage. b. Divorce or annulment—Revokes dispositions of property made under a will to a former spouse. c. Subsequently born child—*It is implied* that the child is entitled to receive the portion of the estate granted under intestacy distribution laws.
Probate Procedures	For smaller estates, most state statutes provide for the distribution of assets without formal probate proceedings. For larger estates, formal probate proceedings are normally undertaken, and the probate court supervises every aspect of the settlement of the decedent's estate.
Property Transfers outside the Probate Process	Estate planning typically involves arranging to transfer certain assets outside the probate process. This can be done in several ways, including holding property as a joint tenancy,

CHAPTER SUMMARY—CONTINUED	
Property Transfers outside the Probate Process—continued	making gifts to children while one is still living, and naming children or others as beneficiaries of pension accounts.
Intestacy Laws	1. Intestacy laws vary widely from state to state. Usually, the law provides that the surviving spouse and children inherit the property of the decedent (after the decedent's debts are paid). The spouse usually will inherit the entire estate if there are no children, one-half of the estate if there is one child, and one-third of the estate if there are two or more children. 2. If there is no surviving spouse or child, then, in order, lineal descendants (grandchildren, brothers and sisters, and—in some states—parents of the decedent) inherit. If there are no lineal descendants, collateral heirs (nieces, nephews, aunts, and uncles of the decedent) inherit.
TRUSTS	
Definition	A trust is any arrangement through which property is transferred from one person to be administered by a trustee for another party's benefit. The essential elements of a trust are (1) a designated beneficiary, (2) a designated trustee, (3) a fund sufficiently identified to enable title to pass to the trustee, and (4) actual delivery to the trustee with the intention of passing title.
Express Trusts	Express trusts are created by expressed terms, usually in writing, and fall into two categories: 1. Inter vivos *trust*—A trust executed by a grantor during his or her lifetime. 2. *Testamentary trust*—A trust created by will and coming into existence on the death of the grantor. 3. *Charitable trust*—A trust designed for the benefit of a public group or the public in general. 4. *Spendthrift trust*—A trust created to provide for the maintenance of a beneficiary by allowing only a certain portion of the total amount to be received by the beneficiary at any one time. 5. *Totten trust*—A trust created when one person deposits funds in his or her own name as a trustee for another.
Implied Trusts	Implied trusts, which are imposed by law in the interests of fairness and justice, include the following: 1. *Resulting trust*—Arises from the conduct of the parties when an *apparent intention* to create a trust is present. 2. *Constructive trust*—Arises by operation of law whenever a transaction takes place in which the person who takes title to property is in equity not entitled to enjoy the beneficial interest therein.
ELDER LAW	
Planning for Disability	Planning for disability often involves one or more of the following: 1. *Durable power of attorney*—This authorizes a person to act on behalf of an incompetent person when he or she becomes incapacitated. 2. *Health-care power of attorney*—This designates a person who will have the power to choose what type of and how much medical treatment a person who is unable to make such a choice will receive. 3. *Living will*—This allows a person to control what medical treatment may be used after a serious accident or illness. Through a living will, a person can designate whether he or she

CHAPTER SUMMARY—CONTINUED

Planning for Disability—continued	wants certain lifesaving procedures to be undertaken in situations in which the treatment will not result in a reasonable quality of life.
Medicaid Planning	The cost of long-term care is a serious problem facing older persons today. Medicaid planning involves transferring to others, such as children and friends, assets that might otherwise have to be forfeited to pay for the cost of nursing-home care.

CASES FOR ANALYSIS

Westlaw. You can access the full text of each case presented below by going to the Westlaw cases on this text's Web site at http://wbl-cs.westbuslaw.com. Each Westlaw case includes the names of all plaintiffs and defendants, the dates on which the case was argued and decided, a brief summary of the issues and decisions in the case, headnotes classifying specific issues in the case according to the West Key Number System, and the court's opinion. Concurring and dissenting opinions, if any, are included as well.

CASE 50.1 REQUIREMENTS FOR A VALID WILL

IN RE ESTATE OF KLAUZER

Supreme Court of South Dakota, 2000.
2000 SD 7,
604 N.W.2d 474.

SABERS, Justice

* * * *

FACTS

On March 26, 1993, Frank [Klauzer] was appointed to act as Guardian and Conservator for his brother, John, who had suffered a severe stroke. In this capacity, Frank was required to inventory, account and manage the property of John and provide an annual accounting of John's estate. Frank was compensated for those services.

On September 9, 1996, John passed away. His estate was valued at $1.4 million. Pursuant to John's will, Frank was appointed personal representative of the estate on October 11, 1996. Wade Klauzer, John's nephew, petitioned for supervised administration and [a South Dakota state] trial court ordered the same.

John's will, dated August 30, 1990, disposed of the majority of his estate in the following residuary clause:

> THIRD: I hereby give, devise and bequeath unto my brother, Thomas Klauzer, my sister, Agnes Blake, my sister, Anna Malenovsky Baker, my brother, Raymond Klauzer, my niece, Jenny Culver, my niece, Judy Klauzer, my niece, Bernice Cunningham, my nephew, Wade Klauzer, my nephew, Jim Klauzer, my niece, Debra Klauzer, friends, Douglas Olson and Fern Olson, and my friends, William Hollister and Shirley Hollister, my brother, Frank Klauzer, and my sister-in-law, Patricia Klauzer, all of my property of every kind and character and wheresoever situated, in equal shares, share and share alike. That should any of the individuals above named predecease me, then their share of my estate shall go to their decedents [descendants] surviving.

On December 22, 1998, the trial court ordered that * * * the residuary clause be distributed in sixteen equal shares * * * . Frank appeals * * * in his personal capacity.

* * * *

Frank argues that the twelve Klauzer relatives named in clause number three should take one share each while friends, Doug and Fern Olson and William and Shirley Hollister, should receive one share per couple resulting in a $\frac{1}{14}$th division of the estate. He relies heavily on what he terms the "grammatical geometrics" of the clause to support his contention: i.e., (1) the placement of the commas between the names of the devisees and the indication of relationship for the twelve heirs, but not for Olsons and Hollisters; [and] (2) the word "and," which connects the spouses' names, is claimed as evidence that John intended for each couple to receive one share * * * .

On the other hand, Olsons and Hollisters argue that all named individuals should take in equal shares resulting in a $\frac{1}{16}$th division of the estate. For support, they point to John's will which: (1) refers to all sixteen heirs as "individuals"; (2) indicates that if any of the "individuals above named" predecease him, their share is to go to their "[descendants] surviving"; and (3) provides that the named parties are to receive his property "in equal shares, share and share alike." * * *

Our goal in interpreting a will is to discern the testator's intent. If the intent is clear from the language used, that intent controls. However, if * * * doubt remains as to decedent's intent, the language used and the circumstances surrounding the execution of the writing will again be examined in light of pertinent rules of construction. Our inquiry is limited to what the testator meant by what he said, not what we think the testator meant to say.

* * * Language is ambiguous when it is reasonably capable of being understood in more than one sense. *An ambiguity is not of itself created simply because the parties differ as to the interpretation of the will.* * * * All the words and provisions appearing in a will must be given effect as far as possible, and none should be cast aside as meaningless. * * * [Emphasis added.]

The third clause in John's will, as set forth above, names each individual followed by their relationship to John. Olsons and Hollisters are referenced as follows: "friends, Douglas Olson and Fern Olson, and my friends, William Hollister and Shirley Hollister * * * ." Each spouse is named as an individual. They are not referred to as "Mr. and Mrs. Olson" nor as "William and Shirley Hollister."

The clause contains other language to support the position that John intended that his estate be divided sixteen ways versus fourteen ways. After naming all sixteen individuals, the clause provides that they should receive his property "in equal shares, share and share alike. That should any of the *individuals* above named predecease me, then their share of my estate shall go to their [descendants] surviving."

First, John refers to his friends as individuals. Second, he requests that they receive his property "in equal shares, share and share alike." Third, he states that if one individual predeceases him, his or her share "shall go to their [descendants] surviving." In this regard, it is important to point out that married couples may have different descendants.

We determine that the testator's intent is clearly expressed within the four corners of the document. We are bound by the unambiguous language of the will. * * *

* * * *

The structure and language of the clause itself * * * convince us that John intended to leave one share to Douglas Olson, one share to Fern Olson, one share to William Hollister and one share to Shirley Hollister. Therefore, we affirm the trial court's order to distribute the estate in sixteen equal shares.

CASE 50.2 PROPERTY TRANSFERS OUTSIDE THE PROBATE PROCESS

BIELAT V. BIELAT

Supreme Court of Ohio, 2000.
87 Ohio St.3d 350,
721 N.E.2d 28.

COOK, J. [Justice]

* * * *

This case concerns the legal effect of two actions taken by a decedent prior to the effective date of Ohio's Transfer-on-Death Security Registration Act. First, in 1983, Chester S. Bielat opened an Individual Retirement Account ("IRA") with Merrill Lynch, Pierce, Fenner & Smith, Inc. In the "Adoption Agreement" that he signed to open this account, Chester named his sister, Stella, as the beneficiary of the account's balance upon his death. Shortly thereafter, Chester made a will containing a clause giving all of his property to his wife, Dorothy, upon his death.

In 1993, three years before Chester's death, the [Ohio] General Assembly codified Ohio's version of the Uniform Transfer-on-Death Security Registration Act ("Act"). The Act provides, *inter alia* [among other things], that "[a]ny transfer-on-death resulting from a registration in beneficiary form * * * is *not testamentary*." Accordingly, the Act removes such transfers on death from the decedent's *testamentary* estate * * * .

Soon after Chester's death in 1996, Dorothy discovered that Chester had named Stella the beneficiary of his IRA. Dorothy filed a complaint in [an Ohio state probate court], seeking a declaratory judgment that she, not Stella, was entitled to the IRA proceeds. * * * Dorothy argued that the Act could not *constitutionally* apply retroactively to Chester's IRA beneficiary clause, which was signed a decade prior to the effective date of the Act. * * *

* * * [T]he probate court ordered the balance of the IRA to pass to Stella under the terms of the beneficiary clause that Mr. Bielat had signed in 1983.

Dorothy appealed this judgment to [a state intermediate appellate court]. * * * The court of appeals affirmed the probate court's decision * * * .

The cause is now before this court * * * .

* * * *

* * * [T]he Ohio Constitution prohibits the General Assembly from passing retroactive laws and protects vested rights from new legislative encroachments. *The retroactivity clause nullifies those new laws that reach back and create new burdens, new duties, new obligations, or new liabilities not existing at the time the statute becomes effective.* [Emphasis added.]

* * * *

I

Because [there is] a presumption that statutes are prospective in operation, our inquiry into whether a statute may constitutionally be applied retrospectively continues only after a threshold finding that the General Assembly expressly intended the statute to apply retrospectively. In this case, by its own terms, [the Act] applies to registrations of securities made "prior to, on, or after" the effective date of the Act. When [its provisions] are read together, therefore, the Act declares that transfers on death resulting from those registrations in beneficiary form described therein are *always* nontestamentary [not part of a will], even if such registrations were made before the statute's effective date. The Act became effective on October 1, 1993, and Chester designated Stella as his IRA beneficiary a decade earlier, in 1983. The General Assembly expressly intended for the Act to reach back in time and apply to Chester's 1983 designation of Stella as his IRA beneficiary.

II

* * * *

* * * Dorothy claims that by reaching back in time and declaring Chester's 1983 beneficiary clause to be nontestamentary, the Act impaired her "right" as the sole beneficiary of Chester's will to take the IRA account balance as part of Chester's probate estate upon his death. Dorothy correctly notes that the constitutional limitations on laws affecting substantive rights prohibit statutes that take away or impair rights, create new obligations, impose new duties, or attach new disabilities with respect to transactions already past.

Ohio courts have consistently held, however, that in order for a retroactive law to unconstitutionally impair a right, not just any asserted "right" will suffice. * * * [A] later enactment will not burden or attach a new disability to a past transaction or consideration in the constitutional sense, *unless the past transaction or consideration, if it did not create a vested right, created at least a reasonable expectation of finality.* * * *

Dorothy cannot claim a vested right to the proceeds of the IRA under the law of contracts, for she was in no way connected to the IRA Adoption Agreement that Mr. Bielat executed with Merrill Lynch. * * * The Adoption Agreement signed by Mr. Bielat and Merrill Lynch placed valid contractual obligations upon them, with Merrill Lynch bound to pay the IRA balance to the beneficiary that Chester designated. The IRA Adoption Agreement created no rights or obligations for Dorothy. Dorothy thus had no vested *contractual* right impaired by the retroactive application of the disputed statutes; she had no contractual rights to impair.

Likewise, at the time of the Act's effective date, Dorothy had no vested right to the IRA proceeds as the sole beneficiary under Chester's will. * * * Until a * * * will has been probated * * *, the legatee under such will has no rights whatever. A mere expectation of property in the future is not a vested right. Because Dorothy's asserted "rights" as an expectant beneficiary of Chester's estate did not vest until his death in 1996, her claim that the 1993 Act retroactively impaired her vested rights is untenable. If Dorothy had no vested rights in the contract that Mr. Bielat executed with Merrill Lynch, and no vested rights in Chester's probate estate until his death, then the Act did not impair any vested rights of hers when it applied retrospectively to validate the pay-on-death beneficiary clause in Chester's preexisting contract with Merrill Lynch.

* * * *

III

* * * Dorothy [also] advances an argument separate from her retroactivity claim. Dorothy submits that to resolve this dispute, we should apply the law in effect at the time Mr. Bielat executed his will, since that is the law that frames the intent of the testator. Dorothy argues that since Chester executed his will prior to the existence of the Act, he must have done so with the expectation that the designation of Stella as the transfer-on-death beneficiary of his IRA was void, since the Act was not yet in place to explicitly validate it. We are not persuaded by this argument. [This argument] represents a correct statement of the law of interpreting wills, but we are not interpreting Chester's will in this case. This is not a will contest action, where the true intent of the testator may be at the heart of the dispute, nor is it a situation where an unclear testamentary provision requires construction by the court. Rather, we are faced with two equally unambiguous acts by Mr. Bielat: (1) the designation of his sister Stella as the beneficiary of his IRA in his contract with Merrill Lynch, and (2) the clause in his will leaving all of his property to Dorothy.

IV

* * * *

For the foregoing reasons, we hold that * * * Ohio's Transfer-on-Death Security Registration Act, as applied to the pay- on-death beneficiary designation in an Individual Retirement Account created prior to the Act's effective date, do not violate the prohibition against retroactive laws in * * * the Ohio Constitution.

Judgment affirmed.

CASE 50.3 CONSTRUCTIVE TRUSTS

ZEIGLER V. CARDONA

United States District Court,
Middle District of Alabama, 1993.
830 F.Supp. 1395.

DE MENT, District Judge.

* * * *

FINDINGS OF FACT

The court finds from the evidence that on or about March 26, 1990, Antonio Suarez, Sr., applied for life insurance on his life in the amount of $50,000.00 with Liberty National Life Insurance Company. The agent taking the application was Winifred Hamilton. Liberty National issued policy number * * * 30798355 effective April 1, 1990. At the time of the issuance of the policy, the only beneficiary listed on the policy of insurance was Guarina Cardona. Guarina Cardona is the mother of the insured, Antonio Suarez, Sr. Ms. Cardona is the grandmother of the two minor children represented by a guardian *ad litem* in this case, *viz.:* Antonio Suarez, Jr., who is nine years old and Ebony Suarez, who is eight years old. * * *

The court finds that in May or June of 1990, Mr. Suarez was a resident of Clanton, Alabama. Mr. Suarez was living in the home of Ruby Zeigler, his aunt by marriage. The evidence reveals that during that time there was a meeting between Ms. Zeigler, Mr. Suarez and Winifred Hamilton. The evidence indicates that at that time, Mr. Suarez attempted to change the primary beneficiary of the Liberty National policy to Ruby Zeigler * * * .

At the time of the discussion regarding changing the beneficiary, Mr. Suarez made a statement to both Ms. Zeigler and Ms. Hamilton that shows he intended that the proceeds of the policy, in the event of his death, be *utilized for the benefit of his two minor children*. There is also evidence, and the court finds that Ms. Zeigler agreed, that the money would be used for the benefit of Mr. Suarez's minor children. * * *

Ms. Zeigler provided a home for Mr. Suarez for a period of three months or more. There is further evidence that Ms. Zeigler maintained the policy in force and paid the premiums during the time that Mr. Suarez lived with her and subsequent to the time Mr. Suarez was incarcerated.

* * * *

According to the Liberty National records, effective as of June 5, 1990, the decedent made a change in the beneficiary designation; however, the change showed only that Ruby Zeigler was made a contingent beneficiary on the Suarez policy. The records reflect that Ms. Guarina Cardona remained the primary beneficiary. The evidence shows however that on June 5, 1990, the decedent was not living at his address to which the letter was addressed.

Taken as a whole, the evidence indicates that although Mr. Suarez intended to change his primary beneficiary, the Liberty National records never properly reflected the change due to a clerical error.

CONCLUSIONS OF LAW

The Change of Beneficiary Issue

* * * *As it relates to changing of beneficiaries, the law of equity regards as having been done that which ought to be done* and the courts will give effect to the intention of the insured by holding that a change of beneficiary has been accomplished where he or she has done all that he or she could do in order to comply with the provisions of the policy. The beneficiary of an insurance policy may be effectively changed if the insured substantially complies with the provisions of the policy for such change of beneficiary. The test of substantial compliance is whether the insured has done everything that he could do to make that change. [Emphasis added.]

In this case, Mr. Suarez met with his insurance agent and requested that the change be made in the beneficiary. Mr. Suarez signed the form necessary to effectuate the change and left it to the agent to submit the form on his behalf. The court is satisfied that due to a clerical error on the part of Liberty National, the beneficiary designation was not correctly changed to reflect the intent of Mr. Suarez.

Based upon these facts and conclusions of law, it is the court's opinion that Mr. Suarez did all that he could do in order to effectuate the change to name Ruby Zeigler as his primary beneficiary. Having found that Mrs. Zeigler is the proper beneficiary on the policy, the court now directs its attention to the issue of constructive trust.

The Constructive Trust Issue

In this case, the minor children of Antonio Suarez, Sr., contend that the proceeds of the policy should be subject to a constructive trust. The evidence is undisputed that Mr. Suarez wanted the proceeds of his life insurance policy to go to the benefit of the children. * * * The children clearly have an equitable interest in the proceeds of the policy since it was their father's intent that the policy proceeds be used for them. A constructive trust may be imposed on life insurance proceeds even though the designated beneficiary is not guilty of fraud or wrongdoing. The court finds that to allow the total proceeds to be turned over to Mrs. Zeigler would not be honoring or effectuating the intent of Mr. Suarez, nor would it comply with the agreement that Mr. Suarez had with Mrs. Zeigler at the time he made her the primary beneficiary of the policy. Although the court does not find actual or intentional fraud on the part of Mrs. Zeigler, *a constructive trust may be imposed to prevent unjust enrichment, without regard to actual fraud.* * * * [Emphasis added.]

The court hereby finds that Mrs. Zeigler did in fact provide a service to Mr. Suarez by providing him with a home and paying the premiums on his life insurance policy for a period of time. Therefore, the court feels that Mrs. Zeigler is entitled to some benefit for her efforts and hereby grants to Mrs. Zeigler the sum of $10,000.00 from the insurance proceeds. The court imposes a constructive trust for the use and benefit of Antonio Suarez, Jr., and Ebony Suarez, on the remainder of the life insurance proceeds * * * . The proceeds of the trust will be administered according to the laws of the State of Alabama by the Probate Court of the county in which said children reside.

CASE PROBLEMS

50–1. H. W. Wolfe died at the age of sixty-seven, leaving personal property worth about $4,000 and more than five hundred acres of land. On July 31, 1911, not long before he died, he properly executed a will that contained the following provision: "I, H. W. Wolfe, will and bequeath to Miss Mary Lilly Luffman, a tract of land near Roaring Gap Post Office, on State Road and South Fork, adjoining the lands of J. M. Royal and others, the land bought by me from H. D. Woodruff. Witness my hand and seal, this thirty-first day of July, 1911." On August 14, 1911, Wolfe wrote another will that provided in part: "I, H. W. Wolfe, do make and declare this to be my last will and testament. I will and bequeath all my effects to my brothers and sisters, to be divided equally among them. Witness my hand and seal, this the fourteenth day of August, 1911." Both wills were properly signed and attested. Who was entitled to what under these wills? [*In re Wolfe's Will,* 185 N.C. 563, 117 S.E. 804 (1923)]

50–2. Tennie Joyner was eighty years old and about to be hospitalized for an illness. To provide for her son, Calvin, Joyner wrote a will and took it to her neighbors for them to type and witness. In the document, she stated that she was giving all her possessions to Calvin because he had taken care of her for years. The will was contested on the basis that Joyner had not met the formal requirement of publication, because she did not tell her neighbors explicitly that the document was her "last will and testament." Joyner had merely told her neighbors that she wanted "a piece of paper fixed up so I can sign it and Calvin will have a place to live." Joyner intended the document to dispose of her property, and the neighbors were fully aware of her intention. Does Joyner's failure to state "this is my last will and testament" invalidate the will? Explain. [*Faith v. Singleton,* 286 Ark. 403, 692 S.W.2d 239 (1985)]

50–3. In 1956, Jack Adams executed a will, the terms of which established a charitable trust. The trust income was to go to the Prince Edward School Foundation as long as the foundation continued to operate and admitted to its schools "only members of the White Race." If the foundation admitted nonwhites to its schools, the trust income was to go to the Miller School, under the same limitation, and so on to two other educational institutions. If all of the successively named educational beneficiaries violated the limitation, the income would go to Hermitage Methodist Homes of Virginia, Inc., without any limitation attending the bequest. In 1968, Adams died. Subsequent to the execution of the will, all of the educational beneficiaries enrolled African American students. The trustee, uncertain as to how to distribute the trust income under these circumstances, sought counsel from the court. Assuming that the racially discriminatory provisions are unconstitutional and void, which, if any, of the named beneficiaries should receive the trust income? Discuss. [*Hermitage Methodist Homes of Virginia, Inc. v. Dominion Trust Co.,* 387 S.E.2d 740 (Va. 1990)]

50–4. An elderly, childless widow had nine nieces and nephews. Her will divided her entire estate equally among two nieces and the husband of one of the nieces, who was also the attorney-draftsman of the will and the executor named in the will. The testator was definitely of sound mind when the will was executed. If you were one of the seven nieces or nephews omitted from the will, could you think of any way to have the will invalidated? [*Estate of Eckert,* 93 Misc.2d 677, 403 N.Y.S.2d 633 (Surrogate's Ct. 1978)]

50–5. Louie Villwok died on November 12, 1984, leaving an executed will that left everything to his present wife, Rose. If Rose had predeceased him, according to the will, his three daughters from a previous marriage would have received a general bequest of money and a portion of the residue of the estate. When the will was offered for probate, the decedent's daughters contested the will. They claimed, among other things, that the will was a result of undue influence on the part of Rose. At the hearing, the daughters presented evidence to show that after Rose married the decedent, the relationship between her and the decedent's children deteriorated; that the decedent drank heavily on a daily basis and was intoxicated most of the time; and that Rose made concerted efforts to come between the decedent and his daughters. Each daughter also testified that her father had made statements to her expressly indicating that he did not want Rose or her children to have his property and that he wanted his daughters to receive all of his property. The probate court entered summary judgment in favor of Rose. What will the appellate court decide? Discuss fully. [*In re Estate of Villwok,* 226 Neb. 693, 413 N.W.2d 921 (1987)]

50–6. Paula Thomas was formerly married to Charles Fales. During their marriage, Charles sold illegal drugs and frequently possessed large amounts of cash resulting from those transactions. To avoid the increasing scrutiny of a neighbor (a police officer), Charles decided to purchase a home (the Winslow property) in another area in September 1983. Allegedly to avert suspicion concerning his drug activity, Charles had his brother Steven purchase the property in Steven's name. Charles, however, provided Steven with the money for the down payment, and Charles and Paula lived in the home and paid the mortgage payments and all other expenses. Eventually, Paula separated from Charles; she left the home, and it was rented to a third party. In 1988, Paula and Charles divorced, and the divorce judgment awarded her all of their right, title, and interest in the Winslow property. Steven refused to convey the property to Paula, contending that he was the legal owner. Paula then brought an action seeking the imposition of a constructive trust on the Winslow property and an order that legal title be conveyed to her. Should the court impose a constructive trust on the Winslow property for Paula's benefit? Discuss fully. [*Thomas v. Fales,* 577 A.2d 1181 (Me. 1990)]

50–7. Billy Putman rented and occupied a house trailer owned by Douglas Sanders. Because Putman damaged the trailer while it was in his possession, Sanders sought and acquired a judgment against Putman for $2,429.36 in damages, plus court costs and interest. Sanders garnished Putman's bank account and learned of a certificate of deposit (CD) worth $20,000, which was held by a trustee (Georgia Putman) on behalf of Billy as the beneficiary. The CD had been purchased with the proceeds from Billy's deceased father's life insurance policy. Sanders claimed that the insurance proceeds—the CD—could be garnished. Putman argued that the CD funds were part of a spendthrift trust and therefore could not be reached by creditors, including Sanders. The only evidence in support of a spendthrift trust was the insurance company's check made payable to Billy Putman's trustee. How should the court decide? Explain. [*Sanders v. Putman,* 315 Ark. 251, 866 S.W.2d 827 (1993)]

50–8. Edwin Fickes died in 1943. His will provided for the creation of a trust, half of which was to be divided, on the death of Fickes's last surviving child, "in equal portions between [the testator's] grandchildren then living." At the time of the death of Fickes's last surviving child, there were four biological grandchildren and four adopted grandchildren living. Two of the adopted grandchildren, both boys, had been adopted prior to Fickes's death. The other two, both girls, had been adopted after Fickes died. The trustee, Connecticut National Bank and Trust Co., sought a court determination of whether the adopted grandchildren were entitled to share in the trust distribution. The trial court found that the testator, Fickes, had intended to include his adopted grandsons as "grandchildren" within the meaning of his will but could not have intended to include his adopted granddaughters as "grandchildren," so they were not entitled to a share of the trust. What will happen on appeal? Discuss fully. [*Connecticut National Bank and Trust Co. v. Chadwick,* 217 Conn. 260, 585 A.2d 1189 (1991)]

50–9. In the last fourteen years of Evelyn Maheras's life, William Cook, a Baptist pastor, became her spiritual adviser and close personal friend. Cook—and no one else—actively participated in helping Maheras draft her will. He gave Maheras a church-sponsored booklet on will drafting, recommended an attorney (a church member) to do the drafting, and reviewed the terms of the will with Maheras. When Maheras died, she left most of her estate to Cook's church. Cook personally received nothing under the will. Maheras's nephew and only heir, Richard Suagee, filed a suit against Cook in an Oklahoma state court to contest the will, arguing that Cook had unduly influenced Maheras. Can a party who receives nothing under a will be regarded as having exercised undue influence over the testator? What should the court in Maheras's case do? [*Estate of Maheras,* 897 P.2d 268 (Okla. 1995)]

50–10. Robert and Everett Kling, two brothers, purchased rental property in Fenton, Missouri. Robert contributed $5,544 and Everett, $5,624 toward the purchase price of $19,005. Title to the property was taken in the name of Everett's wife, Nancy. The brothers maintained an account in which they made deposits and from which they paid expenses related to the rental property. Although each brother had agreed to contribute $20 per month toward the remaining purchase price, Robert never did do so, and Everett consequently increased his contribution to $40 per month. When Robert died, Everett and Nancy claimed 100 percent ownership of the Fenton property. Robert's children, John and Janet, filed suit, claiming that Everett and Nancy held the property as a resulting trust and that they (John and Janet) were entitled to half of the property. Discuss whether a resulting trust had been created and, if so, what the distribution should be. [*Estate of Kling,* 736 S.W.2d 65 (Mo.App. 1987)]

50–11. Myrtle Courziel executed a valid will that provided for the establishment of a scholarship fund designed to encourage the study of corrosion as it affects metallurgical engineering. The recipients were to be students in the upper half of their classes at the University of Alabama. Subsequently, Courziel died. John Calhoun, the eventual administrator of her estate, obtained access to Courziel's safe-deposit box to search for her will. He found the will intact, except that the last page of the will, which had contained Courziel's signature and the signatures of the witnesses, had been removed from the document and was not in the safe-deposit box or anywhere else to be found. Because Courziel had had sole control over the will, should it be presumed that by removing the last page of the will (or allowing it to be removed), she effectively revoked the will? [*Board of Trustees of University of Alabama v. Calhoun,* 514 So.2d 895 (Ala. 1987)]

50–12. Gail MacCallum was the daughter of Anita Seymour. After the death of Gail's father, Anita married Richard Seymour, who adopted Gail the next year, when she was seven years old. The same year, Janet Seymour was born to Richard and Anita. Almost forty years later, when Richard's brother Philip died, both

Gail and Janet sought to share in the estate. A Vermont state court concluded that Gail could not share in the estate because a state statute prohibited "inheritance between the person adopted . . . and collateral kin of the person or persons making the adoption." Gail appealed, arguing that the statute was unconstitutional. Will the court agree? Discuss fully. [*MacCallum v. Seymour,* 686 A.2d. 935 (Vt. 1996)]

50–13. William Laneer urged his son, also William, to join the family business. The son, who was made partner, became suspicious of the handling of the business's finances. He filed a suit against the business and reported it to the Internal Revenue Service. Laneer then executed a will that disinherited his son, giving him one dollar and leaving the balance of the estate equally to Laneer's four daughters, including Bellinda Barrera. Until his death more than twenty years later, Laneer harbored ill feelings toward his son. After Laneer's death, his original copy of the will could not be found. A photocopy was found in his safe-deposit box, however, and his lawyer's original copy was entered for probate in an Arkansas state court. Barrera, who wanted her brother William to share an equal portion of the inheritance, filed a petition to contest the will. Barrera claimed, among other things, that Laneer had revoked the will, and that was why his original copy of the will could not be found. Was the will revoked? If so, to whom would the estate be distributed? [*Barrera v. Vanpelt,* 332 Ark. 482, 965 S.W.2d 780 (1998)]

50–14. Rose Martin died in 1995. At the time, she owned thirty-five of the eighty outstanding shares in Refrigeration Supplies Distributors, Inc. (RSD), a family business that had existed for ninety years. Rose's daughter Alice Karlebach, an RSD officer and director, owned five RSD shares. Karlebach was appointed executor of Rose's estate. Karlebach hired Cronkite & Roda (C&R), an independent professional appraiser, to determine the value of the shares. C&R determined that Rose's RSD shares were worth $9.7 million, or approximately $277,142.86 per share, on the date of Rose's death. To pay the estate's taxes, Karlebach sold 22.5 of the estate's RSD shares to RSD for $6.235 million. Patrick Martin was Rose's grandson, Alice's nephew, and a beneficiary of one-sixth of the residuary estate. Martin filed a petition with the California state probate court that was overseeing the administration of the estate to void the sale of the shares. Martin contended that Karlebach had breached her fiduciary duty to act in the best interests of the estate. How should the court rule? Why? [*Estate of Martin,* 72 Cal.App.4th 148, 86 Cal.Rptr.2d 37 (2 Dist. 1999)]

50–15. A QUESTION OF ETHICS

Heber Burke and his wife Evelyn spent most of their lives in Ohio and jointly accumulated a substantial amount of property there. When Evelyn died in February 1985, the Burkes had been married for fifty-three years and had two children, four grandchildren, and four great-grandchildren. Heber had originally hailed from Pike County, Kentucky, and in June 1985, he returned to Pike County and bought a house there. In the same month, he told his children that he was going to marry Lexie Damron, a widow who attended his church. Lexie and Heber were married on July 20. On July 27, Heber executed a will, which was drawn up by Lexie's attorney, in which he left all of his property to Lexie. Heber died three weeks later. Heber's children, Donald Burke and Beatrice Bates, contested the will, alleging that Heber had lacked testamentary capacity and that Heber's will had resulted from Lexie's undue influence over him. Friends and relatives of Heber in Pike County testified that they had never known Heber to drink and that, although he seemed saddened by his first wife's death, he was not incapacitated by it. According to the children's witnesses, however, after Evelyn's death, Heber allegedly drank heavily and constantly; had frequent crying spells; repeatedly visited his wife's grave; tried to dig her up so that he could talk to her; and had hallucinations, talking to people who were not present and claiming that Evelyn visited him regularly at night, which frightened him into sleeping in the attic. The jury found the will to be invalid on the grounds of undue influence, and Lexie appealed. [*Burke v. Burke,* 801 S.W.2d 691 (Ken.App. 1990)]

1. The appellate court had to weigh two conflicting policies in deciding this issue. What two policies are in conflict here, and what criteria should be used in resolving the matter?
2. Given the circumstances described above, would you infer undue influence on Lexie's part if you were the judge? Would you conclude that Heber lacked testamentary capacity? What would be the fairest solution, in your opinion?
3. Heber's first wife, Evelyn, contributed substantially to the acquisition of the property subject to Heber's will. A natural assumption is that Evelyn would have wanted their children to inherit the jointly acquired property. Yet if the court found that Heber was of sound mind and not the victim of any undue influence, it would let stand a will that totally disregarded the children. Is this fair to Evelyn's presumed intentions? To the children? Is there any solution to the possible unfairness that can result from giving people the right to disregard natural heirs in their wills?

E-LINKS

For updated links to resources available on the Web, as well as a variety of other materials, visit this text's Web site at

http://wbl-cs.westbuslaw.com

The wills of various historical figures and celebrities, including Elvis Presley, Jacqueline Kennedy Onassis, and Richard Nixon, are online at

http://www.ca-probate.com/wills.htm

The Senior Law Web site offers information on a variety of topics, including elder law, estate planning, and trusts. The URL for this site is

http://www.seniorlaw.com

You can find the Uniform Probate Code, as well as links to various state probate statutes, at Cornell Law University's Legal Information Institute. Go to

http://www.law.cornell.edu/uniform/probate.html

LEGAL RESEARCH EXERCISES ON THE WEB

Go to http://wbl-cs.westbuslaw.com, the Web site that accompanies this text. Select "Interactive Study Center," and then click on "Chapter 50." There you will find the following Internet research exercises that you can perform to learn more about wills, trusts, and elder law:

Activity 50–1: Wills and Trusts

Activity 50–2: Elder Law

CHAPTER 51

Liability of Accountants and Other Professionals

PROFESSIONALS SUCH AS ACCOUNTANTS, attorneys, physicians, architects, and others are increasingly faced with the threat of liability. Perhaps this is due to a greater public awareness of the fact that professionals are required to deliver competent services and are obligated to adhere to standards of performance commonly accepted within their professions.

Considering the many potential sources of legal liability that may be imposed on them, accountants, attorneys, and other professionals should be well aware of their legal obligations. In the first part of this chapter, we look at the potential liability of professionals under the common law and then examine the potential liability of accountants under securities laws and the Internal Revenue Code. The chapter concludes with a brief examination of other topics of concern for professionals, including rights to working papers, professional-client privilege, and the increasing use of the limited liability partnership by accountants and other professionals to limit their tort liability.

SECTION 1

Common Law Liability to Clients

Under the common law, professionals may be liable to clients for breach of contract, negligence, or fraud.

LIABILITY FOR BREACH OF CONTRACT

Accountants and other professionals face liability for any breach of contract under the common law. A professional owes a duty to his or her client to honor the terms of the contract and to perform the contract within the stated time period. If the professional fails to perform as agreed in the contract, he or she has breached the contract, and the client has the right to recover damages from the professional. A professional may be held liable for expenses incurred by his or her client in securing another professional to provide the contracted-for services, for penalties imposed on the client for failure to meet time deadlines, and for any other reasonable and foreseeable monetary losses that arise from the professional's breach.

LIABILITY FOR NEGLIGENCE

Accountants and other professionals may also be held liable under the common law for negligence in the performance of their services. As with any negligence claim, the elements that must be proved to establish negligence on the part of a professional are as follows:

1. A duty of care existed.
2. That duty of care was breached.
3. The plaintiff suffered an injury.
4. The injury was proximately caused by the defendant's breach of the duty of care.

All professionals are subject to standards of conduct established by codes of professional standards and ethics, by state statutes, and by judicial decisions. They are also governed by the contracts into which they enter with their clients. In their performance of contracts, professionals must exercise the established standard of care, knowledge, and judgment generally accepted by members of their professional group. We look below at the duty of care owed by two groups of professionals that frequently perform services for business firms: accountants and attorneys.

Accountant's Duty of Care. Accountants play a major role in a business's financial system. Accountants have the necessary expertise and experience in establishing and maintaining accurate financial records to design, control, and audit record-keeping systems; to prepare reliable statements that reflect an individual's or a business's financial status; and to give tax advice and prepare tax returns.

An *audit* is a systematic inspection, by analyses and tests, of a business's financial records. The purpose of an audit is to provide the auditor with evidence to support an opinion on the fairness of the business's financial statements. A normal audit is not intended to uncover fraud or other misconduct. An accountant may be liable for failing to detect misconduct, however, if a normal audit would have revealed it or the auditor agreed to examine the records for evidence of fraud or other misconduct.

After performing an audit, the auditor issues an opinion letter stating whether, in his or her opinion, the financial statements fairly present the business's financial position. The opinion letter is said to certify the financial statements. Normally, an auditor issues an *unqualified opinion,* which means that the audit and the financial statements comply with the principles and standards discussed in the next section.

Standard of Care. Generally, an accountant must possess the skills that an ordinarily prudent accountant would have and must exercise the degree of care that an ordinarily prudent accountant would exercise. The level of skill expected of accountants and the degree of care that they should exercise in performing their services are reflected in what are known as **generally accepted accounting principles (GAAP)** and **generally accepted auditing standards (GAAS).** The Financial Accounting Standards Board (FASB, usually pronounced "faz-bee") determines what accounting conventions, rules, and procedures constitute GAAP at a given point in time. GAAS are standards concerning an auditor's professional qualities and the judgment that he or she exercises in auditing financial records. GAAS are established by the American Institute of Certified Public Accountants. GAAP and GAAS are also reflected in the rules established by the Securities and Exchange Commission (see Chapter 37).

As long as an accountant conforms to GAAP and acts in good faith, he or she normally will not be held liable to the client for incorrect judgment. As mentioned above, an accountant is not required to discover every impropriety, **defalcation**[1] (embezzlement), or fraud in a client's books. If, however, the impropriety, defalcation, or fraud has gone undiscovered because of an accountant's negligence or failure to perform an express or implied duty, the accountant will be liable for any resulting losses suffered by the client. Therefore, an accountant who uncovers suspicious financial transactions and fails to investigate the matter fully or to inform his or her client of the discovery can be held liable to the client for the resulting loss.

A violation of GAAP and GAAS will be considered *prima facie* evidence of negligence on the part of the accountant. Compliance with GAAP and GAAS, however, does not necessarily relieve an accountant from potential legal liability. An accountant may be held to a higher standard of conduct established by state statute and by judicial decisions. If an accountant is found to have been negligent in the performance of accounting services for a client, the client may collect damages for any losses that arose from the accountant's negligence.

Defenses to Negligence. Accountants have several defenses available. Possible defenses include the following allegations:

1. The accountant was not negligent.
2. If the accountant was negligent, this negligence was not the proximate cause of the client's losses.
3. The client was also negligent (depending on whether state law allows contributory negligence or comparative negligence as a defense—see Chapter 5).

Qualified Opinions and Disclaimers. In issuing an opinion letter, an auditor may qualify the opinion or include a disclaimer. An auditor will not be held liable for damages resulting from whatever is qualified or disclaimed. An opinion that disclaims any liability for false or misleading financial statements is too general, however. A qualified opinion or a disclaimer must be specific. For example, an auditor might qualify an opinion, in an audit of a corporation, by stating that there is uncertainty about how a lawsuit against the firm will be resolved. The auditor will not be liable if the result of the suit is bad for the firm. The auditor could still be liable, however, for failing

1. This term, pronounced deh-ful-*kay*-shun, is derived from the Latin *de* ("off") and *falx* ("sickle"—a tool for cutting grain or tall grass). In law, the term refers to the act of a defaulter or of an embezzler. As used here, it means embezzlement.

to discover other problems that an audit in compliance with GAAS and GAAP would have revealed.

Unaudited Financial Statements. Sometimes accountants are hired to prepare unaudited financial statements. (A financial statement is considered unaudited if no auditing procedures have been used in its preparation or if insufficient procedures have been used to justify an opinion.) Accountants may be subject to liability for failing, in accordance with standard accounting procedures, to designate a balance sheet as "unaudited." An accountant will also be held liable for failure to disclose to a client facts or circumstances that give reason to believe that misstatements have been made or that a fraud has been committed.

Attorney's Duty of Care. The conduct of attorneys is governed by rules established by each state and by the American Bar Association's Model Rules of Professional Conduct. All attorneys owe a duty to provide competent and diligent representation. Attorneys are required to be familiar with well-settled principles of law applicable to a case and to discover law that can be found through a reasonable amount of research. The lawyer also must investigate and discover facts that could materially affect the client's legal rights.

Standard of Care. In judging an attorney's performance, the standard used will normally be that of a reasonably competent general practitioner of ordinary skill, experience, and capacity. If an attorney holds himself or herself out as having expertise in a special area of law (for example, domestic relations), the attorney's standard of care in that area is higher than for attorneys without such expertise.

Liability for Malpractice. When an attorney fails to exercise reasonable care and professional judgment, he or she breaches the duty of care and can be held liable for *malpractice* (professional negligence). In malpractice cases—as in all cases involving allegations of negligence—the plaintiff must prove that the attorney's breach of the duty of care actually caused the plaintiff to suffer some injury. For example, if the attorney allows the statute of limitations to lapse on a client's claim, he or she can be held liable for malpractice because the client can no longer file a cause of action in this case and has lost a potential award of damages.

Traditionally, to establish causation, the client normally had to show that "but for" the attorney's negligence, the client would not have suffered the injury. In recent years, however, several courts have held that plaintiffs in malpractice cases need only show that the defendant's negligence was a "substantial factor" in causing the plaintiff's injury.

LIABILITY FOR FRAUD

Recall from Chapter 13 that fraud, or misrepresentation, consists of the following elements:

1. A misrepresentation of a material fact has occurred.
2. There exists an intent to deceive.
3. The innocent party has justifiably relied on the misrepresentation.
4. For damages, the innocent party must have been injured.

A professional may be held liable for *actual* fraud when he or she intentionally misstates a material fact to mislead his or her client and the client justifiably relies on the misstated fact to his or her injury. A material fact is one that a reasonable person would consider important in deciding whether to act.

In contrast, a professional may be held liable for *constructive* fraud whether or not he or she acted with fraudulent intent. For example, constructive fraud may be found when an accountant is grossly negligent in the performance of his or her duties. The intentional failure to perform a duty in reckless disregard of the consequences of such a failure would constitute gross negligence on the part of a professional.

SECTION 2

Liability to Third Parties

Traditionally, an accountant or other professional only owed a duty to those with whom he or she was in *privity of contract*. (Recall from Chapter 15 that privity of contract refers to the relationship that exists between the promisor and the promisee of a contract.) In other words, a professional owed no duty to a third party outside the contractual relationship—a professional's duty was only to his or her client. Violations of statutory laws, fraud, and other intentional or reckless acts of wrongdoing were the only exceptions to this general rule.

Today, numerous third parties—including investors, shareholders, creditors, corporate managers and directors, regulatory agencies, and others—rely on the opinions of auditors (accountants) when making decisions. In view of this extensive reliance, many courts have all but abandoned the privity requirement in regard to accountants' liability to third parties. Like accountants, attorneys may be held liable under the common law to third parties who rely on legal opinions to their detriment. Generally, however, an attorney is not liable to a nonclient unless there is fraud (or malicious conduct) by the attorney. The liability principles stated in Section 552 of the *Restatement (Second) of Torts* (these principles will be discussed shortly), however, may apply to attorneys just as they apply to accountants.

Understanding an auditor's common law liability to third parties is critical, because when a business fails, its independent auditor may be one of the few potentially solvent defendants. The majority of courts now hold that auditors can be held liable to third parties for negligence, but the standard for the imposition of this liability varies. There are generally three different views of accountants' liability to third parties:

1. Accountants should be liable only to those with whom they are in privity or "near privity" of contract (the *Ultramares* rule).
2. Accountants should be liable to foreseen, or known, users of their reports or financial statements (the *Restatement* rule).
3. Accounts should be liable to those whose use of their reports or financial statements is reasonably foreseeable.

We discuss each of these views here.

THE *ULTRAMARES* RULE

The traditional rule regarding an accountant's liability to third parties was enunciated by Chief Judge Benjamin Cardozo in *Ultramares Corp. v. Touche,*[2] a case decided in 1931. In *Ultramares,* Fred Stern & Company (Stern) hired the public accounting firm of Touche, Niven & Company (Touche) to review Stern's financial records and prepare a balance sheet for the year ending December 31, 1923.[3] Touche prepared the balance sheet and supplied Stern with thirty-two certified copies. According to the certified balance sheet, Stern had a net worth (assets less liabilities) of $1,070,715.26. In reality, however, Stern was insolvent—the company's records had been falsified by insiders at Stern to reflect a positive net worth. In reliance on the certified balance sheets, a lender, Ultramares Corporation, loaned substantial amounts to Stern. After Stern was declared bankrupt, Ultramares brought an action against Touche for negligence in an attempt to recover damages.

The New York Court of Appeals (that state's highest court) refused to impose liability on the accountants and concluded that they owed a duty of care only to those persons for whose "primary benefit" the statements were intended. In this case, Stern was the only one for whose primary benefit the statements were intended. The court held that in the absence of privity or a relationship "so close as to approach that of privity," a party could not recover from an accountant.

The court's requirement of privity has since been referred to as the *Ultramares* rule, or the New York rule. The rule was subsequently modified somewhat by courts in some states that held that if a third party has a sufficiently close relationship or nexus (link or connection) with an accountant, the *Ultramares* privity requirement may be satisfied without the establishment of an accountant-client relationship. This modified rule is often referred to as the "near privity" rule.

THE *RESTATEMENT* RULE

Auditors perform much of their work for use by persons who are not parties to the contract; thus, it is asserted that they owe a duty to these third parties. Consequently, there has been an erosion of the *Ultramares* rule, and accountants have increasingly been exposed to potential liability to third parties.

The majority of courts have adopted the position taken by the *Restatement (Second) of Torts,* which states that accountants are subject to liability for negligence not only to their clients but also to foreseen, or *known,* users—or classes of users—of their reports or financial statements. Under Section 552(2) of the *Restatement (Second) of Torts,* an accountant's liability extends to those persons for whose benefit and guidance the accountant "intends to supply the information or knows that the recipi-

2. 255 N.Y. 170, 174 N.E. 441 (1931).

3. Banks, creditors, stockholders, purchasers, and sellers often rely on balance sheets when making decisions relating to a company's business.

4. Only a minority of states have adopted this rule of accountants' liability to third parties.

ent intends to supply it" and to those persons whom the accountant "intends the information to influence or knows that the recipient so intends." In other words, if an accountant prepares a financial statement for a client and knows that the client will submit that statement to a bank to secure a loan, the accountant may be held liable to the bank for negligent misstatements or omissions—because the accountant knew that the bank would rely on the accountant's work product when deciding whether to make the loan.

Westlaw. See Case 51.1 at the end of this chapter. To view the full, unedited case from Westlaw,® go to this text's Web site at **http://wbl-cs.westbuslaw.com**.

LIABILITY TO REASONABLY FORESEEABLE USERS

A small minority of courts hold accountants liable to any users whose reliance on an accountant's statements or reports was *reasonably foreseeable*. This standard has been criticized as extending liability too far. In *Raritan River Steel Co. v. Cherry, Bekaert & Holland*,[5] for example, the North Carolina Supreme Court stated that "in fairness accountants should not be liable in circumstances where they are unaware of the use to which their opinions will be put. Instead, their liability should be commensurate with those persons or classes of persons whom they know will rely on their work. With such knowledge the auditor can, through purchase of liability insurance, setting fees, and adopting other protective measures appropriate to the risk, prepare accordingly."

The North Carolina court's statement echoes the view of the majority of the courts that the *Restatement*'s approach is the more reasonable one because it allows accountants to control their exposure to liability. Liability is "fixed by the accountants' particular knowledge at the moment the audit is published," not by the foreseeability of the harm that might occur to a third party after the report is released.[6]

Even the California courts, which for years had relied on reasonable foreseeability as the standard for determining an auditor's liability to third parties, have changed their position. In a 1992 case, the California Supreme Court held that an accountant "owes no general duty of care regarding the conduct of an audit to persons other than the client." The court went on to say that if third parties rely on an auditor's opinion, "there is no liability even though the [auditor] should reasonably have foreseen such a possibility."[7]

5. 322 N.C. 200, 367 S.E.2d 609 (1988).

6. *Bethlehem Steel Corp. v. Ernst & Whinney*, 822 S.W.2d 592 (Tenn. 1991).

SECTION 3

Liability of Accountants under Securities Laws

Both civil and criminal liability may be imposed on accountants under the Securities Act of 1933, the Securities Exchange Act of 1934, and the Private Securities Litigation Reform Act of 1995.[8]

LIABILITY UNDER THE SECURITIES ACT OF 1933

The Securities Act of 1933 requires registration statements to be filed with the Securities and Exchange Commission (SEC) prior to an offering of securities (see Chapter 37).[9] Accountants frequently prepare and certify the issuer's financial statements that are included in the registration statement.

Liability under Section 11. Section 11 of the Securities Act of 1933 imposes civil liability on accountants for misstatements and omissions of material facts in registration statements. An accountant may be held liable if he or she prepared any financial statements included in the registration statement that "contained an untrue statement of a material fact or omitted to state a material fact required to be stated therein or necessary to make the statements therein not misleading."[10]

Liability to Purchasers of Securities. An accountant may be liable to anyone who acquires a security covered by the registration statement. A purchaser of a

7. *Bily v. Arthur Young & Co.*, 3 Cal.4th 370, 834 P.2d 745, 11 Cal.Rptr.2d 51 (1992).

8. Civil and criminal liability may be imposed on accountants and other professionals under other statutes, including the Racketeer Influenced and Corrupt Organizations Act (RICO). RICO is discussed in Chapter 8.

9. Many securities and transactions are expressly exempted from the 1933 act.

10. 15 U.S.C. Section 77k(a).

security need only demonstrate that he or she has suffered a loss on the security. Proof of reliance on the materially false statement or misleading omission is not ordinarily required, nor is there a requirement of privity between the accountant and the security purchaser.

The Due Diligence Standard. Section 11 imposes a duty on accountants to use **due diligence** in the preparation of financial statements included in the filed registration statements. After the purchaser has proved the loss on the security, the accountant bears the burden of showing that he or she exercised due diligence in the preparation of the financial statements. To avoid liability, the accountant must show that he or she had, "after reasonable investigation, reasonable grounds to believe and did believe, at the time such part of the registration statement became effective, that the statements therein were true and that there was no omission of a material fact required to be stated therein or necessary to make the statements therein not misleading."[11] Further, the failure to follow GAAP and GAAS is also proof of a lack of due diligence.

In particular, the due diligence standard places a burden on accountants to verify information furnished by a corporation's officers and directors. The burden of proving due diligence requires an accountant to demonstrate that he or she did not commit negligence or fraud. The accountants in *Escott v. BarChris Construction Corp.*,[12] for example, were held liable for a failure to detect danger signals in materials that, under GAAS, required further investigation under the circumstances. Merely asking questions is not always sufficient to satisfy the requirement of due diligence.

Defenses to Liability. Besides proving that he or she has acted with due diligence, an accountant may raise the following defenses to Section 11 liability:

1. There were no misstatements or omissions.
2. The misstatements or omissions were not of material facts.
3. The misstatements or omissions had no causal connection to the plaintiff's loss.
4. The plaintiff purchaser invested in the securities knowing of the misstatements or omissions.

Another defense is that an alleged misstatement or omission was not part of a financial statement that the accountant prepared or certified.

Westlaw. See Case 51.2 at the end of this chapter. To view the full, unedited case from Westlaw,® go to this text's Web site at **http://wbl-cs.westbuslaw.com**.

Liability under Section 12(2). Section 12(2) of the Securities Act of 1933 imposes civil liability for fraud on anyone offering or selling a security to any purchaser of the security.[13] Liability is based on communication to an investor, whether orally or in the written prospectus,[14] of an untrue statement or omission of a material fact.

Penalties and Sanctions for Violations. Those who purchase securities and suffer harm as a result of a false or omitted statement, or some other violation, may bring a suit in a federal court to recover their losses and other damages. The U.S. Department of Justice brings criminal actions against those who commit willful violations. The penalties include fines up to $10,000, imprisonment up to five years, or both. The SEC is authorized to seek, against a willful violator, an injunction against further violations. The SEC can also ask a court to grant other relief, such as an order to a violator to refund profits derived from an illegal transaction.

Liability under the Securities Exchange Act of 1934

Under Sections 18 and 10(b) of the Securities Exchange Act of 1934 and Rule 10b-5 of the Securities and Exchange Commission, an accountant may be found liable for fraud. A plaintiff has a substantially heavier burden of proof under the 1934 act than under the 1933 act. Unlike the 1933 act, which provides that an accountant must prove due diligence to escape liability, the 1934 act relieves an accountant from liability if the accountant acted in "good faith."

Liability under Section 18. Section 18 of the 1934 act imposes civil liability on an accountant who

11. 15 U.S.C. Section 77k(b)(3).
12. 283 F.Supp. 643 (S.D.N.Y. 1968).
13. 15 U.S.C. Section 77l.
14. As discussed in Chapter 34, a *prospectus* contains financial disclosures about the corporation for the benefit of potential investors.

makes or causes to be made in any application, report, or document a statement that at the time and in light of the circumstances was false or misleading with respect to any material fact.[15]

Section 18 liability is narrow in that it applies only to applications, reports, documents, and registration statements filed with the SEC. This remedy is further limited in that it applies only to sellers and purchasers. Under Section 18, a seller or purchaser must prove one of the following:

1. That the false or misleading statement affected the price of the security.
2. That the purchaser or seller relied on the false or misleading statement in making the purchase or sale and was not aware of the inaccuracy of the statement.

Even if a purchaser or seller proves these two elements, an accountant can be exonerated of liability by proving good faith in the preparation of the financial statement. To demonstrate good faith, an accountant must show that he or she had no knowledge that the financial statement was false or misleading. Acting in good faith requires the total absence of an intention on the part of the accountant to seek an unfair advantage over, or to defraud, another party. Proving a lack of intent to deceive, manipulate, or defraud is frequently referred to as proving a lack of *scienter* (knowledge on the part of a misrepresenting party that material facts have been misrepresented or omitted with an intent to deceive).

The absence of good faith can be demonstrated not only by proof of *scienter* but also by the accountant's reckless conduct and gross negligence. (Note that "mere" negligence in the preparation of a financial statement does not constitute liability under the 1934 act. This differs from provisions of the 1933 act, under which an accountant is liable for all negligent actions.) In addition to the good faith defense, accountants have available as a defense the buyer's or seller's knowledge that the financial statement was false or misleading.

Under Section 18 of the 1934 act, a court also has the discretion to assess reasonable costs, including attorneys' fees, against accountants.[16] Sellers and purchasers may maintain a cause of action "within one year after the discovery of the facts constituting the cause of action and within three years after such cause of action accrued."[17]

Liability under Section 10(b) and SEC Rule 10b-5. The Securities Exchange Act of 1934 further subjects accountants to potential legal liability in its antifraud provisions. Section 10(b) of the 1934 act and SEC Rule 10b-5 contain the antifraud provisions. As stated in *Herman & MacLean v. Huddleston,*[18] "a private right of action under Section 10(b) of the 1934 act and Rule 10b-5 has been consistently recognized for more than 35 years."

Section 10(b) makes it unlawful for any person, including accountants, to use, in connection with the purchase or sale of any security, any manipulative or deceptive device or contrivance in contravention of SEC rules and regulations.[19] Rule 10b-5 further makes it unlawful for any person, by use of any means or instrumentality of interstate commerce, to do the following:

1. Employ any device, scheme, or artifice to defraud.
2. Make any untrue statement of a material fact or omit to state a material fact necessary to make the statements made, in light of the circumstances, not misleading.
3. Engage in any act, practice, or course of business that operates or would operate as a fraud or deceit on any person, in connection with the purchase or sale of any security.[20]

Accountants may be held liable only to sellers or purchasers under Section 10(b) and Rule 10b-5.[21] The scope of these antifraud provisions is extremely wide. Privity is not necessary for a recovery. Under these provisions, an accountant may be found liable not only for fraudulent misstatements of material facts in written material filed with the SEC but also for any fraudulent oral statements or omissions made in connection with the purchase or sale of any security.

For a plaintiff to recover from an accountant under the antifraud provisions of the 1934 act, he or she must, in addition to establishing status as a pur-

15. 15 U.S.C. Section 78r(a).
16. 15 U.S.C. Section 78r(a).

17. 15 U.S.C. Section 78r(c).
18. 459 U.S. 375, 103 S.Ct. 683, 74 L.Ed.2d 548 (1983).
19. 15 U.S.C. Section 78j(b).
20. 17 C.F.R. Section 240.10b-5.
21. See *Blue Chip Stamps v. Manor Drug Stores,* 421 U.S. 723, 95 S.Ct. 1917, 44 L.Ed.2d 539 (1975).

chaser or seller, prove *scienter*,[22] a fraudulent action or deception, reliance, materiality, and causation. A plaintiff who fails to establish these elements cannot recover damages from an accountant under Section 10(b) or Rule 10b-5.

THE PRIVATE SECURITIES LITIGATION REFORM ACT OF 1995

The Private Securities Litigation Reform Act of 1995 made some changes to the potential liability of accountants and other professionals in securities fraud cases. Among other things, the act imposed a new statutory obligation on accountants. An auditor must use adequate procedures in an audit to detect any illegal acts of the company being audited. If something illegal is detected, the auditor must disclose it to the company's board of directors, the audit committee, or the SEC, depending on the circumstances.[23]

In terms of liability, the 1995 act provides that in most situations, a party is liable only for that proportion of damages for which he or she is responsible.[24] For example, if an accountant actually participated in defrauding investors, he or she could be liable for the entire loss. If the accountant was not aware of the fraud, however, his or her liability could be proportionately less.

The act also stated that aiding and abetting a violation of the Securities Exchange Act of 1934 is a violation in itself. The SEC can enforce this provision by seeking an injunction or money damages against any person who knowingly aids and abets primary violators of the securities law. An accountant aids and abets when he or she is generally aware that he or she is participating in an activity that is improper and knowingly assists the activity. Silence may constitute aiding.

For example, Smith & Jones, an accounting firm, performs an audit for ABC Sales Company that is so inadequate as to constitute gross negligence. ABC uses the materials provided by Smith & Jones as part of a scheme to defraud investors. When the scheme is uncovered, the SEC can bring an action against Smith & Jones for aiding and abetting on the ground that the firm knew or should have known of the material misrepresentations that were in its audit and on which investors were likely to rely.

22. See *Ernst & Ernst v. Hochfelder*, 425 U.S. 185, 96 S.Ct. 1375, 47 L.Ed.2d 668 (1976).

23. 15 U.S.C. Section 78j-1.

24. 15 U.S.C. Section 78u-4(g).

SECTION 4

Potential Criminal Liability of Accountants

An accountant may be found criminally liable for violations of the Securities Act of 1933, the Securities Exchange Act of 1934, the Internal Revenue Code, and both state and federal criminal codes. Under both the 1933 act and the 1934 act, accountants may be subject to criminal penalties for *willful* violations—imprisonment of up to five years and/or a fine of up to $10,000 under the 1933 act and up to ten years and $100,000 under the 1934 act.

The Internal Revenue Code, Section 7206(2),[25] makes aiding or assisting in the preparation of a false tax return a felony punishable by a fine of $100,000 ($500,000 in the case of a corporation) and imprisonment for up to three years. Those who prepare tax returns for others also may face liability under the Internal Revenue Code. Note that one does not have to be an accountant to be subject to liability for tax-preparer penalties. The Internal Revenue Code defines a tax preparer as any person who prepares for compensation, or who employs one or more persons to prepare for compensation, all or a substantial portion of a tax return or a claim for a tax refund.[26]

Section 6694[27] of the Internal Revenue Code imposes on the tax preparer a penalty of $250 per return for negligent understatement of the client's tax liability and a penalty of $1,000 for willful understatement of tax liability or reckless or intentional disregard of rules or regulations. A tax preparer may also be subject to penalties under Section 6695[28] for failing to furnish the taxpayer with a copy of the return, failing to sign the return, or failing to furnish the appropriate tax identification numbers.

Section 6701[29] of the Internal Revenue Code imposes a penalty of $1,000 per document for aiding and abetting an individual's understatement of tax liability (the penalty is increased to $10,000 in corporate cases). The tax preparer's liability is limited to one penalty per taxpayer per tax year. If this penalty is imposed, no penalty can be imposed under Section 6694 with respect to the same document.

25. 26 U.S.C. Section 7206(2).

26. 26 U.S.C. Section 7701(a)(36).

27. 26 U.S.C. Section 6694.

28. 26 U.S.C. Section 6695.

29. 26 U.S.C. Section 6701.

In most states, criminal penalties may be imposed for such actions as knowingly certifying false or fraudulent reports; falsifying, altering, or destroying books of account; and obtaining property or credit through the use of false financial statements.

SECTION 5

Working Papers

Performing an audit for a client involves an accumulation of **working papers**—the various documents used and developed during the audit. These include notes, computations, memoranda, copies, and other papers that make up the work product of an accountant's services to a client. Under the common law, which in this instance has been codified in a number of states, working papers remain the accountant's property. It is important for accountants to retain such records in the event that they need to defend against lawsuits for negligence or other actions in which their competence is challenged. But because an accountant's working papers reflect the client's financial situation, the client has a right of access to them. (An accountant must return to his or her client any of the client's records or journals on the client's request, and failure to do so may result in liability.)

The client must give permission before working papers can be transferred to another accountant. Without the client's permission or a valid court order, the contents of working papers are not to be disclosed. Disclosure would constitute a breach of the accountant's fiduciary duty to the client. On grounds of unauthorized disclosure, the client could initiate a malpractice suit. The accountant's best defense would be that the client gave permission for the papers' release.

SECTION 5

Confidentiality and Privilege

Professionals are restrained by the ethical tenets of their professions to keep all communications with their clients confidential. The confidentiality of attorney-client communications is also protected by law, which confers a *privilege* on such communications. This privilege is granted because of the need for full disclosure to the attorney of the facts of a client's case.

To encourage frankness, confidential attorney-client communications relating to representation are normally held in strictest confidence and protected by law. The attorney and his or her employees may not discuss the client's case with anyone—even under court order—without the client's permission. The client holds the privilege, and only the client may waive it—by disclosing privileged information to someone outside the privilege, for example.

In a few states, accountant-client communications are privileged by state statute. In these states, accountant-client communications may not be revealed even in court or in court-sanctioned proceedings without the client's permission. The majority of states, however, abide by the common law, which provides that, if a court so orders, an accountant must disclose information about his or her client to the court. Physicians and other professionals may similarly be compelled to disclose in court information given to them in confidence by patients or clients.

Communications between professionals and their clients—other than those between an attorney and his or her client—are not privileged under federal law. In cases involving federal law, state-provided rights to confidentiality of accountant-client communications are not recognized. Thus, in those cases, in response to a court order, an accountant must provide the information sought.

SECTION 7

Limiting Professionals' Liability

As mentioned earlier in this chapter, accountants (and other professionals) can limit their liability to some extent by disclaiming it. Depending on the circumstances, a disclaimer that does not meet certain requirements will not be effective, however; and in some situations, a disclaimer may not be effective at all.

Professionals may be able to limit their liability for the misconduct of other professionals with whom they work by organizing the business as a professional corporation (P.C.) or a limited liability partnership (LLP). In some states, a professional who is a member of a P.C. is not personally liable for a co-member's misconduct unless he or she participated in it or supervised the member who acted wrongly. The innocent professional is liable only to the extent of his or her interest in the assets of the firm. This is also true for professionals who are partners in an LLP. P.C.s were discussed in more detail in Chapter 34. LLPs were covered in Chapter 38.

Terms and Concepts to Review

defalcation 1060
due diligence 1064
generally accepted accounting principles (GAAP) 1060
generally accepted auditing standards (GAAS) 1060
working papers 1067

Chapter Summary

COMMON LAW LIABILITY	
Liability to Client	**1.** *Breach of contract*—An accountant or other professional who fails to perform according to his or her contractual obligations can be held liable for breach of contract and resulting damages. **2.** *Negligence*—An accountant or other professional, in performance of his or her duties, must use the care, knowledge, and judgment generally used by professionals in the same or similar circumstances. Failure to do so is negligence. An accountant's violation of generally accepted accounting principles and generally accepted auditing standards is *prima facie* evidence of negligence. An accountant who reveals confidential information or the contents of working papers without the client's permission or a court order can be held liable for malpractice. **3.** *Fraud*—Actual intent to misrepresent a material fact to a client, when the client relies on the misrepresentation, is fraud. Gross negligence in performance of duties is constructive fraud.
Liability to Third Parties	An accountant may be liable for negligence to any third person the accountant knows or should have known will benefit from the accountant's work. The standard for imposing this liability varies, but generally courts follow one of the following three rules: **1.** Ultramares *rule*—Liability will be imposed only if the accountant is in privity, or near privity, with the third party. **2.** Restatement *rule*—Liability will be imposed only if the third party's reliance is foreseen or known or if the third party is among a class of foreseeable or known users. The majority of courts adopt this rule. **3.** *"Reasonably foreseeable user" rule*—Liability will be imposed if the third party's use was reasonably foreseeable.
STATUTORY LIABILITY	
Securities Act of 1933, Sections 11 and 12(2)	Under Section 11 of the 1933 Securities Act, an accountant who makes a false statement or omits a material fact in audited financial statements required for registration of securities under the law may be liable to anyone who acquires securities covered by the registration statement. The accountant's defense is basically the use of due diligence and the reasonable belief that the work was complete and correct. The burden of proof is on the accountant. Willful violations of this act may be subject to criminal penalties. Section 12(2) of the 1933 act imposes civil liability for fraud on anyone offering or selling a security to any purchaser of the security.
Securities Exchange Act of 1934, Sections 10(b) and 18	Under Sections 10(b) and 18 of the 1934 Securities Exchange Act, accountants are held liable for false and misleading applications, reports, and documents required under the act. The burden is on the plaintiff, and the accountant has numerous defenses, including good faith and lack of knowledge that what was submitted was false. Willful violations of this act may be subject to criminal penalties.

CHAPTER SUMMARY—CONTINUED

Internal Revenue Code	1. Aiding or assisting in the preparation of a false tax return is a felony. Aiding and abetting an individual's understatement of tax liability is a separate crime. 2. Tax preparers who negligently or willfully understate a client's tax liability or who recklessly or intentionally disregard Internal Revenue rules or regulations are subject to criminal penalties. 3. Tax preparers who fail to provide a taxpayer with a copy of the return, fail to sign the return, or fail to furnish the appropriate tax identification numbers may also be subject to criminal penalties.

CASES FOR ANALYSIS

Westlaw. You can access the full text of each case presented below by going to the Westlaw cases on this text's Web site at http://wbl-cs.westbuslaw.com. Each Westlaw case includes the names of all plaintiffs and defendants, the dates on which the case was argued and decided, a brief summary of the issues and decisions in the case, headnotes classifying specific issues in the case according to the West Key Number System, and the court's opinion. Concurring and dissenting opinions, if any, are included as well.

CASE 51.1 ACCOUNTANT'S LIABILITY TO THIRD PARTIES

BOYKIN V. ARTHUR ANDERSEN & CO.
Supreme Court of Alabama, 1994.
639 So.2d 504.

SHORES, Justice.

This case involves [in part] claims of * * * professional negligence brought [in an Alabama state court] by two stockholders of Secor Bank against * * * the independent certified public accountants for Secor Bank [and others]. * * * The claims asserted by the plaintiffs are asserted on their own behalf and not derivatively on behalf of the corporation. Secor Bank is not a party.

Samuel H. Boykin, Jr., and Apon, Inc., the plaintiffs, are shareholders in Secor Bank and have been since before 1988. They allege that defendants * * * Arthur Andersen & Company * * * deliberately entered into a scheme to defraud the stockholders of the bank by misrepresenting its true financial condition. Boykin and Apon * * * claim that the defendants knew the true financial condition of Secor and yet failed to mention material losses or liabilities on three years of annual reports. * * *

The trial court granted the defendants' * * * motion to dismiss for failure to state a claim upon which relief can be granted. * * * [T]he trial court held that the plaintiffs' claims failed to meet the "*Credit Alliance* standard" for accountant's liability * * * .

* * * *

* * * The accountants argue that the plaintiffs' claim must be rejected, because, they say, the plaintiffs do not allege an injury to them as individuals for which the law provides a remedy and because, they say, that the only remedy the law provides is a derivative action on behalf of the corporation.

We disagree. * * * [T]he plaintiffs' claims asserted here against Arthur Andersen * * * are not derivative in nature. They do not seek compensation for injury to the bank as a result of negligence or mismanagement. The plaintiffs' claims allege fraud, intentional misrepresentations and omissions of material facts, suppression, conspiracy to defraud, and breach of fiduciary duty. The plaintiffs have asserted that they relied to their detriment on inaccurate financial reports certified by Arthur Andersen; that Arthur Andersen was aware that the annual reports of Secor Bank upon which they placed their certification were to be specifically directed and addressed to the shareholders of the bank; and that the purpose for disseminating the annual reports was to communicate to them, as shareholders, the financial condition of the corporation.

* * * *

The trial court's rationale for dismissing the claims against the accountants was that the test for holding accountants liable for professional negligence in this state includes a "near-privity" [involving a relationship so close as to be equated with privity] requirement, which it says the plaintiffs failed to meet. We believe, however, that the plaintiffs alleged conduct on the part of the accountants that evidences that the accountants understood the shareholders' reliance. They aver that Arthur Andersen certified the 1988, 1989, and 1990 annual reports of Secor Bank in spite of direct knowledge that the bank had serious and material liabilities that were not stated on the reports. * * * .

* * * *

Under the [three-part] test set forth in *Credit Alliance* * * *, these plaintiffs have stated a claim upon which relief can be granted against the accountants, and, thus, the trial court erred in granting the motion to dismiss as to the accountants. Under [the first two parts of the test], the accountants must have been aware that the financial reports were to be used for a particular purpose or purposes, and in the furtherance of which purpose or purposes a known party or parties were intended to rely. Here Arthur Andersen was aware that the annual reports it was certifying were specifically directed to the shareholders of the bank and that they were to be relied upon by the shareholders as stating the true and correct financial status and condition of the bank. *The purpose of having an accounting firm certify a financial statement and annual report is to provide independent certification of the truth of these financial reports for those who must rely upon the reports.* [Emphasis added.]

The trial court held that [part] (3) of the *Credit Alliance* test—that there must have been some conduct on the part of the accountants linking them to that party or parties, which evinces the accountants' understanding of that party or parties' reliance—was not satisfied in this case. The trial court interpreted this language as being a "near-privity" requirement and to mean that unless Arthur Andersen had direct, actual knowledge that plaintiffs Boykin and Apon were relying upon its opinion, Arthur Andersen cannot be held liable to the plaintiffs under Alabama law. This is a misreading of [the test], which does not refer to the accountants' knowledge of reliance on the part of a single, particular individual. * * * There must be simply some conduct on the part of the accountants that evidences the accountants' understanding that their opinion will be relied upon by a reasonably foreseeable and limited class of persons.

In this case, the stockholders who received the certified annual reports were members of a group or class that Arthur Andersen had special reason to expect to be influenced by its certification. Arthur Andersen knew and understood that the annual reports it was certifying were directed to the stockholders of Secor Bank and that those stockholders would rely upon the information contained in those annual reports in making investment decisions.

* * * It is time that Alabama * * * adopt, for determining the professional liability of accountants, the standard set forth in *Restatement (Second) of Torts* [Section] 552 * * * . The *Restatement* rule limits accountants' liability to specifically foreseen and limited groups of third parties for whose benefit and guidance the accounting firm supplied the financial information and who used it as the accounting firm intended it to be used.

* * * [T]he *Restatement* standard is not far afield from the three-pronged test of *Credit Alliance*. The real difference is that the *Restatement* clarifies any confusion as to the question of the privity necessary for the third prong. * * * The *Restatement* represents the moderate view, allowing only a restricted group of third parties to recover for pecuniary losses attributable to inaccurate financial statements. Significantly, the accountants retain control over their liability exposure. The restricted group includes third parties whom the accountants intend to influence and those whom the accountants know their clients intend to influence. Accordingly, liability is fixed by the accountants' particular knowledge at the moment the audit is published, not by the foreseeable path of harm envisioned by jurists years following an unfortunate business decision. * * * The near-privity rule, in other words, requires that the precise identity of the informational consumer be foreseen by the auditors; however, the *Restatement* contemplates identification of a narrow group, not necessarily the specific membership within that group. * * * The *Restatement* adopts the cautious position that an accountant may be liable to a third party with whom the accountant is not in privity, but not every reasonably foreseeable consumer of financial information may recover.

The adoption of the *Restatement* rule for the professional liability of accountants should clarify the confusion exhibited by the trial court in this case as to the privity required by the third prong of the *Credit Alliance* test. * * * Basic principles of justice require that an accounting firm be held liable for its intentional or negligent dissemination of inaccurate financial reports to specifically foreseen and limited groups of third parties for whose benefit and guidance the accounting firm supplied the information.

The plaintiffs have stated a cause of action against * * * the defendant accounting firm, under [*Credit Alliance*] and under the rule of *Restatement (Second) of Torts* [Section] 552. Therefore, the judgment of dismissal is due to be reversed and this cause remanded for an adjudication on the merits.

REVERSED AND REMANDED.

* * * *

MADDOX, Justice (dissenting).

* * * *

On this appeal, we were asked to reconsider our decision * * * to adopt the *Credit Alliance* standard for accountants' professional liability and to adopt in the place of that standard the rule set forth in *Restatement (Second) of Torts* [Section] 552. In [a previous case] the Court carefully considered the different standards for accountants' liability and concluded that the New York view, or *Credit Alliance* standard, was the more reasonable approach to adopt. * * * [I]t appears to me that the reasoning and conclusion there reached were sound. I think that the decision in this case will be construed as overruling, at least in part, the * * * decision [in that case] and that the majority has not stated sufficient legal bases for doing so.

Based on the foregoing, I would affirm the trial court's dismissal * * * for failure to state a claim upon which relief can be granted. * * * I therefore dissent from the majority's opinion.

CASE 51.2 ACCOUNTANT'S LIABILITY UNDER SECURITIES LAWS

ENDO v. ARTHUR ANDERSEN & CO.

United States Court of Appeals,
Seventh Circuit, 1999.
163 F.3d 463.

POSNER, Chief Judge.

In March 1987, Fruit of the Loom, Inc. [FOL], the clothing manufacturer, made an initial public offering of common stock and other securities. Purchasers of these securities who lost money (the share price was $9 at the time of offering and a year later, when the suit was filed, was $6) banded together in a [suit in a federal district court] against * * * [FOL's] former auditor, Arthur Andersen [& Company, and others]. * * * [T]he district judge granted summary judgment for Andersen and the plaintiffs have appealed. The issue on appeal is novel, narrow, esoteric, but potentially important to accountants, to their clients, and to investors. It has to do with the republication by an issuer of securities of audit reports made by the issuer's former auditors. Specifically, we must decide whether a former auditor must condition his consent to republication on the issuer's republishing verbatim all the footnotes that had appeared in the financial statements that the former auditor had approved. * * * [T]he plaintiffs seek to ground this duty [in part] in * * * [S]ection 11(a)(4) of the Securities Act of 1933. This section makes an accountant liable for an untrue statement of fact (or misleading omission) "which purports to have been * * * certified by him" in a registration statement. * * *

Fruit of the Loom had hired Andersen to audit its financial statements for 1985. Andersen did this and reported to Fruit of the Loom's management that the financial statements were complete and accurate so far as Andersen could determine through the use of sound auditing methodology. The statements contain a footnote, reviewed and approved by Andersen as part of the audit, to the effect that FOL is contesting in [federal] Court $105 million in deficiencies assessed by the Internal Revenue Service for a period in the 1970s. The note includes a warning that "the cash payment to the Internal Revenue Service, including interest, may exceed the amount of alleged deficiencies." This warning does not appear in the note on tax liabilities in FOL's 1986 financial statements * * *. The 1986 statements were audited by Ernst & Young, which had replaced Andersen as FOL's auditor.

In the public documents accompanying the 1987 IPO, Fruit of the Loom was required to disclose its financial results for 1985 as well as 1986. It asked Andersen to consent to the republication of the report of the 1985 audit. Sound accounting practice not challenged by Andersen required it to read the offering documents and check with its successor auditor, Ernst & Young, to make sure that Ernst & Young hadn't discovered anything to falsify the 1985 financial statements that Andersen had certified. Andersen duly obtained from Ernst & Young letters certifying that Ernst & Young had discovered nothing that warranted changing the 1985 financial statements. It then consented to the republication of its audit report in the offering documents. The plaintiffs argue that investors would think that Andersen had changed its mind about the danger of the IRS's mulcting Fruit of the Loom for more than $105 million. In fact the IRS did mulct it for more and the plaintiffs argue that this was one cause of the trading losses that they sustained and seek to recoup in this suit.

So far as Andersen's compliance with applicable auditing standards is concerned, there is no issue. It did exactly what those standards require of a former auditor asked to consent to the republication of its audit report: inquire whether any new information had come to light that showed that the report had not been accurate. If investors were misled, it was not because they mistakenly relied on Andersen to exercise reasonable care to discover such information; Andersen used all the requisite care, and discovered no such information—there was none to discover. The question, rather, is whether by permitting FOL to omit from the IPO documents the warning sentence from the footnote to the 1985 financial statements, Andersen misled investors into thinking that the tax-liability picture had brightened—that FOL's *maximum* tax liability for tax years during the 1970s was $105 million.

The key to answering this question lies in the difference between historical and predictive information in a former auditor's audit report. The text, as distinct from the footnotes, of the 1985 financial statements of Fruit of the Loom that Andersen approved shows the revenues and costs that the company actually experienced that year. This was "history" so far as the successor auditor was concerned. Because Fruit of the Loom was required in its IPO documentation to report its 1985 financial results, and because information obtained since Andersen had audited those results might show that they were inaccurate, it was important to FOL and to investors that Andersen, which unlike Ernst & Young had investigated the 1985 results, check to make sure they still were accurate. That is what it did, by checking with Ernst & Young, which had audited the next year's statements and so would know whether anything had happened during that year to require revision of the previous year's statements. The footnotes * * * at issue here * * * talk about the future—specifically, about what might happen as a result of the unresolved litigation in the Tax Court. As to that, Andersen had no continuing responsibility arising from its role as a *former* auditor. The current auditor would know much more about the future.

* * * *

* * * The investor is interested in the *former* auditor's continued confidence in the figures which that auditor had approved, but in the *current* auditor's opinion regarding contingencies that, not yet having materialized, are not reflected in the historical data. The investor who reads the documentation accompanying FOL's IPO sees a column for the company's 1985 financial results, a column for its 1986 results, a set of footnotes dealing with contingent liabilities not reflected in the columns, and notations that Andersen audited the 1985 results and continues to stand by them and that Ernst & Young audited the 1986 results. The investor will assume that Andersen is standing by the numbers in the column for 1985, not standing by the prophecies in the footnotes, which are about today speaking of tomorrow rather than about today speaking of yesterday.

The footnotes are, it is true, a part of the financial statements. But remember that an accountant's liability for misleading representations in a registration statement is limited to the portion of any financial statements which purports to have been prepared or certified by him. Andersen did not purport to certify the footnotes to Fruit of the Loom's 1986 financial statements, though it did purport to certify that, on the basis of information received from Ernst & Young, it had no reason to revise the 1985 financial results shown in the 1986 statements. Nor would any reasonable investor have thought otherwise.

We are reinforced in this conclusion by several additional considerations. One is a desire to avoid disrupting what, so far as we are aware, is a common and (from absence of reported cases or other published discussion) heretofore unquestioned practice of revising the footnotes in the former auditor's report on the basis of new information audited by the current auditor. Another is a disinclination to make registration statements and prospectuses even more bulky and confusing than they are, to the detriment of investors as well as issuers. If the plaintiffs are right, Fruit of the Loom was required to include in the offering documents two footnotes on contingent tax liabilities: one containing Andersen's evaluation of those liabilities as of 1986, when it conducted the audit of FOL's 1985 financial statements, and the other Ernst & Young's evaluation as of 1987, when Ernst & Young audited FOL's 1986 financial statements. The careful reader, juxtaposing the two notes, would notice that the second was more optimistic about the company's tax liabilities for the 1970s. But what would he infer? That Andersen in 1986 knew more about what the future would hold than Ernst & Young in 1987? That is hardly plausible.

Still another, and we think conclusive reason, for our conclusion that Andersen is not responsible for the footnotes is that Ernst & Young is. The investor does not expect the same financial data and estimates to be audited by two separate audit companies. He expects the current data, including the current estimates of contingent liabilities, to be audited by the current auditor, and data for periods prior to the hiring of this auditor to be audited by a former auditor. Ernst & Young did not audit the 1985 financials; Andersen did. Andersen did not audit the 1986 predictions; Ernst & Young did. [The investors also filed a suit against Ernst & Young that was settled out of court.]

AFFIRMED.

CASE PROBLEMS

51–1. Five members of the Hendry family owned property in Arlington, Virginia. When a dispute arose with a developer, the family hired an attorney, Francis Pelland, to represent them. The mother wanted to continue to live in a house on the property. The son and the daughter wanted to preserve the trees on the property. The best interest of the two grandchildren was to maximize the property's long-term value. Pelland advised the family to settle with the developer for $1.5 million, which they did. Unhappy with this result, the Hendrys filed a suit in a federal district court against Pelland for breach of fiduciary duty, seeking in part a refund of the legal fees they had paid. On what basis might the court rule in the Hendrys' favor? Is there any basis on which a court could rule in Pelland's favor? [*Hendry v. Pelland*, 73 F.3d 397 (D.C.Cir. 1996)]

51–2. John and Christine Powell invested in a hotel-condominium development project. When legal problems with the project arose, the attorney representing the Powells was given access to certain documents and correspondence between the project developer, H. E. F. Partnership (HEF), and HEF's own legal counsel. When the project failed, the Powells sued HEF and others involved with the development scheme. In preparation for trial, the Powells sought discovery (see Chapter 3) of the documents and correspondence that HEF had released to them earlier. HEF refused to release the documents, alleging that they were confidential communications and protected under the attorney-client privilege. The Powells filed a motion with the court to compel discovery. How should the court rule on the motion to compel? Explain. [*Powell v. H. E. F. Partnership,* 835 F.Supp. 762 (D.Vt. 1993)]

51–3. The accounting firm of Arthur Young & Co. was employed by DMI Furniture, Inc., to conduct a review of an audit prepared by Brown, Kraft & Co., certified public accountants, for Gillespie Furniture Co. DMI planned to purchase Gillespie and wished to determine its net worth. Arthur Young, by letter, advised DMI that Brown, Kraft had performed a high-quality audit and that Gillespie's inventory on the audit dates was fairly stated on the general ledger. Allegedly as a result of these representations, DMI went forward with its purchase of Gillespie. Subsequently, DMI charged Brown, Kraft & Co., Arthur Young, and Gillespie's former owners with violations of Section 10(b) of the Securities Exchange Act and SEC Rule 10b-5. DMI complained that Arthur Young's review had proved to be materially inaccurate and misleading, primarily because the inventory was grossly overstated in the balance sheet. Arthur Young was charged with "acting recklessly in failing to detect, and thus failing to disclose, material omissions and reckless conduct on the part of Brown, Kraft, and in making affirmative misstatements in its letter" to DMI. Did DMI have a valid cause of action under either Section 10(b) or Rule 10b-5? Discuss. [*DMI Furniture, Inc. v. Brown, Kraft & Co.,* 644 F.Supp. 1517 (C.D.Cal. 1986)]

51–4. Credit Alliance Corp. is a major financial service company engaged primarily in financing the purchase of capital equipment through installment sales and leasing agreements. As a condition of extending additional major financing to L. B. Smith, Credit Alliance required an audited financial statement. Smith provided Credit Alliance with an audited financial statement prepared by the accounting firm of Arthur Andersen & Co. Later, on Smith's petitioning for bankruptcy, it was discovered that Smith, at the time of the audit, had been in a precarious financial position. Credit Alliance filed suit against Arthur Andersen, claiming that Andersen had failed to conduct investigations in accordance with proper auditing standards and that Andersen's recklessness had resulted in misleading statements that caused Credit Alliance to incur damages. In addition, it was claimed that Andersen knew, or should have known, that Credit Alliance would rely on these statements in issuing credit to Smith. Discuss whether Credit Alliance, as a third party, could hold Arthur Andersen liable in a negligence action. [*Credit Alliance Corp. v. Arthur Andersen & Co.,* 65 N.Y.2d 536, 483 N.E.2d 110, 493 N.Y.S.2d 435 (1985)]

51–5. A limited partner brought an action in negligence against the general partners as well as against the firm's accountant. At issue in the case was whether accountants who are retained by a limited partnership to perform both auditing and tax-return services may be held liable for negligence in the carrying out of those professional services. Should accountants be held responsible in these circumstances? [*White v. Guarente,* 43 N.Y.2d 356, 372 N.E.2d 315 (1977)]

51–6. Max Mitchell, a certified public accountant and president of Max Mitchell & Co., went to First Florida Bank, N.A., to negotiate a $500,000 unsecured line of credit for C.M. Systems, Inc. The audited financial statements that Mitchell gave the bank did not indicate that C.M. Systems owed any money. In fact, the company owned at least $750,000 to several banks. First Florida approved the loan, but C.M. Systems never repaid it. The bank filed a suit in Florida state court against Mitchell and his firm, alleging negligence. Because there was no privity between Mitchell and the bank, the court granted Mitchell summary judgment. The bank appealed. On what basis might the appellate court reverse? [*First Florida Bank, N.A. v. Max Mitchell & Co.,* 558 So.2d 9 (Fla. 1990)]

51–7. Ralph W. Moores, Jr., was injured on the job while employed as a dock worker in Maine. After collecting workers' compensation benefits in the amount of $43,000, Moores brought a third party liability suit against the ship owners. Nathan Greenberg was Mooress's attorney. The ship owners informed Greenberg that they would settle the suit, at one point offering $90,000. Greenberg did not inform Moores of the offer because he did not deem it to be sufficiently significant. When Moores lost the case in court, he sued Greenberg, alleging that Greenberg had a duty to inform him of these offers and had breached that duty by not doing so. How should the court rule? Discuss fully. [*Moores v. Greenberg,* 834 F.2d 1105 (1st Cir. 1987)]

51–8. Jerry Barger, Wayne Kennerly, and Harry Young were the shareholders and directors of The Furniture House of North Carolina, Inc. (TFH). They asked David McCoy of the accounting firm of McCoy Hillard & Parks to determine the financial health of TFH. A misapplication of computer data resulted in an overstatement of sales and an understatement of liabilities. Based on these statements, McCoy assured Barger and the others that TFH could repay certain loans. Consequently, Barger and the others personally guaranteed the loans. Ultimately, TFH filed for bankruptcy, and the guarantors were forced to repay the loans with their own money. They filed a suit against the accountants in a North Carolina state court, alleging, in part, fraud. The court granted the accountants' motion for summary judgment. Barger and the others appealed.

What will happen on appeal? Discuss. [*Barger v. McCoy Hillard & Parks,* 120 N.C.App. 326, 462 S.E.2d 252 (1995)]

51–9. The plaintiffs, Harry and Barry Rosenblum, brought an action against Touche Ross & Co., a prominent accounting firm. The plaintiffs alleged that they had relied on the correctness of audits performed by the firm in acquiring Giant common stock in conjunction with the sale of their business to Giant. Giant's financial statements were found to be fraudulent, and the stock that the Rosenblums had acquired proved to be worthless. The plaintiffs alleged that Touche's negligence in conducting the audits was the proximate cause of their loss. There was no statement in the audits limiting to whom the company might disseminate the information. To which third parties should an auditor be liable? Explain. [*H. Rosenblum, Inc. v. Adler,* 93 N.J. 324, 461 A.2d 138 (1983)]

51–10. An accounting firm was engaged by two car rental companies to determine the net worth of those businesses by preparing an audited statement. At the request of their clients, the accountants did not audit the accounts receivable, made appropriate exceptions to the accounts receivable in the balance sheet, and qualified their opinion with a caveat stating that this had been done. After the audit had been performed and on the basis of the figures reflected in the balance sheet, Stephens Industries, Inc., purchased two-thirds of the car rental companies' stock. The car rental businesses thereafter failed, and Stephens Industries brought an action against the accounting firm for allegedly having misrepresented the status of the accounts receivable in the audit. What was the result? [*Stephens Industries, Inc. v. Haskins & Sells,* 438 F.2d 357 (10th Cir. 1971)]

51–11. The plaintiffs were the purchasers of all the stock in companies owned by the defendant sellers. Alleging fraud under the federal securities laws and under the New York common law of fraud, the plaintiffs sued the defendant sellers and their accounting firm. What should be the result with respect to the accounting firm, assuming that the treatment of shipping costs, expenses, and other charges was not in accordance with generally accepted accounting principles and hence created an inaccurate financial picture in the financial statements? [*Berkowitz v. Baron,* 428 F.Supp. 1190 (S.D.N.Y. 1977)]

51–12. Toro Co. was a major supplier of equipment and credit to Summit Power Equipment Distributors. Toro required audited reports from Summit to evaluate the distributor's financial condition. Summit supplied Toro with reports prepared by Krouse, Kern & Co., an accounting firm. The reports allegedly contained mistakes and omissions regarding Summit's financial condition. According to Toro, it extended and renewed large amounts of credit to Summit in reliance on the audited reports. Summit was unable to repay these amounts, and Toro brought a negligence action against the accounting firm and the individual accountants. Evidence produced at the trial showed that Krouse knew that the reports it furnished to Summit were to be used by Summit to induce Toro to extend credit, but no evidence was produced to show either a contractual relationship between Krouse and Toro or a link between these companies evidencing Krouse's understanding of Toro's actual reliance on the reports. The relevant state law follows the *Ultramares* rule. What was the result? [*Toro Co. v. Krouse, Kern & Co.,* 827 F.2d 155 (7th Cir. 1987)]

51–13. Sheila Simpson and the other two shareholders in H. P. Enterprises Corp. decided to sell the corporation and turned to Ed Oliver, an attorney, for assistance. Oliver formed a corporation, Tide Creek, for a group of investors, and Tide Creek then purchased the assets of H. P. Enterprises for $500,000, of which $100,000 was paid at the time of the sale in November 1983. As security for the sellers, Oliver provided a lien on the stock of Tide Creek and personal guaranties of the buyers on the corporation's $400,000 note to the sellers. Oliver was the sole source of legal advice for both parties. About six months after the sale, a fire destroyed Tide Creek's inventory. In October 1984, Oliver left the law firm in which he had been a partner, and one of the other partners, David James, took over the Simpson and Tide Creek accounts. In January 1985, James advised Simpson that Tide Creek was having financial difficulties and suggested that the note be restructured; this was done. When Simpson asked James what he would do if her interests and those of Tide Creek diverged, James replied, "We would have to support you." Tide Creek later filed for bankruptcy, as did the individuals who had personally guaranteed the note, and Simpson and the others received nothing. Did the sellers succeed in a lawsuit against James for negligence? Discuss fully. [*Simpson v. James,* 903 F.2d 372 (5th Cir. 1990)]

51–14. In June 1993, Sparkomatic Corp. agreed to negotiate a sale of its Kenco Engineering division to Williams Controls, Inc. At the end of July, Sparkomatic asked its accountants, Parente, Randolph, Orlando, Carey & Associates, to audit Kenco's financial statements for the previous three years and to certify interim and closing balance sheets to be included with the sale's closing documents. All of the parties knew that these documents would serve as a basis for setting the sale price. Within a few days, Williams signed an "Asset Purchase Agreement" that promised access to Parente's records with respect to Kenco. The sale closed in mid-August. In September, Williams was given the financial statements for Kenco's previous three years and the interim and closing balance sheets, all of which were certified by Parente. Williams's accountant found no errors in the closing balance sheet but did not review any of the other documents. The parties set a final purchase price. Later, however, Williams filed a suit in a federal district court against Parente, claiming negligent misrepresentation, among other things, in connection with Parente's preparation of the financial documents. Parente responded with a motion for summary judgment, asserting that the parties lacked privity. Under the *Restatement (Second) of Torts,* Section 552, how should the court rule? Explain. [*Williams Controls, Inc. v. Parente, Randolph, Orlando, Carey & Associates,* 39 F.Supp.2d 517 (M.D.Pa. 1999)]

51–15. A Question of Ethics

Crawford, a certified public accountant, prepared a financial statement for Erps Construction Co., which was seeking a loan from the First National Bank of Bluefield. Crawford knew at the time he prepared the statement that the bank would rely on the statement in making its decision regarding whether to extend credit to Erps. The bank later sued Crawford, alleging that he had been professionally negligent in preparing the financial statement, on which the bank had relied in determining whether to give the construction company a loan. Crawford defended against the suit by asserting that he could not be liable to the bank because of lack of privity. The trial court ruled that in the absence of contractual privity between the parties, the bank could not recover from the accountant. On appeal, the appellate court adopted the rule enunciated by the *Restatement (Second) of Torts* in regard to a professional's liability to third parties. [*First National Bank of Bluefield v. Crawford,* 386 S.E.2d 310 (W.Va. 1989)]

1. What is the standard of an accountant's liability to third parties under the *Restatement (Second) of Torts*? What ethical reasoning underlies this standard?
2. Do you think that the standard of liability under the *Restatement* adequately balances the rights of accountants and the rights of third parties? Can you think of a fairer standard?
3. A few courts have adopted the principle that accountants should be liable for negligence to all persons who use and rely on their work products, provided that this use and reliance was foreseeable by the accountants at the time they prepared the documents relied on. Does such a standard of liability impose too great a burden on accountants and accounting firms? Why, or why not?

E-Links

For updated links to resources available on the Web, as well as a variety of other materials, visit this text's Web site at

http://wbl-cs.westbuslaw.com

The Web site for the Financial Accounting Standards Board can be found at

http://www.rutgers.edu/Accounting/raw/fasb

For information on the accounting profession, including articles from the *Journal of Accountancy,* go to the Web site for the American Institute of Certified Public Accountants (AICPA) at

http://www.aicpa.org/index.htm

For information on the rules governing the conduct of attorneys, go to the Web site of the American Bar Association at

http://abanet.org

Legal Research Exercises on the Web

Go to http://wbl-cs.westbuslaw.com, the Web site that accompanies this text. Select "Interactive Study Center," and then click on "Chapter 51." There you will find the following Internet research exercise that you can perform to learn more about some of the steps professionals can take to avoid liability:

Activity 51–1: Avoiding Legal Liability

CHAPTER 52

International and Comparative Law

INTERNATIONAL BUSINESS TRANSACTIONS are not unique to the modern world. Indeed, since ancient times independent peoples and nations have traded their goods and wares with one another. What is new in our day is the dramatic growth in world trade and the emergence of a global business community. Today, nearly every major business considers the potential of international markets for its products or services. It is no longer uncommon for a U.S. corporation to have investments or manufacturing plants in a foreign country or for a foreign corporation to have operations in the United States. Because the exchange of goods, services, and ideas on a worldwide level is now routine, students of business law should be familiar with the laws pertaining to international business transactions.

Laws affecting the international legal environment of business include both international law and national law. **International law** can be defined as a body of law—formed as a result of international customs, treaties, and organizations—that governs relations among or between nations. **National law** is the law of a particular nation, such as the United States, Japan, Germany, or Brazil. In this chapter, we examine how both international law and national law frame business operations in the international context.

SECTION 1

International Law

The major difference between international law and national law is the fact that government authorities can enforce national law. What government, however, can enforce international law? By definition, a *nation* is a sovereign entity—which means that there is no higher authority to which that nation must submit. If a nation violates an international law, the most that other countries or international organizations can do (when persuasive tactics fail) is resort to coercive actions—from severance of diplomatic relations and boycotts to, as a last resort, war—against the violating nation.

In essence, international law is the result of centuries-old attempts to reconcile the traditional need of each country to be the final authority over its own affairs with the desire of nations to benefit economically from trade and harmonious relations with one another. Sovereign nations can, and do, voluntarily agree to be governed in certain respects by international law for the purpose of facilitating international trade and commerce, as well as civilized discourse. As a result, a body of international law has evolved. In this section, we examine the primary sources and characteristics of that body of law, as well as some important legal principles and doctrines that have been developed over time to facilitate dealings among nations.

SOURCES OF INTERNATIONAL LAW

Basically, there are three sources of international law: international customs, treaties and international agreements, and international organizations and conferences. We look at each of these sources here.

International Customs. One important source of international law consists of the international customs that have evolved among nations in their relations with one another. In Article 38(1) of the Statute of the International Court of Justice, an international custom is referred to as "evidence of a general practice accepted as law." The legal principles and doctrines that you will read about shortly are rooted in international customs and traditions that evolved over time in the international arena.

Treaties and International Agreements. Treaties and other explicit agreements between or among foreign nations provide another important source of international law. A **treaty** is an agreement or contract between two or more nations that must be authorized and ratified by the supreme power of each nation. Under Article II, Section 2, of the U.S. Constitution, the president has the power "by and with the Advice and Consent of the Senate, to make Treaties, provided two-thirds of the Senators present concur."

A *bilateral* agreement, as the term implies, occurs when two nations form an agreement that will govern their commercial exchanges or other relations with one another. *Multilateral* agreements are those formed by several nations. For example, regional trade associations such as the European Union (EU) and the trading unit established by the North American Free Trade Agreement (NAFTA), both of which are discussed later in this chapter, are the result of multilateral trade agreements. Other regional trade associations that have been created through multilateral agreements include the Association of Southeast Asian Nations (ASEAN) and the Andean Common Market (ANCOM).

International Organizations and Conferences. International organizations and conferences further contribute to international law. In international law, the term **international organization** generally refers to an organization composed mainly of nations and usually established by treaty.

The United States is a member of more than one hundred multilateral and bilateral organizations, including at least twenty through the United Nations (see Exhibit 52–1 on the next page). These organizations adopt resolutions, declarations, and other types of standards that often require a particular behavior of nations. The General Assembly of the United Nations, for example, has adopted numerous nonbinding resolutions and declarations that embody principles of international law. Disputes with respect to these resolutions and declarations may be brought before the International Court of Justice. That court, however, normally has authority to settle legal disputes only when nations voluntarily submit to its jurisdiction.

The United Nations Commission on International Trade Law has made considerable progress in establishing uniformity in international law as it relates to trade and commerce. One of the commission's most significant creations to date is the 1980 Convention on Contracts for the International Sale of Goods (CISG). Recall from Chapters 18 through 23, which cover contracts for the sale of goods, that the CISG is similar to Article 2 of the Uniform Commercial Code in that it is designed to settle disputes between parties to sales contracts. It spells out the duties of international buyers and sellers that will apply if the parties have not agreed otherwise in their contracts. The CISG only governs sales contracts between trading partners in nations that have ratified the CISG, however.

LEGAL PRINCIPLES AND DOCTRINES

Over time, a number of legal principles and doctrines have evolved and have been employed—to a greater or lesser extent—by the courts of various nations to resolve or reduce conflicts that involve a foreign element. The three important legal principles discussed below are based primarily on courtesy and respect and are applied in the interests of maintaining harmonious relations among nations.

The Principle of Comity. Under what is known as the principle of **comity**, one nation will defer and give effect to the laws and judicial decrees of another country, as long as those laws and judicial decrees are consistent with the law and public policy of the accommodating nation. For example, assume that a Swedish seller and an American buyer have formed a contract, which the buyer breaches. The seller sues the buyer in a Swedish court, which awards damages. The buyer's assets, however, are in the United States and cannot be reached unless the judgment is enforced by a U.S. court of law. In such a situation, if a U.S. court determined that the procedures and laws applied in the Swedish court were consistent with U.S. national law and policy, the U.S. court would likely defer to, and enforce, the foreign court's judgment.

The Act of State Doctrine. The **act of state doctrine** is a judicially created doctrine that provides that the judicial branch of one country will not examine the validity of public acts committed by a recognized foreign government within its own territory. This doctrine is premised on the theory that the judicial

EXHIBIT 52–1 MULTILATERAL INTERNATIONAL ORGANIZATIONS IN WHICH THE UNITED STATES PARTICIPATES

NAME	PURPOSE
Customs Cooperation Council	Established in 1950. Supervises the application and interpretation of an international code classifying goods and customs tariffs.
International Bank for Reconstruction and Development	Popularly known as the World Bank; a specialized agency of the United Nations since 1947. Promotes growth, trade, and balance of trade by facilitating and providing technical assistance, particularly in agriculture, energy, transportation, and telecommunications.
International Center for the Settlement of Investment Disputes	Established in 1966. Conciliates and arbitrates disputes between private investors and governments of other countries.
International Civil Aviation Organization	Established in 1947 and became a specialized agency of the United Nations seven months later. Develops international civil aviation by issuing rules and policies for safe and efficient airports and air navigation.
International Court of Justice (World Court)	Established in 1922 and became one of the principal organs of the United Nations in 1945. Jurisdiction comprises all cases that are referred to it. Decides disputes in accord with the rules of international law.
International Maritime Organization	Established in 1948. Promotes cooperation in the areas of government regulation, practices and technical matters of all kinds affecting shipping in international trade, the adoption of standards of maritime safety and efficiency, and the abolition of discrimination and unnecessary restrictions.
International Monetary Fund (IMF)	Created in 1944 at the United Nations Monetary and Financial Conference. Promotes economic stability by aiding the growth of international trade and the stability of currency exchange rates, as well as by providing for a system of international monetary assistance.
International Telecommunications Satellite Organization	Established in 1964. Operates an international public communications satellite system on a commercial, nondiscriminatory basis.
Permanent Court of Arbitration	Established in 1899 to facilitate the settlement of international disputes. The court has jurisdiction over all cases that it is requested to arbitrate.
United Nations (UN)	Established in 1945 to maintain international peace and security. Promotes international cooperation.
World Intellectual Property Organization	Established in 1967 and became a specialized agency of the United Nations in 1974. Promotes protection of intellectual property throughout the world.
World Trade Organization (WTO)	Established in 1994 during the final round of negotiations of the General Agreement on Tariffs and Trade (GATT). The GATT was created in 1947 and was the first global commercial agreement in history. It became the principal instrument for regulating international trade and limiting tariffs and other barriers to world trade on particular commodities and other items. GATT ceased to exist in 1995, when the WTO came into existence to regulate worldwide trade.

branch should not "pass upon the validity of foreign acts when to do so would vex the harmony of our international relations with that foreign nation."[1]

1. *Libra Bank Ltd. v. Banco Nacional de Costa Rica, S.A.*, 570 F.Supp. 870 (S.D.N.Y. 1983).

The act of state doctrine can have important consequences for individuals and firms doing business with, and investing in, other countries. For example, this doctrine is frequently employed in cases involving **expropriation**, which occurs when a government seizes a privately owned business or privately owned goods for a proper public purpose and awards just compensation. When a government seizes private property for an illegal purpose and without just compensation, the taking is referred to as a **confiscation.** The line between these two forms of taking is sometimes blurred because of differing interpretations of what is illegal and what constitutes just compensation. To illustrate: Tim Flaherty, an American businessperson, owns a mine in Brazil. The government of Brazil seizes the mine for public use and claims that the profits Tim has already realized from the mine constitute just compensation. Tim disagrees, but the act of state doctrine may prevent Tim's recovery in a U.S. court of law.

When applicable, both the act of state doctrine and the doctrine of *sovereign immunity,* which we discuss next, tend to shield foreign nations from the jurisdiction of U.S. courts. What this means is that, generally, firms or individuals who own property overseas have little legal protection against government actions in the countries in which they operate.

The Doctrine of Sovereign Immunity. When certain conditions are satisfied, the doctrine of **sovereign immunity** exempts foreign nations from the jurisdiction of the U.S. courts. In 1976, Congress codified this rule in the Foreign Sovereign Immunities Act (FSIA).[2] The FSIA also modified previous applications of the doctrine in certain respects by expanding the rights of plaintiff creditors against foreign nations.

The FSIA exclusively governs the circumstances in which an action may be brought in the United States against a foreign nation. Section 1605 of the FSIA sets forth the major exceptions to the jurisdictional immunity of a foreign state. A foreign state is not immune from the jurisdiction of the courts of the United States when the state has "waived its immunity either explicitly or by implication" or when the state has engaged in actions that are taken "in connection with a commercial activity carried on in the United States by the foreign state" or that have "a direct effect in the United States."

Issues frequently arise as to whether particular entities fall within the category of foreign state. Under Section 1603 of the FSIA, a foreign state is defined to include both a political subdivision of a foreign state and an instrumentality of a foreign state (an agency or entity acting for the state). The question of what is a commercial activity has also been the subject of dispute, because the particulars of what constitutes a commercial activity are not defined in the act. Rather, it is left up to the courts to decide whether a particular activity is governmental or commercial in nature.

2. 28 U.S.C. Sections 1602–1611.

SECTION 2

Doing Business Internationally

A U.S. domestic firm can engage in international business transactions in a number of ways. Contracts for the international purchase and sale of goods were discussed earlier in this text, in Chapters 18 through 23. Here, we look at other aspects of international business transactions, including the ways in which businesspersons typically extend their business operations into the international arena, laws regulating international business activities, and dispute settlement in the international context.

Types of International Business Operations

Most U.S. companies make the initial foray into international business through exporting. There are several other alternatives, however, including those discussed here.

Exporting. The simplest way of entering into international business operations is to seek out foreign markets for domestically produced products. In other words, U.S. firms can **export** their goods and services to foreign markets. Exporting can take two forms: direct exporting and indirect exporting. In *direct exporting,* a U.S. company signs a sales contract with a foreign purchaser that provides for the conditions of shipment and payment for the goods. (How payments are made in international transactions through the use of letters of credit was discussed in Chapter 20.) If business develops sufficiently in foreign countries, a U.S. company may, through the appointment of a foreign agent or a foreign distributor, develop a specialized marketing organization in the foreign market. This is called *indirect exporting.*

When a U.S. firm desires a limited involvement in an international market, it will typically establish an agency relationship with a foreign firm. In an agency relationship, one person (the agent) agrees to act on behalf of, or instead of, another (the principal)—see

Chapter 30. The foreign agent is thereby empowered to enter into contracts in the agent's country on behalf of the U.S. principal.

When a substantial market exists in a foreign country, a U.S. firm may wish to appoint a distributor located in that country. The U.S. firm and the distributor enter into a **distribution agreement**, which is a contract between the seller and the distributor setting out the terms and conditions of the distributorship—for example, price, currency of payment, guarantee of supply availability, and method of payment. The terms and conditions primarily involve contract law. Disputes concerning distribution agreements may involve jurisdictional or other issues, however.

Manufacturing Abroad. An alternative to direct or indirect exporting is the establishment of foreign manufacturing facilities. Typically, U.S. firms want to establish manufacturing plants abroad if they believe that by doing so they will reduce costs—particularly for labor, shipping, and raw materials—and thereby be able to compete more effectively in foreign markets. Apple Computer, IBM, General Motors, and Ford are some of the many U.S. companies that have established manufacturing facilities abroad. Foreign firms have done the same in the United States. Sony, Nissan, and other Japanese manufacturers have established U.S. plants to avoid import duties that the U.S. Congress may impose on Japanese products entering this country.

An American firm can conduct manufacturing operations in other countries in several ways. They include licensing and franchising, as well as investing in a wholly owned subsidiary or a joint venture.

Licensing. A U.S. firm can obtain business from abroad by licensing a foreign manufacturing company to use its copyrighted, patented, or trademarked intellectual property or trade secrets. Like any other licensing agreement (see Chapter 23), a licensing agreement with a foreign-based firm calls for a payment of royalties on some basis—such as so many cents per unit produced or a certain percentage of profits from units sold in a particular geographical territory. For example, the Coca-Cola Bottling Company licenses firms worldwide to use (and keep confidential) its secret formula for the syrup used in that soft drink, in return for a percentage of the income gained from the sale of Coca-Cola by those firms.

The licensing of intellectual property rights benefits all parties to the transaction: the firm that receives the license can take advantage of an established reputation for quality, and the firm that grants the license receives income from the foreign sales of its products, as well as establishing a global reputation. Also, once a firm's trademark is known worldwide, the demand for other products manufactured or sold by that firm may increase—obviously an important consideration.

Franchising. Franchising is a well-known form of licensing. Recall from Chapter 39 that a franchise can be defined as an arrangement in which the owner of a trademark, trade name, or copyright (the franchisor) licenses another (the franchisee) to use the trademark, trade name, or copyright, under certain conditions or limitations, in the selling of goods or services. In return, the franchisee pays a fee, which is usually based on a percentage of gross or net sales. Examples of international franchises include McDonald's, Holiday Inn, Avis, and Hertz.

Investing in a Wholly Owned Subsidiary or a Joint Venture. One way to expand into a foreign market is to establish a wholly owned subsidiary firm in a foreign country. The European subsidiary would likely take the form of a *société anonyme (S.A.),* which is similar to a U.S. corporation. In German-speaking nations, it would be called an *Aktiengesellschaft (A.G.).* When a wholly owned subsidiary is established, the parent company, which remains in the United States, retains complete ownership of all the facilities in the foreign country, as well as total authority and control over all phases of the operation.

The expansion of a U.S. firm into international markets can also take the form of a joint venture. In a joint venture, the U.S. company owns only part of the operation; the rest is owned either by local owners in the foreign country or by another foreign entity. In a joint venture, responsibilities, as well as profits and liabilities, are shared by all of the firms involved in the venture. (See Chapter 39 for a more detailed discussion of joint ventures.)

THE REGULATION OF INTERNATIONAL BUSINESS ACTIVITIES

Doing business abroad can affect the economies, foreign policy, domestic politics, and other national interests of the countries involved. For this reason, nations impose laws to restrict or facilitate international business. Controls may also be imposed by international agreements.

Investing. Investing in foreign nations involves a risk that the foreign government may expropriate the investment property. As mentioned earlier in this chapter, expropriation occurs when property is taken and the owner is paid just compensation for what is taken. This does not violate generally observed principles of international law. Such principles are normally violated, however, when property is confiscated by a government without compensation (or without adequate compensation).

Few remedies are available for confiscation of property by a foreign government. Claims are often resolved by lump-sum settlements after negotiations between the United States and the taking nation. For example, investors whose claims arose out of confiscations following the Russian Revolution in 1917 were offered a lump-sum settlement by the Union of Soviet Socialist Republics in 1974. Still outstanding are $2 billion in claims against Cuba for confiscations that occurred in 1959 and 1960.

To counter the deterrent effect that the possibility of confiscation may have on potential investors, many countries guarantee compensation to foreign investors if property is taken. A guaranty can be in the form of national constitutional or statutory laws or provisions in international treaties. As further protection for foreign investments, some countries provide insurance for their citizens' investments abroad.

Export Control. The U.S. Constitution provides in Article I, Section 9, that "No Tax or Duty shall be laid on Articles exported from any State." Thus, Congress cannot impose any export taxes. Congress can, however, use a variety of other devices to control exports. Congress may set export quotas on various items, such as grain being sold abroad. Under the Export Administration Act of 1979,[3] restrictions can be imposed on the flow of technologically advanced products and technical data. A controversial control in recent years has been the U.S. Department of Commerce's attempt to restrict the export of encryption software.

Devices to stimulate exports and thereby aid domestic businesses include export incentives and subsidies. The Revenue Act of 1971,[4] for example, gave tax benefits to firms marketing their products overseas through certain foreign sales corporations, exempting income produced by the exports. Under the Export Trading Company Act of 1982,[5] U.S. banks are encouraged to invest in export trading companies. An export trading company consists of exporting firms joined together to export a line of goods. The Export-Import Bank provides financial assistance, consisting primarily of credit guaranties given to commercial banks that in turn loan funds to U.S. exporting companies.

Import Control. All nations have restrictions on imports, and the United States is no exception. Restrictions include strict prohibitions, quotas, and tariffs. Under the Trading with the Enemy Act of 1917,[6] for example, no goods may be imported from nations that have been designated enemies of the United States. Other laws prohibit the importation of illegal drugs, books that urge insurrection against the United States, and agricultural products that pose dangers to domestic crops or animals.

Quotas are limits on the amounts of goods that can be imported. At one time, the United States had legal quotas on the numbers of automobiles that could be imported from Japan. Currently, Japan "voluntarily" restricts the numbers of automobiles exported to the United States. **Tariffs** are taxes on imports. A tariff is usually a percentage of the value of the import, but it can be a flat rate per unit (such as per barrel of oil). Tariffs raise the prices of goods, causing some consumers to purchase less expensive, domestically manufactured goods.

The United States has specific laws directed at what it sees as unfair international trade practices. **Dumping**, for example, is the sale of imported goods at "less than fair value." *Fair value* is usually determined by the price of those goods in the exporting country. Dumping is designed to undersell U.S. businesses and obtain a larger share of the U.S. market. To prevent this, an extra tariff—known as an *antidumping duty*—may be assessed on the imports.

The procedure for imposing antidumping duties involves two U.S. government agencies: the International Trade Commission (ITC) and the International Trade Administration (ITA). The ITC is an independent agency that makes recommendations to the president concerning temporary import restrictions. The ITC assesses the effects of dumping on domestic businesses. The ITA is part of the Department of Commerce and decides whether imports were sold

3. 50 U.S.C. App. Sections 2401–2420.

4. 26 U.S.C. Sections 991–994.

5. 15 U.S.C. Sections 4001, 4003.

6. 12 U.S.C. Section 95a.

at less than fair value. The ITA determination establishes the amount of antidumping duties, which are set to equal the difference between the price charged in the United States and the price charged in the exporting country. A duty may be retroactive to cover past dumping.

Westlaw. See Case 52.1 at the end of this chapter. To view the full, unedited case from Westlaw,® go to this text's Web site at **http://wbl-cs.westbuslaw.com**.

International Organizations and Agreements. Over the last decade, countries competing for international trade have become more evenly matched competitors than in earlier years. In part, this is due to the increased use and success of international and regional organizations, such as the World Trade Organization, the European Union, and the North American Free Trade Agreement.

The World Trade Organization. The origins of the World Trade Organization (WTO) date to 1947, when the General Agreement on Tariffs and Trade (GATT) was formed for the purpose of minimizing trade barriers among nations. In subsequent decades, the GATT became the principal instrument for regulating international trade, and over time negotiated tariff reductions on a broad range of products.

In 1994, in a final round of GATT negotiations, called the "Uruguay Round," representatives from over one hundred nations signed agreements relating to investment policies, dispute resolution, and other topics. One of these agreements, the Trade-Related Aspects of Intellectual Property Rights Agreement (TRIPS), was discussed in Chapter 7. The Uruguay Round also established the World Trade Organization (WTO), which replaced the GATT beginning in 1995. Each member country of the WTO agreed to grant **most-favored-nation status** to other member countries. This means that each WTO member must treat other WTO members at least as well as it treats the country that receives its most favorable treatment with regard to imports or exports.)

The European Union (EU). The European Union (EU) arose out of the 1957 Treaty of Rome, which created the Common Market, a free trade zone comprising the nations of Belgium, France, West Germany, Italy, the Netherlands, and Luxembourg. Since 1957, more nations have been added. In 1995, the EU became a single integrated European trading unit made up of fifteen European nations.

The EU has its own governing authorities. One is the Council of Ministers, which coordinates economic policies and includes one representative from each nation. The EU also has a commission that proposes regulations to the council and an elected assembly, which oversees the commission. The EU also has its own court, the European Court of Justice, which can review each nation's judicial decisions and is the ultimate authority on EU law.

The EU has gone far toward creating a new body of law to govern all of the member nations—although some of its efforts to create uniform laws have been confounded by nationalism. The council and the commission issue regulations, or directives, that define EU law in various areas, and these requirements normally are binding on all member countries. EU directives govern such issues as environmental law, product liability, anticompetitive practices, and laws governing corporations. The EU directive on product liability, for example, states that a "producer of an article shall be liable for damages caused by a defect in the article, whether or not he knew or could have known of the defect." Liability extends to anyone who puts a trademark or other identifying feature on an article, and liability may not be excluded, even by contract.

The North American Free Trade Agreement (NAFTA). The North American Free Trade Agreement (NAFTA), which was signed in 1993 and became effective on January 1, 1994, created a regional trading unit consisting of Mexico, the United States, and Canada. The primary goal of NAFTA is to eliminate tariffs among these three nations on substantially all goods over a period of fifteen to twenty years.

NAFTA gives the three countries a competitive advantage by retaining tariffs on goods imported from countries outside the NAFTA trading unit. Additionally, NAFTA provides for the elimination of barriers that traditionally have prevented the cross-border movement of services, such as financial and transportation services. For example, NAFTA provides that, with some exceptions, U.S. firms do not have to relocate in Mexico or Canada to provide services in those countries. NAFTA also attempts to eliminate citizenship requirements for the licensing of accountants, attorneys, physicians, and other professionals.

DISPUTE SETTLEMENT IN THE INTERNATIONAL CONTEXT

Businesspersons who engage in international business transactions normally take special precautions to protect themselves in the event that a party with whom they are dealing in another country breaches an agreement. Recall from Chapter 2 that the arbitration of civil disputes is becoming an increasingly attractive alternative to costly litigation through the court system. This is true on the international level as well. For example, arbitration clauses are frequently found in contracts governing the international sale of goods. By means of such clauses, the parties agree in advance to be bound by the decision of a specified third party in the event of a dispute.

The third party may be a neutral entity (such as the International Chamber of Commerce), a panel of individuals representing both parties' interests, or some other group or organization. The United Nations Convention on the Recognition and Enforcement of Foreign Arbitral Awards[7]—which has been implemented in more than fifty countries, including the United States—assists in the enforcement of arbitration clauses, as do provisions in specific treaties among nations. The American Arbitration Association (discussed in Chapter 2) provides arbitration services for international as well as domestic disputes.

When no arbitration clause is contained in a sales contract, a contract dispute may end in litigation. If the contract includes forum-selection and choice-of-law clauses (discussed in Chapter 18), a court in the specified forum country will hear the lawsuit according to that country's law. If no forum or choice of law has been designated, however, legal proceedings will be more complex and attended by much more uncertainty. For example, litigation may take place in two or more countries, with each country applying its own choice-of-law rules to determine which substantive law will be applied to the particular transactions.

Furthermore, even if a plaintiff wins a favorable judgment in a lawsuit litigated in the plaintiff's country, there is no guarantee that the court's judgment will be enforced by judicial bodies in the defendant's country. As discussed earlier in this chapter, under the principle of comity, the judgment may be enforced in the defendant's country, particularly if the defendant's country is the United States and the foreign court's decision is consistent with U.S. national law and policy. Other nations, however, may not be as accommodating as the United States, and the plaintiff may be left empty-handed.

See Case 52.2 at the end of this chapter. To view the full, unedited case from Westlaw,® go to this text's Web site at **http://wbl-cs.westbuslaw.com**.

SECTION 3

Comparative Law

When doing business in a foreign nation, a company generally will be subject to the jurisdiction and laws of that nation. Therefore, businesspersons will find it helpful to become familiar with the legal systems and laws of foreign nations in which they conduct commercial transactions. We look at some similarities and differences in national legal systems, laws, and cultural and business traditions in this section on **comparative law**, which can be defined as the study and comparison of legal systems and laws across nations.

COMPARATIVE LEGAL SYSTEMS

The legal systems of foreign nations differ, in widely varying degrees, from that of the United States. Additionally, a number of nations have specialized commercial law courts to deal with business disputes (in the United States, some jurisdictions are establishing similar courts). France instituted such courts in 1807, and most nations with commercial codes have done likewise. The United Kingdom also has special commercial courts overseen by judges with expertise in business law.

Common Law and Civil Law Systems. Legal systems around the globe generally are divided into *common law* and *civil law* systems. As discussed in Chapter 1, in a common law system, the courts independently develop the rules governing certain areas of law, such as torts and contracts. These common law rules apply to all areas not covered by statutory law. Although the common law doctrine of *stare decisis* obligates judges to follow precedential decisions in their jurisdictions, courts may modify or even overturn precedents when deemed necessary. Additionally, if there is no case law to

7. June 10, 1958, 21 U.S.T. 2517, T.I.A.S. No. 6997 (the "New York Convention").

guide a court, the court may create a new rule of law. Common law systems exist today in countries that were once a part of the British Empire (such as Australia, India, and the United States).

In contrast to Great Britain and the other common law countries, most of the European nations base their legal systems on Roman civil law, or "code law." The term *civil law,* as used here, refers not to civil as opposed to criminal law but to *codified* law—an ordered grouping of legal principles enacted into law by a legislature or other governing body. In a **civil law system,** the only official source of law is a statutory code. Courts are required to interpret the code and apply the rules to individual cases, but courts may not depart from the code and develop their own laws. In theory, the law code will set forth all the principles needed for the legal system.

Today, civil law systems are followed in most of the continental European countries, as well as in the Latin American, African, and Asian countries that were once colonies of the continental European nations. Japan and South Africa also have civil law systems. Components of the civil law system are found in the Islamic courts of predominantly Muslim countries. In the United States, the state of Louisiana, because of its historical ties to France, has, in part, a civil law system. Exhibit 52–2 lists some of the nations that use common law systems and some that use civil law systems.

Legal Systems Compared. Common law and civil law systems are not wholly distinct. For example, although the United States has a common law system, crimes are defined by statute as in civil law systems. Civil law systems also may allow considerable room for judges to develop law. There is also some variation within common law and civil law systems. The judges of different common law nations have produced differing common law principles. Although the United States and India both derived their legal traditions from England, the common law principles governing contract law vary in some respects between the two countries.

Similarly, the laws of nations that have civil law systems differ considerably. For example, the French code tends to set forth general principles of law, while the German code is far more specific and runs to thousands of sections. In some Middle Eastern countries, codes are grounded in the religious law of Islam, called ***sharia.*** The religious basis of these codes makes them far more difficult to alter.

See Case 52.3 at the end of this chapter. To view the full, unedited case from Westlaw,® go to this text's Web site at **http://wbl-cs.westbuslaw.com**.

Judges and Procedures. Judges play similar roles in virtually all countries: their primary function is the resolution of litigation. The characteristics and qualifications of judges, which are typically set forth in the nation's constitution, can vary widely, however. The U.S. judge normally does not actively participate in a trial, but many foreign judges involve themselves closely in the proceedings, such as by questioning witnesses.

The procedures employed in resolving cases also vary substantially from country to country. A knowledge of a nation's legal procedures is important for a person conducting business transactions in that nation. For example, an American businessperson was on trial in Saudi Arabia for assaulting and slandering a co-worker, an offense for which he might have been jailed or deported. He initially was required to present two witnesses to his version of events, but he had only one. Fortunately, he became aware that he could "demand the oath." In this procedure, he swore before God that he had neither kicked nor slandered the complainant. After taking the oath, he was promptly

EXHIBIT 52–2 THE LEGAL SYSTEMS OF NATIONS

CIVIL LAW	COMMON LAW
Argentina	Australia
Austria	Bangladesh
Brazil	Canada
Chile	Ghana
China	India
Egypt	Israel
Finland	Jamaica
France	Kenya
Germany	Malaysia
Greece	New Zealand
Indonesia	Nigeria
Iran	Singapore
Italy	United Kingdom
Japan	United States
Mexico	Zambia
Poland	
South Korea	
Sweden	
Tunisia	
Venezuela	

adjudged not guilty, as lying under oath is one of the most serious sins under Islamic law. Had he failed to demand the oath, he almost certainly would have been found guilty.

NATIONAL LAWS COMPARED

A businessperson engaging in business operations abroad would be wise to learn about the relevant national laws that may affect those operations. Virtually all nations have laws governing torts, contracts, employment, and other areas. Even when the basic principles are fundamentally similar (as in contract law), there are significant variations in the practical application and effect of these laws across countries. This section summarizes some of the similarities and differences among national laws relating to tort law, contracts, and employment relationships.

Tort Law. Tort law, which allows persons to recover damages for harms or injuries caused by the wrongful actions of others (see Chapters 5 and 6), may vary widely among nations. Common law nations have developed a body of judge-made law regarding what kinds of actions constitute negligence or some other tort that permits recovery. Civil law nations must authorize such recovery in their codes. Exhibit 52–3 shows how the civil law codes of several nations define what constitutes a tort.

Even when the statutory language is similar, the application of tort law varies among nations. For example, which party has the burden of proof in a tort lawsuit differs among countries. In the United States, the burden of proof is on the plaintiff. In Russia, the defendant has the burden of proving that he or she was not at fault. Statutes of limitations (deadlines for filing a lawsuit) in other countries also vary considerably. Generally, the limitations period is longer in other countries than it is in the United States. Additionally, national tort laws vary with respect to certain concepts, including failures to act and damages.

Failures to Act. National tort laws differ considerably with respect to liability for omissions, or failures to act. In some situations, a failure to act will not be regarded as a tort. For example, in the United States, tort law imposes no "duty to rescue," and a person normally is not liable for failing to rescue another person in distress. German law is basically similar. In some countries, though, the failure to rescue another in distress is regarded as negligence.

EXHIBIT 52–3 CIVIL CODE TORT DEFINITIONS

Brazil: He who, by a voluntary act or omission, by negligence or carelessness, violates another's right, or causes him harm, is bound to compensate for the damage.

Egypt: Every culpable act that causes damage to another obliges the person who did it to compensate for it.

The Netherlands: Every unlawful act by which damage is caused to another obliges the person by whose fault the damage occurred to compensate for it.

Spain: He who by act or omission causes damage to another, either by fault or negligence, is obliged to compensate for the damage caused.

Tunisia: Every act a person does without lawful justification that causes willful and voluntary damage—material or moral—to another obliges the person who did it to compensate for the aforesaid damage, when it is shown that the act is the direct cause.

Uruguay: Every unlawful act a person does which causes damage to another imposes on the person whose malice, fault, or negligence brought it about the obligation to compensate for it. When the unlawful act was done maliciously, i.e., with the intention of causing harm—it amounts to a delict [an intentional tort, discussed in Chapter 5, or a crime], when the intention to cause harm is not present, the unlawful act amounts to a quasi-delict [a tort or a crime caused by negligence]. In either case, the unlawful act can be negative or positive according to whether the breach of duty consists of an act or omission.

SOURCE: Andre Tunc, *International Encyclopedia of Comparative Law*, Vol. XI, Chapter 2, pp. 5–6.

Damages. National tort laws also differ in the way in which damages in tort cases are calculated. For example, Swiss law and Turkish law permit a court to reduce damages if an award of full damages would cause undue hardship for a party who was found negligent. In some nations of northern Africa, different amounts of damages are awarded depending on the type of tortious action committed and the degree of intent involved. In the United States, the calculation of actual (compensatory) damages does not depend on whether the tort was negligent or intentional.

Contract Law. Because international business transactions typically involve contracts, businesspersons should familiarize themselves with the contract law of the countries in which they do business. To a degree, the United Nations Convention on Contracts for the International Sale of Goods (CISG), which was described in detail in Chapter 18, has simplified matters for parties to international sales contracts.

For many transactions, however, the CISG may not be applicable. For one thing, the CISG applies only to transactions involving firms in countries that have signed the convention, or agreement, and parties (in nonsignatory nations) that have stipulated in their contracts that the CISG will govern any dispute. When transactions involve firms in countries that are not signatory to the CISG, the contract parties need to determine which nation's law will govern any disputes that may arise under the contract. Additionally, even when the CISG would apply, it does so only if the parties have not agreed otherwise in their contract. For example, parties may agree in their contract that German law or U.S. law or some other nation's law will govern any contract dispute that arises. For these reasons, the contract laws of individual nations remain important to businesspersons involved in international contracts.

Generally, the laws of other nations governing contracts are similar to those in the United States. Recall from Chapter 9 that for a valid contract to be formed, four requirements must be met—agreement, consideration, capacity, and legality. These requirements were discussed at length in Chapters 10 through 12. Additionally, a valid contract may be unenforceable if genuineness of assent was lacking or if the contract was not in the proper form—such as in writing when the law requires that type of contract to be in writing. Many of these requirements exist under other nations' laws as well, but there are some significant differences.

Agreement. The requirement of agreement (offer and acceptance) is common among countries, although what is considered an offer varies by jurisdiction. In the United States, an offer, once made, normally can be revoked (canceled, or taken back) by the offeror at any time prior to the offer's acceptance. Many nations, however, require that an offer must remain open for some minimum period of time. For example, the German Civil Code, which has detailed provisions governing offer and acceptance, requires that a written contractual offer must be held open for a reasonable time, unless the offer specifically states otherwise. Unlike those in the United States, oral contractual offers (those made in person or by telephone) in Germany must be accepted immediately, or they terminate.

Mexico has some special rules for offer and acceptance. If a time for acceptance is not stated in an offer, the offer is deemed to be held open for three days, plus whatever time is necessary for the offer and acceptance to be sent through the mails. If acceptance is desired sooner, the offeror must state the time for acceptance in the offer.

In the United States, a contract's terms must be sufficiently definite that the parties (and a court) can determine whether the contract has been formed (see Chapter 10). For contracts for the sale of goods, however, the Uniform Commercial Code (UCC) has substantially relaxed common law requirements in respect to definiteness of contract terms (see Chapter 18). Mexico also has adopted a commercial code, which, like the UCC, liberalizes the traditional requirements of definiteness in mercantile transactions. Under contract law in some countries, such as Saudi Arabia, however, there are strict requirements about the definiteness of a contract's terms. If the terms of an offer are too vague or indefinite, acceptance of that offer normally will not create a valid contract.

Consideration. In contrast to contract law in the United States, contract law in most civil law countries does not require consideration in order for a contract to be legally binding on the parties. German law, for example, does not require the exchange of consideration. An agreement to make a gift may thus be enforceable by the donee (the gift's recipient). In the United States, because consideration is required for a valid contract, promises to make gifts normally are not enforceable (because the donee does not give consideration for the gift—see Chapter 11).

In other countries, such as Saudi Arabia, consideration is required. Similarly, in India, consideration normally is required, although some contracts may be lawful even when the consideration consists of "past consideration" (that is, consideration that consists of an action that occurred in the past). As noted in Chapter 11, in the United States past consideration is no consideration.

Remedies for Breach of Contract. The types of remedies available for breach of contract vary widely throughout the world. In many countries, as in the United States, the normal remedy is damages—money given to the nonbreaching party to compensate that party for the losses incurred owing to the breach (see Chapter 17). The calculation of damages resulting from a breach of contract, however, may differ from one country to another, as does the calculation of damages under tort law.

National contract laws also differ as to whether and when equitable remedies, such as specific performance (discussed in Chapter 17), will be granted. Germany's typical remedy for a breach of contract is specific performance, which means that the party must go forward and perform the contract. Damages are available only after certain procedures have been employed to seek performance. In contrast, in the United States, the equitable remedy of specific performance will usually not be granted unless the remedy at law (money damages) is inadequate and the subject matter of the contract is unique.

Defenses. As in the United States, contract law in most nations allows parties to defend against contractual liability by claiming that certain requirements for contract enforceability are lacking. For example, many nations, including the United States, have laws requiring that certain types of contracts must be in writing. If such contracts are not in writing, they will not be enforced. In Saudi Arabia, the law strongly encourages parties to put all contracts in writing, and any written contract should be formally witnessed by two males or a male and a female. In that country, it may be difficult to enforce an oral contract.

Another common defense is the assertion that a contract was entered into because of a mistake, fraud, or duress, and thus genuineness of assent to the contract's terms was lacking. In some countries, a party may claim that a contract was not formed because the consideration supporting the contract was inadequate—that is, not *enough* value or money was given in exchange for a contractual promise. Indian courts, for example, look to the adequacy of consideration when determining whether the parties' assent to the contract was truly genuine and therefore whether the contract should be enforced. In the United States, in contrast, courts rarely inquire into the adequacy of consideration. Normally, only in cases in which the consideration is so grossly inadequate as to "shock the conscience of the court" will a court refuse to enforce a contract on this basis.

Employment Law. Employment law is particularly important in many foreign nations. The United States traditionally left the details of the employment relationship to a negotiation between the employer and the employee. Under the common law *employment-at-will doctrine* (discussed in Chapter 41), employers are free to hire and fire employees "at will," meaning that an employee can be fired for any reason or no reason at all. Today, this common law doctrine is less applicable in the United States, because the workplace is regulated extensively by federal and state statutory law. Employment relationships in other nations also are subject to government regulation.

Modifications to the At-Will Doctrine. Many other countries, similar to the United States, have modified their traditional at-will employment rules. In France, for example, the concept of employment at will can be traced back to the original Napoleonic Code. Over the years, the French have modified this doctrine considerably. French courts developed the doctrine of ***abus de droit*** (abuse of rights), which prohibited employers from firing workers for illness, pregnancy, unionization, political beliefs, the exercise of certain rights, or even personal dislike. French courts also began requiring employers to follow customary procedures before terminating workers. French employee-discharge laws were codified in the Dismissal Law of 1973, which also established procedural requirements that employers must follow when discharging workers (to be discussed shortly).

Under the Polish labor code, employment continues to be predominantly "at will." Either party may terminate the employment relationship at any time. Advance notice is generally required, however, and notice requirements vary, depending on the length of the worker's tenure with the employer. An employer may terminate an employee immediately and without notice if the worker has committed a criminal offense, lost a license or other employment qualification, seriously breached his or her duties, or failed to appear regularly at the job site. An employer cannot immediately discharge an employee for the last reason if the employee's absence was due to child-care needs, infectious disease, or entitled sick leave.

Wages and Benefits. One of the reasons U.S. businesspersons decide to establish business operations, such as factories, in other countries is to cut production costs by taking advantage of lower wage rates. Although workers' wages may be lower in some countries than in the United States, typically workers in other countries have many paid holidays, plus vacation time. In addition, employers in other countries may be subject to a variety of requirements not found in the United States.

In Mexico, for example, workers have a right to an annual bonus equal to fifteen days' salary and paid at the end of the year. Mexican law requires a minimum amount of paid vacation time (six days in the first year of employment) and also requires that companies give workers a 25 percent bonus above their ordinary pay rates during those vacations. For example, if a worker's ordinary pay is $200 per week, the vacation pay is $250 per week. Mexican employers also must periodically give training courses to workers. In some countries, such as Egypt, fringe benefits for employees account for as much as 40 percent of an employer's payroll costs.

Equal Employment Opportunity. National laws around the globe vary widely with respect to equal employment opportunity. In the United States, employers are prohibited from discriminating against employees or job applicants on the basis of race, color, national origin, gender, religion, age, or disability. U.S. laws prohibiting discrimination on these bases also apply to all U.S. employees working for U.S. employers abroad. Generally, a U.S. employer must abide by U.S. laws prohibiting employment discrimination *unless* to do so would violate the laws of the country in which the employer's workplace is located. This "foreign laws exception" usually allows U.S. employers abroad to avoid being subjected to conflicting laws.

Some other countries also prohibit discriminatory practices. For example, in Indonesia, the Ministry of Manpower, which implements employment laws and regulations, prohibits discrimination in the workplace. Mexican law forbids employers from discriminating against employees on the basis of race, religion, or gender. The Japanese constitution prohibits discrimination based on race, religion, nationality, or gender.

In contrast, some countries, such as Egypt and Turkey, have no laws requiring equal employment opportunity. In Argentina, racial, religious, or other discrimination is not a political issue or a practice prohibited by law. Similarly, in Brazil, equal opportunity is not a factor in employment relationships.

Generally, in those countries that do prohibit employment discrimination, employers retain some flexibility in hiring and firing managerial personnel. In Mexico, for example, employers traditionally have been allowed to hire and fire "confidential" employees—managerial employees—at their discretion. In Italy, workers classified as managers are also less protected by the law than rank-and-file employees are.

Employment Termination. In many countries, employers find it difficult, and often quite costly, to discharge employees. Employment laws may prohibit the firing of employees for discriminatory reasons, and other laws may also come into play. For example, in France, if an employment contract is for an indefinite term, the employer can fire the worker only for genuine and serious cause or for economic reasons. The law also establishes procedural requirements. Before terminating a worker for cause, the employer must undertake a conciliatory session with labor court mediators. The employer has the burden of proving to the labor court that the cause of the dismissal was serious.

In Egypt, employers commonly use fixed-period employment contracts, which are automatically terminated at the end of the contract period. If an employee continues to work after the end of the contract period and no new contract is created, the employment contract becomes indefinite. It is very difficult to discharge an employee with an indefinite contract. The employee must first commit a serious offense, whereupon the employer must submit a proposal for termination to a committee consisting of representatives of the union, the employer, and the government. Employees may appeal adverse decisions of this committee.

Taiwanese law places clear restrictions on the termination of employment. An employer must provide a reason for discharging an employee. An employer may discharge an employee with advance notice and severance pay for a number of economic reasons or if the worker is incapable of performing the assigned work. Employers may fire employees without notice or severance pay only for certain reasons, such as violence, imprisonment, or extensive absenteeism.

Cultural and Business Traditions

The ability to conduct business successfully in a foreign nation requires not only a knowledge of that nation's laws but also some familiarity with its cultural traditions, economy, and business climate. One obvious cultural difference among nations is language. For example, Rolls-Royce changed the name of its "Silver Mist" in Germany, because in that country, *mist* translates as "manure." In Japan, Esso had difficulty selling gasoline in part because *Esso* sounds like the Japanese word for stalled car. Pepsi's "Come Alive with Pepsi" campaign was translated in Taiwan as "Pepsi brings your ancestors back from the grave."

The meaning of nonverbal language (body movements, gestures, facial expressions, and the like) also varies from culture to culture. In the United States, for example, a nod of the head indicates "yes," while in some countries, such as Greece, the same gesture means "no."

There are also some important ethical differences. In Islamic countries, for example, the consumption of alcohol and certain foods is forbidden by the Koran (the sacred book of the Islamic religion). It would be thoughtless and imprudent to invite a Saudi Arabian business contact out for a drink. Additionally, in many foreign nations, gift giving is a common practice among contracting companies or between companies and government. To Americans, such gift giving may look suspiciously like an unethical (and possibly illegal) bribe. This has been an important source of friction in international business, particularly after the U.S. Congress passed the Foreign Corrupt Practices Act (FCPA) in 1977 (discussed in Chapter 40). The act prohibits American business firms from offering certain side payments to foreign officials to secure favorable contracts.

The role played by women in other countries may present some troublesome ethical problems for U.S. firms doing business internationally. Equal employment opportunity is a fundamental public policy in the United States, and Title VII of the Civil Rights Act of 1964 (discussed in Chapter 42) prohibits discrimination against women in the employment context. Some other countries, however, largely reject any professional role for women, which may cause difficulties for American women conducting business transactions in those countries. For example, when the World Bank sent a delegation including women to negotiate with the Central Bank of Korea, the Koreans were surprised and offended. They thought that the presence of women meant that the Koreans were not being taken seriously.

Terms and Concepts to Review

abus de droit 1087	dumping 1081	quota 1081
act of state doctrine 1077	export 1079	*sharia* 1084
civil law system 1084	expropriation 1078	sovereign immunity 1079
comity 1077	international law 1076	tariff 1081
comparative law 1083	international organization 1077	treaty 1077
confiscation 1079	most-favored-nation status 1082	
distribution agreement 1080	national law 1076	

Chapter Summary

Sources of International Law	Sources of international law include international customs, treaties and international agreements, and international organizations and conferences.
Legal Principles and Doctrines	1. *The principle of comity*—Under this principle, nations give effect to the laws and judicial decrees of other nations for reasons of courtesy and international harmony. 2. *The act of state doctrine*—A doctrine under which American courts avoid passing judgment on the validity of public acts committed by a recognized foreign government within its own territory. 3. *The doctrine of sovereign immunity*—When certain conditions are satisfied, foreign nations are immune from U.S. jurisdiction under the Foreign Sovereign Immunities Act of 1976. Exceptions are made (a) when a foreign state has "waived its immunity either explicitly or by implication" or (b) when the action is "based upon a commercial activity carried on in the United States by the foreign state."

CHAPTER SUMMARY—CONTINUED

Doing Business Internationally	1. *Types of international business operations*—Ways in which U.S. domestic firms engage in international business transactions include (a) exporting, which may involve foreign agents or distributors; (b) manufacturing abroad; (c) licensing arrangements; (d) franchising; and (e) investing in a wholly owned subsidiary or joint venture. 2. *Regulation of international business activities*—Nations impose laws to restrict or facilitate international business. These laws may take the form of investment guaranties, export controls, and import controls. International and regional organizations that have been formed to facilitate trade by reducing tariffs include the World Trade Organization, the European Union, and the North American Free Trade Agreement. 3. *Dispute settlement*—Typically, businesspersons who engage in international business transactions include arbitration clauses in their contracts to facilitate dispute-settlement proceedings should their contracts be breached by foreign parties. International contracts may also include forum-selection and choice-of-law clauses.
Comparative Law	1. *Definition of comparative law*—Comparative law can be defined as the study and comparison of legal systems and laws across nations. 2. *Legal systems*—Legal systems around the globe generally are divided into common law systems and civil law systems. Common law systems, which are based on the common law tradition that evolved in England, exist today in countries that were once a part of the British Empire. Civil law systems, which are based on Roman civil law, or "code law," exist in most of the European nations, as well as in countries that were once colonies of those nations. 3. *National laws*—There are many similarities and differences among national laws relating to tort law, contracts, and employment relationships. When doing business on a global level, it is important that U.S. businesspersons understand the laws of the nations in which they do business. 4. *Cultural and business traditions*—Understanding the cultural and business traditions of other countries is also important to conducting business successfully in foreign nations.

CASES FOR ANALYSIS

Westlaw. You can access the full text of each case presented below by going to the Westlaw cases on this text's Web site at http://wbl-cs.westbuslaw.com. Each Westlaw case includes the names of all plaintiffs and defendants, the dates on which the case was argued and decided, a brief summary of the issues and decisions in the case, headnotes classifying specific issues in the case according to the West Key Number System, and the court's opinion. Concurring and dissenting opinions, if any, are included as well.

CASE 52.1 IMPORT CONTROL

UNITED STATES V. HAGGAR APPAREL CO.

Supreme Court of the United States, 1999.
526 U.S. 380,
119 S.Ct. 1392,
143 L.Ed.2d 480.

Justice *KENNEDY* delivered the opinion of the Court.

* * * *

I

Respondent Haggar Apparel Co. designs, manufactures, and markets apparel for men. This matter arises from a refund proceeding for duties imposed on men's trousers shipped by respondent to this country from an assembly plant it controlled in Mexico. The fabric had been cut in the United States and then shipped to Mexico, along with the thread, buttons, and zippers necessary to complete the garments. There the trousers were sewn and reshipped to the United States. If that had been the full extent of it, there would be no dispute, for if there were mere assembly without other steps, all agree the imported garments would have been eligible for the duty exemption which respondent claims.

Respondent, however, * * * added one other step at the Mexican plant: permapressing. Permapressing is designed to maintain a garment's crease in the desired place and to avoid other creases or wrinkles that detract from its proper appearance. There are various methods and sequences by which permapressing can be accomplished * * *.

For the permapressed garments in question here, respondent purchased fabric in the United States that had been treated with a chemical resin. After the treated fabric had been cut in the United States, shipped to Mexico, and sewn and given a regular pressing there, respondent baked the garments in an oven at the Mexican facility before tagging and shipping them to the United States. The baking operation took some 12 to 15 minutes. With the right heat, the preapplied chemical was activated and the permapress quality was imparted to the garment. If it had delayed baking until the articles returned to the United States, respondent would have had to take extra, otherwise unnecessary steps in the United States before shipping the garments to retailers. In addition, respondent maintained below, there would have been a risk that during shipping unwanted creases and wrinkles might have developed in the otherwise finished garments.

The [U.S.] Customs Service claimed the baking was an added process in addition to assembly, and denied a duty exemption [granted to other imported goods]; respondent claimed the baking was simply part of the assembly process * * *. Respondent's case was made more difficult by a regulation, to be discussed further, that deems all permapressing operations to be an additional step in manufacture, not part of or incidental to the assembly process. The issue before us is the force and effect of the regulation in subsequent judicial proceedings.

After being denied the exemption it sought for the permapressed articles, respondent brought suit for refund in the [U.S.] Court of International Trade. * * * The court ruled in favor of respondent. On review, the [U.S.] Court of Appeals for the Federal Circuit * * * affirmed. We granted *certiorari* * * *.

II

The statute on which respondent relies provides importers a partial exemption from duties otherwise imposed. The exemption extends to:

> "Articles * * * assembled abroad in whole or in part of fabricated components, the product of the United States, which * * * (c) have not been advanced in value or improved in condition abroad except by being assembled and except by operations incidental to the assembly process such as cleaning, lubricating and painting."

The relevant regulation interpreting the statute with respect to permapressed articles provides as follows:

> "Any significant process, operation, or treatment other than assembly whose primary purpose is the fabrication, completion, physical or chemical improvement of a component, or which is not related to the assembly process, whether or not it effects a substantial transformation of the article, shall not be regarded as incidental to the assembly and shall preclude the application of the exemption to such article. The following are examples of operations not considered incidental to the assembly * * *
>
> * * * *
>
> "(4) Chemical treatment of components or assembled articles to impart new characteristics, such as showerproofing, permapressing, sanforizing, dying or bleaching of textiles."

* * *

* * * *

* * * [R]espondent says the regulation binds Customs Service employees when they classify imported merchandise under the tariff schedules but does not bind the importers themselves. The statutory scheme does not support this limited view of the force and effect of the regulation. The Customs Service (which is within the Treasury Department) is charged with the classification of imported goods under the proper provision of the tariff schedules in the first instance. There is specific statutory direction to this effect: "The Customs Service shall, under rules and regulations prescribed by the Secretary [of the Treasury,] * * * fix the final classification and rate of duty applicable to" imported goods. In addition, the Secretary is directed by statute to "establish and promulgate such rules and regulations not inconsistent with the law * * * as may be necessary to secure a just, impartial and uniform appraisement of imported merchandise and the classification and assessment of duties thereon at the various ports of entry." The Secretary, in turn, has delegated to the Commissioner of Customs the authority to issue generally applicable regulations, subject to the Secretary's approval.

Respondent relies on the specific direction to the Secretary to make rules of classification for "the various ports of entry" to argue that the statute authorizes promulgation of regulations that do nothing more than ensure that customs officers in field offices around the country classify goods according to a similar and consistent scheme. The regulations issued under the statute have no bearing, says respondent, on the rights of the importer. We disagree. The phrase in question is explained by the simple fact that classification decisions must be made at the port where goods enter. We shall not assume Congress was concerned only to ensure that customs officials at the various ports of entry make uniform decisions but that it had no concern for uniformity once the goods entered the country and judicial proceedings commenced. *The tariffs do not mean one thing for customs officers and another for importers.* * * * [Emphasis added.]

* * * *

* * * Particularly in light of the fact that the agency utilized the notice-and-comment rulemaking process before issuing the regulations, the argument that they were not intended to be entitled to judicial deference implies a sufficient departure from conventional contemporary administrative practice that we ought not to adopt it absent a different statutory structure and more express language to this effect in the regulations themselves.

III

For the reasons we have given, the statutes authorizing customs classification regulations are consistent with the usual rule that regulations of an administering agency warrant judicial deference; and nothing in the regulation itself persuades us that the agency intended the regulation to have some lesser force and effect. * * *

* * * *

The judgment is vacated, and the case is remanded for further proceedings consistent with this opinion.

It is so ordered.

Justice *STEVENS* * * * dissenting * * * .

* * * *

Respondent's strongest challenge to the judgment of the Customs Service is that the Service has misinterpreted and misapplied one of its excluded examples * * * . Respondent contends that the Service cannot treat pressing-plus-ovenbaking, but not pressing alone, as a species of chemical treatment that is not incidental to the assembly process.

There is a rather obvious answer to this contention. One can certainly discern a meaningful difference between merely pressing a synthetic fabric, on the one hand, and using ovenbaking (or perhaps extended pressing) to treat a fabric to which another substance has been added. Based on that difference, the Service could logically conclude, in accord with its understanding of its own regulation, that only the latter is a form of "chemical treatment" excluded from a duty exemption. Indeed, distinguishing these two operations in this fashion is the product of the kind of line-drawing decisions that must be made by agencies to which Congress has delegated the job of administering legislation that contains ambiguous terms. * * *

In my view, the regulation before us is a reasonable elaboration of the statute, and the Customs Service's denial of a duty allowance in this case was consistent with its regulation and well within the scope of its congressionally delegated authority. * * * I would simply reverse the judgment of the Court of Appeals.

CASE 52.2 CHOICE OF FORUM

GARWARE POLYESTER, LTD. V. INTERMAX TRADING CORP.

United States District Court,
Southern District of New York, 2001.
__ F.Supp.2d __.

CHIN, D.J. [District Judge]

* * * *

BACKGROUND

Garware [Polyester, Ltd.], headquartered in Mumbai, India, develops and manufactures plastics and high-tech polyester film. Intermax [Trading Corp.], a New York corporation, sells and distributes Garware products in North America. In 1987, Intermax became a selling agent for GARFILM and other Garware products. This agency relationship lasted approximately twelve years, and it was governed by four written agreements, dated June 30, 1987, May 30, 1990, May 25, 1993, and May 25, 1996, consecutively (collectively, the "Agency Agreements"). The Agency Agreements set forth the terms and conditions of the relationship, and each included the following forum selection clause:

> *Jurisdiction:* All the terms and conditions of this agreement, unless otherwise specifically provided, are to be observed and performed at Bombay [India]. The courts at Bombay alone will have jurisdiction to try out suits in respect of any claim or dispute arising out of or under this agreement or in any way relating to the same.

Over the course of the twelve-year relationship, sales of Garware products by Intermax in the defined territory were made in two ways: through "direct" sales, where Intermax arranged for customers to order products directly from Garware; or through "warehouse" sales, where Intermax bought products from Garware, housed them in warehouses located in the United States, and then resold them to customers in the territory. For both direct and warehouse sales, Intermax received commissions from Garware.

In the fall of 1998, Intermax fell behind on its payments to Garware. In August 2000, Garware commenced this lawsuit, seeking payment for twenty-two purportedly unpaid invoices. Intermax, however, contends that Garware breached the relationship first, and it raises numerous counter-claims and affirmative defenses.

DISCUSSION

The forum selection clause in the Agency Agreements provides that the "courts at Bombay alone" have jurisdiction over causes of action "in any way relating" to the Agreements. Thus, the Court first considers whether the forum selection clause is valid and enforceable, and then whether the clause applies to the dispute here.

A. Enforceability of the Forum Selection Clause

Forum selection clauses are *prima facie* valid and should be enforced unless enforcement is shown by the resisting party to be unreasonable under the circumstances. In particular, *a forum selection clause is presumed valid where the underlying transaction is international in character.* * * * [I]mportant public policy underlies this presumption: forum selection clauses eliminate uncertainty in international commerce and insure that the parties are not unexpectedly subjected to hostile forums and laws. Moreover, international comity dictates that American courts enforce these sorts of clauses out of respect for the integrity and respect of foreign tribunals. The presumptive validity of forum selection clauses may only be overcome by a strong showing that the clause is unreasonable under the circumstances. [Emphasis added.]

Here, neither party challenges the enforceability of the forum selection clause as it relates to the Agency Agreements, and neither party argues that the clause is unreasonable. Accordingly, I conclude that the forum selection clause is valid and enforceable.

B. The Scope of the Forum Selection Clause

The parties, however, disagree on whether Garware's action here * * * falls within the reach of the forum selection clause, which covers "any claim or dispute arising out of or under this agreement or in any way relating to the same." Garware argues that warehouse sales, which make up all of the twenty-two invoices in question, are not part of and do not relate to the agency relationship formed in 1987, and are therefore not subject to the Agency Agreements' terms and conditions, including the forum selection clause. Rather, Garware contends that the warehouse sales are governed exclusively by the terms and conditions created by the exchange of purchase orders and invoices for each transaction.

I reject this argument. * * * A forum selection clause should not be defeated by artful pleading of claims not based on the contract containing the clause if those claims grow out of the contractual relationship, or if the gist of those claims is a breach of that relationship. Moreover, courts have read forum selection clauses to encompass claims beyond a breach of the contract containing the clause.

Here, the "gist" of Garware's claim is a breach of the Agency Agreements. The warehouse sales in question were made by Intermax for the purpose of selling Garware product in the contractually defined territory. The Agency Agreements specifically relate to Intermax's role as Garware's "selling agents for promoting sales of GARFILM * * * in the United States of America * * * ." Thus, if these sales are not squarely within the scope of the Agency Agreements, they are, at the very least, related to the Agreements. Further, the parties' course of dealing supports the conclusion that the parties themselves believed the Agency Agreements included warehouse sales: as required by the Agreements, Garware paid commissions to Intermax on these sales. Hence, I conclude that the forum selection clause is applicable to Garware's claims.

CONCLUSION

As the forum selection clause contained in the Agency Agreements is valid and enforceable, and as the clause is applicable to the claims Garware raises here, proper venue for this case is in the courts of Bombay. Accordingly, the Clerk of the Court is directed to enter judgment dismissing the complaint * * * and to close the case.

SO ORDERED.

CASE 52.3 COMPARATIVE LAW

UNIVERSE SALES CO. V. SILVER CASTLE, LTD.

United States Court of Appeals,
Ninth Circuit, 1999.
182 F.3d 1036.

BRUNETTI, Circuit Judge:

* * * *

I.

Universe [Sales Company] filed this lawsuit on September 21, 1995 in California state court, seeking restitution for royalties it had paid to [Offshore of California, Inc. (OCI), which was later acquired by Offshore Sportswear, Inc.]—a company that allegedly did not own the two trademarks at issue (the "Marks"). The case was removed to the United States District Court for the Central District of California on October 23, 1995. On November 3, 1995, Sportswear filed an answer together with counterclaims seeking unpaid royalties and $19,008 allegedly due on goods Universe bought from OCI in 1994.

On January 13, 1997, Universe filed a motion for summary judgment. Sportswear filed a cross-motion for summary judgment the next day. * * *

* * * The court * * * granted Universe's summary judgment motion but awarded no damages to Universe. Sportswear appealed.

II.

The district court analyzed the royalty issue that is in dispute under Japanese trademark law, and found that Universe is not obligated to pay royalties to Sportswear. Sportswear argues, *inter alia*, that the district court erred because it failed to consider properly the Declaration of Mitsuhiro Kamiya, a Japanese attorney who specializes in Japanese trademark and contract law. Specifically, Sportswear contends that the Kamiya declaration establishes that Japanese contract law controls in this scenario and that under that body of law the License Agreement executed by [the parties in this case] is a valid and enforceable agreement such that Sportswear is now entitled to receive past royalties due from Universe. According to Sportswear, because the Kamiya declaration has not been not been rebutted by Universe the district court erred in concluding that under Japanese law Universe is not obligated to make royalty payments. We agree with Sportswear's arguments regarding the district court's failure properly to take the Kamiya declaration into account.

The Kamiya declaration states that Japanese contract law, not Japanese trademark law, is controlling in this situation. Under Japanese contract law, explains the declaration, the License Agreement is both valid and enforceable, and as such requires that Universe make royalty payments to Sportswear. According to the declaration, under Japanese contract law a "licensee will be unable to cancel the license agreement or refuse to pay royalties strictly on the grounds that the licensor was not the registered owner of the licensed trademark when the license agreement was executed. In other words, only if the licensor *cannot* acquire proper title from the registered owner of the licensed trademark * * * will the license agreement be terminable." Here, the declaration states, Sportswear can and has obtained proper title of the two trademarks at issue, and therefore is entitled to collect royalty payments from Universe.

The Kamiya declaration is admissible pursuant to Federal Rule of Civil Procedure Rule 44.1, which provides, in relevant part: "The court, in determining foreign law, may consider any relevant material or source, including testimony, whether or not submitted by a party or admissible under the Federal Rules of Evidence." * * *

In this case, the expert testimony of Kamiya, in the form of a declaration with attached exhibits, was submitted by Sportswear. As discussed above, the declaration reasons that Japanese contract law applies, and under that body of law, Universe is obligated to pay royalties to Sportswear. Although Universe had numerous opportunities to present evidence that would rebut this portion of Kamiya's declaration regarding Japanese law, Universe introduced nothing. Also, the district court performed no independent research of Japanese law. The district court should have considered the fact that the Kamiya declaration states that Japanese contract law is controlling. The district court then could have instructed the parties to present further evidence regarding the interpretation of Japanese law on that point; or, the district court may have performed its own research. Because the Kamiya declaration stands as an unrebutted presentation and interpretation of Japanese law, the district court erred in granting summary judgment to Universe.

* * * *

We therefore REVERSE the district court's grant of summary judgment to Universe, GRANT Sportswear's cross-motion for summary judgment, and REMAND to the district court to reconsider consistent with this memorandum any remaining damages issues.

REVERSED and REMANDED.

FERGUSON, Circuit Judge, dissenting:

* * * *

* * * Contrary to the majority's assertions, the district court conducted a thorough inquiry into the Japanese law issue: After determining that the issue of Japanese law was not clear from the parties' initial pleadings, the court requested further evidence and briefing regarding the requirements of Japanese law. The parties submitted such further evidence, and the district court made its determination from a consideration of that evidence. * * * I am at a loss to imagine what more the majority expected the district court to do * * * .

* * * *

* * * [I]t [is] clear that the district court made the correct determination. The Kamiya declaration was before it, and it chose to rely on part of the declaration but not all of it. Instead, the court based its conclusion on other evidence in the record regarding Japanese law, evidence that I find conclusive on the issue. The trademarks at issue here are creatures of Japanese law. Under Japanese law, a transfer in ownership of a trademark must be registered with the Japanese patent office. Likewise, any transfer of a trademark right must also be registered * * * . Thus, the transfer of the right to receive royalties could not have taken place solely in a contract; rather, it must have been registered with the Japanese patent office. * * *

* * * [T]he relevant question in this case is whether the trademark transfer was properly registered with the patent office. It is undisputed that [one of the trademarks] was not properly registered. Regarding [the other] trademark * * * , the district court properly concluded that the evidence submitted by Sportswear did not show that the trademark was registered, as the evidence merely showed that Sportswear (at the time, Offshore of California) was listed as an owner of the trademark. * * *

* * * *

I therefore respectfully dissent.

CASE PROBLEMS

52–1. As part of a plan to stabilize the Republic of Argentina's currency, that country and its central bank (collectively, Argentina) issued bonds that provided for repayment in U.S. dollars. Repayment would be made in several locations, including New York City. When the bonds began to mature, Argentina lacked sufficient funds to cover them, so it unilaterally extended the time for payment and offered bondholders substitute instruments as a means of rescheduling the debts. Weltover, Inc., of Panama, plus another Panamanian corporation and a Swiss bank (collectively, Weltover), declined to accept the rescheduling and insisted on repayment in New York. When Argentina refused, Weltover brought an action for breach of contract in a U.S. district court. Argentina moved to dismiss the action, claiming immunity from the jurisdiction of the U.S. courts under the Foreign Sovereign Immunities Act. Weltover contended that Argentina's sale of the bonds fell under the "commercial activities" exception to sovereign immunity. What should the court decide? Discuss fully. [*Republic of Argentina v. Weltover, Inc.*, 504 U.S. 207, 112 S.Ct. 2160, 119 L.Ed.2d 394 (1992)]

52–2. Sabbatino, an American, contracted with a Cuban corporation that was largely owned by U.S. residents to buy Cuban sugar. When the Cuban government expropriated the corporation's property and rights in retaliation against a U.S. reduction of the Cuban sugar quota, Sabbatino entered into a new contract to make payment for the sugar to Banco Nacional, a government-owned Cuban bank. Sabbatino refused to make the promised payment, and Banco subsequently filed an action in a U.S. district court seeking to recover payment for the sugar. The issue was whether the act of state doctrine should apply when a foreign state violates international law. (If the doctrine were applied, the Cuban government's action would be presumed valid, and thus Banco's claim would be legitimate.) The district court held that the doctrine did not apply and granted summary judgment for Sabbatino. The case was ultimately appealed to the United States Supreme Court. Will the Supreme Court agree that the act of state doctrine should not be applied in these circumstances? Discuss. [*Banco Nacional de Cuba v. Sabbatino*, 376 U.S. 398, 84 S.Ct. 923, 11 L.Ed.2d 804 (1964)]

52–3. While in the United States, Scott Nelson was hired as a monitoring systems engineer for the King Faisal Specialist Hospital in Riyadh, Saudi Arabia. Nelson alleged that in the course of performing his duties under his employment contract with the hospital, he was detained and tortured by agents of the Saudi government in Saudi Arabia for reporting safety violations at the hospital. Nelson brought suit for his injuries against Saudi Arabia, the hospital, and Royspec, a corporation owned and controlled by the government of Saudi Arabia (collectively, Saudi Arabia). Saudi Arabia claimed immunity under the doctrine of sovereign immunity. Nelson contended that because his detention and torture resulted from his recruitment within the United States by an agent of the Saudi government as part of a commercial activity, the district court had subject-matter jurisdiction under the Foreign Sovereign Immunities Act of 1976. What should the court decide? Discuss fully. [*Nelson v. Saudi Arabia*, 923 F.2d 1528 (11th Cir. 1991)]

52–4. The Bank of Jamaica, which is wholly owned by the government of Jamaica, contracted with Chisholm & Company in January 1981 for Chisholm to arrange for lines of credit from various U.S. banks and obtain $50 million in credit insurance from the Export-Import Bank of the United States. This Chisholm successfully did, but subsequently the deals arranged by Chisholm were refused by the Bank of Jamaica. The bank had decided to do its own negotiating while having Chisholm work for it as well. When the bank refused to pay Chisholm for its services, Chisholm brought an action to obtain relief for the bank's breach of the implied contract. The Bank of Jamaica brought a motion to dismiss, claiming, among other things, that it was immune from the jurisdiction of U.S. courts under the doctrine of sovereign immunity. The bank argued that the money was needed for a government purpose. Is the Bank of Jamaica immune from Chisholm's action for breach of contract in a U.S. federal court? Explain fully. [*Chisholm & Co. v. Bank of Jamaica*, 643 F.Supp. 1393 (S.D. Fla. 1986)]

52–5. Alberto-Culver Co., a U.S. firm based in Illinois, bought from Fritz Scherk three business entities that were organized under the laws of Germany and Lichtenstein and that were engaged in the licensing of trademarks for toiletry products. The contract included an arbitration clause, which provided that any claim arising out of the agreement would be referred for arbitration to the International Chamber of Commerce in Paris. When problems developed with the trademarks, Alberto-Culver filed a suit against Scherk in a U.S. federal district court in Illinois. Scherk filed a motion to dismiss the action, contending that the dispute should be arbitrated in accord with the contract. How should the court rule? Discuss. [*Scherk v. Alberto-Culver Co.*, 417 U.S. 506, 94 S.Ct. 2449, 41 L.Ed.2d 270 (1974)]

52–6. Wineworths Group, Ltd., was an Australian company seeking to import Australian-made "champagne" into New Zealand. The French-based Comite Interprofessionel du Vin de Champagne filed suit under New Zealand's Fair Trading Act to prohibit the Australians from referring to their sparkling wine as "champagne," even though Australian wines had been sold under this name in Australia for many years. The trial court held that the French company was entitled to a permanent injunction against the selling of Australian products as champagne, and the defendants appealed. How should the appellate court rule? Discuss. [*Wineworths Group Ltd. v. Comite Interprofessionel du Vin de Champagne,* 1991 2 N.Z.L.R. 327 (C.A. 1991)]

52–7. In November 1967, Zapata Off-Shore Co., a Houston-based American corporation, contracted with Unterwesser, a German corporation, to tow Zapata's drilling rig from Louisiana to Italy. A clause in the contract contained the following provision: "Any dispute arising must be treated before the London Court of Justice." Unterwesser's ship, the *Bremen,* began the towing operation, but a severe storm arose in the Gulf of Mexico. During this storm, the drilling rig was severely damaged, and the rig was towed to the nearest port, which was Tampa, Florida. Zapata, ignoring the contract provision, sued in a U.S. federal district court in Tampa, seeking damages for allegedly negligent towage. Unterwesser argued that U.S. courts lacked jurisdiction because of the contract provision. How should the court rule? [*M/S Bremen v. Zapata Off-Shore Co.,* 407 U.S. 1, 92 S.Ct. 1907, 32 L.Ed.2d 513 (1972)]

52–8. Ronald Riley, an American citizen, wanted to underwrite some insurance policies issued by the Society and Council of Lloyd's, a British insurance corporation with its principal place of business in London. In 1980, Riley and Lloyd's entered into an agreement that allowed Riley to underwrite insurance through Lloyd's and provided that if any dispute arose between Lloyd's and Riley, the courts of England would have exclusive jurisdiction and the laws of England would apply. Over the next decade, some of the parties insured under policies that Riley underwrote experienced large losses, for which they filed claims. Instead of paying his share of the claims, Riley filed a lawsuit in a United States district court, seeking, among other things, rescission of his agreement with Lloyd's. The defendants included Lloyd's and those among its managers and directors—all British citizens or entities—with whom Riley had dealt when he began his association with Lloyd's. Riley alleged that the defendants had violated the Securities Act of 1933, the Securities Exchange Act of 1934, and Rule 10b-5. The defendants asked the court to enforce the forum-selection clause in the agreement. Riley argued that if the clause was enforced, he would be deprived of his rights under the U.S. securities laws. The court ruled that the clause was enforceable, and Riley appealed. What will the appellate court decide? Discuss. [*Riley v. Kingsley Underwriting Agencies, Ltd.,* 969 F.2d 953 (10th Cir. 1992)]

52–9. W. S. Kirkpatrick & Co. learned that the Republic of Nigeria was interested in contracting for the construction and equipping of a medical center in Nigeria. Kirkpatrick, with the aid of a Nigerian citizen, secured the contract as a result of bribing Nigerian officials. Nigerian law prohibits both the payment and the receipt of bribes in connection with the awarding of government contracts, and the U.S. Foreign Corrupt Practices Act (FCPA) of 1977 expressly prohibits U.S. firms and their agents from bribing foreign officials to secure favorable contracts. Environmental Tectonics Corp., International (ETC), an unsuccessful bidder for the contract, learned of the bribery and sued Kirkpatrick in a federal district court for damages. The district court granted summary judgment for Kirkpatrick, because resolution of the case in favor of ETC would require imputing to foreign officials an unlawful motivation (the obtaining of bribes) and accordingly might embarrass the Nigerian government or interfere with the conduct of U.S. foreign policy. Was the district court correct in assuming that the act of state doctrine barred ETC's action against Kirkpatrick? What should happen on appeal? Discuss fully. [*W. S. Kirkpatrick & Co. v. Environmental Tectonics Corp., International,* 493 U.S. 400, 110 S.Ct. 701, 107 L.Ed.2d 816 (1990)]

52–10. George Janini and other former professors and employees of Kuwait University (the plaintiffs) were terminated from their positions following Iraq's invasion of Kuwait in August 1990. Following the invasion, the government of Kuwait issued a decree stating, among other things, that "contracts concluded between the Government and those non-Kuwaiti workers who worked for it . . . shall be considered automatically abrogated because of the impossibility of enforcement due to the Iraqi invasion." The plaintiffs sued Kuwait University in a U.S. court, alleging that their termination breached their employment contracts, which required nine months' notice before termination. The plaintiffs sought back pay and other benefits to which they were entitled under their contracts. The university claimed that, as a government-operated institution, it was immune from the jurisdiction of U.S. courts under the doctrine of sovereign immunity. What exceptions are made to this doctrine? Will an exception apply to the university's activities with respect to the plaintiffs? Discuss fully. [*Janini v. Kuwait University,* 43 F.3d 1534 (D.C. Cir. 1995)]

52–11. Radio Free Europe and Radio Liberty (RFE/RL), a U.S. corporation doing business in Germany, employs more than three hundred U.S. citizens at its principal place of business in Munich, Germany. The concept of mandatory retirement is deeply embedded in German labor policy, and a contract formed in 1982 between RFE/RL and a German labor union contained a clause that required workers to be retired when they reached the age of sixty-five. When William Mahoney and other American employees (the plaintiffs) reached the age of sixty-five, RFE/RL terminated their employment as required under its contract with the labor union. The plaintiffs sued RFE/RL for discriminating against them on the basis of age, in violation of the U.S. Age Discrimination in Employment Act of 1967. Will the plaintiffs succeed in their suit? Discuss fully. [*Mahoney v. RFE/RL, Inc.,* 47 F.3d 447 (D.C. Cir. 1995)]

52–12. Nuovo Pignone, Inc., is an Italian company that designs and manufactures turbine systems. Nuovo sold a turbine system to Cabinda Gulf Oil Co. (CABGOC). The system was manufactured, tested, and inspected in Italy, then sent to Louisiana for mounting on a platform by CABGOC's contractor. Nuovo sent a representative to consult on the mounting. The platform went to a CABGOC site off the coast of West Africa. Marcus Pere, an instrument technician at the site, was killed when a turbine within the system exploded. Pere's widow filed a suit in a federal district court against Nuovo and others. Nuovo claimed sovereign immunity on the ground that its majority shareholder at the time of the explosion was Ente Nazionale Idrocaburi, which was created by the government of Italy to lead its oil and gas exploration and development. Is Nuovo exempt from suit under the doctrine of sovereign immunity? Is it subject to suit under the "commercial activity" exception? Why, or why not? [*Pere v. Nuovo Pignone, Inc.*, 150 F.3d 477 (5th Cir. 1998)]

52–13. In response to a petition filed on behalf of the U.S. pineapple industry, the U.S. Commerce Department initiated an investigation of canned pineapple fruit imported from Thailand. The investigation concerned Thai producers of the canned fruit, including The Thai Pineapple Public Co. The Thai producers also turned out products, such as pineapple juice and juice concentrate, outside the scope of the investigation. These products use separate parts of the same fresh pineapple, and so they share raw material costs. The Commerce Department had to calculate the Thai producers' cost of production, for the purpose of determining fair value and antidumping duties, and in so doing, had to allocate a portion of the shared fruit costs to the canned fruit. These allocations were based on the producers' own financial records, which were consistent with Thai generally accepted accounting principles. The result was a determination that more than 90 percent of the canned fruit sales were below the cost of production. The producers filed a suit in the U.S. Court of International Trade against the federal government, challenging this allocation. The producers argued that their records did not reflect actual production costs, which instead should be based on the weight of fresh fruit used to make the products. Did the Commerce Department act reasonably in determining the cost of production? Why, or why not? [*The Thai Pineapple Public Co. v. United States*, 187 F.3d 1362 (Fed.Cir. 1999)]

52–14. Tonoga, Ltd., doing business as Taconic Plastics, Ltd., is a manufacturer incorporated in Ireland with its principal place of business in New York. In 1997, Taconic entered into a contract with a German construction company to supply special material for a tent project designed to shelter religious pilgrims visiting holy sites in Saudi Arabia. Most of the material was made in, and shipped from, New York. The German company did not pay Taconic and eventually filed for bankruptcy. Another German firm, Werner Voss Architects and Engineers, acting as an agent for the government of Saudi Arabia, guaranteed the payments due Taconic to induce it to complete the project. When Taconic received all but the final payment, the firm filed a suit in a federal district court against the government of Saudi Arabia, claiming a breach of the guaranty and seeking to collect about $3 million. The defendant filed a motion to dismiss based, in part, on the doctrine of sovereign immunity. Under what circumstances does this doctrine apply? What are its exceptions? Should this suit be dismissed under the "commercial activity" exception? Explain. [*Tonoga, Ltd. v. Ministry of Public Works and Housing of Kingdom of Saudi Arabia*, 135 F.Supp.2d 350 (N.D.N.Y. 2001)]

52–15. A Question of Ethics

Gordonsville Industries, Inc., located in Virginia, entered into a contract with American Artos Corp., a North Carolina corporation, for the design, construction, and installation of a textile-drying system. Artos, in turn, contracted with GEA Luftkuhlergesellschaft, a German firm, for the design of a hot-oil boiler, one of the system's integral parts. GEA subcontracted the actual construction of the boiler to Industrial Boiler Co., a Georgia corporation. A forum-selection clause in the Artos–GEA contract specified that in the event of a lawsuit, "it is agreed that the place for litigation shall be the *Amtsgericht* [civil court] in Bochum, Germany." Later, Gordonsville Industries, unhappy with the performance of the textile-drying system, filed suit in a U.S. federal court against Artos to recover damages. Artos then filed a complaint, essentially seeking indemnification (reimbursement), against GEA. GEA moved to dismiss the complaint on the grounds that under the forum-selection clause in the Artos–GEA contract, the dispute should be heard in the specified German court. Artos contended that the clause should not be enforced because the construction of the boiler had taken place in the United States, and all of the relevant records and witnesses were located in the United States, not Germany. [*Gordonsville Industries, Inc. v. American Artos Corp.*, 549 F.Supp. 200 (W.D.Va. 1982)]

1. Discuss whether the circumstances of this case would justify permitting the case to proceed in the U.S. courts.
2. What arguments might Artos raise against having the dispute heard in the German courts?
3. How would you evaluate the argument that strict enforcement of the forum-selection clause is necessary to promote certainty in international commercial transactions?

E-LINKS

For updated links to resources available on the Web, as well as a variety of other materials, visit this text's Web site at

http://cs-alt.westbuslaw.com

An extensive collection of URLs offering access to various international organizations is offered by the Villanova University School of Law at

http://vls.law.vill.edu/students/orgs/ilsa/index.htm

The University of Arizona College of Law has an online collection of various resources relating to international law, as well as to the national laws of some foreign countries. You can access this collection by going to

http://www.law.arizona.edu/library/LibraryInternet/legal_links/topical_links/international_links.htm

The Library of Congress's Global Legal Information Network has information on the national laws of more than thirty-five countries, as well as a comprehensive Guide to Law Online. You can access this site at

http://lcweb2.loc.gov/glin/glinhome.html

LEGAL RESEARCH EXERCISES ON THE WEB

Go to http://wbl-cs.westbuslaw.com, the Web site that accompanies this text. Select "Interactive Study Center," and then click on "Chapter 52." There you will find the following Internet research exercises that you can perform to learn more about international organizations and trade:

Activity 52–1: The World Trade Organization

Activity 52–2: Overseas Business Opportunities

Focus on Legal Reasoning

United States v. Hitt

Chapter 52 mentions the Export Administration Act of 1979, under which restrictions are imposed on the export of technologically advanced products. The United States can charge violators of this act with criminal offenses, including conspiracy. As noted in Chapter 8, however, an indictment must be issued within a certain period—in this case, five years—under the applicable statute of limitations. In this *Focus on Legal Reasoning*, we examine *United States v. Hitt*,[1] a decision that involved these principles.

Case Background

In the early 1990s, McDonnell Douglas Corporation closed a manufacturing plant in Columbus, Ohio, that had produced military aircraft for the United States. McDonnell Douglas and Douglas Aircraft Company (jointly, MDC) entered into an agreement with China National Aero-Technology Import and Export Corporation (CATIC) for the sale of equipment from the plant. This included sophisticated machine tools that were subject to export controls under the Export Administration Act (EAA) of 1979 and required export licenses from the U.S. Department of Commerce. In the applications for licenses to export the equipment, MDC represented that the end user was CATIC Machining Company in Beijing and that the machine tools would be used only to manufacture commercial aircraft.

In September 1994, the U.S. Department of Commerce granted the licenses, which required MDC to verify the equipment's location and usage through quarterly inspections of the CATIC facility. The equipment was shipped to China in March 1995. After the first inspection, MDC reported that the machine tools had been diverted to four different locations, including a factory in Nanchang involved in the manufacture of military equipment.

In October 1999, Robert Hitt, an executive with Douglas Aircraft, and others, were charged in a federal district court with conspiring to violate the EAA. Hitt filed a motion to dismiss the charge against him, arguing that the conspiracy related only to the issuance of the licenses in September 1994 and was therefore barred by a five-year statute of limitations. The government argued that the conspiracy continued until the equipment was shipped in March 1995. The court dismissed the indictment against Hitt. The government appealed to the U.S. Court of Appeals for the District of Columbia Circuit.

1. 249 F.3d 1010 (C.A.D.C. 2001).

Majority Opinion

ROGERS, Circuit Judge.

* * * *

For the indictment to be timely with respect to Hitt, [the government] must show that no more than five years prior to the filing of the indictment (i.e., at a point no earlier than October 19, 1994) (1) the conspiracy, as contemplated by the agreement, still existed, and (2) at least one overt act in furtherance of the conspiracy occurred. In examining whether these conditions are fulfilled, the crucial question * * * is the scope of the conspiratorial agreement, for it is that which determines both the duration of the conspiracy, and whether the act relied on as an overt act may properly be regarded as in furtherance of the conspiracy. Key to determining the scope of the conspiracy * * * is the extent to which there was a "meeting of minds" concerning the object of the conspiracy. * * *

* * * *

* * * Paragraph 43 [of the indictment] describes "THE CONSPIRACY" * * *. Paragraph 43 states:

> From in or about February, 1993 * * * the defendants * * * did unlawfully, willfully and knowingly combine, conspire, confederate and agree together to commit offenses against the United States, that is:
>
> * * *
>
> b. to willfully and knowingly make false and misleading statements and to conceal material facts from the United States Departments of Commerce and Defense in the course of obtaining export licenses * * *;
>
> * * *
>
> e. to buy and sell, before on or about August 20, 1994, machine tools to be exported from the United States subject to the [EAA] with knowledge or reason to know that a violation of the [EAA] is intended to occur * * *.

Paragraph 44 states the "Goal" of the conspiracy:

> A goal of the conspiracy was to obtain export licenses allowing the sale and exportation of machine tools to [China]. [The CATIC defendants'] purpose, among others, was to obtain the Columbus plant machine tools for unrestricted use at undisclosed facilities within [China] * * *. [MDC] and Robert Hitt's purposes, among others, were: (a) to maintain the ongoing commercial relationship between [MDC] and CATIC and to promote the prospects for existing and future business contracts between the parties; and (b) to obtain swift approval from the United States Department of Commerce of export license

applications by presenting seemingly credible and non-controversial justification and end-user information in the license applications, even if such information was not truthful, so that [MDC] could avoid [various] costs * * *.

* * * *

* * * Paragraph 51 lists twenty-five alleged "Overt Acts" committed by the defendants "[i]n furtherance of the conspiracy and to accomplish the objects thereof." * * * Five of these alleged overt acts occurred after the export licenses were issued:

(21) On November 2, 1994, [MDC] signed two separate delivery sheets authorizing the removal of [some licensable machine tools] to destination "red" and [some licensable machine tools] to destination "black."
(22) In or about November 1994, CATIC caused cargo that had been licensed for export to Beijing to be shipped [to and unloaded at two separate locations].
(23) In or about November 1994, CATIC caused another shipment of cargo that had been licensed for export to Beijing to be shipped to and unloaded at two separate ports * * *.
(24) On or about February 18, 1995, CATIC caused * * * a machine tool licensed for export to Beijing[] to be * * * [shipped] to [an unauthorized location].
(25) Between in or about November 1994 and in or about March 1995, CATIC caused six machines licensed for export to Beijing to be delivered to Nanchang.

* * * Only Overt Act No. 21 refers to MDC. The "delivery sheets" that Overt Act No. 21 alleges MDC signed are not alleged to be shipping authorization documents; rather, they are internal MDC records of CATIC's contractually obligated removal of certain machine tools from the Columbus plant. The remaining four overt acts within the statutory period, Overt Acts No. 22 through 25, relate solely to CATIC's efforts to ship the machine tools to unauthorized locations after MDC obtained the requisite export licenses.

From the plain language and structure of [the indictment], it would follow that "The Conspiracy" envisioned by the [indictment] was confined to the defendants' false statements and concealment of information from Commerce Department officials while applying for the export licenses. The "Goal" of the conspiracy, as described in Paragraph 44, did not encompass any event occurring after the export licenses' issuance on September 14, 1994. Because [the indictment] did not allege that MDC and Hitt shared the separate purpose of the CATIC defendants to divert the machine tools in violation of the export licenses, the conspiracy was * * * completed once the export licenses were issued. See * * * *United States v. Krasovich,* 819 F.2d 253 (9th Cir.1987).

* * * *

* * * It is clear from the indictment why MDC and Hitt participated in the fraudulent scheme to obtain the export licenses: They sought to maintain good relations with the Chinese government, especially in light of the substantial financial gain represented by the MDC–CATIC joint venture. MDC would satisfy this objective by selling to CATIC the equipment that it desired, and by obtaining the export licenses that would allow CATIC to transport the machinery to China. Under the Purchase Agreement, that would complete the transaction, as CATIC was responsible for the machinery's removal and transportation. Although the consequence of MDC's alleged fraudulent acquisition of the export licenses might be CATIC's unauthorized use of the machinery, this does not indicate that CATIC's actions upon acquiring the machine tools would be part of the conspiratorial agreement. * * *

* * * *

Accordingly, we affirm the order of the district court dismissing * * * the indictment against Hitt.

QUESTIONS FOR ANALYSIS

1. **Legal Reasoning.** The court in the *Hitt* case cites *United States v. Krasovich*, 819 F.2d 253 (9th Cir. 1987) (see the *E-Links* feature at the end of Chapter 2 for instructions on how to access the opinions of federal courts). How do the facts and the holding of the *Krasovich* case compare to those of the *Hitt* case? Why did the court in the *Hitt* case cite *Krasovich*?

2. **Legal Analysis.** If the contract between MDC and CATIC concerned only obtaining export licenses, how could Hitt and the others be charged with a crime that arguably exceeded this purpose?

3. **Economic Dimension.** Why did MDC and Hitt allegedly participate in a fraudulent scheme to obtain export licenses?

4. **Implications for the Businessperson.** How might a person who does business internationally avoid committing the crime alleged in the Hitt case?

Focus on Legal Reasoning

Westlaw Online Research

Go to this text's companion Web site, at http://wbl-cs.westbuslaw.com, and click on the Westlaw icon. Use your special password to access the full text of this case, including the dissenting opinions. Read through the case, and then answer the following questions.

1. Consider the opinion of the dissent and compare it to the opinion of the majority. What is the basis for the difference in their interpretations of the indictment?
2. Do any of the editors' headnotes relate directly to statements by the dissent? If so, why? If not, why not?
3. As suggested by the *Hitt* case, what ethical duty might support the purposes and actions of MDC in this case?

APPENDIX A

The Constitution of the United States

Preamble

We the People of the United States, in Order to form a more perfect Union, establish Justice, insure domestic Tranquility, provide for the common defence, promote the general Welfare, and secure the Blessings of Liberty to ourselves and our Posterity, do ordain and establish this Constitution for the United States of America.

Article I

Section 1. All legislative Powers herein granted shall be vested in a Congress of the United States, which shall consist of a Senate and House of Representatives.

Section 2. The House of Representatives shall be composed of Members chosen every second Year by the People of the several States, and the Electors in each State shall have the Qualifications requisite for Electors of the most numerous Branch of the State Legislature.

No Person shall be a Representative who shall not have attained to the Age of twenty five Years, and been seven Years a Citizen of the United States, and who shall not, when elected, be an Inhabitant of that State in which he shall be chosen.

Representatives and direct Taxes shall be apportioned among the several States which may be included within this Union, according to their respective Numbers, which shall be determined by adding to the whole Number of free Persons, including those bound to Service for a Term of Years, and excluding Indians not taxed, three fifths of all other Persons. The actual Enumeration shall be made within three Years after the first Meeting of the Congress of the United States, and within every subsequent Term of ten Years, in such Manner as they shall by Law direct. The Number of Representatives shall not exceed one for every thirty Thousand, but each State shall have at Least one Representative; and until such enumeration shall be made, the State of New Hampshire shall be entitled to chuse three, Massachusetts eight, Rhode Island and Providence Plantations one, Connecticut five, New York six, New Jersey four, Pennsylvania eight, Delaware one, Maryland six, Virginia ten, North Carolina five, South Carolina five, and Georgia three.

When vacancies happen in the Representation from any State, the Executive Authority thereof shall issue Writs of Election to fill such Vacancies.

The House of Representatives shall chuse their Speaker and other Officers; and shall have the sole Power of Impeachment.

Section 3. The Senate of the United States shall be composed of two Senators from each State, chosen by the Legislature thereof, for six Years; and each Senator shall have one Vote.

Immediately after they shall be assembled in Consequence of the first Election, they shall be divided as equally as may be into three Classes. The Seats of the Senators of the first Class shall be vacated at the Expiration of the second Year, of the second Class at the Expiration of the fourth Year, and of the third Class at the Expiration of the sixth Year, so that one third may be chosen every second Year; and if Vacancies happen by Resignation, or otherwise, during the Recess of the Legislature of any State, the Executive thereof may make temporary Appointments until the next Meeting of the Legislature, which shall then fill such Vacancies.

No Person shall be a Senator who shall not have attained to the Age of thirty Years, and been nine Years a Citizen of the United States, and who shall not, when elected, be an Inhabitant of that State for which he shall be chosen.

The Vice President of the United States shall be President of the Senate, but shall have no Vote, unless they be equally divided.

The Senate shall chuse their other Officers, and also a President pro tempore, in the Absence of the Vice President, or when he shall exercise the Office of President of the United States.

The Senate shall have the sole Power to try all Impeachments. When sitting for that Purpose, they shall be on Oath or Affirmation. When the President of the United States is tried, the Chief Justice shall preside: And no Person shall be convicted without the Concurrence of two thirds of the Members present.

Judgment in Cases of Impeachment shall not extend further than to removal from Office, and disqualification to hold and enjoy any Office of honor, Trust, or Profit under the United States: but the Party convicted shall nevertheless be liable and subject to Indictment, Trial, Judgment, and Punishment, according to Law.

Section 4. The Times, Places and Manner of holding Elections for Senators and Representatives, shall be prescribed in each State by the Legislature thereof; but the Congress may at any time by Law make or alter such Regulations, except as to the Places of chusing Senators.

The Congress shall assemble at least once in every Year, and such Meeting shall be on the first Monday in December, unless they shall by Law appoint a different Day.

Section 5. Each House shall be the Judge of the Elections, Returns, and Qualifications of its own Members, and a Majority of each shall constitute a Quorum to do Business; but a smaller Number may adjourn from day to day, and may be authorized to compel the Attendance of absent Members, in such Manner, and under such Penalties as each House may provide.

Each House may determine the Rules of its Proceedings, punish its Members for disorderly Behavior, and, with the Concurrence of two thirds, expel a Member.

Each House shall keep a Journal of its Proceedings, and from time to time publish the same, excepting such Parts as may in their Judgment require Secrecy; and the Yeas and Nays of the Members of either House on any question shall, at the Desire of one fifth of those Present, be entered on the Journal.

Neither House, during the Session of Congress, shall, without the Consent of the other, adjourn for more than three days, nor to any other Place than that in which the two Houses shall be sitting.

Section 6. The Senators and Representatives shall receive a Compensation for their Services, to be ascertained by Law, and paid out of the Treasury of the United States. They shall in all Cases, except Treason, Felony and Breach of the Peace, be privileged from Arrest during their Attendance at the Session of their respective Houses, and in going to and returning from the same; and for any Speech or Debate in either House, they shall not be questioned in any other Place.

No Senator or Representative shall, during the Time for which he was elected, be appointed to any civil Office under the Authority of the United States, which shall have been created, or the Emoluments whereof shall have been increased during such time; and no Person holding any Office under the United States, shall be a Member of either House during his Continuance in Office.

Section 7. All Bills for raising Revenue shall originate in the House of Representatives; but the Senate may propose or concur with Amendments as on other Bills.

Every Bill which shall have passed the House of Representatives and the Senate, shall, before it become a Law, be presented to the President of the United States; If he approve he shall sign it, but if not he shall return it, with his Objections to the House in which it shall have originated, who shall enter the Objections at large on their Journal, and proceed to reconsider it. If after such Reconsideration two thirds of that House shall agree to pass the Bill, it shall be sent together with the Objections, to the other House, by which it shall likewise be reconsidered, and if approved by two thirds of that House, it shall become a Law. But in all such Cases the Votes of both Houses shall be determined by Yeas and Nays, and the Names of the Persons voting for and against the Bill shall be entered on the Journal of each House respectively. If any Bill shall not be returned by the President within ten Days (Sundays excepted) after it shall have been presented to him, the Same shall be a Law, in like Manner as if he had signed it, unless the Congress by their Adjournment prevent its Return in which Case it shall not be a Law.

Every Order, Resolution, or Vote, to which the Concurrence of the Senate and House of Representatives may be necessary (except on a question of Adjournment) shall be presented to the President of the United States; and before the Same shall take Effect, shall be approved by him, or being disapproved by him, shall be repassed by two thirds of the Senate and House of Representatives, according to the Rules and Limitations prescribed in the Case of a Bill.

Section 8. The Congress shall have Power To lay and collect Taxes, Duties, Imposts and Excises, to pay the Debts and provide for the common Defence and general Welfare of the United States; but all Duties, Imposts and Excises shall be uniform throughout the United States;

To borrow Money on the credit of the United States;

To regulate Commerce with foreign Nations, and among the several States, and with the Indian Tribes;

To establish an uniform Rule of Naturalization, and uniform Laws on the subject of Bankruptcies throughout the United States;

To coin Money, regulate the Value thereof, and of foreign Coin, and fix the Standard of Weights and Measures;

To provide for the Punishment of counterfeiting the Securities and current Coin of the United States;

To establish Post Offices and post Roads;

To promote the Progress of Science and useful Arts, by securing for limited Times to Authors and Inventors the exclusive Right to their respective Writings and Discoveries;

To constitute Tribunals inferior to the supreme Court;

To define and punish Piracies and Felonies committed on the high Seas, and Offenses against the Law of Nations;

To declare War, grant Letters of Marque and Reprisal, and make Rules concerning Captures on Land and Water;

To raise and support Armies, but no Appropriation of Money to that Use shall be for a longer Term than two Years;

To provide and maintain a Navy;

To make Rules for the Government and Regulation of the land and naval Forces;

To provide for calling forth the Militia to execute the Laws of the Union, suppress Insurrections and repel Invasions;

To provide for organizing, arming, and disciplining, the Militia, and for governing such Part of them as may be employed in the Service of the United States, reserving to the States respectively, the Appointment of the Officers, and the Authority of training the Militia according to the discipline prescribed by Congress;

To exercise exclusive Legislation in all Cases whatsoever, over such District (not exceeding ten Miles square) as may, by Cession of particular States, and the Acceptance of Congress, become the Seat of the Government of the United States, and to exercise like Authority over all Places purchased by the Consent of the Legislature of the State in which the Same shall be, for the Erection of Forts, Magazines, Arsenals, dock-Yards, and other needful Buildings;—And

To make all Laws which shall be necessary and proper for carrying into Execution the foregoing Powers, and all other Powers vested by this Constitution in the Government of the United States, or in any Department or Officer thereof.

Section 9. The Migration or Importation of such Persons as any of the States now existing shall think proper to admit, shall not be prohibited by the Congress prior to the Year one thousand eight hundred and eight, but a Tax or duty may be imposed on such Importation, not exceeding ten dollars for each Person.

The privilege of the Writ of Habeas Corpus shall not be suspended, unless when in Cases of Rebellion or Invasion the public Safety may require it.

No Bill of Attainder or ex post facto Law shall be passed.

No Capitation, or other direct, Tax shall be laid, unless in Proportion to the Census or Enumeration herein before directed to be taken.

No Tax or Duty shall be laid on Articles exported from any State.

No Preference shall be given by any Regulation of Commerce or Revenue to the Ports of one State over those of another: nor shall Vessels bound to, or from, one State be obliged to enter, clear, or pay Duties in another.

No Money shall be drawn from the Treasury, but in Consequence of Appropriations made by Law; and a regular Statement and Account of the Receipts and Expenditures of all public Money shall be published from time to time.

No Title of Nobility shall be granted by the United States: And no Person holding any Office of Profit or Trust under them, shall, without the Consent of the Congress, accept of any present, Emolument, Office, or Title, of any kind whatever, from any King, Prince, or foreign State.

Section 10. No State shall enter into any Treaty, Alliance, or Confederation; grant Letters of Marque and Reprisal; coin Money; emit Bills of Credit; make any Thing but gold and silver Coin a Tender in Payment of Debts; pass any Bill of Attainder, ex post facto Law, or Law impairing the Obligation of Contracts, or grant any Title of Nobility.

No State shall, without the Consent of the Congress, lay any Imposts or Duties on Imports or Exports, except what may be absolutely necessary for executing its inspection Laws: and the net Produce of all Duties and Imposts, laid by any State on Imports or Exports, shall be for the Use of the Treasury of the United States; and all such Laws shall be subject to the Revision and Controul of the Congress.

No State shall, without the Consent of Congress, lay any Duty of Tonnage, keep Troops, or Ships of War in time of Peace, enter into any Agreement or Compact with another State, or with a foreign Power, or engage in War, unless actually invaded, or in such imminent Danger as will not admit of delay.

Article II

Section 1. The executive Power shall be vested in a President of the United States of America. He shall hold his Office during the Term of four Years, and, together with the Vice President, chosen for the same Term, be elected, as follows:

Each State shall appoint, in such Manner as the Legislature thereof may direct, a Number of Electors, equal to the whole Number of Senators and Representatives to which the State may be entitled in the Congress; but no Senator or Representative, or Person holding an Office of Trust or Profit under the United States, shall be appointed an Elector.

The Electors shall meet in their respective States, and vote by Ballot for two Persons, of whom one at least shall not be an Inhabitant of the same State with themselves. And they shall make a List of all the Persons voted for, and of the Number of Votes for each; which List they shall sign and certify, and transmit sealed to the Seat of the Government of the United States, directed to the President of the Senate. The President of the Senate shall, in the Presence of the Senate and House of Representatives, open all the Certificates, and the Votes shall then be counted. The Person having the greatest Number of Votes shall be the President, if such Number be a Majority of the whole Number of Electors appointed; and if there be more than one who have such Majority, and have an equal Number of Votes, then the House of Representatives shall immediately chuse by Ballot one of them for President; and if no Person have a Majority, then from the five highest on the List the said House shall in like Manner chuse the President. But in chusing the President, the Votes shall be taken by States, the Representation from each State having one Vote; A quorum for this Purpose shall consist of a Member or Members from two thirds of the States, and a Majority of all the States shall be necessary to a Choice. In every Case, after the Choice of the President, the Person having the greater Number of Votes of the Electors shall be the Vice President. But if there should remain two or more who have equal Votes, the Senate shall chuse from them by Ballot the Vice President.

The Congress may determine the Time of chusing the Electors, and the Day on which they shall give their Votes; which Day shall be the same throughout the United States.

No person except a natural born Citizen, or a Citizen of the United States, at the time of the Adoption of this Constitution, shall be eligible to the Office of President; neither shall any Person be eligible to that Office who shall not have attained to the Age of thirty five Years, and been fourteen Years a Resident within the United States.

In Case of the Removal of the President from Office, or of his Death, Resignation or Inability to discharge the Powers and Duties of the said Office, the same shall devolve on the Vice President, and the Congress may by Law provide for the Case of Removal, Death, Resignation or Inability, both of the President and Vice President, declaring what Officer shall then act as President, and such Officer shall act accordingly, until the Disability be removed, or a President shall be elected.

The President shall, at stated Times, receive for his Services, a Compensation, which shall neither be increased nor diminished during the Period for which he shall have been elected, and he shall not receive within that Period any other Emolument from the United States, or any of them.

Before he enter on the Execution of his Office, he shall take the following Oath or Affirmation: "I do solemnly swear (or affirm) that I will faithfully execute the Office of President of the United States, and will to the best of my Ability, preserve, protect and defend the Constitution of the United States."

Section 2. The President shall be Commander in Chief of the Army and Navy of the United States, and of the Militia of the several States, when called into the actual Service of the United States; he may require the Opinion, in writing, of the principal Officer in each of the executive Departments, upon any Subject relating to the Duties of their respective Offices, and he shall have Power to grant Reprieves and Pardons for Offenses against the United States, except in Cases of Impeachment.

He shall have Power, by and with the Advice and Consent of the Senate to make Treaties, provided two thirds of the Senators present concur; and he shall nominate, and by and with the Advice and Consent of the Senate, shall appoint Ambassadors, other public Ministers and Consuls, Judges of the supreme Court, and all other Officers of the United States, whose Appointments are not herein otherwise provided for, and which shall be established by Law; but the Congress may by Law vest the Appointment of such inferior Officers, as they think proper, in the President alone, in the Courts of Law, or in the Heads of Departments.

The President shall have Power to fill up all Vacancies that may happen during the Recess of the Senate, by granting Commissions which shall expire at the End of their next Session.

Section 3. He shall from time to time give to the Congress Information of the State of the Union, and recommend to their Consideration such Measures as he shall judge necessary and expedient; he may, on extraordinary Occasions, convene both Houses, or either of them, and in Case of Disagreement between them, with Respect to the Time of Adjournment, he may adjourn them to such Time as he shall think proper; he shall receive Ambassadors and other public Ministers; he shall take Care that the Laws be faithfully executed, and shall Commission all the Officers of the United States.

Section 4. The President, Vice President and all civil Officers of the United States, shall be removed from Office on Impeachment for, and Conviction of, Treason, Bribery, or other high Crimes and Misdemeanors.

Article III

Section 1. The judicial Power of the United States, shall be vested in one supreme Court, and in such inferior Courts as the Congress may from time to time ordain and establish. The Judges, both of the supreme and inferior Courts, shall hold their Offices during good Behaviour, and shall, at stated Times, receive for their Services a Compensation, which shall not be diminished during their Continuance in Office.

Section 2. The judicial Power shall extend to all Cases, in Law and Equity, arising under this Constitution, the Laws of the United States, and Treaties made, or which shall be made, under their Authority;—to all Cases affecting Ambassadors, other public Ministers and Consuls;—to all Cases of admiralty and maritime Jurisdiction;—to Controversies to which the United States shall be a Party;—to Controversies between two or more States;—between a State and Citizens of another State;—between Citizens of different States;—between Citizens of the same State claiming Lands under Grants of different States, and between a State, or the Citizens thereof, and foreign States, Citizens or Subjects.

In all Cases affecting Ambassadors, other public Ministers and Consuls, and those in which a State shall be a Party, the supreme Court shall have original Jurisdiction. In all the other Cases before mentioned, the supreme Court shall have appellate Jurisdiction, both as to Law and Fact, with such Exceptions, and under such Regulations as the Congress shall make.

The Trial of all Crimes, except in Cases of Impeachment, shall be by Jury; and such Trial shall be held in the State where the said Crimes shall have been committed; but when not committed within any State, the Trial shall be at such Place or Places as the Congress may by Law have directed.

Section 3. Treason against the United States, shall consist only in levying War against them, or, in adhering to their Enemies, giving them Aid and Comfort. No Person shall be convicted of Treason unless on the Testimony of two Witnesses to the same overt Act, or on Confession in open Court.

The Congress shall have Power to declare the Punishment of Treason, but no Attainder of Treason shall work Corruption of Blood, or Forfeiture except during the Life of the Person attainted.

Article IV

Section 1. Full Faith and Credit shall be given in each State to the public Acts, Records, and judicial Proceedings of every other State. And the Congress may by general Laws prescribe the Manner in which such Acts, Records and Proceedings shall be proved, and the Effect thereof.

Section 2. The Citizens of each State shall be entitled to all Privileges and Immunities of Citizens in the several States.

A Person charged in any State with Treason, Felony, or other Crime, who shall flee from Justice, and be found in another State, shall on Demand of the executive Authority of the State from which he fled, be delivered up, to be removed to the State having Jurisdiction of the Crime.

No Person held to Service or Labour in one State, under the Laws thereof, escaping into another, shall, in Consequence of any Law or Regulation therein, be discharged from such Service or Labour, but shall be delivered up on Claim of the Party to whom such Service or Labour may be due.

Section 3. New States may be admitted by the Congress into this Union; but no new State shall be formed or erected within the Jurisdiction of any other State; nor any State be formed by the Junction of two or more States, or Parts of States, without the Consent of the Legislatures of the States concerned as well as of the Congress.

The Congress shall have Power to dispose of and make all needful Rules and Regulations respecting the Territory or other Property belonging to the United States; and nothing in this Constitution shall be so construed as to Prejudice any Claims of the United States, or of any particular State.

Section 4. The United States shall guarantee to every State in this Union a Republican Form of Government, and shall protect each of them against Invasion; and on Application of the Legislature, or of the Executive (when the Legislature cannot be convened) against domestic Violence.

Article V

The Congress, whenever two thirds of both Houses shall deem it necessary, shall propose Amendments to this Constitution, or, on the Application of the Legislatures of two thirds of the several States, shall call a Convention for proposing Amendments, which, in either Case, shall be valid to all Intents and Purposes, as part of this Constitution, when ratified by the Legislatures of three fourths of the several States, or by Conventions in three fourths thereof, as the one or the other Mode of Ratification may be proposed by the Congress; Provided that no Amendment which may be made prior to the Year One thousand eight hundred and eight shall in any Manner affect the first and fourth Clauses in the Ninth Section of the first Article; and that no State, without its Consent, shall be deprived of its equal Suffrage in the Senate.

Article VI

All Debts contracted and Engagements entered into, before the Adoption of this Constitution shall be as valid against the United States under this Constitution, as under the Confederation.

This Constitution, and the Laws of the United States which shall be made in Pursuance thereof; and all Treaties made, or which shall be made, under the Authority of the United States, shall be the supreme Law of the Land; and the Judges in every State shall be bound thereby, any Thing in the Constitution or Laws of any State to the Contrary notwithstanding.

The Senators and Representatives before mentioned, and the Members of the several State Legislatures, and all executive and judicial Officers, both of the United States and of the several States, shall be bound by Oath or Affirmation, to support this Constitution; but no religious Test shall ever be required as a Qualification to any Office or public Trust under the United States.

Article VII

The Ratification of the Conventions of nine States shall be sufficient for the Establishment of this Constitution between the States so ratifying the Same.

Amendment I [1791]

Congress shall make no law respecting an establishment of religion, or prohibiting the free exercise thereof; or abridging the freedom of speech, or of the press; or the right of the people peaceably to assembly, and to petition the Government for a redress of grievances.

Amendment II [1791]

A well regulated Militia, being necessary to the security of a free State, the right of the people to keep and bear Arms, shall not be infringed.

Amendment III [1791]

No Soldier shall, in time of peace be quartered in any house, without the consent of the Owner, nor in time of war, but in a manner to be prescribed by law.

Amendment IV [1791]

The right of the people to be secure in their persons, houses, papers, and effects, against unreasonable searches and seizures, shall not be violated, and no Warrants shall issue, but upon probable cause, supported by Oath or affirmation, and particularly describing the place to be searched, and the persons or things to be seized.

Amendment V [1791]

No person shall be held to answer for a capital, or otherwise infamous crime, unless on a presentment or indictment of a Grand Jury, except in cases arising in the land or naval forces, or in the Militia, when in actual service in time of War or public danger; nor shall any person be subject for the same offence to be twice put in jeopardy of life or limb; nor shall be compelled in any criminal case to be a witness against himself, nor be deprived of life, liberty, or property, without due process of law; nor shall private property be taken for public use, without just compensation.

Amendment VI [1791]

In all criminal prosecutions, the accused shall enjoy the right to a speedy and public trial, by an impartial jury of the State and district wherein the crime shall have been committed, which district shall have been previously ascertained by law, and to be informed of the nature and cause of the accusation; to be confronted with the witnesses against him; to have compulsory process for obtaining witnesses in his favor, and to have the Assistance of Counsel for his defence.

Amendment VII [1791]

In Suits at common law, where the value in controversy shall exceed twenty dollars, the right of trial by jury shall be preserved, and no fact tried by jury, shall be otherwise re-examined in any Court of the United States, than according to the rules of the common law.

Amendment VIII [1791]

Excessive bail shall not be required, nor excessive fines imposed, nor cruel and unusual punishments inflicted.

Amendment IX [1791]

The enumeration in the Constitution, of certain rights, shall not be construed to deny or disparage others retained by the people.

Amendment X [1791]

The powers not delegated to the United States by the Constitution, nor prohibited by it to the States, are reserved to the States respectively, or to the people.

Amendment XI [1798]

The Judicial power of the United States shall not be

construed to extend to any suit in law or equity, commenced or prosecuted against one of the United States by Citizens of another State, or by Citizens or Subjects of any Foreign State.

Amendment XII [1804]

The Electors shall meet in their respective states, and vote by ballot for President and Vice-President, one of whom, at least, shall not be an inhabitant of the same state with themselves; they shall name in their ballots the person voted for as President, and in distinct ballots the person voted for as Vice-President, and they shall make distinct lists of all persons voted for as President, and of all persons voted for as Vice-President, and of the number of votes for each, which lists they shall sign and certify, and transmit sealed to the seat of the government of the United States, directed to the President of the Senate;—The President of the Senate shall, in the presence of the Senate and House of Representatives, open all the certificates and the votes shall then be counted;—The person having the greatest number of votes for President, shall be the President, if such number be a majority of the whole number of Electors appointed; and if no person have such majority, then from the persons having the highest numbers not exceeding three on the list of those voted for as President, the House of Representatives shall choose immediately, by ballot, the President. But in choosing the President, the votes shall be taken by states, the representation from each state having one vote; a quorum for this purpose shall consist of a member or members from two-thirds of the states, and a majority of all states shall be necessary to a choice. And if the House of Representatives shall not choose a President whenever the right of choice shall devolve upon them, before the fourth day of March next following, then the Vice-President shall act as President, as in the case of the death or other constitutional disability of the President.—The person having the greatest number of votes as Vice-President, shall be the Vice-President, if such number be a majority of the whole number of Electors appointed, and if no person have a majority, then from the two highest numbers on the list, the Senate shall choose the Vice-President; a quorum for the purpose shall consist of two-thirds of the whole number of Senators, and a majority of the whole number shall be necessary to a choice. But no person constitutionally ineligible to the office of President shall be eligible to that of Vice-President of the United States.

Amendment XIII [1865]

Section 1. Neither slavery nor involuntary servitude, except as a punishment for crime whereof the party shall have been duly convicted, shall exist within the United States, or any place subject to their jurisdiction.

Section 2. Congress shall have power to enforce this article by appropriate legislation.

Amendment XIV [1868]

Section 1. All persons born or naturalized in the United States, and subject to the jurisdiction thereof, are citizens of the United States and of the State wherein they reside. No State shall make or enforce any law which shall abridge the privileges or immunities of citizens of the United States; nor shall any State deprive any person of life, liberty, or property, without due process of law; nor deny to any person within its jurisdiction the equal protection of the laws.

Section 2. Representatives shall be apportioned among the several States according to their respective numbers, counting the whole number of persons in each State, excluding Indians not taxed. But when the right to vote at any election for the choice of electors for President and Vice President of the United States, Representatives in Congress, the Executive and Judicial officers of a State, or the members of the Legislature thereof, is denied to any of the male inhabitants of such State, being twenty-one years of age, and citizens of the United States, or in any way abridged, except for participation in rebellion, or other crime, the basis of representation therein shall be reduced in the proportion which the number of such male citizens shall bear to the whole number of male citizens twenty-one years of age in such State.

Section 3. No person shall be a Senator or Representative in Congress, or elector of President and Vice President, or hold any office, civil or military, under the United States, or under any State, who having previously taken an oath, as a member of Congress, or as an officer of the United States, or as a member of any State legislature, or as an executive or judicial officer of any State, to support the Constitution of the United States, shall have engaged in insurrection or rebellion against the same, or given aid or comfort to the enemies thereof. But Congress may by a vote of two-thirds of each House, remove such disability.

Section 4. The validity of the public debt of the United States, authorized by law, including debts incurred for payment of pensions and bounties for services in suppressing insurrection or rebellion, shall not be questioned. But neither the United States nor any State shall assume or pay any debt or obligation incurred in aid of insurrection or rebellion against the United States, or any claim for the loss or emancipation of any slave; but all such debts, obligations and claims shall be held illegal and void.

Section 5. The Congress shall have power to

enforce, by appropriate legislation, the provisions of this article.

Amendment XV [1870]

Section 1. The right of citizens of the United States to vote shall not be denied or abridged by the United States or by any State on account of race, color, or previous condition of servitude.

Section 2. The Congress shall have power to enforce this article by appropriate legislation.

Amendment XVI [1913]

The Congress shall have power to lay and collect taxes on incomes, from whatever source derived, without apportionment among the several States, and without regard to any census or enumeration.

Amendment XVII [1913]

Section 1. The Senate of the United States shall be composed of two Senators from each State, elected by the people thereof, for six years; and each Senator shall have one vote. The electors in each State shall have the qualifications requisite for electors of the most numerous branch of the State legislatures.

Section 2. When vacancies happen in the representation of any State in the Senate, the executive authority of such State shall issue writs of election to fill such vacancies: *Provided*, That the legislature of any State may empower the executive thereof to make temporary appointments until the people fill the vacancies by election as the legislature may direct.

Section 3. This amendment shall not be so construed as to affect the election or term of any Senator chosen before it becomes valid as part of the Constitution.

Amendment XVIII [1919]

Section 1. After one year from the ratification of this article the manufacture, sale, or transportation of intoxicating liquors within, the importation thereof into, or the exportation thereof from the United States and all territory subject to the jurisdiction thereof for beverage purposes is hereby prohibited.

Section 2. The Congress and the several States shall have concurrent power to enforce this article by appropriate legislation.

Section 3. This article shall be inoperative unless it shall have been ratified as an amendment to the Constitution by the legislatures of the several States, as provided in the Constitution, within seven years from the date of the submission hereof to the States by the Congress.

Amendment XIX [1920]

Section 1. The right of citizens of the United States to vote shall not be denied or abridged by the United States or by any State on account of sex.

Section 2. Congress shall have power to enforce this article by appropriate legislation.

Amendment XX [1933]

Section 1. The terms of the President and Vice President shall end at noon on the 20th day of January, and the terms of Senators and Representatives at noon on the 3d day of January, of the years in which such terms would have ended if this article had not been ratified; and the terms of their successors shall then begin.

Section 2. The Congress shall assemble at least once in every year, and such meeting shall begin at noon on the 3d day of January, unless they shall by law appoint a different day.

Section 3. If, at the time fixed for the beginning of the term of the President, the President elect shall have died, the Vice President elect shall become President. If the President shall not have been chosen before the time fixed for the beginning of his term, or if the President elect shall have failed to qualify, then the Vice President elect shall act as President until a President shall have qualified; and the Congress may by law provide for the case wherein neither a President elect nor a Vice President elect shall have qualified, declaring who shall then act as President, or the manner in which one who is to act shall be selected, and such person shall act accordingly until a President or Vice President shall have qualified.

Section 4. The Congress may by law provide for the case of the death of any of the persons from whom the House of Representatives may choose a President whenever the right of choice shall have devolved upon them, and for the case of the death of any of the persons from whom the Senate may choose a Vice President whenever the right of choice shall have devolved upon them.

Section 5. Sections 1 and 2 shall take effect on the 15th day of October following the ratification of this article.

Section 6. This article shall be inoperative unless it shall have been ratified as an amendment to the Constitution by the legislatures of three-fourths of the several States within seven years from the date of its submission.

Amendment XXI [1933]

Section 1. The eighteenth article of amendment to the Constitution of the United States is hereby repealed.

Section 2. The transportation or importation into any State, Territory, or possession of the United States for delivery or use therein of intoxicating liquors, in violation of the laws thereof, is hereby prohibited.

Section 3. This article shall be inoperative unless it shall have been ratified as an amendment to the

Constitution by conventions in the several States, as provided in the Constitution, within seven years from the date of the submission hereof to the States by the Congress.

Amendment XXII [1951]

Section 1. No person shall be elected to the office of the President more than twice, and no person who has held the office of President, or acted as President, for more than two years of a term to which some other person was elected President shall be elected to the office of President more than once. But this Article shall not apply to any person holding the office of President when this Article was proposed by the Congress, and shall not prevent any person who may be holding the office of President, or acting as President, during the term within which this Article becomes operative from holding the office of President or acting as President during the remainder of such term.

Section 2. This article shall be inoperative unless it shall have been ratified as an amendment to the Constitution by the legislatures of three-fourths of the several States within seven years from the date of its submission to the States by the Congress.

Amendment XXIII [1961]

Section 1. The District constituting the seat of Government of the United States shall appoint in such manner as the Congress may direct:

A number of electors of President and Vice President equal to the whole number of Senators and Representatives in Congress to which the District would be entitled if it were a State, but in no event more than the least populous state; they shall be in addition to those appointed by the states, but they shall be considered, for the purposes of the election of President and Vice President, to be electors appointed by a state; and they shall meet in the District and perform such duties as provided by the twelfth article of amendment.

Section 2. The Congress shall have power to enforce this article by appropriate legislation.

Amendment XXIV [1964]

Section 1. The right of citizens of the United States to vote in any primary or other election for President or Vice President, for electors for President or Vice President, or for Senator or Representative in Congress, shall not be denied or abridged by the United States, or any State by reason of failure to pay any poll tax or other tax.

Section 2. The Congress shall have power to enforce this article by appropriate legislation.

Amendment XXV [1967]

Section 1. In case of the removal of the President from office or of his death or resignation, the Vice President shall become President.

Section 2. Whenever there is a vacancy in the office of the Vice President, the President shall nominate a Vice President who shall take office upon confirmation by a majority vote of both Houses of Congress.

Section 3. Whenever the President transmits to the President pro tempore of the Senate and the Speaker of the House of Representatives his written declaration that he is unable to discharge the powers and duties of his office, and until he transmits to them a written declaration to the contrary, such powers and duties shall be discharged by the Vice President as Acting President.

Section 4. Whenever the Vice President and a majority of either the principal officers of the executive departments or of such other body as Congress may by law provide, transmit to the President pro tempore of the Senate and the Speaker of the House of Representatives their written declaration that the President is unable to discharge the powers and duties of his office, the Vice President shall immediately assume the powers and duties of the office as Acting President.

Thereafter, when the President transmits to the President pro tempore of the Senate and the Speaker of the House of Representatives his written declaration that no inability exists, he shall resume the powers and duties of his office unless the Vice President and a majority of either the principal officers of the executive department or of such other body as Congress may by law provide, transmit within four days to the President pro tempore of the Senate and the Speaker of the House of Representatives their written declaration that the President is unable to discharge the powers and duties of his office. Thereupon Congress shall decide the issue, assembling within forty-eight hours for that purpose if not in session. If the Congress, within twenty-one days after receipt of the latter written declaration, or, if Congress is not in session, within twenty-one days after Congress is required to assemble, determines by two-thirds vote of both Houses that the President is unable to discharge the powers and duties of his office, the Vice President shall continue to discharge the same as Acting President; otherwise, the President shall resume the powers and duties of his office.

Amendment XXVI [1971]

Section 1. The right of citizens of the United States, who are eighteen years of age or older, to vote shall not be denied or abridged by the United States or by any State on account of age.

Section 2. The Congress shall have power to enforce this article by appropriate legislation.

Amendment XXVII [1992]

No law, varying the compensation for the services of the Senators and Representatives, shall take effect, until an election of Representatives shall have intervened.

APPENDIX B

The Uniform Commercial Code

(Adopted in fifty-two jurisdictions; all fifty States, although Louisiana has adopted only Articles 1, 3, 4, 7, 8, and 9; the District of Columbia; and the Virgin Islands.)

The Code consists of the following articles:

Art.

1. General Provisions
2. Sales

2A. Leases

3. Commercial Paper
4. Bank Deposits and Collections

4A. Funds Transfers

5. Letters of Credit
6. Bulk Transfers (including Alternative B)
7. Warehouse Receipts, Bills of Lading and Other Documents of Title
8. Investment Securities
9. Secured Transactions: Sales of Accounts and Chattel Paper
10. Effective Date and Repealer
11. Effective Date and Transition Provisions

Article 1
GENERAL PROVISIONS

Part 1 Short Title, Construction, Application and Subject Matter of the Act

§ 1—101. Short Title.

This Act shall be known and may be cited as Uniform Commercial Code.

§ 1—102. Purposes; Rules of Construction; Variation by Agreement.

(1) This Act shall be liberally construed and applied to promote its underlying purposes and policies.

(2) Underlying purposes and policies of this Act are

(a) to simplify, clarify and modernize the law governing commercial transactions;

(b) to permit the continued expansion of commercial practices through custom, usage and agreement of the parties;

(c) to make uniform the law among the various jurisdictions.

(3) The effect of provisions of this Act may be varied by agreement, except as otherwise provided in this Act and except that the obligations of good faith, diligence, reasonableness and care prescribed by this Act may not be disclaimed by agreement but the parties may by agreement determine the standards by which the performance of such obligations is to be measured if such standards are not manifestly unreasonable.

(4) The presence in certain provisions of this Act of the words "unless otherwise agreed" or words of similar import does not imply that the effect of other provisions may not be varied by agreement under subsection (3).

(5) In this Act unless the context otherwise requires

(a) words in the singular number include the plural, and in the plural include the singular;

(b) words of the masculine gender include the feminine and the neuter, and when the sense so indicates words of the neuter gender may refer to any gender.

§ 1—103. Supplementary General Principles of Law Applicable.

Unless displaced by the particular provisions of this Act, the principles of law and equity, including the law merchant and the law relative to capacity to contract, principal and agent, estoppel, fraud, misrepresentation, duress, coercion, mistake, bankruptcy, or other validating or invalidating cause shall supplement its provisions.

§ 1—104. **Construction Against Implicit Repeal.**

This Act being a general act intended as a unified coverage of its subject matter, no part of it shall be deemed to be impliedly repealed by subsequent legislation if such construction can reasonably be avoided.

§ 1—105. **Territorial Application of the Act; Parties' Power to Choose Applicable Law.**

(1) Except as provided hereafter in this section, when a transaction bears a reasonable relation to this state and also to another state or nation the parties may agree that the law either of this state or of such other state or nation shall govern their rights and duties. Failing such agreement this Act applies to transactions bearing an appropriate relation to this state.

(2) Where one of the following provisions of this Act specifies the applicable law, that provision governs and a contrary agreement is effective only to the extent permitted by the law (including the conflict of laws rules) so specified:

Rights of creditors against sold goods. Section 2—402.

Applicability of the Article on Leases. Sections 2A—105 and 2A—106.

Applicability of the Article on Bank Deposits and Collections. Section 4—102.

Governing law in the Article on Funds Transfers. Section 4A—507.

Letters of Credit, Section 5—116.

Bulk sales subject to the Article on Bulk Sales. Section 6—103.

Applicability of the Article on Investment Securities. Section 8—106.

Perfection provisions of the Article on Secured Transactions. Section 9—103.

§ 1—106. **Remedies to Be Liberally Administered.**

(1) The remedies provided by this Act shall be liberally administered to the end that the aggrieved party may be put in as good a position as if the other party had fully performed but neither consequential or special nor penal damages may be had except as specifically provided in this Act or by other rule of law.

(2) Any right or obligation declared by this Act is enforceable by action unless the provision declaring it specifies a different and limited effect.

§ 1—107. **Waiver or Renunciation of Claim or Right After Breach.**

Any claim or right arising out of an alleged breach can be discharged in whole or in part without consideration by a written waiver or renunciation signed and delivered by the aggrieved party.

§ 1—108. **Severability.**

If any provision or clause of this Act or application thereof to any person or circumstances is held invalid, such invalidity shall not affect other provisions or applications of the Act which can be given effect without the invalid provision or application, and to this end the provisions of this Act are declared to be severable.

§ 1—109. **Section Captions.**

Section captions are parts of this Act.

Part 2 General Definitions and Principles of Interpretation

§ 1—201. **General Definitions.**

Subject to additional definitions contained in the subsequent Articles of this Act which are applicable to specific Articles or Parts thereof, and unless the context otherwise requires, in this Act:

(1) "Action" in the sense of a judicial proceeding includes recoupment, counterclaim, set-off, suit in equity and any other proceedings in which rights are determined.

(2) "Aggrieved party" means a party entitled to resort to a remedy.

(3) "Agreement" means the bargain of the parties in fact as found in their language or by implication from other circumstances including course of dealing or usage of trade or course of performance as provided in this Act (Sections 1—205 and 2—208). Whether an agreement has legal consequences is determined by the provisions of this Act, if applicable; otherwise by the law of contracts (Section 1—103). (Compare "Contract".)

(4) "Bank" means any person engaged in the business of banking.

(5) "Bearer" means the person in possession of an instrument, document of title, or certificated security payable to bearer or indorsed in blank.

(6) "Bill of lading" means a document evidencing the receipt of goods for shipment issued by a person engaged in the business of transporting or forwarding goods, and includes an airbill. "Airbill" means a document serving for air transportation as a bill of lading does for marine or rail transportation, and includes an air consignment note or air waybill.

(7) "Branch" includes a separately incorporated foreign branch of a bank.

(8) "Burden of establishing" a fact means the burden of persuading the triers of fact that the existence of the fact is more probable than its non-existence.

(9) "Buyer in ordinary course of business" means a person who in good faith and without knowledge that the sale to him is in violation of the ownership rights or security interest of a third party in the goods buys in ordinary course from a person in the business of selling goods of that kind but does not include a pawnbroker. All persons who sell minerals or the like (including oil and gas) at wellhead or minehead shall be deemed to be persons in the business of selling goods of that kind. "Buying" may be for cash or by exchange of other property or on secured or unsecured credit and includes receiving goods or documents of title under a pre-existing contract for sale but does not include a transfer in bulk or as security for or in total or partial satisfaction of a money debt.

(10) "Conspicuous": A term or clause is conspicuous when it is so written that a reasonable person against whom it is to operate ought to have noticed it. A printed heading in capitals (as: NON-NEGOTIABLE BILL OF LADING) is conspicuous. Language in the body of a form is "conspicuous" if it is in larger or other contrasting type or color. But in a telegram any stated term is "conspicuous". Whether a term or clause is "conspicuous" or not is for decision by the court.

(11) "Contract" means the total legal obligation which results from the parties' agreement as affected by this Act and any other applicable rules of law. (Compare "Agreement".)

(12) "Creditor" includes a general creditor, a secured creditor, a lien creditor and any representative of creditors, including an assignee for the benefit of creditors, a trustee in bankruptcy, a receiver in equity and an executor or administrator of an insolvent debtor's or assignor's estate.

(13) "Defendant" includes a person in the position of defendant in a cross-action or counterclaim.

(14) "Delivery" with respect to instruments, documents of title, chattel paper, or certificated securities means voluntary transfer of possession.

(15) "Document of title" includes bill of lading, dock warrant, dock receipt, warehouse receipt or order for the delivery of goods, and also any other document which in the regular course of business or financing is treated as adequately evidencing that the person in possession of it is entitled to receive, hold and dispose of the document and the goods it covers. To be a document of title a document must purport to be issued by or addressed to a bailee and purport to cover goods in the bailee's possession which are either identified or are fungible portions of an identified mass.

(16) "Fault" means wrongful act, omission or breach.

(17) "Fungible" with respect to goods or securities means goods or securities of which any unit is, by nature or usage of trade, the equivalent of any other like unit. Goods which are not fungible shall be deemed fungible for the purposes of this Act to the extent that under a particular agreement or document unlike units are treated as equivalents.

(18) "Genuine" means free of forgery or counterfeiting.

(19) "Good faith" means honesty in fact in the conduct or transaction concerned.

(20) "Holder" with respect to a negotiable instrument, means the person in possession if the instrument is payable to bearer or, in the cases of an instrument payable to an identified person, if the identified person is in possession. "Holder" with respect to a document of title means the person in possession if the goods are deliverable to bearer or to the order of the person in possession.

(21) To "honor" is to pay or to accept and pay, or where a credit so engages to purchase or discount a draft complying with the terms of the credit.

(22) "Insolvency proceedings" includes any assignment for the benefit of creditors or other proceedings intended to liquidate or rehabilitate the estate of the person involved.

(23) A person is "insolvent" who either has ceased to pay his debts in the ordinary course of business or cannot pay his debts as they become due or is insolvent within the meaning of the federal bankruptcy law.

(24) "Money" means a medium of exchange authorized or adopted by a domestic or foreign government and includes a monetary unit of account established by an intergovernmental organization or by agreement between two or more nations.

(25) A person has "notice" of a fact when

(a) he has actual knowledge of it; or

(b) he has received a notice or notification of it; or

(c) from all the facts and circumstances known to him at the time in question he has reason to know that it exists.

A person "knows" or has "knowledge" of a fact when he has actual knowledge of it. "Discover" or "learn" or a word or phrase of similar import refers to knowledge rather than to reason to know. The time and circumstances under which a notice or notification may cease to be effective are not determined by this Act.

(26) A person "notifies" or "gives" a notice or notification to another by taking such steps as may be reasonably required to inform the other in ordinary course whether or not such other actually comes to know of it. A person "receives" a notice or notification when

(a) it comes to his attention; or

(b) it is duly delivered at the place of business through which the contract was made or at any other place held out by him as the place for receipt of such communications.

(27) Notice, knowledge or a notice or notification received by an organization is effective for a particular transaction from the time when it is brought to the attention of the individual conducting that transaction, and in any event from the time when it would have been brought to his attention if the organization had exercised due diligence. An organization exercises due diligence if it maintains reasonable routines for communicating significant information to the person conducting the transaction and there is reasonable compliance with the routines. Due diligence does not require an individual acting for the organization to communicate information unless such communication is part of his regular duties or unless he has reason to know of the transaction and that the transaction would be materially affected by the information.

(28) "Organization" includes a corporation, government or governmental subdivision or agency, business trust, estate, trust, partnership or association, two or more persons having a joint or common interest, or any other legal or commercial entity.

(29) "Party", as distinct from "third party", means a person who has engaged in a transaction or made an agreement within this Act.

(30) "Person" includes an individual or an organization (See Section 1—102).

(31) "Presumption" or "presumed" means that the trier of fact must find the existence of the fact presumed unless and until evidence is introduced which would support a finding of its non-existence.

(32) "Purchase" includes taking by sale, discount, negotiation, mortgage, pledge, lien, issue or re-issue, gift or any other voluntary transaction creating an interest in property.

(33) "Purchaser" means a person who takes by purchase.

(34) "Remedy" means any remedial right to which an aggrieved party is entitled with or without resort to a tribunal.

(35) "Representative" includes an agent, an officer of a corporation or association, and a trustee, executor or administrator of an estate, or any other person empowered to act for another.

(36) "Rights" includes remedies.

(37) "Security interest" means an interest in personal property or fixtures which secures payment or performance of an obligation. The retention or reservation of title by a seller of goods notwithstanding shipment or delivery to the buyer (Section 2—401) is limited in effect to a reservation of a "security interest". The term also includes any interest of a buyer of accounts or chattel paper which is subject to Article 9. The special property interest of a buyer of goods on identification of those goods to a contract for sale under Section 2—401 is not a "security interest", but a buyer may also acquire a "security interest" by complying with Article 9. Unless a consignment is intended as security, reservation of title thereunder is not a "security interest," but a consignment is in any event subject to the provisions on consignment sales (Section 2—326).

Whether a transaction creates a lease or security interest is determined by the facts of each case; however, a transaction creates a security interest if the consideration the lessee is to pay the lessor for the right to possession and use of the goods is an obligation for the term of the lease not subject to termination by the lessee, and

(a) the original term of the lease is equal to or greater than the remaining economic life of the goods,

(b) the lessee is bound to renew the lease for the remaining economic life of the goods or is bound to become the owner of the goods,

(c) the lessee has an option to renew the lease for the remaining economic life of the goods for no additional consideration or nominal additional consideration upon compliance with the lease agreement, or

(d) the lessee has an option to become the owner of the goods for no additional consideration or nominal additional consideration upon compliance with the lease agreement.

A transaction does not create a security interest merely because it provides that

(a) the present value of the consideration the lessee is obligated to pay the lessor for the right to possession and use of the goods is substantially equal to or is greater than the fair market value of the goods at the time the lease is entered into,

(b) the lessee assumes risk of loss of the goods, or agrees to pay taxes, insurance, filing, recording, or registration fees, or service or maintenance costs with respect to the goods,

(c) the lessee has an option to renew the lease or to become the owner of the goods,

(d) the lessee has an option to renew the lease for a fixed rent that is equal to or greater than the reasonably predictable fair market rent for the use of the goods for the term of the renewal at the time the option is to be performed, or

(e) the lessee has an option to become the owner of the goods for a fixed price that is equal to or greater than the reasonably predictable fair market value of the goods at the time the option is to be performed.

For purposes of this subsection (37):

(x) Additional consideration is not nominal if (i) when the option to renew the lease is granted to the lessee the rent is stated to be the fair market rent for the use of the goods for the term of the renewal determined at the time the option is to be performed, or (ii) when the option to become the owner of the goods is granted to the lessee the price is stated to be the fair market value of the goods determined at the time the option is to be performed. Additional consideration is nominal if it is less than the lessee's reasonably predictable cost of performing under the lease agreement if the option is not exercised;

(y) "Reasonably predictable" and "remaining economic life of the goods" are to be determined with reference to the facts and circumstances at the time the transaction is entered into; and

(z) "Present value" means the amount as of a date certain of one or more sums payable in the future, discounted to the date certain. The discount is determined by the interest rate specified by the parties if the rate is not manifestly unreasonable at the time the transaction is entered into; otherwise, the discount is determined by a commercially reasonable rate that takes into account the facts and circumstances of each case at the time the transaction was entered into.

(38) "Send" in connection with any writing or notice means to deposit in the mail or deliver for transmission by any other usual means of communication with postage or cost of transmission provided for and properly addressed and in the case of an instrument to an address specified thereon or otherwise agreed, or if there be none to any address reasonable under the circumstances. The receipt of any writing or notice within the time at which it would have arrived if properly sent has the effect of a proper sending.

(39) "Signed" includes any symbol executed or adopted by a party with present intention to authenticate a writing.

(40) "Surety" includes guarantor.

(41) "Telegram" includes a message transmitted by radio, teletype, cable, any mechanical method of transmission, or the like.

(42) "Term" means that portion of an agreement which relates to a particular matter.

(43) "Unauthorized" signature means one made without actual, implied or apparent authority and includes a forgery.

(44) "Value". Except as otherwise provided with respect to negotiable instruments and bank collections (Sections 3—303, 4—210 and 4—211) a person gives "value" for rights if he acquires them

(a) in return for a binding commitment to extend credit or for the extension of immediately available credit whether or not drawn upon and whether or not a chargeback is provided for in the event of difficulties in collection; or

(b) as security for or in total or partial satisfaction of a pre-existing claim; or

(c) by accepting delivery pursuant to a preexisting contract for purchase; or

(d) generally, in return for any consideration sufficient to support a simple contract.

(45) "Warehouse receipt" means a receipt issued by a person engaged in the business of storing goods for hire.

(46) "Written" or "writing" includes printing, typewriting or any other intentional reduction to tangible form.

§1—202. Prima Facie Evidence by Third Party Documents.

A document in due form purporting to be a bill of lading, policy or certificate of insurance, official weigher's or inspector's certificate, consular invoice, or any other document authorized or required by the contract to be issued by a third party shall be prima facie evidence of its own authenticity and genuineness and of the facts stated in the document by the third party.

§ 1—203. Obligation of Good Faith.

Every contract or duty within this Act imposes an obligation of good faith in its performance or enforcement.

§ 1—204. Time; Reasonable Time; "Seasonably".

(1) Whenever this Act requires any action to be taken within a reasonable time, any time which is not manifestly unreasonable may be fixed by agreement.

(2) What is a reasonable time for taking any action depends on the nature, purpose and circumstances of such action.

(3) An action is taken "seasonably" when it is taken at or within the time agreed or if no time is agreed at or within a reasonable time.

§ 1—205. Course of Dealing and Usage of Trade.

(1) A course of dealing is a sequence of previous conduct between the parties to a particular transaction which is fairly to be regarded as establishing a common basis of understanding for interpreting their expressions and other conduct.

(2) A usage of trade is any practice or method of dealing having such regularity of observance in a place, vocation or trade as to justify an expectation that it will be observed with respect to the transaction in question. The existence and scope of such a usage are to be proved as facts. If it is established that such a usage is embodied in a written trade code or similar writing the interpretation of the writing is for the court.

(3) A course of dealing between parties and any usage of trade in the vocation or trade in which they are engaged or of which they are or should be aware give

particular meaning to and supplement or qualify terms of an agreement.

(4) The express terms of an agreement and an applicable course of dealing or usage of trade shall be construed wherever reasonable as consistent with each other; but when such construction is unreasonable express terms control both course of dealing and usage of trade and course of dealing controls usage trade.

(5) An applicable usage of trade in the place where any part of performance is to occur shall be used in interpreting the agreement as to that part of the performance.

(6) Evidence of a relevant usage of trade offered by one party is not admissible unless and until he has given the other party such notice as the court finds sufficient to prevent unfair surprise to the latter.

§ 1—206. **Statute of Frauds for Kinds of Personal Property Not Otherwise Covered.**

(1) Except in the cases described in subsection (2) of this section a contract for the sale of personal property is not enforceable by way of action or defense beyond five thousand dollars in amount or value of remedy unless there is some writing which indicates that a contract for sale has been made between the parties at a defined or stated price, reasonably identifies the subject matter, and is signed by the party against whom enforcement is sought or by his authorized agent.

(2) Subsection (1) of this section does not apply to contracts for the sale of goods (Section 2—201) nor of securities (Section 8—113) nor to security agreements (Section 9—203).

§ 1—207. **Performance or Acceptance Under Reservation of Rights.**

(1) A party who with explicit reservation of rights performs or promises performance or assents to performance in a manner demanded or offered by the other party does not thereby prejudice the rights reserved. Such words as "without prejudice", "under protest" or the like are sufficient.

(2) Subsection (1) does not apply to an accord and satisfaction.

§ 1—208. **Option to Accelerate at Will.**

A term providing that one party or his successor in interest may accelerate payment or performance or require collateral or additional collateral "at will" or "when he deems himself insecure" or in words of similar import shall be construed to mean that he shall have power to do so only if he in good faith believes that the prospect of payment or performance is impaired. The burden of establishing lack of good faith is on the party against whom the power has been exercised.

§ 1—209. **Subordinated Obligations.**

An obligation may be issued as subordinated to payment of another obligation of the person obligated, or a creditor may subordinate his right to payment of an obligation by agreement with either the person obligated or another creditor of the person obligated. Such a subordination does not create a security interest as against either the common debtor or a subordinated creditor. This section shall be construed as declaring the law as it existed prior to the enactment of this section and not as modifying it. Added 1966.

Note: *This new section is proposed as an optional provision to make it clear that a subordination agreement does not create a security interest unless so intended.*

Article 2
SALES

Part 1 Short Title, General Construction and Subject Matter

§ 2—101. **Short Title.**

This Article shall be known and may be cited as Uniform Commercial Code—Sales.

§ 2—102. **Scope; Certain Security and Other Transactions Excluded From This Article.**

Unless the context otherwise requires, this Article applies to transactions in goods; it does not apply to any transaction which although in the form of an unconditional contract to sell or present sale is intended to operate only as a security transaction nor does this Article impair or repeal any statute regulating sales to consumers, farmers or other specified classes of buyers.

§ 2—103. **Definitions and Index of Definitions.**

(1) In this Article unless the context otherwise requires

(a) "Buyer" means a person who buys or contracts to buy goods.

(b) "Good faith" in the case of a merchant means honesty in fact and the observance of reasonable commercial standards of fair dealing in the trade.

(c) "Receipt" of goods means taking physical possession of them.

(d) "Seller" means a person who sells or contracts to sell goods.

(2) Other definitions applying to this Article or to specified Parts thereof, and the sections in which they appear are:

"Acceptance". Section 2—606.
"Banker's credit". Section 2—325.
"Between merchants". Section 2—104.
"Cancellation". Section 2—106(4).

"Commercial unit". Section 2—105.
"Confirmed credit". Section 2—325.
"Conforming to contract". Section 2—106.
"Contract for sale". Section 2—106.
"Cover". Section 2—712.
"Entrusting". Section 2—403.
"Financing agency". Section 2—104.
"Future goods". Section 2—105.
"Goods". Section 2—105.
"Identification". Section 2—501.
"Installment contract". Section 2—612.
"Letter of Credit". Section 2—325.
"Lot". Section 2—105.
"Merchant". Section 2—104.
"Overseas". Section 2—323.
"Person in position of seller". Section 2—707.
"Present sale". Section 2—106.
"Sale". Section 2—106.
"Sale on approval". Section 2—326.
"Sale or return". Section 2—326.
"Termination". Section 2—106.

(3) The following definitions in other Articles apply to this Article:

"Check". Section 3—104.
"Consignee". Section 7—102.
"Consignor". Section 7—102.
"Consumer goods". Section 9—109.
"Dishonor". Section 3—507.
"Draft". Section 3—104.

(4) In addition Article 1 contains general definitions and principles of construction and interpretation applicable throughout this Article.

§ 2—104. Definitions: "Merchant"; "Between Merchants"; "Financing Agency".

(1) "Merchant" means a person who deals in goods of the kind or otherwise by his occupation holds himself out as having knowledge or skill peculiar to the practices or goods involved in the transaction or to whom such knowledge or skill may be attributed by his employment of an agent or broker or other intermediary who by his occupation holds himself out as having such knowledge or skill.

(2) "Financing agency" means a bank, finance company or other person who in the ordinary course of business makes advances against goods or documents of title or who by arrangement with either the seller or the buyer intervenes in ordinary course to make or collect payment due or claimed under the contract for sale, as by purchasing or paying the seller's draft or making advances against it or by merely taking it for collection whether or not documents of title accompany the draft. "Financing agency" includes also a bank or other person who similarly intervenes between persons who are in the position of seller and buyer in respect to the goods (Section 2—707).

(3) "Between merchants" means in any transaction with respect to which both parties are chargeable with the knowledge or skill of merchants.

§ 2—105. Definitions: Transferability; "Goods"; "Future" Goods; "Lot"; "Commercial Unit".

(1) "Goods" means all things (including specially manufactured goods) which are movable at the time of identification to the contract for sale other than the money in which the price is to be paid, investment securities (Article 8) and things in action. "Goods" also includes the unborn young of animals and growing crops and other identified things attached to realty as described in the section on goods to be severed from realty (Section 2—107).

(2) Goods must be both existing and identified before any interest in them can pass. Goods which are not both existing and identified are "future" goods. A purported present sale of future goods or of any interest therein operates as a contract to sell.

(3) There may be a sale of a part interest in existing identified goods.

(4) An undivided share in an identified bulk of fungible goods is sufficiently identified to be sold although the quantity of the bulk is not determined. Any agreed proportion of such a bulk or any quantity thereof agreed upon by number, weight or other measure may to the extent of the seller's interest in the bulk be sold to the buyer who then becomes an owner in common.

(5) "Lot" means a parcel or a single article which is the subject matter of a separate sale or delivery, whether or not it is sufficient to perform the contract.

(6) "Commercial unit" means such a unit of goods as by commercial usage is a single whole for purposes of sale and division of which materially impairs its character or value on the market or in use. A commercial unit may be a single article (as a machine) or a set of articles (as a suite of furniture or an assortment of sizes) or a quantity (as a bale, gross, or carload) or any other unit treated in use or in the relevant market as a single whole.

§ 2—106. Definitions: "Contract"; "Agreement"; "Contract for Sale"; "Sale"; "Present Sale"; "Conforming" to Contract; "Termination"; "Cancellation".

(1) In this Article unless the context otherwise requires "contract" and "agreement" are limited to those relating to the present or future sale of goods. "Contract for sale" includes both a present sale of goods and a contract to sell goods at a future time. A "sale" consists in the passing of title from the seller to the buyer for a price (Section 2—401). A "present sale" means a sale which is accomplished by the making of the contract.

(2) Goods or conduct including any part of a performance are "conforming" or conform to the contract when they are in accordance with the obligations under the contract.

(3) "Termination" occurs when either party pursuant to a power created by agreement or law puts an end to the contract otherwise than for its breach. On "termination" all obligations which are still executory on both sides are discharged but any right based on prior breach or performance survives.

(4) "Cancellation" occurs when either party puts an end to the contract for breach by the other and its effect is the same as that of "termination" except that the cancelling party also retains any remedy for breach of the whole contract or any unperformed balance.

§ 2—107. Goods to Be Severed From Realty: Recording.

(1) A contract for the sale of minerals or the like (including oil and gas) or a structure or its materials to be removed from realty is a contract for the sale of goods within this Article if they are to be severed by the seller but until severance a purported present sale thereof which is not effective as a transfer of an interest in land is effective only as a contract to sell.

(2) A contract for the sale apart from the land of growing crops or other things attached to realty and capable of severance without material harm thereto but not described in subsection (1) or of timber to be cut is a contract for the sale of goods within this Article whether the subject matter is to be severed by the buyer or by the seller even though it forms part of the realty at the time of contracting, and the parties can by identification effect a present sale before severance.

(3) The provisions of this section are subject to any third party rights provided by the law relating to realty records, and the contract for sale may be executed and recorded as a document transferring an interest in land and shall then constitute notice to third parties of the buyer's rights under the contract for sale.

Part 2 Form, Formation and Readjustment of Contract

§ 2—201. Formal Requirements; Statute of Frauds.

(1) Except as otherwise provided in this section a contract for the sale of goods for the price of $500 or more is not enforceable by way of action or defense unless there is some writing sufficient to indicate that a contract for sale has been made between the parties and signed by the party against whom enforcement is sought or by his authorized agent or broker. A writing is not insufficient because it omits or incorrectly states a term agreed upon but the contract is not enforceable under this paragraph beyond the quantity of goods shown in such writing.

(2) Between merchants if within a reasonable time a writing in confirmation of the contract and sufficient against the sender is received and the party receiving it has reason to know its contents, its satisfies the requirements of subsection (1) against such party unless written notice of objection to its contents is given within ten days after it is received.

(3) A contract which does not satisfy the requirements of subsection (1) but which is valid in other respects is enforceable

(a) if the goods are to be specially manufactured for the buyer and are not suitable for sale to others in the ordinary course of the seller's business and the seller, before notice of repudiation is received and under circumstances which reasonably indicate that the goods are for the buyer, has made either a substantial beginning of their manufacture or commitments for their procurement; or

(b) if the party against whom enforcement is sought admits in his pleading, testimony or otherwise in court that a contract for sale was made, but the contract is not enforceable under this provision beyond the quantity of goods admitted; or

(c) with respect to goods for which payment has been made and accepted or which have been received and accepted (Sec. 2—606).

§ 2—202. Final Written Expression: Parol or Extrinsic Evidence.

Terms with respect to which the confirmatory memoranda of the parties agree or which are otherwise set forth in a writing intended by the parties as a final expression of their agreement with respect to such terms as are included therein may not be contradicted by evidence of any prior agreement or of a contemporaneous oral agreement but may be explained or supplemented

(a) by course of dealing or usage of trade (Section 1—205) or by course of performance (Section 2—208); and

(b) by evidence of consistent additional terms unless the court finds the writing to have been intended also as a complete and exclusive statement of the terms of the agreement.

§ 2—203. Seals Inoperative.

The affixing of a seal to a writing evidencing a contract for sale or an offer to buy or sell goods does not constitute the writing a sealed instrument and the law with respect to sealed instruments does not apply to such a contract or offer.

§ 2—204. Formation in General.

(1) A contract for sale of goods may be made in any manner sufficient to show agreement, including conduct by

both parties which recognizes the existence of such a contract.

(2) An agreement sufficient to constitute a contract for sale may be found even though the moment of its making is undetermined.

(3) Even though one or more terms are left open a contract for sale does not fail for indefiniteness if the parties have intended to make a contract and there is a reasonably certain basis for giving an appropriate remedy.

§ 2—205. Firm Offers.

An offer by a merchant to buy or sell goods in a signed writing which by its terms gives assurance that it will be held open is not revocable, for lack of consideration, during the time stated or if no time is stated for a reasonable time, but in no event may such period of irrevocability exceed three months; but any such term of assurance on a form supplied by the offeree must be separately signed by the offeror.

§ 2—206. Offer and Acceptance in Formation of Contract.

(1) Unless other unambiguously indicated by the language or circumstances

(a) an offer to make a contract shall be construed as inviting acceptance in any manner and by any medium reasonable in the circumstances;

(b) an order or other offer to buy goods for prompt or current shipment shall be construed as inviting acceptance either by a prompt promise to ship or by the prompt or current shipment of conforming or nonconforming goods, but such a shipment of nonconforming goods does not constitute an acceptance if the seller seasonably notifies the buyer that the shipment is offered only as an accommodation to the buyer.

(2) Where the beginning of a requested performance is a reasonable mode of acceptance an offeror who is not notified of acceptance within a reasonable time may treat the offer as having lapsed before acceptance.

§ 2—207. Additional Terms in Acceptance or Confirmation.

(1) A definite and seasonable expression of acceptance or a written confirmation which is sent within a reasonable time operates as an acceptance even though it states terms additional to or different from those offered or agreed upon, unless acceptance is expressly made conditional on assent to the additional or different terms.

(2) The additional terms are to be construed as proposals for addition to the contract. Between merchants such terms become part of the contract unless:

(a) the offer expressly limits acceptance to the terms of the offer;

(b) they materially alter it; or

(c) notification of objection to them has already been given or is given within a reasonable time after notice of them is received.

(3) Conduct by both parties which recognizes the existence of a contract is sufficient to establish a contract for sale although the writings of the parties do not otherwise establish a contract. In such case the terms of the particular contract consist of those terms on which the writings of the parties agree, together with any supplementary terms incorporated under any other provisions of this Act.

§ 2—208. Course of Performance or Practical Construction.

(1) Where the contract for sale involves repeated occasions for performance by either party with knowledge of the nature of the performance and opportunity for objection to it by the other, any course of performance accepted or acquiesced in without objection shall be relevant to determine the meaning of the agreement.

(2) The express terms of the agreement and any such course of performance, as well as any course of dealing and usage of trade, shall be construed whenever reasonable as consistent with each other; but when such construction is unreasonable, express terms shall control course of performance and course of performance shall control both course of dealing and usage of trade (Section 1—205).

(3) Subject to the provisions of the next section on modification and waiver, such course of performance shall be relevant to show a waiver or modification of any term inconsistent with such course of performance.

§ 2—209. Modification, Rescission and Waiver.

(1) An agreement modifying a contract within this Article needs no consideration to be binding.

(2) A signed agreement which excludes modification or rescission except by a signed writing cannot be otherwise modified or rescinded, but except as between merchants such a requirement on a form supplied by the merchant must be separately signed by the other party.

(3) The requirements of the statute of frauds section of this Article (Section 2—201) must be satisfied if the contract as modified is within its provisions.

(4) Although an attempt at modification or rescission does not satisfy the requirements of subsection (2) or (3) it can operate as a waiver.

(5) A party who has made a waiver affecting an executory portion of the contract may retract the waiver by reasonable notification received by the other party that strict performance will be required of any term waived, unless the retraction would be unjust in view of a material change of position in reliance on the waiver.

§ 2—210. Delegation of Performance; Assignment of Rights.

(1) A party may perform his duty through a delegate unless otherwise agreed or unless the other party has a substantial interest in having his original promisor perform or control the acts required by the contract. No delegation of performance relieves the party delegating of any duty to perform or any liability for breach.

(2) Unless otherwise agreed all rights of either seller or buyer can be assigned except where the assignment would materially change the duty of the other party, or increase materially the burden or risk imposed on him by his contract, or impair materially his chance of obtaining return performance. A right to damages for breach of the whole contract or a right arising out of the assignor's due performance of his entire obligation can be assigned despite agreement otherwise.

(3) Unless the circumstances indicate the contrary a prohibition of assignment of "the contract" is to be construed as barring only the delegation to the assignee of the assignor's performance.

(4) An assignment of "the contract" or of "all my rights under the contract" or an assignment in similar general terms is an assignment of rights and unless the language or the circumstances (as in an assignment for security) indicate the contrary, it is a delegation of performance of the duties of the assignor and its acceptance by the assignee constitutes a promise by him to perform those duties. This promise is enforceable by either the assignor or the other party to the original contract.

(5) The other party may treat any assignment which delegates performance as creating reasonable grounds for insecurity and may without prejudice to his rights against the assignor demand assurances from the assignee (Section 2—609).

Part 3 General Obligation and Construction of Contract

§ 2—301. General Obligations of Parties.

The obligation of the seller is to transfer and deliver and that of the buyer is to accept and pay in accordance with the contract.

§ 2—302. Unconscionable Contract or Clause.

(1) If the court as a matter of law finds the contract or any clause of the contract to have been unconscionable at the time it was made the court may refuse to enforce the contract, or it may enforce the remainder of the contract without the unconscionable clause, or it may so limit the application of any unconscionable clause as to avoid any unconscionable result.

(2) When it is claimed or appears to the court that the contract or any clause thereof may be unconscionable the parties shall be afforded a reasonable opportunity to present evidence as to its commercial setting, purpose and effect to aid the court in making the determination.

§ 2—303. Allocations or Division of Risks.

Where this Article allocates a risk or a burden as between the parties "unless otherwise agreed", the agreement may not only shift the allocation but may also divide the risk or burden.

§ 2—304. Price Payable in Money, Goods, Realty, or Otherwise.

(1) The price can be made payable in money or otherwise. If it is payable in whole or in part in goods each party is a seller of the goods which he is to transfer.

(2) Even though all or part of the price is payable in an interest in realty the transfer of the goods and the seller's obligations with reference to them are subject to this Article, but not the transfer of the interest in realty or the transferor's obligations in connection therewith.

§ 2—305. Open Price Term.

(1) The parties if they so intend can conclude a contract for sale even though the price is not settled. In such a case the price is a reasonable price at the time for delivery if

(a) nothing is said as to price; or

(b) the price is left to be agreed by the parties and they fail to agree; or

(c) the price is to be fixed in terms of some agreed market or other standard as set or recorded by a third person or agency and it is not so set or recorded.

(2) A price to be fixed by the seller or by the buyer means a price for him to fix in good faith.

(3) When a price left to be fixed otherwise than by agreement of the parties fails to be fixed through fault of one party the other may at his option treat the contract as cancelled or himself fix a reasonable price.

(4) Where, however, the parties intend not to be bound unless the price be fixed or agreed and it is not fixed or agreed there is no contract. In such a case the buyer must return any goods already received or if unable so to do must pay their reasonable value at the time of delivery and the seller must return any portion of the price paid on account.

§ 2—306. Output, Requirements and Exclusive Dealings.

(1) A term which measures the quantity by the output of the seller or the requirements of the buyer means such actual output or requirements as may occur in good faith, except that no quantity unreasonably disproportionate to any stated estimate or in the absence of a stated estimate to any normal or otherwise comparable prior output or requirements may be tendered or demanded.

(2) A lawful agreement by either the seller or the buyer for exclusive dealing in the kind of goods concerned imposes unless otherwise agreed an obligation by the seller to use best efforts to supply the goods and by the buyer to use best efforts to promote their sale.

§ 2—307. Delivery in Single Lot or Several Lots.

Unless otherwise agreed all goods called for by a contract for sale must be tendered in a single delivery and payment is due only on such tender but where the circumstances give either party the right to make or demand delivery in lots the price if it can be apportioned may be demanded for each lot.

§ 2—308. Absence of Specified Place for Delivery.

Unless otherwise agreed

(a) the place for delivery of goods is the seller's place of business or if he has none his residence; but

(b) in a contract for sale of identified goods which to the knowledge of the parties at the time of contracting are in some other place, that place is the place for their delivery; and

(c) documents of title may be delivered through customary banking channels.

§ 2—309. Absence of Specific Time Provisions; Notice of Termination.

(1) The time for shipment or delivery or any other action under a contract if not provided in this Article or agreed upon shall be a reasonable time.

(2) Where the contract provides for successive performances but is indefinite in duration it is valid for a reasonable time but unless otherwise agreed may be terminated at any time by either party.

(3) Termination of a contract by one party except on the happening of an agreed event requires that reasonable notification be received by the other party and an agreement dispensing with notification is invalid if its operation would be unconscionable.

§ 2—310. Open Time for Payment or Running of Credit; Authority to Ship Under Reservation.

Unless otherwise agreed

(a) payment is due at the time and place at which the buyer is to receive the goods even though the place of shipment is the place of delivery; and

(b) if the seller is authorized to send the goods he may ship them under reservation, and may tender the documents of title, but the buyer may inspect the goods after their arrival before payment is due unless such inspection is inconsistent with the terms of the contract (Section 2—513); and

(c) if delivery is authorized and made by way of documents of title otherwise than by subsection (b) then payment is due at the time and place at which the buyer is to receive the documents regardless of where the goods are to be received; and

(d) where the seller is required or authorized to ship the goods on credit the credit period runs from the time of shipment but post-dating the invoice or delaying its dispatch will correspondingly delay the starting of the credit period.

§ 2—311. Options and Cooperation Respecting Performance.

(1) An agreement for sale which is otherwise sufficiently definite (subsection (3) of Section 2—204) to be a contract is not made invalid by the fact that it leaves particulars of performance to be specified by one of the parties. Any such specification must be made in good faith and within limits set by commercial reasonableness.

(2) Unless otherwise agreed specifications relating to assortment of the goods are at the buyer's option and except as otherwise provided in subsections (1)(c) and (3) of Section 2—319 specifications or arrangements relating to shipment are at the seller's option.

(3) Where such specification would materially affect the other party's performance but is not seasonably made or where one party's cooperation is necessary to the agreed performance of the other but is not seasonably forthcoming, the other party in addition to all other remedies

(a) is excused for any resulting delay in his own performance; and

(b) may also either proceed to perform in any reasonable manner or after the time for a material part of his own performance treat the failure to specify or to cooperate as a breach by failure to deliver or accept the goods.

§ 2—312. Warranty of Title and Against Infringement; Buyer's Obligation Against Infringement.

(1) Subject to subsection (2) there is in a contract for sale a warranty by the seller that

(a) the title conveyed shall be good, and its transfer rightful; and

(b) the goods shall be delivered free from any security interest or other lien or encumbrance of which the buyer at the time of contracting has no knowledge.

(2) A warranty under subsection (1) will be excluded or modified only by specific language or by circumstances which give the buyer reason to know that the person selling does not claim title in himself or that he is purporting to sell only such right or title as he or a third person may have.

(3) Unless otherwise agreed a seller who is a merchant regularly dealing in goods of the kind warrants that the goods shall be delivered free of the rightful claim of any

third person by way of infringement or the like but a buyer who furnishes specifications to the seller must hold the seller harmless against any such claim which arises out of compliance with the specifications.

§ 2—313. Express Warranties by Affirmation, Promise, Description, Sample.

(1) Express warranties by the seller are created as follows:

(a) Any affirmation of fact or promise made by the seller to the buyer which relates to the goods and becomes part of the basis of the bargain creates an express warranty that the goods shall conform to the affirmation or promise.

(b) Any description of the goods which is made part of the basis of the bargain creates an express warranty that the goods shall conform to the description.

(c) Any sample or model which is made part of the basis of the bargain creates an express warranty that the whole of the goods shall conform to the sample or model.

(2) It is not necessary to the creation of an express warranty that the seller use formal words such as "warrant" or "guarantee" or that he have a specific intention to make a warranty, but an affirmation merely of the value of the goods or a statement purporting to be merely the seller's opinion or commendation of the goods does not create a warranty.

§ 2—314. Implied Warranty: Merchantability; Usage of Trade.

(1) Unless excluded or modified (Section 2—316), a warranty that the goods shall be merchantable is implied in a contract for their sale if the seller is a merchant with respect to goods of that kind. Under this section the serving for value of food or drink to be consumed either on the premises or elsewhere is a sale.

(2) Goods to be merchantable must be at least such as

(a) pass without objection in the trade under the contract description; and

(b) in the case of fungible goods, are of fair average quality within the description; and

(c) are fit for the ordinary purposes for which such goods are used; and

(d) run, within the variations permitted by the agreement, of even kind, quality and quantity within each unit and among all units involved; and

(e) are adequately contained, packaged, and labeled as the agreement may require; and

(f) conform to the promises or affirmations of fact made on the container or label if any.

(3) Unless excluded or modified (Section 2—316) other implied warranties may arise from course of dealing or usage of trade.

§ 2—315. Implied Warranty: Fitness for Particular Purpose.

Where the seller at the time of contracting has reason to know any particular purpose for which the goods are required and that the buyer is relying on the seller's skill or judgment to select or furnish suitable goods, there is unless excluded or modified under the next section an implied warranty that the goods shall be fit for such purpose.

§ 2—316. Exclusion or Modification of Warranties.

(1) Words or conduct relevant to the creation of an express warranty and words or conduct tending to negate or limit warranty shall be construed wherever reasonable as consistent with each other; but subject to the provisions of this Article on parol or extrinsic evidence (Section 2—202) negation or limitation is inoperative to the extent that such construction is unreasonable.

(2) Subject to subsection (3), to exclude or modify the implied warranty of merchantability or any part of it the language must mention merchantability and in case of a writing must be conspicuous, and to exclude or modify any implied warranty of fitness the exclusion must be by a writing and conspicuous. Language to exclude all implied warranties of fitness is sufficient if it states, for example, that "There are no warranties which extend beyond the description on the face hereof."

(3) Notwithstanding subsection (2)

(a) unless the circumstances indicate otherwise, all implied warranties are excluded by expressions like "as is", "with all faults" or other language which in common understanding calls the buyer's attention to the exclusion of warranties and makes plain that there is no implied warranty; and

(b) when the buyer before entering into the contract has examined the goods or the sample or model as fully as he desired or has refused to examine the goods there is no implied warranty with regard to defects which an examination ought in the circumstances to have revealed to him; and

(c) an implied warranty can also be excluded or modified by course of dealing or course of performance or usage of trade.

(4) Remedies for breach of warranty can be limited in accordance with the provisions of this Article on liquidation or limitation of damages and on contractual modification of remedy (Sections 2—718 and 2—719).

§ 2—317. Cumulation and Conflict of Warranties Express or Implied.

Warranties whether express or implied shall be construed as consistent with each other and as cumulative, but if such construction is unreasonable the intention of the parties shall determine which warranty is dominant. In ascertaining that intention the following rules apply:

(a) Exact or technical specifications displace an inconsistent sample or model or general language of description.

(b) A sample from an existing bulk displaces inconsistent general language of description.

(c) Express warranties displace inconsistent implied warranties other than an implied warranty of fitness for a particular purpose.

§ 2—318. Third Party Beneficiaries of Warranties Express or Implied.

Note: If this Act is introduced in the Congress of the United States this section should be omitted. (States to select one alternative.)

Alternative A

A seller's warranty whether express or implied extends to any natural person who is in the family or household of his buyer or who is a guest in his home if it is reasonable to expect that such person may use, consume or be affected by the goods and who is injured in person by breach of the warranty. A seller may not exclude or limit the operation of this section.

Alternative B

A seller's warranty whether express or implied extends to any natural person who may reasonably be expected to use, consume or be affected by the goods and who is injured in person by breach of the warranty. A seller may not exclude or limit the operation of this section.

Alternative C

A seller's warranty whether express or implied extends to any person who may reasonably be expected to use, consume or be affected by the goods and who is injured by breach of the warranty. A seller may not exclude or limit the operation of this section with respect to injury to the person of an individual to whom the warranty extends. As amended 1966.

§ 2—319. F.O.B. and F.A.S. Terms.

(1) Unless otherwise agreed the term F.O.B. (which means "free on board") at a named place, even though used only in connection with the stated price, is a delivery term under which

(a) when the term is F.O.B. the place of shipment, the seller must at that place ship the goods in the manner provided in this Article (Section 2—504) and bear the expense and risk of putting them into the possession of the carrier; or

(b) when the term is F.O.B. the place of destination, the seller must at his own expense and risk transport the goods to that place and there tender delivery of them in the manner provided in this Article (Section 2—503);

(c) when under either (a) or (b) the term is also F.O.B. vessel, car or other vehicle, the seller must in addition at his own expense and risk load the goods on board. If the term is F.O.B. vessel the buyer must name the vessel and in an appropriate case the seller must comply with the provisions of this Article on the form of bill of lading (Section 2—323).

(2) Unless otherwise agreed the term F.A.S. vessel (which means "free alongside") at a named port, even though used only in connection with the stated price, is a delivery term under which the seller must

(a) at his own expense and risk deliver the goods alongside the vessel in the manner usual in that port or on a dock designated and provided by the buyer; and

(b) obtain and tender a receipt for the goods in exchange for which the carrier is under a duty to issue a bill of lading.

(3) Unless otherwise agreed in any case falling within subsection (1)(a) or (c) or subsection (2) the buyer must seasonably give any needed instructions for making delivery, including when the term is F.A.S. or F.O.B. the loading berth of the vessel and in an appropriate case its name and sailing date. The seller may treat the failure of needed instructions as a failure of cooperation under this Article (Section 2—311). He may also at his option move the goods in any reasonable manner preparatory to delivery or shipment.

(4) Under the term F.O.B. vessel or F.A.S. unless otherwise agreed the buyer must make payment against tender of the required documents and the seller may not tender nor the buyer demand delivery of the goods in substitution for the documents.

§ 2—320. C.I.F. and C. & F. Terms.

(1) The term C.I.F. means that the price includes in a lump sum the cost of the goods and the insurance and freight to the named destination. The term C. & F. or C.F. means that the price so includes cost and freight to the named destination.

(2) Unless otherwise agreed and even though used only in connection with the stated price and destination, the term C.I.F. destination or its equivalent requires the seller at his own expense and risk to

(a) put the goods into the possession of a carrier at the port for shipment and obtain a negotiable bill or bills of lading covering the entire transportation to the named destination; and

(b) load the goods and obtain a receipt from the carrier (which may be contained in the bill of lading) showing that the freight has been paid or provided for; and

(c) obtain a policy or certificate of insurance, including any war risk insurance, of a kind and on terms then current at the port of shipment in the usual amount, in the currency of the contract, shown to cover the same goods covered by the bill of lading and providing for payment of loss to the order of the buyer or for the account of whom it may concern; but the seller may add to the price the amount of the premium for any such war risk insurance; and

(d) prepare an invoice of the goods and procure any other documents required to effect shipment or to comply with the contract; and

(e) forward and tender with commercial promptness all the documents in due form and with any indorsement necessary to perfect the buyer's rights.

(3) Unless otherwise agreed the term C. & F. or its equivalent has the same effect and imposes upon the seller the same obligations and risks as a C.I.F. term except the obligation as to insurance.

(4) Under the term C.I.F. or C. & F. unless otherwise agreed the buyer must make payment against tender of the required documents and the seller may not tender nor the buyer demand delivery of the goods in substitution for the documents.

§ 2—321. C.I.F. or C. & F.: "Net Landed Weights"; "Payment on Arrival"; Warranty of Condition on Arrival.

Under a contract containing a term C.I.F. or C. & F.

(1) Where the price is based on or is to be adjusted according to "net landed weights", "delivered weights", "out turn" quantity or quality or the like, unless otherwise agreed the seller must reasonably estimate the price. The payment due on tender of the documents called for by the contract is the amount so estimated, but after final adjustment of the price a settlement must be made with commercial promptness.

(2) An agreement described in subsection (1) or any warranty of quality or condition of the goods on arrival places upon the seller the risk of ordinary deterioration, shrinkage and the like in transportation but has no effect on the place or time of identification to the contract for sale or delivery or on the passing of the risk of loss.

(3) Unless otherwise agreed where the contract provides for payment on or after arrival of the goods the seller must before payment allow such preliminary inspection as is feasible; but if the goods are lost delivery of the documents and payment are due when the goods should have arrived.

§ 2—322. Delivery "Ex-Ship".

(1) Unless otherwise agreed a term for delivery of goods "ex-ship" (which means from the carrying vessel) or in equivalent language is not restricted to a particular ship and requires delivery from a ship which has reached a place at the named port of destination where goods of the kind are usually discharged.

(2) Under such a term unless otherwise agreed

(a) the seller must discharge all liens arising out of the carriage and furnish the buyer with a direction which puts the carrier under a duty to deliver the goods; and

(b) the risk of loss does not pass to the buyer until the goods leave the ship's tackle or are otherwise properly unloaded.

§ 2—323. Form of Bill of Lading Required in Overseas Shipment; "Overseas".

(1) Where the contract contemplates overseas shipment and contains a term C.I.F. or C. & F. or F.O.B. vessel, the seller unless otherwise agreed must obtain a negotiable bill of lading stating that the goods have been loaded on board or, in the case of a term C.I.F. or C. & F., received for shipment.

(2) Where in a case within subsection (1) a bill of lading has been issued in a set of parts, unless otherwise agreed if the documents are not to be sent from abroad the buyer may demand tender of the full set; otherwise only one part of the bill of lading need be tendered. Even if the agreement expressly requires a full set

(a) due tender of a single part is acceptable within the provisions of this Article on cure of improper delivery (subsection (1) of Section 2—508); and

(b) even though the full set is demanded, if the documents are sent from abroad the person tendering an incomplete set may nevertheless require payment upon furnishing an indemnity which the buyer in good faith deems adequate.

(3) A shipment by water or by air or a contract contemplating such shipment is "overseas" insofar as by usage of trade or agreement it is subject to the commercial, financing or shipping practices characteristic of international deep water commerce.

§ 2—324. "No Arrival, No Sale" Term.

Under a term "no arrival, no sale" or terms of like meaning, unless otherwise agreed,

(a) the seller must properly ship conforming goods and if they arrive by any means he must tender them on arrival but he assumes no obligation that the goods will arrive unless he has caused the non-arrival; and

(b) where without fault of the seller the goods are in part lost or have so deteriorated as no longer to conform to the contract or arrive after the contract time, the buyer may proceed as if there had been casualty to identified goods (Section 2—613).

§ 2—325. "Letter of Credit" Term; "Confirmed Credit".

(1) Failure of the buyer seasonably to furnish an agreed letter of credit is a breach of the contract for sale.

(2) The delivery to seller of a proper letter of credit suspends the buyer's obligation to pay. If the letter of credit is dishonored, the seller may on seasonable notification to the buyer require payment directly from him.

(3) Unless otherwise agreed the term "letter of credit" or "banker's credit" in a contract for sale means an irrevocable credit issued by a financing agency of good repute and, where the shipment is overseas, of good international repute. The term "confirmed credit" means that the credit must also carry the direct obligation of such an agency which does business in the seller's financial market.

§ 2—326. Sale on Approval and Sale or Return; Consignment Sales and Rights of Creditors.

(1) Unless otherwise agreed, if delivered goods may be returned by the buyer even though they conform to the contract, the transaction is

(a) a "sale on approval" if the goods are delivered primarily for use, and

(b) a "sale or return" if the goods are delivered primarily for resale.

(2) Except as provided in subsection (3), goods held on approval are not subject to the claims of the buyer's creditors until acceptance; goods held on sale or return are subject to such claims while in the buyer's possession.

(3) Where goods are delivered to a person for sale and such person maintains a place of business at which he deals in goods of the kind involved, under a name other than the name of the person making delivery, then with respect to claims of creditors of the person conducting the business the goods are deemed to be on sale or return. The provisions of this subsection are applicable even though an agreement purports to reserve title to the person making delivery until payment or resale or uses such words as "on consignment" or "on memorandum". However, this subsection is not applicable if the person making delivery

(a) complies with an applicable law providing for a consignor's interest or the like to be evidenced by a sign, or

(b) establishes that the person conducting the business is generally known by his creditors to be substantially engaged in selling the goods of others, or

(c) complies with the filing provisions of the Article on Secured Transactions (Article 9).

(4) Any "or return" term of a contract for sale is to be treated as a separate contract for sale within the statute of frauds section of this Article (Section 2—201) and as contradicting the sale aspect of the contract within the provisions of this Article on parol or extrinsic evidence (Section 2—202).

§ 2—327. Special Incidents of Sale on Approval and Sale or Return.

(1) Under a sale on approval unless otherwise agreed

(a) although the goods are identified to the contract the risk of loss and the title do not pass to the buyer until acceptance; and

(b) use of the goods consistent with the purpose of trial is not acceptance but failure seasonably to notify the seller of election to return the goods is acceptance, and if the goods conform to the contract acceptance of any part is acceptance of the whole; and

(c) after due notification of election to return, the return is at the seller's risk and expense but a merchant buyer must follow any reasonable instructions.

(2) Under a sale or return unless otherwise agreed

(a) the option to return extends to the whole or any commercial unit of the goods while in substantially their original condition, but must be exercised seasonably; and

(b) the return is at the buyer's risk and expense.

§ 2—328. Sale by Auction.

(1) In a sale by auction if goods are put up in lots each lot is the subject of a separate sale.

(2) A sale by auction is complete when the auctioneer so announces by the fall of the hammer or in other customary manner. Where a bid is made while the hammer is falling in acceptance of a prior bid the auctioneer may in his discretion reopen the bidding or declare the goods sold under the bid on which the hammer was falling.

(3) Such a sale is with reserve unless the goods are in explicit terms put up without reserve. In an auction with reserve the auctioneer may withdraw the goods at any time until he announces completion of the sale. In an auction without reserve, after the auctioneer calls for bids on an article or lot, that article or lot cannot be withdrawn unless no bid is made within a reasonable time. In either case a bidder may retract his bid until the auctioneer's announcement of completion of the sale, but a bidder's retraction does not revive any previous bid.

(4) If the auctioneer knowingly receives a bid on the seller's behalf or the seller makes or procures such as bid, and notice has not been given that liberty for such bidding is reserved, the buyer may at his option avoid the sale or take the goods at the price of the last good faith bid prior to the completion of the sale. This subsection shall not apply to any bid at a forced sale.

Part 4 Title, Creditors and Good Faith Purchasers

§ 2—401. Passing of Title; Reservation for Security; Limited Application of This Section.

Each provision of this Article with regard to the rights, obligations and remedies of the seller, the buyer, purchasers or other third parties applies irrespective of title to the goods except where the provision refers to such title. Insofar as situations are not covered by the other provisions of this Article and matters concerning title became material the following rules apply:

(1) Title to goods cannot pass under a contract for sale prior to their identification to the contract (Section 2—501), and unless otherwise explicitly agreed the buyer acquires by their identification a special property as limited by this Act. Any retention or reservation by the seller of the title (property) in goods shipped or delivered to the buyer is limited in effect to a reservation of a security interest. Subject to these provisions and to the provisions of the Article on Secured Transactions (Article 9), title to goods passes from the seller to the buyer in any manner and on any conditions explicitly agreed on by the parties.

(2) Unless otherwise explicitly agreed title passes to the buyer at the time and place at which the seller completes his performance with reference to the physical delivery of the goods, despite any reservation of a security interest and even though a document of title is to be delivered at a different time or place; and in particular and despite any reservation of a security interest by the bill of lading

(a) if the contract requires or authorizes the seller to send the goods to the buyer but does not require him to deliver them at destination, title passes to the buyer at the time and place of shipment; but

(b) if the contract requires delivery at destination, title passes on tender there.

(3) Unless otherwise explicitly agreed where delivery is to be made without moving the goods,

(a) if the seller is to deliver a document of title, title passes at the time when and the place where he delivers such documents; or

(b) if the goods are at the time of contracting already identified and no documents are to be delivered, title passes at the time and place of contracting.

(4) A rejection or other refusal by the buyer to receive or retain the goods, whether or not justified, or a justified revocation of acceptance revests title to the goods in the seller. Such revesting occurs by operation of law and is not a "sale".

§ 2—402. Rights of Seller's Creditors Against Sold Goods.

(1) Except as provided in subsections (2) and (3), rights of unsecured creditors of the seller with respect to goods which have been identified to a contract for sale are subject to the buyer's rights to recover the goods under this Article (Sections 2—502 and 2—716).

(2) A creditor of the seller may treat a sale or an identification of goods to a contract for sale as void if as against him a retention of possession by the seller is fraudulent under any rule of law of the state where the goods are situated, except that retention of possession in good faith and current course of trade by a merchant-seller for a commercially reasonable time after a sale or identification is not fraudulent.

(3) Nothing in this Article shall be deemed to impair the rights of creditors of the seller

(a) under the provisions of the Article on Secured Transactions (Article 9); or

(b) where identification to the contract or delivery is made not in current course of trade but in satisfaction of or as security for a pre-existing claim for money, security or the like and is made under circumstances which under any rule of law of the state where the goods are situated would apart from this Article constitute the transaction a fraudulent transfer or voidable preference.

§ 2—403. Power to Transfer; Good Faith Purchase of Goods; "Entrusting".

(1) A purchaser of goods acquires all title which his transferor had or had power to transfer except that a purchaser of a limited interest acquires rights only to the extent of the interest purchased. A person with voidable title has power to transfer a good title to a good faith purchaser for value. When goods have been delivered under a transaction of purchase the purchaser has such power even though

(a) the transferor was deceived as to the identity of the purchaser, or

(b) the delivery was in exchange for a check which is later dishonored, or

(c) it was agreed that the transaction was to be a "cash sale", or

(d) the delivery was procured through fraud punishable as larcenous under the criminal law.

(2) Any entrusting of possession of goods to a merchant who deals in goods of that kind gives him power to transfer all rights of the entruster to a buyer in ordinary course of business.

(3) "Entrusting" includes any delivery and any acquiescence in retention of possession regardless of any condition expressed between the parties to the delivery or acquiescence and regardless of whether the procurement of the entrusting or the possessor's disposition of the goods have been such as to be larcenous under the criminal law.

(4) The rights of other purchasers of goods and of lien creditors are governed by the Articles on Secured Transactions (Article 9), Bulk Transfers (Article 6) and Documents of Title (Article 7).

Part 5 Performance

§ 2—501. Insurable Interest in Goods; Manner of Identification of Goods.

(1) The buyer obtains a special property and an insurable interest in goods by identification of existing goods as goods to which the contract refers even though the goods so identified are non-conforming and he has an option to return or reject them. Such identification can be made at any time and in any manner explicitly agreed to by the parties. In the absence of explicit agreement identification occurs

(a) when the contract is made if it is for the sale of goods already existing and identified;

(b) if the contract is for the sale of future goods other than those described in paragraph (c), when goods are shipped, marked or otherwise designated by the seller as goods to which the contract refers;

(c) when the crops are planted or otherwise become growing crops or the young are conceived if the contract is for the sale of unborn young to be born within twelve months after contracting or for the sale of crops to be harvested within twelve months or the next normal harvest season after contracting whichever is longer.

(2) The seller retains an insurable interest in goods so long as title to or any security interest in the goods remains in him and where the identification is by the seller alone he may until default or insolvency or notification to the buyer that the identification is final substitute other goods for those identified.

(3) Nothing in this section impairs any insurable interest recognized under any other statute or rule of law.

§ 2—502. Buyer's Right to Goods on Seller's Insolvency.

(1) Subject to subsection (2) and even though the goods have not been shipped a buyer who has paid a part or all of the price of goods in which he has a special property under the provisions of the immediately preceding section may on making and keeping good a tender of any unpaid portion of their price recover them from the seller if the seller becomes insolvent within ten days after receipt of the first installment on their price.

(2) If the identification creating his special property has been made by the buyer he acquires the right to recover the goods only if they conform to the contract for sale.

§ 2—503. Manner of Seller's Tender of Delivery.

(1) Tender of delivery requires that the seller put and hold conforming goods at the buyer's disposition and give the buyer any notification reasonably necessary to enable him to take delivery. The manner, time and place for tender are determined by the agreement and this Article, and in particular

(a) tender must be at a reasonable hour, and if it is of goods they must be kept available for the period reasonably necessary to enable the buyer to take possession; but

(b) unless otherwise agreed the buyer must furnish facilities reasonably suited to the receipt of the goods.

(2) Where the case is within the next section respecting shipment tender requires that the seller comply with its provisions.

(3) Where the seller is required to deliver at a particular destination tender requires that he comply with subsection (1) and also in any appropriate case tender documents as described in subsections (4) and (5) of this section.

(4) Where goods are in the possession of a bailee and are to be delivered without being moved

(a) tender requires that the seller either tender a negotiable document of title covering such goods or procure acknowledgment by the bailee of the buyer's right to possession of the goods; but

(b) tender to the buyer of a non-negotiable document of title or of a written direction to the bailee to deliver is sufficient tender unless the buyer seasonably objects, and receipt by the bailee of notification of the buyer's rights fixes those rights as against the bailee and all third persons; but risk of loss of the goods and of any failure by the bailee to honor the non-negotiable document of title or to obey the direction remains on the seller until the buyer has had a reasonable time to present the document or direction, and a refusal by the bailee to honor the document or to obey the direction defeats the tender.

(5) Where the contract requires the seller to deliver documents

(a) he must tender all such documents in correct form, except as provided in this Article with respect to bills of lading in a set (subsection (2) of Section 2—323); and

(b) tender through customary banking channels is sufficient and dishonor of a draft accompanying the documents constitutes non-acceptance or rejection.

§ 2—504. Shipment by Seller.

Where the seller is required or authorized to send the goods to the buyer and the contract does not require him to deliver them at a particular destination, then unless otherwise agreed he must

(a) put the goods in the possession of such a carrier and make such a contract for their transportation as may be reasonable having regard to the nature of the goods and other circumstances of the case; and

(b) obtain and promptly deliver or tender in due form any document necessary to enable the buyer to obtain possession of the goods or otherwise required by the agreement or by usage of trade; and

(c) promptly notify the buyer of the shipment.

Failure to notify the buyer under paragraph (c) or to make a proper contract under paragraph (a) is a ground for rejection only if material delay or loss ensues.

§ 2—505. **Seller's Shipment under Reservation.**

(1) Where the seller has identified goods to the contract by or before shipment:

(a) his procurement of a negotiable bill of lading to his own order or otherwise reserves in him a security interest in the goods. His procurement of the bill to the order of a financing agency or of the buyer indicates in addition only the seller's expectation of transferring that interest to the person named.

(b) a non-negotiable bill of lading to himself or his nominee reserves possession of the goods as security but except in a case of conditional delivery (subsection (2) of Section 2—507) a non-negotiable bill of lading naming the buyer as consignee reserves no security interest even though the seller retains possession of the bill of lading.

(2) When shipment by the seller with reservation of a security interest is in violation of the contract for sale it constitutes an improper contract for transportation within the preceding section but impairs neither the rights given to the buyer by shipment and identification of the goods to the contract nor the seller's powers as a holder of a negotiable document.

§ 2—506. **Rights of Financing Agency.**

(1) A financing agency by paying or purchasing for value a draft which relates to a shipment of goods acquires to the extent of the payment or purchase and in addition to its own rights under the draft and any document of title securing it any rights of the shipper in the goods including the right to stop delivery and the shipper's right to have the draft honored by the buyer.

(2) The right to reimbursement of a financing agency which has in good faith honored or purchased the draft under commitment to or authority from the buyer is not impaired by subsequent discovery of defects with reference to any relevant document which was apparently regular on its face.

§ 2—507. **Effect of Seller's Tender; Delivery on Condition.**

(1) Tender of delivery is a condition to the buyer's duty to accept the goods and, unless otherwise agreed, to his duty to pay for them. Tender entitles the seller to acceptance of the goods and to payment according to the contract.

(2) Where payment is due and demanded on the delivery to the buyer of goods or documents of title, his right as against the seller to retain or dispose of them is conditional upon his making the payment due.

§ 2—508. **Cure by Seller of Improper Tender or Delivery; Replacement.**

(1) Where any tender or delivery by the seller is rejected because non-conforming and the time for performance has not yet expired, the seller may seasonably notify the buyer of his intention to cure and may then within the contract time make a conforming delivery.

(2) Where the buyer rejects a non-conforming tender which the seller had reasonable grounds to believe would be acceptable with or without money allowance the seller may if he seasonably notifies the buyer have a further reasonable time to substitute a conforming tender.

§ 2—509. **Risk of Loss in the Absence of Breach.**

(1) Where the contract requires or authorizes the seller to ship the goods by carrier

(a) if it does not require him to deliver them at a particular destination, the risk of loss passes to the buyer when the goods are duly delivered to the carrier even though the shipment is under reservation (Section 2—505); but

(b) if it does require him to deliver them at a particular destination and the goods are there duly tendered while in the possession of the carrier, the risk of loss passes to the buyer when the goods are there duly so tendered as to enable the buyer to take delivery.

(2) Where the goods are held by a bailee to be delivered without being moved, the risk of loss passes to the buyer

(a) on his receipt of a negotiable document of title covering the goods; or

(b) on acknowledgment by the bailee of the buyer's right to possession of the goods; or

(c) after his receipt of a non-negotiable document of title or other written direction to deliver, as provided in subsection (4)(b) of Section 2—503.

(3) In any case not within subsection (1) or (2), the risk of loss passes to the buyer on his receipt of the goods if the seller is a merchant; otherwise the risk passes to the buyer on tender of delivery.

(4) The provisions of this section are subject to contrary agreement of the parties and to the provisions of this Article on sale on approval (Section 2—327) and on effect of breach on risk of loss (Section 2—510).

§ 2—510. **Effect of Breach on Risk of Loss.**

(1) Where a tender or delivery of goods so fails to conform to the contract as to give a right of rejection the risk of their loss remains on the seller until cure or acceptance.

(2) Where the buyer rightfully revokes acceptance he may to the extent of any deficiency in his effective insurance coverage treat the risk of loss as having rested on the seller from the beginning.

(3) Where the buyer as to conforming goods already identified to the contract for sale repudiates or is otherwise in breach before risk of their loss has passed to him, the seller may to the extent of any deficiency in his effective insurance coverage treat the risk of loss as resting on the buyer for a commercially reasonable time.

§ 2—511. Tender of Payment by Buyer; Payment by Check.

(1) Unless otherwise agreed tender of payment is a condition to the seller's duty to tender and complete any delivery.

(2) Tender of payment is sufficient when made by any means or in any manner current in the ordinary course of business unless the seller demands payment in legal tender and gives any extension of time reasonably necessary to procure it.

(3) Subject to the provisions of this Act on the effect of an instrument on an obligation (Section 3—310), payment by check is conditional and is defeated as between the parties by dishonor of the check on due presentment.

§ 2—512. Payment by Buyer Before Inspection.

(1) Where the contract requires payment before inspection non-conformity of the goods does not excuse the buyer from so making payment unless

(a) the non-conformity appears without inspection; or

(b) despite tender of the required documents the circumstances would justify injunction against honor under the provisions of this Act (Section 5—114).

(2) Payment pursuant to subsection (1) does not constitute an acceptance of goods or impair the buyer's right to inspect or any of his remedies.

§ 2—513. Buyer's Right to Inspection of Goods.

(1) Unless otherwise agreed and subject to subsection (3), where goods are tendered or delivered or identified to the contract for sale, the buyer has a right before payment or acceptance to inspect them at any reasonable place and time and in any reasonable manner. When the seller is required or authorized to send the goods to the buyer, the inspection may be after their arrival.

(2) Expenses of inspection must be borne by the buyer but may be recovered from the seller if the goods do not conform and are rejected.

(3) Unless otherwise agreed and subject to the provisions of this Article on C.I.F. contracts (subsection (3) of Section 2—321), the buyer is not entitled to inspect the goods before payment of the price when the contract provides

(a) for delivery "C.O.D." or on other like terms; or

(b) for payment against documents of title, except where such payment is due only after the goods are to become available for inspection.

(4) A place or method of inspection fixed by the parties is presumed to be exclusive but unless otherwise expressly agreed it does not postpone identification or shift the place for delivery or for passing the risk of loss. If compliance becomes impossible, inspection shall be as provided in this section unless the place or method fixed was clearly intended as an indispensable condition failure of which avoids the contract.

§ 2—514. When Documents Deliverable on Acceptance; When on Payment.

Unless otherwise agreed documents against which a draft is drawn are to be delivered to the drawee on acceptance of the draft if it is payable more than three days after presentment; otherwise, only on payment.

§ 2—515. Preserving Evidence of Goods in Dispute.

In furtherance of the adjustment of any claim or dispute

(a) either party on reasonable notification to the other and for the purpose of ascertaining the facts and preserving evidence has the right to inspect, test and sample the goods including such of them as may be in the possession or control of the other; and

(b) the parties may agree to a third party inspection or survey to determine the conformity or condition of the goods and may agree that the findings shall be binding upon them in any subsequent litigation or adjustment.

Part 6 Breach, Repudiation and Excuse

§ 2—601. Buyer's Rights on Improper Delivery.

Subject to the provisions of this Article on breach in installment contracts (Section 2—612) and unless otherwise agreed under the sections on contractual limitations of remedy (Sections 2—718 and 2—719), if the goods or the tender of delivery fail in any respect to conform to the contract, the buyer may

(a) reject the whole; or

(b) accept the whole; or

(c) accept any commercial unit or units and reject the rest.

§ 2—602. Manner and Effect of Rightful Rejection.

(1) Rejection of goods must be within a reasonable time after their delivery or tender. It is ineffective unless the buyer seasonably notifies the seller.

(2) Subject to the provisions of the two following sections on rejected goods (Sections 2—603 and 2—604),

(a) after rejection any exercise of ownership by the buyer with respect to any commercial unit is wrongful as against the seller; and

(b) if the buyer has before rejection taken physical possession of goods in which he does not have a security interest under the provisions of this Article (subsection (3) of Section 2—711), he is under a duty after rejection to hold them with reasonable care at the seller's disposition for a time sufficient to permit the seller to remove them; but

(c) the buyer has no further obligations with regard to goods rightfully rejected.

(3) The seller's rights with respect to goods wrongfully rejected are governed by the provisions of this Article on Seller's remedies in general (Section 2—703).

§ 2—603. Merchant Buyer's Duties as to Rightfully Rejected Goods.

(1) Subject to any security interest in the buyer (subsection (3) of Section 2—711), when the seller has no agent or place of business at the market of rejection a merchant buyer is under a duty after rejection of goods in his possession or control to follow any reasonable instructions received from the seller with respect to the goods and in the absence of such instructions to make reasonable efforts to sell them for the seller's account if they are perishable or threaten to decline in value speedily. Instructions are not reasonable if on demand indemnity for expenses is not forthcoming.

(2) When the buyer sells goods under subsection (1), he is entitled to reimbursement from the seller or out of the proceeds for reasonable expenses of caring for and selling them, and if the expenses include no selling commission then to such commission as is usual in the trade or if there is none to a reasonable sum not exceeding ten per cent on the gross proceeds.

(3) In complying with this section the buyer is held only to good faith and good faith conduct hereunder is neither acceptance nor conversion nor the basis of an action for damages.

§ 2—604. Buyer's Options as to Salvage of Rightfully Rejected Goods.

Subject to the provisions of the immediately preceding section on perishables if the seller gives no instructions within a reasonable time after notification of rejection the buyer may store the rejected goods for the seller's account or reship them to him or resell them for the seller's account with reimbursement as provided in the preceding section. Such action is not acceptance or conversion.

§ 2—605. Waiver of Buyer's Objections by Failure to Particularize.

(1) The buyer's failure to state in connection with rejection a particular defect which is ascertainable by reasonable inspection precludes him from relying on the unstated defect to justify rejection or to establish breach

(a) where the seller could have cured it if stated seasonably; or

(b) between merchants when the seller has after rejection made a request in writing for a full and final written statement of all defects on which the buyer proposes to rely.

(2) Payment against documents made without reservation of rights precludes recovery of the payment for defects apparent on the face of the documents.

§ 2—606. What Constitutes Acceptance of Goods.

(1) Acceptance of goods occurs when the buyer

(a) after a reasonable opportunity to inspect the goods signifies to the seller that the goods are conforming or that he will take or retain them in spite of their nonconformity; or

(b) fails to make an effective rejection (subsection (1) of Section 2—602), but such acceptance does not occur until the buyer has had a reasonable opportunity to inspect them; or

(c) does any act inconsistent with the seller's ownership; but if such act is wrongful as against the seller it is an acceptance only if ratified by him.

(2) Acceptance of a part of any commercial unit is acceptance of that entire unit.

§ 2—607. Effect of Acceptance; Notice of Breach; Burden of Establishing Breach After Acceptance; Notice of Claim or Litigation to Person Answerable Over.

(1) The buyer must pay at the contract rate for any goods accepted.

(2) Acceptance of goods by the buyer precludes rejection of the goods accepted and if made with knowledge of a non-conformity cannot be revoked because of it unless the acceptance was on the reasonable assumption that the non-conformity would be seasonably cured but acceptance does not of itself impair any other remedy provided by this Article for non-conformity.

(3) Where a tender has been accepted

(a) the buyer must within a reasonable time after he discovers or should have discovered any breach notify the seller of breach or be barred from any remedy; and

(b) if the claim is one for infringement or the like (subsection (3) of Section 2—312) and the buyer is sued as a result of such a breach he must so notify the seller within a reasonable time after he receives notice of the litigation or be barred from any remedy over for liability established by the litigation.

(4) The burden is on the buyer to establish any breach with respect to the goods accepted.

(5) Where the buyer is sued for breach of a warranty or other obligation for which his seller is answerable over

(a) he may give his seller written notice of the litigation. If the notice states that the seller may come in and defend and that if the seller does not do so he will be bound in any action against him by his buyer by any determination of fact common to the two litigations, then unless the seller after seasonable receipt of the notice does come in and defend he is so bound.

(b) if the claim is one for infringement or the like (subsection (3) of Section 2—312) the original seller may demand in writing that his buyer turn over to him control of the litigation including settlement or else be barred from any remedy over and if he also agrees to bear all expense and to satisfy any adverse judgment, then unless the buyer after seasonable receipt of the demand does turn over control the buyer is so barred.

(6) The provisions of subsections (3), (4) and (5) apply to any obligation of a buyer to hold the seller harmless against infringement or the like (subsection (3) of Section 2—312).

§ 2—608. Revocation of Acceptance in Whole or in Part.

(1) The buyer may revoke his acceptance of a lot or commercial unit whose non-conformity substantially impairs its value to him if he has accepted it

(a) on the reasonable assumption that its nonconformity would be cured and it has not been seasonably cured; or

(b) without discovery of such non-conformity if his acceptance was reasonably induced either by the difficulty of discovery before acceptance or by the seller's assurances.

(2) Revocation of acceptance must occur within a reasonable time after the buyer discovers or should have discovered the ground for it and before any substantial change in condition of the goods which is not caused by their own defects. It is not effective until the buyer notifies the seller of it.

(3) A buyer who so revokes has the same rights and duties with regard to the goods involved as if he had rejected them.

§ 2—609. Right to Adequate Assurance of Performance.

(1) A contract for sale imposes an obligation on each party that the other's expectation of receiving due performance will not be impaired. When reasonable grounds for insecurity arise with respect to the performance of either party the other may in writing demand adequate assurance of due performance and until he receives such assurance may if commercially reasonable suspend any performance for which he has not already received the agreed return.

(2) Between merchants the reasonableness of grounds for insecurity and the adequacy of any assurance offered shall be determined according to commercial standards.

(3) Acceptance of any improper delivery or payment does not prejudice the party's right to demand adequate assurance of future performance.

(4) After receipt of a justified demand failure to provide within a reasonable time not exceeding thirty days such assurance of due performance as is adequate under the circumstances of the particular case is a repudiation of the contract.

§ 2—610. Anticipatory Repudiation.

When either party repudiates the contract with respect to a performance not yet due the loss of which will substantially impair the value of the contract to the other, the aggrieved party may

(a) for a commercially reasonable time await performance by the repudiating party; or

(b) resort to any remedy for breach (Section 2—703 or Section 2—711), even though he has notified the repudiating party that he would await the latter's performance and has urged retraction; and

(c) in either case suspend his own performance or proceed in accordance with the provisions of this Article on the seller's right to identify goods to the contract notwithstanding breach or to salvage unfinished goods (Section 2—704).

§ 2—611. Retraction of Anticipatory Repudiation.

(1) Until the repudiating party's next performance is due he can retract his repudiation unless the aggrieved party has since the repudiation cancelled or materially changed his position or otherwise indicated that he considers the repudiation final.

(2) Retraction may be by any method which clearly indicates to the aggrieved party that the repudiating party intends to perform, but must include any assurance justifiably demanded under the provisions of this Article (Section 2—609).

(3) Retraction reinstates the repudiating party's rights under the contract with due excuse and allowance to the aggrieved party for any delay occasioned by the repudiation.

§ 2—612. "Installment Contract"; Breach.

(1) An "installment contract" is one which requires or authorizes the delivery of goods in separate lots to be separately accepted, even though the contract contains a clause "each delivery is a separate contract" or its equivalent.

(2) The buyer may reject any installment which is non-conforming if the non-conformity substantially impairs the value of that installment and cannot be cured or if the non-conformity is a defect in the required documents; but if the non-conformity does not fall within subsection (3) and the seller gives adequate assurance of its cure the buyer must accept that installment.

(3) Whenever non-conformity or default with respect to one or more installments substantially impairs the value of the whole contract there is a breach of the whole. But the aggrieved party reinstates the contract if he accepts a non-conforming installment without seasonably notifying of cancellation or if he brings an action with respect only to past installments or demands performance as to future installments.

§ 2—613. Casualty to Identified Goods.

Where the contract requires for its performance goods identified when the contract is made, and the goods suffer casualty without fault of either party before the risk of loss passes to the buyer, or in a proper case under a "no arrival, no sale" term (Section 2—324) then

(a) if the loss is total the contract is avoided; and

(b) if the loss is partial or the goods have so deteriorated as no longer to conform to the contract the buyer may nevertheless demand inspection and at his option either treat the contract as voided or accept the goods with due allowance from the contract price for the deterioration or the deficiency in quantity but without further right against the seller.

§ 2—614. Substituted Performance.

(1) Where without fault of either party the agreed berthing, loading, or unloading facilities fail or an agreed type of carrier becomes unavailable or the agreed manner of delivery otherwise becomes commercially impracticable but a commercially reasonable substitute is available, such substitute performance must be tendered and accepted.

(2) If the agreed means or manner of payment fails because of domestic or foreign governmental regulation, the seller may withhold or stop delivery unless the buyer provides a means or manner of payment which is commercially a substantial equivalent. If delivery has already been taken, payment by the means or in the manner provided by the regulation discharges the buyer's obligation unless the regulation is discriminatory, oppressive or predatory.

§ 2—615. Excuse by Failure of Presupposed Conditions.

Except so far as a seller may have assumed a greater obligation and subject to the preceding section on substituted performance:

(a) Delay in delivery or non-delivery in whole or in part by a seller who complies with paragraphs (b) and (c) is not a breach of his duty under a contract for sale if performance as agreed has been made impracticable by the occurrence of a contingency the nonoccurrence of which was a basic assumption on which the contract was made or by compliance in good faith with any applicable foreign or domestic governmental regulation or order whether or not it later proves to be invalid.

(b) Where the causes mentioned in paragraph (a) affect only a part of the seller's capacity to perform, he must allocate production and deliveries among his customers but may at his option include regular customers not then under contract as well as his own requirements for further manufacture. He may so allocate in any manner which is fair and reasonable.

(c) The seller must notify the buyer seasonably that there will be delay or non-delivery and, when allocation is required under paragraph (b), of the estimated quota thus made available for the buyer.

§ 2—616. Procedure on Notice Claiming Excuse.

(1) Where the buyer receives notification of a material or indefinite delay or an allocation justified under the preceding section he may by written notification to the seller as to any delivery concerned, and where the prospective deficiency substantially impairs the value of the whole contract under the provisions of this Article relating to breach of installment contracts (Section 2—612), then also as to the whole,

(a) terminate and thereby discharge any unexecuted portion of the contract; or

(b) modify the contract by agreeing to take his available quota in substitution.

(2) If after receipt of such notification from the seller the buyer fails so to modify the contract within a reasonable time not exceeding thirty days the contract lapses with respect to any deliveries affected.

(3) The provisions of this section may not be negated by agreement except in so far as the seller has assumed a greater obligation under the preceding section.

Part 7 Remedies

§ 2—701. Remedies for Breach of Collateral Contracts Not Impaired.

Remedies for breach of any obligation or promise collateral or ancillary to a contract for sale are not impaired by the provisions of this Article.

§ 2—702. Seller's Remedies on Discovery of Buyer's Insolvency.

(1) Where the seller discovers the buyer to be insolvent he may refuse delivery except for cash including payment for all goods theretofore delivered under the contract, and stop delivery under this Article (Section 2—705).

(2) Where the seller discovers that the buyer has received goods on credit while insolvent he may reclaim the goods upon demand made within ten days after the receipt, but if misrepresentation of solvency has been made to the particular seller in writing within three months before delivery the ten day limitation does not apply. Except as provided in this subsection the seller may not base a right to reclaim goods on the buyer's fraudulent or innocent misrepresentation of solvency or of intent to pay.

(3) The seller's right to reclaim under subsection (2) is subject to the rights of a buyer in ordinary course or other good faith purchaser under this Article (Section 2—403). Successful reclamation of goods excludes all other remedies with respect to them.

§ 2—703. Seller's Remedies in General.

Where the buyer wrongfully rejects or revokes acceptance of goods or fails to make a payment due on or before delivery or repudiates with respect to a part or the whole, then with respect to any goods directly affected and, if the breach is of the whole contract (Section 2—612), then also with respect to the whole undelivered balance, the aggrieved seller may

(a) withhold delivery of such goods;

(b) stop delivery by any bailee as hereafter provided (Section 2—705);

(c) proceed under the next section respecting goods still unidentified to the contract;

(d) resell and recover damages as hereafter provided (Section 2—706);

(e) recover damages for non-acceptance (Section 2—708) or in a proper case the price (Section 2—709);

(f) cancel.

§ 2—704. Seller's Right to Identify Goods to the Contract Notwithstanding Breach or to Salvage Unfinished Goods.

(1) An aggrieved seller under the preceding section may

(a) identify to the contract conforming goods not already identified if at the time he learned of the breach they are in his possession or control;

(b) treat as the subject of resale goods which have demonstrably been intended for the particular contract even though those goods are unfinished.

(2) Where the goods are unfinished an aggrieved seller may in the exercise of reasonable commercial judgment for the purposes of avoiding loss and of effective realization either complete the manufacture and wholly identify the goods to the contract or cease manufacture and resell for scrap or salvage value or proceed in any other reasonable manner.

§ 2—705. Seller's Stoppage of Delivery in Transit or Otherwise.

(1) The seller may stop delivery of goods in the possession of a carrier or other bailee when he discovers the buyer to be insolvent (Section 2—702) and may stop delivery of carload, truckload, planeload or larger shipments of express or freight when the buyer repudiates or fails to make a payment due before delivery or if for any other reason the seller has a right to withhold or reclaim the goods.

(2) As against such buyer the seller may stop delivery until

(a) receipt of the goods by the buyer; or

(b) acknowledgment to the buyer by any bailee of the goods except a carrier that the bailee holds the goods for the buyer; or

(c) such acknowledgment to the buyer by a carrier by reshipment or as warehouseman; or

(d) negotiation to the buyer of any negotiable document of title covering the goods.

(3) (a) To stop delivery the seller must so notify as to enable the bailee by reasonable diligence to prevent delivery of the goods.

(b) After such notification the bailee must hold and deliver the goods according to the directions of the seller but the seller is liable to the bailee for any ensuing charges or damages.

(c) If a negotiable document of title has been issued for goods the bailee is not obliged to obey a notification to stop until surrender of the document.

(d) A carrier who has issued a non-negotiable bill of lading is not obliged to obey a notification to stop received from a person other than the consignor.

§ 2—706. Seller's Resale Including Contract for Resale.

(1) Under the conditions stated in Section 2—703 on seller's remedies, the seller may resell the goods concerned or the undelivered balance thereof. Where the resale is made in good faith and in a commercially reasonable manner the seller may recover the difference between the resale price and the contract price together with any incidental damages allowed under the provisions of this Article (Section 2—710), but less expenses saved in consequence of the buyer's breach.

(2) Except as otherwise provided in subsection (3) or unless otherwise agreed resale may be at public or private sale including sale by way of one or more contracts to sell or of identification to an existing contract of the seller. Sale may be as a unit or in parcels and at any time and place and on any terms but every aspect of the sale including the method, manner, time, place and terms must be commercially reasonable. The resale must be rea-

sonably identified as referring to the broken contract, but it is not necessary that the goods be in existence or that any or all of them have been identified to the contract before the breach.

(3) Where the resale is at private sale the seller must give the buyer reasonable notification of his intention to resell.

(4) Where the resale is at public sale

(a) only identified goods can be sold except where there is a recognized market for a public sale of futures in goods of the kind; and

(b) it must be made at a usual place or market for public sale if one is reasonably available and except in the case of goods which are perishable or threaten to decline in value speedily the seller must give the buyer reasonable notice of the time and place of the resale; and

(c) if the goods are not to be within the view of those attending the sale the notification of sale must state the place where the goods are located and provide for their reasonable inspection by prospective bidders; and

(d) the seller may buy.

(5) A purchaser who buys in good faith at a resale takes the goods free of any rights of the original buyer even though the seller fails to comply with one or more of the requirements of this section.

(6) The seller is not accountable to the buyer for any profit made on any resale. A person in the position of a seller (Section 2—707) or a buyer who has rightfully rejected or justifiably revoked acceptance must account for any excess over the amount of his security interest, as hereinafter defined (subsection (3) of Section 2—711).

§ 2—707. "Person in the Position of a Seller".

(1) A "person in the position of a seller" includes as against a principal an agent who has paid or become responsible for the price of goods on behalf of his principal or anyone who otherwise holds a security interest or other right in goods similar to that of a seller.

(2) A person in the position of a seller may as provided in this Article withhold or stop delivery (Section 2—705) and resell (Section 2—706) and recover incidental damages (Section 2—710).

§ 2—708. Seller's Damages for Non-Acceptance or Repudiation.

(1) Subject to subsection (2) and to the provisions of this Article with respect to proof of market price (Section 2—723), the measure of damages for non-acceptance or repudiation by the buyer is the difference between the market price at the time and place for tender and the unpaid contract price together with any incidental damages provided in this Article (Section 2—710), but less expenses saved in consequence of the buyer's breach.

(2) If the measure of damages provided in subsection (1) is inadequate to put the seller in as good a position as performance would have done then the measure of damages is the profit (including reasonable overhead) which the seller would have made from full performance by the buyer, together with any incidental damages provided in this Article (Section 2—710), due allowance for costs reasonably incurred and due credit for payments or proceeds of resale.

§ 2—709. Action for the Price.

(1) When the buyer fails to pay the price as it becomes due the seller may recover, together with any incidental damages under the next section, the price

(a) of goods accepted or of conforming goods lost or damaged within a commercially reasonable time after risk of their loss has passed to the buyer; and

(b) of goods identified to the contract if the seller is unable after reasonable effort to resell them at a reasonable price or the circumstances reasonably indicate that such effort will be unavailing.

(2) Where the seller sues for the price he must hold for the buyer any goods which have been identified to the contract and are still in his control except that if resale becomes possible he may resell them at any time prior to the collection of the judgment. The net proceeds of any such resale must be credited to the buyer and payment of the judgment entitles him to any goods not resold.

(3) After the buyer has wrongfully rejected or revoked acceptance of the goods or has failed to make a payment due or has repudiated (Section 2—610), a seller who is held not entitled to the price under this section shall nevertheless be awarded damages for non-acceptance under the preceding section.

§ 2—710. Seller's Incidental Damages.

Incidental damages to an aggrieved seller include any commercially reasonable charges, expenses or commissions incurred in stopping delivery, in the transportation, care and custody of goods after the buyer's breach, in connection with return or resale of the goods or otherwise resulting from the breach.

§ 2—711. Buyer's Remedies in General; Buyer's Security Interest in Rejected Goods.

(1) Where the seller fails to make delivery or repudiates or the buyer rightfully rejects or justifiably revokes acceptance then with respect to any goods involved, and with respect to the whole if the breach goes to the whole contract (Section 2—612), the buyer may cancel and whether or not he has done so may in addition to recovering so much of the price as has been paid

(a) "cover" and have damages under the next section as to all the goods affected whether or not they have been identified to the contract; or

(b) recover damages for non-delivery as provided in this Article (Section 2—713).

(2) Where the seller fails to deliver or repudiates the buyer may also

(a) if the goods have been identified recover them as provided in this Article (Section 2—502); or

(b) in a proper case obtain specific performance or replevy the goods as provided in this Article (Section 2—716).

(3) On rightful rejection or justifiable revocation of acceptance a buyer has a security interest in goods in his possession or control for any payments made on their price and any expenses reasonably incurred in their inspection, receipt, transportation, care and custody and may hold such goods and resell them in like manner as an aggrieved seller (Section 2—706).

§ 2—712. "Cover"; Buyer's Procurement of Substitute Goods.

(1) After a breach within the preceding section the buyer may "cover" by making in good faith and without unreasonable delay any reasonable purchase of or contract to purchase goods in substitution for those due from the seller.

(2) The buyer may recover from the seller as damages the difference between the cost of cover and the contract price together with any incidental or consequential damages as hereinafter defined (Section 2—715), but less expenses saved in consequence of the seller's breach.

(3) Failure of the buyer to effect cover within this section does not bar him from any other remedy.

§ 2—713. Buyer's Damages for Non-Delivery or Repudiation.

(1) Subject to the provisions of this Article with respect to proof of market price (Section 2—723), the measure of damages for non-delivery or repudiation by the seller is the difference between the market price at the time when the buyer learned of the breach and the contract price together with any incidental and consequential damages provided in this Article (Section 2—715), but less expenses saved in consequence of the seller's breach.

(2) Market price is to be determined as of the place for tender or, in cases of rejection after arrival or revocation of acceptance, as of the place of arrival.

§ 2—714. Buyer's Damages for Breach in Regard to Accepted Goods.

(1) Where the buyer has accepted goods and given notification (subsection (3) of Section 2—607) he may recover as damages for any non-conformity of tender the loss resulting in the ordinary course of events from the seller's breach as determined in any manner which is reasonable.

(2) The measure of damages for breach of warranty is the difference at the time and place of acceptance between the value of the goods accepted and the value they would have had if they had been as warranted, unless special circumstances show proximate damages of a different amount.

(3) In a proper case any incidental and consequential damages under the next section may also be recovered.

§ 2—715. Buyer's Incidental and Consequential Damages.

(1) Incidental damages resulting from the seller's breach include expenses reasonably incurred in inspection, receipt, transportation and care and custody of goods rightfully rejected, any commercially reasonable charges, expenses or commissions in connection with effecting cover and any other reasonable expense incident to the delay or other breach.

(2) Consequential damages resulting from the seller's breach include

(a) any loss resulting from general or particular requirements and needs of which the seller at the time of contracting had reason to know and which could not reasonably be prevented by cover or otherwise; and

(b) injury to person or property proximately resulting from any breach of warranty.

§ 2—716. Buyer's Right to Specific Performance or Replevin.

(1) Specific performance may be decreed where the goods are unique or in other proper circumstances.

(2) The decree for specific performance may include such terms and conditions as to payment of the price, damages, or other relief as the court may deem just.

(3) The buyer has a right of replevin for goods identified to the contract if after reasonable effort he is unable to effect cover for such goods or the circumstances reasonably indicate that such effort will be unavailing or if the goods have been shipped under reservation and satisfaction of the security interest in them has been made or tendered.

§ 2—717. Deduction of Damages From the Price.

The buyer on notifying the seller of his intention to do so may deduct all or any part of the damages resulting from any breach of the contract from any part of the price still due under the same contract.

§ 2—718. Liquidation or Limitation of Damages; Deposits.

(1) Damages for breach by either party may be liquidated in the agreement but only at an amount which is reasonable in the light of the anticipated or actual harm caused by the breach, the difficulties of proof of loss, and the

inconvenience or nonfeasibility of otherwise obtaining an adequate remedy. A term fixing unreasonably large liquidated damages is void as a penalty.

(2) Where the seller justifiably withholds delivery of goods because of the buyer's breach, the buyer is entitled to restitution of any amount by which the sum of his payments exceeds

(a) the amount to which the seller is entitled by virtue of terms liquidating the seller's damages in accordance with subsection (1), or

(b) in the absence of such terms, twenty per cent of the value of the total performance for which the buyer is obligated under the contract or $500, whichever is smaller.

(3) The buyer's right to restitution under subsection (2) is subject to offset to the extent that the seller establishes

(a) a right to recover damages under the provisions of this Article other than subsection (1), and

(b) the amount or value of any benefits received by the buyer directly or indirectly by reason of the contract.

(4) Where a seller has received payment in goods their reasonable value or the proceeds of their resale shall be treated as payments for the purposes of subsection (2); but if the seller has notice of the buyer's breach before reselling goods received in part performance, his resale is subject to the conditions laid down in this Article on resale by an aggrieved seller (Section 2—706).

§ 2—719. **Contractual Modification or Limitation of Remedy.**

(1) Subject to the provisions of subsections (2) and (3) of this section and of the preceding section on liquidation and limitation of damages,

(a) the agreement may provide for remedies in addition to or in substitution for those provided in this Article and may limit or alter the measure of damages recoverable under this Article, as by limiting the buyer's remedies to return of the goods and repayment of the price or to repair and replacement of nonconforming goods or parts; and

(b) resort to a remedy as provided is optional unless the remedy is expressly agreed to be exclusive, in which case it is the sole remedy.

(2) Where circumstances cause an exclusive or limited remedy to fail of its essential purpose, remedy may be had as provided in this Act.

(3) Consequential damages may be limited or excluded unless the limitation or exclusion is unconscionable. Limitation of consequential damages for injury to the person in the case of consumer goods is prima facie unconscionable but limitation of damages where the loss is commercial is not.

§ 2—720. **Effect of "Cancellation" or "Rescission" on Claims for Antecedent Breach.**

Unless the contrary intention clearly appears, expressions of "cancellation" or "rescission" of the contract or the like shall not be construed as a renunciation or discharge of any claim in damages for an antecedent breach.

§ 2—721. **Remedies for Fraud.**

Remedies for material misrepresentation or fraud include all remedies available under this Article for non-fraudulent breach. Neither rescission or a claim for rescission of the contract for sale nor rejection or return of the goods shall bar or be deemed inconsistent with a claim for damages or other remedy.

§ 2—722. **Who Can Sue Third Parties for Injury to Goods.**

Where a third party so deals with goods which have been identified to a contract for sale as to cause actionable injury to a party to that contract

(a) a right of action against the third party is in either party to the contract for sale who has title to or a security interest or a special property or an insurable interest in the goods; and if the goods have been destroyed or converted a right of action is also in the party who either bore the risk of loss under the contract for sale or has since the injury assumed that risk as against the other;

(b) if at the time of the injury the party plaintiff did not bear the risk of loss as against the other party to the contract for sale and there is no arrangement between them for disposition of the recovery, his suit or settlement is, subject to his own interest, as a fiduciary for the other party to the contract;

(c) either party may with the consent of the other sue for the benefit of whom it may concern.

§ 2—723. **Proof of Market Price: Time and Place.**

(1) If an action based on anticipatory repudiation comes to trial before the time for performance with respect to some or all of the goods, any damages based on market price (Section 2—708 or Section 2—713) shall be determined according to the price of such goods prevailing at the time when the aggrieved party learned of the repudiation.

(2) If evidence of a price prevailing at the times or places described in this Article is not readily available the price prevailing within any reasonable time before or after the time described or at any other place which in commercial judgment or under usage of trade would serve as a reasonable substitute for the one described may be used, making any proper allowance for the cost of transporting the goods to or from such other place.

(3) Evidence of a relevant price prevailing at a time or place other than the one described in this Article offered by one party is not admissible unless and until he has

given the other party such notice as the court finds sufficient to prevent unfair surprise.

§ 2—724. **Admissibility of Market Quotations.**

Whenever the prevailing price or value of any goods regularly bought and sold in any established commodity market is in issue, reports in official publications or trade journals or in newspapers or periodicals of general circulation published as the reports of such market shall be admissible in evidence. The circumstances of the preparation of such a report may be shown to affect its weight but not its admissibility.

§ 2—725. **Statute of Limitations in Contracts for Sale.**

(1) An action for breach of any contract for sale must be commenced within four years after the cause of action has accrued. By the original agreement the parties may reduce the period of limitation to not less than one year but may not extend it.

(2) A cause of action accrues when the breach occurs, regardless of the aggrieved party's lack of knowledge of the breach. A breach of warranty occurs when tender of delivery is made, except that where a warranty explicitly extends to future performance of the goods and discovery of the breach must await the time of such performance the cause of action accrues when the breach is or should have been discovered.

(3) Where an action commenced within the time limited by subsection (1) is so terminated as to leave available a remedy by another action for the same breach such other action may be commenced after the expiration of the time limited and within six months after the termination of the first action unless the termination resulted from voluntary discontinuance or from dismissal for failure or neglect to prosecute.

(4) This section does not alter the law on tolling of the statute of limitations nor does it apply to causes of action which have accrued before this Act becomes effective.

Article 2A
LEASES

Part 1 General Provisions

§ 2A—101. **Short Title.**

This Article shall be known and may be cited as the Uniform Commercial Code—Leases.

§ 2A—102. **Scope.**

This Article applies to any transaction, regardless of form, that creates a lease.

§ 2A—103. **Definitions and Index of Definitions.**

(1) In this Article unless the context otherwise requires:

(a) "Buyer in ordinary course of business" means a person who in good faith and without knowledge that the sale to him [or her] is in violation of the ownership rights or security interest or leasehold interest of a third party in the goods buys in ordinary course from a person in the business of selling goods of that kind but does not include a pawnbroker. "Buying" may be for cash or by exchange of other property or on secured or unsecured credit and includes receiving goods or documents of title under a pre-existing contract for sale but does not include a transfer in bulk or as security for or in total or partial satisfaction of a money debt.

(b) "Cancellation" occurs when either party puts an end to the lease contract for default by the other party.

(c) "Commercial unit" means such a unit of goods as by commercial usage is a single whole for purposes of lease and division of which materially impairs its character or value on the market or in use. A commercial unit may be a single article, as a machine, or a set of articles, as a suite of furniture or a line of machinery, or a quantity, as a gross or carload, or any other unit treated in use or in the relevant market as a single whole.

(d) "Conforming" goods or performance under a lease contract means goods or performance that are in accordance with the obligations under the lease contract.

(e) "Consumer lease" means a lease that a lessor regularly engaged in the business of leasing or selling makes to a lessee who is an individual and who takes under the lease primarily for a personal, family, or household "purpose [, if" the total payments to be made under the lease contract, excluding payments for options to renew or buy, do not exceed. . . .

(f) "Fault" means wrongful act, omission, breach, or default.

(g) "Finance lease" means a lease with respect to which:

(i) the lessor does not select, manufacture or supply the goods;

(ii) the lessor acquires the goods or the right to possession and use of the goods in connection with the lease; and

(iii) one of the following occurs:

(A) the lessee receives a copy of the contract by which the lessor acquired the goods or the right to possession and use of the goods before signing the lease contract;

(B) the lessee's approval of the contract by which the lessor acquired the goods or the right to possession and use of the goods is a condition to effectiveness of the lease contract;

(C) the lessee, before signing the lease contract, receives an accurate and complete statement designating the promises and warranties, and any disclaimers of warranties, limitations or modifications of remedies, or liquidated damages, including those of a third party, such as the manufacturer of the goods, provided to the lessor by the person supplying the goods in connection with or as part of the contract by which the lessor acquired the goods or the right to possession and use of the goods; or

(D) if the lease is not a consumer lease, the lessor, before the lessee signs the lease contract, informs the lessee in writing (a) of the identity of the person supplying the goods to the lessor, unless the lessee has selected that person and directed the lessor to acquire the goods or the right to possession and use of the goods from that person, (b) that the lessee is entitled under this Article to any promises and warranties, including those of any third party, provided to the lessor by the person supplying the goods in connection with or as part of the contract by which the lessor acquired the goods or the right to possession and use of the goods, and (c) that the lessee may communicate with the person supplying the goods to the lessor and receive an accurate and complete statement of those promises and warranties, including any disclaimers and limitations of them or of remedies.

(h) "Goods" means all things that are movable at the time of identification to the lease contract, or are fixtures (Section 2A—309), but the term does not include money, documents, instruments, accounts, chattel paper, general intangibles, or minerals or the like, including oil and gas, before extraction. The term also includes the unborn young of animals.

(i) "Installment lease contract" means a lease contract that authorizes or requires the delivery of goods in separate lots to be separately accepted, even though the lease contract contains a clause "each delivery is a eparate lease" or its equivalent.

(j) "Lease" means a transfer of the right to possession and use of goods for a term in return for consideration, but a sale, including a sale on approval or a sale or return, or retention or creation of a security interest is not a lease. Unless the context clearly indicates otherwise, the term includes a sublease.

(k) "Lease agreement" means the bargain, with respect to the lease, of the lessor and the lessee in fact as found in their language or by implication from other circumstances including course of dealing or usage of trade or course of performance as provided in this Article. Unless the context clearly indicates otherwise, the term includes a sublease agreement.

(l) "Lease contract" means the total legal obligation that results from the lease agreement as affected by this Article and any other applicable rules of law. Unless the context clearly indicates otherwise, the term includes a sublease contract.

(m) "Leasehold interest" means the interest of the lessor or the lessee under a lease contract.

(n) "Lessee" means a person who acquires the right to possession and use of goods under a lease. Unless the context clearly indicates otherwise, the term includes a sublessee.

(o) "Lessee in ordinary course of business" means a person who in good faith and without knowledge that the lease to him [or her] is in violation of the ownership rights or security interest or leasehold interest of a third party in the goods, leases in ordinary course from a person in the business of selling or leasing goods of that kind but does not include a pawnbroker. "Leasing" may be for cash or by exchange of other property or on secured or unsecured credit and includes receiving goods or documents of title under a pre-existing lease contract but does not include a transfer in bulk or as security for or in total or partial satisfaction of a money debt.

(p) "Lessor" means a person who transfers the right to possession and use of goods under a lease. Unless the context clearly indicates otherwise, the term includes a sublessor.

(q) "Lessor's residual interest" means the lessor's interest in the goods after expiration, termination, or cancellation of the lease contract.

(r) "Lien" means a charge against or interest in goods to secure payment of a debt or performance of an obligation, but the term does not include a security interest.

(s) "Lot" means a parcel or a single article that is the subject matter of a separate lease or delivery, whether or not it is sufficient to perform the lease contract.

(t) "Merchant lessee" means a lessee that is a merchant with respect to goods of the kind subject to the lease.

(u) "Present value" means the amount as of a date certain of one or more sums payable in the future, discounted to the date certain. The discount is determined by the interest rate specified by the parties if the rate was not manifestly unreasonable at the time the transaction was entered into; otherwise, the discount is determined by a commercially reasonable rate that takes into account the facts and circumstances of each case at the time the transaction was entered into.

(v) "Purchase" includes taking by sale, lease, mortgage, security interest, pledge, gift, or any other voluntary transaction creating an interest in goods.

(w) "Sublease" means a lease of goods the right to possession and use of which was acquired by the lessor as a lessee under an existing lease.

(x) "Supplier" means a person from whom a lessor buys or leases goods to be leased under a finance lease.

(y) "Supply contract" means a contract under which a lessor buys or leases goods to be leased.

(z) "Termination" occurs when either party pursuant to a power created by agreement or law puts an end to the lease contract otherwise than for default.

(2) Other definitions applying to this Article and the sections in which they appear are:

"Accessions". Section 2A—310(1).
"Construction mortgage". Section 2A—309(1)(d).
"Encumbrance". Section 2A—309(1)(e).
"Fixtures". Section 2A—309(1)(a).
"Fixture filing". Section 2A—309(1)(b).
"Purchase money lease". Section 2A—309(1)(c).

(3) The following definitions in other Articles apply to this Article:

"Accounts". Section 9—106.
"Between merchants". Section 2—104(3).
"Buyer". Section 2—103(1)(a).
"Chattel paper". Section 9—105(1)(b).
"Consumer goods". Section 9—109(1).
"Document". Section 9—105(1)(f).
"Entrusting". Section 2—403(3).
"General intangibles". Section 9—106.
"Good faith". Section 2—103(1)(b).
"Instrument". Section 9—105(1)(i).
"Merchant". Section 2—104(1).
"Mortgage". Section 9—105(1)(j).
"Pursuant to commitment". Section 9—105(1)(k).
"Receipt". Section 2—103(1)(c).
"Sale". Section 2—106(1).
"Sale on approval". Section 2—326.
"Sale or return". Section 2—326.
"Seller". Section 2—103(1)(d).

(4) In addition Article 1 contains general definitions and principles of construction and interpretation applicable throughout this Article.

As amended in 1990.

§ 2A—104. Leases Subject to Other Law.

(1) A lease, although subject to this Article, is also subject to any applicable:

(a) certificate of title statute of this State: (list any certificate of title statutes covering automobiles, trailers, mobile homes, boats, farm tractors, and the like);

(b) certificate of title statute of another jurisdiction (Section 2A—105); or

(c) consumer protection statute of this State, or final consumer protection decision of a court of this State existing on the effective date of this Article.

(2) In case of conflict between this Article, other than Sections 2A—105, 2A—304(3), and 2A—305(3), and a statute or decision referred to in subsection (1), the statute or decision controls.

(3) Failure to comply with an applicable law has only the effect specified therein.

As amended in 1990.

§ 2A—105. Territorial Application of Article to Goods Covered by Certificate of Title.

Subject to the provisions of Sections 2A—304(3) and 2A—305(3), with respect to goods covered by a certificate of title issued under a statute of this State or of another jurisdiction, compliance and the effect of compliance or noncompliance with a certificate of title statute are governed by the law (including the conflict of laws rules) of the jurisdiction issuing the certificate until the earlier of (a) surrender of the certificate, or (b) four months after the goods are removed from that jurisdiction and thereafter until a new certificate of title is issued by another jurisdiction.

§ 2A—106. Limitation on Power of Parties to Consumer Lease to Choose Applicable Law and Judicial Forum.

(1) If the law chosen by the parties to a consumer lease is that of a jurisdiction other than a jurisdiction in which the lessee resides at the time the lease agreement becomes enforceable or within 30 days thereafter or in which the goods are to be used, the choice is not enforceable.

(2) If the judicial forum chosen by the parties to a consumer lease is a forum that would not otherwise have jurisdiction over the lessee, the choice is not enforceable.

§ 2A—107. Waiver or Renunciation of Claim or Right After Default.

Any claim or right arising out of an alleged default or breach of warranty may be discharged in whole or in part without consideration by a written waiver or renunciation signed and delivered by the aggrieved party.

§ 2A—108. Unconscionability.

(1) If the court as a matter of law finds a lease contract or any clause of a lease contract to have been unconscionable at the time it was made the court may refuse to enforce the lease contract, or it may enforce the remainder of the lease contract without the unconscionable clause, or it may so limit the application of any unconscionable clause as to avoid any unconscionable result.

(2) With respect to a consumer lease, if the court as a matter of law finds that a lease contract or any clause of a lease contract has been induced by unconscionable conduct or that unconscionable conduct has occurred in the collection of a claim arising from a lease contract, the court may grant appropriate relief.

(3) Before making a finding of unconscionability under subsection (1) or (2), the court, on its own motion or

that of a party, shall afford the parties a reasonable opportunity to present evidence as to the setting, purpose, and effect of the lease contract or clause thereof, or of the conduct.

(4) In an action in which the lessee claims unconscionability with respect to a consumer lease:

(a) If the court finds unconscionability under subsection (1) or (2), the court shall award reasonable attorney's fees to the lessee.

(b) If the court does not find unconscionability and the lessee claiming unconscionability has brought or maintained an action he [or she] knew to be groundless, the court shall award reasonable attorney's fees to the party against whom the claim is made.

(c) In determining attorney's fees, the amount of the recovery on behalf of the claimant under subsections (1) and (2) is not controlling.

§ 2A—109. Option to Accelerate at Will.

(1) A term providing that one party or his [or her] successor in interest may accelerate payment or performance or require collateral or additional collateral "at will" or "when he [or she] deems himself [or herself] insecure" or in words of similar import must be construed to mean that he [or she] has power to do so only if he [or she] in good faith believes that the prospect of payment or performance is impaired.

(2) With respect to a consumer lease, the burden of establishing good faith under subsection (1) is on the party who exercised the power; otherwise the burden of establishing lack of good faith is on the party against whom the power has been exercised.

Part 2 Formation and Construction of Lease Contract

§ 2A—201. Statute of Frauds.

(1) A lease contract is not enforceable by way of action or defense unless:

(a) the total payments to be made under the lease contract, excluding payments for options to renew or buy, are less than $1,000; or

(b) there is a writing, signed by the party against whom enforcement is sought or by that party's authorized agent, sufficient to indicate that a lease contract has been made between the parties and to describe the goods leased and the lease term.

(2) Any description of leased goods or of the lease term is sufficient and satisfies subsection (1)(b), whether or not it is specific, if it reasonably identifies what is described.

(3) A writing is not insufficient because it omits or incorrectly states a term agreed upon, but the lease contract is not enforceable under subsection (1)(b) beyond the lease term and the quantity of goods shown in the writing.

(4) A lease contract that does not satisfy the requirements of subsection (1), but which is valid in other respects, is enforceable:

(a) if the goods are to be specially manufactured or obtained for the lessee and are not suitable for lease or sale to others in the ordinary course of the lessor's business, and the lessor, before notice of repudiation is received and under circumstances that reasonably indicate that the goods are for the lessee, has made either a substantial beginning of their manufacture or commitments for their procurement;

(b) if the party against whom enforcement is sought admits in that party's pleading, testimony or otherwise in court that a lease contract was made, but the lease contract is not enforceable under this provision beyond the quantity of goods admitted; or

(c) with respect to goods that have been received and accepted by the lessee.

(5) The lease term under a lease contract referred to in subsection (4) is:

(a) if there is a writing signed by the party against whom enforcement is sought or by that party's authorized agent specifying the lease term, the term so specified;

(b) if the party against whom enforcement is sought admits in that party's pleading, testimony, or otherwise in court a lease term, the term so admitted; or

(c) a reasonable lease term.

§ 2A—202. Final Written Expression: Parol or Extrinsic Evidence.

Terms with respect to which the confirmatory memoranda of the parties agree or which are otherwise set forth in a writing intended by the parties as a final expression of their agreement with respect to such terms as are included therein may not be contradicted by evidence of any prior agreement or of a contemporaneous oral agreement but may be explained or supplemented:

(a) by course of dealing or usage of trade or by course of performance; and

(b) by evidence of consistent additional terms unless the court finds the writing to have been intended also as a complete and exclusive statement of the terms of the agreement.

§ 2A—203. Seals Inoperative.

The affixing of a seal to a writing evidencing a lease contract or an offer to enter into a lease contract does not render the writing a sealed instrument and the law with respect to sealed instruments does not apply to the lease contract or offer.

§ 2A—204. Formation in General.

(1) A lease contract may be made in any manner sufficient to show agreement, including conduct by both parties which recognizes the existence of a lease contract.

(2) An agreement sufficient to constitute a lease contract may be found although the moment of its making is undetermined.

(3) Although one or more terms are left open, a lease contract does not fail for indefiniteness if the parties have intended to make a lease contract and there is a reasonably certain basis for giving an appropriate remedy.

§ 2A—205. Firm Offers.

An offer by a merchant to lease goods to or from another person in a signed writing that by its terms gives assurance it will be held open is not revocable, for lack of consideration, during the time stated or, if no time is stated, for a reasonable time, but in no event may the period of irrevocability exceed 3 months. Any such term of assurance on a form supplied by the offeree must be separately signed by the offeror.

§ 2A—206. Offer and Acceptance in Formation of Lease Contract.

(1) Unless otherwise unambiguously indicated by the language or circumstances, an offer to make a lease contract must be construed as inviting acceptance in any manner and by any medium reasonable in the circumstances.

(2) If the beginning of a requested performance is a reasonable mode of acceptance, an offeror who is not notified of acceptance within a reasonable time may treat the offer as having lapsed before acceptance.

§ 2A—207. Course of Performance or Practical Construction.

(1) If a lease contract involves repeated occasions for performance by either party with knowledge of the nature of the performance and opportunity for objection to it by the other, any course of performance accepted or acquiesced in without objection is relevant to determine the meaning of the lease agreement.

(2) The express terms of a lease agreement and any course of performance, as well as any course of dealing and usage of trade, must be construed whenever reasonable as consistent with each other; but if that construction is unreasonable, express terms control course of performance, course of performance controls both course of dealing and usage of trade, and course of dealing controls usage of trade.

(3) Subject to the provisions of Section 2A—208 on modification and waiver, course of performance is relevant to show a waiver or modification of any term inconsistent with the course of performance.

§ 2A—208. Modification, Rescission and Waiver.

(1) An agreement modifying a lease contract needs no consideration to be binding.

(2) A signed lease agreement that excludes modification or rescission except by a signed writing may not be otherwise modified or rescinded, but, except as between merchants, such a requirement on a form supplied by a merchant must be separately signed by the other party.

(3) Although an attempt at modification or rescission does not satisfy the requirements of subsection (2), it may operate as a waiver.

(4) A party who has made a waiver affecting an executory portion of a lease contract may retract the waiver by reasonable notification received by the other party that strict performance will be required of any term waived, unless the retraction would be unjust in view of a material change of position in reliance on the waiver.

§ 2A—209. Lessee under Finance Lease as Beneficiary of Supply Contract.

(1) The benefit of the supplier's promises to the lessor under the supply contract and of all warranties, whether express or implied, including those of any third party provided in connection with or as part of the supply contract, extends to the lessee to the extent of the lessee's leasehold interest under a finance lease related to the supply contract, but is subject to the terms warranty and of the supply contract and all defenses or claims arising therefrom.

(2) The extension of the benefit of supplier's promises and of warranties to the lessee (Section 2A–209(1)) does not: (i) modify the rights and obligations of the parties to the supply contract, whether arising therefrom or otherwise, or (ii) impose any duty or liability under the supply contract on the lessee.

(3) Any modification or rescission of the supply contract by the supplier and the lessor is effective between the supplier and the lessee unless, before the modification or rescission, the supplier has received notice that the lessee has entered into a finance lease related to the supply contract. If the modification or rescission is effective between the supplier and the lessee, the lessor is deemed to have assumed, in addition to the obligations of the lessor to the lessee under the lease contract, promises of the supplier to the lessor and warranties that were so modified or rescinded as they existed and were available to the lessee before modification or rescission.

(4) In addition to the extension of the benefit of the supplier's promises and of warranties to the lessee under subsection (1), the lessee retains all rights that the lessee may have against the supplier which arise from an agreement between the lessee and the supplier or under other law.

As amended in 1990.

§ 2A—210. Express Warranties.

(1) Express warranties by the lessor are created as follows:

(a) Any affirmation of fact or promise made by the lessor to the lessee which relates to the goods and becomes part of the basis of the bargain creates an express warranty that the goods will conform to the affirmation or promise.

(b) Any description of the goods which is made part of the basis of the bargain creates an express warranty that the goods will conform to the description.

(c) Any sample or model that is made part of the basis of the bargain creates an express warranty that the whole of the goods will conform to the sample or model.

(2) It is not necessary to the creation of an express warranty that the lessor use formal words, such as "warrant" or "guarantee," or that the lessor have a specific intention to make a warranty, but an affirmation merely of the value of the goods or a statement purporting to be merely the lessor's opinion or commendation of the goods does not create a warranty.

§ 2A—211. Warranties Against Interference and Against Infringement; Lessee's Obligation Against Infringement.

(1) There is in a lease contract a warranty that for the lease term no person holds a claim to or interest in the goods that arose from an act or omission of the lessor, other than a claim by way of infringement or the like, which will interfere with the lessee's enjoyment of its leasehold interest.

(2) Except in a finance lease there is in a lease contract by a lessor who is a merchant regularly dealing in goods of the kind a warranty that the goods are delivered free of the rightful claim of any person by way of infringement or the like.

(3) A lessee who furnishes specifications to a lessor or a supplier shall hold the lessor and the supplier harmless against any claim by way of infringement or the like that arises out of compliance with the specifications.

§ 2A—212. Implied Warranty of Merchantability.

(1) Except in a finance lease, a warranty that the goods will be merchantable is implied in a lease contract if the lessor is a merchant with respect to goods of that kind.

(2) Goods to be merchantable must be at least such as

(a) pass without objection in the trade under the description in the lease agreement;

(b) in the case of fungible goods, are of fair average quality within the description;

(c) are fit for the ordinary purposes for which goods of that type are used;

(d) run, within the variation permitted by the lease agreement, of even kind, quality, and quantity within each unit and among all units involved;

(e) are adequately contained, packaged, and labeled as the lease agreement may require; and

(f) conform to any promises or affirmations of fact made on the container or label.

(3) Other implied warranties may arise from course of dealing or usage of trade.

§ 2A—213. Implied Warranty of Fitness for Particular Purpose.

Except in a finance of lease, if the lessor at the time the lease contract is made has reason to know of any particular purpose for which the goods are required and that the lessee is relying on the lessor's skill or judgment to select or furnish suitable goods, there is in the lease contract an implied warranty that the goods will be fit for that purpose.

§ 2A—214. Exclusion or Modification of Warranties.

(1) Words or conduct relevant to the creation of an express warranty and words or conduct tending to negate or limit a warranty must be construed wherever reasonable as consistent with each other; but, subject to the provisions of Section 2A—202 on parol or extrinsic evidence, negation or limitation is inoperative to the extent that the construction is unreasonable.

(2) Subject to subsection (3), to exclude or modify the implied warranty of merchantability or any part of it the language must mention "merchantability", be by a writing, and be conspicuous. Subject to subsection (3), to exclude or modify any implied warranty of fitness the exclusion must be by a writing and be conspicuous. Language to exclude all implied warranties of fitness is sufficient if it is in writing, is conspicuous and states, for example, "There is no warranty that the goods will be fit for a particular purpose".

(3) Notwithstanding subsection (2), but subject to subsection (4),

(a) unless the circumstances indicate otherwise, all implied warranties are excluded by expressions like "as is" or "with all faults" or by other language that in common understanding calls the lessee's attention to the exclusion of warranties and makes plain that there is no implied warranty, if in writing and conspicuous;

(b) if the lessee before entering into the lease contract has examined the goods or the sample or model as fully as desired or has refused to examine the goods, there is no implied warranty with regard to defects that an examination ought in the circumstances to have revealed; and

(c) an implied warranty may also be excluded or modified by course of dealing, course of performance, or usage of trade.

(4) To exclude or modify a warranty against interference or against infringement (Section 2A—211) or any part of it, the language must be specific, be by a writing, and be conspicuous, unless the circumstances, including course of performance, course of dealing, or usage of trade, give the lessee reason to know that the goods are being leased subject to a claim or interest of any person.

§ 2A—215. Cumulation and Conflict of Warranties Express or Implied.

Warranties, whether express or implied, must be construed as consistent with each other and as cumulative, but if that construction is unreasonable, the intention of the parties determines which warranty is dominant. In ascertaining that intention the following rules apply:

(a) Exact or technical specifications displace an inconsistent sample or model or general language of description.

(b) A sample from an existing bulk displaces inconsistent general language of description.

(c) Express warranties displace inconsistent implied warranties other than an implied warranty of fitness for a particular purpose.

§ 2A—216. Third-Party Beneficiaries of Express and Implied Warranties.

Alternative A

A warranty to or for the benefit of a lessee under this Article, whether express or implied, extends to any natural person who is in the family or household of the lessee or who is a guest in the lessee's home if it is reasonable to expect that such person may use, consume, or be affected by the goods and who is injured in person by breach of the warranty. This section does not displace principles of law and equity that extend a warranty to or for the benefit of a lessee to other persons. The operation of this section may not be excluded, modified, or limited, but an exclusion, modification, or limitation of the warranty, including any with respect to rights and remedies, effective against the lessee is also effective against any beneficiary designated under this section.

Alternative B

A warranty to or for the benefit of a lessee under this Article, whether express or implied, extends to any natural person who may reasonably be expected to use, consume, or be affected by the goods and who is injured in person by breach of the warranty. This section does not displace principles of law and equity that extend a warranty to or for the benefit of a lessee to other persons. The operation of this section may not be excluded, modified, or limited, but an exclusion, modification, or limitation of the warranty, including any with respect to rights and remedies, effective against the lessee is also effective against the beneficiary designated under this section.

Alternative C

A warranty to or for the benefit of a lessee under this Article, whether express or implied, extends to any person who may reasonably be expected to use, consume, or be affected by the goods and who is injured by breach of the warranty. The operation of this section may not be excluded, modified, or limited with respect to injury to the person of an individual to whom the warranty extends, but an exclusion, modification, or limitation of the warranty, including any with respect to rights and remedies, effective against the lessee is also effective against the beneficiary designated under this section.

§ 2A—217. Identification.

Identification of goods as goods to which a lease contract refers may be made at any time and in any manner explicitly agreed to by the parties. In the absence of explicit agreement, identification occurs:

(a) when the lease contract is made if the lease contract is for a lease of goods that are existing and identified;

(b) when the goods are shipped, marked, or otherwise designated by the lessor as goods to which the lease contract refers, if the lease contract is for a lease of goods that are not existing and identified; or

(c) when the young are conceived, if the lease contract is for a lease of unborn young of animals.

§ 2A—218. Insurance and Proceeds.

(1) A lessee obtains an insurable interest when existing goods are identified to the lease contract even though the goods identified are nonconforming and the lessee has an option to reject them.

(2) If a lessee has an insurable interest only by reason of the lessor's identification of the goods, the lessor, until default or insolvency or notification to the lessee that identification is final, may substitute other goods for those identified.

(3) Notwithstanding a lessee's insurable interest under subsections (1) and (2), the lessor retains an insurable interest until an option to buy has been exercised by the lessee and risk of loss has passed to the lessee.

(4) Nothing in this section impairs any insurable interest recognized under any other statute or rule of law.

(5) The parties by agreement may determine that one or more parties have an obligation to obtain and pay for insurance covering the goods and by agreement may determine the beneficiary of the proceeds of the insurance.

§ 2A—219. Risk of Loss.

(1) Except in the case of a finance lease, risk of loss is retained by the lessor and does not pass to the lessee. In the case of a finance lease, risk of loss passes to the lessee.

(2) Subject to the provisions of this Article on the effect of default on risk of loss (Section 2A—220), if risk of loss

is to pass to the lessee and the time of passage is not stated, the following rules apply:

(a) If the lease contract requires or authorizes the goods to be shipped by carrier

(i) and it does not require delivery at a particular destination, the risk of loss passes to the lessee when the goods are duly delivered to the carrier; but

(ii) if it does require delivery at a particular destination and the goods are there duly tendered while in the possession of the carrier, the risk of loss passes to the lessee when the goods are there duly so tendered as to enable the lessee to take delivery.

(b) If the goods are held by a bailee to be delivered without being moved, the risk of loss passes to the lessee on acknowledgment by the bailee of the lessee's right to possession of the goods.

(c) In any case not within subsection (a) or (b), the risk of loss passes to the lessee on the lessee's receipt of the goods if the lessor, or, in the case of a finance lease, the supplier, is a merchant; otherwise the risk passes to the lessee on tender of delivery.

§ 2A—220. Effect of Default on Risk of Loss.

(1) Where risk of loss is to pass to the lessee and the time of passage is not stated:

(a) If a tender or delivery of goods so fails to conform to the lease contract as to give a right of rejection, the risk of their loss remains with the lessor, or, in the case of a finance lease, the supplier, until cure or acceptance.

(b) If the lessee rightfully revokes acceptance, he [or she], to the extent of any deficiency in his [or her] effective insurance coverage, may treat the risk of loss as having remained with the lessor from the beginning.

(2) Whether or not risk of loss is to pass to the lessee, if the lessee as to conforming goods already identified to a lease contract repudiates or is otherwise in default under the lease contract, the lessor, or, in the case of a finance lease, the supplier, to the extent of any deficiency in his [or her] effective insurance coverage may treat the risk of loss as resting on the lessee for a commercially reasonable time.

§ 2A—221. Casualty to Identified Goods.

If a lease contract requires goods identified when the lease contract is made, and the goods suffer casualty without fault of the lessee, the lessor or the supplier before delivery, or the goods suffer casualty before risk of loss passes to the lessee pursuant to the lease agreement or Section 2A—219, then:

(a) if the loss is total, the lease contract is avoided; and

(b) if the loss is partial or the goods have so deteriorated as to no longer conform to the lease contract, the lessee may nevertheless demand inspection and at his [or her] option either treat the lease contract as avoided or, except in a finance lease that is not a consumer lease, accept the goods with due allowance from the rent payable for the balance of the lease term for the deterioration or the deficiency in quantity but without further right against the lessor.

Part 3 Effect Of Lease Contract

§ 2A—301. Enforceability of Lease Contract.

Except as otherwise provided in this Article, a lease contract is effective and enforceable according to its terms between the parties, against purchasers of the goods and against creditors of the parties.

§ 2A—302. Title to and Possession of Goods.

Except as otherwise provided in this Article, each provision of this Article applies whether the lessor or a third party has title to the goods, and whether the lessor, the lessee, or a third party has possession of the goods, notwithstanding any statute or rule of law that possession or the absence of possession is fraudulent.

§ 2A—303. Alienability of Party's Interest Under Lease Contract or of Lessor's Residual Interest in Goods; Delegation of Performance; Transfer of Rights.

(1) As used in this section, "creation of a security interest" includes the sale of a lease contract that is subject to Article 9, Secured Transactions, by reason of Section 9—102(1)(b).

(2) Except as provided in subsections (3) and (4), a provision in a lease agreement which (i) prohibits the voluntary or involuntary transfer, including a transfer by sale, sublease, creation or enforcement of a security interest, or attachment, levy, or other judicial process, of an interest of a party under the lease contract or of the lessor's residual interest in the goods, or (ii) makes such a transfer an event of default, gives rise to the rights and remedies provided in subsection (5), but a transfer that is prohibited or is an event of default under the lease agreement is otherwise effective.

(3) A provision in a lease agreement which (i) prohibits the creation or enforcement of a security interest in an interest of a party under the lease contract or in the lessor's residual interest in the goods, or (ii) makes such a transfer an event of default, is not enforceable unless, and then only to the extent that, there is an actual transfer by the lessee of the lessee's right of possession or use of the goods in violation of the provision or an actual delegation of a material performance of either party to the lease contract in violation of the provision. Neither the granting nor the enforcement of a security interest in (i) the lessor's interest under the lease contract or (ii) the lessor's residual interest in the goods is a transfer that materially impairs the prospect of obtaining return performance by, materially changes the duty of, or materially increases the burden or risk imposed on, the lessee

within the purview of subsection (5) unless, and then only to the extent that, there is an actual delegation of a material performance of the lessor.

(4) A provision in a lease agreement which (i) prohibits a transfer of a right to damages for default with respect to the whole lease contract or of a right to payment arising out of the transferor's due performance of the transferor's entire obligation, or (ii) makes such a transfer an event of default, is not enforceable, and such a transfer is not a transfer that materially impairs the prospect of obtaining return performance by, materially changes the duty of, or materially increases the burden or risk imposed on, the other party to the lease contract within the purview of subsection (5).

(5) Subject to subsections (3) and (4):

(a) if a transfer is made which is made an event of default under a lease agreement, the party to the lease contract not making the transfer, unless that party waives the default or otherwise agrees, has the rights and remedies described in Section 2A—501(2);

(b) if paragraph (a) is not applicable and if a transfer is made that (i) is prohibited under a lease agreement or (ii) materially impairs the prospect of obtaining return performance by, materially changes the duty of, or materially increases the burden or risk imposed on, the other party to the lease contract, unless the party not making the transfer agrees at any time to the transfer in the lease contract or otherwise, then, except as limited by contract, (i) the transferor is liable to the party not making the transfer for damages caused by the transfer to the extent that the damages could not reasonably be prevented by the party not making the transfer and (ii) a court having jurisdiction may grant other appropriate relief, including cancellation of the lease contract or an injunction against the transfer.

(6) A transfer of "the lease" or of "all my rights under the lease," or a transfer in similar general terms, is a transfer of rights and, unless the language or the circumstances, as in a transfer for security, indicate the contrary, the transfer is a delegation of duties by the transferor to the transferee. Acceptance by the transferee constitutes a promise by the transferee to perform those duties. The promise is enforceable by either the transferor or the other party to the lease contract.

(7) Unless otherwise agreed by the lessor and the lessee, a delegation of performance does not relieve the transferor as against the other party of any duty to perform or of any liability for default.

(8) In a consumer lease, to prohibit the transfer of an interest of a party under the lease contract or to make a transfer an event of default, the language must be specific, by a writing, and conspicuous.

As amended in 1990.

§ 2A—304. Subsequent Lease of Goods by Lessor.

(1) Subject to Section 2A—303, a subsequent lessee from a lessor of goods under an existing lease contract obtains, to the extent of the leasehold interest transferred, the leasehold interest in the goods that the lessor had or had power to transfer, and except as provided in subsection (2) and Section 2A—527(4), takes subject to the existing lease contract. A lessor with voidable title has power to transfer a good leasehold interest to a good faith subsequent lessee for value, but only to the extent set forth in the preceding sentence. If goods have been delivered under a transaction of purchase the lessor has that power even though:

(a) the lessor's transferor was deceived as to the identity of the lessor;

(b) the delivery was in exchange for a check which is later dishonored;

(c) it was agreed that the transaction was to be a "cash sale"; or

(d) the delivery was procured through fraud punishable as larcenous under the criminal law.

(2) A subsequent lessee in the ordinary course of business from a lessor who is a merchant dealing in goods of that kind to whom the goods were entrusted by the existing lessee of that lessor before the interest of the subsequent lessee became enforceable against that lessor obtains, to the extent of the leasehold interest transferred, all of that lessor's and the existing lessee's rights to the goods, and takes free of the existing lease contract.

(3) A subsequent lessee from the lessor of goods that are subject to an existing lease contract and are covered by a certificate of title issued under a statute of this State or of another jurisdiction takes no greater rights than those provided both by this section and by the certificate of title statute.

As amended in 1990.

§ 2A—305. Sale or Sublease of Goods by Lessee.

(1) Subject to the provisions of Section 2A—303, a buyer or sublessee from the lessee of goods under an existing lease contract obtains, to the extent of the interest transferred, the leasehold interest in the goods that the lessee had or had power to transfer, and except as provided in subsection (2) and Section 2A—511(4), takes subject to the existing lease contract. A lessee with a voidable leasehold interest has power to transfer a good leasehold interest to a good faith buyer for value or a good faith sublessee for value, but only to the extent set forth in the preceding sentence. When goods have been delivered under a transaction of lease the lessee has that power even though:

(a) the lessor was deceived as to the identity of the lessee;

(b) the delivery was in exchange for a check which is later dishonored; or

(c) the delivery was procured through fraud punishable as larcenous under the criminal law.

(2) A buyer in the ordinary course of business or a sublessee in the ordinary course of business from a lessee who is a merchant dealing in goods of that kind to whom the goods were entrusted by the lessor obtains, to the extent of the interest transferred, all of the lessor's and lessee's rights to the goods, and takes free of the existing lease contract.

(3) A buyer or sublessee from the lessee of goods that are subject to an existing lease contract and are covered by a certificate of title issued under a statute of this State or of another jurisdiction takes no greater rights than those provided both by this section and by the certificate of title statute.

§ 2A—306. Priority of Certain Liens Arising by Operation of Law.

If a person in the ordinary course of his [or her] business furnishes services or materials with respect to goods subject to a lease contract, a lien upon those goods in the possession of that person given by statute or rule of law for those materials or services takes priority over any interest of the lessor or lessee under the lease contract or this Article unless the lien is created by statute and the statute provides otherwise or unless the lien is created by rule of law and the rule of law provides otherwise.

§ 2A—307. Priority of Liens Arising by Attachment or Levy on, Security Interests in, and Other Claims to Goods.

(1) Except as otherwise provided in Section 2A—306, a creditor of a lessee takes subject to the lease contract.

(2) Except as otherwise provided in subsections (3) and (4) and in Sections 2A—306 and 2A—308, a creditor of a lessor takes subject to the lease contract unless:

(a) the creditor holds a lien that attached to the goods before the lease contract became enforceable,

(b) the creditor holds a security interest in the goods and the lessee did not give value and receive delivery of the goods without knowledge of the security interest; or

(c) the creditor holds a security interest in the goods which was perfected (Section 9—303) before the lease contract became enforceable.

(3) A lessee in the ordinary course of business takes the leasehold interest free of a security interest in the goods created by the lessor even though the security interest is perfected (Section 9—303) and the lessee knows of its existence.

(4) A lessee other than a lessee in the ordinary course of business takes the leasehold interest free of a security interest to the extent that it secures future advances made after the secured party acquires knowledge of the lease or more than 45 days after the lease contract becomes enforceable, whichever first occurs, unless the future advances are made pursuant to a commitment entered into without knowledge of the lease and before the expiration of the 45-day period.

§ 2A—308. Special Rights of Creditors.

(1) A creditor of a lessor in possession of goods subject to a lease contract may treat the lease contract as void if as against the creditor retention of possession by the lessor is fraudulent under any statute or rule of law, but retention of possession in good faith and current course of trade by the lessor for a commercially reasonable time after the lease contract becomes enforceable is not fraudulent.

(2) Nothing in this Article impairs the rights of creditors of a lessor if the lease contract (a) becomes enforceable, not in current course of trade but in satisfaction of or as security for a pre-existing claim for money, security, or the like, and (b) is made under circumstances which under any statute or rule of law apart from this Article would constitute the transaction a fraudulent transfer or voidable preference.

(3) A creditor of a seller may treat a sale or an identification of goods to a contract for sale as void if as against the creditor retention of possession by the seller is fraudulent under any statute or rule of law, but retention of possession of the goods pursuant to a lease contract entered into by the seller as lessee and the buyer as lessor in connection with the sale or identification of the goods is not fraudulent if the buyer bought for value and in good faith.

§ 2A—309. Lessor's and Lessee's Rights When Goods Become Fixtures.

(1) In this section:

(a) goods are "fixtures" when they become so related to particular real estate that an interest in them arises under real estate law;

(b) a "fixture filing" is the filing, in the office where a mortgage on the real estate would be filed or recorded, of a financing statement covering goods that are or are to become fixtures and conforming to the requirements of Section 9—402(5);

(c) a lease is a "purchase money lease" unless the lessee has possession or use of the goods or the right to possession or use of the goods before the lease agreement is enforceable;

(d) a mortgage is a "construction mortgage" to the extent it secures an obligation incurred for the construction of an improvement on land including the acquisition cost of the land, if the recorded writing so indicates; and

(e) "encumbrance" includes real estate mortgages and other liens on real estate and all other rights in real estate that are not ownership interests.

(2) Under this Article a lease may be of goods that are fixtures or may continue in goods that become fixtures, but no lease exists under this Article of ordinary building materials incorporated into an improvement on land.

(3) This Article does not prevent creation of a lease of fixtures pursuant to real estate law.

(4) The perfected interest of a lessor of fixtures has priority over a conflicting interest of an encumbrancer or owner of the real estate if:

(a) the lease is a purchase money lease, the conflicting interest of the encumbrancer or owner arises before the goods become fixtures, the interest of the lessor is perfected by a fixture filing before the goods become fixtures or within ten days thereafter, and the lessee has an interest of record in the real estate or is in possession of the real estate; or

(b) the interest of the lessor is perfected by a fixture filing before the interest of the encumbrancer or owner is of record, the lessor's interest has priority over any conflicting interest of a predecessor in title of the encumbrancer or owner, and the lessee has an interest of record in the real estate or is in possession of the real estate.

(5) The interest of a lessor of fixtures, whether or not perfected, has priority over the conflicting interest of an encumbrancer or owner of the real estate if:

(a) the fixtures are readily removable factory or office machines, readily removable equipment that is not primarily used or leased for use in the operation of the real estate, or readily removable replacements of domestic appliances that are goods subject to a consumer lease, and before the goods become fixtures the lease contract is enforceable; or

(b) the conflicting interest is a lien on the real estate obtained by legal or equitable proceedings after the lease contract is enforceable; or

(c) the encumbrancer or owner has consented in writing to the lease or has disclaimed an interest in the goods as fixtures; or

(d) the lessee has a right to remove the goods as against the encumbrancer or owner. If the lessee's right to remove terminates, the priority of the interest of the lessor continues for a reasonable time.

(6) Notwithstanding paragraph (4)(a) but otherwise subject to subsections (4) and (5), the interest of a lessor of fixtures, including the lessor's residual interest, is subordinate to the conflicting interest of an encumbrancer of the real estate under a construction mortgage recorded before the goods become fixtures if the goods become fixtures before the completion of the construction. To the extent given to refinance a construction mortgage, the conflicting interest of an encumbrancer of the real estate under a mortgage has this priority to the same extent as the encumbrancer of the real estate under the construction mortgage.

(7) In cases not within the preceding subsections, priority between the interest of a lessor of fixtures, including the lessor's residual interest, and the conflicting interest of an encumbrancer or owner of the real estate who is not the lessee is determined by the priority rules governing conflicting interests in real estate.

(8) If the interest of a lessor of fixtures, including the lessor's residual interest, has priority over all conflicting interests of all owners and encumbrancers of the real estate, the lessor or the lessee may (i) on default, expiration, termination, or cancellation of the lease agreement but subject to the agreement and this Article, or (ii) if necessary to enforce other rights and remedies of the lessor or lessee under this Article, remove the goods from the real estate, free and clear of all conflicting interests of all owners and encumbrancers of the real estate, but the lessor or lessee must reimburse any encumbrancer or owner of the real estate who is not the lessee and who has not otherwise agreed for the cost of repair of any physical injury, but not for any diminution in value of the real estate caused by the absence of the goods removed or by any necessity of replacing them. A person entitled to reimbursement may refuse permission to remove until the party seeking removal gives adequate security for the performance of this obligation.

(9) Even though the lease agreement does not create a security interest, the interest of a lessor of fixtures, including the lessor's residual interest, is perfected by filing a financing statement as a fixture filing for leased goods that are or are to become fixtures in accordance with the relevant provisions of the Article on Secured Transactions (Article 9).

As amended in 1990.

§ 2A—310. **Lessor's and Lessee's Rights When Goods Become Accessions.**

(1) Goods are "accessions" when they are installed in or affixed to other goods.

(2) The interest of a lessor or a lessee under a lease contract entered into before the goods became accessions is superior to all interests in the whole except as stated in subsection (4).

(3) The interest of a lessor or a lessee under a lease contract entered into at the time or after the goods became accessions is superior to all subsequently acquired interests in the whole except as stated in subsection (4) but is subordinate to interests in the whole existing at the time the lease contract was made unless the holders of such interests in the whole have in writing consented to the

lease or disclaimed an interest in the goods as part of the whole.

(4) The interest of a lessor or a lessee under a lease contract described in subsection (2) or (3) is subordinate to the interest of

(a) a buyer in the ordinary course of business or a lessee in the ordinary course of business of any interest in the whole acquired after the goods became accessions; or

(b) a creditor with a security interest in the whole perfected before the lease contract was made to the extent that the creditor makes subsequent advances without knowledge of the lease contract.

(5) When under subsections (2) or (3) and (4) a lessor or a lessee of accessions holds an interest that is superior to all interests in the whole, the lessor or the lessee may (a) on default, expiration, termination, or cancellation of the lease contract by the other party but subject to the provisions of the lease contract and this Article, or (b) if necessary to enforce his [or her] other rights and remedies under this Article, remove the goods from the whole, free and clear of all interests in the whole, but he [or she] must reimburse any holder of an interest in the whole who is not the lessee and who has not otherwise agreed for the cost of repair of any physical injury but not for any diminution in value of the whole caused by the absence of the goods removed or by any necessity for replacing them. A person entitled to reimbursement may refuse permission to remove until the party seeking removal gives adequate security for the performance of this obligation.

§ 2A—311. Priority Subject to Subordination.

Nothing in this Article prevents subordination by agreement by any person entitled to priority.

As added in 1990.

Part 4 Performance Of Lease Contract: Repudiated, Substituted And Excused

§ 2A—401. Insecurity: Adequate Assurance of Performance.

(1) A lease contract imposes an obligation on each party that the other's expectation of receiving due performance will not be impaired.

(2) If reasonable grounds for insecurity arise with respect to the performance of either party, the insecure party may demand in writing adequate assurance of due performance. Until the insecure party receives that assurance, if commercially reasonable the insecure party may suspend any performance for which he [or she] has not already received the agreed return.

(3) A repudiation of the lease contract occurs if assurance of due performance adequate under the circumstances of the particular case is not provided to the insecure party within a reasonable time, not to exceed 30 days after receipt of a demand by the other party.

(4) Between merchants, the reasonableness of grounds for insecurity and the adequacy of any assurance offered must be determined according to commercial standards.

(5) Acceptance of any nonconforming delivery or payment does not prejudice the aggrieved party's right to demand adequate assurance of future performance.

§ 2A—402. Anticipatory Repudiation.

If either party repudiates a lease contract with respect to a performance not yet due under the lease contract, the loss of which performance will substantially impair the value of the lease contract to the other, the aggrieved party may:

(a) for a commercially reasonable time, await retraction of repudiation and performance by the repudiating party;

(b) make demand pursuant to Section 2A—401 and await assurance of future performance adequate under the circumstances of the particular case; or

(c) resort to any right or remedy upon default under the lease contract or this Article, even though the aggrieved party has notified the repudiating party that the aggrieved party would await the repudiating party's performance and assurance and has urged retraction. In addition, whether or not the aggrieved party is pursuing one of the foregoing remedies, the aggrieved party may suspend performance or, if the aggrieved party is the lessor, proceed in accordance with the provisions of this Article on the lessor's right to identify goods to the lease contract notwithstanding default or to salvage unfinished goods (Section 2A—524).

§ 2A—403. Retraction of Anticipatory Repudiation.

(1) Until the repudiating party's next performance is due, the repudiating party can retract the repudiation unless, since the repudiation, the aggrieved party has cancelled the lease contract or materially changed the aggrieved party's position or otherwise indicated that the aggrieved party considers the repudiation final.

(2) Retraction may be by any method that clearly indicates to the aggrieved party that the repudiating party intends to perform under the lease contract and includes any assurance demanded under Section 2A—401.

(3) Retraction reinstates a repudiating party's rights under a lease contract with due excuse and allowance to the aggrieved party for any delay occasioned by the repudiation.

§ 2A—404. Substituted Performance.

(1) If without fault of the lessee, the lessor and the supplier, the agreed berthing, loading, or unloading facilities fail or the agreed type of carrier becomes unavailable or

the agreed manner of delivery otherwise becomes commercially impracticable, but a commercially reasonable substitute is available, the substitute performance must be tendered and accepted.

(2) If the agreed means or manner of payment fails because of domestic or foreign governmental regulation:

(a) the lessor may withhold or stop delivery or cause the supplier to withhold or stop delivery unless the lessee provides a means or manner of payment that is commercially a substantial equivalent; and

(b) if delivery has already been taken, payment by the means or in the manner provided by the regulation discharges the lessee's obligation unless the regulation is discriminatory, oppressive, or predatory.

§ 2A—405. **Excused Performance.**

Subject to Section 2A—404 on substituted performance, the following rules apply:

(a) Delay in delivery or nondelivery in whole or in part by a lessor or a supplier who complies with paragraphs (b) and (c) is not a default under the lease contract if performance as agreed has been made impracticable by the occurrence of a contingency the nonoccurrence of which was a basic assumption on which the lease contract was made or by compliance in good faith with any applicable foreign or domestic governmental regulation or order, whether or not the regulation or order later proves to be invalid.

(b) If the causes mentioned in paragraph (a) affect only part of the lessor's or the supplier's capacity to perform, he [or she] shall allocate production and deliveries among his [or her] customers but at his [or her] option may include regular customers not then under contract for sale or lease as well as his [or her] own requirements for further manufacture. He [or she] may so allocate in any manner that is fair and reasonable.

(c) The lessor seasonably shall notify the lessee and in the case of a finance lease the supplier seasonably shall notify the lessor and the lessee, if known, that there will be delay or nondelivery and, if allocation is required under paragraph (b), of the estimated quota thus made available for the lessee.

§ 2A—406. **Procedure on Excused Performance.**

(1) If the lessee receives notification of a material or indefinite delay or an allocation justified under Section 2A—405, the lessee may by written notification to the lessor as to any goods involved, and with respect to all of the goods if under an installment lease contract the value of the whole lease contract is substantially impaired (Section 2A—510):

(a) terminate the lease contract (Section 2A—505(2)); or

(b) except in a finance lease that is not a consumer lease, modify the lease contract by accepting the available quota in substitution, with due allowance from the rent payable for the balance of the lease term for the deficiency but without further right against the lessor.

(2) If, after receipt of a notification from the lessor under Section 2A—405, the lessee fails so to modify the lease agreement within a reasonable time not exceeding 30 days, the lease contract lapses with respect to any deliveries affected.

§ 2A—407. **Irrevocable Promises: Finance Leases.**

(1) In the case of a finance lease that is not a consumer lease the lessee's promises under the lease contract become irrevocable and independent upon the lessee's acceptance of the goods.

(2) A promise that has become irrevocable and independent under subsection (1):

(a) is effective and enforceable between the parties, and by or against third parties including assignees of the parties, and

(b) is not subject to cancellation, termination, modification, repudiation, excuse, or substitution without the consent of the party to whom the promise runs.

(3) This section does not affect the validity under any other law of a covenant in any lease contract making the lessee's promises irrevocable and independent upon the lessee's acceptance of the goods.

As amended in 1990.

Part 5 **Default**

A. In General

§ 2A—501. **Default: Procedure.**

(1) Whether the lessor or the lessee is in default under a lease contract is determined by the lease agreement and this Article.

(2) If the lessor or the lessee is in default under the lease contract, the party seeking enforcement has rights and remedies as provided in this Article and, except as limited by this Article, as provided in the lease agreement.

(3) If the lessor or the lessee is in default under the lease contract, the party seeking enforcement may reduce the party's claim to judgment, or otherwise enforce the lease contract by self-help or any available judicial procedure or nonjudicial procedure, including administrative proceeding, arbitration, or the like, in accordance with this Article.

(4) Except as otherwise provided in Section 1–106(1) or this Article or the lease agreement, the rights and remedies referred to in subsections (2) and (3) are cumulative.

(5) If the lease agreement covers both real property and goods, the party seeking enforcement may proceed under this Part as to the goods, or under other applicable law as to both the real property and the goods in accordance with that party's rights and remedies in respect of the real property, in which case this Part does not apply.

As amended in 1990.

§ 2A—502. Notice After Default.

Except as otherwise provided in this Article or the lease agreement, the lessor or lessee in default under the lease contract is not entitled to notice of default or notice of enforcement from the other party to the lease agreement.

§ 2A—503. Modification or Impairment of Rights and Remedies.

(1) Except as otherwise provided in this Article, the lease agreement may include rights and remedies for default in addition to or in substitution for those provided in this Article and may limit or alter the measure of damages recoverable under this Article.

(2) Resort to a remedy provided under this Article or in the lease agreement is optional unless the remedy is expressly agreed to be exclusive. If circumstances cause an exclusive or limited remedy to fail of its essential purpose, or provision for an exclusive remedy is unconscionable, remedy may be had as provided in this Article.

(3) Consequential damages may be liquidated under Section 2A—504, or may otherwise be limited, altered, or excluded unless the limitation, alteration, or exclusion is unconscionable. Limitation, alteration, or exclusion of consequential damages for injury to the person in the case of consumer goods is prima facie unconscionable but limitation, alteration, or exclusion of damages where the loss is commercial is not prima facie unconscionable.

(4) Rights and remedies on default by the lessor or the lessee with respect to any obligation or promise collateral or ancillary to the lease contract are not impaired by this Article.

As amended in 1990.

§ 2A—504. Liquidation of Damages.

(1) Damages payable by either party for default, or any other act or omission, including indemnity for loss or diminution of anticipated tax benefits or loss or damage to lessor's residual interest, may be liquidated in the lease agreement but only at an amount or by a formula that is reasonable in light of the then anticipated harm caused by the default or other act or omission.

(2) If the lease agreement provides for liquidation of damages, and such provision does not comply with subsection (1), or such provision is an exclusive or limited remedy that circumstances cause to fail of its essential purpose, remedy may be had as provided in this Article.

(3) If the lessor justifiably withholds or stops delivery of goods because of the lessee's default or insolvency (Section 2A—525 or 2A—526), the lessee is entitled to restitution of any amount by which the sum of his [or her] payments exceeds:

(a) the amount to which the lessor is entitled by virtue of terms liquidating the lessor's damages in accordance with subsection (1); or

(b) in the absence of those terms, 20 percent of the then present value of the total rent the lessee was obligated to pay for the balance of the lease term, or, in the case of a consumer lease, the lesser of such amount or $500.

(4) A lessee's right to restitution under subsection (3) is subject to offset to the extent the lessor establishes:

(a) a right to recover damages under the provisions of this Article other than subsection (1); and

(b) the amount or value of any benefits received by the lessee directly or indirectly by reason of the lease contract.

§ 2A—505. Cancellation and Termination and Effect of Cancellation, Termination, Rescission, or Fraud on Rights and Remedies.

(1) On cancellation of the lease contract, all obligations that are still executory on both sides are discharged, but any right based on prior default or performance survives, and the cancelling party also retains any remedy for default of the whole lease contract or any unperformed balance.

(2) On termination of the lease contract, all obligations that are still executory on both sides are discharged but any right based on prior default or performance survives.

(3) Unless the contrary intention clearly appears, expressions of "cancellation," "rescission," or the like of the lease contract may not be construed as a renunciation or discharge of any claim in damages for an antecedent default.

(4) Rights and remedies for material misrepresentation or fraud include all rights and remedies available under this Article for default.

(5) Neither rescission nor a claim for rescission of the lease contract nor rejection or return of the goods may bar or be deemed inconsistent with a claim for damages or other right or remedy.

§ 2A—506. Statute of Limitations.

(1) An action for default under a lease contract, including breach of warranty or indemnity, must be commenced within 4 years after the cause of action accrued. By the original lease contract the parties may reduce the period of limitation to not less than one year.

(2) A cause of action for default accrues when the act or omission on which the default or breach of warranty is

based is or should have been discovered by the aggrieved party, or when the default occurs, whichever is later. A cause of action for indemnity accrues when the act or omission on which the claim for indemnity is based is or should have been discovered by the indemnified party, whichever is later.

(3) If an action commenced within the time limited by subsection (1) is so terminated as to leave available a remedy by another action for the same default or breach of warranty or indemnity, the other action may be commenced after the expiration of the time limited and within 6 months after the termination of the first action unless the termination resulted from voluntary discontinuance or from dismissal for failure or neglect to prosecute.

(4) This section does not alter the law on tolling of the statute of limitations nor does it apply to causes of action that have accrued before this Article becomes effective.

§ 2A—507. **Proof of Market Rent: Time and Place.**

(1) Damages based on market rent (Section 2A—519 or 2A—528) are determined according to the rent for the use of the goods concerned for a lease term identical to the remaining lease term of the original lease agreement and prevailing at the times specified in Sections 2A–519 and 2A–528.

(2) If evidence of rent for the use of the goods concerned for a lease term identical to the remaining lease term of the original lease agreement and prevailing at the times or places described in this Article is not readily available, the rent prevailing within any reasonable time before or after the time described or at any other place or for a different lease term which in commercial judgment or under usage of trade would serve as a reasonable substitute for the one described may be used, making any proper allowance for the difference, including the cost of transporting the goods to or from the other place.

(3) Evidence of a relevant rent prevailing at a time or place or for a lease term other than the one described in this Article offered by one party is not admissible unless and until he [or she] has given the other party notice the court finds sufficient to prevent unfair surprise.

(4) If the prevailing rent or value of any goods regularly leased in any established market is in issue, reports in official publications or trade journals or in newspapers or periodicals of general circulation published as the reports of that market are admissible in evidence. The circumstances of the preparation of the report may be shown to affect its weight but not its admissibility.

As amended in 1990.

B. Default by Lessor

§ 2A—508. **Lessee's Remedies.**

(1) If a lessor fails to deliver the goods in conformity to the lease contract (Section 2A—509) or repudiates the lease contract (Section 2A—402), or a lessee rightfully rejects the goods (Section 2A—509) or justifiably revokes acceptance of the goods (Section 2A—517), then with respect to any goods involved, and with respect to all of the goods if under an installment lease contract the value of the whole lease contract is substantially impaired (Section 2A—510), the lessor is in default under the lease contract and the lessee may:

(a) cancel the lease contract (Section 2A—505(1));

(b) recover so much of the rent and security as has been paid and is just under the circumstances;

(c) cover and recover damages as to all goods affected whether or not they have been identified to the lease contract (Sections 2A—518 and 2A—520), or recover damages for nondelivery (Sections 2A—519 and 2A—520);

(d) exercise any other rights or pursue any other remedies provided in the lease contract..

(2) If a lessor fails to deliver the goods in conformity to the lease contract or repudiates the lease contract, the lessee may also:

(a) if the goods have been identified, recover them (Section 2A—522); or

(b) in a proper case, obtain specific performance or replevy the goods (Section 2A—521).

(3) If a lessor is otherwise in default under a lease contract, the lessee may exercise the rights and pursue the remedies provided in the lease contract, which may include a right to cancel the lease, and in Section 2A–519(3).

(4) If a lessor has breached a warranty, whether express or implied, the lessee may recover damages (Section 2A—519(4)).

(5) On rightful rejection or justifiable revocation of acceptance, a lessee has a security interest in goods in the lessee's possession or control for any rent and security that has been paid and any expenses reasonably incurred in their inspection, receipt, transportation, and care and custody and may hold those goods and dispose of them in good faith and in a commercially reasonable manner, subject to Section 2A—527(5).

(6) Subject to the provisions of Section 2A—407, a lessee, on notifying the lessor of the lessee's intention to do so, may deduct all or any part of the damages resulting from any default under the lease contract from any part of the rent still due under the same lease contract.

As amended in 1990.

§ 2A—509. **Lessee's Rights on Improper Delivery; Rightful Rejection.**

(1) Subject to the provisions of Section 2A—510 on default in installment lease contracts, if the goods or the

tender or delivery fail in any respect to conform to the lease contract, the lessee may reject or accept the goods or accept any commercial unit or units and reject the rest of the goods.

(2) Rejection of goods is ineffective unless it is within a reasonable time after tender or delivery of the goods and the lessee seasonably notifies the lessor.

§ 2A—510. **Installment Lease Contracts: Rejection and Default.**

(1) Under an installment lease contract a lessee may reject any delivery that is nonconforming if the nonconformity substantially impairs the value of that delivery and cannot be cured or the nonconformity is a defect in the required documents; but if the nonconformity does not fall within subsection (2) and the lessor or the supplier gives adequate assurance of its cure, the lessee must accept that delivery.

(2) Whenever nonconformity or default with respect to one or more deliveries substantially impairs the value of the installment lease contract as a whole there is a default with respect to the whole. But, the aggrieved party reinstates the installment lease contract as a whole if the aggrieved party accepts a nonconforming delivery without seasonably notifying of cancellation or brings an action with respect only to past deliveries or demands performance as to future deliveries.

§ 2A—511. **Merchant Lessee's Duties as to Rightfully Rejected Goods.**

(1) Subject to any security interest of a lessee (Section 2A—508(5)), if a lessor or a supplier has no agent or place of business at the market of rejection, a merchant lessee, after rejection of goods in his [or her] possession or control, shall follow any reasonable instructions received from the lessor or the supplier with respect to the goods. In the absence of those instructions, a merchant lessee shall make reasonable efforts to sell, lease, or otherwise dispose of the goods for the lessor's account if they threaten to decline in value speedily. Instructions are not reasonable if on demand indemnity for expenses is not forthcoming.

(2) If a merchant lessee (subsection (1)) or any other lessee (Section 2A—512) disposes of goods, he [or she] is entitled to reimbursement either from the lessor or the supplier or out of the proceeds for reasonable expenses of caring for and disposing of the goods and, if the expenses include no disposition commission, to such commission as is usual in the trade, or if there is none, to a reasonable sum not exceeding 10 percent of the gross proceeds.

(3) In complying with this section or Section 2A—512, the lessee is held only to good faith. Good faith conduct hereunder is neither acceptance or conversion nor the basis of an action for damages.

(4) A purchaser who purchases in good faith from a lessee pursuant to this section or Section 2A—512 takes the goods free of any rights of the lessor and the supplier even though the lessee fails to comply with one or more of the requirements of this Article.

§ 2A—512. **Lessee's Duties as to Rightfully Rejected Goods.**

(1) Except as otherwise provided with respect to goods that threaten to decline in value speedily (Section 2A—511) and subject to any security interest of a lessee (Section 2A—508(5)):

(a) the lessee, after rejection of goods in the lessee's possession, shall hold them with reasonable care at the lessor's or the supplier's disposition for a reasonable time after the lessee's seasonable notification of rejection;

(b) if the lessor or the supplier gives no instructions within a reasonable time after notification of rejection, the lessee may store the rejected goods for the lessor's or the supplier's account or ship them to the lessor or the supplier or dispose of them for the lessor's or the supplier's account with reimbursement in the manner provided in Section 2A—511; but

(c) the lessee has no further obligations with regard to goods rightfully rejected.

(2) Action by the lessee pursuant to subsection (1) is not acceptance or conversion.

§ 2A—513. **Cure by Lessor of Improper Tender or Delivery; Replacement.**

(1) If any tender or delivery by the lessor or the supplier is rejected because nonconforming and the time for performance has not yet expired, the lessor or the supplier may seasonably notify the lessee of the lessor's or the supplier's intention to cure and may then make a conforming delivery within the time provided in the lease contract.

(2) If the lessee rejects a nonconforming tender that the lessor or the supplier had reasonable grounds to believe would be acceptable with or without money allowance, the lessor or the supplier may have a further reasonable time to substitute a conforming tender if he [or she] seasonably notifies the lessee.

§ 2A—514. **Waiver of Lessee's Objections.**

(1) In rejecting goods, a lessee's failure to state a particular defect that is ascertainable by reasonable inspection precludes the lessee from relying on the defect to justify rejection or to establish default:

(a) if, stated seasonably, the lessor or the supplier could have cured it (Section 2A—513); or

(b) between merchants if the lessor or the supplier after rejection has made a request in writing for a full and final written statement of all defects on which the lessee proposes to rely.

(2) A lessee's failure to reserve rights when paying rent or other consideration against documents precludes recovery of the payment for defects apparent on the face of the documents.

§ 2A—515. **Acceptance of Goods.**

(1) Acceptance of goods occurs after the lessee has had a reasonable opportunity to inspect the goods and

(a) the lessee signifies or acts with respect to the goods in a manner that signifies to the lessor or the supplier that the goods are conforming or that the lessee will take or retain them in spite of their nonconformity; or

(b) the lessee fails to make an effective rejection of the goods (Section 2A—509(2)).

(2) Acceptance of a part of any commercial unit is acceptance of that entire unit.

§ 2A—516. **Effect of Acceptance of Goods; Notice of Default; Burden of Establishing Default after Acceptance; Notice of Claim or Litigation to Person Answerable Over.**

(1) A lessee must pay rent for any goods accepted in accordance with the lease contract, with due allowance for goods rightfully rejected or not delivered.

(2) A lessee's acceptance of goods precludes rejection of the goods accepted. In the case of a finance lease, if made with knowledge of a nonconformity, acceptance cannot be revoked because of it. In any other case, if made with knowledge of a nonconformity, acceptance cannot be revoked because of it unless the acceptance was on the reasonable assumption that the nonconformity would be seasonably cured. Acceptance does not of itself impair any other remedy provided by this Article or the lease agreement for nonconformity.

(3) If a tender has been accepted:

(a) within a reasonable time after the lessee discovers or should have discovered any default, the lessee shall notify the lessor and the supplier, if any, or be barred from any remedy against the party notified;

(b) except in the case of a consumer lease, within a reasonable time after the lessee receives notice of litigation for infringement or the like (Section 2A—211) the lessee shall notify the lessor or be barred from any remedy over for liability established by the litigation; and

(c) the burden is on the lessee to establish any default.

(4) If a lessee is sued for breach of a warranty or other obligation for which a lessor or a supplier is answerable over the following apply:

(a) The lessee may give the lessor or the supplier, or both, written notice of the litigation. If the notice states that the person notified may come in and defend and that if the person notified does not do so that person will be bound in any action against that person by the lessee by any determination of fact common to the two litigations, then unless the person notified after seasonable receipt of the notice does come in and defend that person is so bound.

(b) The lessor or the supplier may demand in writing that the lessee turn over control of the litigation including settlement if the claim is one for infringement or the like (Section 2A—211) or else be barred from any remedy over. If the demand states that the lessor or the supplier agrees to bear all expense and to satisfy any adverse judgment, then unless the lessee after seasonable receipt of the demand does turn over control the lessee is so barred.

(5) Subsections (3) and (4) apply to any obligation of a lessee to hold the lessor or the supplier harmless against infringement or the like (Section 2A—211).

As amended in 1990.

§ 2A—517. **Revocation of Acceptance of Goods.**

(1) A lessee may revoke acceptance of a lot or commercial unit whose nonconformity substantially impairs its value to the lessee if the lessee has accepted it:

(a) except in the case of a finance lease, on the reasonable assumption that its nonconformity would be cured and it has not been seasonably cured; or

(b) without discovery of the nonconformity if the lessee's acceptance was reasonably induced either by the lessor's assurances or, except in the case of a finance lease, by the difficulty of discovery before acceptance.

(2) Except in the case of a finance lease that is not a consumer lease, a lessee may revoke acceptance of a lot or commercial unit if the lessor defaults under the lease contract and the default substantially impairs the value of that lot or commercial unit to the lessee.

(3) If the lease agreement so provides, the lessee may revoke acceptance of a lot or commercial unit because of other defaults by the lessor.

(4) Revocation of acceptance must occur within a reasonable time after the lessee discovers or should have discovered the ground for it and before any substantial change in condition of the goods which is not caused by the nonconformity. Revocation is not effective until the lessee notifies the lessor.

(5) A lessee who so revokes has the same rights and duties with regard to the goods involved as if the lessee had rejected them.

As amended in 1990.

§ 2A—518. **Cover; Substitute Goods.**

(1) After a default by a lessor under the lease contract of the type described in Section 2A—508(1), or, if agreed,

after other default by the lessor, the lessee may cover by making any purchase or lease of or contract to purchase or lease goods in substitution for those due from the lessor.

(2) Except as otherwise provided with respect to damages liquidated in the lease agreement (Section 2A—504) or otherwise determined pursuant to agreement of the parties (Sections 1—102(3) and 2A—503), if a lessee's cover is by lease agreement substantially similar to the original lease agreement and the new lease agreement is made in good faith and in a commercially reasonable manner, the lessee may recover from the lessor as damages (i) the present value, as of the date of the commencement of the term of the new lease agreement, of the rent under the new lease agreement applicable to that period of the new lease term which is comparable to the then remaining term of the original lease agreement minus the present value as of the same date of the total rent for the then remaining lease term of the original lease agreement, and (ii) any incidental or consequential damages, less expenses saved in consequence of the lessor's default.

(3) If a lessee's cover is by lease agreement that for any reason does not qualify for treatment under subsection (2), or is by purchase or otherwise, the lessee may recover from the lessor as if the lessee had elected not to cover and Section 2A—519 governs.

As amended in 1990.

§ 2A—519. Lessee's Damages for Non-Delivery, Repudiation, Default, and Breach of Warranty in Regard to Accepted Goods.

(1) Except as otherwise provided with respect to damages liquidated in the lease agreement (Section 2A—504) or otherwise determined pursuant to agreement of the parties (Sections 1—102(3) and 2A—503), if a lessee elects not to cover or a lessee elects to cover and the cover is by lease agreement that for any reason does not qualify for treatment under Section 2A—518(2), or is by purchase or otherwise, the measure of damages for non-delivery or repudiation by the lessor or for rejection or revocation of acceptance by the lessee is the present value, as of the date of the default, of the then market rent minus the present value as of the same date of the original rent, computed for the remaining lease term of the original lease agreement, together with incidental and consequential damages, less expenses saved in consequence of the lessor's default.

(2) Market rent is to be determined as of the place for tender or, in cases of rejection after arrival or revocation of acceptance, as of the place of arrival.

(3) Except as otherwise agreed, if the lessee has accepted goods and given notification (Section 2A—516(3)), the measure of damages for non-conforming tender or delivery or other default by a lessor is the loss resulting in the ordinary course of events from the lessor's default as determined in any manner that is reasonable together with incidental and consequential damages, less expenses saved in consequence of the lessor's default.

(4) Except as otherwise agreed, the measure of damages for breach of warranty is the present value at the time and place of acceptance of the difference between the value of the use of the goods accepted and the value if they had been as warranted for the lease term, unless special circumstances show proximate damages of a different amount, together with incidental and consequential damages, less expenses saved in consequence of the lessor's default or breach of warranty.

As amended in 1990.

§ 2A—520. Lessee's Incidental and Consequential Damages.

(1) Incidental damages resulting from a lessor's default include expenses reasonably incurred in inspection, receipt, transportation, and care and custody of goods rightfully rejected or goods the acceptance of which is justifiably revoked, any commercially reasonable charges, expenses or commissions in connection with effecting cover, and any other reasonable expense incident to the default.

(2) Consequential damages resulting from a lessor's default include:

(a) any loss resulting from general or particular requirements and needs of which the lessor at the time of contracting had reason to know and which could not reasonably be prevented by cover or otherwise; and

(b) injury to person or property proximately resulting from any breach of warranty.

§ 2A—521. Lessee's Right to Specific Performance or Replevin.

(1) Specific performance may be decreed if the goods are unique or in other proper circumstances.

(2) A decree for specific performance may include any terms and conditions as to payment of the rent, damages, or other relief that the court deems just.

(3) A lessee has a right of replevin, detinue, sequestration, claim and delivery, or the like for goods identified to the lease contract if after reasonable effort the lessee is unable to effect cover for those goods or the circumstances reasonably indicate that the effort will be unavailing.

§ 2A—522. Lessee's Right to Goods on Lessor's Insolvency.

(1) Subject to subsection (2) and even though the goods have not been shipped, a lessee who has paid a part or all of the rent and security for goods identified to a lease contract

(Section 2A—217) on making and keeping good a tender of any unpaid portion of the rent and security due under the lease contract may recover the goods identified from the lessor if the lessor becomes insolvent within 10 days after receipt of the first installment of rent and security.

(2) A lessee acquires the right to recover goods identified to a lease contract only if they conform to the lease contract.

C. Default by Lessee

§ 2A—523. **Lessor's Remedies.**

(1) If a lessee wrongfully rejects or revokes acceptance of goods or fails to make a payment when due or repudiates with respect to a part or the whole, then, with respect to any goods involved, and with respect to all of the goods if under an installment lease contract the value of the whole lease contract is substantially impaired (Section 2A—510), the lessee is in default under the lease contract and the lessor may:

(a) cancel the lease contract (Section 2A—505(1));

(b) proceed respecting goods not identified to the lease contract (Section 2A—524);

(c) withhold delivery of the goods and take possession of goods previously delivered (Section 2A—525);

(d) stop delivery of the goods by any bailee (Section 2A—526);

(e) dispose of the goods and recover damages (Section 2A—527), or retain the goods and recover damages (Section 2A—528), or in a proper case recover rent (Section 2A—529)

(f) exercise any other rights or pursue any other remedies provided in the lease contract.

(2) If a lessor does not fully exercise a right or obtain a remedy to which the lessor is entitled under subsection (1), the lessor may recover the loss resulting in the ordinary course of events from the lessee's default as determined in any reasonable manner, together with incidental damages, less expenses saved in consequence of the lessee's default.

(3) If a lessee is otherwise in default under a lease contract, the lessor may exercise the rights and pursue the remedies provided in the lease contract, which may include a right to cancel the lease. In addition, unless otherwise provided in the lease contract:

(a) if the default substantially impairs the value of the lease contract to the lessor, the lessor may exercise the rights and pursue the remedies provided in subsections (1) or (2); or

(b) if the default does not substantially impair the value of the lease contract to the lessor, the lessor may recover as provided in subsection (2).

As amended in 1990.

§ 2A—524. **Lessor's Right to Identify Goods to Lease Contract.**

(1) After default by the lessee under the lease contract of the type described in Section 2A—523(1) or 2A—523(3)(a) or, if agreed, after other default by the lessee, the lessor may:

(a) identify to the lease contract conforming goods not already identified if at the time the lessor learned of the default they were in the lessor's or the supplier's possession or control; and

(b) dispose of goods (Section 2A—527(1)) that demonstrably have been intended for the particular lease contract even though those goods are unfinished.

(2) If the goods are unfinished, in the exercise of reasonable commercial judgment for the purposes of avoiding loss and of effective realization, an aggrieved lessor or the supplier may either complete manufacture and wholly identify the goods to the lease contract or cease manufacture and lease, sell, or otherwise dispose of the goods for scrap or salvage value or proceed in any other reasonable manner.

As amended in 1990.

§ 2A—525. **Lessor's Right to Possession of Goods.**

(1) If a lessor discovers the lessee to be insolvent, the lessor may refuse to deliver the goods.

(2) After a default by the lessee under the lease contract of the type described in Section 2A—523(1) or 2A—523(3)(a) or, if agreed, after other default by the lessee, the lessor has the right to take possession of the goods. If the lease contract so provides, the lessor may require the lessee to assemble the goods and make them available to the lessor at a place to be designated by the lessor which is reasonably convenient to both parties. Without removal, the lessor may render unusable any goods employed in trade or business, and may dispose of goods on the lessee's premises (Section 2A—527).

(3) The lessor may proceed under subsection (2) without judicial process if that can be done without breach of the peace or the lessor may proceed by action.

As amended in 1990.

§ 2A—526. **Lessor's Stoppage of Delivery in Transit or Otherwise.**

(1) A lessor may stop delivery of goods in the possession of a carrier or other bailee if the lessor discovers the lessee to be insolvent and may stop delivery of carload, truckload, planeload, or larger shipments of express or freight if the lessee repudiates or fails to make a payment due before delivery, whether for rent, security or otherwise under the lease contract, or for any other reason the lessor has a right to withhold or take possession of the goods.

(2) In pursuing its remedies under subsection (1), the lessor may stop delivery until

(a) receipt of the goods by the lessee;

(b) acknowledgment to the lessee by any bailee of the goods, except a carrier, that the bailee holds the goods for the lessee; or

(c) such an acknowledgment to the lessee by a carrier via reshipment or as warehouseman.

(3) (a) To stop delivery, a lessor shall so notify as to enable the bailee by reasonable diligence to prevent delivery of the goods.

(b) After notification, the bailee shall hold and deliver the goods according to the directions of the lessor, but the lessor is liable to the bailee for any ensuing charges or damages.

(c) A carrier who has issued a nonnegotiable bill of lading is not obliged to obey a notification to stop received from a person other than the consignor.

§ 2A—527. **Lessor's Rights to Dispose of Goods.**

(1) After a default by a lessee under the lease contract of the type described in Section 2A—523(1) or 2A–523(3)(a) or after the lessor refuses to deliver or takes possession of goods (Section 2A—525 or 2A—526), or, if agreed, after other default by a lessee, the lessor may dispose of the goods concerned or the undelivered balance thereof by lease, sale, or otherwise.

(2) Except as otherwise provided with respect to damages liquidated in the lease agreement (Section 2A—504) or otherwise determined pursuant to agreement of the parties (Sections 1—102(3) and 2A—503), if the disposition is by lease agreement substantially similar to the original lease agreement and the new lease agreement is made in good faith and in a commercially reasonable manner, the lessor may recover from the lessee as damages (i) accrued and unpaid rent as of the date of the commencement of the term of the new lease agreement, (ii) the present value, as of the same date, of the total rent for the then remaining lease term of the original lease agreement minus the present value, as of the same date, of the rent under the new lease agreement applicable to that period of the new lease term which is comparable to the then remaining term of the original lease agreement, and (iii) any incidental damages allowed under Section 2A—530, less expenses saved in consequence of the lessee's default.

(3) If the lessor's disposition is by lease agreement that for any reason does not qualify for treatment under subsection (2), or is by sale or otherwise, the lessor may recover from the lessee as if the lessor had elected not to dispose of the goods and Section 2A—528 governs.

(4) A subsequent buyer or lessee who buys or leases from the lessor in good faith for value as a result of a disposition under this section takes the goods free of the original lease contract and any rights of the original lessee even though the lessor fails to comply with one or more of the requirements of this Article.

(5) The lessor is not accountable to the lessee for any profit made on any disposition. A lessee who has rightfully rejected or justifiably revoked acceptance shall account to the lessor for any excess over the amount of the lessee's security interest (Section 2A—508(5)).

As amended in 1990.

§ 2A—528. **Lessor's Damages for Non-acceptance, Failure to Pay, Repudiation, or Other Default.**

(1) Except as otherwise provided with respect to damages liquidated in the lease agreement (Section 2A—504) or otherwise determined pursuant to agreement of the parties (Section 1—102(3) and 2A—503), if a lessor elects to retain the goods or a lessor elects to dispose of the goods and the disposition is by lease agreement that for anyreason does not qualify for treatment under Section 2A—527(2), or is by sale or otherwise, the lessor may recover from the lessee as damages for a default of the type described in Section 2A—523(1) or 2A—523(3)(a), or if agreed, for other default of the lessee, (i) accrued and unpaid rent as of the date of the default if the lessee has never taken possession of the goods, or, if the lessee has taken possession of the goods, as of the date the lessor repossesses the goods or an earlier date on which the lessee makes a tender of the goods to the lessor, (ii) the present value as of the date determined under clause (i) of the total rent for the then remaining lease term of the original lease agreement minus the present value as of the same date of the market rent as the place where the goods are located computed for the same lease term, and (iii) any incidental damages allowed under Section 2A—530, less expenses saved in consequence of the lessee's default.

(2) If the measure of damages provided in subsection (1) is inadequate to put a lessor in as good a position as performance would have, the measure of damages is the present value of the profit, including reasonable overhead, the lessor would have made from full performance by the lessee, together with any incidental damages allowed under Section 2A—530, due allowance for costs reasonably incurred and due credit for payments or proceeds of disposition.

As amended in 1990.

§ 2A—529. **Lessor's Action for the Rent.**

(1) After default by the lessee under the lease contract of the type described in Section 2A—523(1) or 2A—523(3)(a) or, if agreed, after other default by the lessee, if the lessor complies with subsection (2), the lessor may recover from the lessee as damages:

(a) for goods accepted by the lessee and not repossessed by or tendered to the lessor, and for conforming goods lost or damaged within a commercially reasonable time after risk of loss passes to the lessee (Section 2A—219), (i) accrued and unpaid rent as of the date of entry of judgment in favor of the lessor (ii) the present value as of the same date of the rent for the then remaining lease term of the lease agreement, and (iii) any incidental damages allowed under Section 2A—530, less expenses saved in consequence of the lessee's default; and

(b) for goods identified to the lease contract if the lessor is unable after reasonable effort to dispose of them at a reasonable price or the circumstances reasonably indicate that effort will be unavailing, (i) accrued and unpaid rent as of the date of entry of judgment in favor of the lessor, (ii) the present value as of the same date of the rent for the then remaining lease term of the lease agreement, and (iii) any incidental damages allowed under Section 2A—530, less expenses saved in consequence of the lessee's default.

(2) Except as provided in subsection (3), the lessor shall hold for the lessee for the remaining lease term of the lease agreement any goods that have been identified to the lease contract and are in the lessor's control.

(3) The lessor may dispose of the goods at any time before collection of the judgment for damages obtained pursuant to subsection (1). If the disposition is before the end of the remaining lease term of the lease agreement, the lessor's recovery against the lessee for damages is governed by Section 2A—527 or Section 2A—528, and the lessor will cause an appropriate credit to be provided against a judgment for damages to the extent that the amount of the judgment exceeds the recovery available pursuant to Section 2A—527 or 2A—528.

(4) Payment of the judgment for damages obtained pursuant to subsection (1) entitles the lessee to the use and possession of the goods not then disposed of for the remaining lease term of and in accordance with the lease agreement.

(5) After default by the lessee under the lease contract of the type described in Section 2A—523(1) or Section 2A—523(3)(a) or, if agreed, after other default by the lessee, a lessor who is held not entitled to rent under this section must nevertheless be awarded damages for non-acceptance under Sections 2A—527 and 2A—528.

As amended in 1990.

§ 2A—530. **Lessor's Incidental Damages.**

Incidental damages to an aggrieved lessor include any commercially reasonable charges, expenses, or commissions incurred in stopping delivery, in the transportation, care and custody of goods after the lessee's default, in connection with return or disposition of the goods, or otherwise resulting from the default.

§ 2A—531. **Standing to Sue Third Parties for Injury to Goods.**

(1) If a third party so deals with goods that have been identified to a lease contract as to cause actionable injury to a party to the lease contract (a) the lessor has a right of action against the third party, and (b) the lessee also has a right of action against the third party if the lessee:

(i) has a security interest in the goods;

(ii) has an insurable interest in the goods; or

(iii) bears the risk of loss under the lease contract or has since the injury assumed that risk as against the lessor and the goods have been converted or destroyed.

(2) If at the time of the injury the party plaintiff did not bear the risk of loss as against the other party to the lease contract and there is no arrangement between them for disposition of the recovery, his [or her] suit or settlement, subject to his [or her] own interest, is as a fiduciary for the other party to the lease contract.

(3) Either party with the consent of the other may sue for the benefit of whom it may concern.

§ 2A—532. **Lessor's Rights to Residual Interest.**

In addition to any other recovery permitted by this Article or other law, the lessor may recover from the lessee an amount that will fully compensate the lessor for any loss of or damage to the lessor's residual interest in the goods caused by the default of the lessee.

As added in 1990.

Revised Article 3
NEGOTIABLE INSTRUMENTS

Part 1 General Provisions and Definitions

§ 3—101. **Short Title.**

This Article may be cited as Uniform Commercial Code—Negotiable Instruments.

§ 3—102. **Subject Matter.**

(a) This Article applies to negotiable instruments. It does not apply to money, to payment orders governed by Article 4A, or to securities governed by Article 8.

(b) If there is conflict between this Article and Article 4 or 9, Articles 4 and 9 govern.

(c) Regulations of the Board of Governors of the Federal Reserve System and operating circulars of the Federal Reserve Banks supersede any inconsistent provision of this Article to the extent of the inconsistency.

§ 3—103. **Definitions.**

(a) In this Article:

(1) "Acceptor" means a drawee who has accepted a draft.

(2) "Drawee" means a person ordered in a draft to make payment.

(3) "Drawer" means a person who signs or is identified in a draft as a person ordering payment.

(4) "Good faith" means honesty in fact and the observance of reasonable commercial standards of fair dealing.

(5) "Maker" means a person who signs or is identified in a note as a person undertaking to pay.

(6) "Order" means a written instruction to pay money signed by the person giving the instruction. The instruction may be addressed to any person, including the person giving the instruction, or to one or more persons jointly or in the alternative but not in succession. An authorization to pay is not an order unless the person authorized to pay is also instructed to pay.

(7) "Ordinary care" in the case of a person engaged in business means observance of reasonable commercial standards, prevailing in the area in which the person is located, with respect to the business in which the person is engaged. In the case of a bank that takes an instrument for processing for collection or payment by automated means, reasonable commercial standards do not require the bank to examine the instrument if the failure to examine does not violate the bank's prescribed procedures and the bank's procedures do not vary unreasonably from general banking usage not disapproved by this Article or Article 4.

(8) "Party" means a party to an instrument.

(9) "Promise" means a written undertaking to pay money signed by the person undertaking to pay. An acknowledgment of an obligation by the obligor is not a promise unless the obligor also undertakes to pay the obligation.

(10) "Prove" with respect to a fact means to meet the burden of establishing the fact (Section 1—201(8)).

(11) "Remitter" means a person who purchases an instrument from its issuer if the instrument is payable to an identified person other than the purchaser.

(b);(c) [Other definitions' section references deleted.]

(d) In addition, Article 1 contains general definitions and principles of construction and interpretation applicable throughout this Article.

§ 3—104. **Negotiable Instrument.**

(a) Except as provided in subsections (c) and (d), "negotiable instrument" means an unconditional promise or order to pay a fixed amount of money, with or without interest or other charges described in the promise or order, if it:

(1) is payable to bearer or to order at the time it is issued or first comes into possession of a holder;

(2) is payable on demand or at a definite time; and

(3) does not state any other undertaking or instruction by the person promising or ordering payment to do any act in addition to the payment of money, but the promise or order may contain (i) an undertaking or power to give, maintain, or protect collateral to secure payment, (ii) an authorization or power to the holder to confess judgment or realize on or dispose of collateral, or (iii) a waiver of the benefit of any law intended for the advantage or protection of an obligor.

(b) "Instrument" means a negotiable instrument.

(c) An order that meets all of the requirements of subsection (a), except paragraph (1), and otherwise falls within the definition of "check" in subsection (f) is a negotiable instrument and a check.

(d) A promise or order other than a check is not an instrument if, at the time it is issued or first comes into possession of a holder, it contains a conspicuous statement, however expressed, to the effect that the promise or order is not negotiable or is not an instrument governed by this Article.

(e) An instrument is a "note" if it is a promise and is a "draft" if it is an order. If an instrument falls within the definition of both "note" and "draft," a person entitled to enforce the instrument may treat it as either.

(f) "Check" means (i) a draft, other than a documentary draft, payable on demand and drawn on a bank or (ii) a cashier's check or teller's check. An instrument may be a check even though it is described on its face by another term, such as "money order."

(g) "Cashier's check" means a draft with respect to which the drawer and drawee are the same bank or branches of the same bank.

(h) "Teller's check" means a draft drawn by a bank (i) on another bank, or (ii) payable at or through a bank.

(i) "Traveler's check" means an instrument that (i) is payable on demand, (ii) is drawn on or payable at or through a bank, (iii) is designated by the term "traveler's check" or by a substantially similar term, and (iv) requires, as a condition to payment, a countersignature by a person whose specimen signature appears on the instrument.

(j) "Certificate of deposit" means an instrument containing an acknowledgment by a bank that a sum of money has been received by the bank and a promise by the bank to repay the sum of money. A certificate of deposit is a note of the bank.

§ 3—105. **Issue of Instrument.**

(a) "Issue" means the first delivery of an instrument by the maker or drawer, whether to a holder or nonholder, for the purpose of giving rights on the instrument to any person.

(b) An unissued instrument, or an unissued incomplete instrument that is completed, is binding on the maker or drawer, but nonissuance is a defense. An instrument that is conditionally issued or is issued for a special purpose is binding on the maker or drawer, but failure of the condition or special purpose to be fulfilled is a defense.

(c) "Issuer" applies to issued and unissued instruments and means a maker or drawer of an instrument.

§ 3—106. Unconditional Promise or Order.

(a) Except as provided in this section, for the purposes of Section 3—104(a), a promise or order is unconditional unless it states (i) an express condition to payment, (ii) that the promise or order is subject to or governed by another writing, or (iii) that rights or obligations with respect to the promise or order are stated in another writing. A reference to another writing does not of itself make the promise or order conditional.

(b) A promise or order is not made conditional (i) by a reference to another writing for a statement of rights with respect to collateral, prepayment, or acceleration, or (ii) because payment is limited to resort to a particular fund or source.

(c) If a promise or order requires, as a condition to payment, a countersignature by a person whose specimen signature appears on the promise or order, the condition does not make the promise or order conditional for the purposes of Section 3—104(a). If the person whose specimen signature appears on an instrument fails to countersign the instrument, the failure to countersign is a defense to the obligation of the issuer, but the failure does not prevent a transferee of the instrument from becoming a holder of the instrument.

(d) If a promise or order at the time it is issued or first comes into possession of a holder contains a statement, required by applicable statutory or administrative law, to the effect that the rights of a holder or transferee are subject to claims or defenses that the issuer could assert against the original payee, the promise or order is not thereby made conditional for the purposes of Section 3—104(a); but if the promise or order is an instrument, there cannot be a holder in due course of the instrument.

§ 3—107. Instrument Payable in Foreign Money.

Unless the instrument otherwise provides, an instrument that states the amount payable in foreign money may be paid in the foreign money or in an equivalent amount in dollars calculated by using the current bank-offered spot rate at the place of payment for the purchase of dollars on the day on which the instrument is paid.

§ 3—108. Payable on Demand or at Definite Time.

(a) A promise or order is "payable on demand" if it (i) states that it is payable on demand or at sight, or otherwise indicates that it is payable at the will of the holder, or (ii) does not state any time of payment.

(b) A promise or order is "payable at a definite time" if it is payable on elapse of a definite period of time after sight or acceptance or at a fixed date or dates or at a time or times readily ascertainable at the time the promise or order is issued, subject to rights of (i) prepayment, (ii) acceleration, (iii) extension at the option of the holder, or (iv) extension to a further definite time at the option of the maker or acceptor or automatically upon or after a specified act or event.

(c) If an instrument, payable at a fixed date, is also payable upon demand made before the fixed date, the instrument is payable on demand until the fixed date and, if demand for payment is not made before that date, becomes payable at a definite time on the fixed date.

§ 3—109. Payable to Bearer or to Order.

(a) A promise or order is payable to bearer if it:

(1) states that it is payable to bearer or to the order of bearer or otherwise indicates that the person in possession of the promise or order is entitled to payment;

(2) does not state a payee; or

(3) states that it is payable to or to the order of cash or otherwise indicates that it is not payable to an identified person.

(b) A promise or order that is not payable to bearer is payable to order if it is payable (i) to the order of an identified person or (ii) to an identified person or order. A promise or order that is payable to order is payable to the identified person.

(c) An instrument payable to bearer may become payable to an identified person if it is specially indorsed pursuant to Section 3—205(a). An instrument payable to an identified person may become payable to bearer if it is indorsed in blank pursuant to Section 3—205(b).

§ 3—110. Identification of Person to Whom Instrument Is Payable.

(a) The person to whom an instrument is initially payable is determined by the intent of the person, whether or not authorized, signing as, or in the name or behalf of, the issuer of the instrument. The instrument is payable to the person intended by the signer even if that person is identified in the instrument by a name or other identification that is not that of the intended person. If more than one person signs in the name or behalf of the issuer of an instrument and all the signers do not intend the same person as payee, the instrument is payable to any person intended by one or more of the signers.

(b) If the signature of the issuer of an instrument is made by automated means, such as a check-writing machine, the payee of the instrument is determined by the intent of the person who supplied the name or identification of the payee, whether or not authorized to do so.

(c) A person to whom an instrument is payable may be identified in any way, including by name, identifying number, office, or account number. For the purpose of determining the holder of an instrument, the following rules apply:

(1) If an instrument is payable to an account and the account is identified only by number, the instrument is payable to the person to whom the account is payable. If an instrument is payable to an account identified by number and by the name of a person, the instrument is payable to the named person, whether or not that person is the owner of the account identified by number.

(2) If an instrument is payable to:

(i) a trust, an estate, or a person described as trustee or representative of a trust or estate, the instrument is payable to the trustee, the representative, or a successor of either, whether or not the beneficiary or estate is also named;

(ii) a person described as agent or similar representative of a named or identified person, the instrument is payable to the represented person, the representative, or a successor of the representative;

(iii) a fund or organization that is not a legal entity, the instrument is payable to a representative of the members of the fund or organization; or

(iv) an office or to a person described as holding an office, the instrument is payable to the named person, the incumbent of the office, or a successor to the incumbent.

(d) If an instrument is payable to two or more persons alternatively, it is payable to any of them and may be negotiated, discharged, or enforced by any or all of them in possession of the instrument. If an instrument is payable to two or more persons not alternatively, it is payable to all of them and may be negotiated, discharged, or enforced only by all of them. If an instrument payable to two or more persons is ambiguous as to whether it is payable to the persons alternatively, the instrument is payable to the persons alternatively.

§ 3—111. Place of Payment.

Except as otherwise provided for items in Article 4, an instrument is payable at the place of payment stated in the instrument. If no place of payment is stated, an instrument is payable at the address of the drawee or maker stated in the instrument. If no address is stated, the place of payment is the place of business of the drawee or maker. If a drawee or maker has more than one place of business, the place of payment is any place of business of the drawee or maker chosen by the person entitled to enforce the instrument. If the drawee or maker has no place of business, the place of payment is the residence of the drawee or maker.

§ 3—112. Interest.

(a) Unless otherwise provided in the instrument, (i) an instrument is not payable with interest, and (ii) interest on an interest-bearing instrument is payable from the date of the instrument.

(b) Interest may be stated in an instrument as a fixed or variable amount of money or it may be expressed as a fixed or variable rate or rates. The amount or rate of interest may be stated or described in the instrument in any manner and may require reference to information not contained in the instrument. If an instrument provides for interest, but the amount of interest payable cannot be ascertained from the description, interest is payable at the judgment rate in effect at the place of payment of the instrument and at the time interest first accrues.

§ 3—113. Date of Instrument.

(a) An instrument may be antedated or postdated. The date stated determines the time of payment if the instrument is payable at a fixed period after date. Except as provided in Section 4—401(c), an instrument payable on demand is not payable before the date of the instrument.

(b) If an instrument is undated, its date is the date of its issue or, in the case of an unissued instrument, the date it first comes into possession of a holder.

§ 3—114. Contradictory Terms of Instrument.

If an instrument contains contradictory terms, typewritten terms prevail over printed terms, handwritten terms prevail over both, and words prevail over numbers.

§ 3—115. Incomplete Instrument.

(a) "Incomplete instrument" means a signed writing, whether or not issued by the signer, the contents of which show at the time of signing that it is incomplete but that the signer intended it to be completed by the addition of words or numbers.

(b) Subject to subsection (c), if an incomplete instrument is an instrument under Section 3—104, it may be enforced according to its terms if it is not completed, or according to its terms as augmented by completion. If an incomplete instrument is not an instrument under Section 3—104, but, after completion, the requirements of Section 3—104 are met, the instrument may be enforced according to its terms as augmented by completion.

(c) If words or numbers are added to an incomplete instrument without authority of the signer, there is an alteration of the incomplete instrument under Section 3—407.

(d) The burden of establishing that words or numbers were added to an incomplete instrument without authority of the signer is on the person asserting the lack of authority.

§ 3—116. Joint and Several Liability; Contribution.

(a) Except as otherwise provided in the instrument, two or more persons who have the same liability on an instrument as makers, drawers, acceptors, indorsers who indorse as joint payees, or anomalous indorsers are jointly and severally liable in the capacity in which they sign.

(b) Except as provided in Section 3—419(e) or by agreement of the affected parties, a party having joint and several liability who pays the instrument is entitled to receive from any party having the same joint and several liability contribution in accordance with applicable law.

(c) Discharge of one party having joint and several liability by a person entitled to enforce the instrument does not affect the right under subsection (b) of a party having the same joint and several liability to receive contribution from the party discharged.

§ 3—117. Other Agreements Affecting Instrument.

Subject to applicable law regarding exclusion of proof of contemporaneous or previous agreements, the obligation of a party to an instrument to pay the instrument may be modified, supplemented, or nullified by a separate agreement of the obligor and a person entitled to enforce the instrument, if the instrument is issued or the obligation is incurred in reliance on the agreement or as part of the same transaction giving rise to the agreement. To the extent an obligation is modified, supplemented, or nullified by an agreement under this section, the agreement is a defense to the obligation.

§ 3—118. Statute of Limitations.

(a) Except as provided in subsection (e), an action to enforce the obligation of a party to pay a note payable at a definite time must be commenced within six years after the due date or dates stated in the note or, if a due date is accelerated, within six years after the accelerated due date.

(b) Except as provided in subsection (d) or (e), if demand for payment is made to the maker of a note payable on demand, an action to enforce the obligation of a party to pay the note must be commenced within six years after the demand. If no demand for payment is made to the maker, an action to enforce the note is barred if neither principal nor interest on the note has been paid for a continuous period of 10 years.

(c) Except as provided in subsection (d), an action to enforce the obligation of a party to an unaccepted draft to pay the draft must be commenced within three years after dishonor of the draft or 10 years after the date of the draft, whichever period expires first.

(d) An action to enforce the obligation of the acceptor of a certified check or the issuer of a teller's check, cashier's check, or traveler's check must be commenced within three years after demand for payment is made to the acceptor or issuer, as the case may be.

(e) An action to enforce the obligation of a party to a certificate of deposit to pay the instrument must be commenced within six years after demand for payment is made to the maker, but if the instrument states a due date and the maker is not required to pay before that date, the six-year period begins when a demand for payment is in effect and the due date has passed.

(f) An action to enforce the obligation of a party to pay an accepted draft, other than a certified check, must be commenced (i) within six years after the due date or dates stated in the draft or acceptance if the obligation of the acceptor is payable at a definite time, or (ii) within six years after the date of the acceptance if the obligation of the acceptor is payable on demand.

(g) Unless governed by other law regarding claims for indemnity or contribution, an action (i) for conversion of an instrument, for money had and received, or like action based on conversion, (ii) for breach of warranty, or (iii) to enforce an obligation, duty, or right arising under this Article and not governed by this section must be commenced within three years after the [cause of action] accrues.

§ 3—119. Notice of Right to Defend Action.

In an action for breach of an obligation for which a third person is answerable over pursuant to this Article or Article 4, the defendant may give the third person written notice of the litigation, and the person notified may then give similar notice to any other person who is answerable over. If the notice states (i) that the person notified may come in and defend and (ii) that failure to do so will bind the person notified in an action later brought by the person giving the notice as to any determination of fact common to the two litigations, the person notified is so bound unless after seasonable receipt of the notice the person notified does come in and defend.

Part 2 Negotiation, Transfer, and Indorsement

§ 3—201. Negotiation.

(a) "Negotiation" means a transfer of possession, whether voluntary or involuntary, of an instrument by a person other than the issuer to a person who thereby becomes its holder.

(b) Except for negotiation by a remitter, if an instrument is payable to an identified person, negotiation requires transfer of possession of the instrument and its indorsement by the holder. If an instrument is payable to bearer, it may be negotiated by transfer of possession alone.

§ 3—202. Negotiation Subject to Rescission.

(a) Negotiation is effective even if obtained (i) from an infant, a corporation exceeding its powers, or a person without capacity, (ii) by fraud, duress, or mistake, or (iii) in breach of duty or as part of an illegal transaction.

(b) To the extent permitted by other law, negotiation may be rescinded or may be subject to other remedies, but those remedies may not be asserted against a subsequent holder in due course or a person paying the instrument in good faith and without knowledge of facts that are a basis for rescission or other remedy.

§ 3—203. Transfer of Instrument; Rights Acquired by Transfer.

(a) An instrument is transferred when it is delivered by a person other than its issuer for the purpose of giving to the person receiving delivery the right to enforce the instrument.

(b) Transfer of an instrument, whether or not the transfer is a negotiation, vests in the transferee any right of the transferor to enforce the instrument, including any right as a holder in due course, but the transferee cannot acquire rights of a holder in due course by a transfer, directly or indirectly, from a holder in due course if the transferee engaged in fraud or illegality affecting the instrument.

(c) Unless otherwise agreed, if an instrument is transferred for value and the transferee does not become a holder because of lack of indorsement by the transferor, the transferee has a specifically enforceable right to the unqualified indorsement of the transferor, but negotiation of the instrument does not occur until the indorsement is made.

(d) If a transferor purports to transfer less than the entire instrument, negotiation of the instrument does not occur. The transferee obtains no rights under this Article and has only the rights of a partial assignee.

§ 3—204. Indorsement.

(a) "Indorsement" means a signature, other than that of a signer as maker, drawer, or acceptor, that alone or accompanied by other words is made on an instrument for the purpose of (i) negotiating the instrument, (ii) restricting payment of the instrument, or (iii) incurring indorser's liability on the instrument, but regardless of the intent of the signer, a signature and its accompanying words is an indorsement unless the accompanying words, terms of the instrument, place of the signature, or other circumstances unambiguously indicate that the signature was made for a purpose other than indorsement. For the purpose of determining whether a signature is made on an instrument, a paper affixed to the instrument is a part of the instrument.

(b) "Indorser" means a person who makes an indorsement.

(c) For the purpose of determining whether the transferee of an instrument is a holder, an indorsement that transfers a security interest in the instrument is effective as an unqualified indorsement of the instrument.

(d) If an instrument is payable to a holder under a name that is not the name of the holder, indorsement may be made by the holder in the name stated in the instrument or in the holder's name or both, but signature in both names may be required by a person paying or taking the instrument for value or collection.

§ 3—205. Special Indorsement; Blank Indorsement; Anomalous Indorsement.

(a) If an indorsement is made by the holder of an instrument, whether payable to an identified person or payable to bearer, and the indorsement identifies a person to whom it makes the instrument payable, it is a "special indorsement." When specially indorsed, an instrument becomes payable to the identified person and may be negotiated only by the indorsement of that person. The principles stated in Section 3—110 apply to special indorsements.

(b) If an indorsement is made by the holder of an instrument and it is not a special indorsement, it is a "blank indorsement." When indorsed in blank, an instrument becomes payable to bearer and may be negotiated by transfer of possession alone until specially indorsed.

(c) The holder may convert a blank indorsement that consists only of a signature into a special indorsement by writing, above the signature of the indorser, words identifying the person to whom the instrument is made payable.

(d) "Anomalous indorsement" means an indorsement made by a person who is not the holder of the instrument. An anomalous indorsement does not affect the manner in which the instrument may be negotiated.

§ 3—206. Restrictive Indorsement.

(a) An indorsement limiting payment to a particular person or otherwise prohibiting further transfer or negotiation of the instrument is not effective to prevent further transfer or negotiation of the instrument.

(b) An indorsement stating a condition to the right of the indorsee to receive payment does not affect the right of the indorsee to enforce the instrument. A person paying the instrument or taking it for value or collection may disregard the condition, and the rights and liabilities of that person are not affected by whether the condition has been fulfilled.

(c) If an instrument bears an indorsement (i) described in Section 4—201(b), or (ii) in blank or to a particular bank using the words "for deposit," "for collection," or other words indicating a purpose of having the instrument collected by a bank for the indorser or for a particular account, the following rules apply:

(1) A person, other than a bank, who purchases the instrument when so indorsed converts the instrument unless the amount paid for the instrument is received by the indorser or applied consistently with the indorsement.

(2) A depositary bank that purchases the instrument or takes it for collection when so indorsed converts the instrument unless the amount paid by the bank with respect to the instrument is received by the indorser or applied consistently with the indorsement.

(3) A payor bank that is also the depositary bank or that takes the instrument for immediate payment over the counter from a person other than a collecting bank converts the instrument unless the proceeds of the instrument are received by the indorser or applied consistently with the indorsement.

(4) Except as otherwise provided in paragraph (3), a payor bank or intermediary bank may disregard the indorsement and is not liable if the proceeds of the instrument are not received by the indorser or applied consistently with the indorsement.

(d) Except for an indorsement covered by subsection (c), if an instrument bears an indorsement using words to the effect that payment is to be made to the indorsee as agent, trustee, or other fiduciary for the benefit of the indorser or another person, the following rules apply:

(1) Unless there is notice of breach of fiduciary duty as provided in Section 3—307, a person who purchases the instrument from the indorsee or takes the instrument from the indorsee for collection or payment may pay the proceeds of payment or the value given for the instrument to the indorsee without regard to whether the indorsee violates a fiduciary duty to the indorser.

(2) A subsequent transferee of the instrument or person who pays the instrument is neither given notice nor otherwise affected by the restriction in the indorsement unless the transferee or payor knows that the fiduciary dealt with the instrument or its proceeds in breach of fiduciary duty.

(e) The presence on an instrument of an indorsement to which this section applies does not prevent a purchaser of the instrument from becoming a holder in due course of the instrument unless the purchaser is a converter under subsection (c) or has notice or knowledge of breach of fiduciary duty as stated in subsection (d).

(f) In an action to enforce the obligation of a party to pay the instrument, the obligor has a defense if payment would violate an indorsement to which this section applies and the payment is not permitted by this section.

§ 3—207. **Reacquisition.**

Reacquisition of an instrument occurs if it is transferred to a former holder, by negotiation or otherwise. A former holder who reacquires the instrument may cancel indorsements made after the reacquirer first became a holder of the instrument. If the cancellation causes the instrument to be payable to the reacquirer or to bearer, the reacquirer may negotiate the instrument. An indorser whose indorsement is canceled is discharged, and the discharge is effective against any subsequent holder.

Part 3 **Enforcement of Instruments**

§ 3—301. **Person Entitled to Enforce Instrument.**

"Person entitled to enforce" an instrument means (i) the holder of the instrument, (ii) a nonholder in possession of the instrument who has the rights of a holder, or (iii) a person not in possession of the instrument who is entitled to enforce the instrument pursuant to Section 3—309 or 3—418(d). A person may be a person entitled to enforce the instrument even though the person is not the owner of the instrument or is in wrongful possession of the instrument.

§ 3—302. **Holder in Due Course.**

(a) Subject to subsection (c) and Section 3—106(d), "holder in due course" means the holder of an instrument if:

(1) the instrument when issued or negotiated to the holder does not bear such apparent evidence of forgery or alteration or is not otherwise so irregular or incomplete as to call into question its authenticity; and

(2) the holder took the instrument (i) for value, (ii) in good faith, (iii) without notice that the instrument is overdue or has been dishonored or that there is an uncured default with respect to payment of another instrument issued as part of the same series, (iv) without notice that the instrument contains an unauthorized signature or has been altered, (v) without notice of any claim to the instrument described in Section 3—306, and (vi) without notice that any party has a defense or claim in recoupment described in Section 3—305(a).

(b) Notice of discharge of a party, other than discharge in an insolvency proceeding, is not notice of a defense under subsection (a), but discharge is effective against a person who became a holder in due course with notice of the discharge. Public filing or recording of a document does not of itself constitute notice of a defense, claim in recoupment, or claim to the instrument.

(c) Except to the extent a transferor or predecessor in interest has rights as a holder in due course, a person does not acquire rights of a holder in due course of an instrument taken (i) by legal process or by purchase in an execution, bankruptcy, or creditor's sale or similar proceeding, (ii) by purchase as part of a bulk transaction not in ordinary course of business of the transferor, or (iii) as the successor in interest to an estate or other organization.

(d) If, under Section 3—303(a)(1), the promise of performance that is the consideration for an instrument has been partially performed, the holder may assert rights as a holder in due course of the instrument only to the fraction of the amount payable under the instrument equal to the value of the partial performance divided by the value of the promised performance.

(e) If (i) the person entitled to enforce an instrument has only a security interest in the instrument and (ii) the person obliged to pay the instrument has a defense, claim in recoupment, or claim to the instrument that may be asserted against the person who granted the security interest, the person entitled to enforce the instrument may assert rights as a holder in due course only to an amount payable under the instrument which, at the time of enforcement of the instrument, does not exceed the amount of the unpaid obligation secured.

(f) To be effective, notice must be received at a time and in a manner that gives a reasonable opportunity to act on it.

(g) This section is subject to any law limiting status as a holder in due course in particular classes of transactions.

§ 3—303. Value and Consideration.

(a) An instrument is issued or transferred for value if:

(1) the instrument is issued or transferred for a promise of performance, to the extent the promise has been performed;

(2) the transferee acquires a security interest or other lien in the instrument other than a lien obtained by judicial proceeding;

(3) the instrument is issued or transferred as payment of, or as security for, an antecedent claim against any person, whether or not the claim is due;

(4) the instrument is issued or transferred in exchange for a negotiable instrument; or

(5) the instrument is issued or transferred in exchange for the incurring of an irrevocable obligation to a third party by the person taking the instrument.

(b) "Consideration" means any consideration sufficient to support a simple contract. The drawer or maker of an instrument has a defense if the instrument is issued without consideration. If an instrument is issued for a promise of performance, the issuer has a defense to the extent performance of the promise is due and the promise has not been performed. If an instrument is issued for value as stated in subsection (a), the instrument is also issued for consideration.

§ 3—304. Overdue Instrument.

(a) An instrument payable on demand becomes overdue at the earliest of the following times:

(1) on the day after the day demand for payment is duly made;

(2) if the instrument is a check, 90 days after its date; or

(3) if the instrument is not a check, when the instrument has been outstanding for a period of time after its date which is unreasonably long under the circumstances of the particular case in light of the nature of the instrument and usage of the trade.

(b) With respect to an instrument payable at a definite time the following rules apply:

(1) If the principal is payable in installments and a due date has not been accelerated, the instrument becomes overdue upon default under the instrument for nonpayment of an installment, and the instrument remains overdue until the default is cured.

(2) If the principal is not payable in installments and the due date has not been accelerated, the instrument becomes overdue on the day after the due date.

(3) If a due date with respect to principal has been accelerated, the instrument becomes overdue on the day after the accelerated due date.

(c) Unless the due date of principal has been accelerated, an instrument does not become overdue if there is default in payment of interest but no default in payment of principal.

§ 3—305. Defenses and Claims in Recoupment.

(a) Except as stated in subsection (b), the right to enforce the obligation of a party to pay an instrument is subject to the following:

(1) a defense of the obligor based on (i) infancy of the obligor to the extent it is a defense to a simple contract, (ii) duress, lack of legal capacity, or illegality of the transaction which, under other law, nullifies the obligation of the obligor, (iii) fraud that induced the obligor to sign the instrument with neither knowledge nor reasonable opportunity to learn of its character or its essential terms, or (iv) discharge of the obligor in insolvency proceedings;

(2) a defense of the obligor stated in another section of this Article or a defense of the obligor that would be available if the person entitled to enforce the instrument were enforcing a right to payment under a simple contract; and

(3) a claim in recoupment of the obligor against the original payee of the instrument if the claim arose from the transaction that gave rise to the instrument; but the claim of the obligor may be asserted against a transferee of the instrument only to reduce the amount owing on the instrument at the time the action is brought.

(b) The right of a holder in due course to enforce the obligation of a party to pay the instrument is subject to defenses of the obligor stated in subsection (a)(1), but is not subject to defenses of the obligor stated in subsection (a)(2) or claims in recoupment stated in subsection (a)(3) against a person other than the holder.

(c) Except as stated in subsection (d), in an action to enforce the obligation of a party to pay the instrument, the obligor may not assert against the person entitled to enforce the instrument a defense, claim in recoupment, or claim to the instrument (Section 3—306) of another person, but the other person's claim to the instrument may be asserted by the obligor if the other person is joined in the action and personally asserts the claim against the person entitled to enforce the instrument. An obligor is not obliged to pay the instrument if the person seeking enforcement of the instrument does not have rights of a holder in due course and the obligor proves that the instrument is a lost or stolen instrument.

(d) In an action to enforce the obligation of an accommodation party to pay an instrument, the accommodation party may assert against the person entitled to enforce the instrument any defense or claim in recoupment under subsection (a) that the accommodated party could assert against the person entitled to enforce the instrument, except the defenses of discharge in insolvency proceedings, infancy, and lack of legal capacity.

§ 3—306. Claims to an Instrument.

A person taking an instrument, other than a person having rights of a holder in due course, is subject to a claim of a property or possessory right in the instrument or its proceeds, including a claim to rescind a negotiation and to recover the instrument or its proceeds. A person having rights of a holder in due course takes free of the claim to the instrument.

§ 3—307. Notice of Breach of Fiduciary Duty.

(a) In this section:

(1) "Fiduciary" means an agent, trustee, partner, corporate officer or director, or other representative owing a fiduciary duty with respect to an instrument.

(2) "Represented person" means the principal, beneficiary, partnership, corporation, or other person to whom the duty stated in paragraph (1) is owed.

(b) If (i) an instrument is taken from a fiduciary for payment or collection or for value, (ii) the taker has knowledge of the fiduciary status of the fiduciary, and (iii) the represented person makes a claim to the instrument or its proceeds on the basis that the transaction of the fiduciary is a breach of fiduciary duty, the following rules apply:

(1) Notice of breach of fiduciary duty by the fiduciary is notice of the claim of the represented person.

(2) In the case of an instrument payable to the represented person or the fiduciary as such, the taker has notice of the breach of fiduciary duty if the instrument is (i) taken in payment of or as security for a debt known by the taker to be the personal debt of the fiduciary, (ii) taken in a transaction known by the taker to be for the personal benefit of the fiduciary, or (iii) deposited to an account other than an account of the fiduciary, as such, or an account of the represented person.

(3) If an instrument is issued by the represented person or the fiduciary as such, and made payable to the fiduciary personally, the taker does not have notice of the breach of fiduciary duty unless the taker knows of the breach of fiduciary duty.

(4) If an instrument is issued by the represented person or the fiduciary as such, to the taker as payee, the taker has notice of the breach of fiduciary duty if the instrument is (i) taken in payment of or as security for a debt known by the taker to be the personal debt of the fiduciary, (ii) taken in a transaction known by the taker to be for the personal benefit of the fiduciary, or (iii) deposited to an account other than an account of the fiduciary, as such, or an account of the represented person.

§ 3—308. Proof of Signatures and Status as Holder in Due Course.

(a) In an action with respect to an instrument, the authenticity of, and authority to make, each signature on the instrument is admitted unless specifically denied in the pleadings. If the validity of a signature is denied in the pleadings, the burden of establishing validity is on the person claiming validity, but the signature is presumed to be authentic and authorized unless the action is to enforce the liability of the purported signer and the signer is dead or incompetent at the time of trial of the issue of validity of the signature. If an action to enforce the instrument is brought against a person as the undisclosed principal of a person who signed the instrument as a party to the instrument, the plaintiff has the burden of establishing that the defendant is liable on the instrument as a represented person under Section 3—402(a).

(b) If the validity of signatures is admitted or proved and there is compliance with subsection (a), a plaintiff producing the instrument is entitled to payment if the plaintiff proves entitlement to enforce the instrument under Section 3—301, unless the defendant proves a defense or claim in recoupment. If a defense or claim in recoupment is proved, the right to payment of the plaintiff is subject to the defense or claim, except to the extent the plaintiff proves that the plaintiff has rights of a holder in due course which are not subject to the defense or claim.

§ 3—309. Enforcement of Lost, Destroyed, or Stolen Instrument.

(a) A person not in possession of an instrument is entitled to enforce the instrument if (i) the person was in possession of the instrument and entitled to enforce it when loss of possession occurred, (ii) the loss of possession was not the result of a transfer by the person or a lawful seizure, and (iii) the person cannot reasonably obtain possession of the instrument because the instrument was destroyed, its whereabouts cannot be determined, or it is in the wrongful possession of an unknown person or a person that cannot be found or is not amenable to service of process.

(b) A person seeking enforcement of an instrument under subsection (a) must prove the terms of the instrument and the person's right to enforce the instrument. If that proof is made, Section 3—308 applies to the case as if the person seeking enforcement had produced the instrument. The court may not enter judgment in favor of the person seeking enforcement unless it finds that the person required to pay the instrument is adequately protected against loss that might occur by reason of a claim by another person to enforce the instrument. Adequate protection may be provided by any reasonable means.

§ 3—310. **Effect of Instrument on Obligation for Which Taken.**

(a) Unless otherwise agreed, if a certified check, cashier's check, or teller's check is taken for an obligation, the obligation is discharged to the same extent discharge would result if an amount of money equal to the amount of the instrument were taken in payment of the obligation. Discharge of the obligation does not affect any liability that the obligor may have as an indorser of the instrument.

(b) Unless otherwise agreed and except as provided in subsection (a), if a note or an uncertified check is taken for an obligation, the obligation is suspended to the same extent the obligation would be discharged if an amount of money equal to the amount of the instrument were taken, and the following rules apply:

(1) In the case of an uncertified check, suspension of the obligation continues until dishonor of the check or until it is paid or certified. Payment or certification of the check results in discharge of the obligation to the extent of the amount of the check.

(2) In the case of a note, suspension of the obligation continues until dishonor of the note or until it is paid. Payment of the note results in discharge of the obligation to the extent of the payment.

(3) Except as provided in paragraph (4), if the check or note is dishonored and the obligee of the obligation for which the instrument was taken is the person entitled to enforce the instrument, the obligee may enforce either the instrument or the obligation. In the case of an instrument of a third person which is negotiated to the obligee by the obligor, discharge of the obligor on the instrument also discharges the obligation.

(4) If the person entitled to enforce the instrument taken for an obligation is a person other than the obligee, the obligee may not enforce the obligation to the extent the obligation is suspended. If the obligee is the person entitled to enforce the instrument but no longer has possession of it because it was lost, stolen, or destroyed, the obligation may not be enforced to the extent of the amount payable on the instrument, and to that extent the obligee's rights against the obligor are limited to enforcement of the instrument.

(c) If an instrument other than one described in subsection (a) or (b) is taken for an obligation, the effect is (i) that stated in subsection (a) if the instrument is one on which a bank is liable as maker or acceptor, or (ii) that stated in subsection (b) in any other case.

§ 3—311. **Accord and Satisfaction by Use of Instrument.**

(a) If a person against whom a claim is asserted proves that (i) that person in good faith tendered an instrument to the claimant as full satisfaction of the claim, (ii) the amount of the claim was unliquidated or subject to a bona fide dispute, and (iii) the claimant obtained payment of the instrument, the following subsections apply.

(b) Unless subsection (c) applies, the claim is discharged if the person against whom the claim is asserted proves that the instrument or an accompanying written communication contained a conspicuous statement to the effect that the instrument was tendered as full satisfaction of the claim.

(c) Subject to subsection (d), a claim is not discharged under subsection (b) if either of the following applies:

(1) The claimant, if an organization, proves that (i) within a reasonable time before the tender, the claimant sent a conspicuous statement to the person against whom the claim is asserted that communications concerning disputed debts, including an instrument tendered as full satisfaction of a debt, are to be sent to a designated person, office, or place, and (ii) the instrument or accompanying communication was not received by that designated person, office, or place.

(2) The claimant, whether or not an organization, proves that within 90 days after payment of the instrument, the claimant tendered repayment of the amount of the instrument to the person against whom the claim is asserted. This paragraph does not apply if the claimant is an organization that sent a statement complying with paragraph (1)(i).

(d) A claim is discharged if the person against whom the claim is asserted proves that within a reasonable time before collection of the instrument was initiated, the claimant, or an agent of the claimant having direct responsibility with respect to the disputed obligation, knew that the instrument was tendered in full satisfaction of the claim.

§ 3—312. Lost, Destroyed, or Stolen Cashier's Check, Teller's Check, or Certified Check.

(a) In this section:

(1) "Check" means a cashier's check, teller's check, or certified check.

(2) "Claimant" means a person who claims the right to receive the amount of a cashier's check, teller's check, or certified check that was lost, destroyed, or stolen.

(3) "Declaration of loss" means a written statement, made under penalty of perjury, to the effect that (i) the declarer lost possession of a check, (ii) the declarer is the drawer or payee of the check, in the case of a certified check, or the remitter or payee of the check, in the case of a cashier's check or teller's check, (iii) the loss of possession was not the result of a transfer by the declarer or a lawful seizure, and (iv) the declarer cannot reasonably obtain possession of the check because the check was destroyed, its whereabouts cannot be determined, or it is in the wrongful possession of an unknown person or a person that cannot be found or is not amenable to service of process.

(4) "Obligated bank" means the issuer of a cashier's check or teller's check or the acceptor of a certified check.

(b) A claimant may assert a claim to the amount of a check by a communication to the obligated bank describing the check with reasonable certainty and requesting payment of the amount of the check, if (i) the claimant is the drawer or payee of a certified check or the remitter or payee of a cashier's check or teller's check, (ii) the communication contains or is accompanied by a declaration of loss of the claimant with respect to the check, (iii) the communication is received at a time and in a manner affording the bank a reasonable time to act on it before the check is paid, and (iv) the claimant provides reasonable identification if requested by the obligated bank. Delivery of a declaration of loss is a warranty of the truth of the statements made in the declaration. If a claim is asserted in compliance with this subsection, the following rules apply:

(1) The claim becomes enforceable at the later of (i) the time the claim is asserted, or (ii) the 90th day following the date of the check, in the case of a cashier's check or teller's check, or the 90th day following the date of the acceptance, in the case of a certified check.

(2) Until the claim becomes enforceable, it has no legal effect and the obligated bank may pay the check or, in the case of a teller's check, may permit the drawee to pay the check. Payment to a person entitled to enforce the check discharges all liability of the obligated bank with respect to the check.

(3) If the claim becomes enforceable before the check is presented for payment, the obligated bank is not obliged to pay the check.

(4) When the claim becomes enforceable, the obligated bank becomes obliged to pay the amount of the check to the claimant if payment of the check has not been made to a person entitled to enforce the check. Subject to Section 4—302(a)(1), payment to the claimant discharges all liability of the obligated bank with respect to the check.

(c) If the obligated bank pays the amount of a check to a claimant under subsection (b)(4) and the check is presented for payment by a person having rights of a holder in due course, the claimant is obliged to (i) refund the payment to the obligated bank if the check is paid, or (ii) pay the amount of the check to the person having rights of a holder in due course if the check is dishonored.

(d) If a claimant has the right to assert a claim under subsection (b) and is also a person entitled to enforce a cashier's check, teller's check, or certified check which is lost, destroyed, or stolen, the claimant may assert rights with respect to the check either under this section or Section 3—309.

Part 4 Liability of Parties

§ 3—401. Signature.

(a) A person is not liable on an instrument unless (i) the person signed the instrument, or (ii) the person is represented by an agent or representative who signed the instrument and the signature is binding on the represented person under Section 3—402.

(b) A signature may be made (i) manually or by means of a device or machine, and (ii) by the use of any name, including a trade or assumed name, or by a word, mark, or symbol executed or adopted by a person with present intention to authenticate a writing.

§ 3—402. Signature by Representative.

(a) If a person acting, or purporting to act, as a representative signs an instrument by signing either the name of the represented person or the name of the signer, the represented person is bound by the signature to the same extent the represented person would be bound if the signature were on a simple contract. If the represented person is bound, the signature of the representative is the "authorized signature of the represented person" and the represented person is liable on the instrument, whether or not identified in the instrument.

(b) If a representative signs the name of the representative to an instrument and the signature is an authorized signature of the represented person, the following rules apply:

(1) If the form of the signature shows unambiguously that the signature is made on behalf of the rep-

resented person who is identified in the instrument, the representative is not liable on the instrument.

(2) Subject to subsection (c), if (i) the form of the signature does not show unambiguously that the signature is made in a representative capacity or (ii) the represented person is not identified in the instrument, the representative is liable on the instrument to a holder in due course that took the instrument without notice that the representative was not intended to be liable on the instrument. With respect to any other person, the representative is liable on the instrument unless the representative proves that the original parties did not intend the representative to be liable on the instrument.

(c) If a representative signs the name of the representative as drawer of a check without indication of the representative status and the check is payable from an account of the represented person who is identified on the check, the signer is not liable on the check if the signature is an authorized signature of the represented person.

§ 3—403. **Unauthorized Signature.**

(a) Unless otherwise provided in this Article or Article 4, an unauthorized signature is ineffective except as the signature of the unauthorized signer in favor of a person who in good faith pays the instrument or takes it for value. An unauthorized signature may be ratified for all purposes of this Article.

(b) If the signature of more than one person is required to constitute the authorized signature of an organization, the signature of the organization is unauthorized if one of the required signatures is lacking.

(c) The civil or criminal liability of a person who makes an unauthorized signature is not affected by any provision of this Article which makes the unauthorized signature effective for the purposes of this Article.

§ 3—404. **Impostors; Fictitious Payees.**

(a) If an impostor, by use of the mails or otherwise, induces the issuer of an instrument to issue the instrument to the impostor, or to a person acting in concert with the impostor, by impersonating the payee of the instrument or a person authorized to act for the payee, an indorsement of the instrument by any person in the name of the payee is effective as the indorsement of the payee in favor of a person who, in good faith, pays the instrument or takes it for value or for collection.

(b) If (i) a person whose intent determines to whom an instrument is payable (Section 3—110(a) or (b)) does not intend the person identified as payee to have any interest in the instrument, or (ii) the person identified as payee of an instrument is a fictitious person, the following rules apply until the instrument is negotiated by special indorsement:

(1) Any person in possession of the instrument is its holder.

(2) An indorsement by any person in the name of the payee stated in the instrument is effective as the indorsement of the payee in favor of a person who, in good faith, pays the instrument or takes it for value or for collection.

(c) Under subsection (a) or (b), an indorsement is made in the name of a payee if (i) it is made in a name substantially similar to that of the payee or (ii) the instrument, whether or not indorsed, is deposited in a depositary bank to an account in a name substantially similar to that of the payee.

(d) With respect to an instrument to which subsection (a) or (b) applies, if a person paying the instrument or taking it for value or for collection fails to exercise ordinary care in paying or taking the instrument and that failure substantially contributes to loss resulting from payment of the instrument, the person bearing the loss may recover from the person failing to exercise ordinary care to the extent the failure to exercise ordinary care contributed to the loss.

§ 3—405. **Employer's Responsibility for Fraudulent Indorsement by Employee.**

(a) In this section:

(1) "Employee" includes an independent contractor and employee of an independent contractor retained by the employer.

(2) "Fraudulent indorsement" means (i) in the case of an instrument payable to the employer, a forged indorsement purporting to be that of the employer, or (ii) in the case of an instrument with respect to which the employer is the issuer, a forged indorsement purporting to be that of the person identified as payee.

(3) "Responsibility" with respect to instruments means authority (i) to sign or indorse instruments on behalf of the employer, (ii) to process instruments received by the employer for bookkeeping purposes, for deposit to an account, or for other disposition, (iii) to prepare or process instruments for issue in the name of the employer, (iv) to supply information determining the names or addresses of payees of instruments to be issued in the name of the employer, (v) to control the disposition of instruments to be issued in the name of the employer, or (vi) to act otherwise with respect to instruments in a responsible capacity. "Responsibility" does not include authority that merely allows an employee to have access to instruments or blank or incomplete instrument forms that are being stored or transported or are part of incoming or outgoing mail, or similar access.

(b) For the purpose of determining the rights and liabilities of a person who, in good faith, pays an instrument or takes it for value or for collection, if an employer entrusted an employee with responsibility with respect to the instrument and the employee or a person acting in concert with the employee makes a fraudulent indorsement of the instrument, the indorsement is effective as the indorsement of the person to whom the instrument is payable if it is made in the name of that person. If the person paying the instrument or taking it for value or for collection fails to exercise ordinary care in paying or taking the instrument and that failure substantially contributes to loss resulting from the fraud, the person bearing the loss may recover from the person failing to exercise ordinary care to the extent the failure to exercise ordinary care contributed to the loss.

(c) Under subsection (b), an indorsement is made in the name of the person to whom an instrument is payable if (i) it is made in a name substantially similar to the name of that person or (ii) the instrument, whether or not indorsed, is deposited in a depositary bank to an account in a name substantially similar to the name of that person.

§ 3—406. Negligence Contributing to Forged Signature or Alteration of Instrument.

(a) A person whose failure to exercise ordinary care substantially contributes to an alteration of an instrument or to the making of a forged signature on an instrument is precluded from asserting the alteration or the forgery against a person who, in good faith, pays the instrument or takes it for value or for collection.

(b) Under subsection (a), if the person asserting the preclusion fails to exercise ordinary care in paying or taking the instrument and that failure substantially contributes to loss, the loss is allocated between the person precluded and the person asserting the preclusion according to the extent to which the failure of each to exercise ordinary care contributed to the loss.

(c) Under subsection (a), the burden of proving failure to exercise ordinary care is on the person asserting the preclusion. Under subsection (b), the burden of proving failure to exercise ordinary care is on the person precluded.

§ 3—407. Alteration.

(a) "Alteration" means (i) an unauthorized change in an instrument that purports to modify in any respect the obligation of a party, or (ii) an unauthorized addition of words or numbers or other change to an incomplete instrument relating to the obligation of a party.

(b) Except as provided in subsection (c), an alteration fraudulently made discharges a party whose obligation is affected by the alteration unless that party assents or is precluded from asserting the alteration. No other alteration discharges a party, and the instrument may be enforced according to its original terms.

(c) A payor bank or drawee paying a fraudulently altered instrument or a person taking it for value, in good faith and without notice of the alteration, may enforce rights with respect to the instrument (i) according to its original terms, or (ii) in the case of an incomplete instrument altered by unauthorized completion, according to its terms as completed.

§ 3—408. Drawee Not Liable on Unaccepted Draft.

A check or other draft does not of itself operate as an assignment of funds in the hands of the drawee available for its payment, and the drawee is not liable on the instrument until the drawee accepts it.

§ 3—409. Acceptance of Draft; Certified Check.

(a) "Acceptance" means the drawee's signed agreement to pay a draft as presented. It must be written on the draft and may consist of the drawee's signature alone. Acceptance may be made at any time and becomes effective when notification pursuant to instructions is given or the accepted draft is delivered for the purpose of giving rights on the acceptance to any person.

(b) A draft may be accepted although it has not been signed by the drawer, is otherwise incomplete, is overdue, or has been dishonored.

(c) If a draft is payable at a fixed period after sight and the acceptor fails to date the acceptance, the holder may complete the acceptance by supplying a date in good faith.

(d) "Certified check" means a check accepted by the bank on which it is drawn. Acceptance may be made as stated in subsection (a) or by a writing on the check which indicates that the check is certified. The drawee of a check has no obligation to certify the check, and refusal to certify is not dishonor of the check.

§ 3—410. Acceptance Varying Draft.

(a) If the terms of a drawee's acceptance vary from the terms of the draft as presented, the holder may refuse the acceptance and treat the draft as dishonored. In that case, the drawee may cancel the acceptance.

(b) The terms of a draft are not varied by an acceptance to pay at a particular bank or place in the United States, unless the acceptance states that the draft is to be paid only at that bank or place.

(c) If the holder assents to an acceptance varying the terms of a draft, the obligation of each drawer and indorser that does not expressly assent to the acceptance is discharged.

§ 3—411. Refusal to Pay Cashier's Checks, Teller's Checks, and Certified Checks.

(a) In this section, "obligated bank" means the acceptor of a certified check or the issuer of a cashier's check or teller's check bought from the issuer.

(b) If the obligated bank wrongfully (i) refuses to pay a cashier's check or certified check, (ii) stops payment of a teller's check, or (iii) refuses to pay a dishonored teller's check, the person asserting the right to enforce the check is entitled to compensation for expenses and loss of interest resulting from the nonpayment and may recover consequential damages if the obligated bank refuses to pay after receiving notice of particular circumstances giving rise to the damages.

(c) Expenses or consequential damages under subsection (b) are not recoverable if the refusal of the obligated bank to pay occurs because (i) the bank suspends payments, (ii) the obligated bank asserts a claim or defense of the bank that it has reasonable grounds to believe is available against the person entitled to enforce the instrument, (iii) the obligated bank has a reasonable doubt whether the person demanding payment is the person entitled to enforce the instrument, or (iv) payment is prohibited by law.

§ 3—412. Obligation of Issuer of Note or Cashier's Check.

The issuer of a note or cashier's check or other draft drawn on the drawer is obliged to pay the instrument (i) according to its terms at the time it was issued or, if not issued, at the time it first came into possession of a holder, or (ii) if the issuer signed an incomplete instrument, according to its terms when completed, to the extent stated in Sections 3—115 and 3—407. The obligation is owed to a person entitled to enforce the instrument or to an indorser who paid the instrument under Section 3—415.

§ 3—413. Obligation of Acceptor.

(a) The acceptor of a draft is obliged to pay the draft (i) according to its terms at the time it was accepted, even though the acceptance states that the draft is payable "as originally drawn" or equivalent terms, (ii) if the acceptance varies the terms of the draft, according to the terms of the draft as varied, or (iii) if the acceptance is of a draft that is an incomplete instrument, according to its terms when completed, to the extent stated in Sections 3—115 and 3—407. The obligation is owed to a person entitled to enforce the draft or to the drawer or an indorser who paid the draft under Section 3—414 or 3—415.

(b) If the certification of a check or other acceptance of a draft states the amount certified or accepted, the obligation of the acceptor is that amount. If (i) the certification or acceptance does not state an amount, (ii) the amount of the instrument is subsequently raised, and (iii) the instrument is then negotiated to a holder in due course, the obligation of the acceptor is the amount of the instrument at the time it was taken by the holder in due course.

§ 3—414. Obligation of Drawer.

(a) This section does not apply to cashier's checks or other drafts drawn on the drawer.

(b) If an unaccepted draft is dishonored, the drawer is obliged to pay the draft (i) according to its terms at the time it was issued or, if not issued, at the time it first came into possession of a holder, or (ii) if the drawer signed an incomplete instrument, according to its terms when completed, to the extent stated in Sections 3—115 and 3—407. The obligation is owed to a person entitled to enforce the draft or to an indorser who paid the draft under Section 3—415.

(c) If a draft is accepted by a bank, the drawer is discharged, regardless of when or by whom acceptance was obtained.

(d) If a draft is accepted and the acceptor is not a bank, the obligation of the drawer to pay the draft if the draft is dishonored by the acceptor is the same as the obligation of an indorser under Section 3—415(a) and (c).

(e) If a draft states that it is drawn "without recourse" or otherwise disclaims liability of the drawer to pay the draft, the drawer is not liable under subsection (b) to pay the draft if the draft is not a check. A disclaimer of the liability stated in subsection (b) is not effective if the draft is a check.

(f) If (i) a check is not presented for payment or given to a depositary bank for collection within 30 days after its date, (ii) the drawee suspends payments after expiration of the 30-day period without paying the check, and (iii) because of the suspension of payments, the drawer is deprived of funds maintained with the drawee to cover payment of the check, the drawer to the extent deprived of funds may discharge its obligation to pay the check by assigning to the person entitled to enforce the check the rights of the drawer against the drawee with respect to the funds.

§ 3—415. Obligation of Indorser.

(a) Subject to subsections (b), (c), and (d) and to Section 3—419(d), if an instrument is dishonored, an indorser is obliged to pay the amount due on the instrument (i) according to the terms of the instrument at the time it was indorsed, or (ii) if the indorser indorsed an incomplete instrument, according to its terms when completed, to the extent stated in Sections 3—115 and 3—407. The obligation of the indorser is owed to a person entitled to enforce the instrument or to a subsequent indorser who paid the instrument under this section.

(b) If an indorsement states that it is made "without recourse" or otherwise disclaims liability of the indorser, the indorser is not liable under subsection (a) to pay the instrument.

(c) If notice of dishonor of an instrument is required by Section 3—503 and notice of dishonor complying with that section is not given to an indorser, the liability of the indorser under subsection (a) is discharged.

(d) If a draft is accepted by a bank after an indorsement is made, the liability of the indorser under subsection (a) is discharged.

(e) If an indorser of a check is liable under subsection (a) and the check is not presented for payment, or given to a depositary bank for collection, within 30 days after the day the indorsement was made, the liability of the indorser under subsection (a) is discharged.

§ 3—416. Transfer Warranties.

(a) A person who transfers an instrument for consideration warrants to the transferee and, if the transfer is by indorsement, to any subsequent transferee that:

(1) the warrantor is a person entitled to enforce the instrument;

(2) all signatures on the instrument are authentic and authorized;

(3) the instrument has not been altered;

(4) the instrument is not subject to a defense or claim in recoupment of any party which can be asserted against the warrantor; and

(5) the warrantor has no knowledge of any insolvency proceeding commenced with respect to the maker or acceptor or, in the case of an unaccepted draft, the drawer.

(b) A person to whom the warranties under subsection (a) are made and who took the instrument in good faith may recover from the warrantor as damages for breach of warranty an amount equal to the loss suffered as a result of the breach, but not more than the amount of the instrument plus expenses and loss of interest incurred as a result of the breach.

(c) The warranties stated in subsection (a) cannot be disclaimed with respect to checks. Unless notice of a claim for breach of warranty is given to the warrantor within 30 days after the claimant has reason to know of the breach and the identity of the warrantor, the liability of the warrantor under subsection (b) is discharged to the extent of any loss caused by the delay in giving notice of the claim.

(d) A [cause of action] for breach of warranty under this section accrues when the claimant has reason to know of the breach.

§ 3—417. Presentment Warranties.

(a) If an unaccepted draft is presented to the drawee for payment or acceptance and the drawee pays or accepts the draft, (i) the person obtaining payment or acceptance, at the time of presentment, and (ii) a previous transferor of the draft, at the time of transfer, warrant to the drawee making payment or accepting the draft in good faith that:

(1) the warrantor is, or was, at the time the warrantor transferred the draft, a person entitled to enforce the draft or authorized to obtain payment or acceptance of the draft on behalf of a person entitled to enforce the draft;

(2) the draft has not been altered; and

(3) the warrantor has no knowledge that the signature of the drawer of the draft is unauthorized.

(b) A drawee making payment may recover from any warrantor damages for breach of warranty equal to the amount paid by the drawee less the amount the drawee received or is entitled to receive from the drawer because of the payment. In addition, the drawee is entitled to compensation for expenses and loss of interest resulting from the breach. The right of the drawee to recover damages under this subsection is not affected by any failure of the drawee to exercise ordinary care in making payment. If the drawee accepts the draft, breach of warranty is a defense to the obligation of the acceptor. If the acceptor makes payment with respect to the draft, the acceptor is entitled to recover from any warrantor for breach of warranty the amounts stated in this subsection.

(c) If a drawee asserts a claim for breach of warranty under subsection (a) based on an unauthorized indorsement of the draft or an alteration of the draft, the warrantor may defend by proving that the indorsement is effective under Section 3—404 or 3—405 or the drawer is precluded under Section 3—406 or 4—406 from asserting against the drawee the unauthorized indorsement or alteration.

(d) If (i) a dishonored draft is presented for payment to the drawer or an indorser or (ii) any other instrument is presented for payment to a party obliged to pay the instrument, and (iii) payment is received, the following rules apply:

(1) The person obtaining payment and a prior transferor of the instrument warrant to the person making payment in good faith that the warrantor is, or was, at the time the warrantor transferred the instrument, a person entitled to enforce the instrument or authorized to obtain payment on behalf of a person entitled to enforce the instrument.

(2) The person making payment may recover from any warrantor for breach of warranty an amount equal to the amount paid plus expenses and loss of interest resulting from the breach.

(e) The warranties stated in subsections (a) and (d) cannot be disclaimed with respect to checks. Unless notice of a claim for breach of warranty is given to the warrantor within 30 days after the claimant has reason to know of the breach and the identity of the warrantor, the liability of the warrantor under subsection (b) or (d) is discharged to the extent of any loss caused by the delay in giving notice of the claim.

(f) A [cause of action] for breach of warranty under this section accrues when the claimant has reason to know of the breach.

§ 3—418. Payment or Acceptance by Mistake.

(a) Except as provided in subsection (c), if the drawee of a draft pays or accepts the draft and the drawee acted on the mistaken belief that (i) payment of the draft had not been stopped pursuant to Section 4—403 or (ii) the signature of the drawer of the draft was authorized, the drawee may recover the amount of the draft from the person to whom or for whose benefit payment was made or, in the case of acceptance, may revoke the acceptance. Rights of the drawee under this subsection are not affected by failure of the drawee to exercise ordinary care in paying or accepting the draft.

(b) Except as provided in subsection (c), if an instrument has been paid or accepted by mistake and the case is not covered by subsection (a), the person paying or accepting may, to the extent permitted by the law governing mistake and restitution, (i) recover the payment from the person to whom or for whose benefit payment was made or (ii) in the case of acceptance, may revoke the acceptance.

(c) The remedies provided by subsection (a) or (b) may not be asserted against a person who took the instrument in good faith and for value or who in good faith changed position in reliance on the payment or acceptance. This subsection does not limit remedies provided by Section 3—417 or 4—407.

(d) Notwithstanding Section 4—215, if an instrument is paid or accepted by mistake and the payor or acceptor recovers payment or revokes acceptance under subsection (a) or (b), the instrument is deemed not to have been paid or accepted and is treated as dishonored, and the person from whom payment is recovered has rights as a person entitled to enforce the dishonored instrument.

§ 3—419. Instruments Signed for Accommodation.

(a) If an instrument is issued for value given for the benefit of a party to the instrument ("accommodated party") and another party to the instrument ("accommodation party") signs the instrument for the purpose of incurring liability on the instrument without being a direct beneficiary of the value given for the instrument, the instrument is signed by the accommodation party "for accommodation."

(b) An accommodation party may sign the instrument as maker, drawer, acceptor, or indorser and, subject to subsection (d), is obliged to pay the instrument in the capacity in which the accommodation party signs. The obligation of an accommodation party may be enforced notwithstanding any statute of frauds and whether or not the accommodation party receives consideration for the accommodation.

(c) A person signing an instrument is presumed to be an accommodation party and there is notice that the instrument is signed for accommodation if the signature is an anomalous indorsement or is accompanied by words indicating that the signer is acting as surety or guarantor with respect to the obligation of another party to the instrument. Except as provided in Section 3—605, the obligation of an accommodation party to pay the instrument is not affected by the fact that the person enforcing the obligation had notice when the instrument was taken by that person that the accommodation party signed the instrument for accommodation.

(d) If the signature of a party to an instrument is accompanied by words indicating unambiguously that the party is guaranteeing collection rather than payment of the obligation of another party to the instrument, the signer is obliged to pay the amount due on the instrument to a person entitled to enforce the instrument only if (i) execution of judgment against the other party has been returned unsatisfied, (ii) the other party is insolvent or in an insolvency proceeding, (iii) the other party cannot be served with process, or (iv) it is otherwise apparent that payment cannot be obtained from the other party.

(e) An accommodation party who pays the instrument is entitled to reimbursement from the accommodated party and is entitled to enforce the instrument against the accommodated party. An accommodated party who pays the instrument has no right of recourse against, and is not entitled to contribution from, an accommodation party.

§ 3—420. Conversion of Instrument.

(a) The law applicable to conversion of personal property applies to instruments. An instrument is also converted if it is taken by transfer, other than a negotiation, from a person not entitled to enforce the instrument or a bank makes or obtains payment with respect to the instrument for a person not entitled to enforce the instrument or receive payment. An action for conversion of an instrument may not be brought by (i) the issuer or acceptor of the instrument or (ii) a payee or indorsee who did not receive delivery of the instrument either directly or through delivery to an agent or a co-payee.

(b) In an action under subsection (a), the measure of liability is presumed to be the amount payable on the instrument, but recovery may not exceed the amount of the plaintiff's interest in the instrument.

(c) A representative, other than a depositary bank, who has in good faith dealt with an instrument or its proceeds on behalf of one who was not the person entitled to enforce the instrument is not liable in conversion to that person beyond the amount of any proceeds that it has not paid out.

Part 5 Dishonor

§ 3—501. Presentment.

(a) "Presentment" means a demand made by or on behalf of a person entitled to enforce an instrument (i) to pay the instrument made to the drawee or a party obliged to pay the instrument or, in the case of a note or accepted draft payable at a bank, to the bank, or (ii) to accept a draft made to the drawee.

(b) The following rules are subject to Article 4, agreement of the parties, and clearing-house rules and the like:

(1) Presentment may be made at the place of payment of the instrument and must be made at the place of payment if the instrument is payable at a bank in the United States; may be made by any commercially reasonable means, including an oral, written, or electronic communication; is effective when the demand for payment or acceptance is received by the person to whom presentment is made; and is effective if made to any one of two or more makers, acceptors, drawees, or other payors.

(2) Upon demand of the person to whom presentment is made, the person making presentment must (i) exhibit the instrument, (ii) give reasonable identification and, if presentment is made on behalf of another person, reasonable evidence of authority to do so, and (. . .) sign a receipt on the instrument for any payment made or surrender the instrument if full payment is made.

(3) Without dishonoring the instrument, the party to whom presentment is made may (i) return the instrument for lack of a necessary indorsement, or (ii) refuse payment or acceptance for failure of the presentment to comply with the terms of the instrument, an agreement of the parties, or other applicable law or rule.

(4) The party to whom presentment is made may treat presentment as occurring on the next business day after the day of presentment if the party to whom presentment is made has established a cut-off hour not earlier than 2 P.M. for the receipt and processing of instruments presented for payment or acceptance and presentment is made after the cut-off hour.

§ 3—502. **Dishonor.**

(a) Dishonor of a note is governed by the following rules:

(1) If the note is payable on demand, the note is dishonored if presentment is duly made to the maker and the note is not paid on the day of presentment.

(2) If the note is not payable on demand and is payable at or through a bank or the terms of the note require presentment, the note is dishonored if presentment is duly made and the note is not paid on the day it becomes payable or the day of presentment, whichever is later.

(3) If the note is not payable on demand and paragraph (2) does not apply, the note is dishonored if it is not paid on the day it becomes payable.

(b) Dishonor of an unaccepted draft other than a documentary draft is governed by the following rules:

(1) If a check is duly presented for payment to the payor bank otherwise than for immediate payment over the counter, the check is dishonored if the payor bank makes timely return of the check or sends timely notice of dishonor or nonpayment under Section 4—301 or 4—302, or becomes accountable for the amount of the check under Section 4—302.

(2) If a draft is payable on demand and paragraph (1) does not apply, the draft is dishonored if presentment for payment is duly made to the drawee and the draft is not paid on the day of presentment.

(3) If a draft is payable on a date stated in the draft, the draft is dishonored if (i) presentment for payment is duly made to the drawee and payment is not made on the day the draft becomes payable or the day of presentment, whichever is later, or (ii) presentment for acceptance is duly made before the day the draft becomes payable and the draft is not accepted on the day of presentment.

(4) If a draft is payable on elapse of a period of time after sight or acceptance, the draft is dishonored if presentment for acceptance is duly made and the draft is not accepted on the day of presentment.

(c) Dishonor of an unaccepted documentary draft occurs according to the rules stated in subsection (b)(2), (3), and (4), except that payment or acceptance may be delayed without dishonor until no later than the close of the third business day of the drawee following the day on which payment or acceptance is required by those paragraphs.

(d) Dishonor of an accepted draft is governed by the following rules:

(1) If the draft is payable on demand, the draft is dishonored if presentment for payment is duly made to the acceptor and the draft is not paid on the day of presentment.

(2) If the draft is not payable on demand, the draft is dishonored if presentment for payment is duly made to the acceptor and payment is not made on the day it becomes payable or the day of presentment, whichever is later.

(e) In any case in which presentment is otherwise required for dishonor under this section and presentment is excused under Section 3—504, dishonor occurs without presentment if the instrument is not duly accepted or paid.

(f) If a draft is dishonored because timely acceptance of the draft was not made and the person entitled to demand acceptance consents to a late acceptance, from the time of acceptance the draft is treated as never having been dishonored.

§ 3—503. Notice of Dishonor.

(a) The obligation of an indorser stated in Section 3—415(a) and the obligation of a drawer stated in Section 3—414(d) may not be enforced unless (i) the indorser or drawer is given notice of dishonor of the instrument complying with this section or (ii) notice of dishonor is excused under Section 3—504(b).

(b) Notice of dishonor may be given by any person; may be given by any commercially reasonable means, including an oral, written, or electronic communication; and is sufficient if it reasonably identifies the instrument and indicates that the instrument has been dishonored or has not been paid or accepted. Return of an instrument given to a bank for collection is sufficient notice of dishonor.

(c) Subject to Section 3—504(c), with respect to an instrument taken for collection by a collecting bank, notice of dishonor must be given (i) by the bank before midnight of the next banking day following the banking day on which the bank receives notice of dishonor of the instrument, or (ii) by any other person within 30 days following the day on which the person receives notice of dishonor. With respect to any other instrument, notice of dishonor must be given within 30 days following the day on which dishonor occurs.

§ 3—504. Excused Presentment and Notice of Dishonor.

(a) Presentment for payment or acceptance of an instrument is excused if (i) the person entitled to present the instrument cannot with reasonable diligence make presentment, (ii) the maker or acceptor has repudiated an obligation to pay the instrument or is dead or in insolvency proceedings, (iii) by the terms of the instrument presentment is not necessary to enforce the obligation of indorsers or the drawer, (iv) the drawer or indorser whose obligation is being enforced has waived presentment or otherwise has no reason to expect or right to require that the instrument be paid or accepted, or (v) the drawer instructed the drawee not to pay or accept the draft or the drawee was not obligated to the drawer to pay the draft.

(b) Notice of dishonor is excused if (i) by the terms of the instrument notice of dishonor is not necessary to enforce the obligation of a party to pay the instrument, or (ii) the party whose obligation is being enforced waived notice of dishonor. A waiver of presentment is also a waiver of notice of dishonor.

(c) Delay in giving notice of dishonor is excused if the delay was caused by circumstances beyond the control of the person giving the notice and the person giving the notice exercised reasonable diligence after the cause of the delay ceased to operate.

§ 3—505. Evidence of Dishonor.

(a) The following are admissible as evidence and create a presumption of dishonor and of any notice of dishonor stated:

(1) a document regular in form as provided in subsection (b) which purports to be a protest;

(2) a purported stamp or writing of the drawee, payor bank, or presenting bank on or accompanying the instrument stating that acceptance or payment has been refused unless reasons for the refusal are stated and the reasons are not consistent with dishonor;

(3) a book or record of the drawee, payor bank, or collecting bank, kept in the usual course of business which shows dishonor, even if there is no evidence of who made the entry.

(b) A protest is a certificate of dishonor made by a United States consul or vice consul, or a notary public or other person authorized to administer oaths by the law of the place where dishonor occurs. It may be made upon information satisfactory to that person. The protest must identify the instrument and certify either that presentment has been made or, if not made, the reason why it was not made, and that the instrument has been dishonored by nonacceptance or nonpayment. The protest may also certify that notice of dishonor has been given to some or all parties.

Part 6 Discharge and Payment

§ 3—601. Discharge and Effect of Discharge.

(a) The obligation of a party to pay the instrument is discharged as stated in this Article or by an act or agreement with the party which would discharge an obligation to pay money under a simple contract.

(b) Discharge of the obligation of a party is not effective against a person acquiring rights of a holder in due course of the instrument without notice of the discharge.

§ 3—602. Payment.

(a) Subject to subsection (b), an instrument is paid to the extent payment is made (i) by or on behalf of a party obliged to pay the instrument, and (ii) to a person entitled to enforce the instrument. To the extent of the payment, the obligation of the party obliged to pay the instrument is discharged even though payment is made with knowledge of a claim to the instrument under Section 3—306 by another person.

(b) The obligation of a party to pay the instrument is not discharged under subsection (a) if:

(1) a claim to the instrument under Section 3—306 is enforceable against the party receiving payment and (i) payment is made with knowledge by the

payor that payment is prohibited by injunction or similar process of a court of competent jurisdiction, or (ii) in the case of an instrument other than a cashier's check, teller's check, or certified check, the party making payment accepted, from the person having a claim to the instrument, indemnity against loss resulting from refusal to pay the person entitled to enforce the instrument; or

(2) the person making payment knows that the instrument is a stolen instrument and pays a person it knows is in wrongful possession of the instrument.

§ 3—603. **Tender of Payment.**

(a) If tender of payment of an obligation to pay an instrument is made to a person entitled to enforce the instrument, the effect of tender is governed by principles of law applicable to tender of payment under a simple contract.

(b) If tender of payment of an obligation to pay an instrument is made to a person entitled to enforce the instrument and the tender is refused, there is discharge, to the extent of the amount of the tender, of the obligation of an indorser or accommodation party having a right of recourse with respect to the obligation to which the tender relates.

(c) If tender of payment of an amount due on an instrument is made to a person entitled to enforce the instrument, the obligation of the obligor to pay interest after the due date on the amount tendered is discharged. If presentment is required with respect to an instrument and the obligor is able and ready to pay on the due date at every place of payment stated in the instrument, the obligor is deemed to have made tender of payment on the due date to the person entitled to enforce the instrument.

§ 3—604. **Discharge by Cancellation or Renunciation.**

(a) A person entitled to enforce an instrument, with or without consideration, may discharge the obligation of a party to pay the instrument (i) by an intentional voluntary act, such as surrender of the instrument to the party, destruction, mutilation, or cancellation of the instrument, cancellation or striking out of the party's signature, or the addition of words to the instrument indicating discharge, or (ii) by agreeing not to sue or otherwise renouncing rights against the party by a signed writing.

(b) Cancellation or striking out of an indorsement pursuant to subsection (a) does not affect the status and rights of a party derived from the indorsement.

§ 3—605. **Discharge of Indorsers and Accommodation Parties.**

(a) In this section, the term "indorser" includes a drawer having the obligation described in Section 3—414(d).

(b) Discharge, under Section 3—604, of the obligation of a party to pay an instrument does not discharge the obligation of an indorser or accommodation party having a right of recourse against the discharged party.

(c) If a person entitled to enforce an instrument agrees, with or without consideration, to an extension of the due date of the obligation of a party to pay the instrument, the extension discharges an indorser or accommodation party having a right of recourse against the party whose obligation is extended to the extent the indorser or accommodation party proves that the extension caused loss to the indorser or accommodation party with respect to the right of recourse.

(d) If a person entitled to enforce an instrument agrees, with or without consideration, to a material modification of the obligation of a party other than an extension of the due date, the modification discharges the obligation of an indorser or accommodation party having a right of recourse against the person whose obligation is modified to the extent the modification causes loss to the indorser or accommodation party with respect to the right of recourse. The loss suffered by the indorser or accommodation party as a result of the modification is equal to the amount of the right of recourse unless the person enforcing the instrument proves that no loss was caused by the modification or that the loss caused by the modification was an amount less than the amount of the right of recourse.

(e) If the obligation of a party to pay an instrument is secured by an interest in collateral and a person entitled to enforce the instrument impairs the value of the interest in collateral, the obligation of an indorser or accommodation party having a right of recourse against the obligor is discharged to the extent of the impairment. The value of an interest in collateral is impaired to the extent (i) the value of the interest is reduced to an amount less than the amount of the right of recourse of the party asserting discharge, or (ii) the reduction in value of the interest causes an increase in the amount by which the amount of the right of recourse exceeds the value of the interest. The burden of proving impairment is on the party asserting discharge.

(f) If the obligation of a party is secured by an interest in collateral not provided by an accommodation party and a person entitled to enforce the instrument impairs the value of the interest in collateral, the obligation of any party who is jointly and severally liable with respect to the secured obligation is discharged to the extent the impairment causes the party asserting discharge to pay more than that party would have been obliged to pay, taking into account rights of contribution, if impairment had not occurred. If the party asserting discharge is an accommodation party not entitled to discharge under subsection (e), the party is deemed to have a right to contribution based on joint and several liability rather than a right to reimbursement. The burden of proving impairment is on the party asserting discharge.

(g) Under subsection (e) or (f), impairing value of an interest in collateral includes (i) failure to obtain or maintain perfection or recordation of the interest in collateral, (ii) release of collateral without substitution of collateral of equal value, (iii) failure to perform a duty to preserve the value of collateral owed, under Article 9 or other law, to a debtor or surety or other person secondarily liable, or (iv) failure to comply with applicable law in disposing of collateral.

(h) An accommodation party is not discharged under subsection (c), (d), or (e) unless the person entitled to enforce the instrument knows of the accommodation or has notice under Section 3—419(c) that the instrument was signed for accommodation.

(i) A party is not discharged under this section if (i) the party asserting discharge consents to the event or conduct that is the basis of the discharge, or (ii) the instrument or a separate agreement of the party provides for waiver of discharge under this section either specifically or by general language indicating that parties waive defenses based on suretyship or impairment of collateral.

ADDENDUM TO REVISED ARTICLE 3

Notes to Legislative Counsel

1. If revised Article 3 is adopted in your state, the reference in Section 2—511 to Section 3—802 should be changed to Section 3—310.

2. If revised Article 3 is adopted in your state and the Uniform Fiduciaries Act is also in effect in your state, you may want to consider amending Uniform Fiduciaries Act § 9 to conform to Section 3—307(b)(2)(iii) and (4)(iii). See Official Comment 3 to Section 3—307.

Revised Article 4
BANK DEPOSITS AND COLLECTIONS

Part 1 General Provisions and Definitions

§ 4—101. **Short Title.**

This Article may be cited as Uniform Commercial Code—Bank Deposits and Collections.

§ 4—102. **Applicability.**

(a) To the extent that items within this Article are also within Articles 3 and 8, they are subject to those Articles. If there is conflict, this Article governs Article 3, but Article 8 governs this Article.

(b) The liability of a bank for action or non-action with respect to an item handled by it for purposes of presentment, payment, or collection is governed by the law of the place where the bank is located. In the case of action or non-action by or at a branch or separate office of a bank, its liability is governed by the law of the place where the branch or separate office is located.

§ 4—103. **Variation by Agreement; Measure of Damages; Action Constituting Ordinary Care.**

(a) The effect of the provisions of this Article may be varied by agreement, but the parties to the agreement cannot disclaim a bank's responsibility for its lack of good faith or failure to exercise ordinary care or limit the measure of damages for the lack or failure. However, the parties may determine by agreement the standards by which the bank's responsibility is to be measured if those standards are not manifestly unreasonable.

(b) Federal Reserve regulations and operating circulars, clearing-house rules, and the like have the effect of agreements under subsection (a), whether or not specifically assented to by all parties interested in items handled.

(c) Action or non-action approved by this Article or pursuant to Federal Reserve regulations or operating circulars is the exercise of ordinary care and, in the absence of special instructions, action or non-action consistent with clearing-house rules and the like or with a general banking usage not disapproved by this Article, is prima facie the exercise of ordinary care.

(d) The specification or approval of certain procedures by this Article is not disapproval of other procedures that may be reasonable under the circumstances.

(e) The measure of damages for failure to exercise ordinary care in handling an item is the amount of the item reduced by an amount that could not have been realized by the exercise of ordinary care. If there is also bad faith it includes any other damages the party suffered as a proximate consequence.

§ 4—104. **Definitions and Index of Definitions.**

(a) In this Article, unless the context otherwise requires:

(1) "Account" means any deposit or credit account with a bank, including a demand, time, savings, passbook, share draft, or like account, other than an account evidenced by a certificate of deposit;

(2) "Afternoon" means the period of a day between noon and midnight;

(3) "Banking day" means the part of a day on which a bank is open to the public for carrying on substantially all of its banking functions;

(4) "Clearing house" means an association of banks or other payors regularly clearing items;

(5) "Customer" means a person having an account with a bank or for whom a bank has agreed to collect items, including a bank that maintains an account at another bank;

(6) "Documentary draft" means a draft to be presented for acceptance or payment if specified documents, certificated securities (Section 8—102) or instructions for uncertificated securities (Section 8—102), or other certificates, statements, or the like are to be received by the drawee or other payor before acceptance or payment of the draft;

(7) "Draft" means a draft as defined in Section 3—104 or an item, other than an instrument, that is an order;

(8) "Drawee" means a person ordered in a draft to make payment;

(9) "Item" means an instrument or a promise or order to pay money handled by a bank for collection or payment. The term does not include a payment order governed by Article 4A or a credit or debit card slip;

(10) "Midnight deadline" with respect to a bank is midnight on its next banking day following the banking day on which it receives the relevant item or notice or from which the time for taking action commences to run, whichever is later;

(11) "Settle" means to pay in cash, by clearing-house settlement, in a charge or credit or by remittance, or otherwise as agreed. A settlement may be either provisional or final;

(12) "Suspends payments" with respect to a bank means that it has been closed by order of the supervisory authorities, that a public officer has been appointed to take it over, or that it ceases or refuses to make payments in the ordinary course of business.

(b);(c) [Other definitions' section references deleted.]

(d) In addition, Article 1 contains general definitions and principles of construction and interpretation applicable throughout this Article.

§ 4—105. **"Bank"; "Depositary Bank"; "Payor Bank"; "Intermediary Bank"; "Collecting Bank"; "Presenting Bank".**

In this Article:

(1) "Bank" means a person engaged in the business of banking, including a savings bank, savings and loan association, credit union, or trust company;

(2) "Depositary bank" means the first bank to take an item even though it is also the payor bank, unless the item is presented for immediate payment over the counter;

(3) "Payor bank" means a bank that is the drawee of a draft;

(4) "Intermediary bank" means a bank to which an item is transferred in course of collection except the depositary or payor bank;

(5) "Collecting bank" means a bank handling an item for collection except the payor bank;

(6) "Presenting bank" means a bank presenting an item except a payor bank.

§ 4—106. **Payable Through or Payable at Bank: Collecting Bank.**

(a) If an item states that it is "payable through" a bank identified in the item, (i) the item designates the bank as a collecting bank and does not by itself authorize the bank to pay the item, and (ii) the item may be presented for payment only by or through the bank.

Alternative A

(b) If an item states that it is "payable at" a bank identified in the item, the item is equivalent to a draft drawn on the bank.

Alternative B

(b) If an item states that it is "payable at" a bank identified in the item, (i) the item designates the bank as a collecting bank and does not by itself authorize the bank to pay the item, and (ii) the item may be presented for payment only by or through the bank.

(c) If a draft names a nonbank drawee and it is unclear whether a bank named in the draft is a co-drawee or a collecting bank, the bank is a collecting bank.

§ 4—107. **Separate Office of Bank.**

A branch or separate office of a bank is a separate bank for the purpose of computing the time within which and determining the place at or to which action may be taken or notices or orders shall be given under this Article and under Article 3.

§ 4—108. **Time of Receipt of Items.**

(a) For the purpose of allowing time to process items, prove balances, and make the necessary entries on its books to determine its position for the day, a bank may fix an afternoon hour of 2 P.M. or later as a cutoff hour for the handling of money and items and the making of entries on its books.

(b) An item or deposit of money received on any day after a cutoff hour so fixed or after the close of the banking day may be treated as being received at the opening of the next banking day.

§ 4—109. **Delays.**

(a) Unless otherwise instructed, a collecting bank in a good faith effort to secure payment of a specific item drawn on a payor other than a bank, and with or without the approval of any person involved, may waive, modify, or extend time limits imposed or permitted by this [act] for a period not exceeding two additional banking days without discharge of drawers or indorsers or liability to its transferor or a prior party.

(b) Delay by a collecting bank or payor bank beyond time limits prescribed or permitted by this [act] or by instructions is excused if (i) the delay is caused by interruption of communication or computer facilities, suspension of payments by another bank, war, emergency conditions, failure of equipment, or other circumstances beyond the control of the bank, and (ii) the bank exercises such diligence as the circumstances require.

§ 4—110. Electronic Presentment.

(a) "Agreement for electronic presentment" means an agreement, clearing-house rule, or Federal Reserve regulation or operating circular, providing that presentment of an item may be made by transmission of an image of an item or information describing the item ("presentment notice") rather than delivery of the item itself. The agreement may provide for procedures governing retention, presentment, payment, dishonor, and other matters concerning items subject to the agreement.

(b) Presentment of an item pursuant to an agreement for presentment is made when the presentment notice is received.

(c) If presentment is made by presentment notice, a reference to "item" or "check" in this Article means the presentment notice unless the context otherwise indicates.

§ 4—111. Statute of Limitations.

An action to enforce an obligation, duty, or right arising under this Article must be commenced within three years after the [cause of action] accrues.

Part 2 Collection of Items: Depositary and Collecting Banks

§ 4—201. Status of Collecting Bank As Agent and Provisional Status of Credits; Applicability of Article; Item Indorsed "Pay Any Bank".

(a) Unless a contrary intent clearly appears and before the time that a settlement given by a collecting bank for an item is or becomes final, the bank, with respect to an item, is an agent or sub-agent of the owner of the item and any settlement given for the item is provisional. This provision applies regardless of the form of indorsement or lack of indorsement and even though credit given for the item is subject to immediate withdrawal as of right or is in fact withdrawn; but the continuance of ownership of an item by its owner and any rights of the owner to proceeds of the item are subject to rights of a collecting bank, such as those resulting from outstanding advances on the item and rights of recoupment or setoff. If an item is handled by banks for purposes of presentment, payment, collection, or return, the relevant provisions of this Article apply even though action of the parties clearly establishes that a particular bank has purchased the item and is the owner of it.

(b) After an item has been indorsed with the words "pay any bank" or the like, only a bank may acquire the rights of a holder until the item has been:

(1) returned to the customer initiating collection; or

(2) specially indorsed by a bank to a person who is not a bank.

§ 4—202. Responsibility for Collection or Return; When Action Timely.

(a) A collecting bank must exercise ordinary care in:

(1) presenting an item or sending it for presentment;

(2) sending notice of dishonor or nonpayment or returning an item other than a documentary draft to the bank's transferor after learning that the item has not been paid or accepted, as the case may be;

(3) settling for an item when the bank receives final settlement; and

(4) notifying its transferor of any loss or delay in transit within a reasonable time after discovery thereof.

(b) A collecting bank exercises ordinary care under subsection (a) by taking proper action before its midnight deadline following receipt of an item, notice, or settlement. Taking proper action within a reasonably longer time may constitute the exercise of ordinary care, but the bank has the burden of establishing timeliness.

(c) Subject to subsection (a)(1), a bank is not liable for the insolvency, neglect, misconduct, mistake, or default of another bank or person or for loss or destruction of an item in the possession of others or in transit.

§ 4—203. Effect of Instructions.

Subject to Article 3 concerning conversion of instruments (Section 3—420) and restrictive indorsements (Section 3—206), only a collecting bank's transferor can give instructions that affect the bank or constitute notice to it, and a collecting bank is not liable to prior parties for any action taken pursuant to the instructions or in accordance with any agreement with its transferor.

§ 4—204. Methods of Sending and Presenting; Sending Directly to Payor Bank.

(a) A collecting bank shall send items by a reasonably prompt method, taking into consideration relevant instructions, the nature of the item, the number of those items on hand, the cost of collection involved, and the method generally used by it or others to present those items.

(b) A collecting bank may send:

(1) an item directly to the payor bank;

(2) an item to a nonbank payor if authorized by its transferor; and

(3) an item other than documentary drafts to a nonbank payor, if authorized by Federal Reserve regulation or operating circular, clearing-house rule, or the like.

(c) Presentment may be made by a presenting bank at a place where the payor bank or other payor has requested that presentment be made.

§ 4—205. **Depositary Bank Holder of Unindorsed Item.**

If a customer delivers an item to a depositary bank for collection:

(1) the depositary bank becomes a holder of the item at the time it receives the item for collection if the customer at the time of delivery was a holder of the item, whether or not the customer indorses the item, and, if the bank satisfies the other requirements of Section 3—302, it is a holder in due course; and

(2) the depositary bank warrants to collecting banks, the payor bank or other payor, and the drawer that the amount of the item was paid to the customer or deposited to the customer's account.

§ 4—206. **Transfer Between Banks.**

Any agreed method that identifies the transferor bank is sufficient for the item's further transfer to another bank.

§ 4—207. **Transfer Warranties.**

(a) A customer or collecting bank that transfers an item and receives a settlement or other consideration warrants to the transferee and to any subsequent collecting bank that:

(1) the warrantor is a person entitled to enforce the item;

(2) all signatures on the item are authentic and authorized;

(3) the item has not been altered;

(4) the item is not subject to a defense or claim in recoupment (Section 3—305(a)) of any party that can be asserted against the warrantor; and

(5) the warrantor has no knowledge of any insolvency proceeding commenced with respect to the maker or acceptor or, in the case of an unaccepted draft, the drawer.

(b) If an item is dishonored, a customer or collecting bank transferring the item and receiving settlement or other consideration is obliged to pay the amount due on the item (i) according to the terms of the item at the time it was transferred, or (ii) if the transfer was of an incomplete item, according to its terms when completed as stated in Sections 3—115 and 3—407. The obligation of a transferor is owed to the transferee and to any subsequent collecting bank that takes the item in good faith. A transferor cannot disclaim its obligation under this subsection by an indorsement stating that it is made "without recourse" or otherwise disclaiming liability.

(c) A person to whom the warranties under subsection (a) are made and who took the item in good faith may recover from the warrantor as damages for breach of warranty an amount equal to the loss suffered as a result of the breach, but not more than the amount of the item plus expenses and loss of interest incurred as a result of the breach.

(d) The warranties stated in subsection (a) cannot be disclaimed with respect to checks. Unless notice of a claim for breach of warranty is given to the warrantor within 30 days after the claimant has reason to know of the breach and the identity of the warrantor, the warrantor is discharged to the extent of any loss caused by the delay in giving notice of the claim.

(e) A cause of action for breach of warranty under this section accrues when the claimant has reason to know of the breach.

§ 4—208. **Presentment Warranties.**

(a) If an unaccepted draft is presented to the drawee for payment or acceptance and the drawee pays or accepts the draft, (i) the person obtaining payment or acceptance, at the time of presentment, and (ii) a previous transferor of the draft, at the time of transfer, warrant to the drawee that pays or accepts the draft in good faith that:

(1) the warrantor is, or was, at the time the warrantor transferred the draft, a person entitled to enforce the draft or authorized to obtain payment or acceptance of the draft on behalf of a person entitled to enforce the draft;

(2) the draft has not been altered; and

(3) the warrantor has no knowledge that the signature of the purported drawer of the draft is unauthorized.

(b) A drawee making payment may recover from a warrantor damages for breach of warranty equal to the amount paid by the drawee less the amount the drawee received or is entitled to receive from the drawer because of the payment. In addition, the drawee is entitled to compensation for expenses and loss of interest resulting from the breach. The right of the drawee to recover damages under this subsection is not affected by any failure of the drawee to exercise ordinary care in making payment. If the drawee accepts the draft (i) breach of warranty is a defense to the obligation of the acceptor, and (ii) if the acceptor makes payment with respect to the draft, the acceptor is entitled to recover from a warrantor for breach of warranty the amounts stated in this subsection.

(c) If a drawee asserts a claim for breach of warranty under subsection (a) based on an unauthorized indorsement of the draft or an alteration of the draft, the warrantor may defend by proving that the indorsement is effective under Section 3—404 or 3—405 or the drawer is precluded under Section 3—406 or 4—406 from asserting against the drawee the unauthorized indorsement or alteration.

(d) If (i) a dishonored draft is presented for payment to the drawer or an indorser or (ii) any other item is presented for payment to a party obliged to pay the item, and the item is paid, the person obtaining payment and a prior transferor of the item warrant to the person making payment in good faith that the warrantor is, or was, at the time the warrantor transferred the item, a person entitled to enforce the item or authorized to obtain payment on behalf of a person entitled to enforce the item. The person making payment may recover from any warrantor for breach of warranty an amount equal to the amount paid plus expenses and loss of interest resulting from the breach.

(e) The warranties stated in subsections (a) and (d) cannot be disclaimed with respect to checks. Unless notice of a claim for breach of warranty is given to the warrantor within 30 days after the claimant has reason to know of the breach and the identity of the warrantor, the warrantor is discharged to the extent of any loss caused by the delay in giving notice of the claim.

(f) A cause of action for breach of warranty under this section accrues when the claimant has reason to know of the breach.

§ 4—209. Encoding and Retention Warranties.

(a) A person who encodes information on or with respect to an item after issue warrants to any subsequent collecting bank and to the payor bank or other payor that the information is correctly encoded. If the customer of a depositary bank encodes, that bank also makes the warranty.

(b) A person who undertakes to retain an item pursuant to an agreement for electronic presentment warrants to any subsequent collecting bank and to the payor bank or other payor that retention and presentment of the item comply with the agreement. If a customer of a depositary bank undertakes to retain an item, that bank also makes this warranty.

(c) A person to whom warranties are made under this section and who took the item in good faith may recover from the warrantor as damages for breach of warranty an amount equal to the loss suffered as a result of the breach, plus expenses and loss of interest incurred as a result of the breach.

§ 4—210. Security Interest of Collecting Bank in Items, Accompanying Documents and Proceeds.

(a) A collecting bank has a security interest in an item and any accompanying documents or the proceeds of either:

(1) in case of an item deposited in an account, to the extent to which credit given for the item has been withdrawn or applied;

(2) in case of an item for which it has given credit available for withdrawal as of right, to the extent of the credit given, whether or not the credit is drawn upon or there is a right of charge-back; or

(3) if it makes an advance on or against the item.

(b) If credit given for several items received at one time or pursuant to a single agreement is withdrawn or applied in part, the security interest remains upon all the items, any accompanying documents or the proceeds of either. For the purpose of this section, credits first given are first withdrawn.

(c) Receipt by a collecting bank of a final settlement for an item is a realization on its security interest in the item, accompanying documents, and proceeds. So long as the bank does not receive final settlement for the item or give up possession of the item or accompanying documents for purposes other than collection, the security interest continues to that extent and is subject to Article 9, but:

(1) no security agreement is necessary to make the security interest enforceable (Section 9—203(1)(a));

(2) no filing is required to perfect the security interest; and

(3) the security interest has priority over conflicting perfected security interests in the item, accompanying documents, or proceeds.

§ 4—211. When Bank Gives Value for Purposes of Holder in Due Course.

For purposes of determining its status as a holder in due course, a bank has given value to the extent it has a security interest in an item, if the bank otherwise complies with the requirements of Section 3—302 on what constitutes a holder in due course.

§ 4—212. Presentment by Notice of Item Not Payable by, Through, or at Bank; Liability of Drawer or Indorser.

(a) Unless otherwise instructed, a collecting bank may present an item not payable by, through, or at a bank by sending to the party to accept or pay a written notice that the bank holds the item for acceptance or payment. The notice must be sent in time to be received on or before the day when presentment is due and the bank must meet any requirement of the party to accept or pay under Section 3—501 by the close of the bank's next banking day after it knows of the requirement.

(b) If presentment is made by notice and payment, acceptance, or request for compliance with a requirement under Section 3—501 is not received by the close of business on the day after maturity or, in the case of demand items, by the close of business on the third banking day after notice was sent, the presenting bank may treat the item as dishonored and charge any drawer or indorser by sending it notice of the facts.

§ 4—213. Medium and Time of Settlement by Bank.

(a) With respect to settlement by a bank, the medium and time of settlement may be prescribed by Federal Reserve regulations or circulars, clearing-house rules, and the like, or agreement. In the absence of such prescription:

(1) the medium of settlement is cash or credit to an account in a Federal Reserve bank of or specified by the person to receive settlement; and

(2) the time of settlement is:

(i) with respect to tender of settlement by cash, a cashier's check, or teller's check, when the cash or check is sent or delivered;

(ii) with respect to tender of settlement by credit in an account in a Federal Reserve Bank, when the credit is made;

(iii) with respect to tender of settlement by a credit or debit to an account in a bank, when the credit or debit is made or, in the case of tender of settlement by authority to charge an account, when the authority is sent or delivered; or

(iv) with respect to tender of settlement by a funds transfer, when payment is made pursuant to Section 4A—406(a) to the person receiving settlement.

(b) If the tender of settlement is not by a medium authorized by subsection (a) or the time of settlement is not fixed by subsection (a), no settlement occurs until the tender of settlement is accepted by the person receiving settlement.

(c) If settlement for an item is made by cashier's check or teller's check and the person receiving settlement, before its midnight deadline:

(1) presents or forwards the check for collection, settlement is final when the check is finally paid; or

(2) fails to present or forward the check for collection, settlement is final at the midnight deadline of the person receiving settlement.

(d) If settlement for an item is made by giving authority to charge the account of the bank giving settlement in the bank receiving settlement, settlement is final when the charge is made by the bank receiving settlement if there are funds available in the account for the amount of the item.

§ 4—214. Right of Charge-Back or Refund; Liability of Collecting Bank: Return of Item.

(a) If a collecting bank has made provisional settlement with its customer for an item and fails by reason of dishonor, suspension of payments by a bank, or otherwise to receive settlement for the item which is or becomes final, the bank may revoke the settlement given by it, charge back the amount of any credit given for the item to its customer's account, or obtain refund from its customer, whether or not it is able to return the item, if by its midnight deadline or within a longer reasonable time after it learns the facts it returns the item or sends notification of the facts. If the return or notice is delayed beyond the bank's midnight deadline or a longer reasonable time after it learns the facts, the bank may revoke the settlement, charge back the credit, or obtain refund from its customer, but it is liable for any loss resulting from the delay. These rights to revoke, charge back, and obtain refund terminate if and when a settlement for the item received by the bank is or becomes final.

(b) A collecting bank returns an item when it is sent or delivered to the bank's customer or transferor or pursuant to its instructions.

(c) A depositary bank that is also the payor may charge back the amount of an item to its customer's account or obtain refund in accordance with the section governing return of an item received by a payor bank for credit on its books (Section 4—301).

(d) The right to charge back is not affected by:

(1) previous use of a credit given for the item; or

(2) failure by any bank to exercise ordinary care with respect to the item, but a bank so failing remains liable.

(e) A failure to charge back or claim refund does not affect other rights of the bank against the customer or any other party.

(f) If credit is given in dollars as the equivalent of the value of an item payable in foreign money, the dollar amount of any charge-back or refund must be calculated on the basis of the bank-offered spot rate for the foreign money prevailing on the day when the person entitled to the charge-back or refund learns that it will not receive payment in ordinary course.

§ 4—215. Final Payment of Item by Payor Bank; When Provisional Debits and Credits Become Final; When Certain Credits Become Available for Withdrawal.

(a) An item is finally paid by a payor bank when the bank has first done any of the following:

(1) paid the item in cash;

(2) settled for the item without having a right to revoke the settlement under statute, clearing-house rule, or agreement; or

(3) made a provisional settlement for the item and failed to revoke the settlement in the time and man-

ner permitted by statute, clearing-house rule, or agreement.

(b) If provisional settlement for an item does not become final, the item is not finally paid.

(c) If provisional settlement for an item between the presenting and payor banks is made through a clearing house or by debits or credits in an account between them, then to the extent that provisional debits or credits for the item are entered in accounts between the presenting and payor banks or between the presenting and successive prior collecting banks seriatim, they become final upon final payment of the item by the payor bank.

(d) If a collecting bank receives a settlement for an item which is or becomes final, the bank is accountable to its customer for the amount of the item and any provisional credit given for the item in an account with its customer becomes final.

(e) Subject to (i) applicable law stating a time for availability of funds and (ii) any right of the bank to apply the credit to an obligation of the customer, credit given by a bank for an item in a customer's account becomes available for withdrawal as of right:

(1) if the bank has received a provisional settlement for the item, when the settlement becomes final and the bank has had a reasonable time to receive return of the item and the item has not been received within that time;

(2) if the bank is both the depositary bank and the payor bank, and the item is finally paid, at the opening of the bank's second banking day following receipt of the item.

(f) Subject to applicable law stating a time for availability of funds and any right of a bank to apply a deposit to an obligation of the depositor, a deposit of money becomes available for withdrawal as of right at the opening of the bank's next banking day after receipt of the deposit.

§ 4—216. Insolvency and Preference.

(a) If an item is in or comes into the possession of a payor or collecting bank that suspends payment and the item has not been finally paid, the item must be returned by the receiver, trustee, or agent in charge of the closed bank to the presenting bank or the closed bank's customer.

(b) If a payor bank finally pays an item and suspends payments without making a settlement for the item with its customer or the presenting bank which settlement is or becomes final, the owner of the item has a preferred claim against the payor bank.

(c) If a payor bank gives or a collecting bank gives or receives a provisional settlement for an item and thereafter suspends payments, the suspension does not prevent or interfere with the settlement's becoming final if the finality occurs automatically upon the lapse of certain time or the happening of certain events.

(d) If a collecting bank receives from subsequent parties settlement for an item, which settlement is or becomes final and the bank suspends payments without making a settlement for the item with its customer which settlement is or becomes final, the owner of the item has a preferred claim against the collecting bank.

Part 3 Collection of Items: Payor Banks

§ 4—301. Deferred Posting; Recovery of Payment by Return of Items; Time of Dishonor; Return of Items by Payor Bank.

(a) If a payor bank settles for a demand item other than a documentary draft presented otherwise than for immediate payment over the counter before midnight of the banking day of receipt, the payor bank may revoke the settlement and recover the settlement if, before it has made final payment and before its midnight deadline, it

(1) returns the item; or

(2) sends written notice of dishonor or nonpayment if the item is unavailable for return.

(b) If a demand item is received by a payor bank for credit on its books, it may return the item or send notice of dishonor and may revoke any credit given or recover the amount thereof withdrawn by its customer, if it acts within the time limit and in the manner specified in subsection (a).

(c) Unless previous notice of dishonor has been sent, an item is dishonored at the time when for purposes of dishonor it is returned or notice sent in accordance with this section.

(d) An item is returned:

(1) as to an item presented through a clearing house, when it is delivered to the presenting or last collecting bank or to the clearing house or is sent or delivered in accordance with clearing-house rules; or

(2) in all other cases, when it is sent or delivered to the bank's customer or transferor or pursuant to instructions.

§ 4—302. Payor Bank's Responsibility for Late Return of Item.

(a) If an item is presented to and received by a payor bank, the bank is accountable for the amount of:

(1) a demand item, other than a documentary draft, whether properly payable or not, if the bank, in any case in which it is not also the depositary bank, retains the item beyond midnight of the banking day of receipt without settling for it or, whether or not it is also the depositary bank, does not pay or return the item or send notice of dishonor until after its midnight deadline; or

(2) any other properly payable item unless, within the time allowed for acceptance or payment of that item, the bank either accepts or pays the item or returns it and accompanying documents.

(b) The liability of a payor bank to pay an item pursuant to subsection (a) is subject to defenses based on breach of a presentment warranty (Section 4—208) or proof that the person seeking enforcement of the liability presented or transferred the item for the purpose of defrauding the payor bank.

§ 4—303. When Items Subject to Notice, Stop-Payment Order, Legal Process, or Setoff; Order in Which Items May Be Charged or Certified.

(a) Any knowledge, notice, or stop-payment order received by, legal process served upon, or setoff exercised by a payor bank comes too late to terminate, suspend, or modify the bank's right or duty to pay an item or to charge its customer's account for the item if the knowledge, notice, stop-payment order, or legal process is received or served and a reasonable time for the bank to act thereon expires or the setoff is exercised after the earliest of the following:

(1) the bank accepts or certifies the item;

(2) the bank pays the item in cash;

(3) the bank settles for the item without having a right to revoke the settlement under statute, clearing-house rule, or agreement;

(4) the bank becomes accountable for the amount of the item under Section 4—302 dealing with the payor bank's responsibility for late return of items; or

(5) with respect to checks, a cutoff hour no earlier than one hour after the opening of the next banking day after the banking day on which the bank received the check and no later than the close of that next banking day or, if no cutoff hour is fixed, the close of the next banking day after the banking day on which the bank received the check.

(b) Subject to subsection (a), items may be accepted, paid, certified, or charged to the indicated account of its customer in any order.

Part 4 Relationship Between Payor Bank and its Customer

§ 4—401. When Bank May Charge Customer's Account.

(a) A bank may charge against the account of a customer an item that is properly payable from the account even though the charge creates an overdraft. An item is properly payable if it is authorized by the customer and is in accordance with any agreement between the customer and bank.

(b) A customer is not liable for the amount of an overdraft if the customer neither signed the item nor benefited from the proceeds of the item.

(c) A bank may charge against the account of a customer a check that is otherwise properly payable from the account, even though payment was made before the date of the check, unless the customer has given notice to the bank of the postdating describing the check with reasonable certainty. The notice is effective for the period stated in Section 4—403(b) for stop-payment orders, and must be received at such time and in such manner as to afford the bank a reasonable opportunity to act on it before the bank takes any action with respect to the check described in Section 4—303. If a bank charges against the account of a customer a check before the date stated in the notice of postdating, the bank is liable for damages for the loss resulting from its act. The loss may include damages for dishonor of subsequent items under Section 4—402.

(d) A bank that in good faith makes payment to a holder may charge the indicated account of its customer according to:

(1) the original terms of the altered item; or

(2) the terms of the completed item, even though the bank knows the item has been completed unless the bank has notice that the completion was improper.

§ 4—402. Bank's Liability to Customer for Wrongful Dishonor; Time of Determining Insufficiency of Account.

(a) Except as otherwise provided in this Article, a payor bank wrongfully dishonors an item if it dishonors an item that is properly payable, but a bank may dishonor an item that would create an overdraft unless it has agreed to pay the overdraft.

(b) A payor bank is liable to its customer for damages proximately caused by the wrongful dishonor of an item. Liability is limited to actual damages proved and may include damages for an arrest or prosecution of the customer or other consequential damages. Whether any consequential damages are proximately caused by the wrongful dishonor is a question of fact to be determined in each case.

(c) A payor bank's determination of the customer's account balance on which a decision to dishonor for insufficiency of available funds is based may be made at any time between the time the item is received by the payor bank and the time that the payor bank returns the item or gives notice in lieu of return, and no more than one determination need be made. If, at the election of the payor bank, a subsequent balance determination is made for the purpose of reevaluating the bank's decision to dishonor the item, the account balance at that time is determinative of whether a dishonor for insufficiency of available funds is wrongful.

§ 4—403. Customer's Right to Stop Payment; Burden of Proof of Loss.

(a) A customer or any person authorized to draw on the account if there is more than one person may stop payment of any item drawn on the customer's account or close the account by an order to the bank describing the item or account with reasonable certainty received at a time and in a manner that affords the bank a reasonable opportunity to act on it before any action by the bank with respect to the item described in Section 4—303. If the signature of more than one person is required to draw on an account, any of these persons may stop payment or close the account.

(b) A stop-payment order is effective for six months, but it lapses after 14 calendar days if the original order was oral and was not confirmed in writing within that period. A stop-payment order may be renewed for additional six-month periods by a writing given to the bank within a period during which the stop-payment order is effective.

(c) The burden of establishing the fact and amount of loss resulting from the payment of an item contrary to a stop-payment order or order to close an account is on the customer. The loss from payment of an item contrary to a stop-payment order may include damages for dishonor of subsequent items under Section 4—402.

§ 4—404. Bank Not Obliged to Pay Check More Than Six Months Old.

A bank is under no obligation to a customer having a checking account to pay a check, other than a certified check, which is presented more than six months after its date, but it may charge its customer's account for a payment made thereafter in good faith.

§ 4—405. Death or Incompetence of Customer.

(a) A payor or collecting bank's authority to accept, pay, or collect an item or to account for proceeds of its collection, if otherwise effective, is not rendered ineffective by incompetence of a customer of either bank existing at the time the item is issued or its collection is undertaken if the bank does not know of an adjudication of incompetence. Neither death nor incompetence of a customer revokes the authority to accept, pay, collect, or account until the bank knows of the fact of death or of an adjudication of incompetence and has reasonable opportunity to act on it.

(b) Even with knowledge, a bank may for 10 days after the date of death pay or certify checks drawn on or before the date unless ordered to stop payment by a person claiming an interest in the account.

§ 4—406. Customer's Duty to Discover and Report Unauthorized Signature or Alteration.

(a) A bank that sends or makes available to a customer a statement of account showing payment of items for the account shall either return or make available to the customer the items paid or provide information in the statement of account sufficient to allow the customer reasonably to identify the items paid. The statement of account provides sufficient information if the item is described by item number, amount, and date of payment.

(b) If the items are not returned to the customer, the person retaining the items shall either retain the items or, if the items are destroyed, maintain the capacity to furnish legible copies of the items until the expiration of seven years after receipt of the items. A customer may request an item from the bank that paid the item, and that bank must provide in a reasonable time either the item or, if the item has been destroyed or is not otherwise obtainable, a legible copy of the item.

(c) If a bank sends or makes available a statement of account or items pursuant to subsection (a), the customer must exercise reasonable promptness in examining the statement or the items to determine whether any payment was not authorized because of an alteration of an item or because a purported signature by or on behalf of the customer was not authorized. If, based on the statement or items provided, the customer should reasonably have discovered the unauthorized payment, the customer must promptly notify the bank of the relevant facts.

(d) If the bank proves that the customer failed, with respect to an item, to comply with the duties imposed on the customer by subsection (c), the customer is precluded from asserting against the bank:

(1) the customer's unauthorized signature or any alteration on the item, if the bank also proves that it suffered a loss by reason of the failure; and

(2) the customer's unauthorized signature or alteration by the same wrongdoer on any other item paid in good faith by the bank if the payment was made before the bank received notice from the customer of the unauthorized signature or alteration and after the customer had been afforded a reasonable period of time, not exceeding 30 days, in which to examine the item or statement of account and notify the bank.

(e) If subsection (d) applies and the customer proves that the bank failed to exercise ordinary care in paying the item and that the failure substantially contributed to loss, the loss is allocated between the customer precluded and the bank asserting the preclusion according to the extent to which the failure of the customer to comply with subsection (c) and the failure of the bank to exercise ordinary care contributed to the loss. If the customer proves that the bank did not pay the item in good faith, the preclusion under subsection (d) does not apply.

(f) Without regard to care or lack of care of either the customer or the bank, a customer who does not within one year after the statement or items are made available to the customer (subsection (a)) discover and report the customer's unauthorized signature on or any alteration on the item is precluded from asserting against the bank the unauthorized signature or alteration. If there is a preclusion under this subsection, the payor bank may not recover for breach or warranty under Section 4—208 with respect to the unauthorized signature or alteration to which the preclusion applies.

§ 4—407. Payor Bank's Right to Subrogation on Improper Payment.

If a payor has paid an item over the order of the drawer or maker to stop payment, or after an account has been closed, or otherwise under circumstances giving a basis for objection by the drawer or maker, to prevent unjust enrichment and only to the extent necessary to prevent loss to the bank by reason of its payment of the item, the payor bank is subrogated to the rights

(1) of any holder in due course on the item against the drawer or maker;

(2) of the payee or any other holder of the item against the drawer or maker either on the item or under the transaction out of which the item arose; and

(3) of the drawer or maker against the payee or any other holder of the item with respect to the transaction out of which the item arose.

Part 5 Collection of Documentary Drafts

§ 4—501. Handling of Documentary Drafts; Duty to Send for Presentment and to Notify Customer of Dishonor.

A bank that takes a documentary draft for collection shall present or send the draft and accompanying documents for presentment and, upon learning that the draft has not been paid or accepted in due course, shall seasonably notify its customer of the fact even though it may have discounted or bought the draft or extended credit available for withdrawal as of right.

§ 4—502. Presentment of "On Arrival" Drafts.

If a draft or the relevant instructions require presentment "on arrival", "when goods arrive" or the like, the collecting bank need not present until in its judgment a reasonable time for arrival of the goods has expired. Refusal to pay or accept because the goods have not arrived is not dishonor; the bank must notify its transferor of the refusal but need not present the draft again until it is instructed to do so or learns of the arrival of the goods.

§ 4—503. Responsibility of Presenting Bank for Documents and Goods; Report of Reasons for Dishonor; Referee in Case of Need.

Unless otherwise instructed and except as provided in Article 5, a bank presenting a documentary draft:

(1) must deliver the documents to the drawee on acceptance of the draft if it is payable more than three days after presentment, otherwise, only on payment; and

(2) upon dishonor, either in the case of presentment for acceptance or presentment for payment, may seek and follow instructions from any referee in case of need designated in the draft or, if the presenting bank does not choose to utilize the referee's services, it must use diligence and good faith to ascertain the reason for dishonor, must notify its transferor of the dishonor and of the results of its effort to ascertain the reasons therefor, and must request instructions.

However, the presenting bank is under no obligation with respect to goods represented by the documents except to follow any reasonable instructions seasonably received; it has a right to reimbursement for any expense incurred in following instructions and to prepayment of or indemnity for those expenses.

§ 4—504. Privilege of Presenting Bank to Deal With Goods; Security Interest for Expenses.

(a) A presenting bank that, following the dishonor of a documentary draft, has seasonably requested instructions but does not receive them within a reasonable time may store, sell, or otherwise deal with the goods in any reasonable manner.

(b) For its reasonable expenses incurred by action under subsection (a) the presenting bank has a lien upon the goods or their proceeds, which may be foreclosed in the same manner as an unpaid seller's lien.

Article 4A
FUNDS TRANSFERS

Part 1 Subject Matter and Definitions

§ 4A—101. Short Title.

This Article may be cited as Uniform Commercial Code—Funds Transfers.

§ 4A—102. Subject Matter.

Except as otherwise provided in Section 4A—108, this Article applies to funds transfers defined in Section 4A—104.

§ 4A—103. Payment Order—Definitions.

(a) In this Article:

(1) "Payment order" means an instruction of a sender to a receiving bank, transmitted orally, electronically, or in writing, to pay, or to cause another bank to pay, a fixed or determinable amount of money to a beneficiary if:

(i) the instruction does not state a condition to payment to the beneficiary other than time of payment,

(ii) the receiving bank is to be reimbursed by debiting an account of, or otherwise receiving payment from, the sender, and

(iii) the instruction is transmitted by the sender directly to the receiving bank or to an agent, funds-transfer system, or communication system for transmittal to the receiving bank.

(2) "Beneficiary" means the person to be paid by the beneficiary's bank.

(3) "Beneficiary's bank" means the bank identified in a payment order in which an account of the beneficiary is to be credited pursuant to the order or which otherwise is to make payment to the beneficiary if the order does not provide for payment to an account.

(4) "Receiving bank" means the bank to which the sender's instruction is addressed.

(5) "Sender" means the person giving the instruction to the receiving bank.

(b) If an instruction complying with subsection (a)(1) is to make more than one payment to a beneficiary, the instruction is a separate payment order with respect to each payment.

(c) A payment order is issued when it is sent to the receiving bank.

§ 4A—104. Funds Transfer—Definitions.

In this Article:

(a) "Funds transfer" means the series of transactions, beginning with the originator's payment order, made for the purpose of making payment to the beneficiary of the order. The term includes any payment order issued by the originator's bank or an intermediary bank intended to carry out the originator's payment order. A funds transfer is completed by acceptance by the beneficiary's bank of a payment order for the benefit of the beneficiary of the originator's payment order.

(b) "Intermediary bank" means a receiving bank other than the originator's bank or the beneficiary's bank.

(c) "Originator" means the sender of the first payment order in a funds transfer.

(d) "Originator's bank" means (i) the receiving bank to which the payment order of the originator is issued if the originator is not a bank, or (ii) the originator if the originator is a bank.

§ 4A—105. Other Definitions.

(a) In this Article:

(1) "Authorized account" means a deposit account of a customer in a bank designated by the customer as a source of payment of payment orders issued by the customer to the bank. If a customer does not so designate an account, any account of the customer is an authorized account if payment of a payment order from that account is not inconsistent with a restriction on the use of that account.

(2) "Bank" means a person engaged in the business of banking and includes a savings bank, savings and loan association, credit union, and trust company. A branch or separate office of a bank is a separate bank for purposes of this Article.

(3) "Customer" means a person, including a bank, having an account with a bank or from whom a bank has agreed to receive payment orders.

(4) "Funds-transfer business day" of a receiving bank means the part of a day during which the receiving bank is open for the receipt, processing, and transmittal of payment orders and cancellations and amendments of payment orders.

(5) "Funds-transfer system" means a wire transfer network, automated clearing house, or other communication system of a clearing house or other association of banks through which a payment order by a bank may be transmitted to the bank to which the order is addressed.

(6) "Good faith" means honesty in fact and the observance of reasonable commercial standards of fair dealing.

(7) "Prove" with respect to a fact means to meet the burden of establishing the fact (Section 1—201(8)).

(b) Other definitions applying to this Article and the sections in which they appear are:

"Acceptance"	Section 4A—209
"Beneficiary"	Section 4A—103
"Beneficiary's bank"	Section 4A—103
"Executed"	Section 4A—301
"Execution date"	Section 4A—301
"Funds transfer"	Section 4A—104
"Funds-transfer system rule"	Section 4A—501
"Intermediary bank"	Section 4A—104
"Originator"	Section 4A—104
"Originator's bank"	Section 4A—104
"Payment by beneficiary's bank to beneficiary"	Section 4A—405
"Payment by originator to beneficiary"	Section 4A—406
"Payment by sender to receiving bank"	Section 4A—403
"Payment date"	Section 4A—401
"Payment order"	Section 4A—103

"Receiving bank"	Section 4A—103
"Security procedure"	Section 4A—201
"Sender"	Section 4A—103

(c) The following definitions in Article 4 apply to this Article:

"Clearing house"	Section 4—104
"Item"	Section 4—104
"Suspends payments"	Section 4—104

(d) In addition, Article 1 contains general definitions and principles of construction and interpretation applicable throughout this Article.

§ 4A—106. Time Payment Order Is Received.

(a) The time of receipt of a payment order or communication cancelling or amending a payment order is determined by the rules applicable to receipt of a notice stated in Section 1—201(27). A receiving bank may fix a cut-off time or times on a funds-transfer business day for the receipt and processing of payment orders and communications cancelling or amending payment orders. Different cut-off times may apply to payment orders, cancellations, or amendments, or to different categories of payment orders, cancellations, or amendments. A cut-off time may apply to senders generally or different cut-off times may apply to different senders or categories of payment orders. If a payment order or communication cancelling or amending a payment order is received after the close of a funds-transfer business day or after the appropriate cut-off time on a funds-transfer business day, the receiving bank may treat the payment order or communication as received at the opening of the next funds-transfer business day.

(b) If this Article refers to an execution date or payment date or states a day on which a receiving bank is required to take action, and the date or day does not fall on a funds-transfer business day, the next day that is a funds-transfer business day is treated as the date or day stated, unless the contrary is stated in this Article.

§ 4A—107. Federal Reserve Regulations and Operating Circulars.

Regulations of the Board of Governors of the Federal Reserve System and operating circulars of the Federal Reserve Banks supersede any inconsistent provision of this Article to the extent of the inconsistency.

§ 4A—108. Exclusion of Consumer Transactions Governed by Federal Law.

This Article does not apply to a funds transfer any part of which is governed by the Electronic Fund Transfer Act of 1978 (Title XX, Public Law 95—630, 92 Stat. 3728, 15 U.S.C. § 1693 et seq.) as amended from time to time.

Part 2 Issue and Acceptance of Payment Order

§ 4A—201. Security Procedure.

"Security procedure" means a procedure established by agreement of a customer and a receiving bank for the purpose of (i) verifying that a payment order or communication amending or cancelling a payment order is that of the customer, or (ii) detecting error in the transmission or the content of the payment order or communication. A security procedure may require the use of algorithms or other codes, identifying words or numbers, encryption, callback procedures, or similar security devices. Comparison of a signature on a payment order or communication with an authorized specimen signature of the customer is not by itself a security procedure.

§ 4A—202. Authorized and Verified Payment Orders.

(a) A payment order received by the receiving bank is the authorized order of the person identified as sender if that person authorized the order or is otherwise bound by it under the law of agency.

(b) If a bank and its customer have agreed that the authenticity of payment orders issued to the bank in the name of the customer as sender will be verified pursuant to a security procedure, a payment order received by the receiving bank is effective as the order of the customer, whether or not authorized, if (i) the security procedure is a commercially reasonable method of providing security against unauthorized payment orders, and (ii) the bank proves that it accepted the payment order in good faith and in compliance with the security procedure and any written agreement or instruction of the customer restricting acceptance of payment orders issued in the name of the customer. The bank is not required to follow an instruction that violates a written agreement with the customer or notice of which is not received at a time and in a manner affording the bank a reasonable opportunity to act on it before the payment order is accepted.

(c) Commercial reasonableness of a security procedure is a question of law to be determined by considering the wishes of the customer expressed to the bank, the circumstances of the customer known to the bank, including the size, type, and frequency of payment orders normally issued by the customer to the bank, alternative security procedures offered to the customer, and security procedures in general use by customers and receiving banks similarly situated. A security procedure is deemed to be commercially reasonable if (i) the security procedure was chosen by the customer after the bank offered, and the customer refused, a security procedure that was commercially reasonable for that customer, and (ii) the customer expressly agreed in writing to be bound by any payment order, whether or not authorized, issued in its name and accepted by the bank in compliance with the security procedure chosen by the customer.

(d) The term "sender" in this Article includes the customer in whose name a payment order is issued if the order is the authorized order of the customer under subsection (a), or it is effective as the order of the customer under subsection (b).

(e) This section applies to amendments and cancellations of payment orders to the same extent it applies to payment orders.

(f) Except as provided in this section and in Section 4A—203(a)(1), rights and obligations arising under this section or Section 4A—203 may not be varied by agreement.

§ 4A—203. Unenforceability of Certain Verified Payment Orders.

(a) If an accepted payment order is not, under Section 4A—202(a), an authorized order of a customer identified as sender, but is effective as an order of the customer pursuant to Section 4A—202(b), the following rules apply:

(1) By express written agreement, the receiving bank may limit the extent to which it is entitled to enforce or retain payment of the payment order.

(2) The receiving bank is not entitled to enforce or retain payment of the payment order if the customer proves that the order was not caused, directly or indirectly, by a person (i) entrusted at any time with duties to act for the customer with respect to payment orders or the security procedure, or (ii) who obtained access to transmitting facilities of the customer or who obtained, from a source controlled by the customer and without authority of the receiving bank, information facilitating breach of the security procedure, regardless of how the information was obtained or whether the customer was at fault. Information includes any access device, computer software, or the like.

(b) This section applies to amendments of payment orders to the same extent it applies to payment orders.

§ 4A—204. Refund of Payment and Duty of Customer to Report with Respect to Unauthorized Payment Order.

(a) If a receiving bank accepts a payment order issued in the name of its customer as sender which is (i) not authorized and not effective as the order of the customer under Section 4A—202, or (ii) not enforceable, in whole or in part, against the customer under Section 4A—203, the bank shall refund any payment of the payment order received from the customer to the extent the bank is not entitled to enforce payment and shall pay interest on the refundable amount calculated from the date the bank received payment to the date of the refund. However, the customer is not entitled to interest from the bank on the amount to be refunded if the customer fails to exercise ordinary care to determine that the order was not authorized by the customer and to notify the bank of the relevant facts within a reasonable time not exceeding 90 days after the date the customer received notification from the bank that the order was accepted or that the customer's account was debited with respect to the order. The bank is not entitled to any recovery from the customer on account of a failure by the customer to give notification as stated in this section.

(b) Reasonable time under subsection (a) may be fixed by agreement as stated in Section 1—204(1), but the obligation of a receiving bank to refund payment as stated in subsection (a) may not otherwise be varied by agreement.

§ 4A—205. Erroneous Payment Orders.

(a) If an accepted payment order was transmitted pursuant to a security procedure for the detection of error and the payment order (i) erroneously instructed payment to a beneficiary not intended by the sender, (ii) erroneously instructed payment in an amount greater than the amount intended by the sender, or (iii) was an erroneously transmitted duplicate of a payment order previously sent by the sender, the following rules apply:

(1) If the sender proves that the sender or a person acting on behalf of the sender pursuant to Section 4A—206 complied with the security procedure and that the error would have been detected if the receiving bank had also complied, the sender is not obliged to pay the order to the extent stated in paragraphs (2) and (3).

(2) If the funds transfer is completed on the basis of an erroneous payment order described in clause (i) or (iii) of subsection (a), the sender is not obliged to pay the order and the receiving bank is entitled to recover from the beneficiary any amount paid to the beneficiary to the extent allowed by the law governing mistake and restitution.

(3) If the funds transfer is completed on the basis of a payment order described in clause (ii) of subsection (a), the sender is not obliged to pay the order to the extent the amount received by the beneficiary is greater than the amount intended by the sender. In that case, the receiving bank is entitled to recover from the beneficiary the excess amount received to the extent allowed by the law governing mistake and restitution.

(b) If (i) the sender of an erroneous payment order described in subsection (a) is not obliged to pay all or part of the order, and (ii) the sender receives notification from the receiving bank that the order was accepted by the bank or that the sender's account was debited with respect to the order, the sender has a duty to exercise ordinary care, on the basis of information available to the sender, to discover the error with respect to the order and to advise the bank of the relevant facts within a reasonable time, not exceeding 90 days, after the bank's notification was received by the sender. If the bank proves that the sender failed to perform that duty, the sender is liable to the bank for the loss the bank proves it incurred as a result of the failure, but the liability of the sender may not exceed the amount of the sender's order.

(c) This section applies to amendments to payment orders to the same extent it applies to payment orders.

§ 4A—206. Transmission of Payment Order through Funds-Transfer or Other Communication System.

(a) If a payment order addressed to a receiving bank is transmitted to a funds-transfer system or other third party communication system for transmittal to the bank, the system is deemed to be an agent of the sender for the purpose of transmitting the payment order to the bank. If there is a discrepancy between the terms of the payment order transmitted to the system and the terms of the payment order transmitted by the system to the bank, the terms of the payment order of the sender are those transmitted by the system. This section does not apply to a funds-transfer system of the Federal Reserve Banks.

(b) This section applies to cancellations and amendments to payment orders to the same extent it applies to payment orders.

§ 4A—207. Misdescription of Beneficiary.

(a) Subject to subsection (b), if, in a payment order received by the beneficiary's bank, the name, bank account number, or other identification of the beneficiary refers to a nonexistent or unidentifiable person or account, no person has rights as a beneficiary of the order and acceptance of the order cannot occur.

(b) If a payment order received by the beneficiary's bank identifies the beneficiary both by name and by an identifying or bank account number and the name and number identify different persons, the following rules apply:

(1) Except as otherwise provided in subsection (c), if the beneficiary's bank does not know that the name and number refer to different persons, it may rely on the number as the proper identification of the beneficiary of the order. The beneficiary's bank need not determine whether the name and number refer to the same person.

(2) If the beneficiary's bank pays the person identified by name or knows that the name and number identify different persons, no person has rights as beneficiary except the person paid by the beneficiary's bank if that person was entitled to receive payment from the originator of the funds transfer. If no person has rights as beneficiary, acceptance of the order cannot occur.

(c) If (i) a payment order described in subsection (b) is accepted, (ii) the originator's payment order described the beneficiary inconsistently by name and number, and (iii) the beneficiary's bank pays the person identified by number as permitted by subsection (b)(1), the following rules apply:

(1) If the originator is a bank, the originator is obliged to pay its order.

(2) If the originator is not a bank and proves that the person identified by number was not entitled to receive payment from the originator, the originator is not obliged to pay its order unless the originator's bank proves that the originator, before acceptance of the originator's order, had notice that payment of a payment order issued by the originator might be made by the beneficiary's bank on the basis of an identifying or bank account number even if it identifies a person different from the named beneficiary. Proof of notice may be made by any admissible evidence. The originator's bank satisfies the burden of proof if it proves that the originator, before the payment order was accepted, signed a writing stating the information to which the notice relates.

(d) In a case governed by subsection (b)(1), if the beneficiary's bank rightfully pays the person identified by number and that person was not entitled to receive payment from the originator, the amount paid may be recovered from that person to the extent allowed by the law governing mistake and restitution as follows:

(1) If the originator is obliged to pay its payment order as stated in subsection (c), the originator has the right to recover.

(2) If the originator is not a bank and is not obliged to pay its payment order, the originator's bank has the right to recover.

§ 4A—208. Misdescription of Intermediary Bank or Beneficiary's Bank.

(a) This subsection applies to a payment order identifying an intermediary bank or the beneficiary's bank only by an identifying number.

(1) The receiving bank may rely on the number as the proper identification of the intermediary or beneficiary's bank and need not determine whether the number identifies a bank.

(2) The sender is obliged to compensate the receiving bank for any loss and expenses incurred by the receiving bank as a result of its reliance on the number in executing or attempting to execute the order.

(b) This subsection applies to a payment order identifying an intermediary bank or the beneficiary's bank both by name and an identifying number if the name and number identify different persons.

(1) If the sender is a bank, the receiving bank may rely on the number as the proper identification of the intermediary or beneficiary's bank if the receiving

bank, when it executes the sender's order, does not know that the name and number identify different persons. The receiving bank need not determine whether the name and number refer to the same person or whether the number refers to a bank. The sender is obliged to compensate the receiving bank for any loss and expenses incurred by the receiving bank as a result of its reliance on the number in executing or attempting to execute the order.

(2) If the sender is not a bank and the receiving bank proves that the sender, before the payment order was accepted, had notice that the receiving bank might rely on the number as the proper identification of the intermediary or beneficiary's bank even if it identifies a person different from the bank identified by name, the rights and obligations of the sender and the receiving bank are governed by subsection (b)(1), as though the sender were a bank. Proof of notice may be made by any admissible evidence. The receiving bank satisfies the burden of proof if it proves that the sender, before the payment order was accepted, signed a writing stating the information to which the notice relates.

(3) Regardless of whether the sender is a bank, the receiving bank may rely on the name as the proper identification of the intermediary or beneficiary's bank if the receiving bank, at the time it executes the sender's order, does not know that the name and number identify different persons. The receiving bank need not determine whether the name and number refer to the same person.

(4) If the receiving bank knows that the name and number identify different persons, reliance on either the name or the number in executing the sender's payment order is a breach of the obligation stated in Section 4A—302(a)(1).

§ 4A—209. **Acceptance of Payment Order.**

(a) Subject to subsection (d), a receiving bank other than the beneficiary's bank accepts a payment order when it executes the order.

(b) Subject to subsections (c) and (d), a beneficiary's bank accepts a payment order at the earliest of the following times:

(1) When the bank (i) pays the beneficiary as stated in Section 4A—405(a) or 4A—405(b), or (ii) notifies the beneficiary of receipt of the order or that the account of the beneficiary has been credited with respect to the order unless the notice indicates that the bank is rejecting the order or that funds with respect to the order may not be withdrawn or used until receipt of payment from the sender of the order;

(2) When the bank receives payment of the entire amount of the sender's order pursuant to Section 4A—403(a)(1) or 4A—403(a)(2); or

(3) The opening of the next funds-transfer business day of the bank following the payment date of the order if, at that time, the amount of the sender's order is fully covered by a withdrawable credit balance in an authorized account of the sender or the bank has otherwise received full payment from the sender, unless the order was rejected before that time or is rejected within (i) one hour after that time, or (ii) one hour after the opening of the next business day of the sender following the payment date if that time is later. If notice of rejection is received by the sender after the payment date and the authorized account of the sender does not bear interest, the bank is obliged to pay interest to the sender on the amount of the order for the number of days elapsing after the payment date to the day the sender receives notice or learns that the order was not accepted, counting that day as an elapsed day. If the withdrawable credit balance during that period falls below the amount of the order, the amount of interest payable is reduced accordingly.

(c) Acceptance of a payment order cannot occur before the order is received by the receiving bank. Acceptance does not occur under subsection (b)(2) or (b)(3) if the beneficiary of the payment order does not have an account with the receiving bank, the account has been closed, or the receiving bank is not permitted by law to receive credits for the beneficiary's account.

(d) A payment order issued to the originator's bank cannot be accepted until the payment date if the bank is the beneficiary's bank, or the execution date if the bank is not the beneficiary's bank. If the originator's bank executes the originator's payment order before the execution date or pays the beneficiary of the originator's payment order before the payment date and the payment order is subsequently cancelled pursuant to Section 4A—211(b), the bank may recover from the beneficiary any payment received to the extent allowed by the law governing mistake and restitution.

§ 4A—210. **Rejection of Payment Order.**

(a) A payment order is rejected by the receiving bank by a notice of rejection transmitted to the sender orally, electronically, or in writing. A notice of rejection need not use any particular words and is sufficient if it indicates that the receiving bank is rejecting the order or will not execute or pay the order. Rejection is effective when the notice is given if transmission is by a means that is reasonable in the circumstances. If notice of rejection is given by a means that is not reasonable, rejection is effective when the notice is received. If an agreement of the sender and receiving bank establishes the means to be used to reject a payment order, (i) any means complying with the agreement is reasonable and (ii) any means not complying is not reasonable unless no significant delay in receipt of the notice resulted from the use of the noncomplying means.

(b) This subsection applies if a receiving bank other than the beneficiary's bank fails to execute a payment order despite the existence on the execution date of a withdrawable credit balance in an authorized account of the sender sufficient to cover the order. If the sender does not receive notice of rejection of the order on the execution date and the authorized account of the sender does not bear interest, the bank is obliged to pay interest to the sender on the amount of the order for the number of days elapsing after the execution date to the earlier of the day the order is cancelled pursuant to Section 4A—211(d) or the day the sender receives notice or learns that the order was not executed, counting the final day of the period as an elapsed day. If the withdrawable credit balance during that period falls below the amount of the order, the amount of interest is reduced accordingly.

(c) If a receiving bank suspends payments, all unaccepted payment orders issued to it are are deemed rejected at the time the bank suspends payments.

(d) Acceptance of a payment order precludes a later rejection of the order. Rejection of a payment order precludes a later acceptance of the order.

§ 4A—211. Cancellation and Amendment of Payment Order.

(a) A communication of the sender of a payment order cancelling or amending the order may be transmitted to the receiving bank orally, electronically, or in writing. If a security procedure is in effect between the sender and the receiving bank, the communication is not effective to cancel or amend the order unless the communication is verified pursuant to the security procedure or the bank agrees to the cancellation or amendment.

(b) Subject to subsection (a), a communication by the sender cancelling or amending a payment order is effective to cancel or amend the order if notice of the communication is received at a time and in a manner affording the receiving bank a reasonable opportunity to act on the communication before the bank accepts the payment order.

(c) After a payment order has been accepted, cancellation or amendment of the order is not effective unless the receiving bank agrees or a funds-transfer system rule allows cancellation or amendment without agreement of the bank.

(1) With respect to a payment order accepted by a receiving bank other than the beneficiary's bank, cancellation or amendment is not effective unless a conforming cancellation or amendment of the payment order issued by the receiving bank is also made.

(2) With respect to a payment order accepted by the beneficiary's bank, cancellation or amendment is not effective unless the order was issued in execution of an unauthorized payment order, or because of a mistake by a sender in the funds transfer which resulted in the issuance of a payment order (i) that is a duplicate of a payment order previously issued by the sender, (ii) that orders payment to a beneficiary not entitled to receive payment from the originator, or (iii) that orders payment in an amount greater than the amount the beneficiary was entitled to receive from the originator. If the payment order is cancelled or amended, the beneficiary's bank is entitled to recover from the beneficiary any amount paid to the beneficiary to the extent allowed by the law governing mistake and restitution.

(d) An unaccepted payment order is cancelled by operation of law at the close of the fifth funds-transfer business day of the receiving bank after the execution date or payment date of the order.

(e) A cancelled payment order cannot be accepted. If an accepted payment order is cancelled, the acceptance is nullified and no person has any right or obligation based on the acceptance. Amendment of a payment order is deemed to be cancellation of the original order at the time of amendment and issue of a new payment order in the amended form at the same time.

(f) Unless otherwise provided in an agreement of the parties or in a funds-transfer system rule, if the receiving bank, after accepting a payment order, agrees to cancellation or amendment of the order by the sender or is bound by a funds-transfer system rule allowing cancellation or amendment without the bank's agreement, the sender, whether or not cancellation or amendment is effective, is liable to the bank for any loss and expenses, including reasonable attorney's fees, incurred by the bank as a result of the cancellation or amendment or attempted cancellation or amendment.

(g) A payment order is not revoked by the death or legal incapacity of the sender unless the receiving bank knows of the death or of an adjudication of incapacity by a court of competent jurisdiction and has reasonable opportunity to act before acceptance of the order.

(h) A funds-transfer system rule is not effective to the extent it conflicts with subsection (c)(2).

§ 4A—212. Liability and Duty of Receiving Bank Regarding Unaccepted Payment Order.

If a receiving bank fails to accept a payment order that it is obliged by express agreement to accept, the bank is liable for breach of the agreement to the extent provided in the agreement or in this Article, but does not otherwise have any duty to accept a payment order or, before acceptance, to take any action, or refrain from taking action, with respect to the order except as provided in this Article or by express agreement. Liability based on acceptance arises only when acceptance occurs as stated in Section 4A—209, and liability is limited to that provided in this Article. A receiving bank is not the agent of the sender or beneficiary of the payment order it accepts, or of any other party to the funds transfer, and the bank owes no duty to any party to the funds transfer except as provided in this Article or by express agreement.

Part 3 Execution of Sender's Payment Order by Receiving Bank

§ 4A—301. Execution and Execution Date.

(a) A payment order is "executed" by the receiving bank when it issues a payment order intended to carry out the payment order received by the bank. A payment order received by the beneficiary's bank can be accepted but cannot be executed.

(b) "Execution date" of a payment order means the day on which the receiving bank may properly issue a payment order in execution of the sender's order. The execution date may be determined by instruction of the sender but cannot be earlier than the day the order is received and, unless otherwise determined, is the day the order is received. If the sender's instruction states a payment date, the execution date is the payment date or an earlier date on which execution is reasonably necessary to allow payment to the beneficiary on the payment date.

§ 4A—302. Obligations of Receiving Bank in Execution of Payment Order.

(a) Except as provided in subsections (b) through (d), if the receiving bank accepts a payment order pursuant to Section 4A—209(a), the bank has the following obligations in executing the order:

(1) The receiving bank is obliged to issue, on the execution date, a payment order complying with the sender's order and to follow the sender's instructions concerning (i) any intermediary bank or funds-transfer system to be used in carrying out the funds transfer, or (ii) the means by which payment orders are to be transmitted in the funds transfer. If the originator's bank issues a payment order to an intermediary bank, the originator's bank is obliged to instruct the intermediary bank according to the instruction of the originator. An intermediary bank in the funds transfer is similarly bound by an instruction given to it by the sender of the payment order it accepts.

(2) If the sender's instruction states that the funds transfer is to be carried out telephonically or by wire transfer or otherwise indicates that the funds transfer is to be carried out by the most expeditious means, the receiving bank is obliged to transmit its payment order by the most expeditious available means, and to instruct any intermediary bank accordingly. If a sender's instruction states a payment date, the receiving bank is obliged to transmit its payment order at a time and by means reasonably necessary to allow payment to the beneficiary on the payment date or as soon thereafter as is feasible.

(b) Unless otherwise instructed, a receiving bank executing a payment order may (i) use any funds-transfer system if use of that system is reasonable in the circumstances, and (ii) issue a payment order to the beneficiary's bank or to an intermediary bank through which a payment order conforming to the sender's order can expeditiously be issued to the beneficiary's bank if the receiving bank exercises ordinary care in the selection of the intermediary bank. A receiving bank is not required to follow an instruction of the sender designating a funds-transfer system to be used in carrying out the funds transfer if the receiving bank, in good faith, determines that it is not feasible to follow the instruction or that following the instruction would unduly delay completion of the funds transfer.

(c) Unless subsection (a)(2) applies or the receiving bank is otherwise instructed, the bank may execute a payment order by transmitting its payment order by first class mail or by any means reasonable in the circumstances. If the receiving bank is instructed to execute the sender's order by transmitting its payment order by a particular means, the receiving bank may issue its payment order by the means stated or by any means as expeditious as the means stated.

(d) Unless instructed by the sender, (i) the receiving bank may not obtain payment of its charges for services and expenses in connection with the execution of the sender's order by issuing a payment order in an amount equal to the amount of the sender's order less the amount of the charges, and (ii) may not instruct a subsequent receiving bank to obtain payment of its charges in the same manner.

§ 4A—303. Erroneous Execution of Payment Order.

(a) A receiving bank that (i) executes the payment order of the sender by issuing a payment order in an amount greater than the amount of the sender's order, or (ii) issues a payment order in execution of the sender's order and then issues a duplicate order, is entitled to payment of the amount of the sender's order under Section 4A—402(c) if that subsection is otherwise satisfied. The bank is entitled to recover from the beneficiary of the erroneous order the excess payment received to the extent allowed by the law governing mistake and restitution.

(b) A receiving bank that executes the payment order of the sender by issuing a payment order in an amount less than the amount of the sender's order is entitled to payment of the amount of the sender's order under Section 4A—402(c) if (i) that subsection is otherwise satisfied and (ii) the bank corrects its mistake by issuing an additional payment order for the benefit of the beneficiary of the sender's order. If the error is not corrected, the issuer of the erroneous order is entitled to receive or retain payment from the sender of the order it accepted only to the extent of the amount of the erroneous order. This subsection does not apply if the receiving bank executes the sender's payment order by issuing a payment order in an amount less than the amount of the sender's order for the purpose of obtaining payment of its charges for services and expenses pursuant to instruction of the sender.

(c) If a receiving bank executes the payment order of the sender by issuing a payment order to a beneficiary different from the beneficiary of the sender's order and the funds transfer is completed on the basis of that error, the sender of the payment order that was erroneously executed and all previous senders in the funds transfer are not obliged to pay the payment orders they issued. The issuer of the erroneous order is entitled to recover from the beneficiary of the order the payment received to the extent allowed by the law governing mistake and restitution.

§ 4A—304. Duty of Sender to Report Erroneously Executed Payment Order.

If the sender of a payment order that is erroneously executed as stated in Section 4A—303 receives notification from the receiving bank that the order was executed or that the sender's account was debited with respect to the order, the sender has a duty to exercise ordinary care to determine, on the basis of information available to the sender, that the order was erroneously executed and to notify the bank of the relevant facts within a reasonable time not exceeding 90 days after the notification from the bank was received by the sender. If the sender fails to perform that duty, the bank is not obliged to pay interest on any amount refundable to the sender under Section 4A—402(d) for the period before the bank learns of the execution error. The bank is not entitled to any recovery from the sender on account of a failure by the sender to perform the duty stated in this section.

§ 4A—305. Liability for Late or Improper Execution or Failure to Execute Payment Order.

(a) If a funds transfer is completed but execution of a payment order by the receiving bank in breach of Section 4A—302 results in delay in payment to the beneficiary, the bank is obliged to pay interest to either the originator or the beneficiary of the funds transfer for the period of delay caused by the improper execution. Except as provided in subsection (c), additional damages are not recoverable.

(b) If execution of a payment order by a receiving bank in breach of Section 4A—302 results in (i) noncompletion of the funds transfer, (ii) failure to use an intermediary bank designated by the originator, or (iii) issuance of a payment order that does not comply with the terms of the payment order of the originator, the bank is liable to the originator for its expenses in the funds transfer and for incidental expenses and interest losses, to the extent not covered by subsection (a), resulting from the improper execution. Except as provided in subsection (c), additional damages are not recoverable.

(c) In addition to the amounts payable under subsections (a) and (b), damages, including consequential damages, are recoverable to the extent provided in an express written agreement of the receiving bank.

(d) If a receiving bank fails to execute a payment order it was obliged by express agreement to execute, the receiving bank is liable to the sender for its expenses in the transaction and for incidental expenses and interest losses resulting from the failure to execute. Additional damages, including consequential damages, are recoverable to the extent provided in an express written agreement of the receiving bank, but are not otherwise recoverable.

(e) Reasonable attorney's fees are recoverable if demand for compensation under subsection (a) or (b) is made and refused before an action is brought on the claim. If a claim is made for breach of an agreement under subsection (d) and the agreement does not provide for damages, reasonable attorney's fees are recoverable if demand for compensation under subsection (d) is made and refused before an action is brought on the claim.

(f) Except as stated in this section, the liability of a receiving bank under subsections (a) and (b) may not be varied by agreement.

Part 4 Payment

§ 4A—401. Payment Date.

"Payment date" of a payment order means the day on which the amount of the order is payable to the beneficiary by the beneficiary's bank. The payment date may be determined by instruction of the sender but cannot be earlier than the day the order is received by the beneficiary's bank and, unless otherwise determined, is the day the order is received by the beneficiary's bank.

§ 4A—402. Obligation of Sender to Pay Receiving Bank.

(a) This section is subject to Sections 4A—205 and 4A—207.

(b) With respect to a payment order issued to the beneficiary's bank, acceptance of the order by the bank obliges the sender to pay the bank the amount of the order, but payment is not due until the payment date of the order.

(c) This subsection is subject to subsection (e) and to Section 4A—303. With respect to a payment order issued to a receiving bank other than the beneficiary's bank, acceptance of the order by the receiving bank obliges the sender to pay the bank the amount of the sender's order. Payment by the sender is not due until the execution date of the sender's order. The obligation of that sender to pay its payment order is excused if the funds transfer is not completed by acceptance by the beneficiary's bank of a payment order instructing payment to the beneficiary of that sender's payment order.

(d) If the sender of a payment order pays the order and was not obliged to pay all or part of the amount paid, the bank receiving payment is obliged to refund payment to the extent the sender was not obliged to pay. Except as provided in Sections 4A—204 and 4A—304, interest is payable on the refundable amount from the date of payment.

(e) If a funds transfer is not completed as stated in subsection (c) and an intermediary bank is obliged to refund payment as stated in subsection (d) but is unable to do so because not permitted by applicable law or because the bank suspends payments, a sender in the funds transfer that executed a payment order in compliance with an instruction, as stated in Section 4A—302(a)(1), to route the funds transfer through that intermediary bank is entitled to receive or retain payment from the sender of the payment order that it accepted. The first sender in the funds transfer that issued an instruction requiring routing through that intermediary bank is subrogated to the right of the bank that paid the intermediary bank to refund as stated in subsection (d).

(f) The right of the sender of a payment order to be excused from the obligation to pay the order as stated in subsection (c) or to receive refund under subsection (d) may not be varied by agreement.

§ 4A—403. Payment by Sender to Receiving Bank.

(a) Payment of the sender's obligation under Section 4A—402 to pay the receiving bank occurs as follows:

(1) If the sender is a bank, payment occurs when the receiving bank receives final settlement of the obligation through a Federal Reserve Bank or through a funds-transfer system.

(2) If the sender is a bank and the sender (i) credited an account of the receiving bank with the sender, or (ii) caused an account of the receiving bank in another bank to be credited, payment occurs when the credit is withdrawn or, if not withdrawn, at midnight of the day on which the credit is withdrawable and the receiving bank learns of that fact.

(3) If the receiving bank debits an account of the sender with the receiving bank, payment occurs when the debit is made to the extent the debit is covered by a withdrawable credit balance in the account.

(b) If the sender and receiving bank are members of a funds-transfer system that nets obligations multilaterally among participants, the receiving bank receives final settlement when settlement is complete in accordance with the rules of the system. The obligation of the sender to pay the amount of a payment order transmitted through the funds-transfer system may be satisfied, to the extent permitted by the rules of the system, by setting off and applying against the sender's obligation the right of the sender to receive payment from the receiving bank of the amount of any other payment order transmitted to the sender by the receiving bank through the funds-transfer system. The aggregate balance of obligations owed by each sender to each receiving bank in the funds-transfer system may be satisfied, to the extent permitted by the rules of the system, by setting off and applying against that balance the aggregate balance of obligations owed to the sender by other members of the system. The aggregate balance is determined after the right of setoff stated in the second sentence of this subsection has been exercised.

(c) If two banks transmit payment orders to each other under an agreement that settlement of the obligations of each bank to the other under Section 4A—402 will be made at the end of the day or other period, the total amount owed with respect to all orders transmitted by one bank shall be set off against the total amount owed with respect to all orders transmitted by the other bank. To the extent of the setoff, each bank has made payment to the other.

(d) In a case not covered by subsection (a), the time when payment of the sender's obligation under Section 4A—402(b) or 4A—402(c) occurs is governed by applicable principles of law that determine when an obligation is satisfied.

§ 4A—404. Obligation of Beneficiary's Bank to Pay and Give Notice to Beneficiary.

(a) Subject to Sections 4A—211(e), 4A—405(d), and 4A—405(e), if a beneficiary's bank accepts a payment order, the bank is obliged to pay the amount of the order to the beneficiary of the order. Payment is due on the payment date of the order, but if acceptance occurs on the payment date after the close of the funds-transfer business day of the bank, payment is due on the next funds-transfer business day. If the bank refuses to pay after demand by the beneficiary and receipt of notice of particular circumstances that will give rise to consequential damages as a result of nonpayment, the beneficiary may recover damages resulting from the refusal to pay to the extent the bank had notice of the damages, unless the bank proves that it did not pay because of a reasonable doubt concerning the right of the beneficiary to payment.

(b) If a payment order accepted by the beneficiary's bank instructs payment to an account of the beneficiary, the bank is obliged to notify the beneficiary of receipt of the order before midnight of the next funds-transfer business day following the payment date. If the payment order does not instruct payment to an account of the beneficiary, the bank is required to notify the beneficiary only if notice is required by the order. Notice may be given by first class mail or any other means reasonable in the circumstances. If the bank fails to give the required notice, the bank is obliged to pay interest to the beneficiary on the amount of the payment order from the day notice should have been given until the day the beneficiary learned of receipt of the payment order by the bank. No other damages are recoverable. Reasonable attorney's fees are also recoverable if demand for interest is made and refused before an action is brought on the claim.

(c) The right of a beneficiary to receive payment and damages as stated in subsection (a) may not be varied by agreement or a funds-transfer system rule. The right of a beneficiary to be notified as stated in subsection (b) may be varied by agreement of the beneficiary or by a funds-transfer system rule if the beneficiary is notified of the rule before initiation of the funds transfer.

§ 4A—405. Payment by Beneficiary's Bank to Beneficiary.

(a) If the beneficiary's bank credits an account of the beneficiary of a payment order, payment of the bank's obligation under Section 4A—404(a) occurs when and to the extent (i) the beneficiary is notified of the right to withdraw the credit, (ii) the bank lawfully applies the credit to a debt of the beneficiary, or (iii) funds with respect to the order are otherwise made available to the beneficiary by the bank.

(b) If the beneficiary's bank does not credit an account of the beneficiary of a payment order, the time when payment of the bank's obligation under Section 4A—404(a) occurs is governed by principles of law that determine when an obligation is satisfied.

(c) Except as stated in subsections (d) and (e), if the beneficiary's bank pays the beneficiary of a payment order under a condition to payment or agreement of the beneficiary giving the bank the right to recover payment from the beneficiary if the bank does not receive payment of the order, the condition to payment or agreement is not enforceable.

(d) A funds-transfer system rule may provide that payments made to beneficiaries of funds transfers made through the system are provisional until receipt of payment by the beneficiary's bank of the payment order it accepted. A beneficiary's bank that makes a payment that is provisional under the rule is entitled to refund from the beneficiary if (i) the rule requires that both the beneficiary and the originator be given notice of the provisional nature of the payment before the funds transfer is initiated, (ii) the beneficiary, the beneficiary's bank, and the originator's bank agreed to be bound by the rule, and (iii) the beneficiary's bank did not receive payment of the payment order that it accepted. If the beneficiary is obliged to refund payment to the beneficiary's bank, acceptance of the payment order by the beneficiary's bank is nullified and no payment by the originator of the funds transfer to the beneficiary occurs under Section 4A—406.

(e) This subsection applies to a funds transfer that includes a payment order transmitted over a funds-transfer system that (i) nets obligations multilaterally among participants, and (ii) has in effect a loss-sharing agreement among participants for the purpose of providing funds necessary to complete settlement of the obligations of one or more participants that do not meet their settlement obligations. If the beneficiary's bank in the funds transfer accepts a payment order and the system fails to complete settlement pursuant to its rules with respect to any payment order in the funds transfer, (i) the acceptance by the beneficiary's bank is nullified and no person has any right or obligation based on the acceptance, (ii) the beneficiary's bank is entitled to recover payment from the beneficiary, (iii) no payment by the originator to the beneficiary occurs under Section 4A—406, and (iv) subject to Section 4A—402(e), each sender in the funds transfer is excused from its obligation to pay its payment order under Section 4A—402(c) because the funds transfer has not been completed.

§ 4A—406. Payment by Originator to Beneficiary; Discharge of Underlying Obligation.

(a) Subject to Sections 4A—211(e), 4A—405(d), and 4A—405(e), the originator of a funds transfer pays the beneficiary of the originator's payment order (i) at the time a payment order for the benefit of the beneficiary is accepted by the beneficiary's bank in the funds transfer and (ii) in an amount equal to the amount of the order accepted by the beneficiary's bank, but not more than the amount of the originator's order.

(b) If payment under subsection (a) is made to satisfy an obligation, the obligation is discharged to the same extent discharge would result from payment to the beneficiary of the same amount in money, unless (i) the payment under subsection (a) was made by a means prohibited by the contract of the beneficiary with respect to the obligation, (ii) the beneficiary, within a reasonable time after receiving notice of receipt of the order by the beneficiary's bank, notified the originator of the beneficiary's refusal of the payment, (iii) funds with respect to the order were not withdrawn by the beneficiary or applied to a debt of the beneficiary, and (iv) the beneficiary would suffer a loss that could reasonably have been avoided if payment had been made by a means complying with the contract. If payment by the originator does not result in discharge under this section, the originator is subrogated to the rights of the beneficiary to receive payment from the beneficiary's bank under Section 4A—404(a).

(c) For the purpose of determining whether discharge of an obligation occurs under subsection (b), if the beneficiary's bank accepts a payment order in an amount equal to the amount of the originator's payment order less charges of one or more receiving banks in the funds transfer, payment to the beneficiary is deemed to be in the amount of the originator's order unless upon demand by the beneficiary the originator does not pay the beneficiary the amount of the deducted charges.

(d) Rights of the originator or of the beneficiary of a funds transfer under this section may be varied only by agreement of the originator and the beneficiary.

Part 5 Miscellaneous Provisions

§ 4A—501. Variation by Agreement and Effect of Funds-Transfer System Rule.

(a) Except as otherwise provided in this Article, the rights and obligations of a party to a funds transfer may be varied by agreement of the affected party.

(b) "Funds-transfer system rule" means a rule of an association of banks (i) governing transmission of payment orders by means of a funds-transfer system of the association or rights and obligations with respect to those orders, or (ii) to the extent the rule governs rights and obligations between banks that are parties to a funds transfer in which a Federal Reserve Bank, acting as an intermediary bank, sends a payment order to the beneficiary's bank. Except as otherwise provided in this Article, a funds-transfer system rule governing rights and obligations between participating banks using the system may be effective even if the rule conflicts with this Article and indirectly affects another party to the funds transfer who does not consent to the rule. A funds-transfer system rule may also govern rights and obligations of parties other than participating banks using the system to the extent stated in Sections 4A—404(c), 4A—405(d), and 4A—507(c).

§ 4A—502. Creditor Process Served on Receiving Bank; Setoff by Beneficiary's Bank.

(a) As used in this section, "creditor process" means levy, attachment, garnishment, notice of lien, sequestration, or similar process issued by or on behalf of a creditor or other claimant with respect to an account.

(b) This subsection applies to creditor process with respect to an authorized account of the sender of a payment order if the creditor process is served on the receiving bank. For the purpose of determining rights with respect to the creditor process, if the receiving bank accepts the payment order the balance in the authorized account is deemed to be reduced by the amount of the payment order to the extent the bank did not otherwise receive payment of the order, unless the creditor process is served at a time and in a manner affording the bank a reasonable opportunity to act on it before the bank accepts the payment order.

(c) If a beneficiary's bank has received a payment order for payment to the beneficiary's account in the bank, the following rules apply:

(1) The bank may credit the beneficiary's account. The amount credited may be set off against an obligation owed by the beneficiary to the bank or may be applied to satisfy creditor process served on the bank with respect to the account.

(2) The bank may credit the beneficiary's account and allow withdrawal of the amount credited unless creditor process with respect to the account is served at a time and in a manner affording the bank a reasonable opportunity to act to prevent withdrawal.

(3) If creditor process with respect to the beneficiary's account has been served and the bank has had a reasonable opportunity to act on it, the bank may not reject the payment order except for a reason unrelated to the service of process.

(d) Creditor process with respect to a payment by the originator to the beneficiary pursuant to a funds transfer may be served only on the beneficiary's bank with respect to the debt owed by that bank to the beneficiary. Any other bank served with the creditor process is not obliged to act with respect to the process.

§ 4A—503. Injunction or Restraining Order with Respect to Funds Transfer.

For proper cause and in compliance with applicable law, a court may restrain (i) a person from issuing a payment order to initiate a funds transfer, (ii) an originator's bank from executing the payment order of the originator, or (iii) the beneficiary's bank from releasing funds to the beneficiary or the beneficiary from withdrawing the funds. A court may not otherwise restrain a person from issuing a payment order, paying or receiving payment of a payment order, or otherwise acting with respect to a funds transfer.

§ 4A—504. Order in Which Items and Payment Orders May Be Charged to Account; Order of Withdrawals from Account.

(a) If a receiving bank has received more than one payment order of the sender or one or more payment orders and other items that are payable from the sender's account, the bank may charge the sender's account with respect to the various orders and items in any sequence.

(b) In determining whether a credit to an account has been withdrawn by the holder of the account or applied to a debt of the holder of the account, credits first made to the account are first withdrawn or applied.

§ 4A—505. Preclusion of Objection to Debit of Customer's Account.

If a receiving bank has received payment from its customer with respect to a payment order issued in the name of the customer as sender and accepted by the bank, and the customer received notification reasonably identifying the order, the customer is precluded from asserting that the bank is not entitled to retain the payment unless the customer notifies the bank of the customer's objection to the payment within one year after the notification was received by the customer.

§ 4A—506. Rate of Interest.

(a) If, under this Article, a receiving bank is obliged to pay interest with respect to a payment order issued to the bank, the amount payable may be determined (i) by agreement of the sender and receiving bank, or (ii) by a funds-transfer system rule if the payment order is transmitted through a funds-transfer system.

(b) If the amount of interest is not determined by an agreement or rule as stated in subsection (a), the amount is calculated by multiplying the applicable Federal Funds rate by the amount on which interest is payable, and then multiplying the product by the number of days for which interest is payable. The applicable Federal Funds rate is the average of the Federal Funds rates published by the Federal Reserve Bank of New York for each of the days for which interest is payable divided by 360. The Federal Funds rate for any day on which a published rate is not available is the same as the published rate for the next preceding day for which there is a published rate. If a receiving bank that accepted a payment order is required to refund payment to the sender of the order because the funds transfer was not completed, but the failure to complete was not due to any fault by the bank, the interest payable is reduced by a percentage equal to the reserve requirement on deposits of the receiving bank.

§ 4A—507. Choice of Law.

(a) The following rules apply unless the affected parties otherwise agree or subsection (c) applies:

(1) The rights and obligations between the sender of a payment order and the receiving bank are governed by the law of the jurisdiction in which the receiving bank is located.

(2) The rights and obligations between the beneficiary's bank and the beneficiary are governed by the law of the jurisdiction in which the beneficiary's bank is located.

(3) The issue of when payment is made pursuant to a funds transfer by the originator to the beneficiary is governed by the law of the jurisdiction in which the beneficiary's bank is located.

(b) If the parties described in each paragraph of subsection (a) have made an agreement selecting the law of a particular jurisdiction to govern rights and obligations between each other, the law of that jurisdiction governs those rights and obligations, whether or not the payment order or the funds transfer bears a reasonable relation to that jurisdiction.

(c) A funds-transfer system rule may select the law of a particular jurisdiction to govern (i) rights and obligations between participating banks with respect to payment orders transmitted or processed through the system, or (ii) the rights and obligations of some or all parties to a funds transfer any part of which is carried out by means of the system. A choice of law made pursuant to clause (i) is binding on participating banks. A choice of law made pursuant to clause (ii) is binding on the originator, other sender, or a receiving bank having notice that the funds-transfer system might be used in the funds transfer and of the choice of law by the system when the originator, other sender, or receiving bank issued or accepted a payment order. The beneficiary of a funds transfer is bound by the choice of law if, when the funds transfer is initiated, the beneficiary has notice that the funds-transfer system might be used in the funds transfer and of the choice of law by the system. The law of a jurisdiction selected pursuant to this subsection may govern, whether or not that law bears a reasonable relation to the matter in issue.

(d) In the event of inconsistency between an agreement under subsection (b) and a choice-of-law rule under subsection (c), the agreement under subsection (b) prevails.

(e) If a funds transfer is made by use of more than one funds-transfer system and there is inconsistency between choice-of-law rules of the systems, the matter in issue is governed by the law of the selected jurisdiction that has the most significant relationship to the matter in issue.

Revised (1995) Article 5
LETTERS OF CREDIT

§ 5—101. Short Title.

This article may be cited as Uniform Commercial Code—Letters of Credit.

§ 5—102. Definitions.

(a) In this article:

(1) "Adviser" means a person who, at the request of the issuer, a confirmer, or another adviser, notifies or requests another adviser to notify the beneficiary that a letter of credit has been issued, confirmed, or amended.

(2) "Applicant" means a person at whose request or for whose account a letter of credit is issued. The

term includes a person who requests an issuer to issue a letter of credit on behalf of another if the person making the request undertakes an obligation to reimburse the issuer.

(3) "Beneficiary" means a person who under the terms of a letter of credit is entitled to have its complying presentation honored. The term includes a person to whom drawing rights have been transferred under a transferable letter of credit.

(4) "Confirmer" means a nominated person who undertakes, at the request or with the consent of the issuer, to honor a presentation under a letter of credit issued by another.

(5) "Dishonor" of a letter of credit means failure timely to honor or to take an interim action, such as acceptance of a draft, that may be required by the letter of credit.

(6) "Document" means a draft or other demand, document of title, investment security, certificate, invoice, or other record, statement, or representation of fact, law, right, or opinion (i) which is presented in a written or other medium permitted by the letter of credit or, unless prohibited by the letter of credit, by the standard practice referred to in Section 5—108(e) and (ii) which is capable of being examined for compliance with the terms and conditions of the letter of credit. A document may not be oral.

(7) "Good faith" means honesty in fact in the conduct or transaction concerned.

(8) "Honor" of a letter of credit means performance of the issuer's undertaking in the letter of credit to pay or deliver an item of value. Unless the letter of credit otherwise provides, "honor" occurs

(i) upon payment,

(ii) if the letter of credit provides for acceptance, upon acceptance of a draft and, at maturity, its payment, or

(iii) if the letter of credit provides for incurring a deferred obligation, upon incurring the obligation and, at maturity, its performance.

(9) "Issuer" means a bank or other person that issues a letter of credit, but does not include an individual who makes an engagement for personal, family, or household purposes.

(10) "Letter of credit" means a definite undertaking that satisfies the requirements of Section 5—104 by an issuer to a beneficiary at the request or for the account of an applicant or, in the case of a financial institution, to itself or for its own account, to honor a documentary presentation by payment or delivery of an item of value.

(11) "Nominated person" means a person whom the issuer (i) designates or authorizes to pay, accept, negotiate, or otherwise give value under a letter of credit and (ii) undertakes by agreement or custom and practice to reimburse.

(12) "Presentation" means delivery of a document to an issuer or nominated person for honor or giving of value under a letter of credit.

(13) "Presenter" means a person making a presentation as or on behalf of a beneficiary or nominated person.

(14) "Record" means information that is inscribed on a tangible medium, or that is stored in an electronic or other medium and is retrievable in perceivable form.

(15) "Successor of a beneficiary" means a person who succeeds to substantially all of the rights of a beneficiary by operation of law, including a corporation with or into which the beneficiary has been merged or consolidated, an administrator, executor, personal representative, trustee in bankruptcy, debtor in possession, liquidator, and receiver.

(b) Definitions in other Articles applying to this article and the sections in which they appear are:

"Accept" or "Acceptance" Section 3—409

"Value" Sections 3—303, 4—211

(c) Article 1 contains certain additional general definitions and principles of construction and interpretation applicable throughout this article.

§ 5—103. Scope.

(a) This article applies to letters of credit and to certain rights and obligations arising out of transactions involving letters of credit.

(b) The statement of a rule in this article does not by itself require, imply, or negate application of the same or a different rule to a situation not provided for, or to a person not specified, in this article.

(c) With the exception of this subsection, subsections (a) and (d), Sections 5—102(a)(9) and (10), 5—106(d), and 5—114(d), and except to the extent prohibited in Sections 1—102(3) and 5—117(d), the effect of this article may be varied by agreement or by a provision stated or incorporated by reference in an undertaking. A term in an agreement or undertaking generally excusing liability or generally limiting remedies for failure to perform obligations is not sufficient to vary obligations prescribed by this article.

(d) Rights and obligations of an issuer to a beneficiary or a nominated person under a letter of credit are independent of the existence, performance, or nonperformance of a contract or arrangement out of which the letter of credit arises or which underlies it, including contracts or arrangements between the issuer and the applicant and between the applicant and the beneficiary.

§ 5—104. Formal Requirements.

A letter of credit, confirmation, advice, transfer, amendment, or cancellation may be issued in any form that is a record and is authenticated (i) by a signature or (ii) in accordance with the agreement of the parties or the standard practice referred to in Section 5—108(e).

§ 5—105. Consideration.

Consideration is not required to issue, amend, transfer, or cancel a letter of credit, advice, or confirmation.

§ 5—106. Issuance, Amendment, Cancellation, and Duration.

(a) A letter of credit is issued and becomes enforceable according to its terms against the issuer when the issuer sends or otherwise transmits it to the person requested to advise or to the beneficiary. A letter of credit is revocable only if it so provides.

(b) After a letter of credit is issued, rights and obligations of a beneficiary, applicant, confirmer, and issuer are not affected by an amendment or cancellation to which that person has not consented except to the extent the letter of credit provides that it is revocable or that the issuer may amend or cancel the letter of credit without that consent.

(c) If there is no stated expiration date or other provision that determines its duration, a letter of credit expires one year after its stated date of issuance or, if none is stated, after the date on which it is issued.

(d) A letter of credit that states that it is perpetual expires five years after its stated date of issuance, or if none is stated, after the date on which it is issued.

§ 5—107. Confirmer, Nominated Person, and Adviser.

(a) A confirmer is directly obligated on a letter of credit and has the rights and obligations of an issuer to the extent of its confirmation. The confirmer also has rights against and obligations to the issuer as if the issuer were an applicant and the confirmer had issued the letter of credit at the request and for the account of the issuer.

(b) A nominated person who is not a confirmer is not obligated to honor or otherwise give value for a presentation.

(c) A person requested to advise may decline to act as an adviser. An adviser that is not a confirmer is not obligated to honor or give value for a presentation. An adviser undertakes to the issuer and to the beneficiary accurately to advise the terms of the letter of credit, confirmation, amendment, or advice received by that person and undertakes to the beneficiary to check the apparent authenticity of the request to advise. Even if the advice is inaccurate, the letter of credit, confirmation, or amendment is enforceable as issued.

(d) A person who notifies a transferee beneficiary of the terms of a letter of credit, confirmation, amendment, or advice has the rights and obligations of an adviser under subsection (c). The terms in the notice to the transferee beneficiary may differ from the terms in any notice to the transferor beneficiary to the extent permitted by the letter of credit, confirmation, amendment, or advice received by the person who so notifies.

§ 5—108. Issuer's Rights and Obligations.

(a) Except as otherwise provided in Section 5—109, an issuer shall honor a presentation that, as determined by the standard practice referred to in subsection (e), appears on its face strictly to comply with the terms and conditions of the letter of credit. Except as otherwise provided in Section 5—113 and unless otherwise agreed with the applicant, an issuer shall dishonor a presentation that does not appear so to comply.

(b) An issuer has a reasonable time after presentation, but not beyond the end of the seventh business day of the issuer after the day of its receipt of documents:

(1) to honor,

(2) if the letter of credit provides for honor to be completed more than seven business days after presentation, to accept a draft or incur a deferred obligation, or

(3) to give notice to the presenter of discrepancies in the presentation.

(c) Except as otherwise provided in subsection (d), an issuer is precluded from asserting as a basis for dishonor any discrepancy if timely notice is not given, or any discrepancy not stated in the notice if timely notice is given.

(d) Failure to give the notice specified in subsection (b) or to mention fraud, forgery, or expiration in the notice does not preclude the issuer from asserting as a basis for dishonor fraud or forgery as described in Section 5—109(a) or expiration of the letter of credit before presentation.

(e) An issuer shall observe standard practice of financial institutions that regularly issue letters of credit. Determination of the issuer's observance of the standard practice is a matter of interpretation for the court. The court shall offer the parties a reasonable opportunity to present evidence of the standard practice.

(f) An issuer is not responsible for:

(1) the performance or nonperformance of the underlying contract, arrangement, or transaction,

(2) an act or omission of others, or

(3) observance or knowledge of the usage of a particular trade other than the standard practice referred to in subsection (e).

(g) If an undertaking constituting a letter of credit under Section 5—102(a)(10) contains nondocumentary conditions, an issuer shall disregard the nondocumentary conditions and treat them as if they were not stated.

(h) An issuer that has dishonored a presentation shall return the documents or hold them at the disposal of, and send advice to that effect to, the presenter.

(i) An issuer that has honored a presentation as permitted or required by this article:

(1) is entitled to be reimbursed by the applicant in immediately available funds not later than the date of its payment of funds;

(2) takes the documents free of claims of the beneficiary or presenter;

(3) is precluded from asserting a right of recourse on a draft under Sections 3—414 and 3—415;

(4) except as otherwise provided in Sections 5—110 and 5—117, is precluded from restitution of money paid or other value given by mistake to the extent the mistake concerns discrepancies in the documents or tender which are apparent on the face of the presentation; and

(5) is discharged to the extent of its performance under the letter of credit unless the issuer honored a presentation in which a required signature of a beneficiary was forged.

§ 5—109. Fraud and Forgery.

(a) If a presentation is made that appears on its face strictly to comply with the terms and conditions of the letter of credit, but a required document is forged or materially fraudulent, or honor of the presentation would facilitate a material fraud by the beneficiary on the issuer or applicant:

(1) the issuer shall honor the presentation, if honor is demanded by (i) a nominated person who has given value in good faith and without notice of forgery or material fraud, (ii) a confirmer who has honored its confirmation in good faith, (iii) a holder in due course of a draft drawn under the letter of credit which was taken after acceptance by the issuer or nominated person, or (iv) an assignee of the issuer's or nominated person's deferred obligation that was taken for value and without notice of forgery or material fraud after the obligation was incurred by the issuer or nominated person; and

(2) the issuer, acting in good faith, may honor or dishonor the presentation in any other case.

(b) If an applicant claims that a required document is forged or materially fraudulent or that honor of the presentation would facilitate a material fraud by the beneficiary on the issuer or applicant, a court of competent jurisdiction may temporarily or permanently enjoin the issuer from honoring a presentation or grant similar relief against the issuer or other persons only if the court finds that:

(1) the relief is not prohibited under the law applicable to an accepted draft or deferred obligation incurred by the issuer;

(2) a beneficiary, issuer, or nominated person who may be adversely affected is adequately protected against loss that it may suffer because the relief is granted;

(3) all of the conditions to entitle a person to the relief under the law of this State have been met; and

(4) on the basis of the information submitted to the court, the applicant is more likely than not to succeed under its claim of forgery or material fraud and the person demanding honor does not qualify for protection under subsection (a)(1).

§ 5—110. Warranties.

(a) If its presentation is honored, the beneficiary warrants:

(1) to the issuer, any other person to whom presentation is made, and the applicant that there is no fraud or forgery of the kind described in Section 5—109(a); and

(2) to the applicant that the drawing does not violate any agreement between the applicant and beneficiary or any other agreement intended by them to be augmented by the letter of credit.

(b) The warranties in subsection (a) are in addition to warranties arising under Article 3, 4, 7, and 8 because of the presentation or transfer of documents covered by any of those articles.

§ 5—111. Remedies.

(a) If an issuer wrongfully dishonors or repudiates its obligation to pay money under a letter of credit before presentation, the beneficiary, successor, or nominated person presenting on its own behalf may recover from the issuer the amount that is the subject of the dishonor or repudiation. If the issuer's obligation under the letter of credit is not for the payment of money, the claimant may obtain specific performance or, at the claimant's election, recover an amount equal to the value of performance from the issuer. In either case, the claimant may also recover incidental but not consequential damages. The claimant is not obligated to take action to avoid damages that might be due from the issuer under this subsection. If, although not obligated to do so, the claimant avoids damages, the claimant's recovery from the issuer must be reduced by the amount of damages avoided. The issuer has the burden of proving the amount of damages avoided. In the case of repudiation the claimant need not present any document.

(b) If an issuer wrongfully dishonors a draft or demand presented under a letter of credit or honors a draft or demand in breach of its obligation to the applicant, the applicant may recover damages resulting from the breach, including incidental but not consequential damages, less any amount saved as a result of the breach.

(c) If an adviser or nominated person other than a confirmer breaches an obligation under this article or an issuer breaches an obligation not covered in subsection (a) or (b), a person to whom the obligation is owed may recover damages resulting from the breach, including incidental but not consequential damages, less any amount saved as a result of the breach. To the extent of the confirmation, a confirmer has the liability of an issuer specified in this subsection and subsections (a) and (b).

(d) An issuer, nominated person, or adviser who is found liable under subsection (a), (b), or (c) shall pay interest on the amount owed thereunder from the date of wrongful dishonor or other appropriate date.

(e) Reasonable attorney's fees and other expenses of litigation must be awarded to the prevailing party in an action in which a remedy is sought under this article.

(f) Damages that would otherwise be payable by a party for breach of an obligation under this article may be liquidated by agreement or undertaking, but only in an amount or by a formula that is reasonable in light of the harm anticipated.

§ 5—112. Transfer of Letter of Credit.

(a) Except as otherwise provided in Section 5–113, unless a letter of credit provides that it is transferable, the right of a beneficiary to draw or otherwise demand performance under a letter of credit may not be transferred.

(b) Even if a letter of credit provides that it is transferable, the issuer may refuse to recognize or carry out a transfer if:

(1) the transfer would violate applicable law; or

(2) the transferor or transferee has failed to comply with any requirement stated in the letter of credit or any other requirement relating to transfer imposed by the issuer which is within the standard practice referred to in Section 5–108(e) or is otherwise reasonable under the circumstances.

§ 5—113. Transfer by Operation of Law.

(a) A successor of a beneficiary may consent to amendments, sign and present documents, and receive payment or other items of value in the name of the beneficiary without disclosing its status as a successor.

(b) A successor of a beneficiary may consent to amendments, sign and present documents, and receive payment or other items of value in its own name as the disclosed successor of the beneficiary. Except as otherwise provided in subsection (e), an issuer shall recognize a disclosed successor of a beneficiary as beneficiary in full substitution for its predecessor upon compliance with the requirements for recognition by the issuer of a transfer of drawing rights by operation of law under the standard practice referred to in Section 5—108(e) or, in the absence of such a practice, compliance with other reasonable procedures sufficient to protect the issuer.

(c) An issuer is not obliged to determine whether a purported successor is a successor of a beneficiary or whether the signature of a purported successor is genuine or authorized.

(d) Honor of a purported successor's apparently complying presentation under subsection (a) or (b) has the consequences specified in Section 5—108(i) even if the purported successor is not the successor of a beneficiary. Documents signed in the name of the beneficiary or of a disclosed successor by a person who is neither the beneficiary nor the successor of the beneficiary are forged documents for the purposes of Section 5—109.

(e) An issuer whose rights of reimbursement are not covered by subsection (d) or substantially similar law and any confirmer or nominated person may decline to recognize a presentation under subsection (b).

(f) A beneficiary whose name is changed after the issuance of a letter of credit has the same rights and obligations as a successor of a beneficiary under this section.

§ 5—114. Assignment of Proceeds.

(a) In this section, "proceeds of a letter of credit" means the cash, check, accepted draft, or other item of value paid or delivered upon honor or giving of value by the issuer or any nominated person under the letter of credit. The term does not include a beneficiary's drawing rights or documents presented by the beneficiary.

(b) A beneficiary may assign its right to part or all of the proceeds of a letter of credit. The beneficiary may do so before presentation as a present assignment of its right to receive proceeds contingent upon its compliance with the terms and conditions of the letter of credit.

(c) An issuer or nominated person need not recognize an assignment of proceeds of a letter of credit until it consents to the assignment.

(d) An issuer or nominated person has no obligation to give or withhold its consent to an assignment of proceeds of a letter of credit, but consent may not be unreasonably withheld if the assignee possesses and exhibits the letter of credit and presentation of the letter of credit is a condition to honor.

(e) Rights of a transferee beneficiary or nominated person are independent of the beneficiary's assignment of the proceeds of a letter of credit and are superior to the assignee's right to the proceeds.

(f) Neither the rights recognized by this section between an assignee and an issuer, transferee beneficiary, or nominated person nor the issuer's or nominated person's payment of proceeds to an assignee or a third person affect the rights between the assignee and any person other than the issuer, transferee beneficiary, or nominated person. The mode of creating and perfecting a security interest in or granting an assignment of a beneficiary's rights to proceeds is governed by Article 9 or other law. Against persons other than the issuer, transferee beneficiary, or nominated person, the rights and obligations arising upon the creation of a security interest or other assignment of a beneficiary's right to proceeds and its perfection are governed by Article 9 or other law.

§ 5—115. Statute of Limitations.

An action to enforce a right or obligation arising under this article must be commenced within one year after the expiration date of the relevant letter of credit or one year after the [claim for relief] [cause of action] accrues, whichever occurs later. A [claim for relief] [cause of action] accrues when the breach occurs, regardless of the aggrieved party's lack of knowledge of the breach.

§ 5—116. Choice of Law and Forum.

(a) The liability of an issuer, nominated person, or adviser for action or omission is governed by the law of the jurisdiction chosen by an agreement in the form of a record signed or otherwise authenticated by the affected parties in the manner provided in Section 5—104 or by a provision in the person's letter of credit, confirmation, or other undertaking. The jurisdiction whose law is chosen need not bear any relation to the transaction.

(b) Unless subsection (a) applies, the liability of an issuer, nominated person, or adviser for action or omission is governed by the law of the jurisdiction in which the person is located. The person is considered to be located at the address indicated in the person's undertaking. If more than one address is indicated, the person is considered to be located at the address from which the person's undertaking was issued. For the purpose of jurisdiction, choice of law, and recognition of interbranch letters of credit, but not enforcement of a judgment, all branches of a bank are considered separate juridical entities and a bank is considered to be located at the place where its relevant branch is considered to be located under this subsection.

(c) Except as otherwise provided in this subsection, the liability of an issuer, nominated person, or adviser is governed by any rules of custom or practice, such as the Uniform Customs and Practice for Documentary Credits, to which the letter of credit, confirmation, or other undertaking is expressly made subject. If (i) this article would govern the liability of an issuer, nominated person, or adviser under subsection (a) or (b), (ii) the relevant undertaking incorporates rules of custom or practice, and (iii) there is conflict between this article and those rules as applied to that undertaking, those rules govern except to the extent of any conflict with the nonvariable provisions specified in Section 5—103(c).

(d) If there is conflict between this article and Article 3, 4, 4A, or 9, this article governs.

(e) The forum for settling disputes arising out of an undertaking within this article may be chosen in the manner and with the binding effect that governing law may be chosen in accordance with subsection (a).

§ 5—117. Subrogation of Issuer, Applicant, and Nominated Person.

(a) An issuer that honors a beneficiary's presentation is subrogated to the rights of the beneficiary to the same extent as if the issuer were a secondary obligor of the underlying obligation owed to the beneficiary and of the applicant to the same extent as if the issuer were the secondary obligor of the underlying obligation owed to the applicant.

(b) An applicant that reimburses an issuer is subrogated to the rights of the issuer against any beneficiary, presenter, or nominated person to the same extent as if the applicant were the secondary obligor of the obligations owed to the issuer and has the rights of subrogation of the issuer to the rights of the beneficiary stated in subsection (a).

(c) A nominated person who pays or gives value against a draft or demand presented under a letter of credit is subrogated to the rights of:

(1) the issuer against the applicant to the same extent as if the nominated person were a secondary obligor of the obligation owed to the issuer by the applicant;

(2) the beneficiary to the same extent as if the nominated person were a secondary obligor of the underlying obligation owed to the beneficiary; and

(3) the applicant to same extent as if the nominated person were a secondary obligor of the underlying obligation owed to the applicant.

(d) Notwithstanding any agreement or term to the contrary, the rights of subrogation stated in subsections (a) and (b) do not arise until the issuer honors the letter of credit or otherwise pays and the rights in subsection

(c) do not arise until the nominated person pays or otherwise gives value. Until then, the issuer, nominated person, and the applicant do not derive under this section present or prospective rights forming the basis of a claim, defense, or excuse.

Transition Provisions

§ [ ]. **Effective Date.**

This [Act] shall become effective on _______, 199__.

§ [ ]. **Repeal.**

This [Act] [repeals] [amends] [insert citation to existing Article 5].

§ [ ]. **Applicability.**

This [Act] applies to a letter of credit that is issued on or after the effective date of this [Act]. This [Act] does not apply to a transaction, event, obligation, or duty arising out of or associated with a letter of credit that was issued before the effective date of this [Act].

§ [ ]. **Savings Clause.**

A transaction arising out of or associated with a letter of credit that was issued before the effective date of this [Act] and the rights, obligations, and interests flowing from that transaction are governed by any statute or other law amended or repealed by this [Act] as if repeal or amendment had not occurred and may be terminated, completed, consummated, or enforced under that statute or other law.

Article 6
BULK TRANSFERS

§ 6—101. **Short Title.**

This Article shall be known and may be cited as Uniform Commercial Code—Bulk Transfers.

§ 6—102. **"Bulk Transfers"; Transfers of Equipment; Enterprises Subject to This Article; Bulk Transfers Subject to This Article.**

(1) A "bulk transfer" is any transfer in bulk and not in the ordinary course of the transferor's business of a major part of the materials, supplies, merchandise or other inventory (Section 9—109) of an enterprise subject to this Article.

(2) A transfer of a substantial part of the equipment (Section 9—109) of such an enterprise is a bulk transfer if it is made in connection with a bulk transfer of inventory, but not otherwise.

(3) The enterprises subject to this Article are all those whose principal business is the sale of merchandise from stock, including those who manufacture what they sell.

(4) Except as limited by the following section all bulk transfers of goods located within this state are subject to this Article.

§ 6—103. **Transfers Excepted From This Article.**

The following transfers are not subject to this Article:

(1) Those made to give security for the performance of an obligation;

(2) General assignments for the benefit of all the creditors of the transferor, and subsequent transfers by the assignee thereunder;

(3) Transfers in settlement or realization of a lien or other security interests;

(4) Sales by executors, administrators, receivers, trustees in bankruptcy, or any public officer under judicial process;

(5) Sales made in the course of judicial or administrative proceedings for the dissolution or reorganization of a corporation and of which notice is sent to the creditors of the corporation pursuant to order of the court or administrative agency;

(6) Transfers to a person maintaining a known place of business in this State who becomes bound to pay the debts of the transferor in full and gives public notice of that fact, and who is solvent after becoming so bound;

(7) A transfer to a new business enterprise organized to take over and continue the business, if public notice of the transaction is given and the new enterprise assumes the debts of the transferor and he receives nothing from the transaction except an interest in the new enterprise junior to the claims of creditors;

(8) Transfers of property which is exempt from execution.

Public notice under subsection (6) or subsection (7) may be given by publishing once a week for two consecutive weeks in a newspaper of general circulation where the transferor had its principal place of business in this state an advertisement including the names and addresses of the transferor and transferee and the effective date of the transfer.

§ 6—104. **Schedule of Property, List of Creditors.**

(1) Except as provided with respect to auction sales (Section 6—108), a bulk transfer subject to this Article is ineffective against any creditor of the transferor unless:

(a) The transferee requires the transferor to furnish a list of his existing creditors prepared as stated in this section; and

(b) The parties prepare a schedule of the property transferred sufficient to identify it; and

(c) The transferee preserves the list and schedule for six months next following the transfer and permits inspection of either or both and copying therefrom at all reasonable hours by any creditor of the transferor, or files the list and schedule in (a public office to be here identified).

(2) The list of creditors must be signed and sworn to or affirmed by the transferor or his agent. It must contain the names and business addresses of all creditors of the transferor, with the amounts when known, and also the names of all persons who are known to the transferor to assert claims against him even though such claims are disputed. If the transferor is the obligor of an outstanding issue of bonds, debentures or the like as to which there is an indenture trustee, the list of creditors need include only the name and address of the indenture trustee and the aggregate outstanding principal amount of the issue.

(3) Responsibility for the completeness and accuracy of the list of creditors rests on the transferor, and the transfer is not rendered ineffective by errors or omissions therein unless the transferee is shown to have had knowledge.

§ 6—105. Notice to Creditors.

In addition to the requirements of the preceding section, any bulk transfer subject to this Article except one made by auction sale (Section 6—108) is ineffective against any creditor of the transferor unless at least ten days before he takes possession of the goods or pays for them, whichever happens first, the transferee gives notice of the transfer in the manner and to the persons hereafter provided (Section 6—107).

§ 6—106. Application of the Proceeds.

In addition to the requirements of the two preceding sections:

(1) Upon every bulk transfer subject to this Article for which new consideration becomes payable except those made by sale at auction it is the duty of the transferee to assure that such consideration is applied so far as necessary to pay those debts of the transferor which are either shown on the list furnished by the transferor (Section 6—104) or filed in writing in the place stated in the notice (Section 6—107) within thirty days after the mailing of such notice. This duty of the transferee runs to all the holders of such debts, and may be enforced by any of them for the benefit of all.

(2) If any of said debts are in dispute the necessary sum may be withheld from distribution until the dispute is settled or adjudicated.

(3) If the consideration payable is not enough to pay all of the said debts in full distribution shall be made pro rata.]

Note: *This section is bracketed to indicate division of opinion as to whether or not it is a wise provision, and to suggest that this is a point on which State enactments may differ without serious damage to the principle of uniformity. In any State where this section is omitted, the following parts of sections, also bracketed in the text, should also be omitted, namely:*

Section 6—107(2)(e).

6—108(3)(c).

6—109(2).

In any State where this section is enacted, these other provisions should be also.

Optional Subsection (4)

[(4) The transferee may within ten days after he takes possession of the goods pay the consideration into the (specify court) in the county where the transferor had its principal place of business in this state and thereafter may discharge his duty under this section by giving notice by registered or certified mail to all the persons to whom the duty runs that the consideration has been paid into that court and that they should file their claims there. On motion of any interested party, the court may order the distribution of the consideration to the persons entitled to it.]

Note: Optional subsection (4) is recommended for those states which do not have a general statute providing for payment of money into court.

§ 6—107. The Notice.

(1) The notice to creditors (Section 6—105) shall state:

(a) that a bulk transfer is about to be made; and

(b) the names and business addresses of the transferor and transferee, and all other business names and addresses used by the transferor within three years last past so far as known to the transferee; and

(c) whether or not all the debts of the transferor are to be paid in full as they fall due as a result of the transaction, and if so, the address to which creditors should send their bills.

(2) If the debts of the transferor are not to be paid in full as they fall due or if the transferee is in doubt on that point then the notice shall state further:

(a) the location and general description of the property to be transferred and the estimated total of the transferor's debts;

(b) the address where the schedule of property and list of creditors (Section 6—104) may be inspected;

(c) whether the transfer is to pay existing debts and if so the amount of such debts and to whom owing;

(d) whether the transfer is for new consideration and if so the amount of such consideration and the time and place of payment; [and]

[(e) if for new consideration the time and place where creditors of the transferor are to file their claims.]

(3) The notice in any case shall be delivered personally or sent by registered or certified mail to all the persons

shown on the list of creditors furnished by the transferor (Section 6—104) and to all other persons who are known to the transferee to hold or assert claims against the transferor.

§ 6—108. **Auction Sales; "Auctioneer".**

(1) A bulk transfer is subject to this Article even though it is by sale at auction, but only in the manner and with the results stated in this section.

(2) The transferor shall furnish a list of his creditors and assist in the preparation of a schedule of the property to be sold, both prepared as before stated (Section 6—104).

(3) The person or persons other than the transferor who direct, control or are responsible for the auction are collectively called the "auctioneer". The auctioneer shall:

(a) receive and retain the list of creditors and prepare and retain the schedule of property for the period stated in this Article (Section 6—104);

(b) give notice of the auction personally or by registered or certified mail at least ten days before it occurs to all persons shown on the list of creditors and to all other persons who are known to him to hold or assert claims against the transferor; [and]

[(c) assure that the net proceeds of the auction are applied as provided in this Article (Section 6—106).]

(4) Failure of the auctioneer to perform any of these duties does not affect the validity of the sale or the title of the purchasers, but if the auctioneer knows that the auction constitutes a bulk transfer such failure renders the auctioneer liable to the creditors of the transferor as a class for the sums owing to them from the transferor up to but not exceeding the net proceeds of the auction. If the auctioneer consists of several persons their liability is joint and several.

§ 6—109. **What Creditors Protected; [Credit for Payment to Particular Creditors].**

(1) The creditors of the transferor mentioned in this Article are those holding claims based on transactions or events occurring before the bulk transfer, but creditors who become such after notice to creditors is given (Sections 6—105 and 6—107) are not entitled to notice.

[(2) Against the aggregate obligation imposed by the provisions of this Article concerning the application of the proceeds (Section 6—106 and subsection (3)(c) of 6—108) the transferee or auctioneer is entitled to credit for sums paid to particular creditors of the transferor, not exceeding the sums believed in good faith at the time of the payment to be properly payable to such creditors.]

§ 6—110. **Subsequent Transfers.**

When the title of a transferee to property is subject to a defect by reason of his noncompliance with the requirements of this Article, then:

(1) a purchaser of any of such property from such transferee who pays no value or who takes with notice of such noncompliance takes subject to such defect, but

(2) a purchaser for value in good faith and without such notice takes free of such defect.

§ 6—111. **Limitation of Actions and Levies.**

No action under this Article shall be brought nor levy made more than six months after the date on which the transferee took possession of the goods unless the transfer has been concealed. If the transfer has been concealed, actions may be brought or levies made within six months after its discovery.

Note to Article 6: *Section 6—106 is bracketed to indicate division of opinion as to whether or not it is a wise provision, and to suggest that this is a point on which State enactments may differ without serious damage to the principle of uniformity.*

In any State where Section 6—106 is not enacted, the following parts of sections, also bracketed in the text, should also be omitted, namely:
Sec. 6—107(2)(e).
6—108(3)(c).
6—109(2).

In any State where Section 6—106 is enacted, these other provisions should be also.

Article 6
Alternative B*

§ 6—101. **Short Title.**

This Article shall be known and may be cited as Uniform Commercial Code—Bulk Sales.

§ 6—102. **Definitions and Index of Definitions.**

(1) In this Article, unless the context otherwise requires:

(a) "Assets" means the inventory that is the subject of a bulk sale and any tangible and intangible personal property used or held for use primarily in, or arising from, the seller's business and sold in connection with that inventory, but the term does not include:

(i) fixtures (Section 9—313(1)(a)) other than readily removable factory and office machines;

(ii) the lessee's interest in a lease of real property; or

(iii) property to the extent it is generally exempt from creditor process under nonbankruptcy law.

(b) "Auctioneer" means a person whom the seller engages to direct, conduct, control, or be responsible for a sale by auction.

*Approved in substance by the National Conference of Commissioners on Uniform State Laws and The American Law Institute. States have the choice of adopting this alternative to the existing Article 6 or repealing Article 6 entirely (Alternative A).

(c) "Bulk sale" means:

(i) in the case of a sale by auction or a sale or series of sales conducted by a liquidator on the seller's behalf, a sale or series of sales not in the ordinary course of the seller's business of more than half of the seller's inventory, as measured by value on the date of the bulk-sale agreement, if on that date the auctioneer or liquidator has notice, or after reasonable inquiry would have had notice, that the seller will not continue to operate the same or a similar kind of business after the sale or series of sales; and

(ii) in all other cases, a sale not in the ordinary course of the seller's business of more than half the seller's inventory, as measured by value on the date of the bulk-sale agreement, if on that date the buyer has notice, or after reasonable inquiry would have had notice, that the seller will not continue to operate the same or a similar kind of business after the sale.

(d) "Claim" means a right to payment from the seller, whether or not the right is reduced to judgment, liquidated, fixed, matured, disputed, secured, legal, or equitable. The term includes costs of collection and attorney's fees only to the extent that the laws of this state permit the holder of the claim to recover them in an action against the obligor.

(e) "Claimant" means a person holding a claim incurred in the seller's business other than:

(i) an unsecured and unmatured claim for employment compensation and benefits, including commissions and vacation, severance, and sick-leave pay;

(ii) a claim for injury to an individual or to property, or for breach of warranty, unless:

(A) a right of action for the claim has accrued;

(B) the claim has been asserted against the seller; and

(C) the seller knows the identity of the person asserting the claim and the basis upon which the person has asserted it; and

(States to Select One Alternative)

Alternative A

[(iii) a claim for taxes owing to a governmental unit.]

Alternative B

[(iii) a claim for taxes owing to a governmental unit, if:

(A) a statute governing the enforcement of the claim permits or requires notice of the bulk sale to be given to the governmental unit in a manner other than by compliance with the requirements of this Article; and

(B) notice is given in accordance with the statute.]

(f) "Creditor" means a claimant or other person holding a claim.

(g)(i) "Date of the bulk sale" means:

(A) if the sale is by auction or is conducted by a liquidator on the seller's behalf, the date on which more than ten percent of the net proceeds is paid to or for the benefit of the seller; and

(B) in all other cases, the later of the date on which:

(I) more than ten percent of the net contract price is paid to or for the benefit of the seller; or

(II) more than ten percent of the assets, as measured by value, are transferred to the buyer.

(ii) For purposes of this subsection:

(A) delivery of a negotiable instrument (Section 3—104(1)) to or for the benefit of the seller in exchange for assets constitutes payment of the contract price pro tanto;

(B) to the extent that the contract price is deposited in an escrow, the contract price is paid to or for the benefit of the seller when the seller acquires the unconditional right to receive the deposit or when the deposit is delivered to the seller or for the benefit of the seller, whichever is earlier; and

(C) an asset is transferred when a person holding an unsecured claim can no longer obtain through judicial proceedings rights to the asset that are superior to those of the buyer arising as a result of the bulk sale. A person holding an unsecured claim can obtain those superior rights to a tangible asset at least until the buyer has an unconditional right, under the bulk-sale agreement, to possess the asset, and a person holding an unsecured claim can obtain those superior rights to an intangible asset at least until the buyer has an unconditional right, under the bulk-sale agreement, to use the asset.

(h) "Date of the bulk-sale agreement" means:

(i) in the case of a sale by auction or conducted by a liquidator (subsection (c)(i)), the date on which the seller engages the auctioneer or liquidator; and

(ii) in all other cases, the date on which a bulk-sale agreement becomes enforceable between the buyer and the seller.

(i) "Debt" means liability on a claim.

(j) "Liquidator" means a person who is regularly engaged in the business of disposing of assets for businesses contemplating liquidation or dissolution.

(k) "Net contract price" means the new consideration the buyer is obligated to pay for the assets less:

(i) the amount of any proceeds of the sale of an asset, to the extent the proceeds are applied in partial or total satisfaction of a debt secured by the asset; and

(ii) the amount of any debt to the extent it is secured by a security interest or lien that is enforceable against the asset before and after it has been sold to a buyer. If a debt is secured by an asset and other property of the seller, the amount of the debt secured by a security interest or lien that is enforceable against the asset is determined by multiplying the debt by a fraction, the numerator of which is the value of the new consideration for the asset on the date of the bulk sale and the denominator of which is the value of all property securing the debt on the date of the bulk sale.

(l) "Net proceeds" means the new consideration received for assets sold at a sale by auction or a sale conducted by a liquidator on the seller's behalf less:

(i) commissions and reasonable expenses of the sale;

(ii) the amount of any proceeds of the sale of an asset, to the extent the proceeds are applied in partial or total satisfaction of a debt secured by the asset; and

(iii) the amount of any debt to the extent it is secured by a security interest or lien that is enforceable against the asset before and after it has been sold to a buyer. If a debt is secured by an asset and other property of the seller, the amount of the debt secured by a security interest or lien that is enforceable against the asset is determined by multiplying the debt by a fraction, the numerator of which is the value of the new consideration for the asset on the date of the bulk sale and the denominator of which is the value of all property securing the debt on the date of the bulk sale.

(m) A sale is "in the ordinary course of the seller's business" if the sale comports with usual or customary practices in the kind of business in which the seller is engaged or with the seller's own usual or customary practices.

(n) "United States" includes its territories and possessions and the Commonwealth of Puerto Rico.

(o) "Value" means fair market value.

(p) "Verified" means signed and sworn to or affirmed.

(2) The following definitions in other Articles apply to this Article:

(a) "Buyer."	Section 2—103(1)(a).
(b) "Equipment."	Section 9—109(2).
(c) "Inventory."	Section 9—109(4).
(d) "Sale."	Section 2—106(1).
(e) "Seller."	Section 2—103(1)(d).

(3) In addition, Article 1 contains general definitions and principles of construction and interpretation applicable throughout this Article.

§ 6—103. **Applicability of Article.**

(1) Except as otherwise provided in subsection (3), this Article applies to a bulk sale if:

(a) the seller's principal business is the sale of inventory from stock; and

(b) on the date of the bulk-sale agreement the seller is located in this state or, if the seller is located in a jurisdiction that is not a part of the United States, the seller's major executive office in the United States is in this state.

(2) A seller is deemed to be located at his [or her] place of business. If a seller has more than one place of business, the seller is deemed located at his [or her] chief executive office.

(3) This Article does not apply to:

(a) a transfer made to secure payment or performance of an obligation;

(b) a transfer of collateral to a secured party pursuant to Section 9—503;

(c) a sale of collateral pursuant to Section 9—504;

(d) retention of collateral pursuant to Section 9—505;

(e) a sale of an asset encumbered by a security interest or lien if (i) all the proceeds of the sale are applied in partial or total satisfaction of the debt secured by the security interest or lien or (ii) the security interest or lien is enforceable against the asset after it has been sold to the buyer and the net contract price is zero;

(f) a general assignment for the benefit of creditors or to a subsequent transfer by the assignee;

(g) a sale by an executor, administrator, receiver, trustee in bankruptcy, or any public officer under judicial process;

(h) a sale made in the course of judicial or administrative proceedings for the dissolution or reorganization of an organization;

(i) a sale to a buyer whose principal place of business is in the United States and who:

(i) not earlier than 21 days before the date of the bulk sale, (A) obtains from the seller a verified and dated list of claimants of whom the seller has notice three days before the seller sends or delivers the list to the buyer or (B) conducts a reasonable inquiry to discover the claimants;

(ii) assumes in full the debts owed to claimants of whom the buyer has knowledge on the date the buyer receives the list of claimants from the seller or on the date the buyer completes the reasonable inquiry, as the case may be;

(iii) is not insolvent after the assumption; and

(iv) gives written notice of the assumption not later than 30 days after the date of the bulk sale by sending or delivering a notice to the claimants identified in subparagraph (ii) or by filing a notice in the office of the [Secretary of State];

(j) a sale to a buyer whose principal place of business is in the United States and who:

(i) assumes in full the debts that were incurred in the seller's business before the date of the bulk sale;

(ii) is not insolvent after the assumption; and

(iii) gives written notice of the assumption not later than 30 days after the date of the bulk sale by sending or delivering a notice to each creditor whose debt is assumed or by filing a notice in the office of the [Secretary of State];

(k) a sale to a new organization that is organized to take over and continue the business of the seller and that has its principal place of business in the United States if:

(i) the buyer assumes in full the debts that were incurred in the seller's business before the date of the bulk sale;

(ii) the seller receives nothing from the sale except an interest in the new organization that is subordinate to the claims against the organization arising from the assumption; and

(iii) the buyer gives written notice of the assumption not later than 30 days after the date of the bulk sale by sending or delivering a notice to each creditor whose debt is assumed or by filing a notice in the office of the [Secretary of State];

(l) a sale of assets having:

(i) a value, net of liens and security interests, of less than $10,000. If a debt is secured by assets and other property of the seller, the net value of the assets is determined by subtracting from their value an amount equal to the product of the debt multiplied by a fraction, the numerator of which is the value of the assets on the date of the bulk sale and the denominator of which is the value of all property securing the debt on the date of the bulk sale; or

(ii) a value of more than $25,000,000 on the date of the bulk-sale agreement; or

(m) a sale required by, and made pursuant to, statute.

(4) The notice under subsection (3)(i)(iv) must state: (i) that a sale that may constitute a bulk sale has been or will be made; (ii) the date or prospective date of the bulk sale; (iii) the individual, partnership, or corporate names and the addresses of the seller and buyer; (iv) the address to which inquiries about the sale may be made, if different from the seller's address; and (v) that the buyer has assumed or will assume in full the debts owed to claimants of whom the buyer has knowledge on the date the buyer receives the list of claimants from the seller or completes a reasonable inquiry to discover the claimants.

(5) The notice under subsections (3)(j)(iii) and (3)(k)(iii) must state: (i) that a sale that may constitute a bulk sale has been or will be made; (ii) the date or prospective date of the bulk sale; (iii) the individual, partnership, or corporate names and the addresses of the seller and buyer; (iv) the address to which inquiries about the sale may be made, if different from the seller's address; and (v) that the buyer has assumed or will assume the debts that were incurred in the seller's business before the date of the bulk sale.

(6) For purposes of subsection (3)(l), the value of assets is presumed to be equal to the price the buyer agrees to pay for the assets. However, in a sale by auction or a sale conducted by a liquidator on the seller's behalf, the value of assets is presumed to be the amount the auctioneer or liquidator reasonably estimates the assets will bring at auction or upon liquidation.

§ 6—104. **Obligations of Buyer.**

(1) In a bulk sale as defined in Section 6—102(1)(c)(ii) the buyer shall:

(a) obtain from the seller a list of all business names and addresses used by the seller within three years before the date the list is sent or delivered to the buyer;

(b) unless excused under subsection (2), obtain from the seller a verified and dated list of claimants of whom the seller has notice three days before the seller sends or delivers the list to the buyer and including, to the extent known by the seller, the address of and the amount claimed by each claimant;

(c) obtain from the seller or prepare a schedule of distribution (Section 6—106(1));

(d) give notice of the bulk sale in accordance with Section 6—105;

(e) unless excused under Section 6—106(4), distribute the net contract price in accordance with the undertakings of the buyer in the schedule of distribution; and

(f) unless excused under subsection (2), make available the list of claimants (subsection (1)(b)) by:

(i) promptly sending or delivering a copy of the list without charge to any claimant whose written request is received by the buyer no later than six months after the date of the bulk sale;

(ii) permitting any claimant to inspect and copy the list at any reasonable hour upon request received by the buyer no later than six months after the date of the bulk sale; or

(iii) filing a copy of the list in the office of the [Secretary of State] no later than the time for giving a notice of the bulk sale (Section 6—105(5)). A list filed in accordance with this subparagraph must state the individual, partnership, or corporate name and a mailing address of the seller.

(2) A buyer who gives notice in accordance with Section 6—105(2) is excused from complying with the requirements of subsections (1)(b) and (1)(f).

§ 6—105. Notice to Claimants.

(1) Except as otherwise provided in subsection (2), to comply with Section 6—104(1)(d) the buyer shall send or deliver a written notice of the bulk sale to each claimant on the list of claimants (Section 6—104(1)(b)) and to any other claimant of which the buyer has knowledge at the time the notice of the bulk sale is sent or delivered.

(2) A buyer may comply with Section 6—104(1)(d) by filing a written notice of the bulk sale in the office of the [Secretary of State] if:

(a) on the date of the bulk-sale agreement the seller has 200 or more claimants, exclusive of claimants holding secured or matured claims for employment compensation and benefits, including commissions and vacation, severance, and sick-leave pay; or

(b) the buyer has received a verified statement from the seller stating that, as of the date of the bulk-sale agreement, the number of claimants, exclusive of claimants holding secured or matured claims for employment compensation and benefits, including commissions and vacation, severance, and sick-leave pay, is 200 or more.

(3) The written notice of the bulk sale must be accompanied by a copy of the schedule of distribution (Section 6—106(1)) and state at least:

(a) that the seller and buyer have entered into an agreement for a sale that may constitute a bulk sale under the laws of the State of ________;

(b) the date of the agreement;

(c) the date on or after which more than ten percent of the assets were or will be transferred;

(d) the date on or after which more than ten percent of the net contract price was or will be paid, if the date is not stated in the schedule of distribution;

(e) the name and a mailing address of the seller;

(f) any other business name and address listed by the seller pursuant to Section 6—104(1)(a);

(g) the name of the buyer and an address of the buyer from which information concerning the sale can be obtained;

(h) a statement indicating the type of assets or describing the assets item by item;

(i) the manner in which the buyer will make available the list of claimants (Section 6—104(1)(f)), if applicable; and

(j) if the sale is in total or partial satisfaction of an antecedent debt owed by the seller, the amount of the debt to be satisfied and the name of the person to whom it is owed.

(4) For purposes of subsections (3)(e) and (3)(g), the name of a person is the person's individual, partnership, or corporate name.

(5) The buyer shall give notice of the bulk sale not less than 45 days before the date of the bulk sale and, if the buyer gives notice in accordance with subsection (1), not more than 30 days after obtaining the list of claimants.

(6) A written notice substantially complying with the requirements of subsection (3) is effective even though it contains minor errors that are not seriously misleading.

(7) A form substantially as follows is sufficient to comply with subsection (3):

Notice of Sale

(1) ________, whose address is ________, is described in this notice as the "seller."

(2) ________, whose address is ________, is described in this notice as the "buyer."

(3) The seller has disclosed to the buyer that within the past three years the seller has used other business names, operated at other addresses, or both, as follows: ________________________________.

(4) The seller and the buyer have entered into an agreement dated ________, for a sale that may constitute a bulk sale under the laws of the State of ______.

(5) The date on or after which more than ten percent of the assets that are the subject of the sale were or will be transferred is ________, and [if not stated in the schedule of distribution] the date on or after which more than ten percent of the net contract price was or will be paid is ________.

(6) The following assets are the subject of the sale: ____________________.

(7) [If applicable] The buyer will make available to claimants of the seller a list of the seller's claimants in the following manner: ____________________.

(8) [If applicable] The sale is to satisfy $ ________ of an antecedent debt owed by the seller to ________ .

(9) A copy of the schedule of distribution of the net contract price accompanies this notice.

[End of Notice]

§ 6—106. **Schedule of Distribution.**

(1) The seller and buyer shall agree on how the net contract price is to be distributed and set forth their agreement in a written schedule of distribution.

(2) The schedule of distribution may provide for distribution to any person at any time, including distribution of the entire net contract price to the seller.

(3) The buyer's undertakings in the schedule of distribution run only to the seller. However, a buyer who fails to distribute the net contract price in accordance with the buyer's undertakings in the schedule of distribution is liable to a creditor only as provided in Section 6—107(1).

(4) If the buyer undertakes in the schedule of distribution to distribute any part of the net contract price to a person other than the seller, and, after the buyer has given notice in accordance with Section 6—105, some or all of the anticipated net contract price is or becomes unavailable for distribution as a consequence of the buyer's or seller's having complied with an order of court, legal process, statute, or rule of law, the buyer is excused from any obligation arising under this Article or under any contract with the seller to distribute the net contract price in accordance with the buyer's undertakings in the schedule if the buyer:

(a) distributes the net contract price remaining available in accordance with any priorities for payment stated in the schedule of distribution and, to the extent that the price is insufficient to pay all the debts having a given priority, distributes the price pro rata among those debts shown in the schedule as having the same priority;

(b) distributes the net contract price remaining available in accordance with an order of court;

(c) commences a proceeding for interpleader in a court of competent jurisdiction and is discharged from the proceeding; or

(d) reaches a new agreement with the seller for the distribution of the net contract price remaining available, sets forth the new agreement in an amended schedule of distribution, gives notice of the amended schedule, and distributes the net contract price remaining available in accordance with the buyer's undertakings in the amended schedule.

(5) The notice under subsection (4)(d) must identify the buyer and the seller, state the filing number, if any, of the original notice, set forth the amended schedule, and be given in accordance with subsection (1) or (2) of Section 6—105, whichever is applicable, at least 14 days before the buyer distributes any part of the net contract price remaining available.

(6) If the seller undertakes in the schedule of distribution to distribute any part of the net contract price, and, after the buyer has given notice in accordance with Section 6—105, some or all of the anticipated net contract price is or becomes unavailable for distribution as a consequence of the buyer's or seller's having complied with an order of court, legal process, statute, or rule of law, the seller and any person in control of the seller are excused from any obligation arising under this Article or under any agreement with the buyer to distribute the net contract price in accordance with the seller's undertakings in the schedule if the seller:

(a) distributes the net contract price remaining available in accordance with any priorities for payment stated in the schedule of distribution and, to the extent that the price is insufficient to pay all the debts having a given priority, distributes the price pro rata among those debts shown in the schedule as having the same priority;

(b) distributes the net contract price remaining available in accordance with an order of court;

(c) commences a proceeding for interpleader in a court of competent jurisdiction and is discharged from the proceeding; or

(d) prepares a written amended schedule of distribution of the net contract price remaining available for distribution, gives notice of the amended schedule, and distributes the net contract price remaining available in accordance with the amended schedule.

(7) The notice under subsection (6)(d) must identify the buyer and the seller, state the filing number, if any, of the original notice, set forth the amended schedule, and be given in accordance with subsection (1) or (2) of Section 6—105, whichever is applicable, at least 14 days before the seller distributes any part of the net contract price remaining available.

§ 6—107. **Liability for Noncompliance.**

(1) Except as provided in subsection (3), and subject to the limitation in subsection (4):

(a) a buyer who fails to comply with the requirements of Section 6—104(1)(e) with respect to a creditor is liable to the creditor for damages in the amount of the claim, reduced by any amount that the creditor would not have realized if the buyer had complied; and

(b) a buyer who fails to comply with the requirements of any other subsection of Section 6—104 with respect to a claimant is liable to the claimant for damages in the amount of the claim, reduced by any amount that the claimant would not have realized if the buyer had complied.

(2) In an action under subsection (1), the creditor has the burden of establishing the validity and amount of the claim, and the buyer has the burden of establishing the amount that the creditor would not have realized if the buyer had complied.

(3) A buyer who:

(a) made a good faith and commercially reasonable effort to comply with the requirements of Section 6—104(1) or to exclude the sale from the application of this Article under Section 6—103(3); or

(b) on or after the date of the bulk-sale agreement, but before the date of the bulk sale, held a good faith and commercially reasonable belief that this Article does not apply to the particular sale

is not liable to creditors for failure to comply with the requirements of Section 6—104. The buyer has the burden of establishing the good faith and commercial reasonableness of the effort or belief.

(4) In a single bulk sale the cumulative liability of the buyer for failure to comply with the requirements of Section 6—104(1) may not exceed an amount equal to:

(a) if the assets consist only of inventory and equipment, twice the net contract price, less the amount of any part of the net contract price paid to or applied for the benefit of the seller or a creditor; or

(b) if the assets include property other than inventory and equipment, twice the net value of the inventory and equipment less the amount of the portion of any part of the net contract price paid to or applied for the benefit of the seller or a creditor which is allocable to the inventory and equipment.

(5) For the purposes of subsection (4)(b), the "net value" of an asset is the value of the asset less (i) the amount of any proceeds of the sale of an asset, to the extent the proceeds are applied in partial or total satisfaction of a debt secured by the asset and (ii) the amount of any debt to the extent it is secured by a security interest or lien that is enforceable against the asset before and after it has been sold to a buyer. If a debt is secured by an asset and other property of the seller, the amount of the debt secured by a security interest or lien that is enforceable against the asset is determined by multiplying the debt by a fraction, the numerator of which is the value of the asset on the date of the bulk sale and the denominator of which is the value of all property securing the debt on the date of the bulk sale. The portion of a part of the net contract price paid to or applied for the benefit of the seller or a creditor that is "allocable to the inventory and equipment" is the portion that bears the same ratio to that part of the net contract price as the net value of the inventory and equipment bears to the net value of all of the assets.

(6) A payment made by the buyer to a person to whom the buyer is, or believes he [or she] is, liable under subsection (1) reduces pro tanto the buyer's cumulative liability under subsection (4).

(7) No action may be brought under subsection (1)(b) by or on behalf of a claimant whose claim is unliquidated or contingent.

(8) A buyer's failure to comply with the requirements of Section 6—104(1) does not (i) impair the buyer's rights in or title to the assets, (ii) render the sale ineffective, void, or voidable, (iii) entitle a creditor to more than a single satisfaction of his [or her] claim, or (iv) create liability other than as provided in this Article.

(9) Payment of the buyer's liability under subsection (1) discharges pro tanto the seller's debt to the creditor.

(10) Unless otherwise agreed, a buyer has an immediate right of reimbursement from the seller for any amount paid to a creditor in partial or total satisfaction of the buyer's liability under subsection (1).

(11) If the seller is an organization, a person who is in direct or indirect control of the seller, and who knowingly, intentionally, and without legal justification fails, or causes the seller to fail, to distribute the net contract price in accordance with the schedule of distribution is liable to any creditor to whom the seller undertook to make payment under the schedule for damages caused by the failure.

§ 6—108. Bulk Sales by Auction; Bulk Sales Conducted by Liquidator.

(1) Sections 6—104, 6—105, 6—106, and 6—107 apply to a bulk sale by auction and a bulk sale conducted by a liquidator on the seller's behalf with the following modifications:

(a) "buyer" refers to auctioneer or liquidator, as the case may be;

(b) "net contract price" refers to net proceeds of the auction or net proceeds of the sale, as the case may be;

(c) the written notice required under Section 6—105(3) must be accompanied by a copy of the schedule of distribution (Section 6—106(1)) and state at least:

(i) that the seller and the auctioneer or liquidator have entered into an agreement for auction or liquidation services that may constitute an agreement to make a bulk sale under the laws of the State of ________ ;

(ii) the date of the agreement;

(iii) the date on or after which the auction began or will begin or the date on or after which the liquidator began or will begin to sell assets on the seller's behalf;

(iv) the date on or after which more than ten percent of the net proceeds of the sale were or will be paid, if the date is not stated in the schedule of distribution;

(v) the name and a mailing address of the seller;

(vi) any other business name and address listed by the seller pursuant to Section 6—104(1)(a);

(vii) the name of the auctioneer or liquidator and an address of the auctioneer or liquidator from which information concerning the sale can be obtained;

(viii) a statement indicating the type of assets or describing the assets item by item;

(ix) the manner in which the auctioneer or liquidator will make available the list of claimants (Section 6—104(1)(f)), if applicable; and

(x) if the sale is in total or partial satisfaction of an antecedent debt owed by the seller, the amount of the debt to be satisfied and the name of the person to whom it is owed; and

(d) in a single bulk sale the cumulative liability of the auctioneer or liquidator for failure to comply with the requirements of this section may not exceed the amount of the net proceeds of the sale allocable to inventory and equipment sold less the amount of the portion of any part of the net proceeds paid to or applied for the benefit of a creditor which is allocable to the inventory and equipment.

(2) A payment made by the auctioneer or liquidator to a person to whom the auctioneer or liquidator is, or believes he [or she] is, liable under this section reduces pro tanto the auctioneer's or liquidator's cumulative liability under subsection (1)(d).

(3) A form substantially as follows is sufficient to comply with subsection (1)(c):

Notice of Sale

(1) ________, whose address is ________, is described in this notice as the "seller."

(2) ______, whose address is ______, is described in this notice as the "auctioneer" or "liquidator."

(3) The seller has disclosed to the auctioneer or liquidator that within the past three years the seller has used other business names, operated at other addresses, or both, as follows: ________________ .

(4) The seller and the auctioneer or liquidator have entered into an agreement dated ________ for auction or liquidation services that may constitute an agreement to make a bulk sale under the laws of the State of __________ .

(5) The date on or after which the auction began or will begin or the date on or after which the liquidator began or will begin to sell assets on the seller's behalf is _________ , and [if not stated in the schedule of distribution] the date on or after which more than ten percent of the net proceeds of the sale were or will be paid is _________ .

(6) The following assets are the subject of the sale: ______________________________ .

(7) [If applicable] The auctioneer or liquidator will make available to claimants of the seller a list of the seller's claimants in the following manner: ________ .

(8) [If applicable] The sale is to satisfy $ ________ of an antecedent debt owed by the seller to ________ .

(9) A copy of the schedule of distribution of the net proceeds accompanies this notice.

[End of Notice]

(4) A person who buys at a bulk sale by auction or conducted by a liquidator need not comply with the requirements of Section 6—104(1) and is not liable for the failure of an auctioneer or liquidator to comply with the requirements of this section.

§ 6—109. What Constitutes Filing; Duties of Filing Officer; Information from Filing Officer.

(1) Presentation of a notice or list of claimants for filing and tender of the filing fee or acceptance of the notice or list by the filing officer constitutes filing under this Article.

(2) The filing officer shall:

(a) mark each notice or list with a file number and with the date and hour of filing;

(b) hold the notice or list or a copy for public inspection;

(c) index the notice or list according to each name given for the seller and for the buyer; and

(d) note in the index the file number and the addresses of the seller and buyer given in the notice or list.

(3) If the person filing a notice or list furnishes the filing officer with a copy, the filing officer upon request shall note upon the copy the file number and date and hour of the filing of the original and send or deliver the copy to the person.

(4) The fee for filing and indexing and for stamping a copy furnished by the person filing to show the date and place of filing is $ ______ for the first page and $ ______ for each additional page. The fee for indexing each name beyond the first two is $ ________ .

(5) Upon request of any person, the filing officer shall issue a certificate showing whether any notice or list with respect to a particular seller or buyer is on file on the date and hour stated in the certificate. If a notice or list is on file, the certificate must give the date and hour of filing of each notice or list and the name and address of each seller, buyer, auctioneer, or liquidator. The fee for the certificate is $ ________ if the request for the certificate is in the standard form prescribed by the [Secretary of State] and otherwise is $ ________ . Upon request of any person, the filing officer shall furnish a copy of any filed notice or list for a fee of $ ________ .

(6) The filing officer shall keep each notice or list for two years after it is filed.

§ 6—110. **Limitation of Actions.**

(1) Except as provided in subsection (2), an action under this Article against a buyer, auctioneer, or liquidator must be commenced within one year after the date of the bulk sale.

(2) If the buyer, auctioneer, or liquidator conceals the fact that the sale has occurred, the limitation is tolled and an action under this Article may be commenced within the earlier of (i) one year after the person bringing the action discovers that the sale has occurred or (ii) one year after the person bringing the action should have discovered that the sale has occurred, but no later than two years after the date of the bulk sale. Complete noncompliance with the requirements of this Article does not of itself constitute concealment.

(3) An action under Section 6—107(11) must be commenced within one year after the alleged violation occurs.

Article 7
Warehouse Receipts, Bills of Lading and Other Documents of Title

Part 1 General

§ 7—101. **Short Title.**

This Article shall be known and may be cited as Uniform Commercial Code—Documents of Title.

§ 7—102. **Definitions and Index of Definitions.**

(1) In this Article, unless the context otherwise requires:

(a) "Bailee" means the person who by a warehouse receipt, bill of lading or other document of title acknowledges possession of goods and contracts to deliver them.

(b) "Consignee" means the person named in a bill to whom or to whose order the bill promises delivery.

(c) "Consignor" means the person named in a bill as the person from whom the goods have been received for shipment.

(d) "Delivery order" means a written order to deliver goods directed to a warehouseman, carrier or other person who in the ordinary course of business issues warehouse receipts or bills of lading.

(e) "Document" means document of title as defined in the general definitions in Article 1 (Section 1—201).

(f) "Goods" means all things which are treated as movable for the purposes of a contract of storage or transportation.

(g) "Issuer" means a bailee who issues a document except that in relation to an unaccepted delivery order it means the person who orders the possessor of goods to deliver. Issuer includes any person for whom an agent or employee purports to act in issuing a document if the agent or employee has real or apparent authority to issue documents, notwithstanding that the issuer received no goods or that the goods were misdescribed or that in any other respect the agent or employee violated his instructions.

(h) "Warehouseman" is a person engaged in the business of storing goods for hire.

(2) Other definitions applying to this Article or to specified Parts thereof, and the sections in which they appear are:

"Duly negotiate". Section 7—501.

"Person entitled under the document". Section 7—403(4).

(3) Definitions in other Articles applying to this Article and the sections in which they appear are:

"Contract for sale". Section 2—106.

"Overseas". Section 2—323.

"Receipt" of goods. Section 2—103.

(4) In addition Article 1 contains general definitions and principles of construction and interpretation applicable throughout this Article.

§ 7—103. **Relation of Article to Treaty, Statute, Tariff, Classification or Regulation.**

To the extent that any treaty or statute of the United States, regulatory statute of this State or tariff, classification or regulation filed or issued pursuant thereto is applicable, the provisions of this Article are subject thereto.

§ 7—104. **Negotiable and Nonnegotiable Warehouse Receipt, Bill of Lading or Other Document of Title.**

(1) A warehouse receipt, bill of lading or other document of title is negotiable

(a) if by its terms the goods are to be delivered to bearer or to the order of a named person; or

(b) where recognized in overseas trade, if it runs to a named person or assigns.

(2) Any other document is nonnegotiable. A bill of lading in which it is stated that the goods are consigned to a

named person is not made negotiable by a provision that the goods are to be delivered only against a written order signed by the same or another named person.

§ 7—105. **Construction Against Negative Implication.**

The omission from either Part 2 or Part 3 of this Article of a provision corresponding to a provision made in the other Part does not imply that a corresponding rule of law is not applicable.

Part 2 Warehouse Receipts: Special Provisions

§ 7—201. **Who May Issue a Warehouse Receipt; Storage Under Government Bond.**

(1) A warehouse receipt may be issued by any warehouseman.

(2) Where goods including distilled spirits and agricultural commodities are stored under a statute requiring a bond against withdrawal or a license for the issuance of receipts in the nature of warehouse receipts, a receipt issued for the goods has like effect as a warehouse receipt even though issued by a person who is the owner of the goods and is not a warehouseman.

§ 7—202. **Form of Warehouse Receipt; Essential Terms; Optional Terms.**

(1) A warehouse receipt need not be in any particular form.

(2) Unless a warehouse receipt embodies within its written or printed terms each of the following, the warehouseman is liable for damages caused by the omission to a person injured thereby:

(a) the location of the warehouse where the goods are stored;

(b) the date of issue of the receipt;

(c) the consecutive number of the receipt;

(d) a statement whether the goods received will be delivered to the bearer, to a specified person, or to a specified person or his order;

(e) the rate of storage and handling charges, except that where goods are stored under a field warehousing arrangement a statement of that fact is sufficient on a nonnegotiable receipt;

(f) a description of the goods or of the packages containing them;

(g) the signature of the warehouseman, which may be made by his authorized agent;

(h) if the receipt is issued for goods of which the warehouseman is owner, either solely or jointly or in common with others, the fact of such ownership; and

(i) a statement of the amount of advances made and of liabilities incurred for which the warehouseman claims a lien or security interest (Section 7—209). If the precise amount of such advances made or of such liabilities incurred is, at the time of the issue of the receipt, unknown to the warehouseman or to his agent who issues it, a statement of the fact that advances have been made or liabilities incurred and the purpose thereof is sufficient.

(3) A warehouseman may insert in his receipt any other terms which are not contrary to the provisions of this Act and do not impair his obligation of delivery (Section 7—403) or his duty of care (Section 7—204). Any contrary provisions shall be ineffective.

§ 7—203. **Liability for Nonreceipt or Misdescription.**

A party to or purchaser for value in good faith of a document of title other than a bill of lading relying in either case upon the description therein of the goods may recover from the issuer damages caused by the nonreceipt or misdescription of the goods, except to the extent that the document conspicuously indicates that the issuer does not know whether any part or all of the goods in fact were received or conform to the description, as where the description is in terms of marks or labels or kind, quantity or condition, or the receipt or description is qualified by "contents, condition and quality unknown", "said to contain" or the like, if such indication be true, or the party or purchaser otherwise has notice.

§ 7—204. **Duty of Care; Contractual Limitation of Warehouseman's Liability.**

(1) A warehouseman is liable for damages for loss of or injury to the goods caused by his failure to exercise such care in regard to them as a reasonably careful man would exercise under like circumstances but unless otherwise agreed he is not liable for damages which could not have been avoided by the exercise of such care.

(2) Damages may be limited by a term in the warehouse receipt or storage agreement limiting the amount of liability in case of loss or damage, and setting forth a specific liability per article or item, or value per unit of weight, beyond which the warehouseman shall not be liable; provided, however, that such liability may on written request of the bailor at the time of signing such storage agreement or within a reasonable time after receipt of the warehouse receipt be increased on part or all of the goods thereunder, in which event increased rates may be charged based on such increased valuation, but that no such increase shall be permitted contrary to a lawful limitation of liability contained in the warehouseman's tariff, if any. No such limitation is effective with respect to the warehouseman's liability for conversion to his own use.

(3) Reasonable provisions as to the time and manner of presenting claims and instituting actions based on the bailment may be included in the warehouse receipt or tariff.

(4) This section does not impair or repeal . . .

Note: *Insert in subsection (4) a reference to any statute which imposes a higher responsibility upon the warehouseman or invalidates contractual limitations which would be permissible under this Article.*

§ 7—205. **Title Under Warehouse Receipt Defeated in Certain Cases.**

A buyer in the ordinary course of business of fungible goods sold and delivered by a warehouseman who is also in the business of buying and selling such goods takes free of any claim under a warehouse receipt even though it has been duly negotiated.

§ 7—206. **Termination of Storage at Warehouseman's Option.**

(1) A warehouseman may on notifying the person on whose account the goods are held and any other person known to claim an interest in the goods require payment of any charges and removal of the goods from the warehouse at the termination of the period of storage fixed by the document, or, if no period is fixed, within a stated period not less than thirty days after the notification. If the goods are not removed before the date specified in the notification, the warehouseman may sell them in accordance with the provisions of the section on enforcement of a warehouseman's lien (Section 7—210).

(2) If a warehouseman in good faith believes that the goods are about to deteriorate or decline in value to less than the amount of his lien within the time prescribed in subsection (1) for notification, advertisement and sale, the warehouseman may specify in the notification any reasonable shorter time for removal of the goods and in case the goods are not removed, may sell them at public sale held not less than one week after a single advertisement or posting.

(3) If as a result of a quality or condition of the goods of which the warehouseman had no notice at the time of deposit the goods are a hazard to other property or to the warehouse or to persons, the warehouseman may sell the goods at public or private sale without advertisement on reasonable notification to all persons known to claim an interest in the goods. If the warehouseman after a reasonable effort is unable to sell the goods he may dispose of them in any lawful manner and shall incur no liability by reason of such disposition.

(4) The warehouseman must deliver the goods to any person entitled to them under this Article upon due demand made at any time prior to sale or other disposition under this section.

(5) The warehouseman may satisfy his lien from the proceeds of any sale or disposition under this section but must hold the balance for delivery on the demand of any person to whom he would have been bound to deliver the goods.

§ 7—207. **Goods Must Be Kept Separate; Fungible Goods.**

(1) Unless the warehouse receipt otherwise provides, a warehouseman must keep separate the goods covered by each receipt so as to permit at all times identification and delivery of those goods except that different lots of fungible goods may be commingled.

(2) Fungible goods so commingled are owned in common by the persons entitled thereto and the warehouseman is severally liable to each owner for that owner's share. Where because of overissue a mass of fungible goods is insufficient to meet all the receipts which the warehouseman has issued against it, the persons entitled include all holders to whom overissued receipts have been duly negotiated.

§ 7—208. **Altered Warehouse Receipts.**

Where a blank in a negotiable warehouse receipt has been filled in without authority, a purchaser for value and without notice of the want of authority may treat the insertion as authorized. Any other unauthorized alteration leaves any receipt enforceable against the issuer according to its original tenor.

§ 7—209. **Lien of Warehouseman.**

(1) A warehouseman has a lien against the bailor on the goods covered by a warehouse receipt or on the proceeds thereof in his possession for charges for storage or transportation (including demurrage and terminal charges), insurance, labor, or charges present or future in relation to the goods, and for expenses necessary for preservation of the goods or reasonably incurred in their sale pursuant to law. If the person on whose account the goods are held is liable for like charges or expenses in relation to other goods whenever deposited and it is stated in the receipt that a lien is claimed for charges and expenses in relation to other goods, the warehouseman also has a lien against him for such charges and expenses whether or not the other goods have been delivered by the warehouseman. But against a person to whom a negotiable warehouse receipt is duly negotiated a warehouseman's lien is limited to charges in an amount or at a rate specified on the receipt or if no charges are so specified then to a reasonable charge for storage of the goods covered by the receipt subsequent to the date of the receipt.

(2) The warehouseman may also reserve a security interest against the bailor for a maximum amount specified on the receipt for charges other than those specified in subsection (1), such as for money advanced and interest. Such a security interest is governed by the Article on Secured Transactions (Article 9).

(3)(a) A warehouseman's lien for charges and expenses under subsection (1) or a security interest under subsection (2) is also effective against any person who so entrusted the bailor with possession of the goods that a pledge of them by him to a good faith purchaser for value would have been valid but is not effective against a person as to whom the document confers no right in the goods covered by it under Section 7—503.

(b) A warehouseman's lien on household goods for charges and expenses in relation to the goods under subsection (1) is also effective against all persons if the depositor was the legal possessor of the goods at the time of deposit. "Household goods" means furniture, furnishings and personal effects used by the depositor in a dwelling.

(4) A warehouseman loses his lien on any goods which he voluntarily delivers or which he unjustifiably refuses to deliver.

§ 7—210. **Enforcement of Warehouseman's Lien.**

(1) Except as provided in subsection (2), a warehouseman's lien may be enforced by public or private sale of the goods in bloc or in parcels, at any time or place and on any terms which are commercially reasonable, after notifying all persons known to claim an interest in the goods. Such notification must include a statement of the amount due, the nature of the proposed sale and the time and place of any public sale. The fact that a better price could have been obtained by a sale at a different time or in a different method from that selected by the warehouseman is not of itself sufficient to establish that the sale was not made in a commercially reasonable manner. If the warehouseman either sells the goods in the usual manner in any recognized market therefor, or if he sells at the price current in such market at the time of his sale, or if he has otherwise sold in conformity with commercially reasonable practices among dealers in the type of goods sold, he has sold in a commercially reasonable manner. A sale of more goods than apparently necessary to be offered to ensure satisfaction of the obligation is not commercially reasonable except in cases covered by the preceding sentence.

(2) A warehouseman's lien on goods other than goods stored by a merchant in the course of his business may be enforced only as follows:

(a) All persons known to claim an interest in the goods must be notified.

(b) The notification must be delivered in person or sent by registered or certified letter to the last known address of any person to be notified.

(c) The notification must include an itemized statement of the claim, a description of the goods subject to the lien, a demand for payment within a specified time not less than ten days after receipt of the notification, and a conspicuous statement that unless the claim is paid within the time the goods will be advertised for sale and sold by auction at a specified time and place.

(d) The sale must conform to the terms of the notification.

(e) The sale must be held at the nearest suitable place to that where the goods are held or stored.

(f) After the expiration of the time given in the notification, an advertisement of the sale must be published once a week for two weeks consecutively in a newspaper of general circulation where the sale is to be held. The advertisement must include a description of the goods, the name of the person on whose account they are being held, and the time and place of the sale. The sale must take place at least fifteen days after the first publication. If there is no newspaper of general circulation where the sale is to be held, the advertisement must be posted at least ten days before the sale in not less than six conspicuous places in the neighborhood of the proposed sale.

(3) Before any sale pursuant to this section any person claiming a right in the goods may pay the amount necessary to satisfy the lien and the reasonable expenses incurred under this section. In that event the goods must not be sold, but must be retained by the warehouseman subject to the terms of the receipt and this Article.

(4) The warehouseman may buy at any public sale pursuant to this section.

(5) A purchaser in good faith of goods sold to enforce a warehouseman's lien takes the goods free of any rights of persons against whom the lien was valid, despite noncompliance by the warehouseman with the requirements of this section.

(6) The warehouseman may satisfy his lien from the proceeds of any sale pursuant to this section but must hold the balance, if any, for delivery on demand to any person to whom he would have been bound to deliver the goods.

(7) The rights provided by this section shall be in addition to all other rights allowed by law to a creditor against his debtor.

(8) Where a lien is on goods stored by a merchant in the course of his business the lien may be enforced in accordance with either subsection (1) or (2).

(9) The warehouseman is liable for damages caused by failure to comply with the requirements for sale under this section and in case of willful violation is liable for conversion.

Part 3 Bills of Lading: Special Provisions

§ 7—301. **Liability for Nonreceipt or Misdescription; "Said to Contain"; "Shipper's Load and Count"; Improper Handling.**

(1) A consignee of a nonnegotiable bill who has given value in good faith or a holder to whom a negotiable bill has been duly negotiated relying in either case upon the description therein of the goods, or upon the date therein shown, may recover from the issuer damages caused by the misdating of the bill or the nonreceipt or misdescription of the goods, except to the extent that the document

indicates that the issuer does not know whether any part of all of the goods in fact were received or conform to the description, as where the description is in terms of marks or labels or kind, quantity, or condition or the receipt or description is qualified by "contents or condition of contents of packages unknown", "said to contain", "shipper's weight, load and count" or the like, if such indication be true.

(2) When goods are loaded by an issuer who is a common carrier, the issuer must count the packages of goods if package freight and ascertain the kind and quantity if bulk freight. In such cases "shipper's weight, load and count" or other words indicating that the description was made by the shipper are ineffective except as to freight concealed by packages.

(3) When bulk freight is loaded by a shipper who makes available to the issuer adequate facilities for weighing such freight, an issuer who is a common carrier must ascertain the kind and quantity within a reasonable time after receiving the written request of the shipper to do so. In such cases "shipper's weight" or other words of like purport are ineffective.

(4) The issuer may by inserting in the bill the words "shipper's weight, load and count" or other words of like purport indicate that the goods were loaded by the shipper; and if such statement be true the issuer shall not be liable for damages caused by the improper loading. But their omission does not imply liability for such damages.

(5) The shipper shall be deemed to have guaranteed to the issuer the accuracy at the time of shipment of the description, marks, labels, number, kind, quantity, condition and weight, as furnished by him; and the shipper shall indemnify the issuer against damage caused by inaccuracies in such particulars. The right of the issuer to such indemnity shall in no way limit his responsibility and liability under the contract of carriage to any person other than the shipper.

§ 7—302. **Through Bills of Lading and Similar Documents.**

(1) The issuer of a through bill of lading or other document embodying an undertaking to be performed in part by persons acting as its agents or by connecting carriers is liable to anyone entitled to recover on the document for any breach by such other persons or by a connecting carrier of its obligation under the document but to the extent that the bill covers an undertaking to be performed overseas or in territory not contiguous to the continental United States or an undertaking including matters other than transportation this liability may be varied by agreement of the parties.

(2) Where goods covered by a through bill of lading or other document embodying an undertaking to be performed in part by persons other than the issuer are received by any such person, he is subject with respect to his own performance while the goods are in his possession to the obligation of the issuer. His obligation is discharged by delivery of the goods to another such person pursuant to the document, and does not include liability for breach by any other such persons or by the issuer.

(3) The issuer of such through bill of lading or other document shall be entitled to recover from the connecting carrier or such other person in possession of the goods when the breach of the obligation under the document occurred, the amount it may be required to pay to anyone entitled to recover on the document therefor, as may be evidenced by any receipt, judgment, or transcript thereof, and the amount of any expense reasonably incurred by it in defending any action brought by anyone entitled to recover on the document therefor.

§ 7—303. **Diversion; Reconsignment; Change of Instructions.**

(1) Unless the bill of lading otherwise provides, the carrier may deliver the goods to a person or destination other than that stated in the bill or may otherwise dispose of the goods on instructions from

(a) the holder of a negotiable bill; or

(b) the consignor on a nonnegotiable bill notwithstanding contrary instructions from the consignee; or

(c) the consignee on a nonnegotiable bill in the absence of contrary instructions from the consignor, if the goods have arrived at the billed destination or if the consignee is in possession of the bill; or

(d) the consignee on a nonnegotiable bill if he is entitled as against the consignor to dispose of them.

(2) Unless such instructions are noted on a negotiable bill of lading, a person to whom the bill is duly negotiated can hold the bailee according to the original terms.

§ 7—304. **Bills of Lading in a Set.**

(1) Except where customary in overseas transportation, a bill of lading must not be issued in a set of parts. The issuer is liable for damages caused by violation of this subsection.

(2) Where a bill of lading is lawfully drawn in a set of parts, each of which is numbered and expressed to be valid only if the goods have not been delivered against any other part, the whole of the parts constitute one bill.

(3) Where a bill of lading is lawfully issued in a set of parts and different parts are negotiated to different persons, the title of the holder to whom the first due negotiation is made prevails as to both the document and the goods even though any later holder may have received the goods from the carrier in good faith and discharged the carrier's obligation by surrender of his part.

(4) Any person who negotiates or transfers a single part of a bill of lading drawn in a set is liable to holders of that part as if it were the whole set.

(5) The bailee is obliged to deliver in accordance with Part 4 of this Article against the first presented part of a bill of lading lawfully drawn in a set. Such delivery discharges the bailee's obligation on the whole bill.

§ 7—305. Destination Bills.

(1) Instead of issuing a bill of lading to the consignor at the place of shipment a carrier may at the request of the consignor procure the bill to be issued at destination or at any other place designated in the request.

(2) Upon request of anyone entitled as against the carrier to control the goods while in transit and on surrender of any outstanding bill of lading or other receipt covering such goods, the issuer may procure a substitute bill to be issued at any place designated in the request.

§ 7—306. Altered Bills of Lading.

An unauthorized alteration or filling in of a blank in a bill of lading leaves the bill enforceable according to its original tenor.

§ 7—307. Lien of Carrier.

(1) A carrier has a lien on the goods covered by a bill of lading for charges subsequent to the date of its receipt of the goods for storage or transportation (including demurrage and terminal charges) and for expenses necessary for preservation of the goods incident to their transportation or reasonably incurred in their sale pursuant to law. But against a purchaser for value of a negotiable bill of lading a carrier's lien is limited to charges stated in the bill or the applicable tariffs, or if no charges are stated then to a reasonable charge.

(2) A lien for charges and expenses under subsection (1) on goods which the carrier was required by law to receive for transportation is effective against the consignor or any person entitled to the goods unless the carrier had notice that the consignor lacked authority to subject the goods to such charges and expenses. Any other lien under subsection (1) is effective against the consignor and any person who permitted the bailor to have control or possession of the goods unless the carrier had notice that the bailor lacked such authority.

(3) A carrier loses his lien on any goods which he voluntarily delivers or which he unjustifiably refuses to deliver.

§ 7—308. Enforcement of Carrier's Lien.

(1) A carrier's lien may be enforced by public or private sale of the goods, in bloc or in parcels, at any time or place and on any terms which are commercially reasonable, after notifying all persons known to claim an interest in the goods. Such notification must include a statement of the amount due, the nature of the proposed sale and the time and place of any public sale. The fact that a better price could have been obtained by a sale at a different time or in a different method from that selected by the carrier is not of itself sufficient to establish that the sale was not made in a commercially reasonable manner. If the carrier either sells the goods in the usual manner in any recognized market therefor or if he sells at the price current in such market at the time of his sale or if he has otherwise sold in conformity with commercially reasonable practices among dealers in the type of goods sold he has sold in a commercially reasonable manner. A sale of more goods than apparently necessary to be offered to ensure satisfaction of the obligation is not commercially reasonable except in cases covered by the preceding sentence.

(2) Before any sale pursuant to this section any person claiming a right in the goods may pay the amount necessary to satisfy the lien and the reasonable expenses incurred under this section. In that event the goods must not be sold, but must be retained by the carrier subject to the terms of the bill and this Article.

(3) The carrier may buy at any public sale pursuant to this section.

(4) A purchaser in good faith of goods sold to enforce a carrier's lien takes the goods free of any rights of persons against whom the lien was valid, despite noncompliance by the carrier with the requirements of this section.

(5) The carrier may satisfy his lien from the proceeds of any sale pursuant to this section but must hold the balance, if any, for delivery on demand to any person to whom he would have been bound to deliver the goods.

(6) The rights provided by this section shall be in addition to all other rights allowed by law to a creditor against his debtor.

(7) A carrier's lien may be enforced in accordance with either subsection (1) or the procedure set forth in subsection (2) of Section 7—210.

(8) The carrier is liable for damages caused by failure to comply with the requirements for sale under this section and in case of willful violation is liable for conversion.

§ 7—309. Duty of Care; Contractual Limitation of Carrier's Liability.

(1) A carrier who issues a bill of lading whether negotiable or nonnegotiable must exercise the degree of care in relation to the goods which a reasonably careful man would exercise under like circumstances. This subsection does not repeal or change any law or rule of law which imposes liability upon a common carrier for damages not caused by its negligence.

(2) Damages may be limited by a provision that the carrier's liability shall not exceed a value stated in the document if the carrier's rates are dependent upon value and the consignor by the carrier's tariff is afforded an opportunity to declare a higher value or a value as lawfully

provided in the tariff, or where no tariff is filed he is otherwise advised of such opportunity; but no such limitation is effective with respect to the carrier's liability for conversion to its own use.

(3) Reasonable provisions as to the time and manner of presenting claims and instituting actions based on the shipment may be included in a bill of lading or tariff.

Part 4 Warehouse Receipts and Bills of Lading: General Obligations

§ 7—401. Irregularities in Issue of Receipt or Bill or Conduct of Issuer.

The obligations imposed by this Article on an issuer apply to a document of title regardless of the fact that

(a) the document may not comply with the requirements of this Article or of any other law or regulation regarding its issue, form or content; or

(b) the issuer may have violated laws regulating the conduct of his business; or

(c) the goods covered by the document were owned by the bailee at the time the document was issued; or

(d) the person issuing the document does not come within the definition of warehouseman if it purports to be a warehouse receipt.

§ 7—402. Duplicate Receipt or Bill; Overissue.

Neither a duplicate nor any other document of title purporting to cover goods already represented by an outstanding document of the same issuer confers any right in the goods, except as provided in the case of bills in a set, overissue of documents for fungible goods and substitutes for lost, stolen or destroyed documents. But the issuer is liable for damages caused by his overissue or failure to identify a duplicate document as such by conspicuous notation on its face.

§ 7—403. Obligation of Warehouseman or Carrier to Deliver; Excuse.

(1) The bailee must deliver the goods to a person entitled under the document who complies with subsections (2) and (3), unless and to the extent that the bailee establishes any of the following:

(a) delivery of the goods to a person whose receipt was rightful as against the claimant;

(b) damage to or delay, loss or destruction of the goods for which the bailee is not liable [, but the burden of establishing negligence in such cases is on the person entitled under the document];

Note: *The brackets in (1)(b) indicate that State enactments may differ on this point without serious damage to the principle of uniformity.*

(c) previous sale or other disposition of the goods in lawful enforcement of a lien or on warehouseman's lawful termination of storage;

(d) the exercise by a seller of his right to stop delivery pursuant to the provisions of the Article on Sales (Section 2—705);

(e) a diversion, reconsignment or other disposition pursuant to the provisions of this Article (Section 7—303) or tariff regulating such right;

(f) release, satisfaction or any other fact affording a personal defense against the claimant;

(g) any other lawful excuse.

(2) A person claiming goods covered by a document of title must satisfy the bailee's lien where the bailee so requests or where the bailee is prohibited by law from delivering the goods until the charges are paid.

(3) Unless the person claiming is one against whom the document confers no right under Sec. 7—503(1), he must surrender for cancellation or notation of partial deliveries any outstanding negotiable document covering the goods, and the bailee must cancel the document or conspicuously note the partial delivery thereon or be liable to any person to whom the document is duly negotiated.

(4) "Person entitled under the document" means holder in the case of a negotiable document, or the person to whom delivery is to be made by the terms of or pursuant to written instructions under a nonnegotiable document.

§ 7—404. No Liability for Good Faith Delivery Pursuant to Receipt or Bill.

A bailee who in good faith including observance of reasonable commercial standards has received goods and delivered or otherwise disposed of them according to the terms of the document of title or pursuant to this Article is not liable therefor. This rule applies even though the person from whom he received the goods had no authority to procure the document or to dispose of the goods and even though the person to whom he delivered the goods had no authority to receive them.

Part 5 Warehouse Receipts and Bills of Lading: Negotiation and Transfer

§ 7—501. Form of Negotiation and Requirements of "Due Negotiation".

(1) A negotiable document of title running to the order of a named person is negotiated by his indorsement and delivery. After his indorsement in blank or to bearer any person can negotiate it by delivery alone.

(2)(a) A negotiable document of title is also negotiated by delivery alone when by its original terms it runs to bearer.

(b) When a document running to the order of a named person is delivered to him the effect is the same as if the document had been negotiated.

(3) Negotiation of a negotiable document of title after it has been indorsed to a specified person requires indorsement by the special indorsee as well as delivery.

(4) A negotiable document of title is "duly negotiated" when it is negotiated in the manner stated in this section to a holder who purchases it in good faith without notice of any defense against or claim to it on the part of any person and for value, unless it is established that the negotiation is not in the regular course of business or financing or involves receiving the document in settlement or payment of a money obligation.

(5) Indorsement of a nonnegotiable document neither makes it negotiable nor adds to the transferee's rights.

(6) The naming in a negotiable bill of a person to be notified of the arrival of the goods does not limit the negotiability of the bill nor constitute notice to a purchaser thereof of any interest of such person in the goods.

§ 7—502. **Rights Acquired by Due Negotiation.**

(1) Subject to the following section and to the provisions of Section 7—205 on fungible goods, a holder to whom a negotiable document of title has been duly negotiated acquires thereby:

(a) title to the document;

(b) title to the goods;

(c) all rights accruing under the law of agency or estoppel, including rights to goods delivered to the bailee after the document was issued; and

(d) the direct obligation of the issuer to hold or deliver the goods according to the terms of the document free of any defense or claim by him except those arising under the terms of the document or under this Article. In the case of a delivery order the bailee's obligation accrues only upon acceptance and the obligation acquired by the holder is that the issuer and any indorser will procure the acceptance of the bailee.

(2) Subject to the following section, title and rights so acquired are not defeated by any stoppage of the goods represented by the document or by surrender of such goods by the bailee, and are not impaired even though the negotiation or any prior negotiation constituted a breach of duty or even though any person has been deprived of possession of the document by misrepresentation, fraud, accident, mistake, duress, loss, theft or conversion, or even though a previous sale or other transfer of the goods or document has been made to a third person.

§ 7—503. **Document of Title to Goods Defeated in Certain Cases.**

(1) A document of title confers no right in goods against a person who before issuance of the document had a legal interest or a perfected security interest in them and who neither

(a) delivered or entrusted them or any document of title covering them to the bailor or his nominee with actual or apparent authority to ship, store or sell or with power to obtain delivery under this Article (Section 7—403) or with power of disposition under this Act (Sections 2—403 and 9—307) or other statute or rule of law; nor

(b) acquiesced in the procurement by the bailor or his nominee of any document of title.

(2) Title to goods based upon an unaccepted delivery order is subject to the rights of anyone to whom a negotiable warehouse receipt or bill of lading covering the goods has been duly negotiated. Such a title may be defeated under the next section to the same extent as the rights of the issuer or a transferee from the issuer.

(3) Title to goods based upon a bill of lading issued to a freight forwarder is subject to the rights of anyone to whom a bill issued by the freight forwarder is duly negotiated; but delivery by the carrier in accordance with Part 4 of this Article pursuant to its own bill of lading discharges the carrier's obligation to deliver.

§ 7—504. **Rights Acquired in the Absence of Due Negotiation; Effect of Diversion; Seller's Stoppage of Delivery.**

(1) A transferee of a document, whether negotiable or nonnegotiable, to whom the document has been delivered but not duly negotiated, acquires the title and rights which his transferor had or had actual authority to convey.

(2) In the case of a nonnegotiable document, until but not after the bailee receives notification of the transfer, the rights of the transferee may be defeated

(a) by those creditors of the transferor who could treat the sale as void under Section 2—402; or

(b) by a buyer from the transferor in ordinary course of business if the bailee has delivered the goods to the buyer or received notification of his rights; or

(c) as against the bailee by good faith dealings of the bailee with the transferor.

(3) A diversion or other change of shipping instructions by the consignor in a nonnegotiable bill of lading which causes the bailee not to deliver to the consignee defeats the consignee's title to the goods if they have been delivered to a buyer in ordinary course of business and in any event defeats the consignee's rights against the bailee.

(4) Delivery pursuant to a nonnegotiable document may be stopped by a seller under Section 2—705, and subject to the requirement of due notification there provided. A bailee honoring the seller's instructions is entitled to be indemnified by the seller against any resulting loss or expense.

§ 7—505. **Indorser Not a Guarantor for Other Parties.**

The indorsement of a document of title issued by a bailee does not make the indorser liable for any default by the bailee or by previous indorsers.

§ 7—506. **Delivery Without Indorsement: Right to Compel Indorsement.**

The transferee of a negotiable document of title has a specifically enforceable right to have his transferor supply any necessary indorsement but the transfer becomes a negotiation only as of the time the indorsement is supplied.

§ 7—507. **Warranties on Negotiation or Transfer of Receipt or Bill.**

Where a person negotiates or transfers a document of title for value otherwise than as a mere intermediary under the next following section, then unless otherwise agreed he warrants to his immediate purchaser only in addition to any warranty made in selling the goods

(a) that the document is genuine; and

(b) that he has no knowledge of any fact which would impair its validity or worth; and

(c) that his negotiation or transfer is rightful and fully effective with respect to the title to the document and the goods it represents.

§ 7—508. **Warranties of Collecting Bank as to Documents.**

A collecting bank or other intermediary known to be entrusted with documents on behalf of another or with collection of a draft or other claim against delivery of documents warrants by such delivery of the documents only its own good faith and authority. This rule applies even though the intermediary has purchased or made advances against the claim or draft to be collected.

§ 7—509. **Receipt or Bill: When Adequate Compliance With Commercial Contract.**

The question whether a document is adequate to fulfill the obligations of a contract for sale or the conditions of a credit is governed by the Articles on Sales (Article 2) and on Letters of Credit (Article 5).

Part 6 Warehouse Receipts and Bills of Lading: Miscellaneous Provisions

§ 7—601. **Lost and Missing Documents.**

(1) If a document has been lost, stolen or destroyed, a court may order delivery of the goods or issuance of a substitute document and the bailee may without liability to any person comply with such order. If the document was negotiable the claimant must post security approved by the court to indemnify any person who may suffer loss as a result of non-surrender of the document. If the document was not negotiable, such security may be required at the discretion of the court. The court may also in its discretion order payment of the bailee's reasonable costs and counsel fees.

(2) A bailee who without court order delivers goods to a person claiming under a missing negotiable document is liable to any person injured thereby, and if the delivery is not in good faith becomes liable for conversion. Delivery in good faith is not conversion if made in accordance with a filed classification or tariff or, where no classification or tariff is filed, if the claimant posts security with the bailee in an amount at least double the value of the goods at the time of posting to indemnify any person injured by the delivery who files a notice of claim within one year after the delivery.

§ 7—602. **Attachment of Goods Covered by a Negotiable Document.**

Except where the document was originally issued upon delivery of the goods by a person who had no power to dispose of them, no lien attaches by virtue of any judicial process to goods in the possession of a bailee for which a negotiable document of title is outstanding unless the document be first surrendered to the bailee or its negotiation enjoined, and the bailee shall not be compelled to deliver the goods pursuant to process until the document is surrendered to him or impounded by the court. One who purchases the document for value without notice of the process or injunction takes free of the lien imposed by judicial process.

§ 7—603. **Conflicting Claims; Interpleader.**

If more than one person claims title or possession of the goods, the bailee is excused from delivery until he has had a reasonable time to ascertain the validity of the adverse claims or to bring an action to compel all claimants to interplead and may compel such interpleader, either in defending an action for nondelivery of the goods, or by original action, whichever is appropriate.

Revised (1994) Article 8
INVESTMENT SECURITIES

Part 1 Short Title and General Matters

§ 8—101. **Short Title.**

This Article may be cited as Uniform Commercial Code—Investment Securities.

§ 8—102. **Definitions.**

(a) In this Article:

(1) "Adverse claim" means a claim that a claimant has a property interest in a financial asset and that it

is a violation of the rights of the claimant for another person to hold, transfer, or deal with the financial asset.

(2) "Bearer form," as applied to a certificated security, means a form in which the security is payable to the bearer of the security certificate according to its terms but not by reason of an indorsement.

(3) "Broker" means a person defined as a broker or dealer under the federal securities laws, but without excluding a bank acting in that capacity.

(4) "Certificated security" means a security that is represented by a certificate.

(5) "Clearing corporation" means:

(i) a person that is registered as a "clearing agency" under the federal securities laws;

(ii) a federal reserve bank; or

(iii) any other person that provides clearance or settlement services with respect to financial assets that would require it to register as a clearing agency under the federal securities laws but for an exclusion or exemption from the registration requirement, if its activities as a clearing corporation, including promulgation of rules, are subject to regulation by a federal or state governmental authority.

(6) "Communicate" means to:

(i) send a signed writing; or

(ii) transmit information by any mechanism agreed upon by the persons transmitting and receiving the information.

(7) "Entitlement holder" means a person identified in the records of a securities intermediary as the person having a security entitlement against the securities intermediary. If a person acquires a security entitlement by virtue of Section 8—501(b)(2) or (3), that person is the entitlement holder.

(8) "Entitlement order" means a notification communicated to a securities intermediary directing transfer or redemption of a financial asset to which the entitlement holder has a security entitlement.

(9) "Financial asset," except as otherwise provided in Section 8—103, means:

(i) a security;

(ii) an obligation of a person or a share, participation, or other interest in a person or in property or an enterprise of a person, which is, or is of a type, dealt in or traded on financial markets, or which is recognized in any area in which it is issued or dealt in as a medium for investment; or

(iii) any property that is held by a securities intermediary for another person in a securities account if the securities intermediary has expressly agreed with the other person that the property is to be treated as a financial asset under this Article.

As context requires, the term means either the interest itself or the means by which a person's claim to it is evidenced, including a certificated or uncertificated security, a security certificate, or a security entitlement.

(10) "Good faith," for purposes of the obligation of good faith in the performance or enforcement of contracts or duties within this Article, means honesty in fact and the observance of reasonable commercial standards of fair dealing.

(11) "Indorsement" means a signature that alone or accompanied by other words is made on a security certificate in registered form or on a separate document for the purpose of assigning, transferring, or redeeming the security or granting a power to assign, transfer, or redeem it.

(12) "Instruction" means a notification communicated to the issuer of an uncertificated security which directs that the transfer of the security be registered or that the security be redeemed.

(13) "Registered form," as applied to a certificated security, means a form in which:

(i) the security certificate specifies a person entitled to the security; and

(ii) a transfer of the security may be registered upon books maintained for that purpose by or on behalf of the issuer, or the security certificate so states.

(14) "Securities intermediary" means:

(i) a clearing corporation; or

(ii) a person, including a bank or broker, that in the ordinary course of its business maintains securities accounts for others and is acting in that capacity.

(15) "Security," except as otherwise provided in Section 8—103, means an obligation of an issuer or a share, participation, or other interest in an issuer or in property or an enterprise of an issuer:

(i) which is represented by a security certificate in bearer or registered form, or the transfer of which may be registered upon books maintained for that purpose by or on behalf of the issuer;

(ii) which is one of a class or series or by its terms is divisible into a class or series of shares, participations, interests, or obligations; and

(iii) which:

(A) is, or is of a type, dealt in or traded on securities exchanges or securities markets; or

(B) is a medium for investment and by its terms expressly provides that it is a security governed by this Article.

(16) "Security certificate" means a certificate representing a security.

(17) "Security entitlement" means the rights and property interest of an entitlement holder with respect to a financial asset specified in Part 5.

(18) "Uncertificated security" means a security that is not represented by a certificate.

(b) Other definitions applying to this Article and the sections in which they appear are:

Appropriate person	Section 8—107
Control	Section 8—106
Delivery	Section 8—301
Investment company security	Section 8—103
Issuer	Section 8—201
Overissue	Section 8—210
Protected purchaser	Section 8—303
Securities account	Section 8—501

(c) In addition, Article 1 contains general definitions and principles of construction and interpretation applicable throughout this Article.

(d) The characterization of a person, business, or transaction for purposes of this Article does not determine the characterization of the person, business, or transaction for purposes of any other law, regulation, or rule.

§ 8—103. Rules for Determining Whether Certain Obligations and Interests Are Securities or Financial Assets.

(a) A share or similar equity interest issued by a corporation, business trust, joint stock company, or similar entity is a security.

(b) An "investment company security" is a security. "Investment company security" means a share or similar equity interest issued by an entity that is registered as an investment company under the federal investment company laws, an interest in a unit investment trust that is so registered, or a face-amount certificate issued by a face-amount certificate company that is so registered. Investment company security does not include an insurance policy or endowment policy or annuity contract issued by an insurance company.

(c) An interest in a partnership or limited liability company is not a security unless it is dealt in or traded on securities exchanges or in securities markets, its terms expressly provide that it is a security governed by this Article, or it is an investment company security. However, an interest in a partnership or limited liability company is a financial asset if it is held in a securities account.

(d) A writing that is a security certificate is governed by this Article and not by Article 3, even though it also meets the requirements of that Article. However, a negotiable instrument governed by Article 3 is a financial asset if it is held in a securities account.

(e) An option or similar obligation issued by a clearing corporation to its participants is not a security, but is a financial asset.

(f) A commodity contract, as defined in Section 9—115, is not a security or a financial asset.

§ 8—104. Acquisition of Security or Financial Asset or Interest Therein.

(a) A person acquires a security or an interest therein, under this Article, if:

(1) the person is a purchaser to whom a security is delivered pursuant to Section 8—301; or

(2) the person acquires a security entitlement to the security pursuant to Section 8—501.

(b) A person acquires a financial asset, other than a security, or an interest therein, under this Article, if the person acquires a security entitlement to the financial asset.

(c) A person who acquires a security entitlement to a security or other financial asset has the rights specified in Part 5, but is a purchaser of any security, security entitlement, or other financial asset held by the securities intermediary only to the extent provided in Section 8—503.

(d) Unless the context shows that a different meaning is intended, a person who is required by other law, regulation, rule, or agreement to transfer, deliver, present, surrender, exchange, or otherwise put in the possession of another person a security or financial asset satisfies that requirement by causing the other person to acquire an interest in the security or financial asset pursuant to subsection (a) or (b).

§ 8—105. Notice of Adverse Claim.

(a) A person has notice of an adverse claim if:

(1) the person knows of the adverse claim;

(2) the person is aware of facts sufficient to indicate that there is a significant probability that the adverse claim exists and deliberately avoids information that would establish the existence of the adverse claim; or

(3) the person has a duty, imposed by statute or regulation, to investigate whether an adverse claim exists, and the investigation so required would establish the existence of the adverse claim.

(b) Having knowledge that a financial asset or interest therein is or has been transferred by a representative imposes no duty of inquiry into the rightfulness of a transaction and is not notice of an adverse claim. However, a person who knows that a representative has transferred a financial asset or interest therein in a transaction that is, or whose proceeds are being used, for the individual benefit of the representative or otherwise in breach of duty has notice of an adverse claim.

(c) An act or event that creates a right to immediate performance of the principal obligation represented by a security certificate or sets a date on or after which the certificate is to be presented or surrendered for redemption or exchange does not itself constitute notice of an adverse claim except in the case of a transfer more than:

(1) one year after a date set for presentment or surrender for redemption or exchange; or

(2) six months after a date set for payment of money against presentation or surrender of the certificate, if money was available for payment on that date.

(d) A purchaser of a certificated security has notice of an adverse claim if the security certificate:

(1) whether in bearer or registered form, has been indorsed "for collection" or "for surrender" or for some other purpose not involving transfer; or

(2) is in bearer form and has on it an unambiguous statement that it is the property of a person other than the transferor, but the mere writing of a name on the certificate is not such a statement.

(e) Filing of a financing statement under Article 9 is not notice of an adverse claim to a financial asset.

§ 8—106. **Control.**

(a) A purchaser has "control" of a certificated security in bearer form if the certificated security is delivered to the purchaser.

(b) A purchaser has "control" of a certificated security in registered form if the certificated security is delivered to the purchaser, and:

(1) the certificate is indorsed to the purchaser or in blank by an effective indorsement; or

(2) the certificate is registered in the name of the purchaser, upon original issue or registration of transfer by the issuer.

(c) A purchaser has "control" of an uncertificated security if:

(1) the uncertificated security is delivered to the purchaser; or

(2) the issuer has agreed that it will comply with instructions originated by the purchaser without further consent by the registered owner.

(d) A purchaser has "control" of a security entitlement if:

(1) the purchaser becomes the entitlement holder; or

(2) the securities intermediary has agreed that it will comply with entitlement orders originated by the purchaser without further consent by the entitlement holder.

(e) If an interest in a security entitlement is granted by the entitlement holder to the entitlement holder's own securities intermediary, the securities intermediary has control.

(f) A purchaser who has satisfied the requirements of subsection (c)(2) or (d)(2) has control even if the registered owner in the case of subsection (c)(2) or the entitlement holder in the case of subsection (d)(2) retains the right to make substitutions for the uncertificated security or security entitlement, to originate instructions or entitlement orders to the issuer or securities intermediary, or otherwise to deal with the uncertificated security or security entitlement.

(g) An issuer or a securities intermediary may not enter into an agreement of the kind described in subsection (c)(2) or (d)(2) without the consent of the registered owner or entitlement holder, but an issuer or a securities intermediary is not required to enter into such an agreement even though the registered owner or entitlement holder so directs. An issuer or securities intermediary that has entered into such an agreement is not required to confirm the existence of the agreement to another party unless requested to do so by the registered owner or entitlement holder.

§ 8—107. **Whether Indorsement, Instruction, or Entitlement Order Is Effective.**

(a) "Appropriate person" means:

(1) with respect to an indorsement, the person specified by a security certificate or by an effective special indorsement to be entitled to the security;

(2) with respect to an instruction, the registered owner of an uncertificated security;

(3) with respect to an entitlement order, the entitlement holder;

(4) if the person designated in paragraph (1), (2), or (3) is deceased, the designated person's successor taking under other law or the designated person's personal representative acting for the estate of the decedent; or

(5) if the person designated in paragraph (1), (2), or (3) lacks capacity, the designated person's guardian, conservator, or other similar representative who has power under other law to transfer the security or financial asset.

(b) An indorsement, instruction, or entitlement order is effective if:

(1) it is made by the appropriate person;

(2) it is made by a person who has power under the law of agency to transfer the security or financial asset on behalf of the appropriate person, including, in the case of an instruction or entitlement order, a person who has control under Section 8—106(c)(2) or (d)(2); or

(3) the appropriate person has ratified it or is otherwise precluded from asserting its ineffectiveness.

(c) An indorsement, instruction, or entitlement order made by a representative is effective even if:

(1) the representative has failed to comply with a controlling instrument or with the law of the State having jurisdiction of the representative relationship, including any law requiring the representative to obtain court approval of the transaction; or

(2) the representative's action in making the indorsement, instruction, or entitlement order or using the proceeds of the transaction is otherwise a breach of duty.

(d) If a security is registered in the name of or specially indorsed to a person described as a representative, or if a securities account is maintained in the name of a person described as a representative, an indorsement, instruction, or entitlement order made by the person is effective even though the person is no longer serving in the described capacity.

(e) Effectiveness of an indorsement, instruction, or entitlement order is determined as of the date the indorsement, instruction, or entitlement order is made, and an indorsement, instruction, or entitlement order does not become ineffective by reason of any later change of circumstances.

§ 8—108. Warranties in Direct Holding.

(a) A person who transfers a certificated security to a purchaser for value warrants to the purchaser, and an indorser, if the transfer is by indorsement, warrants to any subsequent purchaser, that:

(1) the certificate is genuine and has not been materially altered;

(2) the transferor or indorser does not know of any fact that might impair the validity of the security;

(3) there is no adverse claim to the security;

(4) the transfer does not violate any restriction on transfer;

(5) if the transfer is by indorsement, the indorsement is made by an appropriate person, or if the indorsement is by an agent, the agent has actual authority to act on behalf of the appropriate person; and

(6) the transfer is otherwise effective and rightful.

(b) A person who originates an instruction for registration of transfer of an uncertificated security to a purchaser for value warrants to the purchaser that:

(1) the instruction is made by an appropriate person, or if the instruction is by an agent, the agent has actual authority to act on behalf of the appropriate person;

(2) the security is valid;

(3) there is no adverse claim to the security; and

(4) at the time the instruction is presented to the issuer:

(i) the purchaser will be entitled to the registration of transfer;

(ii) the transfer will be registered by the issuer free from all liens, security interests, restrictions, and claims other than those specified in the instruction;

(iii) the transfer will not violate any restriction on transfer; and

(iv) the requested transfer will otherwise be effective and rightful.

(c) A person who transfers an uncertificated security to a purchaser for value and does not originate an instruction in connection with the transfer warrants that:

(1) the uncertificated security is valid;

(2) there is no adverse claim to the security;

(3) the transfer does not violate any restriction on transfer; and

(4) the transfer is otherwise effective and rightful.

(d) A person who indorses a security certificate warrants to the issuer that:

(1) there is no adverse claim to the security; and

(2) the indorsement is effective.

(e) A person who originates an instruction for registration of transfer of an uncertificated security warrants to the issuer that:

(1) the instruction is effective; and

(2) at the time the instruction is presented to the issuer the purchaser will be entitled to the registration of transfer.

(f) A person who presents a certificated security for registration of transfer or for payment or exchange warrants to the issuer that the person is entitled to the registration, payment, or exchange, but a purchaser for value and without notice of adverse claims to whom transfer is registered warrants only that the person has no knowledge of any unauthorized signature in a necessary indorsement.

(g) If a person acts as agent of another in delivering a certificated security to a purchaser, the identity of the principal was known to the person to whom the certificate was delivered, and the certificate delivered by the agent was received by the agent from the principal or received by the agent from another person at the direction of the principal, the person delivering the security certificate warrants only that the delivering person has authority to act for the principal and does not know of any adverse claim to the certificated security.

(h) A secured party who redelivers a security certificate received, or after payment and on order of the debtor delivers the security certificate to another person, makes only the warranties of an agent under subsection (g).

(i) Except as otherwise provided in subsection (g), a broker acting for a customer makes to the issuer and a purchaser the warranties provided in subsections (a) through (f). A broker that delivers a security certificate to its customer, or causes its customer to be registered as the owner of an uncertificated security, makes to the customer the warranties provided in subsection (a) or (b), and has the rights and privileges of a purchaser under this section. The warranties of and in favor of the broker acting as an agent are in addition to applicable warranties given by and in favor of the customer.

§ 8—109. **Warranties in Indirect Holding.**

(a) A person who originates an entitlement order to a securities intermediary warrants to the securities intermediary that:

(1) the entitlement order is made by an appropriate person, or if the entitlement order is by an agent, the agent has actual authority to act on behalf of the appropriate person; and

(2) there is no adverse claim to the security entitlement.

(b) A person who delivers a security certificate to a securities intermediary for credit to a securities account or originates an instruction with respect to an uncertificated security directing that the uncertificated security be credited to a securities account makes to the securities intermediary the warranties specified in Section 8—108(a) or (b).

(c) If a securities intermediary delivers a security certificate to its entitlement holder or causes its entitlement holder to be registered as the owner of an uncertificated security, the securities intermediary makes to the entitlement holder the warranties specified in Section 8—108(a) or (b).

§ 8—110. **Applicability; Choice of Law.**

(a) The local law of the issuer's jurisdiction, as specified in subsection (d), governs:

(1) the validity of a security;

(2) the rights and duties of the issuer with respect to registration of transfer;

(3) the effectiveness of registration of transfer by the issuer;

(4) whether the issuer owes any duties to an adverse claimant to a security; and

(5) whether an adverse claim can be asserted against a person to whom transfer of a certificated or uncertificated security is registered or a person who obtains control of an uncertificated security.

(b) The local law of the securities intermediary's jurisdiction, as specified in subsection (e), governs:

(1) acquisition of a security entitlement from the securities intermediary;

(2) the rights and duties of the securities intermediary and entitlement holder arising out of a security entitlement;

(3) whether the securities intermediary owes any duties to an adverse claimant to a security entitlement; and

(4) whether an adverse claim can be asserted against a person who acquires a security entitlement from the securities intermediary or a person who purchases a security entitlement or interest therein from an entitlement holder.

(c) The local law of the jurisdiction in which a security certificate is located at the time of delivery governs whether an adverse claim can be asserted against a person to whom the security certificate is delivered.

(d) "Issuer's jurisdiction" means the jurisdiction under which the issuer of the security is organized or, if permitted by the law of that jurisdiction, the law of another jurisdiction specified by the issuer. An issuer organized under the law of this State may specify the law of another jurisdiction as the law governing the matters specified in subsection (a)(2) through (5).

(e) The following rules determine a "securities intermediary's jurisdiction" for purposes of this section:

(1) If an agreement between the securities intermediary and its entitlement holder specifies that it is governed by the law of a particular jurisdiction, that jurisdiction is the securities intermediary's jurisdiction.

(2) If an agreement between the securities intermediary and its entitlement holder does not specify the governing law as provided in paragraph (1), but expressly specifies that the securities account is maintained at an office in a particular jurisdiction, that jurisdiction is the securities intermediary's jurisdiction.

(3) If an agreement between the securities intermediary and its entitlement holder does not specify a jurisdiction as provided in paragraph (1) or (2), the securities intermediary's jurisdiction is the jurisdiction in which is located the office identified in an account statement as the office serving the entitlement holder's account.

(4) If an agreement between the securities intermediary and its entitlement holder does not specify a jurisdiction as provided in paragraph (1) or (2) and

an account statement does not identify an office serving the entitlement holder's account as provided in paragraph (3), the securities intermediary's jurisdiction is the jurisdiction in which is located the chief executive office of the securities intermediary.

(f) A securities intermediary's jurisdiction is not determined by the physical location of certificates representing financial assets, or by the jurisdiction in which is organized the issuer of the financial asset with respect to which an entitlement holder has a security entitlement, or by the location of facilities for data processing or other record keeping concerning the account.

§ 8—111. **Clearing Corporation Rules.**

A rule adopted by a clearing corporation governing rights and obligations among the clearing corporation and its participants in the clearing corporation is effective even if the rule conflicts with this [Act] and affects another party who does not consent to the rule.

§ 8—112. **Creditor's Legal Process.**

(a) The interest of a debtor in a certificated security may be reached by a creditor only by actual seizure of the security certificate by the officer making the attachment or levy, except as otherwise provided in subsection (d). However, a certificated security for which the certificate has been surrendered to the issuer may be reached by a creditor by legal process upon the issuer.

(b) The interest of a debtor in an uncertificated security may be reached by a creditor only by legal process upon the issuer at its chief executive office in the United States, except as otherwise provided in subsection (d).

(c) The interest of a debtor in a security entitlement may be reached by a creditor only by legal process upon the securities intermediary with whom the debtor's securities account is maintained, except as otherwise provided in subsection (d).

(d) The interest of a debtor in a certificated security for which the certificate is in the possession of a secured party, or in an uncertificated security registered in the name of a secured party, or a security entitlement maintained in the name of a secured party, may be reached by a creditor by legal process upon the secured party.

(e) A creditor whose debtor is the owner of a certificated security, uncertificated security, or security entitlement is entitled to aid from a court of competent jurisdiction, by injunction or otherwise, in reaching the certificated security, uncertificated security, or security entitlement or in satisfying the claim by means allowed at law or in equity in regard to property that cannot readily be reached by other legal process.

§ 8—113. **Statute of Frauds Inapplicable.**

A contract or modification of a contract for the sale or purchase of a security is enforceable whether or not there is a writing signed or record authenticated by a party against whom enforcement is sought, even if the contract or modification is not capable of performance within one year of its making.

§ 8—114. **Evidentiary Rules Concerning Certificated Securities.**

The following rules apply in an action on a certificated security against the issuer:

(1) Unless specifically denied in the pleadings, each signature on a security certificate or in a necessary indorsement is admitted.

(2) If the effectiveness of a signature is put in issue, the burden of establishing effectiveness is on the party claiming under the signature, but the signature is presumed to be genuine or authorized.

(3) If signatures on a security certificate are admitted or established, production of the certificate entitles a holder to recover on it unless the defendant establishes a defense or a defect going to the validity of the security.

(4) If it is shown that a defense or defect exists, the plaintiff has the burden of establishing that the plaintiff or some person under whom the plaintiff claims is a person against whom the defense or defect cannot be asserted.

§ 8—115. **Securities Intermediary and Others Not Liable to Adverse Claimant.**

A securities intermediary that has transferred a financial asset pursuant to an effective entitlement order, or a broker or other agent or bailee that has dealt with a financial asset at the direction of its customer or principal, is not liable to a person having an adverse claim to the financial asset, unless the securities intermediary, or broker or other agent or bailee:

(1) took the action after it had been served with an injunction, restraining order, or other legal process enjoining it from doing so, issued by a court of competent jurisdiction, and had a reasonable opportunity to act on the injunction, restraining order, or other legal process; or

(2) acted in collusion with the wrongdoer in violating the rights of the adverse claimant; or

(3) in the case of a security certificate that has been stolen, acted with notice of the adverse claim.

§ 8—116. **Securities Intermediary as Purchaser for Value.**

A securities intermediary that receives a financial asset and establishes a security entitlement to the financial asset in favor of an entitlement holder is a purchaser for value of the financial asset. A securities intermediary that acquires a security entitlement to a financial asset from another securities intermediary acquires the security entitlement for value if the securities intermediary acquiring the security entitlement establishes a security entitlement to the financial asset in favor of an entitlement holder.

Part 2 Issue and Issuer

§ 8—201. Issuer.

(a) With respect to an obligation on or a defense to a security, an "issuer" includes a person that:

(1) places or authorizes the placing of its name on a security certificate, other than as authenticating trustee, registrar, transfer agent, or the like, to evidence a share, participation, or other interest in its property or in an enterprise, or to evidence its duty to perform an obligation represented by the certificate;

(2) creates a share, participation, or other interest in its property or in an enterprise, or undertakes an obligation, that is an uncertificated security;

(3) directly or indirectly creates a fractional interest in its rights or property, if the fractional interest is represented by a security certificate; or

(4) becomes responsible for, or in place of, another person described as an issuer in this section.

(b) With respect to an obligation on or defense to a security, a guarantor is an issuer to the extent of its guaranty, whether or not its obligation is noted on a security certificate.

(c) With respect to a registration of a transfer, issuer means a person on whose behalf transfer books are maintained.

§ 8—202. Issuer's Responsibility and Defenses; Notice of Defect or Defense.

(a) Even against a purchaser for value and without notice, the terms of a certificated security include terms stated on the certificate and terms made part of the security by reference on the certificate to another instrument, indenture, or document or to a constitution, statute, ordinance, rule, regulation, order, or the like, to the extent the terms referred to do not conflict with terms stated on the certificate. A reference under this subsection does not of itself charge a purchaser for value with notice of a defect going to the validity of the security, even if the certificate expressly states that a person accepting it admits notice. The terms of an uncertificated security include those stated in any instrument, indenture, or document or in a constitution, statute, ordinance, rule, regulation, order, or the like, pursuant to which the security is issued.

(b) The following rules apply if an issuer asserts that a security is not valid:

(1) A security other than one issued by a government or governmental subdivision, agency, or instrumentality, even though issued with a defect going to its validity, is valid in the hands of a purchaser for value and without notice of the particular defect unless the defect involves a violation of a constitutional provision. In that case, the security is valid in the hands of a purchaser for value and without notice of the defect, other than one who takes by original issue.

(2) Paragraph (1) applies to an issuer that is a government or governmental subdivision, agency, or instrumentality only if there has been substantial compliance with the legal requirements governing the issue or the issuer has received a substantial consideration for the issue as a whole or for the particular security and a stated purpose of the issue is one for which the issuer has power to borrow money or issue the security.

(c) Except as otherwise provided in Section 8—205, lack of genuineness of a certificated security is a complete defense, even against a purchaser for value and without notice.

(d) All other defenses of the issuer of a security, including nondelivery and conditional delivery of a certificated security, are ineffective against a purchaser for value who has taken the certificated security without notice of the particular defense.

(e) This section does not affect the right of a party to cancel a contract for a security "when, as and if issued" or "when distributed" in the event of a material change in the character of the security that is the subject of the contract or in the plan or arrangement pursuant to which the security is to be issued or distributed.

(f) If a security is held by a securities intermediary against whom an entitlement holder has a security entitlement with respect to the security, the issuer may not assert any defense that the issuer could not assert if the entitlement holder held the security directly.

§ 8—203. Staleness as Notice of Defect or Defense.

After an act or event, other than a call that has been revoked, creating a right to immediate performance of the principal obligation represented by a certificated security or setting a date on or after which the security is to be presented or surrendered for redemption or exchange, a purchaser is charged with notice of any defect in its issue or defense of the issuer, if the act or event:

(1) requires the payment of money, the delivery of a certificated security, the registration of transfer of an uncertificated security, or any of them on presentation or surrender of the security certificate, the money or security is available on the date set for

payment or exchange, and the purchaser takes the security more than one year after that date; or

(2) is not covered by paragraph (1) and the purchaser takes the security more than two years after the date set for surrender or presentation or the date on which performance became due.

§ 8—204. **Effect of Issuer's Restriction on Transfer.**

A restriction on transfer of a security imposed by the issuer, even if otherwise lawful, is ineffective against a person without knowledge of the restriction unless:

(1) the security is certificated and the restriction is noted conspicuously on the security certificate; or

(2) the security is uncertificated and the registered owner has been notified of the restriction.

§ 8—205. **Effect of Unauthorized Signature on Security Certificate.**

An unauthorized signature placed on a security certificate before or in the course of issue is ineffective, but the signature is effective in favor of a purchaser for value of the certificated security if the purchaser is without notice of the lack of authority and the signing has been done by:

(1) an authenticating trustee, registrar, transfer agent, or other person entrusted by the issuer with the signing of the security certificate or of similar security certificates, or the immediate preparation for signing of any of them; or

(2) an employee of the issuer, or of any of the persons listed in paragraph (1), entrusted with responsible handling of the security certificate.

§ 8—206. **Completion of Alteration of Security Certificate.**

(a) If a security certificate contains the signatures necessary to its issue or transfer but is incomplete in any other respect:

(1) any person may complete it by filling in the blanks as authorized; and

(2) even if the blanks are incorrectly filled in, the security certificate as completed is enforceable by a purchaser who took it for value and without notice of the incorrectness.

(b) A complete security certificate that has been improperly altered, even if fraudulently, remains enforceable, but only according to its original terms.

§ 8—207. **Rights and Duties of Issuer with Respect to Registered Owners.**

(a) Before due presentment for registration of transfer of a certificated security in registered form or of an instruction requesting registration of transfer of an uncertificated security, the issuer or indenture trustee may treat the registered owner as the person exclusively entitled to vote, receive notifications, and otherwise exercise all the rights and powers of an owner.

(b) This Article does not affect the liability of the registered owner of a security for a call, assessment, or the like.

§ 8—208. **Effect of Signature of Authenticating Trustee, Registrar, or Transfer Agent.**

(a) A person signing a security certificate as authenticating trustee, registrar, transfer agent, or the like, warrants to a purchaser for value of the certificated security, if the purchaser is without notice of a particular defect, that:

(1) the certificate is genuine;

(2) the person's own participation in the issue of the security is within the person's capacity and within the scope of the authority received by the person from the issuer; and

(3) the person has reasonable grounds to believe that the certificated security is in the form and within the amount the issuer is authorized to issue.

(b) Unless otherwise agreed, a person signing under subsection (a) does not assume responsibility for the validity of the security in other respects.

§ 8—209. **Issuer's Lien.**

A lien in favor of an issuer upon a certificated security is valid against a purchaser only if the right of the issuer to the lien is noted conspicuously on the security certificate.

§ 8—210. **Overissue.**

(a) In this section, "overissue" means the issue of securities in excess of the amount the issuer has corporate power to issue, but an overissue does not occur if appropriate action has cured the overissue.

(b) Except as otherwise provided in subsections (c) and (d), the provisions of this Article which validate a security or compel its issue or reissue do not apply to the extent that validation, issue, or reissue would result in overissue.

(c) If an identical security not constituting an overissue is reasonably available for purchase, a person entitled to issue or validation may compel the issuer to purchase the security and deliver it if certificated or register its transfer if uncertificated, against surrender of any security certificate the person holds.

(d) If a security is not reasonably available for purchase, a person entitled to issue or validation may recover from the issuer the price the person or the last purchaser for value paid for it with interest from the date of the person's demand.

Part 3 Transfer of Certificated and Uncertificated Securities

§ 8—301. Delivery.

(a) Delivery of a certificated security to a purchaser occurs when:

(1) the purchaser acquires possession of the security certificate;

(2) another person, other than a securities intermediary, either acquires possession of the security certificate on behalf of the purchaser or, having previously acquired possession of the certificate, acknowledges that it holds for the purchaser; or

(3) a securities intermediary acting on behalf of the purchaser acquires possession of the security certificate, only if the certificate is in registered form and has been specially indorsed to the purchaser by an effective indorsement.

(b) Delivery of an uncertificated security to a purchaser occurs when:

(1) the issuer registers the purchaser as the registered owner, upon original issue or registration of transfer; or

(2) another person, other than a securities intermediary, either becomes the registered owner of the uncertificated security on behalf of the purchaser or, having previously become the registered owner, acknowledges that it holds for the purchaser.

§ 8—302. Rights of Purchaser.

(a) Except as otherwise provided in subsections (b) and (c), upon delivery of a certificated or uncertificated security to a purchaser, the purchaser acquires all rights in the security that the transferor had or had power to transfer.

(b) A purchaser of a limited interest acquires rights only to the extent of the interest purchased.

(c) A purchaser of a certificated security who as a previous holder had notice of an adverse claim does not improve its position by taking from a protected purchaser.

§ 8—303. Protected Purchaser.

(a) "Protected purchaser" means a purchaser of a certificated or uncertificated security, or of an interest therein, who:

(1) gives value;

(2) does not have notice of any adverse claim to the security; and

(3) obtains control of the certificated or uncertificated security.

(b) In addition to acquiring the rights of a purchaser, a protected purchaser also acquires its interest in the security free of any adverse claim.

§ 8—304. Indorsement.

(a) An indorsement may be in blank or special. An indorsement in blank includes an indorsement to bearer. A special indorsement specifies to whom a security is to be transferred or who has power to transfer it. A holder may convert a blank indorsement to a special indorsement.

(b) An indorsement purporting to be only of part of a security certificate representing units intended by the issuer to be separately transferable is effective to the extent of the indorsement.

(c) An indorsement, whether special or in blank, does not constitute a transfer until delivery of the certificate on which it appears or, if the indorsement is on a separate document, until delivery of both the document and the certificate.

(d) If a security certificate in registered form has been delivered to a purchaser without a necessary indorsement, the purchaser may become a protected purchaser only when the indorsement is supplied. However, against a transferor, a transfer is complete upon delivery and the purchaser has a specifically enforceable right to have any necessary indorsement supplied.

(e) An indorsement of a security certificate in bearer form may give notice of an adverse claim to the certificate, but it does not otherwise affect a right to registration that the holder possesses.

(f) Unless otherwise agreed, a person making an indorsement assumes only the obligations provided in Section 8—108 and not an obligation that the security will be honored by the issuer.

§ 8—305. Instruction.

(a) If an instruction has been originated by an appropriate person but is incomplete in any other respect, any person may complete it as authorized and the issuer may rely on it as completed, even though it has been completed incorrectly.

(b) Unless otherwise agreed, a person initiating an instruction assumes only the obligations imposed by Section 8—108 and not an obligation that the security will be honored by the issuer.

§ 8—306. Effect of Guaranteeing Signature, Indorsement, or Instruction.

(a) A person who guarantees a signature of an indorser of a security certificate warrants that at the time of signing:

(1) the signature was genuine;

(2) the signer was an appropriate person to indorse, or if the signature is by an agent, the agent had actual authority to act on behalf of the appropriate person; and

(3) the signer had legal capacity to sign.

(b) A person who guarantees a signature of the originator of an instruction warrants that at the time of signing:

(1) the signature was genuine;

(2) the signer was an appropriate person to originate the instruction, or if the signature is by an agent, the agent had actual authority to act on behalf of the appropriate person, if the person specified in the instruction as the registered owner was, in fact, the registered owner, as to which fact the signature guarantor does not make a warranty; and

(3) the signer had legal capacity to sign.

(c) A person who specially guarantees the signature of an originator of an instruction makes the warranties of a signature guarantor under subsection (b) and also warrants that at the time the instruction is presented to the issuer:

(1) the person specified in the instruction as the registered owner of the uncertificated security will be the registered owner; and

(2) the transfer of the uncertificated security requested in the instruction will be registered by the issuer free from all liens, security interests, restrictions, and claims other than those specified in the instruction.

(d) A guarantor under subsections (a) and (b) or a special guarantor under subsection (c) does not otherwise warrant the rightfulness of the transfer.

(e) A person who guarantees an indorsement of a security certificate makes the warranties of a signature guarantor under subsection (a) and also warrants the rightfulness of the transfer in all respects.

(f) A person who guarantees an instruction requesting the transfer of an uncertificated security makes the warranties of a special signature guarantor under subsection (c) and also warrants the rightfulness of the transfer in all respects.

(g) An issuer may not require a special guaranty of signature, a guaranty of indorsement, or a guaranty of instruction as a condition to registration of transfer.

(h) The warranties under this section are made to a person taking or dealing with the security in reliance on the guaranty, and the guarantor is liable to the person for loss resulting from their breach. An indorser or originator of an instruction whose signature, indorsement, or instruction has been guaranteed is liable to a guarantor for any loss suffered by the guarantor as a result of breach of the warranties of the guarantor.

§ 8—307. Purchaser's Right to Requisites for Registration of Transfer.

Unless otherwise agreed, the transferor of a security on due demand shall supply the purchaser with proof of authority to transfer or with any other requisite necessary to obtain registration of the transfer of the security, but if the transfer is not for value, a transferor need not comply unless the purchaser pays the necessary expenses. If the transferor fails within a reasonable time to comply with the demand, the purchaser may reject or rescind the transfer.

Part 4 Registration

§ 8—401. Duty of Issuer to Register Transfer.

(a) If a certificated security in registered form is presented to an issuer with a request to register transfer or an instruction is presented to an issuer with a request to register transfer of an uncertificated security, the issuer shall register the transfer as requested if:

(1) under the terms of the security the person seeking registration of transfer is eligible to have the security registered in its name;

(2) the indorsement or instruction is made by the appropriate person or by an agent who has actual authority to act on behalf of the appropriate person;

(3) reasonable assurance is given that the indorsement or instruction is genuine and authorized (Section 8—402);

(4) any applicable law relating to the collection of taxes has been complied with;

(5) the transfer does not violate any restriction on transfer imposed by the issuer in accordance with Section 8—204;

(6) a demand that the issuer not register transfer has not become effective under Section 8—403, or the issuer has complied with Section 8—403(b) but no legal process or indemnity bond is obtained as provided in Section 8—403(d); and

(7) the transfer is in fact rightful or is to a protected purchaser.

(b) If an issuer is under a duty to register a transfer of a security, the issuer is liable to a person presenting a certificated security or an instruction for registration or to the person's principal for loss resulting from unreasonable delay in registration or failure or refusal to register the transfer.

§ 8—402. Assurance That Indorsement or Instruction Is Effective.

(a) An issuer may require the following assurance that each necessary indorsement or each instruction is genuine and authorized:

(1) in all cases, a guaranty of the signature of the person making an indorsement or originating an

instruction including, in the case of an instruction, reasonable assurance of identity;

(2) if the indorsement is made or the instruction is originated by an agent, appropriate assurance of actual authority to sign;

(3) if the indorsement is made or the instruction is originated by a fiduciary pursuant to Section 8—107(a)(4) or (a)(5), appropriate evidence of appointment or incumbency;

(4) if there is more than one fiduciary, reasonable assurance that all who are required to sign have done so; and

(5) if the indorsement is made or the instruction is originated by a person not covered by another provision of this subsection, assurance appropriate to the case corresponding as nearly as may be to the provisions of this subsection.

(b) An issuer may elect to require reasonable assurance beyond that specified in this section.

(c) In this section:

(1) "Guaranty of the signature" means a guaranty signed by or on behalf of a person reasonably believed by the issuer to be responsible. An issuer may adopt standards with respect to responsibility if they are not manifestly unreasonable.

(2) "Appropriate evidence of appointment or incumbency" means:

(i) in the case of a fiduciary appointed or qualified by a court, a certificate issued by or under the direction or supervision of the court or an officer thereof and dated within 60 days before the date of presentation for transfer; or

(ii) in any other case, a copy of a document showing the appointment or a certificate issued by or on behalf of a person reasonably believed by an issuer to be responsible or, in the absence of that document or certificate, other evidence the issuer reasonably considers appropriate.

§ 8—403. Demand That Issuer Not Register Transfer.

(a) A person who is an appropriate person to make an indorsement or originate an instruction may demand that the issuer not register transfer of a security by communicating to the issuer a notification that identifies the registered owner and the issue of which the security is a part and provides an address for communications directed to the person making the demand. The demand is effective only if it is received by the issuer at a time and in a manner affording the issuer reasonable opportunity to act on it.

(b) If a certificated security in registered form is presented to an issuer with a request to register transfer or an instruction is presented to an issuer with a request to register transfer of an uncertificated security after a demand that the issuer not register transfer has become effective, the issuer shall promptly communicate to (i) the person who initiated the demand at the address provided in the demand and (ii) the person who presented the security for registration of transfer or initiated the instruction requesting registration of transfer a notification stating that:

(1) the certificated security has been presented for registration of transfer or the instruction for registration of transfer of the uncertificated security has been received;

(2) a demand that the issuer not register transfer had previously been received; and

(3) the issuer will withhold registration of transfer for a period of time stated in the notification in order to provide the person who initiated the demand an opportunity to obtain legal process or an indemnity bond.

(c) The period described in subsection (b)(3) may not exceed 30 days after the date of communication of the notification. A shorter period may be specified by the issuer if it is not manifestly unreasonable.

(d) An issuer is not liable to a person who initiated a demand that the issuer not register transfer for any loss the person suffers as a result of registration of a transfer pursuant to an effective indorsement or instruction if the person who initiated the demand does not, within the time stated in the issuer's communication, either:

(1) obtain an appropriate restraining order, injunction, or other process from a court of competent jurisdiction enjoining the issuer from registering the transfer; or

(2) file with the issuer an indemnity bond, sufficient in the issuer's judgment to protect the issuer and any transfer agent, registrar, or other agent of the issuer involved from any loss it or they may suffer by refusing to register the transfer.

(e) This section does not relieve an issuer from liability for registering transfer pursuant to an indorsement or instruction that was not effective.

§ 8—404. Wrongful Registration.

(a) Except as otherwise provided in Section 8—406, an issuer is liable for wrongful registration of transfer if the issuer has registered a transfer of a security to a person not entitled to it, and the transfer was registered:

(1) pursuant to an ineffective indorsement or instruction;

(2) after a demand that the issuer not register transfer became effective under Section 8—403(a) and the issuer did not comply with Section 8—403(b);

(3) after the issuer had been served with an injunction, restraining order, or other legal process enjoining it from registering the transfer, issued by a court of competent jurisdiction, and the issuer had a reasonable opportunity to act on the injunction, restraining order, or other legal process; or

(4) by an issuer acting in collusion with the wrongdoer.

(b) An issuer that is liable for wrongful registration of transfer under subsection (a) on demand shall provide the person entitled to the security with a like certificated or uncertificated security, and any payments or distributions that the person did not receive as a result of the wrongful registration. If an overissue would result, the issuer's liability to provide the person with a like security is governed by Section 8—210.

(c) Except as otherwise provided in subsection (a) or in a law relating to the collection of taxes, an issuer is not liable to an owner or other person suffering loss as a result of the registration of a transfer of a security if registration was made pursuant to an effective indorsement or instruction.

§ 8—405. Replacement of Lost, Destroyed, or Wrongfully Taken Security Certificate.

(a) If an owner of a certificated security, whether in registered or bearer form, claims that the certificate has been lost, destroyed, or wrongfully taken, the issuer shall issue a new certificate if the owner:

(1) so requests before the issuer has notice that the certificate has been acquired by a protected purchaser;

(2) files with the issuer a sufficient indemnity bond; and

(3) satisfies other reasonable requirements imposed by the issuer.

(b) If, after the issue of a new security certificate, a protected purchaser of the original certificate presents it for registration of transfer, the issuer shall register the transfer unless an overissue would result. In that case, the issuer's liability is governed by Section 8—210. In addition to any rights on the indemnity bond, an issuer may recover the new certificate from a person to whom it was issued or any person taking under that person, except a protected purchaser.

§ 8—406. Obligation to Notify Issuer of Lost, Destroyed, or Wrongfully Taken Security Certificate.

If a security certificate has been lost, apparently destroyed, or wrongfully taken, and the owner fails to notify the issuer of that fact within a reasonable time after the owner has notice of it and the issuer registers a transfer of the security before receiving notification, the owner may not assert against the issuer a claim for registering the transfer under Section 8–404 or a claim to a new security certificate under Section 8–405.

§ 8—407. Authenticating Trustee, Transfer Agent, and Registrar.

A person acting as authenticating trustee, transfer agent, registrar, or other agent for an issuer in the registration of a transfer of its securities, in the issue of new security certificates or uncertificated securities, or in the cancellation of surrendered security certificates has the same obligation to the holder or owner of a certificated or uncertificated security with regard to the particular functions performed as the issuer has in regard to those functions.

Part 5 Security Entitlements

§ 8—501. Securities Account; Acquisition of Security Entitlement from Securities Intermediary.

(a) "Securities account" means an account to which a financial asset is or may be credited in accordance with an agreement under which the person maintaining the account undertakes to treat the person for whom the account is maintained as entitled to exercise the rights that comprise the financial asset.

(b) Except as otherwise provided in subsections (d) and (e), a person acquires a security entitlement if a securities intermediary:

(1) indicates by book entry that a financial asset has been credited to the person's securities account;

(2) receives a financial asset from the person or acquires a financial asset for the person and, in either case, accepts it for credit to the person's securities account; or

(3) becomes obligated under other law, regulation, or rule to credit a financial asset to the person's securities account.

(c) If a condition of subsection (b) has been met, a person has a security entitlement even though the securities intermediary does not itself hold the financial asset.

(d) If a securities intermediary holds a financial asset for another person, and the financial asset is registered in the name of, payable to the order of, or specially indorsed to the other person, and has not been indorsed to the securities intermediary or in blank, the other person is treated as holding the financial asset directly rather than as having a security entitlement with respect to the financial asset.

(e) Issuance of a security is not establishment of a security entitlement.

§ 8—502. Assertion of Adverse Claim against Entitlement Holder.

An action based on an adverse claim to a financial asset, whether framed in conversion, replevin, constructive trust, equitable lien, or other theory, may not be asserted against a person who acquires a security entitlement under Section 8—501 for value and without notice of the adverse claim.

§ 8—503. Property Interest of Entitlement Holder in Financial Asset Held by Securities Intermediary.

(a) To the extent necessary for a securities intermediary to satisfy all security entitlements with respect to a particular financial asset, all interests in that financial asset held by the securities intermediary are held by the securities intermediary for the entitlement holders, are not property of the securities intermediary, and are not subject to claims of creditors of the securities intermediary, except as otherwise provided in Section 8—511.

(b) An entitlement holder's property interest with respect to a particular financial asset under subsection (a) is a pro rata property interest in all interests in that financial asset held by the securities intermediary, without regard to the time the entitlement holder acquired the security entitlement or the time the securities intermediary acquired the interest in that financial asset.

(c) An entitlement holder's property interest with respect to a particular financial asset under subsection (a) may be enforced against the securities intermediary only by exercise of the entitlement holder's rights under Sections 8—505 through 8—508.

(d) An entitlement holder's property interest with respect to a particular financial asset under subsection (a) may be enforced against a purchaser of the financial asset or interest therein only if:

(1) insolvency proceedings have been initiated by or against the securities intermediary;

(2) the securities intermediary does not have sufficient interests in the financial asset to satisfy the security entitlements of all of its entitlement holders to that financial asset;

(3) the securities intermediary violated its obligations under Section 8—504 by transferring the financial asset or interest therein to the purchaser; and

(4) the purchaser is not protected under subsection (e).

The trustee or other liquidator, acting on behalf of all entitlement holders having security entitlements with respect to a particular financial asset, may recover the financial asset, or interest therein, from the purchaser. If the trustee or other liquidator elects not to pursue that right, an entitlement holder whose security entitlement remains unsatisfied has the right to recover its interest in the financial asset from the purchaser.

(e) An action based on the entitlement holder's property interest with respect to a particular financial asset under subsection (a), whether framed in conversion, replevin, constructive trust, equitable lien, or other theory, may not be asserted against any purchaser of a financial asset or interest therein who gives value, obtains control, and does not act in collusion with the securities intermediary in violating the securities intermediary's obligations under Section 8—504.

§ 8—504. Duty of Securities Intermediary to Maintain Financial Asset.

(a) A securities intermediary shall promptly obtain and thereafter maintain a financial asset in a quantity corresponding to the aggregate of all security entitlements it has established in favor of its entitlement holders with respect to that financial asset. The securities intermediary may maintain those financial assets directly or through one or more other securities intermediaries.

(b) Except to the extent otherwise agreed by its entitlement holder, a securities intermediary may not grant any security interests in a financial asset it is obligated to maintain pursuant to subsection (a).

(c) A securities intermediary satisfies the duty in subsection (a) if:

(1) the securities intermediary acts with respect to the duty as agreed upon by the entitlement holder and the securities intermediary; or

(2) in the absence of agreement, the securities intermediary exercises due care in accordance with reasonable commercial standards to obtain and maintain the financial asset.

(d) This section does not apply to a clearing corporation that is itself the obligor of an option or similar obligation to which its entitlement holders have security entitlements.

§ 8—505. Duty of Securities Intermediary with Respect to Payments and Distributions.

(a) A securities intermediary shall take action to obtain a payment or distribution made by the issuer of a financial asset. A securities intermediary satisfies the duty if:

(1) the securities intermediary acts with respect to the duty as agreed upon by the entitlement holder and the securities intermediary; or

(2) in the absence of agreement, the securities intermediary exercises due care in accordance with reasonable commercial standards to attempt to obtain the payment or distribution.

(b) A securities intermediary is obligated to its entitlement holder for a payment or distribution made by the issuer of a financial asset if the payment or distribution is received by the securities intermediary.

§ 8—506. Duty of Securities Intermediary to Exercise Rights as Directed by Entitlement Holder.

A securities intermediary shall exercise rights with respect to a financial asset if directed to do so by an entitlement holder. A securities intermediary satisfies the duty if:

(1) the securities intermediary acts with respect to the duty as agreed upon by the entitlement holder and the securities intermediary; or

(2) in the absence of agreement, the securities intermediary either places the entitlement holder in a position to exercise the rights directly or exercises due care in accordance with reasonable commercial standards to follow the direction of the entitlement holder.

§ 8—507. Duty of Securities Intermediary to Comply with Entitlement Order.

(a) A securities intermediary shall comply with an entitlement order if the entitlement order is originated by the appropriate person, the securities intermediary has had reasonable opportunity to assure itself that the entitlement order is genuine and authorized, and the securities intermediary has had reasonable opportunity to comply with the entitlement order. A securities intermediary satisfies the duty if:

(1) the securities intermediary acts with respect to the duty as agreed upon by the entitlement holder and the securities intermediary; or

(2) in the absence of agreement, the securities intermediary exercises due care in accordance with reasonable commercial standards to comply with the entitlement order.

(b) If a securities intermediary transfers a financial asset pursuant to an ineffective entitlement order, the securities intermediary shall reestablish a security entitlement in favor of the person entitled to it, and pay or credit any payments or distributions that the person did not receive as a result of the wrongful transfer. If the securities intermediary does not reestablish a security entitlement, the securities intermediary is liable to the entitlement holder for damages.

§ 8—508. Duty of Securities Intermediary to Change Entitlement Holder's Position to Other Form of Security Holding.

A securities intermediary shall act at the direction of an entitlement holder to change a security entitlement into another available form of holding for which the entitlement holder is eligible, or to cause the financial asset to be transferred to a securities account of the entitlement holder with another securities intermediary. A securities intermediary satisfies the duty if:

(1) the securities intermediary acts as agreed upon by the entitlement holder and the securities intermediary; or

(2) in the absence of agreement, the securities intermediary exercises due care in accordance with reasonable commercial standards to follow the direction of the entitlement holder.

§ 8—509. Specification of Duties of Securities Intermediary by Other Statute or Regulation; Manner of Performance of Duties of Securities Intermediary and Exercise of Rights of Entitlement Holder.

(a) If the substance of a duty imposed upon a securities intermediary by Sections 8—504 through 8—508 is the subject of other statute, regulation, or rule, compliance with that statute, regulation, or rule satisfies the duty.

(b) To the extent that specific standards for the performance of the duties of a securities intermediary or the exercise of the rights of an entitlement holder are not specified by other statute, regulation, or rule or by agreement between the securities intermediary and entitlement holder, the securities intermediary shall perform its duties and the entitlement holder shall exercise its rights in a commercially reasonable manner.

(c) The obligation of a securities intermediary to perform the duties imposed by Sections 8—504 through 8—508 is subject to:

(1) rights of the securities intermediary arising out of a security interest under a security agreement with the entitlement holder or otherwise; and

(2) rights of the securities intermediary under other law, regulation, rule, or agreement to withhold performance of its duties as a result of unfulfilled obligations of the entitlement holder to the securities intermediary.

(d) Sections 8—504 through 8—508 do not require a securities intermediary to take any action that is prohibited by other statute, regulation, or rule.

§ 8—510. Rights of Purchaser of Security Entitlement from Entitlement Holder.

(a) An action based on an adverse claim to a financial asset or security entitlement, whether framed in conversion, replevin, constructive trust, equitable lien, or other theory, may not be asserted against a person who purchases a security entitlement, or an interest therein, from an entitlement holder if the purchaser gives value, does not have notice of the adverse claim, and obtains control.

(b) If an adverse claim could not have been asserted against an entitlement holder under Section 8—502, the adverse claim cannot be asserted against a person who purchases a security entitlement, or an interest therein, from the entitlement holder.

(c) In a case not covered by the priority rules in Article 9, a purchaser for value of a security entitlement, or an interest therein, who obtains control has priority over a purchaser of a security entitlement, or an interest therein, who does not obtain control. Purchasers who have control rank equally, except that a securities intermediary as purchaser has priority over a conflicting purchaser who has control unless otherwise agreed by the securities intermediary.

§ 8—511. Priority among Security Interests and Entitlement Holders.

(a) Except as otherwise provided in subsections (b) and (c), if a securities intermediary does not have sufficient interests in a particular financial asset to satisfy both its obligations to entitlement holders who have security entitlements to that financial asset and its obligation to a creditor of the securities intermediary who has a security interest in that financial asset, the claims of entitlement holders, other than the creditor, have priority over the claim of the creditor.

(b) A claim of a creditor of a securities intermediary who has a security interest in a financial asset held by a securities intermediary has priority over claims of the securities intermediary's entitlement holders who have security entitlements with respect to that financial asset if the creditor has control over the financial asset.

(c) If a clearing corporation does not have sufficient financial assets to satisfy both its obligations to entitlement holders who have security entitlements with respect to a financial asset and its obligation to a creditor of the clearing corporation who has a security interest in that financial asset, the claim of the creditor has priority over the claims of entitlement holders.

Part 6 Transition Provisions for Revised Article 8

§ 8—601. Effective Date.

This [Act] takes effect....

§ 8—602. Repeals.

This [Act] repeals....

§ 8—603. Savings Clause.

(a) This [Act] does not affect an action or proceeding commenced before this [Act] takes effect.

(b) If a security interest in a security is perfected at the date this [Act] takes effect, and the action by which the security interest was perfected would suffice to perfect a security interest under this [Act], no further action is required to continue perfection. If a security interest in a security is perfected at the date this [Act] takes effect but the action by which the security interest was perfected would not suffice to perfect a security interest under this [Act], the security interest remains perfected for a period of four months after the effective date and continues perfected thereafter if appropriate action to perfect under this [Act] is taken within that period. If a security interest is perfected at the date this [Act] takes effect and the security interest can be perfected by filing under this [Act], a financing statement signed by the secured party instead of the debtor may be filed within that period to continue perfection or thereafter to perfect.

Revised (1999) Article 9
SECURED TRANSACTIONS

Part 1 General Provisions

[Subpart 1. Short Title, Definitions, and General Concepts]

§ 9—101. Short Title.

This article may be cited as Uniform Commercial Code—Secured Transactions.

§ 9—102. Definitions and Index of Definitions.

(a) In this article:

(1) "Accession" means goods that are physically united with other goods in such a manner that the identity of the original goods is not lost.

(2) "Account", except as used in "account for", means a right to payment of a monetary obligation, whether or not earned by performance, (i) for property that has been or is to be sold, leased, licensed, assigned, or otherwise disposed of, (ii) for services rendered or to be rendered, (iii) for a policy of insurance issued or to be issued, (iv) for a secondary obligation incurred or to be incurred, (v) for energy provided or to be provided, (vi) for the use or hire of a vessel under a charter or other contract, (vii) arising out of the use of a credit or charge card or information contained on or for use with the card, or (viii) as winnings in a lottery or other game of chance operated or sponsored by a State, governmental unit of a State, or person licensed or authorized to operate the game by a State or governmental unit of a State. The term includes health-care insurance receivables. The term

does not include (i) rights to payment evidenced by chattel paper or an instrument, (ii) commercial tort claims, (iii) deposit accounts, (iv) investment property, (v) letter-of-credit rights or letters of credit, or (vi) rights to payment for money or funds advanced or sold, other than rights arising out of the use of a credit or charge card or information contained on or for use with the card.

(3) "Account debtor" means a person obligated on an account, chattel paper, or general intangible. The term does not include persons obligated to pay a negotiable instrument, even if the instrument constitutes part of chattel paper.

(4) "Accounting", except as used in "accounting for", means a record:

(A) authenticated by a secured party;

(B) indicating the aggregate unpaid secured obligations as of a date not more than 35 days earlier or 35 days later than the date of the record; and

(C) identifying the components of the obligations in reasonable detail.

(5) "Agricultural lien" means an interest, other than a security interest, in farm products:

(A) which secures payment or performance of an obligation for:

(i) goods or services furnished in connection with a debtor's farming operation; or

(ii) rent on real property leased by a debtor in connection with its farming operation;

(B) which is created by statute in favor of a person that:

(i) in the ordinary course of its business furnished goods or services to a debtor in connection with a debtor's farming operation; or

(ii) leased real property to a debtor in connection with the debtor's farming operation; and

(C) whose effectiveness does not depend on the person's possession of the personal property.

(6) "As-extracted collateral" means:

(A) oil, gas, or other minerals that are subject to a security interest that:

(i) is created by a debtor having an interest in the minerals before extraction; and

(ii) attaches to the minerals as extracted; or

(B) accounts arising out of the sale at the wellhead or minehead of oil, gas, or other minerals in which the debtor had an interest before extraction.

(7) "Authenticate" means:

(A) to sign; or

(B) to execute or otherwise adopt a symbol, or encrypt or similarly process a record in whole or in part, with the present intent of the authenticating person to identify the person and adopt or accept a record.

(8) "Bank" means an organization that is engaged in the business of banking. The term includes savings banks, savings and loan associations, credit unions, and trust companies.

(9) "Cash proceeds" means proceeds that are money, checks, deposit accounts, or the like.

(10) "Certificate of title" means a certificate of title with respect to which a statute provides for the security interest in question to be indicated on the certificate as a condition or result of the security interest's obtaining priority over the rights of a lien creditor with respect to the collateral.

(11) "Chattel paper" means a record or records that evidence both a monetary obligation and a security interest in specific goods, a security interest in specific goods and software used in the goods, a security interest in specific goods and license of software used in the goods, a lease of specific goods, or a lease of specific goods and license of software used in the goods. In this paragraph, "monetary obligation" means a monetary obligation secured by the goods or owed under a lease of the goods and includes a monetary obligation with respect to software used in the goods. The term does not include (i) charters or other contracts involving the use or hire of a vessel or (ii) records that evidence a right to payment arising out of the use of a credit or charge card or information contained on or for use with the card. If a transaction is evidenced by records that include an instrument or series of instruments, the group of records taken together constitutes chattel paper.

(12) "Collateral" means the property subject to a security interest or agricultural lien. The term includes:

(A) proceeds to which a security interest attaches;

(B) accounts, chattel paper, payment intangibles, and promissory notes that have been sold; and

(C) goods that are the subject of a consignment.

(13) "Commercial tort claim" means a claim arising in tort with respect to which:

(A) the claimant is an organization; or

(B) the claimant is an individual and the claim:

(i) arose in the course of the claimant's business or profession; and

(ii) does not include damages arising out of personal injury to or the death of an individual.

(14) "Commodity account" means an account maintained by a commodity intermediary in which a commodity contract is carried for a commodity customer.

(15) "Commodity contract" means a commodity futures contract, an option on a commodity futures contract, a commodity option, or another contract if the contract or option is:

(A) traded on or subject to the rules of a board of trade that has been designated as a contract market for such a contract pursuant to federal commodities laws; or

(B) traded on a foreign commodity board of trade, exchange, or market, and is carried on the books of a commodity intermediary for a commodity customer.

(16) "Commodity customer" means a person for which a commodity intermediary carries a commodity contract on its books.

(17) "Commodity intermediary" means a person that:

(A) is registered as a futures commission merchant under federal commodities law; or

(B) in the ordinary course of its business provides clearance or settlement services for a board of trade that has been designated as a contract market pursuant to federal commodities law.

(18) "Communicate" means:

(A) to send a written or other tangible record;

(B) to transmit a record by any means agreed upon by the persons sending and receiving the record; or

(C) in the case of transmission of a record to or by a filing office, to transmit a record by any means prescribed by filing-office rule.

(19) "Consignee" means a merchant to which goods are delivered in a consignment.

(20) "Consignment" means a transaction, regardless of its form, in which a person delivers goods to a merchant for the purpose of sale and:

(A) the merchant:

(i) deals in goods of that kind under a name other than the name of the person making delivery;

(ii) is not an auctioneer; and

(iii) is not generally known by its creditors to be substantially engaged in selling the goods of others;

(B) with respect to each delivery, the aggregate value of the goods is $1,000 or more at the time of delivery;

(C) the goods are not consumer goods immediately before delivery; and

(D) the transaction does not create a security interest that secures an obligation.

(21) "Consignor" means a person that delivers goods to a consignee in a consignment.

(22) "Consumer debtor" means a debtor in a consumer transaction.

(23) "Consumer goods" means goods that are used or bought for use primarily for personal, family, or household purposes.

(24) "Consumer-goods transaction" means a consumer transaction in which:

(A) an individual incurs an obligation primarily for personal, family, or household purposes; and

(B) a security interest in consumer goods secures the obligation.

(25) "Consumer obligor" means an obligor who is an individual and who incurred the obligation as part of a transaction entered into primarily for personal, family, or household purposes.

(26) "Consumer transaction" means a transaction in which (i) an individual incurs an obligation primarily for personal, family, or household purposes, (ii) a security interest secures the obligation, and (iii) the collateral is held or acquired primarily for personal, family, or household purposes. The term includes consumer-goods transactions.

(27) "Continuation statement" means an amendment of a financing statement which:

(A) identifies, by its file number, the initial financing statement to which it relates; and

(B) indicates that it is a continuation statement for, or that it is filed to continue the effectiveness of, the identified financing statement.

(28) "Debtor" means:

(A) a person having an interest, other than a security interest or other lien, in the collateral, whether or not the person is an obligor;

(B) a seller of accounts, chattel paper, payment intangibles, or promissory notes; or

(C) a consignee.

(29) "Deposit account" means a demand, time, savings, passbook, or similar account maintained with a bank. The term does not include investment property or accounts evidenced by an instrument.

(30) "Document" means a document of title or a receipt of the type described in Section 7—201(2).

(31) "Electronic chattel paper" means chattel paper evidenced by a record or records consisting of information stored in an electronic medium.

(32) "Encumbrance" means a right, other than an ownership interest, in real property. The term includes mortgages and other liens on real property.

(33) "Equipment" means goods other than inventory, farm products, or consumer goods.

(34) "Farm products" means goods, other than standing timber, with respect to which the debtor is engaged in a farming operation and which are:

(A) crops grown, growing, or to be grown, including:

(i) crops produced on trees, vines, and bushes; and

(ii) aquatic goods produced in aquacultural operations;

(B) livestock, born or unborn, including aquatic goods produced in aquacultural operations;

(C) supplies used or produced in a farming operation; or

(D) products of crops or livestock in their unmanufactured states.

(35) "Farming operation" means raising, cultivating, propagating, fattening, grazing, or any other farming, livestock, or aquacultural operation.

(36) "File number" means the number assigned to an initial financing statement pursuant to Section 9—519(a).

(37) "Filing office" means an office designated in Section 9—501 as the place to file a financing statement.

(38) "Filing-office rule" means a rule adopted pursuant to Section 9—526.

(39) "Financing statement" means a record or records composed of an initial financing statement and any filed record relating to the initial financing statement.

(40) "Fixture filing" means the filing of a financing statement covering goods that are or are to become fixtures and satisfying Section 9—502(a) and (b). The term includes the filing of a financing statement covering goods of a transmitting utility which are or are to become fixtures.

(41) "Fixtures" means goods that have become so related to particular real property that an interest in them arises under real property law.

(42) "General intangible" means any personal property, including things in action, other than accounts, chattel paper, commercial tort claims, deposit accounts, documents, goods, instruments, investment property, letter-of-credit rights, letters of credit, money, and oil, gas, or other minerals before extraction. The term includes payment intangibles and software.

(43) "Good faith" means honesty in fact and the observance of reasonable commercial standards of fair dealing.

(44) "Goods" means all things that are movable when a security interest attaches. The term includes (i) fixtures, (ii) standing timber that is to be cut and removed under a conveyance or contract for sale, (iii) the unborn young of animals, (iv) crops grown, growing, or to be grown, even if the crops are produced on trees, vines, or bushes, and (v) manufactured homes. The term also includes a computer program embedded in goods and any supporting information provided in connection with a transaction relating to the program if (i) the program is associated with the goods in such a manner that it customarily is considered part of the goods, or (ii) by becoming the owner of the goods, a person acquires a right to use the program in connection with the goods. The term does not include a computer program embedded in goods that consist solely of the medium in which the program is embedded. The term also does not include accounts, chattel paper, commercial tort claims, deposit accounts, documents, general intangibles, instruments, investment property, letter-of-credit rights, letters of credit, money, or oil, gas, or other minerals before extraction.

(45) "Governmental unit" means a subdivision, agency, department, county, parish, municipality, or other unit of the government of the United States, a State, or a foreign country. The term includes an organization having a separate corporate existence if the organization is eligible to issue debt on which interest is exempt from income taxation under the laws of the United States.

(46) "Health-care-insurance receivable" means an interest in or claim under a policy of insurance which is a right to payment of a monetary obligation for health-care goods or services provided.

(47) "Instrument" means a negotiable instrument or any other writing that evidences a right to the payment of a monetary obligation, is not itself a security agreement or lease, and is of a type that in ordinary course of business is transferred by delivery with any necessary indorsement or assignment. The term does not include (i) investment property, (ii) letters of credit, or (iii) writings that evidence a right to payment arising out of the use of a credit or charge card or information contained on or for use with the card.

(48) "Inventory" means goods, other than farm products, which:

(A) are leased by a person as lessor;

(B) are held by a person for sale or lease or to be furnished under a contract of service;

(C) are furnished by a person under a contract of service; or

(D) consist of raw materials, work in process, or materials used or consumed in a business.

(49) "Investment property" means a security, whether certificated or uncertificated, security entitlement, securities account, commodity contract, or commodity account.

(50) "Jurisdiction of organization", with respect to a registered organization, means the jurisdiction under whose law the organization is organized.

(51) "Letter-of-credit right" means a right to payment or performance under a letter of credit, whether or not the beneficiary has demanded or is at the time entitled to demand payment or performance. The term does not include the right of a beneficiary to demand payment or performance under a letter of credit.

(52) "Lien creditor" means:

(A) a creditor that has acquired a lien on the property involved by attachment, levy, or the like;

(B) an assignee for benefit of creditors from the time of assignment;

(C) a trustee in bankruptcy from the date of the filing of the petition; or

(D) a receiver in equity from the time of appointment.

(53) "Manufactured home" means a structure, transportable in one or more sections, which, in the traveling mode, is eight body feet or more in width or 40 body feet or more in length, or, when erected on site, is 320 or more square feet, and which is built on a permanent chassis and designed to be used as a dwelling with or without a permanent foundation when connected to the required utilities, and includes the plumbing, heating, air-conditioning, and electrical systems contained therein. The term includes any structure that meets all of the requirements of this paragraph except the size requirements and with respect to which the manufacturer voluntarily files a certification required by the United States Secretary of Housing and Urban Development and complies with the standards established under Title 42 of the United States Code.

(54) "Manufactured-home transaction" means a secured transaction:

(A) that creates a purchase-money security interest in a manufactured home, other than a manufactured home held as inventory; or

(B) in which a manufactured home, other than a manufactured home held as inventory, is the primary collateral.

(55) "Mortgage" means a consensual interest in real property, including fixtures, which secures payment or performance of an obligation.

(56) "New debtor" means a person that becomes bound as debtor under Section 9—203(d) by a security agreement previously entered into by another person.

(57) "New value" means (i) money, (ii) money's worth in property, services, or new credit, or (iii) release by a transferee of an interest in property previously transferred to the transferee. The term does not include an obligation substituted for another obligation.

(58) "Noncash proceeds" means proceeds other than cash proceeds.

(59) "Obligor" means a person that, with respect to an obligation secured by a security interest in or an agricultural lien on the collateral, (i) owes payment or other performance of the obligation, (ii) has provided property other than the collateral to secure payment or other performance of the obligation, or (iii) is otherwise accountable in whole or in part for payment or other performance of the obligation. The term does not include issuers or nominated persons under a letter of credit.

(60) "Original debtor", except as used in Section 9—310(c), means a person that, as debtor, entered into a security agreement to which a new debtor has become bound under Section 9—203(d).

(61) "Payment intangible" means a general intangible under which the account debtor's principal obligation is a monetary obligation.

(62) "Person related to", with respect to an individual, means:

(A) the spouse of the individual;

(B) a brother, brother-in-law, sister, or sister-in-law of the individual;

(C) an ancestor or lineal descendant of the individual or the individual's spouse; or

(D) any other relative, by blood or marriage, of the individual or the individual's spouse who shares the same home with the individual.

(63) "Person related to", with respect to an organization, means:

(A) a person directly or indirectly controlling, controlled by, or under common control with the organization;

(B) an officer or director of, or a person performing similar functions with respect to, the organization;

(C) an officer or director of, or a person performing similar functions with respect to, a person described in subparagraph (A);

(D) the spouse of an individual described in subparagraph (A), (B), or (C); or

(E) an individual who is related by blood or marriage to an individual described in subparagraph (A), (B), (C), or (D) and shares the same home with the individual.

(64) "Proceeds", except as used in Section 9—609(b), means the following property:

(A) whatever is acquired upon the sale, lease, license, exchange, or other disposition of collateral;

(B) whatever is collected on, or distributed on account of, collateral;

(C) rights arising out of collateral;

(D) to the extent of the value of collateral, claims arising out of the loss, nonconformity, or interference with the use of, defects or infringement of rights in, or damage to, the collateral; or

(E) to the extent of the value of collateral and to the extent payable to the debtor or the secured party, insurance payable by reason of the loss or nonconformity of, defects or infringement of rights in, or damage to, the collateral.

(65) "Promissory note" means an instrument that evidences a promise to pay a monetary obligation, does not evidence an order to pay, and does not contain an acknowledgment by a bank that the bank has received for deposit a sum of money or funds.

(66) "Proposal" means a record authenticated by a secured party which includes the terms on which the secured party is willing to accept collateral in full or partial satisfaction of the obligation it secures pursuant to Sections 9—620, 9—621, and 9—622.

(67) "Public-finance transaction" means a secured transaction in connection with which:

(A) debt securities are issued;

(B) all or a portion of the securities issued have an initial stated maturity of at least 20 years; and

(C) the debtor, obligor, secured party, account debtor or other person obligated on collateral, assignor or assignee of a secured obligation, or assignor or assignee of a security interest is a State or a governmental unit of a State.

(68) "Pursuant to commitment", with respect to an advance made or other value given by a secured party, means pursuant to the secured party's obligation, whether or not a subsequent event of default or other event not within the secured party's control has relieved or may relieve the secured party from its obligation.

(69) "Record", except as used in "for record", "of record", "record or legal title", and "record owner", means information that is inscribed on a tangible medium or which is stored in an electronic or other medium and is retrievable in perceivable form.

(70) "Registered organization" means an organization organized solely under the law of a single State or the United States and as to which the State or the United States must maintain a public record showing the organization to have been organized.

(71) "Secondary obligor" means an obligor to the extent that:

(A) the obligor's obligation is secondary; or

(B) the obligor has a right of recourse with respect to an obligation secured by collateral against the debtor, another obligor, or property of either.

(72) "Secured party" means:

(A) a person in whose favor a security interest is created or provided for under a security agreement, whether or not any obligation to be secured is outstanding;

(B) a person that holds an agricultural lien;

(C) a consignor;

(D) a person to which accounts, chattel paper, payment intangibles, or promissory notes have been sold;

(E) a trustee, indenture trustee, agent, collateral agent, or other representative in whose favor a security interest or agricultural lien is created or provided for; or

(F) a person that holds a security interest arising under Section 2—401, 2—505, 2—711(3), 2A—508(5), 4—210, or 5—118.

(73) "Security agreement" means an agreement that creates or provides for a security interest.

(74) "Send", in connection with a record or notification, means:

(A) to deposit in the mail, deliver for transmission, or transmit by any other usual means of communication, with postage or cost of transmission provided for, addressed to any address reasonable under the circumstances; or

(B) to cause the record or notification to be received within the time that it would have been received if properly sent under subparagraph (A).

(75) "Software" means a computer program and any supporting information provided in connection with a transaction relating to the program. The term does not include a computer program that is included in the definition of goods.

(76) "State" means a State of the United States, the District of Columbia, Puerto Rico, the United States

Virgin Islands, or any territory or insular possession subject to the jurisdiction of the United States.

(77) "Supporting obligation" means a letter-of-credit right or secondary obligation that supports the payment or performance of an account, chattel paper, a document, a general intangible, an instrument, or investment property.

(78) "Tangible chattel paper" means chattel paper evidenced by a record or records consisting of information that is inscribed on a tangible medium.

(79) "Termination statement" means an amendment of a financing statement which:

(A) identifies, by its file number, the initial financing statement to which it relates; and

(B) indicates either that it is a termination statement or that the identified financing statement is no longer effective.

(80) "Transmitting utility" means a person primarily engaged in the business of:

(A) operating a railroad, subway, street railway, or trolley bus;

(B) transmitting communications electrically, electromagnetically, or by light;

(C) transmitting goods by pipeline or sewer; or

(D) transmitting or producing and transmitting electricity, steam, gas, or water.

(b) The following definitions in other articles apply to this article:

"Applicant"	Section 5—102
"Beneficiary"	Section 5—102
"Broker"	Section 8—102
"Certificated security"	Section 8—102
"Check"	Section 3—104
"Clearing corporation"	Section 8—102
"Contract for sale"	Section 2—106
"Customer"	Section 4—104
"Entitlement holder"	Section 8—102
"Financial asset"	Section 8—102
"Holder in due course"	Section 3—302
"Issuer" (with respect to a letter of credit or letter-of-credit right)	Section 5—102
"Issuer" (with respect to a security)	Section 8—201
"Lease"	Section 2A—103
"Lease agreement"	Section 2A—103
"Lease contract"	Section 2A—103
"Leasehold interest"	Section 2A—103
"Lessee"	Section 2A—103
"Lessee in ordinary course of business"	Section 2A—103
"Lessor"	Section 2A—103
"Lessor's residual interest"	Section 2A—103
"Letter of credit"	Section 5—102
"Merchant"	Section 2—104
"Negotiable instrument"	Section 3—104
"Nominated person"	Section 5—102
"Note"	Section 3—104
"Proceeds of a letter of credit"	Section 5—114
"Prove"	Section 3—103
"Sale"	Section 2—106
"Securities account"	Section 8—501
"Securities intermediary"	Section 8—102
"Security"	Section 8—102
"Security certificate"	Section 8—102
"Security entitlement"	Section 8—102
"Uncertificated security"	Section 8—102

(c) Article 1 contains general definitions and principles of construction and interpretation applicable throughout this article.

§ 9—103. Purchase-Money Security Interest; Application of Payments; Burden of Establishing.

(a) In this section:

(1) "purchase-money collateral" means goods or software that secures a purchase-money obligation incurred with respect to that collateral; and

(2) "purchase-money obligation" means an obligation of an obligor incurred as all or part of the price of the collateral or for value given to enable the debtor to acquire rights in or the use of the collateral if the value is in fact so used.

(b) A security interest in goods is a purchase-money security interest:

(1) to the extent that the goods are purchase-money collateral with respect to that security interest;

(2) if the security interest is in inventory that is or was purchase-money collateral, also to the extent that the security interest secures a purchase-money obligation incurred with respect to other inventory in which the secured party holds or held a purchase-money security interest; and

(3) also to the extent that the security interest secures a purchase-money obligation incurred with respect to software in which the secured party holds or held a purchase-money security interest.

(c) A security interest in software is a purchase-money security interest to the extent that the security interest also secures a purchase-money obligation incurred with respect to goods in which the secured party holds or held a purchase-money security interest if:

(1) the debtor acquired its interest in the software in an integrated transaction in which it acquired an interest in the goods; and

(2) the debtor acquired its interest in the software for the principal purpose of using the software in the goods.

(d) The security interest of a consignor in goods that are the subject of a consignment is a purchase-money security interest in inventory.

(e) In a transaction other than a consumer-goods transaction, if the extent to which a security interest is a purchase-money security interest depends on the application of a payment to a particular obligation, the payment must be applied:

(1) in accordance with any reasonable method of application to which the parties agree;

(2) in the absence of the parties' agreement to a reasonable method, in accordance with any intention of the obligor manifested at or before the time of payment; or

(3) in the absence of an agreement to a reasonable method and a timely manifestation of the obligor's intention, in the following order:

(A) to obligations that are not secured; and

(B) if more than one obligation is secured, to obligations secured by purchase-money security interests in the order in which those obligations were incurred.

(f) In a transaction other than a consumer-goods transaction, a purchase-money security interest does not lose its status as such, even if:

(1) the purchase-money collateral also secures an obligation that is not a purchase-money obligation;

(2) collateral that is not purchase-money collateral also secures the purchase-money obligation; or

(3) the purchase-money obligation has been renewed, refinanced, consolidated, or restructured.

(g) In a transaction other than a consumer-goods transaction, a secured party claiming a purchase-money security interest has the burden of establishing the extent to which the security interest is a purchase-money security interest.

(h) The limitation of the rules in subsections (e), (f), and (g) to transactions other than consumer-goods transactions is intended to leave to the court the determination of the proper rules in consumer-goods transactions. The court may not infer from that limitation the nature of the proper rule in consumer-goods transactions and may continue to apply established approaches.

§ 9—104. Control of Deposit Account.

(a) A secured party has control of a deposit account if:

(1) the secured party is the bank with which the deposit account is maintained;

(2) the debtor, secured party, and bank have agreed in an authenticated record that the bank will comply with instructions originated by the secured party directing disposition of the funds in the deposit account without further consent by the debtor; or

(3) the secured party becomes the bank's customer with respect to the deposit account.

(b) A secured party that has satisfied subsection (a) has control, even if the debtor retains the right to direct the disposition of funds from the deposit account.

§ 9—105. Control of Electronic Chattel Paper.

A secured party has control of electronic chattel paper if the record or records comprising the chattel paper are created, stored, and assigned in such a manner that:

(1) a single authoritative copy of the record or records exists which is unique, identifiable and, except as otherwise provided in paragraphs (4), (5), and (6), unalterable;

(2) the authoritative copy identifies the secured party as the assignee of the record or records;

(3) the authoritative copy is communicated to and maintained by the secured party or its designated custodian;

(4) copies or revisions that add or change an identified assignee of the authoritative copy can be made only with the participation of the secured party;

(5) each copy of the authoritative copy and any copy of a copy is readily identifiable as a copy that is not the authoritative copy; and

(6) any revision of the authoritative copy is readily identifiable as an authorized or unauthorized revision.

§ 9—106. Control of Investment Property.

(a) A person has control of a certificated security, uncertificated security, or security entitlement as provided in Section 8—106.

(b) A secured party has control of a commodity contract if:

(1) the secured party is the commodity intermediary with which the commodity contract is carried; or

(2) the commodity customer, secured party, and commodity intermediary have agreed that the commodity intermediary will apply any value distributed on

account of the commodity contract as directed by the secured party without further consent by the commodity customer.

(c) A secured party having control of all security entitlements or commodity contracts carried in a securities account or commodity account has control over the securities account or commodity account.

§ 9—107. Control of Letter-of-Credit Right.

A secured party has control of a letter-of-credit right to the extent of any right to payment or performance by the issuer or any nominated person if the issuer or nominated person has consented to an assignment of proceeds of the letter of credit under Section 5—114(c) or otherwise applicable law or practice.

§ 9—108. Sufficiency of Description.

(a) Except as otherwise provided in subsections (c), (d), and (e), a description of personal or real property is sufficient, whether or not it is specific, if it reasonably identifies what is described.

(b) Except as otherwise provided in subsection (d), a description of collateral reasonably identifies the collateral if it identifies the collateral by:

(1) specific listing;

(2) category;

(3) except as otherwise provided in subsection (e), a type of collateral defined in [the Uniform Commercial Code];

(4) quantity;

(5) computational or allocational formula or procedure; or

(6) except as otherwise provided in subsection (c), any other method, if the identity of the collateral is objectively determinable.

(c) A description of collateral as "all the debtor's assets" or "all the debtor's personal property" or using words of similar import does not reasonably identify the collateral.

(d) Except as otherwise provided in subsection (e), a description of a security entitlement, securities account, or commodity account is sufficient if it describes:

(1) the collateral by those terms or as investment property; or

(2) the underlying financial asset or commodity contract.

(e) A description only by type of collateral defined in [the Uniform Commercial Code] is an insufficient description of:

(1) a commercial tort claim; or

(2) in a consumer transaction, consumer goods, a security entitlement, a securities account, or a commodity account.

[Subpart 2. Applicability of Article]

§ 9—109. Scope.

(a) Except as otherwise provided in subsections (c) and (d), this article applies to:

(1) a transaction, regardless of its form, that creates a security interest in personal property or fixtures by contract;

(2) an agricultural lien;

(3) a sale of accounts, chattel paper, payment intangibles, or promissory notes;

(4) a consignment;

(5) a security interest arising under Section 2—401, 2—505, 2—711(3), or 2A—508(5), as provided in Section 9—110; and

(6) a security interest arising under Section 4—210 or 5—118.

(b) The application of this article to a security interest in a secured obligation is not affected by the fact that the obligation is itself secured by a transaction or interest to which this article does not apply.

(c) This article does not apply to the extent that:

(1) a statute, regulation, or treaty of the United States preempts this article;

(2) another statute of this State expressly governs the creation, perfection, priority, or enforcement of a security interest created by this State or a governmental unit of this State;

(3) a statute of another State, a foreign country, or a governmental unit of another State or a foreign country, other than a statute generally applicable to security interests, expressly governs creation, perfection, priority, or enforcement of a security interest created by the State, country, or governmental unit; or

(4) the rights of a transferee beneficiary or nominated person under a letter of credit are independent and superior under Section 5—114.

(d) This article does not apply to:

(1) a landlord's lien, other than an agricultural lien;

(2) a lien, other than an agricultural lien, given by statute or other rule of law for services or materials, but Section 9—333 applies with respect to priority of the lien;

(3) an assignment of a claim for wages, salary, or other compensation of an employee;

(4) a sale of accounts, chattel paper, payment intangibles, or promissory notes as part of a sale of the business out of which they arose;

(5) an assignment of accounts, chattel paper, payment intangibles, or promissory notes which is for the purpose of collection only;

(6) an assignment of a right to payment under a contract to an assignee that is also obligated to perform under the contract;

(7) an assignment of a single account, payment intangible, or promissory note to an assignee in full or partial satisfaction of a preexisting indebtedness;

(8) a transfer of an interest in or an assignment of a claim under a policy of insurance, other than an assignment by or to a health-care provider of a health-care-insurance receivable and any subsequent assignment of the right to payment, but Sections 9—315 and 9—322 apply with respect to proceeds and priorities in proceeds;

(9) an assignment of a right represented by a judgment, other than a judgment taken on a right to payment that was collateral;

(10) a right of recoupment or set-off, but:

(A) Section 9—340 applies with respect to the effectiveness of rights of recoupment or set-off against deposit accounts; and

(B) Section 9—404 applies with respect to defenses or claims of an account debtor;

(11) the creation or transfer of an interest in or lien on real property, including a lease or rents thereunder, except to the extent that provision is made for:

(A) liens on real property in Sections 9—203 and 9—308;

(B) fixtures in Section 9—334;

(C) fixture filings in Sections 9—501, 9—502, 9—512, 9—516, and 9—519; and

(D) security agreements covering personal and real property in Section 9—604;

(12) an assignment of a claim arising in tort, other than a commercial tort claim, but Sections 9—315 and 9—322 apply with respect to proceeds and priorities in proceeds; or

(13) an assignment of a deposit account in a consumer transaction, but Sections 9—315 and 9—322 apply with respect to proceeds and priorities in proceeds.

§ 9—110. Security Interests Arising under Article 2 or 2A.

A security interest arising under Section 2—401, 2—505, 2—711(3), or 2A—508(5) is subject to this article. However, until the debtor obtains possession of the goods:

(1) the security interest is enforceable, even if Section 9—203(b)(3) has not been satisfied;

(2) filing is not required to perfect the security interest;

(3) the rights of the secured party after default by the debtor are governed by Article 2 or 2A; and

(4) the security interest has priority over a conflicting security interest created by the debtor.

Part 2 Effectiveness of Security Agreement; Attachment of Security Interest; Rights of Parties to Security Agreement

[Subpart 1. Effectiveness and Attachment]

§ 9—201. General Effectiveness of Security Agreement.

(a) Except as otherwise provided in [the Uniform Commercial Code], a security agreement is effective according to its terms between the parties, against purchasers of the collateral, and against creditors.

(b) A transaction subject to this article is subject to any applicable rule of law which establishes a different rule for consumers and [insert reference to (i) any other statute or regulation that regulates the rates, charges, agreements, and practices for loans, credit sales, or other extensions of credit and (ii) any consumer-protection statute or regulation].

(c) In case of conflict between this article and a rule of law, statute, or regulation described in subsection (b), the rule of law, statute, or regulation controls. Failure to comply with a statute or regulation described in subsection (b) has only the effect the statute or regulation specifies.

(d) This article does not:

(1) validate any rate, charge, agreement, or practice that violates a rule of law, statute, or regulation described in subsection (b); or

(2) extend the application of the rule of law, statute, or regulation to a transaction not otherwise subject to it.

§ 9—202. Title to Collateral Immaterial.

Except as otherwise provided with respect to consignments or sales of accounts, chattel paper, payment intangibles, or promissory notes, the provisions of this article with regard to rights and obligations apply whether title to collateral is in the secured party or the debtor.

§ 9—203. Attachment and Enforceability of Security Interest; Proceeds; Supporting Obligations; Formal Requisites.

(a) A security interest attaches to collateral when it becomes enforceable against the debtor with respect to the collateral, unless an agreement expressly postpones the time of attachment.

(b) Except as otherwise provided in subsections (c) through (i), a security interest is enforceable against the debtor and third parties with respect to the collateral only if:

(1) value has been given;

(2) the debtor has rights in the collateral or the power to transfer rights in the collateral to a secured party; and

(3) one of the following conditions is met:

(A) the debtor has authenticated a security agreement that provides a description of the collateral and, if the security interest covers timber to be cut, a description of the land concerned;

(B) the collateral is not a certificated security and is in the possession of the secured party under Section 9—313 pursuant to the debtor's security agreement;

(C) the collateral is a certificated security in registered form and the security certificate has been delivered to the secured party under Section 8—301 pursuant to the debtor's security agreement; or

(D) the collateral is deposit accounts, electronic chattel paper, investment property, or letter-of-credit rights, and the secured party has control under Section 9—104, 9—105, 9—106, or 9—107 pursuant to the debtor's security agreement.

(c) Subsection (b) is subject to Section 4—210 on the security interest of a collecting bank, Section 5—118 on the security interest of a letter-of-credit issuer or nominated person, Section 9—110 on a security interest arising under Article 2 or 2A, and Section 9—206 on security interests in investment property.

(d) A person becomes bound as debtor by a security agreement entered into by another person if, by operation of law other than this article or by contract:

(1) the security agreement becomes effective to create a security interest in the person's property; or

(2) the person becomes generally obligated for the obligations of the other person, including the obligation secured under the security agreement, and acquires or succeeds to all or substantially all of the assets of the other person.

(e) If a new debtor becomes bound as debtor by a security agreement entered into by another person:

(1) the agreement satisfies subsection (b)(3) with respect to existing or after-acquired property of the new debtor to the extent the property is described in the agreement; and

(2) another agreement is not necessary to make a security interest in the property enforceable.

(f) The attachment of a security interest in collateral gives the secured party the rights to proceeds provided by Section 9—315 and is also attachment of a security interest in a supporting obligation for the collateral.

(g) The attachment of a security interest in a right to payment or performance secured by a security interest or other lien on personal or real property is also attachment of a security interest in the security interest, mortgage, or other lien.

(h) The attachment of a security interest in a securities account is also attachment of a security interest in the security entitlements carried in the securities account.

(i) The attachment of a security interest in a commodity account is also attachment of a security interest in the commodity contracts carried in the commodity account.

§ 9—204. After-Acquired Property; Future Advances.

(a) Except as otherwise provided in subsection (b), a security agreement may create or provide for a security interest in after-acquired collateral.

(b) A security interest does not attach under a term constituting an after-acquired property clause to:

(1) consumer goods, other than an accession when given as additional security, unless the debtor acquires rights in them within 10 days after the secured party gives value; or

(2) a commercial tort claim.

(c) A security agreement may provide that collateral secures, or that accounts, chattel paper, payment intangibles, or promissory notes are sold in connection with, future advances or other value, whether or not the advances or value are given pursuant to commitment.

§ 9—205. Use or Disposition of Collateral Permissible.

(a) A security interest is not invalid or fraudulent against creditors solely because:

(1) the debtor has the right or ability to:

(A) use, commingle, or dispose of all or part of the collateral, including returned or repossessed goods;

(B) collect, compromise, enforce, or otherwise deal with collateral;

(C) accept the return of collateral or make repossessions; or

(D) use, commingle, or dispose of proceeds; or

(2) the secured party fails to require the debtor to account for proceeds or replace collateral.

(b) This section does not relax the requirements of possession if attachment, perfection, or enforcement of a security interest depends upon possession of the collateral by the secured party.

§ 9—206. Security Interest Arising in Purchase or Delivery of Financial Asset.

(a) A security interest in favor of a securities intermediary attaches to a person's security entitlement if:

(1) the person buys a financial asset through the securities intermediary in a transaction in which the person is obligated to pay the purchase price to the securities intermediary at the time of the purchase; and

(2) the securities intermediary credits the financial asset to the buyer's securities account before the buyer pays the securities intermediary.

(b) The security interest described in subsection (a) secures the person's obligation to pay for the financial asset.

(c) A security interest in favor of a person that delivers a certificated security or other financial asset represented by a writing attaches to the security or other financial asset if:

(1) the security or other financial asset:

(A) in the ordinary course of business is transferred by delivery with any necessary indorsement or assignment; and

(B) is delivered under an agreement between persons in the business of dealing with such securities or financial assets; and

(2) the agreement calls for delivery against payment.

(d) The security interest described in subsection (c) secures the obligation to make payment for the delivery.

[Subpart 2. Rights and Duties]

§ 9—207. Rights and Duties of Secured Party Having Possession or Control of Collateral.

(a) Except as otherwise provided in subsection (d), a secured party shall use reasonable care in the custody and preservation of collateral in the secured party's possession. In the case of chattel paper or an instrument, reasonable care includes taking necessary steps to preserve rights against prior parties unless otherwise agreed.

(b) Except as otherwise provided in subsection (d), if a secured party has possession of collateral:

(1) reasonable expenses, including the cost of insurance and payment of taxes or other charges, incurred in the custody, preservation, use, or operation of the collateral are chargeable to the debtor and are secured by the collateral;

(2) the risk of accidental loss or damage is on the debtor to the extent of a deficiency in any effective insurance coverage;

(3) the secured party shall keep the collateral identifiable, but fungible collateral may be commingled; and

(4) the secured party may use or operate the collateral:

(A) for the purpose of preserving the collateral or its value;

(B) as permitted by an order of a court having competent jurisdiction; or

(C) except in the case of consumer goods, in the manner and to the extent agreed by the debtor.

(c) Except as otherwise provided in subsection (d), a secured party having possession of collateral or control of collateral under Section 9—104, 9—105, 9—106, or 9—107:

(1) may hold as additional security any proceeds, except money or funds, received from the collateral;

(2) shall apply money or funds received from the collateral to reduce the secured obligation, unless remitted to the debtor; and

(3) may create a security interest in the collateral.

(d) If the secured party is a buyer of accounts, chattel paper, payment intangibles, or promissory notes or a consignor:

(1) subsection (a) does not apply unless the secured party is entitled under an agreement:

(A) to charge back uncollected collateral; or

(B) otherwise to full or limited recourse against the debtor or a secondary obligor based on the nonpayment or other default of an account debtor or other obligor on the collateral; and

(2) subsections (b) and (c) do not apply.

§ 9—208. Additional Duties of Secured Party Having Control of Collateral.

(a) This section applies to cases in which there is no outstanding secured obligation and the secured party is not committed to make advances, incur obligations, or otherwise give value.

(b) Within 10 days after receiving an authenticated demand by the debtor:

(1) a secured party having control of a deposit account under Section 9—104(a)(2) shall send to the bank with which the deposit account is maintained an authenticated statement that releases the bank from any further obligation to comply with instructions originated by the secured party;

(2) a secured party having control of a deposit account under Section 9—104(a)(3) shall:

(A) pay the debtor the balance on deposit in the deposit account; or

(B) transfer the balance on deposit into a deposit account in the debtor's name;

(3) a secured party, other than a buyer, having control of electronic chattel paper under Section 9—105 shall:

(A) communicate the authoritative copy of the electronic chattel paper to the debtor or its designated custodian;

(B) if the debtor designates a custodian that is the designated custodian with which the authoritative copy of the electronic chattel paper is maintained for the secured party, communicate to the custodian an authenticated record releasing the designated custodian from any further obligation to comply with instructions originated by the secured party and instructing the custodian to comply with instructions originated by the debtor; and

(C) take appropriate action to enable the debtor or its designated custodian to make copies of or revisions to the authoritative copy which add or change an identified assignee of the authoritative copy without the consent of the secured party;

(4) a secured party having control of investment property under Section 8—106(d)(2) or 9—106(b) shall send to the securities intermediary or commodity intermediary with which the security entitlement or commodity contract is maintained an authenticated record that releases the securities intermediary or commodity intermediary from any further obligation to comply with entitlement orders or directions originated by the secured party; and

(5) a secured party having control of a letter-of-credit right under Section 9—107 shall send to each person having an unfulfilled obligation to pay or deliver proceeds of the letter of credit to the secured party an authenticated release from any further obligation to pay or deliver proceeds of the letter of credit to the secured party.

§ 9—209. Duties of Secured Party If Account Debtor Has Been Notified of Assignment.

(a) Except as otherwise provided in subsection (c), this section applies if:

(1) there is no outstanding secured obligation; and

(2) the secured party is not committed to make advances, incur obligations, or otherwise give value.

(b) Within 10 days after receiving an authenticated demand by the debtor, a secured party shall send to an account debtor that has received notification of an assignment to the secured party as assignee under Section 9—406(a) an authenticated record that releases the account debtor from any further obligation to the secured party.

(c) This section does not apply to an assignment constituting the sale of an account, chattel paper, or payment intangible.

§ 9—210. Request for Accounting; Request Regarding List of Collateral or Statement of Account.

(a) In this section:

(1) "Request" means a record of a type described in paragraph (2), (3), or (4).

(2) "Request for an accounting" means a record authenticated by a debtor requesting that the recipient provide an accounting of the unpaid obligations secured by collateral and reasonably identifying the transaction or relationship that is the subject of the request.

(3) "Request regarding a list of collateral" means a record authenticated by a debtor requesting that the recipient approve or correct a list of what the debtor believes to be the collateral securing an obligation and reasonably identifying the transaction or relationship that is the subject of the request.

(4) "Request regarding a statement of account" means a record authenticated by a debtor requesting that the recipient approve or correct a statement indicating what the debtor believes to be the aggregate amount of unpaid obligations secured by collateral as of a specified date and reasonably identifying the transaction or relationship that is the subject of the request.

(b) Subject to subsections (c), (d), (e), and (f), a secured party, other than a buyer of accounts, chattel paper, payment intangibles, or promissory notes or a consignor, shall comply with a request within 14 days after receipt:

(1) in the case of a request for an accounting, by authenticating and sending to the debtor an accounting; and

(2) in the case of a request regarding a list of collateral or a request regarding a statement of account, by authenticating and sending to the debtor an approval or correction.

(c) A secured party that claims a security interest in all of a particular type of collateral owned by the debtor may comply with a request regarding a list of collateral by sending to the debtor an authenticated record including a statement to that effect within 14 days after receipt.

(d) A person that receives a request regarding a list of collateral, claims no interest in the collateral when it receives the request, and claimed an interest in the collateral at an earlier time shall comply with the request within 14 days after receipt by sending to the debtor an authenticated record:

(1) disclaiming any interest in the collateral; and

(2) if known to the recipient, providing the name and mailing address of any assignee of or successor to the recipient's interest in the collateral.

(e) A person that receives a request for an accounting or a request regarding a statement of account, claims no interest in the obligations when it receives the request, and claimed an interest in the obligations at an earlier time shall comply with the request within 14 days after receipt by sending to the debtor an authenticated record:

(1) disclaiming any interest in the obligations; and

(2) if known to the recipient, providing the name and mailing address of any assignee of or successor to the recipient's interest in the obligations.

(f) A debtor is entitled without charge to one response to a request under this section during any six-month period. The secured party may require payment of a charge not exceeding $25 for each additional response.

Part 3 Perfection and Priority

[Subpart 1. Law Governing Perfection and Priority]

§ 9—301. Law Governing Perfection and Priority of Security Interests.

Except as otherwise provided in Sections 9—303 through 9—306, the following rules determine the law governing perfection, the effect of perfection or nonperfection, and the priority of a security interest in collateral:

(1) Except as otherwise provided in this section, while a debtor is located in a jurisdiction, the local law of that jurisdiction governs perfection, the effect of perfection or nonperfection, and the priority of a security interest in collateral.

(2) While collateral is located in a jurisdiction, the local law of that jurisdiction governs perfection, the effect of perfection or nonperfection, and the priority of a possessory security interest in that collateral.

(3) Except as otherwise provided in paragraph (4), while negotiable documents, goods, instruments, money, or tangible chattel paper is located in a jurisdiction, the local law of that jurisdiction governs:

(A) perfection of a security interest in the goods by filing a fixture filing;

(B) perfection of a security interest in timber to be cut; and

(C) the effect of perfection or nonperfection and the priority of a nonpossessory security interest in the collateral.

(4) The local law of the jurisdiction in which the wellhead or minehead is located governs perfection, the effect of perfection or nonperfection, and the priority of a security interest in as-extracted collateral.

§ 9—302. Law Governing Perfection and Priority of Agricultural Liens.

While farm products are located in a jurisdiction, the local law of that jurisdiction governs perfection, the effect of perfection or nonperfection, and the priority of an agricultural lien on the farm products.

§ 9—303. Law Governing Perfection and Priority of Security Interests in Goods Covered by a Certificate of Title.

(a) This section applies to goods covered by a certificate of title, even if there is no other relationship between the jurisdiction under whose certificate of title the goods are covered and the goods or the debtor.

(b) Goods become covered by a certificate of title when a valid application for the certificate of title and the applicable fee are delivered to the appropriate authority. Goods cease to be covered by a certificate of title at the earlier of the time the certificate of title ceases to be effective under the law of the issuing jurisdiction or the time the goods become covered subsequently by a certificate of title issued by another jurisdiction.

(c) The local law of the jurisdiction under whose certificate of title the goods are covered governs perfection, the effect of perfection or nonperfection, and the priority of a security interest in goods covered by a certificate of title from the time the goods become covered by the certificate of title until the goods cease to be covered by the certificate of title.

§ 9—304. Law Governing Perfection and Priority of Security Interests in Deposit Accounts.

(a) The local law of a bank's jurisdiction governs perfection, the effect of perfection or nonperfection, and the priority of a security interest in a deposit account maintained with that bank.

(b) The following rules determine a bank's jurisdiction for purposes of this part:

(1) If an agreement between the bank and the debtor governing the deposit account expressly provides that a particular jurisdiction is the bank's jurisdiction for purposes of this part, this article, or [the Uniform Commercial Code], that jurisdiction is the bank's jurisdiction.

(2) If paragraph (1) does not apply and an agreement between the bank and its customer governing the deposit account expressly provides that the agreement is governed by the law of a particular jurisdiction, that jurisdiction is the bank's jurisdiction.

(3) If neither paragraph (1) nor paragraph (2) applies and an agreement between the bank and its customer governing the deposit account expressly provides that the deposit account is maintained at an office in a particular jurisdiction, that jurisdiction is the bank's jurisdiction.

(4) If none of the preceding paragraphs applies, the bank's jurisdiction is the jurisdiction in which the office identified in an account statement as the office serving the customer's account is located.

(5) If none of the preceding paragraphs applies, the bank's jurisdiction is the jurisdiction in which the chief executive office of the bank is located.

§ 9—305. Law Governing Perfection and Priority of Security Interests in Investment Property.

(a) Except as otherwise provided in subsection (c), the following rules apply:

(1) While a security certificate is located in a jurisdiction, the local law of that jurisdiction governs perfection, the effect of perfection or nonperfection, and the priority of a security interest in the certificated security represented thereby.

(2) The local law of the issuer's jurisdiction as specified in Section 8—110(d) governs perfection, the effect of perfection or nonperfection, and the priority of a security interest in an uncertificated security.

(3) The local law of the securities intermediary's jurisdiction as specified in Section 8—110(e) governs perfection, the effect of perfection or nonperfection, and the priority of a security interest in a security entitlement or securities account.

(4) The local law of the commodity intermediary's jurisdiction governs perfection, the effect of perfection or nonperfection, and the priority of a security interest in a commodity contract or commodity account.

(b) The following rules determine a commodity intermediary's jurisdiction for purposes of this part:

(1) If an agreement between the commodity intermediary and commodity customer governing the commodity account expressly provides that a particular jurisdiction is the commodity intermediary's jurisdiction for purposes of this part, this article, or [the Uniform Commercial Code], that jurisdiction is the commodity intermediary's jurisdiction.

(2) If paragraph (1) does not apply and an agreement between the commodity intermediary and commodity customer governing the commodity account expressly provides that the agreement is governed by the law of a particular jurisdiction, that jurisdiction is the commodity intermediary's jurisdiction.

(3) If neither paragraph (1) nor paragraph (2) applies and an agreement between the commodity intermediary and commodity customer governing the commodity account expressly provides that the commodity account is maintained at an office in a particular jurisdiction, that jurisdiction is the commodity intermediary's jurisdiction.

(4) If none of the preceding paragraphs applies, the commodity intermediary's jurisdiction is the jurisdiction in which the office identified in an account statement as the office serving the commodity customer's account is located.

(5) If none of the preceding paragraphs applies, the commodity intermediary's jurisdiction is the jurisdiction in which the chief executive office of the commodity intermediary is located.

(c) The local law of the jurisdiction in which the debtor is located governs:

(1) perfection of a security interest in investment property by filing;

(2) automatic perfection of a security interest in investment property created by a broker or securities intermediary; and

(3) automatic perfection of a security interest in a commodity contract or commodity account created by a commodity intermediary.

§ 9—306. Law Governing Perfection and Priority of Security Interests in Letter-of-Credit Rights.

(a) Subject to subsection (c), the local law of the issuer's jurisdiction or a nominated person's jurisdiction governs perfection, the effect of perfection or nonperfection, and the priority of a security interest in a letter-of-credit right if the issuer's jurisdiction or nominated person's jurisdiction is a State.

(b) For purposes of this part, an issuer's jurisdiction or nominated person's jurisdiction is the jurisdiction whose law governs the liability of the issuer or nominated person with respect to the letter-of-credit right as provided in Section 5—116.

(c) This section does not apply to a security interest that is perfected only under Section 9—308(d).

§ 9—307. Location of Debtor.

(a) In this section, "place of business" means a place where a debtor conducts its affairs.

(b) Except as otherwise provided in this section, the following rules determine a debtor's location:

(1) A debtor who is an individual is located at the individual's principal residence.

(2) A debtor that is an organization and has only one place of business is located at its place of business.

(3) A debtor that is an organization and has more than one place of business is located at its chief executive office.

(c) Subsection (b) applies only if a debtor's residence, place of business, or chief executive office, as applicable, is located in a jurisdiction whose law generally requires information concerning the existence of a nonpossessory security interest to be made generally available in a filing, recording, or registration system as a condition or result of the security interest's obtaining priority over the rights of a lien creditor with respect to the collateral. If subsection (b) does not apply, the debtor is located in the District of Columbia.

(d) A person that ceases to exist, have a residence, or have a place of business continues to be located in the jurisdiction specified by subsections (b) and (c).

(e) A registered organization that is organized under the law of a State is located in that State.

(f) Except as otherwise provided in subsection (i), a registered organization that is organized under the law of the

United States and a branch or agency of a bank that is not organized under the law of the United States or a State are located:

(1) in the State that the law of the United States designates, if the law designates a State of location;

(2) in the State that the registered organization, branch, or agency designates, if the law of the United States authorizes the registered organization, branch, or agency to designate its State of location; or

(3) in the District of Columbia, if neither paragraph (1) nor paragraph (2) applies.

(g) A registered organization continues to be located in the jurisdiction specified by subsection (e) or (f) notwithstanding:

(1) the suspension, revocation, forfeiture, or lapse of the registered organization's status as such in its jurisdiction of organization; or

(2) the dissolution, winding up, or cancellation of the existence of the registered organization.

(h) The United States is located in the District of Columbia.

(i) A branch or agency of a bank that is not organized under the law of the United States or a State is located in the State in which the branch or agency is licensed, if all branches and agencies of the bank are licensed in only one State.

(j) A foreign air carrier under the Federal Aviation Act of 1958, as amended, is located at the designated office of the agent upon which service of process may be made on behalf of the carrier.

(k) This section applies only for purposes of this part.

[Subpart 2. Perfection]

§ 9—308. When Security Interest or Agricultural Lien Is Perfected; Continuity of Perfection.

(a) Except as otherwise provided in this section and Section 9—309, a security interest is perfected if it has attached and all of the applicable requirements for perfection in Sections 9—310 through 9—316 have been satisfied. A security interest is perfected when it attaches if the applicable requirements are satisfied before the security interest attaches.

(b) An agricultural lien is perfected if it has become effective and all of the applicable requirements for perfection in Section 9—310 have been satisfied. An agricultural lien is perfected when it becomes effective if the applicable requirements are satisfied before the agricultural lien becomes effective.

(c) A security interest or agricultural lien is perfected continuously if it is originally perfected by one method under this article and is later perfected by another method under this article, without an intermediate period when it was unperfected.

(d) Perfection of a security interest in collateral also perfects a security interest in a supporting obligation for the collateral.

(e) Perfection of a security interest in a right to payment or performance also perfects a security interest in a security interest, mortgage, or other lien on personal or real property securing the right.

(f) Perfection of a security interest in a securities account also perfects a security interest in the security entitlements carried in the securities account.

(g) Perfection of a security interest in a commodity account also perfects a security interest in the commodity contracts carried in the commodity account.

Legislative Note: Any statute conflicting with subsection (e) must be made expressly subject to that subsection.

§ 9—309. Security Interest Perfected upon Attachment.

The following security interests are perfected when they attach:

(1) a purchase-money security interest in consumer goods, except as otherwise provided in Section 9—311(b) with respect to consumer goods that are subject to a statute or treaty described in Section 9—311(a);

(2) an assignment of accounts or payment intangibles which does not by itself or in conjunction with other assignments to the same assignee transfer a significant part of the assignor's outstanding accounts or payment intangibles;

(3) a sale of a payment intangible;

(4) a sale of a promissory note;

(5) a security interest created by the assignment of a health-care-insurance receivable to the provider of the health-care goods or services;

(6) a security interest arising under Section 2—401, 2—505, 2—711(3), or 2A—508(5), until the debtor obtains possession of the collateral;

(7) a security interest of a collecting bank arising under Section 4—210;

(8) a security interest of an issuer or nominated person arising under Section 5—118;

(9) a security interest arising in the delivery of a financial asset under Section 9—206(c);

(10) a security interest in investment property created by a broker or securities intermediary;

(11) a security interest in a commodity contract or a commodity account created by a commodity intermediary;

(12) an assignment for the benefit of all creditors of the transferor and subsequent transfers by the assignee thereunder; and

(13) a security interest created by an assignment of a beneficial interest in a decedent's estate.

§ 9—310. When Filing Required to Perfect Security Interest or Agricultural Lien; Security Interests and Agricultural Liens to Which Filing Provisions Do Not Apply.

(a) Except as otherwise provided in subsection (b) and Section 9—312(b), a financing statement must be filed to perfect all security interests and agricultural liens.

(b) The filing of a financing statement is not necessary to perfect a security interest:

(1) that is perfected under Section 9—308(d), (e), (f), or (g);

(2) that is perfected under Section 9—309 when it attaches;

(3) in property subject to a statute, regulation, or treaty described in Section 9—311(a);

(4) in goods in possession of a bailee which is perfected under Section 9—312(d)(1) or (2);

(5) in certificated securities, documents, goods, or instruments which is perfected without filing or possession under Section 9—312(e), (f), or (g);

(6) in collateral in the secured party's possession under Section 9—313;

(7) in a certificated security which is perfected by delivery of the security certificate to the secured party under Section 9—313;

(8) in deposit accounts, electronic chattel paper, investment property, or letter-of-credit rights which is perfected by control under Section 9—314;

(9) in proceeds which is perfected under Section 9—315; or

(10) that is perfected under Section 9—316.

(c) If a secured party assigns a perfected security interest or agricultural lien, a filing under this article is not required to continue the perfected status of the security interest against creditors of and transferees from the original debtor.

§ 9—311. Perfection of Security Interests in Property Subject to Certain Statutes, Regulations, and Treaties.

(a) Except as otherwise provided in subsection (d), the filing of a financing statement is not necessary or effective to perfect a security interest in property subject to:

(1) a statute, regulation, or treaty of the United States whose requirements for a security interest's obtaining priority over the rights of a lien creditor with respect to the property preempt Section 9—310(a);

(2) [list any certificate-of-title statute covering automobiles, trailers, mobile homes, boats, farm tractors, or the like, which provides for a security interest to be indicated on the certificate as a condition or result of perfection, and any non-Uniform Commercial Code central filing statute]; or

(3) a certificate-of-title statute of another jurisdiction which provides for a security interest to be indicated on the certificate as a condition or result of the security interest's obtaining priority over the rights of a lien creditor with respect to the property.

(b) Compliance with the requirements of a statute, regulation, or treaty described in subsection (a) for obtaining priority over the rights of a lien creditor is equivalent to the filing of a financing statement under this article. Except as otherwise provided in subsection (d) and Sections 9—313 and 9—316(d) and (e) for goods covered by a certificate of title, a security interest in property subject to a statute, regulation, or treaty described in subsection (a) may be perfected only by compliance with those requirements, and a security interest so perfected remains perfected notwithstanding a change in the use or transfer of possession of the collateral.

(c) Except as otherwise provided in subsection (d) and Section 9—316(d) and (e), duration and renewal of perfection of a security interest perfected by compliance with the requirements prescribed by a statute, regulation, or treaty described in subsection (a) are governed by the statute, regulation, or treaty. In other respects, the security interest is subject to this article.

(d) During any period in which collateral subject to a statute specified in subsection (a)(2) is inventory held for sale or lease by a person or leased by that person as lessor and that person is in the business of selling goods of that kind, this section does not apply to a security interest in that collateral created by that person.

Legislative Note: This Article contemplates that perfection of a security interest in goods covered by a certificate of title occurs upon receipt by appropriate State officials of a properly tendered application for a certificate of title on which the security interest is to be indicated, without a relation back to an earlier time. States whose certificate-of-title statutes provide for perfection at a different time or contain a relation-back provision should amend the statutes accordingly.

§ 9—312. Perfection of Security Interests in Chattel Paper, Deposit Accounts, Documents, Goods Covered by Documents, Instruments, Investment Property, Letter-of-Credit Rights, and Money; Perfection by Permissive Filing; Temporary Perfection without Filing or Transfer of Possession.

(a) A security interest in chattel paper, negotiable documents, instruments, or investment property may be perfected by filing.

(b) Except as otherwise provided in Section 9—315(c) and (d) for proceeds:

(1) a security interest in a deposit account may be perfected only by control under Section 9—314;

(2) and except as otherwise provided in Section 9—308(d), a security interest in a letter-of-credit right may be perfected only by control under Section 9—314; and

(3) a security interest in money may be perfected only by the secured party's taking possession under Section 9—313.

(c) While goods are in the possession of a bailee that has issued a negotiable document covering the goods:

(1) a security interest in the goods may be perfected by perfecting a security interest in the document; and

(2) a security interest perfected in the document has priority over any security interest that becomes perfected in the goods by another method during that time.

(d) While goods are in the possession of a bailee that has issued a nonnegotiable document covering the goods, a security interest in the goods may be perfected by:

(1) issuance of a document in the name of the secured party;

(2) the bailee's receipt of notification of the secured party's interest; or

(3) filing as to the goods.

(e) A security interest in certificated securities, negotiable documents, or instruments is perfected without filing or the taking of possession for a period of 20 days from the time it attaches to the extent that it arises for new value given under an authenticated security agreement.

(f) A perfected security interest in a negotiable document or goods in possession of a bailee, other than one that has issued a negotiable document for the goods, remains perfected for 20 days without filing if the secured party makes available to the debtor the goods or documents representing the goods for the purpose of:

(1) ultimate sale or exchange; or

(2) loading, unloading, storing, shipping, transshipping, manufacturing, processing, or otherwise dealing with them in a manner preliminary to their sale or exchange.

(g) A perfected security interest in a certificated security or instrument remains perfected for 20 days without filing if the secured party delivers the security certificate or instrument to the debtor for the purpose of:

(1) ultimate sale or exchange; or

(2) presentation, collection, enforcement, renewal, or registration of transfer.

(h) After the 20-day period specified in subsection (e), (f), or (g) expires, perfection depends upon compliance with this article.

§ 9—313. When Possession by or Delivery to Secured Party Perfects Security Interest without Filing.

(a) Except as otherwise provided in subsection (b), a secured party may perfect a security interest in negotiable documents, goods, instruments, money, or tangible chattel paper by taking possession of the collateral. A secured party may perfect a security interest in certificated securities by taking delivery of the certificated securities under Section 8—301.

(b) With respect to goods covered by a certificate of title issued by this State, a secured party may perfect a security interest in the goods by taking possession of the goods only in the circumstances described in Section 9—316(d).

(c) With respect to collateral other than certificated securities and goods covered by a document, a secured party takes possession of collateral in the possession of a person other than the debtor, the secured party, or a lessee of the collateral from the debtor in the ordinary course of the debtor's business, when:

(1) the person in possession authenticates a record acknowledging that it holds possession of the collateral for the secured party's benefit; or

(2) the person takes possession of the collateral after having authenticated a record acknowledging that it will hold possession of collateral for the secured party's benefit.

(d) If perfection of a security interest depends upon possession of the collateral by a secured party, perfection occurs no earlier than the time the secured party takes possession and continues only while the secured party retains possession.

(e) A security interest in a certificated security in registered form is perfected by delivery when delivery of the certificated security occurs under Section 8—301 and remains perfected by delivery until the debtor obtains possession of the security certificate.

(f) A person in possession of collateral is not required to acknowledge that it holds possession for a secured party's benefit.

(g) If a person acknowledges that it holds possession for the secured party's benefit:

(1) the acknowledgment is effective under subsection (c) or Section 8—301(a), even if the acknowledgment violates the rights of a debtor; and

(2) unless the person otherwise agrees or law other than this article otherwise provides, the person does not owe any duty to the secured party and is not required to confirm the acknowledgment to another person.

(h) A secured party having possession of collateral does not relinquish possession by delivering the collateral to a person other than the debtor or a lessee of the collateral from the debtor in the ordinary course of the debtor's business if the person was instructed before the delivery or is instructed contemporaneously with the delivery:

(1) to hold possession of the collateral for the secured party's benefit; or

(2) to redeliver the collateral to the secured party.

(i) A secured party does not relinquish possession, even if a delivery under subsection (h) violates the rights of a debtor. A person to which collateral is delivered under subsection (h) does not owe any duty to the secured party and is not required to confirm the delivery to another person unless the person otherwise agrees or law other than this article otherwise provides.

§ 9—314. Perfection by Control.

(a) A security interest in investment property, deposit accounts, letter-of-credit rights, or electronic chattel paper may be perfected by control of the collateral under Section 9—104, 9—105, 9—106, or 9—107.

(b) A security interest in deposit accounts, electronic chattel paper, or letter-of-credit rights is perfected by control under Section 9—104, 9—105, or 9—107 when the secured party obtains control and remains perfected by control only while the secured party retains control.

(c) A security interest in investment property is perfected by control under Section 9—106 from the time the secured party obtains control and remains perfected by control until:

(1) the secured party does not have control; and

(2) one of the following occurs:

(A) if the collateral is a certificated security, the debtor has or acquires possession of the security certificate;

(B) if the collateral is an uncertificated security, the issuer has registered or registers the debtor as the registered owner; or

(C) if the collateral is a security entitlement, the debtor is or becomes the entitlement holder.

§ 9—315. Secured Party's Rights on Disposition of Collateral and in Proceeds.

(a) Except as otherwise provided in this article and in Section 2—403(2):

(1) a security interest or agricultural lien continues in collateral notwithstanding sale, lease, license, exchange, or other disposition thereof unless the secured party authorized the disposition free of the security interest or agricultural lien; and

(2) a security interest attaches to any identifiable proceeds of collateral.

(b) Proceeds that are commingled with other property are identifiable proceeds:

(1) if the proceeds are goods, to the extent provided by Section 9—336; and

(2) if the proceeds are not goods, to the extent that the secured party identifies the proceeds by a method of tracing, including application of equitable principles, that is permitted under law other than this article with respect to commingled property of the type involved.

(c) A security interest in proceeds is a perfected security interest if the security interest in the original collateral was perfected.

(d) A perfected security interest in proceeds becomes unperfected on the 21st day after the security interest attaches to the proceeds unless:

(1) the following conditions are satisfied:

(A) a filed financing statement covers the original collateral;

(B) the proceeds are collateral in which a security interest may be perfected by filing in the office in which the financing statement has been filed; and

(C) the proceeds are not acquired with cash proceeds;

(2) the proceeds are identifiable cash proceeds; or

(3) the security interest in the proceeds is perfected other than under subsection (c) when the security interest attaches to the proceeds or within 20 days thereafter.

(e) If a filed financing statement covers the original collateral, a security interest in proceeds which remains perfected under subsection (d)(1) becomes unperfected at the later of:

(1) when the effectiveness of the filed financing statement lapses under Section 9—515 or is terminated under Section 9—513; or

(2) the 21st day after the security interest attaches to the proceeds.

§ 9—316. Continued Perfection of Security Interest Following Change in Governing Law.

(a) A security interest perfected pursuant to the law of the jurisdiction designated in Section 9—301(1) or 9—305(c) remains perfected until the earliest of:

(1) the time perfection would have ceased under the law of that jurisdiction;

(2) the expiration of four months after a change of the debtor's location to another jurisdiction; or

(3) the expiration of one year after a transfer of collateral to a person that thereby becomes a debtor and is located in another jurisdiction.

(b) If a security interest described in subsection (a) becomes perfected under the law of the other jurisdiction before the earliest time or event described in that subsection, it remains perfected thereafter. If the security interest does not become perfected under the law of the other jurisdiction before the earliest time or event, it becomes unperfected and is deemed never to have been perfected as against a purchaser of the collateral for value.

(c) A possessory security interest in collateral, other than goods covered by a certificate of title and as-extracted collateral consisting of goods, remains continuously perfected if:

(1) the collateral is located in one jurisdiction and subject to a security interest perfected under the law of that jurisdiction;

(2) thereafter the collateral is brought into another jurisdiction; and

(3) upon entry into the other jurisdiction, the security interest is perfected under the law of the other jurisdiction.

(d) Except as otherwise provided in subsection (e), a security interest in goods covered by a certificate of title which is perfected by any method under the law of another jurisdiction when the goods become covered by a certificate of title from this State remains perfected until the security interest would have become unperfected under the law of the other jurisdiction had the goods not become so covered.

(e) A security interest described in subsection (d) becomes unperfected as against a purchaser of the goods for value and is deemed never to have been perfected as against a purchaser of the goods for value if the applicable requirements for perfection under Section 9—311(b) or 9—313 are not satisfied before the earlier of:

(1) the time the security interest would have become unperfected under the law of the other jurisdiction had the goods not become covered by a certificate of title from this State; or

(2) the expiration of four months after the goods had become so covered.

(f) A security interest in deposit accounts, letter-of-credit rights, or investment property which is perfected under the law of the bank's jurisdiction, the issuer's jurisdiction, a nominated person's jurisdiction, the securities intermediary's jurisdiction, or the commodity intermediary's jurisdiction, as applicable, remains perfected until the earlier of:

(1) the time the security interest would have become unperfected under the law of that jurisdiction; or

(2) the expiration of four months after a change of the applicable jurisdiction to another jurisdiction.

(g) If a security interest described in subsection (f) becomes perfected under the law of the other jurisdiction before the earlier of the time or the end of the period described in that subsection, it remains perfected thereafter. If the security interest does not become perfected under the law of the other jurisdiction before the earlier of that time or the end of that period, it becomes unperfected and is deemed never to have been perfected as against a purchaser of the collateral for value.

[Subpart 3. Priority]

§ 9—317. Interests That Take Priority over or Take Free of Security Interest or Agricultural Lien.

(a) A security interest or agricultural lien is subordinate to the rights of:

(1) a person entitled to priority under Section 9—322; and

(2) except as otherwise provided in subsection (e), a person that becomes a lien creditor before the earlier of the time:

(A) the security interest or agricultural lien is perfected; or

(B) one of the conditions specified in Section 9—203(b)(3) is met and a financing statement covering the collateral is filed.

(b) Except as otherwise provided in subsection (e), a buyer, other than a secured party, of tangible chattel paper, documents, goods, instruments, or a security certificate takes free of a security interest or agricultural lien if the buyer gives value and receives delivery of the collateral without knowledge of the security interest or agricultural lien and before it is perfected.

(c) Except as otherwise provided in subsection (e), a lessee of goods takes free of a security interest or agricultural lien if the lessee gives value and receives delivery of the collateral without knowledge of the security interest or agricultural lien and before it is perfected.

(d) A licensee of a general intangible or a buyer, other than a secured party, of accounts, electronic chattel paper, general intangibles, or investment property other than a certificated security takes free of a security interest if the licensee or buyer gives value without knowledge of the security interest and before it is perfected.

(e) Except as otherwise provided in Sections 9—320 and 9—321, if a person files a financing statement with respect to a purchase-money security interest before or within 20 days after the debtor receives delivery of the collateral, the security interest takes priority over the rights of a buyer, lessee, or lien creditor which arise between the time the security interest attaches and the time of filing.

§ 9—318. No Interest Retained in Right to Payment That Is Sold; Rights and Title of Seller of Account or Chattel Paper with Respect to Creditors and Purchasers.

(a) A debtor that has sold an account, chattel paper, payment intangible, or promissory note does not retain a legal or equitable interest in the collateral sold.

(b) For purposes of determining the rights of creditors of, and purchasers for value of an account or chattel paper from, a debtor that has sold an account or chattel paper, while the buyer's security interest is unperfected, the debtor is deemed to have rights and title to the account or chattel paper identical to those the debtor sold.

§ 9—319. Rights and Title of Consignee with Respect to Creditors and Purchasers.

(a) Except as otherwise provided in subsection (b), for purposes of determining the rights of creditors of, and purchasers for value of goods from, a consignee, while the goods are in the possession of the consignee, the consignee is deemed to have rights and title to the goods identical to those the consignor had or had power to transfer.

(b) For purposes of determining the rights of a creditor of a consignee, law other than this article determines the rights and title of a consignee while goods are in the consignee's possession if, under this part, a perfected security interest held by the consignor would have priority over the rights of the creditor.

§ 9—320. Buyer of Goods.

(a) Except as otherwise provided in subsection (e), a buyer in ordinary course of business, other than a person buying farm products from a person engaged in farming operations, takes free of a security interest created by the buyer's seller, even if the security interest is perfected and the buyer knows of its existence.

(b) Except as otherwise provided in subsection (e), a buyer of goods from a person who used or bought the goods for use primarily for personal, family, or household purposes takes free of a security interest, even if perfected, if the buyer buys:

(1) without knowledge of the security interest;

(2) for value;

(3) primarily for the buyer's personal, family, or household purposes; and

(4) before the filing of a financing statement covering the goods.

(c) To the extent that it affects the priority of a security interest over a buyer of goods under subsection (b), the period of effectiveness of a filing made in the jurisdiction in which the seller is located is governed by Section 9—316(a) and (b).

(d) A buyer in ordinary course of business buying oil, gas, or other minerals at the wellhead or minehead or after extraction takes free of an interest arising out of an encumbrance.

(e) Subsections (a) and (b) do not affect a security interest in goods in the possession of the secured party under Section 9—313.

§ 9—321. Licensee of General Intangible and Lessee of Goods in Ordinary Course of Business.

(a) In this section, "licensee in ordinary course of business" means a person that becomes a licensee of a general intangible in good faith, without knowledge that the license violates the rights of another person in the general intangible, and in the ordinary course from a person in the business of licensing general intangibles of that kind. A person becomes a licensee in the ordinary course if the license to the person comports with the usual or customary practices in the kind of business in which the licensor is engaged or with the licensor's own usual or customary practices.

(b) A licensee in ordinary course of business takes its rights under a nonexclusive license free of a security interest in the general intangible created by the licensor, even if the security interest is perfected and the licensee knows of its existence.

(c) A lessee in ordinary course of business takes its leasehold interest free of a security interest in the goods created by the lessor, even if the security interest is perfected and the lessee knows of its existence.

§ 9—322. Priorities among Conflicting Security Interests in and Agricultural Liens on Same Collateral.

(a) Except as otherwise provided in this section, priority among conflicting security interests and agricultural liens in the same collateral is determined according to the following rules:

(1) Conflicting perfected security interests and agricultural liens rank according to priority in time of filing or perfection. Priority dates from the earlier of the time a filing covering the collateral is first made or the security interest or agricultural lien is first perfected, if there is no period thereafter when there is neither filing nor perfection.

(2) A perfected security interest or agricultural lien has priority over a conflicting unperfected security interest or agricultural lien.

(3) The first security interest or agricultural lien to attach or become effective has priority if conflicting security interests and agricultural liens are unperfected.

(b) For the purposes of subsection (a)(1):

(1) the time of filing or perfection as to a security interest in collateral is also the time of filing or perfection as to a security interest in proceeds; and

(2) the time of filing or perfection as to a security interest in collateral supported by a supporting obligation is also the time of filing or perfection as to a security interest in the supporting obligation.

(c) Except as otherwise provided in subsection (f), a security interest in collateral which qualifies for priority over a conflicting security interest under Section 9—327, 9—328, 9—329, 9—330, or 9—331 also has priority over a conflicting security interest in:

(1) any supporting obligation for the collateral; and

(2) proceeds of the collateral if:

(A) the security interest in proceeds is perfected;

(B) the proceeds are cash proceeds or of the same type as the collateral; and

(C) in the case of proceeds that are proceeds of proceeds, all intervening proceeds are cash proceeds, proceeds of the same type as the collateral, or an account relating to the collateral.

(d) Subject to subsection (e) and except as otherwise provided in subsection (f), if a security interest in chattel paper, deposit accounts, negotiable documents, instruments, investment property, or letter-of-credit rights is perfected by a method other than filing, conflicting perfected security interests in proceeds of the collateral rank according to priority in time of filing.

(e) Subsection (d) applies only if the proceeds of the collateral are not cash proceeds, chattel paper, negotiable documents, instruments, investment property, or letter-of-credit rights.

(f) Subsections (a) through (e) are subject to:

(1) subsection (g) and the other provisions of this part;

(2) Section 4—210 with respect to a security interest of a collecting bank;

(3) Section 5—118 with respect to a security interest of an issuer or nominated person; and

(4) Section 9—110 with respect to a security interest arising under Article 2 or 2A.

(g) A perfected agricultural lien on collateral has priority over a conflicting security interest in or agricultural lien on the same collateral if the statute creating the agricultural lien so provides.

§ 9—323. Future Advances.

(a) Except as otherwise provided in subsection (c), for purposes of determining the priority of a perfected security interest under Section 9—322(a)(1), perfection of the security interest dates from the time an advance is made to the extent that the security interest secures an advance that:

(1) is made while the security interest is perfected only:

(A) under Section 9—309 when it attaches; or

(B) temporarily under Section 9—312(e), (f), or (g); and

(2) is not made pursuant to a commitment entered into before or while the security interest is perfected by a method other than under Section 9—309 or 9—312(e), (f), or (g).

(b) Except as otherwise provided in subsection (c), a security interest is subordinate to the rights of a person that becomes a lien creditor to the extent that the security interest secures an advance made more than 45 days after the person becomes a lien creditor unless the advance is made:

(1) without knowledge of the lien; or

(2) pursuant to a commitment entered into without knowledge of the lien.

(c) Subsections (a) and (b) do not apply to a security interest held by a secured party that is a buyer of accounts, chattel paper, payment intangibles, or promissory notes or a consignor.

(d) Except as otherwise provided in subsection (e), a buyer of goods other than a buyer in ordinary course of business takes free of a security interest to the extent that it secures advances made after the earlier of:

(1) the time the secured party acquires knowledge of the buyer's purchase; or

(2) 45 days after the purchase.

(e) Subsection (d) does not apply if the advance is made pursuant to a commitment entered into without knowledge of the buyer's purchase and before the expiration of the 45-day period.

(f) Except as otherwise provided in subsection (g), a lessee of goods, other than a lessee in ordinary course of business, takes the leasehold interest free of a security interest to the extent that it secures advances made after the earlier of:

(1) the time the secured party acquires knowledge of the lease; or

(2) 45 days after the lease contract becomes enforceable.

(g) Subsection (f) does not apply if the advance is made pursuant to a commitment entered into without knowledge of the lease and before the expiration of the 45-day period.

§ 9—324. Priority of Purchase-Money Security Interests.

(a) Except as otherwise provided in subsection (g), a perfected purchase-money security interest in goods other than inventory or livestock has priority over a conflicting security interest in the same goods, and, except as otherwise provided in Section 9—327, a perfected security interest in its identifiable proceeds also has priority, if the purchase-money security interest is perfected when the debtor receives possession of the collateral or within 20 days thereafter.

(b) Subject to subsection (c) and except as otherwise provided in subsection (g), a perfected purchase-money security interest in inventory has priority over a conflicting security interest in the same inventory, has priority over a conflicting security interest in chattel paper or an instrument constituting proceeds of the inventory and in proceeds of the chattel paper, if so provided in Section 9—330, and, except as otherwise provided in Section 9—327, also has priority in identifiable cash proceeds of the inventory to the extent the identifiable cash proceeds are received on or before the delivery of the inventory to a buyer, if:

(1) the purchase-money security interest is perfected when the debtor receives possession of the inventory;

(2) the purchase-money secured party sends an authenticated notification to the holder of the conflicting security interest;

(3) the holder of the conflicting security interest receives the notification within five years before the debtor receives possession of the inventory; and

(4) the notification states that the person sending the notification has or expects to acquire a purchase-money security interest in inventory of the debtor and describes the inventory.

(c) Subsections (b)(2) through (4) apply only if the holder of the conflicting security interest had filed a financing statement covering the same types of inventory:

(1) if the purchase-money security interest is perfected by filing, before the date of the filing; or

(2) if the purchase-money security interest is temporarily perfected without filing or possession under Section 9—312(f), before the beginning of the 20-day period thereunder.

(d) Subject to subsection (e) and except as otherwise provided in subsection (g), a perfected purchase-money security interest in livestock that are farm products has priority over a conflicting security interest in the same livestock, and, except as otherwise provided in Section 9—327, a perfected security interest in their identifiable proceeds and identifiable products in their unmanufactured states also has priority, if:

(1) the purchase-money security interest is perfected when the debtor receives possession of the livestock;

(2) the purchase-money secured party sends an authenticated notification to the holder of the conflicting security interest;

(3) the holder of the conflicting security interest receives the notification within six months before the debtor receives possession of the livestock; and

(4) the notification states that the person sending the notification has or expects to acquire a purchase-money security interest in livestock of the debtor and describes the livestock.

(e) Subsections (d)(2) through (4) apply only if the holder of the conflicting security interest had filed a financing statement covering the same types of livestock:

(1) if the purchase-money security interest is perfected by filing, before the date of the filing; or

(2) if the purchase-money security interest is temporarily perfected without filing or possession under Section 9—312(f), before the beginning of the 20-day period thereunder.

(f) Except as otherwise provided in subsection (g), a perfected purchase-money security interest in software has priority over a conflicting security interest in the same collateral, and, except as otherwise provided in Section 9—327, a perfected security interest in its identifiable proceeds also has priority, to the extent that the purchase-money security interest in the goods in which the software was acquired for use has priority in the goods and proceeds of the goods under this section.

(g) If more than one security interest qualifies for priority in the same collateral under subsection (a), (b), (d), or (f):

(1) a security interest securing an obligation incurred as all or part of the price of the collateral has priority over a security interest securing an obligation incurred for value given to enable the debtor to acquire rights in or the use of collateral; and

(2) in all other cases, Section 9—322(a) applies to the qualifying security interests.

§ 9—325. Priority of Security Interests in Transferred Collateral.

(a) Except as otherwise provided in subsection (b), a security interest created by a debtor is subordinate to a security interest in the same collateral created by another person if:

(1) the debtor acquired the collateral subject to the security interest created by the other person;

(2) the security interest created by the other person was perfected when the debtor acquired the collateral; and

(3) there is no period thereafter when the security interest is unperfected.

(b) Subsection (a) subordinates a security interest only if the security interest:

(1) otherwise would have priority solely under Section 9—322(a) or 9—324; or

(2) arose solely under Section 2—711(3) or 2A—508(5).

§ 9—326. Priority of Security Interests Created by New Debtor.

(a) Subject to subsection (b), a security interest created by a new debtor which is perfected by a filed financing statement that is effective solely under Section 9—508 in collateral in which a new debtor has or acquires rights is subordinate to a security interest in the same collateral which is perfected other than by a filed financing statement that is effective solely under Section 9—508.

(b) The other provisions of this part determine the priority among conflicting security interests in the same collateral perfected by filed financing statements that are effective solely under Section 9—508. However, if the security agreements to which a new debtor became bound as debtor were not entered into by the same original debtor, the conflicting security interests rank according to priority in time of the new debtor's having become bound.

§ 9—327. Priority of Security Interests in Deposit Account.

The following rules govern priority among conflicting security interests in the same deposit account:

(1) A security interest held by a secured party having control of the deposit account under Section 9—104 has priority over a conflicting security interest held by a secured party that does not have control.

(2) Except as otherwise provided in paragraphs (3) and (4), security interests perfected by control under Section 9—314 rank according to priority in time of obtaining control.

(3) Except as otherwise provided in paragraph (4), a security interest held by the bank with which the deposit account is maintained has priority over a conflicting security interest held by another secured party.

(4) A security interest perfected by control under Section 9—104(a)(3) has priority over a security interest held by the bank with which the deposit account is maintained.

§ 9—328. Priority of Security Interests in Investment Property.

The following rules govern priority among conflicting security interests in the same investment property:

(1) A security interest held by a secured party having control of investment property under Section 9—106 has priority over a security interest held by a secured party that does not have control of the investment property.

(2) Except as otherwise provided in paragraphs (3) and (4), conflicting security interests held by secured parties each of which has control under Section 9—106 rank according to priority in time of:

(A) if the collateral is a security, obtaining control;

(B) if the collateral is a security entitlement carried in a securities account and:

(i) if the secured party obtained control under Section 8—106(d)(1), the secured party's becoming the person for which the securities account is maintained;

(ii) if the secured party obtained control under Section 8—106(d)(2), the securities intermediary's agreement to comply with the secured party's entitlement orders with respect to security entitlements carried or to be carried in the securities account; or

(iii) if the secured party obtained control through another person under Section 8—106(d)(3), the time on which priority would be based under this paragraph if the other person were the secured party; or

(C) if the collateral is a commodity contract carried with a commodity intermediary, the satisfaction of the requirement for control specified in Section 9—106(b)(2) with respect to commodity contracts carried or to be carried with the commodity intermediary.

(3) A security interest held by a securities intermediary in a security entitlement or a securities account maintained with the securities intermediary has priority over a conflicting security interest held by another secured party.

(4) A security interest held by a commodity intermediary in a commodity contract or a commodity account maintained with the commodity intermediary has priority over a conflicting security interest held by another secured party.

(5) A security interest in a certificated security in registered form which is perfected by taking delivery under Section 9—313(a) and not by control under Section 9—314 has priority over a conflicting security interest perfected by a method other than control.

(6) Conflicting security interests created by a broker, securities intermediary, or commodity intermediary which are perfected without control under Section 9—106 rank equally.

(7) In all other cases, priority among conflicting security interests in investment property is governed by Sections 9—322 and 9—323.

§ 9—329. Priority of Security Interests in Letter-of-Credit Right.

The following rules govern priority among conflicting security interests in the same letter-of-credit right:

(1) A security interest held by a secured party having control of the letter-of-credit right under Section 9—107 has priority to the extent of its control over a conflicting security interest held by a secured party that does not have control.

(2) Security interests perfected by control under Section 9—314 rank according to priority in time of obtaining control.

§ 9—330. Priority of Purchaser of Chattel Paper or Instrument.

(a) A purchaser of chattel paper has priority over a security interest in the chattel paper which is claimed merely as proceeds of inventory subject to a security interest if:

(1) in good faith and in the ordinary course of the purchaser's business, the purchaser gives new value and takes possession of the chattel paper or obtains control of the chattel paper under Section 9—105; and

(2) the chattel paper does not indicate that it has been assigned to an identified assignee other than the purchaser.

(b) A purchaser of chattel paper has priority over a security interest in the chattel paper which is claimed other than merely as proceeds of inventory subject to a security interest if the purchaser gives new value and takes possession of the chattel paper or obtains control of the chattel paper under Section 9—105 in good faith, in the ordinary course of the purchaser's business, and without knowledge that the purchase violates the rights of the secured party.

(c) Except as otherwise provided in Section 9—327, a purchaser having priority in chattel paper under subsection (a) or (b) also has priority in proceeds of the chattel paper to the extent that:

(1) Section 9—322 provides for priority in the proceeds; or

(2) the proceeds consist of the specific goods covered by the chattel paper or cash proceeds of the specific goods, even if the purchaser's security interest in the proceeds is unperfected.

(d) Except as otherwise provided in Section 9—331(a), a purchaser of an instrument has priority over a security interest in the instrument perfected by a method other than possession if the purchaser gives value and takes possession of the instrument in good faith and without knowledge that the purchase violates the rights of the secured party.

(e) For purposes of subsections (a) and (b), the holder of a purchase-money security interest in inventory gives new value for chattel paper constituting proceeds of the inventory.

(f) For purposes of subsections (b) and (d), if chattel paper or an instrument indicates that it has been assigned to an identified secured party other than the purchaser, a purchaser of the chattel paper or instrument has knowledge that the purchase violates the rights of the secured party.

§ 9—331. Priority of Rights of Purchasers of Instruments, Documents, and Securities under Other Articles; Priority of Interests in Financial Assets and Security Entitlements under Article 8.

(a) This article does not limit the rights of a holder in due course of a negotiable instrument, a holder to which a negotiable document of title has been duly negotiated, or a protected purchaser of a security. These holders or purchasers take priority over an earlier security interest, even if perfected, to the extent provided in Articles 3, 7, and 8.

(b) This article does not limit the rights of or impose liability on a person to the extent that the person is protected against the assertion of a claim under Article 8.

(c) Filing under this article does not constitute notice of a claim or defense to the holders, or purchasers, or persons described in subsections (a) and (b).

§ 9—332. Transfer of Money; Transfer of Funds from Deposit Account.

(a) A transferee of money takes the money free of a security interest unless the transferee acts in collusion with the debtor in violating the rights of the secured party.

(b) A transferee of funds from a deposit account takes the funds free of a security interest in the deposit account unless the transferee acts in collusion with the debtor in violating the rights of the secured party.

§ 9—333. Priority of Certain Liens Arising by Operation of Law.

(a) In this section, "possessory lien" means an interest, other than a security interest or an agricultural lien:

(1) which secures payment or performance of an obligation for services or materials furnished with respect to goods by a person in the ordinary course of the person's business;

(2) which is created by statute or rule of law in favor of the person; and

(3) whose effectiveness depends on the person's possession of the goods.

(b) A possessory lien on goods has priority over a security interest in the goods unless the lien is created by a statute that expressly provides otherwise.

§ 9—334. Priority of Security Interests in Fixtures and Crops.

(a) A security interest under this article may be created in goods that are fixtures or may continue in goods that become fixtures. A security interest does not exist under this article in ordinary building materials incorporated into an improvement on land.

(b) This article does not prevent creation of an encumbrance upon fixtures under real property law.

(c) In cases not governed by subsections (d) through (h), a security interest in fixtures is subordinate to a conflicting interest of an encumbrancer or owner of the related real property other than the debtor.

(d) Except as otherwise provided in subsection (h), a perfected security interest in fixtures has priority over a conflicting interest of an encumbrancer or owner of the real property if the debtor has an interest of record in or is in possession of the real property and:

(1) the security interest is a purchase-money security interest;

(2) the interest of the encumbrancer or owner arises before the goods become fixtures; and

(3) the security interest is perfected by a fixture filing before the goods become fixtures or within 20 days thereafter.

(e) A perfected security interest in fixtures has priority over a conflicting interest of an encumbrancer or owner of the real property if:

(1) the debtor has an interest of record in the real property or is in possession of the real property and the security interest:

(A) is perfected by a fixture filing before the interest of the encumbrancer or owner is of record; and

(B) has priority over any conflicting interest of a predecessor in title of the encumbrancer or owner;

(2) before the goods become fixtures, the security interest is perfected by any method permitted by this article and the fixtures are readily removable:

(A) factory or office machines;

(B) equipment that is not primarily used or leased for use in the operation of the real property; or

(C) replacements of domestic appliances that are consumer goods;

(3) the conflicting interest is a lien on the real property obtained by legal or equitable proceedings after the security interest was perfected by any method permitted by this article; or

(4) the security interest is:

(A) created in a manufactured home in a manufactured-home transaction; and

(B) perfected pursuant to a statute described in Section 9—311(a)(2).

(f) A security interest in fixtures, whether or not perfected, has priority over a conflicting interest of an encumbrancer or owner of the real property if:

(1) the encumbrancer or owner has, in an authenticated record, consented to the security interest or disclaimed an interest in the goods as fixtures; or

(2) the debtor has a right to remove the goods as against the encumbrancer or owner.

(g) The priority of the security interest under paragraph (f)(2) continues for a reasonable time if the debtor's right to remove the goods as against the encumbrancer or owner terminates.

(h) A mortgage is a construction mortgage to the extent that it secures an obligation incurred for the construction of an improvement on land, including the acquisition cost of the land, if a recorded record of the mortgage so indicates. Except as otherwise provided in subsections (e) and (f), a security interest in fixtures is subordinate to a construction mortgage if a record of the mortgage is recorded before the goods become fixtures and the goods become fixtures before the completion of the construction. A mortgage has this priority to the same extent as a construction mortgage to the extent that it is given to refinance a construction mortgage.

(i) A perfected security interest in crops growing on real property has priority over a conflicting interest of an encumbrancer or owner of the real property if the debtor has an interest of record in or is in possession of the real property.

(j) Subsection (i) prevails over any inconsistent provisions of the following statutes:

[List here any statutes containing provisions inconsistent with subsection (i).]

Legislative Note: States that amend statutes to remove provisions inconsistent with subsection (i) need not enact subsection (j).

§ 9—335. Accessions.

(a) A security interest may be created in an accession and continues in collateral that becomes an accession.

(b) If a security interest is perfected when the collateral becomes an accession, the security interest remains perfected in the collateral.

(c) Except as otherwise provided in subsection (d), the other provisions of this part determine the priority of a security interest in an accession.

(d) A security interest in an accession is subordinate to a security interest in the whole which is perfected by compliance with the requirements of a certificate-of-title statute under Section 9—311(b).

(e) After default, subject to Part 6, a secured party may remove an accession from other goods if the security interest in the accession has priority over the claims of every person having an interest in the whole.

(f) A secured party that removes an accession from other goods under subsection (e) shall promptly reimburse any holder of a security interest or other lien on, or owner of, the whole or of the other goods, other than the debtor, for the cost of repair of any physical injury to the whole or the other goods. The secured party need not reimburse the holder or owner for any diminution in value of the whole or the other goods caused by the absence of the accession removed or by any necessity for replacing it. A person entitled to reimbursement may refuse permission to remove until the secured party gives adequate assurance for the performance of the obligation to reimburse.

§ 9—336. Commingled Goods.

(a) In this section, "commingled goods" means goods that are physically united with other goods in such a manner that their identity is lost in a product or mass.

(b) A security interest does not exist in commingled goods as such. However, a security interest may attach to a product or mass that results when goods become commingled goods.

(c) If collateral becomes commingled goods, a security interest attaches to the product or mass.

(d) If a security interest in collateral is perfected before the collateral becomes commingled goods, the security interest that attaches to the product or mass under subsection (c) is perfected.

(e) Except as otherwise provided in subsection (f), the other provisions of this part determine the priority of a security interest that attaches to the product or mass under subsection (c).

(f) If more than one security interest attaches to the product or mass under subsection (c), the following rules determine priority:

(1) A security interest that is perfected under subsection (d) has priority over a security interest that is unperfected at the time the collateral becomes commingled goods.

(2) If more than one security interest is perfected under subsection (d), the security interests rank equally in proportion to the value of the collateral at the time it became commingled goods.

§ 9—337. Priority of Security Interests in Goods Covered by Certificate of Title.

If, while a security interest in goods is perfected by any method under the law of another jurisdiction, this State issues a certificate of title that does not show that the goods are subject to the security interest or contain a statement that they may be subject to security interests not shown on the certificate:

(1) a buyer of the goods, other than a person in the business of selling goods of that kind, takes free of the security interest if the buyer gives value and receives delivery of the goods after issuance of the certificate and without knowledge of the security interest; and

(2) the security interest is subordinate to a conflicting security interest in the goods that attaches, and is perfected under Section 9—311(b), after issuance of the certificate and without the conflicting secured party's knowledge of the security interest.

§ 9—338. Priority of Security Interest or Agricultural Lien Perfected by Filed Financing Statement Providing Certain Incorrect Information.

If a security interest or agricultural lien is perfected by a filed financing statement providing information described in Section 9—516(b)(5) which is incorrect at the time the financing statement is filed:

(1) the security interest or agricultural lien is subordinate to a conflicting perfected security interest in the collateral to the extent that the holder of the conflicting security interest gives value in reasonable reliance upon the incorrect information; and

(2) a purchaser, other than a secured party, of the collateral takes free of the security interest or agricultural lien to the extent that, in reasonable reliance upon the incorrect information, the purchaser gives value and, in the case of chattel paper, documents, goods, instruments, or a security certificate, receives delivery of the collateral.

§ 9—339 Priority Subject to Subordination.

This article does not preclude subordination by agreement by a person entitled to priority.

[Subpart 4. Rights of Bank]

§ 9—340. Effectiveness of Right of Recoupment or Set-Off against Deposit Account.

(a) Except as otherwise provided in subsection (c), a bank with which a deposit account is maintained may exercise any right of recoupment or set-off against a secured party that holds a security interest in the deposit account.

(b) Except as otherwise provided in subsection (c), the application of this article to a security interest in a deposit account does not affect a right of recoupment or set-off of the secured party as to a deposit account maintained with the secured party.

(c) The exercise by a bank of a set-off against a deposit account is ineffective against a secured party that holds a security interest in the deposit account which is perfected by control under Section 9—104(a)(3), if the set-off is based on a claim against the debtor.

§ 9—341. Bank's Rights and Duties with Respect to Deposit Account.

Except as otherwise provided in Section 9—340(c), and unless the bank otherwise agrees in an authenticated record, a bank's rights and duties with respect to a deposit account maintained with the bank are not terminated, suspended, or modified by:

(1) the creation, attachment, or perfection of a security interest in the deposit account;

(2) the bank's knowledge of the security interest; or

(3) the bank's receipt of instructions from the secured party.

§ 9—342. Bank's Right to Refuse to Enter into or Disclose Existence of Control Agreement.

This article does not require a bank to enter into an agreement of the kind described in Section 9—104(a)(2), even if its customer so requests or directs. A bank that has entered into such an agreement is not required to confirm the existence of the agreement to another person unless requested to do so by its customer.

Part 4 Rights of Third Parties

§ 9—401. Alienability of Debtor's Rights.

(a) as otherwise provided in subsection (b) and Sections 9—406, 9—407, 9—408, and 9—409, whether a debtor's rights in collateral may be voluntarily or involuntarily transferred is governed by law other than this article.

(b) An agreement between the debtor and secured party which prohibits a transfer of the debtor's rights in collateral or makes the transfer a default does not prevent the transfer from taking effect.

§ 9—402. Secured Party Not Obligated on Contract of Debtor or in Tort.

The existence of a security interest, agricultural lien, or authority given to a debtor to dispose of or use collateral, without more, does not subject a secured party to liability in contract or tort for the debtor's acts or omissions.

§ 9—403. Agreement Not to Assert Defenses against Assignee.

(a) In this section, "value" has the meaning provided in Section 3—303(a).

(b) Except as otherwise provided in this section, an agreement between an account debtor and an assignor not to assert against an assignee any claim or defense that the account debtor may have against the assignor is enforceable by an assignee that takes an assignment:

(1) for value;

(2) in good faith;

(3) without notice of a claim of a property or possessory right to the property assigned; and

(4) without notice of a defense or claim in recoupment of the type that may be asserted against a person entitled to enforce a negotiable instrument under Section 3—305(a).

(c) Subsection (b) does not apply to defenses of a type that may be asserted against a holder in due course of a negotiable instrument under Section 3—305(b).

(d) In a consumer transaction, if a record evidences the account debtor's obligation, law other than this article requires that the record include a statement to the effect that the rights of an assignee are subject to claims or defenses that the account debtor could assert against the original obligee, and the record does not include such a statement:

(1) the record has the same effect as if the record included such a statement; and

(2) the account debtor may assert against an assignee those claims and defenses that would have been available if the record included such a statement.

(e) This section is subject to law other than this article which establishes a different rule for an account debtor who is an individual and who incurred the obligation primarily for personal, family, or household purposes.

(f) Except as otherwise provided in subsection (d), this section does not displace law other than this article which gives effect to an agreement by an account debtor not to assert a claim or defense against an assignee.

§ 9—404. Rights Acquired by Assignee; Claims and Defenses against Assignee.

(a) Unless an account debtor has made an enforceable agreement not to assert defenses or claims, and subject to subsections (b) through (e), the rights of an assignee are subject to:

(1) all terms of the agreement between the account debtor and assignor and any defense or claim in recoupment arising from the transaction that gave rise to the contract; and

(2) any other defense or claim of the account debtor against the assignor which accrues before the account debtor receives a notification of the assignment authenticated by the assignor or the assignee.

(b) Subject to subsection (c) and except as otherwise provided in subsection (d), the claim of an account debtor against an assignor may be asserted against an assignee under subsection (a) only to reduce the amount the account debtor owes.

(c) This section is subject to law other than this article which establishes a different rule for an account debtor who is an individual and who incurred the obligation primarily for personal, family, or household purposes.

(d) In a consumer transaction, if a record evidences the account debtor's obligation, law other than this article requires that the record include a statement to the effect that the account debtor's recovery against an assignee with respect to claims and defenses against the assignor may not exceed amounts paid by the account debtor under the record, and the record does not include such a statement, the extent to which a claim of an account debtor against the assignor may be asserted against an assignee is determined as if the record included such a statement.

(e) This section does not apply to an assignment of a health-care-insurance receivable.

§ 9—405. Modification of Assigned Contract.

(a) A modification of or substitution for an assigned contract is effective against an assignee if made in good faith. The assignee acquires corresponding rights under the modified or substituted contract. The assignment may provide that the modification or substitution is a breach of contract by the assignor. This subsection is subject to subsections (b) through (d).

(b) Subsection (a) applies to the extent that:

(1) the right to payment or a part thereof under an assigned contract has not been fully earned by performance; or

(2) the right to payment or a part thereof has been fully earned by performance and the account debtor has not received notification of the assignment under Section 9—406(a).

(c) This section is subject to law other than this article which establishes a different rule for an account debtor who is an individual and who incurred the obligation primarily for personal, family, or household purposes.

(d) This section does not apply to an assignment of a health-care-insurance receivable.

§ 9—406. Discharge of Account Debtor; Notification of Assignment; Identification and Proof of Assignment; Restrictions on Assignment of Accounts, Chattel Paper, Payment Intangibles, and Promissory Notes Ineffective.

(a) Subject to subsections (b) through (i), an account debtor on an account, chattel paper, or a payment intangible may discharge its obligation by paying the assignor until, but not after, the account debtor receives a notification, authenticated by the assignor or the assignee, that the amount due or to become due has been assigned and that payment is to be made to the assignee. After receipt of the notification, the account debtor may discharge its obligation by paying the assignee and may not discharge the obligation by paying the assignor.

(b) Subject to subsection (h), notification is ineffective under subsection (a):

(1) if it does not reasonably identify the rights assigned;

(2) to the extent that an agreement between an account debtor and a seller of a payment intangible limits the account debtor's duty to pay a person other than the seller and the limitation is effective under law other than this article; or

(3) at the option of an account debtor, if the notification notifies the account debtor to make less than the full amount of any installment or other periodic payment to the assignee, even if:

(A) only a portion of the account, chattel paper, or payment intangible has been assigned to that assignee;

(B) a portion has been assigned to another assignee; or

(C) the account debtor knows that the assignment to that assignee is limited.

(c) Subject to subsection (h), if requested by the account debtor, an assignee shall seasonably furnish reasonable proof that the assignment has been made. Unless the assignee complies, the account debtor may discharge its obligation by paying the assignor, even if the account debtor has received a notification under subsection (a).

(d) Except as otherwise provided in subsection (e) and Sections 2A—303 and 9—407, and subject to subsection (h), a term in an agreement between an account debtor and an assignor or in a promissory note is ineffective to the extent that it:

(1) prohibits, restricts, or requires the consent of the account debtor or person obligated on the promissory note to the assignment or transfer of, or the creation, attachment, perfection, or enforcement of a security interest in, the account, chattel paper, payment intangible, or promissory note; or

(2) provides that the assignment or transfer or the creation, attachment, perfection, or enforcement of the security interest may give rise to a default, breach, right of recoupment, claim, defense, termination, right of termination, or remedy under the account, chattel paper, payment intangible, or promissory note.

(e) Subsection (d) does not apply to the sale of a payment intangible or promissory note.

(f) Except as otherwise provided in Sections 2A—303 and 9—407 and subject to subsections (h) and (i), a rule of law, statute, or regulation that prohibits, restricts, or requires the consent of a government, governmental body or official, or account debtor to the assignment or transfer of, or creation of a security interest in, an account or chattel paper is ineffective to the extent that the rule of law, statute, or regulation:

(1) prohibits, restricts, or requires the consent of the government, governmental body or official, or account debtor to the assignment or transfer of, or the creation, attachment, perfection, or enforcement of a security interest in the account or chattel paper; or

(2) provides that the assignment or transfer or the creation, attachment, perfection, or enforcement of the security interest may give rise to a default, breach, right of recoupment, claim, defense, termination, right of termination, or remedy under the account or chattel paper.

(g) Subject to subsection (h), an account debtor may not waive or vary its option under subsection (b)(3).

(h) This section is subject to law other than this article which establishes a different rule for an account debtor who is an individual and who incurred the obligation primarily for personal, family, or household purposes.

(i) This section does not apply to an assignment of a health-care-insurance receivable.

(j) This section prevails over any inconsistent provisions of the following statutes, rules, and regulations:

[List here any statutes, rules, and regulations containing provisions inconsistent with this section.]

Legislative Note: States that amend statutes, rules, and regulations to remove provisions inconsistent with this section need not enact subsection (j).

§ 9—407. Restrictions on Creation or Enforcement of Security Interest in Leasehold Interest or in Lessor's Residual Interest.

(a) Except as otherwise provided in subsection (b), a term in a lease agreement is ineffective to the extent that it:

(1) prohibits, restricts, or requires the consent of a party to the lease to the assignment or transfer of, or the creation, attachment, perfection, or enforcement of a security interest in an interest of a party under the lease contract or in the lessor's residual interest in the goods; or

(2) provides that the assignment or transfer or the creation, attachment, perfection, or enforcement of the security interest may give rise to a default, breach, right of recoupment, claim, defense, termination, right of termination, or remedy under the lease.

(b) Except as otherwise provided in Section 2A—303(7), a term described in subsection (a)(2) is effective to the extent that there is:

(1) a transfer by the lessee of the lessee's right of possession or use of the goods in violation of the term; or

(2) a delegation of a material performance of either party to the lease contract in violation of the term.

(c) The creation, attachment, perfection, or enforcement of a security interest in the lessor's interest under the lease contract or the lessor's residual interest in the goods is not a transfer that materially impairs the lessee's prospect of obtaining return performance or materially changes the duty of or materially increases the burden or risk imposed on the lessee within the purview of Section 2A—303(4) unless, and then only to the extent that, enforcement actually results in a delegation of material performance of the lessor.

§ 9—408. Restrictions on Assignment of Promissory Notes, Health-Care-Insurance Receivables, and Certain General Intangibles Ineffective.

(a) Except as otherwise provided in subsection (b), a term in a promissory note or in an agreement between an account debtor and a debtor which relates to a health-care-insurance receivable or a general intangible, including a contract, permit, license, or franchise, and which term prohibits, restricts, or requires the consent of the person obligated on the promissory note or the account debtor to, the assignment or transfer of, or creation, attachment, or perfection of a security interest in, the promissory note, health-care-insurance receivable, or general intangible, is ineffective to the extent that the term:

(1) would impair the creation, attachment, or perfection of a security interest; or

(2) provides that the assignment or transfer or the creation, attachment, or perfection of the security interest may give rise to a default, breach, right of recoupment, claim, defense, termination, right of termination, or remedy under the promissory note, health-care-insurance receivable, or general intangible.

(b) Subsection (a) applies to a security interest in a payment intangible or promissory note only if the security interest arises out of a sale of the payment intangible or promissory note.

(c) A rule of law, statute, or regulation that prohibits, restricts, or requires the consent of a government, governmental body or official, person obligated on a promissory note, or account debtor to the assignment or transfer of, or creation of a security interest in, a promissory note, health-care-insurance receivable, or general intangible, including a contract, permit, license, or franchise between an account debtor and a debtor, is ineffective to the extent that the rule of law, statute, or regulation:

(1) would impair the creation, attachment, or perfection of a security interest; or

(2) provides that the assignment or transfer or the creation, attachment, or perfection of the security interest may give rise to a default, breach, right of recoupment, claim, defense, termination, right of termination, or remedy under the promissory note, health-care-insurance receivable, or general intangible.

(d) To the extent that a term in a promissory note or in an agreement between an account debtor and a debtor which relates to a health-care-insurance receivable or general intangible or a rule of law, statute, or regulation described in subsection (c) would be effective under law other than this article but is ineffective under subsection (a) or (c), the creation, attachment, or perfection of a security interest in the promissory note, health-care-insurance receivable, or general intangible:

(1) is not enforceable against the person obligated on the promissory note or the account debtor;

(2) does not impose a duty or obligation on the person obligated on the promissory note or the account debtor;

(3) does not require the person obligated on the promissory note or the account debtor to recognize the security interest, pay or render performance to the secured party, or accept payment or performance from the secured party;

(4) does not entitle the secured party to use or assign the debtor's rights under the promissory note, health-care-insurance receivable, or general intangible, including any related information or materials furnished to the debtor in the transaction giving rise to the promissory note, health-care-insurance receivable, or general intangible;

(5) does not entitle the secured party to use, assign, possess, or have access to any trade secrets or confidential information of the person obligated on the promissory note or the account debtor; and

(6) does not entitle the secured party to enforce the security interest in the promissory note, health-care-insurance receivable, or general intangible.

(e) This section prevails over any inconsistent provisions of the following statutes, rules, and regulations:

[List here any statutes, rules, and regulations containing provisions inconsistent with this section.]

Legislative Note: States that amend statutes, rules, and regulations to remove provisions inconsistent with this section need not enact subsection (e).

§ 9—409. Restrictions on Assignment of Letter-of-Credit Rights Ineffective.

(a) A term in a letter of credit or a rule of law, statute, regulation, custom, or practice applicable to the letter of credit which prohibits, restricts, or requires the consent of an applicant, issuer, or nominated person to a beneficiary's assignment of or creation of a security interest in a letter-of-credit right is ineffective to the extent that the term or rule of law, statute, regulation, custom, or practice:

(1) would impair the creation, attachment, or perfection of a security interest in the letter-of-credit right; or

(2) provides that the assignment or the creation, attachment, or perfection of the security interest may give rise to a default, breach, right of recoupment, claim, defense, termination, right of termination, or remedy under the letter-of-credit right.

(b) To the extent that a term in a letter of credit is ineffective under subsection (a) but would be effective under law other than this article or a custom or practice applicable to the letter of credit, to the transfer of a right to draw or otherwise demand performance under the letter of credit, or to the assignment of a right to proceeds of the letter of credit, the creation, attachment, or perfection of a security interest in the letter-of-credit right:

(1) is not enforceable against the applicant, issuer, nominated person, or transferee beneficiary;

(2) imposes no duties or obligations on the applicant, issuer, nominated person, or transferee beneficiary; and

(3) does not require the applicant, issuer, nominated person, or transferee beneficiary to recognize the security interest, pay or render performance to the secured party, or accept payment or other performance from the secured party.

Part 5 Filing

[Subpart 1. Filing Office; Contents and Effectiveness of Financing Statement]

§ 9—501. Filing Office.

(a) Except as otherwise provided in subsection (b), if the local law of this State governs perfection of a security interest or agricultural lien, the office in which to file a financing statement to perfect the security interest or agricultural lien is:

(1) the office designated for the filing or recording of a record of a mortgage on the related real property, if:

(A) the collateral is as-extracted collateral or timber to be cut; or

(B) the financing statement is filed as a fixture filing and the collateral is goods that are or are to become fixtures; or

(2) the office of [ ] [or any office duly authorized by [ ]], in all other cases, including a case in which the collateral is goods that are or are to become fixtures and the financing statement is not filed as a fixture filing.

(b) The office in which to file a financing statement to perfect a security interest in collateral, including fixtures, of a transmitting utility is the office of [ ]. The financing statement also constitutes a fixture filing as to the collateral indicated in the financing statement which is or is to become fixtures.

Legislative Note: The State should designate the filing office where the brackets appear. The filing office may be that of a governmental official (e.g., the Secretary of State) or a private party that maintains the State's filing system.

§ 9—502 Contents of Financing Statement; Record of Mortgage as Financing Statement; Time of Filing Financing Statement.

(a) Subject to subsection (b), a financing statement is sufficient only if it:

(1) provides the name of the debtor;

(2) provides the name of the secured party or a representative of the secured party; and

(3) indicates the collateral covered by the financing statement.

(b) Except as otherwise provided in Section 9—501(b), to be sufficient, a financing statement that covers as-extracted collateral or timber to be cut, or which is filed as a fixture filing and covers goods that are or are to become fixtures, must satisfy subsection (a) and also:

(1) indicate that it covers this type of collateral;

(2) indicate that it is to be filed [for record] in the real property records;

(3) provide a description of the real property to which the collateral is related [sufficient to give constructive notice of a mortgage under the law of this State if the description were contained in a record of the mortgage of the real property]; and

(4) if the debtor does not have an interest of record in the real property, provide the name of a record owner.

(c) A record of a mortgage is effective, from the date of recording, as a financing statement filed as a fixture filing or as a financing statement covering as-extracted collateral or timber to be cut only if:

(1) the record indicates the goods or accounts that it covers;

(2) the goods are or are to become fixtures related to the real property described in the record or the collateral is related to the real property described in the record and is as-extracted collateral or timber to be cut;

(3) the record satisfies the requirements for a financing statement in this section other than an indication that it is to be filed in the real property records; and

(4) the record is [duly] recorded.

(d) A financing statement may be filed before a security agreement is made or a security interest otherwise attaches.

Legislative Note: Language in brackets is optional. Where the State has any special recording system for real property other than the usual grantor-grantee index (as, for instance, a tract system or a title registration or Torrens system) local adaptations of subsection (b) and Section 9—519(d) and (e) may be necessary. See, e.g., Mass. Gen. Laws Chapter 106, Section 9—410.

§ 9—503. Name of Debtor and Secured Party.

(a) A financing statement sufficiently provides the name of the debtor:

(1) if the debtor is a registered organization, only if the financing statement provides the name of the debtor indicated on the public record of the debtor's jurisdiction of organization which shows the debtor to have been organized;

(2) if the debtor is a decedent's estate, only if the financing statement provides the name of the decedent and indicates that the debtor is an estate;

(3) if the debtor is a trust or a trustee acting with respect to property held in trust, only if the financing statement:

(A) provides the name specified for the trust in its organic documents or, if no name is specified, provides the name of the settlor and additional information sufficient to distinguish the debtor from other trusts having one or more of the same settlors; and

(B) indicates, in the debtor's name or otherwise, that the debtor is a trust or is a trustee acting with respect to property held in trust; and

(4) in other cases:

(A) if the debtor has a name, only if it provides the individual or organizational name of the debtor; and

(B) if the debtor does not have a name, only if it provides the names of the partners, members, associates, or other persons comprising the debtor.

(b) A financing statement that provides the name of the debtor in accordance with subsection (a) is not rendered ineffective by the absence of:

(1) a trade name or other name of the debtor; or

(2) unless required under subsection (a)(4)(B), names of partners, members, associates, or other persons comprising the debtor.

(c) A financing statement that provides only the debtor's trade name does not sufficiently provide the name of the debtor.

(d) Failure to indicate the representative capacity of a secured party or representative of a secured party does not affect the sufficiency of a financing statement.

(e) A financing statement may provide the name of more than one debtor and the name of more than one secured party.

§ 9—504. Indication of Collateral.

A financing statement sufficiently indicates the collateral that it covers if the financing statement provides:

(1) a description of the collateral pursuant to Section 9—108; or

(2) an indication that the financing statement covers all assets or all personal property.

§ 9—505. Filing and Compliance with Other Statutes and Treaties for Consignments, Leases, Other Bailments, and Other Transactions.

(a) A consignor, lessor, or other bailor of goods, a licensor, or a buyer of a payment intangible or promissory note may file a financing statement, or may comply with a statute or treaty described in Section 9—311(a), using the terms "consignor", "consignee", "lessor", "lessee", "bailor", "bailee", "licensor", "licensee", "owner", "registered owner", "buyer", "seller", or words of similar import, instead of the terms "secured party" and "debtor".

(b) This part applies to the filing of a financing statement under subsection (a) and, as appropriate, to compliance that is equivalent to filing a financing statement under Section 9—311(b), but the filing or compliance is not of itself a factor in determining whether the collateral secures an obligation. If it is determined for another reason that the collateral secures an obligation, a security interest held by the consignor, lessor, bailor, licensor, owner, or buyer which attaches to the collateral is perfected by the filing or compliance.

§ 9—506. Effect of Errors or Omissions.

(a) A financing statement substantially satisfying the requirements of this part is effective, even if it has minor errors or omissions, unless the errors or omissions make the financing statement seriously misleading.

(b) Except as otherwise provided in subsection (c), a financing statement that fails sufficiently to provide the name of the debtor in accordance with Section 9—503(a) is seriously misleading.

(c) If a search of the records of the filing office under the debtor's correct name, using the filing office's standard search logic, if any, would disclose a financing statement that fails sufficiently to provide the name of the debtor in accordance with Section 9—503(a), the name provided does not make the financing statement seriously misleading.

(d) For purposes of Section 9—508(b), the "debtor's correct name" in subsection (c) means the correct name of the new debtor.

§ 9—507. Effect of Certain Events on Effectiveness of Financing Statement.

(a) A filed financing statement remains effective with respect to collateral that is sold, exchanged, leased, licensed, or otherwise disposed of and in which a security interest or agricultural lien continues, even if the secured party knows of or consents to the disposition.

(b) Except as otherwise provided in subsection (c) and Section 9—508, a financing statement is not rendered ineffective if, after the financing statement is filed, the information provided in the financing statement becomes seriously misleading under Section 9—506.

(c) If a debtor so changes its name that a filed financing statement becomes seriously misleading under Section 9—506:

(1) the financing statement is effective to perfect a security interest in collateral acquired by the debtor before, or within four months after, the change; and

(2) the financing statement is not effective to perfect a security interest in collateral acquired by the debtor more than four months after the change, unless an amendment to the financing statement which renders the financing statement not seriously misleading is filed within four months after the change.

§ 9—508. Effectiveness of Financing Statement If New Debtor Becomes Bound by Security Agreement.

(a) Except as otherwise provided in this section, a filed financing statement naming an original debtor is effective to perfect a security interest in collateral in which a new debtor has or acquires rights to the extent that the financing statement would have been effective had the original debtor acquired rights in the collateral.

(b) If the difference between the name of the original debtor and that of the new debtor causes a filed financing statement that is effective under subsection (a) to be seriously misleading under Section 9—506:

(1) the financing statement is effective to perfect a security interest in collateral acquired by the new debtor before, and within four months after, the new debtor becomes bound under Section 9B—203(d); and

(2) the financing statement is not effective to perfect a security interest in collateral acquired by the new debtor more than four months after the new debtor becomes bound under Section 9—203(d) unless an initial financing statement providing the name of the new debtor is filed before the expiration of that time.

(c) This section does not apply to collateral as to which a filed financing statement remains effective against the new debtor under Section 9—507(a).

§ 9—509. Persons Entitled to File a Record.

(a) A person may file an initial financing statement, amendment that adds collateral covered by a financing statement, or amendment that adds a debtor to a financing statement only if:

(1) the debtor authorizes the filing in an authenticated record or pursuant to subsection (b) or (c); or

(2) the person holds an agricultural lien that has become effective at the time of filing and the financing statement covers only collateral in which the person holds an agricultural lien.

(b) By authenticating or becoming bound as debtor by a security agreement, a debtor or new debtor authorizes the filing of an initial financing statement, and an amendment, covering:

(1) the collateral described in the security agreement; and

(2) property that becomes collateral under Section 9—315(a)(2), whether or not the security agreement expressly covers proceeds.

(c) By acquiring collateral in which a security interest or agricultural lien continues under Section 9—315(a)(1), a debtor authorizes the filing of an initial financing statement, and an amendment, covering the collateral and property that becomes collateral under Section 9—315(a)(2).

(d) A person may file an amendment other than an amendment that adds collateral covered by a financing statement or an amendment that adds a debtor to a financing statement only if:

(1) the secured party of record authorizes the filing; or

(2) the amendment is a termination statement for a financing statement as to which the secured party of record has failed to file or send a termination statement as required by Section 9—513(a) or (c), the debtor authorizes the filing, and the termination statement indicates that the debtor authorized it to be filed.

(e) If there is more than one secured party of record for a financing statement, each secured party of record may authorize the filing of an amendment under subsection (d).

§ 9—510. Effectiveness of Filed Record.

(a) A filed record is effective only to the extent that it was filed by a person that may file it under Section 9—509.

(b) A record authorized by one secured party of record does not affect the financing statement with respect to another secured party of record.

(c) A continuation statement that is not filed within the six-month period prescribed by Section 9—515(d) is ineffective.

§ 9—511. Secured Party of Record.

(a) A secured party of record with respect to a financing statement is a person whose name is provided as the name of the secured party or a representative of the secured party in an initial financing statement that has been filed. If an initial financing statement is filed under Section 9—514(a), the assignee named in the initial financing statement is the secured party of record with respect to the financing statement.

(b) If an amendment of a financing statement which provides the name of a person as a secured party or a representative of a secured party is filed, the person named in the amendment is a secured party of record. If an amendment is filed under Section 9—514(b), the assignee named in the amendment is a secured party of record.

(c) A person remains a secured party of record until the filing of an amendment of the financing statement which deletes the person.

§ 9—512. Amendment of Financing Statement.

[Alternative A]

(a) Subject to Section 9—509, a person may add or delete collateral covered by, continue or terminate the effectiveness of, or, subject to subsection (e), otherwise amend the information provided in, a financing statement by filing an amendment that:

(1) identifies, by its file number, the initial financing statement to which the amendment relates; and

(2) if the amendment relates to an initial financing statement filed [or recorded] in a filing office described in Section 9—501(a)(1), provides the information specified in Section 9—502(b).

[Alternative B]

(a) Subject to Section 9—509, a person may add or delete collateral covered by, continue or terminate the effectiveness of, or, subject to subsection (e), otherwise amend the information provided in, a financing statement by filing an amendment that:

(1) identifies, by its file number, the initial financing statement to which the amendment relates; and

(2) if the amendment relates to an initial financing statement filed [or recorded] in a filing office described in Section 9—501(a)(1), provides the date [and time]

that the initial financing statement was filed [or recorded] and the information specified in Section 9—502(b).

[End of Alternatives]

(b) Except as otherwise provided in Section 9—515, the filing of an amendment does not extend the period of effectiveness of the financing statement.

(c) A financing statement that is amended by an amendment that adds collateral is effective as to the added collateral only from the date of the filing of the amendment.

(d) A financing statement that is amended by an amendment that adds a debtor is effective as to the added debtor only from the date of the filing of the amendment.

(e) An amendment is ineffective to the extent it:

(1) purports to delete all debtors and fails to provide the name of a debtor to be covered by the financing statement; or

(2) purports to delete all secured parties of record and fails to provide the name of a new secured party of record.

Legislative Note: States whose real-estate filing offices require additional information in amendments and cannot search their records by both the name of the debtor and the file number should enact Alternative B to Sections 9—512(a), 9—518(b), 9—519(f), and 9—522(a).

§ 9—513. Termination Statement.

(a) A secured party shall cause the secured party of record for a financing statement to file a termination statement for the financing statement if the financing statement covers consumer goods and:

(1) there is no obligation secured by the collateral covered by the financing statement and no commitment to make an advance, incur an obligation, or otherwise give value; or

(2) the debtor did not authorize the filing of the initial financing statement.

(b) To comply with subsection (a), a secured party shall cause the secured party of record to file the termination statement:

(1) within one month after there is no obligation secured by the collateral covered by the financing statement and no commitment to make an advance, incur an obligation, or otherwise give value; or

(2) if earlier, within 20 days after the secured party receives an authenticated demand from a debtor.

(c) In cases not governed by subsection (a), within 20 days after a secured party receives an authenticated demand from a debtor, the secured party shall cause the secured party of record for a financing statement to send to the debtor a termination statement for the financing statement or file the termination statement in the filing office if:

(1) except in the case of a financing statement covering accounts or chattel paper that has been sold or goods that are the subject of a consignment, there is no obligation secured by the collateral covered by the financing statement and no commitment to make an advance, incur an obligation, or otherwise give value;

(2) the financing statement covers accounts or chattel paper that has been sold but as to which the account debtor or other person obligated has discharged its obligation;

(3) the financing statement covers goods that were the subject of a consignment to the debtor but are not in the debtor's possession; or

(4) the debtor did not authorize the filing of the initial financing statement.

(d) Except as otherwise provided in Section 9—510, upon the filing of a termination statement with the filing office, the financing statement to which the termination statement relates ceases to be effective. Except as otherwise provided in Section 9—510, for purposes of Sections 9—519(g), 9—522(a), and 9—523(c), the filing with the filing office of a termination statement relating to a financing statement that indicates that the debtor is a transmitting utility also causes the effectiveness of the financing statement to lapse.

§ 9—514. Assignment of Powers of Secured Party of Record.

(a) Except as otherwise provided in subsection (c), an initial financing statement may reflect an assignment of all of the secured party's power to authorize an amendment to the financing statement by providing the name and mailing address of the assignee as the name and address of the secured party.

(b) Except as otherwise provided in subsection (c), a secured party of record may assign of record all or part of its power to authorize an amendment to a financing statement by filing in the filing office an amendment of the financing statement which:

(1) identifies, by its file number, the initial financing statement to which it relates;

(2) provides the name of the assignor; and

(3) provides the name and mailing address of the assignee.

(c) An assignment of record of a security interest in a fixture covered by a record of a mortgage which is effective as a financing statement filed as a fixture filing under Section 9—502(c) may be made only by an assignment of record of the mortgage in the manner provided by law of this State other than [the Uniform Commercial Code].

§ 9—515. Duration and Effectiveness of Financing Statement; Effect of Lapsed Financing Statement.

(a) Except as otherwise provided in subsections (b), (e), (f), and (g), a filed financing statement is effective for a period of five years after the date of filing.

(b) Except as otherwise provided in subsections (e), (f), and (g), an initial financing statement filed in connection with a public-finance transaction or manufactured-home transaction is effective for a period of 30 years after the date of filing if it indicates that it is filed in connection with a public-finance transaction or manufactured-home transaction.

(c) The effectiveness of a filed financing statement lapses on the expiration of the period of its effectiveness unless before the lapse a continuation statement is filed pursuant to subsection (d). Upon lapse, a financing statement ceases to be effective and any security interest or agricultural lien that was perfected by the financing statement becomes unperfected, unless the security interest is perfected otherwise. If the security interest or agricultural lien becomes unperfected upon lapse, it is deemed never to have been perfected as against a purchaser of the collateral for value.

(d) A continuation statement may be filed only within six months before the expiration of the five-year period specified in subsection (a) or the 30-year period specified in subsection (b), whichever is applicable.

(e) Except as otherwise provided in Section 9—510, upon timely filing of a continuation statement, the effectiveness of the initial financing statement continues for a period of five years commencing on the day on which the financing statement would have become ineffective in the absence of the filing. Upon the expiration of the five-year period, the financing statement lapses in the same manner as provided in subsection (c), unless, before the lapse, another continuation statement is filed pursuant to subsection (d). Succeeding continuation statements may be filed in the same manner to continue the effectiveness of the initial financing statement.

(f) If a debtor is a transmitting utility and a filed financing statement so indicates, the financing statement is effective until a termination statement is filed.

(g) A record of a mortgage that is effective as a financing statement filed as a fixture filing under Section 9—502(c) remains effective as a financing statement filed as a fixture filing until the mortgage is released or satisfied of record or its effectiveness otherwise terminates as to the real property.

§ 9—516. What Constitutes Filing; Effectiveness of Filing.

(a) Except as otherwise provided in subsection (b), communication of a record to a filing office and tender of the filing fee or acceptance of the record by the filing office constitutes filing.

(b) Filing does not occur with respect to a record that a filing office refuses to accept because:

(1) the record is not communicated by a method or medium of communication authorized by the filing office;

(2) an amount equal to or greater than the applicable filing fee is not tendered;

(3) the filing office is unable to index the record because:

(A) in the case of an initial financing statement, the record does not provide a name for the debtor;

(B) in the case of an amendment or correction statement, the record:

(i) does not identify the initial financing statement as required by Section 9—512 or 9—518, as applicable; or

(ii) identifies an initial financing statement whose effectiveness has lapsed under Section 9—515;

(C) in the case of an initial financing statement that provides the name of a debtor identified as an individual or an amendment that provides a name of a debtor identified as an individual which was not previously provided in the financing statement to which the record relates, the record does not identify the debtor's last name; or

(D) in the case of a record filed [or recorded] in the filing office described in Section 9—501(a)(1), the record does not provide a sufficient description of the real property to which it relates;

(4) in the case of an initial financing statement or an amendment that adds a secured party of record, the record does not provide a name and mailing address for the secured party of record;

(5) in the case of an initial financing statement or an amendment that provides a name of a debtor which was not previously provided in the financing statement to which the amendment relates, the record does not:

(A) provide a mailing address for the debtor;

(B) indicate whether the debtor is an individual or an organization; or

(C) if the financing statement indicates that the debtor is an organization, provide:

(i) a type of organization for the debtor;

(ii) a jurisdiction of organization for the debtor; or

(iii) an organizational identification number for the debtor or indicate that the debtor has none;

(6) in the case of an assignment reflected in an initial financing statement under Section 9—514(a) or an amendment filed under Section 9—514(b), the record does not provide a name and mailing address for the assignee; or

(7) in the case of a continuation statement, the record is not filed within the six-month period prescribed by Section 9—515(d).

(c) For purposes of subsection (b):

(1) a record does not provide information if the filing office is unable to read or decipher the information; and

(2) a record that does not indicate that it is an amendment or identify an initial financing statement to which it relates, as required by Section 9—512, 9—514, or 9—518, is an initial financing statement.

(d) A record that is communicated to the filing office with tender of the filing fee, but which the filing office refuses to accept for a reason other than one set forth in subsection (b), is effective as a filed record except as against a purchaser of the collateral which gives value in reasonable reliance upon the absence of the record from the files.

§ 9—517. Effect of Indexing Errors.

The failure of the filing office to index a record correctly does not affect the effectiveness of the filed record.

§ 9—518. Claim Concerning Inaccurate or Wrongfully Filed Record.

(a) A person may file in the filing office a correction statement with respect to a record indexed there under the person's name if the person believes that the record is inaccurate or was wrongfully filed.

[Alternative A]

(b) A correction statement must:

(1) identify the record to which it relates by the file number assigned to the initial financing statement to which the record relates;

(2) indicate that it is a correction statement; and

(3) provide the basis for the person's belief that the record is inaccurate and indicate the manner in which the person believes the record should be amended to cure any inaccuracy or provide the basis for the person's belief that the record was wrongfully filed.

[Alternative B]

(b) A correction statement must:

(1) identify the record to which it relates by:

(A) the file number assigned to the initial financing statement to which the record relates; and

(B) if the correction statement relates to a record filed [or recorded] in a filing office described in Section 9—501(a)(1), the date [and time] that the initial financing statement was filed [or recorded] and the information specified in Section 9—502(b);

(2) indicate that it is a correction statement; and

(3) provide the basis for the person's belief that the record is inaccurate and indicate the manner in which the person believes the record should be amended to cure any inaccuracy or provide the basis for the person's belief that the record was wrongfully filed.

[End of Alternatives]

(c) The filing of a correction statement does not affect the effectiveness of an initial financing statement or other filed record.

Legislative Note: States whose real-estate filing offices require additional information in amendments and cannot search their records by both the name of the debtor and the file number should enact Alternative B to Sections 9–512(a), 9—518(b), 9—519(f), and 9—522(a).

[Subpart 2. Duties and Operation of Filing Office]

§ 9—519. Numbering, Maintaining, and Indexing Records; Communicating Information Provided in Records.

(a) For each record filed in a filing office, the filing office shall:

(1) assign a unique number to the filed record;

(2) create a record that bears the number assigned to the filed record and the date and time of filing;

(3) maintain the filed record for public inspection; and

(4) index the filed record in accordance with subsections (c), (d), and (e).

(b) A file number [assigned after January 1, 2002,] must include a digit that:

(1) is mathematically derived from or related to the other digits of the file number; and

(2) aids the filing office in determining whether a number communicated as the file number includes a single-digit or transpositional error.

(c) Except as otherwise provided in subsections (d) and (e), the filing office shall:

(1) index an initial financing statement according to the name of the debtor and index all filed records relating to the initial financing statement in a manner that associates with one another an initial financing statement and all filed records relating to the initial financing statement; and

(2) index a record that provides a name of a debtor which was not previously provided in the financing statement to which the record relates also according to the name that was not previously provided.

(d) If a financing statement is filed as a fixture filing or covers as-extracted collateral or timber to be cut, [it must be filed for record and] the filing office shall index it:

(1) under the names of the debtor and of each owner of record shown on the financing statement as if they were the mortgagors under a mortgage of the real property described; and

(2) to the extent that the law of this State provides for indexing of records of mortgages under the name of the mortgagee, under the name of the secured party as if the secured party were the mortgagee thereunder, or, if indexing is by description, as if the financing statement were a record of a mortgage of the real property described.

(e) If a financing statement is filed as a fixture filing or covers as-extracted collateral or timber to be cut, the filing office shall index an assignment filed under Section 9—514(a) or an amendment filed under Section 9—514(b):

(1) under the name of the assignor as grantor; and

(2) to the extent that the law of this State provides for indexing a record of the assignment of a mortgage under the name of the assignee, under the name of the assignee.

[Alternative A]

(f) The filing office shall maintain a capability:

(1) to retrieve a record by the name of the debtor and by the file number assigned to the initial financing statement to which the record relates; and

(2) to associate and retrieve with one another an initial financing statement and each filed record relating to the initial financing statement.

[Alternative B]

(f) The filing office shall maintain a capability:

(1) to retrieve a record by the name of the debtor and:

(A) if the filing office is described in Section 9—501(a)(1), by the file number assigned to the initial financing statement to which the record relates and the date [and time] that the record was filed [or recorded]; or

(B) if the filing office is described in Section 9—501(a)(2), by the file number assigned to the initial financing statement to which the record relates; and

(2) to associate and retrieve with one another an initial financing statement and each filed record relating to the initial financing statement.

[End of Alternatives]

(g) The filing office may not remove a debtor's name from the index until one year after the effectiveness of a financing statement naming the debtor lapses under Section 9—515 with respect to all secured parties of record.

(h) The filing office shall perform the acts required by subsections (a) through (e) at the time and in the manner prescribed by filing-office rule, but not later than two business days after the filing office receives the record in question.

[(i) Subsection[s] [(b)] [and] [(h)] do[es] not apply to a filing office described in Section 9—501(a)(1).]

Legislative Notes:

1. States whose filing offices currently assign file numbers that include a verification number, commonly known as a "check digit," or can implement this requirement before the effective date of this Article should omit the bracketed language in subsection (b).

2. In States in which writings will not appear in the real property records and indices unless actually recorded the bracketed language in subsection (d) should be used.

3. States whose real-estate filing offices require additional information in amendments and cannot search their records by both the name of the debtor and the file number should enact Alternative B to Sections 9—512(a), 9—518(b), 9—519(f), and 9—522(a).

4. A State that elects not to require real-estate filing offices to comply with either or both of subsections (b) and (h) may adopt an applicable variation of subsection (i) and add "Except as otherwise provided in subsection (i)," to the appropriate subsection or subsections.

§ 9—520. Acceptance and Refusal to Accept Record.

(a) filing office shall refuse to accept a record for filing for a reason set forth in Section 9—516(b) and may refuse to accept a record for filing only for a reason set forth in Section 9—516(b).

(b) If a filing office refuses to accept a record for filing, it shall communicate to the person that presented the record the fact of and reason for the refusal and the date and time the record would have been filed had the filing office accepted it. The communication must be made at the time and in the manner prescribed by filing-office rule but [, in the case of a filing office described in Section 9—501(a)(2),] in no event more than two business days after the filing office receives the record.

(c) A filed financing statement satisfying Section 9–502(a) and (b) is effective, even if the filing office is required to refuse to accept it for filing under subsection (a). However, Section 9—338 applies to a filed financing statement providing information described in Section 9—516(b)(5) which is incorrect at the time the financing statement is filed.

(d) If a record communicated to a filing office provides information that relates to more than one debtor, this part applies as to each debtor separately.

Legislative Note: A State that elects not to require real-property filing offices to comply with subsection (b) should include the bracketed language.

§ 9—521. Uniform Form of Written Financing Statement and Amendment.

(a) A filing office that accepts written records may not refuse to accept a written initial financing statement in the following form and format except for a reason set forth in Section 9—516(b):

[NATIONAL UCC FINANCING STATEMENT (FORM UCC)(REV. 7/29/98)]

[NATIONAL UCC FINANCING STATEMENT ADDENDUM (FORM UCC 1Ad)(REV. 07/29/98)]

(b) A filing office that accepts written records may not refuse to accept a written record in the following form and format except for a reason set forth in Section 9—516(b):

[NATIONAL UCC FINANCING STATEMENT AMENDMENT (FORM UCC)(REV. 07/29/98)]

[NATIONAL UCC FINANCING STATEMENT AMENDMENT ADDENDUM (FORM UCC3Ad)(REV. 07/29/98)]

§ 9—522. Maintenance and Destruction of Records.

[Alternative A]

(a) The filing office shall maintain a record of the information provided in a filed financing statement for at least one year after the effectiveness of the financing statement has lapsed under Section 9—515 with respect to all secured parties of record. The record must be retrievable by using the name of the debtor and by using the file number assigned to the initial financing statement to which the record relates.

[Alternative B]

(a) The filing office shall maintain a record of the information provided in a filed financing statement for at least one year after the effectiveness of the financing statement has lapsed under Section 9—515 with respect to all secured parties of record. The record must be retrievable by using the name of the debtor and:

(1) if the record was filed [or recorded] in the filing office described in Section 9—501(a)(1), by using the file number assigned to the initial financing statement to which the record relates and the date [and time] that the record was filed [or recorded]; or

(2) if the record was filed in the filing office described in Section 9—501(a)(2), by using the file number assigned to the initial financing statement to which the record relates.

[End of Alternatives]

(b) Except to the extent that a statute governing disposition of public records provides otherwise, the filing office immediately may destroy any written record evidencing a financing statement. However, if the filing office destroys a written record, it shall maintain another record of the financing statement which complies with subsection (a).

Legislative Note: States whose real-estate filing offices require additional information in amendments and cannot search their records by both the name of the debtor and the file number should enact Alternative B to Sections 9—512(a), 9—518(b), 9—519(f), and 9—522(a).

§ 9—523. Information from Filing Office; Sale or License of Records.

(a) If a person that files a written record requests an acknowledgment of the filing, the filing office shall send to the person an image of the record showing the number assigned to the record pursuant to Section 9—519(a)(1) and the date and time of the filing of the record. However, if the person furnishes a copy of the record to the filing office, the filing office may instead:

(1) note upon the copy the number assigned to the record pursuant to Section 9—519(a)(1) and the date and time of the filing of the record; and

(2) send the copy to the person.

(b) If a person files a record other than a written record, the filing office shall communicate to the person an acknowledgment that provides:

(1) the information in the record;

(2) the number assigned to the record pursuant to Section 9—519(a)(1); and

(3) the date and time of the filing of the record.

(c) The filing office shall communicate or otherwise make available in a record the following information to any person that requests it:

(1) whether there is on file on a date and time specified by the filing office, but not a date earlier than three business days before the filing office receives the request, any financing statement that:

(A) designates a particular debtor [or, if the request so states, designates a particular debtor at the address specified in the request];

(B) has not lapsed under Section 9—515 with respect to all secured parties of record; and

(C) if the request so states, has lapsed under Section 9—515 and a record of which is maintained by the filing office under Section 9—522(a);

(2) the date and time of filing of each financing statement; and

(3) the information provided in each financing statement.

(d) In complying with its duty under subsection (c), the filing office may communicate information in any medium. However, if requested, the filing office shall communicate information by issuing [its written certificate] [a record that can be admitted into evidence in the courts of this State without extrinsic evidence of its authenticity].

(e) The filing office shall perform the acts required by subsections (a) through (d) at the time and in the manner prescribed by filing-office rule, but not later than two business days after the filing office receives the request.

(f) At least weekly, the [insert appropriate official or governmental agency] [filing office] shall offer to sell or license to the public on a nonexclusive basis, in bulk, copies of all records filed in it under this part, in every medium from time to time available to the filing office.

Legislative Notes:

1. *States whose filing office does not offer the additional service of responding to search requests limited to a particular address should omit the bracketed language in subsection (c)(1)(A).*

2. *A State that elects not to require real-estate filing offices to comply with either or both of subsections (e) and (f) should specify in the appropriate subsection(s) only the filing office described in Section 9—501(a)(2).*

§ 9—524. **Delay by Filing Office.**

Delay by the filing office beyond a time limit prescribed by this part is excused if:

(1) the delay is caused by interruption of communication or computer facilities, war, emergency conditions, failure of equipment, or other circumstances beyond control of the filing office; and

(2) the filing office exercises reasonable diligence under the circumstances.

§ 9—525. **Fees.**

(a) Except as otherwise provided in subsection (e), the fee for filing and indexing a record under this part, other than an initial financing statement of the kind described in subsection (b), is [the amount specified in subsection (c), if applicable, plus]:

(1) $[X] if the record is communicated in writing and consists of one or two pages;

(2) $[2X] if the record is communicated in writing and consists of more than two pages; and

(3) $[½X] if the record is communicated by another medium authorized by filing-office rule.

(b) Except as otherwise provided in subsection (e), the fee for filing and indexing an initial financing statement of the following kind is [the amount specified in subsection (c), if applicable, plus]:

(1) $_______ if the financing statement indicates that it is filed in connection with a public-finance transaction;

(2) $_______ if the financing statement indicates that it is filed in connection with a manufactured-home transaction.

[Alternative A]

(c) The number of names required to be indexed does not affect the amount of the fee in subsections (a) and (b).

[Alternative B]

(c) Except as otherwise provided in subsection (e), if a record is communicated in writing, the fee for each name more than two required to be indexed is $_______.

[End of Alternatives]

(d) The fee for responding to a request for information from the filing office, including for [issuing a certificate showing] [communicating] whether there is on file any financing statement naming a particular debtor, is:

(1) $_______ if the request is communicated in writing; and

(2) $_______ if the request is communicated by another medium authorized by filing-office rule.

(e) This section does not require a fee with respect to a record of a mortgage which is effective as a financing statement filed as a fixture filing or as a financing statement covering as-extracted collateral or timber to be cut under Section 9—502(c). However, the recording and satisfaction fees that otherwise would be applicable to the record of the mortgage apply.

Legislative Notes:

1. *To preserve uniformity, a State that places the provisions of this section together with statutes setting fees for other services should do so without modification.*

2. *A State should enact subsection (c), Alternative A, and omit the bracketed language in subsections (a) and (b) unless its indexing system entails a substantial additional cost when indexing additional names.*

§ 9—526. **Filing-Office Rules.**

(a) The [insert appropriate governmental official or agency] shall adopt and publish rules to implement this article. The filing-office rules must be:

(1)] consistent with this article[; and

(2) adopted and published in accordance with the [insert any applicable state administrative procedure act]].

(b) To keep the filing-office rules and practices of the filing office in harmony with the rules and practices of filing offices in other jurisdictions that enact substantially this part, and to keep the technology used by the filing office compatible with the technology used by filing offices in other jurisdictions that enact substantially this part, the [insert appropriate governmental official or agency], so far as is consistent with the purposes, policies, and provisions of this article, in adopting, amending, and repealing filing-office rules, shall:

(1) consult with filing offices in other jurisdictions that enact substantially this part; and

(2) consult the most recent version of the Model Rules promulgated by the International Association of Corporate Administrators or any successor organization; and

(3) take into consideration the rules and practices of, and the technology used by, filing offices in other jurisdictions that enact substantially this part.

§ 9—527. Duty to Report.

The [insert appropriate governmental official or agency] shall report [annually on or before ________] to the [Governor and Legislature] on the operation of the filing office. The report must contain a statement of the extent to which:

(1) the filing-office rules are not in harmony with the rules of filing offices in other jurisdictions that enact substantially this part and the reasons for these variations; and

(2) the filing-office rules are not in harmony with the most recent version of the Model Rules promulgated by the International Association of Corporate Administrators, or any successor organization, and the reasons for these variations.

Part 6 Default

[Subpart 1. Default and Enforcement of Security Interest]

§ 9—601. Rights after Default; Judicial Enforcement; Consignor or Buyer of Accounts, Chattel Paper, Payment Intangibles, or Promissory Notes.

(a) After default, a secured party has the rights provided in this part and, except as otherwise provided in Section 9—602, those provided by agreement of the parties. A secured party:

(1) may reduce a claim to judgment, foreclose, or otherwise enforce the claim, security interest, or agricultural lien by any available judicial procedure; and

(2) if the collateral is documents, may proceed either as to the documents or as to the goods they cover.

(b) A secured party in possession of collateral or control of collateral under Section 9—104, 9—105, 9—106, or 9—107 has the rights and duties provided in Section 9—207.

(c) The rights under subsections (a) and (b) are cumulative and may be exercised simultaneously.

(d) Except as otherwise provided in subsection (g) and Section 9—605, after default, a debtor and an obligor have the rights provided in this part and by agreement of the parties.

(e) If a secured party has reduced its claim to judgment, the lien of any levy that may be made upon the collateral by virtue of an execution based upon the judgment relates back to the earliest of:

(1) the date of perfection of the security interest or agricultural lien in the collateral;

(2) the date of filing a financing statement covering the collateral; or

(3) any date specified in a statute under which the agricultural lien was created.

(f) A sale pursuant to an execution is a foreclosure of the security interest or agricultural lien by judicial procedure within the meaning of this section. A secured party may purchase at the sale and thereafter hold the collateral free of any other requirements of this article.

(g) Except as otherwise provided in Section 9—607(c), this part imposes no duties upon a secured party that is a consignor or is a buyer of accounts, chattel paper, payment intangibles, or promissory notes.

§ 9-602. Waiver and Variance of Rights and Duties.

Except as otherwise provided in Section 9—624, to the extent that they give rights to a debtor or obligor and impose duties on a secured party, the debtor or obligor may not waive or vary the rules stated in the following listed sections:

(1) Section 9—207(b)(4)(C), which deals with use and operation of the collateral by the secured party;

(2) Section 9—210, which deals with requests for an accounting and requests concerning a list of collateral and statement of account;

(3) Section 9—607(c), which deals with collection and enforcement of collateral;

(4) Sections 9—608(a) and 9—615(c) to the extent that they deal with application or payment of noncash proceeds of collection, enforcement, or disposition;

(5) Sections 9—608(a) and 9—615(d) to the extent that they require accounting for or payment of surplus proceeds of collateral;

(6) Section 9-609 to the extent that it imposes upon a secured party that takes possession of collateral without judicial process the duty to do so without breach of the peace;

(7) Sections 9—610(b), 9—611, 9—613, and 9—614, which deal with disposition of collateral;

(8) Section 9—615(f), which deals with calculation of a deficiency or surplus when a disposition is made to the secured party, a person related to the secured party, or a secondary obligor;

(9) Section 9—616, which deals with explanation of the calculation of a surplus or deficiency;

(10) Sections 9—620, 9—621, and 9—622, which deal with acceptance of collateral in satisfaction of obligation;

(11) Section 9—623, which deals with redemption of collateral;

(12) Section 9—624, which deals with permissible waivers; and

(13) Sections 9—625 and 9—626, which deal with the secured party's liability for failure to comply with this article.

§ 9—603. Agreement on Standards Concerning Rights and Duties.

(a) The parties may determine by agreement the standards measuring the fulfillment of the rights of a debtor or obligor and the duties of a secured party under a rule stated in Section 9—602 if the standards are not manifestly unreasonable.

(b) Subsection (a) does not apply to the duty under Section 9—609 to refrain from breaching the peace.

§ 9—604. Procedure If Security Agreement Covers Real Property or Fixtures.

(a) If a security agreement covers both personal and real property, a secured party may proceed:

(1) under this part as to the personal property without prejudicing any rights with respect to the real property; or

(2) as to both the personal property and the real property in accordance with the rights with respect to the real property, in which case the other provisions of this part do not apply.

(b) Subject to subsection (c), if a security agreement covers goods that are or become fixtures, a secured party may proceed:

(1) under this part; or

(2) in accordance with the rights with respect to real property, in which case the other provisions of this part do not apply.

(c) Subject to the other provisions of this part, if a secured party holding a security interest in fixtures has priority over all owners and encumbrancers of the real property, the secured party, after default, may remove the collateral from the real property.

(d) A secured party that removes collateral shall promptly reimburse any encumbrancer or owner of the real property, other than the debtor, for the cost of repair of any physical injury caused by the removal. The secured party need not reimburse the encumbrancer or owner for any diminution in value of the real property caused by the absence of the goods removed or by any necessity of replacing them. A person entitled to reimbursement may refuse permission to remove until the secured party gives adequate assurance for the performance of the obligation to reimburse.

§ 9—605. Unknown Debtor or Secondary Obligor.

A secured party does not owe a duty based on its status as secured party:

(1) to a person that is a debtor or obligor, unless the secured party knows:

(A) that the person is a debtor or obligor;

(B) the identity of the person; and

(C) how to communicate with the person; or

(2) to a secured party or lienholder that has filed a financing statement against a person, unless the secured party knows:

(A) that the person is a debtor; and

(B) the identity of the person.

§ 9—606. Time of Default for Agricultural Lien.

For purposes of this part, a default occurs in connection with an agricultural lien at the time the secured party becomes entitled to enforce the lien in accordance with the statute under which it was created.

§ 9—607. Collection and Enforcement by Secured Party.

(a) If so agreed, and in any event after default, a secured party:

(1) may notify an account debtor or other person obligated on collateral to make payment or otherwise render performance to or for the benefit of the secured party;

(2) may take any proceeds to which the secured party is entitled under Section 9—315;

(3) may enforce the obligations of an account debtor or other person obligated on collateral and exercise the rights of the debtor with respect to the obligation of the account debtor or other person obligated on collateral to make payment or otherwise render performance to the debtor, and with respect to any property that secures the obligations of the account debtor or other person obligated on the collateral;

(4) if it holds a security interest in a deposit account perfected by control under Section 9—104(a)(1), may apply the balance of the deposit account to the obligation secured by the deposit account; and

(5) if it holds a security interest in a deposit account perfected by control under Section 9—104(a)(2) or (3), may instruct the bank to pay the balance of the deposit account to or for the benefit of the secured party.

(b) If necessary to enable a secured party to exercise under subsection (a)(3) the right of a debtor to enforce a mortgage nonjudicially, the secured party may record in the office in which a record of the mortgage is recorded:

(1) a copy of the security agreement that creates or provides for a security interest in the obligation secured by the mortgage; and

(2) the secured party's sworn affidavit in recordable form stating that:

(A) a default has occurred; and

(B) the secured party is entitled to enforce the mortgage nonjudicially.

(c) A secured party shall proceed in a commercially reasonable manner if the secured party:

(1) undertakes to collect from or enforce an obligation of an account debtor or other person obligated on collateral; and

(2) is entitled to charge back uncollected collateral or otherwise to full or limited recourse against the debtor or a secondary obligor.

(d) A secured party may deduct from the collections made pursuant to subsection (c) reasonable expenses of collection and enforcement, including reasonable attorney's fees and legal expenses incurred by the secured party.

(e) This section does not determine whether an account debtor, bank, or other person obligated on collateral owes a duty to a secured party.

§ 9—608. Application of Proceeds of Collection or Enforcement; Liability for Deficiency and Right to Surplus.

(a) If a security interest or agricultural lien secures payment or performance of an obligation, the following rules apply:

(1) A secured party shall apply or pay over for application the cash proceeds of collection or enforcement under Section 9—607 in the following order to:

(A) the reasonable expenses of collection and enforcement and, to the extent provided for by agreement and not prohibited by law, reasonable attorney's fees and legal expenses incurred by the secured party;

(B) the satisfaction of obligations secured by the security interest or agricultural lien under which the collection or enforcement is made; and

(C) the satisfaction of obligations secured by any subordinate security interest in or other lien on the collateral subject to the security interest or agricultural lien under which the collection or enforcement is made if the secured party receives an authenticated demand for proceeds before distribution of the proceeds is completed.

(2) If requested by a secured party, a holder of a subordinate security interest or other lien shall furnish reasonable proof of the interest or lien within a reasonable time. Unless the holder complies, the secured party need not comply with the holder's demand under paragraph (1)(C).

(3) A secured party need not apply or pay over for application noncash proceeds of collection and enforcement under Section 9—607 unless the failure to do so would be commercially unreasonable. A secured party that applies or pays over for application noncash proceeds shall do so in a commercially reasonable manner.

(4) A secured party shall account to and pay a debtor for any surplus, and the obligor is liable for any deficiency.

(b) If the underlying transaction is a sale of accounts, chattel paper, payment intangibles, or promissory notes, the debtor is not entitled to any surplus, and the obligor is not liable for any deficiency.

§ 9—609. Secured Party's Right to Take Possession after Default.

(a) After default, a secured party:

(1) may take possession of the collateral; and

(2) without removal, may render equipment unusable and dispose of collateral on a debtor's premises under Section 9—610.

(b) A secured party may proceed under subsection (a):

(1) pursuant to judicial process; or

(2) without judicial process, if it proceeds without breach of the peace.

(c) If so agreed, and in any event after default, a secured party may require the debtor to assemble the collateral and make it available to the secured party at a place to be designated by the secured party which is reasonably convenient to both parties.

§ 9—610. Disposition of Collateral after Default.

(a) After default, a secured party may sell, lease, license, or otherwise dispose of any or all of the collateral in its present condition or following any commercially reasonable preparation or processing.

(b) Every aspect of a disposition of collateral, including the method, manner, time, place, and other terms, must be commercially reasonable. If commercially reasonable, a secured party may dispose of collateral by public or private proceedings, by one or more contracts, as a unit or in parcels, and at any time and place and on any terms.

(c) A secured party may purchase collateral:

(1) at a public disposition; or

(2) at a private disposition only if the collateral is of a kind that is customarily sold on a recognized market or the subject of widely distributed standard price quotations.

(d) A contract for sale, lease, license, or other disposition includes the warranties relating to title, possession, quiet enjoyment, and the like which by operation of law accompany a voluntary disposition of property of the kind subject to the contract.

(e) A secured party may disclaim or modify warranties under subsection (d):

(1) in a manner that would be effective to disclaim or modify the warranties in a voluntary disposition of property of the kind subject to the contract of disposition; or

(2) by communicating to the purchaser a record evidencing the contract for disposition and including an express disclaimer or modification of the warranties.

(f) A record is sufficient to disclaim warranties under subsection (e) if it indicates "There is no warranty relating to title, possession, quiet enjoyment, or the like in this disposition" or uses words of similar import.

§ 9—611. Notification before Disposition of Collateral.

(a) In this section, "notification date" means the earlier of the date on which:

(1) a secured party sends to the debtor and any secondary obligor an authenticated notification of disposition; or

(2) the debtor and any secondary obligor waive the right to notification.

(b) Except as otherwise provided in subsection (d), a secured party that disposes of collateral under Section 9—610 shall send to the persons specified in subsection (c) a reasonable authenticated notification of disposition.

(c) To comply with subsection (b), the secured party shall send an authenticated notification of disposition to:

(1) the debtor;

(2) any secondary obligor; and

(3) if the collateral is other than consumer goods:

(A) any other person from which the secured party has received, before the notification date, an authenticated notification of a claim of an interest in the collateral;

(B) any other secured party or lienholder that, 10 days before the notification date, held a security interest in or other lien on the collateral perfected by the filing of a financing statement that:

(i) identified the collateral;

(ii) was indexed under the debtor's name as of that date; and

(iii) was filed in the office in which to file a financing statement against the debtor covering the collateral as of that date; and

(C) any other secured party that, 10 days before the notification date, held a security interest in the collateral perfected by compliance with a statute, regulation, or treaty described in Section 9—311(a).

(d) Subsection (b) does not apply if the collateral is perishable or threatens to decline speedily in value or is of a type customarily sold on a recognized market.

(e) A secured party complies with the requirement for notification prescribed by subsection (c)(3)(B) if:

(1) not later than 20 days or earlier than 30 days before the notification date, the secured party requests, in a commercially reasonable manner, information concerning financing statements indexed under the debtor's name in the office indicated in subsection (c)(3)(B); and

(2) before the notification date, the secured party:

(A) did not receive a response to the request for information; or

(B) received a response to the request for information and sent an authenticated notification of disposition to each secured party or other lienholder named in that response whose financing statement covered the collateral.

§ 9—612. Timeliness of Notification before Disposition of Collateral.

(a) Except as otherwise provided in subsection (b), whether a notification is sent within a reasonable time is a question of fact.

(b) In a transaction other than a consumer transaction, a notification of disposition sent after default and 10 days or more before the earliest time of disposition set forth in the notification is sent within a reasonable time before the disposition.

§ 9—613. Contents and Form of Notification before Disposition of Collateral: General.

Except in a consumer-goods transaction, the following rules apply:

(1) The contents of a notification of disposition are sufficient if the notification:

(A) describes the debtor and the secured party;

(B) describes the collateral that is the subject of the intended disposition;

(C) states the method of intended disposition;

(D) states that the debtor is entitled to an accounting of the unpaid indebtedness and states the charge, if any, for an accounting; and

(E) states the time and place of a public disposition or the time after which any other disposition is to be made.

(2) Whether the contents of a notification that lacks any of the information specified in paragraph (1) are nevertheless sufficient is a question of fact.

(3) The contents of a notification providing substantially the information specified in paragraph (1) are sufficient, even if the notification includes:

(A) information not specified by that paragraph; or

(B) minor errors that are not seriously misleading.

(4) A particular phrasing of the notification is not required.

(5) The following form of notification and the form appearing in Section 9—614(3), when completed, each provides sufficient information:

NOTIFICATION OF DISPOSITION OF COLLATERAL

To: [Name of debtor, obligor, or other person to which the notification is sent]

From: [Name, address, and telephone number of secured party]

Name of Debtor(s): [Include only if debtor(s) are not an addressee]

[For a public disposition:]

We will sell [or lease or license, as applicable] the [describe collateral] [to the highest qualified bidder] in public as follows:

Day and Date: _______

Time: _______

Place: _______

[For a private disposition:]

We will sell [or lease or license, as applicable] the [describe collateral] privately sometime after [day and date].

You are entitled to an accounting of the unpaid indebtedness secured by the property that we intend to sell [or lease or license, as applicable] [for a charge of $_______]. You may request an accounting by calling us at [telephone number].

[End of Form]

§ 9—614. Contents and Form of Notification before Disposition of Collateral: Consumer-Goods Transaction.

In a consumer-goods transaction, the following rules apply:

(1) A notification of disposition must provide the following information:

(A) the information specified in Section 9—613(1);

(B) a description of any liability for a deficiency of the person to which the notification is sent;

(C) a telephone number from which the amount that must be paid to the secured party to redeem the collateral under Section 9—623 is available; and

(D) a telephone number or mailing address from which additional information concerning the disposition and the obligation secured is available.

(2) A particular phrasing of the notification is not required.

(3) The following form of notification, when completed, provides sufficient information:

[Name and address of secured party]

[Date]

NOTICE OF OUR PLAN TO SELL PROPERTY

[Name and address of any obligor who is also a debtor]

Subject: [Identification of Transaction]

We have your [describe collateral], because you broke promises in our agreement.

[For a public disposition:]

We will sell [describe collateral] at public sale. A sale could include a lease or license. The sale will be held as follows:

Date: _______

Time: _______

Place: _______

You may attend the sale and bring bidders if you want.

[For a private disposition:]

We will sell [describe collateral] at private sale sometime after [date]. A sale could include a lease or license.

The money that we get from the sale (after paying our costs) will reduce the amount you owe. If we get less money than you owe, you [will or will not, as applicable] still owe us the difference. If we get more money than you owe, you will get the extra money, unless we must pay it to someone else.

You can get the property back at any time before we sell it by paying us the full amount you owe (not just the past due payments), including our expenses. To learn the exact amount you must pay, call us at [telephone number].

If you want us to explain to you in writing how we have figured the amount that you owe us, you may call us at [telephone number] [or write us at [secured party's address]] and request a written explanation. [We will charge you $_______ for the explanation if we sent you another written explanation of the amount you owe us within the last six months.]

If you need more information about the sale call us at [telephone number] [or write us at [secured party's address]].

We are sending this notice to the following other people who have an interest in [describe collateral] or who owe money under your agreement:

[Names of all other debtors and obligors, if any]

[End of Form]

(4) A notification in the form of paragraph (3) is sufficient, even if additional information appears at the end of the form.

(5) A notification in the form of paragraph (3) is sufficient, even if it includes errors in information not required by paragraph (1), unless the error is misleading with respect to rights arising under this article.

(6) If a notification under this section is not in the form of paragraph (3), law other than this article determines the effect of including information not required by paragraph (1).

§ 9—615. Application of Proceeds of Disposition; Liability for Deficiency and Right to Surplus.

(a) A secured party shall apply or pay over for application the cash proceeds of disposition under Section 9—610 in the following order to:

(1) the reasonable expenses of retaking, holding, preparing for disposition, processing, and disposing, and, to the extent provided for by agreement and not prohibited by law, reasonable attorney's fees and legal expenses incurred by the secured party;

(2) the satisfaction of obligations secured by the security interest or agricultural lien under which the disposition is made;

(3) the satisfaction of obligations secured by any subordinate security interest in or other subordinate lien on the collateral if:

(A) the secured party receives from the holder of the subordinate security interest or other lien an authenticated demand for proceeds before distribution of the proceeds is completed; and

(B) in a case in which a consignor has an interest in the collateral, the subordinate security interest or other lien is senior to the interest of the consignor; and

(4) a secured party that is a consignor of the collateral if the secured party receives from the consignor an authenticated demand for proceeds before distribution of the proceeds is completed.

(b) If requested by a secured party, a holder of a subordinate security interest or other lien shall furnish reasonable proof of the interest or lien within a reasonable time. Unless the holder does so, the secured party need not comply with the holder's demand under subsection (a)(3).

(c) A secured party need not apply or pay over for application noncash proceeds of disposition under Section 9—610 unless the failure to do so would be commercially unreasonable. A secured party that applies or pays over for application noncash proceeds shall do so in a commercially reasonable manner.

(d) If the security interest under which a disposition is made secures payment or performance of an obligation, after making the payments and applications required by subsection (a) and permitted by subsection (c):

(1) unless subsection (a)(4) requires the secured party to apply or pay over cash proceeds to a consignor, the secured party shall account to and pay a debtor for any surplus; and

(2) the obligor is liable for any deficiency.

(e) If the underlying transaction is a sale of accounts, chattel paper, payment intangibles, or promissory notes:

(1) the debtor is not entitled to any surplus; and

(2) the obligor is not liable for any deficiency.

(f) The surplus or deficiency following a disposition is calculated based on the amount of proceeds that would have been realized in a disposition complying with this part to a transferee other than the secured party, a person related to the secured party, or a secondary obligor if:

(1) the transferee in the disposition is the secured party, a person related to the secured party, or a secondary obligor; and

(2) the amount of proceeds of the disposition is significantly below the range of proceeds that a complying disposition to a person other than the secured party, a person related to the secured party, or a secondary obligor would have brought.

(g) A secured party that receives cash proceeds of a disposition in good faith and without knowledge that the receipt violates the rights of the holder of a security interest or other lien that is not subordinate to the security interest or agricultural lien under which the disposition is made:

(1) takes the cash proceeds free of the security interest or other lien;

(2) is not obligated to apply the proceeds of the disposition to the satisfaction of obligations secured by the security interest or other lien; and

(3) is not obligated to account to or pay the holder of the security interest or other lien for any surplus.

§ 9—616. Explanation of Calculation of Surplus or Deficiency.

(a) In this section:

(1) "Explanation" means a writing that:

(A) states the amount of the surplus or deficiency;

(B) provides an explanation in accordance with subsection (c) of how the secured party calculated the surplus or deficiency;

(C) states, if applicable, that future debits, credits, charges, including additional credit service charges or interest, rebates, and expenses may affect the amount of the surplus or deficiency; and

(D) provides a telephone number or mailing address from which additional information concerning the transaction is available.

(2) "Request" means a record:

(A) authenticated by a debtor or consumer obligor;

(B) requesting that the recipient provide an explanation; and

(C) sent after disposition of the collateral under Section 9—610.

(b) In a consumer-goods transaction in which the debtor is entitled to a surplus or a consumer obligor is liable for a deficiency under Section 9—615, the secured party shall:

(1) send an explanation to the debtor or consumer obligor, as applicable, after the disposition and:

(A) before or when the secured party accounts to the debtor and pays any surplus or first makes written demand on the consumer obligor after the disposition for payment of the deficiency; and

(B) within 14 days after receipt of a request; or

(2) in the case of a consumer obligor who is liable for a deficiency, within 14 days after receipt of a request, send to the consumer obligor a record waiving the secured party's right to a deficiency.

(c) To comply with subsection (a)(1)(B), a writing must provide the following information in the following order:

(1) the aggregate amount of obligations secured by the security interest under which the disposition was made, and, if the amount reflects a rebate of unearned interest or credit service charge, an indication of that fact, calculated as of a specified date:

(A) if the secured party takes or receives possession of the collateral after default, not more than 35 days before the secured party takes or receives possession; or

(B) if the secured party takes or receives possession of the collateral before default or does not take possession of the collateral, not more than 35 days before the disposition;

(2) the amount of proceeds of the disposition;

(3) the aggregate amount of the obligations after deducting the amount of proceeds;

(4) the amount, in the aggregate or by type, and types of expenses, including expenses of retaking, holding, preparing for disposition, processing, and disposing of the collateral, and attorney's fees secured by the collateral which are known to the secured party and relate to the current disposition;

(5) the amount, in the aggregate or by type, and types of credits, including rebates of interest or credit service charges, to which the obligor is known to be entitled and which are not reflected in the amount in paragraph (1); and

(6) the amount of the surplus or deficiency.

(d) A particular phrasing of the explanation is not required. An explanation complying substantially with the requirements of subsection (a) is sufficient, even if it includes minor errors that are not seriously misleading.

(e) A debtor or consumer obligor is entitled without charge to one response to a request under this section during any six-month period in which the secured party did not send to the debtor or consumer obligor an explanation pursuant to subsection (b)(1). The secured party may require payment of a charge not exceeding $25 for each additional response.

§ 9—617. Rights of Transferee of Collateral.

(a) A secured party's disposition of collateral after default:

(1) transfers to a transferee for value all of the debtor's rights in the collateral;

(2) discharges the security interest under which the disposition is made; and

(3) discharges any subordinate security interest or other subordinate lien [other than liens created under [cite acts or statutes providing for liens, if any, that are not to be discharged]].

(b) A transferee that acts in good faith takes free of the rights and interests described in subsection (a), even if the secured party fails to comply with this article or the requirements of any judicial proceeding.

(c) If a transferee does not take free of the rights and interests described in subsection (a), the transferee takes the collateral subject to:

(1) the debtor's rights in the collateral;

(2) the security interest or agricultural lien under which the disposition is made; and

(3) any other security interest or other lien.

§ 9—618. **Rights and Duties of Certain Secondary Obligors.**

(a) A secondary obligor acquires the rights and becomes obligated to perform the duties of the secured party after the secondary obligor:

(1) receives an assignment of a secured obligation from the secured party;

(2) receives a transfer of collateral from the secured party and agrees to accept the rights and assume the duties of the secured party; or

(3) is subrogated to the rights of a secured party with respect to collateral.

(b) An assignment, transfer, or subrogation described in subsection (a):

(1) is not a disposition of collateral under Section 9—610; and

(2) relieves the secured party of further duties under this article.

§ 9—619. **Transfer of Record or Legal Title.**

(a) In this section, "transfer statement" means a record authenticated by a secured party stating:

(1) that the debtor has defaulted in connection with an obligation secured by specified collateral;

(2) that the secured party has exercised its post-default remedies with respect to the collateral;

(3) that, by reason of the exercise, a transferee has acquired the rights of the debtor in the collateral; and

(4) the name and mailing address of the secured party, debtor, and transferee.

(b) A transfer statement entitles the transferee to the transfer of record of all rights of the debtor in the collateral specified in the statement in any official filing, recording, registration, or certificate-of-title system covering the collateral. If a transfer statement is presented with the applicable fee and request form to the official or office responsible for maintaining the system, the official or office shall:

(1) accept the transfer statement;

(2) promptly amend its records to reflect the transfer; and

(3) if applicable, issue a new appropriate certificate of title in the name of the transferee.

(c) A transfer of the record or legal title to collateral to a secured party under subsection (b) or otherwise is not of itself a disposition of collateral under this article and does not of itself relieve the secured party of its duties under this article.

§ 9—620. **Acceptance of Collateral in Full or Partial Satisfaction of Obligation; Compulsory Disposition of Collateral.**

(a) Except as otherwise provided in subsection (g), a secured party may accept collateral in full or partial satisfaction of the obligation it secures only if:

(1) the debtor consents to the acceptance under subsection (c);

(2) the secured party does not receive, within the time set forth in subsection (d), a notification of objection to the proposal authenticated by:

(A) a person to which the secured party was required to send a proposal under Section 9—621; or

(B) any other person, other than the debtor, holding an interest in the collateral subordinate to the security interest that is the subject of the proposal;

(3) if the collateral is consumer goods, the collateral is not in the possession of the debtor when the debtor consents to the acceptance; and

(4) subsection (e) does not require the secured party to dispose of the collateral or the debtor waives the requirement pursuant to Section 9—624.

(b) A purported or apparent acceptance of collateral under this section is ineffective unless:

(1) the secured party consents to the acceptance in an authenticated record or sends a proposal to the debtor; and

(2) the conditions of subsection (a) are met.

(c) For purposes of this section:

(1) a debtor consents to an acceptance of collateral in partial satisfaction of the obligation it secures only if the debtor agrees to the terms of the acceptance in a record authenticated after default; and

(2) a debtor consents to an acceptance of collateral in full satisfaction of the obligation it secures only if the debtor agrees to the terms of the acceptance in a record authenticated after default or the secured party:

(A) sends to the debtor after default a proposal that is unconditional or subject only to a condition that collateral not in the possession of the secured party be preserved or maintained;

(B) in the proposal, proposes to accept collateral in full satisfaction of the obligation it secures; and

(C) does not receive a notification of objection authenticated by the debtor within 20 days after the proposal is sent.

(d) To be effective under subsection (a)(2), a notification of objection must be received by the secured party:

(1) in the case of a person to which the proposal was sent pursuant to Section 9—621, within 20 days after notification was sent to that person; and

(2) in other cases:

(A) within 20 days after the last notification was sent pursuant to Section 9—621; or

(B) if a notification was not sent, before the debtor consents to the acceptance under subsection (c).

(e) A secured party that has taken possession of collateral shall dispose of the collateral pursuant to Section 9—610 within the time specified in subsection (f) if:

(1) 60 percent of the cash price has been paid in the case of a purchase-money security interest in consumer goods; or

(2) 60 percent of the principal amount of the obligation secured has been paid in the case of a non-purchase-money security interest in consumer goods.

(f) To comply with subsection (e), the secured party shall dispose of the collateral:

(1) within 90 days after taking possession; or

(2) within any longer period to which the debtor and all secondary obligors have agreed in an agreement to that effect entered into and authenticated after default.

(g) In a consumer transaction, a secured party may not accept collateral in partial satisfaction of the obligation it secures.

§ 9—621. Notification of Proposal to Accept Collateral.

(a) A secured party that desires to accept collateral in full or partial satisfaction of the obligation it secures shall send its proposal to:

(1) any person from which the secured party has received, before the debtor consented to the acceptance, an authenticated notification of a claim of an interest in the collateral;

(2) any other secured party or lienholder that, 10 days before the debtor consented to the acceptance, held a security interest in or other lien on the collateral perfected by the filing of a financing statement that:

(A) identified the collateral;

(B) was indexed under the debtor's name as of that date; and

(C) was filed in the office or offices in which to file a financing statement against the debtor covering the collateral as of that date; and

(3) any other secured party that, 10 days before the debtor consented to the acceptance, held a security interest in the collateral perfected by compliance with a statute, regulation, or treaty described in Section 9—311(a).

(b) A secured party that desires to accept collateral in partial satisfaction of the obligation it secures shall send its proposal to any secondary obligor in addition to the persons described in subsection (a).

§ 9—622. Effect of Acceptance of Collateral.

(a) A secured party's acceptance of collateral in full or partial satisfaction of the obligation it secures:

(1) discharges the obligation to the extent consented to by the debtor;

(2) transfers to the secured party all of a debtor's rights in the collateral;

(3) discharges the security interest or agricultural lien that is the subject of the debtor's consent and any subordinate security interest or other subordinate lien; and

(4) terminates any other subordinate interest.

(b) A subordinate interest is discharged or terminated under subsection (a), even if the secured party fails to comply with this article.

§ 9—623. Right to Redeem Collateral.

(a) A debtor, any secondary obligor, or any other secured party or lienholder may redeem collateral.

(b) To redeem collateral, a person shall tender:

(1) fulfillment of all obligations secured by the collateral; and

(2) the reasonable expenses and attorney's fees described in Section 9—615(a)(1).

(c) A redemption may occur at any time before a secured party:

(1) has collected collateral under Section 9—607;

(2) has disposed of collateral or entered into a contract for its disposition under Section 9—610; or

(3) has accepted collateral in full or partial satisfaction of the obligation it secures under Section 9—622.

§ 9—624. Waiver.

(a) A debtor or secondary obligor may waive the right to notification of disposition of collateral under Section 9—611 only by an agreement to that effect entered into and authenticated after default.

(b) A debtor may waive the right to require disposition of collateral under Section 9—620(e) only by an agreement to that effect entered into and authenticated after default.

(c) Except in a consumer-goods transaction, a debtor or secondary obligor may waive the right to redeem collateral under Section 9—623 only by an agreement to that effect entered into and authenticated after default.

[Subpart 2. Noncompliance with Article]

§ 9—625. Remedies for Secured Party's Failure to Comply with Article.

(a) If it is established that a secured party is not proceeding in accordance with this article, a court may order or restrain collection, enforcement, or disposition of collateral on appropriate terms and conditions.

(b) Subject to subsections (c), (d), and (f), a person is liable for damages in the amount of any loss caused by a failure to comply with this article. Loss caused by a failure to comply may include loss resulting from the debtor's inability to obtain, or increased costs of, alternative financing.

(c) Except as otherwise provided in Section 9—628:

(1) a person that, at the time of the failure, was a debtor, was an obligor, or held a security interest in or other lien on the collateral may recover damages under subsection (b) for its loss; and

(2) if the collateral is consumer goods, a person that was a debtor or a secondary obligor at the time a secured party failed to comply with this part may recover for that failure in any event an amount not less than the credit service charge plus 10 percent of the principal amount of the obligation or the time-price differential plus 10 percent of the cash price.

(d) A debtor whose deficiency is eliminated under Section 9—626 may recover damages for the loss of any surplus. However, a debtor or secondary obligor whose deficiency is eliminated or reduced under Section 9—626 may not otherwise recover under subsection (b) for noncompliance with the provisions of this part relating to collection, enforcement, disposition, or acceptance.

(e) In addition to any damages recoverable under subsection (b), the debtor, consumer obligor, or person named as a debtor in a filed record, as applicable, may recover $500 in each case from a person that:

(1) fails to comply with Section 9—208;

(2) fails to comply with Section 9—209;

(3) files a record that the person is not entitled to file under Section 9—509(a);

(4) fails to cause the secured party of record to file or send a termination statement as required by Section 9—513(a) or (c);

(5) fails to comply with Section 9—616(b)(1) and whose failure is part of a pattern, or consistent with a practice, of noncompliance; or

(6) fails to comply with Section 9—616(b)(2).

(f) A debtor or consumer obligor may recover damages under subsection (b) and, in addition, $500 in each case from a person that, without reasonable cause, fails to comply with a request under Section 9—210. A recipient of a request under Section 9—210 which never claimed an interest in the collateral or obligations that are the subject of a request under that section has a reasonable excuse for failure to comply with the request within the meaning of this subsection.

(g) If a secured party fails to comply with a request regarding a list of collateral or a statement of account under Section 9—210, the secured party may claim a security interest only as shown in the list or statement included in the request as against a person that is reasonably misled by the failure.

§ 9—626. Action in Which Deficiency or Surplus Is in Issue.

(a) In an action arising from a transaction, other than a consumer transaction, in which the amount of a deficiency or surplus is in issue, the following rules apply:

(1) A secured party need not prove compliance with the provisions of this part relating to collection, enforcement, disposition, or acceptance unless the debtor or a secondary obligor places the secured party's compliance in issue.

(2) If the secured party's compliance is placed in issue, the secured party has the burden of establishing that the collection, enforcement, disposition, or acceptance was conducted in accordance with this part.

(3) Except as otherwise provided in Section 9—628, if a secured party fails to prove that the collection, enforcement, disposition, or acceptance was conducted in accordance with the provisions of this part relating to collection, enforcement, disposition, or acceptance, the liability of a debtor or a secondary obligor for a deficiency is limited to an amount by which the sum of the secured obligation, expenses, and attorney's fees exceeds the greater of:

(A) the proceeds of the collection, enforcement, disposition, or acceptance; or

(B) the amount of proceeds that would have been realized had the noncomplying secured party proceeded in accordance with the provisions of this part relating to collection, enforcement, disposition, or acceptance.

(4) For purposes of paragraph (3)(B), the amount of proceeds that would have been realized is equal to the

sum of the secured obligation, expenses, and attorney's fees unless the secured party proves that the amount is less than that sum.

(5) If a deficiency or surplus is calculated under Section 9—615(f), the debtor or obligor has the burden of establishing that the amount of proceeds of the disposition is significantly below the range of prices that a complying disposition to a person other than the secured party, a person related to the secured party, or a secondary obligor would have brought.

(b) The limitation of the rules in subsection (a) to transactions other than consumer transactions is intended to leave to the court the determination of the proper rules in consumer transactions. The court may not infer from that limitation the nature of the proper rule in consumer transactions and may continue to apply established approaches.

§ 9—627. Determination of Whether Conduct Was Commercially Reasonable.

(a) The fact that a greater amount could have been obtained by a collection, enforcement, disposition, or acceptance at a different time or in a different method from that selected by the secured party is not of itself sufficient to preclude the secured party from establishing that the collection, enforcement, disposition, or acceptance was made in a commercially reasonable manner.

(b) A disposition of collateral is made in a commercially reasonable manner if the disposition is made:

(1) in the usual manner on any recognized market;

(2) at the price current in any recognized market at the time of the disposition; or

(3) otherwise in conformity with reasonable commercial practices among dealers in the type of property that was the subject of the disposition.

(c) A collection, enforcement, disposition, or acceptance is commercially reasonable if it has been approved:

(1) in a judicial proceeding;

(2) by a bona fide creditors' committee;

(3) by a representative of creditors; or

(4) by an assignee for the benefit of creditors.

(d) Approval under subsection (c) need not be obtained, and lack of approval does not mean that the collection, enforcement, disposition, or acceptance is not commercially reasonable.

§ 9—628. Nonliability and Limitation on Liability of Secured Party; Liability of Secondary Obligor.

(a) Unless a secured party knows that a person is a debtor or obligor, knows the identity of the person, and knows how to communicate with the person:

(1) the secured party is not liable to the person, or to a secured party or lienholder that has filed a financing statement against the person, for failure to comply with this article; and

(2) the secured party's failure to comply with this article does not affect the liability of the person for a deficiency.

(b) A secured party is not liable because of its status as secured party:

(1) to a person that is a debtor or obligor, unless the secured party knows:

(A) that the person is a debtor or obligor;

(B) the identity of the person; and

(C) how to communicate with the person; or

(2) to a secured party or lienholder that has filed a financing statement against a person, unless the secured party knows:

(A) that the person is a debtor; and

(B) the identity of the person.

(c) A secured party is not liable to any person, and a person's liability for a deficiency is not affected, because of any act or omission arising out of the secured party's reasonable belief that a transaction is not a consumer-goods transaction or a consumer transaction or that goods are not consumer goods, if the secured party's belief is based on its reasonable reliance on:

(1) a debtor's representation concerning the purpose for which collateral was to be used, acquired, or held; or

(2) an obligor's representation concerning the purpose for which a secured obligation was incurred.

(d) A secured party is not liable to any person under Section 9—625(c)(2) for its failure to comply with Section 9—616.

(e) A secured party is not liable under Section 9—625(c)(2) more than once with respect to any one secured obligation.

Part 7 Transition

§ 9—701. Effective Date.

This [Act] takes effect on July 1, 2001.

§ 9—702. Savings Clause.

(a) Except as otherwise provided in this part, this [Act] applies to a transaction or lien within its scope, even if the transaction or lien was entered into or created before this [Act] takes effect.

(b) Except as otherwise provided in subsection (c) and Sections 9—703 through 9—709:

(1) transactions and liens that were not governed by [former Article 9], were validly entered into or created before this [Act] takes effect, and would be subject to this [Act] if they had been entered into or created after this [Act] takes effect, and the rights, duties, and interests flowing from those transactions and liens remain valid after this [Act] takes effect; and

(2) the transactions and liens may be terminated, completed, consummated, and enforced as required or permitted by this [Act] or by the law that otherwise would apply if this [Act] had not taken effect.

(c) This [Act] does not affect an action, case, or proceeding commenced before this [Act] takes effect.

§ 9—703. Security Interest Perfected before Effective Date.

(a) A security interest that is enforceable immediately before this [Act] takes effect and would have priority over the rights of a person that becomes a lien creditor at that time is a perfected security interest under this [Act] if, when this [Act] takes effect, the applicable requirements for enforceability and perfection under this [Act] are satisfied without further action.

(b) Except as otherwise provided in Section 9—705, if, immediately before this [Act] takes effect, a security interest is enforceable and would have priority over the rights of a person that becomes a lien creditor at that time, but the applicable requirements for enforceability or perfection under this [Act] are not satisfied when this [Act] takes effect, the security interest:

(1) is a perfected security interest for one year after this [Act] takes effect;

(2) remains enforceable thereafter only if the security interest becomes enforceable under Section 9—203 before the year expires; and

(3) remains perfected thereafter only if the applicable requirements for perfection under this [Act] are satisfied before the year expires.

§ 9—704. Security Interest Unperfected before Effective Date.

A security interest that is enforceable immediately before this [Act] takes effect but which would be subordinate to the rights of a person that becomes a lien creditor at that time:

(1) remains an enforceable security interest for one year after this [Act] takes effect;

(2) remains enforceable thereafter if the security interest becomes enforceable under Section 9—203 when this [Act] takes effect or within one year thereafter; and

(3) becomes perfected:

(A) without further action, when this [Act] takes effect if the applicable requirements for perfection under this [Act] are satisfied before or at that time; or

(B) when the applicable requirements for perfection are satisfied if the requirements are satisfied after that time.

§ 9—705. Effectiveness of Action Taken before Effective Date.

(a) If action, other than the filing of a financing statement, is taken before this [Act] takes effect and the action would have resulted in priority of a security interest over the rights of a person that becomes a lien creditor had the security interest become enforceable before this [Act] takes effect, the action is effective to perfect a security interest that attaches under this [Act] within one year after this [Act] takes effect. An attached security interest becomes unperfected one year after this [Act] takes effect unless the security interest becomes a perfected security interest under this [Act] before the expiration of that period.

(b) The filing of a financing statement before this [Act] takes effect is effective to perfect a security interest to the extent the filing would satisfy the applicable requirements for perfection under this [Act].

(c) This [Act] does not render ineffective an effective financing statement that, before this [Act] takes effect, is filed and satisfies the applicable requirements for perfection under the law of the jurisdiction governing perfection as provided in [former Section 9—103]. However, except as otherwise provided in subsections (d) and (e) and Section 9—706, the financing statement ceases to be effective at the earlier of:

(1) the time the financing statement would have ceased to be effective under the law of the jurisdiction in which it is filed; or

(2) June 30, 2006.

(d) The filing of a continuation statement after this [Act] takes effect does not continue the effectiveness of the financing statement filed before this [Act] takes effect. However, upon the timely filing of a continuation statement after this [Act] takes effect and in accordance with the law of the jurisdiction governing perfection as provided in Part 3, the effectiveness of a financing statement filed in the same office in that jurisdiction before this [Act] takes effect continues for the period provided by the law of that jurisdiction.

(e) Subsection (c)(2) applies to a financing statement that, before this [Act] takes effect, is filed against a transmitting utility and satisfies the applicable requirements for perfection under the law of the jurisdiction governing perfection as provided in [former Section 9—103] only to the extent that Part 3 provides that the law of a jurisdiction other than the jurisdiction in which the financing statement is filed governs perfection of a security interest in collateral covered by the financing statement.

(f) A financing statement that includes a financing statement filed before this [Act] takes effect and a continuation statement filed after this [Act] takes effect is effective only to the extent that it satisfies the requirements of Part 5 for an initial financing statement.

§ 9—706. When Initial Financing Statement Suffices to Continue Effectiveness of Financing Statement.

(a) The filing of an initial financing statement in the office specified in Section 9—501 continues the effectiveness of a financing statement filed before this [Act] takes effect if:

(1) the filing of an initial financing statement in that office would be effective to perfect a security interest under this [Act];

(2) the pre-effective-date financing statement was filed in an office in another State or another office in this State; and

(3) the initial financing statement satisfies subsection (c).

(b) The filing of an initial financing statement under subsection (a) continues the effectiveness of the pre-effective-date financing statement:

(1) if the initial financing statement is filed before this [Act] takes effect, for the period provided in [former Section 9—403] with respect to a financing statement; and

(2) if the initial financing statement is filed after this [Act] takes effect, for the period provided in Section 9—515 with respect to an initial financing statement.

(c) To be effective for purposes of subsection (a), an initial financing statement must:

(1) satisfy the requirements of Part 5 for an initial financing statement;

(2) identify the pre-effective-date financing statement by indicating the office in which the financing statement was filed and providing the dates of filing and file numbers, if any, of the financing statement and of the most recent continuation statement filed with respect to the financing statement; and

(3) indicate that the pre-effective-date financing statement remains effective.

§ 9—707. Amendment of Pre-Effective-Date Financing Statement.

(a) In this section, "Pre-effective-date financing statement" means a financing statement filed before this [Act] takes effect.

(b) After this [Act] takes effect, a person may add or delete collateral covered by, continue or terminate the effectiveness of, or otherwise amend the information provided in, a pre-effective-date financing statement only in accordance with the law of the jurisdiction governing perfection as provided in Part 3. However, the effectiveness of a pre-effective-date financing statement also may be terminated in accordance with the law of the jurisdiction in which the financing statement is filed.

(c) Except as otherwise provided in subsection (d), if the law of this State governs perfection of a security interest, the information in a pre-effective-date financing statement may be amended after this [Act] takes effect only if:

(1) the pre-effective-date financing statement and an amendment are filed in the office specified in Section 9—501;

(2) an amendment is filed in the office specified in Section 9—501 concurrently with, or after the filing in that office of, an initial financing statement that satisfies Section 9—706(c); or

(3) an initial financing statement that provides the information as amended and satisfies Section 9—706(c) is filed in the office specified in Section 9—501.

(d) If the law of this State governs perfection of a security interest, the effectiveness of a pre-effective-date financing statement may be continued only under Section 9—705(d) and (f) or 9—706.

(e) Whether or not the law of this State governs perfection of a security interest, the effectiveness of a pre-effective-date financing statement filed in this State may be terminated after this [Act] takes effect by filing a termination statement in the office in which the pre-effective-date financing statement is filed, unless an initial financing statement that satisfies Section 9—706(c) has been filed in the office specified by the law of the jurisdiction governing perfection as provided in Part 3 as the office in which to file a financing statement.

§ 9—708. Persons Entitled to File Initial Financing Statement or Continuation Statement.

A person may file an initial financing statement or a continuation statement under this part if:

(1) the secured party of record authorizes the filing; and

(2) the filing is necessary under this part:

(A) to continue the effectiveness of a financing statement filed before this [Act] takes effect; or

(B) to perfect or continue the perfection of a security interest.

§ 9—709. **Priority.**

(a) This [Act] determines the priority of conflicting claims to collateral. However, if the relative priorities of the claims were established before this [Act] takes effect, [former Article 9] determines priority.

(b) For purposes of Section 9—322(a), the priority of a security interest that becomes enforceable under Section 9—203 of this [Act] dates from the time this [Act] takes effect if the security interest is perfected under this [Act] by the filing of a financing statement before this [Act] takes effect which would not have been effective to perfect the security interest under [former Article 9]. This subsection does not apply to conflicting security interests each of which is perfected by the filing of such a financing statement.

APPENDIX C

The United Nations Convention on Contracts for the International Sale of Goods (Excerpts)

Part I. SPHERE OF APPLICATION AND GENERAL PROVISIONS

* * * *

Chapter II—General Provisions

* * * *

Article 8

(1) For the purposes of this Convention statements made by and other conduct of a party are to be interpreted according to his intent where the other party knew or could not have been unaware what that intent was.

(2) If the preceding paragraph is not applicable, statements made by and other conduct of a party are to be interpreted according to the understanding that a reasonable person of the same kind as the other party would have had in the same circumstances.

(3) In determining the intent of a party or the understanding a reasonable person would have had, due consideration is to be given to all relevant circumstances of the case including the negotiations, any practices which the parties have established between themselves, usages and any subsequent conduct of the parties.

Article 9

(1) The parties are bound by any usage to which they have agreed and by any practices which they have established between themselves.

(2) The parties are considered, unless otherwise agreed, to have impliedly made applicable to their contract or its formation a usage of which the parties knew or ought to have known and which in international trade is widely known to, and regularly observed by, parties to contracts of the type involved in the particular trade concerned.

* * * *

Article 11

A contract of sale need not be concluded in or evidenced by writing and is not subject to any other requirement as to form. It may be proved by any means, including witnesses.

* * * *

Part II. FORMATION OF THE CONTRACT

Article 14

(1) A proposal for concluding a contract addressed to one or more specific persons constitutes an offer if it is sufficiently definite and indicates the intention of the offeror to be bound in case of acceptance. A proposal is sufficiently definite if it indicates the goods and expressly or implicitly fixes or makes provision for determining the quantity and the price.

(2) A proposal other than one addressed to one or more specific persons is to be considered merely as an invitation to make offers, unless the contrary is clearly indicated by the person making the proposal.

Article 15

(1) An offer becomes effective when it reaches the offeree.

(2) An offer, even if it is irrevocable, may be withdrawn if the withdrawal reaches the offeree before or at the same time as the offer.

Article 16

(1) Until a contract is concluded an offer may be revoked if the revocation reaches the offeree before he has dispatched an acceptance.

(2) However, an offer cannot be revoked:

(a) If it indicates, whether by stating a fixed time for acceptance or otherwise, that it is irrevocable; or

(b) If it was reasonable for the offeree to rely on the offer as being irrevocable and the offeree has acted in reliance on the offer.

Article 17

An offer, even if it is irrevocable, is terminated when a rejection reaches the offeror.

Article 18

(1) A statement made by or other conduct of the offeree indicating assent to an offer is an acceptance. Silence or inactivity does not in itself amount to acceptance.

(2) An acceptance of an offer becomes effective at the moment the indication of assent reaches the offeror. An acceptance is not effective if the indication of assent does not reach the offeror within the time he has fixed or, if no time is fixed, within a reasonable time, due account being taken of the circumstances of the transaction, including the rapidity of the means of communication employed by the offeror. An oral offer must be accepted immediately unless the circumstances indicate otherwise.

(3) However, if, by virtue of the offer or as a result of practices which the parties have established between themselves or of usage, the offeree may indicate assent by performing an act, such as one relating to the dispatch of the goods or payment of the price, without notice to the offeror, the acceptance is effective at the moment the act is performed, provided that the act is performed within the period of time laid down in the preceding paragraph.

Article 19

(1) A reply to an offer which purports to be an acceptance but contains additions, limitations or other modifications is a rejection of the offer and constitutes a counter-offer.

(2) However, a reply to an offer which purports to be an acceptance but contains additional or different terms which do not materially alter the terms of the offer constitutes an acceptance, unless the offeror, without undue delay, objects orally to the discrepancy or dispatches a notice to that effect. If he does not so object, the terms of the contract are the terms of the offer with the modifications contained in the acceptance.

(3) Additional or different terms relating, among other things, to the price, payment, quality and quantity of the goods, place and time of delivery, extent of one party's liability to the other or the settlement of disputes are considered to alter the terms of the offer materially.

* * * *

Article 22

An acceptance may be withdrawn if the withdrawal reaches the offeror before or at the same time as the acceptance would have become effective.

* * * *

Part III. SALE OF GOODS

Chapter I—General Provisions

Article 25

A breach of contract committed by one of the parties is fundamental if it results in such detriment to the other party as substantially to deprive him of what he is entitled to expect under the contract, unless the party in breach did not foresee and a reasonable person of the same kind in the same circumstances would not have foreseen such a result.

* * * *

Article 28

If, in accordance with the provisions of this Convention, one party is entitled to require performance of any obligation by the other party, a court is not bound to enter a judgment for specific performance unless the court would do so under its own law in respect of similar contracts of sale not governed by this Convention.

Article 29

(1) A contract may be modified or terminated by the mere agreement of the parties.

(2) A contract in writing which contains a provision requiring any modification or termination by agreement to be in writing may not be otherwise modified or terminated by agreement. However, a party may be precluded by his conduct from asserting such a provision to the extent that the other party has relied on that conduct.

* * * *

Chapter II—Obligations of the Seller

* * * *

Section II. Conformity of the Goods and Third Party Claims

Article 35

(1) The seller must deliver goods which are of the quantity, quality and description required by the contract and which are contained or packaged in the manner required by the contract.

(2) Except where the parties have agreed otherwise, the goods do not conform with the contract unless they:

(a) Are fit for the purposes for which goods of the same description would ordinarily be used;

(b) Are fit for any particular purpose expressly or impliedly made known to the seller at the time of the conclusion of the contract, except where the circumstances show that the buyer did not rely, or that it was unreasonable for him to rely, on the seller's skill and judgment;

(c) Possess the qualities of goods which the seller has held out to the buyer as a sample or model;

(d) Are contained or packaged in the manner usual for such goods or, where there is no such manner, in a manner adequate to preserve and protect the goods.

(3) The seller is not liable under subparagraphs (a) to (d) of the preceding paragraph for any lack of conformity of the goods if at the time of the conclusion of the contract the buyer knew or could not have been unaware of such lack of conformity.

* * * *

Article 64

(1) The seller may declare the contract avoided:

(a) If the failure by the buyer to perform any of his obligations under the contract or this Convention amounts to a fundamental breach of contract; or

(b) If the buyer does not, within the additional period of time fixed by the seller in accordance with paragraph (1) of article 63, perform his obligation to pay the price or take delivery of the goods, or if he declares that he will not do so within the period so fixed.

(2) However, in cases where the buyer has paid the price, the seller loses the right to declare the contract avoided unless he does so:

(a) In respect of late performance by the buyer, before the seller has become aware that performance has been rendered; or

(b) In respect of any breach other than late performance by the buyer, within a reasonable time:

(i) After the seller knew or ought to have known of the breach; or

(ii) After the expiration of any additional period of time fixed by the seller in accordance with paragraph (1) of article 63, or after the buyer has declared that he will not perform his obligations within such an additional period.

* * * *

Chapter IV—Passing of Risk

* * * *

Article 67

(1) If the contract of sale involves carriage of the goods and the seller is not bound to hand them over at a particular place, the risk passes to the buyer when the goods are handed over to the first carrier for transmission to the buyer in accordance with the contract of sale. If the seller is bound to hand the goods over to a carrier at a particular place, the risk does not pass to the buyer until the goods are handed over to the carrier at that place. The fact that the seller is authorized to retain documents controlling the disposition of the goods does not affect the passage of the risk.

(2) Nevertheless, the risk does not pass to the buyer until the goods are clearly identified to the contract, whether by markings on the goods, by shipping documents, by notice given to the buyer or otherwise.

* * * *

Chapter V—Provisions Common to the Obligations of the Seller and of the Buyer

Section I. Anticipatory Breach and Instalment Contracts

Article 71

(1) A party may suspend the performance of his obligations if, after the conclusion of the contract, it becomes apparent that the other party will not perform a substantial part of his obligations as a result of:

(a) A serious deficiency in his ability to perform or in his creditworthiness; or

(b) His conduct in preparing to perform or in performing the contract.

(2) If the seller has already dispatched the goods before the grounds described in the preceding paragraph become evident, he may prevent the handing over of the goods to the buyer even though the buyer holds a document which entitles him to obtain them. The present paragraph relates only to the rights in the goods as between the buyer and the seller.

(3) A party suspending performance, whether before or after dispatch of the goods, must immediately give notice of the suspension to the other party and must continue with performance if the other party provides adequate assurance of his performance.

Article 72

(1) If prior to the date for performance of the contract it is clear that one of the parties will commit a fundamental breach of contract, the other party may declare the contract avoided.

(2) If time allows, the party intending to declare the contract avoided must give reasonable notice to the other party in order to permit him to provide adequate assurance of his performance.

(3) The requirements of the preceding paragraph do not apply if the other party has declared that he will not perform his obligations.

Article 73

(1) In the case of a contract for delivery of goods by instalments, if the failure of one party to perform any of his obligations in respect of any instalment constitutes a fundamental breach of contract with respect to that instalment, the other party may declare the contract avoided with respect to that instalment.

(2) If one party's failure to perform any of his obligations in respect of any instalment gives the other party good grounds to conclude that a fundamental breach of contract will occur with respect to future instalments, he may declare the contract avoided for the future, provided that he does so within a reasonable time.

(3) A buyer who declares the contract avoided in respect of any delivery may, at the same time, declare it avoided in respect of deliveries already made or of future deliveries if, by reason of their interdependence, those deliveries could not be used for the purpose contemplated by the parties at the time of the conclusion of the contract.

Section II. Damages

Article 74

Damages for breach of contract by one party consist of a sum equal to the loss, including loss of profit, suffered by the other party as a consequence of the breach. Such damages may not exceed the loss which the party in breach foresaw or ought to have foreseen at the time of the conclusion of the contract, in the light of the facts and matters of which he then knew or ought to have known, as a possible consequence of the breach of contract.

Article 75

If the contract is avoided and if, in a reasonable manner and within a reasonable time after avoidance, the buyer has bought goods in replacement or the seller has resold the goods, the party claiming damages may recover the difference between the contract price and the price in the substitute transaction as well as any further damages recoverable under article 74.

Article 76

(1) If the contract is avoided and there is a current price for the goods, the party claiming damages may, if he has not made a purchase or resale under article 75, recover the difference between the price fixed by the contract and the current price at the time of avoidance as well as any further damages recoverable under article 74. If, however, the party claiming damages has avoided the contract after taking over the goods, the current price at the time of such taking over shall be applied instead of the current price at the time of avoidance.

(2) For the purposes of the preceding paragraph, the current price is the price prevailing at the place where delivery of the goods should have been made or, if there is no current price at that place, the price at such other place as serves as a reasonable substitute, making due allowance for differences in the cost of transporting the goods.

Article 77

A party who relies on a breach of contract must take such measures as are reasonable in the circumstances to mitigate the loss, including loss of profit, resulting from the breach. If he fails to take such measures, the party in breach may claim a reduction in the damages in the amount by which the loss should have been mitigated.

APPENDIX D

The Uniform Partnership Act

(Adopted in forty-nine states [all of the states except Louisiana], the District of Columbia, the Virgin Islands, and Guam. The adoptions by Alabama and Nebraska do not follow the official text in every respect, but are substantially similar, with local variations.)

The Act consists of 7 Parts as follows:

I. Preliminary Provisions

II. Nature of Partnership

III. Relations of Partners to Persons Dealing with the Partnership

IV. Relations of Partners to One Another

V. Property Rights of a Partner

VI. Dissolution and Winding Up

VII. Miscellaneous Provisions

An Act to make uniform the Law of Partnerships

Be it enacted, etc.:

Part I Preliminary Provisions

Sec. 1. Name of Act

This act may be cited as Uniform Partnership Act.

Sec. 2. Definition of Terms

In this act, "Court" includes every court and judge having jurisdiction in the case.

"Business" includes every trade, occupation, or profession.

"Person" includes individuals, partnerships, corporations, and other associations.

"Bankrupt" includes bankrupt under the Federal Bankruptcy Act or insolvent under any state insolvent act.

"Conveyance" includes every assignment, lease, mortgage, or encumbrance.

"Real property" includes land and any interest or estate in land.

Sec. 3. Interpretation of Knowledge and Notice

(1) A person has "knowledge" of a fact within the meaning of this act not only when he has actual knowledge thereof, but also when he has knowledge of such other facts as in the circumstances shows bad faith.

(2) A person has "notice" of a fact within the meaning of this act when the person who claims the benefit of the notice:

(a) States the fact to such person, or

(b) Delivers through the mail, or by other means of communication, a written statement of the fact to such person or to a proper person at his place of business or residence.

Sec. 4. Rules of Construction

(1) The rule that statutes in derogation of the common law are to be strictly construed shall have no application to this act.

(2) The law of estoppel shall apply under this act.

(3) The law of agency shall apply under this act.

(4) This act shall be so interpreted and construed as to effect its general purpose to make uniform the law of those states which enact it.

(5) This act shall not be construed so as to impair the obligations of any contract existing when the act goes into effect, nor to affect any action or proceedings begun or right accrued before this act takes effect.

Sec. 5. Rules for Cases Not Provided for in This Act.

In any case not provided for in this act the rules of law and equity, including the law merchant, shall govern.

Part II Nature of Partnership

Sec. 6. Partnership Defined

(1) A partnership is an association of two or more persons to carry on as co-owners a business for profit.

(2) But any association formed under any other statute of this state, or any statute adopted by authority, other than the authority of this state, is not a partnership under this act, unless such association would have been a partnership in this state prior to the adoption of this act; but this act shall apply to limited partnerships except in so far as the statutes relating to such partnerships are inconsistent herewith.

Sec. 7. Rules for Determining the Existence of a Partnership

In determining whether a partnership exists, these rules shall apply:

(1) Except as provided by Section 16 persons who are not partners as to each other are not partners as to third persons.

(2) Joint tenancy, tenancy in common, tenancy by the entireties, joint property, common property, or part ownership does not of itself establish a partnership, whether such co-owners do or do not share any profits made by the use of the property.

(3) The sharing of gross returns does not of itself establish a partnership, whether or not the persons sharing them have a joint or common right or interest in any property from which the returns are derived.

(4) The receipt by a person of a share of the profits of a business is prima facie evidence that he is a partner in the business, but no such inference shall be drawn if such profits were received in payment:

(a) As a debt by installments or otherwise,

(b) As wages of an employee or rent to a landlord,

(c) As an annuity to a widow or representative of a deceased partner,

(d) As interest on a loan, though the amount of payment vary with the profits of the business,

(e) As the consideration for the sale of a good-will of a business or other property by installments or otherwise.

Sec. 8. Partnership Property

(1) All property originally brought into the partnership stock or subsequently acquired by purchase or otherwise, on account of the partnership, is partnership property.

(2) Unless the contrary intention appears, property acquired with partnership funds is partnership property.

(3) Any estate in real property may be acquired in the partnership name. Title so acquired can be conveyed only in the partnership name.

(4) A conveyance to a partnership in the partnership name, though without words of inheritance, passes the entire estate of the grantor unless a contrary intent appears.

Part III Relations of Partners to Persons Dealing with the Partnership

Sec. 9. Partner Agent of Partnership as to Partnership Business

(1) Every partner is an agent of the partnership for the purpose of its business, and the act of every partner, including the execution in the partnership name of any instrument, for apparently carrying on in the usual way the business of the partnership of which he is a member binds the partnership, unless the partner so acting has in fact no authority to act for the partnership in the particular matter, and the person with whom he is dealing has knowledge of the fact that he has no such authority.

(2) An act of a partner which is not apparently for the carrying on of the business of the partnership in the usual way does not bind the partnership unless authorized by the other partners.

(3) Unless authorized by the other partners or unless they have abandoned the business, one or more but less than all the partners have no authority to:

(a) Assign the partnership property in trust for creditors or on the assignee's promise to pay the debts of the partnership,

(b) Dispose of the good-will of the business,

(c) Do any other act which would make it impossible to carry on the ordinary business of a partnership,

(d) Confess a judgment,

(e) Submit a partnership claim or liability to arbitration or reference.

(4) No act of a partner in contravention of a restriction on authority shall bind the partnership to persons having knowledge of the restriction.

Sec. 10. Conveyance of Real Property of the Partnership

(1) Where title to real property is in the partnership name, any partner may convey title to such property by a conveyance executed in the partnership name; but the partnership may recover such property unless the partner's act binds the partnership under the provisions of paragraph (1) of section 9, or unless such property has been conveyed by the grantee or a person claiming through such grantee to a holder for value without knowledge that the partner, in making the conveyance, has exceeded his authority.

(2) Where title to real property is in the name of the partnership, a conveyance executed by a partner, in his own name, passes the equitable interest of the partnership, provided the act is one within the authority of the partner under the provisions of paragraph (1) of section 9.

(3) Where title to real property is in the name of one or more but not all the partners, and the record does not disclose the right of the partnership, the partners in whose name the title stands may convey title to such property, but the partnership may recover such property if the partners' act does not bind the partnership under the provisions of paragraph (1) of section 9, unless the purchaser or his assignee, is a holder for value, without knowledge.

(4) Where the title to real property is in the name of one or more or all the partners, or in a third person in trust for the partnership, a conveyance executed by a partner in the partnership name, or in his own name, passes the equitable interest of the partnership, provided the act is one within the authority of the partner under the provisions of paragraph (1) of section 9.

(5) Where the title to real property is in the names of all the partners a conveyance executed by all the partners passes all their rights in such property.

Sec. 11. Partnership Bound by Admission of Partner

An admission or representation made by any partner concerning partnership affairs within the scope of his authority as conferred by this act is evidence against the partnership.

Sec. 12. Partnership Charged with Knowledge of or Notice to Partner

Notice to any partner of any matter relating to partnership affairs, and the knowledge of the partner acting in the particular matter, acquired while a partner or then present to his mind, and the knowledge of any other partner who reasonably could and should have communicated it to the acting partner, operate as notice to or knowledge of the partnership, except in the case of a fraud on the partnership committed by or with the consent of that partner.

Sec. 13. Partnership Bound by Partner's Wrongful Act

Where, by any wrongful act or omission of any partner acting in the ordinary course of the business of the partnership or with the authority of his co-partners, loss or injury is caused to any person, not being a partner in the partnership, or any penalty is incurred, the partnership is liable therefor to the same extent as the partner so acting or omitting to act.

Sec. 14. Partnership Bound by Partner's Breach of Trust

The partnership is bound to make good the loss:

(a) Where one partner acting within the scope of his apparent authority receives money or property of a third person and misapplies it; and

(b) Where the partnership in the course of its business receives money or property of a third person and the money or property so received is misapplied by any partner while it is in the custody of the partnership.

Sec. 15. Nature of Partner's Liability

All partners are liable

(a) Jointly and severally for everything chargeable to the partnership under sections 13 and 14.

(b) Jointly for all other debts and obligations of the partnership; but any partner may enter into a separate obligation to perform a partnership contract.

Sec. 16. Partner by Estoppel

(1) When a person, by words spoken or written or by conduct, represents himself, or consents to another representing him to any one, as a partner in an existing partnership or with one or more persons not actual partners, he is liable to any such person to whom such representation has been made, who has, on the faith of such representation, given credit to the actual or apparent partnership, and if he has made such representation or consented to its being made in a public manner he is liable to such person, whether the representation has or has not been made or communicated to such person so giving credit by or with the knowledge of the apparent partner making the representation or consenting to its being made.

(a) When a partnership liability results, he is liable as though he were an actual member of the partnership.

(b) When no partnership liability results, he is liable jointly with the other persons, if any, so consenting to the contract or representation as to incur liability, otherwise separately.

(2) When a person has been thus represented to be a partner in an existing partnership, or with one or more persons not actual partners, he is an agent of the persons consenting to such representation to bind them to the same extent and in the same manner as though he were a partner in fact, with respect to persons who rely upon the representation. Where all the members of the existing partnership consent to the representation, a partnership act or obligation results; but in all other cases it is the

joint act or obligation of the person acting and the persons consenting to the representation.

Sec. 17. Liability of Incoming Partner

A person admitted as a partner into an existing partnership is liable for all the obligations of the partnership arising before his admission as though he had been a partner when such obligations were incurred, except that this liability shall be satisfied only out of partnership property.

Part IV Relations of Partners to One Another

Sec. 18. Rules Determining Rights and Duties of Partners

The rights and duties of the partners in relation to the partnership shall be determined, subject to any agreement between them, by the following rules:

(a) Each partner shall be repaid his contributions, whether by way of capital or advances to the partnership property and share equally in the profits and surplus remaining after all liabilities, including those to partners, are satisfied; and must contribute towards the losses, whether of capital or otherwise, sustained by the partnership according to his share in the profits.

(b) The partnership must indemnify every partner in respect of payments made and personal liabilities reasonably incurred by him in the ordinary and proper conduct of its business, or for the preservation of its business or property.

(c) A partner, who in aid of the partnership makes any payment or advance beyond the amount of capital which he agreed to contribute, shall be paid interest from the date of the payment or advance.

(d) A partner shall receive interest on the capital contributed by him only from the date when repayment should be made.

(e) All partners have equal rights in the management and conduct of the partnership business.

(f) No partner is entitled to remuneration for acting in the partnership business, except that a surviving partner is entitled to reasonable compensation for his services in winding up the partnership affairs.

(g) No person can become a member of a partnership without the consent of all the partners.

(h) Any difference arising as to ordinary matters connected with the partnership business may be decided by a majority of the partners; but no act in contravention of any agreement between the partners may be done rightfully without the consent of all the partners.

Sec. 19. Partnership Books

The partnership books shall be kept, subject to any agreement between the partners, at the principal place of business of the partnership, and every partner shall at all times have access to and may inspect and copy any of them.

Sec. 20. Duty of Partners to Render Information

Partners shall render on demand true and full information of all things affecting the partnership to any partner or the legal representative of any deceased partner or partner under legal disability.

Sec. 21. Partner Accountable as a Fiduciary

(1) Every partner must account to the partnership for any benefit, and hold as trustee for it any profits derived by him without the consent of the other partners from any transaction connected with the formation, conduct, or liquidation of the partnership or from any use by him of its property.

(2) This section applies also to the representatives of a deceased partner engaged in the liquidation of the affairs of the partnership as the personal representatives of the last surviving partner.

Sec. 22. Right to an Account

Any partner shall have the right to a formal account as to partnership affairs:

(a) If he is wrongfully excluded from the partnership business or possession of its property by his co-partners,

(b) If the right exists under the terms of any agreement,

(c) As provided by section 21,

(d) Whenever other circumstances render it just and reasonable.

Sec. 23. Continuation of Partnership beyond Fixed Term

(1) When a partnership for a fixed term or particular undertaking is continued after the termination of such term or particular undertaking without any express agreement, the rights and duties of the partners remain the same as they were at such termination, so far as is consistent with a partnership at will.

(2) A continuation of the business by the partners or such of them as habitually acted therein during the term, without any settlement or liquidation of the partnership affairs, is prima facie evidence of a continuation of the partnership.

Part V Property Rights of a Partner

Sec. 24. Extent of Property Rights of a Partner

The property rights of a partner are (1) his rights in specific partnership property, (2) his interest in the partnership, and (3) his right to participate in the management.

Sec. 25. Nature of a Partner's Right in Specific Partnership Property

(1) A partner is co-owner with his partners of specific partnership property holding as a tenant in partnership.

(2) The incidents of this tenancy are such that:

(a) A partner, subject to the provisions of this act and to any agreement between the partners, has an equal right with his partners to possess specific partnership property for partnership purposes; but he has no right to possess such property for any other purpose without the consent of his partners.

(b) A partner's right in specific partnership property is not assignable except in connection with the assignment of rights of all the partners in the same property.

(c) A partner's right in specific partnership property is not subject to attachment or execution, except on a claim against the partnership. When partnership property is attached for a partnership debt the partners, or any of them, or the representatives of a deceased partner, cannot claim any right under the homestead or exemption laws.

(d) On the death of a partner his right in specific partnership property vests in the surviving partner or partners, except where the deceased was the last surviving partner, when his right in such property vests in his legal representative. Such surviving partner or partners, or the legal representative of the last surviving partner, has no right to possess the partnership property for any but a partnership purpose.

(e) A partner's right in specific partnership property is not subject to dower, curtesy, or allowances to widows, heirs, or next of kin.

Sec. 26. Nature of Partner's Interest in the Partnership

A partner's interest in the partnership is his share of the profits and surplus, and the same is personal property.

Sec. 27. Assignment of Partner's Interest

(1) A conveyance by a partner of his interest in the partnership does not of itself dissolve the partnership, nor, as against the other partners in the absence of agreement, entitle the assignee, during the continuance of the partnership, to interfere in the management or administration of the partnership business or affairs, or to require any information or account of partnership transactions, or to inspect the partnership books; but it merely entitles the assignee to receive in accordance with his contract the profits to which the assigning partner would otherwise be entitled.

(2) In case of a dissolution of the partnership, the assignee is entitled to receive his assignor's interest and may require an account from the date only of the last account agreed to by all the partners.

Sec. 28. Partner's Interest Subject to Charging Order

(1) On due application to a competent court by any judgment creditor of a partner, the court which entered the judgment, order, or decree, or any other court, may charge the interest of the debtor partner with payment of the unsatisfied amount of such judgment debt with interest thereon; and may then or later appoint a receiver of his share of the profits, and of any other money due or to fall due to him in respect of the partnership, and make all other orders, directions, accounts and inquiries which the debtor partner might have made, or which the circumstances of the case may require.

(2) The interest charged may be redeemed at any time before foreclosure, or in case of a sale being directed by the court may be purchased without thereby causing a dissolution:

(a) With separate property, by any one or more of the partners, or

(b) With partnership property, by any one or more of the partners with the consent of all the partners whose interests are not so charged or sold.

(3) Nothing in this act shall be held to deprive a partner of his right, if any, under the exemption laws, as regards his interest in the partnership.

Part VI Dissolution and Winding up

Sec. 29. Dissolution Defined

The dissolution of a partnership is the change in the relation of the partners caused by any partner ceasing to be associated in the carrying on as distinguished from the winding up of the business.

Sec. 30. Partnership not Terminated by Dissolution

On dissolution the partnership is not terminated, but continues until the winding up of partnership affairs is completed.

Sec. 31. Causes of Dissolution

Dissolution is caused:

(1) Without violation of the agreement between the partners,

(a) By the termination of the definite term or particular undertaking specified in the agreement,

(b) By the express will of any partner when no definite term or particular undertaking is specified,

(c) By the express will of all the partners who have not assigned their interests or suffered them to be charged for their separate debts, either before or after the termination of any specified term or particular undertaking,

(d) By the expulsion of any partner from the business bona fide in accordance with such a power conferred by the agreement between the partners;

(2) In contravention of the agreement between the partners, where the circumstances do not permit a

dissolution under any other provision of this section, by the express will of any partner at any time;

(3) By any event which makes it unlawful for the business of the partnership to be carried on or for the members to carry it on in partnership;

(4) By the death of any partner;

(5) By the bankruptcy of any partner or the partnership;

(6) By decree of court under section 32.

Sec. 32. Dissolution by Decree of Court

(1) On application by or for a partner the court shall decree a dissolution whenever:

(a) A partner has been declared a lunatic in any judicial proceeding or is shown to be of unsound mind,

(b) A partner becomes in any other way incapable of performing his part of the partnership contract,

(c) A partner has been guilty of such conduct as tends to affect prejudicially the carrying on of the business,

(d) A partner wilfully or persistently commits a breach of the partnership agreement, or otherwise so conducts himself in matters relating to the partnership business that it is not reasonably practicable to carry on the business in partnership with him,

(e) The business of the partnership can only be carried on at a loss,

(f) Other circumstances render a dissolution equitable.

(2) On the application of the purchaser of a partner's interest under sections 28 or 29 [should read 27 or 28];

(a) After the termination of the specified term or particular undertaking,

(b) At any time if the partnership was a partnership at will when the interest was assigned or when the charging order was issued.

Sec. 33. General Effect of Dissolution on Authority of Partner

Except so far as may be necessary to wind up partnership affairs or to complete transactions begun but not then finished, dissolution terminates all authority of any partner to act for the partnership,

(1) With respect to the partners,

(a) When the dissolution is not by the act, bankruptcy or death of a partner; or

(b) When the dissolution is by such act, bankruptcy or death of a partner, in cases where section 34 so requires.

(2) With respect to persons not partners, as declared in section 35.

Sec. 34. Rights of Partner to Contribution from Copartners after Dissolution

Where the dissolution is caused by the act, death or bankruptcy of a partner, each partner is liable to his copartners for his share of any liability created by any partner acting for the partnership as if the partnership had not been dissolved unless

(a) The dissolution being by act of any partner, the partner acting for the partnership had knowledge of the dissolution, or

(b) The dissolution being by the death or bankruptcy of a partner, the partner acting for the partnership had knowledge or notice of the death or bankruptcy.

Sec. 35. Power of Partner to Bind Partnership to Third Persons after Dissolution

(1) After dissolution a partner can bind the partnership except as provided in Paragraph (3).

(a) By any act appropriate for winding up partnership affairs or completing transactions unfinished at dissolution;

(b) By any transaction which would bind the partnership if dissolution had not taken place, provided the other party to the transaction

(I) Had extended credit to the partnership prior to dissolution and had no knowledge or notice of the dissolution; or

(II) Though he had not so extended credit, had nevertheless known of the partnership prior to dissolution, and, having no knowledge or notice of dissolution, the fact of dissolution had not been advertised in a newspaper of general circulation in the place (or in each place if more than one) at which the partnership business was regularly carried on.

(2) The liability of a partner under paragraph (1b) shall be satisfied out of partnership assets alone when such partner had been prior to dissolution

(a) Unknown as a partner to the person with whom the contract is made; and

(b) So far unknown and inactive in partnership affairs that the business reputation of the partnership could not be said to have been in any degree due to his connection with it.

(3) The partnership is in no case bound by any act of a partner after dissolution

(a) Where the partnership is dissolved because it is unlawful to carry on the business, unless the act is appropriate for winding up partnership affairs; or

(b) Where the partner has become bankrupt; or

(c) Where the partner has no authority to wind up partnership affairs; except by a transaction with one who

(I) Had extended credit to the partnership prior to dissolution and had no knowledge or notice of his want of authority; or

(II) Had not extended credit to the partnership prior to dissolution, and, having no knowledge or notice of his want of authority, the fact of his want of authority has not been advertised in the manner provided for advertising the fact of dissolution in paragraph (1bII).

(4) Nothing in this section shall affect the liability under Section 16 of any person who after dissolution represents himself or consents to another representing him as a partner in a partnership engaged in carrying on business.

Sec. 36. Effect of Dissolution on Partner's Existing Liability

(1) The dissolution of the partnership does not of itself discharge the existing liability of any partner.

(2) A partner is discharged from any existing liability upon dissolution of the partnership by an agreement to that effect between himself, the partnership creditor and the person or partnership continuing the business; and such agreement may be inferred from the course of dealing between the creditor having knowledge of the dissolution and the person or partnership continuing the business.

(3) Where a person agrees to assume the existing obligations of a dissolved partnership, the partners whose obligations have been assumed shall be discharged from any liability to any creditor of the partnership who, knowing of the agreement, consents to a material alteration in the nature or time of payment of such obligations.

(4) The individual property of a deceased partner shall be liable for all obligations of the partnership incurred while he was a partner but subject to the prior payment of his separate debts.

Sec. 37. Right to Wind Up

Unless otherwise agreed the partners who have not wrongfully dissolved the partnership or the legal representative of the last surviving partner, not bankrupt, has the right to wind up the partnership affairs; provided, however, that any partner, his legal representative or his assignee, upon cause shown, may obtain winding up by the court.

Sec. 38. Rights of Partners to Application of Partnership Property

(1) When dissolution is caused in any way, except in contravention of the partnership agreement, each partner, as against his co-partners and all persons claiming through them in respect of their interests in the partnership, unless otherwise agreed, may have the partnership property applied to discharge its liabilities, and the surplus applied to pay in cash the net amount owing to the respective partners. But if dissolution is caused by expulsion of a partner, bona fide under the partnership agreement and if the expelled partner is discharged from all partnership liabilities, either by payment or agreement under section 36(2), he shall receive in cash only the net amount due him from the partnership.

(2) When dissolution is caused in contravention of the partnership agreement the rights of the partners shall be as follows:

(a) Each partner who has not caused dissolution wrongfully shall have,

(I) All the rights specified in paragraph (1) of this section, and

(II) The right, as against each partner who has caused the dissolution wrongfully, to damages for breach of the agreement.

(b) The partners who have not caused the dissolution wrongfully, if they all desire to continue the business in the same name, either by themselves or jointly with others, may do so, during the agreed term for the partnership and for that purpose may possess the partnership property, provided they secure the payment by bond approved by the court, or pay to any partner who has caused the dissolution wrongfully, the value of his interest in the partnership at the dissolution, less any damages recoverable under clause (2a II) of the section, and in like manner indemnify him against all present or future partnership liabilities.

(c) A partner who has caused the dissolution wrongfully shall have:

(I) If the business is not continued under the provisions of paragraph (2b) all the rights of a partner under paragraph (1), subject to clause (2a II), of this section,

(II) If the business is continued under paragraph (2b) of this section the right as against his co-partners and all claiming through them in respect of their interests in the partnership, to have the value of his interest in the partnership, less any damages caused to his co-partners by the dissolution, ascertained and paid to him in cash, or the payment secured by bond approved by the court, and to be released from all existing liabilities of the partnership; but in ascertaining the value of the partner's interest the value of the good-will of the business shall not be considered.

Sec. 39. Rights Where Partnership Is Dissolved for Fraud or Misrepresentation

Where a partnership contract is rescinded on the ground of the fraud or misrepresentation of one of the parties thereto, the party entitled to rescind is, without prejudice to any other right, entitled,

(a) To a lien on, or right of retention of, the surplus of the partnership property after satisfying the partnership liabilities to third persons for any sum of money paid by him for the purchase of an interest in the partnership and for any capital or advances contributed by him; and

(b) To stand, after all liabilities to third persons have been satisfied, in the place of the creditors of the partnership for any payments made by him in respect of the partnership liabilities; and

(c) To be indemnified by the person guilty of the fraud or making the representation against all debts and liabilities of the partnership.

Sec. 40. Rules for Distribution

In settling accounts between the partners after dissolution, the following rules shall be observed, subject to any agreement to the contrary:

(a) The assets of the partnership are:

(I) The partnership property,

(II) The contributions of the partners necessary for the payment of all the liabilities specified in clause (b) of this paragraph.

(b) The liabilities of the partnership shall rank in order of payment, as follows:

(I) Those owing to creditors other than partners,

(II) Those owing to partners other than for capital and profits,

(III) Those owing to partners in respect of capital,

(IV) Those owing to partners in respect of profits.

(c) The assets shall be applied in the order of their declaration in clause (a) of this paragraph to the satisfaction of the liabilities.

(d) The partners shall contribute, as provided by section 18(a) the amount necessary to satisfy the liabilities; but if any, but not all, of the partners are insolvent, or, not being subject to process, refuse to contribute, the other partners shall contribute their share of the liabilities, and, in the relative proportions in which they share the profits, the additional amount necessary to pay the liabilities.

(e) An assignee for the benefit of creditors or any person appointed by the court shall have the right to enforce the contributions specified in clause (d) of this paragraph.

(f) Any partner or his legal representative shall have the right to enforce the contributions specified in clause (d) of this paragraph, to the extent of the amount which he has paid in excess of his share of the liability.

(g) The individual property of a deceased partner shall be liable for the contributions specified in clause (d) of this paragraph.

(h) When partnership property and the individual properties of the partners are in possession of a court for distribution, partnership creditors shall have priority on partnership property and separate creditors on individual property, saving the rights of lien or secured creditors as heretofore.

(i) Where a partner has become bankrupt or his estate is insolvent the claims against his separate property shall rank in the following order:

(I) Those owing to separate creditors,

(II) Those owing to partnership creditors,

(III) Those owing to partners by way of contribution.

Sec. 41. Liability of Persons Continuing the Business in Certain Cases

(1) When any new partner is admitted into an existing partnership, or when any partner retires and assigns (or the representative of the deceased partner assigns) his rights in partnership property to two or more of the partners, or to one or more of the partners and one or more third persons, if the business is continued without liquidation of the partnership affairs, creditors of the first or dissolved partnership are also creditors of the partnership so continuing the business.

(2) When all but one partner retire and assign (or the representative of a deceased partner assigns) their rights in partnership property to the remaining partner, who continues the business without liquidation of partnership affairs, either alone or with others, creditors of the dissolved partnership are also creditors of the person or partnership so continuing the business.

(3) When any partner retires or dies and the business of the dissolved partnership is continued as set forth in paragraphs (1) and (2) of this section, with the consent of the retired partners or the representative of the deceased partner, but without any assignment of his right in partnership property, rights of creditors of the dissolved partnership and of the creditors of the person or partnership continuing the business shall be as if such assignment had been made.

(4) When all the partners or their representatives assign their rights in partnership property to one or more third persons who promise to pay the debts and who continue the business of the dissolved partnership, creditors of the dissolved partnership are also creditors of the person or partnership continuing the business.

(5) When any partner wrongfully causes a dissolution and the remaining partners continue the business under the provisions of section 38(2b), either alone or with others, and without liquidation of the partnership affairs, creditors of the dissolved partnership are also creditors of the person or partnership continuing the business.

(6) When a partner is expelled and the remaining partners continue the business either alone or with others, without liquidation of the partnership affairs, creditors of the dissolved partnership are also creditors of the person or partnership continuing the business.

(7) The liability of a third person becoming a partner in the partnership continuing the business, under this section, to the creditors of the dissolved partnership shall be satisfied out of partnership property only.

(8) When the business of a partnership after dissolution is continued under any conditions set forth in this section the creditors of the dissolved partnership, as against the separate creditors of the retiring or deceased partner or the representative of the deceased partner, have a prior right to any claim of the retired partner or the representative of the deceased partner against the person or partnership continuing the business, on account of the retired or deceased partner's interest in the dissolved partnership or on account of any consideration promised for such interest or for his right in partnership property.

(9) Nothing in this section shall be held to modify any right of creditors to set aside any assignment on the ground of fraud.

(10) The use by the person or partnership continuing the business of the partnership name, or the name of a deceased partner as part thereof, shall not of itself make the individual property of the deceased partner liable for any debts contracted by such person or partnership.

Sec. 42. Rights of Retiring or Estate of Deceased Partner When the Business Is Continued

When any partner retires or dies, and the business is continued under any of the conditions set forth in section 41 (1, 2, 3, 5, 6), or section 38(2b) without any settlement of accounts as between him or his estate and the person or partnership continuing the business, unless otherwise agreed, he or his legal representative as against such persons or partnership may have the value of his interest at the date of dissolution ascertained, and shall receive as an ordinary creditor an amount equal to the value of his interest in the dissolved partnership with interest, or, at his option or at the option of his legal representative, in lieu of interest, the profits attributable to the use of his right in the property of the dissolved partnership; provided that the creditors of the dissolved partnership as against the separate creditors, or the representative of the retired or deceased partner, shall have priority on any claim arising under this section, as provided by section 41(8) of this act.

Sec. 43. Accrual of Actions

The right to an account of his interest shall accrue to any partner, or his legal representative, as against the winding up partners or the surviving partners or the person or partnership continuing the business, at the date of dissolution, in the absence of any agreement to the contrary.

Part VII Miscellaneous Provisions

Sec. 44. When Act Takes Effect

This act shall take effect on the ___ day of ___ one thousand nine hundred and ___.

Sec. 45. Legislation Repealed

All acts or parts of acts inconsistent with this act are hereby repealed.

APPENDIX E

The Revised Uniform Partnership Act (Excerpts)

Article 2.
GENERAL PROVISIONS

* * * *

§ 201. Partnership as Entity.

A partnership is an entity.

* * * *

§ 203. Partnership Property.

Property transferred to or otherwise acquired by a partnership is property of the partnership and not of the partners individually.

§ 204. When Property is Partnership Property.

(a) Property is partnership property if acquired in the name of:

(1) the partnership; or

(2) one or more partners with an indication in the instrument transferring title to the property of the person's capacity as a partner or of the existence of a partnership but without an indication of the name of the partnership.

(b) Property is acquired in the name of the partnership by a transfer to:

(1) the partnership in its name; or

(2) one or more partners in their capacity as partners in the partnership, if the name of the partnership is indicated in the instrument transferring title to the property.

(c) Property is presumed to be partnership property if purchased with partnership assets, even if not acquired in the name of the partnership or of one or more partners with an indication in the instrument transferring title to the property of the person's capacity as a partner or of the existence of a partnership.

(d) Property acquired in the name of one or more of the partners, without an indication in the instrument transferring title to the property of the person's capacity as a partner or of the existence of a partnership and without use of partnership assets, is presumed to be separate property, even if used for partnership purposes.

Article 3.
RELATIONS OF PARTNERS TO PERSONS DEALING WITH PARTNERSHIP

* * * *

§ 302. Transfer of Partnership Property.

(a) Subject to the effect of a statement of partnership authority under Section 303:

(1) Partnership property held in the name of the partnership may be transferred by an instrument of transfer executed by a partner in the partnership name.

(2) Partnership property held in the name of one or more partners with an indication in the instru-

ment transferring the property to them of their capacity as partners or of the existence of a partnership, but without an indication of the name of the partnership, may be transferred by an instrument of transfer executed by the persons in whose name the property is held.

(3) A partnership may recover property transferred under this subsection if it proves that execution of the instrument of transfer did not bind the partnership under Section 301, unless the property was transferred by the initial transferee or a person claiming through the initial transferee to a subsequent transferee who gave value without having notice that the person who executed the instrument of initial transfer lacked authority to bind the partnership.

(b) Partnership property held in the name of one or more persons other than the partnership, without an indication in the instrument transferring the property to them of their capacity as partners or of the existence of a partnership, may be transferred free of claims of the partnership or the partners by the persons in whose name the property is held to a transferee who gives value without having notice that it is partnership property.

(c) If a person holds all of the partners' interests in the partnership, all of the partnership property vests in that person. The person may execute a document in the name of the partnership to evidence vesting of the property in that person and may file or record the document.

* * * *

§ 306. Partner's Liability.

All partners are liable jointly and severally for all obligations of the partnership unless otherwise agreed by the claimant or provided by law.

§ 307. Actions by and Against Partnership and Partners.

(a) A partnership may sue and be sued in the name of the partnership.

(b) An action may be brought against the partnership and any or all of the partners in the same action or in separate actions.

(c) A judgment against a partnership is not by itself a judgment against a partner. A judgment against a partnership may not be satisfied from a partner's assets unless there is also a judgment against the partner.

(d) A judgment creditor of a partner may not levy execution against the assets of the partner to satisfy a judgment based on a claim against the partnership unless:

(1) a judgment based on the same claim has been obtained against the partnership and a writ of execution on the judgment has been returned unsatisfied in whole or in part;

(2) an involuntary case under Title 11 of the United States Code has been commenced against the partnership and has not been dismissed within 60 days after commencement, or the partnership has commenced a voluntary case under Title 11 of the United States Code and the case has not been dismissed;

(3) the partner has agreed that the creditor need not exhaust partnership assets;

(4) a court grants permission to the judgment creditor to levy execution against the assets of a partner based on a finding that partnership assets subject to execution are clearly insufficient to satisfy the judgment, that exhaustion of partnership assets is excessively burdensome, or that the grant of permission is an appropriate exercise of the court's equitable powers; or

(5) liability is imposed on the partner by law or contract independent of the existence of the partnership.

(e) This section applies to any partnership liability or obligation resulting from a representation by a partner or purported partner under Section 308.

* * * *

Article 5.
TRANSFEREES AND CREDITORS OF PARTNER

§ 501. Partner's Interest in Partnership Property not Transferable.

A partner is not a co-owner of partnership property and has no interest in partnership property which can be transferred, either voluntarily or involuntarily.

* * * *

Article 6.
PARTNER'S DISSOCIATION

§ 601. Events Causing Partner's Dissociation.

A partner is dissociated from a partnership upon:

(1) receipt by the partnership of notice of the partner's express will to withdraw as a partner or upon any later date specified in the notice;

(2) an event agreed to in the partnership agreement as causing the partner's dissociation;

(3) the partner's expulsion pursuant to the partnership agreement;

(4) the partner's expulsion by the unanimous vote of the other partners if:

(i) it is unlawful to carry on the partnership business with that partner;

(ii) there has been a transfer of all or substantially all of that partner's transferable interest in the partnership, other than a transfer for security purposes, or a court order charging the partner's interest, which has not been foreclosed;

(iii) within 90 days after the partnership notifies a corporate partner that it will be expelled because it has filed a certificate of dissolution or the equivalent, its charter has been revoked, or its right to conduct business has been suspended by the jurisdiction of its incorporation, there is no revocation of the certificate of dissolution or no reinstatement of its charter or its right to conduct business; or

(iv) a partnership that is a partner has been dissolved and its business is being wound up;

(5) on application by the partnership or another partner, the partner's expulsion by judicial determination because:

(i) the partner engaged in wrongful conduct that adversely and materially affected the partnership business;

(ii) the partner willfully or persistently committed a material breach of the partnership agreement or of a duty owed to the partnership or the other partners under Section 404; or

(iii) the partner engaged in conduct relating to the partnership business which makes it not reasonably practicable to carry on the business in partnership with the partner;

(6) the partner's:

(i) becoming a debtor in bankruptcy;

(ii) executing an assignment for the benefit of creditors;

(iii) seeking, consenting to, or acquiescing in the appointment of a trustee, receiver, or liquidator of that partner or of all or substantially all of that partner's property; or

(iv) failing, within 90 days after the appointment, to have vacated or stayed the appointment of a trustee, receiver, or liquidator of the partner or of all or substantially all of the partner's property obtained without the partner's consent or acquiescence, or failing within 90 days after the expiration of a stay to have the appointment vacated;

(7) in the case of a partner who is an individual:

(i) the partner's death;

(ii) the appointment of a guardian or general conservator for the partner; or

(iii) a judicial determination that the partner has otherwise become incapable of performing the partner's duties under the partnership agreement;

(8) in the case of a partner that is a trust or is acting as a partner by virtue of being a trustee of a trust, distribution of the trust's entire transferable interest in the partnership, but not merely by reason of the substitution of a successor trustee;

(9) in the case of a partner that is an estate or is acting as a partner by virtue of being a personal representative of an estate, distribution of the estate's entire transferable interest in the partnership, but not merely by reason of the substitution of a successor personal representative; or

(10) termination of a partner who is not an individual, partnership, corporation, trust, or estate.

* * * *

Article 7. PARTNER'S DISSOCIATION WHEN BUSINESS NOT WOUND UP

§ 701. Purchase of Dissociated Partner's Interest.

(a) If a partner is dissociated from a partnership without resulting in a dissolution and winding up of the partnership business under Section 801, the partnership shall cause the dissociated partner's interest in the partnership to be purchased for a buyout price determined pursuant to subsection (b).

(b) The buyout price of a dissociated partner's interest is the amount that would have been distributable to the dissociating partner under Section 808(b) if, on the date of dissociation, the assets of the partnership were sold at a price equal to the greater of the liquidation value or the value based on a sale of the entire business as a going concern without the dissociated partner and the partnership were wound up as of that date. In either case, the selling price of the partnership assets must be determined on the basis of the amount that would be paid by a willing buyer to a willing seller, neither being under any compulsion to buy or sell, and with knowledge of all relevant facts. Interest must be paid from the date of dissociation to the date of payment.

(c) Damages for wrongful dissociation under Section 602(b), and all other amounts owing, whether or not presently due, from the dissociated partner to the partnership, must be offset against the buyout price. Interest must be paid from the date the amount owed becomes due to the date of payment.

(d) A partnership shall indemnify a dissociated partner against all partnership liabilities incurred before the dissociation, except liabilities then unknown to the partnership, and against all partnership liabilities incurred after the dissociation, except liabilities incurred by an act of the dissociated partner under Section 702. For purposes of this subsection, a liability not known to a partner other than the dissociated partner is not known to the partnership.

(e) If no agreement for the purchase of a dissociated partner's interest is reached within 120 days after a written demand for payment, the partnership shall pay, or cause to be paid, in cash to the dissociated partner the amount the partnership estimates to be the buyout price and accrued interest, reduced by any offsets and accrued interest under subsection (c).

(f) If a deferred payment is authorized under subsection (h), the partnership may tender a written offer to pay the amount it estimates to be the buyout price and accrued interest, reduced by any offsets under subsection (c), stating the time of payment, the amount and type of security for payment, and the other terms and conditions of the obligation.

(g) The payment or tender required by subsection (e) or (f) must be accompanied by the following:

(1) a statement of partnership assets and liabilities as of the date of dissociation;

(2) the latest available partnership balance sheet and income statement, if any;

(3) an explanation of how the estimated amount of the payment was calculated; and

(4) written notice that the payment is in full satisfaction of the obligation to purchase unless, within 120 days after the written notice, the dissociated partner commences an action to determine the buyout price, any offsets under subsection (c), or other terms of the obligation to purchase.

(h) A partner who wrongfully dissociates before the expiration of a definite term or the completion of a particular undertaking is not entitled to payment of any portion of the buyout price until the expiration of the term or completion of the undertaking, unless the partner establishes to the satisfaction of the court that earlier payment will not cause undue hardship to the business of the partnership. A deferred payment must be adequately secured and bear interest.

(i) A dissociated partner may maintain an action against the partnership, pursuant to Section 406(b)(2)(ii), to determine the buyout price of that partner's interest, any offsets under subsection (c), or other terms of the obligation to purchase. The action must be commenced within 120 days after the partnership has tendered payment or an offer to pay or within one year after written demand for payment if no payment or offer to pay is tendered. The court shall determine the buyout price of the dissociated partner's interest, any offset due under subsection (c), and accrued interest, and enter judgment for any additional payment or refund. If deferred payment is authorized under subsection (h), the court shall also determine the security for payment and other terms of the obligation to purchase. The court may assess reasonable attorney's fees and the fees and expenses of appraisers or other experts for a party to the action, in amounts the court finds equitable, against a party that the court finds acted arbitrarily, vexatiously, or not in good faith. The finding may be based on the partnership's failure to tender payment or an offer to pay or to comply with subsection (g).

APPENDIX F

The Revised Uniform Limited Partnership Act

Article 1
GENERAL PROVISIONS

Section 101. Definitions.

As used in this [Act], unless the context otherwise requires:

(1) "Certificate of limited partnership" means the certificate referred to in Section 201, and the certificate as amended or restated.

(2) "Contribution" means any cash, property, services rendered, or a promissory note or other binding obligation to contribute cash or property or to perform services, which a partner contributes to a limited partnership in his capacity as a partner.

(3) "Event of withdrawal of a general partner" means an event that causes a person to cease to be a general partner as provided in Section 402.

(4) "Foreign limited partnership" means a partnership formed under the laws of any state other than this State and having as partners one or more general partners and one or more limited partners.

(5) "General partner" means a person who has been admitted to a limited partnership as a general partner in accordance with the partnership agreement and named in the certificate of limited partnership as a general partner.

(6) "Limited partner" means a person who has been admitted to a limited partnership as a limited partner in accordance with the partnership agreement.

(7) "Limited partnership" and "domestic limited partnership" mean a partnership formed by two or more persons under the laws of this State and having one or more general partners and one or more limited partners.

(8) "Partner" means a limited or general partner.

(9) "Partnership agreement" means any valid agreement, written or oral, of the partners as to the affairs of a limited partnership and the conduct of its business.

(10) "Partnership interest" means a partner's share of the profits and losses of a limited partnership and the right to receive distributions of partnership assets.

(11) "Person" means a natural person, partnership, limited partnership (domestic or foreign), trust, estate, association, or corporation.

(12) "State" means a state, territory, or possession of the United States, the District of Columbia, or the Commonwealth of Puerto Rico.

Section 102. Name.

The name of each limited partnership as set forth in its certificate of limited partnership:

(1) shall contain without abbreviation the words "limited partnership";

(2) may not contain the name of a limited partner unless (i) it is also the name of a general partner or the corporate name of a corporate general partner, or (ii) the business of the limited partnership had been carried on under that name before the admission of that limited partner;

(3) may not be the same as, or deceptively similar to, the name of any corporation or limited partnership organized under the laws of this State or licensed or registered as a foreign corporation or limited partnership in this State; and

(4) may not contain the following words [here insert prohibited words].

Section 103. **Reservation of Name.**

(a) The exclusive right to the use of a name may be reserved by:

(1) any person intending to organize a limited partnership under this [Act] and to adopt that name;

(2) any domestic limited partnership or any foreign limited partnership registered in this State which, in either case, intends to adopt that name;

(3) any foreign limited partnership intending to register in this State and adopt that name; and

(4) any person intending to organize a foreign limited partnership and intending to have it register in this State and adopt that name.

(b) The reservation shall be made by filing with the Secretary of State an application, executed by the applicant, to reserve a specified name. If the Secretary of State finds that the name is available for use by a domestic or foreign limited partnership, he [or she] shall reserve the name for the exclusive use of the applicant for a period of 120 days. Once having so reserved a name, the same applicant may not again reserve the same name until more than 60 days after the expiration of the last 120-day period for which that applicant reserved that name. The right to the exclusive use of a reserved name may be transferred to any other person by filing in the office of the Secretary of State a notice of the transfer, executed by the applicant for whom the name was reserved and specifying the name and address of the transferee.

Section 104. **Specified Office and Agent.**

Each limited partnership shall continuously maintain in this State:

(1) an office, which may but need not be a place of its business in this State, at which shall be kept the records required by Section 105 to be maintained; and

(2) an agent for service of process on the limited partnership, which agent must be an individual resident of this State, a domestic corporation, or a foreign corporation authorized to do business in this State.

Section 105. **Records to Be Kept.**

(a) Each limited partnership shall keep at the office referred to in Section 104(1) the following:

(1) a current list of the full name and last known business address of each partner, separately identifying the general partners (in alphabetical order) and the limited partners (in alphabetical order);

(2) a copy of the certificate of limited partnership and all certificates of amendment thereto, together with executed copies of any powers of attorney pursuant to which any certificate has been executed;

(3) copies of the limited partnership's federal, state and local income tax returns and reports, if any, for the three most recent years;

(4) copies of any then effective written partnership agreements and of any financial statements of the limited partnership for the three most recent years; and

(5) unless contained in a written partnership agreement, a writing setting out:

(i) the amount of cash and a description and statement of the agreed value of the other property or services contributed by each partner and which each partner has agreed to contribute;

(ii) the times at which or events on the happening of which any additional contributions agreed to be made by each partner are to be made;

(iii) any right of a partner to receive, or of a general partner to make, distributions to a partner which include a return of all or any part of the partner's contribution; and

(iv) any events upon the happening of which the limited partnership is to be dissolved and its affairs wound up.

(b) Records kept under this section are subject to inspection and copying at the reasonable request and at the expense of any partner during ordinary business hours.

Section 106. **Nature of Business.**

A limited partnership may carry on any business that a partnership without limited partners may carry on except [here designate prohibited activities].

Section 107. **Business Transactions of Partners with Partnership.**

Except as provided in the partnership agreement, a partner may lend money to and transact other business with the limited partnership and, subject to other applicable law, has the same rights and obligations with respect thereto as a person who is not a partner.

Article 2
FORMATION; CERTIFICATE OF LIMITED PARTNERSHIP

Section 201. **Certificate of Limited Partnership.**

(a) In order to form a limited partnership, a certificate of limited partnership must be executed and filed in the office of the Secretary of State. The certificate shall set forth:

(1) the name of the limited partnership;

(2) the address of the office and the name and address of the agent for service of process required to be maintained by Section 104;

(3) the name and the business address of each general partner;

(4) the latest date upon which the limited partnership is to dissolve; and

(5) any other matters the general partners determine to include therein.

(b) A limited partnership is formed at the time of the filing of the certificate of limited partnership in the office of the Secretary of State or at any later time specified in the certificate of limited partnership if, in either case, there has been substantial compliance with the requirements of this section.

Section 202. Amendment to Certificate.

(a) A certificate of limited partnership is amended by filing a certificate of amendment thereto in the office of the Secretary of State. The certificate shall set forth:

(1) the name of the limited partnership;

(2) the date of filing the certificate; and

(3) the amendment to the certificate.

(b) Within 30 days after the happening of any of the following events, an amendment to a certificate of limited partnership reflecting the occurrence of the event or events shall be filed:

(1) the admission of a new general partner;

(2) the withdrawal of a general partner; or

(3) the continuation of the business under Section 801 after an event of withdrawal of a general partner.

(c) A general partner who becomes aware that any statement in a certificate of limited partnership was false when made or that any arrangements or other facts described have changed, making the certificate inaccurate in any respect, shall promptly amend the certificate.

(d) A certificate of limited partnership may be amended at any time for any other proper purpose the general partners determine.

(e) No person has any liability because an amendment to a certificate of limited partnership has not been filed to reflect the occurrence of any event referred to in subsection (b) of this section if the amendment is filed within the 30-day period specified in subsection (b).

(f) A restated certificate of limited partnership may be executed and filed in the same manner as a certificate of amendment.

Section 203. Cancellation of Certificate.

A certificate of limited partnership shall be cancelled upon the dissolution and the commencement of winding up of the partnership or at any other time there are no limited partners. A certificate of cancellation shall be filed in the office of the Secretary of State and set forth:

(1) the name of the limited partnership;

(2) the date of filing of its certificate of limited partnership;

(3) the reason for filing the certificate of cancellation;

(4) the effective date (which shall be a date certain) of cancellation if it is not to be effective upon the filing of the certificate; and

(5) any other information the general partners filing the certificate determine.

Section 204. Execution of Certificates.

(a) Each certificate required by this Article to be filed in the office of the Secretary of State shall be executed in the following manner:

(1) an original certificate of limited partnership must be signed by all general partners;

(2) a certificate of amendment must be signed by at least one general partner and by each other general partner designated in the certificate as a new general partner; and

(3) a certificate of cancellation must be signed by all general partners.

(b) Any person may sign a certificate by an attorney-in-fact, but a power of attorney to sign a certificate relating to the admission of a general partner must specifically describe the admission.

(c) The execution of a certificate by a general partner constitutes an affirmation under the penalties of perjury that the facts stated therein are true.

Section 205. Execution by Judicial Act.

If a person required by Section 204 to execute any certificate fails or refuses to do so, any other person who is adversely affected by the failure or refusal may petition the [designate the appropriate court] to direct the execution of the certificate. If the court finds that it is proper for the certificate to be executed and that any person so designated has failed or refused to execute the certificate, it shall order the Secretary of State to record an appropriate certificate.

Section 206. Filing in Office of Secretary of State.

(a) Two signed copies of the certificate of limited partnership and of any certificates of amendment or cancellation (or of any judicial decree of amendment or cancellation) shall be delivered to the Secretary of State. A person who executes a certificate as an agent or fiduciary need not exhibit evidence of his [or her] authority as a prerequisite to filing. Unless the Secretary of State finds that any certificate does not conform to law, upon receipt of all filing fees required by law he [or she] shall:

(1) endorse on each duplicate original the word "Filed" and the day, month, and year of the filing thereof;

(2) file one duplicate original in his [or her] office; and

(3) return the other duplicate original to the person who filed it or his [or her] representative.

(b) Upon the filing of a certificate of amendment (or judicial decree of amendment) in the office of the Secretary of State, the certificate of limited partnership shall be amended as set forth therein, and upon the effective date of a certificate of cancellation (or a judicial decree thereof), the certificate of limited partnership is cancelled.

Section 207. Liability for False Statement in Certificate.

If any certificate of limited partnership or certificate of amendment or cancellation contains a false statement, one who suffers loss by reliance on the statement may recover damages for the loss from:

(1) any person who executes the certificate, or causes another to execute it on his behalf, and knew, and any general partner who knew or should have known, the statement to be false at the time the certificate was executed; and

(2) any general partner who thereafter knows or should have known that any arrangement or other fact described in the certificate has changed, making the statement inaccurate in any respect within a sufficient time before the statement was relied upon reasonably to have enabled that general partner to cancel or amend the certificate, or to file a petition for its cancellation or amendment under Section 205.

Section 208. Scope of Notice.

The fact that a certificate of limited partnership is on file in the office of the Secretary of State is notice that the partnership is a limited partnership and the persons designated therein as general partners are general partners, but it is not notice of any other fact.

Section 209. Delivery of Certificates to Limited Partners.

Upon the return by the Secretary of State pursuant to Section 206 of a certificate marked "Filed," the general partners shall promptly deliver or mail a copy of the certificate of limited partnership and each certificate of amendment or cancellation to each limited partner unless the partnership agreement provides otherwise.

Article 3
LIMITED PARTNERS

Section 301. Admission of Additional Limited Partners.

(a) A person becomes a limited partner on the later of:

(1) the date the original certificate of limited partnership is filed; or

(2) the date stated in the records of the limited partnership as the date that person becomes a limited partner.

(b) After the filing of a limited partnership's original certificate of limited partnership, a person may be admitted as an additional limited partner:

(1) in the case of a person acquiring a partnership interest directly from the limited partnership, upon compliance with the partnership agreement or, if the partnership agreement does not so provide, upon the written consent of all partners; and

(2) in the case of an assignee of a partnership interest of a partner who has the power, as provided in Section 704, to grant the assignee the right to become a limited partner, upon the exercise of that power and compliance with any conditions limiting the grant or exercise of the power.

Section 302. Voting.

Subject to Section 303, the partnership agreement may grant to all or a specified group of the limited partners the right to vote (on a per capita or other basis) upon any matter.

Section 303. Liability to Third Parties.

(a) Except as provided in subsection (d), a limited partner is not liable for the obligations of a limited partnership unless he [or she] is also a general partner or, in addition to the exercise of his [or her] rights and powers as a limited partner, he [or she] participates in the control of the business. However, if the limited partner participates in the control of the business, he [or she] is liable only to persons who transact business with the limited partnership reasonably believing, based upon the limited partner's conduct, that the limited partner is a general partner.

(b) A limited partner does not participate in the control of the business within the meaning of subsection (a) solely by doing one or more of the following:

(1) being a contractor for or an agent or employee of the limited partnership or of a general partner or being an officer, director, or shareholder of a general partner that is a corporation;

(2) consulting with and advising a general partner with respect to the business of the limited partnership;

(3) acting as surety for the limited partnership or guaranteeing or assuming one or more specific obligations of the limited partnership;

(4) taking any action required or permitted by law to bring or pursue a derivative action in the right of the limited partnership;

(5) requesting or attending a meeting of partners;

(6) proposing, approving, or disapproving, by voting or otherwise, one or more of the following matters:

(i) the dissolution and winding up of the limited partnership;

(ii) the sale, exchange, lease, mortgage, pledge, or other transfer of all or substantially all of the assets of the limited partnership;

(iii) the incurrence of indebtedness by the limited partnership other than in the ordinary course of its business;

(iv) a change in the nature of the business;

(v) the admission or removal of a general partner;

(vi) the admission or removal of a limited partner;

(vii) a transaction involving an actual or potential conflict of interest between a general partner and the limited partnership or the limited partners;

(viii) an amendment to the partnership agreement or certificate of limited partnership; or

(ix) matters related to the business of the limited partnership not otherwise enumerated in this subsection (b), which the partnership agreement states in writing may be subject to the approval or disapproval of limited partners;

(7) winding up the limited partnership pursuant to Section 803; or

(8) exercising any right or power permitted to limited partners under this [Act] and not specifically enumerated in this subsection (b).

(c) The enumeration in subsection (b) does not mean that the possession or exercise of any other powers by a limited partner constitutes participation by him [or her] in the business of the limited partnership.

(d) A limited partner who knowingly permits his [or her] name to be used in the name of the limited partnership, except under circumstances permitted by Section 102(2), is liable to creditors who extend credit to the limited partnership without actual knowledge that the limited partner is not a general partner.

Section 304. Person Erroneously Believing Himself [or Herself] Limited Partner.

(a) Except as provided in subsection (b), a person who makes a contribution to a business enterprise and erroneously but in good faith believes that he [or she] has become a limited partner in the enterprise is not a general partner in the enterprise and is not bound by its obligations by reason of making the contribution, receiving distributions from the enterprise, or exercising any rights of a limited partner, if, on ascertaining the mistake, he [or she]:

(1) causes an appropriate certificate of limited partnership or a certificate of amendment to be executed and filed; or

(2) withdraws from future equity participation in the enterprise by executing and filing in the office of the Secretary of State a certificate declaring withdrawal under this section.

(b) A person who makes a contribution of the kind described in subsection (a) is liable as a general partner to any third party who transacts business with the enterprise (i) before the person withdraws and an appropriate certificate is filed to show withdrawal, or (ii) before an appropriate certificate is filed to show that he [or she] is not a general partner, but in either case only if the third party actually believed in good faith that the person was a general partner at the time of the transaction.

Section 305. Information.

Each limited partner has the right to:

(1) inspect and copy any of the partnership records required to be maintained by Section 105; and

(2) obtain from the general partners from time to time upon reasonable demand (i) true and full information regarding the state of the business and financial condition of the limited partnership, (ii) promptly after becoming available, a copy of the limited partnership's federal, state, and local income tax returns for each year, and (iii) other information regarding the affairs of the limited partnership as is just and reasonable.

Article 4
GENERAL PARTNERS

Section 401. Admission of Additional General Partners.

After the filing of a limited partnership's original certificate of limited partnership, additional general partners may be admitted as provided in writing in the partnership agreement or, if the partnership agreement does not provide in writing for the admission of additional general partners, with the written consent of all partners.

Section 402. Events of Withdrawal.

Except as approved by the specific written consent of all partners at the time, a person ceases to be a general partner of a limited partnership upon the happening of any of the following events:

(1) the general partner withdraws from the limited partnership as provided in Section 602;

(2) the general partner ceases to be a member of the limited partnership as provided in Section 702;

(3) the general partner is removed as a general partner in accordance with the partnership agreement;

(4) unless otherwise provided in writing in the partnership agreement, the general partner: (i) makes an assignment for the benefit of creditors; (ii) files a voluntary petition in bankruptcy; (iii) is adjudicated a bankrupt or insolvent; (iv) files a petition or answer seeking for him-

self [or herself] any reorganization, arrangement, composition, readjustment, liquidation, dissolution, or similar relief under any statute, law, or regulation; (v) files an answer or other pleading admitting or failing to contest the material allegations of a petition filed against him [or her] in any proceeding of this nature; or (vi) seeks, consents to, or acquiesces in the appointment of a trustee, receiver, or liquidator of the general partner or of all or any substantial part of his [or her] properties;

(5) unless otherwise provided in writing in the partnership agreement, [120] days after the commencement of any proceeding against the general partner seeking reorganization, arrangement, composition, readjustment, liquidation, dissolution, or similar relief under any statute, law, or regulation, the proceeding has not been dismissed, or if within [90] days after the appointment without his [or her] consent or acquiescence of a trustee, receiver, or liquidator of the general partner or of all or any substantial part of his [or her] properties, the appointment is not vacated or stayed or within [90] days after the expiration of any such stay, the appointment is not vacated;

(6) in the case of a general partner who is a natural person,

(i) his [or her] death; or

(ii) the entry of an order by a court of competent jurisdiction adjudicating him [or her] incompetent to manage his [or her] person or his [or her] estate;

(7) in the case of a general partner who is acting as a general partner by virtue of being a trustee of a trust, the termination of the trust (but not merely the substitution of a new trustee);

(8) in the case of a general partner that is a separate partnership, the dissolution and commencement of winding up of the separate partnership;

(9) in the case of a general partner that is a corporation, the filing of a certificate of dissolution, or its equivalent, for the corporation or the revocation of its charter; or

(10) in the case of an estate, the distribution by the fiduciary of the estate's entire interest in the partnership.

Section 403. General Powers and Liabilities.

(a) Except as provided in this [Act] or in the partnership agreement, a general partner of a limited partnership has the rights and powers and is subject to the restrictions of a partner in a partnership without limited partners.

(b) Except as provided in this [Act], a general partner of a limited partnership has the liabilities of a partner in a partnership without limited partners to persons other than the partnership and the other partners. Except as provided in this [Act] or in the partnership agreement, a general partner of a limited partnership has the liabilities of a partner in a partnership without limited partners to the partnership and to the other partners.

Section 404. Contributions by General Partner.

A general partner of a limited partnership may make contributions to the partnership and share in the profits and losses of, and in distributions from, the limited partnership as a general partner. A general partner also may make contributions to and share in profits, losses, and distributions as a limited partner. A person who is both a general partner and a limited partner has the rights and powers, and is subject to the restrictions and liabilities, of a general partner and, except as provided in the partnership agreement, also has the powers, and is subject to the restrictions, of a limited partner to the extent of his [or her] participation in the partnership as a limited partner.

Section 405. Voting.

The partnership agreement may grant to all or certain identified general partners the right to vote (on a per capita or any other basis), separately or with all or any class of the limited partners, on any matter.

Article 5
FINANCE

Section 501. Form of Contribution.

The contribution of a partner may be in cash, property, or services rendered, or a promissory note or other obligation to contribute cash or property or to perform services.

Section 502. Liability for Contribution.

(a) A promise by a limited partner to contribute to the limited partnership is not enforceable unless set out in a writing signed by the limited partner.

(b) Except as provided in the partnership agreement, a partner is obligated to the limited partnership to perform any enforceable promise to contribute cash or property or to perform services, even if he [or she] is unable to perform because of death, disability, or any other reason. If a partner does not make the required contribution of property or services, he [or she] is obligated at the option of the limited partnership to contribute cash equal to that portion of the value, as stated in the partnership records required to be kept pursuant to Section 105, of the stated contribution which has not been made.

(c) Unless otherwise provided in the partnership agreement, the obligation of a partner to make a contribution or return money or other property paid or distributed in violation of this [Act] may be compromised only by consent of all partners. Notwithstanding the compromise, a creditor of a limited partnership who extends credit, or, otherwise acts in reliance on that obligation after the partner signs a writing which reflects the obligation and before the amendment or cancellation thereof to reflect the compromise may enforce the original obligation.

Section 503. Sharing of Profits and Losses.

The profits and losses of a limited partnership shall be allocated among the partners, and among classes of partners, in the manner provided in writing in the partnership agreement. If the partnership agreement does not so provide in writing, profits and losses shall be allocated on the basis of the value, as stated in the partnership records required to be kept pursuant to Section 105, of the contributions made by each partner to the extent they have been received by the partnership and have not been returned.

Section 504. Sharing of Distributions.

Distributions of cash or other assets of a limited partnership shall be allocated among the partners and among classes of partners in the manner provided in writing in the partnership agreement. If the partnership agreement does not so provide in writing, distributions shall be made on the basis of the value, as stated in the partnership records required to be kept pursuant to Section 105, of the contributions made by each partner to the extent they have been received by the partnership and have not been returned.

Article 6 DISTRIBUTIONS AND WITHDRAWAL

Section 601. Interim Distributions.

Except as provided in this Article, a partner is entitled to receive distributions from a limited partnership before his [or her] withdrawal from the limited partnership and before the dissolution and winding up thereof to the extent and at the times or upon the happening of the events specified in the partnership agreement.

Section 602. Withdrawal of General Partner.

A general partner may withdraw from a limited partnership at any time by giving written notice to the other partners, but if the withdrawal violates the partnership agreement, the limited partnership may recover from the withdrawing general partner damages for breach of the partnership agreement and offset the damages against the amount otherwise distributable to him [or her].

Section 603. Withdrawal of Limited Partner.

A limited partner may withdraw from a limited partnership at the time or upon the happening of events specified in writing in the partnership agreement. If the agreement does not specify in writing the time or the events upon the happening of which a limited partner may withdraw or a definite time for the dissolution and winding up of the limited partnership, a limited partner may withdraw upon not less than six months' prior written notice to each general partner at his [or her] address on the books of the limited partnership at its office in this State.

Section 604. Distribution Upon Withdrawal.

Except as provided in this Article, upon withdrawal any withdrawing partner is entitled to receive any distribution to which he [or she] is entitled under the partnership agreement and, if not otherwise provided in the agreement, he [or she] is entitled to receive, within a reasonable time after withdrawal, the fair value of his [or her] interest in the limited partnership as of the date of withdrawal based upon his [or her] right to share in distributions from the limited partnership.

Section 605. Distribution in Kind.

Except as provided in writing in the partnership agreement, a partner, regardless of the nature of his [or her] contribution, has no right to demand and receive any distribution from a limited partnership in any form other than cash. Except as provided in writing in the partnership agreement, a partner may not be compelled to accept a distribution of any asset in kind from a limited partnership to the extent that the percentage of the asset distributed to him [or her] exceeds a percentage of that asset which is equal to the percentage in which he [or she] shares in distributions from the limited partnership.

Section 606. Right to Distribution.

At the time a partner becomes entitled to receive a distribution, he [or she] has the status of, and is entitled to all remedies available to, a creditor of the limited partnership with respect to the distribution.

Section 607. Limitations on Distribution.

A partner may not receive a distribution from a limited partnership to the extent that, after giving effect to the distribution, all liabilities of the limited partnership, other than liabilities to partners on account of their partnership interests, exceed the fair value of the partnership assets.

Section 608. Liability Upon Return of Contribution.

(a) If a partner has received the return of any part of his [or her] contribution without violation of the partnership agreement or this [Act], he [or she] is liable to the limited partnership for a period of one year thereafter for the amount of the returned contribution, but only to the extent necessary to discharge the limited partnership's liabilities to creditors who extended credit to the limited partnership during the period the contribution was held by the partnership.

(b) If a partner has received the return of any part of his [or her] contribution in violation of the partnership agreement or this [Act], he [or she] is liable to the limited partnership for a period of six years thereafter for the amount of the contribution wrongfully returned.

(c) A partner receives a return of his [or her] contribution to the extent that a distribution to him [or her] reduces his [or her] share of the fair value of the net assets of the limited partnership below the value, as set forth in the partnership records required to be kept pursuant to Section 105, of his [or her] contribution which has not been distributed to him [or her].

Article 7
ASSIGNMENT OF PARTNERSHIP INTERESTS

Section 701. Nature of Partnership Interest.

A partnership interest is personal property.

Section 702. Assignment of Partnership Interest.

Except as provided in the partnership agreement, a partnership interest is assignable in whole or in part. An assignment of a partnership interest does not dissolve a limited partnership or entitle the assignee to become or to exercise any rights of a partner. An assignment entitles the assignee to receive, to the extent assigned, only the distribution to which the assignor would be entitled. Except as provided in the partnership agreement, a partner ceases to be a partner upon assignment of all his [or her] partnership interest.

Section 703. Rights of Creditor.

On application to a court of competent jurisdiction by any judgment creditor of a partner, the court may charge the partnership interest of the partner with payment of the unsatisfied amount of the judgment with interest. To the extent so charged, the judgment creditor has only the rights of an assignee of the partnership interest. This [Act] does not deprive any partner of the benefit of any exemption laws applicable to his [or her] partnership interest.

Section 704. Right of Assignee to Become Limited Partner.

(a) An assignee of a partnership interest, including an assignee of a general partner, may become a limited partner if and to the extent that (i) the assignor gives the assignee that right in accordance with authority described in the partnership agreement, or (ii) all other partners consent.

(b) An assignee who has become a limited partner has, to the extent assigned, the rights and powers, and is subject to the restrictions and liabilities, of a limited partner under the partnership agreement and this [Act]. An assignee who becomes a limited partner also is liable for the obligations of his [or her] assignor to make and return contributions as provided in Articles 5 and 6. However, the assignee is not obligated for liabilities unknown to the assignee at the time he [or she] became a limited partner.

(c) If an assignee of a partnership interest becomes a limited partner, the assignor is not released from his [or her] liability to the limited partnership under Sections 207 and 502.

Section 705. Power of Estate of Deceased or Incompetent Partner.

If a partner who is an individual dies or a court of competent jurisdiction adjudges him [or her] to be incompetent to manage his [or her] person or his [or her] property, the partner's executor, administrator, guardian, conservator, or other legal representative may exercise all of the partner's rights for the purpose of settling his [or her] estate or administering his [or her] property, including any power the partner had to give an assignee the right to become a limited partner. If a partner is a corporation, trust, or other entity and is dissolved or terminated, the powers of that partner may be exercised by its legal representative or successor.

Article 8
DISSOLUTION

Section 801. Nonjudicial Dissolution.

A limited partnership is dissolved and its affairs shall be wound up upon the happening of the first to occur of the following:

(1) at the time specified in the certificate of limited partnership;

(2) upon the happening of events specified in writing in the partnership agreement;

(3) written consent of all partners;

(4) an event of withdrawal of a general partner unless at the time there is at least one other general partner and the written provisions of the partnership agreement permit the business of the limited partnership to be carried on by the remaining general partner and that partner does so, but the limited partnership is not dissolved and is not required to be wound up by reason of any event of withdrawal if, within 90 days after the withdrawal, all partners agree in writing to continue the business of the limited partnership and to the appointment of one or more additional general partners if necessary or desired; or

(5) entry of a decree of judicial dissolution under Section 802.

Section 802. Judicial Dissolution.

On application by or for a partner the [designate the appropriate court] court may decree dissolution of a limited partnership whenever it is not reasonably practicable to carry on the business in conformity with the partnership agreement.

Section 803. **Winding Up.**

Except as provided in the partnership agreement, the general partners who have not wrongfully dissolved a limited partnership or, if none, the limited partners, may wind up the limited partnership's affairs; but the [designate the appropriate court] court may wind up the limited partnership's affairs upon application of any partner, his [or her] legal representative, or assignee.

Section 804. **Distribution of Assets.**

Upon the winding up of a limited partnership, the assets shall be distributed as follows:

(1) to creditors, including partners who are creditors, to the extent permitted by law, in satisfaction of liabilities of the limited partnership other than liabilities for distributions to partners under Section 601 or 604;

(2) except as provided in the partnership agreement, to partners and former partners in satisfaction of liabilities for distributions under Section 601 or 604; and

(3) except as provided in the partnership agreement, to partners first for the return of their contributions and secondly respecting their partnership interests, in the proportions in which the partners share in distributions.

Article 9
FOREIGN LIMITED PARTNERSHIPS

Section 901. **Law Governing.**

Subject to the Constitution of this State, (i) the laws of the state under which a foreign limited partnership is organized govern its organization and internal affairs and the liability of its limited partners, and (ii) a foreign limited partnership may not be denied registration by reason of any difference between those laws and the laws of this State.

Section 902. **Registration.**

Before transacting business in this State, a foreign limited partnership shall register with the Secretary of State. In order to register, a foreign limited partnership shall submit to the Secretary of State, in duplicate, an application for registration as a foreign limited partnership, signed and sworn to by a general partner and setting forth:

(1) the name of the foreign limited partnership and, if different, the name under which it proposes to register and transact business in this State;

(2) the State and date of its formation;

(3) the name and address of any agent for service of process on the foreign limited partnership whom the foreign limited partnership elects to appoint; the agent must be an individual resident of this State, a domestic corporation, or a foreign corporation having a place of business in, and authorized to do business in, this State;

(4) a statement that the Secretary of State is appointed the agent of the foreign limited partnership for service of process if no agent has been appointed under paragraph (3) or, if appointed, the agent's authority has been revoked or if the agent cannot be found or served with the exercise of reasonable diligence;

(5) the address of the office required to be maintained in the state of its organization by the laws of that state or, if not so required, of the principal office of the foreign limited partnership;

(6) the name and business address of each general partner; and

(7) the address of the office at which is kept a list of the names and addresses of the limited partners and their capital contributions, together with an undertaking by the foreign limited partnership to keep those records until the foreign limited partnership's registration in this State is cancelled or withdrawn.

Section 903. **Issuance of Registration.**

(a) If the Secretary of State finds that an application for registration conforms to law and all requisite fees have been paid, he [or she] shall:

(1) endorse on the application the word "Filed", and the month, day, and year of the filing thereof;

(2) file in his [or her] office a duplicate original of the application; and

(3) issue a certificate of registration to transact business in this State.

(b) The certificate of registration, together with a duplicate original of the application, shall be returned to the person who filed the application or his [or her] representative.

Section 904. **Name.**

A foreign limited partnership may register with the Secretary of State under any name, whether or not it is the name under which it is registered in its state of organization, that includes without abbreviation the words "limited partnership" and that could be registered by a domestic limited partnership.

Section 905. **Changes and Amendments.**

If any statement in the application for registration of a foreign limited partnership was false when made or any arrangements or other facts described have changed, making the application inaccurate in any respect, the foreign limited partnership shall promptly file in the office of the Secretary of State a certificate, signed and sworn to by a general partner, correcting such statement.

Section 906. Cancellation of Registration.

A foreign limited partnership may cancel its registration by filing with the Secretary of State a certificate of cancellation signed and sworn to by a general partner. A cancellation does not terminate the authority of the Secretary of State to accept service of process on the foreign limited partnership with respect to [claims for relief] [causes of action] arising out of the transactions of business in this State.

Section 907. Transaction of Business Without Registration.

(a) A foreign limited partnership transacting business in this State may not maintain any action, suit, or proceeding in any court of this State until it has registered in this State.

(b) The failure of a foreign limited partnership to register in this State does not impair the validity of any contract or act of the foreign limited partnership or prevent the foreign limited partnership from defending any action, suit, or proceeding in any court of this State.

(c) A limited partner of a foreign limited partnership is not liable as a general partner of the foreign limited partnership solely by reason of having transacted business in this State without registration.

(d) A foreign limited partnership, by transacting business in this State without registration, appoints the Secretary of State as its agent for service of process with respect to [claims for relief] [causes of action] arising out of the transaction of business in this State.

Section 908. Action by [Appropriate Official].

The [designate the appropriate official] may bring an action to restrain a foreign limited partnership from transacting business in this State in violation of this Article.

Article 10
DERIVATIVE ACTIONS

Section 1001. Right of Action.

A limited partner may bring an action in the right of a limited partnership to recover a judgment in its favor if general partners with authority to do so have refused to bring the action or if an effort to cause those general partners to bring the action is not likely to succeed.

Section 1002. Proper Plaintiff.

In a derivative action, the plaintiff must be a partner at the time of bringing the action and (i) must have been a partner at the time of the transaction of which he [or she] complains or (ii) his [or her] status as a partner must have devolved upon him by operation of law or pursuant to the terms of the partnership agreement from a person who was a partner at the time of the transaction.

Section 1003. Pleading.

In a derivative action, the complaint shall set forth with particularity the effort of the plaintiff to secure initiation of the action by a general partner or the reasons for not making the effort.

Section 1004. Expenses.

If a derivative action is successful, in whole or in part, or if anything is received by the plaintiff as a result of a judgment, compromise, or settlement of an action or claim, the court may award the plaintiff reasonable expenses, including reasonable attorney's fees, and shall direct him [or her] to remit to the limited partnership the remainder of those proceeds received by him [or her].

Article 11
MISCELLANEOUS

Section 1101. Construction and Application.

This [Act] shall be so applied and construed to effectuate its general purpose to make uniform the law with respect to the subject of this [Act] among states enacting it.

Section 1102. Short Title.

This [Act] may be cited as the Uniform Limited Partnership Act.

Section 1103. Severability.

If any provision of this [Act] or its application to any person or circumstance is held invalid, the invalidity does not affect other provisions or applications of the [Act] which can be given effect without the invalid provision or application, and to this end the provisions of this [Act] are severable.

Section 1104. Effective Date, Extended Effective Date, and Repeal.

Except as set forth below, the effective date of this [Act] is ______ and the following acts [list existing limited partnership acts] are hereby repealed:

(1) The existing provisions for execution and filing of certificates of limited partnerships and amendments thereunder and cancellations thereof continue in effect until [specify time required to create central filing system], the extended effective date, and Sections 102, 103, 104, 105, 201, 202, 203, 204 and 206 are not effective until the extended effective date.

(2) Section 402, specifying the conditions under which a general partner ceases to be a member of a limited partnership, is not effective until the extended effective date, and the applicable provisions of existing law continue to govern until the extended effective date.

(3) Sections 501, 502 and 608 apply only to contributions and distributions made after the effective date of this [Act].

(4) Section 704 applies only to assignments made after the effective date of this [Act].

(5) Article 9, dealing with registration of foreign limited partnerships, is not effective until the extended effective date.

(6) Unless otherwise agreed by the partners, the applicable provisions of existing law governing allocation of profits and losses (rather than the provisions of Section 503), distributions to a withdrawing partner (rather than the provisions of Section 604), and distributions of assets upon the winding up of a limited partnership (rather than the provisions of Section 804) govern limited partnerships formed before the effective date of this [Act].

Section 1105. Rules for Cases Not Provided For in This [Act].

In any case not provided for in this [Act] the provisions of the Uniform Partnership Act govern.

Section 1106. Savings Clause.

The repeal of any statutory provision by this [Act] does not impair, or otherwise affect, the organization or the continued existence of a limited partnership existing at the effective date of this [Act], nor does the repeal of any existing statutory provision by this [Act] impair any contract or affect any right accrued before the effective date of this [Act].

APPENDIX G

The Revised Model Business Corporation Act (Excerpts)

Chapter 2. INCORPORATION

§ 2.01 Incorporators

One or more persons may act as the incorporator or incorporators of a corporation by delivering articles of incorporation to the secretary of state for filing.

§ 2.02 Articles of Incorporation

(a) The articles of incorporation must set forth:

(1) a corporate name * * * ;

(2) the number of shares the corporation is authorized to issue;

(3) the street address of the corporation's initial registered office and the name of its initial registered agent at that office; and

(4) the name and address of each incorporator.

(b) The articles of incorporation may set forth:

(1) the names and addresses of the individuals who are to serve as the initial directors;

(2) provisions not inconsistent with law regarding:

(i) the purpose or purposes for which the corporation is organized;

(ii) managing the business and regulating the affairs of the corporation;

(iii) defining, limiting, and regulating the powers of the corporation, its board of directors, and shareholders;

(iv) a par value for authorized shares or classes of shares;

(v) the imposition of personal liability on shareholders for the debts of the corporation to a specified extent and upon specified conditions;

(3) any provision that under this Act is required or permitted to be set forth in the bylaws; and

(4) a provision eliminating or limiting the liability of a director to the corporation or its shareholders for money damages for any action taken, or any failure to take any action, as a director, except liability for (A) the amount of a financial benefit received by a director to which he is not entitled; (B) an intentional infliction of harm on the corporation or the shareholders; (C) [unlawful distributions]; or (D) an intentional violation of criminal law.

(c) The articles of incorporation need not set forth any of the corporate powers enumerated in this Act.

§ 2.03 Incorporation

(a) Unless a delayed effective date is specified, the corporate existence begins when the articles of incorporation are filed.

(b) The secretary of state's filing of the articles of incorporation is conclusive proof that the incorporators satisfied all conditions precedent to incorporation except in a proceeding by the state to cancel or revoke the incorporation or involuntarily dissolve the corporation.

§ 2.04 Liability for Preincorporation Transactions

All persons purporting to act as or on behalf of a corporation, knowing there was no incorporation under this Act, are jointly and severally liable for all liabilities created while so acting.

§ 2.05 Organization of Corporation

(a) After incorporation:

(1) if initial directors are named in the articles of incorporation, the initial directors shall hold an organizational meeting, at the call of a majority of the directors, to complete the organization of the corporation by appointing officers, adopting bylaws, and carrying on any other business brought before the meeting;

(2) if initial directors are not named in the articles, the incorporator or incorporators shall hold an organizational meeting at the call of a majority of the incorporators:

(i) to elect directors and complete the organization of the corporation; or

(ii) to elect a board of directors who shall complete the organization of the corporation.

(b) Action required or permitted by this Act to be taken by incorporators at an organizational meeting may be taken without a meeting if the action taken is evidenced by one or more written consents describing the action taken and signed by each incorporator.

(c) An organizational meeting may be held in or out of this state.

* * * *

Chapter 3. PURPOSES AND POWERS

§ 3.01 Purposes

(a) Every corporation incorporated under this Act has the purpose of engaging in any lawful business unless a more limited purpose is set forth in the articles of incorporation.

(b) A corporation engaging in a business that is subject to regulation under another statute of this state may incorporate under this Act only if permitted by, and subject to all limitations of, the other statute.

§ 3.02 General Powers

Unless its articles of incorporation provide otherwise, every corporation has perpetual duration and succession in its corporate name and has the same powers as an individual to do all things necessary or convenient to carry out its business and affairs, including without limitation power:

(1) to sue and be sued, complain and defend in its corporate name;

(2) to have a corporate seal, which may be altered at will, and to use it, or a facsimile of it, by impressing or affixing it or in any other manner reproducing it;

(3) to make and amend bylaws, not inconsistent with its articles of incorporation or with the laws of this state, for managing the business and regulating the affairs of the corporation;

(4) to purchase, receive, lease, or otherwise acquire, and own, hold, improve, use, and otherwise deal with, real or personal property, or any legal or equitable interest in property, wherever located;

(5) to sell, convey, mortgage, pledge, lease, exchange, and otherwise dispose of all or any part of its property;

(6) to purchase, receive, subscribe for, or otherwise acquire; own, hold, vote, use, sell, mortgage, lend, pledge, or otherwise dispose of; and deal in and with shares or other interests in, or obligations of, any other entity;

(7) to make contracts and guarantees, incur liabilities, borrow money, issue its notes, bonds, and other obligations (which may be convertible into or include the option to purchase other securities of the corporation), and secure any of its obligations by mortgage or pledge of any of its property, franchises, or income;

(8) to lend money, invest and reinvest its funds, and receive and hold real and personal property as security for repayment;

(9) to be a promoter, partner, member, associate, or manager of any partnership, joint venture, trust, or other entity;

(10) to conduct its business, locate offices, and exercise the powers granted by this Act within or without this state;

(11) to elect directors and appoint officers, employees, and agents of the corporation, define their duties, fix their compensation, and lend them money and credit;

(12) to pay pensions and establish pension plans, pension trusts, profit sharing plans, share bonus plans, share option plans, and benefit or incentive plans for any or all of its current or former directors, officers, employees, and agents;

(13) to make donations for the public welfare or for charitable, scientific, or educational purposes;

(14) to transact any lawful business that will aid governmental policy;

(15) to make payments or donations, or do any other act, not inconsistent with law, that furthers the business and affairs of the corporation.

* * * *

Chapter 5. OFFICE AND AGENT

§ 5.01 Registered Office and Registered Agent

Each corporation must continuously maintain in this state:

(1) a registered office that may be the same as any of its places of business; and

(2) a registered agent, who may be:

(i) an individual who resides in this state and whose business office is identical with the registered office;

(ii) a domestic corporation or not-for-profit domestic corporation whose business office is identical with the registered office; or

(iii) a foreign corporation or not-for-profit foreign corporation authorized to transact business in this state whose business office is identical with the registered office.

* * * *

§ 5.04 Service on Corporation

(a) A corporation's registered agent is the corporation's agent for service of process, notice, or demand required or permitted by law to be served on the corporation.

(b) If a corporation has no registered agent, or the agent cannot with reasonable diligence be served, the corporation may be served by registered or certified mail, return receipt requested, addressed to the secretary of the corporation at its principal office. Service is perfected under this subsection at the earliest of:

(1) the date the corporation receives the mail;

(2) the date shown on the return receipt, if signed on behalf of the corporation; or

(3) five days after its deposit in the United States Mail, if mailed postpaid and correctly addressed.

(c) This section does not prescribe the only means, or necessarily the required means, of serving a corporation.

Chapter 6.
SHARES AND DISTRIBUTIONS

* * * *

Subchapter B. Issuance of Shares

* * * *

§ 6.21 Issuance of Shares

(a) The powers granted in this section to the board of directors may be reserved to the shareholders by the articles of incorporation.

(b) The board of directors may authorize shares to be issued for consideration consisting of any tangible or intangible property or benefit to the corporation, including cash, promissory notes, services performed, contracts for services to be performed, or other securities of the corporation.

(c) Before the corporation issues shares, the board of directors must determine that the consideration received or to be received for shares to be issued is adequate. That determination by the board of directors is conclusive insofar as the adequacy of consideration for the issuance of shares relates to whether the shares are validly issued, fully paid, and nonassessable.

(d) When the corporation receives the consideration for which the board of directors authorized the issuance of shares, the shares issued therefor are fully paid and nonassessable.

(e) The corporation may place in escrow shares issued for a contract for future services or benefits or a promissory note, or make other arrangements to restrict the transfer of the shares, and may credit distributions in respect of the shares against their purchase price, until the services are performed, the note is paid, or the benefits received. If the services are not performed, the note is not paid, or the benefits are not received, the shares escrowed or restricted and the distributions credited may be cancelled in whole or part.

* * * *

§ 6.27 Restriction on Transfer or Registration of Shares and Other Securities

(a) The articles of incorporation, bylaws, an agreement among shareholders, or an agreement between shareholders and the corporation may impose restrictions on the transfer or registration of transfer of shares of the corporation. A restriction does not affect shares issued before the restriction was adopted unless the holders of the shares are parties to the restriction agreement or voted in favor of the restriction.

(b) A restriction on the transfer or registration of transfer of shares is valid and enforceable against the holder or a transferee of the holder if the restriction is authorized by this section and its existence is noted conspicuously on the front or back of the certificate or is contained in the information statement [sent to the shareholder]. Unless so noted, a restriction is not enforceable against a person without knowledge of the restriction.

(c) A restriction on the transfer or registration of transfer of shares is authorized:

(1) to maintain the corporation's status when it is dependent on the number or identity of its shareholders;

(2) to preserve exemptions under federal or state securities law;

(3) for any other reasonable purpose.

(d) A restriction on the transfer or registration of transfer of shares may:

(1) obligate the shareholder first to offer the corporation or other persons (separately, consecutively, or simultaneously) an opportunity to acquire the restricted shares;

(2) obligate the corporate or other persons (separately, consecutively, or simultaneously) to acquire the restricted shares;

(3) require the corporation, the holders of any class of its shares, or another person to approve the transfer of the restricted shares, if the requirement is not manifestly unreasonable;

(4) prohibit the transfer of the restricted shares to designated persons or classes of persons, if the prohibition is not manifestly unreasonable.

(e) For purposes of this section, "shares" includes a security convertible into or carrying a right to subscribe for or acquire shares.

* * * *

Chapter 7. SHAREHOLDERS

Subchapter A. Meetings

§ 7.01 Annual Meeting

(a) A corporation shall hold annually at a time stated in or fixed in accordance with the bylaws a meeting of shareholders.

(b) Annual shareholders' meetings may be held in or out of this state at the place stated in or fixed in accordance with the bylaws. If no place is stated in or fixed in accordance with the bylaws, annual meetings shall be held at the corporation's principal office.

(c) The failure to hold an annual meeting at the time stated in or fixed in accordance with a corporation's bylaws does not affect the validity of any corporate action.

* * * *

§ 7.05 Notice of Meeting

(a) A corporation shall notify shareholders of the date, time, and place of each annual and special shareholders' meeting no fewer than 10 nor more than 60 days before the meeting date. Unless this Act or the articles of incorporation require otherwise, the corporation is required to give notice only to shareholders entitled to vote at the meeting.

(b) Unless this Act or the articles of incorporation require otherwise, notice of an annual meeting need not include a description of the purpose or purposes for which the meeting is called.

(c) Notice of a special meeting must include a description of the purpose or purposes for which the meeting is called.

(d) If not otherwise fixed * * *, the record date for determining shareholders entitled to notice of and to vote at an annual or special shareholders' meeting is the day before the first notice is delivered to shareholders.

(e) Unless the bylaws require otherwise, if an annual or special shareholders' meeting is adjourned to a different date, time, or place, notice need not be given of the new date, time, or place if the new date, time, or place is announced at the meeting before adjournment. * * *

* * * *

§ 7.07 Record Date

(a) The bylaws may fix or provide the manner of fixing the record date for one or more voting groups in order to determine the shareholders entitled to notice of a shareholders' meeting, to demand a special meeting, to vote, or to take any other action. If the bylaws do not fix or provide for fixing a record date, the board of directors of the corporation may fix a future date as the record date.

(b) A record date fixed under this section may not be more than 70 days before the meeting or action requiring a determination of shareholders.

(c) A determination of shareholders entitled to notice of or to vote at a shareholders' meeting is effective for any adjournment of the meeting unless the board of directors fixes a new record date, which it must do if the meeting is adjourned to a date more than 120 days after the date fixed for the original meeting.

(d) If a court orders a meeting adjourned to a date more than 120 days after the date fixed for the original meeting, it may provide that the original record date continues in effect or it may fix a new record date.

Subchapter B. Voting

§ 7.20 Shareholders' List for Meeting

(a) After fixing a record date for a meeting, a corporation shall prepare an alphabetical list of the names of all its shareholders who are entitled to notice of a shareholders' meeting. The list must be arranged by voting group (and within each voting group by class or series of shares) and show the address of and number of shares held by each shareholder.

(b) The shareholders' list must be available for inspection by any shareholder, beginning two business days after notice of the meeting is given for which the list was prepared and continuing through the meeting, at the corporation's principal office or at a place identified in the meeting notice in the city where the meeting will be held. A shareholder, his agent, or attorney is entitled on written demand to inspect and, subject to the requirements of section 16.02(c), to copy the list, during regular business hours and at his expense, during the period it is available for inspection.

(c) The corporation shall make the shareholders' list available at the meeting, and any shareholder, his agent, or attorney is entitled to inspect the list at any time during the meeting or any adjournment.

(d) If the corporation refuses to allow a shareholder, his agent, or attorney to inspect the shareholders' list before or at the meeting (or copy the list as permitted by subsection (b)), the [name or describe] court of the county where a corporation's principal office (or, if none in this state, its registered office) is located, on application of the shareholder, may summarily order the inspection or copying at the corporation's expense and may postpone the meeting for which the list was prepared until the inspection or copying is complete.

(e) Refusal or failure to prepare or make available the shareholders' list does not affect the validity of action taken at the meeting.

* * * *

§ 7.22 Proxies

(a) A shareholder may vote his shares in person or by proxy.

(b) A shareholder may appoint a proxy to vote or otherwise act for him by signing an appointment form, either personally or by his attorney-in-fact.

(c) An appointment of a proxy is effective when received by the secretary or other officer or agent authorized to tabulate votes. An appointment is valid for 11 months unless a longer period is expressly provided in the appointment form.

* * * *

§ 7.28 Voting for Directors; Cumulative Voting

(a) Unless otherwise provided in the articles of incorporation, directors are elected by a plurality of the votes cast by the shares entitled to vote in the election at a meeting at which a quorum is present.

(b) Shareholders do not have a right to cumulate their votes for directors unless the articles of incorporation so provide.

(c) A statement included in the articles of incorporation that "[all] [a designated voting group of] shareholders are entitled to cumulate their votes for directors" (or words of similar import) means that the shareholders designated are entitled to multiply the number of votes they are entitled to cast by the number of directors for whom they are entitled to vote and cast the product for a single candidate or distribute the product among two or more candidates.

(d) Shares otherwise entitled to vote cumulatively may not be voted cumulatively at a particular meeting unless:

(1) the meeting notice or proxy statement accompanying the notice states conspicuously that cumulative voting is authorized; or

(2) a shareholder who has the right to cumulate his votes gives notice to the corporation not less than 48 hours before the time set for the meeting of his intent to cumulate his votes during the meeting, and if one shareholder gives this notice all other shareholders in the same voting group participating in the election are entitled to cumulate their votes without giving further notice.

* * * *

Subchapter D. Derivative Proceedings

* * * *

§ 7.41 Standing

A shareholder may not commence or maintain a derivative proceeding unless the shareholder:

(1) was a shareholder of the corporation at the time of the act or omission complained of or became a shareholder through transfer by operation of law from one who was a shareholder at that time; and

(2) fairly and adequately represents the interests of the corporation in enforcing the right of the corporation.

§ 7.42 Demand

No shareholder may commence a derivative proceeding until:

(1) a written demand has been made upon the corporation to take suitable action; and

(2) 90 days have expired from the date the demand was made unless the shareholder has earlier been notified that the demand has been rejected by the corporation or unless irreparable injury to the corporation would result by waiting for the expiration of the 90 day period.

* * * *

Chapter 8. DIRECTORS AND OFFICERS

Subchapter A. Board of Directors

* * * *

§ 8.02 Qualifications of Directors

The articles of incorporation or bylaws may prescribe qualifications for directors. A director need not be a resident of this state or a shareholder of the corporation unless the articles of incorporation or bylaws so prescribe.

§ 8.03 Number and Election of Directors

(a) A board of directors must consist of one or more individuals, with the number specified in or fixed in accordance with the articles of incorporation or bylaws.

(b) If a board of directors has power to fix or change the number of directors, the board may increase or decrease by 30 percent or less the number of directors last approved by the shareholders, but only the shareholders may increase or decrease by more than 30 percent the number of directors last approved by the shareholders.

(c) The articles of incorporation or bylaws may establish a variable range for the size of the board of directors by fixing a minimum and maximum number of directors. If a variable range is established, the number of directors may be fixed or changed from time to time, within the minimum and maximum, by the shareholders or the board of directors. After shares are issued, only the shareholders may change the range for the size of the board or change from a fixed to a variable-range size board or vice versa.

(d) Directors are elected at the first annual shareholders' meeting and at each annual meeting thereafter unless their terms are staggered under section 8.06.

* * * *

§ 8.08 Removal of Directors by Shareholders

(a) The shareholders may remove one or more directors with or without cause unless the articles of incorporation provide that directors may be removed only for cause.

(b) If a director is elected by a voting group of shareholders, only the shareholders of that voting group may participate in the vote to remove him.

(c) If cumulative voting is authorized, a director may not be removed if the number of votes sufficient to elect him under cumulative voting is voted against his removal. If cumulative voting is not authorized, a director may be removed only if the number of votes cast to remove him exceeds the number of votes cast not to remove him.

(d) A director may be removed by the shareholders only at a meeting called for the purpose of removing him and the meeting notice must state that the purpose, or one of the purposes, of the meeting is removal of the director.

* * * *

Subchapter B. Meetings and Action of the Board

§ 8.20 Meetings

(a) The board of directors may hold regular or special meetings in or out of this state.

(b) Unless the articles of incorporation or bylaws provide otherwise, the board of directors may permit any or all directors to participate in a regular or special meeting by, or conduct the meeting through the use of, any means of communication by which all directors participating may simultaneously hear each other during the meeting. A director participating in a meeting by this means is deemed to be present in person at the meeting.

* * * *

§ 8.22 Notice of Meeting

(a) Unless the articles of incorporation or bylaws provide otherwise, regular meetings of the board of directors may be held without notice of the date, time, place, or purpose of the meeting.

(b) Unless the articles of incorporation or bylaws provide for a longer or shorter period, special meetings of the board of directors must be preceded by at least two days' notice of the date, time, and place of the meeting. The notice need not describe the purpose of the special meeting unless required by the articles of incorporation or bylaws.

* * * *

§ 8.24 Quorum and Voting

(a) Unless the articles of incorporation or bylaws require a greater number, a quorum of a board of directors consists of:

(1) a majority of the fixed number of directors if the corporation has a fixed board size; or

(2) a majority of the number of directors prescribed, or if no number is prescribed the number in office immediately before the meeting begins, if the corporation has a variable-range size board.

(b) The articles of incorporation or bylaws may authorize a quorum of a board of directors to consist of no fewer than one-third of the fixed or prescribed number of directors determined under subsection (a).

(c) If a quorum is present when a vote is taken, the affirmative vote of a majority of directors present is the act of the board of directors unless the articles of incorporation or bylaws require the vote of a greater number of directors.

(d) A director who is present at a meeting of the board of directors or a committee of the board of directors when corporate action is taken is deemed to have assented to the action taken unless: (1) he objects at the beginning of the meeting (or promptly upon his arrival) to holding it or transacting business at the meeting; (2) his dissent or abstention from the action taken is entered in the minutes of the meeting; or (3) he delivers written notice of his dissent or abstention to the presiding officer of the meeting before its adjournment or to the corporation immediately after adjournment of the meeting. The right of dissent or abstention is not available to a director who votes in favor of the action taken.

* * * *

Subchapter C. Standards of Conduct

§ 8.30 General Standards for Directors

(a) A director shall discharge his duties as a director, including his duties as a member of a committee:

(1) in good faith;

(2) with the care an ordinarily prudent person in a like position would exercise under similar circumstances; and

(3) in a manner he reasonably believes to be in the best interests of the corporation.

(b) In discharging his duties a director is entitled to rely on information, opinions, reports, or statements, including financial statements and other financial data, if prepared or presented by:

(1) one or more officers or employees of the corporation whom the director reasonably believes to be reliable and competent in the matters presented;

(2) legal counsel, public accountants, or other persons as to matters the director reasonably believes are within the person's professional or expert competence; or

(3) a committee of the board of directors of which he is not a member if the director reasonably believes the committee merits confidence.

(c) A director is not acting in good faith if he has knowledge concerning the matter in question that makes reliance otherwise permitted by subsection (b) unwarranted.

(d) A director is not liable for any action taken as a director, or any failure to take any action, if he performed the duties of his office in compliance with this section.

* * * *

Subchapter D. Officers

* * * *

§ 8.41 Duties of Officers

Each officer has the authority and shall perform the duties set forth in the bylaws or, to the extent consistent with the bylaws, the duties prescribed by the board of directors or by direction of an officer authorized by the board of directors to prescribe the duties of other officers.

§ 8.42 Standards of Conduct for Officers

(a) An officer with discretionary authority shall discharge his duties under that authority:

(1) in good faith;

(2) with the care an ordinarily prudent person in a like position would exercise under similar circumstances; and

(3) in a manner he reasonably believes to be in the best interests of the corporation.

(b) In discharging his duties an officer is entitled to rely on information, opinions, reports, or statements, including financial statements and other financial data, if prepared or presented by:

(1) one or more officers or employees of the corporation whom the officer reasonably believes to be reliable and competent in the matters presented; or

(2) legal counsel, public accountants, or other persons as to matters the officer reasonably believes are within the person's professional or expert competence.

(c) An officer is not acting in good faith if he has knowledge concerning the matter in question that makes reliance otherwise permitted by subsection (b) unwarranted.

(d) An officer is not liable for any action taken as an officer, or any failure to take any action, if he performed the duties of his office in compliance with this section.

* * * *

Chapter 11.
MERGER AND SHARE EXCHANGE

§ 11.01 Merger

(a) One or more corporations may merge into another corporation if the board of directors of each corporation adopts and its shareholders (if required * * *) approve a plan of merger.

(b) The plan of merger must set forth:

(1) the name of each corporation planning to merge and the name of the surviving corporation into which each other corporation plans to merge;

(2) the terms and conditions of the merger; and

(3) the manner and basis of converting the shares of each corporation into shares, obligations, or other securities of the surviving or any other corporation or into cash or other property in whole or part.

(c) The plan of merger may set forth:

(1) amendments to the articles of incorporation of the surviving corporation; and

(2) other provisions relating to the merger.

* * * *

§ 11.04 Merger of Subsidiary

(a) A parent corporation owning at least 90 percent of the outstanding shares of each class of a subsidiary corporation may merge the subsidiary into itself without approval of the shareholders of the parent or subsidiary.

(b) The board of directors of the parent shall adopt a plan of merger that sets forth:

(1) the names of the parent and subsidiary; and

(2) the manner and basis of converting the shares of the subsidiary into shares, obligations, or other securities of the parent or any other corporation or into cash or other property in whole or part.

(c) The parent shall mail a copy or summary of the plan of merger to each shareholder of the subsidiary who does not waive the mailing requirement in writing.

(d) The parent may not deliver articles of merger to the secretary of state for filing until at least 30 days after the date it mailed a copy of the plan of merger to each shareholder of the subsidiary who did not waive the mailing requirement.

(e) Articles of merger under this section may not contain amendments to the articles of incorporation of the parent corporation (except for amendments enumerated in section 10.02).

* * * *

§ 11.06 Effect of Merger or Share Exchange

(a) When a merger takes effect:

(1) every other corporation party to the merger merges into the surviving corporation and the separate existence of every corporation except the surviving corporation ceases;

(2) the title to all real estate and other property owned by each corporation party to the merger is vested in the surviving corporation without reversion or impairment;

(3) the surviving corporation has all liabilities of each corporation party to the merger;

(4) a proceeding pending against any corporation party to the merger may be continued as if the merger did not occur or the surviving corporation may be substituted in the proceeding for the corporation whose existence ceased;

(5) the articles of incorporation of the surviving corporation are amended to the extent provided in the plan of merger; and

(6) the shares of each corporation party to the merger that are to be converted into shares, obligations, or other securities of the surviving or any other corporation or into cash or other property are converted and the former holders of the shares are entitled only to the rights provided in the articles of merger or to their rights under chapter 13.

(b) When a share exchange takes effect, the shares of each acquired corporation are exchanged as provided in the plan, and the former holders of the shares are entitled only to the exchange rights provided in the articles of share exchange or to their rights under chapter 13.

* * * *

Chapter 13.
DISSENTERS' RIGHTS

Subchapter A. Right to Dissent and Obtain Payment for Shares

* * * *

§ 13.02 Right to Dissent

(a) A shareholder is entitled to dissent from, and obtain payment of the fair value of his shares in the event of, any of the following corporate actions:

(1) consummation of a plan of merger to which the corporation is a party (i) if shareholder approval is required for the merger by [statute] or the articles of incorporation and the shareholder is entitled to vote on the merger or (ii) if the corporation is a subsidiary that is merged with its parent under section 11.04;

(2) consummation of a plan of share exchange to which the corporation is a party as the corporation whose shares will be acquired, if the shareholder is entitled to vote on the plan;

(3) consummation of a sale or exchange of all, or substantially all, of the property of the corporation other than in the usual and regular course of business, if the shareholder is entitled to vote on the sale or exchange, including a sale in dissolution, but not including a sale pursuant to court order or a sale for cash pursuant to a plan by which all or substantially all of the net proceeds of the sale will be distributed to the shareholders within one year after the date of sale;

(4) an amendment of the articles of incorporation that materially and adversely affects rights in respect of a dissenter's shares because it:

(i) alters or abolishes a preferential right of the shares;

(ii) creates, alters, or abolishes a right in respect of redemption, including a provision respecting a sinking fund for the redemption or repurchase, of the shares;

(iii) alters or abolishes a preemptive right of the holder of the shares to acquire shares or other securities;

(iv) excludes or limits the right of the shares to vote on any matter, or to cumulate votes, other than a limitation by dilution through issuance of shares or other securities with similar voting rights; or

(v) reduces the number of shares owned by the shareholder to a fraction of a share if the fractional share so created is to be acquired for cash * * *; or

(5) any corporate action taken pursuant to a shareholder vote to the extent the articles of incorporation, bylaws, or a resolution of the board of directors provides that voting or nonvoting shareholders are entitled to dissent and obtain payment for their shares.

(b) A shareholder entitled to dissent and obtain payment for his shares under this chapter may not challenge the corporate action creating his entitlement unless the action is unlawful or fraudulent with respect to the shareholder or the corporation.

* * * *

Subchapter B. Procedure for Exercise of Dissenters' Rights

* * * *

§ 13.21 Notice of Intent to Demand Payment

(a) If proposed corporate action creating dissenters' rights under section 13.02 is submitted to a vote at a shareholders' meeting, a shareholder who wishes to assert dissenters' rights (1) must deliver to the corporation before the vote is taken written notice of his intent to demand payment for his shares if the proposed action is effectuated and (2) must not vote his shares in favor of the proposed action.

(b) A shareholder who does not satisfy the requirements of subsection (a) is not entitled to payment for his shares under this chapter.

* * * *

§ 13.25 Payment

(a) * * * [A]s soon as the proposed corporate action is taken, or upon receipt of a payment demand, the corporation shall pay each dissenter * * * the amount the corporation estimates to be the fair value of his shares, plus accrued interest.

* * * *

§ 13.28 Procedure If Shareholder Dissatisfied with Payment or Offer

(a) A dissenter may notify the corporation in writing of his own estimate of the fair value of his shares and amount of interest due, and demand payment of his estimate (less any payment under section 13.25) * * * if:

(1) the dissenter believes that the amount paid under section 13.25 * * * is less than the fair value of his shares or that the interest due is incorrectly calculated;

(2) the corporation fails to make payment under section 13.25 within 60 days after the date set for demanding payment; or

(3) the corporation, having failed to take the proposed action, does not return the deposited certificates or release the transfer restrictions imposed on uncertificated shares within 60 days after the date set for demanding payment.

(b) A dissenter waives his right to demand payment under this section unless he notifies the corporation of his demand in writing under subsection (a) within 30 days after the corporation made or offered payment for his shares.

* * * *

Chapter 14. DISSOLUTION

Subchapter A. Voluntary Dissolution

* * * *

§ 14.02 Dissolution by Board of Directors and Shareholders

(a) A corporation's board of directors may propose dissolution for submission to the shareholders.

(b) For a proposal to dissolve to be adopted:

(1) the board of directors must recommend dissolution to the shareholders unless the board of directors determines that because of conflict of interest or other special circumstances it should make no recommendation and communicates the basis for its determination to the shareholders; and

(2) the shareholders entitled to vote must approve the proposal to dissolve as provided in subsection (e).

(c) The board of directors may condition its submission of the proposal for dissolution on any basis.

(d) The corporation shall notify each shareholder, whether or not entitled to vote, of the proposed shareholders' meeting in accordance with section 7.05. The notice must also state that the purpose, or one of the purposes, of the meeting is to consider dissolving the corporation.

(e) Unless the articles of incorporation or the board of directors (acting pursuant to subsection (c)) require a greater vote or a vote by voting groups, the proposal to dissolve to be adopted must be approved by a majority of all the votes entitled to be cast on that proposal.

* * * *

§ 14.05 Effect of Dissolution

(a) A dissolved corporation continues its corporate existence but may not carry on any business except that appropriate to wind up and liquidate its business and affairs, including:

(1) collecting its assets;

(2) disposing of its properties that will not be distributed in kind to its shareholders;

(3) discharging or making provision for discharging its liabilities;

(4) distributing its remaining property among its shareholders according to their interests; and

(5) doing every other act necessary to wind up and liquidate its business and affairs.

(b) Dissolution of a corporation does not:

(1) transfer title to the corporation's property;

(2) prevent transfer of its shares or securities, although the authorization to dissolve may provide for closing the corporation's share transfer records;

(3) subject its directors or officers to standards of conduct different from those prescribed in chapter 8;

(4) change quorum or voting requirements for its board of directors or shareholders; change provisions for selection, resignation, or removal of its directors or officers or both; or change provisions for amending its bylaws;

(5) prevent commencement of a proceeding by or against the corporation in its corporate name;

(6) abate or suspend a proceeding pending by or against the corporation on the effective date of dissolution; or

(7) terminate the authority of the registered agent of the corporation.

* * * *

Subchapter C. Judicial Dissolution

§ 14.30 Grounds for Judicial Dissolution

The [name or describe court or courts] may dissolve a corporation:

(1) in a proceeding by the attorney general if it is established that:

(i) the corporation obtained its articles of incorporation through fraud; or

(ii) the corporation has continued to exceed or abuse the authority conferred upon it by law;

(2) in a proceeding by a shareholder if it is established that:

(i) the directors are deadlocked in the management of the corporate affairs, the shareholders are unable to break the deadlock, and irreparable injury to the corporation is threatened or being suffered, or the business and affairs of the corporation can no longer be conducted to the advantage of the shareholders generally, because of the deadlock;

(ii) the directors or those in control of the corporation have acted, are acting, or will act in a manner that is illegal, oppressive, or fraudulent;

(iii) the shareholders are deadlocked in voting power and have failed, for a period that includes at least two consecutive annual meeting dates, to elect successors to directors whose terms have expired; or

(iv) the corporate assets are being misapplied or wasted;

(3) in a proceeding by a creditor if it is established that:

(i) the creditor's claim has been reduced to judgment, the execution on the judgment returned unsatisfied, and the corporation is insolvent; or

(ii) the corporation has admitted in writing that the creditor's claim is due and owing and the corporation is insolvent; or

(4) in a proceeding by the corporation to have its voluntary dissolution continued under court supervision.

* * * *

Chapter 16.
RECORDS AND REPORTS

Subchapter A. Records

§ 16.01 Corporate Records

(a) A corporation shall keep as permanent records minutes of all meetings of its shareholders and board of directors, a record of all actions taken by the shareholders or board of directors without a meeting, and a record of all actions taken by a committee of the board of directors in place of the board of directors on behalf of the corporation.

(b) A corporation shall maintain appropriate accounting records.

(c) A corporation or its agent shall maintain a record of its shareholders, in a form that permits preparation of a list of the names and addresses of all shareholders, in alphabetical order by class of shares showing the number and class of shares held by each.

(d) A corporation shall maintain its records in written form or in another form capable of conversion into written form within a reasonable time.

(e) A corporation shall keep a copy of the following records at its principal office:

(1) its articles or restated articles of incorporation and all amendments to them currently in effect;

(2) its bylaws or restated bylaws and all amendments to them currently in effect;

(3) resolutions adopted by its board of directors creating one or more classes or series of shares, and fixing their relative rights, preferences, and limitations, if shares issued pursuant to those resolutions are outstanding;

(4) the minutes of all shareholders' meetings, and records of all action taken by shareholders without a meeting, for the past three years;

(5) all written communications to shareholders generally within the past three years, including the financial statements furnished for the past three years * * *;

(6) a list of the names and business addresses of its current directors and officers; and

(7) its most recent annual report delivered to the secretary of state * * *.

§ 16.02 Inspection of Records by Shareholders

(a) Subject to section 16.03(c), a shareholder of a corporation is entitled to inspect and copy, during regular business hours at the corporation's principal office, any of the records of the corporation described in section 16.01(e) if he gives the corporation written notice of his demand at least five business days before the date on which he wishes to inspect and copy.

(b) A shareholder of a corporation is entitled to inspect and copy, during regular business hours at a reasonable location specified by the corporation, any of the following records of the corporation if the shareholder meets the requirements of subsection (c) and gives the corporation written notice of his demand at least five business days before the date on which he wishes to inspect and copy:

(1) excerpts from minutes of any meeting of the board of directors, records of any action of a committee of the board of directors while acting in place of the board of directors on behalf of the corporation, minutes of any meeting of the shareholders, and records of action taken by the shareholders or board of directors without a meeting, to the extent not subject to inspection under section 16.02(a);

(2) accounting records of the corporation; and

(3) the record of shareholders.

(c) A shareholder may inspect and copy the records identified in subsection (b) only if:

(1) his demand is made in good faith and for a proper purpose;

(2) he describes with reasonable particularity his purpose and the records he desires to inspect; and

(3) the records are directly connected with his purpose.

(d) The right of inspection granted by this section may not be abolished or limited by a corporation's articles of incorporation or bylaws.

(e) This section does not affect:

(1) the right of a shareholder to inspect records under section 7.20 or, if the shareholder is in litigation with the corporation, to the same extent as any other litigant;

(2) the power of a court, independently of this Act, to compel the production of corporate records for examination.

(f) For purposes of this section, "shareholder" includes a beneficial owner whose shares are held in a voting trust or by a nominee on his behalf.

APPENDIX H

The Uniform Limited Liability Company Act (Excerpts)

[ARTICLE] 2. ORGANIZATION

Section 201. Limited liability company as legal entity.

A limited liability company is a legal entity distinct from its members.

Section 202. Organization.

(a) One or more persons may organize a limited liability company, consisting of one or more members, by delivering articles of organization to the office of the [Secretary of State] for filing.

(b) Unless a delayed effective date is specified, the existence of a limited liability company begins when the articles of organization are filed.

(c) The filing of the articles of organization by the [Secretary of State] is conclusive proof that the organizers satisfied all conditions precedent to the creation of a limited liability company.

Section 203. Articles of organization.

(a) Articles of organization of a limited liability company must set forth:

(1) the name of the company;

(2) the address of the initial designated office;

(3) the name and street address of the initial agent for service of process;

(4) the name and address of each organizer;

(5) whether the company is to be a term company and, if so, the term specified;

(6) whether the company is to be manager-managed, and, if so, the name and address of each initial manager; and

(7) whether one or more of the members of the company are to be liable for its debts and obligations under Section 303(c).

(b) Articles of organization of a limited liability company may set forth:

(1) provisions permitted to be set forth in an operating agreement; or

(2) other matters not inconsistent with law.

(c) Articles of organization of a limited liability company may not vary the nonwaivable provisions of Section 103(b). As to all other matters, if any provision of an operating agreement is inconsistent with the articles of organization:

(1) the operating agreement controls as to managers, members, and members' transferees; and

(2) the articles of organization control as to persons, other than managers, members and their transferees, who reasonably rely on the articles to their detriment.

* * * *

Section 208. Certificate of existence or authorization.

(a) A person may request the [Secretary of State] to furnish a certificate of existence for a limited liability company or a certificate of authorization for a foreign limited liability company.

(b) A certificate of existence for a limited liability company must set forth:

(1) the company's name;

(2) that it is duly organized under the laws of this State, the date of organization, whether its duration is at-will or for a specified term, and, if the latter, the period specified;

(3) if payment is reflected in the records of the [Secretary of State] and if nonpayment affects the existence of the company, that all fees, taxes, and penalties owed to this State have been paid;

(4) whether its most recent annual report required by Section 211 has been filed with the [Secretary of State];

(5) that articles of termination have not been filed; and

(6) other facts of record in the office of the [Secretary of State] which may be requested by the applicant.

(c) A certificate of authorization for a foreign limited liability company must set forth:

(1) the company's name used in this State;

(2) that it is authorized to transact business in this State;

(3) if payment is reflected in the records of the [Secretary of State] and if nonpayment affects the authorization of the company, that all fees, taxes, and penalties owed to this State have been paid;

(4) whether its most recent annual report required by Section 211 has been filed with the [Secretary of State];

(5) that a certificate of cancellation has not been filed; and

(6) other facts of record in the office of the [Secretary of State] which may be requested by the applicant.

(d) Subject to any qualification stated in the certificate, a certificate of existence or authorization issued by the [Secretary of State] may be relied upon as conclusive evidence that the domestic or foreign limited liability company is in existence or is authorized to transact business in this State.

* * * *

[ARTICLE] 3.

RELATIONS OF MEMBERS AND MANAGERS TO PERSONS DEALING WITH LIMITED LIABILITY COMPANY

* * * *

Section 303. Liability of members and managers.

(a) Except as otherwise provided in subsection (c), the debts, obligations, and liabilities of a limited liability company, whether arising in contract, tort, or otherwise, are solely the debts, obligations, and liabilities of the company. A member or manager is not personally liable for a debt, obligation, or liability of the company solely by reason of being or acting as a member or manager.

(b) The failure of a limited liability company to observe the usual company formalities or requirements relating to the exercise of its company powers or management of its business is not a ground for imposing personal liability on the members or managers for liabilities of the company.

(c) All or specified members of a limited liability company are liable in their capacity as members for all or specified debts, obligations, or liabilities of the company if:

(1) a provision to that effect is contained in the articles of organization; and

(2) a member so liable has consented in writing to the adoption of the provision or to be bound by the provision.

* * * *

[ARTICLE] 4.

RELATIONS OF MEMBERS TO EACH OTHER AND TO LIMITED LIABILITY COMPANY

* * * *

Section 404. Management of limited liability company.

(a) In a member-managed company:

(1) each member has equal rights in the management and conduct of the company's business; and

(2) except as otherwise provided in subsection (c) or in Section 801(b)(3)(i), any matter relating to the business of the company may be decided by a majority of the members.

(b) In a manager-managed company:

(1) each manager has equal rights in the management and conduct of the company's business;

(2) except as otherwise provided in subsection (c) or in Section 801(b)(3)(i), any matter relating to the business of the company may be exclusively decided by the manager or, if there is more than one manager, by a majority of the managers; and

(3) a manager:

(i) must be designated, appointed, elected, removed, or replaced by a vote, approval, or consent of a majority of the members; and

(ii) holds office until a successor has been elected and qualified, unless the manager sooner resigns or is removed.

(c) The only matters of a member or manager-managed company's business requiring the consent of all of the members are:

(1) the amendment of the operating agreement under Section 103;

(2) the authorization or ratification of acts or transactions under Section 103(b)(2)(ii) which would otherwise violate the duty of loyalty;

(3) an amendment to the articles of organization under Section 204;

(4) the compromise of an obligation to make a contribution under Section 402(b);

(5) the compromise, as among members, of an obligation of a member to make a contribution or return money or other property paid or distributed in violation of this [Act];

(6) the making of interim distributions under Section 405(a), including the redemption of an interest;

(7) the admission of a new member;

(8) the use of the company's property to redeem an interest subject to a charging order;

(9) the consent to dissolve the company under Section 801(b)(2);

(10) a waiver of the right to have the company's business wound up and the company terminated under Section 802(b);

(11) the consent of members to merge with another entity under Section 904(c)(1); and

(12) the sale, lease, exchange, or other disposal of all, or substantially all, of the company's property with or without goodwill.

(d) Action requiring the consent of members or managers under this [Act] may be taken without a meeting.

(e) A member or manager may appoint a proxy to vote or otherwise act for the member or manager by signing an appointment instrument, either personally or by the member's or manager's attorney-in-fact.

* * * *

APPENDIX I

The Securities Act of 1933 (Excerpts)

Definitions

Section 2. When used in this title, unless the context requires—

(1) The term "security" means any note, stock, treasury stock, bond, debenture, evidence of indebtedness, certificate of interest or participation in any profit-sharing agreement, collateral-trust certificate, preorganization certificate or subscription, transferable share, investment contract, voting-trust certificate, certificate of deposit for a security, fractional undivided interest in oil, gas, or other mineral rights, any put, call, straddle, option, or privilege on any security, certificate of deposit, or group or index of securities (including any interest therein or based on the value thereof), or any put, call, straddle, option, or privilege entered into on a national securities exchange relating to foreign currency, or, in general, any interest or participation in, temporary or interim certificate for, receipt for, guarantee of, or warrant or right to subscribe to or purchase, any of the foregoing.

Exempted Securities

Section 3. (a) Except as hereinafter expressly provided the provisions of this title shall not apply to any of the following classes of securities:

* * * *

(2) Any security issued or guaranteed by the United States or any territory thereof, or by the District of Columbia, or by any State of the United States, or by any political subdivision of a State or Territory, or by any public instrumentality of one or more States or Territories, or by any person controlled or supervised by and acting as an instrumentality of the Government of the United States pursuant to authority granted by the Congress of the United States; or any certificate of deposit for any of the foregoing; or any security issued or guaranteed by any bank; or any security issued by or representing an interest in or a direct obligation of a Federal Reserve Bank. * * *

(3) Any note, draft, bill of exchange, or banker's acceptance which arises out of a current transaction or the proceeds of which have been or are to be used for current transactions, and which has a maturity at the time of issuance of not exceeding nine months, exclusive of days of grace, or any renewal thereof the maturity of which is likewise limited;

(4) Any security issued by a person organized and operated exclusively for religious, educational, benevolent, fraternal, charitable, or reformatory purposes and not for pecuniary profit, and no part of the net earnings of which inures to the benefit of any person, private stockholder, or individual;

* * * *

(11) Any security which is a part of an issue offered and sold only to persons resident within a single State or Territory, where the issuer of such security is a person resident and doing business within, or, if a corporation, incorporated by and doing business within, such State or Territory.

(b) The Commission may from time to time by its rules and regulations and subject to such terms and conditions as may be described therein, add any class of securities to the securities exempted as provided in this section, if it finds that the enforcement of this title with respect to such securities is not necessary in the public interest and for the protection of investors by reason of the small amount involved or the limited character of the public offering; but no issue of securities shall be exempted under this subsection where the aggregate amount at which such issue is offered to the public exceeds $5,000,000.

Exempted Transactions

Section 4. The provisions of section 5 shall not apply to—

(1) transactions by any person other than an issuer, underwriter, or dealer.

(2) transactions by an issuer not involving any public offering.

(3) transactions by a dealer (including an underwriter no longer acting as an underwriter in respect of the security involved in such transactions), except—

(A) transactions taking place prior to the expiration of forty days after the first date upon which the security was bona fide offered to the public by the issuer or by or through an underwriter.

(B) transactions in a security as to which a registration statement has been filed taking place prior to the expiration of forty days after the effective date of such registration statement or prior to the expiration of forty days after the first date upon which the security was bona fide offered to the public by the issuer or by or through an underwriter after such effective date, whichever is later (excluding in the computation of such forty days any time during which a stop order issued under section 8 is in effect as to the security), or such shorter period as the Commission may specify by rules and regulations or order, and

(C) transactions as to the securities constituting the whole or a part of an unsold allotment to or subscription by such dealer as a participant in the distribution of such securities by the issuer or by or through an underwriter.

With respect to transactions referred to in clause (B), if securities of the issuer have not previously been sold pursuant to an earlier effective registration statement the applicable period, instead of forty days, shall be ninety days, or such shorter period as the Commission may specify by rules and regulations or order.

(4) brokers' transactions, executed upon customers' orders on any exchange or in the over-the-counter market but not the solicitation of such orders.

* * * *

(6) transactions involving offers or sales by an issuer solely to one or more accredited investors, if the aggregate offering price of an issue of securities offered in reliance on this paragraph does not exceed the amount allowed under Section 3(b) of this title, if there is no advertising or public solicitation in connection with the transaction by the issuer or anyone acting on the issuer's behalf, and if the issuer files such notice with the Commission as the Commission shall prescribe.

Prohibitions Relating to Interstate Commerce and the Mails

Section 5. (a) Unless a registration statement is in effect as to a security, it shall be unlawful for any person, directly or indirectly—

(1) to make use of any means or instruments of transportation or communication in interstate commerce or of the mails to sell such security through the use or medium of any prospectus or otherwise; or

(2) to carry or cause to be carried through the mails or in interstate commerce, by any means or instruments of transportation, any such security for the purpose of sale or for delivery after sale.

(b) It shall be unlawful for any person, directly or indirectly—

(1) to make use of any means or instruments of transportation or communication in interstate commerce or of the mails to carry or transmit any prospectus relating to any security with respect to which a registration statement has been filed under this title, unless such prospectus meets the requirements of section 10, or

(2) to carry or to cause to be carried through the mails or in interstate commerce any such security for the purpose of sale or for delivery after sale, unless accompanied or preceded by a prospectus that meets the requirements of subsection (a) of section 10.

(c) It shall be unlawful for any person, directly, or indirectly, to make use of any means or instruments of transportation or communication in interstate commerce or of the mails to offer to sell or offer to buy through the use or medium of any prospectus or otherwise any security, unless a registration statement has been filed as to such security, or while the registration statement is the subject of a refusal order or stop order or (prior to the effective date of the registration statement) any public proceeding of examination under section 8.

APPENDIX J

The Securities Exchange Act of 1934 (Excerpts)

Definitions and Application of Title

Section 3. (a) When used in this title, unless the context otherwise requires—

* * * *

(4) The term "broker" means any person engaged in the business of effecting transactions in securities for the account of others, but does not include a bank.

(5) The term "dealer" means any person engaged in the business of buying and selling securities for his own account, through a broker or otherwise, but does not include a bank, or any person insofar as he buys or sells securities for his own account, either individually or in some fiduciary capacity, but not as part of a regular business.

* * * *

(7) The term "director" means any director of a corporation or any person performing similar functions with respect to any organization, whether incorporated or unincorporated.

(8) The term "issuer" means any person who issues or proposes to issue any security; except that with respect to certificates of deposit for securities, voting-trust certificates, or collateral-trust certificates, or with respect to certificates of interest or shares in an unincorporated investment trust not having a board of directors or the fixed, restricted management, or unit type, the term "issuer" means the person or persons performing the acts and assuming the duties of depositor or manager pursuant to the provisions of the trust or other agreement or instrument under which such securities are issued; and except that with respect to equipment-trust certificates or like securities, the term "issuer" means the person by whom the equipment or property is, or is to be, used.

(9) The term "person" means a natural person, company, government, or political subdivision, agency, or instrumentality of a government.

Regulation of the Use of Manipulative and Deceptive Devices

Section 10. It shall be unlawful for any person, directly or indirectly, by the use of any means or instrumentality of interstate commerce or of the mails, or of any facility of any national securities exchange—

(a) To effect a short sale, or to use or employ any stop-loss order in connection with the purchase or sale, of any security registered on a national securities exchange, in contravention of such rules and regulations as the Commission may prescribe as necessary or appropriate in the public interest or for the protection of investors.

(b) To use or employ, in connection with the purchase or sale of any security registered on a national securities exchange or any security not so registered, any manipulative or deceptive device or contrivance in contravention of such rules and regulations as the Commission may prescribe as necessary or appropriate in the public interest or for the protection of investors.

APPENDIX K

The Administrative Procedure Act of 1946 (Excerpts)

Section 551. Definitions

For the purpose of this subchapter—

* * * *

(4) "rule" means the whole or a part of an agency statement of general or particular applicability and future effect designed to implement, interpret, or prescribe law or policy or describing the organization, procedure, or practice requirements of an agency and includes the approval or prescription for the future of rates, wages, corporate or financial structures or reorganizations thereof, prices, facilities, appliances, services or allowances therefor or of valuations, costs, or accounting, or practices bearing on any of the foregoing[.]

* * * *

Section 552. Public Information; Agency Rules, Opinions, Orders, Records, and Proceedings

(a) Each agency shall make available to the public information as follows:

(1) Each agency shall separately state and currently publish in the Federal Register for the guidance of the public—

(A) descriptions of its central and field organization and the established places at which, the employees * * * from whom, and the methods whereby, the public may obtain information, make submittals or requests, or obtain decisions;

* * * *

(C) rules of procedure, descriptions of forms available or the places at which forms may be obtained, and instructions as to the scope and contents of all papers, reports, or examinations;

(D) substantive rules of general applicability adopted as authorized by law, and statements of general policy or interpretations of general applicability formulated and adopted by the agency[.] * * *

* * * *

Section 552b. Open Meetings

* * * *

(j) Each agency subject to the requirements of this section shall annually report to Congress regarding its compliance with such requirements, including a tabulation of the total number of agency meetings open to the public, the total number of meetings closed to the public, the reasons for closing such meetings, and a description of any litigation brought against the agency under this section, including any costs assessed against the agency in such litigation * * *.

* * * *

Section 553. Rule Making

* * * *

(b) General notice of proposed rule making shall be published in the Federal Register, unless persons subject thereto are named and either personally served or otherwise have actual notice thereof in accordance with law. * * *

(c) After notice required by this section, the agency shall give interested persons an opportunity to participate in the rule making through submission of written data, views, or arguments with or without opportunity for oral presentation. * * *

* * * *

Section 554. Adjudications

* * * *

(b) Persons entitled to notice of an agency hearing shall be timely informed of—

(1) the time, place, and nature of the hearing;

(2) the legal authority and jurisdiction under which the hearing is to be held; and

(3) the matters of fact and law asserted.

* * * *

(c) The agency shall give all interested parties opportunity for—

(1) the submission and consideration of facts, arguments, offers of settlement, or proposals of adjustment when time, the nature of the proceeding, and the public interest permit; and

(2) to the extent that the parties are unable so to determine a controversy by consent, hearing and decision on notice * * * .

* * * *

Section 555. Ancillary Matters

* * * *

(c) Process, requirement of a report, inspection, or other investigative act or demand may not be issued, made, or enforced except as authorized by law. A person compelled to submit data or evidence is entitled to retain or, on payment of lawfully prescribed costs, procure a copy or transcript thereof, except that in a nonpublic investigatory proceeding the witness may for good cause be limited to inspection of the official transcript of his testimony.

* * * *

(e) Prompt notice shall be given of the denial in whole or in part of a written application, petition, or other request of an interested person made in connection with any agency proceeding. * * *

Section 556. Hearings; Presiding Employees; Powers and Duties; Burden of Proof; Evidence; Record as Basis of Decision

* * * *

(b) There shall preside at the taking of evidence—

(1) the agency;

(2) one or more members of the body which comprises the agency; or

(3) one or more administrative law judges * * * .

* * * *

(c) Subject to published rules of the agency and within its powers, employees presiding at hearings may—

(1) administer oaths and affirmations;

(2) issue subpoenas authorized by law;

(3) rule on offers of proof and receive relevant evidence;

(4) take depositions or have depositions taken when the ends of justice would be served;

(5) regulate the course of the hearing;

(6) hold conferences for the settlement or simplification of the issues by consent of the parties or by the use of alternative means of dispute resolution as provided in subchapter IV of this chapter;

(7) inform the parties as to the availability of one or more alternative means of dispute resolution, and encourage use of such methods;

* * * *

(9) dispose of procedural requests or similar matters;

(10) make or recommend decisions in accordance with * * * this title; and

(11) take other action authorized by agency rule consistent with this subchapter.

* * * *

Section 702. Right of Review

A person suffering legal wrong because of agency action * * * is entitled to judicial review thereof. An action in a court of the United States seeking relief other than money damages and stating a claim that an agency or an officer or employee thereof acted or failed to act in an official capacity or under color of legal authority shall not be dismissed nor relief therein be denied on the ground that it is against the United States or that the United States is an indispensable party. The United States may be named as a defendant in any such action, and a judgment or decree may be entered against the United States: Provided, [t]hat any mandatory or injunctive decree shall specify the [f]ederal officer or officers (by name or by title), and their successors in office, personally responsible for compliance. * * *

* * * *

Section 704. Actions Reviewable

Agency action made reviewable by statute and final agency action for which there is no other adequate remedy in a court are subject to judicial review. A preliminary, procedural, or intermediate agency action or ruling not directly reviewable is subject to review on the review of the final agency action.

APPENDIX L

Digital Millennium Copyright Act of 1998 (Excerpts)

Sec. 1201. Circumvention of Copyright Protection Systems

(a) VIOLATIONS REGARDING CIRCUMVENTION OF TECHNOLOGICAL MEASURES—(1)(A) No person shall circumvent a technological measure that effectively controls access to a work protected under this title. * * *

* * * *

(b) ADDITIONAL VIOLATIONS—(1) No person shall manufacture, import, offer to the public, provide, or otherwise traffic in any technology, product, service, device, component, or part thereof, that—

(A) is primarily designed or produced for the purpose of circumventing protection afforded by a technological measure that effectively protects a right of a copyright owner under this title in a work or a portion thereof;

(B) has only limited commercially significant purpose or use other than to circumvent protection afforded by a technological measure that effectively protects a right of a copyright owner under this title in a work or a portion thereof; or

(C) is marketed by that person or another acting in concert with that person with that person's knowledge for use in circumventing protection afforded by a technological measure that effectively protects a right of a copyright owner under this title in a work or a portion thereof.

* * * *

Sec. 1202. Integrity of Copyright Management Information

(a) FALSE COPYRIGHT MANAGEMENT INFORMATION—No person shall knowingly and with the intent to induce, enable, facilitate, or conceal infringement—

(1) provide copyright management information that is false, or

(2) distribute or import for distribution copyright management information that is false.

(b) REMOVAL OR ALTERATION OF COPYRIGHT MANAGEMENT INFORMATION—No person shall, without the authority of the copyright owner or the law—

(1) intentionally remove or alter any copyright management information,

(2) distribute or import for distribution copyright management information knowing that the copyright management information has been removed or altered without authority of the copyright owner or the law, or

(3) distribute, import for distribution, or publicly perform works, copies of works, or phonorecords, knowing that copyright management information has been removed or altered without authority of the copyright owner or the law, knowing, or, with respect to civil remedies under section 1203, having reasonable grounds to know, that it will induce, enable, facilitate, or conceal an infringement of any right under this title.

(c) DEFINITION—As used in this section, the term "copyright management information" means any of the following information conveyed in connection with copies or phonorecords of a work or performances or displays of a work, including in digital form, except that such term does not include any personally identifying information about a user of a work or of a copy, phonorecord, performance, or display of a work:

(1) The title and other information identifying the work, including the information set forth on a notice of copyright.

(2) The name of, and other identifying information about, the author of a work.

(3) The name of, and other identifying information about, the copyright owner of the work, including the information set forth in a notice of copyright.

(4) With the exception of public performances of works by radio and television broadcast stations, the name of, and other identifying information about, a performer whose performance is fixed in a work other than an audiovisual work.

(5) With the exception of public performances of works by radio and television broadcast stations, in the case of an audiovisual work, the name of, and other identifying information about, a writer, performer, or director who is credited in the audiovisual work.

(6) Terms and conditions for use of the work.

(7) Identifying numbers or symbols referring to such information or links to such information.

(8) Such other information as the Register of Copyrights may prescribe by regulation, except that the Register of Copyrights may not require the provision of any information concerning the user of a copyrighted work.

* * * *

Sec. 512. Limitations on Liability Relating to Material Online

(a) TRANSITORY DIGITAL NETWORK COMMUNICATIONS—A service provider shall not be liable for monetary relief, or, except as provided in subsection (j), for injunctive or other equitable relief, for infringement of copyright by reason of the provider's transmitting, routing, or providing connections for, material through a system or network controlled or operated by or for the service provider, or by reason of the intermediate and transient storage of that material in the course of such transmitting, routing, or providing connections, if—

(1) the transmission of the material was initiated by or at the direction of a person other than the service provider;

(2) the transmission, routing, provision of connections, or storage is carried out through an automatic technical process without selection of the material by the service provider;

(3) the service provider does not select the recipients of the material except as an automatic response to the request of another person;

(4) no copy of the material made by the service provider in the course of such intermediate or transient storage is maintained on the system or network in a manner ordinarily accessible to anyone other than anticipated recipients, and no such copy is maintained on the system or network in a manner ordinarily accessible to such anticipated recipients for a longer period than is reasonably necessary for the transmission, routing, or provision of connections; and

(5) the material is transmitted through the system or network without modification of its content.

APPENDIX M

The Anticybersquatting Consumer Protection Act of 1999 (Excerpts)

[15 U.S.C. Section 1114. **Remedies; Infringement; Innocent Infringement by Printers and Publishers**

* * * *

[(2) Notwithstanding any other provision of this chapter, the remedies given to the owner of a right infringed under this chapter or to a person bringing an action under section 1125(a) or (d) of this title shall be limited as follows:]

* * * *

(D)(i)(I) A domain name registrar, a domain name registry, or other domain name registration authority that takes any action described under clause (ii) affecting a domain name shall not be liable for monetary relief or, except as provided in subclause (II), for injunctive relief, to any person for such action, regardless of whether the domain name is finally determined to infringe or dilute the mark.

(II) A domain name registrar, domain name registry, or other domain name registration authority described in subclause (I) may be subject to injunctive relief only if such registrar, registry, or other registration authority has—

(aa) not expeditiously deposited with a court, in which an action has been filed regarding the disposition of the domain name, documents sufficient for the court to establish the court's control and authority regarding the disposition of the registration and use of the domain name;

(bb) transferred, suspended, or otherwise modified the domain name during the pendency of the action, except upon order of the court; or

(cc) willfully failed to comply with any such court order.

(ii) An action referred to under clause (i)(I) is any action of refusing to register, removing from registration, transferring, temporarily disabling, or permanently canceling a domain name—

(I) in compliance with a court order under section 1125(d) of this title; or

(II) in the implementation of a reasonable policy by such registrar, registry, or authority prohibiting the registration of a domain name that is identical to, confusingly similar to, or dilutive of another's mark.

(iii) A domain name registrar, a domain name registry, or other domain name registration authority shall not be liable for damages under this section for the registration or maintenance of a domain name for another absent a showing of bad faith intent to profit from such registration or maintenance of the domain name.

(iv) If a registrar, registry, or other registration authority takes an action described under clause (ii) based on a knowing and material misrepresentation by any other person that a domain name is identical to, confusingly similar to, or dilutive of a mark, the person making the knowing and material misrepresentation shall be liable for any damages, including costs and attorney's fees, incurred by the domain name registrant as a result of such action. The court may also grant injunctive relief to the domain name registrant, including the reactivation of the domain name or the transfer of the domain name to the domain name registrant.

(v) A domain name registrant whose domain name has been suspended, disabled, or transferred under a policy described under clause (ii)(II) may, upon notice to the mark owner, file a civil action to establish that the registration or use of the domain name by such registrant is not unlawful under this chapter. The court may grant injunctive relief to the domain name registrant, including the reactivation of the domain name or transfer of the domain name to the domain name registrant.

[15 U.S.C. Section 1117. **Recovery for Violation of Rights; Profits, Damages and Costs; Attorney Fees; Treble Damages; Election**]

* * * *

(d) In a case involving a violation of section 1125(d)(1) of this title, the plaintiff may elect, at any time before final judgment is rendered by the trial court, to recover, instead of actual damages and profits, an award of statutory damages in the amount of not less than $1,000 and not more than $100,000 per domain name, as the court considers just.

[15 U.S.C. Section 1125. **False Designations of Origin, False Descriptions, and Dilution Forbidden**]

* * * *

(d) Cyberpiracy prevention

(1)(A) A person shall be liable in a civil action by the owner of a mark, including a personal name which is protected as a mark under this section, if, without regard to the goods or services of the parties, that person

(i) has a bad faith intent to profit from that mark, including a personal name which is protected as a mark under this section; and

(ii) registers, traffics in, or uses a domain name that—

(I) in the case of a mark that is distinctive at the time of registration of the domain name, is identical or confusingly similar to that mark;

(II) in the case of a famous mark that is famous at the time of registration of the domain name, is identical or confusingly similar to or dilutive of that mark; or

(III) is a trademark, word, or name protected by reason of section 706 of Title 18 or section 220506 of Title 36.

(B)(i) In determining whether a person has a bad faith intent described under subparagraph (a), a court may consider factors such as, but not limited to

(I) the trademark or other intellectual property rights of the person, if any, in the domain name;

(II) the extent to which the domain name consists of the legal name of the person or a name that is otherwise commonly used to identify that person;

(III) the person's prior use, if any, of the domain name in connection with the bona fide offering of any goods or services;

(IV) the person's bona fide noncommercial or fair use of the mark in a site accessible under the domain name;

(V) the person's intent to divert consumers from the mark owner's online location to a site accessible under the domain name that could harm the goodwill represented by the mark, either for commercial gain or with the intent to tarnish or disparage the mark, by creating a likelihood of confusion as to the source, sponsorship, affiliation, or endorsement of the site;

(VI) the person's offer to transfer, sell, or otherwise assign the domain name to the mark owner or any third party for financial gain without having used, or having an intent to use, the domain name in the bona fide offering of any goods or services, or the person's prior conduct indicating a pattern of such conduct;

(VII) the person's provision of material and misleading false contact information when applying for the registration of the domain name, the person's intentional failure to maintain accurate contact information, or the person's prior conduct indicating a pattern of such conduct;

(VIII) the person's registration or acquisition of multiple domain names which the person knows are identical or confusingly similar to marks of others that are distinctive at the time of registration of such domain names, or dilutive of famous marks of others that are famous at the time of registration of such domain names, without regard to the goods or services of the parties; and

(IX) the extent to which the mark incorporated in the person's domain name registration is or is not distinctive and famous within the meaning of subsection (c)(1) of this section.

(ii) Bad faith intent described under subparagraph (A) shall not be found in any case in which the court determines that the person believed and had reasonable grounds to believe that the use of the domain name was a fair use or otherwise lawful.

(C) In any civil action involving the registration, trafficking, or use of a domain name under this paragraph, a court may order the forfeiture or cancellation of the domain name or the transfer of the domain name to the owner of the mark.

(D) A person shall be liable for using a domain name under subparagraph (A) only if that person is the domain name registrant or that registrant's authorized licensee.

(E) As used in this paragraph, the term "traffics in" refers to transactions that include, but are not limited to, sales, purchases, loans, pledges, licenses, exchanges of currency, and any other transfer for consideration or receipt in exchange for consideration.

(2)(A) The owner of a mark may file an in rem civil action against a domain name in the judicial district in which the domain name registrar, domain name registry, or other domain name authority that registered or assigned the domain name is located if

(i) the domain name violates any right of the owner of a mark registered in the Patent and Trademark Office, or protected under subsection (a) or (c); and

(ii) the court finds that the owner—

(I) is not able to obtain in personam jurisdiction over a person who would have been a defendant in a civil action under paragraph (1); or

(II) through due diligence was not able to find a person who would have been a defendant in a civil action under paragraph (1) by—

(aa) sending a notice of the alleged violation and intent to proceed under this paragraph to the registrant of the domain name at the postal and e-mail address provided by the registrant to the registrar; and

(bb) publishing notice of the action as the court may direct promptly after filing the action.

(B) The actions under subparagraph (A)(ii) shall constitute service of process.

(C) In an in rem action under this paragraph, a domain name shall be deemed to have its situs in the judicial district in which

(i) the domain name registrar, registry, or other domain name authority that registered or assigned the domain name is located; or

(ii) documents sufficient to establish control and authority regarding the disposition of the registration and use of the domain name are deposited with the court.

(D)(i) The remedies in an in rem action under this paragraph shall be limited to a court order for the forfeiture or cancellation of the domain name or the transfer of the domain name to the owner of the mark. upon receipt of written notification of a filed, stamped copy of a complaint filed by the owner of a mark in a United States district court under this paragraph, the domain name registrar, domain name registry, or other domain name authority shall

(I) expeditiously deposit with the court documents sufficient to establish the court's control and authority regarding the disposition of the registration and use of the domain name to the court; and

(II) not transfer, suspend, or otherwise modify the domain name during the pendency of the action, except upon order of the court.

(ii) The domain name registrar or registry or other domain name authority shall not be liable for injunctive or monetary relief under this paragraph except in the case of bad faith or reckless disregard, which includes a willful failure to comply with any such court order.

(3) The civil action established under paragraph (1) and the in rem action established under paragraph (2), and any remedy available under either such action, shall be in addition to any other civil action or remedy otherwise applicable.

(4) The in rem jurisdiction established under paragraph (2) shall be in addition to any other jurisdiction that otherwise exists, whether in rem or in personam.

[15 U.S.C. Section 1127. Construction and Definitions; Intent of Chapter]

* * * *

The term "domain name" means any alphanumeric designation which is registered with or assigned by any domain name registrar, domain name registry, or other domain name registration authority as part of an electronic address on the Internet.

[15 U.S.C. Section 1129.] Cyberpiracy Protections for Individuals

(1) In general

(A) Civil liability

Any person who registers a domain name that consists of the name of another living person, or a name substantially and confusingly similar thereto, without that person's consent, with the specific intent to profit from such name by selling the domain name for financial gain to that person or any third party, shall be liable in a civil action by such person.

(B) Exception

A person who in good faith registers a domain name consisting of the name of another living person, or a name substantially and confusingly similar thereto, shall not be liable under this paragraph if such name is used in, affiliated with, or related to a work of authorship protected under Title 17, including a work made for hire as defined in section 101 of Title 17, and if the person registering the domain name is the copyright owner or licensee of the work, the person intends to sell the domain name in conjunction with the lawful exploitation of the work, and such registration is not prohibited by a contract between the registrant and the named person. The exception under this subparagraph shall apply only to a civil action brought under paragraph (1) and shall in no manner limit the protections afforded under the Trademark Act of 1946 (15 U.S.C. 1051 et seq.) or other provision of Federal or State law.

(2) Remedies

In any civil action brought under paragraph (1), a court may award injunctive relief, including the forfeiture or cancellation of the domain name or the transfer of the domain name to the plaintiff. The court may also, in its discretion, award costs and attorneys fees to the prevailing party.

(3) Definition

In this section, the term "domain name" has the meaning given that term in section 45 of the Trademark Act of 1946 (15 U.S.C. 1127).

(4) Effective date

This section shall apply to domain names registered on or after November 29, 1999.

APPENDIX N

Electronic Signatures in Global and National Commerce Act of 2000 (Excerpts)

SEC. 101. **General Rule of Validity**

(a) IN GENERAL—Notwithstanding any statute, regulation, or other rule of law (other than this title and title II), with respect to any transaction in or affecting interstate or foreign commerce—

(1) a signature, contract, or other record relating to such transaction may not be denied legal effect, validity, or enforceability solely because it is in electronic form; and

(2) a contract relating to such transaction may not be denied legal effect, validity, or enforceability solely because an electronic signature or electronic record was used in its formation.

* * * *

(d) RETENTION OF CONTRACTS AND RECORDS—

(1) ACCURACY AND ACCESSIBILITY—If a statute, regulation, or other rule of law requires that a contract or other record relating to a transaction in or affecting interstate or foreign commerce be retained, that requirement is met by retaining an electronic record of the information in the contract or other record that—

(A) accurately reflects the information set forth in the contract or other record; and

(B) remains accessible to all persons who are entitled to access by statute, regulation, or rule of law, for the period required by such statute, regulation, or rule of law, in a form that is capable of being accurately reproduced for later reference, whether by transmission, printing, or otherwise.

(2) EXCEPTION—A requirement to retain a contract or other record in accordance with paragraph (1) does not apply to any information whose sole purpose is to enable the contract or other record to be sent, communicated, or received.

(3) ORIGINALS—If a statute, regulation, or other rule of law requires a contract or other record relating to a transaction in or affecting interstate or foreign commerce to be provided, available, or retained in its original form, or provides consequences if the contract or other record is not provided, available, or retained in its original form, that statute, regulation, or rule of law is satisfied by an electronic record that complies with paragraph (1).

(4) CHECKS—If a statute, regulation, or other rule of law requires the retention of a check, that requirement is satisfied by retention of an electronic record of the information on the front and back of the check in accordance with paragraph (1).

* * * *

(g) NOTARIZATION AND ACKNOWLEDGMENT—If a statute, regulation, or other rule of law requires a signature or record relating to a transaction in or affecting interstate or foreign commerce to be notarized, acknowledged, verified, or made under oath, that requirement is satisfied if the electronic signature of the person authorized to perform those acts, together with all other information required to be included by other applicable statute, regulation, or rule of law, is attached to or logically associated with the signature or record.

(h) ELECTRONIC AGENTS—A contract or other record relating to a transaction in or affecting interstate or foreign commerce may not be denied legal effect, validity, or enforceability solely because its formation, creation, or delivery involved the action of one or more electronic agents so long as the action of any such electronic agent is legally attributable to the person to be bound.

(i) INSURANCE—It is the specific intent of the Congress that this title and title II apply to the business of insurance.

(j) INSURANCE AGENTS AND BROKERS—An insurance agent or broker acting under the direction of a party that enters into a contract by means of an electronic record or electronic signature may not be held liable for any deficiency in the electronic procedures agreed to by the parties under that contract if—

(1) the agent or broker has not engaged in negligent, reckless, or intentional tortious conduct;

(2) the agent or broker was not involved in the development or establishment of such electronic procedures; and

(3) the agent or broker did not deviate from such procedures.

* * * *

SEC. 103. Specific Exceptions.

(a) EXCEPTED REQUIREMENTS—The provisions of section 101 shall not apply to a contract or other record to the extent it is governed by—

(1) a statute, regulation, or other rule of law governing the creation and execution of wills, codicils, or testamentary trusts;

(2) a State statute, regulation, or other rule of law governing adoption, divorce, or other matters of family law; or

(3) the Uniform Commercial Code, as in effect in any State, other than sections 1–107 and 1–206 and Articles 2 and 2A.

(b) ADDITIONAL EXCEPTIONS—The provisions of section 101 shall not apply to—

(1) court orders or notices, or official court documents (including briefs, pleadings, and other writings) required to be executed in connection with court proceedings;

(2) any notice of—

(A) the cancellation or termination of utility services (including water, heat, and power);

(B) default, acceleration, repossession, foreclosure, or eviction, or the right to cure, under a credit agreement secured by, or a rental agreement for, a primary residence of an individual;

(C) the cancellation or termination of health insurance or benefits or life insurance benefits (excluding annuities); or

(D) recall of a product, or material failure of a product, that risks endangering health or safety; or

(3) any document required to accompany any transportation or handling of hazardous materials, pesticides, or other toxic or dangerous materials.

APPENDIX O

The Uniform Electronic Transactions Act (Excerpts)

Section 5. Use of Electronic Records and Electronic Signatures; Variations by Agreement.

(a) This [Act] does not require a record or signature to be created, generated, sent, communicated, received, stored, or otherwise processed or used by electronic means or in electronic form.

(b) This [Act] applies only to transactions between parties each of which has agreed to conduct transactions by electronic means. Whether the parties agree to conduct a transaction by electronic means is determined from the context and surrounding circumstances, including the parties' conduct.

(c) A party that agrees to conduct a transaction by electronic means may refuse to conduct other transactions by electronic means. The right granted by this subsection may not be waived by agreement.

(d) Except as otherwise provided in this [Act], the effect of any of its provisions may be varied by agreement. The presence in certain provisions of this [Act] of the words "unless otherwise agreed," or words of similar import, does not imply that the effect of other provisions may not be varied by agreement.

(e) Whether an electronic record or electronic signature has legal consequences is determined by this [Act] and other applicable law.

Section 6. Construction and Application. This [Act] must be construed and applied:

(1) to facilitate electronic transactions consistent with other applicable law; (2) to be consistent with reasonable practices concerning electronic transactions and with the continued expansion of those practices; and

(3) to effectuate its general purpose to make uniform the law with respect to the subject of this [Act] among States enacting it.

Section 7. Legal Recognition of Electronic Records, Electronic Signatures, and Electronic Contracts.

(a) A record or signature may not be denied legal effect or enforceability solely because it is in electronic form.

(b) A contract may not be denied legal effect or enforceability solely because an electronic record was used in its formation.

(c) If a law requires a record to be in writing, an electronic record satisfies the law.

(d) If a law requires a signature, an electronic signature satisfies the law.

* * * *

Section 10. Effect of Change or Error.

If a change or error in an electronic record occurs in a transmission between parties to a transaction, the following rules apply:

(1) If the parties have agreed to use a security procedure to detect changes or errors and one party has conformed to the procedure, but the other party has not, and the nonconforming party would have

detected the change or error had that party also conformed, the conforming party may avoid the effect of the changed or erroneous electronic record.

(2) In an automated transaction involving an individual, the individual may avoid the effect of an electronic record that resulted from an error made by the individual in dealing with the electronic agent of another person if the electronic agent did not provide an opportunity for the prevention or correction of the error and, at the time the individual learns of the error, the individual:

(A) promptly notifies the other person of the error and that the individual did not intend to be bound by the electronic record received by the other person;

(B) takes reasonable steps, including steps that conform to the other person's reasonable instructions, to return to the other person or, if instructed by the other person, to destroy the consideration received, if any, as a result of the erroneous electronic record; and

(C) has not used or received any benefit or value from the consideration, if any, received from the other person.

(3) If neither paragraph (1) nor paragraph (2) applies, the change or error has the effect provided by other law, including the law of mistake, and the parties' contract, if any.

(4) Paragraphs (2) and (3) may not be varied by agreement.

APPENDIX P

The Uniform Computer Information Transactions Act (Excerpts)

Section 104. Mixed Transactions: Agreement to Opt-In or Opt-Out.

The parties may agree that this [Act], including contract-formation rules, governs the transaction, in whole or part, or that other law governs the transaction and this [Act] does not apply, if a material part of the subject matter to which the agreement applies is computer information or informational rights in it that are within the scope of this [Act], or is subject matter within this [Act] under Section 103(b), or is subject matter excluded by Section 103(d)(1) or (2). However, any agreement to do so is subject to the following rules:

(1) An agreement that this [Act] governs a transaction does not alter the applicability of any rule or procedure that may not be varied by agreement of the parties or that may be varied only in a manner specified by the rule or procedure, including a consumer protection statute [or administrative rule]. In addition, in a mass-market transaction, the agreement does not alter the applicability of a law applicable to a copy of information in printed form.

(2) An agreement that this [Act] does not govern a transaction:

(A) does not alter the applicability of Section 214 or 816; and

(B) in a mass-market transaction, does not alter the applicability under [this Act] of the doctrine of unconscionability or fundamental public policy or the obligation of good faith.

(3) In a mass-market transaction, any term under this section which changes the extent to which this [Act] governs the transaction must be conspicuous.

(4) A copy of a computer program contained in and sold or leased as part of goods and which is excluded from this [Act] by Section 103(b)(1) cannot provide the basis for an agreement under this section that this [Act] governs the transaction.

* * * *

Section 107. Legal Recognition of Electronic Record and Authentication; Use of Electronic Agents.

(a) A record or authentication may not be denied legal effect or enforceability solely because it is in electronic form.

(b) This [Act] does not require that a record or authentication be generated, stored, sent, received, or otherwise processed by electronic means or in electronic form.

(c) In any transaction, a person may establish requirements regarding the type of authentication or record acceptable to it.

(d) A person that uses an electronic agent that it has selected for making an authentication, performance, or agreement, including manifestation of assent, is bound by the operations of the electronic agent, even if no individual was aware of or reviewed the agent's operations or the results of the operations.

* * * *

Section 202. Formation in General.

(a) A contract may be formed in any manner sufficient to show agreement, including offer and acceptance or conduct of both parties or operations of electronic agents which recognize the existence of a contract.

(b) If the parties so intend, an agreement sufficient to constitute a contract may be found even if the time of its making is undetermined, one or more terms are left open or to be agreed on, the records of the parties do not otherwise establish a contract, or one party reserves the right to modify terms.

(c) Even if one or more terms are left open or to be agreed upon, a contract does not fail for indefiniteness if the parties intended to make a contract and there is a reasonably certain basis for giving an appropriate remedy.

(d) In the absence of conduct or performance by both parties to the contrary, a contract is not formed if there is a material disagreement about a material term, including a term concerning scope.

(e) If a term is to be adopted by later agreement and the parties intend not to be bound unless the term is so adopted, a contract is not formed if the parties do not agree to the term. In that case, each party shall deliver to the other party, or with the consent of the other party destroy, all copies of information, access materials, and other materials received or made, and each party is entitled to a return with respect to any contract fee paid for which performance has not been received, has not been accepted, or has been redelivered without any benefit being retained. The parties remain bound by any restriction in a contractual use term with respect to information or copies received or made from copies received pursuant to the agreement, but the contractual use term does not apply to information or copies properly received or obtained from another source.

Section 203. Offer and Acceptance in General.

Unless otherwise unambiguously indicated by the language or the circumstances:

(1) An offer to make a contract invites acceptance in any manner and by any medium reasonable under the circumstances.

(2) An order or other offer to acquire a copy for prompt or current delivery invites acceptance by either a prompt promise to ship or a prompt or current shipment of a conforming or nonconforming copy. However, a shipment of a nonconforming copy is not an acceptance if the licensor seasonably notifies the licensee that the shipment is offered only as an accommodation to the licensee.

(3) If the beginning of a requested performance is a reasonable mode of acceptance, an offeror that is not notified of acceptance or performance within a reasonable time may treat the offer as having lapsed before acceptance.

(4) If an offer in an electronic message evokes an electronic message accepting the offer, a contract is formed:

  (A) when an electronic acceptance is received; or
  (B) if the response consists of beginning performance, full performance, or giving access to information, when the performance is received or the access is enabled and necessary access materials are received.

* * * *

Section 209. Mass-Market License.

(a) A party adopts the terms of a mass-market license for purposes of Section 208 only if the party agrees to the license, such as by manifesting assent, before or during the party's initial performance or use of or access to the information. A term is not part of the license if:

(1) the term is unconscionable or is unenforceable under Section 105(a) or (b); or

(2) subject to Section 301, the term conflicts with a term to which the parties to the license have expressly agreed.

(b) If a mass-market license or a copy of the license is not available in a manner permitting an opportunity to review by the licensee before the licensee becomes obligated to pay and the licensee does not agree, such as by manifesting assent, to the license after having an opportunity to review, the licensee is entitled to a return under Section 112 and, in addition, to:

(1) reimbursement of any reasonable expenses incurred in complying with the licensor's instructions for returning or destroying the computer information or, in the absence of instructions, expenses incurred for return postage or similar reasonable expense in returning the computer information; and

(2) compensation for any reasonable and foreseeable costs of restoring the licensee's information processing system to reverse changes in the system caused by the installation, if:

  (A) the installation occurs because information must be installed to enable review of the license; and

  (B) the installation alters the system or information in it but does not restore the system or information after removal of the installed information because the licensee rejected the license.

(c) In a mass-market transaction, if the licensor does not have an opportunity to review a record containing proposed terms from the licensee before the licensor delivers or becomes obligated to deliver the information, and if the licensor does not agree, such as by manifesting assent, to those terms after having that opportunity, the licensor is entitled to a return.

* * * *

Section 211. Pretransaction Disclosures in Internet-Type Transactions.

This section applies to a licensor that makes its computer information available to a licensee by electronic means from its Internet or similar electronic site. In such a case, the licensor affords an opportunity to review the terms of a standard form license which opportunity satisfies Section 112(e) with respect to a licensee that acquires the information from that site, if the licensor:

(1) makes the standard terms of the license readily available for review by the licensee before the information is delivered or the licensee becomes obligated to pay, whichever occurs first, by:

(A) displaying prominently and in close proximity to a description of the computer information, or to instructions or steps for acquiring it, the standard terms or a reference to an electronic location from which they can be readily obtained; or

(B) disclosing the availability of the standard terms in a prominent place on the site from which the computer information is offered and promptly furnishing a copy of the standard terms on request before the transfer of the computer information; and

(2) does not take affirmative acts to prevent printing or storage of the standard terms for archival or review purposes by the licensee.

APPENDIX Q

Spanish Equivalents for Important Legal Terms in English

Abandoned property: bienes abandonados
Acceptance: aceptación; consentimiento; acuerdo
Acceptor: aceptante
Accession: toma de posesión; aumento; accesión
Accommodation indorser: avalista de favor
Accommodation party: firmante de favor
Accord: acuerdo; convenio; arregio
Accord and satisfaction: transacción ejecutada
Act of state doctrine: doctrina de acto de gobierno
Administrative law: derecho administrativo
Administrative process: procedimiento o metódo administrativo
Administrator: administrador (-a)
Adverse possession: posesión de hecho susceptible de proscripción adquisitiva
Affirmative action: acción afirmativa
Affirmative defense: defensa afirmativa
After-acquired property: bienes adquiridos con posterioridad a un hecho dado
Agency: mandato; agencia
Agent: mandatorio; agente; representante
Agreement: convenio; acuerdo; contrato
Alien corporation: empresa extranjera
Allonge: hojas adicionales de endosos
Answer: contestación de la demande; alegato
Anticipatory repudiation: anuncio previo de las partes de su imposibilidad de cumplir con el contrato
Appeal: apelación; recurso de apelación
Appellate jurisdiction: jurisdicción de apelaciones
Appraisal right: derecho de valuación
Arbitration: arbitraje
Arson: incendio intencional
Articles of partnership: contrato social
Artisan's lien: derecho de retención que ejerce al artesano
Assault: asalto; ataque; agresión
Assignment of rights: transmisión; transferencia; cesión
Assumption of risk: no resarcimiento por exposición voluntaria al peligro
Attachment: auto judicial que autoriza el embargo; embargo

Bailee: depositario
Bailment: depósito; constitución en depósito
Bailor: depositante
Bankruptcy trustee: síndico de la quiebra
Battery: agresión; física
Bearer: portador; tenedor
Bearer instrument: documento al portador
Bequest or legacy: legado (de bienes muebles)
Bilateral contract: contrato bilateral
Bill of lading: conocimiento de embarque; carta de porte
Bill of Rights: declaración de derechos
Binder: póliza de seguro provisoria; recibo de pago a cuenta del precio
Blank indorsement: endoso en blanco
Blue sky laws: leyes reguladoras del comercio bursátil
Bond: título de crédito; garantía; caución
Bond indenture: contrato de emisión de bonos; contrato del ampréstito
Breach of contract: incumplimiento de contrato

Brief: escrito; resumen; informe
Burglary: violación de domicilio
Business judgment rule: regla de juicio comercial
Business tort: agravio comercial

Case law: ley de casos; derecho casuístico
Cashier's check: cheque de caja
Causation in fact: causalidad en realidad
Cease-and-desist order: orden para cesar y desistir
Certificate of deposit: certificado de depósito
Certified check: cheque certificado
Charitable trust: fideicomiso para fines benéficos
Chattel: bien mueble
Check: cheque
Chose in action: derecho inmaterial; derecho de acción
Civil law: derecho civil
Close corporation: sociedad de un solo accionista o de un grupo restringido de accionistas
Closed shop: taller agremiado (emplea solamente a miembros de un gremio)
Closing argument: argumento al final
Codicil: codicilo
Collateral: guarantía; bien objeto de la guarantía real
Comity: cortesía; cortesía entre naciones
Commercial paper: instrumentos negociables; documentos a valores commerciales
Common law: derecho consuetudinario; derecho común; ley común
Common stock: acción ordinaria
Comparative negligence: negligencia comparada
Compensatory damages: daños y perjuicios reales o compensatorios
Concurrent conditions: condiciones concurrentes
Concurrent jurisdiction: competencia concurrente de varios tribunales para entender en una misma causa
Concurring opinion: opinión concurrente
Condition: condición
Condition precedent: condición suspensiva
Condition subsequent: condición resolutoria
Confiscation: confiscación
Confusion: confusión; fusión
Conglomerate merger: fusión de firmas que operan en distintos mercados
Consent decree: acuerdo entre las partes aprobado por un tribunal
Consequential damages: daños y perjuicios indirectos
Consideration: consideración; motivo; contraprestación
Consolidation: consolidación
Constructive delivery: entrega simbólica
Constructive trust: fideicomiso creado por aplicación de la ley
Consumer protection law: ley para proteger el consumidor
Contract: contrato
Contract under seal: contrato formal o sellado
Contributory negligence: negligencia de la parte actora
Conversion: usurpación; conversión de valores
Copyright: derecho de autor
Corporation: sociedad anómina; corporación; persona juridica
Co-sureties: cogarantes
Counterclaim: reconvención; contrademanda
Counteroffer: contraoferta
Course of dealing: curso de transacciones
Course of performance: curso de cumplimiento
Covenant: pacto; garantía; contrato
Covenant not to sue: pacto or contrato a no demandar
Covenant of quiet enjoyment: garantía del uso y goce pacífico del inmueble
Creditors' composition agreement: concordato preventivo
Crime: crimen; delito; contravención
Criminal law: derecho penal
Cross-examination: contrainterrogatorio
Cure: cura; cuidado; derecho de remediar un vicio contractual
Customs receipts: recibos de derechos aduaneros

Damages: daños; indemnización por daños y perjuicios
Debit card: tarjeta de dé bito
Debtor: deudor
Debt securities: seguridades de deuda
Deceptive advertising: publicidad engañosa
Deed: escritura; título; acta translativa de domino
Defamation: difamación
Delegation of duties: delegación de obligaciones
Demand deposit: depósito a la vista
Depositions: declaración de un testigo fuera del tribunal
Devise: legado; deposición testamentaria (bienes inmuebles)
Directed verdict: veredicto según orden del juez y sin participación activa del jurado
Direct examination: interrogatorio directo; primer interrogatorio
Disaffirmance: repudiación; renuncia; anulación
Discharge: descargo; liberación; cumplimiento
Disclosed principal: mandante revelado
Discovery: descubrimiento; producción de la prueba
Dissenting opinion: opinión disidente
Dissolution: disolución; terminación
Diversity of citizenship: competencia de los tribunales federales para entender en causas cuyas partes intervinientes son cuidadanos de distintos estados
Divestiture: extinción premature de derechos reales
Dividend: dividendo
Docket: orden del día; lista de causas pendientes
Domestic corporation: sociedad local
Draft: orden de pago; letrade cambio
Drawee: girado; beneficiario
Drawer: librador
Duress: coacción; violencia

Easement: servidumbre
Embezzlement: desfalco; malversación

Eminent domain: poder de expropiación
Employment discrimination: discriminación en el empleo
Entrepreneur: empresario
Environmental law: ley ambiental
Equal dignity rule: regla de dignidad egual
Equity security: tipo de participación en una sociedad
Estate: propiedad; patrimonio; derecho
Estop: impedir; prevenir
Ethical issue: cuestión ética
Exclusive jurisdiction: competencia exclusiva
Exculpatory clause: cláusula eximente
Executed contract: contrato ejecutado
Execution: ejecución; cumplimiento
Executor: albacea
Executory contract: contrato aún no completamente consumado
Executory interest: derecho futuro
Express contract: contrato expreso
Expropriation: expropriación

Federal question: caso federal
Fee simple: pleno dominio; dominio absoluto
Fee simple absolute: dominio absoluto
Fee simple defeasible: dominio sujeta a una condición resolutoria
Felony: crimen; delito grave
Fictitious payee: beneficiario ficticio
Fiduciary: fiduciaro
Firm offer: oferta en firme
Fixture: inmueble por destino, incorporación a anexación
Floating lien: gravamen continuado
Foreign corporation: sociedad extranjera; U.S. sociedad constituída en otro estado
Forgery: falso; falsificación
Formal contract: contrato formal
Franchise: privilegio; franquicia; concesión
Franchisee: persona que recibe una concesión
Franchisor: persona que vende una concesión
Fraud: fraude; dolo; engaño
Future interest: bien futuro

Garnishment: embargo de derechos
General partner: socio comanditario
General warranty deed: escritura translativa de domino con garantía de título
Gift: donación
Gift *causa mortis*: donación por causa de muerte
Gift *inter vivos*: donación entre vivos
Good faith: buena fe
Good faith purchaser: comprador de buena fe

Holder: tenedor por contraprestación
Holder in due course: tenedor legítimo
Holographic will: testamento olográfico
Homestead exemption laws: leyes que exceptúan las casas de familia de ejecución por duedas generales
Horizontal merger: fusión horizontal

Identification: identificación
Implied-in-fact contract: contrato implícito en realidad
Implied warranty: guarantía implícita
Implied warranty of merchantability: garantía implícita de vendibilidad
Impossibility of performance: imposibilidad de cumplir un contrato
Imposter: imposter
Incidental beneficiary: beneficiario incidental; beneficiario secundario
Incidental damages: daños incidentales
Indictment: auto de acusación; acusación
Indorsee: endorsatario
Indorsement: endoso
Indorser: endosante
Informal contract: contrato no formal; contrato verbal
Information: acusación hecha por el ministerio público
Injunction: mandamiento; orden de no innovar
Innkeeper's lien: derecho de retención que ejerce el posadero

Installment contract: contrato de pago en cuotas
Insurable interest: interés asegurable
Intended beneficiary: beneficiario destinado
Intentional tort: agravio; cuasi-delito intenciónal
International law: derecho internaciónal
Interrogatories: preguntas escritas sometidas por una parte a la otra o a un testigo
***Inter vivos* trust**: fideicomiso entre vivos
Intestacy laws: leyes de la condición de morir intestado
Intestate: intestado
Investment company: compañia de inversiones
Issue: emisión

Joint tenancy: derechos conjuntos en un bien inmueble en favor del beneficiario sobreviviente
Judgment *n.o.v.*: juicio no obstante veredicto
Judgment rate of interest: interés de juicio
Judicial process: acto de procedimiento; proceso jurídico
Judicial review: revisión judicial
Jurisdiction: jurisdicción

Larceny: robo; hurto
Law: derecho; ley; jurisprudencia
Lease: contrato de locación; contrato de alquiler
Leasehold estate: bienes forales
Legal rate of interest: interés legal
Legatee: legatario
Letter of credit: carta de crédito
Levy: embargo; comiso
Libel: libelo; difamación escrita
Life estate: usufructo
Limited partner: comanditario
Limited partnership: sociedad en comandita
Liquidation: liquidación; realización
Lost property: objetos perdidos

Majority opinion: opinión de la mayoría
Maker: persona que realiza u ordena; librador

Mechanic's lien: gravamen de constructor
Mediation: mediación; intervención
Merger: fusión
Mirror image rule: fallo de reflejo
Misdemeanor: infracción; contravención
Mislaid property: bienes extraviados
Mitigation of damages: reducción de daños
Mortgage: hypoteca
Motion to dismiss: excepción parentoria
Mutual fund: fondo mutual

Negotiable instrument: instrumento negociable
Negotiation: negociación
Nominal damages: daños y perjuicios nominales
Novation: novación
Nuncupative will: testamento nuncupativo

Objective theory of contracts: teoria objetiva de contratos
Offer: oferta
Offeree: persona que recibe una oferta
Offeror: oferente
Order instrument: instrumento o documento a la orden
Original jurisdiction: jurisdicción de primera instancia
Output contract: contrato de producción

Parol evidence rule: regla relativa a la prueba oral
Partially disclosed principal: mandante revelado en parte
Partnership: sociedad colectiva; asociación; asociación de participación
Past consideration: causa o contraprestación anterior
Patent: patente; privilegio
Pattern or practice: muestra o práctica
Payee: beneficiario de un pago
Penalty: pena; penalidad
***Per capita*:** por cabeza
Perfection: perfeción
Performance: cumplimiento; ejecución
Personal defenses: excepciones personales
Personal property: bienes muebles
***Per stirpes*:** por estirpe
Plea bargaining: regateo por un alegato
Pleadings: alegatos
Pledge: prenda
Police powers: poders de policia y de prevención del crimen
Policy: póliza
Positive law: derecho positivo; ley positiva
Possibility of reverter: posibilidad de reversión
Precedent: precedente
Preemptive right: derecho de prelación
Preferred stock: acciones preferidas
Premium: recompensa; prima
Presentment warranty: garantía de presentación
Price discrimination: discriminación en los precios
Principal: mandante; principal
Privity: nexo jurídico
Privity of contract: relación contractual
Probable cause: causa probable
Probate: verificación; verificación del testamento
Probate court: tribunal de sucesiones y tutelas
Proceeds: resultados; ingresos
Profit: beneficio; utilidad; lucro
Promise: promesa
Promisee: beneficiario de una promesa
Promisor: promtente
Promissory estoppel: impedimento promisorio
Promissory note: pagaré; nota de pago
Promoter: promotor; fundador
Proximate cause: causa inmediata o próxima
Proxy: apoderado; poder
Punitive, or exemplary, damages: daños y perjuicios punitivos o ejemplares

Qualified indorsement: endoso con reservas
Quasi contract: contrato tácito o implícito
Quitclaim deed: acto de transferencia de una propiedad por finiquito, pero sin ninguna garantía sobre la validez del título transferido

Ratification: ratificación
Real property: bienes inmuebles
Reasonable doubt: duda razonable
Rebuttal: refutación
Recognizance: promesa; compromiso; reconocimiento
Recording statutes: leyes estatales sobre registros oficiales
Redress: reporacíon
Reformation: rectificación; reforma; corrección
Rejoinder: dúplica; contrarréplica
Release: liberación; renuncia a un derecho
Remainder: substitución; reversión
Remedy: recurso; remedio; reparación
Replevin: acción reivindicatoria; reivindicación
Reply: réplica
Requirements contract: contrato de suministro
Rescission: rescisión
***Res judicata*:** cosa juzgada; res judicata
***Respondeat superior*:** responsabilidad del mandante o del maestro
Restitution: restitución
Restrictive indorsement: endoso restrictivo
Resulting trust: fideicomiso implícito
Reversion: reversión; sustitución
Revocation: revocación; derogación
Right of contribution: derecho de contribución
Right of reimbursement: derecho de reembolso
Right of subrogation: derecho de subrogación
Right-to-work law: ley de libertad de trabajo
Robbery: robo
Rule 10b-5: Regla 10b-5

Sale: venta; contrato de compreventa
Sale on approval: venta a ensayo; venta sujeta a la aprobación del comprador

Sale or return: venta con derecho de devolución
Sales contract: contrato de compraventa; boleto de compraventa
Satisfaction: satisfacción; pago
Scienter: a sabiendas
S corporation: S corporación
Secured party: acreedor garantizado
Secured transaction: transacción garantizada
Securities: volares; titulos; seguridades
Security agreement: convenio de seguridad
Security interest: interés en un bien dado en garantía que permite a quien lo detenta venderlo en caso de incumplimiento
Service mark: marca de identificación de servicios
Shareholder's derivative suit: acción judicial entablada por un accionista en nombre de la sociedad
Signature: firma; rúbrica
Slander: difamación oral; calumnia
Sovereign immunity: immunidad soberana
Special indorsement: endoso especial; endoso a la orden de una person en particular
Specific performance: ejecución precisa, según los términos del contrato
Spendthrift trust: fideicomiso para pródigos
Stale check: cheque vencido
Stare decisis: acatar las decisiones, observar los precedentes
Statutory law: derecho estatutario; derecho legislado; derecho escrito
Stock: acciones
Stock warrant: certificado para la compra de acciones
Stop-payment order: orden de suspensión del pago de un cheque dada por el librador del mismo
Strict liability: responsabilidad uncondicional
Summary judgment: fallo sumario

Tangible property: bienes corpóreos
Tenancy at will: inguilino por tiempo indeterminado (según la voluntad del propietario)
Tenancy by sufferance: posesión por tolerancia
Tenancy by the entirety: locación conyugal conjunta
Tenancy for years: inguilino por un término fijo
Tenancy in common: specie de copropiedad indivisa
Tender: oferta de pago; oferta de ejecución
Testamentary trust: fideicomiso testamentario
Testator: testador (-a)
Third party beneficiary contract: contrato para el beneficio del tercero-beneficiario
Tort: agravio; cuasi-delito
Totten trust: fideicomiso creado por un depósito bancario
Trade acceptance: letra de cambio aceptada
Trademark: marca registrada
Trade name: nombre comercial; razón social
Traveler's check: cheque del viajero
Trespass to land: ingreso no authorizado a las tierras de otro
Trespass to personal property: violación de los derechos posesorios de un tercero con respecto a bienes muebles
Trust: fideicomiso; trust

Ultra vires: ultra vires; fuera de la facultad (de una sociedad anónima)
Unanimous opinion: opinión unámine
Unconscionable contract or clause: contrato leonino; cláusula leonino
Underwriter: subscriptor; asegurador
Unenforceable contract: contrato que no se puede hacer cumplir
Unilateral contract: contrato unilateral
Union shop: taller agremiado; empresa en la que todos los empleados son miembros del gremio o sindicato
Universal defenses: defensas legitimas o legales
Usage of trade: uso comercial
Usury: usura

Valid contract: contrato válido
Venue: lugar; sede del proceso
Vertical merger: fusión vertical de empresas
Voidable contract: contrato anulable
Void contract: contrato nulo; contrato inválido, sin fuerza legal
Voir dire: examen preliminar de un testigo a jurado por el tribunal para determinar su competencia
Voting trust: fideicomiso para ejercer el derecho de voto

Waiver: renuncia; abandono
Warranty of habitability: garantía de habitabilidad
Watered stock: acciones diluídos; capital inflado
White-collar crime: crimen administrativo
Writ of attachment: mandamiento de ejecución; mandamiento de embargo
Writ of *certiorari*: auto de avocación; auto de certiorari
Writ of execution: auto ejecutivo; mandamiento de ejecutión
Writ of mandamus: auto de mandamus; mandamiento; orden judicial

Glossary

A

Abandoned property Property with which the owner has voluntarily parted, with no intention of recovering it.
Abandonment In landlord-tenant law, a tenant's departure from leased premises completely, with no intention of returning before the end of the lease term.
Abatement A process by which legatees receive reduced benefits if the assets of an estate are insufficient to pay in full all general bequests provided for in the will.
Abus de droit A doctrine developed in the French courts. The doctrine modified employment at will and protected workers exercising their rights from wrongful discharge and other employer abuses.
Acceleration clause A clause in an installment contract that provides for all future payments to become due immediately on the failure to tender timely payments or on the occurrence of a specified event.
Acceptance (1) In contract law, the offeree's notification to the offeror that the offeree agrees to be bound by the terms of the offeror's proposal. Although historically the terms of acceptance had to be the mirror image of the terms of the offer, the Uniform Commercial Code provides that even modified terms of the offer in a definite expression of acceptance constitute a contract. (2) In negotiable instruments law, the drawee's signed agreement to pay a draft when presented.
Acceptor The person (the drawee) who accepts a draft and who agrees to be primarily responsible for its payment.
Access contract A contract formed for the purpose of obtaining, by electronic means, access to another's database or information processing system.
Accession Occurs when an individual adds value to personal property by either labor or materials. In some situations, a person may acquire ownership rights in another's property through accession.
Accommodation party A person who signs an instrument for the purpose of lending his or her name as credit to another party on the instrument.
Accord and satisfaction An agreement for payment (or other performance) between two parties, one of whom has a right of action against the other. After the payment has been accepted or other performance has been made, the "accord and satisfaction" is complete and the obligation is discharged.
Accredited investors In the context of securities offerings, "sophisticated" investors, such as banks, insurance companies, investment companies, the issuer's executive officers and directors, and persons whose income or net worth exceeds certain limits.
Acquittal A certification or declaration following a trial that the individual accused of a crime is innocent, or free from guilt, and is thus absolved of the charges.
Act of state doctrine A doctrine that provides that the judicial branch of one country will not examine the validity of public acts committed by a recognized foreign government within its own territory.
Actionable Capable of serving as the basis of a lawsuit.
Actual authority Authority of an agent that is express or implied.
Actual malice Real and demonstrable evil intent. In a defamation suit, a statement made about a public figure normally must be made with actual malice (with either knowledge of its falsity or a reckless disregard of the truth) for liability to be incurred.
Actus reus (pronounced *ak*-tus *ray*-uhs) A guilty (prohibited) act. The commission of a prohibited act is one of the two essential elements required for criminal liability, the other element being the intent to commit a crime.
Adequate protection doctrine In bankruptcy law, a doctrine that protects secured creditors from losing their security as a result of an automatic stay on legal proceedings by creditors against the debtor once the debtor petitions for bankruptcy relief. In certain circumstances, the bankruptcy court may provide adequate protection by requiring the debtor or trustee to pay the creditor or provide additional guaranties to protect the creditor against the losses suffered by the creditor as a result of the stay.
Adhesion contract A "standard-form" contract, such as that between a large retailer and a consumer, in which the stronger party dictates the terms.
Adjudicate To render a judicial decision. In the administrative process, the proceeding in which an administrative law judge hears and decides on issues that arise when an administrative agency charges a person or a firm with violating a law or regulation enforced by the agency.
Adjudication The process of adjudicating. *See* Adjudicate
Administrative agency A federal or state government agency established to perform a specific function. Administrative agencies are authorized by legislative acts to make and enforce rules to administer and enforce the acts.
Administrative law The body of law created by administrative agencies (in the form of rules, regulations,

orders, and decisions) in order to carry out their duties and responsibilities.

Administrative law judge (ALJ) One who presides over an administrative agency hearing and who has the power to administer oaths, take testimony, rule on questions of evidence, and make determinations of fact.

Administrative process The procedure used by administrative agencies in the administration of law.

Administrator One who is appointed by a court to handle the probate (disposition) of a person's estate if that person dies intestate (without a valid will) or if the executor named in the will cannot serve.

Adverse possession The acquisition of title to real property by occupying it openly, without the consent of the owner, for a period of time specified by a state statute. The occupation must be actual, open, notorious, exclusive, and in opposition to all others, including the owner.

Affidavit A written or printed voluntary statement of facts, confirmed by the oath or affirmation of the party making it and made before a person having the authority to administer the oath or affirmation.

Affirm To validate; to give legal force to. *See also* Ratification

Affirmative action Job-hiring policies that give special consideration to members of protected classes in an effort to overcome present effects of past discrimination.

Affirmative defense A response to a plaintiff's claim that does not deny the plaintiff's facts but attacks the plaintiff's legal right to bring an action. An example is the running of the statute of limitations.

After-acquired evidence A type of evidence submitted in support of an affirmative defense in employment discrimination cases. Evidence that, prior to the employer's discriminatory act, the employee engaged in misconduct sufficient to warrant dismissal had the employer known of it earlier.

After-acquired property Property of the debtor that is acquired after the execution of a security agreement.

Age of majority The age at which an individual is considered legally capable of conducting himself or herself responsibly. A person of this age is entitled to the full rights of citizenship, including the right to vote in elections. In contract law, one who is no longer an infant and can no longer disaffirm a contract.

Agency A relationship between two parties in which one party (the agent) agrees to represent or act for the other (the principal).

Agency by estoppel Arises when a principal negligently allows an agent to exercise powers not granted to the agent, thus justifying others in believing that the agent possesses the requisite agency authority. *See also* Promissory estoppel

Agent A person who agrees to represent or act for another, called the principal.

Aggressor The acquiring corporation in a takeover attempt.

Agreement A meeting of two or more minds in regard to the terms of a contract; usually broken down into two events—an offer by one party to form a contract, and an acceptance of the offer by the person to whom the offer is made.

Alien corporation A designation in the United States for a corporation formed in another country but doing business in the United States.

Alienation In real property law, the voluntary transfer of property from one person to another (as opposed to a transfer by operation of law).

Allegation A statement, claim, or assertion.

Allege To state, recite, assert, or charge.

Allonge (pronounced uh-*lohnj*) A piece of paper firmly attached to a negotiable instrument, on which transferees can make indorsements if there is no room left on the instrument itself.

Alteration In the context of leaseholds, an improvement or change made that materially affects the condition of the property. Thus, for example, erecting an additional structure probably would (and painting interior walls would not) be considered making an alteration.

Alternative dispute resolution (ADR) The resolution of disputes in ways other than those involved in the traditional judicial process. Negotiation, mediation, and arbitration are forms of ADR.

Amend To change and improve through a formal procedure.

American Arbitration Association (AAA) The major organization offering arbitration services in the United States.

Analogy In logical reasoning, an assumption that if two things are similar in some respects, they will be similar in other respects also. Often used in legal reasoning to infer the appropriate application of legal principles in a case being decided by referring to previous cases involving different facts but considered to come within the policy underlying the rule.

Annuity An insurance policy that pays the insured fixed, periodic payments for life or for a term of years, as stipulated in the policy, after the insured reaches a specified age.

Annul To cancel; to make void.

Answer Procedurally, a defendant's response to the plaintiff's complaint.

Antecedent claim A preexisting claim. In negotiable instruments law, taking an instrument in satisfaction of an antecedent claim is taking the instrument for value—that is, for valid consideration.

Anticipatory repudiation An assertion or action by a party indicating that he or she will not perform an obligation that the party is contractually obligated to perform at a future time.

Antitrust law The body of federal and state laws and statutes protecting trade and commerce from unlawful restraints, price discrimination, price fixing, and monopolies. The principal federal antitrust statues are the

Sherman Act of 1890, the Clayton Act of 1914, and the Federal Trade Commission Act of 1914.

Apparent authority Authority that is only apparent, not real. In agency law, a person may be deemed to have had the power to act as an agent for another party if the other party's manifestations to a third party led the third party to believe that an agency existed when, in fact, it did not.

Appeal Resort to a superior court, such as an appellate court, to review the decision of an inferior court, such as a trial court or an administrative agency.

Appellant The party who takes an appeal from one court to another.

Appellate court A court having appellate jurisdiction. Each state court system has at least one level of appellate courts. In the federal court system, the appellate courts are the circuit courts of appeals (intermediate appellate courts) and the United States Supreme Court (the highest appellate court in the federal system).

Appellate jurisdiction Courts having appellate jurisdiction act as reviewing courts, or appellate courts. Generally, cases can be brought before appellate courts only on appeal from an order or a judgment of a trial court or other lower court.

Appellee The party against whom an appeal is taken—that is, the party who opposes setting aside or reversing the judgment.

Appraisal right The right of a dissenting shareholder, if he or she objects to an extraordinary transaction of the corporation (such as a merger or consolidation), to have his or her shares appraised and to be paid the fair value of his or her shares by the corporation.

Appropriation In tort law, the use by one person of another person's name, likeness, or other identifying characteristic without permission and for the benefit of the user.

Arbitrary and capricious test The court reviewing an informal administrative agency action applies this test to determine whether or not that action was in clear error. The court gives wide discretion to the expertise of the agency and decides if the agency had sufficient factual information on which to base its action. If no clear error was made, then the agency's action stands.

Arbitration The settling of a dispute by submitting it to a disinterested third party (other than a court), who renders a decision. The decision may or may not be legally binding.

Arbitration clause A clause in a contract that provides that, in the event of a dispute, the parties will submit the dispute to arbitration rather than litigate the dispute in court.

Arraignment A procedure in which an accused person is brought before the court to plead to the criminal charge in the indictment or information. The charge is read to the person, and he or she is asked to enter a plea—such as "guilty" or "not guilty."

Arson The malicious burning of another's dwelling. Some statutes have expanded this to include any real property regardless of ownership and the destruction of property by other means—for example, by explosion.

Articles of incorporation The document filed with the appropriate governmental agency, usually the secretary of state, when a business is incorporated; state statutes usually prescribe what kind of information must be contained in the articles of incorporation.

Articles of organization The document filed with a designated state official by which a limited liability company is formed.

Articles of partnership A written agreement that sets forth each partner's rights and obligations with respect to the partnership.

Artisan's lien A possessory lien given to a person who has made improvements and added value to another person's personal property as security for payment for services performed.

Assault Any word or action intended to make another person fearful of immediate physical harm; a reasonably believable threat.

Assignee The person to whom contract rights are assigned.

Assignment The act of transferring to another all or part of one's rights arising under a contract.

Assignor The person who assigns contract rights.

Assumption of risk A defense against negligence that can be used when the plaintiff is aware of a danger and voluntarily assumes the risk of injury from that danger.

Attachment (1) In the context of secured transactions, the process by which a security interest in the property of another becomes enforceable. (2) In the context of judicial liens, a court-ordered seizure and taking into custody of property prior to the securing of a judgment for a past-due debt.

Attempted monopolization Any actions by a firm to eliminate competition and gain monopoly power.

Attractive nuisance doctrine A common law doctrine under which a landowner or landlord may be held liable for injuries incurred by children who are lured onto the property by something dangerous and enticing thereon.

Authenticate To sign a record, or with the intent to sign a record, to execute or to adopt an electronic sound, symbol, or the like to link with the record. See *record.*

Authority In agency law, the agent's permission to act on behalf of the principal. An agent's authority may be actual (express or implied) or apparent. *See also* Actual authority; Apparent authority

Authorized means In contract law, the means of acceptance authorized by the offeror.

Automatic stay In bankruptcy proceedings, the suspension of virtually all litigation and other action by creditors against the debtor or the debtor's property; the stay is effective the moment the debtor files a petition in bankruptcy.

Award In the context of litigation, the amount of money awarded to a plaintiff in a civil lawsuit as damages. In the context of arbitration, the arbitrator's decision.

B

B2B transaction A business-to-business transaction conducted via the Internet; an online sale or lease of goods or services from one business party to another.

B2C transaction A business-to-consumer transaction conducted via the Internet; an online sale, or lease of goods or services from a business party to a consumer.

Bail An amount of money set by the court that must be paid by a criminal defendant to the court before the defendant will be released from custody. Bail is set to assure that an individual accused of a crime will appear for further criminal proceedings. If the accused provides bail, whether in cash or in a surety bond, then he or she is released from jail.

Bailee One to whom goods are entrusted by a bailor. Under the Uniform Commercial Code, a party who, by a bill of lading, warehouse receipt, or other document of title, acknowledges possession of goods and contracts.

Bailee's lien A possessory lien, or claim, that a bailee entitled to compensation can place on the bailed property to ensure that he or she will be paid for the services provided. The lien is effective as long as the bailee retains possession of the bailed goods and has not agreed to extend credit to the bailor. Sometimes referred to as an artisan's lien.

Bailment A situation in which the personal property of one person (a bailor) is entrusted to another (a bailee), who is obligated to return the bailed property to the bailor or dispose of it as directed.

Bailor One who entrusts goods to a bailee.

Bait-and-switch advertising Advertising a product at a very attractive price (the "bait") and then informing the consumer, once he or she is in the store, that the advertised product is either not available or is of poor quality; the customer is then urged to purchase ("switched" to) a more expensive item.

Banker's acceptance A negotiable instrument that is commonly used in international trade. A banker's acceptance is drawn by a creditor against the debtor, who pays the draft at maturity. The drawer creates a draft without designating a payee. The draft can pass through many parties' hands before a bank (drawee) accepts it, transforming the draft into a banker's acceptance. Acceptances can be purchased and sold in a way similar to securities.

Bankruptcy court A federal court of limited jurisdiction that handles only bankruptcy proceedings. Bankruptcy proceedings are governed by federal bankruptcy law.

Bargain A mutual undertaking, contract, or agreement between two parties; to negotiate over the terms of a purchase or contract.

Basis of the bargain In contract law, the affirmation of fact or promise on which the sale of goods is predicated, creating an express warranty.

Battery The unprivileged, intentional touching of another.

Beachhead acquistion The gradual accumulation of a bloc of a target corporation's shares by an aggressor during an attempt to obtain control of the corporation.

Bearer A person in the possession of an instrument payable to bearer or indorsed in blank.

Bearer instrument Any instrument that is not payable to a specific person, including instruments payable to the bearer or to "cash."

Beneficiary One to whom life insurance proceeds are payable or for whose benefit a trust has been established or property under a will has been transferred.

Bequest A gift by will of personal property (from the verb—to bequeath).

Beyond a reasonable doubt The standard used to determine the guilt or innocence of a person criminally charged. To be guilty of a crime, one must be proved guilty "beyond and to the exclusion of every reasonable doubt." A reasonable doubt is one that would cause a prudent person to hesitate before acting in matters important to him or her.

Bilateral contract A type of contract that arises when a promise is given in exchange for a return promise.

Bill of lading A document that serves both as evidence of the receipt of goods for shipment and as documentary evidence of title to the goods.

Bill of Rights The first ten amendments to the U.S. Constitution.

Binder A written, temporary insurance policy.

Binding authority Any source of law that a court must follow when deciding a case. Binding authorities include constitutions, statutes, and regulations that govern the issue being decided, as well as court decisions that are controlling precedents within the jurisdiction.

Blank indorsement An indorsement that specifies no particular indorsee and that can consist of a mere signature. An order instrument that is indorsed in blank becomes a bearer instrument.

Blue laws State or local laws that prohibit the performance of certain types of commercial activities on Sunday.

Blue sky laws State laws that regulate the offer and sale of securities.

Bona fide Good faith. A bona fide obligation is one made in good faith—that is, sincerely and honestly.

Bona fide occupational qualification (BFOQ) Identifiable characteristics reasonably necessary to the normal operation of a particular business. These characteristics can include gender, national origin, and religion, but not race.

Bond A certificate that evidences a corporate (or government) debt. It is a security that involves no ownership interest in the issuing entity.

Bond indenture A contract between the issuer of a bond and the bondholder.

Bounty payment A reward (payment) given to a person or persons who perform a certain service—such as informing legal authorities of illegal actions.

Boycott A concerted refusal to do business with a particular person or entity in order to obtain concessions or to express displeasure with certain acts or practices of that person or business. *See also* Secondary boycott

Breach To violate a law, by an act or an omission, or to break a legal obligation that one owes to another person or to society.

Breach of contract The failure, without legal excuse, of a promisor to perform the obligations of a contract.

Bribery The offering, giving, receiving, or soliciting of anything of value with the aim of influencing an official action or an official's discharge of a legal or public duty or (with respect to commercial bribery) a business decision.

Brief A formal legal document submitted by the attorney for the appellant—or the appellee (in answer to the appellant's brief)—to an appellate court when a case is appealed. The appellant's brief outlines the facts and issues of the case, the judge's rulings or jury's findings that should be reversed or modified, the applicable law, and the arguments on the client's behalf.

Browse-Wrap terms Terms and conditions of use that are presented to an Internet user at the time certain products, such as software, are being downloaded but that need not be agreed to (by clicking "I agree," for example) before being able to install the software.

Bulk transfer A bulk sale or transfer, not made in the ordinary course of business, of a major part of the materials, supplies, merchandise, or other inventory of an enterprise.

Bureaucracy A large organization that is structured hierarchically to carry out specific functions.

Burglary The unlawful entry into a building with the intent to commit a felony. (Some state statutes expand this to include the intent to commit any crime.)

Business ethics Ethics in a business context; a consensus of what constitutes right or wrong behavior in the world of business and the application of moral principles to situations that arise in a business setting.

Business invitees Those people, such as customers or clients, who are invited onto business premises by the owner of those premises for business purposes.

Business judgment rule A rule that immunizes corporate management from liability for actions that result in corporate losses or damages if the actions are undertaken in good faith and are within both the power of the corporation and the authority of management to make.

Business necessity A defense to allegations of employment discrimination in which the employer demonstrates that an employment practice that discriminates against members of a protected class is related to job performance.

Business plan A document describing a company, its products, and its anticipated future performance. Creating a business plan is normally the first step in obtaining loans or venture-capital funds for a new business enterprise.

Business tort The wrongful interference with the business rights of another.

Business trust A voluntary form of business organization in which investors (trust beneficiaries) transfer cash or property to trustees in exchange for trust certificates that represent their investment shares. Management of the business and trust property is handled by the trustees for the use and benefit of the investors. The certificate holders have limited liability (are not responsible for the debts and obligations incurred by the trust) and share in the trust's profits.

Buyer in the ordinary course of business A buyer who, in good faith and without knowledge that the sale to him or her is in violation of the ownership rights or security interest of a third party in the goods, purchases goods in the ordinary course of business from a person in the business of selling goods of that kind.

Buy-sell agreement In the context of partnerships, an express agreement made at the time of partnership formation for one or more of the partners to buy out the other or others should the situation warrant—and thus provide for the smooth dissolution of the partnership.

Bylaws A set of governing rules adopted by a corporation or other association.

Bystander A spectator, witness, or person standing nearby when an event occurred and who did not engage in the business or act leading to the event.

C

C.I.F. or C.&F. Cost, insurance, and freight—or just cost and freight. A pricing term in a contract for the sale of goods requiring, among other things, that the seller place the goods in the possession of a carrier before risk passes to the buyer.

C.O.D. Cash on delivery. In sales transactions, a term meaning that the buyer will pay for the goods on delivery and before inspecting the goods.

Callable bond A bond that may be called in and the principal repaid at specified times or under conditions specified in the bond when it is issued.

Cancellation The act of nullifying, or making void. *See also* Rescission

Capital Accumulated goods, possessions, and assets used for the production of profits and wealth; the equity of owners in a business.

Carrier An individual or organization engaged in transporting passengers or goods for hire. *See also* Common carrier

Case law The rules of law announced in court decisions. Case law includes the aggregate of reported cases that interpret judicial precedents, statutes, regulations, and constitutional provisions.

Case on point A previous case involving factual circumstances and issues that are similar to the case before the court.

Cash surrender value The amount that the insurer has agreed to pay to the insured if a life insurance policy is canceled before the insured's death.
Cashier's check A check drawn by a bank on itself.
Categorical imperative A concept developed by the philosopher Immanuel Kant as an ethical guideline for behavior. In deciding whether an action is right or wrong, or desirable or undesirable, a person should evaluate the action in terms of what would happen if everybody else in the same situation, or category, acted the same way.
Causation in fact An act or omission without ("but for") which an event would not have occurred.
Cause of action A situation or state of facts that would entitle a party to sustain a legal action and give the party a right to seek a judicial remedy.
Cease-and-desist order An administrative or judicial order prohibiting a person or business firm from conducting activities that an agency or court has deemed illegal.
Certificate of deposit (CD) A note of a bank in which a bank acknowledges a receipt of money from a party and promises to repay the money, with interest, to the party on a certain date.
Certificate of incorporation The primary document that evidences corporate existence (referred to as articles of incorporation in some states).
Certificate of limited partnership The basic document filed with a designated state official by which a limited partnership is formed.
Certification In negotiable instruments law, the act of certifying a check. *See* Certified check
Certification mark A mark used by one or more persons, other than the owner, to certify the region, materials, mode of manufacture, quality, or accuracy of the owner's goods or services. When used by members of a cooperative, association, or other organization, such a mark is referred to as a collective mark. Examples of certification marks include the "Good Housekeeping Seal of Approval" and "UL Tested."
Certified check A check that has been accepted by the bank on which it is drawn. Essentially, the bank, by certifying (accepting) the check, promises to pay the check at the time the check is presented.
Certiorari *See* Writ of *certiorari*
Chain-style business franchise A franchise that operates under a franchisor's trade name and that is identified as a member of a select group of dealers that engage in the franchisor's business. The franchisee is generally required to follow standardized or prescribed methods of operation. Examples of this type of franchise are McDonald's and most other fast-food chains.
Chancellor An adviser to the king at the time of the early king's courts of England. Individuals petitioned the king for relief when they could not obtain an adequate remedy in a court of law, and these petitions were decided by the chancellor.
Charging order In partnership law, an order granted by a court to a judgment creditor that entitles the creditor to attach profits or assets of a partner on dissolution of the partnership.
Charitable trust A trust in which the property held by a trustee must be used for a charitable purpose, such as the advancement of health, education, or religion.
Charter *See* Corporate charter
Chattel All forms of personal property.
Chattel paper Any writing or writings that show both a debt and the fact that the debt is secured by personal property. In many instances, chattel paper consists of a negotiable instrument coupled with a security agreement.
Check A draft drawn by a drawer ordering the drawee bank or financial institution to pay a certain amount of money to the holder on demand.
Checks and balances The national government is composed of three separate branches: the executive, the legislative, and the judicial branches. Each branch of the government exercises a check on the actions of the others.
Choice-of-language clause A clause in a contract designating the official language by which the contract will be interpreted in the event of a future disagreement over the contract's terms.
Choice-of-law clause A clause in a contract designating the law (such as the law of a particular state or nation) that will govern the contract.
Citation A reference to a publication in which a legal authority—such as a statute or a court decision—or other source can be found.
Civil law The branch of law dealing with the definition and enforcement of all private or public rights, as opposed to criminal matters.
Civil law system A system of law derived from that of the Roman Empire and based on a code rather than case law; the predominant system of law in the nations of continental Europe and the nations that were once their colonies. In the United States, Louisiana is the only state that has a civil law system.
Claim As a verb, to assert or demand. As a noun, a right to payment.
Clearinghouse A system or place where banks exchange checks and drafts drawn on each other and settle daily balances.
Click-On agreement This arises when a buyer, completing a transaction on a computer, is required to indicate his or her assent to be bound by the terms of an offer by clicking on a button that says, for example, "I agree"; sometimes referred to as a *click-on license* or a *click-wrap agreement.*
Close corporation A corporation whose shareholders are limited to a small group of persons, often including only family members. The rights of shareholders of a close corporation usually are restricted regarding the transfer of shares to others.
Closed shop A firm that requires union membership by its workers as a condition of employment. The closed shop was made illegal by the Labor-Management Relations Act of 1947.

Closing The final step in the sale of real estate—also called settlement or closing escrow. The escrow agent coordinates the closing with the recording of deeds, the obtaining of title insurance, and other concurrent closing activities. A number of costs must be paid, in cash, at the time of closing, and they can range from several hundred to several thousand dollars, depending on the amount of the mortgage loan and other conditions of the sale.

Closing argument An argument made after the plaintiff and defendant have rested their cases. Closing arguments are made prior to the jury charges.

Codicil A written supplement or modification to a will. A codicil must be executed with the same formalities as a will.

Collateral Under Article 9 of the Uniform Commercial Code, the property subject to a security interest, including accounts and chattel paper that have been sold.

Collateral promise A secondary promise that is ancillary (subsidiary) to a principal transaction or primary contractual relationship, such as a promise made by one person to pay the debts of another if the latter fails to perform. A collateral promise normally must be in writing to be enforceable.

Collecting bank Any bank handling an item for collection, except the payor bank.

Collective bargaining The process by which labor and management negotiate the terms and conditions of employment, including working hours and workplace conditions.

Collective mark A mark used by members of a cooperative, association, or other organization to certify the region, materials, mode of manufacture, quality, or accuracy of the specific goods or services. Examples of collective marks include the labor union marks found on tags of certain products and the credits of movies, which indicate the various associations and organizations that participated in the making of the movies.

Comity A deference by which one nation gives effect to the laws and judicial decrees of another nation. This recognition is based primarily on respect.

Comment period A period of time following an administrative agency's publication or a notice of a proposed rule during which private parties may comment in writing on the agency proposal in an effort to influence agency policy. The agency takes any comments received into consideration when drafting the final version of the regulation.

Commerce clause The provision in Article I, Section 8, of the U.S. Constitution that gives Congress the power to regulate interstate commerce.

Commercial impracticability A doctrine under which a seller may be excused from performing a contract when (1) a contingency occurs, (2) the contingency's occurrence makes performance impracticable, and (3) the nonoccurrence of the contingency was a basic assumption on which the contract was made. Despite the fact that UCC 2–615 expressly frees only sellers under this doctrine, courts have not distinguished between buyers and sellers in applying it.

Commercial paper *See* Negotiable instrument

Commingle To mix together. To put funds or goods together into one mass so that the funds or goods are so mixed that they no longer have separate identities. In corporate law, if personal and corporate interests are commingled to the extent that the corporation has no separate identity, a court may "pierce the corporate veil" and expose the shareholders to personal liability.

Common area In landlord-tenant law, a portion of the premises over which the landlord retains control and maintenance responsibilities. Common areas may include stairs, lobbies, garages, hallways, and other areas in common use.

Common carrier A carrier that holds itself out or undertakes to carry persons or goods of all persons indifferently, or of all who choose to employ it.

Common law That body of law developed from custom or judicial decisions in English and U.S. courts, not attributable to a legislature.

Common stock Shares of ownership in a corporation that give the owner of the stock a proportionate interest in the corporation with regard to control, earnings, and net assets; shares of common stock are lowest in priority with respect to payment of dividends and distribution of the corporation's assets on dissolution.

Community property A form of concurrent ownership of property in which each spouse technically owns an undivided one-half interest in property acquired during the marriage. This form of joint ownership occurs in only nine states and Puerto Rico.

Comparative law The study and comparison of legal systems and laws across nations.

Comparative negligence A theory in tort law under which the liability for injuries resulting from negligent acts is shared by all parties who were negligent (including the injured party), on the basis of each person's proportionate negligence.

Compensatory damages A money award equivalent to the actual value of injuries or damages sustained by the aggrieved party.

Complaint The pleading made by a plaintiff alleging wrongdoing on the part of the defendant; the document that, when filed with a court, initiates a lawsuit.

Complete performance Performance of a contract strictly in accordance with the contract's terms.

Composition agreement *See* Creditors' composition agreement

Computer crime Any wrongful act that is directed against computers and computer parties, or wrongful use or abuse of computers or software.

Computer information Information in electronic form obtained from or through use of a computer, or that is in digital or an equivalent form capable of being processed by a computer.

Concentrated industry An industry in which a large percentage of market sales is controlled by either a single firm or a small number of firms.

Conciliation A form of alternative dispute resolution in which the parties reach an agreement themselves with the help of a neutral third party, called a conciliator, who facilitates the negotiations.

Concurrent conditions Conditions in a contract that must occur or be performed at the same time; they are mutually dependent. No obligations arise until these conditions are simultaneously performed.

Concurrent jurisdiction Jurisdiction that exists when two different courts have the power to hear a case. For example, some cases can be heard in either a federal or a state court.

Concurrent ownership Joint ownership.

Concurring opinion A written opinion outlining the views of a judge or justice to make or emphasize a point that was not made or emphasized in the majority opinion.

Condition A qualification, provision, or clause in a contractual agreement, the occurrence of which creates, suspends, or terminates the obligations of the contracting parties.

Condition precedent A condition in a contract that must be met before a party's promise becomes absolute.

Condition subsequent A condition in a contract that operates to terminate a party's absolute promise to perform.

Conditional contract A contract subject to a condition that must be met for the contract to be enforceable. *See* Condition precedent

Confession of judgment The act of a debtor in permitting a judgment to be entered against him or her by a creditor, for an agreed sum, without the institution of legal proceedings.

Confiscation A government's taking of privately owned business or personal property without a proper public purpose or an award of just compensation.

Conforming goods Goods that conform to contract specifications.

Confusion The mixing together of goods belonging to two or more owners so that the separately owned goods cannot be identified.

Conglomerate merger A merger between firms that do not compete with each other because they are in different markets (as opposed to horizontal and vertical mergers).

Consent Voluntary agreement to a proposition or an act of another. A concurrence of wills.

Consequential damages Special damages that compensate for a loss that is not direct or immediate (for example, lost profits). The special damages must have been reasonably foreseeable at the time the breach or injury occurred in order for the plaintiff to collect them.

Consideration Generally, the value given in return for a promise. The consideration, which must be present to make the contract legally binding, must be something of legally sufficient value and bargained for and must result in a detriment to the promisee or a benefit to the promisor.

Consignee One to whom goods are delivered on consignment. *See also* Consignment

Consignment A transaction in which an owner of goods (the consignor) delivers the goods to another (the consignee) for the consignee to sell. The consignee pays the consignor for the goods when they are sold by the consignee.

Consignor One who consigns goods to another. *See also* Consignment

Consolidation A contractual and statutory process in which two or more corporations join to become a completely new corporation. The original corporations cease to exist, and the new corporation acquires all their assets and liabilities.

Constitutional law Law that is based on the U.S. Constitution and the constitutions of the various states.

Constructive condition A condition in a contract that is neither expressed nor implied by the contract but rather is imposed by law for reasons of justice.

Constructive delivery An act equivalent to the actual, physical delivery of property that cannot be physically delivered because of difficulty or impossibility; for example, the transfer of a key to a safe constructively delivers the contents of the safe.

Constructive eviction A form of eviction that occurs when a landlord fails to perform adequately any of the undertakings (such as providing heat in the winter) required by the lease, thereby making the tenant's further use and enjoyment of the property exceedingly difficult or impossible.

Constructive trust An equitable trust that is imposed in the interests of fairness and justice when someone wrongfully holds legal title to property. A court may require the owner to hold the property in trust for the person or persons who rightfully should own the property.

Consumer credit Credit extended primarily for personal or household use.

Consumer-debtor An individual whose debts are primarily consumer debts (debts for purchases made primarily for personal or household use).

Consumer goods Goods that are primarily for personal or household use.

Consumer law The body of statutes, agency rules, and judicial decisions protecting consumers of goods and services from dangerous manufacturing techniques, mislabeling, unfair credit practices, deceptive advertising, and so on. Consumer laws provide remedies and protections that are not ordinarily available to merchants or to businesses.

Contingency fee An attorney's fee that is based on a percentage of the final award received by his or her client as a result of litigation.

Continuation statement A statement that, if filed within six months prior to the expiration date of the original financing statement, continues the perfection of the original security interest for another five years.

The perfection of a security interest can be continued in the same manner indefinitely.

Contract An agreement that can be enforced in court; formed by two or more parties, each of whom agrees to perform or to refrain from performing some act now or in the future.

Contract implied in law *See* Quasi contract

Contract under seal A formal agreement in which the seal is a substitute for consideration. A court will not invalidate a contract under seal for lack of consideration.

Contractual agreement *See* Contract

Contractual capacity The threshold mental capacity required by the law for a party who enters into a contract to be bound by that contract.

Contribution *See* Right of contribution

Contributory negligence A theory in tort law under which a complaining party's own negligence contributed to or caused his or her injuries. Contributory negligence is an absolute bar to recovery in a minority of jurisdictions.

Conversion The wrongful taking, using, or retaining possession of personal property that belongs to another.

Convertible bond A bond that can be exchanged for a specified number of shares of common stock under certain conditions.

Conveyance The transfer of a title to land from one person to another by deed; a document (such as a deed) by which an interest in land is transferred from one person to another.

Conviction The outcome of a criminal trial in which the defendant has been found guilty of the crime with which he or she was charged and on which sentencing, or punishment, is based.

Cooperative An association that is organized to provide an economic service to its members (or shareholders). An incorporated cooperative is a nonprofit corporation. It will make distributions of dividends, or profits, to its owners on the basis of their transactions with the cooperative rather than on the basis of the amount of capital they contributed. Examples of cooperatives are consumer purchasing cooperatives, credit cooperatives, and farmers' cooperatives.

Co-ownership Joint ownership.

Copyright The exclusive right of authors to publish, print, or sell an intellectual production for a statutory period of time. A copyright has the same monopolistic nature as a patent or trademark, but it differs in that it applies exclusively to works of art, literature, and other works of authorship, including computer programs.

Corporate charter The document issued by a state agency or authority (usually the secretary of state) that grants a corporation legal existence and the right to function.

Corporate social responsibility The concept that corporations can and should act ethically and be accountable to society for their actions.

Corporation A legal entity formed in compliance with statutory requirements. The entity is distinct from its shareholders-owners.

Cosign The act of signing a document (such as a note promising to pay another in return for a loan or other benefit) jointly with another person and thereby assuming liability for performing what was promised in the document.

Cost-benefit analysis A decision-making technique that involves weighing the costs of a given action against the benefits of the action.

Co-surety A joint surety. One who assumes liability jointly with another surety for the payment of an obligation.

Counteradvertising New advertising that is undertaken pursuant to a Federal Trade Commission order for the purpose of correcting earlier false claims that were made about a product.

Counterclaim A claim made by a defendant in a civil lawsuit that in effect sues the plaintiff.

Counteroffer An offeree's response to an offer in which the offeree rejects the original offer and at the same time makes a new offer.

Course of dealing Prior conduct between parties to a contract that establishes a common basis for their understanding.

Course of performance The conduct that occurs under the terms of a particular agreement; such conduct indicates what the parties to an agreement intended it to mean.

Court of equity A court that decides controversies and administers justice according to the rules, principles, and precedents of equity.

Court of law A court in which the only remedies that could be granted were things of value, such as money damages. In the early English king's courts, courts of law were distinct from courts of equity.

Covenant against encumbrances A grantor's assurance that on land conveyed there are no encumbrances—that is, that no third parties have rights to or interests in the land that would diminish its value to the grantee.

Covenant not to compete A contractual promise to refrain from competing with another party for a certain period of time (not excessive in duration) and within a reasonable geographic area. Although covenants not to compete restrain trade, they are commonly found in partnership agreements, business sale agreements, and employment contracts. If they are ancillary to such agreements, covenants not to compete will normally be enforced by the courts unless the time period or geographic area is deemed unreasonable.

Covenant not to sue An agreement to substitute a contractual obligation for some other type of legal action based on a valid claim.

Covenant of quiet enjoyment A promise by a grantor (or landlord) that the grantee (or tenant) will not be evicted or disturbed by the grantor or a person having a lien or superior title.

Covenant of the right to convey A grantor's assurance that he or she has sufficient capacity and title to convey the estate that he or she undertakes to convey by deed.
Covenant running with the land An executory promise made between a grantor and a grantee to which they and subsequent owners of the land are bound.
Cover Under the Uniform Commercial Code, a remedy of the buyer or lessee that allows the buyer or lessee, on the seller's or lessor's breach, to purchase the goods from another seller or lessor and substitute them for the goods due under the contract. If the cost of cover exceeds the cost of the contract goods, the breaching seller or lessor will be liable to the buyer or lessee for the difference. In obtaining cover, the buyer or lessee must act in good faith and without unreasonable delay.
Cram-down provision A provision of the Bankruptcy Code that allows a court to confirm a debtor's Chapter 11 reorganization plan even though only one class of creditors has accepted it. To exercise the court's right under this provision, the court must demonstrate that the plan does not discriminate unfairly against any creditors and is fair and equitable.
Crashworthiness doctrine A doctrine that imposes liability for defects in the design or construction of motor vehicles that increase the extent of injuries to passengers if an accident occurs. The doctrine holds even when the defects do not actually cause the accident.
Creditor A person to whom a debt is owed by another person (the debtor).
Creditor beneficiary A third party beneficiary who has rights in a contract made by the debtor and a third person. The terms of the contract obligate the third person to pay the debt owed to the creditor. The creditor beneficiary can enforce the debt against either party.
Creditors' composition agreement An agreement formed between a debtor and his or her creditors in which the creditors agree to accept a lesser sum than that owed by the debtor in full satisfaction of the debt.
Crime A wrong against society proclaimed in a statute and, if committed, punishable by society through fines and/or imprisonment—and, in some cases, death.
Criminal act *See Actus reus*
Criminal intent *See Mens rea*
Criminal law Law that defines and governs actions that constitute crimes. Generally, criminal law has to do with wrongful actions committed against society for which society demands redress.
Cross-examination The questioning of an opposing witness during the trial.
Cumulative voting A method of shareholder voting designed to allow minority shareholders to be represented on the board of directors. With cumulative voting, the number of members of the board to be elected is multiplied by the total number of voting shares held. The result equals the number of votes a shareholder has, and this total can be cast for one or more nominees for director.
Cure Under the Uniform Commercial Code, the right of a party who tenders nonconforming performance to correct his or her performance within the contract period.
Cyber crime A crime that occurs online, in the virtual community of the Internet, as opposed to the physical world.
Cyber hate speech Extreme hate speech on the Internet. Racist materials and Holocaust denials disseminated on the Web are examples.
Cyber mark A trademark in cyberspace.
Cyber stalker A person who commits the crime of stalking in cyberspace. Generally, stalking consists of harassing a person and putting that person in reasonable fear for his or her safety or the safety of the person's immediate family.
Cybersquatting An act that occurs when a person registers a domain name that is the same as, or confusingly similar to, the trademark of another and offers to sell the domain name back to the trademark owner.
Cyber terrorist A hacker whose purpose is to exploit a target computer for a serious impact, such as the corruption of a program to sabotage a business.
Cyber tort A tort committed in cyberspace.

D

Damages Money sought as a remedy for a breach of contract or for a tortious act.
Debenture bond A bond for which no specific assets of the corporation are pledged as backing; rather, the bond is backed by the general credit rating of the corporation, plus any assets that can be seized if the corporation allows the debentures to go into default.
Debtor Under Article 9 of the Uniform Commercial Code, a debtor is any party who owes payment or performance of a secured obligation, whether or not the party actually owns or has rights in the collateral.
Debtor in possession (DIP) In Chapter 11 bankruptcy proceedings, a debtor who is allowed to continue in possession of the estate in property (the business) and to continue business operations.
Declaratory judgment A court's judgment on a justiciable controversy when the plaintiff is in doubt as to his or her legal rights; a binding adjudication of the rights and status of litigants even though no consequential relief is awarded.
Decree The judgment of a court of equity.
Deed A document by which title to property (usually real property) is passed.
Defalcation The misuse of funds.
Defamation Any published or publicly spoken false statement that causes injury to another's good name, reputation, or character.
Default The failure to observe a promise or discharge an obligation. The term is commonly used to mean the failure to pay a debt when it is due.

Default judgment A judgment entered by a court against a defendant who has failed to appear in court to answer or defend against the plaintiff's claim.

Default rules Rules that apply under the Uniform Computer Information Transactions Act only in the absence of an agreement between contracting parties to the contrary.

Defendant One against whom a lawsuit is brought; the accused person in a criminal proceeding.

Defense That which a defendant offers and alleges in an action or suit as a reason why the plaintiff should not recover or establish what he or she seeks.

Deficiency judgment A judgment against a debtor for the amount of a debt remaining unpaid after collateral has been repossessed and sold.

Delegatee One to whom contract duties are delegated by another, called the delegator.

Delegation The transfer of a contractual duty to a third party. The party delegating the duty (the delegator) to the third party (the delegatee) is still obliged to perform on the contract should the delegatee fail to perform.

Delegation doctrine A doctrine based on Article I, Section 8, of the U.S. Constitution, which has been construed to allow Congress to delegate some of its power to make and implement laws to administrative agencies. The delegation is considered to be proper as long as Congress sets standards outlining the scope of the agency's authority.

Delegator One who delegates his or her duties under a contract to another, called the delegatee.

Delivery In contract law, the one party's act of placing the subject matter of the contract within the other party's possession or control.

Delivery ex ship Delivery from the carrying ship. A contract term indicating that risk of loss will not pass to the buyer until the goods leave the ship or are otherwise properly unloaded.

Delivery order A written order to deliver goods directed to a warehouser, carrier, or other person who, in the ordinary course of business, issues warehouse receipts or bills of lading [UCC 7–102(1)(d)].

Demand deposit Funds (accepted by a bank) subject to immediate withdrawal, in contrast to a time deposit, which requires that a depositor wait a specific time before withdrawing or pay a penalty for early withdrawal.

Demurrer *See* Motion to dismiss

De novo Anew; afresh; a second time. In a hearing *de novo,* an appellate court hears the case as a court of original jurisidction—that is, as if the case had not previously been tried and a decision rendered.

Depositary bank The first bank to receive a check for payment.

Deposition The testimony of a party to a lawsuit or a witness taken under oath before a trial.

Destination contract A contract for the sale of goods in which the seller is required or authorized to ship the goods by carrier and deliver them at a particular destination. The seller assumes liability for any losses or damage to the goods until they are tendered at the destination specified in the contract.

Devise To make a gift of real property by will.

Dilution With respect to trademarks, a doctrine under which distinctive or famous trademarks are protected from certain unauthorized uses of the marks regardless of a showing of competition or a likelihood of confusion. Congress created a federal cause of action for dilution in 1995 with the passage of the Federal Trademark Dilution Act.

Direct examination The examination of a witness by the attorney who calls the witness to the stand to testify on behalf of the attorney's client.

Directed verdict *See* Motion for a directed verdict

Disaffirmance The legal avoidance, or setting aside, of a contractual obligation.

Discharge The termination of an obligation. (1) In contract law, discharge occurs when the parties have fully performed their contractual obligations or when events, conduct of the parties, or operation of the law releases the parties from performance. (2) In bankruptcy proceedings, the extinction of the debtor's dischargeable debts.

Discharge in bankruptcy The release of a debtor from all debts that are provable, except those specifically excepted from discharge by statute.

Disclosed principal A principal whose identity is known to a third party at the time the agent makes a contract with the third party.

Discovery A phase in the litigation process during which the opposing parties may obtain information from each other and from third parties prior to trial.

Dishonor To refuse to accept or pay a draft or a promissory note when it is properly presented. An instrument is dishonored when presentment is properly made and acceptance or payment is refused or cannot be obtained within the prescribed time.

Disparagement of property An economically injurious falsehood made about another's product or property. A general term for torts that are more specifically referred to as slander of quality or slander of title.

Disparate-impact discrimination A form of employment discrimination that results from certain employer practices or procedures that, although not discriminatory on their face, have a discriminatory effect.

Disparate-treatment discrimination A form of employment discrimination that results when an employer intentionally discriminates against employees who are members of protected classes.

Dissenting opinion A written opinion by a judge or justice who disagrees with the majority opinion.

Dissolution The formal disbanding of a partnership or a corporation. It can take place by (1) acts of the partners or, in a corporation, of the shareholders and board of directors; (2) the death of a partner; (3) the expiration of a time period stated in a partnership agreement or a certificate of incorporation; or (4) judicial decree.

Distributed network A network that can be used by persons located (distributed) around the country or the globe to share computer files.

Distribution agreement A contract between a seller and a distributor of the seller's products setting out the terms and conditions of the distributorship.

Distributorship A business arrangement that is established when a manufacturer licenses a dealer to sell its product. An example of a distributorship is an automobile dealership.

Diversity of citizenship Under Article III, Section 2, of the Constitution, a basis for federal court jurisdiction over a lawsuit between (1) citizens of different states, (2) a foreign country and citizens of a state or of different states, or (3) citizens of a state and citizens or subjects of a foreign country. The amount in controversy must be more than $75,000 before a federal court can take jurisdiction in such cases.

Divestiture The act of selling one or more of a company's parts, such as a subsidiary or plant; often mandated by the courts in merger or monopolization cases.

Dividend A distribution to corporate shareholders of corporate profits or income, disbursed in proportion to the number of shares held.

Docket The list of cases entered on a court's calendar and thus scheduled to be heard by the court.

Document of title Paper exchanged in the regular course of business that evidences the right to possession of goods (for example, a bill of lading or a warehouse receipt).

Domain name The series of letters and symbols used to identify site operators on the Internet; Internet "addresses."

Domestic corporation In a given state, a corporation that does business in, and is organized under the law of, that state.

Domestic relations court A court that deals with domestic (household) relationships, such as adoption, divorce, support payments, child custody, and the like.

Donee beneficiary A third party beneficiary who has rights under a contract as a direct result of the intention of the contract parties to make a gift to the third party.

Double jeopardy A situation occurring when a person is tried twice for the same criminal offense; prohibited by the Fifth Amendment to the Constitution.

Double taxation A feature (and disadvantage) of the corporate form of business. Because a corporation is a separate legal entity, corporate profits are taxed by state and federal governments. Dividends are again taxable as ordinary income to the shareholders receiving them.

Draft Any instrument drawn on a drawee (such as a bank) that orders the drawee to pay a certain sum of money, usually to a third party (the payee), on demand or at a definite future time.

Dram shop act A state statute that imposes liability on the owners of bars and taverns, as well as those who serve alcoholic drinks to the public, for injuries resulting from accidents caused by intoxicated persons when the sellers or servers of alcoholic drinks contributed to the intoxication.

Drawee The party that is ordered to pay a draft or check. With a check, a financial institution is always the drawee.

Drawer The party that initiates a draft (such as a check), thereby ordering the drawee to pay.

Due diligence A required standard of care that certain professionals, such as accountants, must meet to avoid liability for securities violations. Under securities law, an accountant will be deemed to have exercised due diligence if he or she followed generally accepted accounting principles and generally accepted auditing standards and had, "after reasonable investigation, reasonable grounds to believe and did believe, at the time such part of the registration statement became effective, that the statements therein were true and that there was no omission of a material fact required to be stated therein or necessary to make the statements therein not misleading."

Due negotiation The transfer of a document of title in such form that the transferee becomes a holder [UCC 7–501].

Due process clause The provisions of the Fifth and Fourteenth Amendments to the Constitution that guarantee that no person shall be deprived of life, liberty, or property without due process of law. Similar clauses are found in most state constitutions.

Dumping The selling of goods in a foreign country at a price below the price charged for the same goods in the domestic market.

Durable power of attorney A document that authorizes a person to act on behalf of an incompetent person—write checks, collect insurance proceeds, and otherwise manage the disabled person's affairs, including health care—when he or she becomes incapacitated. Spouses often give each other durable power of attorney and, if they are advanced in age, may give a second such power of attorney to an older child.

Duress Unlawful pressure brought to bear on a person, causing the person to perform an act that he or she would not otherwise perform.

Duty of care The duty of all persons, as established by tort law, to exercise a reasonable amount of care in their dealings with others. Failure to exercise due care, which is normally determined by the "reasonable person standard," constitutes the tort of negligence.

E

E-agent According to the Uniform Computer Information Transactions Act, a computer program, or electronic or other automated means used to independently initiate an action or to respond to electronic messages or performances without review by an individual.

E-commerce Business transacted in cyberspace.

E-contract A contract that is formed electronically.

E-money Prepaid funds recorded on a computer or a card (such as a *smart card*).

E-signature An electronic sound, symbol, or process attached to or logically associated with a record and executed or adopted by a person with the intent to sign the record, according to the Uniform Electronic Transactions Act.

Early neutral case evaluation A form of alternative dispute resolution in which a neutral third party evaluates the strengths and weakness of the disputing parties' positions; the evaluator's opinion forms the basis for negotiating a settlement.

Easement A nonpossessory right to use another's property in a manner established by either express or implied agreement.

Ejectment The eviction of a tenant from leased premises. A remedy at common law to which the landlord can resort when a tenant fails to pay rent for leased premises. To obtain possession of the premises, the landlord must appear in court and show that the defaulting tenant is in wrongful possession.

Elder law A relatively new area of legal practice in which attorneys assist older persons in dealing with such problems as disability, long-term health care, age discrimination, grandparents' visitation rights, and other problems relating to age.

Electronic fund transfer (EFT) A transfer of funds with the use of an electronic terminal, a telephone, a computer, or magnetic tape.

Emancipation In regard to minors, the act of being freed from parental control; occurs when a child's parent or legal guardian relinquishes the legal right to exercise control over the child. Normally, a minor who leaves home to support himself or herself is considered emancipated.

Embezzlement The fraudulent appropriation of money or other property by a person to whom the money or property has been entrusted.

Eminent domain The power of a government to take land for public use from private citizens for just compensation.

Employee A person who works for an employer for a salary or for wages.

Employer An individual or business entity that hires employees, pays them salaries or wages, and exercises control over their work.

Employment at will A common law doctrine under which either party may terminate an employment relationship at any time for any reason, unless a contract specifies otherwise.

Employment discrimination Treating employees or job applicants unequally on the basis of race, color, national origin, religion, gender, age, or disability; prohibited by federal statutes.

Enabling legislation A statute enacted by Congress that authorizes the creation of an administrative agency and specifies the name, composition, purpose, and powers of the agency being created.

Encryption The process by which a message (plaintext) is transformed into something (ciphertext) that the sender and receiver intend third parties not to understand.

Endowment insurance A type of insurance that combines life insurance with an investment so that if the insured outlives the policy, the face value is paid to him or her; if the insured does not outlive the policy, the face value is paid to his or her beneficiary.

Entrapment In criminal law, a defense in which the defendant claims that he or she was induced by a public official—usually an undercover agent or police officer—to commit a crime that he or she would otherwise not have committed.

Entrepreneur One who initiates and assumes the financial risks of a new enterprise and who undertakes to provide or control its management.

Entrustment The transfer of goods to a merchant who deals in goods of that kind and who may transfer those goods and all rights to them to a buyer in the ordinary course of business [UCC 2–403(2)].

Environmental impact statement (EIS) A statement required by the National Environmental Policy Act for any major federal action that will significantly affect the quality of the environment. The statement must analyze the action's impact on the environment and explore alternative actions that might be taken.

Environmental law The body of statutory, regulatory, and common law relating to the protection of the environment.

Equal dignity rule In most states, a rule stating that express authority given to an agent must be in writing if the contract to be made on behalf of the principal is required to be in writing.

Equal protection clause The provision in the Fourteenth Amendment to the Constitution that guarantees that no state will "deny to any person within its jurisdiction the equal protection of the laws." This clause mandates that state governments treat similarly situated individuals in a similar manner.

Equitable maxims General propositions or principles of law that have to do with fairness (equity).

Equity of redemption The right of a mortgagor who has breached the mortgage agreement to redeem or purchase the property prior to foreclosure proceedings.

Escheat The transfer of property to the state when the owner of the property dies without heirs.

Escrow account An account that is generally held in the name of the depositor and escrow agent; the funds in the account are paid to a third person only on fulfillment of the escrow condition.

Establishment clause The provision in the First Amendment to the U.S. Constitution that prohibits Congress from creating any law "respecting an establishment of religion."

Estate The interest that a person has in real and personal property.

Estate planning Planning in advance how one's property and obligations should be transferred on one's death. Wills and trusts are two basic devices used in the process of estate planning.

Estop To bar, impede, or preclude.

Estoppel The principle that a party's own acts prevent him or her from claiming a right to the detriment of another who was entitled to and did rely on those acts. *See also* Agency by estoppel; Promissory estoppel

Estray statute A statute defining finders' rights in property when the true owners are unknown.

Ethical reasoning A reasoning process in which an individual links his or her moral convictions or ethical standards to the particular situation at hand.

Ethics Moral principles and values applied to social behavior.

Evidence Proof offered at trial—in the form of testimony, documents, records, exhibits, objects, and so on—for the purpose of convincing the court or jury of the truth of a contention.

Eviction A landlord's act of depriving a tenant of possession of the leased premises.

***Ex parte* contact** Communications with an administrative agency that are not placed in the record.

Ex ship *See* Delivery ex ship

Exclusionary rule In criminal procedure, a rule under which any evidence that is obtained in violation of the accused's constitutional rights guaranteed by the Fourth, Fifth, and Sixth Amendments, as well as any evidence derived from illegally obtained evidence, will not be admissible in court.

Exclusive distributorship A distributorship in which the seller and the distributor of the seller's products agree that the distributor has the exclusive right to distribute the seller's products in a certain geographic area.

Exclusive jurisdiction Jurisdiction that exists when a case can be heard only in a particular court or type of court, such as a federal court or a state court.

Exclusive-dealing contract An agreement under which a seller forbids a buyer to purchase products from the seller's competitors.

Exculpatory clause A clause that releases a contractual party from liability in the event of monetary or physical injury, no matter who is at fault.

Executed contract A contract that has been completely performed by both parties.

Execution An action to carry into effect the directions in a court decree or judgment.

Executive agency An administrative agency within the executive branch of government. At the federal level, executive agencies are those within the cabinet departments.

Executor A person appointed by a testator to see that his or her will is administered appropriately.

Executory contract A contract that has not as yet been fully performed.

Export To sell products to buyers located in other countries.

Express authority Authority expressly given by one party to another. In agency law, an agent has express authority to act for a principal if both parties agree, orally or in writing, that an agency relationship exists in which the agent had the power (authority) to act in the place of, and on behalf of, the principal.

Express contract A contract in which the terms of the agreement are fully and explicitly stated in words, oral or written.

Express warranty A seller's or lessor's oral or written promise, ancillary to an underlying sales or lease agreement, as to the quality, description, or performance of the goods being sold or leased.

Expropriation The seizure by a government of privately owned business or personal property for a proper public purpose and with just compensation.

Extension clause A clause in a time instrument that allows the instrument's date of maturity to be extended into the future.

F

F.A.S. Free alongside. A contract term that requires the seller, at his or her own expense and risk, to deliver the goods alongside the ship before risk passes to the buyer.

F.O.B. Free on board. A contract term that indicates that the selling price of the goods includes transportation costs (and that the seller carries the risk of loss) to the specific F.O.B. place named in the contract. The place can be either the place of initial shipment (for example, the seller's city or place of business) or the place of destination (for example, the buyer's city or place of business).

Family limited liability partnership (FLLP) A limited liability partnership (LLP) in which the majority of the partners are persons related to each other, essentially as spouses, parents, grandparents, siblings, cousins, nephews, or nieces. A person acting in a fiduciary capacity for persons so related could also be a partner. All of the partners must be natural persons or persons acting in a fiduciary capacity for the benefit of natural persons.

Federal form of government A system of government in which the states form a union and the sovereign power is divided between a central government and the member states.

Federal question A question that pertains to the U.S. Constitution, acts of Congress, or treaties. A federal question provides a basis for federal jurisdiction.

Federal Reserve System A network of twelve central banks, located around the country and headed by the Federal Reserve Board of Governors. Most banks in the United States have Federal Reserve accounts.

Federal Rules of Civil Procedure (FRCP) The rules controlling procedural matters in civil trials brought before the federal district courts.

Federal system A system of government in which power is divided by a written constitution between a central government and regional, or subdivisional, governments. Each level must have some domain in which its policies are dominant and some genuine political or constitutional guarantee of its authority.

Fee simple An absolute form of property ownership entitling the property owner to use, possess, or dispose of the property as he or she chooses during his or her lifetime. On death, the interest in the property descends to the owner's heirs; a fee simple absolute.

Fee simple absolute An ownership interest in land in which the owner has the greatest possible aggregation of rights, privileges, and power. Ownership in fee simple absolute is limited absolutely to a person and his or her heirs.

Fellow-servant doctrine A doctrine that bars an employee from suing his or her employer for injuries caused by a fellow employee.

Felony A crime—such as arson, murder, rape, or robbery—that carries the most severe sanctions, usually ranging from one year in a state or federal prison to the forfeiture of one's life.

Fictitious payee A payee on a negotiable instrument whom the maker or drawer does not intend to have an interest in the instrument. Indorsements by fictitious payees are not treated as unauthorized under Article 3 of the Uniform Commercial Code.

Fiduciary As a noun, a person having a duty created by his or her undertaking to act primarily for another's benefit in matters connected with the undertaking. As an adjective, a relationship founded on trust and confidence.

Fiduciary duty The duty, imposed on a fiduciary by virtue of his or her position, to act primarily for another's benefit.

Filtering software A computer program that includes a pattern through which data are passed. When designed to block access to certain Web sites, the pattern blocks the retrieval of a site whose URL or key words are on a list within the program.

Final order The final decision of an administrative agency on an issue. If no appeal is taken, or if the case is not reviewed or considered anew by the agency commission, the administrative law judge's initial order becomes the final order of the agency.

Financial institution An organization authorized to do business under state or federal laws relating to financial institutions. For example, under the Electronic Fund Transfer Act, financial institutions include banks, savings and loan associations, credit unions, and other business entities that directly or indirectly hold accounts belonging to consumers.

Financing statement A document prepared by a secured creditor and filed with the appropriate state or local official to give notice to the public that the creditor claims an interest in collateral belonging to the debtor named in the statement. The financing statement must be signed by the debtor, contain the addresses of both the debtor and the creditor, and describe the collateral by type or item.

Firm offer An offer (by a merchant) that is irrevocable without consideration for a period of time (not longer than three months). A firm offer by a merchant must be in writing and must be signed by the offeror.

Fitness for a particular purpose *See* Implied warranty of fitness for a particular purpose

Fixture A thing that was once personal property but that has become attached to real property in such a way that it takes on the characteristics of real property and becomes part of that real property.

Flame An online message in which one party attacks another in harsh, often personal, terms.

Floating lien A security interest in proceeds, after-acquired property, or property purchased under a line of credit (or all three); a security interest in collateral that is retained even when the collateral changes in character, classification, or location.

Force majeure (pronounced mah-*zhure*) **clause** A provision in a contract stipulating that certain unforeseen events—such as war, political upheavals, acts of God, or other events—will excuse a party from liability for nonperformance of contractual obligations.

Foreclosure A proceeding in which a mortgagee either takes title to or forces the sale of the mortgagor's property in satisfaction of a debt.

Foreign corporation In a given state, a corporation that does business in the state without being incorporated therein.

Foreseeable risk In negligence law, the risk of harm or injury to another that a person of ordinary intelligence and prudence should have reasonably anticipated or foreseen when undertaking an action or refraining from undertaking an action.

Forfeiture The termination of a lease, according to its terms or the terms of a statute, when one of the parties fails to fulfill a condition under the lease and thereby breaches it.

Forgery The fraudulent making or altering of any writing in a way that changes the legal rights and liabilities of another.

Formal contract A contract that by law requires for its validity a specific form, such as executed under seal.

Forum A jurisdiction, court, or place in which disputes are litigated and legal remedies are sought.

Forum-selection clause A provision in a contract designating the court, jurisdiction, or tribunal that will decide any disputes arising under the contract.

Franchise Any arrangement in which the owner of a trademark, trade name, or copyright licenses another to use that trademark, trade name, or copyright, under specified conditions or limitations, in the selling of goods and services.

Franchisee One receiving a license to use another's (the franchisor's) trademark, trade name, or copyright in the sale of goods and services.

Franchisor One licensing another (the franchisee) to use his or her trademark, trade name, or copyright in the sale of goods or services.

Fraud Any misrepresentation, either by misstatement or omission of a material fact, knowingly made with the intention of deceiving another and on which a reasonable person would and does rely to his or her detriment.

Fraud in the execution In the law of negotiable instruments, a type of fraud that occurs when a person is deceived into signing a negotiable instrument, believing that he or she is signing something else (such as a receipt); also called fraud in the inception. Fraud in the execution is a universal defense to payment on a negotiable instrument.

Fraud in the inducement Ordinary fraud. In the law of negotiable instruments, fraud in the inducement occurs when a person issues a negotiable instrument based on false statements by the other party. The issuing party will be able to avoid payment on that instrument unless the holder is a holder in due course; in other words, fraud in the inducement is a personal defense to payment on a negotiable instrument.

Fraudulent misrepresentation (fraud) Any misrepresentation, either by misstatement or omission of a material fact, knowingly made with the intention of deceiving another and on which a reasonable person would and does rely to his or her detriment.

Free exercise clause The provision in the First Amendment to the U.S. Constitution that prohibits Congress from making any law "prohibiting the free exercise" of religion.

Frustration of purpose A court-created doctrine under which a party to a contract will be relieved of his or her duty to perform when the objective purpose for performance no longer exists (due to reasons beyond that party's control).

Full faith and credit clause A clause in Article IV, Section 1, of the Constitution that provides that "Full Faith and Credit shall be given in each State to the public Acts, Records, and Judicial Proceedings of every othere States." The clause ensures that rights established under deeds, wills, contracts, and the like in one state will be honored by the other states and that any judicial decision with respect to such property rights will be honored and enforced in all states.

Full warranty A warranty as to full performance covering generally both labor and materials.

Fungible goods Goods that are alike by physical nature, by agreement, or by trade usage. Examples of fungible goods are wheat, oil, and wine that are identical in type and quality.

G

Garnishment A legal process used by a creditor to collect a debt by seizing property of the debtor (such as wages) that is being held by a third party (such as the debtor's employer).

General jurisdiction Exists when a court's subject-matter jurisdiction is not restricted. A court of general jurisdiction normally can hear any type of case.

General partner In a limited partnership, a partner who assumes responsibility for the management of the partnership and liability for all partnership debts.

General partnership *See* Partnership

Generally accepted accounting principles (GAAP) The conventions, rules, and procedures necessary to define accepted accounting practices at a particular time. The source of the principles is the Federal Accounting Standards Board.

Generally accepted auditing standards (GAAS) Standards concerning an auditor's professional qualities and the judgment exercised by him or her in the performance of an examination and report. The source of the standards is the American Institute of Certified Public Accountants.

Genuineness of assent Knowing and voluntary assent to the terms of a contract. If a contract is formed as a result of a mistake, misrepresentation, undue influence, or duress, genuineness of assent is lacking, and the contract will be voidable.

Gift Any voluntary transfer of property made without consideration, past or present.

Gift *causa mortis* A gift made in contemplation of death. If the donor does not die of that ailment, the gift is revoked.

Gift *inter vivos* A gift made during one's lifetime and not in contemplation of imminent death, in contrast to a gift *causa mortis*.

Good faith Under the Uniform Commercial Code good faith means honesty in fact; with regard to merchants, good faith means honesty in fact *and* the observance of reasonable commercial standards of fair dealing in the trade.

Good faith purchaser A purchaser who buys without notice of any circumstance that would put a person of ordinary prudence on inquiry as to whether the seller has valid title to the goods being sold.

Good Samaritan statute A state statute that provides that persons who rescue or provide emergency services to others in peril—unless they do so recklessly, thus causing further harm—cannot be sued for negligence.

Grand jury A group of citizens called to decide, after hearing the state's evidence, whether a reasonable basis (probable cause) exists for believing that a crime has been committed and whether a trial ought to be held.

Grant deed A deed that simply recites words of consideration and conveyance. Under statute, a grant deed may impliedly warrant that at least the grantor has not conveyed the property's title to someone else.

Grantee One to whom a grant (of land or property, for example) is made.

Grantor A person who makes a grant, such as a transferor of property or the creator of a trust.

Group boycott The refusal to deal with a particular person or firm by a group of competitors; prohibited by the Sherman Act.

Guarantor A person who agrees to satisfy the debt of

another (the debtor) only after the principal debtor defaults; a guarantor's liability is thus secondary.

H

Habitability *See* Implied warranty of habitability

Hacker A person who uses one computer to break into another. Professional computer programmers refer to such persons as "crackers."

Health-care power of attorney A document that designates a person who will have the power to choose what type of and how much medical treatment a person who is unable to make such a choice will receive.

Hearsay An oral or written statement made out of court that is later offered in court by a witness (not the person who made the statement) to prove the truth of the matter asserted in the statement. Hearsay is generally inadmissible as evidence.

Hirfindahl-Hirschman Index (HHI) An index of market power used to calculate whether a merger of two businesses will result in sufficient monopoly power to violate antitrust laws.

Historical school A school of legal thought that emphasizes the evolutionary process of law and that looks to the past to discover what the principles of contemporary law should be.

Holder Any person in the possession of an instrument drawn, issued, or indorsed to him or her, to his or her order, to bearer, or in blank.

Holder in due course (HDC) A holder who acquires a negotiable instrument for value; in good faith; and without notice that the instrument is overdue, that it has been dishonored, that any person has a defense against it or a claim to it, or that the instrument contains unauthorized signatures, alterations, or is so irregular or incomplete as to call into question its authenticity.

Holographic will A will written entirely in the signer's handwriting and usually not witnessed.

Homestead exemption A law permitting a debtor to retain the family home, either in its entirety or up to a specified dollar amount, free from the claims of unsecured creditors or trustees in bankruptcy.

Horizontal merger A merger between two firms that are competing in the same market.

Horizontal restraint Any agreement that in some way restrains competition between rival firms competing in the same market.

Hot-cargo agreement An agreement in which employers voluntarily agree with unions not to handle, use, or deal in nonunion-produced goods of other employers; a type of secondary boycott explicitly prohibited by the Labor-Management Reporting and Disclosure Act of 1959.

Hung jury A jury whose members are so irreconcilably divided in their opinions that they cannot come to a verdict by the requisite number of jurors. The judge in this situation may order a new trial.

I

Identification In a sale of goods, the express designation of the goods provided for in the contract.

Identity theft Occurs when a person steals another's identifying information—such as a name, date of birth, or Social Security number—and uses the information to access the victim's financial resources.

Illusory promise A promise made without consideration, which renders the promise unenforceable.

Immunity A status of being exempt, or free, from certain duties or requirements. In criminal law, the state may grant an accused person immunity from prosecution—or agree to prosecute for a lesser offense—if the accused person agrees to give the state information that would assist the state in prosecuting other individuals for crimes. In tort law, freedom from liability for defamatory speech. *See also* Privilege

Implied authority Authority that is created not by an explicit oral or written agreement but by implication. In agency law, implied authority (of the agent) can be conferred by custom, inferred from the position the agent occupies, or implied by virtue of being reasonably necessary to carry out express authority.

Implied warranty A warranty that the law derives by implication or inference from the nature of the transaction or the relative situation or circumstances of the parties.

Implied warranty of fitness for a particular purpose A warranty that goods sold or leased are fit for a particular purpose. The warranty arises when any seller or lessor knows the particular purpose for which a buyer or lessee will use the goods and knows that the buyer or lessee is relying on the skill and judgment of the seller or lessor to select suitable goods.

Implied warranty of habitability An implied promise by a landlord that rented residential premises are fit for human habitation—that is, in a condition that is safe and suitable for people to live in.

Implied warranty of merchantability A warranty that goods being sold or leased are reasonably fit for the general purpose for which they are sold or leased, are properly packaged and labeled, and are of proper quality. The warranty automatically arises in every sale or lease of goods made by a merchant who deals in goods of the kind sold or leased.

Implied-in-fact contract A contract formed in whole or in part from the conduct of the parties (as opposed to an express contract).

Impossibility of performance A doctrine under which a party to a contract is relieved of his or her duty to perform when performance becomes impossible or totally impracticable (through no fault of either party).

Imposter One who, by use of the mails, telephone, or personal appearance, induces a maker or drawer to issue an instrument in the name of an impersonated payee. Indorsements by imposters are not treated as unauthorized under Article 3 of the Uniform Commercial Code.

In pari delicto At equal fault.

***In personam* jurisdiction** Court jurisdiction over the "person" involved in a legal action; personal jurisdiction.

***In rem* jurisdiction** Court jurisdiction over a defendant's property.

Incidental beneficiary A third party who incidentally benefits from a contract but whose benefit was not the reason the contract was formed; an incidental beneficiary has no rights in a contract and cannot sue to have the contract enforced.

Incidental damages Damages resulting from a breach of contract, including all reasonable expenses incurred because of the breach.

Indemnify To compensate or reimburse another for losses or expenses incurred.

Independent contractor One who works for, and receives payment from, an employer but whose working conditions and methods are not controlled by the employer. An independent contractor is not an employee but may be an agent.

Independent regulatory agency An administrative agency that is not considered part of the government's executive branch and is not subject to the authority of the president. Independent agency officials cannot be removed without cause.

Indictment (pronounced in-*dyte*-ment) A charge by a grand jury that a named person has committed a crime.

Indorsee The person to whom a negotiable instrument is transferred by indorsement.

Indorsement A signature placed on an instrument for the purpose of transferring one's ownership rights in the instrument.

Indorser A person who transfers an instrument by signing (indorsing) it and delivering it to another person.

Industry-wide liability Product liability that is imposed on an entire industry when it is unclear which of several sellers within the industry manufactured a particular product. *See also* Market-share liability

Informal contract A contract that does not require a specified form or formality in order to be valid.

Information A formal accusation or complaint (without an indictment) issued in certain types of actions (usually criminal actions involving lesser crimes) by a law officer, such as a magistrate.

Information return A tax return submitted by a partnership that only reports the income earned by the business. The partnership as an entity does not pay taxes on the income received by the partnership. A partner's profit from the partnership (whether distributed or not) is taxed as individual income to the individual partner.

Infringement A violation of another's legally recognized right. The term is commonly used with reference to the invasion by one party of another party's rights in a patent, trademark, or copyright.

Initial order In the context of administrative law, an agency's disposition in a matter other than a rulemaking. An administrative law judge's initial order becomes final unless it is appealed.

Injunction A court decree ordering a person to do or refrain from doing a certain act or activity.

Innkeeper An owner of an inn, hotel, motel, or other lodgings.

Innkeeper's lien A possessory or statutory lien allowing the innkeeper to take the personal property of a guest, brought into the hotel, as security for nonpayment of the guest's bill (debt).

Innocent misrepresentation A false statement of fact or an act made in good faith that deceives and causes harm or injury to another.

Insider A corporate director or officer, or other employee or agent, with access to confidential information and a duty not to disclose that information in violation of insider-trading laws.

Insider trading The purchase or sale of securities on the basis of "inside information" (information that has not been made available to the public) in violation of a duty owed to the company whose stock is being traded.

Insolvent Under the Uniform Commercial Code, a term describing a person who ceases to pay "his debts in the ordinary course of business or cannot pay his debts as they become due or is insolvent within the meaning of federal bankruptcy law" [UCC 1–201(23)].

Installment contract Under the Uniform Commercial Code, a contract that requires or authorizes delivery in two or more separate lots to be accepted and paid for separately.

Instrument *See* Negotiable instrument

Insurable interest An interest either in a person's life or well-being or in property that is sufficiently substantial that insuring against injury to (or the death of) the person or against damage to the property does not amount to a mere wagering (betting) contract.

Insurance A contract in which, for a stipulated consideration, one party agrees to compensate the other for loss on a specific subject by a specified peril.

Intangible property Property that is incapable of being apprehended by the senses (such as by sight or touch); intellectual property is an example of intangible property.

Integrated contract A written contract that constitutes the final expression of the parties' agreement. If a contract is integrated, evidence extraneous to the contract that contradicts or alters the meaning of the contract in any way is inadmissible.

Intellectual property Property resulting from intellectual, creative processes. Patents, trademarks, and copyrights are examples of intellectual property.

Intended beneficiary A third party for whose benefit a contract is formed; an intended beneficiary can sue the promisor if such a contract is breached.

Intentional tort A wrongful act knowingly committed.

***Inter vivos* gift** *See* Gift *inter vivos*

***Inter vivos* trust** A trust created by the grantor (settlor) and effective during the grantor's lifetime (that is, a trust not established by a will).

Intermediary bank Any bank to which an item is transferred in the course of collection, except the depositary or payor bank.

International law The law that governs relations among nations. International customs and treaties are generally considered to be two of the most important sources of international law.

International organization In international law, a term that generally refers to an organization composed mainly of nations and usually established by treaty. The United States is a member of more than one hundred multilateral and bilateral organizations, including at least twenty through the United Nations.

Interpretive rule An administrative agency rule that is simply a statement or opinion issued by the agency explaining how it interprets and intends to apply the statutes it enforces. Such rules are not automatically binding on private individuals or organizations.

Interrogatories A series of written questions for which written answers are prepared and then signed under oath by a party to a lawsuit, usually with the assistance of the party's attorney.

Intestacy laws State statutes that specify how property will be distributed when a person dies intestate (without a valid will); statutes of descent and distribution.

Intestate As a noun, one who has died without having created a valid will; as an adjective, the state of having died without a will.

Investment company A company that acts on behalf of many smaller shareholder-owners by buying a large portfolio of securities and professionally managing that portfolio.

Invitee A person who, either expressly or impliedly, is privileged to enter onto another's land. The inviter owes the invitee (for example, a customer in a store) the duty to exercise reasonable care to protect the invitee from harm.

Irrevocable offer An offer that cannot be revoked or recalled by the offeror without liability. A merchant's firm offer is an example of an irrevocable offer.

Issue The first transfer, or delivery, of an instrument to a holder.

J

Joint and several liability In partnership law, a doctrine under which a plaintiff may sue, and collect a judgment from, one or more of the partners separately (severally, or individually) or all of the partners together (jointly). This is true even if one of the partners sued did not participate in, ratify, or know about whatever it was that gave rise to the cause of action.

Joint liability Shared liability. In partnership law, partners incur joint liability for partnership obligations and debts. For example, if a third party sues a partner on a partnership debt, the partner has the right to insist that the other partners be sued with him or her.

Joint stock company A hybrid form of business organization that combines characteristics of a corporation (shareholder-owners, management by directors and officers of the company, and perpetual existence) and a partnership (it is formed by agreement, not statute; property is usually held in the names of the members; and the shareholders have personal liability for business debts). Usually, the joint stock company is regarded as a partnership for tax and other legally related purposes.

Joint tenancy The joint ownership of property by two or more co-owners in which each co-owner owns an undivided portion of the property. On the death of one of the joint tenants, his or her interest automatically passes to the surviving joint tenants.

Joint venture A joint undertaking of a specific commercial enterprise by an association of persons. A joint venture is normally not a legal entity and is treated like a partnership for federal income tax purposes.

Judgment The final order or decision resulting from a legal action.

Judgment *n.o.v.* *See* Motion for judgment *n.o.v.*

Judgment rate of interest A rate of interest fixed by statute that is applied to a monetary judgment from the moment the judgment is awarded by a court until the judgment is paid or terminated.

Judicial lien A lien on property created by a court order.

Judicial process The procedures relating to, or connected with, the administration of justice through the judicial system.

Judicial review The process by which courts decide on the constitutionality of legislative enactments and actions of the executive branch.

Jurisdiction The authority of a court to hear and decide a specific action.

Jurisprudence The science or philosophy of law.

Justiciable (pronounced jus-*tish*-a-bul) **controversy** A controversy that is not hypothetical or academic but real and substantial; a requirement that must be satisfied before a court will hear a case.

K

King's court A medieval English court. The king's courts, or *curiae regis,* were established by the Norman conquerors of England. The body of law that developed in these courts was common to the entire English realm and thus became known as the common law.

L

Laches The equitable doctrine that bars a party's right to legal action if the party has neglected for an unreasonable length of time to act on his or her rights.

Landlord An owner of land or rental property who leases it to another person, called the tenant.
Landlord's lien A landlord's remedy for a tenant's failure to pay rent. When permitted under a statute or the lease agreement, the landlord may take and keep or sell whatever of the defaulting tenant's property is on the leased premises.
Larceny The wrongful taking and carrying away of another person's personal property with the intent to permanently deprive the owner of the property. Some states classify larceny as either grand or petit, depending on the property's value.
Last clear chance A doctrine under which a plaintiff may recover from a defendant for injuries or damages suffered, notwithstanding the plaintiff's own negligence, when the defendant had the opportunity—a last clear chance—to avoid harming the plaintiff through the exercise of reasonable care but failed to do so.
Law A body of enforceable rules governing relationships among individuals and between individuals and their society.
Lawsuit The litigation process. *See* Litigation
Lease In real property law, a contract by which the owner of real property (the landlord, or lessor) grants to a person (the tenant, or lessee) an exclusive right to use and possess the property, usually for a specified period of time, in return for rent or some other form of payment.
Lease agreement In regard to the lease of goods, an agreement in which one person (the lessor) agrees to transfer the right to the possession and use of property to another person (the lessee) in exchange for rental payments.
Leasehold estate An estate in realty held by a tenant under a lease. In every leasehold estate, the tenant has a qualified right to possess and/or use the land.
Legacy A gift of personal property under a will.
Legal positivists Adherents to the positivist school of legal thought. This school holds that there can be no higher law than a nation's positive law—law created by a particular society at a particular point in time. In contrast to the natural law school, the positivist school maintains that there are no "natural" rights; rights come into existence only when there is a sovereign power (government) to confer and enforce those rights.
Legal rate of interest A rate of interest fixed by statute as either the maximum rate of interest allowed by law or a rate of interest applied when the parties to a contract intend, but do not fix, an interest rate in the contract. In the latter case, the rate is frequently the same as the statutory maximum rate permitted.
Legal realism A school of legal thought that was popular in the 1920s and 1930s and that challenged many existing jurisprudential assumptions, particularly the assumption that subjective elements play no part in judicial reasoning. Legal realists generally advocated a less abstract and more realistic approach to the law, an approach that would take into account customary practices and the circumstances in which transactions take place. The school left a lasting imprint on American jurisprudence.
Legal reasoning The process of reasoning by which a judge harmonizes his or her decision with the judicial decisions of previous cases.
Legatee One designated in a will to receive a gift of personal property.
Legislative rule An administrative agency rule that carries the same weight as a congressionally enacted statute.
Lessee A person who acquires the right to the possession and use of another's property in exchange for rental payments.
Lessor A person who sells the right to the possession and use of property to another in exchange for rental payments.
Letter of credit A written instrument, usually issued by a bank on behalf of a customer or other person, in which the issuer promises to honor drafts or other demands for payment by third persons in accordance with the terms of the instrument.
Leveraged buyout (LBO) A corporate takeover financed by loans secured by the acquired corporation's assets or by the issuance of corporate bonds, resulting in a high debt load for the corporation.
Levy The obtaining of money by legal process through the seizure and sale of property, usually done after a writ of execution has been issued.
Liability Any actual or potential legal obligation, duty, debt, or responsibility.
Libel Defamation in writing or other form (such as in a videotape) having the quality of permanence.
License A revocable right or privilege of a person to come on another person's land.
Licensee One who receives a license to use, or enter onto, another's property.
Lien (pronounced leen) An encumbrance on a property to satisfy a debt or protect a claim for payment of a debt.
Lien creditor One whose claim is secured by a lien on particular property, as distinguished from a general creditor, who has no such security.
Life estate An interest in land that exists only for the duration of the life of some person, usually the holder of the estate.
Limited jurisdiction Exists when a court's subject-matter jurisdiction is limited. Bankruptcy courts and probate courts are examples of courts with limited jurisdiction.
Limited liability Exists when the liability of the owners of a business is limited to the amount of their investments in the firm.
Limited liability company (LLC) A hybrid form of business enterprise that offers the limited liability of the corporation but the tax advantages of a partnership.
Limited liability limited partnership (LLLP) A type of limited partnership. The difference between a limited

partnership and an LLLP is that the liability of the general partner in an LLLP is the same as the liability of the limited partner. That is, the liability of all partners is limited to the amount of their investments in the firm.

Limited liability partnership (LLP) A form of partnership that allows professionals to enjoy the tax benefits of a partnership while limiting their personal liability for the malpractice of other partners.

Limited partner In a limited partnership, a partner who contributes capital to the partnership but has no right to participate in the management and operation of the business. The limited partner assumes no liability for partnership debts beyond the capital contributed.

Limited partnership A partnership consisting of one or more general partners (who manage the business and are liable to the full extent of their personal assets for debts of the partnership) and one or more limited partners (who contribute only assets and are liable only to the extent of their contributions).

Limited-payment life A type of life insurance for which premiums are payable for a definite period, after which the policy is fully paid.

Limited warranty A written warranty that fails to meet one or more of the minimum standards for a full warranty.

Liquidated damages An amount, stipulated in the contract, that the parties to a contract believe to be a reasonable estimation of the damages that will occur in the event of a breach.

Liquidated debt A debt that is due and certain in amount.

Liquidation (1) In regard to bankruptcy, the sale of all of the nonexempt assets of a debtor and the distribution of the proceeds to the debtor's creditors. Chapter 7 of the Bankruptcy Code provides for liquidation bankruptcy proceedings. (2) In regard to corporations, the process by which corporate assets are converted into cash and distributed among creditors and shareholders according to specific rules of preference.

Litigant A party to a lawsuit.

Litigation The process of resolving a dispute through the court system.

Living will A document that allows a person to control the methods of medical treatment that may be used after a serious accident or illness.

Loan workout *See* Workout

Long arm statute A state statute that permits a state to obtain personal jurisdiction over nonresident defendants. A defendant must have "minimum contacts" with that state for the statute to apply.

Lost property Property with which the owner has involuntarily parted and then cannot find or recover.

M

Magistrate's court A court of limited jurisdiction that is presided over by a public official (magistrate) with certain judicial authority, such as the power to set bail.

Mailbox rule A rule providing that an acceptance of an offer becomes effective on dispatch (on being placed in a mailbox), if mail is, expressly or impliedly, an authorized means of communication of acceptance to the offeror.

Main purpose rule A rule of contract law under which an exception to the Statute of Frauds is made if the main purpose in accepting secondary liability under a contract is to secure a personal benefit. If this situation exists, the contract need not be in writing to be enforceable.

Majority *See* Age of majority

Majority opinion A court's written opinion, outlining the views of the majority of the judges or justices deciding the case.

Maker One who promises to pay a certain sum to the holder of a promissory note or certificate of deposit (CD).

Malpractice Professional misconduct or the failure to exercise the requisite degree of skill as a professional. Negligence—the failure to exercise due care—on the part of a professional, such as a physician or an attorney, is commonly referred to as malpractice.

Manufacturing or processing-plant franchise A franchise that is created when the franchisor transmits to the franchisee the essential ingredients or formula to make a particular product. The franchisee then markets the product either at wholesale or at retail in accordance with the franchisor's standards. Examples of this type of franchise are Coca-Cola and other soft-drink bottling companies.

Marine insurance Insurance protecting shippers and vessel owners from losses or damages sustained by a vessel or its cargo during the transport of goods or materials by water.

Mark *See* Trademark

Market concentration A situation that exists when a small number of firms share the market for a particular good or service. For example, if the four largest grocery stores in Chicago accounted for 80 percent of all retail food sales, the market clearly would be concentrated in those four firms.

Market power The power of a firm to control the market price of its product. A monopoly has the greatest degree of market power.

Marketable title Title to real estate that is reasonably free from encumbrances, defects in the chain of title, and other events that affect title, such as adverse possession.

Market-share liability A method of sharing liability among several firms that manufactured or marketed a particular product that may have caused a plaintiff's injury. This form of liability sharing is used when the true source of the product is unidentifiable. Each firm's liability is proportionate to its respective share of the relevant market for the product. Market-share liability applies only if the injuring product is fungible, the true manufacturer is unidentifiable, and the unknown character of the manufacturer is not the plaintiff's fault.

Market-share test The primary measure of monopoly power. A firm's market share is the percentage of a market that the firm controls.

Marshalling assets The arrangement or ranking of assets in a certain order toward the payment of debts. In equity, when two creditors have recourse to the same property of the debtor, but one has recourse to other property of the debtor, that creditor must resort first to those assets of the debtor that are not available to the other creditor.

Mass-market license An e-contract that is presented with a package of computer information in the form of a *click-on license* or a *shrink-wrap license*.

Material alteration *See* Alteration

Material fact A fact to which a reasonable person would attach importance in determining his or her course of action. In regard to tender offers, for example, a fact is material if there is a substantial likelihood that a reasonable shareholder would consider it important in deciding how to vote.

Mechanic's lien A statutory lien on the real property of another, created to ensure payment for work performed and materials furnished in the repair or improvement of real property, such as a building.

Mediation A method of settling disputes outside of court by using the services of a neutral third party, called a mediator. The mediator acts as a communicating agent between the parties and suggests ways in which the parties can resolve their dispute.

Member The term used to designate a person who has an ownership interest in a limited liability company.

Mens rea (pronounced *mehns ray*-uh) Mental state, or intent. A wrongful mental state is as necessary as a wrongful act to establish criminal liability. What constitutes a mental state varies according to the wrongful action. Thus, for murder, the *mens rea* is the intent to take a life; for theft, the *mens rea* must involve both the knowledge that the property belongs to another and the intent to deprive the owner of it.

Merchant A person who is engaged in the purchase and sale of goods. Under the Uniform Commercial Code, a person who deals in goods of the kind involved in the sales contract; for further definitions, see UCC 2–104.

Merger A contractual and statutory process in which one corporation (the surviving corporation) acquires all of the assets and liabilities of another corporation (the merged corporation). The shareholders of the merged corporation receive either payment for their shares or shares in the surviving corporation.

Meta tags Words inserted into a Web site's key words field to increase the site's appearance in search engine results.

Minimum-contacts requirement The requirement that before a state court can exercise jurisdiction over a foreign corporation, the foreign corporation must have sufficient contacts with the state. A foreign corporation that has its home office in the state or that has manufacturing plants in the state meets this requirement.

Minimum wage The lowest wage, either by government regulation or union contract, that an employer may pay an hourly worker.

Mini-trial A private proceeding in which each party to a dispute argues its position before the other side and vice versa. A neutral third party may be present and act as an adviser if the parties fail to reach an agreement.

Mirror image rule A common law rule that requires, for a valid contractual agreement, that the terms of the offeree's acceptance adhere exactly to the terms of the offeror's offer.

Misdemeanor A lesser crime than a felony, punishable by a fine or imprisonment for up to one year in other than a state or federal penitentiary.

Mislaid property Property with which the owner has voluntarily parted and then cannot find or recover.

Misrepresentation A false statement of fact or an action that deceives and causes harm or injury to another. *See also* Fraudulent misrepresentation (fraud); Innocent misrepresentation

Mitigation of damages A rule requiring a plaintiff to have done whatever was reasonable to minimize the damages caused by the defendant.

Money laundering Falsely reporting income that has been obtained through criminal activity as income obtained through a legitimate business enterprise—in effect, "laundering" the "dirty money."

Monopolization The possession of monopoly power in the relevant market and the willful acquisition or maintenance of the power, as distinguished from growth or development as a consequence of a superior product, business acumen, or historic accident.

Monopoly A term generally used to describe a market in which there is a single seller or a limited number of sellers.

Monopoly power The ability of a monopoly to dictate what takes place in a given market.

Moral minimum The minimum degree of ethical behavior expected of a business firm, which is usually defined as compliance with the law.

Mortgage A written instrument giving a creditor (the mortgagee) an interest in (a lien on) the debtor's (mortgagor's) property as security for a debt.

Mortgage bond A bond that pledges specific property. If the corporation defaults on the bond, the bondholder can take the property.

Mortgagee Under a mortgage agreement, the creditor who takes a security interest in the debtor's property.

Mortgagor Under a mortgage agreement, the debtor who gives the creditor a security interest in the debtor's property in return for a mortgage loan.

Most-favored-nation status A status granted in an international treaty by a provision stating that the citizens of the contracting nations may enjoy the privileges accorded by either party to citizens of the most favored nations. Generally, most-favored-nation clauses are designed to establish equality of international treatment.

Motion A procedural request or application presented by an attorney to the court on behalf of a client.

Motion for a directed verdict In a jury trial, a motion for the judge to take the decision out of the hands of the jury and direct a verdict for the moving party on the ground that the other party has not produced sufficient evidence to support his or her claim; referred to as a motion for judgment as a matter of law in the federal courts.
Motion for a new trial A motion asserting that the trial was so fundamentally flawed (because of error, newly discovered evidence, prejudice, or other reason) that a new trial is necessary to prevent a miscarriage of justice.
Motion for judgment *n.o.v.* A motion requesting the court to grant judgment in favor of the party making the motion on the ground that the jury verdict against him or her was unreasonable and erroneous.
Motion for judgment on the pleadings A motion by either party to a lawsuit at the close of the pleadings requesting the court to decide the issue solely on the pleadings without proceeding to trial. The motion will be granted only if no facts are in dispute.
Motion for summary judgment A motion requesting the court to enter a judgment without proceeding to trial. The motion can be based on evidence outside the pleadings and will be granted only if no facts are in dispute.
Motion to dismiss A pleading in which a defendant asserts that the plaintiff's claim fails to state a cause of action (that is, has no basis in law) or that there are other grounds on which a suit should be dismissed.
Multiple product order An order issued by the Federal Trade Commission to a firm that has engaged in deceptive advertising by which the firm is required to cease and desist from false advertising not only in regard to the product that was the subject of the action but also in regard to all the firm's other products.
Municipal court A city or community court with criminal jurisdiction over traffic violations and, less frequently, with civil jurisdiction over other minor matters.
Mutual assent The element of agreement in the formation of a contract. The manifestation of contract parties' mutual assent to the same bargain is required to establish a contract.
Mutual fund A specific type of investment company that continually buys or sells to investors shares of ownership in a portfolio.
Mutual rescission An agreement between the parties to cancel their contract, releasing the parties from further obligations under the contract. The object of the agreement is to restore the parties to the positions they would have occupied had no contract ever been formed. *See also* Rescission

N

National law Law that pertains to a particular nation (as opposed to international law).
Natural law The belief that government and the legal system should reflect universal moral and ethical principles that are inherent in human nature. The natural law school is the oldest and one of the most significant schools of legal thought.
Necessaries Necessities required for life, such as food, shelter, clothing, and medical attention; may include whatever is believed to be necessary to maintain a person's standard of living or financial and social status.
Necessity In criminal law, a defense against liability; under Section 3.02 of the Model Penal Code, this defense is justifiable if "the harm or evil sought to be avoided" by a given action "is greater than that sought to be prevented by the law defining the offense charged."
Negligence The failure to exercise the standard of care that a reasonable person would exercise in similar circumstances.
Negligence *per se* An act (or failure to act) in violation of a statutory requirement.
Negligent misrepresentation Any manifestation through words or conduct that amounts to an untrue statement of fact made in circumstances in which a reasonable and prudent person would not have done (or failed to do) that which led to the misrepresentation. A representation made with an honest belief in its truth may still be negligent due to (1) a lack of reasonable care in ascertaining the facts, (2) the manner of expression, or (3) the absence of the skill or competence required by a particular business or profession.
Negotiable instrument A signed writing that contains an unconditional promise or order to pay an exact sum of money, on demand or at an exact future time, to a specific person or order, or to bearer.
Negotiation (1) In regard to dispute settlement, a process in which parties attempt to settle their dispute without going to court, with or without attorneys to represent them. (2) In regard to instruments, the transfer of an instrument in such a way that the transferee (the person to whom the instrument is transferred) becomes a holder.
Nominal damages A small monetary award (often one dollar) granted to a plaintiff when no actual damage was suffered.
Nonconforming goods Goods that do not conform to contract specifications.
No-par shares Corporate shares that have no face value—that is, no specific dollar amount is printed on their face.
Notary public A public official authorized to attest to the authenticity of signatures.
Note A written instrument signed by a maker unconditionally promising to pay a fixed amount of money to a payee or a holder on demand or on a specific date.
Notice-and-comment rulemaking An administrative rulemaking procedure that involves the publication of a notice of a proposed rulemaking in the *Federal Register*, a comment period for interested parties to express their views on the proposed rule, and the publication of the agency's final rule in the *Federal Register*.

Notice of Proposed Rulemaking A notice published (in the *Federal Register*) by an administrative agency describing a proposed rule. The notice must give the time and place for which agency proceedings on the proposed rule will be held, a description of the nature of the proceedings, the legal authority for the proceedings (which is usually the agency's enabling legislation), and the terms of the proposed rule or the subject matter of the proposed rule.

Novation The substitution, by agreement, of a new contract for an old one, with the rights under the old one being terminated. Typically, there is a substitution of a new person who is responsible for the contract and the removal of an original party's rights and duties under the contract.

Nuisance A common law doctrine under which persons may be held liable for using their property in a manner that unreasonably interferes with others' rights to use or enjoy their own property.

Nuncupative will An oral will (often called a deathbed will) made before witnesses; usually limited to transfers of personal property.

O

Objective theory of contracts A theory under which the intent to form a contract will be judged by outward, objective facts (what the party said when entering into the contract, how the party acted or appeared, and the circumstances surrounding the transaction) as interpreted by a reasonable person, rather than by the party's own secret, subjective intentions.

Obligee One to whom an obligation is owed.

Obligor One that owes an obligation to another.

Offer A promise or commitment to perform or refrain from performing some specified act in the future.

Offeree A person to whom an offer is made.

Offeror A person who makes an offer.

Omnibus clause A provision in an automobile insurance policy that protects the vehicle owner who has taken out the insurance policy and anyone who drives the vehicle with the owner's permission.

Online dispute resolution (ODR) The resolution of disputes with the assistance of organizations that offer dispute-resolution services via the Internet.

Opening statement A statement made to the jury at the beginning of a trial by a party's attorney, prior to the presentation of evidence. The attorney briefly outlines the evidence that will be offered and the legal theory that will be pursued.

Operating agreement In a limited liability company, an agreement in which the members set forth the details of how the business will be managed and operated.

Operation of law A term expressing the manner in which certain rights or liabilities may be imposed on a person by the application of established rules of law to the particular transaction, without regard to the actions or cooperation of the party himself or herself.

Opinion A statement by the court expressing the reasons for its decision in a case.

Optimum profits The amount of profits that a business can make and still act ethically, as opposed to maximum profits, defined as the amount of profits a firm can make if it is willing to disregard ethical concerns.

Option contract A contract under which the offeror cannot revoke his or her offer for a stipulated time period, and the offeree can accept or reject the offer during this period without fear that the offer will be made to another person. The offeree must give consideration for the option (the irrevocable offer) to be enforceable.

Order for relief A court's grant of assistance to a complainant. In bankruptcy proceedings, the order relieves the debtor of the immediate obligation to pay the debts listed in the bankruptcy petition.

Order instrument A negotiable instrument that is payable "to the order of an identified person" or "to an identified person or order."

Ordinance A law passed by a local governing unit, such as a municipality or a county.

Original jurisdiction Courts having original jurisdiction are courts of the first instance, or trial courts—that is, courts in which lawsuits begin, trials take place, and evidence is presented.

Output contract An agreement in which a seller agrees to sell and a buyer agrees to buy all or up to a stated amount of what the seller produces.

Overdraft A check written on a checking account in which there are insufficient funds to cover the amount of the check.

P

Parent-subsidiary merger A merger of companies in which one company (the parent corporation) owns most of the stock of the other (the subsidiary corporation). A parent-subsidiary merger (short-form merger) can use a simplified procedure when the parent corporation owns at least 90 percent of the outstanding shares of each class of stock of the subsidiary corporation.

Parol evidence A term that originally meant "oral evidence," but which has come to refer to any negotiations or agreements made prior to a contract or any contemporaneous oral agreements made by the parties.

Parol evidence rule A substantive rule of contracts under which a court will not receive into evidence the parties' prior negotiations, prior agreements, or contemporaneous oral agreements if that evidence contradicts or varies the terms of the parties' written contract.

Partially disclosed principal A principal whose identity is unknown by a third person, but the third person knows that the agent is or may be acting for a principal at the time the agent and the third person form a contract.

Partner A co-owner of a partnership.

Partnering agreement An agreement between a seller and a buyer who frequently do business with each other on the terms and conditions that will apply to all subsequently formed electronic contracts.

Partnership An agreement by two or more persons to carry on, as co-owners, a business for profit.

Partnership by estoppel A judicially created partnership that may, at the court's discretion, be imposed for purposes of fairness. The court can prevent those who present themselves as partners (but who are not) from escaping liability if a third person relies on an alleged partnership in good faith and is harmed as a result.

Par-value shares Corporate shares that have a specific face value, or formal cash-in value, written on them, such as one dollar.

Past consideration An act done before the contract is made, which ordinarily, by itself, cannot be consideration for a later promise to pay for the act.

Patent A government grant that gives an inventor the exclusive right or privilege to make, use, or sell his or her invention for a limited time period. The word *patent* usually refers to some invention and designates either the instrument by which patent rights are evidenced or the patent itself.

Payee A person to whom an instrument is made payable.

Payor bank The bank on which a check is drawn (the drawee bank).

Peer-to-peer (P2P) networking A technology that allows Internet users to access files on other users' computers.

Penalty A sum inserted into a contract, not as a measure of compensation for its breach but rather as punishment for a default. The agreement as to the amount will not be enforced, and recovery will be limited to actual damages.

Per capita A Latin term meaning "per person." In the law governing estate distribution, a method of distributing the property of an intestate's estate in which each heir in a certain class (such as grandchildren) receives an equal share.

Per curiam By the whole court; a court opinion written by the court as a whole instead of being authored by a judge or justice.

Per se A Latin term meaning "in itself" or "by itself."

***Per se* violation** A type of anticompetitive agreement—such as a horizontal price-fixing agreement—that is considered to be so injurious to the public that there is no need to determine whether it actually injures market competition; rather, it is in itself (*per se*) a violation of the Sherman Act.

Per stirpes A Latin term meaning "by the roots." In the law governing estate distribution, a method of distributing an intestate's estate in which each heir in a certain class (such as grandchildren) takes the share to which his or her deceased ancestor (such as a mother or father) would have been entitled.

Perfect tender rule A common law rule under which a seller was required to deliver to the buyer goods that conformed perfectly to the requirements stipulated in the sales contract. A tender of nonconforming goods would automatically constitute a breach of contract. Under the Uniform Commercial Code, the rule has been greatly modified.

Perfection The legal process by which secured parties protect themselves against the claims of third parties who may wish to have their debts satisfied out of the same collateral; usually accomplished by the filing of a financing statement with the appropriate government official.

Performance In contract law, the fulfillment of one's duties arising under a contract with another; the normal way of discharging one's contractual obligations.

Periodic tenancy A lease interest in land for an indefinite period involving payment of rent at fixed intervals, such as week to week, month to month, or year to year.

Personal defense A defense that can be used to avoid payment to an ordinary holder of a negotiable instrument but not a holder in due course (HDC) or a holder with the rights of an HDC.

Personal identification number (PIN) A number given to the holder of an access card (debit card, credit card, ATM card, or the like) that is used to conduct financial transactions electronically. Typically, the card will not provide access to a system without the number, which is meant to be kept secret to inhibit unauthorized use of the card.

Personal jurisdiction *See In personam* jurisdiction

Personal property Property that is movable; any property that is not real property.

Personalty Personal property.

Petition in bankruptcy The document that is filed with a bankruptcy court to initiate bankruptcy proceedings. The official forms required for a petition in bankruptcy must be completed accurately, sworn to under oath, and signed by the debtor.

Petitioner In equity practice, a party that initiates a lawsuit.

Petty offense In criminal law, the least serious kind of criminal offense, such as a traffic or building-code violation.

Pierce the corporate veil To disregard the corporate entity, which limits the liability of shareholders, and hold the shareholders personally liable for a corporate obligation.

Plaintiff One who initiates a lawsuit.

Plea In criminal law, a defendant's allegation, in response to the charges brought against him or her, of guilt or innocence.

Plea bargaining The process by which a criminal defendant and the prosecutor in a criminal case work out a mutually satisfactory disposition of the case, subject to court approval; usually involves the defendant's pleading guilty to a lesser offense in return for a lighter sentence.

Pleadings Statements made by the plaintiff and the defendant in a lawsuit that detail the facts, charges, and defenses involved in the litigation; the complaint and answer are part of the pleadings.

Pledge A common law security device (retained in Article 9 of the Uniform Commercial Code) in which personal property is turned over to the creditor as security for the payment of a debt and retained by the creditor until the debt is paid.

Police powers Powers possessed by states as part of their inherent sovereignty. These powers may be exercised to protect or promote the public order, health, safety, morals, and general welfare.

Policy In insurance law, a contract between the insurer and the insured in which, for a stipulated consideration, the insurer agrees to compensate the insured for loss on a specific subject by a specified peril.

Positive law The body of conventional, or written, law of a particular society at a particular point in time.

Positivist school A school of legal thought whose adherents believe that there can be no higher law than a nation's positive law—the body of conventional, or written, law of a particular society at a particular time.

Possessory lien A lien that allows one person to retain possession of another's property as security for a debt or obligation owed by the owner of the property to the lienholder. An example of a possessory lien is an artisan's lien.

Potential competition doctrine A doctrine under which a conglomerate merger may be prohibited by law because it would be injurious to potential competition.

Potentially responsible party (PRP) A potentially liable party under the Comprehensive Environmental Response, Compensation and Liability Act (CERCLA). Any person who generated the hazardous waste, transported the hazardous waste, owned or operated a waste site at the time of disposal, or currently owns or operates a site may be responsible for some or all of the clean-up costs involved in removing the hazardous chemicals.

Power of attorney A written document, which is usually notarized, authorizing another to act as one's agent; can be special (permitting the agent to do specified acts only) or general (permitting the agent to transact all business for the principal).

Preauthorized transfer A transaction authorized in advance to recur at substantially regular intervals. The terms and procedures for preauthorized electronic fund transfers through certain financial institutions are subject to the Electronic Fund Transfer Act.

Precedent A court decision that furnishes an example or authority for deciding subsequent cases involving identical or similar facts.

Predatory pricing The pricing of a product below cost with the intent to drive competitors out of the market.

Preemption A doctrine under which certain federal laws preempt, or take precedence over, conflicting state or local laws.

Preemptive rights Rights held by shareholders that entitle them to purchase newly issued shares of a corporation's stock, equal in percentage to shares presently held, before the stock is offered to any outside buyers. Preemptive rights enable shareholders to maintain their proportionate ownership and voice in the corporation.

Preference In bankruptcy proceedings, property transfers or payments made by the debtor that favor (give preference to) one creditor over others. The bankruptcy trustee is allowed to recover payments made both voluntarily and involuntarily to one creditor in preference over another.

Preferred stock Classes of stock that have priority over common stock both as to payment of dividends and distribution of assets on the corporation's dissolution.

Prejudgment interest Interest that accrues on the amount of a court judgment from the time of the filing of a lawsuit to the court's issuance of a judgment.

Preliminary hearing An initial hearing used in many felony cases to establish whether or not it is proper to detain the defendant. A magistrate reviews the evidence and decides if there is probable cause to believe that the defendant committed the crime with which he or she has been charged.

Premium In insurance law, the price paid by the insured for insurance protection for a specified period of time.

Prenuptial agreement An agreement made before marriage that defines each partner's ownership rights in the other partner's property. Prenuptial agreements must be in writing to be enforceable.

Preponderance of the evidence A standard in civil law cases under which the plaintiff must convince the court that, based on the evidence presented by both parties, it is more likely than not that the plaintiff's allegation is true.

Presentment The act of presenting an instrument to the party liable on the instrument to collect payment; presentment also occurs when a person presents an instrument to a drawee for acceptance.

Presentment warranties Implied warranties, made by any person who presents an instrument for payment or acceptance, that (1) the person obtaining payment or acceptance is entitled to enforce the instrument or is authorized to obtain payment or acceptance on behalf of a person who is entitled to enforce the instrument, (2) the instrument has not been altered, and (3) the person obtaining payment or acceptance has no knowledge that the signature of the drawer of the instrument is unauthorized.

Pretrial conference A conference, scheduled before the trial begins, between the judge and the attorneys litigating the suit. The parties may settle the dispute, clarify the issues, schedule discovery, and so on during the conference.

Pretrial motion A written or oral application to a court for a ruling or order, made before trial.

Price discrimination Setting prices in such a way that two competing buyers pay two different prices for an identical product or service.

Price-fixing agreement An agreement between competitors in which the competitors agree to fix the prices of products or services at a certain level; prohibited by the Sherman Act.

***Prima facie* case** A case in which the plaintiff has produced sufficient evidence of his or her conclusion that the case can go to to a jury; a case in which the evidence compels the plaintiff's conclusion if the defendant produces no evidence to disprove it.

Primary liability In negotiable instruments law, absolute responsibility for paying a negotiable instrument. Makers and acceptors are primarily liable.

Principal In agency law, a person who agrees to have another, called the agent, act on his or her behalf.

Principle of rights The principle that human beings have certain fundamental rights (to life, freedom, and the pursuit of happiness, for example). Those who adhere to this "rights theory" believe that a key factor in determining whether a business decision is ethical is how that decision affects the rights of others. These others include the firm's owners, its employees, the consumers of its products or services, its suppliers, the community in which it does business, and society as a whole.

Privatization The replacement of government-provided products and services by private firms.

Privilege In tort law, the ability to act contrary to another person's right without that person's having legal redress for such acts. Privilege may be raised as a defense to defamation.

Privileges and immunities clause Special rights and exceptions provided by law. Article IV, Section 2, of the Constitution requires states not to discriminate against one another's citizens. A resident of one state cannot be treated as an alien when in another state; he or she may not be denied such privileges and immunities as legal protection, access to courts, travel rights, or property rights.

Privity of contract The relationship that exists between the promisor and the promisee of a contract.

Pro rata Proportionately; in proportion.

Probable cause Reasonable grounds to believe the existence of facts warranting certain actions, such as the search or arrest of a person.

Probate The process of proving and validating a will and the settling of all matters pertaining to administration, guardianship, and the like.

Probate court A state court of limited jurisdiction that conducts proceedings relating to the settlement of a deceased person's estate.

Procedural due process The requirement that any government decision to take life, liberty, or property must be made fairly. For example, fair procedures must be used in determining whether a person will be subjected to punishment or have some burden imposed on him or her.

Procedural law Rules that define the manner in which the rights and duties of individuals may be enforced.

Procedural unconscionability Occurs when, due to one contractual party's vastly superior bargaining power, the other party lacks a knowledge or understanding of the contract terms due to inconspicuous print or the lack of an opportunity to read the contract or to ask questions about its meaning. Procedural unconscionability often involves an *adhesion contract,* which is a contract drafted by the dominant party and then presented to the other—the adhering party—on a take-it-or-leave-it basis.

Proceeds Under Article 9 of the Uniform Commercial Code, whatever is received when the collateral is sold or otherwise disposed of, such as by exchange.

Product liability The legal liability of manufacturers, sellers, and lessors of goods to consumers, users, and bystanders for injuries or damages that are caused by the goods.

Product misuse A defense against product liability that may be raised when the plaintiff used a product in a manner not intended by the manufacturer. If the misuse is reasonably foreseeable, the seller will not escape liability unless measures were taken to guard against the harm that could result from the misuse.

Professional corporation A corporation formed by professional persons, such as physicians, lawyers, dentists, and accountants, to gain tax benefits. Subject to certain exceptions (when a court may treat a professional corporation as a partnership for liability purposes), the shareholders of a professional corporation have the limited liability characteristic of the corporate form of business.

Profit In real property law, the right to enter onto and remove things from the property of another (for example, the right to enter onto a person's land and remove sand and gravel therefrom).

Promise A declaration that something either will or will not happen in the future.

Promisee A person to whom a promise is made.

Promisor A person who makes a promise.

Promissory estoppel A doctrine that applies when a promisor makes a clear and definite promise on which the promisee justifiably relies; such a promise is binding if justice will be better served by the enforcement of the promise. *See also* Estoppel

Promissory note A written promise made by one person (the maker) to pay a fixed sum of money to another person (the payee or a subsequent holder) on demand or on a specified date.

Promoter A person who takes the preliminary steps in organizing a corporation, including (usually) issuing a prospectus, procuring stock subscriptions, making contract purchases, securing a corporate charter, and the like.

Property Legally protected rights and interests in anything with an ascertainable value that is subject to ownership.

Prospectus A document required by federal or state securities laws that describes the financial operations of the corporation, thus allowing investors to make informed decisions.

Protected class A class of persons with identifiable characteristics who historically have been victimized

by discriminatory treatment for certain purposes. Depending on the context, these characteristics include age, color, gender, national origin, race, and religion.
Proximate cause Legal cause; exists when the connection between an act and an injury is strong enough to justify imposing liability.
Proxy In corporation law, a written agreement between a stockholder and another under which the stockholder authorizes the other to vote the stockholder's shares in a certain manner.
Proxy fight A conflict between an individual, group, or firm attempting to take control of a corporation and the corporation's management for the votes of the shareholders.
Public figures Individuals who are thrust into the public limelight. Public figures include government officials and politicians, movie stars, well-known businesspersons, and generally anybody who becomes known to the public because of his or her position or activities.
Public policy A government policy based on widely held societal values and (usually) expressed or implied in laws or regulations.
Public prosecutor An individual, acting as a trial lawyer, who initiates and conducts criminal cases in the government's name and on behalf of the people.
Puffery A salesperson's often exaggerated claims concerning the quality of property offered for sale. Such claims involve opinions rather than facts and are not considered to be legally binding promises or warranties.
Punitive damages Money damages that may be awarded to a plaintiff to punish the defendant and deter future similar conduct.
Purchase-money security interest (PMSI) A security interest that arises when a seller or lender extends credit for part or all of the purchase price of goods purchased by a buyer.

Q

Qualified indorsement An indorsement on a negotiable instrument in which the indorser disclaims any contract liability on the instrument; the notation "without recourse" is commonly used to create a qualified indorsement.
Quantum meruit (pronounced *kwahn*-tuhm *mehr*-oowuht) Literally, "as much as he deserves"—an expression describing the extent of liability on a contract implied in law (quasi contract). An equitable doctrine based on the concept that one who benefits from another's labor and materials should not be unjustly enriched thereby but should be required to pay a reasonable amount for the benefits received, even absent a contract.
Quasi contract A fictional contract imposed on parties by a court in the interests of fairness and justice; usually, quasi contracts are imposed to avoid the unjust enrichment of one party at the expense of another.
Question of fact In a lawsuit, an issue involving a factual dispute that can only be decided by a judge (or, in a jury trial, a jury).
Question of law In a lawsuit, an issue involving the application or interpretation of a law; therefore, the judge, and not the jury, decides the issue.
Quiet enjoyment. *See* Covenant of quiet enjoyment
Quitclaim deed A deed intended to pass any title, interest, or claim that the grantor may have in the property but not warranting that such title is valid. A quitclaim deed offers the least amount of protection against defects in the title.
Quorum The number of members of a decision-making body that must be present before business may be transacted.
Quota An assigned import limit on goods.

R

Ratification The act of accepting and giving legal force to an obligation that previously was not enforceable.
Reaffirmation agreement An agreement between a debtor and a creditor in which the debtor reaffirms, or promises to pay, a debt dischargeable in bankruptcy. To be enforceable, the agreement must be made prior to the discharge of the debt by the bankruptcy court.
Real defense *See* Universal defense
Real property Land and everything attached to it, such as foliage and buildings.
Reasonable care The degree of care that a person of ordinary prudence would exercise in the same or similar circumstances.
Reasonable doubt *See* Beyond a reasonable doubt
Reasonable person standard The standard of behavior expected of a hypothetical "reasonable person." The standard against which negligence is measured and that must be observed to avoid liability for negligence.
Rebuttal The refutation of evidence introduced by an adverse party's attorney.
Receiver In a corporate dissolution, a court-appointed person who winds up corporate affairs and liquidates corporate assets.
Record Information that is either inscribed in a tangible medium or stored in an electronic or other medium and that is retrievable, according to the Uniform Electronic Transaction Act. The Uniform Computer Information Transactions Act uses *record* instead of *writing*.
Recording statutes Statutes that allow deeds, mortgages, and other real property transactions to be recorded so as to provide notice to future purchasers or creditors of an existing claim on the property.
Red herring A preliminary prospectus that can be distributed to potential investors after the registration statement (for a securities offering) has been filed with

the Securities and Exchange Commission. The name derives from the red legend printed across the prospectus stating that the registration has been filed but has not become effective.

Redemption A repurchase, or buying back. In secured transactions law, a debtor's repurchase of collateral securing a debt after a creditor has taken title to the collateral due to the debtor's default but before the secured party disposes of the collateral.

Reformation A court-ordered correction of a written contract so that it reflects the true intentions of the parties.

Regulation E A set of rules issued by the Federal Reserve System's board of governors under the authority of the Electronic Fund Transfer Act to protect users of electronic fund transfer systems.

Regulation Z A set of rules promulgated by the Federal Reserve Board to implement the provisions of the Truth-in-Lending Act.

Reimbursement *See* Right of reimbursement

Rejection In contract law, an offeree's express or implied manifestation not to accept an offer. In the law governing contracts for the sale of goods, a buyer's manifest refusal to accept goods on the ground that they do not conform to contract specifications.

Rejoinder The defendant's answer to the plaintiff's rebuttal.

Release A contract in which one party forfeits the right to pursue a legal claim against the other party.

Relevant evidence Evidence tending to make a fact at issue in the case more or less probable than it would be without the evidence. Only relevant evidence is admissible in court.

Remainder A future interest in property held by a person other than the original owner.

Remanded Sent back. If an appellate court disagrees with a lower court's judgment, the case may be remanded to the lower court for further proceedings in which the lower court's decision should be consistent with the appellate court's opinion on the matter.

Remedy The relief given to an innocent party to enforce a right or compensate for the violation of a right.

Remedy at law A remedy available in a court of law. Money damages are awarded as a remedy at law.

Remedy in equity A remedy allowed by courts in situations where remedies at law are not appropriate. Remedies in equity are based on settled rules of fairness, justice, and honesty, and include injunction, specific performance, rescission and restitution, and reformation.

Remitter A person who sends money, or remits payment.

Rent The consideration paid for the use or enjoyment of another's property. In landlord-tenant relationships, the payment made by the tenant to the landlord for the right to possess the premises.

Rent escalation clause A clause providing for an increase in rent during a lease term.

Repair-and-deduct statutes Statutes providing that a tenant may pay for repairs and deduct the cost of the repairs from the rent, as a remedy for a landlord's failure to maintain leased premises.

Replevin (pronounced ruh-*pleh*-vin) An action to recover specific goods in the hands of a party who is wrongfully withholding them from the other party.

Reply Procedurally, a plaintiff's response to a defendant's answer.

Reporter A publication in which court cases are published, or reported.

Repudiation The renunciation of a right or duty; the act of a buyer or seller in rejecting a contract either partially or totally. *See also* Anticipatory repudiation

Requirements contract An agreement in which a buyer agrees to purchase and the seller agrees to sell all or up to a stated amount of what the buyer needs or requires.

Res ipsa loquitur (pronounced *rehs ehp*-suh *low*-quuh-duhr) A doctrine under which negligence may be inferred simply because an event occurred, if it is the type of event that would not occur in the absence of negligence. Literally, the term means "the facts speak for themselves."

Resale price maintenance agreement An agreement between a manufacturer and a retailer in which the manufacturer specifies the minimum retail price of its products. Resale price maintenance agreements are illegal *per se* under the Sherman Act.

Rescind (pronounced reh-*sihnd*) To cancel. *See also* Rescission

Rescission (pronounced reh-*sih*-zhen) A remedy whereby a contract is canceled and the parties are returned to the positions they occupied before the contract was made; may be effected through the mutual consent of the parties, by their conduct, or by court decree.

Residuary The surplus of a testator's estate remaining after all of the debts and particular legacies have been discharged.

Respondeat superior (pronounced ree-*spahn*-dee-uht soo-*peer*-ee-your) In Latin, "Let the master respond." A doctrine under which a principal or an employer is held liable for the wrongful acts committed by agents or employees while acting within the course and scope of their agency or employment.

Respondent In equity practice, the party who answers a bill or other proceeding.

Restitution An equitable remedy under which a person is restored to his or her original position prior to loss or injury, or placed in the position he or she would have been in had the breach not occurred.

Restraint on trade Any contract or combination that tends to eliminate or reduce competition, effect a monopoly, artificially maintain prices, or otherwise hamper the course of trade and commerce as it would be carried on if left to the control of natural economic forces.

Restrictive covenant A private restriction on the use of land that is binding on the party that purchases the property originally as well as on subsequent purchasers. If its benefit or obligation passes with the land's ownership, it is said to "run with the land."

Restrictive indorsement Any indorsement on a negotiable instrument that requires the indorsee to comply with certain instructions regarding the funds involved. A restrictive indorsement does not prohibit the further negotiation of the instrument.

Resulting trust An implied trust arising from the conduct of the parties. A trust in which a party holds the actual legal title to another's property but only for that person's benefit.

Retained earnings The portion of a corporation's profits that has not been paid out as dividends to shareholders.

Retaliatory eviction The eviction of a tenant because of the tenant's complaints, participation in a tenant's union, or similar activity with which the landlord does not agree.

Reverse To reject or overrule a court's judgment. An appellate court, for example, might reverse a lower court's judgment on an issue if it feels that the lower court committed an error during the trial or that the jury was improperly instructed.

Reverse discrimination Discrimination against majority groups, such as white males, that results from affirmative action programs, in which preferences are given to minority members and women.

Reversible error An error by a lower court that is sufficiently substantial to justify an appellate court's reversal of the lower court's decision.

Reversionary interest A future interest in property retained by the original owner.

Revocation In contract law, the withdrawal of an offer by an offeror. Unless an offer is irrevocable, it can be revoked at any time prior to acceptance without liability.

Right of contribution The right of a co-surety who pays more than his or her proportionate share on a debtor's default to recover the excess paid from other co-sureties.

Right of entry The right to peaceably take or resume possession of real property.

Right of first refusal The right to purchase personal or real property—such as corporate shares or real estate—before the property is offered for sale to others.

Right of redemption *See* Equity of redemption; Redemption

Right of reimbursement The legal right of a person to be restored, repaid, or indemnified for costs, expenses, or losses incurred or expended on behalf of another.

Right of subrogation The right of a person to stand in the place of (be substituted for) another, giving the substituted party the same legal rights that the original party had.

Right-to-work law A state law providing that employees are not to be required to join a union as a condition of obtaining or retaining employment.

Risk A prediction concerning potential loss based on known and unknown factors.

Risk management Planning that is undertaken to protect one's interest should some event threaten to undermine its security. In the context of insurance, risk management involves transferring certain risks from the insured to the insurance company.

Robbery The act of forcefully and unlawfully taking personal property of any value from another; force or intimidation is usually necessary for an act of theft to be considered a robbery.

Rule of four A rule of the United States Supreme Court under which the Court will not issue a writ of *certiorari* unless at least four justices approve of the decision to issue the writ.

Rule of reason A test by which a court balances the positive effects (such as economic efficiency) of an agreement against its potentially anticompetitive effects. In antitrust litigation, many practices are analyzed under the rule of reason.

Rule 10b-5 *See* SEC Rule 10b-5

Rulemaking The process undertaken by an administrative agency when formally adopting a new regulation or amending an old one. Rulemaking involves notifying the public of a proposed rule or change and receiving and considering the public's comments.

Rules of evidence Rules governing the admissibility of evidence in trial courts.

S

S corporation A close business corporation that has met certain requirements as set out by the Internal Revenue Code and thus qualifies for special income tax treatment. Essentially, an S corporation is taxed the same as a partnership, but its owners enjoy the privilege of limited liability.

Sale The passing of title from the seller to the buyer for a price.

Sale on approval A type of conditional sale in which the buyer may take the goods on a trial basis. The sale becomes absolute only when the buyer approves of (or is satisfied with) the goods being sold.

Sale or return A type of conditional sale in which title and possession pass from the seller to the buyer; however, the buyer retains the option to return the goods during a specified period even though the goods conform to the contract.

Sales contract A contract for the sale of goods under which the ownership of goods is transferred from a seller to a buyer for a price.

Satisfaction *See* Accord and satisfaction

Scienter (pronounced *sy-en-*ter) Knowledge by the misrepresenting party that material facts have been falsely represented or omitted with an intent to deceive.

Search warrant An order granted by a public authority, such as a judge, that authorizes law enforcement personnel to search particular premises or property.

Seasonably Within a specified time period, or, if no period is specified, within a reasonable time.
SEC Rule 10b-5 A rule of the Securities and Exchange Commission that makes it unlawful, in connection with the purchase or sale of any security, to make any untrue statement of a material fact or to omit a material fact if such omission causes the statement to be misleading.
Secondary boycott A union's refusal to work for, purchase from, or handle the products of a secondary employer, with whom the union has no dispute, for the purpose of forcing that employer to stop doing business with the primary employer, with whom the union has a labor dispute.
Secondary liability In negotiable instruments law, the contingent liability of drawers and indorsers. A secondarily liable party becomes liable on an instrument only if the party that is primarily liable on the instrument dishonors it or, in regard to drafts and checks, the drawee fails to pay or to accept the instrument, whichever is required.
Secured party A lender, seller, or any other person in whose favor there is a security interest, including a person to whom accounts or chattel paper has been sold.
Secured transaction Any transaction in which the payment of a debt is guaranteed, or secured, by personal property owned by the debtor or in which the debtor has a legal interest.
Securities Generally, corporate stocks and bonds. A security may also be a note, debenture, stock warrant, or any document given as evidence of an ownership interest in a corporation or as a promise of repayment by a corporation.
Security agreement An agreement that creates or provides for a security interest between the debtor and a secured party.
Security interest Any interest "in personal property or fixtures which secures payment or performance of an obligation" [UCC 1–201(37)].
Self-defense The legally recognized privilege to protect one's self or property against injury by another. The privilege of self-defense protects only acts that are reasonably necessary to protect one's self or property.
Seniority system In regard to employment relationships, a system in which those who have worked longest for the company are first in line for promotions, salary increases, and other benefits; they are also the last to be laid off if the work force must be reduced.
Service mark A mark used in the sale or the advertising of services, such as to distinguish the services of one person from the services of others. Titles, character names, and other distinctive features of radio and television programs may be registered as service marks.
Service of process The delivery of the complaint and summons to a defendant.
Settlor One creating a trust.
Sexual harassment In the employment context, the granting of job promotions or other benefits in return for sexual favors or language or conduct that is so sexually offensive that it creates a hostile working environment.
Sham transaction A false transaction without substance that is undertaken with the intent to defraud a creditor or the government. An example of a sham transaction is the sale of assets to a friend or relative for the purpose of concealing assets from creditors or a bankruptcy court.
Share A unit of stock. *See also* Stock
Shareholder One who purchases shares of a corporation's stock, thus acquiring an equity interest in the corporation.
Shareholder's derivative suit A suit brought by a shareholder to enforce a corporate cause of action against a third person.
Sharia Civil law principles of some Middle Eastern countries that are based on the Islamic directives that follow the teachings of the prophet Mohammed.
Shelter principle The principle that the holder of a negotiable instrument who cannot qualify as a holder in due course (HDC), but who derives his or her title through an HDC, acquires the rights of an HDC.
Sheriff's deed The deed given to the purchaser of property at a sheriff's sale as part of the foreclosure process against the owner of the property.
Shipment contract A contract for the sale of goods in which the seller is required or authorized to ship the goods by carrier. The buyer assumes liability for any losses or damage to the goods after they are delivered to the carrier.
Short-form merger A merger between a subsidiary corporation and a parent corporation that owns at least 90 percent of the outstanding shares of each class of stock issued by the subsidiary corporation. Short-form mergers can be accomplished without the approval of the shareholders of either corporation.
Short-swing profits Profits made by officers, directors, and certain large stockholders resulting from the use of nonpublic (inside) information about their companies; prohibited by Section 12 of the 1934 Securities Exchange Act.
Shrink-wrap agreement An agreement whose terms are expressed in a document located inside a box in which goods are packaged; sometimes called a *shrink-wrap license*.
Sight draft In negotiable instruments law, a draft payable on sight—that is, when it is presented for payment.
Signature Under the Uniform Commercial Code, "any symbol executed or adopted by a party with a present intention to authenticate a writing."
Slander Defamation in oral form.
Slander of quality (trade libel) The publication of false information about another's product, alleging that it is not what its seller claims.
Slander of title The publication of a statement that denies or casts doubt on another's legal ownership of

any property, causing financial loss to that property's owner.

Small claims courts Special courts in which parties may litigate small claims (usually, claims involving $2,500 or less). Attorneys are not required in small claims courts, and in many states attorneys are not allowed to represent the parties.

Smart card Prepaid funds recorded on a microprocessor chip embedded on a card. One type of *e-money*.

Sociological school A school of legal thought that views the law as a tool for promoting justice in society.

Sole proprietorship The simplest form of business, in which the owner is the business; the owner reports business income on his or her personal income tax return and is legally responsible for all debts and obligations incurred by the business.

Sovereign immunity A doctrine that immunizes foreign nations from the jurisdiction of U.S. courts when certain conditions are satisfied.

Spam Bulk, unsolicited ("junk") e-mail.

Special indorsement An indorsement on an instrument that indicates the specific person to whom the indorser intends to make the instrument payable; that is, it names the indorsee.

Special warranty deed A deed in which the grantor only covenants to warrant and defend the title against claims and demands of the grantor and all persons claiming by, through, and under the grantor.

Specific performance An equitable remedy requiring exactly the performance that was specified in a contract; usually granted only when money damages would be an inadequate remedy and the subject matter of the contract is unique (for example, real property).

Spendthrift trust A trust created to prevent the beneficiary from spending all the money to which he or she is entitled. Only a certain portion of the total amount is given to the beneficiary at any one time, and most states prohibit creditors from attaching assets of the trust.

Spot zoning Granting a zoning classification to a parcel of land that is different from the classification given to other land in the immediate area.

Stale check A check, other than a certified check, that is presented for payment more than six months after its date.

Standing to sue The requirement that an individual must have a sufficient stake in a controversy before he or she can bring a lawsuit. The plaintiff must demonstrate that he or she either has been injured or threatened with injury.

Stare decisis (pronounced *ster*-ay dih-*si*-ses) A common law doctrine under which judges are obligated to follow the precedents established in prior decisions.

Statute of Frauds A state statute under which certain types of contracts must be in writing to be enforceable.

Statute of limitations A federal or state statute setting the maximum time period during which a certain action can be brought or certain rights enforced.

Statute of repose Basically, a statute of limitations that is not dependent on the happening of a cause of action. Statutes of repose generally begin to run at an earlier date and run for a longer period of time than statutes of limitations.

Statutory law The body of law enacted by legislative bodies (as opposed to constitutional law, administrative law, or case law).

Statutory lien A lien created by statute.

Statutory period of redemption A time period (usually set by state statute) during which the property subject to a defaulted mortgage, land contract, or other contract can be redeemed by the debtor after foreclosure or judicial sale.

Stock An equity (ownership) interest in a corporation, measured in units of shares.

Stock certificate A certificate issued by a corporation evidencing the ownership of a specified number of shares in the corporation.

Stock option *See* Stock warrant

Stock warrant A certificate that grants the owner the option to buy a given number of shares of stock, usually within a set time period.

Stockholder *See* Shareholder

Stop-payment order An order by a bank customer to his or her bank not to pay or certify a certain check.

Strict liability Liability regardless of fault. In tort law, strict liability may be imposed on defendants in cases involving abnormally dangerous activities, dangerous animals, or defective products.

Strike An extreme action undertaken by unionized workers when collective bargaining fails; the workers leave their jobs, refuse to work, and (typically) picket the employer's workplace.

Subject-matter jurisdiction Jurisdiction over the subject matter of a lawsuit.

Sublease A lease executed by the lessee of real estate to a third person, conveying the same interest that the lessee enjoys but for a shorter term than that held by the lessee.

Subpoena A document commanding a person to appear at a certain time and place or give testimony concerning a certain matter.

Subrogation *See* Right of subrogation

Subscriber An investor who agrees, in a subscription agreement, to purchase capital stock in a corporation.

Substantial evidence test The test applied by a court reviewing an administrative agency's informal action. The court determines whether the agency acted unreasonably and overturns the agency's findings only if unsupported by a substantial body of evidence.

Substantial performance Performance that does not vary greatly from the performance promised in a contract; the performance must create substantially the same benefits as those promised in the contract.

Substantive due process A requirement that focuses on the content, or substance, of legislation. If a law or other governmental action limits a fundamental right, such as the right to travel or to vote, it will be held to violate substantive due process unless it promotes a compelling or overriding state interest.

Substantive law Law that defines the rights and duties of individuals with respect to each other, as opposed to procedural law, which defines the manner in which these rights and duties may be enforced.

Substantive unconscionability Results from contracts, or portions of contracts, that are oppressive or overly harsh. Courts generally focus on provisions that deprive one party of the benefits of the agreement or leave that party without remedy for nonperformance by the other. An example of substantive unconscionability is the agreement by a welfare recipient with a fourth-grade education to purchase a refrigerator for $2,000 under an installment contract.

Suit *See* Lawsuit; Litigation

Summary judgment *See* Motion for summary judgment

Summary jury trial (SJT) A method of settling disputes in which a trial is held, but the jury's verdict is not binding. The verdict acts only as a guide to both sides in reaching an agreement during the mandatory negotiations that immediately follow the summary jury trial.

Summons A document informing a defendant that a legal action has been commenced against him or her and that the defendant must appear in court on a certain date to answer the plaintiff's complaint. The document is delivered by a sheriff or any other person so authorized.

Superseding cause An intervening force or event that breaks the connection between a wrongful act and an injury to another; in negligence law, a defense to liability.

Supremacy clause The provision in Article VI of the Constitution that provides that the Constitution, laws, and treaties of the United States are "the supreme Law of the Land." Under this clause, state and local laws that directly conflict with federal law will be rendered invalid.

Surety A person, such as a cosigner on a note, who agrees to be primarily responsible for the debt of another.

Suretyship An express contract in which a third party to a debtor-creditor relationship (the surety) promises to be primarily responsible for the debtor's obligation.

Surviving corporation The remaining, or continuing, corporation following a merger. The surviving corporation is vested with the merged corporation's legal rights and obligations.

Syllogism A form of deductive reasoning consisting of a major premise, a minor premise, and a conclusion.

Symbolic speech Nonverbal conduct that expresses opinions or thoughts about a subject. Symbolic speech is protected under the First Amendment's guarantee of freedom of speech.

Syndicate An investment group of persons or firms brought together for the purpose of financing a project that they would not or could not undertake independently.

T

Tag A key word in a document that can serve as an index reference to the document. On the Web, search engines return results based, in part, on the tags in Web documents.

Takeover The acquisition of control over a corporation through the purchase of a substantial number of the voting shares of the corporation.

Taking The taking of private property by the government for public use. Under the Fifth Amendment to the Constitution, the government may not take private property for public use without "just compensation."

Tangible property Property that has physical existence and can be distinguished by the senses of touch, sight, and so on. A car is tangible property; a patent right is intangible property.

Target corporation The corporation to be acquired in a corporate takeover; a corporation to whose shareholders a tender offer is submitted.

Tariff An tax on imported goods.

Technology licensing Allowing another to use and profit from intellectual property (patents, copyrights, trademarks, innovative products or processes, and so on) for consideration. In the context of international business transactions, technology licensing is sometimes an attractive alternative to the establishment of foreign production facilities.

Teller's check A negotiable instrument drawn by a bank on another bank or drawn by a bank and payable at or payable through a bank.

Tenancy at sufferance A type of tenancy under which one who, after rightfully being in possession of leased premises, continues (wrongfully) to occupy the property after the lease has been terminated. The tenant has no rights to possess the property and occupies it only because the person entitled to evict the tenant has not done so.

Tenancy at will A type of tenancy under which either party can terminate the tenancy without notice; usually arises when a tenant who has been under a tenancy for years retains possession, with the landlord's consent, after the tenancy for years has terminated.

Tenancy by the entirety The joint ownership of property by a husband and wife. Neither party can transfer his or her interest in the property without the consent of the other.

Tenancy for years A type of tenancy under which property is leased for a specified period of time, such as a month, a year, or a period of years.

Tenancy in common Co-ownership of property in which each party owns an undivided interest that passes to his or her heirs at death.

Tenancy in partnership Co-ownership of partnership property.

Tenant One who has the temporary use and occupation of real property owned by another person, called the landlord; the duration and terms of the tenancy are usually established by a lease.

Tender An unconditional offer to perform an obligation by a person who is ready, willing, and able to do so.

Tender of delivery Under the Uniform Commercial Code, a seller's or lessor's act of placing conforming goods at the disposal of the buyer or lessee and giving the buyer or lessee whatever notification is reasonably necessary to enable the buyer or lessee to take delivery.

Tender offer An offer to purchase made by one company directly to the shareholders of another (target) company; often referred to as a "takeover bid."

Term insurance A type of life insurance policy for which premiums are paid for a specified term. Payment on the policy is due only if death occurs within the term period. Premiums are less expensive than for whole life or limited-payment life, and there is usually no cash surrender value.

Testamentary trust A trust that is created by will and therefore does not take effect until the death of the testator.

Testate The condition of having died with a valid will.

Testator One who makes and executes a will.

Third party beneficiary One for whose benefit a promise is made in a contract but who is not a party to the contract.

Time draft A draft that is payable at a definite future time.

Tippee A person who receives inside information.

Title insurance Insurance commonly purchased by a purchaser of real property to protect against loss in the event that the title to the property is not free from liens or superior ownership claims.

Tombstone ad An advertisement, historically in a format resembling a tombstone, of a securities offering. The ad informs potential investors of where and how they may obtain a prospectus.

Tort A civil wrong not arising from a breach of contract. A breach of a legal duty that proximately causes harm or injury to another.

Tortfeasor One who commits a tort.

Totten trust A trust created by the deposit of a person's own money in his or her own name as a trustee for another. It is a tentative trust, revocable at will until the depositor dies or completes the gift in his or her lifetime by some unequivocal act or declaration.

Toxic tort Failure to use or to clean up properly toxic chemicals that cause harm to a person or society.

Trade acceptance A draft that is drawn by a seller of goods ordering the buyer to pay a specified sum of money to the seller, usually at a stated time in the future. The buyer accepts the draft by signing the face of the draft, thus creating an enforceable obligation to pay the draft when it comes due. On a trade acceptance, the seller is both the drawer and the payee.

Trade dress The image and overall appearance of a product—for example, the distinctive decor, menu, layout, and style of service of a particular restaurant. Basically, trade dress is subject to the same protection as trademarks.

Trade fixture The personal property of a commercial tenant that has been installed or affixed to real property for a business purpose. When the lease ends, the tenant can remove the fixture but must repair any damage to the real property caused by the fixture's removal.

Trade libel The publication of false information about another's product, alleging it is not what its seller claims; also referred to as slander of quality.

Trade name A term that is used to indicate part or all of a business's name and that is directly related to the business's reputation and goodwill. Trade names are protected under the common law (and under trademark law, if the name is the same as the firm's trademarked property).

Trade secret Information or a process that gives a business an advantage over competitors who do not know the information or process.

Trademark A distinctive mark, motto, device, or implement that a manufacturer stamps, prints, or otherwise affixes to the goods it produces so that they may be identified on the market and their origins made known. Once a trademark is established (under the common law or through registration), the owner is entitled to its exclusive use.

Transfer warranties Implied warranties, made by any person who transfers an instrument for consideration to subsequent transferees and holders who take the instrument in good faith, that (1) the transferor is entitled to enforce the instrument, (2) all signatures are authentic and authorized, (3) the instrument has not been altered, (4) the instrument is not subject to a defense or claim of any party that can be asserted against the transferor, and (5) the transferor has no knowledge of any insolvency proceedings against the maker, the acceptor, or the drawer of the instrument.

Transferee In negotiable instruments law, one to whom a negotiable instrument is transferred (delivered).

Transferor In negotiable instruments law, one who transfers (delivers) a negotiable instrument to another.

Traveler's check A check that is payable on demand, drawn on or payable through a bank, and designated as a traveler's check.

Treasure trove Money or coin, gold, silver, or bullion found hidden in the earth or other private place, the owner of which is unknown; literally, treasure found.

Treasury shares Corporate shares that are authorized by the corporation but that have not been issued.

Treaty An agreement formed between two or more independent nations.

Treble damages Damages consisting of single damages determined by a jury and tripled in amount in certain cases as required by statute.

Trespass to land The entry onto, above, or below the surface of land owned by another without the owner's permission or legal authorization.

Trespass to personal property The unlawful taking or harming of another's personal property; interference with another's right to the exclusive possession of his or her personal property.

Trespasser One who commits the tort of trespass in one of its forms.

Trial court A court in which trials are held and testimony taken.

Trust An arrangement in which title to property is held by one person (a trustee) for the benefit of another (a beneficiary).

Trust indorsement An indorsement for the benefit of the indorser or a third person; also known as an agency indorsement. The indorsement results in legal title vesting in the original indorsee.

Trustee One who holds title to property for the use or benefit of another (the beneficiary).

Tying arrangement An agreement between a buyer and a seller in which the buyer of a specific product or service becomes obligated to purchase additional products or services from the seller.

U

U.S. trustee A government official who performs certain administrative tasks that a bankruptcy judge would otherwise have to perform.

Ultra vires (pronounced *uhl*-trah *vye*-reez) A Latin term meaning "beyond the powers"; in corporate law, acts of a corporation that are beyond its express and implied powers to undertake.

Unanimous opinion A court opinion in which all of the judges or justices of the court agree to the court's decision.

Unconscionable (pronounced un-*kon*-shun-uh-bul) **contract or clause** A contract or clause that is void on the basis of public policy because one party, as a result of his or her disproportionate bargaining power, is forced to accept terms that are unfairly burdensome and that unfairly benefit the dominating party. *See also* Procedural unconscionability; Substantive unconscionability

Underwriter In insurance law, the insurer, or the one assuming a risk in return for the payment of a premium.

Undisclosed principal A principal whose identity is unknown by a third person, and the third person has no knowledge that the agent is acting for a principal at the time the agent and the third person form a contract.

Unenforceable contract A valid contract rendered unenforceable by some statute or law.

Uniform law A model law created by the National Conference of Commissioners (NCC) on Uniform State Laws and/or the American Law Institute for the states to consider adopting. If the state adopts the law, it becomes statutory law in that state. Each state has the option of adopting or rejecting all or part of a uniform law.

Unilateral contract A contract that results when an offer can only be accepted by the offeree's performance.

Union shop A place of employment in which all workers, once employed, must become union members within a specified period of time as a condition of their continued employment.

Unitary system A centralized governmental system in which local or subdivisional governments exercise only those powers given to them by the central government.

Universal defense A defense that is valid against all holders of a negotiable instrument, including holders in due course (HDCs) and holders with the rights of HDCs. Universal defenses are also called real defenses.

Universal life A type of insurance that combines some aspects of term insurance with some aspects of whole life insurance.

Unlawful detainer The unjustifiable retention of the possession of real property by one whose right to possession has terminated—as when a tenant holds over after the end of the lease term in spite of the landlord's demand for possession.

Unliquidated debt A debt that is uncertain in amount.

Unreasonably dangerous product In product liability, a product that is defective to the point of threatening a consumer's health and safety. A product will be considered unreasonably dangerous if it is dangerous beyond the expectation of the ordinary consumer or if a less dangerous alternative was economically feasible for the manufacturer, but the manufacturer failed to produce it.

Usage of trade Any practice or method of dealing having such regularity of observance in a place, vocation, or trade as to justify an expectation that it will be observed with respect to the transaction in question.

Usurpation In corporation law, the taking advantage of a corporate opportunity by a corporate officer or director for his or her personal gain and in violation of his or her fiduciary duties.

Usury Charging an illegal rate of interest.

Utilitarianism An approach to ethical reasoning in which ethically correct behavior is not related to any absolute ethical or moral values but to an evaluation of the consequences of a given action on those who will be affected by it. In utilitarian reasoning, a "good" decision is one that results in the greatest good for the greatest number of people affected by the decision.

V

Valid contract A contract that results when elements necessary for contract formation (agreement, consideration, legal purpose, and contractual capacity) are present.

Validation notice An initial notice to a debtor from a collection agency informing the debtor that he or she has thirty days to challenge the debt and request verification.

Vendee One who purchases property from another, called the vendor.

Vendor One who sells property to another, called the vendee.
Venture capital Funds that are invested in, or that are available for investment in, a new corporate enterprise.
Venture capitalist A person or entity that seeks out promising entrepreneurial ventures and funds them in exchange for equity stakes.
Venue (pronounced *ven*-yoo) The geographical district in which an action is tried and from which the jury is selected.
Verdict A formal decision made by a jury.
Vertical merger The acquisition by a company at one stage of production of a company at a higher or lower stage of production (such as a company merging with one of its suppliers or retailers).
Vertical restraint Any restraint on trade created by agreements between firms at different levels in the manufacturing and distribution process.
Vertically integrated firm A firm that carries out two or more functional phases (manufacture, distribution, retailing, and so on) of a product.
Vesting The creation of an absolute or unconditional right or power.
Vicarious liability Legal responsibility placed on one person for the acts of another.
Virtual courtroom A courtroom that is conceptual and not physical. In the context of cyberspace, a virtual courtroom could be a location on the Internet at which judicial proceedings take place.
Virtual property Property that, in the context of cyberspace, is conceptual, as opposed to physical. Intellectual property that exists on the Internet is virtual property.
Void contract A contract having no legal force or binding effect.
Voidable contract A contract that may be legally avoided (canceled, or annulled) at the option of one of the parties.
Voidable preference In bankruptcy law, a preference that may be avoided, or set aside, by the trustee.
Voir dire (pronounced *vwahr deehr*) A French phrase meaning, literally, "to see, to speak." In jury trials, the phrase refers to the process in which the attorneys question prospective jurors to determine whether they are biased or have any connection with a party to the action or with a prospective witness.
Voting trust An agreement (trust contract) under which legal title to shares of corporate stock is transferred to a trustee who is authorized by the shareholders to vote the shares on their behalf.

W

Waiver An intentional, knowing relinquishment of a legal right.
Warehouse receipt A document of title issued by a bailee-warehouser to cover the goods stored in the warehouse.
Warehouser One in the business of operating a warehouse.
Warranty A promise that certain facts are truly as they are represented to be.
Warranty deed A deed in which the grantor guarantees to the grantee that the grantor has title to the property conveyed in the deed, that there are no encumbrances on the property other than what the grantor has represented, and that the grantee will enjoy quiet possession of the property; a deed that provides the greatest amount of protection for the grantee.
Warranty disclaimer A seller's or lessor's negation or qualification of a warranty.
Warranty of fitness *See* Implied warranty of fitness for a particular purpose
Warranty of merchantability *See* Implied warranty of merchantability
Warranty of title An implied warranty made by a seller that the seller has good and valid title to the goods sold and that the transfer of the title is rightful.
Waste The abuse or destructive use of real property by one who is in rightful possession of the property but who does not have title to it. Waste does not include ordinary depreciation due to age and normal use.
Watered stock Shares of stock issued by a corporation for which the corporation receives, as payment, less than the stated value of the shares.
Wetlands Areas of land designated by government agencies (such as the Army Corps of Engineers or the Environmental Protection Agency) as protected areas that support wildlife and that therefore cannot be filled in or dredged by private contractors or parties.
Whistleblowing An employee's disclosure to government, the press, or upper-management authorities that the employer is engaged in unsafe or illegal activities.
White-collar crime Nonviolent crime committed by individuals or corporations to obtain a personal or business advantage.
Whole life A life insurance policy in which the insured pays a level premium for his or her entire life and in which there is a constantly accumulating cash value that can be withdrawn or borrowed against by the borrower. Sometimes referred to as straight life insurance.
Will An instrument directing what is to be done with the testator's property on his or her death, made by the testator and revocable during his or her lifetime. No interests in the testator's property pass until the testator dies.
Willful Intentional.
Winding up The second of two stages involved in the termination of a partnership or corporation. Once the firm is dissolved, it continues to exist legally until the process of winding up all business affairs (collecting and distributing the firm's assets) is complete.
Workers' compensation laws State statutes establishing an administrative procedure for compensating workers' injuries that arise out of—or in the course of—their employment, regardless of fault.

Working papers The various documents used and developed by an accountant during an audit. Working papers include notes, computations, memoranda, copies, and other papers that make up the work product of an accountant's services to a client.

Workout An out-of-court agreement between a debtor and his or her creditors in which the parties work out a payment plan or schedule under which the debtor's debts can be discharged.

Writ of attachment A court's order, prior to a trial to collect a debt, directing the sheriff or other officer to seize nonexempt property of the debtor; if the creditor prevails at trial, the seized property can be sold to satisfy the judgment.

Writ of *certiorari* (pronounced sur-shee-uh-*rah*-ree) A writ from a higher court asking the lower court for the record of a case.

Writ of execution A court's order, after a judgment has been entered against the debtor, directing the sheriff to seize (levy) and sell any of the debtor's nonexempt real or personal property. The proceeds of the sale are used to pay off the judgment, accrued interest, and costs of the sale; any surplus is paid to the debtor.

Wrongful discharge An employer's termination of an employee's employment in violation of an employment contract or laws that protect employees.

Z

Zoning The division of a city by legislative regulation into districts and the application in each district of regulations having to do with structural and architectural designs of buildings and prescribing the use to which buildings within designated districts may be put.

Table of Cases

C

D

E

T

X

Y

Z

INDEX

B

C

F

O

Q

U

V

Y

Z

Sample Sales Contract for Purchase of Green Coffee

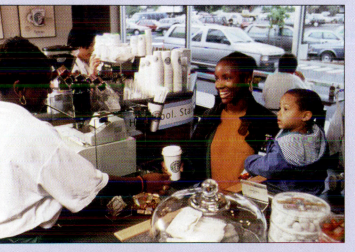

Starbucks Coffee Company was founded in 1971, opening its first store in Seattle's Pike Place Market. Today, Starbucks is North America's leading roaster and retailer of specialty coffee beans and operates more than four hundred stores around the country. In greater Seattle alone, more than a quarter of a million people buy their coffee at Starbucks stores every week.

"Our mission as a company," states Howard Schultz, chairman and CEO of Starbucks, "is to establish Starbucks as the premier purveyor of the finest coffees in the world." When Schultz first joined the company in the early 1980s as director of retail operations, Starbucks was a local, highly respected roaster and retailer of whole bean and ground coffees. A business trip to Italy opened his eyes to the rich tradition of the espresso bar. Espresso drinks became an irreplaceable element of Schultz's vision for the company, and when Schultz purchased Starbucks, with the support of local investors, in 1987, Starbucks started brewing. Coffee lovers can now enjoy Starbucks coffee in fine restaurants in several areas of the United States as well as in a variety of other carefully chosen locations, including high above the ground on Horizon Air flights, at sea with the Washington State Ferry System, and at all major games and events in the Seattle Kingdome. In addition, Starbucks operates a mail-order business. Starbucks coffee and Pepsi-Cola have joined to create unique coffee-based beverages that are now in the same outlets as Pepsi-Cola soft drinks.

Schultz is committed to maintaining the quality, integrity, and great taste of Starbucks as the company grows. "I take great pride," continues Schultz, "not in the number of stores we have opened, but in the growth and development of our people." The unusual dedication of Starbucks to investment in its people, believes Schultz, guarantees exceptional quality for the company's customers. The Starbucks mission statement, while recognizing the need for profitability, pledges that the company will make decisions that foster "respect and dignity" in the workplace. Each employee becomes part of an extensive training program that facilitates strong coffee knowledge, product expertise, a commitment to customer service, and well-developed interpersonal skills.

Dedicated to active support of the communities in which it operates, Starbucks helps organizations that benefit children's welfare, AIDS outreach, and increase environmental awareness.

Starbucks is involved in a variety of community cultural events, including jazz and film festivals. The company also has become the largest corporate sponsor of the international aid and relief organization, CARE. Programs, developed through the partnership of Starbucks with CARE, work toward reducing malnutrition in Guatemala, supporting education and literacy programs in Kenya, and lowering the mortality rate of children in Indonesia.

Photo Credit: Jill Doran for Starbucks Coffee

1. This is a contract for a sale of coffee to be *imported* internationally. If the parties have their principal places of business located in different countries, the contract may be subject to the United Nations Convention on Contracts for the International Sale of Goods (CISG). If the parties' principal places of business are located in the United States, the contract may be subject to the Uniform Commercial Code (UCC).

2. Quantity is one of the most important terms to include in a contract. Without it, a court may not be able to enforce the contract. See Chapter 18.

3. Weight per unit (bag) can be exactly stated or approximately stated. If it is not so stated, usage of trade in international contracts determines standards of weight.

4. Packaging requirements can be conditions for acceptance and payment. Bulk shipments are not permitted without the consent of the buyer. See Chapter 20, for an explanation of the different types of conditions.

5. A description of the coffee and the "Markings" constitute express warranties. Warranties in contracts for domestic sales of goods are discussed generally in Chapter 22. International contracts rely more heavily on descriptions and models or samples.

6. Under the UCC, parties may enter into a valid contract even though the price is not set. See Chapter 18. Under the CISG, a contract must provide for an exact determination of the price.

7. The terms of payment may take one of two forms: credit or cash. Credit terms can be complicated. A cash term can be simple, and payment may be by any means acceptable in the ordinary course of business (for example, a personal check or a letter of credit). If the seller insists on actual cash, the buyer must be given a reasonable time to get it. See Chapter 20.

8. *Tender* means the seller has placed goods that conform to the contract at the buyer's disposition. What constitutes a valid tender is explained in Chapter 20. This contract requires that the coffee meet all import regulations and that it be ready for pickup by the buyer at a "Bonded Public Warehouse." (A *bonded warehouse* is a place in which goods can be stored without paying taxes until the goods are removed.) For a discussion of the responsibilities of the parties when goods are in a warehouse, see Chapter 46.

9. The delivery date is significant because, if it is not met, the buyer may hold the seller in breach of the contract. Under this contract, the seller can be given a "period" within which to deliver the goods, instead of a specific day, which could otherwise present problems. The seller is also given some time to rectify goods that do not pass inspection (see the "Guarantee" clause on page two). For a discussion of the remedies of the buyer and seller, see Chapter 21.

10. As part of a proper tender, the seller (or its agent) must inform the buyer (or its agent) when the goods have arrived at their destination. The responsibilities of agents are set out in Chapters 31 and 32.

11. In some contracts, delivered and shipped weights can be important. During shipping, some loss can be attributed to the type of goods (spoilage of fresh produce, for example) or to the transportation itself. A seller and buyer can agree on the extent to which either of them will bear such losses. See Chapter 46 for a discussion of the liability of common carriers for loss during shipment.

12. Documents are often incorporated in a contract by reference, because including them word for word can make a contract difficult to read. If the document is later revised, the whole contract might have to be reworked. Documents that are typically incorporated by reference include detailed payment and delivery terms, special provisions, and sets of rules, codes, and standards.

13. In international sales transactions, and for domestic deals involving certain products, brokers are used to form the contracts. When so used, the brokers are entitled to a commission. See Chapter 31.

OVERLAND COFFEE IMPORT CONTRACT
OF THE
GREEN COFFEE ASSOCIATION
OF
NEW YORK CITY, INC.*
Effective May 9, 1991

SOLD BY: XYZ Co.

TO: Starbucks

QUANTITY: Five Hundred (500) Tons of (Bags)
weighing about 152.117 lbs. per ba

PACKAGING: Coffee must be packed in clean sound bags of uniform similar woven material, without inner lining or outer and/or machine.
Bulk shipments are allowed if agreed by mutual cons

DESCRIPTION: High grown Mexican Altura

PRICE: At Ten/$10.00 dollars U. S
Upon delivery in Bonded Public Warehouse at

PAYMENT: Cash against warehouse receipts

Bill and tender to DATE when all import requiremer and coffee delivered or discharged (as per contract te calendar days free time in Bonded Public Warehouse

ARRIVAL: During December via truck
(Period)
from Mexico for
(Country of Exportation)
Partial shipments permitted.

ADVICE OF ARRIVAL: Advice of arrival with warehouse name and location place of entry, must be transmitted directly, or throu Broker. Advice will be given as soon as known but at the named warehouse. Such advice may be giver same day.

WEIGHTS: (1) DELIVERED WEIGHTS: Coffee covered by th tender. Actual tare to be allowed.
(2) SHIPPING WEIGHTS: Coffee covered by this weight exceeding 1/2 percent at location nan
(3) Coffee is to be weighed within fifteen (15) cale account of seller

MARKINGS: Bags to be branded in English with the name of Co regulations of the Country of Importation, in effect merchandise. Any expense incurred by failure to c Exporter/Seller.

RULINGS: The "Rulings on Coffee Contracts" of the Green C the date this contract is made, is incorporated for a herewith, constitute the entire contract. No variatio parties to the contract.
Seller guarantees that the terms printed on the reve are identical with the terms as printed in By-Laws York City, Inc., heretofore adopted.
Exceptions to this guarantee are:

ACCEPTED:
XYZ Co. Seller
BY Agent
Starbucks Buyer
BY Agent

When this contract is executed by a person acting fully authorized to commit his principal.

* Reprinted with permission of The Green Coffee Association of New York

Contract Seller's No.: 504617
Buyer's No.: P9264
Date: 9/11/00

Mexican coffee

ze made of sisal, henequen, jute, burlap, or
ering of any material properly sewn by hand

of Buyer and Seller.

urrency, per lb. net, (U.S. Funds)
edo, TX
(City and State)

d governmental regulations have been satisfied,
. Seller is obliged to give the Buyer two (2)
wing but not including date of tender.

ethod of Transportation)
al at Laredo, TX
(Country of Importation)

ther with the quantity, description, marks and
ler's Agent/Broker, to the Buyer or his Agent/
er than the fifth business day following arrival
lly with written confirmation to be sent the

ract is to be weighed at location named in

t is sold on shipping weights. Any loss in
ender is for account of Seller at contract price.
ys after tender. Weighing expenses, if any, for
(Seller or Buyer)
Origin and otherwise to comply with laws and
me of entry, governing marking of import
with these regulations to be borne by

sociation of New York City, Inc., in effect on
es as a part of this agreement, and together
ition hereto shall be valid unless signed by the

f, which by reference are made a part hereof,
s of the Green Coffee Association of New

SSION TO BE PAID BY:
ler

Brokerage
Broker(s)
r, such person hereby represents that he is

---

14 Arbitration is the settling of a dispute by submitting it to a disinterested party (other than a court) that renders a decision. The procedures and costs can be provided for in an arbitration clause or incorporated through other documents. To enforce an award rendered in an arbitration, the winning party can "enter" (submit) the award in a court "of competent jurisdiction." For a general discussion of arbitration and other forms of dispute resolution (other than courts), see Chapter 2.

15 When goods are imported internationally, they must meet certain import requirements before being released to the buyer. Because of this, buyers frequently want a guaranty clause that covers the goods not admitted into the country and that either requires the seller to replace the goods within a stated time or allows the contract for those goods not admitted to be void. See Chapter 20.

16 In the "Claims" clause, the parties agree that the buyer has a certain time within which to reject the goods. The right to reject is a right by law and does not need to be stated in a contract. If the buyer does not exercise the right within the time specified in the contract, the goods will be considered accepted. See Chapter 20.

17 Many international contracts include definitions of terms so that the parties understand what they mean. Some terms are used in a particular industry in a specific way. Here, the word "chop" refers to a unit of like-grade coffee bean. The buyer has a right to inspect ("sample") the coffee. If the coffee does not conform to the contract, the seller must correct the nonconformity. See Chapter 20.

18 The "Delivery," "Insurance," and "Freight" clauses, with the "Arrival" clause on page one, indicate that this is a destination contract. The seller has the obligation to deliver the goods to the destination, not simply deliver them into the hands of a carrier. Under this contract, the destination is a "Bonded Public Warehouse" in a specific location. The seller bears the risk of loss until the goods are delivered at their destination. Typically, the seller will have bought insurance to cover the risk. See Chapter 19 for a discussion of delivery terms and the risk of loss, and Chapter 49 for a general discussion of insurance.

19 Delivery terms are commonly placed in all sales contracts. Such terms determine who pays freight and other costs, and, in the absence of an agreement specifying otherwise, who bears the risk of loss. International contracts can use delivery terms as provided under the UCC (see Chapter 19),or can use INCOTERMS, which are published by the International Chamber of Commerce. INCOTERMS differ slightly from UCC terms in legal effect. For example, the INCOTERM "DDP" ("delivered duty paid") requires the seller to arrange shipment, obtain and pay for import or export permits, and get the goods through customs to a named destination.

20 Exported and imported goods are subject to duties, taxes, and other charges imposed by the governments of the countries involved. International contracts spell out who is responsible for these charges.

21 This clause protects a party if the other party should become financially unable to fulfill the obligations under the contract. Thus, if the seller cannot afford to deliver, or the buyer cannot afford to pay, for the stated reasons, the other party can consider the contract breached. This right is subject to "11 USC 365(e)(1)," which refers to a specific provision of the U.S. Bankruptcy Code dealing with executory contracts. Bankruptcy provisions are covered in Chapter 30.

22 In the "Breach or Default of Contract" clause, the parties agreed that the remedies under this contract are the remedies (except for consequential damages) provided by the UCC, as in effect in the state of New York. The amount and "ascertainment" of damages, as well as other disputes about relief, are to be determined by arbitration. UCC remedies are discussed in Chapter 21. Breach of contract under the UCC is explained in Chapter 20.

23 Three clauses frequently included in international contracts are omitted here. There is no "Choice of Language" clause designating the official language to be used in interpreting the contract terms. There is no "Choice of Forum" clause designating the place in which disputes will be litigated, except for arbitration (law of New York State). Finally, there is no "*Force Majeure*" clause relieving the sellers or buyers from nonperformance due to events beyond their control.

TERMS AND CONDITIONS

ARBITRATION: All controversies relating to, in connection with, or arising out of this contract, its modification, making or the authority or obligations of the signatories hereto, and whether involving the principals, agents, brokers, or others who actually subscribe hereto, shall be settled by arbitration in accordance with the "Rules of Arbitration" of the Green Coffee Association of New York City, Inc., as they exist at the time of the arbitration (including provisions as to payment of fees and expenses). Arbitration is the sole remedy hereunder, and it shall be held in accordance with the law of New York State, and judgment of any award may be entered in the courts of that State, or in any other court of competent jurisdiction. All notices or judicial service in reference to arbitration or enforcement shall be deemed given if transmitted as required by the aforesaid rules.

GUARANTEE: (a) If all or any of the coffee is refused admission into the country of importation by reason of any violation of governmental laws or acts, which violation existed at the time the coffee arrived at Bonded-Public Warehouse, seller is required, as to the amount not admitted and as soon as possible, to deliver replacement coffee in conformity to all terms and conditions of this contract, excepting only the Arrival terms, but not later than thirty (30) days after the date of the violation notice. Any payment made and expenses incurred for any coffee denied entry shall be refunded within ten (10) calendar days of denial of entry, and payment shall be made for the replacement delivery in accordance with the terms of this contract. Consequently, if Buyer removes the coffee from the Bonded Public Warehouse, Seller's responsibility as to such portion hereunder ceases.
(b) Contracts containing the overstamp "No Pass-No Sale" on the face of the contract shall be interpreted to mean: If any or all of the coffee is not admitted into the country of Importation in its original condition by reason of failure to meet requirements of the government's laws or Acts, the contract shall be deemed null and void as to that portion of the coffee which is not admitted in its original condition. Any payment made and expenses incurred for any coffee denied entry shall be refunded within ten (10) calendar days of denial of entry.

CONTINGENCY: This contract is not contingent upon any other contract.

CLAIMS: Coffee shall be considered accepted as to quality unless within *fifteen* (15) calendar days after delivery at Bonded Public Warehouse or within *fifteen* (15) calendar days after all Government clearances have been received, whichever is later, either:
(a) Claims are settled by the parties hereto, or,
(b) Arbitration proceedings have been filed by one of the parties in accordance with the provisions hereof.
(c) If neither (a) nor (b) has been done in the stated period or if any portion of the coffee has been removed from the Bonded Public Warehouse before representative sealed samples have been drawn by the Green Coffee Association of New York City, Inc., in accordance with its rules, Seller's responsibility for quality claims ceases for that portion so removed.
(d) Any question of quality submitted to arbitration shall be a matter of allowance only, unless otherwise provided in the contract.

DELIVERY: (a) No more than three (3) chops may be tendered for each lot of 250 bags.
(b) Each chop of coffee tendered is to be uniform in grade and appearance. All expense necessary to make coffee uniform shall be for account of seller.
(c) Notice of arrival and/or sampling order constitutes a tender, and must be given not later than the fifth business day following arrival at Bonded Public Warehouse stated on the contract.

INSURANCE: Seller is responsible for any loss or damage, or both, until Delivery and Discharge of coffee at the Bonded Public Warehouse in the Country of Importation.

All Insurance Risks, costs and responsibility are for Seller's Account until Delivery and Discharge of coffee at the Bonded Public Warehouse in the Country of Importation.

Buyer's insurance responsibility begins from the day of importation or from the day of tender, whichever is later.

FREIGHT: Seller to provide and pay for all transportation and related expenses to the Bonded Public Warehouse in the Country of Importation.

EXPORT DUTIES/TAXES: Exporter is to pay all Export taxes, duties or other fees or charges, if any, levied because of exportation.

IMPORT DUTIES/TAXES: Any Duty or Tax whatsoever, imposed by the government or any authority of the Country of Importation, shall be borne by the Importer/Buyer.

INSOLVENCY OR FINANCIAL FAILURE OF BUYER OR SELLER: If, at any time before the contract is fully executed, either party hereto shall meet with creditors because of inability generally to make payment of obligations when due, or shall suspend such payments, fail to meet his general trade obligations in the regular course of business, shall file a petition in bankruptcy or, for an arrangement, shall become insolvent, or commit an act of bankruptcy, then the other party may at his option, expressed in writing, declare the aforesaid to constitute a breach and default of this contract, and may, in addition to other remedies, decline to deliver further or make payment or may sell or purchase for the defaulter's account, and may collect damage for any injury or loss, or shall account for the profit, if any, occasioned by such sale or purchase.

This clause is subject to the provisions of (11 USC 365 (e) 1) if invoked.

BREACH OR DEFAULT OF CONTRACT: In the event either party hereto fails to perform, or breaches or repudiates this agreement, the other party shall subject to the specific provisions of this contract be entitled to the remedies and relief provided for by the Uniform Commercial Code of the State of New York. The computation and ascertainment of damages, or the determination of any other dispute as to relief, shall be made by the arbitrators in accordance with the Arbitration Clause herein.

Consequential damages shall not, however, be allowed.

A Sample Court Case

Clark County School Dist. v. Breeden

532 U.S. 268
121 S.Ct. 1508.
149 L.Ed.2d 509

* * *

April 23, 2001. * * *

* * * *

School district employee sued district under **Title VII** [of the Civil Rights Act of 1964], alleging retaliation for engaging in protected activities. The United States District Court for the District of Nevada, Hagen, J., granted **summary judgment** for district. The Ninth Circuit Court of Appeals reversed. On grant of petition for writ of *certiorari*, the [United States] Supreme Court held that: (1) no reasonable person could have believed that single incident of alleged sexual harassment violated Title VII, precluding retaliation claim based on employee's internal complaints about incident, and (2) fact that **Equal Employment Opportunity Commission** (EEOC) issued right-to-sue letter to employee three months before employee's supervisor announced she was contemplating employee's transfer was insufficient to establish causation element of retaliation claim.

Reversed.

* * * *

[3] KeyCite Notes

345 Schools

345II Public Schools

345II(C) Government, Officers, and District Meetings

345k63 District and Other Local Officers

345k63(1) k. Appointment, Qualification, and Tenure. Most Cited Cases

No reasonable person could have believed that Title VII sex discrimination provision was implicated by single incident during school district's review of job applicants' profiles, in which male supervisor, in presence of one male and one female employee who were also participating in review, read aloud sexually explicit statement attributed to one applicant, stated that he did not know what it meant, and was told by male employee, "I'll tell you later," at which both men laughed; thus, incident did not support female employee's Title VII retaliation claim alleging that adverse actions followed her internal complaints about exchange.

* * * *

Carol Davis Zucker, Kamer, Zucker & Abbott, Las Vegas, Nevada, Kathy M. Banke, Crosby, Heafey, Roach & May, Oakland, California, for Petitioner.

Richard Segerblom, Las Vegas, Nevada, for Respondent.

PER CURIAM.

Under Title VII of the Civil Rights Act of 1964, it is unlawful "for an employer to discriminate against any of his employees * * * because [the employee] has opposed any practice made an unlawful employment practice by [Title VII], or because [the employee] has made a charge, testified, assisted, or participated in any manner in an investigation, proceeding, or hearing under [Title VII]." In 1997, **respondent** filed a retaliation claim against **petitioner** Clark County School District. The claim as eventually amended alleged that petitioner had taken two separate adverse employment actions against her in response to two different protected activities in which she had engaged. The **District Court** granted **summary judgment** to petitioner, but a panel of the Court of Appeals for the Ninth Circuit reversed * * * . We grant the writ of *certiorari* and reverse.

On October 21, 1994, respondent's male supervisor met with respondent and another male employee to review the psychological evaluation reports of four job applicants. The report for one of the applicants disclosed that the applicant had once commented to a co-worker, "I hear making love to you is like making love to the Grand Canyon." At the meeting respondent's supervisor read the comment aloud, looked at respondent and stated, "I don't know what that means." The other employee then said, "Well, I'll tell you later," and both men chuckled. Respondent later complained about the comment to the offending employee, to Assistant Superintendent George Ann Rice, the employee's supervisor, and to another assistant superintendent of petitioner. Her first claim of retaliation asserts that she was punished for these complaints.

The Court of Appeals for the Ninth Circuit has applied [Title VII] to protect employee "oppos[ition]" not just to practices that are actually "made * * * unlawful" by Title VII, but also to practices that the employee could reasonably believe were unlawful. We have no occasion to rule on the propriety of this interpretation, because even assuming it is correct, no one could reasonably believe that the incident recounted above violated Title VII.

[1][2] Title VII forbids actions taken on the basis of sex that "discriminate against any individual with respect to his compensation, terms, conditions, or privileges of employment." Just three **Terms** ago, we reiterated, what was plain from our previous decisions, that sexual harassment is actionable under Title

Citations indicating the reporters in which this case has been published and the relevant volume and page numbers in each reporter.

The date on which the decision in this case was issued.

A federal statute that prohibits employment discrimination based on race, color, national origin, religion, or gender.

The case synopsis: a brief summary of the issues and decisions in the case, prepared by the West editors.

The federal administrative agency that handles claims of employment discrimination.

An appellate court will reverse a lower court's judgment if the lower court erred in some way.

On Westlaw, this is a link to a list of cases in which this headnote is discussed or cited.

This number refers to the place in the text of the opinion where the point of law summarized in this headnote is discussed.

These numbers and headings classify this headnote in the West Key Number System, which provides access to all other American cases on the point of law dealt with in this headnote. On Westlaw, these cases can be accessed by clicking on the appropriate links.

This is a link, on Westlaw, to a list of the cases that the courts cite most often on this point of law.

headnote: a paragraph consisting of a brief statement of facts and a brief statement of the rule of law that the court applied to the facts. A case will have as many headnotes as there are points of law in the opinion. This is the third headnote in this case.

Attorneys for the parties to the case. The links are to these attorneys' entries in West's Legal Directory.

By the whole court. This line states the name of the justice who wrote the Court's opinion. In this case, the opinion was written by the Court as a whole.

The first paragraph of the opinion summarizes the legal, factual, and procedural background of the case.

The party against whom the appeal was brought.

The party who appealed the decision.

A federal trial court in which a lawsuit is initiated.

A judgment entered without a trial, in response to a motion for summary judgment.

A Latin term meaning that the Court ordered the lower court to send it the record of the case for review.

This paragraph sets out the factual background of the case.

A reference and links to the headnotes that summarize the points of law discussed in this part of the opinion.

A term is the time prescribed by law during which a court hears cases. The Supreme Court hears cases in an annual term that begins on the first Monday in October and normally ends in the first week of July.

VII only if it is "so 'severe or pervasive' as to 'alter the conditions of [the victim's] employment and create an abusive working environment.'" Workplace conduct is not measured in isolation; instead, whether an environment is sufficiently hostile or abusive must be judged by looking at all the circumstances, including the frequency of the discriminatory conduct; its severity; whether it is physically threatening or humiliating, or a mere offensive utterance; and whether it unreasonably interferes with an employee's work performance. Hence, a recurring point in our opinions is that simple teasing, offhand comments, and isolated incidents (unless extremely serious) will not amount to discriminatory changes in the "terms and conditions of employment."

This part of the Court's opinion expands on the point of law summarized in the headnote set out earlier in this exhibit.

[3] No reasonable person could have believed that the single incident recounted above violated Title VII's standard. The ordinary terms and conditions of respondent's job required her to review the sexually explicit statement in the course of screening job applicants. Her co-workers who participated in the hiring process were subject to the same requirement, and indeed, in the District Court respondent "conceded that it did not bother or upset her" to read the statement in the file. Her supervisor's comment, made at a meeting to review the application, that he did not know what the statement meant; her co-worker's responding comment; and the chuckling of both are at worst an isolated incident that cannot remotely be considered extremely serious, as our cases require. The holding of the Court of Appeals to the contrary must be reversed.

The Court's conclusion on the first issue reviewed in this opinion.

[4] Besides claiming that she was punished for complaining to petitioner's personnel about the alleged sexual harassment, respondent also claimed that she was punished for filing charges against petitioner with the **Nevada Equal Rights Commission** and the Equal Employment Opportunity Commission (EEOC) and for filing the present suit. Respondent filed her lawsuit on April 1, 1997; on April 10, 1997, respondent's supervisor, Assistant Superintendent Rice, mentioned to Allin Chandler, Executive Director of plaintiff's union, that she was contemplating transferring plaintiff to the position of Director of Professional Development Education, and this transfer was carried through in May. In order to show, as her defense against summary judgment required, the existence of a causal connection between her protected activities and the transfer, respondent relied wholly on the **temporal proximity** of the filing of her complaint on April 1, 1997 and Rice's statement to plaintiff's union representative on April 10, 1997 that she was considering transferring plaintiff to the new position. The District Court, however, found that respondent did not **serve** petitioner with the **summons** and **complaint** until April 11, 1997, one day *after* Rice had made the statement, and Rice filed an **affidavit** stating that she did not become aware of the lawsuit until after April 11, a claim that respondent did not challenge. Hence, the court concluded, respondent "ha[d] not shown that any causal connection exists between her protected activities and the adverse employment decision."

A state administrative agency that handles claims of employment discrimination.

Nearness in time.

To deliver a copy of the summons and complaint. This is usually done by a sheriff or other authorized person.

A document informing a defendant that a legal action has been commenced against him or her and that he or she must appear in court on a certain date to answer the complaint.

A document alleging wrongdoing on the part of a defendant. A complaint initiates a lawsuit when it is filed with a court.

A statement of facts, confirmed by the oath of the party making it and made before a person having the authority to administer the oath.

The Court of Appeals reversed, relying on two facts: The EEOC had issued a **right-to-sue letter** to respondent three months before Rice announced she was contemplating the transfer, and the actual transfer occurred one month after Rice learned of respondent's suit. The latter fact is immaterial in light of the fact that petitioner concededly was contemplating the transfer before it learned of the suit. Employers need not suspend previously planned transfers upon discovering that a Title VII suit has been filed, and their proceeding along lines previously contemplated, though not yet definitively determined, is no evidence whatever of causality.

A letter from the EEOC to a victim of alleged discrimination stating that the EEOC has decided not to file a suit on the victim's behalf but that the victim may bring his or her own suit.

The Court's conclusion on the first part of the second issue considered in this opinion.

[5] As for the right-to-sue letter: * * * [t]he Ninth Circuit's opinion did not adopt respondent's utterly implausible suggestion that the EEOC's issuance of a right-to-sue letter—an action in which the employee takes no part—is a protected activity of the employee. Rather, the opinion suggests that the letter provided petitioner with its first notice of respondent's charge before the EEOC, and hence allowed the inference that the transfer proposal made three months later was petitioner's reaction to the charge. This will not do.

First, there is no indication that Rice even knew about the right-to-sue letter when she proposed transferring respondent. And second, if one presumes she knew about it, one must also presume that she (or her predecessor) knew *almost two years earlier* about the protected action (filing of the EEOC complaint) that the letter supposedly disclosed. (The complaint had been filed on August 23, 1995, and both Title VII and its implementing regulations require that an employer be given notice within 10 days of filing.) The cases that accept mere temporal proximity between an employer's knowledge of protected activity and an adverse employment action as sufficient evidence of causality to establish a *prima facie* case uniformly hold that the temporal proximity must be "very close." Action taken (as here) 20 months later suggests, by itself, no causality at all.

The Court's conclusion on the second part of the second issue discussed in this opinion.

In short, neither the grounds that respondent presented to the District Court, nor the ground she added on appeal, nor even the ground the Court of Appeals developed on its own, sufficed to establish a dispute substantial enough to withstand the motion for summary judgment. The District Court's granting of that motion was correct. The judgment of the Court of Appeals is reversed.

It is so ordered.

The Court summarizes its conclusions and gives its order in the final part of this opinion.